Schofield & Sims

The Complete Primary Dictionary

Michael Janes

Published by **Schofield & Sims Ltd**, Dogley Mill, Fenay Bridge, Huddersfield HD8 0NQ, UK
Telephone 01484 607080
www.schofieldandsims.co.uk

Copyright © Schofield & Sims Ltd 2016

Author: **Michael Janes**
Michael Janes has asserted his moral right under the Copyright, Designs and Patents Act, 1988, to be identified as the author of this work.

British Library Cataloguing in Publication Data
A catalogue record for this book is available from the British Library.

All rights reserved. No part of this publication may be reproduced, stored in a retrieval system, or transmitted in any form or by any means, electronic, mechanical, photocopying, recording or otherwise, without either the prior permission of the publisher or a licence permitting restricted copying in the United Kingdom issued by the Copyright Licensing Agency Ltd, Saffron House, 6–10 Kirby Street, London EC1N 8TS.

Headwords that Schofield & Sims believes to be trademarks are identified by this label: (trademark). However, neither the presence nor the absence of such a label affects the legal status of any trademark. Trademarks, registered trademarks, product names and brands referred to within definitions and examples are not identified but remain the property of their respective trademark holders.

Michael Janes would like to express his gratitude to freelance commissioning editor **Carolyn Richardson** (www.publiserve.co.uk) for her guidance, support and insightful comments and to copy-editor **Pat Dunn** for her meticulousness, enthusiasm and dedication; he would also like to thank proofreaders **Sally Critchlow** and **Susie Millard** for their skilful reading and attention to detail.

Michael Janes is also grateful to his family, Susan, Leah and Daniel, who lived and breathed the dictionary with him for more than five years.

Designed by **Oxford Designers & Illustrators Ltd**
Front cover designed by **Ledgard Jepson Ltd**

Printed in Spain by **Gráficas Díaz Tuduri, S.L.**

ISBN 978 07217 1371 7

Contents

Introduction — iv

How to use this book — v

Dictionary

A	1
B	27
C	55
D	106
E	137
F	158
G	189
H	206
I	227
J	247
K	253
L	258
M	279
N	307
O	319
P	334
Q	387
R	390
S	427
T	515
U	551
V	563
W	571
X	595
Y	595
Z	597

Parts of speech — 599

Punctuation — 600

Introduction

The Complete Primary Dictionary is one of the first completely new English dictionaries of the twenty-first century. The dictionary was specially written for primary school children. It took more than five years to write.

Clear and precise

The language used is clear and simple. Each definition uses easy words, rather than difficult words that you need to look up. Clear examples show you how the words are used. Some words have several meanings or mean different things in different situations. These variations are known as 'senses'. The dictionary defines all the senses of a word that are appropriate to your age group. If you look up the word 'cell', for example, you will find that it has five different senses. The everyday sense is 'a small room in a prison or police station where prisoners are kept', but the other important senses – which you will come across in science and in maths – are also given.

Each definition is precise and gives you the specific information you need. For example, crows and ravens belong to the same family of birds and are similar, but this dictionary tells you that a raven is very large, has shiny feathers and a heavy sharp beak and lives in mountainous areas, which will help you to identify it.

Phrases and idioms

Some English words are used with other words to make phrases or idioms. Idioms have a special meaning that is not the same as the usual meaning. This meaning too is included in the dictionary. For example, the noun 'blink' refers to the action of closing your eyes and opening them again quickly, but the dictionary also gives the meaning of two idioms – 'in the blink of an eye' (meaning very quickly) and 'on the blink' (a way of saying that a piece of equipment is not working very well).

New and old

Language is always changing. This dictionary includes many new words and also recognises the value of older words that you find in your favourite classics – words like 'dell' (a small valley) and 'tidings' (news). Such words widen your vocabulary and improve your understanding of the world.

Words across the curriculum

The Complete Primary Dictionary will help you in your schoolwork across all the National Curriculum subjects. Scientific terms such as 'ecosystem' and 'polymer', mathematical terms like 'composite number' and 'order of operations', words to do with language such as 'phoneme' and 'grapheme' – all these are clearly explained.

Proper nouns, such as the names of countries, and other names such as those referring to historical periods, are usually found only in encyclopedias. This dictionary, however, defines many of these nouns as used in the National Curriculum. So you can look up 'Neolithic Age' and 'Industrial Revolution', for example, as well as 'Greenwich Mean Time' and 'Ghana'.

Origins

Did you know that the letter J entered English in 1066, for use in words borrowed from French? Or that the letter O still looks just as it did 3000 years ago? Each letter section opens with a short history of the shape of the capital letter. Other 'Origin' panels tell you about words with an interesting history – look up the origin of 'denim', for example – and 'Culture note' panels provide extra information about some words, with facts about traditions, history and famous people.

British and American English

Britain and America are sometimes described as two nations divided by a common language, because they occasionally use the same words in different ways. As many British children see American films and websites, this dictionary includes some words clearly labelled as American – with notes about differences in meaning where needed. Did you know, for example, that Americans refer to the ground floor of a building as the 'first floor'? Many possible confusions like these are explained.

How to use this book

Reading for meaning

To find the meaning of a word, look at its first letter and turn to the relevant alphabetical section in the dictionary. Next, look at the second and then the third letter of your word while also reading the guide words in the top outside corners of the dictionary pages. Continue with the other letters until you find your word. If the word has more than one numbered sense (meaning), use the definition and examples to help you choose the most suitable one. Then return to the text you are reading. If the sense you have found does not seem right, try another. The correct sense is the one that *makes sense*.

Use all the dictionary features to improve your understanding of definitions. For example, cross-references encourage you to compare the word with other words. Synonyms (which mean the same) and antonyms (which mean the opposite) help you to understand meanings too.

Sometimes you know the meaning of a word but don't know how to say it aloud. The dictionary shows you how to say some words that are difficult to pronounce.

Checking your spelling

To find a word that you cannot spell, listen to its sound and work out the first few letters. Use these letters as described at the top of this page. If you cannot find the word, make another guess at the first few letters. Write them down. Do they look right? If you get stuck, ask yourself:

- Is there another spelling for the opening sound? The 'f' sound may be spelt 'ph', the 'r' sound 'rh', the 's' sound 'c' and the 'j' sound 'g' (as in 'gem'). The 'kw' sound is usually spelt 'qu'.
- Does the word start with a silent letter? Letter 'k' is silent in words beginning 'kn', 'w' is silent in 'wr' words and 'h' is silent in some 'ho' words (such as 'honest').
- Can you spell another word in the same family? For example, to spell 'knowledge', go to 'know' and look for 'knowledge' nearby.
- Does the word start with a prefix? For example, 'un' is a prefix added to 'lucky' to make 'unlucky'. Most prefixes are easy to spell and take you quickly to the correct part of the dictionary.
- Does the word represent a particular sound, for example 'aargh', 'eek' or 'oink'? If so, its spelling may be so closely related to its sound that it does not follow spelling rules.

Word origins can help you remember correct spellings, so be sure to read the 'Origin' panels.

Using correct grammar

Use this book to improve your grammar. Each headword is labelled with its part of speech (for example noun, adjective, verb). If the word is a noun, its plural is given. If the word is an adjective (for example 'good'), its comparative ('better') and superlative ('best') are provided. If the word is a verb, some important tenses are given. Some of the 'Language extra' panels give you extra grammar information and more examples. Pages 599 and 600 bring together in one place all the information that the dictionary provides on parts of speech and punctuation.

Improving your writing

Using this book regularly will widen your vocabulary. For example, synonyms can make your writing less repetitive. Similes (phrases that compare one thing with another) strengthen your descriptions and inspire you to make comparisons of your own. Before using a word for the first time, study any examples and check for guidance on how to use the word – for example, a word labelled 'slang' is not usually suitable for writing in your schoolwork. Finally, read any 'Culture note' panels to learn more about unfamiliar words and improve your general knowledge.

Now turn over and look at some dictionary pages. The labels point out the important features and will help you to find your way around.

Finding your way around

Here are two pages of the dictionary. The green labels show you the most important things to look out for when you are finding your way around the book. The other labels give examples of some more of the dictionary's features.

> The big green letters show the start of a **new section**.

> The **guide words** in the top outside corners tell you the first and last words on the page. They help you to find your way around the book.

a–abreast

a A

> The **Origin** panel at the start of each new section tells you the history of the shape of the capital letter.

ORIGIN the capital letter A started life as a picture of the head of an ox in ancient Egyptian hieroglyphics. The Phoenicians changed it so that it looked more like an A but on its side with its point facing left. They called the shape *aleph* meaning 'ox'. The ancient Greeks turned the letter to the right to stand on its two feet like modern A and called it *alpha*, where the first part of the word 'alphabet' comes from. Letter A then passed into Roman and into our own alphabet without any more important changes.

a *indefinite article*
1 one or any one of something *We waited a day. I don't have a bike. A boy bumped into me.*
2 each of something *They cost £2 a kilo.*

LANGUAGE EXTRA *a* is used before a word beginning with a consonant, and *an* before a word beginning with a vowel sound, for example *an ear*

> **Language extra** panels give useful information on alternative spellings and word forms, different ways of using the word, grammar, common errors and points to remember. Look out for **Pronunciation rule** panels, such as the one about 'kn' on page 256.

aardvark *noun* aardvarks
an animal from Africa with a long nose and tongue and a heavy tail. It lives under the ground and eats small insects.

aargh [rhymes with 'are'] *interjection*
a word used for showing that you're angry *Aargh! I forgot my key.*

aback *adverb*
if you are taken aback by something, you are surprised by it, usually in an unpleasant way

abacus *noun* abacuses
a frame with lots of small balls on metal wires. You slide the balls along the wires to help you count and do simple sums.

ORIGIN from Latin *abacus* and Greek *abax* 'board with sand on it for doing calculations'

> The words in black are called **headwords**. They are shown in alphabetical order.

abandon *verb*
abandons, abandoning, abandoned
1 to go away and leave someone or something and never come back *Someone abandoned an old car in my road.*
2 to stop doing something *I abandoned French after two terms.*

abbess *noun* abbesses
a woman in charge of an abbey of nuns

abbey *noun* abbeys
a large church and the buildings around it where monks and nuns live, or used to live in the past

abbot *noun* abbots
a man in charge of an abbey of monks

abbreviate *verb*
abbreviates, abbreviating, abbreviated
to make a word or expression shorter *Physical education is usually abbreviated to PE.*

> The descriptions under the headwords are called **definitions**. They tell you what the word means. All the information given about each headword is called a **dictionary entry**. See **Taking a closer look** for more about dictionary entries.

abbreviation *noun* abbreviations
a shorter form of a word or expression

LANGUAGE EXTRA some examples of *abbreviations* are: *Dr* (Doctor), *Rd* (Road), *Oct* (October) and *RAF* (Royal Air Force)

ABC *noun*
a way of talking about the alphabet and all its letters *Do you know your ABC?*

abdomen *noun* abdomens
1 the front part of your body below your chest, where your stomach is
2 the abdomen of an insect such as a grasshopper is the back part of its body

abdominal *adjective*
connected with the abdomen *abdominal pains*

abduct *verb*
abducts, abducting, abducted
to abduct someone is to take them away using force **abduction** *noun*

SYNONYM to kidnap

abide *verb*
abides, abiding, abided
1 if you abide by the rules, you accept and obey them
2 if you can't abide someone or something, you do not like them even a little bit

ability *noun*
1 being able to do something *Having a comfortable bed can improve your ability to sleep.*
2 (*plural* abilities) the skill to do something, or a particular skill *a singer of great ability; painters of all abilities*

ablaze *adjective*
burning with lots of flames *The whole house was ablaze.*

able *adjective* abler, ablest
1 if you are able to do something, you know how to do it or it is possible for you to do it *Are you able to ride a bike? I was able to get to school on time.*
2 good at doing something *a very able footballer*

-able *suffix*
used for making adjectives that show something that can be done or a particular quality that something or someone has *drinkable; comfortable; likeable*

ably *adverb*
if you do something ably, you do it very well

abnormal *adjective*
different from normal in a way that is strange or worrying

abnormality *noun* abnormalities
a part of something that is abnormal, especially a part of the body

aboard *adverb & preposition*
if you go aboard a ship, plane or train, you go onto it *What time do we go aboard? All the passengers were aboard the ship.*

abode *noun* abodes
the place where someone lives

abolish *verb*
abolishes, abolishing, abolished
to get rid of something that people often consider to be bad *Slavery was abolished more than 200 years ago.* **abolition** *noun*

abominable *adjective*
very bad

CULTURE NOTE some people believe there is a frightening creature called the *abominable snowman* that looks like a hairy person and lives in the Himalayan mountains

> **Culture note** panels tell you fascinating facts about history, traditions and other topics.

Aboriginal *noun* Aboriginals
another word for an Aborigine
Aboriginal *adjective*

Aborigine ['ab-er-rij-ern-ee'] *noun* Aborigines
an Australian man or woman belonging to the group of people who were living in Australia before the Europeans arrived

> **Proper nouns** like these are given, together with other names such as those referring to historical periods.

abort *verb*
aborts, aborting, aborted
1 to stop something from happening on your computer *Do you want to abort the print command?*
2 to stop an activity that has already begun *The space mission was aborted.*

abound *verb*
abounds, abounding, abounded
if things or animals abound, there are lots of them *Deer abound in Epping Forest.*

about *preposition*
1 used when mentioning a subject or the reason for something, or something connected with something else *a film about monsters; I'm worried about my exams. I've been thinking about what you said. I don't know what to do about it.*
2 all around something *Toys lay scattered about the room.*

about *adverb*
1 slightly more or less than something such as a number or amount *about 25 people; about half an hour*
2 in many different places *Don't leave your school things lying about. The kids were running about.*
3 used for saying that someone is near to where you are or that something exists *Is David about? There's a lot of flu about.*
4 to be about to do something is to be going to do it straightaway or very soon *I'm about to leave.*

above *preposition & adverb*
higher than something *The temperature was above 20 degrees. There was banging coming from the room above.*

above board *adjective*
honest and legal

abracadabra *interjection*
a word people say before doing a magic trick to make it successful

ORIGIN from Greek *abrasadabra*, a word used by an early Christian sect when asking God for help

abrasive *adjective*
1 very rude *an abrasive manner*
2 an abrasive material, such as sandpaper, is rough and used for rubbing surfaces

abreast *adverb*
1 side by side, going in the same direction *We were walking four abreast.*

1

> A **synonym** is a word that **means the same** as another word – 'to kidnap' means the same as 'to abduct'. An **antonym** is a word that **means the opposite** to another word. For example, see page 2, where the antonym of 'abundant' is given as 'scarce'. Many synonyms and antonyms are given in this dictionary.

> **Interjections** are words used for showing feelings or when greeting someone. It is useful to know how to spell them, especially if you are writing down what someone says.

> A **suffix** is added to the **end of a word** to change its meaning. A **prefix** is added to the **beginning of a word** to change its meaning, for example see 'bi-' on page 37. Important suffixes and prefixes are given as headwords in this dictionary.

vi

Important **faith words** from all the main religions are included. Other faith words in the first part of the book include 'Adi Granth', 'Advent', 'Buddha', 'Chanukah', 'Diwali' and 'Eid'.

alias – allowed

Origin panels for some words tell you where the word comes from. Knowing the origin of a word sometimes helps you to spell it.

alias ['ay-lee-ers] *noun* aliases
a name that someone uses instead of their real name, for example because they are a spy or criminal

alias ['ay-lee-ers] *preposition*
used when giving another name that someone uses, for example in a film or TV show *James Bond, alias 007*

alibi ['a-li-bye] *noun* alibis
something that proves someone did not commit a crime because it shows they were somewhere else when the crime happened

ORIGIN from Latin *alibi* 'somewhere else'

You will come across **old words** and some **old ways of using words** throughout the dictionary. This meaning of 'alien' was still used in the 20th century, but some words in the dictionary are much older, for example 'alas' (see page 10), and 'dale' and 'damsel' (page 107).

alien *noun* aliens
1 in stories, an alien is a being from another planet
2 an old-fashioned word for someone who is not a citizen of the country where they live

alien *adjective*
1 very different from what you know and understand *These ideas are completely alien to me.*
2 connected with beings from another planet *An alien spaceship has landed.*
3 foreign

ORIGIN from Latin *alienus* 'belonging to something or someone else'

alienate *verb*
alienates, alienating, alienated
if someone or something alienates you, you have bad feelings about them or are made to feel that you are not wanted

alienation *noun*
the feeling of not being wanted or when you have bad feelings about something *the alienation of young people*

alight *adjective*
1 burning
2 to set something alight is to start a fire in or on it *Some vandals set his car alight.*

alight *verb*
alights, alighting, alighted
to alight from a train or bus is to get off

align *verb*
aligns, aligning, aligned
to align objects is to arrange them in a straight line *The boxes were neatly aligned along the wall.*

alike *adverb*
in the same way *Anil and his brother were dressed alike.*

alike *adjective*
similar in some way *We're alike, you and I.*

SIMILE 'as alike as two peas in a pod' means very similar to each other

A **simile** is a way of describing something by comparing it to something else. Look out for **Simile** panels throughout this book.

alive *adjective*
1 living and not dead *Is the goldfish still alive?*
2 full of energy or activity *You feel so alive when you walk around London. The town comes alive in August.*

This dictionary includes most of the specialist words relating to all the **school curriculum subjects**. Here is a word from the science curriculum. See if you can find on this page a word from the English curriculum.

alkali ['al-ker-lye] *noun* alkalis
a chemical substance that forms a salt when mixed with an acid. Alkalis turn litmus paper blue.

alkaline ['al-ker-lyne] *adjective*
an alkaline substance contains an alkali

all *adjective, adverb & pronoun*
1 the whole of something *I've eaten all the chocolate – all of it. All is well.*
2 every person or thing *All my friends came. All books must be returned to the library.*
3 the only thing *That's all I'm saying*
4 completely *My homework is all finished.*
5 **all along** from the beginning *I've known all along that she was hiding something.*
6 (*informal*) **all in** very tired *I'm all in after that swim.*
7 **all of a sudden** suddenly
8 **all the best** used for saying you hope things are good for someone, for example as a friendly way of saying goodbye, often at the end of an email or letter
9 **all the same** when something doesn't make any difference *Caleb doesn't like me but I want to be his friend all the same.*
10 (*informal*) **not all there** slightly mad *Your brother's not all there!*

Allah *noun*
the name people give to God in the Muslim religion

all-clear *noun*
1 a sound or signal that tells you a situation is not dangerous any more
2 if someone gets the all-clear, they are told they can go ahead with their plan
3 if a sick person gets the all-clear, a doctor tells them they no longer need to worry about their health

allegation *noun* allegations
if you make an allegation, you say someone has done something wrong

allege [rhymes with 'edge'] *verb*
alleges, alleging, alleged
to say that someone has done something wrong but without proving that this is true *She alleged that I hit her little brother.*

allegedly ['er-lej-id-lee] *adverb*
if you say something allegedly happened, you mean it is true that it happened because you or others say so but you have no proof *The meeting allegedly took place last year.*

allegiance ['er-lee-jerns] *noun* allegiances
support that you give to a person, country or group because of a feeling of duty and love

allegory *noun* allegories
a story, poem or painting where the different characters, places or things are symbols of something else, such as religious or political ideas **allegorical** *adjective*

allergic *adjective*
1 if you're allergic to something like dust or milk, you have an allergy to it
2 (*informal*) if you don't like something, for example work or PE or travelling on buses, you can say you're allergic to it

allergy *noun* allergies
a medical condition where you become ill or get spots on your skin when you eat, drink or touch something or when you breathe something in *He has an allergy to milk.*

alley *noun* alleys
1 a very narrow street with buildings on both sides
2 a bowling alley is a place where people go to play the game of bowling

alleyway *noun* alleyways
another word for an alley

alliance ['er-lye-erns] *noun* alliances
an agreement between countries or political groups to help each other and to work together

Allied *adjective*
connected with the countries that fought on the same side as Britain, France and the US in the First and Second World Wars *Allied soldiers*

Allies *noun plural*
see: **ally**

alligator *noun* alligators
a large animal like a crocodile with a long body, short legs and a large mouth with sharp teeth. Alligators live in rivers and lakes in the United States and China.

ORIGIN from Spanish *el lagarto* 'the lizard'

alliteration *noun*
when a writer or poet uses the same sound at the beginning of several words in a sentence *Poppy painted a pretty picture.*

allocate *verb*
allocates, allocating, allocated
to allocate something to someone is to give it to them, especially when someone makes an official decision to do it

allocation *noun*
1 (*plural* allocations) something that has been allocated *an allocation of tickets*
2 the action of allocating something

allot *verb*
allots, allotting, allotted
to allot something to someone is to give it to them, often as part of their share of something

allotment *noun* allotments
a small piece of ground that someone rents for growing vegetables on

allow *verb*
allows, allowing, allowed
1 to give someone permission to do something or let them do it *She allowed us to go out to play. Am I allowed to watch TV?*
2 to let someone have something *My parents allow me pocket money every week. Allow yourself plenty of time.*
3 to make it possible for something to happen *The police officer turned round, which allowed the prisoner to escape.*
4 to allow for something is to take something into consideration, for example in order to deal with it

allowance *noun* allowances
1 an amount of money that someone gives you regularly for a particular purpose
2 if you make allowances for someone, you forgive their behaviour

allowed *adjective*
1 used for saying that you can do something in a particular situation or in a game because the rules say that you can do it *Playing football in the playground is allowed. Is this move allowed in chess?*

This is a **cross-reference**. It tells you to go to the headword 'ally' to find out about 'Allies'. Some cross-references use the word *compare* instead of *see*, for example look at 'A level' on page 10. Comparing similar words can help you to understand them.

Precise definitions give you the information you need and help you to tell the difference between similar things, for example different kinds of animals, birds or trees.

If the word is used in a particular way, for example if it is a **slang** word or an **informal** word, this is shown.

Words about **parts of the body**, **health** and **illnesses** are explained in a direct way that you will understand easily.

vii

Taking a closer look

Here is some text taken from another part of the dictionary. The green labels show you the most important things to look out for at each dictionary entry. The other labels show you examples of some more features.

The *black italic* word next to a headword tells you the part of speech. For example, 'strategy' is a noun. Which other parts of speech can you find on this page and in **Finding your way around**?

Words that belong to the same word family as the headword are sometimes given in bold at the end of an entry. Their part of speech is shown beside them.

The *green italic* text gives you examples. You can see how the word is used in one or more phrases or sentences.

The text in square brackets helps you with pronunciation. It tells you how to say the word. If part of it is in **bold** (like '**strah**' in '**strah**-term'), you say this part more strongly. Don't mix up pronunciation with spelling. The spelling is always given in the headword.

The dictionary defines all the senses (different meanings) of a word that are useful for you. Each sense is numbered.

If the headword is a noun, the word in black after the part of speech shows you the plural. For example, the plural of 'strawberry' is 'strawberries'.

If the headword is a verb, you are given the third person singular in the present tense (for example 'He or she **strays**'), the **present participle** ('I am **straying**'), and the **past tense** and **past participle** ('I **strayed**', 'I have **strayed**').

If the headword is an adjective, special comparative and superlative forms may be given. The comparative of 'streaky' is 'streakier' and the superlative is 'streakiest'.

---

strategy *noun*
1 (*plural* **strategies**) a plan or plans for doing something important that needs a lot of careful thinking over a long period of time
2 the skill or activity of making important plans, for example in a game of chess or a computer game
strategic *adjective*

stratosphere *noun*
the stratosphere is the air and gases in the atmosphere around the earth, between 10 and 50 kilometres above the earth

stratum ['strah-term] *noun*
strata ['strah-ter]
in geology, a stratum is a layer of rock or earth

straw *noun*
1 the dry cut yellow stems of some plants that produce grain such as wheat or oats. Straw is used, for example, for making things such as mats and baskets, for giving to animals such as cows to eat or sleep on, and for wrapping around things to protect them. *an old mattress filled with straw; a straw hat*
2 (*plural* **straws**) a long thin tube of plastic or paper that you use for drinking cold drinks by sucking the liquid up into your mouth *He was drinking lemonade through a straw.*
3 **the last straw** or **the final straw** used about another bad thing that someone has just done or that has just happened, which makes someone decide they can no longer put up with a bad situation *This is the seventh day you've behaved badly and that's the last straw – no pocket money for two weeks!*

strawberry *noun* **strawberries**
a small soft red fruit that you eat. It has lots of yellow dots on its skin that look like seeds. Strawberries grow on plants close to the ground.

stray *verb*
strays, straying, strayed
1 if a person or animal strays, they move away from the place where they should be or from the path they should be following *Don't stray too far from the campsite. Your dog has strayed into our garden.*
2 to talk about something different from what you should be talking about *We seem to have strayed from the subject.*
3 to think about something different from what you should be thinking about *I was bored in class and my mind kept straying.*
4 to move somewhere or move about without ... *My eyes strayed ...*

2 used for talking about one particular quality of someone's character, often an unpleasant one *My uncle has a mean streak.*
3 used for talking about the number of times someone wins or loses, for example in a game or sport, when these happen one after the other *Our team had a lucky (or winning) streak (for example, won several matches one after the other). Dad's playing cards and he's on a losing streak.*

streak *verb*
streaks, streaking, streaked
1 to make thin marks or lines of a different colour go onto or into something *cheeks streaked with tears; My dad has black hair streaked with grey. My sister had her hair streaked (the hairdresser put coloured lines in it using special chemicals).*
2 to move somewhere very fast

streaky *adjective* **streakier, streakiest**
1 marked with streaks *streaky windows*
2 streaky bacon is bacon (meat from a pig) with thin lines of fat in it

stream *noun* **streams**
1 a small narrow river
2 used about something that keeps moving or flowing without stopping, for example water in a pipe or traffic on a road *A stream of water was pouring out of the gutter. There's been a steady stream of visitors going into the exhibition.*

stream *verb*
streams, streaming, streamed
1 used about a liquid that flows strongly and without stopping *Tears were streaming down her face. Blood streamed from the soldier's wounded leg.*
2 if people or things stream somewhere, large numbers or amounts of them go there quickly and without stopping *Football fans were streaming out of the stadium. Emails are streaming into the BBC about last night's film. Sally opened the curtains and sunlight came streaming into the room.*
3 if you stream something such as a film, programme or song on your computer, you watch or listen to it straight from the internet instead of downloading it first, or you watch or listen to it at the same time as it is being downloaded *Click on this icon to start streaming the song. Don't disconnect the router – my film is streaming.*

streamer *noun* **streamers**
streamers are long strips of coloured paper

2 **down** (or **up** or **along**) **the street** ... short distance away in the same street *My uncle lives down the street.*
3 **across the street** on the opposite side of the street
4 (*informal*) **up your street** used about something such as an activity that you know a lot about and that you are interested in

streetcar *noun* **streetcars**
the American word for a tram

streetlight *noun* **streetlights**
a light at the top of a tall post that stands at the side of a street

LANGUAGE EXTRA you can also say **streetlamp**

strength *noun*
1 the power you have to do things with your body such as lift, move, push and pull heavy things or hit things hard, or the power that a part of your body has to do these things *My sister kicked me with all her strength. The lion killed the antelope because of its greater strength. Look at the strength of the boxer's arms. I didn't have the strength to get up from the chair.*
2 the power something has to move or hold something heavy or to be treated roughly without breaking or getting damaged *We used ropes of great strength to hold down the sails. Because of its strength, the fence didn't fall down in the wind.*
3 having a lot of something such as heat, light, speed or sound *the strength of the sun's rays; the strength of the wind; The boat capsized because of the strength of the current*
4 the influence that someone or something has *The strength of the Labour Party is mainly in the north of England.*
5 (*plural* **strengths**) a good quality that someone or something has *Being able to run fast is one of David's strengths (one of the things he's good at). My new tablet has more strengths than weaknesses.*

strengthen *verb*
strengthens, strengthening, strengthened
1 to make something or someone stronger *Cycling is good for strengthening your leg muscles. If I stay over at Ben's, it will help to strengthen our friendship.*
2 to become stronger *The wind strengthened during the night.*

strenuous *adjective*
needing or showing a lot of hard work and energy *strenuous exercises. They made ...*

Idioms have a meaning that is different from the usual meaning. The idiom 'up your street' has nothing to do with a street.

Some **American words** are given as headwords or are mentioned in **Language extra** or **Culture note** panels.

In some examples and definitions, you will see black text inside brackets. This **explains the meaning** of words used in the example or definition.

For some **nouns**, the **plural** is not shown after the part of speech. Instead, it is shown in one or more of the different senses. This tells you which senses can be used in the plural. For example, only sense 5 of 'strength' can be used in the plural.

New uses of old words and completely **new words** are always being invented. When this book was first published, words such as 'phablet', 'selfie' and 'chillax' were quite new – as was this use of the verb 'stream'.

viii

a A

ORIGIN the capital letter A started life as a picture of the head of an ox in ancient Egyptian hieroglyphics. The Phoenicians changed it so that it looked more like an A but on its side with its point facing left. They called the shape *aleph* meaning 'ox'. The ancient Greeks turned the letter to the right to stand on its two feet like modern A and called it *alpha*, where the first part of the word 'alphabet' comes from. Letter A then passed into Roman and into our own alphabet without any more important changes.

a *indefinite article*
1 one or any one of something *We waited a day. I don't have a bike. A boy bumped into me.*
2 each of something *They cost £2 a kilo.*

LANGUAGE EXTRA *a* is used before a word beginning with a consonant, and *an* before a word beginning with a vowel sound, for example *an ear*

aardvark *noun* **aardvarks**
an animal from Africa with a long nose and tongue and a heavy tail. It lives under the ground and eats small insects.

aargh [rhymes with 'are'] *interjection*
a word used for showing that you're angry *Aargh! I forgot my key.*

aback *adverb*
if you are taken aback by something, you are surprised by it, usually in an unpleasant way

abacus *noun* **abacuses**
a frame with lots of small balls on metal wires. You slide the balls along the wires to help you count and do simple sums.

ORIGIN from Latin *abacus* and Greek *abax* 'board with sand on it for doing calculations'

abandon *verb*
abandons, abandoning, abandoned
1 to go away and leave someone or something and never come back *Someone abandoned an old car in my road.*
2 to stop doing something *I abandoned French after two terms.*

abbess *noun* **abbesses**
a woman in charge of an abbey of nuns

abbey *noun* **abbeys**
a large church and the buildings around it where monks and nuns live, or used to live in the past

abbot *noun* **abbots**
a man in charge of an abbey of monks

abbreviate *verb*
abbreviates, abbreviating, abbreviated
to make a word or expression shorter *Physical education is usually abbreviated to PE.*

abbreviation *noun* **abbreviations**
a shorter form of a word or expression

LANGUAGE EXTRA some examples of *abbreviations* are: *Dr* (Doctor), *Rd* (Road), *Oct* (October) and *RAF* (Royal Air Force)

ABC *noun*
a way of talking about the alphabet and all its letters *Do you know your ABC?*

abdomen *noun* **abdomens**
1 the front part of your body below your chest, where your stomach is
2 the abdomen of an insect such as a grasshopper is the back part of its body

abdominal *adjective*
connected with the abdomen *abdominal pains*

abduct *verb*
abducts, abducting, abducted
to abduct someone is to take them away using force **abduction** *noun*

SYNONYM to kidnap

abide *verb*
abides, abiding, abided
1 if you abide by the rules, you accept and obey them
2 if you can't abide someone or something, you do not like them even a little bit

ability *noun*
1 being able to do something *Having a comfortable bed can improve your ability to sleep.*
2 (*plural* **abilities**) the skill to do something, or a particular skill *a singer of great ability*; *painters of all abilities*

ablaze *adjective*
burning with lots of flames *The whole house was ablaze.*

able *adjective* **abler, ablest**
1 if you are able to do something, you know how to do it or it is possible for you to do it *Are you able to ride a bike? I was able to get to school on time.*
2 good at doing something *a very able footballer*

-able *suffix*
used for making adjectives that show something that can be done or a particular quality that something or someone has *drinkable*; *comfortable*; *likeable*

ably *adverb*
if you do something ably, you do it very well

abnormal *adjective*
different from normal in a way that is strange or worrying

abnormality *noun* **abnormalities**
a part of something that is abnormal, especially a part of the body

aboard *adverb & preposition*
if you go aboard a ship, plane or train, you go onto it *What time do we go aboard? All the passengers were aboard the ship.*

abode *noun* **abodes**
the place where someone lives

abolish *verb*
abolishes, abolishing, abolished
to get rid of something that people often consider to be bad *Slavery was abolished more than 200 years ago.* **abolition** *noun*

abominable *adjective*
very bad

CULTURE NOTE some people believe there is a frightening creature called the *abominable snowman* that looks like a hairy person and lives in the Himalayan mountains

Aboriginal *noun* **Aboriginals**
another word for an Aborigine
Aboriginal *adjective*

Aborigine ['ab-er-rij-ern-ee'] *noun* **Aborigines**
an Australian man or woman belonging to the group of people who were living in Australia before the Europeans arrived

abort *verb*
aborts, aborting, aborted
1 to stop something from happening on your computer *Do you want to abort the print command?*
2 to stop an activity that has already begun *The space mission was aborted.*

abound *verb*
abounds, abounding, abounded
if things or animals abound, there are lots of them *Deer abound in Epping Forest.*

about *preposition*
1 used when mentioning a subject or the reason for something, or something connected with something else *a film about monsters*; *I'm worried about my exams. I've been thinking about what you said. I don't know what to do about it.*
2 all around something *Toys lay scattered about the room.*

about *adverb*
1 slightly more or less than something such as a number or amount *about 25 people*; *about half an hour*
2 in many different places *Don't leave your school things lying about. The kids were running about.*
3 used for saying that someone is near to where you are or that something exists *Is David about? There's a lot of flu about.*
4 to be about to do something is to be going to do it straightaway or very soon *I'm about to leave.*

above *preposition & adverb*
higher than something *The temperature was above 20 degrees. There was banging coming from the room above.*

above board *adjective*
honest and legal

abracadabra *interjection*
a word people say before doing a magic trick to make it successful

ORIGIN from Greek *abrasadabra*, a word used by an early Christian sect when asking God for help

abrasive *adjective*
1 very rude *an abrasive manner*
2 an abrasive material, such as sandpaper, is rough and used for rubbing surfaces

abreast *adverb*
1 side by side, going in the same direction *We were walking four abreast.*

abridged–accept

2 to keep abreast of something is to know all about the latest things happening *It's hard to keep abreast of developments in computing.*

abridged *adjective*
an abridged edition of a book or play is one that is shorter than the original

abroad *adverb*
in or to another country *Have you ever been abroad?*

abrupt *adjective*
1 very rude to people *Dad is often abrupt when people disturb him at work.*
2 sudden and unexpected *The conversation came to an abrupt end.*
abruptly *adverb* **abruptness** *noun*

abscess *noun* **abscesses**
a swelling on the skin or inside the body. It is filled with a yellowish liquid called pus and is usually painful.

abscond *verb*
absconds, absconding, absconded
if someone absconds from a place where they must stay, such as a prison, they run away from there

abseil ['ab-sayl'] *verb*
abseils, abseiling, abseiled
to climb down a large rock or tall building using a rope

ORIGIN from German *abseilen* 'to go down by rope' (*ab* 'down' and *Seil* 'rope')

absence *noun*
1 (plural **absences**) a period of time when you are not in a place where you should be or where you normally are *My grandparents returned home after an absence of three weeks. Ms Singh warned me about my absences* (told me I'd been away from school too many times). *Mum gave me an absence note* (message to the teacher explaining the reason for not being at school).
2 when something or someone does not exist *We were surprised by the absence of our team from the football league.*

absent *adjective*
if you are absent, you are not in a place where you should be, such as school or work, for example because you are ill

absentee *noun* **absentees**
someone who is absent, for example from school or work

absent-minded *adjective*
if you are absent-minded, you forget things easily

absent-mindedly *adverb*
without paying attention to what you're doing

absolute *adjective*
complete *That's absolute nonsense!*

absolutely *adverb*
1 used for giving special importance to a word *I know absolutely nothing about football. Are you absolutely sure?*

SYNONYM completely

2 used as a way of saying yes or when you agree with what someone says *'Do you like Shakespeare?' – 'Absolutely.'*

absorb *verb*
absorbs, absorbing, absorbed
1 if something absorbs something else such as a liquid or light, it takes it into itself *Plants absorb food from the soil.*
2 to learn completely *We have to absorb lots of facts for history.*
3 if someone is absorbed in something, they are so interested in it that they don't pay attention to anything else *I was completely absorbed in my book.*
absorption *noun*

absorbent *adjective*
material that is absorbent takes in liquid easily, like a sponge

abstract *adjective*
1 not connected with things, people or actions but based on ideas *abstract thinking*
2 in abstract paintings or art there are shapes or patterns instead of things or people

LANGUAGE EXTRA abstract nouns are connected with ideas, not things or people, for example *intelligence*, *happiness* and *beauty*

abstract *noun* **abstracts**
a short piece of writing that briefly describes the main points of something such as a book or article

absurd *adjective*
stupid and not making any sense *an absurd idea* **absurdity** *noun* **absurdly** *adverb*

abundance *noun*
a large amount of something *an abundance of spiders*

abundant *adjective*
used for describing something that there is a lot of or things that there are lots of *abundant rainfall*; *Jobs are abundant in this part of the country.*

ANTONYM scarce

abuse ['erb-yooz'] *verb*
abuses, abusing, abused
1 to abuse someone is to cause them pain by treating them in a very cruel or violent way *The poor boy was abused as a child.*
2 to say very rude things to someone *He was sent home from school for abusing his teacher.*
3 to abuse something is to use it in a harmful way or for bad reasons *Don't abuse your body by taking drugs.*

abuse ['erb-yooss'] *noun*
1 cruel or violent treatment that causes pain or harm to someone *He suffered months of abuse.*
2 very rude words said to someone *She shouted abuse at me.*
3 (plural **abuses**) using something in a harmful way or for bad reasons *abuses of power*

abusive *adjective*
1 saying very rude words to someone *He became very abusive.*
2 treating someone in a cruel or violent way *an abusive father*

abysmal *adjective*
very bad *The exam results were abysmal.*
abysmally *adverb*

abyss *noun* **abysses**
1 a deep hole that has no bottom
2 a very frightening and terrible situation *a country on the brink of an abyss*

academic *adjective*
1 connected with education, schools or universities *the academic year* (period from autumn to summer when students go to school or university)
2 good at learning things *He's not very academic.*
3 if something someone says is academic, it is not worth talking about because it is not connected to anything that really happened or is going to happen *The question of when I'm going to visit Grandma is academic as I don't have any time.*

academic *noun* **academics**
someone who teaches or does research at a university

academy *noun* **academies**
1 a school or college
2 an organisation of scholars that encourages learning *the Royal Academy of Arts*

ORIGIN from the Greek *Akademeia*, the gardens near Athens that belonged to *Akademos*, a hero of Greek mythology. Plato taught his school of philosophy there.

accelerate *verb*
accelerates, accelerating, accelerated
1 to go faster *The car accelerated when it reached the motorway.*
2 to make something go faster
acceleration *noun*

accelerator *noun* **accelerators**
a pedal in a car that a driver presses down with his or her foot to make the car start to move or to make it go faster

accent ['ak-sent'] *noun* **accents**
1 a particular way of pronouncing words that shows where you come from *He has a Welsh accent.*
2 the part of a word that you pronounce more strongly *In 'sunshine' the accent is on 'sun'.*
3 if a letter in a foreign word has an accent, it has a special mark above or below it, usually to show how it is pronounced *In the French word 'château' there's an accent on the 'a'.*

accent ['erk-sent'] *verb*
accents, accenting, accented
to accent part of a word is to pronounce it more strongly

accept *verb*
accepts, accepting, accepted
1 to take something that someone offers you or say yes to it *I accepted the prize. Will you accept the invitation?*
2 to recognise that something is true, right or correct *The police officer wouldn't accept Jo's explanation. Mum accepted my apology. We had a class quiz but not many of my answers were accepted.*
3 to recognise a situation that you cannot change *He must accept that he won't see his best friend again.*
4 to allow someone to become part of something *I was accepted into a good school.*

acceptable – accusation

5 to recognise that something is good and often decide to do something, for example use it *My poem has been accepted by the school magazine. My friends accepted my suggestion to play football instead.*
6 to recognise something as being official or trusted *The US dollar is accepted all over the world.*
7 to say that you are responsible for something or that something is your fault *Jack fully accepted his mistakes.*
8 if a machine accepts something such as a coin, ticket or card, you put this particular thing into the machine to make it work
acceptance *noun*

acceptable *adjective*
1 good enough to be accepted or good enough to be considered very reasonable *acceptable behaviour; Your ideas are acceptable.*
2 reasonable but not very good *The food was acceptable but not very tasty.*

access *verb*
accesses, accessing, accessed
to find information on a computer or to get into a computer program *I can't access my mailbox.*

access *noun*
1 the opportunity or right to have, use or get to something *The internet gives us access to lots of information.*
2 a way of getting to a place *Access to the castle is on foot.*

accessible *adjective*
1 an accessible place is easy to get to
2 easy for everyone to have, use or understand *accessible information*
3 an accessible person is easy to talk to
accessibility *noun*

accession *noun*
1 the accession of a king or queen is the time when he or she starts to rule
2 the accession of a country is the time when it joins other countries to form a group *Ireland's accession to the EU*

accessory *noun* accessories
1 an extra part added to something to make it more useful or attractive *car accessories; On my laptop you find the calculator in the Accessories folder.*
2 something such as a handbag, belt or piece of jewellery that goes with your clothes to give them more style *a fashion accessory*

accident *noun* accidents
1 an accident is when a road vehicle, train or aircraft hits something or someone, or when something bad happens suddenly that causes damage, injury or death *a helicopter accident; a skiing accident*
2 something that happens by chance and without planning *Penicillin was discovered by accident.*
3 if someone is accident prone, they are clumsy and likely to have more accidents than other people

accidental *adjective*
happening by chance, not done on purpose

accidentally *adverb*
to do something accidentally is to do it when you didn't mean to

acclaim *verb*
acclaims, acclaiming, acclaimed
if someone or something is acclaimed, they are praised by many people *Her latest film was widely acclaimed.*

acclaim *noun*
great praise from many people

acclimatise *verb*
acclimatises, acclimatising, acclimatised
to get used to something new *They're trying to acclimatise to the cold British winters.*

LANGUAGE EXTRA also spelt *acclimatize*

accommodate *verb*
accommodates, accommodating, accommodated
1 to provide someone with somewhere to stay or live
2 to find space for someone or something *Two more students can be accommodated on the bus.*

LANGUAGE EXTRA be careful to spell *accommodate* with two cs and two ms, not one

accommodation *noun*
a place to stay or live *student accommodation*

accompaniment *noun* accompaniments
a musical accompaniment is music played by an instrument that supports the main tune *a piano accompaniment*

accompanist *noun* accompanists
someone who plays a musical instrument while someone else plays or sings the main tune

accompany *verb*
accompanies, accompanying, accompanied
1 to go somewhere with someone *All children must be accompanied by an adult.*
2 to play a musical instrument such as the piano or violin while someone else plays or sings the main tune *My sister accompanied me on the violin.*

accomplice *noun* accomplices
a person who helps someone commit a crime

accomplish *verb*
accomplishes, accomplishing, accomplished
to accomplish something is to be able to do something difficult that you try very hard to do *You've accomplished a lot this term.*

accomplished *adjective*
doing something very well *an accomplished painter*

accomplishment *noun* accomplishments
1 something difficult that you have done very well *Passing these exams is a great accomplishment.*
2 a skill that you are good at *He has many accomplishments.*

accord *noun*
if you do something of your own accord, you decide to do it yourself without anyone telling you

accordingly *adverb*
1 in a way that is decided by a situation *This dog is dangerous and should be treated accordingly.*
2 for that reason, therefore

according to *preposition*
1 used for showing the person or place that a piece of information or an idea comes from *According to the book, Harry is 10 years old.*
2 in a way that follows a set of rules or a plan *We must play according to the rules.*
3 in a way that is decided by something else *Your place in the team will be decided according to how hard you work.*

accordion *noun* accordions
a musical instrument shaped like a box, with keys (long narrow bars) like a piano at one side and buttons at the other side. You play it by holding it in both hands and squeezing it in and out while pressing the keys and buttons.

account *noun* accounts
1 a description of something that happens *He gave a detailed account of the accident.*
2 if you have a bank account, you have an agreement with a bank to look after your money *I have £100 in my account.*
3 a way of using something on the internet, for example email or a website such as Facebook, by making an agreement with an internet company and giving them information about yourself *How do you create an email account? My brother signed up for a Facebook account.*
4 a piece of paper showing amounts of money that people have spent and received and especially amounts that people owe *Please pay your account by Friday.*
5 if you take something into account, you consider it when making a decision
6 **on account of** because of
7 **on no account** used for saying that someone must definitely not do something *On no account cross the road by yourself.*

account *verb*
accounts, accounting, accounted
to account for something is to explain the reason for it *They're having a party and that accounts for the loud music.*

accountant *noun* accountants
someone whose job is to prepare and check people's money records and to work out people's taxes **accountancy** *noun*

accumulate *verb*
accumulates, accumulating, accumulated
1 if you accumulate things, you get more of them as time passes
2 if things accumulate, they gradually increase as time passes
accumulation *noun*

accurate *adjective*
1 exactly right *The numbers are accurate.*
2 exactly done *an accurate aim*
accuracy *noun*

accurately *adverb*
exactly *Mum set the time accurately.*

accusation *noun* accusations
words accusing someone of doing something wrong *He denied the accusation.*

3

accuse – act

accuse *verb*
accuses, accusing, accused
to say that someone has done something wrong *They accused me of cheating.*

accustomed *adjective*
if you are accustomed to something, you think it is normal because you have done it so many times or have known it for so long *She's accustomed to the cold Scottish winters.*

SYNONYM 'to be used to' means the same as 'to be accustomed to'

ace *noun* aces
1 in a game of cards, an ace is a card that has just one symbol on it. It is usually the card with the highest value. *the ace of diamonds*
2 a very skilful person *He's an ace at quizzes.*

ace *adjective*
very skilful *an ace pilot*

ache *noun* aches
a steady pain in a part of your body *a tummy ache*

ache *verb*
aches, aching, ached
to hurt *My arm is aching.*

achieve *verb*
achieves, achieving, achieved
to be successful in getting or doing something after a lot of hard work *You've achieved excellent results in your exams.*

LANGUAGE EXTRA remember that *i* comes before *e* in achieve

achievement *noun* achievements
something important that you have done successfully after a lot of hard work *an outstanding achievement*

achiever *noun* achievers
a high achiever is someone who is very successful because they work hard

achoo *interjection*
the sound you make when you sneeze

LANGUAGE EXTRA also spelt *atchoo*

achy *adjective* achier, achiest (informal)
1 if you're achy, you have steady pains in your body
2 if a part of your body is achy, you feel a pain in it

acid *noun* acids
1 a chemical substance that contains hydrogen and turns litmus paper red. Strong acids can hurt your skin.
2 a chemical in the stomach that helps you to digest food (change it so your body can use it)

acid *adjective*
tasting sour, like an apple that is not ripe

acidic *adjective*
sour *an acidic taste*

acid rain *noun*
rain that contains acid and is caused by chemicals in the air, for example from factories and cars. It damages buildings, plants and trees.

acknowledge *verb*
acknowledges, acknowledging, acknowledged
1 to say that something is true *You must acknowledge your mistakes.*
2 to tell someone that you have received something, such as a letter or email
3 to thank someone for what they have done *I wish to acknowledge the help that my teachers have given me.*
4 to give a sign to someone that you have seen them, for example by smiling or waving

acknowledgement *noun* acknowledgements
1 a letter or message telling someone that you have received something from them
2 an action recognising that something is true
3 thanks given to someone for what they have done

LANGUAGE EXTRA also sometimes spelt *acknowledgment*

acne ['ak-nee'] *noun*
a medical problem that causes red spots on the face. It mainly affects young people.

ORIGIN from Greek *akme* 'point'

acorn *noun* acorns
an oval-shaped nut that is the fruit of an oak tree. Its base has a cover shaped like a cup.

acoustic ['er-koo-stik'] *adjective*
1 connected with sound
2 an acoustic musical instrument is one that does not have its sound made louder by an electrical amplifier *an acoustic guitar*

acoustics *noun plural*
the particular qualities of a room or building, such as size or shape, that affect the way sound is heard there *The acoustics of the Royal Albert Hall are excellent.*

acquaintance *noun* acquaintances
1 someone you know but not very well
2 to make someone's acquaintance is to meet that person for the first time and get to know them

acquainted *adjective*
1 if people are acquainted, they know each other slightly *Are you acquainted with my friend?*
2 if you are acquainted with something, you know it

acquire *verb*
acquires, acquiring, acquired
to get something *Children acquire knowledge very fast.*

LANGUAGE EXTRA be careful to spell *acquire* with a *c* before the *q*

acquisition *noun*
1 (plural acquisitions) something that someone buys or gets
2 the action of acquiring something

acquisitive *adjective*
an acquisitive person is greedy and likes to get and keep lots of things

acquit *verb*
acquits, acquitting, acquitted
1 to acquit someone of a crime is to decide in a court of law that they are not guilty

ANTONYM to convict

2 to acquit yourself well is to do something difficult very well

acquittal *noun* acquittals
in a court of law, a decision that someone is not guilty

acre ['ay-ker'] *noun* acres
a unit for measuring an area of land, equal to 4047 square metres

ORIGIN from Old English *æcer* 'field', 'open land'. It later came to mean an amount of land that a pair of oxen could plough in one day.

acrobat *noun* acrobats
someone who performs skilful actions with their body such as jumping through the air or walking on their hands, usually in a circus **acrobatic** *adjective*

ORIGIN from Greek *akrobatos* 'walking on tiptoe'

acrobatics *noun plural*
skilful exercises of the body such as jumping and balancing

acronym *noun* acronyms
a word made up of the first letters of a name or phrase *'Radar' is an acronym from 'radio detection and ranging'.*

ORIGIN from Greek *akros* 'tip' and *onym* 'name'

across *preposition & adverb*
1 from one side of something to the other *I walked across the road. We have to swim across.*
2 on the other side of something *The school is across the road.*
3 in many parts of something *They have offices across England and Wales.*

acrostic *noun* acrostics
a poem or word puzzle where the first letter of the first word of each line forms a word or phrase

acrylic *adjective*
used about cloth or paint made from an acid by a chemical process

act *noun* acts
1 an action that someone does *a brave act*; *He was caught in the act* (while doing something wrong).
2 a short performance by an entertainer *The comedian had a very funny act.*
3 someone who performs on stage *They're an act that everyone likes.*
4 one of the main parts of a play or opera *Act 1, Scene 3*
5 someone's behaviour that doesn't show their true feelings *I think she was just putting on an act.*
6 a new law made in a parliament
7 if someone gets their act together, they become better organised and can achieve more things

act *verb*
acts, acting, acted
1 to do something *Our teachers acted very fast when the fire alarm went off.*
2 to do things in a certain way *She was acting strangely.*
3 to take part in a play or film
4 to act up is to behave badly

4

action – adequate

action noun
1 (plural **actions**) something that someone does
2 (plural **actions**) a movement made with your body
3 the events of a film or play *The action takes place in Madrid.*
4 exciting things happening, for example in a place or film *There's plenty of action in this western.*
5 fighting in war *Her brother was killed in action.*
6 if something is out of action, it is broken and not working
7 if someone is out of action, they are not able to do what they usually do, for example because they are ill
8 to put something into action is to start it *Tomorrow we'll put our plan into action.*
9 to take action is to deal with something in a very strong way

activate verb
activates, activating, activated
to activate software or a machine is to start using it *You can activate the program by keying in a number code.*

active adjective
1 lively and busy, for example moving about a lot or doing lots of different things *a classroom full of active children*
2 doing a particular activity *He's an active member of our club.*
3 an active volcano is one that can explode at any moment
4 if your mind is active, you keep it healthy by using it a lot, for example by reading, writing or learning a new skill
5 in grammar, the active voice describes a verb where the subject of a sentence does the action. In 'Jack ate the cake', the subject is 'Jack' and 'ate' is an active verb.
compare: **passive**

actively adverb
1 in a way that shows that you really want to do something *My brother is actively looking for a job.*
2 in a very strong way *My parents actively encouraged me to start swimming.*

activity noun
1 when people are busy doing lots of things at the same time *There's a lot of activity in the classroom in the mornings.*
2 (plural **activities**) something that people do for a reason *What's your favourite activity?*
3 activities are things that people do for pleasure or as a sport *I enjoy indoor activities such as swimming and gym.*

actor noun **actors**
a person who plays a part in a film or play

LANGUAGE EXTRA an *actor* can be a woman or girl as well as a man or boy

actress noun **actresses**
a woman or girl who plays a part in a film or play

actual adjective
real *This was Shakespeare's actual house.*

actually adverb
1 really *I've never actually met him.*
2 used for adding something more exact to what you've already said *I play a musical instrument, actually the guitar.*

acupuncture ['ak-yoo-punk-cher] noun
a way of taking away pain and treating illness by putting special needles into parts of a person's body

ORIGIN from Latin *acu* 'with a needle'. Acupuncture started in ancient China.

acute adjective
1 very strong *acute pain*
2 very serious *an acute shortage; The problem has become acute.*
3 very good and sharp *an acute sense of smell*
4 in maths, an acute angle is one that is less than 90 degrees
compare: **obtuse**, **reflex** and **straight**
5 an acute accent is the symbol ´ above a letter in some languages such as French or Spanish, for example é or ó

ad noun **ads**
short for **advertisement**

AD
used for showing a date after the birth of Jesus Christ *Boudicca died in AD 62.*
short for: Anno Domini 'in the year of the Lord'

Adam's apple noun **Adam's apples**
a man's Adam's apple is the lump at the front of his neck

ORIGIN some people say it comes from the biblical story of Adam and Eve, in which a piece of the *apple* that Eve offered to *Adam* got stuck in his throat

adapt verb
adapts, adapting, adapted
1 to change your behaviour to deal with a new situation *She's having trouble adapting to her new school.*
2 to change something to make it suitable for a different purpose *The car has been adapted for a disabled person.*
3 to change a book or play so that it can be turned into a film or television programme

adaptable adjective
able to change your behaviour to deal with new situations

adaptation noun **adaptations**
a film or television programme made from a book or play

adapted adjective
if animals or plants are adapted to their environment, they have developed special features that help them to survive

adapter noun **adapters**
a small object such as a plug for connecting two or more pieces of equipment

LANGUAGE EXTRA also spelt *adaptor*

add verb
adds, adding, added
1 to put numbers together to make a total *If you add five to twenty, you get twenty-five (20 + 5 = 25).*
2 to put something together with something else *She added her name to the list.*
3 to give something extra or make something more *The flowers add colour to the room. That adds to the price.*
4 to say something else *The teacher added that we must be very quiet.*
5 if you add up numbers or if they add up, the numbers are put together to make a total *Seven and nine add up to sixteen.*
6 if things don't add up, they don't make sense *These facts just don't add up.*

adder noun **adders**
a type of snake, usually poisonous

ORIGIN from Old English *nædre* 'snake'

addict noun **addicts**
1 someone who puts harmful drugs into their body and who cannot stop doing it
2 someone who cannot stop doing something because they like it so much *a chocolate addict*

addicted adjective
if someone is addicted to something, such as taking drugs or eating chocolate, they cannot stop doing it **addiction** noun

addictive adjective
if something is addictive, people like doing it so much that they cannot stop *The internet is very addictive.*

addition noun **additions**
1 putting numbers together to make a total or putting something together with something else
2 something added to something else *This book is a useful addition to our library.*
3 in addition to as well as

additional adjective
extra *For additional information go to 'About Us'.*

additive noun **additives**
a substance added to food *free from artificial additives*

add-on noun **add-ons**
in computing, an add-on is a small program or a piece of equipment that you add to your system to make it work better

address noun **addresses**
1 the number of the house or flat where someone lives or works, and other details such as the name of the street and town
2 in computing, an address is the series of letters, numbers and symbols used for finding a website or sending someone an email *What is your email address?*
3 an important speech

address verb
addresses, addressing, addressed
1 to write an address on an envelope or parcel before posting it
2 to say or write something directly to someone *Any comments should be addressed to the head teacher.*
3 to talk to someone directly or make an important speech to them *The prime minister will address parliament.*

adenoids noun plural
a mass of flesh at the back of your throat that sometimes becomes swollen

adequate adjective
1 good enough *The school has an adequate number of teachers.*
2 fairly good but not very good *The food was adequate.*
adequately adverb

adhere – adulthood

adhere verb
adheres, adhering, adhered
1 to stick to something *The omelette has adhered to the pan.*
2 to adhere to something such as a rule or belief is to obey or follow it

adhesive noun adhesives
a substance such as glue, used for sticking things together

adhesive adjective
something that is adhesive sticks to things or makes them stick *adhesive labels*

Adi Granth ['ah-dee-grunt'] noun
the holy book of the Sikh religion

> ORIGIN *Adi Granth* means 'first book' and is written in Punjabi. It is also known as the *Guru Granth Sahib*.

adjacent ['er-jay-sernt] adjective
next to something *an adjacent building*; *adjacent angles*

> ORIGIN from Latin *ad* 'near' and *jacere* 'to lie'

adjective noun adjectives
a word that describes a noun or pronoun, for example 'happy' or 'short'
adjectival adjective

> LANGUAGE EXTRA an *adjective* comes before a noun (*a small house*) or after a verb (*My house is small*). There are many different kinds, for example adjectives that describe size (*a big cat*); age (*an old man*); colour (*a blue shirt*); number or quantity (*nine boys, many books*); feelings (*an angry farmer*); opinions (*my favourite film*); state of health (*a sick girl*); qualities (*a clever son*); nationality (*an Italian singer*); what something is made of (*a plastic box*).
> Many adjectives have two forms: the comparative and the superlative. The comparative is used for comparing two things: *This tree is taller than that one. Peter's drawing is good but Abdul's is better.* The superlative is used for describing the most of a particular quality: *This tree is the tallest one. Anne's is the best drawing in the class.*

adjoining adjective
an adjoining room or building is one that is next to another

adjourn verb
adjourns, adjourning, adjourned
to end something or to come to an end for a short time *The meeting was adjourned until Monday.*

adjust verb
adjusts, adjusting, adjusted
1 to change something or the position of something slightly in order to make it better *I adjusted my glasses. Please adjust the sound on your TV.*
2 to get used to a new situation *She can't adjust to living in London.*
adjustable adjective

adjustment noun adjustments
a small change in something to make it better

ad-lib verb
ad-libs, ad-libbing, ad-libbed
to say something that you haven't prepared, for example when giving a speech or acting a part in a play

ad-lib adverb & adjective
without any preparation

administer verb
administers, administering, administered
1 to be in charge of something such as a business or organisation and to run it
2 to be responsible for providing something such as justice or exams
3 to give someone a medicine or drug

administration noun
1 the activity of running something such as a business, organisation or country
2 the people involved in this activity *The administration accepted responsibility.*
3 (plural **administrations**) the government of a country, especially in the USA *the Obama administration*

administrative adjective
connected with running a business or organisation *My dad's job is mainly administrative.* **administrator** noun

admirable adjective
excellent and of the highest quality *That was an admirable thing to do.*
admirably adverb

admiral noun admirals
an officer of the highest rank in the navy *Admiral Lord Nelson*

> ORIGIN from Arabic *amir-al* 'commander of' (as in the title *amir-al-bahr* 'commander of the sea'). The *d* between the *a* and *m* of *admiral* comes from another word – the Latin *admirabilis* 'admirable'.

admiration noun
a feeling of great respect for someone or something *He's full of admiration for what you do.*

admire verb
admires, admiring, admired
1 to have great respect for someone because you think they do good things or they do something very well *We all admire Churchill.*
2 to have great respect for something because you think it is very good *I admire the way you work and study at the same time.*
3 to enjoy looking at something beautiful *to admire the view*

admirer noun

admission noun admissions
1 being allowed into a place such as a theatre, school or hospital *There's no admission to the show after six o'clock. Admission costs £10.*
2 when someone says something is true, especially something bad *That's an admission of failure.*

admit verb
admits, admitting, admitted
1 to say that something is true, often something that you did not want people to know *I admit that I can't swim. She admitted to being very scared.*
2 to admit someone is to allow them to get into a place *This ticket admits two people. He was admitted to hospital.*

admittance noun
being allowed into a place such as a theatre or club *No admittance without a ticket.*

admittedly adverb
used for saying that something is true *Admittedly it's late but let's read a story.*

ado ['er-doo] noun
if you do something without further ado, you do it straightaway without waiting

adolescent noun adolescents
someone who is too old to be a child and too young to be an adult (between the ages of about 12 and 18) **adolescence** noun

> ORIGIN from Latin *adolescere* 'to grow up'

adopt verb
adopts, adopting, adopted
1 if a grown-up adopts a child, they take the child into their home and bring him or her up as their son or daughter *He's their adopted son.*
compare: **foster**
2 to start using, doing or having something, such as an idea, plan or name *You've adopted some strange habits!*
adoption noun

adoptive adjective
adoptive parents are people who have adopted a child or children

adorable adjective
really lovely and attractive

adore verb
adores, adoring, adored
to love someone or something very much *He adores his children.* **adoration** noun

adorn verb
adorns, adorning, adorned
to decorate *My room is adorned with colourful posters.*

adornment noun adornments
decoration

adrenalin noun
a substance produced by your body. It gives you more energy, for example when you're angry, afraid or excited.

> LANGUAGE EXTRA also spelt *adrenaline*

adrift adverb
1 if a boat is adrift or if someone is adrift in a boat, the boat is not tied to anything and goes wherever the wind takes it
2 if someone is adrift in their life, they are lonely and don't know what to do

adult noun adults
a grown-up person or fully grown animal

adult adjective
1 connected with being an adult *He's been poor all his adult life.*
2 fully grown *an adult tiger*

adultery noun
a love relationship between a married person and someone who is not his or her husband or wife *to commit adultery*

adulthood noun
the period of time when someone is an adult

advance noun advances
1 progress *scientific advances*
2 moving forward towards something *The armies continued their advance on the capital city.*
3 money for work paid to someone before they have done all the work *The author asked for an advance on payment for his book.*
4 **in advance** before something *You must book tickets a month in advance* (before the show).

advance verb
advances, advancing, advanced
1 to move forward
2 to make progress *Computers have advanced in the last 10 years.*
3 to develop something such as knowledge or ideas

advance adjective
happening or done before something else *an advance warning*

advanced adjective
1 at a high level of progress or knowledge *Our old computer isn't very advanced. My brother is doing an advanced course in Arabic.*
2 an advanced student or learner is one who studies a subject at a high level
3 knowing a lot or knowing more than other people of your age *Her daughter is very advanced.*
4 an advanced illness is so far forward that it cannot be cured

advantage noun advantages
1 something good and useful, especially something that helps you to be more successful *Knowing a second language is a great advantage.*
2 to take advantage of someone is to treat them very badly and selfishly by getting them to do what you want or by taking something from them
3 to take advantage of something is to use it because it will be good for you *We took advantage of the nice weather to play football.*

Advent noun
1 in the Christian religion, Advent is the four weeks just before Christmas
2 an Advent calendar is a big card with flaps like small doors that you open to show Christmas pictures

ORIGIN from Latin *adventus* 'coming', meaning the coming or second coming of Jesus Christ

adventure noun
1 (plural adventures) an exciting happening *He described his adventures travelling round India.*
2 doing exciting things *the love of adventure*
3 an adventure film or novel is a type of film or novel in which lots of exciting things happen
4 an adventure playground is a place outside with things such as climbing structures, ropes and tyres where children play

adventurous adjective
if someone is adventurous, they like doing exciting things

adverb noun adverbs
a word that describes a verb, an adjective or another adverb or gives more information about them, for example 'quickly', 'always', 'very'

LANGUAGE EXTRA there are at least five different kinds of *adverbs*, showing: how (*I walked slowly*); when (*It rained yesterday*); where (*I hurt myself here*); how often (*Meena sometimes plays the piano*); to what extent (*He arrived very late*).
Most adverbs of the 'how' type are formed by adding *-ly* to an adjective, for example *brightly, softly, pleasantly.*

adverbial noun adverbials
1 a group of words used like an adverb
2 another word for an adverb

adverbial adjective
used like an adverb *an adverbial phrase*

adversary ['ad-ver-se-ree'] noun adversaries
someone who is against you in a competition, argument or war

adverse adjective
bad or unpleasant *adverse weather conditions*

adversity noun
a bad situation causing someone a lot of problems

advert noun adverts
short for **advertisement**

advertise verb
advertises, advertising, advertised
1 to advertise something you sell is to tell people about it, for example on television, on the internet or in newspapers, to try to make them buy it
2 to advertise a job is to tell people about it so they will apply for it
3 to advertise an event such as a film show is to tell people about it so they will come along

advertisement noun advertisements
something such as a short television film or an announcement on the internet or in a newspaper. It tells people about things to buy, jobs to apply for or events to go to.

advice noun
something that someone tells you to help you decide what you should do

advisable adjective
if something is advisable, you should do it to avoid having problems later on

advise verb
advises, advising, advised
to tell someone what you think is the best thing they should do

adviser noun advisers
someone who gives advice to other people, for example in politics or business

advisor noun advisors
another spelling of **adviser**

advisory adjective

advocate ['ad-ver-kayt'] verb
advocates, advocating, advocated
to say that you strongly support something *Gandhi advocated non-violence.*

advocate ['ad-ver-kert'] noun advocates
a strong supporter of something *an advocate of women's rights*

adware noun
software that puts an advertisement on your computer, usually without you wanting it or knowing about it
compare: **malware** and **spyware**

aerial noun aerials
a long thin piece of metal, used for sending out or receiving radio or television signals, or a piece of equipment made of two or more long pieces of metal. Aerials come in different shapes and sizes. They are used indoors, for example fixed onto radio sets and routers (equipment for connecting computers to the internet) and outdoors, for example fixed onto the roofs of buildings and cars.

aerial adjective
1 from an aircraft *an aerial photo*
2 in the air *aerial combat*

aerobatics noun plural
skilful movements made in the air by aircraft, such as flying in a complete circle
aerobatic adjective

aerobics ['air-oh-biks'] noun plural
a type of very energetic exercise for strengthening the heart and lungs

aerodrome noun aerodromes
a small airport

aeronautics noun plural
the science of making and flying aircraft
aeronautical adjective

aeroplane noun aeroplanes
a vehicle that has wings and one or more engines and that flies through the air

SYNONYM plane

aerosol noun aerosols
a small metal container of liquid with a button at the top that you press to make the liquid come out in a spray of small drops. Aerosols contain things such as deodorant or paint.

aesthetic ['ees-thet-ik' or 'es-thet-ik'] adjective
connected with beauty, for example in art, literature or music

affair noun affairs
1 an event, subject or situation *The whole affair made lots of people angry. We've been invited to a family affair.*
2 someone's private business *That's entirely his affair.*
3 if two people are having an affair, they have a love relationship without being married to each other

affect verb
affects, affecting, affected
1 if something affects something else, it changes it in some way *A new airport would affect many people's lives.*
2 to have something to do with something or someone in some way *There was an internet problem affecting some customers.*
3 to harm someone or something in some way *Drugs usually affect your health.*

affected – aggression

4 to have a strong influence on someone's feelings, for example by making someone very sad *The accident affected the whole school.*

> **LANGUAGE EXTRA** be careful not to confuse the verb *affect* with the noun *effect* (influence). Verb: *It affected us all.* Noun: *It had an effect on us all.*

affected *adjective*
1 if someone or something is affected by something, they experience changes because of it *We're all affected by the new rules.*
2 not sincere or real *an affected smile*

affection *noun* **affections**
a feeling of love *He has great affection for the city. You have a special place in my affections.*

affectionate *adjective*
an affectionate person or animal shows love towards someone in a pleasant and gentle way

affix *noun* **affixes**
in grammar, an affix is a part added to the beginning or end of a word, such as 'un-' (unlock) or '-ness' (softness)
compare: **prefix** and **suffix**

afflict *verb*
afflicts, afflicting, afflicted
if you are afflicted by something bad, you suffer from it *a country afflicted by drought*

affliction *noun* **afflictions**
a serious problem or illness that causes suffering

affluence *noun*
when people have a lot of money

affluent *adjective*
rich *an affluent neighbourhood*

> **ORIGIN** from Latin *ad* 'to' and *fluere* 'to flow', suggesting the idea that lots of good things are 'flowing towards you'

afford *verb*
affords, affording, afforded
1 to have enough money to pay for something *My parents can't afford a car.*
2 to have enough time to do something *I'm not coming because I can't afford the time.*
3 if you say that you cannot afford something or cannot afford to do something, you also mean that you don't want something to happen or you don't want to do something because it will cause problems for you *I just can't afford to wait any longer. We can't afford any more mistakes.*
4 to provide something such as protection or an opportunity *This computer guarantee affords peace of mind.*

afforestation *noun*
the planting of trees to make a forest

Afghanistan *noun*
a country in West Asia
Afghan *adjective & noun*

afield *adverb*
far afield far away *People came from far afield to visit our town.*

afloat *adjective & adverb*
1 floating on water
2 having enough money to keep you out of debt

afraid *adjective*
1 frightened *Are you afraid of spiders?*
2 **I'm afraid** used for saying you're sorry when you tell someone something that they might not like to hear *I have to go to bed now, I'm afraid.*

afresh *adverb*
to do something afresh is to do it all over again *Let's start afresh.*

Africa *noun*
a continent south of the Mediterranean that includes countries such as Egypt and Algeria in the north and South Africa and Mozambique in the south

African *adjective*
connected with Africa

African *noun* **Africans**
someone from Africa

African American *noun*
African Americans
someone from the United States of America with dark skin, whose family came from Africa, usually a long time ago
African American *adjective*

after *preposition & adverb*
1 later than something or someone *I went to bed after ten o'clock. I'll go first and you can go after me. Will you do it after?*
2 following someone *I ran after her.*
3 further than something *Turn right after the post office.*
4 because of something or when you have considered something *After what you did, I'm not speaking to you.*
5 looking for something *I'm after a good dictionary.*
6 used with nouns for showing a large number of something or something that happens a lot *There were traffic jams for mile after mile. It rained day after day.*
7 **after all** used for saying something different from what you said before or for giving a reason for something *I'm not going to your party after all. I'm very tired – after all, I've been running around all day.*

afternoon *noun* **afternoons**
1 the time of the day between morning and evening
2 **good afternoon** a polite way of saying hello to someone in the afternoon

afters *noun plural*
an informal word for the last part of a meal

> **SYNONYM** dessert

afterwards *adverb*
after something else

again *adverb*
1 one more time *Say that again.*
2 as before *I climbed the hill and came down again.*
3 **again and again** many times

against *preposition*
1 touching a surface *Put your hands against the wall.*
2 if you're against something, you think it's bad or wrong *Most parents are against children drinking alcohol.*
3 fighting or competing with someone *England against Germany*
4 aimed at someone *That bully made threats against me.*
5 not allowed by something *It's against the rules.*
6 protecting someone or something from harm *Have you been vaccinated against measles?*
7 in the opposite direction to something *We're driving against the wind.*

age *noun* **ages**
1 the number of years you've lived, or how old you have to be to do something *I'm 10 years of age. Many children go to a new school around the age of 11.*
2 the number of years something has existed, for example a house or a computer
3 a period of history *the Tudor age*
4 being or becoming old *People's hearing gets worse with age.*
5 **ages** used when you mean a very long time *I've been standing here for ages.*

age *verb*
ages, ageing, aged
to become older or to look older *You've aged since I last saw you.*

aged *adjective*
1 ['ayjd'] having a certain age. If you are aged 10, for example, you are 10 years old.
2 ['ay-jid'] very old *She has aged parents.*

age gap *noun* **age gaps**
the age gap between two people is the difference between their ages

age group *noun* **age groups**
all of the people between two particular ages *a dictionary for the 9 to 13 age group*

ageing *adjective*
becoming old *an ageing rock star*

agency *noun* **agencies**
a business that provides different types of services for people *an employment agency*

agenda *noun* **agendas**
all the important things that people must do or talk about, for example in an organisation, business or meeting

> **ORIGIN** from Latin *agenda* 'things to be done', a part of the verb *agere* 'to do'

agent *noun* **agents**
1 someone who represents someone else in a business and organises things for them *a travel agent*
2 a spy who works for a government *a secret agent*

aggravate *verb*
aggravates, aggravating, aggravated
1 to aggravate someone is to make them angry
2 to aggravate something is to make it worse

aggravation *noun*
1 problems and difficulties *I've had a lot of aggravation today.*
2 violent behaviour or fighting *They're trying to start some aggravation.*

aggression *noun*
1 angry feelings that make people violent
2 attacking a country or a group of people without any reason

aggressor *noun*

aggressive – aircraft carrier

aggressive *adjective*
1 if a person or animal is aggressive, they have angry feelings that make them violent
2 also used for describing something such as an action that is angry and violent *aggressive behaviour; an aggressive look*
3 if someone such as a business person or politician is aggressive, they use lots of energy in their activities to try to be successful
4 also used for describing something done or said by someone such as a business person or politician who uses lots of energy *an aggressive political campaign*

aggro *noun*
an informal word for aggravation *I don't want any aggro.*

aghast *adjective*
very shocked about something *We were all aghast when we heard the news.*

agile *adjective*
an agile person or animal moves quickly and easily **agility** *noun*

agitate *verb*
agitates, agitating, agitated
1 to make someone feel nervous and worried *The longer he waited, the more agitated he became.*
2 to take part in political activity to get something done
3 to shake something
agitation *noun*

agitator *noun* **agitators**
someone who takes part in political activity to get something done

agnostic *noun* **agnostics**
someone who believes that it is not possible to know whether God exists

ago *adverb*
used for saying that something happened in the past or has just happened *She changed schools four years ago. I saw him five minutes ago.*

agonising *adjective*
1 if something such as a decision or choice is agonising, it is very difficult to make
2 very unpleasant or painful *a long agonising wait; an agonising death*

> **LANGUAGE EXTRA** also spelt *agonizing*

agony *noun*
1 very great pain *I was in agony with my toothache.*
2 a very unpleasant experience *It was agony waiting for our exam results.*

agree *verb*
agrees, agreeing, agreed
1 to think the same as someone else *I agree with you. We both agree on what to do.*
2 to say yes to something because you think it's good *He asked me to do it and I agreed. I didn't agree to it. Do you agree with these ideas?*
3 to be the same as something else *Her story doesn't agree with the facts.*
4 if a situation or a food agrees with you, you like it and it does you good *Living beside the sea really agrees with me.*

agreeable *adjective*
1 acceptable to someone or to everyone *an agreeable solution*
2 ready to say yes to something *Are you agreeable?*
3 pleasant *a very agreeable young man*

agreement *noun*
1 (*plural* **agreements**) a decision between two or more people or groups about what to do *We came to an agreement.*
2 when people or groups think the same as each other *We're all in agreement.*
3 when you say yes to something *We need the teacher's agreement.*
4 (*plural* **agreements**) a document listing the things that people have agreed to

agriculture *noun*
growing crops and keeping animals for food
agricultural *adjective*

aground *adverb*
if a boat or ship goes aground, it gets stuck in sand or on rocks because the water is not deep enough

ah *interjection*
a word used for showing a feeling such as surprise or happiness

ahead *adverb*
1 in front of someone or something *a few miles ahead*
2 in the future *to plan ahead*
3 more advanced than someone *Josh is ahead of everyone else in maths.*
4 winning *Our team's ahead.*
5 to get ahead is to make good progress, for example in your studies
6 if you tell someone to go ahead, you give them permission to do something
7 if something goes ahead, it happens, and if you go ahead with something, you allow it to happen or make it happen *The school trip went ahead in spite of the bad weather.*

ahoy *interjection*
a word that sailors shout to get someone's attention

aid *noun*
1 help *No-one came to his aid.*
2 money, food and other things that a country or organisation sends to a country to help the people there
3 (*plural* **aids**) something that helps someone to do something better, such as a piece of equipment *a hearing aid*
4 **in aid of** in order to help someone or something

aid *verb*
aids, aiding, aided
another way of saying to help

AIDS or **Aids** *noun*
a serious disease that stops the body from protecting itself against infections
short for: Acquired Immune Deficiency Syndrome

ailing *adjective*
in very bad shape and with a lot of problems *the ailing British car industry*

ailment *noun* **ailments**
a slight illness

aim *noun*
1 (*plural* **aims**) someone's aim is what they hope to do *My aim is to go on to university.*
2 (*plural* **aims**) the reason for something and what it is supposed to do *The aim of this computer program is to teach you how to type.*
3 skill in hitting something, for example when kicking a ball or shooting a gun *Your aim wasn't very good.*

aim *verb*
aims, aiming, aimed
1 to point something such as a gun at someone or something
2 to throw or kick something such as a ball towards a particular thing or person
3 to say, write or do something for a particular person or reason *a book aimed at young children; a program aiming to teach people how to draw*
4 to hope to achieve something or get somewhere *What is she aiming to do?*

aimless *adjective*
not knowing what to do and without any clear plan *He was aimless in his life.*
aimlessly *adverb*

air *noun*
1 air is the space all around us and above the ground
2 air is also the oxygen and other gases that you breathe
3 the look of something or the feeling connected with something *The old house had an air of mystery about it.*
4 (*plural* **airs**) a tune
5 if something is in the air, it is happening now or will happen soon *Change is in the air.*
6 if someone puts on airs, they behave as if they are more important than they really are
7 if a plan is up in the air, you haven't decided exactly what to do
8 **by air** in an aeroplane
9 **on air** or **on the air** on the radio or television

air *verb*
airs, airing, aired
1 to air clothes is to make them feel fresh by putting them in a place with warm or moving air
2 to air a room is to let fresh air in by opening the windows and doors
3 to air opinions or views is to tell people about them

airbag *noun* **airbags**
a type of bag in front of the driver or passenger of a car. In an accident, the bag fills with air to protect the driver or passenger.

airborne *adjective*
flying or moving in the air *Our plane is now airborne.*

air conditioning *noun*
an electrical system for keeping the air cool inside a room, building or car in hot weather **air-conditioned** *adjective*

aircraft *noun* **aircraft**
an aeroplane *Thousands of aircraft use London Gatwick.*

aircraft carrier *noun* **aircraft carriers**
a ship belonging to a country's military forces. This type of ship carries planes, which can take off from it and land on it.

9

airfield–algorithm

airfield noun airfields
a small place where military or private planes take off and land

air force noun air forces
the part of a country's fighting force of soldiers that uses planes

air gun noun air guns
a type of gun that uses air under pressure to fire pellets (small pieces of metal like tubes) or small metal balls like bullets

LANGUAGE EXTRA also spelt *airgun*

airhead noun airheads
an informal word for someone you think is not very clever

airing cupboard noun airing cupboards
a warm cupboard in a house or flat where you keep clothes and other materials such as sheets and towels

airlift verb
airlifts, airlifting, airlifted
if someone is airlifted, they are taken by plane or helicopter away from a place because they are in danger

airline noun airlines
a business that owns aircraft for flying passengers or goods

airliner noun airliners
a large plane for carrying passengers

airlock noun airlocks
a small amount of air in a pipe that stops liquid flowing through it

airmail noun
1 the system of sending letters by plane *by airmail*
2 letters sent by plane

airman noun airmen
a man who belongs to a country's air force

airplane noun airplanes
the American word for an aeroplane

airport noun airports
a place where planes take off and land, with buildings where passengers go when they travel by plane

air raid noun air raids
a bomb attack by planes, for example on a town

airship noun airships
a very large flying vehicle like a balloon with engines, for carrying people or goods

airsick adjective
someone who is airsick feels ill when they travel by plane **airsickness** noun

airspace noun
the sky above a country that belongs to that particular country *British airspace*

airstrip noun airstrips
a long and narrow piece of land specially prepared for planes to take off from and land on

airtight adjective
if something is airtight, it is so tightly closed that no air can get in or out *an airtight container*

air traffic controller noun
air traffic controllers
a person at an airport whose job is to give instructions to pilots about landing and taking off

airwoman noun airwomen
a woman who belongs to a country's air force

airy adjective airier, airiest
1 an airy room or building has lots of fresh air
2 done in a way that shows you don't take something seriously *airy promises*
airily adverb

aisle [rhymes with 'pile'] noun aisles
a long space for walking along between rows of seats, for example in a cinema or train, or between shelves, for example in a supermarket *Eggs are in aisle 4.*

ajar adverb & adjective
if a door is ajar, it is slightly open

akela ['ah-kay-ler'] noun akelas
a leader in the Cub Scouts

ORIGIN from a Hindi word meaning 'alone'; used by Rudyard Kipling in the *Jungle Books* for a wolf that was the leader of a pack

alarm noun
1 (plural **alarms**) a piece of equipment that warns you of danger by making a loud noise *The burglar alarm went off.*
2 a feeling you have when you are afraid something bad might happen *The whole town was in a state of alarm.*
3 if you raise the alarm, you warn people that something bad might happen
4 (plural **alarms**) an alarm clock *Mum set the alarm for eight o'clock.*

alarm verb
alarms, alarming, alarmed
to make someone feel worried or frightened that something bad might happen *I was very alarmed.*

alarm clock noun alarm clocks
a clock that can be made to ring or beep at a particular time to wake you up

alarming adjective
very frightening

alas interjection
an old-fashioned word used for showing that you are sad about something

Albania noun
a country in South-East Europe
Albanian adjective & noun

albatross noun albatrosses
a large white seabird with very long wings

albeit conjunction
another way of saying although

album noun albums
1 a book for keeping a collection of things in, for example photos, stamps or autographs
2 a collection of songs or pieces of music as a computer file, on a CD or, especially in the past, on a record or cassette *She's just released a new album.*
compare: **single**

ORIGIN from Latin *album/albus* 'white'; used about a blank (or white) tablet on which ancient Roman officials recorded public matters

alcohol noun
1 drinks such as beer or wine containing a substance that can make you drunk
2 a chemical substance in drinks such as beer or wine made from sugars that have been fermented (changed by bacteria or micro-organisms)

alcoholic adjective
an alcoholic drink contains alcohol

alcoholic noun alcoholics
someone who keeps drinking too much alcohol and cannot stop doing this

alcoholism noun
an illness caused when people drink too much alcohol

alcopop noun alcopops
a sweet fizzy drink like lemonade that contains alcohol

alcove noun alcoves
an alcove in a room is a small part of a wall that is built further back from the rest of the wall

ORIGIN from French *alcôve* and Spanish *alcoba*, taken from Arabic words meaning 'the vault'

ale noun ales
another word for beer, especially when it is made in the traditional way

alert adjective
1 if you are alert, you are watching out for something and are ready to act
2 if you are alert or your mind is alert, you are able to think quickly and in an intelligent way
alertness noun

alert verb
alerts, alerting, alerted
to tell someone about a danger or problem *The teachers alerted the children to some of the dangers of the internet.*

alert noun alerts
1 a warning about a danger *a flood alert*
2 if you are on the alert for something, you are watching out for it because it is dangerous and you are ready to act

A level noun A levels
an examination that students take in English, Welsh and Northern Irish schools and colleges around the age of 18. It allows them to apply to university.
compare: **AS level**

algae ['al-gee'] noun
a kind of plant that grows in water, for example seaweed

algebra noun
a type of maths that uses letters and symbols instead of numbers

ORIGIN from the Arabic words *al-jabr* 'the putting together of broken parts', used in the title of a 9th-century book from Baghdad on equations

Algeria noun
a country in North-West Africa
Algerian adjective & noun

algorithm noun algorithms
in maths and computing, an algorithm is a series of instructions that you follow in a particular order to find the answer to a problem

alias – allowed

alias ['ay-lee-ers'] *noun* **aliases**
a name that someone uses instead of their real name, for example because they are a spy or criminal

alias ['ay-lee-ers'] *preposition*
used when giving another name that someone uses, for example in a film or TV show *James Bond, alias 007*

alibi ['a-li-bye'] *noun* **alibis**
something that proves someone did not commit a crime because it shows they were somewhere else when the crime happened

ORIGIN from Latin *alibi* 'somewhere else'

alien *noun* **aliens**
1 in stories, an alien is a being from another planet
2 an old-fashioned word for someone who is not a citizen of the country where they live

alien *adjective*
1 very different from what you know and understand *These ideas are completely alien to me.*
2 connected with beings from another planet *An alien spaceship has landed.*
3 foreign

ORIGIN from Latin *alienus* 'belonging to something or someone else'

alienate *verb*
alienates, alienating, alienated
if someone or something alienates you, you have bad feelings about them or are made to feel that you are not wanted

alienation *noun*
the feeling of not being wanted or when you have bad feelings about something *the alienation of young people*

alight *adjective*
1 burning
2 to set something alight is to start a fire in or on it *Some vandals set his car alight.*

alight *verb*
alights, alighting, alighted
to alight from a train or bus is to get off

align *verb*
aligns, aligning, aligned
to align objects is to arrange them in a straight line *The boxes were neatly aligned along the wall.*

alike *adverb*
in the same way *Anil and his brother were dressed alike.*

alike *adjective*
similar in some way *We're alike, you and I.*

SIMILE 'as alike as two peas in a pod' means very similar to each other

alive *adjective*
1 living and not dead *Is the goldfish still alive?*
2 full of energy or activity *You feel so alive when you walk around London. The town comes alive in August.*

alkali ['al-ker-lye'] *noun* **alkalis**
a chemical substance that forms a salt when mixed with an acid. Alkalis turn litmus paper blue.

alkaline ['al-ker-lyne'] *adjective*
an alkaline substance contains an alkali

all *adjective, adverb & pronoun*
1 the whole of something *I've eaten all the chocolate – all of it. All is well.*
2 every person or thing *All my friends came. All books must be returned to the library.*
3 the only thing *That's all I'm saying*
4 completely *My homework is all finished.*
5 **all along** from the beginning *I've known all along that she was hiding something.*
6 (*informal*) **all in** very tired *I'm all in after that swim.*
7 **all of a sudden** suddenly
8 **all the best** used for saying you hope things are good for someone, for example as a friendly way of saying goodbye, often at the end of an email or letter
9 **all the same** when something doesn't make any difference *Caleb doesn't like me but I want to be his friend all the same.*
10 (*informal*) **not all there** slightly mad *Your brother's not all there!*

Allah *noun*
the name people give to God in the Muslim religion

all-clear *noun*
1 a sound or signal that tells you a situation is not dangerous any more
2 if someone gets the all-clear, they are told they can go ahead with their plan
3 if a sick person gets the all-clear, a doctor tells them they no longer need to worry about their health

allegation *noun* **allegations**
if you make an allegation, you say someone has done something wrong

allege [rhymes with 'edge'] *verb*
alleges, alleging, alleged
to say that someone has done something wrong but without proving that this is true *She alleged that I hit her little brother.*

allegedly ['er-lej-id-lee'] *adverb*
if you say something allegedly happened, you mean it is true that it happened because you or others say so but you have no proof *The meeting allegedly took place last year.*

allegiance ['er-lee-jerns'] *noun* **allegiances**
support that you give to a person, country or group because of a feeling of duty and love

allegory *noun* **allegories**
a story, poem or painting where the different characters, places or things are symbols of something else, such as religious or political ideas **allegorical** *adjective*

allergic *adjective*
1 if you're allergic to something like dust or milk, you have an allergy to it
2 (*informal*) if you don't like something, for example work or PE or travelling on buses, you can say you're allergic to it

allergy *noun* **allergies**
a medical condition where you become ill or get spots on your skin when you eat, drink or touch something or when you breathe something in *He has an allergy to milk.*

alley *noun* **alleys**
1 a very narrow street with buildings on both sides
2 a bowling alley is a place where people go to play the game of bowling

alleyway *noun* **alleyways**
another word for an alley

alliance ['er-lye-erns'] *noun* **alliances**
an agreement between countries or political groups to help each other and to work together

Allied *adjective*
connected with the countries that fought on the same side as Britain, France and the US in the First and Second World Wars *Allied soldiers*

Allies *noun plural*
see: **ally**

alligator *noun* **alligators**
a large animal like a crocodile with a long body, short legs and a large mouth with sharp teeth. Alligators live in rivers and lakes in the United States and China.

ORIGIN from Spanish *el lagarto* 'the lizard'

alliteration *noun*
when a writer or poet uses the same sound at the beginning of several words in a sentence *Poppy painted a pretty picture.*

allocate *verb*
allocates, allocating, allocated
to allocate something to someone is to give it to them, especially when someone makes an official decision to do it

allocation *noun*
1 (*plural* **allocations**) something that has been allocated *an allocation of tickets*
2 the action of allocating something

allot *verb*
allots, allotting, allotted
to allot something to someone is to give it to them, often as part of their share of something

allotment *noun* **allotments**
a small piece of ground that someone rents for growing vegetables on

allow *verb*
allows, allowing, allowed
1 to give someone permission to do something or let them do it *She allowed us to go out to play. Am I allowed to watch TV?*
2 to let someone have something *My parents allow me pocket money every week. Allow yourself plenty of time.*
3 to make it possible for something to happen *The police officer turned round, which allowed the prisoner to escape.*
4 to allow for something is to take something into consideration, for example in order to deal with it

allowance *noun* **allowances**
1 an amount of money that someone gives you regularly for a particular purpose
2 if you make allowances for someone, you forgive their behaviour

allowed *adjective*
1 used for saying that you can do something in a particular situation or in a game because the rules say that you can do it *Playing football in the playground is allowed. Is this move allowed in chess?*

11

alloy–alternative

2 used for saying that someone can go somewhere or that you can have something or bring something somewhere because the rules say that you can or because someone has given you permission *Granddad's feeling better so visitors are allowed. Your own food isn't allowed in the canteen. Are plaits and ponytails allowed in school?*

alloy *noun* **alloys**
a metal made from mixing two or more other metals together

all right *adjective & adverb*
1 fairly good, but not excellent *I thought the film was all right.*
2 very good *Everything has been all right for the past week.*
3 well *My eyes are tired but I can see all right.*
4 not hurt or ill *I fell over but I'm all right.*
5 safe and well *Go into his room to see if he's all right.*
6 used for saying yes or for agreeing to something *'Are you coming?' – 'All right!' If I come to your house at ten o'clock, is that all right for you?*
7 used for asking permission *Is it all right to close the door?*
8 used as an exclamation *All right, I've had enough!*

> LANGUAGE EXTRA also spelt *alright*, but some people think this spelling should not be used in careful writing

all-round *adjective*
good at lots of different things *an all-round athlete* **all-rounder** *noun*

allude *verb*
alludes, alluding, alluded
to allude to something is to mention it but not directly

allusion *noun* **allusions**
an indirect mention of something

ally [rhymes with 'eye'] *noun* **allies**
1 a country or political group that has agreed to help another, for example in a war
2 someone who helps you, especially when others are against you
3 the Allies are the countries that fought on the same side as Britain, France and the US in the First and Second World Wars
compare: **Axis**

ally [rhymes with 'eye'] *verb*
allies, allying, allied
to ally oneself with someone is to agree to help them and work with them

almighty *adjective*
1 an informal word for very great or loud *an almighty crash*
2 Almighty God another name for God, used for saying that God has lots of power

almond ['ah-mernd'] *noun* **almonds**
a flat brown nut with an oval shape and a slightly sweet taste

almost *adverb*
1 not completely but not far from it *I've almost finished.*
2 used for saying that something is not true always but not far from it *I go swimming almost every day.*

> SYNONYM nearly

aloft *adverb*
high in the air

alone *adjective & adverb*
1 with no-one with you *I was all alone.*
2 lonely and unhappy *I was feeling all alone.*
3 without anything else *The introduction alone comes to 80 pages.*
4 to leave someone alone is to keep away from them and stop making them angry or upset *Go away and leave me alone!*
5 to leave something alone is to keep away from it or stop touching it *I want you to leave those chocolates alone.*

along *preposition & adverb*
1 going forward towards the end of something *I was walking along the street. Move along!*
2 from one end to the other of something *all the towns along the coast*
3 with someone *Bring your friend along.*
4 to a particular place *Jason will be along soon.*
5 all along from the beginning
6 along with as well as *He was rescued along with his dog.*

alongside *adverb*
1 next to something *The motorbike pulled up alongside our car.*
2 together with something or someone, or at the same time or place *People of all religions worked alongside each other.*

aloof *adjective*
if someone is aloof, they are distant from other people and are considered unfriendly

aloud *adverb*
in a loud enough voice for people to hear

alphabet *noun* **alphabets**
all the letters of a language arranged in order. The English alphabet has 26 letters, going from A to Z.

> ORIGIN from Greek *alpha* and *beta*, the first two letters of the Greek alphabet

alphabetical *adjective*
arranged in the order of the alphabet, from A to Z *The names of the trees are given in alphabetical order.* **alphabetically** *adverb*

alpine *adjective*
connected with the Alps

Alps *noun plural*
a group of high mountains in Switzerland and countries nearby

already *adverb*
1 before now or before a particular time *I've already had lunch.*
2 sooner than expected *Are you leaving already?*
3 used for saying that a situation exists at the present time *We're late already.*

alright *adjective & adverb*
another spelling of **all right**

> LANGUAGE EXTRA some people think the spelling *alright* should not be used in careful writing

Alsatian *noun* **Alsatians**
a big dog like a wolf, often used for guarding buildings, as a guide dog (helping someone who cannot see) or by the police

> SYNONYM German shepherd

> ORIGIN the name *Alsatian* started to be used in 1917 instead of *German shepherd* to avoid the word 'German', as Britain was at war with Germany. The dog has no connection with Alsace, a region in eastern France.

also *adverb*
1 used for talking about something or someone extra or for adding something extra to what you say *She is also my favourite author. Take me along also.*
2 used for saying that the same thing is true about something or someone else *Rashid went to my school and Joanna did also.*

> SYNONYM too

Alt *noun*
a key on a computer keyboard that you press, usually together with another key, to perform an action on screen *Press Alt F4 to shut down your program.*

altar *noun* **altars**
a raised table for religious ceremonies, for example in the Christian church

alter *verb*
alters, altering, altered
to change something or to become changed

alteration *noun* **alterations**
a change made to something, for example a book or piece of clothing

alternate ['ol-**terr**-nert'] *adjective*
1 happening on one day or in one week, month or year but not the next, as part of a regular pattern *Mum works on alternate Sundays.*
2 coming one after the other as part of a regular pattern *alternate green and yellow stripes*
alternately *adverb*

> LANGUAGE EXTRA be careful not to use *alternate* instead of *alternative* when you mean 'offering a different choice from something else', as this is American usage

alternate ['ol-ter-nayt'] *verb*
alternates, alternating, alternated
if two things alternate or if you alternate them, one comes first then the other one, as part of a regular pattern *Blue stripes alternated with red ones.*

alternating current *noun*
electric current that keeps changing direction *compare:* **direct current**

alternative *noun* **alternatives**
a choice between two or more different things *We have no alternative but to wait for a bus.*

alternative *adjective*
offering a different choice from something else *Is there an alternative way of getting home?*

> SYNONYM another

alternatively–amino acid

alternatively *adverb*
used for showing a choice between two different things *You can wait here or alternatively walk home with me.*

although *conjunction*
used for connecting two parts of a sentence when the second part introduces a very different idea from the first part, for example a surprising idea *Although Granddad is old, he walks more than two miles a day. I love France although I've never been to Paris.*

altitude *noun* altitudes
the height of something above the sea

alto *noun* altos
1 a woman with a low singing voice
2 a man with the highest singing voice
3 an alto voice or musical instrument

altogether *adverb*
1 completely *Things are altogether different now.*
2 used for showing a total amount *There are nine of us altogether.*
3 used for saying something is really true *The food is altogether much better in France.*
4 used for mentioning your final idea about something *Altogether, it was quite a good film.*

> LANGUAGE EXTRA be careful not to confuse *altogether* with *all together* meaning 'all people together', for example *We walked home from school all together.*

aluminium *noun*
a silver-coloured metal that is not very heavy. It is used for making things such as cans or saucepans.

> LANGUAGE EXTRA the American word is *aluminum*

always *adverb*
1 all the time or at all times *I always tell the truth.*
2 very often *You're always complaining.*
3 used for making a suggestion *You could always ask your mum to help you.*

am
first person singular present tense of **be**

a.m.
used for showing the time after midnight and before midday *It's 7.00 a.m.*

> ORIGIN from Latin *ante meridiem* 'before midday'

amalgamate *verb*
amalgamates, amalgamating, amalgamated
if things amalgamate or if you amalgamate them, they join together to form a single large thing *Our bank has amalgamated with a Dutch bank.* **amalgamation** *noun*

amateur ['am-er-ter] *noun* amateurs
1 someone who plays a game or does an activity because they like doing it, not because it is their job *an amateur chess player*

> ANTONYM professional

2 someone who doesn't do an activity very well

> ORIGIN from French *amateur*, which comes from Latin *amator* 'lover'

amateurish *adjective*
1 if something is amateurish, it is not done very well
2 if someone is amateurish, they don't do things very well

amaze *verb*
amazes, amazing, amazed
if someone or something amazes you, they make you very surprised, often in a way that makes you happy *She amazed us all by the way she sang. It amazes me how silly some boys can be.*

amazement *noun*
1 very great surprise
2 a feeling of great respect, pleasure and surprise, for example when you see something beautiful, large or good

amazing *adjective*
1 really surprising *It's amazing how noisy your class is.*
2 really good *an amazing bit of luck; Isabella has an amazing voice.*
3 really great or large *an amazing effort*
4 if you think that someone is amazing, you really like and admire them *Your brother is amazing!*

amazingly *adverb*
1 extremely *My sister is amazingly hard-working.*
2 extremely well *He sang truly amazingly.*
3 used when something is hard to believe *Amazingly, I came top of the class.*

Amazon *noun*
a very long river in South America

ambassador *noun* ambassadors
someone who lives in a foreign country and represents the government of his or her own country. An ambassador lives in an embassy. *the British ambassador to Mexico*

amber *noun*
1 a yellow-brown substance for making jewellery or ornaments
2 a yellow-brown colour, such as the colour in traffic lights between red and green *an amber shirt*

ambiguity *noun* ambiguities
1 something that is not clear because people understand it in different ways *Your essay is full of ambiguities.*
2 the ambiguity of something is when it is not clear *Try to avoid ambiguity.*

ambiguous *adjective*
if something such as a word or phrase is ambiguous, it is not clear because it means two or more different things *Her answer is slightly ambiguous.* **ambiguously** *adverb*

ambition *noun*
1 (*plural* ambitions) if you have an ambition to do something, you want to do it very much *My ambition is to be a teacher.*
2 ambition is also the wish to be successful *Don't you have any ambition?*

ambitious *adjective*
1 if you're ambitious, you want very much to be successful *ambitious students*
2 an ambitious idea or plan is one where you want to achieve something big and good that needs lots of effort

amble *verb*
ambles, ambling, ambled
to walk without hurrying, in a relaxed way *We were just ambling along aimlessly.*

> ORIGIN from Latin *ambulare* 'to walk'

ambulance *noun* ambulances
a vehicle for taking people to and from hospital

ambush *verb*
ambushes, ambushing, ambushed
if you ambush someone, you attack them suddenly after hiding and waiting for them

ambush *noun* ambushes
a sudden attack on someone from a hiding place

amen *interjection*
a word used at the end of a prayer, especially in the Christian religion

amend *verb*
amends, amending, amended
to change something such as a word in a document or written agreement

amendment *noun* amendments
a change to something such as a document or agreement

amends *noun plural*
to make amends for something bad you've done is to show that you are sorry by doing something good

amenities *noun plural*
things that make it better or easier to live in a place, such as parks, public toilets, shops or libraries *Our house is close to all the local amenities.*

America *noun*
1 another name for the United States of America
2 a continent that includes North, South and Central America and contains countries such as the United States, Canada, Mexico, Brazil and Argentina

American *adjective*
1 connected with the United States of America
2 connected with North, South and Central America *the American continent*

American *noun* Americans
someone from the United States of America

amiable *adjective*
an amiable person is pleasant and easy to like **amiability** *noun* **amiably** *adverb*

amicable *adjective*
friendly *an amicable agreement*
amicably *adverb*

amid *preposition*
used for saying that something else is happening at the same time *The army was called in amid fears of a terrorist attack.*

amidst *preposition*
an old-fashioned word for amid

amino acid ['er-mee-noh] *noun*
amino acids
one of the substances in animals and plants. Amino acids join together to make proteins (needed by the body to help it grow and stay healthy).

13

amiss – anarchy

amiss *adverb*
if you say something is amiss, you mean something is wrong

ammonia *noun*
a gas or liquid with a very strong smell, used for example in cleaning or hair-colouring products

ammunition *noun*
things such as bullets, rockets or bombs that can be fired from weapons or used as weapons in fighting

amnesty *noun* **amnesties**
a decision made by a government not to punish someone or to stop punishing someone who has committed a crime

amoeba ['er-mee-ber] *noun* **amoebas**
a tiny creature that only has one cell (smallest unit of living matter) and can be found in water and soil

among or **amongst** *preposition*
1 in the middle of a group of people or things, or surrounded by them *Can you see the ball among the daffodils? You're among friends.*
2 used for talking about something that is included in a larger group *He has a signed copy of 'Goodnight Mister Tom' among his books.*
3 used for talking about a group of people that something is happening to *There are lots of problems among the children in his class.*
4 between *Let's divide the sweets among us.*

amount *noun* **amounts**
1 a quantity of something *a small amount of information*
2 a sum of money *Can you pay the full amount by tomorrow?*

amount *verb*
amounts, amounting, amounted
1 to come to a particular total *The hours I spent on this project amounted to more than 30.*
2 to be the same as something else *What I feel amounts to much more than disappointment.*

amp *noun* **amps**
a unit for measuring electric current *a 13-amp plug*

> ORIGIN from André-Marie *Ampère*, French 18th-century mathematician and scientist

ampersand *noun* **ampersands**
the & sign, sometimes used instead of 'and' in writing

amphibian *noun* **amphibians**
an animal like a frog or newt that can live in water and on land

> ORIGIN from Greek *amphibios* 'living two lives' (*amphi* 'both' and *bios* 'life'), because amphibians live both in water and on the land

amphibious *adjective*
1 an amphibious animal can live in water and on land
2 an amphibious vehicle can travel in water and on land

amphitheatre *noun* **amphitheatres**
a large circular or oval building without a roof, with rows of seats built above each other going all around it. Amphitheatres are used for events such as sports competitions, plays or concerts and have existed since ancient Greek and Roman times.

> ORIGIN from Greek *amphi-* 'on both sides' and *theatron* 'place for seeing'. Theatres were normally in the shape of a semicircle so an amphitheatre was like two theatres put together.

ample *adjective*
1 more than enough *You'll have ample time to ask questions later.*
2 large in size *There's an ample fridge in the kitchen.*

amplifier *noun* **amplifiers**
a piece of electrical equipment for making sounds louder, for example the sound of an electric guitar

amplify *verb*
amplifies, amplifying, amplified
1 to amplify a sound is to make it louder
2 to amplify something such as a remark or idea is to give more information about it
amplification *noun*

amply *adverb*
extremely well *an amply illustrated book*; *They are amply paid.*

amputate *verb*
amputates, amputating, amputated
to cut off a part of someone's body, such as an arm or leg, in a medical operation
amputation *noun*

amuse *verb*
amuses, amusing, amused
1 to make someone laugh or smile, or to please someone with something enjoyable *My teacher was amused when he read my homework.*
2 to keep someone interested in something so that they don't get bored *Can you amuse yourself for an hour until I get back?*

amusement *noun*
1 the feeling you have when something is funny or enjoyable *She looked at me in amusement.*
2 (*plural* **amusements**) something you like doing
3 amusements are things for people's pleasure such as video games or machines for riding on or for winning prizes, usually at a funfair
4 an amusement park is a large outside area where people go to enjoy themselves. There are games to play, machines such as merry-go-rounds and Ferris wheels for riding on and other activities such as riding in trains, on roller coasters and on boats.

amusing *adjective*
funny and enjoyable *an amusing book*

an *indefinite article*
one or any one of something, or each of something *an elephant*; *an hour*

> LANGUAGE EXTRA *an* is used before a word beginning with a vowel sound, and *a* before a word beginning with a consonant, for example *a girl*

anachronism *noun* **anachronisms**
1 something that belongs to the past and not the present
2 something that appears in a film or play set in the past that did not exist at that time

anaemia ['er-nee-mee-er] *noun*
a condition of the blood that makes people feel tired and look pale **anaemic** *adjective*

anaesthetic *noun* **anaesthetics**
a drug that a doctor gives someone before an operation so that they feel no pain or go to sleep. A general anaesthetic makes the whole body feel no pain, and a local anaesthetic makes someone stop feeling pain in one part of the body.

anaesthetise *verb*
anaesthetises, anaesthetising, anaesthetised
to give someone an anaesthetic

> LANGUAGE EXTRA also spelt *anaesthetize*

anaesthetist *noun* **anaesthetists**
a doctor who gives someone an anaesthetic before an operation

anagram *noun* **anagrams**
a word or phrase that you make by putting the letters of another word or phrase in a different order. For example, 'canoe' is an anagram of 'ocean', and 'dormitory' is an anagram of 'dirty room'.

analogous *adjective*
similar in some way

analogue *adjective*
an analogue clock or watch has hands that move around a dial, instead of numbers that change as in a digital clock or watch
compare: **digital**

analogy *noun* **analogies**
a comparison between two things that seem similar in some way *The teacher drew an analogy between the human brain and a computer.*

analyse *verb*
analyses, analysing, analysed
1 to examine something carefully to understand and explain it *We need to analyse the results.*
2 to examine a substance carefully to see what it is made of

analysis *noun* **analyses**
a careful examination of something
analytical *adjective*

analyst *noun* **analysts**
1 someone who analyses things and provides information about them to other people
2 a doctor who helps people with problems that affect their mind or feelings

anarchist ['a-ner-kist] *noun* **anarchists**
someone who believes that there should not be any laws, rules or governments
anarchism *noun*

anarchy ['a-ner-kee] *noun*
1 when there are no laws, rules or government in a country
2 when people behave badly without any control over what they do *There was complete anarchy in the classroom.*

anatomy *noun*
1 the study of the body or of a part of it *the anatomy of the neck*
2 the human body itself
anatomical *adjective*

ancestor *noun* **ancestors**
someone in your family who lived before you were born

ancestral *adjective*
1 connected with your ancestors
2 an ancestral home is a large house that has belonged to a family for very many years

ancestry *noun*
all your ancestors

anchor *noun* **anchors**
1 a heavy weight at the end of a chain that is dropped from a boat or ship to the bottom of the sea. It stops the boat or ship from moving.
2 a person who presents a television or radio news programme

anchor *verb*
anchors, anchoring, anchored
to drop the anchor from a boat or ship to stop it from moving *The 'Beagle' was anchored off the Galapagos Islands.*

anchovy ['an-cher-vee' or 'an-choh-vee'] *noun* **anchovies**
a very small fish with a salty taste, often sold in a tin

ancient ['ayn-shernt'] *adjective*
1 belonging to a time very long ago *the ancient Greeks*
2 very old *an ancient tradition*
3 ancient history is the study of civilisations that existed very long ago, especially those of Greece and Rome

and *conjunction*
used for joining together words and sentences *apples and oranges; Come in and sit down. Add 4 and 6 to make 10.*

android *noun*
1 (*plural* **androids**) in science fiction, a machine that looks completely human
2 Android (trademark) is also an operating system used on many smartphones and tablet computers

ORIGIN from Greek *androeides* 'like a human'

anecdote *noun* **anecdotes**
a short story about something that happened to you

anemone ['er-nem-er-nee'] *noun* **anemones**
a plant with white, red or blue flowers like little cups

anew *adverb*
to do something anew is to do it again, often in a new way *Let's begin anew.*

angel *noun* **angels**
1 a being that some people believe lives in heaven and has been sent by God. In paintings, angels often appear as people with wings, dressed in white.
2 someone who is very kind or very beautiful *Be an angel and make me a cup of tea.*

ORIGIN from ancient Greek *angelos* 'messenger'

angelic *adjective*
very beautiful and kind *an angelic smile*

anger *noun*
a strong feeling that you have when someone has done something you don't like. It makes you want to say bad things, such as swearing at them or quarrelling with them, or do bad things, such as hitting them or shaking your fists.

angle *noun* **angles**
1 the shape made when two straight lines join or cross each other at a point. Angles are measured in degrees. *an acute angle*
2 the direction that you look at something from or that something comes from *The photo was taken from a strange angle.*
3 a way of looking at a problem or question
4 **at an angle** used for describing something that is not horizontal (going in the same direction as the ground) or vertical (pointing straight up) but in between these two positions

angle *verb*
angles, angling, angled
1 to move something in a particular direction so that it is not pointing straight in front of you *Angle the mirror to the side.*
2 to present something such as information or news from a particular point of view *The headline was angled to show the Conservatives in a more favourable light.*

angler *noun* **anglers**
someone who catches fish with a fishing rod
angling *noun*

Anglican *noun* **Anglicans**
a Christian who belongs to the Church of England **Anglican** *adjective*

Anglo- *prefix*
connected with England or Britain

Anglo-Saxon *noun*
1 (*plural* **Anglo-Saxons**) the Anglo-Saxons were a people made up of Angles, Saxons and Jutes. They came to England in the 5th century, from parts of what is now Germany and Denmark, and ruled until the Norman Conquest in 1066.
2 the old English language of the Anglo-Saxons
Anglo-Saxon *adjective*

angry *adjective* **angrier, angriest**
feeling anger *What you said made me very angry.* **angrily** *adverb*

SYNONYM furious

anguish *noun*
great suffering

anguished *adjective*
showing great suffering *an anguished cry*

angular *adjective*
1 an angular part of the body is one where you can see the shape of the bones *an angular face*
2 an angular shape has sharp corners

animal *noun* **animals**
1 a living creature that is not a plant. The word 'animals' does not usually include human beings. *I love animals, especially cats, dogs and horses.*
2 someone who behaves in a very violent way *The person who did that is just an animal.*

animate ['an-i-mert] *adjective*
living *animate beings*

animate ['an-i-mayt] *verb*
animates, animating, animated
1 to make something or someone more lively *The class became quite animated.*
2 an animated film or cartoon is made by showing different pictures of the same thing one after the other so it looks as if they are moving

animation *noun*
1 the method of making animated films and cartoons
2 (*plural* **animations**) an animated film or cartoon *It's a 3-D animation.*
3 being lively *She spoke with great animation.*

animosity *noun* **animosities**
a strong feeling of disliking someone

aniseed *noun*
the seeds of the anise plant, used for giving a liquorice taste to sweets and alcoholic drinks

ankle *noun* **ankles**
the part of your body where your leg joins your foot

annex *verb*
annexes, annexing, annexed
to annex a country is to take it from someone by force and make it a part of your own country **annexation** *noun*

annexe *noun* **annexes**
a separate building added to a larger one

annihilate *verb*
annihilates, annihilating, annihilated
1 to destroy something completely *The whole population was annihilated.*
2 to beat someone completely in a game or competition
annihilation *noun*

anniversary *noun* **anniversaries**
1 a date that you celebrate because of something important that happened on the same day in an earlier year *the anniversary of the Battle of Waterloo*
2 a date that you celebrate because someone got married on the same day in an earlier year *Today is my parents' tenth anniversary. I gave them an anniversary card.*

announce *verb*
announces, announcing, announced
to tell people about something, especially in an official way *My brother announced his wedding in the newspaper.*

announcement *noun* **announcements**
something that people are told, especially in an official way *The head teacher is about to make an important announcement.*

announcer *noun* **announcers**
someone who announces television or radio programmes

annoy *verb*
annoys, annoying, annoyed
1 if someone annoys you, they make you feel slightly angry, for example by doing something you don't want them to do *Leave me alone – you're annoying me!*

annoyance – anticyclone

2 if something annoys you, you don't like it or you don't like doing it, for example because it makes you feel slightly uncomfortable or slightly angry *That noise is beginning to annoy me* (for example by giving me a headache or stopping me relaxing). *Your question annoyed Mum* (made her slightly angry).

annoyance *noun*
1 annoyance is when you are annoyed *To my annoyance, I found that all the doors were locked.*
2 (plural **annoyances**) an annoyance is something that annoys you

annoying *adjective*
1 making you feel slightly angry *We just missed the bus – that's annoying! My brother is annoying* (for example because he's always doing things I don't like).
2 making you feel slightly uncomfortable *Having planes flying over every few minutes is really annoying* (for example because they give you a headache or stop you from relaxing).

annoyingly *adverb*

annual *adjective*
1 happening once every year *the annual sports day*
2 an annual amount is worked out over the whole year *an annual salary*
3 lasting a whole year *an annual season ticket*

annually *adverb*

annual *noun* **annuals**
1 a book that comes out once every year, especially a children's book with stories
2 a plant that lives for one year or less
compare: **perennial**

anonymous *adjective*
1 if something is anonymous, it is by someone whose name you don't know *an anonymous gift*
2 if someone is anonymous, you don't know their name *They want to remain anonymous.*

anonymity *noun* **anonymously** *adverb*

ORIGIN from Greek *anonumos* (*an* 'without' and *onoma* 'name')

anorak *noun* **anoraks**
a short coat with a hood

ORIGIN from Inuit *anoraq*, the warm waterproof coat worn by the Inuit in places such as Greenland

anorexia *noun*
an illness that makes people not want to eat because they think they will get fat

ORIGIN from Greek *an* 'without' and *orexis* 'appetite'

anorexic *adjective*
if someone is anorexic, they suffer from anorexia

another *adjective & pronoun*
1 one more thing or person *Could I have another chocolate?*
2 a different thing or person *This scarf is too heavy – I would like to try another.*

answer *noun* **answers**
1 something you say when someone asks you a question

2 something you write to someone, for example when they send you a letter or email or when you're dealing with an advertisement
3 when someone opens the front door of their house or flat if the doorbell rings, or when they pick up their phone if it rings *There was no answer.*
4 a way of solving a problem *There's no easy answer to the country's problems.*

answer *verb*
answers, answering, answered
1 to say something to someone after they have said something to you or asked you a question *'Can you hear me?' – 'Yes,' I answered. Would you please answer my question?*
2 to answer something such as a letter or advertisement is to write back
3 to answer the door or the phone is to open the front door of your house or flat or to pick up the phone to speak to whoever is there
4 to answer back is to say something rude to someone instead of obeying them
5 to answer for something is to be responsible for it and explain it to other people

answerphone *noun* **answerphones**
a piece of equipment that records your phone calls when you are out or when you do not wish to answer them

ant *noun* **ants**
a very small insect that lives in large groups under the ground

antagonise *verb*
antagonises, antagonising, antagonised
if you antagonise someone, you make them feel angry and negative towards you

LANGUAGE EXTRA also spelt *antagonize*

antagonism *noun*
strong dislike between people or groups

antagonistic *adjective*
if you are antagonistic towards someone, you are very unfriendly to them because you dislike them very much

Antarctic *noun*
the Antarctic is the very cold region at the most southern point of the world. The region at the most northern point is the Arctic.

LANGUAGE EXTRA also called *Antarctica*

anteater *noun* **anteaters**
a South American animal. It has a very long nose and tongue, and eats small insects.

antelope *noun* **antelopes**
an African and Asian animal with long legs and horns. Antelopes can run very fast.

antenna *noun* **antennae**
one of the two long thin feelers on the head of an insect or animal such as a snail or shrimp

antenna *noun* **antennas**
1 another word for an aerial
2 a round piece of equipment shaped like a dish, used for receiving radio or television signals, for example from satellites

anthem *noun* **anthems**
an anthem is the official song of a particular country or group *The French national anthem is 'La Marseillaise'.*

anther *noun* **anthers**
the part of a flower that contains pollen. It is the top part of the stamen of the flower.

anthill *noun* **anthills**
a pile of earth that ants make over the place where they live in the ground

anthology *noun* **anthologies**
a book of stories, poems or songs written by different people

ORIGIN from Greek *anthologia* 'collection of flowers' (from *anthos* 'flower')

anthracite *noun*
a very hard type of coal

anthropology *noun*
the study of people and how they live and behave **anthropological** *adjective* **anthropologist** *noun*

ORIGIN from Greek *anthropos* 'man' and *logos* 'word' or 'study'

anti- *prefix*
1 against something or someone *anti-European*
2 the opposite of something *an anti-hero*

ANTONYM pro-

antibiotic *noun* **antibiotics**
a drug used for killing bacteria (tiny harmful living things) that cause infections

antibody *noun* **antibodies**
a substance in your blood that fights illnesses

anticipate *verb*
anticipates, anticipating, anticipated
1 if you anticipate something, you expect it to happen *We're anticipating very good exam results for our class.*
2 to be ready to deal with something because you are expecting it *They're anticipating trouble at tomorrow's match.*
3 to be excited about something that is going to happen *The whole town was eagerly anticipating the president's visit.*

anticipation *noun*
1 great excitement about something that is going to happen *When the coach arrived, the children were full of anticipation.*
2 when you're expecting something to happen *There's an anticipation of trouble at tomorrow's game.*

anticlimax *noun* **anticlimaxes**
1 when you're disappointed because something you thought would be good or exciting is not what you expected *The ending of the film was a real anticlimax.*
2 something that is not as good or exciting as something else that happened before it *Living at home is bound to be an anticlimax compared to three years at university.*

anticlockwise *adverb & adjective*
moving in the direction that is opposite to the way the hands of a clock move

ANTONYM clockwise

antics *noun plural*
silly or annoying behaviour

anticyclone *noun* **anticyclones**
an area of high air pressure that keeps the weather fine and calm

antidote – apostrophe

antidote *noun* **antidotes**
a substance that stops a poison from having a bad effect

antifreeze *noun*
a chemical added to the cooling water in a car engine that stops it from freezing in cold weather

antiglare *adjective*
an antiglare screen is a special type of computer screen that allows you to spend a long time watching it without getting your eyes tired

antipathy *noun*
a strong feeling of disliking someone

Antipodes ['an-ti-per-deez'] *noun plural*
the Antipodes are Australia and New Zealand

> ORIGIN from Greek *antipodes* 'with feet opposite' (*anti* 'opposite' and plural of *pous* 'foot'), because people in Australia and New Zealand have their feet on the opposite side of the world to people in Europe

antiquated *adjective*
old-fashioned and not useful

antique *noun* **antiques**
an old object such as a piece of furniture or jewellery that is valuable, for example because it is well made or beautiful

antique *adjective*
old and valuable

antiquity *noun*
1 ancient times, especially before the Middle Ages
2 antiquities are objects made in ancient times *The British Museum has a collection of Roman antiquities.*

antiseptic *noun* **antiseptics**
a substance that you put on injured skin to stop infections **antiseptic** *adjective*

antisocial *adjective*
an antisocial person is not friendly or does not care about other people

antivirus *noun*
software that finds and removes viruses from your computer

> LANGUAGE EXTRA also called *antivirus software*

antler *noun* **antlers**
one of the two horns on the head of a male deer and some other animals

antonym *noun* **antonyms**
a word that has the opposite meaning to another word *'Happy' is the antonym of 'sad'.*

> ORIGIN from Greek *anti-* 'opposite' and *onoma* 'name'

anus ['ay-ners'] *noun* **anuses**
the opening in your bottom that gets rid of solid waste from your body

anvil *noun* **anvils**
a block of iron on which red hot pieces of metal are hammered into shape

anxiety *noun*
1 (plural **anxieties**) the feeling of being worried or something that worries you *His behaviour has caused us a lot of anxiety. It's better to talk about your anxieties.*
2 a strong feeling of wanting to do something or wanting something to happen *my anxiety to get top marks in the exam*

anxious *adjective*
1 worried about something *We're anxious about the exams. Mum gave me an anxious look.*
2 an anxious time is a time when you worry
3 if you're anxious to do something, you want to do it very much

anxiously *adverb*

any *adjective & pronoun*
1 every *Any teacher could have helped you.*
2 some *Do you have any problems?*
3 used for saying that it is not important which one *Come and see me any morning.*

any *adverb*
1 even a small amount *Are you feeling any better?*
2 used in negatives with 'more' or 'longer' to mean something has stopped happening *I don't like her any more. He doesn't play the piano any longer.*

anybody *pronoun*
anyone

anyhow *adverb*
1 anyway
2 carelessly *She just does her work anyhow.*

anyone *pronoun*
any person

anything *pronoun*
any kind of thing, situation, action or idea

anyway *adverb*
1 no matter what happens *Dad has said no, but I'm going to do it anyway.*
2 used for mentioning something else or another reason for something *He hasn't invited me to his party and anyway I don't want to go.*
3 used for saying something more clearly or correctly or in a different way *The doctor said I should stay in bed for a week – or for at least five days anyway.*
4 used for changing the subject *Anyway, tell me about your holidays.*

anywhere *adverb*
1 in, at or to any place *I can't see it anywhere.*
2 any place *Do you have anywhere to stay?*

apart *adverb*
1 if two or more things are apart from each other, there is an amount of space or time between them *I planted the seeds a few inches apart. My brother and I were born two years apart.*
2 into pieces *It came apart when I touched it.*
3 if people's ideas or opinions are apart, there is a difference between them *The two sides are as far apart as ever.*
4 to set someone or something apart from someone or something else is to make them different *What sets me apart from my brother is my love of football.*
5 **apart from** except for

apartment *noun* **apartments**
1 another word for a flat *an apartment block*
2 a number of rooms used for a special purpose by someone important *the president's private apartments*

apathetic *adjective*
if someone is apathetic, they have no interest in something

apathy *noun*
the feeling of not being interested in something

apatosaurus *noun* **apatosauruses**
a large plant-eating dinosaur with a small head and long neck

ape *noun* **apes**
a large animal like a monkey without a tail or with a very short tail, such as a chimpanzee or gorilla

apex *noun* **apexes**
the highest part of something *the apex of a triangle*

aphid ['ay-fid'] *noun* **aphids**
a tiny insect that lives on plants and feeds on their juices

apiece *adverb*
each *Old books were selling at £5 apiece.*

apocalypse *noun*
a time when the world comes to an end

apologetic *adjective*
if someone is apologetic, they are sorry for something **apologetically** *adverb*

apologise *verb*
apologises, apologising, apologised
if you apologise to someone, you tell them you're sorry

> LANGUAGE EXTRA also spelt *apologize*

apology *noun* **apologies**
a word or words that you say to someone to show that you're sorry for something

apostle *noun* **apostles**
1 one of the 12 men that Jesus told to go and tell people about the Christian religion
2 someone who believes in an idea and tries to get other people to believe in it

apostrophe ['er-pos-trer-fee'] *noun* **apostrophes**
a punctuation mark written like this '

> LANGUAGE EXTRA you use an *apostrophe* for showing that one or more letters have been left out of a word, for example *I'm* (for *I am*) or *they'll* (for *they will*). The apostrophe stands for the missing part of the word.
>
> An apostrophe is also used for showing that something belongs to someone or to something else – this is the possessive use of the apostrophe. In the sentence *This is the girl's book*, the *'s* shows that the book belongs to *the girl* (one girl), and in the sentence *These are the girls' books* the *s'* shows that the books belong to *the girls* (more than one girl). Be careful to put the apostrophe in the correct place – before the *s* when there is only one and after the *s* when there is more than one.
>
> Take care also not to confuse *'s* with plural *s*. Write *I can see the girls*, not *I can see the girl's*.

17

app–appreciative

app *noun* **apps**
a software program, used especially in mobile equipment such as smartphones and tablets *short for:* application

appal *verb*
appals, appalling, appalled
if something or someone appals you, you are very shocked by them *We were appalled by his behaviour.*

appalling *adjective*
very bad and shocking *appalling behaviour; appalling weather* **appallingly** *adverb*

apparatus *noun* **apparatuses**
equipment used for a special purpose *Put the gym apparatus back when you're finished.*

apparent *adjective*
1 completely clear and very easy to see *After a while the difficulty becomes apparent.*
2 appearing to be true although it may not be true *We were delighted by her apparent love of music.*

apparently *adverb*
used for saying that something appears to be true but may not be true *Apparently, she's left the country.*

appeal *verb*
appeals, appealing, appealed
1 to appeal for something such as help, money or information is to ask people for it urgently *The Red Cross has appealed for blankets for the earthquake victims.*
2 if something appeals to you, you like it or you are interested in it *These computer games really appeal to children.*
3 to appeal against a decision is to ask someone to change it, especially in a court of law *The prisoner decided not to appeal.*

appeal *noun*
1 (*plural* **appeals**) asking for something urgently *He made an appeal for the kidnappers to release his son.*
2 the quality that makes people like something *Football has a lot of appeal for young boys.*
3 (*plural* **appeals**) asking for someone to change a decision *The prisoner lost his appeal.*

appealing *adjective*
very interesting and attractive *These ideas are appealing.*

appear *verb*
appears, appearing, appeared
1 to start to be seen *She suddenly appeared in front of me.*
2 to be written down somewhere *The story appeared in the newspaper.*
3 if something appears to be true, you have the feeling or an opinion that it is true *He appears to be tired. Nothing appeared to go right.*

> SYNONYM to seem

4 to appear in a play, film, show or other event is to take part in it

appearance *noun* **appearances**
1 the way someone or something looks *He's always worried about his appearance.*
2 when something or someone starts to be seen *the appearance of mountains in the distance*
3 the look of something that is different from the way it really is *There was an appearance of calm.*
4 when someone takes part in a play, film, show or other event

appease *verb*
appeases, appeasing, appeased
to appease someone is to give them what they want and be nice to them in order to make them less angry **appeasement** *noun*

appendicitis *noun*
a painful illness in which someone's appendix becomes infected (full of germs)

appendix *noun* **appendixes**
a small tube near the end of your intestines

appendix *noun* **appendices**
['er-pen-di-seez']
a section that gives extra information at the end of a book or document

appetiser *noun* **appetisers**
something you eat or drink before the start of a meal

> LANGUAGE EXTRA also spelt *appetizer*

appetising *adjective*
food that is appetising looks, smells and tastes good

> LANGUAGE EXTRA also spelt *appetizing*

appetite *noun* **appetites**
1 a feeling of being hungry *He has a huge appetite.*
2 a feeling of wanting something *an appetite for learning*

applaud *verb*
applauds, applauding, applauded
1 to clap your hands to show that you like someone's speech or performance, for example in a play or concert
2 to praise something such as an idea or decision

applause *noun*
when you applaud someone *There was loud applause.*

apple *noun* **apples**
a hard round fruit that is red, green or yellow on the outside and white on the inside

applet *noun* **applets**
a small computer program that works on a web page

appliance *noun* **appliances**
a piece of electrical equipment that people have at home, such as a television or washing machine

applicable *adjective*
if something is applicable to something else, it has something to do with it *These rules are applicable to all children in the school. What you said is not applicable.*

applicant *noun* **applicants**
someone who applies for something, especially a job

application *noun* **applications**
1 a letter you write or a form you fill in to ask for something important
2 a particular use that something can have *a technology with lots of practical applications*
3 a software program for a particular purpose *a word-processing application*
4 hard work *You need lots of application to pass your exams.*

applied *adjective*
used about a subject that you study for its practical use *applied mathematics*

apply *verb*
applies, applying, applied
1 to ask for something such as a job, a passport or money by writing a letter or filling in a form *My mum has applied for a job as a teacher. My sister has applied to three universities.*
2 to have something to do with someone or something *Does this rule apply to me?*
3 to put something on to something else *Apply the paint thickly to all the walls.*
4 to use something such as a word, method or activity *The head teacher has applied some new ideas to the problem.*
5 if you apply yourself to something, you work hard at it

appoint *verb*
appoints, appointing, appointed
1 to choose someone for a job *They've appointed a new science teacher.*
2 to choose a particular time or place for something to happen

appointment *noun* **appointments**
1 a meeting with someone arranged for a particular time and place *Try to keep your doctor's appointment and be on time.*
2 a job, or being chosen for a job *This is her first appointment as a teacher.*

apposition *noun*
used about a noun that appears next to another and means the same thing. For example, in the sentence 'My brother Alan lives here', 'my brother' and 'Alan' are nouns in apposition.

appraise *verb*
appraises, appraising, appraised
to give an opinion about the value or quality of something **appraisal** *noun*

appreciate *verb*
appreciates, appreciating, appreciated
1 to be grateful for something *I really appreciate all your help.*
2 to understand something completely
3 to understand the good qualities of something or someone *Not enough people appreciate good food.*
4 to go up in value, for example a house or antique

appreciation *noun*
1 a feeling of being grateful *She expressed her appreciation.*
2 an understanding of something good that gives you pleasure *an appreciation of music*
3 an understanding of the importance of something *an appreciation of other cultures*
4 an increase in the value of something

appreciative *adjective*
1 grateful for something *We're very appreciative of all your help.*
2 showing that you understand something or that you like something very much *an appreciative audience*

apprehensive adjective
if you are apprehensive, you are worried about something or afraid something bad might happen *We're all slightly apprehensive about the exams.* **apprehension** noun

apprentice noun **apprentices**
someone who works with someone else to learn the skills of their job *an apprentice bricklayer*

apprenticeship noun **apprenticeships**
1 the job of an apprentice
2 the time someone spends as an apprentice

approach verb
approaches, approaching, approached
1 to get closer to something or someone
2 to ask someone about something or to ask someone to do something
3 to be almost the same amount, size or value as something *temperatures approaching 30 degrees*
4 to deal with something *How should we approach this question?*

approach noun **approaches**
1 a way of dealing with something
2 when something gets closer *the approach of winter*
3 when you ask someone about something or ask someone to do something *He made a direct approach to the prime minister.*
4 a road or path leading to a building
5 the part of a plane's flight just before it lands

approachable adjective
someone who is approachable is friendly and easy to talk to

appropriate adjective
suitable **appropriately** adverb

approval noun
1 someone's agreement
2 a positive feeling that shows you like someone or think something is good or right *a nod of approval*

approve verb
approves, approving, approved
1 if you approve of something, you think it is good or right
2 if you approve of someone, you like them and have a good opinion of them
3 if an official person or organisation approves something, they agree to it *The government has not yet approved the plan.*

approximate adjective
not exactly right but roughly correct *What is the approximate number of children in the school?*

approximately adverb
not exactly but roughly *approximately 200 people*

approximation noun **approximations**
something such as a number, amount or size that is only roughly correct

apricot noun **apricots**
a small round yellow or orange fruit with a big hard seed inside called a stone

April noun
the fourth month of the year, between March and May. April has 30 days.

ORIGIN from Latin *Aprilis* '(the month) of Venus', from Greek *Aphro* 'Aphrodite', the goddess of love. Venus is the Roman name for this goddess.

April Fool's Day noun
the first day of April every year, a day when people play tricks on each other. The person you play the trick on is called an April fool.

apron noun **aprons**
a piece of clothing you wear at the front of your body and tie around your waist. You wear it to protect your clothes, especially if you're cooking.

apt adjective
1 exactly right *a very apt description*
2 if you're apt to do something, you're likely to do it *My teacher is apt to be late on a Friday.*
3 an apt pupil or student is quick to learn
aptly adverb

aptitude noun **aptitudes**
the talent for doing something or a particular talent *She has an aptitude for languages.*

aquarium noun **aquariums**
1 a glass or plastic container for keeping living fish in
2 a building with lots of aquariums where you go to look at fish and other water animals

ORIGIN from Latin *aquarius* 'connected with water', from *aqua* 'water'

aquatic adjective
connected with water *aquatic plants; aquatic sports*

aqueduct noun **aqueducts**
a bridge that carries water across a valley or river

Arab noun **Arabs**
someone from an important ethnic group in the Middle East and North Africa who speaks Arabic

Arabia noun
a peninsula in South-West Asia that includes countries such as Saudi Arabia and Yemen **Arabian** adjective

Arabic noun
the language spoken by most people in the Middle East and North Africa

Arabic adjective
connected with Arabic *the Arabic language*

Arabic numeral noun **Arabic numerals**
any one of the written numbers 1, 2, 3, 4, 5, 6, 7, 8, 9 and 0. The numerals were first used by Indian and Arab mathematicians.
compare: **Roman numeral**

arable adjective
1 connected with the growing of crops *arable farming*
2 arable land is land that is suitable for growing crops

arachnid ['er-rak-nid'] noun **arachnids**
another word for a spider

arbiter noun **arbiters**
1 a judge who decides disputes between people
2 someone who influences many people's opinions

arbitrary adjective
done or decided for no good reason, and often not fair *His decision was completely arbitrary.*

arbitrate verb
arbitrates, arbitrating, arbitrated
to decide a dispute between people by considering all the facts carefully
arbitration noun **arbitrator** noun

arc noun **arcs**
1 a curved shape
2 part of the curved line that forms the outside (or circumference) of a circle

arcade noun **arcades**
1 an amusement arcade is a large room for playing video games or playing on machines where you can win prizes
2 a shopping arcade is a covered place to walk with shops on either side

arcane adjective
secret and mysterious

arch noun **arches**
a part of a building or bridge with a curved top and straight sides

arch verb
arches, arching, arched
to curve like an arch *The cat arched its back.*

archaeologist noun **archaeologists**
someone who studies archaeology, usually by digging in the ground to find objects from the past

archaeology ['ah-kee-ol-er-jee'] noun
the study of ancient peoples by examining objects found in the ground such as parts of their buildings, tools and bones
archaeological adjective

ORIGIN from Greek *arkhaios* 'ancient' and *logos* 'word' or 'study'

archaic adjective
very old and no longer used *an archaic word*

archbishop noun **archbishops**
a Christian priest of the highest rank in charge of churches in a whole region

arch-enemy noun **arch-enemies**
someone's main enemy

archer noun **archers**
someone who shoots with a bow and arrow

archery noun
the sport of shooting with a bow and arrow

archipelago ['ah-kee-pel-er-goh'] noun **archipelagos**
a group of small islands

architect ['ah-kee-tekt'] noun **architects**
someone who designs buildings
architectural adjective

architecture noun
1 the style of designing buildings or a particular style of a building *the architecture of Rome*
2 the study and work of designing buildings

archive noun **archives**
1 a collection of historical documents or of documents that are no longer looked at often
2 a place where old documents are kept *the National Archives*
3 a copy of information stored on the internet for people to use

archway–around

archway *noun* **archways**
an entrance with an arch over it

arctic *adjective*
extremely cold *an arctic wind*

Arctic *noun*
1 the Arctic is the very cold region at the most northern point of the world. The region at the most southern point is the Antarctic.
2 the Arctic Circle is an imaginary line going around the earth in the Arctic region

ardent *adjective*
showing a very strongly positive feeling about something *an ardent supporter of Manchester United*

arduous *adjective*
very difficult *an arduous task*

are
second person singular and first, second and third person plural present tense of **be**

area *noun* **areas**
1 a part of a place such as a country or town *Do you live in this area?*
2 a part of a building or piece of land used for a special purpose *the kitchen area*
3 a part of the surface of something *a painful area of the skin*
4 a particular subject or group of subjects *What's your area of interest?*
5 in maths, the amount of space that something covers *an area of 100 square miles*

arena ['er-ree-ner'] *noun* **arenas**
a large building with seats all around where sports events take place

aren't
short for 'are not' or for 'am not' in questions ('aren't I?')

Argentina *noun*
a country in South America
Argentinian *adjective & noun*

arguable *adjective*
if something is arguable, it is not certain because people can have different opinions about it

SYNONYM debatable

argue *verb*
argues, arguing, argued
1 to talk to someone in an angry way because you do not agree with them *My brother and sister were arguing again.*
2 to give clear reasons for or against something *All the parents argued that a new computer room should be built.*

argument *noun* **arguments**
1 an angry talk with someone that you don't agree with *We had an argument about the price.*
2 a discussion with someone who has a different opinion *Did you win the argument?*
3 a reason or a number of reasons that someone gives for or against something *a good argument against smoking*

argumentative *adjective*
an argumentative person often argues angrily with people

arid *adjective*
arid land is very dry and plants do not grow there

arise *verb*
arises, arising, arose, arisen
1 to start to appear or happen *A problem has arisen.*
2 (old-fashioned) to stand up or get up

aristocracy *noun* **aristocracies**
a class of people such as lords or dukes who have the highest rank in a society and who may have lots of money or land
aristocratic *adjective*

aristocrat *noun* **aristocrats**
a member of an aristocracy

arithmetic *noun*
the study of the basic mathematical calculations of addition, subtraction, multiplication and division
arithmetical *adjective*

Ark *noun*
in the Bible, the Ark is a boat that Noah built to save his family and the animals from the flood

arm *noun* **arms**
1 one of the two parts of your body between your shoulder and your hand
2 the sleeve of a piece of clothing
3 the arm of a chair is the part at the side that you rest your arm on
4 the arm of an animal such as an octopus is one of the long body parts that it uses for holding and feeding
5 the arms of a tool such as tongs or compasses are the two thin bars that it is made of

arm *verb*
arms, arming, armed
to give weapons to people *They armed themselves with knives.*

armada *noun* **armadas**
a large group of ships, especially ready for war

CULTURE NOTE the *Spanish Armada* was a group of warships sent by King Philip II to attack the English in 1588

armadillo *noun* **armadillos**
a small animal from South America with a body covered in a hard shell made of scales

ORIGIN from Spanish *armadillo* 'little armed man'

Armageddon *noun*
a huge battle that will destroy the world

ORIGIN from the place of the final battle between good and evil mentioned in the New Testament

armaments *noun plural*
weapons

armband *noun* **armbands**
a piece of cloth that you wear around your arm as a sign of something, such as belonging to a group or because someone has just died

armchair *noun* **armchairs**
a big comfortable chair with sides to rest your arms on

armed *adjective*
if someone is armed, they are carrying a gun

armed forces *noun plural*
a country's army, navy and air force

armful *noun* **armfuls**
an amount of something you can hold in your arms *She was carrying an armful of twigs.*

armistice *noun* **armistices**
1 an agreement between enemies to stop fighting
2 Armistice Day is 11 November, the anniversary of the date the First World War ended in 1918

armour *noun*
1 a metal covering for protecting a soldier's body in past times *a suit of armour*
2 strong metal layers for protecting vehicles such as tanks

armoured *adjective*
covered in strong metal layers *an armoured vehicle*

armour-plated *adjective*
covered in a thin layer of strong metal as a protection

armoury *noun* **armouries**
1 a place where weapons are kept
2 the amount of weapons a country has

armpit *noun* **armpits**
the part of your body under your arm where your arm joins your shoulder

arms *noun plural*
1 weapons *nuclear arms*
2 a design on a shield that represents an important family, town or organisation. It is also called a coat of arms.

army *noun* **armies**
1 the part of a country's fighting force of soldiers that fights on land *He joined the army.*
2 any large group of soldiers *a rebel army*
3 any large group of people *an army of volunteers*

A-road *noun* **A-roads**
a main road in the UK that is smaller than a motorway but larger than a B-road

aroma *noun* **aromas**
a pleasant smell, for example coming from food *the aroma of fresh coffee*

aromatic *adjective*
if something is aromatic, it has a pleasant smell *aromatic herbs*

arose
past tense of **arise**

around *preposition & adverb*
1 on all sides of something *I put a string around the parcel.*
2 in or to lots of different places *There are many museums around London. Stop following me around. Can I have a look around? Pass the sweets around* (to different people).
3 in a particular direction or in the opposite direction *She lives around the corner. Turn around so I can see you.*
4 nearby *Is there a school around here?*
5 used for saying that something exists *There isn't much money around.*

6 used for saying that someone is in a place without doing much *He just sits around all day.*
7 slightly more or less than something such as a number, amount or time *around £300; around three o'clock*

arouse *verb*
arouses, arousing, aroused
1 to cause a particular feeling or attitude *Your idea has aroused a lot of interest.*
2 to make someone wake up

arrange *verb*
arranges, arranging, arranged
1 to put things in a particular order *Arrange the chairs in a circle.*
2 if you arrange something such as a visit, meeting or party, you make plans for it to happen *My parents have arranged to go on holiday to Spain.*
3 to make sure something happens *Can you arrange to pick me up at the airport?*

arrangement *noun* arrangements
1 things in a particular order or the way they are ordered *a lovely arrangement of flowers*
2 an agreement *I have an arrangement with my uncle to pick me up after school.*
3 the way something is organised *What are the sleeping arrangements?*

array *noun* arrays
a large group of things displayed for people to see *a dazzling array of colours*

arrears *noun plural*
1 money that someone owes because they haven't made a regular payment at the correct time
2 if you are in arrears, you are late in making a regular payment *We're three weeks in arrears with our rent.*

arrest *verb*
arrests, arresting, arrested
1 if the police arrest someone, they take them to the police station because they think they have committed a crime
2 to stop something *The doctors couldn't arrest the bleeding.*

arrest *noun* arrests
1 when the police arrest someone *The police have made an arrest.*
2 if someone is under arrest, they have been arrested by the police

arrival *noun* arrivals
1 when someone or something gets somewhere *They're waiting for the arrival of the prime minister.*
2 when something happens *the arrival of summer*
3 someone who has just arrived *The head teacher showed the new arrivals around.*
4 a baby who has just been born
5 arrivals are planes or trains that have just arrived *Check the arrivals board.*

arrive *verb*
arrives, arriving, arrived
1 to arrive somewhere is to get there from somewhere else *The train arrived at Euston at noon.*
2 to happen *Winter arrived early this year.*

3 to come by post *Your birthday card has arrived.*
4 to be born *Her little sister arrived last week.*

arrogant *adjective*
used for describing someone who behaves rudely (or someone's rude behaviour or feelings) because they think they are more important than other people
arrogance *noun*

arrow *noun* arrows
1 a thin straight piece of wood with a sharp point that people shoot from a bow as a weapon or for sport
2 a sign shaped like an arrow for pointing in the direction of something
3 the arrow keys on a computer keyboard are the four keys marked with up, down, left and right arrows that show ways to move the cursor

arsenal *noun* arsenals
1 a large amount of weapons that someone has
2 a building where weapons are stored

arsenic *noun*
a strong poison made from a chemical element and used for killing insects and small animals

arson *noun*
a crime in which someone deliberately sets fire to a building *an arson attack*
arsonist *noun*

art *noun* arts
1 painting, drawing and sculpture as activities, objects or creative products *Leah is good at art. It's a great work of art. My dad is an art teacher.*
2 arts or arts subjects are subjects such as literature, music, history and languages that are not scientific
3 a creative skill *the art of writing short stories*

Art Deco *noun*
a style in art and architecture of the 1920s and 1930s that uses simple strong lines and shapes

artefact *noun* artefacts
an object such as a tool or weapon made by people in the past and considered important to study

artery *noun* arteries
a tube that carries blood from the heart to the rest of the body

artful *adjective*
very good at tricking people in order to get what you want **artfully** *adverb*

arthritis ['ah-thry-ters'] *noun*
an illness that makes the joints in the body swollen and painful *Gran has arthritis in her hand.* **arthritic** *adjective*

Arthur *noun*
in stories, an ancient king of the Britons who fought the Saxons in the 6th century AD and led a group of soldiers called the Knights of the Round Table
Arthurian *adjective*

artichoke *noun* artichokes
a round green vegetable with thick pointed leaves that you cook and eat the bottom part of

article *noun* articles
1 a particular thing *an article of clothing*
2 a piece of writing in a newspaper or magazine
3 in grammar, an article is a word that refers to a particular example of something using 'the' (for example 'the school') or to a general example using 'a' or 'an' (for example 'a school'). The word 'the' is called the definite article, and 'a' or 'an' is the indefinite article.

articulate ['ah-tik-yoo-lert'] *adjective*
if someone is articulate, they can express their thoughts very clearly and easily in words

articulate ['ah-tik-yoo-layt'] *verb*
articulates, articulating, articulated
1 to pronounce a word or words very clearly so that the person listening can easily understand
2 to express thoughts and feelings very clearly in words
articulation *noun*

articulated lorry *noun*
articulated lorries
a lorry made up of two parts, a driver's cab and a trailer, so that it can go round corners more easily

artificial *adjective*
1 not real but made by people or machines, and often made to look like something real *artificial flowers*
2 artificial intelligence is when machines and computers are used for doing things that people do such as thinking
3 artificial respiration is when someone blows into someone else's mouth to try to make them start breathing again after they have stopped breathing, for example after an accident

artificially *adverb*
not naturally but in a way that is done or made by people or machines *an artificially created environment*

artillery *noun*
1 large and powerful guns that are used by an army
2 the section of an army that uses these guns

artist *noun* artists
1 someone who creates a work of art, especially a painting or drawing *Tate Britain has paintings by Turner and other famous artists.*
2 a performer such as a dancer, musician or actor

artiste ['ah-teest'] *noun* artistes
an entertainer such as a singer or dancer *a cabaret artiste*

artistic *adjective*
1 connected with art, beauty and culture *artistic activities*
2 good at painting or drawing *Susan is very artistic.*
3 attractive and done with skill *an artistic display*

artistry *noun*
artistic skill *a work of great artistry*

artwork *noun*
pieces of art such as drawings or paintings

as–assess

as conjunction, preposition & adverb
1 at the same time as something else *I bumped into Robert as I got off the bus.*
2 used for describing what someone or something is, does or looks like *As a teacher, he was very helpful. She was dressed up as an angel.*
3 in a particular way *Do as I do.*
4 used when you compare things *You're as tall as me.*
5 used in similes *as brave as a lion*
6 another word for because *I'm going to bed as I'm very tired.*
7 **as if** or **as though** used for showing that something may be true *It looks as if she'll be late.*
8 **as for** used for introducing a different subject, but one that you were talking about earlier *As for my sister, she left school and became a doctor.*
9 **as soon as** at the same time as or immediately after something else *As soon as Holly comes home, she puts on the TV.*
10 **as well** used when you mean something or someone extra *Can Sarah come as well?*

SYNONYMS too, also

11 **as well** also used when you mean the same thing is true about something or someone else *We live in York and Grandma does as well.*

SYNONYMS too, also

asbestos noun
a building material that was used in the past to protect against fire and heat. It is made of fibres that do not burn.

ASBO noun ASBOs
an official document from a court of law that orders someone to stop behaving badly or in a particular way, for example to stop bullying someone

ORIGIN an acronym from *AntiSocial Behaviour Order*

ascend verb
ascends, ascending, ascended
1 to climb up something such as a hill or stairs
2 if a plane ascends, it goes up into the air
3 an ascending order or sequence is one where the numbers get larger, for example 1, 2, 3, 4 and so on

ascent noun ascents
1 a climb up something *the ascent of Everest*
2 the ascent of a plane is when it goes up into the air

asexual reproduction noun
when new plants or animals are produced from one single plant or animal without male and female cells joining together

ash noun ashes
1 the grey powder that is left after something has burnt *cigarette ash*
2 an ash tree is a large tree with a thin grey bark and oval leaves that come to a point. Each of its seeds is shaped like a small wing.

ashamed adjective
1 sad and embarrassed about something you've done or about a particular thing or situation *I'm ashamed of what I said. My dad is ashamed of his bald head.*
2 if you're ashamed of someone, you feel sad and embarrassed about something they have done *My brother hit my best friend – I feel so ashamed.*
3 if you're ashamed to do something, you feel sad and embarrassed about doing it *I'm ashamed to show Ms Singh my homework this week (I don't want to show it to her, for example because it's so bad).*

ashen adjective
very pale, for example because you're ill or frightened

ashore adverb
1 on land, not on the sea or on a river *We have two days ashore.*
2 onto the land or shore *We go ashore at two o'clock.*

ashtray noun ashtrays
a small flat bowl where people put ash from their cigarettes

Asia noun
a continent south of the Arctic Ocean, north of the Indian Ocean and linked to Europe in the east. It includes countries such as Russia, China and India.

Asian noun Asians
1 someone from Asia
2 someone from India, Pakistan, Bangladesh or Sri Lanka
Asian adjective

aside adverb
1 to one side *Move aside and let me pass.*
2 used about money or time that you keep for doing something in the future *I'm putting some money aside every week to buy a bike. Ms Blake told us to put an hour a day aside for our homework.*
3 **aside from** except for

ask verb
asks, asking, asked
1 to say something to someone as a question in order to get an answer from them *I asked them the way to the station.*
2 if you ask for something, you say politely that you want someone to give it to you *I asked my sister for some advice.*
3 if you ask someone to do something, you say politely that you want them to do it
4 if you ask someone to a place or to something such as a party, you say politely that you want them to come *He asked me round to play a video game.*
5 if you say that someone is asking for it, you mean they deserve something bad that happens to them *It's your own fault – you were asking for it.*
6 if someone asks you out, they invite you to go somewhere with them, for example to the cinema

asleep adjective
1 sleeping *He's fast asleep.*
2 if your foot or another part of your body is asleep, you can't feel anything in it

AS level noun AS levels
an examination that students take in English, Welsh and Northern Irish schools and colleges around the age of 17. It is part of their A levels.
compare: A level

asparagus noun
a long thin green vegetable with a pointed end

aspect noun aspects
1 a particular part of something or way of looking at a situation *The new head teacher will look at all aspects of the school.*
2 the direction a room or building faces
3 an appearance *We were frightened by the stranger's sinister aspect.*

asphalt ['ass-falt'] noun
a black substance used for making roads and other hard surfaces

aspire verb
aspires, aspiring, aspired
if someone aspires to something, they want very much to be, do or have something, for example in a job *My sister aspires to be a lawyer. My brother is an aspiring actor.*

aspirin noun
1 a medicine that reduces pain or fever
2 (plural **aspirins**) a tablet of this medicine

ass noun asses
1 a stupid fool
2 a donkey

assassin noun assassins
someone who murders an important person

assassinate verb
assassinates, assassinating, assassinated
to murder an important person such as a king or president **assassination** noun

assault noun assaults
an attack on someone *He was sent to prison for assault.*

assault verb
assaults, assaulting, assaulted
to assault someone is to attack them and hurt them

assemble verb
assembles, assembling, assembled
1 to come together in one place *The children assembled in front of the school.*
2 to bring people together in one place
3 to put the parts of something together in order to build something *Dad is trying to assemble the chest of drawers.*

assembly noun assemblies
1 a meeting of people who have come together for a particular reason
2 a school assembly is a regular meeting of all the students and teachers
3 an official group of people who meet together to make decisions, for example in a government
4 the action of assembling parts in order to build something such as a car

assent noun
an agreement to something *Do you think they will give their assent?*

assert verb
asserts, asserting, asserted
to say strongly that something is true *She asserted her innocence.* **assertion** noun

assertive adjective
someone who is assertive says what they think very strongly so that people take notice of them

assess verb
assesses, assessing, assessed
to consider something carefully and give an opinion about it

assessment – atlas

assessment *noun* assessments
1 when someone considers something carefully
2 someone's opinion about something that they have considered

asset *noun* assets
1 someone or something that is very helpful to you *She's an asset to the school.*
2 someone's assets are all the money and property that they own

assign *verb*
assigns, assigning, assigned
1 to give someone something to do as a job or activity, or to give someone something they can use *We were assigned homework to do over the weekend. Everyone in the class was assigned a tablet computer.*
2 to put or send someone somewhere *I was assigned to the highest group in maths.*
3 to make someone responsible for someone else *They assigned a partner to every student.*

assignment *noun* assignments
a piece of work that a student must do or that is a part of someone's job *Hand in your assignments before the end of the week.*

assist *verb*
assists, assisting, assisted
to help someone or something *Teachers can assist pupils with their homework.*

assistance *noun*
help or support *No-one came to his assistance.*

assistant *noun* assistants
1 someone who helps someone else in their job
2 a shop assistant is someone who serves customers in a shop

associate ['ers-oh-si-ayt'] *verb*
associates, associating, associated
1 to connect something with something else in your mind *We associate the Eiffel Tower with Paris.*
2 if you associate with someone, you spend time with them or are friends with them *My sister associates with lots of artists.*

associate ['ers-oh-si-ert'] *noun* associates
a person that someone works with

association *noun* associations
1 a group of people with the same aims or jobs who have joined together
2 when you associate with someone *They don't approve of her association with artists.*
3 a connection between two things
4 a memory or feeling connected with something, for example with an idea or word

assonance *noun*
in literature or poetry, assonance is the use of the same vowel sound in words that are near each other, for example 'On either side the river lie' (The Lady of Shalott)

assorted *adjective*
of different kinds or colours, sizes or shapes *a box full of assorted books*; *apples of assorted sizes*

assortment *noun* assortments
a group of different things

assume *verb*
assumes, assuming, assumed
if you assume that something is true, you believe it is reasonable to think it is true even though there is no proof

assumed name *noun* assumed names
a name that a person uses that is not their real name

assumption *noun* assumptions
something that it is reasonable to think is true even though there is no proof *I made an assumption but I was wrong.*

assurance *noun*
1 (*plural* **assurances**) a promise that something is definitely true *She gave me an assurance.*
2 a feeling that you are right about something *an air of assurance*
3 another word for insurance

assure *verb*
assures, assuring, assured
if you assure someone of something, you tell them it is definitely true so that they will be less worried *I assure you I will do all I can to help.*

asterisk *noun* asterisks
a mark like a small star * used in writing for drawing someone's attention to something

> **ORIGIN** from Latin *asteriscus* and Greek *asteriskos* 'small star'

asteroid *noun* asteroids
one of thousands of very large rocks much smaller than planets that move around the sun. Most asteroids are found in the asteroid belt between Jupiter and Mars.

asthma ['ass-mer'] *noun*
an illness that makes it difficult for you to breathe

asthmatic *adjective*
suffering from asthma **asthmatic** *noun*

astonish *verb*
astonishes, astonishing, astonished
to surprise someone very much *I was astonished at his behaviour.*

astonishing *adjective*
1 very surprising
2 extremely good *She achieved an astonishing result.*
astonishingly *adverb*

astonishment *noun*
very great surprise

astound *verb*
astounds, astounding, astounded
to make someone extremely surprised

astray *adverb*
1 to go astray is to get lost
2 to lead someone astray is to make them behave badly

astride *adverb*
if someone is astride something, they have one leg on either side of it *I was sitting astride the garden wall.*

astrology *noun*
the study of the movements of planets and stars and how some people think they influence people's lives **astrologer** *noun*
astrological *adjective*

astronaut *noun* astronauts
someone who travels in space

> **ORIGIN** from Greek *astron* 'star' and *nautes* 'sailor'

astronomical *adjective*
1 connected with astronomy
2 extremely high or large *Prices were astronomical.*

astronomy *noun*
the study of the stars and planets and other objects in the universe **astronomer** *noun*

astute *adjective*
very clever and good at making judgements

asunder *adverb*
if someone tears something asunder, they put it into pieces and destroy it

asylum ['er-sye-lerm'] *noun*
when someone is given protection by a country and allowed to live there because it is too dangerous or difficult to continue living in their own country. Someone who needs this protection is called an asylum seeker.

at *preposition*
1 used for showing where or when *He's at school. It happened at five o'clock.*
2 used for showing a situation *The country is at war.*
3 used for showing a measurement or price *tickets at £10*
4 towards *She looked at me. I'm annoyed at you.*
5 the symbol @ used in email addresses

at all *adverb*
1 used in negative sentences to make the meaning stronger *I have no money at all.*
2 used in questions to mean 'even a little bit' *Can you hear at all?*

atchoo *interjection*
the sound you make when you sneeze

> **LANGUAGE EXTRA** also spelt *achoo*

ate
past tense of **eat**

atheist ['ay-thee-ist'] *noun* atheists
someone who does not believe in God
atheism *noun*

athlete *noun* athletes
1 someone who does athletics
2 someone who is good at sports

athletic *adjective*
1 connected with athletics
2 strong and good at sports

athletics *noun*
1 the sports of running, jumping and throwing
2 physical exercises and sports

Atlantic *noun*
the Atlantic or Atlantic Ocean is the sea that separates North and South America from Europe and Africa **Atlantic** *adjective*

atlas *noun* atlases
a book of maps

> **ORIGIN** from *Atlas*, a Titan god in Greek mythology, whose punishment for fighting against the god Zeus was to carry the heavens on his shoulders. In early maps from the 16th century, Atlas is shown holding up the world.

23

atmosphere – audience

atmosphere noun
1 (plural **atmospheres**) the air and gases around the earth or around other planets
2 the air inside a room
3 the particular feeling you get from a place, event or period *There was a lovely atmosphere at the party.*

atmospheric adjective
1 connected with the earth's atmosphere
2 something atmospheric gives you a particular feeling *atmospheric music*

atoll noun **atolls**
an island shaped like a ring and made of coral

atom noun **atoms**
1 an atom is the smallest part of a chemical element
2 a tiny amount of something

at once adverb
1 immediately *Get out of here at once!*
2 at the same time *Don't eat your cake all at once.*

atrocious adjective
extremely bad *atrocious weather*

atrocity noun **atrocities**
a very violent action, such as killing lots of people, especially during a war *There were atrocities on both sides.*

at sign noun **at signs**
the symbol @ used in email addresses

attach verb
attaches, attaching, attached
1 to fix, join or connect something to something else *I attached the balloon to the door handle.*
2 to send a computer file with an email
3 to attach importance to something is to think that it is important

attached adjective
if you are attached to someone or something, you've gradually come to like them very much *They are very attached.*

attachment noun **attachments**
1 an extra part that is fixed to a piece of equipment for doing a particular job *The vacuum cleaner comes with all sorts of attachments.*
2 a strong liking for someone or something
3 a computer file that you send to someone with an email

attack verb
attacks, attacking, attacked
1 to use violence against a person or animal, for example by hitting, shooting or jumping on them *He was attacked with a knife. The cat attacked the mouse.*
2 to use weapons such as guns or bombs against a place or enemy *The battleship was attacked by helicopters. The soldiers attack by night.*
3 to damage something, for example using a weapon or tool *A crazy person attacked the painting with a hammer.*
4 to go into a place to steal money or goods *Thieves attacked the jewellery shop during the night.*
5 to say bad things about someone or something using strong words
6 in football and other games, to try to score points or goals by getting the ball into the correct position and moving forward

attacker noun

attack noun **attacks**
1 an act of violence against someone
2 an act of using weapons against a place or country, for example in a war
3 when someone uses strong words to say bad things about someone or something *This will be seen as an attack on the government.*
4 a sudden short illness *a heart attack*
5 when a player tries to score points or goals against another player or team, for example in football

attain verb
attains, attaining, attained
to achieve or reach something such as a level, amount or grade *The adult crocodile can attain an enormous size.*

attainment noun

attempt verb
attempts, attempting, attempted
to attempt to do something is to try to do it

attempt noun **attempts**
an attempt to do something is when you try to do it

attend verb
attends, attending, attended
1 to attend somewhere such as a school or club is to go there regularly as a student or a member *Jacob's sister attends university.*
2 to attend a meeting, event or performance is to be or go there
3 to attend to something that needs to be done is to deal with it
4 to attend to someone is to look after them, for example because they are ill

attendance noun **attendances**
1 going somewhere regularly or being present somewhere
2 the number of people who go somewhere or who are present there *Attendance at the match was very high* (lots of people came).

attendant noun **attendants**
1 someone who helps people in a public place *a car park attendant*
2 someone who goes with an important person and looks after them

attention noun
1 interest in something *The Harry Potter books have received a lot of attention.*
2 when you notice something *Try and walk out of the room without attracting attention* (without anyone noticing). *Can I draw your attention to this little icon?* (make you notice it)
3 care given to something or someone *attention to detail; The teacher gave her a lot of attention to help her catch up.*
4 if you pay attention, you listen or watch carefully, or you take care over something or take care to read or obey something *Pay attention to what I say. Pay attention – there are cars coming! I wasn't paying attention to the instructions.*
5 if soldiers stand to attention, they stand up straight with their feet together

attentive adjective
1 listening or watching carefully *an attentive audience*
2 showing an interest in someone and trying to help them

attic noun **attics**
a room at the top of a house just under the roof

> ORIGIN from the design around the top storey of buildings in *Attica*, the region around Athens in ancient Greece

attitude noun **attitudes**
your attitude is the way you feel about something and the way you behave because of this *I don't like your attitude.*

attract verb
attracts, attracting, attracted
1 if something attracts you, it makes you interested *Going to Spain really attracts me.*
2 if you're attracted to someone, you like them very much
3 to make someone or something come to a place or move closer to something *London attracts lots of visitors. These smells attract flies.*
4 to get something or make it happen *I'm trying to attract his attention. We need to attract support for the idea.*

attraction noun **attractions**
1 something interesting that people like to see or go to, such as a museum or funfair *tourist attractions*
2 a quality that makes you like something or someone *The main attraction of this software is that it's free.*
3 in science, attraction is a force that makes something move towards something else, for example magnetism (the power of a magnet to make iron or steel move towards it)

attractive adjective
1 very pleasant to look at *an attractive girl; an attractive house*
2 very interesting in a way that makes you like something *an attractive offer*

attractiveness noun

aubergine noun **aubergines**
a large dark purple vegetable with a smooth shiny skin and white flesh

auburn adjective
auburn hair is of a reddish-brown colour

auction noun **auctions**
a type of public event where people meet somewhere or go online to buy something that is sold to the person offering the most money

auction verb
auctions, auctioning, auctioned
to sell something at an auction

auctioneer noun **auctioneers**
a person in charge of an auction

audacious adjective
something that is audacious involves lots of risks so you have to be very brave to do it *an audacious plan to send a man to the moon*

audible adjective
if something is audible, you can hear it *Her voice was barely audible.*

audience noun **audiences**
1 all the people who watch or listen to a film, play, concert, television programme or some other performance *a theatre audience*

24

2 a meeting with someone important *The prime minister was granted an audience with the King.*

audio *adjective*
connected with sound that is recorded with electronic equipment *an audio book*

audiovisual *adjective*
audiovisual aids or materials use recorded sounds and pictures

audition *noun* **auditions**
a short performance in which someone does something creative such as sing, dance, act or play music. Judges decide if they are good enough to be in the show, film, play or band, for example.

audition *verb*
auditions, auditioning, auditioned
to take part in an audition

auditorium *noun* **auditoriums**
an auditorium is the part of a theatre, cinema or concert hall where the audience sits

August *noun*
the eighth month of the year, between July and September. August has 31 days.

> ORIGIN from *Augustus*, the name of the first emperor of Rome (27 BC)

aunt *noun* **aunts**
someone's aunt is the sister of their father or mother, or the wife of their uncle

auntie or **aunty** *noun* **aunties**
an informal word for an aunt

au pair ['oh-pair'] *noun* **au pairs**
a young person who stays with a family in another country, looking after the children and doing the housework, so that he or she can learn a foreign language

> ORIGIN from French *au pair* 'on an equal footing', because an au pair helps in the house instead of paying for meals and a place to stay

aura *noun* **auras**
a particular feeling that you get from a place or person *There was an aura of mystery surrounding the old house.*

aural *adjective*
connected with hearing *The film has some strange aural effects.*

> LANGUAGE EXTRA be careful not to confuse *aural* and *oral*. *Oral* means 'connected with speaking', as in *a Spanish oral exam*.

austere *adjective*
1 simple and without anything pleasant or comfortable *the austere life of a monk*
2 plain and simple *the austere style of the old church*
3 someone who is austere is very strict

austerity *noun*
1 a government policy of reducing the money it spends *tough austerity measures*
2 a time when people are poorer because the money situation of a country is bad

Australia *noun*
a continent and country south-east of Asia and south of the Equator

Australian *adjective*
connected with Australia

Australian *noun* **Australians**
someone from Australia

Austria *noun*
a country in Central Europe

Austrian *adjective*
connected with Austria

Austrian *noun* **Austrians**
someone from Austria

authentic *adjective*
1 real *an authentic painting by Matisse; authentic Italian food*
2 correct in every way *an authentic description of the Battle of Hastings*
authenticity *noun*

authenticate *verb*
authenticates, authenticating, authenticated
to prove that something is not false, such as a painting or computer software

author *noun* **authors**
someone who writes a book or something else such as an article, poem or report

authorisation *noun* **authorisations**
official permission

> LANGUAGE EXTRA also spelt *authorization*

authorise *verb*
authorises, authorising, authorised
to give official permission for something *Who authorised the class to leave?*

> LANGUAGE EXTRA also spelt *authorize*

authority *noun* **authorities**
1 the power to tell people what to do *You have no authority to order me around.*
2 the authorities are the people in charge of a country, area or town, such as the police or the government
3 an organisation that controls a public service *She complained about the noise to the local authority.*
4 a person that people trust because he or she knows a lot about a subject *My teacher is an authority on Dickens.*
5 a book that has a lot of very accurate information about something

autistic *adjective*
if someone is autistic, they have a disability that makes it difficult for them to communicate with other people
autism *noun*

auto- *prefix*
1 of or done by yourself *autobiography*
2 working by itself *automatic*

autobiography *noun* **autobiographies**
a book someone writes about their own life
autobiographical *adjective*

> LANGUAGE EXTRA a book someone writes about someone else's life is called a *biography*

autograph *noun* **autographs**
a famous person's name that they write down somewhere, for example in a book, for someone else to keep so that they remember the famous person

> SYNONYM signature

> ORIGIN from Greek *autographos* (*autos* 'self' and *graphos* 'written')

automate *verb*
automates, automating, automated
to make computers and machines do something instead of people *a fully automated office*

automatic *adjective*
1 working by itself *an automatic door*
2 an automatic action that someone does is one done without thinking
3 if something that someone gets or gives is automatic, it happens because of a rule or a particular situation and nothing can stop it happening *an automatic fine*
4 an automatic car is one in which the gears change by themselves

automatically *adverb*
1 if something such as a machine works automatically, it works by itself without people doing anything
2 without thinking *I automatically answered the phone.*
3 because of a rule or a particular situation *You automatically receive a £10 voucher.*

automation *noun*
using computers and machines to do work instead of people

automobile *noun* **automobiles**
an American word for a car

autopsy *noun* **autopsies**
an examination of someone's dead body to find out how they died

> SYNONYM post-mortem

autumn ['ort-erm'] *noun* **autumns**
the season between summer and winter when the leaves fall off trees and the weather starts to get cold **autumnal** *adjective*

auxiliary *adjective*
1 an auxiliary worker helps another worker *an auxiliary nurse*
2 an auxiliary piece of equipment helps the main equipment to work or makes it work again if it stops working *an auxiliary engine*
3 an auxiliary verb helps other verbs, for example to form different tenses

> LANGUAGE EXTRA in English, an *auxiliary verb* is a very common verb such as *to have, to be* or *to do*. You use auxiliary verbs to make tenses such as *I have eaten, she is running* or *they did go*, or passive forms such as *you were seen*.

compare: **modal verb**

auxiliary *noun* **auxiliaries**
1 an auxiliary worker
2 an auxiliary verb

> ORIGIN from Latin *auxilium* 'help'

availability *noun*
1 the availability of something is when you can find, use or buy it
2 the availability of someone is when they are not busy and are able to do something

available *adjective*
1 if something is available, you can find it, use it or buy it somewhere *Tickets are available now. Information is available online.*
2 if someone is available, they are not busy and they are able to do something *The head teacher is available to speak to us this afternoon.*

avalanche – awkward

avalanche ['av-er-lahnch'] *noun*
avalanches
a large amount of snow, ice, rocks or earth falling down the side of a mountain

avarice *noun*
another word for greed

avatar *noun* avatars
a picture of a person or animal that you display on a computer screen to represent you, for example in a computer game or chat room

> ORIGIN from Sanskrit *avatara* 'going down', describing a Hindu god who 'goes down' to take on a human or animal form

avenge *verb*
avenges, avenging, avenged
to punish someone because they have harmed or insulted you or a friend or family member *The soldiers avenged the King's death.*

avenue *noun* avenues
a wide and straight road, usually with trees on both sides

average *adjective*
1 of a level or amount that most people would consider normal *I'm of average height. Your work this term has been average.*
2 normal and like others of the same kind *How many times do you play football in an average week?*
3 not very good but not bad either *The latest 'Doctor Who' was just average.*

average *noun* averages
1 in maths, an average is a number you get by adding together a set of numbers and dividing the total by the amount of these numbers *The average of 3, 6 and 12 is 7* (21 divided by 3).
2 a level or amount that most people would consider normal *Sally's exam mark was above average.*
3 **on average** used for describing something that often happens when you consider lots of examples of it, but doesn't always happen *On average I sleep eight hours a night.*

average *verb*
averages, averaging, averaged
to average is to have or do something as an average *The ship averaged 400 miles a day.*

averse *adjective*
if you are not averse to something, you like it or like doing it *My dad's not averse to an ice cream in summer.*

avert *verb*
averts, averting, averted
1 to stop something bad happening *The pilot averted a disaster.*
2 if someone averts their eyes, they look in the other direction and away from something

avi ['a-vee']
the ending of a computer filename. An .avi contains sound and pictures.
short for: Audio–Video Interleave

aviary ['ayv-yer-ee'] *noun* aviaries
a large cage for keeping birds in

aviation *noun*
1 the industry that makes aircraft
2 the study of flying in aircraft

aviator *noun* aviators
an old-fashioned word for a pilot

avid *adjective*
used for describing someone who really likes doing something and does it as much as possible *I'm an avid reader.*

avocado *noun* avocados
a pear-shaped fruit with a green or dark purple skin, a very big hard seed inside called a stone and light green flesh

avoid *verb*
avoids, avoiding, avoided
1 to keep away from someone or something *I don't like Ben so I try to avoid him in the playground.*
2 to stop something from happening *To avoid an accident, don't go near the edge.*
3 to not do something or deal with something *You'll do anything to avoid going to school. She avoided the question.*

avoidance *noun*

avoidable *adjective*
if something bad is avoidable, it doesn't have to happen or it can be stopped from happening *This tragedy was completely avoidable.*

await *verb*
awaits, awaiting, awaited
1 if you await something, you're waiting for it *We're awaiting a decision.*
2 if something awaits you, it is waiting to happen to you *A little treat awaits you in the kitchen.*

awake *adjective*
1 not sleeping *I kept awake until midnight.*
2 if someone can't keep awake, they fall asleep

awake *verb*
awakes, awaking, awoke, awoken
to wake up or wake someone up

awaken *verb*
awakens, awakening, awakened
1 to make someone have a feeling or an interest *This awakened our curiosity.*
2 to wake up or wake someone up

> LANGUAGE EXTRA in everyday language, you use *wake up* rather than *awake* or *awaken*. For example, you say *I woke up at seven o'clock* rather than *I awoke at seven o'clock* or (rarely) *I awakened at seven o'clock*.

awakening *noun* awakenings
1 when you suddenly realise something
2 a rude awakening is a very unpleasant surprise

award *noun* awards
1 a prize or money that someone gets when they have done something successful *She won an award for her paintings.*
2 money that someone gets, for example from the government, to be able to do something *My brother has applied for an award to continue his studies.*

award *verb*
awards, awarding, awarded
to award someone something is to give them an award

aware *adjective*
1 to be aware of something is to know about it *I'm aware of the problem.*
2 to be aware of something is also to notice it because you can see, hear, feel or smell it *I was aware of a strange smell coming from the basement. He became aware that someone was following him.*
3 to make someone aware of something is to tell them about it

awareness *noun*
1 knowledge and understanding of something
2 when you notice something

awash *adjective*
covered with water or liquid *The whole village is awash with muddy water.*

away *adverb*
1 from a place, or not in a place *Please go away. Yesterday our teacher was away* (not in school).
2 in the right place or a safe place *Put your books away in your desk.*
3 not near someone or something *Keep that bully away from me. The hat needs to be away from the baby's eyes.*
4 from now *Christmas is only a few weeks away.*
5 from achieving something *He was just a few votes away from becoming head boy.*
6 used for showing that something disappears *The water has boiled away.*
7 used for showing that something continues *I've been working away all day.*
8 if a sports team plays away, they play at their opponents' sports field, not at home

away *adjective*
an away game is one played at the opponents' sports field. If a team plays at their own field, they play at home.

awe *noun*
a feeling of great respect, sometimes mixed with fear *We looked up at the huge statue with awe.*

awesome *adjective*
1 very great or serious and often frightening *an awesome responsibility*
2 an informal word meaning excellent *Your friend is simply awesome!*

awful *adjective*
1 extremely bad *That was an awful thing to say.*
2 used for saying how big something is or how much of something there is *an awful lot of people; I looked an awful idiot.*
3 sad or ill *You look awful. I feel awful about what happened.*
4 ugly *I'm glad you got rid of those awful glasses.*

awfully *adverb*
1 extremely *Rachel is awfully lucky.*
2 very much *Would you mind awfully making less noise?*
3 extremely badly *You behaved awfully.*

awhile *adverb*
for a short time

awkward *adjective*
1 difficult to deal with *an awkward question; Stop being so awkward.*
2 feeling uncomfortable and embarrassed *I feel awkward if someone watches me.*

26

3 clumsy *I'm very awkward – I'm always bumping into things.*
4 an awkward time is a time of the day that is not good for you *Come back later – this is an awkward time.*

awkwardly *adverb*

awning *noun* **awnings**
a piece of cloth above the window or door of a building such as a shop, which protects it from the rain and sun

awoke
past tense of **awake**

awoken
past participle of **awake**

awry ['er-rye', to rhyme with 'eye'] *adjective*
if something goes awry, it goes wrong *All our plans have gone awry.*

axe *noun* **axes**
a tool with a long wooden handle fixed to a heavy metal blade. It is used for chopping wood.

axe *verb*
axes, axing, axed
to get rid of something such as someone's job or a television programme, to save money

axis ['ak-siss] *noun* **axes** ['ak-seez]
1 an imaginary line through the middle of a round object, around which it turns *The earth spins on its axis.*
2 a line through the middle of a shape such as a circle or square that divides it into two equal halves
3 one of the two sides of a graph or chart (mathematical diagram) where the measurements are given *I've given the amounts on the vertical axis* (or *y-axis*) *and the dates along the horizontal axis* (or *x-axis*).

Axis *noun*
the Axis countries are the countries such as Germany and Japan that fought against Britain, France and the US in the Second World War *Axis soldiers*
compare: **Allies** (see: **ally**)

axle *noun* **axles**
an axle is the bar that joins the centres of a pair of wheels on a vehicle

aye [rhymes with 'eye'] *interjection*
yes

LANGUAGE EXTRA this word is used mainly in Scotland

azalea ['er-zay-lee-er] *noun* **azaleas**
a bush with attractive pink or purple flowers that grows in gardens and parks

Aztec *noun* **Aztecs**
the Aztecs were an Indian people who lived in Central and South Mexico before they were destroyed in the 16th century during the Spanish Conquest **Aztec** *adjective*

azure ['az-yoo-er' or 'az-yer'] *adjective*
bright blue *an azure sky*

ORIGIN the letter B grew out of a shape representing a shelter in ancient Egyptian hieroglyphics. Many years later, the Phoenicians changed it to something that looked like a P but faced left instead of right. They called the shape *beth* meaning 'house'. Eventually the letter passed into Greek with the name *beta*. The Greeks turned it to face right and added a second loop. From Greek, B passed into Roman, and from there into our own alphabet.

baa *noun*
the sound that a sheep or lamb makes

babble *verb*
babbles, babbling, babbled
1 to talk like a baby, or without making much sense
2 to make the sound of water flowing gently *a babbling brook*

babble *noun*
a noise that is difficult to understand, such as people talking at the same time

baboon *noun* **baboons**
a big monkey from Africa or Asia with a long face and short tail

baby *noun* **babies**
1 a very young child between the time he or she is born and the age of about one or two
2 a child that is still developing in his or her mother's body
3 a very young animal

babyish *adjective*
1 behaving like a silly child
2 only suitable for a baby or child, not for a grown-up

babysit *verb*
babysits, babysitting, babysat
to look after a child (or children) when the parents are not at home **babysitting** *noun*

babysitter *noun* **babysitters**
someone who babysits

bachelor *noun* **bachelors**
a man who isn't married
compare: **spinster**

back *adverb*
1 behind you, or in the opposite direction *I looked back. Lean back.*
2 where something or someone was before *Let's go back to school. Put it back on the shelf. Give my book back.*
3 how something or someone was before *Dad took his laptop apart and can't put it back. Things are back to normal.*
4 used when you do something to someone after they have done something to you *I hit him back. Phone me back later.*
5 used when you do the same thing you've already done *I went back over my homework.*
6 used when referring to a distance, or a time away from now *Move back! I can't think back that far.*

back *noun* **backs**
1 the part of your body between your shoulders and your buttocks
2 a similar part of the body of an animal, bird or insect *The boy was riding on the back of an elephant.*
3 the part furthest away from the front *the back of the house; the back of the book*
4 the side of something such as a page, photo or sweater that is not the main side *Write your name on the back of your library card.*
5 the back of a chair or seat is the part that you rest your back against
6 a player in a football team who has the job of stopping players from the other team from scoring goals
7 if something such as a piece of clothing is back to front, it is the wrong way round because the back part is where the front part should be

back *adjective*
at the back *the back seat*

back *verb*
backs, backing, backed
1 to support someone
2 to make a car move backwards *Dad backed up slowly. Back the car out of the garage.*
3 to back up a computer file or disk is to make a copy of it in case it is lost
4 to put money as a bet on a person or animal in a race or competition because you think they have a chance of winning. If they win, you get more money back.
5 if you back down in an argument, you say you are wrong

backache *noun* **backaches**
a pain in the back

backbone *noun* **backbones**
the long row of bones down the middle of your back

SYNONYM spine

backfire *verb*
backfires, backfiring, backfired
1 if a car backfires, it makes a loud noise from its exhaust (pipe at the back where gas from the engine comes out)
2 to go wrong *Our plans backfired.*

background *noun* **backgrounds**
1 the part of a picture or scene that is furthest away from you

ANTONYM foreground

2 if you hear a sound in the background, you hear it in the distance
3 if a computer program runs in the background, it is always working on your computer but does not appear on the screen
4 information for understanding a situation completely *What's the background to the fighting between the two countries?*
5 someone's background refers to things such as their education, family life, culture and religion *What's her family background?*
6 an image or pattern used as decoration on the screen of a computer or mobile phone. It is also called wallpaper.

backing *noun*
1 support
2 material for making the back of something, such as a picture to be framed
3 music that supports a main singer's voice

27

backlog – baking powder

backlog noun backlogs
work that should have been done that you still have to do *to clear the backlog*

backpack noun backpacks
a bag that you carry on your back. It has straps that go over your shoulders.

SYNONYM rucksack

backpacker noun backpackers
a person who travels around a country carrying a backpack

backside noun backsides
an informal word for the buttocks

backspace noun
1 a key on a computer keyboard that you press to move one space back when writing text
2 the action of moving one space back by pressing the backspace key

backstroke noun
a way of swimming on your back

backup noun backups
1 a copy of a computer file or disk that you make in case the first one is lost
2 extra help

backward adjective
1 slow to develop *a backward region*
2 in the direction that is behind you *a backward glance*

backwards adverb
1 in the opposite way to what is normal *He was walking backwards. Can you count backwards?*
2 behind you, or towards the back *Lean backwards.*

backyard noun backyards
1 the land behind your house, usually covered with a hard surface
2 in American English, a backyard is a garden behind your house

bacon noun
meat from the back or sides of a pig that has been salted and smoked (made to last longer by using salt and smoke). It is usually eaten in long thin slices.

bacteria noun plural
tiny organisms (living things) that you can usually see only through a microscope. Some bacteria cause disease but others are good for our bodies and the environment. Bacteria are sometimes added to food such as yoghurt.

bad adjective worse, worst
1 not good, for example when talking about something or someone you don't like or something you can't do very well *bad weather*; *a bad film*; *bad behaviour*; *Nandita is a bad swimmer. I'm bad at maths.*
2 causing harm *Too much sugar is bad for you.*
3 cruel, evil or wicked *He's a bad man and should be in prison.*
4 serious *a bad accident* (for example injuring or killing someone); *a bad mistake* (a big one that causes problems)
5 painful or unhealthy *a bad leg*; *Grandpa is feeling bad today.*
6 not fresh *These plums have gone bad.*
7 **not bad** quite good *This film isn't bad.*

baddie noun baddies
a bad person in a film, play or book

LANGUAGE EXTRA also spelt *baddy*

badge noun badges
1 a small round object with words or a picture on it that you pin onto your clothes
2 a piece of plastic, metal or cloth that you wear as a sign that you belong to something such as your school or a club

badger noun badgers
a grey animal that has a white face with black stripes, lives in the ground and comes out at night

badger verb
badgers, badgering, badgered
to make someone angry by asking them to do something lots of times

badly adverb
1 in a way that is not good *to behave badly*; *to sing badly*
2 seriously *to be badly hurt*
3 if you need to do something badly, you want to do it very much *I need a haircut badly.*

bad-mannered adjective
behaving badly when you are with other people

ANTONYM well-mannered

badminton noun
a game like tennis played indoors with a shuttlecock (round cork with feathers sticking out of it)

ORIGIN named after *Badminton House*, the country house of the Duke of Beaufort in Gloucestershire. The game started in India among British soldiers but was played for the first time in England at the Duke of Beaufort's house in the 19th century.

bad-tempered adjective
a bad-tempered person gets angry a lot of the time

baffle verb
baffles, baffling, baffled
if something baffles you, you can't understand it, for example because it's so strange

SYNONYM to puzzle

bag noun bags
1 a container made of paper, plastic, fabric or leather, used for carrying things
2 **bags of** a lot of *We've got bags of time.*

bag verb
bags, bagging, bagged
to get something before someone else does *I bagged a seat near the window.*

bagel noun bagels
a hard round bread roll with a hole in the middle

ORIGIN from Yiddish *beygl* 'ring'

baggage noun
bags and cases used when travelling

baggy adjective baggier, baggiest
baggy clothes, such as trousers, are big and have lots of room around the body

bagpipes noun plural
a Scottish musical instrument. You play it by blowing air through a pipe into a bag, and then squeezing air out from the bag through different pipes.

baguette ['ba-get'] noun baguettes
a long thin loaf of bread that is crusty on the outside. It is a French style of bread and is usually at least two feet long.

ORIGIN from French *baguette* 'little stick'

Bahamas noun
the Bahamas is a country made up of many islands in the Atlantic, south-east of the United States and close to the state of Florida **Bahamian** adjective & noun

bail noun
1 money given to a court so that someone can be freed from prison until their trial *The suspect was released on bail.*
2 (plural **bails**) one of the two small pieces of wood lying flat on top of the stumps (upright sticks) in cricket

bail verb
bails, bailing, bailed
1 to empty water from the bottom of a boat using a container
2 if someone is bailed, they are freed from prison until their trial because money has been paid

bailiff noun bailiffs
an official who takes away people's property from their home if they owe money

Bairam ['by-ram'] noun
a Muslim festival at the end of Ramadan (Lesser Bairam) and another (Greater Bairam) that takes place 70 days later at the end of the Islamic year

Baisakhi ['by-sa-kee'] noun
a Sikh festival that takes place in April to celebrate the new year

LANGUAGE EXTRA also spelt *Vaisakhi*

bait noun
food that you put on a hook or in a trap to catch a fish or animal

bait verb
baits, baiting, baited
to put food on a hook or in a trap to catch a fish or animal

bake verb
bakes, baking, baked
1 to cook food in an oven
2 to make cakes or bread in an oven *My stepdad bakes every Sunday.*
3 to make something such as clay hard by heating it in an oven called a kiln, for example to make pottery, bricks or tiles
4 to be very hot *It's baking in here.*

baked beans noun plural
beans in tomato sauce, sold in a tin. The beans are usually haricot beans.

baker noun bakers
a person who makes and sells bread and cakes

bakery noun bakeries
a place where bread and cakes are made and sold

baking powder noun
a powder that makes cakes swell up (or rise) when they are baked

balaclava–banister

balaclava *noun* balaclavas
a soft covering for the head and neck and most of the face, usually worn to keep warm

> ORIGIN from the name of a small port near Sebastopol in Russia. The *Balaclava helmet* was a head covering made of wool worn by soldiers in the Crimean War (1853–56).

balance *verb*
balances, balancing, balanced
1 to keep something steady without dropping it or to stay steady without falling *I balanced a cup on my head. Jason is balancing on one foot.*
2 if two weights balance, they are equal

balance *noun*
1 the feeling of being steady and upright *Be careful not to lose your balance.*
2 a situation where different things are in a good relationship with each other *It's hard to get the right balance between work and play.*
3 (*plural* **balances**) the amount of money you have in your bank account, or the amount left that you owe someone after you've paid back some of their money
4 (*plural* **balances**) a piece of equipment for weighing, usually containing an upright bar in the middle that supports another bar going across. This bar has a little tray hanging from each end where you put the things to be weighed.

balanced *adjective*
1 a balanced diet contains many different healthy and fresh ingredients
2 in science, balanced forces are forces that are the same size but act in opposite directions

balcony *noun* balconies
1 an outdoor platform that you get to from an upstairs floor of a building. It sticks out from a wall and has metal bars or a wall going around it.
2 an upstairs area where people sit in a theatre or cinema

bald *adjective* balder, baldest
someone who is bald has no hair or very little hair on their head

bale *noun* bales
a large amount of something tied together tightly *a big bale of hay*

bale *verb*
bales, baling, baled
to bale out of a plane is to jump out using a parachute

Balkans *noun plural*
the Balkans are a group of countries (including Albania, Bulgaria, Greece and part of Turkey, for example) in a large area of South-East Europe known as the Balkan Peninsula

ball *noun* balls
1 a round object used in games
2 any round shape *a ball of wool*
3 an important event where people dressed in smart clothes go to dance

ballad *noun* ballads
a long song or poem that tells a story

ballerina *noun* ballerinas
a woman or girl who dances in a ballet

ballet ['ba-lay'] *noun*
a form of artistic dancing that usually tells a story set to music *a ballet dancer*

balloon *noun* balloons
1 a small container of thin rubber that you blow air into and use as a toy or decoration
2 a large soft container filled with gas or hot air, with a big basket hanging from it. It is used for travelling through the air and carrying people. *a hot-air balloon* (with air heated by a flame so that it rises)
3 a circle around the speaking words of a character in a cartoon. It is also called a speech bubble or a bubble.

balloonist *noun* balloonists
someone who travels through the air in a hot-air balloon or gas balloon

ballot *noun* ballots
a secret vote to choose someone, usually by making a mark on a ballot paper that is put into a ballot box

ballpoint *noun* ballpoints
a ballpoint or ballpoint pen is a pen with a tiny metal ball at the end through which the ink comes out

ballroom *noun* ballrooms
a very large room for dancing

balsa ['bol-ser'] *noun*
balsa wood is a very light wood used for making models

bamboo *noun* bamboos
a kind of grass with hard hollow stems used for building things such as fences or furniture

ban *verb*
bans, banning, banned
to ban someone from doing something is to say that they must not do it *Playing football in the corridor is banned.*

ban *noun* bans
if there is a ban on something, you must not do it

banana *noun* bananas
a long curved fruit with a yellow skin

band *noun* bands
1 a group of people who play rock, pop or jazz music together
2 any group of people *a band of outlaws*
3 a small strip of material for putting around something or for decoration *a hair band*
4 a line of something that is different from what is around it, for example having a different colour or design or being lighter or darker *a circle with an orange band around the edge*

band *verb*
bands, banding, banded
to band together is to come together as a group

bandage *noun* bandages
a strip of material for winding around a cut or injury to protect it

bandage *verb*
bandages, bandaging, bandaged
to put a bandage around a cut or injury

Band-Aid *noun* Band-Aids (trademark)
a plaster for putting on a cut or injury to protect it

bandit *noun* bandits
a thief who attacks travellers and steals from them, usually as a member of a gang

bandstand *noun* bandstands
a platform, usually with a roof, where musicians play their music, for example in a park

bandwagon *noun*
to jump on the bandwagon to do the same activity as other people in order to be fashionable or successful

bandy *adjective* bandier, bandiest
bandy legs are curved outwards at the knees

> LANGUAGE EXTRA a person with *bandy legs* is called *bandy-legged* or *bow-legged*

bang *noun* bangs
1 a short loud noise
2 a heavy knock *I felt a bang on my arm.*

bang *verb*
bangs, banging, banged
1 to hit something or someone hard *Don't bang me over the head with that piece of wood!*
2 to hit something hard against something else, for example a part of your body that you hit accidentally *He fell and banged his head.*
3 to hit something hard with a loud noise *I banged on the window. The door was banging in the wind.*
4 to close something with a loud noise *Don't bang that door!*
5 (informal) to bang someone up is to put them in prison

bang *adverb*
an informal way of saying exactly at a particular place or time or of giving special importance to a word *a village bang in the middle of Scotland; You're bang on time. My homework is bang up to date.*

> SYNONYM right

banger *noun* bangers
1 a firework that makes a loud noise when it goes off

> SYNONYM firecracker

2 an informal word for an old car
3 an informal word for a sausage *bangers and mash*

Bangladesh *noun*
a country in South-East Asia
Bangladeshi *adjective & noun*

bangle *noun* bangles
a metal or wooden ring worn around the wrist

> ORIGIN from Hindi *bangli* 'glass ring'

banish *verb*
banishes, banishing, banished
to send someone away as a punishment, especially for a long time or for ever *Napoleon was banished to the Isle of Elba in 1814.*

banister *noun* banisters
a rail to hold on to at the side of stairs

> LANGUAGE EXTRA also spelt *bannister*

banjo–barista

banjo *noun* **banjos**
a musical instrument like a small circular guitar

bank *noun* **banks**
1 a place that looks after people's money. People go to banks, for example, to put money in to save for the future, to take money out, to borrow money or to pay bills.
2 the bank of a river is the ground along the side of it
3 a pile of earth, sand or snow with sloping sides
4 a number of things arranged in a row, such as pieces of equipment *a bank of computers*
5 a place where blood or other things from the body can be stored safely *a blood bank*

> ORIGIN sense 1 comes from Italian *banca* 'bench', because in medieval Italy moneylenders did their business sitting on benches

bank *verb*
banks, banking, banked
1 if someone banks with a particular bank, they have put their money in that bank
2 if a plane banks, the pilot puts one wing lower than the other to change direction
3 to bank on something is to expect or hope very much that it will happen

banker *noun* **bankers**
someone who works in a bank and has an important position

bank holiday *noun* **bank holidays**
a public holiday when shops, offices and banks are closed

banknote *noun* **banknotes**
a piece of paper money

bankrupt *adjective*
if a person or company is bankrupt, they don't have enough money to pay what they owe people **bankruptcy** *noun*

> ORIGIN from Italian *banca rotta* 'broken bench'. In medieval Italy the moneylender's bench that he used for his business was broken up when he had no more money to lend.

banner *noun* **banners**
1 a long piece of cloth or paper with a message, pattern or picture on it, usually fixed to a pole or to poles at both ends, or tied to something with rope
2 a long narrow shape used as a design or for decoration, or as an advertisement across a web page

banquet *noun* **banquets**
a formal meal for many people, usually for a special occasion or to honour someone important

bap *noun* **baps**
a soft bread roll

baptise *verb*
baptises, baptising, baptised
to welcome someone into the Christian religion by pouring water over them or covering them in water

> LANGUAGE EXTRA also spelt *baptize*

baptism *noun* **baptisms**
a ceremony for baptising someone

Baptist *noun* **Baptists**
a Christian who believes that only grown-ups and not babies should be baptised

bar *noun* **bars**
1 a long piece of metal *an iron bar*
2 a piece of something hard *a bar of soap*
3 a place or a counter where drinks are served
4 a short division in music containing a number of beats (regular patterns of sounds)
5 a long strip along the top, side or bottom of a computer screen, for example with symbols, icons or menus that you click on
6 something that stops something else happening *a bar to success*

bar *verb*
bars, barring, barred
1 to bar someone from a place is to say they must not go there *He's been barred from our club.*
2 to bar someone from doing something is to say they must not do it
3 if you bar someone's way, you stop them from going past
4 if you bar a door, you stop it from being opened by putting something in front of it or fixing something across it

barbarian *noun* **barbarians**
a cruel and violent person with no education

> ORIGIN from Greek *barbaros* 'non-Greek' or 'foreigner'

barbaric *adjective*
cruel and violent

barbarity *noun*
great cruelty and violence

barbecue *noun* **barbecues**
1 a meal that is cooked and eaten outdoors using a metal frame called a barbecue
2 a thin metal frame for cooking food, such as meat, outdoors over a fire
3 barbecue sauce is a brown sauce that gives a strong and smoky flavour to food, especially meat. It can have many ingredients including spices, tomatoes, sugar and vinegar (sour liquid made from wine).

> ORIGIN from Spanish and Haitian *barbacoa*, which comes from a South American Indian word meaning 'frame of sticks'

barbed wire *noun*
strong twisted wires with lots of sharp points, used for making fences

barber *noun* **barbers**
a person who cuts men's hair

> ORIGIN from Latin *barba* 'beard'

bar chart *noun* **bar charts**
a diagram where amounts are shown as long rectangles (or bars) of different lengths

> LANGUAGE EXTRA you can also say *bar graph*

barcode *noun* **barcodes**
a pattern of printed lines on products that you buy. The lines can be read by a computer to give information such as price.

> LANGUAGE EXTRA also spelt *bar code*

bard *noun* **bards**
an old-fashioned word for a poet

> LANGUAGE EXTRA Shakespeare is sometimes known as *the Bard*

bare *adjective* **barer, barest**
1 with no clothes on *bare feet; bare arms*
2 not covered or decorated with anything *a bare wall*
3 empty *The cupboard is bare.*
4 used for describing the least amount of something, with nothing extra *In some countries they don't have the bare essentials to live.*

barefoot *adjective & adverb*
with no shoes or socks on

barely *adverb*
only just *I was so tired I could barely walk.*

bargain *noun* **bargains**
1 something of good value that you buy cheaply
2 a bargain between two people is an agreement in which each person has to do something for the other *Don't forget to keep your part of the bargain.*
3 **into the bargain** also *He fell over and hurt his leg, and broke his smartphone into the bargain.*

bargain *verb*
bargains, bargaining, bargained
1 to argue with someone to get a better price or agreement
2 if you get more than you bargained for, you get something that you didn't expect, especially something bad

barge *noun* **barges**
a boat with a flat bottom, used on a canal or river

barge *verb*
barges, barging, barged
1 to barge in on someone is to interrupt them while they are talking *I'm sorry to barge in like this.*
2 to barge into a place is to rush into it in a rude way and interrupt the people already there
3 to barge into a person is to bump into them in a rough way

bargepole *noun*
if you say you wouldn't touch something or someone with a bargepole, you mean you don't want to have anything to do with them

bar graph *noun* **bar graphs**
a diagram where amounts are shown as long rectangles (or bars) of different lengths

> LANGUAGE EXTRA you can also say *bar chart*

barista ['ber-ree-ster] *noun* **baristas**
someone who serves customers in a coffee shop and who is skilled at making different types of coffee such as cappuccino and espresso

> ORIGIN from Italian *barista* 'person who serves drinks in a bar'

baritone *noun* baritones
a man with a fairly deep singing voice, lower than a tenor but higher than a bass

bark *noun*
1 (*plural* **barks**) a bark is the sound of a dog barking
2 bark is the hard covering around a tree or branch

bark *verb*
barks, barking, barked
1 when a dog barks, it makes a short loud noise that is its own special sound
2 if a person barks, they say something in a very loud voice

barley *noun*
a plant with seeds used as food and for making drinks such as beer and whisky

barmaid *noun* barmaids
a woman who serves drinks in a bar

barman *noun* barmen
a man who serves drinks in a bar

bar mitzvah *noun* bar mitzvahs
a Jewish religious ceremony for a boy at the age of 13, when he accepts the religious duties of an adult
compare: bat mitzvah

ORIGIN from Hebrew words meaning 'son of the law or the commandment'

barmy *adjective* barmier, barmiest
not sensible and very silly

barn *noun* barns
a building on a farm, used for storing crops or farm machines or for keeping animals such as pigs or chickens

barnacle *noun* barnacles
a small sea animal with a shell that fixes itself to the bottom of boats and to rocks

barometer *noun* barometers
an instrument that shows you the changes in the weather by measuring air pressure

baron *noun* barons
in the UK, a man of the lowest noble rank

baroness *noun* baronesses
in the UK, a woman of the lowest noble rank, or the wife of a baron

baroque *adjective*
connected with a detailed and complicated style of art and music, for example, that was popular in the 17th and 18th centuries

barrack *verb*
barracks, barracking, barracked
to interrupt someone speaking in public by shouting at them

barracks *noun* barracks
an army barracks is the place where soldiers live

ORIGIN from French *baraque* and Catalan *barraca* 'hut'

barrage ['ba-rahj'; 'j' has the middle sound of 'pleasure'] *noun* barrages
1 an attack from lots of guns firing for a long period of time in war
2 a large amount of questions or complaints aimed at someone all at the same time *The prime minister faced a barrage of questions.*
3 a wall across a river to control the level of water

barrel *noun* barrels
1 a big container for liquids, made of wood, metal or plastic. It has the shape of a cylinder (tube with flat ends shaped like circles) and is sometimes curved outwards in the middle.
2 the barrel of a gun is the tube through which the bullet comes out

barrel organ *noun* barrel organs
a big instrument that produces music when you turn a handle

barren *adjective*
barren land is where no plants grow because the soil is of bad quality

barricade *noun* barricades
a structure or a number of large objects placed across a street to stop people getting past

barricade *verb*
barricades, barricading, barricaded
1 to barricade a street is to put a barricade across it
2 if you barricade yourself in a room or building, you block the door to stop people getting in

barrier *noun* barriers
1 a fence, gate or wall that stops people going somewhere
2 something that stops something else happening *Having dyslexia should not be a barrier to success.*

barring *preposition*
except for *We'll arrive tomorrow, barring accidents.*

barrister *noun* barristers
a lawyer in England and Wales who represents people in higher courts

barrow *noun* barrows
1 a small cart that you push

SYNONYM wheelbarrow

2 a large cart from which goods are sold in the street

barter *verb*
barters, bartering, bartered
if you barter, you exchange goods for other goods instead of using money

base *noun* bases
1 the bottom part of something
2 a place where an organisation, group or person operates from *an army base*
3 in maths, a base is a number that forms a system of counting, for example the number 10 in the decimal system
4 in science, a base is a substance that forms a salt and water when it is mixed with an acid

base *verb*
bases, basing, based
1 if someone bases something on something else, they get their idea or information from it or they use it as a starting point *In my story I based the main character on someone I knew. The film is based on Roald Dahl's book. Celsius is a system for measuring temperature based on the metric system.*
2 if you are based somewhere, you live there and operate from there

baseball *noun*
1 an American game like rounders, played between two teams. Each player has to hit a ball with a bat and run around four 'bases'.
2 (*plural* **baseballs**) the small hard ball used in the game of baseball

based on *conjunction & preposition*
used for mentioning that there is an important fact or situation that influences something *Based on what happened to you last time, I think you were right to complain. We were put into groups based on our knowledge of maths.*

basement *noun* basements
a floor of a building built below the level of the ground *a basement flat*

bash *verb*
bashes, bashing, bashed
to hit something or someone hard *I slipped over and bashed my head on the door. Park on the driveway if you don't want anyone bashing into the car. The front of the bus is all bashed in* (damaged from hitting something).

bash *noun* bashes
1 a hard hit *a bash on the head*
2 to have a bash at something is to try to do it

bashful *adjective*
shy

basic *adjective*
1 forming the most important or most needed part of something *Reading and writing are basic skills. My cousin has a basic knowledge of Spanish.*
2 very simple and without anything extra *very basic accommodation*

basically *adverb*
used for talking about the most important detail of something *The book is basically a horror story. Basically, it can't be done.*

basil ['ba-zerl'] *noun*
a plant with a strong sweet smell, used for making food taste better

basilica *noun* basilicas
1 a large Roman Catholic church shaped like a rectangle with a round end
2 a large ancient Roman building, used for example as a public meeting place

basin *noun* basins
1 a large container for washing your hands and face

SYNONYM washbasin

2 a deep round container for food
3 a river basin is the land around the river where it gets its water from

basis *noun* bases ['bay-seez']
1 a particular way of doing something *He visits his grandparents on a regular basis.*
2 the most important part of something that you start from and build into something better or bigger *These ideas form the basis for J. K. Rowling's new book.*
3 an important fact or idea that supports something and helps to make it successful *This argument has no basis.*
4 the reason for something *You have no basis for saying that.*

bask–bazaar

bask *verb*
basks, basking, basked
to bask in the sun is to let the sun warm you as you are lying or sitting

basket *noun* baskets
1 a container, with or without a handle, used for carrying or storing things. It is often made from thin pieces of wood, wire, plastic or straw that are twisted together.
2 the place on a shopping website where you put the things you want to buy

basketball *noun*
1 a game in which two teams try to throw a ball through a high net fixed to a metal ring
2 (*plural* **basketballs**) the large ball used in the game of basketball

bass ['bayss'] *adjective*
producing a very deep sound *a bass guitar*

bass ['bayss'] *noun* basses
a voice, singer or instrument (for example a guitar) that produces a very deep sound *They have someone famous on bass.*

bass clef *noun* bass clefs
a symbol at the beginning of a line of music that shows the low pitch (or quality) of the notes

bassoon *noun* bassoons
a musical instrument in the shape of a long tube that you blow into to produce very low sounds

bat *noun* bats
1 a piece of wood that you use to hit the ball in games such as cricket, baseball and table tennis. Different shapes of bat are used for different games.
2 a small animal like a mouse with wings that flies at night
3 to do something off your own bat is to decide to do it yourself, not because someone told you to do it

bat *verb*
bats, batting, batted
1 to hit the ball with a bat in games such as cricket or baseball
2 if you say someone didn't bat an eyelid or didn't bat an eye, you mean they were not surprised or upset by something

batch *noun* batches
a group of things done at the same time, or people doing something at the same time *Send me the files in batches, not one at a time. The next batch of pupils came into the room.*

bated *adjective*
with bated breath worried or excited because you badly want to know about something *The whole class was waiting for the news with bated breath.*

> **LANGUAGE EXTRA** remember that the correct spelling is *bated*. Do not write *baited*.

> **ORIGIN** from an old word *bate* 'to slow down'. The idea is that you hold your breath (or 'slow down' your breathing) while waiting to hear about something very important. The expression was first used by Shakespeare in *The Merchant of Venice* (1596).

bath *noun* baths
1 a water container that you lie in or sit in to wash yourself
2 the action of washing yourself in the bath, or the water you wash yourself with *to have a bath*; *The bath is cold.*

bath *verb*
baths, bathing, bathed
to wash someone in the bath

bathe *verb*
bathes, bathing, bathed
1 to bathe in the sea or a river is to swim or play in the water
2 to bathe a wound or a part of your body is to wash it carefully

bathe *noun*
the action of swimming or playing in the water *to go for a bathe*

bathrobe *noun* bathrobes
a soft loose coat that people wear indoors, for example before or after having a shower

bathroom *noun* bathrooms
1 a room with a bath or shower and a sink for washing
2 in American English, a bathroom is a room with a toilet *to go to the bathroom*

baths *noun plural*
1 a public indoor swimming pool
2 a public building where people go to wash themselves *Roman baths*

bathtub *noun* bathtubs
the American word for a bath (water container that you wash yourself in)

bat mitzvah *noun* bat mitzvahs
a Jewish religious ceremony for a girl at the age of 12 or 13, when she accepts the religious duties of an adult
compare: **bar mitzvah**

> **ORIGIN** from Hebrew words meaning 'daughter of the law or the commandment'

baton *noun* batons
1 a thin stick used by a conductor to conduct an orchestra
2 a short stick that runners pass to each other in a relay race
3 a thick stick that a police officer carries as a weapon

> **SYNONYM** truncheon

4 a thin stick that someone walking in front of a musical group in a procession spins and throws in the air
see: **majorette**
5 a thin loaf of bread that is hard on the outside, like a small baguette

batsman *noun* batsmen
a batsman in cricket is a player who hits the ball using a bat

battalion *noun* battalions
a large group of soldiers. A battalion contains two or more companies and is a part of a regiment or brigade.

batten *noun* battens
a piece of wood for fixing something down

batten *verb*
battens, battening, battened
if something is battened down, it is fixed down tightly

batter *verb*
batters, battering, battered
to hit many times *The victim was battered to death.*

batter *noun*
a mixture of flour, eggs and water, used for example for making pancakes or frying fish *plaice in batter*

battery *noun* batteries
1 a small container for storing electricity, for example to make a radio, mobile phone or computer work. A battery is made up of two or more electric cells (pieces of equipment for making electricity out of chemicals).
2 a car battery is a big square box that stores the electricity to give power to a car, for example to make it start
3 a group of things of the same type, such as large guns or tests *He's had a whole battery of tests at the hospital.*
4 a group of cages for animals such as chickens or cows on a farm (called a battery farm). Large numbers of animals are kept in very small spaces so that the food from these animals can be sold as cheaply as possible. *battery eggs* (produced by battery chickens)
compare: **free-range**

battle *noun* battles
1 a fight between armies in a war
2 a fight or great effort to get something done, or for or against something *a battle to attract customers*; *a battle against cancer*

battlefield *noun* battlefields
a place where a battle is going on or where one took place in the past

battlements *noun plural*
a wall at the top of a castle with gaps for firing weapons such as arrows

battleship *noun* battleships
a very large ship with guns

batty *adjective* battier, battiest (informal)
slightly crazy or behaving in a slightly strange way

bawl *verb*
bawls, bawling, bawled
to shout or cry loudly

bay *noun* bays
1 a place where the coast curves in
2 an area used for special purposes *a parking bay*; *a cargo bay*
3 to keep something at bay is to keep it away from you so that it doesn't harm you

bayonet *noun* bayonets
a long blade fixed at the end of a rifle for attacking someone with

bay window *noun* bay windows
a large window that sticks out from the main wall of a house

bazaar *noun* bazaars
1 a market in an Eastern country
2 a sale of goods to raise money, for example for a school or charity (group that helps people)

> **ORIGIN** from Persian *bazar* 'market'

BBC *noun*
a British organisation that broadcasts television and radio programmes. It is also the name of the channels operated by the BBC. *It's on BBC1 tonight.*
short for: British Broadcasting Corporation

BC
used for showing a date before the birth of Jesus Christ *Plato was born in 427 BC.*
short for: before Christ

BCE
used for showing a date before the birth of Jesus Christ
short for: before common era

> **LANGUAGE EXTRA** some people, for example from non-Christian religions, use *BCE* instead of *BC* so as not to mention Christ

be *verb*
am, are, is; being; was, were; been
1 used for linking different parts of a sentence, or giving a description *It is Daniel. I am happy. She is a doctor.*
2 used for forming continuous tenses *They are playing football.*
3 used for forming the passive *The picture was painted by Van Gogh.*
4 used for saying that something exists *There is a tree in the playground.*
5 used instead of the verbs 'to go' or 'to come' when talking about the past *I've never been to Spain. Has the window cleaner been?*

beach *noun* **beaches**
the land by the sea covered with sand or small stones

beacon *noun* **beacons**
a light or fire on a hill for warning of danger

bead *noun* **beads**
1 a small round piece of coloured glass, plastic or wood with a hole through the middle. It can be put on a string with others to make a necklace or bracelet.
2 a tiny drop of liquid *beads of sweat*

beady *adjective* **beadier, beadiest**
beady eyes are small and bright in a way that is often seen as a sign of something unpleasant, such as being greedy or dishonest

beagle *noun* **beagles**
a dog with short hair, long ears and short legs

beak *noun* **beaks**
the hard pointed mouth of a bird

beaker *noun* **beakers**
1 a tall plastic drinking cup without a handle
2 a glass or plastic container with a lip (pointed part) for pouring liquids, used in a laboratory

beam *noun* **beams**
1 a long and heavy piece of wood or metal, usually for supporting a roof
2 a long line of light, for example from the headlights of a car *a laser beam*

beam *verb*
beams, beaming, beamed
1 to send out light or radio signals *Pictures were beamed to the other side of the world.*
2 to smile with a big smile because you're very happy *My parents were beaming when I told them I'd passed my exams.*

bean *noun* **beans**
1 a seed you can eat from different kinds of plants, for example a kidney bean or haricot bean. The seed grows inside a pod (long narrow container).
2 the pod that contains the beans, for example a runner bean or green bean
3 a plant that produces beans

beansprout *noun* **beansprouts**
a type of bean seed with its stem that is eaten as food

> **LANGUAGE EXTRA** also spelt *bean sprout*

beanstalk *noun* **beanstalks**
the stem of a bean plant

> **CULTURE NOTE** most people know the word *beanstalk* from the English fairy story *Jack and the Beanstalk*

bear *noun* **bears**
an animal with a big heavy body, thick fur and short thick legs

bear *verb*
bears, bearing, bore, borne
1 if you can't bear something or someone, it means you dislike them very much
2 to support or carry *The floor can't bear the weight of all these boxes. Demonstrators bearing slogans marched down the street.*
3 to have or show *The room bore the signs of a struggle. She bears no resemblance to her mother.*
4 to bear children is to give birth to them *She bore two daughters.*
5 to bear something in mind means that you must remember it because it is important *Bear in mind that I haven't eaten since breakfast.*
6 to bear with someone is to ask them to be patient with you *Bear with me while I put on my shoes.*

bearable *adjective*
something bearable is not pleasant but you can accept it without complaining

beard *noun* **beards**
hair growing on a man's chin and cheeks

bearded *adjective*
a bearded man has a beard

bearings *noun plural*
1 if you lose your bearings, you don't know where you are or where to go next
2 if you get or find your bearings, you find out where you are and where to go next

beast *noun* **beasts**
1 an animal, especially a big or dangerous one *a wild beast*
2 a cruel or violent person

beastly *adjective*
unpleasant

beat *verb*
beats, beating, beat, beaten
1 to hit someone or something very many times *The bully was trying to beat me with a stick. The musicians were beating the drums. The rain was beating against the window.*
2 to do better than someone in a game or competition and become the winner
3 to beat eggs or other food is to mix them using a fork or piece of equipment such as a mixer
4 when your heart beats, it makes regular movements as it pumps blood
5 if the sun beats down, the sun's heat is strong and the weather is very hot
6 to beat someone up is to hit them or kick them in a very violent way

beat *noun* **beats**
1 a regular sound that a heart makes as it pumps blood
2 a regular pattern of sounds in music or poetry
3 the area a police officer must walk around while on duty

beating *noun* **beatings**
1 when someone is hit very many times *I was given a beating by the class bully.*
2 when someone loses badly, for example in a game, competition or battle *Our football team took a real beating.*

beautiful *adjective*
1 very pleasant to look at *a beautiful girl*
2 extremely good and pleasing *beautiful weather*

beautifully *adverb*
in a very pleasing way

beauty *noun*
1 the quality of being beautiful *the beauty of the countryside*
2 (*plural* **beauties**) a very beautiful girl or woman
3 a very good advantage that something has *That's the beauty of living in the city.*

beaver *noun* **beavers**
1 a furry animal with a wide flat tail that builds dams in streams
2 a Beaver in the Scouts is a boy who belongs to the youngest section, for boys aged 6 to 8. The next section is known as the Cubs, for boys aged 8 to 10.

became
past tense of **become**

because *conjunction*
used for giving a reason for something *We can't go out because it's raining. We can't go out because of the rain.*

beckon *verb*
beckons, beckoning, beckoned
to beckon to someone is to make a sign, usually with your hand, to ask them to come over to you

become *verb*
becomes, becoming, became, become
1 to start being something *I was becoming tired. She became a teacher.*
2 if you ask what has become of something or someone, you want to know what has happened to them *What became of Mr Adams?*
3 (old-fashioned) if something becomes you, it makes you look good *That suit becomes you.*

bed *noun* **beds**
1 a piece of furniture for sleeping on, or the place where you sleep *It's time to go to bed.*
2 a part of a garden for growing plants
3 the bottom of the sea or a river

33

bedclothes – beige

bedclothes *noun plural*
the sheets and blankets you put over yourself when you go to bed

bedding *noun*
the sheets and blankets needed for making a bed

bedlam *noun*
great noise and confusion *There was bedlam in the classroom.*

> ORIGIN from *Bethlehem*, the name of a lunatic asylum (home for people with an illness of the mind) in London in the 15th century

bedraggled *adjective*
if someone is bedraggled, they look untidy and often sad, for example because they are wet from being out in the rain

bedridden *adjective*
not able to get out of bed because you are ill or disabled

bedroom *noun* **bedrooms**
a room with a bed or beds for sleeping in

bedside *noun*
the area next to a bed or next to the bed of a sick person *a bedside table*; *We were called to Granddad's bedside in the middle of the night.*

bedsit *noun* **bedsits**
a room that people such as students rent for living and sleeping in

> SYNONYM bedsitter

bedspread *noun* **bedspreads**
a cover on the top of a bed, used mainly for decoration

bedstead *noun* **bedsteads**
the frame of an old-fashioned bed

bedtime *noun*
1 (*plural* **bedtimes**) the time when you normally go to bed *It's past my bedtime. Tell me a bedtime story.*
2 the time when you must go straight to bed *'Bedtime – now!' shouted Mum.*

bee *noun* **bees**
a flying insect that makes honey and can sting. It makes a buzzing sound and its body has black and yellow stripes.

> SIMILE 'as busy as a bee' means very busy

beech *noun* **beeches**
a tree with smooth grey bark and shiny leaves

beef *noun*
meat from a cow or bull

beefburger *noun* **beefburgers**
minced beef in a flat round shape that is fried and eaten in a bread roll

Beefeater *noun* **Beefeaters**
a guard at the Tower of London

> CULTURE NOTE *Beefeaters* traditionally wear a red uniform with a black hat. This uniform dates back to the 16th century.

beefy *adjective* **beefier, beefiest**
a beefy person has a big body and strong muscles

beehive *noun* **beehives**
a structure where bees live and make honey

beeline *noun*
to make a beeline for a place is to go there as fast as you can

been
past participle of **be**

beep *noun* **beeps**
a short high sound made by a car horn or a piece of electronic equipment such as a mobile phone or computer

beep *verb*
beeps, beeping, beeped
1 to make a short high sound *The timer is beeping.*

> SYNONYM to bleep

2 to call someone such as a doctor or nurse by sending a signal to their beeper

> SYNONYMS to bleep, to page

beeper *noun* **beepers**
a small piece of electronic equipment that you carry around. It makes a beeping sound to tell you that you must phone someone.

> SYNONYMS bleeper, pager

beer *noun*
1 an alcoholic drink made from barley and hops
2 (*plural* **beers**) a glass or bottle of beer

beet *noun* **beet** or **beets**
a plant used for producing sugar and as a vegetable

beetle *noun* **beetles**
1 an insect with four wings. The outer two wings fold to form a hard cover when it is not flying.
2 any insect that looks like a beetle, for example a cockroach

beetroot *noun* **beetroot** or **beetroots**
a dark red vegetable from the root of one type of beet. It is sometimes used in salads.

before *preposition & adverb*
1 earlier than something or someone *I got up before nine o'clock. Arun finished his homework before me. I'm busy until next week – I can't see you before.*
2 used for talking about something that has already happened or been done in the past *Have you been there before?*
3 in front of someone or something *He stood up before the whole class.*
4 up until the time something happens *It was a week before she replied to my email.*

beforehand *adverb*
earlier *Why didn't you tell me beforehand?*

beg *verb*
begs, begging, begged
1 to ask people for money or food because you are poor
2 to beg someone is to ask them to do something or to ask them for something, for example many times, because it is something you want very much *She begged me not to go swimming as I had a cold. He begged for mercy.*
3 **I beg your pardon?** used for asking someone to repeat something because you didn't hear or understand
4 **I beg your pardon!** used for saying sorry, for example if you bump into someone

began
past tense of **begin**

beggar *noun* **beggars**
1 someone who lives by asking for money or food in the street
2 an informal word for a person (only used with a small number of adjectives, for example 'lucky', 'cheeky', 'silly', 'poor') *You lucky beggar!*

begin *verb*
begins, beginning, began, begun
another way of saying to start *I'll begin my homework tomorrow. My stepmum has begun to study Spanish. The day began cloudy.*

beginner *noun* **beginners**
someone who has just started to learn something or has not learnt much yet in a subject

beginning *noun* **beginnings**
the start of something

begrudge *verb*
begrudges, begrudging, begrudged
1 to begrudge someone something worth having is to think they don't deserve it and to feel unhappy that they have it *I don't begrudge him that big house – he's worked for it!*
2 to feel angry about something you have done or have to do *I begrudge every minute I have to spend waiting for that bus.*

begun
past participle of **begin**

behalf *noun*
on behalf of
1 instead of someone *Mr Brown spoke to the head teacher on behalf of the parents.*
2 in order to help someone and do good things for them *a sponsored walk on behalf of sick children*

behave *verb*
behaves, behaving, behaved
1 to act in a certain way *Sam behaved very well but Sophia behaved badly.*
2 to act in a polite way *They always behave in class. Behave yourself!*

behaviour *noun*
the way people or animals behave

behead *verb*
beheads, beheading, beheaded
to cut off someone's head as a punishment

> SYNONYM to decapitate

behind *adverb & preposition*
1 at the back of something or someone *Look behind the door. Mum walked first and Dad followed on behind.*
2 doing something later or more slowly than you should *Try not to get behind in your studies.*
3 supporting someone *The whole class was behind him.*
4 if someone is behind bars, they are in prison
5 if you do something behind someone's back, you do it without them knowing

behind *noun* **behinds**
buttocks

beige ['bayj'; 'j' has the middle sound of 'pleasure'] *adjective & noun*
a light colour that is a mixture of brown and yellow

being–bereaved

being
present participle of **be**

being *noun* **beings**
1 any living thing *human beings; a being from another planet*
2 to come into being is to start to exist

Belarus ['bel-er-rooss'] *noun*
a country in North-East Europe
Belarusian *adjective & noun*

belch *verb*
belches, belching, belched
1 to make a loud noise from your mouth caused by air coming up from your stomach

SYNONYM to burp

2 to produce a lot of something such as smoke, fumes or flames *factories belching thick clouds of smoke*

belch *noun* **belches**
the action or sound of belching

belfry *noun* **belfries**
a tower with a bell in it, for example on top of a church

ORIGIN from Latin *belfredus*. In medieval times a belfry was a tall tower that could be pushed around by soldiers to fire weapons over city walls. It had nothing to do with bells but its shape was similar to a modern belfry.

Belgian *adjective*
connected with Belgium

Belgian *noun* **Belgians**
someone from Belgium

Belgium *noun*
a country in North-West Europe

belief *noun* **beliefs**
1 the feeling of being sure that something is true
2 a religious or political idea that you feel strongly to be true *Many people have deep religious beliefs.*

believable *adjective*
something believable can be believed because it seems possible, true or real *a completely believable story*

believe *verb*
believes, believing, believed
1 to be sure that something is true, or to think that it is true without being completely sure *I believed what he said. It's about ten o'clock, I believe.*
2 to be sure that someone is telling the truth *Do you believe me?*
3 to believe in something is to think that it exists (for example ghosts) or is really important (for example hard work)
4 to believe in someone is to think they are good or will do good things

believer *noun* **believers**
1 someone who feels strongly that their god or religion is very important or is the true one
2 someone who feels strongly about a political or other idea *a great believer in exercise*

bell *noun* **bells**
1 a metal object that makes a ringing noise. It is usually shaped like an upside-down cup and has a piece of metal hanging inside it. *the school bell; a bicycle bell*
2 a piece of electrical equipment that rings when a button is pressed

bellow *verb*
bellows, bellowing, bellowed
to shout loudly and in a deep voice

bellows *noun plural*
an object for blowing air into a fire to make it burn better

belly *noun* **bellies**
1 (informal) the soft front part of your body below your chest that contains your stomach
2 (informal) the stomach itself when talking about food *Charlie went to bed with a full belly.*
3 the under part of an animal's body
4 a belly button is an informal name for the small round hollow place in the middle of the stomach known as the navel

bellyache *noun* **bellyaches**
an informal word for a pain in the stomach (front part of the body below the chest)

belong *verb*
belongs, belonging, belonged
1 if something belongs to you, it's your own *This book belongs to me.*
2 if you belong to a group, you are part of it *She belongs to the film club.*
3 to be in the right place *Put the coat on the peg where it belongs.*

belongings *noun plural*
your belongings are things that are your own, especially things you can carry *He picked up his belongings and left.*

beloved ['bi-luv-id'] *adjective*
loved very much

below *adverb & preposition*
lower than something *I can hear someone down below. It was two degrees below zero.*

belt *noun* **belts**
1 a thin piece of leather or cloth that you wear around your waist
2 a flat circular band of rubber that turns something in a machine *a supermarket checkout belt*
3 an area of land usually surrounding something *a commuter belt*
4 any long thin area *a belt of rain*

belt *verb*
belts, belting, belted
1 to move very fast *They were belting along the motorway at 90 miles an hour.*
2 to hit someone hard

bench *noun* **benches**
1 a long seat, usually made of wood or metal
2 a heavy work table *a carpenter's bench*

bend *verb*
bends, bending, bent
1 to pull, press or move something so that it becomes curved, crooked or no longer straight *Don't bend your library card. I can't bend my arm.*
2 to become curved, crooked or not straight *The road bends to the right.*
3 to move your head or the top of your body downwards *I bent down (or over) to pick up the ball.*

bend *noun* **bends**
a place where something curves *a bend in the road*

bendy *adjective* **bendier, bendiest**
easy to bend or with lots of bends in it *a bendy straw; a bendy road*

beneath *adverb & preposition*
1 under something
2 used for talking about something that is not good enough or is not suitable for someone *My brother doesn't want to work in a shop – he thinks that's beneath him.*

beneficial *adjective*
something beneficial is good for you and helps you *Eating lots of fruit can be beneficial.*

benefit *verb*
benefits, benefiting, benefited
if you benefit from something, or if it benefits you, it does you good and helps you

benefit *noun* **benefits**
1 something that does you good or helps you *the benefits of going to university; It's of benefit to the whole school.*

SYNONYM advantage

2 money from the government for someone who is out of work, ill or poor *Her mum's partner is on benefits.*
3 a benefit concert or match is for raising money, for example for a charity (group that helps people)
4 to give someone the benefit of the doubt is to accept what they say or do even though you think they might not be telling the truth or doing what they should

Benelux *noun*
the group of countries made up of Belgium, the Netherlands and Luxembourg

benevolent *adjective*
helpful, kind and generous
benevolence *noun*

Bengali *noun*
the language of Bangladesh

bent
past tense & past participle of **bend**

bent *adjective*
1 with a curved or crooked shape, not straight
2 an informal word for dishonest
3 to be bent on doing something is to want very much to do it, especially something bad *aliens bent on destroying the world*

bequeath *verb*
bequeaths, bequeathing, bequeathed
if you bequeath something to someone, you sign an official document saying that the thing will be given to that person after you die

bequest *noun* **bequests**
money or property that you leave to another person after you die

bereaved *adjective & noun*
if someone is bereaved, it means that one of their family members or friends died a short time ago *a support group for the bereaved*

35

bereavement – bewitch

bereavement *noun*
when a member of someone's family or someone's friend has died

bereft *adjective*
to be bereft of something means to be completely without it *a country bereft of hope*

beret ['ber-ray] *noun* berets
a soft flat round hat that fits tightly around the head

> ORIGIN from French *béret*. This type of hat was worn in France and Spain especially in the 19th and 20th centuries.

Bermuda *noun*
a country in the West Atlantic made up of many islands **Bermudan** *adjective & noun*

berry *noun* berries
a small juicy fruit with tiny seeds inside

berserk *adjective*
to go berserk is to get very angry and violent

> ORIGIN from old Scandinavian words *bjorn* 'bear' and *serkr* 'shirt'. When a Viking soldier wore a 'bear shirt', he fought like a crazy wild animal.

berth *noun* berths
1 a place to sleep in a boat or on a train
2 a place for a boat to stop and be tied up
3 to give something or someone a wide berth is to avoid them on purpose

beside *preposition*
1 next to *Stand beside your sister.*
2 if something is beside the point, it has nothing to do with what you're talking about *That's completely beside the point.*
3 to be beside yourself is to be very angry, upset or worried *Dad was beside himself with worry.*

besides *adverb*
used for mentioning something else or another reason for something *Besides, it's late. For my birthday I got a chess set, a pair of shoes and lots more besides.*

besides *preposition*
1 as well as something or someone *I have lots of friends besides Jon.*
2 except for something or someone *Besides football, he doesn't have any hobbies.*

besiege *verb*
besieges, besieging, besieged
1 if soldiers besiege a place, they surround it and wait to take control of the people inside *The president's palace was besieged by Russian soldiers.*
2 if lots of people besiege a place, they surround it in a threatening way, for example because they are angry *Dozens of customers besieged the offices of British Airways.*
3 to form a crowd around someone famous *Madonna was besieged by fans.*

best *adjective*
superlative of **good**
better than anything or anyone else *the best teacher*

best *adverb*
superlative of **well**
1 in a way that is better than anything or anyone else *Harry sings best.*
2 used for saying that something should be done *It's best if you stay here.*

best *noun*
1 the person or thing that is better than all the others *For me Beckham is the best.*
2 to do or try your best is to try as hard as you can *I did my best not to fall over.*
3 to make the best of something is to try to make a bad situation as pleasant as possible

best man *noun* best men
a friend of the bridegroom who helps him at his wedding

bestseller *noun* bestsellers
a popular book or other product that very many people buy

> LANGUAGE EXTRA also spelt *best-seller*

bet *verb*
bets, betting, bet
1 to bet on something is to give someone money and tell them what you think will happen, for example who will win in a race or competition. If you are right, you get back extra money, but if you are wrong, you lose your money. *My dad bet £10 on his favourite horse. My mum never bets.*
2 to be sure that something will happen *I bet he will pass the entry test.*

bet *noun* bets
1 an agreement that someone makes when they bet money *My nan made a bet on our team winning.*
2 an amount of money that someone bets *How much was the bet? She lost the bet.*
3 **best bet** someone's best bet is the best thing they can do in a particular situation *Your best bet is to wait till it stops raining before going out.*

beta version ['bee-ter] *noun*
beta versions
a software program that is not finished because people are still testing it

> ORIGIN from *beta*, the second letter of the Greek alphabet

betray *verb*
betrays, betraying, betrayed
1 to cause harm to someone and destroy the trust they have in you *My best friend betrayed me by giving away my secrets. They betrayed him to the police.*
2 to betray someone's secret is to tell people what it is
3 to betray a feeling is to show it
betrayal *noun*

better *adjective*
comparative of **good**
1 nicer, more pleasant, more useful or more able *better weather; You're better at French than me.*
2 of higher quality *My school report is better than it was last term.*
3 less ill than you were, or feeling completely well *Is she better yet?*

better *adverb*
comparative of **well**
1 in a way that is nicer, more pleasant or more useful, or in a more able way *You play much better than I do.*
2 to feel better is to feel less ill than you were or to feel completely well
3 if something gets better, for example the weather or a skill, then it is nicer, more pleasant or of a higher quality than it used to be *It was raining in London but it got better when we reached Leeds. My maths is getting better.*
4 if you say that you had better do something, you mean that you should do it *I'd better go to bed now.*
5 if someone is better off doing something, it means that it would be better for them to do it, for example because they would be happier or have more money *Some students are better off living with their parents.*

better *noun*
1 someone or something that is better *I can't decide which is the better of the two.*
2 to get the better of someone is to be more clever than they are, for example by beating them in a game

between *preposition*
1 between two things or people means in the middle of them *Hasan stood between John and Anil.*
2 between two places or times means within the distance or the period of time separating them *We cycled between Leeds and York. Come round between two and four o'clock.*
3 used for showing things that are connected, shared or done together *the friendship between brother and sister; We shared out the sweets between the five of us. Between the four of them they ended up eating the whole cake.*
4 used for showing a range in numbers or in several different things *Think of a number between 10 and 20. It's hard to choose between these colours.*

> LANGUAGE EXTRA you can also use *in between* for some meanings, for example *Hasan stood in between John and Anil.*

between *adverb*
in the middle of two things or people, or within two periods of time or two numbers *Hasan stood in between. We have a ten-minute break in between.*

> LANGUAGE EXTRA when *between* is an adverb, it is usually used with *in*

beverage *noun* beverages
a drink, often a hot drink *a hot beverage*

beware *verb*
used for warning people to be very careful *Beware of the dog.*

> LANGUAGE EXTRA used only in the form *beware*

bewilder *verb*
bewilders, bewildering, bewildered
if something bewilders you, you can't understand it and you are very confused
bewilderment *noun*

> SYNONYM to puzzle

bewitch *verb*
bewitches, bewitching, bewitched
1 to make someone very interested in you and have strong feelings about you *He was bewitched by her great beauty.*
2 to put a magic spell on someone

beyond *adverb & preposition*
1 further on or further on from something *the river beyond*; *There's a house beyond the trees. It's beyond midnight.*
2 if something is beyond you, it's too difficult for you to understand
3 used for saying that something cannot be done or a particular situation cannot be changed *Our TV is beyond repair* (cannot be repaired). *The ball was beyond reach* (we couldn't reach it). *We were late due to circumstances beyond our control* (we could do nothing to change the situation).

bi- *prefix*
twice or two *bilingual* (speaking two languages); *bicycle* (a cycle with two wheels); *bimonthly* (twice a month or once every two months)

bias *noun* **biases**
a feeling or opinion that shows you prefer a person or thing to someone or something else without any good reason *a bias in favour of women*; *a bias against science*

biased *adjective*
showing that you prefer someone or something without any good reason

bib *noun* **bibs**
a piece of plastic or cloth tied under a baby's chin to keep its clothes clean during meals

Bible *noun* **Bibles**
1 the holy book of the Christian religion, made up of the Old and New Testaments
2 the holy book of the Jewish religion

ORIGIN from Latin and Greek *biblia* 'books', based on another Greek word meaning 'papyrus' (a tall plant that grows in water and is similar to grass)

biblical *adjective*
connected with the Bible

bibliography *noun* **bibliographies**
a list of books on a particular subject

bicentenary ['by-sen-teen-er-ee] *noun* **bicentenaries**
a day or year that is 200 years after an event such as the birth of someone famous

biceps *noun* **biceps**
the big muscle in your arm between your shoulder and elbow

bicker *verb*
bickers, bickering, bickered
to argue about things that are not important

bicycle *noun* **bicycles**
a vehicle with two wheels that you ride by sitting on it and using your feet to push pedals round

ORIGIN from *cycle* and *bi-* 'a cycle with two wheels' (from Greek *kyklos* 'circle' or 'wheel' and Latin *bi-* 'twice')

bid *noun* **bids**
1 to make a bid is to offer an amount of money to buy something, usually at an auction
2 when you try to do something *Obama made a successful bid for the presidency.*

bid *verb*
bids, bidding, bid
1 to bid an amount of money is to offer it to buy something, usually at an auction
2 to bid someone goodbye or good night, for example, is to say these words to them

bide *verb*
bides, biding, bided
to bide your time to wait for the right time to do something

big *adjective* **bigger, biggest**
1 more than the normal size or amount *a big tree*; *a big slice of cake*

SYNONYM large

2 more important than normal *a big problem*; *a big difference*; *a big change*
3 older than someone *my big brother*
4 used for giving extra importance to a word *You're just a big coward!*
5 used when you mean someone does something a lot *I'm a big eater.*

big *verb* (slang)
bigs, bigging, bigged
if someone bigs someone up or bigs something up, they tell people how excellent someone or something is and how much respect they have for them

bigamy *noun*
having more than one husband or wife at the same time

big-head *noun* **big-heads** (informal)
someone who thinks they are more intelligent or more important than they really are **big-headed** *adjective*

bike *noun* **bikes**
1 a bicycle or motorcycle
2 **On your bike!** used for telling someone to go away and leave you alone

bikini *noun* **bikinis**
a swimming costume for women and girls made of two pieces covering the top and bottom parts of the body

ORIGIN from *Bikini*, one of the Marshall Islands where the USA first tested the atomic bomb

bile *noun*
a bitter yellow-green liquid produced by the liver. It helps the body to digest fats (change them into substances the body can use).

bilingual *adjective*
1 a bilingual person knows two languages equally well
2 in two languages *a bilingual dictionary*

bill *noun* **bills**
1 a piece of paper that shows the amount of money you must pay for something *the electricity bill*; *The waiter asked Jack to pay the bill.*
2 in a parliament, a bill is a written document to bring in a new law, which members of parliament must discuss and vote on
3 in the theatre, a bill is a list of things and people in the show *Who's on the bill tonight?*
4 a bird's beak
5 the American word for a banknote
6 (slang) **the bill** or **the old bill** the police

billboard *noun* **billboards**
a structure with a large flat surface that has an advertisement on it, for example at the side of a road

billiards *noun*
a game played on a cloth-covered table in which players use a cue (long stick) to hit three balls against each other or into holes *compare*: snooker and pool

billion *noun* **billions**
1 a thousand million (1 000 000 000)
2 a very large number of something *I've told you this a billion times.*

LANGUAGE EXTRA in British English, a *billion* used to mean a million million but is rarely used with that meaning now

billionaire *noun* **billionaires**
an extremely rich person who has at least a billion pounds, dollars or euros

billow *verb*
billows, billowing, billowed
1 to rise up into the air like a cloud *There was smoke billowing out of chimneys.*
2 if something made of cloth billows, it fills with air and swells out *Her skirt billowed out in the wind like a sail.*

billow *noun* **billows**
a billow of smoke is a large cloud of it moving through the air

billy goat *noun* **billy goats**
a male goat

LANGUAGE EXTRA a female goat is called a *nanny goat*

bin *noun* **bins**
1 a container for putting rubbish in
2 a container for storing things *a bread bin*

binary *adjective*
in computing, a binary number is a number based on the binary system of counting, which uses only numbers 0 and 1

bind *verb*
binds, binding, bound
1 to tie up or tie together *They bound the prisoner's hands with rope. We found a bunch of old papers bound with string.*
2 to wrap something round with a piece of cloth *They cleaned and bound the wound.*
3 to bind a book is to fasten the pages together inside a cover
4 to bind someone to do something is to say that they must do it *This agreement binds you to pay £10 a week. We're bound to keep our plans secret* (we must keep them secret).
5 if something binds people together, they share something in common *War and suffering bound us closer together.*

binder *noun* **binders**
a hard cover made of cardboard or plastic that holds together loose sheets of paper or copies of magazines

binge *verb*
binges, bingeing, binged
to eat or drink too much *Every Saturday she binged on chocolate.*

binge *noun* **binges**
a short period when someone eats or drinks too much or spends too much money *He went on a chocolate binge. Mum warned us about the problems of binge drinking and binge eating* (drinking and eating too much).

bingo – blab

bingo *noun*
a game in which players try to match numbers on a card with numbers that someone calls out. The player who is first to match all the numbers on his or her card wins money or a prize.

bin liner *noun* **bin liners**
a plastic bag that goes inside a bin to hold the rubbish

binman *noun* **binmen**
someone who comes to your house to empty your dustbin

LANGUAGE EXTRA also called a *refuse collector*

binoculars *noun plural*
a piece of equipment with two small telescopes, one for each eye, used for making faraway objects appear closer

biodegradable *adjective*
if something that you throw away, such as a plastic bag, is biodegradable, it can be changed by bacteria (tiny living things) into substances that cause no harm to the environment

biographer *noun* **biographers**
someone who writes a biography

biography *noun* **biographies**
a book about someone's life that is written by someone else **biographical** *adjective*

LANGUAGE EXTRA a book written by someone about their own life is called an *autobiography*

biologist *noun* **biologists**
a scientist who studies living things

biology *noun*
the science of living things, often studied as a school subject **biological** *adjective*

biome ['by-ohm'] *noun* **biomes**
a large area with its own climate and special qualities, for example a rainforest or desert, where particular types of plants, animals and insects live

bionic *adjective*
a bionic arm, leg or other part of the body is artificial and worked by electronic equipment

biopsy *noun* **biopsies**
if someone has a biopsy, a doctor removes some cells (smallest units of living matter) from their body to check that they are healthy

biosphere *noun*
the part of the surface and atmosphere of the world where animals and plants can live

biped ['by-ped'] *noun* **bipeds**
an animal that walks on two legs. Bipeds include human beings.
compare: **quadruped**

birch *noun* **birches**
a birch or silver birch is a tall thin tree with a silvery-coloured bark and thin branches

bird *noun* **birds**
1 an animal with feathers, two wings, two legs and a beak. Most birds can fly.
2 a bird of prey is a large bird, such as a vulture, that kills other birds and eats them

birdseed *noun*
seeds for feeding birds

bird's-eye view *noun*
a view of something from high above it *a bird's-eye view of the Thames seen from the London Eye*

biriani *noun* **birianis**
an Indian meal of rice and spices together with meat, fish, vegetables or eggs

biro *noun* **biros** (trademark)
a type of ballpoint pen

ORIGIN from the name of László *Biró*, its Hungarian inventor

birth *noun*
1 (*plural* **births**) the time when a person or animal is born
2 to give birth to a baby is to produce a baby *The mother gave birth to a baby boy.*
3 a birth certificate is a document that shows where and when you were born and who your parents are
4 birth control is when a man and woman control the number of children they have, for example by using contraceptives so that the woman doesn't become pregnant
compare: **family planning**

birthday *noun*
1 (*plural* **birthdays**) the day of the year when you were born, when people often have a party with a cake and receive cards and presents *They wished me a happy birthday.*
2 used for describing something you do, have or give for a birthday, for example a party, present or greeting *a birthday cake*; *a birthday card*

birthmark *noun* **birthmarks**
a red or brown mark on the skin that someone has had since they were born

birthplace *noun* **birthplaces**
the place where someone was born, especially someone famous

biscuit *noun* **biscuits**
a small flat cake that is hard and is for just one person to eat

ORIGIN from Old French words meaning 'bread twice cooked': *pain bescuit* (*pain* 'bread', *bes* 'twice' and *cuit* 'cooked')

bisect *verb*
bisects, bisecting, bisected
to divide something into two equal parts

bishop *noun* **bishops**
1 a Christian priest in charge of churches in a large area, such as a whole city
2 a piece in the game of chess. It is shaped like a bishop's hat and moves across the board in a diagonal line (in a straight line from one corner of a square to the opposite corner, either one square or more than one square at a time).

bison *noun* **bison**
a wild animal like a big cow with long hair

SYNONYM **buffalo**

bit
past tense of **bite**

bit *noun* **bits**
1 a small part or amount of something *a bit of bread*; *What was your favourite bit of the book? Do you want a bit of lunch?*
2 the smallest piece of information used by a computer *Eight bits make up one byte.*
3 a piece of metal fixed to the bridle (leather straps) of a horse and put into the horse's mouth. It is used for controlling the horse.
4 if something falls to bits or is smashed to bits, it breaks or is broken into many small parts, often so that it is completely destroyed
5 **a bit** slightly *I'm a bit cold. Do you want a bit more?*
6 **quite a bit** a lot *He spent quite a bit of time in Paris.*
7 **bit by bit** gradually
8 **bits and pieces** or **bits and bobs** small things of different kinds
9 (*informal*) **to do your bit** to do your share of something that needs to be done

bitch *noun* **bitches**
a female dog

bitchy *adjective* **bitchier, bitchiest**
very cruel or unpleasant *a bitchy remark*

bite *verb*
bites, biting, bit, bitten
1 to cut or press something with your teeth
2 if an insect or animal bites you, it hurts you by making a small hole in your skin
3 if a fish bites, it eats food from a hook that you throw into the water to catch the fish
4 if an object bites into something, it presses into it hard *The wire bit into the prisoner's wrists.*

bite *noun* **bites**
1 the action of biting *I took a bite of the apple.*
2 a small injury made by an insect or animal biting you
3 a bite (or a bite to eat) is a small meal *I went home for a bite.*

biting *adjective*
very cold and unpleasant *a biting wind*

bitmap *noun* **bitmaps**
a computer file of a picture made up of many small points, called bits

bitten
past participle of **bite**

bitter *adjective*
1 tasting strong and not sweet, sometimes in an unpleasant way *Coffee is bitter.*
2 angry, especially because of a bad experience *She felt very bitter about it.*
3 showing strong feelings of dislike *bitter enemies*
4 very unpleasant *a bitter disappointment*
5 very cold *a bitter wind*
bitterness *noun*

bitterly *adverb*
1 very much and in a very angry way *bitterly disappointed*; *He complained bitterly.*
2 **bitterly cold** extremely cold in a way that makes you feel uncomfortable *a bitterly cold wind*

bizarre *adjective*
very strange **bizarrely** *adverb*

blab *verb*
blabs, blabbing, blabbed
to tell people about something secret *Don't go blabbing to your friends.*

blabber *verb*
blabbers, blabbering, blabbered
to talk too much *What are you blabbering on about?*

black *adjective* blacker, blackest
1 having the darkest possible colour, like coal
2 having skin that is dark, not light-coloured
3 connected with people who have skin that is dark *a black neighbourhood*
4 very sad, angry or gloomy *a black look*; *a black day*
5 without milk *black coffee*
6 if someone is black and blue, they have lots of bruises
blackness *noun*

black *noun* blacks
1 the colour black
2 someone with dark skin

black and white *adjective*
used for describing something such as a photo or film that has or shows no colours but is in black, white and grey *a black and white TV*
black and white *noun*

blackberry *noun* blackberries
a small juicy fruit that grows on a thorny bush (with sharp points on it)

BlackBerry *noun* (trademark)
a small computer that you hold in your hand. It can also be used as a mobile phone.

blackbird *noun* blackbirds
a common European and American bird. The male has black feathers.

blackboard *noun* blackboards
a big black or dark-coloured surface used for writing on with chalk, which can later be rubbed out. Blackboards are used by teachers in some classrooms.

Black Country *noun*
the Black Country is a part of the Midlands in the UK where there used to be lots of factories. Some factories made the air smoky, which is the reason for the name 'Black'.

blackcurrant *noun* blackcurrants
a very small dark purple fruit

Black Death *noun*
the Black Death was the disease in Europe and Asia in the 14th century that killed millions of people. It was spread by rats and is also known as the Plague.

blacken *verb*
blackens, blackening, blackened
to make something black or to become black

black eye *noun* black eyes
an eye with a dark bruise around it where you have been hit

black hole *noun* black holes
a region in space where the gravity is so strong that it pulls everything into it, including light. It is made by the collapse of a star.

black ice *noun*
thin ice on a road or path. It is very dangerous because it's difficult to see.

blackmail *verb*
blackmails, blackmailing, blackmailed
to blackmail someone is to tell them that unless they pay you money or do something else that you want, you will tell people about their secrets
blackmailer *noun*

blackmail *noun*
the action or crime of blackmailing someone

black market *noun*
1 illegal buying and selling of goods
2 if you buy or sell something on the black market, you buy or sell it illegally

black out *verb*
blacks out, blacking out, blacked out
to black out is to become unconscious suddenly for several minutes

blackout *noun* blackouts
1 a short period when the electricity in a building is cut off or, in a war, when the lights are turned off in a whole town
2 when someone suddenly becomes unconscious for several minutes

black sheep *noun* black sheep
a black sheep in a family is someone that other family members do not like because they have done something bad

blacksmith *noun* blacksmiths
someone who works with iron, making and repairing things and putting shoes on horses

bladder *noun* bladders
the part of your body that is like a bag and holds urine (waste liquid that is passed from the body)

blade *noun* blades
1 the part of a knife, tool or sword used for cutting
2 the blades of a fan or propeller are the long flat parts that go round
3 a blade of grass is a single leaf of grass

blame *verb*
blames, blaming, blamed
1 to say that someone or something is responsible when something bad has happened *I blame Ruby for knocking over the paint* (it's Ruby's fault). *Don't blame all your problems on your school.*
2 if you say something is to blame for something, you mean it is the reason why something bad has happened *The bad weather is to blame for the floods.*
3 if you say someone is to blame for something, you mean they have caused something bad to happen and should accept that they are wrong *'Look at this mess!' – 'Lewis is the one to blame.'* (Lewis made the mess.)
4 if you say you don't blame someone, you mean you think someone is right to do what they do *'It was snowing again so I decided not to go to school.' – 'I don't blame you.'*

blame *noun*
the responsibility for something bad happening *I always get the blame* (people say it's my fault). *Some people put the blame on fast food* (say fast food is responsible). *You and Oliver must share the blame* (you are both responsible).

blameless *adjective*
if someone is blameless, they are not responsible for anything bad that has happened

bland *adjective* blander, blandest
food that is bland doesn't have much taste

blank *adjective*
1 empty, with no writing, pictures or information on it *a blank sheet of paper; a blank screen; a blank disk*
2 showing no feeling or understanding *a blank look*
3 if your mind goes blank, you cannot remember something at that moment
blankly *adverb*

ORIGIN from Old French *blanc* 'white'

blank *noun* blanks
1 an empty space *I left a blank next to my name on the form.*
2 in a gun, a blank is the container for the bullet but without a bullet in it. When the gun is fired, it makes a noise but no bullet comes out.

blank *verb*
blanks, blanking, blanked
to blank someone is to ignore them instead of going to speak to them

blanket *noun* blankets
1 a piece of cloth, usually thick, used as a covering for a bed
2 a thick covering of something *a blanket of snow*

blank verse *noun*
poetry made up of lines that do not rhyme

blare *verb*
blares, blaring, blared
to make a sound that is loud and unpleasant *The sirens were blaring.*

blast *noun* blasts
1 an explosion *Ten people died in the blast.*
2 a sudden loud noise
3 a sudden rush of wind or air *We felt an icy blast.*

blast *verb*
blasts, blasting, blasted
1 to break up or damage with explosives *A huge bomb blasted the enemy's headquarters.*
2 to shoot *Someone blasted a passer-by with a shotgun.*
3 to criticise *The trade union blasted the government over the rise in the number of people out of work.*

blast-off *noun*
the moment when a spacecraft leaves the ground

blaze *verb*
blazes, blazing, blazed
1 to burn strongly or shine brightly *The fire was blazing. The sun was blazing down.*
2 if guns blaze away, they keep on firing bullets
3 **to blaze a trail** to discover something new that other people will develop further later on

blaze *noun* blazes
1 a very big fire
2 a blaze of colour or light means a lot of bright colours or light

blazer–blizzard

blazer noun blazers
a jacket that is sometimes part of a school or club uniform, with a badge on its top pocket

bleach noun bleaches
a strong chemical for cleaning things or for making cloth white or lighter in colour

bleach verb
bleaches, bleaching, bleached
to make something white or lighter in colour, such as cloth or hair

bleak adjective bleaker, bleakest
1 if a place is bleak, it is unfriendly and unpleasant and often looks empty *a bleak landscape*
2 if something such as the weather is bleak, it is unpleasant and cold and often windy *a bleak December day*
3 very bad and without hope *The future looks bleak.*

bleakness noun

bleary adjective blearier, bleariest
if someone has bleary eyes, they cannot see completely clearly, usually because they are tired **bleary-eyed** adjective

bleat verb
bleats, bleating, bleated
when a sheep or goat bleats, it makes a high sound

bleat noun bleats
the high sound made by a sheep or goat

bleed verb
bleeds, bleeding, bled
to lose blood from your body because of an injury

bleep noun bleeps
a short high sound made by electronic equipment

bleep verb
bleeps, bleeping, bleeped
1 to make a short high sound *My watch is bleeping.*

SYNONYM to beep

2 to call someone such as a doctor or nurse by sending a signal to their bleeper

SYNONYMS to beep, to page

bleeper noun bleepers
a small piece of electronic equipment that you carry around. It makes a bleeping sound to tell you that you must phone someone.

SYNONYMS beeper, pager

blemish noun blemishes
1 a small mark on the surface of something that spoils the way it looks
2 a blemish on someone's character or reputation is something that spoils it

blend verb
blends, blending, blended
1 to mix things together smoothly to form a single thing *Blend the eggs and the sugar. His music blends jazz and rock.*
2 to join things together in a way that works well, or to become joined together in this way *This film blends fact and fiction. Fact and fiction blend together very well.*

3 if you blend the sounds of a word together, or if they blend together, you put the sounds together to make a word *The sounds 'ch', 'a' and 't' blend together to make 'chat'.*
compare: segment

blend noun blends
a mixture of different things that go well together

blender noun blenders
a piece of kitchen equipment that mixes foods and turns them into liquid

SYNONYM liquidiser

bless verb
blesses, blessing, blessed
1 if a religious person blesses you, he or she asks God or a particular god to help and protect you
2 to be blessed with something is to be lucky enough to have it *blessed with a first-class brain*
3 **Bless you!** used as a polite way of wishing someone well when they have just sneezed

blessing noun blessings
1 something you are happy about *The mobile phone is a blessing.*
2 the help and protection of God or a particular god, or a prayer asking for this

blew
past tense of **blow**

blight verb
blights, blighting, blighted
to spoil or harm very seriously *a landscape blighted by factory chimneys*

blight noun blights
something that spoils or harms in a very serious way *Violence has been a blight on their lives.*

blimp noun blimps
a large flying vehicle like a balloon with engines, used for example for advertising. A blimp is a type of airship.

blind adjective
1 not able to see
2 used about beliefs or feelings people have even though they are not reasonable *blind faith; blind panic*
3 **blind drunk** completely drunk
4 **not a blind bit of** not any at all *It didn't make a blind bit of difference.*

blindness noun

blind verb
blinds, blinding, blinded
1 if a bright light blinds someone, they cannot see for a short time *I was blinded by the headlights.*
2 to make someone blind *blinded in an accident*

blind noun blinds
a cover that can be pulled over a window on the inside of a building

blind alley noun blind alleys
a small street that leads nowhere because it is closed at one end

blindfold noun blindfolds
a piece of cloth covering someone's eyes to stop them from seeing

blindfold verb
blindfolds, blindfolding, blindfolded
to put a blindfold over someone's eyes

blindfold adjective
1 wearing a blindfold
2 if someone says they can do something blindfold, they mean they can do it very easily, often because they've done it many times before

blindly adverb
without thinking *Don't obey your friends blindly.*

bling noun (slang)
shiny and expensive jewellery, for example gold and diamonds, that someone wears to attract people's attention

ORIGIN first used in hip-hop music to suggest the sound you could imagine light making when it hits shiny jewellery

blink verb
blinks, blinking, blinked
1 to close your eyes and open them again very quickly
2 if a light blinks, it keeps going on and off

blink noun blinks
1 an action of blinking
2 **in the blink of an eye** very quickly *She was gone in the blink of an eye.*
3 **on the blink** an informal way of saying that a piece of equipment is not working very well

blip noun blips
a slight problem, for example when something gets worse for a short time and then gets better

bliss noun
great happiness, especially when it goes on for a long time

blissful adjective
1 very happy *We spent a blissful week on a Greek island.*
2 making you feel very happy *Sitting on the beach reading was blissful.*

blissfully adverb
used for showing that someone is completely happy, or completely happy about a situation *blissfully happy; blissfully ignorant*

SYNONYM completely

blister noun blisters
a small swelling on the skin with liquid inside it. It is caused by burning or rubbing.

blitz noun
1 if you have a blitz on something that needs to be done, you make a great effort to try to deal with it *I had a blitz on the mess in my bedroom.*
2 (plural **blitzes**) a bombing attack by planes on a city
3 **the Blitz** the night-time bombing of British cities by Germany (1940–41)

ORIGIN from German *Blitzkrieg* 'lightning war'

blizzard noun blizzards
a storm with strong winds and heavy snow

bloated–blow

bloated *adjective*
1 swollen *a bloated face*
2 if you feel bloated, you have an uncomfortable feeling in your stomach because it is too full

blob *noun* blobs
a small round amount of something thick or sticky *a blob of glue*

block *noun* blocks
1 a thick piece of something such as wood or stone
2 a large building divided into flats or offices, or one part of a large building *a block of flats; a prison block*
3 a group of buildings with streets on all sides *We went for a walk around the block.*
4 an amount of something *to highlight a block of text*

block *verb*
blocks, blocking, blocked
1 to stop someone getting past *Two police officers blocked our way. Some fallen rocks had blocked the road.*
2 to get in the way of something *A tree blocked my view. Move over – you're blocking out the sun.*
3 to stop something such as a liquid, gas or air flowing through or out of something *The pipe is blocked. Leaves have blocked the gutter. Our sink is blocked up with hairs. Granny's oxygen tube got blocked.*
4 to fill something such as a hole or gap, for example so that nothing or no-one can get through *The old house had all its windows blocked up.*
5 to block someone or something in is to stop them from getting out or to surround them so that they cannot move *Mum's car is blocked in. The police blocked the protesters in.*
6 to stop someone getting in touch with you online, for example when you use email or a service such as Facebook *George used to be my friend but I've blocked him.*
7 to stop something reaching you on a phone or online, for example a mobile number or email address *I've blocked all the calls from that number.*

blockade *noun* blockades
the action of stopping people or goods from getting into or out of a place such as a town **blockade** *verb*

blockage *noun* blockages
something that stops something else passing or flowing through it *a blockage in a pipe* (for example, water, gas or air cannot flow); *a blockage in an artery* (blood cannot flow properly)

block capitals or **block letters** *noun plural*
letters in capitals, for example A, B, C

block graph *noun* block graphs
a type of graph (mathematical diagram) that uses blocks joined together to make columns or rows, which are often put side by side to show data (information)

blog *noun* blogs
a website where you can read someone's diary, find out about their opinions and experiences or see examples of their work. The writer should keep the blog up to date so you always have the latest information.

ORIGIN from *web* and *log*

blog *verb*
blogs, blogging, blogged
if someone blogs, they write things in their blog **blogger** *noun*

bloke *noun* blokes
an informal word for a man

blond or **blonde** *adjective*
used for describing hair that is light yellow in colour or someone who has this hair colour *a little blond boy; a little blonde girl*

LANGUAGE EXTRA use *blond* for boys and men, and *blonde* for girls and women

blonde *noun* blondes
a girl or woman with light yellow hair

blood *noun*
1 the red liquid that flows around the body and is pumped by the heart
2 the family group someone belongs to *a rich man of noble blood*
3 a blood test is a sample of blood taken from the body. It is examined to see if you have an illness.
4 **in cold blood** in a very cruel way

blood cell *noun* blood cells
one of the cells (smallest units of living matter) in your blood. The red blood cells carry oxygen around the body and the white cells fight infection.

blood donor *noun* blood donors
someone who gives a small amount of their blood to treat people who are ill

blood group *noun* blood groups
the type of blood a person has. The four main groups are A, B, AB and O.

bloodhound *noun* bloodhounds
a big dog with a very good sense of smell. Bloodhounds are often used for finding people or animals.

blood pressure *noun*
a measure of how hard your heart pumps blood around your body and how hard the blood presses on your arteries (tubes carrying the blood). Blood pressure can be high (it presses too hard on the arteries) or low (it doesn't press hard enough).

bloodshed *noun*
when people are killed or injured *We must avoid bloodshed.*

bloodshot *adjective*
if someone's eyes are bloodshot, they are red in the parts that should be white, for example because that person is very tired

bloodstream *noun*
another word for blood when it flows around the body

bloodthirsty *adjective*
bloodthirstier, bloodthirstiest
1 enjoying killing or injuring people *a bloodthirsty prince*
2 describing lots of killing *a bloodthirsty battle*

blood vessel *noun* blood vessels
one of the very narrow tubes in your body that blood flows through

bloody *adjective* bloodier, bloodiest
1 covered with blood or with blood coming out *a bloody nose*
2 a bloody battle or war is one where lots of people are killed and injured

bloom *noun* blooms
1 a flower, often on a tree or bush
2 **in (full) bloom** with lots of flowers *The cherry tree was in full bloom.*

bloom *verb*
blooms, blooming, bloomed
to produce flowers

blossom *noun* blossoms
a flower or flowers, usually on a tree or bush

blossom *verb*
blossoms, blossoming, blossomed
1 to produce flowers
2 to become something better *He has blossomed into a great actor.*

blot *noun* blots
1 a dirty mark made by ink
2 to be a blot on something is to spoil it *That building is a blot on the landscape.*

blot *verb*
blots, blotting, blotted
1 to blot a wet surface is to dry it using soft paper
2 to blot ink is to dry it using blotting paper
3 to blot something out is to hide it or get rid of it *The smoke completely blotted out the sun. He couldn't blot out the memory of that terrible day.*

blotch *noun* blotches
a red mark, usually on the skin
blotchy *adjective*

blotting paper *noun*
soft thick paper for drying ink after writing with a cartridge pen or fountain pen

blouse *noun* blouses
a light piece of clothing that girls and women wear on the top half of their body, similar to a man's shirt

blow *noun* blows
1 a hit made with the hand or an object *a blow to the head*
2 something unpleasant that makes you very unhappy or disappointed *Not winning the match was a big blow.*
3 the action of blowing

blow *verb*
blows, blowing, blew, blown
1 to make air come out of your mouth with force *Blow on your tea if it's too hot.*
2 if the wind blows, the air moves quickly, or if something blows in the wind, it moves quickly in the air *A strong wind was blowing. The flag was blowing in the wind.*
3 if the wind blows something or someone, it makes them move in the air or fall down *The wind blew my hat off. I was blown over by the wind.*
4 to blow a whistle is to make a sound from it with the air that comes out of your mouth
5 to destroy something by an explosion or kill someone by shooting *The explosion blew a big hole in the wall. The robbers said they would blow our heads off.*
6 to blow your nose is to clean it by making air go through it onto a tissue or handkerchief
7 if a light bulb or fuse blows, a thin wire in it breaks and it no longer works

41

blowtorch – bobble

8 to blow up is to destroy something or to be destroyed by an explosion *They blew up the bridge. The plane blew up in mid-air.*
9 to blow up a balloon is to fill it with air

blowtorch *noun* **blowtorches**
a piece of equipment with a flame used for burning paint off surfaces

SYNONYM blowlamp

blue *adjective* **bluer, bluest**
1 having the colour of the sky without clouds
2 an informal word for very sad *Listen to music if you're feeling blue.*

blue *noun* **blues**
1 the colour blue
2 **out of the blue** suddenly and without being expected *He rang me out of the blue.*

bluebell *noun* **bluebells**
a wild plant with small blue flowers that look like bells. Bluebells appear in spring.

blueberry *noun* **blueberries**
a small blue-black fruit that you eat

bluebottle *noun* **bluebottles**
a large blue fly that has a shiny body and buzzes as it flies

blueprint *noun* **blueprints**
a drawing that shows how something is going to be built

blues *noun plural*
1 (informal) if you have the blues, you feel sad
2 a type of sad music from the south of the US

Bluetooth *noun* (trademark)
a system for connecting computers, mobile phones and other devices using radio waves over short distances *a Bluetooth mouse*

bluff *noun*
an attempt to trick someone by bluffing *He said he would tell Dad but it was just bluff.*

bluff *verb*
bluffs, bluffing, bluffed
to make someone believe that you know something (even if you don't know it) or that you will do something (even if you don't intend to do it)

ORIGIN from Dutch *bluffen* 'to boast'

bluish *adjective*
slightly blue

blunder *noun* **blunders**
a stupid mistake **blunder** *verb*

blunt *adjective* **blunter, bluntest**
1 with an edge that cannot cut *a blunt knife*
2 with a round point, not a sharp one *a blunt pencil*
3 if someone is blunt, they say what they think and do not care if this upsets people
bluntness *noun*

bluntly *adverb*
if you tell someone something bluntly, you say it in a very direct and rough way

blur *verb*
blurs, blurring, blurred
1 to make something unclear, for example an image or the edge of a shape
2 to blur the difference or the line between two things is to make the difference between them less clear

blur *noun*
if something like a shape or a memory is a blur, it isn't clear *I can't see clearly – everything's a blur. My days in playschool are a bit of a blur.*

Blu-ray *noun* (trademark)
a way of storing films, video games and data on a disc that can hold much more information than a normal DVD and produce much clearer images

blurb *noun* **blurbs**
information about a book that is written on its cover to make people interested in buying it

blurred *adjective*
not clear *The picture is blurred.*

LANGUAGE EXTRA you can also say *blurry*

blurt *verb*
blurts, blurting, blurted
if someone blurts something out, they say it suddenly and without thinking

blush *verb*
blushes, blushing, blushed
to go red in the face because you are ashamed, excited or shy **blush** *noun*

bluster *verb*
blusters, blustering, blustered
to speak in a loud and boastful way, often because you are angry

blustery *adjective*
very windy *blustery weather*

Blu-Tack *noun* (trademark)
a soft blue substance for sticking things, for example pieces of paper, to surfaces such as walls

bmp
the ending of a computer filename. A .bmp file contains a picture.
short for: **bitmap**

BMX *noun* **BMXes**
a strong bicycle with small wheels and a low frame. It is often used for racing over rough ground where it makes special movements like jumping in the air.

ORIGIN from *bicycle motocross*

boa *noun* **boas**
a boa or boa constrictor is a very long snake that kills animals by wrapping itself around them and crushing them

boar *noun* **boars**
1 a boar or wild boar is a type of pig that is large and has long hair
2 a male pig for breeding (kept for producing baby pigs)

board *noun* **boards**
1 a long flat piece of wood, for example for building things
2 a flat piece of wood, cardboard or plastic for playing games on or for doing things on *a snakes and ladders board; a cutting board; a chessboard*
3 a big flat surface for showing information *a train departure board*
4 in a classroom, a board is short for **blackboard** (black surface you write on with chalk) or **whiteboard** (white surface you write on with a pen)
5 short for **noticeboard** (wood or other material that you display things such as announcements on)
6 a long narrow piece of special metal or plastic hanging over a swimming pool. It is used for diving into the water from. *a diving board*
7 a group of people who control a business or organisation
8 board is the food you get when you pay to stay somewhere *The price of the activity break includes board and lodging.*
9 **on board** on a ship or plane

board *verb*
boards, boarding, boarded
1 to get on a train, bus, ship or plane *We boarded the train at noon.*
2 to live somewhere and pay to live there and have your meals provided *Rupa boards at a school in Oxfordshire.*
3 to board up is to cover with wooden boards, for example a window or door *All the shops were boarded up.*

boarder *noun* **boarders**
1 a boy or girl who lives at a boarding school during term time
2 someone who pays money to live in someone else's home

board game *noun* **board games**
any game played on a board, such as chess or ludo

boarding school *noun* **boarding schools**
a school where students live during term time

boast *verb*
boasts, boasting, boasted
to talk about the good things that you have done, or that someone else has done, or about the wonderful things that belong to you, often to make people have a better opinion of you **boast** *noun*

SYNONYM to brag

boastful *adjective*
a boastful person is often or always boasting

boat *noun* **boats**
1 an object for carrying people or things on water. It uses a motor, sails or oars (long poles with flat ends) to move along.
2 **to be in the same boat** to have the same problems as other people and to try to sort them out together *We're all in the same boat.*

boatload *noun* **boatloads**
a large number of people or amount of things that are carried in a boat

bob *verb*
bobs, bobbing, bobbed
to bob up and down is to move up and down like something that floats on water

bob *noun* **bobs**
a style of hair for girls and women. The hair is cut evenly all the way round the head at the level of the neck and chin, often with a fringe (hair cut level over the forehead).

bobble *noun* **bobbles**
1 a small ball of soft material such as wool, often used for decorating clothes

bobsleigh–boo

2 a tiny untidy piece of material such as wool that appears on something that has been worn or used a lot, for example a sweater or cushion **bobbly** *adjective*

bobsleigh *noun* **bobsleighs**
a sledge for two or more people, used for racing over snow on special tracks

> LANGUAGE EXTRA the American word is *bobsled*

bodice *noun* **bodices**
the part of a dress from the waist upwards

bodily *adjective*
connected with the body *bodily injury*

bodily *adverb*
by moving someone's whole body *He was lifted bodily out of the chair.*

body *noun* **bodies**
1 the whole of a person or animal, used when talking about the flesh, bones and organs or when you mean the shape or appearance *The heart pumps blood around the body. Look at the shape of the seahorse's body.*
2 the middle part of the body that does not include the head, arms and legs *long legs and a short body*
3 a dead person
4 a group of people *the governing body of our school*
5 the main part of something such as a car, book or guitar

bodyguard *noun* **bodyguards**
someone who has the job of protecting an important person

boffin *noun* **boffins**
someone who knows a lot about a subject, especially a scientific subject *a computer boffin*

bog *noun* **bogs**
an area of wet and muddy ground
boggy *adjective*

bog down *verb*
bogs down, bogging down, bogged down
if someone gets bogged down in something such as details, they are stuck and not able to make progress

bogeyman *noun* **bogeymen**
an evil and scary creature that only exists in children's stories or in the imagination

bogus *adjective*
false *a bogus address*

> ORIGIN from *bogus*, a machine once used for making counterfeit ('false') money

boil *verb*
boils, boiling, boiled
1 if you boil a liquid or if it boils, it becomes very hot and starts to bubble and turn into steam
2 to boil food is to cook it in very hot bubbling water

boil *noun*
1 (*plural* **boils**) a small painful swelling on the skin that is filled with a yellowish liquid called pus
2 to bring something to the boil is to heat it up until it starts to boil

boiler *noun* **boilers**
a big container that heats water and provides hot water and heating in a house or building

boiling *adjective*
very hot *I'm boiling. It's a boiling hot day.*

boiling point *noun* **boiling points**
the temperature at which a liquid boils

boisterous *adjective*
noisy and full of energy

bold *adjective* **bolder, boldest**
1 brave and not afraid of taking risks
2 feeling sure of yourself and of the things you can do
3 strong, clear and easy to see *bold colours*
4 printed in a thicker and darker way than ordinary letters *bold letters*; *a bold paragraph*
boldly *adverb* **boldness** *noun*

> SIMILE 'as bold as brass' means very bold (sense 2)

bold *noun*
letters in a book or written document that are printed in a thicker and darker way than ordinary letters *The letter **b** is in bold.*

Bolivia *noun*
a country in central South America
Bolivian *adjective & noun*

bollard *noun* **bollards**
1 a short thick post used for stopping cars from driving somewhere such as into a street or on the pavement
2 a short thick post for tying a boat to

Bollywood *noun*
the film-making business in India *I love Bollywood films.*

> ORIGIN from *Bombay* (the centre of film-making in India) and *Hollywood* (the main centre of film-making in the US). Bombay is now called Mumbai.

bolster *verb*
bolsters, bolstering, bolstered
to make something stronger or better

bolt *noun* **bolts**
1 a sliding metal bar that keeps a door or gate shut
2 a thick metal screw that fits into a ring called a nut and is used for fastening things together
3 a bolt of lightning is a sudden flash of bright light that appears in the sky
4 **a bolt from the blue** something that happens suddenly that you weren't expecting

bolt *verb*
bolts, bolting, bolted
1 to lock a door or gate with a bolt
2 to run away suddenly and very fast, for example because you are frightened *There was a loud noise and the horse bolted.*
3 to bolt down food is to eat it very quickly

bomb *noun* **bombs**
a weapon that explodes when dropped to the ground from an aircraft or when it hits something, or that is made to explode at a particular time

bomb *verb*
bombs, bombing, bombed
to attack a place by dropping bombs on it or by putting a bomb somewhere in it

bombard *verb*
bombards, bombarding, bombarded
1 to bombard someone with something is to give, do or send so much of the particular thing to them that they have trouble dealing with it *They bombarded the teacher with questions.*
2 to bombard a place is to attack it with heavy guns or with bombs over a long time
bombardment *noun*

bomber *noun* **bombers**
1 someone who puts a bomb somewhere
2 an aircraft that drops bombs

bombshell *noun* **bombshells**
an unexpected and often bad piece of news

bond *noun* **bonds**
1 a relationship that brings people or groups closer together *the bond between father and son*
2 a document from a company or the government promising to pay back the money it borrows *Premium Bonds*

bondage *noun*
when someone is a slave and has no freedom

bone *noun* **bones**
1 one of the hard parts of the body that make up the skeleton
2 if you have a bone to pick with someone, you are angry with them and want to talk to them about why you are angry

bonfire *noun* **bonfires**
a large fire built in the open air

> ORIGIN from *bone* and *fire*, because bones were once used as fuel

Bonfire Night *noun* **Bonfire Nights**
the night of 5 November, when British people light bonfires and set off fireworks to celebrate the day in 1605 when Guy Fawkes tried but failed to blow up the Houses of Parliament

> SYNONYM Guy Fawkes' Night

bonkers *adjective*
an informal word for mad or crazy *You're completely bonkers!*

bonnet *noun* **bonnets**
1 a bonnet is the cover over the front part of a car where the engine is
2 a type of hat, usually with strings tied under the chin and worn by babies, girls and women

bonus *noun* **bonuses**
1 money added to your usual pay for good work
2 something good you get in addition to something else *I got an extra box of chocolates as a bonus.*

bony *adjective* **bonier, boniest**
1 a bony fish has lots of little bones in it
2 a bony body or part of the body is very thin so that you can see the shape of the bones *bony fingers*

boo *verb*
boos, booing, booed
if someone in an audience or crowd boos, they shout 'boo' loudly, for example when they don't like what an actor, speaker or politician has said or done *Everyone started booing. The singer was booed loudly.*

boo *noun* **boos**
1 the sound 'boo' shouted loudly, for example by an audience in a theatre or a crowd around a politician
2 the noise made by someone to frighten someone else as a joke

booby prize *noun* **booby prizes**
a joke prize given to someone who comes last in a competition

booby trap *noun* **booby traps**
a hidden bomb, for example in a car or building, which is set off when touched
booby-trap *verb*

book *noun* **books**
1 a number of printed pages fastened together inside a cardboard, plastic or thick paper cover *The book fell on the floor.*
2 something similar with empty pages for writing in *an exercise book*
3 a text someone writes that contains printed pages or that appears as an electronic document or on a website *I'm reading a book by Dickens.*
4 a number of small things held together inside a paper cover *a book of stamps*
5 if you're in someone's good books, they are pleased with you, and if you're in their bad books, they are angry with you

book *verb*
books, booking, booked
1 to arrange to have something kept for you at some future time, for example a seat at the theatre or on a train or a room in a hotel *We've booked our tickets to see 'Hamlet'.*

SYNONYM to reserve

2 to arrange something for the future *to book a holiday*
3 to book a player in a sport is to write down their name in a book as a punishment
4 to book in at a hotel (or to book into a hotel) is to arrive and tell someone who works there that you have arrived. You often sign your name on a piece of paper or in a book to show who you are.

bookcase *noun* **bookcases**
a piece of furniture with shelves for books

booked up *adjective*
1 to be booked up means there are no more of certain things, such as seats on a train, rooms in a hotel, tables in a restaurant or tickets for a show
2 if someone is booked up, they are very busy and have no time

booking *noun* **bookings**
1 when you arrange for something to be kept for you, for example a seat at the theatre, room in a hotel or ticket to travel somewhere *Have you made a booking to see the show yet?*

SYNONYM reservation

2 a booking office is a place where you buy train or bus tickets or tickets for the theatre

bookkeeping *noun*
when someone keeps a record of all the money that comes into and goes out of a business **bookkeeper** *noun*

booklet *noun* **booklets**
a small thin book with information on one subject

bookmaker *noun* **bookmakers**
a person whose job is to take people's bets, usually on horses, and to pay them if they win

bookmark *noun* **bookmarks**
1 a piece of paper or cloth that you put inside a book to mark the page that you're up to
2 a web page whose address you've saved to your computer so you can find it again easily. It is also called a favorite.

bookmark *verb*
bookmarks, bookmarking, bookmarked
1 to bookmark a web page is to save its address on your computer so you can find it again easily
2 to mark the page that you're up to in a book, by putting a piece of paper or cloth there

bookshelf *noun* **bookshelves**
a shelf in a bookcase or fixed to a wall, used for putting books on

boom *noun* **booms**
1 an increase in business or in the success of something *an economic boom*
2 a very loud deep sound

boom *verb*
booms, booming, boomed
1 if something such as an activity or country is booming, it is very successful and getting more successful as time goes by *the booming market for second-hand cars*
2 to make a very loud deep sound *The teacher's voice boomed out from the other end of the hall. We could hear the booming noise of a dozen planes.*

boomerang *noun* **boomerangs**
a curved weapon from Australia that is thrown into the air and flies back in a circular movement to where the thrower stands

boost *verb*
boosts, boosting, boosted
to make something bigger, better or stronger *They tried to boost his confidence.*

boost *noun* **boosts**
1 an action or event that helps to make something bigger, better or stronger *a boost to the film industry*
2 something that makes you feel happier and more confident *Passing my exams has given me a real boost.*

booster *noun* **boosters**
1 something that boosts something *a confidence booster*
2 a small extra amount of a type of medicine called a vaccine that is usually put into your skin with a needle *a tetanus booster*
3 an extra engine on a spacecraft

boot *noun* **boots**
1 a strong shoe that comes up over your ankle or part of your leg
2 a covered place for luggage at the back of a car
3 if someone gives you the boot, they get rid of you because they don't want you any more
4 if someone quakes in their boots, they are very frightened

boot *verb*
boots, booting, booted
1 if you boot up a computer or if it boots up, the operating system comes on and the computer starts working
2 to boot someone out is to get rid of them, for example because they've done something wrong

booth *noun* **booths**
a small structure with walls, a roof and a door or a structure that is partly open, usually big enough for one person. There are many types of booths, for example for making a phone call, voting, having your photo taken or getting information from. *a photo booth; an information booth*

border *noun* **borders**
1 the border between two countries or regions is the line that divides them
2 a pattern or colour that goes around the edge of something, such as a picture
3 a narrow area along the edge of a garden for growing plants

border *verb*
borders, bordering, bordered
1 if one country or region borders another, it lies next to it
2 if something such as a feeling borders on something else, it is very close to it *a dislike bordering on fear*

borderline *adjective*
in between being acceptable and not acceptable *borderline results; I didn't pass the exam but I was borderline.*

bore *verb*
bores, boring, bored
1 to make someone feel fed up and impatient, for example by talking about things in a way that is not interesting
2 to bore a hole is to make a hole in something, for example with a drill

bore *noun* **bores**
a person or thing that is not interesting

bore
past tense of **bear**

bored *adjective*
fed up and impatient, for example because you're not interested in what someone is saying or you have nothing to do

LANGUAGE EXTRA you say *bored with* or *bored by* something. Do not say *bored of.*

boredom *noun*
a feeling of being fed up and impatient

boring *adjective*
used about something or someone that is not interesting or that makes you feel fed up and impatient *a boring film; a boring teacher*

born *adjective*
when a baby or animal is born, it comes out of the mother's body and begins its life *I was born on 24th March.*

borne
past participle of **bear**

> LANGUAGE EXTRA be careful not to confuse *borne* and *born*. *Borne* is used with parts of 'to have' and is a form of the verb 'to bear', for example *She has borne a son.*

borough ['bu-rer'; 'u' rhymes with 'u' in 'cup'] *noun* **boroughs**
a town, or part of a large town, with its own council that is responsible for many things, such as schools and hospitals

borrow *verb*
borrows, borrowing, borrowed
1 to take or use something belonging to someone else and agree to give it back later
2 if someone borrows money from a bank, the bank gives them money that they agree to pay back later with interest (extra regular amounts of money)
3 to borrow an idea, word or way of doing something is to copy it and use it yourself *a phrase borrowed from French*
borrower *noun*

Bosnia *noun*
a country in South-East Europe
Bosnian *adjective & noun*

> LANGUAGE EXTRA short for *Bosnia and Herzegovina*

bosom *noun* **bosoms**
a woman's breasts

boss *noun* **bosses**
a person in charge of a group of people at work or in charge of a whole business *She's my boss. He's the boss of the BBC.*

boss *verb*
bosses, bossing, bossed
to boss someone around is to keep telling them what to do even though you have no power to make them obey you

bossy *adjective* **bossier, bossiest**
a bossy person likes telling people what to do

botanical *adjective*
1 connected with plants
2 a botanical garden is a large area with lots of different plants for people to go and see

botanist *noun* **botanists**
a scientist who studies plants

botany *noun*
the scientific study of plants

botch *verb*
botches, botching, botched
to botch something or botch something up is to do it badly

both *adjective & pronoun*
used when you mean two people or things and not just one *Take it with both hands. I've read both these books.*

> LANGUAGE EXTRA when *both* is a pronoun, you can use it with *of*, for example *I've read both of these books.* You often do this to show that the word *both* is especially important.

both *conjunction*
used with 'and' for saying that two things are true *She knows both Spanish and French.*

bother *verb*
bothers, bothering, bothered
1 to make someone feel worried, upset or frightened
2 to make someone slightly angry, especially by interrupting them, pestering them or using up their time
3 to cause someone pain *My leg's bothering me.*
4 if you don't bother to do something or if you can't be bothered to do something, you don't make any effort to do it *He didn't even bother to say goodbye. He couldn't even be bothered to say goodbye.*
5 if you're not bothered about something, you don't care about it

bother *noun*
trouble *I'm having some bother with my leg. I'll help you – it's no bother.*

bottle *noun* **bottles**
a glass or plastic container with a narrow opening, used for liquids

bottle *verb*
bottles, bottling, bottled
1 to put something into a bottle in a factory
2 to bottle up a feeling is to hide it inside you and not let anyone know about it

bottle bank *noun* **bottle banks**
a large container for putting empty bottles and jars into so that the glass can be recycled (used again)

bottleneck *noun* **bottlenecks**
a place in a road where the traffic has to go slow, for example because the road has become narrow or different lines of traffic meet

bottom *noun* **bottoms**
1 the lowest part of something
2 the part of something furthest away from you *My friend lives at the bottom of the street.*
3 the part of your body that you sit on
4 to get to the bottom of something is to find out the reason for it
5 bottoms are soft loose trousers for doing exercises in or for wearing in bed. What you wear with the bottoms is called the top. *jogging bottoms; pyjama bottoms*

bottom *adjective*
lowest or in the lowest place or position *the bottom drawer; She came bottom of the class in the test.*

bottomless *adjective*
very deep and almost without end

bough [rhymes with 'brow'] *noun* **boughs**
a word used in books and poems for a large branch of a tree

bought
past tense & past participle of **buy**

boulder *noun* **boulders**
a very large piece of rock

bounce *verb*
bounces, bouncing, bounced
1 if a ball or another object bounces or if you bounce it, it springs back after hitting a surface like a wall or the ground *The ball bounced (or bounced back) off the fence and hit me on the arm. Fatima was bouncing a tennis ball up and down.*
2 if a person bounces, they jump up and down *I was bouncing on the bed.*
3 if someone bounces back, they become healthy or successful again
4 if an email bounces back, it comes back to you because there is a problem
bounce *noun*

bouncing *adjective*
a bouncing baby is a healthy one

bouncy *adjective* **bouncier, bounciest**
1 a bouncy person is happy and full of energy

> SYNONYM bubbly

2 if something such as a ball is bouncy, it is good for bouncing because it springs back strongly
3 soft enough to be pressed or bent but going back to its normal shape afterwards *a bouncy bed*

bouncy castle *noun* **bouncy castles**
a big soft plastic structure filled with air that children bounce up and down on

bound *adjective*
1 **bound to** certain to *It's bound to happen.*
2 to feel bound to do something is to feel that you must do it
3 to be bound for somewhere means to be going there *The plane is bound for Rome.*

bound *verb*
bounds, bounding, bounded
to move quickly and with large steps and lots of energy **bound** *noun*

bound
past tense & past participle of **bind**

boundary *noun* **boundaries**
1 a line where one piece of land touches another
2 a limit
3 the boundary between activities or ideas is the point that separates them
4 the outside edge of a cricket field

bounds *noun plural*
1 limits
2 **out of bounds** used for describing a place where you're not allowed to go *The staff room is out of bounds to students.*

bouquet ['boo-kay'] *noun* **bouquets**
an attractive bunch of different flowers that you give to someone

> ORIGIN from an Old French word meaning 'little wood'

bout *noun* **bouts**
1 a short period, especially when you're ill *a bout of flu*
2 a fight in boxing or wrestling

boutique ['boo-teek'] *noun* **boutiques**
a small shop selling fashionable clothes

> ORIGIN from French *boutique* 'shop'

bow [rhymes with 'throw'] *noun* **bows**
1 a knot with two loops or curved parts and two loose ends
2 a weapon for shooting arrows, made of a long curved piece of wood and a tight string *a bow and arrow*
3 a special stick with a tight string stretched along it that is used for playing a violin, viola or cello

bow–brain

bow [rhymes with 'brow'] *noun* **bows**
the front part of a boat

> **LANGUAGE EXTRA** the back part of a boat is called the *stern*

bow [rhymes with 'brow'] *verb*
bows, bowing, bowed
1 to bend forward from the waist, or to bend your head forward, for example to show respect to someone important such as a king or queen *I bowed to the King. He bowed his head in shame.*
2 to bow down is to bend your body completely forward, for example to touch the ground when you are already kneeling

bow [rhymes with 'brow'] *noun* **bows**
the action of bending your body or your head *At the end of the show the actors took a bow.*

bowels *noun plural*
the tubes inside your body that carry food from the stomach towards the anus (the place where it comes out of your body)

> **ORIGIN** from Latin *botellus* 'little sausage'

bowl *noun* **bowls**
1 a deep round dish *a cereal bowl*
2 something in a bowl *I ate two bowls of rice.*
3 something shaped like a bowl *a toilet bowl*
4 a ball used in the game of bowls

bowl *verb*
bowls, bowling, bowled
1 in cricket, to bowl is to throw the ball towards the person who is batting (hitting the ball) to try to hit the wicket (three upright sticks)
2 if you are bowled over by something, you are surprised and delighted by it

bow-legged *adjective*
if you are bow-legged, your legs are curved outwards at the knees

> **SYNONYM** bandy-legged

bowler *noun* **bowlers**
1 a person in cricket who bowls the ball
2 a bowler or bowler hat is a hard round black hat that businessmen wore in the past

bowling *noun*
1 an indoor game in which people roll a large heavy ball down a narrow track to knock down wooden objects called pins *Let's go bowling.*

> **LANGUAGE EXTRA** also called *tenpin bowling*

2 a bowling alley is the place where people go to play the game of bowling

bowls *noun plural*
an outdoor game where people roll a large heavy ball along grass and try to get it as close as possible to a small ball called the jack

> **ORIGIN** from French *boule* 'ball' or 'round object', and Latin *bulla* 'bubble'

bow tie *noun* **bow ties**
a man's tie in the shape of a bow (knot with two loops and loose ends), usually worn on special occasions

box *noun* **boxes**
1 a container for putting things in, with straight sides and often a lid, usually made of cardboard, plastic or wood
2 something in a box *You've eaten the whole box of chocolates.*
3 a small space on a printed form or web page for writing something in or putting a tick in, or a space on a page or computer screen where information is given
4 a small structure for a particular purpose *a post box*

box *verb*
boxes, boxing, boxed
1 to fight with the fists (hands with closed fingers) in the sport of boxing
2 to box something up is to put it into a box
3 if someone in a car is boxed in, they cannot move their car because another car has parked in the way

boxer *noun* **boxers**
1 a fighter who takes part in boxing
2 a big dog with a flat face and short hair
3 boxers or boxer shorts are a type of cotton underwear for men. They look like short trousers.

boxing *noun*
a sport in which two fighters hit each other with their fists. They wear big leather gloves, called boxing gloves. The place where they fight is called a boxing ring.

Boxing Day *noun* **Boxing Days**
the day that follows Christmas Day. It is a national holiday.

> **ORIGIN** from the 19th-century tradition of giving *Christmas boxes* (small gifts of money) to employees and servants. Many people still give Christmas boxes to people who deliver their post or newspapers.

box office *noun* **box offices**
a place in a theatre or cinema where you buy tickets

box room *noun* **box rooms**
a small room in a house or flat, used for example as a bedroom or for storing things

boy *noun* **boys**
a male child

boy band *noun* **boy bands**
a pop band made up of attractive young men who sing and dance

boycott *verb*
boycotts, boycotting, boycotted
to refuse to buy or use something or go somewhere, usually to try to get someone to change their mind about something *The whole class boycotted the canteen because the food was so bad.* **boycott** *noun*

> **ORIGIN** from Captain C. C. *Boycott*, who caused the first *boycott* in 19th-century Ireland because of the bad way he treated people there

boyfriend *noun* **boyfriends**
someone's boyfriend is the boy they are going out with

boyish *adjective*
behaving or looking like a boy

Boy Scout *noun* **Boy Scouts**
a boy, usually aged 11 to 18, who belongs to the Scout Association. This organisation teaches boys useful skills.

bra *noun* **bras**
a piece of underwear for supporting the breasts

> **ORIGIN** from Old French *braciere* 'protector or shield for the arm' (used by soldiers), which comes from *bras* 'arm'

brace *noun* **braces**
1 an object for supporting something, for example a part of your body *a leg brace*
2 if you have a brace or braces on your teeth, you have wires to straighten them

brace *verb*
braces, bracing, braced
to brace yourself for something is to get ready for something powerful and often bad, for example bad news

bracelet *noun* **bracelets**
a piece of jewellery worn around the wrist or arm, for example shaped like a chain

> **ORIGIN** from an Old French word meaning 'little arm'

braces *noun plural*
straps worn over the shoulders for holding up trousers

bracken *noun*
a plant with leaves like large feathers. It often grows in forests.

bracket *noun* **brackets**
1 one of a pair of punctuation marks that are either round like this ( ), square [ ] or curly { }
2 a support for a shelf or a light that is fixed to a wall

> **LANGUAGE EXTRA** you can put *brackets* around words to give extra information in a sentence, for example *My bike cost a lot of money (more than my parents could afford).*
> In maths, you often use brackets to group numbers together. For example, in $5 + (2 \times 4)$, you work out the numbers in brackets first ($2 \times 4 = 8$) and then do the rest of the calculation ($5 + 8 = 13$).

brag *verb*
brags, bragging, bragged
to boast

braid *noun* **braids**
1 a narrow piece of twisted material for decorating clothes or furniture
2 another word for a plait

braille ['brayl'] *noun*
a printing system for blind people that uses raised dots, which can be read by touching them with the fingers

> **LANGUAGE EXTRA** also spelt *Braille*

> **ORIGIN** from Louis *Braille*, the blind 19th-century French musician and teacher who invented it

brain *noun* **brains**
1 the organ inside your head used for thinking and feeling

2 your intelligence, or someone with intelligence *She has brains. He's the brains of the family.*

brain-dead *adjective*
1 someone who is brain-dead has a brain that is no longer working because of an injury or illness
2 completely stupid, or with a mind that doesn't seem to be working, for example because you're so tired

brainwash *verb*
brainwashes, brainwashing, brainwashed
to make someone believe something false by repeating it so many times that they accept it as being true

brainwave *noun* brainwaves
a good idea that comes to you suddenly

brainy *adjective* brainier, brainiest
intelligent

brake *noun* brakes
a piece of equipment for making a car or another machine slow down and stop

brake *verb*
brakes, braking, braked
to put on the brakes, for example in a car

bramble *noun* brambles
1 a bush that blackberries grow on that has lots of thorns (sharp points) on it
2 a blackberry

bran *noun*
the small brown flakes from the outside of grain, such as wheat, that are separated from the grain when flour is made

branch *noun* branches
1 a part of a tree on which the leaves grow
2 an office or shop that is part of a large business
3 a smaller part of something such as a river or road, for example, that leaves the main part
4 a branch of a family is a part of it where all the members are closely related

branch *verb*
branches, branching, branched
1 to branch off is to go off in a different direction from the main part of something
2 to branch out is to start to do something new and different

brand *noun* brands
a particular kind of product made by one company *I don't like this brand of chocolate.*

brand *verb*
brands, branding, branded
to brand someone something is to describe them in that way (often in an unkind way) *They branded him a liar.*

brandish *verb*
brandishes, brandishing, brandished
to wave something about in a dangerous way, especially a weapon such as a knife

brand-new *adjective*
completely new

brandy *noun* brandies
a strong alcoholic drink made from wine

brass *noun*
1 a yellowish metal made from mixing copper and zinc
2 in an orchestra, the brass are the musical instruments made of brass, such as trumpets, trombones and tubas *a brass band*

brassed off *adjective* (informal)
fed up and annoyed

brat *noun* brats
an informal word for a child who behaves badly

brave *adjective* braver, bravest
1 not afraid to face danger, pain or difficult things *a very brave little boy*
2 also used about the behaviour of a brave person *That was a very brave thing to do.*
bravely *adverb* **bravery** *noun*

SIMILE 'as brave as a lion' means very brave

brawl *noun* brawls
a rough and noisy fight **brawl** *verb*

brawn *noun*
a strong body and big muscles *Carrying luggage needs brawn, not brains.*
brawny *adjective*

bray *verb*
brays, braying, brayed
when a donkey brays, it makes a loud rough noise that is its own special sound

brazen *adjective*
someone who is brazen does things that are not moral or good and doesn't care what other people think

Brazil *noun*
a country in South America
Brazilian *adjective & noun*

brazil nut *noun* brazil nuts
a large curved brown nut that you can eat. It has a very hard grey-brown shell with three sides.

LANGUAGE EXTRA also spelt *Brazil nut*

breach *verb*
breaches, breaching, breached
1 to break a rule or agreement
2 to make a hole in something like a wall *The water breached the dam.*
breach *noun*

bread *noun*
a baked food made from flour and water

breadcrumbs *noun plural*
1 tiny pieces that fall off bread when you cut it or eat it
2 tiny pieces of dry bread used in cooking, for example for covering or putting on top of food

breaded *adjective*
covered in breadcrumbs and cooked *breaded fish*

breadth *noun* breadths
the breadth of something is the distance from one side to the other

SYNONYM width

breadwinner *noun* breadwinners
the person in a family who earns most of the money that the family needs to live

break *verb*
breaks, breaking, broke, broken
1 if something breaks, or if someone or something breaks it, it falls into two or more pieces *The plate hit the floor and broke. I broke my leg. A tree fell down and broke our roof.*
2 if a machine or other piece of equipment breaks or if you break it, it stops working *I think I've broken my camera.*
3 if you break a rule or the law, you do not obey it
4 if you break a promise or your word, you do not do what you have said you will do
5 if news breaks or if you break news to someone, it becomes known *Breaking news: an earthquake has hit Chile.*
6 to stop doing something and have a rest *They broke for lunch.*
7 if the weather breaks, hot weather suddenly becomes cold
8 to break a record is to do something better than anyone has done it before *She broke the record for the fastest time in the marathon.*
9 if a boy's voice breaks, he begins to have the deeper voice of a man, usually between the ages of 12 and 15
10 if waves break, they hit the shore or the rocks as they come in
11 if a vehicle or machine breaks down, it stops working
12 if someone breaks down a door, they make it fall down by hitting it hard
13 if you break something down into parts, you divide it into smaller parts, for example to understand it better *Our teacher showed us how to break down words into separate sounds.*
14 if thieves break in, they use force to go into a building or car to steal things
15 to break off something is to end it or not do it any more *My sister broke off her engagement.*
16 if something bad breaks out, such as a fire, a disease or fighting, it starts and gets worse
17 if a school breaks up, students and teachers stop working because it is the start of a school holiday
18 if two people break up, they do not see each other or live with each other any more *Charlie's sister broke up with her boyfriend.*

break *noun* breaks
1 a short time when something stops before it starts again, such as a short rest when you're working or playing a game *Let's have a five-minute break.*
2 a break during the school day is a short time between classes, for example for playing
3 a break in a TV or radio programme is a short period where there are advertisements
4 a break in something like a bone is the place where it is broken
5 a piece of luck that you need to be successful *I had a lucky break.*

breakable *adjective*
easy to break, like glass or china

breakdown *noun* breakdowns
1 when a vehicle or machine stops working *We had a breakdown on a country road. Dad called the breakdown lorry* (to pull or carry our car to a place where it can be repaired).

breaker–brief

2 if there is a breakdown in something such as a system or relationship, it no longer works *a breakdown in communication*
3 when someone becomes ill and depressed *He had a nervous breakdown.*
4 a detailed list of something so that people can understand it easily *Give me a breakdown of all the different figures.*

breaker *noun* **breakers**
a big wave that comes onto the seashore

breakfast *noun* **breakfasts**
the first meal of the day. You have it in the morning.

> ORIGIN from the 15th-century English word *brekfast*, meaning 'break' (put an end to) and 'fast' (going without food and drink). You go without food and drink when you sleep, and start eating and drinking when you wake up.

break-in *noun* **break-ins**
when thieves go into a building or car to steal things

breakneck *adjective*
very fast in a dangerous way *at breakneck speed*

breakthrough *noun* **breakthroughs**
a very important development, for example in science or in a police investigation

break-up *noun* **break-ups**
when two people stop seeing or living with each other

breakwater *noun* **breakwaters**
a wall going out into the sea to protect the shore from the waves

breast *noun* **breasts**
1 a woman's breasts are the two parts on her chest that produce milk when she has a baby
2 the front part of the body of a bird *a robin red breast*
3 the meat from the front part of a bird or other animal *a chicken breast; a breast of pork*

breaststroke *noun*
a frog-like way of swimming where you push your arms forward and back while bending your knees and kicking

breath *noun* **breaths**
1 the air that goes in and out of your lungs as you breathe
2 to hold your breath is to breathe air into your lungs and not to breathe again for a few seconds or minutes
3 if you are out of breath, you breathe very fast, for example after running or doing exercise
4 to catch your breath is to gradually begin to breathe again normally after you've been out of breath
5 if you are short of breath, you are having trouble breathing, for example because you are ill or old or after doing exercise
6 if you say something under your breath, you say it very quietly to yourself so that no-one can hear you

breathalyser *noun* **breathalysers**
a piece of equipment that the police ask car drivers to blow into to check the amount of alcohol in their body **breathalyse** *verb*

breathe *verb*
breathes, breathing, breathed
to take air into your lungs through your mouth and nose ('breathe in') and let it out again ('breathe out')

> LANGUAGE EXTRA be careful not to confuse *breath* and *breathe*. *Breath* is a noun (pronounced 'breth') and *breathe* is a verb (pronounced 'breethe').

breather *noun* **breathers**
a short rest from working or playing a game

breathless *adjective*
if someone is breathless, they are having trouble breathing

breathtaking *adjective*
very beautiful *breathtaking views*

bred
past tense & past participle of **breed**

breeches ['britch-iz] *noun plural*
short trousers that come down to the knees *riding breeches*

breed *verb*
breeds, breeding, bred
1 if animals breed, they come together to produce baby animals
2 if people breed animals, they keep them to make them produce baby animals, usually with the special qualities they want them to have
3 to produce or cause something, usually something bad, for example germs, disease or violence

breed *noun* **breeds**
a type of animal with its own special qualities *The German shepherd is an intelligent breed of dog.*

breeder *noun* **breeders**
someone who breeds animals

breeding *noun*
1 the business of making animals produce new animals with special qualities *cattle breeding*
2 a breeding ground is a place that provides conditions to help something happen, usually something bad *This estate is a breeding ground for crime.*

breeze *noun* **breezes**
a gentle wind

breeze block *noun* **breeze blocks**
a type of very large brick used for making buildings. It is made from cement and cinders (the ashes from coal).

breezy *adjective* **breezier, breeziest**
1 with a gentle wind blowing
2 happy and lively *a breezy smile*

brethren *noun plural*
an old word meaning 'brothers', used for referring to male members of a group, such as a religious group

breve ['breev'] *noun* **breves**
a musical note that is twice as long as a semibreve

brevity *noun*
the quality of being brief

brew *verb*
brews, brewing, brewed
1 to brew tea or coffee is to make it by pouring hot water over it
2 if tea or coffee is brewing, it is being made and the flavour is gradually going into the water
3 to brew beer is to make it in a brewery
4 if something bad is brewing, it will happen very soon *Trouble is brewing.*
brewer *noun*

brewery *noun* **breweries**
a place or company that makes beer

briar *noun* **briars**
a wild thorny bush (with sharp points on it). There are different types of briars, for example the wild rose.

bribe *verb*
bribes, bribing, bribed
to give someone a bribe

bribe *noun* **bribes**
money or a present you give to someone so that they will do something, usually something dishonest

bribery *noun*
the action or crime of offering someone a bribe

brick *noun* **bricks**
1 a small block of baked clay used for making walls and buildings
2 a very small block of plastic or wood used as a toy for building things

brick *verb*
bricks, bricking, bricked
if someone bricks up a space in a wall, for example where a window or door is, they block it up by filling it with bricks

bricklayer *noun* **bricklayers**
someone who builds walls with bricks

bridal *adjective*
connected with brides *bridal gown*

bride *noun* **brides**
a woman on her wedding day

bridegroom *noun* **bridegrooms**
a man on his wedding day

bridesmaid *noun* **bridesmaids**
a girl or young woman who helps a bride on her wedding day

bride-to-be *noun* **brides-to-be**
a woman who will soon be getting married

bridge *noun* **bridges**
1 a structure built to let you cross over a river, road or railway
2 the platform on a ship where the captain stands. The captain controls the ship from the bridge.
3 a card game for four people
4 the bridge of your nose is the hard part between your eyes

bridle *noun* **bridles**
1 a number of connected leather strips put on a horse's head to control it. The bridle is connected to the reins (leather straps held in your hand).
2 a bridle path is a path used by people riding horses

brief *adjective* **briefer, briefest**
1 short *a brief visit*
2 if someone is brief, they use few words to say what they need to say
3 **in brief** using few words

brief – broad-minded

brief *noun* briefs
instructions that someone gives you about a job that you must do

brief *verb*
briefs, briefing, briefed
to brief someone on something is to give them all the information they need to know about it *The prime minister was briefed on the plan.*

briefcase *noun* briefcases
a small case, often flat, for carrying documents

briefly *adverb*
1 for a short time
2 in few words

briefs *noun plural*
short underwear for the lower part of the body

brier *noun* briers
another spelling of **briar**

brigade *noun* brigades
1 a very large group of soldiers. A brigade contains between three and five battalions and is part of a division.
2 a group of organised people such as the fire brigade

brigadier *noun* brigadiers
an army officer usually in charge of a brigade and with a higher rank than a colonel

bright *adjective* brighter, brightest
1 used for describing something that produces a lot of strong light *bright sunshine*; *a bright light*; *a bright room*
2 used for describing something that reflects the light *bright white paper*; *The steel had a bright polished surface.*
3 a bright colour is strong, clear and easy to see *a bright red sweater*
4 intelligent *She's one of the bright pupils in the class.*
5 likely to be successful *a bright future*
6 happy and lively *bright eyes*
brightness *noun*

SIMILE 'as bright as a button' means very bright (senses 4 & 6)

brighten *verb*
brightens, brightening, brightened
1 to give something more light or colour, or to start to have more light or colour *The sun brightened up the room. The weather is brightening up.*
2 to make or become more attractive, pleasant or happy *These drawings on the wall will brighten up the classroom.*

brightly *adverb*
1 with lots of strong light *The sun shone brightly.*
2 reflecting the light *The diamonds sparkled brightly.*
3 strongly *a brightly coloured painting*
4 in a happy and lively way *Her eyes shone brightly.*

brilliance *noun*
1 great intelligence or skill
2 the strong light or colour of something, such as the sun

brilliant *adjective*
1 very intelligent or skilful *a brilliant student*; *a brilliant musician*
2 (informal) excellent *That book was brilliant.*
3 very bright and strong *brilliant sunshine*

brilliantly *adverb*
1 really well *She danced brilliantly.*
2 strongly *brilliantly coloured*

brim *noun* brims
1 the top edge of a container *The glass was filled to the brim.*
2 the flat bottom part of a hat that sticks out at the edge and usually goes all the way around the hat

brim *verb*
brims, brimming, brimmed
1 if a container is brimming over with a liquid, the liquid is spilling out because the container is full
2 to have lots of something *The children were brimming with excitement.*

brine *noun*
salty water used for preserving food

bring *verb*
brings, bringing, brought
1 if you bring someone or something to a place, you come or go to the place with that person or thing *My brother brought me to school. I've brought my new pen with me.*
2 to go and get something *Bring me a cup of tea.*
3 to cause something or make it happen *to bring something to an end*; *The president brought peace to the country.*
4 to bring something about is to make it happen
5 to bring something back is to make sure it goes to the place where it was before or to the person who had it before
6 to bring something off is to manage to do something difficult
7 to bring out a product such as a book is to produce it
8 to bring someone round is to wake them up after they have fainted
9 to bring up a child is to take care of and educate the child until he or she is grown up
10 to bring something up on a computer screen is to make it appear
11 to bring something up in a conversation is to talk about it

brink *noun*
if you are on the brink of something, something very important is about to happen *a country on the brink of war*

brisk *adjective* brisker, briskest
1 quick and lively *a brisk walk*
2 if business is brisk, for example in a shop, it is very busy
3 if someone is brisk, they are efficient and only do or say what is necessary
briskly *adverb* **briskness** *noun*

bristle *noun* bristles
a short stiff hair like those on a brush or a man's chin **bristly** *adjective*

Brit *noun* Brits
an informal word for a Briton

Britain *noun*
England, Scotland and Wales

LANGUAGE EXTRA *Britain* is also called *Great Britain*. The *United Kingdom* (or *UK* for short) includes England, Scotland, Wales and Northern Ireland.

British *adjective*
connected with Britain

British Isles *noun plural*
the British Isles are the islands made up of Britain, Ireland and other small islands around the coast

Briton *noun* Britons
someone from Britain

brittle *adjective*
hard but easily broken

broad *adjective* broader, broadest
1 wide *He has broad shoulders.*
2 including lots of different things *a broad range of subjects*
3 not detailed *a broad outline of the subject*
4 if something happens in broad daylight, especially a crime or something bad, it happens during the day when it's light and anyone can see it

B-road *noun* B-roads
a main road in the UK that is smaller than an A-road

broadband *noun*
a way of connecting computers to the internet for sending and receiving information, sound and pictures very quickly

broad bean *noun* broad beans
a round flat pale green bean

broadcast *verb*
broadcasts, broadcasting, broadcast
1 to send out something such as a radio or television programme using radio waves *The Olympics were broadcast all around the world. The BBC will be broadcasting from Glasgow.*
2 to take part in a programme that is broadcast *During his visit to the UK, the Pope broadcast from London.*
3 to tell lots of people something, especially something secret *Please don't broadcast this to all your friends.*

broadcast *noun* broadcasts
a radio or television programme

broadcaster *noun* broadcasters
1 someone who takes part in and is in charge of a radio or television programme
2 a company that makes radio or television programmes

broaden *verb*
broadens, broadening, broadened
1 to make something more general and include more things *We need to broaden our knowledge of other countries.*
2 to make something wider, for example a road
3 if you say that something such as travelling broadens the mind, you mean that it makes you understand people better

broadly *adverb*
broadly or broadly speaking means in a very general way *Our ideas are broadly similar. Broadly speaking, you're right.*

broad-minded *adjective*
if someone is broad-minded, they understand and accept other people's behaviour and are not easily shocked

49

broccoli–brute

broccoli *noun*
a vegetable with thick pale green stems and lots of green or purple heads (top parts where the buds grow)

> ORIGIN from Italian *broccolo* 'little sprout'

brochure ['broh-sher] *noun* **brochures**
a small book with thin paper covers that gives information and pictures, for example about things to buy or places to visit *a holiday brochure*

> ORIGIN from an 18th-century French word meaning 'stitching', because the pages were stitched together. The pronunciation has the same 'sh' sound as in French.

brogue *noun* **brogues**
a strong accent, especially an Irish one

broil *verb*
broils, broiling, broiled
in American English, to broil is to grill food under direct heat

broke
past tense of **break**

broke *adjective* (informal)
if you're broke, you have no money

broken
past participle of **break**

broken *adjective*
1 not working *My mobile is broken.*
2 in two or more pieces, or in many pieces *broken glass*
3 if someone speaks in broken English, they make lots of mistakes and have a foreign accent
4 if a child comes from a broken home, his or her parents no longer live together
5 a broken line is a line with spaces in it, like this – – – –

brolly *noun* **brollies**
an informal word for an umbrella

bronchitis ['bron-kye-ters] *noun*
an illness of the lungs caused by an infection that makes you cough

brontosaurus *noun* **brontosauruses**
a large plant-eating dinosaur with a small head and long neck

> LANGUAGE EXTRA also called an *apatosaurus*

bronze *noun*
1 a reddish-brown metal made from mixing copper and tin
2 a reddish-brown colour
3 a bronze medal is given to someone who comes third in a race or competition. A gold medal goes to the winner and a silver one to the person who comes second.
4 the Bronze Age is the period between the Stone Age and the Iron Age, around 4000 to 1000 BC, when people used bronze to make tools and weapons

brooch ['broach'] *noun* **brooches**
a small object that can be pinned to your clothes. It is worn as jewellery, usually by women.

brood *noun* **broods**
a family of young birds born at the same time

brood *verb*
broods, brooding, brooded
1 to think deeply and to worry about something when it will not help to do so *She sat brooding over the exam results.*
2 if a bird broods, it sits on its eggs until the young birds hatch out

broody *adjective* **broodier, broodiest**
a broody person is someone who often sits quietly and worries about things, or who is thinking and worrying about a particular thing

brook *noun* **brooks**
a small stream

broom *noun*
1 (*plural* **brooms**) a brush with a long handle, used for sweeping
2 a wild bush with lots of tiny yellow flowers and small leaves

broom cupboard *noun*
broom cupboards
1 a small cupboard built into a wall, where you keep small things used in a house or flat, for example things for cleaning such as brooms, brushes and mops
2 an informal word for a very small room

broomstick *noun* **broomsticks**
in children's stories, a broomstick is a broom with a brush made from sticks and small branches that witches and wizards use to fly on

broth *noun* **broths**
a soup made from meat or fish and vegetables *chicken broth*

brother *noun* **brothers**
1 a boy or man who has the same parents as you
2 the title given to someone such as a monk who belongs to a Christian religious group *Brother Arnold*

brother-in-law *noun* **brothers-in-law**
someone's brother-in-law is their sister's husband, or the brother of their own husband or wife, or the husband of their husband's sister or of their wife's sister

brought
past tense & past participle of **bring**

brow *noun* **brows**
1 the part of your face above your eyes

> SYNONYM forehead

2 the brow of a hill is the top of it where the hill starts to be flatter

brown *adjective* **browner, brownest**
1 having the colour of earth or chocolate
2 suntanned

brown *noun* **browns**
the colour brown

browned off *adjective* (informal)
fed up and annoyed

brownie *noun* **brownies**
a flat chocolate cake

Brownie *noun* **Brownies**
a girl who belongs to the youngest section of the Guides (or Guide Association), for girls aged 7 to 10

brownish *adjective*
slightly brown

browse *verb*
browses, browsing, browsed
1 to look at things in a shop, for example a bookshop, or to look through the pages of a book or magazine in a relaxed way
2 to browse a web page or the internet is to look for information there
3 if an animal such as a goat or deer browses, it eats leaves or plants

browse *noun*

browser *noun* **browsers**
a computer program that allows you to look at sites on the internet

bruise *noun* **bruises**
a dark mark on the skin where it has been hit

bruise *verb*
bruises, bruising, bruised
to get a bruise on your skin by hitting it on something, or to make someone have a bruise on their skin *My leg is badly bruised.*

brunch *noun* **brunches**
a meal usually eaten in the late morning instead of breakfast and lunch

> ORIGIN from *breakfast* and *lunch*

brunette *noun* **brunettes**
a girl or woman with brown or black hair *Is she a blonde or a brunette?*

brush *noun* **brushes**
1 an object with hairs, bristles or wires fixed to a handle. Brushes come in many different shapes and sizes. You use them for many different things such as making your hair tidy, painting, sweeping, scrubbing or cleaning your teeth.
2 the action of brushing *I gave my teeth a good brush.*
3 the thick tail of a fox

brush *verb*
brushes, brushing, brushed
1 to brush something is to clean it or make it tidy or smooth with a brush *Have you brushed your teeth?*
2 if you brush past or against something or someone, you touch them very slightly as you pass
3 to push *He brushed the crumbs off the table.*
4 to brush aside what someone says is to refuse to listen to it
5 to brush something up or to brush up on something, for example a skill you learnt in the past, is to improve your knowledge of it *I need to brush up on my Urdu.*

Brussels sprout *noun* **Brussels sprouts**
a vegetable like a very small cabbage

brutal *adjective*
1 very violent *a brutal death*
2 very unpleasant and cruel *a brutal remark*

brutality *noun* **brutally** *adverb*

brute *noun* **brutes**
1 a very violent person, especially a man
2 a big strong man
3 a very unpleasant and cruel man

brute *adjective*
brute force great strength

50

BSE *noun*
a brain disease in cows that causes their death
short for: bovine spongiform encephalopathy

SYNONYM mad cow disease

bubble *noun* bubbles
1 a small ball of air or gas inside a liquid *When the water boils you can see the bubbles.*
2 a small ball of air with a thin covering of soap. It can float in the air or on water. *I was blowing bubbles in the bath.*
3 a ball blown from bubble gum
4 a bubble or speech bubble is a circle around the speaking words of a character in a cartoon. It is also called a balloon.

bubble *verb*
bubbles, bubbling, bubbled
to produce bubbles, like water when it boils

bubble and squeak *noun*
a dish made of cold leftover potatoes, cabbage and sometimes meat, usually fried in a large pan

bubble gum *noun*
a type of chewing gum that you can blow into to make a big bubble

bubble wrap *noun*
thin plastic with lots of bubbles in it filled with air, used for wrapping around objects to protect them, for example when sending them by post. Bubble wrap usually comes in transparent sheets.

bubbly *adjective* bubblier, bubbliest
1 happy and full of energy *a bubbly personality*

SYNONYM bouncy

2 full of bubbles

buccaneer *noun* buccaneers
a pirate, especially in the 17th and 18th centuries

buck *noun* bucks
1 the male of a rabbit or deer
2 in American English, a buck is a dollar, and bucks can mean money
3 **to pass the buck** to take no responsibility for dealing with something because you think that someone else should be responsible

buck *verb*
bucks, bucking, bucked
1 if a horse bucks, it kicks into the air wildly with its back legs
compare: rear
2 to buck someone up is to make them happier

SYNONYM to cheer up

3 if you tell someone to buck up their ideas, you mean they must improve and try harder, for example in their schoolwork

bucket *noun* buckets
a container with an open top and a handle, used for carrying liquids and other things such as sand or earth

bucketful *noun* bucketfuls
an amount of something that you can carry in a bucket

Buckingham Palace *noun*
the London home of the British king or queen

buckle *noun* buckles
a metal object on the end of a strap, used for fastening something such as a belt, bag or shoe

buckle *verb*
buckles, buckling, buckled
1 to fasten something or be fastened with a buckle
2 to bend or become bent because of pressure or great heat *My bicycle wheel has buckled.*
3 to buckle down is to start working seriously and hard

bud *noun* buds
a small pointed or round lump on a plant or tree. A bud opens out to become a flower or leaf.

bud *verb*
buds, budding, budded
to produce buds

Buddha ['Budd' rhymes with 'could'] *noun*
the title given to the Indian philosopher Siddhartha Gautama (563–483 BC), who founded Buddhism

Buddhism *noun*
a religion of Asia that has developed from the teachings of Buddha

Buddhist *noun* Buddhists
someone who follows the teachings of Buddha **Buddhist** *adjective*

budding *adjective*
used about someone who is just starting a creative activity such as painting or music and will probably be successful at it later *a budding artist*

buddy *noun* buddies
1 a friend
2 someone from a group who is selected to help you or look after you

budge *verb*
budges, budging, budged
1 to move *He stood in front of me and wouldn't budge.*
2 to change your mind, even slightly *I asked Dad to give me permission but he wouldn't budge.*

budgerigar *noun* budgerigars
a brightly coloured bird like a small parrot that people keep as a pet

ORIGIN from an Australian Aboriginal word *budgeri* 'good' and *gar* 'cockatoo'

budget *noun* budgets
1 an amount of money that a person or organisation has ready to spend on something *a family on a tight budget* (without much money to spend)
2 a plan for showing how this money will be spent

budget *verb*
budgets, budgeting, budgeted
to plan how much money you will spend and how you will spend it

budget *adjective*
very cheap *budget prices*

budgie *noun* budgies
an informal word for a budgerigar

buff *adjective*
having a yellow-brown colour, like the colour of sand *a buff envelope*

buff *noun* buffs
someone who is interested in and usually knows a lot about a subject *a film buff*

buffalo *noun* buffalo or buffaloes
1 a wild African animal like a big cow with curved horns
2 a wild American animal like a big cow with long hair. It is also called a bison.

buffer *noun* buffers
1 the buffers on a train (or at the end of a railway line) are big metal discs on springs that protect the train if it hits something
2 something or someone that protects something or someone else from being harmed
3 a part of a computer's memory where information can be stored for a short time

buffer *verb*
buffers, buffering, buffered
if your computer buffers while you are watching a film or TV programme, the image on the screen stops for a short time because the computer does not have enough data to continue showing the film or programme smoothly

buffet ['buf-fay'] *noun* buffets
1 a café at a railway station or bus station
2 a meal where people choose their own food from a table and eat it somewhere else, either sitting down or standing up

buffoon *noun* buffoons
a very stupid, funny or annoying person

bug *noun* bugs
1 a small insect
2 an illness, but not a serious one, or the germ that causes it *I picked up a bug on holiday.*
3 an error in a computer program
4 a tiny hidden microphone

bug *verb*
bugs, bugging, bugged
1 to annoy *That noise is really bugging me.*
2 to pester *I keep bugging Mum to buy me a bike.*
3 to hide a small microphone somewhere to listen to what people are saying

bug-eyed *adjective*
with eyes that seem to stick out

buggy *noun* buggies
a light chair with wheels for pushing a baby or young child in when you are walking. It folds up flat when it is not being used.

SYNONYM pushchair

bugle ['byoo-gerl'] *noun* bugles
a brass musical instrument like a small trumpet **bugler** *noun*

build–bun

build *verb*
builds, building, built
1 to make something such as a building or machine by putting all the different parts together
2 to gradually make or develop something *She is building up a reputation.*
3 to build someone up is to make them more healthy *Exercise and good food will soon build you up.*
4 if things such as work, dust or feelings build up, they start to increase *Thick layers of dust have built up in the corners. Tensions have recently built up.*

build *noun* builds
your build is the size and shape of your body *He's of slim build.*

builder *noun* builders
someone who puts up or repairs buildings

building *noun*
1 (*plural* buildings) something such as a house, school or block of flats that has been built
2 the action or business of building things *This land is for building.*
3 a building site is a piece of land that people are building on

building society *noun* building societies
a type of bank that people can pay money into or borrow money from to buy a house or flat

build-up *noun*
1 a slow increase in the size of something *a build-up of traffic on the motorway*
2 the build-up to something important is the period before it where people prepare for it *Shoppers were very busy in the build-up to Christmas.*

built
past tense & past participle of **build**

built *adjective*
used for describing the shape and size that someone's body has *My brother is strongly built* (has a big and strong body).

built-in *adjective*
something that is built-in is a fixed part of it and not separate from it *built-in cupboards*

built-up *adjective*
a built-up area is one that has lots of houses or buildings in it

bulb *noun* bulbs
1 the glass part of an electric light that shines
2 a root shaped like an onion that a flower grows from, for example a tulip or daffodil

Bulgaria *noun*
a country in South-East Europe
Bulgarian *adjective & noun*

bulge *verb*
bulges, bulging, bulged
1 to stick out or swell
2 to be bulging with something is to be very full of something *Her pockets were bulging with sweets.*

bulge *noun* bulges
a lump or swelling

bulk *noun*
1 (*plural* bulks) the large size of someone or something
2 the bulk of something is most of it *The bulk of your term's work has been very good.*
3 if people buy or sell things in bulk, they buy or sell in large quantities

bulky *adjective* bulkier, bulkiest
big and heavy

bull *noun* bulls
1 an adult male of the cow family
2 the male of some other animals such as an elephant or whale

bulldog *noun* bulldogs
a strong dog that has a large head with a flat nose, a short thick neck and short hair on its body

bulldoze *verb*
bulldozes, bulldozing, bulldozed
to clear an area or destroy a building with a bulldozer

bulldozer *noun* bulldozers
a heavy vehicle like a tractor with a large container at the front for moving earth or destroying buildings

bullet *noun* bullets
1 a small piece of metal with a pointed or round end that is shot from a gun
2 a bullet or bullet point is a black dot written in front of things on a list as a way of showing each of them separately and clearly. Each item on the list is also called a bullet point.

bulletin *noun* bulletins
1 a news report on television or on the radio
2 a short news announcement
3 a newspaper or letter produced by a group to give information to its members

bulletin board *noun* bulletin boards
1 a place on the internet where you can leave and read messages
2 the American word for a noticeboard

bulletproof *adjective*
something that is bulletproof stops bullets going through it

bullfight *noun* bullfights
an entertainment in Spain and Mexico where someone called a matador tries to kill a bull **bullfighter** *noun*

bullion *noun*
gold or silver bars

bullock *noun* bullocks
a young bull that cannot breed (produce baby animals)

bull's-eye *noun* bull's-eyes
the circle at the centre of a target in sports and games such as archery and darts

bully *verb*
bullies, bullying, bullied
1 if someone bullies you, they frighten or hurt you because they are stronger or more powerful than you are
2 to bully someone into doing something is to make them do it by saying you will do bad things to them, such as hurt them, if they don't do it
bullying *noun*

bully *noun* bullies
someone who bullies people

bulrush *noun* bulrushes
a tall plant like a reed (stiff type of grass) that grows in or near water

bulwark ['bul-werk'; 'bul' rhymes with 'bull'] *noun* bulwarks
1 a bulwark against something is something that protects you from a bad situation
2 a strong wall built to protect people

bum *noun* bums (informal)
1 the buttocks
2 in American English, a bum is someone who has no home or job, or who is lazy

bum around *verb* (informal)
bums around, bumming around, bummed around
to bum around is to go from place to place with no particular plans

bumblebee *noun* bumblebees
a large hairy bee that makes a loud buzzing sound

bump *noun* bumps
1 a sudden knock of something hitting something else *I felt a bump on my head.*
2 a lump or swelling, for example on the skin, or a raised part, for example in the road
3 an unpleasant movement up and down *The flight was uncomfortable because of the bumps.*

bump *verb*
bumps, bumping, bumped
1 to hit something accidentally against something else, for example a part of your body *I slipped over and bumped my head. I wasn't looking and bumped into a tree.*
2 to bump along is to go along a road with up and down movements, for example because the road has holes in it
3 to bump into someone is to meet them accidentally
4 (informal) to bump someone off is to kill them

bumper *noun* bumpers
a bar or part at the front and back of a vehicle that protects it from knocks

bumper *adjective*
much larger than usual *a bumper crop of strawberries*

bumper car *noun* bumper cars
a small electric car at a funfair that you drive around in and use for deliberately hitting other cars. Bumper cars are also called dodgems.

bumptious *adjective*
used for describing someone who annoys you because they think they are very important, for example someone who continually gives their opinions in an unpleasant way

bumpy *adjective* bumpier, bumpiest
1 a bumpy surface such as a road has lots of bumps
2 a bumpy journey or ride is uncomfortable because of movements up and down, for example caused by bumps in a road
3 a bumpy flight is uncomfortable because the plane moves suddenly up and down

bun *noun* buns
1 a small round cake or bread roll
2 if a girl or woman wears her hair in a bun, she makes it into a tight ball at the back of her head

bunch *noun* **bunches**
1 several things joined together *a bunch of flowers; a bunch of grapes*
2 a group of people *a nice bunch of friends*
3 an informal word for a large number or amount *There are a bunch of books I'd like to read.*
4 **bunches** used for describing a girl's hair when two parts on either side of her head have been tied so that they hang down separately *Hannah wears her hair in bunches.*
compare: **plait** and **pigtail**

bunch *verb*
bunches, bunching, bunched
if people are bunched up, they are sitting or standing very close to each other in a group *The boys were all bunched up at one end of the room and the girls at the other.*

bundle *noun* **bundles**
a bundle of things such as newspapers, exam papers, clothes or twigs is a number of them tied or fastened together

bundle *verb*
bundles, bundling, bundled
1 to bundle things up is to tie or fasten them together to make a bundle
2 to bundle someone somewhere is to push them in a rough way *They quickly bundled the criminal into a police car.*

bung *verb*
bungs, bunging, bunged
1 an informal way of saying to throw or to put *Can you bung me a pen? Bung this suitcase in the car.*
2 if something is bunged up, it is blocked *The sink's bunged up again.*
3 if someone is bunged up, their nose is blocked and they have trouble breathing because they have a cold

bung *noun* **bungs**
a stopper for closing the hole in a container such as a barrel

bungalow *noun* **bungalows**
a house with no upstairs floors

ORIGIN from Hindi *bangla*, referring to a house 'belonging to Bengal'

bungee jumping *noun*
a sport where someone jumps from a high place with a long piece of elastic tied to their legs to stop them hitting the ground or the water below

bungle *verb*
bungles, bungling, bungled
to do something badly *a bungled police investigation*

bunk *noun* **bunks**
1 a narrow bed fixed to a wall in a ship or train
2 each of two beds joined together with one above the other

SYNONYM **bunk bed**

3 (slang) **to do a bunk** to run away without telling anyone

bunk bed *noun* **bunk beds**
each of two beds joined together with one above the other

bunker *noun* **bunkers**
1 a bunker or coal bunker is a place or container for storing coal
2 a strongly built shelter for soldiers, usually underground

bunny *noun* **bunnies**
a bunny or bunny rabbit is a children's word for a rabbit

Bunsen burner *noun* **Bunsen burners**
a gas burner used in laboratories

ORIGIN named after the German 19th-century chemist R. W. *Bunsen*, who invented it

bunting *noun*
small cloth or paper flags fixed or sewn onto long strings and usually shaped like triangles. Bunting is used for decorating places for special occasions such as school fairs.

buoy ['boy'] *noun* **buoys**
a floating object that shows ships the places where it is safe or dangerous to go

buoyant *adjective*
1 lively and happy *in a buoyant mood*
2 if something like cork is buoyant, it can float
buoyancy *noun*

burden *noun* **burdens**
1 a heavy responsibility that causes serious worry to someone *Granddad doesn't want to be a burden on his family.*
2 a heavy load that is very difficult to carry
burden *verb* **burdensome** *adjective*

bureau ['byoo-roh'] *noun* **bureaus** or **bureaux**
1 an organisation or office that provides a particular service *an employment bureau*
2 a desk with drawers and a writing table that is closed up when it is not being used

ORIGIN from 17th-century French *bureau* 'office' and Old French *burel* 'cloth for covering desks'. The plural ends in *-x* because the word is French.

burger *noun* **burgers**
a round flat cake of minced meat or vegetables that is fried and eaten in a bread roll *a veggie burger*
short for: **hamburger**

burglar *noun* **burglars**
a thief who uses force to go into a building to steal things

burglary *noun* **burglaries**
the crime of going into a building to steal things

burgle *verb*
burgles, burgling, burgled
to burgle someone is to go into their home by force to steal things

burial *noun* **burials**
when a dead body is put into a grave in the ground at a funeral

burka *noun* **burkas**
a piece of clothing that covers the whole body including the head, with a space only for the eyes. It is worn in public by some Muslim women.

burly *adjective* **burlier, burliest**
with a big and strong body

Burma *noun*
a country in South-East Asia, now officially called Myanmar **Burmese** *adjective & noun*

burn *verb*
burns, burning, burnt or **burned**
1 to produce fire *A bonfire was burning in the garden.*
2 to be on fire or set something on fire *The forest was burning. The soldiers burnt down their house.*
3 to hurt someone or a part of the body with heat, or to feel very hot and painful *The sun was burning my arms. Inside the train it was burning hot. After that curry my tongue was burning.*
4 if food burns or you burn it, you cook it for too long and it gets spoilt *Don't burn the toast.*
5 to leave the lights burning is to leave them switched on
6 to burn a disc such as a CD or DVD is to copy information onto it using a computer or CD burner

burn *noun* **burns**
1 a burn on your skin is where something very hot has caused an injury
2 a mark on a surface left by something very hot *burn marks on the carpet*

burner *noun* **burners**
1 the burners on a cooker are the round parts on the top of it that produce the heat or flame for heating pans
2 the burner in an oven, boiler or heater is the part that produces the flame

burning *adjective*
1 on fire *a burning house*
2 very hot *I had this burning feeling on my arm.*
3 very strong *burning ambition*

burnt
a past tense & past participle of **burn**. You can also say 'burned'.

burnt *adjective*
1 spoilt or hurt by burning *burnt toast; I've got burnt arms from sitting in the sun.*
2 if something such as a car or building is burnt out, it has been completely destroyed by fire

burp *verb*
burps, burping, burped
to make a noise from your mouth caused by air coming up from your stomach

SYNONYM **to belch**

burp *noun* **burps**
the action or sound of burping

burrow *noun* **burrows**
a tunnel or hole in the ground dug by an animal such as a rabbit or fox

burrow *verb*
burrows, burrowing, burrowed
1 if an animal burrows into the ground, it digs a burrow
2 to dig deeply somewhere *He burrowed in his pockets for some change.*

burst *verb*
bursts, bursting, burst
1 if something bursts or if you burst it, it breaks suddenly because there is too much inside it or because something hits it *He burst my balloon.*

burst – butterfly

2 to do something or to happen suddenly or quickly *She burst into the room. The car burst into flames. They all burst out laughing.*
3 to burst into tears is to suddenly start crying
4 to be bursting with something is to have lots of it *The children were bursting with excitement.*

burst *noun* **bursts**
1 something sudden that happens and lasts for a short time, such as a feeling, energy or a noise *a burst of energy; a burst of gunfire*
2 a break where something has burst *a burst in the pipes*

bury *verb*
buries, burying, buried
1 to put something in a hole in the ground and cover it over
2 to put a dead body into a grave in the ground at a funeral
3 to hide *My library card was buried under a pile of books.*
4 to bury the hatchet to stop arguing and become friends

bus *noun* **buses**
a large road vehicle, often with an upstairs floor, that passengers pay to travel in

ORIGIN from early 19th-century French *voiture omnibus* 'a carriage for everyone' (from Latin *omnibus* 'for all')

bus *verb*
busses, bussing, bussed
to bus people is to take them somewhere by bus

bush *noun*
1 (*plural* **bushes**) a plant like a small tree with lots of branches growing closely together
2 in Africa or Australia, the bush is land in its natural state where people have not planted crops

bushy *adjective* **bushier, bushiest**
very thick *bushy hair; a bushy tail*

busily *adverb*
in a busy way *We're busily revising for exams.*

business ['biz-niss'] *noun*
1 selling goods or services in order to make money *My dad is not very good at business.*
2 (*plural* **businesses**) a company, shop, factory or organisation that makes money by selling goods or services *They have a small family business.*
3 a particular area of business *She's in the music business.*
4 the customers of a business *Our shop is losing business.*
5 something that concerns a particular person and no-one else *That's none of your business.*
6 a subject, situation or event *It's a nasty business.*
7 to go about your business is to do the things you normally do
8 if someone goes out of business, they put an end to their job of selling things because they are not making enough money
9 if someone means business, they really mean what they say and intend to do it even though other people might not like it

ORIGIN from *busy* and *ness* 'the quality of being busy' (*y* changes to *i* before *-ness*)

businesslike *adjective*
serious and efficient

businessman *noun* **businessmen**
a man who works in business

businesswoman *noun* **businesswomen**
a woman who works in business

busker *noun* **buskers**
someone who plays music in a public place to get money from people who pass by
busk *verb*

busload *noun* **busloads**
a large number of people who are carried in a bus

bus shelter *noun* **bus shelters**
a small place with a roof where people can sit or stand while waiting for a bus

bus stop *noun* **bus stops**
a place at the side of the road where buses stop to let passengers get on and off

bust *noun* **busts**
1 a statue of someone's head and shoulders *a bust of Dickens*
2 a woman's breasts

bust *verb*
busts, busting, bust or **busted**
an informal way of saying to break *I've busted my mobile phone.*

bust *adjective*
1 if a company goes bust, it doesn't have enough money and puts an end to its business

SYNONYM bankrupt

2 an informal word for broken *The TV's bust.*

bustle *verb*
bustles, bustling, bustled
to rush about because you're very busy

bustle *noun*
the noise and movements made by lots of people rushing about *the hustle and bustle of a large city*

bust-up *noun* **bust-ups**
an informal word for a big argument or fight

busy *adjective* **busier, busiest**
1 doing something or giving attention to something now or at a particular time *Dad's busy with his car. The cat was busy chasing the mouse.*
2 having lots of things to do and no time to spare *I can't come over this week – I'm too busy.*
3 a busy place is full of people and activity *a busy railway station*
4 a busy road is full of traffic
5 a busy time is full of work or when lots of things are happening *Next week is a very busy week.*
6 if someone's telephone is busy, they are already speaking to someone else
7 if someone keeps busy, they find things to do

busybody *noun* **busybodies**
someone who acts badly by getting involved in other people's private activities

but *conjunction*
1 used for connecting two parts of a sentence when the second part introduces a different idea from the first part *My brother is clever but lazy. I wanted to play in the garden but it was raining.*
2 used when apologising or interrupting someone in a polite way *Sorry, but I can't do it. Excuse me, but could you tell me the time?*

but *preposition*
except *no-one but you; My friend lives in the next house but one* (not the next house but the one after that).

butcher *noun* **butchers**
1 someone who works in a shop that sells meat, or who kills and cuts up animals for meat
2 someone who kills lots of people in a violent way

butcher *verb*
butchers, butchering, butchered
to kill people in a violent way
butchery *noun*

butler *noun* **butlers**
the most important male servant in the house of a rich person

butt *noun* **butts**
1 the butt of a gun is the end part of its handle
2 an informal word for the buttocks
3 if you are the butt of someone's jokes, they often make jokes about you

butt *verb*
butts, butting, butted
1 to butt someone is to hit them with your head

SYNONYM to head-butt

2 to butt in is to interrupt someone rudely while they are speaking

butter *noun*
a soft yellow food made from cream. You put it on bread or toast and use it in cooking.

butter *verb*
butters, buttering, buttered
to put butter on something such as bread or toast *a slice of buttered toast*

butter bean *noun* **butter beans**
a large flat pale yellow or white bean

buttercup *noun* **buttercups**
a small yellow wild flower

butterfingers *noun*
an informal word for someone who often drops things

butterfly *noun*
1 (*plural* **butterflies**) a flying insect with a thin body and four large wings, often brightly coloured. A butterfly develops from a caterpillar.
2 a way of swimming on your front. You move both arms together over your head while kicking your legs up and down.
3 if you have or get butterflies in your stomach, you are nervous, for example because you think you might not do something well *I always get butterflies before school tests.*

butterscotch noun
a type of toffee made from butter and sugar

buttocks noun plural
the part of your body that you sit on

button noun buttons
1 a button on one side of a piece of clothing like a coat, shirt or cardigan is a small round object that you pass through a hole on the other side to fasten it
2 a button on a piece of equipment such as a computer or phone is a small switch that you press to make it work or perform a particular action
3 a button in a computer program is a small square or symbol that you touch or click on to perform an action *a toolbar button*

button verb
buttons, buttoning, buttoned
to fasten with buttons *I buttoned up my shirt. This dress buttons up at the back.*

buttonhole noun buttonholes
1 a narrow hole for a button to pass through on a piece of clothing
2 a flower that people wear on the collar of a jacket, for example at a wedding

buttress noun buttresses
a buttress on the wall of a building is a structure that supports it

buy verb
buys, buying, bought
to get something by giving someone money for it

buy noun buys
something you buy, especially if it's worth buying *It was a good buy.*

buyer noun buyers
1 someone who buys something
2 someone who works for a store and buys products from factories to sell in the store

buzz noun
1 (plural **buzzes**) a buzzing sound made by an insect such as a bee when it flies, or a similar sound made by a piece of equipment
2 a feeling of excitement

buzz verb
buzzes, buzzing, buzzed
1 to make a continuous low sound like an insect such as a bee when it flies, or to make the similar sound that is made by a piece of equipment such as a TV or computer *Flies were buzzing all around. Computers were buzzing in every classroom.*
2 to be buzzing with activity or excitement means there is a lot of activity or excitement
3 to move about in a busy way *Lots of waiters were buzzing around offering drinks.*
4 to press a buzzer, for example in a quiz
5 (informal) if you tell someone to buzz off, you want them to go away

buzzard noun buzzards
a large bird like a hawk that kills other birds and small animals for food

buzzer noun buzzers
a small object shaped like a button that makes a buzzing noise when you press it. It is used for getting someone's attention or showing that you know the answer in a quiz show.

by preposition
1 showing who or what does something or makes it happen *I was praised by my teacher. My hat was blown off by the wind.*
2 showing a particular way of doing something *You'll pass your exams by working hard. She was holding me by the hand.*
3 showing a particular way of travelling somewhere *I went by bike. We travelled by train.*
4 near or past something *Go and stand by the door. We walked by your house.*
5 visiting someone or something *I dropped by the sweet shop.*
6 before *School finished by three o'clock.*
7 at a particular time *by night*
8 showing a change that happens slowly *bit by bit*

by adverb
1 past *He just walked by.*
2 at someone's home *Can you stop by* (or **drop by**) *after school?*
3 **by and large** mostly
4 **by the way** used for changing the subject of a conversation

bye or **bye-bye** interjection
an informal way of saying goodbye

by-election noun by-elections
an election of a new member of parliament in one small area only

bypass noun bypasses
a road that takes traffic around a town or village instead of going through it

bypass verb
bypasses, bypassing, bypassed
to avoid going through a particular place or dealing with a particular person *Mum took the motorway to bypass the town. He bypassed his teacher and went straight to the head.*

by-product noun by-products
something that happens to be produced when another product is made

bystander noun bystanders
someone who is in a place by chance when something happens but takes no part in it

byte noun bytes
a piece of information used by a computer, for example for measuring the size of a file or program. A byte is made up of eight bits.

Byzantine adjective
1 connected with Byzantium, the ancient Greek city that was later called Constantinople and is now called Istanbul (in Turkey)
2 connected with the Byzantine Empire, the Roman Empire in the East *a Byzantine church*

butterscotch–cable

C C

ORIGIN the letter C started life as a shape representing a 'throwing stick' or 'boomerang' and looked like an upside-down capital L facing left. C was the third letter of the Phoenician alphabet but instead of having the 'c' sound of 'cat' it had the sound of 'g' in 'good' and its name was *gimel*. The Etruscans first changed the sound from 'g' to 'c' (as in 'cat') because there was no 'g' sound in their language. They also turned the letter to face right and made it more curved, like a crescent. The letter then passed into Greek with the name *gamma* (the Greeks kept the original 'g' sound) and into Roman where its curve became gradually rounder, ending up as the C of our own alphabet.

C
1 short for **centigrade** or **Celsius**
2 the Roman numeral for 100

cab noun cabs
1 a taxi
2 a place where the driver sits, for example in a lorry, train or bus

ORIGIN from 18th-century French *cabriolet* 'light vehicle with two wheels pulled by a horse'

cabaret ['kab-er-ray'] noun cabarets
a show in a restaurant or nightclub where people sing, dance and play music

cabbage noun cabbages
a large round vegetable made up of layers of thick green leaves. The leaves can be boiled, steamed or eaten raw in salads.

cabin noun cabins
1 a small room for sleeping in on a boat or ship
2 a small house, usually built of wood, in a forest or on a mountain *a log cabin*
3 the long part of a plane where the passengers sit

cabin crew noun cabin crews
the people on a plane who look after the passengers, for example by serving them food

cabinet noun cabinets
1 a small cupboard for holding things or displaying attractive objects *a kitchen cabinet; a medicine cabinet*
2 the cabinet in a government is the group of people, called ministers, who help the leader of a government make important decisions

cable noun cables
1 a thick wire for carrying electricity, television programmes or telephone calls *My laptop is connected to my printer with a cable.*
2 a thick metal rope often made of wires twisted together, for example for lifting, moving or tying things

55

cable car–call

3 cable or cable television is a system of broadcasting television programmes using cables that go under the ground

cable car *noun* **cable cars**
a large container that hangs down from a cable, for example for carrying people up and down mountains and hills

cache *noun* **caches**
1 a quantity of things that someone has hidden away, usually weapons *a cache of explosives*
2 the part of a computer memory where information that is often needed is stored for a short time

> **ORIGIN** from French *cacher* 'to hide'

cackle *verb*
cackles, cackling, cackled
1 when a hen cackles, it makes a loud high sound after laying an egg
2 to laugh in a loud unpleasant way
3 to talk in a loud and stupid way
cackle *noun*

cactus *noun* **cactuses** or **cacti** ['cak-tie']
a prickly plant with a thick stem. Cactuses usually grow in deserts.

CAD ['kad'] *noun*
the use of computers to design things such as equipment or buildings
short for: computer-aided (or -assisted) design

caddie or **caddy** *noun* **caddies**
someone who carries golf clubs for a golf player

caddy *noun* **caddies**
a small container for tea

cadet ['ker-det'] *noun* **cadets**
someone training to be a police officer or an officer in the army, navy or air force

cadge *verb* (informal)
cadges, cadging, cadged
to ask someone to give you something because you cannot or do not want to pay for it

café ['ka-fay'] *noun* **cafés**
a small restaurant where you can buy drinks and sometimes eat a simple meal

> **ORIGIN** from French *café* 'coffee' as well as 'coffee shop'

cafeteria ['ka-fi-**teer**-ee-er] *noun* **cafeterias**
a restaurant, for example in a college, factory or hospital, where you choose the food yourself from a counter and take it to your own table

caffeine ['ka-feen'] *noun*
a substance in drinks such as coffee, tea and cola that makes you feel more active

caftan *noun* **caftans**
a long loose piece of clothing like a coat, often worn in the Middle East

> **LANGUAGE EXTRA** also spelt *kaftan*

cage *noun* **cages**
a container or room made of wires or metal bars for keeping birds or animals in

cage *verb*
cages, caging, caged
to put an animal or bird into a cage

cagey *adjective* **cagier, cagiest**
if someone is cagey, they don't say much about something because they don't want anyone to know *He was a bit cagey about his age.*

cagoule ['ker-gool'] *noun* **cagoules**
a light thin jacket with a hood that keeps you dry when it rains

> **ORIGIN** from French *cagoule* 'hood covering head and face'

cairn *noun* **cairns**
a heap of loose stones built as a landmark or monument

cajole *verb*
cajoles, cajoling, cajoled
to persuade someone to do something by being extremely nice

cake *noun* **cakes**
1 a sweet food made from flour, eggs, sugar and butter, baked in an oven
2 a type of food formed into a flat round shape and cooked *a fish cake*
3 a small hard lump of something *a cake of soap*
4 to be a piece of cake to be very easy to do *Last week's homework was a piece of cake.*
5 to have your cake and eat it to enjoy having two things at the same time when it is usually only possible to have one of them

caked *adjective*
to be caked in (or with) something is to be covered with something soft that has dried to form a hard layer *My shoes are caked in mud.*

calamine *noun*
calamine or calamine lotion is a pink liquid that you put on sore skin to make it feel cooler and better

calamity *noun* **calamities**
a terrible event that causes great damage and suffering **calamitous** *adjective*

> **SYNONYM** disaster

calcium *noun*
a silver-white chemical element that is very important in bones and teeth. It is contained in some rocks such as chalk and marble.

calculate *verb*
calculates, calculating, calculated
1 to find out an amount or measurement by using numbers. You do this in your head, by writing the numbers down, or with a calculator. *I'm trying to calculate how much I owe my dad.*
2 to make a careful judgement about something that you expect to happen based on all the facts *Scientists calculate that the spaceship will pass Venus in 10 years' time.*
3 to calculate on something is to expect something to happen

> **ORIGIN** from Latin *calculus* 'pebble', because pebbles were used for counting in Roman times

calculation *noun* **calculations**
1 numbers that you use when finding out an amount or measurement *Your calculations are correct.*
2 the action of calculating something *I made a quick calculation.*
3 a careful judgement about something you expect to happen

calculator *noun* **calculators**
a small piece of electronic equipment for adding, subtracting, multiplying and dividing, and solving other number problems

calendar *noun* **calendars**
1 a printed page or series of pages that shows the days, weeks and months of the year arranged in rows
2 a particular system for measuring time *the Roman calendar*
3 a list of all the events in a year for a particular activity *Tomorrow is an important date in the football calendar.*

calf *noun* **calves**
1 a young cow or bull, or another young animal such as an elephant, seal or whale
2 the soft back part of your leg between your knee and ankle

calibration *noun*
in science, when a measuring instrument such as scales or a thermometer is officially checked against something to make sure it is completely correct

call *noun* **calls**
1 when you speak to someone on the phone *There's a phone call for you.*
2 the sound of something that you say in a loud voice to attract someone's attention

> **SYNONYM** shout

3 a short visit *We're going to pay a call on Grandma.*
4 a message at an airport telling someone their plane is about to leave *Final call for flight 601 to Athens.*
5 if someone is on call, they are ready to help as part of their job or they are working now to help people *There's always a doctor on call at this hotel.*

call *verb*
calls, calling, called
1 to say something loudly *Mum called me and I came downstairs.*
2 to ask someone to come to you *The teacher called me over.*
3 to phone someone *I'll call you tomorrow.*
4 to visit someone or to stop somewhere for a short time *I'll call round after school. We called on my aunty last weekend. The train to Edinburgh calls at York.*
5 to give someone or something a name *What do you call your dog?*
6 to be called something is to have something as a name *The picture on the screen is called an icon.*
7 to describe someone or something in a certain way *She called me a liar. He's always calling me names* (using rude names when talking to me).
8 to organise something such as a meeting or election
9 to call for someone is to go to someone's home and then go somewhere with them
10 if something calls for something, it needs it *Studying French calls for a lot of hard work.*
11 if someone calls for something, they ask for it in a very strong way *Many parents called for the bully to be expelled from school.*

12 to call something off, such as a trip, football match or meeting, is to tell people it will not happen
13 to call something up on a computer screen is to make it appear
14 in American English, to call someone up is to phone them
15 to call it a day to stop working, for example because you have worked enough

call centre *noun* **call centres**
a large office where workers using telephones provide information or services to customers or take orders from customers who want to buy things

caller *noun* **callers**
someone who makes a phone call

calligraphy *noun*
beautiful handwriting using special pens or brushes **calligrapher** *noun*

ORIGIN from Greek *kalli* 'beautiful' and *graphein* 'to write'

calling *noun* **callings**
1 a strong feeling that makes you want to do a particular job, especially a job that people respect
2 a job that people respect *Teaching is his calling.*

callipers *noun plural*
a tool for measuring how thick something is or how wide a round object is. It is usually made up of two thin pieces of metal joined at the top.

callous *adjective*
a callous person does not care about other people's feelings or their problems or suffering

calltime *noun*
the calltime on a mobile phone is the amount of time you have for making calls

calm *adjective* **calmer, calmest**
1 not excited, angry or worried *He was very calm after the accident.*

SYNONYM *relaxed*

2 quiet and still *a calm sea*
calmly *adverb* **calmness** *noun*

calm *verb*
calms, calming, calmed
1 if you calm someone down or if someone calms down, they become less excited, angry or worried
2 if a situation calms down, things become better and less difficult

calorie *noun* **calories**
a unit for measuring the amount of energy you get from food

calves
plural of **calf**

calypso ['ker-lip-soh'] *noun* **calypsos**
a type of music from the Caribbean where the singer usually sings about local people and events. The words are often made up as the singer goes along.

Cambodia *noun*
a country in South-East Asia
Cambodian *adjective & noun*

camcorder *noun* **camcorders**
a camera for recording moving pictures and sounds

SYNONYM *video camera*

ORIGIN from *cam* (the first part of *camera*) and *corder* (the second part of *recorder*)

came
past tense of **come**

camel *noun* **camels**
a large animal with one or two humps on its back and a long neck. It is used for carrying people and goods in the desert and can live for long periods without food and water.

camellia *noun* **camellias**
a plant with shiny green leaves and white, pink or red flowers like roses

cameo *noun* **cameos**
if someone famous such as an actor or writer plays a cameo in a film or play, they play a very small part in it

CULTURE NOTE the director Alfred Hitchcock played a *cameo role* in many of his films

camera *noun* **cameras**
1 a small piece of equipment for taking photos
2 a large piece of equipment, used by a camera operator, for making films or recording television programmes

ORIGIN from Latin *camera* 'room' or 'chamber'. It became the usual word for a 'picture-taking machine' around 1840 because of the *camera obscura* – a 'dark room' with a lens that could project images of external objects.

camera operator *noun*
camera operators
a person who operates a television or film camera

LANGUAGE EXTRA you can also say *cameraman* or *camerawoman*

camomile *noun*
a plant whose leaves and small white flowers are used for making a type of tea

LANGUAGE EXTRA also spelt *chamomile*

camouflage ['ka-mer-flahj'; 'j' has the middle sound of 'pleasure'] *noun*
1 something such as leaves or branches used for covering or hiding people or things to make them look like part of the surroundings. You can describe the face paint and painted clothing of a soldier as camouflage.
2 the particular colour or shape of an animal such as a chameleon that makes it look like part of the surroundings

camouflage *verb*
camouflages, camouflaging, camouflaged
to camouflage something is to cover or hide it using something that makes it look like part of the surroundings *a camouflaged army tank*

ORIGIN from French *camoufler* and Italian slang *camuffare* 'to disguise'

camp *noun* **camps**
1 a place with tents or shelters where people live for a short time *a holiday camp*; *a refugee camp*
2 a place where soldiers live and train

camp *verb*
camps, camping, camped
1 to stay somewhere in a tent or shelter for a short time
2 to put up a tent or shelter *Let's camp by the river.*
3 to go camping is to stay in a tent, for example in the countryside or the mountains, as a pleasure activity or for your holiday

campaign *noun* **campaigns**
1 a series of actions to achieve something, for example in business or politics, by persuading people to support you *a campaign for a new school*; *an election campaign*
2 a series of advertisements to persuade people to buy something
3 a series of actions by soldiers to try to win a war

campaign *verb*
campaigns, campaigning, campaigned
to persuade people to support you in order to achieve something *They were campaigning against the building of a road through the village.*

camper *noun* **campers**
1 someone who goes camping
2 a camper or camper van is a vehicle with beds and cooking equipment. People live in campers when they're on holiday.

campfire *noun* **campfires**
a fire outside made by people who are camping

camping *noun*
the activity of staying in a tent *a camping holiday*; *a camping stove*

campsite *noun* **campsites**
a place where people stay in tents, often with toilets, shops and other comforts

campus *noun* **campuses**
an area of land and all the main buildings that belong to a university

can *verb*
present tense **can**, past tense **could**
1 to be able to do something *You can succeed if you try.*
2 to know how to do something *I wanted to know if she could swim.*
3 used for asking someone to do something or give you something *Can you shut the door? Can I have an ice cream?*
4 used for giving permission *You can leave now.*
5 used for saying that something is possible or happens sometimes *It can get very hot in summer.*

can *noun* **cans**
1 a metal container for drink or food, or for other things such as paint or hair spray. It often has the shape of a cylinder (tube with flat ends shaped like circles). *a can of beans*
2 something in a can *I drank a can of lemonade.*

LANGUAGE EXTRA you often use *tin* instead of *can*, for example *a tin of beans*, but you don't use *tin* for drinks, for example you don't say *a tin of lemonade*

Canada–capable

Canada *noun*
a country in North America
Canadian *adjective & noun*

canal *noun* **canals**
1 a man-made river, usually for boats to travel along
2 a narrow tube in the body, for example for carrying food or air

canary *noun* **canaries**
a small yellow bird that sings and that people keep as a pet

> ORIGIN from the *Canary Islands*, where the bird comes from

cancel *verb*
cancels, cancelling, cancelled
1 to cancel something planned such as a trip or meeting is to tell people it will not happen
2 to cancel something such as a flight or train is to stop it from leaving *The two o'clock flight to Brussels has been cancelled.*
3 to cancel something such as an action, instruction or agreement is to stop it because you no longer want to do something *Press Undo on your keyboard to cancel the last action.*
4 to cancel something that you have agreed to pay for is to tell people you no longer want it *Mum cancelled the grocery order.*
5 to cancel a postage stamp or a train or bus ticket is to make marks on it so that it cannot be used again

> ORIGIN from Latin *cancellare* 'to cross out a piece of writing by using *cancelli* (a pattern of crossed lines)'

cancellation *noun* **cancellations**
1 a decision to cancel something
2 something such as a hospital appointment that someone has cancelled. It can then be given to someone else.

cancer *noun* **cancers**
a very serious illness caused by cells (smallest units of living matter) in the body that grow in a way that is not normal. This usually causes a lump called a tumour to grow in a part of the body.
cancerous *adjective*

> ORIGIN from Latin *cancer* and Greek *karkinos* 'crab', because Greek doctors such as Galen thought the swollen veins around some tumours looked like crabs

candid *adjective*
someone who is candid tells the truth in a very direct way

candidate *noun* **candidates**
1 someone who has applied for a job
2 someone who takes part in a competition, exam or election

> ORIGIN from Latin *candidatus* 'dressed in white', because people who applied for official jobs in ancient Rome had to wear a white toga (long piece of loose clothing)

candle *noun* **candles**
a stick of wax (a substance like fat that is soft when hot and hard when cold) with a thin string through the middle called a wick. When the wick is lit, it burns to provide light.

candlelight *noun*
the light from a candle *We walked around the old house by candlelight.*

candlestick *noun* **candlesticks**
an object for holding a candle

candy *noun* **candies**
the American word for a sweet or sweets *Do you want a candy?*

candyfloss *noun*
long thin pieces of sugar produced by a special machine and wrapped round a stick for eating

cane *noun* **canes**
1 the hollow stem of a plant such as bamboo. It is used for making furniture such as chairs or for making sticks to support plants in a garden.
2 a long thin stick used by people to help them walk
3 a stick that was used in the past to punish children in school

cane *verb*
canes, caning, caned
to punish children in school by hitting them with a cane, as sometimes happened in the past

canine ['kay-nine'] *adjective*
connected with dogs

> ORIGIN from Latin *canis* 'dog'

canine ['kay-nine'] *noun* **canines**
a canine or canine tooth is one of the four pointed teeth towards the front of the mouth

canister *noun* **canisters**
1 a round metal container for holding gases or chemicals
2 a metal container for storing things such as food

canned *adjective*
food that is canned is put in a sealed metal container to preserve it *canned pears*

cannibal *noun* **cannibals**
someone who eats human flesh
cannibalism *noun*

cannon *noun* **cannons**
a large gun, usually on wheels, used in past times to fire heavy metal balls called cannonballs

cannonball *noun* **cannonballs**
a heavy metal ball fired from a cannon

cannot *verb*
can not *We cannot agree.*

canoe ['ker-noo'] *noun* **canoes**
a light narrow boat that is moved along by using a paddle (pole with a flat part at one end)

canoe ['ker-noo'] *verb*
canoes, canoeing, canoed
to travel along in the water using a canoe
canoeist *noun*

canopy *noun* **canopies**
1 a cloth cover that hangs over something such as a bed
2 a covering high above something, for example leaves and branches in a forest

can't
short for **cannot** *I can't do it.*

cantaloupe ['kan-ter-loop'] *noun* **cantaloupes**
a type of melon with a greyish-green skin and orange flesh

> LANGUAGE EXTRA also spelt *cantaloup*

canteen *noun* **canteens**
1 a restaurant, for example in a school, office or factory, where you can buy a cheap meal that you choose yourself from a counter and take to your own table
2 a small container for water that people carry with them, for example when going on long walks
3 a canteen of cutlery is a box containing a set of knives, forks and spoons

canter *verb*
canters, cantering, cantered
if a horse canters, it runs fairly fast. It runs faster than when it trots but not as fast as when it gallops. **canter** *noun*

Cantonese *adjective*
connected with Southern China and the Chinese language spoken there
Cantonese *noun*

canvas *noun* **canvases** or **canvasses**
1 a strong cotton cloth for making things such as tents, sails, shoes and bags
2 this cloth or another strong cloth used by artists for painting on, or the painting itself *a canvas by Monet*

canvass *verb*
canvasses, canvassing, canvassed
to canvass people, for example in an election, is to go to their homes and persuade them to vote for you or support you

canyon *noun* **canyons**
a very deep valley with sides made of rock, usually with a river through it

cap *noun* **caps**
1 a soft hat with a hard flat curved part at the front called a peak *a baseball cap*
2 a covering that fits tightly over your head to protect your hair *a swimming cap*
3 a part that fits over the top or end of something to protect it *a bottle cap*
4 a cap in a toy gun is a small piece of paper with a tiny explosive inside it that makes it go bang

cap *verb*
caps, capping, capped
1 to cover something *a snow-capped mountain*
2 in sports, to be capped is to be selected to play for your country in a team game such as football, cricket or rugby *He's been capped for England 13 times.*
3 to follow something with something better or bigger *a fantastic achievement that is difficult to cap*

capability *noun* **capabilities**
1 the qualities, power or skill to do something
2 if something is beyond someone's capabilities, it is not possible for them to do it

capable *adjective*
1 if someone or something is capable of doing something, it is possible for them to do it or they know how to do it

58

2 if someone is capable of something bad, they have the sort of character that allows them to do bad things *When his dad is drunk, he's capable of anything.*
3 good at doing something *a very capable teacher*

capably *adverb*
if you do something capably, you do it well

capacity *noun* **capacities**
1 being capable of doing something *She has a great capacity for learning languages.*
2 the amount that something can hold, for example a container or computer disk *The capacity of the bottle is two litres.*
3 if you do something in a particular capacity, you do it as part of your job or because you represent something *in your mother's capacity as a parent*

cape *noun* **capes**
1 a piece of land that sticks out into the sea *Cape Horn*
2 another word for a cloak

caper *noun* **capers**
1 an activity that is not serious or that wastes time *the cartoon capers of Mickey Mouse*
2 an illegal activity
3 a jumping movement

caper *verb*
capers, capering, capered
to run and jump about in a happy way

capillary *noun* **capillaries**
a very small blood vessel (narrow tube) that carries blood to and from cells (smallest units of living matter) in the body

capital *noun*
1 (*plural* **capitals**) a capital or capital city is the main city of a country, where the government is
2 (*plural* **capitals**) a capital or capital letter is a large letter (such as A, B or C). Capital letters are used at the beginning of names and sentences.
3 money or property that can be used in business for making more money

ORIGIN from Latin *caput* 'head'

capital *adjective*
used for describing a large letter *You spell London with a capital L.*

capitalism *noun*
a political system where property and businesses are owned by people and not by the government **capitalist** *adjective & noun*

capital punishment *noun*
the punishment by law of killing someone if they have committed a serious crime

cappuccino ['kap-per-**chee**-noh'] *noun*
1 a drink made from espresso (strong coffee made with a special machine) and hot milk and with cinnamon or chocolate powder on top
2 (*plural* **cappuccinos**) a cup or mug of cappuccino

ORIGIN from Italian *cappuccino* 'small hood', referring to the brown colour of the hoods worn by a community of monks called Capuchins

capsize *verb*
capsizes, capsizing, capsized
if a boat capsizes, it turns upside down in the water

caps lock *noun*
a key on a computer keyboard that you press when you want to use capital letters only

capsule *noun* **capsules**
1 a very small tube containing medicine that you swallow whole with water
2 a capsule or space capsule is the part of a spacecraft where the astronauts live

captain *noun* **captains**
1 the person in charge of a ship or aircraft
2 an officer in the army or navy
3 the player in charge of a sports or quiz team

captain *verb*
captains, captaining, captained
to captain a team is to be in charge of it

caption *noun* **captions**
the words next to a picture, for example in a book or magazine, that explain what the picture is about

captivate *verb*
captivates, captivating, captivated
to captivate someone is to be so interesting, good or attractive that they cannot take their attention away *Her singing captivated the audience. He gave me a captivating smile.*

captive *noun* **captives**
a prisoner

captive *adjective*
1 kept as a prisoner *He was held captive for a month.*
2 kept in a cage or zoo *captive animals*

captivity *noun*
1 when someone is kept as a prisoner *The soldier died in captivity.*
2 when an animal is kept in a cage or zoo *Many animals in captivity don't live long.*

captor *noun* **captors**
someone who keeps a person as a prisoner

capture *verb*
captures, capturing, captured
1 to catch a person or animal and keep them so that they cannot escape
2 to take control of a place, property or equipment belonging to an enemy in war *The British captured 20 tanks.*
3 in computing, to capture information or a picture is to put it into a form that a computer can understand

capture *noun*

car *noun* **cars**
1 a private road vehicle for one driver and usually three or four passengers
2 a railway carriage *a buffet car*

caramel *noun*
1 (*plural* **caramels**) a chewy brown sweet made from sugar, butter and milk
2 burnt sugar used for giving a taste and colour to food

carat *noun* **carats**
1 a unit for measuring how pure gold is *a 22 carat gold ring*
2 a unit for measuring how heavy jewels are *a 15 carat diamond*

caravan *noun* **caravans**
1 a vehicle that people live in, for example on holiday. Caravans can be pulled by a car or remain fixed in one place.
2 a group of people who travel together across a desert

caravan site *noun* **caravan sites**
a place where people park their caravans for a short time while on holiday or where they stay in caravans that are permanently fixed to the ground

caraway *noun*
a plant used in cooking. Caraway seeds are used for giving extra taste to bread and cakes.

carbohydrate *noun* **carbohydrates**
a substance consisting of oxygen, hydrogen and carbon in foods such as bread, potatoes and sugar. Carbohydrates give heat and energy to your body.

carbon *noun*
a chemical element in diamonds, coal, petrol and other substances as well as in all living things

carbonated *adjective*
a carbonated drink is one that has lots of small bubbles in it

SYNONYM fizzy

ANTONYM still

carbon dioxide *noun*
a gas produced when humans and animals breathe out or when carbon is burnt

carbon monoxide *noun*
a colourless and poisonous gas produced mainly by the engines of vehicles

car boot sale *noun* **car boot sales**
an event at which people sell private goods from the back of a car. Car boot sales usually take place in a large open area such as a field.

carburettor *noun* **carburettors**
the part of a vehicle engine that mixes petrol and air to provide power

carcass *noun* **carcasses**
the body of a dead animal

LANGUAGE EXTRA also spelt *carcase*

card *noun* **cards**
1 a type of stiff paper that is not as thick as cardboard
2 a piece of stiff paper, usually folded, for sending greetings or a personal message *a birthday card; a thank you card*
3 a small piece of stiff paper or plastic with information on it or for writing information on *a library card; a score card*
4 a small piece of plastic for getting money from a bank or for paying for things, for example in a shop or on the internet *a credit card*
5 a card or playing card is a small piece of stiff paper with numbers and pictures on it, used for playing games. In some of the most common games, there are 52 cards, called a pack, divided into four different groups, called hearts, diamonds, spades and clubs. *The grown-ups were playing cards.*

cardboard – Carroll diagram

6 a card in a computer is a piece of electronic equipment that makes a particular part of the computer work *a graphics card*
7 **on the cards** likely to happen *Rain is on the cards for Saturday.*

> ORIGIN from Latin *charta* 'leaf of papyrus'. Papyrus is paper made from plants that was used in ancient Egypt.

cardboard noun
thick stiff paper, usually brown or grey, used especially for making boxes

cardigan noun **cardigans**
a knitted jacket with buttons or a zip down the front

> ORIGIN from James Thomas Brudenell, 7th Earl of *Cardigan*, who was in charge of an army in the Crimean War (1853–56). His men were the first to wear woollen cardigans to keep warm.

cardinal noun **cardinals**
a priest with a very high rank in the Catholic Church, below the rank of Pope

cardinal number noun **cardinal numbers**
a number used for counting, such as 1, 2 or 3
compare: **ordinal number**

care noun
1 looking after someone or something *We get good care from our doctor.*
2 if you **take care of** someone, you look after them
3 if you **take care of** something belonging to someone, you keep it safe for them, for example while they are away *Take care of my laptop while I go to the toilet.*
4 if you **take care of** something that needs to be done, you deal with it *Dad takes care of all the problems.*
5 being careful *She held the baby's hand with great care.*
6 if you **take care**, you are very careful *Take care when crossing the road.*
7 (plural **cares**) a worry or problem *He doesn't have a care in the world.*
8 **care of** used when writing to someone at the address of someone else. It is often shortened to c/o. *Dan Smith, care of (or c/o) Daljit Singh*

care verb
cares, caring, cared
1 to be interested in something because you think it is important *Simon only cares about football. I don't care what happens. Who cares?* (it's not important and I'm not interested)
2 to like someone or something very much and want to look after them *We all care about Grandma.*
3 to care for someone such as a sick person or for an animal or for something that needs to be kept in good condition is to look after them *I'm learning how to care for my dog. Your laptop is well cared for.*
4 to care for someone such as a friend is to really like them or love them *I think Isabel really cares for you.*
5 to care for something is also to want or to like it *Would you care for an ice cream?*

career noun **careers**
a job or profession that you learn and that you spend a long period of your life working at *a teaching career*

career verb
careers, careering, careered
to move along very fast, usually in a careless way *A car careered off the road and hit a garden wall.*

carefree adjective
completely happy and without any cares or worries

careful adjective
1 if you are careful, you pay attention to things and try to do them well so as to avoid problems, mistakes or danger *Be careful when you cross the road. Your spelling isn't very careful* (you've made lots of mistakes).
2 if people are careful with money, they pay attention to how much they spend because they don't have much money

carefully adverb
1 if you do something carefully, you do it very well and pay attention so as to avoid problems, mistakes or danger *I wrote the poem carefully in my exercise book.*
2 if you think carefully about something, you try very hard to understand it, for example in order to make a decision or solve a problem *Dad thought carefully for a few moments then decided it wasn't a good idea.*

care home noun **care homes**
a place where people who are old or ill are looked after

careless adjective
1 if you are careless, you don't pay attention to things so you have problems and make mistakes *I was careless and dropped my mobile.*
2 used about something you do that shows you are careless *a careless piece of homework; a careless mistake*
carelessly adverb **carelessness** noun

carer noun **carers**
someone who looks after an old or sick person or a child

caress verb
caresses, caressing, caressed
to move your hand gently along a part of someone's body to show your love *She caressed his hair.* **caress** noun

caretaker noun **caretakers**
someone who looks after a building, such as a block of flats or a school

cargo noun **cargoes**
things carried on a ship or plane *a cargo of bananas*

Caribbean ['ka-rib-bee-yern'] adjective
connected with the islands of the Caribbean Sea and the surrounding countries. The Caribbean Sea lies between the West Indies, Central America and South America.

caricature noun **caricatures**
a drawing of someone that makes them look funny because they are drawn uglier or bigger, for example, than they really are *'The Times' has a caricature of the prime minister.*

> ORIGIN from Italian *caricare* 'to exaggerate'

caricaturist noun **caricaturists**
someone who draws caricatures

caring adjective
kind, helpful and loving *a caring father*

carload noun **carloads**
a number of people or amount of things that someone carries in a car

carnation noun **carnations**
a pink, white or red garden flower with a sweet smell

carnival noun **carnivals**
a festival where people in fancy dress go through the streets playing music and dancing

carnivore noun **carnivores**
an animal that eats other animals
carnivorous adjective
compare: **herbivore** and **omnivore**

carol noun **carols**
a Christmas song

carp noun **carp**
a large fish that lives in rivers and lakes and can be eaten

car park noun **car parks**
an area outside or inside a building with spaces for people to leave their cars

carpenter noun **carpenters**
someone who makes things from wood and repairs things made of wood, especially things that are parts of buildings
carpentry noun

> ORIGIN from Latin *carpentarius* 'maker of carriages'

carpet noun **carpets**
1 a thick soft covering for a floor
2 a layer of something covering the ground *a thick carpet of leaves*

carriage noun **carriages**
1 one of the separate long parts of a train where the passengers sit

> SYNONYM **coach**

2 a vehicle pulled by horses that was used in past times

> SYNONYM **coach**

3 in American English, a carriage or baby carriage is a small vehicle on wheels for carrying a baby around when you are walking

> LANGUAGE EXTRA the British word for sense 3 is *pram*

carriageway noun **carriageways**
one side of an important road such as a motorway where the cars travel in one direction *They've closed the northbound carriageway of the M11.*

carrier noun **carriers**
a carrier or carrier bag is a large bag, usually made of thin plastic, for carrying shopping, for example from a supermarket

Carroll diagram noun **Carroll diagrams**
a diagram in maths that uses rectangles for grouping numbers or objects. It describes things in two different ways, for example as 'being something' and 'not being something'. A simple Carroll diagram

might show 'even' numbers (2, 4, 6) in one rectangle and 'not even' numbers (1, 3, 5) in another.
compare: **Venn diagram**

ORIGIN invented by the 19th-century author and mathematician Lewis *Carroll*

carrot noun **carrots**
a long hard pointed orange-coloured vegetable. Carrots grow in the ground.

carry verb
carries, carrying, carried
1 to hold something or someone and take them somewhere *I carried my books into my room. The school bus can carry 30 children.*
2 to have something with you *The police in France carry guns.*
3 to carry a disease is to pass it on to people *Mosquitoes carry malaria.*
4 if a sound carries, you can hear it a long way away
5 in adding up columns of numbers, if you carry a number you move it into the next column to the left, for example from units to tens
6 if someone gets carried away, they become so excited or interested in something that they can't control their behaviour
7 to carry on is to continue doing something *We carried on after lunch. Carry on as far as the post office then turn left.*
8 to carry something out is to do it, for example some work or an order from someone *The class carried out an experiment.*

carrycot noun **carrycots**
a small bed for carrying a baby in

carsick adjective
someone who is carsick feels ill when they travel by car **carsickness** noun

cart noun **carts**
1 a small vehicle for carrying things. It has no roof and is usually pulled by a horse or horses.
2 the place on a shopping website where you put the things you want to buy
3 the American word for a trolley (at a supermarket or airport, or for serving food and drinks)
4 **to put the cart before the horse** to do two things in the wrong order

cart verb (informal)
carts, carting, carted
to carry something around or to a particular place, especially something heavy *I've been carting my laptop around all day.*

carthorse noun **carthorses**
a big strong horse used in the past for pulling carts

cartilage noun
a strong substance that surrounds the joints in the body and forms parts of the nose and ears. It is softer than bone but harder than muscle.

cartography noun
the making of maps **cartographer** noun

carton noun **cartons**
1 a small container for liquids, made of stiff paper *a carton of orange juice*
2 a cardboard box for carrying things

cartoon noun **cartoons**
1 a funny drawing in a magazine, book or newspaper
2 a series of funny drawings that tell a story

SYNONYM **comic strip**

3 a film made with characters and things that are drawn rather than with real people and things *a Disney cartoon*
cartoonist noun

cartridge noun **cartridges**
1 a small container of ink for a printer or tube of ink for a pen *a cartridge pen*
2 a small piece of equipment that goes inside something to make it work *a computer game cartridge*
3 a small metal tube containing a bullet for a gun

cartwheel noun **cartwheels**
an acrobatic movement that consists of moving sideways on your hands, bringing your legs over in a circular motion, like the wheels of a cart, and landing on your feet

carve verb
carves, carving, carved
1 to make an object or shape out of wood or stone by cutting it with special tools
2 if you carve something such as a letter or word into something, you cut it into the surface *He carved his name into the desk.*
3 to cut meat into slices *Dad carved the chicken.*
4 to carve something up is to divide it *The country was carved up after the war.*

car wash noun **car washes**
a place with special brushes and equipment for automatically washing cars

cascade noun **cascades**
1 a waterfall
2 a large amount of something, especially something that hangs down like hair

cascade verb
cascades, cascading, cascaded
to fall, hang or flow down *Water and rocks cascaded down into the valley.*

case noun **cases**
1 a container or box for keeping or carrying things in. Cases come in different shapes and sizes and are made out of different materials. *a glasses case; a guitar case*
2 a container, usually made of plastic, that the different parts of a piece of equipment such as a computer are built into
3 another word for a suitcase
4 a particular situation or example *The teacher made an exception in my case. 'I'm busy tomorrow.' – 'In that case come to my house on Friday.'*
5 a crime being investigated, for example by the police or a private detective *This is a case for Sherlock Holmes.*
6 a matter that is decided by a court of law *Our lawyer won the case.*
7 **in any case** no matter what happens *In any case I'm definitely not going.*
8 **in any case** also used for mentioning something else or another reason for something *She ought to be in school now in any case.*

9 **in case** or **just in case** used for explaining the reason for something *Take your coat in case it gets cold. I'll take my umbrella just in case.*

cash noun
money in banknotes and coins

ORIGIN from Old Italian *cassa* 'money box'

cash verb
cashes, cashing, cashed
if someone cashes a cheque, for example in a bank, they get money for it

cashew noun **cashews**
a small light-coloured nut that is curved and has a strong sweet taste

cashier noun **cashiers**
someone in a shop, bank or office who receives and pays out the money

cash machine noun **cash machines**
a machine, for example at a bank or supermarket, for taking money out of a bank account. The machine works when you put a small plastic card into it and key in a special number.

cash register noun **cash registers**
a machine used in a shop for storing the money received and recording everything that is sold

casino noun **casinos**
a place where people go to try to win money by taking part in games such as card games or roulette or by using game machines

cask noun **casks**
a container for liquids. It has the shape of a cylinder (tube with flat ends shaped like circles) but is curved outwards in the middle.

SYNONYM **barrel**

casket noun **caskets**
1 a small box for keeping valuable things in, such as jewels
2 in American English, a casket is a coffin

casserole noun **casseroles**
1 a stew, for example of meat and vegetables, that is baked in a casserole dish in an oven
2 a large dish with a lid, used for cooking food in an oven

cassette noun **cassettes**
a small flat plastic container with magnetic tape inside for playing and recording sounds and pictures, used especially in the past

cassette recorder noun **cassette recorders**
a piece of electrical equipment for playing and recording cassettes (containers with magnetic tape inside), used especially in the past

cast verb
casts, casting, cast
1 to cast someone in a play or film is to select them for a particular part *In the school play I was cast as Willy Wonka.*
2 to make something by pouring liquid metal, plastic or plaster into a mould *a Henry Moore sculpture cast in bronze*
3 an old-fashioned way of saying to throw

cast – catchment area

4 to put *The wicked witch cast a spell on the princess. You must cast these ideas from your head.*
5 to cast doubt on something is to make it less certain or less good
6 to cast a vote is to vote in an election
7 to cast a shadow is to make a shadow appear *I saw the shadow cast on the wall by the huge animal.*
8 to cast a glance at something is to have a quick look at it
9 to cast off is to untie the ropes holding a boat and to start sailing

> **LANGUAGE EXTRA** be careful to use the correct form of the past tense – *cast*. Do not say *casted*.

cast noun **casts**
1 the actors in a play, film or TV programme
2 a cast or plaster cast is a hard cover placed around a broken part of the body such as an arm or leg. It is made from a white powder called plaster of Paris that dries quickly when mixed with water.
3 a shape made from liquid metal, plastic or plaster that has become hard in a mould

castanets noun plural
a type of musical instrument used in Spanish dancing. It is made up of two small round pieces of wood or plastic tied together. Dancers hold these in one hand and make a clicking sound by knocking one piece against the other.

> **ORIGIN** from Spanish *castañetas* 'little chestnuts', because they look like empty chestnut shells

castaway noun **castaways**
someone who has been left in a lonely place or on an island when their ship has sunk

caster noun **casters**
a small wheel fixed to the bottom of a piece of furniture for moving it around

> **LANGUAGE EXTRA** also spelt *castor*

caster sugar noun
white sugar with very small grains

castle noun **castles**
1 a large building with strong stone walls, built in the past to keep out enemies. Castles usually have battlements along the top – a wall with gaps for firing weapons from.
2 a piece in the game of chess that is shaped like a round castle. It can only move in a straight line across the board. It is also called a rook.

cast-offs noun plural
clothes that someone doesn't wear any more and that are given to someone else

castor noun **castors**
a small wheel fixed to the bottom of a piece of furniture for moving it around

> **LANGUAGE EXTRA** also spelt *caster*

castor oil noun
an oil made from the seeds of a plant. It was used in the past as a medicine.

casual adjective
1 relaxed and friendly *a casual atmosphere*
2 casual clothes, such as jeans or T-shirts, are worn in relaxed situations and are comfortable to wear
3 done (or doing something) without thinking or paying attention *a casual remark*; *a casual observer*
4 happening (or doing something) by chance, not in a regular way *a casual meeting*; *a casual visitor*; *a casual worker*
5 not based on strong feelings, for example when you like someone or something only slightly *a casual friend*; *a casual friendship*
casually adverb

casualty noun
1 (plural **casualties**) someone killed or injured in an accident or war *The enemy suffered heavy casualties.*
2 the part of a hospital where people go if they have an accident or become ill and need to see a doctor urgently

cat noun **cats**
1 a small furry animal that people keep as a pet or for catching mice. Cats have whiskers and the sound they make is a miaow.
2 a big wild animal that belongs to the cat family, for example a tiger or lion
3 **to be the cat's whiskers** to be better than anyone else
4 **to let the cat out of the bag** to tell people something that should be kept secret, usually without meaning to

Catalan noun
a language similar to Spanish that people speak in the area around Barcelona in the north-east of Spain

catalogue noun **catalogues**
a book or list that gives details of everything you can find in a library, exhibition or museum or of all the goods you can buy from a store *a mail order catalogue*

catalyst noun **catalysts**
1 a substance that speeds up a chemical reaction (change when one chemical is put together with another) but does not change itself
2 something or someone that causes an important change to happen

catamaran noun **catamarans**
a boat or ship with sails or an engine, made up of two or more main sections called hulls. Small catamarans look like two boats put together and large ones are often used as ferries to transport passengers.

> **ORIGIN** from *kattumaram* 'logs tied together' in Tamil (a language of south India and Sri Lanka)

catapult noun **catapults**
1 a small weapon used by children for firing stones. It is made from a Y-shaped piece of branch with a rubber band tied to the top of the Y shape.
2 a large weapon used in past times for throwing heavy stones or iron balls

catastrophe [´ker-tas-trer-fee´] noun **catastrophes**
1 a terrible event, such as an earthquake, that causes great damage, suffering and death
2 any very bad event *It will be a catastrophe if he isn't in the England team.*

catastrophic adjective
1 causing great damage, suffering and death *catastrophic floods*
2 very bad *catastrophic exam results*

catch verb
catches, catching, caught
1 to find someone or run after someone and stop them so that they cannot escape *Catch me if you can!*
2 to use something like a net or hook to hold an animal or fish and stop it from escaping
3 to stop something like a ball while it is moving through the air
4 to get hold of something with your hand *I caught hold of his arm to stop him falling.*
5 to be just in time to get on something such as a train, bus or plane before it leaves, or to be just in time to do something like speak to someone *We just caught the head before she went home.*
6 to get an illness *Jamie caught the flu.*
7 to find someone doing something wrong *I caught my best friend stealing my pen.*
8 to hear something *I'm sorry I didn't catch your name.*
9 if something gets caught somewhere or you catch it somewhere, it gets stuck *I nearly caught my finger in the door.*
10 if a piece of clothing gets caught on something, it accidentally touches something sharp and gets damaged or torn
11 if you get caught in a particular situation, you find yourself suddenly in that situation *I got caught in the rain.*
12 if something catches your eye or your attention, you can't help looking at it
13 to catch fire is to start burning
14 if you catch the sun, your skin becomes red because of the sun
15 if something like an idea or fashion catches on, it becomes popular
16 if you catch someone out, you make them make a mistake, for example by tricking them
17 to catch up is to reach the same level or place as someone else who is ahead of you *I've missed a lesson but I'll catch up. She ran fast and caught up with me.*

catch noun **catches**
1 the action of catching a ball that someone has thrown or hit *Good catch!*
2 if you play catch, you play at throwing the ball to someone
3 something caught or good to catch, especially fish
4 a hidden problem with something that seems very good *What's the catch?*
5 something that fastens a door or window so it can't open

catching adjective
if an illness is catching, you can catch it easily through the air or by touching someone

> **SYNONYMS** infectious, contagious

catchment area noun **catchment areas**
the area close to a school where all the students who go to the school must live. It can also mean the area close to any place that provides a service, such as a hospital.

62

catchphrase *noun* **catchphrases**
a short phrase said by many people, for example because a famous person often uses it or it is connected with a particular group

catchy *adjective* **catchier, catchiest**
easy to remember and very pleasant
a catchy tune

category *noun* **categories**
a group of things or people of the same type *What category does the band's music fit into?*

cater *verb*
caters, catering, catered
to cater for people is to provide them with the things they need *It's a supermarket catering mainly for the Bangladeshi community.*

caterer *noun* **caterers**
a person or business that provides food at important events such as parties, weddings and meetings

catering *noun*
the business of providing food at important events *My auntie is doing the catering for my sister's wedding.*

caterpillar *noun* **caterpillars**
a long thin insect like a worm with legs that turns into a butterfly or moth. Caterpillars are often brightly coloured or hairy.

ORIGIN from Old French *catepelose* 'hairy cat'

cathedral *noun* **cathedrals**
a very large church that is the most important one in a particular area. It is under the control of a bishop.

Catherine wheel *noun* **Catherine wheels**
a flat circular firework with a spiral tube inside. It is fixed to something such as a wooden post and spins round when it burns.

ORIGIN from Saint *Catherine*, who declared her Christian faith in Alexandria (Egypt) in the 4th century. For this she was tied to a wheel and tortured.

Catholic *noun* **Catholics**
a Christian who is a member of the Roman Catholic Church. Catholics accept the Pope as their leader. **Catholic** *adjective*

Catholicism *noun*
the religion of Catholics

catkin *noun* **catkins**
a kind of fluffy flower that hangs down from the branches of some trees such as willows, birches and hazels

Catseye *noun* **Catseyes** (trademark)
a small object made of glass or plastic, which is fixed into the surface of a main road. It reflects light coming from vehicles at night. Catseyes are placed in lines in the middle of roads to help drivers see the different parts of the road more clearly.

cattle *noun plural*
cows and bulls

cattle grid *noun* **cattle grids**
a series of metal bars across a hole in the ground to stop cows and other animals from going somewhere

catwalk *noun* **catwalks**
a raised structure that fashion models walk along at a show

caught
past tense & past participle of **catch**

cauldron *noun* **cauldrons**
a large round metal pot for cooking over a fire. Cauldrons are often used by witches in stories for boiling things to make magic spells.

cauliflower *noun* **cauliflowers**
a vegetable like a cabbage with a large hard white flower that you eat

cause *verb*
causes, causing, caused
to make something happen, usually something bad *The fire caused a lot of damage.*

cause *noun* **causes**
1 something that makes something happen, or the reason why something happens *Your behaviour is the cause of all our problems.*
2 a reason for doing something or feeling in a certain way, for example worried or happy *You have no cause to be angry with your sister.*
3 an aim or idea that a group of people believe in and work for, for example in politics or because they want to help people *We want to raise money for a good cause.*

caution *noun*
1 when you pay attention to avoid danger, problems or mistakes *We must act with caution.*
2 a warning telling someone to be careful *Here's a word of caution.*

cautious *adjective*
if someone is cautious, they pay attention to avoid danger, problems or mistakes
cautiously *adverb*

Cavalier *noun* **Cavaliers**
someone who supported King Charles I in the English Civil War of the 17th century
compare: **Roundhead**

cavalry *noun*
1 the part of an army in the past made up of soldiers who rode horses
2 the part of a modern army that uses tanks

cave *noun* **caves**
a large hollow place in a rock or under the ground

cave in *verb*
caves in, caving in, caved in
if something such as a roof, wall or building caves in, it falls down

caveman *noun* **cavemen**
a man who lived in a cave in prehistoric times

cavern *noun* **caverns**
a large deep cave

cavernous *adjective*
very large and often dark like a cave *a cavernous room*

cavewoman *noun* **cavewomen**
a woman who lived in a cave in prehistoric times

caving *noun*
the activity of going into caves

cavity *noun* **cavities**
1 a hole or space inside something
2 a hole in a tooth where it has gone bad

CCTV *noun*
a system of cameras that allows people to see on TV screens what is happening in different parts of a building, town or road
short for: closed-circuit television

CD *noun* **CDs**
a round flat piece of plastic used for storing and recording computer information, sounds and pictures
short for: compact disc

CD burner *noun* **CD burners**
a piece of equipment for burning (copying) information onto a CD

LANGUAGE EXTRA also called a *CD writer*

CD player *noun* **CD players**
a piece of equipment for playing music CDs

C drive *noun* **C drives**
the main hard disk drive inside a computer

CD-ROM *noun* **CD-ROMs**
a round flat piece of plastic used for storing large amounts of computer information, such as an encyclopedia or dictionary
short for: compact disc read-only memory

CE
used for showing a date after the birth of Jesus Christ
short for: common era

LANGUAGE EXTRA some people, for example from non-Christian religions, use *CE* instead of *AD* so as not to mention Christ

cease *verb*
ceases, ceasing, ceased
1 if something ceases, it stops happening
2 if someone ceases doing something, they stop doing it

ceasefire *noun* **ceasefires**
an agreement between enemies to stop fighting each other for a period of time

ceaseless *adjective*
happening all the time, without stopping
ceaseless efforts

cedar *noun* **cedars**
a large tree with hard red wood and leaves shaped like needles that do not fall off in winter

cedilla ['ser-dill-er] *noun* **cedillas**
a mark at the bottom of the letter *c* in some languages such as French or Portuguese, used for showing that *c* is pronounced with an 's' sound, not a 'k' sound. It is written ç.

ceilidh ['kay-lee] *noun* **ceilidhs**
an event where people play Scottish and Irish music, with singing and dancing

ceiling *noun* **ceilings**
1 the top flat part of a room, above your head
2 a ceiling on something is a top limit or the largest amount of something that is allowed *a ceiling of £300; The government has put a ceiling on wages.*

celeb *noun* **celebs**
an informal word for a celebrity *a TV celeb*

63

celebrate – centre

celebrate *verb*
celebrates, celebrating, celebrated
1 if someone celebrates or celebrates an event, they do something special because it is an important occasion and they want to remember it *I'm having a party to celebrate my birthday. People were celebrating in the streets* (for example dancing, singing, shouting happily).
2 to perform a religious ceremony *The Pope celebrated Mass.*

celebrated *adjective*
famous and admired by lots of people *a celebrated artist*

celebration *noun* **celebrations**
1 a special event such as a party to remember something important like a birthday or passing exams
2 the action of celebrating something *There was celebration in every town and village.*
3 an event where people praise and admire someone's life *a celebration of John Lennon's life*

celebrity *noun*
1 (*plural* **celebrities**) a famous person, especially in films, on television or in sport
2 being famous

celery *noun*
a vegetable with long whitish-green stalks that can be eaten raw or cooked

celestial *adjective*
1 connected with the sky or space
2 celestial bodies are objects in space such as the planets and stars

> ORIGIN from Latin *caelum* 'heaven'

cell *noun* **cells**
1 a small room in a prison or police station where prisoners are kept
2 in humans, animals and plants, a cell is the smallest unit of living matter that can live by itself. Millions of cells make up each human, animal or plant.
3 a piece of equipment for making electricity out of chemicals. Two or more cells together make a battery.
4 a small square in a spreadsheet or table, for writing a number or word in
5 a small area of land with electronic equipment for providing radio signals used by mobile phones

cellar *noun* **cellars**
a room under a building for storing things in

cello ['chel-oh'] *noun* **cellos**
a wooden musical instrument with strings that looks like a large violin. You stand it up on the floor between your knees while you are sitting down and play it by moving a special stick (called a bow) across the strings. **cellist** *noun*

cellophane *noun* (trademark)
a thin transparent material for wrapping things in, for example sandwiches

cell phone *noun* **cell phones**
a small phone that you carry around with you

> SYNONYM mobile phone

> ORIGIN short for *cellular phone*, because it uses radio signals from areas called *cells*

cellular *adjective*
1 made of cells or connected with cells *a cellular structure*
2 connected with cell phones or the networks of radio stations they use

celluloid *noun*
a thin plastic used in the past for making films used in cameras

cellulose *noun*
a substance that makes up the outer layers of cells (smallest units of living matter) in plants, used for making things such as plastics, paper and films

Celsius *noun*
a system for measuring temperature based on the metric system. Water freezes at 0 degrees and boils at 100 degrees. compare: Fahrenheit

> ORIGIN named after the Swedish 18th-century astronomer Anders *Celsius* who invented it

Celt ['kelt'] *noun* **Celts**
a member of an ancient people who lived in Britain before the time of the Romans

Celtic ['kel-tik'] *adjective*
1 connected with the Celts
2 connected with the modern Welsh, Scottish and Irish people whose ancestors were the ancient Celts

cement *noun*
1 a grey powder made from a chalky substance (called lime) and clay. It becomes hard when mixed with sand and water. Cement is used for making parts of buildings such as floors and for sticking bricks together.
2 a cement mixer is a machine with a large drum for mixing cement with sand and water

cement *verb*
cements, cementing, cemented
1 to cover or fix something with cement
2 to cement something such as a friendship is to make it stronger

cemetery *noun* **cemeteries**
an area of land where people who have died are buried

cenotaph *noun* **cenotaphs**
a monument to remind people of all the soldiers and others who died in a country's wars

> ORIGIN from Greek meaning 'empty tomb' (*kenos* 'empty' and *taphos* 'tomb'), because a cenotaph is in a different place from where people are buried

> CULTURE NOTE the people killed in Great Britain's wars are remembered each year at the *Cenotaph* in Whitehall, London. This takes place on Remembrance Sunday, on or close to Armistice Day on 11 November.

censor *verb*
censors, censoring, censored
if officials censor something such as a film, play, book or document, they examine it carefully and get rid of parts they think are not suitable for people to see, hear or read. They do this, for example, because they think these parts are dangerous or will lead people to behave badly.

censor *noun* **censors**
someone who censors things, especially films, plays or books *a film censor*
censorship *noun*

census *noun* **censuses**
a census or population census is when a government counts all the people living in a country and finds out some details about them

cent *noun* **cents**
a coin and small unit of money in the USA, Canada, Europe, Australia and some other countries. There are 100 cents in a dollar and in a euro.

centaur *noun* **centaurs**
in ancient Greek stories, a creature with the head, arms and chest of a man and the lower body and legs of a horse

centenary ['sen-teen-er-ee'] *noun* **centenaries**
a day or year that is 100 years after a particular event *Many people celebrated the centenary of the artist's birth.*

centigrade *noun*
another way of saying Celsius *20 degrees centigrade*

centimetre *noun* **centimetres**
a unit for measuring length in the metric system. There are 100 centimetres in a metre.

centipede *noun* **centipedes**
a long small crawling creature with lots of legs

> ORIGIN from Latin *centum* 'a hundred' and *pedes* 'feet'

central *adjective*
1 in or near the middle of something *He lives in central France.*
2 in or near the centre of town *Our school is very central.*
3 important *Education is central.*
4 making important decisions affecting a larger group *central government*
centrally *adverb*

Central America *noun*
the narrow part of the American continent between Mexico and Colombia
Central American *adjective & noun*

central heating *noun*
a system of heating a building where water or air is heated in one place and sent around the whole building through pipes

centre *noun* **centres**
1 the middle of something
2 an important place where a particular activity is done *Oxford and Cambridge are centres of learning.*
3 a building where people go for a particular purpose *an information centre; a sports centre; a shopping centre*
4 if a political party is in the centre, it does not support extreme ideas

centre *verb*
centres, centring, centred
1 to put something in the centre of something else, for example a word on a page in a computer document *Click on this icon to centre your heading.*

centre forward–challenge

2 to centre around something or someone is to have that thing or person as the main subject of interest or the main purpose *Their activities centred* (or *were centred*) *around helping poor people.*
3 if something centres around a particular place, it happens there *The celebrations will be centred around Trafalgar Square.*

centre forward noun **centre forwards**
a player who plays in the middle of the line of attack in a football team

centre of gravity noun **centres of gravity**
the point in an object on which it balances

centrifugal force noun
a force that moves something or parts of it outwards from the centre when it is spinning around

centurion noun **centurions**
an army officer in ancient Rome in charge of 100 soldiers

century noun **centuries**
1 a period of 100 years *in the twentieth century*
2 a score of 100 runs by one batsman in cricket

ORIGIN from Latin *centum* 'a hundred'

ceramic noun **ceramics**
something made from baked clay
ceramic adjective

ceramics noun
the art of making things from baked clay

SYNONYM pottery

cereal noun **cereals**
1 food made from seeds called grain. People usually eat cereal for breakfast.
2 a plant that produces grain used for food

ORIGIN from Latin *cerealis* 'connected with growing plants that produce grain'. *Ceres* was the Roman goddess of agriculture.

ceremonial adjective
connected with a ceremony *ceremonial duties*

ceremonious adjective
1 serious or polite, such as someone's actions in a ceremony
2 having the appearance of being in a ceremony *a ceremonious look*

ceremony noun
1 (plural **ceremonies**) an important, official or religious occasion when things have to be done following special rules *a prize-giving ceremony*; *a wedding ceremony*; *a religious ceremony* (for example when people pray or sing religious songs together)
2 the special actions done at an important or official occasion *The soldiers marched with great ceremony.*

certain adjective
1 if you're certain about something, you know it has happened or is true or correct (or you know or believe it will happen) *I'm certain you've made a mistake. I'm certain of where he lives. Em is certain we'll have better luck next time.*
2 used about something that you know will happen or be true or correct (or that is very likely to happen or be true or correct) *One thing is certain – I'll always be your friend. You're certain of a warm welcome. Touch that wire and it's certain death.*
3 used for talking about things but without saying exactly what they are *The swimming pool is only open at certain times.*
4 used for talking about an amount of something, usually a small amount *There was a certain disappointment in her voice.*

SYNONYM some

5 if you make certain of something or make certain you do something, you do what needs to be done so that something can happen or be true *Arrive early at the theatre to make certain of getting a ticket. I made certain I arrived early to get a ticket. Close the window to make certain the rain can't come in.*
6 to make certain you do something also means to pay attention to doing it so that you know it is done properly *Make certain you take your packed lunch* (you mustn't forget to take it).
7 **for certain** used when you mean that something you know, say or do is really true or will happen (or has happened) *I can't say for certain what I did with my umbrella.*

certainly adverb
1 used for saying that something will or did happen or is true *It will certainly rain tomorrow.*
2 used for saying in a very strong way that, in your opinion, something is really true *It's certainly very hot.*
3 used for agreeing or giving permission *'Can I come in?' – 'Certainly!'*

certainty noun
1 (plural **certainties**) something that will happen *A change of government in the next month is a certainty.*
2 when you know that something will happen or is true *She said this with complete certainty.*

certificate noun **certificates**
an official piece of paper that says something important has happened, such as someone's birth or marriage or someone passing an exam *a GCSE certificate*

ORIGIN from Latin *certificare* 'to make certain'

certify verb
certifies, certifying, certified
to certify something is to say that it is true in an official document

cesspit noun **cesspits**
1 a hole or container in the ground where waste from people's toilets is stored
2 a place where people behave in a very bad way

CFC noun
a gas that damages the earth's ozone layer (part of the earth's atmosphere). It was used in the past in fridges and aerosols.
short for: chlorofluorocarbon

chafe verb
chafes, chafing, chafed
if something chafes a part of your body, it rubs against it and makes it sore *My collar is chafing.*

chaffinch noun **chaffinches**
a small bird with black and white wings

chain noun **chains**
1 a series of metal rings joined together, for example for fastening or pulling things or for wearing as jewellery
2 a series of rings made from materials such as paper or plastic and joined together *paper chains for Christmas*
3 a group of shops, restaurants or other businesses that belong to the same company *McDonald's is a chain. There are lots of chain stores in our town.*
4 a number of things that are connected *a chain of events; a mountain chain*

chain reaction noun **chain reactions**
a series of events that happen very fast and where one event causes the next one to happen

chain saw noun **chain saws**
a tool for cutting wood, made from a circular chain worked by a motor

chair noun **chairs**
1 a piece of furniture for one person to sit on. It has a back and legs (supports). Some chairs, such as armchairs, also have arms (side parts for resting your arms on).
2 the person in charge of a meeting or official group

chairlift noun **chairlifts**
a line of seats that hang down from a moving wire, used for carrying people up and down a mountain, for example to go skiing

chairperson noun **chairpersons**
the person in charge of a meeting or official group

LANGUAGE EXTRA you can also say *chairman*, *chairwoman* or *chair*

chalet ['sha-lay'] noun **chalets**
1 a house made of wood and with a big sloping roof. A chalet is usually built on a mountain, for example in Switzerland.
2 a small house in a holiday camp

chalk noun
1 a soft white rock formed from the shells of small sea creatures
2 (plural **chalks**) a stick of this type of rock used for writing or drawing, for example on a blackboard or wall
chalky adverb

SIMILE 'as different as chalk and cheese' means very different from each other

chalk verb
chalks, chalking, chalked
to write or draw something with chalk

challenge noun **challenges**
1 something new and interesting that needs a lot of skill and effort *I'm looking forward to the challenge of learning Urdu.*
2 when someone asks you to try to beat them in a competition or fight *Dan accepted the challenge.*

challenge verb
challenges, challenging, challenged
1 to ask someone to try to beat you in a competition or fight

65

challenger – Chanukah

2 to refuse to accept something as true or right *The soldiers challenged the King's authority.*
3 to give someone something to do that needs a lot of skill and effort *Maths is the subject that will really challenge the class.*

challenger noun challengers
someone who tries to win a competition or sporting event

challenging adjective
if something is challenging, it needs a lot of skill and effort but it is interesting and worth doing *Mandarin is a challenging language.*

chamber noun chambers
1 a room used for meetings in a public building or a room used for a special purpose *a torture chamber*
2 an enclosed space
3 an old word for a room or bedroom

chamber music noun
classical music written for and played by a small group of musicians

chameleon ['ker-**mee**-lee-ern'] noun chameleons
a lizard that changes its colour so that it has the same colour as the things around it and cannot easily be seen

> ORIGIN from Greek *khamaileon* 'lion on the ground'

chamomile noun
a plant whose leaves and small white flowers are used for making a type of tea

> LANGUAGE EXTRA also spelt *camomile*

champ noun champs
short for **champion**

champagne ['sham-**payn**'] noun
a white wine from France with lots of bubbles in it. People often drink champagne to celebrate a special occasion.

champion noun champions
1 the winner in a sport or competition
2 someone who fights for an aim or idea they believe in or for a group of people they support *a great champion of disabled people*

champion verb
champions, championing, championed
to fight for an aim or idea or for a group of people

championship noun championships
a competition or sporting event to find a winning person or team

chance noun chances
1 a time when you can do something you want to do *I had the chance to go on a school trip to Italy.*
2 when something happens that you're not expecting *It was chance that brought us together. A cure was found thanks to a chance discovery.*
3 when something might happen *There's a chance of snow tomorrow.*
4 to take a chance means to do something although you know that something bad might happen or you might not get what you want

> SYNONYM to chance it

5 someone's chances are how likely they are to get what they want *Your chances of passing the exam are good.*
6 by chance without knowing about something before or without meaning to do something *We found this toy shop by chance.*
7 No chance! used when you mean something could never happen *'Do you think our team can win?' – 'No chance!'*

chance verb
chances, chancing, chanced
to chance it means to do something even though you know that something bad might happen or you might not get what you want

> SYNONYM to take a chance

chancellor noun chancellors
1 short for **Chancellor of the Exchequer**
2 the leader of the government in some countries, such as Germany

Chancellor of the Exchequer noun Chancellors of the Exchequer
the member of the British government in charge of money and taxes

chandelier ['shan-der-**leer**'] noun chandeliers
a large light that hangs from a ceiling. It is made up of a round frame with lots of branches for holding small light bulbs.

change verb
changes, changing, changed
1 to become different, or to make something or someone different *Nothing has changed. The leaves are changing colour. Success has really changed him. Caterpillars change into butterflies.*
2 to stop one thing and start or go to something else instead *My mum's partner has changed his job.*
3 to change trains, buses or planes is to get off one and get on another *You change at King's Cross.*
4 to put something in the place of something else *I changed the batteries in the camera.*
5 to put on different clothes *She went upstairs to change. Dad is changing the baby* (putting a new nappy on the baby).
6 to give someone something and take something else instead *If the shoes don't fit, we'll change them.*
7 to give someone coins or banknotes and get coins or notes of smaller value instead *Can you change a £10 note?*
8 to change money in a bank is to hand over the money of one country and get the money of another instead *Can I change 100 dollars, please?*
9 to change places or seats with someone is to let them sit in your seat while you go and sit in theirs

change noun changes
1 when things are different from what they were before *There have been lots of changes in our school.*
2 when something is put in the place of something else *a change of clothes*
3 a new situation that you think is good *It's hot today – that makes a change. Let's take our bikes to school for a change.*
4 money that you get back, for example in a shop, when you buy something that costs less than the money you gave for it

5 when you get off one train, bus or plane and get on another *For the six o'clock train to London, there's one change at York.*

changeable adjective
changing very often *The weather's very changeable.*

Changing of the Guard noun
a ceremony that takes place in front of Buckingham Palace (the London home of the British king or queen) when a new group of soldiers take over from the previous group to guard the Palace

changing room noun changing rooms
1 a room where people change their clothes, for example before playing sports
2 a room in a store where people try on clothes before buying them

channel noun channels
1 a television station with all its programmes *Mum changed channels to watch the news.*
2 a narrow area of water, for example connecting two seas
3 a long narrow space along the ground for water to flow along *an irrigation channel*
4 a way of doing something or getting information *To complain you need to go through the right channels.*

channel verb
channels, channelling, channelled
to control or organise something in a particular way *Craig channelled all his energies into football.*

Channel noun
the Channel is the area of water between the south coast of England and the north coast of France

> LANGUAGE EXTRA also called the *English Channel*

channel-hopping noun
when you keep changing from one television channel to another using the remote control
channel-hop verb

> SYNONYM channel-surfing

Channel Islands noun plural
a group of islands in the English Channel. The two largest islands are Jersey and Guernsey.

Channel Tunnel noun
the train tunnel under the Channel between England and France

chant verb
chants, chanting, chanted
to say words aloud very many times, often using a special rhythm *The protesters were chanting slogans.*

chant noun chants
1 a word or phrase said aloud very many times
2 a religious song using a few notes only

Chanukah ['**hah**-noo-ker'] noun
an eight-day Jewish holiday in November or December. It is also known as the 'festival of lights'. Candles are lit to celebrate the time when the Jews took back the Holy Temple in Jerusalem about 2200 years ago.

> LANGUAGE EXTRA also spelt *Hanukkah*

chaos ['kay-oss'] *noun*
a situation where things are not organised and everything is confused *There was complete chaos in the classroom.*

> **ORIGIN** from Greek *khaos* 'bottomless hole'

chaotic ['kay-ot-ik] *adjective*
very confused and not organised

chap *noun* **chaps**
an informal word for a man

chapatti *noun* **chapattis**
a thin flat round Indian bread made without yeast (substance that makes bread swell up)

chapel *noun* **chapels**
1 a small church
2 a room where Christians pray, for example in a hospital or prison

chapped *adjective*
if your skin or lips are chapped, they are sore or bleeding because of cold weather

chaps *noun plural*
sore or bleeding areas on the skin, for example the hands, because of cold weather

chapter *noun* **chapters**
1 one of the parts that a book is divided into
2 a period in history or in someone's life

char *verb*
chars, charring, charred
if something chars or is charred, it becomes burnt and black on the outside

character *noun* **characters**
1 the special qualities of someone or something that make them what they are *The English and the French have very different characters.*
2 a person in a play, book or film
3 the opinion people have about you as a good and honest person *a man of good character*
4 an unusual and interesting person, or a person of a particular type *Your friend is quite a character.*
5 a letter, number or symbol used in writing or on computers *Chinese characters*

characterise *verb*
characterises, characterising, characterised
1 to describe someone or something in a certain way
2 if something characterises something else, that thing or quality makes up an important part of it *A normal school day is characterised by lots of hard work.*
characterisation *noun*

> **LANGUAGE EXTRA** also spelt *characterize* and *characterization*

characteristic *noun* **characteristics**
a special quality that belongs to someone or something and makes them different *Strange faces are a characteristic of Picasso's paintings.*

characteristic *adjective*
used about a particular quality that is often seen in someone or something *The snail moves along with characteristic slowness.*

charades ['sher-rahdz'] *noun plural*
a game where players have to guess a word or phrase that another player tries to tell them by using movements only, without speaking any words

charcoal *noun*
a black substance made from burnt wood. It can be used as a fuel for cooking, and sticks of charcoal can be used for drawing.

charge *noun* **charges**
1 money that you must pay for something *There's a charge to use wi-fi. There's no charge for children to travel on the buses.*
2 when someone is accused of a crime or of doing something bad *She was found guilty of all charges.*
3 an attack by people or animals running towards you *There was a sudden charge by the King's soldiers.*
4 the amount of electricity inside a piece of equipment, or a type of electrical force *My mobile is on charge. Electrons have a negative charge.*
5 if you are in charge of someone or something, you are responsible for looking after them or dealing with them, or for making decisions about them *Our teacher is in charge of 30 children. The nurse is in charge of giving the injections.*
6 to take charge of something is to start being responsible for it

charge *verb*
charges, charging, charged
1 to ask someone to pay money for something *How much do you charge for an ice cream?*
2 to run somewhere suddenly or run towards someone to attack them *The elephant came charging towards us.*
3 to accuse someone of a crime *He was charged with murder.*
4 to put electricity into a piece of equipment by connecting it to an electrical plug or a computer port *I'm charging my phone. My phone is charging.*

ChargeBox *noun* **ChargeBoxes**
(trademark)
a piece of equipment in a public place such as a shopping centre or railway station, used for charging a mobile phone or small computer such as a tablet. It contains a series of small boxes with cables and plugs inside that you put your phone or computer into. Each box has a key so that you can lock it.

> **LANGUAGE EXTRA** also called a *charge box*

charger *noun* **chargers**
a piece of electrical equipment for putting electricity into something such as a battery *a phone charger*

chariot *noun* **chariots**
a small vehicle with no roof, pulled by a horse or horses. It was used in ancient times in battles or for racing.

charioteer *noun* **charioteers**
a driver of a chariot

charitable *adjective*
1 helping people who are poor or who need help badly *a charitable organisation*
2 kind and understanding

charity *noun*
1 (plural **charities**) an organisation that helps people who are poor or who need help, for example by giving them money or goods that they get from other people
2 money, goods or help given to people who need it

charity shop *noun* **charity shops**
a shop belonging to a charity. Charity shops sell things that people have given to them for free.

charm *noun* **charms**
1 a special quality that someone or something has that makes you like them
2 a small object that people wear, for example on a chain around the wrist *a good luck charm*
3 words with special magic powers

charm *verb*
charms, charming, charmed
if someone or something charms you, they make you like them and they give you great pleasure

charming *adjective*
very pleasant or attractive

charred *adjective*
burnt and black on the outside

chart *noun* **charts**
1 a drawing or diagram that gives information about something
2 a map that gives information about the sea or stars
3 a mathematical diagram with amounts shown as long rectangles (a bar chart or graph) or divided into parts of a circle (a pie chart)
4 the charts are lists of the most popular music that people have bought

chart *verb*
charts, charting, charted
1 to record how something moves and develops *Scientists chart the spaceship's progress.*
2 to make a map of something or a plan of action

charter *noun*
1 (plural **charters**) an official document explaining the duties and aims of an organisation or the rights and benefits that people have *the UN charter; Does the NHS have a patient's charter?*
2 when someone pays money to a company to use their aircraft or vehicle for a special purpose
3 a charter plane or flight is a plane or plane journey for people going on holiday. It is paid for by a travel company.

charter *verb*
charters, chartering, chartered
to pay money to use an aircraft or vehicle belonging to a company *Our school chartered a plane to take the football team to Scotland.*

chase *verb*
chases, chasing, chased
1 to follow someone or something quickly, usually to try to catch them
2 to make someone or something go away *I chased the flies away with my hand.*
3 to hurry somewhere *We've been chasing around the town all day.*

chase *noun* **chases**
when you follow someone or something quickly, usually to try to catch them *a car chase*

chasm – cheerleader

chasm ['ka-zerm'] *noun* **chasms**
1 a deep hole in the ground between rocks
2 a big difference between people

chassis ['shass-ee'] *noun* **chassis**
the frame, wheels and engine of a vehicle, which support the body (main part of the vehicle)

chat *noun* **chats**
a friendly talk with someone

chat *verb*
chats, chatting, chatted
1 to talk to someone in a friendly way
2 to exchange written messages with someone on the internet, using a program that shows immediately the messages that you receive

chateau ['sha-toh'] *noun* **chateaux**
a large house in France

ORIGIN from French *château* 'castle'. The plural ending in -*x* is because the word is French.

chat room *noun* **chat rooms**
a place on the internet where you can exchange written messages with people and receive immediate replies to the messages you send

LANGUAGE EXTRA also spelt *chatroom*

chat show *noun* **chat shows**
a television or radio programme where someone called a host asks famous people questions about themselves

SYNONYM talk show

chatter *verb*
chatters, chattering, chattered
1 to talk quickly and without stopping, usually about things that are not important
2 if your teeth are chattering, they are knocking against each other because you are cold or frightened

chatterbox *noun* **chatterboxes**
someone who does a lot of chatting to people

chatty *adjective* **chattier, chattiest**
someone who is chatty does a lot of chatting to people or likes chatting to people

chauffeur ['shoh-fer'] *noun* **chauffeurs**
a person whose job is to drive someone around in a car. Chauffeurs usually wear a uniform.

ORIGIN from an old French meaning of *chauffeur* as 'stoker' – someone who heated a furnace (*chauffer* means 'to heat'). The *chauffeur* later became the person who heated the engine of an old steam car and then the one who drove it.

cheap *adjective* **cheaper, cheapest**
1 if something is cheap, it doesn't cost much money
2 very bad in quality *This laptop looks cheap.*
cheaply *adverb*

cheap *noun*
on the cheap if you buy something or do something on the cheap, you spend less money but get something that is not of good quality

cheat *verb*
cheats, cheating, cheated
1 to behave or do something in a way that goes against the rules, usually in order to try to win a game or do well in an exam
2 to cheat someone is to make them believe something that isn't true or to behave in a dishonest way towards them so that they lose something *You've cheated me out of all my pocket money!*

cheat *noun* **cheats**
someone who cheats

LANGUAGE EXTRA the American word is *cheater*

check *verb*
checks, checking, checked
1 to look at something carefully to make sure it is all right or as it is supposed to be *Check your spelling before sending the email.*
2 to find out about or be sure about something *Before going out check that you have an umbrella.*
3 to stop something or someone from doing something or from getting worse *I wanted to cry but I checked myself. How can we check the spread of malaria?*
4 to check into a hotel is to arrive and tell someone who works there that you have arrived. You usually sign your name on a piece of paper or in a register (book) to show who you are. *Have you checked in?*
5 to check in at an airport is to arrive there and show your ticket
6 to check your luggage in is to give it to someone who puts it somewhere such as on a plane
7 to check on someone is to find out if they are all right *Go upstairs and check on the baby.*
8 to check up on someone is to find out if they are doing what they are supposed to be doing
9 to check something or someone out is to find out about them to see if they are good or suitable *Check him out before you invite him round.*
10 to check out of a hotel is to pay the bill and leave

check *noun* **checks**
1 when you check something *a spelling check; a health check*
2 a pattern of small squares *a check jacket*
3 to hold or keep something in check is to keep it under control
4 in chess, when your king is in check, it is being attacked by another piece
5 a check or check mark is the same as a tick
6 in American English, a check is a piece of paper showing the amount of money you must pay for food or drinks in a restaurant
7 the American spelling of **cheque**

checkbox *noun* **checkboxes**
a small square on a computer screen where you choose something by clicking in it with your mouse

checkers *noun*
the American word for draughts

checkmate *noun*
in chess, checkmate is when one player's king cannot move because it is being attacked by another piece and so the other player wins
compare: **stalemate**

ORIGIN from Persian *shah mat* 'the king is dead'

checkout *noun* **checkouts**
a place in a supermarket where you pay for your shopping

checkpoint *noun* **checkpoints**
a place where police officers, soldiers or other officials stop vehicles to check them, for example on a road or at a border between countries

check-up *noun* **check-ups**
an examination by a doctor or dentist to make sure you are healthy *a dental check-up*

cheddar *noun* **cheddars**
a hard smooth yellow cheese

ORIGIN from the Somerset village of *Cheddar*

cheek *noun*
1 (*plural* **cheeks**) one of the two sides of your face between your ears and mouth
2 rude behaviour or talk that shows no respect for the person you are speaking to

cheeky *adjective* **cheekier, cheekiest**
not polite or not showing respect, but usually in a pleasant or friendly way
cheekily *adverb*

cheep *verb*
cheeps, cheeping, cheeped
when a small bird such as a chick cheeps, it makes a short high sound **cheep** *noun*

cheer *verb*
cheers, cheering, cheered
1 to shout loudly and happily as a way of showing you like someone or support them *We all cheered the school team.*
2 if you are cheered by something such as good news, you feel happier because of it
3 to cheer up is to become less sad or make someone less sad *Cheer up – tomorrow we're going on holiday! I told her some jokes to cheer her up.*

cheer *noun* **cheers**
1 a shout of happiness to show you like someone or support them
2 **Three cheers for … !** used for telling people to shout loudly three times, for example saying 'Hip, hip, hooray!', to show their happiness and support for someone or something

cheerful *adjective*
1 happy *a cheerful smile*
2 pleasant or bright *cheerful colours*
cheerfully *adverb*

cheerio *interjection*
an informal way of saying goodbye

cheerleader *noun* **cheerleaders**
a person, usually a woman or girl, who is one of a group of people at a sports event in the USA who support their team by dancing and getting the crowd to cheer loudly. Cheerleaders wear uniforms and in each hand they often carry a pompom (ball of loose strips of paper, cloth or plastic).

cheers *interjection*
1 used as a friendly wish just before people drink a glass of alcohol
2 an informal way of saying thank you

cheese *noun* **cheeses**
a hard or soft food make from milk. Cheese is usually yellow like cheddar or white like cottage cheese.

cheeseburger *noun* **cheeseburgers**
a round flat cake of minced meat that is fried and has a piece of cheese on top

cheesecake *noun* **cheesecakes**
a cake made from soft white cheese

cheesed off *adjective* (informal)
slightly angry or unhappy about something

cheesy *adjective* **cheesier, cheesiest**
1 tasting or smelling of cheese
2 (informal) cheap or unpleasant
3 (informal) a cheesy grin is a big smile that looks false

cheetah *noun* **cheetahs**
a big wild cat with yellow fur and black spots. Cheetahs can run very fast.

> ORIGIN from Hindi *cita* 'leopard' and Sanskrit *citrakaya* (*citra* means 'bright' or 'spotty' and *kaya* means 'body')

chef ['shef'] *noun* **chefs**
the main cook in a restaurant or hotel

> ORIGIN from French *chef de cuisine* 'head of the kitchen'

chemical *noun* **chemicals**
in science, a substance that is produced when other substances are put together

chemical *adjective*
connected with chemistry or with substances that are put together in a scientific way *a chemical reaction*

chemist *noun* **chemists**
1 someone who prepares and sells medicines in a shop or supermarket. A chemist's shop also sells products for the body such as cosmetics, toothpaste and soap.
2 a scientist who studies chemistry

chemistry *noun*
the science of substances and how they change when put together with other substances. Chemistry is often studied as a school subject.

cheque *noun* **cheques**
a piece of printed paper that people write an amount of money on and use to pay for things

chequered *adjective*
1 if something is chequered or has a chequered pattern, it has lots of small squares
2 in motor racing, a chequered flag with black and white squares is waved at the start and finish of a race

cherish *verb*
cherishes, cherishing, cherished
1 to love someone or something and look after them
2 to consider that someone or something is very important to you

cherry *noun* **cherries**
a small round red or black fruit with a hard seed inside called a stone

chess *noun*
a game for two people on a board of 64 squares. Each player has 16 pieces: a king and queen, two castles (or rooks), two bishops, two knights and eight pawns. The aim is to trap the other player's king so that it can no longer move.

chessboard *noun* **chessboards**
a square board of 64 black and white squares for playing chess

chesspiece *noun* **chesspieces**
one of the 16 pieces that each player has in a game of chess

chest *noun* **chests**
1 the upper front part of your body between your neck and stomach
2 a large strong box
3 a chest or chest of drawers is a piece of furniture with drawers, usually for keeping clothes in
4 **to get something off your chest** to tell someone about something that worries you because it makes you feel better when someone else knows about it

chestnut *noun*
1 (*plural* **chestnuts**) a large round reddish-brown nut that you can eat. Chestnuts grow on a chestnut tree.
2 a reddish-brown colour *chestnut hair*

chesty *adjective* **chestier, chestiest**
if you have a chesty cough, you have an infection in your lungs

chew *verb*
chews, chewing, chewed
1 to chew food is to break it up with your teeth into little pieces so that you can swallow it
2 to keep biting something to get a taste from it or because you are nervous *You're allowed to chew gum in the playground. Stop chewing your nails.*

chewing gum *noun*
a kind of sticky sweet, often flavoured with mint, that you chew to taste its flavour but do not swallow

chewy *adjective* **chewier, chewiest**
if food is chewy, it is tough or sticky and you have to chew it for a long time before you can swallow it *a very chewy steak*

chick *noun* **chicks**
1 a young bird
2 a baby chicken

chicken *noun*
1 (*plural* **chickens**) a bird kept for its eggs and meat, usually on a farm. The female chicken is called a hen and the male is called a rooster. The sound a chicken makes is a cluck.
2 the meat of the chicken

chicken *adjective* (informal)
too frightened or not brave enough to do something

chicken out *verb* (informal)
chickens out, chickening out, chickened out
if someone chickens out of something, they change their mind and say they don't want to do it because they are frightened

chickenpox *noun*
an illness that produces lots of red itchy spots on your skin and a slight temperature. Chickenpox is catching but you only get it once.

chickpea *noun* **chickpeas**
a large round bean, often light brown, that is cooked and eaten as a vegetable

chief *noun* **chiefs**
1 the person in charge of something such as an organisation *the Police Chief*
2 the leader of a tribe (group of related families) *a Native American Indian chief*

chief *adjective*
1 most important *That was the chief reason.*

> SYNONYM main

2 most likely *The lawyer was the chief suspect.*

> SYNONYM main

3 highest in rank *chief constable* (police officer in charge of the police of a large area)

chiefly *adverb*
mainly *My gran has travelled a lot, chiefly in Europe.*

chieftain ['cheef-tern'] *noun* **chieftains**
the leader of a tribe (related families) or Scottish clan (families with the same name)

chilblain *noun* **chilblains**
a sore and itchy area on a finger or toe. People sometimes get chilblains during cold weather.

child *noun* **children**
1 someone from the time they are born until they start to become an adult (for example around the ages of 12 to 14)
2 someone's son or daughter, of any age *My uncle has two grown-up children.*

childcare *noun*
help provided by a person or organisation in looking after someone's children when their parents are at work

childhood *noun*
the time of your life when you're a child

childish *adjective*
1 behaving like a silly child *My brother is very childish.*
2 silly in a way that makes you think of a child *childish behaviour*

childlike *adjective*
a childlike quality makes you think of a child in a very nice way *a childlike sense of wonder*

childminder *noun* **childminders**
someone who is paid to look after children when the children's parents are at work

childproof *adjective*
if something is childproof, it has been specially made so that it cannot be opened, used or broken by a child *a childproof lock*

children
plural of **child**

Chile *noun*
a country in South America
Chilean *adjective & noun*

chill–cholera

chill *noun* **chills**
1 a feeling of being too cold
2 a slight illness with a temperature and headache that makes you shake because you are cold
3 a feeling of being afraid

chill *verb*
chills, chilling, chilled
1 to chill something such as a drink is to make it cold *Water is best served chilled.*
2 to make someone feel cold
3 to chill or chill out is to relax when you are tired, angry or worried

chillax *verb* (slang)
chillaxes, chillaxing, chillaxed
to relax when you've been feeling tired, angry or worried

ORIGIN from *chill* and *relax*

chilli *noun* **chillies**
a chilli or chilli pepper is a small red or green seed pod (long narrow container) with a very spicy taste

chilly *adjective* **chillier, chilliest**
1 slightly cold in a way that makes you feel uncomfortable *It was a chilly September night.*
2 unfriendly *We received a rather chilly reply.*

chime *verb*
chimes, chiming, chimed
if a bell or clock chimes, it makes a high ringing sound *The station clock chimes every hour.*

chime *noun* **chimes**
a high ringing sound made by a bell or clock

chimney *noun* **chimneys**
1 a big tube that gets rid of smoke from a fire inside a building. It takes the smoke up through the building into the roof and out into the air.
2 the part of a chimney that you see coming out of a roof *tall factory chimneys*

chimney pot *noun* **chimney pots**
the short piece of pipe at the top of a chimney

chimney sweep *noun* **chimney sweeps**
someone whose job is to clean the inside of chimneys. This job was more common in the past than it is today.

chimpanzee *noun* **chimpanzees**
an intelligent ape with brown or black fur, a face without hair, and big ears

chin *noun* **chins**
the part of your face below your bottom lip

china *noun*
1 a type of thin hard clay for making things such as cups and plates
2 cups, saucers, plates and other dishes made from china

ORIGIN from Persian *chini* 'baked clay from China'

China *noun*
a country in East Asia

Chinese *adjective*
connected with China or the Chinese language

Chinese *noun*
1 one of the languages people speak in China, especially Mandarin
2 the Chinese are people from China

chink *noun* **chinks**
1 a small opening or hole in something that lets the light through *a chink in the curtains*
2 a ringing sound, for example when glass or small metal objects touch each other

chinos *noun plural*
trousers made from strong cotton cloth

chip *noun* **chips**
1 a long piece of potato fried in oil and eaten hot
2 a chip or silicon chip is a very small piece of silicon (grey substance from rocks and sand) with electrical connections in it. It is used mainly in electronic equipment such as computers and allows the equipment to work and store information.
3 a place on something, such as a cup or a piece of furniture, where a small piece has broken off
4 a small piece that has broken off something larger
5 a round piece of plastic used instead of money in some games played in casinos, for example roulette
6 if someone has a chip on their shoulder, they get angry about a particular thing because it is connected with something bad that happened to them in the past
7 the American word for a crisp (thin potato slice fried in oil and eaten cold)

chip *verb*
chips, chipping, chipped
1 if you chip something or if it chips, a small piece of it breaks off *I dropped the plate and it chipped. I threw away a chipped cup.*
2 if someone chips in with money, they pay money towards something
3 if someone chips in while people are talking, they add something to the conversation

chip shop *noun* **chip shops**
a shop that sells fried fish and chips and other fried food to take away

chirp *verb*
chirps, chirping, chirped
when a small bird or insect chirps, it makes a short high sound *We could hear the grasshoppers chirping.* **chirp** *noun*

chirpy *adjective* **chirpier, chirpiest**
happy and lively

chisel *noun* **chisels**
a sharp steel tool used for cutting wood or stone

chisel *verb*
chisels, chiselling, chiselled
to chisel wood or stone is to cut it with a chisel

chit-chat *noun*
when people talk about things that are not important *There was a lot of chit-chat about last night's TV programme.*

chivalry *noun*
polite behaviour, especially of men towards women in the past **chivalrous** *adjective*

chives *noun plural*
the long thin green leaves of a plant used for giving flavour to food. Chives taste like onions.

chlorine ['klor-een'] *noun*
a chemical with a strong smell used for keeping water clean, for example in swimming pools

chlorophyll ['klor-er-fill'] *noun*
the substance in plants that gives them their green colour

ORIGIN from Greek *khloros* 'green' and *phyllon* 'leaf'

choc-ice *noun* **choc-ices**
a small block of ice cream covered with a layer of chocolate

chock-a-block *adjective*
completely full so there is no room for anything else *The train was chock-a-block with students.*

chock-full *adjective*
completely full in a way that you find very pleasant *The book is chock-full of wonderful stories.*

chocolate *noun*
1 a sweet hard food made from cocoa beans. Chocolate is usually brown but sometimes white.
2 (*plural* **chocolates**) a small sweet made from chocolate *a box of chocolates*
3 (*plural* **chocolates**) a drink made from chocolate *a hot chocolate*

ORIGIN from *chocolatl*, a word in Nahuatl, a Central American language

choice *noun* **choices**
1 the action of choosing something or the opportunity to choose between different things *Have you made a choice? We have no choice.*
2 something you choose *This blue dress is my choice.*
3 a number of different things you can choose from *The shop has a wide choice of T-shirts.*

choir ['kwire', to rhyme with 'wire'] *noun* **choirs**
a group of people who sing together, for example in a school or church. Someone who sings in a choir is a chorister.

choke *verb*
chokes, choking, choked
1 to find it hard to breathe, for example because there is not enough air *I'm choking in all this smoke.*
2 to stop breathing, for example because of something stuck in your throat, or to stop someone breathing *He nearly choked on a fish bone. She was so angry she wanted to choke me!*
3 to block something *The drain was completely choked with leaves.*

cholera ['kol-er-rer'] *noun*
a serious illness affecting the stomach and intestines. It is caused by drinking water or eating food containing bacteria (tiny harmful living things), often from waste from the human body.

cholesterol ['ker-lest-er-ol'] *noun*
a substance in the fat, blood and cells (smallest units of living matter) of the body. Too much of it can cause an illness in the heart and make it harder for blood to flow through the arteries (tubes that carry blood from the heart).

chomp *verb*
chomps, chomping, chomped
to chomp on food is to eat it in a noisy way

choose *verb*
chooses, choosing, chose, chosen
1 if you choose something or someone from among two or more things or people, you decide which of them you want *I chose the green shirt, not the blue one.*
2 if you choose to do something, you do it because you want to

choosy *adjective* choosier, choosiest
if someone is choosy, they are hard to please because they only want the things that they like very much and will not accept anything else

chop *verb*
chops, chopping, chopped
1 to cut something into pieces, for example wood, using an axe, or food, using a knife or chopper *First, chop up the onions.*
2 to cut something with a heavy sharp tool *They chopped down the tree.*

chop *noun* chops
1 a small piece of meat on a bone, usually from a pig or lamb *a pork chop*
2 a karate chop is hitting someone hard with the side of the hand
3 a chopping action

chopper *noun* choppers
1 a big knife with a square blade for cutting meat
2 an informal word for a helicopter

choppy *adjective* choppier, choppiest
a choppy sea has lots of waves because of winds or storms

chopstick *noun* chopsticks
one of the two thin sticks used for eating Chinese food and the food of many East Asian countries. Chopsticks are usually made of wood or plastic and are held in one hand.

ORIGIN from *chop* 'quick' (from Cantonese *kap*) and English *stick*

choral ['kor-erl'] *adjective*
connected with the music sung by a choir *choral music*

chord ['kord'] *noun* chords
musical notes played together that produce a pleasant sound

LANGUAGE EXTRA be careful not to confuse *chord* with *cord* (thick string)

chore *noun* chores
1 household chores are regular and sometimes boring activities that people have to do, such as shopping, cleaning or doing the washing-up
2 a boring and unpleasant activity that you have to do *My teacher says writing reports can be a real chore.*

chorister ['kor-iss-ter'] *noun* choristers
someone who sings in a choir

chortle *verb*
chortles, chortling, chortled
to laugh loudly

ORIGIN from *chuckle* and *snort*, invented by the author Lewis Carroll in 1871

chorus ['chor' is pronounced 'core'] *noun* choruses
1 a part of a song containing words that you repeat after singing each of the main parts (or verses) of the song
2 a large group of singers
3 a piece of music sung by a large group of singers
4 a group of dancers, singers and actors in a play
5 a group of people speaking at the same time

chose
past tense of choose

chosen
past participle of choose

chow mein [pronounce 'mein' like 'main'] *noun*
a Chinese dish of noodles with small pieces of meat and vegetables

Christ *noun*
the founder of Christianity. He is also known as Jesus Christ or Jesus.

christen *verb*
christens, christening, christened
to welcome a baby into the Christian religion and give him or her a name

christening *noun*
the ceremony of welcoming a baby into the Christian religion and giving him or her a name. During the ceremony the baby is baptised (water is poured over him or her).

Christian *noun* Christians
someone who believes in Jesus Christ

Christian *adjective*
connected with the religion of Christians

Christianity *noun*
the religion of Christians

Christmas *noun*
1 a religious holiday on 25 December when Christians celebrate the birth of Jesus
2 a public holiday on 25 December when many people give each other presents

LANGUAGE EXTRA 25 December is also called *Christmas Day*

Christmas box *noun* Christmas boxes
money given at Christmas to people who provide services, such as a hairdresser or a person who delivers the newspaper to your home

Christmas Eve *noun*
the day before Christmas

Christmas tree *noun* Christmas trees
a fir tree, or part of a tree, decorated with lights to celebrate Christmas. Some Christmas trees are not real trees, for example they are made out of plastic. People usually have them in their homes during Christmas.

chrome *noun*
a metal mixed with chromium, used for covering other metals to give them a shiny finish *chrome taps*

chromium *noun*
a hard shiny metal element

chromosome *noun* chromosomes
the part of a living cell (smallest unit of living matter) containing the genes (information) that control the shape, size and special qualities of a human, animal or plant

chronic *adjective*
1 a chronic illness or pain is one that lasts for a long time without getting better
2 a chronic problem is one that keeps happening *a chronic shortage of good teachers*
3 a slang way of saying very bad

chronically *adverb*
if someone is chronically ill, they have a serious illness that will not get better

chronicle *noun* chronicles
a record of historical events with their dates

chronological *adjective*
arranged in the order that things happened *The police officer wrote down the events in chronological order.* **chronologically** *adverb*

chronology *noun*
1 the order that events happen in, for example in history
2 (*plural* chronologies) a description of events in the order that they happen

chrysalis ['kriss-er-liss'] *noun* chrysalises
the hard cover around a caterpillar before it turns into a butterfly or moth

chrysanthemum ['kriz-an-ther-merm'] *noun* chrysanthemums
a garden plant with brightly coloured flowers

chubby *adjective* chubbier, chubbiest
slightly fat, often in a way that looks pleasant

chuck *verb*
chucks, chucking, chucked
an informal way of saying to throw *Chuck the ball to me. I chucked out my old exercise books.*

chuckle *verb*
chuckles, chuckling, chuckled
to laugh quietly *Dad was chuckling to himself.* **chuckle** *noun*

chuffed *adjective* (informal)
pleased about something

chug *verb*
chugs, chugging, chugged
to make a low heavy sound, like the sound made by a car engine or a train running slowly *The old car was chugging up the hill.*

chum *noun* chums
an informal word for a friend

chummy *adjective* chummier, chummiest
an informal way of saying friendly

chunk *noun* chunks
a big piece of something, often cut off from something larger

chunky *adjective* chunkier, chunkiest
big, thick and heavy

church *noun* churches
1 a building where Christians pray and celebrate their religion
2 the Christian religion or a particular type of it *He belongs to the Church of England.*

churchyard–civilised

churchyard *noun* **churchyards**
the land around a church where people are buried

churn *verb*
churns, churning, churned
1 to move liquid about quickly
2 to make butter in a churn
3 to churn things out is to produce lots of them very quickly *This author churns out two novels a year.*

churn *noun* **churns**
1 a container for making milk into butter
2 a big container for milk

chute ['shoot'] *noun* **chutes**
1 a long tube for sliding things down *a rubbish chute*
2 a long slope for people to slide down *a water chute*

chutney *noun*
a sauce made from fruit, spices and sugar. Chutney is eaten with meat or cheese.

cider *noun* **ciders**
a strong alcoholic drink made from apples

cigar *noun* **cigars**
a tube made from rolled-up tobacco leaves that people smoke

cigarette *noun* **cigarettes**
a small thin tube of paper with tobacco inside that people smoke

cinder *noun* **cinders**
1 a piece of coal or wood that has been almost completely burnt
2 if something is burnt to a cinder, it is completely burnt

cinema *noun*
1 (*plural* **cinemas**) a place where films are shown
2 the business or art of making films *the cinema of Walt Disney*
3 films in general that you see in a cinema *My brother loves the cinema.*

cinnamon *noun*
a brown spice used for giving a taste to cakes and other sweet things

circle *noun* **circles**
1 a completely round flat shape like the letter O
2 a group of people, usually people who have the same interests *a circle of friends*
3 the first floor seats upstairs in a cinema or theatre

> **ORIGIN** from Latin *circulus* 'little ring' (from *circus* 'ring')

circle *verb*
circles, circling, circled
1 to move or travel in a circle around something *The plane was circling the airport.*
2 to put a circle around something such as a word *The teacher has circled all the spelling mistakes.*

circuit ['serr-kit'] *noun* **circuits**
1 the places that someone visits regularly, often for their job *He's a famous author who gives talks on the school circuit.*
2 an electrical circuit is the path an electric current travels round
3 a round track for racing cars or bicycles
4 a circular journey

circuitous ['ser-kyoo-it-ers'] *adjective*
a circuitous route between two places is not the shortest and quickest way but a longer and more complicated way

> **SYNONYM** roundabout

circular *adjective*
1 round like a circle *a circular mirror*
2 going round in a circle *a circular bus route*

circular *noun* **circulars**
an official document or advertisement sent to lots of people

circulate *verb*
circulates, circulating, circulated
1 to move all around something or to make something do this *Blood circulates in the veins. Our fan circulates cool air around the room.*
2 to send something such as a letter to a lot of people
3 if information or rumours circulate, they gradually become known to lots of people

circulation *noun*
1 the circulation of blood is when it moves around the body
2 the total number of copies of a newspaper or magazine that are sold, for example each day, week or month
3 when something is used by lots of people *There are lots of these coins in circulation.*

circulatory *adjective*
connected to the movement of blood around the body *circulatory problems*; *the circulatory system* (for example the heart, arteries and veins)

circumference *noun* **circumferences**
the outside edge of a circle or of any round shape

> **ORIGIN** from Latin *circum* 'around' and *ferre* 'to carry'

circumflex *noun* **circumflexes**
a circumflex or circumflex accent is the symbol ^ above a letter in some languages such as French, for example ê or ô

circumstance *noun* **circumstances**
1 the special facts connected with a particular event or situation *Under the circumstances, I think you did the right thing.*
2 someone's circumstances are the amount of money they have to live on and their type of life *Let the school know if your circumstances change.*

circus *noun* **circuses**
a travelling show of clowns and acrobats and sometimes animals such as elephants, horses and lions. It usually takes place in a large tent called a big top.

> **ORIGIN** from Latin *circus* 'ring'. This is the shape of the central area of the circus where the show is performed.

cistern *noun* **cisterns**
1 a container for supplying water to a building
2 a water container for flushing a toilet

citadel *noun* **citadels**
a strong building in the past where people could go to be safe if their city was attacked

citizen *noun* **citizens**
1 someone who lives in a particular country or town
2 someone who was born in a particular country and has the benefits and responsibilities of that country

citizenship *noun*
1 the right to live in a particular country *He applied for British citizenship.*
2 the behaviour and responsibilities of a good citizen *All students must study citizenship.*

citric acid *noun*
a weak acid in citrus fruits such as oranges, lemons and limes

citrus fruit *noun* **citrus fruits**
a juicy fruit such as an orange, lemon, lime or grapefruit

city *noun* **cities**
1 a large and important town
2 the City is the business and banking centre in London

> **LANGUAGE EXTRA** also called the *City of London*

civic *adjective*
1 connected with a city *civic leaders*
2 connected with the citizens of a country or town *civic duties*

civil *adjective*
1 polite *Be more civil to your teachers.*
2 connected with ordinary people *civil unrest* (trouble caused by ordinary people)
3 not criminal *a civil court*
4 not religious *a civil wedding*
5 not connected with soldiers or fighting *an aircraft for civil use*

civility *noun*

civil engineer *noun* **civil engineers**
someone who designs and builds roads, bridges and large buildings
civil engineering *noun*

civilian *noun* **civilians**
someone who is not a soldier or police officer *civilian casualties*

civilisation *noun*
1 (*plural* **civilisations**) a particular society with a high level of organisation *ancient Greek civilisation*
2 human society in general with its high level of organisation *A nuclear war might mean the end of civilisation.*
3 a place where there are lots of people *After months at sea, the sailor wanted to get back to civilisation.*

> **LANGUAGE EXTRA** also spelt *civilization*

civilise *verb*
civilises, civilising, civilised
1 to get people to behave in a polite and reasonable way
2 to give people the knowledge and skills of a civilised society

> **LANGUAGE EXTRA** also spelt *civilize*

civilised *adjective*
1 a civilised society or country is well organised and has laws that are fair to all
2 polite *He's always very civilised.*

civil rights – classic

3 reasonable *Eight o'clock in the morning is a civilised time to get up.*
4 pleasant to an educated person *They spent a very civilised afternoon talking about books.*

> LANGUAGE EXTRA also spelt *civilized*

civil rights noun plural
the rights that all people should have to be free, to be treated in a fair and equal way in law and to be allowed to vote

civil service noun
the different sections of a country's government and all the people who work for them (called civil servants)

civil war noun civil wars
a war between different groups of people in the same country

> CULTURE NOTE important *civil wars* of the past include the *English Civil War* (1642–51), the *American Civil War* (1861–65) and the *Spanish Civil War* (1936–39)

clack verb
clacks, clacking, clacked
to make the short loud sound of a hard object hitting another, often when this sound is repeated *We heard the sound of shoes clacking across the playground.*
clack noun

clad adjective (old-fashioned)
wearing or covered in something *a figure clad in black*

claim verb
claims, claiming, claimed
1 to ask for something that belongs to you or that you think you should be allowed to have *If you can't come, you can claim a refund.*
2 to say that something is true even though you can't prove it *She claimed she had lost her smartphone.*
3 to win something *He claimed first prize in the competition.*
4 to get back your luggage at an airport when you've been on a flight

claim noun claims
1 when you claim something that is yours *Fill in this form to make a claim.*
2 when you say that something is true *The claims of every scientist must be checked.*

claimant noun claimants
someone who asks for money, especially from the government *benefit claimants*

clam noun clams
a shellfish that you can eat. It has a soft body with a small foot and lives inside a shell made up of two parts joined together.

clamber verb
clambers, clambering, clambered
to climb somewhere using your hands as well as your feet because it is not easy *I clambered over the wall.*

clammy adjective clammier, clammiest
wet and sticky in a way that you find unpleasant *clammy hands*

clamp noun clamps
1 a tool for holding things together
2 a metal object put on one wheel of a car to stop someone driving it

clamp verb
clamps, clamping, clamped
1 to hold or put something tightly against something else
2 to hold two things together using a clamp
3 to put a clamp on the wheel of a car to stop someone driving it, usually because it has been parked in the wrong place
4 to clamp down on something is to stop something bad or to stop people doing something bad *The police are clamping down on people using their mobiles while driving.*

> SYNONYM for sense 4: to crack down on

clan noun clans
1 a group of families with the same family name, especially in Scotland *He belongs to the MacDonald clan.*
2 a very big family

> ORIGIN from Scottish Gaelic *clann* 'family'

clang verb
clangs, clanging, clanged
to make the loud ringing noise of big metal objects hitting each other *We heard the church bells clanging in the distance.*
clang noun

clank verb
clanks, clanking, clanked
to make the short loud noise of heavy metal objects or machines *Old trams clanked along the streets of Vienna.* **clank** noun

clap verb
claps, clapping, clapped
1 if you clap or clap your hands, you hit the palms of your hands together many times to show that you like something or agree with what someone has said
2 to put something somewhere quickly *He clapped his hand over his mouth.*

clap noun claps
1 the action of clapping your hands *We gave the singer a loud clap.*
2 a clap of thunder is the sudden loud noise made by thunder

clapped-out adjective (informal)
old and not working properly *a clapped-out computer running very old software*

clapper noun clappers
the loose metal part inside a bell that hits the sides of the bell to make it ring

clapperboard noun clapperboards
an object used in film-making consisting of two connected pieces of wood with numbers on them. The pieces of wood are banged together at the start of a film scene. This makes it easier to match the sound and the pictures.

clarify verb
clarifies, clarifying, clarified
to explain something clearly
clarification noun

clarinet noun clarinets
a musical instrument made up of a long tube that you play by blowing into it over a reed (thin strip of wood that vibrates). You press keys (small buttons or levers) along the tube to change the notes.
clarinettist noun

clarity noun
1 the quality of being able to be seen or heard clearly *the clarity of the photo*
2 the quality of explaining or understanding something clearly *Our teacher talked about the poem with great clarity.*

clash verb
clashes, clashing, clashed
1 if two events or TV or radio programmes clash, they happen at the same time, which causes you a problem *The film I wanted to see clashes with the news.*
2 if metal objects clash, they make a loud ringing noise when hitting each other, like cymbals or swords
3 if colours clash, they don't look right together
4 if people clash, they start arguing or fighting with each other

clash noun clashes
1 a problem caused by events or programmes happening at the same time
2 a loud ringing noise made by metal objects hitting each other
3 an argument or fight between people
4 when people or groups are so different from each other that they cannot both exist in the same place *There's a clash of personality between the two teachers.*

clasp noun
1 (plural **clasps**) a small metal object for fastening things such as a bag, watch or piece of jewellery
2 the action of holding something or someone tightly

clasp verb
clasps, clasping, clasped
to hold something or someone tightly

class noun classes
1 a group of children or students taught together
2 a period of time when children or students are taught together *The class starts at two o'clock.*
3 a group of things, people or animals that are similar to each other *These butterflies belong to a different class altogether.*
4 the level or quality of something or someone, or the group they are put into *to travel by second class*; *Dalí is an artist in a class of his own.*
5 the high level of quality or skill that someone has that makes them attractive or special *She's a dancer with lots of class.*
6 one of the groups in society based on people's jobs, education, the amount of money they have and the activities they like doing *Politicians try to please the middle classes.*

> ORIGIN from Latin *classis*, one of the divisions of the ancient Roman people

class verb
classes, classing, classed
to put people or things into a particular group *As a singer he is classed as one of the best.*

classic adjective
1 if something is classic, it happens a lot *a classic example*

> SYNONYMS common, usual

classic–clear

2 a classic film or piece of writing or music is popular and considered very good and important by most people at different periods of history *Melville's classic novel 'Moby Dick'*
3 simple and beautiful, and not having changed much with time *He was wearing a classic black suit.*
4 another way of saying excellent *a classic performance by the school team*

classic *noun*
1 (*plural* **classics**) something such as a film, book, song or TV programme that is popular and considered very good and important by most people at different periods of history
2 classics is the study of the language, history and literature of ancient Greece and Rome

classical *adjective*
1 classical music is serious music, usually written a long time ago by musicians such as Beethoven and Mozart, that people consider to be of high quality *My auntie prefers classical to modern composers.*
2 connected to the old or original style of something *classical ballet*; *classical Arabic*
3 connected with ancient Greece and Rome *classical mythology*

classification *noun*
1 putting things or people into groups
2 (*plural* **classifications**) a group that things or people are put into

classified *adjective*
1 a classified ad is a small advertisement that someone puts into a newspaper when they want to sell something
2 classified information is secret, for example known only by people in a government

classify *verb*
classifies, classifying, classified
to put things or people into groups

classmate *noun* **classmates**
someone in the same class as you at school

classroom *noun* **classrooms**
a room at school where you have lessons

classwork *noun*
the work that you do in the classroom

classy *adjective* **classier, classiest**
1 if a place such as a hotel or restaurant is classy, it is fashionable and attractive and usually expensive
2 if someone is classy, they have a high level of quality and skill and very good judgement

clatter *verb*
clatters, clattering, clattered
to make the short loud noise of objects banging against something *We could hear football boots clattering across the playground.* **clatter** *noun*

clause *noun* **clauses**
1 a clause in grammar is a part of a sentence with its own verb
compare: **phrase**

2 a legal clause is part of a document on a particular subject

LANGUAGE EXTRA a *clause* contains a subject and a verb. There are two types of clauses: main clauses and subordinate clauses. In the sentence *I went to bed after we finished dinner*, the main clause is *I went to bed* (subject *I* and verb *went*) and the subordinate clause is *after we finished dinner* (subject *we* and verb *finished*).
Main clauses are complete sentences and make sense by themselves. Subordinate clauses only make sense when you read them next to the main clause.

claustrophobia *noun*
the frightened feeling of not having enough room when you're in a small or crowded space

claw *noun* **claws**
1 one of the pointed curved nails on the feet of birds or animals such as cats
2 one of the large pointed parts at the end of the front legs of sea animals such as crabs and lobsters

claw *verb*
claws, clawing, clawed
to scratch or cut something or someone with claws or fingernails

clay *noun*
a kind of heavy sticky earth. It is used for making bricks and pottery. **clayey** *adjective*

clean *adjective* **cleaner, cleanest**
1 if something or someone is clean, they have no trace of dirt, dust or marks *a clean house*
2 if clothes or fabrics are clean, they have been washed *Please put on a clean shirt.*
3 if air and water are clean, they are pure and have no harmful substances in them
4 doing things to keep yourself clean *She's a very clean person.*
5 a clean sheet of paper has nothing written on it
6 showing that nothing wrong has been done *a clean driving licence*
7 done according to the rules *a clean fight*
8 clean language is not rude and doesn't upset people *Keep your jokes clean.*
9 smooth and regular *a clean cut*
10 to come clean about something is to start to tell the truth about it

SIMILE 'as clean as a whistle' means very clean (especially senses 1, 2, 6 & 9)

clean *verb*
cleans, cleaning, cleaned
1 to get rid of dirt, dust or marks from something
2 to clean your teeth is to brush them with a toothbrush and toothpaste
3 to clean people's houses *She cleans for several people in Oxford.*
4 to clean a place up is to make it clean and tidy *It's time to clean up your room.*
5 to get rid of something dirty or untidy *Please clean up the mess.*
6 to clean yourself up is to wash yourself

clean *noun*
the action of cleaning something *Dad gave the cupboard a good clean.*

clean *adverb*
an informal way of saying completely *The thief got clean away.*

cleaner *noun* **cleaners**
1 someone who cleans the inside of offices or houses
2 something used for cleaning *a vacuum cleaner*
3 a cleaner or cleaner's is a shop that cleans clothes

cleanliness ['klen-lee-ners'] *noun*
when you keep yourself and other things clean *Jo has high standards of cleanliness.*

cleanly *adverb*
completely, smoothly and with one movement *He broke the stick cleanly in half.*

cleanse ['klenz'] *verb*
cleanses, cleansing, cleansed
to make something like your skin or a cut completely clean, for example by using special liquids or antiseptics

cleanser ['klenz-er'] *noun* **cleansers**
a special liquid for cleaning the skin, for example by removing make-up or dirt

clear *adjective* **clearer, clearest**
1 easy to see *The picture is very clear.*
2 easy to hear *The sound isn't very clear.*
3 easy to understand *The instructions are clear.*
4 certain that you understand something *Are you clear about what to do? I don't really have a clear idea* (good idea).
5 certain, and impossible to be mistaken about *It's clear we're going to be late.*
6 not blocked by anything *The road ahead is completely clear.*
7 if a place or area such as a room, garden or table is clear, things that you didn't want to be there have been taken away
8 not busy *Keep Friday clear for our trip to the museum.*
9 a clear sky has no clouds in it
10 clear skin is smooth and healthy-looking
11 if a liquid or if glass or plastic is clear, you can see through it
12 if medical tests are clear, they show nothing wrong

SIMILES 'as clear as a bell' (sense 2) and 'as clear as day' (senses 1 & 3) mean very clear; 'as clear as mud' (sense 3) means not clear at all

clear *verb*
clears, clearing, cleared
1 to get rid of things from somewhere where they are not wanted *Let's clear the table. I've cleared all the toys from the floor.*
2 if fog or smoke clears, it goes away
3 if the weather clears, the rain and clouds go away and it gets better
4 if someone is cleared of a crime, they are told that they are not guilty
5 to go over something without touching it *The horse easily cleared the fence.*
6 to clear work or a backlog is to do all the work that you have to do
7 to clear off or out is to go away from a place
8 to clear out a container or room is to empty it to make it clean and tidy

9 to clear up is to make a room look better by putting things back in the places where they should be
10 if an illness clears up, it gets better

clear *adverb*
1 away from something *Keep clear of the edge of the platform.*
2 completely *He threw the ball clear across the playground.*
3 clearly *I can hear you loud and clear.*

clearance *noun* **clearances**
1 official permission to do something
2 the clearance between two objects is the space between them that stops one object touching the other

clear-cut *adjective*
used about something people can be certain about *There's a clear-cut difference between my parents' ideas and those of my teacher.*

clearing *noun* **clearings**
a small space without trees in a forest

clearly *adverb*
1 in a way that you can see, hear or understand easily *Can you speak clearly?*
2 used for saying that something is definitely true *You're clearly wrong.*
3 if you think clearly, your thoughts are reasonable and logical

clef *noun* **clefs**
a symbol at the beginning of a line of music that shows the high or low quality (or pitch) of the notes

clementine *noun* **clementines**
a fruit like a small orange

clench *verb*
clenches, clenching, clenched
to hold your fists, teeth or another part of your body closely together *She was so angry she clenched her fists.*

clergy *noun plural*
the people in charge of religious activities, especially in the Christian church. A man who is a member of the clergy is known as a clergyman and a woman is known as a clergywoman.

cleric *noun* **clerics**
a religious leader *a Muslim cleric*

clerical *adjective*
1 connected with office work *clerical workers*; *a clerical error* (mistake made by someone working in an office)
2 connected with the clergy, especially in the Christian religion

clerk ['klahk'] *noun* **clerks**
1 someone who works in an office or bank, for example looking after documents or keeping records
2 in American English, a clerk is someone who works in a shop or at the desk of a hotel

> **LANGUAGE EXTRA** the American pronunciation of *clerk* rhymes with 'circ' in 'circle'

clever *adjective* **cleverer, cleverest**
1 intelligent, and quick to learn and understand things
2 good at doing things, for example with your hands *She's clever at designing and making clothes.*
3 good at getting what you want, for example by making someone believe something or being nice to them or by being dishonest *a clever politician*; *It was a clever trick to steal the money.*
4 done or made with skill *a clever gadget*
5 excellent, and showing that you've thought carefully about something *What a clever idea!*

cleverly *adverb* **cleverness** *noun*

cliché ['klee-shay'] *noun* **clichés**
a phrase or idea that has been used so many times that people may feel it is no longer interesting or useful

click *verb*
clicks, clicking, clicked
1 if something clicks or you click it, it makes a short hard sound *I clicked the switch to turn on the light.*
2 if you click your tongue, you make a small sound with it, for example when you do not like something
3 to press the left or right button on your computer mouse to make your computer do something *Click on the icon to open the Start menu.*
4 to suddenly understand something *I was trying to figure it out all day and then it clicked!*

click *noun* **clicks**
1 a short hard sound
2 when you make your computer do something by clicking the mouse *Help is only a mouse click away.*

clickable *adjective*
if something on a computer screen is clickable, you can click on it with the mouse to make an action happen *This link is not clickable.*

client *noun* **clients**
someone who uses the services of a company or of a professional person such as a lawyer or accountant

cliff *noun* **cliffs**
a very steep rock, usually next to the sea *the White Cliffs of Dover*

cliffhanger *noun* **cliffhangers**
an exciting part at the end of a TV programme, film or story where you do not know what is going to happen next

> **ORIGIN** at the end of old films and stories, the main character was often left *hanging* over the edge of a *cliff* and people had to wait for the next episode to see what happened

climate *noun* **climates**
the sort of weather that a particular country or area usually has **climatic** *adjective*

climax *noun* **climaxes**
the climax of something such as a story, film or event is the most exciting part of it, often near the end *The climax of the match came when he scored the only goal.*

climb *verb*
climbs, climbing, climbed
1 to go up somewhere *We climbed onto the bus. Be careful when you climb up the ladder.*
2 if you climb down somewhere, you go down *Climb down slowly or you might fall.*
3 to go up to a higher level *Temperatures have been climbing all week.*
4 if you climb down, for example in an argument, you say you are wrong
5 if a plant climbs, it grows tall by attaching itself to something such as a fence, wall or pole

climb *noun* **climbs**
the action of climbing *It was a difficult climb to the top of the mountain.*

climber *noun* **climbers**
1 someone who climbs mountains or rocks as a sport
2 a person, animal or plant that climbs

cling *verb*
clings, clinging, clung
1 if you cling to something or someone, you hold on to them tightly
2 if something clings to something, it sticks to it *My wet jeans clung to my legs.*

clingfilm *noun*
thin transparent plastic for putting around food to keep it fresh

clinic *noun* **clinics**
1 a place where people go to see a doctor or nurse
2 the period of time when you can see a doctor or nurse *The doctor's clinic starts at two o'clock.*

clinical *adjective*
connected with illness or people who are ill *clinical symptoms*

clink *verb*
clinks, clinking, clinked
to make the short ringing noise of glass or a small metal object hitting something *We clinked our glasses.* **clink** *noun*

clip *noun* **clips**
1 a small metal or plastic object that fastens things together or that fastens something to something else *a paper clip*
2 if people show a clip of a film or TV programme, they show a short part of it by itself

clip *verb*
clips, clipping, clipped
1 to fasten something with a clip *I clipped my mobile to my belt.*
2 to be fastened with a clip *This badge clips on to your sweater.*
3 to cut something to make it tidier, for example with scissors or clippers *My stepdad clips his beard once a week.*
4 to remove something by cutting it *Clip these pictures from the magazine.*

clip art *noun*
pictures that you copy from computer programs, CD-ROMs or the internet for using on your own computer *a clip art gallery*

> **LANGUAGE EXTRA** also spelt *clipart*

clipboard *noun* **clipboards**
1 a small hard board with a clip on top used for holding paper to write on while you are moving around
2 the clipboard of a computer is the part of its memory where information or a picture is stored as you copy it from one place to another on your computer

clip-clop – cloth

clip-clop noun
the sound made by a horse's hooves when it walks on a hard surface **clip-clop** verb

clipper noun **clippers**
a fast ship with sails, used especially in the 19th century

clippers noun plural
a tool with small blades, pressed or moved together, that you use for cutting small amounts off things to make them tidy. Clippers come in different shapes and sizes and are used especially for cutting nails, hair or hedges (thick bushes). *nail clippers*

clipping noun **clippings**
something cut from a newspaper or magazine, for example an article or picture

cloak noun **cloaks**
a type of loose coat without sleeves that hangs from the shoulders and is fastened around the neck

cloakroom noun **cloakrooms**
1 a room in a building for leaving things such as your coat, bag or umbrella
2 a polite word for a toilet

clobber verb (informal)
clobbers, clobbering, clobbered
1 to hit someone hard
2 to beat someone very easily in a game or sport *Our team has got clobbered again.*

clock noun **clocks**
1 a piece of equipment for showing what time it is
2 **around the clock** all day and all night without stopping

clock verb
clocks, clocking, clocked
if someone clocks in (or off) at work, they record the time they start (or finish) work onto a special card *Rashid clocks in at seven every morning.*

clockwise adverb & adjective
moving in the same direction as the hands of a clock

> ANTONYM anticlockwise

clockwork noun
1 clockwork toys or machines have springs inside. You make them work by winding them up with a special key. *an old clockwork soldier*
2 if something happens like clockwork, it happens without problems or regularly, in the same way each time

clod noun **clods**
an informal word for a stupid or clumsy fool

clog verb
clogs, clogging, clogged
to block something, such as a pipe or road, so that it is difficult or impossible for anything to pass through *clogged drains; The motorway is getting clogged up.*

clog noun **clogs**
a shoe with a wooden sole and usually without a part covering the heel

cloister noun **cloisters**
cloisters are paths covered with a roof that go round the sides of an open square area at the centre of a building such as a cathedral or church

clone noun **clones**
an animal or plant that is the exact copy of another because it is created from the cells (smallest units of living matter) of the other animal or plant

clone verb
clones, cloning, cloned
to create an animal or plant by copying it exactly

close ['klohss'] adjective closer, closest
1 not far away *My school is very close. Our house is close to the school.*

> SYNONYM near

2 not far away in time *The end of term is quite close.*

> SYNONYM near

3 very careful and paying attention to details *I'm going to have a close look at your homework.*
4 if people are close or if someone is close to someone else, they like each other very much *She has a handful of close friends.*
5 a close relative is someone related to you directly such as a parent, brother or sister
6 hot and sticky and without much fresh air *The weather's very close tonight.*
7 almost, or similar to something *Your answer isn't quite right but it's close enough. The number is close to a hundred.*
8 if someone has a close haircut, their hair is so short that it is almost at the level of their skin
9 if you say that something was close or a close shave, you mean that something bad or dangerous almost happened
10 if a game, competition or election is close, one side wins but only just *Jack won the class vote but the result was very close.*
11 if something is a close fit, it is very tight *We managed to squeeze in an extra desk, but it was a close fit.*

close ['klohss'] adverb closer, closest
not far away *Come closer. Don't walk too close to the edge. There are no houses close by. The picture was clearer close up.*

> SYNONYM near

close ['klohz'] verb
closes, closing, closed
1 if you close something, you move it so that an empty space or a gap is covered and it is no longer open *I closed the door. Can I close the curtains? Close your eyes.*
2 if something closes by itself, it moves so that an empty space or a gap is covered *The door closed behind me.*
3 if you close something such as a book or umbrella, you move its parts together so that no empty space is left between them and you cannot use it
4 to stop doing business or being open to the public, for example at the end of a working day *The bank closes at 5 p.m.*
5 to stop people from going into and out of somewhere, or from passing through somewhere *They've closed the school because of the snow.*
6 if an event or activity closes, or if someone closes it, it stops happening and comes to an end *The play closed last week.*
7 if you close a computer program or if it closes, it stops operating *Close down all programs before turning off your laptop.*
8 if a shop, company or public building closes down, it stops doing business completely and will not open again *Our local hospital has closed down.*
9 if the police or soldiers close in on someone, they get closer to them because they want to stop them from escaping

Close ['klohss'] noun
used in names of streets, especially streets that are closed at one end *He lives at 10 Cherry Close.*

closed adjective
1 covering an empty space or a gap *a closed door*
2 if something such as a book or umbrella is closed, its parts have been moved together and you cannot use it
3 if something such as a building or road is closed, people cannot go into it or out of it, or pass through it
4 if a shop or office is closed, it is not open to people for doing business
5 if someone's mind is closed, they do not want to accept new ideas

closely ['klohss-lee'] adverb
1 very carefully and paying a lot of attention *You have to watch the baby closely.*
2 having a strong connection with someone or something *We're closely related because he's my brother.*
3 very much *Humans closely resemble chimpanzees.*
4 without much time or distance between things *The teacher left, closely followed by the rest of the class. We were closely packed together on the tube.*

closet ['klo-zit'] noun **closets**
in American English, a piece of furniture or a small room built into a wall. It is used for storing things such as clothes.

close-up ['klohss-up'] noun **close-ups**
1 a photo or part of a film that shows the image of something or someone to be very big because the camera is very close or because special equipment such as a zoom lens is used
2 on a computer, a picture that is made bigger using software. For example, you can remove the part you don't want from a larger picture and make the rest of the image bigger.

closure ['kloh-jer'; 'j' has the middle sound of 'pleasure'] noun **closures**
the closure of a shop, company or public building is when it stops doing business completely

clot noun **clots**
1 a thick lump of something, especially blood *a blood clot*
2 an informal word for a stupid fool

clot verb
clots, clotting, clotted
if blood or another liquid clots, it forms a thick lump or lumps

cloth noun
1 material for making things such as clothes, curtains or blankets. It is made from substances such as cotton, wool or silk.

76

2 (*plural* **cloths**) a piece of cloth, for example for cleaning a surface or covering a table

clothe *verb*
clothes, clothing, clothed
to put clothes on someone

clothed *adjective*
wearing clothes *clothed in white*; *fully clothed* (wearing all your clothes)

clothes *noun plural*
the things you wear on your body, such as jeans, shirts or socks

clothesline *noun* clotheslines
a long rope that you put outdoors for hanging wet clothes on when they have just been washed

SYNONYM washing line

clothing *noun*
another word for clothes

cloud *noun* clouds
1 a white or grey shape in the sky that contains a mass of tiny drops of water
2 a mass of something floating in the sky, for example smoke, dust or insects
3 the cloud is a place on the internet where files and programs are stored

cloud *verb*
clouds, clouding, clouded
if the sky clouds over, it becomes dark and full of clouds

cloudburst *noun* cloudbursts
a short period when a lot of rain falls

SYNONYM downpour

cloud computing *noun*
a type of computing where you run programs and store files on the internet instead of on your own computer

cloudless *adjective*
a cloudless day or sky is bright and clear because there are no clouds

cloudy *adjective* cloudier, cloudiest
1 full of clouds
2 if a liquid is cloudy, you cannot see through it

clout *verb* (informal)
clouts, clouting, clouted
to hit someone hard with your hand
clout *noun*

clove *noun* cloves
1 a clove of garlic is one of the parts that make up the bulb of a garlic plant
2 a flower bud from a tropical tree. The bud is dried (water has been removed) and used as a spice.

clover *noun*
a small flowering plant that has leaves made up of three round parts of the same size

clown *noun* clowns
1 an entertainer in a circus who makes people laugh by doing and saying silly things. Clowns wear funny clothes with big shoes, lots of make-up on their face and a big red nose.
2 someone who makes people laugh, for example by making jokes
3 a very stupid or annoying person
clownish *adjective*

clown *verb*
clowns, clowning, clowned
to clown around is to do silly things

club *noun* clubs
1 a heavy stick for hitting people or animals
2 a golf club is a thin metal stick with a curved end for hitting the ball
3 a group of people with the same interests who meet to take part in activities *I've joined a chess club.*
4 the building where members of a club meet
5 a team of professional sports players *West Ham Football Club*
6 a place where people go to relax and enjoy themselves, for example by dancing or listening to music *a jazz club*
7 in a game of cards, a club is one of the four types of cards. It has a black picture of three round clover leaves. The other three types of playing cards are hearts, diamonds and spades.

club *verb*
clubs, clubbing, clubbed
1 to hit a person or animal with a heavy stick
2 if people club together, they get together to do something, especially to give money to buy something

clubbing *noun*
the activity of going out in the evenings to clubs for dancing and drinking

club soda *noun* club sodas
water with bubbles in it that can be drunk by itself or added to alcoholic drinks

SYNONYM soda water

cluck *verb*
clucks, clucking, clucked
when a chicken clucks, it makes a short low noise **cluck** *noun*

clue *noun* clues
1 a piece of information that helps you to find the answer to a puzzle or problem or that helps a police officer to solve a crime
2 if someone doesn't have a clue about something, they know nothing or have no idea about it

clueless *adjective*
if someone is clueless, they have no idea or understanding about something *When it comes to football, I'm clueless.*

clump *noun* clumps
1 a group of trees, bushes or plants that grow closely together
2 a small lump of something such as earth or hair

clumsy *adjective* clumsier, clumsiest
a clumsy person moves or does things in a careless way, such as bumping into things or knocking things over **clumsily** *adverb*
clumsiness *noun*

clung
past tense & past participle of **cling**

clunky *adjective* clunkier, clunkiest
big and heavy in an ugly way *clunky shoes*

cluster *noun* clusters
a group of things or people in the same place *a cluster of red flowers*

cluster *verb*
clusters, clustering, clustered
to form a group *Lots of students were clustering around the noticeboard.*

clutch *verb*
clutches, clutching, clutched
1 to hold something or someone tightly
2 to suddenly reach out to grab hold of something or someone *I slipped over and clutched at Dad's coat.*

clutch *noun* clutches
1 a piece of equipment in a car that a driver presses with one foot to change gear
2 a clutch of eggs is the number of eggs laid by a chicken at one time
3 a tight hold of something
4 to escape someone's clutches is to escape the power that they have over you

clutter *noun*
a mess that people make, for example in a room or building, by leaving lots of things lying around

clutter *verb*
clutters, cluttering, cluttered
to make a place untidy by leaving lots of things lying around

cm
short for **centimetre** or **centimetres**

c/o
short for **care of** (usually on an envelope or parcel) *T. Smith, c/o J. Evans*

Co.
short for **Company** *S. Patel & Co.*

coach *noun* coaches
1 a large road vehicle, with no upstairs floor, that passengers pay to travel in over long distances
2 one of the separate long parts of a train where the passengers sit

SYNONYM carriage

3 a vehicle pulled by horses, used especially in past times

SYNONYM carriage

4 a person who gives someone training in a sport or skill *a football coach*

ORIGIN from Hungarian *kocsi szekér* 'carriage from Kocs', a town in Hungary where coaches to be pulled by horses were first made in the 16th century

coach *verb*
coaches, coaching, coached
to train someone in a sport or skill

coal *noun*
1 a hard black rock that is dug out of the ground and burnt to make heat
2 a coal mine is a place in the ground from where coal is dug

coalition *noun* coalitions
a government made up of people from two or more different political parties

coarse *adjective* coarser, coarsest
1 having a rough surface *coarse cloth*
2 rude *a coarse joke*
3 thick or made up of thick pieces *coarse hair*; *coarse salt*
coarsely *adverb* **coarseness** *noun*

coast–coffee

coast *noun* coasts
1 the area of a country next to the sea *a visit to the Norfolk coast*
2 the piece of land, made up of sand and rocks, that runs along the edge of the sea *I love walking along the coast.*

SYNONYM seashore

3 if you tell someone that the coast is clear, you mean that it's safe to do something, such as run away, without being seen

coast *verb* coasts, coasting, coasted
to ride on a bicycle without pedalling or in a car with the engine switched off *I coasted down the hill on my bike.*

coastal *adjective*
near the coast *a coastal town*

coaster *noun* coasters
a thin flat object for putting under glasses or hot cups. A coaster protects a table from the liquid and the heat.

coastguard *noun* coastguards
someone who belongs to an organisation that helps people or boats in danger near the coast. Coastguards also watch the coast carefully to stop people smuggling.

coastline *noun* coastlines
the line showing the shape of the coast, for example on a map or seen from the air

coat *noun* coats
1 a piece of clothing with long sleeves that you wear over your other clothes to keep you warm. Long coats (for example overcoats) reach down to your knees and short ones (for example jackets) reach to the top of your legs.
2 an animal's coat is the hair that covers its body
3 a coat of paint is a thin layer of it that you put on something
4 a coat of arms is a design on a shield used by a family, organisation or town as their own special sign

coat *verb* coats, coating, coated
to cover something with a layer of something else *A choc-ice is an ice cream coated with chocolate.*

coating *noun* coatings
a layer of something

coatstand *noun* coatstands
a pole or frame with hooks at the top for hanging coats on

LANGUAGE EXTRA also spelt *coat stand*

coax *verb* coaxes, coaxing, coaxed
to persuade someone to do something by being extremely nice

cob *noun*
corn on the cob is the long hard part of the maize plant where the yellow seeds grow, which people cook and eat

cobalt *noun*
a silver-white metal and chemical element that is often mixed with other metals or used for giving substances a blue colour

cobble *verb* cobbles, cobbling, cobbled
to cobble something together is to produce it very quickly and without giving it a lot of attention

cobble *noun* cobbles
another word for a cobblestone

cobbled *adjective*
covered with cobblestones *a cobbled street*

cobbler *noun* cobblers
an old-fashioned word for someone who makes and repairs shoes

cobblestone *noun* cobblestones
cobblestones are round stones used in the past for making roads in towns

cobra *noun* cobras
a big poisonous snake from Africa or Asia. It spreads the skin of its neck when it is frightened.

cobweb *noun* cobwebs
a net of thin threads that a spider spins to catch insects. Cobwebs are often covered with dust and seen inside old buildings or hanging from ceilings in rooms that have not been cleaned.

ORIGIN from Middle English *copweb*, from *coppe* 'spider' and *web*

Coca-Cola *noun* (trademark)
a sweet brown fizzy drink

cock *noun* cocks
1 a male chicken

SYNONYM rooster

2 any male bird

cock-a-doodle-doo *noun*
the loud sound that a male chicken makes

cockatoo *noun* cockatoos
a large Australian parrot with a lot of feathers on its head

cockerel *noun* cockerels
a young male chicken

cocker spaniel *noun* cocker spaniels
a small dog with soft hair and long ears that hang down

cockle *noun* cockles
a small shellfish that you can eat

cockney *noun*
1 (*plural* **cockneys**) someone born in London, especially East London, who has a particular way of speaking and whose family sometimes has very little money
2 the type of English and the particular way of speaking used by cockneys

cockney *adjective*

ORIGIN from 14th-century English *cokeney* 'cock's egg' (an egg without a yolk – something considered useless). The word was originally used about anyone born in London within the sound of Bow Bells (the bells of St Mary-le-Bow Church in the old City of London).

cockpit *noun* cockpits
1 the place at the front of an aircraft where the pilot or pilots sit
2 the place in a racing car where the driver sits

cockroach *noun* cockroaches
a large dark brown insect like a beetle that lives in houses and comes out at night

cocktail *noun* cocktails
an alcoholic drink made from mixing different drinks together

cocky *adjective* cockier, cockiest
if someone is cocky, they do not show respect because they think they know better than other people

cocoa *noun*
1 a brown powder made from cocoa beans (the seeds of a tropical tree). This powder is used for making chocolate.
2 a hot drink with a chocolate taste made from cocoa powder, milk and sugar

coconut *noun*
1 (*plural* **coconuts**) a large brown hairy nut that is white inside and contains a clear liquid called milk, which you can drink. It grows on a special kind of palm tree.
2 the thick white flesh inside a coconut, which you can eat

cocoon *noun* cocoons
a silky covering that insects make around themselves as they change into their adult form

cod *noun* cod
a large sea fish with white flesh that is used as food

code *noun* codes
1 a system of letters, numbers and symbols for sending secret messages
2 a set of rules *Our school has a dress code* (rules about what to wear in school).
3 numbers, symbols, letters or colours that give information about something *a bar code* (pattern of lines printed on a product that give information about the product)
4 the part of a telephone number that shows where someone lives *The area code for central London is 0207.*
5 computer code is a list of instructions that tell a computer what to do

code *verb* codes, coding, coded
1 to give instructions to a computer to create your own website, software or app (program for a tablet or smartphone, for example) *I'm learning to code.*
2 to code a message is to put it into a secret code so that only the person receiving it knows what it means
3 to put numbers, symbols, letters or colours on something as a way of giving information about it

coder *noun* **coding** *noun*

codeine ['koh-deen'] *noun*
a substance that people swallow to get rid of pain

cod-liver oil *noun*
a yellow oil made from fish. People swallow a small amount of it regularly to stay healthy.

coeducational ['koh-ed-yoo-kay-sher-nerl'] *adjective*
a coeducational school is one where boys and girls are taught together

coeducation *noun*

coffee *noun*
1 a hot drink made from the seeds of a tropical tree called the coffee tree. The seeds, called coffee beans, are roasted (heated and dried) and then crushed.

2 a powder made from crushed coffee seeds, used for making this drink *a jar of coffee*
3 (*plural* **coffees**) a cup or mug of coffee

ORIGIN from Arabic *kahwa* and Turkish *kahve*

coffee shop *noun* **coffee shops**
a restaurant or shop where you can buy hot drinks such as coffee and tea and sometimes light meals or sandwiches. A coffee shop is sometimes inside another building such as a department store or railway station.

coffee table *noun* **coffee tables**
a small low table, usually in a living room. It is used for putting cups of tea or coffee on, for example.

coffin *noun* **coffins**
a box used for burying or cremating a dead person

cog *noun* **cogs**
1 a wheel in a machine with small teeth (or points) around its edge. The teeth fit into those of another wheel, so that when one wheel turns it makes the other wheel turn too.
2 one of the small teeth of a cog

cohesion *noun*
1 used for describing the quality of a piece of writing in which you connect words and ideas in a logical and thoughtful way so that it is clear how all the different meanings fit together
2 used for describing a way of putting things together in a thoughtful and sensible way

coil *noun* **coils**
1 something such as a wire or rope twisted into lots of small spiral loops *The telephone coil has got twisted again.*
2 one single loop of a coil

coil *verb*
coils, coiling, coiled
to twist something like a wire or rope around itself or around something else lots of times *The snake coiled itself around the tree.*

coin *noun* **coins**
a piece of metal used as money, usually flat and round

coin *verb*
coins, coining, coined
to invent a new word or expression

coinage *noun*
1 (*plural* **coinages**) a word or expression that someone has invented
2 the coins used in a particular country or place

coincide ['koh-in-side'] *verb*
coincides, coinciding, coincided
if two or more things coincide, they happen at the same time *My birthday coincides with the first day of exams.*

coincidence ['koh-in-sid-erns'] *noun* **coincidences**
when things happen accidentally at the same time or when surprising things become known *'I come from Leeds.' – 'What a coincidence! So do I.'*

coincidental *adjective*

coke *noun*
a hard grey fuel made out of coal

Coke *noun* **Cokes** (trademark)
a type of sweet brown fizzy drink
short for: **Coca-Cola**

cola *noun* **colas**
a sweet brown fizzy drink

colander ['kol-ern-der' or 'kul-ern-der'] *noun* **colanders**
a metal or plastic bowl with holes in it, used for example for washing vegetables or getting rid of liquid from food

cold *adjective* **colder, coldest**
1 if something is cold, it has a low temperature, for example below about 10–15 degrees Celsius (such as ice, snow, the climate at the North or South Poles or the weather in winter). Cold things can feel pleasant (like a cold drink) or unpleasant (like a cold room).
2 if someone is cold, they feel uncomfortable because the surrounding temperature is too low for them
3 unfriendly and not showing normal human feelings *Your cousins are very cold. I received a cold reply to my email.*

SIMILE 'as cold as ice' means very cold

cold *noun*
1 (*plural* **colds**) a slight illness, caused by a virus, that makes you sneeze and gives you a headache and runny nose
2 cold air or weather *I don't like the cold.*

cold *adverb*
completely and suddenly *The boxer was knocked out cold.*

cold-blooded *adjective*
1 a cold-blooded animal changes the temperature of its body to match its surroundings. All animals are cold-blooded except mammals and birds.
compare: **warm-blooded**
2 very cruel and evil, and showing no feelings

coldly *adverb*
if someone behaves coldly, they behave in an unfriendly way

coldness *noun*
when someone is unfriendly

cold snap *noun* **cold snaps**
a sudden very short period of cold weather

cold spell *noun* **cold spells**
a period of cold weather, for example lasting days or weeks

Cold War *noun*
the situation of dislike and distrust that existed between the former Soviet Union and the United States (and other countries who were friendly with these two countries). It lasted from the Second World War up to the 1980s.

coleslaw *noun*
a salad made from raw cabbage and carrots cut into thin pieces and mixed with mayonnaise

collaborate *verb*
collaborates, collaborating, collaborated
1 if people collaborate, they work together *I collaborated with Ed to write the school play.*
2 if someone collaborates with an enemy, they help them in secret, for example by giving them information
collaboration *noun*

collaborator *noun* **collaborators**
1 someone who works with someone else *The author had two collaborators on the book.*
2 someone who helps an enemy in secret

collage ['ko-lahj'; 'j' has the middle sound of 'pleasure'] *noun* **collages**
a picture made by sticking different things together on a surface, for example pieces of paper or cloth or pictures from newspapers stuck onto card

collapse *verb*
collapses, collapsing, collapsed
1 to fall down and break suddenly *The roof collapsed in the wind.*
2 if a person collapses, they fall to the ground because they suddenly become ill or weak
3 if someone collapses onto a chair or bed, they let themselves fall because they are very tired
4 if a piece of furniture such as a chair collapses, it is specially made so that it can be folded up easily

collapse *noun*
1 when something suddenly comes to an end *the collapse of the Soviet Union*
2 when something or someone collapses

collapsible *adjective*
if something is collapsible, it can be folded up *a collapsible table*

collar *noun* **collars**
1 the folded part of a shirt, coat, dress or something else that you wear that goes around your neck
2 a leather, metal or plastic band around the neck of a dog or cat

collate *verb*
collates, collating, collated
to collect and organise information and compare it with other information *The police computer collates data from across the country.*

colleague *noun* **colleagues**
1 a person someone works with
2 someone who does the same type of job as someone else *Teachers from our school will visit their colleagues in Hungary.*

collect *verb*
collects, collecting, collected
1 to get something, usually from different places *Go and collect some twigs to make a camp fire.*
2 to get and keep things as a hobby *Do you collect stamps?*
3 to get different things such as information, someone's rent or debts or a passenger's ticket *This website collects details about the people who use it.*
4 to go and get someone or something and bring them somewhere *Mum collected me from school today.*
5 to ask for money to help people *She's collecting for the Salvation Army.*
6 if something collects in a place, it gradually increases *Rain collects in this bucket.*
7 to gradually get more and more of something *These books have been collecting dust for years.*

collection *noun* **collections**
1 a group of things, for example things collected as a hobby *a stamp collection*
2 pieces of writing brought together in one book *a collection of short stories*
3 the action of collecting things
4 the action of asking for money, for example in the street or a church, in order to help people *The collection raised £1000 towards a new music room.*

collective *adjective*
including everyone or everything in a particular group *a collective decision*
collectively *adverb*

collective noun *noun* **collective nouns**
a singular noun that refers to several people or things considered as a group, such as 'family', 'team', 'army' or 'flock'. Collective nouns can usually be followed by either a singular or a plural verb, for example 'The team has won' or 'The team have won'.

collector *noun* **collectors**
1 someone who collects things as a hobby *a stamp collector*
2 someone who collects things such as rent, debts or passengers' tickets

college *noun* **colleges**
1 a place where students study for different types of qualifications after they leave school *a sixth-form college*; *an art college*
2 one of the parts that some large universities are divided into *Clare College, Cambridge*

collide *verb*
collides, colliding, collided
if people or things collide, they hit each other while they are moving *A bus has collided with a motorbike.*

collie *noun* **collies**
a dog with long hair and a long face, often used for looking after sheep

collision *noun* **collisions**
an accident in which a road vehicle or train hits something *The road is blocked because of a collision between several lorries.*

colloquial *adjective*
colloquial words and expressions are used in ordinary conversation but not in careful speaking or writing or in serious situations *'Brolly' is a colloquial word for 'umbrella'.*

Colombia *noun*
a country in South America
Colombian *adjective & noun*

colon *noun* **colons**
1 a punctuation mark consisting of two dots, one above the other, like this :
2 the lower part of the bowels (tubes inside the body that carry waste food out of the body)

> **LANGUAGE EXTRA** you use a *colon* before an explanation, quotation or list of different things. For example, *There's something I want you to know: I can't play chess* (explanation). *It was Shakespeare who wrote: 'To be or not to be. That is the question'* (quotation). *I speak three languages: English, French and Spanish* (list).

colonel ['kerr-nerl'] *noun* **colonels**
an army officer usually in charge of a regiment and with a lower rank than a brigadier

> **ORIGIN** from Old Italian *colonnello* 'column of soldiers'

colonial *adjective*
connected with a country that rules other countries *colonial rule*

colonise *verb*
colonises, colonising, colonised
1 if a country colonises another country, it takes control of it and sends some of its own people to live there
2 if animals colonise a place, they start living there in large numbers

> **LANGUAGE EXTRA** also spelt *colonize*

colony *noun* **colonies**
1 a country ruled by another country, usually one that is far away. The ruling country sends some of its own people to live there.
2 a group of people who live together or the place where they live *an artists' colony*
3 a group of animals, birds or insects that live together *an ant colony*

colossal *adjective*
very big *a colossal mistake*

> **SYNONYMS** huge, enormous

> **ORIGIN** from Greek *kolossos* 'giant statue', used about the statues of ancient Egypt and also about the bronze statue of the Greek god Apollo built in the 3rd century on the island of Rhodes. This statue was known as the *Colossus of Rhodes*.

colour *noun* **colours**
1 the colour of something is the way it reflects light. Red, blue, yellow and green are the names of some of the most important colours.
2 colours in general *Flowers add colour to the room. I watched an old film that wasn't in colour* (showed no colours but was in black, white and grey).
3 a paint or dye (a special liquid that gives colour to clothes) *Wash the jeans separately because the colour might run.*
4 if someone feels off colour, they feel slightly ill

colour *adjective*
1 using or showing different colours *colour printing*; *a colour palette* (for choosing colours in a computer program)
2 made up of a particular colour *colour ink* (for example in a printer)

colour *verb*
colours, colouring, coloured
1 if you colour a picture or colour it in, you use pencils, crayons or paints to put colour into the shapes that make up the picture
2 to change the colour of something *Use this chemical to colour the water blue.*

colour-blind *adjective*
if someone is colour-blind, they can't see the difference between some colours, usually red and green **colour-blindness** *noun*

colour-coded *adjective*
having different colours for showing different uses *The wires in a plug are colour-coded.*

coloured *adjective*
1 having any colour except black or white *a coloured shirt*
2 having a colour (or colours) of a particular kind *a brightly coloured room* (with strong colours); *a light-coloured T-shirt* (not dark)

colourfast *adjective*
used for describing a piece of clothing that will not lose its colour when it is washed

> **LANGUAGE EXTRA** you can also write *colour fast*

colourful *adjective*
1 having lots of different colours, especially bright ones
2 exciting and interesting *a colourful life*
colourfully *adverb*

colouring *noun*
1 (*plural* **colourings**) a substance that is added to food to give it a certain colour
2 the colour of someone's hair and skin
3 the activity of adding colours to pictures *a colouring book*

colourless *adjective*
something colourless has no colour *a colourless gas*

colt *noun* **colts**
a young male horse

> **LANGUAGE EXTRA** a young female horse is a *filly*

column *noun* **columns**
1 one of the tall stone posts that hold up a building or that are used for decorating it *the columns of the British Museum*
2 a tall post used as a monument to remember a person or event *Nelson's Column*
3 a block of words written under each other on a page, for example in a book or newspaper
4 a line of numbers or words written under each other, for example in a spreadsheet or table
compare: row (sense 3)
5 a regular article in a newspaper or magazine *My mum writes a music column in our local paper.*
6 a long line of something *a column of smoke rising into the air*; *a column of soldiers marching into battle*

columnist *noun* **columnists**
someone who writes a regular article in a newspaper or magazine

coma ['koh-mer'] *noun* **comas**
if someone is in a coma, they are unconscious because of an accident or illness, usually for a long time

comb *noun* **combs**
a piece of flat plastic or metal with little teeth (points) on one side that you use for making your hair tidy

comb *verb*
combs, combing, combed
1 to move a comb through your hair or someone else's hair to make it tidy
2 to search somewhere or something very carefully *The police combed the town looking for the little girl. I spent hours combing through Wikipedia trying to find information for my school project.*

combat noun combats
fighting, usually in a war

combat verb
combats, combating, combated
to fight against something bad, for example crime or global warming, in order to try to stop it

combination noun combinations
1 putting things together or when things are put together
2 two or more things together *a combination of wind and rain*
3 numbers or letters for opening a combination lock
4 a combination lock is a lock with numbers or letters on a dial (round part that you turn, on something such as a safe). You can only open it if you know what the numbers and letters are.

combine verb
combines, combining, combined
1 to put things together *We combined a week in Newcastle with a few days in Manchester. Try and combine all these ideas into one or two paragraphs.*
2 if things combine, they join together *The rain and wind combined to spoil our holiday.*

combine harvester noun
combine harvesters
a large machine that farmers use for cutting, separating and cleaning grain

combustible adjective
if a material is combustible, it burns easily

combustion noun
the series of actions that happen when a material burns

come verb
comes, coming, came, come
1 to move to the place where someone or something is *Come to the desk. I'll come back to your house tomorrow.*
2 to go somewhere with someone *Are you coming?*
3 to reach somewhere, something or someone *Has the letter come yet? The bus comes every 10 minutes.*
4 to move a certain distance *He's come a long way.*
5 to happen *The time has come for me to leave.*
6 to be in a certain position *I came first in the exam.*
7 to come about is to happen
8 to come across someone or something is to meet someone or find something by chance
9 to come along, come by or come over is to meet someone somewhere, for example at their home
10 if something that has happened before comes back, it happens again *The snow has come back.*
11 if you come by something hard to get, you manage to get it *I've come by an old map of Scotland.*
12 if someone comes from a place, they were born there or have their home there *She comes from Birmingham.*
13 if something comes from something else, that is where it started *This word comes from French.*
14 if something comes off, it stops being fixed to something *A button has come off my jacket.*
15 if something such as paint or dirt comes off, you can get rid of it easily
16 if someone comes off something such as a medicine, they stop taking it
17 if something such as news comes out, it becomes known
18 if a book comes out, it is printed and sold
19 if a film comes out, it is shown in cinemas
20 if someone comes round or comes to, they wake up after being unconscious
21 if something comes to a certain amount or number, it reaches a total *If you add 6 and 3, it comes to 9.*
22 if a problem comes up, it happens
23 if something comes up in a conversation or meeting, it is mentioned
24 if someone comes up with an idea or suggestion, they think of it

comeback noun comebacks
if someone (such as a film star) or something (such as a fashion) makes a comeback, they become popular again after a period when they were not popular

comedian noun comedians
someone who makes people laugh by telling jokes and funny stories

SYNONYM comic

comedy noun
1 (*plural* comedies) a particular film, play or TV programme that makes people laugh
2 the films, plays and TV programmes in general that make people laugh *There's a lot of comedy on this channel.*
3 a style of writing or way of speaking in which you write or say funny things to make people laugh

comet noun comets
an object that moves in space, made of gas, dust and ice. It often looks like a bright ball with a tail (long thin end).

comfort noun
1 a pleasant physical feeling that you get, for example, from wearing comfortable clothes or because there is nothing hurting or worrying you
2 when someone tries to understand how you feel and to help you feel less sad or worried *The police offered comfort to the injured people.*
3 someone's comforts are the things in their home that they enjoy having because they make their life easier

comfort verb
comforts, comforting, comforted
to comfort someone is to make them feel better and less sad or worried by showing them kindness *comforting words*

comfortable adjective
1 if something such as clothes or a piece of furniture is comfortable, it gives you a pleasant and happy feeling, for example because it is soft
2 if someone is comfortable, they feel good and relaxed, for example because there is nothing hurting or worrying them or because they are sitting or lying on something soft
3 having enough money to live well *My teacher comes from a comfortable family.*
4 if someone is comfortable with something, they are happy with it
comfortably adverb

comfy adjective comfier, comfiest
an informal word for comfortable

comic noun comics
1 a comic or comic book is a magazine for children with stories told in pictures
2 someone who makes people laugh by telling jokes and funny stories. A comic is also called a comedian.

comic adjective
1 funny *The play had a comic ending.*
2 connected with comedy *a comic actor*

comical adjective
funny **comically** adverb

comic strip noun comic strips
a series of drawings inside little boxes that tell a funny story, for example in a newspaper

SYNONYM cartoon

coming adjective
happening next *My parents will be seeing the head teacher in the coming week.*

comings and goings noun plural
the busy activity of lots of people arriving and leaving somewhere

comma noun commas
a punctuation mark like this ,

LANGUAGE EXTRA commas help to make reading a sentence easier because they separate the different parts of the sentence (*As you can see, it's raining*).
   Commas are also used for separating parts of a sentence that contain extra information about the main sentence (*My mobile phone, which I bought last week, doesn't work*). You can easily leave out the part between the commas without changing the basic meaning of the sentence.
   You also use commas for separating different things in a list (*I love apples, pears, oranges and bananas*).

command noun commands
1 an order telling someone or an animal to do something *The dog obeyed my command.*
2 an instruction telling a computer to do something
3 the power someone has over something such as a group of people or soldiers *His regiment is under the command of Colonel Roberts.*
4 your command of a foreign language is how well you know and speak it *My sister has a good command of Welsh.*
5 in grammar, a command is a type of sentence used for telling someone to do something, for example 'Go!', 'Sit down!' or 'Eat up!'

command verb
commands, commanding, commanded
1 if someone important or official commands someone to do something, they tell them to do it and expect to be obeyed *The captain commanded his soldiers to attack at dawn.*

commander–communication

2 to be in charge of a group of people or a particular activity *He's a general who commanded our troops during the war.*
3 to command respect is to get respect from people

commander *noun* **commanders**
an officer in charge of a group of soldiers

commandment *noun* **commandments**
in the Christian and Jewish religions, one of the rules describing how people should behave, given by God to Moses. These rules are known as the Ten Commandments.

commando *noun* **commandos**
a soldier specially trained to attack in areas controlled by an enemy

commemorate *verb*
commemorates, commemorating, commemorated
if people commemorate a person or event, they do something to show that they remember them and have respect for them *They've built a monument to commemorate the soldiers who died in Iraq.*
commemoration *noun*

commence *verb*
commences, commencing, commenced
another way of saying to begin, especially in official language *The meeting commences at 3.00 p.m.* **commencement** *noun*

commend *verb*
commends, commending, commended
1 to commend someone or something is to praise them, for example in an official ceremony or by giving them a prize
2 to commend something to someone is to suggest that they will think it is very good and should give it their attention *I commend this fascinating book to anyone interested in music.*

commendable *adjective*
deserving great praise

commendation *noun* **commendations**
official praise or an official prize for doing something good

comment *noun*
1 (*plural* **comments**) something someone says, such as an opinion *That's an interesting comment.*
2 general discussion about something, for example in a newspaper *There's lots of comment on the front page.*

comment *verb*
comments, commenting, commented
to say something or to give an opinion about something *Lots of people commented on the way she was dressed.*

commentary *noun* **commentaries**
1 if someone gives a commentary on an event, for example a football match on television, they describe what is happening as the event takes place
2 an article or book about a particular subject

commentator *noun* **commentators**
someone who gives a commentary *a sports commentator*

commerce *noun*
the activity of buying and selling things, for example goods from shops or websites or services from banks, lawyers or accountants

commercial *adjective*
1 connected with commerce *This town is a big commercial centre.*
2 a commercial television or radio station makes its money by selling advertisements
commercially *adverb*

commercial *noun* **commercials**
a short television film or radio announcement telling people about things to buy

SYNONYM advertisement

commission *noun* **commissions**
a small amount of extra money that a bank charges someone, for example for changing money into a foreign currency

commit *verb*
commits, committing, committed
1 to do something that is against the law or wrong *to commit a crime*
2 to commit suicide is to kill yourself
3 if you commit yourself to something, you say you will definitely do it
4 if you don't want to commit yourself on a particular subject, you mean you don't want to make a decision about it or to say what you really think

commitment *noun*
1 believing something is very important and being willing to work very hard for it *My sister shows great commitment to the team.*
2 (*plural* **commitments**) when you say you will definitely do something *He asked me to join the team but I haven't made a commitment yet.*
3 someone's commitments are the things they have to do, for example because of their job or family *My dad won't be going on holiday because of work commitments.*

committed *adjective*
if someone is committed to something, they think it is very important and they are willing to work very hard *Jason isn't very committed to schoolwork. I'm a committed footballer.*

committee *noun* **committees**
a group of people representing a larger group, who meet to make decisions and organise things *My parents are on the school committee.*

commodity *noun* **commodities**
a basic product that people buy, for example food or petrol

common *adjective* **commoner, commonest**
1 happening a lot *This mistake is very common.*
2 existing in large numbers *Snails are common at this time of year.*
3 shared by two or more people *a common interest*; *Hindi was the language common to most people in our group.*
4 not special in any way *Life was hard for the common people in the sixteenth century.*
5 (old-fashioned) used for describing someone who does not have good manners and who cannot recognise things of good quality, or for describing something such as their behaviour *The way he talks is very common.*

LANGUAGE EXTRA *common nouns* name things or people, for example *computer*, *boy* or *sadness*. They include *concrete nouns* (things you can see or hear, for example *computer*, *boy*) and *abstract nouns* (words connected with ideas or feelings, for example *sadness*, *love*).
Names of people or places (such as *Daniel* or *Cambridge*) are written with capital first letters and are known as *proper nouns*.

common *noun*
1 (*plural* **commons**) open land covered in grass, in a town or village, where people can walk or play games
2 if people have something in common, they share the same interests, ideas or experiences *I have a lot in common with my brother.*
3 if things have something in common, they share something that makes them different from other things *Spanish and Italian have a lot of words in common.*

common knowledge *noun*
if something is common knowledge, everyone knows it

commonly *adverb*
often *This word is commonly used in Wales.*

commonplace *adjective*
happening a lot or in many places *Travelling by bike has become commonplace in London.*

common room *noun* **common rooms**
a room in a school for teachers or students to relax in

Commons *noun*
the Commons is short for the **House of Commons**

common sense *noun*
if someone has common sense, they know how to behave in a sensible way and make good and useful decisions

commonwealth *noun* **commonwealths**
1 a group of countries that have joined together because they have many interests in common
2 the Commonwealth is a group of countries made up of Great Britain and other places, such as Australia or Canada, that were ruled by Britain in the past

commotion *noun* **commotions**
a lot of loud and unpleasant noises that happen suddenly

communal *adjective*
1 shared by lots of people *a communal garden*
2 connected with a whole community

commune *noun* **communes**
a group of people who live and work together and share all their possessions *a hippie commune*

communicate *verb*
communicates, communicating, communicated
1 to exchange information *I communicate with my grandparents by email.*
2 to make someone understand an idea or feeling *Our German teacher communicated her love of languages to us.*

communication *noun*
1 the exchange of information *The mobile phone is a great means of communication.*
2 (*plural* **communications**) a message from someone *We've received a communication from the head teacher.*
3 communications are ways of sending information using different technologies such as computers or telephones

4 **communications** are also the different ways people use to travel between places, for example roads, railways and rivers *Communications are very good in most parts of the US.*

communicative *adjective*
if someone is communicative, they like talking to people

Communion *noun*
a ceremony in the Christian religion where bread and wine are given to people to remember the death of Christ

communism *noun*
a political belief that all people are equal, that the government should provide all goods and food to everyone equally and that there should be no private property

communist *noun* **communists**
someone who believes in communism
communist *adjective*

community *noun* **communities**
1 all the people who live in a place
2 a group of people who have something in common such as an interest, religion, nationality or job *the Polish community in London*

commute *verb*
commutes, commuting, commuted
if someone commutes, they travel from their home to and from work, usually by train, bus or car **commuter** *noun*

compact *adjective*
1 if something is compact, it is small but built or organised in a way that uses space well *a compact car*
2 with its parts pushed tightly together *a compact bundle of newspapers*

compact disc *noun* **compact discs**
a round flat piece of plastic used for storing and recording computer information, sounds and pictures. It is usually called a CD.

companion *noun* **companions**
1 someone you spend time with, for example a friend *a travelling companion*
2 a book that gives useful information on a subject, used especially as a title *'A Companion to English Poetry'*

ORIGIN from Latin *companio* 'someone who eats bread with you' (Latin *com* 'with' and *panis* 'bread')

companionship *noun*
spending time with someone, for example because you are their friend

company *noun*
1 when you have another person or other people with you *I really enjoy your company.*
2 other people such as your friends or the guests who come to your home *My parents have company on Sunday.*
3 (*plural* **companies**) an organisation that makes money by selling things such as goods or information and advice

SYNONYM business

4 (*plural* **companies**) a group of actors, singers or dancers who work together
5 (*plural* **companies**) a group of soldiers, smaller than a battalion, made up of two or more platoons

comparable ['kom-prer-berl'] *adjective*
1 similar *The two towns are comparable in size.*
2 equally good *She's a good painter but isn't comparable to someone like David Hockney.*

comparative *adjective*
1 compared to something else, for example compared to a situation that existed before or compared to other similar things *In the UK we live in comparative freedom.*
2 used about things you can compare *a comparative study of Shakespeare and Milton*

comparative *noun* **comparatives**
the form of an adjective or adverb that is used for comparing two things (or people) when the second thing (or person) has more of a particular quality than the first one

LANGUAGE EXTRA to form the *comparative* of adjectives and adverbs, you add *-er*, for example *small – smaller, fast – faster*. If a word ends in *-y* (like *happy*), then you change *y* to *i* (*happier*). Words that end in a single consonant (for example *big, hot* or *thin*) usually double that consonant before *-er* (*bigger, hotter, thinner*).
Some very common words are exceptions to this *-er* rule: for example, *good* changes to *better*, not *gooder*!
For longer adjectives and for adverbs ending in *-ly*, you usually put 'more' before the word, for example *difficult – more difficult, slowly – more slowly*.

compare: **superlative**

comparatively *adverb*
1 compared to something else, for example a situation that existed before, or compared to what is normal *Going to bed at nine o'clock is comparatively early for me.*
2 not completely but to a certain extent *Our teacher said she was comparatively happy with the results.*

SYNONYMS for sense 2: fairly, rather

compare *verb*
compares, comparing, compared
1 if you compare two or more things or people, you see how they are alike and how they are different *Let's compare our answers.*
2 if something compares with something else, it is equally good (or bad) *He plays the guitar well but he can't compare with Paul McCartney.*

comparison *noun* **comparisons**
1 when you compare things or people to see how they are alike or different
2 when you try to find something in common between things or people *Our science teacher made comparisons between the two materials.*
3 if you say there's no comparison between two things, you mean one thing is much better than the other

compartment *noun* **compartments**
1 a separate section of something larger for storing things, such as a freezer compartment in a fridge or a luggage compartment in a bus
2 a separate section of a railway carriage *a second-class compartment*

compass *noun* **compasses**
a round instrument for finding the direction you are facing. It has a magnetic needle that always points north.

compasses *noun plural*
compasses (also called a pair of compasses) are used for drawing circles. They are made up of two thin bars (called arms) joined at the top in an upside-down V shape. One of the bars is pointed and the other holds a pencil or pen.

compassion *noun*
a strong feeling of being sad when you see someone suffering or someone having problems, because you care about their feelings **compassionate** *adjective*

compatible *adjective*
1 if things such as ideas or laws are compatible, they can exist together
2 if pieces of computer equipment or software are compatible, they can be used together
3 if people are compatible, they like each other and behave well towards each other
compatibility *noun*

compel *verb*
compels, compelling, compelled
to make someone do something

compensate *verb*
compensates, compensating, compensated
1 to pay someone money because they have lost something, had problems or been hurt
2 to do something to make a bad situation better *What can I do to compensate for not inviting you to my party?*

compensation *noun*
1 money paid to someone because of something bad that has happened to them
2 (*plural* **compensations**) something that helps to make a bad situation better

compère ['kom-pair'] *noun* **compères**
someone who introduces the people performing in a show, for example on TV

compete *verb*
competes, competing, competed
1 to take part in a sports event or competition
2 to try to do better than someone or be more successful than other people *School leavers often have to compete for jobs* (have to try to get a job that lots of others want).
3 if businesses compete, they try to sell more than other businesses

competent *adjective*
1 if someone is competent to do something, they have enough skill to do it well
2 if something that you do is competent, you do it well *a very competent piece of homework*
competence *noun* **competently** *adverb*

competition *noun*
1 (*plural* **competitions**) an event or game where you try to do better than other people and win a prize
2 when people try to get something that lots of other people also want *competition for university places*
3 when businesses try to sell more than other businesses

competitive – compound

competitive *adjective*
1 trying hard to do better than everyone else *Iqbal is a very competitive chess player.*
2 connected with businesses that try to sell more than other businesses *Japan is very competitive.*
3 competitive prices are cheaper than other people's prices for the same thing

competitor *noun* **competitors**
1 someone who takes part in a race or game
2 in business, a competitor is someone who sells the same things as someone else and tries to sell more of them

compilation *noun*
1 (*plural* **compilations**) a collection of things such as songs or poems by different people
2 the action of compiling something

compile *verb*
compiles, compiling, compiled
to write something such as a list or a book that you have put together using information from different places *A lexicographer is someone who compiles a dictionary.* **compiler** *noun*

complacent *adjective*
if someone is complacent, they are happy with what they have achieved or with the way things are and they make no effort to make things better **complacency** *noun*

complain *verb*
complains, complaining, complained
1 to say you're not happy about something or someone, for example to get someone to do something about it *I complained to my teacher that I was being bullied.*
2 to complain of something is to say you have a pain *She was complaining of a headache.*

complaint *noun* **complaints**
1 words that you say or write when you're not happy about something or someone *My parents made a complaint to the school.*
2 a medical problem, usually not serious *a chest complaint*

complement *noun* **complements**
1 something that goes well with something else or that is added to it to complete it *Use these spices as a complement to the meal.*
2 the number of things or people needed to complete something *Our school has a full complement of teachers.*
3 in grammar, a complement of a verb is a word or words needed to complete the meaning of a sentence. For example, in 'I am sleepy' and 'Chris became head boy', the complements are 'sleepy' and 'head boy'.

LANGUAGE EXTRA be careful not to confuse *complement* and *compliment* (kind words)

complementary *adjective*
1 used about things that go well together or that are added to make something complete *Her musical skills are complementary to her painting.*
2 in maths, complementary angles are two angles that together come to 90 degrees
compare: **supplementary angles**
3 complementary medicine is a type of medical care that uses unusual methods such as needles (acupuncture) or drugs from plants (herbal medicine)

complete *adjective*
1 used for describing the whole of something and not just part of it *We spent a complete day travelling.*
2 having all the parts that something is supposed to have *The list is now complete.*
3 used for giving extra importance to a word, for example when you mean that something or someone is as big or as great as can be *It was a complete shock. You're a complete idiot!*
4 finished *Work on the new stadium is complete.*

complete *verb*
completes, completing, completed
1 to finish doing something
2 to make something whole by adding to it something that was missing *Complete the following sentence.*
3 to write information in the spaces of a form or questionnaire

completely *adverb*
1 used for giving special importance to a word or for saying that something is very true *I completely forgot. We're completely lost.*
2 in every way or when talking about every part of something *I want you to tidy your room completely. It's completely new.*

SYNONYMS entirely, totally

completion *noun*
1 being finished *Work is nearing completion* (nearly finished).
2 the action of finishing something *You'll get a certificate on completion of the course.*

complex *adjective*
if something is complex, it has lots of different parts and needs a lot of study or attention to be understood *The rules are very complex.* **complexity** *noun*

complex *noun* **complexes**
1 a group of buildings of a particular kind, for example used for shopping or playing sports *a sports complex*
2 a problem that exists in someone's mind that makes them more worried or frightened about something than they should be *Josh has a complex about his ginger hair.*

complexion *noun* **complexions**
the natural appearance of the skin on someone's face *Grandma doesn't go out much so she has a pale complexion.*

complicate *verb*
complicates, complicating, complicated
to make something more difficult

complicated *adjective*
if something is complicated, it has lots of different parts and is difficult to deal with or understand *Using a program for the first time is quite complicated.*

complication *noun* **complications**
1 a problem that makes a situation more difficult
2 a medical problem that happens because of something else such as an illness or operation *Eye problems can be a complication of diabetes.*

compliment ['kom-pli-mernt'] *noun* **compliments**
1 kind words that someone says about someone else
2 an action that shows you have great respect for someone *They paid my teacher a compliment by naming the sports hall after her.*

LANGUAGE EXTRA be careful not to confuse *compliment* and *complement* (something that goes well with something else)

compliment ['kom-pli-ment'] *verb*
compliments, complimenting, complimented
to say kind words about someone

complimentary *adjective*
1 saying kind words about someone *Mr Clark was very complimentary about my essay.*
2 given to someone without asking them to pay for it *complimentary tickets*

comply *verb*
complies, complying, complied
to do what someone asks you to do, for example by obeying a rule

component *noun* **components**
one of the parts that something is made up of, such as a piece of equipment or a system *Cells, bulbs and switches are components of a circuit.*

compose *verb*
composes, composing, composed
1 to write something, especially a piece of music
2 to be composed of things or people is to be made up of them *Our team is composed of both boys and girls.*

composer *noun* **composers**
someone who writes music, usually classical music

composite number *noun* **composite numbers**
a number larger than 1 that can be divided exactly by one or more other numbers (other than 1 or itself). For example, 4 (2 × 2), 6 (2 × 3), 8 (2 × 4) and 9 (3 × 3) are composite numbers.
compare: **prime number**

composition *noun* **compositions**
1 a piece of music *a composition by Beethoven*
2 a piece of written work, for example an essay done in school
3 the action of writing something
4 the way something is made up *chemical composition*

compost *noun*
a mixture of leaves, grass and dead plants that is put into the ground to make things grow better

compound *noun* **compounds**
1 a chemical substance that is made up of two or more parts
2 an area with buildings surrounded by a wall *a prison compound*

comprehend–concern

3 in grammar, a compound is a word made up of two or more other words

> **LANGUAGE EXTRA** a *compound* is formed from two or more words. There are three main types: nouns such as *blackbird* or *ice cream*; verbs such as *channel-hop* or *overtake*; adjectives such as *old-fashioned* or *olive green*.
> Compounds are written as one word, two words (except verbs) or with a hyphen. Use this dictionary to check a spelling.

comprehend *verb*
comprehends, comprehending, comprehended
to understand something, especially something difficult

comprehensible *adjective*
easy to understand

comprehension *noun*
1 understanding something
2 (*plural* **comprehensions**) a language exercise or activity that helps students understand a piece of writing. Students read or listen to the piece of writing and are given questions to answer about it.

comprehensive *adjective*
1 including everything that is needed *a comprehensive guide to the theatre*
2 comprehensive education describes the teaching of students in comprehensive schools

comprehensive *noun* comprehensives
short for **comprehensive school** *My sister goes to a comprehensive.*

comprehensive school *noun*
comprehensive schools
a school for students aged 11 to 18 of all different levels of natural learning ability

compress *verb*
compresses, compressing, compressed
1 to press something so that it becomes smaller and takes up less space
2 to compress a computer file is to make it smaller using a special program, for example to make it easier to download or to send by email

> **SYNONYM** for sense 2: to zip

compression *noun*

comprise *verb*
comprises, comprising, comprised
1 to comprise something (or to be comprised of something) is to be made up of different things or people *The crowd mainly comprised students* (or *was mainly comprised of students*). *The house comprises six rooms.*
2 to make up a part of a bigger group *Boys comprise half the class.*

> **LANGUAGE EXTRA** be careful to say *comprise*, not *comprise of*. For example, do not say *The house comprises of six rooms*.

compromise ['kom-prer-myze] *verb*
compromises, compromising, compromised
if two or more people compromise, they agree to stop an argument between them. They agree to accept less than they really want because they know that they cannot have everything they want.

compromise ['kom-prer-myze] *noun*
compromises
an agreement between people where each person accepts less than they want in order to stop an argument *We reached a compromise.*

compulsory *adjective*
if something is compulsory, you have to do it or have it because it is the law or a rule *The school uniform is compulsory.*
compulsorily *adverb*
compare: optional

computer *noun* computers
a piece of electronic equipment, usually with a screen, that stores information and uses special instructions called programs to make it work. It can be used for lots of purposes such as writing and printing documents, doing calculations and drawing shapes as well as using the internet, sending emails, watching films and making phone calls.

> **ORIGIN** from Latin *computare* 'to calculate'

computerise *verb*
computerises, computerising, computerised
to use computers for something such as doing different types of work *All our medical records are now computerised.*

> **LANGUAGE EXTRA** also spelt *computerize*

computer science *noun*
the study of computers and ways of using them

computing *noun*
the activity of using a computer

comrade *noun* comrades
a friend, for example from someone's time in the army or in a difficult job

comradeship *noun*
friendship *Granddad talked about the comradeship of his army friends.*

con *verb* (*informal*)
cons, conning, conned
to get money out of someone or make someone do something by telling them something that isn't true

> **LANGUAGE EXTRA** a *conman* or *conwoman* is someone who tries to get money out of people in this way

concave *adjective*
curved inwards like the inside of a ball

> **ANTONYM** convex

conceal *verb*
conceals, concealing, concealed
another way of saying to hide
concealment *noun*

concede *verb*
concedes, conceding, conceded
1 to admit that something is true
2 to concede something to someone is to give it to them

conceit *noun*
the way in which a conceited person behaves

conceited *adjective*
used for describing someone who has a very high opinion of their own qualities, such as being intelligent or attractive, and who makes sure other people know about these qualities

conceivable *adjective*
if something is conceivable, it is possible to think about it *It's conceivable that he missed the last train.*

conceive *verb*
conceives, conceiving, conceived
1 to think of something such as an idea or plan
2 to imagine something *I couldn't conceive of living in a big town.*
3 if a woman conceives, she becomes pregnant

concentrate *verb*
concentrates, concentrating, concentrated
1 to give all your attention to something, for example by thinking hard, listening or watching carefully *Go away, I'm trying to concentrate. Have you been concentrating on your homework?*
2 if something is concentrated somewhere, there is more of it there than anywhere else *The schools are concentrated in the north of the town.*

concentrated *adjective*
if a liquid is concentrated, it has been made stronger because water has been removed from it *concentrated apple juice*

concentration *noun*
1 when you give all your attention to something *I lost my concentration for a moment.*
2 (*plural* **concentrations**) when there is more of something in one area than anywhere else *There's a concentration of theatres in the West End of London.*

concentric *adjective*
concentric circles are two or more circles inside each other with the same centre

concept *noun* concepts
a general idea about something *We're studying the basic concepts of science.*

conception *noun*
1 (*plural* **conceptions**) an idea about something in your own mind
2 when something was first thought of, such as an idea or plan
3 when a woman becomes pregnant

concern *verb*
concerns, concerning, concerned
1 if something concerns someone, it is important to them because it is connected with them in some way *This problem concerns us all.*
2 to be about a particular subject *The book concerns a boy wizard.*
3 if someone is concerned about something or if it concerns them, they are worried about it *Mum said she wasn't too concerned.*

concern *noun* concerns
1 a feeling of worry or something that worries you *There's a lot of concern about the new teacher. Getting home after dark is my main concern.*

85

concerning – cone

2 something that is important to you *Our concern is the children's safety.*
3 something that is your own responsibility and no-one else's *That's none of your concern.*
4 a feeling of wanting someone to be healthy and happy *Our doctor shows a lot of concern for her patients.*
5 a business or company

concerning *preposition*
used when mentioning a particular subject *I have a question concerning the exams.*

> SYNONYM about

concert *noun* **concerts**
an event with music, or with music and singing, in front of an audience. A concert may be given by one musician only, a group of musicians or an orchestra. *a rock concert; a concert of classical music*

concertina *noun* **concertinas**
a musical instrument similar to an accordion but smaller. You hold it in both hands and play it by squeezing it in and out like bellows and pressing buttons at each end.

concerto ['kern-**cherrt**-oh'] *noun*
concertos or **concerti**
a piece of classical music written for one instrument only and an orchestra *Beethoven's Violin Concerto*

concession *noun* **concessions**
1 when you are allowed to have something or do something because someone wants to be helpful to you or wants to reach an agreement *As a special concession, you won't have to wear school uniform tomorrow.*
2 when you are allowed to buy something such as a ticket for less than the normal price *Do you have a student travel concession?*

concise *adjective*
a concise piece of writing or speech is short and contains lots of information without using any unnecessary words

concisely *adverb*
using few words *He told us everything clearly and concisely.*

conclude *verb*
concludes, concluding, concluded
1 to decide something after considering all the facts carefully *The police officer concluded there was enough evidence to charge him.*
2 to end something, or to come to an end *The author concluded the chapter with a quotation from Kipling.*

conclusion *noun* **conclusions**
1 a decision you make after you have thought about something carefully
2 the end of something

concrete *noun*
a hard substance for building things. It is made by mixing cement with sand, stones and water.

concrete *adjective*
1 made out of concrete *a concrete path*
2 clear, definite or exact *concrete plans; concrete proof*

> LANGUAGE EXTRA *concrete nouns* name real things that you can see, hear or touch, not ideas or feelings, for example *house*, *cat*, *tree* or *friend*

concussion *noun*
if someone has concussion, something hard hits their head and they become dizzy or unconscious for a short period

condemn *verb*
condemns, condemning, condemned
1 to say very strongly that something or someone is bad or wrong *The head teacher made a speech condemning all bullying.*
2 to punish someone who has committed a crime *The terrorist was condemned to death.*
3 if a building is condemned, people have decided officially that it is not safe to be used

condemnation *noun*
when people say very strongly that something or someone is bad or wrong *There was international condemnation of the attack.*

condensation *noun*
drops of water on windows or walls. Condensation forms when warm air or steam changes into liquid.

condense *verb*
condenses, condensing, condensed
1 to make something shorter, for example a piece of writing
2 if a gas condenses, or if something such as steam (tiny drops of water) condenses, it changes into liquid *The mist had condensed on the car windows.*

condensed *adjective*
a condensed liquid is made thicker, for example by removing some of the water *condensed milk*

condiment *noun* **condiments**
used for describing salt, pepper or sauce that you put on food

condition *noun* **conditions**
1 the condition of something is how good or bad it is or what it is like compared to how it should be *My laptop is old but in good condition* (for example, it works well and looks good). *I don't like the condition of your bike – it's rusty.*
2 someone's condition is how healthy they are *She had an accident and is in a serious condition in hospital* (she's badly hurt).
3 something that must happen first before something else can be done *I'll be your friend on condition that you say sorry.*
4 something that you must agree to *He'll never accept your conditions.*
5 conditions are all the things affecting people's lives or affecting a particular situation *Poor people in many countries live in terrible conditions. The driving conditions were good.*

conditional *adjective*
if something is conditional, something else must happen first before it can happen *My brother's place at Oxford is conditional* (he has to do well in his exams first).

> LANGUAGE EXTRA a *conditional clause* describes a clause that begins with 'if' or 'unless', showing a condition that must happen first before something else can happen, for example *If it is sunny* (conditional clause), *I'll go out.*

conditioner *noun* **conditioners**
a liquid that you put on your hair after you've washed it to make it softer

condolence *noun* **condolences**
when you tell someone you are very sorry that a member of their family or a friend has just died *We sent Harry a condolence card.*

condom *noun* **condoms**
a thin rubber tube that a man puts on his penis when he has sex, to stop a woman from getting pregnant or to stop infection

condor *noun* **condors**
a very big South American bird like a vulture

conduct ['kern-dukt'] *verb*
conducts, conducting, conducted
1 to conduct a particular activity such as an experiment, interview or campaign is to do it

> SYNONYM to carry out

2 to conduct an orchestra or choir is to stand in front of it and organise the way the music should be played or sung
3 if something, such as a metal, conducts electricity or heat, it allows electricity or heat to pass through it
4 if someone is conducted somewhere, they are taken there *a conducted tour* (a tour of a place such as a town or building where someone is taken by a guide who points out interesting information)

conduct ['kon-dukt'] *noun*
someone's conduct is their behaviour

conduction *noun*
when electricity or heat passes through something such as metal or wires

conductor *noun* **conductors**
1 someone in charge of an orchestra or choir who conducts the music
2 someone who sells and checks tickets on a bus
3 something that allows electricity or heat to pass through it *Copper is a good conductor of heat.*

cone *noun* **cones**
1 a shape that has a circle at one end, sloping sides and a point at the other end
2 a cone-shaped container for ice cream made from a very thin dry biscuit that you eat with the ice cream
3 a traffic cone is a hollow piece of plastic shaped like a cone with its point at the top and usually coloured orange. Traffic cones are put in the road to stop cars driving or parking there or to warn people about something.
4 the large hard brown fruit of the pine tree. It has the rough shape of a cone (sloping sides, point at one end and circle at the other end).

confectioner – confusion

confectioner noun confectioners
someone who sells sweets and chocolates in a shop

confectionery noun
sweets and chocolates that are sold in a shop

Confederacy noun
in the American Civil War (1861–65), the Confederacy was the group of southern states that fought the northern states
compare: **Union**

Confederate adjective
connected with the Confederacy in the American Civil War (1861–65) *the Confederate flag*

confer verb
confers, conferring, conferred
1 to confer with someone is to discuss something with them
2 to confer something on someone, such as an honour or title, is to give it to them officially

conference noun conferences
a meeting where people discuss important matters

confess verb
confesses, confessing, confessed
1 to say it is true that you have done something wrong, especially a crime *Ella confessed to stealing my bike.*
2 to say something is true that you didn't really want people to know, for example because you're embarrassed *I confess I don't know much about gardening.*

confession noun confessions
1 someone's spoken or written words saying it is true that they have committed a crime *He made a full confession to the police* (said everything is true).
2 saying something is true that you didn't really want people to know *I have a little confession to make.*

confetti noun plural
very small pieces of coloured paper that you throw at people to celebrate something, especially at a bride and groom after their wedding ceremony

ORIGIN from Italian *confetti* 'small round sweets'. People often threw these during carnivals in Italy from the beginning of the 19th century.

confide verb
confides, confiding, confided
if you confide in someone, you tell them your private thoughts and feelings that you don't want anyone else to know

confidence noun
1 if someone has confidence, they have good feelings about themselves and know very well how to do things successfully
2 confidence in someone or something is believing that they are good and can be trusted
3 a feeling that something is certainly true or will certainly happen *I can say with confidence that Sam is the smartest person in the class.*
4 if you tell someone something in confidence, you tell them a private thought or feeling

5 a confidence trick is when someone gets money out of someone by telling them something that isn't true

confident adjective
1 certain that something will happen just as you expect it to happen *I'm very confident that I'll do well in the exams.*
2 a confident person is someone who knows very well how to do things successfully and who behaves boldly and calmly
3 also used about what a person says or does *a confident smile*

confidently adverb

confidential adjective
if something is confidential, such as a letter or piece of information, it must be kept secret **confidentially** adverb

configure verb
configures, configuring, configured
in computing, to configure a program is to make it work exactly how you want it to work, for example by changing settings

confine verb
confines, confining, confined
1 if something is confined to something else such as a place or group of people, it does not exist or happen anywhere else *The Welsh language is confined mainly to North Wales.*

SYNONYM to limit

2 to confine someone to a place is to make them stay there and not let them leave *My brother has been naughty and has been confined to his room.*

confined adjective
a confined space is a very small space where there is not much room to move

confinement noun
when someone is made to stay in a place, for example a prisoner in a cell

confirm verb
confirms, confirming, confirmed
1 to show or say that something is true *Bring along some ID to confirm your age. My teacher confirmed that I'd won the top prize.*
2 to confirm something you've agreed to do or pay for is to say you will definitely do it or pay for it *I am writing to confirm our meeting on Saturday. Click 'Finish' to confirm your order.*

confirmation noun
1 someone's spoken or written words saying that something is true *We're waiting for confirmation that our flight has been cancelled.*
2 a message such as a letter or email saying that something you've agreed to do or pay for is certain to happen *The hotel sent us a confirmation of the booking.*

confiscate verb
confiscates, confiscating, confiscated
to take away something that belongs to someone in order to punish them or because they are not allowed to have it *The teacher confiscated George's penknife.*

confiscation noun

conflict ['kon-flikt'] noun **conflicts**
1 an argument between people or groups

2 fighting between groups *The United Nations tried to end the conflict between the two countries.*
3 when it is difficult for two different things, for example ideas or personalities, both to exist at the same time

SYNONYM clash

conflict ['kern-flikt'] verb
conflicts, conflicting, conflicted
if two things such as ideas or pieces of information conflict, they both cannot be true at the same time *The opinion you just gave conflicts with what you said yesterday.*

conform verb
conforms, conforming, conformed
1 to behave in the same way as other people *Ruby hates conforming.*
2 to obey a rule or law *All electrical equipment must conform to safety standards.*

confront verb
confronts, confronting, confronted
1 to go up to someone in order to argue or fight with them, or to compete with them in a sport or competition *I decided to confront the bully.*
2 if you confront a problem or something difficult, or if a problem confronts you, you have to deal with it

confrontation noun confrontations
a serious argument or fight between people or groups *a confrontation with the police*

confuse verb
confuses, confusing, confused
1 if something or someone confuses you, they make it difficult for you to understand something *Stop confusing me with all those long words.*
2 to make the mistake of thinking that something or someone is something or someone else *A DVD should not be confused with a CD as they are different.*

confused adjective
1 not able to understand something *Please explain what you mean – I'm confused.*
2 not knowing what is happening or what to do *Dad told me to walk home but Mum said she'd pick me up so I'm confused.*
3 not knowing what is happening around you and not able to behave normally or sensibly *Sometimes Granddad gets a bit confused.*
4 if something such as an idea or situation is confused, it is not well explained or organised and people cannot understand it clearly

confusing adjective
difficult to understand

confusion noun
1 when you do not understand something or know what is happening or know what to do *What the doctor said has caused a lot of confusion. There was confusion about who really won the race.*
2 when you do not know what is happening around you and are not able to behave normally or sensibly *I was shaken up after the accident and had a strong feeling of confusion.*

congested–conscious

3 when you make the mistake of thinking that something or someone is something or someone else *To avoid confusion, the twins wore different clothes.*
4 a situation that is not well organised, for example one where things are untidy, there is a lot of noise and lots of things are happening at the same time *After the bomb exploded, there was complete confusion.*

congested *adjective*
1 with too many cars and other vehicles *congested roads*
2 with too many people *congested railway stations*
congestion *noun*

congratulate *verb*
congratulates, congratulating, congratulated
to tell someone you're very pleased about something they've done or about something nice that has happened to them *Lots of people congratulated my sister on the birth of her baby.*

congratulations *noun plural*
words telling someone you're very pleased about something

congregate *verb*
congregates, congregating, congregated
if people congregate somewhere, they come together and form a group

congregation *noun* **congregations**
1 the people taking part in a religious service, for example in a church, mosque or synagogue
2 the people who usually go to religious services

congress *noun* **congresses**
1 a meeting of people from different groups or countries
2 Congress is the government of the USA

congressman *noun* **congressmen**
a man who is a member of the US Congress
compare: **senator** and **Representative**

congresswoman *noun* **congresswomen**
a woman who is a member of the US Congress
compare: **senator** and **Representative**

congruent *adjective*
in maths, congruent shapes have exactly the same shape and size *congruent triangles*
congruence *noun*

conical *adjective*
shaped like a cone (circle at one end, sloping sides and point at the other end)

conifer *noun* **conifers**
a type of tree, such as a pine tree, with thin pointed leaves that stay green in winter. Conifers usually produce brown cones (fruits) with seeds in them.
coniferous *adjective*

conjugate *verb*
conjugates, conjugating, conjugated
to conjugate a verb is to say or write down all the different forms it has. The forms of a verb change with its subject (for example I, you, he) and with its tense (past, present, future). For example, the verb 'to go' is conjugated as follows: I go, you go, he goes (and so on); I went, you went, he went (and so on); I will go, you will go, he will go (and so on). **conjugation** *noun*

conjunction *noun* **conjunctions**
a word that joins other words or parts of a sentence together, for example 'and' or 'but'

> **LANGUAGE EXTRA** *conjunctions* such as *and* and *or* are used for joining individual words together, for example *reading, writing and spelling; red or blue*. Conjunctions used for joining parts of sentences together include *and, or, but, because, that* and *so*, for example *I'm tired but I don't want to go to bed. She didn't go to school because she was ill.*

conjunctivitis *noun*
an infection that makes the inside of your eyelid (skin above and below your eyes) painful and swollen

conjure *verb*
conjures, conjuring, conjured
to perform magic tricks, such as making something suddenly appear or disappear *a conjuring trick*

conjurer *noun* **conjurers**
someone who performs magic tricks

> **LANGUAGE EXTRA** also spelt *conjuror*

conk *verb* (informal)
conks, conking, conked
1 if you conk your head, you hit it on something
2 if a machine or car conks out, it stops working

conker *noun* **conkers**
1 a big brown hard and shiny nut that grows on a horse chestnut tree
2 conkers is a game children play using a conker tied onto a piece of string through a hole in its middle. Each player takes turns to try to break the other's conker by hitting it with their own.

> **ORIGIN** from Latin *concha* and Greek *konkhe* meaning 'the shell of a sea creature', because the game was originally played with the shell of a snail on a string

conman *noun* **conmen** (informal)
a man who tries to get money out of someone by telling them something that isn't true

connect *verb*
connects, connecting, connected
1 to join things together *Connect the cable to the laptop and then to the printer.*
2 if things or people are connected, or if people connect them, they have something to do with each other *This idea is connected with what I was saying earlier. The police were trying to connect my cousin to the crime.*
3 to allow someone to join a computer or telephone network, or to join something to this kind of network *Click here to connect to the internet. Our phone isn't connected yet.*

connection *noun* **connections**
1 when something has to do with something else *The police said there was no connection between the two crimes.*

> **SYNONYM** link

2 the people or things connected with something or someone *He has no family connections.*
3 a way of joining a computer or telephone network *Do you have a broadband connection?*
4 something joined to something else, or the action of joining something to something else *There's a loose connection in the plug.*
5 a plane, train or bus that lets you continue your journey *Be careful not to miss your connection.*
6 a road or railway that joins places *Manchester has good connections with the rest of the country.*

connective *noun* **connectives**
a word or phrase that connects other words or parts of a sentence together, for example 'and', 'therefore' and 'in addition'

> **LANGUAGE EXTRA** *connectives* can be conjunctions like *and, but* or *because* (words that join individual words or parts of sentences). They can also be adverbs like *therefore, firstly* (*secondly, finally,* and so on) or *in addition* (words or phrases that join parts of sentences).

connoisseur ['kon-er-**serr**'] *noun* **connoisseurs**
someone who knows a lot about art, music or food *a connoisseur of French wines*

> **ORIGIN** from Old French *conoiseor* 'person who knows'

conquer *verb*
conquers, conquering, conquered
1 to win a war against a country or group of people and take control of them *England was conquered by the Normans in 1066.*
2 to deal successfully with a problem *I conquered my fear of spiders.*
3 to climb to the top of a mountain *Hillary and Tenzing conquered Everest in 1953.*

conqueror *noun* **conquerors**
someone who conquers a country or group of people *William the Conqueror*

conquest *noun* **conquests**
1 when an army or country wins a war and takes control of a country or group of people *the Norman conquest of England*
2 the action of climbing to the top of a mountain *the conquest of Everest*

conscience ['**kon**-sherns'] *noun*
the feeling of what is right and what is wrong that controls people's actions and thoughts *I have a guilty conscience* (a bad feeling because I have done something wrong).

> **ORIGIN** from Latin *conscientia* 'knowledge within yourself' (from *com* 'with' and *scire* 'to know')

conscientious ['kon-shee-**en**-shers'] *adjective*
someone who is conscientious works very hard and pays a lot of attention to their work **conscientiously** *adverb*

conscious ['**kon**-shers'] *adjective*
1 awake and able to hear, see and understand *The patient is now conscious.*
2 to be conscious of something is to know it, to know about it or to notice that it is happening *I was conscious of the whole class staring at me.*

> **SYNONYM** aware

consciously–consonant

3 done on purpose *I made a conscious effort to finish my homework before bedtime.*

ORIGIN from Latin *conscius* 'knowing something' (from *com* 'with' and *scire* 'to know')

consciously adverb
if you do something consciously, you know that you are doing it and you do it on purpose

consciousness noun
1 being awake and able to hear, see and understand *The patient lost consciousness* (stopped being awake and went into a deep sleep).
2 knowledge and understanding of something

SYNONYM for sense 2: awareness

conscription noun
when young people are made to join the army for a certain amount of time

consecutive adjective
things that are consecutive, such as numbers or periods of time, come after each other with nothing in between *He's been late for school on four consecutive days.*

consensus noun
an agreement between most people or everyone *There was a general consensus in our team that we needed more practice.*

consent noun
someone's consent is when they say yes and let someone do something *You need the teacher's consent to go home early.*

SYNONYM permission

consent verb
consents, consenting, consented
to say yes to something, for example something important or something you think about carefully *My parents finally consented to my brother getting married.*

consequence noun
1 (plural consequences) something that happens because of something else *She slipped over and, as a consequence, bruised her knee. I'm afraid of the consequences* (of what might happen).
2 importance *What you say is of no consequence.*

consequently adverb
because of something, or because of something happening *Our team is practising three times a week and consequently we've won some matches.*

conservation noun
the protection of nature and our surroundings, including animals and plants and old buildings

conservationist noun conservationists
someone who believes that nature, our surroundings and old buildings are important and spends time trying to protect them

conservative adjective
1 if someone is conservative, they do not like new things, such as new ideas
2 a conservative estimate or guess is a number that may be a bit less than the true number

Conservative noun Conservatives
someone who is a member of or who supports the Conservative Party, one of the main political parties in the UK

conservatory noun conservatories
an extra room at the back of or next to a house, with walls and a roof built from glass. It is used for living in or growing plants in.

conserve verb
conserves, conserving, conserved
1 to prevent a part of nature such as a forest from being damaged
2 to use just a small amount of something such as water or electricity so that it is not wasted

consider verb
considers, considering, considered
1 to think about something carefully *I'm still considering what to do. My mum's considering changing her job* (she hasn't decided yet).
2 to say something that is your opinion or to think about something or someone in a particular way *I consider Jo my best friend. You consider everything to be a joke!*
3 to be kind to someone, for example by showing an interest in them *You never consider your little sister.*

considerable adjective
1 used when you mean a lot of something or something very large *a considerable sum of money; a considerable distance; Birmingham is a town of considerable importance. The cat was in considerable pain.*
2 used when you mean a large number of things *There are considerable differences between the two poems.*

considerably adverb
a lot *She's considerably taller than her brother.*

considerate adjective
if someone is considerate, they think about other people's feelings, for example they may want to help them

considerately adverb

SYNONYM thoughtful

consideration noun
1 when you think carefully about something, especially before making a decision *After a lot of consideration, I decided not to join their group.*

SYNONYM thought

2 (plural considerations) something you must think about before making a decision *When you plan your holiday, the weather is an important consideration.*
3 behaviour that shows that you think about other people's feelings *Children don't always have enough consideration for old people.*
4 if you take something into consideration, you think about it carefully before making a decision

considering conjunction & preposition
used for mentioning an important fact or situation that influences what you say or gives the reason for something *Considering how clever he is, he should have done better in the exam. You speak French well, considering that you've only been learning it for a month. Considering the weather, we decided to go home early.*

consist verb
consists, consisting, consisted
to consist of something is to be made up of different things or people *Breakfast consisted of cereal, a roll and a cup of tea.*

consistency noun
1 behaviour or ideas that are always the same
2 (plural consistencies) the consistency of a liquid or substance is how thick and smooth it is *I don't like the consistency of this soup.*
3 the consistency of a text is when things such as spellings of the same word are always the same

consistent adjective
1 always behaving in the same way and not changing in your ideas
2 if things such as facts or ideas are consistent, they are all true and there are no differences between them
3 if things such as spellings in a text are consistent, all the same words are spelt in the same way, for example 'adviser' is always spelt 'adviser' and not sometimes 'advisor'

consistently adjective
always doing the same thing *You've consistently lied to me.*

consolation noun consolations
1 something to make you feel better when you are disappointed or unhappy
2 a consolation prize in a competition is a small prize given to someone who has not won to make them feel better

console ['kern-sohl'] verb
consoles, consoling, consoled
to make someone feel better when they are disappointed or unhappy

console ['kon-sohl'] noun consoles
a board with buttons and switches for controlling a piece of equipment such as a computer, often used for playing video games on a screen

consonant noun consonants
a letter of the alphabet such as *b* or *g* that is not a vowel

LANGUAGE EXTRA the *consonants* in English are the following letters: *b, c, d, f, g, h, j, k, l, m, n, p, q, r, s, t, v, w, x, y* and *z*. The *vowels* are: *a, e, i, o, u* and *y*. The letter *y* can be both a consonant and a vowel – it is a consonant in 'yellow' and a vowel in 'rhyme'.
A consonant sound is made when the air through your mouth is blocked so the sound cannot last very long, as a vowel sound can. For example, the 'i' sound of 'big' can be made to last longer but the 'b' and the 'g' sounds cannot: 'b-i-i-i-i-i-i-g'.

ORIGIN from Latin *consonans* 'sounding together', because a consonant can only be 'sounded' with a vowel

conspicuous – contaminate

conspicuous adjective
1 if something or someone is conspicuous, they are easy to see *The parrot has a conspicuous red tail.*
2 if someone feels conspicuous, they feel different and think that other people can notice them easily
conspicuously adverb

conspiracy noun conspiracies
a plan to do something, often something bad, made in secret by a group of people
conspirator noun

SYNONYM plot

conspire verb
conspires, conspiring, conspired
1 if people conspire to do something, for example something bad, they plan in secret to do it
2 if things conspire to produce a particular result, especially a bad one, they happen at the same time *The snow and the wind conspired to make the roads very dangerous.*

constable noun constables
an ordinary police officer

constant adjective
1 something that is constant happens all the time or is always there *the constant noise of the traffic*
2 if something like an amount, rate or level is constant, it stays the same for a period of time *Mum drove at a constant speed of 50 miles an hour.*

constant noun constants
in maths, a constant is a number or amount that always stays the same

constantly adverb
all the time *She's constantly talking in class.*

constellation noun constellations
a group of stars that form a pattern in the sky and have been given a name, such as the Great Bear

ORIGIN from Latin *com* 'together' and *stella* 'star'

consternation noun
a feeling of being worried or afraid

constipated adjective
if someone is constipated, they have trouble going to the toilet to get rid of waste from their bowels **constipation** noun

constituency noun constituencies
an area of the country that elects a member of parliament

constituent noun constituents
1 someone who lives in a constituency and votes for a member of parliament
2 one of the parts that something is made up of

constitute verb
constitutes, constituting, constituted
1 if people or things constitute something, they form part of the whole of something *Young people constitute 20 per cent of the population.*
2 to be considered to be something *What Jack did doesn't constitute a reason to be angry.*

constitution noun constitutions
1 the laws and rules that describe the way a country or organisation operates *the Constitution of the United States*
2 a person's general health and strength *My brother has a strong constitution.*
constitutional adjective

construct verb
constructs, constructing, constructed
1 to build something such as a road or school
2 to create something such as a sentence, idea or piece of writing

construction noun
1 the action of constructing something
2 the way something is constructed
3 (plural **constructions**) a building *Tower Bridge is a wonderful construction.*

constructive adjective
if something such as advice or criticism is constructive, it is very useful and helps to make a situation successful

consul noun consuls
a government official from one country who lives in a foreign country. Consuls look after the citizens of their own country if they need help.
consular adjective

consulate noun consulates
the building where a consul works *the Egyptian consulate in London*

consult verb
consults, consulting, consulted
1 to ask someone for information *You must consult your doctor.*
2 to look for information in something, for example in a book or online *I always consult Wikipedia.*
3 to talk about something with someone

consultant noun consultants
1 someone who gives professional advice on a particular subject
2 a hospital doctor of the highest rank who is an expert in a medical subject

consultation noun consultations
1 a meeting with someone, such as a doctor or teacher, to ask for information
2 a conversation with someone about something *The decision was made in consultation with the head teacher.*

consume verb
consumes, consuming, consumed
1 to eat or drink something *People often consume too much sugar.*
2 to use something such as electricity or energy
3 to destroy something completely, for example by fire

consumer noun consumers
1 someone who buys and uses things

SYNONYM customer

2 in biology, a consumer is an animal that eats plants and other animals
compare: **producer**

consumption noun
1 the amount of something that people use, such as electricity or energy
2 the action of eating and drinking *This meal is not fit for consumption* (is not safe to eat).
3 the action of buying and using things

contact noun
1 exchange of information, for example by talking or writing *I'm in contact with my grandparents every week* (I talk to or email them). *I've lost contact with some of my friends* (we don't talk or write to each other any more).
2 when people or things touch each other *Make sure this chemical doesn't come into contact with your skin* (doesn't touch your skin).
3 (plural **contacts**) a person you know, often someone who can help you, for example in a particular job

contact verb
contacts, contacting, contacted
to contact someone is to talk to them, for example by phone, or to write to them, for example by email *You can always contact me on my mobile.*

contact lens noun contact lenses
a small plastic disc that you wear in your eye to help you see better

contactless adjective
connected with equipment such as mobile phones or smart cards (small plastic cards that store information a computer can read) that use radio waves for making payments, for example when someone buys something in a shop or uses the London Underground *a contactless card; a contactless payment*

contact number noun contact numbers
a phone number where people can talk to you or send you a text message

contagious ['kern-tay-jers'] adjective
1 if an illness is contagious, you can catch it easily through the air or by touching someone
2 if someone is contagious, they have an illness that you can catch easily

SYNONYMS infectious, catching

contain verb
contains, containing, contained
1 if something contains something else, it has that thing inside it *The box contained lots of presents.*
2 if something like a book, film or speech contains something, it includes that thing as a part of it *This letter contains important information.*
3 if someone contains a feeling, they hide it *The children couldn't contain their excitement.*

container noun containers
1 something that you use for keeping things in, such as a box, bottle or tin
2 a very big metal box for carrying goods by ship or on a truck *a container ship*

contaminate verb
contaminates, contaminating, contaminated
to make something dirty, for example when chemical or harmful substances go into it or onto it *Bacteria have contaminated the water. This part of the coast is contaminated.* **contamination** noun

contemplate – contradict

contemplate verb
contemplates, contemplating, contemplated
1 to think about something or about doing something in the future *He sat down and contemplated the idea. My sister is contemplating going to university.*
2 to think about something being possible in the future *Another war is too horrible to contemplate.*
contemplation noun

contemporary adjective
1 belonging to the present time *contemporary music*

SYNONYM modern

2 belonging to the same time as something else *These paintings are contemporary with those of Rembrandt.*
contemporary noun contemporaries
someone who is alive at the same time as someone else *Shakespeare and his contemporaries*

contempt noun
a strong feeling of dislike towards someone or something because you have no respect for them and think there is nothing good about them

contemptible adjective
if someone or something is contemptible, you have no respect for them because they are very bad

contemptuous adjective
showing no respect and a strong feeling of dislike *a contemptuous laugh; He was contemptuous of my suggestion.*

contend verb
contends, contending, contended
1 to try to get something or win something by struggling against someone or being more successful than they are *Several teams are contending for the top prize.*
2 to contend with something difficult is to deal with it *We had some very bad weather to contend with.*

contender noun contenders
someone who takes part in a competition, sports event or quiz

content ['kern-tent] adjective
if someone is content, they are happy with a particular situation or with things as they are *I wouldn't be content to stay at home and do nothing.*

content ['kon-tent] noun
1 the content of something such as a piece of writing, TV programme or course of study is everything that it deals with
2 the content of a website is all the information it contains *To read the magazine on your tablet you have to pay for the online content.*
3 the amount of a substance that something contains *butter with a low salt content*

contented adjective
happy with things as they are or with your life **contentment** noun

contents ['kon-tents] noun plural
1 the things that are inside something such as a container, room or building *I emptied out the contents of the box.*
2 the contents of a piece of writing are the things written in it *Keep the contents of my email secret.*

contest ['kon-test] noun contests
1 a competition
2 a struggle between people for power, especially in politics

contest ['kern-test] verb
contests, contesting, contested
1 to try to win something such as a sporting title
2 to say officially that you think something such as a decision is wrong

contestant noun contestants
someone who takes part in a competition or quiz

context noun contexts
1 the words that come before and after another word or sentence and make its meaning easier to understand
2 the things connected with something, such as an event, that make it easier to understand *the historical context of the English Civil War*

continent noun continents
1 a very large area of land that is surrounded (or almost surrounded) by sea and usually consists of several countries. There are seven continents: Europe, Asia, Africa, North America, South America, Australia and Antarctica.
2 the Continent is the main part of the continent of Europe, not including the British Isles

continental adjective
1 connected with any of the seven continents *continental USA* (the main land area, not including the islands)
2 connected with Europe *The euro is the main continental currency.*
3 making you think of the warm countries of Europe, such as France, Italy or Spain *Do you like the continental way of life?*
4 a continental breakfast consists of food such as French bread, butter, jam and croissants, with coffee to drink

continual adjective
1 happening all the time or lots of times *Stop your continual complaining!*
2 happening for a long time without stopping *continual rain*
continually adverb
compare: continuous

continue verb
continues, continuing, continued
1 to keep on doing something or keep on happening *The rain continued all day.*
2 to start doing something again after stopping *Let's continue after the break.*
3 to keep moving in a certain direction *We continued for another mile along the road.*

continuity noun
a situation where things continue smoothly and without big changes *Teachers aim for continuity between primary and secondary schools.*

continuous adjective
1 happening without stopping *a continuous noise*
2 continuing without any holes or spaces in between *a continuous line*
3 in grammar, the continuous form of the verb is made from the auxiliary verb 'to be' and a present participle (for example 'I am eating', 'she was playing', 'it has been raining', 'I'll be running'). It shows that an action is, was, has been or will be continuing. This form is also called the progressive form.
continuously adverb

LANGUAGE EXTRA *continuous* and *continual* can both mean 'happening without stopping' but only *continual* can mean 'happening again after stopping'. For example, *continuous rain* is rain that never stops, but *continual rain* is rain that happens for a very long time but can sometimes stop.

contorted adjective
twisted in a very strange way *the acrobat's contorted body*

contour noun contours
1 the contours of something are the lines around its edges that show its shape *We could see the contours of a camel's back.*
2 the contours of a map are lines that show things of the same height above or below sea level. They are used for showing hills, mountains and valleys.

contraceptive noun contraceptives
something that stops a woman from getting pregnant, such as a pill (taken by a woman) or a condom (used by a man)

contract ['kon-trakt] noun contracts
an official agreement between people, for example about money when someone works for someone or sells something to someone *The film star signed a three-year contract with her studio.*

contract ['kern-trakt] verb
contracts, contracting, contracted
1 if something contracts, it gets smaller or shorter *Hot metal contracts as it cools down.*
2 if someone contracts a serious illness, they get it *He contracted AIDS and died.*
3 to contract to do something is to officially agree to do it

contraction noun contractions
1 when something gets smaller or shorter. For example, your arm muscles contract when you raise your hand.
2 in grammar, a contraction is a short form of a word that you make by leaving out one or more of its letters

LANGUAGE EXTRA you use *contractions* in spoken or everyday language, usually between a pronoun or noun and a verb. For example, *I'm* is a contraction of *I am*, *he's* is a contraction of *he is* or *he has*, and *Jack's* is a contraction of *Jack is* or *Jack has* (*Jack's late, Jack's got a cold*). You use the apostrophe for showing that one or more letters have been left out.
Be careful not to confuse *it's* (*It's blue*) with *its*, which is a possessive adjective (*The dog has lost its bone*).

contradict verb
contradicts, contradicting, contradicted
1 if you contradict someone, you say the opposite of what they say or you say that what they say is not true

contradiction–conventionally

2 if something that someone says contradicts something else, both things cannot be true because the facts in them are different

contradiction noun contradictions
when two things that someone says cannot both be true because the facts in them are different *There's a contradiction between what you said this morning and what you're saying now.*

contradictory adjective
if two or more things that people say are contradictory, they cannot both or all be true because the facts in them are different

contralto noun contraltos
1 a woman with the lowest singing voice
2 a contralto voice

contraption noun contraptions
a piece of equipment or a machine that looks strange or complicated

contrary ['kon-trer-ree'] adjective
1 if something is contrary to something else, it is completely different from it or opposite to it *My brother and I have contrary opinions on this subject.*
2 **contrary to** used for saying that something is true even though most people think that the opposite is true or will happen *Contrary to expectations, our school won last Saturday's football match.*

contrary ['kon-trer-ree'] noun
1 the contrary is the opposite of something
2 **on the contrary** used when you disagree with what someone says or for saying no very strongly *'Do you think I'm lying?' – 'On the contrary, I think you're telling the truth.'*

contrast ['kon-trahst'] noun
1 (plural **contrasts**) a difference between things or people that is easy to see
2 (plural **contrasts**) something that is different from something else in a way that is easy to see
3 the amount of difference in light or colour in a picture or on a screen *Adjust the contrast of your webcam as I can't see you clearly.*

contrast ['kern-trahst'] verb
contrasts, contrasting, contrasted
1 if something contrasts with something else, there is a difference between them that you can see clearly *The beauty of the town contrasts with the unfriendliness of the people.*
2 if you contrast something with something else, you show that there is a difference between them

contrasting adjective
different from each other *contrasting colours*

contribute ['kern-trib-yoot' or 'kon-tri-byoot'] verb
contributes, contributing, contributed
1 to give money, things or something else such as your time or advice in order to help with something *My parents contributed £70 towards the school trip.*
2 to help to make something successful or to make it happen *We all contributed to the project. Smoking contributed to his illness.*
3 to write articles for a newspaper or magazine

contributor noun

contribution noun contributions
1 money or things that you give to help with something *a £100 contribution to the school funds*
2 something you do that helps to make something successful *Stephen Hawking's outstanding contribution to science*

contrive verb
contrives, contriving, contrived
1 to contrive to do something, for example something difficult, dangerous or surprising, is to manage to do it
2 to make something happen or to invent something, especially in a very clever way

control noun
1 being able to make things or people do what you want or being in charge of them *Our teacher is always in control of the class. I lost control of my bike. The rebels have control over this part of the city.*
2 (plural **controls**) stopping something from getting worse or bigger *In China they need stricter controls on air pollution.*
3 if something is under control, people are dealing with it correctly and making it do what they want *The fire is under control.*
4 if something is out of control, people cannot make it do what they want *Noah's behaviour is out of control.*
5 if someone takes control of a thing or place, that thing or place starts to belong to them or they start having the power to do whatever they want with it *The police took control of the town centre.*
6 the controls of something such as a plane, boat, car or piece of equipment are the buttons, switches and levers that you press, turn or move to operate it
7 on a computer keyboard, control is the name of a key that you press, usually together with another key, to make the computer do something. It is also called the control key. *Press Control P to print.*

control verb
controls, controlling, controlled
1 to make something or someone do what you want *Our teacher has trouble controlling the class.*
2 to make a piece of equipment work *You control the computer with a mouse.*
3 to be in charge of someone or something *This part of Berlin was controlled by the British army.*
4 to stop something from getting worse or bigger *The government has taken measures to control drugs.*
5 if you control your feelings or yourself, you do not show that you are angry or excited *Try and control your temper!*

controller noun controllers
someone whose job is to be in charge of something *an air traffic controller*

control panel noun control panels
a board with buttons, switches and levers for controlling machines and equipment. On a computer, the control panel is a piece of software for controlling the basic operations of the computer.

control room noun control rooms
a room with lots of equipment, for example for controlling something such as a spaceship or submarine

control tower noun control towers
a building at an airport where people called air traffic controllers give instructions to planes to help them land and take off

controversial adjective
if something or someone is controversial, lots of people have strong and very different opinions about them *The prime minister gave a controversial speech about education.*

controversy ['kon-trer-verr-see' or 'kon-trov-er-see'] noun controversies
when people disagree strongly about something or someone, often over a long period of time *There's a lot of controversy surrounding how the film star died.*

conundrum noun conundrums
a difficult problem that is hard to understand and solve

convalescence noun
a period of time that people spend getting better after an illness

convection noun
a way of making heat by moving around tiny molecules in the air or a liquid

convector noun convectors
an electrical heater that moves warm air around a room

convenience noun
1 (plural **conveniences**) something or a situation that makes things easier for you or saves you time *I like the convenience of living near the school. We have a new kitchen with all the conveniences.*
2 conveniences are public toilets. You can also say a convenience.
3 convenience food is food that is easy to make because it has been cooked already so it only has to be heated up

convenient adjective
1 if something is convenient, it makes things easier for you or saves you time, for example by being useful or close by *Going to school by bike is very convenient. The local shops are very convenient.*
2 used about a time when you are free to do something *Come and see me tomorrow if it's convenient.*

conveniently adverb

convent noun convents
a building or group of buildings where nuns (religious women) live and pray

convention noun conventions
1 a way of doing things that most people think is right and normal
2 an agreement, usually between countries *the Geneva Convention* (an agreement about how to treat enemy prisoners during a war)

conventional adjective
1 of the usual type, not new or original *Blu-ray Discs hold a lot more than conventional DVDs.*
2 if someone is conventional, they have the same opinions and behaviour as most other people

conventionally adverb
in the usual way

converge verb
converges, converging, converged
if things or people converge, they come together from different directions *Several tube lines converge at King's Cross station. Millions converged on the city for the Olympic Games.*

conversation noun
1 (plural **conversations**) a talk between people, especially a private or friendly one *I had a conversation with my teacher.*
2 talking between people *Conversation is difficult because the mobile signal is poor.*

conversational adjective
1 if the way you speak or write is conversational, it is friendly, just as when you have a conversation with someone
2 connected with talking *Her conversational Arabic is very good.*

conversationalist noun
conversationalists
someone who loves talking and has interesting things to say

converse ['kern-verrs'] verb
converses, conversing, conversed
to converse with someone is to talk to them

converse ['kon-verss'] noun
the converse of something is the opposite of it

conversely adverb
used for saying that one part of a sentence is the opposite of another *In the UK they drive on the left; conversely, in France they drive on the right.*

conversion noun conversions
the action of converting something or someone or of being converted

convert ['kern-verrt'] verb
converts, converting, converted
1 to change something into something else, for example so that it has a different form or use *My parents converted the loft into a bedroom. Convert this fraction into a decimal. I converted the file to a pdf.*
2 to be changed into something else *The sofa opens out and converts into a bed.*
3 to change your religion or persuade someone to change theirs *My friend converted to Catholicism.*
4 in rugby, to convert a try is to score a goal by kicking the ball over the crossbar

convert ['kon-vert'] noun converts
someone who has changed their religion or beliefs *a convert to Buddhism*

convertible adjective
if something is convertible, it can be changed into something else *a convertible sofa*

convertible noun convertibles
a car with a roof that you can fold back or open

convex adjective
curved outwards like the outside of a ball

ANTONYM concave

convey verb
conveys, conveying, conveyed
1 to convey something to someone is to make it known to them, for example by showing or giving it to them, telling them about it or making them understand it *Convey my best wishes to your uncle. The painting conveys a feeling of joy.*
2 to convey someone or something to a place is to take them there, for example by car or train

conveyor belt noun conveyor belts
a long flat band, usually made of rubber or metal, that moves things without stopping. It is used, for example, for moving goods in a factory or luggage at an airport.

convict ['kon-vikt'] noun convicts
a criminal in prison

convict ['kern-vikt'] verb
convicts, convicting, convicted
to convict someone of a crime is to decide in a court of law that they are guilty and to punish them *Her brother was convicted of theft.*

ANTONYM to acquit

conviction noun convictions
1 the decision by a court of law that someone is guilty of a crime
2 a strong belief that something is true, for example a political or religious idea *My dad has deep political convictions. He said he didn't do it but without much conviction.*

convince verb
convinces, convincing, convinced
1 if you convince someone of something, you make them believe it's true *He convinced me that he knew how to fix my laptop.*
2 if you convince someone to do something, you get them to want to do it *I'll try and convince her to join the team.*

convinced adjective
if you're convinced about something, you're certain of it

convincing adjective
1 if something such as an argument or explanation is convincing, you believe it's true
2 very well done and of high quality, or doing something very well *She plays a convincing part in the play. He was very convincing as Hamlet.*

convoluted adjective
very complicated

convoy noun convoys
a group of ships or vehicles travelling together. Ships or vehicles often travel in a convoy because it is safer than travelling separately.

conwoman noun conwomen (informal)
a woman who tries to get money out of someone by telling them something that isn't true

coo verb
coos, cooing, cooed
when a pigeon coos, it makes a soft low noise **coo** noun

cook verb
cooks, cooking, cooked
1 if you cook food, you make it ready and heat it up before eating it
2 if food cooks, it heats up
3 to cook up something such as an excuse or reason is to make up a false one
4 to cook up a plan is to plan something clever but dishonest
5 (informal) **What's cooking?** used when you want to know what's happening

cook noun cooks
someone who cooks food

cooker noun cookers
a large piece of equipment with an oven and burners that provide heat for cooking food *a gas cooker*

cookery noun
the activity of cooking *a cookery book* (a book with recipes in)

cookie noun cookies
1 another word for a biscuit
2 in computing, a cookie is a small file that a website you visit puts on your computer so that it remembers you if you visit again

ORIGIN from Dutch *koekje* 'little cake'

cooking noun
1 when you make food ready and heat it up *My dad does most of the cooking. Put the vegetables into the cooking pot.*
2 the type of food that you cook *I love home cooking.*
3 a cooking apple is a large green apple with a strong taste that you cook or that you bake in an oven

cool adjective cooler, coolest
1 if something is cool, it has a low temperature but it is not too cold
2 cool clothes are made of thin material to stop you feeling too hot *a cool cotton shirt*
3 not excited, nervous or angry *Stay cool whatever happens!*

SYNONYMS calm, relaxed

4 unfriendly *a very cool welcome*
5 (informal) used for showing that you like someone because they do the latest things or dress in a modern way or that you like something because it is fashionable *You look really cool in your new jeans and trainers. Do you think my new glasses are cool?*
6 (informal) good or interesting *I think your idea is very cool.*
7 (informal) used for saying that you agree with something *Is it cool with you if I go to Tom's house tomorrow?*
coolness noun

SIMILE 'as cool as a cucumber' means very cool (sense 3)

cool verb
cools, cooling, cooled
to become cooler or make something cooler *Let your coffee cool down for a minute or two.*

cool noun
1 the cool is a pleasant temperature that is not too cold *in the cool of the evening*
2 if someone keeps their cool, they stay calm and do not get excited or angry

cool head noun
if someone has a cool head, they know how to stay calm in a difficult situation
cool-headed adjective

coolly adverb
1 calmly
2 in an unfriendly way

coop *noun* **coops**
a small building for keeping chickens or other animals in

cooped up *adjective*
if someone is cooped up, they've been in a small place for too long *I need to go for a walk – I've been cooped up in the flat all day.*

cooperate ['koh-op-er-ayt'] *verb*
cooperates, cooperating, cooperated
1 to work with other people or groups and help them to do something *Daniel cooperated with Ed on the school history project.*
2 to do what someone asks you to do

cooperation ['koh-op-er-ray-shern'] *noun*
1 when you work with other people or groups *There's a lot of cooperation between Britain and France.*
2 when you do what someone asks you to do *Thank you for your cooperation.*

cooperative ['koh-op-er-rer-tiv'] *adjective*
happy to cooperate

SYNONYM *helpful*

coordinate ['koh-or-di-nayt'] *verb*
coordinates, coordinating, coordinated
to organise something, for example so that people connected with it can work together *The police will coordinate the rescue operation.* **coordinator** *noun*

coordinates ['koh-or-di-nerts'] *noun plural*
the numbers that give the position of points on a map or graph (mathematical diagram)

coordination ['koh-or-di-nay-shern'] *noun*
1 the organisation of things, for example so that people connected with them can work together
2 the coordination of parts of the body, such as muscles, is when you control them and make them work together

cop *noun* **cops**
1 an informal word for a police officer
2 (slang) **not much cop** not very good

cop *verb* (slang)
cops, copping, copped
1 to get something you don't want *I was the one who copped the blame.*
2 **to cop it** to get into trouble or be punished
3 **to cop out** to avoid doing something that you should do **cop-out** *noun*

ORIGIN from Latin *capere* 'to take'

cope *verb*
copes, coping, coped
to deal with something difficult *I'm coping very well with all my homework.*

co-pilot *noun* **co-pilots**
a pilot who helps the main pilot to fly a plane

copious ['koh-pee-ers'] *adjective*
used for describing a large amount of something *Dylan drank copious amounts of lemonade at the party.* **copiously** *adverb*

copper *noun*
1 a soft reddish-brown metal, used for example for making pipes, wires and coins
2 a reddish-brown colour
3 coppers are coins made from copper or bronze, for example the one penny and two pence coins
4 (*plural* **coppers**) an informal word for a police officer

ORIGIN from Latin *cyprium* '(metal) of Cyprus', the place where the copper usually came from in ancient times

copse *noun* **copses**
a group of trees growing together

LANGUAGE EXTRA also called a *coppice*

copy *noun* **copies**
1 something that someone makes that is exactly the same as something else *I've saved a copy of the file to my computer.*
2 something such as one single book, newspaper or CD (out of many that are all exactly the same) *I bought a copy of 'Private Peaceful'.*

copy *verb*
copies, copying, copied
1 to make something that is exactly the same as something else *You use a photocopier to copy documents.*
2 if you copy information, for example from a book or the internet, you write it out again somewhere else *We all copied out the poem from the whiteboard.*
3 to do something in exactly the same way as someone else *Stop copying me!*
4 if you copy something that belongs to someone else, such as their ideas, you use it just as if it's your own
5 if you copy in an exam, you cheat

copycat *noun* **copycats**
an informal word for someone who copies something from someone else, for example their behaviour or ideas

coral *noun*
1 a hard substance from the bones of small sea creatures called corals
2 a coral reef is a structure like a line of rocks just below the surface of the sea, made from millions of corals

cord *noun* **cords**
a piece of thick string or thin rope

LANGUAGE EXTRA be careful not to confuse *cord* with *chord* (musical notes)

cordial *adjective*
friendly and warm **cordially** *adverb*

ORIGIN from Latin *cordialis* 'connected with the heart'

cordial *noun* **cordials**
a sweet fruit juice that you mix with water before drinking it

cordless *adjective*
if a piece of equipment is cordless, it works without wires *a cordless phone*

cordon *noun* **cordons**
a line of people, such as police officers, who stand around a place to stop people going there or coming from there

cordon *verb*
cordons, cordoning, cordoned
if police officers or soldiers cordon off a place, they surround it or put ropes around it to stop people going there or coming from there

corduroy ['kor-der-oy'] *noun*
a heavy cotton cloth with raised lines on the outside, used for making clothes such as jackets and trousers

core *noun* **cores**
1 the part in the centre of something *an apple core*
2 the most important part of something *That's the core of the problem.*

corgi ['kor-gee'] *noun* **corgis**
a small dog with a thick body, short legs and large pointed ears

coriander ['kor-i-an-der'] *noun*
a plant whose seeds are used as a spice for giving flavour to food

cork *noun*
1 the soft light bark of a tree called the cork oak. It is used for making many things such as bulletin boards and floors.
2 (*plural* **corks**) a piece of cork or plastic that is pushed into the top of a bottle, for example a wine bottle, to close it

corkscrew *noun* **corkscrews**
a tool made of a piece of twisted metal that you put into the cork of a bottle to pull it out

cormorant *noun* **cormorants**
a big black seabird with a long neck. Cormorants dive into the sea to catch fish.

corn *noun*
1 a plant such as wheat, barley or oats *a field of corn*
2 the seeds of this plant used for making flour *a sack of corn*
3 the yellow seeds of the maize plant that can be cooked and eaten. The seeds are also called sweetcorn.
see: **cob**
4 the American word for the maize plant
5 (*plural* **corns**) a small piece of hard skin on your foot or toe

corned beef *noun*
cooked beef that is stored in salty water and sold in a tin

corner *noun* **corners**
1 the place where two roads, walls or edges meet *Our school is on the corner. She lives around the corner* (nearby).
2 a small area, usually where it's quiet *Let's find a corner where we can talk.*
3 a faraway place *They came from every corner of the country.*
4 in sports such as football or hockey, a corner is when a player on the opposite team kicks or hits the ball from a corner of the field to try to score a goal

corner *verb*
corners, cornering, cornered
1 to corner a person or animal is to get them into a place that they cannot get out of
2 to go up to someone and speak to them even though they may not know you or want to speak to you
3 if a car corners, it goes around a corner *The car cornered too fast and skidded.*

cornet–cosmology

cornet *noun* **cornets**
1 a container for ice cream that has the shape of a cone (circle at the top, sloping sides and point at the bottom). It is made from a very thin dry biscuit that you eat with the ice cream.

SYNONYM cone

2 a musical instrument like a small trumpet, used for example in military bands

cornfield *noun* **cornfields**
a field planted with corn

cornflakes *noun plural*
a breakfast cereal made of small toasted pieces of maize that you eat with milk

cornflour *noun*
a white flour made from maize, often used for making sauces thicker

cornflower *noun* **cornflowers**
a small wild plant usually with a blue flower

Cornish *adjective*
1 connected with Cornwall
2 a Cornish pasty is a pie for one person, shaped like a semicircle and with meat and vegetables inside

Cornwall *noun*
a county in the south-west of England

corny *adjective* **cornier, corniest**
if something you say or do is corny, people have said or done it lots of times before, so repeating it may sound silly *a corny joke*; *'My sister got married on St Valentine's Day.' – 'How corny!'*

coronation *noun* **coronations**
a ceremony where someone becomes a king or queen and is given their crown

ORIGIN from Latin *corona* 'crown'

coroner *noun* **coroners**
an official in charge of an investigation into how someone died, especially when their death is unusual

corporal *noun* **corporals**
a soldier of low rank in the army or air force, just below the rank of sergeant

corporal punishment *noun*
punishing someone by hitting them, for example in schools in the past

corporation *noun* **corporations**
1 a large company
2 a group of people who control the public services of a town

corps ['kor'] *noun* **corps** ['korz']
1 a group in an army that has special duties *the medical corps*
2 an official group of people who do a special job *the press corps*

ORIGIN from French *corps* 'body'. As in French, the final 'ps' is not pronounced.

corpse *noun* **corpses**
a dead body

ORIGIN from French *corps* 'body'

corpuscle ['kor-pus-erl'] *noun* **corpuscles**
one of the cells (tiny units of living matter) in the blood. Corpuscles are either red cells that carry oxygen or white cells that fight infection.

corral ['ker-rahl'] *noun* **corrals**
an area surrounded by a fence where cows or horses are kept, usually in the US

correct *adjective*
1 with no mistakes *a correct answer*

SYNONYM right

2 used for describing something you should do or have, the position or situation where something should be or the time when something should be done *a correct decision*; *the correct tools*; *What's the correct way to shut down a computer?* *I put the book back in its correct place. This is not the correct time.*

SYNONYM right

3 behaving in the way you should behave among people *It's not very correct to shout at your teachers.*

SYNONYM polite

correct *verb*
corrects, correcting, corrected
1 to correct something such as homework or spelling is to put the mistakes right by marking them in writing
2 to correct something that is wrong or bad is to put it right *It's a problem that's easy to correct.*
3 to correct someone who is wrong is to give them the right information

correction *noun*
1 (*plural* **corrections**) a word or mark that someone puts in writing, for example on homework, to show what the correct answer should be
2 the action of correcting something or someone *These are serious errors that need correction.*

correctly *adverb*
1 without mistakes *I answered correctly.*
2 in the right way, or in the way something should happen or be done *You decided correctly to go home straightaway. The TV isn't working correctly.*
3 in the way things should be done among people *The prize-giving began correctly with a speech by the head teacher.*

correspond *verb*
corresponds, corresponding, corresponded
1 if something corresponds to something else, the two things are closely connected because something in one of them is similar to something in the other *The description corresponds to the first picture.*
2 to be equivalent to or very similar to something *The French word 'château' corresponds to the English word 'castle'.*
3 if you correspond with someone, you send them letters or emails and they send them to you

correspondence *noun*
1 sending or receiving letters or emails
2 the letters and emails sent and received *I have a file on my computer with all our correspondence in it.*
3 a connection between two or more things

correspondent *noun* **correspondents**
1 someone who writes letters or emails to someone
2 someone working for a newspaper or TV station who sends in news from a particular place or on a particular subject *This report is from our sports correspondent.*

corridor *noun* **corridors**
1 a long narrow passage in a building such as a hotel or school. It has doors on one or both sides that open into rooms.
2 a narrow passage on a train with doors on one side that open into compartments (separate sections)

corrode *verb*
corrodes, corroding, corroded
if metal corrodes or if something corrodes it, it is gradually destroyed by something such as chemicals, rust or water **corrosion** *noun*

corrosive *adjective*
if something is corrosive, it contains chemicals that make things such as metals or plastics corrode

corrugated *adjective*
shaped into small waves or folds for extra strength *a corrugated metal roof*

corrupt *adjective*
1 if someone people trust such as a politician, judge or police officer is corrupt, they behave in a way that is dishonest or wrong in order to get money or power *The corrupt official was seen taking a bribe.*
2 if a computer file or program is corrupt, it doesn't work properly because some of its data (information) has been changed or has mistakes in it

corrupt *verb*
corrupts, corrupting, corrupted
1 to corrupt someone is to make them behave dishonestly or badly
2 to change something and make it worse *Some people are afraid these foreign words will corrupt our language.*
3 to change a computer file or program or put mistakes in it so that it doesn't work properly

corruption *noun*
1 dishonest or bad behaviour by someone people trust
2 the action of corrupting something

corset *noun* **corsets**
a piece of underwear that women wear tightly around the middle part of the body to make them look thinner. Corsets were worn especially in the past.

cosh *noun* **coshes**
a short thick stick used as a weapon

cosmetic *adjective*
connected with making people look more attractive *a cosmetic product*; *cosmetic surgery*

cosmetics *noun plural*
substances such as creams or lipstick that people use on their face and skin to make them look more attractive

cosmic *adjective*
connected with space or the universe *cosmic rays* (radioactive particles that reach the earth from outer space)

cosmology *noun*
the study of the origin and structure of the universe **cosmologist** *noun*

95

cosmonaut *noun* **cosmonauts**
someone who travels in space on the Russian space programme

ORIGIN from Greek *kosmos* 'order', 'universe', and *nautes* 'sailor'

cosmopolitan *adjective*
a place that is cosmopolitan has people from many different countries living there *London is a very cosmopolitan city.*

cosmos *noun*
the cosmos is the universe

cosset *verb*
cossets, cosseting, cosseted
to give someone lots of attention and protect them from anything unpleasant

cost *noun* **costs**
1 how much you have to pay to buy or do something *The cost of a taxi is very high.*
2 the cost of living is the amount of money people need to pay for the things they must have to live, such as food, clothes and a home
3 **at all costs** whatever happens *We will win at all costs.*

cost *verb*
costs, costing, cost
1 if something costs a certain amount of money, that's what you have to pay for it *This pair of shoes costs £50.*
2 if something costs you something of great value, you end up losing it *His bad behaviour cost him his job.*

costly *adjective* **costlier, costliest**
costing a lot of money

SYNONYM expensive

costume *noun* **costumes**
1 clothes from a particular place, such as a country or region, or from a particular time in history *a television costume drama*
2 clothes that an actor wears or that people wear to make them look like someone else *We all wore costumes to the fancy dress party.*
3 a swimming costume is a piece of clothing for swimming in, usually worn by girls and women

cosy *adjective* **cosier, cosiest**
1 comfortable and warm (usually used about small things) *a nice cosy little house*
2 friendly and pleasant *a cosy weekend at home*

cosy *noun* **cosies**
a cloth cover you put over a teapot to stop the tea from getting cold too quickly *a tea cosy*

cot *noun* **cots**
a bed with high sides for a baby or young child

cottage *noun* **cottages**
a small individual house, often in the country and sometimes with a thatched roof (covered with dry plants such as straw)

cottage cheese *noun*
a soft white cheese without much fat in it

cottage pie *noun* **cottage pies**
a pie made of minced meat, usually beef, with mashed potato on top. It is baked in an oven.

cotton *noun*
1 a light cloth made from the white fibres of a plant called the cotton plant
2 a thread used for sewing, usually made from the cotton plant *a cotton reel*
3 a plant that grows in warm countries and produces white fibres for making cotton

couch *noun* **couches**
a soft seat with a back and arms. It is made for more than one person to sit on.

SYNONYMS sofa, settee

couch potato *noun* **couch potatoes**
(informal)
someone who spends most of their time sitting and watching television

cough *noun* **coughs**
1 an illness where you cough a lot *I have a nasty cough.*
2 the action or sound of coughing

cough *verb*
coughs, coughing, coughed
1 to make a loud noise when you force air from your chest and lungs. People cough, for example, when they are ill, when they have something stuck in their throat or to attract someone's attention.
2 (informal) to cough up is to give someone money to pay for something, especially when you don't want to

could *verb*
past tense of **can**
1 used for saying you were able or knew how to do something *I could swim when I was six.*
2 used for saying that something was possible or that it happened or would happen sometimes *It could get very cold in winter.*
3 used when you ask someone politely to do something *Could you help me across the road, please?*
4 used for making a suggestion *You could ask your mum if you don't know the answer.*

couldn't
short for 'could not' *I couldn't see her.*

council *noun* **councils**
1 a group of people chosen to be in charge of an area such as a town or county and to control public services *My dad works for the local council.*
2 a group of people chosen to give advice and make decisions *the United Nations Security Council*
3 a council house or flat is a house or flat that people rent from their local council
4 council tax is a tax that people pay to their local council. It pays for things such as schools, libraries and the police.

councillor *noun* **councillors**
someone chosen to be a member of a local council in charge of a town or county

LANGUAGE EXTRA be careful not to confuse *councillor* with *counsellor* (someone who gives advice)

counsel *noun*
1 a lawyer who represents someone in a court of law
2 an old-fashioned word for advice

counsel *verb*
counsels, counselling, counselled
to give someone advice and help, especially with particular problems **counsellor** *noun*

LANGUAGE EXTRA be careful not to confuse *counsellor* with *councillor* (member of a local council)

count *verb*
counts, counting, counted
1 to name the numbers one after another in the proper order *Can you count up to 100?*
2 to work out the total number of things or people by using numbers *I counted how many people there were in my class.*
3 to include something or to be included in a total *Marks given for homework count towards your final score. There are six of us in our group, not counting me.*
4 to be important *What counts is working hard in class and doing your homework on time.*
5 if you count on someone, you trust them to do something for you and expect them to do it *We're counting on Isaac to score at least one of the goals.*

count *noun* **counts**
1 the action of counting *Come and get me after a count of 20.*
2 the total number of things you get when you count
3 the amount of a substance in something else *the pollen count* (the amount of pollen measured in the air)
4 if you lose count of something, you can't remember how many of something you have counted or how often something has happened
5 the title of a foreign nobleman. The British title is earl.

ORIGIN sense 5 is from Old French *conte* 'count' and Latin *comes* 'someone who goes with the emperor'. It has nothing to do with counting.

countable *adjective*
in grammar, a countable noun is one that can be used in the plural, for example picture (pictures), child (children). In this dictionary, the plural is shown for all countable nouns.

ANTONYM uncountable

countdown *noun* **countdowns**
when people count numbers backwards, for example from 10 to 0, especially before launching a spacecraft

countenance *noun* **countenances**
someone's face or the look on their face

counter *noun* **counters**
1 a table where customers pay for things or do business in a place like a shop or bank
2 a small plastic or cardboard disc that you use to play some indoor games such as ludo

counterclockwise *adverb*
the American word for anticlockwise

counterfeit ['kown-ter-fit'] *adjective*
if something is counterfeit, it looks exactly like something else but is false *The shopkeeper was fooled by the counterfeit money.*

counterfeit–cover

counterfeit ['kown-ter-fit'] *verb*
counterfeits, counterfeiting, counterfeited
to make an exact copy of something in order to trick someone

counterpart *noun* **counterparts**
someone's counterpart is the person who does the same job as them but in a different country or organisation

countess *noun* **countesses**
a woman who has the same rank as a count or earl

countless *adjective*
too many to count *I've told you countless times to behave.*

country *noun*
1 (plural **countries**) one of the areas of land that the world is divided into, with its own government, flag and borders *France and Spain are two of my favourite countries.*
2 all the people who live in a country
3 another word for countryside *We usually spend our holidays in the country.*

country dancing *noun*
a type of old English dancing in which groups made up of pairs of male and female dancers dance together in rows or circles
country dance *noun*

countryside *noun*
the area of land away from towns and cities, for example with fields, forests and hills

county *noun* **counties**
one of the regions that some countries are divided into, with its own council responsible for things such as schools and hospitals. Examples of counties are Devon (England), Angus (Scotland), Flintshire (Wales) and Antrim (Northern Ireland).

coup ['koo'] *noun* **coups** ['kooz']
an event when a group of soldiers or an army suddenly takes control of the government of a country

ORIGIN from French *coup d'état* 'a blow or attack against the state' (a state is a nation or country)

couple *noun*
1 two things or people
2 a very small number of things or people, for example about two, three, four or more *I'll be back in a couple of minutes.*
3 (plural **couples**) two people who are married or who go out together

couple *verb*
couples, coupling, coupled
to couple two things is to join them together

couplet *noun* **couplets**
two lines of poetry together of the same length *a rhyming couplet*

coupon *noun* **coupons**
1 a piece of paper that you exchange for something of value or that allows you to pay less for something

SYNONYM voucher

2 a form that you fill in with your name and address

courage *noun*
when you are not afraid to face danger or pain, for example because you know that what you are doing is good

courageous *adjective*
1 not afraid to face danger or pain *The soldier was given a medal for being courageous.*
2 also used about something that someone does *a very courageous decision*
courageously *adverb*

courgette *noun* **courgettes**
a long green vegetable that looks like a small cucumber and is a type of marrow. Courgettes are usually eaten cooked.

courier ['koo-ree-er'] *noun* **couriers**
1 a person or company that delivers parcels and documents
2 someone who works for a travel company and looks after holidaymakers as they travel around

course *noun* **courses**
1 a number of lessons for learning a particular subject *I took a Spanish course before I went on holiday.*
2 one part of a meal *The first course was soup, the main course chicken and the third course cheese and biscuits.*
3 an amount of medicine that you must take regularly *a course of antibiotics*
4 a large area of land where certain sports take place such as horse racing, cycling or golf *a golf course*
5 the direction something takes *The ship changed course.*
6 a period of time when something happens *In the course of the next few weeks, I became very good at maths.*
7 a course of study refers to the subjects that someone studies, for example at college
8 **of course** used as a polite or very strong way of saying yes *'Could you open the window?' – 'Of course.' 'You weren't late, were you?' – 'Of course not.'* (no)

SYNONYM certainly

9 **of course** also used when you say something that you think is known to the person you're speaking to or to everyone *Of course, I can't be in two places at once.*

SYNONYM obviously

court *noun* **courts**
1 a court or court of law is a place where a judge or jury decides whether someone is guilty of a crime or deals with disagreements between people *My dad went to court because his boss didn't pay him.*
2 the people in a court, for example the judge and jury
3 the place where a king or queen lives
4 a king or queen together with the people who live with them, help them and work for them
5 a piece of ground marked with lines for playing certain sports such as tennis, squash or basketball *a tennis court*
6 another word for a courtyard

courteous ['kerr-tee-ers'] *adjective*
if someone is courteous, they are polite and show respect towards other people
courteously *adverb*

courtesy ['kerr-ter-see'] *noun*
polite behaviour and respect towards other people

SYNONYM politeness

courtier *noun* **courtiers**
someone who lives at the court of a king or queen

court martial *noun* **courts martial**
a military court where soldiers decide whether other soldiers are guilty of a crime

court-martial *verb*
court-martials, court-martialling, court-martialled
1 to judge a soldier in a military court and decide whether he or she is guilty
2 if a solder has been court-martialled, he or she has been judged in a military court and found guilty

courtyard *noun* **courtyards**
an open space with a hard flat surface surrounded by buildings or walls *He lives in an old part of town with a cobbled courtyard.*

couscous ['cous' rhymes with 'puss' or 'goose'] *noun*
a food made from crushed grains of wheat that are cooked in steam or boiling water. It is eaten hot or cold, usually with vegetables or meat.

ORIGIN from Arabic *kaskasa* 'to crush until fine'. Couscous was first eaten in North African countries such as Morocco, Algeria and Tunisia and is still the most popular food in those countries.

cousin *noun* **cousins**
a son or daughter of your aunt or uncle

cove *noun* **coves**
a small area of the coast that curves inwards so that the sea is surrounded partly by land. A cove is smaller than a bay.

cover *verb*
covers, covering, covered
1 to put something on something else or all over it, for example to protect, hide, decorate or close it *Cover your head when you go out. Grandma covered the cake with icing. Mum covered the pot* (put a lid on it).
2 to be on top of something or all around something *Snow covered the ground. Forests cover an area of hundreds of miles.*
3 to deal with a particular subject, or to talk about it *The history course covers the reign of Elizabeth I.*
4 to travel over a particular distance *We've covered over 200 miles today.*
5 to pay for something *My sister has a student grant to cover her expenses.*
6 to protect someone by being ready to use a gun and shoot someone else who might attack them
7 to point a gun towards someone to stop them from moving or towards a place to stop someone from escaping *The police covered all the exits.*
8 if you cover someone in a sport, you stay close to a person in the opposite team to stop him or her getting the ball
9 if a singer or musician covers a song or piece of music that was first recorded by someone else, they sing, play or record a new version of it themselves

97

cover – cram

10 to cover for someone is to do their job or work instead of them, for example because they are ill or busy doing something else
11 if you cover up a bad action or event, you hide the truth about it

cover *noun*
1 (*plural* **covers**) something that goes on top of something else, for example to protect it or close it *Put the cover on the saucepan.*
2 (*plural* **covers**) the outside front or back part of a book or magazine
3 a place where you go to protect yourself from something *I ran for cover under a bridge when the rain started.*
4 the covers are the sheets and blankets on a bed

coverage *noun*
when an event is described, for example on TV, on the internet or in the newspapers, or the amount of time spent describing it *live coverage of the tennis at Wimbledon; The plane crash has received a lot of coverage.*

covering *noun* **coverings**
1 a layer that covers something *a covering of dust*
2 something such as a piece of material that goes on top of something *A cap is a covering that fits over your head.*

cover-up *noun* **cover-ups**
when important people hide the truth about something from the public *a government cover-up*

cow *noun* **cows**
1 a large female animal that people keep on farms and use for providing milk and meat, called beef. A male of this type of animal is a bull and a young cow or bull is a calf. The sound a cow makes is a moo.
2 the female of some other animals such as an elephant, seal or whale

coward *noun* **cowards**
someone who is too afraid to face danger or difficulties **cowardice** *noun*

cowardly *adjective*
1 too afraid to face danger or difficulties
2 also used about something that someone does *cowardly behaviour*
3 cruel towards someone weaker than you are *a cowardly attack on an old man*

cowboy *noun* **cowboys**
1 a man who rides a horse and looks after cows on a farm in America. Cowboys often appear in films called westerns, where they do not usually look after cows but do things such as fight Indians or rob banks.
2 someone who does manual work for other people that is of bad quality or someone who is dishonest in business *a cowboy builder*

cowgirl *noun* **cowgirls**
a woman who rides a horse and looks after cows on a farm in America

cowpat *noun* **cowpats**
solid waste that a cow's body get rids of, which dries on the ground into a flat round shape

cowshed *noun* **cowsheds**
a building on a farm where people keep cows

cowslip *noun* **cowslips**
a wild plant with yellow bell-shaped flowers

cox *noun* **coxes**
someone who tells people the correct direction to steer in when they are rowing a boat in a race

coy *adjective*
1 pretending to be shy *Don't be so coy!*
2 if someone is coy about something, they don't want to talk about it, for example because they are too embarrassed
coyly *adverb*

coyote ['koy-oh-tee'] *noun* **coyotes**
an animal like a small wolf that lives in deserts and prairies in North America

CPU ['see-pee-yoo'] *noun* **CPUs**
the main part of a computer that controls how it works
short for: central processing unit

crab *noun* **crabs**
a sea animal with a hard shell, five pairs of legs and big claws (pointed parts) on its front legs

crab apple *noun* **crab apples**
a small apple that is very sour

crack *noun* **cracks**
1 a line in something hard such as glass, a wall or a plate, where it is broken but still in one piece
2 a small gap between things *a crack in the curtains*
3 a short loud noise, for example of something being broken or of a gun being fired
4 a heavy knock on part of the body *Something fell off the roof and gave me a crack on the head.*
5 a joke
6 when someone tries to do something *I had a crack at playing my friend's clarinet.*
7 at the crack of dawn very early in the morning or when the sun rises

crack *verb*
cracks, cracking, cracked
1 if you crack something or it cracks, it breaks slightly and a line appears in it *I dropped the mug and it cracked.*
2 to hit something very hard, for example so that it breaks or breaks open *Be careful not to fall and crack your head.*
3 to make a short loud noise or to make something make this noise *The lion tamer cracked his whip.*
4 to find an answer to something such as a code
5 to crack a joke is to tell it
6 to get cracking is to start doing something, or to continue doing something but more quickly than before
7 to crack down on something is to start dealing with a problem more strongly *The school has cracked down on bullying.*

SYNONYM to clamp down on

8 to crack on is to carry on doing something
9 if someone cracks up, they become ill in their mind, for example because they have too much work or too many problems

cracker *noun* **crackers**
1 a cardboard tube covered with coloured paper, used when you have a party. When two people pull each of its ends apart, it makes a bang and a small gift falls out. *a Christmas cracker*
2 a thin dry biscuit that is not sweet and is sometimes eaten with cheese

crackers *adjective*
an informal word for mad

SYNONYM crazy

crackle *verb*
crackles, crackling, crackled
if something crackles, it makes short loud noises like a fire burning or an old radio
crackle *noun* **crackly** *adjective*

crackling *noun*
1 a crackling sound
2 the hard skin on a piece of cooked meat from a pig

crackpot *noun* **crackpots**
a crazy person **crackpot** *adjective*

cradle *noun* **cradles**
1 a bed for a baby. You can rock the cradle gently, from side to side.
2 a structure for supporting or lifting something heavy
3 the cradle of something is where something important and good started a long time ago *That country was considered the cradle of civilisation.*

craft *noun*
1 (*plural* **crafts**) an activity where you make something artistic with your hands that needs a lot of skill, for example wood-carving, pottery or origami
2 crafts are artistic objects that people make
3 the skill to do a particular job *Mozart was a master of his craft.*
4 (*plural* **craft**) a small boat *There were lots of craft on the river.*

craftsman *noun* **craftsmen**
a man who makes artistic objects with his hands using great skill

craftsmanship *noun*
1 the skill of making artistic objects with your hands
2 the quality of an artistic object that has been made with skill

craftswoman *noun* **craftswomen**
a woman who makes artistic objects with her hands using great skill

crafty *adjective* **craftier, craftiest**
1 clever at getting what you want, for example by making people believe things that aren't true *Crafty so-and-so!*
2 also used about someone's actions or ideas *That's a really crafty idea!*
craftily *adverb* **craftiness** *noun*

crag *noun* **crags**
a steep rough rock or part of a mountain

craggy *adjective* **craggier, craggiest**
1 steep and with lots of rough rocks
2 a craggy face looks rough with lots of lines in it

cram *verb*
crams, cramming, crammed
1 to put lots of things or people into something so that there is no space left *I crammed all my clothes into one suitcase.*

98

2 if people cram into a place such as a room, they go into it but there is no space left
3 to study for an exam by learning a lot of information quickly

cramp *noun* **cramps**
1 a pain in a muscle of the body, for example in the leg, when it becomes very hard and tight
2 cramps are pains in the stomach

cramped *adjective*
1 if a place is cramped, it is too small and you feel that there is not enough room
2 if someone feels cramped, they feel that there is not enough room

cranberry *noun* **cranberries**
a tiny red juicy berry that is very sour *cranberry sauce*

crane *noun* **cranes**
1 a very tall machine for lifting and moving heavy things, used especially to build large buildings
2 a large bird with long legs and a long neck. Cranes live near water.

crane *verb*
cranes, craning, craned
if someone cranes their neck, they stretch it to try to see something better, for example by looking over the heads of other people in a crowd

crane fly *noun* **crane flies**
a flying insect with long thin legs and a thin body

crank *noun* **cranks**
1 a handle shaped like the letter L that turns a machine to make it start working
2 someone who has strange ideas about something and does not deserve your attention or respect

cranky *adjective* **crankier, crankiest**
1 strange, or different in a strange way *He has some pretty cranky ideas.*
2 easily upset or annoyed by things, for example because you are tired or working too hard

cranny *noun* **crannies**
1 a small narrow hole, for example in a wall
2 if you talk about every nook and cranny, you mean everywhere in a particular place *I've looked for my keys in every nook and cranny.*

crash *noun* **crashes**
1 a very loud noise, usually when things hit each other or when something heavy falls or breaks
2 an accident caused by a road vehicle, train or aircraft hitting something

crash *verb*
crashes, crashing, crashed
1 if a road vehicle, train or aircraft crashes or if someone crashes it, it hits something and causes damage *A motorcycle has crashed into a tree. The pilot crashed his plane.*
2 if someone or something crashes somewhere such as into, onto or through something, they hit it with a loud noise *The ladder crashed to the floor. Parts of the ceiling came crashing down.*
3 if a computer or computer program crashes, it stops working

crash course *noun* **crash courses**
a course in a particular subject where you learn a lot in a short amount of time

crash helmet *noun* **crash helmets**
a hard hat that protects someone's head when they drive a motorcycle or racing car or ride a bicycle

crash landing *noun* **crash landings**
when a plane has to land suddenly and in a dangerous way because it has a problem flying

crate *noun* **crates**
1 a large box used for moving or storing things
2 a smaller container for carrying things such as bottles or fruit

crater *noun* **craters**
1 a hole in the ground caused by a bomb or by something hitting it from the sky such as a meteorite
2 the round open top of a volcano

crave *verb*
craves, craving, craved
if someone craves something or craves for something, they want it very much and they are always trying to get it

craving *noun* **cravings**
a strong feeling of wanting something

crawl *verb*
crawls, crawling, crawled
1 if someone such as a baby crawls, they move along the ground using their hands and knees
2 if an insect such as an ant or spider crawls, it moves slowly along the ground
3 if cars crawl, they move very slowly, for example because there is too much traffic
4 if something is crawling with insects or people such as tourists or police officers, there are lots of them everywhere *The whole room was crawling with ants.*

crawl *noun*
1 a very slow speed *The traffic was at a crawl.*
2 a fast way of swimming lying on your front. You move one arm over your head and then the other and at the same time kick your legs.

crayon *noun* **crayons**
a stick of coloured wax (a substance like fat that is soft when hot and hard when cold) for drawing with, like a small pencil

craze *noun* **crazes**
1 something that people like very much but that only lasts for a short time *Long hair was a craze in the 1960s.*

SYNONYM **fad**

2 a big interest in something that only lasts for a short time *There was a craze for that type of music a few years ago.*

crazy *adjective* **crazier, craziest**
1 stupid *That's a crazy idea.*
2 strange *Our neighbour seems a bit crazy.*
3 to drive someone crazy is to make them angry
4 if someone is crazy about something or someone, they like them very much
crazily *adverb* **craziness** *noun*

creak *verb*
creaks, creaking, creaked
if something creaks, it makes a high noise, for example when it is moved, like old stairs that you walk on or an old chair that you sit on **creak** *noun*

creaky *adjective* **creakier, creakiest**
1 making a creaking noise *a creaky door*
2 old and not working very well *Granddad's bones are getting creaky.*

cream *noun* **creams**
1 a thick yellowy-white substance in milk that contains fat. If you leave fresh milk, after a time the cream rises to the top.
2 any food that contains cream or looks like cream
3 a soft substance for rubbing on skin to protect it or make it better *sun cream*
4 a colour between yellow and white *a cream shirt*

cream cheese *noun*
a soft white cheese made from cream

cream cracker *noun* **cream crackers**
a type of thin dry biscuit. It is not sweet and is sometimes eaten with cheese.

cream tea *noun* **cream teas**
a small meal with scones, jam, cream and a pot of tea

creamy *adjective* **creamier, creamiest**
1 like cream, for example thick and smooth *creamy soup*
2 containing a lot of cream *creamy coffee*

crease *noun* **creases**
1 a regular line that you make in paper or cloth when you fold it
2 if there are creases in cloth or paper, there are irregular marks or lines in it, for example where it has been crushed
3 the line on a cricket pitch (or ground) where the batsman stands to hit the ball

crease *verb*
creases, creasing, creased
1 to make a crease or creases in cloth or paper *a neatly creased pair of trousers; The book's pages are creased.*
2 to become creased with irregular marks or lines *My dress creases very easily.*

create *verb*
creates, creating, created
1 to make something new *Click here to create a folder. How do you create an email address?*
2 to cause something or make something happen *This creates a big problem.*
3 to design, invent, write or paint something using skill *He's created a beautiful sculpture.*

creation *noun*
1 the action of creating something
2 (*plural* **creations**) something created, especially with imagination and skill *Sherlock Holmes is a creation of Conan Doyle.*

creative *adjective*
1 showing lots of imagination and skill in producing new things *She's a very creative musician.*
2 creative writing is writing stories and poetry, especially when people are taught how to do this in a class with other students
creativity *noun*

creator *noun* **creators**
someone who creates something

creature – crisis

creature *noun* **creatures**
a living thing, such as an animal, fish, bird or insect, but not a plant

crèche ['kresh'] *noun* **crèches**
a place where people look after babies and young children whose parents are working or busy

credible *adjective*
if something or someone is credible, you can believe them and trust them
credibility *noun*

credit *noun*
1 a way of buying something by paying for it in small amounts of money. People buy things in this way when they don't have enough money to pay in one go. *My parents bought their car on credit.*
2 praise that you give someone for something good they've done
3 (plural **credits**) an amount of money added to someone's bank account or the money in someone's account *My brother's account is in credit* (there is money in it).
4 the credits of a film, TV programme or play are the list of the people who helped to make it. The credits are usually shown at the end but sometimes at the beginning.

credit *verb*
credits, crediting, credited
1 to believe something *Would you credit it?*
2 to add an amount of money to someone's bank account *Dad will be credited with £100 at the end of the month.*

credit card *noun* **credit cards**
a small plastic card that people use for borrowing money to pay for things, for example in shops and supermarkets. They pay back later the money that they borrow, usually in small amounts.

creditor *noun* **creditors**
a person or company that people owe money to

creed *noun* **creeds**
someone's creed is the religious or political ideas they feel strongly to be true *people of all nationalities and creeds*

creek *noun* **creeks**
1 a long narrow strip of water that comes a long way into the land
2 an American word for a narrow river or stream
3 (informal) **up the creek** in trouble

creep *verb*
creeps, creeping, crept
1 to go somewhere, moving very slowly and quietly *I crept downstairs.*
2 to creep up on someone is to surprise them by going up to them very quietly from behind

creep *noun* **creeps** (informal)
1 a very nasty person
2 if something or someone gives you the creeps, you feel frightened and uncomfortable

creepy *adjective* **creepier, creepiest** (informal)
if someone or something is creepy, they make you feel frightened and uncomfortable, for example because they are strange

creepy-crawly *noun* **creepy-crawlies**
an informal word for an insect

cremate *verb*
cremates, cremating, cremated
if a dead body is cremated, it is burnt in a special way after a funeral ceremony
cremation *noun*

crematorium *noun* **crematoria**
a building where dead bodies are cremated

creosote ['kree-er-soht'] *noun*
a brown liquid that people paint or spray onto wooden things, for example fences or sheds, to protect them from the weather

crepe ['krayp'] *noun*
1 a thin cloth with tiny lines or folds in it, made from cotton, silk or wool *a crepe bandage*
2 (plural **crepes**) a large thin French pancake
3 crepe paper is a very thin coloured paper often used for decorating things

> **LANGUAGE EXTRA** also spelt *crêpe*

crept
past tense & past participle of **creep**

crescendo ['krer-shen-doh'] *noun* **crescendos**
a piece of music or a sound that gradually gets louder and louder

crescent *noun* **crescents**
1 a shape made up of two curved lines like parts of the edges of circles, joined together at the ends. It is wide in the middle and pointed at both ends. The crescent is the shape of a new moon (one of the phases of the moon).
2 a curved street *15 Maple Crescent*

cress *noun*
a plant with very small green leaves, eaten raw in salads

crest *noun* **crests**
1 the top of something, especially of a hill or wave
2 a bunch of feathers that stick up on the top of a bird's head

cretin *noun* **cretins**
an informal and very insulting word for a stupid person

crevasse *noun* **crevasses**
a very large deep crack in ice or a rock

crevice *noun* **crevices**
a narrow crack in a rock

crew *noun* **crews**
1 the people who do the work of sailing a boat or ship or flying a plane or spacecraft
2 a group of people with special skills *a television camera crew; an ambulance crew*
3 an informal or insulting word for any group of people

crib *noun* **cribs**
1 a bed for a baby or young child
2 a piece of paper or a book giving information or answers, used for cheating in an exam

crib *verb*
cribs, cribbing, cribbed
to copy schoolwork from someone, for example in an exam

crick *noun* **cricks**
if you have a crick in your neck, you have a pain caused by the neck muscles becoming stiff

cricket *noun*
1 an outdoor game played between two teams of people, where each team has a turn to hit a small hard ball with a bat. Points called runs are scored when the batsman hits the ball and then runs between two places called wickets.
2 (plural **crickets**) a small brown insect that jumps like a grasshopper and makes a noise with its wings

cricketer *noun* **cricketers**
a person who plays cricket

cried
past tense & past participle of **cry**

crime *noun*
1 (plural **crimes**) a particular action that is against the law *The thief committed a serious crime.*
2 all actions that are against the law *There's a lot of crime in the city centre.*
3 a bad action that someone can be blamed for but one that isn't against the law *It's a crime to throw away all that food.*

criminal *noun* **criminals**
someone who has committed a crime or more than one crime

criminal *adjective*
1 connected with crime or criminals *criminal behaviour*
2 very wrong *Hitting a cat is really criminal.*

crimson *adjective*
very dark red **crimson** *noun*

cringe *verb*
cringes, cringing, cringed
1 to move away suddenly from something unpleasant because you're afraid *She cringed when I showed her the spider.*
2 to feel very embarrassed or angry at something *When people say 'bored of' instead of 'bored with', it makes me cringe.*

crinkle *verb*
crinkles, crinkling, crinkled
1 to make small lines or folds in something such as paper or cloth, for example by crushing it slightly
2 if something like paper or cloth crinkles, it gets small lines or folds put into it
crinkle *noun*

crinkly *adjective* **crinklier, crinkliest**
with lots of small lines or folds in it *crinkly paper*

cripple *verb*
cripples, crippling, crippled
1 if someone is crippled, for example in an accident, they are badly hurt and can no longer walk
2 to cause something great harm or a serious problem that lasts for a long time *After the war, the economy was crippled.*

cripple *noun* **cripples**
an old-fashioned or insulting word for a disabled person who finds it difficult to walk

crippling *adjective*
1 causing great harm or serious problems that last for a long time *crippling debts*
2 causing great pain *a crippling illness*

crisis ['kry-siss'] *noun* **crises** ['kry-seez']
a difficult or dangerous situation when someone or something is faced with urgent problems to deal with

crisp adjective **crisper, crispest**
1 if something is crisp, it is hard and makes a pleasant sound when it is broken, stepped on or crushed *I love walking on the crisp deep snow.*
2 crisp food is hard but pleasant to eat *a crisp green apple*
3 crisp weather or air is cold and dry in a pleasant way
4 new and clean *a crisp £5 note*
5 if a picture or sound is crisp, it is very clear

crisp noun **crisps**
a thin round slice of potato fried in oil and eaten cold *a packet of crisps*

crispy adjective **crispier, crispiest**
crispy food is hard on the outside but pleasant to eat

criss-cross verb
criss-crosses, criss-crossing, criss-crossed
1 if lines criss-cross, they form a pattern of many lines that cross each other
2 if people or things criss-cross a place, they go everywhere from one side to the other *The police criss-crossed the country searching for the escaped murderer.*

criss-cross adjective
a criss-cross pattern is a pattern of many crossing lines

critic noun **critics**
1 someone who criticises someone or something
2 someone who works for a newspaper, magazine or TV station giving their opinion about artistic things such as books, music, films or plays *a music critic*

critical adjective
1 criticising someone or something *My teacher is very critical of the head teacher's plans for the school.*
2 very important *Success is critical for the future of the whole school.*
3 very serious and causing people to worry about what will happen *The situation of the country is critical.*
4 connected with the opinions of critics *The play was a critical success.*

critically adverb
1 seriously *critically ill*
2 when you are criticising someone or something *He spoke very critically of the prime minister.*

criticise verb
criticises, criticising, criticised
to say what you think is wrong about someone or something, or to say what you think someone is doing wrong

LANGUAGE EXTRA also spelt *criticize*

criticism noun
1 (plural **criticisms**) a particular opinion or people's opinions in general about what is wrong about someone or something, or about what someone is doing wrong *He didn't like your criticism of the way he sings. He doesn't like criticism.*
2 written opinions about artistic things such as books, music, films or plays *film criticism*

croak verb
croaks, croaking, croaked
1 when a frog croaks, it makes a low rough sound
2 if a person croaks, he or she speaks in a deep rough voice
croak noun **croaky** adjective

Croatia noun
a country in South-East Europe
Croatian adjective & noun

crochet ['kroh-shay'] noun
a way of making clothes and other things from wool or cotton using a special needle with a hook at the end **crochet** verb

> ORIGIN from Old French *crochet* 'little hook'

crock noun **crocks** (informal)
an old crock is something that is old and broken or someone old and weak

crockery noun
plates, mugs, bowls and other dishes used for eating and drinking

crocodile noun **crocodiles**
a big dangerous animal with a long thick body and tail, short legs and a very large mouth with sharp teeth. Crocodiles live in rivers and lakes in many hot parts of the world.

> ORIGIN from Latin *crocodilus* and Greek *krokodeilos* – from *kroke* 'pebble' and *drilos* 'worm' – because it is like a big worm that likes to lie on pebbles

crocodile tears noun plural
if someone sheds crocodile tears, they look very sad but are not really sad at all

crocus noun **crocuses**
a small yellow, purple or white flower that usually appears in spring in gardens and parks and grows close to the ground

croft noun **crofts**
a very small farm in Scotland **crofter** noun

croissant ['krwah-son'] noun **croissants**
a small piece of light and flaky sweet bread in the shape of a curve. It is often heated up and eaten for breakfast.

> ORIGIN from French *croissant* 'crescent', because the shape is similar

crook noun **crooks**
1 a dishonest person or someone who has committed a crime
2 a shepherd's crook is a tall stick shaped like a hook at one end. It was used especially in the past for controlling sheep.
3 the crook of your arm is the soft inner part where you bend it

crook verb
crooks, crooking, crooked
if you crook a part of your body such as your finger, you bend it inwards

crooked [pronounce '-ed' like '-id'] adjective
1 not straight *crooked teeth*; *a crooked picture on the wall*
2 not honest *a crooked lawyer*
crookedly adverb

croon verb
croons, crooning, crooned
to sing in a soft and gentle voice

crop noun **crops**
1 something that farmers grow for food, such as wheat, rice or potatoes
2 an amount of these plants that farmers grow in a particular year *We had a good crop of strawberries.*
3 a group of things happening at the same time or of people arriving somewhere at the same time *this year's crop of new students*

crop verb
crops, cropping, cropped
1 to crop a picture or computer image is to make it smaller by cutting a part of it away *I cropped the photo so that you can only see my face.*
2 to crop someone's hair is to cut it short
3 to make something shorter, for example grass or plants, by cutting it as farmers do or eating it as animals do
4 to crop up is to appear or to happen, for example suddenly or in different places *The word 'dinosaur' cropped up several times in the story.*

cross noun **crosses**
1 a mark or shape that looks like + or like the letter X
2 an X mark that you write against something such as an answer to show that it's wrong
3 an X mark that you write against something in a list to show that you've chosen something
4 a shape that looks like † that is used as a Christian symbol
5 a mixture of things or qualities *A mule is a cross between a horse and a donkey. He made a sound that was a cross between a yawn and a laugh.*

cross verb
crosses, crossing, crossed
1 if you cross something like a road or river, you go from one side of it to the other
2 to go towards something and then go past it *We crossed the French border at Strasbourg. This is the place where the two roads cross.*
3 if you cross your arms or legs, you put one arm on top of the other arm or one leg on top of the other leg
4 if you say you will keep your fingers crossed, you mean that you wish for good luck for yourself or someone else. Sometimes people put their middle finger over their first finger when they say this.
5 if something crosses your mind, you think of it *It suddenly crossed my mind that I'd forgotten to phone my parents.*
6 if you cross something out, you draw a mark such as a line or X through it, for example because it is wrong

cross adjective
angry *Dad is very cross with you.*
crossly adverb

cross- prefix
connected with something that goes from one side to another *a cross-Channel ferry*

crossbar noun **crossbars**
1 a long piece of metal, wood or plastic joining the top of two upright posts
2 in football, a long piece of wood joining the top of two goalposts

crossbow–crummy

crossbow noun **crossbows**
a weapon used in the past for shooting arrows. It is a small bow fixed to a piece of wood and has a trigger that shoots the arrows.

cross-country adjective
a cross-country race is one where the runners run through fields and forests, not on roads or tracks

cross-examine verb
cross-examines, cross-examining, cross-examined
to cross-examine someone in a court of law is to ask them questions about what they have already said to see if they are telling the truth **cross-examination** noun

cross-eyed adjective
if someone is cross-eyed, their eyes look inwards towards each other

crossing noun **crossings**
1 a place where you can cross a road, railway line or river safely. Road crossings usually have black and white stripes going across the road.
2 a journey across a sea or river

cross-legged adjective
sitting with one leg under the other and your knees pointing outwards, usually on the floor

crossroads noun **crossroads**
1 a place where one road crosses another
2 a time when someone has to make an important decision that will change their future

cross-section noun **cross-sections**
1 something cut in half to show what it is like on the inside
2 a drawing of something such as a machine that shows what it would be like inside if it were cut in half
3 a group of people or things that is an example of all of them *A cross-section of the children wanted more time to spend on sports.*

crossword noun **crosswords**
a word puzzle where you have to find answers to questions (called clues) and write each letter of the answer in a different square. The squares are joined in rows or columns that sometimes cross each other so that some letters of an answer are shared.

crotchet ['krotch-it] noun **crotchets**
a musical note that is twice as long as a quaver

crouch verb
crouches, crouching, crouched
to bend your legs, lean forward and lower your body close to the ground *I crouched down to pick up my pen from the floor. He was crouching behind a wall so as not to be seen.*

crow noun **crows**
1 a large black bird that makes a loud rough noise
2 **as the crow flies** used for talking about the shortest distance between two places, which is the distance it would be if someone could go in a straight line

crow verb
crows, crowing, crowed
1 when a cock crows, it makes a loud high sound, usually early in the morning
2 if someone crows about something, they let other people know how pleased they are about it but they do so in a way that is very annoying

SYNONYM for sense 2: to boast

crowbar noun **crowbars**
an iron bar with a curved end, used for lifting heavy things or forcing things open

crowd noun **crowds**
1 a large group of people together in one place
2 a particular group of people such as your friends *They went to see the football match with their usual crowd.*

crowd verb
crowds, crowding, crowded
1 to go somewhere all together at the same time *People crowded onto platforms and into trains. Fans crowded round the footballer as he left the match.*
2 if people crowd a place, they go there in large numbers *Tourists crowded Trafalgar Square for the event.*

crowded adjective
full of people

crown noun **crowns**
1 a circular decoration, usually made of gold and jewels, worn by kings and queens on their head to show their power
2 something shaped like a crown worn on the head as a decoration or a special honour
3 the crown as a symbol of a king or queen *The crown passed to his son.*
4 the Crown means the king or queen of a country or their government *These lands belong to the Crown.*
5 the top part of something, especially your head or a hill

ORIGIN from Latin *corona* 'crown' or 'garland'

crown verb
crowns, crowning, crowned
1 to make someone a king or queen by putting a crown on their head in a special ceremony
2 to give someone a title when they win a competition *She was crowned dance champion.*
3 to make something successful or complete by achieving something greater than before *His efforts were crowned by the winning of a Nobel Prize.*

crown jewels noun plural
the crown and all the jewels belonging to a king or queen, which they wear for ceremonies

crow's nest noun **crow's nests**
a small place for standing at the top of a ship's mast where a sailor can look out over the sea

crucial ['kroo-sherl] adjective
very important *My teacher's help has been crucial in getting me through the exam.*
crucially adverb

crucifix noun **crucifixes**
a model of Jesus on the cross, which is a symbol of the Christian religion

crucify verb
crucifies, crucifying, crucified
to kill someone by fixing their hands and feet to a cross. The ancient Romans punished criminals in this way. **crucifixion** noun

crud noun
an informal word for dirt

crude adjective **cruder, crudest**
1 made in a rough and simple way, without any skill *a crude weapon*
2 not very exact *I have a crude idea of what it's like.*

SYNONYM rough

3 very rude *crude jokes; Your brother is vulgar and crude.*
4 crude oil is natural oil before it has been changed by any chemical process
crudely adverb

cruel adjective **crueller, cruellest**
1 causing a lot of pain in the body of a person or animal *He was cruel to his little sister and her pet goldfish.*
2 causing a lot of pain in someone's mind or in the mind of animals such as dogs or cats *I think your uncle is very cruel.*
3 also used about something that someone does or says *cruel words*
cruelly adverb

cruelty noun **cruelties**
when someone causes a lot of pain to people or animals through their words or actions *The boys' cruelty to the cat must be punished.*

cruise noun **cruises**
1 a holiday on a ship called a cruise ship, during which people visit different places or countries
2 a journey by boat for pleasure

cruise verb
cruises, cruising, cruised
1 to have a holiday on a ship
2 to travel at a slow but steady speed, for example in a boat or on a plane

cruiser noun **cruisers**
1 a large boat with an engine and a cabin where people live and sleep

LANGUAGE EXTRA also called a *cabin cruiser*

2 a large fast warship *a battle cruiser*

crumb noun **crumbs**
a tiny piece that falls off something such as bread or cake, for example when you cut it or eat it

crumble verb
crumbles, crumbling, crumbled
1 if something crumbles, or if you crumble it, it breaks into little pieces
2 if a building is crumbling, small parts of it keep falling off, for example because it is old and has not been looked after

crumble noun **crumbles**
a baked dish made of fruit and covered with a dry mixture of butter, flour and sugar *an apple crumble*

crumbly adjective **crumblier, crumbliest**
if something such as cheese or an old brick is crumbly, it breaks easily into little pieces

crummy adjective **crummier, crummiest**
a slang word for bad *I'm feeling crummy today.*

crumpet *noun* **crumpets**
a small flat round food like bread, with tiny holes in the top. You toast it and eat it warm, for example with butter or jam.

crumple *verb*
crumples, crumpling, crumpled
1 to crumple something such as paper is to crush it so that it becomes smaller and full of lots of irregular folds and marks
2 if something crumples, it becomes crushed and smaller

crunch *verb*
crunches, crunching, crunched
1 if you crunch something, you make the noise of something being crushed, for example when eating hard food, like nuts, or when walking on snow or dry twigs
2 if something crunches, it makes the noise of being crushed

crunch *noun* **crunches**
1 the noise of something being crushed, such as hard food, snow or dry twigs
2 **the crunch** a difficult situation, often when you have to make an important decision

crunchy *adjective* **crunchier, crunchiest**
crunchy food is hard, like nuts, crisps or an apple, and makes a loud sound when you eat it **crunchiness** *noun*

crusade *noun* **crusades**
someone's efforts over a long period of time to achieve something they think is good or to stop something they think is bad
crusader *noun*

ORIGIN from French *croisade* and Old French *crois* 'cross' – the Christian symbol. The *Crusades* were wars fought in the Middle Ages between Christian and Muslim armies, who were fighting over Palestine.

crush *verb*
crushes, crushing, crushed
1 to press or hit something very hard so that it gets completely broken, badly damaged or destroyed, or so that it completely loses its shape and gets flatter or bent *A brick fell and crushed his toe. The car was crushed when it hit a tree. I sat on the hat and crushed it.*
2 to kill or injure a person, animal or insect *Did you have to crush that spider?*
3 to beat someone easily in a game or completely in a battle *The French were crushed at Waterloo.*

crush *noun*
1 a large crowd of people so close together that they can hardly move
2 (*plural* **crushes**) a strong feeling of love towards someone *My sister has a crush on a boy at school.*

crust *noun* **crusts**
1 the brown part on the outside of bread that is harder than the rest of the bread
2 the hard outer part of something baked such as a pizza or pie
3 the earth's crust is its hard outer surface
4 any hard part or layer on top of something softer

crustacean ['krus-tay-shern] *noun* **crustaceans**
a sea animal with a shell, such as a crab, shrimp or lobster

crusty *adjective* **crustier, crustiest**
bread that is crusty has a hard crust but is pleasant to eat *a crusty baguette*

crutch *noun* **crutches**
crutches are special sticks to help you walk, for example if you've hurt one or both of your legs. You put them under your arms and lean on them.

cry *verb*
cries, crying, cried
1 if you cry, tears come out of your eyes, usually because you're unhappy or hurt
2 if a baby cries, it makes a loud sound because it wants something
3 to say something very loudly *Someone cried out my name in the street. 'I'm over here,' she cried.*

SYNONYM to shout

4 if someone cries off something, they suddenly change their mind and decide they no longer want to do it or have it

cry *noun* **cries**
1 a shout
2 the high sound made by an animal or bird *the cry of the giraffe*
3 if someone has a cry, they let tears come out of their eyes

crybaby *noun* **crybabies**
if you say someone is a crybaby, you think they cry too much, for example when they are not allowed to do something

crypt *noun* **crypts**
a room under a church where dead people were buried in the past

crystal *noun*
1 (*plural* **crystals**) a tiny piece of a substance with a natural regular shape and many sides *ice crystals*
2 a type of glass of very good quality *a crystal wine glass*
3 (*plural* **crystals**) a mineral like glass that you can see through
4 a crystal ball is a glass ball that some people look into, for example fortune-tellers, because they think it will show them what will happen in the future
crystalline *adjective*

crystallise *verb*
crystallises, crystallising, crystallised
if a substance such as ice or snow crystallises, it forms crystals

LANGUAGE EXTRA also spelt *crystallize*

Ctrl *noun*
a key on a computer keyboard that you press, usually together with another key, to make the computer do something
short for: control

cub *noun* **cubs**
1 a young animal such as a lion, tiger, fox, wolf or bear
2 a Cub in the Scouts is a boy who belongs to the junior section, for boys aged 8 to 10. The earlier section is known as the Beavers, for boys aged 6 to 8.

Cuba *noun*
an island and country in the Caribbean Sea, south of the United States and not far from the state of Florida
Cuban *adjective & noun*

cubbyhole *noun* **cubbyholes**
1 one of the small open boxes, for example in a piece of furniture with shelves, for putting things into *There was a letter in my cubbyhole.*
2 a small space for storing things

cube *noun* **cubes**
1 a solid object like a box with six equal square sides *a sugar cube*
2 in maths, the cube of a number is the number you get when you multiply that number by itself twice. For example, the cube of 2 is 8 (2 × 2 × 2).
3 in maths, the cube root of a number is the number that you multiply by itself twice to get the bigger number. For example, the cube root of 8 is 2.

cube *verb*
cubes, cubing, cubed
1 in maths, if you cube a number, you multiply that number by itself twice. For example, 3 cubed is 27 (3 × 3 × 3).
2 if you cube food such as cheese, you cut it into small cubes

cubic *adjective*
connected with measuring volume (the amount of space inside an object). For example, a cubic metre is the volume of a cube where each side is one metre long.

cubicle *noun* **cubicles**
a small part of a room that is divided from the rest of the room, for example by a thin wall or a curtain *a shower cubicle; a toilet cubicle*

Cubism *noun*
a style of art of the early part of the 20th century that uses simple shapes, for example straight lines and angles, to represent objects and people **Cubist** *adjective & noun*

cuboid *noun* **cuboids**
a shape like a rectangular box with six sides

cuckoo *noun* **cuckoos**
a bird that lays its eggs in other birds' nests and makes a sound like its name

cucumber *noun* **cucumbers**
a long dark green vegetable that you cut into slices and eat raw, for example in sandwiches or salads

cud *noun*
if an animal such as a cow or sheep chews the cud, it brings back into its mouth from its stomach the food that it has swallowed so that it can chew it again

cuddle *verb*
cuddles, cuddling, cuddled
if you cuddle someone or something such as a doll, you put your arms around them and hold them tight in a way that shows that you love them **cuddle** *noun*

cuddly *adjective* **cuddlier, cuddliest**
a cuddly person, animal or thing looks nice to cuddle, for example because they are soft and round *a cuddly teddy bear*

cudgel *noun* **cudgels**
a short thick stick for hitting people or animals

cue *noun* **cues**
1 a sign for someone such as an actor to start doing or saying something
2 a long thin stick for hitting the ball in games such as snooker or billiards

cuff–current

cuff *noun* **cuffs**
1 the end part of a sleeve that goes around your wrist
2 to give someone a cuff is to cuff them

cuff *verb*
cuffs, cuffing, cuffed
to hit someone with your open hand, usually lightly on the side of the head

cufflink *noun* **cufflinks**
cufflinks are small fasteners used instead of buttons to join the cuffs of a man's shirt

cul-de-sac ['kul-der-sak'] *noun*
cul-de-sacs
a short road closed at one end so that traffic cannot pass through

> ORIGIN from French *cul-de-sac* 'bottom of the bag or sack'

culminate *verb*
culminates, culminating, culminated
if an action or event culminates in something, that thing is the final or most important part of it *These attacks culminated in war between the two countries.*

culmination *noun*
the final or most important part of something

culprit *noun* **culprits**
someone who is to blame for doing something wrong or bad

cult *noun* **cults**
1 a religious group, especially one with ideas that people think are strange
2 great interest that people show in something or someone at a particular time *the cult of Princess Diana*
3 used for describing something or someone that people show great interest in at a particular time *a cult film; a cult hero*

cultivate *verb*
cultivates, cultivating, cultivated
1 to grow crops on land *This land is too dry to cultivate. Rice is cultivated in the north of the country.*
2 to develop something gradually and carefully, for example a quality or someone's friendship
cultivation *noun*

cultural *adjective*
1 connected with literature, painting, music and the other arts *Liverpool is a major cultural centre.*
2 connected with the ideas and ways of behaving of a particular society *the cultural differences between Europe and America*
culturally *adverb*

culture *noun*
1 activities that develop your mind such as literature, painting, music and the other arts
2 (*plural* **cultures**) the ideas and ways of behaving of a particular society *ancient Greek culture*
3 (*plural* **cultures**) a particular society with its own ideas and ways of behaving *China is a very different culture from our own.*

cultured *adjective*
a cultured person is well-educated, knows a lot about things such as literature, painting and music, and has good manners

cumbersome *adjective*
1 large and difficult to carry *an old and cumbersome computer*
2 slow and complicated *Getting a passport can be very cumbersome.*

cunning *adjective*
1 if someone is cunning, they are clever at getting what they want, for example by making people believe things that aren't true
2 cunning actions are clever at helping people get what they want *a cunning plan*
cunningly *adverb*

> SIMILE 'as cunning as a fox' means very cunning

cup *noun* **cups**
1 a small round container with a handle, used for drinking hot drinks such as tea or coffee
2 something in a cup, for example a hot drink *I drank two cups of coffee.*
3 a big cup made of silver or another metal, usually with two handles. It is given as a prize to people who win a game or competition.

cup *verb*
cups, cupping, cupped
if you cup your hands, you hold them together to form a cup shape *She showed off the little chick in her cupped hands.*

cupboard ['kub-erd'] *noun* **cupboards**
a piece of furniture or a small area in the wall of a room with a door and usually shelves for storing things

> ORIGIN from 14th-century *cup board* 'a board for putting cups on'

cupcake *noun* **cupcakes**
a small round cake, usually with icing (sugar, water and other ingredients) on it

cup final *noun* **cup finals**
the last and most important match in a football competition

cupful *noun* **cupfuls**
an amount of something that is contained in a cup

curator *noun* **curators**
someone who works in a museum or art gallery and is in charge of the objects or paintings

curb *verb*
curbs, curbing, curbed
to control something such as your feelings or the spread of an illness **curb** *noun*

curd *noun* **curds**
curds are thick lumps in milk when it becomes sour

curdle *verb*
curdles, curdling, curdled
if milk curdles, it forms thick lumps when it becomes sour, for example if it is left in the sun

cure *noun* **cures**
something that makes a sick person better or that makes an illness or something bad go away

cure *verb*
cures, curing, cured
1 if a doctor or medical treatment cures someone who is ill, it makes them better
2 to cure an illness or something bad is to make it go away
3 to cure food such as fish or meat is to make it last longer by drying it, hanging it in smoke and covering it with salt

curfew *noun* **curfews**
1 a particular time, for example from the evening until the following morning, when people are not allowed to go out of their homes
2 the government law that decides on the curfew and how long it will last

> ORIGIN from Old French *cuevrefeu* 'cover the fire' – the time in the evening when people had to put out their fires

curiosity *noun*
1 a feeling that you want to know more about something
2 (*plural* **curiosities**) something unusual and strange

curious *adjective*
1 if you are curious about something, you want to know more about it
2 unusual and strange
curiously *adverb*

curl *noun* **curls**
1 a part of your hair that forms a curve or circle
2 a shape like a curve or circle

curl *verb*
curls, curling, curled
1 if your hair curls, you have lots of curls in it
2 if someone such as a hairdresser curls your hair, they put curls in it
3 to curl round something is to twist around it with lots of curved shapes like a snake
4 to curl up is to put your body into a comfortable round shape with your legs bent and pulled towards your body

curler *noun* **curlers**
a small plastic or metal tube for putting curls in your hair

curly *adjective* **curlier, curliest**
1 full of curls or having curls in your hair *long curly hair*
2 shaped like a curl *Pigs have curly tails.*

currant *noun* **currants**
1 a small grape that is dried (water has been removed). Currants are often used in puddings and cakes. *a currant bun*
2 a small red, black or white berry that grows on a bush

> ORIGIN from Old French *rayson de Corannte* 'raisin of Corinth' – a city in ancient Greece where currants first came from

currency *noun* **currencies**
the type of money used in a particular country *The French currency is the euro.*

current *noun* **currents**
1 a steady flow of water or air *Their boat was swept out to sea in the strong current.*
2 a flow of electricity through something such as a wire

current – cutting

current *adjective*
if something is current, it exists or happens now *our current head teacher; my current address*

> ORIGIN from Old French *corant* 'running', 'flowing' (from Latin *currere* 'to run')

currently *adverb*
at the present time

curriculum *noun* curricula or curriculums
the subjects students study at school *English and maths are on the curriculum.*

curry *noun* curries
a cooked Indian food made from vegetables or from meat and vegetables, with a sauce that has a very strong taste. It is usually eaten with rice.

> ORIGIN from *kari* 'spicy sauce for rice' in Tamil (a language of south India and Sri Lanka)

curse *noun* curses
1 if someone puts a curse on someone or something, they say special magic words to get bad things to happen to them *The wicked witch put a curse on the Princess.*
2 a bad thing that causes people a lot of trouble
3 a swear word

curse *verb*
curses, cursing, cursed
1 to swear
2 to say bad things about someone or something

cursor *noun* cursors
a symbol on a computer screen that you can move using a mouse or keyboard or by touch. The cursor shows you the place on the screen where you do something, for example type text, open or close a program or move to another web page.

curtain *noun* curtains
1 a piece of cloth that hangs down in front of a window, used for example to stop people from seeing into a room
2 a heavy piece of cloth that hangs down in front of the stage of a theatre and is raised up when the performance begins

curtsy *verb*
curtsies, curtsying, curtsied
if a woman or girl curtsies, she lowers her body slightly and bends her knees to show respect to someone important *I curtsied to the Queen.* **curtsy** *noun*

> LANGUAGE EXTRA also spelt *curtsey*

curve *noun* curves
a line or shape with a gradual bend in it like a part of a circle

curve *verb*
curves, curving, curved
to form a curve *The river curved to the right.*

curved *adjective*
forming a curve *the curved top of an arch*

cushion *noun* cushions
a square or circle of cloth with soft material inside, used on chairs for making them more comfortable to sit on

cushion *verb*
cushions, cushioning, cushioned
if something soft cushions someone or something, it protects them when they hit something *I slipped over but the soft carpet cushioned my fall.*

cushy *adjective* cushier, cushiest (informal)
if something like a job is cushy, it is easy and you don't have to work very hard

> ORIGIN from Hindi *khush* 'pleasant', 'happy'

custard *noun* custards
a yellow sauce made from eggs, milk, sugar and flour or cooked from a special powder. It is eaten with sweet food or fruit.

custom *noun*
1 (plural customs) a way of doing things that people accept as normal because they have been behaving that way for a very long time *It's the custom to shake hands when you are introduced to someone.*
2 when you buy things from someone as a customer *All these shops want your custom.*

customary *adjective*
usual, for example because of a custom *It's customary to leave a tip in a restaurant.*

customer *noun* customers
1 someone who buys something, for example from a shop or website *supermarket customers*
2 someone who uses someone's services *a bank customer*

customise *verb*
customises, customising, customised
to customise something is to change it so that it works or looks the way you want it to *On this computer, you customise the desktop by clicking on Properties.*

> LANGUAGE EXTRA also spelt *customize*

custom-made *adjective*
specially made for a particular person

customs *noun plural*
the place at a border, port or airport where officials check your luggage to see if you have any goods that you are not allowed to bring into the country

cut *verb*
cuts, cutting, cut
1 to divide something or to take a piece out of something using a sharp object like a knife or scissors *Who wants to cut the cake?*
2 if something cuts, it is sharp enough to cut things *These scissors don't cut.*
3 to make something shorter using something like a knife, scissors or a blade *I hate cutting the grass.*
4 to hurt a part of your body with something sharp *I cut my finger on some glass.*
5 to make something smaller or less, such as a price, an amount or the size of something *Our school is trying to cut costs. I've cut down on the sweets I eat.*
6 if you cut text or a picture in a computer file, you remove it from the screen *Highlight this paragraph, press Control X to cut it and Control V to paste it into a new document.*
7 if a baby cuts a tooth, a new tooth starts to grow
8 to go somewhere as a shortcut *I usually cut through the park to get to school.*
9 to stop doing something or to stop something happening or working *They've cut (or cut off) the phone lines. The electricity has been cut off. You should cut out sugar.*
10 if you cut in, you interrupt someone speaking
11 if someone in a vehicle such as a car or motorbike cuts in, they go past another vehicle and then drive in front of it in a dangerous way
12 to cut something off is to remove it by cutting it, usually with a knife *The tree branch was sticking out so Dad cut it off.*
13 if something such as a snowstorm or flood cuts a place or person off, it means it is not possible to reach that place or person in the usual way, for example by road or train or on foot *It's been snowing for two days and we're completely cut off* (we can't leave our house, for example, and no-one can reach us).
14 if someone is cut off from other people, for example their friends or family, they miss being with other people and talking to them *Mira's from London and she feels cut off in the countryside.*
15 to cut someone off while they are speaking on the phone or making an internet call is to stop the line from working so they cannot continue speaking
16 to cut something out is to remove it from something bigger, usually with scissors *Cut out a triangle from this piece of card.*

cut *noun* cuts
1 a small injury to your body or a mark or narrow opening made by something sharp *I got a nasty cut on my finger.*
2 the action of cutting something *My hair needs a cut.*
3 cuts are when something such as prices or amounts are made less *There are lots of price cuts today in the supermarket.*
4 someone's share of an amount of money

cute *adjective* cuter, cutest
attractive and very nice *a cute little baby*

cutlass *noun* cutlasses
a short curved sword, for example used by sailors in the past

cutlery *noun*
knives, forks and spoons for eating with

cutlet *noun* cutlets
a flat slice of meat with its bone *a lamb cutlet*

cutout *noun* cutouts
a shape cut out of paper or card *a cardboard cutout of the prime minister*

cut-price *adjective*
if something you buy is cut-price, it is cheap

cutting *noun* cuttings
1 an article cut out of a newspaper or magazine
2 a piece cut from a plant that you put in the soil so that it can grow into a new plant

105

cyan ['cy' rhymes with 'eye'] noun
a greenish-blue colour. It is one of the main colours used in colour printing.
cyan adjective

cyber- ['cy' rhymes with 'eye'] prefix
connected with the internet

> ORIGIN from *cybernetics* 'the study of how machines, electronic equipment and human brains work'

cyberbully noun **cyberbullies**
a person who bullies someone over the internet, for example by saying bad things to or about them or by making them feel embarrassed or look stupid. Cyberbullies use different ways of communicating such as chat rooms, email and text messages.
cyberbullying noun

cybercafé noun **cybercafés**
a shop or café with computers where you pay to use the internet

cybercrime noun **cybercrimes**
crime that people commit using the internet

cyberspace noun
the internet considered as a place where information exists and is exchanged between computers *Your email must have got lost in cyberspace.*

cyborg noun **cyborgs**
in science fiction, a creature that is part human and part machine

> ORIGIN from *cybernetic* and *organism*

cycle noun **cycles**
1 a series of events that keep happening again in the same order *the cycle of the seasons*
2 a bicycle *a cycle path*

> ORIGIN from Greek *kyklos* 'circle', 'wheel'

cycle verb
cycles, cycling, cycled
to ride a bicycle *My brother cycles to school.* **cyclist** noun

cyclical ['sik-li-kerl'] adjective
happening in cycles

cyclone ['cy' rhymes with 'eye'] noun
cyclones
a bad storm where the wind goes round in a circle **cyclonic** adjective

Cyclops ['cy' rhymes with 'eye'] noun
a giant with one eye in the middle of the forehead in ancient Greek stories

cygnet ['sig-nit'] noun **cygnets**
a young swan

cylinder ['sil-in-der'] noun **cylinders**
1 a long object like a tube, can or pipe. It has straight sides and two flat ends shaped like circles, and both ends are the same size.
2 the tube in an engine where a piece of metal called the piston moves up and down, making part of the engine move
cylindrical adjective

cymbal ['sim-berl'] noun **cymbals**
a large thin disc made of brass used as a musical instrument. You play it by hitting it with a stick or by banging two of them together to make a loud ringing noise.

cynical ['sin-ik-erl'] adjective
if someone is cynical, they believe that people are not good and only care about themselves **cynic** noun

cypress ['cy' rhymes with 'eye'] noun
cypresses
a tall tree with dark green leaves. It is a type of conifer and its leaves stay green in winter.

Cyprus ['cy' rhymes with 'eye'] noun
a country in the eastern Mediterranean, south of Turkey **Cypriot** adjective & noun

Cyrillic ['si-ril-ik'] adjective
the Cyrillic alphabet is the one used for writing Russian and some other languages

> ORIGIN from Saint *Cyril*, the 9th-century Greek Christian saint who invented this alphabet

czar ['zahr'] noun **czars**
the name given to the emperor of Russia until 1917

> LANGUAGE EXTRA also spelt *tsar*

> ORIGIN from the Latin name *Caesar*, first used in Russia by Emperor Ivan IV in 1547

Czech Republic ['chek'] noun
a country in Central Europe
Czech adjective & noun

d D

> ORIGIN the letter D comes from a shape representing either a door or a fish – no-one knows for sure. In the Phoenician alphabet, the letter looked like a curious triangle with curved angles and its name was *dalet* meaning 'door'. When the Greeks borrowed the letter, they called it *delta* and changed it in two important ways. Some Greek cities turned it into a perfect triangle with equal sides and others into a semicircle shape with its curve facing left. When the Romans began to use the letter, they preferred the semicircle but changed it so that the curve faced right – the shape we recognise as our own D.

D
the Roman numeral for 500

dab verb
dabs, dabbing, dabbed
1 to touch something lightly a few times with a piece of cloth or a tissue
2 to dab something onto something is to put it on lightly *Take a tissue and dab some antiseptic on your cut.*

dab noun **dabs**
1 a small amount of something that you put onto something else
2 a light touch with a piece of cloth or a tissue

dabble verb
dabbles, dabbling, dabbled
1 to dabble in an activity is to do it because you enjoy it but not to spend much time or effort on it *It's the story of a little girl who dabbles in magic.*
2 to move your hands and feet about in water

dachshund ['daks-ernd'] noun
dachshunds
a small dog with very short legs and a long body

> ORIGIN from German *Dachs* 'badger' and *Hund* 'dog', because they were used in Germany to hunt badgers

dad noun **dads**
an informal word for a father

daddy noun **daddies**
an informal word for a father (used mainly by young children or when you are speaking to young children)

daddy-long-legs noun **daddy-long-legs**
a flying insect with long thin legs and a thin body. Its proper name is crane fly.

daffodil noun **daffodils**
a yellow or yellow and white flower that appears in spring. The centre of the flower is shaped like a trumpet. A daffodil grows from a bulb (root shaped like an onion).

daft adjective **dafter, daftest**
silly or crazy

dagger–dark

dagger *noun* **daggers**
1 a short pointed knife with a blade on both sides used as a weapon, especially in past times
2 **to look daggers at someone** to look at someone in an angry way

dahlia ['day-lee-er'] *noun* **dahlias**
a large garden plant with big flowers of many different colours and a very thick root

daily *adjective & adverb*
happening every day *Andrew goes for a daily swim. Our post is delivered daily.*

dainty *adjective* **daintier, daintiest**
1 small and attractive, with many fine details *dainty hands*
2 small and done in an attractive and careful way *She walks with dainty steps.*
daintily *adverb* **daintiness** *noun*

dairy *noun* **dairies**
1 a place on a farm where butter and cheese are made from milk and cream
2 a place where milk is put into bottles and sold
3 dairy products are things made from milk such as butter, cheese and yoghurt

daisy *noun* **daisies**
a small flower with a yellow centre and pinkish-white petals

Dalai Lama ['da-lye-lah-mer'] *noun*
the name given to the leader of the Tibetan Buddhist religion

dale *noun* **dales**
an old-fashioned word for a valley

dally *verb*
dallies, dallying, dallied
if someone dallies in doing something, such as making a decision, they take too much time doing it

Dalmatian *noun* **Dalmatians**
a large dog with short white hair and black spots

dam *noun* **dams**
a structure such as a wall built across a river or stream to stop the water flowing

dam *verb*
dams, damming, dammed
to build a dam across a river or stream

damage *noun*
1 something bad that is done to something so that it gets broken or made worse in some way *The wind caused a lot of damage to our house. We sent the laptop back because there was damage on the outside* (it was dented, scratched or cracked, for example). *Losing every match this year caused damage to our team's reputation* (people's opinion of the team has become worse).
2 damages are money that a court of law says must be paid to someone because of something bad that has happened to them

damage *verb*
damages, damaging, damaged
to cause something bad to happen to something so that it gets broken or made worse in some way *Fire damaged a number of buildings. My laptop is damaged. This sort of behaviour will damage your good name* (make your reputation worse).

damaging *adjective*
causing damage or a bad effect *This news is very damaging to the government.*

SYNONYM **harmful**

dame *noun* **dames**
a comic woman character played by a man in a pantomime (Christmas play for children)

Dame *noun* **Dames**
the title of a woman given a special honour by the British government. The title is similar to a knighthood for a man. *Dame Vera Lynn sang to the troops in the Second World War.*
compare: **Sir**

ORIGIN from Old French *dame* 'lady', 'wife', and Latin *domina* 'lady', 'mistress of the house' (Latin *domus* 'house')

damp *adjective* **damper, dampest**
1 slightly wet, often used for talking about something that should be dry *a damp basement*
2 if the weather is damp, the air is slightly wet in an unpleasant way *a grey and damp London morning; I hate the damp* (damp weather).
dampness *noun*

dampen *verb*
dampens, dampening, dampened
1 to make something slightly wet
2 to make a feeling less strong *Nothing could dampen the crowd's enthusiasm.*

damsel *noun* **damsels**
in old stories, a damsel is a young woman who is not married

damson *noun* **damsons**
a small purple plum

dance *noun* **dances**
1 the action of dancing *Paula did a little dance for us.*
2 the movements you make with your body and feet when you dance, or the piece of music you dance to *an Irish dance*
3 the art of dancing, for example when it is taught as a school subject *a dance class; The story was told through song and dance.*
4 a party where people dance

dance *verb*
dances, dancing, danced
1 to move your body and feet in a special way that follows the sound of music
2 to do a particular type of dance *Can you dance the salsa?*
dancer *noun*

dandelion *noun* **dandelions**
a wild plant with a bright yellow flower and jagged leaves. When the flower dies, it leaves a white fluffy ball of seeds.

ORIGIN from Old French *dent de lion* 'lion's tooth', because of the tooth-like shapes along the edges of the leaves

dandruff *noun*
tiny white pieces of dry skin from someone's head that you see in their hair

Dane *noun* **Danes**
someone from Denmark

danger *noun* **dangers**
1 a situation where someone can be hurt or killed *Let's go home – we're in danger here.*
2 something or someone that can hurt or kill you *That old building is a real danger.*
3 a situation where something bad can happen *We're in danger of losing the match.*

dangerous *adjective*
if something or someone is dangerous, they can harm or kill you *a dangerous elephant; He has a gun and he's dangerous. It's dangerous to cross the road here.*

dangerously *adverb*
1 in a way that can cause someone to be harmed or killed *That person was driving dangerously.*
2 in a way that can cause something bad to happen *Your cup of tea is dangerously close to the edge of the table.*

dangle *verb*
dangles, dangling, dangled
if something dangles or if you dangle it, it hangs down or it swings gently without anything to stop it *Lights dangled from the ceiling of the old house.*

Danish *adjective*
1 connected with Denmark or the Danish language
2 a Danish pastry is a flat sweet cake for one person. It has fruit or jam inside and often has icing (sugar, water and other ingredients) on the top. It is made from several layers of dough (flour and water).

Danish *noun*
the language people speak in Denmark

dank *adjective* **danker, dankest**
if something such as air or a room is dank, it is cold, smells unpleasant and is slightly wet

dappled *adjective*
marked by areas of lighter and darker colours *a dappled horse*

dare *verb*
dares, daring, dared
1 if you dare to do something, you're not afraid to do it although it could get you into trouble or be dangerous
2 if you dare someone to do something, you ask them to prove to you that they're not afraid to do it although it could get them into trouble or be dangerous

dare *noun* **dares**
when someone dares you to do something dangerous or bad *Why don't you knock that man's hat off, for a dare?*

daredevil *noun* **daredevils**
someone who likes doing dangerous things

daring *adjective*
if someone is daring or does something daring, they're not afraid of doing it although it could be dangerous or could upset or surprise people *a daring plan*

daring *noun*
when you are not afraid of doing something dangerous or something that could upset or surprise people

SYNONYMS **courage, boldness**

dark *adjective* **darker, darkest**
1 if something is dark, there isn't enough light to see properly or there's no light at all *a dark cave*

107

dark–daybreak

2 when the night has come *I don't like going out when it's dark.*
3 black or brown, or a colour that is close to black or stronger than another colour *a dark pair of trousers; dark hair (either black or brown); This part of the painting is slightly darker.*
4 used for describing colours that are strong and not pale *Cucumbers have a dark green skin.*
5 bad or mysterious *a dark secret*

dark *noun*
1 when there isn't enough light or there's no light at all *Please turn the light on – I don't want to sit here in the dark.*
2 the night-time *Don't stay out after dark.*

Dark Ages *noun plural*
the period of European history after the end of the Roman Empire, from about AD 480 to about AD 1000

darken *verb*
darkens, darkening, darkened
1 to become dark or darker *The sky darkened.*
2 to make something dark or darker

darkness *noun*
1 when there is no light *The whole town was in darkness.*
2 the night-time *Darkness fell.*
3 the dark colour of something

darling *noun* **darlings**
someone you love very much

darn *verb*
darns, darning, darned
to mend a hole in a piece of clothing by sewing stitches across the hole *My brother hates darning socks.* **darn** *noun*

dart *noun* **darts**
1 a small pointed object that people throw at a round board in the game of darts
2 a small pointed object that people throw as a weapon or fire from a gun. A dart with a poison or drug in its tip can be used for capturing an animal by making it unconscious.

dart *verb*
darts, darting, darted
to move suddenly and quickly somewhere *A dog darted out in front of my bicycle.*

dartboard *noun* **dartboards**
a round board placed against a wall that people throw darts at in the game of darts. Points are scored depending on what part of the board the dart hits.

dash *verb*
dashes, dashing, dashed
1 to go somewhere quickly *I dashed downstairs to open the door. She had to dash off* (leave suddenly).
2 to throw something strongly against something else, usually so that it breaks *The wind dashed the boat against the rocks.*
3 to dash someone's hopes is to disappoint someone by destroying their hopes of doing something

dash *noun* **dashes**
1 when you go somewhere quickly *We all made a dash for the exit.*
2 a short line like this – used in writing

3 a small amount of something *Add a dash of lemon juice to the fish.*

LANGUAGE EXTRA you use a *dash* to separate parts of a sentence when you add an explanation or opinion or say something strongly.
You can use a dash on its own, for example *When I grow up, there's one thing I want to be – happy.* Or you can use two dashes in one sentence, for example *There is nowhere – nowhere in the world – I'd want to live except Scotland.*
A dash is used in a similar way to a comma but often separates a part of the sentence that is very different from the main sentence and doesn't belong to it (such as *nowhere in the world* in the last example).

dashboard *noun* **dashboards**
the part of a car in front of the driver where there are instruments such as the speedometer

dashing *adjective*
very attractive and dressed in nice clothes (often used in stories) *a dashing young prince*

data ['day-ter'] *noun plural*
information, for example for making calculations or stored on a computer *You can store a lot of data on a Blu-ray Disc.*

LANGUAGE EXTRA *data* is usually used with a singular verb (*The data is wrong*) but can be used with a plural verb in maths and in scientific language (*The data are given in the spreadsheet*)

database *noun* **databases**
a large store of information on a computer. It is organised so that you can find any piece of information easily.

date *noun* **dates**
1 a particular day of the month or year, often shown by a number *Today's date is 24th March. The date of the Battle of Hastings was 14th October 1066. Do you know the date and time of the match?*
2 when you meet someone you want to go out with, such as a boyfriend or girlfriend *My brother has a date* (is meeting someone to go out with).
3 a small sticky brown fruit with a hard seed inside called a stone. Dates grow on palm trees.

date *verb*
dates, dating, dated
1 to write the date on something *The letter is dated 5th June.*
2 to find out the date of something *They dated the coin to the time of Napoleon.*
3 if two people are dating, or if someone is dating someone else, they are going out together
4 if something dates from or back to a particular time, it has existed since that time *These Roman coins date from the third century. The school's records date back to the nineteenth century.*

dated *adjective*
if something such as a style or word is dated, it is no longer modern *Your jacket looks a bit dated.*

daub *verb*
daubs, daubing, daubed
1 to spread something liquid or very soft on a surface, often in a careless way *The naughty children daubed paint on the school gates.*
2 to draw or write on a surface, often in a careless way, with something liquid *Someone daubed graffiti on the wall.*
daub *noun*

daughter *noun* **daughters**
the daughter of a mother or father is their female child

daughter-in-law *noun* **daughters-in-law**
the wife of someone's son

daunt *verb*
daunts, daunting, daunted
if you are daunted by something, you are worried by it or nervous or upset because of it, for example because it is a big problem *I was daunted by the amount of homework to do.*

daunting *adjective*
if something is daunting, it makes you feel worried, nervous or upset, for example because it is a big problem *The job of clearing up my room is pretty daunting.*

dawdle *verb*
dawdles, dawdling, dawdled
to waste time by doing something or walking somewhere too slowly *Come straight back, and don't dawdle!*

dawn *noun*
the beginning of the day when it starts to get light as the sun rises

SYNONYMS daybreak, sunrise

ANTONYMS dusk, sunset

dawn *verb*
dawns, dawning, dawned
1 if a day dawns, it starts to get light as the sun rises *A bright day was dawning.*
2 to start to exist *The age of the internet has dawned.*
3 if something dawns on you, you think of it or understand it for the first time

day *noun* **days**
1 a period of time that lasts 24 hours *We spent two days in Paris.*
2 the part of the day when it's light outside *During the day I go to school.*
3 the time that someone spends at school or at work or doing an activity *I had a good day at school.*
4 a period of time in the future or past *One day you'll be a grown-up. The day came when England went to war. In those days things were different. People didn't have computers in the old days.*
5 these days used for talking about the present *These days Granddad doesn't go out much.*

day boy or **girl** *noun* **day boys** or **girls**
a boy or girl who goes to a boarding school but does not live there during term time

daybreak *noun*
the early morning when it first starts to get light

SYNONYMS dawn, sunrise

ANTONYMS dusk, sunset

day care *noun*
when a person or organisation looks after old people or young children during the day, for example when the old people's families can no longer look after them or when the children's parents are at work *a day care centre*

daydream *verb*
daydreams, daydreaming, daydreamed
if someone is daydreaming, they are thinking pleasant thoughts instead of paying attention to more serious things
daydream *noun* **daydreamer** *noun*

Day-Glo *noun* (trademark)
a colour such as yellow or green that appears to shine brightly in the light *a Day-Glo jacket*

daylight *noun*
the light from the sun during the day or the time of the day when it's light *Don't play outside – there isn't enough daylight now.*

day return *noun* **day returns**
a train or bus ticket that is cheaper than normal because you go somewhere and come back on the same day

daytime *noun*
the part of the day when it's light outside

day-to-day *adjective*
happening every day *my day-to-day routine*

daze *noun*
in a daze looking as if you can't understand what is going on around you or as if you don't know where you are

dazed *adjective*
not able to understand what is going on around you, for example because you are shocked or hurt

dazzle *verb*
dazzles, dazzling, dazzled
if a light dazzles you, you cannot see for a short time because it shines so brightly in your eyes

SYNONYM **to blind**

de- *prefix*
used for giving a word an opposite meaning, for example by showing that something is taken away or made less *decompression*; *decontaminate*; *desperate* (without hope)

dead *adjective*
1 no longer living
2 no longer working *My phone battery is dead.*
3 if a place is dead, nothing much happens there *The centre of town is dead after six o'clock.*
4 complete *The car came to a dead stop. When it comes to football, I'm a dead loss* (completely useless).
5 exact *This point is the dead centre of the room.*

SIMILE 'as dead as a doornail' means very definitely dead (senses 1, 2 & 3)

dead *adverb*
1 completely *You're dead right! The bus arrived dead on time.*
2 very *It's dead easy.*

deaden *verb*
deadens, deadening, deadened
to make something less strong, for example a pain

dead end *noun* **dead ends**
a road or passage closed at one end so that traffic or people cannot pass through

dead heat *noun* **dead heats**
a race or competition where there are two or more winners who finish at the same time or have the same number of points

deadline *noun* **deadlines**
a date or time by which you must finish doing something

deadlock *noun*
a situation in which people who are discussing something cannot agree

deadly *adjective* **deadlier, deadliest**
1 likely to kill you or harm you *a deadly poison*; *He's my deadly enemy.*
2 complete *deadly silence*

deadly *adverb*
very *The teacher's lesson was deadly boring.*

deaf *adjective* **deafer, deafest**
not able to hear **deafness** *noun*

deafen *verb*
deafens, deafening, deafened
if a noise deafens you, it is very loud so that you can't hear anything else

deafening *adjective*
very loud *the deafening sound of aircraft*

deal *verb*
deals, dealing, dealt ['delt']
1 to deal with something or someone is to give them your attention by doing what needs to be done *I'll deal with my emails later. My teacher is very good at dealing with the class.*
2 to deal with something or someone is also to be in charge of them or make decisions about them *It's the school nurse who deals with injections. Mum deals with* (looks after) *my baby brother during the day and Dad deals with him in the evenings.*
3 to deal with something such as someone's problem or complaint is to sort it out or try to sort it out *Please just deal with my question* (answer it).
4 if something such as a book or person deals with a subject, that particular subject is the one that is mentioned *The next chapter deals with the solar system.*
5 if a person or company deals in something, they buy or sell it. If a person or company deals with someone, they buy from or sell to them or they use their services. *This shop deals in old books. My parents don't deal with this bank any more.*
6 to deal cards or to deal them out is to give them out to every player in a game of cards

deal *noun* **deals**
1 a decision about something made between people, for example in business *The two companies have made a deal.*

SYNONYM **agreement**

2 a good or great deal of something means a lot of it *I spent a great deal of time learning fractions. She's travelled a great deal.*
3 (informal) if you say something is a big deal, you mean it's important *It's a big deal when you have to change schools. No big deal!* (that's not important); *If you lose the match, big deal!* (or *no big deal!*) (it really doesn't matter at all)
4 if something you buy is a good deal, you get it for a good price
5 when someone gives out the cards to players in a game of cards *It's your deal.*

dealer *noun* **dealers**
1 someone who buys and sells something *a car dealer*
2 someone who deals the cards to players in a game of cards

dealing *noun*
1 buying or selling things *arms dealing* (buying and selling weapons)
2 if someone has dealings with someone else, they have something to do with them, for example they buy from them or sell to them or are often in contact with them

dealt ['delt]
past tense & past participle of **deal**

dean *noun* **deans**
1 an important official in charge of a part of a university
2 an important priest in charge of a church

dear *adjective* **dearer, dearest**
1 used about someone you love or like very much *my dear uncle*
2 costing a lot of money

SYNONYM **expensive**

3 used as one way of starting a letter or email to someone *Dear Leah*

dear *noun* **dears**
1 used about someone you love or when you want to be friendly to someone you don't know *Can I help you, dear?*
2 a kind person *Be a dear and make me a cup of tea.*

dear *interjection*
Oh dear! used for showing that you're upset, surprised or slightly angry *Oh dear, I've broken the window!*

dearly *adverb*
very much *We would dearly like to know what happened.*

death *noun*
1 the time when you stop living *The animal starved to death.*
2 (*plural* **deaths**) a particular time when someone dies *There were two deaths on the motorway.*
3 if you're bored or scared to death, you're very bored or scared

deathly *adjective & adverb*
making you think of death or a dead person *a deathly silence*; *deathly pale*

death toll *noun*
the number of people killed at a particular time, for example in an accident

death trap *noun* **death traps**
something such as a car or building that is in such a bad condition that it could kill you

debatable – decisively

debatable *adjective*
if something is debatable, it is not certain because people can have different opinions about it

> SYNONYM arguable

debate *verb*
debates, debating, debated
1 to talk about something seriously before making a decision

> SYNONYM to discuss

2 to think about something before making a decision *I was debating whether to go to Rick's party or not.*

debate *noun* debates
a discussion where people give lots of different opinions

debris ['deb-ree'] *noun*
pieces left over when something has been destroyed, for example in an accident or fire *The debris from the aircraft was scattered all over the field.*

debt ['det'] *noun* debts
1 money that someone owes
2 if someone is in debt, they owe money
debtor *noun*

debug *verb*
debugs, debugging, debugged
to debug a computer program is to remove the bugs (or errors) from it so that it works properly

debut ['day-byoo'] *noun* debuts
the debut of someone such as an actor or sports player is the first time that they appear in front of people

debut ['day-byoo'] *verb*
debuts, debuting, debuted
to be seen by people for the first time

decade *noun* decades
a period of 10 years

> ORIGIN from Greek *deka* 'ten'

decaffeinated *adjective*
decaffeinated coffee or tea has had the caffeine taken out

decapitate *verb*
decapitates, decapitating, decapitated
to cut off someone's head

> SYNONYM to behead

> ORIGIN from Latin *de-* (showing something taken off) and *caput* 'head'

decathlon ['di-kath-lon'] *noun* decathlons
a sports competition where someone takes part in 10 different sports
compare: **pentathlon** and **triathlon**

decay *verb*
decays, decaying, decayed
1 if something that is or was living decays, it goes bad because tiny organisms feed off it *The apples fell off the trees and were left to decay.*

> SYNONYM to rot

2 if something such as a building or city decays, its condition is bad and it gets worse because people don't look after it

decay *noun*
1 when something goes bad because tiny organisms feed off it *tooth decay*
2 the part of something that has gone bad
3 the bad condition of something such as a building or city

deceased *adjective*
a deceased person is someone who has recently died

deceit ['di-seet'] *noun*
dishonest behaviour or making people believe something that isn't true
deceitful *adjective* **deceitfully** *adverb*

deceive *verb*
deceives, deceiving, deceived
if you deceive someone, you make them believe something that isn't true or you behave in a dishonest way towards them

December *noun*
the twelfth month of the year, between November and January. December has 31 days.

> ORIGIN from Latin *decem* 'ten', because it was the tenth month of the ancient Roman year

decency *noun*
good behaviour that shows respect towards other people

decent *adjective*
1 of a good enough standard *Are there any decent programmes on TV this weekend?*
2 behaving well towards people *We have a very decent head teacher.*

> SYNONYM kind

3 ordinary and good *They are decent hard-working people.*
4 used for describing what most people think is the correct way of doing things *People said that wasn't a very decent thing to do.*

decently *adverb*
1 in a good enough way *a decently cooked meal*
2 behaving well towards people *She treated us very decently.*

deception *noun* deceptions
making someone believe something that isn't true

deceptive *adjective*
if something is deceptive, it looks like one thing but it is really something else

decibel *noun* decibels
a unit for measuring how loud a sound is

decide *verb*
decides, deciding, decided
1 to think about something first before doing or not doing it, or before saying you will or won't do it *I've decided to do my homework tonight. I decided against going to school in the heavy snow* (decided not to go).
2 to form an opinion about something *I decided English was more interesting than maths. 'Tea or coffee?' – 'I can't decide.'* (I don't know)
3 if something decides you to do something, it is the reason for it *What decided us to move to Wales was the beautiful scenery.*
4 if something decides something else, it makes a particular result happen or makes something exist in a particular way *These exams will decide your future.*
5 if someone decides a question or argument, they think about it carefully before saying what should be done
6 to decide on something is to choose it, and to decide against something is not to choose it *I've decided on the green dress and against the red one.*

deciduous *adjective*
if a tree is deciduous, all its leaves fall off in the autumn. Oak, horse chestnut and plane trees, for example, are deciduous.

> ANTONYM evergreen

decimal *adjective*
1 connected with a way of counting using the number 10. This way of counting is known as a decimal system.
2 a decimal place is the number of positions after a decimal point (the dot in a decimal number). For example, 2.564 has three decimal places.

decimal *noun* decimals
a number in a system of counting using the number 10. It is a number with a fraction written as a dot followed by one or more numbers. The dot is called a decimal point and the first number after the point shows the number of tenths. For example, 2.5 is 2 and 5 tenths (2$\frac{1}{2}$).

> ORIGIN from Latin *decima* 'tenth'

decimalise *verb*
decimalises, decimalising, decimalised
to change the money of a country or a measurement so that it uses the decimal system based on the number 10
decimalisation *noun*

> LANGUAGE EXTRA also spelt *decimalize* and *decimalization*

decipher ['di-sye-fer'] *verb*
deciphers, deciphering, deciphered
to find the meaning of something that is difficult to read, for example because it is written in a secret code or because the handwriting is careless

decision *noun* decisions
a choice you make or an opinion you give after thinking about something carefully *The head teacher took an important decision.*

decisive *adjective*
1 if something is decisive, it is very important and has a strong influence on making something else happen *the decisive battle of the war; The firefighters took decisive action to stop the flames spreading.*
2 completely certain *There's a decisive link between smoking and bad health.*
3 if someone is decisive, they are not afraid to make decisions quickly and they do not change their mind *a decisive leader*

decisively *adverb*
1 in a way that shows that you are not afraid to make decisions quickly *The prime minister acted decisively.*
2 completely, certainly or easily *Eva beat me decisively at chess.*

deck–deepen

3 in a way that shows that you will not change your mind *'I'm not going,' she said decisively.*

deck *noun* **decks**
1 a floor of a boat, bus or plane *I like travelling on the upper deck of the bus.*
2 the outside top part of a boat that passengers can walk on or sit on
3 a deck of cards is the complete number of 52 playing cards. It is also called a pack of cards.

deck *verb*
decks, decking, decked
to decorate *All the streets were decked out (or were decked) with flags.*

deckchair *noun* **deckchairs**
a folding chair with a cloth part to sit on. People use deckchairs for sitting outside, for example on a beach.

> **ORIGIN** deckchairs get their name because they have been used since the 19th century on the decks of big passenger ships

declaration *noun* **declarations**
something that people say in an official way

declare *verb*
declares, declaring, declared
1 to say in an official way that a particular situation is true *War was declared in 1939.*
2 to say something strongly, especially when you want everyone to know *Peter declared that he was angry with us all.*
3 if a cricket team declares, it ends its turn in the game by saying that its batsmen will not continue playing

decline *verb*
declines, declining, declined
1 to become less *The number of students studying German has declined.*
2 to become worse *Standards of behaviour have declined.*
3 to say no very politely when someone gives you or asks you something *My parents declined the invitation.*

decline *noun*
when something becomes less or worse *the decline of the Roman Empire*

decode *verb*
decodes, decoding, decoded
to find the meaning of something that is written in a secret code

decompose *verb*
decomposes, decomposing, decomposed
if something like a plant or animal decomposes, it is gradually destroyed because of chemical changes **decomposition** *noun*

> **SYNONYM** to rot

decompression *noun*
when the body of someone who has been diving deep under the sea is allowed to return gradually to normal air pressure, usually in a special room called a decompression chamber

decontaminate *verb*
decontaminates, decontaminating, decontaminated
to remove the chemical or harmful substances from something such as land or water **decontamination** *noun*

decorate *verb*
decorates, decorating, decorated
1 to put attractive or colourful things on or in something to make it look better *For the party we decorated the room with balloons.*
2 to decorate a room or building is to paint it or to put wallpaper on the walls
3 to give someone a medal because they have done something brave, for example in a war

decoration *noun*
1 (*plural* **decorations**) something attractive or colourful that you put on or in something *Mum put a lovely decoration on my birthday cake.*
2 decorations are things such as colourful pieces of paper or balloons that you put in a room for a special occasion *We're putting up the party decorations.*
3 the way something is decorated or the action of decorating it *These paper flowers are for decoration.*
4 (*plural* **decorations**) a medal for doing something brave

decorative *adjective*
looking very attractive, often in an artistic way *a decorative pattern*

decorator *noun* **decorators**
someone whose job is to paint rooms and buildings and to put up wallpaper

> **LANGUAGE EXTRA** also called a *painter and decorator*

decoy ['dee-koy'] *noun* **decoys**
something or someone used for tricking someone by making them go somewhere or do something, for example to catch them in a trap

decrease ['di-kreess'] *verb*
decreases, decreasing, decreased
to become less, or to make something less *The number of children staying for school dinners has decreased. You have to decrease the medicine gradually.*

decrease ['dee-kreess'] *noun* **decreases**
1 when something becomes less *a decrease in smoking*
2 the amount by which something is less *a decrease of £100*

decree *noun* **decrees**
an official order, for example made by a ruler such as a king or queen

decree *verb*
decrees, decreeing, decreed
to give an official order

decrepit ['di-krep-it'] *adjective*
old and no longer in good condition *Our school is looking a bit decrepit.*

> **ORIGIN** from Latin *decrepitus* 'creaking'

dedicate *verb*
dedicates, dedicating, dedicated
1 to spend time doing something because you are really interested in it *Mother Teresa dedicated her life to looking after the poor. He wants to dedicate himself to his hobbies.*

> **SYNONYM** to devote

2 if someone dedicates a book, song or film to someone, they name that person, at the beginning of it, as a special honour *This poem is dedicated to Wordsworth's best friend.*
3 to use something in a particular way *The magazine dedicated many pages to the royal wedding.*

> **SYNONYM** to devote

dedication *noun*
1 a lot of time, hard work and effort doing something that you are really interested in *My parents praised my teacher's dedication to the job.*
2 (*plural* **dedications**) a message at the beginning of something such as a book in which you name someone as a special honour

deduce *verb*
deduces, deducing, deduced
to find out something in a logical way after carefully considering the information you have *From my shaky handwriting, the teacher deduced that I was nervous.*

deduct *verb*
deducts, deducting, deducted
if you deduct an amount or number from something, you take it away from a total *Mum deducted £2 from my pocket money for bad behaviour.*

deduction *noun* **deductions**
1 an amount or number taken away from something
2 something that you find out in a logical way, or the action of finding it out *the powers of deduction of Sherlock Holmes*

deed *noun* **deeds**
1 something that someone has done, often something good *Florence Nightingale's good deeds*
2 an official document that shows that someone owns a building or some land *the house deeds*

deep *adjective & adverb* **deeper, deepest**
1 going a long way down from the ground or from the top of something *a deep river; a deep bowl; deep under the ground*
2 going a long way back from the front of something *a deep cupboard; We walked deep into the forest.*
3 used for saying the distance that something goes down or back *a cupboard three feet deep*
4 deep feelings are very strong ones *She felt deep anger.*
5 a deep sound is very low *My brother has a deep voice.*
6 a deep colour is dark and strong *deep blue*
7 a deep sleep is when it is difficult to wake up *Dad didn't hear the alarm – he's in a deep sleep.*
8 very big, serious or important *Take a deep breath. You're in deep trouble.*

deepen *verb*
deepens, deepening, deepened
1 to become stronger or greater, or to make something stronger or greater *Their love for each other deepened. I want to deepen my understanding of history.*
2 if something such as a river or the sea deepens, the amount of water in it increases as the distance from the top to the bottom gets larger *The swimming pool deepens towards the end.*

deep-freeze noun deep-freezes
a large piece of equipment like a fridge where food is stored at a temperature below freezing

SYNONYM freezer

deeply adverb
1 very *Grandma was deeply shocked.*
2 very much *Her behaviour upset me deeply.*
3 a long way into something *The arrow went in deeply.*

deer noun deer
a large wild animal that has long legs and can run fast. The adult male, called a stag, has big twisted horns on its head called antlers.

deface verb
defaces, defacing, defaced
if someone defaces a building, monument or wall, they make it look bad by writing on it or causing damage to it

default noun defaults
1 the way something is shown on a computer screen before you make any changes to it *We changed some of the program's default settings.*
2 a default program is the usual program your computer uses for a particular activity such as surfing the internet *My default browser is Firefox.*

defeat verb
defeats, defeating, defeated
1 to win a battle or war against someone *Germany was defeated in the Second World War.*
2 to do better than someone in a game or competition and become the winner

defeat noun defeats
1 when someone loses a battle or war or a game or competition *the French defeat at Agincourt in 1415*
2 a lost battle or war, or a lost game or competition *England suffered three defeats in a row.*

defect ['dee-fekt] noun defects
something wrong with someone or something that makes them less good than they should be *My tablet computer has a defect.*

defect ['di-fekt] verb
defects, defecting, defected
if someone defects, they leave the country or organisation they belong to and join an opposing one **defector** noun

defective adjective
not working properly, or not as good as it should be *a defective battery*

SYNONYM faulty

defence noun
1 the action of protecting someone or something from being hurt, attacked or criticised *Anne came to my defence.*
2 (plural **defences**) something that protects you *Hadrian's Wall was built in the second century as a defence against invaders from the north.*
3 arguments to support something, or when someone argues to support something *We listened to the head teacher's defence of his ideas.*

4 the defence in a team game such as football means the players whose job is to stop the other team from scoring points or goals

defenceless adjective
if a person or animal is defenceless, they are not able to protect themselves if someone wants to hurt them

defend verb
defends, defending, defended
1 to protect someone or something from being hurt, attacked or criticised
2 to use arguments to support something such as an idea or opinion
3 to stop something being taken away *Teachers are marching to parliament to defend their jobs.*
4 in football and other games, to try to stop players from the opposite team from scoring points or goals
defender noun

defendant noun defendants
someone accused of a crime in a court of law

defensive adjective
1 used for protecting someone or something *These weapons are defensive.*
2 upset or worried because you think someone might be saying something bad about you or saying that you have done something bad *Don't be so defensive when I ask you a question.*

defer verb
defers, deferring, deferred
to defer something such as a decision or payment is to say you will do it later or it will happen later *The prime minister's decision has been deferred.*

SYNONYM to delay

defiant adjective
if someone is defiant, they are angry and do not do what you tell them or do not obey the rules **defiance** noun **defiantly** adverb

deficiency noun deficiencies
1 a shortage of something that you need
2 a fault or problem with something

SYNONYM for sense 2: shortcoming

deficient adjective
to be deficient in something is not to have enough of something that is needed *a diet deficient in the essential vitamins*

define verb
defines, defining, defined
1 to describe exactly what something is or is like *His ideas are hard to define.*
2 to define a word or phrase is to explain exactly what it means

defined adjective
if a shape is well defined, it has edges that you can see clearly

definite adjective
1 if something is definite, it is completely true or will happen, or it is impossible to be mistaken about it *It's definite you're not getting any pocket money this week. Tom's birthday party isn't definite. I have a definite idea about what I want for Christmas.*

SYNONYM certain

2 used about something that is fixed and will not change *He gave me a definite answer. Is there a definite date for the test yet?*

definite article noun definite articles
the word 'the' used in grammar. It is called the definite article because it refers to a particular example of a noun. For example, 'the house' refers to a particular house, not just any house.
compare: **indefinite article**

definitely adverb
1 used for saying something will or did happen or is true or for making a meaning stronger *I'll definitely email you tomorrow. Jack is definitely my favourite uncle. I definitely didn't see her leave.*
2 used for agreeing with someone *'Isn't this film awful?' – 'Yes, definitely!'*

definition noun
1 (plural **definitions**) an explanation of the exact meaning of a word or phrase *Look up the definition of 'school' in this dictionary.*
2 when a shape has edges that you can see clearly *high-definition television*

deflate verb
deflates, deflating, deflated
if someone deflates a tyre or balloon, they let the air out of it and it becomes smaller

deflect verb
deflects, deflecting, deflected
to make something move in a different direction by hitting it *The ball hit the post and was deflected into the goal.*
deflection noun

deforestation noun
when people cut down or burn down trees in an area of land, for example to sell the wood from the trees or to grow crops

deformed adjective
if something such as a hand or toe is deformed, it has an unusual shape, for example because of illness or because it has not grown properly

deformity noun deformities
a part of the body with an unusual shape

defrag verb
defrags, defragging, defragged
if you defrag your computer, you use a program to organise the information stored on it by putting the broken (or fragmented) files together. Defragging helps to make your hard disk work better.
short for: **defragment**

defraud verb
defrauds, defrauding, defrauded
to get money from someone in a dishonest way by committing the crime of fraud

defriend verb
defriends, defriending, defriended
if you defriend someone on an internet site such as Facebook, you remove them from your list of friends

SYNONYM to unfriend

defrost verb
defrosts, defrosting, defrosted
1 if you defrost frozen food, or if it defrosts, it warms up slowly so that it is not frozen any more. You defrost food by leaving it in a warm kitchen or using a microwave oven.

deft–delightful

2 if you defrost a fridge or freezer, you turn it off so that the ice inside it melts

deft *adjective* **defter, deftest**
quick and showing a lot of skill *We cheered the footballer's deft movements.*
deftly *adverb*

defuse *verb*
defuses, defusing, defused
1 to stop a bomb going off by taking out its fuse (the electrical part inside a bomb that makes it explode)
2 to make a situation better by making people less worried or angry and by trying to solve any problems

defy *verb*
defies, defying, defied
1 if you defy someone or something such as an order, you don't do what you are told

> SYNONYM to disobey

2 if you say that something defies description or belief, you mean that it is impossible to describe or believe, for example because it is so strange or beautiful or ugly or big
3 to go against something *That defies the law of gravity.*
4 if you defy someone to do something, you ask them to do it so as to prove to you that it can be done

degenerate *verb*
degenerates, degenerating, degenerated
to become worse or turn into something worse *The lesson degenerated into an argument between me and the teacher.*

degradation *noun*
1 when people show no respect towards others as human beings
2 a situation where people feel ashamed, for example because they are poor or being treated badly *poverty and degradation*

degrade *verb*
degrades, degrading, degraded
to show no respect towards someone as a human being *a TV programme that degrades children*

degree *noun* **degrees**
1 a unit for measuring temperature and angles. It is written as the symbol ° after a number. *20 degrees* (or *20°*) *Celsius*; *An equilateral triangle has three angles of 60 degrees* (or *60°*).
2 an amount or level of something *a high degree of success*; *You're right to a certain degree* (partly but not completely).
3 a course of study at a university or college *Daniel is doing a history degree.*
4 an official piece of paper that someone at a university or college receives when they finish their studies and pass their exams

dehydrated *adjective*
1 if someone is dehydrated, they are weak because they do not have enough water in their body
2 if food is dehydrated, all the water has been taken out of it so that it will last longer
dehydration *noun*

de-ice *verb*
de-ices, de-icing, de-iced
to get rid of the ice from something such as the windscreen of a car or wings of an aircraft

de-icer *noun* **de-icers**
a substance in a small metal container that you spray onto a car's windscreen to get rid of the ice

deity ['day-er-tee' or 'dee-er-tee'] *noun*
deities
a god or goddess

dejected *adjective*
unhappy and without any feeling of hope
dejection *noun*

delay *verb*
delays, delaying, delayed
1 to wait until a later time before you decide to do something *If you delay, you might not be able to get any tickets.*
2 to do something at a later time or say you will do it at a later time *Granddad has delayed his departure because he doesn't feel well.*

> SYNONYM to put off

3 to make someone late *I don't want to delay you any more.*
4 if something such as a plane or train is delayed, it is late

delay *noun* **delays**
1 a period of time that you have to wait because something happens later than it should *The plane had about an hour's delay.*
2 waiting before you do something *Go and see the head teacher without delay.*
3 a period of time between two events *There's a delay of 30 seconds between switching on my laptop and the Windows logo appearing.*

delectable *adjective*
extremely good, pleasing or delicious

> SYNONYM delightful

delegate ['del-i-gayt'] *verb*
delegates, delegating, delegated
to give some of your work responsibilities to someone or ask them to do something that you are responsible for *I was delegated the task of washing the dishes. The teacher delegated me to fetch the register.*

delegate ['del-i-gert'] *noun* **delegates**
someone chosen to attend an event such as a meeting or conference, often someone who represents a group of people

delete *verb*
deletes, deleting, deleted
1 to get rid of something on a computer *Press the delete key on your laptop to delete a file or folder.*
2 to cross something out that is written down

> ORIGIN from Latin *deletus* 'destroyed' (from *delere* 'to destroy')

deletion *noun*
1 the action of deleting something on a computer or something that is written down
2 (*plural* **deletions**) something deleted *The teacher made lots of deletions in my story.*

deli *noun* **delis**
short for **delicatessen**

deliberate ['di-li-ber-ert'] *adjective*
1 not happening by chance but done on purpose *I made a deliberate mistake.*
2 if a movement is deliberate, it is slow and careful

deliberate ['di-li-ber-ayt'] *verb*
deliberates, deliberating, deliberated
to think about something or discuss something carefully **deliberation** *noun*

deliberately *adverb*
to do something deliberately is to do it because you want to

delicacy *noun*
1 (*plural* **delicacies**) a food that costs a lot of money to buy and has a delicious taste
2 the quality of being delicate *the delicacy of the butterfly's wings*
3 when you behave in a careful way *The teacher dealt with the bully with delicacy.*

delicate *adjective*
1 easy to break or damage, for example because it is thin or small *the delicate wings of a butterfly*
2 attractive and thin or small *a baby's delicate hands*
3 done or made with lots of attractive details and great care *a delicate pattern*; *a delicate instrument*
4 pleasant and not too strong *an ice cream with a delicate flavour*
5 a delicate situation or matter is a difficult one where you need to be very careful
6 a delicate person is someone who is weak and easily becomes ill

delicately *adverb*
1 in a careful or gentle way *I placed the vase delicately on the shelf. The situation must be handled delicately.*
2 in an attractive way, for example with lots of details *a delicately shaped leaf*
3 in a way that is pleasant and not too strong *a delicately flavoured milkshake*

delicatessen *noun* **delicatessens**
a shop selling food of good quality that is already prepared, such as cooked meats. The food often comes from another country.

> ORIGIN from German *Delikatessen* 'delicacies that you eat'

delicious *adjective*
if something you eat or drink is delicious, it tastes or smells very good *This fish tastes delicious.* **deliciously** *adverb*

delight *verb*
delights, delighting, delighted
to make someone very happy *We were all delighted to see Oliver back at school.*

delight *noun*
1 a feeling of great happiness
2 (*plural* **delights**) something that makes you very happy

delightful *adjective*
1 very pleasant *That's a delightful way to pass the time.*
2 very attractive *Leah drew a delightful picture.*
delightfully *adverb*

113

delinquent–denim

delinquent *noun* delinquents
a young person who breaks the law or behaves very badly **delinquency** *noun*

delirious *adjective*
1 if someone is delirious, their mind is not working properly because they are ill or have a fever and they say strange things or make strange noises
2 behaving in a very happy or excited way
deliriously *adverb*

delirium *noun*
1 the condition of someone who is delirious because they are ill or have a fever
2 great happiness or very excited behaviour

ORIGIN from Latin *delirium* 'madness'

deliver *verb*
delivers, delivering, delivered
1 to take something somewhere, for example letters or newspapers to someone's home *What time do they deliver the post?*
2 if a shop or business delivers goods that you have bought, it sends them to your home
3 to give something such as a speech or warning
4 to deliver a punch or blow to a part of someone's body is to hit them hard
5 to deliver a baby is to help a woman when her baby is being born

delivery *noun* deliveries
1 when someone takes or sends something somewhere, for example to someone's home *Allow two weeks for the delivery of your tablet computer.*
2 goods that you buy and that someone sends to your home *The lorry is carrying deliveries of fresh fruit.*
3 when a woman gives birth to a baby

dell *noun* dells
an old-fashioned word for a small valley

delta *noun* deltas
an area shaped like a triangle where a river divides into a number of smaller rivers before it joins the sea *the Nile Delta*

ORIGIN from *delta*, the fourth letter of the Greek alphabet, because of its triangular shape

delude *verb*
deludes, deluding, deluded
if someone is deluded or if they delude themselves, they believe something that isn't true

deluge *verb*
deluges, deluging, deluged
if someone is deluged with things, they get lots of them *The head teacher has been deluged with complaints.*

deluge *noun* deluges
1 a large number of things that someone gets at the same time *a deluge of questions*
2 a very heavy fall of rain
3 a flood

delusion *noun* delusions
an idea that someone has about something that isn't true

de luxe ['di-lucks'] *adjective*
of high quality and more expensive than other things *a de luxe car*

ORIGIN from French *de luxe* 'of luxury'

demand *verb*
demands, demanding, demanded
1 to ask for something in a very strong way because you want it or need it very much *She demanded an apology.*
2 if something demands something else, it needs it *Painting a picture demands skill and hard work.*

demand *noun*
1 (*plural* **demands**) when you ask for something that you want or need very much *This letter is a demand for money that you owe.*
2 if there is a demand for something that people buy, it means that a lot of people want to buy it *There's a lot of demand for ice cream during the summer.*
3 demands are also the things that people must do *A teacher's job has lots of demands.*
4 if something or someone is in demand, lots of people want them or like them *Shakespeare's plays are always in demand.*

demanding *adjective*
1 if something like a job or hobby is demanding, it needs a lot of time and hard work and is difficult to do
2 if someone is demanding, they need a lot of attention and are difficult to deal with *Babies are very demanding.*
3 hard to please and expecting people to work hard *Our teacher is very demanding.*

demeanour *noun*
the way someone behaves

demented *adjective*
behaving in a very strange or stupid way

demerara ['dem-er-air-rer'] *noun*
a type of light brown sugar

demise [rhymes with 'prize'] *noun*
the time when something ends *the demise of the floppy disk*

demist *verb*
demists, demisting, demisted
to remove drops of water from a car windscreen using air or heat

demister *noun* demisters
a piece of equipment in a car for blowing air or heat onto the windscreen to remove drops of water

demo *noun* demos
short for **demonstration**

democracy *noun*
1 a system of governing a country where people choose their leaders by voting for them freely
2 (*plural* **democracies**) a country governed in this way

democrat *noun* democrats
1 someone who thinks democracy is very important
2 a Democrat in the USA is someone who supports the Democratic Party (one of the two main US political parties)
compare: Republican

democratic *adjective*
1 using a system where people choose their leaders by voting for them freely *a democratic country*
2 following the idea that everyone should be allowed to decide how something is organised *Our school is very democratic.*

democratically *adverb*

demolish *verb*
demolishes, demolishing, demolished
to completely destroy something such as a building or wall **demolition** *noun*

SYNONYM to knock down

demon *noun* demons
1 an evil spirit
2 a very cruel person

ORIGIN from Greek *daimon* 'spirit' or 'god'

demonstrate *verb*
demonstrates, demonstrating, demonstrated
1 to show someone how to do something *I will demonstrate the correct way to shut down your computer.*
2 to show or prove something clearly
3 if people demonstrate, lots of them join together in a public place. They do this usually to show that they are not happy about something but sometimes to show that they support something.

demonstration *noun* demonstrations
1 when you show someone how to do something *The teacher gave us a practical demonstration.*
2 an event, such as a march, in which people join together to show that they are not happy about something or that they support something *a demonstration against closing the local library*
3 the action of showing or proving something clearly

demonstrator *noun* demonstrators
1 someone who shows people how to do something
2 someone who takes part in a demonstration with other people

demoralise *verb*
demoralises, demoralising, demoralised
to make someone lose hope and want to give up because they feel they will not be successful

LANGUAGE EXTRA also spelt *demoralize*

demote *verb*
demotes, demoting, demoted
1 to give a soldier or police officer a lower rank, or to give someone a less important job, usually because they have done something wrong
2 to make a sports team play in a lower division
demotion *noun*
compare: promote

den *noun* dens
1 the place where a wild animal lives *a lion's den*
2 a hiding place for children
3 a secret place where something bad or dishonest happens *a gambling den*
4 a small room in a house where someone can be alone and relax or work

denial *noun*
1 (*plural* **denials**) words or a written document saying that something isn't true
2 when someone doesn't give something to someone else *the denial of freedom*

denim *noun*
1 strong cotton cloth, usually blue, for making jeans

2 **denims** are clothes made of denim, especially jeans

ORIGIN from French *de Nîmes* 'of Nîmes', referring to the type of cloth (serge) that was first produced in this southern French town

Denmark *noun*
a country in Northern Europe

denominator *noun* **denominators**
1 in maths, the denominator is the bottom number in a fraction. It tells you how many parts the whole has been divided into. The top number in a fraction is the numerator. *In $\frac{1}{3}$, the denominator is 3.*
2 in maths, the lowest common denominator is the smallest whole number that can be divided exactly by all the denominators of two or more fractions *The lowest common denominator of $\frac{1}{2}$ and $\frac{1}{3}$ is 6.*

denote *verb*
denotes, denoting, denoted
to be a sign of something or to mean something *An S on the map denotes a school.*

denounce *verb*
denounces, denouncing, denounced
1 to say officially that you think something or someone is bad *He strongly denounced the government's actions. She was denounced as a spy.*
2 to tell the people in charge, such as the police or the government, that someone has committed a crime *He denounced her to the police.*

dense *adjective* **denser, densest**
1 very thick and difficult to see through *dense fog; dense smoke*
2 made up of many things or people in a small space *a dense forest* (with lots of trees); *a dense crowd*
3 an informal word for stupid

densely *adverb*
with many things or people in a small space *England is a densely populated country.*

density *noun*
1 the amount of things or people in a particular place *Scotland has a low population density.*
2 (*plural* **densities**) a scientific measurement of how much space is filled by a particular amount of something. To work out the density of something, you divide its mass (matter or substance) by its volume (size).

dent *noun* **dents**
a place on the surface of something that goes inwards because something has hit it or pushed it hard *There's a dent in the car's bumper.*

dent *verb*
dents, denting, dented
to make a dent in something *a dented car door*

dental *adjective*
connected with teeth or with the work of a dentist

dentist *noun* **dentists**
someone whose job is to look after people's teeth, for example by filling the holes in decayed teeth

dentistry *noun*
the medical study of teeth, or the work of looking after people's teeth *a school of dentistry*

dentures *noun plural*
false teeth

denunciation *noun* **denunciations**
1 when someone says officially that they think something or someone is bad
2 when someone tells the people in charge, such as the police or the government, that someone has committed a crime

deny *verb*
denies, denying, denied
1 to say that something isn't true *She denied saying that I was a liar.*
2 to deny someone something is not to give it to them *My parents denied me sweets when I was naughty.*
3 if someone denies a request, they say no to it

deodorant *noun* **deodorants**
a substance that people put on their skin, for example under the arms, to make them smell better

depart *verb*
departs, departing, departed
to leave a place and go away or go on a journey *Our plane departs at six o'clock.*

department *noun* **departments**
1 one of the sections of a big organisation such as a government, hospital or university *We're looking for the X-ray department.*
2 an area that sells a particular type of thing inside a big store *the shoe department*
3 a department store is a big store that sells lots of different things and is divided into separate departments

departure *noun* **departures**
1 the action of leaving a place and going away, or the time when you do this *We're waiting for the departure of our train.*
2 when someone leaves an organisation, job or group *After her departure from the BBC, she joined the government.*
3 a plane, train, bus or boat that leaves at a particular time *There are 10 departures a day between London and Madrid.*
4 the departure lounge at an airport is the area where people sit and wait for their plane to leave

depend *verb*
depends, depending, depended
1 if something depends on something else, it is influenced by it or it is the reason why it happens *Your exam results depend on how hard you work.*
2 if something depends on someone, it will happen only if that person allows it to happen *'Can we have a pizza tonight?' – 'That depends on Dad.'*
3 to need something or someone or their help in order to live or to be successful *The Lake District depends on tourists.*
4 to trust someone to help you *I know I can depend on you if I have a problem.*

SYNONYM to rely on

5 **it depends** used when you're not sure about something because your answer is influenced by different things *'Are you going to the party?' – 'It depends. If it's on Sunday I can, but only if my parents say yes.'*

dependable *adjective*
1 if someone is dependable, you can trust them to behave well, always do what they should do and do what you ask them to do
2 if something such as a piece of equipment is dependable, you can trust it to do what it should be doing

SYNONYM reliable

dependant *noun* **dependants**
someone such as a child who depends on someone else, for example his or her parents, for food, money, clothes and a place to live *His son is his only dependant.*

LANGUAGE EXTRA be careful to spell the noun with *-ant* at the end and the adjective with *-ent* at the end

dependent *adjective*
1 needing someone or someone's help in order to live or to be successful *dependent children; Her two daughters are dependent on her.*
2 if something is dependent on something else, it depends on it *Success is dependent on hard work. Seaside towns are dependent on tourists.*

dependence *noun*

depending on *preposition*
in a way that is influenced or decided by something else *You'll be selected for the team depending on how well you play.*

SYNONYM according to

depict *verb*
depicts, depicting, depicted
1 to describe something or someone, for example in a story or film
2 to show something or someone in a painting, a drawing or another art form *St Michael is depicted as an angel.*

depiction *noun*

SYNONYM to portray

depleted *adjective*
if something is depleted, there is less of it than there was before *The soldiers' food supplies were depleted.*

deplorable *adjective*
very bad *Alan's behaviour is deplorable.*

deplore *verb*
deplores, deploring, deplored
to dislike something very much because you think it is wrong or bad *We all deplore violence.*

ORIGIN from Latin *de-* 'completely' and *plorare* 'to weep'

deport *verb*
deports, deporting, deported
to send someone out of a country because they do not have the right to be there

deportation *noun*

115

deposit – describe

deposit *noun* **deposits**
1 an amount of money someone pays into a bank account *Grandma made a deposit of £50 into my account.*
2 if someone puts down a deposit on something they buy, such as a house or car, they pay an amount of money as the first payment. They borrow the rest of the money and pay it back over a period of time, for example a little bit every month.
3 a deposit is also an amount of money that someone pays to the owner of a house or flat when they start to rent the house or flat. The money is given back when they stop renting it.
4 a layer of something, for example something on the inside or bottom of a container or something in the ground formed by a chemical process *gold deposits*

deposit *verb*
deposits, depositing, deposited
1 to pay money into a bank account, usually your own account *I deposited £10.*
2 to put something valuable in a safe place
3 to put or leave something somewhere *Chris deposited his backpack on the chair.*

depot ['dep-oh'] *noun* **depots**
1 a place where large amounts of goods or equipment are stored, such as fuel or weapons
2 a large building where buses or trains are kept and repaired

depress *verb*
depresses, depressing, depressed
to make someone feel very sad

depressed *adjective*
1 very sad about something *Robin didn't pass the exam and feels depressed.*
2 suffering from an illness of the mind that makes you so sad that you cannot live your life normally

depressing *adjective*
making you feel very sad *I didn't like the film – it was too depressing.*

depression *noun* **depressions**
1 a feeling of being very sad
2 if someone suffers from depression, they have an illness of the mind that makes them so sad that they cannot live their life normally
3 a long period of time when many people are poor and have no jobs because there is not much business activity *the Great Depression of the 1930s*
4 a large area where the air pressure is low, causing rain and low temperatures
5 a part of the ground that is lower than the surrounding area

deprivation *noun* **deprivations**
1 when people are poor and do not have the things they need for a normal and happy life

SYNONYM poverty

2 being deprived of something such as sleep or food

deprive *verb*
deprives, depriving, deprived
if you deprive someone of something, you stop them from having it or you take it away from them *They deprived the prisoners of food.*

deprived *adjective*
1 not having the things that you need for a normal and happy life or not having enough of them, for example money, food, love or education
2 used about the places where deprived people live *This is a deprived area of London.*

depth *noun* **depths**
1 the depth of something is how deep it is *The water in the pool reaches a depth of three metres.*
2 the depth of something such as knowledge is a great amount of it *We admire the depth of our teacher's understanding.*
3 if something is done in depth, it is done with a lot of details *We discussed our plans in depth.*
4 **out of your depth** used when you mean that someone is in water that is too deep for them or has to do something that is too difficult for them

deputise *verb*
deputises, deputising, deputised
if you deputise for someone, usually someone who has a more important job than you, you do their work instead of them for a short time

LANGUAGE EXTRA also spelt *deputize*

deputy *noun* **deputies**
someone who is the second most important person in a job and is in charge when the most important person is not there

derail *verb*
derails, derailing, derailed
if a train derails or if something derails it, it comes off the track

deranged *adjective*
if someone is deranged, they are mentally ill and behave in a dangerous way

derby ['dar-bee'] *noun* **derbies**
1 a sports match between teams from the same area or city *We enjoyed yesterday's derby between Manchester City and Manchester United.*
2 used in the name of some horse races. The Derby is a well-known race that takes place in Epsom in England every May or June.

ORIGIN named after the 12th Earl of *Derby* who started the famous horse race in the 18th century

derelict ['dair-rer-likt'] *adjective*
a building or place that is derelict is empty and usually in a bad condition because people stopped using it a long time ago

deride *verb*
derides, deriding, derided
to say something about someone or something that shows you have no respect for them and think they are silly or not important *She was derided for her ideas on music.*

SYNONYM to mock

derision *noun*
when you show you have no respect for someone or something and think they are silly or not important *Her opinions were treated with derision.*

derivation *noun* **derivations**
the derivation of a word is where it comes from *In English there are thousands of words of Latin derivation.*

derive *verb*
derives, deriving, derived
1 to get something from something else *I derived a lot of pleasure from the book.*
2 to come from something else *This word is derived from French.*

derogatory *adjective*
if something you say is derogatory, it shows that you have no respect for the person or thing you are talking about and that you think they are bad *He made derogatory remarks about the teacher.*

derrick *noun* **derricks**
1 a tall tower built over an oil well. It holds the equipment used for drilling the hole.
2 a very tall machine for lifting heavy things, especially from ships

ORIGIN named after *Derrick*, the surname of a well-known hangman at Tyburn (a place where criminals were hanged in 17th-century London). At first, *derrick* meant 'hangman', then 'gallows' and later 'machine for lifting'.

descale *verb*
descales, descaling, descaled
to remove the hard substance (called scale) from the inside of a kettle or pipe. Scale is formed when there are lots of chemicals in the water. **descaler** *noun*

descant *noun* **descants**
in music, a descant is a second tune that is higher than the main one and that is sung or played at the same time

descend *verb*
descends, descending, descended
1 to go down something such as a hill or stairs
2 if a plane descends, it comes down towards the ground and prepares to land
3 if night descends, it starts to get dark
4 if people descend on a place, lots of them arrive at the same time *Hundreds of students descended on Trafalgar Square.*
5 if you're descended from someone, you belong to the same family as someone who lived before you were born
6 a descending order is one where the numbers get smaller, for example 4, 3, 2, 1

descendant *noun* **descendants**
someone alive now who belongs to the same family as someone who lived before they were born *The modern Welsh, Scottish and Irish people are descendants of the ancient Celts.*

descent *noun* **descents**
1 a climb down something *He fell during the descent from Snowdon.*
2 the descent of a plane is when it comes down and prepares to land
3 a path that goes down from somewhere
4 your family origin *She's of Irish descent.*

describe *verb*
describes, describing, described
1 to give details about someone or something, for example to show how they look or what type of person or thing they

are *Describe the house where you live. Would you describe Tony as a happy boy?*
2 to explain or say something with details *Describe what happened next.*

description noun
1 (plural **descriptions**) words giving details about someone or something, for example to show how they look or what they are like *The book gives a description of life in Victorian England.*
2 the action of describing something *Dickens has great powers of description.*

descriptive adjective
if something is descriptive, it gives a description *This passage of the book is very descriptive.*

desert ['dez-ert] noun **deserts**
a large area of land with very hot and dry weather, almost no water, plants or trees and usually a lot of sand *the Sahara Desert*

desert ['di-zerrt] verb
deserts, deserting, deserted
1 to go away and leave someone or something and never come back
2 if someone such as a soldier deserts, he or she leaves the army (or navy or air force) without permission

deserted adjective
if a place is deserted, there are no people there *At night the streets are deserted.*

deserter noun **deserters**
someone such as a soldier who leaves the army (or navy or air force) without permission

desertion noun **desertions**
when someone such as a soldier leaves the army (or navy or air force) without permission

desert island noun **desert islands**
a small and beautiful tropical island that has no-one living there

deserts ['di-zerrts] noun plural
if someone gets their just deserts, they get the punishment they deserve

deserve verb
deserves, deserving, deserved
if someone or something deserves something, it is right for them to have it or for something to happen to them, often something good *Our team has worked hard and they deserve to win. The film is excellent and deserves all the praise it got.*

deservedly ['di-zerr-vid-lee] adverb
used for saying that it is right for something to have happened or to be the way it is *It's described as the best museum in our town, and deservedly.*

SYNONYM **rightly**

deserving adjective
if you say that someone or something is deserving, you mean they should be helped because there are good things about them *Our school is raising money to help deserving children from the refugee camps.*

desiccated adjective
desiccated food has had all the water removed to preserve it *desiccated coconut*

design noun **designs**
1 the way that something is made or organised and how it works and looks *I really like the colour and design of your laptop.*
2 a drawing of something that shows how it will be made or organised and how it will look
3 lines and shapes that decorate something

SYNONYM **pattern**

4 the activity or study of designing things *Her brother studies software design.*

design verb
designs, designing, designed
1 to make or to organise something, for example by doing a drawing of it first with the details of how it will work or look *An architect is someone who designs buildings.*
2 if something is well designed, it has been made very carefully
3 if something is designed to do something, or if it is designed for something or someone, it was made or intended for that particular reason or person *The rules were designed to help people with disabilities. It's a laptop designed for children.*

designate verb
designates, designating, designated
1 to choose something or someone, for example for a particular purpose *A section of the playground has been designated for ball games.*
2 to describe or to show something or someone in a certain way

designer noun **designers**
1 someone who designs things *a fashion designer*
2 designer clothes cost a lot of money because they are modern and made by famous fashion designers

desirable adjective
if something is desirable, it is good and you want it or like it or you want to do it *Friendliness and intelligence are desirable qualities. This is a desirable part of town* (people want to live there). *A visit to Nan would be desirable this weekend as I know she's feeling lonely.*

desire noun **desires**
a strong feeling of wanting something *My sister has a great desire to be a nurse.*

desire verb
desires, desiring, desired
to want something very much

desk noun **desks**
1 a table, for example in a school or office, where you sit and do your reading, writing or work *I keep my pens and notebooks in my desk drawer.*
2 a place, for example in a hotel or airport, where customers get information or receive a service *an airport check-in desk*

desktop noun **desktops**
1 the main screen on a computer where icons of programs are shown and where you can start programs and find information
2 a desktop computer is a small computer that you keep on your desk because it cannot be carried around like a laptop
3 desktop publishing is the use of computers for producing documents containing words and pictures, for example for a newspaper or magazine

desolate adjective
1 a desolate place is empty and looks unpleasant because there are no people or buildings there *We imagined the desolate streets of Coventry after it was bombed in the Second World War.*
2 a desolate person is sad and lonely
desolation noun

despair noun
the feeling that you have lost all hope because there is nothing you can do to change a situation *Our poor teacher was in despair.*

despair verb
despairs, despairing, despaired
to lose all hope because you feel that there is nothing you can do to change a situation

ORIGIN from Latin *desperare* 'to have no hope' (from *de-* 'without' and *sperare* 'to hope')

despatch verb
despatches, despatching, despatched
1 to send something or someone *The parcel was despatched yesterday.*
2 to get rid of someone, for example by beating them in a game or by killing them

LANGUAGE EXTRA also spelt *dispatch*

desperate adjective
1 very worried about a bad situation because you don't know how to make it better *The missing girl's parents were desperate.*
2 ready to do anything to change a situation that is bad for you *a desperate criminal*
3 if something someone does is desperate, it is the only thing they can think of to make a bad situation better *It was a desperate attempt to save his life.*
4 wanting something very much *His family is desperate for money. I need to go to the loo – I'm desperate!*
5 very bad or serious *There's a desperate shortage of teachers.*

ORIGIN from Latin *desperatus* 'not having any hope' (from *de-* 'without' and *sperare* 'to hope')

desperately adverb
1 with lots of energy and because you can't think of anything else to make a bad situation better *I was trying desperately to phone my parents.*
2 very much *We desperately need your help.*
3 very *She was desperately sad.*

desperation noun
being very worried about a situation that is bad for you because you don't know how to make it better *a look of desperation*

despicable adjective
very bad or cruel

SYNONYM **horrible**

despise verb
despises, despising, despised
if you despise someone, you dislike them very much and have no respect for them

SYNONYM **to hate**

despite–deterrent

despite preposition
used for saying that something you mention does not stop something else happening *David is my friend despite his bad behaviour.*

dessert ['di-zerrt'] noun **desserts**
something sweet such as cake, ice cream or fruit that you eat at the end of a meal

> LANGUAGE EXTRA be careful not to confuse *dessert* with *desert* (area of land)

dessertspoon noun **dessertspoons**
1 a fairly large spoon, for example for eating desserts. A dessertspoon is bigger than a teaspoon and smaller than a tablespoon.
2 the amount of food or liquid that a dessertspoon can hold, used for measuring

destination noun **destinations**
the place where someone is travelling to or where goods are sent

destined adjective
if something is destined to happen, it must happen because that is the way things are meant to be *He was destined to meet his future wife in Manchester. Shakespeare was destined for greatness.*

destiny noun **destinies**
what will happen to someone or what someone will do in the future, especially because things are meant to be that way

> SYNONYM fate

destitute adjective
if someone is destitute, they have no money or possessions

destroy verb
destroys, destroying, destroyed
1 to cause something so bad to happen to something or someone that they no longer exist *Fire damaged some buildings and destroyed others.*
2 to take something away or stop it from happening or continuing *These decisions will destroy our hopes and dreams.*
3 to spoil someone's life *If he doesn't win the cup, he'll be completely destroyed.*

destroyer noun **destroyers**
a small fast ship with guns for fighting in a war

destruction noun
the action of destroying something or of being destroyed

destructive adjective
causing a lot of damage to things or people *Volcanoes can be very destructive.*

detach verb
detaches, detaching, detached
to remove something from something else that it is fixed or joined to *Detach the form by cutting along the dotted line.*

detachable adjective
if something is detachable, you can remove it and put it back again *a detachable hood*

detached adjective
1 if someone is detached, they are not interested in other people or influenced by an event or situation *The soldiers were detached from the suffering around them.*
2 a detached house is one that is not joined to another house
compare: **terraced house** and **semi-detached house**

detachment noun
1 a feeling of not being interested in other people or influenced by an event or situation
2 (*plural* **detachments**) a group of soldiers from a larger group who are ordered to do a particular job

detail noun **details**
1 one of many small pieces of information in something *I've read the book twice and know every detail about it.*
2 all the small parts or pieces of information in something *Look at the artist's amazing attention to detail.*
3 details are all the information about something *Send off this form to get further details.*
4 your details are the information about yourself that you give to someone, for example your name and address
5 a detail of something such as a picture or pattern is one small part of it
6 **in detail** carefully and with lots of small pieces of information *He explained in detail what happened.*

detail verb
details, detailing, detailed
to give all the details about something

detailed adjective
1 with lots of small pieces of information *I read a detailed study of the English Civil War.*
2 with lots of small or complicated parts *Amesh's drawing is very detailed.*

detain verb
detains, detaining, detained
1 to keep someone in a place such as a hospital or police station *After the accident she was detained in hospital overnight. The thief was detained.*
2 to keep someone somewhere longer than they expected
3 to keep someone waiting

detect verb
detects, detecting, detected
1 to notice something that is hard to see or hear *I detected a slight smile on my teacher's face.*
2 to find something when it is not easy to find, for example by using scientific instruments *The doctors detected a small cancer.*

detection noun
1 finding something that is not easy to find *early detection of cancers*
2 being found *Turn off your mobile to avoid detection.*

detective noun **detectives**
1 a police officer who has the job of finding information about crimes and catching criminals
2 a detective or private detective is a person someone pays to find information about a crime or another activity
3 a detective story is a story about a detective (or detectives) trying to solve a crime (or crimes)

detector noun **detectors**
a piece of equipment for finding something *a metal detector* (for finding metal objects in the ground); *a smoke detector* (for finding smoke and warning people that there is a fire)

detention noun
1 (*plural* **detentions**) a punishment in which a teacher makes a child stay at school for a short time when the other children have gone home *My brother was put in detention last week.*
2 the action of keeping someone in a place

deter verb
deters, deterring, deterred
to stop someone from doing something, for example by making them think it is too difficult or that bad things could happen to them

> ORIGIN from Latin *de-* 'away' and *terrere* 'to frighten'

detergent noun **detergents**
a powder or liquid for washing clothes or cleaning dishes

deteriorate verb
deteriorates, deteriorating, deteriorated
to get worse *Grandma's health is beginning to deteriorate.* **deterioration** noun

determination noun
the special quality of not letting anything stop you from doing what you want to do *The teacher praised my determination to do well in spite of all my problems.*

determine verb
determines, determining, determined
1 to find something out *The police are trying to determine the cause of the accident.*
2 if something determines something else, it controls what it will be *These exams could determine your future.*

> SYNONYM to decide

3 to decide something officially *The jury determined that he was not guilty.*

determined adjective
if you are determined to do something, you really want to do it and nothing will stop you

determiner noun **determiners**
a word used before a noun (or a noun plus an adjective) to show which thing or person you mean

> LANGUAGE EXTRA a *determiner* is a word such as the indefinite article *a* or *an*, the definite article *the*, or a number, for example *a hat*, *an empty glass*, *the girls* or *four books*. Determiners show which thing or person you are referring to and whether you mean just one or more than one. Some more examples of determiners are *this* (*that*, *these* and *those*), *each*, *every*, *some*, *all*, *many*, and *my* (*your*, *his*, *her* and so on).

deterrent noun **deterrents**
something that is meant to stop someone from doing something because it makes them think bad things could happen to them if they do it *Sending students home if they use a mobile during exams is a big deterrent.*

detest verb
detests, detesting, detested
to dislike someone or something very much

SYNONYM to hate

detestable adjective
very unpleasant

SYNONYM horrible

detonate verb
detonates, detonating, detonated
if someone detonates something such as a bomb, they make it explode

detonator noun detonators
a piece of equipment that makes a bomb explode

detour noun detours
if you make a detour to get to a place, you go by a way that is longer than usual, for example because you want to avoid something

ORIGIN from French *détour* and Old French *destor* 'side road'

detract verb
detracts, detracting, detracted
if something detracts from something else, it makes it appear to be less good or important than it should be

detrimental adjective
causing damage or a bad effect *Overeating can be detrimental to your health.*

SYNONYM harmful

deuce ['dyooss'] noun
a score in tennis when both of the players have 40 points

devalue verb
devalues, devaluing, devalued
if a country devalues its currency, it makes it worth less compared to the money of other countries

Devanagari ['day-ver-**nah**-ger-ree'] noun
the alphabet used for writing Hindi, Sanskrit and some other Indian languages

ORIGIN 'town writing of the gods', from Sanskrit *Deva* 'god' and *nagari* 'of the town'

devastate verb
devastates, devastating, devastated
1 to damage a place very badly, or to destroy it completely *The city was devastated by the Great Fire of London in 1666.*
2 to make someone very sad, especially when something bad happens suddenly *We were devastated when our pet dog was run over.*

devastation noun

develop verb
develops, developing, developed
1 to gradually become bigger, better or stronger or to change into something bigger, better or stronger *Caterpillars develop into butterflies. Their friendship has developed in the last year.*
2 to make something bigger, better or stronger *Swimming helps to develop your muscles. Aishah is developing her computer skills.*
3 to become a better, happier and more successful person, for example by doing things in a way that you think is natural and good *Young children develop best if you let them play and explore by themselves.*
4 to spend time gradually producing something such as an idea, story or new product, or to produce something that you've spent a lot of time working on
5 to start to happen, or to make something happen *A problem has developed. My tablet has developed a problem.*
6 if you develop something such as an illness, feeling or liking, or if something such as an illness, feeling or liking develops, you start to have it *I've developed a liking for strawberry ice cream. A rash has developed on the baby's body.*
7 to develop land or an area is to build houses or put up buildings there or make other changes such as creating parks and roads *They're going to develop the centre of town.*

developer noun developers
1 someone who buys land and builds new houses or buildings on it
2 someone who creates new products such as computer software
3 a late developer is someone whose body or mind takes longer to develop but who becomes as fully grown or intelligent as anyone else

developing adjective
a developing country or nation is poor but is gradually making progress in producing things that it can sell, so that the people who live there can earn more money

development noun developments
1 changing into or making something bigger or better or stronger *I read lots of books for the development of my mind.*
2 producing something such as an idea, story or new product
3 a new product that has been produced *Our teacher explained the new developments in computing.*
4 a new event that happens *Have there been any developments since yesterday?*
5 building houses or putting buildings on land
6 a group of houses or buildings that have been built together *a new housing development in the suburbs*

deviate verb
deviates, deviating, deviated
to deviate from something is to start doing something different and unexpected or to start moving away from something *Our teacher started talking about the environment but then deviated from the subject. The spacecraft has deviated from its path.*

device noun devices
1 a piece of equipment or machine *A tap is a device for controlling the flow of water in a pipe.*
2 a piece of electronic equipment such as a computer or something inside a computer or connected to one, for example a printer or router (for connecting a computer to the internet)
3 a bomb *a nuclear device*
4 a special way of creating an effect, for example in a book or film *A simile is a literary device.*
5 **to leave someone to their own devices** to leave someone alone and let them do whatever they want or think best

devil noun devils
1 an evil spirit or person who exists in some religions such as Christianity
2 someone who behaves very badly *Rosa can be a bit of a devil.*

devilish adjective
1 naughty in a playful way *a devilish smile*

SYNONYM mischievous

2 evil and cruel

devious adjective
1 if someone is devious, they behave in a dishonest or complicated way to get what they want
2 also used about someone's behaviour or actions *a devious scheme*
3 not direct *They took a devious route to avoid the police.*

deviously adverb

devise verb
devises, devising, devised
to think of a way of doing something, for example a new method or plan

devoid adjective
devoid of without having any of something *This paragraph is completely devoid of meaning.*

devolution noun
when the government of a country gives away some of its power to a smaller government in a local area

devote verb
devotes, devoting, devoted
1 if you devote yourself or your time, effort or energy to something, you spend a lot of time doing it, usually because you are interested in it *I devote most of my time to my schoolwork. She devoted herself to looking after her grandmother.*
2 to use something in a particular way *The teacher devoted the whole lesson to Shakespeare.*

SYNONYM to dedicate

devoted adjective
1 giving someone great love and support *a devoted daughter*
2 **devoted to** dealing with something or doing something *a concert devoted to Mozart; an afternoon devoted to playing games*

devotion noun
1 great love towards someone and support for them *She looked after him with devotion.*
2 a lot of time and effort that you spend doing something

devour verb
devours, devouring, devoured
1 to eat something quickly because you are very hungry
2 if you devour books, you read them with great interest

devout adjective
very religious

dew noun
tiny drops of water that you see on things such as grass and leaves. Dew forms during the night as the air gets cooler.

dewy adjective

dexterity – diet

dexterity *noun*
skill with your hands or your mind

dexterous *adjective*
skilful

LANGUAGE EXTRA also spelt *dextrous*

diabetes ['dye-er-bee-teez'] *noun*
an illness in which someone has too much sugar in their blood

diabetic *adjective*
1 someone who is diabetic has diabetes
2 connected with diabetes *diabetic foot problems*
3 for diabetic people to eat *diabetic biscuits*

diabetic *noun*

diabolical *adjective*
1 very bad *The acting in the film was diabolical.*
2 evil and cruel

diabolically *adverb*
1 very badly *You behaved diabolically.*
2 very *diabolically awful food*

diagnose *verb*
diagnoses, diagnosing, diagnosed
1 to find out what sort of illness someone has so that they can be treated properly
2 to find out what is wrong with a piece of equipment or computer software *Run a troubleshooter to diagnose the problem.*

diagnosis *noun* **diagnoses**
when doctors find out what sort of illness someone has *Has Dr Patel made a diagnosis yet?*

diagonal *adjective*
a diagonal line is a straight line joining the opposite corners of a square or rectangle

diagonally *adverb*

diagonal *noun* **diagonals**
a diagonal line

diagram *noun* **diagrams**
a drawing showing what something looks like or how it works. Diagrams can include words and numbers.

dial *verb*
dials, dialling, dialled
if you dial a number on a phone, you press the buttons to make a call

dial *noun* **dials**
1 a round part on the front of a piece of equipment that shows measurements
2 the front part of a clock or watch that shows the time
3 a round part on a piece of equipment that you turn to choose a particular action, for example to choose a station on a radio

dialect *noun* **dialects**
the form of a language that is only used by a group of people in one part of a country *Scouse is the dialect spoken in Liverpool.*

dialogue *noun* **dialogues**
1 a conversation between people, for example to solve a problem *a dialogue between the police and the kidnappers*
2 the words spoken by characters in a book, film or play
3 a dialogue box is a small space on a computer screen for selecting an option or typing an instruction in a program

diameter *noun* **diameters**
1 a line through the middle of a circle from one side to the other, connecting two points on the circumference (or outside edge). It is twice the radius of a circle.
2 the length of this line

diamond *noun* **diamonds**
1 a hard stone that looks like glass and sparkles. It is a very valuable jewel and is used, for example, in rings and necklaces.
2 a flat shape with four equal straight sides. Its sides are sloping and it has no right angles (angles of 90 degrees). It is usually shown with one of its two thin angles pointing upwards and the opposite one pointing downwards. A diamond is sometimes called a rhombus.
3 a red diamond shape in a game of cards. A diamond is one of the four types of playing cards. The other three types are hearts, clubs and spades.

diaper *noun* **diapers**
the American word for a baby's nappy

diaphragm ['dye-er-fram'] *noun* **diaphragms**
the large muscle between your lungs and your stomach that helps you to breathe

diarrhoea ['dye-er-ree-er'] *noun*
an illness that makes you go to the toilet often. The waste that you pass is more liquid than solid.

diary *noun* **diaries**
1 a book with spaces for each day of the year in which you write things that you have to do
2 a book with empty pages in which you write your private thoughts and the dates on which you have these thoughts

dice *noun* **dice**
a small cube of plastic or wood with six sides. Each side has one to six dots on it. You throw the dice to find a number between one and six in games such as snakes and ladders.

LANGUAGE EXTRA *die* was once the singular of *dice* but now *dice* is used for both the singular and the plural

dice *verb*
dices, dicing, diced
to cut up food into small square pieces *diced carrots*

Dickensian *adjective*
used about things or people that make you think about descriptions in the novels of Charles Dickens, for example buildings or places that are unpleasant and look poor and old or people who are comical in an exaggerated or unpleasant way *The film shows the horrors of Dickensian London.*

ORIGIN from Charles *Dickens* (1812–70)

Dictaphone *noun* **Dictaphones** (trademark)
a piece of equipment that records someone's voice so that someone else can listen to it later and type out the recorded message. Dictaphones were used especially in the past.

dictate *verb*
dictates, dictating, dictated
1 to say something out loud for someone to write down *His boss is dictating a letter.*
2 to tell someone what to do and how to do it *I don't like people dictating to me.*

dictation *noun*
1 the action of saying something out loud for someone to write down
2 the action of writing down what someone says out loud
3 (*plural* **dictations**) an exercise where students write down what the teacher reads out *a French dictation*

dictator *noun* **dictators**
someone who has taken over a country by using force and who controls it with complete power **dictatorial** *adjective*

dictatorship *noun* **dictatorships**
a country controlled by a dictator

dictionary *noun* **dictionaries**
1 a book like this one that gives words in alphabetical order and their meanings, usually with examples
2 a book that gives words in one language with their translations in another, usually with examples *an English–Spanish dictionary*
3 a book that gives the meanings of words in a particular subject or that gives information about a list of things in a particular subject *a maths dictionary; a dictionary of quotations*
4 a list of words stored in a computer program so that you can check meanings and spellings, for example using a spellchecker

did
past tense of **do**

diddle *verb*
diddles, diddling, diddled
an informal way of saying to cheat *He was diddled out of all his money.*

didn't
short for 'did not' *I didn't know.*

die *verb*
dies, dying, died
1 to stop living
2 to die down is to become less strong *After a while the noise died down.*
3 to die out is to become less common and then disappear *These traditions are beginning to die out.*
4 if an animal or plant dies out, it becomes extinct (there are no more living examples of it) *When did the dinosaurs die out?*
5 (informal) to be dying for something or to do something is to want to have it or do it very much *I'm dying for a cup of tea. I'm dying to see your new bike.*

diesel ['dee-zerl'] *noun*
1 (*plural* **diesels**) a type of engine in which fuel is burnt when air is kept under pressure
2 an oil used instead of petrol in diesel engines. It comes from petroleum (a thick liquid from under the ground).
3 (*plural* **diesels**) a vehicle that uses diesel oil

diet *noun* **diets**
1 a way of eating that includes special foods or a different amount of food from usual, for example to help you to become thinner or healthier *I'm on a diet.*
2 the food that a person or animal normally eats

diet – dim

diet *verb*
diets, dieting, dieted
to eat special foods or a different amount of food, for example because you want to become thinner or healthier

dietitian *noun* dietitians
someone who gives people advice about the food they should eat

LANGUAGE EXTRA also spelt *dietician*

differ *verb*
differs, differing, differed
1 to differ from something or someone is not to be the same as they are *Arabic differs from English in being written from right to left.*
2 to disagree with someone about something

difference *noun* differences
1 the way in which things or people are different from each other *There's a big difference between your school and mine. The word 'set' has many differences of meaning* (many different meanings).
2 the amount between two numbers or measurements *The difference between 16 and 10 is 6.*
3 differences between people are when they disagree about something

SYNONYM disagreements

4 if something makes a difference to someone or something, it makes a situation better *Having my own laptop has made a big difference to me.*
5 if something makes no difference, it is not important *'Shall I pick the red ball or the blue one?' – 'It makes no difference.'*

different *adjective*
1 not the same as something or someone else *Mandy is very different from her sister.*
2 not the same as something or someone was before *You look different.*
3 used for talking about separate things of the same type *At weekends, I do my homework at different times of the day.*

SIMILE 'as different as chalk and cheese' means very different from each other

LANGUAGE EXTRA you can say *different from* or *different to* but some people think that *different from* is better

differentiate *verb*
differentiates, differentiating, differentiated
to show or recognise the difference between things or people *Who can differentiate between a crocodile and an alligator?*

differently *adverb*
in a different way

difficult *adjective*
1 needing a lot of effort to do, understand or deal with *a difficult exercise; a difficult question* (not easy to answer)

ANTONYM easy

2 needing a lot of effort to control or make better *a difficult child; difficult behaviour*
3 not easy to please *My teacher is very difficult.*
4 with lots of problems *a difficult situation*

difficulty *noun*
1 when you need a lot of effort to do something *I had difficulty walking in the snow.*

SYNONYM trouble

2 (plural **difficulties**) a problem *Some children in the class have learning difficulties.*

diffident *adjective*
shy

diffuse *verb*
diffuses, diffusing, diffused
if something diffuses or is diffused, it spreads over a wide area or through something

dig *verb*
digs, digging, dug
1 to dig the ground is to move the earth or to make holes in it, for example with a spade
2 to dig a hole is to make a hole in the ground
3 to dig the snow is to move it away, for example with a shovel
4 to push something hard into someone or something *Stop digging me with your elbow. I dug my teeth into an apple.*
5 if something digs into something else, it presses hard into it *I feel something digging into my leg.*
6 (informal) if you dig in, or if you dig into some food, you start to eat the food that's in front of you *We're hungry so let's dig in!*
7 to dig something up is to remove it from the ground
8 to dig up information is to find it after searching very hard

dig *noun* digs
1 when you push something hard into someone or something *I gave him a dig in the ribs with my elbow.*
2 an archaeological dig is a place where you dig in the ground to find objects from the past
3 an unpleasant thing that someone says, often as a joke *The comedian made a dig at the royal family.*

digest *verb*
digests, digesting, digested
1 to digest food is to change it in your stomach into substances that your body can use
2 to digest information is to gradually understand it because there is so much of it

digestible *adjective*
easy to digest

digestion *noun*
the series of gradual changes in your stomach when you digest food

digestive *adjective*
1 connected with digestion *the digestive system* (stomach, tubes and other parts of the body for digesting food)
2 a digestive biscuit is a slightly sweet biscuit made from wholemeal flour

digger *noun* diggers
a large machine that digs holes and moves earth

digit ['di-jit'] *noun* digits
1 one of the 10 symbols used for writing numbers (from 0 to 9)
2 a finger or toe

ORIGIN from Latin *digitus* 'finger' or 'toe'

digital *adjective*
1 used about information that is stored as numbers or electronic signals and about the equipment that stores information in this way *a digital image; a digital camera*
2 also used about a piece of equipment with a display, such as a timer or scales, that shows information as a row of numbers, instead of by a pointer that moves around a dial
3 a digital clock or watch shows time as a row of numbers, instead of by hands that move around a dial as in an analogue clock or watch
compare: **analogue**
4 connected with buying and selling things on the internet *digital sales*

digitally *adverb*

digitise *verb*
digitises, digitising, digitised
to put information into an electronic form, for example so that people can use it on the internet *digitised books*

LANGUAGE EXTRA also spelt *digitize*

dignified *adjective*
1 if someone is dignified, they behave with dignity
2 if someone looks dignified, they look serious and important so people respect them
3 also used about someone's behaviour, actions or appearance *He gave a very dignified speech.*

dignity *noun*
1 behaviour that people respect because you control your feelings and do not get excited or angry in a difficult situation
2 the respect that someone deserves *You should treat old people with dignity.*

digress *verb*
digresses, digressing, digressed
to talk about something different from the subject that you are supposed to be talking about

dike *noun* dikes
a long wall built to stop water from flooding an area of land

LANGUAGE EXTRA also spelt *dyke*

dilapidated *adjective*
if something such as a building or piece of furniture is dilapidated, it is old and in bad condition

dilemma *noun* dilemmas
a situation in which you have to make a difficult choice between two or more actions

diligent *adjective*
if someone is diligent, they work hard and produce good work

dilute *verb*
dilutes, diluting, diluted
to add water to a liquid to make it less strong

dim *adjective* dimmer, dimmest
1 not bright enough and hard to see *We saw the dim lights of the town in the distance.*
2 slight and not very good *a dim memory*
3 an informal word for not very intelligent

dim–directness

dim *verb*
dims, dimming, dimmed
if a light dims or if you dim it, it becomes less bright

dime *noun* dimes
a coin worth 10 cents in the USA or Canada

dimension *noun* dimensions
1 the dimensions of something are its size, for example its length, width and height
2 a particular way of looking at a situation

diminish *verb*
diminishes, diminishing, diminished
1 to become less *The popularity of the book has not diminished.*
2 to make something less

diminutive ['di-min-yer-tiv'] *adjective*
tiny

diminutive ['di-min-yer-tiv'] *noun*
diminutives
a word formed by adding a group of letters to show that something is smaller than other things of the same type, for example 'duckling' (small duck), 'piglet' (young pig)

dimly *adverb*
1 if something is dimly lit, there is not much light
2 not very much or very well *He dimly remembered her face.*

dimple *noun* dimples
a small hollow place on your chin or cheek

din *noun*
a loud and unpleasant noise

dine *verb*
dines, dining, dined
to have dinner

diner *noun* diners
1 someone eating in a restaurant
2 a small restaurant in the US that sells cheap meals. It looks like an American railway carriage.

ding-dong *noun*
the noise that a bell makes

dinghy ['din-gee'] *noun* dinghies
a small open boat of various types, used for example for sailing or racing

dingy ['din-jee'] *adjective* dingier, dingiest
dark and dirty *a dingy hotel room*

dining car *noun* dining cars
a carriage on a train where there is a restaurant

dining room *noun* dining rooms
a room in a house, flat or hotel where you eat your meals

dining table *noun* dining tables
a table where you eat your meals

dinner *noun* dinners
1 the main meal of the day, which people eat in the evening or in the middle of the day
2 school dinners are meals that you eat at school in the middle of the day
3 an official or important occasion when many people get together to eat a meal, for example to celebrate something

dinnertime *noun*
the time in the evening or middle of the day when people usually have dinner or when someone is having their dinner

dinosaur *noun* dinosaurs
a reptile that lived millions of years ago, especially a giant one like a tyrannosaurus

ORIGIN from Greek *deinos* 'terrible and big' and *sauros* 'lizard'

dip *verb*
dips, dipping, dipped
1 if you dip something in liquid, you put it in and take it out again
2 if something such as a road dips, it slopes downwards
3 if something such as an amount or level dips, it goes down slightly
4 to dip the headlights of a car is to make them point downwards to stop them shining into the eyes of other drivers

dip *noun* dips
1 if you go for a dip, you go for a quick swim
2 a place in a surface where it slopes downwards *Be careful – there's a dip in the road.*
3 a sauce in which you dip food such as crisps or biscuits before eating it
4 a slight drop in the amount or level of something

diphtheria ['dip-theer-ree-er'] *noun*
a serious illness that makes it difficult for someone to breathe and swallow

diphthong ['dip-thong'] *noun* diphthongs
a vowel sound made by blending two vowels together, for example the 'ou' sound in 'shout'

diplodocus *noun* diplodocuses
a very large plant-eating dinosaur with a very long thin neck and tail and a very small head

diploma *noun* diplomas
1 an official piece of paper that says someone has passed an exam or followed a course

SYNONYM certificate

2 a course of study at a university or college, for example in a subject that teaches you skills for a particular job

diplomacy *noun*
1 the job of keeping a friendly relationship with other countries
2 skill in dealing with other people and keeping them happy

diplomat *noun* diplomats
an official who represents his or her government in another country because both countries want to keep a friendly relationship

diplomatic *adjective*
1 connected with diplomacy
2 showing skill in dealing with other people

SYNONYM for sense 2: tactful

diplomatically *adverb*

dire *adjective* direr, direst
1 very serious *a dire situation*
2 saying that something very bad will happen in the future *a dire warning*
3 an informal word for very bad *The food in our school canteen is dire.*

direct *adjective*
1 going straight from one place to another *a direct road; a direct flight* (where the plane does not stop on the way)
2 not including anything or anyone else *There's a direct connection between the two events.*
3 exact *This is a direct quotation from the book.*
4 saying what you really think in an honest way *She gave me a direct answer to a direct question.*

direct *verb*
directs, directing, directed
1 to tell or show someone how to get somewhere *Could you direct me to the station, please?*
2 to say, write or do something for a particular person or reason *These harsh words were directed at you.*
3 to point something somewhere or make it go somewhere *Can you direct the light away from my eyes?*
4 to be in charge of an activity or group of people
5 to direct a film or play is to make it, for example by telling the actors what to do

direct *adverb*
1 going straight from one place to another without stopping *We flew from Mumbai to Paris direct.*
2 not including anything or anyone else *I went to see the head teacher direct.*

direct current *noun*
electric current that flows in one direction only
compare: **alternating current**

direction *noun* directions
1 an imaginary line that someone or something goes along to get to a place *Are we walking in the right direction? The car suddenly changed direction* (stopped going towards one place and started going towards a different place).

SYNONYM way

2 a place or a point of the compass that the front of something points to *Our house faces in a westerly direction.*
3 the way things gradually move and change *My teacher likes the direction my story is going in.*
4 directing something such as a film or play
5 directions are information about how to do something or how to get to a place

directly *adverb*
1 going straight to a place without stopping *Go home directly without going to the sweet shop.*
2 immediately *I went to Sam's house directly after school.*
3 exactly *She sat directly opposite me.*
4 without including anything or anyone else *You can buy it directly from the factory.*
5 if you say something directly, you say what you really think in an honest way

directness *noun*
when you say what you really think in an honest way

122

direct object – disconcerting

direct object *noun* direct objects
in grammar, the direct object is the noun or pronoun that receives the direct action of a verb. For example, in the sentence 'I like chocolate', 'chocolate' is the direct object of 'like'.
compare: **indirect object**

director *noun* directors
1 someone who is in charge of something such as a company, activity or organisation
2 someone who makes a film or play

directory *noun* directories
1 a book with information in it such as people's names, addresses and phone numbers *a telephone directory*
2 an old name for a computer file that stores other files and programs. A directory is now usually called a folder.

direct speech *noun*
in grammar, direct speech refers to the exact words that someone says when they are written down somewhere, such as in a book. You write these words inside quotation marks, for example 'I'm tired,' in the following example: *'I'm tired,' said Peter.*
compare: **indirect speech**

dirt *noun*
earth, mud, dust, marks or any substance that makes something dirty

dirty *adjective* dirtier, dirtiest
1 if something or someone is dirty, they have marks on them that are not supposed to be there, coming from many different things such as earth, mud, dust, grease or stains *dirty fingernails*; *a dirty plate* (with bits of food on it)
2 connected with sex *a dirty joke*

SYNONYM **rude**

3 bad, unfair or dishonest *a dirty trick*
dirtiness *noun*

dis- *prefix*
used for giving a word an opposite meaning *dislike*; *disloyal*

disability *noun* disabilities
a medical problem that affects the way someone uses their body or brain

disabled *adjective*
someone who is disabled finds it difficult to do some things with their body (such as walk) or with their brain (such as talk or read)

disadvantage *noun* disadvantages
something bad that causes a problem or makes things more difficult for you *One of the disadvantages of our school is that it's far away from where we live.*

disagree *verb*
disagrees, disagreeing, disagreed
1 to have a different opinion from someone else
2 if a situation or food disagrees with you, you don't like it and it doesn't do you any good *Strawberries disagree with me.*

disagreeable *adjective*
unpleasant

disagreement *noun* disagreements
1 a situation in which people have different opinions about something
2 an angry talk with someone that you disagree with

SYNONYM for sense 2: **argument**

disappear *verb*
disappears, disappearing, disappeared
1 if someone or something disappears, they go somewhere where you can't see or find them any more *My gloves have disappeared*

SYNONYM **to vanish**

2 to stop happening or existing *Has the pain disappeared?*

disappearance *noun* disappearances
when something or someone disappears *the disappearance of the rainforest*

disappoint *verb*
disappoints, disappointing, disappointed
to make someone sad because what they hope for doesn't happen or because something they expect to be good is not good *I'm disappointed that we're not going on holiday this year. He disappointed me* (for example by not doing what I hoped he would do).

disappointing *adjective*
making someone feel disappointed

disappointment *noun*
1 the feeling of being disappointed
2 (*plural* disappointments) something or someone that disappoints you because they are not as good as you expect

disapproval *noun*
a feeling that shows you dislike someone or think something is bad or wrong

disapprove *verb*
disapproves, disapproving, disapproved
1 if you disapprove of something, you think it is bad or wrong
2 if you disapprove of someone, you dislike them and have a bad opinion of them

disarm *verb*
disarms, disarming, disarmed
1 to take a weapon or weapons away from someone
2 if a country disarms, it makes the size of its army smaller or it gets rid of it completely
3 if a group disarms, it gets rid of its own weapons

disarmament *noun*
when a country makes the size of its army smaller or gets rid of it completely

disaster *noun* disasters
1 a very bad event that causes great damage and often suffering and death, for example a forest fire, flood or earthquake
2 any very bad event
3 someone or something that is not successful *I was a disaster at school.*

disastrous *adjective*
1 very bad
2 causing great damage and often suffering and death *a disastrous flood*
3 not successful in any way *I tried to learn French but my efforts were disastrous.*
disastrously *adverb*

disband *verb*
disbands, disbanding, disbanded
if a group of people such as a music group disband, they stop working together

disbelief *noun*
a feeling of great surprise when you do not believe something is true

disc *noun* discs
1 a round flat object *A coin is a small metal disc.*
2 a CD or DVD

LANGUAGE EXTRA do not confuse *disc* with *disk*. A *disk* is used inside a computer.

discard *verb*
discards, discarding, discarded
to get rid of something that you do not want

SYNONYM **to throw away**

discharge *verb*
discharges, discharging, discharged
1 to allow someone to leave somewhere such as a hospital or the army *Grandma was discharged from hospital today.*
2 to allow something such as a liquid or smoke to go somewhere *Sewage used to be discharged into the sea.*

disciple *noun* disciples
someone who has great respect for and interest in the ideas of an important person such as a religious or political leader

discipline *noun*
1 making people obey rules of good behaviour and punishing them if they do not *The discipline in our school is very good* (students behave well).
2 the control over your behaviour or mind that you need to make yourself do something that you should do, for example study, work or practise something *David doesn't have the discipline to learn a foreign language.*

discipline *verb*
disciplines, disciplining, disciplined
1 to teach someone to obey rules of good behaviour
2 to punish someone who has behaved badly
3 to control your own behaviour in order to study or work properly

disc jockey *noun* disc jockeys
someone who introduces and plays music on the radio or in a place such as a club, for example using CDs or a record player

LANGUAGE EXTRA often written as *DJ*

disclose *verb*
discloses, disclosing, disclosed
if you disclose something to someone, you tell them about it even if it is secret *She disclosed the information to the police.*
disclosure *noun*

disco *noun* discos
a place or event where people dance to pop music

discoloured *adjective*
if something is discoloured, its colour has changed so that it looks worse than it did before *the discoloured pages of an old book* **discolour** *verb*

discomfort *noun*
a feeling of slight pain

disconcerting *adjective*
making someone feel worried, confused or upset *I'm supposed to meet Tom at noon but he's not here – that's rather disconcerting.*

123

disconnect – dishonest

disconnect *verb*
disconnects, disconnecting, disconnected
1 to disconnect something from something else is to stop it being joined *I disconnected the cable from my laptop.*
2 to disconnect someone is to stop them joining a computer or telephone network *I dialled the number but was disconnected.*
3 to stop being connected to this type of network *Click here to disconnect from the internet.*
disconnection *noun*

discontent *noun*
a feeling of unhappiness because something is not as good as it should be
discontented *adjective*

discontinue *verb*
discontinues, discontinuing, discontinued
to stop doing, giving or selling something *Our supermarket has discontinued my favourite biscuits.*

discount *noun* discounts
the amount by which the price of something is less *There's a £200 discount on this laptop until the end of the month.*

discounted *adjective*
1 a discounted price is less than the usual price
2 a discounted product is sold for less than the usual price

discourage *verb*
discourages, discouraging, discouraged
1 to take away someone's hopes and make them less interested in doing something
2 to stop (or try to stop) something from happening or someone from doing something, for example because you think it is difficult or not a good idea *The snowy weather discouraged some of my friends from coming to my party.*

discouraged *adjective*
sad and losing interest in something because your hopes are being taken away

discouragement *noun*
1 the feeling of being discouraged
2 the action of discouraging something from happening or someone from doing something

discouraging *adjective*
making you feel sad because your hopes are being taken away

discover *verb*
discovers, discovering, discovered
1 to find something out
2 to find something for the first time *I discovered some Roman coins in a field.*

discovery *noun* discoveries
1 when you find something out *Scientists have made an important discovery.*
2 when you find something for the first time *the discovery of a new planet*
3 something that is found out or found for the first time *The Sutton Hoo treasure is a spectacular discovery.*

discreet *adjective*
careful about what you say or do, for example because you do not want someone to know something or to notice you doing something, or because you do not want to upset someone
discreetly *adverb*

discriminate *verb*
discriminates, discriminating, discriminated
1 to discriminate against someone is to treat them in a different and worse way from someone else, for example because they belong to a different religion or country
2 to discriminate between one thing and another is to notice that they are different *Some learners have trouble discriminating between these two vowel sounds.*

discrimination *noun*
1 treating someone in a different and worse way, for example because of their religion or sex or the country they come from *racial discrimination*; *sexual discrimination* (when girls and women, or boys and men, are treated badly)
2 being able to know the difference between things, especially between something that is good and something that is not good

discus ['dis-kers'] *noun* discuses
a heavy round flat object used in sport. People try to throw it as far as they can.

discuss *verb*
discusses, discussing, discussed
1 to talk about something with someone
2 to talk about a subject with lots of details, for example in a book or in order to make a decision

discussion *noun* discussions
1 an important conversation about something, usually with lots of details
2 an important piece of writing in which someone gives lots of details or different opinions about a subject

disease *noun* diseases
an illness, especially a serious one, that affects a person, animal or plant

diseased *adjective*
if something such as a plant or animal is diseased, it has a disease

disembark *verb*
disembarks, disembarking, disembarked
to get off a boat or plane
disembarkation *noun*

disentangle *verb*
disentangles, disentangling, disentangled
1 to get rid of the knots from something such as a rope or shoelace
2 to separate something from something else that has got twisted around it

disfigured *adjective*
if someone is disfigured, or if their face is disfigured, something very bad has changed their normal appearance, for example an accident

disgrace *noun*
1 when someone no longer has the respect of other people because they have done something bad *Oliver's behaviour has brought disgrace on the whole school.*
2 something or someone that you should feel ashamed of because they are very bad *Your homework is a disgrace.*

disgrace *verb*
disgraces, disgracing, disgraced
to disgrace someone is to do something bad that takes away people's respect for them *You've disgraced your family by this behaviour.*

disgraceful *adjective*
if something is disgraceful, it is so bad that people should feel ashamed of it
disgracefully *adverb*

disguise *noun* disguises
something you wear or a change you make to the way you look, so that people don't recognise you *We went to the party in disguise.*

disguise *verb*
disguises, disguising, disguised
1 to make changes to someone or something so that people don't recognise them
2 if someone is disguised, they are wearing something or have made a change to the way they look, so that people don't recognise them *My teacher was disguised as a wizard.*

disgust *verb*
disgusts, disgusting, disgusted
if something or someone disgusts you, you dislike them very much and they make you feel very shocked or upset

disgust *noun*
a very strong feeling of dislike about something or someone

disgusted *adjective*
feeling very shocked or upset about something bad

disgusting *adjective*
1 bad enough to make you feel sick *a disgusting taste*
2 bad enough to really shock you or upset you *disgusting behaviour*
3 extremely unpleasant *We've had disgusting weather all week.*
disgustingly *adverb*

dish *noun* dishes
1 a container with low sides for cooking or serving food in
2 the food cooked in a dish
3 food cooked as part of a meal *Our family prefers vegetarian dishes.*
4 the dishes are the plates, bowls, cups and other things used for cooking and eating meals *It's your turn to wash the dishes.*

dish *verb*
dishes, dishing, dished
1 (informal) to dish something out is to give something to lots of people, especially in a careless way
2 to dish out food or a meal, or to dish it up, is to serve it to someone *Dish out a few more beans, please. Dad's dishing up dinner.*

dishcloth *noun* dishcloths
a cloth for washing dishes or for drying them

disheartened *adjective*
if you are disheartened, you lose interest in something because you have less hope than before **disheartening** *adjective*

dishevelled ['dis-shev-erld'] *adjective*
if you are dishevelled, you have untidy hair and you look untidy

dishonest *adjective*
behaving in a very bad way, for example by stealing, going against the rules or telling lies **dishonesty** *noun*

dishwasher – displace

dishwasher noun dishwashers
a large piece of equipment where you put dirty dishes to be washed automatically

disillusioned adjective
sad because something or someone is not as good as you thought they were

disinfect verb
disinfects, disinfecting, disinfected
to clean something such as a wound or surface by using chemicals to kill germs

disinfectant noun disinfectants
a chemical that kills germs and cleans things

disintegrate verb
disintegrates, disintegrating, disintegrated
1 to be destroyed by breaking up into very small pieces
2 to be destroyed after gradually getting weaker and more useless *Eventually the Soviet Union disintegrated.*
disintegration noun

disinterested adjective
1 if someone is disinterested, they are able to give a fair opinion in a particular situation because they have no personal feelings towards anyone connected with the situation
2 also used about something that someone does or says *a disinterested opinion*

LANGUAGE EXTRA be careful not to confuse *disinterested* with *uninterested*, which means 'not interested in something'

disk noun disks
1 a round flat object inside a computer that the computer uses to store information on. It is usually made of metal and other materials in a rectangular container.

SYNONYM hard disk

2 a round flat piece of plastic used for storing and recording computer information, sounds and pictures, for example a CD or DVD
3 a disk drive is a piece of equipment, either inside a computer or connected to a computer, that stores information onto a hard disk and uses information from it

LANGUAGE EXTRA do not confuse *disk* with *disc*. A *disc* can be any round flat object. A CD or DVD is usually called a *disc* but the spelling *disk* can also be used.

dislike verb
dislikes, disliking, disliked
if you dislike someone or something, you don't like them but you don't hate them either

dislike noun
1 a feeling that you don't like someone or something
2 dislikes are things you don't like

dislocate verb
dislocates, dislocating, dislocated
if you accidentally dislocate a bone, it comes away from its normal place in your body **dislocation** noun

dislodge verb
dislodges, dislodging, dislodged
to move something from the place where it is fixed

disloyal adjective
if you are disloyal, for example to a person or your country, you do not behave towards them as a good person and you do not support them in the way that you should **disloyalty** noun

dismal adjective
1 if something is dismal, it makes you feel sad because it is very bad or without hope *The situation looks dismal at the moment.*
2 dark and unpleasant *a dismal winter's morning*

ORIGIN from Latin *dies mali* 'evil days', referring to what the Romans believed were the two unlucky days in every month

dismally adverb
very badly *We failed dismally.*

dismantle verb
dismantles, dismantling, dismantled
to separate the different parts that make up a machine or structure

dismay verb
dismays, dismaying, dismayed
to make someone feel upset, disappointed or worried and often surprised

dismay noun
a feeling of being upset, disappointed or worried and often surprised

dismiss verb
dismisses, dismissing, dismissed
1 to tell someone to leave *My uncle was dismissed from his job.*
2 to say that something is not good enough to consider *They dismissed my idea as stupid.*

dismissal noun dismissals
telling someone to leave their job

dismount verb
dismounts, dismounting, dismounted
to get off a bicycle or horse

disobedient adjective
deliberately not doing what someone tells you to do **disobedience** noun

disobey verb
disobeys, disobeying, disobeyed
1 not to do what someone tells you to do *He always disobeys his parents.*
2 if you disobey a rule or law, you don't do what it says you must do

disorder noun
1 (plural **disorders**) an illness or medical problem
2 a situation in which things are badly organised or untidy
3 a situation in which people make a lot of noise and behave badly

disorderly adjective
1 untidy *a disorderly pile of books*
2 making a lot of noise and behaving badly *a disorderly crowd*

disorganised adjective
1 bad at organising things or keeping things tidy
2 badly planned *The school outing was a bit disorganised.*

LANGUAGE EXTRA also spelt *disorganized*

disorientated adjective
1 not knowing where you are or where to go next, for example because you are lost
2 not knowing what is happening around you and not able to behave normally, for example because you've been in an accident

disown verb
disowns, disowning, disowned
to say that you don't want to have anything to do with someone or something *Your parents will disown you if your behaviour doesn't get better.*

dispatch verb
dispatches, dispatching, dispatched
1 to send something or someone *Your order was dispatched yesterday.*
2 to get rid of someone, for example by beating them in a game or by killing them

LANGUAGE EXTRA also spelt *despatch*

dispel verb
dispels, dispelling, dispelled
to show that something such as an idea or belief is wrong

dispense verb
dispenses, dispensing, dispensed
1 if a machine dispenses something, it gives it out to you *Put £1 in the machine and it will dispense a cold drink.*
2 if a chemist dispenses medicine, he or she prepares it and gives it to you
3 to dispense with something is to not use or do something that you usually use or do

dispenser noun dispensers
a container or machine that gives out a small amount of something, for example when you press a button or type in a special number *a cash dispenser*

disperse verb
disperses, dispersing, dispersed
1 if people disperse or if someone disperses them, they go away in different directions *The police dispersed the crowd.*
2 if something such as fog or smoke disperses, it gradually becomes less and goes away
3 if things such as seeds or clouds disperse or if something disperses them, they spread over a large area
dispersal noun

dispirited adjective
if you are dispirited, you no longer have the hope or interest you had before

SYNONYM disheartened

displace verb
displaces, displacing, displaced
1 to take the place of something or move it from its place *The computer has completely displaced the typewriter.*
2 to take the place of someone, for example someone with an official position, or to take someone's place using force *Our school has displaced Oakdale School at the top of the league tables.*
3 a displaced person is someone who has been forced to leave their country, for example because of a war

125

display–distraction

display *verb*
displays, displaying, displayed
1 to show something or put something somewhere so that people can see it easily
2 to show a particular feeling or behaviour *She displayed a talent for music from the age of seven.*
3 to show information on a computer screen

display *noun* displays
1 things put or arranged somewhere so that people can look at them *a beautiful display of Chinese vases; Children's artwork was on display in the hall.*
2 when people do things in front of an audience to entertain them *a firework display*
3 when someone shows a particular feeling or behaviour
4 a piece of equipment that shows information, for example a computer screen

displease *verb*
displeases, displeasing, displeased
to make someone slightly angry

SYNONYM to annoy

disposable *adjective*
if something is disposable, you throw it away after using it

disposal *noun*
1 getting rid of something
2 **at someone's disposal** ready for someone to use at any time

dispose *verb*
disposes, disposing, disposed
to dispose of something is to get rid of it

disposed *adjective*
1 ready to behave in a certain way *He was well disposed towards us.*
2 if you are disposed to do something, you are ready and happy to do it

disposition *noun* dispositions
1 someone's special qualities that make them what they are *She has a friendly disposition.*
2 the way someone is likely to behave

disproportionate *adjective*
too large or too great when compared to something else *My sister earns a disproportionate amount of money considering she hardly does any work.*
disproportionately *adverb*

disprove *verb*
disproves, disproving, disproved
to prove that something is not true

dispute *noun* disputes
a situation in which people are angry and have very different opinions about something

SYNONYM quarrel

disqualify *verb*
disqualifies, disqualifying, disqualified
1 to make someone leave a race or competition or to stop them taking part because they have broken the rules
2 to disqualify someone from driving is to take away their driving licence because they have broken the law while driving
disqualification *noun*

disregard *verb*
disregards, disregarding, disregarded
to take no notice of something
disregard *noun*

disrespect *noun*
the way that someone feels about something or someone when they have no respect for them **disrespectful** *adjective*

disrespect *verb*
disrespects, disrespecting, disrespected
to show disrespect to someone or something by saying or doing something unpleasant

disrupt *verb*
disrupts, disrupting, disrupted
to cause problems that make it difficult for something to keep going or for someone to do something in the normal way *The snow has disrupted our plans.* **disruption** *noun*

disruptive *adjective*
causing problems that stop people from doing things in the normal way *Jason is very disruptive in class.*

diss *verb* (informal)
disses, dissing, dissed
to diss someone is to show disrespect by saying unpleasant things to or about them

dissatisfied *adjective*
not pleased because something is not as good as you thought it would be *Dad was very dissatisfied with the meal.*
dissatisfaction *noun*

dissect *verb*
dissects, dissecting, dissected
if someone dissects something, such as a dead animal, they cut it up in order to study it **dissection** *noun*

dissertation *noun* dissertations
a long piece of writing that a student chooses to do on a particular subject as part of a university degree

dissolve *verb*
dissolves, dissolving, dissolved
if something dissolves or you dissolve it, it mixes with a liquid and becomes part of it *Salt dissolves in water.*

dissuade *verb*
dissuades, dissuading, dissuaded
to persuade someone not to do something

distance *noun* distances
1 the space between two places, things or people
2 when things or people are far away from each other *We didn't want to go on holiday to Australia because of the distance.*
3 **in the distance** far away from where you are but still able to be seen or heard

distant *adjective*
1 far away from where you are
2 far away in time in the past or the future
3 not friendly or not wanting to be with other people

distil *verb*
distils, distilling, distilled
to make a liquid pure by heating it so that it becomes a vapour (tiny drops in the air) and then letting it cool down until it becomes a liquid again *distilled water*
distillation *noun*

distillery *noun* distilleries
a factory that makes alcoholic drinks such as whisky by distilling them

distinct *adjective*
1 different in a way that you can notice *The Liverpool accent is quite distinct from the Newcastle one.*
2 easy to see, hear, taste or smell *There's a distinct outline of a tree in the background.*
3 if something such as a feeling, idea or quality is distinct, it is impossible to be mistaken about it *a distinct possibility*

SYNONYM for senses 2 & 3: definite

distinction *noun*
1 (*plural* distinctions) a clear difference between two things
2 (*plural* distinctions) a very high mark in an exam
3 a special quality that makes something or someone different *Our school has the distinction of being the oldest in the county.*
4 the excellent quality of someone or something *Constable is a painter of distinction.*

distinctive *adjective*
if something is distinctive, there is something special about it that makes it different from all others and easy to notice *Peter has a distinctive laugh.*

distinctly *adverb*
1 very clearly *I can see your face distinctly on the webcam.*
2 definitely and completely *The teacher was distinctly worried about Simon's behaviour.*

distinguish *verb*
distinguishes, distinguishing, distinguished
1 to tell the difference between things or people *My little brother can't distinguish between right and wrong.*
2 to be the thing that makes something or someone special and different *Theo's intelligence distinguishes him from the rest of the class.*
3 to see or hear something clearly

distinguished *adjective*
1 looking serious and important, and deserving people's respect

SYNONYM dignified

2 successful and respected by many people *a distinguished playwright*

distort *verb*
distorts, distorting, distorted
1 to change something so that it looks or sounds strange *This is a bad phone line – your voice sounds distorted.*
2 to change information so that it is not completely true *You've distorted the truth.*
distortion *noun*

distract *verb*
distracts, distracting, distracted
to take away someone's attention from something *Don't distract me when I'm working.*

distraction *noun* distractions
1 something that takes away your attention and stops you doing what you are supposed to do
2 an activity you do for pleasure

SYNONYM diversion

distraught – divorce

distraught adjective
very sad and worried

distress noun
1 a feeling of being very unhappy or worried *She arrived home in distress.*
2 great trouble or pain
3 if a plane or ship is in distress, it is in very real danger

distress verb
distresses, distressing, distressed
to make someone very unhappy or worried

distribute verb
distributes, distributing, distributed
1 to give something out to lots of people *Can you distribute the exercise books, Amesh?*
2 to share things out among people *Our school distributes food and clothes to homeless people.*
3 to spread something over a certain area *These butterflies are distributed throughout the whole of Wales.*
4 to supply goods to shops or companies
distribution noun **distributor** noun

district noun districts
a part of a town or country

distrust verb
distrusts, distrusting, distrusted
to think that someone or something cannot be trusted

distrust noun
a feeling of not being able to trust someone or something **distrustful** adjective

disturb verb
disturbs, disturbing, disturbed
1 to stop someone doing something, for example by making a noise or talking to them *Try not to disturb me when I'm working.*
2 to worry or upset someone very much *I was really disturbed by those pictures on TV.*
3 to move something from its position, for example by touching it or knocking it *Don't disturb any of my books.*

disturbance noun disturbances
1 something that stops someone doing something
2 noisy or violent behaviour in a public place

disturbing adjective
making you feel very worried or upset, for example because you have seen something bad or shocking *disturbing images*

disused adjective
empty and no longer used *a disused warehouse*

ditch noun ditches
a long hole in the ground for holding water, for example by the side of a road or field

ditch verb
ditches, ditching, ditched
an informal way of saying to get rid of something

dither verb
dithers, dithering, dithered
if you dither, you cannot decide something because you are not sure

SYNONYM to hesitate

ditto noun
a punctuation mark " that you write under a word in a list to repeat that word. The ditto mark means 'the same again' and saves you from having to write the word again.

ditty noun ditties
a short and very simple song or poem

divan noun divans
1 a sofa without a back or arms
2 a very simple bed that looks like this

dive verb
dives, diving, dived
1 to jump into the water with your head first and your arms stretched out in front of you
2 to go under the water, usually with breathing equipment
3 to move somewhere very quickly, usually downwards *When I heard the thunder, I dived under the table.*

dive noun dives
1 a very quick movement, usually downwards *The plane went into a dive.*
2 the action of jumping into the water or going under the water *Let's go for a dive.*

diver noun divers
1 someone who goes under the water, usually with breathing equipment
2 a swimmer who dives into the water

diverge verb
diverges, diverging, diverged
if things such as lines or paths diverge, they start to go in different directions after they have been going in the same direction

diverse adjective
very different from each other, or made up of many different things or people *a diverse range of after-school activities*

diversify verb
diversifies, diversifying, diversified
1 if a shop or business diversifies, it develops and tries to sell different products
2 to change and become different *Animal species have diversified over millions of years.*

diversion noun diversions
1 a different way that traffic must go because the usual road is closed
2 something that someone does to take away your attention from something that they don't want you to notice
3 an activity you do for pleasure

SYNONYM for senses 2 & 3: distraction

diversity noun
when there are many different kinds of things or people *the rich diversity of London's population*

divert verb
diverts, diverting, diverted
1 to change the direction that something moves in
2 if you divert someone's attention, you do something to take away their attention from something so that they don't think about it or notice it
3 if a phone call is diverted, it automatically goes to a second number because it cannot be answered at the first number

divide verb
divides, dividing, divided
1 to separate something into two or more parts
2 to form two or more separate parts
3 in maths, if you divide one number by another number (usually a smaller one), you work out how many times the second number can fit into the first one *Thirty divided by six is five* (30 ÷ 6 = 5, or $\frac{30}{6} = 5$).
4 to share something *They divided up the money between them.*

dividend noun dividends
1 in maths, a dividend is a number divided by another number
compare: **divisor** and **quotient**
2 money given to someone who has shares in a company

dividers noun plural
an instrument for measuring angles and distances. It is made up of two thin pointed pieces of metal joined at the top in an upside-down V shape.

divine adjective
1 coming from or connected with God or a god
2 an informal word for excellent, beautiful or delicious
divinely adverb

diving noun
1 the activity or sport of swimming under the water, usually with breathing equipment *My uncle goes diving off the Cornish coast.*
2 the activity or sport of jumping into the water with your head first *a diving board* (for jumping into the water, usually from the side of a swimming pool)

divisible adjective
in maths, if a number is divisible, it can be divided by another number *12 is divisible by 3.*

division noun divisions
1 the action or result of dividing one number by another in maths
2 separating something into two or more parts
3 a part into which something such as an organisation, group or sports team is divided *The football team I support is in the Second Division.*
4 a very large group of soldiers. A division is usually made up of several regiments or brigades. *a tank division*
5 a big difference or disagreement between groups of people *the divisions between rich and poor*
6 the division sign is the symbol ÷ used between two numbers to show that one is divided by the other. In computing, for example in spreadsheets, the symbol / (a slash) is usually used.

divisor noun divisors
in maths, a divisor is a number that you divide into another number
compare: **dividend** and **quotient**

divorce verb
divorces, divorcing, divorced
if a man and woman, or two partners, divorce or get divorced, they end their marriage by law **divorce** noun

divorced–dogged

divorced *adjective*
if someone is divorced, they are no longer married

divulge *verb*
divulges, divulging, divulged
if you divulge something to someone, you tell them about it even if it is secret

SYNONYM to disclose

Diwali ['di-wah-lee'] *noun*
a Hindu and Sikh festival in October or November. It is known as the 'festival of lights' and celebrates an important victory of the god Rama.

DIY
short for **do-it-yourself**

dizzy *adjective* dizzier, dizziest
feeling as if things are going round and round in your head and that you might fall
dizziness *noun*

DJ *noun* DJs
someone who introduces and plays music on the radio or in a place such as a club, for example using CDs or a record player
short for: **disc jockey**

do *verb*
does, doing, did, done
1 if you do something, you start an action or you start it and then complete it *I'm doing my homework. I've done my homework.*

LANGUAGE EXTRA *do* is often used instead of another verb and can mean many different things. For example: *Dad's doing (preparing) some sandwiches. Nathan has a lot of emails to do (write). I've done (brushed) my teeth. This painting was done (painted) by Monet.*

2 used for talking about someone's health *How are you doing?* (How are you?)
3 used for talking about how successful someone is *My sister is doing really well.*
4 used for making a question or negative sentence *Do you like football? I don't like ice cream.*
5 used for giving special importance to a verb or to refer back to a verb *I do like my teacher. She knows more about computers than you do* (know).
6 to do away with something is to get rid of it
7 (informal) to do someone in is to kill them
8 to do something up, such as your coat or buttons, is to fasten them
9 to do something up, such as a house or room, is to paint it and repair it
10 if someone or something has something to do with you, they are connected with you in some way *That broken window is nothing to do* (not connected) *with me.*
11 if you say you could do with something, you mean that you need it *I could really do with a nice cup of tea.*
12 to do without something is to carry on in the usual way without having it
13 to do without someone is to carry on in the usual way without someone being there or without someone doing the good things they usually do *Everyone likes the music teacher – we couldn't do without her.*

do *noun* dos or do's
1 an event in which people get together to enjoy themselves

SYNONYM party

2 dos and don'ts are things that you should and should not do *Here are some dos and don'ts when you're using your computer for the first time.*

Doberman *noun* Dobermans
a large dog with black or brown hair, often used for guarding buildings

doc *noun* docs
1 an informal word for a doctor
2 the ending of a computer filename. A .doc file contains text or text and pictures.
short for: **document**

docile *adjective*
a child or animal that is docile behaves very well and is easy to control

ORIGIN from Latin *docilis* 'easily taught', from *docere* 'to teach'

dock *noun* docks
1 a place in a harbour where ships stay while they are loaded, unloaded or repaired
2 the dock is the place where an accused person stands in a court of law
3 a piece of equipment that connects a digital player such as an iPod to something else such as a computer

dock *verb*
docks, docking, docked
1 if a ship docks, it comes into a dock
2 if two spacecraft dock, they join together in space

docker *noun* dockers
someone who loads and unloads ships in a dock

dockyard *noun* dockyards
a place in a harbour where people build and repair ships

SYNONYM shipyard

doctor *noun* doctors
someone who has studied medicine and whose job is to make sick people better

ORIGIN from Latin *doctor* 'teacher', from *docere* 'to teach'

document *noun* documents
1 a piece of paper with important information written on it
2 a piece of information containing text or pictures that you save on a computer, disk or drive *I've saved my homework as a document on my flash drive.*

documentary *noun* documentaries
a film, TV or radio programme that deals with a particular subject taken from real life *a documentary about the rainforest in Brazil* **documentary** *adjective*

documentation *noun*
1 documents that prove something is true
2 instructions that tell you how to use a piece of equipment or a computer program

docx
the ending of a computer filename. A .docx file contains text or text and pictures.
short for: **document xml** (extensible markup language)

doddering *adjective*
shaking slightly when you move or walk because of old age *a doddering old man*

LANGUAGE EXTRA you can also say *doddery*

doddle *noun* (informal)
if you say that something is a doddle, you mean that it's easy to do

dodge *verb*
dodges, dodging, dodged
1 to move quickly to get away from something or someone *She threw a stick at me but I managed to dodge it.*
2 to avoid dealing with something, especially by being clever or dishonest *You've dodged the question.*
dodge *noun*

dodgems *noun plural*
small electric cars at a funfair that children or grown-ups drive around in and use for deliberately hitting other cars

SYNONYM bumper cars

dodgy *adjective* dodgier, dodgiest (informal)
1 dishonest *Don't buy anything from him – he's dodgy.*
2 bad *My grammar is a bit dodgy.*
3 in bad condition or not working properly *dodgy tyres; a dodgy computer*
4 dangerous *It's dodgy walking around the town centre at night.*
5 false *a dodgy address; a dodgy £10 note*

dodo *noun* dodos
a large bird that could not fly and no longer exists. The dodo lived on the island of Mauritius, in the Indian Ocean, until the 17th century.

SIMILE 'as dead as a dodo' means very definitely dead

doe *noun* does
a female deer or rabbit

does
third person singular present tense of **do**

doesn't
short for 'does not'

dog *noun* dogs
a small, medium-sized or large animal that people keep as a pet or for other activities such as guarding buildings or helping blind people. Dogs have short or long hair and the sound they make is a bark.

dog *verb*
dogs, dogging, dogged
if someone is dogged by something, that thing causes them lots of problems all of the time *He was dogged by bad luck all his life.*

dog-eared *adjective*
1 if a page of a book is dog-eared, it has its corner turned down, for example to mark someone's place
2 if a book is dog-eared (or if its pages are dog-eared), the corners of some pages are turned down or damaged because it has been used so much

dogged ['dog-id'] *adjective*
really wanting to do something and not letting anything stop you *dogged determination* **doggedly** *adverb*

128

d'oh–doorstop

d'oh *interjection* (informal)
used when you realise that you've just done or said something wrong

> **ORIGIN** used by Homer Simpson in the TV cartoon *The Simpsons*

doing *noun*
if something bad is someone's doing, it is their fault *My smartphone won't work, and it's your doing.*

do-it-yourself *noun*
the activity of doing or fixing things yourself in the home, instead of having to pay someone else to do it

do-it-yourself *adjective*
1 a do-it-yourself store sells things such as tools and equipment for doing or fixing things yourself
2 if something such as a piece of furniture is do-it-yourself, it can be made or put together in the home, instead of having to buy it already made

doldrums *noun plural*
1 if someone is in the doldrums, they are feeling sad
2 if a company or activity is in the doldrums, it is not successful or not making progress

> **LANGUAGE EXTRA** the *doldrums* are a part of the ocean near the Equator where there is very little wind

dole *noun* (informal)
money that the government pays to people who don't have a job *My mum's on the dole* (getting money from the government because she doesn't have a job).

dole out *verb*
doles out, doling out, doled out
to dole out something such as money or food is to give it to a group of people

doll *noun* **dolls**
1 a small toy that looks like a person, usually a baby or child
2 a doll's house is a toy house with toy furniture that children play with

> **ORIGIN** from *Doll*, a nickname for *Dorothy*, used originally about a female pet

dollar *noun* **dollars**
a unit of money in the USA, Canada, Australia and some other countries. A dollar is worth 100 cents, and the symbol $ is the dollar sign.

dolly *noun* **dollies**
an informal word for a doll

dolphin *noun* **dolphins**
a large sea animal like a fish, with a pointed nose and a mouth with teeth. Dolphins are very intelligent and friendly.

domain *noun* **domains**
1 an area of land that is ruled by someone, such as a king
2 an area of activity of a particular person *My sister's domain is painting.*
3 a domain or domain name is an address on the internet, such as www.schofieldandsims.co.uk

dome *noun* **domes**
a round roof on a building shaped like the top half of a ball

domestic *adjective*
1 connected with the home *He lives a quiet domestic life.*
2 connected with a particular country *To fly from Edinburgh to London you take a domestic flight.*
3 a domestic animal, such as a cat or dog, is one that lives in someone's home

domesticated *adjective*
1 a domesticated animal is one that people have trained to work for them or live with them *The horse is a domesticated animal.*
2 if a person is domesticated, he or she enjoys doing things in the home, such as cooking and cleaning

dominant *adjective*
1 most important *the dominant idea in the book*
2 strongest *a dominant personality*
3 easiest to see or notice *Blue is the dominant colour.*

dominance *noun*

dominate *verb*
dominates, dominating, dominated
1 to have power over someone or something and control them
2 to be the most important thing or person or have the strongest effect in a particular situation *The crash dominated the newspapers.*
3 to be bigger than everything else and easier to see *Paris is dominated by the Eiffel Tower.*

domination *noun*
power and control over people

dominion *noun*
dominion over something, such as a country, is the power to rule over it

domino *noun* **dominoes**
one of the small oblong pieces of plastic or wood used in the game of dominoes. Each half of a domino usually has a group of dots on it (from one to six) or a blank space.

donate *verb*
donates, donating, donated
to give something, for example money, to help an organisation or person *My parents donated £50 to the school.*

donation *noun* **donations**
something that someone donates to an organisation or person

done
past participle of **do**

done *adjective*
1 finished *I'm not done yet.*
2 cooked *Are the eggs done?*

doner kebab *noun* **doner kebabs**
a food made up of flat pieces of cooked meat such as lamb served in pitta (oval-shaped flat bread), often with salad

> **ORIGIN** from Turkish *doner* 'turning or spinning' and *kebap* 'roast meat'

dongle *noun* **dongles**
1 a small piece of equipment that you must connect to a computer to make a program work
2 also used about any small piece of equipment that connects to a computer *a Bluetooth dongle*

donkey *noun* **donkeys**
an animal like a small horse with very long ears. The sound that a donkey makes is braying.

donor *noun* **donors**
1 someone who gives something from their body to help another person *a blood donor*; *a kidney donor*
2 someone who gives something such as money to help an organisation or person

don't
short for 'do not'

doodle *verb*
doodles, doodling, doodled
to draw simple shapes or patterns, for example because you're bored

doodle *noun*

doom *noun*
a terrible event such as death or destruction that is certain to happen in the future

doom *verb*
dooms, dooming, doomed
if someone or something is doomed to something bad, that particular thing is certain to happen *Our team was doomed to failure.*

door *noun* **doors**
1 a large flat object that you open or close to go into or out of somewhere such as a room, building, vehicle or lift
2 a similar object for opening or closing a cupboard or wardrobe

doorbell *noun* **doorbells**
a button at the front door of a house or flat that rings when you press it so that someone inside knows you're there

doorknob *noun* **doorknobs**
a round handle on a door for opening or closing the door

doorknocker *noun* **doorknockers**
a metal object fixed to a door, with a moving part for hitting the door to let someone inside know you're there

doorman *noun* **doormen**
someone who stands in front of the main door of a building, such as a hotel, to help people when they go in and come out

doormat *noun* **doormats**
a small piece of material inside or outside the main door of a building, used for cleaning the bottom of your shoes

doornail *noun*

> **SIMILE** 'as dead as a doornail' means very definitely dead

doorstep *noun* **doorsteps**
1 a small step outside the front door of a building
2 if something such as a school or the shops is on your doorstep, it is very close to where you live

doorstop *noun* **doorstops**
1 something that you put against or under a door to stop it from closing
2 something fixed to a wall to stop a door from hitting the wall when you open it

doorway–downcast

doorway noun doorways
the space in a wall where a door opens and closes *I saw my teacher standing in the doorway.*

doorwoman noun doorwomen
a woman who stands in front of the main door of a building, such as a hotel, to help people when they go in and come out

dope noun dopes
an informal word for a stupid fool

dopey adjective dopier, dopiest (informal)
1 stupid
2 feeling tired or sleepy, for example because of a drug or medicine

dormant adjective
1 if something such as a virus is dormant, it is not growing now but may grow in the future
2 a dormant volcano is one that is not exploding now but may explode in the future

dormitory noun dormitories
1 a large room with many beds, for example in a boarding school
2 in American English, a dormitory is a building at a college where students live

ORIGIN from Latin *dormitorium*, from *dormire* 'to sleep'

dormouse noun dormice
an animal that looks like a mouse with a long furry tail

dose noun doses
1 an amount of medicine that is measured and that someone takes at one time
2 an amount of something *a dose of good luck*

doss verb (informal)
dosses, dossing, dossed
to sleep somewhere

dot noun dots
1 a tiny round mark
2 a point that you write in an internet or email address. For example, you say .com as 'dot com' and you say .co.uk as 'dot co dot uk'.
3 **on the dot** exactly at a particular time *The lesson started at nine o'clock on the dot.*

dot verb
dots, dotting, dotted
1 to put a dot on the letter *i* or *j*
2 if a place is dotted with things, there are lots of them everywhere *There are many castles dotted around this part of Scotland.*

dotted line noun dotted lines
a printed line made up of lots of dots *Cut out the coupon along the dotted line.*

dotty adjective dottier, dottiest
an informal word for slightly mad or crazy

double adjective & adverb
1 twice the amount or size or number of something *Amy's house is double the size of mine.*
2 made up of two things of the same type *Don't park on the double yellow lines.*
3 for two people or things, or connected with two things *a double bed*; *a double meaning*
4 used for repeating a letter or number *'Book' is spelt 'b', double 'o', 'k'.*

double noun doubles
1 something that is twice the amount or size or number of something *That's not enough pocket money – I want double!*
2 a person who looks almost exactly the same as you
3 if you play doubles in tennis, you play with someone else against two other people. If you play against one other person only, you play singles.

double verb
doubles, doubling, doubled
1 to become twice as big or twice as much *The number of children in the school has doubled.*
2 to make something twice as big or twice as much *Think of a number, then double it.*
3 to double something over, such as a sheet of paper, is to fold it in two
4 to be doubled over or up, for example with pain, is to be bent forwards

double bass ['bayss] noun
double basses
a wooden musical instrument with strings. It looks like a large cello.

double-check verb
double-checks, double-checking, double-checked
to check something a second time, for example to make sure it's correct

double-click verb
double-clicks, double-clicking, double-clicked
to quickly click twice with the left button of your computer mouse, for example to open a program or to highlight text
double click noun

double-cross verb
double-crosses, double-crossing, double-crossed
to cheat someone, for example after you have planned to do something dishonest with them

double-decker noun double-deckers
a bus that has an upstairs and a downstairs where people sit
compare: single-decker

double glazing noun
two layers of glass on a window or door for keeping a building quiet and warm

doubly adverb
1 much more than usual *I was doubly afraid that night.*
2 in two ways *My sister is doubly talented – she can sing and dance.*

doubt verb
doubts, doubting, doubted
to think that something is not likely to be true *I doubt that George will come to your party.*

doubt noun doubts
1 a feeling of not being sure about something *I don't have any doubts about what I want for my birthday.*
2 if you are in doubt about something, you are not sure about it
3 **without a doubt** used for saying something is certain

doubtful adjective
1 not being sure about something *I was doubtful that she would win.*
2 not likely to be true or to happen *It's doubtful we'll get to school on time in this snow.*

doubtless adverb
used for saying something is true or will happen

SYNONYM certainly

dough noun
1 a mixture of flour and water for making cakes or bread
2 a slang word for money

doughnut noun doughnuts
a small cake shaped like a ring or ball. It is made from dough, often has jam inside and is cooked by frying.

dour [rhymes with 'sure'] adjective
if someone is dour, they are serious and unfriendly

douse verb
douses, dousing, doused
1 to pour a liquid over something or someone
2 to douse a fire is to pour water over it to stop it from burning

dove noun doves
a bird like a small white pigeon. Doves are often used as a symbol of peace.

dowdy adjective dowdier, dowdiest
if someone is dowdy, or if their clothes are dowdy, they are not fashionable or pleasant to look at

down adverb & preposition
1 to a lower position or level *Come down! I climbed down the ladder.*
2 in a lower position or level *The fence is down again.*
3 towards the south *My cousin is down from Manchester.*
4 along *We walked down the street.*
5 used when talking about a place that is close by *I saw him down at the library.*
6 used when talking about doing something completely or thoroughly *Can you wash down the shower?*
7 used when you mean something is less *Turn the radio down* (make it quieter). *Prices have come down* (they are lower).
8 used when talking about writing something *Please put my name down for the football team.*
9 used when talking about fastening something *Tie down the luggage.*
10 in or into the stomach when eating or drinking *Drink down the rest of your lemonade.*
11 not working *My computer is down.*
12 sad *My sister's been feeling very down.*
13 **down with** used for saying you don't like someone or something *Down with racists!*
14 **down under** in or to Australia or New Zealand

down noun
1 very soft feathers on a bird
2 very soft hairs

downcast adjective
1 sad
2 if your eyes are downcast, you are looking down, for example because you are sad

downfall–drastically

downfall *noun*
1 someone's downfall is when they lose all their power or money or everything they have achieved
2 the reason for someone's downfall *Gambling was his downfall.*
3 (*plural* **downfalls**) a heavy fall of rain or snow

downhill *adverb*
1 down a slope *You don't have to pedal your bike if you go downhill.*
2 if an organisation or someone such as an old or sick person goes downhill, they get worse *Our school has been going downhill for years.*
downhill *adjective*

Downing Street *noun*
1 the home of the British prime minister in London
2 the British government or the office of the British prime minister

CULTURE NOTE short for *Number 10 Downing Street*, in Westminster

download ['down-lohd'] *verb*
downloads, downloading, downloaded
if you download software or a file, or if it downloads, you copy it to your computer from the internet or from another computer
downloadable *adjective*

download ['down-lohd'] *noun* **downloads**
1 downloading a file or program *The download took 10 minutes.*
2 a downloaded file or program

downpour *noun* **downpours**
a sudden and heavy fall of rain

downright *adverb*
very *He's downright naughty.*

LANGUAGE EXTRA *downright* is used in front of adjectives that show something unpleasant, for example *rude*, *dangerous* or *greedy*

downright *adjective*
complete *My brother is a downright nuisance.*

downs *noun plural*
low hills covered with grass

downstairs *adverb*
1 to or on a lower floor of a building
2 to or on the ground floor of a building
downstairs *adjective*

downstairs *noun*
the ground floor of a building

downstream *adverb*
in the direction that a river flows

down-to-earth *adjective*
if someone is down-to-earth, they are sensible and make good decisions in real situations

downward *adjective*
going towards a lower level *a downward slope*

downwards *adverb*
towards a lower level *I looked downwards.*

downy *adjective* **downier, downiest**
covered in very soft hairs or feathers

doze *verb*
dozes, dozing, dozed
1 to sleep, usually for a short time
2 if you doze off, you fall asleep, usually without meaning to
doze *noun*

dozen *noun* **dozens**
1 twelve *a dozen eggs*
2 **half a dozen** about six
3 **dozens** lots of things or people *I've done this dozens of times.*

dozy *adjective* **dozier, doziest**
1 feeling sleepy
2 an informal word for stupid

Dr
short for **Doctor**

drab *adjective* **drabber, drabbest**
1 not colourful or attractive *drab clothes*
2 boring *Her life sounds so drab.*

draft *noun* **drafts**
a rough plan of something that you write *This is the first draft of my essay.*

LANGUAGE EXTRA be careful not to confuse *draft* with *draught*, which means 'cold air'

draft *verb*
drafts, drafting, drafted
to write a rough plan of something

drag *verb*
drags, dragging, dragged
1 to pull something along the ground, for example something heavy
2 to pull something or someone somewhere, using a lot of strength *I dragged her out of the water.*
3 to make someone go somewhere when they don't want to *Mum had to drag my sister to school today.*
4 to move something such as a file or text on a computer screen using your mouse or by touch *Drag and drop this folder into the Recycle Bin.*
5 to drag a river, canal or lake is to look for something in it by pulling a net along the bottom of it

drag *noun* (informal)
something or someone very annoying or boring *Doing homework every day is such a drag.*

dragon *noun* **dragons**
in stories, an animal like a giant crocodile with wings. Dragons breathe out fire.

ORIGIN from Greek *drakon* 'serpent'

dragonfly *noun* **dragonflies**
a flying insect with a long thin body and two pairs of thin wings. Dragonflies usually live near water.

drain *noun* **drains**
1 a pipe that takes away dirty water and waste from a building or from many buildings
2 an opening, for example in a street, that leads to one of these pipes
3 something that uses up a lot of something such as money or energy *These expenses are a big drain on the school.*
4 (informal) **down the drain** wasted *All that time and money down the drain!*

drain *verb*
drains, draining, drained
1 if you drain liquid from something or if liquid drains from something, you get rid of all the liquid by letting it flow away
2 to drain something such as a glass is to get rid of all the liquid in it, for example by drinking it
3 to use up a lot of or all of something, for example energy, money or resources *Surfing the Net will drain your laptop battery.*
4 to take away someone's energy and make them very tired *After doing my homework I feel completely drained.*

draining board *noun* **draining boards**
a place next to a kitchen sink where you put washed dishes until they are dry

drainpipe *noun* **drainpipes**
a pipe going down the side of a building to take rainwater from the roof to the ground or to the drains

drake *noun* **drakes**
a male duck

drama *noun*
1 (*plural* **dramas**) a play, for example in the theatre or on TV
2 acting in plays or writing plays *We study drama at our school.*
3 used for talking about plays in general *I like drama more than films.*
4 (*plural* **dramas**) an exciting event or lots of exciting events *A police officer's job is full of drama.*

dramatic *adjective*
1 very sudden and big or easy to see *a dramatic change*
2 very exciting *a dramatic event*
3 connected with drama

dramatically *adverb*
suddenly and very much *Her behaviour has improved dramatically.*

dramatisation *noun* **dramatisations**
a play or film made from a story

LANGUAGE EXTRA also spelt *dramatization*

dramatise *verb*
dramatises, dramatising, dramatised
1 to make a story or event into a play or film *'Great Expectations' by Charles Dickens has been dramatised for TV.*
2 to make a situation seem more important or exciting than it really is

LANGUAGE EXTRA also spelt *dramatize*

dramatist *noun* **dramatists**
someone who writes plays

SYNONYM playwright

drank
past tense of **drink**

drape *verb*
drapes, draping, draped
if you drape something made of cloth somewhere, you put it there so that it hangs loosely *He unfolded the flag and draped it over the arm of the chair.*

drapes *noun plural*
in American English, long heavy curtains

drastic *adjective*
very serious, important and urgent *drastic changes*

drastically *adverb*
very much *Our school is trying to cut costs drastically.*

draught–dressing-up

draught *noun* draughts
a flow of cold air into a room that makes you feel cold

> **LANGUAGE EXTRA** be careful not to confuse *draught* with *draft*, which means 'a rough plan'

draughts *noun plural*
a game that two people play with 24 small round pieces on a board of 64 squares

draughtsman *noun* draughtsmen
someone who draws plans of things to be built, especially buildings

draughtswoman *noun* draughtswomen
a woman who draws plans of things to be built, especially buildings

draughty *adjective*
draughtier, draughtiest
a draughty place has lots of draughts *My bedroom is draughty and cold.*

draw *verb*
draws, drawing, drew, drawn
1 to make a picture, shape or line, usually with a pencil or pen *I drew a picture of a tree. Leah draws very well.*
2 if you draw someone's attention to something, you make them notice it
3 to pull or move something or someone *Draw your chair up to the table.*
4 to go or move somewhere *He drew a bit closer to the screen.*
5 to make someone want to come or go somewhere *The film drew a big crowd.*
6 to draw the curtains is to close them if they are open or to open them if they are closed
7 to draw a sword or gun is to take it out and be ready to use it
8 to get something *Aisha's schoolwork drew praise from her teachers.*
9 to make something such as a comparison, conclusion or distinction
10 if two sides in a game draw, they end the game with the same number of points so neither side wins

draw *noun* draws
1 the result of a game between two sides in which neither side wins because they both have the same number of points
2 a competition in which tickets with numbers or names on them are picked by chance to win money or a prize *a prize draw*
3 the action of picking by chance a winning ticket or a team to play against another team, for example in a football match
4 an event or person such as an actor or singer that lots of people come to see

drawback *noun* drawbacks
something bad that causes a problem or makes something less good

> **SYNONYM** disadvantage

drawbridge *noun* drawbridges
a bridge that can be lifted up and dropped down to stop enemies attacking, for example a bridge over a moat in front of a castle

drawer *noun* drawers
a sliding part of a piece of furniture shaped like a box, used for keeping things in. You pull it to open it and push it to close it.

drawing *noun*
1 (*plural* **drawings**) a picture of something, usually made with a pencil or pen
2 the skill or activity of drawing pictures *Katie is good at drawing.*

drawing pin *noun* drawing pins
a small metal pin with a round flat top, used for fixing a piece of paper or card to a wall or noticeboard
compare: **push pin**

drawing room *noun* drawing rooms
(old-fashioned)
a room in a big house with comfortable chairs for relaxing in

drawl *noun* drawls
a slow way of speaking in which vowel sounds continue longer than they usually do **drawl** *verb*

drawn
past participle of **draw**

dread *verb*
dreads, dreading, dreaded
if you dread something, you feel very worried about it or worried that it might happen *I'm really dreading the exams.*

dreadful *adjective*
1 extremely bad *dreadful weather*
2 ill *Go straight to bed – you look dreadful.*
3 sad *I feel dreadful about what happened.*
4 ugly *That's a dreadful shirt you're wearing.*

dreadfully *adverb*
1 extremely *It's dreadfully late.*
2 very much *He suffered dreadfully.*
3 extremely badly *You behaved dreadfully.*

dreadlocks *noun plural*
a hairstyle in which your hair is twisted into long thick pieces. This way of arranging hair is popular with Rastafarians.

dream *noun* dreams
1 images and thoughts that you have in your mind when you're asleep
2 something that you really want to do or want to happen in the future *My dream is to fly a plane.*
3 a dream world is a pleasant and exciting place that only exists in the imagination

dream *verb*
dreams, dreaming, dreamt or dreamed
1 to have images and thoughts in your mind when you're asleep *I dreamt about you last night.*
2 to think a lot about something that you really want to do or want to happen *I dream of becoming an astronaut.*
3 to not pay attention *I didn't see you waving to me – I must have been dreaming.*
4 not to dream about something is not to think about something ever happening *I never dreamt I would be famous one day.*

dreamer *noun*

dreamy *adjective* dreamier, dreamiest
looking or behaving as if you are in a dream and not paying attention to things *a dreamy look*

dreary *adjective* drearier, dreariest
1 if something is dreary, it makes you feel sad because it is not interesting, pleasant or attractive *My teacher's lessons are so dreary.*
2 not bright *dreary weather*

dreariness *noun*

dredge *verb*
dredges, dredging, dredged
to dredge a river is to take away mud or sand from the bottom of it, for example to make it deeper or to look for something

dredger *noun* dredgers
a boat or piece of equipment for dredging a river

dregs *noun plural*
the small pieces and drops left over in a cup or glass after someone has drunk something such as tea, coffee or wine

drench *verb*
drenches, drenching, drenched
to make someone or something very wet *We were caught in the rain and got drenched.*

dress *noun*
1 (*plural* **dresses**) a piece of clothing that girls and women wear, covering the top half of the body and hanging down from the waist over the legs. Dresses can be short (reaching above or below the knees) or long (reaching to the ankles or the ground).
2 clothes of a particular type *We went to the party in fancy dress.*

dress *verb*
dresses, dressing, dressed
1 to put your clothes on
2 to wear clothes of a particular type *At the weekend I like to dress in jeans.*
3 to put clothes on someone such as a baby or doll
4 if you dress up, you put on special clothes, for example to look different or to look nicer *Jess dressed up as a witch for Halloween.*
5 to put a bandage or piece of soft material on a wound after cleaning it

dressed *adjective*
1 wearing clothes, or wearing clothes of a particular type *Are you dressed? Granddad was smartly dressed in a suit.*
2 to get dressed is to put your clothes on

dresser *noun* dressers
a large piece of furniture with open shelves at the top and drawers and cupboards at the bottom

dressing *noun* dressings
1 a sauce that you put on a salad, for example made from oil and vinegar (sour liquid made from wine)
2 a bandage or piece of soft material that covers a wound

dressing gown *noun* dressing gowns
a soft loose coat that someone wears indoors, for example over their pyjamas or a nightdress

dressing room *noun* dressing rooms
1 a room where someone such as an actor gets ready before appearing in front of an audience
2 a room where sports players get ready for a game

dressing table *noun* dressing tables
a piece of furniture made up of a table with drawers and a large mirror, for example for doing your hair or putting on make-up

dressing-up *noun*
a game in which children put on different clothes and pretend to be someone else, such as a nurse or soldier

dressmaker–drop

dressmaker *noun* **dressmakers**
someone who makes clothes for other people, especially for women or children

drew
past tense of **draw**

dribble *verb*
dribbles, dribbling, dribbled
1 to let liquid slowly come out of your mouth *The baby was dribbling.*
2 if you dribble in a game such as football, you move the ball along with your feet as you run past a player from the other team
dribble *noun*

dribs and drabs *noun plural*
used about something that happens or that you do a little bit at a time *The children handed in their homework in dribs and drabs.*

dried
past tense & past participle of **dry**

dried *adjective*
dried plants or flowers or food such as fruit or pasta have had the water removed from them, for example to make them last longer

drier *noun* **driers**
a piece of equipment for drying things, such as a tumble drier for drying clothes

> LANGUAGE EXTRA also spelt *dryer*

drift *verb*
drifts, drifting, drifted
1 if a boat drifts, it floats slowly on the water and goes wherever the tide or the wind takes it
2 if snow or sand drifts, it forms big piles that are made by the wind
3 if someone drifts somewhere, they go there without having any real reason or without knowing why *We were just drifting around the museum passing the time.*
4 if someone drifts off, they slowly fall asleep or stop paying attention to someone or something

drift *noun*
1 (*plural* **drifts**) a big pile of snow or sand made by the wind
2 a slow movement of something or of many people away from somewhere
3 (informal) the meaning of something

driftwood *noun*
wood floating in the sea or a river, or wood that has come onto the shore

drill *noun* **drills**
1 a tool for making a hole in something hard such as wood or stone
2 a tool used by a dentist for removing the bad parts of people's teeth
3 an exercise or lots of exercises to teach people something, for example by making them practise the same thing many times *a fire drill*; *French grammar drill*

drill *verb*
drills, drilling, drilled
1 to make a hole or holes in something with a drill *The carpenter drilled a hole through the wood. They were drilling for oil.*
2 to teach someone something by making them practise it many times *Our teacher has been drilling us in French grammar.*

drink *verb*
drinks, drinking, drank, drunk
1 to drink a liquid is to take it into your mouth and swallow it
2 if someone drinks, they drink alcohol such as wine or beer *My parents don't drink.*
3 to drink up is to finish drinking all of your drink
drinker *noun*

drink *noun* **drinks**
1 liquid that you drink *You can take your drink with you.*
2 the action of drinking *I had a drink of water.*
3 an alcoholic drink such as wine or beer

drinkable *adjective*
good or safe to drink

drinking water *noun*
water that is safe to drink

drip *verb*
drips, dripping, dripped
1 to fall in small drops *Water was dripping from the ceiling.*
2 to let liquid fall in small drops *The tap is dripping.*

drip *noun* **drips**
1 a drop of liquid that falls from something
2 the sound of drops of liquid falling

dripping *adjective*
dripping wet very wet

> SYNONYM soaking wet

dripping *noun*
the fat that comes from meat when it is cooked or fried

drive *verb*
drives, driving, drove, driven
1 to make a vehicle such as a car or bus move along *My mum drives her car to work. My dad also drives.*
2 to go somewhere or go a certain distance by car *We drove to Scotland. We drove more than 500 miles.*
3 if a vehicle drives somewhere, it goes there *The bus drove off* (it left). *The taxi drove up to* (it arrived at) *the front door.*
4 to take someone somewhere in a vehicle *My brother drives me to school.*
5 to make someone do something or go somewhere *The bullying drove me to ask my teacher for help. My brother has driven all my friends away.*
6 to make someone become very angry or excited or have another strong feeling *You're driving me mad!*
7 to provide the power that makes something work *The wheels are driven by an electric motor.*

drive *noun* **drives**
1 a journey in a vehicle such as a car or lorry *We went for a drive.*
2 a path for a car going from the street to someone's house, or a small area for parking a car between the street and someone's house

> SYNONYM driveway

3 if someone has drive, they have lots of energy and a strong feeling of wanting to be successful
4 a piece of computer equipment that stores information onto a hard disk and uses information from it. A drive may be inside a computer (such as the C drive) or connected to a computer from the outside (an external drive).
5 also used in names of streets, for example long or wide streets with big houses *She lives at 215 Sandy Drive.*

driver *noun* **drivers**
1 someone who drives a vehicle
2 a piece of software that makes something work with a computer, for example a printer or mouse *a webcam driver*

driveway *noun* **driveways**
a path for a car going from the street to someone's house, or a small area for parking a car between the street and someone's house

> SYNONYM drive

driving *noun*
1 the activity of driving a vehicle *driving lessons*
2 a driving licence is a special document that proves someone knows how to drive
3 a driving test is the official test that someone must pass to be able to drive a vehicle alone. It includes driving on roads and answering questions about driving.

drizzle *noun*
light rain **drizzly** *adjective*

drizzle *verb*
drizzles, drizzling, drizzled
to rain lightly

dromedary *noun* **dromedaries**
a type of camel with one hump on its back

drone *noun*
1 a low humming noise, for example made by a plane
2 (*plural* **drones**) a male honeybee that doesn't do any work
3 (*plural* **drones**) a small aircraft that flies without a pilot. It is controlled by a computer inside it or by someone on the ground.

drone *verb*
drones, droning, droned
1 to make a low humming noise
2 if someone drones on, they talk for a long time in a boring voice

drool *verb*
drools, drooling, drooled
1 to let liquid come out of the mouth *The dog was drooling.*
2 if someone drools over something, such as a picture in a magazine, they look at it for a long time and with a lot of pleasure

droop *verb*
droops, drooping, drooped
to hang down *I watered the flowers because they were drooping.* **droopy** *adjective*

drop *noun* **drops**
1 a small amount of liquid shaped like a little ball
2 a small amount of something that you drink *There wasn't a drop of tea left in the pot.*
3 a drop in something such as a price or the temperature means that it goes down

> SYNONYM for sense 3: fall

133

drop *verb*
drops, dropping, dropped
1 to fall, or to let something fall
2 to become less or lower, or to go down *The wind has dropped. The number of students learning French has dropped.*
3 to make something less or lower *They've dropped their prices.*
4 if you drop someone or something somewhere, you take them there by car *My dad dropped me off at the school gate.*
5 to stop doing something or not to continue with something any longer *I dropped French after one term.*
6 to drop someone a line is to write to them
7 (informal) if someone drops dead, they die suddenly, for example from a heart attack (their heart stops working)
8 if you drop in on someone or if you drop by, you visit someone
9 if you drop off, you fall asleep
10 if you drop out, you stop taking part in an activity or you stop going to school or university

drop-down menu *noun*
drop-down menus
a list of detailed things in a computer program that you can ask a computer to do. When you choose a word or name from the menu bar (strip usually at the top of the screen listing the main things the computer can do), the list drops down (or appears) under the word or name.

LANGUAGE EXTRA also spelt *dropdown menu*

dropout *noun* **dropouts**
someone who stops going to school or university

droppings *noun plural*
the waste matter from the bodies of birds or animals *pigeon droppings*

drought *noun* **droughts**
a long period of time when no rain falls and there is not enough water for people, animals and plants

drove
past tense of **drive**

droves *noun plural*
in droves used when talking about large numbers of people *Fans turned out in droves to see their favourite rock star.*

drown *verb*
drowns, drowning, drowned
1 to drown or to be drowned is to die from being under water without air to breathe
2 to drown someone is to kill them by keeping them under water without air
3 if one sound drowns out another, it is so loud that you can't hear the other sound

drowsy *adjective* **drowsier, drowsiest**
sleepy **drowsily** *adverb* **drowsiness** *noun*

drug *noun* **drugs**
1 a chemical for treating an illness or medical problem *a cancer drug*
2 a harmful substance that some people put into their body to make them feel good *He never takes drugs.*
3 a drug addict is someone who cannot stop putting drugs into their body

drug *verb*
drugs, drugging, drugged
1 to give someone a drug or drugs, for example to make them unconscious
2 to put a drug in someone's food or drink

drugstore *noun* **drugstores**
in American English, a shop or supermarket that sells medicines, products for the body such as toothpaste or soap and some products for the home

Druid ['droo-id'] *noun* **Druids**
1 a priest in an ancient Celtic religion in Britain, France and Ireland
2 someone who follows the religion of the ancient Druids

drum *noun* **drums**
1 a round musical instrument that has the shape of a short cylinder (tube with flat ends shaped like circles). It has a special skin stretched over one or both ends. You play a drum by beating it (hitting it) with sticks or sometimes with your hands.
2 a round container shaped like a cylinder, for example for holding liquids or used as part of a machine *an oil drum; a washing machine drum* (for holding clothes)

drum *verb*
drums, drumming, drummed
1 to make light hitting sounds against something *The rain was drumming against the window.*
2 to play a drum or drums
3 if someone drums something into you, they make you learn it by repeating it lots of times

drummer *noun*

drumstick *noun* **drumsticks**
1 a stick used for playing a drum
2 the lower part of a chicken's leg when it has been cooked

drunk
past participle of **drink**

drunk *adjective*
if someone is drunk, they have drunk too much alcohol and they can't control their actions properly

drunk *noun* **drunks**
someone who is drunk or who often gets drunk

drunken *adjective*
1 drunk or often getting drunk *a drunken driver*
2 used about the actions of people who are drunk *a drunken fight* (between drunk people)

dry *adjective* **drier, driest**
1 if something is dry, there is no water or liquid on it or in it
2 used about something such as paint, ink or glue that has been put onto a surface and is no longer in liquid form *Leave the paint for 24 hours until it's dry.*
3 used about the weather or about a place when you mean there is no rain *Yesterday was dry. The Sahara Desert is dry all year round.*
4 if food is dry, it doesn't have enough natural liquid or is not covered with anything *This cake is a bit dry. I had a piece of dry toast* (with no butter or jam on it).
5 if your hair or skin is dry, it doesn't have enough natural oil
6 thirsty *I get very dry when I run.*
7 boring or too serious *a dry book on algebra*
dryness *noun*

SIMILES 'as dry as a bone' (mainly sense 1) and 'as dry as dust' (mainly sense 7) mean very dry

dry *verb*
dries, drying, dried
1 to make something or someone dry *Help me dry the dishes.*
2 to become dry
3 if something such as a river dries up, all the water disappears from it
4 if something such as money, work or a conversation dries up, there is no more of it and it comes to an end

dry-clean *verb*
dry-cleans, dry-cleaning, dry-cleaned
to clean clothes with special equipment using chemicals instead of water

dry-cleaner's *noun* **dry-cleaner's**
a shop where people take their clothes to be dry-cleaned

dryer *noun* **dryers**
a piece of equipment for drying things, such as a tumble dryer for drying clothes

LANGUAGE EXTRA also spelt *drier*

dual *adjective*
1 having two of something, for example two parts *I have dual nationality* (I'm a citizen of two countries).
2 a dual carriageway is a road with two lanes of traffic going in each direction. It is separated in the middle by a narrow piece of ground that sometimes has grass and bushes on it.

LANGUAGE EXTRA be careful not to confuse *dual* with the noun *duel* (fight between two people)

dub *verb*
dubs, dubbing, dubbed
1 if a film is dubbed, the voices of the actors have been changed so that the words they speak are in a different language *I went to see a French film dubbed into English.*
2 to give someone or something a name or nickname *King Richard I, dubbed the Lionheart*

dubious *adjective*
1 not sure about something *I'm a bit dubious about going ahead.*

SYNONYM doubtful

2 not completely honest
3 not to be trusted or believed *What she said about her teacher seems very dubious to me.*
4 not very good or safe *a dubious part of town*

duchess *noun* **duchesses**
1 a woman of very high noble rank, just below that of princess
2 the wife or widow of a duke

duck *noun*
1 (*plural* **ducks**) a bird that has short legs, webbed feet (skin between the toes) and a round flat beak. Ducks live on water. A male duck is called a drake.
2 the meat of the duck eaten as food

duck–dusk

duck *verb*
ducks, ducking, ducked
1 if you duck, you move your head or body down quickly, for example to avoid being hit by something or being seen
2 to move somewhere quickly *We ducked into a doorway to get out of the rain.*

duckling *noun* ducklings
a young duck

duct *noun* ducts
a tube, for example that liquid or air passes through

dud *noun* duds
if something is a dud, it is useless, for example because it doesn't work properly

due *adjective*
1 expected to arrive or to happen *What time is the plane due?*
2 if something is due by a certain time, you must do it by that time *My homework is due next Monday.*
3 if money is due, you must pay it by a certain time
4 **due to** used for giving a reason for something *I didn't get to school due to the snow.*

SYNONYM for sense 4: because of

due *adverb*
used with points of the compass to mean exactly in a particular direction *My village is due east of Bristol.*

duel *noun* duels
a fight between two people. Each person uses the same kind of weapon, usually a gun or sword.

LANGUAGE EXTRA be careful not to confuse *duel* with the adjective *dual* (having two of something)

duet *noun* duets
a song or piece of music for two people

duff *adjective*
a slang word for useless, bad or broken

duffel *noun*
1 a strong thick cloth
2 a duffel bag is a large bag made from duffel or another type of strong cloth. It often has the shape of a cylinder (tube with flat ends shaped like circles) and has a string at the top that you pull to close it.
3 a duffel coat is a coat made from duffel or another type of strong cloth. It has a hood and long buttons shaped like tubes.

LANGUAGE EXTRA also spelt *duffle*, for example *duffle bag* and *duffle coat*

ORIGIN from *Duffel*, a town in Belgium, where the cloth first came from

CULTURE NOTE Paddington Bear, in Michael Bond's *Paddington Bear* books, often wears a *duffel coat*

dug
past tense & past participle of **dig**

dugout *noun* dugouts
1 a hole or tunnel in the ground, for example where soldiers hide to protect themselves
2 a boat made by cutting out the inside of a tree trunk

duke *noun* dukes
a man of very high noble rank, just below that of prince. The wife of a duke is called a duchess.

dull *adjective* duller, dullest
1 boring *Our maths lessons are so dull.*
2 not bright *a dull winter's day*
3 not strong in colour or not shiny *dull colours*
4 not loud or clear *a dull thud*
5 if a pain or ache is dull, it is not strong but lasts a long time
6 an old-fashioned word for stupid
dullness *noun*

SIMILES 'as dull as dishwater' and 'as dull as ditchwater' mean very dull (sense 1)

dull *verb*
dulls, dulling, dulled
to make something less, for example a pain or sound *Take this medicine to dull the pain.*

duly *adverb*
1 just as expected *Our team played well and duly won the match.*
2 in the correct way

dumb *adjective* dumber, dumbest
1 an informal word for stupid
2 not able to speak, for example because you are so shocked or angry
dumbly *adverb*

dumbfounded *adjective*
very surprised by something

dumbstruck *adjective*
so surprised by something that you can't speak

dummy *noun* dummies
1 a small rubber object that a baby sucks to make him or her feel better
2 a model of a person's body, for example for showing clothes on
3 an informal word for a stupid person

dump *noun* dumps
1 a place where people take rubbish to be recycled (used again) or thrown away *a rubbish dump*

SYNONYMS tip, recycling centre

2 (informal) a dirty, untidy or unpleasant place *Please tidy your room – it's a dump! The village I live in is a dump* (an unpleasant place to live).
3 (informal) **down in the dumps** feeling very sad

dump *verb*
dumps, dumping, dumped
1 to put something somewhere in a careless way, for example something heavy or big *Just dump your coat on the chair.*
2 to get rid of something or someone that you don't want

dumpling *noun* dumplings
a small round lump of dough (flour and water) that is boiled or baked. It is eaten with meat, for example, or in a stew.

dumpy *adjective* dumpier, dumpiest
an informal word for short and fat

dune *noun* dunes
a hill of sand formed by the wind on a beach or in a desert

dung *noun*
the waste matter from the bodies of large animals *cow dung*

dungarees *noun plural*
a piece of clothing made up of trousers and a part covering the chest. It is fastened to the body by straps that go over the shoulders.

ORIGIN from Hindi *Dungri*, the area in Mumbai, India, where the cloth for making dungarees first came from

dungeon ['dun-jern'] *noun* dungeons
an underground prison, for example a prison built in the past underneath a castle

dunk *verb*
dunks, dunking, dunked
if you dunk something in liquid, you put it in and take it out again, usually something to eat *I dunked my biscuit in the hot tea.*

duo *noun* duos
two people who do things together in front of an audience, such as play music, sing, dance or act *Morecambe and Wise were a famous comedy duo in the twentieth century.*

ORIGIN from Latin *duo* 'two'

dupe *verb*
dupes, duping, duped
to make someone believe something that isn't true or to behave in a dishonest way towards them

SYNONYM to deceive

duplicate ['dyoo-pli-kert] *noun* duplicates
an exact copy of something

duplicate ['dyoo-pli-kert] *adjective*
used for describing something that is an exact copy of something else *a duplicate key*

duplicate ['dyoo-pli-kayt] *verb*
duplicates, duplicating, duplicated
to make an exact copy of something

ORIGIN from Latin *duo* 'two' and *plicare* 'to fold'

durable *adjective*
lasting for a long time *Plastic is a strong and durable material.* **durability** *noun*

duration *noun*
the time something lasts

ORIGIN from Latin *durare* 'to last'

during *preposition*
1 for the whole of a period of time *I slept during the flight.*
2 at one moment in a period of time *Come and see me during the lunch break.*

dusk *noun*
the end of the day when it starts to get dark as the sun sets

SYNONYM sunset

ANTONYMS dawn, daybreak, sunrise

dust – dyslexic

dust *noun*
1 tiny pieces of soft dirt made up of fibres, hairs, pollen, dead insects and other things in the air. Dust forms on surfaces inside buildings.
2 tiny pieces of earth or sand or of another material such as coal *a cloud of dust; coal dust*

dust *verb*
dusts, dusting, dusted
1 to clean the dust off something, for example with a cloth
2 to put a fine powder over something *The cakes were dusted with sugar.*

dustbin *noun* **dustbins**
a large container for rubbish that you keep outside your house

dustcart *noun* **dustcarts**
a large vehicle with a big container for carrying the rubbish from people's dustbins

duster *noun* **dusters**
a cloth for cleaning the dust off things

dustman *noun* **dustmen**
someone who comes to your house to empty dustbins and get rid of rubbish

> LANGUAGE EXTRA also called a *refuse collector*

dustpan *noun* **dustpans**
a small flat container that you put dust into with a brush

dusty *adjective* **dustier, dustiest**
covered with dust *a dusty table; a dusty road*

Dutch *adjective*
connected with the Netherlands or the Dutch language

Dutch *noun*
1 the language people speak in the Netherlands
2 the Dutch are people from the Netherlands

Dutchman *noun* **Dutchmen**
a man from the Netherlands

Dutchwoman *noun* **Dutchwomen**
a woman from the Netherlands

duty *noun* **duties**
1 someone's duty is something they have to do because it is their responsibility to do it *It's your duty to look after your children.*
2 someone's duties are what they have to do in their job *a teacher's duties*
3 if someone such as a doctor or nurse is on duty, they are working now
4 a special kind of tax on something that you buy

duty-free *adjective*
used for describing things that you buy, for example at an airport or port, when you travel from one country to another. The prices are lower than usual because there is less tax to pay on them. *a duty-free bottle of perfume; a duty-free shop*

duvet *noun* **duvets**
a type of cover for a bed. It is filled with feathers or other soft materials and is used instead of a blanket.
compare: **eiderdown**

> ORIGIN from French *duvet* 'down' (soft feathers)

DVD *noun* **DVDs**
a disc that looks like a CD and is used for storing and recording large amounts of computer information such as sounds, pictures and films
short for: digital versatile (or video) disc

DVD player *noun* **DVD players**
a piece of equipment for playing DVDs, used especially for playing films

dwarf *noun* **dwarfs** or **dwarves**
1 an imaginary small person in children's stories
2 a plant or animal that is much smaller than others of the same type

dwarf *verb*
dwarfs, dwarfing, dwarfed
to make something or someone look much smaller *They're building a new skyscraper that will dwarf all the others.*

dwell *verb*
dwells, dwelling, dwelt or **dwelled**
1 to live somewhere
2 to dwell on something is to talk about it or think about it all the time

dwelling *noun* **dwellings**
a place where someone lives

dwindle *verb*
dwindles, dwindling, dwindled
to gradually get smaller and smaller

dye *noun* **dyes**
a special liquid for changing the colour of something

dye *verb*
dyes, dyeing, dyed
to change the colour of something such as cloth or someone's hair by putting it into a dye or putting a dye on it

dying
present participle of **die**

dyke *noun* **dykes**
a long wall built to stop water from flooding an area of land

> LANGUAGE EXTRA also spelt *dike*

dynamic *adjective*
a dynamic person is full of energy and really wants to be successful
dynamism *noun*

dynamite *noun*
a substance used for making things explode

dynamo *noun* **dynamos**
a piece of equipment that changes movement into electricity

dynasty *noun* **dynasties**
1 a family of kings and queens or other leaders who have ruled a country for very many years *the Habsburg dynasty in Austria and Hungary*
2 the period of time when a dynasty rules

dysfunctional *adjective*
if a group such as a family is dysfunctional, the people in it don't behave in a normal way and their behaviour is sometimes bad *Our teacher can't control the children and the class is completely dysfunctional.*

dyslexia *noun*
a difficulty with reading, spelling and writing because of a particular way the brain is organised. Children and grown-ups with dyslexia have normal or high intelligence.

> ORIGIN from Greek *dys-* 'bad', 'difficult', and *lexis* 'word', 'speaking'

dyslexic *noun* **dyslexics**
someone who has dyslexia
dyslexic *adjective*

e E

ORIGIN the letter E started life, in ancient Egyptian hieroglyphics, as the shape of a human figure with arms raised at the elbows, as if shouting to someone or praying. In the Phoenician alphabet, the letter no longer looked like a shouting person. It had the shape of an E but facing left with its vertical line sticking down like a tail beyond the bottom horizontal line. The Phoenician E was a consonant with the sound of our letter H. When E passed into Greek, its sound changed to a vowel similar to our 'e' sound. By the time the Romans began using the letter, E had the shape we know today. It had been turned to the right and its short tail had fallen off.

each *adjective & pronoun*
1 used when talking about all the things or people in a group but mentioning them separately *Each letter in the alphabet has a different sound. Sonia, Tom and Ahmed each have 10 points.*
2 **each other** used when you mean that every person or thing in a group (of two or more) does something to the others or is connected to them in some way *John and I looked at each other. The three girls sat next to each other.*

eager *adjective*
1 really wanting to do something *I'm very eager to learn to read and write.*
2 very happy about something that will happen soon *The children had eager faces as they waited for the show to start.*
eagerly *adverb* **eagerness** *noun*

SYNONYM **keen**

eagle *noun* **eagles**
a very large bird with a curved beak and eyes that see clearly from a great distance. It is a bird of prey that eats small animals and other birds. Its nest is called an eyrie.

eagle-eyed *adjective*
if someone is eagle-eyed, they notice things that are difficult to see or that other people don't see

ear *noun* **ears**
1 your ears are the parts on either side of your head that you use for hearing
2 if you have an ear for something, you have the skill to learn and understand sounds easily *Aisha has a good ear for music.*
3 an ear of corn or wheat is the top part of the plant where the seeds are

earache *noun* **earaches**
a pain in the ear, usually caused by an infection

earbuds *noun plural*
earphones (small round speakers) that you put into your ears. Earbuds are joined to each other by a wire that hangs down and is connected to a radio or computer, for example, so that you can listen to things such as music or programmes.

ear drops *noun plural*
small drops of medicine that you put in your ear, for example to get rid of an infection

eardrum *noun* **eardrums**
a thin piece of tight skin inside your ear that vibrates when there is a sound, which allows you to hear the sound

earl *noun* **earls**
a British nobleman with a very high rank

earlobe *noun* **earlobes**
the soft part that hangs from the bottom of your ear

LANGUAGE EXTRA also spelt *ear lobe*

early *adverb & adjective* **earlier, earliest**
1 before the usual time, or before the time you expect something to happen *We came home from school early. I caught the early bus.*
2 near the beginning of something such as a period of time *I'll come to your house early next week. It's very early* (right at the beginning of the morning). *We went to Spain in early August.*
3 **at** (or **from**) **an early age** when (or from the time when) you are very young
4 **to have** (or **get**) **an early night** to go to bed before the usual time
5 **to have** (or **get** or **make**) **an early start** to start to do something or go somewhere in the first part of the morning

early bird *noun* **early birds** (informal)
someone who gets up early in the morning

earmuffs *noun plural*
two round pieces of soft cloth to keep your ears warm, joined together by a band that you wear over your head

earn *verb*
earns, earning, earned
1 to get money by working *How much money does your brother earn?*
2 to earn a living is to get enough money to live by working
3 to get something good because you've worked hard for it *You've earned a place in the school football team.*

earnest *adjective*
1 if someone is earnest, they are serious and mean what they say
2 earnest actions are serious and important *He made earnest efforts to succeed.*
3 **in earnest** seriously or properly *The work has begun in earnest.*
4 **in earnest** also means serious *I was in earnest when I said that.*
earnestly *adverb*

earnings *noun plural*
money that someone earns by working

earphones *noun plural*
two small round speakers that you put over or into your ears, used for listening to things on a radio, computer or other device. The speakers are connected to the device, for example by a wire or by Bluetooth (a system using radio waves). They are sometimes joined by a narrow curved piece that goes over your head.

earpiece *noun* **earpieces**
a small piece of electronic equipment that you put into or close to your ear so that you can listen to something

earplug *noun* **earplugs**
a small piece of soft material such as rubber that you put into your ear to protect it from water or loud noises

earring *noun* **earrings**
a jewel that people wear on their ear

earshot *noun*
if a sound is within earshot, it is close enough to hear; if it is out of earshot, it is too far away to hear

ear-splitting *adjective*
extremely loud

earth *noun*
1 the planet that we live on. It is the third closest one to the sun, between Venus and Mars.

LANGUAGE EXTRA also spelt *Earth*

2 the soil that plants and trees grow in

SYNONYM **ground**

3 the land or surface that we live on *The earth shook.*

SYNONYM **ground**

4 (*plural* **earths**) an electrical wire that connects a piece of equipment to the ground to make it safe
5 (informal) if something costs the earth or if someone charges the earth for something, it costs a lot of money or someone makes you pay a lot of money for it
6 **on earth** used for giving special importance to a word or for showing that you are surprised or angry about something *Why on earth did you do that?*

earthenware *noun*
plates, cups, saucers and other dishes made of baked clay

earthling *noun* **earthlings**
in science fiction, a human who lives on earth

earthly *adjective*
connected with life on earth

earthquake *noun* **earthquakes**
a sudden and violent shaking of the ground that usually causes a lot of damage. It happens when pressure builds up inside the earth's crust (its hard outer surface). The strength of an earthquake is measured by a number on the Richter scale from 0 to over 8.

earthworm *noun* **earthworms**
a long thin brown worm that lives in the soil

earthy *adjective* **earthier, earthiest**
1 like earth, for example in the way something smells or looks
2 an earthy colour is dark brown, like the colour of earth
3 earthy language or humour deals with subjects connected with the body in a direct and open way

earwax *noun*
a soft yellow or brown substance that forms inside your ears

earwig – ecological

earwig noun earwigs
a long thin brown insect with pincers at the end of its body

> ORIGIN from Old English *eare* 'ear' and *wicga* 'insect', because people once believed it crawled into your ear

ease noun
1 **with ease** easily and without much effort *We downloaded the files with ease.*
2 **at ease** feeling good and relaxed *Our teacher is completely at ease in front of the class.*

ease verb
eases, easing, eased
1 to make something less bad, or to become less bad *The doctor gave me something to ease the pain. The fighting between the two countries has eased.*
2 to make something less tight, or to become less tight *Please ease your grip on my arm.*
3 to make something easier
4 to move something or yourself carefully into another position *I eased myself slowly into the front seat.*

easel noun easels
a frame that holds a painting while you are painting it

easily adverb
1 without any problem *We won the match easily.*
2 used for saying that something might be true *You could easily forget to take your umbrella.*
3 used for saying that something is definitely true *Marie-Claude is easily the most intelligent person in the class.*
4 quickly *I don't give up easily even if it's hard.*

east noun
1 the direction that is straight ahead of you if you face the rising sun (as it appears in the sky in the early morning). The east is on your right if you face north and is also on the right of most maps, which have the north at the top.
2 the part of a country or town that is in the east *We live in the east of town.*
3 the East refers to the countries of Asia, for example China, Japan or India

east adverb
towards the east *Our house faces east.*

east adjective
in or from the east *the east coast; an east wind*

East End noun
the East End is a part of East London. In the past, many of the people who lived there worked in places such as factories, shops and warehouses (buildings where goods are stored). These people were sometimes known as cockneys. Today the East End has many modern offices, pleasant homes and fashionable areas, for example with restaurants and shops.
see: cockney
compare: West End

Easter noun
1 a Christian holiday in March or April. It celebrates the time when Jesus Christ died and returned to life.
2 an Easter egg is a chocolate egg given as a present at Easter, especially to children

easterly adjective
towards or from the east *an easterly wind*

eastern adjective
in or connected with the east *eastern France*

Eastern adjective
in or connected with the East, for example China, Japan or India *Eastern traditions*

eastwards adverb
towards the east *eastward* adjective

easy adjective easier, easiest
1 not causing you any problems or needing a lot of effort to do, understand or deal with *This week's homework was easy.*

> ANTONYM difficult

2 quick *There are no easy answers.*
3 comfortable *My grandparents live in Spain and have an easy life.*

> SIMILES 'as easy as ABC' and 'as easy as pie' mean very easy (sense 1)

easy adverb
1 to go easy on something is not to use, eat or drink too much of it *Go easy on the sweets!*
2 to go easy on someone is to treat them in a kind and gentle way *Josh behaved badly but the teacher went easy on him* (for example didn't punish him).
3 to take it easy is to rest and not do too much *The doctor told me to take it easy for a few days.*
4 if you tell someone to take it easy, you also mean that you want them to be careful about something or not to get excited or angry *Take it easy! – You nearly knocked me over! Take it easy! – Sit down and tell me what happened.*

easy-going adjective
if someone is easy-going, they don't get excited, angry or worried very easily

eat verb
eats, eating, ate, eaten
1 to put food into your mouth, chew it and swallow it
2 to have a meal *What time are we going to eat?*
3 to eat something away is to gradually destroy it *The front of the old building is being eaten away by pollution.*
4 to eat out is to eat in a restaurant
5 to eat something up is to use a lot of something *Texting eats up all my time.*
6 to eat up is also to finish eating all of your food

eater noun

eaves noun plural
the edge of a roof that sticks out beyond the wall of a building

eavesdrop verb
eavesdrops, eavesdropping, eavesdropped
to eavesdrop on people is to listen to what they are saying without them knowing that you are listening

ebb noun
1 the flow of the sea away from the coast that happens when the tide goes out
2 **at a low ebb** very weak *Our teacher's popularity is at a low ebb.*
3 **ebb and flow** a situation in which something changes all the time, for example getting stronger then weaker or bigger then smaller

> LANGUAGE EXTRA the flow of the sea away from and back towards the coast is sometimes called the *ebb and flow* of the tide

ebb verb
ebbs, ebbing, ebbed
1 if the tide ebbs, the sea flows away from the coast and its level becomes lower
2 to gradually become weaker or less *Grandma's strength is ebbing away.*

ebony noun
a hard black wood, used for making furniture

ebony adjective
black *ebony hair*

e-book noun e-books
a book that you read on a computer or on a special electronic reader that you hold in your hand
short for: electronic book

eccentric ['ik-sen-trik'] adjective
1 if someone is eccentric, they behave in a slightly strange way compared to how most people behave
2 also used about someone's actions *eccentric behaviour*

eccentric noun **eccentrically** adverb

> ORIGIN from Greek *ek-* 'out of' and *kentron* 'centre'

eccentricity noun
1 a slightly strange way of behaving
2 (plural **eccentricities**) a slightly strange thing that someone does or says

echo noun echoes
a noise that repeats itself when the sound waves bounce off a surface such as the wall of a cave or a tall building

echo verb
echoes, echoing, echoed
1 if a noise echoes, it makes an echo *The howling of wolves echoed across the valley.*
2 if a place or building echoes, noises echo there *The valley echoed with the howling of wolves.*
3 to agree with and repeat someone's words or ideas *Most parents echoed the opinions of the head teacher.*

éclair ['ay-klair'] noun éclairs
a soft cake shaped like a small tube. It is filled with cream and usually covered with chocolate.

eclipse noun eclipses
a short period of darkness when you cannot see the sun or when the earth's shadow falls on the moon. An eclipse of the sun (or solar eclipse) happens when the moon moves between the earth and the sun. An eclipse of the moon (or lunar eclipse) happens when the earth moves between the moon and the sun.

> LANGUAGE EXTRA in a *total eclipse of the sun*, you cannot see any of the sun because it is completely hidden by the moon. In a *partial eclipse of the sun*, you can see part of the sun.
> In a *total eclipse of the moon*, the moon appears very dark because the earth's shadow covers it. In a *partial eclipse*, only part of the earth's shadow falls on the moon.

ecological adjective
1 connected with ecology *an ecological disaster*

ecology – effigy

2 wanting to protect people's natural surroundings and quality of life *an ecological group*

ecology *noun*
the way people, animals and plants live together in their surroundings, and the scientific study of this **ecologist** *noun*

e-commerce *noun*
the activity of buying and selling goods on the internet

economic ['eek-er-**nom**-ik' or 'ek-er-**nom**-ik'] *adjective*
1 connected with the economy of a country or region *Scotland's economic development*
2 connected with money *economic developments*
3 bringing in money *They got rid of the number 26 bus route because it wasn't economic.*
economically *adverb*

economical ['eek-er-**nom**-ik-erl' or 'ek-er-**nom**-ik-erl'] *adjective*
using money carefully *Mum's car is economical to run.* **economically** *adverb*

economics ['eek-er-**nom**-iks' or 'ek-er-**nom**-iks'] *noun*
the study of how goods and services are produced and sold and how money is used **economist** *noun*

economise ['ik-**on**-er-myze'] *verb*
economises, economising, economised
to save money by spending it carefully or more carefully than in the past *My dad goes to work by bus to economise on petrol.*

> LANGUAGE EXTRA also spelt *economize*

economy ['ik-**on**-er-mee'] *noun*
1 (plural **economies**) the economy of a country or region is the way goods and services are produced and sold and the way money is used
2 (plural **economies**) the economy of a country or region is also all the money it gets from producing goods and services
3 the careful use of something such as money
4 if someone makes economies, they save money by being careful about what they spend

ecosystem *noun* **ecosystems**
all the animals, insects and plants in a particular place and the way they live together

ecstasy *noun* **ecstasies**
a feeling of very great happiness

ecstatic *adjective*
1 if someone is ecstatic, they are extremely happy
2 also used about what people say or do to show that they are extremely happy *The school play received ecstatic praise from all the parents.*
ecstatically *adverb*

Ecuador *noun*
a country in South America
Ecuadorian *adjective & noun*

eczema ['ek-ser-mer'] *noun*
a medical problem that makes your skin red, rough, itchy and sometimes painful

edge *noun* **edges**
1 the part or the line at the end of something where it stops *Don't stand too close to the edge of the platform.*
2 in maths, the edge of a 3-D shape is where two faces (surfaces) meet
3 the sharp part of a blade
4 an advantage that makes you more successful than someone else *If you already know French, you'll have the edge over all the other students in the class.*
5 if you are on edge (or if your nerves are on edge), you are nervous and worried
6 if you are on the edge of your seat, you are very interested in something and want to know what happens next

edge *verb*
edges, edging, edged
1 to move somewhere very slowly and carefully *I edged towards the door.*
2 if something is edged with something, that particular thing forms the edge of it *Her dress was edged with ribbon.*

edgy *adjective* **edgier, edgiest**
1 nervous and worried
2 fashionable and exciting *People think the band's music is very edgy.*

edible *adjective*
1 safe to eat *edible mushrooms*
2 good enough to eat *The food in the school canteen is only just edible.*

edifice *noun* **edifices**
a building, usually a large and important one

edit *verb*
edits, editing, edited
1 to edit something such as a book or newspaper is to get it ready to be printed or read online, for example by correcting mistakes in it
2 to edit something such as a film or video is to get it ready to be shown, for example by getting rid of parts that are not good enough
3 to put together a book by selecting, organising and discussing a piece of writing by a particular author or authors *'Shakespeare's Sonnets', edited by Tim Browne*
4 to edit a document or file on a computer is to make changes to it

edition *noun* **editions**
1 all the copies of something such as a book or newspaper that are ready at the same time, for example they are printed or you can read them online or on a device such as an e-reader *The latest edition of the dictionary has just come out.*
2 one version or form of something such as a book or newspaper *I use the paperback edition.*
3 a TV or radio programme that is part of a series *today's edition of 'Sesame Street'*

editor *noun* **editors**
1 someone in charge of a newspaper or a section of it
2 someone who gets something such as a book ready to be printed or read online, for example by correcting mistakes in it
3 someone who gets something such as a film ready to be shown
4 someone who selects, organises and discusses a piece of writing in a book by a particular author or authors

editorial *adjective*
connected with editing

educate *verb*
educates, educating, educated
1 to teach someone, especially in a school, college or university
2 to teach someone about something useful *Parents need to educate children about the bad effects of smoking.*

> ORIGIN from Latin *ex-* 'out' and *ducere* 'to lead'

educated *adjective*
an educated person has been taught lots of things at a high level

education *noun*
1 learning and teaching, especially in a school, college or university
2 someone's personal experience of learning *He went to Edinburgh to get an education.*

educational *adjective*
1 connected with education
2 teaching you something useful *That TV programme was very educational.*

Edwardian *adjective*
connected with the time of King Edward VII (1901–10) *an Edwardian house*

eek *interjection*
a word used for showing that you have been frightened and surprised by something

eel *noun* **eels**
a long thin fish that looks like a snake. Eels can be cooked and eaten as food.

eerie [rhymes with 'weary'] *adjective*
eerier, eeriest
strange and frightening *The streets were dark and eerie.*

eerily *adverb*
in a strange and frightening way *The wolves howled eerily in the night.*

effect *noun* **effects**
1 a change that something causes in something else or in someone *Going to bed late can have a bad effect on your concentration.*

> SYNONYM influence

2 an idea or appearance produced by someone such as an artist *The red and orange create an effect of warmth.*
3 sound effects are the sounds used in a film or TV or radio programme, for example a door closing or a glass breaking
4 special effects are unusual images or sounds in a film or TV programme that are specially created by technical experts
5 if something such as a law comes into effect or takes effect, it starts
6 if a medicine takes effect, it starts to work

> LANGUAGE EXTRA be careful not to confuse the noun *effect* with the verb *affect*.
> Noun: *It had an effect on us all.*
> Verb: *It affected us all.*

effective *adjective*
working well and producing good results *This is a very effective way of getting rid of computer viruses.* **effectively** *adverb*
effectiveness *noun*

efficient *adjective*
working well and not wasting time, money or energy *The people in the school office are efficient. Our old electric heater isn't very efficient.* **efficiency** *noun* **efficiently** *adverb*

effigy *noun* **effigies**
1 a model of someone, for example a statue of a famous person

effort–elect

2 a model of someone that people make and then destroy to show that they do not like that person

effort *noun*
1 the hard work and strength needed to do something *It takes a lot of effort to play football.*
2 (*plural* **efforts**) when you try very hard to do something *I made an effort to finish my homework on time.*

effortless *adjective*
if something is effortless, it doesn't need much hard work for you to do it successfully *Our team had an effortless win.*
effortlessly *adverb*

e.g.
for example *List your hobbies, e.g. reading, playing football, painting.*

> ORIGIN from Latin *exempli gratia* 'for the sake of example'

egg *noun* **eggs**
1 a round or oval object laid (produced) by a female bird, in which a young bird develops before hatching (breaking out). Most reptiles, fish, amphibians and insects also lay eggs. Different creatures lay eggs of different shapes and sizes.
2 the egg of a chicken used as food
3 a cell (smallest unit of living matter) in a woman or female animal that can develop into a baby or baby animal

egg *verb*
eggs, egging, egged
to egg someone on is to keep telling them that they should do something, especially something they don't want to do

eggcup *noun* **eggcups**
a small container that holds a boiled egg while you eat it

eggplant *noun* **eggplants**
the American word for an aubergine

eggshell *noun* **eggshells**
the hard outside layer of a bird's egg

egg-timer *noun* **egg-timers**
a small glass container with sand in it, used for measuring the time it takes to boil an egg (usually three minutes)

Egypt *noun*
a country in North-East Africa
Egyptian *adjective & noun*

eh ['ay'] *interjection*
a word used for asking someone to repeat something or for saying that you don't understand something

Eid ['eed'] *noun*
the short name of two important Muslim festivals. Eid ul-Fitr celebrates the end of the fast of Ramadan. Eid ul-Adha remembers the prophet Ibrahim who was ready to kill his son Ishmael for God.

eiderdown ['ei' rhymes with 'eye'] *noun*
eiderdowns
a thick cover for a bed. It is filled with feathers or other soft materials and is put on top of the blankets.
compare: **duvet**

> ORIGIN originally filled with the *down* (feathers) of the female *eider duck*, a duck that lives in the Arctic

Eiffel Tower *noun*
a tall pointed tower made of iron, in Paris. People often think of it as a symbol of France.

> CULTURE NOTE it was built by Gustave Eiffel for the World's Fair of 1889 and is still the tallest building in Paris

eight *adjective & noun* **eights**
the number 8

eighteen *adjective & noun* **eighteens**
the number 18
eighteenth *adjective & noun*

eighth *adjective & noun*
1 used about something or someone that comes in place number 8 *in the eighth month*
2 (*plural* **eighths**) one of 8 equal parts of something *an eighth of the cake*

eighty *adjective & noun* **eighties**
1 the number 80
2 the eighties are the eightieth to eighty-ninth years of a century, for example 1980 to 1989
3 if someone is in their eighties, they are between 80 and 89 years old
eightieth *adjective & noun*

either *adjective & pronoun*
1 only one thing or person or the other *You can choose either T-shirt. Would either of you fetch the register?*
2 both *There are windows at either end of the classroom. Both answers are correct so you can give either.*

either *conjunction*
only one thing or person or the other *You can choose either the red dress or the blue one. Either you stay or you leave.*

> LANGUAGE EXTRA used with *or* for showing two possibilities

either *adverb*
also *My sister can't sing and I can't either.*

eject *verb*
ejects, ejecting, ejected
1 to make someone leave a place *The noisy children were ejected from the hall.*
2 to make something come out of a piece of equipment, for example by pressing a button *I ejected the CD after listening to it.*
3 if a pilot ejects, he or she uses an ejector seat to be thrown out of an aircraft that is about to crash
ejection *noun*

eke out *verb*
ekes out, eking out, eked out
if someone ekes out a living, they get just enough money or food to live

elaborate ['i-lab-er-ert'] *adjective*
1 with lots of small or different parts that are carefully put together *an elaborate pattern*
2 planned carefully and with a lot of attention to small details *elaborate preparations*

elaborate ['i-lab-er-ayt'] *verb*
elaborates, elaborating, elaborated
1 if you elaborate on something, you give extra information about it

2 to elaborate something such as a plan is to develop it carefully

elapse *verb*
elapses, elapsing, elapsed
if a period of time elapses, it passes *Two years elapsed before I saw her again.*

elastic *noun*
a rubber material that stretches and then goes back to its normal length. It is often used in clothes to keep them tight against the body.

elastic *adjective*
1 made of elastic *an elastic cord*
2 able to stretch and then go back to its normal length *This material is very elastic.*
3 an elastic band is a thin ring of rubber that stretches, used for holding things together such as sheets of paper. It is also called a rubber band.

elasticity *noun*
the quality that something has of being able to stretch and then go back to its normal length

Elastoplast *noun* **Elastoplasts**
(trademark)
a plaster for putting on a cut or injury to protect it

elated *adjective*
extremely happy

elbow *noun* **elbows**
1 the joint in the middle of your arm, where your arm bends
2 (informal) elbow grease is hard work that is needed to clean something

elbow *verb*
elbows, elbowing, elbowed
to push your elbow into someone

elder *adjective & noun*
older than someone else, especially your brother or sister *I have an elder sister. Joanna is the elder of the two.*

elderberry *noun* **elderberries**
a small black berry that grows on a tree called the elder tree *elderberry wine*

elderly *adjective & noun*
another way of saying old, when talking about a person *my elderly grandparents; The government has promised extra money to help the elderly.*

eldest *adjective & noun*
oldest, when talking about the children in a family *She's the eldest daughter. I'm the eldest in the family.*

El Dorado *noun*
an imaginary place, for example in stories, where people go to become rich because there is money everywhere

> ORIGIN from Spanish meaning 'the Golden One'. Spanish explorers of the 16th century thought there was a city of gold somewhere in South America.

elect *verb*
elects, electing, elected
to choose someone to do a special job by voting for them *She was elected Member of Parliament.*

140

election – elude

election *noun*
1 (*plural* **elections**) an event when people choose a government or leader by voting for them
2 the action of electing someone

electorate *noun* **electorates**
all the people of a country or region who are allowed to vote in an election

electric *adjective*
using, carrying or producing electricity *an electric kettle*; *an electric wire*

> ORIGIN from Greek *elektron* 'amber', because static electricity was first produced by rubbing this substance with something else

electrical *adjective*
using electricity or connected with electricity *electrical goods*; *an electrical fault* **electrically** *adverb*

electrician *noun* **electricians**
someone whose job is to repair or connect electrical equipment

electricity *noun*
a type of energy that flows through wires and around a circuit. It is used for making light bulbs work and equipment such as computers, washing machines and heaters.

electrify *verb*
electrifies, electrifying, electrified
1 to make a railway line work with electric cables and electric rails, so that the trains run faster *The west coast line is electrified.*
2 to give something an electric charge *an electrified fence*
3 to make someone very excited and happy *The singer electrified the audience.*
electrification *noun*

electrifying *adjective*
if something that someone does such as acting or singing is electrifying, you like it so much that you are very excited by it

electrocute *verb*
electrocutes, electrocuting, electrocuted
if someone is electrocuted, they are killed when a large amount of electricity passes through their body **electrocution** *noun*

electron *noun* **electrons**
a part of an atom that has a negative electrical charge
compare: **neutron** and **proton**

electronic *adjective*
1 if a piece of equipment is electronic, it uses electricity and computer chips to make it work *an electronic calculator*
2 connected with computers *electronic mail*

electronically *adverb*
using a computer or computers *I've sent you a message electronically.*

electronics *noun*
1 the science of using and making electronic equipment
2 (*noun plural*) electronic equipment

elegant *adjective*
1 if someone is elegant, they are attractive, well-dressed and behave in a pleasing and controlled way
2 if something is elegant, it is attractive, fashionable and of a high quality *an elegant pair of shoes*; *an elegant restaurant*
elegance *noun* **elegantly** *adverb*

elegy *noun* **elegies**
a sad poem, usually about someone who has died

element *noun* **elements**
1 a part of something, especially an important part
2 a simple chemical substance made up of one type of atom only. Two or more elements together are called a compound. There are 105 known elements.
3 a small amount of something *There's an element of truth in what you say.*
4 an element in something such as a heater is the metal part that gives out heat
5 if you talk about the elements, you mean the weather, especially the bad weather such as rain and wind *There's no bus shelter – we're just exposed to the elements.*
6 the elements of a subject are the first things you need to learn about it *He taught us the elements of early American history.*
7 if you are in your element, you are happy in a particular situation or doing a particular thing

elementary *adjective*
1 forming the most important or most needed part of something *elementary exercises in English grammar*
2 very simple *an elementary mistake*

> SYNONYM basic

elephant *noun* **elephants**
a very heavy animal with big ears, a trunk (long nose) and tusks (big pointed teeth). The sound it makes is a trumpeting sound. Elephants live in Africa and India.

elevate *verb*
elevates, elevating, elevated
to move or lift something or someone to a higher level or position

elevation *noun*
1 the height of something above sea level
2 the action of elevating something or someone

elevator *noun* **elevators**
the American word for a lift (for taking people or goods between floors in a building)

eleven *adjective & noun* **elevens**
the number 11

eleventh *adjective & noun*
1 used about something or someone that comes in place number 11 *in the eleventh month*
2 (*plural* **elevenths**) one of 11 equal parts of something

elf *noun* **elves**
in stories, an imaginary creature with magic powers. Elves are usually small with pointed ears and sometimes play tricks on people, but they may be beautiful creatures too.

eligible *adjective*
if someone is eligible for something, the rules say that they are allowed to do it or get it *You're not eligible to vote because you're only nine.* **eligibility** *noun*

eliminate *verb*
eliminates, eliminating, eliminated
1 to get rid of something or someone
2 if someone is eliminated from a game or competition, they are not allowed to continue because they have lost
elimination *noun*

elite *noun* **elites**
a small group of people allowed to have a lot of influence or do special things, for example because they are rich or powerful, or intelligent or skilful

Elizabethan *adjective*
connected with the time when Elizabeth I was Queen of England (1558–1603)

elk *noun* **elks**
an animal like a large deer. Elks live mainly in Europe and Asia.

ellipse *noun* **ellipses** [′il-**lip**-siz]
an oval shape, like a circle that has been made flatter and longer **elliptical** *adjective*

ellipsis *noun* **ellipses** [′il-**lip**-seez]
1 in grammar, if you use ellipsis, you leave out a part of a sentence when the sentence is clear without that part. An example of ellipsis is if you say 'You play football but I don't' instead of 'You play football but I don't play football'.
2 a punctuation mark like this ... consisting of three dots. It is used in writing to show that a word or some words have been left out of a sentence.

elm *noun* **elms**
a tall tree that has round leaves with rough edges. Its wood is often used for furniture.

elocution *noun*
the action or skill of pronouncing words clearly and in the correct way *Some actors think it's good to have elocution lessons.*

elongated *adjective*
longer than normal *an elongated face*

eloquent *adjective*
if someone is eloquent, they express their ideas very well, using clear and well-chosen words **eloquence** *noun*

> ORIGIN from Latin *eloqui* 'to speak out' (*e-* 'out' and *loqui* 'to speak')

else *adverb*
1 used when you mean another person or thing besides the one you've mentioned or that you're thinking about *I can't see anything else.*

> SYNONYM more

2 also used for another person, thing or place that is different from the one you've mentioned or that you're thinking about *Let's sit somewhere else.*
3 **or else** used for saying that if you don't do something, another thing will happen *Hurry or else we'll be late for school.*

> SYNONYM if not

4 **or else** also used for showing another possibility *You can choose the red pen or else the green one.*

elsewhere *adverb*
in or to another place or other places

elude *verb*
eludes, eluding, eluded
1 to avoid being caught by someone *The thief eluded the police by jumping onto a train.*

141

elusive – emotion

2 if something eludes you, you don't get it, remember it or understand it *The exact meaning of the word eludes me.*

elusive adjective
1 difficult to find, see or get *This film star is very elusive.*
2 difficult to remember or understand *elusive memories*

elves
plural of **elf**

emaciated adjective
extremely thin because of illness or not enough food

email noun
1 a system for sending and receiving messages over the internet using a computer or another piece of equipment such as a mobile phone
2 (*plural* **emails**) a message that you send or receive in this way
short for: electronic mail

> LANGUAGE EXTRA also spelt *e-mail*

email verb
emails, emailing, emailed
to send a message to someone by email

> LANGUAGE EXTRA also spelt *e-mail*

embankment noun embankments
a wall of earth or stone built to support a railway or road or to stop water from flooding the land

embark verb
embarks, embarking, embarked
1 to go onto a ship or plane
2 to embark on something is to start to do something important or difficult
embarkation noun

> ORIGIN from French *em-* 'in' and *barque* 'boat'

embarrass verb
embarrasses, embarrassing, embarrassed
1 to make someone feel silly and worried about what people think, for example by behaving badly or not doing something well *You've embarrassed your parents by being so rude. The team played so badly they embarrassed the school.*
2 to make someone feel silly, nervous and uncomfortable *Someone asked her a question about her scar, which embarrassed her. It embarrasses me to stand up and read in class.*

embarrassed adjective
1 feeling silly or worried about what people think *I played some wrong notes on the piano and was embarrassed.*
2 feeling silly, nervous and uncomfortable *He looked awkward and embarrassed when I asked him where he'd been.*

embarrassing adjective
1 making someone feel silly or worried about what people think *Your son's behaviour was embarrassing.*
2 making someone feel silly, nervous and uncomfortable *an embarrassing question*
3 so bad that you should be embarrassed *The way the team played was embarrassing.*

embarrassment noun
1 a feeling of being embarrassed
2 (*plural* **embarrassments**) someone or something that makes you feel embarrassed

embassy noun embassies
a building in a foreign country where an ambassador lives and works, and where the people who work for him or her have their offices. An ambassador is someone who represents the government of his or her own country in a foreign country. *the British embassy in Japan*

embellish verb
embellishes, embellishing, embellished
1 to decorate something, for example with patterns or flowers, to make it look nicer
2 to add extra details that are not true to something such as a piece of writing

> ORIGIN from Old French *embelir* (from *bel* 'beautiful')

embellishment noun embellishments
1 a decoration to make something look nicer
2 an extra detail that is not true that is added to something

embers noun plural
small pieces of coal or wood in a fire that stay red and burning after the fire has gone out *glowing embers*

embezzle verb
embezzles, embezzling, embezzled
to steal money from a person or company when you should be looking after it for them

emblem noun emblems
a picture, shape or thing that represents something *The leek is one of the national emblems of Wales.*

> SYNONYM symbol

embrace verb
embraces, embracing, embraced
1 to put your arms around someone or hold them in your arms because you like them or love them
2 to start believing in a new idea or religion
3 to include something

> ORIGIN from Old French *embracier* 'to hold tightly in the arms' (*em-* 'in' and *brace* 'arms')

embroider verb
embroiders, embroidering, embroidered
to sew patterns or pictures onto cloth *a tablecloth embroidered with flowers*

embroidery noun
1 (*plural* **embroideries**) a pattern or picture sewn onto cloth
2 the art of sewing patterns or pictures onto cloth

embryo ['em-bree-oh'] noun embryos
a human or animal baby as it starts to grow in its mother's body
compare: **foetus**

emerald noun
1 (*plural* **emeralds**) a bright green jewel
2 emerald or emerald green is a bright green colour

emerge verb
emerges, emerging, emerged
1 to come out from somewhere *The caterpillar emerges as a butterfly.*
2 to become known
emergence noun

emergency noun
1 (*plural* **emergencies**) something very bad that happens suddenly and must be dealt with immediately
2 the emergency services are the organisations that deal with emergencies, especially the police, fire brigade and ambulance service
3 the American word for casualty (the part of a hospital where people go if they have an accident or suddenly become ill)
emergency adjective

emery board noun emery boards
a long narrow piece of thick paper with a rough surface. It is used for giving your fingernails or toenails a round and smooth shape.

emigrant noun emigrants
someone who leaves their country to go and live in another country
compare: **immigrant**

emigrate verb
emigrates, emigrating, emigrated
if someone emigrates, they leave their country to go and live in another country
emigration noun

> LANGUAGE EXTRA be careful not to confuse *emigrate* and *immigrate* (to come into a country from another country)

eminent adjective
if someone is eminent, they are famous and people respect them for the important things they have done in their work *an eminent scientist* **eminence** noun

emission noun
1 (*plural* **emissions**) a substance such as a gas that is produced or let out, usually into the air
2 the action of producing something such as a gas, light, heat or sound

emit verb
emits, emitting, emitted
to produce something such as a gas, light, heat or sound

emoji ['i-moh-jee'] noun emoji or emojis
a small image or moving picture that you put into an email, text message or computer document. An emoji is used for showing any object or idea, for example a person's head, a building or a colour. It is different from an emoticon, which only shows how someone feels.

> ORIGIN from a Japanese word meaning 'picture character'

emoticon noun emoticons
a symbol that you put into an email, text message or computer document to show how you feel. For example, ☺ and :) are emoticons that show you are happy.

emotion noun emotions
a very strong feeling such as anger, fear, happiness or sadness, love or hatred *His voice was full of emotion* (for example because he was sad, happy or angry).

142

emotional *adjective*
1 connected with human feelings *emotional problems*
2 showing your feelings *She became very emotional and started to cry.*
3 making someone have strong feelings such as happiness, sadness or anger *Seeing him again after all these years was very emotional.*
emotionally *adverb*

emperor *noun* **emperors**
a man who rules an empire

emphasis *noun* **emphases** ['em-fer-seez']
1 extra importance given to a particular thing *In our school the emphasis is on good behaviour.*
2 if you put emphasis on a word or part of a word in a sentence, you say it more strongly because you want people to take more notice of it. In the following example, the emphasis is on 'not': *'I will NOT do it,' she said.*

emphasise *verb*
emphasises, emphasising, emphasised
1 to give extra importance to a particular thing *My parents have always emphasised the need for good manners.*
2 to say or mention something strongly because it is especially important *Our teacher emphasised that we must hand in our homework by Monday.*
3 to say a word or part of a word more strongly or loudly *In the word 'together' the second syllable is emphasised.*

LANGUAGE EXTRA also spelt *emphasize*

emphatic *adjective*
1 showing that you have a very strong opinion about something, which will not change *Dad was emphatic – no pocket money this week.*
2 done or said in a very strong way *That was a very emphatic 'no'!*
emphatically *adverb*

empire *noun* **empires**
1 a group of countries under the same ruler or government *the Roman Empire*
2 a large group of businesses controlled by one person or one company *an international media empire*

employ *verb*
employs, employing, employed
1 to employ someone is to give them a job and pay them for doing it
2 to use something

employee ['im-**ploy**-ee] or ['im-ploy-**ee**'] *noun* **employees**
someone who works for a person, business or organisation and gets paid regularly

employer *noun* **employers**
a person, business or organisation that gives someone a job and pays them regularly

employment *noun*
work that someone is paid regularly to do *Mum's looking for employment (a job).*

empress *noun* **empresses**
a woman who rules an empire, or the wife of an emperor

empty *adjective*
1 with nothing at all inside *an empty box*
2 with no-one at all inside *an empty house*
3 not being used by anyone *an empty chair*
4 only being used by a few people *The motorway is empty at this time of day.*
5 without meaning, or without producing any effect *empty promises*
emptiness *noun*

empty *verb*
empties, emptying, emptied
1 to take out or take away everything that is in something *I emptied the bag. I emptied the sweets from the bag. Empty your glass* (pour out the liquid in it).
2 if a place empties, everyone leaves it *The shops emptied at six o'clock.*

empty-handed *adjective*
without getting anything when you were hoping to get something *The burglars left the house empty-handed.*

emu ['ee-myoo'] *noun* **emus**
a large Australian bird that cannot fly but can run fast. It is similar to an ostrich but smaller.

ORIGIN from Portuguese *ema* 'ostrich'

emulate *verb*
emulates, emulating, emulated
to do the same as someone or something else, for example because you have great respect for them

emulsion *noun* **emulsions**
a type of paint used on walls and ceilings that is not shiny when it dries

enable *verb*
enables, enabling, enabled
to make something possible *A better laptop will enable you to surf the internet faster.*

enamel *noun*
1 a type of shiny paint made from glass. It is put onto pottery or metal to decorate or protect it
2 the hard shiny surface of your teeth

encampment *noun* **encampments**
a place with lots of tents or shelters, for example where soldiers live for a short time

enchant *verb*
enchants, enchanting, enchanted
if something or someone enchants you, they give you great pleasure *We were enchanted by the view from the hotel window.*

enchanted *adjective*
changed by a magic spell *an enchanted castle*

enchanting *adjective*
very attractive

encircle *verb*
encircles, encircling, encircled
to completely surround something or someone *The demonstrators encircled the King's palace.*

enclose *verb*
encloses, enclosing, enclosed
1 to put something inside something else such as an envelope, parcel or box that you send to someone *My grandparents enclosed some money with their birthday card.*
2 if a place is enclosed by something such as a fence or wall, it is surrounded by it *Our playground is enclosed by a high wall.*

enclosure *noun* **enclosures**
an area of land surrounded by a fence or wall *the giraffe enclosure at the zoo*

encore ['on-kor'] *noun* **encores**
when an audience at a concert or show asks an entertainer to come back onto the stage after he or she has finished, to play some more music or sing some more songs

ORIGIN from French *encore* 'again'

encounter *verb*
encounters, encountering, encountered
1 if you encounter something such as a problem, you have it or find it *I encountered lots of difficulties in my homework.*
2 to encounter someone is to meet them

encounter *noun* **encounters**
1 a meeting
2 a time when you get to know something for the first time *In the film a little boy had a close encounter with an alien.*

encourage *verb*
encourages, encouraging, encouraged
1 to speak or behave in a way that helps someone to do something or that helps something to happen, usually something that you think is good *My parents encouraged me to learn to play the piano. Our teachers have always encouraged sport.*
2 to give someone hope *Dad's words encouraged us all.*
3 to make something happen or likely to happen *Some TV programmes encourage bad behaviour.*

encouraged *adjective*
happy and having a lot of hope *We were all encouraged when our team finally won.*

ANTONYM dejected

encouragement *noun*
words or actions that help someone to do something, help something to happen or give someone hope *I got plenty of encouragement in school.*

SYNONYM support

encouraging *adjective*
if something or someone is encouraging, they give you hope *The news was encouraging.*

encrypted *adjective*
used for describing computer information, such as a file or email, that has been changed into a special code called encryption (secret letters, numbers or symbols) so that no-one can understand the information except the person it is meant for

encyclopedia *noun* **encyclopedias**
a book (or books), website or DVD containing a lot of information about many different things, usually given in alphabetical order. Encylopedias can be general (about many subjects) or specialised (about particular subjects such as science, art or music).

LANGUAGE EXTRA also spelt *encyclopaedia*

ORIGIN from Greek *enkuklios paideia* 'general education'

encyclopedic–engagement

encyclopedic *adjective*
1 used for showing that someone knows a lot about many different things or about a particular subject *Bradley has an encyclopedic knowledge of cars.*
2 used about something that shows a lot of information about a subject *an encyclopedic volume*

LANGUAGE EXTRA also spelt *encyclopaedic*

end *noun* **ends**
1 the part of something such as an activity, period or event that comes after the first part of it and all the rest of it. It is the point after which that particular thing no longer exists or when it stops happening. *It's the end of the holidays. What happens at the end of the book?*
2 the part of an object or place that is furthest away from where it starts or from the first part of it. It is the point where that particular thing or place stops. *There's a shed at the end of the garden.*
3 the point where an object or place stops compared to where you are, for example the point closest to you or furthest away from you *I'm sitting at this end of the table and Andy's at the other end. Amy lives at the other end of Scotland.*
4 the lowest or highest part of a range of different numbers or things *Dad bought me a laptop at the bottom end of the price range.*
5 a situation in which someone or something no longer exists *He fell through the ice and that was the end of him. It was the end of our hopes and dreams.*
6 to come to an end is to stop happening *One day all my problems will come to an end.*
7 to put an end to something or bring something to an end is to make it stop happening
8 **in the end** after a long time *In the end I just gave up.*

SYNONYM finally

9 **on end** without stopping *It rained for days on end.*

end *verb*
ends, ending, ended
1 to stop happening or existing *School ends at 3.30 p.m. The chapter ends with a picture of Alice.*
2 to stop something or stop doing something *Don't forget to end the sentence with a full stop.*
3 to make something stop happening *The teacher ended a fight between the two boys.*
4 to reach the part of a period of time that comes after the first part and all the rest of it *We ended the day with a walk through the park.*
5 to end up doing something is to do something, after a certain amount of time, that you were not expecting to do *After listening to classical music all weekend, I ended up liking it.*
6 to end up somewhere or with something is to be somewhere or get something, after a certain amount of time, that you were not expecting to *We took a bus and ended up in Rome. I spent all my pocket money and ended up with nothing.*

7 to end up in a certain way is to be that way at the end *After many years of hard work, my uncle ended up a millionaire.*

endanger *verb*
endangers, endangering, endangered
1 to endanger someone's life is to put someone in a situation where they can be hurt or killed
2 to cause something very bad to happen to something *Cutting down trees will endanger the whole island. Tigers are an endangered species* (may soon disappear completely from the world).

endearing *adjective*
1 used for describing someone who has a special way of making people like them
2 also used for describing what someone does or says or the sort of character someone has *an endearing smile; Your grandma has some endearing qualities.*

endeavour *verb*
endeavours, endeavouring, endeavoured
to try hard *You must endeavour to be a better student next term.*

endeavour *noun* **endeavours**
an effort to do something, for example something difficult or artistic

end game *noun* **end games**
1 the last part of a game of chess when there are very few pieces left on the board
2 the last part of something such as a battle or debate that makes a particular result happen

ending *noun* **endings**
1 the ending of something such as a book or film is what happens in the last part of it or the way the last part of it is put together *a story with a happy ending*
2 the last letter or letters of a word *To form the plural of a noun you usually add the ending 's'.*
3 when someone stops something *The workers voted for the ending of their strike.*

endless *adjective*
1 going on for a very long time or never stopping *This film seems to be endless!*
2 also used for describing a very large number of things or amount of something *an endless flow of cars on the motorway*

SYNONYM never-ending

endlessly *adverb*
without stopping

endurance *noun*
being able to accept something difficult or unpleasant or to continue doing it for a very long time *Running in the marathon was a real endurance test* (really difficult to do).

endure *verb*
endures, enduring, endured
1 to accept something unpleasant such as pain or suffering, often without complaining
2 to last for a very long time

enemy *noun* **enemies**
1 someone who hates you and tries to harm you

ANTONYM friend

2 a country or army fighting in a war with another country or army *enemy aircraft* (belonging to an enemy)

ORIGIN from Old French *enemi* 'enemy' (from Latin *in-* 'not' and *amicus* 'friend')

energetic *adjective*
1 having a lot of energy and not getting tired easily *My brother is very energetic.*

SYNONYM active

2 really wanting to do something and doing it with a lot of energy *My dad is an energetic supporter of West Ham.*
3 if an activity is energetic, it needs a lot of energy *the energetic movements of the acrobats*

energetically *adverb*
with a lot of energy

energise *verb*
energises, energising, energised
to energise someone is to make them really want to do something and feel that they have the energy to do it

LANGUAGE EXTRA also spelt *energize*

energy *noun*
1 the power that you have to move your body and do things without getting tired *You need lots of energy to play football.*
2 (*plural* **energies**) the power that you have to do things you really want to do *I put all my energy* (or *energies*) *into studying maths.*

SYNONYM enthusiasm

3 a power, such as electricity, oil or gas, that makes things work or provides heat or light *solar energy* (the power that comes from the sun)

enervating *adjective*
making you feel very tired

enforce *verb*
enforces, enforcing, enforced
to make sure people obey a rule or law *The head teacher enforces the wearing of the school uniform.* **enforcement** *noun*

engage *verb*
engages, engaging, engaged
1 to get someone interested in something
2 to give someone a job
3 to start to fight with an enemy
4 to engage in something is to take part in it or do it

engaged *adjective*
1 if two people are engaged, they have decided that they are going to get married
2 if a phone or phone number is engaged, someone is already speaking when you call

SYNONYM busy

3 if a toilet is engaged, someone is already using it

engagement *noun* **engagements**
1 a decision by two people that they are going to get married *My brother broke off his engagement* (decided he no longer wanted to get married). *She put on her engagement ring* (a ring that shows that the person wearing it is engaged).

engaging–ensign

2 the time between two people deciding to get married and their wedding day *a short engagement*
3 a meeting with someone or an occasion when you have to do something
4 a battle between enemies

engaging *adjective*
very pleasant in an interesting way *an engaging smile*

engine *noun* **engines**
1 a machine that uses energy, for example from petrol, electricity or steam, to make something move *a car engine*; *a jet engine*
2 a vehicle that pulls a train. This type of engine is also called a locomotive. *an engine driver* (someone who drives a train)

ORIGIN from Old French *engin* 'skill' and Latin *ingenium* 'talent' and also 'ingenious machine'

engineer *noun* **engineers**
1 someone who designs things such as machines, roads or bridges
2 someone who repairs machines or electrical equipment such as televisions or computers
3 a software engineer is someone who designs computer programs

engineering *noun*
the work of designing things such as machines, roads or bridges. Engineering is also studied as a subject, for example at university.

England *noun*
a country in North-West Europe. England is a part of the island of Great Britain together with Scotland and Wales.

English *adjective*
1 connected with England or the English language
2 an English breakfast consists of food such as eggs, bacon, sausages, tomatoes and toast with tea or coffee
3 the English Channel is the area of water between the south coast of England and the north coast of France

English *noun*
1 the language people speak in England, the United States, Australia, Canada, New Zealand and many other countries
2 the English are people from England

Englishman *noun* **Englishmen**
a man from England

Englishwoman *noun* **Englishwomen**
a woman from England

engrave *verb*
engraves, engraving, engraved
to cut words or pictures into something such as glass, metal or wood using a special tool *The trophy was engraved with the name of our school.*

engraver *noun*

engraving *noun* **engravings**
1 a picture cut into a hard surface
2 a picture printed onto paper using a thin piece of metal with the picture cut into it

engrossed *adjective*
if someone is engrossed in something, they are so interested in it that they don't pay attention to anything else *I was so engrossed in the TV programme that I forgot to do my homework.*

SYNONYM absorbed

engulf *verb*
engulfs, engulfing, engulfed
1 to cover something or someone suddenly and completely and cause destruction or great damage *The whole village was engulfed in flames.*
2 to affect the whole of something, used when talking about something bad *Fighting soon engulfed the whole country.*

enhance *verb*
enhances, enhancing, enhanced
to make something better or more attractive *My laptop has enhanced the quality of my life.*

enhancement *noun* **enhancements**
something that makes a thing better or more attractive

enigmatic *adjective*
difficult to understand or explain

SYNONYM mysterious

enjoy *verb*
enjoys, enjoying, enjoyed
1 to like something very much or to like doing something
2 if you enjoy yourself, you're happy in a particular situation because you're doing something you like

enjoyable *adjective*
if something is enjoyable, you like it very much and it makes you happy

SYNONYM pleasant

enjoyment *noun*
the happy feeling you get from doing or having something you like *Listening to Mozart gives me a lot of enjoyment.*

SYNONYM pleasure

enlarge *verb*
enlarges, enlarging, enlarged
to make something bigger

enlargement *noun*
1 (*plural* **enlargements**) a photo or document that has been copied to make it bigger than the original

ANTONYM reduction

2 the action of making something bigger

enlist *verb*
enlists, enlisting, enlisted
1 to join the army, navy or air force
2 to enlist someone's help is to ask or get them to help you *Our teacher enlisted the help of a classroom assistant.*

enliven *verb*
enlivens, enlivening, enlivened
to make something more interesting

SYNONYM to liven up

enormity *noun*
1 how bad something is *The government tried to hide the enormity of the problem.*
2 how big something is *the enormity of the task ahead*

enormous *adjective*
very big

SYNONYM huge

ORIGIN from Latin *enormis* 'shapeless' (from *ex-* 'out of' and *norma* 'rule' or 'pattern')

enormously *adverb*
1 very *enormously lucky*
2 very much *I enjoyed myself enormously.*

enough *adjective*
1 as much or as many as needed *We have enough time. There aren't enough books.*
2 quite a lot of *I've got enough problems.*

enough *pronoun*
1 as much or as many as needed *You haven't done enough. Enough of them were left.*
2 quite a lot *I've got enough to worry about.*
3 if you've had enough of something or someone, you're angry about a situation and don't want it to continue

enough *adverb*
1 as much as needed *I'm not tall enough.*
2 quite a lot *She's happy enough at school.*

SYNONYMS for sense 2: fairly, quite

enquire *verb*
enquires, enquiring, enquired
to ask about something *She enquired what time it was.*

LANGUAGE EXTRA also spelt *inquire*

enquiry *noun* **enquiries**
a question someone asks to get information about something *The school gets lots of enquiries from parents.*

LANGUAGE EXTRA also spelt *inquiry*

enrage *verb*
enrages, enraging, enraged
to make someone very angry

enraged *adjective*
very angry

enrich *verb*
enriches, enriching, enriched
1 to make the quality of something better *Reading Shakespeare has enriched my life.*
2 to make someone rich

enrichment *noun*

enrol *verb*
enrols, enrolling, enrolled
to put your name or someone else's name on a list of people who want to become members of something such as a class, club or school *I enrolled on a course to learn Spanish. Mum enrolled me for the chess club.* **enrolment** *noun*

ensemble ['on-som-berl'] *noun* **ensembles**
a group of musicians, actors or dancers who appear together in front of an audience

ensign *noun* **ensigns**
a flag on a ship that shows the country it belongs to

enslave–entrust

enslave *verb*
enslaves, enslaving, enslaved
1 to make someone a slave
2 to put a people or country in a situation that they cannot escape from

ensure *verb*
ensures, ensuring, ensured
to make sure that something happens *All their coaches have seat belts to ensure the safety of passengers.*

LANGUAGE EXTRA be careful not to confuse *ensure* with *insure* (buy insurance for something)

entail *verb*
entails, entailing, entailed
if something entails something else, it makes that particular thing necessary *Learning Arabic entails a lot of hard work.*

SYNONYM to involve

entangle *verb*
entangles, entangling, entangled
if something or someone is entangled in something, they are caught in it because it has got twisted around them *A pigeon had got entangled in the net.*
entanglement *noun*

enter *verb*
enters, entering, entered
1 to go or come into a place *Harry entered the room. The thief entered through the window.*
2 to start to work somewhere or to become part of or take part in something *My brother entered the army and my sister entered university.*
3 to write something somewhere, for example on a list or by pressing keys on a computer *Enter your password.*
4 to put your name or someone else's name on a list of people who want to take part in a race, competition or exam *My friends have entered the competition so I'm going to enter too. Dad entered me for an exam to get into Elmdale School.*
5 if something enters your mind, you think of it *The thought of giving up had never entered my mind.*

enter *noun*
on a computer keyboard, enter (or the enter key) is a key that you press to make the computer do something, for example to make a program start or to accept an option *Press Enter to start a new paragraph.*

enterprise *noun*
1 if someone has enterprise, they have the imagination to think of new ideas and are not afraid to take risks to make their ideas successful
2 (*plural* **enterprises**) an important, new or difficult task *a scientific enterprise*
3 (*plural* **enterprises**) a company or organisation that makes money by selling goods or services

enterprising *adjective*
1 full of new ideas and the energy to make them successful *an enterprising student*
2 new and put into action with a lot of energy *an enterprising plan*

entertain *verb*
entertains, entertaining, entertained
1 if someone entertains you, for example by playing music, singing or dancing (or if something such as a book or film entertains you), they make you happy and keep you interested *The latest Disney cartoon entertained us all.*
2 to make someone laugh by telling jokes or doing silly things *The clowns entertained the children.*
3 if you entertain people as guests, you have invited them to your home, for example to have a meal *My parents are entertaining my aunt and uncle.*

entertainer *noun* entertainers
someone who entertains people, for example a singer, comedian, clown or musician

entertaining *adjective*
enjoyable and interesting

entertainment *noun* entertainments
something that entertains people, for example activities such as singing, dancing, playing music or telling jokes or things such as books or films *A magician will provide the entertainment at Jim's party.*

enthralled *adjective*
if someone is enthralled by something, they think it is so interesting that they give it all their attention

enthralling *adjective*
really interesting and enjoyable

enthusiasm *noun*
1 a feeling of liking something very much and being really interested in it *My enthusiasm for reading has never left me.*
2 a feeling of wanting to do something *Mum asked me to help but I didn't show much enthusiasm.*
3 strong feelings of liking something or someone, which you show by behaving in a certain way *The children were playing in the snow with lots of enthusiasm* (for example shouting, laughing, jumping, sliding).

ORIGIN from Greek *enthousiasmos* 'possessed by a god', from *entheos* 'possessed' (*en-* 'in' and *theos* 'god')

enthusiast *noun* enthusiasts
someone who is very interested in something and spends a lot of time on it *a computer enthusiast*

enthusiastic *adjective*
1 liking something very much and being really interested in it *Most of the parents were enthusiastic about the school play.*
2 really wanting to do something *When I asked Dad to play football with me, he didn't sound too enthusiastic.*
3 showing strong feelings of liking something or someone by behaving in a certain way *When the film stars arrived, there was an enthusiastic crowd waiting for them* (for example shouting, smiling, clapping, waving arms).

enthusiastically *adverb*
1 in a way that shows you like something very much or really want to do something *They supported me enthusiastically.*

SYNONYM very much

2 in a way that shows the strong feelings you have about something or someone you like *The crowd were singing and dancing enthusiastically.*

entice *verb*
entices, enticing, enticed
to get someone to do something or go somewhere by giving them something good that they want

enticing *adjective*
if something is enticing, it is so good that you want it

SYNONYMS interesting, attractive

entire *adjective*
the whole of something *They're digging up the entire road.*

entirely *adverb*
1 used for giving special importance to a word or for saying that something is very true *I entirely agree with you. That's entirely wrong.*
2 in every way or when talking about every part of something *You will have to redo your homework entirely. It's entirely new.*

SYNONYMS completely, totally

entirety *noun*
the whole of something

entitle *verb*
entitles, entitling, entitled
1 to let someone have or do something officially *This coupon entitles you to a free ice cream.*
2 if you are entitled to something or entitled to do, have or be something, you are allowed to have it, do it or be that way *You've finished your homework so you're entitled to an ice cream. You're entitled to be angry* (you are right to be angry).
3 if a book or play is entitled something, that is its title (or name) *a book by Dickens entitled 'Oliver Twist'*

entrance ['en-trəns] *noun* entrances
1 the place where you go into a building, room or area
2 when someone goes into a place
3 when someone comes onto the stage in a play or show *The clown made a noisy entrance.*
4 when someone is allowed to go into a place such as a museum *This ticket gives you free entrance.*

SYNONYM for senses 2, 3 & 4: entry

entrance ['in-trahns] *verb*
entrances, entrancing, entranced
to give someone great pleasure by being very beautiful or good *The beauty of the landscape entranced us.*

entrant *noun* entrants
someone who enters for an exam or competition

entrust *verb*
entrusts, entrusting, entrusted
to give someone the responsibility for something *Can we entrust the care of the children to our neighbour?*

entry noun entries
1 when someone goes into a place *to make an entry*
2 when someone is allowed to go into a place *No entry* (sign saying no-one is allowed in).
3 becoming part of or taking part in something *Britain's entry into the war*
4 something you do to try to win a competition, for example writing, drawing or painting something or answering questions
5 a piece of writing, usually short, that is one of many pieces written in a list or diary *Look up the dictionary entry for 'chrysalis'.*

SYNONYM for senses 1, 2 & 3: entrance

E number noun E numbers
the number of a chemical that is added to food. It begins with the letter E and is written on the outside of the food container or wrapper.

enunciate verb
enunciates, enunciating, enunciated
to pronounce a word or words very carefully **enunciation** noun

SYNONYM to articulate

envelop ['in-vel-erp'] verb
envelops, enveloping, enveloped
to cover something or someone completely *The whole forest was enveloped in mist.*

envelope ['en-ver-lohp'] noun envelopes
1 a paper cover in which you put a letter, document or card that you send by post
2 a thin layer that surrounds something

envious adjective
if you are envious of someone, you wish you could have what they have or do what they do *My best friend has a new bike and I'm so envious.* **enviously** adverb

SYNONYM jealous

environment noun
1 (plural environments) the place where people, animals and plants live, and everything and everyone that affects them *Children quickly get used to their new environment when they move to another country.*
2 (plural environments) the situation affecting someone's life at a particular time and place *The school has created the right environment for learning.*
3 the air, land, water, plants and animals that make up the natural world *We must protect the environment.*
environmental adjective

environmentalist noun
environmentalists
someone who wants to protect the natural environment

environmentally adverb
1 in a way that is connected with the natural environment
2 if something is environmentally friendly, it does not harm the environment

envisage verb
envisages, envisaging, envisaged
to think that something is likely to happen in the future

envy noun
the bad feeling of wishing you could have something that someone else has or do something that they do

SYNONYM jealousy

envy verb
envies, envying, envied
to wish you could have what someone else has or do what they do *I really envy you!*

epic noun epics
a long poem, book or film about the actions of heroes and brave people in the past *a Hollywood epic*

ORIGIN from Greek *epikos*, from *epos* 'word', 'song'

epic adjective
1 an epic poem, book or film is one about the actions of heroes and brave people in the past
2 very long, difficult and with lots of exciting events *an epic journey through Africa*
3 very big

epidemic noun epidemics
1 a situation in which very many people suffer from a disease *An epidemic of flu spread quickly to all parts of the country.*
2 a situation in which something bad happens quickly and affects lots of people *an epidemic of crime*

epigram noun epigrams
a short poem or sentence that says something in a funny or clever way

epigraph noun epigraphs
a few words or short sentences written at the beginning of a book, for example, or on a building

epilepsy noun
a medical problem that affects the brain. It makes someone suddenly become unconscious and they can't control the movements of their body.

epileptic adjective
caused by epilepsy *an epileptic fit*

epileptic noun epileptics
someone who has epilepsy

epilogue ['ep-ee-log'] noun epilogues
a piece of writing at the end of a book or play
compare: prologue

episode noun episodes
1 one of the parts that a TV or radio programme is divided into. Each episode is a part of a series. It may continue the same story or tell a different story with the same characters.
2 an event, for example one that is part of a story or someone's life *The next chapter deals with another episode in Gulliver's life.*
3 an event that is one of a number of similar events *This was one of the most deadly episodes of the war.*

epitaph noun epitaphs
a few words or short sentences about a dead person, written on a gravestone or memorial

epoch ['ee-pok'] noun epochs
a long and important period of time, usually in the past *the Victorian epoch*

equal adjective
1 the same in size, number, quality or importance *A kilo is equal to about two and a quarter pounds. The two teams are equal* (have the same number of points).
2 if you think that people are equal, you think that no-one is better or worse than anyone else so you behave in the same way towards everyone
3 if someone is equal to an activity, they are good enough to do it and be successful at it *Do you think he'll be equal to the task?*

equal noun equals
someone who is just as good as someone else and who deserves the same amount of respect *She treated me as an equal.*

equal verb
equals, equalling, equalled
1 to be the same as something else in size, number, quality or importance *Four plus four equals eight* (written as 4 + 4 = 8).
2 to reach the same level as someone else *I didn't quite equal his score.*

equalise verb
equalises, equalising, equalised
to score a goal or point in a match or game that makes your score the same as someone else's

LANGUAGE EXTRA also spelt *equalize*

equaliser noun equalisers
a goal or point scored in a match or game that makes the scores equal

LANGUAGE EXTRA also spelt *equalizer*

equality noun
a situation in which people are equal to each other and deserve the same amount of respect

equally adverb
1 in the same way *to treat people equally*
2 to the same amount or level *Ruth and Steve are equally good at maths.*
3 in parts that are the same *Mum divided the cake equally between the five of us.*
4 used for showing that the second thing you say is just as important as the first *You must respect your parents but equally you should listen to your teachers.*

equals sign noun equals signs
the sign = that shows that numbers are equal, for example 2 + 3 = 5

equation ['i-kway-jern'; 'j' has the middle sound of 'pleasure'] noun equations
in maths, an equation is a group of numbers (or letters and numbers) in which an equals sign shows that two amounts are the same, for example $5x + 9 = 18 + 11$. Equations are sometimes referred to as number sentences and are often used in algebra.

Equator ['i-kway-ter'] noun
an imaginary line going around the earth. It is halfway between the North and South Poles.

LANGUAGE EXTRA also spelt *equator*

equatorial ['ek-wer-tor-ee-erl'] adjective
connected with the Equator

equestrian–Eskimo

equestrian *adjective*
connected with horse riding

> ORIGIN from Latin *equestris* 'of a horseman', from *equus* 'horse'

equidistant *adjective*
at the same distance from two places

equilateral ['ee-kwi-lat-er-erl'] *adjective*
an equilateral triangle has three sides of the same length and three angles of 60 degrees
compare: **isosceles** and **scalene**

equilibrium *noun*
1 a balance between different people or influences
2 a situation in which you control your feelings and you are not excited or angry

equinox *noun* **equinoxes**
one of the two days in the year (around 21 March and 23 September) when day and night last the same amount of time *the spring equinox*

> ORIGIN from Latin *aequinoctium*, from *aequi-* 'equal' and *nox* 'night'

equip *verb*
equips, equipping, equipped
1 to provide someone or something with what is needed *The head teacher wants to equip the school with a new computer room.*
2 to be equipped with something is to have something that is needed *My laptop is equipped with a special antiglare screen. The soldiers were well equipped.*

equipment *noun*
1 things needed for a particular activity. Equipment includes tools, machines, electrical and electronic goods, things with moving parts and things with different parts that are put together. *playground equipment* (for example slides, swings, seesaws); *camping equipment* (for example tents, sleeping bags, stoves); *office equipment* (for example punches, desks, photocopiers)
2 a piece of equipment is something needed for a particular activity, especially something that works with electricity or silicon chips such as a television, computer or camera

equivalent *adjective*
if something is equivalent to something else, it has the same size, amount, importance or meaning **equivalence** *noun*

equivalent *noun* **equivalents**
something that is the same as something else in meaning, importance, size or amount *This word has no equivalent in English.*

equivalent fractions *noun plural*
in maths, fractions that have the same value even though each has a different numerator (top number) and denominator (bottom number). For example, $\frac{1}{2}$ (a half), $\frac{2}{4}$ (two quarters) and $\frac{3}{6}$ (three sixths) all have exactly the same value so they are equivalent fractions.
compare: **proper fraction** and **improper fraction**

era ['ee-rer'] *noun* **eras**
an important period of time *This is the era of the internet.*

eradicate *verb*
eradicates, eradicating, eradicated
to get rid of something completely
eradication *noun*

erase *verb*
erases, erasing, erased
1 to get rid of something, especially something stored on a computer *I accidentally erased the file.*
2 to get rid of a pencil mark from paper using a rubber
3 to get rid of a mark made on a blackboard with chalk or on a whiteboard with a marker (pen with a thick soft point) using a piece of cloth or plastic

eraser *noun* **erasers**
1 a small piece of special rubber, or rubber mixed with other substances, for getting rid of pencil marks from paper

> SYNONYM rubber

2 a piece of cloth or an object with a soft material fixed to it, used for getting rid of marks made on a blackboard with chalk or on a whiteboard with a marker (pen with a thick soft point)

e-reader *noun* **e-readers**
a piece of electronic equipment that you hold in your hand, used for reading digital books called e-books

> LANGUAGE EXTRA also called an *e-book reader*

erect *adjective*
standing straight up

> SYNONYM upright

erect *verb*
erects, erecting, erected
1 to build something, for example a monument or big building
2 to fix something so that it stands straight up *to erect a tent*
erection *noun*

ERNIE ['err-nee'] *noun*
a piece of equipment that selects the prize-winning numbers of Premium Bonds
short for: Electronic Random Number Indicator Equipment

erode *verb*
erodes, eroding, eroded
if something such as a rock erodes or if something such as water erodes it, its surface is gradually destroyed *The sea is eroding the coast near Dover.* **erosion** *noun*

errand *noun* **errands**
a short journey to get something for someone or take something from them to give to someone else

erratic ['i-rat-ik'] *adjective*
not following a regular pattern, so that you do not know what will happen next *erratic behaviour* (for example sometimes noisy and sometimes quiet) **erratically** *adverb*

error *noun* **errors**
1 a mistake *Your homework contains lots of grammatical errors.*
2 a computer problem when something has gone wrong with a program *There's an error message on the computer.*
3 **in error** by mistake

erupt *verb*
erupts, erupting, erupted
1 if a volcano erupts, it explodes and lava (liquid rock) comes out of it
2 if something bad erupts, such as fighting or an argument, it starts suddenly and often gets worse
eruption *noun*

Esc *noun*
a key on a computer keyboard that you press to make the computer stop an action
short for: escape

escalate *verb*
escalates, escalating, escalated
to become much more serious *The fighting has escalated.* **escalation** *noun*

escalator *noun* **escalators**
a moving staircase that takes people from one level to another in a building such as a shopping centre or airport

escape *verb*
escapes, escaping, escaped
1 if someone escapes, they get away from somewhere they do not want to be, for example because they are in danger *The bully was hitting me but I managed to escape.*
2 to avoid something bad *When the car crashed, Aziz was lucky to escape. I hope the thief doesn't escape punishment.*
3 if something such as gas or oil escapes from something, it comes out
4 if something escapes you, you can't remember it *Her name escapes me.*

escape *noun* **escapes**
1 the action of getting away from somewhere or avoiding something bad *There's been an escape of prisoners. I had a lucky escape* (for example, I avoided being hurt).
2 an amount of something such as gas or oil that has escaped *an escape of gas*
3 a way of not thinking about the unpleasant things in your life *For me, books are an escape.*
4 on a computer keyboard, escape (or the escape key) is a key that you press to make the computer stop an action *Press Escape to return to the previous page.*

escort ['es-kort'] *noun* **escorts**
1 a person (or a group of people) who goes with someone to protect them or stop them from escaping
2 a boat, road vehicle or aircraft (or a group of them) that goes with other boats, road vehicles or aircraft to protect them or stop them from escaping

escort ['i-skort'] *verb*
escorts, escorting, escorted
to go somewhere with someone, or to go somewhere with a boat, road vehicle or aircraft (or group of them), to protect them or stop them from escaping

Eskimo *noun* **Eskimos**
an old name for a member of a group of people who live in the cold areas of North America, Greenland and Siberia

> LANGUAGE EXTRA the *Eskimos* who live in North America and Greenland are now usually called *Inuit*

especially–etiquette

especially adverb
1 used for giving special importance to a word *I'm especially angry about missing the train.*

SYNONYM particularly

2 used for saying something is more true about one particular person or thing than it is about others *We're all hungry, especially Dad.*

SYNONYM particularly

3 for a particular person and no other *I did this especially for you.*

SYNONYM specially

4 **not especially** not really *'Did you like my friend?' – 'Not especially.'*

espionage ['es-pee-er-nahj'; 'j' has the middle sound of 'pleasure'] noun
the activity of trying to find out secret information about someone or something and passing that information to someone else, for example an enemy

SYNONYM spying

esplanade noun esplanades
a wide road beside the sea where people walk

espresso noun
1 strong coffee made using a special machine and served without milk
2 (plural **espressos**) a small cup of espresso

ORIGIN from Italian *caffè espresso* 'pressed coffee' or 'quick coffee'

Esq.
a title used after a man's surname on letters, especially in the past *Jack Clark Esq.*
short for: esquire ('someone who held the shield' for a knight in medieval England)

-ess suffix
1 used for making nouns refer to women or girls *actress*
2 used for making nouns refer to female animals *lioness*

essay noun essays
a short piece of written work on a particular subject, for example by a student in school or by an author

essence noun
1 the essence of something is its most important quality
2 (plural **essences**) a liquid that comes from a plant and has a strong taste or smell *vanilla essence*

essential adjective
1 if something is essential, you must do it, have it or use it *It's essential to wear a helmet when you ride a bike.*

SYNONYM necessary

2 if someone is essential, you need them and can't do without them *Ricardo is an essential member of our team.*

SYNONYM very important

3 forming the most important part of something *Describe the essential ideas in Wordsworth's poem.*

SYNONYM basic

essentially adverb
used for talking about the most important detail, idea or fact about something *The film is essentially about a boy wizard.*

establish verb
establishes, establishing, established
1 to start something that you want to last for a long time *Our school was established 100 years ago.*
2 to be successful in getting or doing something *He's established a reputation for being a clown.*
3 to find out something *The police are trying to establish the truth.*
4 to prove something *The medical tests established her innocence.*

established adjective
used about someone or something that is accepted or well-known because they have been doing something for a long time or because they have existed for a long time *an established artist*; *This is an established way of putting up a tent.*

establishment noun
1 (plural **establishments**) a business or organisation *an eating establishment* (restaurant or café)
2 establishing something
3 the people in a country or group with power and influence. *The establishment do not usually want anything to change.*

estate noun estates
1 an area of land with lots of houses or blocks of flats on it that were built at the same time
2 an area of land with businesses and factories on it
3 a very large area of land with a big house on it that belongs to one person

estate agent noun estate agents
someone who has a business buying, selling and renting houses, flats, offices and land for other people

estate car noun estate cars
a long car with a door at the back and lots of room. It has back seats that fold down or can be taken out.

esteem noun
a feeling of respect for someone *Our head teacher is held in great esteem* (is greatly respected by everyone).

esteemed adjective
respected by everyone

estimate ['es-ti-mayt'] verb
estimates, estimating, estimated
1 to say roughly how much, how big or how long, for example, something will be *I estimate that this homework will take me about 30 minutes.*

SYNONYM guess

2 to work something out roughly such as an amount, value or size *I estimated I would need another £30 before I had enough for a bike. An estimated 200 children were there* (about 200).

estimate ['es-ti-mert'] noun estimates
1 a rough calculation about something such as an amount, value or size

SYNONYM guess

2 something someone says or writes to let you know how much it is going to cost to do a piece of work, for example to repair something *The engineer sent me a written estimate for fixing the computer.*

estimation noun
1 (plural **estimations**) a rough calculation about something such as an amount, value or size

SYNONYM estimate

2 an opinion about someone or something

Estonia noun
a country in North-East Europe
Estonian adjective & noun

estuary ['es-tyoo-er-ee'] noun estuaries
the wide part of a large river where it joins the sea *the Thames estuary*

etc.
used at the end of a list to show that there are other things that you haven't mentioned
short for: et cetera (Latin *et* 'and' and *cetera* 'rest')

SYNONYM and so on

etch verb
etches, etching, etched
to cut words, patterns or pictures into a hard surface using acid or a special tool

etching noun etchings
a picture printed from a thin piece of metal that has the picture cut into it with acid

eternal adjective
1 lasting for ever *the dream of eternal life*
2 unpleasant and lasting for a very long time *The school put a stop to those eternal fights in the playground.*
3 going on for a very long time in a certain way *My brother is the eternal student.*

eternally adverb
1 for ever
2 for a very long time

eternity noun
1 the whole of time that lasts for ever
2 a very long time *We waited for an eternity.*

ether ['ee-ther'] noun
1 a colourless liquid used for changing solid substances into liquid. It was used in the past as an anaesthetic to put people to sleep.
2 the ether is the air that computer signals and radio waves go through

Ethernet noun
a system for connecting computers to each other with wires *an Ethernet cable*

Ethiopia noun
a country in East Africa
Ethiopian adjective & noun

ethnic adjective
connected with people who have the same culture or whose family share the same ancestors *an ethnic group*

ORIGIN from Greek *ethnos* 'nation'

etiquette ['et-i-ket'] noun
rules for behaving correctly towards other people in different situations or online *chat room etiquette*

149

Etruscan – event

Etruscan *noun* Etruscans
someone who belonged to an ancient people of central Italy. The Etruscans influenced the Romans and played an important part in how the letters of the alphabet developed.

etymology *noun*
1 the study of where words come from and how they change
2 (*plural* **etymologies**) the etymology of a particular word is the description of where it has come from and how it has changed
etymological *adjective*

> ORIGIN from Greek *etymon* 'true sense' and *logos* 'word'

EU *noun*
short for **European Union** *Britain is a member of the EU.*

eucalyptus ['yoo-ker-**lip**-ters'] *noun* eucalyptuses
a tall tree from Australia with leaves that stay green in winter. It produces an oil used in medicines.

euphemism ['**yoo**-fer-miz-erm'] *noun* euphemisms
a polite word or expression used instead of a more usual but less pleasant one. You use a euphemism when you don't want to upset or shock someone. *'Chubby' can be considered a euphemism for 'fat'.*

euphoria ['yoo-**for**-ee-er'] *noun*
a feeling of great happiness, usually among a group of people

euphoric ['yoo-**for**-ik'] *adjective*
if people are euphoric, they are extremely happy

> SYNONYM ecstatic

eureka ['yoo-**ree**-ker'] *interjection*
used for showing how happy you are when you suddenly find something or find out the answer to a problem

> ORIGIN from Greek *heureka* 'I have found it'. These words were said by the Greek philosopher Archimedes in the 3rd century BC after he discovered the answer to a complicated mathematical question.

euro *noun* euros
a unit of money in France, Ireland, Spain, Germany, Italy and most countries of the European Union. A euro is worth 100 cents, and its symbol is €.

Europe *noun*
a continent between Asia and the Atlantic Ocean that includes countries such as Iceland and Finland in the north and Spain and Greece in the south

European *adjective*
connected with Europe

European *noun* Europeans
someone from Europe

European Union *noun*
an organisation of European countries for developing business activities, friendship and common laws and rules between members

Eurostar *noun* (trademark)
a fast train between Britain, France and Belgium. It uses the Channel Tunnel to cross between England and France.

euthanasia ['yoo-ther-**nay**-zee-er'] *noun*
the killing of a very sick person without causing him or her any pain. This is done in order to stop the person suffering any more.

evacuate *verb*
evacuates, evacuating, evacuated
1 to move someone away from a place because it is too dangerous *My great-grandparents were evacuated from London to the countryside during the war.*
2 to evacuate a building or area is to move everyone away from it because it is too dangerous
evacuation *noun*

evacuee *noun* evacuees
someone who is moved away from their home during a war because it is too dangerous

evade *verb*
evades, evading, evaded
1 to not deal with something or not do something that you should *He evaded the question.*
2 to not let yourself get caught by someone *So far the thief has evaded the police.*
3 to get away from someone or something that you consider unpleasant *The film star left through the back door to evade the crowds.*

> SYNONYM to avoid

evaluate *verb*
evaluates, evaluating, evaluated
to consider something in order to decide how good, useful or important it is
evaluation *noun*

evaporate *verb*
evaporates, evaporating, evaporated
if liquid evaporates, it changes into steam or vapour (tiny drops in the air) and disappears **evaporation** *noun*

evasion *noun*
1 when you do not deal with something or do not do something that you should
2 (*plural* **evasions**) an answer that does not deal with the question that someone asks you

evasive *adjective*
1 not dealing with a question as you should, for example by telling lies or talking about something that has nothing to do with the question *an evasive answer*
2 **to take evasive action** to do something very quickly to stop a dangerous situation happening

eve *noun* eves
the day before a holiday or important event *Christmas Eve; New Year's Eve*

even *adverb*
1 used about something that you don't expect or that you think is surprising *Anyone can make a mistake, even the teacher.*
2 used for saying strongly that something is more than something else *I go to bed late but my sister goes to bed even later!*
3 used for adding something stronger to what you've already said *Anisha is a good student, brilliant even.*
4 **even if** used for saying that although one thing is true or could happen, another thing will still be true *Even if you don't come with me, I'm going to the football match tomorrow.*
5 **even so** used for saying that although one thing is true, the second thing is also true, but it may be surprising *I had the flu but, even so, I went to the cinema.*
6 **even though** although *I jumped into the pool even though I was fully dressed!*

even *adjective*
1 flat and smooth *an even surface*
2 not changing *an even temperature*
3 equal *Our scores are even now.*
4 having the same size and position *My sister has beautiful even teeth.*
5 not excited or angry *an even tone*
6 used for describing a number that can be divided exactly by 2, for example 4, 6 and 8 are even numbers
compare: **odd** (sense 2)
7 if two people are even, they don't owe each other anything
8 to get even with someone is to do the same bad thing to them as they've done to you

even *verb*
evens, evening, evened
1 to make something equal *That goal has evened the score.*
2 if things even out or if you even them out, they become more equal *The differences between the north and the south have evened out.*

evening *noun* evenings
1 the time of the day between afternoon and night
2 an event that takes place in the evening *a poetry evening*
3 **good evening** a polite way of saying hello to someone in the evening
4 **evening dress** smart clothes that people wear in the evening to go to important events such as weddings or official meals

evenly *adverb*
1 including all parts of something in the same way *Spread the jam evenly on the bread. The fish is evenly cooked.*
2 used when talking about equal amounts of something *Dad shared out the sweets evenly among us. The vote was evenly split between John and Mary* (John and Mary both had the same number of votes).

> SYNONYM equally

3 used when talking about equal amounts of space or time *evenly spaced lines; Granddad wasn't breathing very evenly.*

> SYNONYM regularly

evenness *noun*
1 when something is flat and smooth *the evenness of the road*
2 when something has the same size and position *the evenness of the spaces between the rows*

event *noun* events
1 something that happens, for example something important or unusual
2 an occasion when people meet to take part in something *a sports event; Our school organised a Christmas event for parents.*
3 one part of a sports competition *Sol won the 100 metres event.*
4 **in any event** no matter what happens

> SYNONYMS for sense 4: anyway, in any case

eventful *adjective*
full of things happening, for example exciting or dangerous things *an eventful journey*

eventual *adjective*
happening at the end of a period of time or after many things have happened *Lots of children took part but Rachel was the eventual winner.*

eventually *adverb*
after a period of time or after many things have happened

SYNONYMS in the end, finally

ever *adverb*
1 at any time *Have you ever been to Manchester? Go there if ever you have the chance.*
2 used for giving extra importance to a word *You're the best dad ever! Why ever did you do it? I've never ever been to Leeds. Don't ever say that again!*
3 all the time or at all times *That's all I ever wanted. The giant's footsteps were getting ever closer.*
4 **ever so** or **ever such** very *That's ever so nice of you. He's ever such a good footballer.*
5 **for ever** for all time in the future or for a very long time *I hope we don't have to wait for ever.*

evergreen *adjective*
an evergreen tree or plant has leaves that stay green all year round. A conifer is an evergreen tree.

ANTONYM deciduous

evergreen *noun* **evergreens**
a tree or plant that has leaves that stay green all year round

everlasting *adjective*
1 lasting for ever
2 lasting for a very long time or for the whole of your life *everlasting memories*

every *adjective*
1 used when talking about all the things or people in a group or of a particular kind *Every boy and girl in my class can read and write.*
2 used when talking about how often something happens or what distance there is between things or people *every day* (at least once a day); *There were soldiers standing every few feet* (a few feet away from each other, for example in a line).
3 **every other** used when talking about something such as a day, week or month when something happens on one of them but not the next, as part of a regular pattern *We go swimming every other Thursday* (one Thursday in two).
4 **every other** also used when talking about a regular pattern affecting one thing but not the next *There was a flag in the window of every other house* (for example in the first house but not the second, in the third one but not the fourth).

everybody *pronoun*
1 all the people in a group *The teacher told everybody to be quiet.*
2 people in general *Everybody needs a holiday.*

SYNONYM everyone

everyday *adjective*
connected with normal life, for example happening or used a lot *an everyday event; everyday language*

SYNONYMS ordinary, usual

everyone *pronoun*
1 all the people in a group *Everyone in my family speaks Hindi.*
2 people in general *Everyone can learn to swim.*

SYNONYM everybody

everything *pronoun*
1 all the things to do with a particular situation *I dropped everything on the floor.*
2 things in general *Everything is fine.*
3 the most important thing or things *Money isn't everything.*
4 all the things that you need, for example to be happy *He's a film star who has everything.*

everywhere *adverb & conjunction*
1 in all places *I've looked everywhere. Everywhere I went, he followed.*
2 to all places *My sister has travelled everywhere in England.*

everywhere *pronoun*
all places *Everywhere was closed.*

evict *verb*
evicts, evicting, evicted
to make someone move out of their house or flat according to the law *The family were evicted for not paying their rent.*

eviction *noun*

evidence *noun*
1 information or signs that prove (or could prove) that something is true *Are these footprints evidence of the yeti?*
2 information in a court of law that proves (or could prove) that someone is guilty or innocent

evident *adjective*
easy to see *It's evident that he's not telling the truth.*

SYNONYMS obvious, clear

evidently *adverb*
1 used for saying that something is true because it is easy to see *The injured soldier was evidently in great pain.*

SYNONYMS obviously, clearly

2 used for saying that something appears to be true but may not be true *Evidently, Craig didn't go to school today.*

SYNONYM apparently

evil *adjective*
1 doing very bad and cruel things *an evil dictator*
2 also used about something that an evil person does or says *an evil smile*
3 very wrong and causing a lot of suffering *Slavery is evil.*
4 very unpleasant *the evil effects of smoking*
5 an evil spirit is an imaginary being with no body who does bad and cruel things

evil *noun*
1 very bad or cruel things *The King was known for the evil he did.*
2 the power to do evil things *a struggle between good and evil*
3 (*plural* **evils**) a very bad thing *Poverty is a great evil.*

evoke *verb*
evokes, evoking, evoked
to make you think of a particular feeling, idea or memory

evolution ['ee-ver-loo-shern'] *noun*
1 the way in which humans, animals and plants develop from a more simple form of life and gradually change over long periods of time *the theory of evolution*
2 the way in which something develops and gradually changes *the evolution of the English language*

evolve *verb*
evolves, evolving, evolved
1 to develop and gradually change *Language evolves all the time.*
2 to evolve from something is to gradually develop from it *Did the birds evolve from the dinosaurs?*

ewe ['yoo'] *noun* **ewes**
a female sheep. A male sheep is called a ram.

ex- *prefix*
used before a noun for showing that someone is no longer what the noun says they are *an ex-teacher; an ex-serviceman* (a man no longer in a country's army, navy or air force)

exacerbate *verb*
exacerbates, exacerbating, exacerbated
to make something such as a problem even worse

exact *adjective*
1 correct in every detail *Do you have the exact time?*
2 the same as something else in every detail *I have an exact copy at home.*
3 used about something when you mean just that thing and no other *This is the exact spot where it happened.*
4 if someone or something is the exact opposite, they are completely different *I'm the exact opposite of my brother.*

exactly *adverb*
1 in every way or detail *Tell me exactly what happened.*
2 used when you mean no more and no less than a particular number or amount *I went to bed at exactly eight o'clock.*
3 used in maths when you mean that a number can be divided by another number without a remainder (an amount left over) *10 can be divided exactly by 2 and 5.*
4 used when you mean a particular thing or place and no other *I'm sitting exactly where I want to sit.*
5 used when you agree with what someone says *'Let's get rid of exams.' – 'Exactly!'*
6 **not exactly** used for saying that something is not completely true *'Is yellow your favourite colour?' – 'Not exactly, I prefer orange.'*
7 **not exactly** also used when you mean the opposite of something *Bob isn't exactly stupid* (he's very clever).

exactness – exchange

exactness *noun*
being correct or the same as something in every detail

exaggerate *verb*
exaggerates, exaggerating, exaggerated
to say more about something or someone than is really true, for example that they are bigger, better, worse or more important than they really are *Sarah always exaggerates the number of friends she has.*

exaggeration *noun* exaggerations
1 words or a description that exaggerates something *To say that Tom and I are good friends is a slight exaggeration – we hardly know each other.*
2 the action of exaggerating something

exam *noun* exams
1 a series of questions to find out your knowledge of a subject. You usually write your answers on paper or using a computer.
2 an exam board is an organisation that produces the exams you take at secondary school. It also marks them (corrects mistakes and gives you a number or letter to show how well you have done) and gives you certificates if you are successful. An exam board is also called an awarding body.

examination *noun* examinations
1 an exam
2 a careful look at something
3 when a doctor checks your body to see if you are healthy

examine *verb*
examines, examining, examined
1 to look at something carefully
2 if a doctor examines you, he or she checks your body to see if you are healthy
3 to give someone an exam to find out their knowledge of a subject

examiner *noun* examiners
someone whose job is to find out your knowledge of a subject by making up or marking an exam or by talking to you directly

example *noun* examples
1 a thing or person that is one of a number of things or people of the same kind *Daffodils and crocuses are examples of spring flowers.*
2 a particular thing or person that helps you to explain the type of thing or person that you mean *The teacher wrote some examples on the whiteboard.*
3 a way of behaving that you should copy because it is good *You should set an example to your little sister* (behave well so that she will do the same).
4 someone whose behaviour is good and should be copied *Anisha is an example to us all.*
5 a sentence or expression that shows how a word is used *a dictionary example*
6 **for example** used when mentioning something as an example *There are many types of spring flowers, for example daffodils and crocuses.*

exasperate *verb*
exasperates, exasperating, exasperated
to make someone feel angry and impatient because something they want is not happening or something bad is continuing to happen **exasperation** *noun*

excavate *verb*
excavates, excavating, excavated
1 to dig in the ground to look for objects from the past *Archaeologists have excavated the ancient Italian city of Pompeii.*
2 to dig a hole in the ground in order to build things such as houses or blocks of flats
excavation *noun*

excavator *noun* excavators
1 a large machine for digging and moving earth
2 someone such as an archaeologist who digs in the ground to look for objects from the past

exceed *verb*
exceeds, exceeding, exceeded
1 to be more than a number or amount *If the temperature exceeds 30 degrees, we will have to cancel sports day.*
2 to be or do better than something *This year's sales have exceeded last year's.*
3 to go above a particular limit that is allowed *Cars mustn't exceed the speed limit near the school.*

exceedingly *adverb*
extremely *Katie works exceedingly hard.*

excel *verb*
excels, excelling, excelled
1 to be very good at something *Olivia excels at maths.*
2 to do very well *You've excelled this year, Daniel.*

excellence *noun*
the quality of being very good *Our school is known for its academic excellence* (the very good quality of its teaching).

excellent *adjective*
very good

excellently *adverb*
very well

except *preposition*
used when you mean that you don't include something or someone in what you say *We go to school every day except Saturday and Sunday. She was dressed all in green except for her hat.*

except *conjunction*
used for connecting two parts of a sentence when you give a reason why something you have just mentioned cannot happen or isn't true *I would help you with your homework except I'm no good at maths.*

exception *noun* exceptions
1 something or someone not included in a rule or in something you say *You form the plural of most nouns by adding 's' but 'child' is an exception. I don't usually let people ride my bike but I'll make an exception for Ava* (I won't include Ava in the rule).
2 if you take exception to something, you do not like it because it upsets you or makes you angry

exceptional *adjective*
1 unusual and very good or great *Einstein was a person of exceptional intelligence.*
2 unusual and not likely to happen again or to happen often *an exceptional situation*
3 very great *I took exceptional care in cutting out the hexagon.*

SYNONYM extraordinary

exceptionally *adverb*
1 extremely *Jack's answers were exceptionally good.*
2 extremely and not what you normally expect *The weather's exceptionally cold for this time of year.*
3 when something or someone is not included in a rule *Exceptionally, you can stay up until ten o'clock.*

excerpt *noun* excerpts
a short piece taken from something much longer such as a book, film or piece of music

SYNONYM extract

excess *noun* excesses
1 an amount of something that is more than is needed or allowed *An excess of coffee can be harmful.*
2 **in excess of** more than *Mum was driving in excess of 60 miles an hour.*

excess *adjective*
1 more than needed or allowed *excess baggage* (more bags and cases than you are allowed to take on a plane)
2 extra *You haven't paid enough for your ticket so you need to pay an excess fare.*

excessive *adjective*
1 more or greater than is needed or allowed *The soldiers used excessive force.*
2 more or greater than seems reasonable or usual *These prices are excessive.*

excessively *adverb*
1 too much *You've been watching TV excessively this week.*
2 too *I've been excessively tired today.*

exchange *verb*
exchanges, exchanging, exchanged
1 to give something to someone and get something else back from them *The two boys exchanged names and addresses.*
2 if you exchange things such as words, messages or letters with someone, you say, write or send them and the other person does the same
3 to take or send something back to a shop and get something else instead *This shirt is too small so I will exchange it.*

SYNONYM to change

4 to give someone the money of one country and get the money of another country instead *Dad exchanged 200 euros at the bank.*

SYNONYM to change

exchange *noun* exchanges
1 the action of doing something, for example giving, saying, writing or sending something to someone, and getting something back from them *an exchange of messages*
2 a building or place where telephone lines are connected when you make a call or use the internet
3 the action of exchanging the money of one country for the money of another country *What's the exchange rate of the euro?* (What is the euro worth in another country's money?)
4 the action of exchanging something for something else, for example in a shop *If you buy a dress in the sale, no exchanges are allowed.*

5 a short or long stay by students from different countries who visit each other as part of a school or university programme

excitable *adjective*
easily becoming worried or angry, or easily becoming very happy, and often showing this in your behaviour, for example by running about or doing lots of quick movements

excite *verb*
excites, exciting, excited
1 if something excites you or makes you excited, it makes you very happy, for example about something that is going to happen, or it makes you really want to do something *We were all excited about the trip to Paris. I was so excited by the football match that I asked if I could join the team.*
2 to cause something such as a particular feeling or attitude *This book has excited a lot of interest.*

excited *adjective*
1 very happy about something, or really wanting to do something, and often showing the way you feel by your behaviour, for example not being able to keep still *The train was full of excited children* (for example happy children running about and shouting).

SYNONYM enthusiastic

2 worried or angry about something *Don't get excited – things could be worse.*
excitedly *adverb*

excitement *noun*
1 when someone feels very happy about something or really wants to do something *There was a feeling of great excitement among the children as they watched the race.*
2 very great interest *The author's new book has caused a lot of excitement.*
3 strong feelings of pleasure, for example when someone does something dangerous *If you want excitement, try scuba diving.*
4 a situation or period when someone does exciting things

exciting *adjective*
if something is exciting, it makes you very happy and often makes you show your feelings in a strong way, for example because it is so interesting or good *exciting news*; *an exciting adventure* (full of things happening)

exclaim *verb*
exclaims, exclaiming, exclaimed
to say something loudly and suddenly, for example because you are surprised, upset or angry

SYNONYM to shout out

exclamation *noun* exclamations
a word or sentence that you say, often loudly and suddenly, that shows a strong feeling such as anger, surprise, or liking or disliking something. Examples are 'Aargh!', 'Wow!', 'Stop it!' and 'I can't believe it!' In this dictionary, exclamations are called interjections.

exclamation mark *noun*
exclamation marks
a punctuation mark like this ! used after an exclamation in a sentence

> LANGUAGE EXTRA you use an *exclamation mark* after a word, phrase or sentence as a way of showing a particular feeling. For example, you can show that you are angry (*I'll never speak to you again!*); surprised (*Look at that!*); disappointed (*Pity!*); happy about something (*What a beautiful dress!*); unhappy about something (*Sorry!*); agreeing (*Yes!*) or disagreeing (*No!*).
> You can also use an exclamation mark with a command (*Go away! Don't run! Help me!*) and to give special importance to a word or sentence (*I've been to Spain three times!*).
> In informal writing, a number of exclamation marks can be used together to show that your feelings are very strong (*Your plan is completely crazy!!!*).

exclude *verb*
excludes, excluding, excluded
1 to make sure something or someone is not a part of something else *Vegetarians exclude meat from their diet.*

SYNONYM to leave out

2 to stop someone or something from going into a place or from being connected with something *Ella has been excluded from the race.*

SYNONYM to keep out

3 to say that something should not be considered *The police have excluded bad driving as a reason for the accident.*

SYNONYM to rule out

exclusion *noun*

ORIGIN from Latin *excludere* 'to shut out' (*ex-* 'out' and *claudere* 'to shut')

excluding *preposition*
used when you mean that something or someone is not a part of something else *There are 20 children in the class, excluding me.*

SYNONYM not counting

ANTONYM including

exclusive *adjective*
1 if something is exclusive, it belongs to or is for a particular group only and it is not shared with anyone else *The staff room is for the exclusive use of the teachers. This special offer is exclusive to readers of our magazine* (only for them and not for anyone else).
2 if something such as a shop, club or part of a town is exclusive, it is very expensive and suitable only for a few people, for example people who have lots of money
exclusiveness *noun*

exclusively *adverb*
only *Madame Duval taught her lesson exclusively in French.*

excrement *noun*
the waste matter that your body gets rid of from your bowels

excrete *verb*
excretes, excreting, excreted
to get rid of waste from the body, for example by going to the toilet
excretion *noun*

excruciating *adjective*
1 really painful *an excruciating headache*
2 really bad or unpleasant *The film was excruciating.*

excruciatingly *adverb*
really (used when talking about things that are unpleasant or bad) *an excruciatingly boring lesson*

excursion *noun* excursions
a short journey that you make for pleasure, for example to visit a place *Our school went on an excursion to Stonehenge.*

excusable *adjective*
if something is excusable, you can forgive someone for doing it

excuse ['iks-kyooss'] *noun* excuses
1 a reason for not doing something that you should have done or for explaining why you did something bad. You give someone an excuse so that they will understand your behaviour and forgive you. *Holly's late again – what's her excuse?*
2 a reason for doing something you really want to do, or for avoiding something you don't want to do *Saying you have a headache is just an excuse for not going to school.*

excuse ['iks-kyooz'] *verb*
excuses, excusing, excused
1 to forgive someone for doing something bad *Please excuse me for being late.*
2 to be a good reason for bad behaviour *You're only eight but that doesn't excuse what you did.*
3 to give someone permission not to do something *Ask your teacher if you can be excused from football.*
4 **excuse me** used as a polite way of interrupting someone, saying you don't agree with someone or showing you're sorry for doing something *Excuse me, but I've got to go home now.*
5 **excuse me** also used as a polite way of getting someone's attention when you want to ask them something *Excuse me, can you tell me the way to Oxford Street?*

exe ['eks-ee']
the ending of a computer filename. An .exe file runs a program on a computer.
short for: executable

executable *adjective*
an executable file is one that starts running a program on your computer when you click on it

execute *verb*
executes, executing, executed
1 to kill someone as a punishment
2 to do or produce something, especially something difficult *The ballet dancer executed a perfect movement.*

execution–exotic

execution *noun*
1 (*plural* **executions**) the killing of someone as a punishment, which is still done in some countries *Do they still have executions in Texas?*
2 the action of doing or producing something

executioner *noun* **executioners**
someone who has the job of executing criminals

executive *noun* **executives**
someone with a lot of responsibility and power in a business or organisation *My mum's a senior executive in a bank.*

exemplary *adjective*
excellent and good enough to be copied by other people *Charlie's behaviour was exemplary.*

exemplify *verb*
exemplifies, exemplifying, exemplified
to be an example of something

exempt *adjective*
if you are exempt from something, you don't have to do something that other people have to do such as obey a rule or pay money *It costs £5 to see the exhibition but children are exempt* (they don't have to pay).

exempt *verb*
exempts, exempting, exempted
to give someone permission not to do something that others must do or not to pay money that others must pay

exemption *noun* **exemptions**
permission not to do something or pay money *It costs £5 to get in and there are no exemptions.*

exercise *noun* **exercises**
1 movements that you make (for example stretching or bending) or activities that you do (for example running or swimming) to keep your body healthy *I don't get enough exercise.*
2 a piece of work you do to learn or practise something, for example one that has a number of questions that you write answers to
3 a particular activity or action *a military exercise* (for training soldiers); *a pointless exercise* (something that is a waste of time)

exercise *verb*
exercises, exercising, exercised
1 to move your body in different ways or do activities such as running or swimming in order to keep healthy *Granddad exercises every day. My wrist is painful so I have to exercise it.*
2 to let an animal run or walk to stay healthy *Have you exercised the dog today?*
3 to use something such as a quality, power or skill or do something such as a duty *Mr Taylor doesn't exercise enough control over the class.*

exercise book *noun* **exercise books**
a book for doing your schoolwork or homework in. It has empty pages or pages with lines on for you to write on.

exert *verb*
exerts, exerting, exerted
1 if you exert yourself, you make a lot of effort to do something
2 to use something such as influence, pressure or control to make something happen

exertion ['ig-**zerr**-shern'] *noun* **exertions**
very great effort

exhale *verb*
exhales, exhaling, exhaled
to let air go out from your lungs through your mouth

SYNONYM to breathe out

ANTONYM to inhale

exhaust *verb*
exhausts, exhausting, exhausted
1 to make someone very tired
2 to use all of something *The soldiers have exhausted all their food.*
3 to say all there is to say about something *We've exhausted the subject.*
4 to think about every way of looking at something or doing something *Every possibility has been exhausted.*

exhaust *noun* **exhausts**
1 the gas produced from an engine, for example in a car or motorbike *The exhaust fumes from the traffic gave me a headache.*
2 an exhaust or exhaust pipe is a pipe that allows the gas from an engine to come out

exhausted *adjective*
1 if someone is exhausted, they are very tired
2 if something is exhausted, all of it has been used *Natural gas is almost exhausted.*

exhaustion *noun*
a feeling of being very tired

exhibit *verb*
exhibits, exhibiting, exhibited
1 to show something, for example in an art gallery or museum, so that people can spend time looking at it
2 to show a particular feeling or behaviour
3 to show something, especially something you're pleased with *She exhibited a pair of gold earrings.*

SYNONYM to display

exhibit *noun* **exhibits**
something such as a painting, photo or sculpture shown in a gallery or an object shown in a museum

exhibition *noun* **exhibitions**
1 an event where people show things such as paintings, photos or sculptures
2 when someone shows a particular feeling or behaviour

SYNONYM display

exhibitor *noun* **exhibitors**
1 a person who exhibits his or her work, for example in an art gallery
2 a person or company that exhibits and sells their new products at an event called a fair

exhilarating *adjective*
making you feel happy and full of energy

exhort *verb*
exhorts, exhorting, exhorted
to try very hard to get someone to do something by giving them good reasons why they should

exile *noun*
1 when someone is forced to leave their country and live somewhere else *The president lived in exile for many years.*
2 (*plural* **exiles**) someone who is exiled

exile *verb*
exiles, exiling, exiled
to make someone leave their country and live somewhere else *Napoleon was exiled to the island of Saint Helena.*

exist *verb*
exists, existing, existed
1 to be something that you can find somewhere in the world *These strange creatures exist at the bottom of the sea.*
2 to happen in a particular situation *The problem hasn't existed before.*
3 to live, especially when you don't have enough of something *The prisoners had to exist on bread and water.*

existence *noun*
1 when something exists somewhere in the world *How long has your school been in existence?*
2 (*plural* **existences**) a way of living, especially one that is very hard *Many people in that country lead a terrible existence.*

existing *adjective*
used for describing something that exists or happens now *The existing rules are not fair.*

exit *noun* **exits**
1 a door or space you go through to leave a place such as a room or building
2 the action of leaving a place *The actors made their exit to the right of the stage.*
3 a small road that leads away from a motorway. A driver takes an exit to leave the motorway.

exit *verb*
exits, exiting, exited
1 to leave a place *The burglar exited through a window. Exit Julius Caesar* (used in a play to tell a character when to leave the stage).
2 to close a computer program *Click on X to exit the program.*

exodus *noun*
a situation in which lots of people leave a place at the same time

exorbitant *adjective*
if an amount of money such as the cost of something is exorbitant, it is much more than it should be *exorbitant prices*

exorcise *verb*
exorcises, exorcising, exorcised
to get rid of evil spirits from someone or from a place, for example in a religious ceremony

LANGUAGE EXTRA also spelt *exorcize*

exorcist *noun* **exorcists**
someone who gets rid of evil spirits, for example in a religious ceremony
exorcism *noun*

exotic *adjective*
if something is exotic, it is interesting or unusual because it is connected with a distant country or makes you think of distant countries *Our zoo has lots of brightly coloured exotic birds.*

ORIGIN from Greek *exotikos* 'foreign'

expand – exploration

expand *verb*
expands, expanding, expanded
to become bigger or more important, or to make something bigger or more important *Our school is expanding in size and influence.* **expansion** *noun*

expanse *noun* expanses
a very large area of something, for example of land, sea or sky

expect *verb*
expects, expecting, expected
1 to think that something will happen *They're expecting trouble at the football match.*
2 to think that it is right that something should happen *Our teacher expects everyone to do their homework on time.*
3 to think that something is true *I expect you're tired. I expect so* (I think so).
4 to think that someone or something will arrive soon or within a certain amount of time *We're expecting the post at any moment. A bigger crowd is expected next year.*
5 if a woman is expecting a baby, she is pregnant

expectant *adjective*
1 full of hope because you think something good will happen
2 an expectant mother is a woman who is going to have a baby soon
expectantly *adverb*

expectation *noun* expectations
1 a hope that something good will happen *My sister has expectations of going to university.*
2 what someone thinks will happen or should happen *Our team isn't very good so the expectation is that we won't win.*

expedition *noun* expeditions
1 a journey to a place to find out more about it *an expedition to the North Pole*
2 a group of people who go on an expedition
3 a journey made for pleasure *a skiing expedition*

expel *verb*
expels, expelling, expelled
1 to make someone leave a place, organisation or country, for example because they have behaved badly *My brother was expelled from school.*
2 to force something such as a liquid or gas to come out of something *Air is expelled from the lungs.*

expendable *adjective*
if something or someone is expendable, they are not needed and can be got rid of

expenditure *noun*
spending money or the money that is spent

expense *noun* expenses
the money you have to pay to buy or do something *We went to Leeds to play the match and the school paid our expenses* (for example train fare, hotel, food).

expensive *adjective*
1 costing a lot of money *expensive clothes*
2 selling things for a lot of money or making people pay a lot of money *Mayfair in London has lots of expensive shops and hotels.*
3 used for describing a place where it costs a lot of money to live *Chelsea is an expensive part of London.*
4 used for describing something such as tastes or ideas suitable only for people who like to spend a lot of money

expensively *adverb*
in a way that shows you have a lot of money *an expensively dressed tourist*

experience *noun*
1 what you learn from doing a particular activity or job for a certain amount of time *My mum has 10 years' experience as a dentist.*

SYNONYM skill

2 (*plural* experiences) something that happens to you or that you do *I had a nasty experience on the way to school.*
3 what you have learnt from the things that have happened to you in your life *Dad says he speaks from experience when he tells us not to smoke.*

experience *verb*
experiences, experiencing, experienced
1 to have something *I'm experiencing problems with my laptop.*
2 to feel something *We experienced a lot of excitement when the plane took off.*
3 to let something have an effect on you or give you pleasure *A live concert is a great way to experience music.*

experienced *adjective*
if someone is experienced, they have learnt a lot from doing a particular activity or job for a long time

SYNONYM skilled

experiment *noun* experiments
a scientific test to find out what happens to something *We carried out an experiment on light and shadow.*

experiment *verb*
experiments, experimenting, experimented
1 to do a scientific test or tests to find out what happens to something
2 to try out new ideas or ways of doing things to see what happens *The children love experimenting with different paints and brushes.*

experimental *adjective*
1 using new ideas or ways of doing things, not always with complete success *experimental music*
2 connected with scientific experiments

experimentation *noun*
when someone tries out new ideas or ways of doing things to see what happens

expert *noun* experts
someone who knows a lot about something or has a lot of skill in something *She's an expert on computers.*

expert *adjective*
1 knowing a lot or having a lot of skill *an expert dog trainer*
2 coming from or belonging to an expert *expert advice*

expertise *noun*
skill or knowledge that you get from practice

expire *verb*
expires, expiring, expired
1 if something such as a ticket or passport expires, it cannot be used later than the date written on it *Your library card has expired. I threw away the expired ticket.*

SYNONYM to run out

2 if someone expires, they die

expiry *noun*
the time when something expires *What's the expiry date on your passport?*

explain *verb*
explains, explaining, explained
1 to tell someone something very clearly so that they can understand it *Our teacher explained to us how a light bulb works.*
2 to give a reason or reasons for something *I hope this explains her behaviour.*

ORIGIN from Latin *explanare* 'to make flat or smooth' (from *planus* 'flat', 'smooth')

explanation *noun* explanations
1 a reason or reasons why something has happened or why someone has done something
2 words that describe clearly how to do something, how something works or what something means *John's homework provided an excellent explanation of Wordsworth's poem.*

explanatory *adjective*
explaining something clearly so that you can understand it *an explanatory note*

explode *verb*
explodes, exploding, exploded
1 if something such as a bomb explodes, it bursts with a very loud bang and causes a lot of damage
2 if something such as a plane or road vehicle explodes, it breaks up into small pieces with a very loud bang, for example because it has been hit by a bomb
3 to explode a bomb is to make it burst with a loud bang
4 to get bigger or become more important very quickly *In the sixteenth century, London's population exploded.*
5 if someone explodes, they suddenly show a strong feeling, usually anger *Ben exploded when I told him the truth.*

exploit ['eks-ployt'] *noun* exploits
someone's exploits are the brave, interesting or important things that they have done

exploit ['iks-ployt'] *verb*
exploits, exploiting, exploited
1 to develop natural resources such as oil, coal, land or forests
2 to exploit someone is to treat them badly, for example by making them work for you without paying them properly or by using their ideas as your own
exploitation *noun*

exploration *noun* explorations
1 the action of going somewhere to explore it or the journeys made to explore it *What's the future of space exploration?*
2 when you look at or think about something carefully, for example a subject or idea
3 the action of searching for something *oil exploration*

155

explore – extinguish

explore *verb*
explores, exploring, explored
1 to go to a place you don't know and travel around it to find out what it is like *Scott explored the Antarctic.*
2 to look at or think about something carefully, for example by discussing it *Keats explores the subject of beauty in this poem.*
3 to search for something *The company is exploring for oil in this part of Scotland.*

explorer *noun*
1 (*plural* **explorers**) someone who travels around an unknown place to find out what it is like
2 Windows Explorer (trademark) is a computer program that is part of the Windows operating system (software that makes a computer work). It lets you see the files you have on your computer.

explosion *noun* **explosions**
1 when something explodes with a loud bang *a gas explosion*
2 when something gets bigger or becomes more important very quickly *a population explosion*

explosive *noun* **explosives**
a substance or object that can explode

explosive *adjective*
1 able to explode or cause an explosion *an explosive substance*
2 likely to become very dangerous at any moment *The situation in Brazil's slums is explosive.*

exponent *noun* **exponents**
in maths, the exponent is a small number written to the right of another number that tells you how many times to multiply that number by itself. For example, in 5^3 the exponent is 3. It tells you that 5 must be multiplied 3 times (5 × 5 × 5, which equals 125).

export ['eks-port] *noun*
1 (*plural* **exports**) a product sent to another country to be sold
2 the business of exporting products to other countries, or the action of exporting a product

export [ɪks-port] *verb*
exports, exporting, exported
1 to send products to another country in order to sell them
2 to copy computer information from one place to another, for example from a program or file to another program or file. When the information is copied, it is often stored in a different format.

exporter *noun*

expose *verb*
exposes, exposing, exposed
1 to show something that is usually covered
2 to let people know about something bad *The newspapers exposed the film star as a liar.*
3 if you are exposed to something bad or dangerous, you are made to experience it *The astronaut was exposed to the harmful rays of the sun.*

exposure *noun*
1 being exposed to something bad or dangerous *Avoid too much exposure to the sun.*
2 the harm that very cold weather causes to your body *The skier died of exposure.*

express *verb*
expresses, expressing, expressed
1 to tell someone what your ideas or feelings are by talking or writing about them *Everyone should be allowed to express their opinions. Alfie can express himself clearly* (say what he means) *in French.*
2 to describe something using particular words *Words can't express the horror of the accident.*
3 to show something *Her face expressed a deep feeling of anger.*

express *adjective*
1 very fast *an express train*
2 sent using a very fast system *an express letter*
3 clear, and impossible to be mistaken about *He came with the express purpose of annoying me.*

express *noun* **expresses**
a train or bus that travels very fast between two places

expression *noun* **expressions**
1 the way your face looks at a particular time to show what you are thinking or feeling *Amy had a strange expression on her face.*

SYNONYM look

2 a word or group of words *'To bury the hatchet' is an idiomatic expression.*
3 showing ideas, opinions or feelings, for example in words, art or music *Poetry is a form of artistic expression.*

expressionist *adjective*
connected with a style of art, writing, music, cinema and theatre that expresses feelings. It was popular at the start of the 20th century. **expressionism** *noun*

expressive *adjective*
1 clearly showing your feelings *a wonderfully expressive face*
2 showing meaning in a very strong and interesting way *The word 'humongous' is very expressive.*
expressively *adverb* **expressiveness** *noun*

expressly *adverb*
1 for a particular purpose *My parents came expressly to see the head teacher.*
2 **expressly forbidden** definitely not allowed

expulsion *noun* **expulsions**
when someone is made to leave a place, organisation or country, for example because they have behaved badly

exquisite *adjective*
1 extremely delicate and beautiful *exquisite hands; an exquisite pattern*
2 extremely good or great *exquisite taste; exquisite joy*
exquisitely *adverb*

extend *verb*
extends, extending, extended
1 to continue over a certain distance *This road extends all the way to the Scottish border.*
2 to continue for a certain time *The holidays extend until Monday.*
3 to make something bigger or longer, for example a house or road
4 to make something last longer *Your library card can be extended for another year.*
5 to give someone something such as a greeting or thanks *The mayor extended a warm welcome to the foreign students.*

SYNONYM for sense 5: to offer

extension *noun* **extensions**
1 an extra room or rooms added on to a building
2 a part of a road or railway line added on to the existing one
3 an extra phone or phone line that is added to the main one
4 extra time for something, for example to finish a piece of homework
5 an extension lead is an electrical wire added to another one to make it longer
6 making something bigger or longer

extensive *adjective*
1 used when you mean a very great amount of something or a very large number of things *extensive damage; extensive changes*
2 covering a very big area *The hotel has extensive gardens.*

extensively *adverb*
very much *My sister has travelled extensively.*

extent *noun* **extents**
1 the amount of something *We don't know the extent of the damage.*
2 how big something is *He was surprised by the extent of the problem.*
3 **to a great extent** mainly
4 **to a certain extent** partly

exterior *noun* **exteriors**
the outside of something

ANTONYM interior

exterior *adjective*
outside *an exterior wall*

ANTONYM interior

exterminate *verb*
exterminates, exterminating, exterminated
to kill all the insects, animals or people of a particular group or in a particular place
extermination *noun*

exterminator *noun* **exterminators**
someone whose job is to kill harmful animals such as rats, or insects such as cockroaches

external *adjective*
connected with the outside of something *an external wall* **externally** *adverb*

extinct *adjective*
1 if an animal, plant or language is extinct, there are no more living examples of it
2 if a volcano is extinct, it will never again erupt (explode)

extinction *noun*
a situation in which there are no more living examples of an animal, plant or language

extinguish *verb*
extinguishes, extinguishing, extinguished
1 to put out a fire
2 to turn off a light

156

extinguisher noun **extinguishers**
a large metal tube containing a chemical that you spray onto a small fire to put it out

> LANGUAGE EXTRA also called a *fire extinguisher*

extol verb
extols, extolling, extolled
to praise something or someone very much

extra adjective
1 used when you mean more of something of the same kind *Do you want an extra blanket? These two blankets are extra* (left over).

> SYNONYM additional

2 also used when you mean that something costs more *It's extra if you want to sit in the front row.*

extra adverb
1 more than usual *Be extra careful.*

> SYNONYM very

2 more money *That costs extra.*

extra noun **extras**
1 something more that you can buy *I bought some extras for my laptop, for example a mouse and memory stick.*
2 someone who plays a very small part in a film, for example in a crowd

extra- prefix
outside something *extraordinary* (outside what is ordinary)

extract ['eks-trakt] noun **extracts**
1 a short piece taken from something longer such as a book, film or piece of music

> SYNONYM excerpt

2 a substance taken from something else, usually a plant *vanilla extract*

extract ['iks-trakt] verb
extracts, extracting, extracted
1 to take something out of something else

> SYNONYM to remove

2 to get information from someone who doesn't want to give it

> ORIGIN from Latin *ex-* 'out' and *trahere* 'to drag' or 'to draw'

extraction noun
1 (plural **extractions**) extracting something from something else
2 used for talking about where the people in your family come from, for example a particular country or part of a country *Manuel is of Spanish extraction.*

extracurricular adjective
connected with activities that you do at school that are not part of your normal schoolwork, such as learning to play a musical instrument

extraordinarily adverb
1 extremely *Jo was extraordinarily brave at the dentist's.*
2 in a very unusual or surprising way

extraordinary adjective
1 really good and much better than usual *an extraordinary stroke of luck; extraordinary beauty*
2 very unusual or surprising *What happened was pretty extraordinary.*
3 much more than usual *I took extraordinary care over my homework.*

> SYNONYM exceptional

extraterrestrial adjective
connected with things that exist in or come from another planet

extraterrestrial noun **extraterrestrials**
a living being that comes from another planet

extravagant adjective
1 spending too much money *My sister is very extravagant.*
2 costing too much money *an extravagant birthday present*
3 much more, greater or bigger than seems reasonable *an extravagant use of the school's resources*
extravagance noun **extravagantly** adverb

extreme adjective
1 used when you mean the greatest possible amount of something *The people in these slums live in extreme poverty.*
2 very unusual, and often a long way from what is reasonable or normal *extreme weather; My uncle has some extreme opinions. The book is about an extreme example of an unhappy school.*
3 furthest away *Our classroom is at the extreme end of the corridor.*
4 an extreme sport is one that is dangerous but very exciting, for example bungee jumping

extreme noun **extremes**
1 something that is as different from something else as it is possible to be *We're looking for a middle way that is somewhere between the two extremes.*
2 something that is the opposite of something else or at the opposite end of something else *extremes of heat and cold; extremes of temperature*
3 if you do something to extremes, you do it much more than is reasonable

extremely adverb
a stronger way of saying very *extremely late.*

extremity ['iks-trem-er-tee] noun **extremities**
1 your extremities are the end parts of your body, for example your feet or hands
2 the part of something at the very end of it *a small village at the southern extremity of the island*

extricate verb
extricates, extricating, extricated
to get someone or yourself out of a bad or dangerous situation or place *The driver extricated himself from the blazing car.*

exuberant adjective
happy and full of energy **exuberance** noun

eye noun **eyes**
1 your eyes are the two parts in your face that you use for seeing
2 if you have an eye for something, you have the skill for noticing things that are not easy to see *Mohammed has an eye for detail.*
3 the tiny hole at the top of a needle
4 the eye of a storm is the calm area at its centre
5 if you keep an eye on something or someone, you watch them carefully, for example to make sure they are safe
6 if you keep an eye out for someone or something, you remember to keep looking for them even while you are doing something else

eye verb
eyes, eyeing, eyed
to look at someone or something closely *The crowd eyed me suspiciously.*

eyeball noun **eyeballs**
the round ball shape that forms the whole of your eye

eyebrow noun **eyebrows**
your eyebrows are the curved lines of hair above your eyes

eye-catching adjective
if something is eye-catching, it is easily noticed, for example because it is attractive, big or unusual

eye chart noun **eye charts**
a chart (or drawing) used by an optician or an eye doctor for measuring how well someone can see. It usually has letters of the alphabet of different sizes on different lines – one big letter at the top, two smaller letters on the next line, three even smaller ones underneath and so on. The bottom line has very small letters.

eye drops noun plural
small drops of medicine that you put in your eye, for example to get rid of an infection

eyelash noun **eyelashes**
your eyelashes are the hairs on the edges of your eyelids

eyelid noun **eyelids**
your eyelids are the pieces of skin above and below your eyes that cover your eyes when you close them

eyepiece noun **eyepieces**
the piece of glass at the end of a telescope or microscope that you look through

eye shadow noun
a substance for colouring the eyelids

eyesight noun
the natural ability you have to see *I have good eyesight.*

eyesore noun **eyesores**
something such as a building or place that is ugly to look at

eyewitness noun **eyewitnesses**
someone who has seen something happen, for example a crime or accident, and can describe it to the police

eyrie [rhymes with 'weary'] noun **eyries**
the nest of a bird of prey such as an eagle. It is built in a very high place such as on a mountain.

e-zine ['ee-zeen] noun **e-zines**
a magazine that you read online

f F

ORIGIN F, U, V and W all come from the same letter in the Phoenician alphabet. The letter looked like a Y and represented either a peg or a hook. It had the sound of 'w' and was called *waw* because the Phoenicians did not have the sound 'f' in their language. When the letter passed into the Greek alphabet, the Greeks changed its shape to something similar to an F but facing left. Eventually the Greeks got rid of the letter altogether as they had another letter for their 'f' sound. However, the Romans found a good use for it in their Latin language. They changed the sound of the letter from 'w' to 'f' and turned the F to face right – giving us the shape we know today.

F
short for **Fahrenheit**

FA *noun*
the organisation in charge of football in England and Wales
short for: **Football Association**

fable *noun* **fables**
a short story or poem that teaches you a lesson about how you should behave. It often uses animal characters.

ORIGIN from Latin *fabula* 'story' (from *fari* 'to speak')

fabric *noun*
1 (plural **fabrics**) another word for cloth *a fabric shop* (shop selling cloth)
2 the walls, roof and windows of a building

SYNONYM for sense 2: **structure**

fabricate *verb*
fabricates, fabricating, fabricated
1 to make up something that isn't true, for example an excuse *to fabricate stories* (to tell lies)
2 to make a product in a factory

fabrication *noun* **fabrications**
a piece of information that isn't true

fabulous *adjective*
1 extremely good *fabulous weather*
2 extremely large and rich *a fabulous palace*
3 extremely great *fabulous wealth*
4 not real but in stories only *The griffin is a fabulous creature.*

fabulously *adverb*
1 extremely well *You danced fabulously.*
2 extremely *She's fabulously rich.*

facade ['fer-**sahd**'] *noun* **facades**
the front of a large house

LANGUAGE EXTRA also spelt **façade**

face *noun* **faces**
1 the front of your head
2 an expression on your face showing how you feel or what you're like *Lily has a sad face. Ahmed has a friendly face.*
3 a way of moving your face to show what you think or to get someone to do something *Charlie pulled a face* (showed he disliked something, for example by pushing out his lips). *The clowns made funny faces* (to make people laugh).
4 the side of a mountain, rock or cliff *a steep cliff face*
5 the front part of something *a clock face*
6 in maths, a face is the flat or curved surface of a 3-D shape such as a sphere, cone or cube *A cube has six faces.*
7 the open part at the front of a goal in football
8 **face down** with the front of something downwards or with your face downwards
9 **face to face** used when you mean you're meeting someone or you're with someone in the same place as they are *Dad wanted to meet my teacher face to face, not speak to her over the phone.*

face *verb*
faces, facing, faced
1 to look towards someone or something or in a particular direction *I turned and faced the door. Our school faces east.*
2 to turn or be turned in a particular direction *Can you face the computer screen towards me?*
3 if you face something (or face up to something) or if it faces you, you have to accept it and deal with it *Children must face up to their responsibilities. There are many problems and dangers that face us. I was faced with a difficult choice.*
4 to talk to someone after something bad has happened that you're ashamed of *I won't be able to face my uncle again.*
5 if you can't face doing something, you strongly dislike the idea of doing it

Facebook *noun* (trademark)
the name of a particular website that people use for keeping in touch with friends, for example by giving information about themselves and posting or exchanging messages

facebook *verb*
facebooks, facebooking, facebooked
1 to use Facebook
2 to find out about someone by using Facebook *I didn't know who he was so I facebooked him.*

facecloth *noun* **facecloths**
a small cloth for washing your face

faceless *adjective*
if someone or something is faceless, they have no special quality but are considered to be exactly the same as all the others of the same type *faceless office workers*

facelift *noun* **facelifts**
1 if someone has a facelift, they have a medical operation to make their face look younger
2 work to make something such as a building look more attractive

face paint *noun* **face paints**
a special paint used for painting marks or designs on someone's face, for example to make them look like a princess or a tiger

face painting *noun*

facet ['**fas**-it'] *noun* **facets**
a particular part of something such as a situation or someone's character *We will be studying every facet of life in China.*

facetious ['fer-**see**-shers'] *adjective*
saying something that is supposed to be funny but is not funny at all *a facetious remark*

facial *adjective*
connected with the face *facial muscles*

facilitate *verb*
facilitates, facilitating, facilitated
to make something easier or more likely to happen

facility *noun*
1 (plural **facilities**) something provided for someone to use, for example equipment or an area, room or building *cooking facilities; Our gym has facilities for basketball.*
2 a natural skill to do something *Michael has a facility for languages.*

facing *preposition*
opposite *Facing the school there's a post office.*

fact *noun* **facts**
1 something that is true or that really happened *The Guinness World Records website is full of facts. The story is based on historical fact.*
2 **in fact** or **as a matter of fact** used for saying that something is really true or for adding something to what you've already said
3 **the facts of life** information about sex and the way babies are made

ORIGIN from Latin *factum* 'event', 'thing done', from *facere* 'to do'

factor *noun* **factors**
1 one of a number of things that help to make something happen or that are needed to produce a particular result *The fog was a factor in the plane crash.*
2 in maths, a factor is a whole number that divides exactly into another number without a remainder (an amount left over) *The factors of 12 are 1, 2, 3, 4, 6 and 12.*
compare: **multiple**
3 in science, a factor is one of the parts that make up an experiment

ORIGIN from Latin *factor* 'doer', 'maker', from *facere* 'to do'

factory *noun* **factories**
a large building with lots of machines or electronic equipment for making things, for example cars, computers or clothes *Dad works in a furniture factory.*

fact sheet *noun* **fact sheets**
a piece of paper or an electronic file giving important information about something

factual *adjective*
1 based on or containing facts only, not ideas or opinions *a factual TV programme*
2 connected with facts *a factual error*

factually *adverb*
connected with facts *factually correct*

FA Cup *noun*
the most important football competition for English and Welsh teams. It is run by the Football Association.

fad noun **fads**
something that people like very much but that only lasts for a short time *Do you think this music is just a passing fad?*

SYNONYM craze

fade verb
fades, fading, faded
1 if something fades or its colour fades, or if the sunlight fades something, it gradually becomes less bright *She wore a pair of faded jeans. The light is fading* (it's getting dark).
2 to gradually become less strong, clear or loud *My scar has faded. After a while the sound of the music faded away.*
3 if a flower fades, it becomes less fresh and dies
4 if someone fades away, they begin to lose their strength and gradually die

faeces ['fee-seez'] noun plural
the waste matter that your body gets rid of from your bowels

faff verb (informal)
faffs, faffing, faffed
if you faff about, you waste time doing things badly or doing things that are not important

fag noun **fags**
an informal word for a cigarette

faggot noun **faggots**
a meatball usually made from pig's meat and bread

Fahrenheit noun
a system for measuring temperature, in which water freezes at 32 degrees and boils at 212 degrees
compare: **Celsius**

ORIGIN named after the German–Polish 18th-century scientist Daniel Gabriel *Fahrenheit* who invented it

fail verb
fails, failing, failed
1 if you fail, you cannot do something that you try to do *Mum tried to fix my laptop but she failed.*

ANTONYM to succeed

2 to not do something that you should do *Granddad failed to tell us he was in hospital.*
3 if you fail an exam or test, you are not successful

ANTONYM to pass

4 if something fails or fails to do something, what you expect to happen does not happen *Our plans failed. The letter failed to arrive* (did not arrive).
5 to stop working properly *The plane's engines failed.*
6 to become weaker *Grandma's health is beginning to fail.*
7 to stop growing *The crops failed because there was no rain.*
8 if a business or relationship fails, it has become bad and is unable to continue

fail noun **fails**
1 when you are not successful in an exam or test *Did you get a pass or a fail in maths?*
2 **without fail** used for saying that something always happens or must definitely happen *We go and see Granddad every Sunday without fail. Be here tomorrow at nine o'clock without fail.*

failed adjective
not successful *a failed experiment*

failing noun **failings**
the bad part of something such as someone's character

SYNONYMS fault, weakness

failure noun **failures**
1 a situation in which someone or something is not successful *Our talks ended in failure.*

ANTONYM success

2 someone or something that is not successful *Try not to see yourself as a failure.*

ANTONYM success

3 when something stops working (or stops working properly) *heart failure*
4 when something such as a business has become bad and cannot continue
5 when you do not do something that you should do *I was disappointed by your failure to tell me.*

faint adjective **fainter, faintest**
1 not very easy to see, hear, smell or feel *a faint voice; a faint outline*

SYNONYM weak

2 not very easy to remember *a faint recollection*
3 very small *Your chances of winning are faint. I don't have the faintest idea* (I really don't know).
4 if you feel faint, you become very weak and feel that you are going to become unconscious, for example because you are ill, hot or hungry

faintness noun

faint verb
faints, fainting, fainted
to suddenly feel very weak and become unconscious for a short period, for example because you are ill, hot or hungry

SYNONYM to pass out

faint-hearted adjective
1 not very brave or not feeling very sure of yourself
2 if you say something is not for the faint-hearted, you mean it is not for anyone who is easily shocked, frightened or afraid of difficulties

faintly adverb
1 in a way that is not very easy to see, hear, smell or feel *'Yes,' she said, faintly.*
2 slightly *Dad was faintly amused.*

fair adjective **fairer, fairest**
1 if you have fair hair or if you are fair, the colour of your hair is light yellow or very light brown
2 if you have fair skin or if you are fair, the colour of your skin is very light
3 if you are fair to people or if a situation is fair, everyone is treated the same and in a very good and reasonable way *You gave Chloe an ice cream but not me — that's not fair!*
4 reasonable or right *That's a fair price for a computer. It's not fair to blame me without knowing what really happened.*
5 large but not too large *Our house is a fair size.*
6 neither good nor bad but somewhere in between *You have a fair chance of passing the exam. Ethan's reading is fair.*
7 used when you mean quite a lot of something *There's a fair amount of work to do.*
8 if the weather is fair, it is dry and pleasant
9 if something such as a fight, game or match is fair, it is played or done according to the rules
10 in science, a fair test is an experiment in which you only change one factor (or part of the experiment) at a time
11 an old-fashioned word for beautiful, used especially in stories and poems *a fair maiden*
12 **fair enough** used for saying that what someone says sounds reasonable and is OK with you *'I can't play any more because I'm tired.' – 'Fair enough.'*

fair noun **fairs**
1 an outside area where people go to have fun. There are games to play and machines such as merry-go-rounds for riding on and bumper cars for driving in.

SYNONYM funfair

2 an event where you go to look at or buy products that people or companies are selling *a book fair*
3 an event, usually outside, organised by a group such as a school or club to make money. There are games and things to buy including food and drinks. This type of fair is also called a fête.

ORIGIN from Latin *feriae* 'religious holidays'

fairground noun **fairgrounds**
an area of land that is used for a funfair

fair-haired adjective
if you are fair-haired, the colour of your hair is light yellow or very light brown

fairly adverb
1 not very but still enough or quite a lot *Granddad is fairly old* (old enough but not very old). *Daniel plays the piano fairly well* (not very well but well enough).

SYNONYMS quite, rather

2 in a good and reasonable way so that everyone is treated the same *Does your teacher treat everyone in the class fairly?*

fair-minded adjective
reasonable in the way you treat people or consider situations

fairness noun
when something or someone is reasonable or right *the fairness of a decision*

159

fairy – falsify

fairy noun fairies
1 in stories, a fairy is a small imaginary creature with wings and with magic powers. Fairies can be good or bad.
2 in stories, a fairy godmother is a fairy who helps people with her magic powers, especially people who are in trouble
3 a fairy cake is a very small round cake, usually with icing (sugar, water and other ingredients) on it. It is like a small cupcake.
4 fairy lights are very small lights for decorating a Christmas tree
5 a fairy tale or story is a story in which magic things happen

fairyland noun
an imaginary land where fairies live

faith noun
1 a strong feeling that someone or something is good and can be trusted *We all have faith in our head teacher.*
2 a strong feeling that a particular god exists and a love for that god
3 (plural **faiths**) another word for religion *People of many different faiths live in London.*
4 if you do something in good faith, you believe that what you do is honest and the right way to behave

faithful adjective
1 if you are faithful to someone or something, you stay with them and support them because they are important to you *a faithful friend*
2 also used about someone's actions *Ms Thomas has given years of faithful service.*
3 exactly right and true to the original *a faithful copy*

faithfulness noun

faithfully adverb
1 in a way that shows support and liking or love towards someone or something *Ms Thomas has faithfully served the school.*
2 exactly *It's copied faithfully from the book.*
3 really and truly *I promise faithfully that I will help you.*

fake adjective
1 not real *a fake name*

SYNONYM **false**

2 if an object such as a painting or diamond is fake, it is not real but looks like it is real

fake noun fakes
something not real, especially something that looks like it is real *This painting is a fake.*

fake verb
fakes, faking, faked
1 to pretend to have a certain feeling *He faked a headache so that he could stay home from school.*
2 to try to make something look as if it really happened (when it didn't) or look real (when it isn't) *The criminal faked his own death. She faked her dad's signature.*

faker noun

falafel ['fer-lahf-erl'] noun
a Middle Eastern food made from chickpeas (large round beans) that are cooked, mashed, formed into balls and fried. Falafel is usually eaten in pitta (flat or oval bread that you open to make a pocket).

falcon noun falcons
a large bird like a hawk. It is a bird of prey that eats small animals and other birds and can be trained to hunt them.

fall verb
falls, falling, fell, fallen
1 to move down quickly from a higher position to a lower one *I slipped and fell. The snow is still falling.*
2 if things such as amounts, numbers or prices fall, they become lower or less *It's cooler now – the temperature has fallen.*
3 to change from the way someone or something is at a particular time to something different, or to become something *My brother fell ill. I fell asleep. Dad fell silent. My old bike is falling to bits* (or *to pieces*) (is becoming broken).
4 to go onto something *The shadow from the big tree fell across the playground. The stress falls on the first syllable of the word.*
5 to go into something *We fell into a trap.*
6 to belong to something, for example a group *Man falls into the group known as 'Homo sapiens'.*
7 to happen *My birthday falls on a Sunday this year. We reached safety before darkness fell.*
8 to become quieter *Her voice fell.*

ANTONYM **to rise**

9 if a town or country falls in a war or battle, it is captured by the enemy
10 if a soldier falls in a war or battle, he or she dies
11 if something falls apart, it breaks up into pieces
12 if you fall back on something or someone, you use something or trust someone to help you if you have a problem, for example something you have used before or someone who has helped you before
13 if you fall behind with something, for example your schoolwork, you are not doing things as well or as quickly as you should
14 if someone or something falls down, they fall accidentally *I fell down and hurt my leg while jogging.*
15 if a building is falling down, it is in bad condition and needs to be repaired
16 if you fall for someone, you start to love them
17 if you fall for a trick, you believe something that isn't true
18 if something such as a roof falls in, it breaks and falls suddenly
19 if someone falls in with someone, they become friends with them *He fell in with a bad crowd at school.*
20 if something falls off, it stops being fixed to something *A button has fallen off my coat.*
21 if something such as your hair or a tooth falls out, it comes away from your body
22 if you fall out with someone, you have an argument with them
23 if someone or something falls over, they fall accidentally *I fell over while running.*
24 if something such as a plan falls through, it does not happen

fall noun falls
1 when someone or something falls *Granddad had a fall.*
2 a fall in something such as a price or the temperature means that it goes down

SYNONYM **drop**

3 when a person or country loses their power *the fall of the Roman Empire*
4 the American word for autumn *We're going to England in the fall.*
5 **falls** another word for a waterfall, especially in names *Niagara Falls*

fallacy noun fallacies
a false idea that many people think is true

fallen
past participle of **fall**

fallout noun
dangerous radioactive dust that falls to the ground after the explosion of a nuclear bomb

fallow adjective
land that is fallow has been dug with a plough or ploughs but does not have anything growing on it yet

false adjective
1 if something is false, it does not exist as a real thing or did not happen *a false address; I didn't kick Sophia – that's false!*
2 completely wrong or mistaken *a false idea; Your answer is false.*
3 not real but made by people or machines and made to look like something real *false teeth; a suitcase with a false bottom*

SYNONYM **artificial**

4 if someone is false, or if their behaviour is false, they are not honest or open and you don't know what they are really like *Emily is so false. Tom gave a false smile.*
5 if you make a false move, you make a mistake or a movement with your body that causes something very serious to happen

falseness noun

false alarm noun false alarms
when you think something bad is going to happen but it doesn't happen after all

falsehood noun
1 (plural **falsehoods**) words that are not true

SYNONYM **lie**

2 when something is not true *We all prefer truth to falsehood.*

falsely adverb
1 wrongly or by mistake *I was falsely accused of cheating.*
2 in a way that doesn't show what someone is really like *He smiled falsely.*

falsetto noun falsettos
a man's singing or speaking voice that is very high

falsify verb
falsifies, falsifying, falsified
to change something such as a document so that it contains false information

falsification noun

falter – fantastic

falter *verb*
falters, faltering, faltered
1 if someone falters (or if something someone does falters), they almost stop doing something, for example because they become less certain or weaker *Her steps faltered as she approached the head teacher's office* (she almost stopped walking).
2 to become weaker or less or to be unable to continue as before *Ava's determination to do well has never faltered.*

faltering *adjective*
weak or becoming weaker or less successful *a faltering voice*; *the country's faltering economy*

fame *noun*
being famous *Dickens achieved world fame as a writer.*

famed *adjective*
known to lots of people

SYNONYM famous

familiar *adjective*
1 if something or someone is familiar, you recognise them or know them *a familiar face*; *He looks familiar to me.*

SYNONYM well-known

2 happening a lot *a familiar problem*

SYNONYM common

3 if you're familiar with something, you know it or know something about it *Grandma isn't very familiar with the latest music.*
4 very friendly *Don't be too familiar with your teachers.*
familiarly *adverb*

ORIGIN from Latin *familiaris* 'connected with people living together in the same house', for example family members

familiarise *verb*
familiarises, familiarising, familiarised
1 if you familiarise yourself with something, you learn it (for example a rule) or you learn about it (for example a computer)
2 if you familiarise someone with something, you help them to learn it or learn about it
familiarisation *noun*

LANGUAGE EXTRA also spelt *familiarize* and *familiarization*

familiarity *noun*
1 knowing something or knowing about something *Ella has some familiarity with Spanish.*
2 the pleasant feeling you have towards someone or something because you know them so well
3 very friendly behaviour towards someone

family *noun* families
1 a group of people who are related to each other, especially a mother and father and their children *There's a quiet family living next door.*
2 all the people related to each other *My family comes from Poland.*
3 in science, a group of things such as animals or plants that are similar to each other *The tiger belongs to the cat family.*

ORIGIN from Latin *familia* 'servants and other people living in the same house' (from *famulus* 'servant')

family name *noun* family names
the last part of your name that you share with all the people in your close family

SYNONYMS surname, last name

family planning *noun*
using contraceptives to stop a woman from becoming pregnant and to control how many children a man and woman have and when they have them
compare: birth control

family tree *noun* family trees
a drawing that shows how the people in a family are related to each other

famine *noun* famines
a situation in a country or region in which people do not have enough food for a long time *Many people died in the famine.*

famished *adjective*
very hungry

SYNONYM starving

famous *adjective*
if something or someone is famous, lots of people know about them

SYNONYM well-known

famously *adverb*
used when you mean lots of people know about something *Winston Churchill famously smoked cigars.*

fan *noun* fans
1 a piece of equipment with blades (long flat parts) that go round, used for making the air cooler. Fans come in many shapes and sizes. They are used for keeping people cool and for stopping equipment or engines from getting too hot.
2 a flat object made of paper or plastic that you wave in your hand to keep cool
3 someone who is very interested in a famous person or in a famous group such as a music band or sports team *a Beatles fan*
4 a person who likes watching things such as sports or films or listening to things such as music or the radio *a football fan*

fan *verb*
fans, fanning, fanned
1 to wave a flat object in front of your face to keep yourself cool *I fanned my face with my exercise book.*
2 to make a fire burn more strongly by blowing air onto it *The wind was fanning the flames.*
3 if a group of people fan out, they move forwards and spread out in all directions

fanatic *noun* fanatics
1 someone whose opinions about something are so strong that they behave in an unreasonable way
2 someone who really likes a particular thing or doing a particular activity *a cycling fanatic*

fanatical *adjective*
1 strongly interested in something or someone or in doing something *I'm fanatical about football. My cousins are fanatical supporters of the president.*
2 very unreasonable, or behaving in a very unreasonable way *fanatical opinions*
fanatically *adverb*

fanciful *adjective*
if something such as an idea is fanciful, it is silly and not serious because it is not based on reason or fact

fan club *noun* fan clubs
a group of people who are fans of someone famous such as a pop star or actor. Members of the group share information and take part in activities.

fancy *verb*
fancies, fancying, fancied
1 to want something or to want to do something *Do you fancy some fish and chips? I really don't fancy doing my homework.*
2 to like something *I don't fancy the idea of staying at home by myself.*
3 to think that someone is attractive and want to be their friend
4 to imagine something that is or might be true *Fancy Raj winning the race!*

fancy *adjective* fancier, fanciest
1 made in a complicated way, for example with lots of decorations, extra parts or different colours *a fancy handbag*

ANTONYM plain

2 able to do lots of extra things, used for example when talking about equipment or computer software *This program has very fancy graphics.*
3 expensive *a fancy restaurant*
4 complicated or difficult *Don't use any fancy words in your homework.*

fancy *noun* fancies
1 imagination or an imaginary idea
2 a feeling of wanting something *It was just a passing fancy.*

fancy dress *noun*
clothes that you wear to look like someone else when you go to an event called a fancy dress party

fanfare *noun* fanfares
a short tune, usually played by trumpets, to announce something special on an important occasion

fang *noun* fangs
one of the long pointed teeth in some animals such as tigers, dogs and snakes. Fangs are used for catching animals and biting them hard. Some imaginary creatures such as vampires and dragons also have fangs.

ORIGIN from Old English *fang* 'something caught' and Old Norse *fang* 'a capture'

fantastic *adjective*
1 extremely good *Leah did a fantastic drawing.*
2 extremely large *a fantastic amount of money*
3 strange, magical or imaginary *There are many fantastic creatures in the paintings of Hieronymus Bosch.*

161

fantastically – fashion

fantastically adverb
1 extremely well *He played fantastically.*
2 extremely *You were fantastically brave at the dentist's.*

fantasy noun **fantasies**
1 a pleasant and exciting situation that someone wants to happen but that usually never happens *Leela's fantasy is to fly a plane.*
2 a situation or idea based on the imagination *I think you live in a fantasy world* (where things are not real).
3 a story, film or play based on the imagination

fanzine ['fan-zeen'] noun **fanzines**
a magazine for fans interested in subjects such as music, sports or science fiction

FAQ ['ef-ay-kyoo'] noun **FAQs**
a list of questions and answers that give useful information about something such as a particular subject, product or company
short for: Frequently Asked Questions

far adverb
further or **farther**, **furthest** or **farthest**
1 used when talking about distance, especially a great distance *Don't go far from the house. My dad lives far away. It's not far.*

SYNONYM a long way

2 used for giving extra importance to a word, for example for showing how different things are in a comparison *His home is far bigger than mine* (much bigger). *You read far better than you used to* (a lot better). *There were far more children than last time* (lots more children).
3 used when talking about a long time ago in the past or a long time ahead in the future *People used this word as far back as the sixteenth century. Don't plan too far ahead.*
4 used when talking about progress *I haven't got very far with my homework.*
5 **as far as** all the way to a particular place *We went by train as far as Leeds.*
6 **so far** up until now
7 **by far** used in comparisons for showing how different things or situations are, for example how much bigger or better something is *Our school is by far the best one around. Great-Granddad is by far the oldest member of the family.*
8 **as far as I know** or **as far as I can see** used when you mean that you think something is true but you are not completely sure about it
9 **far and wide** used when talking about a very large distance *People travelled far and wide to see her.*

far adjective
further or **farther**, **furthest** or **farthest**
1 used for describing something that is the greatest distance away from you *Mum was sitting at the far end of the table.*
2 used for describing a place that is beyond the left or the right, or a point of the compass that is beyond the north, south, east or west *That's me at the far left of the photo. Angus lives in the far north of Scotland.*

faraway adjective
a long way from where you are *a faraway country*

SYNONYMS distant, far-off

farce noun
1 an event or situation that is ridiculous, for example because it is badly organised or not very good *The school concert was a farce.*
2 (plural **farces**) a film, play or TV programme that makes people laugh. Farces deal with silly and complicated situations.
3 the particular style of acting or writing in a farce

farcical adjective
if something is farcical, it is ridiculous or bad and you cannot take it seriously

fare noun **fares**
the money you pay for a ticket to travel somewhere, for example by train, bus or plane *How much is the air fare?* (to travel by plane)

fare verb
fares, faring, fared
used for saying how well or how badly someone or something does *He didn't fare too well in his exams.*

SYNONYM to do

Far East noun
a region in the eastern part of Asia that includes more than 20 countries, for example China, Japan and Indonesia

farewell interjection
an old-fashioned way of saying goodbye to someone when you don't think you will see them again or for a long time

far-fetched adjective
if something is far-fetched, you have trouble believing it is true, for example because it seems very strange or does not seem possible

farm noun **farms**
1 an area of land and buildings for keeping animals for food (for example cows, chickens or sheep) or for growing plants and vegetables (for example wheat or potatoes) *farm animals*
2 the house in which a farmer lives
3 a place for producing a particular type of animal for food *a salmon farm*

farm verb
farms, farming, farmed
to use land for keeping animals for food or for growing plants and vegetables *My uncle has farmed in Kent for years. My brother dreams of farming the land.*

farmer noun **farmers**
a person who owns or looks after a farm

farmhouse noun **farmhouses**
the house in which a farmer lives

farming noun
the activity of a farmer

farmland noun
land used for keeping animals for food or for growing plants and vegetables

farmyard noun **farmyards**
an open area near a farmhouse and farm buildings, often surrounded by a fence or wall. Animals such as chickens or pigs sometimes live there.

far-off adjective
1 a long way from where you are *a far-off land*

SYNONYMS distant, faraway

2 a long way from the present time *It happened in the far-off days of Julius Caesar.*

farther adverb & adjective
used when talking about a greater distance than something else *Anisha lives a long way from the school but Olivia lives even farther away.*

SYNONYM further

farthest adverb & adjective
used when talking about the greatest distance away from something else *Let's see who can throw the ball farthest. Neptune is the farthest planet from the sun.*

SYNONYM furthest

farthing noun **farthings**
an old British coin that was worth a quarter of one penny

fascinate verb
fascinates, fascinating, fascinated
if something or someone fascinates you, they really interest you and you think about them a lot *Jo is fascinated by the stories of Roald Dahl.*

ORIGIN from Latin *fascinare* 'to cast a magic spell over' (from *fascinum* 'magic spell')

fascinating adjective
really interesting

fascination noun
1 the power that someone or something has to really interest you *Italy holds a fascination for me.*
2 being really interested in someone or something *My brother has a fascination for comic books.*

fascism ['fash-iz-erm'] noun
a political belief that the government should have complete control over people's lives and that people should not be free to express their opinions

fascist ['fash-ist'] noun **fascists**
someone who believes in fascism
fascist adjective

fashion noun **fashions**
1 the type of clothes that many people like to wear at a particular time *It's the latest fashion. Fashions change every year.*
2 the activity or business of making clothes that many people like to wear *a fashion designer*
3 when something is popular at a particular time *This kind of music is in fashion now.*
4 a particular way of doing something *These two machines work in a similar fashion.*

162

fashion verb
fashions, fashioning, fashioned
to make something in a particular way and with great skill

fashionable adjective
1 if clothes are fashionable, many people at a particular time want to wear them because they think they are attractive
2 if a place is fashionable, many people at a particular time want to go there or live there, for example because they think it is pleasant or because they like expensive things *a fashionable restaurant*; *Mayfair is a fashionable part of London.*

SYNONYM classy

3 if an activity or object is fashionable, many people at a particular time want to do it, use it or have it *Jogging is very fashionable. A new mobile app may quickly become fashionable.*
4 if something such as an idea or opinion is fashionable, many people at a particular time are really interested in it
5 if a person is fashionable, he or she likes to wear clothes that are popular at a particular time

fashionably adverb

fast adjective faster, fastest
1 moving quickly *a fast car*
2 doing something quickly or done quickly *That was fast! It was a fast journey.*

SYNONYM quick

3 letting something move quickly *a fast road*; *a fast speed*
4 if a watch or clock is fast, the time it shows is later than the correct time

fast adverb faster, fastest
1 quickly
2 if you make something fast, for example a boat or tent, you fix it tightly to something
3 if you hold fast to something, you hold on to it tightly
4 if something or someone is stuck fast, they cannot move
5 **fast asleep** sleeping very deeply

fast verb
fasts, fasting, fasted
to eat no food or hardly any food for a short period of time

fast noun fasts
a short period of time when you eat no food or hardly any food

fasten verb
fastens, fastening, fastened
1 to close something, for example by joining the two ends of it or sides of it together *Fasten your seat belt. Could you fasten my necklace?*
2 to be joined together by its two ends or sides *This skirt fastens at the back.*
3 to fix or join something to something else *I fastened my bike to the school railings. Fasten these papers with a paperclip.*

fastener noun fasteners
something such as a button, zip or Velcro, used for fastening a piece of clothing

LANGUAGE EXTRA also called a *fastening*

fast food noun
hot food, such as burgers and chips, that is served quickly from a restaurant, stall or vehicle. People often take fast food away to eat somewhere else.

fast-forward verb
fast-forwards, fast-forwarding, fast-forwarded
to press a button or click an icon to make something such as a video or DVD go forwards to another position without playing it

ANTONYM to rewind

fat adjective fatter, fattest
1 a fat person or animal has a big heavy body that weighs too much
2 big and thick *a fat book*; *fat legs*

SIMILE 'as fat as a pig' means very fat (sense 1)

fat noun
1 (plural **fats**) an oily substance in food *This yoghurt has too much fat. We're trying to cut down on fat* (or fats).
2 (plural **fats**) an oily substance from animals or plants, used for cooking
3 the substance under the skin of a person or animal that stores energy and keeps them warm
4 the soft white parts in meat *Cut off the fat before you eat this lamb chop.*

fatal adjective
1 causing someone to die *a fatal accident*
2 causing something very bad to happen *a fatal mistake*

fatality noun fatalities
the death of someone that is caused suddenly, for example by an accident or in a war

fatally adverb
if someone is fatally wounded or injured, their injuries are so bad that they die

fate noun
1 (plural **fates**) someone's fate is what happens to them, especially something bad
2 an imaginary power that controls everything that happens in someone's life

fat-free adjective
containing no fat *a fat-free ice cream*

father noun fathers
1 a man who has a son or daughter
2 the title given to a male Christian leader such as a priest or monk, especially in the Roman Catholic Church or in the Orthodox Church (Eastern Europe, Russia and Greece) *Father John*

Father Christmas noun
an imaginary man with a red coat and white beard who brings presents to children at Christmas. He is sometimes called Santa Claus.

fatherhood noun
being a father and looking after a child or children

father-in-law noun fathers-in-law
the father of someone's husband or wife

fatherly adjective
connected with the feelings and behaviour of a loving father *fatherly advice*

Father's Day noun Father's Days
a special day for honouring fathers when people give cards and presents to their father. It is usually celebrated in June.

fathom verb
fathoms, fathoming, fathomed
to fathom something out is to understand something difficult or mysterious

fathom noun fathoms
a unit for measuring the depth of water, equal to about 1.8 metres

fatigue ['fer-teeg'] noun
a feeling of being very tired

ORIGIN from 17th-century French *fatigue* 'tiredness'

fatigued adjective
very tired

fatten verb
fattens, fattening, fattened
1 to give an animal a lot of food to make it fat
2 to fatten someone up is to give them more food because you think they are too thin

fattening adjective
if a particular food is fattening, it will make you fat or fatter

fatty adjective fattier, fattiest
containing a lot of fat *fatty food*

fatwa ['fat-wah'] noun fatwas
an order given by a Muslim religious leader

faucet noun faucets
the American word for a tap (something you turn to control water or gas)

fault noun faults
1 the responsibility for something bad happening *I was late through no fault of my own. The lorry driver was at fault* (responsible, for example for an accident).
2 if something is someone's fault, they have done something bad, or not done something that they should have done, and they should be blamed for it *I broke the window – it's my fault.*
3 something that is wrong with something or someone *My mobile isn't working – it has a fault. We all have our faults* (things wrong with our character).
4 in science, a fault is a deep crack in the rocks below the surface of the earth where earthquakes sometimes happen *the San Andreas fault in California*

fault verb
faults, faulting, faulted
to find something bad or wrong with someone or something

faultless adjective
if something is faultless, there is nothing wrong with it and it is perfect

faultlessly adverb

SYNONYM flawless

faulty adjective faultier, faultiest
if something is faulty, there is something wrong with it and it doesn't work properly

fauna [rhymes with 'corner'] noun
all the animals that live in a particular place or at a particular time in history. The plants of a place or time are called the flora.

favorite–feed

favorite noun favorites
a web page whose address you've saved to your computer so you can find it again easily

SYNONYM bookmark

LANGUAGE EXTRA *favorite* is the American spelling of *favourite*

favour noun
1 (plural **favours**) something kind that you do to help someone *Can I ask you a little favour?*
2 a feeling that shows that people like someone or something and think they are good *Most countries look on the idea of freedom with favour.*
3 if someone is in favour of something, they want it and support it *We're all in favour of less homework.*
4 if something or someone is in favour, people like them *These ideas are very much in favour now.*
5 (plural **favours**) a party favour is a small present you get for going to a party, for example a birthday party

favour verb
favours, favouring, favoured
1 to like something or someone more than something or someone else *Spain is a country favoured by British holidaymakers.*
2 to treat someone better than someone else *She favoured her eldest son.*
3 to help someone or something *These new rules favour trade between countries.*

favourable adjective
1 if something is favourable, it is good *He made a favourable impression on the class.*
2 helping you in some way *We went skiing because the weather was quite favourable.*
3 also used for showing that you like something *We were all favourable to the plan.*

favourably adverb
1 in a way that shows that someone likes something *He replied favourably to my letter.*
2 in a way that shows that something is good *Our team compares very favourably to yours.*
3 very or very well *favourably impressed*; *favourably treated*

favourite adjective
your favourite thing or person is the one you like most of all *What's your favourite sport?*

favourite noun favourites
the thing or person you like most of all

favouritism noun
treating someone better than someone else because you like them more

fawn noun
1 (plural **fawns**) a young deer
2 a light brown colour

fawn adjective
light brown

fax noun
1 (plural **faxes**) a piece of equipment for sending and receiving paper messages as electronic information through a telephone line. A fax is also called a fax machine.
2 (plural **faxes**) a message that you send or receive on paper using a fax machine or as an electronic file using a computer
3 a system for sending and receiving messages using a fax machine or computer

ORIGIN from *facsimile* meaning 'exact copy' (from Latin *fac simile* 'make similar')

fax verb
faxes, faxing, faxed
to send a message to someone using a fax machine or computer

fear noun fears
a very strong and unpleasant feeling you have when you think something bad might happen, for example when you are in danger

fear verb
fears, fearing, feared
1 to feel very worried or sad because you think something bad might happen or has happened *If I take my bike in the snow, Mum fears there could be an accident.*
2 to be frightened of someone because you think they will do something bad

fearful adjective
frightened

fearless adjective
not frightened of anything at all *These dogs are fearless.* **fearlessly** adverb

fearsome adjective
very frightening *a fearsome warrior*

feasible adjective
1 that can be done *Meeting next week just isn't feasible.*

SYNONYM possible

2 likely to be successful *a feasible plan*

feast noun feasts
1 a delicious meal for lots of people, usually for a special occasion *a wedding feast*
2 any delicious meal

feast verb
feasts, feasting, feasted
1 to eat and drink a lot *The guests feasted on beef and roast potatoes.*
2 to feast your eyes on something is to look at it for a long time and with a feeling of pleasure

feat noun feats
something important, difficult or brave that someone does, for example something that needs lots of skill or strength

feather noun feathers
one of the soft parts that cover the body and wings of a bird. A feather is made up of a long stiff centre with hairs on either side.

feathery adjective
soft and light like a feather or feathers *The clouds were very high and feathery.*

feature noun features
1 an important part or quality of something or someone, for example that makes them different or more attractive *A special feature of this smartphone is its powerful camera. The tourists admired the natural features of the landscape* (for example hills, rivers and forests).
2 your features are all the different parts that make up your face, for example your eyes, nose and mouth *Leah has long hair and delicate features.*
3 a piece of writing on a particular subject, for example in a newspaper or magazine
4 a programme on a particular subject, for example on TV, the radio or the internet

feature verb
features, featuring, featured
1 if something features something or someone, it includes them as an important part of itself *The exhibition features paintings by Monet.*
2 to be an important part of something *The film star featured in a documentary about the environment.*

February noun
the second month of the year, between January and March. February has 28 days but 29 days in a leap year (a year with one extra day).

ORIGIN from Latin *februarius* '(the month) of purification', referring to a Roman festival (called *Februa*) of washing and cleaning the body

feckless adjective
if someone is feckless, they are not responsible and are too weak or lazy to do anything properly

fed
past tense & past participle of **feed**

federal adjective
connected with a country or type of government in which different regions are allowed to make their own laws and decisions *the federal government of the United States*

federation noun federations
1 a country or region made up of a group of regions that have joined together *Germany is a federation.*
2 an organisation made up of a group of organisations that have joined together

fed up adjective
unhappy or slightly angry about something, especially something that has been going on for too long *I'm fed up with telling you to turn down that music.*

LANGUAGE EXTRA you say *fed up with*. Do not say *fed up of*.

fee noun fees
1 the money you pay someone, such as a doctor, lawyer or teacher, for work that they do for you *school fees*
2 the money you pay to be allowed to do something such as join a club or visit a museum *an entrance fee*

feeble adjective feebler, feeblest
if someone or something is feeble, they are weak *Granddad has become quite feeble. 'Help,' she said, in a feeble voice.*
feebly adverb

ORIGIN from Old French *feble* 'weak' (from Latin *flebilis* 'causing tears' and *flere* 'to cry')

feed verb
feeds, feeding, fed
1 to give food to someone or to an animal
2 to feed a baby is to give it milk

164

feed–ferment

3 to eat food *The chimpanzees go to the back of the cage to feed. Caterpillars feed on leaves.*
4 to put something into something, for example through a hole or opening *I kept feeding the printer with paper.*
5 to provide something or someone with something *The criminals fed false information to the police.*

feed *noun* **feeds**
1 an occasion when someone feeds a baby
2 food for animals
3 in computing, a feed is a way of storing the latest information about something and sending it to people's computers *Amy subscribes to the BBC news feed.*

feedback *noun*
useful information someone gives you about something, usually so that you know whether or not that thing is good or whether or not someone likes it *Ms Singh gave me positive feedback on my homework* (she said it was good and told me why). *The latest episode of 'Doctor Who' got some pretty bad feedback* (people didn't like it).

feel *verb*
feels, feeling, felt
1 to have a feeling (in your mind or body) or to be in a particular way because of a feeling (such as happiness, fear, hunger or weakness) *I felt anger. Do you feel any pain? Dad is feeling tired and hungry.*
2 to give someone a feeling of something *If I put my hand in the water, it feels cold.*
3 to touch something *Feel this material – it's really soft.*
4 to notice something, for example something touching you or happening to you *I felt someone push me. I felt that I was falling.*
5 to have an opinion about something *My parents feel that I have too much homework.*
6 to be affected or influenced by something *We'll soon be feeling the effects of the head teacher's changes.*
7 if you feel like something, you want to have it or do it *Do you feel like an ice cream? I feel like watching TV.*
8 if you feel up to doing something, you have enough energy or interest to really want to do it

feel *noun*
1 the feeling that something has when you touch it *I like the feel of this scarf.*
2 a particular quality that something has *These sculptures have a modern feel.*

feeler *noun* **feelers**
one of the two long thin parts on the head of an insect or animal such as a snail. Feelers are used, for example, for touching, seeing and smelling.

SYNONYM **antenna**

feeling *noun* **feelings**
1 something that exists in your mind and makes you behave in a certain way. Feelings are such things as happiness (or sadness), love (or hatred), liking (or dislike), anger, hope or worry.
2 something that exists in your body and makes you behave in a certain way *a feeling of tiredness; I have a painful feeling in my leg.*
3 when you are able to touch things or feel something with your body *I have no feeling in my left hand.*
4 someone's particular thought, idea or opinion about something *My feeling is that we should wait and see. There's a strong feeling against the president.*
5 to hurt someone's feelings is to make them feel upset, for example by saying something bad to them

feet
plural of **foot**

feign *verb*
feigns, feigning, feigned
to pretend to have a particular feeling or medical problem *She feigned illness.*

feline ['fee-line'] *adjective*
connected with cats

ORIGIN from Latin *feles* 'cat'

fell
past tense of **fall**

fell *verb*
fells, felling, felled
1 to cut down a tree
2 to knock someone to the ground with great strength

fell *noun* **fells**
an area of hilly ground or mountains, for example in the north of England

fellow *noun* **fellows**
1 another word for a man or boy *Ajit is a nice fellow.*
2 someone you share an activity or experience with, for example someone who goes to the same school as you

fellow *adjective*
used about someone you share an activity or experience with *a fellow traveller* (someone you travel with)

fellowship *noun*
1 a feeling of friendship
2 (*plural* **fellowships**) a group of people who share the same interests

felt
past tense & past participle of **feel**

felt *noun*
1 a thick soft cloth made from wool *a felt hat*
2 roofing felt is a thick building material made from paper and tar (thick sticky liquid). It is used for covering roofs.

felt-tip *noun* **felt-tips**
a felt-tip or felt-tip pen is a pen with a piece of felt at the end through which the ink comes out

female *adjective*
1 connected with girls or women *Over half our class is female.*
2 belonging to the sex that has babies (or baby animals) or produces eggs *a female cat*

ANTONYM **male**

female *noun* **females**
1 a girl or woman
2 an animal belonging to the sex that has baby animals or produces eggs

ANTONYM **male**

feminine *adjective*
1 connected with girls or women *a feminine point of view*
2 connected with the qualities people sometimes think of when they think about girls or women *She gave the room a feminine touch* (made it look attractive, for example).
3 used about the form of a part of speech, such as a pronoun, noun or adjective, that is different from the masculine form in some languages *'She' is a feminine pronoun.*
femininity *noun*

ANTONYM **masculine**

feminism *noun*
a belief that women should have the same power and opportunities as men

feminist *noun* **feminists**
a woman who believes in feminism
feminist *adjective*

fen *noun* **fens**
an area of flat and very wet land, for example in eastern England

fence *noun* **fences**
1 a structure made of wood or wire that is built around a piece of land such as a garden or field, for example to keep people out
2 a structure made of wood or a group of bushes that horses jump over in horse racing or show jumping

fence *verb*
fences, fencing, fenced
1 to build a fence around something, for example a field *The farmer has fenced in his animals.*
2 to fight with a special light sword in the sport of fencing
fencer *noun*

fencing *noun*
a sport in which two people fight each other with a special light sword

fend *verb*
fends, fending, fended
1 if you fend for yourself, you do things for yourself without anyone's help
2 if you fend something or someone off, you defend yourself, for example against an attack or difficult questions

fennel *noun*
a light green plant whose leaves, bulb and seeds are used for giving flavour to food

feral *adjective*
a feral animal is one that in the past lived among people but now lives as a wild animal *a feral cat*

ORIGIN from Latin *fera* 'wild animal'

ferment ['fer-ment'] *verb*
ferments, fermenting, fermented
if someone ferments a drink such as wine or beer, or if a drink ferments, a chemical change happens, produced by bacteria or micro-organisms that change the sugar into alcohol **fermentation** *noun*

ferment ['ferr-ment'] *noun*
when people behave in a noisy, excited and violent way, for example because they want to change a political situation *At the end of the eighteenth century France was in ferment.*

fern – fiancé

fern noun **ferns**
a plant with very big leaves shaped like feathers but with no flowers

ferocious adjective
1 violent and terrifying *a ferocious lion*; *He was killed in a ferocious attack.*
2 showing lots of energy or strong feelings such as anger *a ferocious critic*
3 very great and strong *The house burnt down in a ferocious blaze.*
ferociously adverb

ferocity noun
1 violence and horror *the ferocity of the attack*
2 great energy and strong feelings *the ferocity of their arguments*
3 great amount and strength *the ferocity of the fire*

ferret noun **ferrets**
a small furry animal with a long thin body. People sometimes use ferrets for hunting, for example rabbits, or they keep them as pets.

ferret verb
ferrets, ferreting, ferreted
1 if you ferret about for something, you look for something hidden among lots of other small things
2 if you ferret something out, you find something that is difficult to find, such as a piece of information

Ferris wheel noun **Ferris wheels**
a big upright wheel, usually at an amusement park. It has seats or passenger cars all around it that stay level as the wheel turns.

> ORIGIN from George W. G. *Ferris*, the engineer who built the first one in Chicago in 1893

> CULTURE NOTE the London Eye is one of the world's tallest *Ferris wheels*

ferry noun **ferries**
a boat that carries people, goods and cars across a river or for a short distance across a sea

ferry verb
ferries, ferrying, ferried
to take people or things for a short distance between two places, usually by boat, car or plane, and especially when this happens regularly *My stepdad ferries me to school every day.*

fertile adjective
1 good for growing things, especially plants for food *This land is very fertile.*

> ANTONYM sterile

2 a fertile person is able to produce babies, and a fertile animal can produce young animals

> ANTONYM sterile

3 a fertile imagination or mind produces interesting and original ideas
fertility noun

fertilise verb
fertilises, fertilising, fertilised
1 to put chemicals or manure (waste matter from animals such as horses or cows) on soil so that plants grow better
2 if a human or animal egg is fertilised, a male cell (smallest unit of living matter) called a sperm goes into it so that it grows into a new person or animal

3 if a plant is fertilised, a powder called pollen goes into it so that it produces seeds that grow into a new plant
fertilisation noun

> LANGUAGE EXTRA also spelt *fertilize* and *fertilization*

fertiliser noun **fertilisers**
a chemical substance or waste matter from animals (manure) that is put on soil so that plants grow better

> LANGUAGE EXTRA also spelt *fertilizer*

fervent adjective
showing a very strong feeling about something that you like or want *a fervent supporter of West Ham*; *a fervent hope*
fervently adverb

fervour noun
a very strong and enthusiastic feeling *religious fervour*

festival noun **festivals**
1 a series of events and activities that people organise, for example in which films or plays are shown or where people play music or dance. A festival often happens at the same time and in the same place every year. *The Edinburgh Festival takes place in August.*
2 a day or period for celebrating something, usually a religious event *Diwali is a Hindu festival.*

festive adjective
1 connected with celebrating *All the children love birthdays and other festive occasions.*
2 colourful, noisy or exciting because people are celebrating something *The school looked very festive.*
3 connected with Christmas *We're going to Italy for the festive season.*

festivities noun plural
events such as parties and shows for celebrating something

festooned adjective
if a thing or place is festooned with something, it is decorated with lots of that particular thing *The streets were festooned with flags.*

> ORIGIN from 17th century Italian *festone* 'ornament for a feast' (from Italian *festa* 'feast')

feta ['fet-er'] noun
feta or feta cheese is a type of white crumbly cheese from Greece, usually made from sheep's milk

fetch verb
fetches, fetching, fetched
1 to go and get something or someone
2 to come and get someone *I'm waiting in the playground – please fetch me now.*
3 to be sold for a particular amount of money *We sold all our books but they didn't fetch much.*

fête ['fayt'] noun **fêtes**
an event, usually outside, organised by a group such as a school or club to make money. There are games and things to buy including food and drinks.

> SYNONYM fair

> LANGUAGE EXTRA also spelt *fete*

fetid adjective
having a very bad smell *the fetid smell of rotten meat*

fetters noun plural
chains around a prisoner's ankles

fetus ['fee-ters'] noun **fetuses**
a human or animal baby that is developing in its mother's body. In humans an embryo becomes a fetus at around 10 weeks.

> LANGUAGE EXTRA also spelt *foetus*

compare: embryo

feud ['fyood'] noun **feuds**
a strong disagreement between two people or groups that lasts for a long time *a family feud*

feud ['fyood'] verb
feuds, feuding, feuded
if people feud, they have a strong disagreement that lasts for a long time

feudal ['fyoo-derl'] adjective
connected with feudalism *a feudal lord*

feudalism ['fyoo-der-liz-erm'] noun
a way of organising society in the Middle Ages. Ordinary people were allowed to live on land that belonged to rich people if they agreed to work and fight for them.

fever noun
1 (plural **fevers**) an illness that makes the body hot *Ayesha didn't go to school because she has a fever.*
2 a feeling of being very excited about something

feverish adjective
1 if someone is feverish, they feel ill and their body feels hot
2 feverish activity is something that you do very quickly because you are very excited *We were working at a feverish pace.*
feverishly adverb

few adjective & pronoun **fewer, fewest**
1 used when talking about a small number of things or people *I have a few things to do. Theo reads fewer books than his brother* (a smaller number of them). *A few of my friends came to my party.*
2 used when you mean only a small number of things or people or hardly any at all *Our team has few supporters.*
3 **quite a few** or **a good few** used when talking about a number of things or people that is large but not very large

> LANGUAGE EXTRA be careful not to confuse *a few* (a small number, for example *I have a few friends*) with *few* (not many at all, for example *I have few friends*)

fez noun **fezzes**
a small round red hat with sloping sides and a flat top and usually with a tassel (a group of hanging threads). Fezzes are sometimes worn by men in Muslim countries such as Turkey.

> ORIGIN from Turkish *fes* and the name *Fez*, a city in Morocco where fezzes were first made

fiancé ['fee-on-say'] noun **fiancés**
the man someone is engaged to and is going to marry

fiancée–fight

fiancée ['fee-on-say'] *noun* **fiancées**
the woman someone is engaged to and is going to marry

fiasco ['fee-ass-koh'] *noun* **fiascos**
something that is not successful, often something someone is ashamed about *Our school play was a complete fiasco.*

fib *noun* **fibs**
a lie someone tells about something that is not very important

fib *verb*
fibs, fibbing, fibbed
to tell a lie or tell lies about things that are not very important **fibber** *noun*

fibre ['fy-ber'] *noun*
1 (*plural* **fibres**) a long thin thread, used for example for making cloth or ropes
2 (*plural* **fibres**) a material such as cloth made up of long thin threads
3 a substance in fruit, vegetables and grains that your body cannot digest (change in the stomach). Fibre is useful because it helps food pass more quickly through the body. *a high-fibre diet* (with lots of fruit, vegetables and grains)

SYNONYM **roughage**

4 fibre optics is a technology that uses cables made of glass fibres to send information at very fast speeds

fibreglass *noun*
a type of light but strong plastic that contains thin threads of glass, used for example for making cars and boats

fickle *adjective*
1 if someone is fickle, they say they want or like something and then change their mind and say they don't want or like it
2 if the weather is fickle, it keeps changing

fiction *noun*
1 books and stories about people and things that are not real, for example novels and fairy stories
2 something that is not true or did not really happen *Sol won £1000! – Is that fact or fiction?*

fictional *adjective*
only happening in a work of fiction *Alice is a fictional character in Lewis Carroll's book.*

SYNONYM **imaginary**

fictitious *adjective*
not true or real *He registered online with a fictitious address. The events in this film are fictitious.*

fiddle *verb*
fiddles, fiddling, fiddled
1 to keep moving or touching something with your fingers *Stop fiddling with your pen!*
2 if you fiddle around with something, such as a machine, you keep doing things to it, for example to make it work or to make it work better
3 to give false information about something in order to get or to save money *My mum's boss has been fiddling his expenses for years.*
4 to play the violin, for example for playing folk music

fiddle *noun* **fiddles**
1 a dishonest way of getting or saving money by giving false information *Charlie's dad is on the fiddle.*
2 another word for a violin

fiddler *noun* **fiddlers**
1 someone who plays the violin, for example to play folk music
2 a dishonest person who gives false information to get or to save money

fiddly *adjective* **fiddlier, fiddliest**
if something is fiddly, it is difficult to do or to use because you have to pay attention to very small details or deal with very small things *Eating with chopsticks can be a bit fiddly. Your mobile is very fiddly* (the screen is too small, for example).

fidelity *noun*
being faithful to someone or something

fidget *verb*
fidgets, fidgeting, fidgeted
1 to keep making small movements with your body, for example because you're bored, nervous or uncomfortable
2 if you fidget with something, you keep moving or touching it

fidget *noun* **fidgets**
someone who keeps fidgeting all the time

fidgety *adjective*
fidgeting all the time

field *noun* **fields**
1 a piece of land in the countryside where farmers grow plants or keep animals or which is covered in grass
2 an area of land covered in grass and painted with lines where people play sports such as football *a sports field*
3 an area of land where something such as coal or gas is found *a coal field*
4 a particular subject or type of work *What field is your dad in?*
5 a space in a database or in a form on a website for one piece of information, such as a name or address *I typed my user name and password into the correct fields.*
6 a field trip is an occasion when you go with your school to learn about things such as plants or rocks in their own environment or about the history of a place *We went to Belgium on a field trip to study the history of the Battle of Waterloo.*

field *verb*
fields, fielding, fielded
1 in cricket, baseball or rounders, the team that fields is the one that throws and tries to catch the ball and not the team that hits it
2 in cricket, baseball or rounders, to field a ball is to catch it or pick it up
fielder *noun*

field marshal *noun* **field marshals**
an army officer with the highest possible rank, above the rank of general

fieldwork *noun*
practical work and study that is done outside school *geography fieldwork*

fiend *noun* **fiends**
1 a very evil and cruel person

SYNONYM **monster**

2 an evil spirit

3 someone who really likes a particular thing or doing a particular activity *a football fiend*

SYNONYM **fanatic**

fiendish *adjective*
1 very evil and cruel
2 very clever but bad *a fiendish plan*
3 very difficult *In the quiz we had some really fiendish questions.*

fiendishly *adverb*
extremely, especially in a way that shows that you think a situation is bad *fiendishly difficult; Watch out, he's fiendishly clever.*

fierce *adjective* **fiercer, fiercest**
1 violent and angry *a fierce dog*
2 showing strong feelings such as anger *a fierce argument*
3 very strong *fierce winds; fierce competition*
fierceness *noun*

fiercely *adverb*
1 violently and angrily *The dog attacked him fiercely.*
2 very strongly *The winds were blowing fiercely.*
3 very *fiercely competitive*

fiery ['fier' rhymes with 'higher'] *adjective*
fierier, fieriest
1 showing feelings very easily, for example feelings of anger or enthusiasm *He has a fiery temper.*
2 angry *a fiery debate*
3 very bright, red or hot like a fire *a fiery sunset; The sun is a fiery ball of gas.*

fiesta *noun* **fiestas**
an occasion when Spanish-speaking people celebrate something, for example with music and dancing, especially a religious festival

fifteen *adjective & noun* **fifteens**
the number 15 **fifteenth** *adjective & noun*

fifth *adjective & noun*
1 used about something or someone that comes in place number 5 *on the fifth day*
2 (*plural* **fifths**) one of 5 equal parts of something *a fifth of the class*

fifty *adjective & noun* **fifties**
1 the number 50
2 the fifties are the fiftieth to fifty-ninth years of a century, for example 1950 to 1959
3 if someone is in their fifties, they are between 50 and 59 years old
fiftieth *adjective & noun*

fifty-fifty *adverb & adjective*
1 in two equal parts *We shared the money fifty-fifty.*
2 if there is a fifty-fifty chance of something happening, there is the same chance of it happening as there is of it not happening

fig *noun* **figs**
a soft sweet fruit full of tiny seeds. Figs have a green or purple skin and are often eaten dried (the water has been removed).

fight *verb*
fights, fighting, fought
1 if people or animals fight, they try to hurt each other, for example by hitting
2 to take part in a war or battle against an enemy, for example using weapons *In 1939 Britain was fighting Germany. There are many battles to fight. Who are they fighting against?*

fight – filly

3 to take part in something that you want to win *to fight an election*
4 to try very hard to do, get or stop something *When the fire broke out, we fought our way out of the building. Our team is fighting for a place in the semi-final. A doctor's job is to fight disease.*
5 to talk to someone in a very angry way *I'm always fighting with my sister.*

> SYNONYM to argue

6 if someone is fighting for their life, they are very ill or badly hurt and trying very hard to stay alive

fight *noun* **fights**
1 a situation in which people or animals try to hurt each other *There's a fight in the corridor.*
2 a situation in which enemies attack each other with weapons in a war

> SYNONYM battle

3 a great effort to do, get or stop something *a fight to get the truth*; *the fight against cancer*

> SYNONYM battle

4 an argument *I had a fight with my parents.*

fighter *noun* **fighters**
1 someone who fights, for example in a war or to try to do or get something
2 a small plane that destroys other planes *My great-granddad was a fighter pilot.*

figment *noun* **figments**
if something is a figment of your imagination, it only exists in your mind

figurative *adjective*
used for describing the meaning of a word or expression that is different from its usual meaning, for example the word 'heart' in 'the heart of the problem'. The usual meaning is known as the literal meaning.

> LANGUAGE EXTRA *figurative language* uses *figures of speech*. Some of the main figures of speech are: comparisons such as similes (*Grandma is as old as the hills*) and metaphors (*Isla's face was a blank page*); exaggeration (*I have a sky-high pile of books to read*); personification (*The sea danced in the moonlight*).
> You use words in a figurative way to make your writing more interesting and to create a particular image in the mind of the reader.

figuratively *adverb*
used for saying that the way you use a word or expression is different from the way it is usually used *I was dead, figuratively speaking.*

figure *noun* **figures**
1 one of the symbols that represent the numbers 0 to 9 *Write your age in figures not letters.*
2 an official number or amount of something *The school produced a list of facts and figures.*
3 the shape of a person's body *A tall figure with long hair appeared at the window.*
4 a model of a person or of an animal in art *a bronze figure of Julius Caesar*

5 an important person *He's a famous figure in British music.*
6 a character in a play or book *Hamlet is shown as a sad and tragic figure.*
7 a shape in mathematics *An octagon is an eight-sided figure.*
8 a drawing in a book *Figure 5 shows Alice talking to the Cheshire Cat.*
9 a figure of eight is the shape 8. It is used for describing types of knots or ways of dancing or ice-skating, for example.

figure *verb*
figures, figuring, figured
1 to think that something is likely to be true *I figured it was time to go home.*
2 to be included in something *The hero doesn't figure in the first chapter.*
3 if you figure something out, you manage to understand it *I couldn't figure out what the teacher was saying.*

figurehead *noun* **figureheads**
1 someone who leads a country or organisation but has no real power
2 a painted model, usually of a person or animal, that was fixed to the front of an old-fashioned sailing ship

figure of speech *noun* **figures of speech**
an expression that uses words in an unusual way, for example in a meaning that is different from its usual meaning, to make your writing more interesting. Figures of speech include similes, metaphors, hyperbole (exaggeration), personification and alliteration.
see: figurative

figure skating *noun*
a type of skating on ice in which skaters make movements such as spinning and jumping

figurine *noun* **figurines**
a small model of a person or animal, made for example out of wood, china or stone

filament *noun* **filaments**
a very thin piece of something such as the wire inside a light bulb

filch *verb*
filches, filching, filched
an informal way of saying to steal something, especially something small or not very important

file *noun* **files**
1 a piece of information stored on a computer, with its own name and often kept inside a folder (a folder for a group of files). Files have a special ending, called a file extension, written as three or four letters following a dot (for example .jpeg). The extension tells you what type of file it is, for example a picture file or word file.
2 a container such as a folded envelope or a box where you store letters and documents
3 a steel tool with a flat rough side, shaped like a stick with a handle. It is used for making wood or metal surfaces smooth.
4 a small thin tool with a flat rough side, used for rubbing on your fingernails or toenails to give them a round and smooth shape
5 *in single file* standing one behind the other in a line

file *verb*
files, filing, filed
1 to store a document or letter in a container
2 if people file somewhere, they walk there one behind the other
3 if you file something down, you rub it with a tool to make it smooth

filename *noun* **filenames**
the name you give to a computer file

filing cabinet *noun* **filing cabinets**
a piece of office furniture like a chest of drawers, usually made of metal. It is used for storing documents in.

Filipino *adjective*
connected with the Philippines

Filipino *noun* **Filipinos**
someone from the Philippines

fill *verb*
fills, filling, filled
1 to make something full so that it can hold no more *I filled the cup with tea.*
2 to put lots of something into something *The teacher filled my head with facts.*
3 to go into all parts of something *Music filled the air.*
4 to give someone a strong feeling of something *What she said filled me with anger.*
5 if something fills or fills up, it becomes full *The park filled with people enjoying the sunshine. The cinema filled up quickly.*
6 to put something into a hole so that there is no hole left *The dentist filled my tooth.*
7 if you fill in or fill out a form, you put information on it, for example your name and address
8 if you fill someone up, you give them enough food so that they are not hungry
9 if a meal or particular food fills you up, you no longer feel hungry after eating it

fill *noun*
if you eat your fill, you eat enough of something

filler *noun* **fillers**
a substance used for repairing holes, for example in wood, plastic or walls

fillet *noun* **fillets**
a piece of fish or meat with the bones taken out

filling *adjective*
if food is filling, you no longer feel hungry after eating it or it makes you full quickly

filling *noun* **fillings**
1 the action of a dentist filling the hole in someone's tooth, or the material (such as metal or plastic) that the dentist uses for this *Tomorrow I'm having a filling.*
2 the food that you put inside something such as a pie, cake or sandwich *a pie with an apple filling*
3 the soft material inside something such as a cushion
4 a filling station is a place where someone buys petrol or diesel for their car

filly *noun* **fillies**
a young female horse

> LANGUAGE EXTRA a young male horse is *a colt*

film–fine

film *noun* films
1 a moving picture that you watch in a cinema, on TV or online

SYNONYM movie

2 a thin layer on the surface of something *The statue was covered by a film of dirt.*
3 a thin plastic strip or roll used by a camera for taking photos or making moving pictures, especially in the past

film *verb* films, filming, filmed
1 to make a moving picture of something to be shown in a cinema, on TV or online *They're going to film 'Great Expectations'.*
2 to take moving pictures of something using something such as a camcorder or mobile phone camera *Mum filmed Harry's birthday party.*

filmgoer *noun* filmgoers
someone who goes to see films a lot

film-maker *noun* film-makers
someone who makes a film
film-making *noun*

SYNONYM director

film star *noun* film stars
a very famous actor in films

filter *noun* filters
1 an object or piece of equipment that separates something from something else, for example by allowing very small things or liquids to pass through it *a dust filter; filter paper* (used for making coffee, for example); *You can separate sand and water using a filter.*
2 a computer program or tool for performing different sorts of actions, such as removing or blocking unwanted information, changing an image or changing the order of things in a list

filter *verb* filters, filtering, filtered
1 to pass something through a filter, for example to remove small things or liquids or to get rid of unwanted things
2 to remove unwanted information on a computer, for example by organising it in a particular way in an email or spreadsheet program or by checking and blocking it *My antivirus filters everything I download. My email program filters out the spam.*
3 if something such as news or light filters somewhere, only a little of it reaches a person or place *News of the earthquake is beginning to filter through. A ray of light filtered through the curtains.*
4 if people filter somewhere, they go there slowly *At the sound of the bell, children started to filter into the classrooms.*

filth *noun*
another word for dirt, especially when there is a lot of it and it is very unpleasant

filthy *adjective* filthier, filthiest
1 very dirty *The kitchen floor was filthy.*
2 very bad *filthy weather*
3 connected with sex *a filthy joke*
filthiness *noun*

fin *noun* fins
1 one of the thin flat parts of a fish that stick out from its body. A fish uses its fins for swimming and balancing.
2 one of the two rubber shoes that swimmers and divers use to help them to swim

SYNONYM flipper

3 a part on the back of an aircraft that sticks up and helps it to fly

final *adjective*
1 coming at the end of something or after all the others *the final score of the match; my final day in school*

SYNONYM last

2 if something such as a decision, answer or offer is final, it is the very last one and cannot be changed
3 finishing or putting an end to something *We're making the final arrangements.*
4 used for telling someone that you definitely won't change your mind *I'm not going to bed, and that's final!*

final *noun* finals
the last game or race in a whole series of games or races that make up a competition. The winner of the final is the winner of the competition.

finale ['fi-nah-lee'] *noun* finales
the last part of a show or piece of music, especially when this includes a lot of exciting things happening or lots of people

finalise *verb* finalises, finalising, finalised
to finish the last details of something, for example a plan, agreement or piece of writing, so that it is complete

LANGUAGE EXTRA also spelt *finalize*

finalist *noun* finalists
a player or team that reaches the final in a competition

finally *adverb*
1 after a long time *The letter finally arrived.*
2 used when talking about the last action that comes after all the others *I lost my balance, fell over and finally banged my head.*
3 used when talking about the last thing you want to say *Finally, I want to thank my teachers.*

finance *noun*
1 the activity of dealing with money, for example how money is spent, saved, borrowed and lent
2 the money needed to pay for something
3 someone's finances are the amount of money they have and how well it is organised *The school's finances are good* (the school has lots of money and is spending it well).

finance *verb* finances, financing, financed
to pay money for something or to someone

financial *adjective*
connected with money *Megan's parents have financial problems.*

financially *adverb*
used when talking about money *financially successful* (having lots of money); *Financially, things are bad* (there isn't much money).

finch *noun* finches
a small bird with a short strong beak

find *verb* finds, finding, found
1 to get or see something that you've been looking for *I've found my keys.*
2 to get or see something by chance *Evie found a spider in the bathroom.*
3 to get something that you want, for example something you've been looking for or thinking about *My brother has found work. At last I've found an explanation.*
4 to have a particular situation happen by chance *When I got home, I found the house empty.*
5 to learn something that you didn't know before *I found that there were lots of mistakes in the book.*
6 to have an opinion about something or think in a certain way *I find these ideas amazing. We find this difficult to believe.*
7 to have a particular feeling *I find it difficult to walk.*
8 if you find time or money to do something, you have enough time or money to do it
9 if you find something out, you learn something you didn't know before *They found out the truth. I want to find out how she did it.*
10 if you find someone out, you learn that they have done something wrong

find *noun* finds
something that someone finds by chance, especially something good

find and replace *noun*
a tool on a computer that you use to find particular letters, words, numbers or symbols in a text document and replace them with others

findings *noun plural*
information that someone has found out after studying all the facts of a particular subject

fine *adjective* finer, finest
1 very good *Amit is a really fine player. This is Turner's finest painting* (best painting).
2 good enough *Your test results are not brilliant but they're fine.*
3 if the weather is fine, it is pleasant and not raining
4 in good health *I'm feeling fine.*
5 not hurt *I slipped over but I'm fine.*
6 used for saying yes or for agreeing to something *'Do you want to play football?' – 'Fine!'*
7 very thin *a fine hair*
8 attractive, small and thin *She has fine hands.*

SYNONYM delicate

9 made up of very small parts or drops *This sugar is very fine. It's raining but it's just a fine drizzle.*

fine *adverb*
well or well enough *With these new glasses I can see fine. Granddad was ill but he's doing fine* (getting on well).

fine *noun* fines
1 money someone must pay as a punishment, usually for breaking the law *a parking fine; The motorcycle driver got a fine* (had to pay money).

169

fine – fire station

2 money someone must pay to a library for returning a book (or something else they borrow) after the date it is supposed to be returned

fine *verb*
fines, fining, fined
to make someone pay money as a punishment, usually for breaking the law

finely *adverb*
1 into small thin pieces *Slice the cucumber finely.*
2 in a careful and attractive way, for example with lots of details *a finely drawn picture of a tree*

SYNONYM **delicately**

3 very well *finely dressed*

finery *noun*
beautiful clothes and jewels

fine-tune *verb*
fine-tunes, fine-tuning, fine-tuned
to make very small changes to something to finish it completely and make it as good as it can be

finger *noun* **fingers**
1 one of the four long thin parts at the end of your hand next to your thumb
2 something shaped like a finger

finger *verb*
fingers, fingering, fingered
to touch something with your fingers

fingermark *noun* **fingermarks**
a dirty mark on something made with your fingers

LANGUAGE EXTRA also spelt *finger mark*

fingernail *noun* **fingernails**
the hard smooth part at the end of each of your fingers

fingerprint *noun* **fingerprints**
a mark made on something by the pattern of lines in the skin at the end of your finger *The thief's fingerprints were on the gun.*

fingertip *noun* **fingertips**
1 your fingertips are the ends of your fingers
2 if you have something at your fingertips, for example information or facts, you can find it and use it very easily

finicky *adjective*
if someone is finicky, they are difficult to please because they pay too much attention to little things or small details *My sister is a finicky eater* (she only eats some types of food, for example).

finish *verb*
finishes, finishing, finished
1 to do or deal with the last part of something so that there is nothing left to do *I've finished my homework. Have you finished eating? I want to finish off the last chapter quickly before I go to bed.*
2 if something finishes, it stops or stops happening *School finishes at three o'clock.*
3 to be in a certain position, for example in a race *She finished third.*

SYNONYM **to come**

4 to eat or drink all or the rest of something *I was so hungry I finished off the cake. Finish* (or *finish up*) *your dinner before you eat any sweets.*

5 to finish someone off is to do something very bad to them such as kill them or destroy their reputation
6 to finish up somewhere or with something is to be in a place or get something, after a certain amount of time, that you were not expecting to *We took a train and finished up in Paris. I fell over and finished up with a bruise.*

SYNONYM **to end up**

7 if you've finished with something, you don't need it or are not using it any longer

finish *noun* **finishes**
1 the end of something
2 the way something looks or feels on the surface *This table has a rough finish.*

finished *adjective*
1 if something is finished, it has been done
2 if someone is finished, they're not doing something any longer *Are you finished?*
3 if someone is finished with something, they're not using it any longer *I'm finished with the book.*
4 not able to continue any longer, for example because you are in serious trouble *After what happened, he's finished as a footballer.*

finishing line *noun* **finishing lines**
a line marked on the ground to show where a race ends. It is sometimes called a finish line.
compare: **winning post**

finite [rhymes with 'highlight'] *adjective*
in grammar, a finite verb is a verb form that shows its person and tense. For example, 'I do', 'he does' and 'they did' are finite forms but 'doing', 'to do' and 'done' are not.

ORIGIN from Latin *finitus* 'finished'

Finland *noun*
a country in Northern Europe

Finn *noun* **Finns**
someone from Finland

Finnish *adjective*
connected with Finland or the Finnish language

Finnish *noun*
the language people speak in Finland

fiord ['fee-ord'] *noun* **fiords**
a narrow part of the sea between steep cliffs, usually in Norway

LANGUAGE EXTRA also spelt *fjord*

fir *noun* **firs**
a tall tree with thin pointed leaves that stay green in winter

fire *noun* **fires**
1 the flames and heat that come from something burning and that usually destroy or damage something *The plane's engine caught fire* (started burning).
2 a small area where someone burns something, such as wood or coal, for example to get heat or cook food *The Scouts lit a fire beside the river.*
3 something that heats a room using electricity or gas *a gas fire*
4 shooting from a gun or guns *The soldiers opened fire* (started to shoot).
5 if something is on fire, it is burning *The roof was on fire.*
6 if you set fire to something, you make it start burning

fire *verb*
fires, firing, fired
1 if someone fires or fires a gun (or if a gun fires), one or more bullets are shot from it *The soldiers fired on the crowd.*
2 to tell someone to leave their job *My dad's just been fired.*

SYNONYM **to sack**

3 to fire questions at someone is to ask them lots of questions

fire alarm *noun* **fire alarms**
a piece of equipment that warns you of a fire by making a loud noise

firearm *noun* **firearms**
another word for a gun, especially a small one

fire brigade *noun* **fire brigades**
a group of people whose job is to put out fires and rescue people, for example from fires or car accidents

firecracker *noun* **firecrackers**
a firework that makes a loud noise when it goes off

SYNONYM **banger**

fire drill *noun* **fire drills**
an exercise in which people pretend that a building is on fire and that they have to get out safely

fire engine *noun* **fire engines**
a vehicle that firefighters use to take them to where a fire is and to carry their equipment

fire escape *noun* **fire escapes**
a metal staircase on the outside of a building that people use to get out of the building if there is a fire

fire extinguisher *noun* **fire extinguishers**
a large metal tube containing a chemical that you spray onto a small fire to put it out

firefighter *noun* **firefighters**
someone whose job is to put out fires and rescue people, for example from fires or car accidents. A male firefighter is also called a fireman and a female firefighter is called a firewoman.

fireplace *noun* **fireplaces**
1 an opening in the wall of a room where people make a fire to heat the room
2 a frame, for example of tiles or bricks, that surrounds this opening

fireproof *adjective*
if something is fireproof, it cannot burn or be damaged by fire

fireside *noun*
the area in a room that is close to the fire *I fell asleep at the fireside.*

fire station *noun* **fire stations**
the building where fire engines are kept and where firefighters wait until they are needed

firewall–fishy

firewall *noun* firewalls
1 a piece of computer software or hardware that protects your computer when you use the internet or another network. It stops people using your computer or stealing information from it.
2 a strong wall that stops fire from spreading from one part of a building to another

firewood *noun*
small pieces of wood for burning in a fire

firework *noun* fireworks
a small object containing chemicals that explode with a loud noise when someone lights it. Fireworks send sparks or bright lights into the air and people use them to celebrate important events. *a 5th November firework display*

firing squad *noun* firing squads
a group of soldiers who shoot and kill someone as a punishment

firm *adjective* firmer, firmest
1 if something is firm, it is fairly hard but not completely hard *I like firm tomatoes in my salad.*
2 if something that is able to move is firm, it is fixed or held in a place so that it no longer moves *Hold the ladder to make sure it's firm.*

SYNONYM steady

3 done with a lot of strength *a firm grip; a firm handshake*
4 not likely to change *a firm decision*
5 based on facts *We're waiting for firm news.*
6 very strong or strongly felt *a firm belief; Dad's a firm believer in homework.*
7 if you are firm with someone, you say what you think very strongly so they take notice of you

firmness *noun*

firm *noun* firms
a business or company *My mum works for a firm of solicitors.*

firmly *adverb*
1 very strongly *She held my arm firmly.*
2 showing your feelings very strongly in what you say *Mum told me firmly that I had to tidy up my room.*
3 safely and completely *Make sure your seat belt is firmly attached.*

firmware *noun*
a type of software that makes a piece of electronic equipment work, for example a mobile phone, digital camera or remote control

first *adjective*
1 coming before the others or before another

ANTONYM last

2 if you do something for the first time, you have never done it before
3 if you do something first thing, you do it early in the morning before doing anything else
4 most important *A teacher's first duty is to his or her pupils.*
5 the first prize is the prize given to the person who wins a competition

6 **at first sight** when you have a quick look at someone or something and before you've looked at them more closely

first *adverb*
1 before anything else *You can watch TV but you must do your homework first. First of all wash your hands* (before doing anything at all).
2 before the others or before another *Mohammed arrived first.*

ANTONYM last

3 used about something that has never happened before *I first met him in Durham.*
4 if you put something first, you think of it as the most important thing *You must put your schoolwork first.*

first *noun*
1 the person who comes before the others or who does something before the others *Ava was the first to finish.*

ANTONYM last

2 the thing that comes before the others or happens before anything else *Our school was the first to be built.*

ANTONYM last

3 something that has never happened before *Our team won – that was a first!*
4 **at first** at the beginning of something

first aid *noun*
simple medical help that is given quickly to someone injured or ill

first class *noun*
the best and most expensive way of sending something by post or travelling somewhere, for example by train or plane *Use first class if you want the letter to arrive the next day. I've never travelled in first class before.*

first class *adverb*
used about a first-class way of sending something or travelling *to send a letter first class; to travel first class*

first-class *adjective*
1 used for describing a level, quality or person of the highest standard *a first-class piece of homework; a first-class teacher*

SYNONYM first-rate

2 connected with the best and most expensive way of sending something by post or travelling somewhere, for example by train or plane *a first-class stamp; a first-class seat*

first cousin *noun* first cousins
a son or daughter of your aunt or uncle

first floor *noun* first floors
the floor of a building that is above the floor at the bottom level

LANGUAGE EXTRA in American English, the *first floor* is the floor at the bottom level of a building. The bottom floor is called the *ground floor* in British English.

first footing *noun*
a tradition, mainly in Scotland, of visiting someone's home to bring them luck as soon as a New Year starts

first-hand *adjective & adverb*
if you get first-hand information, or get information first-hand from someone, you get it directly through speaking to someone, not from other people

firstly *adverb*
used when talking about the first thing that happened or that you want to say *Firstly, let me say sorry, and secondly, I want to explain what happened.*

LANGUAGE EXTRA used in careful speaking or writing instead of *first*

first name *noun* first names
the first part of your name that you were given when you were born. Some examples of first names are Isabella, Emily, Daniel and Kareem.

first-rate *adjective*
used for describing a level, quality or person of the highest standard *a first-rate football player*

SYNONYM first-class

firth *noun* firths
a place where a river flows into the sea, especially in Scotland *the Firth of Forth*

fish *noun*
1 (*plural* fish or fishes) an animal that lives in water. Fish use fins to swim and gills to breathe.
2 the flesh of a fish eaten as food

fish *verb*
fishes, fishing, fished
1 to try to catch fish to eat or as a sport
2 to try to find something inside a small space *Mum was fishing for her keys in her bag.*
3 to try to get someone to tell you something *Josh was fishing for information.*
4 to fish something out is to pull it or take it out from somewhere *I fished out a pen from my pocket. A body was fished out of the river.*

fishcake *noun* fishcakes
a small round cake made of cooked fish and mashed potato

fisherman *noun* fishermen
someone who catches fish for their job or as a sport

fisherwoman *noun* fisherwomen
a woman who catches fish for her job or as a sport

fish finger *noun* fish fingers
a piece of fish shaped like a rectangle and about the size of a finger. It is covered in breadcrumbs, cooked and frozen, and sold with others in a packet.

fishing *noun*
1 the sport or business of catching fish
2 a fishing rod is a long thin pole for catching fish, usually made from glass fibres (long thin threads) or bamboo (grass with hard hollow stems). It has a string attached to it with a hook at the end.

fishmonger *noun* fishmongers
someone who sells fish, usually in a shop

fishy *adjective* fishier, fishiest
1 making you feel that something is wrong or dishonest *There's something a bit fishy about her.*

171

fist – flagship

2 a fishy smell or taste is a smell or taste of fish

fist *noun* **fists**
a hand with the fingers closed tightly into the palm, for example for hitting someone or for showing that you're angry *The bully made a fist.*

fit *adjective* **fitter, fittest**
1 if someone is fit, they are in very good health, for example because they do exercises to keep their body strong
2 good enough for something *a feast fit for a king*; *This fish is not fit to eat.*
3 well enough to do something *Mum's tired and not fit to drive.*
4 having good enough qualities to do something *Alfie's behaviour is so bad he's not fit to be in our team.*
5 ready to do something *I'd walked so much I was fit to drop* (so tired I was about to fall over).
6 a slang word for good-looking
7 if you see or think fit to do something, you think that is the best thing to do *My parents saw fit to keep me home from school.*

> SIMILE 'as fit as a fiddle' means very fit (sense 1)

fit *verb*
fits, fitting, fitted
1 to be the right size or shape for something or someone *These shoes fit me nicely.*
2 to put something or someone into a certain place, for example because they are the right size or shape to go there or because there is enough room for them *Can we fit some more books in the box?*
3 if something or someone fits somewhere, they go into that place, for example because they have the right size or shape to go there *Does the key fit the lock?*
4 to add something or fix something somewhere, for example a piece of equipment *My parents want to fit a burglar alarm to our house.*
5 to be similar to or connected with something or right for something *She fits the description of the person I saw. The punishment should fit the crime.*

> SYNONYM to match

6 if someone in a group does not fit in, they do not belong there *The new girl had trouble fitting in.*
7 if someone who is very busy (such as a doctor or dentist) fits someone in, they have just enough time to deal with that person

fit *noun* **fits**
1 a short period when you cannot control an action of your body (such as coughing or laughing) or when you have a strong feeling (such as anger or panic) that you cannot control *I had a sneezing fit. She slammed the door in a fit of anger.*
2 a sudden illness in which someone becomes unconscious for a short time *an epileptic fit*
3 something being the right size or shape *These jeans are a good fit.*
4 **in fits and starts** stopping and starting lots of times *My sister does her homework in fits and starts.*

fitness *noun*
very good health, which you get by exercising, for example *Harry walks to school to improve his fitness.*

fitted *adjective*
1 made to fit a particular space exactly *a fitted carpet* (covers a whole room or area); *a fitted kitchen* (for example with cupboards, cooker, fridge and sink as a fixed part of it)
2 if something is fitted with something, it already has it *These new houses are fitted with solar panels.*

fitter *noun* **fitters**
someone whose job is to put together, make or install machines and equipment

fitting *adjective*
right or suitable *That was a fitting end to a lovely day.*

fitting *noun* **fittings**
1 a small part connected to something such as a piece of equipment
2 a piece of equipment fixed inside a building, for example a washing machine or cooker. Fittings can be moved if you move house.
compare: **fixture**
3 when you try on a piece of clothing to see how it looks *a fitting room* (for example in a department store)

five *adjective & noun* **fives**
the number 5

fiver *noun* **fivers** (informal)
a piece of paper money worth £5

five-star *adjective*
of the highest possible quality *a five-star hotel*

fix *verb*
fixes, fixing, fixed
1 to make something work again or to make it as good as it was before *Mum fixed the computer.*

> SYNONYM to repair

2 to put something somewhere so that it doesn't move *I fixed the star onto the Christmas tree with ribbon.*
3 to make plans for something to happen *We've fixed up a meeting for tomorrow.*
4 to decide or choose something and not change it later *They've fixed a date to deliver the new laptop.*
5 to fix something up, such as a house or room, is to paint it and repair it

> SYNONYM to do up

6 in American English, to fix a meal or drink is to prepare it *I'll fix dinner tonight.*

fix *noun* **fixes**
1 a difficult situation *Ben's in a fix.*
2 to get a fix on something such as a ship is to find its exact position with measurements and a compass or using a computer with GPS (a system using radio waves from satellites)
3 **a quick fix** an easy solution to a problem

fixation *noun* **fixations**
a very strong and sometimes strange interest in something or someone. A fixation is not normal.

fixed *adjective*
used for describing something that does not change *fixed prices*; *fixed ideas*; *They've taken on an extra teacher for a fixed period of one term.*

fixture *noun* **fixtures**
1 a sports event planned for a certain date and time *a list of the latest football fixtures*
2 something fixed inside a building, for example a cupboard or bath. Fixtures cannot be moved if you move house.
compare: **fitting**

fizz *verb*
fizzes, fizzing, fizzed
if liquid fizzes, it produces small bubbles and makes a soft hissing sound **fizz** *noun*

fizzle *verb*
fizzles, fizzling, fizzled
1 if something fizzles, it makes a hissing sound
2 if something fizzles out, for example a flame, relationship or hope, it gradually disappears or stops happening

fizzy *adjective* **fizzier, fizziest**
a fizzy drink is one that has lots of small bubbles in it

> SYNONYM carbonated

> ANTONYM still

fjord ['fee-ord'] *noun* **fjords**
a narrow part of the sea between steep cliffs, usually in Norway

> LANGUAGE EXTRA also spelt *fiord*

flab *noun*
loose flesh on the body, for example around the stomach

flabbergasted *adjective*
very surprised about something

flabby *adjective* **flabbier, flabbiest**
having loose flesh on the body *He's quite flabby. Granddad has a flabby stomach.*
flabbiness *noun*

flag *noun* **flags**
1 a piece of cloth, usually shaped like a rectangle, with special colours and a special pattern, shape or picture on it. Flags are used for representing countries and organisations, for example.
2 a piece of coloured cloth, used for giving a signal, for example, or for decoration

flag *verb*
flags, flagging, flagged
1 to become weak or get less *Interest is beginning to flag.*
2 to become tired *After three hours' homework I began to flag.*
3 if you flag down a car or taxi, you wave your hand to make it stop

flagpole *noun* **flagpoles**
a tall pole at the top of which hangs a flag. A flagpole is usually attached to something such as a building or fixed to the ground.

flagship *noun* **flagships**
1 the most important ship of a group of ships belonging to a country's navy
2 the most important store or product of a group of stores or products *The company's flagship store is on Oxford Street.*

flagstone *noun* **flagstones**
a flat stone for making things such as paths, patios and walls. Flagstones come in different shapes and sizes.

flair *noun*
1 if you have a flair for something, you have a natural skill that makes you good at it *My brother has a flair for languages.*
2 a way of doing things that shows you have style and imagination

flake *noun* **flakes**
1 a small thin piece that comes off something
2 flakes of snow are pieces of falling snow

flake *verb*
flakes, flaking, flaked
1 to come off in small thin pieces *The walls are flaking.*
2 (informal) to flake out is to fall asleep or be unable to concentrate, for example because you're so tired

flaky *adjective* **flakier, flakiest**
1 coming off in small thin pieces *flaky skin*
2 breaking into small thin pieces *flaky pastry*
3 (informal) if someone is flaky, they are slightly strange

flame *noun* **flames**
hot bright gas that comes from something burning. Flames are often long and narrow and are different colours (for example white, yellow, orange or blue) depending on what is burning and how hot it is. *The flame of the burner is too high. The building went up in flames* (caught fire).

flamenco *noun*
1 (*plural* **flamencos**) a type of Spanish dance
2 the type of guitar playing that goes with flamenco dancing

flamingo *noun* **flamingos**
a large bird with long legs, a long neck and usually pink and white feathers. Flamingos live near water.

flammable *adjective*
easy to catch fire

flan *noun* **flans**
an open pie that has a pastry base (bottom part made from a mixture of flour, water and fat) and is filled with things such as cheese, fruit or vegetables

Flanders *noun*
a region in Belgium

flank *noun* **flanks**
the side of something such as a mountain or an animal's body

flannel *noun*
1 (*plural* **flannels**) a soft cloth that soaks up water, used for washing your face or body
2 a soft material made from wool or cotton, used for making clothes

flap *noun* **flaps**
1 a thin flat part of something, such as cloth, paper or wood, that can be moved up or down or from side to side because it is fixed to something along one of its sides only *a cat flap* (for letting cats go in and out of a house)
2 the noise of something flapping, such as the wings of a bird
3 the flaps of an aircraft are the parts that move up and down along the back of the wings. The flaps allow the pilot to control speed.
4 (informal) if someone is in a flap about something, they have feelings of fear, worry or nervousness

flap *verb*
flaps, flapping, flapped
1 to move quickly up and down or from side to side *The bird flapped its wings. The bird's wings were flapping.*
2 to move about noisily, for example in the wind *My coat was flapping about as I ran.*
3 (informal) to behave in a worried or nervous way

flapjack *noun* **flapjacks**
a biscuit in the shape of a rectangle made of oats, butter, sugar and syrup

flare *noun* **flares**
1 a flame that is shot into the sky using special equipment. It is used as a signal, for example to show that someone is in danger.
2 a shape that gets wider at the end, for example in trousers or skirts

flare *verb*
flares, flaring, flared
1 to suddenly start burning or shining brightly *The fire flared up when I threw twigs on it.*
2 if something bad flares up, for example an illness, fighting or anger, it starts and quickly gets worse
3 to get wider or to make something wider *The horse's nostrils flared.*

flare-up *noun* **flare-ups**
1 a situation in which something bad suddenly happens, for example fighting or violence
2 a situation in which you suddenly start to have an illness that you haven't had for a long time *George has had another flare-up of his asthma.*

flash *noun* **flashes**
1 a bright light that suddenly shines then stops *a flash of lightning*
2 a sudden feeling or idea *a flash of genius*
3 **in a flash** or **as quick as a flash** very quickly

flash *verb*
flashes, flashing, flashed
1 to shine with a bright light for a short time and then stop, or to do this lots of times *I saw a light flash in the distance. The lights on the police car were flashing.*
2 to make a light shine on someone and then off, usually lots of times *The car behind was flashing its headlights at us.*
3 to show something very fast or to be shown very fast *The BBC flashed a message on the screen. Images of the earthquake flashed across our screens.*
4 to move very fast *Lightning flashed across the sky.*

flashback *noun* **flashbacks**
a part of a film, play or book that describes something that happened earlier in the story *The hero was shown as a young man in flashback.*

flashcard *noun* **flashcards**
a small card with something such as a picture, word, number or date on it, used for teaching

flash drive *noun* **flash drives**
a small piece of computer equipment that stores information and that you carry around with you. It plugs into a computer using a type of connection known as USB.

flashlight *noun* **flashlights**
the American word for a torch (electric light that you carry in your hand)

flashy *adjective* **flashier, flashiest**
1 if something you have is flashy, it is bright, colourful or expensive, especially in a way that is likely to make people take notice of you *a flashy shirt; My uncle drives a flashy car.*
2 if someone is flashy, they wear flashy clothes or jewels

flask *noun* **flasks**
1 a container shaped like a tube, with hollow walls that have no air between them. Flasks are used for keeping liquids hot or cold.

SYNONYMS vacuum flask, Thermos

2 a bottle shaped like a triangle with a narrow opening, used in a laboratory

flat *adjective* **flatter, flattest**
1 not bumpy, curved or sloping up or down *This part of the country is flat. Our school has a flat roof.*
2 stretched out so that all of something is touching a surface *I was flat on my back.*
3 complete and certain *I hadn't done my homework so I told a flat lie and said I'd left it at home.*
4 not interesting *Our teacher has a rather flat voice.*
5 a flat tyre is one that has a hole in it and doesn't have any air or enough air in it
6 a flat battery is one that doesn't have any power
7 a flat drink is one that doesn't have any bubbles in it

ANTONYM fizzy

8 if someone has flat feet, the middle parts of their feet are not curved so their feet are completely flat on the ground
9 in music, a note that is flat is one that is played or sung slightly lower than the correct note. A note that is slightly higher is called a sharp.

SIMILE 'as flat as a pancake' means very flat (sense 1)

flat *adverb*
1 stretched out so that all of something is touching a surface *I was lying flat on the ground.*
2 exactly *I finished my homework in 10 minutes flat.*
3 completely *They turned me down flat.*
4 in a way that is slightly lower than the correct note in music *You played that note flat.*

ANTONYM sharp

5 if you do something such as work or run flat out, you do it with as much energy and speed as possible

flat – flinch

flat *noun* **flats**
1 a place for people to live in, made up of a number of rooms all on one level inside a large building *a block of flats*

> SYNONYM apartment

2 a musical note that is slightly lower than the correct note

> ANTONYM sharp

3 another word for a flat tyre *I had a flat on the motorway.*

flatly *adverb*
very strongly *He flatly refused to say sorry.*

flatness *noun*
the quality of being flat *the flatness of Norfolk*

flatten *verb*
flattens, flattening, flattened
1 to make something flat, or to become flat *They were flattening the metal with a hammer. I sat on the hat and it flattened.*
2 to destroy something completely *Coventry was flattened during the Second World War.*

flatter *verb*
flatters, flattering, flattered
1 to say nice things to or about someone, often things that are not true, in order to please them or get them to do something
2 if something flatters you, it makes you look good or better *This dress really flatters you.*

flatterer *noun*

> ORIGIN from Old French *flater* 'to flatten down' or 'to stroke with your hand'

flattering *adjective*
1 making someone look good or better *a very flattering hat*
2 if someone's words are flattering, they make someone feel pleased, although they are often not true *a flattering remark*

flattery *noun*
words that flatter someone

flaunt *verb*
flaunts, flaunting, flaunted
to make people notice something you're very pleased about, such as your money or beauty, for example to make them like you more

> SYNONYM to show off

flautist *noun* **flautists**
someone who plays the flute

flavour *noun* **flavours**
1 the taste of something *I prefer ice cream with a strawberry flavour.*
2 a special quality that something has *This part of town has a strongly French flavour.*

flavour *verb*
flavours, flavouring, flavoured
to give something a particular flavour *a curry flavoured with ginger; banana-flavoured milkshake*

flavouring *noun* **flavourings**
a substance put in food or drink to give it a certain flavour

flaw *noun* **flaws**
1 a mistake in something, usually at a deep level, that makes it less good *I downloaded the new browser but there's a flaw in it.*
2 a mark in something, such as a diamond or glass, that makes it less perfect

flawed *adjective*
1 having a serious mistake or mistakes *a flawed argument*
2 with a mark in it *a flawed diamond*

flawless *adjective*
if something is flawless, there is nothing wrong with it and it is perfect

flawlessly *adverb*

> SYNONYM faultless

flax *noun*
a plant with blue flowers. It is used for making rope and cloth and its seeds are used for making oil.

flea *noun* **fleas**
a tiny jumping insect that bites people and animals

fleck *noun* **flecks**
1 a small area of colour *The horse was grey with flecks of white.*
2 a small piece of something *flecks of dust*

flecked *adjective*
marked with flecks of something *Granddad has grey hair flecked with white.*

fledgling *noun* **fledglings**
a young bird that is just learning how to fly

flee *verb*
flees, fleeing, fled
to run away from somewhere, for example because you are in danger or you might be caught *A little boy rang the doorbell and fled. After the earthquake most people fled their homes.*

fleece *noun*
1 (*plural* **fleeces**) the wool that covers a sheep or goat
2 a soft artificial material, used for example for making jackets
3 (*plural* **fleeces**) a warm jacket or sweater made from artificial fleece

fleece *verb*
fleeces, fleecing, fleeced
1 to cheat someone in order to get their money
2 to cut the wool off a sheep

fleecy *adjective* **fleecier, fleeciest**
soft like fleece *These boots are warm and fleecy inside.*

fleet *noun* **fleets**
1 all the ships belonging to a country's navy
2 a group of vehicles, boats or planes belonging to an organisation or person *The injured people were taken to hospital in a fleet of ambulances.*

fleeting *adjective*
not lasting very long *We caught a fleeting glimpse of the film star.*

> SYNONYM brief

Flemish *adjective*
connected with Flanders in Belgium

Flemish *noun*
the language that people speak in the Belgian region of Flanders. It is a type of Dutch.

flesh *noun*
1 the soft part of the body of a person or animal that covers the bones
2 the skin of a person *He had scratches on his flesh.*
3 the soft part of a fruit such as a peach, melon or avocado or the part inside a vegetable such as a potato or squash

fleshy *adjective* **fleshier, fleshiest**
1 if a part of the body is fleshy, it has a lot of flesh on it *thick fleshy arms*
2 a fleshy fruit, for example a peach, has a soft and thick inside part

flew
past tense of **fly**

flex *noun* **flexes**
an electrical wire covered with plastic

flex *verb*
flexes, flexing, flexed
to stretch or bend a muscle or part of your body

flexible *adjective*
1 easy to bend or stretch
2 easy to change *The date is flexible.*
3 able to change your behaviour to deal with a new situation

flexibility *noun*

flick *verb*
flicks, flicking, flicked
1 to make something move quickly, for example by hitting it with your finger or pushing it with your hand *I flicked the dust off my shirt.*
2 to move something up and down or from side to side *I flicked the switch to turn off the light.*
3 to flick through something such as a book is to look at it quickly

flick *noun* **flicks**
1 a quick movement
2 if you have a flick through something, you have a quick look at it

flicker *verb*
flickers, flickering, flickered
1 if a light flickers, it keeps going on and off
2 if a flame flickers, it does not burn normally but keeps burning weakly and then strongly again or keeps shaking slightly

flicker *noun*

flight *noun* **flights**
1 a journey by plane or a journey into space *We're on the next flight to Amsterdam.*
2 the movement of flying *I saw a group of geese in flight.*
3 a group of birds or planes flying
4 the action of running away *The fox took flight when the children approached.*
5 a flight of stairs is a group of stairs between one floor of a building and the next

flight attendant *noun* **flight attendants**
someone who helps and looks after people on a plane

flimsy *adjective* **flimsier, flimsiest**
1 light and thin, or made of a light and thin material *flimsy cotton; a flimsy dress*
2 not well made, for example because the things used for making it are too thin *This chair is rather flimsy.*
3 weak and not easy to believe *a flimsy excuse*

flinch *verb*
flinches, flinching, flinched
to suddenly make a slight movement with your head or body, for example to get away from something because you're in pain

fling – floppy

fling *verb*
flings, flinging, flung
1 to throw something quickly or using a lot of strength *I flung all my toys on the floor.*
2 to move, push or put something or someone quickly or suddenly into a particular position *I flung open the window. The bully flung me to the ground.*

flint *noun*
1 a type of hard grey stone. It makes a tiny flame when it is hit with a piece of steel. Flint was used in prehistoric times for making tools.
2 (*plural* flints) a piece of flint

flip *verb*
flips, flipping, flipped
1 to turn something over, for example so that it is upside down, or to get turned over *Dad flipped the omelette in the frying pan. The car skidded round the corner and flipped over.*
2 to move something with a quick movement, for example to open something or make something start *I flipped open the lid of the box. Flip the switch and the light will come on.*
3 to flip through something such as a book is to look at it quickly

> SYNONYM to flick through

4 to move quickly between different activities or ideas *Please stop flipping through the TV channels.*
5 to change the position of things *Flip these two letters around and you have the correct spelling.*

> SYNONYM to swap

6 to flip a coin is to throw it into the air to see which side it comes down, for example to decide who will win or lose something *'Tails!' she shouted, after flipping the coin.*

> SYNONYM to toss

7 to flip out (or to flip) is an informal way of saying to become very angry

flip *noun* flips
1 a quick movement, for example in which something or someone turns over
2 if you have a flip through something, you have a quick look at it

flip-flop *noun* flip-flops
a type of summer shoe made up of a rubber sole (bottom part) and a V-shaped strap that goes between the toes

> ORIGIN from the sound that people make when they walk in *flip-flops*

flippant *adjective*
if you describe someone as flippant, you think they are not being serious about something when they should be
flippancy *noun* **flippantly** *adverb*

flipper *noun* flippers
1 one of two body parts like arms that some animals use for swimming, for example penguins and seals
2 one of the two flat wide rubber shoes that swimmers and divers use to help them to swim

> SYNONYM for sense 2: fin

flirt *verb*
flirts, flirting, flirted
1 to flirt with someone is to behave towards them in a way that shows you want a love relationship with them but not a serious one
2 to flirt with something such as an idea is to think about it but not very seriously

flirt *noun* flirts
someone who likes flirting

flit *verb*
flits, flitting, flitted
1 to fly quickly from one place to another, for example with short light movements *Birds were flitting from branch to branch.*
2 to move from one place to another without staying very long in any place *My brother spent a year flitting from country to country.*

float *verb*
floats, floating, floated
1 to stay or move slowly on the surface of water or a liquid without sinking
2 to move slowly in the air, for example like a bubble, cloud or balloon
3 to make something float on water or a liquid

float *noun* floats
1 an object that floats on water, for example one that helps you to swim
2 a float or milk float is a special vehicle for carrying milk to deliver to people's homes
3 a decorated truck used in a carnival or parade for carrying people or objects to display

flock *noun* flocks
a group of birds, sheep or goats *a flock of geese*

flock *verb*
flocks, flocking, flocked
if lots of people flock somewhere, they go there, for example because there is something interesting to see *Every day tourists flock to Buckingham Palace.*

flog *verb*
flogs, flogging, flogged
1 to hit a person or animal very hard and many times with a whip or stick
2 (informal) to flog something is to sell it, for example cheaply *I flogged my bike for a tenner.*

flood *noun* floods
1 a very large amount of water covering a part of the land that is usually dry, for example from a river that overflows because of too much rain *The town was cut off by floods.*
2 a small amount of water covering a surface, for example because of a pipe that bursts *The washing machine broke and now there's a flood on the kitchen floor.*
3 a large number of things or people *The head teacher received a flood of complaints.*

flood *verb*
floods, flooding, flooded
1 to cover something with water or to be covered with water *The river flooded the village. The basement floods every time it rains. The kitchen was flooded.*
2 if a river floods, water flows over its edges and onto the land
3 if water floods somewhere, it flows there in large amounts *Water flooded through the open door.*
4 if things or people flood somewhere, they go there quickly and in large numbers *The gates opened and the football fans flooded in.*

floodlight *noun* floodlights
a very bright light, used for example for lighting up buildings or sports grounds at night
compare: **searchlight** and **spotlight**

floodlit *adjective*
lit up at night by floodlights

floor *noun* floors
1 the part of a room that you walk on
2 one level in a building *The toy department is on the next floor.*
3 the ground, for example at the bottom of a cave or the sea

> CULTURE NOTE the floor at the bottom level of a building is called the *ground floor* in British English and the *first floor* in American English. The next floor up is called the *first floor* in British English and the *second floor* in American English, and so on.

floor *verb*
floors, flooring, floored
1 if you're floored by something, you don't know what to say or do because you're so surprised by it or you can't understand it *I was completely floored by the last exam question.*
2 to hit someone so hard that they fall over

floorboard *noun* floorboards
one of the long flat pieces of wood that make up the wooden floor in a building

flooring *noun*
material used for making or covering a floor *Our kitchen has vinyl flooring.*

flop *verb*
flops, flopping, flopped
1 to let yourself drop suddenly and with all the weight of your body onto something *I was tired and just flopped onto the bed.*
2 to fall or hang down loosely or heavily *Don't let the baby's head flop back.*
3 (informal) if something such as a play, idea or new product flops, it is not successful

> SYNONYM for sense 3: to fail

flop *noun* flops
1 (informal) something that is not successful *The film was a flop.*

> SYNONYM failure

2 the noise of something or someone falling onto something soft *The rag doll fell onto the sofa with a flop.*

floppy *adjective* floppier, floppiest
1 if something soft is floppy, it hangs down loosely or heavily *My dog has big floppy ears.*
2 a floppy disk is a small square piece of plastic with a magnetic disc inside for storing computer information, used especially in the past

175

flora–flush

flora *noun*
all the plants that grow in a particular place or at a particular time in history. The animals of a place or time are called the fauna.

floral *adjective*
made of or decorated with flowers or with flower patterns on it *a floral dress*

florist *noun* **florists**
someone who sells flowers, usually in a shop

floss *noun*
floss or dental floss is a thin thread for cleaning between your teeth

floss *verb*
flosses, flossing, flossed
to clean between your teeth with floss

flotilla *noun* **flotillas**
a small group of boats or ships

flounce *noun* **flounces**
a wide strip of material with folds in it used as a decoration, for example on a dress

flounder *verb*
flounders, floundering, floundered
1 to move about with great difficulty, for example because you are trying not to sink in water or fall over into deep mud
2 not to know what to say or do, for example because you are confused
3 to have problems and no longer be successful

flounder *noun* **flounder** or **flounders**
a flat sea fish that is used as food

flour *noun*
a powder made from crushing grains of wheat. It is used for making bread, cakes and pasta.

flourish *verb*
flourishes, flourishing, flourished
1 to be very successful *Our school is flourishing.*
2 to grow well and strongly, used for example about plants, animals and babies
3 to wave something in your hand so that people see it clearly

flourish *noun* **flourishes**
1 a curved line or a number of curved lines used as decoration, for example in someone's signature
2 a strong movement, usually with your hands, that you do so that people take notice of you

floury *adjective*
1 covered with flour
2 looking or tasting like flour

flow *verb*
flows, flowing, flowed
1 to move along smoothly, for example like water in a river or through a pipe or like air through a tunnel
2 if electricity flows, it moves through a wire
3 if people or things flow somewhere, they go there without stopping *Tourists are still flowing into the country.*
4 if hair or clothes flow, they hang down loosely and in a pleasant way *Her long hair flowed over her shoulders.*

flow *noun* **flows**
1 the movement of something that continues smoothly without stopping, such as water in a river or through a pipe or electricity through a wire *the flow of blood around the body*; *the flow of traffic on the motorway*
2 when people or things go somewhere without stopping *There has been a steady flow of visitors to the BBC studios.*
3 a flow chart is a drawing that uses shapes, words, lines and arrows to show the different actions and choices needed to achieve a particular result

flower *noun* **flowers**
1 the brightly coloured or white part of a plant that produces seeds or fruit. A flower is usually made up of lots of petals. Some trees also produce flowers, usually called blossoms or blooms.
2 a flower with its stem *a bunch of flowers*
3 a plant that people grow for its flowers
4 **in flower** with flowers growing on it

flower *verb*
flowers, flowering, flowered
if a plant or tree flowers, it produces flowers

flowerbed *noun* **flowerbeds**
a place for growing flowers, for example in a garden or park

flowerpot *noun* **flowerpots**
a container for growing plants in

flowery *adjective*
1 decorated with flower patterns *a flowery dress*
2 flowery language is made up of unusual or difficult words to make it seem more attractive

flowing *adjective*
hanging down loosely and in a pleasant way *She had long flowing hair.*

flown
past participle of **fly**

flu *noun*
an illness like a very bad cold that makes you feel weak, hot or cold and ache all over
short for: influenza

fluctuate *verb*
fluctuates, fluctuating, fluctuated
if something such as a price or number fluctuates, it keeps changing
fluctuation *noun*

ORIGIN from Latin *fluctus* 'wave'

flue *noun* **flues**
a large pipe that takes fumes and smoke away from something such as a stove or boiler

fluent *adjective*
1 if you're fluent in a language, you can speak it very well *I'm fluent in Spanish.*
2 also used about a language itself *I speak fluent Spanish.*
3 if you're a fluent reader, you can read very well
fluency *noun*

ORIGIN from Latin *fluens* 'flowing'

fluently *adverb*
very well *I speak Spanish fluently.*

fluff *noun*
small soft pieces of something such as cloth or hair that can fly about and become mixed with dust

fluffy *adjective* **fluffier, fluffiest**
1 covered with or made from something that is very light and soft to touch *a fluffy sweater*; *a fluffy little chick*
2 looking very light and soft, for example because there is air in it *a fluffy pancake*; *a fluffy cloud*
fluffiness *noun*

fluid *noun* **fluids**
another word for a liquid

fluid *adjective*
smooth and attractive in the way something or someone moves *the fluid movements of a ballet dancer*

fluke *noun* **flukes**
an informal word for a piece of good luck that you were not expecting

flummoxed *adjective*
an informal way of saying confused by something

flung
past tense & past participle of **fling**

flunk *verb* (informal)
flunks, flunking, flunked
if you flunk something such as an exam, you are not successful

LANGUAGE EXTRA used mainly in American English

fluorescent *adjective*
1 a fluorescent light is a very bright light (produced by a special gas) inside a lamp shaped like a tube
2 a fluorescent colour appears to shine brightly in the light *The police officer was wearing a fluorescent jacket.*

fluoride *noun*
a chemical added to water and toothpaste to stop your teeth from going bad

flurry *noun* **flurries**
1 a small amount of something blown about in the wind, for example snow, leaves or dust
2 a short period with a lot of things happening somewhere *a flurry of activity*

flush *verb*
flushes, flushing, flushed
1 if someone flushes, they go red in the face
2 if you flush a toilet or if it flushes, you make the water go down it to clean it, for example by pressing a handle or pushing a button
3 if you flush something down the toilet, you get rid of it by putting it in the toilet and making the water go down
4 to clean something by pouring lots of water through it or in it

flush *noun* **flushes**
1 a slight red colour that appears on the face
2 a part of a toilet that allows the water to go down it

flush *adjective*
1 completely level with something so that there is nothing sticking out *These shelves are flush with the wall.*

flushed–folk

2 (informal) if someone is flush with money, they have lots of it

flushed *adjective*
if your face or cheeks are flushed, they are red

flustered *adjective*
if you are flustered, you are nervous and not able to do something properly

flute *noun* **flutes**
a musical instrument made up of a long thin tube that you play by holding it to one side of your mouth and blowing into it. You press buttons or cover holes along the tube to change the notes.

LANGUAGE EXTRA someone who plays the flute is called a *flautist* in British English or a *flutist* in American English

flutter *verb*
flutters, fluttering, fluttered
1 if a bird or insect flutters its wings, it moves them gently or quickly up and down
2 to fly somewhere with a gentle movement of the wings *Butterflies were fluttering around the lettuces.*
3 to move about gently in the air *Leaves were fluttering in the breeze.*

flutter *noun* **flutters**
1 the noise or movement of something fluttering
2 (informal) to have a flutter is to have a small bet, for example in a horse race, to try to win money
3 **in a flutter** excited or nervous about something

fly *verb*
flies, flying, flew, flown
1 to move in or through the air, for example with wings like a bird or plane
2 to be a passenger in a plane, or to take someone or something by plane *We're flying to Spain for our holiday. The injured girl was flown to hospital.*
3 to control a plane *My uncle can fly a plane.*
4 to make something move in or through the air, for example a kite or flag
5 to move, go or do something very quickly *The door flew open. Time flies. Dad flew into a rage.*
6 to send something or someone flying is to knock them through the air, for example by hitting them or in an explosion
7 **to fly off the handle** to become very angry

fly *noun* **flies**
1 a small flying insect with wings
2 the part that opens at the front of a pair of trousers. You can also say flies.

flyer *noun* **flyers**
1 a piece of paper that gives information about something such as an event or product
2 someone who flies in a plane

flying *adjective*
1 moving fast through the air, for example because of an explosion or after being thrown *Many people were hurt by flying glass.*
2 a flying saucer is a flat round spacecraft shaped like a saucer that comes from another planet, especially in science fiction

3 the Flying Squad is a special group of police officers who investigate serious crimes such as robberies
4 a flying visit is a very short one

flyover *noun* **flyovers**
a bridge that takes a road over another road

foal *noun* **foals**
a young horse

LANGUAGE EXTRA a young male horse is a *colt* and a young female horse is a *filly*

foam *noun*
1 lots of bubbles on the surface of a liquid *sea foam*

SYNONYM froth

2 a liquid or substance that produces lots of white bubbles, used for example for washing, shaving or putting out fires *bath foam; shaving foam; a foam fire extinguisher*
3 a soft rubber or plastic material with lots of small holes in it, used for example in cushions and seats

foamy *adjective*

foam *verb*
foams, foaming, foamed
1 if water or the sea foams, it produces lots of bubbles
2 if an animal or person foams at the mouth, small white bubbles come out, for example because they are ill or very angry

SYNONYM to froth

focus *noun*
1 the focus of an image is how clear it is when you look at it through a camera or telescope, for example. You can change the focus usually by turning a part of the camera or telescope. If an image is in focus, it is clear.
2 the particular attention you pay to something *Your focus should be on your schoolwork.*
3 (plural **focuses**) the particular thing or person that you pay attention to *It's my birthday so I'm the main focus of attention.*

ORIGIN from Latin *focus* 'fireplace' or 'hearth', which was the centre of a Roman household

focus *verb*
focuses, focusing, focused or
focusses, focussing, focussed
1 to focus on something is to give all your attention to it
2 if you focus your efforts or energy on something, you work very hard on that particular thing and not on anything else
3 to turn a part in something such as a camera or telescope so that you can see an image clearly
4 if you focus your eyes or if your eyes focus, you look at something until it becomes clear

fodder *noun*
food for farm animals such as cows, pigs and horses

foe *noun* **foes**
an old-fashioned word for an enemy

foetus ['fee-ters'] *noun* **foetuses**
a human or animal baby that is developing in its mother's body. In humans an embryo becomes a foetus at around 10 weeks.

LANGUAGE EXTRA also spelt *fetus*

compare: embryo

fog *noun* **fogs**
a thick cloud formed by tiny drops of water. Fog hangs close to the ground (or the sea) and makes it difficult to see.

fogey ['foh-gee'] *noun* **fogeys**
a fogey or old fogey is someone with old-fashioned ideas who doesn't like change

foggy *adjective* **foggier, foggiest**
if the weather or a place is foggy, there is lots of fog

foghorn *noun* **foghorns**
a piece of equipment on a ship that makes a loud noise when it is foggy. The sound of the foghorn tells other ships to be careful.

foil *noun*
1 sheets of metal that are as thin as paper, used for example for wrapping food to keep it fresh
2 a piece of foil *Mum put some foil around my cake.*

SYNONYM tinfoil

foil *verb*
foils, foiling, foiled
if you foil something such as someone's plan, you stop it from being successful

fold *verb*
folds, folding, folded
1 to bend something such as paper or cloth so that one part of it goes over another part *Fold your clothes neatly before going to bed.*
2 if you fold something or if it folds, for example a chair or umbrella, you bend some parts of it so that it takes up less room *Fold the deckchair and put it away. The kitchen table folds down.*
3 if you fold your arms, you put one arm over the other and hold them close to your body

fold *noun* **folds**
1 a line that you make in paper or cloth when you fold it
2 folds in cloth are parts of the cloth that hang down loosely over other parts *the regular folds of the curtains*
3 a place surrounded by a fence or wall for keeping sheep in

folder *noun* **folders**
1 a large cover for papers. It is made of thin cardboard or plastic that is folded over.
2 a place on a computer for storing groups of files and programs. Folders are shown on the screen as a particular icon. You can give each folder its own name.

foliage *noun*
the leaves on a tree or plant

ORIGIN from Old French *feuille* 'leaf'

folk *noun*
1 (plural **folks**) another word for people *They're nice folk. What are you folks doing?*
2 folk music *a folk festival*

177

folk – foothold

folk *adjective*
1 connected with the way people in a particular country or region usually do things such as dance, sing and play music *a folk dance; a folk song; folk music*

SYNONYM traditional

2 folk music is also a type of modern music that people play mainly on acoustic guitars (not electric ones). They often sing songs about important subjects and events.

folklore *noun*
old stories and beliefs from a particular country or region

follow *verb*
follows, following, followed
1 to go or come behind someone or something, for example when walking, running or driving
2 to come or happen after something *Sunday follows Saturday.*
3 to do something after someone has done it *My sister started at Redlands Secondary School this term and I will follow next year.*
4 to go along something or in the same direction as something *Follow the path to the house. I cut out a triangle by following the dotted lines on the paper.*
5 to do the same as someone *Your sister is a good example to follow.*
6 to pay attention to something or someone *Have you been following what the teacher was saying?*
7 to understand someone or something *I'm sorry – I don't follow.*
8 to obey something such as a rule, instruction or advice or to do what you are supposed to do *Follow these directions to get to the station. Are you still following that diet?*
9 to study a subject or do a course of study *My brother is following a course in German.*
10 to happen because of something *I changed schools and a lot of problems followed.*
11 to have or show an interest in something or someone, or to support them *Which team do you follow? My sister has 30 people following her blog* (interested in reading the latest things she writes about). *Click here to follow him on Twitter* (to be allowed to receive his messages).
12 to happen in a particular way *The animal's behaviour follows a pattern.*
13 to keep doing a particular activity over a period of time, for example watching a programme on TV, so that you have the latest information about something *They've been following the news. We follow 'Doctor Who'.*
14 to describe something that happens over a period of time *The book follows the adventures of a boy called Harry.*
15 if you follow your instincts or feelings, you do what you feel is best without having to think about it

follower *noun* followers
1 someone who supports someone or something such as a team or sport
2 someone who has or shows an interest in someone else's ideas, for example the ideas of a religious or political leader or someone who writes a blog
3 someone who is interested in receiving the messages that someone writes on a website such as Twitter
4 someone who believes in something such as a religion or a particular idea

following *preposition & adjective*
1 after something *Following the party, we played football.*
2 used when talking about something that comes next *The following day was a holiday.*
3 also used when talking about the things or people you are going to mention next *The following pupils got top marks: Priyanka, Rahul and Sam.*

follow-up *noun* follow-ups
something that continues something else *The author is writing a follow-up to her novel.*

folly *noun* follies
a really stupid action or idea

ORIGIN from Old French *folie* 'madness'

fond *adjective* fonder, fondest
1 if you are fond of something or someone, you like them very much *I'm very fond of cooking.*
2 showing love or showing that you like something very much *a fond look; My dad has fond memories of school.*
fondly *adverb* **fondness** *noun*

font *noun* fonts
1 the letters and numbers of a particular style and size, used for computer documents and in printing *Change the font from Arial bold to Times New Roman italic.*
2 a stone container in a church, used for holding water for the Christian ceremony of baptism

food *noun*
1 (*plural* foods) what people and animals eat to stay alive and to get enough energy to grow. Food includes things such as meat, fish, fruit and vegetables.
2 what plants need to grow
3 a food chain is a group of animals and plants that are connected to each other because each one is eaten as food by the living thing that is above it in the chain. Food chains always start with a plant.
4 a food processor is a piece of kitchen equipment for cutting, slicing, crushing and mixing food

fool *noun* fools
1 someone who doesn't behave in a sensible way *I was a fool not to do my homework.*
2 someone who behaves in a silly way, for example to annoy people *Stop playing the fool!*

fool *verb*
fools, fooling, fooled
1 to make someone believe something that isn't true

SYNONYM to deceive

2 to fool around or about is to behave in a silly way

foolhardy *adjective*
if someone is foolhardy, they don't think properly about what they do, for example they may do something dangerous

foolish *adjective*
1 not sensible or wise

SYNONYM stupid

2 behaving in a silly way *Stop being foolish!*

SYNONYM silly

3 embarrassed *I got stuck in the gate and felt very foolish!*
foolishness *noun*

foolishly *adverb*
1 in a foolish way *Try not to act foolishly when Grandma comes over.*
2 used for saying that you've done something foolish *Foolishly, I forgot to take my umbrella.*

foolproof *adjective*
if something such as a plan is foolproof, it is so good that it cannot go wrong

foot *noun* feet
1 the part of your leg that you use for standing, walking, running and kicking
2 the lowest part of something *I'll wait for you at the foot of the stairs.*
3 a unit for measuring length. There are 12 inches in a foot (about 30 centimetres).
4 a unit of rhythm in poetry made up of two or more syllables
5 if you put your feet up, you relax, for example by sitting down and resting your feet on something
6 if you put your foot down, you say no to something in a very strong way
7 if you set foot somewhere, you go there, for example for the first time *Men first set foot on the moon in 1969.*
8 **on foot** or **by foot** walking somewhere *I go to school on foot.*

football *noun*
1 a game in which two teams of 11 players kick a ball around a pitch (ground covered in grass) and try to kick it into the other team's goal

SYNONYM soccer

2 (*plural* footballs) the big round ball used in football

CULTURE NOTE in the USA, *football* is a game in which two teams of 11 players throw, carry and kick a ball

footballer *noun* footballers
someone who plays football

LANGUAGE EXTRA also called a *football player*

footbridge *noun* footbridges
a small bridge, for example over a railway line, road or river, for people to walk across

foothills *noun plural*
small hills close to a mountain or group of mountains

foothold *noun* footholds
1 a small position in something such as an organisation, which you use as a starting point to become more successful
2 a small place on the surface of a rock or mountain, where you put your foot when climbing

178

footie *noun*
an informal word for the game of football

footing *noun*
1 the position of your feet when you are standing safely on something
2 if you lose your footing, you lose your balance and fall over
3 the particular way people or things are connected to each other *He wants to be put on an equal footing with his older brother.*

footlights *noun plural*
a row of lights along the front edge of a theatre stage

footnote *noun* **footnotes**
a note at the bottom of a page in a book that refers to a part of the text and gives more information about it

footpath *noun* **footpaths**
a path for walking along, for example in the countryside

footprint *noun* **footprints**
a mark made by a foot or shoe, for example in something soft such as earth, sand or snow

footstep *noun* **footsteps**
1 the sound of someone walking or running as their feet or shoes touch the ground
2 another word for a footprint
3 if you follow in someone's footsteps, you do the same work or activities as someone else before you

for *preposition*
1 used for showing where something or someone is supposed to go, or who or what is supposed to get something *We have a new teacher for our class. This present is for you.*
2 used for showing a reason or purpose *He only does it for the money. It's a machine for making ice cream.*
3 used for showing a price *I bought my bike for £50.*
4 used for showing a direction *Where can I get a train for Leeds?*
5 used for showing a time *The match is planned for two o'clock.*
6 used for showing that someone or something is connected to someone or something else *My brother works for the BBC. It's a problem for us all.*
7 used for showing that something helps someone *Could you tidy the room for me?*
8 used when you give something and get something else back *Swap my bag of crisps for your ice cream?*
9 used for showing the whole time that something happens *It rained for three hours.*
10 used for showing that something is done over a particular distance *They ran for two miles.*
11 used for showing that you support something or someone *Are you for me or against me?*

for *conjunction*
an old-fashioned way of saying because *The soldiers fought many battles, for they were very brave.*

forbid *verb*
forbids, forbidding, forbade, forbidden
1 to tell someone they are not allowed to do something *Dad has forbidden us to play in the street.*
2 to say that something is not allowed *Wearing jeans to school is forbidden.*

forbidding *adjective*
looking frightening and unfriendly *the forbidding landscape of the Russian steppes*

force *verb*
forces, forcing, forced
1 to make someone do something they don't want to do, for example by using your strength or your power to tell them what to do *My mum forced me to tell the truth.*
2 to push or move something or someone using a lot of strength *The crowds forced me into a corner. The police forced their way in.*
3 to break open something using a lot of strength, for example a door or lock

force *noun* **forces**
1 a lot of strength *The police used force to break down the door.*
2 in science, a force is a power that makes things move or changes the way they move, for example pushing, pulling or hitting *the force of gravity*
3 the strong influence that something or someone has, or something or someone with a strong influence *the force of an argument*; *The film's hero battles supernatural forces.*
4 a group of people who are trained for a particular job, for example police officers or soldiers *My uncle's in the police force.*
5 if something such as a rule is in force, it exists now and must be obeyed

forceful *adjective*
very strong and powerful *a forceful argument* **forcefully** *adverb*

forcemeter *noun* **forcemeters**
in science, an instrument with a spring used for measuring forces. The units for measuring the forces are called newtons.

forceps *noun* **forceps**
a medical tool for holding and pulling, with two narrow parts like a pair of scissors

forcible *adjective*
done using a lot of strength **forcibly** *adverb*

ford *noun* **fords**
a place in a river where the water is not deep so that you can easily go across it

forearm *noun* **forearms**
the part of your arm between your elbow and your wrist

foreboding *noun*
a strong feeling that something bad will happen *I had a sense of foreboding when the head called me into his office.*

forecast *noun* **forecasts**
a description of something likely to happen in the future, using information that you have now *a weather forecast* (describing what the weather is likely to be)

forecast *verb*
forecasts, forecasting, forecast or **forecasted**
to say what is likely to happen in the future, using information that you have now *They're forecasting rain for the weekend.*

forecourt *noun* **forecourts**
1 the place in a petrol station where the pumps are and where people park their cars and fill them with fuel
2 an open area in front of a building

forefathers *noun plural*
the people in your family who lived before you were born

SYNONYM **ancestors**

forefinger *noun* **forefingers**
the finger next to your thumb. It's the finger you use for pointing.

SYNONYM **index finger**

foreground *noun* **foregrounds**
the part of a picture or scene that is closest to you

ANTONYM **background**

forehead ['for-hed' or 'fo-rid'] *noun* **foreheads**
the part of your face above your eyes and below your hair

foreign ['fo-rern'] *adjective*
1 from or in another country *Dutch is a foreign language.*
2 connected with another country *foreign aid*
3 if something is foreign to someone, it is strange and completely different to anything they already know *Your way of doing things is foreign to me.*

foreigner *noun* **foreigners**
someone from another country

foreleg *noun* **forelegs**
one of the two front legs of an animal that has four legs
compare: **hind leg**

foreman *noun* **foremen**
a worker who is in charge of a group of other workers, for example in a factory

foremost *adjective*
the most important *She's one of the foremost actors in the country.*

forename *noun* **forenames**
your first name. Some examples of forenames are Olivia, Hannah, Jack and Mohammed.

forerunner *noun* **forerunners**
something that existed in the past from which something newer has developed *The museum displayed the forerunner of the modern telephone.*

foresee *verb*
foresees, foreseeing, foresaw, foreseen
to think that something is likely to happen in the future

foreseeable *adjective*
1 if something such as an event is foreseeable, you think it is likely to happen in the future
2 **in the foreseeable future** in the future but fairly soon
3 **for the foreseeable future** for quite a long time

foresight *noun*
the good judgement to be ready for something that may happen in the future *I had the foresight to bring a raincoat.*

forest *noun* **forests**
a large area where lots of trees grow close together

forestry–former

forestry noun
the science of looking after forests and planting new ones

forever adverb
1 for all time in the future *Our life has changed forever.*
2 for a very long time *I've been waiting forever.*
3 always *You're forever complaining.*

LANGUAGE EXTRA senses 1 and 2 are also spelt **for ever**

forewoman noun **forewomen**
a female worker in charge of a group of other workers, for example in a factory

forfeit ['for-fit'] noun **forfeits**
something you have to pay or give or something you lose, for example because you have done something wrong

forfeit ['for-fit'] verb
forfeits, forfeiting, forfeited
to lose something or to have to pay or give something, for example because you have done something wrong

forgave
past tense of **forgive**

forge noun **forges**
a place where metal goods are made. Pieces of metal are heated and then hammered or poured into different shapes.

forge verb
forges, forging, forged
1 to copy something in a dishonest way, for example a document, signature or passport, in order to trick someone *The police officer showed us a forged £10 note.*
2 to start a new relationship and gradually make it stronger *Britain has forged close links with China.*

SYNONYM to establish

3 to heat metal and hammer it or pour it into different shapes
4 to forge ahead is to make very good progress, for example in your studies

forger noun **forgers**
a criminal who copies things to trick people, for example paintings or money

forgery noun
1 (plural **forgeries**) a copy of something made in a dishonest way to trick someone
2 the crime of copying something to trick someone

forget verb
forgets, forgetting, forgot, forgotten
1 if you forget something, you don't know it any more although you did know it in the past *Sorry, I've forgotten how to shut down the computer.*
2 not to do something that you should do *I forgot to brush my teeth.*
3 not to take something with you that you should have *I forgot my schoolbag.*
4 to deliberately stop thinking about something or someone *Forget all your problems.*
5 used when you mean that doing or having something isn't possible *You've behaved badly so you can forget about going to the match on Saturday.*
6 if you forget yourself, you behave in a very stupid way

forgetful adjective
having trouble thinking of things that you knew in the past **forgetfulness** noun

forget-me-not noun **forget-me-nots**
a plant that has small blue flowers with yellow centres

ORIGIN the name comes from Old French. In the 15th century, the flower was supposed to mean that a lady wearing it would never be forgotten by the man she loved.

forgivable adjective
used for describing something bad someone does or says that you can forgive because it's not serious *a forgivable mistake*

forgive verb
forgives, forgiving, forgave, forgiven
1 to stop being angry with someone even though they've done something wrong, or to tell them you're not angry with them any more *Dad forgave me for breaking the window. OK, I forgive you this time.*
2 **forgive me** used as a polite way of saying sorry because you don't want to seem rude *Forgive me but I think you're wrong.*

forgiveness noun
the action of forgiving someone

forgot
past tense of **forget**

forgotten
past participle of **forget**

fork noun **forks**
1 something used for picking up your food and eating it. It consists of a handle and three or four points (or prongs) at the other end.
2 a fork or garden fork is a large tool with a similar shape used for digging earth, or a small tool used for example for getting rid of weeds
3 a place in a road or river where it divides into two parts

fork verb
forks, forking, forked
1 if a road or river forks, it divides into two parts
2 to move or dig something with a garden fork
3 if you fork out money, you spend it on something *Your parents will have to fork out a lot to buy that bike.*

fork-lift truck noun **fork-lift trucks**
a small vehicle with metal bars at the front for lifting and moving heavy objects

forlorn adjective
1 if someone is forlorn, they look sad and lonely
2 if something such as an attempt is forlorn, it will not be successful

form noun **forms**
1 a type of something *This insect is a form of beetle.*
2 the shape of something *A strange form appeared at the window.*
3 used for describing the particular way something is *Send your reply in the form of an email* (as an email).
4 a printed or online document with questions and spaces for you to write answers in
5 a class in a school *What form are you in? We all like our form teacher.*
6 in grammar, a form is a part of something such as a verb, noun or adjective that has a number of different parts *Geese is the plural form of goose.*

form verb
forms, forming, formed
1 to start to exist or make something start to exist *Ice is forming on the roads.*
2 to make a particular shape or thing *Can you please form a circle?*
3 to be something *These ideas form an important part of the book.*
4 to make something such as a part of a verb, noun or adjective *You add '-ed' to form the past tense of most verbs.*

formal adjective
1 very polite and serious, for example in a way that seems unfriendly *formal language; Our teacher is too formal.*
2 official or important *The head teacher invited the parents to a formal dinner.*
formally adverb

formality noun
1 (plural **formalities**) something that must be done because it is usually done, even though it doesn't have much meaning *Showing your passport is just a formality – no-one looks at it.*
2 very polite and serious behaviour or language

format noun **formats**
1 the size or shape of something such as a newspaper or book
2 the way that something is organised or made, for example a TV or radio programme or an exam
3 a way of storing information on a computer about how something works or what type of thing it is. For example, the format of a file is shown by its extension (three or four letters following a dot), and disc formats include CD, DVD and Blu-ray.
4 a computer command used in word processing that allows you to change the way your text is presented

format verb
formats, formatting, formatted
1 to prepare a computer disk so that it can be used with a particular operating system
2 to present text in a certain way in a computer document

formation noun **formations**
1 the action of forming something or the way something is formed
2 something formed in a particular way *rock formations*
3 a pattern in a moving group of people or things *The planes are flying in formation.*

formatting noun
the formatting of text is the way you present it in a computer document. It includes such things as fonts (style and size of letters), spacing of lines and colour.

former adjective
1 used about something that existed or belonged to someone in the past *the former Soviet Union; The former home of Jane Austen is in Chawton.*
2 used about the job or position that someone had in the past *the former prime minister*

former *pronoun*
used when talking about the first of two things or people that you have already mentioned *If the choice is between watching TV or doing homework, I'll choose the former.*

ANTONYM **latter**

formerly *adverb*
in the past

formidable *adjective*
1 very important or powerful *a formidable influence*
2 very large and often frightening *a formidable amount of work*; *The formidable prison building loomed before us.*
3 very difficult *a formidable task*

formidably *adverb*
extremely *formidably intelligent*

formless *adjective*
without any proper shape

formula *noun* **formulas** or **formulae**
1 a group of letters or numbers that make up a rule in maths *What's the formula for the area of a circle? Enter this formula into your spreadsheet formula bar.*
2 a list of substances that something consists of, for example a chemical, medicine or drink, or the symbols representing these substances *O₂ is the formula for oxygen.*
3 a plan or series of actions needed to be successful in something *Eating fruit and vegetables is a formula for good health.*
4 in car racing, formulas are rules for putting cars into different groups, for example based on the size of their engines *a Formula One race*

formulate *verb*
formulates, formulating, formulated
1 to produce something carefully and with lots of details, for example a plan or guidelines
2 to express something carefully, for example an opinion, idea or question
formulation *noun*

forsake *verb*
forsakes, forsaking, forsook, forsaken
1 to go away and leave someone or something, especially when you should have stayed
2 to stop doing, having or using something, for example a belief, interest, idea or method

fort *noun* **forts**
a strong building or group of buildings in which soldiers live, which protects them from attack

ORIGIN from Latin *fortis* 'strong'

forth *adverb*
an old-fashioned word for forwards or out *You can switch back and forth between the two. Blood poured forth from the wound.*

forthcoming *adjective*
coming or happening soon *I can't wait for her forthcoming film.*

forthright *adjective*
saying what you really think in an honest way

SYNONYM **direct**

forties *noun plural*
1 the forties are the fortieth to forty-ninth years of a century, for example 1940 to 1949
2 if someone is in their forties, they are between 40 and 49 years old

fortifications *noun plural*
strong buildings or structures such as walls and towers built around a place to protect it from attack

fortify *verb*
fortifies, fortifying, fortified
1 to protect a place from being attacked by putting strong buildings or structures around it
2 to make someone feel stronger or give them more energy *The driver stopped for a coffee to fortify him for the journey.*

ORIGIN from Latin *fortis* 'strong' and *facere* 'to make'

fortnight *noun* **fortnights**
a period of two weeks

fortnightly *adjective*
happening every two weeks *a fortnightly game of football*

fortnightly *adverb*
every two weeks *I play tennis fortnightly.*

fortress *noun* **fortresses**
a very strong building such as a castle that is difficult for enemies to attack

fortunate *adjective*
1 lucky *You're fortunate to have such a good teacher.*
2 used about someone who has better things in their life than other people *In some countries less fortunate* (poorer) *children don't go to school.*

fortunately *adverb*
used when talking about something good happening *Fortunately, we didn't get lost.*

SYNONYM **luckily**

fortune *noun*
1 (plural **fortunes**) a lot of money *My uncle has made a fortune in his job.*
2 luck *I had the good fortune to win a prize.*
3 someone's fortunes are the things that happen to them, which may affect how successful they are
4 to tell someone's fortune is to tell them what will happen to them in the future, for example using magic

fortune cookie *noun* **fortune cookies**
a thin biscuit with a paper message inside telling you what will happen to you in the future. Fortune cookies are served as desserts in Chinese restaurants.

fortune-teller *noun* **fortune-tellers**
someone who tells you what will happen to you in the future, for example by looking at your hands **fortune-telling** *noun*

forty *adjective & noun* **forties**
1 the number 40
2 the forties are the fortieth to forty-ninth years of a century, for example 1940 to 1949
3 if someone is in their forties, they are between 40 and 49 years old
fortieth *adjective & noun*

forum *noun* **forums**
1 a website where you can write down your opinions or ask questions and receive replies from other people
2 an open area in the middle of an ancient Roman town in which people met to discuss important matters

forward or **forwards** *adverb*
1 in the direction that is in front of you *Lean forwards. The cars were moving forward slowly.*
2 towards the front of something, such as a train or room *To get to the dining car you have to go forward.*
3 towards something better in the future *Passing the exam would be a big step forward for Ruby.*
4 used about a period time from which something starts *From this day forward, I'll be good to my sister.*

forward *adjective*
1 in the direction in front of you *a forward movement*
2 towards the front *I prefer to sit in the forward part of the train.*
3 if someone is forward, they are too friendly and say what they really think

forward *verb*
forwards, forwarding, forwarded
1 if you forward an email you've received, you send it to someone else
2 if you forward a letter or parcel to someone, you send it on to them (or to someone else) at a different address

forward *noun* **forwards**
a player in a game such as football or hockey whose position at the front is closest to the other team. A forward's job is to attack and score goals.

fossil *noun* **fossils**
an animal or plant from prehistoric times that is preserved in a rock or whose shape is preserved in a rock

ORIGIN from Latin *fossilis* 'obtained from digging up'

fossilised *adjective*
preserved in a rock or whose shape is preserved in a rock *a fossilised dinosaur*

LANGUAGE EXTRA also spelt *fossilized*

foster *verb*
fosters, fostering, fostered
if a grown-up fosters someone else's child, they take the child into their home and look after him or her for a period of time
compare: **adopt**

foster *adjective*
connected with fostering a child. The child is called a foster child and the person who looks after the child is called a foster parent. The foster parent's home is called a foster home.

fought
past tense & past participle of **fight**

foul *adjective*
1 very unpleasant or dirty *a foul smell*; *Dad's in a foul mood.*

SYNONYM **disgusting**

2 not allowed by the rules of a sport or game *a foul move*

181

foul–frank

foul *noun* **fouls**
an action that isn't allowed by the rules of a sport or game

foul *verb*
fouls, fouling, fouled
to do something to another player in a sport or game that isn't allowed by the rules

found
past tense & past participle of **find**

found *verb*
founds, founding, founded
to start something such as an organisation, religion or hospital, for example by providing the money for it *Our school was founded in 1906.*

foundation *noun*
1 the foundations of a building are the parts of it under the ground that support it
2 (*plural* **foundations**) a very important thing or group of things, for example ideas, actions or situations, from which something can develop *Our teacher has given us a good foundation in grammar.*
3 the founding of something *The foundation of the cathedral goes back to the thirteenth century.*

founder *noun* **founders**
someone who founds something *Buddhism was founded by Siddhartha Gautama.*

founder *verb*
founders, foundering, foundered
1 if something such as a plan or action founders, it goes wrong and fails
2 if a ship founders, it fills up with water and sinks

foundry *noun* **foundries**
1 a factory where metal is heated and poured into different shapes
2 a glass foundry is a factory where glass objects are made, for example by heating and pouring glass

fountain *noun* **fountains**
1 a structure with a stream or streams of water going up into the air, used for example in a park to make it look more attractive
2 a piece of equipment in an office or public place that produces a small stream of water to drink
3 a fountain pen is a pen with a cartridge of ink inside it or with a rubber tube inside that you fill with ink

four *adjective & noun* **fours**
1 the number 4
2 if you're on all fours, you have your hands and knees on the ground *Stop crawling on all fours like a baby.*

four-star *adjective*
of high quality *a four-star restaurant*

fourteen *adjective & noun* **fourteens**
the number 14 **fourteenth** *adjective & noun*

fourth *adjective & noun*
1 used about something or someone that comes in place number 4 *in the fourth row*
2 (*plural* **fourths**) in American English, a fourth is one of 4 equal parts of something *a fourth of the class*

fourthly *adverb*
in fourth place

fowl *noun* **fowls** or **fowl**
a bird such as a chicken that is kept for its eggs and meat

fox *noun* **foxes**
a wild animal that looks like a dog with a pointed face and long thick tail

fox *verb*
foxes, foxing, foxed
if something foxes you, you don't understand it

foxglove *noun* **foxgloves**
a tall plant with lots of purple or white flowers shaped like bells

foxy *adjective* **foxier, foxiest**
if someone is foxy, they are clever at getting what they want, for example by tricking people

> SYNONYM cunning

> LANGUAGE EXTRA in books and fables, foxes are often shown as clever creatures, as in the simile *as cunning as a fox*

foyer ['foy-yay'] *noun* **foyers**
the large open space when you go into a building such as a hotel or theatre

> SYNONYM lobby

> ORIGIN from Old French *foier* 'fireplace'

fracking *noun*
a way of removing gas from under the ground by drilling straight down very deep into the earth and then across into the rock where the gas is. Water, sand and chemicals are forced into the rock to make the gas come out.

fraction *noun* **fractions**
1 a tiny amount or part of something
2 in maths, a fraction is part of something that has been split into equal parts. Fractions are written using two numbers, one on top of the other, for example $\frac{1}{2}$ (a half) and $\frac{1}{3}$ (one third). The top number is the numerator (it shows the number of parts you're talking about). The bottom number is the denominator (it tells you how many parts the whole has been split into).

fractionally *adverb*
by a tiny amount *Kala's mark was fractionally higher than mine.*

fracture *verb*
fractures, fracturing, fractured
if you fracture a bone in your body, for example your leg or arm, you break it

fracture *noun* **fractures**
a break in a bone of your body

fragile *adjective*
if something is fragile, it can be broken or damaged easily **fragility** *noun*

fragment *noun* **fragments**
a small piece or part of something larger *I dropped the vase and it broke into fragments.*

fragmented *adjective*
if computer files are fragmented, there are small parts of them all over the hard disk, which slows down a computer

fragrance ['fray-grerns'] *noun* **fragrances**
1 a pleasant smell, especially a sweet one
2 a liquid that people put on the body to smell pleasant

fragrant ['fray-grernt'] *adjective*
having a pleasant smell, especially a sweet one

frail *adjective* **frailer, frailest**
if someone is frail, they are weak, for example because they are very old **frailty** *noun*

frame *noun* **frames**
1 a piece of wood, plastic or metal that goes around the edge of something, such as a picture or window, to hold it in place
2 a structure that supports something *a bicycle frame; a climbing frame* (metal or wooden bars for practising climbing on)
3 the plastic or metal part of a pair of glasses that holds the glass in place
4 the shape and size of a person's body *The footballer has a big frame.*
5 your frame of mind is the way you feel at a particular time *I'll be in a better frame of mind tomorrow.*

> SYNONYM for sense 5: mood

frame *verb*
frames, framing, framed
1 to put something such as a picture or certificate into a frame, for example so that it can be displayed on a wall
2 to frame someone is to make it look as if they have committed a crime, for example by lying to the police about them

framework *noun* **frameworks**
1 a structure, usually made of steel or wood, that supports something, for example a building, and gives it its shape
2 the ideas or rules that someone uses as a guide to help them do something such as make a decision
3 a particular way of doing something

franc *noun* **francs**
a unit of money in Switzerland and some other countries, especially in Africa. The franc was used in France and Belgium before the euro.

> ORIGIN from the Latin words *Francorum Rex* 'King of the Franks', which was written on French gold coins in the 14th century. The Franks were a tribe that gave its name to France, a country they conquered in the 6th century.

France *noun*
a country in Western Europe between the English Channel and the Mediterranean

franchise *noun* **franchises**
1 a shop or business that has permission to sell products belonging to a larger organisation *McDonald's is a franchise.*
2 the permission or agreement a shop or business has to sell these products

Franco- *prefix*
connected with France

frank *adjective* **franker, frankest**
1 if you are frank, you tell people the truth or tell them what you really think in an honest way, even if they don't like what you say

2 also used about what someone says or writes *a frank answer*

frankness *noun*

frank *verb*
franks, franking, franked
to print an official mark on a letter or parcel to show that you've paid the postage *a franking machine*

frankly *adverb*
1 used when you mean that you're saying what you really think, even if someone doesn't like it *Frankly, you're wrong!*
2 in a way that shows that you're telling the truth *Our teacher spoke frankly about her life in Australia* (she told us all the details about it).

frantic *adjective*
1 if someone is frantic, they're so worried or frightened about something that they can't control their feelings
2 if something someone does is frantic, they do it with lots of energy and in a hurry but they can't think clearly about it because they are so worried *There was a frantic search for the missing boy.*

frantically *adverb*
with lots of energy, for example because you're worried or frightened about something or because you're in a hurry *Charlotte was running frantically to catch the bus.*

fraternal *adjective*
between friends or between brothers *fraternal feelings*

ORIGIN from Latin *frater* 'brother'

fraud *noun* **frauds**
1 the crime of getting money from someone in a dishonest way, for example by using someone's credit card or cheating the government
2 someone who tricks people by pretending to be something they are not or to have qualities they don't have

fraudulent *adjective*
dishonest

fraught *adjective*
1 full of something bad such as worry, problems or danger *a fraught situation*; *Travelling to this part of the country is fraught with danger.*
2 if someone is fraught, they are very worried

fray *noun*
an activity such as a fight, argument or competition *Everyone in the room entered the fray* (started fighting, for example).

frayed *adjective*
1 if something such as a piece of clothing or a rope is frayed, its threads become loose at the edges, for example because it is old
2 if people's nerves or tempers are frayed, they are upset or angry, usually because of a bad situation that has gradually got worse *Tempers were becoming frayed in the hot weather.*

frazzled *adjective* (informal)
if you are frazzled, you are tired, confused or upset and can't deal with things properly

freak *noun* **freaks**
1 a person or animal that looks strange and abnormal

2 someone who behaves strangely or differently from other people
3 (informal) someone who really likes a particular thing or doing a particular activity *a computer freak*

SYNONYM for sense 3: **fanatic**

freak *adjective*
used about something that is so unusual that it almost never happens *He was killed in a freak accident.*

freak *verb* (informal)
freaks, freaking, freaked
to become or to make someone become very frightened, surprised, worried or upset *Take off that Halloween mask — you're freaking me out! I was late home from school and Mum just freaked.*

freakish *adjective*
very unusual or abnormal *freakish weather*

freaky *adjective* **freakier, freakiest**
very strange and often frightening

SYNONYM **weird**

freckle *noun* **freckles**
one of the tiny light-brown marks that some people have on their skin, especially on the face, arms and shoulders

freckled *adjective*
if a part of your body is freckled, it has freckles on it *a freckled face*

LANGUAGE EXTRA you can also say *freckly*

free *adjective* **freer, freest**
1 allowed to do or say what you want or go where you like, without anyone stopping you *You're free to go home now.*
2 also used about something such as a country or election in which no-one stops you from doing something *There is free movement of goods in the EU.*
3 not kept somewhere, for example as a prisoner or in a cage *He set the monkey free.*
4 not fixed, caught or tied somewhere *Isla's dress got caught in the door and she struggled to get it free.*
5 not costing any money *I've got some free tickets to the match.*
6 not being used by anyone *Is this seat free?*
7 not doing anything at a certain time *Are you free to come over tomorrow? I have lots of free time this weekend.*
8 not having something bad *Grandma took her medicine and is now free of pain.*
9 giving people more of something than is usual, for example money, advice or opinions *My brother's very free with his money.*

SIMILE 'as free as a bird' means free to go anywhere

free *adverb*
1 free or free of charge means without paying any money *We got into the museum free. Children can travel free of charge on the buses.*
2 without anyone stopping you *The children were running free in the park.*

free *verb*
frees, freeing, freed
1 to stop keeping a person or animal as a prisoner or in a cage *The captured soldiers were finally freed.*
2 to help a person or animal to get out of a situation where they are fixed, caught or tied somewhere *After the accident the police had to free many people from their cars.*
3 to take away something bad from someone *Teachers want to be freed from too much paperwork.*

-free *suffix*
used for making adjectives that mean without something, usually something bad *fat-free cheese*; *duty-free goods*; *My laptop has been trouble-free for six months.*

freebie *noun* **freebies**
an informal word for something someone gives you that you don't have to pay for

freedom *noun*
1 a situation in which you are allowed to do or say what you want or go where you like *freedom of speech* (being allowed to say what you like without being put in prison)
2 a situation in which you are no longer kept somewhere, for example as a prisoner
3 a situation in which you do not have something bad *freedom from disease*

freehand *adjective*
a freehand drawing is one done by hand without using tools such as tracing paper, stencils or rulers

freehand *adverb*
to draw freehand is to draw by hand without using tools

free kick *noun* **free kicks**
when there is a free kick in a football match, a player is allowed to kick the ball freely on one occasion because a player in the other team has done something wrong

freely *adverb*
1 if you do something freely, no-one stops you from doing it or controls you in any way *Everyone can speak freely in this country.*
2 easily and without any problems *The motorway traffic is moving freely. This software is freely available on the internet.*
3 honestly and without hiding anything *I freely admit I've been a bad student.*
4 in a way that shows you are willing *A volunteer is someone who gives his or her time freely.*

free period *noun* **free periods**
a part of the school day when a student does not have a lesson

free-range *adjective*
free-range farm animals such as chickens are allowed to move around freely outside instead of being kept in cages *free-range eggs* (produced by free-range chickens) compare: **battery** (sense 4)

freestyle *noun*
a swimming race in which swimmers can use any style of swimming. Most swimmers choose the crawl because it is the fastest way of swimming.

free verse *noun*
a type of poetry that does not rhyme

freeware *noun*
computer software that you can get free, for example by downloading it from the internet
compare: **shareware**

freeway *noun* **freeways**
a very wide road in the USA on which cars travel very fast

freewheel *verb*
freewheels, freewheeling, freewheeled
to ride a bicycle without using the pedals, usually when going down a slope

freeze *verb*
freezes, freezing, froze, frozen
1 if water or another liquid freezes or if something freezes it, it becomes so cold that it turns into ice
2 if something such as a pond freezes, it becomes covered with ice
3 if a pipe freezes, the water inside it turns into ice
4 if something such as a lock freezes, it no longer works because the weather is so cold
5 to feel extremely cold *You'll freeze if you go out without a scarf.*
6 if someone freezes food, they put it into a freezer to make it very cold and hard so that it will last for a long time
7 to stop moving suddenly and keep completely still, for example because you are afraid *'Freeze!' said the police officer.*
8 if a computer or computer program freezes, it stops working and does not respond to any normal action, for example by a mouse or keyboard
9 if the government or a company freezes prices or wages, it keeps them at the same level

freeze *noun* **freezes**
1 a period when the temperature falls below freezing
2 a period when prices or wages are kept at the same level

freezer *noun* **freezers**
a large piece of equipment like a refrigerator (or a small piece that is a part of a refrigerator) in which people freeze food so that it will last for a long time

freezing *adjective*
extremely cold *The classroom is freezing. I'm freezing cold!*

freezing *noun*
1 the temperature at which water freezes (0 degrees Celsius) *It's below freezing outside.*
2 a freezing point is the temperature at which water or another liquid freezes

freight ['frayt'] *noun*
goods that are carried by road vehicles, trains, ships or planes

French *adjective*
1 connected with France or the French language
2 French bread is a long thin loaf of bread that is crusty on the outside

SYNONYM **baguette**

3 French fries are long thin pieces of potato fried in oil and eaten hot

SYNONYM **chips**

4 a French horn is a brass musical instrument made up of a long narrow tube bent round and round inside a circular shape. You blow into a short piece of tube that sticks out at one end and the sound comes out of a wide opening at the other end.
5 French windows (or French doors) are a pair of glass doors that open onto a garden or balcony

French *noun*
1 the language people speak in France, Belgium, Switzerland, parts of Canada and some other countries
2 the French are people from France

Frenchman *noun* **Frenchmen**
a man from France

Frenchwoman *noun* **Frenchwomen**
a woman from France

frenzied *adjective*
done by someone who cannot control their feelings *a frenzied attack*

frenzy *noun* **frenzies**
1 the behaviour of someone who cannot control their feelings *The whole crowd was in a frenzy.*
2 a period of time when a lot of things happen quickly *a frenzy of activity*

frequency *noun*
1 the number of times something happens
2 when something happens lots of times *These acts of bullying have happened with great frequency.*
3 (*plural* **frequencies**) in physics, the frequency of a sound or radio wave is the number of times it vibrates every second

frequent ['free-kwernt'] *adjective*
happening a lot or doing something a lot

ANTONYM **occasional**

frequent ['fri-kwent'] *verb*
frequents, frequenting, frequented
to go somewhere lots of times *I frequent the swimming pool three times a week.*

frequently *adverb*
lots of times

SYNONYM **often**

ANTONYM **occasionally**

fresh *adjective* **fresher, freshest**
1 if food is fresh, it looks good and is good to eat because it has recently been prepared, picked, caught or killed. Fresh food is not tinned or frozen. *fresh fish*; *Put the strawberries in the fridge to keep them fresh.*
2 if flowers are fresh, they have recently been picked but still look as good as when they were growing
3 used about something that has happened or was done recently *My sister still has fresh memories of school. There were fresh footprints outside the window.*
4 completely new *We need to take a fresh look at the problem.*
5 replacing or adding to something else *Can you give me a fresh cup of tea?*
6 feeling clean or cool in a very pleasant way *The weather is fresher today. I need some fresh air* (the pleasant air outside).
7 slightly cold in a way that makes you feel uncomfortable *Wrap up well – it's very fresh today. A fresh wind was blowing from the north.*

SYNONYM **chilly**

8 full of energy *I woke up after my nap feeling relaxed and fresh.*
9 fresh water is water in rivers, lakes and ponds that does not have any salt in it like the sea
10 if someone is fresh from somewhere, they were in that place a short time before *My parents are fresh from a meeting with the head teacher.*

freshness *noun*

SIMILE 'as fresh as a daisy' means very fresh (sense 8)

freshen *verb*
freshens, freshening, freshened
1 to make something feel or look cleaner, more pleasant or better *They freshened up our classroom by painting it.*
2 to make yourself cleaner, for example by washing your hands and face *I'm very hot – I need to freshen up.*
3 to become chilly *The wind is freshening.*

freshly *adjective*
used about something that happened a short time ago *a freshly prepared meal*

SYNONYM **recently**

freshwater *adjective*
1 not salty *a freshwater lake*
2 living in the water of rivers, lakes or ponds, which is not salty *freshwater fish*

fret *verb*
frets, fretting, fretted
to worry about something

fretful *adjective*
worried or unhappy about something
fretfully *adverb*

frets *noun plural*
thin metal strips across the long narrow part of a guitar (called the neck) where you press your fingers to change the notes

friar *noun* **friars**
a member of one of several types of Christian religious groups. Friars live in poverty and travel around teaching the Christian religion.

ORIGIN from French *frère* 'brother'

friary *noun* **friaries**
a building where friars live

friction *noun*
1 (*plural* **frictions**) angry feelings between people or groups, for example because they don't agree with each other
2 when something rubs against something else *The friction of the rope against the wall caused it to break.*
3 in science, friction is a force that slows down moving objects by stopping one surface moving easily over another. For example, a rough surface has more friction than a smooth one.

Friday – frolic

Friday noun Fridays
the day of the week between Thursday and Saturday. It is the last day of the school week or working week before the weekend.

ORIGIN from Old English *Frigedæg* 'Frigg's day'. In Old Norse, Frigg was the goddess of love.

fridge noun fridges
a piece of equipment like a large box with shelves and a door, used for keeping food cold

SYNONYM refrigerator

friend noun friends
1 someone you like and know well and want to spend your time with but who is not a member of your family
2 a person or country that shares the same interests as another and likes to help them *Britain and America are friends.*

ANTONYM enemy

3 someone who creates a link with you on an internet site such as Facebook even though they may not be your friend. Friends can see each other's posts (information such as messages) and send posts to each other. *Lucy has 500 friends on Facebook.*
4 if you're friends with someone, you're that person's friend *Dan is friends with Jake.*

friend verb
friends, friending, friended
if you friend someone on an internet site such as Facebook, you add them to your list of friends by creating a link with them

ANTONYMS to unfriend, to defriend

friendless adjective
feeling sad because you have no friends

friendly adjective friendlier, friendliest
1 if someone is friendly, they are very pleasant, kind and helpful towards someone *a friendly police officer*
2 also used about someone's words and actions and about places *Dad gave me some friendly advice* (very helpful advice). *Our school is really friendly* (very pleasant and kind towards students).
3 if you're friendly with someone, you like them quite a lot but they may not be your friend
4 a friendly country is one that has a good relationship with another
5 a friendly game or match is one that is played for fun and is not part of a competition

friendship noun friendships
1 being someone's friend, or the feelings that friends have for each other *Hannah and Jess have a close friendship.*
2 a good relationship with another country or group

fries noun plural
long thin pieces of potato fried in oil and eaten hot

SYNONYMS French fries, chips

frieze noun friezes
a wide strip around the top of a building or wall, decorated with designs or images and usually carved out of stone. Ancient Greek and Roman buildings often have friezes.

frigate noun frigates
a small fast warship often used for protecting bigger ships

fright noun
a sudden strong feeling of being frightened or very upset *I got a fright when I saw her with blood all over her arm.*

frighten verb
frightens, frightening, frightened
1 to make someone feel worried, for example because they think they might get hurt or something bad might happen *We heard a loud bang that frightened us. I was lost in the forest and felt frightened. Emma was frightened to go home by herself.*
2 to make someone very upset, uncomfortable and shocked *Take off that mask – it frightens me!*
3 if you're frightened of something or someone, they frighten you
4 if you frighten a person or animal away, they go away quickly because they don't want anything bad to happen to them

frightening adjective
1 making you feel worried, for example because you think you might get hurt or something bad might happen *It was frightening going home after dark.*
2 making you feel very upset, uncomfortable and shocked *Lots of people think spiders are frightening.*

frighteningly adverb

frightful adjective
1 extremely bad *frightful weather*
2 used for saying strongly that something or someone is as you say they are, especially when they are bad *You've made a frightful mess. She's a frightful bore.*

frightfully adverb
extremely *a frightfully hot day*

frill noun frills
1 a strip of material with small folds in it used as a decoration, for example on the edge of a dress *a lace frill*
2 **no frills** used about something that is plain and simple and has no extra features or comforts *We stayed in a hotel with no frills. Jo had a no-frills birthday party.*

frilly adjective frillier, frilliest
decorated with frills

fringe noun fringes
1 a line of short hair on your head that has been cut so that it hangs down over your forehead
2 fringes are small thin threads of material such as cotton or wool that hang loosely from the edges of something such as a piece of clothing, cushion or rug. They are used as a decoration.
3 the part of a something furthest from its centre *Our school is on the southern fringe of the city.*

Frisbee noun (trademark)
1 (*plural* **Frisbees**) a piece of plastic shaped like a large saucer that you throw to someone to catch
2 the game of throwing a Frisbee

ORIGIN the name comes from the pie tins of the *Frisbie Bakery* in Connecticut in the USA. College students started throwing the tins around as a game in the 1930s.

frisk verb
frisks, frisking, frisked
if someone frisks you, for example at an airport, they search you with their hands to see if you are carrying something against the law, such as a gun

frisky adjective friskier, friskiest
lively and full of fun *a frisky kitten*
friskily adverb **friskiness** noun

fritter noun fritters
food such as a piece of fruit or meat that is covered with batter (flour, eggs and water) and cooked in hot fat

fritter verb
fritters, frittering, frittered
to waste time or money on things that are not important *I've frittered away the whole day playing games on the computer.*

frivolity noun frivolities
an action, thing or someone's behaviour that is not serious

frivolous adjective
1 if someone is frivolous, they do not behave in a serious way when someone expects them to be serious
2 also used about someone's words or actions *a frivolous question* (one that is silly or not important)
frivolously adverb

ANTONYM serious

frizzy adjective frizzier, frizziest
frizzy hair has lots of small stiff curls

fro adverb
to and fro backwards and forwards

frock noun frocks
an old-fashioned word for a girl's or woman's dress

frog noun frogs
a small green jumping animal with a smooth body and big eyes. Frogs live in water and on land and develop from tiny water animals called tadpoles.

frogman noun frogmen
someone who swims and works under the water using breathing equipment. Frogmen are often police officers or soldiers.

SYNONYM diver

frogspawn noun
a substance like jelly containing the eggs of a frog

frogwoman noun frogwomen
a woman who swims and works under the water using breathing equipment. Frogwomen are often police officers or soldiers.

frolic verb
frolics, frolicking, frolicked
if people or animals frolic, they run around and play happily and with lots of energy

from – frustration

from *preposition*
1 used for showing where something or someone starts, or where something or someone is before it is taken, sent or given *I took the pen from my pocket. My mum comes from France.*
2 used for showing when something starts *The English lesson is from nine to ten o'clock.*
3 used for showing a distance between places or people *We live two miles from the school. Get away from me!*
4 used for showing a range of different things or numbers *They sell everything from books to food. The exercises go from pages 6 to 8.*
5 used for showing what something is made of *The nest is built from twigs.*
6 because of something *I suffer from hay fever. I'm tired from working so hard.*
7 used when you stop or protect something or someone *I stopped her from running across the road. We're protected from the rain.*
8 used for showing a difference *I'm very different from my sister.*

front *noun* **fronts**
1 the part of something that faces forwards *The front of the school was decorated with flags.*
2 the part of your body between your neck and legs, especially your chest
3 a similar part of the body of an animal, bird or insect
4 the part of something that is at or near the beginning *the front of the book*
5 a road going along the edge of the sea for people to walk along
6 a place where two armies fight each other in a war
7 a weather front is where masses of air of different temperatures meet. A mass of cold air is called a cold front and a mass of warm air is called a warm front.
8 if someone or something is in front or in front of you, they are in a position in which you are looking straight at them *Walk in front and I'll follow behind. She stood in front of me smiling.*
9 if someone or something is in front (or in the front), they are in or near the front part of something *On short journeys I prefer to sit in front (or in the front). The engine is in the front.*
10 if you do or say something in front of someone, they can see and hear you clearly *Say your 12 times table in front of the class.*
11 if you are in front of something, or if you do something in front of something, the front part of that thing is turned towards you *I'm sitting in front of the computer.*

front *adjective*
at the front *the front seat*; *the front door* (main door of a house or building); *the front room* (main room in a house, where people sit and relax); *the front page* (first page of a newspaper or book)

front *verb*
fronts, fronting, fronted
in grammar, if you front a word, phrase or sentence, you move it from its normal position after a verb and put it before the verb instead. For example, in the sentence 'I go swimming every Monday', you can put 'every Monday' before the verb: 'Every Monday I go swimming.' When it is before the verb, it is called a fronted phrase. **fronting** *noun*

frontier *noun* **frontiers**
the line that divides two countries

SYNONYM **border**

frost *noun*
1 a powder of ice that covers things outside in freezing weather
2 (*plural* **frosts**) a period of freezing weather when frost is formed

frost *verb*
frosts, frosting, frosted
1 if something such as a car window frosts up or gets frosted up, it becomes covered in frost
2 frosted glass is glass with a rough surface that you can't see through

frostbite *noun*
a serious medical problem in which freezing weather damages parts of the body such as fingers or toes

frostbitten *adjective*
damaged by the freezing weather *frostbitten toes*

frosting *noun*
the American word for icing

frosty *adjective* **frostier, frostiest**
1 very cold with temperatures below freezing *a frosty night*
2 covered with frost *frosty windows*
3 not very friendly *a frosty welcome*

froth *noun*
1 lots of tiny bubbles on the surface of a liquid such as beer or coffee
2 tiny white bubbles around the mouth of an animal or person

SYNONYM **foam**

froth *verb*
froths, frothing, frothed
1 if a liquid such as beer or coffee froths, it produces lots of tiny bubbles
2 if an animal or person froths at the mouth, tiny white bubbles come out of their mouth, for example because they are ill

SYNONYM **to foam**

frothy *adjective* **frothier, frothiest**
1 with lots of tiny bubbles on top *frothy coffee*
2 not serious but good fun *a light and frothy comedy*

frown *noun* **frowns**
the particular expression on your face that you make when you frown

frown *verb*
frowns, frowning, frowned
1 to make lines in your forehead by moving your eyebrows closer together because you are worried, confused, angry or thinking very hard
2 if someone frowns on something, they think it is wrong or bad

froze
past tense of **freeze**

frozen
past participle of **freeze**

frozen *adjective*
1 turned into ice *frozen water*
2 covered with ice *a frozen lake*
3 containing frozen water *frozen pipes*
4 frozen food is made very cold so that it will last for a long time
5 feeling extremely cold *Put on the heat – I'm frozen!*

frugal *adjective*
1 if someone is frugal, they spend very little money
2 also used about someone's meals and way of life *a frugal lunch* (small and simple and not costing much); *a frugal life* (simple because very little money is spent)
frugality *noun*

fruit *noun* **fruit** or **fruits**
1 something that grows on a plant or tree and contains the seeds of the plant, for example an apple, orange or tomato. Fruit is often used as food.
2 a piece of fruit is one single fruit such as an apple or banana
3 the good things that come from something such as hard work or effort *Granddad is enjoying the fruits of many years of work.*
4 a fruit machine is a machine for playing a game to win money. When you put in a coin, three pictures appear and if they are the same you win.

SYNONYM **slot machine**

5 a fruit salad is a mixture of small pieces of different kinds of fruit, for example eaten as a dessert

fruitcake *noun* **fruitcakes**
a cake made with dried fruits such as raisins, often with nuts and spices in it

fruitful *adjective*
producing good results *My mum had a fruitful meeting with my teacher.*
fruitfully *adverb*

SYNONYM **successful**

fruitless *adjective*
not producing any results at all *a fruitless search*

SYNONYM **unsuccessful**

fruitlessly *adverb*
without any success

SYNONYM **unsuccessfully**

fruity *adjective* **fruitier, fruitiest**
1 tasting or smelling like fruit *a fruity taste*
2 deep, strong and pleasant *a fruity voice*

frumpy *adjective* **frumpier, frumpiest**
1 not fashionable *frumpy clothes*
2 wearing frumpy clothes *a frumpy old lady*

frustrate *verb*
frustrates, frustrating, frustrated
1 to make someone feel angry or sad because they can't do or have something or change a bad situation *I'm frustrated because I can't sing. Not being able to sing is quite frustrating.*
2 to stop something or someone from being successful *The snow has completely frustrated our plans.*

frustration *noun* **frustrations**
an angry or sad feeling because you can't do or have something or change a bad situation

fry–fund

fry *verb*
fries, frying, fried
1 to cook something in hot oil or fat
2 to be cooked in hot oil or fat *The fish is frying in the pan.*

frying pan *noun* frying pans
a round pan that has a long handle and is not very deep, used for frying food

ft
short for **foot** or **feet** *I'm 5 ft tall.*

fuddled *adjective*
confused in the mind, for example because of feeling sleepy or being out in the sun for too long

fuddy-duddy *noun* fuddy-duddies
someone with old-fashioned ideas

fudge *noun* fudges
a soft brown sweet made from butter, sugar and milk

fuel *noun* fuels
1 something such as coal, oil or gas that makes heat or power when it is burnt
2 petrol or diesel, used for example in vehicles or aircraft

fuel *verb*
fuels, fuelling, fuelled
1 to provide something with a fuel such as coal, oil or gas for heat or power
2 to put fuel into a vehicle or aircraft

fugitive [ˈfyoo-ji-tiv] *noun* fugitives
someone who is hiding, usually from the police, for example because they have committed a crime

-ful *suffix*
used for showing the amount of something that fills a particular container or that can be carried by a part of the body *a basketful of flowers*; *an armful of twigs*

fulfil *verb*
fulfils, fulfilling, fulfilled
1 to do something that you are supposed to do, such as a duty or promise
2 to do something that you want to do, such as an ambition or hope
3 to do what someone needs *My laptop fulfils all my requirements.*

fulfilled *adjective*
happy because you are doing what you want in your life or in a particular situation, for example something interesting, important or good

fulfilling *adjective*
if something such as a job is fulfilling, it makes you happy because it gives you what you want, for example it lets you do something interesting, important or good

full *adjective* fuller, fullest
1 with no more room for anything or anyone else *The hotel is full.*
2 having lots of something or many people *a book full of pictures*; *a room full of children*
3 complete *Can you give me the full details?*
4 used for describing the greatest amount of something *Turn the radio up full* (as loud as possible). *The train was travelling at full speed.*
5 with lots of things happening *I've had a very full day.*
6 if you're full or full up, you've eaten enough food
7 if a piece of clothing is full, it contains a lot of material *a full skirt*
8 if a taste or sound is full, it is strong and pleasant *the full flavour of fresh coffee*
9 **in full** completely *Dad paid the bill in full.*
10 **in full swing** happening now and having started some time ago *The party is in full swing.*
11 **to the full** as much as possible *My brother enjoys life to the full.*
12 **full of beans** full of energy
fullness *noun*

full *adverb*
completely *He hit me full in the face. You know full well what I mean.*

full board *noun*
if you have full board in a hotel, you have all your meals there

full-fat *adjective*
full-fat milk, cream, cheese or yoghurt has all its natural fat with none of it removed
compare: **semi-skimmed** and **skimmed**

full house *noun*
when there are no empty seats left in a place such as a cinema or sports stadium

full moon *noun* full moons
1 the moon when it appears in the sky as a complete circle
2 the time when this happens

full name *noun* full names
your whole name including your first, middle and family name

full-scale *adjective*
1 used about a model or drawing of something that is the same size as the original thing
2 complete, or as big as can be *a full-scale investigation*

full-size *adjective*
used about an object that is the same size as a normal object of that type and no smaller *a full-size statue of Mandela*

> **LANGUAGE EXTRA** you can also say *full-sized*

full stop *noun* full stops
a punctuation mark that looks like a dot

> **LANGUAGE EXTRA** a *full stop* is used for showing the end of a sentence (but you do not use one after a question mark or exclamation mark). It is always followed by a capital letter at the beginning of the first word of the next sentence.
> A full stop is sometimes used in words that have been shortened, for example *etc.* (short for Latin *et cetera* 'and so on') or *p.* (short for page).

full-time *adjective & adverb*
for all the hours in a week that people normally work or study *My mum has a full-time job. My sister studies full-time.*

fully *adverb*
completely *fully dressed* (with all your clothes on); *The hotel is fully booked.*

fumble *verb*
fumbles, fumbling, fumbled
to do something in a clumsy way using your hands, for example look for something or move around *I was fumbling around in the dark for the torch.*

fume *verb*
fumes, fuming, fumed
to be fuming is to be very angry about something

fumes *noun plural*
smoke or gas that has a strong and unpleasant smell and can make you ill if you breathe it *dangerous car fumes*

> **ORIGIN** from Latin *fumus* 'smoke'

fun *noun*
1 an activity that you really like doing or the happy feeling you get from doing it *Maths is fun. Ismail plays the guitar for fun* (because he likes doing it, not for any serious reason). *It's not much fun being indoors by yourself.*

> **SYNONYM** enjoyment

2 great energy and enthusiasm *The children are full of fun.*
3 if you have fun, you enjoy yourself
4 if someone is fun, you like being with them *My uncle's great fun!*
5 if you make fun of someone or something, you think they're silly and you laugh at them and say unkind things

fun *adjective*
enjoyable *Going to the beach is a fun thing to do.*

function *noun* functions
1 the job that something or someone is supposed to do
2 an official event such as a party
3 a basic operation performed by a computer or calculator
4 a function key on a computer keyboard is a key that you press to perform an action on screen. Function keys are usually at the top of the keyboard and are marked with the letter F and a number, for example F4.
5 in grammar, function words are words such as 'and', 'the', 'with' or 'she' that show relationships between words in a sentence

function *verb*
functions, functioning, functioned
1 to work correctly or in a particular way
2 to do the job of a particular thing *This room also functions as a spare bedroom.*

functional *adjective*
1 working correctly and well *The central heating isn't functional.*
2 useful rather than attractive *functional buildings*
functionally *adverb*

fund *noun* funds
an amount of money collected or saved for a special purpose *The school has started a fund to buy new textbooks. My sister is raising funds for the school* (collecting money from people to give to the school).

fund *verb*
funds, funding, funded
to provide money for something *My trip to Paris was funded by the school* (the school paid all the money for it).

fundamental–fuss

fundamental *adjective*
very important or more important than anything else *fundamental changes*

fundamentally *adverb*
in a very important way, or in many important ways *My sister and I are fundamentally different.*

funeral *noun* **funerals**
a ceremony where someone who has just died is buried or cremated

funfair *noun* **funfairs**
an outside area where people go to have fun. There are games to play and machines such as merry-go-rounds for riding on and bumper cars for driving in.

SYNONYM fair

fungus ['fun-gers'] *noun* **fungi** ['fun-gye']
a type of plant without any green colour, leaves or flowers. Fungi grow in wet places and live on other plants or rotten surfaces. Mushrooms and toadstools are fungi.

funicular *noun* **funiculars**
a small railway, usually with a single carriage, for carrying people up or down a steep slope or mountain. The carriage is pulled by a cable.

fun-loving *adjective*
a fun-loving person really likes to enjoy himself or herself

funnel *noun* **funnels**
1 the chimney on a boat, ship or old-fashioned steam train
2 a narrow tube with a wide top, used for pouring something such as a liquid or powder into a narrow container

funnily *adverb*
1 in an unusual or strange way *He seemed to be walking funnily.*
2 **funnily enough** used for saying that something is surprising or that something is definitely true even though it seems surprising *Funnily enough, I bumped into her this morning.*

funny *adjective* **funnier, funniest**
1 making someone laugh *a funny joke; a funny clown; Having chickenpox isn't funny* (it's serious).
2 unusual or strange *What's that funny noise?*
3 slightly ill *I feel funny. I've got a funny tummy* (a stomach upset).
4 not working properly *My phone has gone funny.*
5 your funny bone is the outside part of your elbow that hurts and gives you a funny feeling if you knock it

fur *noun*
1 the soft hair that covers some animals such as cats and dogs
2 (plural **furs**) the skin of an animal with its soft hair, used for making things such as clothes, or a material that looks and feels like this *I was wearing warm gloves with fur inside. The film star wore a fur coat.*
3 a hard light grey substance that forms in places that are always wet, such as pipes and kettles

furious *adjective*
1 very angry
2 using a lot of energy and effort *There's a furious battle between the two teams.*
3 very fast *at a furious pace*

furiously *adverb*
1 in a very angry way *'Go away,' said Ben, furiously.*
2 with a lot of energy and effort *They were running furiously to catch the bus.*

furlong *noun* **furlongs**
a unit for measuring length, equal to 201 metres, used mainly in horse racing. There are eight furlongs in a mile.

furnace *noun* **furnaces**
1 a large container with a very hot fire inside, used for example for heating metal, making glass or burning rubbish
2 in American English, a furnace is a container for burning fuel to provide heating in a house or building

ORIGIN from Latin *fornax* 'oven'

furnish *verb*
furnishes, furnishing, furnished
1 to put furniture into a room, house, flat or building *a furnished flat* (with the furniture already in it)
2 to furnish someone with something is to give them something that they need

SYNONYM for sense 2: to provide

furniture *noun*
large objects such as tables, chairs, beds or bookcases that you need in a building in order to be able to live or work there

furrow *noun* **furrows**
1 a long line that is dug in the ground with a plough so that a farmer can grow crops there
2 a deep line, especially in someone's forehead

furrow *verb*
furrows, furrowing, furrowed
if you furrow your brow, you make deep lines appear in it when you frown (move your eyebrows closer together)

furry *adjective* **furrier, furriest**
covered with fur or with a material that looks and feels like fur *a furry animal; furry slippers*

further *adverb & adjective*
1 used when talking about a greater distance than something else *I can't walk any further.*

SYNONYM farther

2 used when talking about more progress when compared to something else *You're further ahead than me. George never got further than page 5.*
3 more of something *You can get further details from our website. There's been a further delay.*
4 further education is study or training for people who have left school but who are not at a university

further *verb*
furthers, furthering, furthered
to make something more successful, better or stronger *They work to further the cause of Welsh speakers.*

furthermore *adverb*
used for adding something extra to what you say

SYNONYM also

furthest *adverb & adjective*
used when talking about the greatest distance away from something else *Megan is the one who travels furthest to school. What's the furthest star you can see from earth?*

SYNONYM farthest

furtive *adjective*
done secretly, or connected with someone who behaves as if they have something to hide *a furtive glance; furtive behaviour*

furtively *adverb*

fury *noun*
very strong anger

ORIGIN from Latin *furia* ('rage' or 'madness'), which comes from *Furiae* 'Furies'. The Furies were three winged goddesses with snakes for hair, who chased and punished evil people.

fuse *noun* **fuses**
1 a tiny tube with a piece of wire inside, used in the plug of a piece of electrical equipment. The wire melts if there is an electrical problem, which makes the equipment stop working and prevents fires and explosions.
2 a piece of material such as a string connected to a bomb or firework. The string is lit and burns slowly along its length so that the bomb or firework explodes at a safe distance.
3 the electrical part inside a bomb that makes it explode after a certain amount of time or when it hits something

fuse *verb*
fuses, fusing, fused
1 if a piece of electrical equipment fuses, or if someone fuses it, it stops working because the wire inside the plug's fuse has melted *The lights have fused.*
2 if things fuse or if something or someone fuses them, they become joined together *These bones fuse together as you get older.*

fuselage ['fyoo-zer-lahj'; 'j' has the middle sound of 'pleasure'] *noun* **fuselages**
the main part of an aircraft, for example where the crew and passengers sit

fuss *noun*
1 behaviour or activity that shows that someone is worried or angry about something, usually something not very important *What's all the fuss about? My brother took his medicine without any fuss* (without worrying about it or creating a problem).
2 interest shown by other people in something *The film star's wedding took place without any fuss.*
3 if you make (or kick up) a fuss about something, you get angry or complain about it
4 if you make a fuss of someone, you treat them very well because you like them or love them

fuss *verb*
fusses, fussing, fussed
1 to be worried or angry about something, usually something not very important *Stop fussing – it's only a broken glass!*
2 if you fuss over someone, you pay too much attention to them

fusspot *noun* fusspots
an informal word for someone who pays too much attention to little things

fussy *adjective* fussier, fussiest
1 if you're fussy, you pay a lot of attention to things because you like them to be just right *I'm very fussy about my food.*
2 if you say you're not fussy, you mean you don't mind about a particular choice *'Do you want tea or coffee?' – 'I'm not fussy.'*
3 if something such as a pattern or piece of clothing is fussy, it has too many small details or decorations
fussily *adverb* **fussiness** *noun*

futile ['fyoo-tile] *adjective*
completely useless *Our efforts to save her were futile.* **futility** *noun*

futon ['foo-ton] *noun* futons
a mattress that can be used either as a bed or as a sofa for sitting on. Futons were first used in Japan. The Japanese futon is a mattress used only for sleeping on.

future *noun*
1 the time that will happen after the present time *In the future, I hope to go to college.*
2 what will happen to someone or something after the present time *You've got a great future ahead of you.*
3 in grammar, the future or future tense is the form of a verb that shows what is going to happen but has not happened yet. The future is usually formed using the words 'will' or 'shall' ('I shall do it later', 'he will see you tomorrow') or the contractions (short forms) 'I'll', 'you'll', 'he'll', 'she'll' and so on ('I'll do it later', 'he'll see you tomorrow').
4 **in future** from now on *In future, ask my permission before using my tablet.*

future *adjective*
happening or existing in the future *my future school*

futurist *adjective*
connected with a style of art, writing and music that gives importance to modern objects such as cars and planes and ideas such as speed and violence. It was popular at the start of the 20th century.
futurism *noun*

fuzz *noun*
thin soft hairs that cover something such as a part of the body

fuzzy *adjective* fuzzier, fuzziest
1 if something such as a picture, sound or idea is fuzzy, it is not clear
2 with lots of soft short hairs *a fuzzy little kitten*
3 with lots of short tight curls *My hair went fuzzy in the rain.*
fuzziness *noun*

g G

ORIGIN the letter G started life in the same way as C, as a shape representing a 'throwing stick' (an upside-down capital L facing left). In the Phoenician alphabet, this shape had the sound of 'g' in 'good' and its name was *gimel*. When the Etruscans borrowed the letter, they changed its sound from 'g' to 'c' (as in 'cat') because there was no 'g' sound in their language. By the time the letter passed into the Roman alphabet, it looked something like C and was used for making both 'c' and 'g' sounds. Much later, around the 3rd century BC, the Romans decided they wanted a separate letter for each of these two sounds so they added a little line to the bottom curve of C to create the letter G.

g
short for **gram** or **grams**

gabble *verb*
gabbles, gabbling, gabbled
to speak very quickly and in a way that is difficult to understand **gabble** *noun*

gable *noun* gables
the top part of the outside wall of a building between the two sloping parts of the roof. A gable is shaped like a triangle.

gad *verb*
gads, gadding, gadded
if you gad about, you go around visiting different places and having a good time

gadget *noun* gadgets
1 a small tool, machine or piece of equipment that does something useful *A graphics tablet is a handy gadget for your computer.*
2 a software gadget is a tiny program that displays something on your computer screen, for example a clock or the weather

Gaelic ['gay-lik in Ireland; 'ga-lik in Scotland] *noun*
a Celtic language with different forms that are spoken in parts of Ireland and Scotland
Gaelic *adjective*

gag *noun* gags
1 something such as a piece of cloth that is put over or into someone's mouth to stop them from speaking or calling for help
2 a joke, especially one that is told by a comedian in front of an audience

gag *verb*
gags, gagging, gagged
1 to put a gag over or into someone's mouth to stop them from speaking or calling for help
2 to have a feeling in your throat as if you are going to be sick *The smell was so bad it made me gag.*

gaggle *noun* gaggles
1 a gaggle of geese is a noisy group of geese
2 a noisy group of people

gaiety *noun*
happiness

gaily *adverb*
1 happily *They were gaily clapping to the music.*
2 brightly *a gaily painted mural*

gain *verb*
gains, gaining, gained
1 to get something, for example something useful or something you have tried very hard to get *Mira gained a good mark for her essay.*
2 to get more of something *My bike gains speed when I go downhill. These old comics have gained in value.*
3 if a clock or watch gains, it works too fast so the time it shows is later than the correct time
4 if you gain on someone, for example someone you are chasing, you gradually get closer to them

gain *noun* gains
1 an increase in something, for example an amount, weight or speed
2 money that people make

SYNONYM profit

3 getting something useful *The gains in going to a good school are obvious.*

gait *noun*
the way that someone walks

gala ['gah-ler] *noun* galas
1 a public event that celebrates a special occasion, for example with performances by singers, actors or musicians
2 a series of sports events, especially in swimming

galaxy *noun* galaxies
1 a very large group of stars
2 the Galaxy is the large group of stars that contains the sun, the earth and the other planets of the solar system
galactic *adjective*

ORIGIN from Latin *galaxias* 'Milky Way' and Greek *gala* 'milk'

gale *noun* gales
a very strong wind

gallant *adjective*
1 not afraid to face danger or difficult things *a gallant knight*

SYNONYM brave

2 used about a man who is very polite towards women
gallantly *adverb* **gallantry** *noun*

galleon *noun* galleons
a large sailing ship with three or more masts (poles holding the sails), used mainly by European sailors in the 16th and 17th centuries

ORIGIN from Old French *galion* 'little ship'

gallery *noun* galleries
1 a building or large room used for showing pictures or sculptures *Have you been to the National Gallery in Trafalgar Square?*
2 a series of photos or clip art on a website *You can upload your own picture to our photo gallery.*

galley – garden

3 the highest floor in a theatre or cinema, with the cheapest seats
4 a raised area inside a building such as a hall, court of law or church. It goes around the walls and provides extra space for people to sit or stand in.
5 a narrow passage under the ground, for example in a cave

galley *noun* **galleys**
1 a kitchen in a ship or on a plane
2 a long ship that was moved by sails and oars. Galleys were used by sailors in the past, for example in ancient Greek and Roman times.

Gallic *adjective*
connected with French or the French people

> ORIGIN from Latin *Gallicus* 'connected with ancient Gaul'

gallon *noun* **gallons**
a unit for measuring liquid, equal to about 4.5 litres. There are eight pints in a gallon.

> CULTURE NOTE in the USA, a *gallon* is equal to about 3.8 litres

gallop *verb*
gallops, galloping, galloped
if a horse gallops, it runs very fast so that some of the time none of its feet are touching the ground. It runs faster than when it canters and much faster than when it trots.

gallop *noun*
1 the fastest speed that a horse can run *We went off at a gallop.*
2 (*plural* **gallops**) a very fast ride on a horse

gallows *noun plural*
a frame made of wood with a rope hanging down from it. In the past, it was used for killing criminals by putting the rope around their neck.

galore *adverb* (informal)
used when you mean lots of something *There was ice cream galore at Leela's party.*

> ORIGIN from Irish *go leór* 'enough'

galoshes *noun plural*
rubber shoes or boots worn over ordinary shoes, for example in the rain or snow

gambit *noun* **gambits**
a series of moves at the beginning of a game of chess in which you try to get an advantage

gamble *verb*
gambles, gambling, gambled
1 if someone gambles in a game such as cards, they pay money to take part. If they win, they get more money, but if they lose the game, they lose the money they pay.
2 if someone gambles on something such as a horse race, they pay someone money to let them choose a winner. If they get it right, they get more money, but if they get it wrong, they lose their money.
3 to take a chance that something good will happen *We're gambling on nice weather for the barbecue.*
4 to do something that might lead to something bad happening *If you don't fix the electrical fault, you're gambling with people's lives.*

gambler *noun*

gamble *noun* **gambles**
1 an action that you take hoping something good will happen but that includes a risk of something bad happening *My dad took a gamble when he left his job to become a musician.*
2 the action of gambling to try to win money *Grandma has a little gamble every Saturday.*

game *noun* **games**
1 something that you play and try to win, with rules that you must obey *a chess game; a game of Scrabble*
2 the things or equipment needed to play a game *I put all my games into this big box.*
3 a sport that you play and try to win, for example football, tennis or cricket, or part of a competition for that sport *West Ham have played five games this season.*
4 an activity that you do for fun *The children were playing games with their toys.*
5 games are sports that children do at school *Who takes you for games?*
6 wild animals or birds that people kill as a sport or for food *Many tourists go to Africa to hunt game. A pheasant is a game bird.*

game *adjective*
ready to do something, especially something new or difficult *Are you game for a walk into town?*

gamekeeper *noun* **gamekeepers**
someone whose job is to look after wild animals and birds on a piece of land and to stop people killing them

game show *noun* **game shows**
a television or radio programme where people answer questions or play games to win a prize

gaming *noun*
the activity of playing games on a computer, for example using the internet

gammon *noun*
salted or smoked meat from the leg of a pig, similar to bacon

gander *noun* **ganders**
a male goose

gang *noun* **gangs**
1 a group of young people who do things together, often bad things
2 a group of criminals
3 a group of young friends

gang *verb*
gangs, ganging, ganged
if people gang up on someone, they join together against them, for example to frighten them or get them to do something

gangling *adjective*
someone who is gangling is tall and thin and moves in a clumsy way

> LANGUAGE EXTRA you can also say *gangly*

gangplank *noun* **gangplanks**
a long flat piece of wood between a boat and the land, used for walking onto or off the boat

gangrene *noun*
a serious medical problem when a part of the body goes bad and dies because the blood has stopped flowing to it

gangster *noun* **gangsters**
a violent criminal who belongs to a gang of criminals

gangway *noun* **gangways**
1 a long space for walking along between rows of seats, for example in a bus, train or cinema *You're blocking the gangway.*
2 a bridge, usually of metal, between a ship and the land, used for walking onto or off the ship

gaol [pronounced the same as 'jail'] *noun* **gaols**
an old-fashioned spelling of **jail gaoler** *noun*

gap *noun* **gaps**
1 an empty space in something or between two things *I slipped through a gap in the fence. I have a gap between two of my teeth.*
2 a period of time when you stop doing something *Jo was in hospital but came back to school after a gap of six weeks.*
3 a big difference between things or people *There's a big age gap between my mum and my dad* (one is much older than the other).

gape *verb*
gapes, gaping, gaped
1 to look at something or someone with your mouth wide open, usually because you're surprised
2 if something gapes, it is or becomes wide open *He stood there with his shirt gaping.*

gaping *adjective*
very wide *a gaping hole*

garage ['ga-ridj', 'ga-rahdj' or 'ga-rahj'; the 'j' in 'ga-rahj' has the middle sound of 'pleasure'] *noun* **garages**
1 a building for keeping someone's car safe in, usually next to or close to their home
2 a place where someone goes to get their car repaired or checked
3 a place with fuel pumps where someone goes to buy petrol or diesel for their car
4 a place that sells new or used cars

garbage *noun*
1 things that are not wanted that you throw away

> SYNONYM rubbish

2 things that are no good because they are of really bad quality *There's a lot of garbage on TV.*

> SYNONYM rubbish

3 words or ideas that are false or stupid *What he said about me was garbage.*

> SYNONYM nonsense

4 a garbage can is the American word for a dustbin
5 a garbage collector is the American word for a dustman or refuse collector
6 a garbage truck is the American word for a dustcart

garden *noun* **gardens**
1 a piece of land next to your house, for example with grass on it or where plants, vegetables or trees grow
2 **gardens** used for describing a large area open to the public where lots of different plants and trees are grown *The house and gardens are open until six o'clock. We visited Kew Gardens in London.*

190

garden centre–Gaul

3 Gardens used in the name of streets *We live at 36 Acacia Gardens.*

garden centre noun **garden centres**
a place where you buy plants and equipment for your garden

gardener noun **gardeners**
1 someone who looks after a garden as their job
2 someone who likes growing plants in their garden

gardening noun
the activity or job of growing plants in a garden and looking after it

gargle verb
gargles, gargling, gargled
to put liquid in your mouth and make a bubbling sound with it at the back of your throat. You do this in order to clean your mouth or to make a sore throat feel better.

gargle noun **gargles**
1 a liquid that you use for gargling
2 the action of gargling

gargoyle noun **gargoyles**
a stone carving of an ugly or strange face that sticks out from the roof of an old building such as a church. It is mainly used for carrying rainwater away from the side of the building through its open mouth.

> ORIGIN from Old French *gargouille* 'throat'

garish ['gair-ish'] adjective
having lots of bright colours that you don't like *a garish wallpaper*

garland noun **garlands**
a ring of flowers and leaves, for example for wearing around your neck or for decorating something

garlic noun
a small white bulb of a plant that belongs to the onion family. It is divided into parts called cloves and is used in cooking for its very strong taste.

garment noun **garments**
a piece of clothing

garnish verb
garnishes, garnishing, garnished
to add to a dish of cooked food a small amount of another food, for example to make it look nicer or taste better *fish garnished with lemon slices*

garnish noun **garnishes**
a food such as salad or parsley that is put on a dish of cooked food, for example to make it look nicer or taste better

garret noun **garrets**
a small room under the roof of a house

garrison noun **garrisons**
1 a group of soldiers who live in a town or building in order to guard it
2 the buildings in which the soldiers live

garter noun **garters**
a band of elastic material worn by women around their stockings or by men around their socks to stop them falling down, especially in the past

gas noun
1 (*plural* **gases**) a substance like air that is neither solid nor liquid. Oxygen and carbon dioxide are examples of gases. Solids, liquids and gases are the three states of matter (what everything in the world is made of).
2 a gas that is burnt as a fuel and used for heating and cooking *There's a smell of gas.*
3 a type of gas used for harming people *tear gas; a gas mask* (covering for the face to protect you from harmful gases)
4 air in your stomach or bowels (tubes that carry waste food out of the body). This air makes you feel uncomfortable.

> SYNONYM wind

5 a gas fire is a piece of equipment that heats a room using gas
6 gas (or gasoline) is the American word for petrol

> ORIGIN from Greek *khaos* 'vast empty space' or 'bottomless hole', probably invented in the 17th century by the Flemish chemist J. B. van Helmont

gas verb
gasses, gassing, gassed
to make someone breathe a poisonous gas in order to kill or injure them

gash noun **gashes**
a deep cut in the skin, especially a long one

gash verb
gashes, gashing, gashed
if you gash a part of the body, you accidentally make a deep cut in it

gasman noun **gasmen**
someone who comes to your home to check how much gas you've used or to repair a piece of equipment that uses gas

> LANGUAGE EXTRA someone who checks how much gas you've used is also called a *meter reader*. Someone who repairs gas equipment is also called a *gas engineer*.

gasp verb
gasps, gasping, gasped
1 to breathe in suddenly, for example because you're surprised *Mum gasped when she saw the mess in my room.*
2 to have trouble breathing, for example because you're tired or ill or there isn't enough air *There was so much smoke that I was gasping for air.*
3 to say something when you're out of breath *'Help me,' she gasped.*
4 (informal) to be gasping for something is to want it very much *I'm gasping for a glass of water.*

gasp noun **gasps**
1 the noise you make when you gasp
2 the action of gasping

gastric adjective
connected with the stomach

gasworks noun
a factory where coal is made into gas for heating and cooking (especially in the past)

gate noun **gates**
1 a flat metal or wooden object like a door in a fence or outside wall. You open or close it to go into or out of a place, for example a garden, field or school. *We were all waiting at the school gate.*
2 the place where you go into a large building or sports stadium *The museum gates were shut.*
3 the place at an airport that you go through to get on a plane *Flight 26 is now boarding at gate 13.*

gateau ['ga-toh'] noun **gateaux**
a large cake filled with cream, chocolate or fruit

> ORIGIN from French *gâteau* 'cake'. The plural ending in *-x* is because the word is French.

gatecrash verb
gatecrashes, gatecrashing, gatecrashed
if someone gatecrashes a party or event, they go there and try to get in even though they haven't been invited

gateway noun **gateways**
a way into a place or building through a gate

gather verb
gathers, gathering, gathered
1 to come together in a group *We gathered in front of the school gates.*
2 to get things, people or information from different places *I gathered my toys, which were lying around the house. You can gather details from the website.*
3 to get more of something *The train is beginning to gather speed* (go faster). *These comics have been gathering dust in the shed.*
4 if you say 'I gather', you mean you've just found out some information and you think it's true *I gather you're going to Sweden for your holidays.*
5 if a piece of clothing is gathered, small folds are made in it by pulling the cloth together

gather noun **gathers**
a small fold in a piece of clothing made by pulling the cloth together

gathering noun **gatherings**
1 a group of people who come together
2 an occasion when a group of people come together

gauche ['gohsh'] adjective
behaving in an awkward way when you are with other people

> ORIGIN from French *gauche* 'left'

gaudy adjective **gaudier, gaudiest**
if something is gaudy, its colour is bright in a way that is very unpleasant
gaudily adverb

gauge ['gayj'] noun **gauges**
1 a piece of equipment for measuring the amount of something *a petrol gauge*
2 a way of describing how thick something is, for example a wire or needle

gauge ['gayj'] verb
gauges, gauging, gauged
1 to say roughly what you think something is, for example someone's feelings, or what someone might say or do
2 to say roughly what something is, such as an amount, distance, size or weight *Hold this envelope in your hand to gauge its weight.*
3 to measure something using a piece of equipment *Use this thermometer to gauge how hot the water is.*

Gaul noun
an ancient region in Western Europe that included France and Belgium, most of Switzerland and parts of Germany, Italy and the Netherlands

gaunt – generation

gaunt *adjective*
very thin, for example because you are ill, tired or hungry *a gaunt face*

gauze *noun*
a very thin cloth with many tiny holes in it, used for example as a bandage or for making curtains

gave
past tense of **give**

gawky *adjective* **gawkier, gawkiest**
someone who is gawky moves in a clumsy way, for example because they are tall and thin

gawp *verb*
gawps, gawping, gawped
to look at someone or something in a stupid way, for example with your mouth open

gay *adjective*
1 a gay person is someone who has or wants a love relationship with a person of the same sex
2 an old-fashioned word for happy or bright *gay colours*

gaze *verb*
gazes, gazing, gazed
to look at someone or something for a long time

> SYNONYM to stare

gaze *noun*
a way of looking at someone or something

gazelle *noun* **gazelles**
an animal like a small brown deer that lives in Africa or Asia

gazette *noun* **gazettes**
another word for a newspaper, used mainly in the titles of newspapers

gazetteer *noun* **gazetteers**
a dictionary that gives information about names of places such as towns and villages

GB
1 short for **Great Britain**
2 short for **gigabyte** or **gigabytes**

GCSE *noun* **GCSEs**
an examination that students take in English, Welsh and Northern Irish schools at the age of about 16
short for: General Certificate of Secondary Education

gear *noun*
1 (*plural* **gears**) the part of a vehicle or machine that uses power from its engine to make the vehicle move or the machine work. Gears consist of connecting wheels with small teeth (or points) around the edge. *The car is in gear* (one of its gears is connected so that the wheels of the car are turning).
2 (*plural* **gears**) the part of a bicycle used for changing the speed at which the wheels turn
3 the special clothes and equipment you need for something, for example to play a sport *football gear*
4 an informal word for clothes *My brother wears the latest gear.*

gee *interjection*
used for showing that you're surprised, upset or that you really like something

geek *noun* **geeks** (informal)
1 an expert in something, or someone who spends a lot of time doing something, especially something technical *a computer geek*
2 someone who doesn't wear fashionable clothes or know how to behave properly with other people, especially someone very clever

geeky *adjective*

geese
plural of **goose**

gee up *interjection*
used for telling a horse to go faster

geezer *noun* **geezers**
a slang word for a man

Geiger counter ['gye-ger'] *noun*
Geiger counters
a piece of equipment that measures how much radioactivity there is in a place

> ORIGIN named after the German scientist Hans Geiger who, with Ernest Rutherford and later Walther Müller, invented it at the beginning of the 20th century

gel *noun* **gels**
a liquid like jelly used on your hair or body, for example to clean it or to treat a skin problem *shower gel*

gelatine *noun*
a substance used for making jellies. Gelatine has no taste or colour and often comes as a powder.

> LANGUAGE EXTRA also spelt *gelatin*

gem *noun* **gems**
1 a beautiful stone that is cut into a regular shape to make a jewel
2 someone or something really special and good *Your sister's a real gem!*

gender *noun* **genders**
in grammar, gender is used for describing the masculine, feminine or neuter form of a part of speech such as a pronoun, noun or adjective

> LANGUAGE EXTRA some languages, such as French and Spanish, have two *genders* (masculine and feminine); others, such as Latin and German, have three (masculine, feminine and neuter).
> In English only a few words have a gender, for example the pronoun forms *he*, *him* or *his* (masculine), *she*, *her* or *hers* (feminine) and *it* or *its* (neuter). Nouns that show gender are mainly those ending in *-ess* (*actress*, *giantess*). Note also the ending *-oine* in *heroine* (female hero).

gene ['jeen'] *noun* **genes**
a part of a cell (smallest unit of living matter) containing all the information that controls how a living thing grows and what it looks like. In humans, genes are passed from parents to children.

genealogy *noun*
1 the study of the history of families
2 (*plural* **genealogies**) a drawing or list showing the past and present members of a family and how they are related to each other

general *adjective*
1 used for describing the main things of something without any detail *a general idea*
2 connected with the whole or most of something *a general problem*
3 shared by most people *That's the general opinion of the class.*
4 dealing with different things *general knowledge*; *a general hospital*
5 ordinary *the general reader*
6 **in general** usually *In general I prefer cats to dogs.*
7 **in general** also used when talking about the whole of something *How are you feeling in general?*

general *noun* **generals**
an army officer with a high rank, below the rank of field marshal

general election *noun* **general elections**
an event when all the people in a country are allowed to vote to choose a government

generalisation *noun* **generalisations**
something someone says that may or may not be true in most or all cases, for example because they do not have all the details *Tom's always making generalisations about people.*

> LANGUAGE EXTRA also spelt *generalization*

generalise *verb*
generalises, generalising, generalised
1 to say something, about the whole of a group of people or things, that may or may not be true because you do not have all the details *I don't want to generalise and say our school is the best one in the county.*
2 to take something such as a fact, idea, example or rule and connect it to a larger number of them *This rule can be generalised beyond the English language.*

> LANGUAGE EXTRA also spelt *generalize*

generally *adverb*
1 usually *I generally do my homework before dinner.*
2 considering the whole of something without going into detail *I'm feeling generally tired.*
3 used for talking about most people *My teachers generally say that my sister works harder than me.*

general practitioner *noun*
general practitioners
a doctor who deals with people who have all types of illnesses and sends them to hospital if they need special treatment

> SYNONYM GP

generate *verb*
generates, generating, generated
to make something happen or cause it to exist

> SYNONYM to produce

generation *noun* **generations**
1 all the people in a family or society who are about the same age *The book is about three generations of the Taylor family: children, parents and grandparents. The younger generation tries to be different from the older generation.*

2 a period of about 20 to 30 years (from people's birth until the birth of their own children) *These events took place many generations ago.*

generator *noun* **generators**
a piece of equipment that produces electricity

generous *adjective*
1 if you are generous, you give someone something (or you like giving someone something) such as money or help because you are kind *Thanks for the gift – you were very generous. My uncle is always so generous.*
2 also used about something kind that someone says or does *generous praise; That was a very generous thing to do.*
3 larger or better than you might expect *a generous amount; a generous gift*
generosity *noun*

generously *adverb*
1 more than you might expect *My grandparents always give generously* (for example more money or better gifts than you might expect).
2 in a friendly and helpful way *Mum generously offered to drive me back to school.*
3 used for talking about large amounts of something *Spread the jam generously over the top of the cake.*

genetic *adjective*
connected with genes *a genetic defect* (passed from parents to children)
genetically *adverb*

genetics *noun*
the study of how special qualities of living things are passed on in their genes (tiny parts of living matter that contain information about how something grows)

genial *adjective*
friendly and pleasant **genially** *adverb*

genie *noun* **genies**
in stories from Arabia, a genie is a magical spirit that will do whatever the person who controls it tells it to do

genius *noun*
1 (*plural* **geniuses**) someone who has a much higher level of intelligence or skill than other people *Einstein was a mathematical genius.*
2 very great intelligence or skill *Planting apple trees in the garden was a stroke of genius* (a very intelligent idea).

genre ['jon-rer'; 'j' has the middle sound of 'pleasure'] *noun* **genres**
a particular style, for example in writing, art, music or films *My favourite genre is the thriller.*

gent *noun* **gents**
1 an old-fashioned word for a man
2 **the gents** the men's toilet in a public place

gentle *adjective* **gentler**, **gentlest**
1 kind, pleasant or careful *a gentle smile; Be gentle with the baby.*
2 calm and quiet *'Yes,' she said in a gentle voice.*
3 not strong *a gentle breeze; In PE we did some gentle exercises.*
4 not steep or big but slight *a gentle slope; a gentle curve*

gentleness *noun*

SIMILE 'as gentle as a lamb' means very gentle (sense 1)

gentleman *noun* **gentlemen**
1 a polite word for a man
2 a man whose behaviour is polite and who shows respect towards other people

gentlemanly *adjective*
polite and showing respect towards other people

gently *adverb*
1 carefully *Open the box very gently.*
2 in a kind, pleasant or calm way *He told me gently to sit down.*
3 not strongly *The wind was blowing gently.*
4 slightly *The river curved gently to the left.*

genuine *adjective*
1 real or true, not fake *This painting is a genuine Picasso. Dad's surprise was genuine.*
2 if someone is genuine, they are honest, good and you can trust them *Ruby is a very genuine person.*

genuinely *adverb*
really *I'm genuinely sorry.*

genus ['jee-ners'] *noun* **genera** ['jen-er-er']
in science, a group of animals or plants that are similar to each other. A genus is smaller than a family and the animals and plants are more closely related.

geographical *adjective*
1 connected with an area you can see on a map *a geographical region*
2 connected with geography *geographical studies*
geographically *adverb*

geography *noun*
the study of the surface of the earth including its features such as forests, rivers, seas and mountains, and the study of the countries of the world including people and cities. Geography is often studied as a school subject.

ORIGIN from Greek *geographia* 'description of the surface of the earth', from *geo* 'earth' and *graphia* 'description' or 'writing'

geological *adjective*
connected with geology *geological studies; a geological period* (a period of time in the past when rocks were formed)
geologically *adverb*

geologist *noun* **geologists**
a scientist who studies geology

geology *noun*
the study of the earth's crust (its hard outer surface), especially the rocks and soil and how they were formed

geometric or **geometrical** *adjective*
1 used about simple and regular shapes such as squares, triangles and angles
2 used about patterns and designs that have simple and regular shapes
3 connected with geometry
geometrically *adverb*

geometry *noun*
the mathematical study of lines, angles, curves and surfaces

ORIGIN from Greek *geometria* 'measurement of land'

geranium ['jer-ray-nee-erm'] *noun* **geraniums**
a plant with red, pink or white flowers and round leaves. Geraniums are grown in gardens or pots in people's homes.

gerbil *noun* **gerbils**
a furry animal like a big mouse that people often keep as a pet

germ *noun* **germs**
a tiny organism (living thing) that causes disease. Bacteria and viruses are germs.

German *adjective*
1 connected with Germany or the German language
2 a German shepherd is a big dog like a wolf, often used for guarding buildings, as a guide dog or by the police. It is also called an Alsatian.

German *noun*
1 the language people speak in Germany, Austria, Switzerland, Luxembourg and some other countries
2 (*plural* **Germans**) someone from Germany

Germany *noun*
a country in Western and Central Europe

germinate *verb*
germinates, germinating, germinated
if a seed germinates, it starts to grow
germination *noun*

gestate *verb*
gestates, gestating, gestated
1 if a baby or animal gestates, it spends time developing and growing inside its mother's body
2 to carry a baby or animal inside the body until it is born

gestation *noun*
the time that a baby or animal needs to develop and grow inside its mother's body before it can be born. In humans gestation lasts about 40 weeks.

LANGUAGE EXTRA you can also say *gestation period*

gesticulate *verb*
gesticulates, gesticulating, gesticulated
to make movements with your hands and arms while you speak, for example to make your words clearer or give extra importance to them **gesticulation** *noun*

gesture *noun* **gestures**
1 a movement, usually with your body, hands or head, for example to help you say what you mean or feel
2 an action you do that shows the way you feel about something, especially when you have good feelings *We gave flowers to our teacher as a gesture of thanks.*

gesture *verb*
gestures, gesturing, gestured
to make a gesture, for example to help you say what you mean or feel *Jon gestured towards the door.*

get–gigabyte

get *verb*
gets, getting, got
1 if you get something you don't have, you do something in order to have it, such as taking it, buying it or earning it *I got an ice cream from the fridge. Do teachers get much money?*
2 to be given something *Sam got lots of presents.*

SYNONYM to receive

3 to start being something (used with an adjective) *I'm getting angry.*

SYNONYM to become

4 to start making someone become something (used with an adjective) *You're getting me angry.*

SYNONYM to make

5 to start having something such as an idea, feeling or illness *I got a surprise when I opened the letter. Stay indoors if you get a cold.*
6 used for saying that something happens to or is done to someone or something *Scotland gets a lot of rain. My laptop got broken.*
7 to go into a certain position, or to go somewhere *I got onto my bike. Isabelle got to school late.*
8 to put something into a certain position, or to put something somewhere *Get your coat on. I got the ball in the net.*
9 to make something happen, or to make someone do something *I have to get my jeans cleaned. Dad got me to tidy my room.*
10 to travel somewhere, for example by bus, train or plane *I get the bus to school.*
11 (informal) to understand something *Dad didn't get the joke.*
12 if people get along or get on, they are friendly towards each other *I get on well with my teacher. My teacher and I get along well.*
13 if you say that someone gets along or gets on in a particular way, you mean they are dealing with a situation in that way *Fatima is getting along well in her new school. How are you getting on?*
14 if you get away with something, you are not punished for doing something bad
15 if you get by, you have just enough of something to deal successfully with a particular situation *I know just enough French to get by in Paris.*
16 if something gets you down, it makes you feel sad *This very cold weather has been getting me down.*
17 to get on with something such as your work is to continue doing it *Don't talk – get on with your homework.*
18 to get out of something that you don't want to do is to avoid doing it *How can I get out of doing PE?*
19 to get over an illness is to become well again
20 to get over something such as a difficulty is to deal with it successfully
21 to get through a situation is to deal with it successfully *I got through the whole year without seeing the doctor.*
22 to get through something such as a test, an exam or your work is to complete it successfully
23 to get through money or an amount of something is to use it all up
24 if people get together, they meet
25 to get up is to get onto your feet, for example from a sitting position
26 to get up when you've been sleeping is to wake up and get out of bed
27 to get up to something is to do something, especially something bad *What are you two getting up to?*

getaway *noun*
an escape from somewhere *The robbers made their getaway in a white van.*

get-together *noun* **get-togethers**
an occasion when people come together for a particular purpose

geyser ['gee-zer'] *noun* **geysers**
a hole in the ground from which a stream of hot water comes out and goes up into the air

Ghana *noun*
a country in West Africa
Ghanaian *adjective & noun*

ghastly *adjective* **ghastlier, ghastliest**
1 extremely bad *ghastly weather*
2 bad enough to really shock you *a ghastly death*
3 ugly *She was wearing a ghastly hat.*
4 ill or sad *You look ghastly.*

gherkin *noun* **gherkins**
a small cucumber that is put in vinegar (sour liquid made from wine) or salty water to make it last longer. Gherkins are eaten cold.

ghetto *noun* **ghettos** or **ghettoes**
an area of a town where a certain group of people live, for example people who belong to a particular nationality or religion. The people who live in a ghetto are often poor.

ORIGIN from Italian *ghetto*. The Ghetto was an area of Venice where Jewish people were forced to live in the 16th century.

ghost *noun* **ghosts**
the image of a dead person that someone sees or whose presence someone feels

ghostly *adjective* **ghostlier, ghostliest**
1 reminding you of a ghost, for example pale or transparent *We saw a ghostly outline.*
2 frightening because it doesn't seem real *a ghostly voice*

ghoul ['gool'] *noun* **ghouls**
in old Arabian stories, an imaginary evil creature that eats dead bodies

ghoulish ['gool-ish'] *adjective*
connected with or interested in death in a way that is frightening *ghoulish behaviour; The character in the film is very ghoulish.*

giant *noun* **giants**
1 in stories, an extremely tall man, often someone who is evil
2 someone who is much taller or something that is much larger than usual
3 a very famous person, such as a musician, actor or artist, who is much more successful than other famous people

ORIGIN from Old French *geant* 'giant' and Greek *gigas*. In Greek stories, the *gigantes* were the very big and strong sons of Uranus (god of the heavens) and Gaia (goddess of the earth).

giant *adjective*
extremely large *a giant screen*

giantess *noun* **giantesses**
in stories, an extremely tall woman, often someone who is evil

gibberish *noun*
words that have no meaning

SYNONYM nonsense

gibbon *noun* **gibbons**
an animal like a monkey with long arms. Gibbons live in South-East Asia.

gibe *noun* **gibes**
words that someone says in order to insult someone or make them look stupid

LANGUAGE EXTRA also spelt *jibe*

Gibraltar *noun*
a British territory at the tip of southern Spain **Gibraltarian** *adjective & noun*

giddy *adjective* **giddier, giddiest**
feeling as if things are going round and round in your head and that you might fall
giddiness *noun*

gif ['gif' or 'jif'] *noun* **gifs**
the ending of a computer filename. A .gif file contains an image or images and is also used for small animated films or cartoons. *short for:* Graphics Interchange Format

LANGUAGE EXTRA also spelt *GIF*

gift *noun* **gifts**
1 something that someone gives to someone, usually for a special occasion

SYNONYM present

2 a natural skill that someone has for doing something well *My brother has a gift for languages.*

SYNONYM talent

3 a gift card or gift certificate is the same as a gift voucher
see: voucher (sense 1)

gifted *adjective*
if someone is gifted, they have a very great natural skill *She's in a class for gifted children.*

gift-wrapped *adjective*
if something is gift-wrapped, it is covered in attractive paper (called gift wrap) so that it can be given as a gift *a gift-wrapped box of chocolates*

gig *noun* **gigs**
a performance of modern music, for example rock, pop or jazz *My brother is playing a gig in Leeds.*

gigabyte *noun* **gigabytes**
a unit for measuring how much information a piece of computer equipment can store. A gigabyte is made up of 1024 megabytes. *a 500 gigabyte hard drive*

gigantic–glamour

gigantic *adjective*
extremely big

> **SYNONYMS** huge, enormous

giggle *verb*
giggles, giggling, giggled
to laugh in a nervous or silly way, often when you can't control your laughing

giggle *noun* giggles
1 a nervous or silly laugh *She has the giggles* (she can't stop laughing).
2 a silly thing that someone does for fun *Let's do some face painting for a giggle.*

giggly *adjective* gigglier, giggliest
laughing all the time in a nervous or silly way *There are some giggly boys in the back row.*

gilded *adjective*
covered with a thin layer of gold or something that looks like gold *a gilded picture frame*

> **LANGUAGE EXTRA** you can also say *gilt*

gills *noun plural*
the parts on the head of a fish that allow it to breathe

gimmick *noun* gimmicks
something that someone does or uses to attract people's interest, for example to get them to buy something. People do not usually consider gimmicks very serious, useful or important. *a sales gimmick*

gimmicky *adjective*

gin *noun* gins
a strong alcoholic drink made from small fruits called juniper berries

ginger *noun*
1 the root of a tropical plant. It is used in cooking to give food and drink a strong taste.
2 an orange-brown or reddish-brown colour

ginger *adjective*
1 orange-brown or reddish-brown *ginger hair*
2 containing or tasting of ginger *ginger biscuits*; *ginger cake*

gingerbread *noun*
1 a cake or biscuit with ginger in it
2 a gingerbread man is a biscuit made of gingerbread in the shape of a little man

gingerly *adverb*
very carefully and slowly *I tiptoed gingerly upstairs so as not to make any noise.*

gipsy *noun* gipsies
a member of a group of people living mainly in Europe but originally from India. Gipsies usually travel around, for example in caravans, instead of living in one place.

> **LANGUAGE EXTRA** also spelt *gypsy*

> **ORIGIN** from Middle English *gypcian* 'Egyptian', because people believed (wrongly) that gipsies came from Egypt

giraffe *noun* giraffes
an animal with a very long neck, long legs and large brown spots on its body. Giraffes live in Africa.

> **ORIGIN** from Italian *giraffa* and Arabic *zarafa*

girder *noun* girders
a long and heavy piece of metal, used for supporting a floor, roof or bridge, for example

girdle *noun* girdles
a piece of underwear that women wore in the past around their waist to make them look thinner

girl *noun* girls
1 a female child
2 a young woman

girl band *noun* girl bands
a pop band made up of attractive young women who sing and dance

girlfriend *noun* girlfriends
someone's girlfriend is the girl they are going out with

girlish *adjective*
behaving or looking like a girl

giro ['jy-roh'] *noun* giros
a cheque paid by the government, especially in the past, for example to people who have no job or who cannot work because of an illness

girth *noun* girths
the measurement around something thick such as a tree or someone's body

gist ['jist'] *noun*
the gist of something that someone says or writes is its general meaning but not every detail *I got the gist of what the head teacher said.*

give *verb*
gives, giving, gave, given
1 to put something in someone's hand *Give me the pen.*
2 to let someone have something, for example as a present or to help them or allow them to do something *We gave Mum a radio for her birthday. Can you give me some advice? Dad gave me permission to stay up late.*
3 to do something *He gave a smile.*
4 to make someone have something, for example when talking about a particular action being done to them or a particular feeling *She gave me a push. Those words gave me a shock.*
5 to make something have something, for example when talking about a particular action being done to it or a particular quality *I gave the shower a good clean. The salt gives flavour to the fish.*
6 to tell someone something *Can you give Chloe a message?*
7 to organise something *The school is giving a concert.*
8 to pay money for something *How much will you give me for my bike?*
9 if something gives, it bends or stretches *The rope gave under the weight.*
10 if you give something away, you let someone have it because you don't want it
11 if a company or shop gives something away, they let you have it without paying for it
12 if you give in, you agree to do or accept something
13 if you give something in, you give it to someone in charge *We gave in our homework to the teacher.*
14 if something gives off something such as a smell, gas or heat, it produces it
15 if you give things out, you give them to different people *Miss Miller gave out the exercise books.*
16 if something gives out heat or light, it produces it
17 if you give up, you stop trying to do or have something *I don't know the answer – I give up!*
18 if you give something up, you stop doing or having it *Raj has given up playing video games. We never gave up hope.*
19 if something such as a branch or roof gives way, it breaks suddenly and falls down
20 if a cyclist or driver gives way, he or she allows other cyclists or drivers to go past before moving onto a road

given *adjective*
1 used for talking about a particular thing, time, amount or situation *This could happen at any given time.*
2 already agreed *You will choose your essay from one of the given subjects.*

gizmo ['giz-moh'] *noun* gizmos
an informal word for a small piece of equipment *an electronic gizmo*

glacier ['glas-ee-er'] *noun* glaciers
a very large mass of ice that moves slowly on land, for example down a mountain valley

> **ORIGIN** from French *glace* 'ice'

glad *adjective* gladder, gladdest
1 happy about something *I'm glad to know he's all right.*

> **SYNONYM** pleased

2 happy to have something, or happy that someone does something for you *Take your scarf – you'll be glad of it.*

> **SYNONYM** grateful

glade *noun* glades
a small area without trees in a forest

gladiator *noun* gladiators
a man who fought with a sword against other men or wild animals at a public show in ancient Roman times

> **ORIGIN** from Latin *gladius* 'sword'

gladiolus *noun* gladioli
a tall garden plant with pointed leaves and lots of flowers growing along its stem

gladly *adverb*
when you are happy to do something *I will gladly help you.*

glamorous *adjective*
1 a glamorous place or activity is exciting and interesting *a glamorous job*
2 a glamorous person is attractive and often rich and successful

glamour *noun*
a special quality that makes a person, place or activity exciting, interesting and attractive. Glamour is often connected with money and success. *Some actors enjoy the glamour of working in films.*

glance – gloriously

glance *verb*
glances, glancing, glanced
1 to look at something or someone quickly and then look away *I glanced around the room but couldn't see anyone I knew.*
2 if something such as a ball or bullet glances off something, it hits it at an angle and then moves away in a different direction

glance *noun* glances
a quick look

gland *noun* glands
a part of the body that produces many different substances that the body uses, for example hormones, proteins or sweat

glandular *adjective*
1 connected with the glands
2 glandular fever is an illness affecting some of the glands in the body (lymph glands). It makes you feel tired and weak.

glare *verb*
glares, glaring, glared
1 to shine with a very strong light *The sun was glaring in my eyes.*
2 to look at someone in an angry way, often for a long time *My teacher glared angrily at me as if I'd done something wrong.*

glare *noun*
1 a very strong light
2 (*plural* **glares**) an angry look

glaring *adjective*
1 a glaring light shines so strongly that you cannot see

SYNONYM dazzling

2 a glaring mistake is so obvious that you should be able to see it easily

glaringly *adverb*
if something is glaringly obvious, it is completely obvious for everyone to see

glass *noun*
1 a hard material that you can usually see through, used for making things such as windows and bottles
2 (*plural* **glasses**) a round container made of glass, used for drinking
3 (*plural* **glasses**) the drink in a glass *I drank a glass of milk.*

glasses *noun plural*
two pieces of special glass or plastic fixed to a frame that you wear in front of your eyes to see better

SYNONYM spectacles

glassful *noun* glassfuls
an amount of something that is contained in a glass

glassy *adjective* glassier, glassiest
1 a glassy look is one that is empty and shows no interest or feeling
2 smooth and shiny like glass

glaze *noun* glazes
1 a liquid put onto food to make it look shiny
2 a liquid put onto a painting or clay object to protect it and make it look shiny
3 the surface of food, a painting or a clay object with a glaze on it

196

glaze *verb*
glazes, glazing, glazed
1 if someone's eyes glaze over, they stop showing any interest or feeling, for example because of boredom or illness
2 to give something such as food or a painting a shiny surface

glazed *adjective*
1 a glazed look is one that is empty and shows no interest or feeling
2 with glass in it *a glazed door*

glazier ['glay-zee-er'] *noun* glaziers
someone whose job is to put glass into windows and doors

gleam *verb*
gleams, gleaming, gleamed
1 to shine with a soft light *Mum polished the trophy until it gleamed.*
2 to show a particular feeling such as happiness *My parents' eyes were gleaming with pride.*

gleam *noun* gleams
1 a soft light
2 a look that you can see in someone's eyes *a gleam of pride*

glee *noun*
1 a feeling of happiness
2 a feeling of pleasure when something bad happens to someone else

gleeful *adjective*
happy **gleefully** *adverb*

glen *noun* glens
a long valley, especially in Scotland or Ireland

glide *verb*
glides, gliding, glided
1 to move smoothly and easily along a surface or in the air
2 to fly without an engine, using the wind to move

glider *noun* gliders
a light plane that has no engine and uses the wind to move

glimmer *noun* glimmers
1 a soft weak light
2 a slight sign of something *a glimmer of hope*

glimmer *verb*
glimmers, glimmering, glimmered
to shine with a soft weak light

glimpse *noun* glimpses
when you see someone or something for a short time only *I caught a glimpse of him in the crowd* (saw him for a short time).

glimpse *verb*
glimpses, glimpsing, glimpsed
to see someone or something for a short time only

glint *verb*
glints, glinting, glinted
1 if a shiny surface glints, it shines with small flashes of light *The sea glinted in the moonlight.*
2 if someone's eyes glint, they show an unfriendly feeling, such as anger

glint *noun* glints
1 a small flash of light
2 a look in your eyes showing an unfriendly feeling

glisten *verb*
glistens, glistening, glistened
if something glistens, it shines because it is wet *My face was glistening with sweat.*

glitch *noun* glitches
a small problem with something such as a piece of equipment or computer software

glitter *verb*
glitters, glittering, glittered
if something glitters, light shines from it with small bright flashes

glitter *noun*
1 tiny pieces of metal or plastic used for decorating things such as greetings cards or pictures
2 small bright flashes of light

gloat *verb*
gloats, gloating, gloated
if someone gloats, they show, in an unpleasant way, that they are happy because they are successful or lucky or because someone else is not successful or lucky

global *adjective*
1 including or connected with the whole world *global trade; a global problem*
2 connected with all the parts of something or with a situation *I did a global search for 'tiger' and replaced it with 'lion'.*
globally *adverb*

global warming *noun*
an increase in the temperature of the air around the earth caused by large amounts of gases such as carbon dioxide (produced when carbon is burnt). The gases cannot escape because of pollution. This is known as the greenhouse effect.

globe *noun*
1 (*plural* **globes**) an object shaped like a ball, especially one with a map of the world on it
2 the globe is the world *Who was the first pilot to fly around the globe?*

gloom *noun*
a feeling of great sadness because there is no hope

gloomy *adjective* gloomier, gloomiest
1 dark and unpleasant, and making you feel sad *gloomy weather*
2 feeling sad and without hope or making you feel sad and without hope *You're very gloomy today. The future looks rather gloomy.*
gloomily *adverb* **gloominess** *noun*

glorify *verb*
glorifies, glorifying, glorified
1 to make something or someone seem much better than they really are *This film seems to glorify war.*
2 to praise and honour someone
glorification *noun*

glorious *adjective*
1 extremely beautiful *The theatre is a truly glorious building.*
2 extremely good and pleasing *We had glorious weather* (for example warm and sunny). *I spent a glorious day with my grandparents.*
3 deserving praise and honour *a glorious victory*

gloriously *adverb*
in a very pleasing way *a gloriously decorated cake; It was gloriously sunny* (very sunny and pleasing).

glory – goalpost

glory *noun*
1 praise and honour for someone who has done something important
2 great beauty
3 (*plural* **glories**) something that deserves praise and honour

gloss *noun*
the shine on the surface of something such as paper

glossary *noun* **glossaries**
a list of difficult words or phrases in alphabetical order with their meanings explained (or with their translations in another language). Glossaries often appear at the end of a book.

glossy *adjective* **glossier, glossiest**
smooth and shiny

glove *noun* **gloves**
1 a covering for the hand with a separate place for each finger and for the thumb
2 a glove puppet is a puppet made of cloth that you put over your hand and move with your fingers

glow *verb*
glows, glowing, glowed
to shine or burn with a small and steady light *The baby's nightlight glows in the dark. The campfire was still glowing* (burning with a small light but without any flames).

glow *noun*
1 a small and steady light, for example from a lamp or computer screen
2 the orange light from a fire burning without a flame
3 a happy feeling *My parents felt a glow of pride after speaking to my teacher.*

glower [rhymes with 'tower'] *verb*
glowers, glowering, glowered
to look in an angry way *He glowered at me.*

SYNONYM to glare

glow-worm *noun* **glow-worms**
an insect that produces a small light from a part of its body such as its tail

glucose *noun*
a type of sugar that exists in plants, animals and humans

glue *noun* **glues**
a thick substance for sticking things together, such as paper

glue *verb*
glues, gluing, glued
1 to stick something with glue
2 if someone or someone's eyes are glued to something, they look at it and pay attention to nothing else *We were all glued to the TV.*

gluey *adjective*
1 sticky
2 covered with glue

glum *adjective* **glummer, glummest**
feeling or looking sad, and not saying much
glumly *adverb*

glutton *noun* **gluttons**
1 someone who eats and drinks too much
2 if someone is a glutton for punishment, they are ready to do something unpleasant or difficult that they don't have to do
gluttonous *adjective*

ORIGIN from Latin *gluttire* 'to swallow'

gluttony *noun*
the habit of eating and drinking too much

GMT *noun*
the time at Greenwich in South London that is used as the standard for international time zones
short for: Greenwich Mean Time

gnarled ['nahld'] *adjective*
rough and twisted, for example because of old age *a gnarled tree trunk; gnarled fingers*

gnash ['nash'] *verb*
gnashes, gnashing, gnashed
if you gnash your teeth, you bite them together, for example because you are angry or in pain

gnat ['nat'] *noun* **gnats**
a tiny flying insect that bites

gnaw ['nor'] *verb*
gnaws, gnawing, gnawed
to keep biting something, for example to make a hole in it *The dog was gnawing on a bone.*

gnome ['nohm'] *noun* **gnomes**
1 in stories, an imaginary creature that lives under the ground and looks like a small man, usually with a beard and pointed hat
2 a garden gnome is a model of a gnome used for making a garden more attractive

go *verb*
goes, going, went, gone
1 to leave somewhere and move somewhere else *I went to school. Mia has gone. Go back to your desk.*
2 to move somewhere in a particular way *I go by bike. His fingers kept going up and down.*
3 if something such as a road or railway goes through or to a place, it is built starting somewhere and ending somewhere else *The motorway goes through the forest. The path goes to the beach.*
4 used for saying where something should be put *The chairs go under the table.*

SYNONYM to belong

5 to be sent somewhere or to someone *The letter went to the head teacher.*
6 to do an activity *to go for a walk; to go shopping*
7 if something such as a piece of equipment or a machine goes, it works *The clock is going again.*
8 to become *I think you've gone mad!*
9 to stop happening, existing or being somewhere *The pain has gone now. My keys have gone.*

SYNONYM to disappear

10 to get weaker or damaged or begin to stop working properly *Granddad's eyesight is going. The carpet on the stairs is starting to go. The battery's gone* (no longer works).
11 used for saying how well or how badly something happens *Our plans are going well.*
12 to make a noise *The bell has gone. The balloon went bang. I went 'Ouch!'*
13 if you are going to do something, you will do it very soon
14 to go away means to leave somewhere
15 to go for someone or something is to go somewhere to get them
16 to go for someone is also to attack them *The dog went for me.*
17 to go in for something such as an exam or competition is to take part in it
18 if one number goes into another number, the second number is divided by the first
19 if a bomb goes off, it explodes
20 if an alarm goes off, it rings
21 to go on doing something is to continue doing it
22 if something goes on, it happens *What's going on?*
23 if someone goes out, they leave a place such as a room or building to go somewhere else, or they leave their home to go somewhere to have fun *I closed the door as I went out. We're going out to play. My big sister likes going out* (going to places such as cinemas or restaurants for fun).
24 if someone goes out with someone else, they have a love relationship with that person
25 if a fire goes out, it stops burning, and if a light goes out, it stops shining
26 to go through money or an amount of something is to use it all up
27 to go through something such as a drawer or document is to search through it trying to find something
28 if something such as a price or level goes up, it increases

go *noun*
1 (*plural* **goes**) when you take part in an activity or try to do something *Could I have a go on your bike? If you can't do it first time, have another go.*
2 (*plural* **goes**) the time when you must play in a game, such as chess or ludo *It's my go now.*

SYNONYM turn

3 an informal word for energy *My baby sister is always full of go.*
4 **on the go** busy doing things

go-ahead *noun*
permission to do something *Mum gave me the go-ahead to buy a new bike.*

goal *noun* **goals**
1 the place between two poles where the ball must go to score a point in a game such as football or hockey
2 a point that you get by making the ball go between the two poles of a goal *Our team scored two goals.*
3 something that you hope to do in the future

SYNONYM for sense 3: aim

goalie *noun* **goalies**
an informal word for a goalkeeper

goalkeeper *noun* **goalkeepers**
a player in a game such as football or hockey whose position is in front of the goal. A goalkeeper's job is to stop the other team scoring goals.

goalpost *noun* **goalposts**
one of the two posts on either side of a goal in games such as football or hockey

goat – good-natured

goat *noun* **goats**
an animal that looks similar to a sheep but usually has horns and a beard. Goats are kept on farms and also live wild on mountains.

gob *noun* **gobs**
a slang word for a mouth

gobble *verb*
gobbles, gobbling, gobbled
to eat food too quickly and often noisily

gobbledegook *noun*
1 language that you cannot understand, for example because it is too technical, complicated or badly written
2 words or symbols that make no sense at all *The email attachment was in gobbledegook.*

LANGUAGE EXTRA also spelt *gobbledygook*

goblet *noun* **goblets**
a drinking glass made of metal or glass, used for example for drinking wine. It has a stem (thin part) standing on a base (bottom part) but has no handle.

goblin *noun* **goblins**
in stories, an imaginary evil creature that usually looks like a small ugly person with big ears

gobsmacked *adjective* (informal)
very surprised about something

god *noun* **gods**
a male being in religions such as Hinduism and the religions of ancient Greece and Rome. Gods control a part of the universe or life and people pray to them. *Poseidon, the Greek god of the sea*

God *noun*
God is what people pray to in their religion, especially in the Christian, Jewish and Muslim religions. In these religions God is the creator of the universe.

godchild *noun* **godchildren**
a child that a godparent promises to take care of. A male child is called a godson and a female child is called a goddaughter.

goddess *noun* **goddesses**
a female being in religions such as Hinduism and the religions of ancient Greece and Rome. Goddesses control a part of the universe or life and people pray to them. *Minerva, the Roman goddess of wisdom*

godparent *noun* **godparents**
a person who promises to take care of a child and teach him or her how to be a good person if the child's real parents die. In the Christian religion, the promise is usually made during the baptism ceremony. A man who makes this promise is called a godfather and a woman is called a godmother.

godsend *noun* **godsends**
something or someone that comes just at the right time to help you in a difficult situation

-goer *suffix*
used for making nouns that mean someone likes going somewhere and usually goes there a lot *cinemagoer*; *filmgoer*; *opera goer*

goes
third person singular present tense of **go**

goggles *noun plural*
large glasses that fit tightly around your eyes and protect you from things such as dust, water or wind

going *noun*
used for talking about how well, quickly or easily you do something *My homework is very slow going.*

gold *noun*
1 a very valuable yellow metal, used for example for making jewellery or medals
2 an orange-yellow colour

gold *adjective*
1 made of gold *a gold bracelet*
2 having the orange-yellow colour of gold *We painted the room gold.*
3 a gold medal is given to the winner in a race or competition. A silver medal goes to the person who comes second and a bronze one to the person who comes third.

golden *adjective*
1 having the orange-yellow colour of gold *golden hair*
2 made of gold
3 very special, happy and successful *the golden days of childhood*
4 a golden opportunity is an excellent chance to do something
5 a golden rule is an important thing you should do to be successful in a particular situation

goldfish *noun* **goldfish**
a small orange fish that people keep as a pet

goldmine *noun* **goldmines**
a place under the ground where gold is dug out of rocks

gold-plated *adjective*
covered with a very thin layer of gold

golf *noun*
a game in which someone uses a stick, called a club, to hit a small white ball into a hole. Golf is played on a large area of land called a golf course.

golfer *noun* **golfers**
someone who plays golf

golfing *adjective*
connected with golf *golfing equipment*

Goliath ['ger-lye-erth'] *noun*
a very big and important organisation or person

ORIGIN from the Bible story about how a boy called David killed a giant called Goliath

gondola ['gon-der-ler] *noun* **gondolas**
1 a long narrow boat with curved ends that point upwards. Someone stands in the boat and moves it through the water using a pole with a long flat part at one end. Gondolas are used on the canals of Venice.
2 the hanging part that you travel in in something such as a ski lift or Ferris wheel

gondolier ['gon-der-leer] *noun* **gondoliers**
someone who stands at the back of a gondola and moves it through the water with a long pole

gone
past participle of **go**

gong *noun* **gongs**
a large metal disc inside a frame. The disc makes a loud deep noise when you hit it.

goo *noun*
any sticky or thick substance that is unpleasant

good *adjective* **better, best**
1 used for showing that you like something or think it is of a high standard *a good piece of homework*; *My Spanish is not very good.*
2 used for showing that you like someone or think they are helpful or kind *a good friend*; *You've been good to me.*
3 used for showing something you want or that makes you happy *good news*; *We had a good holiday.* 'Dad's home.' – 'That's good.'
4 doing something well *a good singer*; *I'm good at languages.*
5 behaving properly *Be good when I'm out.*
6 used for showing something that can help you or have a successful result *a good plan*; *Walking is good for you. What's the best way to the library?*
7 used for showing something that is sensible or can be trusted *good advice*; *a good reason*
8 feeling healthy 'How are you?' – 'I'm good!'
9 used for giving extra importance to something *You need a good rest* (a long rest). *Take a good look* (look very carefully).
10 used for describing a large amount, size or number of something *I waited a good hour* (at least an hour). *A good many of the children* (a lot of them) *come by bus.*
11 used for showing something that can still be used *Your ticket is still good.*

SIMILE 'as good as gold' means very good (sense 5)

good *noun*
1 something good that helps someone *My new school has done me a lot of good. Shouting won't do any good* (isn't useful).
2 very good actions *My uncle is a rich man who tries to do good.*
3 the power to do good things *a struggle between good and evil*
4 **no good** useless *It's no good shouting. I'm no good at football.*
5 **for good** for all time in the future *That teacher has left for good.*

goodbye *interjection*
a word you say when you leave someone or stop speaking to them, for example on the phone

good-for-nothing *noun* **good-for-nothings**
a lazy and useless person

Good Friday *noun*
the Friday before the Christian holiday of Easter

goodies *noun plural*
an informal word for things that are nice to eat or to have

good-looking *adjective*
very attractive

good-natured *adjective*
friendly and kind

goodness – graduated

goodness noun
1 the things in food that are good for your health, for example vitamins and proteins
2 the quality of being good

goods noun plural
1 things that people buy, for example from shops or the internet *electrical goods*; *a goods train* (carrying goods, not people)
2 things that people own

goodwill noun
friendly and helpful feelings towards people

gooey adjective
soft and sticky in an unpleasant way

Google noun (trademark)
the name of an internet search engine (computer program that finds information)

google verb
googles, googling, googled
to search for a word, phrase or picture on the internet using a search engine such as Google

goose noun
1 (plural **geese**) a large water bird that is similar to a duck. A male goose is called a gander and a young goose is called a gosling.
2 the meat of a goose eaten as food
3 goose pimples or goose bumps are tiny points that appear on your skin when you are cold or frightened

gooseberry ['guz-bree; 'u' has the same vowel sound as 'wood'] noun **gooseberries**
a small round green fruit with a sour taste, used for example in pies and jam

gore verb
gores, goring, gored
if an animal such as a bull or elephant gores a person or animal, it injures that person or animal with its horns or tusks

gorge noun **gorges**
a narrow valley with steep sides, usually made by a river

gorge verb
gorges, gorging, gorged
if you gorge yourself, you keep eating until you can't eat any more *Don't gorge yourself on all those sweets or you'll be sick.*

gorgeous adjective
1 extremely beautiful *You look gorgeous in that dress.*
2 extremely good and pleasing *a gorgeous meal*; *gorgeous weather* (for example warm and sunny)

gorilla noun **gorillas**
a very big and strong animal like a monkey that lives in the forests of Central Africa

gorse noun
a prickly bush with small yellow flowers. Gorse grows wild in the countryside.

gory adjective **gorier, goriest**
1 with a lot of blood and killing *a gory horror film*
2 covered in blood

gosh interjection
an old-fashioned word used for showing that you're surprised or slightly angry

gosling noun **goslings**
a young goose

gospel noun
1 (plural **Gospels**) the Gospel is one of the four books of the Christian Bible about the life of Jesus Christ
2 the gospel is the life of Jesus and the things he taught
3 if you take something as gospel, you believe it is completely true

gossip verb
gossips, gossiping, gossiped
to talk about other people's lives and behaviour, usually in an unpleasant way

gossip noun
1 words that people say or write about other people's lives and behaviour *a nasty piece of gossip*
2 (plural **gossips**) someone who talks about other people's lives and behaviour, usually in an unpleasant way

got
past tense & past participle of **get**

goth noun
1 a type of music similar to punk rock, often with words about death
2 (plural **goths**) someone who likes goth music and often wears black clothes

Gothic adjective
1 connected with a style of building, for example churches, that includes pointed arches and tall columns. It was popular between the 12th and 16th centuries.
2 connected with a style in novels and films about frightening and mysterious things

gouge ['gowj'] verb
gouges, gouging, gouged
1 to gouge something out is to cut or dig into a surface, for example to get something out
2 to gouge a hole is to make a hole in a surface

gout noun
an illness that makes the joints in the feet, knees or hands swollen and painful

govern verb
governs, governing, governed
1 to be in charge of a country, area, group or organisation
2 to influence the way something happens *What are the rules that govern football?*

government noun
1 (plural **governments**) a group of people chosen to be in charge of a country or area
2 the way a country or area is governed *Is democracy the best type of government?*

governor noun **governors**
1 someone in charge of something such as a part of a country or a state in the USA
2 someone who is a member of a group of people in charge of something such as a school or hospital

gown noun **gowns**
1 a long dress for special occasions *a wedding gown*
2 a long piece of loose clothing worn over other clothes *a university gown*

GP noun **GPs**
a doctor who deals with people who have all types of illnesses and sends them to hospital if they need special treatment
short for: **general practitioner**

GPS noun
a system that provides information about where someone or something is, using radio waves from satellites that go round the earth
short for: *Global Positioning System*

grab verb
grabs, grabbing, grabbed
1 to take something quickly and roughly with your hand or hands *I grabbed my schoolbag and ran.*
2 to put your hand or hands on someone quickly and roughly, for example to pull them or take them away *I slipped but Mum grabbed me and stopped me falling.*
3 an informal way of saying to get *Let's grab something to eat.*

grace noun
1 a beautiful and gentle way of moving
2 a kind, friendly and pleasant way of behaving

graceful adjective
1 if someone is graceful, they move in a beautiful and gentle way *a graceful dancer*
2 a graceful movement or shape is beautiful and gentle *the graceful curve of a swan's neck*

gracefully adverb

gracious adjective
pleasant and polite **graciously** adverb

grade noun **grades**
1 a number or letter that shows how good someone's schoolwork is or how good their answers in an exam are
2 a level in the quality of something *This coffee is of a high grade.*
3 a level in a job

grade verb
grades, grading, graded
1 to give a number or letter to someone's schoolwork or their answers in an exam to show how good they are
2 to sort things into different groups according to their quality

gradient ['gray-dee-ernt'] noun **gradients**
1 the size of the angle of a slope *a steep gradient*
2 a slope

gradual adjective
1 happening slowly, for example over a period of time *a gradual change in the climate*
2 slight *a gradual slope*

ORIGIN from Medieval Latin *gradualis* 'with steps' (from Latin *gradus* 'step')

gradually adverb
1 slowly, for example over a period of time
2 slightly *The ground slopes gradually down to the sea.*

graduate ['grad-joo-ert'] noun **graduates**
someone who has a degree from a university or college

graduate ['grad-joo-ayt'] verb
graduates, graduating, graduated
to finish your studies and get a degree from your university or college

graduated adjective
if something such as a ruler or container is graduated, it has small marks on it that show measurements

graduation–graph paper

graduation noun
1 the time when you get a degree from your university or college
2 the ceremony where you receive your degree certificate

graffiti noun
words or pictures drawn on a wall or other surface in a public place *The train was covered in graffiti.*

LANGUAGE EXTRA in English, *graffiti* can be either singular or plural. For example, you can say *This graffiti is awesome* or *These graffiti are awesome.*

ORIGIN from the Italian plural *graffiti* 'little scribbles'

grain noun
1 seeds from a plant such as wheat or rice that people eat as food
2 plants such as wheat or rice
3 (plural **grains**) one hard seed from a plant such as wheat or rice
4 (plural **grains**) a grain of something such as salt or sand is one tiny hard piece of it
5 a tiny amount of a quality such as truth or common sense *There isn't a grain of truth in what you say.*
6 the pattern of small lines in a material such as wood, cloth or rock

gram noun grams
a unit for measuring weight in the metric system. There are 1000 grams in a kilogram.

LANGUAGE EXTRA also spelt *gramme*

ORIGIN from Latin and Greek *gramma* 'small weight'

grammar noun
1 the rules for using words in a language *English grammar*
2 the knowledge of how to use words in a language *My grammar isn't very good.*
3 (plural **grammars**) a book explaining the rules for using words *I bought an English grammar.*

ORIGIN from Greek *grammatikos* 'connected with letters'

grammar school noun grammar schools
a school for students aged 11 to 18. You have to pass a special exam to go there.

grammatical adjective
1 obeying the rules of grammar *a grammatical sentence*
2 connected with grammar *a grammatical mistake*

grammatically adverb
1 in a way that obeys the rules of grammar *In school we learn to write grammatically.*
2 if something is grammatically correct, it obeys the rules of grammar

gran noun grans
an informal word for a grandmother

grand adjective grander, grandest
1 very big and important *a grand house in the country*; *grand ideas*
2 important, rich and attractive *He looked very grand in his uniform.*
3 very pleasant *We had a grand day out.*
4 used in names for showing that something is very big and important *the Grand Canal* (the main canal in Venice)
5 very good *You've made a grand job of your homework.*
6 a grand total is the total of everything added together

grandchild noun grandchildren
the child of a person's son or daughter

granddad noun granddads
an informal word for a grandfather

LANGUAGE EXTRA also spelt *grandad*

granddaughter noun granddaughters
the daughter of a person's son or daughter

grandfather noun grandfathers
1 the father of a person's father or mother
2 a grandfather clock is a large clock that stands on the floor inside a tall wooden box or container

grandiose ['gran-dee-ohz' or 'gran-dee-ohs'] adjective
1 very big and important-looking *a grandiose building*
2 if something such as an idea or plan is grandiose, it is meant to achieve something big and important but is not very good or practical

grandly adverb
1 if someone says or does something grandly, they behave in a way that shows they want to appear important
2 in a rich and attractive way *a grandly furnished house*

grandma noun grandmas
an informal word for a grandmother

grandmother noun grandmothers
the mother of a person's father or mother

grandpa noun grandpas
an informal word for a grandfather

grandparent noun grandparents
the father or mother of a person's father or mother

grand piano noun grand pianos
a large piano with a container at the back with horizontal strings in it and a lid that opens up. Grand pianos are used for concerts.

grandson noun grandsons
the son of a person's son or daughter

grandstand noun grandstands
a building that is open at the front and has rows of seats from which people watch sports events such as horse racing

granite ['gran-it'] noun
a very hard rock with small grains in it, used for buildings and monuments

ORIGIN from Italian *granito* 'having small grains'

granny noun grannies
an informal word for a grandmother

granola noun
a breakfast food made from baked grains, nuts and honey that you eat with milk

grant noun grants
money that the government or an organisation gives you for a particular purpose, for example to study at a university

grant verb grants, granting, granted
1 to allow someone to have something that they have asked for
2 if you take something for granted, you simply believe that it is true without thinking about it *I took it for granted that she would come to my party.*

granulated sugar noun
sugar in small grains

grape noun grapes
a small juicy fruit with a green or purple skin, which is eaten or used for making wine. Grapes grow on a plant called a vine.

grapefruit noun grapefruits
a yellow fruit like a large orange but with a sour taste

grapevine noun grapevines
1 a climbing plant on which grapes grow
2 if you hear a piece of news on the grapevine, you hear it from someone you know who has heard it from someone else

graph noun graphs
a mathematical diagram with lines or curves that show how numbers or measurements are related to each other. Most graphs have a horizontal axis (or line) along the bottom and a vertical axis along the side where the measurements are given.

grapheme noun graphemes
in grammar, a grapheme is the smallest written unit that represents a particular sound or meaning in a language. For example, the letter 'g' is a grapheme that represents both the sound in the word 'good' and the sound in 'gentle'.
compare: **phoneme**

graphic adjective
1 very clear and with lots of details, often unpleasant ones *The police gave a graphic description of the accident.*
2 connected with drawing or pictures *a graphic designer* (someone who designs words and pictures, for example in a magazine)

ORIGIN from Greek *graphein* 'to write'

graphically adverb
very clearly and with lots of details *His photos graphically show the horrors of war.*

graphics noun plural
1 pictures and drawings on a computer
2 a graphics card is the part in a computer that produces the picture shown on the screen
3 a graphics tablet is a piece of equipment with a flat surface that is connected to a computer. You draw on the surface with a special pen (called a stylus) to put a picture into the computer. It can also be used instead of a mouse.

graphite noun
a dark grey substance that is a form of carbon. It is used, for example, in the middle of pencils.

graph paper noun
paper with small squares printed on it. It is used, for example, for drawing graphs (mathematical diagrams).

200

grapple – greedy

grapple *verb*
grapples, grappling, grappled
1 to fight with someone, while holding them very tightly *The two boys were grappling with each other on the floor.*
2 to grapple with a problem is to try to solve it

grasp *verb*
grasps, grasping, grasped
1 to take something with your hand or hands and hold it tightly
2 to understand something

grasp *noun*
1 a tight hold on something *His hand slipped out of my grasp.*
2 an understanding of something *My brother has a good grasp of French.*
3 if something is within your grasp, it is very possible that you will achieve it *The gold medal is within your grasp.*

grasping *adjective*
interested in money and nothing else

grass *noun*
1 a plant with long thin green leaves that grows close to the ground. It covers places such as gardens, parks and fields.
2 an area of ground covered with grass *Keep off the grass.*

grass *verb* (informal)
grasses, grassing, grassed
to tell someone such as a teacher or police officer that someone else has done something bad *Tom grassed on me to the head teacher.*

grasshopper *noun* grasshoppers
an insect that jumps using its long back legs and makes a short high sound

grassy *adjective* grassier, grassiest
covered with grass

grate *verb*
grates, grating, grated
1 if you grate something such as cheese, you rub it against a grater to break it into small pieces
2 to make a rough and unpleasant noise by rubbing against a hard surface *As I got up, my chair grated on the floor.*

grate *noun* grates
a frame of metal bars that holds coal and wood in a fireplace

grateful *adjective*
1 wanting to thank someone because they have helped you or been kind to you *I'm grateful to you for all you've done.*
2 very happy that something good happens to you *I'm grateful to be alive.*

gratefully *adverb*
showing thanks to someone *All gifts will be gratefully accepted.*

grater *noun* graters
a metal tool used in cooking. It has lots of holes with sharp edges that you rub food against to break it into small pieces. *a cheese grater*

grating *noun* gratings
a frame with metal bars across it that covers an opening such as a drain

grating *adjective*
a grating noise is one that is rough and unpleasant

gratitude *noun*
pleasant feelings towards someone because they have helped you or been kind to you

grave ['grayv'] *noun* graves
a place in the ground where a dead person is buried

grave ['grayv'] *adjective* graver, gravest
serious in a way that makes you very worried *The situation is grave.*

grave accent ['grahv'] *noun*
grave accents
a grave accent is the symbol ` above a letter in some languages such as French or Italian, for example à or ù

gravedigger *noun* gravediggers
someone whose job is to dig holes in the ground for graves

gravel *noun*
small pieces of stone, used for example for making paths

gravely *adverb*
1 seriously *gravely ill*
2 in a serious voice *'She's dead,' he said gravely.*

gravestone *noun* gravestones
a large piece of stone lying over or standing next to a grave. It has on it the name of the person buried there and the dates when he or she was born and died.

graveyard *noun* graveyards
an area of land where people who have died are buried, often next to a church

gravitation *noun*
a force that pulls all things in the universe towards each other

gravity *noun*
1 a force that pulls things towards each other, especially the force that pulls everything towards the earth. Gravity is what makes things fall to the ground if you drop them.
2 the seriousness of something

gravy *noun*
a brown sauce made using the liquid from cooked meat

graze *verb*
grazes, grazing, grazed
1 to accidentally rub the surface of your skin and make it bleed *I fell down and grazed my elbow on the pavement.*
2 if something grazes a surface, it touches it lightly
3 if animals graze, they eat grass that is growing somewhere, for example in a field

graze *noun* grazes
a place on your body where the skin has been accidentally rubbed

grease *noun*
1 soft animal fat that comes from cooking meat
2 an oily substance that comes from food when it contains a lot of butter or vegetable fat
3 an oily substance produced by the skin
4 a thick oil for making machine parts work better together

grease *verb*
greases, greasing, greased
1 to put a small amount of something such as oil, fat or butter into a pan or container before cooking something in it
2 to put oil onto a machine part to make it work better

greaseproof paper *noun*
a strong thin paper that does not allow oily substances to pass through, used in cooking and for wrapping food

greasy *adjective* greasier, greasiest
1 with lots of grease on it or in it *greasy hair*; *a greasy doughnut*
2 slippery, for example because something oily has been spilt on it *The kitchen floor is a bit greasy.*

great *adjective* greater, greatest
1 used when you mean a lot of something *He's in great pain. I had great difficulty seeing. This is a poem of great beauty. I have a great many friends* (lots of them).
2 very good *We had a great day visiting London. It's great that you can come to my party.*
3 important *Napoleon was a great leader. 'The Haywain' is a great painting by Constable.*
4 very big *a great distance*; *a great big house*; *I saw a great crowd outside the library.*
5 used in names to mean big or important *the Great Fire of London*; *Catherine the Great of Russia*
6 used when you mean someone does something a lot *I'm a great reader of the Dr Seuss books.*

great- *prefix*
used with names such as grandfather or granddaughter to show that they are the next generation *my great-grandmother* (the mother of my grandmother); *her great-grandson* (the son of her grandson)

Great Britain *noun*
England, Scotland and Wales

> **LANGUAGE EXTRA** called *Britain* for short. The *United Kingdom* (or *UK* for short) includes England, Scotland, Wales and Northern Ireland.

greatly *adverb*
very much *Your homework has greatly improved.*

greatness *noun*
used when you mean a lot of success or importance *What are the reasons for Rembrandt's greatness?*

Greece *noun*
a country in South-East Europe

greed *noun*
when someone wants more food, money or power than they need

greedily *adverb*
in a way that shows you are greedy *He was eating the cake greedily* (quickly and noisily, for example, because he wanted more).

greedy *adjective* greedier, greediest
if someone is greedy, they want more food, money or power than they need

Greek–grind

Greek *adjective*
connected with Greece or the Greek language

Greek *noun*
1 (*plural* **Greeks**) someone from modern or ancient Greece
2 the language of modern or ancient Greece

green *adjective* **greener, greenest**
1 having the colour of grass and leaves
2 covered with grass, trees and plants *There are lots of green spaces in London.*
3 not ripe *green bananas*
4 connected with the environment (the natural world) and with protecting it *Electricity is greener than petrol.*
5 pale or ill *You look a bit green.*

SIMILE 'as green as grass' means very green (sense 1)

green *noun* **greens**
1 the colour green
2 an area covered by grass for people to use, for example for walking or playing on
3 greens are cooked green vegetables, especially ones with leaves such as cabbage

green bean *noun* **green beans**
a long thin green bean that is cooked and eaten as a vegetable

SYNONYM string bean

greenery *noun*
green plants, leaves or branches

greengage *noun* **greengages**
a green plum with a sweet taste

greengrocer *noun* **greengrocers**
someone who sells fruit and vegetables, usually from a shop

greenhouse *noun* **greenhouses**
a glass building used for growing plants and vegetables that need to be kept warm and protected from bad weather

greenhouse effect *noun*
a problem caused by an increase in the amounts of gases such as carbon dioxide (produced when carbon is burnt) in the air around the earth. The gases, called greenhouse gases, cannot escape because of pollution. This makes the temperature of the air increase and is known as global warming.

greenish *adjective*
slightly green

green tea *noun* **green teas**
a type of tea from China and Japan that is made with fewer chemicals than normal tea. It has a yellow-green colour and you drink it without milk.

Greenwich Mean Time *noun*
the time at Greenwich in South London that is used as the standard for international time zones

LANGUAGE EXTRA also called **GMT**

greet *verb*
greets, greeting, greeted
1 to behave in a polite way towards someone when you meet them, for example by saying particular words (such as hello) or by doing a particular action (such as smiling)
2 to behave in a certain way towards something or someone *We greeted the news with shouts of joy.*

greeting *noun* **greetings**
1 a polite word (or words) that you say or a polite action that you do when you meet someone
2 greetings are good wishes that you send or give to someone, for example for their birthday or at Christmas *a greetings card*

gremlin *noun* **gremlins**
a small imaginary evil creature that people often blame for getting inside machines or equipment and making them stop working

grenade *noun* **grenades**
a small bomb that someone throws by hand or fires with a special gun

grew
past tense of **grow**

grey *adjective* **greyer, greyest**
1 having a colour halfway between black and white, for example the colour of ashes
2 if someone is grey, they have grey hair
3 used about the weather or sky when there are lots of clouds *a grey December day*

grey *noun* **greys**
the colour grey

greyed out *adjective*
in computer software, if something such as a command or option is greyed out, the words appear in a very light shade of grey to show that you cannot use it

greyhound *noun* **greyhounds**
a tall dog with a thin body, long thin legs and smooth hair. Greyhounds can run very fast and are used especially in races.

greyish *adjective*
slightly grey

grid *noun* **grids**
1 a pattern of straight lines that cross each other and form squares, for example on a map or spreadsheet
2 a metal structure with bars that go across it
3 a grid reference on a map is a group of one or more letters joined to one or more numbers, for example G9 or SE287338. It is used for finding where something or someone is on a map that is divided into a grid (or squares).

grief *noun*
1 very great sadness, for example when someone dies
2 an informal word for problems *Her son has given her a lot of grief.*
3 if someone comes to grief, something very bad happens to them, such as having an accident or not passing an exam

grief-stricken *adjective*
extremely sad

grievance *noun* **grievances**
1 something that someone is angry about because they think they have been treated badly
2 an angry feeling

grieve *verb*
grieves, grieving, grieved
to feel very sad because someone has died

grievous *adjective*
1 very serious
2 making you very sad
grievously *adverb*

griffin *noun* **griffins**
in stories, an imaginary creature with the head and wings of an eagle and the body of a lion

grill *noun* **grills**
1 the part of a cooker that produces a flame or heat that you put food under to be cooked
2 food cooked under a grill
3 a frame with metal bars across it for cooking food over a flame
4 a restaurant that serves grilled food

grill *verb*
grills, grilling, grilled
1 to cook food close to the heat using a grill
2 to ask someone lots of questions for a long period of time *He was grilled by the police for five hours.*

grille *noun* **grilles**
a frame with metal bars or wires across it

LANGUAGE EXTRA also spelt **grill**

grim *adjective* **grimmer, grimmest**
1 unpleasant and making you feel sad *The news is grim.*
2 frightening and ugly *The town looks grim.*
3 serious and unfriendly *a grim expression*
grimly *adverb* **grimness** *noun*

grimace ['grim-ers] *noun* **grimaces**
a very unpleasant or ugly expression on your face, for example showing pain or dislike

grimace ['grim-ers] *verb*
grimaces, grimacing, grimaced
to make a very unpleasant or ugly expression with your face, for example showing pain or dislike

grime *noun*
thick dirt on something *The walls of the old building were covered in grime.*

grimy *adjective* **grimier, grimiest**
very dirty

grin *noun* **grins**
a big smile, usually showing your teeth. A grin can be a false smile rather than a happy and friendly one.

grin *verb*
grins, grinning, grinned
1 to smile with a grin
2 **to grin and bear it** to accept a bad situation without complaining

grind *verb*
grinds, grinding, ground
1 to press something between hard surfaces so that it gets broken into small pieces or made into a powder
2 to press the edge of something such as a knife against a hard surface to make it sharper or smoother
3 to rub against something and make an unpleasant sound *You could hear the parts of the machine grinding against each other.*
4 to grind your teeth is to rub your top teeth against your bottom ones

grind–group

5 if something such as a machine or vehicle grinds to a halt, it stops moving, usually making a lot of noise at the same time
6 if something such as an activity grinds to a halt, it slows down and stops

grind *noun*
hard and boring work, especially work that you have to do every day *the daily grind*

grinding *adjective*
1 a grinding noise is an unpleasant one made by hard things rubbing against each other
2 grinding poverty is when someone is extremely poor

grip *verb*
grips, gripping, gripped
1 to hold something very tightly
2 if something such as fear or panic grips you, you feel it strongly
3 if something such as a story, film or event grips you, it keeps you interested *The whole country was gripped by the royal wedding.*

grip *noun* grips
1 a tight hold on something
2 a part of a handle with a rough surface that makes it easier for you to hold it tightly
3 to get to grips with something such as a problem is to make an effort to deal with it

gripping *adjective*
very interesting

grisly *adjective* grislier, grisliest
shocking and horrible (usually to do with dead people) *a grisly murder*

SYNONYM **gruesome**

gristle *noun*
a rubbery substance around the bones in meat, which is hard to chew

gristly *adjective*

grit *noun*
1 small pieces of stone or sand
2 if someone has grit, they are brave and don't let anything stop them from doing something even if it is difficult

grit *verb*
grits, gritting, gritted
1 to put small pieces of stone or sand on a road to stop it becoming icy
2 to grit your teeth is to bite them together, for example because you're angry or in pain
3 to grit your teeth is also to accept a difficult situation

gritty *adjective* grittier, grittiest
1 containing grit, or rough like grit
2 brave

grizzly bear *noun* grizzly bears
a large brown bear that lives in North America

groan *verb*
groans, groaning, groaned
to make a long deep sound, for example because you're in pain or upset about something **groan** *noun*

grocer *noun* grocers
someone who has a shop selling food and other things for the home

grocery *noun* groceries
1 an old-fashioned word for a grocer's shop
2 groceries are food and other things for the home that you buy from a supermarket or grocer's shop

groggy *adjective* groggier, groggiest
feeling weak or slightly ill

groin *noun* groins
the place where your legs join the front of your body

groom *noun* grooms
1 a man on his wedding day

SYNONYM **bridegroom**

2 a person who looks after horses in a stable

groom *verb*
grooms, grooming, groomed
1 to brush and clean an animal, especially a horse
2 if you groom your hair, you keep it neat and tidy

groomed *adjective*
having a neat and tidy appearance *She's always nicely groomed.*

groove *noun* grooves
a long narrow space made in a surface, for example for something to slide along *Slide the back of the mobile phone along these grooves.*

grope *verb*
gropes, groping, groped
to feel with your hands in order to get somewhere or find something *I was groping around in the dark trying to find my way out.*

gross *adjective* grosser, grossest
1 very unpleasant or disgusting *That food looks gross.*
2 very bad *gross incompetence*
3 very rude *He's always so gross.*
4 a gross amount of money is the total amount before any other money has been taken away from it

gross *noun* gross
a counting unit equal to 12 dozen or 144 *'How many elastic bands do you want?' – 'Two gross.'*

grossly *adverb*
1 extremely *That's grossly unfair.*
2 very much *You're grossly exaggerating!*
3 very rudely *You behaved grossly last night.*

gross out *verb* (informal)
grosses out, grossing out, grossed out
if someone or something grosses you out, they make you feel disgusted *Stop talking about dead insects – you're grossing me out!*

grotesque *adjective*
1 ugly and frightening *a grotesque Halloween mask*
2 very insulting *Those opinions are grotesque.*

grotesquely *adverb*

grotto *noun* grottos or grottoes
a small cave, especially one with nicely shaped rocks or one that has been specially built, for example in a garden

grotty *adjective* grottier, grottiest (informal)
1 unpleasant *a grotty part of town*
2 of bad quality *My phone is pretty grotty.*
3 dirty or untidy *Your room looks a bit grotty.*

grottiness *noun*

grouch *noun* grouches (informal)
someone who complains a lot **grouch** *verb*

grouchy *adjective* grouchier, grouchiest (informal)
angry and complaining a lot

SYNONYM **grumpy**

ground *noun*
1 the surface of the land *The ground shook.*

SYNONYM **earth**

2 the soil under the land's surface *I was digging in the ground.*

SYNONYM **earth**

3 (*plural* **grounds**) a particular area of land, for example for playing sports *a football ground*; *There's some waste ground next to our school.*
4 a subject or an area of knowledge *We've covered this ground in our history lessons.*
5 progress *You were behind but you've now gained ground* (made progress).

ground
past tense and past participle of **grind**

grounded *adjective*
1 if an aircraft is grounded, it is not allowed to fly, for example because of bad weather
2 if a child is grounded, he or she is not allowed to go out, as a punishment

ground floor *noun* ground floors
the floor of a building that is at the bottom and is level with the ground

LANGUAGE EXTRA in American English, this floor is called the *first floor*

grounds *noun plural*
1 the land and gardens around a building such as a large house or a hospital
2 grounds for something are a reason or reasons for it *The teacher had grounds for thinking that Imogen had cheated.*

groundsheet *noun* groundsheets
a piece of waterproof material that you put on the ground, for example in a tent. You put your sleeping bag on top of it.

groundsman *noun* groundsmen
someone who looks after a sports ground

groundswoman *noun* groundswomen
a woman who looks after a sports ground

group *noun* groups
1 a number of people, animals or things together
2 a number of musicians who play together *a rock group*
3 an age group is all the people between two particular ages *the 7 to 11 age group*
4 a blood group is the type of blood a person has. The four main groups are A, B, AB and O.

203

group–guerrilla

group verb
groups, grouping, grouped
1 to put people, animals or things into a group *We grouped eight marbles into four groups of two.*
2 to form a group *We grouped around our teacher in the playground.*

grouse verb (informal)
grouses, grousing, groused
to complain, often in an angry way

grouse noun grouse
a fat brown, black or grey bird that is hunted for sport or food. In the UK, grouse live especially on the Scottish moors.

grove noun groves
a group of trees growing close together, for example orange or olive trees

Grove noun
used in the names of streets and other places *She lives at 35 Maple Grove.*

grovel verb
grovels, grovelling, grovelled
1 if you grovel to someone, you praise them too much or behave as if you are their servant, for example because you want something from them or are afraid of them
2 to move around on the ground on your hands and knees

grow verb
grows, growing, grew, grown
1 if people, animals or plants grow, they gradually get bigger with time
2 to get bigger in amount or numbers, or to get stronger *Our fears are growing. The number of internet users is growing.*
3 to get longer, or to allow something to get longer *Look at Emma – her hair has really grown. My brother is growing a beard.*
4 if plants grow somewhere, they exist there and develop in the soil by getting bigger and producing leaves *There were weeds growing everywhere. Not many trees grow in this part of the country.*
5 if someone grows plants, they put them in the soil and look after them as they develop *We grow runner beans.*
6 if animals grow something such as a part of their body, that part of their body starts and gets bigger *All these insects grow wings.*
7 to become *The noise is growing louder.*
8 to change gradually into something bigger, better or stronger *The caterpillar grew into a butterfly.*
9 if something grows on you, you start to like it more *This music seems to grow on you.*
10 if you grow out of something, you become too big or old for it *I've grown out of these shoes.*
11 if you grow up, you change from being a young child to an older one or you become an adult
12 if you grow up somewhere, you spend your time as a child in that place *I grew up in Leeds.*

growing adjective
getting bigger or stronger *growing numbers of people*; *the growing popularity of e-books*

growl verb
growls, growling, growled
to make a low, rough and frightening sound, like an angry dog **growl** noun

grown
past participle of **grow**

grown-up noun grown-ups
someone who is no longer a child

SYNONYM adult

grown-up adjective
1 no longer a child *a grown-up daughter*
2 behaving or looking like someone who is no longer a child *Ethan is very grown-up. You look very grown-up in that dress.*

growth noun
1 when people, animals or plants get bigger with time *We need good food for healthy growth.*
2 an increase in the amount, numbers or strength of something *the growth of social media*
3 (plural **growths**) a lump growing inside or on the body

grub noun
1 an informal word for food
2 (plural **grubs**) an insect before it has grown wings or legs. It looks like a small white worm.

grubby adjective grubbier, grubbiest
dirty **grubbiness** noun

grudge noun grudges
a strong feeling of anger towards someone who has treated you badly *He's had a grudge against his brother for many years.*

grudge verb
grudges, grudging, grudged
1 to feel angry about something you have done or have to do *I grudge every minute I spent helping her.*
2 if you don't grudge someone something, you mean you don't feel angry that they have it *I don't grudge him his success.*

SYNONYM to begrudge

grudgingly adjective
if you do something grudgingly, you only do it because you have to

gruelling adjective
very difficult *Mum had a gruelling day in the office.*

gruesome adjective
shocking and horrible (usually to do with dead people) *The newspaper had a gruesome description of the murder.*

SYNONYM grisly

gruff adjective gruffer, gruffest
1 unfriendly and rude *a gruff reply*
2 a gruff voice is one that is low and unfriendly
gruffly adverb

grumble verb
grumbles, grumbling, grumbled
1 to complain, especially to complain a lot of the time *My cousin is always grumbling about his teacher.*
2 if your stomach grumbles, it makes low unpleasant noises, for example because you're hungry
grumble noun

grumpy adjective grumpier, grumpiest
angry and complaining a lot
grumpily adverb

grunt verb
grunts, grunting, grunted
1 when a pig grunts, it makes a deep rough noise that is its own special sound
2 to make a similar sound with your voice, for example because you're angry or in pain
grunt noun

guarantee verb
guarantees, guaranteeing, guaranteed
1 to promise that something will definitely be done or will happen or be true *Our school guarantees that we'll get a good education. I can guarantee that this is a good choice.*
2 if something guarantees something else, it makes certain that it happens
3 to promise to repair or change a product if it goes wrong within a certain time *How long is my laptop guaranteed for?*

guarantee noun guarantees
1 a written document from a company that promises to repair or change a product, such as a TV or washing machine, if it goes wrong within a certain time
2 a promise that something will definitely be done or will happen

guard verb
guards, guarding, guarded
1 to keep a person, place or thing safe from harm or danger
2 to watch someone to stop them from escaping *The prisoners are guarded night and day.*
3 to guard against something is to stop it from happening

guard noun guards
1 someone whose job is to keep a person, place or thing safe or to stop someone from escaping
2 a group of guards
3 the action of keeping a person, place or thing safe *I'm on guard tonight* (guarding something or someone). *A police officer stood guard outside the door.*
4 someone whose job is to be in charge of a train, especially in the past
5 something that keeps you safe from something dangerous such as a fire, blade or piece of equipment *a fire guard*
6 a guard dog is a dog that looks after a place or building

guardian noun guardians
a person in charge of someone who cannot look after themselves, for example a child whose parents have died **guardianship** noun

guardrail noun guardrails
a bar along the edge of something such as a bridge or cliff, put there to stop people falling

guerrilla ['ge-ri-ler'] noun guerrillas
someone who belongs to a small group of fighters who use surprise attacks against the official army of a country

LANGUAGE EXTRA also spelt *guerilla*

ORIGIN from Spanish *guerrilla* 'little war'

guess–gunpowder

guess *verb*
guesses, guessing, guessed
1 to give an answer or opinion about something (that may or may not be correct) when you don't know all the details *I don't know what happened – I'm just guessing. Guess what time it is.*
2 to give the right answer or to be correct about something when you don't know all the details *I guessed her age.*
3 **I guess** used when you mean something is probably true *I guess you must be tired.*

guess *noun* **guesses**
an answer or opinion about something (that may or may not be correct) when you don't know all the details *I had a guess but I was wrong.*

guesswork *noun*
when you try to find the answer to something by guessing *If we're successful, it will be by pure guesswork.*

guest *noun* **guests**
1 someone you invite to your home, for example for a meal or to stay with you
2 someone invited somewhere, for example to a party, wedding or restaurant
3 someone staying in a hotel
4 someone invited to take part in a TV or radio show
5 a guest room is a bedroom in your home for a guest to sleep in

guesthouse *noun* **guesthouses**
a private house where people pay to spend the night, like a hotel

guffaw ['gɜː-fɔː] *verb*
guffaws, guffawing, guffawed
to laugh loudly **guffaw** *noun*

guidance *noun*
help and information about how to do something or deal with a particular situation

guide *verb*
guides, guiding, guided
1 to go with someone to show them the way or to show them from place to place *I guided my parents round the school.*
2 to help someone go somewhere or show them where to go *She took my hand and guided me across the road. These lights guide the ships at night.*
3 to move something in a particular direction *I guided my wheelchair carefully along the corridor.*
4 to show someone the correct way to do something

guide *noun* **guides**
1 someone who shows you a place or shows you the way *Jo will be your guide around the school. My mum's a tour guide* (showing people interesting places in a town, country or building).
2 something that helps you do something or form an opinion
3 a book with useful information about something such as a place or subject
4 a Guide is a girl who belongs to the section of the Guides for girls aged 10 to 14. The Guides (or Guide Association) is an organisation that teaches girls useful skills.
5 a guide dog is a dog that helps someone who cannot see to move around safely

guidebook *noun* **guidebooks**
a book with information about a place

guided tour *noun* **guided tours**
a visit in which someone shows you around a building or place

guidelines *noun plural*
information about how to do something or about what something should be

guillotine *noun* **guillotines**
1 a machine for cutting off people's heads, used in France from the time of the French Revolution (1789). It consisted of a tall frame with a sharp blade sliding down it.
2 a tool for cutting paper. It consists of a board with a long blade fixed to it.

ORIGIN named after Joseph *Guillotin*, an 18th-century French doctor who was the first person to suggest using the guillotine

guilt *noun*
1 someone's guilt is the fact that they have done something wrong *The thief stood up in court and admitted his guilt.*

ANTONYM innocence

2 the sad and unpleasant feeling someone has when they have done something wrong

guilty *adjective* **guiltier, guiltiest**
1 if someone is guilty, they have done something wrong *He was found guilty of swearing at a police officer.*

ANTONYM innocent

2 if you feel guilty, you feel sad because you know you have done something wrong

guinea pig *noun* **guinea pigs**
1 a small furry animal with short ears, short legs and no tail. It is often kept as a pet.
2 a person used in a scientific experiment

Guinness World Records *noun*
a website that lists the greatest world records (for example best and worst achievements, biggest and smallest, longest and shortest). The records are also included in a book.

guitar *noun* **guitars**
a musical instrument that usually has six strings, which you play by pulling them with your fingers or with a small piece of plastic called a plectrum. A guitar has a main part (or body) that is usually shaped like the number eight and a long narrow top part (or neck).

guitarist *noun* **guitarists**
someone who plays a guitar

gulf *noun* **gulfs**
1 a large area of sea that is mainly surrounded by land *the Gulf of Mexico*
2 a big difference between people or groups

gull *noun* **gulls**
a big grey and white bird with long wings that lives near the sea

SYNONYM seagull

gullet *noun* **gullets**
the tube that food goes down from your throat to your stomach

SYNONYM oesophagus

gullible *adjective*
if someone is gullible, they are easily tricked because they are ready to believe everything that people tell them

gully *noun* **gullies**
a small valley or large ditch with steep sides. Gullies are usually made by water flowing along them.

LANGUAGE EXTRA also spelt *gulley*. The plural of *gulley* is *gulleys*.

gulp *verb*
gulps, gulping, gulped
1 if you gulp something down, you swallow large amounts of it quickly
2 to make a swallowing noise, for example because you are surprised, nervous or afraid

gulp *noun* **gulps**
1 a quick swallow
2 a swallowing noise

gum *noun*
1 (*plural* **gums**) the pink fleshy part of your mouth where your teeth grow
2 a kind of sticky sweet that you chew to taste its flavour but do not swallow

SYNONYM chewing gum

3 a glue for sticking papers together

gum *verb*
gums, gumming, gummed
1 to stick something to something else with gum
2 to cover something with gum

gum tree *noun* **gum trees**
a tall tree from Australia with leaves that stay green in winter. It produces an oil used in medicines.

SYNONYM eucalyptus

gun *noun* **guns**
1 a small weapon that fires bullets
2 a large weapon that fires shells (metal containers with explosives in them)
3 a small gun used in sports to make a bang that shows the start of a race
4 a tool that forces something such as liquid from a container *a spray gun*

gun *verb*
guns, gunning, gunned
to gun someone down is to shoot them with a gun

gunboat *noun* **gunboats**
a small warship with lots of large guns

gunfire *noun*
1 bullets shot from guns
2 the noise of guns being fired

gunge or **gunk** *noun* (*informal*)
any soft and dirty substance that is unpleasant

gunman *noun* **gunmen**
a male criminal who uses a gun

gunpoint *noun*
if someone holds a person at gunpoint, they threaten to kill him or her with a gun

gunpowder *noun*
a type of powder that explodes, used in fireworks and old-fashioned guns

205

gunshot–hacker

gunshot *noun* **gunshots**
1 a bullet shot from a gun *The police fired gunshots. He had a gunshot wound* (from a bullet or bullets).
2 the noise of a gun being fired

gunwoman *noun* **gunwomen**
a female criminal who uses a gun

guppy *noun* **guppies**
a small brightly coloured fish, often kept as a pet

gurdwara ['gerd-wah-rer] *noun* **gurdwaras**
a building where Sikhs pray and celebrate their religion

gurgle *verb*
gurgles, gurgling, gurgled
1 to make a bubbling noise like water being poured from a bottle
2 if a baby gurgles, it makes a low sound at the back of its throat *The baby was gurgling happily.*
gurgle *noun*

gurn *verb*
gurns, gurning, gurned
to make a very ugly or unusual expression with your face by pulling or twisting your face muscles **gurn** *noun*

guru ['goo-roo] *noun* **gurus**
1 a Hindu or Sikh religious teacher
2 an expert that people go to for particular advice on something

ORIGIN from Hindi *guru* 'teacher' or 'priest'

Guru Granth Sahib ['goo-roo-grunt-sah-heeb'] *noun*
the holy book of the Sikh religion

LANGUAGE EXTRA also known as *Adi Granth*

gush *verb*
gushes, gushing, gushed
1 if a liquid gushes or gushes out, it comes out of somewhere quickly and strongly
2 to express a feeling such as pleasure, liking or respect in a way that is very strong or too strong *'You're the best friend I've ever had,' she gushed.*
gush *noun*

gust *noun* **gusts**
a sudden strong wind *I was almost blown over by a gust of wind.* **gusty** *adjective*

gut *noun* **guts**
1 the tube in the body that carries food from the stomach. The parts of this tube are also called the intestines.
2 a person's or animal's guts are the organs inside their body, especially those around the stomach
3 **guts** is an informal word for courage *I didn't have the guts to climb to the top of the ladder.*

gut *verb*
guts, gutting, gutted
1 to gut a fish is to remove its insides before cooking it
2 to destroy the inside of a building *The library was gutted by fire.*

gutted *adjective*
an informal way of saying extremely disappointed

gutter *noun* **gutters**
1 an open pipe along the edge of a roof that takes the rainwater away
2 the edge of a road where the rainwater flows away

guy *noun* **guys**
1 an informal word for a man
2 a model of Guy Fawkes that is burnt on a bonfire on Guy Fawkes' Night
3 **guys** an informal way of talking to a group of people *See you later, guys!*

Guy Fawkes' Night *noun*
the night of 5 November, when British people light bonfires and set off fireworks to celebrate the day in 1605 when Guy Fawkes tried but failed to blow up the Houses of Parliament

SYNONYM Bonfire Night

guzzle *verb*
guzzles, guzzling, guzzled
to eat or drink large amounts of something quickly

gym *noun*
1 (*plural* **gyms**) a large room or special building with equipment such as wall bars and ropes for doing exercises
2 (*plural* **gyms**) a building or club where people go to do exercises such as running, cycling or swimming to keep their bodies strong
3 the exercises that you do in a gym

gymkhana *noun* **gymkhanas**
a sports event at which people ride horses and take part in jumping and racing

gymnasium *noun* **gymnasiums**
a word sometimes used for a gym (senses 1 & 2)

gymnast *noun* **gymnasts**
a person skilled in gymnastics

gymnastics *noun plural*
a sport, using equipment such as bars and ropes, in which people do difficult exercises with their body

gypsy *noun* **gypsies**
a member of a group of people living mainly in Europe but originally from India. Gypsies usually travel around, for example in caravans, instead of living in one place.

LANGUAGE EXTRA also spelt *gipsy*

ORIGIN from Middle English *gypcian* 'Egyptian', because people believed (wrongly) that gypsies came from Egypt

hH

ORIGIN the letter H started life as the shape of a simple fence (two rectangles or boxes) in the Phoenician alphabet. Some people think its origin goes back to a more complicated fence shape in Egyptian hieroglyphics – a series of little boxes. In Phoenician, the two boxes sat on top of each other with vertical side bars sticking out like the side parts of a ladder. At that time the letter had the sound of 'ch' as in Scottish 'loch' and was called *khet*. When the letter passed into Greek, the shape became simpler – just two boxes – and the sound changed to that of a long A. When the Romans began using the letter, the horizontal bars at the top and bottom had disappeared and H had become the shape we use today, with a similar sound.

habit *noun* **habits**
1 something you do many times or regularly, sometimes without thinking about it *I wake up at seven o'clock out of habit.*
2 something bad you do often, usually because you can't stop yourself doing it *It's time to break your habit of picking your nose.*
3 to get **into a habit** is to start doing something regularly
4 to get **out of a habit** is to stop doing something regularly

habitable *adjective*
if a place is habitable, it is good enough to be lived in

ANTONYM uninhabitable

habitat *noun* **habitats**
the place where an animal or insect usually lives or where a plant usually grows

ORIGIN from Latin *habitat* 'it lives' or 'it dwells'

habitual *adjective*
1 if something is habitual, it often happens or is often done *his habitual friendliness*
2 doing something because you have a bad habit *Myra is a habitual liar.*
habitually *adverb*

hack *verb*
hacks, hacking, hacked
1 to cut or break something in a rough way with a lot of force, for example with an axe or heavy knife *The butcher hacked the meat into small pieces.*
2 to use a computer to break into someone else's computer without their permission, for example to steal information *Someone has hacked into my laptop.*
3 to break into someone's phone, for example to steal their voice messages

hacker *noun* **hackers**
1 someone who uses a computer to break into someone else's computer without their permission, for example to steal information

2 someone who breaks into someone's phone, for example to steal their voice messages

hacksaw *noun* **hacksaws**
a metal saw with a thin blade for cutting through metal

had
past tense & past participle of **have**

haddock *noun* **haddock**
a sea fish with white flesh that is used as food

hadn't
short for 'had not'

hag *noun* **hags**
an ugly old woman

haggard *adjective*
looking very tired or ill

haggis *noun* **haggises**
a Scottish food that looks like a round sausage, made from the skin of a sheep's stomach. It contains chopped sheep's meat with oatmeal and spices.

haggle *verb*
haggles, haggling, haggled
to argue about something such as the price of something you want to buy or the details of an agreement

ha-ha *interjection*
used for representing the sound people make when they laugh

LANGUAGE EXTRA also spelt *ha ha*

haiku *noun* **haikus** or **haiku**
a very short Japanese poem consisting of three lines. The first line has five syllables, the second has seven and the last has five.

ORIGIN from Japanese *hai* 'amusement' and *ku* 'sentence'

hail *noun*
1 frozen rain that comes down like small balls of ice
2 a hail of something such as bullets or stones is a large number of them that fall down on someone

hail *verb*
hails, hailing, hailed
1 if it hails or is hailing, small balls of frozen rain come down from the sky
2 to call out to someone or make a signal to them to attract their attention *Mum hailed a taxi.*

hailstone *noun* **hailstones**
a small ball of frozen rain

hair *noun*
1 the large amount of long thin parts like threads that grow on the top of your head, or the long thin parts that grow on other areas of your body
2 (*plural* **hairs**) a hair is one of these long thin parts *My dad has a few grey hairs. I found a hair in my food.*
3 the soft covering on the skin of some animals such as cats and dogs

SYNONYM fur

4 the hairs of a paintbrush are the mass of stiff threads used for putting paint on

SYNONYM bristles

5 to make someone's hair stand on end is to make them very frightened

hairbrush *noun* **hairbrushes**
a brush for making your hair tidy

haircut *noun* **haircuts**
1 when someone's hair is cut *You need a haircut.*
2 the way someone's hair is cut *I like your haircut.*

hairdo *noun* **hairdos**
an informal word for the way someone's hair is cut and shaped

SYNONYM hairstyle

hairdresser *noun* **hairdressers**
someone who cuts and arranges your hair

hairdryer *noun* **hairdryers**
a piece of electrical equipment that blows out hot air for drying your hair after it has been washed

LANGUAGE EXTRA also spelt *hairdrier*

-haired *suffix*
used for making an adjective that describes hair *a long-haired girl; a ginger-haired boy*

hairpin *noun* **hairpins**
1 a pin for holding part of your hair in place, often made of a thin wire in the shape of the letter U
2 a hairpin bend is a very sharp bend in a road

hair-raising *adjective*
frightening and sometimes dangerous

hair slide *noun* **hair slides**
a small plastic or metal object such as a clip that girls and women put in their hair to make it look pretty or to keep it out of their eyes

hairstyle *noun* **hairstyles**
the way someone's hair is cut and shaped

hairy *adjective* **hairier, hairiest**
1 having lots of hair
2 (*informal*) frightening and sometimes dangerous, often in an exciting way

SIMILE 'as hairy as a gorilla' means very hairy (sense 1)

haj [rhymes with 'badge'] *noun* **hajes**
a journey to the city of Mecca in Saudi Arabia that Muslims make as a religious duty

LANGUAGE EXTRA also spelt *hajj*

hake *noun* **hake**
a small sea fish with white flesh that is used as food

halal *adjective*
1 halal meat is from an animal that has been killed in the correct way according to Muslim law
2 also used for describing a person or place selling this meat *a halal butcher*

half *noun* **halves**
1 one of the two equal parts that make up the whole of something *A half of 10 is 5. I waited half an hour.*
2 used when you mean a lot of something *He complains half the time.*

half *adjective*
1 used for describing one of the two equal parts that make up the whole of something *I waited a half-hour. Many smartphones are at half price.*
2 a half day is a time when someone goes to school or to work either in the morning or the afternoon
3 if you are someone's half brother or half sister, you have either the same mother or the same father

half *adverb*
1 not completely but about halfway *The door was half open.*
2 nearly *I half believed him when he told me that. You're not half as clever as your sister.*
3 **half past** used when you mean 30 minutes later than a particular hour *I left my house at half past three.*
4 (*slang*) **not half** used for giving extra importance to a particular word or phrase *We weren't half late* (we were very late). *'Do you like ice cream?' – 'Yes, not half!'* (yes, very much)

half-baked *adjective* (*informal*)
a half-baked plan or idea is one that has not been thought about carefully

half-hearted *adjective*
used for describing something you do or the way you do something without being very interested in it *He made a half-hearted attempt to close the window.*

half-heartedly *adverb*

half-hour *noun*
a period of time that is 30 minutes long

LANGUAGE EXTRA also spelt *half hour*

half-hourly *adverb*
happening every half-hour

half-mast *noun*
if a flag is at half-mast, it has been moved from the top of its pole to halfway down the pole, usually to show respect for someone who has died

half-price *adjective & adverb*
at half the usual price *a half-price ticket; Children can travel half-price.*

half-term *noun* **half-terms**
a very short holiday from school in the middle of each of the school terms

half-time *noun & adjective*
a short period of rest between the two halves of a game such as football

halfway *adverb & adjective*
1 at an equal distance from two places or points *My house is halfway between the school and the park. I've reached the halfway point in my book.*
2 in the middle of something *I left halfway through the lesson.*

halibut *noun* **halibut**
a flat sea fish with white flesh that is used as food

hall *noun* **halls**
1 the space in a house or flat inside the front door

SYNONYM hallway

2 a very large room used for many different things such as school assemblies, exhibitions, concerts or sports *a concert hall*

hallo–handicapped

3 a very large and important building *a town hall*; *the Royal Albert Hall*
4 a hall of residence is a building at a university where students live

hallo *interjection*
an old-fashioned way of spelling **hello**

Halloween *noun*
the night of 31 October when children sometimes dress up as witches or ghosts and go to people's homes asking for sweets

> LANGUAGE EXTRA also spelt *Hallowe'en*

> ORIGIN from *All Hallow Even* 'evening before All Saints' Day' (1 November) in the Christian religion. 'Hallow' comes from an old English word meaning 'saint' or 'holy person'. People used to think that witches and ghosts appeared on this day.

hallucinate *verb*
hallucinates, hallucinating, hallucinated
to see or hear something that is not there, for example because you are ill

hallucination *noun*
1 (*plural* **hallucinations**) something you can see or hear although it is not there, for example because you are ill
2 the feeling of seeing or hearing something that is not there

hallway *noun* **hallways**
1 the space in a house or flat inside the front door

> SYNONYM hall

2 a long narrow passage in a building with doors on one or both sides that open into rooms

halo ['hay-loh'] *noun* **halos**
1 a ring of light around the head of a holy person or an angel in religious paintings and drawings
2 a ring of light around something, for example the sun or moon

halt *verb*
halts, halting, halted
another way of saying to stop or stop moving *How can we halt the spread of the disease?* *'Halt!' shouted the soldier.*

halt *noun*
when something stops *The snow has brought the trains to a halt* (made them stop). *The traffic has ground* (or *come*) *to a halt* (slowed down and stopped).

halter *noun* **halters**
a series of ropes or leather straps around the head of an animal such as a horse, used for controlling it

halting *adjective*
if something is halting, such as a movement or conversation, it stops and starts again lots of times **haltingly** *adverb*

halve *verb*
halves, halving, halved
1 to divide into two equal parts
2 to make something smaller so that it is half its original size or number
3 to become smaller so that something is half its original size or number

halves
plural of **half**

ham *noun*
1 meat from the top part of the leg of a pig preserved with salt or smoke
2 (*plural* **hams**) a bad actor who has a way of speaking and moving that does not seem real

hamburger *noun* **hamburgers**
a round flat cake of minced meat that is fried and eaten in a bread roll

> ORIGIN probably from *Hamburg* in Germany where the meat was prepared in this way. It was originally called a *hamburger steak* around the end of the 19th century.

hammer *noun* **hammers**
a tool with a heavy metal head (or top) on a long handle. It is used for knocking nails into wood and also, for example, for breaking or shaping things.

hammer *verb*
hammers, hammering, hammered
1 to hit something with a hammer
2 to hit something hard and many times with a very loud noise *Someone was hammering on the door.*
3 (informal) to beat someone easily and completely in a game or competition *Our hockey team was hammered by Mayville School.*

hammock *noun* **hammocks**
a bed made of cloth or net (thin material with lots of small spaces in it). Each end is tied to something such as a pole or tree so that it swings above the ground.

hamper *noun* **hampers**
1 a basket with a lid, usually rectangular, used for taking food on a picnic, for example
2 the American word for a laundry basket

hamper *verb*
hampers, hampering, hampered
to make it difficult for someone to do something or for something to be done

hamster *noun* **hamsters**
a furry animal like a big mouse with a short tail. People often keep hamsters as pets.

> LANGUAGE EXTRA be careful not to spell *hamster* with a *p*. Do not write *hampster*.

hand *noun* **hands**
1 the part of your body at the end of your arm that you use, for example, for touching, holding and moving things
2 one of the long thin parts that point to the time as they move around the face (front part) of a clock or watch *the hour hand*; *the second hand*
3 someone who works in a factory or on a farm or ship *a farm hand*
4 if you give or lend someone a hand, you help them
5 if you do or make something by hand, you do it with your hands
6 if you give someone something by hand, you don't send it to them but give it to them by putting it in their hand
7 if someone's hands are full, they are very busy doing something
8 at hand close by
9 hands up used for asking if anyone knows the answer to a question or for finding out how many people want to have or do a particular thing *Hands up if you can do this sum!*
10 out of hand used when talking about something that you cannot control

hand *verb*
hands, handing, handed
1 to give something to someone by putting it in their hand *Hand me my scarf.*
2 to hand something in is to give it to someone in charge *I handed in my homework to my teacher.*
3 to hand things out is to give them to different people *Aarav, hand out the exercise books, please.*

handbag *noun* **handbags**
a small bag used mainly by women for carrying important things such as money or keys

handbook *noun* **handbooks**
a small book that gives details about how to do something or useful information about a subject

handcuff *verb*
handcuffs, handcuffing, handcuffed
1 to put handcuffs on someone
2 to attach someone to someone or something with handcuffs

handcuffs *noun plural*
a pair of rings, usually made of metal, joined by a short chain. They are used for putting around someone's wrists or for attaching their wrist to someone or something.

handful *noun*
1 a small number of things or people *There are just a handful of mistakes in your homework.*
2 (*plural* **handfuls**) a handful of something is what you can hold in your hand
3 (informal) if you call a child a handful, you mean he or she is not easy to control

hand-held *adjective*
if something is hand-held, it is small enough to be held and used with one or both hands *a hand-held computer*

handicap *noun* **handicaps**
1 something bad that causes a problem or makes things more difficult for you

> SYNONYM disadvantage

2 (old-fashioned) a medical problem that affects the way someone uses their body or brain

> SYNONYM disability

handicap *verb*
handicaps, handicapping, handicapped
to make it more difficult for someone to do something *In Italy we were handicapped by not knowing the language.*

handicapped *adjective* (old-fashioned)
if someone is handicapped, they have a medical problem that affects the way they use their body or brain

> SYNONYM disabled

handicraft–happen

handicraft noun handicrafts
1 an activity where you make something artistic with your hands that needs a lot of skill, for example embroidery or pottery
2 handicrafts are artistic objects that you make with your hands, for example to sell them

handiwork noun
something artistic that you have made with your hands using a lot of skill

handkerchief ['han-ker-cheef'] noun handkerchiefs or handkerchieves
a small square piece of cloth for wiping your nose or eyes

handle noun handles
1 the part of something that you hold, turn or pick up with your hand. Handles come in different shapes and sizes. Many different things have handles, for example a door or drawer (for opening and closing), a cup or suitcase (for picking up and carrying) and a broom or brush (for holding when you use it).
2 a small box at the corner of a computer image that you click on and drag with the mouse, or that you move by touching it, to make the image bigger or smaller
3 if someone flies off the handle, they suddenly get very angry

handle verb
handles, handling, handled
1 to touch something with your hands
2 to control or use something, especially something that can be difficult *Have you ever handled a digital camera?*
3 to deal with something or someone *If you can't handle this situation, you must let your teacher know. Megan is often naughty but Miss Turner can handle her.*

handlebars noun plural
the curved metal bar at the front of a bicycle or motorcycle that you use for steering it

hand luggage noun
a bag or bags that you are allowed to bring with you onto a plane or bus

handmade adjective
made by hand, not by a machine

handout noun handouts
a piece of paper with information about a particular subject, for example given to students in a class

handrail noun handrails
a long bar that you hold on to for safety, for example when going up or down stairs

handset noun handsets
1 the outside part of a mobile phone
2 the part of a landline phone (fixed in one place) that you hold in your hand next to your ear and mouth. It is used for listening and for speaking into.

handshake noun handshakes
when you take someone's right hand in your right hand and move it up and down in a friendly way, for example when you first meet them

handsome adjective
1 very pleasant to look at *a handsome boy*

SYNONYM attractive

2 very large or important *a handsome reward; a handsome victory*

ORIGIN from 15th-century English *handsom* 'easy to handle'

handsomely adverb
1 with a lot of money *My uncle is paid handsomely.*
2 attractively *The room was handsomely decorated.*

hands-on adjective
1 if someone has hands-on experience, they have done an activity themselves
2 used about someone who does an activity themselves rather than letting other people do everything *My dad's boss is very much hands-on.*

handstand noun handstands
a movement in which someone puts their hands on the ground and balances their body with their legs straight up in the air

handwriting noun
1 the way you write using a pen or pencil *Mohammed's handwriting is very neat.*
2 the activity of writing with a pen or pencil *We learn handwriting in school.*

handwritten adjective
written using a pen or pencil, not typed on a computer or printed

handy adjective handier, handiest
1 if something is handy, it is useful and it helps you to do something *This dictionary might come in handy* (be useful).
2 close by and easy to get to *I always keep a pen handy.*
3 good at using something such as a tool
4 good at doing things *My dad is handy around the house.*

handyman noun handymen
a man who does small jobs in someone's home, such as repairing things

handywoman noun handywomen
a woman who does small jobs in someone's home, such as repairing things

hang verb
hangs, hanging, hung
1 to fix the top of something somewhere, leaving the rest of it loose so that it can move *I hung my jacket on the peg.*
2 if something hangs somewhere, it is fixed there from the top but the rest of it is loose and can move *The Christmas decorations were hanging down from the ceiling.*
3 if you hang wallpaper, you stick it to a wall
4 to stay in the air without moving much *The smoke from the fire still hung over the town.*
5 to hang about or around is to wait somewhere or to spend time somewhere *We hung about* (or *around*) *for an hour at the bus stop.*
6 to hang on to something is to hold on to it tightly *Hang on to the strap as the bus goes round the corner.*
7 to hang on is to wait, usually for a short time *Hang on – I'm coming!*
8 to hang up is to stop using the phone after you've been speaking to someone
9 to hang up a piece of clothing is to hang it on a hook or peg *Hang up your coat when you come in.*

hang verb
hangs, hanging, hanged
1 to kill someone by putting a rope fixed to something high around their neck and making them fall *He was hanged for murder.*
2 to be killed in this way *The judge didn't think the killer should hang.*

hang noun
if you get the hang of something, you learn how to do it or use it *I can't get the hang of this new smartphone.*

hangar noun hangars
a large building where aircraft are kept

hanger noun hangers
a hanger or coat hanger is a curved piece of plastic, wood or wire used for hanging clothes on so that they keep their shape

hang-glider noun hang-gliders
a frame with a cloth wing above it that is used by a pilot to fly through the air. It floats with the wind and is steered by moving the body in different directions.

hang-gliding noun
the activity of using a hang-glider

hangman noun
1 (plural hangmen) in the past, someone whose job was to kill criminals by hanging them
2 a game played with a pencil and paper in which one person tries to guess the word the other person is thinking of. The game uses the diagram of a man being hanged.

hangover noun hangovers
a feeling of being ill after drinking too much alcohol

hang-up noun hang-ups
a problem that exists in someone's mind that makes them more worried about something than they should be *Alfie has a hang-up about his skinny legs.*

SYNONYM complex

hanker verb
hankers, hankering, hankered
to hanker after something is to want it very much

hankering noun
a strong feeling of wanting something

SYNONYM yen

hankie noun hankies
an informal word for a handkerchief

LANGUAGE EXTRA also spelt *hanky*

Hanukkah ['hah-noo-ker'] noun
an eight-day Jewish holiday in November or December. It is also known as the 'festival of lights'. Candles are lit to celebrate the time when the Jews took back the Holy Temple in Jerusalem about 2200 years ago.

LANGUAGE EXTRA also spelt *Chanukah*

haphazard ['hap-haz-erd'] adjective
not planned or organised in any way at all *Some of the teaching in my cousin's school is haphazard.* **haphazardly** adverb

happen verb
happens, happening, happened
1 if something happens, it starts to exist and continues before stopping *The Battle of Hastings happened in 1066. What's happening?* (What action has started and is still going on?)

happenings–harm

2 if you say something happens to someone or something, you mean that something is done that affects them or changes them in some way *Something has happened to my computer screen* (for example, the picture has disappeared). *I hope nothing has happened to my teacher* (for example, I hope she isn't hurt).
3 if you ask what happens to someone or something, you are asking what is done that affects them or changes them in some way *What has happened to Grace?* (For example, where is she or why is she wearing a bandage?)
4 used when you mean that an action is done by chance or something is the way it is by chance *It so happened there was no-one in when I got home. I happen to have an extra pen on me.*
5 if you happen to do something, you do it by chance *I happened to bump into her in the library.*

happenings *noun plural*
things that happen, especially unusual things *There have been strange happenings in my village.*

happily *adverb*
1 used when talking about something good happening *Happily, I wasn't hurt.*

> SYNONYM luckily

2 in a happy way *We all sat around chatting happily.*
3 because you want to *I will happily show your parents around the school.*

> SYNONYM willingly

happiness *noun*
the feeling of being happy

happy *adjective* **happier, happiest**
1 if someone is happy, they have the pleasant feeling you get when something good has happened or when a situation, person or thing is good *My sister came top and is very happy. She's happy about it.*
2 used about something that gives you this pleasant feeling or that shows you have this feeling *the happiest day of my life; a story with a happy ending; a happy smile*
3 used in greetings when you want someone to be happy and enjoy themselves *Happy Birthday!*
4 if you're happy with something or someone, you think they are good *I'm very happy with my new school.*

> SYNONYM pleased

5 if you're happy to do something, you want to do it or are ready to do it *I'm happy to help you.*
6 lucky *a happy coincidence*

> SIMILES 'as happy as a lark' and 'as happy as a sandboy' mean very happy (sense 1)

happy-go-lucky *adjective*
not worrying about things and enjoying life

harass *verb*
harasses, harassing, harassed
if someone harasses you, they make your life unpleasant, for example by insulting you or bullying you

> ORIGIN from Old French *harer* 'to set a dog on someone'

harassment *noun*
the behaviour or action of someone who harasses you

harbour *noun* **harbours**
a part of the sea at the coast, often partly enclosed by walls, where boats stop and can be left safely

harbour *verb*
harbours, harbouring, harboured
to harbour someone such as a criminal or terrorist is to protect them and hide them

hard *adjective* **harder, hardest**
1 feeling like something such as wood, metal or stone when you touch it. Something hard can't be pressed in, bent or broken easily or at all.

> ANTONYM soft

2 thicker than normal or thicker than other parts of something *I have some hard skin on my foot. There are some hard lumps in the paint.*

> ANTONYM soft

3 if food is hard, it is difficult to cut or to eat, for example because it is not cooked enough or because it is stale or not ready to be eaten *My potatoes are hard. The bread is hard. This melon is still hard.*

> ANTONYM soft

4 needing a lot of effort to do, understand or deal with *hard work; a hard question*

> ANTONYM easy

5 with lots of problems *a hard life*

> ANTONYM easy

6 using a lot of energy *She gave me a hard push and I fell over. I'm a hard worker.*
7 strict or cruel *My parents have always been very hard on me.*
8 very cold and bad *a hard frost*
9 hard of hearing not able to hear very well
10 (*informal*) **hard up** not having much money

hardness *noun*

> SIMILE 'as hard as a rock' (senses 1 & 3) and 'as hard as nails' (senses 1, 3 & 7) mean very hard

hard *adverb* **harder, hardest**
1 with a lot of effort *Ellie works very hard. Think hard and you'll get the right answer.*
2 strongly *He hit me hard. It's raining hard.*

hardback *noun* **hardbacks**
a book with a strong stiff cover

> ANTONYM paperback

hardboard *noun*
a type of wood made by pressing very small pieces of wood together and shaping them into thin flat pieces

hard-boiled *adjective*
a hard-boiled egg is one that has been cooked in boiling water until the white and yellow parts inside are hard

hard disk *noun* **hard disks**
a stiff disk inside a computer, used for storing information

hard drive *noun* **hard drives**
a piece of equipment inside a computer that stores information onto a hard disk and uses information from it

harden *verb*
hardens, hardening, hardened
1 to become hard *Cement hardens when you mix it with sand and water.*
2 to make something hard

hardly *adverb*
1 almost not at all *You've hardly done any work. I hardly ever* (almost never) *play out in the street.*
2 only just *I'd hardly gone to bed when I was woken up by a loud noise.*
3 definitely not *You can hardly blame me.*

> SYNONYM scarcely

hardship *noun*
1 great suffering, for example caused by not having enough money
2 (*plural* **hardships**) something that causes great suffering

hard shoulder *noun* **hard shoulders**
an area at the side of a motorway where a driver can stop in an emergency

hardware *noun*
1 the equipment that makes up a computer, for example silicon chips, the hard disk or the monitor. The information needed for making a computer and programs work is the software.
2 tools and other equipment for the home or garden, such as hammers, scissors, plugs or spades

hard-wearing *adjective*
if clothes or shoes are hard-wearing, they are strong and last a long time

hardwood *noun*
hard strong wood, mainly from trees that are deciduous (their leaves fall off in the autumn), for example oak, beech or maple

hard-working *adjective*
if someone is hard-working, they work a lot and with a lot of effort

hardy *adjective* **hardier, hardiest**
1 if someone is hardy, they are strong and can put up with bad conditions such as pain
2 a hardy plant is strong enough to live outside throughout the whole year

hare *noun* **hares**
an animal like a large rabbit that can run very fast

haricot bean ['ha-ree-koh'] *noun*
haricot beans
a small white bean that is cooked and eaten as a vegetable. Haricot beans are usually sold dried (hard and with the water removed), not fresh.

hark *verb*
harks, harking, harked
1 an old-fashioned way of saying to listen
2 if someone harks back to something in the past, they talk about it

harm *verb*
harms, harming, harmed
1 to hurt someone or do something bad to them *I won't harm you if you do as I say. Can too much TV harm you?*

2 to damage something *These chemicals can harm the quality of the water in the river.*

harm noun
1 something bad done to something *Smoke causes a lot of harm to the environment.*

SYNONYM damage

2 something bad done to someone, such as hurting them *I don't want any harm to come to you. Smoking causes harm.*
3 if you say that doing something wouldn't do someone any harm, you mean they should do it *It wouldn't do you any harm to tidy up your room!*
4 if you say there's no harm in doing something, you mean it's not a bad idea to do it and nothing bad will happen anyway if you do it *He'll probably say no but there's no harm in asking.*

harmful adjective
causing harm *Smoking is very harmful to the lungs.*

harmless adjective
if something or someone is harmless, they don't cause any harm *a harmless spider; a harmless joke*

SIMILE 'as harmless as a dove' means completely harmless (used about a person)

harmonica noun harmonicas
a small rectangular musical instrument that you play with your mouth. You blow and suck air through holes along one of its long sides to make the notes.

SYNONYM mouth organ

harmonious adjective
1 friendly and peaceful, for example when talking about relationships between people, groups or countries
2 pleasant to listen to because the notes blend together well *harmonious music*
3 pleasant to look at because the parts and colours blend together well *a harmonious painting*
harmoniously adverb

harmonise verb
harmonises, harmonising, harmonised
1 if things harmonise, or if someone harmonises them, they blend together well *The wallpaper harmonises perfectly with the furniture.*
2 to play or sing musical notes at the same time as the main tune. The notes are different from the main tune but produce a pleasant sound.

LANGUAGE EXTRA also spelt *harmonize*

harmony noun
1 when people, groups or countries have friendly and peaceful relationships with each other *In our town, people from many countries and backgrounds live together in harmony.*
2 (plural **harmonies**) musical notes played or sung at the same time to produce a pleasant sound

harness noun harnesses
1 a series of leather straps around the head, neck and body of an animal such as a horse. They are used for controlling it or attaching it to something such as a cart or sleigh.
2 a series of straps around a person, for example to keep them safe or stop them from falling *a baby harness; a safety harness*

harness verb
harnesses, harnessing, harnessed
1 to put a harness around an animal or person
2 to control and use a natural power such as the wind or the water of a river

harp noun harps
a musical instrument shaped like a large triangle with a curved top. It has strings across it from top to bottom, which you play by pulling them with your fingers. You stand it on the floor next to you and play it while you are sitting down.

harp verb
harps, harping, harped
to harp on about something is to talk about it lots of times in a way that is very annoying

harpist noun harpists
someone who plays a harp

harpoon noun harpoons
a long spear fixed to a rope, used for hunting whales and large fish. It can be thrown by hand or fired from a special gun.
harpoon verb

harpsichord noun harpsichords
a musical instrument like a small piano with one, two or sometimes three keyboards. The sound is produced when you press a key (long narrow bar) that plucks a string (pulls it then lets it go).

harrowing adjective
if something is harrowing, it causes you great pain and suffering

harsh adjective harsher, harshest
1 very difficult to live in or put up with, for example because of being so bad or so different from what is usual *a harsh climate; harsh conditions; These are harsh times.*

SYNONYM severe

2 very strong and unpleasant *a harsh light; a harsh voice; harsh words*
3 cruel or strict *a harsh punishment; Your parents seem very harsh.*
harshly adverb **harshness** noun

harvest noun harvests
1 the time of the year when farmers collect their crops from the fields, or the activity of collecting them *They're getting ready for the potato harvest.*
2 the crops collected from the fields or the amount of them

harvest verb
harvests, harvesting, harvested
if a farmer harvests crops, such as wheat or potatoes, he or she collects them from the fields

has
third person singular present tense of **have**

hash noun
1 (plural **hashes**) the symbol # or a key marked with this symbol, for example on a telephone keypad or computer keyboard
2 a dish made of small pieces of meat, potatoes and vegetables
3 a hash brown is a fried food made from potato cut into tiny pieces and formed into a flat shape, for example round or oblong
4 if you make a hash of something, you do it very badly

hashtag noun hashtags
a word that you write after a hash symbol (#), for example #dictionary, used with some web services such as Twitter to help you search for this word in messages

hasn't
short for 'has not'

hassle noun (informal)
trouble or something that causes trouble *Getting a passport is a lot of hassle.*

hassle verb (informal)
hassles, hassling, hassled
1 to bother or annoy someone *I'll do my homework when I'm ready – don't hassle me!*
2 if you feel hassled, you feel unhappy, for example because you're annoyed, upset or have too much work

haste noun
1 doing things quickly *They left in haste (quickly).*
2 to make haste is to hurry

hasten ['hay-sern'] verb
hastens, hastening, hastened
1 to make something happen more quickly
2 to hasten to do or say something is to do or say it quickly

hasty adjective hastier, hastiest
1 done quickly or too quickly *a hasty decision; a hasty departure*
2 doing things quickly or too quickly *Don't be so hasty!*
hastily adverb **hastiness** noun

hat noun hats
1 a covering that you wear on your head
2 if you keep something under your hat, you keep it secret

hatch verb
hatches, hatching, hatched
1 to come out of an egg and be born *These chicks have just hatched.*
2 if an egg hatches, it breaks to allow a baby animal to be born
3 to hatch an egg is to keep it warm until a baby animal comes out
4 to hatch something such as a plan is to make it in secret

hatch noun hatches
a small opening, for example in a wall, ceiling or floor *an escape hatch*

hatchback noun hatchbacks
a car with a door at the back that you lift up to open it

hatchet noun hatchets
a tool that has a heavy metal blade with a small wooden handle fixed to it. It looks like a small axe and is used for cutting and chopping things.

211

hate – head

hate verb
hates, hating, hated
1 to have a very strong feeling of dislike and anger towards someone
2 to not like something or doing something at all *My sister hates swimming.*

hate noun
1 a very strong feeling of dislike and anger towards someone

SYNONYM hatred

2 (*plural* **hates**) a hate or pet hate is something or someone that you have a very strong feeling of dislike for

hateful adjective
extremely unpleasant *That was a really hateful thing to say!* **hatefully** adverb

hatred ['hay-trid'] noun
a very strong feeling of dislike and anger towards someone

SYNONYM hate

hatstand noun hatstands
a pole with hooks at the top for hanging hats and coats on

LANGUAGE EXTRA also spelt *hat stand*

hat trick noun hat tricks
1 three goals scored by the same person in a game such as football
2 three wickets hit by the same bowler in cricket
3 three wins that someone has one after the other in any game

haughty [rhymes with 'naughty'] adjective
haughtier, haughtiest
behaving in an unfriendly way because you think you are more important than other people **haughtily** adverb **haughtiness** noun

haul verb
hauls, hauling, hauled
1 to pull something or someone with a lot of effort *The police hauled the car out of the river.*
2 to carry something heavy using a lot of strength *Dad hauled the suitcases up the stairs.*

haul noun hauls
1 a large amount of something, for example something stolen or not legal *A haul of guns was found hidden inside a lorry.*
2 the amount of fish caught in a net at one time

haunt verb
haunts, haunting, haunted
1 if a ghost haunts a place, it appears there lots of times
2 if something such as an unpleasant image or memory haunts you, you think about it often and it makes you feel sad and worried

haunted adjective
if a building or place is haunted, ghosts often appear there

have verb
has, having, had
1 if you have something or have got something, it belongs to you, is yours in some way or is with you *I have a bike. I've got a cup of tea here.*
2 used for talking about something such as a quality, power, activity or event that is connected with something or someone *Lucy has got blue eyes. These flowers have a lovely smell. Our teacher doesn't have much control over the class. We had a holiday in Croatia. I've got a few things to do.*
3 used for talking about a part of something or something that affects something *Most cups have handles. Our house has five rooms* (there are five rooms in it). *This CD has got a scratch* (there's a scratch on it).
4 used for talking about something that happens to something or someone *My laptop is having problems. I had a good idea. Vijay had an accident.*
5 used for talking about something that you do, eat or drink *I'm going to have a shower. Could I have a look? Have a seat* (sit down). *Oliver had a sandwich and a glass of milk.*
6 used for talking about the time for doing something *Come and see me if you have time. You have one hour to do the test.*
7 used for talking about something or someone that comes to you *I had a letter this morning. We've got friends at our house this weekend.*
8 used for talking about something that you organise *I'm going to have a party tomorrow.*
9 if you have to do something, you must do it because you feel it's right or because someone makes you do it *I've got to go now or I'll be late for school.*
10 if you have something done, you make it happen or get someone to do it *I need to have my bike fixed. I had my hair cut.*

LANGUAGE EXTRA you can also use the verb *to have* as an auxiliary verb (one used with other verbs) to show that an action has already happened, for example *I have seen her* or *Has he finished his book?*

haven ['hay-vern'] noun havens
1 a safe place for people or animals
2 a haven of peace or calm is a peaceful place

haven't
short for 'have not'

haversack noun haversacks
a large strong bag with a strap or straps for carrying on your shoulder or back

havoc noun
1 a situation where everything is confused *The rail strike played havoc with our holiday plans.*
2 a situation where lots of damage is caused *The storm caused havoc up and down the country.*

ORIGIN from Norman French *crier havok* 'to cry havoc', a sign for soldiers at war to attack and steal

hawk noun hawks
1 a large bird with a sharp beak, very good eyesight and a long tail. It is a bird of prey that eats small animals and other birds.
2 if you watch someone like a hawk, you watch them very carefully, for example to stop them escaping or doing something bad

hawk verb
hawks, hawking, hawked
to sell things on the street or in a public place **hawker** noun

hawthorn noun hawthorns
a small tree with lots of thorns (sharp points) on it. It has white or pink flowers and small red berries.

hay noun
long grass that is cut, dried (usually in the sun) and given as food to animals

hay fever noun
an illness like a cold that you get when you breathe in the pollen from grass or plants

LANGUAGE EXTRA also spelt *hayfever*

haystack noun haystacks
a large pile of hay in a field

haywire adjective
if something goes haywire, it suddenly stops working properly *My computer has gone haywire.*

hazard noun hazards
something that is dangerous or causes damage

hazardous adjective
dangerous

haze noun
a thin cloud, formed for example by heat, smoke, dust or tiny drops of water

hazel noun
1 (*plural* **hazels**) a small tree with brown nuts that you can eat
2 a light green-brown colour (used especially about people's eyes)

hazelnut noun hazelnuts
a small round brown nut with a hard shell that comes from the hazel tree

hazy adjective hazier, haziest
1 not clear because of heat, smoke, dust or tiny drops of water in the air
2 not clear because you don't remember something well *a hazy memory*
3 if you are hazy about something, it is not clear to you because there is something you don't understand
hazily adverb **haziness** noun

HD
short for **high-definition**

HDTV noun
a type of television that displays an extremely clear picture
short for: high-definition television

he pronoun
a male person or animal that someone has mentioned before, for example in an earlier sentence *He went into the room.*

head noun heads
1 the part of the body above the neck with the eyes, nose, ears and mouth and the brain in it
2 your mind *An idea just came into my head. Chloe has a good head for figures* (is good at doing sums).
3 someone in charge of something such as a school or government *If you have a problem, it's best to see the head* (head teacher).

212

4 the top part or beginning of something, for example a nail, page, vegetable or bed *cauliflower heads*; *Joshua is standing at the head of the queue.*
5 if something such as a problem or situation comes to a head, it reaches a very difficult or dangerous point
6 if someone keeps their head, they stay calm and relaxed. If they lose their head, they are excited, nervous or angry.
7 if you say someone is off their head, you mean they are crazy or stupid
8 a head or **per head** for each person *It costs £5 per head.*
9 heads used when throwing a coin in the air to decide something. Heads is the side of a coin with a picture of someone's head on it. The other side is called tails. *'Heads!' she shouted, as I tossed the coin.*

head *verb*
heads, heading, headed
1 to go somewhere *We're heading for* (going to) *the gym.*
2 to hit the ball with your head in football
3 to be in charge of a group or organisation *He heads a big firm in the City.*
4 if a name heads a list, it appears at the top of it

headache *noun* **headaches**
1 a pain in the head
2 an informal word for a problem

headband *noun* **headbands**
a narrow piece of cloth that you wear around your head, for example to keep your hair out of your eyes

head boy *noun* **head boys**
a boy in a school such as a comprehensive or public school who is chosen to be a leader and to represent the school at events

head-butt *verb*
head-butts, head-butting, head-butted
to hit someone with your head

headdress *noun* **headdresses**
a decorated covering for the head, usually worn for special occasions

-headed *suffix*
used with another word to make adjectives describing someone's head *a bald-headed man*; *a two-headed monster*

header *noun* **headers**
1 when you hit the ball with your head in football
2 a word or words, such as a title or name, at the top of every page of a document or book

head-first *adverb*
with your head going before the rest of your body *She dived into the pool head-first.*

LANGUAGE EXTRA also spelt *headfirst*

head girl *noun* **head girls**
a girl in a school such as a comprehensive or public school who is chosen to be a leader and to represent the school at events

heading *noun* **headings**
a word or words at the start of a piece of writing such as an essay or a chapter or section of a book. It describes what the piece of writing is about.

headland *noun* **headlands**
a narrow piece of land that sticks out into the sea

head lice *noun plural*
very small insects that live in some people's hair

headlight *noun* **headlights**
a very strong light at the front of a vehicle such as a car or motorbike *We were driving with our headlights dipped* (pointing downwards).

headline *noun* **headlines**
1 words printed in large letters at the start of an article in a newspaper or magazine, describing what the article is about
2 the news headlines are the main facts about the most important stories in the news that you get from the television, radio or internet

headlong *adverb*
1 with your head going before the rest of your body *He fell headlong down the stairs.*
2 very quickly and usually without thinking *They rushed headlong into the crowd.*

headmaster *noun* **headmasters**
a male teacher in charge of a school

LANGUAGE EXTRA you can also say *head teacher*

headmistress *noun* **headmistresses**
a female teacher in charge of a school

LANGUAGE EXTRA you can also say *head teacher*

head-on *adjective & adverb*
with the front parts bumping into each other *a head-on collision*; *The two cars hit each other head-on.*

headphones *noun plural*
two small round speakers that you put over your ears, used for listening to things on a radio, computer or other device. The speakers are connected to the device, for example by a wire or Bluetooth (a system using radio waves). They are joined by a narrow curved piece that goes over your head.

headquarters *noun plural*
the main building of an organisation or business *The headquarters of the United Nations are in New York.*

headscarf *noun* **headscarves**
a piece of cloth worn by girls and women over the head

headset *noun* **headsets**
a piece of equipment consisting of a small speaker or speakers that you put over or into one or both ears. It is often connected to a part that you speak into. *a Bluetooth headset*

headstand *noun* **headstands**
a movement in which someone puts their hands and head on the ground and balances their body with their legs straight up in the air

head start *noun* **head starts**
something useful that helps you to be more successful, for example in your life or in a race

SYNONYM *advantage*

headstone *noun* **headstones**
a large piece of stone standing at one end of a grave. It has on it the name of the person buried there and the dates when he or she was born and died.

headstrong *adjective*
if someone is headstrong, they don't listen to other people and you can't stop them from doing what they want

head teacher *noun* **head teachers**
a teacher in charge of a school

LANGUAGE EXTRA also spelt *headteacher*

headway *noun*
progress towards getting something done *Charlotte has made headway in her school project.*

headword *noun* **headwords**
a word given in alphabetical order in a dictionary with its meaning explained or with its translation in another language. The headword is the word that you look up in the dictionary.

heal *verb*
heals, healing, healed
1 if an injury heals, it gets better *The cut on my finger has completely healed up.*
2 to make someone or a part of someone's body better *It's a special cream for healing bruises. It's a doctor's job to heal sick people.*
3 if a bad situation heals or someone heals it, it gets better and ends

healer *noun* **healers**
someone who heals sick people

health *noun*
1 someone's health is how strong and well or how weak and ill their body is *Grandma is not in good health* (she is weak and ill). *Liam has a health problem* (something is making him ill).
2 being well and strong *We're poor but we have our health.*
3 health food is food that is good for you because it only contains natural substances

healthily *adverb*
in a way that shows you pay attention to staying well *Our family try to eat healthily.*

healthy *adjective* **healthier, healthiest**
1 well and strong *Walking and running help to keep you healthy.*
2 good for you *healthy food*
3 showing that you are strong and well *a healthy appetite*

heap *noun* **heaps**
1 an untidy pile of things placed one on top of another
2 (informal) **heaps of** lots of *We've got heaps of time before the film starts.*

heap *verb*
heaps, heaping, heaped
1 to put lots of something somewhere in an untidy pile *Mum heaped peas on my plate.*
2 to give someone lots of something *My teacher heaped praise on me in my school report.*

hear *verb*
hears, hearing, heard
1 to take the sound that something or someone makes into your brain through your ears *Don't shout – I can hear you. Turn up the TV – I can't hear.*

213

hearing–heavyweight

2 to listen to something or someone *I heard a programme about animals on the radio today.*
3 to be told something such as a piece of news *We've heard that our teacher is leaving. Have you heard about the burglary?*
4 if you hear from someone, they contact you, for example by phone, letter or email, and give you some news
5 if you've heard of someone or something, you know that someone or something exists *Have you ever heard of the Eiffel Tower?*

hearing noun
1 the natural ability you have to hear
2 (plural **hearings**) an official meeting, for example in a court of law, to find out the truth about something
3 if someone is hard of hearing, they can't hear very well
4 a hearing aid is a small object that someone wears in their ear or next to it to make sounds louder and clearer

hearken ['har-kern'] verb
hearkens, hearkening, hearkened
an old-fashioned way of saying to listen

hearse noun **hearses**
a large car that carries a dead person in a coffin to a funeral

heart noun **hearts**
1 the organ inside your chest that pumps blood around your body
2 the centre or most important part of something *The festival took place in the heart of Sheffield.*
3 used for talking about the part of a person where his or her feelings are *His heart was full of sadness* (he was feeling very sad). *My aunt has a kind heart* (she is very kind).
4 a shape like this ♥ with two curved parts at the top and a v-shape at the bottom. It is often used as the symbol of love and is coloured pink or red.
5 a red heart shape in a game of cards. A heart is one of the four types of playing cards. The other three types are diamonds, clubs and spades.
6 if you break someone's heart, you make them very sad
7 if you do something to your heart's content, you do it as much or as often as you want
8 if your heart sinks, you suddenly feel sad or disappointed
9 **by heart** used for talking about something that you've learnt word for word *I know the poem by heart* (I've learnt every word of it).
10 **to lose heart** to lose hope and become unhappy
11 **to take heart** to feel happy or fairly happy about something

heart attack noun **heart attacks**
a very serious medical problem when someone's heart stops working properly, which causes a lot of pain, or stops working completely, which causes death

heartbeat noun **heartbeats**
the sound or movement that the heart makes as it pumps blood around the body

heartbroken adjective
extremely sad

hearten verb
heartens, heartening, heartened
to give someone hope

SYNONYM to encourage

hearth noun **hearths**
1 the area around a fireplace
2 the floor of a fireplace

heartily adverb
1 loudly and in a friendly way *We laughed heartily.*
2 completely *I heartily agree.*
3 with great enjoyment *The children were eating heartily.*

heartless adjective
cruel and showing no feelings towards other people

hearty adjective **heartier, heartiest**
1 very friendly and warm *a hearty welcome*
2 strong and loud in a friendly way *a hearty laugh*; *hearty cheers*
3 large and good *a hearty meal*; *I have a hearty appetite* (I enjoy eating and I eat a lot).

heat noun
1 hot air or weather *I don't like the summer heat.*
2 the quality of being hot *the heat of the sun*
3 the hot part of a cooker or oven, for example where the flame is *Take the saucepan off the heat.*
4 the temperature of something such as central heating or the hot part of a cooker *Boil the pasta on a low heat* (for example with a small flame).
5 a system of heating a building *We have no heat.*

SYNONYM heating

6 (plural **heats**) one of the races or competitions that someone has to win to take part in the final

heat verb
heats, heating, heated
1 to make something hot or warm *Can you heat up my soup in the microwave?*
2 to become hot or warm *The house takes a long time to heat* (or *to heat up*).

heated adjective
made warm, for example with a heater or heating system *a heated swimming pool*

heater noun **heaters**
a piece of equipment for making a room or car warm or for making water hot

heath noun **heaths**
a wild area of land covered with grass, plants and small bushes such as heather

heather noun
a small bush with purple, pink or white flowers. It grows wild, for example on hills and heaths.

heating noun
a system of heating a building *Turn on the heating – it's very cold.*

SYNONYM heat

heatstroke noun
a medical problem caused by being in the sun for too long

SYNONYM sunstroke

heatwave noun **heatwaves**
a period of very hot weather

heave verb
heaves, heaving, heaved
1 to move something heavy with a lot of effort, for example by pulling, pushing or lifting it *Dad heaved the luggage into the boot of the car.*
2 to throw something heavy *He heaved a brick at the window.*
3 to move up and down *Her shoulders heaved as she wept.*
4 (informal) to have a feeling in your throat as if you are going to be sick *That horrible smell makes me heave.*
5 **to heave a sigh of relief** to suddenly feel very happy, for example because something good has happened

heave noun

heaven noun
1 in some religions, heaven is the place, for example in the sky, where God lives or where the gods live, and where good people go after they die
compare: hell
2 a place or situation that makes you feel very happy *I was relaxing on the beach – it was just heaven!*

heavenly adjective
1 connected with heaven or the sky
2 extremely pleasant or beautiful *The countryside in Kent is heavenly.*
3 extremely delicious *Your cake is heavenly.*
4 a heavenly body is a star, planet or moon

heavily adverb
1 very much *It's raining heavily.*
2 very *a heavily populated part of town*
3 loudly and slowly *Granddad was breathing heavily.*
4 hitting something hard *I slipped and fell heavily.*

heaviness noun
the heaviness of something is how heavy it is *the heaviness of the suitcase*; *the heaviness of the snowfall*

heavy adjective **heavier, heaviest**
1 weighing a lot and often hard to lift or move *This dictionary is heavy. How heavy is your suitcase?* (How much does it weigh?)
2 used when you mean a lot of something *There was heavy snow last night. We ate a heavy meal* (with a lot of food).
3 used when you mean someone does something a lot or with a lot of strength or effort *My uncle is a heavy drinker. He received a heavy blow to his arm. Lifting boxes is heavy work.*
4 very thick *a heavy coat*; *heavy clouds*
5 very difficult *Shakespeare is often heavy going. I never take anything heavy to read on holiday.*
6 having very big waves *heavy seas*
7 **with a heavy heart** with a feeling of great sadness

SIMILE 'as heavy as lead' means very heavy (sense 1)

heavyweight noun **heavyweights**
1 a boxer in the heaviest weight group (usually around 90 kilos)
2 a very important and serious person such as a famous writer or politician

214

Hebrew ['hee-broo'] *adjective*
1 connected with the Hebrew language
2 connected with the Jewish people *Hebrew traditions*

Hebrew ['hee-broo'] *noun*
1 one of the languages people speak in Israel
2 the language of the ancient Jews

heckle *verb*
heckles, heckling, heckled
to interrupt someone who is speaking or doing something in front of an audience, for example by shouting at them
heckler *noun* **heckling** *noun*

hectare ['hek-tair'] *noun* **hectares**
a unit for measuring an area of land, equal to 10 000 square metres. A hectare is almost 2½ acres.

hectic *adjective*
used about a situation in which there are lots of things happening *I had a hectic day in the classroom. Things are very hectic at the moment.*

SYNONYM busy

he'd
short for 'he had' or 'he would'

hedge *noun* **hedges**
a line of bushes growing together. Hedges usually separate pieces of land such as gardens and fields or are planted along the sides of roads.

hedgehog *noun* **hedgehogs**
a small animal with prickles on its back that rolls itself into a ball when it is in danger

hedgerow *noun* **hedgerows**
a line of bushes, small trees and plants growing together, usually along the sides of roads or between fields

heed *verb*
heeds, heeding, heeded
to pay attention to something, especially advice or a warning

heed *noun*
if you pay heed to something, you pay attention to it

heel *noun* **heels**
1 the back part of your foot
2 the thick part of a shoe that goes under your heel
3 the part of a sock that goes round your heel
4 if you are hard or hot on the heels of someone, you follow close behind them

hefty *adjective* **heftier, heftiest**
1 big and heavy *a hefty suitcase*; *My brother's quite hefty.*
2 large *a hefty sum of money*
3 done with a lot of strength *a hefty blow*

heifer ['hef-er'] *noun* **heifers**
a young cow, usually under three years old

height *noun* **heights**
1 the height of something is how high it is *The wall is more than three metres in height.*
2 the height of someone is how tall they are
3 the particular distance something is from the ground or a surface *The town was built at a height of 50 metres above sea level.*
4 a high place *I'm afraid of heights.*
5 the most important part or the highest level of something *We went on holiday at the height of summer. A head teacher is someone who has reached the height of his or her career.*

heighten *verb*
heightens, heightening, heightened
1 to make something such as a feeling stronger *These attacks only heightened our fears of going out.*
2 to become stronger

heinous ['hee-ners' or 'hay-ners'] *adjective*
evil and shocking *a heinous crime*

heir ['air'] *noun* **heirs**
someone who receives another person's property when that person dies

heiress ['air-ess'] *noun* **heiresses**
a woman or girl who receives another person's property when that person dies

held
past tense & past participle of **hold**

helicopter *noun* **helicopters**
a vehicle without wings that flies through the air using large metal blades on top that spin round. It can take off and land vertically, stay in one place in the air and fly backwards and sideways as well as forwards.

ORIGIN from Greek *helix* 'spiral' or 'twisted' and *pteron* 'wing'

helipad *noun* **helipads**
a place where helicopters land and take off, often on top of a building

heliport *noun* **heliports**
a small airport for helicopters

helium ['hee-li-erm'] *noun*
a gas that is lighter than air and has no colour or smell. It is sometimes used for lifting balloons and airships and making them move through the air.

helix ['hee-liks'] *noun* **helices** ['hee-lis-eez']
a curve that goes round and round a central point in three dimensions like a coil or screw thread

hell *noun*
1 in some religions, hell is the place where evil people go after they die to be punished for the bad things they have done
compare: **heaven**
2 a place, thing or situation that is as bad or as difficult as can be *I love school but my brother thinks it's hell.*

he'll
short for 'he will'

Hellenic *adjective*
connected with Greece, especially ancient Greece

hellish *adjective*
extremely bad or difficult

hello *interjection*
a word used when you meet someone, begin saying something to them, for example on the phone or in an email, or when you want to get their attention

helm *noun* **helms**
1 a wheel or handle for steering a boat
2 **at the helm** in charge of something such as a team or organisation

helmet *noun* **helmets**
a hard hat, usually of plastic or metal, that protects your head

help *verb*
helps, helping, helped
1 to do something good and useful for someone to make things easier for them, for example by doing some of their work, giving them advice or money or saving them from danger *Mum helped me to cross the road.*
2 to make a situation better *Recycling helps the environment. Complaining won't help.*
3 to give someone more food or to take more food *I helped myself to some more potatoes. Can I help you to some more fruit?*
4 if you can't help doing something, you can't stop yourself from doing that particular thing *I couldn't help laughing.*
helper *noun*

help *noun*
1 something good and useful that you do for someone to make things easier for them
2 someone or something that helps *You've been a great help.*
3 (plural **helps**) someone who helps with the housework *My grandparents have a home help.*
4 a part of a computer program or website that helps you by giving information about how to use it. You click on a help menu to call up a help screen.

helpful *adjective*
1 if someone is helpful, they help you in some way or are ready to help you *My teacher is always helpful.*
2 if something is helpful, it is useful and helps you in some way *helpful advice*

helping *noun* **helpings**
an amount of food that someone gives you or that you take yourself at a meal

SYNONYM portion

helpless *adjective*
if someone is helpless, they can't do anything for themselves or for anyone else

SIMILE 'as helpless as a baby' means completely helpless

helplessly *adverb*
without being able to do anything, for example to stop something bad happening *We watched helplessly as the river flooded the whole village.*

helplessness *noun*
the sad feeling you have of not being able to do anything to stop something bad happening

helpline *noun* **helplines**
a phone number you ring to get advice about something

helter-skelter *noun* **helter-skelters**
a tall tower at a fairground with a slide going around the outside. You slide down it for fun.

hem *noun* **hems**
an edge of cloth that is folded over and stitched, for example at the bottom of something such as trousers or a skirt

215

hem–hey

hem *verb*
hems, hemming, hemmed
1 to fold over and stitch the edge of a piece of clothing or cloth
2 to hem someone or something in is to surround them so that they cannot move easily *We were hemmed in on all sides by a group of noisy students.*

hemisphere *noun* hemispheres
1 one of the two halves of the world, divided into north and south by the Equator *the northern hemisphere; the southern hemisphere*
2 one of the two halves of the brain, divided into left and right
3 a 3-D shape that is exactly one half of a sphere (ball shape)

ORIGIN from Greek *hemi-* 'half' and *sphaira* 'sphere'

hemp *noun*
a plant that produces fibres for making rope and cloth

hen *noun* hens
1 a female chicken kept for its eggs and meat, usually on a farm. A male chicken is called a rooster.
2 the female of any bird

hence *adverb*
1 used for showing the reason for something *Dan's on holiday and hence won't be at my party.*
2 from now *The work will be finished in time for the Olympics, three years hence.*

henceforth *adverb*
from this time on

heptagon *noun* heptagons
a shape with seven straight sides
heptagonal *adjective*

her *pronoun*
a female person or animal that someone has just mentioned, for example in an earlier sentence *Do you know her? I have a present for her.*

her *adjective*
belonging to or connected with a female person or animal that someone has just mentioned *her parents; Her homework is always good.*

herald *verb*
heralds, heralding, heralded
1 to be a sign of something that will happen
2 to announce that something is a sign of what will happen

herald *noun* heralds
1 a person who carried messages for a king or queen in the past
2 a sign of something that will happen *Falling leaves are the heralds of autumn.*

heraldry *noun*
the study of coats of arms (designs on shields used by families)
heraldic *adjective*

herb *noun* herbs
a plant used for making food taste better or for making medicines

herbal *adjective*
made from herbs *herbal tea; herbal medicine*

herbivore *noun* herbivores
an animal that eats only plants
herbivorous *adjective*
compare: **carnivore** and **omnivore**

herd *noun* herds
a large group of animals that live and move around together *a herd of cattle*

herd *verb*
herds, herding, herded
to make animals or people move together as a group

here *adverb*
1 in, at or to this place or the place where you are now *I like it here in Leeds. Come here.*
2 at a particular point while doing something *Let's stop here and start playing again tomorrow.*
3 used when you mean something or someone has come *Summer is here.*
4 used when you mean you've just found something or someone *Here's my mobile – it was under the bed.*
5 used when you're giving someone something *Here's a cup of tea.*
6 used when you're making someone or something known *Here's Simon – he's my brother. Here's a good idea.*
7 **here and there** in a few different places
8 **here and now** straightaway

hereabouts *adverb*
somewhere near this particular place

hereditary *adjective*
passed from parent to child, for example in their genes (tiny parts of living matter that contain information about how someone grows) *a hereditary disease*

heredity ['her-red-er-tee'] *noun*
the passing of special qualities from parents to children in their genes

heritage *noun*
all the important things, people, ideas and ways of behaving of a particular society that exist from the past *Plays by Shakespeare, paintings by Turner and the music of Edward Elgar are all part of the British heritage.*

hermit *noun* hermits
a person who lives on his or her own, usually in a lonely place. Hermits are sometimes religious people, for example Christians or Hindus.

ORIGIN from Greek *eremites* 'of the desert' (from *eremia* 'desert' or 'lonely place')

hermitage *noun* hermitages
a place where religious hermits live

hero *noun* heroes
1 someone you have great respect for, for example for doing something very brave or important or for their very good qualities
2 the main male person in a play, book or film

ORIGIN from Greek *heros* 'person of very great strength, half man and half god'

heroic *adjective*
very brave **heroically** *adverb*

heroine *noun* heroines
1 a girl or woman you have great respect for because she has done something very brave or does things that are very brave
2 the main female person in a play, book or film

heroism *noun*
when someone has done something very brave or does very brave things

heron *noun* herons
a large bird with long legs, a long neck and a long pointed beak. Herons live near water.

herring *noun* **herrings** or **herring**
a long silver-coloured fish that you can eat. Herrings swim in large groups in the sea.

hers *pronoun*
used about something belonging to or connected with a female person or animal that someone has just mentioned *Hers are the best. These shoes are hers.*

herself *pronoun*
1 used when a female person or animal that someone has just mentioned does an action and that action is also directed back onto her *She fell and hurt herself. She bought herself an ice cream.*
2 used when you mean a particular female person or animal that someone has just mentioned and no-one else *Ruth came herself. She did it herself – no-one helped her.*
3 **by herself** without anyone else being there, or without the help of anyone else *She was at home all by herself. Ava lifted the parcel by herself.*

he's
short for 'he is' or 'he has'

hesitant *adjective*
doing or saying something slowly, for example because you're not sure about it or you're nervous **hesitantly** *adverb*

hesitate *verb*
hesitates, hesitating, hesitated
1 to be slow to start saying or doing something (or to stop saying or doing something for a moment), for example because you're not sure or you're nervous
2 if you tell someone not to hesitate to do something, you mean they should do it straightaway and that it's the right thing for them to do *If you need anything, don't hesitate to ask me.*

hesitation *noun* hesitations
1 a short wait before saying or doing something
2 a short time when you stop saying or doing something
3 a feeling that you shouldn't do something

heterosexual *adjective*
if someone is heterosexual, they have or want a love relationship with a person of the opposite sex

het up *adjective* (informal)
worried, nervous or angry about something

hexagon *noun* hexagons
a shape with six straight sides
hexagonal *adjective*

hey *interjection*
a word used for getting someone's attention or for showing a feeling such as surprise or anger

hey presto *interjection*
a word used when something happens so quickly that it seems like magic

hi *interjection*
a word used when you meet someone or begin saying something to them, for example in an email

hibernate ['hy-ber-nayt'] *verb*
hibernates, hibernating, hibernated
1 if an animal hibernates, it spends the winter sleeping
2 if a computer hibernates, it turns off its programs to save energy but is still connected to the power
hibernation *noun*

ORIGIN from Latin *hibernare* 'to spend the winter' (from *hiems* 'winter')

hiccup *noun* **hiccups**
a loud swallowing sound that you make in your throat when you eat or drink something too quickly *I've got the hiccups.*

hiccup *verb*
hiccups, hiccupping, hiccupped
to make a hiccupping sound or sounds after eating or drinking too quickly

hide *verb*
hides, hiding, hid, hidden
1 to put something or someone in a place where no-one can see them or find them
2 to go somewhere where no-one can see you or find you *I hid behind the door.*
3 to stop something from being seen *I use make-up to hide the scar.*
4 to stop something from being known *He couldn't hide his anger any longer. You've hidden the truth from your parents.*

hide *noun* **hides**
the strong skin of a large animal such as a cow, used for making leather

hide-and-seek *noun*
a game in which everyone hides except one player who must try to find them

hideaway *noun* **hideaways**
a place where someone goes when they want to get away from other people

hideous *adjective*
1 ugly or not nice to look at *That's a hideous pair of glasses. I look hideous in that photo.*
2 terrible to look at and frightening *a hideous monster; a hideous scar*
3 extremely bad *hideous weather; hideous food*
4 ill *Are you OK? You look hideous!*

hideously *adverb*
1 very badly *He was hideously scarred.*
2 extremely, in a way that upsets you *Their house is hideously expensive.*

hideout *noun* **hideouts**
a place where someone goes to hide from other people, for example from the police

hiding *noun*
1 (*plural* **hidings**) to give someone a good hiding means to punish them by hitting them lots of times
2 **in hiding** in a place where you can't be found, for example because you are afraid of being caught *Anne Frank was in hiding in Amsterdam during the Second World War.*

3 **to go into hiding** to go somewhere where you can't be found

hieroglyphics ['hy-rer-glif-iks'] *noun plural*
a type of writing that uses pictures and symbols instead of words. It was used mainly in ancient Egypt.

hi-fi ['high-fye'] *noun* **hi-fis**
a piece of equipment for playing music, used especially in the past

ORIGIN an acronym from *high fidelity*

higgledy-piggledy *adjective & adverb*
mixed up in an untidy way

high *adjective* **higher, highest**
1 going a long way up from the ground *a high wall; a high mountain*
2 at a distance a long way above the ground *The helicopter was high in the sky.*
3 used for saying the distance that something goes up from the ground *a building 200 metres high*
4 close to the top of something *Her name is high on the list.*
5 used for talking about an amount, number or level that is much larger than the usual amount, number or level of something *a high price; high temperatures; I got high marks for my homework.*
6 very important *a police officer of high rank; He achieved the country's highest honour.*
7 used about the quality of something that is very good *My teacher praised the high standard of my homework.*
8 a high sound is one that is near the top of the range of sounds, for example the sound made by a whistle or small bird
9 high winds are very strong winds
10 if someone is high on a drug, they are not behaving in a normal way because they have put a harmful substance into their body to make them feel good
11 if you say it's high time that someone does something, you mean it's time for them to do it now because they should have started it much sooner
12 **in high spirits** happy, full of energy and having fun

high *adverb* **higher, highest**
1 a long way above the ground or above a particular position *I kicked the ball high into the air. Books were piled high on the table.*
2 to a much bigger level than the usual level of something *Prices are going up very high* (very much). *I got a good score but Evie scored higher* (more).

high *noun*
1 (*plural* **highs**) used about the level something reaches that is much bigger than the usual level *The temperature reached a high of 30 degrees in central London.*
2 **High** used in the name of some schools in the UK for students aged 11 to 18 *She goes to Chelmsford County High.*

high chair *noun* **high chairs**
a chair with long legs that a baby or young child sits in to eat. It has a small table attached to it.

high-definition *adjective*
used about something such as a TV or computer with a screen that is very clear because it has a high resolution (a lot of detail) *a high-definition television*

higher *adjective*
1 used about subjects or studies at a more advanced level than usual *a higher university degree*
2 higher education is study at a university or college

higher *noun* **highers**
a school examination in Scotland taken by students between the ages of 16 and 18

high five *noun* **high fives**
when you open one of your hands, raise it into the air and hit someone else's open hand in a friendly way. It is a sign that you are happy about something, for example when you win a competition or your team scores a goal.

LANGUAGE EXTRA you can also say *give me five* when you want someone to open one of their hands in this way

high heels *noun plural*
shoes with high heels worn by girls and women

high jump *noun*
a sport in which people jump over a high bar supported by two poles

highland *adjective*
connected with highlands or with the Scottish Highlands

Highlander *noun* **Highlanders**
someone from the Scottish Highlands

highlands *noun plural*
an area of a country with lots of hills or mountains *the Scottish Highlands*

highlight *verb*
highlights, highlighting, highlighted
1 to give extra importance to a particular thing

SYNONYM to emphasise

2 if you highlight words on paper with a special coloured pen, you mark them so they are easy to see
3 if you highlight words on a computer screen, you make them change colour, for example so you can delete or move them

highlight *noun* **highlights**
the best or most interesting part of something *Going to the top of the Shard was the highlight of our trip to London.*

highlighter *noun* **highlighters**
a special pen with an ink that is fluorescent (brightly coloured) for marking words on paper so they are easy to see

highly *adverb*
1 very *highly successful*
2 very well or very much *highly paid; highly respected*
3 if you think or speak highly of someone, you think or say that they are very good

highly strung *adjective*
if someone is highly strung, they become upset or nervous very easily

LANGUAGE EXTRA also spelt *highly-strung*

Highness *noun* **Highnesses**
a title used for a royal person, especially a prince or princess

high-pitched – historic

high-pitched *adjective*
a high-pitched sound or voice is near the top of the range of sounds

high-resolution *adjective*
used about a printed picture or a TV, computer or video image that is very clear because it has a lot of detail *a high-resolution photo*

high rise *noun* **high rises**
a tall building with lots of floors
high-rise *adjective*

High Road *noun*
used in the name of main streets, for example in parts of London *Chiswick High Road*

High School *noun*
used in the name of some schools in the UK for students aged 11 to 18 *He goes to Ilford County High School.*

high street *noun* **high streets**
the main street in a town or part of a town where most of the shops and banks are

high-tech *adjective*
using the most up-to-date electronic features or equipment *a high-tech gadget*

LANGUAGE EXTRA also spelt *hi-tech*

high tide *noun* **high tides**
the time when the sea or a river reaches its highest level. This usually happens about every 12 hours.

highway *noun* **highways**
1 an official word for a road *the Highway Code* (a book of rules about driving in the UK)
2 a road that goes between cities in the United States

highwayman *noun* **highwaymen**
in the past, a man with a gun who rode a horse and stopped people travelling along roads so that he could rob them

hijab ['hi-jahb' or 'hi-jab'] *noun* **hijabs**
a headscarf worn by some Muslim girls and women

hijack *verb*
hijacks, hijacking, hijacked
1 to take control of a plane, road vehicle or ship using violent behaviour
2 to take over someone's computer using software to control it from a distance *My browser was hijacked because I had no antivirus installed.*
hijacker *noun*

hike *noun* **hikes**
a long walk in the countryside

hike *verb*
hikes, hiking, hiked
to go for a long walk in the countryside
hiker *noun* **hiking** *noun*

hilarious *adjective*
very funny

hilariously *adverb*
1 extremely *hilariously funny*
2 in a way that makes you laugh *a hilariously bad film*

hill *noun* **hills**
a piece of land that is higher than the land around it. A hill is not as high as a mountain.

hillside *noun* **hillsides**
the land on the side of a hill

hilly *adjective* **hillier, hilliest**
with lots of hills

hilt *noun* **hilts**
the handle of a weapon such as a sword

him *pronoun*
a male person or animal that someone has just mentioned, for example in an earlier sentence *Have you seen him? I'll go with him.*

himself *pronoun*
1 used when a male person or animal that someone has just mentioned does an action and that action is also directed back onto him *He's washing himself. He made himself a cup of tea.*
2 used when you mean a particular male person or animal that someone has just mentioned and no-one else *Ethan gave me the book himself.*
3 **by himself** without anyone else being there, or without the help of anyone else *He walked to school all by himself. Ahmed tidied his room by himself.*

hind [rhymes with 'kind'] *noun* **hinds**
a female deer

hinder *verb*
hinders, hindering, hindered
to make it more difficult for someone to do something or for something to be done *The snow hindered the efforts of the police to find the missing boy.*

Hindi ['hin-dee'] *noun*
one of the main languages of India

hind leg *noun* **hind legs**
one of the two back legs of an animal that has four legs
compare: **foreleg**

hindrance *noun* **hindrances**
something that makes it more difficult for someone to do something

Hindu ['hin-doo'] *noun* **Hindus**
someone who follows the religion of Hinduism **Hindu** *adjective*

Hinduism *noun*
the main religion of India. It has many gods and includes many different beliefs.

hinge *noun* **hinges**
an object, usually of metal or plastic, that joins a flat part such as a door or lid to a fixed part such as a frame or box. The hinge allows the flat part to swing so that it can be opened or closed.

hinge *verb*
hinges, hinging, hinged
if something hinges on something else, it depends on it *Getting pocket money this week hinges on how you behave.*

hint *noun* **hints**
1 something you say or do that gives someone an idea about something but without you mentioning it clearly *Our teacher dropped a hint that she was leaving* (she didn't say she was leaving but gave some information that made us think she was leaving).
2 a piece of advice that helps you with something *My sister gave me some handy hints on how to use my new phone.*

hint *verb*
hints, hinting, hinted
to say or do something that gives someone an idea about something but without you mentioning it clearly *I hinted that I'd like a new tablet for my birthday.*

hip *noun* **hips**
your hips are the two bony parts on either side of your body at the top of your legs

hip, hip, hooray *interjection*
words shouted out by a group of people to celebrate something such as someone's birthday or as a way of showing that they like what someone has done

hip-hop *noun*
a type of popular music with spoken words and a simple beat (regular pattern of sounds)

LANGUAGE EXTRA also spelt *hip hop*

hippie *noun* **hippies**
someone from the 1960s who was against war and many of the usual ways of behaving. Hippies often had long hair and wore unusual clothes.

hippo *noun* **hippos**
short for **hippopotamus**

hippopotamus *noun* **hippopotamuses**
a very heavy African animal with thick grey skin, short legs and a long head with a wide mouth. Hippopotamuses live near water.

ORIGIN from the Greek words *hippos* 'horse' and *potamos* 'river' (a river horse)

hire *verb*
hires, hiring, hired
1 to borrow something for a short time and pay to use it
2 to pay for someone to do a job for you

hire *noun*
borrowing something for a short time and paying to use it *This bicycle is for hire* (can be borrowed and paid for).

his *adjective*
belonging to or connected with a male person or animal that someone has just mentioned *his parents*; *This is his house.*

his *pronoun*
used about something belonging to or connected with a male person or animal that someone has just mentioned *His are over there. This book is his.*

hiss *verb*
hisses, hissing, hissed
1 to make a sound like the letter S repeated lots of times
2 if someone in an audience or crowd hisses, they make a hissing sound loudly because they don't like what an actor or speaker has said or done
hiss *noun*

historian *noun* **historians**
someone who studies history or writes about it

historic *adjective*
1 important and old *the historic city of Bath*
2 important at a particular time in history *a historic meeting between two leaders*

historical – hog

historical *adjective*
1 connected with the past or the study of past events *a building of historical interest*
2 used about someone or something that really existed *Was King Arthur a historical figure?*

historically *adverb*
1 used about a situation that existed in the past or that still exists from the past *Historically, the two countries have been enemies.*
2 used about events, people or places from the past, especially important ones *The Battle of Hastings is historically important* (an important event from the past).

history *noun*
1 used for talking about the whole period of time before the present time and all the events that happened in the past *The year 1969 was the first time in history that humans had landed on the moon.*
2 past events connected with a particular country, place or group of people, or the study of these past events from written records *It's a film about the history of the English Civil War. Ms Campbell teaches Scottish history.*
3 past changes or events connected with a particular object, building or idea *a history of the Houses of Parliament*; *a history of the ghost story*
4 (*plural* **histories**) a description of past changes and events connected with something or someone *I'm reading a history of the postcard.*

ORIGIN from Greek *historia* 'learning by asking' (from *histor* 'wise man')

hit *verb*
hits, hitting, hit
1 if you hit someone or something, you move your hand or something in your hand onto them using a lot of force *Don't hit your sister!*
2 to make something move by hitting it with something *I hit the ball over the net.*
3 to go onto or into something or someone with a lot of force, for example accidentally *I slipped and my head hit the floor. I hit the floor with my head. A bike hit me as I was crossing the road.*
4 to attack something or someone, for example with a bullet or bomb *The soldier was hit by a bullet in the leg.*
5 to happen to someone or something and have a bad effect on them *Japan was hit by an earthquake and tsunami.*
6 to reach a level or place *The sales of the dictionary have hit a million. The singer had trouble hitting the high notes.*
7 (informal) if two people hit it off, they like each other from the time they first meet
8 to hit on an idea is to suddenly think of it
9 to hit out at someone or something is to say what you think is wrong about them

hit *noun* hits
1 something that people like very much, for example a song, film or show, or a singer or actor *This album was a hit about 10 years ago. Dad's cake was delicious – it was a real hit. He was a hit in Pinter's play at the National Theatre.*
2 the action of hitting someone or something *I got a hit on the head.*
3 when something such as a bullet or bomb hits someone
4 a visit to a web page on the internet *Our website got 50 hits yesterday.*
5 a piece of information you get when you do a computer search *The word 'happiness' gets millions of hits on Google.*

hitch *noun* hitches
a problem, usually a slight one *Our plans went without a hitch.*

hitch *verb*
hitches, hitching, hitched
1 to fix or join something to something else with a hook or rope
2 to move or pull something up, for example a piece of clothing
3 if someone hitches somewhere or hitches a lift or a ride, they travel in someone's car or ask someone to take them in their car, without paying any money

hitchhike *verb*
hitchhikes, hitchhiking, hitchhiked
to travel somewhere by asking someone to take you in their car without paying them any money. You usually show that you are hitchhiking by standing at the side of a road and holding up your thumb. **hitchhiker** *noun*

hi-tech *adjective*
using the most up-to-date electronic features or equipment *a hi-tech gadget*

LANGUAGE EXTRA also spelt *high-tech*

hither *adverb*
an old word meaning 'here' *hither and thither* (here and there, in different directions)

HIV *noun*
a virus that weakens someone's body and causes the serious disease of AIDS
short for: human immunodeficiency virus

hive *noun* hives
1 a structure where bees live and make honey

SYNONYM beehive

2 all the bees that live in a hive
3 **a hive of activity** a place where there are lots of people working hard

hives *noun*
a medical problem in which red spots appear on your skin

hmm *interjection*
a sound you make when you are not sure of something or when you are thinking about something

LANGUAGE EXTRA also spelt *hm*

HMS
used as part of the name of a ship in the British navy *HMS Victoria*
short for: His or Her Majesty's Ship

hoard *noun* hoards
a large amount of something that someone has saved or hidden somewhere

LANGUAGE EXTRA be careful not to confuse *hoard* with *horde* (crowd of people)

hoard *verb*
hoards, hoarding, hoarded
to save large amounts of something and hide it somewhere **hoarder** *noun*

hoarding *noun* hoardings
a structure with a large flat surface that has an advertisement on it, for example at the side of a road

hoarfrost *noun*
pieces of ice like needles that form on objects outside when it is cold

hoarse *adjective* hoarser, hoarsest
if you are hoarse or you have a hoarse voice, you speak in a low unpleasant voice because of a sore throat or too much talking **hoarsely** *adverb* **hoarseness** *noun*

hoax *noun* hoaxes
a trick in which someone is told that something will happen, usually something bad, but it isn't true *Someone called the fire brigade but it was a hoax.*

hoax *verb*
hoaxes, hoaxing, hoaxed
to trick someone by telling them that something bad will happen but it is not going to happen

hob *noun* hobs
a flat surface in a kitchen, sometimes on the top of a cooker, where the burners for heating pans are

hobble *verb*
hobbles, hobbling, hobbled
to walk with difficulty, for example because your feet are sore

hobby *noun* hobbies
an activity you like doing when you're not studying or working. Hobbies usually need imagination or skill, for example painting, playing music or doing sports.

hobgoblin *noun* hobgoblins
in stories, an imaginary ugly creature that can cause people harm

hobo *noun* hobos
in American English, a hobo is someone who has no home or job and who travels around from place to place

hockey *noun*
a game between two teams of 11 players in which each team tries to hit a small hard ball into the other team's goal using a stick that is curved at one end (called a hockey stick)
compare: polo

hodgepodge *noun*
if something is a hodgepodge, it is made up of different things that do not go together

LANGUAGE EXTRA also spelt *hotchpotch*

hoe *noun* hoes
a garden tool with a small metal blade fixed to a long handle. It is used for getting rid of weeds and breaking up the soil.

hoe *verb*
hoes, hoeing, hoed
to break up the soil and get rid of weeds with a hoe

hog *noun* hogs
1 a male pig
2 if someone goes the whole hog, they do a particular thing or action completely

hog – home

hog *verb*
hogs, hogging, hogged
to use or take too much of something (or the whole of something) in a way that is not fair to other people *My brother's always hogging the computer* (using it for a long time so that no-one else can use it).

Hogmanay *noun*
the evening of 31 December in Scotland when New Year's Eve celebrations happen

hoist *verb*
hoists, hoisting, hoisted
1 to lift something heavy
2 to lift something using ropes or special equipment

hoist *noun* **hoists**
a piece of equipment with ropes for lifting something

hold *verb*
holds, holding, held
1 to take and keep something or someone in your hand, hands or arms *Can you hold my book? Hold me tight.*
2 to have something or someone in your hand, hands or arms *I was holding the baby.*
3 to put or keep something somewhere using another part of the body *Hold the thermometer under your arm.*
4 to keep something or someone in a certain position or place *She held the door open for me. They held him prisoner. A brick on top of the dustbin holds it down in the wind.*
5 to not let something or someone go *The story held our attention. Hold the bully until the head gets here.*
6 to organise something such as a meeting or event *The school will be holding its end-of-year party next week.*
7 to have something inside or to be able to fit something inside *This bottle holds two litres.*
8 to be strong enough to support the weight of something or someone *Can the shelf hold all these books?*
9 to have something *My sister holds some strange ideas. This story holds a fascination for children.*
10 to have a particular job, title or record *He holds the position of prime minister. She holds the record for fastest swimmer.*
11 to continue in the same way *I hope my good luck holds.*
12 if you hold someone back, you stop them from going somewhere, doing something or making progress
13 to hold on is to wait *Hold on – don't go without me!*
14 to hold on to something is to keep it *You can hold on to this pen – I've got lots more.*
15 if you hold on to something or someone, you hold them tightly and don't let go *Hold on tight as we go round the corner.*
16 to hold out is to continue or last *I can't hold out much longer without water.*
17 if you hold something out such as your hand, you move it towards someone, for example so they can give you something *Hold out your glass and I'll give you some more lemonade.*
18 if something or someone holds you up, they stop you carrying on with something or travelling somewhere *We were held up by an accident on the tube.*
19 if someone holds up a bank or shop, they steal from it using a gun or other weapon
20 **hold it** used for telling someone to stop moving, to keep still or to wait

hold *noun*
1 the action of holding something or someone *Take hold of my arm. Get (or grab) hold of him before he runs away.*
2 (*plural* **holds**) the place in a plane or ship where luggage or goods are carried
3 to get hold of something is to find or get it *Where can I get hold of a cricket bat?*
4 to get hold of someone is to find them and speak to them *I can't get hold of Jamie.*

holdall *noun* **holdalls**
a large bag with handles, for example for carrying clothes when you're travelling

holder *noun* **holders**
1 someone who has something such as a ticket *Are you a ticket holder?*
2 someone who has a title or record *an Olympic record holder*
3 something for putting objects in *a mobile phone holder*

hold-up *noun* **hold-ups**
1 a situation that stops you carrying on with something
2 a situation in which traffic stops moving or moves very slowly *There are often traffic hold-ups on the M1 motorway.*
3 a situation in which a robber in a bank or shop uses a gun or other weapon in order to steal

hole *noun* **holes**
1 an empty space in the ground
2 an empty space that goes all the way or part of the way through something *There's a hole in the roof.*

Holi ['hoh-lee'] *noun*
a spring festival celebrated by Hindus, in which people throw coloured powder or water over each other

holiday *noun* **holidays**
1 a time when you don't go to school or people don't go to work *Tomorrow is the start of the summer holiday* (or *holidays*).
2 a time when you go away somewhere to enjoy yourself *She's on holiday in Belgium* (has gone there for a time to enjoy herself). *I want to go on holiday* (go away somewhere for a time to enjoy myself).
3 a holiday camp is a place where families pay to spend their holiday. The price includes food and lots of organised activities.

ORIGIN from Old English *haligdæg* 'holy day', because in the past a holiday was a religious festival only

holidaymaker *noun* **holidaymakers**
a person who is on holiday somewhere

Holland *noun*
a country in North-West Europe, officially known as the Netherlands

hollow *adjective*
1 something that is hollow has a hole or empty space inside it *a hollow tube*
2 hollow eyes or cheeks seem to go deeply inwards, for example because someone is ill or tired
hollowness *noun*

SIMILE 'as hollow as a drum' means very hollow (sense 1)

hollow *noun* **hollows**
a place in the ground or in a surface where it slopes inwards to form a slight hole

hollow out *verb*
hollows out, hollowing out, hollowed out
to hollow something out is to make an empty space inside it by taking out the part that is inside

holly *noun*
a tree with dark green prickly leaves and red berries. Some people use the leaves as part of their Christmas decorations.

Hollywood *noun*
the centre of the US film-making business *He's a famous Hollywood star.*

holocaust ['hol-er-korst'] *noun* **holocausts**
1 a situation in which a great number of people are killed and things destroyed, especially by fire *a nuclear holocaust*
2 **the Holocaust** the killing of millions of Jews and other people during the Second World War

ORIGIN from Greek *holos* 'whole' and *kaustos* 'burnt'

hologram *noun* **holograms**
a type of image made by a laser beam (line of light). The image changes when you look at it from different angles so it looks as if it is not flat but real.

holster *noun* **holsters**
a leather container for a gun. It is worn as part of a belt.

holy *adjective* **holier, holiest**
1 important in a particular religion *a holy book; the holy city of Mecca*
2 following the rules of a religion *She leads a holy life.*
3 **the Holy Land** the part of the Middle East that includes countries such as Israel and Egypt, where the events mentioned in the Bible happened
holiness *noun*

homage *noun*
something special that you do or say as a sign of the great respect you have for someone *Fans paid homage* (showed respect) *to the footballer who died last week.*

home *noun* **homes**
1 the place where you live, usually your house or flat
2 the town, country or region where you were born or where you feel that you belong
3 a house or flat that people buy or sell *They're building new homes in this part of York.*
4 the family you come from *I come from a happy home.*

5 a special place for people or animals that need looking after *a home for elderly people*; *a dogs' home*
6 a place in a game or sport that a player must reach to score a point
7 the first page of a website that gives information about the site

SYNONYM homepage

8 if you're at home, you're in your house or flat
9 if you feel at home or you are at home in a particular place, you feel comfortable in that place *'Make yourself at home,' he said.*
10 if a sports team play at home, they play at their own sports field

home *adjective*
1 connected with your home or done at home *home cooking*; *home life* (family life); *a home movie* (a film you make about your family's activities)
2 connected with the town or country where you were born *Sunderland is my home town.*
3 played or playing at a team's own sports field. If a team play at their opponents' sports field, they play away. *a home game*; *a home team*
4 home economics is the study of subjects and skills that are useful if you are in charge of a home, for example cooking, healthy eating and dealing with money
5 a home help is someone who helps with the housework

home *adverb*
1 to or at the place where you live *I want to go home. Lily's not home yet.*
2 to bring something home to someone is to make someone realise how serious something is

Home Counties *noun plural*
the counties around London, such as Hertfordshire and Kent

homeless *adjective*
a homeless person has no place to live

homely *adjective* homelier, homeliest
simple and pleasant in a way that makes you feel at home

homemade *adjective*
made at home and not bought from a shop *a homemade cake*

homepage *noun* homepages
1 the first page of a website that gives information about the site
2 a web page that you choose to be the page that appears when you connect to the internet

LANGUAGE EXTRA also spelt *home page*

homesick *adjective*
feeling unhappy because you are away from home and miss your family
homesickness *noun*

hometime *noun*
the time when you go home from school

homeward *adjective & adverb*
towards home *a homeward journey*

homework *noun*
schoolwork that you do at home

homogenised ['her-moj-er-nyzd'] *adjective*
used about milk in which the cream (thick fat substance that forms on the top of it) is mixed in with the milk

LANGUAGE EXTRA also spelt *homogenized*

homograph *noun* homographs
a word spelt the same as another but with a different meaning, for example 'desert' (land) and 'desert' (go away and leave someone). Homographs may have the same or a different pronunciation.

homonym *noun* homonyms
a word spelt the same as another but with a different meaning, for example 'bank' (place for money) and 'bank' (side of a river)

homophone *noun* homophones
a word that sounds the same as another but has a different spelling and usually a different meaning, for example 'pair' and 'pear'

homosexual *noun* homosexuals
someone who has or wants a love relationship with a person of the same sex
homosexual *adjective*

honest *adjective*
1 an honest person always tells the truth and doesn't steal or cheat, and you can trust what he or she says or does
2 also used about something that someone says or does *He gave me his honest opinion* (he told the truth and said what he really thought). *Aruna made an honest mistake* (she really made a mistake and was not trying to cheat anyone).

honestly *adverb*
1 used when you mean that you're saying what you really think, even if someone doesn't like it *Honestly, I think you're wrong.*
2 in a way that shows you don't steal or cheat *Our cashiers always behave honestly.*
3 in a way that is good and proper *Our teacher dealt with the problem honestly and fairly.*

honesty *noun*
1 an honest quality or honest behaviour or words
2 someone's honest character *a man of great honesty*

honey *noun*
a sweet, thick and sticky substance made by bees and used as food. Bees produce honey from nectar (a sweet liquid) made by flowers.

honeybee *noun* honeybees
a flying insect that makes honey and can sting. It makes a buzzing sound and its body has black and yellow stripes. Its name is usually shortened to bee.

honeycomb *noun* honeycombs
a type of container made by bees where they store honey and eggs in small holes called cells. It is made of wax (a fatty yellowish substance that the bees produce).

honeymoon *noun* honeymoons
a special holiday spent together by two people who have just got married

honeysuckle *noun*
a climbing plant with yellow or pink flowers that smell sweet and are usually shaped like bells

honk *verb*
honks, honking, honked
1 if a car horn honks, or if someone honks it, it makes a loud noise
2 if a goose honks, it makes a loud rough noise that is its own special sound

honk *noun* honks
the sound made by a car horn or a goose

honour *noun*
1 great respect or a sign of great respect for someone or something
2 doing what you think is right and good *a woman of honour*
3 something you are very proud of and that makes people show you great respect *It was an honour to read my poem in front of the school.*
4 (*plural* **honours**) something such as a prize or title that someone gets because of the good things they have done *She got a special honour for her work with disabled children. My brother has an honours degree* (an official piece of paper showing that he has finished his studies).

honour *verb*
honours, honouring, honoured
1 to show great respect to someone or something
2 to make someone very proud
3 to give someone something such as a prize or title because of the good things they have done
4 to do what something such as a promise or agreement says you should do *Tell me you will honour your promise.*

honourable *adjective*
if someone or something is honourable, they are good and deserve respect *an honourable decision* **honourably** *adverb*

hood *noun* hoods
1 the part of a coat or sweatshirt that you pull up to cover the back and top of your head
2 a piece of cloth that covers the whole head, for example so that you cannot be recognised
3 a cloth cover that you pull up, for example on a pram or pushchair, for protection against the weather
4 a piece of equipment that covers something
5 the American word for the bonnet of a car (the cover over the front part)

hooded *adjective*
wearing a coat or jacket with the hood pulled up

hoodie *noun* hoodies
1 someone who wears a sweatshirt usually with the hood pulled up
2 a sweatshirt with a hood

hoof *noun* hoofs or hooves
the hard part at the bottom of the foot of an animal such as a horse, cow or sheep

hook *noun* hooks
1 a curved piece of metal or plastic used for holding things such as clothes or pictures, fastening things or taking and catching things

hook–horrify

2 if a phone is off the hook, the part you hold next to your ear is not in its place and the phone cannot ring

hook *verb*
hooks, hooking, hooked
1 to fasten something with a hook or fix something on a hook
2 to take or catch something with a hook, for example a fish
3 if you hook something up to something else, for example a piece of equipment or a classroom, you connect it to something such as the electricity or the internet *All the school computers are hooked up to the internet.*

hooked *adjective*
if someone is hooked on something, they like it too much or they can't stop doing it *My brother is hooked on football.*

hooky *noun*
in American English, if you play hooky, you don't go to school when you should go to school

> SYNONYM to play truant

hooligan *noun* hooligans
someone who behaves very badly and often damages things *a football hooligan*

hoop *noun* hoops
a big ring usually made of wood, plastic or metal. Hoops are used for many different things such as for jumping through or swinging around the waist.

hooray *interjection*
a word that you shout out to show you're very happy

> LANGUAGE EXTRA also spelt *hurray*

hoot *verb*
hoots, hooting, hooted
1 if someone in a car hoots or hoots the horn, they make a loud noise by pressing the car horn
2 if an owl hoots, it makes a deep noise, for example like 'oo', that is its own special sound
3 to make a loud high sound *We hooted with laughter.*

hoot *noun* hoots
1 the sound made by a car horn or an owl
2 a loud high sound *hoots of laughter*

hooter *noun* hooters
a piece of equipment that makes a loud noise as a signal or warning. For example, you press a hooter in a car to tell other people you are there.

hoover *noun* hoovers (trademark)
a piece of equipment for cleaning carpets and floors. It uses air to suck up dust and dirt.

> SYNONYM vacuum cleaner

hoover *verb*
hoovers, hoovering, hoovered
to clean a carpet or floor with a hoover

> SYNONYM to vacuum

hop *verb*
hops, hopping, hopped
1 to move along by jumping on one foot

2 if animals or birds hop, they move along by jumping with small quick jumps
3 to go or come somewhere quickly *We hopped over to France for the weekend.*
4 to go from one thing or place to another *Dad is always hopping from one channel to another when he watches TV.*
5 if you hop on a bus, plane or train, you get on it
6 (informal) **Hop it!** used for telling someone to go away

hop *noun* hops
1 a jump on one foot
2 a jump by an animal or bird
3 a short journey
4 hops are the flowers of the hop plant. They are used in beer making for giving beer its bitter taste.

hope *verb*
hopes, hoping, hoped
1 to really want something to be true or to happen *I hope Amelia is all right. We're hoping for good weather.*
2 to want something and think that it will happen *My parents are hoping to see the head tomorrow.*

> SYNONYM to expect

3 used as a polite way of saying or asking something *I hope you don't mind if I ask you to close the window.*

hope *noun* hopes
1 a feeling that something good will happen in the future *They have no hope that things will get better.*
2 a feeling that you really want something to be true or to happen *My hope is to win the top prize for my drawing.*
3 the chance of something happening *There's still hope that he might change his mind.*
4 something or someone that makes you feel good about the future *You're my only hope.*

hopeful *adjective*
1 full of hope *Our team are hopeful that they might win next Saturday.*
2 giving you hope *That's a really hopeful sign.*

hopefully *adverb*
1 used, usually at the beginning of a sentence, to mean that you really want something to be true or to happen *Hopefully, Granddad will soon be out of hospital.*
2 in a way that shows hope *She smiled hopefully when her name was called.*

hopeless *adjective*
1 without any chance of hope and not likely to be successful *The situation is hopeless.*
2 very bad at something *I'm hopeless at maths. He's a hopeless swimmer.*
hopelessness *noun*

hopscotch *noun*
a game in which you throw a stone onto squares drawn on the ground and jump into the empty squares to get the stone back

horde *noun* hordes
a large crowd of people, usually moving somewhere

> LANGUAGE EXTRA be careful not to confuse *horde* with *hoard* (large amount of something)

horizon ['her-rye-zern'] *noun*
a line in the distance where the sky and the land or sea seem to touch *I can see a ship on the horizon.*

horizontal ['hor-i-zon-terl'] *adjective*
1 flat or level *A dead body lay horizontal on the ground.*
2 straight and going in the same direction as a level surface or the ground. Something is vertical when it points or goes straight up from a surface. *a horizontal line*
horizontally *adverb*

hormone *noun* hormones
a chemical produced in one part of the body that influences the way another part of the body works. For example, adrenalin is a hormone that can make the heart beat faster.

horn *noun* horns
1 one of the hard pointed parts that grow out of the head of an animal such as a cow, bull or goat
2 a piece of equipment in a car that makes a loud noise when you press it, for example as a warning
3 a musical instrument made of brass that you blow through

hornet *noun* hornets
a type of large wasp with a very painful sting

horoscope *noun* horoscopes
a description of what is likely to happen to someone in the future. It comes from studying the positions of planets and stars on the date the person was born.

horrendous *adjective*
1 extremely bad or shocking *horrendous damage*
2 extremely large in a way that upsets you *Our school has horrendous problems.*

horrendously *adverb*
extremely *horrendously difficult*

horrible *adjective*
1 extremely bad *That was a horrible thing to say.*
2 terrible to look at and frightening *a horrible monster*
3 ugly *You look horrible in that hat.*
4 very rude or unpleasant to someone *Don't be so horrible to your sister.*
5 sad or ill *Go and see the doctor – you look horrible. I feel horrible about what happened.*

horribly *adverb*
1 very badly *You behaved horribly to your brother.*
2 extremely, in a way that upsets you *We're horribly late.*
3 in a frightening way that really shocks you *A person was found horribly murdered.*

horrid *adjective*
extremely bad or unpleasant *He's a horrid little boy. What's that horrid smell?*
horridly *adverb*

horrific *adjective*
extremely bad and shocking *a horrific accident* **horrifically** *adverb*

horrify *verb*
horrifies, horrifying, horrified
to shock someone very much *I was horrified to discover a hair in my soup.*

horrifying adjective
shocking **horrifyingly** adverb

horror noun
1 a very strong feeling of being frightened or shocked *We watched in horror as he fell off the ladder.*
2 how shocking or frightening something is *She survived the horror of being trapped inside the lift.*
3 horrors are frightening or shocking things *the horrors of war*
4 (plural **horrors**) a boy or girl who behaves badly *You little horror!*
5 a horror film or story is one that is supposed to frighten you, for example because it is about evil or strange creatures

horse noun horses
1 a large animal that people use for riding on, or for pulling something such as a cart or coach (especially in the past). The sound a horse makes is a neigh.
2 an object that you jump over for exercise
3 a horse chestnut is a large tree that grows dark brown nuts inside a prickly covering. The nuts are called conkers.

horseback noun
on horseback riding on a horse

horseman noun horsemen
someone skilled at riding a horse

horsemanship noun
skill at riding horses

horsepower noun horsepower
a unit for measuring the amount of power an engine has

> LANGUAGE EXTRA originally a measurement that compared the power of an engine to the *power* of a strong *horse*

horseshoe noun horseshoes
a piece of metal shaped like the letter U that is fixed to the bottom of a horse's hoof to protect it

horsewoman noun horsewomen
a woman who is skilled at riding a horse

horticulture noun
the study and activity of growing plants, fruits and vegetables

> ORIGIN from Latin *hortus* 'garden' and *cultura* 'growing' or 'cultivation'

hose noun hoses
a long tube of rubber or soft plastic for carrying water, used for example for putting out fires

hose verb
hoses, hosing, hosed
to aim water at something using a hose *The firefighters hosed down the fence to stop the fire spreading.*

hosepipe noun hosepipes
a hose

hospice noun hospices
a hospital for people who are dying, for example people who have cancer

hospitable adjective
1 friendly towards someone, for example inviting them into your home and giving them food and a place to stay
2 providing good conditions for something or someone to live and grow *The Sahara Desert is not a very hospitable place.*
hospitably adverb

> ORIGIN from Latin *hospitare* 'to receive as a guest', from *hospes* 'guest'

hospital noun hospitals
a place where sick and injured people go to be looked after by doctors and nurses until they get better

> ORIGIN originally not a place for sick people but 'a place for receiving guests' (Latin *hospitale*, from *hospes* 'guest')

hospitality noun
friendly behaviour towards someone, for example inviting them into your home and giving them food and a place to stay

host noun hosts
1 someone who invites people to their home or to a meal or party
2 someone who introduces or talks to people who take part in a TV or radio programme *a chat show host*
3 a large number of things or people *a host of new gadgets*

host verb
hosts, hosting, hosted
1 to organise a special event, party or meal *London hosted the Olympics in 2012.*
2 to host a TV or radio programme is to introduce it or talk to the people who take part in it

hostage noun hostages
a person taken as a prisoner by someone who will not let him or her go unless they get what they want

hostel noun hostels
1 a building or large house where people such as students or young people can stay cheaply *a student hostel; a youth hostel*
2 a building or large house where people with no home can live without paying anything *a Salvation Army hostel*

hostess noun hostesses
1 a woman who invites people to her home or to a meal or party
2 a woman who introduces or talks to people who take part in a TV or radio programme *a chat show hostess*
3 a hostess or air hostess is an old-fashioned word for a woman who is a flight attendant (someone who helps and looks after people on a plane)

hostile adjective
1 very unfriendly and angry *a hostile crowd*
2 behaving like or belonging to an enemy *a hostile country*
3 not liking something or someone *All the students were hostile to the idea.*

hostility noun
1 unfriendliness and anger
2 a strong dislike of something or someone *There was a lot of hostility towards the new teacher.*

hot adjective hotter, hottest
1 if something is hot, it has a high temperature, for example above about 30 degrees Celsius (such as the climate at the Equator or the weather in summer), or a very high temperature, for example above or very much above 60 degrees (such as an oven, fire or cup of tea)
2 if someone is hot, they feel uncomfortable because the surrounding temperature is too high for them or their body temperature is too high
3 used about food that has a burning taste, such as mustard or a chilli

> SYNONYM spicy

4 if someone has a hot temper, they get angry very easily
5 a hot dog is a long bread roll with a hot sausage inside it
6 **in hot water** in trouble *My brother's in hot water again!*
7 **to sell like hot cakes** used about things that lots of people want to buy *The new phones were selling like hot cakes.*

> SIMILE 'as hot as a furnace' means very hot (sense 1)

hot verb
hots, hotting, hotted
to hot up is to become more exciting *The competition is starting to hot up.*

hotchpotch noun
if something is a hotchpotch, it is made up of different things that do not go together

> LANGUAGE EXTRA also spelt *hodgepodge*

hot-cross bun noun hot-cross buns
a small and sweet round bread roll with the mark of a cross on the top of it

> CULTURE NOTE it is traditional to eat *hot-cross buns* at Easter

hotel noun hotels
a building where you pay to stay in a room for the night and where you can eat meals

hotheaded adjective
doing things too quickly and without thinking

> LANGUAGE EXTRA also spelt *hot-headed*

hothouse noun hothouses
a heated glass building, like a greenhouse, for growing plants and vegetables in

hotline noun hotlines
a phone number you ring to get information, to talk to someone, for example in an emergency, or to order goods

hotly adverb
with a lot of energy and with strong feelings such as anger or enthusiasm *She hotly denied that she had cheated.*

hotplate noun hotplates
a round metal part in a kitchen, for example on the top of an electric cooker, that produces the heat for heating pans

hotpot noun hotpots
a meal of meat and vegetables cooked together in the same container in an oven

hot spell noun hot spells
a period of hot weather, for example lasting days or weeks

hotspot noun **hotspots**
a place in a public building with a wireless network (equipment using radio signals, not wires) that allows you to connect something such as your laptop or smartphone to the internet

> LANGUAGE EXTRA also called a *wireless* or *wi-fi hotspot*

hot-water bottle noun **hot-water bottles**
a type of rubber bag that you fill with hot water and put into your bed to make it warm

houmous ['ou' in 'houm' rhymes with 'u' in 'put'] noun
a Middle Eastern food made from chickpeas (large round beans) that are cooked and made into a soft paste with oil, lemon juice and garlic

> LANGUAGE EXTRA also spelt *hummus*

hound noun **hounds**
a dog used for hunting other animals

hound verb
hounds, hounding, hounded
to follow someone all the time in a very annoying way *The film star was hounded by photographers.*

hour noun **hours**
1 a period of 60 minutes. There are 24 hours in a day.
2 a particular time during the day or night *At this hour you should be asleep*
3 a fixed period of time for something *It's my lunch hour. The library's opening hours are from nine to three o'clock.*
4 **hours** used when you mean a very long time *We've been waiting for hours.*

> ORIGIN from Greek *hora* 'time of day' or 'season'

hourglass noun **hourglasses**
a glass object containing sand, used in the past for measuring one hour of time. The sand takes an hour to pass from the top part of the container to the bottom through a narrow tube.

hour hand noun **hour hands**
a long thin part that moves around the face (front part) of a clock or watch and shows the time in hours. It is shorter than the minute hand.

hourly adjective & adverb
happening or done every hour *hourly buses; Dad took my temperature hourly.*

house ['howss'] noun **houses** ['how-ziz]
1 a building where people live, usually built for one family
2 all the people who live in a house *The noise woke up the whole house.*
3 a building used for a particular purpose *a hen house; an opera house*
4 the audience, for example in a theatre *There was a full house for 'Hamlet'.*
5 a government organisation that makes laws, or the building where people meet to make laws *the Houses of Parliament* (the UK Parliament); *the House of Commons* (the part of the UK Parliament for politicians chosen by the people); *the House of Lords* (the part of the UK Parliament for politicians chosen not by the people but by the government)
6 an important royal family *The UK royal family belongs to the House of Windsor.*
7 a group that children are put in at school for competitions and sports events

house ['howz'] verb
houses, housing, housed
1 to give a person or animal somewhere to live
2 if a building or place houses something, that thing is kept there *The museum houses some of Van Gogh's best paintings.*

houseboat noun **houseboats**
a boat that someone lives in as a home

household noun **households**
all the people who live together in the same house or flat

householder noun **householders**
someone who own or rents a house or flat

house husband noun **house husbands**
a man who doesn't go out to work but stays at home and looks after the house or flat where he lives

housekeeper noun **housekeepers**
someone who looks after someone else's house or flat by doing the cleaning and often the cooking

housekeeping noun
1 all the work that needs to be done to look after a house or flat, such as cleaning, cooking and buying food
2 money to pay for things you need in a house or flat, such as food and electricity

housemaster noun **housemasters**
a male teacher in a boarding school who is in charge of a group of children and the area where they sleep

> LANGUAGE EXTRA a female teacher who is in charge of children in this way is called a *housemistress*

houseproud adjective
if someone is houseproud, they always keep their home clean and tidy

house-trained adjective
used about a pet that has been taught not to go to the toilet inside someone's home

house-warming noun **house-warmings**
a party that you have after moving into a new house or flat

housewife noun **housewives**
a woman who doesn't go out to work but stays at home and looks after the house or flat where she lives

housework noun
the work that needs to be done in a house or flat, such as cleaning, tidying, washing and cooking

housing noun
1 buildings that people live in
2 a housing estate is an area of land with lots of houses or blocks of flats that were built at the same time

hovel noun **hovels**
a small and dirty house

hover verb
hovers, hovering, hovered
1 to stay in one place in the air *A helicopter was hovering overhead.*
2 to stay near someone or something, for example to keep an eye on them or because you're waiting for something *My parents were hovering around me in the park to make sure I didn't wander off.*

hovercraft noun **hovercrafts** or **hovercraft**
a vehicle that moves over both water and land. It travels just above the surface, supported by a current of air.

how adverb & conjunction
1 used when asking or talking about what way something is done *How do you connect to the internet? Do it how you like.*
2 used when asking or talking about a size, amount, age or distance *How big is your house? Tell me how much you want. I don't know how old my granddad is.*
3 used when asking or talking about a quality *She showed me how tidy her homework was.*
4 used when asking or talking about someone's feelings or health *How are you today?*
5 used when asking or talking about what something or someone is like *How was the film? Tell us how your new teacher is.*
6 **How about ... ?** used for asking about something or someone, or for asking if someone wants something or wants to do something *How about Chloe? – Is she coming? How about an ice cream?*
7 **How do you do?** polite words used when you first meet someone

however adverb
1 used for saying that something does not matter, for example how you do something or how something is, because it will not change something else such as a particular situation *However hard you work, you won't be able to catch up.*

> SYNONYM no matter how

2 used for connecting two sentences when the second sentence introduces something surprising or a different idea from the first *It was raining hard. However, I went to school without an umbrella.*

however conjunction
used for saying that something does not matter *Do it however you want.*

howl verb
howls, howling, howled
1 to make a long, loud and high sound like a wolf or wild dog
2 to cry very loudly, for example like a baby who is in pain
3 if the wind howls, it blows very hard and noisily
4 to howl with laughter is to laugh very loudly

howl noun

howler noun **howlers**
an informal word for a stupid mistake

HQ noun
short for **headquarters**

hub noun **hubs**
1 the centre part of a wheel
2 a centre for a particular activity or business
3 a piece of equipment that connects to a computer and allows you to connect two or more other pieces of equipment to the computer *a USB hub*

hubbub–hung

4 a piece of equipment that connects a computer and other pieces of equipment to the internet or to a network (computers connected to each other for sharing information) *an Ethernet hub*

hubbub *noun*
the noise made by lots of people talking at the same time or rushing around

huddle *verb*
huddles, huddling, huddled
if people or animals huddle together, they come together closely in a group, for example to keep warm or because they are frightened *We all huddled together around the fire.*

hue ['hyoo'] *noun* **hues**
another word for a colour *the beautiful hues of the autumn countryside*

huff *noun*
in a huff angry

huff *verb*
huffs, huffing, huffed
if someone huffs and puffs, they breathe in and out loudly and with difficulty

hug *verb*
hugs, hugging, hugged
1 to put or hold your arms round someone and press them tightly to show that you like or love them
2 to stay or move along close to something *This path hugs the coast.*

hug *noun* **hugs**
when you put or hold your arms round someone *She gave me a hug.*

huge *adjective*
very big

SYNONYM enormous

hugely *adverb*
1 very *hugely important*
2 very much *The standard of Tom's work has improved hugely.*

hulk *noun* **hulks**
1 a very tall and heavy person
2 the main part of something such as an old ship or building that still exists after the rest has been destroyed

hulking *adjective*
very big and heavy

hull *noun* **hulls**
the main part of a ship that floats on the water. A large part of the hull usually goes under the water.

hullabaloo *noun*
a lot of loud and unpleasant noise, for example made by people shouting

hullo *interjection*
an old-fashioned way of spelling **hello**

hum *verb*
hums, humming, hummed
1 to make the sound of a tune with your lips closed *My stepdad was humming a tune.*
2 to make a continuous low sound (used about a machine or piece of equipment, for example) *On entering the shop, we heard the freezers humming in the background.*

hum *noun*

human *adjective*
1 connected with people *the human body*
2 showing the feelings and behaviour of people *Sometimes my dog seems almost human.*
3 a human being is a man, woman or child

human *noun* **humans**
a man, woman or child

humane ['hyoo-**mayn**'] *adjective*
showing kindness towards people or animals and not wishing to cause them pain
humanely *adverb*

humanitarian *adjective*
connected with helping people who are suffering, for example because of a war, earthquake or flood *Humanitarian aid will be provided by the UN.*

humanities *noun plural*
subjects that people study such as literature, history and languages. Humanities subjects are not scientific.

SYNONYM arts

humanity *noun*
1 all the people in the world
2 kindness towards people or animals *They treated the prisoners with humanity.*

humankind *noun*
all the human beings in the world, both men and women

humanoid *noun* **humanoids**
in science fiction, a creature that looks like a human

humble *adjective* **humbler, humblest**
1 not behaving as if you are better than other people
2 not important but just ordinary *She's just a humble cleaner.*
3 very simple *Although he is a celebrity, he lives in a humble little flat.*
humbly *adverb*

humid *adjective*
1 if the weather is humid, the air is warm and slightly wet in an unpleasant way
2 also used about a place *Cairo is often very humid.*

humidity *noun*
1 warm and slightly wet weather
2 the amount of water there is in the air

humiliate *verb*
humiliates, humiliating, humiliated
to make someone feel embarrassed or stupid in front of other people

humiliation *noun*
1 the feeling of being embarrassed or stupid in front of other people
2 (*plural* **humiliations**) something that makes you feel embarrassed or stupid in front of other people

humility *noun*
the special good quality of not behaving as if you are better than other people

hummingbird *noun* **hummingbirds**
a tiny bird with brightly coloured feathers and a long thin beak. It moves its wings so fast that it makes a humming sound. It can stay still in one place in the air and can also move backwards.

hummus ['u' in 'hum' rhymes with 'u' in 'put'] *noun*
a Middle Eastern food made from chickpeas (large round beans) that are cooked and made into a soft paste with oil, lemon juice and garlic

LANGUAGE EXTRA also spelt *houmous*

humongous *adjective* (slang)
extremely big

humorous *adjective*
funny *The author gives us a humorous description of life in a British school.*
humorously *adverb*

humour *noun*
1 humour or a sense of humour is a special quality that makes you see the funny side of things
2 the special quality that makes something funny *This poem is full of humour.*

humour *verb*
humours, humouring, humoured
to please someone by doing what they want so that they don't become angry

hump *noun* **humps**
1 a round lump on the back of a camel or person
2 a part of a road or surface that rises like a round lump above the ground
3 (informal) if someone has the hump, they feel angry about something

hump *verb*
humps, humping, humped
to carry something heavy, usually on your back

hunch *noun* **hunches**
a feeling that something is true or will happen

hunch *verb*
hunches, hunching, hunched
to bend your back and shoulders forwards *We sat hunched over the fire.*

hunchback *noun* **hunchbacks**
1 an old-fashioned or insulting word for a person with a large round lump on his or her back
2 a back with a large round lump on it

hundred *noun* **hundreds**
1 the number 100
2 in maths, hundreds are the numbers from 1 to 9 used in sums that include numbers above 99. The numbers are written in the hundreds column to the left of the tens (numbers from 10 to 99). For example, 435 is made up of four hundreds, three tens and five units (whole numbers from 0 to 9).
3 **hundreds of** used when describing large numbers of people, animals or things *Hundreds of people went to the concert.* 'How many books do you have at home?' – 'Hundreds!'

hundredth *adjective & noun*

hung
a past tense & past participle of **hang**

LANGUAGE EXTRA remember that when *hang* means to kill someone, the past tense and past participle are *hanged*

Hungary – hydrogen

Hungary noun
a country in Central Europe
Hungarian adjective & noun

hunger noun
1 the feeling you have when you need to eat something
2 not having enough food *Many people still die of hunger.*

hungry adjective **hungrier, hungriest**
1 feeling that you need to eat something or eat more food
2 without having enough food to eat *The hungry boy stole a loaf of bread.*
hungrily adverb

> SIMILES 'as hungry as a horse (or bear or wolf)' means very hungry

hunk noun **hunks**
a large piece of something, especially food *a hunk of cheese*

hunt verb
hunts, hunting, hunted
1 to try very hard to find something or someone *The police are still hunting the criminal. I've been hunting everywhere for my keys.*

> SYNONYMS to look for, to search for

2 to chase animals to try to catch them or kill them for food or sport
hunting noun

hunt noun **hunts**
1 a search for something or someone *I'll have a hunt for it later.*
2 a time when people hunt animals for food or sport

hunter noun **hunters**
1 someone who hunts for sport
2 someone who tries to find something *He said he was a treasure hunter.*

hunter-gatherer noun **hunter-gatherers**
a member of a group of people who get their food by hunting animals, killing fish and gathering plants rather than by keeping animals or growing plants themselves (usually used for describing human beings who lived in ancient societies thousands of years ago)

hurdle noun **hurdles**
1 a frame or fence that runners jump over in a race
2 a problem you must deal with before you can make progress

hurl verb
hurls, hurling, hurled
1 to throw something as hard as you can
2 to shout something such as insults or abuse at someone

hurly-burly noun
the noise and movements made by lots of people rushing about

hurrah interjection
an old-fashioned way of saying hooray

hurray interjection
a word that you shout out to show you're very happy

> LANGUAGE EXTRA also spelt *hooray*

hurricane ['hu-rik-ern' or 'hu-rik-ayn'] noun **hurricanes**
a very strong wind that can blow down trees and destroy buildings

> ORIGIN from Spanish *huracán*, which came from the name *Juracán*, a Caribbean god who blew strong winds when he was angry

hurriedly adverb
quickly

hurry verb
hurries, hurrying, hurried
1 to do something or go somewhere quickly *Let's hurry up – the bus is coming!*
2 to make someone do something or go somewhere quickly *Don't hurry me – I can't go any faster.*
3 to make something go faster *Don't hurry your homework or you'll make mistakes.*

hurry noun
1 if you do something in a hurry, you do it quickly because you don't have time to do it properly
2 if you are in a hurry, you want to get somewhere or do something quickly
3 **no hurry** used for telling someone that they don't need to do something quickly

hurt verb
hurts, hurting, hurt
1 to make a person, animal or part of the body feel pain *I slipped and hurt my knee.*
2 if a part of your body hurts, you feel pain there
3 to hurt someone or to hurt someone's feelings is to make them feel upset, for example by saying something unkind or rude to them or not showing respect

hurt adjective
1 injured or in pain *Are you hurt?*
2 upset *My sister is feeling very hurt.*

hurtful adjective
if someone says or does something hurtful, they make you feel upset

> SYNONYM cruel

hurtle verb
hurtles, hurtling, hurtled
to move very fast, usually in a dangerous way *A brick came hurtling through the window.*

husband noun **husbands**
a man that a woman is married to

> ORIGIN from Old English *husbonda* 'master of a house' (from *hus* 'house' and *bondi* 'peasant who owns his own house')

hush verb
hushes, hushing, hushed
1 if you hush someone or hush them up, you tell them to keep quiet *Hush! The baby's sleeping.*
2 to hush something up is to stop people knowing about it

hush noun
silence *There was a sudden hush when the teacher walked into the room.*

hushed adjective
silent or very quiet

hush-hush adjective (informal)
if something is hush-hush, people are not allowed to know about it

husk noun **husks**
the dry outside covering of some types of seeds or fruits

husky adjective **huskier, huskiest**
1 if you have a husky voice, your voice is deep as if you have a sore throat. A husky voice often sounds pleasant.
2 in American English, a husky man or boy is big and strong
huskily adverb **huskiness** noun

husky noun **huskies**
a large dog with thick fur. Huskies are used for pulling sledges over the snow, for example in Canada.

hustle verb
hustles, hustling, hustled
to make someone move somewhere quickly, for example by pushing them

hustle noun
hustle and bustle the noise and movements made by lots of people rushing about

hut noun **huts**
a very small building built in a simple way, often of wood, for example for taking shelter in or living in

hutch noun **hutches**
a box, usually made of wood and with a wire front, for keeping a rabbit or small pet in

hyacinth ['hy-er-sinth'] noun **hyacinths**
a spring plant with a very pleasant smell that grows from a bulb (root shaped like an onion). It has lots of white, pink or blue flowers growing along its stem

> ORIGIN from Greek *hyakinthos*. According to Greek legend, Hyakinthos was a young man accidentally killed by the god Apollo. Apollo made a flower grow on the spot where Hyakinthos died.

hybrid noun **hybrids**
1 an animal or plant produced from two different kinds of animals or plants. For example, a mule is produced from a donkey and a horse.
2 a mixture of two different things

hydrangea ['hyd-rayn-jer'] noun **hydrangeas**
a garden bush with large pink, white or blue balls of flowers made up of many smaller flowers

hydrant noun **hydrants**
a water tap in a street connected to the main water system, used by the fire brigade for dealing with fires

hydraulic adjective
used about something such as a pump or lift that needs the movement of water to make it work

hydroelectric adjective
using the power of water to produce electricity

hydrofoil noun **hydrofoils**
a boat that travels quickly just above the surface of the water using special supports fixed to its bottom

hydrogen noun
the lightest of all gases, which mixes with oxygen to make water. It has no colour, taste or smell.

hyena–ice cream

hyena *noun* **hyenas**
a wild animal from Africa and Asia that looks like a dog and hunts other animals in groups. Hyenas make a loud high sound like an unpleasant human laugh.

hygiene ['hy-jeen'] *noun*
keeping your body and the things around you very clean and free of germs so that you can stay healthy

hygienic ['hy-jeen-ik'] *adjective*
1 very clean and free of germs *Our kitchen is very hygienic.*
2 doing things in a very clean way *Eating food from the floor is not hygienic.*
hygienically *adverb*

hygienist ['hy-jeen-ist'] *noun* **hygienists**
someone who works with a dentist and cleans people's teeth

hymn *noun* **hymns**
a religious song, usually sung by people of the Christian religion

hyperactive *adjective*
if someone is hyperactive, they cannot keep still for very long or concentrate properly because they seem to have too much energy

hyperbole ['hy-perr-ber-lee'] *noun*
words that say more about something or someone than is really true, for example that they are bigger, better or more important than they really are

hyperlink *noun* **hyperlinks**
in a computer document or on a web page, a word or image that takes you to another document or web page when you click on it or touch it

hypermarket *noun* **hypermarkets**
a large supermarket, usually outside a town

hyphen *noun* **hyphens**
a short line like this -

LANGUAGE EXTRA a *hyphen* is used as a punctuation mark in writing for joining words or parts of words together (*old-fashioned, merry-go-round*).
It is also used when there is not enough room for a whole word at the end of a line of writing. The word then has to be divided into two parts: the first part is at the end of the line with a hyphen after it and the rest is at the beginning of the next line.

hyphenate *verb*
hyphenates, hyphenating, hyphenated
to put a hyphen in a word or spell it with a hyphen *'Great-grandmother' is always hyphenated.* **hyphenation** *noun*

hypnosis ['hip-noh-siss'] *noun*
1 a type of sleep in which you can still hear someone's voice and you do what they tell you to do
2 the action of putting someone into this type of sleep

ORIGIN from Greek *hypnos* 'sleep'

hypnotise ['hip-ner-tyze'] *verb*
hypnotises, hypnotising, hypnotised
to put someone into a type of sleep in which they do what you tell them

LANGUAGE EXTRA also spelt *hypnotize*

hypnotist ['hip-ner-tist'] *noun* **hypnotists**
someone who hypnotises people
hypnotism *noun*

hypochondriac *noun* **hypochondriacs**
someone who is always worried about their health and thinks they are ill even though there is nothing wrong with them

hypocrisy ['hip-ok-rer-see'] *noun*
the bad behaviour of someone who is a hypocrite **hypocritical** *adjective*

hypocrite ['hip-er-krit'] *noun* **hypocrites**
someone who wants people to think that they behave in a good way with high standards although they don't really behave in a good way at all

hypodermic *adjective*
a hypodermic needle is one that is used for putting drugs into someone's body under the skin

hypotenuse ['hy-pot-er-nyooz'] *noun* **hypotenuses**
the longest side in a triangle that has one angle of 90 degrees

hypothermia *noun*
a serious medical problem in which someone's body temperature is too low because they have been in a cold place for too long

hypothesis ['hy-poth-er-siss'] *noun* **hypotheses** ['hy-poth-er-seez']
an idea that helps to explain something. The idea may or may not be true.

hypothetical *adjective*
if something is hypothetical, it isn't real but it seems possible *a hypothetical example*

hysteria *noun*
a situation in which someone or many people have strong feelings such as fear or anger that make them behave in a way they cannot control

hysterical *adjective*
1 behaving in a way that you cannot control, for example because you are so upset, angry or afraid
2 extremely funny *His last joke was hysterical.*

hysterically *adverb*
1 in a way that you cannot control *She was crying hysterically.*
2 extremely *hysterically funny*

hysterics *noun plural*
1 behaviour such as crying or shouting that someone cannot control because they are so upset, angry or afraid
2 laughter that you cannot control *The show was so funny we were in hysterics.*

I i

ORIGIN the letter I started life as a shape representing an arm together with its hand. In the Phoenician alphabet, it looked like an F facing left with a little hook at the bottom and also appeared as a Z shape with a small vertical line through the middle. The Phoenicians called the letter *yod* ('hand') and it had the sound of our letter 'y' in 'yes'. When the letter passed into Greek, the shape had become simpler – a crooked line pointing upwards. In Greek it had the sound of the short 'i' of 'bit' as well as the 'ee' sound of 'beat'. The Greeks made the shape even simpler, straightening the zigzag into a vertical line. The shape and the two sounds of the Greek letter passed almost unchanged into the Roman alphabet, giving us the I shape and one of the sounds (the short 'i' of 'bit') that the letter has today in English.

I *pronoun*
a word that you use when you are talking about yourself *I don't know*

I
the Roman numeral for the number 1

-ible *suffix*
used for making adjectives that show something that can be done or a particular quality that something or someone has *edible*; *possible*; *flexible*

-ical *suffix*
used for making adjectives that mean connected with something *musical*; *comical*

ice *noun*
water that is frozen and has become hard

ice *verb*
ices, icing, iced
1 if something ices over or ices up, it becomes covered in ice *The pond has iced over.*
2 to ice a cake is to put icing on it

Ice Age *noun* **Ice Ages**
a long period of time in the past when ice covered many northern countries

iceberg *noun* **icebergs**
a very large lump of ice that floats on the sea. You can only see a small part of it because most of it is under the surface of the water.

ORIGIN from Dutch *ijsberg* 'ice mountain' (*ijs* 'ice' and *berg* 'mountain')

ice cap *noun* **ice caps**
a large area covered with ice around the North or South Pole

ice-cold *adjective*
extremely cold

ice cream *noun*
1 a cold food made from frozen milk or cream with different flavours added
2 (*plural* **ice creams**) a portion of ice cream for one person *Do you want a strawberry ice cream?*

ice cube–igneous

ice cube noun ice cubes
a very small block of ice for putting in a drink to make it cold

iced adjective
used about drinks that have pieces of ice in them to make them cold *iced tea*

ice hockey noun
a game like hockey that is played on ice between two teams of six players

Iceland noun
a country in Northern Europe in the North Atlantic **Icelandic** adjective

ice lolly noun ice lollies
a piece of ice on a stick with a flavour added to it, for example strawberry

ice rink noun ice rinks
a floor of ice, usually inside a building, for people to skate on

ice skate noun ice skates
a special shoe with a metal blade at the bottom for moving or dancing on ice

ice-skate verb
ice-skates, ice-skating, ice-skated
to move or dance on ice using ice skates
ice-skating noun

icicle noun icicles
a pointed piece of ice that hangs down from something. It is formed from dripping water.

icily adverb
in an unfriendly way

icing noun
a mixture of sugar, water and other ingredients such as butter or egg whites, used for covering cakes

icky adjective ickier, ickiest (informal)
very unpleasant *What an icky taste!*

icon noun icons
1 a small picture or sign on the screen of a computer, mobile phone or other device. You click on or touch the icon to perform an action.
2 a famous person or thing that represents an important idea
3 a painting of a holy person in the Christian religion, especially in Russia or Greece

ORIGIN from Greek *eikon* 'image' or 'portrait'

iconic adjective
famous as a symbol representing an important idea

ICT noun
1 the study of computers and the internet and the activity of using them *We study ICT at school.*
2 connected with computers and the internet *ICT skills*
short for: information and communication technology

icy adjective icier, iciest
1 covered with ice *icy roads*
2 very cold *icy weather*
3 unfriendly *He gave me an icy look.*

ID noun
an official document or card with your name on it and information about who you are, often with a photo
short for: **identification** or **identity**

I'd
short for 'I would' or 'I had'

idea noun ideas
1 a plan or picture you have in your mind, or a thought about something *What a great idea!*
2 an opinion about something or someone *I have an idea you're not telling the truth.*
3 information or knowledge that is not detailed but very general *Give me an idea of what the film was like. 'Where's Dad?' – 'I have no idea.'* (I don't know)

ideal adjective
the best that something or someone can be *This spot is ideal for a picnic.*

SYNONYM perfect

ideal noun ideals
1 the best example of what someone or someone should be *Ms Rennie is my ideal of all that a teacher should be.*
2 a high standard of behaviour

ideally adverb
1 used for describing something you would like to happen if things were perfect *Ideally, I'd watch TV all day.*
2 in a perfect way *Our school is ideally situated near the park.*

identical adjective
1 exactly the same *My new bike is identical to the old one.*
2 identical twins are brothers or sisters born from the same egg and looking the same

identically adverb
in exactly the same way

identification noun
1 an official document or card with your name on it and information about who you are, often with a photo

SYNONYM ID

2 the action of identifying someone or something

identify verb
identifies, identifying, identified
1 to recognise someone or something and describe exactly who or what they are
2 if you identify with someone, you understand them and share their feelings

identity noun identities
1 who a person is *We don't know the identity of the winner of the school quiz.*
2 an identity card is an official card saying who you are

idiom noun idioms
a group of words with a special meaning that is different from the usual meaning of each word in the group, for example 'to have cold feet' (to suddenly feel scared about doing something)

idiomatic adjective
1 used about a way of speaking or writing that is natural and correct *Manuel's English is fluent and idiomatic.*
2 an idiomatic expression or phrase is an idiom

idiot noun idiots
a stupid person or someone who behaves in a stupid way

ORIGIN from Greek *idiotes* 'person without skill' or 'ignorant person'

idiotic adjective
stupid **idiotically** adverb

idle adjective
1 if something such as a machine or factory is idle, it is not being used
2 not wanting to work or do anything *My brother is bone idle* (never wants to do anything).

SYNONYM lazy

3 not having any work to do *Many workers in our town are idle.*
4 not serious or useful *idle gossip*
idleness noun

idle verb
idles, idling, idled
to waste time doing nothing *I spent the whole day idling away the time.*

idly adverb
1 without any particular reason *She was looking idly out of the window.*
2 without doing anything *He stood there idly while I did all the washing-up.*

idol noun idols
1 a famous person that lots of people have great respect and feelings of love for *a pop idol*
2 an image or statue that people pray to as part of their religion

idolise verb
idolises, idolising, idolised
to have great respect and love for someone

LANGUAGE EXTRA also spelt *idolize*

i.e.
used for explaining exactly what something is or what you mean by something *When was the oldest bridge across the Thames, i.e. London Bridge, first built?*

ORIGIN from Latin *id est* 'that is'

if conjunction
1 used for talking about something that will happen only after something else happens *If you tell me your secret, then I'll tell you mine. You will be successful if you try.*
2 used for describing a situation that is always true *If you leave your ice cream in the sun, it will melt.*
3 used when talking about a possible situation when there is another situation that is possible too *Tell me if you want to come for a sleepover sometime. I wonder if I should take an umbrella or not.*
4 used when asking someone politely to do something or when asking permission *If you don't mind, could you close the window?*
5 **if only** used when you mean you would be happy if a particular situation were different *If only I could swim!*

igloo noun igloos
a small round house made out of blocks of snow that Inuit people sometimes live in

ORIGIN from Inuit *iglu* 'house'

igneous ['ig-nee-ers'] adjective
used about rocks (like granite) formed from magma or lava (hot liquid from inside volcanoes)

ignite–immature

ignite *verb*
ignites, igniting, ignited
to catch fire or make something catch fire

ORIGIN from Latin *ignis* 'fire'

ignition *noun*
1 the electrical system that makes the engine of a vehicle start to burn fuel when it is switched on
2 the action of catching fire or making something catch fire

ignorance *noun*
1 not knowing the things you should know
2 not realising something

ignorant *adjective*
1 if someone is ignorant, they don't know the things they should know and they may appear stupid
2 not realising something *We were ignorant of the dangers ahead.*
3 not knowing how to behave properly

ignore *verb*
ignores, ignoring, ignored
1 to pretend not to see or hear something or someone, or to pay no attention to them
2 to take no notice of something *The children ignored the warning signs.*

iguana *noun* iguanas
a large lizard with a row of sharp points down its back. It lives in tropical places such as Central America and China.

ill *adjective*
1 not feeling well *Grandma has fallen ill* (become ill).
2 bad *ill health*; *ill will* (unfriendly or angry feelings towards someone)

ill- *prefix*
badly or bad *ill-treated* (badly treated); *ill-treatment* (bad treatment)

I'll
short for 'I will' or 'I shall'

illegal *adjective*
not allowed by the law **illegally** *adverb*

illegible *adjective*
impossible to read, for example because of not being clear or tidy *My doctor's handwriting is illegible.* **illegibly** *adverb*

illegitimate ['il-i-jit-i-mert'] *adjective*
(old-fashioned)
having parents who are not married to each other

illiterate ['i-lit-er-ert'] *adjective*
not able to read and write **illiteracy** *noun*

illness *noun*
1 when someone has something wrong with their body *Jo's off school because of illness.*
2 (*plural* **illnesses**) a particular health problem that someone suffers from. Some illnesses (for example the flu) are caused by germs that you can catch. Others (for example diabetes) have different causes. *Granddad has a serious illness.*

illogical *adjective*
not logical or reasonable **illogically** *adverb*

illuminate *verb*
illuminates, illuminating, illuminated
1 to light something up with bright lights *The streets are illuminated at night.*
2 to make something easier to understand by explaining it

illumination *noun*
1 the light that comes from something such as a lamp or the moon
2 illuminations are the lights that make a place such as a street bright and colourful *We went to London to see the Christmas illuminations.*

illusion *noun* illusions
1 an appearance of something that you think is real but it is not real at all
2 a false idea about something *I have no illusions about my singing* (I know that I can't sing well).

illustrate *verb*
illustrates, illustrating, illustrated
1 to put pictures in something such as a book or magazine *an illustrated catalogue*
2 to show the truth of something *Your rash illustrates the dangers of sunbathing.*
3 to make something easier to understand by giving examples or drawing pictures

illustration *noun* illustrations
1 a picture in something such as a book or magazine
2 an example or picture that helps to make something easier to understand

illustrator *noun* illustrators
someone who draws pictures, usually for books

illustrious ['il-us-tree-ers'] *adjective*
famous and greatly respected

im- *prefix*
used for showing the opposite of something
impossible; *impolite*

I'm
short for 'I am'

image *noun* images
1 a picture, for example on a computer screen or TV or seen through a camera
2 the picture of yourself or of someone or something else that you see in a mirror
3 a picture of something that you see in your mind
4 a copy or model of someone or something, for example made out of wood or stone *a wooden image of a Hindu god*
5 what people think of someone or something *Our school needs to improve its image.*
6 to be the image of someone is to look like them almost exactly *Adam is the image of his brother.*

imagery *noun*
1 the use of words, for example in books or poems, to produce a picture or idea in someone's mind
2 the use of pictures, for example in films or paintings, to produce an idea in someone's mind

imaginable *adjective*
1 used for saying that something includes every example of something you can think of *There were birds with feathers of every imaginable colour.*
2 used about something that it is possible to imagine *Space travel wasn't even imaginable 150 years ago.*

imaginary *adjective*
not real but existing in your mind only

imagination *noun*
1 the power to form pictures in your mind
2 the power to think for yourself and produce new, clever and exciting ideas *Leo's essay shows lots of imagination.*
3 thinking that something is real when it exists in your mind only *That wasn't a ghost – it was just your imagination.*

imaginative *adjective*
1 new, clever or exciting *an imaginative way to teach maths*
2 producing new, clever or exciting ideas *an imaginative book*; *Be more imaginative in your homework.*

imagine *verb*
imagines, imagining, imagined
1 to form a picture of something or someone in your mind
2 to understand or realise something *Just imagine how I felt.*
3 to think that something is probably true *I imagine you must be tired.*
4 to think that something is possible *Back then, no-one could've imagined travelling to Mars.*
5 to think that something is real when it exists in your mind only *I didn't hear a noise – you must've imagined it.*

imam *noun* imams
a Muslim religious or community leader

ORIGIN from Arabic *imam* 'leader' (from *amma* 'go first')

imbecile ['im-ber-seel'] *noun* imbeciles
a stupid person

SYNONYM idiot

ORIGIN from Latin *imbecillus* 'weak'

imitate *verb*
imitates, imitating, imitated
to do the same as someone or something else **imitator** *noun*

imitation *noun* imitations
1 when you do the same as someone or something else
2 a copy of something, usually not as good as the thing that is copied

immaculate *adjective*
1 extremely clean and tidy *My auntie's house is immaculate.*

SYNONYM spotless

2 perfect in every way *Megan gave an immaculate reading of the poem.*

immaculately *adverb*
1 used for saying that something is extremely clean or tidy *immaculately clean*; *an immaculately tidy room*
2 in a perfect way *immaculately dressed*

immature *adjective*
1 if someone is immature, they behave in a childish way that is not reasonable for someone of their age
2 also used about someone's behaviour, actions or words *What an immature thing to say!*
3 not yet completely grown *an immature animal*

immaturity *noun*

immediate–impersonal

immediate adjective
1 used about something that happens or is done at once without any waiting *I got an immediate reply to my email.*
2 used about something that exists now *What are your immediate plans?*
3 used about something or someone that is close to a particular place *There are no food shops in the immediate area.*

immediately adverb
1 right now without any waiting, or at a particular time without any waiting *Go home immediately. I got a text from home and replied immediately.*

SYNONYMS at once, straightaway

2 very close to someone or something, for example a particular place or time *Turn left immediately after the post office. I received a text message immediately before lunch.*

SYNONYM just

immediately conjunction
if one thing happens immediately another thing happens, the second thing happens after it and without any waiting time *Immediately the bell went, we rushed to the door.*

SYNONYM as soon as

immense adjective
very big

SYNONYMS huge, enormous

ORIGIN from Latin *immensus* 'not measured'

immensely adverb
1 very *immensely rich*
2 very much *I enjoyed myself immensely.*

immensity noun
the very large size of something

immerse verb
immerses, immersing, immersed
1 to put something in a liquid so that it is completely covered
2 if someone is immersed in something, they are very interested in it and spend a lot of time doing it

immersion noun
1 the action of immersing something in a liquid
2 an immersion heater is a type of electric heater that provides hot water in the home

immigrant noun immigrants
someone who comes into a foreign country to live there
compare: emigrant

immigrate verb
immigrates, immigrating, immigrated
to come into a foreign country to live there
immigration noun

LANGUAGE EXTRA be careful not to confuse *immigrate* and *emigrate* (to leave your country to go and live in another country)

imminent adjective
about to happen very soon *A storm is imminent.*

immobile adjective
1 not moving *He sat there immobile.*
2 not able to move *I broke my leg and will be immobile for a few weeks.*
immobility noun

immobilise verb
immobilises, immobilising, immobilised
to stop something or someone from moving

LANGUAGE EXTRA also spelt *immobilize*

immoral adjective
1 if something is immoral, it is wrong and against the usual standards of behaviour
2 if someone is immoral, they behave in a way that goes against the usual standards of behaviour
immorality noun

immortal adjective
living for ever and never dying
immortality noun

immune adjective
if you are immune to an illness, you cannot catch it because you are protected by substances you have in your blood
immunity noun

immunise verb
immunises, immunising, immunised
to protect someone from an illness, usually by giving them an injection of a substance containing a safe form of the germs of that illness **immunisation** noun

LANGUAGE EXTRA also spelt *immunize* and *immunization*

imp noun imps
1 in stories, an imp is a small ugly creature with magic powers that behaves badly
2 a child who is naughty and full of fun

impact noun impacts
1 when one object hits another
2 a powerful effect that something has on something or someone *What is the impact of too much TV on children?*

impair verb
impairs, impairing, impaired
to make something weaker or less good, or to affect something in a bad way *All that smoking has impaired Granddad's lungs.*

impale verb
impales, impaling, impaled
to push a pointed object through something or someone

impart verb
imparts, imparting, imparted
to give someone something such as news or information

impartial adjective
showing that you are fair to people and that you don't let your own likes or dislikes affect your behaviour or decisions *an impartial judge; impartial advice*
impartiality noun **impartially** adverb

impassive adjective
not expressing any feeling in your face or voice *The murderer was impassive during the whole trial.* **impassively** adverb

impatience noun
1 the angry feeling you get when you have to wait too long for something to happen
2 the excited feeling you get when you want something to happen as soon as possible

impatient adjective
1 if you are impatient, you get angry very quickly when you have to wait too long for something to happen
2 wanting something to happen as soon as possible *I'm really impatient to get started on my school project.*
impatiently adverb

impeccable adjective
perfect in every way *Chantal's English is impeccable.* **impeccably** adverb

impede verb
impedes, impeding, impeded
to make more difficult the progress or movement of something *The storm impeded our progress.*

impending adjective
about to happen very soon (usually used when talking about something bad) *an impending disaster*

imperative adjective
1 if something is imperative, it is very important and needs to be done
2 in grammar, the imperative form of a verb is the one used for giving commands, for example 'Listen!', 'Eat!' or 'Shut up!'

imperative noun imperatives
the form of a verb used for giving commands, such as 'Sit!' or 'Stop!'

imperceptible adjective
almost impossible to see, hear, feel, smell or taste, for example because of being too small, weak or slow

imperceptibly adverb
in such a way that something is almost impossible to see, hear, feel, smell or taste

imperfect adjective
having a fault or faults and not being perfect *This dress is imperfect* (for example, some of the pattern is wrong).
imperfectly adverb

imperfection noun imperfections
1 a fault or something bad in something or someone
2 a small mark or damaged area that spoils something

imperial adjective
1 connected with or belonging to an empire (group of countries ruled by an emperor) *Britain's imperial past*
2 connected with or belonging to an emperor or empress (ruler of an empire) *the imperial family*
3 connected with a system of measuring things that uses British units such as inches, feet and miles, ounces and pounds, pints and gallons *imperial units*
compare: metric

impermeable adjective
used in science for describing a material that does not let a substance such as liquid or gas pass through it

impersonal adjective
1 not showing any human or friendly feeling *an impersonal email*
2 not caring about people or their needs *a very impersonal hotel*

230

impersonate *verb*
impersonates, impersonating, impersonated
1 to pretend to be someone else in order to trick someone
2 to copy the way someone (usually someone famous) speaks, looks and behaves in order to entertain people
impersonation *noun*

impersonator *noun* impersonators
someone who copies the way someone speaks, looks and behaves in order to entertain people

impertinent *adjective*
rude and not showing respect to someone
impertinence *noun* **impertinently** *adverb*

impetuous *adjective*
if someone is impetuous, they do things suddenly without thinking about them properly

impetus *noun*
something that makes something else happen more quickly by putting new energy into it *The president's visit gave fresh impetus to the building of stronger links between the two countries.*

impish *adjective*
naughty and full of fun

implement ['im-pli-mernt'] *noun*
implements
a tool or something used for doing something *A fork is an eating implement.*

implement ['im-pli-ment'] *verb*
implements, implementing, implemented
to make something such as a plan or a change start to happen
implementation *noun*

implication *noun* implications
1 words that make someone think something is true by the way they are said
2 how an action or decision will affect something in the future *If the head teacher leaves, what are the implications for our school?*

implore *verb*
implores, imploring, implored
to ask someone to do something and to ask this many times and with lots of energy

imply *verb*
implies, implying, implied
1 to make someone think something is true by the way you say it, or to give someone an idea about something without actually mentioning it *Are you implying that I'm stupid?*
2 to mean something in a logical way *If your brother has a car, that implies he can drive.*

impolite *adjective*
rude *It's impolite to talk during lessons.*

import ['im-port'] *noun*
1 (*plural* imports) a product brought in from another country to be sold
2 the business of importing products from other countries, or the action of importing a product

import ['im-port'] *verb*
imports, importing, imported
1 to bring in products from another country in order to sell them
2 to copy and bring in computer information, for example from one program or computer to another
importer *noun*

importance *noun*
when something or someone is important *I attach a lot of importance to my schoolwork (I think it is important).*

important *adjective*
1 if something is important, it is of great value or quality and can have an influence on people or things *This email is very important. 'Hamlet' is an important work by Shakespeare.*
2 used about something to pay attention to or consider carefully *My homework is important. It was an important decision.*
3 used about something that you should or must do *It's important to get to school on time. Listen carefully – that's important.*
4 used about something or someone that is needed or extremely useful *A car is important if you live in the country. Patience is an important quality if you work with children.*
5 used about someone or something that you love or like very much *My family is very important to me. Her teddy is so important to her – she takes it everywhere.*
6 used about someone or something that has a lot of power and influence *an important country; A head teacher is an important person.*

importantly *adverb*
used for showing that you think something is important *It's snowing and, more importantly, the roads are slippery.*

impose *verb*
imposes, imposing, imposed
1 to force someone to accept something *My parents never impose their opinions on me.*
2 to make someone obey something such as a rule *The head teacher imposed a ban on ball games in the playground.*
3 to want someone to do something that they don't want to do, such as invite you to their home *Are you sure I can come and stay? – I don't want to impose.*
imposition *noun*

imposing *adjective*
if something such as a building is imposing, it is large and fills you with feelings of respect and wonder

impossible *adjective*
1 if something is impossible, it can't be done or can't happen
2 very difficult to deal with *We're in an impossible situation. Your sister is impossible!*
impossibility *noun*

impossibly *adverb*
extremely *My mum works impossibly long hours.*

impostor *noun* impostors
someone who pretends to be someone else in order to trick people

impractical *adjective*
1 if someone is impractical, they are not good at doing useful things, especially things with their hands
2 if something such as a plan or idea is impractical, it is not likely to work properly
3 not very useful in a particular situation *These shoes are impractical for walking along the beach.*

impress *verb*
impresses, impressing, impressed
1 if someone or something impresses you, you have great respect for them, for example because you think they are very good *Rohan impressed us with his singing.*
2 to impress something on someone is to make them understand the importance of something

impression *noun* impressions
1 an opinion or general idea about someone or something, for example when you don't know someone very well or don't know much about something *I have the impression that she works hard. The school made a good impression on me* (I liked it and thought it was good).
2 when someone copies the way a person speaks, looks and behaves in order to entertain people *Can you do an impression of the prime minister?*

impressionist *adjective*
connected with a style of painting in which light and colour give a general impression of the picture and exact detail is not used. It began in France in the middle of the 19th century. **impressionism** *noun*

impressive *adjective*
if someone or something is impressive, you have great respect for them, for example because you think they are very good or important or because they are very big *an impressive skyscraper; Sherlock Holmes looked impressive in his hat and cloak.*

impressively *adverb*
extremely well *Theo played football impressively.*

imprison *verb*
imprisons, imprisoning, imprisoned
to put someone in prison
imprisonment *noun*

improbable *adjective*
not likely to happen or be true
improbability *noun*

impromptu ['im-promp-tyoo'] *adjective*
used about something that is done or said without being prepared or planned *an impromptu meeting*

improper *adjective*
1 dishonest
2 not right or suitable
3 rude or shocking *an improper remark*
improperly *adverb*

improper fraction *noun*
improper fractions
in maths, a fraction in which the numerator (top number) is larger than the denominator (bottom number), for example $\frac{7}{3}$. Improper fractions are worth more than one whole. *compare*: **proper fraction** and **equivalent fractions**

improve *verb*
improves, improving, improved
1 to become better *Your German has improved.*
2 to feel better after an illness *Grandma's in hospital but she's improving.*
3 to make something better *Lauren needs to improve her schoolwork.*
4 to improve something such as a part of a town is to do things such as repair older buildings and put up new ones

improvement – incidentally

improvement *noun*
1 when something becomes better or when you make it better
2 when someone feels better after an illness *Granddad's in less pain so there has been a slight improvement.*
3 (*plural* **improvements**) a change to something that makes it better *My parents made some improvements to our house* (for example getting new windows or a new roof, or building an extra room).

improvisation *noun* **improvisations**
1 when someone such as an actor or musician performs without preparing first
2 when you make or do something quickly using whatever material you can find

improvise *verb*
improvises, improvising, improvised
1 to make up something such as words or music as you go along, without preparing it first *In this play the actors improvise a lot.*
2 to make or do something quickly when you need to, using whatever material you can find

impudent *adjective*
very rude and not showing respect to someone **impudence** *noun*

impulse *noun* **impulses**
1 a sudden strong feeling that you want to do or have something
2 a short electrical signal that travels along a nerve or a wire, for example

impulsive *adjective*
if someone is impulsive, they do things suddenly without thinking carefully
impulsively *adverb*

impure *adjective*
of lower quality or not pure, for example because of being mixed with other substances *impure gold*

impurity *noun* **impurities**
something in a substance that makes its quality lower or that means it is not pure

in *preposition*
1 used for showing where something or someone is when there is something all around them *She's in school. I left my bag in the classroom.*
2 used for showing where something or someone goes to or is moved to *I jumped in the water. Put this in the box.*

SYNONYM **into**

3 used for showing when something happens *in June; in the morning*
4 used for showing the end of a period of time or one moment in a period of time *Come and see me in a week. I'll do it in the lunch break.*
5 used for showing in what way something is done or happens *Write your answer in pencil. I was dressed in blue. He was behaving in a strange way. We sat in a circle.*
6 used for showing that something or someone forms a part of something *He's in our team. Are you in the queue? There are 1000 metres in a kilometre.*
7 used for talking about a particular situation or feeling *I'm in a hurry. She looked at me in horror. My bike's in good condition.*

8 also used in many idiomatic expressions such as: *in all* (with everything included, for example when buying things in a shop); *in doubt* (not sure about something); *in tears* (crying); *in your twenties* (between the ages of 20 and 29)

in *adverb*
1 used for showing that something or someone has something all around them *The battery isn't in properly. Please make some room in the lift – I'm not in.*
2 used for showing where something or someone goes to or is moved to *Put the money in. Come in!*
3 used when you mean at home or at work *Is Peter in?*
4 included in something, for example a team, group or programme *For Saturday's game, Kyra is in but Grace is out.*
5 to be in for something is to be likely to get it *We're in for some cold weather.*
6 to be in on something is to be connected with it or know about it *Is Jake in on the secret? Many parents want to be in on the decision.*

in- *prefix*
used for showing the opposite of something *indirect*; *inequality*

inability *noun*
not being able to do something

inaccessible *adjective*
1 an inaccessible place is one that is very difficult to get to
2 difficult to understand
3 impossible to use or get *My mailbox and emails are inaccessible.*

inaccuracy *noun*
1 (*plural* **inaccuracies**) a piece of information that is not accurate
2 when something is not accurate

inaccurate *adjective*
not accurate or correct **inaccurately** *adverb*

inaction *noun*
not doing something that you should do

inactive *adjective*
1 not doing any exercise
2 not doing anything
3 an inactive volcano is one that will not explode
inactivity *noun*

inadequate *adjective*
1 not good enough or not enough *The school's heating is inadequate when it gets really cold. The food was inadequate for a whole family.*
2 feeling that other people are better, cleverer or more able to do things than you are
inadequacy *noun* **inadequately** *adverb*

inanimate ['in-an-i-mert'] *adjective*
not living *an inanimate object*

inappropriate *adjective*
not suitable or right **inappropriately** *adverb*

inarticulate ['in-ah-tik-yoo-lert'] *adjective*
not able to express your thoughts very clearly or easily in words

inattentive *adjective*
not listening or paying attention
inattention *noun*

inaudible *adjective*
if something is inaudible, you cannot hear it
inaudibly *adverb*

inbox *noun* **inboxes**
1 a folder on a computer where email messages are received and stored
2 a folder on a mobile phone where text messages are received and stored
compare: **outbox**

incapable *adjective*
1 not able to do something *I'm incapable of walking past a bookshop without going in.*
2 having the sort of character that doesn't allow you to do something *Ellie is such a nice person she's incapable of telling lies.*

incapacitated *adjective*
too ill or weak to be able to do things normally *He was incapacitated for six months after the accident.*

incapacity *noun*
1 when you are too ill or weak to be able to do things normally
2 not being able to do something

incarcerate *verb*
incarcerates, incarcerating, incarcerated
to put someone in prison

SYNONYM **to imprison**

incense ['in-sens'] *noun*
a substance that people burn to produce a sweet smell, often used in religious ceremonies

incense ['in-sens'] *verb*
incenses, incensing, incensed
to make someone very angry

incentive *noun* **incentives**
something that makes you want to do something that you don't really feel like doing *Earning more money is an incentive for working harder.*

incessant *adjective*
happening all the time without ever stopping, often in a way that annoys you *the incessant noise of the dogs barking*

incessantly *adverb*
all the time *The rain fell incessantly.*

inch *noun* **inches**
1 a unit for measuring length, equal to about $2\frac{1}{2}$ centimetres. There are 12 inches in a foot.
2 a very small amount or distance *The train stopped inches from the car.*

inch *verb*
inches, inching, inched
to move very slowing *The traffic is inching along because of the roadworks.*

incident *noun* **incidents**
an event, usually a bad or strange one *There was a shooting incident in the city centre.*

incidental *adjective*
connected with something but less important than that particular thing *What you say is true but incidental to the main question.*

incidentally *adverb*
1 used for changing the subject of a conversation
2 used for adding some information to what has been said, which is connected with it but less important

incinerate–incredulous

incinerate *verb*
incinerates, incinerating, incinerated
to burn something completely, for example hospital waste products and other kinds of rubbish

incinerator *noun* incinerators
a furnace (container with a very hot fire inside) for burning rubbish

incisor ['in-sye-zer] *noun* incisors
one of four pairs of teeth that are thin and flat and used for cutting food. The incisors are at the front of the mouth, in front of the canines.

incite *verb*
incites, inciting, incited
to make someone want to do something bad such as commit a crime, for example by getting them angry **incitement** *noun*

inclination *noun* inclinations
a feeling that makes someone want to do something or behave in a particular way

incline ['in-klyne] *verb*
inclines, inclining, inclined
to bend your head or body slightly forward

incline ['in-klyne] *noun* inclines
another word for a slope

inclined *adjective*
1 feeling that you want to do something *I'm inclined to leave now.*
2 often behaving in a particular way *William is inclined to be silly.*

include *verb*
includes, including, included
1 if something includes something or someone, they are a part of it *Our poetry book includes poems by Wordsworth and Keats.*
2 if you include something or someone, you add them as a part of something *Don't forget to include Nandita in the team.*
inclusion *noun*

ORIGIN from Latin *includere* 'to shut in' (*in-* 'in' and *claudere* 'to shut')

including *preposition*
used when you mean that something or someone is a part of something else *There were 15 children on the trip, including me.*

ANTONYM excluding

inclusive *adjective*
1 used about a price or cost that includes everything
2 including the first and last day, date or number *I'll be on holiday from Tuesday to Friday inclusive.*
3 used for describing something that includes everyone, for example boys and girls, young and old people, and people of all religions and beliefs, where everyone is treated equally *an inclusive society*

incognito ['in-kog-**neet**-oh] *adverb*
without letting anyone know who you are, for example by changing your appearance and name *The King often travelled incognito.*

ORIGIN from Italian *incognito* 'unknown'

income *noun* incomes
1 the money someone earns, for example from their work or savings
2 income tax is a tax that people pay to the government on the money they earn

incoming *adjective*
coming in *incoming emails*

ANTONYM outgoing

incompatible *adjective*
1 if things such as ideas or laws are incompatible, they cannot exist together
2 if pieces of computer equipment or software are incompatible, they cannot be used together
3 if people are incompatible, they are very different from each other and cannot live or work well together
incompatibility *noun*

incompetence *noun*
when someone doesn't have the skill to do something properly

incompetent *adjective*
not very good at doing something such as your job *an incompetent teacher*
incompetently *adverb*

incomplete *adjective*
1 not having all the parts that something is supposed to have *an incomplete list*
2 not finished *The new shopping centre is still incomplete.*

incomprehensible *adjective*
impossible to understand

incomprehension *noun*
not being able to understand something

incongruous *adjective*
looking wrong or unusual because of being different from the other things or people in a particular situation *He looked incongruous in the photo as he was the only one without a uniform.*
incongruously *adverb*

inconsiderate *adjective*
1 if someone is inconsiderate, they are thoughtless and do not think about other people's feelings
2 also used about someone's behaviour
inconsiderately *adverb*

inconsistency *noun*
1 behaviour or ideas that are not always the same in the ways that they should be
2 (*plural* **inconsistencies**) something such as a fact or spelling that is different from something else when it should be the same or should agree with it *There are lots of inconsistencies in your essay.*

inconsistent *adjective*
1 not always behaving in the same way and often changing your ideas
2 if things such as facts or ideas are inconsistent, there are differences between them, which means they cannot all be true
3 if things such as spellings in a text are inconsistent, the same words are not always spelt in the same way, for example 'adviser' is sometimes spelt 'advisor'
inconsistently *adverb*

inconspicuous *adjective*
1 not easy to see
2 not wanting to attract attention
inconspicuously *adverb*

inconvenience *noun* inconveniences
a problem or difficulty, for example one that makes you late for something or causes you extra work or effort *'The train is running one hour late. We apologise for any inconvenience.'*

inconvenience *verb*
inconveniences, inconveniencing, inconvenienced
to cause a problem or difficulty for someone

inconvenient *adjective*
if something is inconvenient, it causes you problems or difficulties
inconveniently *adverb*

incorporate *verb*
incorporates, incorporating, incorporated
1 if something incorporates something, that thing is a part of it *The sports centre incorporates a swimming pool.*
2 if you incorporate something, you add it as a part of something *The school will incorporate our class photo in its next blog.*

SYNONYM to include

incorrect *adjective*
1 if something is incorrect, it is wrong or has a mistake or mistakes in it *an incorrect answer*; *an incorrect email address*
2 not acceptable *incorrect behaviour*

incorrectly *adverb*
wrongly *You've spelt this word incorrectly.*

increase ['in-kreess] *verb*
increases, increasing, increased
to become larger or more, or to make something larger or more *Prices have increased. Click here to increase the text size. Mum has increased my pocket money.*

increase ['in-kreess] *noun* increases
1 when something becomes larger or more *an increase in crime*; *Cases of flu are on the increase* (getting more).
2 the amount by which something is more *an increase of £50*

increased *adjective*
larger or more *There's been an increased level of activity on my website.*

increasingly *adverb*
getting more all the time *Dad was getting increasingly angry.*

SYNONYM more and more

incredible *adjective*
1 almost impossible to believe *an incredible story*; *It's incredible how he's changed.*
2 extremely good *The singer has an incredible voice. We had an incredible time.*
3 extremely large *an incredible amount of money*; *Stop that incredible noise!*

incredibly *adverb*
1 extremely *incredibly difficult*
2 extremely well *She dances incredibly.*
3 used when something is almost impossible to believe *Incredibly, I came first in the race.*

incredulous *adjective*
if you are incredulous, you think it is almost impossible to believe someone or something **incredulously** *adverb*
incredulity *noun*

incubate–indirect

incubate *verb*
incubates, incubating, incubated
1 if a bird incubates its eggs, or if its eggs incubate, the bird keeps the eggs warm until baby birds come out
2 if you incubate an illness, the germs that produce the illness grow in your body but you do not yet show any sign of the illness
incubation *noun*

incubator *noun* incubators
1 a special container used in hospitals for keeping babies alive when they are born too early
2 a special container for keeping birds' eggs at the right temperature until the young birds can break out of their shells

incurable *adjective*
an incurable illness is one that cannot be cured

indebted *adjective*
if you are indebted to someone, you are extremely grateful to them

indecent *adjective*
shocking or rude **indecency** *noun*
indecently *adverb*

indecision *noun*
not being good at making decisions or not being able to make a decision at a particular time *Dad finally made up his mind after two weeks of indecision.*

indecisive *adjective*
1 if someone is indecisive, they are not good at making decisions or they cannot make a decision at a particular time
2 if something such as a battle is indecisive, it is not certain which side has won

indeed *adverb*
1 another way of saying really or certainly *It's very cold indeed.*
2 used for giving special importance to the whole sentence *Indeed it would be a good idea if you phoned your parents.*
3 used as a way of saying yes *'Is this your bike?' – 'It is indeed.'*

indefinite *adjective*
1 continuing into the future without a fixed end *The canteen will be closed for an indefinite period of time.*
2 not exact or clear *Our plans are indefinite.*

indefinite article *noun* indefinite articles
the word 'a' (or 'an') used in grammar. It is called the indefinite article because it does not refer to a particular example of a noun. For example, 'a house' refers to any example of a house, not a particular house.
compare: **definite article**

indefinitely *adverb*
for a period of time continuing into the future without a fixed end *The library is closed indefinitely.*

indelible *adjective*
1 impossible to remove, for example by washing or rubbing *indelible ink*; *an indelible mark*
2 impossible to forget *an indelible memory*
indelibly *adverb*

indent ['in-dent'] *verb*
indents, indenting, indented
if you indent a line of writing, you make it start further in from the edge of the page than the other lines

indent ['in-dent'] *noun* indents
the extra space at the left of a page made by indenting a line of writing

indentation *noun* indentations
a mark, hole or cut made in the surface of something

independence *noun*
1 the freedom of not being controlled or influenced by another country *India won independence in 1947.*
2 when you are free to do what you like or live as you want without being controlled by other people *My brother is travelling around and enjoying his independence.*
3 when something is not controlled or influenced by or connected to something else

independent *adjective*
1 free to do what you like or live as you want without being controlled by other people *My sister's at university and is very independent.*
2 doing things for yourself without accepting help from other people *Granddad is very independent.*
3 having enough money to live without asking for money from other people
4 if something is independent, it is not controlled or influenced by other people, countries or events *France is an independent country. You need some independent advice from an expert.*
5 not controlled or paid for by the government *an independent school; an independent TV company*
6 separate and not connected in any way to something or someone else *These two facts are completely independent. Grandma has seen three independent doctors about her illness.*

independently *adverb*
1 if you live independently, you live as you like without being controlled by other people or without asking for help or money
2 if you do something independently, you do it without asking for help or without being connected in any way to someone or something else

indescribable *adjective*
if something is indescribable, it is impossible to describe it because it is so good or so bad

index *noun* indexes
1 an alphabetical list of subjects or names, usually at the end of a book, with the pages where they are mentioned in the book
2 your index finger is the finger next to your thumb. It's the finger you use for pointing.

ORIGIN from Latin *index* 'forefinger', 'pointer' (from *indicare* 'to point out')

India *noun*
a country in South Asia

Indian *adjective*
1 connected with India
2 an Indian summer is a period of warm weather at the beginning of autumn

Indian *noun* Indians
1 someone from India
2 an old-fashioned word for a Native American *Let's play cowboys and Indians.*

indicate *verb*
indicates, indicating, indicated
1 to show something or show that something exists *This error message indicates a serious problem with your laptop.*
2 to point something out or make something clear *Please indicate your choice by ticking the box.*
3 to point to something or someone, for example with your finger or head
4 if someone in a vehicle indicates, they make lights flash on one side of their vehicle to show they are changing direction *Watch out – there's a car indicating left.*

indication *noun* indications
a sign of something

indicative *adjective*
being a sign that something is true or of what something is like *Ben's behaviour is indicative of someone who's having problems.*

indicator *noun* indicators
1 one of the four flashing lights on each side of a road vehicle at the front and back. It shows that someone is turning left or right.
2 a light on a piece of equipment such as a washing machine that shows something such as whether it is switched on
3 a piece of equipment that shows or measures something such as a level or amount *a speed indicator; a temperature indicator*
4 a sign that shows a particular situation

indifference *noun*
when you do not care about something or someone

indifferent *adjective*
1 not caring about something or someone *My brother seems to be indifferent to me.*
2 not very good *an indifferent football player*

indifferently *adverb*
1 without caring about something or someone *They just looked on indifferently while the bully hit me.*
2 not very well *Molly plays chess indifferently.*

indigestible *adjective*
not easy to digest (change into a substance the body can use)

indigestion *noun*
pain in the stomach caused by food that your body has trouble digesting (changing into substances the body can use)

indignant *adjective*
angry, for example because something bad has been done to you **indignantly** *adverb*

indignation *noun*
a feeling of great anger, for example because something bad has been done to you

indigo *adjective*
having a dark bluish-purple colour
indigo *noun*

ORIGIN from Spanish *indico* and Greek *indikon* 'Indian thing', because the colour came from the dye of a plant grown in India

indirect *adjective*
1 not going straight from one place to another *an indirect route*

SYNONYM roundabout

2 not caused by something or connected to something in an obvious way but often in a complicated way *an indirect connection between two events*; *His illness was an indirect result of smoking.*
3 not saying what you think in a clear or honest way *an indirect answer*

SYNONYM roundabout

indirectly *adverb*
1 not in an obvious way but often in a complicated way *The head teacher was indirectly responsible for what happened.*
2 not going straight from one place to another
3 not saying what you think in a clear or honest way *I answered her question indirectly.*

indirect object *noun* **indirect objects**
in grammar, the indirect object is the noun or pronoun that receives the action of a verb in an indirect way because something is given 'to' them or done 'for' them. For example, in the sentence 'I gave him a chocolate', there are two objects: 'a chocolate' is the direct object of 'gave', and 'him' is the indirect object.
compare: **direct object**

indirect speech *noun*
in grammar, indirect speech refers to the words that someone says when they are written down or spoken by someone else. The form of the words is changed slightly in indirect speech, for example if Anil says 'I am tired' (direct speech), this changes to 'Anil said that he was tired' (indirect speech). Indirect speech is also called reported speech.
compare: **direct speech**

indispensable *adjective*
if something or someone is indispensable, they are so good or important that you can't do without them

SYNONYM essential

indistinct *adjective*
1 not easy to see or hear *an indistinct shape*; *an indistinct sound*
2 not easy to remember *an indistinct memory*
indistinctly *adverb*

indistinguishable *adjective*
if something is indistinguishable from something else, you cannot see any difference between them

individual *adjective*
1 for or belonging to one person only *Children have their individual packed lunches. Each of us got individual attention.*
2 separate or connected with a separate person or thing *There are many individual parts that make up a computer.*
3 different or unusual *In this role, the actor has an individual way of speaking.*

individual *noun* **individuals**
1 another word for a person *Every individual should be treated with respect.*
2 a particular person *We're looking for a very special individual.*

individuality *noun*
the special quality that makes someone different from other people

individually *adverb*
separately, not together *The teacher spoke to each of us individually.*

Indo- *prefix*
connected with India

indoctrinate *verb*
indoctrinates, indoctrinating, indoctrinated
to repeat an idea or opinion so often to someone that they accept it as being true *They've been indoctrinated by TV to think that swearing is normal.*
indoctrination *noun*

Indonesia *noun*
a country in South-East Asia
Indonesian *adjective & noun*

indoor *adjective*
1 done or built inside a building *an indoor swimming pool*; *indoor exercises*
2 used inside a building *an indoor plant*

ANTONYM outdoor

indoors *adverb*
inside a house or building

ANTONYM outdoors

induce *verb*
induces, inducing, induced
1 to cause something to happen
2 to persuade someone to do something

indulge *verb*
indulges, indulging, indulged
1 to let someone have or do things they enjoy or to give them things they want *My grandparents really indulge me.*
2 if you indulge in something, you are nice to yourself by doing something you enjoy or giving yourself something you want *At the party we indulged in some mince pies.*

indulgent *adjective*
being nice to someone by letting them have or do things they enjoy or by giving them things they want **indulgence** *noun*

industrial *adjective*
1 connected with industry *an industrial town*; *industrial development*
2 industrial action is when people who work show they are unhappy about their jobs by doing something such as stopping work *The London tube drivers took industrial action* (stopped work).
3 the Industrial Revolution is the period in the 18th and 19th centuries when machines were used for producing goods. Important changes happened in people's lives because of this.

industrialise *verb*
industrialises, industrialising, industrialised
to develop a lot of industries
industrialisation *noun*

LANGUAGE EXTRA also spelt *industrialize* and *industrialization*

industrious *adjective*
very hard-working **industriously** *adverb*

industry *noun*
1 the work of making goods, especially in factories
2 the people and companies that make goods
3 (*plural* **industries**) a particular business that makes goods or sells a service *the tourist industry*

inedible *adjective*
1 not good enough to eat *The food in the canteen is inedible.*
2 not safe to eat

ineffective *adjective*
useless because not producing good results
ineffectively *adverb*

ineffectual *adjective*
if someone or something is ineffectual, they don't do what they are supposed to do *Our teacher is ineffectual at keeping the class quiet.*

inefficient *adjective*
not working in the best way and wasting time, energy or money **inefficiency** *noun*
inefficiently *adverb*

inept *adjective*
not very good at doing something *Dad dealt with the problem in an inept way.*
ineptly *adverb*

inequality *noun* **inequalities**
a situation in which people are not equal to each other, for example because some people have more money, power or opportunities than others

inert *adjective*
not moving or able to move

inertia ['in-err-sher'] *noun*
1 a feeling of not wanting to do or change anything
2 in science, inertia is a force that keeps something in the same position or moving in the same direction until it is stopped

inevitable *adjective*
certain to happen *It's inevitable that some students will fail their exams.*
inevitability *noun* **inevitably** *adverb*

inexcusable *adjective*
if something is inexcusable, it is so bad that you cannot forgive someone for doing it *His behaviour was inexcusable.*

inexhaustible *adjective*
existing in large amounts that you cannot use up *an inexhaustible supply*

inexpensive *adjective*
not costing much money

SYNONYM cheap

inexpensively *adverb*
without spending much money *You can live inexpensively in that part of the world.*

inexperience *noun*
when someone doesn't have any or enough experience

inexperienced *adjective*
not having any or enough experience

inexplicable *adjective*
impossible to explain **inexplicably** *adverb*

infallible *adjective*
1 never wrong or making a mistake
2 working every time *an infallible remedy*; *He has an infallible way of making money.*
infallibility *noun* **infallibly** *adverb*

infamous ['in-fer-mers'] *adjective*
famous because of something bad *an infamous criminal*

infancy *noun*
the time of your life when you're a baby or very young child

infant – influential

infant *noun* **infants**
1 a baby or very young child
2 a child who goes to an infant school
3 an infant school is a school for children between the ages of about four and seven

> ORIGIN from Latin *infantem* 'very young child' (from *infans* 'not able to speak')

infantile *adjective*
making you think of a child who behaves in a silly way *infantile behaviour*

> SYNONYM childish

infantry *noun*
the part of an army made up of soldiers who fight on foot, not in tanks or on horses

infect *verb*
infects, infecting, infected
1 to give an illness or disease to a person, animal or plant by spreading germs
2 to put germs onto or into something *If you touch your cut, you might infect it. He has an infected finger.*
3 if a virus infects your computer, it damages programs and files so that it is difficult or impossible to use the computer

infection *noun*
1 (*plural* **infections**) an illness caused by germs that spread from one person to another *a throat infection*
2 becoming infected *Wash your hands to protect yourself against infection.*

infectious *adjective*
1 if an illness is infectious, it is caused by germs that spread from one person to another

> SYNONYM catching

2 if someone is infectious, they have an illness that can spread from one person to another
3 if something such as a feeling is infectious, it makes other people feel the same way *The laughter was infectious* (everyone laughed and they couldn't help it).

infer *verb*
infers, inferring, inferred
to form an opinion about something from the information you have *I inferred from her expression that she was angry.*

inference *noun* **inferences**
an opinion that you form from the information you have *Sol pulled a face, the inference being that he disliked the film.*

inferior *adjective*
1 not as good as something or someone else *My cousin's school is inferior to mine.*
2 bad or of bad quality *The smartphones they make are inferior.*
3 less than something else *They lost the battle because of their inferior numbers.*
4 if someone feels inferior, they feel less important or think they deserve less respect than other people
5 having a lower position or rank than someone else

inferior *noun* **inferiors**
someone who has a lower position or rank than someone else

inferiority *noun*
when someone feels inferior to other people

infernal *adjective*
an old-fashioned word for describing something unpleasant or annoying *Stop that infernal noise!*

inferno *noun* **infernos**
a very big fire that causes a lot of destruction

infested *adjective*
if something is infested with insects or animals such as mice or rats, it has lots of them *Our kitchen is infested. Their school has a rat-infested drain.* **infestation** *noun*

infiltrate *verb*
infiltrates, infiltrating, infiltrated
to join a group or get into a place in order to get information secretly about someone such as an enemy or criminal **infiltrator** *noun*

infinite ['in-fin-ert'] *adjective*
1 if something is infinite, it has no end *The universe is infinite.*
2 used when describing a very large amount of something that seems to have no limit *The teacher explained the poem with infinite patience.*

infinitely *adverb*
very or very much (used especially for saying something very strongly or for showing how big a difference there is between things or people) *I'm infinitely grateful. She's infinitely more intelligent than me.*

infinitive ['in-fin-it-iv'] *noun* **infinitives**
in grammar, the infinitive is the basic form of a verb. In English it usually includes the preposition 'to' (for example 'to play' in 'I want to play') but 'to' is not always used (for example 'play' in 'I can play' or 'Watch me play').

infinity *noun*
1 an infinite amount or number of things
2 space or time that has no end *the infinity of the universe*

infirm *adjective*
if someone is infirm, they are weak or ill because they are old

infirmary *noun* **infirmaries**
1 a room, for example in a school, where people who are ill or injured go to be treated
2 used in the name of some hospitals in the UK *Edinburgh Royal Infirmary*

infirmity *noun*
1 bad health because of being old
2 (*plural* **infirmities**) an illness someone gets when they are old

inflame *verb*
inflames, inflaming, inflamed
1 to make a situation worse by making people more angry
2 to make strong feelings such as anger even stronger

inflamed *adjective*
if a part of the body is inflamed, it is red, painful and swollen, usually because of an infection

inflammable *adjective*
easy to catch fire

> SYNONYM flammable

> ANTONYM non-flammable

inflammation *noun* **inflammations**
a place on the body that is red, painful and swollen, usually because of an infection

inflammatory *adjective*
inflammatory words are words that are likely to make people angry

inflatable *adjective*
used about something you must fill with air before you can use it *an inflatable beach ball; an inflatable boat*

inflate *verb*
inflates, inflating, inflated
1 to make something bigger, such as a tyre or balloon, by filling it with air
2 to become bigger by being filled with air
3 to make a price bigger than it should be
4 to say that something is bigger or more important than it really is *The numbers of teachers taking part in the march were inflated.*

inflation *noun*
a situation in which prices keep going up in a country or region

inflection *noun* **inflections**
in grammar, an inflection is a change in the form of a word depending on how it is used in a sentence, for example when a noun changes from singular to plural ('book' to 'books', 'man' to 'men') or when a verb changes from present tense to past ('go' to 'went', 'jump' to 'jumped')

inflexible *adjective*
1 if something such as a rule or opinion is inflexible, it is impossible to change it, for example because the person who makes the rule or has the opinion does not want to change it
2 if someone is inflexible, they do not want to change anything such as their rules, ideas or behaviour
inflexibility *noun* **inflexibly** *adverb*

inflict *verb*
inflicts, inflicting, inflicted
to make something very bad or unpleasant happen to someone or something *He inflicted a lot of pain and suffering on those poor children.*

influence *noun* **influences**
1 the power to change someone's behaviour, ideas or opinions or to change actions or events *Teachers have a lot of influence on the way we learn.*
2 a person or thing that has this power *Your cousin is a good influence on you.*

influence *verb*
influences, influencing, influenced
1 to change what someone does or thinks or the way something happens *The hot weather influences people's behaviour.*
2 to make someone do something by being a reason for it *What influenced you to become a teacher?*
3 to be something that helps to make something happen *Mum's illness influenced our decision not to go on holiday.*

> ORIGIN from Latin *influentia* 'power from the stars' (from *influere* 'to flow in')

influential *adjective*
having a lot of influence over people's behaviour, ideas or opinions or over actions or events

influenza – initiate

influenza ['in-floo-en-zer'] *noun*
an illness like a very bad cold that makes you feel weak, hot or cold and ache all over

SYNONYM flu

influx *noun* influxes
a large number of people or things coming in at the same time *The country expects an influx of tourists for the Olympic Games.*

ORIGIN from Latin *influxus* 'a flowing in'

info *noun*
an informal word for information

inform *verb*
informs, informing, informed
1 to tell someone something *Please inform your teacher if you wish to go on the school trip.*
2 to inform on someone is to give secret information about them to someone else, for example a teacher or the police

informal *adjective*
1 friendly and relaxed, and not done in an official or serious way *an informal chat; an informal meeting*
2 informal clothes are clothes that make you feel relaxed, for example when you're at home or with friends
3 an informal word, expression or meaning is one that you use when speaking or writing to friends or people in your family, for example 'to chuck', 'Daddy', 'hop it'. Informal language is not used in careful speaking or writing, such as news reports or textbooks, or in serious situations.

informality *noun*

informally *adverb*
1 in a friendly and relaxed way
2 wearing clothes that make you feel relaxed *He was informally dressed.*
3 to speak or write informally is to use the kinds of words and meanings you use when speaking or writing to friends or people in your family

informant *noun* informants
someone who gives information to someone else. Sometimes this may be secret information.

information *noun*
1 facts that you learn from someone or something such as a book or the internet *Go to the information desk to find out when the shopping centre closes. The history lesson was full of useful information.*
2 symbols, numbers and words used by a computer, for example to make it work or provide answers to calculations *This information is stored in the computer's memory.*
3 particular things to know about something such as its size, length, shape, weight or the amount of it *To solve this maths problem I need more information. The shoe size information is written on the box.*

information technology *noun*
the study of how to use and store information on computers and other electronic equipment

SYNONYM IT

informative *adjective*
giving useful information *an informative TV programme*

informed *adjective*
if you are informed about something, you know about it *The school kept us informed about the dates of the concert.*

informer *noun* informers
someone who gives secret information to someone else, for example the police

infra-red *adjective*
used about a type of light that produces heat but cannot be seen, used in many products such as cameras for seeing at night, thermometers and lamps

LANGUAGE EXTRA also spelt *infrared*

infrequent *adjective*
not happening a lot or not doing something a lot

infrequently *adverb*
not often

infuriate *verb*
infuriates, infuriating, infuriated
to make someone very angry or annoyed

infuriating *adjective*
very annoying

ingenious *adjective*
1 if something such as an idea, plan or piece of equipment is ingenious, it is very clever or original
2 if someone is ingenious, they have very clever or original ideas or plans, or they are very good at making clever or original things

ingeniously *adverb* **ingenuity** *noun*

ingot *noun* ingots
a lump of metal, especially gold or silver, shaped like a brick

ingrained *adjective*
1 fixed under the surface and difficult to get rid of *There was ingrained dirt in the carpet.*
2 existing for so long that it is difficult to change *Granddad had an ingrained fear of heights.*

ingratitude *noun*
behaviour that shows you are not grateful for something

ingredient ['in-gree-di-ernt'] *noun*
ingredients
1 one of the foods you use together with others to make something such as a cake or a meal
2 something that forms a part of something else together with other things

inhabit *verb*
inhabits, inhabiting, inhabited
to live in a place *The North Pole is inhabited by polar bears.*

inhabitant *noun* inhabitants
1 a person who lives somewhere such as a town or country *a city of 10 million inhabitants*
2 an animal that lives in a particular place such as the jungle or forest

inhale *verb*
inhales, inhaling, inhaled
1 to take air into your lungs through your mouth and nose *Inhale before you speak.*
2 to take something such as smoke or medicine into your lungs

SYNONYM to breathe in

inhaler *noun* inhalers
a tube with a medicine inside that you inhale to make you feel better, for example if you have asthma

inherent *adjective*
existing as a natural or permanent part of something *There are dangers inherent in the sport of motor racing.* **inherently** *adverb*

inherit *verb*
inherits, inheriting, inherited
1 to receive something such as a house or money from someone who has died
2 to be born with the same special quality as one of your parents or grandparents *Lewis inherited his mother's blue eyes.*

inheritance *noun* inheritances
something you inherit from someone who has died

inhibited *adjective*
1 not relaxed enough to behave in the normal way
2 too embarrassed to show your feelings or to say or do something

inhibition *noun* inhibitions
a feeling of being too embarrassed to show your feelings or to say or do something

inhospitable *adjective*
1 not friendly towards someone who comes to visit
2 not providing good conditions for something or someone to live and grow *Mount Everest is a very inhospitable place.*
inhospitably *adverb*

inhuman *adjective*
1 extremely cruel *inhuman treatment*
2 not human in any normal way *inhuman strength*

inhumane ['in-hyoo-mayn'] *adjective*
causing pain and suffering to people or animals **inhumanely** *adverb*

inhumanity *noun*
extremely cruel behaviour

initial *noun* initials
1 the first letter of your name, especially your first name, for example J. Smith
2 your initials are the first letters of all of your names *Someone carved their initials JS into the desk.*

initial *adjective*
happening or coming first or at the beginning *My initial feeling was surprise. What's the initial letter of the word 'hat'?*

initial *verb*
initials, initialling, initialled
to write your initials on something such as a document

initially *adverb*
at the beginning

initiate ['in-ish-ee-ayt'] *verb*
initiates, initiating, initiated
1 to start something or make it happen
2 to accept someone into a group, usually with a special ceremony
3 to introduce someone to a particular skill or activity

initiation *noun*

237

initiative – inquiry

initiative ['in-ish-er-tiv'] *noun*
1 the power to start things and get them done on your own and to make your own decisions about them *Seema is full of initiative. Try and show a bit more initiative.*
2 the first action that someone takes towards getting something done *Ethan took the initiative in organising a new team.*
3 (*plural* **initiatives**) an action towards solving a problem

inject *verb*
injects, injecting, injected
to put a medicine or another substance into someone's body using a special needle *Anaya has to inject herself every day because she has diabetes. The nurse injected me with the flu vaccine.*

ORIGIN from Latin *injectus* 'thrown in' (from *in-* 'in' and *jacere* 'to throw')

injection *noun* **injections**
when someone such as a nurse or doctor puts a medicine into your body with a special needle

injure *verb*
injures, injuring, injured
to cause pain to a person or animal by doing something bad to a part of their body, for example breaking a bone or cutting the skin *Dad has injured his back again. Are you injured?*

SYNONYM to hurt

injury *noun* **injuries**
something bad done to a person's or animal's body that causes pain, for example because of an accident or attack

injustice *noun*
1 when people treat other people unfairly *We must fight injustice in the world.*
2 (*plural* **injustices**) a situation in which someone is treated unfairly *My parents suffered many injustices in their home country.*

ink *noun* **inks**
a black or coloured liquid used for writing, printing or drawing

ORIGIN from Latin *encaustum* (Greek *enkauston*) 'purple or red ink', used for example by Roman emperors to sign documents

inkjet printer *noun* **inkjet printers**
a type of electronic printer that prints using tiny dots of ink

inkling *noun* **inklings**
a very slight idea that something might be true or might happen *Mum didn't have any inkling she would get such a lovely present.*

inky *adjective* **inkier, inkiest**
if something is inky, it has ink marks on it or is covered with ink *inky fingers*

inland *adjective & adverb*
in or towards the inner part of a country and away from the sea

in-laws *noun plural*
the parents (or other relatives) of someone's husband or wife

inlet *noun* **inlets**
a long strip of water that goes into the land from a sea or lake

inmate *noun* **inmates**
someone who is locked up in a place such as a prison

inn *noun* **inns**
1 a pub with rooms for people to stay the night, usually in the countryside
2 used in the names of hotels *Holiday Inn*

inner *adjective*
1 inside something or close to the centre of it *an inner pocket; inner London*

ANTONYM outer

2 secret or hidden *an inner meaning; my inner feelings*
3 the inner city is an area near the centre of a big town. Sometimes the buildings are old and not looked after and some of the people living there are poor and have difficult lives. *an inner-city school*

innermost *adjective*
1 closest to the centre of something
2 the most secret or hidden *my innermost thoughts*

innings *noun* **innings**
a period in a game of cricket during which a player or team does the batting (hitting the ball)

innkeeper *noun* **innkeepers**
a person in charge of an inn, especially in the past

innocence *noun*
1 when someone has done nothing wrong *She stood up in court and proclaimed her innocence* (said she was innocent).

ANTONYM guilt

2 when someone doesn't know anything about the unpleasant or evil side of life

innocent *adjective*
1 if someone is innocent, they have not committed any crime or done anything wrong

ANTONYM guilty

2 not meant to harm anyone *an innocent remark; an innocent gesture*
3 not knowing anything about the unpleasant or evil side of life *an innocent child*

SIMILES 'as innocent as a lamb' and 'as innocent as a baby' mean very innocent (sense 3)

innocently *adverb*
1 without doing anything wrong *Some children were playing innocently in the street.*
2 pretending to know nothing about a situation or pretending you have done nothing wrong *'Did I throw the ball at the window?' he asked innocently.*

innocuous *adjective*
completely harmless

innovate *verb*
innovates, innovating, innovated
to produce ideas for creating new and original things or equipment **innovator** *noun*

innovation *noun*
1 (*plural* **innovations**) something new and original that someone creates, such as a piece of equipment or a way of doing something
2 the skill and imagination to produce new and original things and ideas

innovative ['in-er-ver-tiv' or 'in-ov-er-tiv'] *adjective*
1 new and original *innovative designs*
2 having the skill and imagination to produce new and original things and ideas
innovatively *adverb*

innumerable *adjective*
too many to be counted

inoculate *verb*
inoculates, inoculating, inoculated
to protect someone against an illness by giving them a weak form of it, usually with an injection *Have you been inoculated against measles?* **inoculation** *noun*

inoffensive *adjective*
harmless and not likely to upset anyone *He's a quiet and inoffensive sort of person. It was an inoffensive remark.*

inpatient *noun* **inpatients**
someone who stays in a hospital while they are having their treatment

input *noun*
1 something such as hard work, ideas or information that someone puts into an activity *My teacher thanked me for my input into the project.*
2 information put into a computer
compare: output
3 (*plural* **inputs**) the place on a computer for connecting a piece of equipment such as a microphone or scanner. The equipment sends information to the computer through the input.

input *verb*
inputs, inputting, input
to put information into a computer, for example using a keyboard or microphone
compare: output

inquest *noun* **inquests**
an event organised by an official such as a judge to find out the exact cause of someone's death

inquire *verb*
inquires, inquiring, inquired
1 to ask about something *He inquired as to whether we wanted to go with him.*
2 to inquire into something is to try to find out all the facts about it

LANGUAGE EXTRA sense 1 is also spelt *enquire*

inquiry *noun* **inquiries**
1 a question someone asks to get information about something *The police are making inquiries* (asking questions).
2 when an official such as a judge examines something such as an accident or crime to try to find out the facts about it

LANGUAGE EXTRA sense 1 is also spelt *enquiry*

inquisitive *adjective*
1 asking lots of questions, for example because you want to learn about different things
2 asking too many questions because you are more interested in something or someone than you should be, for example when someone wants to keep something private
inquisitively *adverb* **inquisitiveness** *noun*

ins and outs *noun plural*
all the small details about something such as a subject or situation

insane *adjective*
1 completely stupid or crazy
2 (old-fashioned) having an illness that affects the way you think and behave
3 to drive someone insane is to make them angry

SYNONYM mad

insanely *adverb*
in a way that is extreme and not sensible *insanely jealous*

insanitary *adjective*
dirty and likely to make you ill *insanitary conditions*

insanity *noun*
1 completely stupid or crazy behaviour that often causes harm or serious problems
2 (old-fashioned) when someone has an illness that affects the way they think and behave

SYNONYM madness

inscribe *verb*
inscribes, inscribing, inscribed
1 to cut a letter or word into the surface of something *The name of our school was inscribed on the trophy.*
2 to write something in a book, usually at the front, for example to honour someone *Our names were inscribed in the yearbook.*

inscription *noun* inscriptions
1 a word or words cut into the surface of something such as a monument or coin
2 words written in a book, usually at the front, for example to honour someone

insect *noun* insects
1 a very small creature with six legs, a body divided into three parts and often with wings. Ants, flies and butterflies are insects.
2 any very small creature that looks similar to an insect

ORIGIN from Latin *insectum* 'cut up' or 'divided' (from *insectare* 'to cut up')

insecticide *noun* insecticides
a chemical for killing insects

insecure *adjective*
1 not having good feelings about yourself and often feeling afraid or worried
2 not safe or not protected *The windows are insecure. Your browser is insecure.*
3 not steady or fixed to a place *The ladder is very insecure.*
insecurely *adverb*

insecurity *noun*
when someone doesn't have good feelings about themselves and often feels afraid or worried

insensitive *adjective*
1 if someone is insensitive, they show no understanding of other people's feelings and do not realise that they are upsetting them
2 also used about something that someone does or says *insensitive words*
insensitively *adverb* **insensitivity** *noun*

inseparable *adjective*
1 if two or more people are inseparable, they are very good friends and spend most of their time together
2 if things such as facts or ideas are inseparable, they are very closely connected and cannot be considered separately

inseparably *adverb*
if things are inseparably linked, they are very closely connected and cannot be considered separately

insert *verb*
inserts, inserting, inserted
1 to put something into something else
2 to add a piece of text, an image or number into a computer file such as a document or spreadsheet *Press Control V to insert the missing text.*

SYNONYM for sense 2: to paste

insertion *noun*
1 the action of inserting something
2 (plural **insertions**) something added, for example to a document or spreadsheet

inside *preposition & adverb*
1 in or into something and usually surrounded by it *My sandwiches are inside my lunchbox. Mum called me and I went inside* (into the house). *Look inside* (for example in the room or box).
2 if something such as a piece of clothing is inside out, it is the wrong way round because the inside part is where the outside part should be
3 if someone knows something inside out, they know everything about it

inside *adjective*
on the inside of something *an inside pocket*

inside *noun* insides
1 the part of something surrounded by something else (such as sides or walls) or the part of something towards the middle of it *the inside of a box; the inside of an apple*
2 the part of something that faces inwards or towards the back *I have a scratch on the inside of my arm.*
3 a person's or animal's insides are the organs inside their body, especially those around the stomach

insight *noun* insights
1 an insight into something or someone is an understanding of them, or it is something that allows you to learn from them
2 if someone has insight, they are able to understand people and situations very well

insignia *noun* insignia
a badge or sign that shows what official group someone belongs to or what rank they have *royal insignia*

insignificant *adjective*
1 not very important *He's an insignificant character in the book.*
2 not very big *an insignificant amount of money*

insignificance *noun*

insincere *adjective*
1 if someone is insincere, they do not mean what they say
2 used about feelings, actions or words that do not show what someone really feels *an insincere apology*
insincerely *adverb* **insincerity** *noun*

insist *verb*
insists, insisting, insisted
to say something very strongly or lots of times because you really want someone to believe it or something to happen *I insist I didn't do it. Dad insisted that I go to the doctor. I insist on inviting Granddad to my party.*

insistent *adjective*
saying very strongly or lots of times that something is true or must happen *Cathy wanted an ice cream – she was quite insistent.* **insistence** *noun*

insolent *adjective*
very rude and not showing respect to someone **insolence** *noun* **insolently** *adverb*

insoluble ['in-sol-yoo-berl'] *adjective*
1 impossible to solve *an insoluble problem*
2 an insoluble substance is one that does not dissolve in a liquid

insomnia *noun*
a medical problem that makes it difficult for someone to sleep

ORIGIN from Latin *insomnis* 'sleepless' (from *in-* 'not' and *somnus* 'sleep')

inspect *verb*
inspects, inspecting, inspected
1 to examine something carefully, for example to check that it is in good condition or to get information about it
2 to visit a place such as a school or restaurant to check that the people who work there are doing what they should do

inspection *noun*
1 the action of examining something carefully
2 (plural **inspections**) a visit to a place to check that the people who work there are doing what they should do

inspector *noun* inspectors
1 someone whose job is to make an inspection *a school inspector*
2 a police officer above a sergeant and below a chief inspector

inspiration *noun* inspirations
1 an idea for doing something or a feeling of wanting to do it
2 someone or something that gives you an idea for doing something or makes you want to do it

inspire *verb*
inspires, inspiring, inspired
1 to give someone a feeling of wanting to do something *Our teacher inspired the whole class to read Dickens.*
2 to give someone a particular feeling *My mum inspired a love of music in the whole family.*
3 to give someone an idea for doing something such as writing a book or making a drawing *Many writers have been inspired by Shakespeare.*

instability–intact

instability *noun*
when something such as a situation keeps changing in a way that causes lots of problems

install *verb*
installs, installing, installed
1 to connect a piece of equipment such as a cooker or dishwasher so that it is ready to be used
2 to put a program or piece of software onto a computer so that you can use it
3 to officially put someone into an important job *Mr Shaw was installed as the new head teacher.*

installation *noun*
1 when something is installed such as a piece of equipment or a computer program
2 (*plural* **installations**) a piece of art made up of different objects and including things such as sound, light or movement to create a particular effect

instalment *noun* instalments
1 a regular amount of money that someone pays when they buy something. It is one part of the total cost of something. Paying for something in instalments means that the total cost doesn't have to be paid at the same time.
2 one of the parts that something such as a story or TV programme is divided into. The parts are connected to each other, for example they deal with the same story or with the same subject, but they appear or are shown separately over a period of time.

instance *noun* instances
1 something that happens that is one of a number of things of the same kind *I searched the text for every instance of the word 'honeycomb'.*

> SYNONYM example

2 **for instance** used when mentioning something as an example

> SYNONYM for example

instant *adjective*
1 used about something that happens or is done at once without any waiting *Charlie took an instant dislike to the new teacher.*
2 instant food or drink can be made very quickly by adding hot water *instant coffee*

instant *noun* instants
1 a very short period of time, for example lasting a second or a few seconds *For an instant I thought you were my dad.*

> SYNONYM moment

2 instant messaging is a way of communicating with someone over the internet using messages that are sent and received immediately
3 **this instant** at once without any waiting *Come here this instant!*

instantaneous *adjective*
used about something that happens or is done at once without any waiting
instantaneously *adverb*

> SYNONYM instant

instantly *adverb*
right now without any waiting

> SYNONYMS immediately, at once

240

instead *adverb*
used for talking about something else, for example when the first thing mentioned is not done, used or wanted, or when the first person mentioned does not do, use or want something *I don't want a pear – please give me an apple instead. Jake couldn't go to the party so I went instead. I went instead of him.*

> ORIGIN from Middle English *in stede* 'in place'

instep *noun* insteps
the middle part of the foot, which is slightly curved

instil *verb*
instils, instilling, instilled
to put an idea or feeling into someone's mind by telling them about it often and over a long period of time

instinct *noun* instincts
1 a way of behaving in which a person or animal does something without thinking because of a quality they are born with *A cat's instinct is to chase a mouse.*
2 the skill to know what to do in a particular situation without thinking *When I saw the fire my instinct was to run.*

instinctive *adjective*
done without thinking because of a quality you are born with or a particular skill *Running away was an instinctive reaction.*

instinctively *adverb*
without having to think about something *I knew instinctively that something had gone wrong.*

institute *noun* institutes
1 an organisation where people study something
2 the buildings an institute uses

institution *noun* institutions
1 a large organisation, for example a university, bank or prison
2 a place where people are looked after for a long time, such as a hospital or children's home
3 something that is important in a particular society and has existed for a long time, or a way of organising things that has become important in a particular society *Sport, the family and the pub are three popular institutions in Britain.*

instruct *verb*
instructs, instructing, instructed
1 to tell someone to do something
2 to teach someone something or show them how to do something

instruction *noun*
1 (*plural* **instructions**) something that someone tells you to do
2 the teaching of a skill or subject
3 instructions are information about how to do or use something *The cooking instructions are on the packet.*

instructive *adjective*
giving useful information

> SYNONYM informative

instrument *noun* instruments
1 an object that you play to make musical sounds, for example a guitar, clarinet or drum
2 a tool for doing scientific or medical work *a surgical instrument*
3 a piece of equipment for measuring something such as speed or temperature *The pilot of a plane must check lots of instruments.*
4 an instrument panel is a board where all the instruments are, used for example by a pilot or captain for controlling a plane or ship

instrumental *adjective*
1 instrumental music uses instruments only and no singing
2 helping to make something happen *My teacher was instrumental in entering me for a scholarship.*

insufficient *adjective*
not enough *We had insufficient time to do the homework.* **insufficiently** *adverb*

insulate *verb*
insulates, insulating, insulated
to cover something with a material that stops heat, sound or cold getting in or out, or stops electrical currents passing through
insulation *noun*

insulator *noun* insulators
something that does not allow electricity or heat to pass through it *Wood and plastic are good insulators.*

insulin ['in-syoo-lin'] *noun*
a chemical produced in the body that controls how much sugar there is in the blood. If someone doesn't have enough insulin, there is too much sugar in their blood and they get diabetes.

insult ['in-sult'] *verb*
insults, insulting, insulted
1 to say something rude or unpleasant to someone or about them
2 to upset someone by doing something that does not show respect towards them

insult ['in-sult'] *noun* insults
1 something rude or unpleasant that you say to someone or about them
2 something that upsets someone because it does not show respect towards them

insulting *adjective*
rude or not showing respect towards someone *insulting words*

insurance *noun*
1 an agreement with a company that if you pay them money, they will give you money or will help you if something bad happens to you, for example if you lose or damage something or have an accident
2 the money (called a premium) that someone pays to an insurance company

insure *verb*
insures, insuring, insured
to protect something or someone by buying or providing insurance for them *Is your smartphone insured?*

> LANGUAGE EXTRA be careful not to confuse *insure* with *ensure* (make sure something happens)

intact *adjective*
not damaged, or without any parts missing *The plane hit the water but survived intact.*

intake – interest

intake *noun*
1 the amount of food or drink taken into the body
2 the number of students accepted by a school or university

integer ['in-ti-jer'] *noun* **integers**
in maths, an integer is a whole number (such as 0, 1, 2, 25) and not a fraction or decimal

integral ['in-tig-rerl'] *adjective*
forming a necessary and important part of something *The library is an integral part of the school.*

integrate *verb*
integrates, integrating, integrated
1 to mix with other people in a group *The new boy is having trouble integrating.*
2 to get people to mix with others in a group and become a part of it
3 to get one or more things to become a part of something bigger, for example so that the whole of it is more successful *The pictures are well integrated into the book.*
integration *noun*

integrity ['in-teg-ri-tee'] *noun*
the special quality of always behaving very well and honestly so that people respect you

intellect *noun* **intellects**
the power of your mind to think in an intelligent way

intellectual *adjective*
1 connected with the mind and its power to think in an intelligent way
2 if someone is intellectual, they like to use their mind, for example by studying serious subjects such as science or literature
intellectually *adverb*

intellectual *noun* **intellectuals**
an intellectual person

intelligence *noun*
1 the power to use your mind, learn and understand things quickly and make good judgements
2 secret information, for example about an enemy or foreign government

intelligent *adjective*
1 if you're intelligent, you're good at using your mind, learning and understanding things quickly and making good judgements
2 showing that you're good at using your mind *an intelligent question*
intelligently *adverb*

intelligible *adjective*
if something such as a word or answer is intelligible, it is clear enough for you to understand it *Her email was barely intelligible.* **intelligibility** *noun*

intelligibly *adverb*
if you speak or write intelligibly, people can understand you easily

intend *verb*
intends, intending, intended
1 if you intend to do something, you have thought about it and decided you're going to do it *I'm intending to go to Kareem's party tomorrow.*

SYNONYM to plan

2 to want something or to have a plan for something or someone *I didn't intend you to go there by yourself.*

3 to give your words or actions a particular meaning *That was intended as a joke.*
4 to say, write, do or make something for a particular person or reason *The letter was intended for me.*

intense *adjective*
1 very strong or great *the intense cold of the Antarctic*
2 if someone is intense, they concentrate very hard and look very serious or they show strong feelings

intensely *adverb*
1 very strongly or very much *I think Holly dislikes me intensely.*
2 very *intensely competitive*
3 in a serious way or in a way that shows strong feelings *He looked at me intensely.*

intensify *verb*
intensifies, intensifying, intensified
to increase by making something stronger or more or by becoming stronger or more *The police intensified their efforts to find the missing boy. The fighting between the two countries intensified.* **intensification** *noun*

intensity *noun*
1 the quality of being very strong *We were surprised by the intensity of the storm.*

SYNONYM strength

2 the quality of being very serious or showing strong feelings *The author spoke with intensity about her novel.*

intensive *adjective*
1 very careful and needing a lot of effort *an intensive search*
2 needing a lot of teaching over a short period *I did an intensive course to learn Spanish.*
intensively *adverb*

intensive care *noun*
the part of a hospital that gives special medical care to people who are badly hurt or seriously ill

intent *adjective*
1 if you are intent on doing something, you really want to do it and nothing will stop you

SYNONYM determined

2 paying a lot of attention to something *There was an intent look on his face.*

intent *noun*
what someone intends to do *Spending so long on my homework was not my intent.*

intention *noun* **intentions**
1 what someone has decided they're going to do

SYNONYM plan

2 if someone has good intentions, the things that they want to do are good

intentional *adjective*
not happening by chance but done on purpose *I knocked over the glass but it wasn't intentional.*

SYNONYM deliberate

intentionally *adverb*
to do something intentionally is to do it because you want to

SYNONYM deliberately

intently *adverb*
with a lot of attention *The whole class was listening intently.*

inter- *prefix*
between things or people *international; intercity train*

interact *verb*
interacts, interacting, interacted
1 if two or more people interact, they mix with each other, exchange information and influence each other
2 if you interact with something such as a computer program or TV show, you communicate with it or take part in it by exchanging information with it
3 if things such as different chemicals interact, they change each other in some way when they are put together

interaction *noun* **interactions**
1 the activity of interacting, for example with other people
2 the changes that happen when things such as different chemicals are put together

interactive *adjective*
used about something you communicate with or take part in by exchanging information, such as a computer program (for example by giving instructions to it), a TV show (for example by using your remote control or by phoning in) or a museum event (for example by pressing buttons on exhibits) **interactively** *adverb*

intercept *verb*
intercepts, intercepting, intercepted
to stop someone or something before they reach a particular place **interception** *noun*

interchange *noun* **interchanges**
a place where two or more roads are connected so that you can change from one road to another *a motorway interchange*

interchangeable *adjective*
if two things are interchangeable, you can put one thing in the place of the other without making any difference *The words 'wonderful' and 'fantastic' are often interchangeable.*

intercity *adjective*
used about a train or bus that goes from one big town to another without stopping many times

intercom *noun* **intercoms**
a piece of equipment that people use for speaking to each other over short distances, for example in different parts of a building or aircraft

interconnected *adjective*
if things such as problems, facts or events are interconnected, they are closely connected with each other

interest *noun*
1 a feeling or quality that makes you want to know more about something or someone or to take part in something *Thomas shows a lot of interest in football. York has lots of places of interest.*
2 (*plural* **interests**) something you like doing, for example swimming, reading or playing music

SYNONYM for sense 2: hobby

interest–intersect

3 regular money that you pay to a bank as the cost of borrowing money from them, or regular money that a bank pays you if you save money with them

interest *verb*
interests, interesting, interested
1 if something or someone interests you, or if you're interested in them, you want to know more about them
2 if something or someone interests you, they keep your attention, for example because they are unusual, full of new ideas or tell you things you don't know *The lesson about King Henry VIII really interested me.*
3 to interest someone in something is to make them want to know more about it or take part in it *The head teacher tried to interest us in playing a musical instrument.*

interested *adjective*
1 wanting to know more about something *I'm interested to know what you think.*
2 wanting to do or have something *I have an extra ice cream – are you interested?*

interesting *adjective*
1 if something or someone is interesting, you want to know more about them *What you say sounds very interesting.*
2 also used about something or someone that keeps your attention, for example because they are unusual or different, full of new or important ideas or tell you things that you don't know *I've read an interesting book about dinosaurs. Megan wore an interesting outfit to the Halloween party.*

interestingly *adverb*
1 used when giving information that you think is interesting or unusual *Interestingly, my dad is our head teacher's cousin.*
2 in a way that keeps people's attention *Our teacher spoke interestingly about the Vikings.*

interface *noun* **interfaces**
1 a connection between a person and a computer *This version of the browser has a new user interface.*
2 a connection between two pieces of computer hardware or software

interfere *verb*
interferes, interfering, interfered
1 to try to change some part of something or take part in it even though it has nothing to do with you *Stop interfering in my plans.*
2 to stop something from happening in the way that it should or to get in the way of something *You can watch TV as long as it doesn't interfere with your homework.*

interference *noun*
1 when someone interferes in something
2 unusual noise or electronic signals that stop you from getting a good picture or sound, for example on a TV or on the radio

interior *noun* **interiors**
the inside of something such as a car or building

ANTONYM **exterior**

interior *adjective*
inside *an interior wall*

ANTONYM **exterior**

interjection *noun* **interjections**
a word or words used for showing a feeling such as pain ('ouch') or surprise ('oh dear'), when meeting someone ('hi') or saying goodbye ('cheerio'), or for expressing unusual noises ('shh', 'oink'). Interjections are often followed by an exclamation mark ('ouch!').

ORIGIN from Latin *interiectionem* 'throwing between' (from *inter-* 'between' and *iacere* 'to throw')

interlock *verb*
interlocks, interlocking, interlocked
if things interlock, they fit into each other *The pieces of a jigsaw puzzle interlock.*

interlude *noun* **interludes**
1 a short period of time between two events
2 a short break, for example during a play, concert or film

SYNONYM **interval**

intermediate *adjective*
1 coming in between two places, levels or stages *an intermediate point on the map*
2 at a level of study between high and low *an intermediate course in Italian*
3 an intermediate student is one who studies a subject at a level between high and low

interminable ['in-terr-min-er-berl'] *adjective*
going on for a very long time or never stopping

SYNONYM **endless**

intermission *noun* **intermissions**
a short break during a film, play, concert or opera

SYNONYM **interval**

intermittent *adjective*
1 stopping and then starting again *intermittent rain; an intermittent sound*
2 happening sometimes but not all the time *an intermittent problem*
intermittently *adverb*

intern ['in-terrn'] *noun* **interns**
a student or someone who has recently completed their studies, who works in a job for a short time to get experience but doesn't get paid

intern ['in-terrn'] *verb*
interns, interning, interned
to lock someone up, for example in a prison camp during a war, because they have the same nationality as your enemy or you don't like their political opinions
internment *noun*

internal *adjective*
existing or happening inside something or inside the body *an internal wall; an internal injury* **internally** *adverb*

international *adjective*
1 connected with different countries *an international organisation*
2 between different countries *an international football match*

internationally *adverb*
in different countries *He's an internationally famous footballer.*

internet *noun*
1 the internet is a system that connects millions of computers to each other all over the world and allows people to receive and share information, for example by using websites or email
2 an internet café is a café or shop with computers where you pay to use the internet

LANGUAGE EXTRA also spelt *Internet*

ORIGIN from Latin *inter-* 'between' or 'among' and *network* 'group of connected computers'

interplanetary *adjective*
between planets *interplanetary travel*

Interpol *noun*
an international organisation that helps the police in different countries to catch criminals
short for: International Police

interpret *verb*
interprets, interpreting, interpreted
1 to translate someone's words into another language while they are speaking
2 to explain what something means
3 to understand the meaning of something in a particular way

interpretation *noun* **interpretations**
an explanation of what something means

interpreter *noun* **interpreters**
a person who translates someone's words into another language while they are speaking

interrogate *verb*
interrogates, interrogating, interrogated
to ask someone lots of questions, usually over a long period of time, to get as much information as possible *The police interrogated the criminal for hours.*
interrogation *noun* **interrogator** *noun*

interrogative *noun* **interrogatives**
in grammar, a word such as 'what' or 'when' that is used for asking a question

interrupt *verb*
interrupts, interrupting, interrupted
1 if you interrupt someone, you stop them while they're talking or doing something
2 if something or someone interrupts something, they make it stop happening *The rain interrupted playtime. We interrupted our holidays because Granddad was ill.*

ORIGIN from Latin *interruptus* 'broken apart' (from *inter-* 'between' or 'among' and *rumpere* 'to break')

interruption *noun* **interruptions**
1 something that someone says or does that stops someone talking or doing something
2 when someone or something stops something happening *It rained all day without interruption.*

intersect *verb*
intersects, intersecting, intersected
1 if things such as lines or roads intersect, they cross each other

2 if something intersects something else, it crosses or divides it *This line intersects the circle at two places.*

> ORIGIN from Latin *intersectus* 'cut into parts' (from *inter-* 'between' or 'among' and *secare* 'to cut')

intersection *noun* **intersections**
1 a place where roads join or cross each other
2 a place, for example on a mathematical diagram such as a graph, where lines cross each other, or on a Venn diagram where circles cross each other

interval *noun* **intervals**
1 a short period of time between two events
2 a short break, for example between the first and second parts of a play, concert or film
3 **at intervals** happening or done at different times or places, usually with a regular amount of time or space in between *There were lamp-posts placed at intervals along the street.*

intervene *verb*
intervenes, intervening, intervened
1 to do something to change a bad situation, for example to stop it from continuing *Our teacher had to intervene in the fight between the two boys.*
2 to come between two events *Two years intervened until I saw him again.*
3 to happen in a way that interrupts something *My great-granddad didn't go to university because the war intervened.*
intervention *noun*

interview *noun* **interviews**
a meeting at which someone asks you questions, for example to find out things about you or to talk about your ideas *My mum had an interview for a new job* (to find out if she was suitable).

interview *verb*
interviews, interviewing, interviewed
to ask someone questions in an interview

interviewer *noun* **interviewers**
someone who asks you questions, for example in a television or radio interview

intestine *noun* **intestines**
1 your intestines are the tubes inside your body that carry food from the stomach to the anus (the place where it comes out of your body). They are also called your bowels.
2 your small intestine is the part of your body made up of tubes where food goes after passing through your stomach. It is the place where nutrients (substances needed to grow and stay healthy) are moved into your blood.
3 your large intestine is the large tube from the small intestine to the anus. It is the place where water is removed from food and where food is changed into solid waste.

intimacy *noun*
1 a close friendship between people
2 the private quality of something such as a thought
3 the friendly quality of something such as a place or atmosphere

intimate *adjective*
1 used about friends who like each other very much or about things connected with them *She has one or two intimate friends. They have an intimate friendship.*
2 friendly in a way that makes you feel comfortable and relaxed (often used about small things or places) *It's a small family guesthouse with an intimate atmosphere.*
3 private or secret *He never talked about his intimate thoughts. The book described the intimate details of the film star's life.*
4 complete and including lots of details *an intimate knowledge of something*

intimately *adverb*
1 very strongly *These two ideas are intimately connected.*
2 extremely well *Our teacher knows Edward Lear's poems intimately.*
3 in a private or secret way *She wrote intimately in her diary.*

intimidate *verb*
intimidates, intimidating, intimidated
1 to frighten someone by telling them you will do bad things to them if they don't do what you want
2 to make someone feel nervous
intimidation *noun*

intimidating *adjective*
1 making you feel nervous *Rohan's first day at school was a bit intimidating.*
2 making you feel frightened *The bully ran up to me – he looked very intimidating.*

into *preposition*
1 used for showing where something or someone goes to or is moved to *I fell into the hole. Throw this into the box.*

> SYNONYM **in**

2 used for showing a change to a different type of thing *The pumpkin was turned into a coach. Translate 'good' into French.*
3 used for showing a movement in which something or someone hits something or someone else *I walked into the door.*
4 used in maths for showing division *Two into six goes three times.*
5 used when finding out about something *an investigation into the murder*
6 used for showing something that goes on for a long time *We stayed up talking late into the night.*
7 used for showing that someone has a lot of interest in something *My sister's really into painting.*

intolerable *adjective*
if something is intolerable, it is so bad that you just can't deal with it *an intolerable situation* **intolerably** *adverb*

intolerant *adjective*
if someone is intolerant, they do not like or understand people whose ideas or behaviour are different from their own or they do not accept other people's faults
intolerance *noun*

intonation *noun* **intonations**
the way your voice rises (becomes higher) or falls (becomes lower) as you speak. For example, your voice rises when you ask a question.

intoxicate *verb*
intoxicates, intoxicating, intoxicated
to make someone drunk **intoxication** *noun*

intoxicated *adjective*
if someone is intoxicated, they are drunk

intransitive *adjective*
in grammar, an intransitive verb is one used on its own without a direct object (a noun or pronoun that receives the direct action of the verb) and a transitive verb is one used with a direct object. For example, 'look' is intransitive ('Ethan looked all around') and 'bring' is transitive ('Bring me my glasses'). Many verbs are both intransitive and transitive. For example, 'change' is intransitive in 'Joel has changed' but transitive in 'Riya has changed her phone'.

intrepid *adjective*
not afraid to face danger or very difficult things **intrepidly** *adverb*

intricacy *noun*
1 the quality of something that has lots of small or complicated parts
2 the intricacies of something are its complicated details

intricate *adjective*
1 done or made with lots of small or complicated parts *an intricate pattern*
2 with lots of different parts and difficult to deal with or understand *an intricate problem*; *The play has an intricate plot.*
intricately *adverb*

intrigue ['in-treeg'] *noun* **intrigues**
the making of secret plans to harm someone

intrigue ['in-treeg'] *verb*
intrigues, intriguing, intrigued
if something or someone intrigues you, you want to know more about them, for example because there is something unusual about them

intriguing *adjective*
interesting, for example because of something unusual

introduce *verb*
introduces, introducing, introduced
1 to tell someone's name to another person or to other people when they meet for the first time *The teacher introduced Nisha to the class. I introduced myself* (told someone or other people my name).
2 to put something into use or make something happen for the first time *The head teacher has introduced new rules about the school uniform.*
3 to say a few words about someone such as a speaker or musician before he or she begins speaking or performing, or about something such as a play or TV programme before it begins
4 if a person or book introduces you to a subject or activity, they get you to start to learn about it *Children are introduced to maths from an early age.*

introduction *noun* **introductions**
1 when something is put into use for the first time
2 when you tell someone's name to another person when they meet for the first time
3 the first part of something
4 something written at the beginning of a book that tells you what it is about

introductory – invitation

5 something such as a book that gets you to start to learn about a subject or activity

introductory *adjective*
1 getting you to start to learn about something *an introductory course in Polish*
2 coming at the beginning of something *an introductory chapter*

intrude *verb*
intrudes, intruding, intruded
to go into a situation in which you are not supposed to be *I hope I'm not intruding on your meeting.* **intrusion** *noun*

intruder *noun* intruders
1 someone such as a burglar who goes into a building to steal things
2 someone who goes into a situation in which they are not supposed to be

intuition ['in-tyoo-ish-ern'] *noun* intuitions
a feeling that gives you the power to know something without having to learn it or think about it

intuitive ['in-tyoo-er-tiv'] *adjective*
1 if someone is intuitive, they use intuition
2 if something such as a feeling or idea is intuitive, you know that it is true without having to think about it

Inuit ['in-yoo-it' or 'in-oo-it'] *noun*
Inuit or Inuits
a member of a group of people who live in the cold areas of North America and Greenland

inundate *verb*
inundates, inundating, inundated
1 if someone is inundated with things (for example phone calls, complaints or presents), they get so many of them that they have trouble dealing with them all
2 to cover an area with water

> **SYNONYM** for sense 2: to flood

inundation *noun*

invade *verb*
invades, invading, invaded
1 to attack a country in order to take control of it *The Normans invaded Britain in 1066.*
2 to go into a place in large numbers *Edinburgh is invaded by tourists every August.*

invader *noun* invaders
1 an army or country that attacks a country in order to take control of it
2 invaders are the soldiers who invade a country

invalid ['in-ver-lid'] *noun* invalids
someone who is ill or disabled and usually needs to be looked after

invalid ['in-val-id'] *adjective*
if a document such as a ticket or passport is invalid, it cannot be used because there is something wrong with it

invaluable *adjective*
extremely useful and important

> **LANGUAGE EXTRA** *invaluable* means 'of great value' and is not the opposite of *valuable*

invariable *adjective*
if something is invariable, it never changes but always stays the same

invariably *adjective*
always *The school bus is invariably late.*

invasion *noun* invasions
1 a time when an army or country attacks a country in order to take control of it *In history we are learning about the Norman invasion of 1066.*
2 when a large number of people go into a place *There was an invasion of Christmas shoppers in town today.*

invent *verb*
invents, inventing, invented
1 to be the first person to think of something and usually to make it *Alexander Graham Bell invented the telephone.*
2 to think of something such as an excuse or story that is not true

invention *noun*
1 (*plural* inventions) something such as a machine or tool that someone has thought of or made for the first time
2 the action of inventing something
3 (*plural* inventions) something such as an excuse or story that is not true

inventive *adjective*
good at thinking of new ideas or new ways to do things

inventor *noun* inventors
1 someone who invents something
2 someone whose job is to invent things

inverse *adjective*
opposite to something else *In maths, addition is the inverse operation of subtraction.*

inverse *noun*
if something is the inverse of something else, it is the opposite of it *In maths, multiplication is the inverse of division.*

inversely *adverb*
in the opposite way to something else

invert *verb*
inverts, inverting, inverted
1 to put something upside down
2 to change the order of two things *If you invert the word order of 'he is', you make the question 'is he?'*

inversion *noun*

invertebrate ['in-verr-tib-rert' or 'in-verr-tib-rayt'] *noun* invertebrates
an animal without a backbone, for example a worm or fly
compare: **vertebrate**

inverted commas *noun plural*
punctuation marks like this ' ' or this " "

> **LANGUAGE EXTRA** you use either single ' ' or double " " *inverted commas* around words to show they are the exact words that someone is using ('I'm hungry,' said Ben. "What time is it?" asked Jo).
> Inverted commas can also be used around titles, for example of books, films or paintings (*We're reading 'War Horse'. "Guernica" is a famous painting by Picasso*).
> You also use them to show that words have a meaning that is slightly different from their usual meaning (*If I were you, I wouldn't eat the 'food' she put on your plate*).
> Inverted commas can also be called *quotation marks* or *speech marks*.

invest *verb*
invests, investing, invested
1 to put money into a business or bank in order to try to make more money
2 to spend money on something to make it better *The government should invest more in education.*
3 if you invest in something that you really need, you buy it even though it costs a lot of money *My parents have invested in a new car.*

investor *noun*

investigate *verb*
investigates, investigating, investigated
1 to find out (or try to find out) as much information as possible in order to learn the truth about something or someone *The police are investigating what happened.*
2 to find out (or try to find out) about something scientifically, for example how it works or what it is made of

investigator *noun*

investigation *noun* investigations
1 a search to find out the truth about something or someone *He's under investigation by the police* (they are investigating him).
2 a search to find out scientific information

investment *noun* investments
1 the activity of putting money into a business or bank to try to make more money
2 money invested in a business or bank
3 something that someone invests their money in *Education is a good investment for the future.*

invigilate *verb*
invigilates, invigilating, invigilated
to watch students while they are doing an exam, for example to make sure they don't cheat **invigilation** *noun* **invigilator** *noun*

invigorate *verb*
invigorates, invigorating, invigorated
to give someone more energy or make them feel wide awake

invigorating *adjective*
if something is invigorating, such as a walk or cup of coffee, it gives you more energy or makes you feel wide awake

invincible *adjective*
1 if a person or team is invincible, you cannot beat them in a game

> **SYNONYM** unbeatable

2 if something such as an army or country is invincible, you cannot win a battle or war against them because they are too strong

invisible *adjective*
if something or someone is invisible, they cannot be seen **invisibility** *noun*

invisibly *adverb*
in such a way that something cannot be seen *These changes are happening almost invisibly.*

invitation *noun* invitations
written or spoken words politely asking someone to come somewhere or do something

invite – irrational

invite *verb*
invites, inviting, invited
1 to politely ask someone to come somewhere such as to a party, your home or the cinema
2 to politely ask someone to do something *The head teacher invited new parents to visit the school.*
3 to behave in a way that makes it likely that something bad will happen *If you don't punish their bad behaviour, you're just inviting trouble.*

inviting *adjective*
if something is inviting, it is very pleasant or attractive, for example in a way that makes you want to be near it, in it or on it or to want to try it *The beach looked rather inviting. That looks like a nice inviting cup of tea.* **invitingly** *adverb*

invoice *noun* **invoices**
a piece of paper that shows the amount of money you must pay for something, for example something that you've bought or work that someone has done for you

involuntary *adjective*
1 if something such as a movement is involuntary, it is done without thinking because it is something you cannot control
2 not done on purpose

involve *verb*
involves, involving, involved
1 if something involves something, that thing is a part of it *Passing the test involves a lot of hard work.*
2 if you involve someone, you allow them to take part in something *Our teacher involves us all in classroom activities.*
3 to be connected with something in some way *There was an accident involving a lorry and a bus. A lorry and a bus were involved in an accident. I don't want to be involved in your problems.*

involved *adjective*
complicated and difficult to understand *The film was so involved I didn't know what was happening.*

involvement *noun*
taking part in something *We're happy about the team's involvement in the championship.*

inward *adjective*
1 towards the inside of something *an inward flow*

ANTONYM **outward**

2 used about something inside you such as a thought or feeling that you do not show to other people

inwardly *adverb*
in your mind or thoughts

ANTONYM **outwardly**

inwards *adverb*
towards the inside of something

LANGUAGE EXTRA you can also say *inward*

ANTONYM **outwards**

iodine ['**eye**-er-dyne' or '**eye**-er-deen'] *noun*
a dark blue chemical element that is used in medicine to kill germs

ion ['eye-on'] *noun* **ions**
an atom with an electrical charge, formed when an electron is added or taken away from it

-ion *suffix*
used for making nouns that show an action, quality or the way something is *organisation; condition; attraction*

iPad ['i' rhymes with 'eye'] *noun* **iPads** (trademark)
a small computer connected to the internet that you can carry around with you. It uses a screen that you touch to make programs work.

iPhone ['i' rhymes with 'eye'] *noun* **iPhones** (trademark)
a mobile phone that can connect to the internet, play music and take photos

iPod ['i' rhymes with 'eye'] *noun* **iPods** (trademark)
a small piece of electronic equipment for listening to music using headphones

IQ *noun* **IQs**
the level of someone's intelligence that is measured by a special test *My sister has a very high IQ* (she's very intelligent).
short for: intelligence quotient

ir- *prefix*
used with words starting with 'r' for showing the opposite meaning, for example 'irregular' means not regular

Iran *noun*
a country in South-West Asia
Iranian *adjective & noun*

Iraq *noun*
a country in South-West Asia
Iraqi *adjective & noun*

irate ['i' rhymes with 'eye'] *adjective*
very angry

Ireland *noun*
1 a country in North-West Europe
2 an island in North-West Europe that is a part of the British Isles. Great Britain and the small islands around the coast form the rest of the British Isles.

iris *noun* **irises**
1 the coloured part of the eye. It forms the large circle around the small black circle in the middle, called the pupil.
2 a tall plant with long pointed leaves and large blue, yellow or white flowers. Irises often grow in wet places such as near rivers.

ORIGIN from Latin and Greek *iris* 'rainbow'

Irish *adjective*
connected with Ireland

Irish *noun*
1 a language spoken by some people in Ireland
2 the Irish are people from Ireland

Irishman *noun* **Irishmen**
a man from Ireland

Irishwoman *noun* **Irishwomen**
a woman from Ireland

iron *noun*
1 a very strong hard metal, used with carbon for making steel. Iron is magnetic. *an iron bar; an iron bridge*
2 the tiny amount of this material that is found in food and in the blood. The body needs iron to stay healthy. *iron tablets*
3 (*plural* **irons**) a small electric tool with a flat part underneath. It is heated up and pressed onto clothes to make them smooth.
4 the Iron Age is the period after the Bronze Age around 1000 BC, when people used iron to make tools and weapons
5 the Iron Curtain is the name that was used for the border between the communist countries of Eastern Europe and the rest of Europe from the Second World War up to the 1980s

iron *verb*
irons, ironing, ironed
1 to make clothes smooth with an iron
2 if you iron out problems or difficulties, you deal with them successfully

ironic or **ironical** ['eye-**ron**-ik', 'eye-**ron**-ik-erl'] *adjective*
1 if someone is ironic, they say something that is the opposite of or different from what they really mean, often to be funny
2 also used about what someone says or does *an ironic remark*
3 if something that happens or that you do is ironic, it is unusual or funny because it is the opposite of or different from what you expect

ironically *adverb*
1 in a way that shows that you mean the opposite of or something different from what you say
2 used about a situation that is unusual or funny because something happens that is different from or the opposite of what you expect *Ironically, I got the best mark for the homework that I spent the least time on!*

ironing *noun*
1 the activity of making clothes smooth with an iron
2 clothes that are waiting to be ironed or that you've just ironed
3 an ironing board is a narrow table with a soft top that is used for ironing clothes on

ironmonger *noun* **ironmongers**
an old-fashioned word for someone who sells tools and equipment for the house and garden

irony ['**eye**-rer-nee'] *noun*
1 a way of speaking that shows you really mean the opposite of what you are saying or something different from what you are saying. People often speak this way to be funny. For example, if you say 'That was clever' when someone breaks a cup, you are using irony.
compare: **sarcasm**
2 (*plural* **ironies**) an unusual or funny situation in which something unexpected happens or the opposite of what is expected is true *The irony is that the older he gets, the sillier he becomes!*

ORIGIN from Greek *eironeia* 'pretending not to know'

irrational [ir-**rash**-ern-erl'] *adjective*
not reasonable or logical
irrationally *adverb*

irregular–IT

irregular *adjective*
1 having different shapes, sizes or patterns, or with parts that have different shapes, sizes or patterns *an irregular shape; irregular teeth*
2 not smooth or straight *an irregular surface; an irregular line*
3 not happening with equal periods or spaces in between *He often eats at irregular times.*
4 unusual or not following the usual rules *irregular behaviour*
5 not following the usual patterns of grammar *'To go' is an irregular verb. The plural of 'child' is irregular* (it's 'children', not 'childs').
irregularly *adverb*

irregularity *noun* **irregularities**
1 when something is irregular *the irregularity of his eating times*
2 irregularities are things that are wrong because someone has not followed the usual rules *There were irregularities in the way the football team was selected.*

irrelevant ['i-**rel**-erv-ernt'] *adjective*
not useful or important in a particular situation, for example because of having nothing to do with what someone is saying *These facts are irrelevant.* **irrelevance** *noun*

irresistible *adjective*
1 so strong that something cannot be stopped *He felt an irresistible desire to laugh.*
2 if something or someone is irresistible, they are so pleasant or attractive that you cannot stop yourself from liking them *The chocolates were irresistible.*

irresponsible *adjective*
1 if someone is irresponsible, they are not sensible and do not think about what might happen because of the things that they do
2 also used about what someone does or says *irresponsible behaviour*
irresponsibility *noun*

irresponsibly *adverb*
to act or behave irresponsibly is to behave badly without thinking about what might happen because of your behaviour

irreverent *adjective*
not showing any respect towards people, things or religion **irreverence** *noun*
irreverently *adverb*

irreversible *adjective*
1 if a situation is irreversible, it cannot be changed to how it was before
2 in science, an irreversible change is one that cannot be made to go backwards, such as cooking food or burning something

irrigate *verb*
irrigates, irrigating, irrigated
to bring water to land so that crops and plants can grow, for example by digging long narrow holes along the sides of fields for the water to flow along **irrigation** *noun*

irritable *adjective*
angry, or getting angry very easily
irritability *noun* **irritably** *adverb*

irritant *noun* **irritants**
a substance that causes a painful or sore feeling in a part of the body

irritate *verb*
irritates, irritating, irritated
1 to make someone angry
2 to make a part of your body slightly painful or sore *This cream is irritating my skin.*

irritating *adjective*
making you angry, for example because someone does something you don't like *an irritating habit*

irritation *noun*
1 feeling angry
2 (plural **irritations**) something that makes you feel angry
3 (plural **irritations**) a painful or sore feeling in a part of the body

is
third person singular present tense of **be**

-ise *suffix*
used for making verbs that mean to become, make or put *organise; finalise; hospitalise*

-ish *suffix*
1 used with adjectives to give them the weaker meaning of 'slightly' or 'not completely but still quite a lot' *Grandma is oldish* (old but not very old). *The sky was reddish* (slightly red).
2 used with numbers to give them the meaning of 'not exactly but about' *I got home from school around fourish.*

Islam ['**iz**-lahm' or '**iss**-lahm'] *noun*
the religion of Muslims

Islamic ['iz-**lam**-ik'] *adjective*
connected with Islam

island ['**eye**-lernd'] *noun* **islands**
1 a piece of land surrounded by water
2 an island or traffic island is a small piece of pavement in the middle of a road where you can stand safely while crossing the road

islander ['**eye**-lern-der'] *noun* **islanders**
someone who lives on an island

isle [rhymes with 'pile'] *noun* **isles**
another word for an island, used for example in names such as the British Isles

Isle of Man *noun*
an island in the British Isles between England and Ireland

isn't
short for 'is not'

isobar ['**eye**-ser-bah'] *noun* **isobars**
a line on a weather map that connects all the places that have the same air pressure

isolate *verb*
isolates, isolating, isolated
1 to keep someone away from other people *The children with chickenpox were isolated until they got better.*
2 to separate something from something else or from everything else *Many houses were isolated by the flood water.*

isolated *adjective*
1 an isolated place is one that is a long way from all other places *They live in an isolated house in the middle of the forest.*
2 kept away from other people *Prisoners who behave badly are isolated.*
3 happening only once *an isolated event*

4 feeling lonely and unhappy, for example because you have no friends or no-one to talk to

isolation *noun*
1 when someone feels lonely and unhappy, for example because they have no friends or no-one to talk to
2 being isolated from other places or people

isosceles ['eye-**sos**-er-leez'] *adjective*
in an isosceles triangle, two of the three sides are the same length and two of the three angles are equal
compare: **equilateral** and **scalene**

isotope ['**eye**-ser-tohp'] *noun* **isotopes**
a form of a chemical element with the same number of protons in its nucleus (central part) as other forms of the same element but a different number of neutrons. The forms have the same chemical properties (qualities) as each other but different physical ones.

ISP ['**eye**-ess-pee'] *noun* **ISPs**
a company that provides customers with a connection to the internet
short for: internet service provider

Israel *noun*
a country in South-West Asia
Israeli *adjective & noun*

issue *noun* **issues**
1 a subject or problem that people talk about *This is an important issue for our school.*
2 all the copies of a newspaper or magazine that are ready at the same time, for example they are printed or you can read them online *The June issue has just come out.*
3 one copy of a newspaper or magazine *Dad was reading today's issue of 'The Guardian'.*
4 when something is given out or provided officially *I bought the new stamps on the day of issue.*

issue *verb*
issues, issuing, issued
1 to officially give something out or provide people with something *Your passport will be issued next week.*
2 if something issues from somewhere, it comes out from that place *There was smoke issuing from the burning engine.*

> ORIGIN from Latin *exire* 'to go out'
> (*ex-* 'out' and *ire* 'to go')

isthmus ['**is**-mers'] *noun* **isthmuses**
a narrow piece of land with water on each side that connects two larger pieces of land

it *pronoun*
1 a thing, place or animal that someone has mentioned before, for example in an earlier sentence *It's on the table. Did you hear it? What shall I do with it?*
2 used when talking about a situation *It's true. She found it very strange.*
3 used when talking about the weather, time, day of the week or date *It was snowing. It's two o'clock. It's Saturday.*

IT *noun*
1 the study of computers and the activity of using them *My brother is studying IT.*

246

Italian–jackdaw

2 connected with computers *IT skills*; *the IT department*
short for: **information technology**

Italian *adjective*
connected with Italy or the Italian language

Italian *noun*
1 the language people speak in Italy
2 (*plural* **Italians**) someone from Italy

italic *adjective*
written in letters that lean over to the right *This is italic.*

italics *noun plural*
letters in a book or written document that lean over to the right compared to ordinary letters *This sentence is in italics.*

Italy *noun*
a country in Southern Europe

itch *verb*
itches, itching, itched
1 if something itches (for example your skin, a part of your body or a piece of clothing), you get a feeling that makes you want to scratch your skin (rub it, usually with your nails) *My leg is itching badly.*
2 (informal) if you're itching to do something, you want to do it very much

itch *noun* **itches**
1 a feeling on your skin that makes you want to scratch it
2 (informal) if you have an itch to do something, you want to do it very much

itchy *adjective* **itchier, itchiest**
if you feel itchy or if something such as your skin, your arm or a piece of clothing is itchy, you get a feeling that makes you want to scratch your skin **itchiness** *noun*

it'd
short for 'it had' or 'it would'

item *noun* **items**
1 a thing that is one of a group of things, for example on a list *There are lots of items on the menu.*
2 a piece of news, for example on TV or in a newspaper
3 a single piece of something such as clothing, furniture or jewellery *an item of clothing*

> ORIGIN from Latin *item* 'in the same way', used for example to introduce each new thing on a list

itinerary ['eye-tin-er-rer-ree'] *noun* **itineraries**
a plan that someone makes of a journey, including the route to take and places to visit

-itis ['eye-ters'] *suffix*
used in the names of illnesses and infections *tonsillitis*

it'll
short for 'it will'

its *adjective*
belonging to a thing, place or animal that someone has just mentioned *I love London and its museums.*

it's
short for 'it is' or 'it has'

itself *pronoun*
1 used when a thing or animal that someone has just mentioned does an action and that action is also directed back onto it *The laptop switches itself off. The dog hurt itself.*
2 used for giving special importance to a word *Manchester itself is a lovely town.*
3 **by itself** without any other thing, animal or person being there, or without the help of anything or anyone else *There was a computer by itself in a corner. The rabbit got out of the hutch by itself.*

ITV *noun*
a British organisation that broadcasts television programmes paid for by advertisements. It is also the name of the channels operated by ITV. *There's a good programme on ITV1.*
short for: **Independent Television**

I've
short for 'I have'

ivory *noun*
1 the hard yellow-white bone that forms the tusks of an elephant
2 a yellow-white colour

ivory *adjective*
having the yellow-white colour of the tusks of an elephant

ivy *noun*
a climbing plant that grows along the ground and up walls and trees. Its leaves stay green all year round.

-ize *suffix*
used for making verbs that mean to become, make or put *organize*; *finalize*; *hospitalize*

Jj

> ORIGIN the letter J started life as the same shape as the capital I, representing an arm together with its hand. In Latin a little hook was often added to an I – making it look like a J – when letter I stood at the beginning or end of a word. This was done to make the letter look more attractive. In the 16th century, separate sounds were given to I and J in languages such as Italian and French. Letter J entered English around the time of the Norman Conquest (1066), mainly to show words borrowed from French. At that time, J already had the sound that it has today. By the middle of the 17th century, J was being used in the spelling of other words too, not just words that came from French.

jab *verb*
jabs, jabbing, jabbed
1 to push something pointed into something or someone *She jabbed her elbow into me.*
2 to hit someone with something pointed *She jabbed me with her elbow.*

jab *noun* **jabs**
1 a hit with something pointed *I felt a jab in the back.*
2 an injection to stop you from getting ill *a flu jab*

jabber *verb*
jabbers, jabbering, jabbered
to talk quickly or without stopping, often in a way that people cannot understand **jabber** *noun*

jack *noun* **jacks**
1 a piece of equipment for lifting something very heavy off the ground, for example a car in order to change a tyre
2 in a game of cards, a jack is a card with a picture of a young man on it. Its value is less than the cards with pictures of a king or queen on them. *the jack of clubs*
3 an electrical plug with a metal piece for connecting things such as headphones and speakers, for example to a computer
4 a hole, for example in the side of a laptop, that a jack fits into *a headphone jack*

jack *verb*
jacks, jacking, jacked
to jack up something heavy is to use a jack for lifting it off the ground

jackal *noun* **jackals**
a wild animal that looks like a dog. Jackals have long legs and pointed ears and live in Africa and Asia.

jackass *noun* **jackasses**
1 an informal word for a very stupid person
2 a male donkey

jackdaw *noun* **jackdaws**
a bird like a small crow with a black and grey body. Jackdaws sometimes steal shiny objects, which they take to their nests.

jacket–jazz

jacket *noun* jackets
1 a short coat for wearing indoors or outdoors. It covers the body from the shoulder to the waist or hip.
2 a book jacket is a paper cover for a book
3 a jacket potato or a potato in its jacket is one that is cooked whole in an oven without being peeled first

Jack Frost *noun*
an imaginary person who brings the ice and the freezing weather of winter

jack-in-the-box *noun* jack-in-the-boxes
a toy consisting of a box with the figure of a little person inside that jumps up on a spring when the box is opened

jack-knife *verb*
jack-knifes, jack-knifing, jack-knifed
if a lorry with two connected parts jack-knifes, it goes out of control because one part (the driver's cab) swings round towards the other part (the trailer)

LANGUAGE EXTRA also spelt *jackknife*

jackpot *noun* jackpots
1 a large amount of money that is the biggest prize in a competition or game
2 **to hit the jackpot** to be very lucky and successful, for example by winning the biggest amount of money in a competition or getting lots of money for something

jacks *noun*
a game for children in which you pick up small objects called jacks while bouncing and catching a ball

Jacuzzi ['jer-koo-zee'] *noun* Jacuzzis
(trademark)
a large bath for relaxing in. It has streams of hot water that flow in through small holes and produce lots of bubbles.

LANGUAGE EXTRA also spelt *jacuzzi*

ORIGIN named after Candido *Jacuzzi*, an Italian American who invented it in the mid-20th century

jade *noun*
a hard green stone often used for making jewellery or ornaments

jaded *adjective*
if someone is jaded, they are no longer interested in something because they have had too much of it or because they are very tired

jagged ['jag-id'] *adjective*
1 if something such as an edge, line or shape is jagged, it has lots of pointed parts
2 if an object is jagged, it has edges with lots of pointed parts that can make it look as if it is broken *a jagged rock*
jaggedly *adverb*

jaguar *noun* jaguars
a big wild animal of the cat family. It looks like a large leopard and has yellow fur with black spots on it. Jaguars live mainly in Central and South America.

jail *noun* jails
a place where criminals are kept to punish them

SYNONYM prison

jail *verb*
jails, jailing, jailed
to put someone in prison

jailer *noun* jailers
someone in charge of a prison or a group of prisoners

Jain *noun* Jains
someone who follows the religion of Jainism

Jainism *noun*
an important religion of India. It includes many different beliefs, for example not harming any person or living creature and always speaking the truth.

jam *noun* jams
1 a sweet sticky food made from boiling fruit with sugar. People eat it on bread or in cakes.
2 a jam or traffic jam is a long line of vehicles close together that cannot move or can only move slowly
3 a situation in which there are so many people or things close together that moving is very difficult
4 a situation in which something is stuck in a piece of equipment and stopping it from working *There's a paper jam in the printer.*
5 a difficult situation *Alfie has got himself into a jam.*

jam *verb*
jams, jamming, jammed
1 if someone or something jams something, that thing cannot move or work *A few sheets of paper have jammed the printer. My keys got jammed in the lock.*
2 if something jams, it cannot move or work *The drawer has jammed.*
3 used about crowds of people that fill a place *Hundreds of people jammed the museum to see the exhibition. Trafalgar Square was jammed with young people.*
4 to press or push something using a lot of strength *I jammed all my school things into my bag.*

Jamaica *noun*
an island and country in the West Indies
Jamaican *adjective & noun*

jamboree ['jam-ber-ree'] *noun* jamborees
1 an event organised for many people as a celebration
2 a meeting of Scouts or Guides

jammy *adjective* jammier, jammiest
1 covered with jam
2 (slang) lucky, especially because something good has happened to you that people think you don't deserve

jam-packed *adjective*
completely full or crowded

jangle *verb*
jangles, jangling, jangled
to make the noise of small metal objects hitting each other *My keys were jangling in my pocket.* **jangle** *noun*

janitor *noun* janitors
someone who looks after a building

SYNONYM caretaker

January *noun*
the first month of the year, between December and February. January has 31 days.

ORIGIN from Latin *Ianuarius*, named after *Ianus* 'Janus', the god of gates and doors, because January opens like a door to the start of the year

Japan *noun*
a country in East Asia

Japanese *adjective*
connected with Japan or the Japanese language

Japanese *noun*
1 the language people speak in Japan
2 the Japanese are people from Japan

jar *noun* jars
1 a container with a wide opening at the top for keeping food in. It is usually made of glass and has the shape of a cylinder (tube with flat ends shaped like circles).
2 something in a jar *The boys have eaten the whole jar of jam.*

jar *verb*
jars, jarring, jarred
1 if something jars with something else, the two things do not look right together
2 if something such as a sound or word jars, it produces an unpleasant feeling *That screeching sound is beginning to jar on my ears.*

jargon *noun*
special words used by a particular group of people, for example people who do the same kind of work or have the same type of life *computer jargon; medical jargon*

jarring *adjective*
if something is jarring, it is very unpleasant, and often has something unexpected about it *jarring colours; a jarring sound*

jaundice ['jorn-diss'] *noun*
an illness in which someone's skin becomes slightly yellow

jaunt ['jornt'] *jaunts* *noun*
a short journey someone makes for pleasure

jaunty ['jorn-tee'] *adjective*
jauntier, jauntiest
1 if someone is jaunty, they are happy, full of energy and feeling confident
2 also used about what a person says or does *We walked along with jaunty steps.*
jauntily *adverb* **jauntiness** *noun*

javelin *noun* javelins
a long pointed stick for throwing in a sports competition

jaw *noun* jaws
1 the lower part of your face that includes your bottom teeth and your chin *She punched me on the jaw.*
2 your jaws are the two bones in your mouth that your teeth are fixed into. The bones are called the upper jaw and lower jaw.
3 the jaws of an animal are its mouth, especially when it is big, strong and frightening *The crocodile opened its jaws.*
4 the jaws of something such as a tool or machine are the parts that open and close like a mouth in order to hold or pick up something

jay *noun* jays
a medium-sized brightly coloured bird that lives in Europe, North America and Asia

jazz *noun*
a style of music with a strong regular pattern of sounds. It was started by black American musicians at the beginning of the 20th century.

jazz up–jive

jazz up verb (informal)
jazzes up, jazzing up, jazzed up
if you jazz something up, you make it more lively, interesting or colourful

jazzy adjective jazzier, jazziest
very colourful

jealous adjective
1 if you're jealous or if you're jealous of someone, you're unhappy because you want what someone else has or you want to do what they do *I'm jealous of my sister's good looks* (I wish I had her good looks).

SYNONYM envious

2 unhappy because you think someone loves the person that you love or because you think the person that you love loves someone else

jealously adverb
in a way that shows that you're jealous of someone

jealousy noun
the bad feeling of wishing you could have what someone else has or do what they do

SYNONYM envy

jeans noun plural
trousers usually made from strong blue cotton cloth called denim. Jeans are worn in relaxed situations and are comfortable to wear.

ORIGIN from French *jean*, a type of cotton cloth first made in the Italian city of Genoa (Old French *Janne*)

jeep noun jeeps (trademark)
a small powerful car for driving over rough ground, often used by the army

jeer verb
jeers, jeering, jeered
if you jeer someone or jeer at them, you shout rude and insulting things because you don't like them *The crowd jeered him* (or *at him*) *as he tried to speak. When the footballer missed the goal, we all jeered.*

jeers noun plural
rude and insulting things shouted at someone you don't like

jellied adjective
used about fish or meat that is covered in a jelly made from its own juices

jelly noun jellies
1 a soft sweet food that shakes when you move it and is usually eaten as a dessert. It is made from fruit juice, sugar and a substance called gelatine that makes it thick.
2 a thin jam that does not contain pieces of fruit
3 any soft substance that shakes when you move it

jellyfish noun jellyfish
a sea animal with a round body like jelly that you can see through

jerk noun jerks
1 a short sudden movement
2 an informal word for a very stupid person

jerk verb
jerks, jerking, jerked
1 to move or to move something with a short sudden movement *Mum started the car and it jerked forward.*
2 to pull or push something with a short sudden movement

jerky adjective jerkier, jerkiest
1 short and sudden *a jerky movement*
2 with lots of short and sudden movements *a jerky ride*

jerkily adverb

jersey noun jerseys
1 a piece of knitted clothing that you wear over a shirt or T-shirt to keep the top of your body and arms warm

SYNONYMS sweater, jumper

2 a shirt that people wear for playing sports *a football jersey*

ORIGIN from *jersey*, a type of knitted cloth that was made in Jersey, one of the Channel Islands

jest noun jests
1 something you say or do to be funny

SYNONYM joke

2 if you say something in jest, you don't mean it but say it to be funny

jest verb
jests, jesting, jested
to say something you don't mean, just to be funny

jester noun jesters
a person who in the past was employed by someone such as a king or queen to make people laugh by telling jokes or doing silly things

Jesus Christ noun
the founder of Christianity (the Christian religion). He is also known as Jesus or Christ.

jet noun jets
1 a strong stream of liquid or gas that comes out of a small hole
2 a small hole in a piece of equipment that a stream of liquid or gas comes out of
3 a plane with a very powerful engine called a jet engine
4 a jet engine is a very powerful engine used in a plane. It moves the plane forward by forcing out a jet of hot gas from behind.
5 jet lag is the feeling of being tired when you travel a long way by plane to a place where the time is different

jet verb
jets, jetting, jetted
to fly somewhere by plane *My brother's jetting off to America.*

jet-black adjective
completely black *jet-black hair*

ORIGIN from *jet*, a hard black stone used for making jewels and ornaments

jet-propelled adjective
if something is jet-propelled, it is moved forward by a jet engine that forces out a jet of hot gas from behind

jetty noun jetties
a narrow structure built out into the sea or a river from the edge of the land. It is used as a place for boats to stop at.

Jew noun Jews
someone who believes in Judaism or who belongs to a group of people whose religion has been Judaism since ancient times

jewel noun jewels
1 a beautiful and valuable stone, such as a diamond, used mainly for decorating things you wear, for example rings and necklaces
2 something made with jewels such as a ring or necklace

jeweller noun jewellers
someone who sells or makes jewellery

jewellery noun
objects such as rings, necklaces or brooches. Jewellery is often made from gold or silver and decorated with valuable stones such as diamonds.

Jewish adjective
connected with Jews or with the religion of Jews

jibe noun jibes
words that someone says in order to insult someone or make them look stupid

LANGUAGE EXTRA also spelt *gibe*

jiffy noun
an informal way of saying a very short time *I'll be back in a jiffy.*

Jiffy bag noun Jiffy bags (trademark)
a large thick envelope for sending by post something that needs to be protected

jig noun jigs
1 a traditional dance in Great Britain and Ireland with a lot of jumping steps *an Irish jig*
2 the music that is played for a jig

jiggle verb
jiggles, jiggling, jiggled
to move or shake something with quick and tiny movements, for example to get something to work or to get something loose

jigsaw noun jigsaws
a jigsaw or jigsaw puzzle is a picture that has been cut up into lots of tiny pieces with different shapes. You have to fit the pieces together to make the whole picture appear.

jingle verb
jingles, jingling, jingled
to make the gentle ringing sound of small metal objects knocking against each other *The little bells were jingling on Father Christmas's hat.*

jingle noun jingles
1 a gentle ringing sound
2 a short simple tune, often with words, used for advertising something, for example on TV or on the radio

jitters noun plural
if you have the jitters, you feel very nervous before an important event such as a school test **jittery** adjective

jive noun jives
a type of fast dance for young people that was popular in the 1940s and 1950s

249

job–journal

job noun jobs
1 regular work that someone does to get money *My dad's looking for a job.*
2 a piece of work that needs to be done or has just been done *Your first job is to clean your room. You've done a fantastic job.*
3 something someone has to do because it's their responsibility to do it *It's not my job to look after the baby.*
4 when a lot of effort is needed to do something *I had a job getting to school in the snow.*

SYNONYMS trouble, problem

5 an action that a piece of equipment does, for example a printer *There are a few more print jobs in the queue.*
6 if you say that it's a good job something happens, you mean it's lucky something happens *It's a good job you didn't fall.*
7 if you say that something is just the job, you mean it's perfect for that particular situation

Jobcentre noun
a UK government office where people looking for work get information and help in finding a job

jockey noun jockeys
someone who rides a horse in a race

jocular adjective
1 funny *a jocular poem*
2 used about someone who likes to make jokes

jodhpurs ['jod-perz'] noun plural
trousers that you wear when you ride a horse. They fit tightly to the legs from the knee to the ankle.

ORIGIN from the city of *Jodhpur* in North-West India, where jodhpurs were worn as part of the traditional way of dressing

joey noun joeys
a young kangaroo or wallaby

jog verb
jogs, jogging, jogged
1 to push, knock or shake someone or something very slightly, for example with your arm *He jogged my elbow and I spilt my tea.*
2 to run slowly for exercise
3 if you jog someone's memory, you help them remember something

jog noun jogs
a slow run that you do for exercise *I went for a jog around the playground.*

jogger noun joggers
1 someone who goes jogging
2 joggers are soft trousers that you wear for doing exercises such as jogging

jogging noun
the activity of running slowly for exercise *My sister goes jogging every morning.*

join verb
joins, joining, joined
1 to join things or to join something to something else is to put them together, usually so they are fixed *We joined the paper chains and hung them from the ceiling. Everybody join hands!* (hold each other's hands)
2 if something joins something else, the two things come together *This is where the river joins the sea.*
3 if you join something such as a group, you become part of it *Two new boys joined the class. I joined the queue.*
4 if you join someone, you do an activity with them *Come and join us at our table* (for example to eat something with us). *I'll join you later* (meet you in order to do an activity).
5 to go to someone *Go and join Ava in the corridor.*
6 to go to something such as a road, train or ship in order to travel on it *We joined the train at Dover.*
7 if you join in something, you take part in it *Everyone joined in the song. Can I join in?*

join noun joins
a place where things are joined together, for example pieces of wallpaper (by gluing) or clothing (by sewing)

joiner noun joiners
someone who makes the wooden parts of buildings, for example doors, stairs, windows and shelves **joinery** noun

joint noun joints
1 a place in the body where two bones meet *the elbow joint*
2 a large piece of meat for cooking in an oven, or one that has been cooked in an oven
3 a place where things are joined together, for example pipes or pieces of wood

joint adjective
done or shared by two or more people or groups *a joint decision; a joint bank account*

jointly adverb
used about two or more people or groups doing something together *The two countries are working jointly on the project.*

joke noun jokes
1 something you say or do to make people laugh, for example a funny story or a trick *He made a joke about a dead parrot. I played a joke on my parents* (did something to trick them).
2 something or someone that is not very good and does not deserve any respect or attention *School food is a joke. My aunt thinks her new boss is a joke.*

joke verb
jokes, joking, joked
1 to say funny things
2 to say something that isn't true and that you're only saying to be funny *She joked that the cat was lost. I was only joking! Are you joking?* (Is what you're saying true?)

joker noun jokers
1 someone who likes to say or do things to make people laugh
2 in some games of cards, a joker is a card that has a picture on it of someone who looks like a clown

jokey adjective jokier, jokiest
funny or not serious

LANGUAGE EXTRA also spelt *joky*

jokingly adverb
if you say or do something jokingly, you are being funny, not serious

jolly adjective jollier, jolliest
1 happy *She was in quite a jolly mood.*
2 attractive *The room looked bright and jolly.*
jollity noun

jolly adverb (informal)
1 very *Mum says I go to a jolly good school.*
2 jolly well used for giving special importance to words in a sentence, for example when you're angry *I will jolly well go out if I want to!*

Jolly Roger noun
the Jolly Roger is a black flag with a picture of a skull and bones on it. It was used in the past on a ship belonging to pirates.

jolt noun jolts
1 a sudden strong movement *The car moved forward with a jolt.*
2 a sudden shock

jolt verb
jolts, jolting, jolted
1 to move or to move something or someone with a sudden strong movement *The train suddenly jolted. I was jolted forward when the bus stopped.*
2 to give someone a sudden shock

Jordan noun
a country in South-West Asia
Jordanian adjective & noun

jostle verb
jostles, jostling, jostled
to push roughly, for example because you are trying to get past someone *Some people jostled me as they came out of the lift. Fans jostled to get closer to the film star.*

jot verb
jots, jotting, jotted
to jot something down is to write it down quickly

jot noun
used when you mean a tiny amount *He doesn't have a jot of good sense* (he has none at all).

ORIGIN from the name of the Greek letter *iota*, the smallest letter in the Greek alphabet, corresponding to English *i*

jotter noun jotters
a small notebook

joule noun joules
in science, a joule is a unit for measuring the amount of energy used or work done

ORIGIN after the 19th-century English scientist James P. *Joule*, who studied the connection between heat and energy

journal noun journals
1 a magazine, especially one about a serious subject
2 a newspaper. (This word is used mainly in the titles of newspapers.)
3 a diary for writing down what happens to you every day

ORIGIN from Old French *jurnal* 'daily' or 'day' and Latin *diurnalis* 'daily'

journalism–jumbo

journalism *noun*
1 the work of writing, mainly about the news, for newspapers or magazines or for TV, radio or the internet
2 the business of running newspapers or magazines

journalist *noun* **journalists**
someone who writes for a newspaper or magazine or for TV, radio or the internet, mainly about the news **journalistic** *adjective*

journey *noun* **journeys**
when you travel from one place to another *The class will be going on a journey to Scotland. It's a 500-mile journey* (distance covered). *Our journey took a week.*

ORIGIN from Old French *jornee* 'day' or 'day's travel'

journey *verb*
journeys, journeying, journeyed
to travel somewhere

joust ['jowst'] *verb*
jousts, jousting, jousted
to ride on a horse while using a lance (long pole with a pointed end) to hit other people on horses. Knights jousted in medieval times, usually as a sport. **joust** *noun*

jovial *adjective*
happy and friendly **joviality** *noun*

ORIGIN from Latin *jovialis* 'connected with the planet Jupiter', because people used to think of Jupiter as a place where happiness comes from

joy *noun*
1 the feeling of being very happy
2 (plural **joys**) something that makes you feel very happy

joyful *adjective*
1 very happy
2 making you feel very happy
joyfully *adverb* **joyfulness** *noun*

joyous *adjective*
full of happiness **joyously** *adverb*
joyousness *noun*

joyride *noun* **joyrides**
if someone goes on a joyride, they go for a drive in a car that they have stolen. They usually drive fast or dangerously.
joyrider *noun* **joyriding** *noun*

joystick *noun* **joysticks**
1 a handle that you use for controlling the way things move on a computer screen, especially when playing games
2 a handle that a pilot uses for controlling the direction of a plane

jpeg ['jay-peg'] *noun* **jpegs**
the ending of a computer filename. A .jpeg file contains an image (or images) such as a photo.
short for: Joint Photographic Experts Group

LANGUAGE EXTRA also spelt *JPEG* and *jpg*

jubilant *adjective*
extremely happy, for example because of being successful or winning in a game or competition *The football fans were jubilant.*
jubilantly *adverb*

ORIGIN from Latin *jubilans* 'shouting for joy' (from *jubilum* 'wild shout')

jubilation *noun*
behaviour that shows that someone is feeling extremely happy

jubilee *noun* **jubilees**
a date people celebrate because of something important that happened on that day in an earlier year – either 25 years ago (silver jubilee), 50 years ago (golden jubilee) or 60 years ago (diamond jubilee)

Judaism *noun*
the religion of Jews based on part of the Bible and the written words of rabbis (religious leaders and teachers)

judder *verb*
judders, juddering, juddered
if something judders, it shakes with lots of small strong movements

judge *noun* **judges**
1 an important person in a court of law who decides things, for example whether someone is guilty of a crime, or who deals with disagreements between people
2 someone who decides the winner in a competition
3 someone who understands things or people and is able to make good and sensible decisions about them *Granddad is a good judge of character.*

judge *verb*
judges, judging, judged
1 to decide the winner in a competition
2 to give an opinion about something or someone *Don't judge people by their appearance.*
3 to work something out roughly, for example a distance or amount

SYNONYMS to guess, to estimate

4 to blame someone or say what you think is wrong about them *You're always judging me!*
5 to decide whether or not someone is guilty in a court of law
6 **judging by** or **judging from** used for giving the reason for something *Judging by your dirty knees, you must have fallen over.*

judgement *noun* **judgements**
1 an opinion about something or someone, usually one you have thought about carefully
2 understanding things or people and being able to make decisions about them, for example good and sensible decisions
3 being able to work something out roughly, for example a distance or amount
4 the decision of a judge in a court of law

LANGUAGE EXTRA also sometimes spelt *judgment*

judicial ['joo-**dish**-erl'] *adjective*
connected with judges or courts of law *a judicial decision*

judicious ['joo-**dish**-ers'] *adjective*
showing understanding and good judgement

judo ['**joo**-doh'] *noun*
a sport in which two people fight and throw each other to the ground

ORIGIN from Japanese *ju* and *do* 'gentle art'

jug *noun* **jugs**
1 a container for holding liquids such as water or milk. It has a handle and a lip (pointed part at the top) for pouring.
2 the liquid that is in a jug

juggernaut *noun* **juggernauts**
a very large and heavy lorry

ORIGIN from Sanskrit *Jagannatha* 'lord of the world', a name given to the Hindu god Krishna. Once a year since the 14th century, in a festival in the Indian town of Puri, an image of Krishna is carried through the town on a huge vehicle.

juggle *verb*
juggles, juggling, juggled
if someone juggles objects such as balls, they throw them up in the air, catch them as they fall down and throw them up again so that the objects are always moving

juggler *noun* **jugglers**
someone who entertains people by juggling, for example in a circus or fair

juice *noun* **juices**
1 the liquid that comes from fruit or vegetables when you squeeze them
2 a drink made from this liquid *apple juice*
3 the liquid that comes from meat when you cook it
4 the liquid in your stomach that helps you to digest food (change it into substances your body can use)

juicy *adjective* **juicier, juiciest**
1 full of juice *a juicy orange*
2 interesting and slightly shocking *juicy news*
juiciness *noun*

jukebox *noun* **jukeboxes**
a piece of equipment that plays music when you put a coin in it, used especially in the past in bars and restaurants

July *noun*
the seventh month of the year, between June and August. July has 31 days.

ORIGIN from Latin *Iulius*, named in 44 BC after the Roman general *Julius* Caesar who was born in this month

jumble *verb*
jumbles, jumbling, jumbled
if you jumble things up, you mix them up in an untidy way *The socks were all jumbled up in the drawer. In this puzzle the letters of the alphabet are jumbled up* (not in their correct order).

jumble *noun*
1 a lot of things all mixed up
2 a jumble sale is an event at which people sell old clothes and other things they don't want, for example to get money for places such as schools or hospitals

jumbo *adjective*
1 used for describing something that is bigger than other things of the same kind *a jumbo packet of crisps*
2 a jumbo jet is a very big plane that carries lots of passengers

ORIGIN from *Jumbo*, the name of an elephant that belonged to London Zoo in the 19th century. Jumbo stood 12 feet high and was eventually sold to an American circus.

jump–jut out

jump verb
jumps, jumping, jumped
1 to use your legs to push yourself off the ground and into the air
2 to push yourself from a high place (or from a place above the ground) so that you drop to the ground *The pilot jumped out of the plane. Jump down from the chair.*
3 to go over something by jumping *I jumped over the puddle. The horse jumped the fence.*
4 to move, go or get somewhere quickly *I jumped out of the way when I saw the car coming. We all jumped on the bus.*
5 to make a sudden movement with your body because you're surprised or frightened *A sudden loud noise made me jump.*
6 if something such as a price or amount jumps, it increases suddenly
7 if you jump at something such as a chance or offer, you're very happy to accept it
8 **to jump for joy** to be extremely happy
9 **to jump the queue** to go in front of people already waiting in a queue

jump noun jumps
1 a movement into the air from the ground or from a place above the ground *a parachute jump*
2 a sudden movement you make with your body because you're surprised or frightened
3 a sudden increase in something such as a price or amount

jumper noun jumpers
a piece of knitted clothing that you wear over a shirt or T-shirt to keep the top of your body and arms warm

SYNONYMS sweater, jersey

jumpsuit noun jumpsuits
a piece of clothing made in one piece that covers the body and legs and sometimes the arms

jumpy adjective jumpier, jumpiest
nervous, for example because you're frightened or you've done something wrong

junction noun junctions
1 a place where roads or railway lines join or cross each other
2 a place where you join or leave a motorway *Exit at Junction 13 for Cambridge.*

June noun
the sixth month of the year, between May and July. June has 30 days.

ORIGIN from Latin *Iunius*, named after *Juno*, the Roman goddess of women and marriage

jungle noun jungles
1 a large forest in a hot country with lots of trees and plants growing close to each other
2 a place such as a garden covered thickly with plants and weeds

ORIGIN from Hindi *jangal* 'wild land'

junior adjective
1 for or connected with young people *a junior football team*
2 connected with children who go to junior school *a junior pupil*
3 having a lower position in a job than someone else *a junior doctor*
4 a junior school is a school for children between the ages of 7 and 11

junior noun juniors
1 a young person *music lessons for juniors*
2 a child at school between the ages of 7 and 11 *Juniors have the day off.*
3 someone who has a lower position in their job than someone else
4 if you are someone's junior, you are younger than they are

juniper noun
a bush or tree with small purple fruits (called berries) that are used in cooking or for making a strong alcoholic drink called gin. It has thin pointed leaves that stay green in winter.

junk noun
1 things that are of no use and are often thrown away, for example old or broken things *Your room is full of junk. This old bed is a piece of junk.*

SYNONYM rubbish

2 things that are no good because they are of really bad quality *There's a lot of junk on TV. Your laptop is a piece of junk.*

SYNONYM rubbish

3 (plural **junks**) a Chinese sailing boat with a flat bottom and usually with square sails
4 junk food is food with lots of fat, salt and sugar in it. It is unhealthy but quick to prepare and eat.
5 junk mail is an email (or emails) or a letter (or letters) that you have not asked to receive and that you don't want, often an advertisement to buy something
6 a junk shop is one that sells used furniture and other things that do not have much value

junkyard noun junkyards
a place where people take things that they don't want, for example from their home or garden, to be recycled (used again) or thrown away

SYNONYMS rubbish dump, recycling centre

Jupiter noun
the fifth planet from the sun, after Mars and before Saturn. It is the largest planet in the solar system (group of planets going round the sun).

Jurassic adjective
connected with the period about 200 million years ago when the dinosaurs lived

juror noun jurors
a member of a jury

jury noun juries
1 a group of people chosen from ordinary members of the public to listen to a trial in a court of law and decide whether someone is guilty or not guilty
2 a group of judges who decide the winner in a competition

just adverb
1 in every way or detail *I look just like my mum.*

SYNONYM exactly

2 used when you mean a particular thing, place or person and no other *That's just what I'm looking for. You're just the person to help me with my maths.*

SYNONYM exactly

3 used for giving special importance to a word or phrase *You're just jealous! I just love ice cream!*
4 at this moment or at a particular moment *I'm just coming. Just then the phone rang.*
5 a short moment ago *Dad has just come home. What were you doing just now?*
6 only *He's just a little boy. I live just next door to the school.*
7 used about something that almost doesn't happen *We just caught the train before it left. These jeans only just fit.*
8 used about something that someone has but almost doesn't have *There's just enough food for us all.*
9 used when you mean a very short distance or time away from something *I was walking just behind him. She went home just after lunch.*

just adjective
1 reasonable or right, or treating everyone in a very good and reasonable way *a just decision; a just ruler*

SYNONYM fair

2 used about something that someone deserves *a just punishment*

justice noun
1 treating people in a way that is reasonable or right, or being treated in this way
2 the quality of being reasonable or right
3 the law by which people are judged in a court of law *The criminals must be brought to justice* (caught, judged and punished).

justifiable adjective
if something is justifiable, there is a good reason for it **justifiably** adverb

justification noun justifications
a good reason for something

justify verb
justifies, justifying, justified
1 to give or be a good reason for something *Can you justify your behaviour? Getting up late doesn't justify staying home from school.*
2 if you are justified in doing or saying something, you have a good reason for doing or saying it

justly adverb
1 in a good and reasonable way *The police officer treated everyone justly.*
2 used when talking about something that is deserved *Scotland is justly proud of its traditions.*

jute noun
a fibre that comes from the jute plant, used for making rope or cloth

jut out verb
juts out, jutting out, jutted out
if something juts out, it sticks out more than something around it or beyond an edge or surface *The pipe juts out from the wall.*

juvenile ['joo-ver-nyle'] *adjective*
1 connected with young people *a juvenile delinquent* (young person who breaks the law)
2 silly, or behaving like a silly child *juvenile behaviour*; *Charlie is so juvenile.*

juvenile ['joo-ver-nyle'] *noun* **juveniles**
a young person

K k

ORIGIN the letter K began in Egyptian hieroglyphics as the shape of a hand with fingers stretched out. This was later simplified to make a shape like a letter U (for the hand) with two upright lines in the middle (for the fingers). Just like letter K, it was made up of three parts and its name also started with a 'k' sound (*kaph* meaning 'palm of the hand'). In the Phoenician alphabet, the letter became even simpler with a number of different shapes, all of them made up of three strokes – for example a V shape with a line through the middle (showing three fingers spread out) and a similar shape with the middle line going down past the point of the V (showing the wrist). Then came a shape like a crooked K facing left. The Greeks turned this to face right and straightened it out to produce the letter K we know today.

kaftan *noun* **kaftans**
a long loose piece of clothing like a coat, often worn in the Middle East

LANGUAGE EXTRA also spelt *caftan*

kaleidoscope ['ker-lye-der-skohp'] *noun* **kaleidoscopes**
1 a toy shaped like a tube that you look through to see coloured patterns formed by pieces of glass and mirrors. The patterns change when you turn the end of the tube.
2 any pattern or situation that keeps changing

ORIGIN from Greek *kalos* 'beautiful', *eidos* 'shape' and *skopein* 'to look at'

kangaroo *noun* **kangaroos**
a large Australian animal with a long tail, two short front legs and two long back legs that it uses for jumping. A female kangaroo carries its baby in a pocket of skin called a pouch at the front of its body.

karaoke ['ka-ree-oh-kee'] *noun*
an activity in which people play the music of popular songs but without the words so that they can sing the words themselves

ORIGIN from Japanese *kara* and *oke* 'empty orchestra'. This form of entertainment started in Japan in the 20th century.

karate ['ker-ah-tee'] *noun*
a sport in which people fight using their hands, elbows, feet and legs in particular ways. Someone who does karate wears a white uniform and a coloured belt. The colour of the belt shows their level of skill.

ORIGIN from Japanese *kara* 'empty' and *te* 'bare hand'

kayak *noun* **kayaks**
a canoe (light narrow boat) for one or two people with a covering over the top. It is moved along by using a paddle (pole with a flat part at both ends).

ORIGIN from *qayak* 'small boat of skins' in a Greenland Inuit language

KB
short for **kilobyte** or **kilobytes**

kebab *noun* **kebabs**
1 a kebab or shish kebab is a food made up of small pieces of meat and vegetables cooked on a stick called a skewer

ORIGIN from Turkish *sis* 'skewer' and *kebap* 'roast meat'

2 a kebab or doner kebab is a food made up of flat pieces of cooked meat such as lamb served in pitta (oval-shaped flat bread), often with salad

ORIGIN from Turkish *doner* 'turning or spinning' and *kebap* 'roast meat'

keel *noun* **keels**
a long piece of wood or metal that runs along the middle of the bottom of a ship. It is built onto the ship's hull (the main part of the ship).

keel over *verb*
keels over, keeling over, keeled over
if someone keels over, they fall over from a standing or sitting position, often sideways

keen *adjective* **keener, keenest**
1 really wanting to do something *I'm very keen to learn to ride a bike.*

SYNONYM eager

2 really interested in something *Kareem is a keen footballer. Are you keen on chess?*
3 very strong or great *She's a good teacher and has a keen interest in her pupils.*
4 very good (used when talking about something such as hearing, eyesight or smell) *Dogs have very keen hearing. Leah has a keen eye for detail* (a skill for noticing things that are not easy to see).
5 very sharp *a keen blade*
6 a keen wind is one that is very cold
keenness *noun*

SIMILE 'as keen as mustard' means very keen (senses 1 & 2)

keenly *adverb*
1 very strongly *Josh is keenly interested in table tennis.*
2 very much *The exam results are keenly awaited.*
3 very well *Eagles can see very keenly.*

keep *verb*
keeps, keeping, kept
1 to have something for ever and not give it back or get rid of it *You can keep that pen – I've got another one.*
2 to have something and not lose it *Dad lost his job but Mum kept hers.*
3 to not use something but to have it so that you or someone else can use it in the future *I'll be home late so can you keep some dinner for me? Dad keeps his black shoes for special occasions.*

253

keep–kickoff

4 to put or leave something in its normal place when you're not using it *I keep my laptop in this drawer.*
5 to stay a particular way *We can't keep warm. Goodbye and keep well! Fish won't keep very long* (keep fresh without going bad).
6 to make something or someone stay a particular way *Keep the window open. Our teacher keeps us all busy.*
7 to make someone or something stay in a particular place *My parents kept me at home because I had the flu.*
8 to have an animal and look after it *Lots of people keep dogs.*
9 if you keep doing something (or keep on doing something), you do it lots of times or you do it without stopping *I kept asking him to sit down. Keep moving! We kept on playing in the rain.*
10 if you keep someone doing something, you make them do it, for example without stopping *She kept me talking for a long time.*
11 if you keep a promise or your word, you do what you've said you will do
12 if you keep an appointment, you meet someone at the time you've arranged
13 if someone keeps you in, they make you stay late at school or they keep you indoors
14 if someone keeps off something, they stay away from it *Keep off the grass.*
15 if the rain keeps off, it doesn't rain
16 if you keep out of a place (or keep someone out of it), you don't go into it (or you don't let someone into it) *Danger – keep out!*
17 if you keep up with someone, you move just as fast or make the same progress as they do *I walk fast – can you keep up? Holly finds it difficult to keep up in class.*
18 if you keep something up (or keep up with something), such as an activity, you don't stop doing it *Dad wants me to keep up my guitar lessons.*

keep *noun*
1 someone's keep is the cost of food, clothes and a place to live *Everyone needs to earn* (or *pay for*) *their keep.*
2 (*plural* **keeps**) the strong tower at the centre of a castle
3 **for keeps** for ever *I don't want it back – it's yours for keeps.*

keeper *noun* **keepers**
1 someone who looks after animals *a zoo-keeper*
2 someone in charge of something such as a park or lighthouse *a park keeper*
3 an informal word for a goalkeeper, for example in football

keeping *noun*
1 if something is in someone's keeping, it is being looked after safely by them

SYNONYM **safekeeping**

2 **in keeping with** used for saying that something is suitable in a particular situation

keepsake *noun* **keepsakes**
a small present someone gives you so that you will remember them

keg *noun* **kegs**
a small barrel, usually for beer. It has the shape of a cylinder (tube with flat ends shaped like circles) and is often curved outwards in the middle.

kennel *noun* **kennels**
1 a small hut for a dog to sleep in
2 **kennels** a place where dogs are looked after

kenning *noun* **kennings**
a figure of speech (expression using words in an unusual way) that uses two words to describe a noun without saying what it is, for example 'skin burner' (the sun) or 'whale road' (the sea). Kennings were first used in Icelandic and Old English poetry.

Kenya *noun*
a country in East Africa
Kenyan *adjective & noun*

kept
past tense & past participle of **keep**

kerb *noun* **kerbs**
the edge of a pavement nearest the road. It is formed by a row of stones.

kernel *noun* **kernels**
the soft part inside the shell of a nut

kestrel *noun* **kestrels**
a bird like a small falcon. It is a bird of prey that eats small animals and large insects.

ketchup *noun*
a thick red sauce made from tomatoes that you eat with food such as burgers and chips

kettle *noun* **kettles**
1 a metal or plastic container for boiling water in. It has a handle and a spout (pointed part or tube at or near the top) for pouring.
2 the water that is in a kettle

kettledrum *noun* **kettledrums**
a large metal drum shaped like a bowl, played mainly in an orchestra

key *noun* **keys**
1 a small piece of shaped metal that you put into a lock and turn, for example to open and close a door or start a car
2 a button with a letter, number or symbol on it that you press with your finger on a keyboard or keypad, for example to write something on a computer or mobile phone screen
3 a small object shaped like a tube with a handle for winding up a clockwork toy or machine or an old-fashioned clock
4 one of the long narrow bars that you press on a musical instrument such as a piano to produce a sound
5 one of the small buttons or levers that you press on a musical instrument such as a clarinet or saxophone to change the notes
6 a group of musical notes that begin with one particular note *the key of A minor*
7 something that gives an answer to something such as a mystery or code *That's the key to the whole problem.*
8 a list of things such as colours or symbols, used for example on a map or in a book. It explains what each colour or symbol means.
9 in biology, a system such as a list of questions used for helping you to see the difference between living things, for example so that you know what species (group) they belong to

key *verb*
keys, keying, keyed
if you key something in, you type it on a keyboard or keypad so that it appears somewhere such as on a computer screen

keyboard *noun* **keyboards**
1 a piece of computer equipment with keys (buttons) on it for typing things into a computer
2 the part of a musical instrument with keys (long narrow bars) on it that you press to produce a sound
3 an electronic musical instrument similar to a piano

keyhole *noun* **keyholes**
a hole, usually in a door, that you put a key into to lock or unlock the door

keypad *noun* **keypads**
1 a small keyboard, for example on a mobile phone, remote control or calculator
2 the group of keys on the right side of a computer keyboard with numbers and other symbols on them *the numeric keypad*

key ring *noun* **key rings**
a metal ring for keeping your keys on

keystroke *noun* **keystrokes**
the action of pressing a computer key

keyword *noun* **keywords**
1 a word that is of particular importance in a piece of text
2 a word that you type into a Search box on a computer

kg
short for **kilogram** or **kilograms**

khaki ['kah-kee'] *noun*
a yellowish-brown or light greenish-brown colour, often used for soldiers' uniforms

ORIGIN from Urdu *kaki* 'dusty' or 'dust-coloured'

kibbutz ['butz' rhymes with 'puts'] *noun*
kibbutzim
a community in Israel where people live and work together and often make their money by farming

kick *verb*
kicks, kicking, kicked
1 if you kick someone or something, you hit them with your foot or feet *Mohammed kicked the ball into the goal.*
2 to move your feet and legs about with a lot of energy *We were splashing and kicking in the water.*
3 if you kick someone around, you treat them very badly
4 if a football match kicks off, it starts at a particular time *The game kicked off at three o'clock.*
5 if something or someone kicks off, they start or start doing something
6 to kick someone out is to make them leave a place, group or job

SYNONYM **to throw out**

7 **to kick up a fuss** to get angry or complain about something
8 **to kick the bucket** an informal way of saying to die

kick *noun* **kicks**
1 the action of kicking someone or something *The horse gave him a kick.*
2 if someone gets a kick out of doing something, they like doing it very much

kickoff *noun* **kickoffs**
the time when a football match starts

LANGUAGE EXTRA also spelt *kick-off*

kid – kip

kid *noun* **kids**
1 an informal word for a child or young person
2 a young goat

kid *adjective* (informal)
your kid sister or brother is your younger sister or brother

kid *verb*
kids, kidding, kidded
1 to say something that isn't true, just to be funny *I was just kidding! You're kidding me!*
2 to kid someone about something is to make jokes about them in a friendly way, because of how they look or something they do *She's always kidding me about my freckles.*

kidnap *verb*
kidnaps, kidnapping, kidnapped
to take someone away using force and usually ask for money for releasing them
kidnapper *noun*

kidnapping *noun* **kidnappings**
the crime of kidnapping someone

kidney *noun* **kidneys**
one of the two small organs in the lower part of your back that take waste liquids from your blood and produce urine (waste liquid that is passed from the body). A kidney is shaped like an oval with a curve going inwards in the middle of one of the sides.

kidney bean *noun* **kidney beans**
a small dark red bean that is cooked and eaten as a vegetable. It is shaped like a kidney.

kill *verb*
kills, killing, killed
1 to make someone or something die
2 to stop something *Grandma took some medicine to kill the pain.*
3 (informal) to give someone a lot of pain *My feet are killing me.*
4 (informal) to be very angry with someone *Dad will kill you if you touch his computer!*
killer *noun*

killjoy *noun* **killjoys**
someone who spoils someone else's fun, for example by complaining or saying unpleasant things

kiln *noun* **kilns**
an oven for baking pottery and bricks to make them hard

ORIGIN from Latin *culina* 'kitchen' or 'cooking stove'

kilo *noun* **kilos**
short for kilogram

kilo- *prefix*
one thousand (used in units of measurement) *a kilometre*

kilobyte *noun* **kilobytes**
a unit for measuring the size of data on a computer. A kilobyte is equal to 1024 bytes.

LANGUAGE EXTRA be careful – the meaning is not usually 1000 bytes

kilogram *noun* **kilograms**
a unit for measuring weight in the metric system. A kilogram is equal to 1000 grams or about 2.2 pounds.

LANGUAGE EXTRA also spelt *kilogramme*

kilometre ['kil-om-it-er' or 'kil-er-mee-ter'] *noun* **kilometres**
a unit for measuring distance in the metric system. A kilometre is equal to 1000 metres or about 0.6 of a mile.

kilowatt *noun* **kilowatts**
a unit for measuring electrical power, equal to 1000 watts

kilt *noun* **kilts**
1 a kind of heavy skirt for men and boys worn in Scotland as part of the national costume. It is made of woollen cloth with a pattern called tartan (coloured stripes that cross each other to make squares and rectangles).
2 a similar skirt with a tartan pattern worn by women and girls as part of their normal clothes

kimono ['ki-moh-noh'] *noun* **kimonos**
a piece of clothing like a long loose coat with wide sleeves. Kimonos were first worn in Japan.

kin *noun*
1 all your family and relatives
2 **next of kin** the person or people most closely related to you

kind *adjective* **kinder, kindest**
1 if someone is kind, they think about other people's feelings and are very pleasant towards them and want to help them

SYNONYMS considerate, thoughtful

2 also used about someone's words, actions and appearance *She has a kind face.*
3 not causing any harm *You should be kind to animals.*
kindness *noun*

kind *noun* **kinds**
1 a group of things or people that are similar to each other and different from other groups *Pears and apples are different kinds of fruit.*

SYNONYM sort

2 used for describing or asking about what someone or something is like *What kind of person is your dad? Jack is a very sporty kind of boy.*

SYNONYM sort

3 **kind of** used when you don't want to use a word or phrase in its exact meaning because it is too strong *Your idea is kind of stupid.*

SYNONYM sort of

4 **one of a kind** used about someone or something that is so special that they are the only one of their kind *You'll never find another teacher like Ms Patel – she's one of a kind.*

kindergarten ['kin-der-gah-tern'] *noun* **kindergartens**
a school for young children under the age of five

ORIGIN from German *Kindergarten* 'garden of children' (*Kinder* 'children' and *Garten* 'garden')

kind-hearted *adjective*
very kind towards other people

kindle *verb*
kindles, kindling, kindled
1 to start a fire burning, for example by lighting paper or wood
2 to cause a feeling or idea in someone, such as love or interest *The story kindled his imagination.*

kindly *adverb*
1 in a kind way
2 used instead of 'please' for asking or telling someone to do something politely *Would you kindly stop making a noise? Kindly shut the door.*

kindly *adjective* **kindlier, kindliest**
another word for kind *a kindly old lady*
kindliness *noun*

king *noun* **kings**
1 a man who rules a country, usually because he is the son of the person who ruled the country before. He is made the ruler by having a crown put on his head in a special ceremony called a coronation. *King Henry VIII*
2 if a person or animal is the king of something, they are the best or most important one of a group or at doing a particular thing *The lion is the king of the jungle. He's the king of rock music.*
3 the most important piece in the game of chess that must be captured to win the game. A king can move in any direction on the board but only one square at a time.
4 in a game of cards, a king is a card with a picture of a king on it. It has a value less than an ace but more than a queen. *the king of spades*

kingdom *noun* **kingdoms**
1 a country ruled by a king or queen
2 a group that contains all the animals or plants in the world *the animal and plant kingdoms*

kingfisher *noun* **kingfishers**
a small blue and orange bird with a long beak that lives near water and catches fish

kingly *adjective*
connected with a king or like a king

king-size *adjective*
used for describing something that is bigger than other things of the same kind *a king-size burger*

LANGUAGE EXTRA you can also say *king-sized*

kink *noun* **kinks**
a twisted or bent part in something that should be straight, such as a wire or rope

kiosk *noun* **kiosks**
a very small building, for example in the street or a station, where people sell things such as newspapers and sweets

ORIGIN from Turkish *kiushk* 'pavilion' (garden building where people relax)

kip *noun*
a slang word for a short sleep

kip *verb*
kips, kipping, kipped
a slang way of saying to sleep *You can kip down on my floor for tonight.*

255

kipper – knock

kipper *noun* **kippers**
a herring (long silver-coloured fish) that is cut open, salted and smoked (preserved in salt and hung up in smoke)

kiss *noun* **kisses**
1 the action of kissing someone *Give Mum a kiss. I gave Dad a goodnight kiss.*
2 the action of two people kissing
3 **the kiss of life** when someone blows into someone else's mouth to try to make them start breathing again after they have stopped breathing, for example after an accident

kiss *verb*
kisses, kissing, kissed
1 if someone kisses someone, they touch them with their lips, usually on their face or lips, for example because they love them or as a greeting
2 if two people kiss, they kiss each other

kit *noun* **kits**
1 equipment or clothes needed for doing something such as a particular activity, job or sport *a first-aid kit; football kit*
2 a collection of parts that you fit together to make something *My parents bought me a model aircraft kit.*

kitchen *noun* **kitchens**
1 a room used for cooking food
2 kitchen roll is soft thick paper on a roll that is used in the kitchen, for example for cleaning surfaces

kite *noun* **kites**
1 a toy for flying in the wind made of a frame covered with paper, plastic or cloth. You pull the kite along by a long string fixed to one end.
2 a large bird like a hawk with very long wings. It is a bird of prey that eats small animals and other birds.
3 in maths, a quadrilateral (flat shape with four straight sides) that has two short sides and two longer sides. The short sides are adjacent (next to each other) and of equal length and the longer sides are also adjacent and of equal length.

kitted out *adjective*
if you are kitted out, you have all the clothes or equipment you need for doing something such as a particular activity, job or sport *Mark was kitted out for his football match.*

kitten *noun* **kittens**
a young cat

kitty *noun* **kitties**
1 an amount of money that is saved up from lots of small amounts given by different people. It is used for spending on something that everyone agrees about.
2 an informal way of talking to a cat or kitten *Here kitty!*

kiwi *noun* **kiwis**
1 a bird from New Zealand that cannot fly. It has brown feathers, short wings and a very long beak.
2 a kiwi or kiwi fruit is a small brown hairy fruit that is shaped like an oval. It is green and soft inside with small black seeds.

km
short for **kilometre** or **kilometres**

PRONUNCIATION RULE when you see the letters *kn* at the beginning of a word, say 'n'. The *k* is silent.

knack *noun*
a special skill for doing something easily and well *Lucy has a knack for choosing the right colours.*

knapsack *noun* **knapsacks**
a bag that you carry on your back, for example for going on long walks in the countryside

knave *noun* **knaves**
1 an old-fashioned word for a very bad and dishonest man
2 in a game of cards, a knave is another word for a jack (a card with a picture of a young man on it)

ORIGIN from Old English *cnafa* 'boy'

knead *verb*
kneads, kneading, kneaded
to keep pressing, stretching and folding something such as dough or clay in order to mix together all the ingredients

knee *noun* **knees**
the joint in the middle of your leg, where your leg bends

kneecap *noun* **kneecaps**
the thick round bone at the front of the knee

kneel *verb*
kneels, kneeling, knelt
1 if you kneel or kneel down, you put one or both of your knees on the ground
2 if you're kneeling or kneeling down, you have one or both of your knees on the ground

knew
past tense of **know**

knickers *noun plural*
underwear that girls and women wear to cover the lower part of the body from the hips to the top of the legs

knife *noun* **knives**
a piece of metal with a handle and blade used for cutting, for spreading food such as butter or as a weapon

knife *verb*
knifes, knifing, knifed
to kill or injure someone with a knife

knight *noun* **knights**
1 in medieval times, a knight was a man with a high rank in society who rode a horse, wore armour (metal covering to protect the body) and fought for his king or queen
2 a piece in the game of chess shaped like a horse's head. It moves on the board two squares in one direction and then one square to the side.
3 a man given a special honour by the British government in a ceremony performed by a British king or queen. The honour allows him to use the title 'Sir' before his name.

knight *verb*
knights, knighting, knighted
to give a man the special honour of being a knight

knighthood *noun* **knighthoods**
a special honour given to a man by the British government that allows him to use the title 'Sir' before his name. A woman given this honour uses the title 'Dame'.

knit *verb*
knits, knitting, knitted
1 to make clothes out of wool, usually using knitting needles to join loops of wool into rows
2 if you knit your brow, you frown (make lines in your forehead by moving your eyebrows closer), for example because you are worried, angry or thinking hard

knitting *noun*
1 the activity of making clothes by knitting
2 something that you're knitting at the moment
3 a knitting needle is a plastic, metal or wooden stick with a pointed end that is used with another one for knitting

knives
plural of **knife**

knob *noun* **knobs**
1 a round handle that you turn (to open or close a door) or that you pull or push (to open or close a drawer)
2 a round switch that you turn, on something such as a piece of equipment, for example to turn it on or off
3 a small round shape, for example at the end of something
4 a small lump of something such as butter

knobbly *adjective* **knobblier, knobbliest**
having lots of small hard lumps *knobbly knees*

knock *verb*
knocks, knocking, knocked
1 to hit something or someone and usually make them move or fall *I accidentally knocked over a bottle of milk. Mum knocked a nail into the wood. He knocked me on the arm with a cricket bat.*
2 to bump into something or someone, for example with a part of your body *I slipped and knocked my head on the chair. Seema knocked into the table as she was running.*
3 if you knock on a door, you hit the door with your hand or a knocker to make a sound so that someone inside knows you're there *Who's that knocking?*
4 to make a noise by hitting something *Stop knocking on the table. I can hear someone knocking in the house next door.*
5 if someone knocks someone down or over in a vehicle, they hit them *I nearly got knocked down* (or *knocked over*) *by a bus while crossing the road.*
6 if someone knocks down a building or wall, they completely destroy it
7 (informal) if you knock off, you stop working
8 if someone or something knocks you out, they hit you so that you become unconscious
9 if a person or team is knocked out of a competition, they are beaten and can no longer take part
10 if something such as an effort or medicine knocks you out, it makes you tired or sleepy

knock *noun* **knocks**
1 the sound of someone knocking on a door *I heard a knock.*
2 the action or noise of something hitting something else *I got a knock on my head.*

knocker *noun* **knockers**
a metal object fixed to a door, with a moving part that you hit the door with to let someone inside know you're there

knockout *noun* **knockouts**
1 a knockout in boxing is when one boxer hits the other so hard that he or she falls to the ground and cannot get up
2 a type of competition in which only the winner of each part goes through to the next part of the competition

knot *noun* **knots**
1 a join in something such as string, ribbon or a piece of cloth where you tie the ends together or where you twist it around itself
2 a lump in something such as hair or rope where it has become accidentally twisted around itself
3 a small round area or lump on a piece of wood where a branch was joined to the tree
4 a unit for measuring the speed of ships and aircraft or the movements of winds and water. A knot is equal to 1.85 kilometres an hour or just over a mile an hour.

knot *verb*
knots, knotting, knotted
1 to tie the ends of something together *I knotted my shoelaces.*
2 to tie a knot or knots in something *She knotted the ribbon around her hat.*

knotty *adjective* **knottier, knottiest**
1 a knotty problem is one that is difficult and complicated
2 having lots of knots *knotty wood*

know *verb*
knows, knowing, knew, known
1 to have information about something in your mind *I know where he is. I know about his problems.*
2 used for asking someone to give you some information *Do you know the time?*
3 to be certain about something *I know you will like your new school.*
4 to have learnt something *I know a few words of French. Do you know how to swim? Daniel knows about computers.*
5 to recognise someone because you have met them before *Do you know my sister?*
6 to be friendly with someone *I know Ava well. We've known each other for years.*
7 to have been to a place *Do you know Madrid?*
8 to have learnt a lot about a place, for example because you've lived there *Granddad knows Madrid very well.*
9 to have heard about something or someone *She doesn't know that book. Do you know* (or *know of*) *Picasso?*
10 to have an understanding of something or someone *Our teacher knows Shakespeare very well.*
11 if you know someone or something as something, you call them by a particular name *My name's Robert but people know me as Bob.*

know *noun*
if someone is in the know, they have information about something that other people don't have

know-all *noun* **know-alls**
someone who is unpleasant because they think they know a lot more things than other people

know-how *noun*
the skill and knowledge to do practical things such as making and fixing things

knowing *adjective*
showing that you know about something *a knowing look*

knowingly *adverb*
1 if you do something knowingly, you do it because you want to even though you know you could be doing something bad

> SYNONYM **deliberately**

2 in a way that shows you know about something *He glanced at me knowingly.*

knowledge ['nol-ij'] *noun*
1 the information that someone knows about something *We had no knowledge of what was going on.*
2 what someone has learnt about something *My knowledge of maths isn't very good.*
3 what people know about things in general *Our teachers have lots of knowledge.*

knowledgeable ['nol-ij-er-berl'] *adjective*
1 knowing lots of things
2 knowing a lot about something
knowledgeably *adverb*

known
past participle of **know**

known *adjective*
1 used about someone or something that people know or know about *He's a known criminal. Our teacher is known for her kindness and patience.*
2 if you make something known, you tell people about it

knuckle *noun* **knuckles**
your knuckles are the joints in your hand where your fingers bend, especially the place where the fingers join the hand

koala ['koh-ah-ler'] *noun* **koalas**
a koala or koala bear is an Australian animal that lives in trees and looks like a small bear with thick ears and grey fur. A female koala carries its baby in a pocket of skin called a pouch at the front of its body.

kookaburra ['koo-ker-bur-rer'] *noun* **kookaburras**
a large Australian bird with bright feathers and a fairly large beak. Kookaburras make a sound similar to a person laughing.

Koran ['kor-ahn'] *noun*
the Koran is the holy book of Islam (the religion of Muslims)

> LANGUAGE EXTRA also spelt *Qur'an*

> ORIGIN from an Arabic word meaning 'reading'

Korea ['ker-ee-er'] *noun*
North and South Korea are countries in East Asia **Korean** *adjective & noun*

kosher ['koh-sher'] *adjective*
1 kosher meat is from an animal that has been killed in the correct way according to Jewish law
2 also used for describing a person or place selling this meat *a kosher butcher*

Kremlin *noun*
the Kremlin is the government of Russia or its buildings in Moscow

> ORIGIN from Old Russian *kreml* 'fortress'

kung fu ['kung' rhymes with 'sung' and 'fu' with 'boo'] *noun*
a Chinese sport in which people fight using their hands and feet in particular ways

Kuwait *noun*
a country in South-West Asia
Kuwaiti *adjective & noun*

L l

> **ORIGIN** the letter L is from a shape the Phoenicians called *lamedh* representing a cattle prod (a stick for poking cattle). The sound of the letter has always been 'l'. At first the shape had a curved part at one end and looked like a sloping J – sometimes pointing left and sometimes right. This curved foot was later straightened by the Phoenicians and made even more regular by the Greeks, still sloping and looking sometimes left and sometimes right. When the shape passed into Latin, the straightened foot was facing right, in the direction of the writing flow, and the long line was made to stand upright. The shape now looked just like our letter L – the bottom left part of a rectangle.

L
the Roman numeral for 50

lab *noun* **labs**
short for **laboratory**

label *noun* **labels**
1 a piece of paper, cloth or other material, usually stuck or tied to something, that gives information about it. A label usually explains what something is (for example on a tin of food), who it belongs to (for example on a suitcase) or how much it costs to buy, or it gives instructions about something (for example on clothes – how to wash or dry them).
2 a word or phrase used for describing a particular quality of someone or something

label *verb*
labels, labelling, labelled
1 to put a label on something *The box was labelled 'fragile'.*
2 to use a word or phrase that describes someone or something in a particular way *You don't want people to label you an idiot.*

laboratory ['ler-bor-er-tree'] *noun*
laboratories
a room or building with scientific equipment in it, where experiments are done or medicines produced

laborious *adjective*
if something is laborious, it needs a lot of time and effort and is often boring
laboriously *adverb*

labour *noun*
1 work, for example hard work done using your hands
2 work that someone does to repair or make something or get something ready to be used
3 people who work with their hands
4 the time when a baby is being born and a woman pushes the baby out of her body *My big sister is in labour.*

Labour *noun*
one of the main political parties in the UK

> **LANGUAGE EXTRA** also called *the Labour Party*

labourer *noun* **labourers**
someone who does hard work with their hands, for example digging up roads or working on a farm

Labrador *noun* **Labradors**
a large dog with short yellow-brown, dark brown or black hair and a strong body

> **ORIGIN** named after *Labrador*, an area of eastern Canada where the dog was bred

laburnum *noun* **laburnums**
a small tree with lots of yellow flowers that hang down

labyrinth *noun* **labyrinths**
a place made up of lots of paths or passages in which you can easily get lost

> **SYNONYM** maze

> **ORIGIN** from *labyrinthos*, the word in Greek mythology for the complicated building with lots of passages built at Knossos to hold the Minotaur (half man, half bull)

lace *noun*
1 a delicate cloth with a pattern of open holes in it made by hand or machine
2 (*plural* **laces**) a strong string for fastening a shoe or boot *Please do up your laces!*

lace *verb*
laces, lacing, laced
1 to fasten a shoe or boot with a lace by tying a knot in it *His boots are laced up.*
2 to put a lace through the holes of a shoe or boot *Do you know how to lace a pair of shoes?*

lack *verb*
lacks, lacking, lacked
if you lack something, you don't have it or you don't have enough of it although you need it *My brother lacks common sense.*

lack *noun*
when you don't have something or enough of it *We didn't go on holiday this year because of lack of money.*

lacking *adjective*
if something is lacking, it doesn't exist or there isn't enough of it *Hard work is what's lacking in Ms Campbell's class.*

lacquer *noun*
a liquid painted onto wood or metal to make it shiny

lacquer *verb*
lacquers, lacquering, lacquered
to put lacquer onto wood or metal

lacrosse *noun*
a game in which players in two teams try to catch, carry and throw a ball using a long stick (called a crosse) with a net at the end. They try to get the ball into the other team's goal.

lacy *adjective* **lacier, laciest**
1 made of lace or decorated with lace
2 looking like lace

lad *noun* **lads**
another word for a boy or young man

ladder *noun* **ladders**
1 a frame for climbing up or down made of two long pieces of wood or metal joined by steps called rungs
2 a long thin hole in a pair of tights or a stocking

laden ['lay-dern'] *adjective*
1 carrying a lot of something *Mum came back from France laden with presents.*
2 full of something *a tree laden with apples*

ladle *noun* **ladles**
a big spoon that is shaped like a bowl and has a long handle. It is used mainly for serving soup.

lady *noun* **ladies**
1 another word for a woman, used especially when you want to be polite *Ask the young lady at the desk. This shop sells ladies' clothes.*
2 a woman or girl whose behaviour is polite and who shows respect towards other people *My sister always behaves like a lady.*
3 a woman or girl of high rank in British society who uses the title 'Lady' in front of her name. A man or boy of the same rank uses the title 'Lord'. *Lord and Lady Mountbatten*
4 **the ladies** the women's toilet in a public place

ladybird *noun* **ladybirds**
a small round flying insect that is usually red with black spots

ladybug *noun* **ladybugs**
the American word for a ladybird

ladylike *adjective*
polite and showing respect towards other people

lag *verb*
lags, lagging, lagged
1 if you lag behind, you are not making good enough progress or moving as fast as you should be *I'm lagging behind the others in maths. Most of us were walking as fast as our teacher but two of the girls were lagging behind* (they were some distance behind the rest of us).
2 to cover something such as a water pipe with a special material, for example to stop the water in it from freezing

lager ['lah-ger'] *noun* **lagers**
a type of beer, usually with a light colour and with lots of bubbles in it. It is fermented (sugar is changed into alcohol) for longer than beer.

lagoon *noun* **lagoons**
a large area of calm water that is cut off from the sea by something such as a long pile of sand or line of rocks

laid
past tense & past participle of **lay**

laid-back *adjective* (informal)
not worried about anything

> **SYNONYM** relaxed

lain
past participle of **lie** (be in a flat position)

lair *noun* **lairs**
1 the place where a wild animal lives *a fox's lair*
2 a place where someone hides or can be alone

lake *noun* **lakes**
a large area of water surrounded by land

Lake District–language

Lake District *noun*
an area of lakes, mountains and forests in North-West England

lama *noun* lamas
a priest or monk in the Tibetan Buddhist religion

> LANGUAGE EXTRA be careful not to confuse *lama* and *llama*. A *llama* (with *ll* at the beginning) is a large South American animal.

lamb *noun*
1 (*plural* lambs) a young sheep
2 the meat from a young sheep

lame *adjective* lamer, lamest
1 not able to walk properly *a lame dog*
2 very weak and difficult to believe *a lame excuse*
lameness *noun*

lamely *adverb*
if you say something lamely, it is difficult for people to believe you because you don't sound as if you mean what you say

lament *verb*
laments, lamenting, lamented
to express sadness about something that has happened, for example someone's death or the loss of something

lament *noun* laments
something that expresses sadness, especially an artistic creation such as a poem, song or piece of music

lamentable *adjective*
so bad that you feel very sad and angry about it *a lamentable piece of homework*
lamentably *adverb*

laminated *adjective*
1 if paper or a card is laminated, it has been covered with a thin layer of plastic for protection
2 used about something such as wood or plastic that is made up of thin layers stuck together

lamp *noun* lamps
1 an object that uses electricity to give light, especially one that stands on a desk or the ground *a table lamp*
2 an object that uses gas or oil to give light, especially a small one that you carry around *an oil lamp*

lamp-post *noun* lamp-posts
a tall post with a light at the top that stands at the side of a road or in a public place

> LANGUAGE EXTRA also spelt *lamp post* or *lamppost*

lampshade *noun* lampshades
a cover for an electric light bulb, used for decoration or to make the light less bright

LAN [rhymes with 'man'] *noun* LANs
a way of connecting computers together in one place such as a school, home or office, so that information and equipment can be shared
short for: local area network

lance *noun* lances
a long pole with a pointed end, used as a weapon in the past by soldiers riding horses

lance *verb*
lances, lancing, lanced
if a doctor or nurse lances a part of your skin such as a boil, they cut it open to get rid of the pus (yellowish liquid with germs inside it)

lance corporal *noun* lance corporals
a soldier of low rank in the army, just below the rank of corporal

land *noun*
1 the solid part of the surface of the world that is not covered by water, or one small area of this solid surface *Less than a third of our planet is land. We travelled to Turkey by land* (for example in a car or train but not in a boat or plane). *The ship finally reached land.*
2 the ground that is used for something such as building or growing things on
3 used for talking about farms and the countryside *Not many people in Britain work on the land.*
4 (*plural* lands) an area of ground that belongs to someone *The farmer told me to get off his land.*
5 (*plural* lands) an old-fashioned word for a country *My friend lives in a distant land.*

land *verb*
lands, landing, landed
1 if something such as an aircraft lands or if someone lands it, it comes down to the ground from the air *Their plane has landed. The pilot landed the helicopter safely.*
2 to arrive somewhere by plane or boat *We landed at Edinburgh at two o'clock.*
3 to come down to the ground after falling or jumping *I slipped over and landed on my back. A branch landed on the car.*
4 to get something good, especially when you're not expecting to get it *My brother has landed a job as a waiter.*
5 to make something bad happen to someone *This behaviour will land her in trouble.*
6 to end up in a place or situation, usually where you don't want to be *He landed up in prison.*
7 to land someone with something is to give them something that they don't want to deal with *I was landed with the washing-up.*

landfill *noun* landfills
a large hole in the ground where rubbish from homes and businesses is buried

landing *noun* landings
1 the floor at the top of the stairs in a house, for example leading to bedrooms
2 a floor between different sections of stairs in a building
3 when an aircraft lands on the ground *We fastened our seat belts for the landing.*

> ANTONYM take-off

4 a landing stage is a platform, usually of wood, built along the edge of an area of water, where people and goods are taken on or off a boat

landlady *noun* landladies
1 a woman that someone (called a tenant) pays money to (called rent) for letting them live in a house, flat or room that she owns
2 a woman who is in charge of a pub

landline *noun* landlines
a phone that is fixed in one place and is usually connected to the phone system by wires
compare: mobile phone

landlocked *adjective*
a landlocked country is one that is surrounded by other countries and has no sea coast

landlord *noun* landlords
1 a man that someone (called a tenant) pays money to (called rent) for letting them live in a house, flat or room that he owns
2 a man who is in charge of a pub

landmark *noun* landmarks
a building or place that you can easily recognise and that can help you to see where you are, for example when moving around a town *Tower Bridge is a famous landmark in London.*

landmine *noun* landmines
a bomb that is put on or under the ground and explodes if someone steps on it or if a vehicle drives over it

landowner *noun* landowners
someone who owns a lot of land

landscape *noun*
1 (*plural* landscapes) a large area of land and everything you can see in it, for example hills, trees and buildings *I love the flat landscape of eastern England.*
2 (*plural* landscapes) a large area of land in the countryside that is attractive to look at *Constable has painted some wonderful landscapes.*
3 a way of printing a document from a computer in which the long sides of the page are at the top and bottom. If the short sides are at the top and bottom, it is called portrait.
4 landscape gardening is the activity of designing areas of land around buildings to make them attractive

landslide *noun* landslides
1 a large amount of rocks and earth falling down the side of a hill or mountain
2 a win in an election in which one person or group gets a lot more votes than anyone else *The president won by a landslide.*

lane *noun* lanes
1 a narrow road, often in the countryside *a country lane*
2 used in the names of streets, especially narrow ones *Petticoat Lane in the East End of London*
3 a strip of a main road for a single line of vehicles. It is separated from other strips by painted lines. *The fast lane of the motorway is for overtaking. If you have a bicycle, you must use the cycle lane.*
4 a long narrow section in a swimming pool or on a running track for one swimmer or runner to stay in

language *noun*
1 a way of communicating using sounds, words and grammar *Daniel has good language skills.*
2 a particular way of speaking or writing *Our teacher doesn't like bad language* (very rude words).

259

languish–last

3 (plural **languages**) the words that people in a particular country or area speak and write *the English language*
4 (plural **languages**) the words or symbols used by a particular group *medical language*
5 (plural **languages**) instructions for programming a computer *Java is a computer language.*
6 a language laboratory is a special classroom with equipment for students to listen to a foreign language and practise speaking it

> ORIGIN from Latin *lingua* 'tongue'

languish *verb*
languishes, languishing, languished
to continue to exist in a bad situation, usually for a long time *He languished in a foreign prison for many years.*

lanky *adjective* lankier, lankiest
very tall and thin, sometimes in a clumsy way *lankiness noun*

lantern *noun* lanterns
a container with a handle for carrying a light to help you see your way, often used in the past

lanyard *noun* lanyards
a string, rope or piece of cloth worn around the neck with something fixed to it such as a name badge, key or whistle *She was wearing a BBC lanyard.*

lap *noun* laps
1 the flat area of your body from the waist to the knees when you are sitting down
2 one complete journey around a racetrack

lap *verb*
laps, lapping, lapped
1 if an animal such as a cat laps up a liquid, it drinks it with its tongue
2 to hit something gently with a splashing sound *The waves lapped the rocks.*
3 if you lap someone in a race, you pass in front of them when they are still on an earlier lap

lapel ['ler-pel'] *noun* lapels
one of the two top parts of a jacket or coat that are joined to the collar and folded back. People sometimes wear things such as a badge or flower on their lapel.

lapse *noun* lapses
1 a short period when you forget something or do not do something *a lapse of memory; a lapse of concentration*
2 a short period when you do not behave the way you should *a lapse of control*
3 a period of time that has passed, for example between two events *My uncle visited us again after a lapse of six years.*

lapse *verb*
lapses, lapsing, lapsed
1 if something such as a document or agreement lapses, it is not accepted after a particular date because the time that it lasts has come to an end *a lapsed passport; Your membership lapsed last month.*

> SYNONYM to expire

2 if something such as a quality or standard lapses, it gets worse

3 if something such as concentration or a custom lapses, it gets weaker or stops *Don't let your concentration lapse during the exam.*
4 if someone lapses into something, they change from the way they are to something different or worse *He lapsed into a coma. My little sister has lapsed into her bad habits again.*

laptop *noun* laptops
a small computer that you can carry around with you

lapwing *noun* lapwings
a medium-sized bird, often black and white, with large wings and raised feathers on its head

> SYNONYM peewit

larch *noun* larches
a tall conifer tree with needle-shaped leaves that fall off in the autumn

lard *noun*
a white substance used in cooking, made from the fat of pigs

larder *noun* larders
a cupboard or small room for storing food, usually in a kitchen

large *adjective* larger, largest
1 more than the normal size *a large house*
2 more than the normal amount or number *a large amount of snow; a large number of students*
3 if someone such as a prisoner or animal is at large, they have escaped and have not yet been caught
largeness noun

> SIMILE 'as large as life' doesn't mean very large. You use it when you can't believe you are seeing someone or something near you, for example *I hadn't seen my aunt for years but there she was sitting in the kitchen, as large as life!*

largely *adverb*
almost completely *The fog has largely disappeared.*

> SYNONYM mainly

lark *noun* larks
1 a small brown bird that sings as it flies high in the air

> SYNONYM skylark

2 (informal) something you do or say for fun *I hid Dad's slippers for a lark.*

lark *verb* (informal)
larks, larking, larked
to lark around or about is to behave in a silly way

larva *noun* larvae ['lah-vee']
a part of the life cycle of some insects or animals when they first come out of an egg and before changing into their adult form. Caterpillars are the larvae of butterflies and tadpoles are the larvae of frogs.

> ORIGIN from Latin *larva* 'ghost'

lasagne ['ler-zan-yer'] *noun*
1 pasta in the shape of long wide strips
2 an Italian food made from layers of this pasta with meat (or vegetables), cheese and a sauce

> ORIGIN from Latin *lasanum* 'pot'

laser ['lay-zer'] *noun* lasers
a piece of equipment that produces a very powerful beam (long line of light). It is used for many things, for example cutting metal, printing, reading computer disks and performing medical operations. *a laser printer*

> ORIGIN *laser* is an acronym from *light amplification by stimulated emission of radiation*

lash *verb*
lashes, lashing, lashed
1 to hit very hard, often with something long such as a rope or stick *The cruel man lashed the dog with a belt. Rain lashed against the window.*
2 to tie something tightly with something strong such as rope
3 if an animal lashes its tail, or if its tail lashes, it moves its tail from side to side quickly and angrily
4 to lash out at someone is to attack them angrily
5 to lash out at someone is also to say in an angry way what you think is wrong about them

lash *noun* lashes
1 another word for an eyelash
2 a hit with a whip or stick as a punishment

lass *noun* lasses
another word for a girl or young woman (used especially in Scotland and the north of England)

lasso ['la-soo'] *noun* lassos
a long rope with a loop at the end for catching animals such as horses and cows. It is thrown around the animal's head or another part of the body and pulled tight. Lassos are often used by cowboys and cowgirls in America.

lasso ['la-soo'] *verb*
lassoes, lassoing, lassoed
to catch an animal with a lasso

last *adjective*
1 coming after all the others or at the end of something *I've come last again. It's the last day of the holidays.*

> ANTONYM first

2 the most recent *That was the last thing she said.*

> ANTONYM first

3 used for talking about someone or something before this one *My last teacher was Welsh. He left last year.*
4 used when you mean the only one left *Can I have the last piece of cake?*
5 used when you mean that something or someone is not wanted *A computer problem right now is the last thing I need.*
6 if you do something for the last time, you will never do it again
7 if you do something last thing, you do it late in the day after doing everything else, for example before going to bed

last *adverb*
1 after everything else *He always does his homework last, just before going to bed.*

> ANTONYM first

last–laughter

2 after all the others or at the end of something *Holly arrived last. She was standing last in the queue.*

ANTONYM first

3 used about the most recent time that something happened *I last met her in Paris.*
4 last of all after everything else *I brush my teeth last of all.*
5 last of all also used when you have said several things already and you want to say one more thing *Last of all, remember that tomorrow the school is closed.*

last *noun*
1 the person who comes after all the others or does something after the others *Charlie was the last to finish.*

ANTONYM first

2 the thing that comes after all the others or happens after everything else *This room was the last to be painted.*

ANTONYM first

3 at last used about something you've been waiting for for a long time *It's stopped raining at last. At last we're home!*

last *verb*
lasts, lasting, lasted
1 to continue for a period of time *The film lasted over two hours.*
2 to continue to be good or to be enough for a period of time *I hope these shoes last longer than six months. We have enough food to last another week.*

lasting *adjective*
continuing for a very long time *a lasting impression*; *a lasting friendship*

lastly *adverb*
used when you have said several things already and you want to say one more thing *Lastly, I want to thank everyone for their help.*

last name *noun* last names
the last part of your name that you share with all the people in your close family

SYNONYMS surname, family name

latch *noun* latches
a type of lock for fastening a door or window, consisting of a metal bar that fits into a slot or hole

late *adverb & adjective* later, latest
1 after the usual time, or after the time you expect something to happen *I was late for school. The train to Cardiff is running late.*
2 near the end of something such as a period of time *Mum came home late at night. It's very late* (at the end of the evening or far on into the night). *We went to France in late June.*
3 happening a short time ago *Here's some late news just in.*

SYNONYM recent

4 to have a late night to go to bed after the usual time
5 to have (or **get** or **make**) **a late start** to start to do something or go somewhere after the expected time

lateness *noun*

late *adjective*
used about someone who has died *His late uncle was a teacher.*

latecomer *noun* latecomers
someone who arrives late

lately *adverb*
at the time just before the present *I've been ill lately.*

SYNONYM recently

latent *adjective*
if something is latent, it is hidden but may become clear to see in the future *Ms Harvey is trying to develop our latent talents.*

later *adverb & adjective*
1 at a time shortly after the present time or after a particular time *See you later! She left five minutes later. We caught a later train.*
2 newer or more modern *My laptop is old – I need a later model.*
3 near the end of a period of time or someone's life *His later years were spent in Ireland.*
4 later on another way of saying later *Come and see me later on.*

lateral *adjective*
1 connected with the side of something *a lateral view*
2 going in a sideways direction *a lateral movement*

latest *adjective*
newest *Do you have the latest software on your computer?*

lathe [rhymes with 'bathe'] *noun* lathes
a machine that holds a piece of wood or metal and turns it around while shaping, smoothing or cutting it

lather *noun*
the bubbles formed when you mix soap and water

lather *verb*
lathers, lathering, lathered
1 to cover someone or something with lather
2 to produce a lather

Latin *noun*
the language spoken in ancient Rome
Latin *adjective*

ORIGIN from Latin *Latinus* 'connected with *Latium*'. *Latium* was the ancient name of the region of Italy around Rome.

Latin America *noun*
the part of the American continent made up of South America, Central America and Mexico **Latin American** *adjective & noun*

latitude *noun* latitudes
the position on a map north or south of the Equator measured in degrees, from 0° to 90°
compare: longitude

latte ['lah-tay'] *noun*
1 a drink made from espresso (strong coffee made with a special machine) and milk
2 (*plural* **lattes**) a cup or mug of latte

ORIGIN from Italian *latte* 'milk' (short for *caffè latte* 'milk coffee')

latter *adjective*
near the end of something *the latter part of the week*

latter *pronoun*
used when talking about the second of two things or people that you have already mentioned *If the choice is between tidying my room and washing the dishes, I'll choose the latter.*

ANTONYM former

latterly *adverb*
at the time just before the present

SYNONYMS lately, recently

lattice *noun* lattices
1 a framework made of long strips of something such as wood or plastic that are crossed over each other with spaces in between
2 a pattern of lines that cross over each other

Latvia *noun*
a country in North-East Europe
Latvian *adjective & noun*

laugh *verb*
laughs, laughing, laughed
1 to make sounds with your voice while giving a big smile when you think something is funny
2 to show that you think someone or something is silly, for example by saying something unkind and laughing *When I told her my plan, she just laughed. If I go to school with this hat, everyone will laugh at me.*
3 no laughing matter very serious *Exams are no laughing matter.*

laugh *noun* laughs
1 the sound you make when you laugh or the action of laughing
2 something that is not very serious and is lots of fun *The trip to the seaside was a laugh. We played a trick on him for a laugh.*
3 if someone is a laugh, you really like being with them, for example because they are funny *My cousin's a good laugh!*

laughable *adjective*
very silly *Jo's plan is laughable.*

SYNONYM ridiculous

laughingly *adverb*
1 used for showing that you think something is silly *'Your idea won't work,' he said laughingly.*
2 used about something that you don't think deserves to be described in such a good way *What Dad laughingly calls his study is hardly bigger than a broom cupboard.*

laughing stock *noun* laughing stocks
someone that people think is very silly

laughter *noun*
1 the sound of someone laughing *We heard loud laughter coming from the classroom.*
2 the action of laughing when you think something is funny *The audience roared with laughter.*

261

launch – lb

launch *verb*
launches, launching, launched
1 to send something such as a rocket or satellite into space
2 to put a boat in the water for the first time
3 to begin something such as an attack or project
4 to make something start on a computer *Click here to launch the program.*
5 to start selling something or putting it into use, for example a product or fashion

launch *noun* launches
1 the launching of something into space or a boat in the water
2 an event when something such as a product or fashion is launched
3 the beginning of something such as an attack or project
4 a medium-sized or large boat with an engine, used for carrying passengers
5 a launch pad is a place for launching something such as a rocket or satellite into space

launderette *noun* launderettes
a shop with big washing machines and tumble dryers where people pay to wash and dry their own clothes

laundry *noun*
1 things such as clothes, towels or sheets that are dirty and need to be washed or that have just been washed
2 (*plural* **laundries**) a shop or business where things such as clothes, towels or sheets are washed for you
3 a laundry basket is a container for keeping dirty clothes in until you wash them or for carrying clothes that have just been washed

laurel *noun* laurels
a small tree with dark green shiny leaves that stay green in winter

lava *noun*
1 the hot liquid rock that flows from a volcano. It is also called molten lava.
2 the solid rock formed by liquid lava after it has cooled

lavatory *noun* lavatories
another word for a toilet

> **ORIGIN** from Latin *lavatorium* 'washing place' (from *lavare* 'to wash')

lavender *noun*
1 a plant with small light purple flowers and a very sweet smell. It is used as a garden plant and for making perfumes and soaps.
2 a light purple colour

lavish *adjective*
1 giving someone lots of something *My parents were lavish with their presents.*
2 much larger, more or more expensive than normal *The food was lavish.*
lavishness *noun*

lavish *verb*
lavishes, lavishing, lavished
to give someone lots of something *My teacher lavished praise on me for my homework.*

lavishly *adverb*
1 in a way that costs a lot of money *The palace was lavishly decorated.*

> **SYNONYM** expensively

2 in a way that is much more than normal *a lavishly illustrated book* (with lots more pictures than normal); *We've spent lavishly this Christmas.*

law *noun*
1 (*plural* **laws**) a rule that everyone must obey, for example in a country or organisation *In Britain the laws are made by Parliament.*
2 all the rules together that people must obey *I've never broken the law* (done something wrong that is a crime). *It's against the law* (not allowed by the laws of a country).
3 the study of a country's laws and how they work *My sister is studying law at university.*
4 (*plural* **laws**) a rule in science that says something always happens in the same way *the law of gravity*

law court *noun* law courts
a place where a judge or jury decides whether someone is guilty of a crime or deals with disagreements between people

> **SYNONYM** court of law

lawful *adjective*
allowed by the law **lawfully** *adverb*

lawless *adjective*
1 if a place such as a country is lawless, the people there do not obey the law
2 if people are lawless, they do not obey the law *a lawless crowd*

lawn *noun* lawns
an area with short grass in a garden or park

lawn mower *noun* lawn mowers
a machine or piece of equipment for cutting grass on a lawn. There are many types, for example with a motor, electrical or pushed by hand.

> **LANGUAGE EXTRA** also spelt *lawnmower*

lawsuit *noun* lawsuits
a problem or quarrel to be decided by a court of law

lawyer *noun* lawyers
someone who gives people advice about the law and who helps them if they have problems, for example if they are accused of a crime

lax *adjective*
1 not paying much attention to rules and good behaviour or to doing something that you should do *My teacher is too lax. The police were lax in investigating the crime.*
2 if something is lax, it is not strong enough or controlled in the way it should be *lax discipline*

laxative *noun* laxatives
a medicine that makes you go to the toilet to get rid of waste from the bowels

lay
past tense of **lie** (be in a flat position)

> **LANGUAGE EXTRA** be careful not to confuse *lay* (past tense of *lie*) with *laid* (past tense of *lay*). For example, say *I lay awake thinking.* Do not say *I laid awake thinking.*

lay *verb*
lays, laying, laid
1 if a bird, insect or fish lays an egg, the egg comes out of its body
2 if you lay a table, you put things on it to make it ready for a meal, for example a tablecloth, knives, forks and plates
3 to put something or someone down, often carefully *Lay your head down on the pillow.*
4 to fix something such as a carpet or pipes in the correct place on the ground
5 to prepare something such as a plan
6 to lay the blame on someone is to blame them for something bad
7 to lay your hands on something is to find it *I looked for the book everywhere but couldn't lay my hands on it.*
8 to lay someone off is to make them leave their job
9 to lay something on, for example food, an activity or a bus service, is to provide it
10 to lay something out is to arrange it in a particular way, for example neatly or according to a plan

> **LANGUAGE EXTRA** be careful not to confuse *lay* and *lie*. Remember that the verb *lay* always has a direct object (a noun or pronoun that receives the direct action of the verb), for example *I'm going to lay the blanket down* (the direct object is 'blanket'). The verb *lie* does not have a direct object, for example *I'm going to lie down.* Do not say *I'm going to lay down.*

layabout *noun* layabouts
a lazy person who doesn't want to work

lay-by *noun* lay-bys
an area at the side of a road where vehicles are allowed to stop

layer *noun* layers
1 a substance or amount of something on top of a surface *There was a layer of dust on the table.*
2 a substance or material going through something, which is different from the substances or materials above and below it *The earth is made up of different layers.*

layout *noun* layouts
the way that something is organised and how it looks *I like the layout of the screen on my new smartphone.*

layperson *noun* laypersons
someone who does not have any special knowledge of a particular subject

> **LANGUAGE EXTRA** you can also say *layman* and *laywoman*

laze *verb*
lazes, lazing, lazed
to relax and not do anything *I spent all day lazing about in the garden.*

lazy *adjective* lazier, laziest
not wanting to work or make any effort
lazily *adverb* **laziness** *noun*

> **SIMILE** 'as lazy as a pig' means very lazy

lazybones *noun* lazybones
an informal word for a very lazy person

lb
short for **pound** or **pounds** in weight

> **ORIGIN** from Latin *libra* 'pound'

LCD – learning

LCD *noun*
a type of thin screen, for example on a watch, calculator or computer, where the numbers and letters can be seen when an electric current is passed through it
short for: liquid crystal display

lead ['leed'] *verb*
leads, leading, led
1 to go in front of someone or something
2 to show someone the way, for example by going in front of them *You lead (or you lead the way) and I'll follow.*
3 to take someone somewhere *She led me across the road.*
4 to be in charge of something such as an activity, group of people, country or organisation *The soldiers were led by Napoleon.*
5 to be winning in a competition or race
6 if something such as a road leads somewhere, it goes there *Where does this path lead to?*
7 to have a certain type of life *He leads a normal life although he's in a wheelchair.*
8 to make someone do something *You led me to believe that Chloe had left the country.*
9 to lead to something is to make it happen *His behaviour might lead to problems later on.*

lead ['leed'] *noun* leads
1 the first place in a competition or race *Rick's in the lead. Sarah took the lead* (went into first place).
2 a strap or chain that is fixed onto a dog's collar, used for holding the dog so that it can't run away
3 when you show someone what to do *Follow my lead.*
4 a piece of information that helps you to find the answer to a problem
5 an electrical wire covered in plastic

lead ['led'] *noun*
1 a soft heavy grey metal *a lead pipe*
2 (*plural* **leads**) a substance in the middle of a pencil, used for making a mark on paper. It is made of graphite (a dark grey form of carbon).

leader ['lee-der'] *noun* leaders
1 someone in charge of something such as a group of people, country or organisation
2 someone who is winning in a competition or race

leadership *noun*
1 the quality of being a good leader
2 the position of being a leader

leading *adjective*
1 very important *My mum played a leading part in developing the new software.*
2 most important *the world's leading car maker*

leaf *noun* leaves
1 one of the flat green parts of a tree or plant. Leaves grow from the branches of a tree or from the stem of a plant.
2 a thin sheet of paper, for example in a notebook
3 an extra part fixed to the end of a table by hinges. You can move it up level with the table to make the table longer.
4 **to turn over a new leaf** to start behaving in a different and better way

leaf *verb*
leafs, leafing, leafed
to leaf through something such as a book is to turn the pages quickly without paying much attention

> SYNONYM 'to flick through' means the same as 'to leaf through'

leaflet *noun* leaflets
a printed sheet of paper, or several sheets of paper, giving information about something

leafy *adjective* leafier, leafiest
1 a leafy place is one that is very pleasant because it has lots of trees *a leafy suburb*
2 a leafy tree is one that has lots of leaves

league *noun* leagues
1 a group of teams that play games against each other to find a winner *a football league*
2 a group of countries or organisations that have joined together
3 a group of organisations or places compared to each other and put in order of how good they are *a league table* (a list showing how good one organisation or place is compared to another); *As a seaside town, Brighton is top of the league.*
4 **not in the same league** not as good as someone or something *Our school is not in the same league as yours.*
5 **in a different league** much better than someone or something *Your school is in a different league from ours.*

leak *verb*
leaks, leaking, leaked
1 if something such as a pipe, container or roof leaks, there is a hole or gap in it and liquid or gas comes out or through *The bucket's leaking all over the carpet.*
2 if liquid or gas leaks, it escapes from a hole or gap in something *Oil is leaking from Dad's car.*
3 to give secret information to people such as journalists

leak *noun* leaks
1 a hole or gap in something such as a pipe, container or roof that liquid or gas comes out of or comes through
2 liquid or gas escaping from a hole or gap in something *We had a gas leak.*

leakage *noun*
1 (*plural* **leakages**) liquid or gas escaping from a hole or gap in something

> SYNONYM leak

2 the leaking of liquid or gas from something

leaky *adjective* leakier, leakiest
having a hole or gap that allows liquid or gas to come out or through *a leaky tap*

lean *verb*
leans, leaning, leant ['lent'] or leaned
1 to bend your body, or the top part of your body, in a certain direction *I leant out of the window. Lean your head forward so I can comb your hair.*
2 to rest your body on something *I was leaning against the wall.*
3 to rest the weight of something on something else *Lean your bike against the wall.*
4 if something such as a tree or post leans, it is not straight but sloping to one side *The garden wall was leaning dangerously.*

lean *adjective* leaner, leanest
1 if meat is lean, it doesn't have much fat or doesn't have any fat
2 if a person is lean, he or she is thin and looks healthy

lean-to *noun* lean-tos
a simple building, usually with a sloping roof, built against the side of a bigger building

leap *verb*
leaps, leaping, leapt ['lept'] or leaped
1 another way of saying to jump, especially when talking about jumping high, a long way or quickly *I leapt out of bed. Can you leap over the stream?*
2 if something such as a price leaps, it increases suddenly and very much
3 if you leap at something such as a chance or offer, you accept it quickly and are very happy about it

leap *noun* leaps
1 another word for a jump, especially when it is high, a long way or quick *The deer got over the stream in one leap.*
2 a sudden and big increase in something such as a price

leapfrog *noun*
a children's game in which someone jumps with their legs apart over someone else who is bending over

leap year *noun* leap years
a year that has one more day (29 February) than a normal year. It happens every four years, every time you can divide the year number by four.

> ORIGIN the name *leap year* was probably chosen because from March onwards in a leap year, festival dates *leap* ahead one extra day in the week

learn *verb*
learns, learning, learnt or learned
1 to get to understand something and make yourself remember it (or remember things about it), for example by teaching yourself or when someone else teaches you *I'm learning Spanish. I'm learning about the English Civil War in school.*
2 to get to understand how to do something and to keep getting better at doing it *He's learning to swim.*
3 to get to understand that you must do something, for example change your behaviour *I quickly learnt not to answer my teacher back.*
4 to be told something such as a fact or piece of news *We were all upset to learn about the accident.*

learned ['lerr-nid'] *adjective*
knowing a lot about a subject *a learned professor*

learner *noun* learners
1 someone who is learning something such as a foreign language
2 someone who is learning how to do something such as drive a car

learning *noun*
1 the activity of learning and getting knowledge through reading and studying *Learning is fun.*

263

lease – left

2 what people have learnt and the knowledge they've got through reading and studying *Our head teacher is a person of great learning.*
3 a learning curve is the amount of things you have to understand and remember and the progress you make when learning a new skill

lease noun **leases**
1 an official agreement in which someone pays money to someone else in order to use something, such as a flat, car or computer, for a fixed period of time
2 if someone has a new lease of life, something happens to make them more energetic or happier than before. If something has a new lease of life, it is more useful or successful than before. *Putting more memory into my old computer has given it a new lease of life.*

lease verb

leash noun **leashes**
a strap or chain that is fixed onto a dog's collar, used for holding the dog so that it can't run away

SYNONYM **lead**

least adjective & adverb
1 less than anything or anyone else *I like her least of all my teachers. She's my least favourite teacher.*

ANTONYM **most**

2 smallest in amount, importance or size *It's the least important of my problems. I'm the one with the least ice cream.*

ANTONYM **most**

3 at least not less than a certain amount or number, or even more *The school library has at least a thousand books.*
4 at least also used when you mention something that is good in a bad situation *It was a bad accident but at least you weren't hurt.*
5 at least also used when you mention the smallest thing that should be done in a particular situation *When I can't do my homework, you should at least try and help me.*

least pronoun
1 the smallest or smallest amount *That's the least of my worries. Dad earns the least of anyone.*
2 the smallest thing that should be done in a particular situation *The least you can do is to say sorry.*

ANTONYM **most**

leather noun
a strong material made from the skin of an animal such as a cow. Leather is used for making things such as shoes, clothes and bags.

leathery adjective
if something is leathery, it feels or looks like leather *The farmer had thick leathery hands.*

leave verb
leaves, leaving, left
1 to move from a place and go to another place *He left without saying goodbye.*

2 if you leave something or someone or if you leave a place, you go to another place *I leave the house at eight o'clock to go to school.*
3 to stop going somewhere, being somewhere or doing something *My sister has just left school. My brother left home to live with his friends. Mum is thinking of leaving her job.*
4 to go somewhere without taking something or someone, either on purpose or accidentally *I didn't need my umbrella so I left it at home. Sorry, Miss Clarke, I've left my homework at home.*
5 to go somewhere and let something or someone stay in a certain place or in a certain way *I left my books lying on the floor. Mum left the kids watching TV.*
6 to not deal with something or not do something *Don't leave your homework until it's too late.*
7 to let something remain, for example without having it or using it all yourself *Please leave a few chocolates for me. Six take away two leaves four.*
8 to give something to someone and ask them to give it to someone else who isn't there at that moment *Can I leave a message for Alex?*
9 to put something somewhere for someone to get later *Your aunt left this book for you. Dinner was left in the oven.*
10 to record a message for someone to get later *Anisha left a message on the answerphone.*
11 to let someone do something *I'll leave that decision to you.*
12 to make someone have a certain feeling *Your behaviour has left me very angry.*
13 if something is left (or left over), it is still there, for example when the rest of it is used up or eaten *There's a little bit of cake left (or left over).*
14 if someone from a group of people is left, they are still there, for example after the others have gone
15 to leave someone alone is to keep away from them and stop making them angry
16 to leave something alone is to keep away from it or stop touching it *Leave my laptop alone when I'm out.*
17 if you leave something or someone behind, you go somewhere without taking them
18 if you leave someone behind, for example in a race or in your schoolwork, you make much faster progress
19 if you leave off doing something, you stop doing it
20 if you leave something or someone out, you don't include them *I accidentally left out the 'g' in 'strength'.*

leave noun
1 time away from a job or from the army, navy or air force, for example because of a holiday or illness *My mum's on leave for two weeks. He's on sick leave from the navy.*
2 permission to be away from a job or from the army, navy or air force

leaves
plural of **leaf**

Lebanon noun
a country in South-West Asia
Lebanese adjective & noun

lectern noun **lecterns**
a tall piece of furniture with a sloping part at the top for putting a book or document on, used for reading from when giving a speech

lecture noun **lectures**
1 a talk to a group of people on a particular subject, especially to students at a university
2 a serious talk that warns someone, for example about a danger or problem, or tells someone not to do bad things any more

ORIGIN from Latin *lectura* 'a reading'

lecture verb
lectures, lecturing, lectured
1 to give a lecture or a series of lectures, for example at a university *Professor Adams lectures on French history.*
2 to give someone a lecture, for example about a danger or problem, or about not doing bad things any more *Stop lecturing me!*

lecturer noun **lecturers**
someone who gives a lecture or lectures, usually at a university

led
past tense & past participle of **lead**

ledge noun **ledges**
a narrow shelf that sticks out from a surface, usually a wall *a window ledge*

lee noun
the side of something such as a hill or wall that gives shelter from the wind

leech noun **leeches**
a kind of fat worm that lives in wet places. It sticks to the skin of animals or humans and can feed off their blood.

leek noun **leeks**
a vegetable that tastes like an onion. It has a long thick white stem with flat green leaves at the end of it.

leer verb
leers, leering, leered
to look at someone and smile at them in an evil way *He was leering at me from the other side of the room.*

leeward adjective
the leeward side of something such as a hill or ship is the side that gives shelter from the wind

ANTONYM **windward**

leeway noun
the freedom to do things as you want to but within certain limits

left
past tense & past participle of **leave**

left adjective
1 your left side or your left hand, leg, arm, ear or eye are on the side of your body where your heart is
2 on the left side of something. In the number 25, 2 is on the left side of 5. *Go to the end of the road and take a left turn.*

left adverb
towards the left side *We turned left at the traffic lights.*

left noun
1 the left side or direction *My classroom is the first one on the left.*

264

2 the left or **the Left** political groups who believe that money and power should be shared between more people in society

left-click *verb*
left-clicks, left-clicking, left-clicked
to press the left button on your computer mouse to make your computer do something *If you left-click on a word, the cursor moves there.*

left-hand *adjective*
on the left side of something *What's that icon in the left-hand corner of the screen?*

left-handed *adjective*
if someone is left-handed, they use their left hand for writing and most other things

left-handed *adverb*
with your left hand *Daniel writes left-handed.*

left luggage office *noun*
left luggage offices
a place at a station or airport where you can safely leave your luggage for a short time

leftover *adjective*
used about something that has not been eaten or used *There's some leftover rice.*

leftovers *noun plural*
food that has not been eaten at the end of a meal

leg *noun* legs
1 one of the two parts of your body that you use for standing, walking and running
2 one of the parts of an animal's or insect's body that it uses for moving or crawling *A spider has eight legs.*
3 one of the two parts of a piece of clothing that you put your legs into *trouser legs*
4 one of the parts of a table or chair that stand on the floor and support it
5 one part of a journey, competition or race
6 if something is on its last legs, it is so old or in such a bad condition that it will not last or work for much longer
7 if someone is on their last legs, they are very tired or about to die
8 if you pull someone's leg, you tell someone something that isn't true, as a joke

legacy *noun* legacies
1 something such as money that you get from someone after they die
2 a situation that exists now because of what happened in the past or a situation that will exist in the future because of what happens now *The Olympic Games left a legacy of pride throughout the country.*
3 used for talking about the influence and achievements of someone important, such as a politician, after they die, for example all the changes they have made to their country

legal *adjective*
1 if something is legal, it is allowed or you are allowed to do it because the law does not think it is wrong
2 connected with the law or with lawyers *legal advice*
legality *noun*

legalise *verb*
legalises, legalising, legalised
to allow something by making a new law

LANGUAGE EXTRA also spelt *legalize*

legally *adverb*
according to the law

legend *noun* legends
1 a very old story about people or events in the past that may or may not be true *the legend of King Arthur*
2 a very famous person who is liked and respected because he or she is very good at something *Everyone has heard of football legend David Beckham.*
3 a list of words or things such as colours or symbols, used for example on a map or spreadsheet. A legend explains something, such as what each colour or symbol means.

ORIGIN from Latin *legenda* 'things to read'

legendary *adjective*
1 described in legends *the legendary King Arthur*
2 very famous *the legendary David Beckham*

-legged *suffix*
used with adjectives and numbers for describing people, animals and things with particular types of legs *a long-legged boy; an eight-legged creature*

leggings *noun plural*
trousers made from a material that fits closely to the legs, usually worn by women and girls

legible *adjective*
easy to read *Susan's writing is very neat and legible.* **legibility** *noun*

legibly *adverb*
if you write legibly, your writing is easy to read

legion *noun* legions
1 a large group of soldiers who made up part of an army in ancient Rome
2 a group of foreign soldiers in the French army *the French Foreign Legion*

legislate *verb*
legislates, legislating, legislated
to make a new law **legislator** *noun*

legislation *noun*
a new law or series of laws

legitimate ['li-jit-im-ert'] *adjective*
1 used for describing something that is reasonable or something that it is right to do *You don't have a legitimate excuse. It's legitimate to ask why Sam behaved this way.*
2 allowed by the law or the rules *Moving your bishop forwards in a straight line is not a legitimate move in chess.*
legitimacy *noun*

legitimately *adverb*
1 reasonably *You could legitimately complain about it.*
2 in a way that is allowed by the law or the rules *How can you make lots of money legitimately?*

legless *adjective*
an informal word for very drunk

Lego *noun* (trademark)
a toy that consists of small plastic blocks and other small parts such as wheels and models of people. You fit the blocks and other parts together to build things. *a Lego train; a Lego soldier*

legroom *noun*
room for your legs in front of your seat, for example on a plane or bus

leisure [rhymes with 'pleasure'] *noun*
1 time when you are not working and can do what you like, such as relax and enjoy yourself *My dad doesn't have much leisure time.*
2 leisure activities are things people do to relax and enjoy themselves, for example swimming, reading or playing music
3 if you do something at leisure or at your leisure, you do it when you have time and without hurrying

leisurely *adjective*
used about something that is done without hurrying *We had a leisurely walk home from school.*

lemon *noun*
1 (plural lemons) a fruit like a small orange with a thick yellow skin and a very sour taste
2 a bright yellow colour

lemonade *noun* lemonades
a sweet drink with lots of bubbles, a slight taste of lemon and usually no colour

lend *verb*
lends, lending, lent
1 to let someone have something belonging to you for a certain time and expect them to give it back to you later *Millie asked if she could borrow my bike so I lent it to her for the weekend.*
2 if a bank lends someone money, it gives them money that they agree to pay back later with interest (extra regular amounts of money)
3 to give someone help *Can you lend me a hand?* (Can you help me?); *I lent her my support.*
lender *noun*

length *noun* lengths
1 the length of something is the distance from one end to the other. The length is always measured along the longest side. *My ruler is 30 centimetres in length.*
2 a piece of something long, for example string, wire or a pipe *a length of rope*
3 the distance from one end of a swimming pool to the other *I swam three lengths yesterday.*
4 the time something lasts *What's the length of the film? I can't concentrate for any length of time* (for a long time).
5 the size of a piece of writing such as a book or essay *This maths exercise is twice the length of the one we did yesterday.*
6 **at length** used about something someone does that has lots of details or goes on for a long time *She has talked and written at length about her adventures.*

lengthen *verb*
lengthens, lengthening, lengthened
to make something longer, or to become longer *My skirt was too short so Mum lengthened it for me. Shadows lengthen in the late afternoon.*

lengthways *adverb*
in the direction of the longest side of something *Cut the runner beans in half lengthways.*

LANGUAGE EXTRA you can also say *lengthwise*

lengthy–level

lengthy *adjective* **lengthier, lengthiest**
very long *We had a lengthy wait.*

lenient ['lee-nee-ernt'] *adjective*
if someone or something is lenient, they do not punish someone enough *You're too lenient with this naughty boy. Three months in prison is a lenient sentence for this crime.*
leniency *noun* **leniently** *adverb*

lens *noun* **lenses**
1 a curved piece of glass or plastic, used in things such as glasses, cameras and telescopes. Different types of lenses change the light in different ways so that objects look bigger, smaller or clearer.
2 the part of the eye behind the pupil (black round part in the middle of the eye)

> ORIGIN from Latin *lens* 'lentil', because a lens is the same shape as the bean that is the seed of the lentil plant

lent
past tense & past participle of **lend**

Lent *noun*
a period of 40 days before Easter during which, in the Christian religion, people are supposed to stop doing something that they like doing

lentil *noun* **lentils**
a small round bean that is cooked and eaten, for example in soups. It is the seed of the lentil plant.

leopard ['lep-erd'] *noun* **leopards**
a big wild animal of the cat family. It has yellow fur with small black spots on it and lives mainly in Africa.

leotard ['lee-er-tahd'] *noun* **leotards**
a piece of clothing that fits closely to the body but does not cover the legs or usually the arms. It is worn, for example, by dancers and acrobats.

> ORIGIN named after the French 19th-century acrobat Jules *Léotard*, who wore this style of clothing and made it popular

leper *noun* **lepers**
someone who has leprosy

leprechaun ['lep-ri-korn'] *noun* **leprechauns**
in old Irish stories, a leprechaun is an imaginary creature with magic powers who usually looks like a small man with a beard

leprosy *noun*
a disease, caused by an infection, that affects a person's skin, nerves, eyes and bones and causes serious damage

lesbian *noun* **lesbians**
a woman who has or wants a love relationship with another woman **lesbian** *adjective*

less *adjective*
not as much of something *I've got less cake than you.*

> ANTONYM more

> LANGUAGE EXTRA try not to confuse *less* and *fewer*. Use *less* when talking about something that is singular, for example *I've got less cake than you*. Use *fewer* when talking about plural things, for example *I've got fewer sweets than you*.
> In informal speech, people often use *less* when they should really say *fewer*, for example *I've got less sweets than you*. Many people think this is wrong, so it is best to use *fewer* with a plural noun, especially in writing or in careful speech.

less *adverb & pronoun*
1 not so much *Amelia is less tired than before. You should talk less and work more. I've got less than an hour to finish my homework.*
2 **less and less** used about something such as an amount that keeps getting smaller, or about something that keeps happening but not as much as before *I'm doing less and less exercise. Grandma is reading less and less.*

> ANTONYM more

less *preposition*
used when you are taking a number or amount away from another *The police found all the money, less a few hundred pounds.*

> SYNONYM minus

-less *suffix*
used for making nouns into adjectives meaning 'without something' or 'not having something' *homeless*; *careless*; *wingless*

lessen *verb*
lessens, lessening, lessened
1 to make something not as much or not as strong *Working hard will lessen your chances of failing.*
2 to become not as much or not as strong *His interest in football has lessened this year.*

lesser *adjective & adverb*
1 smaller or not as important *I still take the bus but to a lesser extent* (not as much).
2 not as much *He is one of the country's lesser-known heroes.*

lesson *noun* **lessons**
1 a period of time when someone is taught something, for example in school
2 a part of a book that teaches you about a subject *Lesson 5 starts on page 20.*
3 what you learn from something that happens to you in your life, especially something that makes you behave better in the future *I fell while running down the stairs – that taught me a lesson.*

lest *conjunction*
an old-fashioned word used when explaining that you want (or don't want) to do something because you think it will make something bad happen *The children were afraid to talk lest they should be punished.*

let *verb*
lets, letting, let
1 to say that someone can do something, for example by giving them permission *Will you let me come with you? Let me see the email.*
2 to perform an action so that someone can do something *Let me come in* (for example by opening the door). *Someone has let the dog out. They let him go* (for example by not keeping him as a prisoner so that he can be free).
3 if you let something happen, you don't stop it from happening *Why did you let the glass fall on the floor?*
4 to do nothing so that something can happen *Let the paint dry for a few minutes.*
5 you use 'let's' or 'let us' for suggesting an idea or asking for something *Let's go out and play. Let us ask for some help.*
6 to let a building or room is to allow someone to live there or use it if they pay money
7 if you let someone have something, you give it to them (or do something such as send it to them or tell them) *Let me have your address.*
8 if you let someone know something, you tell them
9 to let go of something or someone is to stop holding them
10 to let someone down is to disappoint them
11 to let someone off is to not punish them or not punish them enough *The teacher let Manuel off with a warning.*
12 to let something off is to make it explode, for example a firework or bomb
13 to let on is to tell someone something secret *It was Jo who broke the window but don't let on.*
14 to let up is to stop doing something *The rain didn't let up all morning. Holly's been moaning all day – she won't let up.*

-let *suffix*
used for making nouns that mean smaller or less important than something else *droplet*; *piglet*

letdown *noun*
something or someone that disappoints you

> SYNONYM disappointment

lethal *adjective*
if something is lethal, it can kill you

lethargic *adjective*
if someone is lethargic, they do not feel like doing anything because they do not have much energy

letter *noun* **letters**
1 a sign used for writing the words of a language. Letters usually represent the sounds of the alphabet (for example 'c', 'a' and 't' in 'cat') but are sometimes silent (for example 'g' in 'length').
2 a written message that you send to someone, usually by post in an envelope

letterbox *noun* **letterboxes**
1 a metal container in the street with a hole at the top for posting letters
2 a hole in the door or wall of a building where letters are delivered

lettering *noun*
letters that are formed carefully and in a particular way *The prize winner's name was in gold lettering in the book.*

lettuce ['let-iss'] *noun* **lettuces**
a round or long vegetable made up of lots of large green leaves that are eaten raw in salads

leukaemia ['loo-kee-mee-yer'] *noun*
a serious disease of the blood in which there are too many white cells (tiny units of living matter that fight infection)

level *adjective*
1 completely flat *Use your laptop on a level surface.*
2 not leaning to one side or sloping *The picture on the wall isn't level.*
3 at the same height as something or someone *The milk is almost level with the top of the glass.*

4 having the same score or number of points *The two teams are level.*

SYNONYM equal

5 at the same position as something or someone, not in front or behind *A second cyclist came along and drew level with the first.*

level *noun* levels
1 the height of something, often measured against or compared to something else *Make sure the bath water doesn't go past this level.*
2 the amount of something, often measured against or compared to something else *What's the level of dust in the air?*
3 the quality or standard of someone's skill measured against or compared to someone else's *Mr Duval teaches French at beginner's level.*
4 a stage that someone must reach in a sport or game of skill, such as a computer game, before going on to the next stage *What level are you on?*
5 a floor in a building *The new art gallery is built on three levels.*
6 a rank or job that someone has, for example in an organisation *My mum works for a big company at a very high level.*
7 a way of understanding something *You can explain this poem on two different levels.*
8 on the level telling the truth *Are you on the level when you say that?*

level *verb*
levels, levelling, levelled
1 to make something flat *Level out the sand before building your sandcastle.*
2 to become flat or horizontal *The plane stopped climbing and levelled off at 20 000 feet.*
3 to make something equal, such as a score
4 to destroy something such as a town or building
5 to stop going up or down and stay the same *Prices have now levelled off.*

level crossing *noun* level crossings
a place where a railway line and road cross each other. It usually has gates that stop people and vehicles crossing when the train passes.

lever *noun* levers
1 a stick or handle that you push, pull or turn, for example to make a machine work
2 a stick or tool that you put under something, for example to lift it or open it

lexical *adjective*
connected with words *a lexical database*

lexicographer *noun* lexicographers
someone who writes a dictionary

lexicon *noun* lexicons
1 all the words and expressions of a language
2 a list of words on a particular subject

liability *noun* liabilities
1 someone's responsibility for something according to the law
2 something or someone that can or does cause you problems and will cause more problems in the future

liable *adjective*
1 used about something that is likely to happen *If you rush your homework, you're liable to make mistakes.*
2 responsible for something according to the law *Your school is liable if you have an accident in the playground.*

liar *noun* liars
someone who tells lies

Lib Dem *noun* Lib Dems
short for **Liberal Democrat**

liberal *adjective*
1 allowing people to have different opinions and different types of behaviour *Great Britain is a very liberal country.*
2 giving lots of something *At the party they were very liberal with the cakes and sweets.*
3 used about a great amount of something *They served us liberal helpings of ice cream.*

Liberal Democrat *noun*
Liberal Democrats
someone who is a member of or who supports the Liberal Democrats, one of the main political parties in the UK

liberally *adverb*
used for talking about large amounts of something *Spread the butter liberally on the toast.*

liberate *verb*
liberates, liberating, liberated
to help someone or a place to become free *British soldiers liberated the town in 1944.*
liberation *noun*

liberty *noun*
1 the freedom to do or say what you want or go where you like
2 the freedom from being kept somewhere, for example as a prisoner
3 (*plural* **liberties**) behaviour that shows no respect for someone, for example doing something without permission *Using my mobile to call your friends is a real liberty. My brother's always taking liberties* (behaving badly by doing things without permission).

librarian *noun* librarians
1 someone who works in a library
2 someone who is in charge of a library

library *noun* libraries
1 a building or room for keeping books and other things in, for example newspapers, CDs, DVDs or records. You go to the library to use them or borrow them.
2 a collection of books or other things such as CDs, DVDs, records or computer files
3 a room in someone's home for keeping and reading books in

ORIGIN from Latin *librarius* 'connected with books' (from *liber* 'book')

libretto *noun* librettos
the words of an opera or musical

Libya *noun*
a country in North Africa
Libyan *adjective & noun*

lice
plural of **louse**

licence *noun* licences
1 an official document that gives someone permission to do or use something *a driving licence; a dog licence*
2 an electronic document that gives someone permission to use a piece of software

license *verb*
licenses, licensing, licensed
to give someone official permission to do or use something *This restaurant is not licensed to sell alcoholic drinks.*

license plate *noun* license plates
the American word for a number plate

lichen ['lye-kern'] *noun* lichens
a type of small soft plant like a fungus that grows on walls, rocks and trees

lick *verb*
licks, licking, licked
1 to move your tongue over something, for example when eating something or to make something wet *I was licking an ice cream.*
2 (informal) to beat someone easily, for example in a competition
lick *noun*

lid *noun* lids
a cover for something such as a box, jar or saucepan, which can be lifted or taken off

lie *verb*
lies, lying, lay, lain
1 to be in a flat position *She was lying on the beach sunbathing.*
2 to put yourself into a flat position *He went upstairs to lie on the bed.*
3 to be in a certain place or in a certain way *The town lies to the east. Her book lay open on the desk.*
4 if a person or animal lies in wait, they hide somewhere and wait, for example ready to catch or attack *Lots of fans were lying in wait for the film star.*
5 if something lies in wait for you, usually something bad, it is waiting for you or waiting to happen to you
6 if you lie low, you hide or try not to be noticed
7 if something is lying around, someone has left it somewhere instead of putting it in the right place *Don't leave your toys lying around on the floor.*
8 if someone lies around, they spend time relaxing and being lazy
9 if you lie down, you put yourself flat, usually in bed to go to sleep
10 if you lie in, you stay in bed in the morning for longer than usual

LANGUAGE EXTRA be careful not to confuse *lie* and *lay*. Remember that the verb *lay* always has a direct object (a noun or pronoun that receives the direct action of the verb), for example *to lay an egg* (the direct object is 'egg'), *to lay something down* (the direct object is 'something'). The verb *lie* does not have a direct object, for example *I'm going to lie down*. Do not say *I'm going to lay down*.
Be careful also not to confuse *lay* (past tense of *lie*) with *laid* (past tense of *lay*). For example, say *I lay awake thinking*. Do not say *I laid awake thinking*.

lie – light

lie *verb*
lies, lying, lied
to say something that isn't true *You're lying! My cousin always lies* (says lots of things that aren't true).

lie *noun* lies
something someone says that isn't true *She's always telling lies.*

lie-down *noun*
a rest on your bed when you lie down flat and go to sleep *Granddad often has a lie-down in the afternoon.*

lie-in *noun*
when you stay in bed in the morning longer than usual *Tomorrow I'm having a lie-in.*

lieutenant *noun* lieutenants
1 ['lef-**ten**-ernt'] an officer of low or middle rank in the army, navy or air force of many countries
2 ['loo-**ten**-ernt'] a police officer of middle rank in the US

life *noun*
1 (*plural* **lives**) the time when a person or animal is alive *It's an illness people have for life. He lost his life* (died) *in an accident.*
2 (*plural* **lives**) a particular way of living and all the things that happen to you *Her life is very hard. My family life is very happy.*
3 the quality that people, animals and plants have that makes them different from objects *He gave no sign of life.*
4 living things *Is there life on other planets? It's too cold for animal or plant life in this region.*
5 the time something lasts, such as a piece of equipment or an organisation *These batteries have a life of 20 hours.*
6 energy and enthusiasm *Holly is full of life.*
7 exciting and interesting things *The centre of town is always full of life.*
8 to bring something to life is to make it interesting *This book really brings the English Civil War to life.*
9 if you have the time of your life, you really enjoy yourself somewhere or doing something

life belt *noun* life belts
a large ring filled with air so that it floats. It is used for supporting someone's body in water and stopping them from drowning.

LANGUAGE EXTRA also spelt *lifebelt*. You can also use *life buoy* or *lifebuoy* with the same meaning.

lifeboat *noun* lifeboats
1 a small boat kept on a ship, used for leaving the ship if it sinks or is not safe
2 a large boat that goes out to sea to save people, for example from a sinking ship

life cycle *noun* life cycles
the important changes that happen to a living thing during its life *Changing into a butterfly is part of the life cycle of the caterpillar.*

lifeguard *noun* lifeguards
someone whose job is to look after swimmers at a swimming pool or beach and to rescue them if they are in danger

life jacket *noun* life jackets
a type of jacket without sleeves filled with air or foam so that it floats. It is used for supporting someone in water and stopping them from drowning.

LANGUAGE EXTRA also spelt *lifejacket*

lifeless *adjective*
1 dead or almost dead *a lifeless body*
2 not showing any sign of human, animal or plant life *a lifeless landscape*
3 not showing any sign of exciting or interesting things *Our town is lifeless on Saturday nights.*
4 not showing any energy or enthusiasm
lifelessly *adverb*

lifelike *adjective*
looking like a real person or thing *a lifelike statue*

lifeline *noun* lifelines
1 something or someone that is very important to you as a way of getting help when you need it *Grandma's mobile phone is her lifeline.*
2 a rope that is thrown to someone to save them from danger, for example someone who has fallen into the sea

lifelong *adjective*
lasting for the whole of someone's life *a lifelong friend*

life process *noun* life processes
something that all living things do, for example grow, move, take in food, use oxygen and reproduce (produce young animals or plants)

life-size or **life-sized** *adjective*
used about a model or picture of someone or something that is the same size as they really are

lifespan *noun* lifespans
1 the length of time that a person, animal or plant lives or is likely to live
2 the length of time that something lasts or is likely to last

lifestyle *noun* lifestyles
the particular way that someone lives and the activities they do *Grace has a very healthy lifestyle.*

lifetime *noun* lifetimes
1 the period of time when someone is alive
2 the period of time that something lasts
3 **of a lifetime** used about something that is the best someone has in their whole life *We had the holiday of a lifetime.*

lift *verb*
lifts, lifting, lifted
1 to move something or someone to a higher position by picking them up *I lifted up the lid and looked inside the box.*
2 to move something to a higher position, for example a part of your body *Lift your feet off the ground.*
3 if something such as fog or mist lifts, it disappears
4 if someone lifts something such as a ban or rule, they get rid of it
5 an informal way of saying to steal
6 if a spacecraft lifts off, it goes up into the air

lift *noun* lifts
1 a piece of equipment like a small room, usually for taking people or goods between the floors of a large building
2 a ride in a car or other vehicle that you don't have to pay for *Can you give me a lift to the station?*
3 a lifting movement

lift-off *noun* lift-offs
when a spacecraft goes up into the air

ligament *noun* ligaments
a strong substance inside the body that connects one bone to another to form a joint

light *noun* lights
1 the power that allows you to see things, which comes for example from the sun, a lamp or a fire *These plants need plenty of light.*
2 a piece of equipment that gives light, usually one that uses electricity, such as a lamp or bulb *Turn off the light.*
3 something that produces a flame, for example the burner on a gas cooker
4 to set light to something is to make it start to burn
5 one of the lights in traffic lights (red, green and orange lights for controlling traffic), especially the red light *The car went through a light* (or *red light*) *without stopping. The school bus stopped at the lights* (the traffic lights were at red).

light *adjective* lighter, lightest
1 if something such as a room is light, there is enough light to see properly, usually light from the sun *Our classroom is very light.*
2 used for talking about the time during the day when there is light from the sun *It gets light at six o'clock. It's ten o'clock in the evening and it's still light.*
3 used for describing colours that are pale or not strong *a light green dress*; *This part of the painting is much lighter. She has light hair* (for example light yellow).
4 not weighing very much and usually easy to lift or move *My schoolbag is very light.*
5 not very thick *She put on a very light dress.*
6 used when you mean there isn't very much of something *a light meal* (without much food); *It's only light rain so you can still walk to school.*
7 used when you mean someone doesn't do something much or they do something without much strength or effort *I'm a light eater. She gave me a light tap on my shoulder. Granddad does some light work around the house.*
8 used about something that isn't very serious but that you like very much *I took some light reading on holiday.*

SIMILE 'as light as a feather' means very light (senses 4 & 5)

light *verb*
lights, lighting, lit
1 to make something start burning *Dad lit a fire. We lit the candles on Granddad's birthday cake.*
2 to start burning *The oven won't light.*
3 to give light to something *Fireworks lit up the sky. The buildings were lit by floodlights.*

268

4 if a light lights up, it comes on
5 if someone's face or eyes light up, they show that someone is happy

light bulb *noun* **light bulbs**
the glass part of an electric light that shines

lighten *verb*
lightens, lightening, lightened
1 to make something less difficult or less heavy *Having less homework will lighten our burden this term.*
2 to become lighter or brighter *After the rain it lightened up a bit.*
3 (informal) **to lighten up** used for telling someone to be less worried or serious *Lighten up a bit, Dad!*

lighter *noun* **lighters**
a small object that produces a flame for lighting something such as an oven

light-headed *adjective*
very weak and feeling as if you might fall, for example because you are ill or hungry
light-headedness *noun*

light-hearted *adjective*
not serious *a light-hearted TV programme*
light-heartedly *adverb*

lighthouse *noun* **lighthouses**
a tall thin building next to the sea, with a strong light at the top to warn ships of danger

lighting *noun*
1 the lights that light up a place such as a room or street
2 the quality of light *The lighting in the classroom is too bright.*

lightly *adverb*
1 not strongly or very much *It was raining lightly. He touched me lightly on the arm.*
2 if food is lightly cooked, it is cooked for a short time only
3 carefully and without putting your foot down hard *I stepped lightly out of the room.*
4 if someone gets off lightly, they are not punished as much as they could be

lightning *noun*
1 a flash of bright light (or flashes of bright light) in the sky during a thunderstorm. Lightning is caused by electricity between clouds or between a cloud and the ground.
2 a lightning conductor is a metal bar fixed to the top of a building to protect it from lightning. The conductor takes the electricity from the lightning to the ground through a wire connected to it.

LANGUAGE EXTRA remember that the correct spelling is *lightning*. Do not write *lightening*, with an extra *e* in the middle.

light source *noun* **light sources**
something that gives out light, such as the sun or a light bulb

lightweight *adjective*
1 not weighing very much *a lightweight raincoat*
2 not very serious or important *a lightweight author*

lightweight *noun* **lightweights**
1 someone such as an author or politician who is not very serious or important
2 a boxer in one of the lightest weight groups (usually around 60 kilos)

light year *noun* **light years**
a unit for measuring distances in space, equal to the distance light travels in one year (about six million million miles)

like *verb*
likes, liking, liked
1 if you like someone or something, there is something about them that makes you happy, for example a quality (of a person, book or film), a sound (of a voice or music), a taste (of food), colours and shapes (of a painting) *I like my teachers* (for example because they have good qualities such as being friendly and helpful).
2 if you like doing something, you do it because you want to and it makes you happy *We like to visit Gran on Sundays.*
3 to want something or want to do something in a particular way, or to want someone to do something in a particular way *I like my tea milky. Mum likes me to do my homework before dinner. I'll help you if you like* (if you want me to do that).
4 used for saying that someone can do or have anything they want *Have whatever you like. Leave whenever you like.*
5 used with 'how' to ask someone's opinion about something or someone *How did you like the film?*
6 used with 'would' for saying politely what you want or asking politely what someone wants *I would like an ice cream, please. He would like to go home. Would you like a lemonade?*
7 if you like something on a website such as Facebook, you click on or touch an icon to show that you think it is good or interesting and worth telling other people about *If you enjoyed this video, please take a moment to like us.*

like *preposition*
1 similar to or almost the same as something or someone else *You're like your mum. Like my sister I'm good at languages.*
2 in a way that is similar to or almost the same as something or someone else *Dad eats like a horse. Don't talk like that.*
3 used for giving an example *Dark colours, like brown and purple, look best on me.*

SYNONYM such as

4 used for describing a particular kind of behaviour you expect from someone *Cathy is late again – that's just like her. It's not like Yussuf to be late* (this is something that doesn't usually happen).
5 used for asking someone to describe someone or something to you *What's your teacher like?*
6 **like mad** or **like crazy** very fast or very much *She rides her bike like crazy.*

SIMILE 'as like as two peas in a pod' means two people or things very similar to each other ('like' is short for 'alike')

like *conjunction*
1 used for showing that something may be true or may happen *It looks like Jack has gone. It looks like rain* (looks as if it will rain). *It sounds like you're sad.*
2 (informal) in the same way as someone else *No-one can play football like you can.*

like *noun*
1 (plural **likes**) your likes and dislikes are the things you like and the ones you don't like
2 **and the like** used when giving examples, when you want to say there are similar things or people that you have not included in the list *There are lots of animals on the farm – cows, pigs, sheep, chickens and the like.*

-like *suffix*
used for making nouns into adjectives meaning similar to something or someone *a cup-like flower; childlike behaviour*

likeable *adjective*
very friendly and easy to like

LANGUAGE EXTRA also spelt *likable*

likelihood *noun*
the chance that something will happen or be true *There isn't much likelihood of falling over if you don't run.*

likely *adjective* **likelier, likeliest**
1 if something is likely, it will probably happen or it is probably true *It's likely that our team will win tomorrow's match. Snow was the likely cause of the accident.*
2 suitable for something *This is a likely place to stop and rest.*

liken *verb*
likens, likening, likened
if you liken something or someone to something or someone else, you show that they are similar

likeness *noun*
1 being similar to someone or something in the way you look *You and your sister share a family likeness.*
2 (plural **likenesses**) a picture or model of someone, especially one that looks exactly like them *This drawing is a good likeness of Sanjay.*

likewise *adverb*
in the same way *Pick up the toys in your room and likewise the ones in the garden. I'll do likewise* (I'll do the same).

liking *noun*
a feeling that you like someone or something *Samuel has a real liking for maths. This kind of book isn't to my liking* (I don't like it).

lilac ['lye-lerk'] *noun*
1 (plural **lilacs**) a bush or small tree with pale purple or white flowers that have a strong sweet smell, or the flower of the lilac bush
2 a pale purple colour

lily *noun* **lilies**
a plant belonging to a family of tall plants that grow from bulbs and have big flowers. The flowers are often shaped like bells or trumpets and have a strong sweet smell.

limb *noun* **limbs**
an arm or leg of a person or animal

limber *verb*
limbers, limbering, limbered
if someone limbers up, they do exercises such as stretching their muscles, for example while waiting to take part in a sport

lime – liner

lime noun
1 (plural **limes**) a fruit like a small lemon with a hard green skin and very sour taste
2 (plural **limes**) a large tree with yellow flowers and leaves shaped like hearts
3 a white or grey powdery substance from limestone. It is used in making cement and for putting on land to make crops grow better.
4 a bright green colour

limelight noun
in the limelight getting a lot of attention from people, for example in newspapers and on TV

limerick noun **limericks**
a funny or nonsense poem that has five lines and a particular rhyming pattern

> ORIGIN from a 19th-century party game in which people sang a poem with the line *Will you come up to Limerick?* Limerick is the name of a county and city in Ireland.

limescale noun
a hard white material that forms inside water pipes and kettles

limestone noun
a white or grey rock used for building and for making cement

limit noun **limits**
1 a point that represents the biggest amount or number of something that is possible or allowed *There's a limit to the number of times you can play computer games in one day. Thirty miles per hour is the speed limit here* (the fastest speed someone is allowed to drive).
2 the biggest amount of something that is enough for someone *Two apples a day are my limit. I've reached my limit* (used when you can't do something any more, for example eat, run, play games or work).
3 the edge of something where it stops *This fence marks the limit of the playground.*
4 **off limits** used about a place where someone is not allowed to go *The sports ground is off limits to children from other schools.*

limit verb
limits, limiting, limited
1 to make sure the amount or number of something does not get bigger than a particular amount or number *Our school has limited the size of classes to 30 pupils.*
2 to stop someone going beyond a certain amount or number *You should limit yourself to no more than two bags of crisps a week. Children are limited to one ice cream a day.*
3 to make something less, fewer or worse *Buying food from one supermarket only will limit your choice.*

limited adjective
1 used when you mean not much of something or not many of some things, for example because it is not possible to go beyond a certain amount or number *Tickets to the school concert are limited. Hurry up – my time is limited.*
2 not very good, for example because the amount or number of something is small *limited resources*

limitless adjective
without any limit or end *a limitless choice; The universe is limitless.*

limousine noun **limousines**
a very large car, often for an important person to travel in. It is driven by a chauffeur (someone whose job is to drive the important person around).

limp verb
limps, limping, limped
1 to walk with difficulty and in a way that is not steady because you have a problem with your leg or foot
2 if something such as a vehicle, plan or organisation limps somewhere or limps along, it moves ahead slowly or with difficulty, or in a way that is not very successful

limp noun **limps**
the way someone walks if they have a problem with their leg or foot

limp adjective **limper, limpest**
1 if something is limp, it is fairly weak and not as strong or stiff as it should be *a limp handshake*
2 without any strength and not moving *a limp body*

limpet noun **limpets**
a small sea animal that fixes itself to rocks. It has a shell roughly shaped like a small cone (circle at the bottom, sloping sides and point or round part at the top).

limply adverb
weakly or loosely *Some branches on the tree were hanging down limply.*

linctus noun
a sweet liquid medicine for curing a cough

line noun **lines**
1 a long thin mark or shape *Draw a straight line. I drew a wavy line to show the sea.*
2 a long thin straight shape made up of people or things close to each other *The children walked to their classrooms in a line. There was a line of trees along the edge of the road.*
3 a group of people or vehicles waiting for something one behind the other *The line for cinema tickets goes all the way round the corner.*

> SYNONYM queue

4 the direction that something moves along *The plane flies from London to Paris in a straight line.*
5 a long thin piece of something such as rope or wire *a washing line*
6 a phone connection or service *a phone line; a chat line* (where many people can talk to each other)
7 the tracks that a train travels along *This railway line goes from London to Chester.*
8 a long thin straight shape made up of words in a text *The first paragraph contains 20 lines.*
9 the words of a song, poem, film or play *The film has some very funny lines.*
10 a long thin mark or imaginary place that forms the edge of something and divides things or places *We've crossed the line between England and Scotland.*
11 a thin mark on the face that appears as someone gets older

> SYNONYM wrinkle

12 a company that runs a transport service *a shipping line*
13 a type of work or activity *What line is your dad in?*
14 to drop someone a line is to write to them
15 in maths, a line of symmetry is a line that divides the halves or parts of a shape that are mirror images of each other
see: reflection (sense 2)
16 **in line** forming a straight line or (especially in American English) standing in a queue *We've been waiting in line for an hour.*
17 **on line** if you do something on line or something happens on line, it is done using the internet *We bought a new laptop on line. Are your grandparents on line?* (connected to the internet at home)

> LANGUAGE EXTRA the usual spelling is *online*

line verb
lines, lining, lined
1 to stand along the edge of something in a long line *Crowds lined the streets waiting for the prime minister. The road was lined with tall trees.*
2 to cover the inside of something with a layer of a different material *The dustbin was lined with a black bag. The cake tin was lined with greaseproof paper.*
3 if people line up, they form a queue *We all lined up in the playground.*
4 if you line things or people up, you put them into a straight line *My toys were lined up against the wall.*

linear adjective
in maths, a linear number sequence is a pattern of numbers that goes up or down by the same amount every time. For example, the numbers 3, 6, 9 and 12 go up by 3 every time. The difference between each of the numbers is called the common difference. In the pattern 3, 6, 9, 12, the common difference is 3.

> ORIGIN from Latin *linearis* 'belonging to a line', because this pattern can be shown by a straight line on a graph

lined adjective
1 with printed lines to help you write *lined paper*
2 with a layer of different material on the inside *a lined skirt; a fur-lined coat*
3 with lots of wrinkles *Grandma's face is more lined than it used to be.*

line graph noun **line graphs**
a drawing or diagram that uses lines to show how pieces of information are connected

linen noun
1 a strong thin cloth made from the flax plant, used for making things such as sheets and tablecloths
2 things made of cloth or linen that are used in your home, for example sheets, tablecloths and pillowcases *bed linen*
3 a linen basket is a container for keeping dirty clothes in until you wash them

liner noun **liners**
1 a big ship for carrying passengers, for example on cruises (holidays when people visit different places or countries)

2 something such as a piece of plastic that protects the inside of something *a dustbin liner*

linesman *noun* **linesmen**
a man who watches the line that marks the edge of the playing area in sports such as football and tennis. He decides whether the ball has gone over the line.

LANGUAGE EXTRA a woman who does this job is called a *lineswoman*

linger *verb*
lingers, lingering, lingered
1 if someone lingers in a place, they stay there longer *A few children lingered in the classroom after the bell had gone.*
2 to take a longer amount of time doing something *Don't linger over breakfast.*
3 to take a long time to disappear *The smell of fried eggs lingered in the kitchen.*

lingerie ['lahn-jer-ree'; 'j' has the middle sound of 'pleasure'] *noun*
underwear and nightclothes (clothes worn in bed) for women

lingering *adjective*
used about something that continues to exist or goes on for a long time *lingering doubts*

lingo *noun* **lingoes** or **lingos**
a slang word for a language, especially a foreign language

linguist *noun* **linguists**
1 someone who studies and speaks foreign languages
2 someone who is an expert in linguistics

linguistic *adjective*
connected with words or languages

linguistics *noun*
the study of languages, for example how they work or how people use them

lining *noun* **linings**
a material or substance that forms a layer covering the inside of something *a coat with a fur lining*

link *noun* **links**
1 one of the rings that join together to form a chain
2 when something has to do with something else *There's a direct link between these two ideas.*

SYNONYM connection

3 a relationship between people or groups *There are close links between Britain and France.*
4 in a computer document or on a web page, a word or image that takes you to another document or web page when you click on it or touch it

SYNONYM hyperlink

5 a way of travelling or communicating between places *a rail link; a satellite link*

link *verb*
links, linking, linked
1 if events, facts or people are linked, or if people link them, they have something to do with each other *The two crimes are not linked.*

SYNONYM to connect

2 to show a relationship between people or things *A love of books is what links us together.*
3 to join things or places together *The Dartford Crossing links Essex with Kent. The school linked up all the computers to form a network. The word 'and' links the two parts of the sentence.*
4 if people or things link up, they come together *The two groups linked up in the Highlands.*

linking word *noun* **linking words**
a word such as 'and', 'but' or 'because' that links two ideas or pieces of information in a sentence

lino ['lye-noh] *noun*
a smooth stiff material used for covering floors
short for: *linoleum*

lint *noun*
1 a soft material for protecting cuts or burns on the skin
2 small soft pieces of cloth or wool that can fly about and become mixed with dust

Linux ['lin-erks' or 'lye-nerks'] *noun* (trademark)
a computer operating system (software that makes a computer work) that is given away free on the internet

lion *noun* **lions**
1 a large wild animal of the cat family that has yellow-brown fur and lives in Africa or Asia. A male lion has a mane (long thick hair around its head). The sound a lion makes is a roar.
2 **the lion's share** the largest amount of something *Ben was hungry so he got the lion's share of the cake.*

lioness *noun* **lionesses**
a female lion

lip *noun* **lips**
1 one of the two soft parts round the edge of your mouth where the skin is slightly darker
2 a pointed part at the top of something such as a jug, used for pouring liquids
compare: *spout*

lip-read *verb*
lip-reads, lip-reading, lip-read
to understand what someone is saying by watching how they move their mouth, not by hearing them speak **lip-reading** *noun*

lipstick *noun*
1 a coloured substance in a small tube, used for putting on the lips to make them more attractive
2 (*plural* **lipsticks**) a tube of lipstick

liquid *noun* **liquids**
a substance that flows, such as water or oil. Solids, liquids and gases are the three states of matter (what everything in the world is made of).

liquid *adjective*
used about a substance that flows because it is in the form of a liquid *liquid soap*

liquidise *verb*
liquidises, liquidising, liquidised
to crush solid foods, such as fruit and vegetables, into a liquid using equipment such as a liquidiser

LANGUAGE EXTRA also spelt *liquidize*

liquidiser *noun* **liquidisers**
a piece of kitchen equipment that crushes solid foods and turns them into a liquid

SYNONYM blender

LANGUAGE EXTRA also spelt *liquidizer*

liquor ['lick-er'] *noun* **liquors**
1 another word for an alcoholic drink, especially a strong one
2 a liquor store is the American word for an off-licence (a shop where people buy alcoholic drinks to drink at home)

liquorice ['lick-er-ish] *noun*
1 a substance with a strong taste that comes from the dried root of a plant. It is used for giving a flavour to food.
2 a soft sweet, usually black, made from liquorice

ORIGIN from Greek *glykyrrhiza* 'sweet root' (*glykys* 'sweet' and *rhiza* 'root')

lisp *noun* **lisps**
a way of pronouncing words in which someone uses the 'th' sound instead of the 's' and 'z' sounds

lisp *verb*
lisps, lisping, lisped
to speak with a lisp

list *noun* **lists**
1 a series of words (such as names) or numbers (such as dates or times) written underneath each other on a different line or next to each other on the same line *Have you put flapjacks on the shopping list?*
2 a series of words or numbers that are said one after another
3 things that you think of as being important or not important *Getting a haircut is on my list of things to do. Tidying my room is right at the bottom of my list* (not important at all).

list *verb*
lists, listing, listed
1 to write things down in a list
2 to say things from a list
3 to show things in a list *The monument lists all the soldiers who died.*
4 if a ship lists, it leans over to one side, usually because it is damaged
5 a listed building is one that cannot be changed or knocked down because it is important for its history or beauty

listen *verb*
listens, listening, listened
1 if you listen to something or someone, you use your ears to hear the sounds they make or words they say *We like listening to podcasts.*
2 to try to hear something *I was listening for a knock on the door.*
3 to obey someone or follow their advice *I told Oliver to be quiet but he wouldn't listen. Listen to me for once.*
4 to listen in is to listen to a radio programme
5 to listen in also means to listen to a conversation between other people

listener *noun* **listeners**
someone who listens, especially to a radio programme

listless – llama

listless adjective
if someone is listless, they have no energy and do not want to do anything
listlessly adverb

lit
past tense & past participle of **light**

literacy noun
being able to read and write
compare: **numeracy**

literal adjective
1 used for describing the most basic and usual meaning of a word or expression, for example if you talk about 'cold weather' you mean that the temperature is very low. The meaning that is different from the usual one is known as the figurative meaning, for example if you talk about 'a cold person' you usually mean that the person is very unfriendly.
2 a literal translation is one in which every word in the first language is translated by one word in the second language, so that it often sounds wrong

literally adverb
1 used for showing that the way you use a word or expression is exactly as it is usually used in its most basic meaning *I was so cold I had to literally jump up and down to keep warm.*
2 also used for showing that something is really true, even though it is so surprising or unusual that it does not seem true *When I saw the dog coming at me, I literally climbed up a tree.*
3 also used for giving extra importance to a word or phrase that cannot be true in the basic meaning of the word *I've got such a bad headache that my head is literally falling off.*
4 if you translate something literally, you translate every word by a word in the second language, so that it often sounds wrong

literary adjective
connected with literature

literate ['lit-er-rert'] adjective
1 if someone is literate, they can read and write
compare: **numerate**
2 if someone is computer literate, they know how to use a computer

literature noun
stories, plays and poems of good artistic quality *Shakespeare's 'Hamlet' is a great work of literature.*

Lithuania noun
a country in North-East Europe
Lithuanian adjective & noun

litmus noun
1 a chemical substance used for showing whether something is an acid or alkali
2 litmus paper is a small strip of paper coloured with litmus. It turns red when it touches an acid and blue when it touches an alkali.

litre ['lee-ter'] noun **litres**
a unit for measuring liquids in the metric system. It is equal to about 1¾ British pints.

litter noun
1 waste paper and small pieces of rubbish that people leave lying around on the ground
2 (plural **litters**) a group of baby animals such as cats or dogs born at the same time *a litter of kittens*
3 small grains in a container used as a toilet by pets, especially cats

litter verb
litters, littering, littered
1 to be left lying around *The park was littered with papers and tin cans.*
2 to leave rubbish lying around *Please don't litter.*
3 if something is littered with things, there are lots of those things in it *Andrew's homework is littered with mistakes.*

little adjective
1 small in size or less than the normal size *a little box*
2 used when you mean a small amount of something *Do you need a little help?*
3 not much of something *We've got very little money left.*
4 not very important *a little problem*
5 younger than someone *my little sister*
6 used for giving extra importance to a word *I had a lovely little holiday in Wales. That was a nasty little trick to play on me!*

little adverb
1 **a little** slightly or to a small degree *I'm a little tired. He was shaking a little.*
2 not very much *She eats very little.*
3 **little by little** gradually

little pronoun
1 a small amount *'More cake?' – 'Just a little.' I read a little of the book.*
2 not very much *His parents are poor – they have very little.*

little finger noun **little fingers**
the smallest finger on your hand. It is at the opposite end of the hand to the thumb.

live ['liv'] verb
lives, living, lived
1 if you live somewhere, you have your home there *We live in a small house in Sheffield.*
2 to be alive or have life *Henry VIII lived in the sixteenth century.*
3 to continue living *Grandpa had a heart attack but the doctors think he will live.*
4 to get enough money to stay alive *How will she live if she doesn't have a job?*
5 to spend your life in a particular way *He lives like a king.*
6 if you live off someone, they provide you with the money and food you need to live
7 if you live on a certain food, you eat that food often *He lives on fish and chips!*
8 if you live on a certain amount of money, you use that money to live
9 if you live through something, you continue to live after being in a very bad situation *My great-grandparents lived through the war.*

live ['lyve'] adjective
1 if something such as a show or concert is live, you watch it as it is happening, for example in a theatre, on TV or on the internet, or you listen to it on the radio as it is happening

ANTONYM **recorded**

2 living *We saw a tank of live fish in the middle of the restaurant.*
3 if something such as a wire is live, it has electricity going through it

live ['lyve'] adverb
if something is broadcast live, you watch it or listen to it as it is happening, for example on TV, the internet or the radio or at the cinema

livelihood noun **livelihoods**
someone's work that provides a way for them to earn the money they need to live

lively adjective **livelier, liveliest**
1 if someone is lively, they are full of energy, are happy and show lots of interest in things
2 if something is lively, it is full of energy and often exciting *a lively atmosphere* (for example people talking loudly, music playing); *lively music* (loud and quick)
liveliness noun

liven verb
livens, livening, livened
to liven something up is to make it more interesting or attractive

liver noun
1 (plural **livers**) a large organ inside the body that keeps the blood clean and produces bile (a yellow-green liquid that helps the body to digest fats)
2 the liver of an animal, such as a calf, lamb or chicken, used as food

lives
plural of **life**

livestock noun
farm animals such as cows, pigs, sheep and chickens

livid adjective
if someone is livid, they are extremely angry

living adjective
1 used about someone or something that has life (the quality that makes them different from objects) *living creatures*
2 used about someone whose life is going on at the present time (or was going on at a particular time in the past) *She's the country's most famous living writer.*

living noun
1 work that someone does to get money to live, or the money that they get by working *He earns a living as a teacher. Ava's family is having trouble making a living* (earning enough money to live).
2 the particular way that someone lives *My uncle is a model of healthy living.*

living room noun **living rooms**
the main room in a house or flat, for example where you can relax, sit and talk or watch TV

SYNONYM **sitting room**

lizard noun **lizards**
a small or medium-sized animal with four short legs, a long body and tail, and thick skin. Lizards often live in hot countries.

llama noun **llamas**
a large South American animal with thick woolly fur and a long neck. It is similar to a camel but doesn't have any humps.

LANGUAGE EXTRA be careful to spell *llama* with *ll* at the beginning. A *lama* (with one *l*) is a priest or monk in the Tibetan Buddhist religion.

load–lodger

load *noun* **loads**
1 something that is being carried or that can be carried, especially when it is heavy *Grandma was carrying a heavy load of shopping.*
2 the clothes washed in a washing machine or dried in a tumble dryer at one time, or the dishes washed in a dishwasher at one time
3 (informal) **a load** or **loads** a lot *I've got a load to do. There were a load of children in the cinema. I have loads of time.*

load *verb*
loads, loading, loaded
1 to put lots of things into or onto something to be carried somewhere *We've loaded up the car with all the luggage. Have they loaded the furniture into the van?*
2 to give someone a lot of or too much of something to carry *I was loaded down with presents.*
3 to put a lot of or too much of something onto something *Dad loaded my plate with potatoes.*
4 to give someone too much of something, for example work, problems or responsibility *Our teacher loaded us with homework.*
5 to put something into a piece of equipment so that the equipment can do what it is supposed to do *Help me load up the dishwasher. The soldiers loaded their guns* (put more bullets into them).
6 used about information that is put into a computer *How do I load this file? The program took a long time to load.*

loaf *noun* **loaves**
bread that is shaped and baked in one big piece. It can be cut into slices and is enough for several people. *a loaf of bread*

loaf *verb*
loafs, loafing, loafed
if someone loafs about, they spend their time doing nothing instead of working or doing useful things **loafer** *noun*

loan *noun* **loans**
1 money that someone borrows, for example from a bank, and that has to be paid back
2 when someone lends something to someone *I have five books on loan* (borrowed from the library).
3 something that is lent to someone *This Picasso is a loan from the National Gallery.*

loan *verb*
loans, loaning, loaned
another way of saying to lend something to someone *Could you loan me your bike?*

loathe *verb*
loathes, loathing, loathed
to dislike someone or something very much

SYNONYM **to hate**

loathing *noun*
a strong feeling of dislike

loathsome *adjective*
completely horrible *They were shocked by the loathsome behaviour of the bully.*

loaves
plural of **loaf**

lob *verb*
lobs, lobbing, lobbed
to throw something somewhere, for example over a wall or high up into the air

lobby *noun* **lobbies**
the large open space when you go into a hotel, theatre or other large building

lobe *noun* **lobes**
the soft part that hangs from the bottom of your ear

SYNONYM **earlobe**

lobster *noun*
1 (*plural* **lobsters**) a sea animal with a long body and hard shell, eight legs and big claws (pointed parts) at the front of its body
2 the flesh of a lobster eaten as food

local *adjective*
1 near to, from or connected with a particular small area, for example the place where you live *I go to the local school. My brother works for a local authority* (an organisation that controls public services in a small area).
2 affecting one part of the body only *a local anaesthetic*

local *noun* **locals**
1 someone who lives in a particular small area *The locals come here for their fish and chips.*
2 a pub near to where someone lives

locality *noun* **localities**
a place such as a town, suburb or village

locally *adverb*
in the area where someone lives

locate *verb*
locates, locating, located
1 to find the exact place of something or someone *Has the engineer located the fault with your laptop?*
2 if a place or building is located somewhere, that is where it is *The supermarket is located on the edge of town.*

location *noun* **locations**
1 a place, especially an exact place where something or someone is
2 a place away from a studio where a film or TV show is filmed *The director wants to film some scenes on location.*

loch *noun* **lochs**
a lake in Scotland

LANGUAGE EXTRA pronounce the 'ch' sound in *loch* with a rough sound as if you want to get rid of something from your throat

lock *noun* **locks**
1 an object fixed onto or into something such as a door, drawer or suitcase, used for keeping it shut. You open and close it with a key.
2 a section of a canal with gates, used for moving boats up or down between parts of the canal where the water is at different levels
3 a way of holding someone or a part of someone's body in a fight to stop them from moving
4 a lock of hair is a small piece of someone's hair, often cut off and kept by someone else

lock *verb*
locks, locking, locked
1 if you lock something such as a door, drawer or suitcase, you shut it and make sure it stays shut by turning the key in the lock
2 if something locks, it can be kept shut when you turn the key in the lock *The bathroom door doesn't lock.*
3 if something locks into a certain position, it becomes fixed in that position
4 to lock something somewhere is to keep it safe there by turning the key in the lock
5 to lock someone in a place such as a room or building is to stop them from leaving by locking a door
6 to lock someone out is to stop them from going into a building or room by locking a door *Chris has locked himself out again.*
7 to lock someone up is to put them in prison
8 if you lock up, or lock something up such as a house or shop, you lock all the doors and windows *Don't forget to lock up before you leave for school.*

locker *noun* **lockers**
a small cupboard, usually metal, for keeping things safe, for example books or clothes. Places such as schools or sports centres often have lockers.

locket *noun* **lockets**
a small container with a picture of someone or lock of hair in it. It is worn as jewellery on a chain around the neck.

locksmith *noun* **locksmiths**
someone whose job is to fix locks, usually on doors

locomotive *noun* **locomotives**
a vehicle that pulls a train

SYNONYM **engine**

locus ['loh-kers'] *noun* **loci** ['loh-sye']
in maths, a locus is a line or curve made by moving a point according to a rule. For example, a circle is the locus of a point that moves at an equal distance from a fixed point.

locust *noun* **locusts**
an insect like a large grasshopper with wings that lives in Africa and Asia. It flies in large groups called swarms and destroys plants by eating them.

lodge *verb*
lodges, lodging, lodged
1 to live in someone's home and pay them money to live there
2 if something lodges somewhere, it becomes fixed there *A chicken bone got lodged in his throat.*
3 to do something in the proper way, for example by complaining officially *My parents lodged a complaint with the school.*

lodge *noun* **lodges**
1 a small house in the countryside where people stay, for example when they are on holiday or doing sports *a ski lodge*
2 a small house on land that belongs to a large house
3 a small room at the entrance to a larger building
4 used in the names of places such as hotels and homes *They live in a small house near Oxford called Willow Lodge.*

lodger *noun* **lodgers**
someone who lives in someone's home and pays them money to live there

273

lodgings–long-life

lodgings *noun plural*
a room or rooms in a person's home that someone pays money to live in

loft *noun* **lofts**
the space under the roof of a building, often used for storing things or made into a room

lofty *adjective* **loftier, loftiest**
1 if something such as a mountain or building is lofty, it is high
2 if something such as an idea or aim is lofty, it deserves respect because it is based on good and serious qualities such as being honest and helpful
loftily *adverb*

log *noun* **logs**
1 a thick piece of wood from the trunk or branch of a tree that has fallen off or been cut off *a log cabin* (small house made from tree trunks)
2 written information or a book with information about things that happen every day, for example on a journey by ship or plane *The ship's log is kept by the captain.*
3 information stored in a file on a computer, for example showing important changes that are made to programs or settings

log *verb*
logs, logging, logged
1 to write information down, usually in an official document or computer file *The police officer logged details of the crime.*
2 if someone logs on, they start using a computer (for example after typing a password). If they log off, they stop using it (for example by clicking on an icon or button to exit).
3 if someone logs in, they start using a computer program or website (for example after typing a password). If they log out, they stop using it (for example by clicking on an icon or button to exit).

SYNONYMS for sense 3: to sign in, to sign out

log book *noun* **log books**
1 a book with information about things that happen every day, for example on a journey by ship or plane
2 a document with information about a road vehicle and the person who owns it

LANGUAGE EXTRA also spelt *logbook*

loggerheads *noun plural*
if people are at loggerheads, they do not agree with each other

logic *noun*
a way of thinking that gives good and sensible reasons for things and comes from understanding things and people

logical *adjective*
1 reasonable or sensible *Leaving now is the logical thing to do.*
2 based on an intelligent way of thinking *a logical argument*
logically *adverb*

login *noun*
a place on a computer screen that you click on or touch to use a program or website, for example after typing a password

logo *noun* **logos**
a symbol designed by a company or organisation so that people can recognise it easily. Logos are used, for example, in advertising.

loiter *verb*
loiters, loitering, loitered
1 to stand somewhere or move around slowly without doing anything in particular
2 to waste time by walking somewhere too slowly

LOL ['loll' or 'ell-oh-ell'] (informal)
used in text, email and online messages when you think something is funny or when you have nothing else to say
short for: laughing out loud

LANGUAGE EXTRA some people use *LOL* to mean *lots of love*, as a very friendly way of saying goodbye at the end of a message

loll *verb*
lolls, lolling, lolled
to sit or lie somewhere in a lazy way *They were lolling around on the beach all day long.*

lollipop *noun* **lollipops**
1 a hard sweet on a stick
2 a lollipop man or woman is someone who helps children cross the road near a school by making the traffic stop. They hold up a long stick, like a big lollipop, with a circular sign at the top saying 'Stop'.

lolly *noun*
1 (*plural* **lollies**) a piece of ice on a stick eaten as a sweet. It comes in many different flavours.
2 (*plural* **lollies**) a hard sweet on a stick
3 a slang word for money

London Eye *noun*
the London Eye is a big upright wheel next to the River Thames in London. It has large passenger cars for people to stand in as the wheel turns round, so that they get a good view of London.

CULTURE NOTE the *London Eye* is one of the world's tallest Ferris wheels

lone *adjective*
with no-one else with you *He was the lone survivor of the crash.*

loneliness *noun*
the feeling of being unhappy because you have no-one to be with or talk to

lonely *adjective* **lonelier, loneliest**
1 if someone is lonely, they feel unhappy because they have no-one to be with or they have no friends or no family
2 also used about a time or situation when you feel unhappy *It was a lonely night.*
3 a lonely place is one that is a long way from where people live or go *The car broke down on a lonely road in the country.*

loner *noun* **loners**
someone who spends a lot of time on their own, avoids other people and usually has trouble making friends

long *adjective* **longer, longest**
1 measuring a large amount of space from one end to the other *A giraffe has a long neck. I walked a long distance* (a large amount of space).
2 used for saying the space that something measures from one end to the other *Our garden is 60 feet long.*
3 lasting a lot of time *a long walk; I waited a long time* (a large amount of time).
4 used about something that has a lot of pages or words *a long book; a long message*
5 if someone has a long face, they look sad or serious

long *adverb* **longer, longest**
1 a lot of time *Have you been waiting long? How long does it take?* (How much time?)
2 a lot of time before or after *This happened long ago. They'll be listening to his music long after he's gone.*
3 used for describing the whole of a period of time *I've been waiting all day long.*
4 if you say you won't be long, you mean you'll be ready or finished soon or coming back soon
5 **as long as** or **so long as** used when you mean that something can or will happen only after something else happens *You can ride my bike as long as you wear a helmet.*
6 **before long** soon *Your baby sister will be talking before long.*
7 **no longer** or **not any longer** used when you mean something has stopped happening or isn't true now *Ben no longer walks to school – he takes the bus. Jo doesn't misbehave any longer.*

long *verb*
longs, longing, longed
to want something or someone very much *I longed to see him. He was longing for the chance to play football again.*

long- *prefix*
used for showing something that goes on for a long time *a long-lasting friendship; a long-awaited visit* (that you've been waiting for for a long time)

long-distance *adjective*
1 travelling or covering a long distance *a long-distance lorry; a long-distance flight*
2 a long-distance phone call is one that is made to a place far away

long division *noun*
in maths, long division is a way of dividing one number by another, especially when using longer numbers, and writing down all the different parts of the calculation
compare: **short division**

longing *noun* **longings**
a strong feeling of wanting something or someone **longingly** *adverb*

longitude ['lon-gi-tyood' or 'lon-ji-tyood'] *noun* **longitudes**
the position on a map east or west of the prime meridian (imaginary line through Greenwich in South London). Longitude is measured in degrees, from 0° to 180° east and 0° to 180° west.
compare: **latitude**

long jump *noun*
a sport in which people jump as far as they can along the ground

long-life *adjective*
used about products that last longer than normal ones because they have been made or changed in a certain way *long-life milk*

long-range – lordly

long-range *adjective*
1 able to be sent a long distance *a long-range missile*
ANTONYM **short-range**
2 connected with the future *long-range plans*

long-sighted *adjective*
if someone is long-sighted, they can see things clearly when they are far away but not when they are close
ANTONYM **short-sighted**

long-term *adjective*
continuing for a long time
ANTONYM **short-term**

longways *adverb*
in the direction of the longest side of something *I folded the paper longways.*

long-winded ['wind' rhymes with 'pinned'] *adjective*
long and complicated, and often boring *a long-winded explanation*

loo *noun* **loos**
an informal word for a toilet

look *verb*
looks, looking, looked
1 to use your eyes to see something or someone *We were looking at the teacher.*
2 to turn your eyes to see something or someone *Can you look out of the window? Look to the left.*
3 to make someone think that something is true or that something or someone is the way you describe them *That exercise looks hard. Evie looks sad. It looks like we've won the match. How does he look?* (How would you describe his face or body, for example happy, thin, ill, tired, attractive?)
SYNONYM **to seem**
4 to try to find something or someone *I've looked everywhere but I can't find my glasses. Mum's looking for you.*
5 to face in a particular direction *My window looks out onto the garden.*
6 to be careful about something *I was looking where I was going. Look out – there's a car coming!*
7 if you look after someone or something, you are responsible for them, for example by making sure they are safe, not damaged or have what they need
8 if you look after something you use (for example a bike or computer) or something you wear, you deal with it carefully so it stays in good condition
9 if you look down on someone, you do not respect them because you think they are less important than you
10 if you look forward to something, you want something to happen or be done soon and you feel happy about it
11 if you look in on someone, you visit them for a short time, for example to check that they are well or safe
12 if you look into something such as a problem or situation, you try to find out all the facts about it
13 if you look like someone, you're similar to them in the shape of your face or in your face and body
14 if you look out for someone or something, you pay attention to the situation so you will notice them as soon as they appear *I'll look out for your brother in the park.*
15 if you look over something such as a document, you examine it quickly
16 if you look something up such as a word in a dictionary, you try to find information about it, for example what it means
17 if you look up to someone, you respect them because you think they are important

look *noun* **looks**
1 when you look at something or someone *Can I have a look at the photo? I took a quick look at the time.*
2 the way your face looks at a particular time to show what you are thinking or feeling *She had a look of anger in her eyes.*
SYNONYM **expression**
3 what something or someone makes you think, for example when you look at them *I don't like the look of that cut on your finger* (for example, there's something wrong). *I like the look of the new teacher* (for example, he or she seems friendly and intelligent).
SYNONYM **appearance**

lookalike *noun* **lookalikes**
a person who looks like someone famous
LANGUAGE EXTRA also spelt *look-alike*

looking glass *noun* **looking glasses**
an old-fashioned word for a mirror

lookout *noun*
1 (*plural* **lookouts**) someone who watches for danger and warns other people
2 (*plural* **lookouts**) a high place from where someone watches for danger
3 when you watch for danger *Keep a lookout for broken pieces of glass.*
4 **it's your lookout** or **that's your lookout** used when you mean something is someone's own responsibility and no-one else's *If you fail, that's your lookout.*

looks *noun plural*
how attractive someone's face is *She's someone of great intelligence and good looks.*

loom *verb*
looms, looming, loomed
1 to appear suddenly as a large frightening shape
2 if an event looms, it gets closer and makes you very worried *The exams are looming.*

loom *noun* **looms**
a machine for making cloth by weaving (crossing threads over each other)

loop *noun* **loops**
1 a shape like a curve or circle made in something such as a piece of string or formed by a river or letter of the alphabet *a loop of string; Make a big loop in the letter g.*
2 a thin strip of material such as cloth or wire shaped like a curve or circle, used for carrying or holding something *a belt loop; Hang your coat up by its loop.*

loop *verb*
loops, looping, looped
to make a loop or make a loop in something *The river loops round the town. Our PE teacher looped the rope over the bar.*

loophole *noun* **loopholes**
something left out in a law that lets people do things that are not allowed

loose *adjective* **looser, loosest**
1 not fixed in its place *A button on my shirt has come loose.*
2 loose clothes are big and not tight against your body
3 if a rope or string is loose, it is not pulled tight
4 not tied or kept somewhere, for example in a cage or prison *The rabbit got loose. The prisoner broke loose from his handcuffs.*
5 not in a pack or box *We bought some loose chocolates.*
6 if someone is at a loose end, they have nothing to do
7 if a person or animal is on the loose, they have escaped from somewhere
looseness *noun*

loosely *adverb*
1 in a way that is not fixed or tied *You've wrapped the present too loosely.*
2 in a way that is not tight against your body *She wore a scarf loosely around her neck.*

loosen *verb*
loosens, loosening, loosened
1 to make something loose, or to become loose *Loosen your belt if it's too tight. The screws holding the drawer have loosened.*
2 to loosen your grip is to hold something less tightly
3 to loosen up is to do exercises to make your muscles less tight
4 (informal) to loosen up is also to become less nervous or worried and more relaxed

loot *noun*
money or goods that have been stolen

loot *verb*
loots, looting, looted
to steal things from shops, houses or businesses *Many shops and homes were looted during the riots.* **looter** *noun* **looting** *noun*

lop *verb*
lops, lopping, lopped
if someone lops something off such as a branch from a tree, they cut it off

lopsided *adjective*
if something is lopsided, one side of it is bigger, higher or heavier than the other *Sally had a bandage on one shoulder, which made her look lopsided.*

lord *noun* **lords**
1 a man or boy of high rank in British society who uses the title 'Lord' in front of his name. A woman or girl of the same rank uses the title 'Lady'. *Lord and Lady Cavendish*
2 a man in the Middle Ages who owned a lot of land *a feudal lord*
3 a man or animal of great power *The tiger is the lord of the jungle.*
4 Lord is a name that Christians give to God or to Jesus Christ
5 the Lords is short for the **House of Lords**

lordly *adjective*
1 used about someone who thinks they are better than other people *lordly behaviour*
2 suitable for a lord *a lordly feast*

lorry–low

lorry *noun* **lorries**
a large road vehicle for carrying goods
SYNONYM truck

lose *verb*
loses, losing, lost
1 if you lose something, you don't have it any more because you don't know where it is or it has been taken away from you *I've lost my glasses. My uncle lost his house in a fire.*
2 if you lose someone, you can't find them *Ben's not on the bus – I think we've lost him.*
3 to put something where it can't be found *Be careful not to lose your pen.*
4 to be beaten, for example in a game, race or battle *We lost yesterday's match. Our school has lost again. When I argue with my brother, I always lose.*
5 to have less of something or get rid of something *Dad's losing his hair. I need to lose a few pounds* (become thinner).
6 to stop having or feeling something, for example patience or interest *Jack is losing interest in maths.*
7 used for talking about when someone dies *He lost his life* (died). *Alice lost her stepdad* (he died).
8 if you lose your balance, you fall over or almost fall
9 if you lose time, you waste it
10 if a watch or clock loses time, it goes more slowly than it is supposed to
11 if you lose your way, you don't know where you are

loser *noun* **losers**
1 a person or team that loses a game
2 a person who is not successful in anything that they do

loss *noun* **losses**
1 when you lose something *I was upset about the loss of my mobile.*
2 when a person, shop or business has less money than before *Our shop made a loss last year.*
3 if someone is at a loss, they don't know what to say or do

lost
past tense & past participle of **lose**

lost *adjective*
1 if something or someone is lost, no-one knows where they are *Our cat is lost.*
SYNONYM missing
2 if you are lost, you don't know where you are or how to find your way

lot *noun* **lots**
1 an amount of something or group of people *Dad has done two lots of washing today. Take the next lot of children into the playground.*
2 an area of land *a parking lot*
3 something being sold in an auction (sale to the public) *Lot 5 is a rare coin.*
4 **a lot** or **lots** a large amount or number of things or people *I've got a lot of homework to do. Our school has lots of computers. You have a lot* (or *lots*) *to think about.*
5 **a lot** very much or very often *I'm feeling a lot better today. Do you see your grandparents a lot?*
6 **the lot** or **the whole lot** everything or everyone *There's nothing left – he's eaten the lot. Her friends are silly – she's fed up with the lot of them.*

lotion *noun* **lotions**
a thick liquid that you put on your skin, for example to protect it *a suntan lotion*

lottery *noun* **lotteries**
a game in which people buy tickets with numbers on them. If your number is chosen, you win money or a prize.

lotto *noun*
a game in which players try to match numbers on a card with numbers that someone takes out of a container. The player who is first to match all the numbers wins.

loud *adjective* **louder, loudest**
1 used about something that makes a lot of noise *a loud voice*; *The TV's too loud.*
2 a loud noise or sound is one that is strong and easy to hear
3 used about colours or clothes that are bright in an unpleasant way *Dad was wearing a loud tie.*
loudness *noun*

loud *adverb* **louder, loudest**
1 in a loud way *You speak too loud.*
2 if you say or read something out loud, you say or read it so that everyone can hear

loudly *adverb*
making a lot of noise *I shouted loudly for help.*

loudspeaker *noun* **loudspeakers**
a piece of equipment that makes sounds louder, for example music or voices, by changing electrical signals into sounds

lounge *noun* **lounges**
1 a room in a house or flat where you can relax, sit and talk or watch TV
2 a room in a public place such as a hotel or airport where you can relax or wait

lounge *verb*
lounges, lounging, lounged
to sit, lie or stand somewhere in a lazy way and not do anything *I've been lounging around the house all day.*

louse *noun* **lice**
a very small insect that lives on the skin and in the hair of some people and animals

lousy *adjective* **lousier, lousiest** (informal)
1 very bad *The weather's lousy today.*
2 used for giving extra importance to a word when you're very angry or upset *I almost won the quiz – I was only a lousy five points behind the winner!*

lout *noun* **louts**
a young man who behaves very badly or in a violent way

lovable *adjective*
if a person or animal is lovable, they have qualities that make you like them very much *a lovable little kitten*
LANGUAGE EXTRA also spelt *loveable*

love *verb*
loves, loving, loved
1 if you love someone, you have very strong feelings of liking for them
2 if you love something, you like it very much or you enjoy doing it *I love ice cream. My sister loves swimming.*
3 used with 'would' for saying politely that you want something very much *I would love a cup of tea. Evie would love to visit us tomorrow.*

love *noun*
1 a very strong feeling of liking someone *Our parents show us lots of love.*
2 when you like something very much *Rohan shares my love of cricket.*
3 (plural **loves**) a person someone loves *She's my uncle's only love.*
4 (plural **loves**) something you like very much *Ballet is her great love.*
5 a score in tennis that shows someone has no points *It's forty-love.*
6 if someone is in love with someone, they have a love relationship with that person. If they fall in love, they start to have a love relationship.

lovely *adjective* **lovelier, loveliest**
1 beautiful *She was wearing a lovely dress.*
2 pleasant *We had a lovely holiday.*
3 friendly and kind *The head teacher is a lovely person.*
4 good *Lovely to meet you! 'I'll see you at the party.' – 'Lovely!'*
5 used about something good that you want to give special importance to *The water is lovely and warm.*
loveliness *noun*

lover *noun* **lovers**
1 someone who loves something *She's a great lover of nature. It's a magazine for music lovers.*
2 someone who has a love relationship with someone *Shakespeare's most famous lovers are Romeo and Juliet.*

loving *adjective*
showing love *My parents are very loving.*
lovingly *adverb*

low *adjective* **lower, lowest**
1 reaching a short way up from the ground *a low wall*
2 at a distance a short way above the ground *low clouds*
3 close to the bottom of something *My name is low on the list.*
4 used for talking about an amount, number or level that is much less than the usual amount, number or level of something *low prices*; *a low temperature*; *My exam marks were very low.*
5 producing a small amount of light or heat *The lights were low. The radiator is on a low heat.*
6 used for talking about something when there isn't much of it left *My mobile battery is getting low. We're low on bread.*
7 not very important *a soldier of low rank*
8 used about the quality of something to show that it is bad *My standard in maths is very low.*
9 quiet *Speak in a low voice so as not to wake the baby. Turn up the TV – it's too low.*
10 a low sound is one that is near the bottom of the range of sounds, for example the sound of a cello
11 very sad *His brother has been feeling low.*
12 without much energy *I felt low after the flu but I'm fine now.*

low–lump

low *adverb* **lower, lowest**
1 a short way above the ground *The plane was flying too low.*
2 less than something or less than the usual level of something *I got a bad score but Oliver scored even lower. Turn the volume down low.*

low *noun* **lows**
used about the level something reaches that is much less than the usual level *Temperatures reached a low of minus 10 degrees in Aberdeen.*

low *verb*
lows, lowing, lowed
when a cow lows, it makes a long deep sound

low- *prefix*
often used for describing food that contains less of something such as fat, salt or sugar *a low-fat yoghurt; a low-salt diet*

lower *verb*
lowers, lowering, lowered
1 to move something or someone down to a lower position
2 to make something less or less big *They've lowered the price of laptops. She lowered her umbrella.*
3 to make something quieter *Please lower your voice.*

lower *adjective*
1 below something of the same kind *the lower lip*
2 at the bottom part of something *the lower floors of the building*

lower case *noun*
letters of the alphabet that are written as small letters (for example a, b, c, d), not as capital (or large) letters *I used lower case letters in my text message.*
compare: **upper case**

lower school *noun* **lower schools**
1 a school (or part of a school), in some parts of the UK, for children between the ages of about 5 and 8
2 a part of a secondary school for children between the ages of about 11 and 14

lowest common denominator *noun*
in maths, the smallest whole number that can be divided exactly by the denominators (bottom numbers) of two or more fractions

lowlands *noun plural*
an area of a country that is flatter than the area around it *the Scottish Lowlands*
lowland *adjective*

lowly *adjective* **lowlier, lowliest**
not important (used about a person or the work they do) *He's a lowly bank clerk.*

low-pitched *adjective*
a low-pitched sound or voice is deep and near the bottom of the range of sounds

low tide *noun* **low tides**
the time when the sea or a river reaches its lowest level. This usually happens about every 12 hours.

loyal *adjective*
1 if you are loyal to someone or something, you stay with them and support them because they are important to you *a loyal friend*
2 also used about someone's actions *My aunt has given years of loyal service.*

loyally *adverb*
in a way that shows great support for someone or something *He has loyally supported Arsenal for many years.*

loyalty *noun*
the quality of being loyal to someone or something

lozenge *noun* **lozenges**
1 a medicine shaped like a small flat sweet. You suck it if you have a cough or sore throat.
2 a shape with four sloping sides like a diamond. It has two thin points, one facing upwards and the opposite one downwards.

L-plate *noun* **L-plates**
a white sign with a red L for 'Learner' on it. It is fixed onto the car of someone learning to drive.

lubricate *verb*
lubricates, lubricating, lubricated
to put something such as oil onto a piece of machinery to make it work better
lubrication *noun*

lucid *adjective*
1 easy to understand *a lucid description*
2 able to understand things well and express ideas clearly *She's 98 but still very lucid.*
lucidity *noun*

ORIGIN from Latin *lucidus* 'light' or 'bright' (from *lucere* 'to shine')

lucidly *adverb*
very clearly *He spoke lucidly about what happened.*

luck *noun*
1 a good thing or good things that happen to you for no particular reason *I never have much luck. I won £100 – what a stroke of luck! That number brought me good luck.*
2 when something good or bad happens to you for no particular reason *You might be successful – it's a matter of luck. I missed the bus – just my luck!*
3 bad luck is a bad thing or bad things that happen to you for no particular reason
4 if you're in luck, you can have or do something you want, often when you didn't think that was likely to happen
5 if you wish someone good luck, you tell them you hope they'll be successful *Good luck with your exam!*

luckily *adverb*
used when you mean something good happens for no particular reason *Luckily, no-one was hurt.*

SYNONYM fortunately

lucky *adjective* **luckier, luckiest**
1 having a good thing or good things happen to you for no particular reason *You're lucky to have such a nice teacher.*
2 happening because of good luck *Jack scored a lucky goal. Arun had a lucky escape* (something bad didn't happen to him).
3 bringing good luck *Seven is my lucky number.*

ludicrous ['loo-dik-rers'] *adjective*
completely unreasonable or stupid

ORIGIN from Latin *ludicrus* 'connected with playing' (from *ludere* 'to play')

ludicrously *adverb*
1 in a way that seems completely unreasonable *ludicrously expensive shoes*
2 in a way that seems completely stupid *He wore a huge hat that looked ludicrously out of place in school.*

ludo *noun*
a game you play on a square board using dice. You move counters (plastic or cardboard discs) or pieces around the board from a starting to a finishing place.

ORIGIN from Latin *ludo* 'I play'

lug *verb*
lugs, lugging, lugged
to carry or move something heavy

luggage *noun*
1 bags or suitcases (or a bag or suitcase) that you take with you when you travel somewhere *I have one piece of luggage.*
2 a luggage rack is a shelf on a train, bus or bicycle for your luggage

lugubrious ['loo-goo-bree-ers'] *adjective*
very sad and serious *a lugubrious face*

lukewarm *adjective*
1 slightly warm, often when you want something to be warmer *Make me another tea – this one is lukewarm.*
2 not showing much enthusiasm *a lukewarm welcome*

lull *noun* **lulls**
a short quiet period in which nothing much happens

lull *verb*
lulls, lulling, lulled
to make someone feel calm and relaxed *The sound of the waves lulled me to sleep.*

lullaby *noun* **lullabies**
a quiet song for making a baby go to sleep

lumber *verb*
lumbers, lumbering, lumbered
1 to move along in a slow and clumsy way because of being big and heavy
2 (informal) to make someone deal with something or someone when they don't want to *I've been lumbered with the washing-up. Mum lumbered us with Gran.*

lumber *noun*
1 things that are of no use such as old furniture that is stored somewhere
2 cut wood that is used for building

lumberjack *noun* **lumberjacks**
someone who cuts down trees and takes them away to be used for building

luminous ['loo-min-ers'] *adjective*
1 shining in the dark *The hands of my watch are luminous.*
2 having a colour that appears to shine brightly in the light *luminous clothing*
luminosity *noun*

lump *noun* **lumps**
1 a big or small piece of something solid without any particular shape *a lump of wood; The soup is full of lumps.*
2 a small hard part on or in the body

lump – lyrics

lump *verb*
lumps, lumping, lumped
to lump different things or people together is to put them in the same group and deal with them in the same way

lumpy *adjective* lumpier, lumpiest
having lots of lumps *a lumpy cushion*

lunacy *noun*
really stupid behaviour that often causes something bad or dangerous to happen

lunar *adjective*
connected with the moon *a lunar eclipse*

> ORIGIN from Latin *luna* 'moon'

lunatic *noun* lunatics
someone who behaves in a very stupid or dangerous way

> ORIGIN from Latin *luna* 'moon', because in ancient times it was thought that the full moon (when it appears as a complete circle) affected people's brains and made them behave strangely

lunch *noun* lunches
1 a meal that you eat in the middle of the day
2 a lunch break is a time when you have a short rest from your work or lessons to have lunch

lunch *verb*
lunches, lunching, lunched
to eat lunch

lunchbox *noun* lunchboxes
a container for taking your lunch to school

lunchtime *noun*
the time in the middle of the day when people usually have lunch or when someone is having their lunch

lung *noun* lungs
your lungs are the two organs inside your chest that you use for breathing

lunge *verb*
lunges, lunging, lunged
to move forward suddenly, for example to attack someone or to grab something

lunge *noun*

lupin *noun* lupins
a garden plant that has long stems with many pink, purple or blue flowers growing along them

lurch *verb*
lurches, lurching, lurched
to move in a way that is not steady or normal, for example like someone who is drunk

lurch *noun*
1 to leave someone in the lurch is to go away and leave them in a difficult situation
2 (*plural* **lurches**) a lurching movement

lure *verb*
lures, luring, lured
1 to get someone to go somewhere or do something by tricking them or by giving them something they want
2 to trick an animal so that it goes into a trap

lurgy *noun*
a slang word for any kind of illness that you might catch from someone *Don't go near him – he's got the dreaded lurgy!*

278

lurk *verb*
lurks, lurking, lurked
1 to wait or hide somewhere, often before doing something bad *We saw someone lurking around the school.*
2 if you lurk on the internet, you go into a chat room and read other people's messages without letting anyone know you're there

luscious *adjective*
if food is luscious, it tastes delicious and is often juicy

lush *adjective* lusher, lushest
a lush area of land is very green because it has lots of grass, plants and trees growing there

lustre ['lus-ter'] *noun*
the shiny quality of something such as hair

lustrous *adjective*
if a surface or someone's hair is lustrous, it is shiny

lute *noun* lutes
a musical instrument with strings like a guitar but with a main part (or body) that is rounder. It was played mainly in the past.

luxurious *adjective*
very expensive and comfortable

luxury *noun*
1 (*plural* **luxuries**) something expensive that someone does not need but that makes them very happy *A new car is a luxury we can't afford.*
2 a situation that makes someone very happy because they are surrounded by expensive things *My uncle lives a life of luxury. We stayed in a luxury hotel* (an expensive and comfortable hotel).

-ly *suffix*
1 used for making adjectives into adverbs meaning in a particular way *Walk slowly* (in a slow way).
2 used for making nouns into adverbs showing a particular time *I go swimming weekly* (every week).
3 used for making nouns into adjectives meaning like or connected with someone or something or showing a particular time *cowardly behaviour*; *a monthly magazine*

> LANGUAGE EXTRA when an adjective or noun ends in *y*, the *y* is changed to *i* before the *-ly* is added. For example, *angry* becomes *angrily* and *day* becomes *daily*.

Lycra ['lye-krer'] *noun* (trademark)
a thin material that stretches easily. It is used especially for making clothes that fit tightly on the body, for example cycling shorts or leggings.

lying
present participle of **lie**

lymph gland *noun* lymph glands
one of the small round parts in the body that store white blood cells (tiny units of living matter) and help you to fight infections

lynch *verb*
lynches, lynching, lynched
to kill someone, usually by hanging them with a rope around the neck, even though they have not been judged in a court of law

lyre *noun* lyres
a musical instrument shaped like the letter U with a bar across the top that strings are fixed to. It was used in ancient Greece.

lyric ['li-rik'] *adjective*
expressing strong feelings such as love, using words that might be used in a song *a lyric poem*

lyrical ['li-rik-erl'] *adjective*
expressing strong feelings in a beautiful way, using words that might be used in a song *a lyrical description of the countryside*

lyrics ['li-riks'] *noun plural*
the words of a song

m M

ORIGIN the letter M has not changed much since it started life in Egyptian hieroglyphics as a zigzag shape, like several Vs put together – vvvvv. This symbol of a wavy line, which also sometimes appeared in the vertical position, represented a wave of water. When the letter passed into the Phoenician alphabet, it was called *mem* meaning 'water' and took the 'm' sound that its name began with. The Phoenicians made the zigzag shorter so it looked similar to a modern M but with the last upright line of the M continuing downwards to form a long handle. The letter passed into Greek without much change. Under the Romans, the handle was made shorter and the shape made neater so that its two halves matched each other, giving us the letter M we use today.

m
1 short for **metre** or **metres**
2 short for **mile** or **miles**
3 short for **million**

M
1 the Roman numeral for 1000
2 short for **motorway** *The M25 goes around London.*

mac *noun* macs
a thin coat that you wear to protect you when it rains
short for: mackintosh

Mac *noun* Macs (trademark)
a type of computer that people use at home or in their office
short for: Macintosh

macabre ['mer-kahbr'] *adjective*
horrible and strange, for example because of being connected with dead people

macaroni *noun*
1 pasta in the shape of small tubes
2 a food made from these tubes, often cooked with a cheese sauce

machete ['mer-shet-ee'] *noun* machetes
a knife with a short handle and a long wide blade. It is used as a tool, for example for cutting trees in the jungle, or as a weapon.

machine *noun* machines
1 an object with many parts that work together to do a particular job. Machines are made out of metal, plastic or another material. They use power such as electricity or steam to make them work. *a washing machine* (for washing clothes); *an answering machine* (for recording phone calls when you are out)
2 another word for a computer
3 an informal word for a motorbike

machine gun *noun* machine guns
a large gun that fires lots of bullets very quickly

machinery *noun*
1 another word for machines, especially large ones *farm machinery*
2 the moving parts inside a machine, especially a large one *Don't get your hand caught in the machinery.*

mackerel *noun* mackerel
a sea fish with wavy lines on its body and oily flesh that is used as food

mackintosh *noun* mackintoshes
an old-fashioned word for a mac (coat you wear when it rains)

ORIGIN named after the Scottish chemist Charles *Macintosh* (there is no *k* in his name). He invented the special cloth that protects you from the rain, which is used for making mackintoshes.

mad *adjective* madder, maddest
1 completely stupid *I won't cross the road if cars are coming – I'm not mad.*
2 very angry *She's mad at me. That noise is driving me mad* (making me angry).
3 (old-fashioned) having an illness that affects the way you think and behave *The British King George III went mad.*

SYNONYM insane

4 strange *From the way he behaves, he seems a bit mad.*
5 excited and happy *When the singer came on stage, the audience went mad.*
6 if someone is mad about something or someone, they like them very much *Andrew is mad about football.*
7 used about something done in a hurry, with lots of energy and without thinking *There was a mad rush for the door.*
8 if you do something like mad, you do it a lot, very quickly or with lots of energy *I'm working like mad to finish my homework.*

SIMILES 'as mad as a hatter' and 'as mad as a March hare' mean completely mad (senses 1, 3 & 4)

madam *noun*
a polite word to call a woman when you don't know her name, used for example in a shop or restaurant *Here is your tea, Madam.*

mad cow disease *noun*
a brain disease in cows that causes their death

SYNONYM BSE

maddening *adjective*
making you feel very angry *It's maddening when you have to wait an hour for the bus.*
maddeningly *adverb*

made
past tense & past participle of **make**

made-to-measure *adjective*
used for describing something that is specially made, for example clothes to fit a particular person *a made-to-measure suit*

made-up *adjective*
not true *a made-up story*

madly *adverb*
1 very quickly or with lots of energy *The children were rushing around madly.*
2 very much *She's madly in love with him.*
3 very *Everyone was madly excited.*

madman *noun* madmen
1 a man who behaves in a stupid or dangerous way *Be careful – that driver is a madman.*
2 an old-fashioned word for a man who has an illness that affects the way he thinks and behaves

madness *noun*
1 used when talking about behaviour or ideas that are stupid or dangerous *It's madness to cross the road without looking.*
2 (old-fashioned) when someone has an illness that affects the way they think and behave

SYNONYM for sense 2: insanity

madwoman *noun* madwomen
1 a woman who behaves in a stupid or dangerous way
2 an old-fashioned word for a woman who has an illness that affects the way she thinks and behaves

magazine *noun* magazines
1 a thin book with a paper cover and large pages containing articles, stories and photos on a particular subject. Magazines are printed at regular times such as every week or month.
2 a radio or TV programme about different events or people

ORIGIN from French *magasin* and Arabic *makhzan* 'place for storing things, such as guns'

magenta *noun*
a purple-red colour. It is one of the main colours used in colour printing.
magenta *adjective*

maggot *noun* maggots
a small creature like a fat worm that changes into a fly. Maggots live in rotten food and dead bodies.

magic *noun*
1 a special power that makes impossible things happen that cannot be explained, for example in stories and films *The prince was turned into a frog by magic.*
2 the skill of using magic to do clever tricks, for example to make things appear or disappear
3 **as if by magic** in a surprising way that cannot be explained *My missing textbook suddenly appeared as if by magic on my desk.*

magic *adjective*
1 using magic or doing something by magic *a magic spell; a magic wand; magic powers*
2 used for describing something such as a number or word that is important in a particular situation or will make something happen *Say the magic word 'please' and I'll get you an ice cream.*

magical *adjective*
1 using magic or connected with magic *The old woman had magical powers* (was able to use magic).
2 used for describing something that is wonderful and has a mysterious or exciting quality *Our holiday in Thailand was magical.*

magically – mainland

magically *adverb*
1 used about something impossible that happens by magic *The rabbit magically disappeared.*
2 used about something surprising that happens in a way that cannot be explained

magician *noun* **magicians**
1 someone who does magic tricks in front of an audience
2 someone who has a special power to make impossible things happen

magistrate *noun* **magistrates**
a judge in a court of law who deals with crimes that are not serious and decides whether someone is guilty or not

magma *noun*
hot liquid formed from rocks and chemicals inside the earth's crust (hard outer surface). When a volcano erupts (explodes), the hot magma that flows out is called lava.

Magna Carta *noun*
an important historical document written in England in 1215. In it King John agrees to give up some of his powers and give more freedom to English people.

> ORIGIN from Latin *magna* 'great' and *carta* 'charter' (an official document explaining someone's rights)

magnesium *noun*
a silver-white metal and chemical element. A powder made from magnesium burns strongly with a bright flame and is used in fireworks.

magnet *noun* **magnets**
1 a piece of iron or steel that can make other pieces of iron or steel move towards it and stick to it. A magnet can also push away another magnet.
2 a fridge magnet is a small magnet with a picture or message on it that you stick onto your fridge

magnetic *adjective*
1 if a piece of metal is magnetic, it is pulled towards a magnet *Iron is a magnetic material.*
2 having the power of a magnet *a magnetic force*
3 a magnetic field is the area around a magnet (or another object with magnetic power) that it uses for pulling things towards it
4 a magnetic strip is a thin layer of a special substance with magnetic qualities, for example on a credit card, for storing information on
5 a magnetic tape is a thin plastic strip covered with a special substance with magnetic qualities. It is used for recording sounds, images or computer information.

magnetise *verb*
magnetises, magnetising, magnetised
to make a piece of metal magnetic

> LANGUAGE EXTRA also spelt *magnetize*

magnetism *noun*
the power of a magnet to make pieces of iron or steel move towards it

magnificent *adjective*
1 very beautiful to look at and deserving great respect *a magnificent building*
2 extremely good *He's a magnificent dancer.*

magnificence *noun*

magnificently *adverb*
1 in a very beautiful way *a magnificently decorated room*
2 extremely well *She sings magnificently.*

magnifier *noun* **magnifiers**
something you use to make things look bigger, especially a computer tool that makes an area of the screen easier to see

magnify *verb*
magnifies, magnifying, magnified
1 to make something look bigger, for example by looking at it through equipment such as a microscope
2 a magnifying glass is a piece of round or square glass, fixed to a handle, that you use to make things look bigger

magnification *noun*

magnitude *noun*
1 the size or importance of something
2 (*plural* **magnitudes**) the strength of an earthquake

magnolia *noun* **magnolias**
a small or medium-sized tree with large mainly white or pink flowers and pointed leaves

> ORIGIN it is named after Pierre *Magnol*, a French 17th-century botanist

magpie *noun* **magpies**
a large black and white bird with a long tail. Magpies often decorate their nests with shiny objects such as coins, jewellery or pieces of tinfoil.

mahogany ['mer-hog-er-nee'] *noun*
a hard brown or dark brown wood used for making furniture

maid *noun* **maids**
1 a woman who cleans rooms in a hotel
2 a woman who does the cleaning, cooking and washing in someone's home

maiden *noun* **maidens**
1 an old word for a girl
2 a maiden name is the family name of a woman who changes her name to her husband's name when she gets married

maiden *adjective*
used for describing the first time something is done, such as a journey *a maiden voyage*

mail *noun*
1 letters and parcels (or a letter or parcel) sent or received by post

> SYNONYM post

2 messages (or a message) sent or received over the internet, for example using a computer

> SYNONYMS emails, email

3 a system for sending or receiving letters and parcels. To send them, you usually stick stamps on them and put them in a postbox or take them to a post office. *Granddad sent me a present by mail.*

> SYNONYM post

mail *verb*
mails, mailing, mailed
1 to send something by post to someone's home or office
2 to send something to someone by email *Can you mail the picture to me as an attachment?*

mailbag *noun* **mailbags**
a large strong bag used by postal workers for carrying letters and parcels

mailbox *noun* **mailboxes**
1 a folder on a computer where email messages are received and stored
2 the American word for a postbox
3 in American English, a mailbox is also a small box outside someone's house for receiving letters and parcels

mailing list *noun* **mailing lists**
a list of people that emails or letters are sent to

mailman *noun* **mailmen**
the American word for a postman

> LANGUAGE EXTRA a man or woman who delivers the mail in the US is also called a *mail carrier* or *letter carrier*

mail order *noun*
a way of buying goods, for example by phone or over the internet, and receiving them by post

maim *verb*
maims, maiming, maimed
to hurt someone so badly that their body is damaged for their whole life *The soldiers were maimed by a bomb* (for example, a bomb blew their legs or arms off).

main *adjective*
1 most important *That's the main reason I'm leaving.*
2 largest *the main entrance to the school*
3 most likely *Who are the main suspects in the robbery?*
4 a main line is the most important railway line between cities
5 a main road is an important road used by lots of traffic

main *noun* **mains**
1 a large pipe that carries water or gas to a building, or waste materials away from a building, usually under the ground *a burst water main*; *Dad turned off the water at the mains* (place where the water pipe from your home meets the public water pipe).
2 a large wire that carries electricity to a building *Our new flat isn't on the mains yet* (connected to the electricity wire). *I plugged my laptop into the mains* (place on a wall where you connect an electric plug).

main clause *noun* **main clauses**
a complete sentence that is a part of a larger sentence. For example, in the sentence 'I'll go out to play if it stops raining', the main clause is 'I'll go out to play'.
compare: **subordinate clause**

mainland *noun*
the land that forms the main part of a country or continent, not the islands close to it

mainly – malicious

mainly adverb
1 almost always *I mainly go to bed at ten o'clock.*
2 used when you mean the biggest or most important part of something or almost all of something *My dress is mainly green.*
3 used when you mean the most important reason for something *I don't take the bus to school mainly because I like walking.*
4 almost but not quite *I'm mainly ready.*

maintain verb
maintains, maintaining, maintained
1 to look after something such as a building, road or piece of equipment so that it stays in good condition
2 to continue to have something or to not allow something to become worse or less *Eat lots of fruit and vegetables to maintain your health.*
3 to say strongly that something is true or that you believe something *The head teacher maintains that the playground is safe.*
4 to provide a person with what they need to live, for example food, clothes and a place to stay *My mum and dad have four children to maintain.*

maintenance noun
1 work done to look after something such as a building or road so that it stays in good condition
2 money paid to someone to provide what they need to live

maisonette noun maisonettes
a flat on two floors that is part of a bigger building. A maisonette usually has its own door to the outside.

maize noun
a tall plant with yellow seeds that can be cooked and eaten

majestic adjective
looking beautiful or powerful in a way that deserves great respect *a majestic building*
majestically adverb

majesty noun
1 (plural **Majesties**) Majesty is the title used when speaking to or about a king or queen *Yes, Your Majesty. Their Majesties, the King and Queen of Sweden.*
2 the quality of looking beautiful or powerful in a way that deserves great respect

major adjective
1 important or big *There are some major mistakes in your homework.*
2 most important or biggest of all *That's my major problem.*
3 in music, a major scale (series of notes) is one in which the third note is two tones higher than the first

major noun majors
an officer in the army just above the rank of captain

majorette noun majorettes
a woman or girl who walks in front of a musical group in a procession while spinning and throwing a thin stick called a baton

majority noun
1 most of a group of people or things *The majority of the children have laptops at home.*
2 the difference in the number of votes between someone who wins a vote or election and someone who comes second *Alex was voted class monitor by a majority of five.*

make verb
makes, making, made
1 to put materials or substances together in a certain way so as to be responsible for the existence of something *I've made a cake. He made the box out of cardboard. Bees make honey.*
2 used with many different nouns to show that someone or something does the particular action corresponding to the noun *I made a phone call. The washing machine is making a noise. What a nice model you've made!*
3 used with many different adjectives to show how someone or something becomes *The results made us happy. Fold the paper to make it smaller.*
4 to make someone or something do something is to be the reason why they do it *The loud noise made me jump. Lots of sunlight makes the flowers grow.*
5 to make someone or something do something is also to use strength or power as a way of getting it done *Dad made me tell the truth.*
6 to organise something in a certain way, for example by putting different parts together *It's time to make the bed. Hitchcock made a famous film called 'The Birds'.*
7 to make money is to get it by working or in some other way *My brother makes £500 a week. How much does your mum make?*
8 used when saying or asking what the time is *I make it six o'clock.*
9 to be successful in getting somewhere *I've made it to the end of the book.*
10 to choose someone, for example for a job or responsibility *Mr Solomon was made head teacher.*
11 if you make do, you accept something even though it's not what you really want *We don't have any tea or coffee so you'll have to make do with water.*
12 if you make for a place, you go there *When the bell went, everyone made for the exit.*
13 if someone makes off, they leave a place quickly, for example after stealing something *The burglars made off with my laptop.*
14 if you make something or someone out, you can see, hear or understand them but not very easily *You can just about make out the shape of a person in the distance.*
15 if you make something up such as an excuse or reason, you give someone an excuse or reason that isn't true
16 if you make something up such as a poem, joke or story, you are the first person to think of it
17 if people or things make up something, they form part of the whole of something *Girls make up half the class. These ideas make up an important part of the book.*
18 to make up is also to become friends with someone again after an argument *Let's make up!*
19 to make up for something is to do something to make a bad situation better *What can I do to make up for being late?*

make noun makes
1 the name of a product made by a particular company *Always buy a good make of computer.*
2 the name of the company that makes this product *What's the make of your bike?*

make-believe noun
imagining that something is real when it is not real *Lots of people live in a world of make-believe.*

maker noun makers
1 a company or person that makes something *a computer maker*
2 a piece of equipment that makes something *a coffee maker*

makeshift adjective
used for a short time only or prepared quickly because there is nothing better *After the earthquake many people had to live in makeshift tents.*

make-up noun
things such as powders, creams or lipstick that someone puts on their face to make them look better or different

LANGUAGE EXTRA also spelt *makeup*

mal- prefix
used with nouns, adjectives and verbs to mean bad or badly *malfunction; malformed*

malaria ['mer-lair-ee-er'] noun
a serious illness that people get by being bitten by a certain type of mosquito. It is common in many hot countries.

Malaysia noun
a country in South-East Asia
Malaysian adjective & noun

male adjective
1 connected with boys or men *Most of the football team are male.*
2 belonging to the sex that does not have babies (or baby animals) or produce eggs *a male horse*

ANTONYM female

male noun males
1 a boy or man
2 an animal belonging to the sex that does not have baby animals or produce eggs

ANTONYM female

malevolent ['mer-lev-er-lernt'] adjective
1 doing or wanting to do very bad or cruel things *a malevolent witch*
2 also used about something that someone does or says *a malevolent smile*
malevolence noun **malevolently** adverb

malfunction verb
malfunctions, malfunctioning, malfunctioned
if something such as a piece of equipment malfunctions, it doesn't work properly
malfunction noun

malice noun
the wish to do bad things to someone or be unkind to them

malicious adjective
1 wanting to do bad things to someone or be unkind to them *Don't be so malicious!*
2 also used about something that someone does or says *a malicious look*

mall–man-made

3 used about software that harms your computer, for example because it contains a virus *I accidentally downloaded a malicious app.*
maliciously adverb

mall noun **malls**
a large building with lots of shops and restaurants and often a cinema, usually built on two or more levels

> **LANGUAGE EXTRA** also called a *shopping mall*

mallet noun **mallets**
1 a large wooden hammer, usually with a large heavy head that is also made of wood, used for example to knock pieces of wood together
2 a long stick with a wooden part at the end that looks like a fat tube, used for hitting a ball in sports such as polo

malnutrition noun
a medical problem that makes someone's body weak because they haven't had enough food

malt noun
dried grains of the barley plant, used for example in making beer and vinegar (sour liquid made from wine)

Malta noun
a country made up of islands in the Mediterranean south of Sicily
Maltese adjective & noun

malware noun
software that harms your computer, for example because it contains a virus or allows someone to take control of your computer
short for: *malicious software*
compare: **adware** and **spyware**

mama noun **mamas**
an informal word for a mother

mammal noun **mammals**
an animal that belongs to a class of animals including humans. The babies of mammals are born from their mother's body, not from eggs, and are fed with their mother's milk.

mammoth noun **mammoths**
a kind of large elephant covered with hair and with very long curved tusks (big pointed teeth). Mammoths existed in the past until about 5000 years ago.

mammoth adjective
used for describing something that is very big *a mammoth task*

> **SYNONYM** huge

man noun **men**
1 a grown-up male person
2 a male person who works somewhere *We're waiting for the TV repair man. The man from the council is at the door.*
3 people in general *prehistoric man; We're studying the history of man.*
4 one of the pieces that you move in a board game such as chess

man verb
mans, manning, manned
if people man something, they work at it, operate it or are in charge of it *The phones are manned between nine and six o'clock.*

man interjection
used for showing a feeling such as being surprised, angry or happy

manage verb
manages, managing, managed
1 to be able to do something even though it may be difficult *I managed to finish my homework on time. The team managed two wins one after the other. Mum's in hospital but Dad's managing well* (dealing well with a difficult situation).
2 to be in charge of something such as a business, shop, sports team or music group and organise the way it works
3 to organise or control something you are responsible for *Our teacher often has trouble managing the class. With so much work to do, you'll have to learn how to manage your time.*

manageable adjective
easy to deal with *Let's break this work into smaller more manageable tasks.*

management noun
1 being in charge of something such as a business or shop
2 the people in charge of a business or shop

manager noun **managers**
someone in charge of something such as a business, shop, sports team or music group

mandarin noun **mandarins**
a type of small orange with loose skin that is easy to peel

Mandarin noun
one of the languages spoken in China and the official language of China

mane noun **manes**
the long thick hair around the head of a horse or male lion

manger ['mayn-jer] noun **mangers**
a long open container in a stable that animals such as horses and cows feed from

mangetout ['monj-too'] noun **mangetouts**
a type of small flat green pea that you eat as a vegetable

> **ORIGIN** from French *mange tout* 'eat everything', because you eat the pod (container) of the pea as well as the seeds

mangle verb
mangles, mangling, mangled
to destroy something or damage it badly by twisting or crushing it *The car was completely mangled in the accident.*

mango noun **mangoes**
an oval-shaped fruit with a smooth green skin, soft orange-yellow flesh and a very big hard seed inside called a stone. Mangoes grow in hot countries.

mangrove noun **mangroves**
a tree that grows near water in hot countries. It has twisted roots that you can see above the ground.

mangy ['mayn-jee] adjective
mangier, mangiest
an informal word for describing something old and dirty *The beggar was wearing a mangy old coat.*

> **SYNONYM** manky

manhandle verb
manhandles, manhandling, manhandled
to push, pull or move someone or something in a rough way

manhole noun **manholes**
an opening with a lid on top in the surface of something such as a road or pavement. It is used for going under the ground, for example for checking or repairing pipes or drains.

mania noun **manias**
1 a very strong interest in something, especially one shared by lots of people *Football mania is spreading across the country.*
2 an illness that makes someone very worried about something or makes them think about one particular thing all the time

maniac noun **maniacs**
1 someone who behaves in a dangerous or violent way *My brother drives like a maniac.*
2 someone who has a very strong interest in something *I'm a football maniac.*
3 if you do something such as work, study or practise like a maniac, you do it with lots of energy

manic adjective
if someone is manic, they do things in a rush and with lots of energy because they are excited or nervous

manicure noun **manicures**
beauty treatment for the hands, for example cutting and smoothing the nails

manifest verb
manifests, manifesting, manifested
if someone manifests something such as a feeling, they show it

manifesto noun **manifestos**
a document written by a group or political party that gives information about its aims and plans

manipulate verb
manipulates, manipulating, manipulated
1 if someone manipulates someone or something, they use skill to deal with them to dishonestly get something they want
2 to control something using your hands
manipulation noun

manipulative adjective
using skill to deal with people to dishonestly get what you want

mankind noun
all the human beings in the world, both men and women *This is an important discovery for the future of mankind.*

manky adjective **mankier, mankiest**
an informal word for describing something old and dirty *a manky old carpet*

> **SYNONYM** mangy

manly adjective **manlier, manliest**
1 having qualities that some people think a man should have *a manly voice* (for example deep)
2 doing something that some people think a man should do *Is it manly to show your feelings?*
manliness noun

man-made adjective
not natural but made by people or machines *a man-made lake; Nylon is a man-made material.*

manned–march

manned *adjective*
connected with vehicles or aircraft that people travel in *a manned spacecraft*; *the history of manned flight*

manner *noun* **manners**
1 a way of doing something or the way that something happens *Press here to shut down your laptop in the normal manner.*
2 the way someone behaves towards other people and speaks to them *Our doctor has a very gentle manner.*
3 manners are ways of behaving when you are with other people, especially polite ways that show respect to them *My sister needs to learn manners. She has bad manners* (her behaviour shows no respect to others).

-mannered *suffix*
used for making adjectives that describe the behaviour someone has when they are with other people *bad-mannered*; *well-mannered* (having good behaviour)

manoeuvre ['mer-noo-ver'] *verb*
manoeuvres, manoeuvring, manoeuvred
to move somewhere or to move something somewhere using a lot of skill *Mum manoeuvred the car into the garage. We've no room to manoeuvre in our tiny flat.*

manoeuvre ['mer-noo-ver'] *noun*
manoeuvres
1 an action or movement that needs a lot of skill
2 a clever action to trick someone and get what you want

manor *noun* **manors**
an old word for a large old house in the country with a lot of land around it

mansion *noun* **mansions**
a very large and expensive house with very many rooms

> ORIGIN from Anglo-Norman *mansion* 'staying place' (from Latin *manere* 'to stay')

manslaughter ['man-slor-ter'] *noun*
the crime of accidentally killing someone

mantelpiece *noun* **mantelpieces**
a shelf that forms the top part of a fireplace (a frame around an opening in a wall where people make a fire)

mantle *noun* **mantles**
1 an old-fashioned word for something that covers a surface *The streets were buried beneath a mantle of snow.*
2 a type of loose coat without sleeves worn mainly in the past

manual *noun* **manuals**
a book or electronic file that gives details about how to do something, especially how to use a piece of equipment *a computer manual*

manual *adjective*
1 used for describing something you do with your hands or a piece of equipment you operate using your hands *manual work*; *an old manual typewriter*
2 used for describing someone who works with their hands *a manual worker*
manually *adverb*

> ORIGIN from Latin *manualis* 'connected with the hand' (from *manus* 'hand')

manufacture *verb*
manufactures, manufacturing, manufactured
to make something with equipment using different materials, usually in a factory *Dad's car was manufactured in Japan. Paper and plastics are manufactured materials.* **manufacturer** *noun*

manufacture *noun*
making things with equipment, usually in large quantities in a factory

manure *noun*
waste matter from animals that is put on soil so that plants grow better

manuscript *noun* **manuscripts**
1 a piece of writing such as a book or article before it is printed
2 a very old book or document written by hand before printing was invented

> ORIGIN from Latin *manu* 'by hand' and *scriptus* 'written'

Manx *adjective*
connected with the Isle of Man

many *adjective & pronoun* **more, most**
1 used when talking about a large number of things or people *We read many books in school. Many of my friends have laptops at home.*
2 **a good many** a large number but not a very large number *I've eaten a good many biscuits already.*
3 **a great many** a very large number
4 **as many as** used for showing how large a number is *I have as many as a hundred books at home.*
5 **how many** used when asking or talking about an amount or number *How many friends do you have?*

Maori ['Mao' rhymes with 'cow'] *noun*
1 (plural **Maoris**) a man or woman belonging to the group of people who were living in New Zealand before the Europeans arrived
2 the language of the Maori people

map *noun* **maps**
1 a drawing of a large area such as a country, continent or the whole world, showing important things such as rivers, towns, mountains and roads
2 a drawing of a smaller area such as a town, village, railway or school to help you find your way *a street map*; *the London tube map*
3 a simple drawing that shows someone how to get to a place *Dad drew me a map to get from the school to the station.*
4 a drawing that gives information or the position of something *a weather map*; *a map of the stars in the sky*

map *verb*
maps, mapping, mapped
1 to make a map of an area *This part of Brazil has not yet been mapped.*
2 to map something out is to plan it carefully, for example a route or someone's future

maple *noun* **maples**
1 a tall tree with attractive wide leaves that have five points. It grows mainly in northern countries. The maple leaf is the symbol of Canada and appears on its flag.
2 maple syrup is a sweet sticky liquid from the maple tree. It is often eaten with pancakes.

mapping *noun*
digital or computer mapping is using computer software to produce detailed maps and images of a place, which people can use on a satnav, computer or smartphone

mar *verb*
mars, marring, marred
to make something less good, attractive or interesting

> SYNONYM to spoil

marathon *noun* **marathons**
1 a race in which people run for a distance of 26 miles
2 an event or activity that lasts a very long time

> ORIGIN from *Marathon*, the name of a plain near Athens in Greece. In 490 BC, a Greek hero ran from there to Athens, about 26 miles away, to bring news of a Greek victory in a battle with the Persians.

marauding *adjective*
used for describing people who go from place to place attacking and killing people and stealing, damaging and destroying things **marauder** *noun*

marble *noun*
1 a very hard rock that is smooth and shiny when it is cut and polished. Marble is usually white with a pattern of small lines called grains. It is used in building and for making statues.
2 (plural **marbles**) a small coloured or transparent ball, usually made of glass, used in children's games
3 marbles is a children's game in which marbles are rolled along the ground

> ORIGIN from Greek *marmaros* 'shining stone'

march *verb*
marches, marching, marched
1 to walk with regular steps as part of a group of people *The soldiers marched through the town.*
2 if someone marches in a demonstration, they walk with other people to show they are not happy about something or that they support something
3 to walk somewhere quickly without letting anything stop you, for example because you are angry *Mum marched into my room and told me to stop watching TV.*

> ORIGIN from Old French *marchier* 'to walk' or 'to tread'

march *noun* **marches**
1 an event in which people walk together through the streets to show that they are not happy about something or that they support something
2 a walk by people such as soldiers who move together with regular steps
3 a piece of music with a strong rhythm, for example suitable for soldiers while they are marching

March–marsh

March noun
the third month of the year, between February and April. March has 31 days.

> ORIGIN from Latin *Martius* '(the month) of Mars', referring to the Roman god of war

mare noun mares
an adult female horse or donkey

> LANGUAGE EXTRA an adult male horse is called a *stallion*

margarine ['mar-jer-reen'] noun
a soft yellow food usually made from vegetable fat. It is used like butter in cooking and for putting on bread or toast.

marge noun
an informal word for margarine

margin noun margins
1 the empty space down the side or along the top of a page of writing or pictures *I made some notes in the margin of my textbook.*
2 the difference between two amounts, for example points in a competition or votes in an election *We won the competition by a margin of 10 points.*

marginal adjective
very small and not important *a marginal improvement*

marginally adverb
very slightly *Grandma is feeling marginally better today.*

marigold noun marigolds
a garden plant that has yellow, gold or orange flowers with lots of petals and a strong smell

marina ['mer-ree-ner'] noun marinas
a part of the sea at the coast where yachts and small boats stop and can be left safely. There are often shops, restaurants and hotels near a marina.

marine ['mer-reen'] adjective
connected with the sea *marine animals*

> ORIGIN from Latin *marinus* 'of the sea' (from *mare* 'sea')

marine ['mer-reen'] noun marines
a soldier who fights on land and sea

mariner ['ma-ri-ner'] noun mariners
an old-fashioned word for a sailor

marionette noun marionettes
a puppet controlled by strings or wires that someone holds from above

> ORIGIN from French *marionnette* 'little Marion' or 'little tiny Mary'

mark noun marks
1 a small area on the surface of something where it is dirty or damaged. Stains, scratches and burns are marks. *finger marks; There's a mark on the lid of my laptop. I've got a red mark on my hand where I burnt myself.*
2 an area that is different from the rest of a surface, for example in its colour or shape. Stripes and dots are marks. *This bird has black marks on its body. Freckles are little round marks on the face and arms.*
3 a shape, object or action that represents something or gives information about something *a question mark* (written symbol showing that a word or phrase is a question); *These marks on the map show towns. I took off my shoes as a mark of respect* (sign showing respect to someone).
4 a number or letter that someone such as a teacher gives to a piece of work or an exam to show how good it is *Mohammed got full* (or *top*) *marks for his maths homework* (for example the highest possible number, such as 20 out of 20, because all his answers were correct). *Jess got a bad* (or *low*) *mark in the test* (for example a letter such as D because she got lots of things wrong).
5 a point that you get for answering a question correctly, for example in an exam or quiz *You get two marks for each correct answer.*
6 a particular level that something reaches *Fill the kettle up to the halfway mark.*
7 a unit of money in Germany before the euro
8 **On your marks, get set, go!** used for telling runners in a race to go into their starting place, get ready and start running

mark verb
marks, marking, marked
1 to put a mark on a surface that makes it dirty or leaves it damaged, for example by staining, scratching or burning it *The cup fell on the table and marked it. His hand was marked with burns.*
2 to put a mark on a surface that shows a different colour or shape *Zebras are marked with stripes.*
3 to put a mark (such as a shape, written symbol or word) on something to give information about it *Mum has marked my schoolbag with my name.*
4 used about something that gives information *An X marks the spot on the map where the treasure is buried. Clocks and watches mark the time.*
5 used about something such as an event, shape, object or action that represents something *This concert marks an important date in the school calendar.*
6 to celebrate an event *We marked our parents' anniversary by going to the theatre.*
7 if someone such as a teacher marks a piece of work or an exam, they correct mistakes in it and give someone a number or letter to show how good it is
8 if you mark someone in a sport such as football, you stay close to a person in the opposite team to stop him or her getting the ball
9 **mark my words** used for telling someone to listen carefully to what you are saying

marker noun markers
1 a pen with a thick soft point
2 an object used for showing the position of something *I put a marker in my book to keep my place.*

market noun markets
1 a place, usually outside, where people sell things, often cheaply from tables called stalls
2 the people who want to buy a particular product *China is our biggest market. There's a big market for second-hand clothes* (lots of people want to buy them).

market verb
markets, marketing, marketed
to sell goods using advertising and other ways to make people buy them

marketplace noun marketplaces
an area in a town or village where there is a market

markings noun plural
1 a pattern of shapes or colours on the fur of an animal or feathers of a bird
2 things painted or written on something such as a road or vehicle *The snow covered up the yellow markings on the road.*

marksman noun marksmen
someone trained to shoot a gun very carefully *a police marksman*

markswoman noun markswomen
a woman trained to shoot a gun very carefully

marmalade noun
a jam made from oranges, lemons, limes or grapefruits

> ORIGIN from 15th-century Portuguese *marmelada* 'quince jam', because it was originally made from quinces (hard yellow fruits like apples)

marmoset noun marmosets
a tiny monkey with large eyes that lives in South America

maroon noun
a very dark red colour *maroon* adjective

maroon verb
maroons, marooning, marooned
if someone is marooned, they are left in a place they can't escape from, far away from other people

marquee ['mah-kee'] noun marquees
a large tent used for events such as parties or exhibitions

marriage noun marriages
1 the life that two married people share
2 the ceremony in which two people make promises to each other and get married

married adjective
if someone is married, they have made promises to someone in a marriage ceremony and have become this person's husband, wife or partner

marrow noun
1 (plural **marrows**) a large long vegetable that is white inside, usually with a hard dark green skin
2 marrow or bone marrow is the soft substance inside bones

marry verb
marries, marrying, married
1 to become someone's husband, wife or partner in a ceremony called a marriage or wedding *Mum and Dad got married a long time ago.*
2 if an official person marries two people, he or she performs the ceremony of marriage

Mars noun
the fourth planet from the sun, after the earth and before Jupiter. It is the closest one to the earth.

marsh noun marshes
flat ground near a river, lake or the sea that is wet and muddy

marshal – masterly

marshal noun marshals
1 an official person who helps to control people at a public event such as a demonstration or sports event
2 an officer in the army or air force with a very high rank or top rank, such as a field marshal
3 a title given to a police officer of the highest rank in some parts of the USA

marshmallow noun marshmallows
a type of soft sweet that is thick and round and is usually made in white or pink colours

ORIGIN from the name of a plant, also called *marshmallow*, because the sweet was first made from a soft substance taken from its root

marshy adjective marshier, marshiest
used about ground that is flat, wet and muddy

marsupial ['mah-**soop**-yerl'] noun marsupials
an animal such as a kangaroo or koala bear. The female carries its baby in a pocket of skin called a pouch at the front of its body.

martial adjective
connected with fighting or with soldiers *martial art* (a fighting sport such as karate or judo); *martial law* (controlling a country with soldiers)

Martian noun Martians
in stories, a Martian is a creature from the planet Mars **Martian** adjective

martyr ['**mah**-ter'] noun martyrs
someone very brave who is killed or suffers great pain because of their religion or political ideas. People praise and respect martyrs.

martyrdom noun
the death or great pain of a martyr

marvel verb
marvels, marvelling, marvelled
if you marvel at something, you have a feeling of great respect for it or you are very surprised by it, for example because it is so beautiful, large or good *We marvelled at the sight of the Eiffel Tower before us.*

marvel noun marvels
something that fills you with great respect or surprise, for example because it is so beautiful, large or good

SYNONYM wonder

marvellous adjective
extremely good *We had a marvellous holiday.*

SYNONYM wonderful

marvellously adverb
1 extremely well *She dances marvellously.*
2 extremely *a marvellously soft armchair*

Marxism noun
a political and economic belief that people in society will become equal in the future as a result of the struggle between different classes

ORIGIN from the name of the German writer Karl *Marx* (1818–83) who developed the idea with Friedrich Engels (1820–95)

Marxist noun Marxists
someone who believes in Marxism
Marxist adjective

marzipan noun
a soft sweet food made from almonds, sugar and eggs, used for putting on cakes and making sweets

mascot noun mascots
an object or animal that belongs, for example, to a person or team taking part in a sport or competition and is supposed to bring them good luck

masculine adjective
1 connected with boys or men *a masculine appearance*
2 connected with the qualities people sometimes think of when they think about boys or men *My brother loves the masculine atmosphere of competitiveness.*
3 used about the form of a part of speech, such as a pronoun, noun or adjective, that is different from the feminine form in some languages *'He' is a masculine pronoun.*
masculinity noun

ANTONYM feminine

mash noun
another word for mashed potatoes

mash verb
mashes, mashing, mashed
to crush food into pieces after cooking it until it becomes a soft mass *I love mashed potatoes.*

mask noun masks
something you wear to cover all or part of your face, for example to hide it, protect it or as a decoration *The robbers were wearing masks. The soldiers wore gas masks* (against harmful gases).

mask verb
masks, masking, masked
1 to hide something *He masked his face with his hand.*
2 to stop something such as a smell, taste or sound from being noticed *Dad cut open some onions to mask the smell of the burnt toast.*

mason noun masons
someone whose job is to cut and use stone for building things

SYNONYM stonemason

masonry noun
the bricks and stone parts that a building is made of *My uncle was injured by some falling masonry.*

mass noun
1 (plural **masses**) a large amount or number of things or people *My aunt has a mass of books to give away. There were masses of people in the streets. I've got masses to do.*
2 (plural **masses**) a lump of something solid without any particular shape *A mass of concrete fell off a building.*
3 in science, mass is the amount of matter (or substance) in an object, liquid or gas. It shows the weight of something and is measured in grams and kilograms.
4 if you talk about the masses, you mean ordinary people in society, not rich people or political leaders *Gandhi was loved by the masses.*

mass verb
masses, massing, massed
to come together in very large numbers *Enemy soldiers were massing at the country's border.*

Mass noun Masses
a religious ceremony in some Christian churches, for example the Roman Catholic Church. Bread and wine are given to people to remind them of Christ's last meal with his disciples.

LANGUAGE EXTRA also spelt mass

massacre ['**mass**-er-ker'] verb
massacres, massacring, massacred
to kill a lot of people at the same time or in a short period of time

massacre ['**mass**-er-ker'] noun massacres
the killing of a lot of people

massage ['**mass**-ahj'; 'j' has the middle sound of 'pleasure'] verb
massages, massaging, massaged
to rub and press someone's body or a part of it to get rid of pain or make someone feel better **massage** noun

massive adjective
1 very big *There's a massive spider in the bathroom.*

SYNONYMS huge, enormous

2 very big and heavy *We could see the massive shape of the mosque in the distance.*

massively adverb
1 very *massively successful*
2 very much *The number of mistakes has increased massively.*

mass-produced adjective
mass-produced goods are made in very large quantities using equipment in factories
mass production noun

mast noun masts
1 a tall pole used for holding up the sails of a ship or boat
2 a pole that a flag hangs from
3 a tall pole or structure for supporting a radio, TV or mobile phone aerial

master noun masters
1 someone who is in charge of something *Who is the master of this house?*
2 someone who is very good at something *She's a master at her craft. This painting is by an old master* (famous painter from long ago). *My aunt is a master chef.*
3 a word sometimes used for a male teacher
4 someone who owns and looks after a dog
5 Master is an old-fashioned word for talking to or about a young boy *Here's young Master John.*

master verb
masters, mastering, mastered
1 to learn something or how to do something very well so that you are very good at it *It took my sister five years to master French.*
2 to learn to control a feeling or difficulty

masterly adjective
very skilful or done in a very skilful way *a masterly performance*

285

mastermind–matter

mastermind noun masterminds
someone who organises a complicated activity or a crime **mastermind** verb

masterpiece noun masterpieces
1 a piece of work that is of a very high quality, for example a painting, book, film or piece of music
2 the best piece of work produced by someone such as a painter, writer, film-maker or musician

mastery noun
1 very great knowledge of something or skill in something *Rosie is proud of her mastery of Spanish.*
2 complete control of something such as a situation

mat noun mats
1 a piece of material such as cloth or plastic that covers part of a floor to protect it or as a decoration
2 a small piece of material inside or outside the main door of a building, used for cleaning the bottom of your shoes

> SYNONYM doormat

3 a small piece of material that you put inside or outside a shower or bath to stop you from slipping *We always use a rubber bath mat in the shower.*
4 a small piece of material such as plastic or wood that you put underneath something, for example a hot dish or mug, to protect the surface it is on *a table mat*

matador noun matadors
someone in Spain or Mexico who takes part in a bullfight and tries to kill the bull

> ORIGIN from Spanish *matar* 'to kill'

match noun matches
1 a short thin piece of wood with a chemical substance at one end that catches fire when you rub it against something. It is used for lighting something such as a fire, gas burner or candle.
2 a game between two teams of people (for example a football match) or between two people (for example a boxing match)
3 something that is similar to something else, for example in its shape, colour or pattern, and looks good with it *We're trying to find a match for this green paint.*

match verb
matches, matching, matched
1 if something matches something else or if two things match, the two things are closely connected because something in one of them is similar to something in the other *Put the correct letters and pictures together, for example A matches the apple. These two symbols match.*
2 if something matches something else or if two things match, it also means that the two things look good or attractive together *Do my jacket and trousers match? Your shoes match your dress.*
3 to put similar things together *Can you match the words and the pictures?*
4 to be as good as something else or do the same thing as someone else *Chloe scored 50 points – I could never match that!*
5 to be equivalent in importance to something else *The punishment must always match the crime.*

matchbox noun matchboxes
a small box that contains matches

matching adjective
1 similar to something else, for example in its shape, colour or pattern *Draw a line between the matching shapes.*
2 looking good or attractive with something else *James is looking for a shirt and a matching tie.*

matchstick noun matchsticks
1 a single wooden match, usually after it has been used *Someone left a pile of matchsticks on the pavement.*
2 a matchstick man or woman is a simple drawing of a man or woman with lines for the body, arms and legs and a circle for the head

mate noun mates
1 an informal word for a friend
2 the partner of an animal that it produces baby animals with
3 someone who helps a skilled worker in their job *a plumber's mate*
4 an officer on a ship, usually a ship transporting goods or passengers

mate verb
mates, mating, mated
if animals mate, they produce baby animals together

material noun materials
1 another word for cloth *You need a lot of material to make a coat.*
2 any substance, especially when it can be used for making something. Materials include plastics, paper and glass (manufactured) and wood, stone and wool (natural).
3 information or ideas used for writing something such as a book or producing something such as a piece of music
4 equipment or documents used for a particular activity *teaching materials*

materialistic adjective
if someone is materialistic, they are only interested in having money and owning things

maternal adjective
1 connected with being a mother or with the qualities some people think a mother should have *maternal feelings* (for example being kind and loving)
2 connected with your mother's side of the family *Granddad John is my maternal grandfather.*

> ORIGIN from Latin *mater* 'mother'

maternity adjective
connected with or suitable for women who are having a baby *maternity clothes*; *a maternity hospital* (where mothers go to give birth to their baby); *maternity leave* (when women are allowed to be away from their job before and after giving birth)

mathematical adjective
connected with mathematics, for example using calculations, measurements and symbols *a mathematical formula*; *Sophie has good mathematical skills.*

mathematician ['math-er-mer-**tish**-ern'] noun mathematicians
someone who studies numbers, quantities, shapes and space or who is an expert in mathematics

mathematics noun
the study of numbers, quantities, shapes and space and the way they are connected to each other

> ORIGIN from Greek *mathema* 'something learnt' or 'science' (from *manthanein* 'to learn')

maths noun
short for **mathematics**

matinée ['**mat**-in-ay'] noun matinées
an afternoon performance of a play or film in a theatre or cinema

> LANGUAGE EXTRA also spelt matinee

> ORIGIN from French *matinée* 'morning period', because in 19th-century France this word included the whole period until about six o'clock in the evening

matrimony noun
another word for marriage
matrimonial adjective

matrix noun matrices ['**may**-tris-eez']
in maths, a matrix is a group of numbers or symbols usually in rows and columns inside in a rectangle. It is used for solving mathematical problems.

matron noun matrons
1 an old-fashioned word for a senior female nurse in a hospital
2 a female nurse in charge of health in some schools

matt adjective
1 used for describing something such as a surface or colour that is not bright and shiny
2 a matt paint is one that does not give a shine to a surface when it dries

matted adjective
twisted together in an untidy way *matted hair*

matter verb
matters, mattering, mattered
if something matters, it is important *Does it matter where we sit? We're late but it doesn't matter.*

matter noun
1 (plural matters) a subject or situation that someone deals with or thinks about *Can you tell me a bit more about this matter? Ed's behaviour made matters worse* (made things worse).
2 things of a particular type *printed matter* (for example books or documents)
3 in science, matter is the substance that all objects in the universe are made of
4 **the matter** used when talking or asking about something bad such as a problem or pain or a situation in which something doesn't work *What's the matter?* (What's wrong?); *Is there anything the matter with your leg? There's nothing the matter with my laptop.*
5 **no matter** used for saying that something is not important because it makes no difference to a situation *No matter how hard I try, I'll never be able to ride a bike.*
6 **as a matter of fact** used for saying that something is really true or for adding something to what you've already said

286

matting–meander

matting *noun*
strong thick material, for example made from rope or straw, used for covering floors

mattress *noun* **mattresses**
the part of a bed that you lie on, made of a cloth cover forming a thick layer that is filled with a soft material

mature *adjective*
1 a mature person is someone who is very sensible and behaves like an adult
2 also used about what a mature person does or says *mature behaviour*
3 a mature person is also someone who is no longer young and who looks like an adult *My sister is a mature adult.*
4 a mature animal or plant is fully grown and will not grow any bigger

mature *verb*
matures, maturing, matured
1 to start to behave like an adult or look like an adult
2 to become fully grown *The young birds mature very quickly.*

maturity *noun*
1 the quality of being sensible and behaving like a grown-up
2 when someone looks like an adult
3 when an animal or plant is fully grown

maul *verb*
mauls, mauling, mauled
if someone is mauled by an animal, they are attacked and injured by its teeth and claws (curved nails)

mauve ['mohv'] *adjective*
light purple *Seema was wearing a mauve blouse.* **mauve** *noun*

ORIGIN from Latin *malva* 'mallow', because the flowers of the mallow plant have this colour

maximise *verb*
maximises, maximising, maximised
to change the way a program or document appears on a computer screen by making the image as big as the screen *Click on the plus sign to maximise the window.*

LANGUAGE EXTRA also spelt *maximize*

maximum *noun* **maximums** or **maxima**
the largest amount or number of something that is possible or allowed *The maximum is 50.*

maximum *adjective*
largest possible or allowed *The maximum score you can get is 250.*

may *verb*
present tense **may**, past tense **might**
1 used for asking and giving permission *May I close the door? You may come in now.*
2 used for saying that something is possible *I may go over to Granddad's tonight. He might have already left.*
3 used for expressing a wish *May you have lots of luck.*

May *noun*
the fifth month of the year, between April and June. May has 31 days.

ORIGIN from Latin *Maius*, named after Maia, the Roman goddess of the earth

maybe *adverb*
1 used for saying that something is possible or could be true *Maybe I'll be late for school.*
2 used for suggesting something *Maybe you should try again.*
3 used when answering a question when you don't want to say yes or no *'Coming to my party tomorrow?' – 'Maybe.'*

SYNONYMS perhaps, possibly

mayday *noun* **maydays**
a radio signal sent from an aircraft or ship when it needs help

ORIGIN from the French *m'aider* 'help me' (pronounced 'may-day'), which comes from the phrase *venez m'aider* 'come and help me'

May Day *noun*
the first day of May when people celebrate the beginning of spring. There is a holiday in the UK on or near this date with traditional dancing around a decorated pole called a maypole.

mayhem ['**may**-hem] *noun*
a situation where everything is confused

mayonnaise ['may-er-**nayz**'] *noun*
a thick white or yellow sauce made from oil, vinegar (sour liquid made from wine) and the yellow parts of eggs. It is often used on salads.

mayor *noun* **mayors**
a person chosen to be the leader of the group of people in charge of a town or city

mayoress *noun* **mayoresses**
1 a female mayor
2 the wife or partner of a mayor

maypole *noun* **maypoles**
a tall pole fixed in the ground and decorated with coloured ribbons (long strips of cloth) that are tied to the top. People hold the ends of the ribbons and do traditional dances around the maypole on the first day of May.

maze *noun* **mazes**
1 a specially built area, for example in a park, with lots of paths separated by bushes or walls. You walk into it for fun and try to find your way out again. *Hampton Court Palace has a famous maze.*
2 a place made up of lots of similar passages or streets in which you can easily get lost
3 a type of puzzle with a drawing of a maze that you are supposed to find your way through

MB
short for **megabyte** or **megabytes**

me *pronoun*
a word that you use when you are talking about yourself *Did you ask me? He's sitting behind me.*

meadow *noun* **meadows**
a field with grass and wild flowers in it

meagre ['**mee**-ger] *adjective*
very small and not enough *There was a meagre amount of food on the table.*

meal *noun*
1 (*plural* **meals**) the food that you eat at one time, especially at a certain time of the day for breakfast, lunch or dinner
2 (*plural* **meals**) an occasion when you eat this food *We went to my uncle's for a meal.*
3 a powder made from crushing plant seeds. It is used as flour or as food for animals.

mean *verb*
means, meaning, meant
1 if something means something or if you mean something, that is the way you explain it, or that is the idea or information that it represents *The word 'excellent' means 'very good'. What do you mean by smiling like that?*
2 used for giving special importance to something you say *No pocket money for you this week and I mean it.*
3 used for saying that something happens as a result of something else *Going by bus means I can get to school in 10 minutes. More homework means less time for TV.*
4 if you mean to do something, you have thought about it and decided that's what you want to do or what you're going to do *I meant to come to your house but I was too tired. Sorry, I didn't mean to bump into you.*

SYNONYM to intend

5 to say, write, do or make something for a particular person or for a particular idea or reason *This email was meant for me. That was meant as a joke.*

SYNONYM to intend

6 used for saying that something or someone is important *Doing well in school means a lot to me* (is very important to me). *Friends don't mean much to him* (are not very important to him).

mean *adjective* **meaner, meanest**
1 unkind and unpleasant *a mean trick; Don't be mean to your little sister.*
2 not wanting to spend money or give money to other people *My uncle is rich but very mean.*

SYNONYM stingy

3 not wanting to give things or share things with other people *Don't be so mean – let me have some sweets.*

SYNONYM stingy

4 frightening *That dog looks very mean.*
5 in maths, a mean value (such as a number, distance, age or weight) is the value you get by adding all the values and dividing by the total number of values

mean *noun*
in maths, the mean is a number you get by adding together a set of numbers and dividing the total by the amount of these numbers *The mean of 5, 9 and 10 is 8 (24 divided by 3).*

SYNONYM average

meander ['mee-an-der] *verb*
meanders, meandering, meandered
if something such as a river or road meanders, it follows a path with lots of bends in it

ORIGIN from the name of a winding river that flows through modern Turkey. It was known to the ancient Greeks as *Maiandros*.

287

meaning–meditate

meaning *noun*
1 (*plural* **meanings**) the way you understand and explain something, or the idea or information that it represents *The word 'cool' has lots of meanings.*
2 the special importance that something has *Having a best friend has given her life a new meaning.*
3 **What's the meaning of this?** used when you're angry and you want to ask someone to explain something you don't like

meaningful *adjective*
1 showing how someone feels or what they think without words being said *He gave me a meaningful look.*
2 important or useful *Kareem has lots of meaningful friendships.*
3 easy to understand and making good sense *This sentence isn't very meaningful.*

meaningfully *adverb*
in a way that shows how someone feels or what they think without words being said or without an explanation being given *He looked at me meaningfully* (I knew what he meant by the way he looked at me).

meaningless *adjective*
1 not having any meaning *This sentence is meaningless.*
2 not having any importance or purpose *a meaningless gesture*

meanly *adverb*
in an unkind and unpleasant way *He always behaves meanly to me.*

meanness *noun*
when someone doesn't want to spend money or give money to other people

means *noun* **means**
1 a way of doing something *We have no means of escaping. We communicated by means of email* (using email).
2 **by all means** used as a polite way of giving permission or saying yes to someone

SYNONYMS certainly, of course

3 **by no means** not at all *My parents are by no means rich.*

means *noun plural*
money, especially money that is needed for doing something *They don't have the means to send their children to a private school. Mum said the bike was beyond their means* (too expensive to buy).

meantime *noun*
in the meantime used when talking about the time between now and a particular thing happening in the future

meanwhile *adverb*
1 in the time between now and a particular thing happening in the future *Your teacher isn't here yet so meanwhile you can carry on playing in the playground.*
2 while something else is happening at the same time *I was washing the dishes and meanwhile my sister was doing her homework.*

measles *noun*
an illness caused by a virus, in which you have small red spots on your body, a high fever, cough and runny nose

measly *adjective* **measlier, measliest**
an informal way of describing something that is very small or not enough *All I got for my birthday was a measly pair of socks.*

measure *verb*
measures, measuring, measured
1 to find out something such as how long or tall something is or how much of it there is *Can you measure the fridge to see if it will fit in this corner? Use a measuring jug to measure exactly the right amount of liquid.*
2 to be a particular size *My laptop screen measures 15 inches.*
3 to show something such as a particular size, amount, weight or speed *A thermometer measures temperature. A clock measures time.*

measure *noun* **measures**
1 a way of dealing with a situation or solving a problem *The head teacher has taken measures to stop bullying.*
2 an amount or unit in a system for measuring things *A foot is a measure of length.*
3 something such as a container for measuring something *a glass measure for liquids*
4 a certain amount of something *I've had a measure of success.*

measurement *noun* **measurements**
1 the size, length or amount of something that you find out by measuring it *Do you know your waist measurement?*
2 the action of measuring something done by a person or piece of equipment

meat *noun*
1 flesh from an animal or bird that is eaten as food
2 (*plural* **meats**) a particular type of meat

meaty *adjective* **meatier, meatiest**
containing a lot of meat or having the taste of meat

Meccano *noun* (trademark)
a toy made of metal or plastic parts that you fit together to build models of things such as cars and planes *a Meccano set*

mechanic *noun* **mechanics**
someone who repairs vehicles and machines *a car mechanic*

mechanical *adjective*
1 connected with machines and engines *mechanical parts* (parts for machines); *a mechanical problem*
2 if someone does something in a mechanical way, they do it without thinking

mechanically *adverb*

mechanics *noun*
the science that deals with forces such as gravity and the way they affect objects

mechanism *noun* **mechanisms**
1 a part of a piece of equipment that does a particular job *a car's steering mechanism*
2 the parts of a piece of equipment that work together *The clock mechanism is broken.*

medal *noun* **medals**
a small piece of metal, usually round and fixed to a strip of cloth, that is given to someone for doing something special, such as winning a race or competition or doing a brave action *She won an Olympic gold medal in swimming.*

medallion *noun* **medallions**
a metal disc worn as decoration around the neck on a chain or string

medallist *noun* **medallists**
someone who wins a medal in a sport *He's a silver medallist.*

meddle *verb*
meddles, meddling, meddled
to try to change a situation or influence someone even though it has nothing to do with you *You're always meddling in what I do.*

SYNONYM to interfere

meddlesome *adjective*
used about someone who meddles in other people's business in an annoying way

media ['mee-di-er'] *noun*
1 the media are organisations such as newspapers, radio, television and the internet that communicate information to the public
2 plural of **medium**

median *noun* **medians**
in maths, the median is the middle value (or number) in a whole set of values that are arranged in order *In the set 2, 2, 7, 9 and 10, the median is 7.* **median** *adjective*

media player *noun* **media players**
a piece of electronic equipment for storing music, sounds, images or videos, for example an iPod. Music is copied from a computer or downloaded from the internet in different file formats (ways of storing information as a file), and you listen to it using headphones.

LANGUAGE EXTRA also called a *digital* or *portable media player*

medical *adjective*
connected with doctors and the treatment of illnesses and injuries *medical care* (care you need if you are ill); *a medical problem* (something that makes you ill); *a medical student* (someone studying to be a doctor)
medically *adverb*

medicinal ['mer-dis-in-erl'] *adjective*
used for describing substances that help to treat illnesses *medicinal herbs*

medicine *noun*
1 (*plural* **medicines**) a substance that you swallow to make you better when you are ill *a cough medicine* (liquid for treating a cough)
2 the treatment or study of illnesses and injuries

medieval ['med-i-ee-verl'] *adjective*
connected with the Middle Ages (the period of history from about the 5th century to the 15th century)

mediocre ['mee-di-oh-ker'] *adjective*
not very good but not very bad either
mediocrity *noun*

meditate *verb*
meditates, meditating, meditated
1 to sit in silence and think pleasant thoughts in order to relax, for example as part of a religious activity
2 to think seriously about something, usually for a long period of time
meditation *noun*

Mediterranean–memorable

Mediterranean ['med-it-er-**ray**-ni-ern']
noun
the Mediterranean or Mediterranean Sea is the sea between the countries of Southern Europe, North Africa and the Middle East

Mediterranean ['med-it-er-**ray**-ni-ern']
adjective
connected with the people or countries around the Mediterranean Sea

medium *adjective*
1 used for describing something halfway between sizes, amounts or levels such as big and small or high and low *I'm of medium height. Take your bath when the water reaches a medium temperature.*
2 neither good nor bad *This painting is of medium quality.*
3 neither light nor dark *My new dress is medium blue.*

medium *noun*
1 (*plural* **media** or **mediums**) a way of communicating something *The internet is a great medium for spreading ideas.*
2 (*plural* **media** or **mediums**) a substance used for a particular purpose, for example something that something else lives in or moves through *Blood is the medium that carries oxygen around the body.*
3 (*plural* **media**) an object, such as a DVD or flash drive, used for storing computer information on

medium *noun* **mediums**
someone who says they can receive messages from people who have died

medium-sized *adjective*
neither big nor small

> LANGUAGE EXTRA you can also say *medium-size*

meek *adjective* **meeker, meekest**
gentle, quiet and not wanting to disagree with people or complain **meekness** *noun*

> SIMILE 'as meek as a lamb' means very meek

meekly *adverb*
in a gentle and quiet way without disagreeing or complaining *He accepted the blame meekly.*

meerkat *noun* **meerkats**
a small furry animal from southern Africa with a long body and long tail. It can stand on its back legs, using its tail to balance. Meerkats eat insects, small animals and plants.

meet *verb*
meets, meeting, met
1 to go to the same place as someone because you have arranged to see them there *I met Dad in front of the school gates. We met in front of the school gates.*
2 to accidentally find yourself in the same place as someone *I met my teacher as I was walking to the library.*
3 to see someone somewhere and speak to them for the first time *Charlie met Rohan in Leicester. When did you first meet?*
4 to come together, or to go and see someone, for a particular reason such as to talk about something *The teachers are meeting to discuss Bill's behaviour. My mum is meeting the head teacher tomorrow.*
5 if things such as surfaces, roads, rivers or lines meet, they come together at a particular place *The two roads meet at Norwich. There's a dirty mark where the ceiling meets the wall.*
6 if people or teams in a competition or game meet or meet each other, they play against each other
7 to do what is needed or promised *My new mobile meets all my needs. I'm trying to meet the deadline for my homework* (finish it by a certain time).
8 to pay money needed for something or promised to someone, for example expenses or debts *It's difficult meeting the school fees.*

meeting *noun* **meetings**
1 an occasion when people come together for a particular reason such as to talk about something. A meeting can happen between people who are in the same place or in different places using a computer and the internet, for example.
2 when two people meet accidentally or for the first time *I had a chance meeting with my cousin.*
3 a sports competition, for example between two teams

mega *adjective*
an informal word for very big *The town was buried beneath a mega snowstorm.*

mega- *prefix*
1 used before a noun to give it the meaning of very big *a mega-city; a megastore*
2 used before an adjective to give it the meaning of very *mega-famous*

> ORIGIN from Greek *megas* 'large', 'huge'

megabyte *noun* **megabytes**
a piece of information used by a computer, for example for measuring the size of a file or program. A megabyte is made up of about a million bytes.

megaphone *noun* **megaphones**
an object shaped like a cone (circle at one end, sloping sides and point at the other end) that you hold in your hand and speak into. It is used for making your voice sound louder.

megastar *noun* **megastars**
a very famous actor, musician or singer

melancholy *adjective*
feeling or looking sad, or making you feel sad *She had a melancholy expression on her face.*

melancholy *noun*
great sadness

mellow *adjective* **mellower, mellowest**
1 a mellow colour or light is not bright but warm and pleasant
2 a mellow sound is not loud but gentle and pleasant

melodic ['mer-**lod**-ik'] *adjective*
used for describing music that has a pleasant tune or a sound that is pleasant like music

melodious *adjective*
used for describing a sound or voice that sounds pleasant like music

melodrama *noun* **melodramas**
a story, play or film full of adventure and excitement, in which the characters show very strong feelings

melodramatic *adjective*
1 if someone is melodramatic, they show much stronger feelings than they need to in a normal situation, for example feelings of great anger, sadness or excitement
2 a melodramatic story is full of adventure and excitement

melody *noun* **melodies**
a tune or song

melon *noun* **melons**
a large round fruit with a hard yellow or green skin. It is soft and juicy inside and has lots of seeds.

melt *verb*
melts, melting, melted
1 if something melts, it changes into a liquid because of heat *The snow has melted.*
2 to make something change into a liquid *Melt the butter in the frying pan.*
3 to melt away is to disappear very slowly *The crowds melted away.*

member *noun* **members**
1 someone who belongs to a group such as a club, family or organisation
2 a country or organisation that belongs to a group, for example a political group *The UK is a member of the European Union.*
3 an animal or plant that belongs to a scientific group *The lion is a member of the cat family.*

Member of Parliament *noun*
Members of Parliament
someone chosen by the people to represent them in a parliament

> LANGUAGE EXTRA also spelt *member of parliament*

membership *noun*
1 being a member of a group
2 the people who are members of a group

membrane *noun* **membranes**
a thin covering or piece of skin that connects parts of the body

memento *noun* **mementos**
something you keep to remind you of a person, place or event

> ORIGIN from Latin *memento* 'remember'

memo *noun* **memos**
a short message that someone sends to someone else who works in the same company

> ORIGIN from Latin *memorandum* 'to be remembered'

memoir ['**mem**-wah'] *noun* **memoirs**
1 a book or article describing someone's life or particular events
2 someone's memoirs are a book that an important or famous person writes describing his or her own life

memorable *adjective*
1 likely to be remembered for a long time, for example because of being so good *Jo's birthday was a memorable occasion.*
2 easy to remember, for example a name, word or quote

289

memorably–merely

memorably *adverb*
in a way that people are likely to remember for a long time

memorial *noun* **memorials**
an object, usually of stone, built to remind people of an important person who has died or a past event *a war memorial*

memorial *adjective*
used for describing something that honours someone who has died *a memorial service*

memorise *verb*
memorises, memorising, memorised
to learn something so that you remember it exactly without looking at it *I've memorised the poem word for word.*

> **LANGUAGE EXTRA** also spelt *memorize*

memory *noun*
1 the power to remember things *Neil has an excellent memory.*
2 (*plural* **memories**) something you remember from the past *What sort of memories of school does your brother have?*
3 the part of your mind where the things you remember are stored *I sang the whole song from memory.*
4 when you remember someone, especially someone who has died *Dad said a prayer in memory of his grandparents.*
5 the part of a computer where it stores information or the size of this part of a computer *You need more memory for your laptop as it only has 500 megabytes of memory.*

memory stick *noun* **memory sticks**
a small piece of computer equipment that stores information and that you carry around with you. It plugs into a computer using a type of connection known as USB.

> **SYNONYM** flash drive

> **ORIGIN** the name comes from *Memory Stick* (trademark), a type of flat computer card for storing information

men
plural of **man**

menace *verb*
menaces, menacing, menaced
to do something that might make bad things happen, or to be likely to make bad things happen *She felt menaced by some of the children in the playground.*

menace *noun*
1 something or someone likely to make bad things happen *These dogs are a menace to people in the park.*
2 a particular quality that makes you think someone is likely to do something bad *His voice was full of menace.*
3 (*plural* **menaces**) a person who is very annoying and likely to do bad things *Your brother is a real menace!*

menacing *adjective*
1 making you think that someone is likely to do something bad *a menacing look*
2 making you think that something bad is likely to happen *menacing storm clouds*
menacingly *adverb*

mend *verb*
mends, mending, mended
1 to make something that is broken as good as it was before *Someone is coming to mend the TV.*

> **SYNONYMS** to repair, to fix

2 to fix a hole or tear in a piece of clothing

mend *noun*
to be on the mend to be getting better after an illness

meningitis ['men-in-**jye**-ters'] *noun*
a serious illness that affects the brain

menstruation *noun*
the natural flow of blood from a woman's womb (the part of her body where a baby grows) for a few days every month
menstrual *adjective* **menstruate** *verb*

menswear *noun*
clothes for men

mental *adjective*
1 connected with the mind *a mental picture* (a picture you have in your mind); *mental arithmetic* (calculations you do in your mind); *I've made a mental note* (used about something you must remember or remember to do).
2 connected with the health of the mind *mental illness*
3 a slang word for crazy or stupid

mentality *noun*
someone's particular way of thinking, especially one that you don't like

mentally *adverb*
1 connected with the health of the mind *He's mentally ill.*
2 used about something that is done or imagined in the mind *Try to add up the numbers mentally. Mentally I have a picture of her as being tall with long hair.*

mention *verb*
mentions, mentioning, mentioned
1 to talk or write briefly about something or someone *I mentioned you in my email.*
2 to say something *Did I mention that I saw Paul at the library?*
3 **Don't mention it!** used as a polite reply when someone says thank you to you

mention *noun* **mentions**
when something or someone is mentioned *My sister saved a dog from drowning and got a mention on the local news.*

mentor *noun* **mentors**
a person with particular knowledge and experience who helps and teaches someone else

menu *noun* **menus**
1 a list of different kinds of food and drink you can choose from in a restaurant, café or pub
2 a list of different things in a computer program that you can ask a computer to do. For example, by clicking on a word or name in the list with your mouse (or by touching it), you can make the computer do something or make a more detailed menu appear in a column under the word or name. *Click on the Edit menu and select Copy.*
3 a menu option is one of the choices listed on a computer menu
4 a menu bar is a long strip, usually at the top of a computer screen, that lists different things that you can ask a computer to do

MEP ['em-ee-**pee**] *noun* **MEPs**
a politician who represents an area of one of the countries that belong to the European Union
short for: Member of the European Parliament

mercenary *noun* **mercenaries**
a soldier who fights for any country for money

mercenary *adjective*
if someone is mercenary, they do something only because they are interested in the money

merchandise *noun*
goods that people buy or sell

merchant *noun* **merchants**
1 someone who buys and sells goods, usually in large quantities *a grain merchant*
2 a merchant navy is a country's ships (called merchant ships) that are used for transporting goods and not for fighting. The sailors on merchant ships are called merchant seamen.

merciful *adjective*
used about someone who shows kindness to someone that they have the power to punish

mercifully *adverb*
1 used when you mean you are happy that something good has happened, when something bad could easily have happened instead *Mercifully no-one was killed.*
2 in a kind way, for example by not punishing someone

merciless *adjective*
very cruel and without showing any mercy
mercilessly *adverb*

mercury *noun*
a chemical element and silver-coloured metal that is liquid at ordinary temperatures. It is used in some thermometers for measuring temperatures.

Mercury *noun*
one of the planets. It is the closest one to the sun, between the sun and Venus.

mercy *noun*
1 kindness shown to a person that someone has the power to punish, for example by forgiving them and letting them go free or by not punishing them very hard *The King showed mercy to the captured soldiers.*
2 (*plural* **mercies**) something good that happens that you are happy about *We should be grateful for small mercies. It's a mercy that no-one was hurt.*
3 if you are at the mercy of someone, they have the power to do whatever they want to you, such as punish you

mere *adjective*
used when you mean something or someone is small or not important *I've got a mere 20 pence left. He's a mere boy.*

merely *adverb*
only *I was merely trying to help.*

merge – methane

merge *verb*
merges, merging, merged
1 if something merges with something else or if things merge, they come together, for example to form a single thing *Our two schools are thinking of merging. In the painting, the blue of the sky merges into the green of the fields* (the blue gradually changes to green).
2 to merge something with something else, or to merge things, is to put them together, for example to form a single thing *For our computer homework we have to merge some pictures with a text.*

merger *noun* mergers
when two businesses come together to form a bigger one

meridian ['mer-**rid**-i-ern'] *noun* meridians
one of the imaginary lines going around the earth from the North Pole to the South Pole, used for helping to show the position of a place

meringue ['mer-**rang**'] *noun* meringues
a very light white-coloured sweet food made by mixing the white parts of eggs with sugar and then baking it, usually until it is slightly hard on the outside

merit *noun* merits
1 a good quality or good qualities that something or someone has *This book has great merit. There isn't much merit in your suggestion* (it isn't very good). *What are the merits of eating lots of fruit and vegetables?* (the good reasons for doing this)
2 a special mark that you get in school for good work or behaviour

merit *verb*
merits, meriting, merited
if something or someone merits something such as praise or attention, they deserve it *This book is so good it merits another reading.*

mermaid *noun* mermaids
in stories, an imaginary creature with the head and body of a woman and the tail of a fish instead of legs

merrily *adverb*
in a happy way *We were all singing merrily.*

merry *adjective* merrier, merriest
1 an old-fashioned word for happy *merry laughter*
2 an informal word for slightly drunk
3 **Merry Christmas!** used as a greeting when you want someone to have a happy time at Christmas

merry-go-round *noun* merry-go-rounds
a large round machine, usually at a fairground, that goes round and round. It has toy horses, cars or other vehicles that you ride on.

mesh *noun* meshes
a material with lots of tiny holes in it like a net, made from threads or wires twisted together *a fence of wire mesh*

mess *noun*
1 a situation in which something is dirty or untidy *I hate mess.*
2 something dirty or untidy *Clean up the mess in your room. My room is a real mess* (really untidy).
3 if something is in a mess, it is dirty or untidy *The children have left the classroom in a mess.*
4 a situation with lots of problems *How did you get into this mess? When our teacher left suddenly, the head had to deal with the mess.*
5 the waste matter from the body of an animal *Don't step in the dog's mess on the pavement.*
6 (*plural* **messes**) a room or building where soldiers or sailors eat their meals and relax
7 if you make a mess of something, for example your homework or exams, you do it badly

mess *verb*
messes, messing, messed
1 if someone messes about or around, they waste time, for example doing silly things, or they spend their time doing different things, usually things that are not important *Stop messing about and do your homework! My brother's messing around on the computer.*
2 if someone messes something up, they do it badly or spoil it *I've messed up all the answers to the maths questions.*
3 if someone messes something up, it also means they make it untidy or dirty *You've messed up your room again!*

message *noun* messages
1 a piece of information sent or given to someone when you are not there to speak to them directly *an email message*
2 the most important idea that is communicated in something such as a book, film, poem or speech
3 a message board is a web page where you can leave a message or reply to a message left by someone else

messaging *noun*
a way of communicating over the internet using messages that are sent and received immediately *Twitter is a well-known messaging service.*

messenger *noun* messengers
someone who takes a message from one person to another

messiah ['mer-**sye**-er'] *noun*
1 in some religions, a leader who people believe will save the world and solve all its problems
2 in the Christian religion, the Messiah is Jesus Christ. In the Jewish religion, the Messiah is someone that God will send.

messy *adjective* messier, messiest
1 untidy *They've left the classroom very messy. Ben's a very messy eater.*
2 dirty *Wash your hands – they're messy.*
3 complicated and unpleasant *a messy situation*
messily *adverb* **messiness** *noun*

met
past tense & past participle of **meet**

metal *noun* metals
a chemical element that is usually hard and shiny, such as gold, silver, iron or lead. Heat and electricity can travel through metals.

metallic *adjective*
1 made of metal
2 used for describing a sound like metal being hit
3 used for describing a colour that shines like metal *a metallic blue car*

metalwork *noun*
making things out of metal *My dad's favourite subject at school was metalwork.*

metamorphosis ['met-er-**mor**-fer-siss'] *noun* metamorphoses ['met-er-**mor**-fer-seez']
the complete change made by some insects and animals as they develop from a young form into an adult form. For example, a caterpillar changes into a butterfly and a tadpole into a frog.

metaphor *noun* metaphors
a way of describing something or someone as if they are really something else or as if they have something that they cannot really have. It is used for showing that the thing or person you describe has a similar quality to the other thing. For example, 'Your house is a dream' is a metaphor because the house is not really a dream but it seems like one because it has the wonderful quality of a dream. If you say 'Charlie has arms of steel', you are using a metaphor because Charlie's arms are not really made of steel but they are very strong, just like steel.
compare: **simile**

metaphorical *adjective*
used for describing language that contains metaphors **metaphorically** *adverb*

meteor ['**mee**-ti-or'] *noun* meteors
a piece of rock from space that burns with a bright light when it enters the earth's atmosphere

> ORIGIN from Greek *meteoros* 'high up in the sky'

meteoric *adjective*
used for describing something that happens very quickly *The pop star's rise to fame was meteoric.*

meteorite ['**mee**-ti-er-ite'] *noun* meteorites
a piece of rock that has fallen from space and landed on earth

meteorologist ['mee-ti-er-**ol**-er-jist'] *noun* meteorologists
a scientist who studies the weather

meteorology ['mee-ti-er-**ol**-er-jee'] *noun*
the scientific study of the weather
meteorological *adjective*

meter *noun* meters
1 a piece of equipment for measuring the amount of something being used, for example gas, electricity or water *a gas meter*; *a taxi meter* (for showing how much passengers have to pay for their journey)
2 short for **parking meter**

> LANGUAGE EXTRA be careful not to confuse *meter* with *metre* (a unit of length)

methane ['**mee**-thayn'] *noun*
a gas that has no colour or smell. It is the main part of natural gas (a gas that exists in rocks under the ground) and is often used for heating and cooking. Methane is also produced from the waste that comes from dead plants and animals.

method–middle finger

method noun
1 (plural **methods**) a particular way of doing something, often a way that is carefully organised or planned *Do you have a method for learning your times tables?*
2 when you do things in a careful and organised way *Ben needs a bit more method in the way he works.*

methodical ['mer-thod-ik-erl'] adjective
1 if someone is methodical, they do things in a careful and organised way
2 also used about someone's actions *a very methodical piece of homework*
methodically adverb

Methodism noun
the religion and beliefs of Methodists

Methodist noun **Methodists**
a Christian belonging to a group started by John and Charles Wesley in the 18th century **Methodist** adjective

meticulous adjective
very careful and giving great attention to small details **meticulously** adverb

metre noun **metres**
1 a unit for measuring length in the metric system, equal to about 39 inches. There are 100 centimetres in a metre.
2 a pattern or patterns of sounds in poetry, for example a strong regular sound followed by a weak one

> **LANGUAGE EXTRA** be careful not to confuse *metre* with *meter* (a piece of equipment)

metric adjective
1 connected with the metric system *metric scales*; *a metric ton* (1000 kilos)
2 the metric system is a way of measuring things using units such as metres, kilograms and litres. It is based on the decimal system (a way of counting using the number 10).
compare: **imperial** (sense 3)

metro noun **metros**
a railway that goes under the ground in tunnels, in some cities such as Paris or Moscow

> **LANGUAGE EXTRA** also spelt *Metro*

metropolis noun **metropolises**
a very large city, often the capital city of a country **metropolitan** adjective

> **ORIGIN** from Greek *metropolis* 'mother city' (from *meter* 'mother' and *polis* 'city')

mew ['myoo'] verb
mews, mewing, mewed
when a cat mews, it makes a short high noise that is its own special sound
mew noun

> **SYNONYM** to miaow

Mexico noun
a country in North America
Mexican adjective & noun

miaow ['mee-ow'] verb
miaows, miaowing, miaowed
when a cat miaows, it makes a short high noise that is its own special sound
miaow noun

> **SYNONYM** to mew

mice
plural of **mouse**

micro- prefix
used before a noun to give it the meaning of very small *a microchip*

> **ORIGIN** from Greek *mikros* 'small'

microbe ['my-krohb'] noun **microbes**
a tiny organism (living thing) that you can only see through a microscope. Microbes often cause disease.

microblogging noun
a way of communicating over the internet using short messages. Twitter is an example of a microblogging service.

microchip noun **microchips**
a very small piece of silicon (grey substance from rocks and sand) with electrical connections in it, used mainly in electronic equipment such as computers. It allows the equipment to work and store information.

micro-habitat noun **micro-habitats**
the small place where an animal or insect usually lives or where a plant usually grows that is different from the larger surrounding place or thing. For example, a bird living in a nest in a tree has a different micro-habitat from a beetle living in the bark of the same tree.

> **LANGUAGE EXTRA** also spelt *microhabitat*

micro-organism noun **micro-organisms**
a tiny organism (living thing) that you can only see through a microscope. Micro-organisms are used in making food such as yoghurt but they also cause disease and make living things decay (go bad).

microphone noun **microphones**
a small piece of equipment for recording sounds or making them louder, for example if you are speaking or singing to lots of people. It is also used for speaking into, for example if you are talking to someone on the internet.

microprocessor noun **microprocessors**
a very small piece of electronic equipment made up of chips (pieces of silicon with electrical connections). It forms the main part of a computer (or other equipment) and makes it work.

> **SYNONYM** processor

microscope noun **microscopes**
a piece of equipment with lenses (curved pieces of glass or plastic) for making small objects look bigger. It stands upright on a surface and you look down through the lenses to study objects scientifically.

> **ORIGIN** from Greek *mikros* 'small' and *skopein* 'to look at'

microscopic adjective
1 used about something that is so small you can only see it through a microscope *a microscopic sea creature*
2 very small *Daniel's handwriting is microscopic.*

microwave noun **microwaves**
1 a microwave or microwave oven is an electric oven that cooks or heats food very quickly using waves of energy
2 a type of electrical and magnetic wave similar to a radio wave, used for cooking and sending information

microwave verb
microwaves, microwaving, microwaved
to cook or heat food in a microwave oven
microwavable or **microwaveable** adjective

mid- prefix
used for making nouns that mean the middle part of something *in mid-June; It was midwinter. Granddad is in his mid-seventies.*

mid-air noun
in mid-air up in the air or the sky *The planes hit each other in mid-air. There was a mid-air collision.*

midday noun
the middle of the day at or around twelve o'clock

> **SYNONYM** noon

middle noun **middles**
1 the place or part of something exactly between its sides or edges or between its two ends *Put a dot in the middle of the circle. There's a knot in the middle of the rope.*
2 the place or part exactly between the beginning and end of something *Letter M is in the middle of the alphabet. It happened in the middle of April.*
3 something such as a number, shape or word exactly between other numbers, shapes or words *In the group 2, 7 and 9, the number 7 is in the middle.*
4 someone's middle is their waist *Your school shirt is too short – it shows your middle.*
5 if someone is in the middle of something such as an activity or event, they are busy doing it or it is happening now *Come back later – I'm in the middle of eating. Our school is in the middle of a crisis.*

middle adjective
in or near the middle of something *the middle shelf; Jack is the middle brother* (not the youngest or the oldest).

middle-aged adjective
no longer young but not old yet *He's a middle-aged teacher in his fifties.*

Middle Ages noun plural
the period of European history from about the 5th century to the 15th century

middle class noun
a group in society between the working class and the upper class. It includes people who have been to university and have jobs such as teachers, doctors, lawyers and managers of businesses.
middle-class adjective

> **LANGUAGE EXTRA** you can also say *middle classes*

Middle East noun
a region in the western part of Asia and North Africa made up of almost 20 countries from Egypt to Iran, including Israel, Jordan, Lebanon, Saudi Arabia and Turkey

middle finger noun **middle fingers**
the longest finger on your hand. It is in the middle of the other fingers next to the forefinger.

middle name–millennium

middle name *noun* **middle names**
the middle part of a name that some people are given when they are born. It comes between the first name and family name.

middle school *noun* **middle schools**
a school (or part of a school), in some parts of the UK, for children between the ages of about 8 and 13

midge *noun* **midges**
a tiny flying insect. Midges usually fly in groups and live near water.

midget *noun* **midgets**
an insulting word for a very small person

midget *adjective*
used for describing something very small *a midget car*

Midlands *noun or noun plural*
the Midlands is the middle part of England. It includes cities such as Birmingham and Nottingham. **Midland** *adjective* **Midlands** *adjective*

midnight *noun*
twelve o'clock at night

midst *noun*
1 to be in the midst of something such as an event means that it is happening now *a country in the midst of war*
2 if someone or something is in your midst, they are among you or with you *He feels a stranger in our midst.*

midsummer *noun*
1 the period in the middle of summer when the weather is hottest
2 the day of the year on which it is light for the longest amount of time, around 21 June in the UK

midway *adverb & adjective*
1 halfway between two places or points *I stopped reading midway through the book.*
2 halfway through a period of time *We walked out midway through the film.*

midweek *noun, adverb & adjective*
used when talking about the middle of the week, for example from Tuesday to Thursday *By midweek, I was feeling better. We have a football match midweek.*

midwife *noun* **midwives**
someone with special training to look after a woman while she is giving birth to a baby

ORIGIN from Old English *mid* 'with' and *wif* 'woman', describing the person who is with the woman having the baby

miffed *adjective* (informal)
slightly angry, especially about the way someone has behaved towards you

might *verb*
past tense of **may**
1 used for saying that something is possible in the future or could have been possible in the past *I might do my homework after tea. I might have helped you if you had asked.*
2 used for suggesting what someone should do or should have done, especially when you're angry *Ben might turn his laptop off for once. You might have told me you were coming home late.*

might *noun*
1 great power, for example of an army or country *the might of the Roman Empire*
2 an old-fashioned word for great strength *He tried with all his might to move the huge rock.*

mighty *adjective* **mightier, mightiest**
very strong, powerful or big *a mighty army*

migraine ['my-grayn' or 'mee-grayn'] *noun* **migraines**
a very bad pain in the head, especially one where you have trouble seeing

migrant ['my-grernt'] *noun* **migrants**
someone who travels to another region or country, for example to get work or have a better life

migrate ['my-grayt'] *verb* **migrates, migrating, migrated**
1 if birds or animals migrate, they travel to another place, for example where the weather is warmer *Swallows migrate to Africa during the winter.*
2 if people migrate, they travel to another region or country, for example to get work or have a better life

migration *noun* **migratory** *adjective*

mike *noun* **mikes**
an informal word for a microphone

mild *adjective* **milder, mildest**
1 not very bad or serious *a mild illness; a mild punishment*
2 not very strong *a mild breeze; This cheese has a mild taste.*
3 not very cold *The weather is mild today.*
4 calm and quiet *Our teacher is a very mild person. 'That's good,' he said in a mild voice.*

mildness *noun*

mildly *adverb*
1 slightly or to a small degree *I was mildly interested in what he was saying.*
2 not very much or not very seriously *I had flu last week but only mildly.*
3 calmly and quietly *'I've done nothing wrong,' she replied mildly.*

mile *noun* **miles**
1 a unit for measuring distance, equal to about 1.6 kilometres *I live two miles away from school. Mum was driving at 30 miles an hour* (the speed of a vehicle measured by the number of miles it travels in an hour).
2 **miles** used when you mean a very long distance *My cousins live miles away.*
3 **miles** also used as an informal way of saying 'very much' *Our school is miles better than yours.*

mileage *noun* **mileages**
1 the number of miles a vehicle has travelled *My dad has done a high mileage* (lots of miles).
2 the number of miles a vehicle can travel using a particular amount of fuel

milestone *noun* **milestones**
1 an important event or stage in someone's life or in the history of something *Learning to walk is a milestone in children's lives.*
2 a stone at the side of a road showing the number of miles to a place, usually to the nearest town. Milestones were used especially in the past.

militant *adjective*
1 used about a person or group that fights hard or in a violent way to make something happen that they believe in, for example to change something in society
2 also used about what someone does or says *a militant speech*
militant *noun*

military *adjective*
connected with a country's army, navy or air force *The country took military action* (for example used soldiers to fight an enemy). *In many countries people have to do military service* (spend time in the army, navy or air force).

milk *noun*
1 a white liquid from cows, goats and sheep, used for drinking, cooking and making things such as butter
2 a liquid from women and female animals, used for feeding babies and baby animals
3 the clear liquid produced by some trees and plants *coconut milk*

milk *verb*
milks, milking, milked
to get milk from an animal such as a cow

milk chocolate *noun*
chocolate made with milk. Chocolate that is made without milk is called plain chocolate.

milk float *noun* **milk floats**
a special vehicle for carrying milk to deliver to people's homes

milkman *noun* **milkmen**
someone who delivers milk to people's homes, usually very early in the morning

milkshake *noun* **milkshakes**
a thick drink made from milk and ice cream *a chocolate milkshake*

LANGUAGE EXTRA also spelt *milk shake*

milk tooth *noun* **milk teeth**
your milk teeth are your first teeth that fall out when your adult teeth begin to grow

milky *adjective* **milkier, milkiest**
1 containing a lot of milk *a milky tea*
2 looking or tasting like milk *a milky liquid; a milky white colour*

Milky Way *noun*
the large group of stars that appear as a strip of pale light in the night sky

mill *noun* **mills**
1 a building where grain is crushed to make flour
2 a large machine for crushing grain to make flour *a flour mill*
3 a small tool used in the kitchen for crushing things to make a powder *a coffee mill; a pepper mill*
4 a factory for making a particular material such as steel or cotton *a paper mill*

mill *verb*
mills, milling, milled
1 to crush something to make flour or a powder
2 to mill around is to move around slowly, for example among a crowd of people *Crowds were milling around waiting for the film star to appear.*

millennium *noun*
millennia or **millenniums**
1 a period of 1000 years
2 the start of a new period of 1000 years

ORIGIN from Latin *mille* 'thousand' and *annus* 'year'

miller – mingle

miller *noun* millers
someone who is in charge of a mill for making flour

millet *noun*
a type of grain often used for feeding birds or animals

milli- *prefix*
used for forming nouns that mean a thousandth part of something *a millisecond*

ORIGIN from Latin *mille* 'thousand'

milligram *noun* milligrams
a unit for measuring weight in the metric system. There are 1000 milligrams in a gram.

LANGUAGE EXTRA also spelt *milligramme*

millilitre ['mil-ee-lee-ter] *noun* millilitres
a unit for measuring liquids in the metric system. There are 1000 millilitres in a litre.

millimetre *noun* millimetres
a unit for measuring length in the metric system. There are 1000 millimetres in a metre.

million *noun* millions
1 a thousand times a thousand (1 000 000)
2 used when describing a very large number of things *I've explained this to you millions of times.*

millionth *adjective & noun*

millionaire *noun* millionaires
a very rich person who has at least a million pounds, dollars or euros

millstone *noun*
if something is a millstone around your neck, it is a very heavy responsibility that you can't get rid of and that causes you worry

ORIGIN from the name of the huge flat round stone used in the past for crushing grain in flour mills

mime *verb*
mimes, miming, mimed
to express ideas or feelings or to tell a story by using movements of the hands and body without speaking

mime *noun*
1 using movements of the hands and body to express ideas or feelings or to tell a story without speaking
2 (*plural* mimes) a play in which no words are spoken and the story is told by movements of the hands and body
3 (*plural* mimes) an actor in a mime

mimic *verb*
mimics, mimicking, mimicked
1 to copy the way someone speaks or behaves, for example to make fun of them or make people laugh
2 to behave exactly like something or someone else

mimicry *noun*

mimic *noun* mimics
someone who is good at mimicking people

minaret *noun* minarets
a tall tower built as part of a mosque (a building where Muslims pray). It is used as a place for calling Muslims to prayer.

ORIGIN from Arabic *manarah* 'lamp' or 'lighthouse' (from *nar* 'fire')

mince *verb*
minces, mincing, minced
1 to cut food such as meat into very small pieces, for example with a mincer or food processor
2 if you say someone doesn't mince their words, you mean they say what they think even if someone else doesn't like it

mince *noun*
1 meat such as beef or chicken that has been cut into very small pieces
2 a mince pie is a small round sweet pie made from mincemeat (dried fruits) covered with pastry. Mince pies are often eaten at Christmas.

mincemeat *noun*
1 meat that has been minced
2 a sweet spicy food made from different dried fruits such as raisins, currants, apple and lemon peel cut into small pieces

mincer *noun* mincers
a machine or piece of electrical equipment for cutting food into very small pieces

mind *verb*
minds, minding, minded
1 to be careful about something *Mind your head – the ceiling is low. Mind that you don't fall.*
2 to be upset or annoyed by something *Do you think Dad would mind if I did my homework tomorrow?*
3 used as a polite way of asking someone to do or not do something *Do you mind closing the window? Would you mind making less noise?*
4 used as a polite way of saying that you are happy to do or not do something, or that you are equally happy to have something or something else *'Will you help me in the kitchen?' – 'Yes, I don't mind.' 'Would you like yoghurt or ice cream?' – 'I don't mind.'*
5 used for saying politely what you want *I wouldn't mind an ice cream.*
6 to look after someone or something *Could you mind the dog if I go out?*
7 **mind out** used when telling someone to be careful, usually when there is danger *Mind out – someone's riding their bike on the pavement!*
8 **mind your own business** used for telling someone not to ask questions about something you don't want them to know
9 **never mind** used when you mean something isn't important *'I forgot to bring my schoolbag.' – 'Never mind!'*

mind *noun* minds
1 the part inside your head that is used for thinking, feeling and understanding things *Ben's mind is always full of ideas. I said the first thing that came into my mind* (the first thing I thought of). *My sister has a good mind* (a lot of intelligence).

SYNONYM brain

2 the attention that you give to things *Keep your mind on your work.*
3 to bear something in mind or keep something in mind means that you must remember it because it is important
4 if something such as an idea or name comes to mind, it's the first thing you think of *'Do you have any suggestions?' – 'No, nothing comes to mind.'*
5 if you change your mind, you change what you think and make a different decision or the opposite decision *I said I'd come but I've changed my mind* (I won't come).
6 if you have a good mind to do something, you have a strong feeling that you want to do it
7 if you have something at the back of your mind, you're not thinking of it now but you might think of it at any moment
8 if you have something on your mind, there's something you're thinking or worrying about *I've got a lot on my mind* (I'm very worried).
9 if you're in two minds about something, you're not able to make a decision about something because you're not sure
10 if you lose your mind, you become mad or confused
11 if you're out of your mind, you're crazy or stupid
12 if you make your mind up, you think about something or about doing something and then make a decision *'Are you coming?' – 'I haven't made up my mind yet.'*
13 if something takes your mind off something unpleasant, it stops you thinking about it *I go swimming to take my mind off my problems in school.*

mindless *adjective*
if something is mindless, it is stupid, for example because there is no reason for it or it has no meaning *mindless violence*

mine *pronoun*
used about something belonging to or connected with the person speaking *This bike is mine.*

mine *noun* mines
1 a deep hole in the ground that people dig to look for things such as coal, metals, gold, silver or diamonds *a coal mine*
2 a bomb hidden under or on the ground or in the sea that explodes if someone or something touches it

mine *verb*
mines, mining, mined
1 to dig something such as coal, metals or diamonds out of the ground
2 to hide bombs under or on the ground or in the sea *The roads into the capital have been mined.*

minefield *noun*
1 (*plural* minefields) an area of land or of the sea where bombs have been hidden
2 used for describing a situation that has lots of hidden dangers or problems

miner *noun* miners
someone who works in a mine *a coal miner*

mineral *noun* minerals
1 a natural substance such as coal, gold or salt that is dug out of the ground
2 a chemical substance in food and in the blood, for example iron or calcium, that the body needs to stay healthy
3 mineral water is water from a spring that comes out of the ground. It contains some of the minerals that the body needs to stay healthy and can be bought in bottles from shops.

mingle *verb*
mingles, mingling, mingled
1 to become mixed with something or mixed together *The smells of fish and meat don't mingle very well.*

mingy–mirth

2 if people mingle, they move around, for example at a party, and talk to other people

mingy ['min-jee'] *adjective*
mingier, mingiest (informal)
1 not wanting to give money to other people or share things with them

SYNONYM mean

2 used for describing something that is very small or not enough *They gave me a mingy portion of ice cream.*

SYNONYM measly

mini- *prefix*
used before a noun to give it the meaning of small or short *a mini-pizza; a miniskirt*

ORIGIN from *miniature*

miniature ['min-er-cher'] *adjective*
used for describing something that is very small, especially when it is a copy of something larger *a miniature railway; a miniature dog*

miniature ['min-er-cher'] *noun* **miniatures**
a very small painting, usually of a person

ORIGIN from Italian *miniatura* 'small picture used for decorating medieval books'

minibeast *noun* **minibeasts**
any small creature such as a spider, snail, butterfly or worm. A minibeast does not have a backbone (row of bones down the middle of the back).

minibus *noun* **minibuses**
a large vehicle usually with seats for between 8 and 15 people

minicab *noun* **minicabs**
a taxi that you call by phone, for example from your house

minim *noun* **minims**
a musical note that is half as long as a semibreve

minimal *adjective*
very small or not very much *Your efforts in school have been minimal.*

minimise *verb*
minimises, minimising, minimised
1 to make something not as much or not as great *If you work hard, you'll minimise your chances of failing.*
2 to change the way a program or document appears on a computer screen by making the image very small when you are not using it *Click on the minus sign to minimise the window.*
3 to make something seem less important

LANGUAGE EXTRA also spelt *minimize*

minimum *noun* **minimums** or **minima**
the smallest amount or number of something that is possible or allowed *The minimum is 20.*

minimum *adjective*
smallest possible or allowed *What's the minimum number of hours I should spend on my homework?*

mining *noun*
the action or work of digging things such as coal, metals, gold, silver or diamonds out of the ground *Dad was born in a Welsh mining town.*

miniskirt *noun* **miniskirts**
a very short skirt

minister *noun* **ministers**
1 a member of a government in charge of an important section called a department *Who is the minister in charge of transport?*
2 a person in charge of a church

ministry *noun*
1 (*plural* **ministries**) a section of a government responsible for a particular area of work *the Ministry of Justice*
2 the work of a person in charge of a church or the period of time when he or she does this work

minivan *noun* **minivans**
a vehicle like a large car with seats for about six to eight people

mink *noun*
1 (*plural* **minks**) a small furry animal with a long thin body. People hunt minks for their fur.
2 the fur from a mink used for making expensive coats *a mink coat*

minnow *noun* **minnows**
a very small fish that lives in streams, lakes and ponds

minor *adjective*
1 small and not very important or serious *a minor problem; a minor injury*
2 in music, a minor scale (series of notes) is one in which the third note is three semitones (half tones) higher than the first

minority ['my-nor-er-tee'] *noun*
1 a group of people or things that make up less than half (or much less than half) the size of a larger group *'How many children have been to New York?' – 'Only a minority.'* (very few)
2 (*plural* **minorities**) a group of people in a society who are different from most people in the society, for example because they have a different religion

minstrel *noun* **minstrels**
a musician who travelled around the country playing music and singing songs, especially during the period from about the 13th century to the 15th century

mint *noun*
1 (*plural* **mints**) a sweet with a very strong fresh taste
2 a plant with a strong fresh smell whose leaves are used for giving flavouring to food or toothpaste
3 (*plural* **mints**) a factory where the new coins and paper money of a country are produced *the Royal Mint* (the place where UK coins are produced)
4 if something is in mint condition, it is new or as good as it was when it was new

mint *verb*
mints, minting, minted
to mint a coin is to produce it in a mint for the government of a country *I've got a newly minted 50 pence piece.*

minus *preposition*
1 used for showing that you are taking a number away from another number. It is written as the symbol –. *Seven minus five equals two* $(7 - 5 = 2)$.
2 used for showing that a number or temperature is less than zero *Four minus six is minus two* $(4 - 6 = -2)$. *It's minus three outside.*
3 the minus sign is the symbol – used instead of the word 'minus' when numbers are used

minute ['min-it'] *noun* **minutes**
1 a period of 60 seconds. There are 60 minutes in an hour.
2 used when talking about a very short period of time *I'm going out but I'll be back in a minute. Mum will be home any minute* (very soon).
3 a particular time when something happens *At that minute someone rang the doorbell.*
4 a minute hand is a long thin part that moves around the face (front part) of a clock or watch and shows the time in minutes. It is longer than the hour hand.
5 **the minute** or **the minute that** as soon as *Let me know the minute you have any news.*
6 **this minute** used for telling someone to do something immediately *Turn the TV off this minute!*

minute ['my-nyoot'] *adjective*
1 extremely small

SYNONYM tiny

2 done in a very careful and detailed way *a minute examination*
minutely *adverb*

miracle *noun* **miracles**
1 a wonderful thing that happens that is impossible to explain by science because it is so strange and surprising
2 used about anything really good that is very surprising *It was a miracle you weren't hurt.*

miraculous *adjective*
1 used for describing something really good that is very surprising *Grandma was very ill but she's made a miraculous recovery.*
2 making miracles happen *This magical stone has miraculous powers.*
miraculously *adverb*

mirage ['mir-ahj'; 'j' has the middle sound of 'pleasure'] *noun* **mirages**
something that someone thinks they can see but is not really there, for example an image of water in a desert

mirror *noun* **mirrors**
1 a piece of glass covered with a special substance to form a shiny surface, used for producing a clear image of anything in front of it
2 a mirror image is something that looks exactly the same as something else but with its left side on the right and its right side on the left. This is the type of image you see when you look in the mirror.

ORIGIN from Old French *mirer* 'to look at'

mirth *noun*
an old-fashioned word for laughter or happiness

mis- – mission

mis- *prefix*
used with verbs, nouns and adjectives to mean badly (or bad) or wrongly (or wrong) or to give an opposite meaning *to misbehave; to mishear; a mistake; misleading; mistrust*

misbehave *verb*
misbehaves, misbehaving, misbehaved
to behave badly **misbehaviour** *noun*

miscarriage *noun* miscarriages
when a woman gives birth to a baby that dies because it has not developed enough to be able to live
miscarry *verb*

miscellaneous ['mis-er-lay-nee-ers'] *adjective*
used for talking about things or groups made up of many different types *My dad has a miscellaneous collection of old books. The drawer was full of miscellaneous toys* (all kinds of different toys).

mischief ['mis-chif] *noun*
1 slightly bad behaviour by someone who wants to have fun *My little brother is always up to some mischief* (doing something slightly bad). *Go and watch TV – that will keep you out of mischief* (stop you behaving badly).
2 the feeling of wanting to have fun by doing something slightly bad *I could see a look of mischief on his face.*

mischievous ['mis-chiv-ers] *adjective*
1 if someone is mischievous, they want to have fun by doing slightly bad things
2 also used about something that someone does or says or the way someone looks *a mischievous prank; He had a mischievous look on his face.*
mischievously *adverb*

LANGUAGE EXTRA be careful not to spell *mischievous* with an extra *i* before the *o*. Do not write *mischievious*. Be careful also not to pronounce it with an extra *i*. Do not say 'mis-**cheev**-ee-ers'.

miser *noun* misers
someone who likes to have money but doesn't like spending it

miserable *adjective*
1 very unhappy *I'm miserable because I don't have any friends.*
2 always complaining *Your granddad is such a miserable old man.*
3 very bad and making you feel unhappy *miserable weather; I have a cold and feel miserable.*
4 very small and not enough *Lily gave me a miserable £10 for my birthday.*

miserably *adverb*
1 very or completely, in a way that makes you feel unhappy *My brother failed his exam miserably. The weather is miserably cold today.*
2 in a way that shows you are unhappy *The baby was crying miserably.*

miserly *adjective*
1 not wanting to spend money
SYNONYM mean
2 very small and not enough *a miserly sum of money*

misery *noun*
1 great suffering or unhappiness *a life of misery; Snow caused misery for thousands of motorists. The bully made my life a misery* (made me very unhappy).
2 (*plural* **miseries**) a situation that causes great suffering or unhappiness *My grandparents had lived through the miseries of war.*
3 (*plural* **miseries**) someone who is always complaining

misfire *verb*
misfires, misfiring, misfired
1 to go wrong *Our plans misfired.*
2 if a gun misfires, no bullet comes out of it

misfit *noun* misfits
someone who is not allowed to belong to a particular group, for example because their behaviour is different or unusual

misfortune *noun* misfortunes
a bad thing or bad things that happen to you *I had the misfortune to miss the train. We should try to learn from our misfortunes.*
SYNONYM bad luck

misgivings *noun plural*
a feeling of being worried about whether something is right or good *Lucy was beginning to have misgivings about our plan.*

mishap ['mis-hap'] *noun* mishaps
an accident or unlucky event but not a very serious one *The party went off without mishap* (without any problems).

misinform *verb*
misinforms, misinforming, misinformed
to give someone wrong information

misjudge *verb*
misjudges, misjudging, misjudged
1 to form a wrong opinion about someone or something
2 to guess something wrongly, for example a distance, amount or speed

mislay *verb*
mislays, mislaying, mislaid
to lose something by forgetting where you put it
SYNONYM to misplace

mislead *verb*
misleads, misleading, misled
to make someone believe something that isn't true

misleading *adjective*
used about something that someone says or writes when it makes you believe something that isn't true *misleading information*

misplace *verb*
misplaces, misplacing, misplaced
to lose something by forgetting where you put it
SYNONYM to mislay

misprint *noun* misprints
a mistake such as a spelling mistake in a printed text *That book is full of misprints.*

miss *verb*
misses, missing, missed
1 to feel sad because someone is no longer with you or because you no longer have something *I'll miss my friends when I'm in Spain. I miss my laptop – it's being repaired.*
2 to not hit, catch or reach something or someone *The ball missed my head. I tried to catch the ball but I missed.*
3 to not hear or see something or someone *Say that again – I missed it. Sorry I missed you.*
4 to arrive too late to get on a bus, train or plane *We've missed the school bus again!*
5 to not go to something or be somewhere, for example a lesson, class, party or concert *I don't want to miss school today.*
6 to not use something such as an opportunity that would be good for you *You've missed your chance to go on the school trip.*
7 to not have or get something that you would like *You're missing all the fun.*
8 to notice that something is missing *When did you first miss your mobile phone?*
9 to avoid something bad *Dad goes to work early to miss the crowds on the train.*
10 if you miss something or miss something out, you don't include it or do it, either on purpose or accidentally, for example because you don't notice it *When you painted the door there's a bit you missed* (or *missed out*). *You've missed out my name from the list.*

miss *noun* misses
1 not hitting something or someone, or not scoring in a game *I threw the ball towards the net but it was a miss.*
2 if you give something a miss, you don't do it, have it or go there *Let's give the British Museum a miss because there isn't enough time.*

Miss *noun* Misses
1 a title you put in front of the name of a woman who isn't married *The nurse's name is Miss Williams.*
2 a title that children use when they talk to a woman teacher *Please, Miss, I have a question.*

misshapen *adjective*
if something is misshapen, it has an unusual shape

missile *noun* missiles
1 a weapon like a rocket that is fired into the air over a long distance. It explodes when it hits the place it has been aimed at.
2 an object thrown through the air and aimed at someone or something

missing *adjective*
1 used about something or someone that you can't find because they are not where they should be *My cat has gone missing.*
2 used about something that should be fixed to something or a part of something but is not there *Sanjay's book has a few missing pages.*
3 used about something or someone not included in something *Joshua's name is missing from the list.*

mission *noun* missions
1 an important job that someone has to do, usually when they have to travel somewhere

296

2 an important journey, for example into space or by military aircraft *Are they planning a mission to Mars?*
3 work that someone wants to do because they think it is their responsibility to do it *Ava's mission in life is to help poor people.*
4 the place where missionaries live

missionary *noun* **missionaries**
someone who travels to a foreign country to teach people about a religion, usually the Christian religion

misspell *verb*
misspells, misspelling, misspelt or misspelled
to spell a word wrongly

misspelling *noun* **misspellings**
a word that is wrongly spelt

mist *noun*
1 (*plural* **mists**) a thin cloud formed by tiny drops of water. Mist stays close to the ground (or the sea) and makes it difficult to see.
2 tiny drops of water on a window or mirror, formed when warm air or steam changes into liquid

mistake *noun* **mistakes**
1 something wrong that you do or say *a spelling mistake*
2 something that you think is wrong *It would be a mistake to watch TV instead of doing your homework.*
3 if you make a mistake, you do or say something wrong
4 if you do something by mistake, you do it when you should not have done it or when you didn't mean to do it

mistake *verb*
mistakes, mistaking, mistook, mistaken
1 to be wrong about something *I mistook the date and arrived on the wrong day.*
2 to think that someone or something is someone or something else *I mistook you for your brother.*

mistaken *adjective*
wrong about something or someone *I'm not Ben – you must be mistaken. I was mistaken about what happened. You've got a mistaken opinion of her.*

mistakenly *adverb*
wrongly *I mistakenly thought you knew how to swim.*

mister *noun*
an informal way of talking to or calling to a man whose name you don't know *Please, mister, can I fetch my ball?*

LANGUAGE EXTRA written as *Mr* when used as a title in front of a man's name, for example *Mr Clark*

mistletoe *noun*
a plant with small round white fruits and leaves that stay green all year round. Mistletoe attaches itself to trees and grows on the branches or trunks (main stems). It is often used as a Christmas decoration.

mistook
past tense of **mistake**

mistreat *verb*
mistreats, mistreating, mistreated
to treat a person or animal badly

mistreatment *noun*

mistress *noun* **mistresses**
1 a woman who is in charge of something *She's the mistress of the house.*
2 a word sometimes used for a female teacher
3 a woman who owns and looks after a dog

mistrust *verb*
mistrusts, mistrusting, mistrusted
to think that someone or something cannot be trusted

mistrust *noun*
a feeling of not being able to trust someone or something **mistrust** *verb*

misty *adjective* **mistier, mistiest**
1 if the weather or a place is misty, there is a lot of mist and it is difficult to see
2 if a window or mirror is misty, it is difficult to see through it or in it because it is covered with mist
3 misty eyes are eyes that are full of tears

misunderstand *verb*
misunderstands, misunderstanding, misunderstood
1 to not understand someone and not know the meaning of what they say *Sorry, I misunderstood you – I thought you meant something else.*
2 to not understand something and not know the meaning of it *I misunderstood the question.*

misunderstanding *noun* **misunderstandings**
1 when you don't understand someone or something, or the problem caused by this
2 a small argument with someone

misunderstood *adjective*
if someone is misunderstood, people don't know what they are really like and the good qualities that they have

misuse ['mis-yooz'] *verb*
misuses, misusing, misused
1 to use something in the wrong way *People often misuse the word 'disinterested'.*
2 to use something in an unsuitable or dishonest way *My brother completely misused the money Dad gave him.*
3 to treat something badly *If you misuse your computer this way, it could easily break.*

misuse ['mis-yooss'] *noun*
1 using something in the wrong way *the misuse of power*
2 using something in an unsuitable or dishonest way *the misuse of the money*
3 treating something badly

mite *noun* **mites**
1 a tiny insect that lives in many different places such as on plants, animals or food. Dust mites live in dust, for example, inside carpets and mattresses.
2 an old-fashioned word for a child that someone feels sorry for *Poor little mite!*
3 **a mite** an old-fashioned way of saying slightly *You look a mite uncomfortable.*

mitre ['my-ter] *noun* **mitres**
a tall pointed hat worn by a bishop (Christian priest)

mitt *noun* **mitts**
1 a thick glove that has a part for the thumb and another part for all the fingers *oven mitts*
2 a glove that covers the whole hand except for the fingers. It is used by people who need to have their fingers free. *cycling mitts*
3 a thick leather glove for catching the ball in baseball
4 a slang word for a hand *Keep your mitts off my cake.*

mitten *noun* **mittens**
1 a glove that has a part for the thumb and another part for all the fingers. It is worn, for example, by children or in sports. *ski mittens*
2 a glove that covers the whole hand except for the fingers

mix *verb*
mixes, mixing, mixed
1 to put different substances together to form a single thing, for example by stirring, shaking or beating *Mix the eggs and flour in a bowl. You mix the blue paint with the yellow to get green.*
2 if different substances mix, they join together to form a single thing *Oil and water don't mix.*
3 to put different things together, for example in a way that works well, or to be put together in this way *This book mixes fact and fiction. These ideas don't really mix.*
4 to spend time talking to people and being friendly with them *Nisha mixes well with the other children.*
5 if you mix things up, you change the order of things in a way that is confusing *Mix up the letters of the alphabet in this box and then make the word 'elephant'.*
6 if you mix up a thing or person with another, you're confused and think that something or someone is something or someone else *I mixed her up with her sister.*

mix *noun*
1 a group of things or people that are put together *Our school has a mix of children from different countries.*
2 the action of mixing things *Give the eggs and flour a good mix.*
3 (*plural* **mixes**) a powder or substance that you mix with liquid to make something such as food *a cake mix*
4 (*plural* **mixes**) a piece of music that you change, for example using a computer, in order to make a different piece of music

mixed *adjective*
1 used about people who are very different from each other, for example people of different ages, countries or religions *a mixed population*
2 used about something that is for both boys and girls *a mixed school*
3 in maths, a mixed number is one such as $4\frac{1}{2}$ that contains a whole number (4) and a fraction ($\frac{1}{2}$)

mixed up *adjective*
confused about something, for example when you have to remember many details *I always get mixed up when I do fractions.*

mixer *noun* **mixers**
1 a piece of electrical kitchen equipment that mixes food such as eggs by beating it with wire loops
2 a similar piece of equipment that is not electrical, for example with a handle that you turn
3 any type of machine that mixes something *a cement mixer*

297

mixture – moderation

mixture *noun*
1 used when talking about different things or people together *The concert included a mixture of old and new songs.*
2 (*plural* **mixtures**) a substance or liquid made by mixing different things together *Shake the cough mixture before you take it.*

mix-up *noun* **mix-ups**
a mistake made by someone who is confused, for example when someone gives you the wrong thing *There was a mix-up over the tickets – the dates are completely wrong.*

mm
short for **millimetre** or **millimetres**

mnemonic ['ner-mon-ik'] *noun* **mnemonics**
a short sentence or poem that helps you remember something. For example, 'I before E except after C' reminds you to spell words like 'receive' with 'ei', not with 'ie'.

ORIGIN from Greek *mnemonikos* 'connected with memory'

moan *verb*
moans, moaning, moaned
1 to complain, for example about something that is not very important
2 to make a long deep sound, usually because you're in pain or very sad

moan *noun*

moat *noun* **moats**
a deep hole filled with water going all the way round a castle. Moats were used in the past to protect castles from being attacked.

mob *noun* **mobs**
1 a large crowd of angry people who are often violent
2 a group of people who do things together, often bad things

mob *verb*
mobs, mobbing, mobbed
if a group of people mob someone, they surround them or go very close to them *The film star was mobbed by fans who wanted his autograph.*

mobile *adjective*
1 able to move easily *After his accident, it was a long time until Granddad was mobile again.*
2 able to be moved or carried around easily *smartphones and other mobile devices*
3 travelling from place to place *a mobile library; a mobile X-ray unit*

mobile *noun* **mobiles**
1 short for **mobile phone**
2 a decoration or work of art made of small objects tied to pieces of string or wire. The objects hang down from a frame so that they move about in the air. *There's a mobile above my baby sister's cot.*

mobile home *noun* **mobile homes**
a type of building or a caravan that people live in. It usually remains fixed in one place although it can be moved to another place.

mobile phone *noun* **mobile phones**
a small phone that you carry around with you

SYNONYM **cell phone**

compare: **landline**

mobility *noun*
1 being able to travel from place to place
2 being able to move or be moved

moccasin *noun* **moccasins**
a flat shoe, usually brown, made from soft leather with stitches all the way round the front part

ORIGIN from *makasin* 'shoe' in Powhatan, a Native American language. Native Americans were the first to use moccasins.

mocha ['mock-er'] *noun*
1 (*plural* **mochas**) a hot drink made from coffee and chocolate
2 a type of small coffee bean

mock *verb*
mocks, mocking, mocked
to show that you think someone or something is silly, for example by saying something unkind or by copying them in an unkind way *She mocked me because I had a hole in my sock.*

mock *adjective*
1 not real *'Really?' he said, with mock surprise.*
2 a mock exam or test is one that you do for practice before the real one

mockery *noun*
1 when someone mocks someone or something in an unkind way
2 if someone makes a mockery of something such as a plan or event, they make it look completely useless or stupid

mock-up *noun* **mock-ups**
a model of something such as a building or car, used for example to teach people about it or show people what it looks like before it is built

LANGUAGE EXTRA also spelt *mockup*

modal *noun* **modals**
another name for a modal verb

modal verb *noun* **modal verbs**
a verb used with other verbs to add a special meaning to them, for example to talk about the action of the verb as being possible or necessary

LANGUAGE EXTRA a *modal verb* is a verb such as *may, might, can, could, will, would, shall, should* or *must*. You use modal verbs to express different meanings such as possibility (*It may be too long*), being able to do something (*They can swim*), intending to do something (*I will do it*) or saying that it is important to do something (*You must obey*).

compare: **auxiliary verb** (*see*: **auxiliary** *adjective*)

mode *noun* **modes**
1 a way of doing something *Cycling is my favourite mode of transport.*
2 a particular way in which a piece of equipment or a computer program works *Use your printer in colour mode.*
3 used about a particular fashion in clothes or style, for example in art or literature
4 in maths, the mode is the number that appears the most times in a list of numbers *The mode of 10, 2, 7, 9 and 2 is 2.*

model *noun* **models**
1 a copy of something such as a building or car that is usually smaller than the real thing. It can help us to understand how the real thing looks or works. *a model of the Eiffel Tower*
2 someone or something that people copy because they have such good qualities *Amy is a model for the class because she works hard and is well-behaved.*
3 a certain type of equipment or car made by a particular company *What model is your computer?*
4 someone whose job is to wear new clothes to show to people *a fashion model*
5 someone whose job is to be painted by an artist or photographed by a photographer

model *adjective*
1 used for describing something that is a smaller copy of the real thing *a model railway*
2 used for describing someone that people copy because of their good qualities *Amy is a model pupil.*

model *verb*
models, modelling, modelled
1 to wear new clothes for a fashion designer
2 to work as an artist's or photographer's model
3 to make a small object or model out of a material such as clay or wood
4 if something is modelled on something else, the first thing uses the second as its pattern or model *This building is modelled on the British Museum.*

modem *noun* **modems**
a piece of equipment that connects a computer to a phone line

moderate ['mod-er-ert'] *adjective*
1 halfway between amounts, sizes, levels or extremes such as high and low, big and small or hot and cold *Bake the potatoes on a moderate heat. I'm a moderate eater (I don't eat too much or too little).*
2 neither good nor bad *a moderate success*
3 used for describing something such as a political opinion or speech that is reasonable and not extreme so that many people can agree with it

moderate ['mod-er-ayt'] *verb*
moderates, moderating, moderated
1 to make something less strong or extreme
2 if someone moderates a discussion, for example in a chat room on the internet, they make sure the rules are followed and people are polite to each other

moderately *adverb*
1 not very but still quite a lot *a moderately successful book; I speak French moderately well.*

SYNONYM **fairly**

2 not very much but still quite a lot *Grandma has improved moderately.*
3 not too much or too little *I always eat moderately.*

moderation *noun*
when you do something in a reasonable way, for example not too much or too little of it *I always eat in moderation.*

298

moderator–mongoose

moderator *noun* **moderators**
someone in charge of a discussion, for example in a chat room on the internet, who makes sure the rules are followed and people are polite to each other

modern *adjective*
1 belonging to the present time and not to the past *a modern city*; *modern art*
2 very new, or using the latest ideas, designs or equipment *Our school has very modern computers.*
3 having the latest ideas and opinions *Great-Gran was very modern and loved to send me texts.*
4 modern languages are ones spoken today and often studied in school or university, for example French or Spanish

modernise *verb*
modernises, modernising, modernised
1 to make something more modern, for example by replacing old ideas, designs or equipment with new ones *My uncle is modernising his house. Our school is trying to modernise its image.*
2 to become more modern *After the war the country needed to modernise.*
modernisation *noun*

> LANGUAGE EXTRA also spelt *modernize* and *modernization*

modest *adjective*
1 not very large or great *My parents earn a modest salary and we live in a modest house* (not an expensive house). *My sister had very modest success as an actor.*
2 if someone is modest, they don't like to talk about how good they are or the good things they've done
modesty *noun*

modestly *adverb*
1 in a way that shows you don't like to talk about how good you are or the good things you've done *'That's true,' she replied modestly.*
2 without spending much money *We live very modestly.*
3 not very (or not very much) but still quite a lot *modestly successful*; *Mum bought me a modestly priced backpack* (not very expensive). *He's paid modestly.*

modification *noun* **modifications**
a slight change made to something

modify *verb*
modifies, modifying, modified
1 to change something slightly, especially to improve it
2 in grammar, if you use an adjective before a noun or an adverb with a verb to give more information about the noun or verb (for example 'a happy face' or 'I run quickly'), you can say that the adjective modifies the noun and the adverb modifies the verb

module *noun* **modules**
1 a separate part of something such as a piece of equipment or a building
2 a separate part of a spacecraft that can operate on its own *a lunar module*
3 a separate part of a course of study that can be studied on its own

Mohammed *noun*
the name of the prophet (religious leader) who founded the religion of Islam

> LANGUAGE EXTRA also spelt *Muhammad*

moist *adjective* **moister, moistest**
slightly wet, often in a pleasant way *This cake is lovely and moist.*

moisten ['moy-sern'] *verb*
moistens, moistening, moistened
to make something slightly wet

moisture *noun*
tiny drops of water in the air or on a surface

moisturiser *noun* **moisturisers**
a cream you put on your skin to make it softer and less dry

> LANGUAGE EXTRA also spelt *moisturizer*

molar ['moh-ler'] *noun* **molars**
one of the large teeth at the back of the mouth, used for chewing food

mole *noun* **moles**
1 a small dark mark or lump on someone's skin
2 a small furry animal that is almost blind and lives in holes that it digs under the ground

molecule ['mol-ik-yool'] *noun* **molecules**
the smallest part of a chemical element that can exist by itself. A molecule is made up of two or more atoms.

molehill *noun* **molehills**
to make a mountain out of a molehill to make a small problem seem like a big one by giving it too much importance

> ORIGIN from the image of a *molehill* looking like a *mountain*, which is thousands of times bigger. A molehill is a pile of earth just a few inches high dug out of the ground by moles. The expression dates from about the 16th century.

mollusc *noun* **molluscs**
an animal with a soft body without bones that is usually covered by a shell. Molluscs include snails and oysters.

> ORIGIN from Latin *mollis* 'soft'

molten *adjective*
used for describing something such as rock, metal or glass that has become liquid because of great heat *Molten lava flowed from the volcano.*

mom *noun* **moms**
the American word for mum

moment *noun* **moments**
1 a very short period of time, for example lasting a few seconds or a minute or two *I'll help you in a moment. Jack will be back any moment* (very soon).
2 a particular time when something happens *At that moment we heard a loud bang.*
3 **at the moment** now *Suresh isn't here at the moment.*
4 **for the moment** used when describing a situation now that might be different soon *I don't need anything for the moment.*
5 **the moment** or **the moment that** as soon as *Tell me the moment you get any news.*

momentarily *adverb*
1 for a very short time only *I was momentarily confused.*
2 used in American English to mean very soon *I'll be back momentarily.*

momentary ['moh-mern-ter-ee'] *adjective*
lasting for a very short time only

momentous ['moh-men-ters'] *adjective*
used for describing something that is very important because it influences things that happen in the future *a momentous decision*

momentum ['moh-men-term'] *noun*
1 in science, the force that makes something keep moving
2 when something keeps moving or developing more and more quickly *Support for the president is gaining momentum* (getting stronger).

mommy *noun* **mommies**
the American word for mummy

Monaco *noun*
a country in Southern Europe on the Mediterranean coast of France

monarch ['mon-erk'] *noun* **monarchs**
a king or queen

monarchy ['mon-er-kee'] *noun* **monarchies**
1 a country ruled by a king or queen
2 a type of government in which a king or queen rules the country

monastery *noun* **monasteries**
a building or group of buildings where monks (religious men) live alone and pray

> ORIGIN from Greek *monazein* 'to live alone' (from *monos* 'alone')

monastic *adjective*
connected with monks or monasteries *monastic life*

Monday *noun* **Mondays**
the day of the week between Sunday and Tuesday. It is the first day of the school or working week after the weekend.

> ORIGIN from Old English *Monandæg* 'day of the moon'

money *noun*
1 pieces of paper and coins with values on them, used for buying things
2 the amount of these that you have or that you get, for example by working or putting them in the bank *My parents don't have much money. My uncle makes a lot of money in his job* (earns it by working).

> ORIGIN from Latin *moneta* 'money' or 'coins', from *Moneta*, another name of the Roman goddess Juno, because it was in Juno's temple that coins were made

moneybox *noun* **moneyboxes**
a small container for putting coins into, usually through a hole in the top, when you want to save up to buy something
compare: **piggy-bank**

Mongolia *noun*
a country in East Asia
Mongolian *adjective & noun*

mongoose *noun* **mongooses**
a small furry animal from Africa and Asia with a long body and tail and short legs. It kills and eats poisonous snakes.

mongrel–moor

mongrel *noun* **mongrels**
a dog that is bred (produced) from two or more different types of dogs
SYNONYM mutt

monitor *noun* **monitors**
1 another word for a screen, for example the screen of a computer *a 17-inch monitor*
2 a piece of equipment that checks something, for example to see how it is working, and shows something about it such as its level or speed *a heart monitor* (for showing how fast the heart beats)
3 a student who is given a responsible job to do by the teacher *a playground monitor* (to make sure children behave well)

monitor *verb*
monitors, monitoring, monitored
1 to check something for a period of time, for example to see how it is working or if everything is happening as it should
2 to watch someone closely for a period of time to see how they behave
3 to listen secretly to something such as someone's phone calls

monk *noun* **monks**
a religious man who belongs to a group of men who live on their own in a building called a monastery

monkey *noun* **monkeys**
a hairy animal with long arms and legs, a long tail, and hands and feet similar to those of a human. Monkeys climb trees and live in hot countries.

monkey *verb* (informal)
monkeys, monkeying, monkeyed
if someone monkeys around, they behave in a silly way

mono- *prefix*
one or single *monorail*; *monolingual* (speaking or connected with one language only)

monocle *noun* **monocles**
a round piece of special glass worn in front of one eye in order to see better, especially in the past

monogram *noun* **monograms**
a design made up of one letter or a small group of letters, for example the first letters of someone's name. It is usually sewn on clothing or put on something else that belongs to you.

monologue *noun* **monologues**
a long speech by one person, for example by a character in a play or film

monopolise *verb*
monopolises, monopolising, monopolised
1 to take complete control of a business activity and not let anyone else do it
2 to not let anyone else use or have something or take part in an activity
LANGUAGE EXTRA also spelt *monopolize*

monopoly *noun* **monopolies**
complete control of a business activity, or a company or person that has this control

Monopoly *noun* (trademark)
a game you play on a square board using dice. You move pieces around the board and use fake money to buy streets, houses and hotels.

monorail *noun* **monorails**
1 a type of railway where the trains travel along a single rail (long metal bar)
2 a train that travels along this single rail

monosyllable *noun* **monosyllables**
a word made up of only one syllable (vowel sound), such as 'big', 'jump' or 'dog'
monosyllabic *adjective*

monotonous ['mer-not-er-ners'] *adjective*
if something is monotonous, it is boring because it is always the same *a monotonous voice*; *Our school dinners are very monotonous.* **monotonously** *adverb*

monotony ['mer-not-er-nee'] *noun*
when something is boring because it is always the same *Dad doesn't like the monotony of his job.*

monsoon *noun* **monsoons**
a season of heavy rain and strong winds during the summer, usually in the hot countries of southern Asia
ORIGIN from Arabic *mawsim* 'season'

monster *noun* **monsters**
1 an imaginary creature that is very large and usually ugly and frightening
2 used for describing something that is very large *That's a real monster of a cucumber. That's a monster cucumber.*
3 an extremely cruel and bad person
ORIGIN from Latin *monstrum* 'sign of bad things to come' (from *monere* 'to warn')

monstrosity *noun* **monstrosities**
an object or building that is very large and ugly

monstrous *adjective*
1 extremely cruel and bad *a monstrous crime*
2 very large *We were shocked by the creature's monstrous size.*
3 very ugly and frightening *He had a monstrous look on his face.*

month *noun* **months**
1 one of the 12 periods of time, starting with January and ending with December, that make up a year. All the months last 30 or 31 days except February (which has 28 days but 29 in a leap year). *Finish your homework by the end of the month.*
2 any period of time that lasts four weeks or about four weeks *We have exams in a couple of months.*

monthly *adjective*
1 happening once every month *a monthly visit*; *a monthly magazine*
2 used for describing the total amount of something for a whole month *What's the monthly rainfall in London?*
3 lasting a whole month *a monthly season ticket*

monthly *adverb*
happening once every month *We visit our grandparents monthly.*

monthly *noun* **monthlies**
a magazine that comes out once every month

monty *noun*
(slang) **the full monty** used for describing everything connected with a particular thing or situation *'What sort of birthday party is it?' – 'The full monty – all my friends, lots of cakes and ice cream, a bouncy castle and a magician!'*

monument *noun* **monuments**
1 a structure such as a building or statue built to make people remember a person or event *a monument to soldiers who died in the war*
2 a very old structure or building that is important in a country's history *an ancient monument*

monumental *adjective*
1 used for describing strongly how good, bad or big something is *a monumental piece of good luck*; *a monumental mistake*; *Moving to a new house is a monumental task.*
2 used for describing strongly how big and important something is *Dr Johnson's dictionary is a monumental work.*

monumentally *adverb*
extremely (used about something either good or bad) *'Hamlet' is a monumentally important play by Shakespeare. Not doing your homework was a monumentally bad idea!*

moo *verb*
moos, mooing, mooed
when a cow moos, it makes a long deep noise that is its own special sound **moo** *noun*

mood *noun* **moods**
1 the way you feel and behave at a particular time, for example whether you are happy, sad, angry or worried *Everyone in the class was in a holiday mood* (feeling excited because of the holidays).
2 **in a good mood** feeling happy and pleasant
3 **in a bad mood** feeling sad or angry

moody *adjective* **moodier, moodiest**
1 angry or unhappy
2 unfriendly because you're angry or unhappy
3 often becoming angry or unhappy suddenly and for no reason
moodily *adverb* **moodiness** *noun*

moon *noun*
1 the moon is the round object in the sky that moves around the earth and shines at night. The light that shines from the moon is reflected light from the sun.
2 (plural **moons**) a similar round object that moves around another planet *Mars has two moons.*

moonlight *noun*
the light from the moon

moonlit *adjective*
lit up with the light from the moon *a moonlit sky*

moor *noun* **moors**
an area of land covered with rough grass and small bushes such as heather, where the soil is not good enough for growing plants for food

moor *verb*
moors, mooring, moored
to stop a boat from moving by tying it with ropes or cables to a structure fixed on the land, for example a post, or by fixing it to the bottom of the sea with an anchor

moorhen–mortgage

moorhen *noun* **moorhens**
a medium-sized black or brown bird with a red beak. Moorhens live near rivers and lakes.

mooring *noun* **moorings**
a structure or place for mooring a boat so that it does not move

moose *noun* **moose**
an animal like a large deer with a big nose and large wide antlers. Moose live mainly in North America.

mop *noun* **mops**
1 a long handle with a sponge or thick strings at the end, used mainly for washing floors
2 a short handle with thick strings at the end, used for washing dishes
3 a mop of hair is a thick mass of hair on someone's head

mop *verb*
mops, mopping, mopped
1 to wash something such as a floor with a mop
2 to use a cloth or tissue to get rid of sweat from your forehead *It was so hot he kept mopping his brow.*
3 if you mop something up, such as a liquid, you get rid of it from a surface with a mop or cloth *I spilt the milk and had to mop it up.*

mope *verb*
mopes, moping, moped
to behave in a way that shows you are unhappy, for example by not being interested in anything or not wanting to do anything *My brother has been moping around the house all day.*

moped ['moh-ped'] *noun* **mopeds**
a type of bicycle with a small engine, or a light motorcycle with a less powerful engine than the one on a normal motorcycle

moral *adjective*
1 connected with how people behave and what is right or wrong *a moral question*
2 if someone is moral, they behave in the right way because they follow standards of good behaviour
3 if something that someone does, says or believes is moral, it is based on what people think is right

moral *noun* **morals**
1 a lesson that you learn from a story or event about how to behave in a particular situation
2 morals are standards about how to behave

morale ['mer-ahl'] *noun*
a feeling of being happy about a situation and hopeful about the future *Morale is low in our class* (children are unhappy).

morality *noun*
1 people's behaviour and whether it is right or wrong
2 standards of good behaviour

morally *adverb*
1 behaving or done in the right way following standards of good behaviour
2 based on what people think is right *Stealing is morally wrong.*

morbid *adjective*
showing too much interest in unpleasant things such as death or disease
morbidly *adverb*

ORIGIN from Latin *morbus* 'disease'

more *adjective*
used for describing a bigger amount or number of something *Evie has more cake than me. I read more books than I used to.*

ANTONYM less

more *adverb & pronoun*
1 very much when compared to something else *My sister is more intelligent than me.*

ANTONYM less

2 used for describing something done in a bigger, better or stronger way, or for a greater amount of time or number of times *You'll have to work more to pass your exams. Push more to get the toothpaste out. May I watch TV a bit more?*

ANTONYM less

3 used for describing a bigger amount of something *I've got more than a week to do my homework.*

ANTONYM less

4 **more and more** used about something such as an amount that keeps getting bigger, or about something that keeps happening for a greater amount of time or number of times *I'm eating more and more cake. I told him to stop but he just hit me more and more.*
5 **more or less** not completely but almost, or not always but almost always *I'm more or less ready. I do my homework more or less every day.*
6 **more or less** also used about a number or amount that is not exact but is roughly correct *My bike cost £200, more or less.*

SYNONYM approximately

7 **not any more** or **no more** used when you mean something has stopped happening or isn't true now *I don't play football any more. 'Is Jodie still your friend?' – 'No, no more!'*

moreover *adverb*
used for adding something extra to what you say

SYNONYM also

morgue *noun* **morgues**
a place, for example in a hospital, where dead bodies are kept until they are buried or cremated

SYNONYM mortuary

Mormon *noun* **Mormons**
someone who belongs to a religious group that was started in the United States in 1830 **Mormon** *adjective*

morning *noun* **mornings**
1 the part of the day from when it gets light until twelve o'clock midday when the afternoon starts *I don't always eat breakfast in the morning.*
2 the part of the night-time from midnight onwards *Mum was still working at two o'clock in the morning.*
3 **in the morning** used when you mean tomorrow morning *Bye, Sally, I'll see you in the morning.*
4 **good morning** a polite way of saying hello to someone in the morning

Morocco *noun*
a country in North-West Africa
Moroccan *adjective & noun*

moron ['more-on'] *noun* **morons**
an informal and very insulting word for a stupid person

ORIGIN from Greek *moros* 'foolish'

moronic ['mer-on-ik'] *adjective*
an informal and very insulting word for stupid

morose ['mer-ohs'] *adjective*
unhappy and not wanting to speak to anyone

morris dancing *noun*
a type of old English dancing. It is usually done by men wearing special clothes decorated with ribbons and bells and often carrying handkerchiefs and sticks.
morris dance *noun* **morris dancer** *noun*

Morse code *noun*
a way of sending messages using dots (short signals) and dashes (long signals) for each of the letters of the alphabet and the numbers 0 to 9. The signals are sent as sounds or flashes of light.

LANGUAGE EXTRA also called *Morse*

ORIGIN named after the American Samuel F. B. *Morse* who invented the code in the 19th century

morsel *noun* **morsels**
a very small piece of something, especially food

mortal *adjective*
1 having to die at some time because you cannot live for ever
2 causing someone's death *a mortal blow*
3 used about a great danger or fear, for example when you think you could die or something bad could happen to you *Every day we live in mortal danger.*
mortality *noun*

mortal *noun* **mortals**
an ordinary person

mortally *adverb*
if someone is mortally wounded or injured, their injuries are so bad that they die

mortar *noun*
1 a mixture of substances such as sand and water. It is used when building something for joining bricks or stones together.
2 (*plural* **mortars**) a small heavy gun for firing bombs into the air over a short distance

mortgage ['mor-gij'] *noun* **mortgages**
1 an agreement, for example with a bank, to borrow money to buy a house or flat and pay it back over many years
2 the amount of money that someone borrows when they have this agreement

mortuary – mount

mortuary *noun* **mortuaries**
a place, for example in a hospital, where dead bodies are kept until they are buried or cremated

SYNONYM morgue

mosaic ['moh-**zay**-ik] *noun* **mosaics**
a picture or pattern made up of small pieces of coloured stone or glass *an ancient Roman mosaic floor*

mosque ['mosk'] *noun* **mosques**
a building where Muslims pray and celebrate their religion

mosquito *noun* **mosquitoes** or **mosquitos**
a small flying insect that bites the skin and sucks blood. In hot countries mosquitoes can cause a serious illness called malaria.

ORIGIN from Spanish *mosquito* 'little fly'

moss *noun* **mosses**
a dark green plant without flowers that grows as a soft thick mass along hard surfaces such as paths or trees

mossy *adjective* **mossier, mossiest**
covered with moss

most *adjective*
1 used for describing the biggest amount or number of something *Ben has eaten the most chocolate. I've got the most toys.*

ANTONYM least

2 almost all *I watch TV most evenings. Most children like ice cream.*

most *adverb & pronoun*
1 more than anything or anyone else *Today is the most exciting day ever. Of all my friends I like you most (or the most).*

ANTONYM least

2 almost all *Most of the film was boring. I understood most of the questions.*
3 extremely *a most important decision*
4 to make the most of something is to enjoy it or use it as much as possible, for example when talking about something that may not last long *Make the most of the nice weather – tomorrow it's supposed to rain.*
5 at most not more than a particular amount or number *'How many friends are coming to your party?' – 'Ten at most.'*

mostly *adverb*
1 used when you mean the biggest or most important part of something or almost all of something *Our class is made up mostly of boys.*
2 almost always *Pandas live mostly in China.*
3 used when you mean the most important reason for something *I don't eat fish – mostly because I don't like the smell.*
4 almost but not quite *I'm mostly finished.*

MOT *noun* **MOTs**
a test that road vehicles must pass every year when they reach a particular age to show they are safe to drive

ORIGIN from the first letters of *Ministry of Transport*, the part of the government responsible for this test in the past

motel ['moh-**tel**'] *noun* **motels**
a hotel near a main road with lots of spaces for people to park their car, often close to the room they are staying in

ORIGIN from *motor* and *hotel*

moth *noun* **moths**
an insect with large wings like a butterfly that flies mainly at night. Moths are attracted by the light.

mothball *noun* **mothballs**
a small white ball made from a chemical with a strong smell. Mothballs are put near clothes to keep moths away.

mother *noun* **mothers**
a woman who has given birth to a son or daughter

motherboard *noun* **motherboards**
the big flat surface inside a computer that contains the CPU (the main part that makes it work) and all the electrical connections to it

motherhood *noun*
being a mother and looking after a child or children

mother-in-law *noun* **mothers-in-law**
the mother of someone's husband or wife

motherly *adjective*
connected with the feelings and behaviour of a loving mother *motherly love*

Mother's Day *noun* **Mother's Days**
a special day for honouring mothers when people give cards and presents to their mother. It is usually celebrated in March.

mother-to-be *noun* **mothers-to-be**
a woman who is expecting a baby

motif ['moh-**teef**'] *noun* **motifs**
a pattern that is repeated to make a decoration, for example on clothes or wallpaper *a dress with a floral motif*

motion *noun* **motions**
1 the action of something or someone moving *the gentle motion of the boat*
2 a particular action *He made a motion with his hand.*
3 to set something in motion is to get it to slowly start happening

motion *verb*
motions, motioning, motioned
to move your hand or head towards something, for example as a way of telling someone to do something or showing what you want *The teacher motioned for me to sit down.*

motionless *adjective*
without moving at all

SYNONYM still

motivate *verb*
motivates, motivating, motivated
1 to make someone really want to do something by making them feel happy about doing it *Mr Brown is good at motivating his pupils* (makes them happy about wanting to learn).
2 if someone is motivated by something, that thing is the reason for the way they behave *My uncle is motivated by greed* (his behaviour shows that he is greedy).

motivation *noun*
1 enthusiasm for doing something
2 (*plural* **motivations**) the reason for doing something

motive *noun* **motives**
the reason for doing something

motor *noun* **motors**
1 a machine that uses electricity or fuel to make something work
2 an old-fashioned word for a car

motorbike *noun* **motorbikes**
another word for a motorcycle

motorboat *noun* **motorboats**
a small boat with an engine

motor car *noun* **motor cars**
an old-fashioned word for a car

motorcycle *noun* **motorcycles**
a powerful vehicle with two wheels and an engine that you ride by sitting on it
motorcyclist *noun*

motoring *noun*
the activity of driving a car

motorist *noun* **motorists**
someone who drives a car

motor racing *noun*
a sport in which fast cars are used for racing round a track

motor vehicle *noun* **motor vehicles**
a vehicle with an engine, for example a car or lorry

motorway *noun* **motorways**
a wide road on which traffic travels very fast between towns

mottled *adjective*
if something is mottled, it has a pattern of light and dark areas with different shapes

motto *noun* **mottos** or **mottoes**
a word, group of words or short sentence that expresses a belief or rule about how to behave *Our school motto is: 'Achieving excellence together'.*

mould *noun*
1 a green, black or grey substance that grows on food that has gone bad or on damp surfaces such as walls
2 (*plural* **moulds**) a container of a particular shape, used for example for making jelly or plaster models. Liquid is poured into the container, and the liquid becomes hard. When it is taken out of the container, it has the same shape as the container.

mould *verb*
moulds, moulding, moulded
to make a soft substance such as clay or dough into a particular shape *We moulded the sand into a sandcastle.*

mouldy *adjective* **mouldier, mouldiest**
with mould on it *mouldy bread*

moult ['molt'] *verb*
moults, moulting, moulted
when a bird or animal moults, it loses its feathers, skin or fur and grows new feathers, skin or fur

mound *noun* **mounds**
1 a large pile of something, for example earth, stones or papers
2 a small hill

mount *verb*
mounts, mounting, mounted
1 to get on a bicycle or horse

mount–movie

2 to climb up onto something such as a platform or ladder
3 to get bigger, stronger or worse *Excitement was mounting in the audience. If you don't do your homework, it will start to mount up.*
4 to fix something onto something else, for example in order to use it or display it *Mount your webcam at the top of the screen. The photos were mounted on card and pinned to the wall.*
5 to organise or start something, for example an attack or exhibition

mount *noun* **mounts**
1 something such as stiff paper, used for fixing a picture or photo onto
2 used in the names of mountains *Mount Everest*

mountain *noun* **mountains**
1 a very high piece of land that is much larger than a hill. The top of a mountain is often covered in snow.
2 a large pile or amount of something *Our teacher has a mountain of homework to mark.*
3 a mountain bike is a strong bicycle with thick tyres that can be used for riding over bumpy ground

mountaineer *noun* **mountaineers**
someone who climbs mountains
mountaineering *noun*

mountainous *adjective*
with lots of mountains

mourn *verb*
mourns, mourning, mourned
to feel very sad because someone has died and show how sad you feel by the way you behave *We're mourning for Gran.*

mourner *noun* **mourners**
someone at the funeral of a person who has died

mournful *adjective*
very sad **mournfully** *adverb*

mourning *noun*
1 great sadness that people feel when someone has died *Granddad is in mourning for Grandma.*
2 the period of time when you show how sad you feel by the way you behave

mouse *noun* **mice**
1 a small furry animal with a long tail and a pointed nose. Mice live in fields or in buildings and people's homes.
2 a small piece of equipment connected to a computer by a wire or radio signal. You move it with your hand in order to move a pointer or cursor (small symbol) on the screen and control what the computer does.

mousetrap *noun* **mousetraps**
a small object with a spring that is used inside buildings for catching and killing mice

moussaka ['moo-**sah**-ker'] *noun*
a Greek food usually made from slices of aubergines with other vegetables and chopped meat and with cheese on top

mousse ['mooss'] *noun* **mousses**
1 a cold sweet food made with eggs and cream that is eaten as a dessert *chocolate mousse*
2 a white creamy substance or a substance with lots of small bubbles in it, used on your hair to make it keep its shape

moustache *noun* **moustaches**
a line of hair growing above a man's upper lip

mousy *adjective* **mousier, mousiest**
1 used for describing hair that is light or medium brown and often dull or not attractive
2 a mousy person is quiet and shy

mouth *noun* **mouths**
1 the opening in the face of a person or animal where the lips, teeth and tongue are, used for eating, drinking, breathing, speaking or making noises
2 the place where a river flows into a sea or lake
3 the entrance to something such as a cave or tunnel
4 used when talking about someone saying something or speaking *Keep your mouth shut* (don't say anything). *You're very quiet – you haven't opened your mouth once* (haven't spoken once). *Don't tell Harry anything – he's a big mouth* (he'll tell other people things that are secret).

mouthful *noun* **mouthfuls**
an amount of food or drink that you put in your mouth at one time

mouth organ *noun* **mouth organs**
a small rectangular musical instrument that you play with your mouth. You blow and suck air through holes along one of its long sides to make the notes.

SYNONYM **harmonica**

mouthpiece *noun* **mouthpieces**
1 the part of something such as a musical instrument or a diver's breathing equipment that goes in the mouth
2 the part of a phone that you hold near your mouth and speak into

mouthwash *noun* **mouthwashes**
a liquid you use in your mouth for making it clean and fresh

mouth-watering *adjective*
used for describing food that looks or smells very good

SYNONYM **delicious**

mov ['mov']
the ending of a computer filename. A .mov file contains sound and moving pictures.
short for: **movie**

movable *adjective*
if something is movable, it can be moved

LANGUAGE EXTRA also spelt *moveable*

move *verb*
moves, moving, moved
1 to change the position of something or take it from one place to another *I can't move my fingers. Please move your chair over to the table.*
2 if someone or something moves, they change their position or go from one place to another *Stay still – you keep moving. Please move to the next seat. The wheels are moving. In chess, a rook moves in a straight line* (goes in a straight line across the board).
3 to go to live in another home or place *We're moving next week. Moving house is a lot of trouble.*
4 to travel fast *Look at that train – it's really moving!*
5 to change the time or date of something *We've moved my birthday party to next Thursday.*
6 to make progress or make progress with something *Lucy is beginning to move ahead in her studies. We're moving forward with our plans.*
7 to have a strong influence on someone's feelings, for example by making them very happy or sad *When the medal was presented to the wounded soldier, we were all very moved.*
8 if someone moves in, they start living in a new home
9 if something such as a bus moves off, it goes away
10 if someone moves out, they leave their home and go to live somewhere else
11 if you move over or up, for example when you're sitting somewhere, you make room for someone by going closer to the person next to you

move *noun* **moves**
1 the action of moving *Try not to make a move* (keep still). *It's time to make a move* (to leave). *You'll fall into the water if you make one false move* (bad movement with your body).
2 when you change the position of a piece in a game such as chess, or the time when it is your turn to do this *That move isn't allowed. Is it my move now?*
3 an action that you do, for example because you hope something good will happen *Getting extra lessons after school is a smart move.*
4 if someone or something is on the move, they are moving, for example after stopping, or they are moving from place to place or making progress
5 **get a move on** used for saying that you have to hurry or for telling someone to hurry *It's late – let's get a move on!*

movement *noun* **movements**
1 when you move a part of your body or when your body moves in a certain way *I made a sudden movement and knocked over the glass.*
2 when something changes its position or moves (or is moved) to another place *the movement of parts in a machine*; *This port deals with the movement of goods across the Channel.*
3 a group of people who have the same aims and who work together to achieve something
4 one of the main divisions of a long piece of classical music *a Beethoven symphony in four movements*

movie *noun* **movies**
1 a moving picture that you watch in a cinema or on TV

SYNONYM **film**

2 a movie theatre is the American word for a cinema
3 **the movies** the cinema *On Sunday we're going to the movies.*
4 **the movies** also used about the business or art of making films

303

moviegoer–multiple

moviegoer noun moviegoers
someone who goes to the cinema to watch movies

moving adjective
1 making someone have strong feelings such as sadness or great happiness
2 used for describing something that moves *a moving train*

mow verb
mows, mowing, mowed, mown
1 to mow grass or a lawn is to cut the grass with a lawn mower
2 to mow people down is to kill them by shooting them or knocking them over with a vehicle

mower noun mowers
a machine or piece of equipment for cutting grass on a lawn

SYNONYM lawn mower

MP noun MPs
someone chosen by the people to represent them in a parliament
short for: Member of Parliament

mph
a unit for measuring speed based on how many miles something travels in an hour
short for: miles per hour

Mr ['mis-ter']
used as a title in front of a man's name *Mr Patel*

Mrs ['mis-iz']
used as a title in front of the name of a married woman *Mrs Williams*

Ms ['merz' or 'miz']
used as a title in front of a woman's name *Ms Thompson*

much adjective & pronoun more, most
1 used when talking about a large amount of something, especially when you mean there isn't a large amount of it *There isn't much cake left. That's not much – is that all you've done? I've read much of the book.*
2 used when asking about an amount of something *Have you done much work?*
3 **as much as** used for saying how large an amount is *It weighs as much as 10 kilos.*
4 **how much** used when asking or talking about an amount *How much does it cost?*
5 **so much** used when talking about a very large amount *You've put so much salt on the chips that I can't eat them.*
6 **too much** used when talking about an amount that is more than is wanted or more than there should be *I've got too much homework.*

much adverb
1 used for showing that something or someone is different from something or someone else by a large amount *I'm much taller than my sister. My brother eats much less than me.*
2 used for giving extra importance to a word *You're much too nice to me. This jacket is much too small* (too small by a large amount).
3 used for saying that something is not done or does not happen to a high level or degree *I don't like carrots much. Things don't change much at school. I never eat too much.*
4 used for asking if something is done or happens to a high level or degree *Do you like carrots much?*
5 used for saying that something doesn't happen often or for asking if it happens often *I don't visit my uncle much. Do you visit your uncle much?*
6 **more or less** *Things are much the same.*
7 **much to** used for showing a certain feeling that someone feels strongly *I passed the exam, much to my surprise* (I was very surprised).

muck noun
1 dirt
2 waste matter from an animal's body *dog's muck*

muck verb (informal)
mucks, mucking, mucked
1 if someone mucks about or around, they waste time, for example doing silly things
2 if someone mucks something up, they do it badly or spoil it *I've mucked up my homework.*
3 if someone mucks something up, it also means they make it dirty or untidy *Take your shoes off – don't muck up the carpet.*

mucky adjective muckier, muckiest
dirty *mucky shoes*

mucus ['myoo-kers'] noun
a thick liquid or sticky substance in some parts of the body such as the nose

mud noun
soft wet earth *My boots got stuck in the mud.*

muddle noun
1 a situation where someone is confused or things are untidy or not well organised *Dad usually gets into a muddle* (becomes confused) *when he helps me with maths. You've left everything – books, papers and clothes – in a muddle in your room.*
2 a mistake made by someone who is confused *There's been a muddle over the dates.*

muddle verb
muddles, muddling, muddled
1 to make things untidy or put them in the wrong order *I need to sort out my books again – you've muddled everything up.*
2 to make someone confused about something or someone *I always get Kate and Mia muddled* (I think Kate is Mia and Mia is Kate).

muddled adjective
1 untidy *a muddled pile of clothes*
2 confused *Your ideas are a bit muddled.*

muddy adjective muddier, muddiest
1 covered with mud
2 containing lots of mud *a muddy puddle*

mudguard noun mudguards
a curved piece of metal or plastic that covers the top of a bicycle wheel or motorcycle wheel. It stops mud and water from hitting you as you ride.

muesli ['myooz-lee'] noun
a breakfast food made from oats, nuts and dried fruit that you eat with milk

muezzin ['moo-ez-in' or 'mwez-in'] noun muezzins
a person who calls Muslims to prayer, often from a minaret (the tower of a mosque)

muffin noun muffins
1 a soft and flat round bread roll that is usually cut in half, toasted and eaten with butter or margarine

LANGUAGE EXTRA also called an *English muffin*

2 a small round soft cake with pieces of fruit in it *a blueberry muffin*

muffle verb
muffles, muffling, muffled
1 to make a sound quieter and more difficult to hear, for example by covering up the thing that makes the sound *We heard the muffled sounds of people inside the building shouting for help.*
2 if someone is muffled up, they wear thick warm clothes

mug noun mugs
1 a large cup with a handle and usually straight sides, used for drinking hot drinks such as tea or coffee
2 something in a mug, for example a hot drink *I drank a whole mug of coffee.*
3 an informal word for a stupid person who is easily tricked
4 an informal word for someone's face *an ugly mug*

mug verb
mugs, mugging, mugged
to attack someone in the street or another place and steal something from them
mugger noun **mugging** noun

muggy adjective muggier, muggiest
used for describing the weather when it is warm in an unpleasant way and the air is wet **mugginess** noun

Muhammad noun
the name of the prophet (religious leader) who founded the religion of Islam

LANGUAGE EXTRA also spelt *Mohammed*

mulberry noun mulberries
1 a tree that produces a small soft purple, black or white berry that can be eaten
2 the berry that grows on the mulberry tree

mule noun mules
an animal that is produced from a male donkey and a female horse

multi- prefix
many *multicoloured* (having many colours); *multilingual* (speaking many or several languages); *multiracial* (including people of many races)

multimedia adjective
using several different ways of giving computer information, including sound, images, video and text *multimedia software*

multinational noun multinationals
a large company with offices, shops or factories in many different countries
multinational adjective

multiple adjective
very many of the same type of thing or of a different thing *multiple injuries*

multiple noun multiples
in maths, a multiple is a whole number that can be divided exactly by a smaller number without a remainder (an amount left over) *12 is a multiple of 4.*
compare: **factor**

304

multiplication *noun*
1 (*plural* **multiplications**) the action or result of multiplying two or more numbers in maths
2 the multiplication sign is the symbol × used between numbers to show that they are multiplied. In computing, for example in spreadsheets, the symbol * (an asterisk) is usually used.
3 a multiplication table is a list showing the results of multiplying one number by another between 1 and 12

SYNONYM for sense 3: times table

multiply *verb*
multiplies, multiplying, multiplied
1 in maths, if you multiply one number by another number, you add the first number to itself the number of times shown by the second number (or the second number to itself the number of times shown by the first number) *Three multiplied by five is fifteen* (3 × 5 = 15, or 3 + 3 + 3 + 3 + 3 = 15).
2 to increase by a large number or amount *Germs multiply in the hot weather.*

multi-storey *adjective*
used for describing a building that has many floors *a multi-storey car park*

multitasking *noun*
being able to do two or more things at the same time, for example watch TV, speak on the phone and type an email

ORIGIN from the computing meaning of *multitasking* (running many programs at the same time)

multitude *noun* **multitudes**
1 a very large number of things or people
2 a large crowd of people

mum *noun* **mums**
an informal word for a mother

mumble *verb*
mumbles, mumbling, mumbled
to speak or say something quietly and in a way that is not clear so that people have trouble understanding you **mumble** *noun*

mummify *verb*
mummifies, mummifying, mummified
to treat a dead body with chemicals to keep it in good condition, for example as happened in ancient Egypt

mummy *noun* **mummies**
1 an informal word for a mother (used mainly by young children or when you are speaking to young children)
2 used about a dead body, usually from ancient Egypt, that has been wrapped in strips of cloth like bandages and treated with chemicals to keep it in good condition

mumps *noun*
an illness caused by a virus in which the glands in your neck become swollen and painful

mum-to-be *noun* **mums-to-be**
an informal word for a woman who is expecting a baby

munch *verb*
munches, munching, munched
to eat something in a noisy way, for example something hard such as crisps or an apple

munchies *noun plural* (informal)
1 small things to eat that you can pick up easily, for example biscuits, crisps or nuts
2 if you have the munchies, you feel like eating something, especially light food

mundane *adjective*
ordinary and often boring *We live a very mundane life.*

municipal ['myoo-nis-ip-erl'] *adjective*
connected with a town or city that has its own local government *a municipal swimming pool*

mural *noun* **murals**
a large picture painted on a wall or building

ORIGIN from Latin *muralis* 'of a wall' (from *murus* 'wall')

murder *noun* **murders**
1 the crime of deliberately killing a person
2 (informal) if you say something is murder, you mean it is really bad or difficult *It was murder getting to school today in the traffic.*

murder *verb*
murders, murdering, murdered
to kill a person deliberately **murderer** *noun*

murderous *adjective*
used for describing a person or action that is likely to kill someone or that has already killed someone *a murderous dictator*; *This was a murderous attack on innocent people.*

murky *adjective* **murkier, murkiest**
1 if something such as a liquid is murky, it is difficult to see through it, for example because it is dirty
2 if something such as the weather is murky, it is difficult to see clearly because there is not enough light *It was a murky December morning in London.*
murkiness *noun*

murmur *verb*
murmurs, murmuring, murmured
to say something in a very quiet voice

murmur *noun* **murmurs**
1 something said in a very quiet voice *'I don't believe you,' he said in a murmur.*
2 a quiet sound that continues for a period of time *We heard the murmur of voices in the next room.*

muscle *noun* **muscles**
1 one of many pieces of flesh inside the body that allows a part of the body to move by becoming tight and then looser *stomach muscles*
2 one of the lumps on someone's arms, legs or chest that show how strong they are *My dad flexed his muscles* (bent his arm muscles to make them tight).
3 if you pull a muscle, you injure it so that it becomes painful

ORIGIN from Latin *musculus* 'little mouse' (from *mus* 'mouse'), because the biceps (big muscle in the arm) looks like a little mouse

muscle in *verb*
muscles in, muscling in, muscled in
if someone muscles in on an activity, they use their power or influence to force their way into it

muscular *adjective*
1 having lots of strong muscles *He has very muscular legs.*
2 connected with muscles *muscular aches and pains*

museum *noun* **museums**
a building for keeping important or interesting things from the past or things connected with science, art or the study of living things. People go to museums to look at these things and learn about them.

mush *noun*
a thick soft substance, for example food that has been cooked for too long
mushy *adjective*

mushroom *noun* **mushrooms**
a small plant with a short stem and a body that is often shaped like the top of a ball. Some types of mushrooms can be eaten. Mushrooms are fungi (plants with no green colour, leaves or flowers that grow in wet places) and grow very quickly.

mushroom *verb*
mushrooms, mushrooming, mushroomed
1 to grow or increase very quickly
2 to appear suddenly and grow quickly *After the war, housing estates mushroomed up and down the country.*

music *noun*
1 sounds that are arranged in a very pleasant pattern, made by instruments such as pianos, guitars or trumpets or by someone singing
2 the art of creating music *I love my music lessons.*
3 the way music is written down using symbols to represent particular sounds *Amy is good at reading music* (understanding what the symbols mean).

ORIGIN from Greek *mousikos* 'connected with the Muses', the nine goddesses in charge of arts and sciences in ancient Greek stories

musical *adjective*
1 connected with music *musical notes* (sounds used in music)
2 good at playing or singing music
3 a musical instrument is an object that you play to make musical sounds, for example a guitar, clarinet, piano or drum
4 musical chairs is a game in which people walk around chairs while music plays. There are always more people than chairs. When the music stops, everyone tries to sit down quickly on a chair and anyone who doesn't find a chair is out of the game.
musically *adverb*

musical *noun* **musicals**
a play or film where all or part of the story is told by singing, music and often dancing

musician *noun* **musicians**
someone who plays a musical instrument, usually as their job

musket *noun* **muskets**
a very long gun similar to a rifle, used in the past

musketeer *noun* **musketeers**
a soldier in the past who carried and used a musket

Muslim – mystery

Muslim ['u' in 'mus' rhymes with 'u' in 'put'] *noun* **Muslims**
someone who believes in the religion of Islam founded by the prophet (religious leader) Mohammed. Muslims follow the teachings of Mohammed given in the Koran (the holy book of Islam).
Muslim *adjective*

muslin ['muz-lin] *noun*
a very thin cotton cloth, used for example for making dresses and curtains

mussel *noun* **mussels**
a shellfish that you can eat. It has a black or dark blue shell made up of two parts that fit tightly together.

must *verb*
1 used for saying strongly that it is very important to do something and that it should be done, for example because there is a need to do it, you have a responsibility to do it or someone orders you to do it *We must go to the supermarket today – we have no food. We must all respect our parents. You must answer all my questions.*

> SYNONYM to have to

2 used for saying that something should be done because of a rule *In English the adjective must come before the noun.*

> SYNONYM to have to

3 used for saying that you think something is true or very likely but you're not sure *You must be tired. It must have been hard walking to school in this snow.*
4 used for making a suggestion *You must come to my house next week.*

must *noun*
something that is very important to have or do, for example because there is a need to have or do it *An umbrella is a must in this weather.*

mustard *noun*
a yellow or brown paste with a very strong taste that gives flavour to food such as meat. It comes from the seeds of the mustard plant.

muster *verb*
musters, mustering, mustered
1 to come together in a group or get things or people to come together *Our teacher mustered all the pupils at the school gate. The soldiers mustered on the hill, ready for battle.*
2 to get as much of a particular feeling or thing as possible *I mustered enough courage to ask a question.*

mustn't
short for 'must not'

musty *adjective* mustier, mustiest
if something is musty, it does not smell clean but smells unpleasant and slightly wet, for example because it is old or has no fresh air *a musty old book; a musty room*
mustiness *noun*

mutant *noun* **mutants**
an animal or plant that is different from other animals or plants of the same type because of chemical changes in its genes (tiny parts of living matter that contain information about how something grows)

mutation *noun* **mutations**
a chemical change in the genes of an animal or plant that makes it different from other animals or plants of the same type

mute *adjective*
1 not speaking or not wanting to speak
2 (old-fashioned) not able to speak because of an illness
mutely *adverb*

mute *noun* **mutes**
1 an object fitted onto or into a musical instrument to make the sound quieter
2 an old-fashioned word for someone who cannot speak because of an illness

muted *adjective*
1 quiet or quieter than usual *muted voices*
2 not bright or less bright than usual *a muted light*

mutilate *verb*
mutilates, mutilating, mutilated
to badly damage the body (or part of the body) of a person or animal by cutting it or cutting something off **mutilation** *noun*

mutineer *noun* **mutineers**
someone who takes part in a mutiny

mutiny *noun* **mutinies**
when people stop obeying the orders of those in charge of them, for example when soldiers or sailors no longer do what their officers want them to do

mutiny *verb*
mutinies, mutinying, mutinied
to take part in a mutiny *The sailors mutinied against their officers.*

mutt *noun* **mutts** (informal)
a dog that is bred (produced) from two or more different types of dogs

> SYNONYM mongrel

mutter *verb*
mutters, muttering, muttered
to speak or say something in a very quiet voice, for example when complaining about something *I was muttering to myself about Dad not being helpful.*

mutton *noun*
the meat from a sheep that is eaten as food

mutual *adjective*
1 used for describing a feeling that is felt in the same way by two or more people *Paul and Sam have mutual respect* (Paul respects Sam and Sam respects Paul).
2 used for describing the same thing done by two or more people *We ended our friendship by mutual agreement.*
3 used about something such as an interest or someone such as a friend that two or more people have *Seema is our mutual friend* (for example, she is my friend and your friend).

mutually *adverb*
1 used for showing that two or more people feel the same about each other *We mutually respect each other.*
2 used for showing something affecting two or more people in the same way *Let's find a mutually convenient time* (for example, a time that is convenient for you and for me).

muzzle *noun* **muzzles**
1 the mouth and nose of an animal such as a dog
2 an object, for example made of straps or wires, put over a dog's mouth to stop it biting or eating
3 the muzzle of a gun is the end of the barrel (tube) through which the bullet comes out

muzzle *verb*
muzzles, muzzling, muzzled
1 to stop someone expressing their ideas and opinions freely
2 to muzzle a dog is to put a muzzle over its mouth to stop it biting or eating

my *adjective*
a word that you use when you are talking about something or someone belonging to or connected with yourself *Have you seen my drawing?*

Myanmar *noun*
the official name of Burma, a country in South-East Asia

myriad *noun* **myriads**
a very large number *I had a myriad of questions for my new teacher.*

myself *pronoun*
1 used when talking about an action you do when that action is also directed back onto you *I'm washing myself. I bought myself some sweets.*
2 used when you mean you yourself and no-one else *I gave Sarah the present myself.*
3 **by myself** without anyone else being there, or without the help of anyone else *I spent the whole afternoon by myself. I baked the cake all by myself.*

mysterious *adjective*
1 strange and not understood or explained (or difficult to understand or explain) *The ship sank in mysterious circumstances. The Mona Lisa has a mysterious smile.*
2 strange and not known *There's a mysterious man walking up and down the street.*
3 not telling anyone anything, which people think is strange *Don't be so mysterious and tell us who your friend is.*

mysteriously *adverb*
1 strangely and in a way that can't be understood or explained (or is difficult to understand or explain) *My mobile has mysteriously disappeared. She smiled mysteriously.*
2 used for showing that you don't understand what someone means *'I might come or I might not,' he said mysteriously.*

mystery *noun*
1 (plural **mysteries**) something strange that cannot be explained or has not been explained yet *No-one knows how Stonehenge was formed – it's a complete mystery. It's a mystery to me why Jack would behave in this way* (I can't explain why).
2 a strange quality that someone or something has *Those glasses give you an air of mystery!*
3 used about someone or something that is secret and you don't know anything about *Why is there so much mystery about your plans? Can you tell me anything about your mystery friend?*
4 (plural **mysteries**) a book, film, play or story about a crime or murder in which lots of things happen that are not explained until the end *a mystery by Agatha Christie*

mystify *verb*
mystifies, mystifying, mystified
if something or someone mystifies you, you are very confused and do not understand something *I was mystified by her strange behaviour.*

mystifying *adjective*
very strange and difficult to understand *The plot of the novel is mystifying.*

myth *noun* myths
1 a story from ancient history about gods, heroes (very brave people) and magic. Myths often try to explain events from the past or how things in the world came into existence. *I love reading Greek myths.*
2 an idea that is not true but that many people believe is true

mythical *adjective*
1 existing only in myths *mythical heroes and creatures*
2 not real but existing in the mind only

> SYNONYM imaginary

mythological *adjective*
connected with myths *a mythological creature, half man and half beast*

mythology *noun*
myths, especially ones connected with a particular place or religion *We're studying classical mythology* (the stories from ancient Greece and Rome).

n N

> ORIGIN the letter N started life in Egyptian hieroglyphics as a simple wavy line representing a snake. The Phoenicians made the line more pointed like an N facing left and lying on its side. They used this symbol for their 'n' sound because their word for snake began with this sound. As in English, N followed M and looked and sounded similar. Because the Phoenician word for fish was *nun* and because M, the previous letter, was the symbol for water, the Phoenicians eventually changed the name of N from snake to fish. The close relationship between M and N continued as the letter passed into the Greek, Etruscan and Roman alphabets. The N shape gradually became more regular and upright and it was the Romans who turned the centre line to face from left to right as in English.

naan ['nahn'] *noun*
naan or naan bread is a type of thick flat bread, usually round. It is eaten with food from India or South Asia.

> LANGUAGE EXTRA also spelt *nan*

> ORIGIN from Persian *nan* 'bread'

nab *verb* (informal)
nabs, nabbing, nabbed
1 to catch someone *The police nabbed the thief before he could escape.*
2 to take or get something quickly *I nabbed my coat and ran out.*

naff *adjective* (informal)
1 silly and unfashionable *The way she dresses is really naff.*
2 not showing good judgement in the way you behave or look or in what you say *He said a few naff words.*

nag *verb*
nags, nagging, nagged
1 to annoy someone by often asking them to do something *I'll do the washing-up if you stop nagging me.*
2 to keep saying to someone that you're not happy about something, for example to get them to change a particular situation *Dad kept nagging me about my long hair.*

nag *noun* nags
1 an informal word for someone who keeps nagging
2 an old-fashioned word for a horse, especially one that is old or sick

nagging *adjective*
1 complaining often about something *a nagging voice*
2 used about something that continues for a long time in an annoying way *nagging doubts*

nail *noun* nails
1 the thin hard shiny part at the end of a finger or toe
2 a small thin piece of metal with a point at one end and a flat top at the other end that is hit with a hammer, for example to fix something to a piece of wood
3 a nail file is a small thin tool with a flat rough side, used for rubbing on your fingernails or toenails to give them a round and smooth shape. It is made out of thick paper or out of steel.
4 nail polish or nail varnish is a transparent or coloured liquid painted onto the fingernails or toenails to make them look attractive

nail *verb*
nails, nailing, nailed
1 to fix something with a nail or nails, for example to a piece of wood *I nailed the lid onto the box.*
2 (informal) to prove that someone is guilty of a crime *They nailed him for stealing from his own business.*

nail-biting *adjective*
used for describing a situation such as a race or film that is very exciting because you don't know what will happen next or at the end

naive ['nye-eev'] *adjective*
1 ready to trust people because you think all people are good, and ready to believe what people say because you think they always tell the truth. Naive people don't know much about the unpleasant side of life.
2 also used about what someone does, says or thinks *a naive opinion*
naively *adverb* **naivety** *noun*

naked ['nay-kid'] *adjective*
1 not wearing any clothes
2 if you can see something with the naked eye, you can see it without using a telescope or microscope
nakedness *noun*

name *noun* names
1 the word or words used for saying who someone is or what something is *I know everyone in my class by name* (by their names).
2 if someone calls you names, they use bad words to insult you
3 the opinion that people have about someone or something *Don't spoil the good name of the school.*
4 a famous person *My cousin is a big name on TV.*

> LANGUAGE EXTRA your *first name* is the first part of your name that you were given when you were born (for example Emma or Harry). Your *last name* (or *family name* or *surname*) is the last part of your name that you share with the people in your close family (for example Clark or Smith).

name *verb*
names, naming, named
1 to give someone or something a name *We named our dog Peppy.*
2 to say what the name of something or someone is *Can you name three types of fruit?*
3 to decide which person or thing you want *They named Indira head girl. Name the time and I'll meet you at the pool.*

> SYNONYM to choose

307

nameless – nationally

4 to name after to give someone or something the same name as someone or something else *Mark was named after his grandfather.*
5 named used for saying a person's name *A boy named Raj put up his hand.*

nameless *adjective*
1 if someone or something is nameless, they have no name or their name is not known *This book was written by a nameless author from the sixteenth century.*
2 also used about someone who has done something wrong and whose name you know but don't want to say *Someone, who will be nameless, has spilt milk on the carpet.*

namely *adverb*
used when someone gives more information to explain something that has just been said or written *Only one friend can't come to my party, namely Sam.*

nan *noun* **nans**
an informal word for a grandmother

nanny *noun* **nannies**
1 a woman whose job is to look after a child or children of a particular family and who usually lives in the family home
2 an informal word for a grandmother

nanny goat *noun* **nanny goats**
a female goat

> LANGUAGE EXTRA a male goat is called a *billy goat*

nap *noun* **naps**
a short sleep *Grandma usually has a nap in the afternoon.*

nap *verb*
naps, napping, napped
to sleep, usually for a short time

nape *noun* **napes**
the back of the neck

napkin *noun* **napkins**
a square piece of paper or cloth used when you eat a meal for keeping your clothes clean and wiping your mouth and hands on

> ORIGIN from a 15th-century word meaning 'little tablecloth' (Old French *nappe* 'tablecloth' and Middle English ending *-kin* 'little')

nappy *noun* **nappies**
a piece of thick soft paper or cloth put round a baby's bottom and between its legs to hold liquid and solid waste from its body

> ORIGIN from the word *napkin*, although napkin is no longer used with this meaning

narcissus ['nah-siss-ers] *noun*
narcissi ['nah-siss-eye]
a yellow and white flower that appears in spring. The centre of the flower is shaped like a trumpet. Daffodils are a type of narcissus.

narrate *verb*
narrates, narrating, narrated
1 to tell a story or to describe something that happens *The story is narrated by the main character in the book.*
2 if someone narrates a film or TV programme, they say the words describing what is happening *a documentary about ancient Greece narrated by a famous professor*

narration *noun*

narrative *noun* **narratives**
a story or description of something that happens

narrator *noun* **narrators**
1 someone who tells a story
2 someone who says the words describing what is happening in a film or TV programme

narrow *adjective* **narrower, narrowest**
1 measuring a short amount of space from one side of something to the other side, especially compared to how long it is *Oxford Street in London is long and narrow.*
2 used for describing something that you only just manage to do *We had a narrow escape* (we escaped from danger but only just).
3 not including very many different things, for example different ideas, choices or meanings *a narrow* (small) *range of subjects; Granddad's interests are very narrow – only TV and football. This is a very narrow meaning of the word* (for example, it is only one meaning when there are other ones).

narrowness *noun*

narrow *verb*
narrows, narrowing, narrowed
1 to become narrow or make something narrow *Be careful, the road narrows after the lights.*
2 to narrow things down is to make the number of them smaller by taking away some of them, for example the ones that are less important, less likely or not wanted *Dad gave me a list of suggestions for birthday presents and told me to narrow it down. The police narrowed down the list of suspects to three.*

narrowly *adverb*
used for saying that you only just manage to do something or that something only just manages to happen *I narrowly escaped being hurt in the accident. The stone narrowly missed my head.*

narrow-minded *adjective*
if someone is narrow-minded, they do not understand or accept ideas or behaviour different from their own

nasal *adjective*
1 connected with the nose *a nasal spray*
2 used for describing a sound that comes through the nose or a person that makes this type of sound *a nasal voice; You sound nasal – do you have a cold?*

nasturtium ['ner-sterr-sherm] *noun*
nasturtiums
a garden plant with round leaves and large flowers that are usually bright yellow, red or orange. It grows very low along the ground.

nasty *adjective* **nastier, nastiest**
1 bad or unpleasant *nasty weather; a nasty accident; I've got a nasty cold.*
2 unkind *He's always so mean and nasty to his brother.*
3 angry or frightening *That dog looks very nasty. When I asked him to be quiet, he got nasty.*

nastily *adverb* **nastiness** *noun*

nation *noun* **nations**
a country and all the people living in it, especially when you think of the people as having the same language, history and government *France is an independent nation.*

> ORIGIN from Latin *natio* 'something born'

national *adjective*
1 connected with a whole country and not just a part of it *a national holiday*
2 connected with a particular country and not other countries *The British have a national liking for fish and chips.*
3 connected with the traditions of a particular country *The dancers were dressed in national costume.*
4 a national anthem is the official song of a particular country
5 a national curriculum is a programme of subjects taught at schools all over a country to make sure that all students learn the most important things
6 national curriculum tests (or national tests) are tests in some subjects, taken in schools all over a country. They compare the skills of students of the same age from all over that country.
7 national service is the time young people have to spend in the army, navy or air force in some countries

nationalise *verb*
nationalises, nationalising, nationalised
if a government nationalises a company or industry, it takes control of it and it becomes the property of the country
nationalisation *noun*

> LANGUAGE EXTRA also spelt *nationalize* and *nationalization*

compare: **privatise**

nationalism *noun*
1 a political belief that people in a particular area who have the same language and history should have their own government and should not be controlled by another country *Scottish nationalism*
2 a political belief that your country is better than other countries

nationalist *noun* **nationalists**
someone who believes in nationalism
nationalist *adjective*

nationality *noun* **nationalities**
1 belonging to a particular country, usually the country where you were born *'What's Miguel's nationality?' – 'He's Spanish.'*
2 a group of people who belong to a particular country or who live in a particular area and have the same language and history *Our school has 30 different nationalities.*

nationally *adverb*
1 used when talking about a whole country and not just a part of it *She's an actor who is well-known nationally.*
2 used when talking about a particular country and not other countries *He plays football nationally but not internationally.*

nationwide *adjective & adverb*
in all the parts of a country *a nationwide chain of supermarkets*; *The TV programme was shown nationwide.*

native *noun* **natives**
1 someone who was born in a particular place *My friend is a native of Portugal.*
2 an animal or plant that has always lived or grown in a particular place

native *adjective*
1 connected with or used about the place where someone was born *She went on holiday to her native New York.*
2 used about an animal or plant that has always lived or grown in a particular place *This bird is native to England.*
3 used about the language that you learnt when you first started to speak *Alain's native language is French. I'm a native speaker of English.*

ORIGIN from Latin *natus* 'born'

Native American *noun* **Native Americans**
a man or woman belonging to the group of people who were living in North or South America before the Europeans arrived

Nativity *noun*
among Christians, the Nativity is the birth of Jesus Christ. This event is celebrated at Christmas.

natter *verb* (informal)
natters, nattering, nattered
to talk, usually about things that are not important and for a long time

natural *adjective*
1 connected with nature or existing because of nature and not because it was made or done by people *the natural beauty of the English countryside*
2 normal and just as you would expect something to be *It's natural to be nervous before an exam.*
3 used about something such as a talent or feeling that you are born with *I have a natural fear of spiders.*
4 used about food or drink that has no chemicals added to it *This flour only contains natural ingredients.*
5 in music, a note that is natural is one that is normal, not flat or sharp
6 the natural world is the world made up of all the natural things in it, for example the air, land, water, plants and animals

natural *noun* **naturals**
1 someone who is very good at doing something and was born that way *Ben is a natural at football.*
2 a musical note that is normal, not flat or sharp

natural gas *noun*
gas that exists in rocks under the ground or the sea. It is used for heating and cooking.

natural history *noun*
the scientific study of plants and animals, especially in their natural environments

naturalist *noun* **naturalists**
someone who studies natural history

naturally *adverb*
1 just as you would expect *Naturally, I was very sad when my dog died.*
2 in a completely normal and relaxed way *Try and behave naturally as if nothing has happened.*
3 another way of saying yes, especially when you mean something is certainly true *'Were you shocked?' – 'Naturally.'*
4 used for showing that something exists or happens because of nature and not because it was made or done by people *These plants grow naturally in this kind of soil. My hair is naturally curly.*
5 used for showing something such as a talent, feeling or quality that you are born with *My brother is naturally grumpy.*

nature *noun*
1 all the things in the world that are not made by people. Nature includes all the living things such as animals, plants and insects as well as all the substances and forces, for example land, water, air and weather.
2 the special qualities of a person or animal that they are born with *My brother is by nature very kind and gentle.*
3 the basic quality of something that makes it what it is *The nature of elastic is to stretch when you pull it.*
4 a particular type of thing *I like cricket and rounders and games of that nature.*
5 a nature trail is a path in the countryside with signs telling you about animals and plants that live and grow there and interesting things that you pass

naughty *adjective* **naughtier, naughtiest**
1 if you are naughty, you behave badly *Alfie is always naughty and never does what he's told.*
2 also used about what someone does *naughty behaviour*
3 rude or not showing respect for people *Rachel used a naughty word.*
naughtily *adverb* **naughtiness** *noun*

nausea ['nor-zee-er] *noun*
a feeling as if you are going to be sick

nauseating ['nor-zee-ay-ting] *adjective*
1 bad enough to make you feel sick *a nauseating smell*
2 bad enough to really shock you or upset you *a nauseating picture*

nauseous ['nor-shers' or 'nor-zee-ers'] *adjective*
if you feel nauseous, you feel as if you are going to be sick

SYNONYM queasy

nautical *adjective*
1 connected with boats, ships and sailing *nautical rope*
2 a nautical mile is a unit for measuring distances at sea, equal to exactly 1852 metres

naval *adjective*
connected with a country's navy *a naval battle* (a battle at sea)

nave *noun* **naves**
the long area in the centre of a church or cathedral where people sit. It goes from the entrance to the altar (raised table for ceremonies).

navel *noun* **navels**
a small round hollow place in the middle of the stomach just below the waist. This is where a baby is joined to the inside of its mother's body by a long soft tube called an umbilical cord, which is cut away when the baby is born.

navigable *adjective*
used for describing a river or other area of water that is deep and wide enough for a boat to sail on

navigate *verb*
navigates, navigating, navigated
1 to move from one place to another on a computer, for example on a web page, document or spreadsheet *The school's website is very easy to navigate.*
2 if someone navigates a boat, ship, plane or road vehicle, they control it so that it goes in a particular direction or they use maps to find the correct direction for it to go in *Mum drives the car and I navigate.*
3 to sail on an area of water *Only small ships can navigate this river.*
4 to know how to find the correct direction to go in *Dolphins navigate through the water using sounds.*
navigation *noun*

navigator *noun* **navigators**
someone whose job is to use maps and equipment to find the correct direction for a plane or ship to go in

navy *noun*
1 (plural **navies**) the part of a country's fighting force of soldiers that uses ships *My sister has joined the navy.*
2 navy blue or navy is a very dark blue colour that is almost black

navy blue *adjective*
having a very dark blue colour that is almost black

LANGUAGE EXTRA you can also say *navy*

near *adjective & adverb* **nearer, nearest**
1 not far away *Our school is very near. You're standing too near to the edge. Where are the nearest shops?*

SYNONYM close

2 not far away in time *Christmas is getting quite near. My parents plan to get me a puppy in the near future* (fairly soon).

SYNONYM close

3 **near enough** almost *I've near enough finished.*

near *preposition*
1 not far away from something or someone *She was sitting near me.*
2 not far away in time *I can't go now but I will go nearer the time.*
3 **nowhere near** far from somewhere *The ball went nowhere near the goal.*
4 **nowhere near** also used for describing something that is a lot less when compared to something else *Leeds is nowhere near as big as London* (a lot less big than London).

near *verb*
nears, nearing, neared
to get close or closer to something such as a particular place or time *Work is nearing completion* (nearly finished).

nearby *adverb & adjective*
not far away from somewhere *My grandparents have friends nearby. We went into a nearby shop to buy some sweets.*

nearly–negative

nearly *adverb*
1 not completely but not far from it *I'm nearly ready.*

SYNONYM **almost**

2 used for saying that something is not true always but not far from it *I visit my grandparents nearly every week.*

SYNONYM **almost**

3 **not nearly** used for describing something that is a lot less when compared to something else *She's not nearly as clever as her sister* (a lot less clever than her sister). *I want a new bike but I don't have nearly enough money* (a lot less money than I need).

near miss *noun* **near misses**
when something almost hits something or someone *The stone didn't hit my head but it was a near miss.*

neat *adjective* **neater, neatest**
1 arranged or done in a very careful way and looking nice *a neat and tidy house; neat handwriting*
2 simple and clever, or cleverly done *a neat solution to the problem; That was a neat move* (for example in a game).
3 a neat person is someone who likes things arranged in a very careful way *Grandma is very neat* (has a neat and tidy house).
4 an American word for good *Your birthday party was really neat!*

neatness *noun*

neatly *adverb*
1 very carefully so that things look nice or well organised *I've put my toys away neatly in the drawer. Chloe writes very neatly. He was neatly dressed* (his clothes looked nice).
2 in a simple and clever way *You've solved this maths problem very neatly.*

necessarily *adverb*
not necessarily used about something that may not be true or may not always be true *A more expensive computer is not necessarily better.*

SYNONYM **not always**

necessary *adjective*
1 used about something that you must do, have or use because it is important or is needed for a particular purpose *It's necessary to work hard if you want to pass your exams. Good food is necessary to stay healthy. Our team scored the necessary number of points to get to the final.*
2 used in negatives (sentences with a word such as 'no', 'not' or 'never') for showing that something should not be done or used, for example because it is not right *I don't think that kind of behaviour is necessary.*

necessity *noun*
1 when something needs to happen because it is very important *the necessity of eating good food; My mum works out of necessity* (because she must work).
2 (*plural* **necessities**) something you must have, for example in order to live or to do something *A computer is a necessity now.*

310

neck *noun* **necks**
1 the part of the body between the head and the shoulders
2 the part of a piece of clothing, such as a sweater, that goes around the neck
3 the narrow part at the top of something such as a bottle
4 the long narrow part of a musical instrument such as a guitar, where you press the strings to produce different notes
5 **neck and neck** used about two people in a race or competition who are very close to each other so that either could win

neckerchief *noun* **neckerchiefs**
a square piece of cloth that is folded to form a triangle and worn around the neck, for example as part of the uniform of a Scout

necklace *noun* **necklaces**
a string of jewels or beads, or a gold or silver chain, that is worn around the neck *a pearl necklace*

nectar *noun*
a sweet liquid produced by flowers. Bees and other insects drink nectar, and bees use it to make honey.

ORIGIN from Greek *nektar* 'drink of the gods'

nectarine *noun* **nectarines**
a soft round fruit like a peach with a smooth skin

need *verb*
needs, needing, needed
1 if someone or something needs something, they must have it or should have it *You need an umbrella in this weather. My trainers need a good clean. Humans, animals and plants need food to live.*
2 if someone or something needs to do something, they must or should do it *I need to go to bed. My soup needs to cool down. It needs lots of hard work to be a good chess player.*
3 if something needs something done to it, that thing must or should be done *Your room needs to be tidied.*
4 if someone needs someone, they must have that person with them, for example because they cannot live or work or play properly without them *A baby needs its mother. You're my best friend, Ruby – I need you. To win tomorrow, we need Ben in our team.*
5 if you say that someone or something need not do something or does not need to do something, you mean that there is no reason why that particular thing should happen *'You needn't be afraid,' said the giant.*

need *noun*
1 something that someone or something must or should have or do *There's a need for more chairs in the classroom. You can phone Dad in the office if need be* (if you must do it).
2 when someone doesn't have something they should have in order to live or live properly *These children are in need of food and a place to live. My cousin went to Africa to help people in need* (people who don't have money to live).

3 (*plural* **needs**) something that someone should have in order to live or live properly *Food and water are basic needs.*
4 the needs of someone such as a student, worker or customer are the things they need to be happy and successful *The school meets all our needs, for example helpful teachers, no bullying and lots of books and computers.*
5 (*plural* **needs**) a strong feeling of wanting something *Ethan has a need for lots of friends.*
6 a reason for something *You can leave now – there's no need to wait.*

needle *noun* **needles**
1 a small thin piece of metal used for sewing. It has a sharp point at one end and a tiny hole (called an eye) at the other end for the thread.
2 a tube with a thin sharp point at one end that is stuck into someone's body to give them a medicine or take out blood
3 a small thin piece of metal that points to something such as a number in a measuring tool or the direction in a compass
4 an acupuncture needle is a small thin piece of metal put into a part of the body to take away pain and treat illness
5 a knitting needle is a plastic, metal or wooden stick with a pointed end that is used with another one for knitting
6 a pine needle is a long thin leaf that grows on a pine tree

needless *adjective*
used for describing something that you don't need to have or do or something that doesn't need to happen *Not phoning your parents when you're away will cause them needless worry.* **needlessly** *adverb*

SYNONYM **unnecessary**

needlework *noun*
1 the activity of sewing, especially sewing patterns or pictures onto cloth
2 the things that are made by sewing

needn't
short for 'need not' *You needn't worry.*

needy *adjective* **needier, neediest**
1 very poor and without enough money to live
2 needing too much attention and love *My little sister is very needy.*

negative *adjective*
1 a negative answer or reply is one that says no
2 used in grammar for describing a word such as 'no', 'not', 'never' or 'nothing' or a sentence that contains words such as these
3 bad or considering only the bad things about someone or something *a negative influence; Some children have negative feelings towards the school* (they don't like it). *Oliver's parents are so negative* (for example, they are always saying bad things about him).
4 a negative number is one that is less than zero
5 used for describing the result of a medical test that someone has, for example to see if they are ill. A negative result means that the test has found nothing bad or different from usual.

negative–nestle

6 used for describing a type of electrical charge that electrons have. In a battery, for example, electrons flow from the negative pole (end) to the positive pole. compare: **positive**

negative noun **negatives**
a special piece of film for producing a photo, used mainly in the past. It shows the dark areas as light and the light areas as dark.

negatively adverb
1 badly or in a way that considers only bad things *Poor exam results will affect the school negatively. Don't think so negatively about your classmates.*
2 to answer or reply negatively is to say no

neglect verb
neglects, neglecting, neglected
1 if you neglect someone or something, you don't give them enough attention or you don't give them any attention at all *I've neglected my homework this week. Our garden is very neglected* (for example, grass and weeds are growing). *She was a neglected child* (wasn't looked after by her parents).
2 if you neglect to do something, you don't do it even though you should

neglect noun
1 when someone doesn't give enough or any attention to someone or something
2 a bad situation because someone or something has been neglected *The house was in a terrible state of neglect* (for example, it had holes in the roof, broken windows and damp walls).

neglectful adjective
not giving enough or any attention to someone or something

negligent adjective
not being careful enough and not giving enough attention to your responsibilities, especially when something bad happens because of this *The zoo-keeper was negligent and allowed the monkey to escape.* **negligence** noun

negligible adjective
used for describing something that is very small or hardly exists at all *The amount of homework you've done today is negligible.*

negotiate ['ner-goh-shee-ayt] verb
negotiates, negotiating, negotiated
1 to discuss something with someone to try to come to an agreement
2 to manage to move or travel somewhere, especially when this is difficult to do *Granddad successfully negotiated the stairs.*

negotiation noun **negotiations**
a discussion with someone to try to come to an agreement

neigh ['nay'] verb
neighs, neighing, neighed
when a horse neighs, it makes a long high noise that is its own special sound
neigh noun

neighbour noun **neighbours**
someone who lives very near you, for example in the same street or block of flats *Our next-door neighbour is very friendly.*

neighbourhood noun **neighbourhoods**
a small part of a town or city where people live

neighbouring adjective
neighbouring places such as countries or towns are next to each other or near each other

neighbourly adjective
friendly, especially towards someone who lives near you

neither adjective & pronoun
not one thing or person nor the other *Neither book is funny. Neither of my parents helps* (or *help*) *me with my homework. Neither can be good.*

LANGUAGE EXTRA you can use either a singular verb or a plural verb when *neither* refers to the subject of a sentence, for example *Neither of my parents helps* (or *help*) *me with my homework. Neither Seema nor Lewis were* (or *was*) *at school today.* In writing it is better to use the singular (which is more serious) but when speaking people often use the plural (which is more friendly).

neither conjunction
not one thing or person nor the other *I can neither swim nor ride a bike. Neither Seema nor Lewis were* (or *was*) *at school today.*

neither adverb
used in negatives (sentences with a word such as 'no', 'not' or 'never') for showing that the same thing is true about something or someone else *My brother doesn't like football and neither do I.*

Neolithic adjective
1 connected with the Neolithic Age *Neolithic tools*
2 the Neolithic Age is the period when people used advanced tools and weapons made of stone and started to grow plants and keep animals for food. It was the last part of the Stone Age, from around 10 000 BC to around 2000 BC.

neon ['nee-on] noun
a gas that has no colour or smell. It is used in some electric lights because it produces a bright light when electricity flows through it. *a neon sign*

Nepal noun
a country in South Asia
Nepalese adjective & noun

nephew noun **nephews**
the son of someone's brother or sister

Neptune noun
the eighth planet from the sun. It comes after Uranus and is the furthest one away from the sun.

nerd noun **nerds** (informal)
1 someone who is boring and who behaves in an awkward way with other people
2 someone who is interested in technical and scientific things *a computer nerd*
nerdy adjective

nerve noun
1 (plural **nerves**) one of the parts in your body that look like long thin strings. Nerves carry information between your brain and the rest of your body and control how your body feels and moves.
2 a special feeling of not being afraid to do something difficult or dangerous *It took a lot of nerve to say the poem by heart in front of the class. Don't lose your nerve* (Stay calm).
3 when someone does something bad that upsets someone *Richard had a lot of nerve coming to school in jeans.*
4 if someone gets on your nerves, they annoy you
5 **nerves** used when you mean you're worried or frightened about something, especially about not doing something well *Hannah suffers from nerves when she reads out loud. We have school tests next week and I'm a bundle of nerves.*

nerve-racking adjective
used about something difficult or bad that makes you feel worried, frightened or annoyed *Exam time is always nerve-racking. That noise is really nerve-racking!*

LANGUAGE EXTRA also spelt *nerve-wracking*

nervous adjective
1 worried or frightened about something, for example about not doing something well or about something bad that might happen *We have a school test tomorrow and I'm really nervous. My sister is nervous about going out by herself.*
2 also used for showing that someone is nervous *a nervous laugh; a nervous look*
3 getting worried, frightened or upset very easily *If you're a nervous child, don't go and see that film.*
4 connected with the nerves in the body *a nervous twitch; the nervous system* (the brain and all the nerves in the body)
5 a nervous breakdown is an illness of the mind that makes you so sad and tired that you cannot live your life normally
nervously adverb **nervousness** noun

-ness suffix
used for making adjectives into nouns meaning a quality or situation *smoothness; fullness*

LANGUAGE EXTRA when an adjective ends in *y*, the *y* changes to *i*, for example *happy* becomes *happiness*

nest noun **nests**
1 a home that a bird makes to lay eggs in and keep them warm until baby birds come out. Nests are usually made of things such as twigs and leaves.
2 a place where insects or small animals live *a wasps' nest*
3 a nest egg is an amount of money that someone has saved up over a long period of time

nest verb
nests, nesting, nested
to live in a nest or build a nest *We have birds nesting in our roof.*

nestle verb
nestles, nestling, nestled
to be in a comfortable position or put something or someone in a comfortable position *It was so cold that I nestled up to my brother under the blankets.*

311

net–newspaper

net *noun* **nets**
1 a material or piece of material made of strings or ropes twisted together with spaces between them. Nets are used, for example, for catching fish or in games such as tennis, basketball or football (for hitting the ball over, through or into).
2 a very thin material or piece of material made of threads twisted together with lots of tiny spaces between them *net curtains*; *a mosquito net* (for keeping mosquitoes away from you)
3 in maths, a net is a flat pattern made up of the sides of a 3-D shape such as a cube. If you draw the pattern on paper or cardboard, you can cut it out and fold it to make the 3-D shape.
4 **the net** or **the Net** another word for the internet (a system connecting computers to each other all over the world)

net *adjective*
1 a net amount of money is the amount left after all other amounts have been taken away from it
2 the net weight of something is what it weighs without its container

netball *noun*
1 a game in which two teams of seven players try to throw a ball through a high net fixed to a metal ring. Netball is similar to basketball but a smaller ball is used.
2 (*plural* **netballs**) the ball used in the game of netball

Netherlands *noun*
the Netherlands is a country in North-West Europe

netiquette ['net-i-ket] *noun*
rules for behaving correctly towards other people online, for example in a chat room or when writing an email

netspeak *noun*
the words and abbreviations people use when they communicate with each other online

netting *noun*
a material made of strings, threads or wires twisted together with spaces between them *Our fruit bushes are surrounded by wire netting.*

nettle *noun* **nettles**
a wild plant with leaves shaped like hearts. It has tiny hairs on its leaves and stems that sting (hurt) you if you touch them. *a stinging nettle*

network *noun* **networks**
1 a large number of long thin parts that are connected to each other so that things can move between them, for example roads, railway lines, wires or pipes *a telephone network*; *a network of tunnels*
2 a number of computers connected to each other so that information can be shared between them
3 a group of people or organisations that work together *The United Nations has a network of offices throughout the world.*
4 a group of radio or TV stations that broadcast the same programmes in different places

network *verb*
networks, networking, networked
if computers are networked, they are connected to each other so that information can be shared between them

neuter ['nyoo-ter] *adjective*
used about the form of a part of speech, such as a noun, pronoun or adjective, that is used in some languages. Neuter words have forms that are different from masculine and feminine forms. *'It' is a neuter pronoun.*

neuter ['nyoo-ter] *verb*
neuters, neutering, neutered
to remove part of the body of an animal, such as a cat or dog, especially a male animal, so that it can no longer produce baby animals

neutral ['nyoo-trerl] *adjective*
1 not supporting any side such as a team, person or country, for example in a fight, competition or war
2 a neutral colour is one that is not strong, for example cream
3 a neutral voice is one that does not show any feeling
4 a neutral substance is a chemical that is not an acid or an alkali
neutrally *adverb*

neutralise *verb*
neutralises, neutralising, neutralised
to stop something having an effect *Mixing an acid and an alkali can neutralise their effects.*

LANGUAGE EXTRA also spelt *neutralize*

neutron ['nyoo-tron] *noun* **neutrons**
a part of an atom that has no electrical charge
compare: **electron** and **proton**

never *adverb*
1 not at any time in the past, present or future *I've never been to Italy.*
2 not in any situation *Shouting never does any good.*
3 another way of saying not *I never knew you could swim.*
4 **never ever** used for saying very strongly that you mean never *Ismail would never ever be naughty.*

never-ending *adjective*
1 going on for a very long time or never stopping *This rain looks like it's never-ending.*
2 also used about a very large number or amount of something *a never-ending stream of visitors*

SYNONYM endless

nevertheless *adverb*
used for saying that something you have just mentioned does not stop something else from happening or being true, usually something contrasting or surprising *Granddad is old but nevertheless plays football every Saturday.*

SYNONYM still

new *adjective* **newer, newest**
1 made a short time ago or having started to exist a short time ago *Is your bike new? My favourite author has written a new book.*
2 bought or received a short time ago *Can I show you my new game?*
3 never used before *My dad's shop sells both new and used books. Start a new page.*
4 different from before or different from others *I have some new friends now. Do you have any new ideas?*
5 not known or seen before *Why don't you learn a new language? They've discovered a new planet. The head teacher gave the school new hope.*
6 used for describing someone who has just come somewhere or started something such as a new school, job or activity *Alex is a new boy. Rupa needs more practice – she's new to netball.*
newness *noun*

newbie *noun* **newbies**
an informal word for someone who has just started a new activity, especially one connected with computers such as playing an online game or joining a chat room (where you exchange messages online)

newcomer *noun* **newcomers**
someone who has just come somewhere or started something such as a new school, job or activity

newly *adverb*
used for talking about something that was done or that happened only a short time ago *I play in the newly formed football team.*

SYNONYM recently

new moon *noun* **new moons**
1 the moon when it appears in the sky as a thin crescent (curve)
2 the time when this happens

news *noun*
1 new information about what has happened or is happening *Do you have any news about Granddad? I've got a piece of good news for you.*
2 important information about events or people, for example printed in newspapers, watched on TV or the internet or listened to on the radio *a news item* (piece of news); *Education is in the news* (being talked about by people).
3 **the news** a programme, for example on TV or the radio, giving important information about events or people *Our head teacher was on the news* (appeared in a news programme).

newsagent *noun* **newsagents**
1 a shop that sells newspapers, magazines and other things, for example sweets and some kinds of food
2 someone who owns or works in this type of shop

newsletter *noun* **newsletters**
a printed or electronic document sent to members of a group, giving information about the activities of the group

newspaper *noun*
1 (*plural* **newspapers**) a number of large sheets of folded paper printed with news and pictures about events and people. Newspapers also have other information such as advertisements and are usually sold or given away free every day or week.

312

2 the paper from a newspaper *My fish and chips were wrapped up in newspaper.*

newsreader noun **newsreaders**
someone who reads the news on TV or the radio

newsstand noun **newsstands**
a very small shop, for example in the street or at a station, where people sell newspapers and magazines

newsworthy adjective
newsworthier, newsworthiest
important enough to be mentioned in the news, for example in a newspaper or on TV

newsy adjective **newsier, newsiest**
if something such as a letter is newsy, it contains a lot of news, usually about small private things

newt noun **newts**
a small animal like a lizard with four short legs and a long soft body and tail. Newts live in or near water.

New Testament noun
the second part of the Christian Bible (holy book of the Christian religion). It describes the life of Jesus Christ and what he taught. compare: **Old Testament**

newton noun **newtons**
in science, a unit for measuring forces including weights

LANGUAGE EXTRA named after the English scientist Sir Isaac *Newton* (1642–1727)

New Year noun
1 the beginning of the year that has just begun or will begin soon
2 the time at the beginning of a year when people celebrate *Our teacher wished us Happy New Year.*
3 a New Year resolution is an important decision that you make to start behaving in a better way or doing something good from 1 January

New Year's Day noun
the first day of the year (1 January)

New Year's Eve noun
the last day of the year (31 December)

New Zealand noun
a country south-east of Asia and south of the Equator **New Zealander** noun

next adjective
1 used for describing something that comes straight after the present thing in time *We break up next week. The next bus will be along in 10 minutes. The next concert is in two days' time.*
2 used for describing someone who comes straight after someone else in time *Who will be the next head teacher?*
3 used for describing a thing, place or person that is the nearest to where someone or something is *My grandparents live in the next village. The next person in the queue was my cousin.*

next adverb
1 straight afterwards *What happened next? Next, Kennedy became president.*
2 used about the time straight after the present time or a particular time *When you next speak to Granddad, ask him if I can come round. When I saw him next, he looked ill.*

next pronoun
the person or thing that comes straight after another person or thing *You're next to see the doctor. We're going on holiday the week after next* (not this coming week but the week after that).

next door adverb
in the house, flat or room next to yours or to someone else's *My uncle lives next door.*

next-door adjective
1 used for describing the house, flat or room next to yours or to someone else's *He lives in the next-door house.*
2 someone's next-door neighbour is the person who lives in the house or flat next to them

next to preposition
used about a thing, place or person that is the nearest to something or someone with no other thing, place or person in between *I was standing next to the window. Piccadilly Circus is next to Leicester Square on the London tube map.*

NHS noun
the organisation in the UK that provides free medical care for everyone *My dad is an NHS doctor.*
short for: National Health Service

nib noun **nibs**
the pointed metal part at the end of a pen, for example a fountain pen. The nib is the part that you write with.

nibble verb
nibbles, nibbling, nibbled
1 to eat something with lots of very small bites *Dad was nibbling a biscuit. The donkey was nibbling on a carrot.*
2 to bite something quickly and lots of times *The rabbit was nibbling my finger.*
3 (informal) to eat small things between meals *Chloe doesn't like big meals but she's always nibbling.*

nibble noun **nibbles**
1 a very small bite of something *I took a nibble of the chocolate.*
2 (informal) nibbles are small things to eat between meals, such as crisps, raisins or nuts

nice adjective **nicer, nicest**
1 pleasant or good *nice weather; We had a nice time.*
2 attractive or pleasant to look at *a nice dress; nice flowers*
3 friendly and kind *Our teacher is very nice. It was nice of you to help me.*
4 used about something good that you want to give special importance to *The weather is nice and warm.*

niceness noun

nice-looking adjective
very attractive

nicely adverb
1 well *I'm getting on nicely at school.*
2 attractively *The flowers were nicely arranged.*
3 in a friendly and pleasant way *If you ask me nicely, I'll tell you.*

nick noun **nicks**
1 a small cut *The wire made a nick in my skin.*
2 in the nick of time just in time, for example to stop something bad happening
3 (slang) **in good nick** in good condition
4 (slang) **the nick** a prison or police station

nick verb
nicks, nicking, nicked
1 to make a small cut in something
2 a slang word for to steal

nickel noun
1 a hard silver-white metal
2 (plural **nickels**) a coin worth five cents in the USA or Canada

nickname noun **nicknames**
a name used for someone instead of their real name, for example a short form of their real name or a name based on a part of their character

nicotine noun
a poisonous substance in tobacco (leaves of a plant that are smoked in cigarettes, for example). Nicotine makes people want to keep smoking even though it is very harmful.

niece noun **nieces**
the daughter of someone's brother or sister

nifty adjective **niftier, niftiest** (informal)
clever, or cleverly done or made *a nifty gadget*

Nigeria noun
a country in West Africa
Nigerian adjective & noun

niggardly adjective
1 not wanting to spend money

SYNONYM mean

2 very small and not enough *a niggardly amount of money*

niggling adjective
used for describing something such as a feeling, suspicion or problem that worries you slightly and usually continues for a long time *I had niggling doubts about whether he was telling the truth.*

night noun **nights**
1 the part of each day when it's dark because there's no light from the sun *My sister doesn't like going out at night. I slept well last night* (yesterday during the night).
2 the time in the evening before you go to sleep *Dad and I went to a football match last night.*
3 the time you spend sleeping *Grandma had a good night* (slept well). *We had a late night* (went to sleep after the usual time).
4 a time in the evening when a particular event happens, for example a play or concert *It's the first night of the pantomime tomorrow.*
5 good night you say this to someone when you are going to bed or when they are going to bed. It is also used for saying goodbye to someone in the evening.

LANGUAGE EXTRA *good night* is also spelt *goodnight*

nightclothes noun plural
clothes that you wear in bed, such as your pyjamas

nightclub noun **nightclubs**
a place where grown-ups go at night to relax and enjoy themselves, for example by dancing, listening to music, eating and drinking

nightdress–nomad

nightdress *noun* **nightdresses**
a thin loose dress that girls and women wear to sleep in

nightfall *noun*
the end of the day when it starts to get dark as the sun sets

SYNONYM dusk

nightie *noun* **nighties** (informal)
a thin loose dress that girls and women wear to sleep in

nightingale *noun* **nightingales**
a small brown bird that sings at night as well as during the day

ORIGIN from Old English *nihtegale* 'night singer' (from *niht* 'night' and *galan* 'to sing')

nightly *adjective & adverb*
happening every night

nightmare *noun* **nightmares**
1 a very upsetting or frightening dream
2 used for describing a situation that is really horrible or difficult *Getting to school in this snow was a nightmare.*

nightmarish *adjective*

ORIGIN from *night* and Old English *mare* 'evil spirit or monster harming people as they sleep'

nightshirt *noun* **nightshirts**
a loose piece of clothing like a long shirt that people wear to sleep in. In the past, nightshirts were only worn by men, often with a loose hat called a nightcap.

night-time *noun*
the part of the day when it's dark outside

nil *noun*
nothing, used especially in sports results *Our team won two–nil (2–0).*

ORIGIN from Latin *nihil* 'nothing'

nimble *adjective* **nimbler, nimblest**
able to move quickly and easily *nimble fingers* **nimbly** *adverb*

nine *adjective & noun* **nines**
the number 9

nineteen *adjective & noun* **nineteens**
the number 19

nineteenth *adjective & noun*

ninety *adjective & noun* **nineties**
1 the number 90
2 the nineties are the ninetieth to ninety-ninth years of a century, for example 1990 to 1999
3 if someone is in their nineties, they are between 90 and 99 years old

ninetieth *adjective & noun*

ninth *adjective & noun*
1 used about something or someone that comes in place number 9 *on the ninth day*
2 (*plural* **ninths**) one of 9 equal parts of something *one ninth of the circle*

nip *verb*
nips, nipping, nipped
1 (informal) to go somewhere quickly and for a very short time *I nipped into the shop.*
2 to bite someone or something gently or squeeze them hard *A squirrel nipped me on the hand.*

nip *noun* **nips**
1 a gentle bite or hard squeeze
2 if you say there's a nip in the air, you mean the weather is cold but not too cold

nipple *noun* **nipples**
the nipples are the small circular parts of darker flesh on a woman's breasts or a man's chest

nippy *adjective* **nippier, nippiest** (informal)
1 cold but not too cold (used about the weather) *It's a bit nippy today.*
2 able to move quickly *a nippy little car*

niqab ['ni-kahb' or 'ni-kab'] *noun* **niqabs**
a piece of cloth that covers the face, with a space for the eyes. It is worn in public by some Muslim women.

nit *noun* **nits**
the egg of a tiny insect called a louse that sometimes lives in people's hair

nitpicking *noun* (informal)
when someone says what they think is wrong about something by paying too much attention to small details that are not important **nitpicking** *adjective*

LANGUAGE EXTRA also spelt *nit-picking*

nitrogen *noun*
a gas that is a part of all living things and is the main part of the earth's atmosphere. It has no colour, taste or smell.

nitwit *noun* **nitwits**
an informal word for a stupid person

no *adverb*
1 used in an answer when you don't agree with what a question is asking or when what a question is asking is not true *'Do you like ice cream?' – 'No.' 'Have you finished?' – 'No.'*
2 used when you refuse something or refuse to do something *'Help me with my homework.' – 'No.'*
3 used when you tell someone not to do something *No, don't switch the TV off yet.*
4 used when you mean not in any way or not at all *She's feeling no better.*
5 used when you're unhappy or surprised about something *Oh no – I've lost again!*

no *adjective*
1 used when you mean there isn't any amount of something or there isn't even one thing or person *I have no sweets left. No school has won as many matches as ours.*
2 used when you mean something isn't allowed *No ball games in the corridor. No smoking* (sign in a building or on a train, for example).
3 **no end** an informal way of saying 'a lot' *Being selected for the football team cheered me up no end. My mum has had no end of problems with her car* (a lot of problems with it).
4 **No way!** an informal way of saying no very strongly *'Can you help me with my homework?' – 'No way!'*

no *noun* **noes**
an answer in which someone says no *Was that a yes or a no?*

Nobel Prize *noun* **Nobel Prizes**
a very important international prize. It is given each year to people who have been successful in their work and have achieved things of the highest quality. *Malala Yousafzai won the Nobel Peace Prize at the age of 17.*

ORIGIN named after the Swedish chemist Alfred *Nobel* (1833–96)

nobility *noun*
1 people who belong to a very high rank in society
2 the quality of being noble

noble *adjective* **nobler, noblest**
1 used for describing someone or something extremely good or kind and deserving great respect *a noble leader; a noble gesture*
2 beautiful in a way that deserves great respect *a noble building*
3 belonging to a very high rank in society

noble *noun* **nobles**
someone who belongs to a very high rank in society

LANGUAGE EXTRA a man with a high rank is called a *nobleman* and a woman with a high rank is called a *noblewoman*

nobly *adverb*
in an extremely good or kind way *He nobly gave up his seat to the old man.*

nobody *pronoun*
no person *Nobody laughed. We saw nobody else* (no other person).

SYNONYM no-one

nobody *noun* **nobodies**
someone who has no important qualities *That person is just a nobody.*

nocturnal *adjective*
1 active at night *The owl is a nocturnal bird.*
2 happening at night or connected with the night *We went for a nocturnal walk.*

ORIGIN from Latin *nocturnus* 'connected with the night' (from *nox* 'night')

nod *verb*
nods, nodding, nodded
1 to move your head down and then up once or several times, as a way of saying yes or of giving a signal to someone
2 if you nod off, you fall asleep, often without meaning to
nod *noun*

no-go area *noun* **no-go areas**
a place where you are not allowed to go, or an area in a town or region where it is dangerous to go, for example because there are people with weapons there

noise *noun* **noises**
a sound, usually an unpleasant or loud one *The boys were making a lot of noise.*

noisily *adverb*
to do something noisily is to make a lot of noise doing it *The children were playing noisily in the garden.*

noisy *adjective* **noisier, noisiest**
1 making a lot of noise *a noisy crowd; a noisy car*
2 full of noise *a noisy classroom*

nomad ['noh-mad'] *noun* **nomads**
someone who belongs to a group of people who spend their lives moving from one

place to another, usually with their animals *This tribe of nomads lives in the Sahara Desert.* **nomadic** ['noh-mad-ik'] *adjective*

nominate *verb*
nominates, nominating, nominated
1 to suggest that someone should be given something such as a job, honour or prize *We nominated Arushi to be class monitor.*
2 to suggest that something such as a book or film should be given a prize
3 to choose someone for a particular job or task
nomination *noun*

non- *prefix*
used for making words with the meaning of 'not' *non-flammable*; *non-living*; *non-member*; *non-smoker*

none *pronoun*
1 not one *None of my friends come* (or *comes*) *round any more. 'How many do you have?' – 'None.'*
2 not any part of something *None of the apple juice is left.*

LANGUAGE EXTRA you can use either a plural verb or a singular verb when *none* refers to a group of things or people, for example *None of my friends come* (or *comes*) *round any more.* In writing it is better to use the singular (which is more serious) but when speaking people often use the plural (which is more friendly).

none *adverb*
not at all *Dad was none too happy about it.*

nonetheless *adverb*
another way of saying nevertheless

LANGUAGE EXTRA also spelt *none the less*

non-existent *adjective*
used for describing something that does not exist, often when you think it should exist *Our team's chances of winning tomorrow's match are non-existent.*

non-fiction *noun*
books based on facts such as science or maths books, or books about real people, things and events, rather than books that tell a story

nonsense *noun*
1 words or ideas that are stupid or not true *Never believe the nonsense people say or write about you.*
2 stupid behaviour *Stop that nonsense and go up to bed.*
3 words that make no sense and cannot be understood *a nonsense poem*

nonsensical *adjective*
stupid or not true *That was a nonsensical thing to say.*

nonstop *adjective & adverb*
1 happening without stopping *nonstop rain*; *It's been raining nonstop since this morning.*
2 without stopping anywhere on the way *a nonstop flight between Glasgow and Athens*; *Our train goes from London to Exeter nonstop.*

LANGUAGE EXTRA also spelt *non-stop*

non-verbal reasoning *noun*
the skill of understanding and using visual information such as pictures, shapes, diagrams and colours, for example to solve problems and make decisions. There are exercises to help you develop this skill and tests to help teachers find out how good your skill is.

noodles *noun plural*
long thin pieces of pasta (flour, water and eggs) eaten in soups and Chinese meals, for example

nook and cranny *noun*
nooks and crannies
1 a small hidden part of something such as a place or building *The British Museum is full of interesting nooks and crannies.*
2 **every nook and cranny** used for talking about every part of something

noon *noun*
twelve o'clock in the middle of the day

SYNONYM midday

no-one *pronoun*
no person *No-one knows. I trust Amy but no-one else* (no other person).

SYNONYM nobody

LANGUAGE EXTRA also spelt *no one*

noose *noun* **nooses**
a loop at the end of a rope that is made tighter by pulling, used for catching animals such as horses and, especially in the past, for killing people by hanging them

nor *conjunction*
1 used in negatives (sentences with a word such as 'no', 'not' or 'never') for showing that the same thing is true about something or someone else *I can't speak a foreign language and nor can my parents.*
2 used with 'neither' for showing two things that are not true *I can neither sing nor dance* (I can't sing and I can't dance).

Nordic *adjective*
connected with Sweden, Norway, Denmark, Finland and Iceland (countries in Northern Europe)

normal *adjective*
1 if something is normal, it is completely usual and as it should be *It's normal to get nervous before school tests. Rain is normal at this time of year.*
2 if someone or something is normal, they are no different from others *My sister's a normal person who likes going out with her friends. It's just a normal bike.*
3 used for describing someone or something that is the same as usual *Who's your normal doctor? My normal pocket money is £20 a week.*
4 healthy *She gave birth to a normal baby boy.*

normality *noun*
a situation in which everything is happening as it should

normally *adverb*
1 in the way that happens most often *I normally do my homework on the day that I get it.*

SYNONYM usually

2 in the usual way or the way you would expect, or in the same way as always *The trains are running normally now.*

Norman *adjective*
1 connected with the Normans (a people from northern France) who attacked and took control of England in 1066 *the Norman invasion*
2 made or built by the Normans *a Norman church*
Norman *noun*

Norman Conquest *noun*
the period of English history when Norman soldiers beat the English in 1066 at the Battle of Hastings and took control of England

Norse *noun*
Old Norse was a language spoken by people in Scandinavia between the 8th and 10th centuries

north *noun*
1 the direction on your left if you face the sun as it rises in the east. On most maps the north is at the top.
2 the part of a country or town that is in the north *My grandparents live in the north of Cambridge.*
3 the North is the northern part of England. It includes cities such as Manchester and Newcastle upon Tyne.

north *adverb*
towards the north *Our school faces north.*

north *adjective*
in or from the north *the north coast*; *a north wind*

North America *noun*
the part of the American continent that contains the United States, Canada and Mexico **North American** *adjective & noun*

north-east *noun, adjective & adverb*
the direction that is between north and east

LANGUAGE EXTRA also spelt *northeast*

northerly *adjective*
towards or from the north *a northerly wind*

northern *adjective*
in or connected with the north *northern Spain*

northerner *noun* **northerners**
someone from the northern part of a country or region

Northern Ireland *noun*
a region in North-West Europe that is a part of the United Kingdom

North Korea ['ker-ee-er'] *noun*
a country in East Asia
North Korean *adjective & noun*

North Pole *noun*
the place on the surface of the earth that is the furthest north

North Sea *noun*
the part of the Atlantic Ocean between the east coast of Britain and countries such as Norway, Denmark, Germany, Holland and Belgium

northwards *adverb*
towards the north **northward** *adjective*

north-west *noun, adjective & adverb*
the direction that is between north and west

LANGUAGE EXTRA also spelt *northwest*

Norway – noticeboard

Norway noun
a country in Northern Europe

Norwegian adjective
connected with Norway or the Norwegian language

Norwegian noun
1 the language people speak in Norway
2 (plural **Norwegians**) someone from Norway

nose noun **noses**
1 the part of your face that sticks out above your mouth, used for smelling and breathing
2 the front part of an aircraft or spacecraft

nose verb
noses, nosing, nosed
1 if someone noses around, they look in different places to try to find something or find out some information *I found my brother nosing around in my bedroom.*
2 if a vehicle noses forward, it moves carefully and slowly *Dad was nosing out gently into the traffic.*

nosebleed noun **nosebleeds**
when you have blood coming out of your nose

nosedive noun **nosedives**
a sudden movement towards the ground made by an aircraft with its nose (front part) pointing downwards

nosedive verb
nosedives, nosediving, nosedived
1 if an aircraft nosedives, it makes a nosedive
2 to go down very fast *Prices have nosedived.*

nosey adjective **nosier, nosiest**
another spelling of **nosy**

nosh noun (slang)
1 an old-fashioned word for food or a meal
2 a small amount of food eaten between meals

nosh verb (slang)
noshes, noshing, noshed
1 an old-fashioned way of saying to eat
2 to eat a small amount of food between meals

nostalgia noun
remembering pleasant things from the past and wishing that things now were just as pleasant **nostalgic** adjective **nostalgically** adverb

nostril noun **nostrils**
your nostrils are the two openings at the end of your nose

ORIGIN from Old English *nosthyrl* 'hole in the nose' (from *nosu* 'nose' and *thyrel* 'hole')

nosy adjective **nosier, nosiest**
1 trying to find out things about someone or something that you shouldn't know about
2 a nosy parker is an informal way of saying a nosy person

LANGUAGE EXTRA also spelt *nosey*

not adverb
1 used for changing the meaning of something to the opposite meaning *I'm not going to do my homework tonight.*
2 used instead of repeating a verb or phrase when you want to give the opposite meaning *Will you help me or not? 'Is it raining?' – 'I hope not.'*
3 **not at all** used for making the opposite meaning stronger *I'm not at all disappointed.*
4 **Not at all!** used as a polite reply to someone, for example when they say thank you or something nice to you, or as a polite way of saying yes when someone asks you to do something *'You're very kind!' – 'Not at all!' 'Would you mind closing the window?' – 'Not at all.'*

LANGUAGE EXTRA *not* is often shortened to *n't* with verbs such as *to be, to have, to do, will* and *can* (for example *isn't, hadn't, don't*)

notable adjective
used about something that is important or important enough to be mentioned
notably adverb

notch noun **notches**
a small cut in the surface of something, shaped like the letter V

note noun **notes**
1 a short letter to someone *a thank-you note* (thanking someone for something); *an absence note* (explaining why someone has not been at school); *Mum wrote a note to the school to ask about holiday dates.*
2 something you write down to remind someone or yourself about something *I stuck a note on the mirror telling Dad I'd gone to the park. Lily grabbed a pen and made a note of my address.*
3 used when you remind yourself about something without writing it down *I won't forget – I've made a note of the date. I've made a mental note to do it.*
4 something you write down to help you understand things or provide information *study notes; We all took notes when the teacher explained the poem.*
5 a short explanation, for example in a book *See the note on page 25.*
6 a sound used in music or the sign that represents this sound *She can sing the high notes but not the low notes I played a few notes on the piano.*
7 a piece of paper used as money *a £10 note*
8 a particular quality or feeling such as sadness, anger or doubt *The head's talk ended on a serious note* (in a serious way).
9 **to take note** to pay attention to something *Take note of what your parents say.*

note verb
notes, noting, noted
1 to notice something or become aware of it
2 to pay attention to something
3 to say or write something
4 if you note something down, you write it down so you will remember it

notebook noun **notebooks**
1 a book with empty pages for writing in
2 another word for a laptop (small computer that you can carry around with you)

notepad noun **notepads**
a number of sheets of empty pages fastened together for writing on

notepaper noun
paper that you use for writing letters or notes

nothing pronoun
1 not a single thing *I have nothing to do. He said nothing else* (no other thing).
2 **nothing like** very different from someone or something *I'm nothing like my brother.*
3 **nothing to do with** not connected in any way with something or someone *My little sister knocked over her juice – I had nothing to do with it.*
4 **for nothing** without paying any money or being paid any money *We got the tickets for nothing. I worked for nothing mowing Granddad's lawn.*
5 **for nothing** also means for no reason, for example because there is no successful result *I did all that work for nothing. They don't call Aberdeen the Granite City for nothing.*

notice verb
notices, noticing, noticed
1 to see something or someone that you haven't seen before or start paying attention to them or to something about them *I've just noticed the time – it's late. Have you noticed my new shirt? We all noticed how tall he's grown.*
2 to realise for the first time that something exists or is happening *I noticed someone was following me. Have you noticed a funny smell from the kitchen?*

notice noun
1 (plural **notices**) something written that provides information and is displayed in a public place *There was a notice on the library door saying it was closed.*
2 a warning that something is going to happen *Miss Williams is leaving and has given the school a month's notice* (has said she will stop working in a month).
3 used about listening or watching carefully and paying attention *She didn't take any notice of* (listen to) *what I said. I was waving my arms but no-one took any notice* (no-one saw or looked). *Take no notice of him* (don't look at him, or don't listen to what he says).
4 used about telling someone something *Ella brought the problem to the teacher's notice* (told the teacher about it).
5 if something such as a fact or detail escapes your notice, you don't realise it

noticeable adjective
1 easy to see *a noticeable scar; a noticeable improvement*
2 easy to feel, smell or hear *a noticeable change in the weather; a noticeable smell of fish*

noticeably adverb
1 in a way that you can see easily *This blue is noticeably darker.*
2 in a way that you can feel, smell or hear easily *a noticeably stronger smell; a noticeably louder noise*

noticeboard noun **noticeboards**
a large flat piece of wood or other material such as cork, often fixed to a wall, used for showing information such as announcements or advertisements

LANGUAGE EXTRA also spelt *notice board*

notify–number

notify *verb*
notifies, notifying, notified
to tell someone something officially *All parents have been notified by email about sports day.* **notification** *noun*

notion *noun* notions
an idea about something or an understanding of something *Do you have any notion of what the author means?*

notorious *adjective*
famous because of something bad *a notorious criminal*; *This street is notorious for accidents.*

notoriously *adverb*
extremely (used about something or someone that is famous because of something bad) *It's a notoriously difficult race.*

nougat ['**nug**-ert' or '**noo**-gah'] *noun*
a hard chewy sweet made from sugar, honey, eggs and nuts

nought ['nort'] *noun* noughts
the number 0 or zero

noughties ['**nor**-teez'] *noun plural* (informal)
used for referring to the years between 2000 and 2009

noughts and crosses *noun*
a game for two players that is played on a pattern of nine squares drawn on a piece of paper. One player writes 0s (noughts) in the squares and the other writes Xs (crosses). The winner is the one who gets three noughts or three crosses in a line.

noun *noun* nouns
a word used as the name of a thing, place or person

LANGUAGE EXTRA there are many different kinds of *nouns*, for example *common nouns* and *proper nouns*.
Common nouns name things or people (*table, man, cat, happiness, anger*). They can be divided into *concrete nouns*, which name anything you can see, hear or touch (*table, man, cat*) and *abstract nouns*, which name ideas or feelings (*happiness, anger*).
Proper nouns (written with a capital first letter) name particular people or places (*George, Leeds, Ireland*).

nourish *verb*
nourishes, nourishing, nourished
to give food to a person, animal or plant to make them grow and keep them healthy

nourishing *adjective*
if a particular food or drink is nourishing, it is good for you and you feel full after eating or drinking it

nourishment *noun*
food needed to grow and stay healthy

novel *noun* novels
a book that tells a story about people and events that never really existed *'The Hobbit' is a novel by J. R. R. Tolkien.*

ORIGIN from Italian *novella* 'new story' (from Latin *novella* 'new things')

novel *adjective*
new and different from anything else *Holly has a novel way of solving the problem.*

ORIGIN from Latin *novellus* 'new'

novelist *noun* novelists
someone who writes novels

novelty *noun*
1 (*plural* **novelties**) something new and unusual *At the start of the twenty-first century, the internet was still a novelty to some people.*
2 the interesting quality about something new and different *The novelty of living in a foreign country soon disappeared.*
3 (*plural* **novelties**) a small cheap object such as a toy, often given to someone as a gift

November *noun*
the eleventh month of the year, between October and December. November has 30 days.

ORIGIN from Latin *novem* 'nine', because it was the ninth month of the ancient Roman year

novice *noun* novices
someone who is just starting to learn an activity or job *Sailing off the Kent coast is not for novices.*

now *adverb*
1 at the present time, not in the past or future *I go to school in Edinburgh now.*
2 immediately *Go to bed now!*
3 used in stories for describing a time in the past *We were lost in the forest and it was now getting dark.*
4 used when you understand the reason for something for the first time or when you first understand what something is *I now know why Joel behaves in that way.*
5 used at the start of a sentence for explaining something or talking about something new *Now, you must remember, I was only six when this happened. Now, sit down, I want to show you something.*
6 used when warning someone or telling someone to do something *Be careful now! Stop doing that now!*
7 **by now** before this time *The plane should have landed by now.*
8 **for now** for a short period of time *Leave your coat on the chair for now. Goodbye for now* (I'll see you soon).
9 **from now on** starting from the present time
10 **just now** a short moment ago or at the present time *What did you say just now? I can't answer the phone just now – I'm busy.*
11 **now and again** or **now and then** sometimes but not often
12 **right now** at the present time or immediately *Right now I'm happy at school. Stop that right now!*

now *conjunction*
used for explaining something such as a new situation *Now that you're older, you can go to school by yourself. You can stay for dinner now you're here.*

nowadays *adverb*
at the present time compared to the past *Nowadays children are much smarter.*

nowhere *adverb*
1 not in or to any place *You're going nowhere until you've finished your homework. This plant exists nowhere in the British Isles. You find this word in Shakespeare but nowhere else* (in no other place).
2 **no place** *I have nowhere to sit.*
3 **in the middle of nowhere** a long way from where people live

nozzle *noun* nozzles
a narrow part at the end of a tube or hosepipe for controlling the way the liquid or air comes out of it

nuclear ['**nyoo**-klee-er'] *adjective*
connected with the power produced when the structure of an atom is changed by dividing its nucleus (central part) or joining it to another nucleus *nuclear energy*; *nuclear weapons*

nucleus ['**nyoo**-klee-ers'] *noun*
nuclei ['**nyoo**-klee-eye']
1 the central part of an atom (smallest part of a chemical element) or of a cell (smallest unit of living matter)
2 the most important part of a group of people or things

nude *adjective*
not wearing any clothes

nude *noun* nudes
1 a person with no clothes on, especially as a work of art, for example in a painting or as a sculpture
2 **in the nude** not wearing any clothes
nudity *noun*

nudge *verb*
nudges, nudging, nudged
to touch or push someone gently, usually with your elbow **nudge** *noun*

nugget ['**nug**-it'] *noun* nuggets
1 a small lump of metal such as gold that is found in the ground
2 a small lump of food, usually covered in breadcrumbs and fried *chicken nuggets*

nuisance *noun*
1 something or someone that annoys you or causes you problems *The library's closed – that's a nuisance* (that's annoying).
2 if you make a nuisance of yourself, you annoy people or cause them problems

numb *adjective*
number ['**num**-er'], **numbest** ['**num**-ist']
1 if a part of your body is numb, you can't feel anything in it for a short time *My fingers are numb with cold.*
2 not able to show your feelings, usually because you are so frightened, upset or shocked *When Tom saw the giant, he was numb with fear.*
numbness *noun*

number *noun* numbers
1 a sign or word showing how many. 0, 1, 2, 3, 4, 5, 6, 7, 8, 9 are numbers.
2 one or more of these signs used for showing something such as a position or order or for recognising and describing something or someone *We live at number 34. I put a tick against number 5 on the list. What's your ticket number?*
3 an amount of things or people *The total number of children at my party was 18. I have a number of questions* (a few questions). *At the zoo we saw a large number of reptiles* (many reptiles). *Every week I visit my grandparents quite a number of times* (quite a lot of times).
4 a phone number *I dialled the wrong number.*

number–nymph

5 a song or tune *She sang a little Scottish number.*
6 a copy of a magazine or newspaper
7 an even number is one that can be divided exactly by 2 (for example 2, 4, 6) and an odd number is one that cannot (for example 1, 3, 5)

number *verb*
numbers, numbering, numbered
1 to give a number to something *All the seats in the cinema are numbered.*
2 to come to a total number *The audience numbered more than 200.*

number plate *noun* **number plates**
a metal or plastic sign at the front and back of a road vehicle. It has numbers and letters on it that show the driver it belongs to.
compare: registration number

Number Ten *noun*
an informal way of referring to the office of the prime minister of the UK

> ORIGIN from *Number 10 Downing Street* in London where the prime minister lives

numeracy *noun*
being able to understand and use numbers and do simple mathematics
compare: literacy

numeral *noun* **numerals**
one of the symbols that represent the numbers 0 to 9. Arabic numerals are 1, 2, 3 and so on, and Roman numerals are I, V, X, L, C, D, M.

numerate *adjective*
if someone is numerate, they can understand and use numbers and do simple mathematics
compare: literate

numerator *noun* **numerators**
in maths, the numerator is the top number in a fraction. It tells you how many of the parts that the whole is divided into (the denominator) are included in the fraction. *In $\frac{3}{4}$, the numerator is 3.*

numerical *adjective*
connected with numbers or using numbers
in numerical order, numerical skills
numerically *adverb*

numeric keypad *noun* **numeric keypads**
a small section on the right of a computer keyboard that has keys with numbers on them

numerous *adjective*
very many *I made numerous mistakes in my homework.*

num lock ['num'] *noun*
a key on a computer keyboard that you press when you want to use numbers on the numeric keypad

nun *noun* **nuns**
a religious woman who belongs to a group of women who live on their own in a building called a convent

nurse *noun* **nurses**
someone whose job is to look after people who are ill or injured, usually in a hospital

nurse *verb*
nurses, nursing, nursed
1 to look after someone who is ill or injured
2 to hold a young child in your arms to make him or her feel better

nursery *noun* **nurseries**
1 a place where people look after babies and young children whose parents are somewhere else, for example working
2 a child's bedroom or room for playing in
3 a place where plants and trees are grown and usually sold
4 a nursery rhyme is a simple poem or song for children
5 a nursery school is a school for young children under the age of five

nursing home *noun* **nursing homes**
a place where old people live if they can no longer look after themselves

nurture *verb*
nurtures, nurturing, nurtured
1 to look after and feed a child, animal or plant so that they grow well
2 to encourage someone or something so that they can develop and be successful

nut *noun* **nuts**
1 a fruit with a very hard shell that grows on a tree or bush
2 the dry fruit inside the hard shell, which you can usually eat
3 a metal ring, usually with six sides, that fits onto a screw called a bolt and is used for fastening things together
4 an informal word for your head
5 an informal word for a crazy person or for someone really interested in a particular activity *a football nut*

nutcase *noun* **nutcases**
an informal word for a crazy or stupid person

nutcracker *noun* **nutcrackers**
a small tool for breaking open the shell of a nut, usually made of a pair of levers or arms that you press onto the nut with your hand

nutmeg *noun*
a brown powder used as a spice for food. It comes from the seed of a tropical tree.

nutrient ['nyoo-tree-ernt'] *noun* **nutrients**
any substance in food that plants, animals and people need to grow and stay healthy

nutrition ['nyoo-trish-ern'] *noun*
the food you eat that is needed so you can grow and stay healthy *Exercise and good nutrition are essential for children.*
nutritional *adjective*

nutritious *adjective*
if food or a meal is nutritious, it helps you to grow and stay healthy

nuts *adjective*
an informal word for crazy

nutshell *noun* **nutshells**
1 the hard shell of a nut
2 **in a nutshell** used for saying something in a simple way using very few words *Well, to put it in a nutshell, you must do your homework again.*

nutty *adjective* **nuttier, nuttiest**
1 containing nuts or tasting of nuts *a nutty cake*
2 an informal word for crazy

> SIMILE 'as nutty as a fruitcake' means completely crazy

nuzzle *verb*
nuzzles, nuzzling, nuzzled
if a person or animal nuzzles someone, they press their nose or face against them in a loving way, as pet animals often do *My dog nuzzled against my cheek.*

nylon *noun*
a strong artificial material used for making many things such as clothes, sheets, ropes and brushes *nylon socks*

nymph *noun* **nymphs**
in ancient Greek stories, a goddess who looks like a girl and lives in places such as trees, rivers or mountains

o O

ORIGIN of all the letters of the alphabet, O has changed the least. It looked almost exactly the same 3000 years ago when the Phoenicians started using it. O started life in Egyptian hieroglyphics as a picture of the human eye – a horizontal oval shape with a small circle inside. Gradually its shape changed from oval to round with just a dot in the middle and then to a circle with no dot. Its name was *ayin* ('eye') but it had the sound of a consonant. When the letter passed into Greek, the shape did not change but the Greeks used it for their vowel sound 'o'. The shape was copied unchanged into the Roman alphabet to represent both a short 'o' sound (for example 'pot') and a long one (for example 'home') – as in English today.

oaf *noun* **oafs**
someone who is very clumsy, rude or stupid
oafish *adjective*

oak *noun*
1 (*plural* **oaks**) a large tree that produces a small oval-shaped fruit called an acorn and a fluffy flower called a catkin
2 the hard wood of the oak tree, used for making things such as furniture and doors

OAP ['oh-ay-pee'] *noun* **OAPs**
an informal word for an older person, for example someone over the age of 65

LANGUAGE EXTRA short for *old age pensioner*, which means someone who gets a pension (regular money) from the government when they reach old age

oar *noun* **oars**
a long pole with a flat part at one end called a blade, used for rowing a boat (moving it through the water). You usually hold an oar in each hand and each oar is supported by the side of the boat.
compare: **paddle**

oarsman *noun* **oarsmen**
a man who rows a boat, especially in a race

oarswoman *noun* **oarswomen**
a woman who rows a boat, especially in a race

oasis ['oh-ay-siss'] *noun* **oases** ['oh-ay-seez']
1 a place in a desert where there is water and where trees and plants grow
2 a quiet and pleasant place in a noisy area *This hotel is an oasis of calm in the busy city centre.*

oat *adjective*
made from oats or containing oats *oat biscuits*

oath *noun* **oaths**
1 a serious promise to do something or to tell the truth, for example in a court of law
2 an old-fashioned word for a swear word

oatmeal *noun*
oats that are crushed and used in cooking or as a breakfast food

oats *noun plural*
seeds from a plant that is similar to grass (the oat plant). The seeds are crushed and used for making food such as porridge (boiled breakfast food) or biscuits and for feeding to animals such as horses.

obedience *noun*
when a person or animal does what they are told to do

obedient *adjective*
if a person or animal is obedient, they do what they are told to do *an obedient little boy* **obediently** *adverb*

obese ['oh-beess'] *adjective*
having a heavy body that weighs too much, which can be dangerous for your health
obesity *noun*

obey *verb*
obeys, obeying, obeyed
1 to do what you are told to do by someone *You should always obey your parents.*
2 to do what something such as a rule, law or order says you must do *Criminals don't obey the law.*
3 if something obeys a rule or law, it behaves in the way it is supposed to because of that rule or law *Falling objects obey the laws of gravity.*

obituary *noun* **obituaries**
an announcement in a newspaper or magazine that someone has just died, usually with details about their life

ORIGIN from Latin *obitus* 'going down', 'death'

object ['ob-jekt'] *noun* **objects**
1 a thing that you can see or touch and that is not a living thing *Someone broke the window with a heavy object.*
2 the reason for something or what it is supposed to do *The object of the exhibition was to show what life was like in ancient Egypt.*
3 something that someone hopes to do *My object is to win the game.*
4 in grammar, the object of a verb is the noun or pronoun that receives the direct or indirect action of the verb, for example 'John' in 'I saw John' (direct) or 'her' in 'I told her the reason' (indirect)
compare: **subject** (sense 5)

object ['erb-jekt'] *verb*
objects, objecting, objected
to say that you do not like or agree with something or someone *I object to the word you just used. I'll open the window if no-one objects.*

objection *noun* **objections**
1 a reason for not liking or agreeing with something or someone *Dad's main objection to the new sports hall is that it will cost too much.*
2 something you say that shows you do not like or agree with something or someone

objectionable *adjective*
extremely unpleasant or bad

objective *noun* **objectives**
something that someone plans to do or tries hard to do *My mum has achieved her objectives* (is successful in doing what she wanted to do).

objective *adjective*
showing that you are not influenced by ideas or feelings but only by facts. Subjective means not influenced by facts but by ideas and feelings instead. *The police officer gave an objective report of what had happened.* **objectively** *adverb*
objectivity *noun*

obligation *noun* **obligations**
something that someone has to do because they have a responsibility to do it *We all have an obligation to do our homework.*

obligatory *adjective*
1 if something is obligatory, you have to do it or have it because of a rule or the law *In many countries it is obligatory for cyclists to wear a helmet.*

SYNONYM compulsory

2 used for describing something that happens or is done so often that people expect it *Many tourists make the obligatory trip to Oxford or Cambridge.*

oblige *verb*
obliges, obliging, obliged
1 to make someone do something, for example because a rule or their duty tells them they should do it or because a situation makes it necessary *People who work are obliged to pay their taxes. The rain obliged us to take shelter under a tree.*
2 to help someone by doing what they ask you to do *Granddad asked someone for their seat on the train and they obliged.*

obliged *adjective*
1 grateful to someone for doing something to help you *Thank you – I'm much obliged.*
2 feeling that you should do something because you think it is the right thing to do *'Why did you give up your seat to that old person?' – 'I felt obliged.'*

obliging *adjective*
helpful **obligingly** *adverb*

oblique *adjective*
1 used for describing something straight such as a line that slopes at an angle so that it is neither horizontal nor vertical *You can write a fraction with an oblique stroke, for example 4/5.*
2 not saying or doing something in a direct way so that people have trouble understanding *an oblique remark*

SYNONYM indirect

3 not looking straight at someone *an oblique glance*
obliquely *adverb*

oblong *noun* **oblongs**
a flat shape with four straight sides and square ends. It has two long sides and two short ones.

SYNONYM rectangle

oblong *adjective*
1 having an oblong shape

SYNONYM rectangular

319

obnoxious – occupation

2 shaped similar to an oblong *Dad takes one of the round pills and two of the oblong ones.*

obnoxious *adjective*
extremely unpleasant, often in a way that makes you feel sick or really shocks you *an obnoxious smell*; *obnoxious behaviour*

> ORIGIN from Latin *ob-* 'towards' and *noxa* 'harm'

oboe *noun* **oboes**
a musical instrument made up of a long thick tube that you play by blowing into it over two reeds (thin strips of wood that vibrate). You press keys along the tube to change the notes. An oboe can play very high and loud sounds.
oboist *noun*

> ORIGIN from French *hautbois* 'high wood' (*haut* 'high' and *bois* 'wood'), because of its very high sound

obscene *adjective*
1 very shocking or rude *an obscene word*
2 used for describing something that shocks and upsets you because it is so large *an obscene amount of money*
obscenely *adverb*

obscure *adjective*
1 difficult to understand, for example because of being unusual or having lots of details *an obscure word*; *This poem is written in a very obscure way.*
2 difficult to see *an obscure figure in the distance*
3 not known or not known about by many people *an obscure author*; *an obscure detail*
obscurely *adverb*

obscure *verb*
obscures, obscuring, obscured
1 to stop something from being seen clearly *The sun was obscured by the clouds.*
2 to stop something from being known and understood *These long words obscure the meaning of the poem.*

obscurity *noun*
not being known or not being known about by many people *Van Gogh is a famous painter but he died in obscurity* (no-one knew him when he died).

observance *noun*
1 when people obey something such as a law or tradition
2 (*plural* **observances**) a ceremony for celebrating a holiday or religious event

observant *adjective*
good at noticing things or quick to notice something *An observant neighbour remembered the car's number and called the police.*

observation *noun*
1 when you watch someone or something carefully or notice something or someone *My sister has good powers of observation.*
2 (*plural* **observations**) something someone notices or something someone says when they notice something *These are interesting scientific observations. My teacher made an observation about my handwriting being untidy.*

observatory *noun* **observatories**
a building with equipment such as telescopes for studying such things as the stars, planets and weather conditions

observe *verb*
observes, observing, observed
1 to watch someone or something carefully, for example in order to find out information *Dad bought a telescope to observe the stars.*
2 to notice something or someone *She observed a look of surprise on his face. He was observed leaving the theatre by the back door.*
3 to say something about something you notice *'It's getting dark early,' Sanjay observed.*
4 to obey something such as a rule, agreement or tradition

observer *noun* **observers**
someone who sees, watches or notices something

obsessed *adjective*
thinking about something or someone all the time *My sister is obsessed with football.*

obsession *noun*
1 when someone thinks about something all the time *None of us can understand his obsession with the way he looks.*
2 (*plural* **obsessions**) something that someone thinks about all the time *Computer games have become an obsession.*

obsolete *adjective*
old and not used any longer *an obsolete computer*

obstacle *noun* **obstacles**
1 something that is in the way and makes it difficult for someone or something to move forward *The train driver saw an obstacle on the line.*
2 something that makes it difficult for someone to be successful in doing something *The biggest obstacle I had in Madrid was not knowing Spanish.*

obstinacy *noun*
the quality of being obstinate

> SYNONYM stubbornness

obstinate *adjective*
1 if someone is obstinate, they have an idea in their mind about something they really want to do (or something they really don't want to do) and nothing will make them change their mind or behave in a different way
2 also used about someone's behaviour *I was upset by her obstinate refusal to talk to me.*

> SYNONYM stubborn

> SIMILE 'as obstinate as a mule' means very obstinate

obstinately *adverb*
in a way that shows nothing will make someone change their mind and behave in a different way *He obstinately refused to leave his room.*

obstruct *verb*
obstructs, obstructing, obstructed
1 to stop someone getting past by getting in the way *A group of children were obstructing the path.*
2 to stop something moving *An accident obstructed the traffic.*
3 to stop someone seeing something *Someone's head was obstructing my view of the stage.*
4 to stop something happening

obstruction *noun*
1 when someone or something gets in the way, for example by stopping you getting past or stopping you seeing something
2 (*plural* **obstructions**) someone or something that gets in the way *There was an obstruction on the railway line.*

obstructive *adjective*
trying to stop someone doing something by causing problems for them

obtain *verb*
obtains, obtaining, obtained
to get something *You have to obtain permission from your parents.*

obtainable *adjective*
if something is obtainable, you can get it somewhere *Information is obtainable online.*

obtuse *adjective*
in maths, an obtuse angle is one that is between 90 and 180 degrees
compare: **acute, reflex** and **straight**

obvious *adjective*
1 easy to see or understand *an obvious mistake*
2 reasonable or sensible *Leaving now is the obvious thing to do.*

obviously *adverb*
used for saying that something is true because it is easy to see or understand *The tree was obviously dead. Obviously, you need to work hard to do well at school.*

occasion *noun* **occasions**
1 a time when something happens *On this occasion she was very helpful.*
2 a special event such as a birthday, anniversary or wedding *The opening of the Scottish Parliament was a historic occasion.*

occasional *adjective*
happening sometimes or doing something sometimes

> ANTONYM frequent

occasionally *adverb*
sometimes but not often

> ANTONYMS frequently, often

occupant *noun* **occupants**
1 someone who lives in a place *All the occupants of the house were Greek.*
2 someone who is in a place, such as a car or room, at a certain time *None of the occupants of the minibus had been hurt.*

occupation *noun*
1 (*plural* **occupations**) a job or profession *On the form my dad put 'teacher' as his occupation.*
2 (*plural* **occupations**) an activity you do often, such as a hobby
3 when people take control of a place, for example a place belonging to an enemy in a war, or the period of time that this control lasts *In France during the occupation many people went hungry.*

320

occupy – off

occupy *verb*
occupies, occupying, occupied
1 to live in a place *Who occupies the flat upstairs?*
2 to fill a particular space *A table occupied the centre of the room.*
3 to sit in a seat *Most of the seats on the bus were occupied.*
4 to use something such as a room, toilet or bed *All the hotel rooms are occupied.*
5 to fill a period of time *My baby sister occupies all my parents' time.*
6 to keep someone or yourself busy doing something *How can we occupy the kids during the journey? We occupied ourselves by singing songs.*
7 to take control of a place such as a country, city or building, for example a place belonging to an enemy in a war *Britain was occupied by the ancient Romans. A group of angry students occupied the university.*

occur *verb*
occurs, occurring, occurred
1 if something occurs, it happens, usually in an unexpected way *Problems can occur if you forget to shut down your computer properly.*
2 if something occurs somewhere, it exists there *This illness mainly occurs in babies.*
3 if something such as an idea occurs to you, you start to think of it *The thought of asking for help never occurred to me.*

occurrence *noun*
1 (*plural* **occurrences**) something that happens *Delays on the tube are a common occurrence.*
2 the existence of something *Many scientists monitor the occurrence of earthquakes in Japan.*

ocean *noun* **oceans**
1 the sea *I love swimming in the ocean.*
2 one of the five main areas that the sea is divided into. These are the Atlantic, Pacific, Indian, Arctic and Antarctic Oceans.

o'clock *adverb*
used when telling the time when you want to give the particular hour that is shown on the clock *It's nine o'clock.*

ORIGIN short for *of the clock*

octagon *noun* **octagons**
a shape with eight straight sides
octagonal *adjective*

octave *noun* **octaves**
a group of eight musical notes in a scale (series of notes). The last note is the same as the first but it has a different pitch (sound quality).

October *noun*
the tenth month of the year, between September and November. October has 31 days.

ORIGIN from Latin *octo* 'eight', because it was the eighth month of the ancient Roman year

octopus *noun* **octopuses**
a sea creature with a soft oval body and eight long arms called tentacles that it uses for holding and feeding

ORIGIN from Greek *oktopous* 'with eight feet' (from *okto* 'eight' and *pous* 'foot')

odd *adjective* **odder, oddest**
1 different from what is usual, for example in a way that is surprising or that you don't understand *There was an odd sound coming from the computer.*

SYNONYMS strange, unusual

2 used for describing a number that cannot be divided exactly by 2, for example 1, 3 and 5 are odd numbers
compare: **even** (sense 6)
3 used about something that happens or is done or seen sometimes but not often *I haven't eaten much – just the odd biscuit. When we did the charity run, the odd person gave a really big donation.*

SYNONYM occasional

4 used about pairs of things such as socks, shoes or gloves that should be similar in their size, shape, colour or pattern but are not

ANTONYM matching

5 used about something that consists of different types, for example different sizes or shapes *Amy made a lovely birthday card out of odd bits of paper. Dad likes doing odd jobs* (small things in the home or office, for example fixing or painting things).
6 **the odd one out** a person or thing that is different from the other people or things in a group so does not really belong there
oddness *noun*

-odd *suffix* (*informal*)
used with a number for showing that you don't know the exact number or when you mean a slightly bigger number *My grandparents have lived here 30-odd years* (about 30 years or more).

oddly *adverb*
1 in a way that is different from what is usual *She was behaving rather oddly.*

SYNONYMS strangely, unusually

2 used for saying that something is true but surprising *Oddly, he decided to stay when all the others had left.*

oddments *noun plural*
small things of different kinds, especially things such as pieces of cloth left over after something has been made

odds *noun plural*
1 used for saying how likely it is that something will happen *The odds of our team winning today are not very good.*

SYNONYM chances

2 if the odds are against someone, that person is not likely to be successful in doing something
3 **at odds with** not agreeing with someone or something *What you just said is at odds with the facts.*
4 **odds and ends** small things of different kinds, usually things that are not very important

odour *noun* **odours**
a smell, usually a bad one

odourless *adjective*
with no smell, for example a gas or liquid

oesophagus ['ee-**sof**-er-gers'] *noun*
oesophaguses or **oesophagi** ['ee-**sof**-er-gye']
the tube in your body that carries food from your mouth to your stomach

SYNONYM gullet

compare: **windpipe**

of *preposition*
1 belonging to or connected with something or someone *the wheels of my bike; the father of my best friend*
2 made or done by someone or something *the plays of Shakespeare; the flow of the river*
3 done to someone or something *I was upset by the killing of the spider.*
4 containing something *a box of chocolates*
5 showing an amount of something *a kilo of oranges*
6 made from something *a dress of beautiful lace; It's made of wood.*
7 having something *a footballer of great skill; London is a city of huge size.*
8 showing a reason for something *to die of starvation*
9 mentioning the subject of something *Our teacher read us the story of Captain Scott.*
10 away from something *We live within two miles of the school.*
11 used with numbers, for example for showing ages and dates *a girl of 10; It happened on the second of March.*
12 used when a second word or idea explains what type of thing the first one is *a feeling of anger; the city of York; the skill of playing the piano*
13 used for completing the meaning of an adjective or verb *I'm afraid of spiders. Ben is afraid of swimming in the sea. It tastes of lemon. I've thought of an idea.*

of course *adverb*
1 used as a polite or strong way of saying yes *'Could you close the door?' – 'Of course.' 'You weren't angry, were you?' – 'Of course not.'* (no)

SYNONYM certainly

2 used when you say something that you think is known to the person you're speaking to or to everyone *Of course, no-one can be in two places at once.*

SYNONYM obviously

off *preposition*
1 away from or down from something *Take your coat off the table. I was off school last week. Alex fell off the top bunk.*
2 out of something such as a vehicle, train or plane *I got off the bus.*
3 no longer eating or drinking something *I've been off fish for a long time. She's off her food* (no longer feeling hungry).
4 used when talking about removing something that is fixed or joined to something else *I can't get the top off the bottle.*
5 used when talking about taking money from a price to make it less *The sales assistant took £10 off the price.*

321

off – off limits

6 near somewhere *a small island off the coast; We live just off the main road.*

off *adverb*
1 away from or down from something *The bird flew off. I stepped on the ladder but nearly fell off. Mum sent me off to school* (away from the house).
2 out of something such as a vehicle, train or plane *The bus stopped and I got off.*
3 no longer fixed or joined to something *One of my shirt buttons is off. Some of the ink has come off. Cut off the bad part of the apple.*
4 no longer on top of or lying against something *The blankets fell off. My coat is off* (I'm not wearing it). *Take your jacket off.*
5 used when talking about something such as a piece of equipment when it has been made to stop working *The lights were off. I turned the TV off.*
6 used when talking about distance or about time in the future or past *a long way off; Ramadan is just a few weeks off.*
7 no longer going to happen *Next Saturday's match is off.*
8 not at school or work *I was off last week. My dad was off sick yesterday* (not at work because he was ill).
9 going somewhere *We're off to school* (going to school). *Where are you off to? I'm off* (leaving).
10 if food or drink is off, it smells too bad to eat or drink *This fish is off.*
11 used when money is taken from a price to make it less *Special offer today: £10 off.*
12 used when talking about separating a place from another place, for example so that people cannot go there *Several streets around the building were closed off.*
13 doing something completely so there is nothing left *I finished off the whole cake. The school has paid off all its debts.*
14 if you feel off, you don't feel as well as you normally feel

off-chance *noun*
on the off-chance hoping something is possible even though it is not likely *My parents came to the school on the off-chance of speaking to the head.*

> LANGUAGE EXTRA also spelt *off chance*

off-colour *adjective*
feeling slightly ill

off-duty *adjective*
if someone such as a police officer, soldier or doctor is off-duty, he or she is not working at a particular time

offence *noun*
1 (*plural* **offences**) an action that is against the law *She committed a minor driving offence.*
2 feelings of being angry and upset *His behaviour caused offence* (made people angry and upset). *When my teacher said I wasn't paying attention, I took offence* (felt angry and upset).

offend *verb*
offends, offending, offended
1 to make someone angry and upset
2 to do an action that is against the law

offender *noun* **offenders**
someone guilty of an action that is against the law

offensive *adjective*
1 very rude and making someone feel angry and upset *offensive language; The comedian was offensive to foreigners.*
2 an offensive weapon is one that is used for attacking someone, for example a knife or gun

offensively *adverb*

offer *verb*
offers, offering, offered
1 to say or show that you are ready to give someone something if they want it *I got up and offered the elderly lady my seat on the bus.*
2 to give someone something *This book offers useful advice on how to look after a cat.*
3 to say that you are ready to do something if someone wants you to *I offered to help her. 'I'll take the dog for a walk,' she offered eagerly.*
4 to hold something out so that someone can take it (or take some of it) if they want it *Mum offered our guests some cakes.*
5 to offer money is to say how much you are ready to pay someone for something *My cousin offered me £100 for my bike.*

offer *noun* **offers**
1 when you say you are ready to give someone something if they want it or to do something if they want you to *Do you want to accept my offer of help?*
2 an amount of money you are ready to pay someone for something
3 a price that is cheaper than the usual price of something *There were many special offers at the supermarket today.*

off-guard *adjective*
if someone or something catches you off-guard, you are completely surprised by something they do or say or by what happens

offhand *adjective*
not at all friendly or polite *Granddad was a bit offhand with me.*

offhand *adverb*
right now and without spending time finding out about something *I don't know offhand how many children there are in my school.*

office *noun* **offices**
1 a room where someone works sitting at a desk, usually with a computer and phone *The head teacher's office is on the first floor.*
2 a building where people in a business or organisation work sitting at desks *My mum works in the office of a big music company.*
3 a room or building where you go for a particular purpose such as to get information or tickets *a tourist office; a ticket office*
4 an important job, for example in an organisation or government *The president has been in office for two years.*
5 an office block is a large building with lots of offices
6 office hours are the times during the day when people who work in an office usually do their work

officer *noun* **officers**
1 an officer or police officer is a member of the police force
2 someone in charge of other people in the army, navy or air force
3 someone with an important job in an organisation *a prison officer*

official *adjective*
1 connected with important people, for example people with responsible jobs in a government, an organisation or the police *Number Ten Downing Street is the official London residence of the prime minister. Our head teacher has lots of official papers to read.*
2 done by a government or by important people, or happening as part of important people's jobs *an official investigation; French is an official language of Belgium* (accepted by the government of Belgium). *The mayor made an official visit to Wales.*
3 used for describing something that people responsible for something announce or accept as being true or right *The referee's official decision is that it wasn't a goal. The school's official advice is to stay at home if it snows. My sister's getting married next year – it's official!*
4 used for describing something that is what it is supposed to be or is the correct and proper thing you should do or have *We bought the official programme of the concert. Click here to go to the school's official website. These are the official rules of the game* (correct rules that you must obey).

official *noun* **officials**
an important person, for example someone with a responsible job in a government or organisation *a trade union official*

officially *adverb*
1 in a way that is accepted by a government or by important people *The fighting between the two countries ended officially at midnight.*
2 done by important people, or by people responsible for something, as part of their job *The new school was officially opened by the mayor. The police officer officially requested more help.*
3 if information is announced or mentioned officially, it is given by important people or by people responsible for something *My sister's wedding was officially announced in the local paper.*
4 used for saying that something should be true, because people responsible say it is, but it is not really true *Officially, Mrs Jordan is in charge when the head teacher is away but Mr Patel is the person who's really in charge.*

officious *adjective*
an officious person is someone unpleasant who likes bothering people, telling them what to do and giving them help or advice that they don't want

off-licence *noun* **off-licences**
a shop that sells alcohol such as wine and beer

off limits *adjective*
used about a place where someone is not allowed to go *This part of the park is off limits to the public.*

> LANGUAGE EXTRA also spelt *off-limits*

322

offline *adjective & adverb*
1 not connected to the internet or to a computer at a particular time *My laptop is offline. The printer is offline.*
2 if you do something offline, you do it when you are not connected to the internet *I read my emails offline.*

ANTONYM online

off-putting *adjective*
slightly unpleasant in a way that makes you feel uncomfortable about something or someone *The colour of the soup is off-putting but it tastes fine.*

offset *verb*
offsets, offsetting, offset
if one thing offsets another thing, it balances it so that in the end things do not change very much *If school were to finish 30 minutes earlier, this would probably be offset by more homework.*

offshore *adjective & adverb*
in the sea but not far from the coast *an offshore island; Ben swam out a mile or two offshore.*

offside *adjective*
used for describing a position, in a sport such as football or hockey, that is not allowed by the rules *The England player was offside.*

offspring *noun plural*
children or young animals *This dog has produced many offspring.*

often *adverb*
1 many times *I've been to Edinburgh often but to Glasgow more often* (more times). *How often* (how many times) *do you go swimming? I go there often enough* (enough times). *My dad complains too often* (too many times).
2 used for saying something is true but not always true *June is often wet* (wet much of the time). *Pupils arriving late are the ones who often cause these problems* (cause them on many occasions).
3 **every so often** sometimes but not very many times

ogre ['oh-ger'] *noun* ogres
1 in stories, an imaginary creature that looks like an ugly giant and often eats people
2 a cruel and frightening person

oh *interjection*
1 used for showing one of many different feelings such as surprise, happiness, sadness, anger or disappointment
2 used when telling someone something you've just remembered *Oh, and here's your umbrella.*
3 used when you're not sure what to say next

oil *noun* oils
1 a thick liquid that comes mainly from plants, used for cooking *vegetable oil*
2 a thick liquid from plants that is used for rubbing onto the skin, for example to protect the skin from the sun *suntan oil*
3 a thick liquid from under the ground that is used for making petrol or for making machine parts work better together or is burnt for heating *an oil rig* (a structure, usually in the sea, with equipment for drilling for oil); *an oil well* (a deep hole in the ground or sea for getting oil)
4 a thick liquid from plants that is used as a paint *a landscape by Constable painted in oils; an oil painting by Turner*
5 a greasy substance produced by glands in the skin
6 a substance produced in the bodies of fish, used for example as a medicine *fish oils; cod-liver oil*

oil *verb*
oils, oiling, oiled
1 to put oil onto something such as a hinge or machine part to make it work better
2 to put oil into a pan or container before cooking something in it so that the food doesn't stick

oilfield *noun* oilfields
an area under the ground or sea where there is a lot of oil

oilskin *noun* oilskins
a piece of clothing such as a coat treated with a special oil to make it waterproof. Oilskins are often worn by fishermen and fisherwomen.

oily *adjective* oilier, oiliest
1 with lots of oil on it or in it *oily hair; an oily sauce*
2 used for describing particular types of fish that contain a lot of oil *Eating oily fish such as herring is good for you.*
3 slippery, for example because oil or grease has been spilt on it *The kitchen floor is rather oily.*
4 too polite or friendly in a way that is false and unpleasant *He has an oily manner.*

oink *interjection*
used for representing the low rough sound made by a pig **oink** *noun*

ointment *noun* ointments
an oily substance that you rub onto your skin, for example if it is sore or dry

OK *adjective & adverb*
1 fairly good, but not very good *I thought the book was OK but nothing special.*
2 good in an acceptable way *My teacher is very pleased with my schoolwork – she says it has been OK this term.*
3 well *My legs ache but I can walk OK.*
4 not hurt or ill *I fell flat on my face but I'm OK.*
5 safe and well *Go into her room to check if she's OK.*
6 used for saying yes or for agreeing to something *'Do you want to leave now?' – 'OK!' I want to see the film at two o'clock, if that's OK with you.*
7 used for asking someone if what you say is true or if they agree with what you say *I'll come over to your house tomorrow, OK?*
8 used for asking permission *Is it OK to watch TV?*
9 used as an exclamation, for example for getting someone's attention or changing the subject *OK, let's go! OK, that's enough!*
10 (informal) you use 'I'm OK' (or 'we're OK') as a polite way of saying no *'More cake?' – 'I'm OK, thanks.'*

LANGUAGE EXTRA also spelt **okay**

old *adjective* older, oldest
1 made a long time ago or having started to exist a long time ago *an old car; This poem has lots of old words in it.*
2 having lived for a long time *Great-Grandma is very old. We have an old oak tree in the garden.*
3 used for describing something that has been used by someone for a long time or was used by them in the past *My sister threw out her old clothes.*
4 used for describing or asking someone's age *I'm nine years old. How old are you? I'm six and I have an older brother* (for example a brother who is eight).
5 connected with someone or something in the past *I went to see my old teacher at my old school.*
6 used about someone that you've known or been connected with for a long time *We're old friends. Professor Moriarty is an old enemy of Sherlock Holmes.*

SIMILE 'as old as the hills' means very old (senses 1, 2 & 3)

old age *noun*
the time when someone is old

old boy *noun* old boys
a man who used to be a student at a particular school in the past

old-fashioned *adjective*
1 used for describing something connected with the past, for example something that people no longer like to have, do, use or wear *old-fashioned ideas; an old-fashioned dress*
2 used for describing someone who has respect for things from the past or likes to do things connected with the past *Miss Adams is an old-fashioned teacher.*

old girl *noun* old girls
a woman who used to be a student at a particular school in the past

old master *noun* old masters
a famous European painter from long ago, especially one from the 13th to the 17th or 18th century

Old Testament *noun*
the first part of the Christian Bible (holy book of the Christian religion). It tells the story of the Jewish people and their relationship to God.
compare: **New Testament**

olive *noun*
1 (*plural* **olives**) a small dark green or black oval-shaped fruit with a hard seed inside called a stone. Olives are eaten as food or used for making an oil (olive oil) used in cooking. They grow on a medium-sized tree called an olive tree, which has leaves that stay green all year round.
2 olive green or olive is a slightly yellowish dark green colour

olive *adjective*
having a slightly yellowish dark green colour

Olympic ['er-lim-pik'] *adjective*
connected with the Olympic Games *She's an Olympic gold medallist.*

323

Olympic Games – ongoing

Olympic Games *noun plural*
an international sports competition that happens once every four years, in a different country each time

LANGUAGE EXTRA also called the *Olympics*

ORIGIN from *Olympia*, a town in ancient Greece, where games took place every four years to honour the Greek god Zeus

omelette *noun* **omelettes**
a food made by mixing together the yellow and clear parts of eggs and cooking them in a frying pan. Other foods are often added. *a cheese omelette*

omen ['oh-mern'] *noun* **omens**
something that happens or that someone does that you think will tell you something about the future *Our team won the match – that's a good omen* (it shows they might win again in the future).

SYNONYM sign

OMG ['oh-em-**jee**']
used in text, email and online messages when you're surprised, shocked or excited about something
short for: Oh my God!

ominous ['o-min-ers'] *adjective*
making you think something bad is going to happen *The clouds look ominous* (it looks like it's going to rain).
ominously *adverb*

omission *noun*
1 (*plural* **omissions**) something or someone that is not included in something when they should be included, or something that is not done when it should be done *My homework had lots of errors and omissions.*
2 when something or someone is not included, or when something is not done *Was that omission of my name deliberate or accidental?*

omit *verb*
omits, omitting, omitted
1 if you omit something or someone, you don't include them in something, either because you don't want to or by mistake *Meena's name was omitted from the list.*
2 if you omit to do something, you don't do it, often when you should do it *Our teacher omitted to mention that she was leaving.*

omnivore *noun* **omnivores**
an animal that eats plants as well as other animals **omnivorous** *adjective*
compare: **carnivore** and **herbivore**

on *preposition*
1 showing that something or someone is in a position touching a surface or goes into a position touching a surface *I'm sitting on a chair. There's snow on the ground. He came up and stood on my foot.*
2 showing a place or object where something or someone is, or a particular part of the land such as a hill, coast or river *on the opposite side of the road*; *on the coast*; *a ship on the sea*; *I used to live on a farm.*
3 showing a place or object where something is written, stored or recorded *on page 25*; *There are too many programs on your computer.*
4 used about something such as a programme or film that you see or listen to somewhere *There's a good film on TV tonight. What's on the radio?*
5 using something such as a piece of equipment *I'm on the computer.*
6 showing a particular time when something happens or when it always happens *Come to my house on Monday* (next Monday). *We play football on Saturdays* (every Saturday).
7 showing a particular way of doing something *He was hopping on one foot. I went to school on my bike.*
8 into something such as a vehicle, train or plane *We got on the bus.*
9 fixed or attached to something *There's a lid on the jar. The dog was on a lead.*
10 about something *We're reading a book on the history of the alphabet.*
11 showing that someone or something forms a part of something *Ali's on our team. Fish is on the menu.*
12 towards something or someone *The soldiers marched on the town. All eyes were on the teacher.*
13 soon after something *On arriving I went straight to bed.*
14 carrying something *Do you have any money on you?*
15 also used in many idiomatic expressions such as: *on foot* (walking somewhere); *on holiday* (taking a holiday); *on purpose* (meaning to do something); *on time* (not late)

on *adverb*
1 in a position touching a surface *The baby's falling off the seat – he's not on properly. The blankets are on now.*
2 wearing something *I was glad I had my coat on. Put your glasses on.*
3 into something such as a vehicle, train or plane *Get on quickly!*
4 fixed or attached to something *The lid isn't on.*
5 used about something such as a piece of equipment to show that it is working or being used *My tablet is on. Switch the light on.*
6 happening as planned *Tomorrow's match is still on.*
7 used about something such as a programme or film that you see, for example on TV, or listen to, for example on the radio *What's on? There's a good film on tomorrow.*
8 used about something that continues *The arguments are still going on. The smell lingered on all day.*
9 going forward or making progress *Please read on. Can you move on?*

once *adverb*
1 one time only *The train stops once between Leeds and Manchester. I gave the right answer for once* (this time only, though usually this doesn't happen).
2 at a particular time in the past *My mum lived in the USA once.*
3 **all at once** suddenly *All at once we heard a loud bang.*
4 **all at once** also means at the same time *You're trying to do too many things all at once.*
5 **at once** at the same time *Everyone in the class was talking at once.*
6 **at once** also means immediately *Go to bed at once!*
7 **once again** or **once more** used for saying strongly that something has happened before *Once again he would not say hello to me.*
8 **once and for all** used when you want to deal with something now so that you don't have to deal with it again in the future *Let's decide once and for all where to go for our holiday.*

once *conjunction*
at the same time as or immediately after something else *You'll like my friend once you've met her.*

SYNONYM as soon as

one *adjective & noun* **ones**
1 the number 1 *I have one brother and two sisters.*
2 a particular person or thing *Nobody can tell the difference between one twin and the other.*
3 a single person or thing *We didn't see one car on the road.*
4 used for talking about some time in the future or past *One day I want to go to university. I bumped into my teacher in the park one evening.*

one *pronoun*
1 used when talking about something or someone already mentioned or known *Which shirt do you prefer – the green one or the blue one? Seema is the one with the yellow dress. In our class the ones who work hardest are the girls.*
2 people in general *One should be careful in the snow. It's important to respect one's parents.*
3 **one another** used when you mean that every person or thing in a group does something to the others or is connected to them in some way *The four boys looked at one another. All my friends live near one another.*
4 **one at a time** each person or thing separately *The children went into the classroom one at a time.*

oneself *pronoun*
1 used with the pronoun 'one' (people in general) for talking about an action people do that is also directed back onto them *How can one protect oneself?*
2 used when people mean themselves and no-one else *One has to do the homework oneself.*
3 **by oneself** without anyone else being there, or without the help of anyone else *It's no fun sitting alone in the house by oneself.*

one-way *adjective*
1 going in one direction only or allowing vehicles to go in one direction only *one-way traffic*; *a one-way street*
2 a one-way ticket is one that allows you to travel to a place but not to come back again. It is also called a single ticket.
compare: **return ticket**

ongoing *adjective*
used for describing something that is still happening or that still exists *I'm having ongoing problems with my computer.*

onion – opening

onion *noun* **onions**
1 a hard round vegetable with a very strong smell and taste. It is usually brown or dark red on the outside and white on the inside and is made up of lots of different layers.
2 an onion ring is a slice of onion covered with flour, egg and breadcrumbs and fried

online *adjective & adverb*
1 connected to the internet or to a computer *Is the printer online? We moved into our new flat but we're still not online.*

ANTONYM offline

2 connected with the internet *online messaging*; *an online bookstore*
3 if you do something online or something happens online, it is done using the internet *We played a game online.*

ANTONYM offline

onlooker *noun* **onlookers**
someone who watches something that happens, usually in a public place, for example an accident or someone playing music in the street

only *adjective*
1 used for saying that there is no other thing or no other person besides the thing or person you mention *Italy is the only foreign country I've been to. I was the only boy on the bus.*
2 an only child is someone who has no brothers or sisters

only *adverb*
1 not more than a particular amount or number that is usually small *He only has three pages left to read. I'm only nine.*
2 no other thing, no other person or in no other way besides the thing, person or way you mention *This is only the beginning. Only Parminder knows the answer. Our house is only small.*
3 no other place or time *I'm only going to Scotland. This only happened once.*
4 no other reason *I only went to bed because I was bored.*
5 no other activity *I was only joking.*
6 a very short time ago *She's only just come home.*

only *conjunction*
used for connecting two parts of a sentence when you give a reason why something you have just mentioned cannot happen or isn't true *I would invite you to my party only we already have too many people.*

onomatopoeia ['on-er-mat-er-**pee**-er'] *noun*
1 a word that is supposed to sound like the particular noise of the thing or animal it refers to, for example 'miaow' (the sound a cat makes) or 'achoo' (the sound of a sneeze)
2 when someone uses such a word, for example in a poem or novel
onomatopoeic *adjective*

ORIGIN from Greek *onoma* 'name' and *poiein* 'to make'

onset *noun*
the beginning of something, often something unpleasant such as winter, war or an illness

onto *preposition*
1 used for showing that something or someone moves or is moved to somewhere else *The cat climbed onto the roof. She threw the ball onto the ground.*
2 into a vehicle, train or plane *We stepped onto the bus. I brought my bag onto the plane.*
3 used for showing that something is added to something else, for example to a word or list *To form the adverb, you add -ly onto the end of the adjective.*
4 used for showing a direction that something goes in *Don't shine the torch onto my face.*
5 used for showing the direction that something such as a window or building faces *My room looks out onto the garden.*
6 used for showing that something is put next to or against something else *There was a horseshoe fixed onto the wall.*

LANGUAGE EXTRA also sometimes spelt *on to*

onward *adjective*
moving forward to another place or a later time *We're flying to Madrid then taking an onward flight.*

onwards *adverb*
1 starting at a certain time and then continuing *From tomorrow onwards we'll be on holiday.*
2 moving forward to another place *The explorers continued onwards towards the mountains.*

ooh *interjection*
used for showing a feeling such as pleasure or surprise

oops *interjection*
used when you make a small mistake or when a small accident happens, such as someone falling over

ooze *verb*
oozes, oozing, oozed
if a liquid oozes from something, or if something oozes a liquid, the liquid flows out of it slowly *Blood was oozing out of my cut and through the bandage.*

ooze *noun*
any thick unpleasant liquid such as soft mud

opaque ['oh-**payk**'] *adjective*
if something such as glass or a liquid is opaque, you can't see through it

ANTONYM transparent

open *adjective*
1 in a position showing an empty space or a gap that allows someone or something to go through, in or out *an open door*; *an open box*
2 in a position showing the parts of something moved away from each other or spread out, for example so that it can be used or can work *an open book*; *an open umbrella*; *The wings of the butterfly were open. My eyes were open* (the eyelids were apart and I could see).
3 if something such as a computer program or document is open, it is displayed on the screen and is being used
4 if something such as a building or road is open, people can go into it or out of it, or pass through it
5 if a shop or office is open, people can go there to buy things or do business
6 not covered by a roof, for example a car or courtyard
7 used for describing a place or event that anyone is allowed to go to *The school concert is open to the public. Tomorrow is the school's open day* (when people can visit and look around).
8 open land is land with no buildings on it *open spaces* (gardens and parks); *Our house is surrounded by open fields.*
9 if you do something in the open air, you do it outside, not indoors
10 if someone is open, they are honest and friendly and have nothing to hide

open *verb*
opens, opening, opened
1 if you open something such as a door, you change its position so that there is an empty space that allows something or someone to go in, out or through
2 if something opens by itself, it changes its position in this way *This window doesn't open.*
3 if you open something such as a book or umbrella, you move its parts away from each other or spread them out, for example so that it can be used or can work *We opened the deckchairs. I opened my eyes* (moved my eyelids apart so I could see).
4 if you open something such as a box or bottle, you take something away from it so that you can get to what's inside *I opened my birthday presents.*
5 if you open a computer program or document, or if it opens, it is displayed on the screen and starts being used
6 to start doing business, for example at the beginning of a working day *The bank opens at nine o'clock.*
7 to allow people to come in, use something or start using something *Our school opened yesterday after the holidays. They've opened the motorway after the accident. A new museum is opening in our town.*
8 if an event or activity opens, it starts happening *The play opens tomorrow at the Garrick Theatre.*
9 to open something such as a meeting or concert is to start it

open-air *adjective*
used for describing something that is outside, not indoors *an open-air swimming pool*

opener *noun* **openers**
a tool used for opening something such as a tin or bottle *a can opener*

opening *noun* **openings**
1 a hole or space in something *an opening in the fence*
2 when something such as a new building or event opens, often as a special occasion that people celebrate *the opening of the new school*; *Tomorrow is the opening night of the play.*
3 the amount of time a shop or business is open *Our supermarket has 24-hour opening. What are the restaurant's opening times?*

325

openly – optical

4 the beginning of something *The opening of the novel is very exciting.*
5 a job for someone to do *The store has no openings at the moment.*

openly adverb
1 in an honest way without hiding any thoughts or feelings
2 in a way that is obvious for everyone to see

open-minded adjective
if someone is open-minded, they are ready to accept new ideas

openness noun
the quality of being honest and not hiding your thoughts or feelings *The head teacher spoke with openness about the school's problems.*

opera noun
1 (plural **operas**) a musical play in which people sing all or most of the words
2 used for talking about musical plays in general *Caleb likes opera more than the theatre.*

operatic adjective

operate verb
operates, operating, operated
1 if someone operates a piece of equipment, they control it and make it work
2 if a piece of equipment operates, it works and does what it is supposed to do
3 if something such as an organisation, system or service operates, it works or exists in a certain way. If someone operates it, they control it and make it work that way. *This bank operates in many countries. The trains don't operate on Sundays. My dad operates a taxi service to the airport.*
4 if a doctor operates on you, he or she cuts into your body in order to remove or repair an injured or diseased part

operating adjective
1 an operating system is a large computer program that allows a computer to work by controlling all its important software and hardware
2 an operating theatre is a room in a hospital where doctors operate on patients

operation noun **operations**
1 an occasion when a doctor cuts into your body in order to remove or repair an injured or diseased part *She had an operation on her leg.*
2 an activity with a particular aim in which lots of people take part *There's a big police operation to capture the escaped prisoner.*
3 an action performed by a computer or another piece of equipment
4 an action in maths in which a calculation is made to change a number or quantity. The four main types of operations are addition, subtraction, multiplication and division.
see: **order of operations**
5 an organisation or business
6 in operation used for describing something such as a piece of equipment that works as it is supposed to, or something such as a rule that exists

operational adjective
working properly *The school's computer room will be operational by Monday.*

operator noun **operators**
1 someone who works for a phone company and helps people with their calls
2 someone who controls and works a piece of equipment *a computer operator*

opinion noun **opinions**
1 what someone thinks or says that shows their feelings or beliefs about something or someone, for example how good or bad they are or what they are like *What's your opinion of our new head teacher? In my opinion you're wrong* (I think you're wrong).
2 if you have a high opinion of someone or something, you think they are good. If you have a low opinion of them, you think they are bad.

opponent noun **opponents**
1 someone who takes part in a competition or game and plays against you
2 someone who does not agree with something such as an idea or law and tries to get people to change their mind about it

opportunity noun **opportunities**
1 a time when it is possible for you to do something *I had the opportunity to play football for the school.*

SYNONYM **chance**

2 opportunities are when people are allowed to do things to make their lives better, for example to get good jobs

oppose verb
opposes, opposing, opposed
1 to disagree with something such as an idea, decision or law, for example in order to try to change it or stop it *Some teachers oppose the plan to build a new gym. We all oppose the closing of the library.*
2 to disagree with someone whose ideas you don't like and often fight against them *Many people oppose the cruel dictator.*
3 if you are opposed to something or someone, you are against them *My parents are not opposed to my learning French.*
4 as opposed to instead of *We want action as opposed to promises.*

opposing adjective
1 playing or fighting against someone *opposing teams; opposing armies*
2 completely different *My brother and I have opposing views.*

opposite adjective
1 used for describing a part of a particular area, such as an end, side or corner of it, that is in front of you but on the other side of the same area or further away *on the opposite side of the road* (the other side); *We were sitting at opposite ends of the sofa.*
2 used for describing a part of a particular area, such as an end, side or corner of it, that is as far away from you as can be but within the same area *My cousin and I live at opposite ends of the country.*
3 next to something *There's a picture on the opposite page.*
4 as different as possible *A bus was coming towards us from the opposite direction* (from the direction in front of us). *I said goodbye to Chloe and we went off in opposite directions* (I went one way and she went another way that was directly away from me). *We hoped that the medicine would make her better but it had the opposite effect* (instead of making her better, it made her worse).
5 a person of the opposite sex is a girl or woman if you are a boy or man, or a boy or man if you are a girl or woman

ORIGIN from Latin *oppositus* 'on the other side of something' or 'opposed to something'

opposite preposition & adverb
1 in front of someone or something but on the other side of a particular area or further away *She sat opposite me at the table. There's a tree opposite our house. My uncle lives in the house opposite.*
2 next to something *Write your address in the space opposite your name. There's a poem on the page opposite.*

opposite noun **opposites**
something or someone that is as different from something or someone else as can be, for example having exactly the qualities that the other thing or person does not have *'Big' is the opposite of 'small'. 'Good' is the opposite of 'bad'. My brother and I are complete opposites.*

opposition noun
1 when people disagree with something such as an idea or law or with someone whose ideas they don't like *There was strong opposition to the head teacher's plan.*
2 in the UK, the Opposition is the main political party fighting the party that controls the government

oppress verb
oppresses, oppressing, oppressed
1 to treat someone or a group of people in a cruel or unfair way and stop them from being free
2 to make someone feel worried
oppression noun **oppressor** noun

oppressive adjective
1 cruel or unfair *an oppressive government*
2 if the weather is oppressive, it is extremely hot in an unpleasant way *The heat at midday is oppressive.*

opt verb
opts, opting, opted
1 if you opt for something, you choose it instead of something else *David opted for the green uniform.*
2 if you opt to do something, you do it because you want to *I opted to study Spanish rather than German.*
3 if you opt out of something, you decide that you don't want to be connected with it *She was allowed to opt out of PE for religious reasons.*

optic adjective
a fibre optic cable is one made of glass fibres that sends information at very fast speeds

optical adjective
1 connected with the eyes or with light *an optical instrument; an optical mouse* (computer mouse that uses light to make it work)

optician–ordinal number

2 an optical disc is a computer disc such as a CD, DVD or Blu-ray Disc that works using a laser beam (line of light)
3 an optical illusion is an image that tricks the eyes and makes someone see something in a different way or see something that is not really there

optician *noun* **opticians**
someone who checks your eyes and sells glasses and contact lenses

optimist *noun* **optimists**
someone who is hopeful about the future because they think good things are more likely to happen than bad ones
optimism *noun*
compare: **pessimist**

optimistic *adjective*
1 hopeful about the future because you think good things are more likely to happen than bad ones
2 used about something that gives you hope for the future *an optimistic sign*
compare: **pessimistic**

optimistically *adverb*
in a way that shows you are hopeful about the future *'Will you win?' – 'Of course,' he said optimistically.*

option *noun* **options**
1 something that you choose from among two or more different choices *There are only two options – walk or go by bike.*
2 one of the choices listed on a computer menu *Select the Print option on the File menu.*
3 one of the subjects you choose to study at school
4 being allowed to make your own choice *You'll always have the option of saying no. I had to tell a lie – I had no option* (there was nothing else I could do).

optional *adjective*
if something is optional, you can choose whether you want to do it, have it or buy it but you don't have to if you don't want to *We have to study maths but music is optional.* **optionally** *adverb*
compare: **compulsory**

opulent *adjective*
used for describing something that looks very rich and expensive or is connected with very rich people *an opulent palace*; *an opulent lifestyle* **opulence** *noun*

or *conjunction*
1 used for showing or asking about two or more possibilities or choices *I'm going to visit Granddad on Monday or Tuesday. Will you tidy your room or shall I?*
2 used when you mean not one thing and not the other *I can't swim or ride a bike.*
3 used for giving a reason for something *You should do your homework or you'll get into trouble.*
4 used for showing a number that is not exact *I've mentioned this three or four times already.*
5 used for correcting or explaining something *Don't go out now – it's raining, or rather hailing.*

oral *adjective*
1 used about something that is said or spoken but not written *an oral exam*
2 connected with the mouth *an oral vaccine*
orally *adverb*

> **LANGUAGE EXTRA** be careful not to confuse *oral* and *aural*. *Aural* means 'connected with hearing'.

oral *noun* **orals**
an examination in which someone speaks the answers to questions instead of writing them, for example an examination in a foreign language

orange *noun* **oranges**
1 a round fruit that has lots of juice and is divided into parts inside called segments. It has a thick skin whose colour is between red and yellow.
2 a colour between red and yellow

> **ORIGIN** from *naranga* 'orange' in Sanskrit, an ancient language of India

orange *adjective*
having a colour between red and yellow

orangeade *noun* **orangeades**
a sweet drink with lots of bubbles and a slight taste of oranges

orang-utan ['o-rang-yoo-tan'] *noun*
orang-utans
a large intelligent ape with reddish-brown hair. Orang-utans live in the rainforests of South-East Asia.

> **LANGUAGE EXTRA** also spelt *orang-utang*

orator ['or-er-ter'] *noun* **orators**
someone who is good at making speeches in public

orbit *noun* **orbits**
the curved path followed by something going round and round another object *the earth's orbit around the sun; The satellite is in orbit around Mars* (going round Mars).
orbital *adjective*

orbit *verb*
orbits, orbiting, orbited
to go round and round following a curved path *A helicopter was orbiting the crash site. How often does the satellite orbit?*

orchard *noun* **orchards**
an area of land where people grow fruit trees, for example apple or cherry trees

orchestra ['or-ker-strer'] *noun* **orchestras**
a large group of musicians who use many different instruments and usually play classical music (music of high quality written a long time ago). The person in charge of an orchestra is called a conductor.
orchestral *adjective*

orchid ['or-kid'] *noun* **orchids**
a plant with brightly coloured flowers and a pleasant smell. There are many types of orchids and their flowers come in different shapes and sizes.

ordeal *noun* **ordeals**
something difficult and unpleasant *Climbing the stairs with a broken leg is quite an ordeal.*

order *noun*
1 the careful way things or people are organised or dealt with next to each other or one after the other, for example first, second, third and so on *A dictionary is a list of words in alphabetical order. A timeline is a list of dates in chronological order.*
2 (*plural* **orders**) something that someone tells you to do and that you must do *The general gave his soldiers the order to start firing.*
3 (*plural* **orders**) when you tell someone you want to buy something, for example in a shop or restaurant or from a website. An order is also the thing that you buy. *The waiter took our order* (we told him what we wanted). *The order took a week to arrive.*
4 a situation in which things are well organised or tidy *There isn't much order among these papers.*
5 a situation in which people behave well and obey the law *Mr Lewis has trouble keeping order in the classroom. The job of the police is to keep law and order.*
6 in maths, an order (or order of rotation symmetry) is the number of times you can fit a shape, such as a square or triangle, into the same shape when you rotate it through 360 degrees. For example, a triangle with three equal sides fits into the same triangle three times so you say that it has an order of rotation symmetry of 3.
7 **in order** in the correct order or in a tidy way *Don't touch these books – they're all arranged in order.*
8 **in order** also used when you mean something is correct and as it is supposed to be *Your passport is in order.*
9 **in order to** used when you give the reason for something *We left at seven in order to get to school early.*
10 **out of order** not in the correct order *The pages of the newspaper are all out of order.*
11 **out of order** if a piece of equipment is out of order, it is not working
12 **out of order** also used when you mean that someone, or something someone does or says, is bad or completely wrong *Your behaviour last night was out of order.*

order *verb*
orders, ordering, ordered
1 to tell someone to do something and expect them to do it
2 to tell someone you want to buy something that they are selling *We went into a restaurant and ordered fish and chips. Dad ordered me some books online.*
3 to put things in a particular order *All the emails are ordered by date.*

orderly *adjective*
1 well-behaved *an orderly queue; We filed out of the classroom in an orderly fashion.*
2 organised in a neat and tidy way *an orderly pile of books; an orderly mind*

order of operations *noun*
in maths, the order in which operations (calculations) should be done. Numbers in brackets, for example (2 × 4), are done first. If there are no brackets, you do multiplications and divisions first and you do additions and subtractions next.

ordinal number *noun* **ordinal numbers**
a number, such as first, second or third, used for showing in what order something or someone comes, for example in a list
compare: **cardinal number**

ordinarily – other

ordinarily *adverb*
used for saying something is usually true or happens most often

SYNONYMS normally, usually

ordinary *adjective*
normal and not different in any way *It was an ordinary Monday morning. My parents are ordinary people.*

ore *noun*
a type of rock that contains metal *iron ore*

organ *noun* **organs**
1 a part of the body that has a special job to do, for example the heart, brain or liver. Each organ forms part of a system, for example the liver is part of the digestive system (helps the body to use food).
2 a large musical instrument with a keyboard and many pipes of different sizes. To play it you sit in front and press keys (long narrow bars) with your hands or feet. Air is forced through the pipes to produce the sound.

organic *adjective*
1 used for describing something such as food or ways of producing food without artificial chemicals when growing plants or keeping animals *organic milk*; *organic farming*
2 made from or connected with living things *organic matter*

organically *adverb*

organisation *noun*
1 (*plural* **organisations**) a group of people who work together and share the same ideas, for example a business, political group or charity (group that helps people) *The United Nations is a large organisation.*
2 the way that something is organised *Our parents were surprised by the bad organisation of the class outing.*
3 the action of organising something

LANGUAGE EXTRA also spelt *organization*

organise *verb*
organises, organising, organised
1 to make plans for something to happen or be done *It's hard work organising a birthday party.*
2 to arrange or do something in a careful or sensible way *You've organised your ideas well in this essay. Try and organise your homework so you do a little every day.*
3 to put things in a particular order *The display of pupils' work was organised by year group.*

organiser *noun*

LANGUAGE EXTRA also spelt *organize* and *organizer*

organised *adjective*
1 planning things carefully or sensibly *My dad is very organised.*
2 arranged carefully or sensibly *Our classroom isn't very well organised.*
3 used for describing something that has been thought about and carefully planned *an organised trip to the museum*; *organised demonstrations in central London*

LANGUAGE EXTRA also spelt *organized*

organism *noun* **organisms**
a living thing such as a human, animal, plant or microbe (tiny thing you can only see through a microscope)

organist *noun* **organists**
someone who plays an organ, for example as their job

oriental *adjective*
connected with the countries of East Asia, for example China and Japan

orienteering *noun*
a sport in which you have to find how to get somewhere using a map and compass (instrument with a needle that points north), usually in the countryside

origami ['o-ri-**gah**-mee'] *noun*
the art of making models out of sheets of paper by folding them in different ways

ORIGIN from Japanese *ori* 'folding' and *kami* 'paper'. Origami started in Japan in the 17th century.

origin *noun* **origins**
1 where something starts to exist or comes from *The origin of the word 'bouquet' is French.*
2 the cause of something *The origin of your cough is a virus.*
3 someone's origin is the country where they were born *I'm of Polish origin.*
4 in maths, the origin is the centre point of a graph (diagram) where the axes (measurement lines) cross

original *adjective*
1 used for describing something or someone that has existed from the beginning *That was the original plan. This part of the building is new but the rest is original. My original maths teacher was Mr Sims.*
2 used for describing the actual thing produced by someone or the first form of something *You're looking at an original painting by Picasso. This is a photocopy of the original certificate.*
3 used for describing something that is new and different from what anyone has thought of or done before *It's not easy to come up with an original idea for a book.*
4 used for describing someone who thinks of new and different ideas *Einstein was an original thinker.*

original *noun* **originals**
the actual thing produced by someone or the first form of something *This painting is the original by Picasso. Send photocopies rather than the originals of your certificates.*

originality *noun*
1 the quality of being new and different from what anyone has thought of or done before
2 being able to produce new and different ideas or things such as works of art

originally *adverb*
at the beginning *Originally, I didn't want to go on the school trip but I changed my mind.*

originate *verb*
originates, originating, originated
1 to come from a particular place or person *This fashion originated in America.*
2 to start at a particular time or in a particular way *Hip-hop music originated in the 1970s.*
3 to start something or make it happen for the first time *Who originated the expression 'the full monty'?*

originator *noun*

ornament *noun* **ornaments**
a small attractive object used as a decoration, especially in someone's home or garden *Christmas tree ornaments*

ornamental *adjective*
looking attractive and used as a decoration *a hand-painted ornamental ceiling*; *ornamental trees* (for example shaped in a particular way)

ornithology *noun*
the scientific study of birds

ornithologist *noun*

orphan *noun* **orphans**
a child whose father and mother have both died

orphanage *noun* **orphanages**
a home where orphans are looked after

orthodontist *noun* **orthodontists**
a dentist whose job is to make people's teeth straight and regular

orthodox *adjective*
1 accepted by most people as being correct or normal *orthodox opinions*; *an orthodox treatment for cancer*
2 the Orthodox Church is a large church made up of Christians living mainly in Eastern Europe, Russia and Greece

Oscar *noun* **Oscars** (trademark)
one of many cinema prizes given each year in the US to actors and to people who make films *The famous director won an Oscar for best film.*

oscillate *verb*
oscillates, oscillating, oscillated
to keep moving from side to side without stopping *an oscillating fan*

ostrich *noun* **ostriches**
a very large African bird with long legs, a long neck and a small head. Ostriches cannot fly but they can run extremely fast, faster than any other bird.

other *adjective & pronoun*
1 used when talking about more of the same kind of thing or person that you have already mentioned *Mohammed and Ethan are here but not the other boys. Rupa and Lily have arrived but I don't know where the others are.*
2 used when talking about the second of two similar things *Hold the ball in your other hand. George was wearing odd socks – one was blue and the other red.*
3 a different thing or person *These jeans don't fit – I'll try the other pair. I don't like spinach but other people do. If these ideas don't work, I have some others.*
4 used for describing a part of a particular area, such as an end, side or corner of it, that is not the part nearest to you but a part that is further away *Her house is on the other side of the street.*

SYNONYM opposite

328

5 used for describing a part of a particular area, such as an end, side or corner of it, that is as far away from you as can be but within the same area *My aunt lives at the other end of the country.*

SYNONYM **opposite**

6 the other day or **the other week** used when you mean very recently, just a few days or weeks ago *I saw Harry the other day.*
7 the other way or **in the other direction** or **from the other direction** used when you mean in or from the opposite direction *I didn't see the bicycle coming the other way* (towards me).
8 other than as well as *What languages are you studying other than French?*
9 other than also means except *I don't have anything to say other than what I've already said.*

otherwise adverb
1 used for saying that if you don't do something or if something doesn't happen, another thing will happen instead *Be quiet, otherwise I won't be able to hear the TV.*

SYNONYM **or else**

2 except for one or more particular things *I had a few cuts but otherwise I wasn't hurt.*
3 differently *You're my best friend and I've never said otherwise.*

otter noun **otters**
an animal with a long body and brown fur. Otters live near rivers, swim and eat fish.

ouch [rhymes with 'pouch'] interjection
a word used for showing that you have a sudden pain

ought verb
1 used for saying that someone should do something because it is the right or best thing to do *You ought to finish your homework before going out.*
2 used for saying something is likely to happen or to have happened *He left an hour ago so he ought to be there by now.*
3 used for making a suggestion *We ought to go to the cinema one day next week.*

ounce noun **ounces**
1 a unit for measuring weight, equal to about 28 grams. There are 16 ounces in a pound.
2 also used when you mean a small amount of something *Your brother doesn't have an ounce of common sense.*

our adjective
belonging to us (when you are the person speaking or writing and you also include one or more other people) *Our teacher is really cool.*

ours pronoun
used about something belonging to the person speaking or writing and to one or more other people *These books are ours.*

ourselves pronoun
1 used when talking about an action you do that one or more other people also do and when that action is also directed back onto you *We're washing ourselves.*
2 used when you mean you yourself and one or more other people and no-one else *Ravi and I did all the work ourselves.*

3 by ourselves without anyone else being there, or without the help of anyone else *We sat in the empty classroom by ourselves. This time we did the homework all by ourselves.*

out adverb
1 used for showing a position or movement away from something or from the inside of something *All my toys are out on my bed. I knocked over the bag and the crisps fell out. Don't stick your hand out of the window. The bus arrived at school and we all jumped out* (got off). *Stay out of the sun.*
2 not at home or not in a building or room *Sorry, my sister is out. Wait for me out in the corridor. Mum went out early. Go out and close the door. The head teacher is out of his office.*
3 used about leaving your home to go somewhere to do something you like doing *My big sister goes out a lot. We don't eat out much.*
4 not included in something, for example a team, group or programme *For tomorrow's match Noah is out and Kareem is in.*
5 used about someone doing a particular job, for example in a public place *The police and the army were out on the streets.*
6 used when something disappears or is removed so that nothing is left *The candle is out. I can't get this ink stain out. All the tickets have sold out. The money on my phone has run out.*
7 used when something appears *The stars are out. These flowers come out in spring.*
8 if someone is out in a game or sport, they are not allowed to play any longer, for example because they have lost or had their turn
9 if something such as a book, film or DVD is out, it is ready to be bought or seen
10 used for showing that a book or DVD is being borrowed from a library *I have three books out at the moment.*
11 completely *Please clean out the toy box. I'm tired out.*
12 loudly *She shouted out to me from the other side of the road.*
13 a long way away *My brother lives out in the country.*
14 out of used when there is nothing left of something *We're out of bread.*
15 out of also used when you mean from something or from a particular material *I drank the milk out of the bottle. The nest was built out of leaves and twigs.*
16 out of also means because of a particular feeling *We went inside out of curiosity.*
17 out of doors outside, not indoors

out-and-out adjective
complete *My sister is an out-and-out liar.*

outback noun
the outback in Australia is a huge area of very dry land a long way from the towns where people live. It covers much of the inner part of the country.

outbox noun **outboxes**
1 a folder on a computer where email messages are stored until you send them
2 a folder on a mobile phone where text messages are stored until you send them
compare: **inbox**

outbreak noun **outbreaks**
when something very bad or dangerous starts suddenly, for example a war or disease *There was an outbreak of fighting on the border.*

outbuilding noun **outbuildings**
a building belonging to a bigger building but separate from it, used for example for storing things

outburst noun **outbursts**
when something starts suddenly, such as a strong feeling *an outburst of anger*

outcast noun **outcasts**
someone who is not accepted by a group such as a family or by a whole society, for example because people think they are different or have done something wrong

outcome noun **outcomes**
a situation that exists at the end of something such as an election, meeting or discussion *My dad went to see the head but I don't know the outcome* (what happened).

SYNONYM **result**

outcry noun **outcries**
a feeling of great anger shown by many people, for example because the people who are in charge, such as a government, have done something bad *There was a public outcry at the big rise in tube fares.*

outdated adjective
1 old-fashioned and no longer good or useful *an outdated computer*
2 no longer correct because information has changed *an outdated map*
3 no longer good because an official date has passed *an outdated passport*

SYNONYM **out-of-date**

outdo verb
outdoes, outdoing, outdid, outdone
to be better than someone else at doing something

outdoor adjective
1 done or built outside a building *an outdoor swimming pool; an outdoor concert*
2 used outside *outdoor clothing*

ANTONYM **indoor**

outdoors adverb
outside a house or building

ANTONYM **indoors**

outer adjective
1 outside something or away from the centre of it *the outer walls of the castle; outer London*

ANTONYM **inner**

2 outer space is the area of the universe that is far away from the earth, for example where the stars and all the other planets are

outfit noun **outfits**
1 clothes that are worn together, usually for a particular event or activity *a wedding outfit; a cowboy outfit*
2 a group of people who work together

outgoing–outside

outgoing *adjective*
going out *outgoing emails*

ANTONYM **incoming**

outgrow *verb*
outgrows, outgrowing, outgrew, outgrown
1 to grow too big to fit into something such as your clothes
2 to grow bigger and faster than someone
3 to no longer do something or like something that you did or liked in the past because you are older and have changed *Charlotte has outgrown the habit of drinking through a straw.*

outhouse *noun* outhouses
a building belonging to a bigger building but usually separate from it, used for example for storing things

outing *noun* outings
a short trip that you make with other people away from your school or home *The whole class went on an outing to the seaside.*

outlast *verb*
outlasts, outlasting, outlasted
to exist for longer or to continue to be good for longer than something or someone else *My brown shoes are older but they've outlasted my black ones.*

outlaw *noun* outlaws
a criminal, especially one who in the past moved from one place to another so as not to be caught

outlaw *verb*
outlaws, outlawing, outlawed
if a government or important person or organisation outlaws something, they decide that the law will not allow it *Smoking is outlawed in trains, restaurants and public buildings.*

outlet *noun* outlets
1 a pipe or hole that allows a liquid or gas to flow out of something
2 a place such as a shop that sells a particular product or only sells the products from a particular company *a fast food outlet*
3 a place, for example on a wall, where you connect a piece of electrical equipment

LANGUAGE EXTRA you can also say a *power outlet*

4 a way for someone to express their feelings or get rid of their energy

outline *noun* outlines
1 a line around the edge of something that shows its main shape without any details *We saw the outline of a ship in the distance.*
2 a short description of something without many details
3 a plan or list showing the main points of a piece of writing, for example a story, before someone writes it

outline *verb*
outlines, outlining, outlined
1 to draw or show a line around the edge of something showing its main shape *A figure was moving towards us, outlined against the moonlit sky.*
2 to outline something such as a plan or idea is to describe it without giving many details or without using many words

outlive *verb*
outlives, outliving, outlived
to live longer than someone

outlook *noun*
1 what people think a situation is likely to be in the future, for example whether things will get better or worse *The outlook for jobs looks gloomy* (for example fewer jobs in the future).
2 the way you feel about something and the way you behave because of this *Granddad has an up-to-date outlook on life* (behaves in a modern way).

outlying *adjective*
1 a long way from a town or city *Children arrived by coach from outlying villages.*
2 a long way from the centre of a town or city *an outlying district of Manchester*

outnumber *verb*
outnumbers, outnumbering, outnumbered
if people or things in one group outnumber those in another, there are more people or things in the first group than the second *In our class the boys outnumber the girls. We're outnumbered* (there are more of them than of us).

out-of-date *adjective*
1 old-fashioned and no longer good or useful *We have an out-of-date computer that belonged to Mum's stepdad.*
2 no longer correct because information has changed *an out-of-date map*
3 no longer good because an official date has passed *an out-of-date passport*

SYNONYM **outdated**

out-of-the-way *adjective*
used for describing a place that is a long way from other places, for example from places where people live or go *My cousin lives in an out-of-the-way village in the mountains.*

SYNONYM **isolated**

LANGUAGE EXTRA usually spelt *out of the way* when it comes after a noun, for example *My uncle's house is a bit out of the way.*

outpatient *noun* outpatients
someone who receives treatment in a hospital but doesn't sleep there at night

outpost *noun* outposts
a place such as a group of buildings a long way from a main town or centre, for example for doing military activities or business activities *an army outpost*

output *noun*
1 the amount of goods produced, for example by a factory or country
2 information produced by a computer or other device
compare: **input**
3 the amount of electricity produced by a circuit (the path that electricity travels around) or by a piece of electrical equipment

output *verb*
outputs, outputting, output
to produce information (used about a computer or other device)
compare: **input**

outrage *noun*
1 a feeling of great anger and shock
2 (*plural* **outrages**) something that causes a feeling of great anger and shock *It's an outrage that so many libraries have been closed.*

outrage *verb*
outrages, outraging, outraged
to make someone feel very angry and shocked

outrageous *adjective*
1 making you feel very shocked and angry *Hitting your little sister is an outrageous thing to do.*
2 shocking because of being strange or unreasonable *He was wearing outrageous clothes. The prices were outrageous* (much too high).

outrageously *adverb*

outright *adverb*
1 completely *Smoking on the tube has been banned outright.*
2 with everything done at the same time *My parents bought their new car outright* (they paid the total amount for it).
3 immediately *The motorbike hit a fox and killed it outright.*

outright *adjective*
complete *an outright lie; There was no outright winner.*

outrun *verb*
outruns, outrunning, outran, outrun
to run faster than someone

outset *noun*
at the outset or **from the outset** at or from the beginning of something

outside *preposition & adverb*
1 not in a building or room but very close to it or moving away from it *She was waiting outside. I ran outside into the street. He left the parcel outside the front door.*
2 not in a building but in the space where the sun, wind and rain are *Outside the sun was shining. It's dark outside.*
3 away from a particular place *This actor is not very well known outside the UK.*
4 not in something *Pile up the books outside the box before you put them in. You can phone the school on this number outside school hours.*

outside *adjective*
1 on the outside of something *an outside pocket; an outside light* (for example outside a block of flats)
2 from or connected with other people *outside help*
3 not connected with your studies or work *Aaron has lots of outside interests like swimming and music.*
4 an outside chance is a slight chance that something will happen
5 the outside world is the rest of the world or society in general

outside *noun* outsides
1 the part of something furthest away from the middle of it *The outside of the car was dirty.*
2 the part of something that faces outwards or towards the front *I have a cut on the outside of my hand.*

outsider *noun* outsiders
1 someone who is not connected with a particular group
2 someone who feels that they do not belong to a particular group
3 a person or animal that only has a slight chance of winning a race

outskirts *noun plural*
the parts of a town or city that are furthest from its centre or just outside its furthest edge

outsmart *verb*
outsmarts, outsmarting, outsmarted
to be cleverer than someone, for example by getting them to do what you want, by taking something from them or by tricking them

SYNONYM to outwit

outspoken *adjective*
saying what you really think in an honest way and without worrying about upsetting people

outstanding *adjective*
1 really and truly excellent *Kareem is an outstanding pupil.*
2 used for describing something that has not been dealt with yet *outstanding problems*

outstandingly *adverb*
used for saying how really good something is or how really well something is done *Venice is an outstandingly beautiful city. He played outstandingly last week.*

outstretched *adjective*
reaching out as far as possible, for example towards someone *She ran up to me with arms outstretched.*

outward *adjective*
1 used about something that you can see from the outside *Your laptop shows no outward sign of a problem.*
2 towards the outside of something *an outward flow*

ANTONYM inward

3 used about a journey away from a particular place such as your home. The journey back is called the return journey.

outwardly *adverb*
used about the way something seems from the outside although this may not be the way something really is *Outwardly, he looked happy and relaxed.*

outwards *adverb*
towards the outside of something

LANGUAGE EXTRA you can also say *outward*

ANTONYM inwards

outweigh *verb*
outweighs, outweighing, outweighed
if something outweighs something else, the first thing is more important than the second one *Do the benefits of jogging outweigh the risks?*

outwit *verb*
outwits, outwitting, outwitted
to be cleverer than someone, for example by getting them to do what you want, by taking something from them or by beating them in a game

SYNONYM to outsmart

outwith *preposition & adverb*
a Scottish English word for outside *My cousin goes to school outwith Edinburgh.*

oval *adjective*
shaped like an egg or a circle that has been made flatter and longer

oval *noun* ovals
an oval shape

ORIGIN from Latin *ovum* 'egg'

ovary *noun* ovaries
1 one of the two organs inside the body of a woman or a female animal that produces cells called eggs (tiny units of living matter that can develop into babies or baby animals)
2 the part of a plant that produces seeds

ORIGIN from Latin *ovum* 'egg'

oven *noun* ovens
1 a piece of kitchen equipment, shaped like a box with a door, that is sometimes part of a cooker. It is used for baking and heating food.
2 an oven glove is a thick glove, or a small cloth bag that you put your hand into, used for taking hot things out of an oven

over *preposition*
1 higher than something *There was a helicopter hovering over us.*

SYNONYM above

2 on something or covering something *I put my hands over my ears. I spilt some milk over the floor.*
3 from one side of something to the other *a bridge over the river; I climbed over the fence.*
4 on the other side of something *Our school is just over the road.*

SYNONYM across

5 in many parts of something *I'd love to travel all over Scotland.*
6 down from something, for example when talking about falling, hanging or looking *I slipped over the edge of the swimming pool. My legs were hanging over the side of the bed.*
7 more than something *We've read over 50 pages. It's a competition for children over the age of 10. I waited for over an hour.*
8 used when mentioning a subject or the reason for something *They were fighting over the last piece of cake.*

SYNONYM about

9 for the whole or a part of something such as a period of time *What are you doing over the summer? Mum reads the newspaper over breakfast.*

SYNONYM during

10 used for talking about something that is finished *We had a lot of problems but we're over them now. My dog is not better yet but she's over the worst.*
11 used for showing that someone or something has power to make people do things *Mr Bradshaw doesn't have much control over the class. The government has a lot of influence over people.*
12 using a piece of equipment *He told me this over the phone.*

SYNONYM on

13 used in maths for showing that you are dividing one number by another *21 over 9 is 2.3* (21 over 9 is usually written $\frac{21}{9}$).

over *adverb*
1 down, for example when talking about falling or bending *I fell over. She knocked the bottle over. He bent over to pick up the book.*
2 from one side to the other *I saw the puddle and jumped over.*
3 from one place to another *Come over here. Move over – there's no room for me. This weekend Olivia is coming over* (to my house).
4 in another place *Who's that girl over by the window?*
5 so that the other side of something shows *Turn the pancake over.*
6 above *Several planes flew over.*
7 so that something takes the place of something else *This cup is dirty – could you change it over?*
8 more than a certain number *The race is open to children of 12 and over.*
9 finished *Is the film over yet?*
10 not used *After the party there wasn't much food over.*
11 **over and done with** used about something unpleasant that is completely finished *I'm glad this week's homework is over and done with.*
12 **over and over** very many times *I read the poem over and over until I knew it by heart.*

over *noun* overs
in cricket, a series of six actions by a bowler. In each action, the bowler throws the ball towards a batsman (someone from the other team who hits the ball).

over- *prefix*
1 used with verbs, adjectives and nouns to mean too much *to overeat; overambitious; overpaid; overoptimism; over-protective*
2 used with nouns to mean more than *There's free travel on the buses for the over-sixties* (people aged 60 and over).

overall *adjective*
connected with the whole of something or the whole of a particular situation *The head teacher has overall responsibility for the school. Jack was the overall winner* (the person who won the whole competition, for example).

overall *adverb*
when every detail of something is considered or included *The captain of our team played very well overall.*

overall *noun* overalls
1 a very thin coat that someone wears over ordinary clothes to keep them clean, for example when doing the housework
2 overalls are trousers and a jacket joined together as a single piece. They are worn over ordinary clothes to keep them clean when dirty work is being done. *Workers in blue overalls were repairing pipes in the street.*

overboard–oversleep

overboard *adverb*
in or into the water from a boat or ship *Someone has fallen overboard. There are two people overboard.*

overcast *adjective*
with lots of clouds and not much light *Monday was overcast. The sky is overcast.*

overcharge *verb*
overcharges, overcharging, overcharged
if someone overcharges you, they make you pay too much money for something

overcoat *noun* overcoats
a long thick coat that you wear in the cold weather

overcome *verb*
overcomes, overcoming, overcame, overcome
1 to try very hard and deal successfully with something that is causing you a problem *After many years Rohan overcame his fear of heights.*
2 if you are overcome by something such as smoke or heat, that thing makes you ill *Many people were overcome by fumes from the bus.*
3 if you are overcome with a feeling, that feeling has a strong influence on you *We were overcome with fear.*

overcook *verb*
overcooks, overcooking, overcooked
to cook something for too long

overcrowded *adjective*
if a thing or place is overcrowded, there are too many people in it *an overcrowded bus*

overcrowding *noun*
when there are too many people in a thing or place *Overcrowding on the tube is a big problem.*

overdo *verb*
overdoes, overdoing, overdid, overdone
1 to do something too much, for example by using it, giving it or saying it too much *When you write a story, try not to overdo the long words.*
2 to overdo food is to cook it for too long

overdose *noun* overdoses
too much of a medicine or drug that someone takes at one time

overdue *adjective*
1 used about something that should have happened or been done before *My homework is overdue – I was supposed to give it in last week. Your library book is overdue* (the date to return it to the library has passed).
2 used about something such as a bus or train that has not arrived yet
3 used about something such as a bill that has not been paid yet *The school fees are overdue.*

overflow *verb*
overflows, overflowing, overflowed
1 if something such as a river or bath overflows, there is so much water in it that the water comes over the edges
2 also used about other liquids that come over the edges of something *I poured too much lemonade into the glass and it overflowed onto the table.*

Overground *noun*
a railway system in London in which the trains travel above the ground, not under it

overgrown *adjective*
if something such as a garden is overgrown, it is full of weeds and of plants that have grown too big

overhang *verb*
overhangs, overhanging, overhung
if something such as the branch of a tree or a rock overhangs something, it sticks out above it

overhaul *verb*
overhauls, overhauling, overhauled
to thoroughly check a piece of equipment or a vehicle and fix any parts that are not working or not working properly
overhaul *noun*

overhead *adjective & adverb*
1 above your head *an overhead cable*; *A helicopter was hovering overhead.*
2 an overhead projector is a piece of equipment that shines light through a photographic film so that the words and pictures on the film can be seen much larger on a screen or wall

overheads *noun plural*
the money that must be paid for the things needed to operate a business, for example electricity, telephones and computers

overhear *verb*
overhears, overhearing, overheard
1 to hear something people say to each other that you are not supposed to hear *Luke overheard a joke on the bus.*
2 to hear people say things to each other that you are not supposed to hear *I overheard two boys saying nasty things about the school.*

overheat *verb*
overheats, overheating, overheated
to get too hot *Switch off your laptop as it's starting to overheat.*

overjoyed *adjective*
very happy about something

overland *adjective & adverb*
going across the land, for example by car or train, not by boat or plane *an overland journey*; *We're going to travel overland to Spain.*

overlap *verb*
overlaps, overlapping, overlapped
if one thing overlaps another, or if two things overlap, a part of one of them covers a part of the other or lies over the edge of the other *a pattern of overlapping circles*; *The curtains overlap in the middle.*

overload *verb*
overloads, overloading, overloaded
to put too many things or people in or on something *Don't overload the dishwasher. The boat sank because it was overloaded.*

overlook *verb*
overlooks, overlooking, overlooked
1 to pay no attention to something, especially something you should pay attention to *Your teachers mustn't overlook safety when organising a school trip.*
2 to not notice something, for example something small that is easy to miss *I'm sorry – I overlooked one small detail.*
3 if someone says they will overlook something such as a mistake or bad behaviour, they mean they will not do anything about it, for example they will not punish someone or tell them off *'You're late but I'll overlook it this time,' said Ms Kumar.*
4 if something such as a room or window overlooks a place, you can see that place from there *My bedroom overlooks the garden.*

overnight *adverb*
1 for the whole of a night *We stayed overnight in a small hotel.*
2 during the night *The fog got thicker overnight.*
3 in an extremely short amount of time *You can't learn a foreign language overnight.*

overnight *adjective*
1 happening during the night, or connected with the night *an overnight stay in a hotel*; *an overnight bus*
2 happening in an extremely short amount of time *The book was an overnight success.*

overpass *noun* overpasses
a bridge that takes a road over another road, or one that allows people to cross a busy road safely

overpower *verb*
overpowers, overpowering, overpowered
if someone overpowers someone else, they fight with them and win because they are stronger *The thief was chased and overpowered by a police officer.*

overpowering *adjective*
1 if a smell or taste or something such as heat is overpowering, it is very strong and unpleasant
2 if a feeling is overpowering, it is so strong that you have trouble controlling it
3 if a person is overpowering, he or she tries to control people or has a very strong and unpleasant character

overpriced *adjective*
if something is overpriced, it costs more money than it should

overrun *verb*
overruns, overrunning, overran, overrun
1 to fill a place in large numbers (used about animals or people that you consider unpleasant) *The whole kitchen was overrun with mice. Hundreds of tourists overran the town centre.*
2 to go on for longer than expected *We're late because the lesson overran by 15 minutes.*

overseas *adverb*
in or to another country *My cousins live overseas.*

SYNONYM abroad

overseas *adjective*
from, in or to other countries or another country *an overseas student*; *The army has many overseas bases.*

oversight *noun* oversights
a mistake someone makes by not noticing something or by not doing something they should have done

oversleep *verb*
oversleeps, oversleeping, overslept
to sleep for too long and wake up late

overtake *verb*
overtakes, overtaking, overtook, overtaken
1 to catch up with and go past a vehicle or person going in the same direction *Drive faster, Dad, and overtake the car in front!*
2 to make more progress, be more successful or increase more quickly than someone or something else *The girls have overtaken the boys in English.*

overthrow *verb*
overthrows, overthrowing, overthrew, overthrown
to get rid of someone by force, for example a leader, ruler or government, by taking away their power **overthrow** *noun*

overtime *noun*
time someone spends working in their job after they have finished working their normal hours *My mum often works overtime.*

overtired *adjective*
very tired, often in a way that means you have trouble getting to sleep

overture *noun* overtures
the first part of a long piece of classical music (such as an opera) that is written as an introduction to it

overturn *verb*
overturns, overturning, overturned
1 to turn something over or knock something over so that the top or side of it is at the bottom *The wind has overturned the dustbin.*
2 if something such as a car overturns, it turns over so that the top of it is at the bottom

overuse *verb*
overuses, overusing, overused
to use something too much or too often, such as a word or expression

overview *noun* overviews
a short description of something that gives the most important details only

overweight *adjective*
used about someone or something that weighs more than they should *overweight luggage*; *Dad is getting a little overweight.*

overwhelm *verb*
overwhelms, overwhelming, overwhelmed
1 if something such as a feeling overwhelms you, it affects you in a very strong way *We were overwhelmed with excitement when Miss Patel announced our trip to the coast. We thanked our uncle for his overwhelming kindness* (great kindness that made us very happy).
2 to surprise someone very much
3 to be too much or too many for someone to deal with *There were so many visitors that they overwhelmed the little museum. The little museum was completely overwhelmed* (for example, it was unable to deal with so many visitors). *Their numbers were overwhelming* (there were too many of them).
4 to win a battle against someone by using a lot more force, or to beat someone in a sport or game, for example by scoring many more points or goals

overwork *verb*
overworks, overworking, overworked
to work too much or make someone work too much

overwork *noun*
too much work, especially when it makes someone ill or very tired

ovum ['oh-verm'] *noun* ova ['oh-ver']
1 a cell (smallest unit of living matter) inside a plant that can grow into a seed from which another plant grows
2 a cell in a woman or female animal that can develop into a baby or baby animal. This ovum is also called an egg.

ORIGIN from Latin *ovum* 'egg'

ow [rhymes with 'now'] *interjection*
a word used for showing that you have a sudden pain

owe *verb*
owes, owing, owed
1 if you owe someone money, you have borrowed money from them and you still have to pay the money back to them (or you have bought something from them and still have to pay them). You pay the money either in one go or in smaller amounts over a period of time. *I owe my mum £20.*
2 to have a responsibility to give someone something or do something for someone, because they have given you something or done something for you or because it is the right thing to do *He owes me a favour. I owe you an apology.*
3 to have something only because of someone or something else *My dad owes his life to a stranger who saved him from drowning.*

owing to *preposition*
used for giving a reason for something *We couldn't go to school today owing to the snow.*

SYNONYM because of

owl *noun* owls
a bird with a flat face, large round eyes and a short curved beak. It is a bird of prey that flies at night and eats small animals and other birds. The sound it makes is a hoot.

own *adjective & pronoun*
1 used for describing something connected with someone or something, or for describing a particular thing that someone or something has *I've got my own mobile. This part of the house has its own entrance. I now have a friend of my own. This book is my own – it's not yours.*
2 used for showing that a particular person does something himself or herself *From now on you'll have to do your own homework* (without anyone helping you).
3 if you do something on your own, you do it without anyone else being there, or without the help of anyone else *Harry walks to school on his own. I made a cup of tea all on my own.*
4 if you get your own back on someone, you do something bad to them because they have done something bad to you

own *verb*
owns, owning, owned
1 to have something that belongs to you according to the law, usually something you have bought that is important *My parents own their flat but don't own a car. Do you own a dog?*
2 to own up is to say it is true that you have done something wrong *Come on, own up to breaking the window.*

owner *noun* owners
someone who owns something, usually something important such as a house, flat, car or dog

ownership *noun*
when you own something, usually something important that you have bought *In this part of the country, there's a lot of home ownership* (people own their own homes).

ox *noun* oxen
an adult male cow, used especially in the past for doing heavy work on farms, for example pulling carts

oxygen *noun*
a gas in the air that has no colour, taste or smell. People and animals need oxygen to breathe, and plants and trees need it to grow.

oyster *noun* oysters
a shellfish that you can eat. It lives in a rough shell made up of two parts that fit tightly together. Some types of oysters produce pearls (small white balls used in jewellery).

Oyster card *noun* Oyster cards
(trademark)
a small plastic card used as a way of paying to travel on buses, trains and the underground in London. You continue using the card by topping it up (adding more money), for example online.

oz
short for **ounce** or **ounces**

ozone *noun*
1 a poisonous gas that is a type of oxygen. It has a strong smell but no colour.
2 the ozone layer is an area of ozone high above the earth and all around it. It protects the earth from the harmful effects of the sun.

ORIGIN from Greek *ozein* 'to smell'

p P

ORIGIN the letter P has changed its shape completely since it started life in the Phoenician alphabet as a symbol like an upside-down J or a curved hook facing left. The letter was called *pe* (pronounced 'pay'), which meant 'mouth', even though it looked nothing like a mouth. When the letter passed into the early Roman alphabet, the curved part of the hook was turned to face right but still left open. Eventually the Romans decided to close the loop – perhaps to make P look more like B, which has a similar sound – producing the P shape we use today.

p
short for **penny** or **pence**

pace *noun*
1 (*plural* **paces**) a step that you take in walking or running *Take two paces forward.*
2 (*plural* **paces**) the distance covered by a step *She was standing a few paces away from me.*
3 the speed at which someone or something moves *Dad was walking at a fast pace.*
4 the speed at which something happens or is done *The pace of life is slow in our village.*
5 if someone or something keeps pace with someone or something else, they make the same progress or move just as fast

pace *verb*
paces, pacing, paced
1 to walk around a small area, for example going in one direction and then the other, often because you are worried or waiting for something *Dad was pacing up and down the room waiting for the phone to ring.*
2 to pace yourself is to do something at the correct speed, not too fast or too slowly, so that you can do it properly

pacemaker *noun* **pacemakers**
a small piece of medical equipment put into someone's chest to make sure that their heart beats in a regular way

Pacific *noun*
the Pacific or Pacific Ocean is the sea that separates Asia and Australia from North and South America **Pacific** *adjective*

pacifier *noun* **pacifiers**
a small rubber object that a baby sucks to make him or her feel better

> **SYNONYM** dummy

pacifism *noun*
a belief that people should not fight in wars because wars are always wrong

pacifist *noun* **pacifists**
someone who believes in pacifism
pacifist *adjective*

pacify *verb*
pacifies, pacifying, pacified
to stop someone from feeling angry or upset and make them feel happier and more relaxed

pack *verb*
packs, packing, packed
1 to put things into a bag, suitcase, box or other container so that they can be carried or sent somewhere *My brother has packed his clothes into his backpack. I packed up my things and left. We're going on holiday but we haven't packed yet. The parcel is packed and can be taken to the post office.*
2 if people pack a place or pack into a place, they fill it completely *Hundreds of fans packed the cinema to watch the film.*
3 if someone packs people into a place, they fill it completely with them *The teacher managed to pack more than 30 children into our small classroom.*
4 if someone packs in a lot of something, they do a lot of it in a short amount of time *We packed a lot of sightseeing into our week in Paris.*
5 (*informal*) if someone packs something in or up, they stop doing it *My brother hated his job so he packed it in* (or *up*). *Pack it in* (stop annoying me) *– I'm trying to work!*
6 (*informal*) if a piece of equipment or a car packs up, it stops working
7 (*informal*) if someone in a job packs up, they finish work at the end of the day

pack *noun* **packs**
1 a group or collection of things, for example things tied or wrapped together and sold *a pack of envelopes*
2 a group of documents *an information pack*
3 a group of wild animals that live or hunt together *a pack of wolves*
4 the complete number of 52 playing cards *a pack of cards*

> **SYNONYM** deck

5 a bag that you carry on your back

> **SYNONYM** backpack

6 a group of boys who belong to the Scouts or girls who belong to the Guides *a Cub pack; a Brownie pack*
7 a group of people that you do not like or respect *a pack of thieves*

package *noun* **packages**
1 an object or objects wrapped in paper and usually sent by post

> **SYNONYM** parcel

2 a number of things, for example ideas or products, that are offered all together as a group *My laptop came with a software package that included several useful programs.*

packaging *noun*
the materials containing or wrapped around products sold in shops, for example cardboard boxes, plastic bags or trays, or pieces of paper

packed *adjective*
1 full of people *a packed bus*

> **SYNONYM** crowded

2 if someone is packed, they have packed up their belongings and are ready to take or send them somewhere
3 a packed lunch is a light meal, such as sandwiches and a drink, that you carry with you in a lunchbox or bag, for example to school or on an outing

packet *noun* **packets**
a small paper, cardboard or thin plastic box or bag containing a number of similar things *a packet of crisps; a packet of cereal*

packing *noun*
the action of packing things up, such as your belongings, so that they are ready to be taken or sent somewhere *I'll do the packing tomorrow.*

pact *noun* **pacts**
an agreement between two or more people or groups

pad *noun* **pads**
1 a number of pieces of paper fixed together at the top or side, used for writing or drawing on *a sketch-pad*
2 a small piece of soft material, for example for protecting or cleaning something *a shin pad* (for protecting the legs, for example in football); *a cotton wool pad* (used for example for cleaning a wound); *an ink pad* (for pressing a rubber stamp onto)
3 a place where helicopters land and take off, often on top of a building

> **SYNONYM** helipad

4 a place for launching something such as a rocket or satellite into space

> **SYNONYM** launch pad

pad *verb*
pads, padding, padded
1 to put soft material in or on something *My shoes are padded with foam to make them more comfortable.*
2 to walk somewhere with small quiet steps
3 if someone pads something out, such as a piece of writing, they make it longer by adding words that are not useful or necessary

padded *adjective*
with soft material inside, often a layer of it for protection *a padded chair; a cyclist's padded helmet*

padding *noun*
1 soft material, for example for protecting something or making something more comfortable
2 unnecessary words added to something such as a piece of writing just to make it longer

paddle *verb*
paddles, paddling, paddled
1 to walk about in water that isn't very deep with no shoes or socks on *Children were having fun paddling in the sea.*
2 if someone paddles a boat, they move it through the water using a paddle
3 a paddling pool is a very small swimming pool for young children to play in. A very common type is made of plastic and must be filled with air before you can use it.

paddle – pal

paddle *noun*
1 (plural **paddles**) a short pole with a flat part at one end called a blade, used for moving a small boat such as a canoe through the water. You hold the paddle in both hands and it is not supported by the side of the boat. A kayak paddle has flat parts at both ends.
compare: **oar**
2 when you walk about in water that isn't very deep *We took our shoes and socks off and went for a paddle.*

paddock *noun* **paddocks**
a small field where horses are kept

paddy *noun* **paddies**
a paddy or paddy field is a field where rice is grown in water

padlock *noun* **padlocks**
a metal lock for fastening things such as bicycles, gates and doors. It has a bar shaped like an upside-down U that opens and closes with a key or when particular numbers are chosen on a dial (round part).

pagan ['pay-gern'] *noun* **pagans**
someone who doesn't believe in any of the main religions of the world (especially in the past) **pagan** *adjective*

page *noun* **pages**
1 one of the pieces of paper that make up something such as a book, newspaper or magazine *Someone tore out a page from my exercise book.*
2 one side of one of the pieces of paper in something such as a book, newspaper or magazine *Turn to page 25.*
3 the words or images that you can see at one time on a computer screen or that make up one part of a computer document or website *a web page*
4 in medieval times, a page was a boy who worked as a servant

page *verb*
pages, paging, paged
1 to call someone such as a doctor or nurse by sending a signal to their pager

SYNONYMS **to bleep, to beep**

2 to call someone in a public place using a loudspeaker (equipment that makes sounds louder)
3 to press a key on a computer to go forward or back through something such as a document or website, one page at a time *I paged down a few times until I reached the end of the story.*

pageant ['paj-ernt'] *noun* **pageants**
a large public event such as a procession, show or concert at which people wear costumes from a particular time in history and celebrate important things and people from the past

pageantry *noun*
the special traditions, costumes, shows, music and processions connected with pageants

pager *noun* **pagers**
a small piece of electronic equipment that you carry around. It makes a sound to tell you that you must phone someone.

SYNONYMS **bleeper, beeper**

pagoda ['per-goh-der'] *noun* **pagodas**
a tall building, for example in China or Japan, used especially by Buddhists to celebrate their religion. Each floor has a separate roof that sticks out and is curved and decorated.

paid
past tense and past participle of **pay**

paid *adjective*
1 used for describing how much money someone gets for doing their job *Doctors are well paid* (get a lot of money). *My brother is a badly paid office worker.*
2 used for describing something that you are given money for *paid work; paid holidays*

pail *noun* **pails**
a container with an open top and a handle, used for example for carrying liquids

SYNONYM **bucket**

pain *noun*
1 (plural **pains**) an unpleasant feeling in your body caused by an illness or medical problem or by something bad done to you, for example something or someone hitting you, cutting your skin or breaking a bone *stomach pains; He's in pain* (he has a pain or pains somewhere).
2 very great sadness *It's hard to describe the pain Ben suffered when his puppy died.*
3 if someone takes pains, they make a lot of effort, for example to do something or to do it properly *Our teacher took pains to explain how the solar system works. I took great pains over this week's homework.*
4 (informal) if you say someone is a pain (or a pain in the neck), you mean they are very annoying

pain *verb*
pains, paining, pained
if something pains you, it makes you very sad

painful *adjective*
1 if a part of your body is painful, you feel a pain in it
2 if something such as a cut, injection or knock on the head is painful, it gives you pain
3 making you feel very sad *a painful memory*
4 making you feel ashamed *It was painful watching our team lose the match.*
5 very difficult *It was very painful for my mum to go back to the country where she was born.*

painfully *adverb*
1 in a way that causes pain *He was squeezing my hand painfully.*
2 extremely, in a way that shows how bad you think something is *painfully slow progress; Charlie looks painfully thin.*

painkiller *noun* **painkillers**
a medicine, such as aspirin, used for making a pain less strong or making it go away

painless *adjective*
1 not giving you any pain *a painless injection*
2 not causing you any difficulties *Living in France is a painless way to learn French.*
painlessly *adverb*

painstaking *adjective*
very careful and giving great attention to small details *Building an Eiffel Tower with Lego took months of painstaking work.*
painstakingly *adverb*

paint *noun* **paints**
1 a liquid that you put on something, for example with a brush, to give it a colour *a tin of yellow paint*
2 paints are small pieces of dried paint or small tubes of paint that you use for painting pictures *a box of paints*
3 a paint program or paint software is a piece of software for making pictures on a computer using different colours

paint *verb*
paints, painting, painted
1 to put paint on something to change its colour *I painted my bike blue.*
2 to make something such as an image, line or sign using paint *A worker is painting yellow lines on the road.*
3 to make a picture using paints *Kareem painted a beautiful picture. George painted his sister sitting on a chair. Nisha paints very well.*

paintbox *noun* **paintboxes**
a box containing paints, often pieces of dried paint, for painting pictures

paintbrush *noun* **paintbrushes**
1 a brush used for painting pictures, for example with a long thin handle and a small mass of hairs at the end
2 a brush used for putting paint on something to change its colour, for example with a short thick handle and a thick or wide mass of hairs at the end

painter *noun* **painters**
1 an artist who makes pictures using paints
2 someone whose job is to paint rooms and buildings

painting *noun*
1 (plural **paintings**) a picture someone has painted
2 the skill or activity of painting pictures *Ava is good at painting. We do a lot of painting at school.*
3 the activity of painting things to change their colour *In our new flat we do all the painting ourselves.*

pair *noun* **pairs**
1 two things of the same kind that are used together *a pair of shoes; The chairs were arranged in pairs* (groups of two).
2 something made up of two similar parts joined together *a pair of trousers; a pair of scissors*
3 two people, especially when they do something together *You'll need to do this homework in pairs. What have you pair been up to?*
4 two animals of the same kind *We saw a pair of foxes.*

pajamas *noun plural*
the American spelling of **pyjamas**

Pakistan *noun*
a country in South Asia
Pakistani *adjective & noun*

pal *noun* **pals**
an informal word for a friend

ORIGIN from the English Gypsy word *phal* 'brother'

335

palace – panic-stricken

palace *noun* palaces
a large building that is the official home of a ruler such as a king, queen or president

palate ['pal-ert] *noun* palates
1 the top part of the inside of the mouth
2 someone's liking for particular types of food or drink *The restaurant serves food to suit every palate.*

pale *adjective* paler, palest
1 having less colour in your face than usual, for example because you're ill, worried, frightened or don't go out in the sun *You look very pale today. My face went pale when I saw him. Granddad has a pale complexion.*
2 used for describing light or a colour that is not very bright *the pale light of the moon; a pale blue dress*
paleness *noun*

SIMILES 'as pale as death' and 'as pale as a ghost' mean extremely pale (sense 1)

pale *verb*
pales, paling, paled
to become pale *His face paled when he saw me and he almost fainted.*

palette ['pal-it] *noun* palettes
1 a thin flat piece of wood or plastic with a curved shape that an artist holds in his or her hand and uses for mixing paints on. Palettes have a hole in them so they can be held easily.
2 the particular colours used by an artist
3 a tool in a computer program containing a selection of colours to choose from

pall *noun* palls
a thick cloud of something such as smoke or dust

pall *verb*
palls, palling, palled
to disappear or become less with time *My interest in classical music gradually palled.*

pallid *adjective*
pale in a way that does not look attractive or healthy *pallid skin*

pallor *noun*
the pale colour of something such as someone's face or skin, for example because of illness or worry

palm *noun* palms
1 the flat inside part of your hand between your wrist and fingers
2 a palm or palm tree is a tree that usually grows in hot countries. It has a thin trunk with large pointed leaves at the top but no branches. *a coconut palm*

palm *verb* (informal)
palms, palming, palmed
to palm something off is to get rid of it by giving or selling it to someone because you don't want it and because you don't think it's worth keeping *I palmed off my old mobile on my cousin.*

palmistry *noun*
telling what will happen to someone in the future by looking at the lines on the inside of their hands

palpable *adjective*
very easy to notice or feel *The excitement in the crowd was palpable.* **palpably** *adverb*

paltry *adjective*
used for describing something very small, especially an amount of money *I worked all day for a paltry £20.*

SYNONYM measly

pampas *noun plural*
1 a large area of flat land in the southern part of South America. The pampas are covered with grass and are very fertile (good for growing things).
2 pampas grass is a very tall grass with sharp leaves and white fluffy flowers that look like very large feathers

pamper *verb*
pampers, pampering, pampered
to treat a person or animal in a very kind way and make sure they have everything they need to be as happy and comfortable as possible *All her children are pampered.*

pamphlet *noun* pamphlets
a thin book with paper covers and just a few pages. It gives information or an opinion about something and is given away free.

ORIGIN from Middle French *Pamphilet* – the name given to a famous Latin love poem from the 12th century about someone called Pamphilus

pan *noun* pans
1 a round metal container with a handle, used for cooking things in *a frying pan*
2 the part of a toilet that is shaped like a big bowl
3 (informal) if something is or goes down the pan, it is or gets completely wasted or destroyed

pancake *noun* pancakes
1 a thin round food made from flour, milk and eggs and fried on both sides
2 Pancake Day is an informal name for Shrove Tuesday. It is the day before the start of the Christian period of Lent (a period lasting 40 days before Easter) when pancakes are often eaten.

panda *noun* pandas
a large animal with black and white fur that looks like a bear. Pandas eat bamboo leaves and stems and live in China.

pandemonium *noun*
a situation where everything is confused and people can no longer control their behaviour, for example they rush around noisily, shout or push *There was pandemonium in the building when the fire broke out.*

ORIGIN from *Pandæmonium* (Greek *pan* 'all' and *daimon* 'demon'), invented in the 17th century by John Milton to mean the capital of hell in his poem *Paradise Lost*

pander *verb*
panders, pandering, pandered
1 if someone panders to a person or group, they do whatever that person or group wants even if it is not reasonable *He said the government was pandering to rich people.*
2 if someone panders to something such as wishes, needs or tastes, they make sure they are dealt with and satisfied even if they are not reasonable

pane *noun* panes
1 a flat piece of glass in a window or door
2 an area of a computer window for looking at something, for example for previewing files or folders (looking at them before you open them)

panel *noun* panels
1 a long flat piece of wood, plastic, metal, glass or other material that forms a part of something larger, for example a door, fence, window or piece of equipment such as a computer or washing machine *Mum took off the side panel of the computer to add some more memory.*
2 a small group of people chosen to do a particular job such as make decisions, give advice, discuss important ideas and questions or take part in a quiz *a panel of experts; a panel of judges*
3 a board with things such as buttons, switches and instruments on it, used for controlling or checking something, for example a piece of equipment, car or plane *the control panel; an instrument panel*
4 a rectangular shape drawn in a dictionary or reference book, like the LANGUAGE EXTRA panels and other panels in this book. They give information to help you understand something such as how to use a particular word.

panellist *noun* panellists
one of a group of people chosen to do something such as make a decision, give advice or take part in a discussion or quiz

pang *noun* pangs
1 a sudden strong feeling of something unpleasant or sad *a pang of jealousy*
2 a sudden strong pain *a pang of hunger*

panic *noun*
1 a sudden feeling of fear that people get, especially when there are many people together in one place, that makes them unable to control their behaviour *Panic spread through the crowd and everyone started shouting, pushing and rushing around.*
2 a sudden feeling of great worry that someone has when they don't know how to deal with a particular situation and so cannot behave normally *Josh is in a panic about his exams.*

panic *verb*
panics, panicking, panicked
1 if people panic, they suddenly feel very frightened and can no longer control their behaviour so they do things such as rush around, shout and push *The audience panicked when the lights suddenly went out.*
2 if someone panics, they feel very worried and can no longer behave normally because they don't know how to deal with a particular situation *The exams are next week and I'm beginning to panic.*

panicky *adjective*
an informal way of saying very worried or frightened *I'm getting a bit panicky.*

panic-stricken *adjective*
1 very frightened *Panic-stricken crowds were running in all directions.*
2 very worried *Tom looks panic-stricken – he has to hand in his homework today and he hasn't finished it.*

336

panorama – paradox

panorama *noun* **panoramas**
a view where you can see over a very large area, for example of the countryside or a city

ORIGIN from Greek *pan* 'all' and *horama* 'view'. The word was invented in the 18th century by Irish painter Robert Barker to describe his long paintings of views of Edinburgh.

panoramic *adjective*
showing a very large area *a panoramic view; a panoramic photo*

pansy *noun* **pansies**
a small garden plant with flowers of many different colours that are made up of large round petals

pant *verb*
pants, panting, panted
1 to breathe very fast with an open mouth, for example after running or doing exercise
2 to say something while you are panting *'I just can't run any more,' he panted.*

panther *noun* **panthers**
1 a leopard (big wild animal of the cat family) that has black fur and lives mainly in Africa
2 a jaguar (big wild animal of the cat family) that has black fur and lives mainly in Central and South America

panties *noun plural*
underwear that girls and women wear to cover the lower part of the body from the hips to the top of the legs

SYNONYM knickers

panto *noun* **pantos**
an informal word for a pantomime

pantomime *noun* **pantomimes**
a play for children with music, singing and lots of silly jokes. Most pantomimes are based on fairy stories and are performed in the theatre around Christmas time.

pantry *noun* **pantries**
a small room for storing food, usually near a kitchen

pants *noun plural*
1 underwear that covers the lower part of the body from the hips to the top of the legs
2 the American word for trousers

papa *noun* **papas**
an informal word for a father

paper *noun*
1 a material made into very thin sheets, used for many things such as writing, printing, drawing and painting on, wrapping things in or making things with. It is made from crushing fibres (threads) from wood and cloth. *Write your address on a piece of paper. Dad was wearing a paper hat.*
2 (*plural* **papers**) a single sheet of paper *There were papers all over the floor.*
3 (*plural* **papers**) large folded sheets of paper printed with news stories and pictures

SYNONYM newspaper

4 (*plural* **papers**) an exam or part of an exam *We have a maths paper this afternoon.*
5 paper for covering the walls of a room *The paper in Gran's house is old-fashioned.*

SYNONYM wallpaper

6 papers are official documents such as a passport *The police asked for my papers.*

ORIGIN from Latin *papyrus* and Greek *papyros*, used for describing the writing material from ancient Egypt that was made from the papyrus plant (a tall plant that grows in water and is similar to grass)

paper *verb*
papers, papering, papered
to cover a wall or room with wallpaper

paperback *noun* **paperbacks**
a book with a soft paper cover

ANTONYM hardback

paperboy *noun* **paperboys**
a boy who delivers newspapers to people's homes, usually early in the morning

LANGUAGE EXTRA also spelt *paper boy*

paperclip *noun* **paperclips**
a small piece of wire bent into the shape of two loops, used for holding pieces of paper together

LANGUAGE EXTRA also spelt *paper clip*

paper girl *noun* **paper girls**
a girl who delivers newspapers to people's homes, usually early in the morning

paper round *noun* **paper rounds**
the job of delivering newspapers to people's homes, usually early in the morning

paperwork *noun*
an activity or part of a job connected with paper documents, for example filling in forms, writing letters or reports and keeping copies

papier-mâché ['pap-yay mash-ay] *noun*
paper mixed with glue or with flour and water, used for making models or objects *a papier-mâché mask*

ORIGIN from French *papier mâché* 'chewed paper'. French people were the first in Europe to make papier-mâché when it came to France from China in the 17th century.

paprika *noun*
a red powder made from peppers (type of vegetable) that are dried (water has been removed from them). It is used for giving a flavour to food, often a strong flavour.

papyrus ['per-pie-rers'] *noun*
1 a plant like very tall grass. It grows in water in hot countries.
2 a type of paper that was made from this plant by the ancient Egyptians

parable *noun* **parables**
a simple story that teaches an important lesson about right and wrong or an important religious idea

paracetamol *noun*
1 a medicine that reduces pain or fever
2 (*plural* **paracetamols**) a tablet (round pill) or capsule (small tube) of this medicine

parachute *noun* **parachutes**
a large piece of special cloth attached with strings to a person's back or to an object. It opens into the shape of a big umbrella when dropped from an aircraft to allow the person or object to come down slowly and safely to the ground.

ORIGIN from French *parachute*. The word was invented in the 18th century by Jean-Pierre Blanchard, a balloonist (flyer in a gas balloon), to mean 'something that protects against a fall' (*para* 'against' and *chute* 'fall').

parachute *verb*
parachutes, parachuting, parachuted
1 to jump from an aircraft using a parachute
2 to drop something or someone from an aircraft with a parachute

parachutist *noun* **parachutists**
someone who jumps from an aircraft using a parachute

parade *noun* **parades**
1 a large group of people walking or riding in vehicles through a town or village to celebrate an event. People often play music and wear colourful clothes and costumes from a particular place or time in history. *We went to see the St Patrick's Day parade in Dublin.*
2 a group of soldiers marching together through a public place, often with music playing, as a way of celebrating something
3 if soldiers are on parade, they march or stand in front of important people who check them carefully
4 a row of shops. (This word is often used as a street name.) *Queen's Parade*

parade *verb*
parades, parading, paraded
1 to walk, march or ride in vehicles to celebrate an event *Crowds paraded through the streets of Edinburgh.*
2 to walk through the streets because you are not happy about something *Angry teachers paraded down The Mall and into Trafalgar Square.*
3 to walk around so that people will look at you *Lucy was parading around the playground in her fancy new dress.*
4 if soldiers parade in front of important people, they march and practise exercises

paradise *noun*
1 a place or situation of complete happiness *Lying on the beach is my dad's idea of paradise.*
2 a place that has everything you could wish for *This store is a toy lover's paradise.*
3 in some religions, paradise is a place where good people go after they die

ORIGIN from Greek *paradeisos* 'garden' or 'park', which came from the Persian word *pairidaeza* 'enclosed area'

paradox *noun* **paradoxes**
a situation (or something that someone says) that is difficult to understand because it includes ideas or facts that are very different *It's a paradox that such a famous film star can't find a job.*

paradoxical *adjective* **paradoxically** *adverb*

paraffin – park

paraffin *noun*
a clear liquid with a very strong smell, used as a fuel for heating or in lamps. It comes from petroleum (a thick liquid from under the ground).

paragraph *noun* **paragraphs**
a short part of a piece of writing consisting of one or more sentences that deal with one particular idea. Every paragraph begins on a new line.

Paraguay ['pa-rer-gwye] *noun*
a country in South America
Paraguayan *adjective & noun*

parakeet *noun* **parakeets**
a brightly coloured bird like a small parrot that people sometimes keep as a pet. Budgerigars are a type of parakeet.

parallel *adjective*
if two or more lines or objects are parallel, they go in the same direction and the distance between them always stays the same so that the lines or objects never meet. Parallel lines can be straight, curved or circular. Railway tracks have both straight and curved parallel lines. *These two streets run parallel to each other.*

parallel *noun* **parallels**
1 used for talking about different things that are similar to each other *The police said there were parallels between the two crimes.*

> **SYNONYM** similarity

2 if you draw a parallel between two things or people, you make a comparison between them

> **LANGUAGE EXTRA** be careful to spell *parallel* with *ll* followed by *l*. The spelling *paralell* is wrong.

parallelogram *noun* **parallelograms**
a flat shape with four straight sides. Opposite sides are parallel to each other, have the same length and can be sloping or not sloping. If the opposite sides are not sloping, the parallelogram is a rectangle or square.

Paralympics ['pa-rer-lim-piks] *noun plural*
an international sports competition for people with a physical disability. It happens once every four years, in a different country each time. It takes place after the Olympic Games in the same country.

> **LANGUAGE EXTRA** also called the *Paralympic Games*

paralyse *verb*
paralyses, paralysing, paralysed
1 if something such as an illness or accident paralyses someone, it makes them unable to move all or part of their body *My uncle was paralysed in a car accident.*
2 if something such as fear paralyses someone, it makes them unable to move, speak or behave normally *As the footsteps approached, we were paralysed with fear.*
3 if something paralyses something such as a place, system or organisation, it stops it from operating properly *Snow completely paralysed London for a whole week.*

paralysis ['per-ral-er-siss] *noun*
1 when you are not able to move all or part of your body, for example because of an illness or accident
2 when something is not able to operate normally *They are trying to avoid paralysis on the trains.*

paramedic *noun* **paramedics**
someone whose job is to give medical treatment to sick and injured people but who does not have the same skill as a doctor or nurse

parapet *noun* **parapets**
a low wall that runs along the edge of something such as a roof, balcony or bridge, for example to stop someone from falling off

paraphernalia ['pa-rer-fer-nayl-ee-er] *noun*
all the objects and equipment needed for a particular activity

> **ORIGIN** from Latin *parapherna* 'things belonging to a married woman'

paraphrase *noun* **paraphrases**
a sentence or expression that means the same as another sentence or expression but uses different words to make it easier to understand or shorter *We didn't understand what the author meant so our teacher gave us a paraphrase.*

paraphrase *verb*
paraphrases, paraphrasing, paraphrased
to repeat something using different words, for example to make it easier to understand or shorter

parasite *noun* **parasites**
an animal or plant that lives on or inside another animal or plant of a different type and gets all its food from it
parasitic *adjective*

> **ORIGIN** from Greek *parasitos* 'someone who eats at someone else's table' (from *para* 'beside' and *sitos* 'grain' or 'food')

parasol *noun* **parasols**
1 a light umbrella for protection against the sun. You hold it over your head when walking or standing.
2 a large heavy umbrella for protection against the sun. It is fixed to the ground on a beach or put over a table. *a beach parasol*

> **ORIGIN** from Italian *parasole*, from *para* 'against' and *sole* 'sun'

paratroops *noun plural*
soldiers who have been trained to jump out of planes using parachutes
paratrooper *noun*

parcel *noun* **parcels**
an object or objects wrapped in paper and usually sent by post

parched *adjective*
1 very dry *parched land*; *parched lips*
2 very thirsty

parchment *noun*
1 a material made from the dried skin of some animals such as calves or goats, used in the past for writing on
2 a type of thick paper that looks like animal parchment because of its pattern of light areas and slightly darker ones

pardon *interjection*
1 a polite way of asking someone to repeat something because you didn't hear or understand
2 a polite way of saying sorry, for example after making a rude sound with your body such as burping
3 used for showing someone that they've said something you didn't like *'Your brother's an idiot.' – 'Pardon?'*

pardon *verb*
pardons, pardoning, pardoned
1 to forgive someone for something, or for saying or doing something *Pardon the mess – I haven't tidied my room today. Pardon me for interrupting.*
2 to allow someone who has committed a crime and is in prison to go free *The thief was pardoned by the King.*

pardon *noun* **pardons**
1 a decision or order from someone important such as a king or president to pardon someone
2 *I beg your pardon?* used for asking someone to repeat something because you didn't hear or understand
3 *I beg your pardon!* used for saying sorry, for example if you bump into someone

parent *noun* **parents**
your parents are your mother and father

parental ['per-ren-terl] *adjective*
connected with parents *parental responsibilities*

parenthesis ['per-ren-ther-siss] *noun*
parentheses ['per-ren-ther-seez]
1 extra information that you add to a sentence, for example if you want to provide an explanation or opinion. It is separated from the main part of the sentence by brackets, dashes or commas, as in 'He phoned me (three weeks later) to say sorry.'
2 one of a pair of round punctuation marks that look like this ( ). It is also called a bracket.

parenthood *noun*
being a parent and looking after a child or children

parish *noun* **parishes**
1 a small area in England with its own council (group of people who control public services)
2 among Christians, a parish is an area with its own church and priest

parishioner *noun* **parishioners**
1 someone who lives in a parish
2 a Christian who goes to a particular church in a parish

park *noun* **parks**
1 a large area of land in a town with grass, flowers and trees in it, where people go to relax, walk, run or play games. Parks are usually surrounded by a wall or fence. *a park keeper* (someone in charge of a park)
2 an area of land surrounding a large house in the countryside

338

park–particular

park verb
parks, parking, parked
1 to leave a vehicle somewhere for a certain time *Dad parked the car outside the school. We can't find a place to park.*
2 to move a vehicle carefully into a place where it can be left for a certain time *My mum is good at parking.*
3 (informal) to put yourself or something in a particular place, especially when this annoys someone *She parked herself right in front of me and I couldn't see the screen.*

parka noun parkas
a long jacket with a hood

parking noun
1 leaving or being able to leave a vehicle somewhere *Parking is difficult here on a Saturday. No parking* (sign saying no-one can park here).
2 the skill of moving a vehicle carefully into a place where it can be left *Parking in a small space isn't easy.*
3 the place where a vehicle can be left *There's plenty of parking over there. Is this a parking space?*

parking lot noun parking lots
an outside area, especially in the US, with spaces for people to leave their cars

LANGUAGE EXTRA in the UK, it is usually called a *car park*

parking meter noun parking meters
a piece of equipment in a public place that someone puts money into so that they can leave their car somewhere for a certain period of time

parking ticket noun parking tickets
an official document put on the windscreen of a vehicle to tell the driver that he or she must pay a fine (money as a punishment) for parking in the wrong place or for too long

parliament ['par-ler-mernt'] noun
1 (plural **parliaments**) a group of people in some countries who make laws for their country
2 Parliament is the group of people in the UK who make the laws. It consists of the House of Commons (politicians chosen by the people) and the House of Lords (politicians chosen by the government).
3 (plural **parliaments**) the period of time that a parliament exists for
4 the place where a parliament meets *There was a big protest outside the French parliament.*

parliamentary adjective

parlour noun parlours
1 a shop that sells a particular type of thing *a pizza parlour*
2 an old-fashioned word for a room in a house where people sit and relax

parody noun parodies
something such as a book, play, film or poem, or an action done by someone, that copies someone else's style in a way that is meant to be funny *This play is a parody of Shakespeare's 'Hamlet'. The comedian did a parody of the US president.*

parody verb
parodies, parodying, parodied
to copy the style of something or someone in a way that is meant to be funny

parole ['per-rohl'] noun
special permission for a prisoner to be let out of prison early. He or she must agree to behave well in order to remain free. *He was released on parole after six months.*

parrot noun parrots
a brightly coloured bird with a very strong curved beak. Some parrots can copy the human voice. Parrots live in many of the hot countries of the world.

parsley noun
a plant with curly or flat green leaves, used for making food taste better or for decorating food

parsnip noun parsnips
a long hard pointed vegetable similar to a carrot but with a yellow-white colour. Parsnips grow in the ground.

part noun parts
1 some of a particular thing but not the whole of it *I threw away the bad part of the banana. Parts of Mohammed's homework are brilliant.*
2 one of the separate things that the whole of something is made up of *This part of the laptop is where the battery goes. What part of town do you live in?*
3 a part in a play or film is the character that an actor plays, or all the words and actions of a character in a play or film *Who wants to play the part of the wicked witch? I had a small part in our school play.*
4 a piece in a car or machine that is needed to make it work *My dad can't get parts for his old car.*
5 used for showing that someone or something belongs to a group *Ben wants to be a part of our football team.*
6 used for showing that something or someone is connected with something, or used about the influence that something or someone has on something *Alan confessed to his part in stealing the money. My grandparents play an important part in my life. Luck played no part in our team's victory.*
7 to take part in something is to do or be in an activity together with other people, for example a race, competition or conversation *Daniel always takes part when there's a class quiz.*
8 **the best part of** or **the better part of** most of *I've wasted the best part of an hour looking for my glasses.*

part verb
parts, parting, parted
1 if people part, they say goodbye and leave each other *We parted at the railway station.*
2 if you are parted from someone, you are separated from them and not allowed to be with them *He's only four and doesn't like to be parted from his mother.*
3 if two sides of something part, or if someone parts them, they move away from each other *The curtains parted and the actors walked onto the stage.*
4 if you part your hair, you make a straight line in it (called a parting) by combing or brushing it in opposite directions
5 if you part with something, you give it to someone although you want to keep it

part adverb
used for saying that someone or something is both of the things you mention *My mum is part English and part American.*

partial adjective
1 used for describing just a part of something and not the whole of it and for showing that there is more to come or to be done *a partial payment; Dad has made a partial recovery.*

ANTONYM complete

2 if you are partial to something, you like it *He's partial to oat biscuits.*
3 showing that you prefer someone to someone else *A judge should not be partial.*

partiality noun
a partiality for something is a liking for it

partially adverb
not completely *You're partially to blame.*

participant noun participants
someone who does an activity with other people

participate verb
participates, participating, participated
to take part in an activity with other people or an activity that other people also do *I don't participate much in sport.*

participation noun

participle noun participles
a part of a verb that is used with the verbs 'to have' or 'to be' to form tenses or to make adjectives

LANGUAGE EXTRA there are two *participles* in English.
The *present participle* ends in -ing (*running, growing*) and is used in present and past tenses, for example *I am running* and *it was growing*.
The *past participle* usually ends in -ed (*looked, danced*) but often has other endings too (*learnt, eaten, been, gone*) or the main stem of the verb is changed (*begun, sung*). It is used in past tenses, for example *I have looked* and *it was eaten*.
Both participles can be used as adjectives, for example *a frightened dog*, *a growing problem*.

particle noun particles
1 a tiny amount of something *dust particles*
2 in science, a particle is a tiny part of an atom, for example an electron or neutron
3 in grammar, a particle is a word such as 'up' that is used with a verb, usually to give the verb a different meaning, as in 'My parents brought up two children.'

particular adjective
1 used for describing one thing or person (or one kind of thing or person) and no other one *I can't remember what I was doing at that particular time. What particular books have you read this year?*
2 used for describing something that is connected with one person or thing and no other one *Sanjay painted the picture in his own particular style.*

particularly–passage

3 used for describing something special or different from normal *Pay particular attention to what I'm going to say. Ben knows lots of people but George is his particular friend.*
4 if someone is particular about something, they pay a lot of attention to it because they like it to be just right *She's very particular about what she eats.*

SYNONYM fussy

5 in particular especially or special *Fran likes lots of subjects, in particular English. I'm not doing anything in particular on Saturday.*

particularly adverb
1 used for giving special importance to a word *I'm particularly upset about the broken window. 'Did you enjoy the match?' – 'Not particularly.'* (not really)
2 used for saying something is more true about one particular thing or person than it is about others *Everyone's homework was good, particularly Kareem's.*

SYNONYM especially

particulars noun plural
1 details about something or someone *Email us if you want further particulars.*
2 someone's particulars are details such as their name and address

parting noun **partings**
1 a straight line that you make in your hair by combing or brushing it in opposite directions
2 when people say goodbye and leave each other *a sad parting; They said a few parting words.*

partition noun
1 (plural **partitions**) something such as a wall or screen that divides a room into two parts
2 dividing something such as a country into separate parts

partly adverb
1 used for talking about a part of something but not the whole of it *The flag of that country is partly green but mainly red. The fish is only partly cooked.*
2 used for giving only one reason for something when there are other reasons too *I take the bus to school partly because I don't like walking.*
3 used when you mean between quite a lot and just a little bit *I was only partly aware of what was going on. Granddad is partly deaf.*
4 used when mentioning one person or thing when there are other people or things too *The bike belongs partly to my sister* (for example, it also belongs to my brother). *She gave a sigh, partly of relief.*

partner noun **partners**
1 one of two people who do an activity together, for example playing a game or sport, working or dancing
2 someone who is married to someone or who lives with them as though they are married
3 a person or group that someone is connected with, for example in business or politics

4 someone who owns a business with someone else

ORIGIN from Old French *parçon* 'sharing' or 'division'

partnership noun
when two people or groups do things together or work together in a friendly way *There's a close partnership between our school and Lakeside Junior.*

part of speech noun **parts of speech**
one of the groups that the words of a language belong to, depending on how they are used in a sentence. The parts of speech in English are noun, verb, adjective, adverb, pronoun, preposition, conjunction and interjection. In this dictionary the part of speech is shown for all headwords (words that you look up).

SYNONYM word class

partridge noun **partridges**
a bird with a large round body, short tail and small head. It is sometimes hunted for food or sport.

part-time adjective & adverb
for only some of the hours in a week that people normally work or study *My sister has a part-time job. My brother studies part-time.*

partway adverb & adjective
1 some of the distance to or from a place *The bus was going to Leeds but it broke down partway.*
2 some of the way through a period of time *We left partway through the film.*

party noun **parties**
1 a time when people come together to enjoy themselves, for example by eating, drinking and playing games and often to celebrate something *a birthday party; We're going to a fancy dress party* (wearing clothes to look like someone else).
2 a group of people who travel somewhere together or do an activity together *a party of schoolchildren; a search party* (looking for a missing person)
3 an organisation of people with the same political ideas. Parties fight against other parties to win votes in elections to control the government of a country, region or town. *the Labour and Conservative Parties*
4 a person or people connected with a matter of law such as a crime or argument between people *Who is the guilty party?*

party favour noun **party favours**
a small present you get for going to a party, for example a birthday party

partygoer noun **partygoers**
1 someone who goes to parties a lot
2 someone who is at a particular party

party pooper noun **party poopers** (informal)
someone who stops other people from having fun, for example by not wanting to take part in a game or activity

pass verb
passes, passing, passed
1 to go up to someone or something and then go past them *I passed my teacher in the street. We passed the Houses of Parliament on the bus.*

2 to catch up with and then go past a vehicle going in the same direction *A motorcycle passed us doing 70 miles an hour.*

SYNONYM to overtake

3 to go from one place to another *The train passes through Newcastle on its way to Edinburgh. Please move to let us pass.*
4 to move something from one place to another *She passed her hand through her hair.*
5 to give something to someone *Can you pass me another cake?*
6 if you pass an exam or test, you are successful in it

ANTONYM to fail

7 if you pass the ball to someone in a game, you kick it or throw it to them
8 if time passes, it happens or it starts and then ends *Time passes slowly when you're standing in a queue. Three years passed before I saw him again.*
9 if you pass time, you spend time doing something *I passed the time reading and sunbathing.*
10 if something such as a pain or feeling passes, it goes away
11 to go beyond a certain date, number, amount or level *Don't eat food that has passed its sell-by date. The number of girls playing football has passed 50 for the first time.*
12 if a government or country or someone such as a president or king passes a law, they make it official so that people must obey it
13 to pass away is to die
14 to pass by is to go past or to go past something *We didn't go into the museum but we passed by. We passed by the museum without going in.*
15 to pass out is to faint, for example because you are ill, hot or hungry
16 to pass something round is to give it to someone in a group, who gives it to the next person, who does the same thing *Could you pass round the chocolates, please?*

pass noun **passes**
1 a pass in an exam or test is a successful result
2 an official document such as a card or ticket that allows you to do something such as get into a building or travel on a train or bus *My grandparents have a bus pass* (giving free travel on the buses).
3 the action of kicking or throwing the ball to someone in a game such as football
4 a path or road that goes between two mountains

passable adjective
not very good but good enough *The food was passable.*

passage noun **passages**
1 a long narrow area that connects rooms to each other or connects one building or place to another
2 a short part of a piece of writing such as a book or poem, or a short part of a piece of music
3 a way through somewhere *The soldiers cleared a passage through the jungle.*

passageway–pat

4 a tube in the body that air or liquid passes through
5 a journey, usually by sea
6 the passage of time is the slow action of time that passes

passageway *noun* **passageways**
a long narrow area that connects one room or building to another

passcode *noun* **passcodes**
a secret number or secret symbols that someone must use, for example to log into a website or online bank account

passenger *noun* **passengers**
someone who travels in a road vehicle, train, ship or plane but who is not the driver and not one of the people who work on it or who are in charge of it

passer-by *noun* **passers-by**
someone who happens to be walking past a place, often when something unusual happens

passing *adjective*
1 used for describing someone who happens to be passing by *Dad stopped a passing motorist to ask for help.*
2 used for describing something that lasts only a short time *a passing interest*

passion *noun* **passions**
1 a very strong feeling of love towards someone
2 a very strong feeling such as anger *She spoke with passion about hungry children in Africa.*
3 a feeling of liking something very much *He has a great passion for football.*
4 something that you like or like doing very much *Music is my dad's passion.*

passionate *adjective*
1 showing very strong feelings *a passionate speaker*
2 showing great liking for something *My brother is passionate about sport.*
3 used for describing something such as an interest or belief that is very strong *He has a passionate interest in music.*

passive *adjective*
1 letting things happen to you rather than doing anything or controlling a situation yourself *He was a passive victim of the attack.*
2 in grammar, the passive voice describes a verb where the subject of a sentence receives the action. In 'The email was written by Jack', the subject is 'the email' and 'was written' is a passive verb. The passive is formed from a part of the verb 'to be' (for example 'was') and a past participle (for example 'written').
compare: **active**

passively *adverb*
without doing anything or controlling a situation yourself *He just sat there passively watching.*

Passover *noun*
a Jewish festival in March or April that lasts seven or eight days. It celebrates the escape of the ancient Jews from Egypt where they were kept as slaves.

passport *noun* **passports**
a special book with your photo in it that you need to travel to another country. It gives information about who you are, for example your name, age and where you were born.

password *noun* **passwords**
1 a secret word (or letters and numbers put together) that you must type into a computer to be allowed to use the computer or a particular program or website
2 a secret word you must tell someone before they will let you into a building, area or room

past *preposition & adverb*
1 further on from a place *My cousin lives just past the post office.*
2 towards someone or something and then going further on *He caught up with the athlete in front and ran past him. The car drove past our house* (in front of it). *She walked past without stopping.*
3 further on from something such as a point in time, level or number *It's past my bedtime. The cheese is past its sell-by date. The tulips are past their best* (not as fresh or good as before). *I didn't get past page 6.*
4 used for talking about the time on the clock when you mean a certain number of minutes after the hour *It's ten past six.*
5 (informal) **past it** used for describing someone who is too old to do something

past *adjective*
1 used about the time just before now and up until the present *I've had a lot of homework in the past week.*
2 used about time that is finished *People's lives were very short in centuries past.*
3 used about something that happened or existed in the past *past achievements; past test papers*
4 used about the position or job that someone had in the past *She's a past winner of an Olympic gold medal.*
5 connected with the past tense *'Begun' is a past form of 'begin'.*

past *noun*
1 the time before the present time *In the past things were different.*
2 what happened to someone or something before the present time *He's proud of his past as a football player.*
3 in grammar, the past is another way of saying the past tense

pasta *noun*
an Italian food made from flour, water and often eggs. Pasta is sold either fresh or dried (hard and with the water removed). It is made into many different shapes such as spaghetti (long thin pieces), macaroni (small tubes) and lasagne (wide layers).

ORIGIN from Italian and Latin *pasta* 'dough' or 'paste'

paste *noun*
1 a soft thick substance made by mixing water with a powder such as flour, usually to make a type of glue
2 a soft thick food made by crushing vegetables, fish, fruit or meat. It is added to other food or spread onto bread. *tomato paste; anchovy paste*

paste *verb*
pastes, pasting, pasted
1 to stick something with paste, usually paper onto another piece of paper
2 to insert a piece of text, an image or number into a computer file such as a document or spreadsheet *Press Control V to paste the missing word into your file.*

pastel *noun* **pastels**
1 a small coloured stick of a material like chalk, used for drawing with
2 a very light colour such as pale blue, green or pink

pastel *adjective*
having a very light colour *pastel blues*

pasteurised ['pahs-cher-ryzed] *adjective*
used for describing a liquid such as milk that is heated in a special way to kill harmful bacteria (tiny living things)

LANGUAGE EXTRA also spelt *pasteurized*

ORIGIN named after the 19th-century French chemist Louis *Pasteur*, who invented this method of making liquids safe to drink

pastille ['pas-terl] *noun* **pastilles**
a small round sweet, often containing a medicine for a sore throat

pastime *noun* **pastimes**
an activity you like doing when you're not studying or working, for example playing sports or reading

past participle *noun* **past participles**
a form of a verb used with the verbs 'to have' and 'to be' and as an adjective. You usually add '-ed' ('played') or '-d' ('danced') but there are other endings too ('learnt', 'eaten', 'been', 'gone') or the main stem of the verb is changed ('begun', 'sung'). It is used in past tenses (for example 'I have played' and 'it was eaten') and for making adjectives (as in 'a worried look').

pastry *noun*
1 a mixture of flour, water and fat that is rolled until it is flat and used for making the outside part of food such as pies. Food made with pastry is cooked in an oven.
2 (plural **pastries**) a small cake that is made from this mixture

past tense *noun* **past tenses**
a form of a verb that shows what happened or existed before the present time. It is usually formed by adding the endings '-ed', '-d' or '-t' to the main part of a verb ('I jumped', 'I have jumped'; 'I danced', 'I have danced'; 'I learnt', 'I have learnt') or by changing the main stem of a verb ('I sang', 'I have sung'; 'I went', 'I have gone').

pasture *noun* **pastures**
land covered with grass and small plants. It is used for keeping animals such as cows, sheep and horses, which eat the grass and plants.

pasty ['pas-tee] *noun* **pasties**
a small pie filled with meat, vegetables or cheese that is baked in an oven and eaten hot or cold. The most common type of pasty is a Cornish pasty, shaped like a semicircle and with meat and vegetables inside.

pasty ['pays-tee] *adjective* **pastier, pastiest**
used for describing someone's face or skin that looks pale and unhealthy

pat *verb*
pats, patting, patted
1 to touch a person or animal several times with the flat part of your hand in a gentle or friendly way

341

pat–patron

2 to touch something several times in a gentle way using something soft such as paper *Pat the tomatoes dry with a piece of kitchen roll.*

pat noun **pats**
1 a gentle touch with the flat part of your hand
2 a small flat piece of butter
3 **a pat on the back** praise that you give to someone for doing something good

patch noun **patches**
1 a small part of an area that is different from the rest *Our dog is grey with a few black patches. Dad has a bald patch* (a small part of his head that has no hair on it). *Be careful – there are icy patches* (small areas of ice on something such as a road or pavement).
2 a small piece of cloth that has been sewn over a hole in clothes or other material
3 a small piece of cloth for covering someone's injured eye *The soldier was wearing an eye patch.*
4 a small piece of ground for growing things, especially vegetables *a cabbage patch*
5 a small free computer program that repairs a problem with a piece of software *You can download the patch from the Microsoft website.*
6 a bad or difficult patch is a difficult period of time *Evie's dad is in hospital so she's going through a bad patch at school.*

patch verb
patches, patching, patched
1 to sew a small piece of cloth over a hole in clothes or other material *She was wearing patched jeans.*
2 to patch something up is to repair it quickly but not properly
3 if two people patch things up, they become friends again after an argument

patchwork noun
1 a sewing activity in which lots of small pieces of cloth, usually square pieces, are sewn together in a pattern to make something such as a quilt or cushion
2 a pattern or design of small pieces of cloth sewn together, or the things that are made in this way
3 a mixture of lots of different things

patchy adjective **patchier, patchiest**
1 existing only in some parts but not others *London will have patchy rain tomorrow.*
2 good in some parts but not in others *Service on the tube is patchy on Sundays.*
3 used for describing something that is only partly known *Details of what happened are patchy.*

pâté ['pat-ay] noun
a thick soft food made from meat, fish or vegetables that have been minced (cut up into tiny pieces). It is often spread on bread.

patent ['pay-ternt] or ['pat-ernt] noun **patents**
an official document that allows someone to make or sell something they have invented and stops anyone else from copying it
patent verb

paternal adjective
1 connected with being a father or with the qualities some people think a father should have *paternal feelings* (for example being kind and loving)
2 connected with your father's side of the family *Grandma Alice is my paternal grandmother.*

ORIGIN from Latin *pater* 'father'

paternity leave noun
a time when a father is allowed to be away from his job after his wife or partner has given birth to their baby

path noun **paths**
1 a narrow way that people walk or ride along, for example through a park *a garden path* (for example from the street to the front door of a house); *a cycle path* (for bicycles)
2 the direction that something moves in *Be careful, you're standing in the path of that bus! The scientists tracked the path of the satellite around the earth.*
3 a way through somewhere *The police cleared a path through the crowds.*
4 the full name of a computer file that shows where it is stored on a computer
5 a way that leads to a particular result *the path to success*

pathetic adjective
1 making you feel sad and upset, for example because a person or animal looks weak or helpless *The injured dog looked pathetic. We watched Ben struggling to finish the race – it was a pathetic sight.*
2 used for describing something that is bad or weak, for example because someone shows no effort or skill in doing it or making it better *a pathetic excuse; Your room is in a pathetic state! Yesterday's football match was pathetic.*
3 used for describing someone you feel no respect towards, for example because they behave badly *You're a liar and you're pathetic!*

pathetically adverb
1 in a way that makes you feel sad and upset *The baby was crying pathetically.*
2 in a way that makes you feel no respect, for example because someone can't do something properly *He really played pathetically* (badly) *in yesterday's match. She made a pathetically small effort.*

patience noun
1 the special quality of being able to wait for something without complaining or getting angry *Have patience and wait a bit longer.*
2 the special quality of being able to take plenty of time doing something difficult without getting angry or losing interest *You need lots of patience when teaching children. Dad lost his patience with me* (became angry with me).
3 a game played with cards by one person only

ORIGIN from Latin *patientia* 'acceptance of pain', from *pati* 'to suffer'

patient adjective
1 being able to wait for something without complaining or getting angry, especially when something takes a long time
2 taking the time to deal with a difficult situation without getting angry or losing interest, even if the difficulties keep happening *Our teacher is very patient with me although I'm no good at maths.*

SIMILES 'as patient as Job' (pronounced 'johb') means very patient. Job was a man in the Bible who was very patient in all his suffering. You can also say 'as patient as a saint'.

patient noun **patients**
1 someone who is receiving medical care by a doctor or nurse *a hospital patient; a cancer patient* (someone treated for cancer)
2 someone who uses the services of a particular doctor or dentist *All the members of our family are patients at the Plainview Medical Centre.*

patiently adverb
1 without complaining or getting angry *We were waiting patiently.*
2 in a way that shows you take the time to deal with a situation without getting angry or worried *He explained to me patiently what the author meant.*

patio ['pat-ee-oh] noun **patios**
an outside area with a stone or brick floor at the back of a house where you sit and relax

ORIGIN from Spanish *patio* 'courtyard' (open space surrounded by buildings or walls)

patriot ['pay-tree-ert] or ['pat-ree-ert] noun **patriots**
someone who loves their country
patriotism noun

patriotic ['pay-tree-ot-ik] or ['pat-ree-ot-ik] adjective
1 used about someone who loves their country
2 also used about something someone does or says *a patriotic speech*
patriotically adverb

patrol verb
patrols, patrolling, patrolled
if people such as soldiers, guards or the police patrol a place, they go round it to make sure there is no trouble *The shopping centre is patrolled by security guards.*

patrol noun **patrols**
1 a group of two or more people, vehicles or boats that go round a place to make sure there is no trouble *an army patrol; a patrol boat*
2 the action of patrolling a place *a routine patrol; Many soldiers were on patrol in the town centre.*
3 a small group of Scouts or Guides led by someone called a patrol leader

patron ['pay-trern] noun **patrons**
1 someone who helps and gives money to artistic people such as musicians, writers or painters, or to groups or organisations that people respect such as charities (groups that help people who need help)
2 someone who often buys from a particular shop or goes somewhere often, such as to a particular restaurant or club
patronage noun

patronise ['pay-trer-nyze' or 'pat-rer-nyze'] *verb*
patronises, patronising, patronised
1 to talk to someone as if you are better or more intelligent than they are

SYNONYM to talk down to

2 if someone patronises a place such as a shop or restaurant, they go there often

LANGUAGE EXTRA also spelt *patronize*

patron saint *noun* **patron saints**
a holy person who is believed by Christians to help or protect a particular place, group or activity *St Thomas Aquinas is the patron saint of students and teachers.*

patter *verb*
patters, pattering, pattered
if something patters against a surface, it makes short quiet sounds as it hits the surface many times *We heard the rain pattering against the window.*

patter *noun*
1 the sound of something making short quiet sounds as it hits a surface *I heard the patter of tiny feet running down the hallway.*
2 a way of speaking that is fast, often used by someone who wants to sell you something or by an entertainer such as a comedian or magician who wants to be funny

pattern *noun* **patterns**
1 lines, shapes or colours arranged in a regular way, for example used for decorating something such as a dress, a curtain or wallpaper
2 a group of things such as sounds, words or numbers arranged in a regular way *This poem by Wordsworth has a simple rhyming pattern.*
3 a particular way in which something usually happens or is done *The summer weather in England doesn't seem to follow a pattern.*
4 a drawing or shape that you copy in order to make something *a dress pattern*

paunch *noun* **paunches**
a fat stomach **paunchy** *adjective*

pauper *noun* **paupers**
an old-fashioned word for a very poor person

pause *verb*
pauses, pausing, paused
1 to stop doing something for a short time, such as talking, moving or working, before starting again *Chloe paused to catch her breath.*
2 if you pause something such as a film or piece of music, for example on a DVD player or computer, you press a button or click on an icon to make it stop playing for a short time

pause *noun* **pauses**
a short time when you stop doing something, such as talking, moving or working, before starting again

pave *verb*
paves, paving, paved
1 to cover an area of ground, for example a road or path, with hard materials such as concrete, blocks of stone or bricks *Our front garden has been paved over so my parents can park their car.*
2 if something paves the way for something else, it makes it easier for the other thing to happen

pavement *noun* **pavements**
a path with a hard surface at the side of a road, specially made for people to walk on

pavilion *noun* **pavilions**
1 a building on a sports ground for players to use, for example for changing their clothes or storing equipment
2 a building or tent at an outdoor event such as an exhibition
3 a building in a park or large garden for people to sit in

paving stone *noun* **paving stones**
a flat, often square, block of stone used for making surfaces to walk on such as paths, pavements and patios

paw *noun* **paws**
the foot of an animal, such as a cat, dog or bear, that has claws (curved nails)

paw *verb*
paws, pawing, pawed
if an animal paws something, it touches it with its paw

pawn *noun* **pawns**
1 the smallest and least important piece in the game of chess. Each player has eight pawns, which are all the same size and shape.
2 a person who is used and controlled by someone else

pawn *verb*
pawns, pawning, pawned
to leave an object with a pawnbroker, who gives you money for it

pawnbroker *noun* **pawnbrokers**
a shopkeeper who lends money to people when they leave an important object with him or her, for example a watch or ring. If the people do not pay the money back and pay extra money, the pawnbroker will sell the object and keep the money.

pay *verb*
pays, paying, paid
1 to give someone money when you buy something from them, for example in a shop or online *Please pay the cashier. You have to pay at the checkout.*
2 to give someone money when they do work for you *Dad paid the gardener £30 for cutting the grass. My brother's job doesn't pay very well* (he doesn't get much money).
3 if you pay for something, you give someone money in order to buy it *Have you paid for the ice cream?*
4 if someone pays something such as a bill, they pay the money they owe, for example to a person, company or government *Mum paid the phone bill. People who work must pay tax.*
5 if something pays, it does you good or helps you and is something that should be done *It pays to learn a foreign language if you want to be successful.*
6 if someone pays for something bad that they've done, someone else makes them suffer because of it *Dad made me pay for my mistake.*
7 used about something that you do, give or say *He paid me a compliment* (said kind words). *I paid Granddad a visit.*
8 if you pay attention, you listen or watch carefully or you take care over something or take care to read or obey something *Pay attention to what I say. Pay attention – there are cars coming! I wasn't paying attention to the instructions.*
9 if you pay something back, you give someone the money that you borrowed from them

pay *noun*
money someone gets for doing their job

payment *noun*
1 (*plural* **payments**) an amount of money that someone pays to someone else
2 the action of paying money *My sister is asking for payment of the money I owe her.*

PC *noun* **PCs**
1 a small or medium-sized computer for one person to use at home, at school or in an office
short for: personal computer
2 an ordinary police officer *PC Wilkins gave a talk at the school.*
short for: police constable

pdf *noun* **pdfs**
the ending of a computer filename. A .pdf file contains text or text and pictures. It can be opened on any computer and will always look the same.
short for: portable document format

PE *noun*
classes at school in which you do exercises and play sport
short for: physical education

pea *noun* **peas**
1 a small round green seed that you cook and eat as a vegetable. It grows inside a pod (long narrow container) on a climbing plant.
2 if two people are like two peas in a pod, they are very similar to each other

peace *noun*
1 a time when there is no war or violence in a country or region and when people live together in a friendly way *The two countries have made peace* (have agreed to stop fighting each other).
2 a place, situation or time in which everything is quiet and no-one bothers you or talks to you *I need peace and quiet to do my homework. Leave me in peace* (go away and leave me alone).
3 a time when you have no worries *You'll never have any peace unless you get me a bike.*

peaceful *adjective*
1 without any noise, activity or excitement *It's peaceful in the park. We spent a peaceful afternoon in the garden.*

SYNONYM quiet

2 without any violence *a peaceful demonstration*
3 without any worry or upset *He had a peaceful look on his face.*
peacefulness *noun*

peacefully *adverb*
1 without any violence *The demonstrators marched peacefully.*
2 in a friendly and happy way *People of different religions live together peacefully in India.*

peach–peel

3 without any noise, activity or excitement *We walked peacefully through the park.*
4 without any worry or upset *She was sleeping peacefully.*

peach *noun* **peaches**
a round juicy fruit with a soft yellow and red skin covered in tiny soft hairs. It has a big hard seed inside called a stone.

peacock *noun* **peacocks**
a large male bird with beautiful green and blue feathers on its tail that it can lift up and spread out like a fan. The feathers have patterns on them shaped like eyes. A female peacock is called a peahen.

peak *noun* **peaks**
1 the pointed part at the top of a mountain
2 the hard flat curved part that sticks out at the front of a cap (soft hat)
3 the highest level of something *The traffic reaches its peak around nine o'clock in the morning. Try to avoid the tube at peak times* (when most people travel).

peak *verb*
peaks, peaking, peaked
if something peaks, it reaches its highest level *In the summer, temperatures can peak at around 30 degrees Celsius.*

peaky *adjective* **peakier, peakiest**
pale and slightly ill *You look peaky today.*

peal *noun* **peals**
1 the sound made by large bells ringing
2 the sound of thunder or loud laughter

peal *verb*
peals, pealing, pealed
if bells peal, they make a loud ringing sound

LANGUAGE EXTRA be careful not to confuse *peal* with *peel* (to remove the skin of fruit or vegetables)

peanut *noun* **peanuts**
1 a small oval seed that you can eat. It grows under the ground inside a thin brown shell.
2 peanut butter is a soft thick food made by crushing peanuts that have been heated and dried (the water has been removed from them). It is often spread onto bread.
3 (informal) **peanuts** used for describing a tiny amount of money *My brother earns peanuts in his job.*

pear *noun* **pears**
a fruit with a round shape that gets narrower at the top. It is white on the inside and usually green, yellow or brown on the outside. Pears are usually eaten when they are soft and juicy.

pearl *noun* **pearls**
a small hard white and shiny ball produced inside the shells of some types of sea creatures called oysters. Pearls are used in jewellery, for example for making necklaces (strings worn around the neck).

pearly *adjective* **pearlier, pearliest**
white and shiny like a pearl *pearly teeth*

peasant *noun* **peasants**
someone who works on the land as a farmer, belongs to a low class in society and is usually poor. This word is usually used about someone from a poor country or someone who lived in the past.

344

peat *noun*
a type of soil made up of plants that have died. It is burnt as a fuel, for example to produce heat or electricity, or is put around plants in gardens to help them grow.

pebble *noun* **pebbles**
a small stone made smooth by water. You see pebbles on beaches and at the bottom of rivers.

pebbly *adjective*
containing lots of pebbles *a pebbly beach*

pecan ['pee-kan'] *noun* **pecans**
a long brown nut with an oval shape and long narrow spaces inside its surface. It grows in a thin smooth shell and has a sweet taste.

peck *verb*
pecks, pecking, pecked
1 if a bird pecks something or pecks at something, it hits it, picks it up or eats it with its beak
2 if someone pecks at their food, they eat small amounts of it, for example because they are not hungry

peck *noun* **pecks**
1 the action of pecking or a mark made by a bird when it pecks something
2 an informal word for a quick kiss

peckish *adjective*
an informal word for hungry

pecs *noun plural*
an informal word for the muscles of the chest
short for: pectorals

peculiar *adjective*
1 strange and unpleasant *What's that peculiar noise?*
2 used for describing something that is connected with a particular person or thing and no other one *Lydia got all the maths answers right but worked them out in her own peculiar way. These houses are peculiar to the north of Scotland.*

peculiarity *noun* **peculiarities**
1 a strange or particular quality that something or someone has and that other things or people do not
2 a strange habit or way of behaving

peculiarly *adverb*
1 in a strange or unpleasant way *You've been behaving peculiarly all day!*
2 used for giving special importance to a word or for saying something is very true about something or someone *It's a peculiarly difficult poem to read.*

pedal *noun* **pedals**
1 one of the two parts on a bicycle that you push round with your feet to make it go
2 a flat part that you press with your foot to make a piece of equipment or a vehicle do something such as start, move or stop *an accelerator pedal* (for example for making a car go faster); *a brake pedal* (for example for making a car stop)
3 a flat part on a piano that you press with your foot to make the sound change

pedal *verb*
pedals, pedalling, pedalled
to push round the pedals of a bicycle with your feet to make it go *You have to pedal harder when you go up a hill.*

peddle *verb*
peddles, peddling, peddled
if someone peddles things, they go to different places, such as streets, markets or people's houses, to try to sell them *An old man was peddling sun hats on the beach.*

pedestal *noun* **pedestals**
a tall thin post or structure that supports something such as a statue or table top

pedestrian *noun* **pedestrians**
someone who walks in a town or city, not someone who travels in a vehicle or rides a bicycle, for example

pedestrian *adjective*
1 used by people who walk in a town or city *a pedestrian bridge*
2 a pedestrian crossing is a place in a road where people can cross it safely. It has black and white stripes going across the road and vehicles must stop to allow people to cross.

pedigree *noun* **pedigrees**
1 the parents and other family members of an animal, or a list of them used for showing that the animal has been bred with good or special qualities
2 the pedigree of a person refers to his or her family members from the past and to his or her education and achievements, used for showing the good or special qualities of that person

pedlar *noun* **pedlars**
someone who goes to different places, such as streets, markets or people's houses, to try to sell small things

LANGUAGE EXTRA be careful not to use the spelling *peddler*, which is used in American English only

peek *verb*
peeks, peeking, peeked
1 to look at something or someone quickly, for example something you shouldn't see *Don't peek at the presents when I'm out of the room.*
2 if something peeks out, it sticks out slightly so that a bit of it can be seen *I saw someone's head peek out from behind a bush.*

peek *noun* **peeks**
a quick look at something or someone *Could I have a peek at your drawing?*

peel *noun*
the skin of a fruit such as a banana, apple or orange or of a vegetable such as a potato or onion, usually after it has been removed

peel *verb*
peels, peeling, peeled
1 to remove the skin from a fruit or vegetable, usually with a knife
2 if you peel something off, back or away, you hold one part of it and slowly pull it off, back or away from the thing that it is stuck to *Gently peel off the plaster on your leg* (or *peel the plaster off your leg*) *before having a bath.*
3 if something covering something else peels, it slowly comes off *The wallpaper is peeling away from the damp wall.*

peelings–penetrate

peelings *noun plural*
pieces of skin that have been removed from a fruit or vegetable *potato peelings*

peep *verb*
peeps, peeping, peeped
1 to look at something or someone quickly, for example when you don't want someone to see you *Grandma peeped through the curtains at the boys playing in the street.*
2 to appear from behind or under something *The sun was peeping out from behind the clouds.*

peep *noun* **peeps**
a quick look at something or someone

peer *verb*
peers, peering, peered
to look carefully, for example because something or someone is difficult to see or because you are interested in something *I peered at the road sign but I couldn't make out the words. The teacher peered over his glasses.*

peer *noun* **peers**
1 someone who is similar to someone else, for example is the same age or does the same activities *At school Kayla is very popular with her peers.*
2 someone who belongs to a very high rank in British society and who has a title such as 'Lord' or 'Lady'

peerage *noun* **peerages**
1 the rank of peer in British society
2 a special honour given to someone by the British government that allows them to have the rank of peer

peeved *adjective*
slightly angry or upset

peewit *noun* **peewits**
a medium-sized bird, often black and white, with large wings and raised feathers on its head

SYNONYM *lapwing*

peg *noun* **pegs**
1 a small hook or stick of wood, plastic or metal that sticks out from a wall or surface, used for hanging things on such as clothes *Take your coat off and hang it on the peg.*
2 a small piece of plastic or wood for fixing clothes that have just been washed onto a washing line (long rope) to let them dry. Pegs are usually made of two similar parts connected by a spring.

LANGUAGE EXTRA also called a *clothes peg*

3 a small stick of metal, plastic or wood with a hook at one end and a point at the other, used for fixing something such as a tent to the ground

peg *verb*
pegs, pegging, pegged
to fix something with pegs *The gardener pegged a plastic sheet to the ground to protect the lettuce seeds.*

pejorative *adjective*
if something such as a word or expression is pejorative, it shows that the person or thing mentioned is not good or important and that you have no respect for them *'Yankee' is a pejorative word for an American. Were you using 'fat' in a pejorative sense?*

Pekinese ['peek-in-*eez*'] *noun* **Pekinese**
a small dog with long hair and a small head with a flat face and large eyes

ORIGIN also spelt *Pekingese*, because this type of dog comes from China and was brought by British soldiers from the palace of the Chinese emperor (ruler) in *Peking*, now called Beijing

pelican *noun* **pelicans**
1 a large water bird that has a very long beak with a large bag of skin under it where it keeps the fish it catches
2 a pelican crossing is a place in a road with traffic lights where people can cross the road safely. People press a button on a piece of equipment fixed to the traffic light pole to turn the lights from green to red. This makes the vehicles stop so that people can cross.

pellet *noun* **pellets**
a small object shaped like a ball or tube and made of metal, paper, plastic or any other substance *food pellets for fish; air gun pellets*

pelt *verb*
pelts, pelting, pelted
1 to throw lots of a particular thing at someone or something *The children pelted each other with snowballs.*
2 to run very fast *Someone hit me then pelted across the playground and disappeared.*
3 to rain heavily *It's pelting down outside.*

pelt *noun* **pelts**
the skin and fur of a dead animal

pelvis *noun* **pelvises**
the group of bones that connect the bottom of your back to the top of your legs. It includes several large round bones such as the hip bones.

pen *noun* **pens**
1 a long thin object with a pointed end used for writing with ink. There are different types of pens, for example a ballpoint with a tiny metal ball at the end through which the ink comes out or a fountain pen with a part inside that you fill up with ink.
2 an object shaped like a pen that you use with a computer for selecting information on the screen or for putting information into the computer, for example by drawing a picture on a piece of equipment called a graphics tablet
3 a place with a fence around it where farmers keep animals such as sheep, pigs or cows

ORIGIN the name of the object that you write with comes from Old French *penne* 'quill pen' (from Latin *penna* 'feather'). Goose feathers were often used in the past for writing with.

pen *verb*
pens, penning, penned
to write something *a poem penned by Edward Lear*

penalise *verb*
penalises, penalising, penalised
1 to punish someone, for example because they have done something against the rules

2 to treat someone in an unfair way, for example by causing them a problem that other people don't have

LANGUAGE EXTRA also spelt *penalize*

penalty *noun* **penalties**
1 a punishment for doing something against the rules or against the law, or for not doing what an agreement says you must do
2 a chance to score a goal or point in sports such as football or rugby because someone in the other team has done something against the rules *Our team has just won a penalty.*

pence
plural of **penny** when it means the unit of money, not the coin. When it means the coin, the plural is 'pennies'.

pencil *noun* **pencils**
1 a long thin object, usually made of wood, with a point at the end used for writing or drawing. The point is made from a grey substance called graphite or a special coloured substance such as chalk, which goes through the middle of the pencil. *I wrote my homework in pencil* (with a pencil).
2 a pencil case is a container for carrying pens, pencils and other small things needed for writing such as sharpeners and erasers
3 a pencil sharpener is a small tool for making the ends of pencils more pointed so that they write properly

ORIGIN from Old French *pincel* 'artist's paintbrush', because brushes were used for writing before pencils

pencil *verb*
pencils, pencilling, pencilled
to write or draw something with a pencil

pendant *noun* **pendants**
a piece of jewellery that hangs at the bottom of a chain or string that you wear around your neck

ORIGIN from Old French *pendant* 'hanging down' (from Latin *pendere* 'to hang down')

pendulum *noun* **pendulums**
1 a long thin bar of metal or stick of wood with a heavy object fixed to the end that hangs down from a clock. It swings from side to side and keeps the moving parts of the clock working.
2 a long thin metal bar or chain with a heavy object fixed to the end that hangs down from something and swings from side to side. It is usually used as a scientific instrument, for example for showing the earth going round.

ORIGIN from Latin *pendulus* 'hanging down' (from *pendere* 'to hang down')

penetrate *verb*
penetrates, penetrating, penetrated
if something penetrates something, for example something hard or something where it shouldn't go, it goes right into it or through it *This drill penetrates rock. A piece of glass has penetrated the skin of my thumb. The rain has penetrated the roof.*

penetration *noun*

345

pen friend–perceptible

pen friend *noun* **pen friends**
someone, usually in another country, that you write letters or emails to in order to get to know them as a friend and learn about different places and people

SYNONYM pen pal

LANGUAGE EXTRA also spelt *penfriend*

penguin *noun* **penguins**
a large seabird with a white body and black head, wings and back. It cannot fly and uses its wings like arms (or flippers) for swimming. Penguins live in the Antarctic (the cold region at the most southern point of the world).

penicillin *noun*
a type of antibiotic (drug for killing tiny living things called bacteria that cause infections). It is made from a fungus (plant living in wet places or on rotten surfaces).

peninsula *noun* **peninsulas**
a long area of land that sticks out from a larger area into the sea or a lake so that it is almost completely surrounded by water. For example, Italy is a peninsula.
peninsular *adjective*

penis *noun* **penises**
the part of the body of a male person or animal used for getting rid of urine (waste liquid) and for sex

penitent *adjective*
1 if someone is penitent, they feel sorry for something bad they have done
2 also used about something such as someone's feelings or behaviour
penitence *noun*

penknife *noun* **penknives**
a small knife with a blade or blades that fold into the handle. It is usually carried around in a pocket.

pennant *noun* **pennants**
a flag shaped like a triangle, usually a long triangle. It is often used by ships or sports teams.

penniless *adjective*
if someone is penniless, they have no money and are very poor

Pennines *noun plural*
a long series of hills and mountains reaching from central England to the Scottish border

penny *noun*
1 (*plural* **pence**) a small unit of money in the UK. There are 100 pence in a pound.
2 (*plural* **pennies**) a small coin in the UK worth the same amount of money *I've got too many pennies in my pocket.*

penny-farthing *noun* **penny-farthings**
a bicycle, used at the end of the 19th century, that had a very big front wheel and much smaller back wheel

ORIGIN the name comes from two old British coins – the large *penny* and the much smaller *farthing* (worth a quarter of a penny)

pen pal *noun* **pen pals**
someone, usually in another country, that you write letters or emails to in order to get to know them as a friend and learn about different places and people

SYNONYM pen friend

pension *noun* **pensions**
a regular amount of money that someone gets, usually every month, when they no longer work, for example because they have reached a particular age or because they are ill *My granddad gets a government pension.*

pensioner *noun* **pensioners**
someone who gets a pension from the government because they have reached a particular age

pensive *adjective*
1 if someone is pensive, they look very serious because they are thinking very hard about something
2 also used about someone's appearance *a pensive expression*

ORIGIN from Old French *penser* 'to think'

pentagon *noun* **pentagons**
1 a shape with five straight sides
2 the Pentagon is a large building with five sides in the United States. It is the headquarters of the part of the government that controls the country's army, navy and air force.

pentagonal *adjective*

pentathlon ['pen-tath-lon'] *noun* **pentathlons**
a sports competition where someone takes part in five different sports
compare: **decathlon** and **triathlon**

penthouse *noun* **penthouses**
1 a very expensive flat at the top of a tall building
2 a very expensive and comfortable group of rooms at the top of a hotel

penultimate *adjective*
used for describing something that is next to the last one in a series *Y is the penultimate letter of the alphabet.*

peony ['pee-er-nee'] *noun* **peonies**
a garden plant with large pink, white, red or yellow flowers made up of many petals like roses

people *noun plural*
1 living beings of any age, for example men, women or children *There were lots of people at my party.*
2 living beings who belong to a particular group or who have their own particular character *British people*; *young people*; *Your mum and dad are lovely people.*
3 people in general *What do people think about the new head teacher?*
4 ordinary men and women *The people won't vote for him – he's not very popular.*

people *noun* **peoples**
a nation or group of people who have something in common, such as a religion *These ideas are shared by many peoples of the world.*

pepper *noun*
1 a black, grey or white powder from the crushed seeds of the pepper plant, used for giving a strong flavour to food. It is often used together with salt.
2 (*plural* **peppers**) a round green, red, yellow or orange vegetable that is hollow inside. It is eaten raw, for example in salads, or cooked.
3 (*plural* **peppers**) a pepper or chilli pepper is a small red or green seed pod (long narrow container) with a very spicy taste

pepper *verb*
peppers, peppering, peppered
if something such as a piece of writing is peppered with things, there are lots of those things in it *Amy's homework is peppered with quotations from Shakespeare.*

peppermint *noun*
1 a substance from the leaves of a type of mint (plant with a strong fresh smell) used for giving flavouring to food, drink or toothpaste *peppermint tea*
2 (*plural* **peppermints**) a hard sweet with a strong fresh taste that comes from the mint plant

pepperoni *noun*
a type of Italian sausage with a strong taste, used in pizzas. It is usually made from beef (meat from a cow) or pork (meat from a pig).

peppery *adjective*
1 peppery food has the strong flavour of pepper
2 a peppery taste is a taste like pepper

per *preposition*
used for talking about each of something *Dad pays the gardener £15 per hour.*

perceive *verb*
perceives, perceiving, perceived
1 to think of someone or something in a particular way *Most people perceive teachers to be very hard-working.*
2 to notice something or to realise that something exists, for example something that is not easy to see or understand *We perceived the faint outline of a person in the distance. I perceived some sadness in his voice.*

per cent *adverb & noun*
used when talking about amounts when you mean a particular amount out of 100 equal parts (or in maths a fraction of the whole of something that is divided by 100). The mathematical symbol for per cent is %. *Prices have gone up ten per cent (10%) this year. I've done about fifty per cent (50%) of my homework.*

ORIGIN from Latin *per centum* 'out of a hundred'

percentage *noun* **percentages**
1 an amount out of 100 equal parts (or in maths a fraction of the whole of something that is divided by 100) *What percentage of people are left-handed?*
2 used when you mean an amount of people or things but not one divided into 100 equal parts *A large percentage of the pupils looked bored.*

perceptible *adjective*
1 used about something you can see, hear, feel, smell or taste if you pay careful attention *There's a slight but perceptible difference in colour.*
2 also used about something you can see, hear, feel, smell or taste clearly *Tommy was walking with a perceptible limp.*
perceptibly *adverb*

perception noun
1 (plural **perceptions**) the opinion people have about someone or something or the particular way people think of someone or something
2 the quality of being able to notice something

perceptive adjective
1 quick to notice and understand things *a perceptive student*
2 used for describing something such as an idea or piece of writing that shows you are good at understanding things *a perceptive remark*

perch noun **perches**
1 a stick that a bird stands on in a cage
2 a place that a bird uses for resting on, for example a branch

perch noun **perch**
a fish, often with stripes on its body, that lives in rivers and lakes and is used as food

perch verb
perches, perching, perched
1 to sit, stand or rest on or near the edge of something *He came over and perched on the arm of my chair. Move your cup – it's perched right at the edge of the table.*
2 to sit on something high up *We had to eat our sandwiches at the bar perched on stools.*
3 if a place or building is perched somewhere, it is in a position high up something and near the edge of it *The village is perched high up in the mountains.*

percolator noun **percolators**
a container for making coffee in. Water is heated inside it and is pushed up through a tube so that it passes through crushed coffee beans.

percussion noun
a group of musical instruments that you play by hitting them or shaking them. Percussion instruments include drums, cymbals and tambourines. **percussionist** noun

perennial adjective
used for describing something that always exists or keeps happening all the time *Not having enough money is a perennial problem.*

perennial noun **perennials**
a plant that lives for many years
compare: **annual**

perennially adverb
all the time or very often *My grandparents are perennially short of money.*

perfect ['perr-fikt] adjective
1 if something or someone is perfect, they are as good as they can be and cannot be made any better
2 used for giving extra importance to a word *Dexter was talking to a perfect stranger.*

perfect ['perr-fikt] noun
in grammar, the perfect or perfect tense is the form of a verb that shows what has happened in the past but still has some importance in the present time. The perfect is formed using the words 'have' or 'has' ('I have finished', 'she has done her homework') or the contractions (short forms) 'I've', 'you've', 'he's', 'she's' and so on ('I've drawn a picture', 'he's fallen over').

perfect ['per-fekt] verb
perfects, perfecting, perfected
to make something as good as it can be *My sister spent a year in Paris to perfect her French.*

perfectly adverb
1 used for giving extra importance to a word *It looks funny but it's perfectly safe to eat* (completely safe). *I know perfectly well what you mean.*
2 as well as something can and in a way that cannot be better *These shoes fit me perfectly.*

perforated adjective
if something is perforated, it has very small holes in it. For example, perforated paper can be separated easily by tearing it.

perforations noun plural
very small holes in paper, for example where you can tear it off *Tear the stamp off along the perforations.*

perform verb
performs, performing, performed
1 to do a particular action, for example an experiment, piece of work or ceremony *The doctors are performing the operation tomorrow. These computers perform thousands of calculations a minute.*
2 to do something such as play music, sing, dance or act in a play in front of an audience, for example in a theatre, circus or concert hall *The orchestra performed a symphony by Beethoven. He's a film actor who has never performed on stage before.*
3 used for talking about how successful someone or something is at doing what they are supposed to do *I don't know how our team will perform* (whether they will be successful or not). *My new smartphone performs very well* (works successfully).

performance noun **performances**
1 an occasion when someone does something such as play music, sing, dance or act in a play, usually in front of an audience *The performance is about to start.*
2 the action of doing something such as playing music, singing, dancing or acting in a play *I'm giving a performance as the wicked witch.*
3 the way someone or something does what they are supposed to do and how successful they are at doing it *The swimmer's performance in the race wasn't very good.*
4 when someone or something does a particular action *This happened during the performance of the ceremony.*
5 used for talking about something that gives you a lot of trouble *What a performance getting my baby brother to bed!*

performer noun **performers**
1 someone who performs in front of an audience, for example a singer, musician, dancer, comedian or magician
2 someone who does what they are supposed to do, either well or badly *Mohammed was one of the best performers in the race.*

perfume noun **perfumes**
1 a liquid with a very pleasant smell that is put onto the skin, for example the neck or wrists
2 the very pleasant smell of something such as a flower

perhaps adverb
1 used for saying that something is possible or could be true *Perhaps Gran missed the bus.*
2 used for suggesting something *Perhaps we could go swimming tomorrow.*
3 used when answering a question when you don't want to say yes or no *'Can you help me with the dishes?' – 'Perhaps.'*

SYNONYMS maybe, possibly

peril noun **perils**
a great danger *If you go through the forest, your life will be in peril.*

perilous adjective
very dangerous *These mountain roads are perilous.* **perilously** adverb

perimeter ['per-rim-it-er] noun **perimeters**
1 the outside edge of an area of land surrounded by a fence, wall or trees, for example an airport or camp *a perimeter fence*
2 the outside edge of a flat shape such as a square or the distance around it

period noun **periods**
1 an amount of time that can be long or short *Mum was in hospital for a period of six months. We had a period of very hot weather.*
2 a particular time in history or in someone's life *We're studying the Victorian period. My teenage brother is going through a difficult period.*
3 a time in the school day when a teacher teaches a particular subject *We've got a maths period after lunch.*
4 the natural bleeding from a woman's womb (part of the body where a baby grows) that happens for a few days every month
5 the American word for a full stop

periodic adjective
happening in a fairly regular way but only sometimes **periodically** adverb

periodical noun **periodicals**
a magazine or newspaper, usually on a serious subject, that is printed at regular times, for example every week or month

periscope noun **periscopes**
an instrument with a long vertical tube and mirrors at both ends for looking over the top of something. Periscopes are used especially in submarines for seeing if there is anything above the water.

perish verb
perishes, perishing, perished
1 to die, for example in an accident or war or because of an illness
2 if something such as leather or rubber perishes, it becomes weak and breaks into small pieces

perishables noun plural
food that goes bad quickly if it is not kept in a fridge **perishable** adjective

perished adjective (informal)
feeling extremely cold

perk–person

perk *noun* **perks**
an extra thing such as money or a car given to someone who has a job, for example to make them feel happier and work better

perk up *verb*
perks up, perking up, perked up
1 to perk up is to become happier or make someone happier *Mum perked up when I told her Granddad was coming over. The news really perked her up.*
2 to perk up is also to get more energy or give someone more energy *Ben perked up after that coffee. He needed a coffee to perk him up.*

perky *adjective* **perkier, perkiest**
1 happy
2 full of energy
perkiness *noun*

perm *noun* **perms**
1 a way of cutting and shaping someone's hair using special chemicals to make it curly and stay curly for a long time
2 someone's hair when it has been done in this way
short for: **permanent wave**

perm *verb*
perms, perming, permed
if someone has their hair permed, a hairdresser cuts and shapes it using special chemicals to make it curly

permanent *adjective*
existing or lasting for ever or for a very long time *The coffee left a permanent stain on the carpet. My sister is looking for a permanent job. We now have a permanent head teacher.* **permanence** *noun*

ANTONYM temporary

permanently *adverb*
1 for all time in the future *The swimming pool has closed permanently.*

ANTONYM temporarily

2 all the time *Rupa feels permanently tired.*

permeable *adjective*
used in science for describing a material that lets a substance such as liquid or gas pass through it

permissible *adjective*
if something is permissible, it is allowed by the rules

permission *noun*
1 used for talking about the words said by someone in charge telling someone they can do something they want to do, for example something that is not usually allowed by a rule *My teacher gave me permission to leave early* (said I could leave early). *If you want to play cricket in the playground, you have to ask permission* (ask if you can).
2 when someone in an important position writes words in a document telling someone that they are allowed to do something *The politician obtained government permission to enter the country.*

permissive *adjective*
allowing someone to behave in whatever way they want and even do things that other people don't like *Sally has very permissive parents.* **permissiveness** *noun*

permit ['per-mit'] *verb*
permits, permitting, permitted
1 to allow someone to do something or let someone do something *Shouting in the library isn't permitted.*
2 to let someone have something *The rules don't permit mobile phones in the classroom.*
3 to make something possible *We're going to play football this afternoon if the weather permits* (or *weather permitting*).

permit ['perr-mit'] *noun* **permits**
an official document that gives someone permission to do something *You need a permit to park in our street.*

perpendicular *adjective*
1 used in maths for describing a line or surface that is at an angle of 90 degrees to another line or surface
2 used for describing something that is tall and goes straight up from a surface *perpendicular cliffs*

perpetual *adjective*
used for describing something that lasts for ever or keeps happening all the time *People in that country live in perpetual fear of an earthquake.*

perpetually *adverb*
all the time *Oliver is perpetually late for school.*

perplex *verb*
perplexes, perplexing, perplexed
if something perplexes you, you are confused and you don't understand it
perplexity *noun*

perplexed *adjective*
if someone is perplexed, they don't understand something

perplexing *adjective*
difficult to understand

persecute *verb*
persecutes, persecuting, persecuted
if someone persecutes someone, they treat them very badly and cruelly, for example because they don't like their religion or political ideas **persecution** *noun*
persecutor *noun*

perseverance *noun*
the quality of really wanting to do something and continuing to do it even though it is difficult *If you want to learn Spanish, you need hard work and perseverance.*

persevere *verb*
perseveres, persevering, persevered
to continue doing something even though it is difficult and you have problems *I have trouble understanding decimals but I decided to persevere with my maths homework.*

Persia *noun*
an ancient country in South-West Asia, now called Iran

Persian *adjective*
1 connected with ancient Persia or modern Iran
2 connected with the language spoken in modern Iran

Persian *noun*
the language people speak in modern Iran

persist *verb*
persists, persisting, persisted
1 to keep on doing something all the time without wanting to stop, even though you might be annoying someone or doing something bad *He persists in phoning me although I don't want to speak to him.*
2 to continue, for example for a long time *If your headache persists, I'll call the doctor.*

persistence *noun*
1 a situation in which something continues or continues for a long time *the persistence of the rain*
2 the quality of really wanting to do something and continuing to do it even though it may be difficult *He was rewarded for his persistence.*

persistent *adjective*
1 if someone is persistent, they keep on doing something even though they might be annoying someone or doing something bad
2 also used about something someone does or for describing what someone is like *a persistent refusal* (when someone keeps on refusing); *a persistent burglar* (who keeps on stealing things)
3 used for describing something that continues for a long time *persistent rain*

persistently *adverb*
1 all the time *It's been raining persistently all day.*
2 every time *She has persistently refused to help me.*
3 in a way that shows you really want to do something and you keep doing it, for example even though it may be difficult *My sister has been working very hard and persistently on her homework.*

person *noun*
1 (*plural* **people**) a living being of any age, for example a man, woman or child *There's a person at the front door.*
2 (*plural* **people**) someone with their own particular character or who belongs to a particular group *My teacher is a very kind person. He's a young person who loves football.*
3 if you do something in person, you do it yourself or go somewhere to do it yourself
4 (*plural* **persons**) in grammar, person is used for showing what form of a pronoun and verb you are referring to

LANGUAGE EXTRA in grammar, there are three types of *person*.
The *first person* refers to the person or people speaking about themselves. For example, *I, we, me* and *us* are first person pronouns, and *am* and *are* are first person forms of the verb 'to be'.
The *second person* is used for the person or people that you're speaking to. For example, *you* is a second person pronoun (both singular and plural), and *are* is used here as a second person form (singular and plural) of the verb 'to be'.
The *third person* refers to the person or people that you're speaking about. For example, *he, she, it, him, her, they* and *them* are third person pronouns, and *is* and *are* are third person forms of the verb 'to be'.
Some forms of a verb only belong to one person (for example, *am* is first person only) but other forms (such as *are*) belong to many different persons.

personal–petrol

personal *adjective*
1 connected with or belonging to a particular person or group of people *personal belongings*; *This is my personal opinion* (my own opinion). *The mayor made a personal appearance at our school* (came himself or herself to our school).
2 made for or used by one person *a personal computer*
3 connected with the body *personal hygiene*
4 connected with the part of someone's life that is private or connected with someone's feelings *This computer file contains personal information. My uncle and aunt have personal problems.*
5 in grammar, a personal pronoun is a word such as 'I', 'me', 'she', 'her', 'they' or 'them' that is used instead of a noun referring to a person

personality *noun*
1 (*plural* **personalities**) the special qualities that someone is born with that make them what they are *He has a lively and friendly personality.*
2 the special quality of being lively and interesting *You need a lot of personality to be a film star.*
3 (*plural* **personalities**) a famous person *She's a well-known TV personality.*

personally *adverb*
1 used when talking about something you do yourself or about going somewhere to do something yourself *I had to go to the head to apologise personally.*
2 used when talking about yourself *I don't know Peter personally.*
3 meant for you yourself and no-one else *The letter was addressed to me personally.*
4 used when you want to give your own opinion about something *Personally, I think Dad is wrong.*

personification *noun*
a way of telling a story or showing something in a painting using a thing or animal as if it were a person, or a way of showing an idea or quality as if it were a person (or as if it could do something that only a person can do). Examples of personification are 'the moon smiled at me' or 'the White Rabbit checked his watch'.

personify *verb*
personifies, personifying, personified
if something such as an idea or quality is personified, for example in poems, stories or art, it is shown as if it were a person or animal *Wisdom is often personified as an owl.*

personnel ['per-ser-**nel**'] *noun*
the people who work in an organisation, office or factory

perspective *noun*
1 (*plural* **perspectives**) the particular way you think about something *Let's consider Shakespeare's play from a historical perspective.*

> SYNONYM point of view

2 a way of drawing or painting objects on a flat surface that makes them look as if they have the same shape and distance from each other as if they were real. For example, objects further away are shown smaller and usually higher.

3 a particular way of considering something and deciding, once you look at the whole situation, whether it is important or not *Let's put this problem in perspective* (consider it and decide that it may not be important, for example).

perspiration *noun*
another word for sweat

perspire *verb*
perspires, perspiring, perspired
to produce liquid through tiny holes in your skin called pores when you do exercises or when you are hot, frightened, nervous or ill

> SYNONYM to sweat

persuade *verb*
persuades, persuading, persuaded
1 to get someone to want to do something by giving them good reasons why they should do it *I persuaded Dad to lend me £10 to buy a present for Mum.*
2 to get someone to believe that something is true by explaining the reasons why it is true *She persuaded me that she was not the person who broke the window.*
3 to be the reason why something happens or why someone does something *The heavy snow persuaded us to stay home from school yesterday.*

persuasion *noun*
when you talk to someone and give them good reasons for doing or believing something *After a lot of persuasion, Dad lent me the money.*

persuasive *adjective*
giving you good reasons for doing or believing something *a persuasive argument*; *I didn't want to help Dad with the dishes but he was very persuasive.*

Peru *noun*
a country in South America
Peruvian *adjective & noun*

pervade *verb*
pervades, pervading, pervaded
to spread through all parts of something *A smell of paint pervaded the whole house.*

> ORIGIN from Latin *per* 'through' and *vadere* 'to go'

perverse ['per-**verrss**'] *adjective*
not reasonable (or showing that someone is not reasonable), usually when someone does the opposite of what they are told to do or when someone doesn't do a normal or expected thing *The teacher told them to stop playing in the corridor but they carried on just to be perverse. Tony took a perverse pleasure in seeing his brother lose.*
perversely *adverb* **perversity** *noun*

peseta ['per-**say**-ter'] *noun* **pesetas**
a unit of money in Spain before the euro

pessimist *noun* **pessimists**
someone who is not hopeful about the future because they think bad things are more likely to happen than good ones
pessimism *noun*
compare: **optimist**

pessimistic *adjective*
1 not hopeful about the future because you think bad things are more likely to happen than good ones

2 used about something that gives you no hope for the future *a pessimistic speech*
compare: **optimistic**

pessimistically *adverb*
in a way that shows you are not hopeful about the future *'Will Jack pass his exam?' – 'Of course he won't,' she replied pessimistically.*

pest *noun* **pests**
1 an insect or small or medium-sized animal that destroys things such as plants or food or that spreads disease. Mice, fleas and mosquitoes are pests.
2 someone who annoys you *Stop being a pest and leave me alone.*

pester *verb*
pesters, pestering, pestered
if you pester someone, you annoy them, usually by keeping on asking them for something or asking them to do something

pesticide *noun* **pesticides**
a chemical used for killing insects

pesto *noun*
a thick green sauce for putting on pasta. It is made from olive oil, basil, garlic and pine nuts.

pet *noun* **pets**
1 an animal, such as a cat, dog or budgerigar, that lives in someone's home *a pet rabbit*; *a pet shop* (one that sells pets)
2 a person that someone likes more than everyone else and treats better than everyone else *Holly is the teacher's pet.*
3 a pet hate is something or someone that you have a very strong feeling of dislike for
4 a pet peeve is the American way of saying a pet hate

pet *verb*
pets, petting, petted
if you pet an animal, you touch or stroke it in a gentle and friendly way

petal *noun* **petals**
one of the brightly coloured or white leaf-like parts that grow around the centre of a flower and make up most of the flower

> ORIGIN from Greek *petalon* 'leaf'

peter out *verb*
peters out, petering out, petered out
if something peters out, for example a storm or conversation, it slowly becomes less or weaker until there is nothing left or until it stops

petition *noun* **petitions**
an official document signed by many people asking someone in charge to do something *Thousands of people signed an online petition to stop the new road from being built.*

petrify *verb*
petrifies, petrifying, petrified
to frighten someone very much *The whole class were so petrified that they couldn't speak.*

> ORIGIN from Latin *petrificare* 'to change something into stone' (from *petra* 'stone')

petrol *noun*
1 a liquid made from petroleum that is put inside the engines of cars and other vehicles to make them work

petroleum – phone book

2 a petrol station is a place with fuel pumps where someone goes to buy petrol or diesel for their vehicle

petroleum ['per-troh-lee-erm'] *noun*
a thick dark liquid from under the ground used for making petrol, diesel oil and paraffin, for example

petticoat *noun* **petticoats**
a piece of women's or girls' clothing like a loose skirt that hangs from the waist underneath a dress or skirt

petty *adjective* **pettier, pettiest**
1 not important or serious (used for example about problems, rules and arguments) *Another petty quarrel between Grandpa and Grandma!*
2 paying attention to things that are not important or serious, often in a way that is mean to someone *Don't tell the teacher I said a swear word – that would be petty!*
3 used for describing someone whose job or activities are not very important or serious *a petty criminal*
pettiness *noun*

pew *noun* **pews**
a long wooden seat with a high back that people sit on, usually in a religious building such as a church

pewter *noun*
a blue-grey metal made from mixing tin and another metal such as copper or lead *a pewter plate*

phablet *noun* **phablets**
a small computer that is connected to the internet and also works as a mobile phone. It is bigger than a smartphone and smaller than a tablet.

ORIGIN from *phone* and *tablet*

phantom *noun* **phantoms**
another word for a ghost (image of a dead person)

phantom *adjective*
used for describing something that you think is real but that does not exist, for example because you have imagined it *My cousin often has a phantom pain in his missing leg.*

pharaoh ['fair-oh'] *noun* **pharaohs**
a king in ancient Egypt

pharmacist *noun* **pharmacists**
someone who prepares and sells medicines in a shop, hospital or supermarket

pharmacy *noun*
1 (*plural* **pharmacies**) a shop where medicines are prepared and sold. It also sells products for the body such as cosmetics, toothpaste and soap.
2 (*plural* **pharmacies**) a place in a hospital or supermarket where medicines are prepared and sold
3 the study of preparing medicines for treating illnesses and injuries

phase *noun* **phases**
1 a period that is one part of a longer period during which something happens *It's the final phase of the building work.*
2 a period when someone behaves in a strange or bad way *Don't worry – it's a phase your brother is going through.*

3 the phases of the moon are the changes in the moon's shape that appear in the sky at different times of the month, for example a new moon (when it appears as a thin crescent or curve)

phase *verb*
phases, phasing, phased
to make something happen gradually over a certain period of time *The changes to the school timetables will be phased in over a few months. During the coming months the old software will be phased out* (got rid of gradually).

pheasant ['fez-ernt'] *noun* **pheasants**
a large wild bird that people kill as a sport or for food. It has a round body with a long tail. Male pheasants have brightly coloured feathers and are usually larger than the females.

phenomenal ['fer-nom-in-erl'] *adjective*
1 really good, often in a surprising way *a phenomenal stroke of good luck*
2 really great or large, often in a surprising way *The book was a phenomenal success. My uncle earns a phenomenal amount of money.*
3 very unusual or surprising *What happened to me next was pretty phenomenal.*

phenomenally ['fer-nom-in-er-lee'] *adverb*
1 extremely, often in a surprising way *a phenomenally successful rock group*
2 very much *My brother's homework has improved phenomenally.*

phenomenon ['fer-nom-in-ern'] *noun*
phenomena
1 something that happens or exists, for example something unusual, interesting or connected with nature *Volcanoes and thunderstorms are natural phenomena.*
2 something or someone very special or successful

phew ['fyoo'] *interjection*
1 used for showing that you're happy something difficult is finished or something bad will not happen
2 also used for showing that you're hot or tired or have other feelings such as shock or dislike

philately ['fil-at-er-lee'] *noun*
collecting postage stamps and the study of postal history **philatelist** *noun*

Philippines *noun*
the Philippines is a country in East Asia

philosopher *noun* **philosophers**
someone who studies and writes about philosophy

philosophical *adjective*
1 connected with philosophy *philosophical ideas*
2 if someone is philosophical, they are ready to accept an unpleasant situation without getting angry or excited because they know they can't change it *My brother was philosophical about failing his exam.*
philosophically *adverb*

philosophy *noun*
1 the study of all the basic things connected with life and the world and of the behaviour and beliefs of human beings
2 (*plural* **philosophies**) the particular beliefs of a philosopher or group of philosophers *the philosophy of Plato*

3 (*plural* **philosophies**) someone's ideas about life or about how to behave in a particular situation *Work hard in school and go on to university – that's my parents' philosophy.*

phishing ['fish-ing'] *noun*
the crime of sending someone an email to trick them into giving information about their internet bank account such as their password or PIN number (secret number). With this information someone steals money from their account. *Dad received a phishing email.*

phlegm ['flem'] *noun*
a thick yellow or green substance produced from your throat when you have a cough or cold

phobia ['foh-bee-er'] *noun* **phobias**
a very strong fear of something *I have a phobia about spiders.*

Phoenician ['fer-nee-shern'] *noun*
Phoenicians
someone who belonged to an ancient people of the Middle East. The Phoenicians played an important part in how the letters of the alphabet developed and were among the first people to use an alphabet. The Phoenician alphabet greatly influenced the Greek and Roman alphabets.

phoenix ['fee-niks'] *noun* **phoenixes**
in the stories of ancient Greece, Egypt, China and many other countries, a phoenix is an imaginary bird that lives for 500 years and dies by setting fire to itself. A new phoenix is then born from its ashes (the powder left after its body has burnt).

phone *noun*
1 (*plural* **phones**) a piece of electronic equipment for speaking to someone in another place. A mobile phone uses radio signals and is carried around with you. A landline phone is usually connected to the phone system by wires and stays in one place. *Seema is on the phone* (talking to someone using a phone).
2 (*plural* **phones**) the part of a landline phone that you hold next to your ear and mouth *The phone is off the hook* (not in its place so it cannot ring)
3 a system for talking to someone who is in another place *Mum spoke to the head teacher by phone.*

phone *verb*
phones, phoning, phoned
1 to speak to someone using a phone *I'll phone you after school. Did anyone phone up while I was out? Granddad phoned for a taxi* (asked for a taxi using the phone).
2 to phone back is to phone someone that you have already phoned or someone who has already phoned you
3 to phone in is to phone someone where you work or study to give them a message *Mum phoned in to school to say I wasn't well.*
4 to phone in is also to phone someone on a TV or radio programme, for example to ask a question or give an opinion

phone book *noun* **phone books**
a book that lists the phone numbers of people and businesses together with their names and addresses

350

phone booth noun **phone booths**
a very small structure with walls, a roof and a door, or a structure that is partly open, with a phone inside that people pay to use

phone box noun **phone boxes**
a very small structure with walls, a roof and a door, and with a phone inside that people pay to use

phone call noun **phone calls**
when you speak to someone on the phone *I made a phone call to Granddad.*

phone-in noun **phone-ins**
a TV or radio programme where you phone someone, for example to ask a question or give an opinion

phoneme ['foh-neem'] noun **phonemes**
in grammar, a phoneme is the smallest unit of sound in a language. For example, the word 'chat' has four letters but three phonemes (or sounds): 'ch', 'a' and 't'.
compare: **grapheme**

phone number noun **phone numbers**
the number you dial (press buttons on a phone) to connect to another phone that belongs to the person you want to speak to

phoney adjective (informal)
if something is phoney, it isn't real *a phoney French accent*

SYNONYMS false, fake

phonics noun
a way of teaching children how to read and write by getting them to understand how sounds and letters are connected to each other

phosphorescent adjective
shining in the dark with a very weak light

photo noun **photos**
1 a picture of someone or something produced using a camera or other equipment such as a mobile phone *My sister took a photo of me in the garden.*
2 a photo booth is a very small structure with walls and a roof and with a seat inside, for example in a railway station or supermarket. While you are sitting, a digital camera takes your photo and special equipment then produces it on paper.
3 a photo finish is the end of a race when two or more of the people or animals go across the finishing line (place where the race ends) almost at the same time. People must then look at a photo to see who the winner is.

photocopier noun **photocopiers**
a piece of equipment for making paper copies of documents or pictures, usually using a special type of camera

photocopy verb
photocopies, photocopying, photocopied
to make a paper copy of a document or picture using a photocopier

photocopy noun **photocopies**
a paper copy of a document or picture made by a photocopier

photogenic ['foh-toh-jen-ik'] adjective
if someone is photogenic, they look good in photos

photograph noun **photographs**
a picture of someone or something produced using a camera or other equipment such as a mobile phone

photograph verb
photographs, photographing, photographed
to take a picture of someone or something using a camera or mobile phone, for example

photographer noun **photographers**
someone who takes pictures using a camera, often as their job

photographic adjective
1 connected with taking pictures using a camera *photographic equipment*
2 if you have a photographic memory, you can remember things or people you see very clearly and with lots of details

photography noun
1 the activity, skill or job of taking pictures using a camera
2 the activity, skill or job of producing films or videos using a film camera

photosynthesis noun
the way that green plants use light and energy from the sun to make the food they need from air and water in order to grow

phrasal verb noun **phrasal verbs**
a type of verb made up of a main verb together with an adverb (for example 'cross out') or preposition (for example 'look after'), or with both an adverb and preposition (for example 'do away with'). A phrasal verb usually has a different meaning from the meaning of the main verb.

phrase noun **phrases**
1 a group of words *I don't like the phrase you used to describe our school.*
2 a phrase in grammar is a part of a sentence that does not have a verb

LANGUAGE EXTRA a *phrase* is a part of a sentence that does the job of a particular part of speech (such as a noun, verb or adjective). For example, the sentence *I saw people with big umbrellas* contains the noun phrase *people with big umbrellas*. It is a noun phrase because all the words together do the job of one part of speech (the noun *people*).

compare: **clause**

phrase verb
phrases, phrasing, phrased
to use particular words to say something *How can we phrase that idea in a different way?*

phrasebook noun **phrasebooks**
a small book for someone travelling to a foreign country. It gives lists of useful words and sentences in your own language with translations in the foreign language. It also contains words and sentences in the foreign language with translations in your language. *a Spanish phrasebook*

LANGUAGE EXTRA also spelt *phrase book*

physical adjective
1 connected with the body *Granddad does physical exercises every day.*
2 used for describing something that you can see and touch *a physical object*

physical education noun
classes at school in which you do exercises and play sport

LANGUAGE EXTRA usually called *PE* for short

physically adverb
1 in a way that is connected with the body or the way people look *My brother is physically strong. My sister is physically attractive. Gardening is hard work physically* (it makes the body tired).
2 in a way that is connected with things that you can see and touch or with the laws of nature *The two countries are separated physically by a mountain range. Touching the moon is physically impossible!*

physician noun **physicians**
another word for a doctor

physicist noun **physicists**
a scientist who is an expert in physics

physics noun
the scientific study of matter (the substance that all objects are made of) and of energy, including light, heat and sound

physiology noun
the scientific study of the way the body works or the way different parts of the body work, for example the eye, heart or liver **physiological** adjective

pianist noun **pianists**
someone who plays the piano, often as their job

piano noun **pianos**
a large musical instrument that you sit in front of to play. It has a row of black and white keys that you press with your fingers to produce the sounds. It also has pedals that you press with your feet to change the quality of the sounds.

ORIGIN from Italian *piano* (short for *piano e forte* 'quiet and loud'), because it plays sounds both quietly and loudly

piccolo noun **piccolos**
a musical instrument that is like a very small flute and plays high notes

pick verb
picks, picking, picked
1 to decide you want something or someone and not something or someone else *They picked David for the football team.*

SYNONYM to choose

2 to remove something from something, for example with your fingers *I picked some dust off my shirt.*
3 to pick a flower or fruit is to cut it or break it off a plant or tree
4 to pick a fight, argument or quarrel with someone is to start it
5 to pick a lock is to open something locked such as a door or suitcase without a key, for example with a piece of wire
6 to pick your nose is to use your finger to remove mucus (thick liquid or sticky substance from inside the nose)
7 if someone picks someone's pocket, they steal things that are inside that person's pocket

8 if someone picks on you, they are very unpleasant towards you and treat you badly *Pick on someone your own size* (used for telling someone to stop being unpleasant to someone smaller and weaker than they are).
9 if you pick something or someone out, you recognise them or find them in a group of different things or people *Can you pick out the shape that looks different from all the others?*
10 to pick something up is to take it from somewhere with your hands, for example something that is on the ground *I bent down and picked up a 50 pence coin from the pavement. Pick up the phone – Jack wants to speak to you.*
11 to pick something up is also to get something, for example a prize, bargain or illness *Mum picked up a newspaper on her way home.*
12 to pick someone or something up is to go and get someone or something that is waiting for you and bring them somewhere *Dad picked me up at school* (came to take me home, for example by car). *I have a book to pick up at the library.*
13 to pick yourself up is to stand up after falling over
14 to pick up speed is to go faster
15 if something such as a situation, someone's health or a book picks up, it gets better *The film was slow but it picked up towards the end.*

pick noun
1 a choice *Take your pick* (choose whatever you want).
2 used about the best things or people of a particular type *For our homework we have to discuss the pick of the week's news stories.*
3 (plural **picks**) a small flat piece of plastic or metal that you hold between your thumb and fingers and use for playing the strings of a musical instrument such as a guitar

> SYNONYM plectrum

4 (plural **picks**) another word for a pickaxe

pickaxe noun **pickaxes**
a tool with a heavy metal head (or top) fixed to a long wooden handle. The metal part is pointed at one end and flat at the other. It is used for breaking hard surfaces such as concrete and digging up hard ground.

picket noun **pickets**
a group of people who stand outside a building to show their anger about something and to stop people going in, usually during a strike (when workers stop work because they are not happy)
picket verb

pickings noun plural
money or other good things that people can get easily *There are rich pickings for burglars in this part of town.*

pickle noun **pickles**
1 a sauce made from vegetables kept for a long time in vinegar (sour liquid made from wine) or salty water *a cheese and pickle sandwich*
2 an informal word for a situation with lots of problems *My brother's in a bit of a pickle.*

pickle verb
pickles, pickling, pickled
to preserve food such as vegetables by keeping them in vinegar (sour liquid made from wine) or salty water for a long time

pickpocket noun **pickpockets**
a thief who steals things from people's pockets and bags

pick-up noun **pick-ups**
1 a pick-up or pick-up truck is a small vehicle for carrying things. It has a flat open part at the back with low sides.
2 a time or place at which someone or something is collected *For tomorrow's outing, the coach will be outside the school for a nine o'clock pick-up.*

> LANGUAGE EXTRA also spelt *pickup*

picky adjective **pickier, pickiest**
if someone is picky, they are hard to please because they only want the things they like and will not accept anything else

picnic noun **picnics**
a meal that you eat outside, for example in the countryside or a park

picnic verb
picnics, picnicking, picnicked
to have a picnic **picnicker** noun

pictogram noun **pictograms**
1 a simple picture or symbol that represents an idea with a particular meaning
2 in maths, a pictogram is a graph (mathematical diagram for comparing things) in which the numbers and words are shown by simple pictures or symbols

pictorial adjective
connected with pictures or photos, or shown using pictures or photos *a pictorial history of Scotland in the nineteenth century*
pictorially adverb

picture noun **pictures**
1 something that someone draws or paints *Do you like my picture of a house?*

> SYNONYMS drawing, painting

2 something that someone produces with a camera *The picture you took is a bit blurred.*

> SYNONYM photo

3 what you see on a TV, cinema or computer screen
4 something or someone that you see in your mind *I have a picture of him as someone tall with long hair.*
5 another word for a film *'War Horse' won an award for best picture.*
6 the pictures an old-fashioned word for the cinema

picture verb
pictures, picturing, pictured
1 to form an idea of something or someone in your mind
2 to understand or realise something *Try and picture what life was like in the Middle Ages.*
3 to show someone or something in a photo or painting *The film star was pictured sunbathing on the beach.*

picturesque ['pik-cher-esk'] adjective
1 if something such as a place or building is picturesque, it is very pleasant to look at and often also old and interesting *a picturesque village*
2 used for describing a word or expression that is interesting and unusual

pie noun **pies**
1 a food made from fruit, meat or vegetables usually covered with or surrounded by pastry (flour, water and fat) and baked in an oven *an apple pie*
2 in maths, a pie chart is a type of graph (diagram for comparing things) shaped like a circle. It shows the total amount of something divided from the centre into several parts like the slices of a pie.

> SIMILE 'as easy as pie' means very easy

piece noun **pieces**
1 some of a particular thing, or some of a thing of a particular kind *a piece of cheese; a piece of advice*
2 a single thing or a single thing of a particular kind *a piece of paper; I cut the cake into six pieces.*
3 an example of something artistic, musical or written *a piece of music; a piece of writing*
4 a part that is connected to another part *My jigsaw has 200 pieces. Dad fixed the broken pieces of the vase. To move the table you have to take it to pieces* (separate the different parts).
5 an object that you move on a board with your hands to play a game such as chess or Monopoly
6 another word for a coin *a 50 pence piece*
7 if something comes or falls to pieces or is smashed to pieces, it breaks or is broken into many small parts, often so that it is completely destroyed
8 in one piece not hurt or damaged in any way *Some children threw stones at us but we arrived home in one piece.*

piece verb
pieces, piecing, pieced
1 if you piece something together, you make it or put it together by joining different things or parts *Mum made a scarf by piecing together some leftover bits of cloth.*
2 if you piece events or details together, you try to find out about something that happened

piecemeal adverb & adjective
used about something that is done not all at once but a bit at a time *The town was built piecemeal over a period of 30 years.*

pier noun **piers**
a narrow structure built out from the edge of the land into the sea, a river or a lake. It usually has shops, restaurants and places of entertainment on it or is used as a place for boats to stop at.

pierce verb
pierces, piercing, pierced
1 to make a hole in or through something with a sharp point
2 if someone gets a part of their body pierced, they get a small hole made in it so that they can wear jewellery there *Amy wants to have her ears pierced.*

piercing–pin

piercing *adjective*
1 used for describing a noise that is high like the sound of a whistle and very unpleasant *a piercing scream*
2 used for describing something such as the wind or a light that is very strong and unpleasant
3 if someone has piercing eyes, you feel as if they are looking right through you

piffling *adjective*
extremely small or not important

pig *noun* **pigs**
1 an animal with a smooth fat body, short legs, a large nose and large ears, and a short curly tail. People keep pigs on farms and use them for providing meat, called pork. The sound that pigs make is an oink.
2 an insulting word for someone who eats too much or wants more things than they need or for someone who is very unpleasant

pig *verb* (informal)
pigs, pigging, pigged
if someone pigs out, they eat too much food *Lewis has been pigging out on ice cream all day.*

pigeon *noun* **pigeons**
a large bird with a fat body that is usually grey. Pigeons often live in towns and the sound they make is a coo.

pigeonhole *noun* **pigeonholes**
one of the small open sections with a person's name on it in a piece of furniture that is usually fixed to a wall. Other people, for example who work in the same office, put messages, letters or small objects in it for that person to take.

ORIGIN originally one of the small open boxes in a specially built structure for *pigeons* to rest in

piggy *noun* **piggies**
an informal word for a little pig

piggy *adjective* **piggier, piggiest** (informal)
if someone is piggy, they eat too much or want more things than they need

SYNONYM greedy

piggyback *noun* **piggybacks**
a ride on someone's back in which you have your arms around their shoulders while their arms support your legs

LANGUAGE EXTRA also called a *piggyback ride*

piggyback *adverb*
if you ride piggyback, you ride on someone's back

piggy-bank *noun* **piggy-banks**
a small container, often shaped like a pig, used mainly by children for putting coins into when they want to save up to buy something. It is a type of moneybox.

LANGUAGE EXTRA also spelt *piggy bank*

pig-headed *adjective*
if someone is pig-headed, they will not change their mind about something even though other people think their behaviour is stupid and unreasonable

pig-headedness *noun*

piglet *noun* **piglets**
a young pig

pigment *noun* **pigments**
a substance that gives colour to something, for example to paint or ink or to the skin or hair of people and animals

pigsty *noun* **pigsties**
1 an informal word for a place that is very untidy or dirty, for example a room or house
2 a place on a farm where pigs live

pigtail *noun* **pigtails**
a long thick piece of hair that hangs down behind the head, or one of two long thick pieces that hang down on either side of the head. Pigtails are formed by twisting together many threads of hair. *Ella wears her hair in pigtails.*
compare: **plait** and **bunches**

pike *noun*
1 (plural **pike**) a large fish with a long body and sharp teeth that lives in rivers and lakes and is sometimes eaten
2 (plural **pikes**) a long pole with a pointed end, used as a weapon in the past by soldiers on foot

pilchard *noun* **pilchards**
a small silver-coloured sea fish with oily flesh that is eaten as food. Pilchards are often bought in tins.

pile *noun* **piles**
1 a number of things on top of each other put together carefully *Put the books neatly in a pile on the table.*
2 a number of things on top of each other put together in an untidy way or an amount of something like a small hill *Alex left a pile of dirty clothes on his bed. There was a pile of rubbish outside the school.*
3 an informal way of saying a lot of something *I have a pile of* (or *piles of*) *homework to do. My uncle has piles of money.*
4 a strong thick pole made of wood, metal or concrete that is pushed deep into the ground. It is used for supporting something such as a building or bridge.

pile *verb*
piles, piling, piled
1 to put things on top of each other *DVDs were piled up in a corner.*
2 to put lots of something somewhere, for example in an untidy way *Pile some more pasta onto my plate.*
3 if something piles up, or if things pile up, there is gradually more of it or them as time passes *If you don't clean your room, the dust will just pile up. The bills are piling up.*
4 if people pile into something, for example a building or car, they all rush in at the same time, often in a clumsy way

pile-up *noun* **pile-ups**
a road accident in which many vehicles crash into each other

LANGUAGE EXTRA also spelt *pileup*

pilfer *verb*
pilfers, pilfering, pilfered
to steal something small, for example something from a shop or office

pilfering *noun*

pilgrim *noun* **pilgrims**
someone who travels for religious reasons to a place that is important in their religion, often a place far away

pilgrimage *noun* **pilgrimages**
a journey that someone makes for religious reasons to a place that is important in their religion

pill *noun* **pills**
1 a very small hard piece of medicine, often round and flat, that you swallow with water *For his backache, Dad took* (swallowed) *a pill.*
2 **the pill** a special type of pill that a woman swallows every day if she has a boyfriend or husband and does not want to have a baby

pillage *verb*
pillages, pillaging, pillaged
to steal something from a place using violence and causing damage, as soldiers sometimes do in a war *Many important paintings were pillaged from the town in the 1940s.* **pillage** *noun*

pillar *noun* **pillars**
1 one of the tall round posts made of stone, concrete or wood that support a structure such as the roof of a building or a bridge or that are used for decorating it
2 a long line of something pointing upwards *a pillar of smoke*
3 a pillar box is a large red container, usually round, that stands in a street and is used for posting letters in

pillion *adverb*
if someone rides pillion, they ride on a motorcycle sitting behind the driver and holding on to him or her for support. The place where they sit is called a pillion seat.

pillow *noun* **pillows**
a rectangle of cloth with soft material inside, used on beds for putting your head on

pillowcase *noun* **pillowcases**
a thin cloth cover for a pillow that you can take off and wash

pilot *noun* **pilots**
1 someone who controls a plane or helicopter and makes it fly somewhere
2 a ship's pilot is someone who guides a ship through a difficult part of the water near a coast such as a harbour or river mouth (where a river flows into a sea)

pilot *verb*
pilots, piloting, piloted
1 to pilot a plane or helicopter is to be its pilot and make it fly somewhere
2 to pilot a ship is to guide it through a difficult part of the water

pimple *noun* **pimples**
a very small round swelling on the skin, often on the face

SYNONYM spot

pimply *adjective*
having lots of pimples

pin *noun* **pins**
1 a small thin piece of metal with a round head (top) and a sharp point at the other end. It is especially used for holding pieces of cloth or paper together.

353

pin–pipeline

2 a small thin piece of metal with a sharp point and a tiny head (top) shaped in different ways, such as round, flat or like a cylinder (tube). It is used, for example, for fixing something to a noticeboard or marking a place on a map.
3 a thin piece of metal for holding things together or connecting things *a three-pin plug* (for connecting equipment to the electricity); *Tony has a pin in his broken leg* (for fixing the bones together).
4 one of the 10 objects shaped like bottles that you knock down with a heavy ball in the game of tenpin bowling
5 a small object pinned to your clothes, worn for example as jewellery (used mainly in American English)
6 pins and needles if you have pins and needles, you have lots of tiny sharp pains in your hands or feet because you have kept them in one position for a long time
7 you could hear a pin drop used when talking about a situation where there is complete silence and no-one is talking

pin *verb*
pins, pinning, pinned
1 to fasten something with a pin *There's a message from the head teacher pinned to the noticeboard.*
2 to hold someone in a fixed position so they can't move *The bully pinned Alfie to the ground and started kicking him. They pinned down the burglar until the police arrived.*
3 to say that someone is responsible for something, usually something bad *She tried to pin the blame on me.*
4 if you pin your hopes on something or someone, you really want them to be successful in the future or to help you
5 on a computer, if you pin an icon or symbol to a part of the screen such as a taskbar (strip usually along the bottom), you fix it there so that it can be used as a shortcut to open a program

PIN ['pin'] *noun* **PINs**
a PIN or PIN number is a secret number that someone uses with a special plastic card for taking money out of their bank account using a cash machine. It is also used when someone pays for something using a card, for example in a shop or restaurant.
short for: personal identification number

pinafore *noun* **pinafores**
1 a loose dress with no sleeves worn over a blouse or sweater
2 a piece of clothing with no sleeves worn at the front of your body to keep your other clothes clean

pinball *noun*
a game that someone plays on a machine, called a pinball machine, that looks like a large box on four legs. The player must hit small balls against different parts of the machine to score points and try to stop the balls falling into a hole.

pincer *noun* **pincers**
one of the large pointed parts at the end of the front legs of sea animals such as crabs and lobsters

SYNONYM claw

pincers *noun plural*
a small metal tool with two handles at one end like scissors and curved parts at the other end. When you press the handles together, the curved parts hold things tightly. Pincers are used especially for pulling things out, such as nails out of wood.

pinch *verb*
pinches, pinching, pinched
1 to squeeze someone's skin tightly between your first finger and thumb *Sol pinched my arm and really hurt me.*
2 an informal way of saying to steal

pinch *noun* **pinches**
1 a small amount of something, for example an amount you can pick up between your first finger and thumb *Do you want a pinch of salt on your eggs?*
2 the action of pinching someone's skin *She gave me a pinch.*

pincushion *noun* **pincushions**
a small soft object used in sewing for sticking pins and needles into so that they can be stored safely

pine *noun*
1 (*plural* **pines**) a tall tree with thin pointed leaves that stay green in winter. It produces a large hard brown fruit called a cone.
2 the wood of the pine tree, used for making things such as furniture and shelves

pine *verb*
pines, pining, pined
to feel extremely sad, and sometimes weak or ill, because someone is no longer with you or because you no longer have something that you really want *After three weeks abroad, Rohan was pining for home. Emma was still pining away for her dog, which died last week.*

pineapple *noun* **pineapples**
a large oval-shaped fruit with a thick rough yellow-brown skin that forms a pattern of lines crossing each other. It has pointed leaves sticking out at the top, and inside it is yellow, sweet and juicy. Pineapples grow in hot countries.

ORIGIN originally *pineapple* meant 'pine cone' (the fruit of the pine tree) because it looked like a very big pine cone

ping *verb*
pings, pinging, pinged
if something pings, it makes a short high ringing sound, like the sound of a small bell *The pizza's ready – the timer's pinging.*

ping-pong *noun*
a game like tennis that is played indoors on a table. One or two players stand at either end of the table holding wooden bats. They use the bats for hitting a small ball to each other across a low net in the middle of the table.

LANGUAGE EXTRA also spelt *Ping-Pong* (trademark). It is also called *table tennis*.

pink *adjective* **pinker, pinkest**
having a light red colour between red and white

pink *noun* **pinks**
the colour pink

pinkie *noun* **pinkies**
an informal word for the little finger (the smallest finger on the hand)

LANGUAGE EXTRA also spelt *pinky*

pinkish *adjective*
slightly pink

pinpoint *verb*
pinpoints, pinpointing, pinpointed
to find out or say exactly what or where something is *The firefighters had trouble pinpointing the source of the fire.*

pint *noun* **pints**
1 a unit for measuring liquid, equal to about 0.57 litres. There are eight pints in a gallon.

CULTURE NOTE in the USA, a *pint* is equal to about 0.47 litres

2 an informal way of saying a pint of beer

pioneer *noun* **pioneers**
one of the first people to do something important such as study a new subject or develop a new activity or skill *Louis Pasteur was a pioneer of modern medicine.*
pioneer *verb*

pious ['pie-ers'] *adjective*
very religious **piously** *adverb*

pip *noun* **pips**
1 one of the small hard seeds inside a fruit such as an apple or orange
compare: **stone** (sense 5)
2 the pips a series of short high sounds used on the radio for showing the exact time at the start of an hour *We heard the pips for the six o'clock news.*

pipe *noun* **pipes**
1 a long tube for carrying liquid (such as water or oil), gas or air from one place to another, for example inside a building or under the ground *a burst water pipe*
2 a small tube, usually made of wood, with a bowl at one end containing tobacco that people smoke
3 a very simple musical instrument made up of one or more tubes that you blow through
4 one of the tubes of an organ (large musical instrument with a keyboard) that produce sounds when air is forced through them
5 pipes another word for bagpipes

pipe *verb*
pipes, piping, piped
1 if a liquid is piped somewhere, it goes there through a pipe or pipes *Hot water is piped to every flat in the building.*
2 if music is piped somewhere, it is played there because electrical equipment and wires have been connected there *You could hear piped music in every part of the hotel.*
3 to say something in a high voice
4 (informal) if someone pipes down, they stop making a noise *Pipe down, will you!*

pipeline *noun* **pipelines**
1 a large pipe that carries oil, gas or water over a long distance, usually under the ground
2 in the pipeline used for describing something that someone is preparing and that will be finished soon or will happen in the future

354

piper noun **pipers**
a musician who plays a pipe or the bagpipes

piping noun
1 a piece of pipe *The plumber put in two metres of copper piping.*
2 all the pipes in a particular place

piping hot adjective
used for describing food or drink that is very hot

piracy noun
1 the crime of making copies of things such as computer programs, music or films
2 the crime of attacking ships and stealing from them

piranha ['per-rah-ner'] noun **piranhas**
a dangerous fish with a large round body and sharp teeth. Piranhas live in South American rivers.

pirate noun **pirates**
1 someone who sails in a ship and attacks other ships in order to steal from them
2 someone who makes copies of things such as computer programs, music or films, which is against the law *Some boys were selling pirate DVDs in the market.*

pirate verb
pirates, pirating, pirated
if someone pirates something such as a computer program, film or piece of music that belongs to someone else, they make a copy of it without permission, which is against the law *We never use pirated computer games.*

pistachio ['pis-tash-ee-oh'] noun
1 (plural **pistachios**) a small green nut that you can eat. It has a hard light brown shell.
2 the green colour of the pistachio nut, used for example when referring to the green colour of ice cream *Ben was eating a pistachio ice cream.*

pistil noun **pistils**
used for describing the different female parts of a flower that produce the seeds
see: **ovary**, **style** and **stigma**

pistol noun **pistols**
a small gun that is held in one hand

piston noun **pistons**
a piece of metal that goes up and down inside a cylinder (tube with flat ends shaped like circles) to make parts of an engine move, for example a car engine. The piston has the same shape as the cylinder so that it fits inside it.

pit noun **pits**
1 a large hole in the ground
2 a place in the ground from where something such as coal or clay is dug *Iestyn's dad used to work down the pit* (in a coal mine).
3 a very small hole in a surface, for example in someone's skin because of an illness such as chickenpox
4 (informal) a dirty or untidy place such as someone's room
5 the American word for a stone (big hard seed) in fruits such as cherries or peaches
6 (slang) **the pits** used for describing something or someone that is really bad *This week's homework is the pits!*

pit verb
pits, pitting, pitted
1 if something is pitted with holes or marks, it has lots of holes or marks all over *The moon is pitted with craters. My bike is pitted with rust.*
2 if someone is pitted against someone or something else, they fight against them or try to beat them in a game *Murray was pitted against his brother in the tennis match.*

pit bull terrier noun **pit bull terriers**
a very strong and dangerous medium-sized dog with short hair

pitch noun
1 (plural **pitches**) an area of land covered in grass and painted with lines, where people play sports such as football, rugby or cricket
2 the high or low quality of a musical sound *My brother raised the pitch of his guitar by tightening the string.*
3 the high level or quality of a feeling or activity *By the time the school coach arrived in Paris, our excitement had reached fever pitch* (a very high level).
4 (plural **pitches**) a small piece of ground for doing something such as putting up a tent
5 a thick black sticky substance usually made from petroleum (liquid from under the ground), used for example on roofs or boats for stopping water from coming through

pitch verb
pitches, pitching, pitched
1 to put up a tent or make a camp somewhere *We pitched our tent beside the river.*
2 to throw something such as a stone or ball
3 to move suddenly in a certain direction *The bus suddenly stopped and we all pitched forward. The boat was pitching up and down in the rough sea.*
4 to aim something so that it is suitable for a particular group of people or for a particular purpose *This book is pitched at very young children.*
5 if people pitch in, they help each other to do something *All my friends pitched in to tidy up after the party.*

pitch-dark adjective
used for describing somewhere that is completely dark *It was pitch-dark outside and we couldn't see a thing.*

LANGUAGE EXTRA you can also say *pitch-black*

pitcher noun **pitchers**
1 a large container for holding liquids such as water. It has a handle (or sometimes two handles) and a lip (pointed part at the top) for pouring.
2 the liquid that is in a pitcher

pitchfork noun **pitchforks**
a large fork with a long handle and three or four points (or prongs) at the other end. It is used by farmers for lifting and moving hay (cut long grass).

pitfall noun **pitfalls**
a problem, mistake or danger that may happen in the future

pith noun
the pith of a citrus fruit such as an orange is the white substance under its skin

pitiful adjective
1 making you feel great sadness *a pitiful sight*
2 used for saying strongly that something is not good enough or is not enough *Charlie made a pitiful attempt to ride a bike. My brother earns a pitiful amount of money.*
3 used for describing something that you strongly dislike or someone's behaviour that you think is very bad *The bully showed a pitiful lack of respect for her teachers.*

pitifully adverb
1 in a way that makes you feel great sadness *The dog looked pitifully weak and thin.*
2 extremely, and showing that something is not enough or not good enough *Dad's wages are pitifully low. Our internet connection is pitifully slow.*

pitiless adjective
cruel and showing no feelings towards other people **pitilessly** adverb

pitta ['pee-ter' or 'pi-ter'] noun
pitta or pitta bread is a type of round or oval-shaped flat bread, originally from the Middle East. It can be cut open and filled with food such as meat or salad.

pity noun
1 used for saying that you are sad and disappointed about something *It's a pity you can't come to my party. What a pity!*

SYNONYM shame

2 feeling sorry for someone because they are unhappy or suffering *We all felt pity for the little boy begging on the street. When I was lost, a kind person took pity on me* (helped me) *and brought me back home.*

pity verb
pities, pitying, pitied
to feel sorry for someone

pivot noun **pivots**
in science, a pivot is a fixed central point that something turns or balances on

pivot verb
pivots, pivoting, pivoted
to turn or balance on a pivot

pix noun plural
an informal word for pictures or photos, especially digital pictures or photos

pixel noun **pixels**
one of the tiny squares or dots forming the smallest part of an image on a computer screen or in a digital camera
short for: picture element

pixie noun **pixies**
in stories, an imaginary creature with magic powers. Pixies are usually small with pointed ears and a pointed hat. They sometimes play tricks on people.

LANGUAGE EXTRA also spelt *pixy*

pizza ['peet-ser'] noun **pizzas**
an Italian food made from a type of flat round bread baked in an oven with different toppings (foods on top) such as cheese, tomatoes, vegetables and meat

pizzeria – plainly

pizzeria ['peet-ser-ree-er'] *noun* **pizzerias**
a restaurant that sells pizzas

placard *noun* **placards**
a large notice with a message on it, for example one that someone carries in a demonstration showing they support or do not support something

place *noun* **places**
1 any part of space or any piece of land where something or someone is or which is suitable for something *Let's stop in this place and have a picnic. The cup is broken in two places. This is a safe place to swim.*
2 any kind of building *Our school is a great place to study and learn. For my birthday meal my parents took me to a lovely place* (for example restaurant). *You can buy these sweets in just about any place* (for example shop).
3 any kind of area such as a town, village or country *What place do you come from?*
4 a house, flat or home *Come round to my place tomorrow. Granddad wants to buy a little place in the country.*
5 a seat, for example on a bus or in a cinema *Don't sit in my place.*
6 a particular point that has been reached, for example in a book or queue *I've lost my place. Dan's in fourth place in the queue.*
7 any part of a computer screen or any website *You can bookmark all the places you've visited.*
8 used for talking about where something belongs *I put the books back in their place on the shelf.*
9 used for talking about the order in which people complete a race or competition *I finished the race in second place.*
10 used for talking about a chance to take part in something or to join something *There's one place left on tomorrow's trip to the museum.*
11 another word for a situation *If I were in your place, I wouldn't go to her party. My brother has had lots of problems and is not in a good place.*
12 all over the place in or to many different places or parts of something *I spilt the tea and it's gone all over the place. My sister has travelled all over the place.*
13 all over the place also used when you mean untidy *Tidy up your room – your toys are all over the place.*
14 to change places or **swap places** to let someone sit in your seat while you go and sit in theirs
15 to change places or **swap places** also used when you mean to put yourself in the situation that someone is in and let them put themselves in your situation *The prince changed places with the pauper.*
16 in place in the correct position *My uncle had burglars but they left everything in place.*
17 out of place in the wrong position *Some of the letters of the alphabet were out of place.*
18 out of place also used when you mean not right in a particular situation, for example something looking odd or someone feeling uncomfortable *My dad's motorbike looked out of place in the school car park. I was the only one wearing jeans so I felt out of place.*
19 in place of instead of something
20 in the first place used for talking about what happened or what someone did (or should have done) at the beginning of a situation *I wish I'd never met Ruby in the first place.*
21 in the first place also used when talking about the first thing that you want to say *In the first place I want to thank everyone who helped me.*
22 to take place to happen *The cricket match will take place this weekend.*
23 to take someone's place to do what someone else did before, or to be as special or important as someone else *No-one can take my mum's place.*
24 to take the place of something to be used for doing what something else did before *Email has taken the place of the written letter.*
25 no place nowhere (used mainly in American English) *We're going no place until it stops raining.*

place *verb*
places, placing, placed
1 another way of saying to put *I placed my schoolbag in the corner. If you do this, you could place us all in danger.*
2 to remember exactly who someone is or what something is *I've seen her before but I just can't place her.*
3 if someone places an order, they tell someone they want to buy something, for example from a shop or website

place mat *noun* **place mats**
a small piece of material such as plastic or wood that you put underneath someone's plate on a table. It is used as a decoration or for protecting the surface of the table.

LANGUAGE EXTRA also spelt *placemat*

placenta ['pler-sen-ter'] *noun* **placentas**
an organ inside the body of a mother. It is joined to a foetus (developing baby) by a tube called an umbilical cord and provides food to the foetus through this tube.

place value *noun* **place values**
a place value in maths is what a digit (number symbol such as 1, 2 or 3) is worth depending on its position in a number, for example whether it is 'placed' in the units, tens or hundreds column *In the number 525, 5 has two different place values.*

placid *adjective*
1 if a person or animal is placid, they have a gentle character and do not get excited or angry
2 also used about someone's character, appearance or behaviour *a placid smile*
3 quiet and still *a placid river*
placidly *adverb*

plague *noun* **plagues**
1 a very serious illness that spreads quickly and kills lots of people *a plague of cholera*
2 used about a large number of animals or insects that cause harm and damage *a plague of rats; a plague of caterpillars*
3 the Plague was the disease in Europe and Asia in the 14th century that killed millions of people. It was spread by rats and is also known as the Black Death.
4 if you avoid someone or something like the plague, you keep well away from them and want nothing to do with them

plague *verb*
plagues, plaguing, plagued
1 to cause serious problems for someone or something over a long period of time *My uncle has been plagued by ill health for many years. This part of the coast is plagued by strong winds.*
2 to annoy someone very much, for example by keeping on asking them questions or asking them for something

plaice *noun* **plaice**
a round flat fish that lives in the sea and usually has small orange spots on its body. It has white flesh and is used as food.

plaid ['plad'] *noun*
cloth with a pattern of coloured stripes that cross each other to make squares and rectangles

plain *adjective* **plainer, plainest**
1 simple and without any pattern, decoration or writing *a plain brown envelope; a plain blue shirt; plain paper* (with no lines on it); *The carpet was very fancy but the curtains were plain.*
2 simple and ordinary *I like plain food best. Give me a strawberry yoghurt, not a plain one* (one with nothing added to it, for example no fruit or sugar).
3 easy to see *The anger on his face was quite plain.*
4 easy to understand *Can you say that again in plain English?*
5 if someone is plain, they look ordinary and not particularly attractive
6 showing what someone really thinks in an honest way *Give me a plain answer to my question.*
7 used for giving special importance to a word *That's plain stupidity!*
plainness *noun*

SIMILE 'as plain as day' means very plain (senses 3 & 4)

plain *noun* **plains**
a large area of flat land usually covered by grass and without many trees

plain *adverb*
used for giving special importance to a word *Going out in this weather is plain stupid.*

SYNONYM completely

plain chocolate *noun*
chocolate with a bitter taste that is made without milk. Chocolate that is made with milk is called milk chocolate.

plain-clothes *adjective*
used for describing a police officer who wears ordinary clothes instead of a uniform

plainly *adverb*
1 in a way that is easy to see, hear or smell *You could plainly see she was angry. I could hear the music plainly in the next room.*
2 in a way that is easy to understand *This behaviour is plainly wrong.*
3 honestly *Can I speak plainly?*
4 in a simple way, for example without anything extra such as decoration or jewellery *She was dressed plainly.*

plaintive *adjective*
if a sound or voice is plaintive, it sounds sad *We could hear the plaintive cries of wounded soldiers.* **plaintively** *adverb*

plait ['plat'] *noun* **plaits**
one of usually two long thick pieces of hair that hang down on either side of the head. Plaits are formed by twisting together many threads of hair. *Amelie wears her hair in plaits.*
compare: **pigtail** and **bunches**

plait ['plat'] *verb*
plaits, plaiting, plaited
to divide many threads of hair or rope into three or more parts that are twisted together to make one long piece

plan *noun* **plans**
1 a way of doing something in the future that someone has thought about carefully, or someone's idea for doing this *The head teacher has a plan to attract more students. Everything is going according to plan* (the way it is supposed to be going).
2 something that someone decides they're going to do *Do you have any plans for Saturday?*
3 a drawing showing the details of how something is arranged, for example a building or machine
4 a map of something such as a town or region *a street plan*
5 if someone makes plans for something or to do something, they decide they're going to do it and they get ready for it

plan *verb*
plans, planning, planned
1 to decide you're going to do something and, for example, to get ready for it and think about what to do *My parents are planning our holidays. The school has planned a visit to the British Museum.*
2 if you plan to do something or plan on doing something, you've decided you're going to do it *I plan to learn Spanish next term. I'm planning on having a smaller party this year.*
3 if something is planned for a certain time or date, that is when it is supposed to happen *Mum's meeting with the head teacher is planned for tomorrow.*
4 to plan something that is going to be built or created, such as a building, book or painting, is to write or draw the details of how it will look before it is started *Granddad asked a builder to plan his new kitchen.*
planner *noun* **planning** *noun*

plane *noun* **planes**
1 a vehicle that has wings and one or more engines and that flies through the air
2 a hand tool with a flat bottom that has a blade in it. It is used for cutting small strips of wood from a surface in order to make the wood smaller or smoother.
3 in maths, a plane is a flat surface with no thickness
4 a plane or plane tree is a tall tree that has large leaves with pointed edges and fruits that form a soft hairy ball. It is often planted along streets and in parks.

plane *verb*
planes, planing, planed
to plane wood is to make it smaller and smoother using a plane (tool with a flat bottom and a blade)

planeload *noun* **planeloads**
a large number of people or amount of things carried in a plane

planet *noun* **planets**
a very large round object in space, for example made of rock or gas, that orbits (goes round) the sun or another star. There are eight planets in our solar system (group of planets going round the sun). They are: Mercury, Venus, Earth, Mars, Jupiter, Saturn, Uranus and Neptune. **planetary** *adjective*

ORIGIN from Greek *planetes* 'wandering stars', because they looked as if they were moving in the sky

planetarium ['plan-er-**tair**-ree-erm'] *noun* **planetariums**
a building with a ceiling like a dome (top half of a ball) on which pictures of the stars in the sky are shown using special equipment

plank *noun* **planks**
a long flat piece of wood, used for example for building things or for walking on to get from one side of something to the other

plankton *noun*
tiny plants and animals that float on or close to the surface of the sea and are eaten by fish and other sea creatures

plant *noun*
1 (*plural* **plants**) a living thing that grows in the earth and has roots and leaves and usually a stem and flowers. A bush is a plant that has branches growing closely together.
2 (*plural* **plants**) a factory for making things or a place where things such as nuclear power or chemicals are produced
3 machines and equipment, used for example in factories

plant *verb*
plants, planting, planted
1 to put a plant, tree or seed into the ground or into a container of earth so that it will grow there
2 if someone plants an area of land with plants or trees, they put them into the ground there *We passed an orchard planted with cherry trees.*
3 to put something or someone somewhere, often in a clear and strong way or in a way that is bad *He planted his feet on the seat opposite. A terrorist planted a bomb in the marketplace.*
4 to secretly put something somewhere so that someone will be accused of a crime *A nasty person planted a stolen mobile in my coat pocket.*

plantain ['**plan**-tin'] *noun* **plantains**
a type of fruit like a green banana that is usually eaten after it has been cooked

plantation *noun* **plantations**
an area of land in a hot country where crops are grown, for example bananas, cotton, tea or sugar

plaque ['plak' or 'plahk'] *noun*
1 (*plural* **plaques**) a flat object, usually rectangular or round and made of metal or stone, that is fixed to a wall. It is used for giving information about someone or something or for decoration. *There's a blue plaque outside the house where Agatha Christie lived.*
2 a substance containing bacteria (tiny harmful living things) that forms on the surface of people's teeth

plasma *noun*
1 a yellowish watery liquid that makes up over half of the blood in the body
2 a plasma TV or computer screen is a flat screen that shows a very clear picture. It is made using different types of gases between two sheets of glass.

plaster *noun*
1 (*plural* **plasters**) a small piece of thin material that you stick over a cut or injury on your skin to protect it

SYNONYMS Elastoplast, Band-Aid

2 a special material made of white powder and water that dries quickly and becomes hard as it dries. It is put around a broken bone and is used for keeping the bone in its place until it heals. This type of plaster is also called plaster of Paris. *Lucy had her arm in plaster.*
3 a mixture of sand, water and lime (white or grey powdery substance) used for covering walls and ceilings to make them smooth
4 **plaster of Paris** a special material made of white powder and water that becomes hard as it dries. It is poured into moulds (shaped containers) to make statues or models, or it is put around broken bones to keep them in their place.

plaster *verb*
plasters, plastering, plastered
1 to cover something completely with something else *Harry's room was plastered with pictures and posters.*
2 to cover a wall or ceiling with plaster to make it smooth
plasterer *noun*

plastered *adjective*
an informal word for very drunk

plastic *noun* **plastics**
a strong but light material that is produced with chemicals such as oil. It can be made into many different shapes and has many uses. *a plastic bag; My computer mouse is made of plastic.*

ORIGIN from Greek *plastikos* 'able to be shaped'

Plasticine *noun* (trademark)
a soft substance like clay, produced in many different colours. It is used by children for making models.

LANGUAGE EXTRA also spelt *plasticine*

plastic surgery *noun*
an operation or operations by a doctor (called a plastic surgeon) to make someone look better, for example by repairing a part of the body that is injured or has an unusual shape or by making a part of the body bigger, smaller, smoother or straighter

plate *noun* **plates**
1 an almost flat usually round object with very low sides, used for eating or serving food on. Plates are made of china, glass, plastic, metal or earthenware (baked clay).
2 the food on a plate *I've eaten two plates of potatoes.*

plateau – plea

3 a flat piece of something hard such as metal *There's a plate on the back of the computer with the serial number on. The wounded soldier has a metal plate in his skull* (for protecting the brain).
4 a picture in a book, printed on special paper and on a separate page
5 if you have a lot on your plate, you have a lot of things to deal with and worry about

LANGUAGE EXTRA you can also say *enough on your plate* or *too much on your plate*

plateau ['plat-oh'] *noun* **plateaus** or **plateaux**
a large area of high ground that is flat or nearly flat

ORIGIN from French *plateau* 'flat land' (from *plat* 'flat'). The plural ending in *-x* is because the word is French.

-plated *suffix*
used for making adjectives describing something covered in a thin layer of metal *armour-plated*; *gold-plated*

plateful *noun* **platefuls**
an amount of food contained on a plate

platform *noun* **platforms**
1 a long flat area at a railway station beside the rails, where you get on and off a train
2 a raised structure for standing on, for example when giving a speech in front of an audience, when workers repair a building or when tourists admire a landscape
3 a structure built above the sea with equipment for drilling under the sea for something such as gas or oil (thick liquid, for example for making petrol) *an oil platform*

platinum *noun*
a silver-white metal used for making expensive jewellery and for making many types of products and equipment

platoon *noun* **platoons**
a group of about 25 to 50 soldiers. A lieutenant is usually in charge of a platoon.

platypus *noun* **platypuses**
a strange-looking animal with a flat beak like a duck, thick fur, a long body with webbed feet (skin between the toes) and a wide flat tail. Platypuses live in Australia in rivers and streams.

play *verb*
plays, playing, played
1 to do an activity for fun, for example running about, using toys, throwing or kicking a ball or going on equipment such as merry-go-rounds and slides *Lots of children were playing in the park. Megan is playing with her dolls.*
2 to take part in an organised activity such as a particular game or sport, often for fun *James loves playing chess. You played very well in yesterday's match. Do you want to play a game of table tennis?*
3 if you play someone or play against someone, you take part in a game or sport where you try to beat the other person and become the winner *Next Saturday West Ham are playing Manchester United.*
4 to make sounds come out of a musical instrument *Lily plays the violin. Mark doesn't play very well.*

5 if you play music or a particular type of music, you make the sounds of it, for example with an instrument, or you listen to the sounds of it, for example on a media player or laptop *Dan plays rock music on his guitar. My dad likes playing jazz while he's working. What sort of music does that station play?*
6 if you play something such as a DVD, film or video, you make it produce sounds or pictures *Gran was playing an old record from the 1980s.*
7 if something such as a DVD, video or the radio plays, it produces sounds or pictures. If something such as a play or film plays somewhere, it is shown in that place. *I put the disc in but it won't play. There's a Harry Potter film playing at the local Odeon.*
8 if you play a message or play back, for example on a mobile phone or answerphone, you listen to it after it has been recorded by someone
9 if you play a part in a play or film, you do the actions and say the words of a particular character *Who wants to play the pirate in the school play? I've never played in front of an audience before.*
10 used for describing a particular way that someone behaves, for example by pretending to be something they are not *If the teacher asks you any questions, just play dumb. Must you always play the fool?*
11 if you play a trick or joke on someone, you do something stupid to annoy them, make them feel silly or make them believe something that isn't true
12 if someone plays about or around, they behave in a silly way or they waste time *Stop playing around and help me with the dishes.*
13 if you play around with something such as a computer or mobile, you spend time using it to do different things that are not very important
14 (informal) if someone plays up or plays someone up, they behave badly and in an annoying way *Charlie is playing up again!*
15 (informal) if something plays up, it causes someone problems, for example by not working properly *The TV has been playing up all day!*
16 if someone plays with something, they keep moving or touching it with their fingers *Stop playing with your food and eat up!*

play *noun*
1 (*plural* **plays**) a story where actors in a theatre or radio or TV programme say the words and do the actions of the characters
2 when children play and have fun *a play area*; *It's time for play.*
3 a play on words is a funny and clever use of words, for example when someone uses a word that has more than one meaning

Play-Doh *noun* (trademark)
a soft substance like clay, produced in many different colours. It is used by children for making shapes and models.

LANGUAGE EXTRA also spelt *play dough*

player *noun* **players**
1 someone who plays a sport or game
2 someone who plays a musical instrument
3 a piece of equipment for playing music, sounds, images or videos that are stored on something such as a DVD or as a digital file *a CD player*; *a media player*

playful *adjective*
1 if a person or animal is playful, they like having fun and playing *a playful kitten*
2 showing that a person or animal likes having fun and playing *playful behaviour*; *You're in a playful mood today!*
3 not serious *a playful remark*
playfully *adverb* **playfulness** *noun*

playground *noun* **playgrounds**
an area where children play, especially at school

playgroup *noun* **playgroups**
a place where children between the ages of about two and five go to play and learn while being looked after and taught by grown-ups

SYNONYM playschool

playing card *noun* **playing cards**
a small piece of stiff paper with numbers and pictures on it, used for playing games. In some of the most common games, there are 52 cards, called a pack, divided into four different groups, called hearts, diamonds, spades and clubs.

playing field *noun* **playing fields**
an area of land covered in grass and painted with lines, where people play sports such as football

playlist *noun* **playlists**
a list of songs or other pieces of music that someone creates, for example in a music software program, so that they can listen to the songs and music again

playmate *noun* **playmates**
a friend that a child often plays games with

play-off *noun* **play-offs**
an extra game played between two teams or two players to decide who is going to win

playpen *noun* **playpens**
a piece of furniture, usually rectangular, with bars or a net around it and open at the top, where a baby or small child can play safely

playschool *noun* **playschools**
a place where children between the ages of about two and five go to play and learn while being looked after and taught by grown-ups

SYNONYM playgroup

plaything *noun* **playthings**
another word for a toy

playtime *noun*
the time when children at school go out to play in the playground

playwright *noun* **playwrights**
someone who writes plays

SYNONYM dramatist

plaza ['plah-zer'] *noun* **plazas**
a large open area in a town, surrounded by shops or other buildings

plea *noun* **pleas**
1 when someone asks for something urgently, often expressing strong feelings such as worry or sadness *The parents made a plea for help to find their missing son.*

358

2 when someone says in a court of law whether they are guilty or not guilty of a crime

plead *verb*
pleads, pleading, pleaded
1 to ask for something urgently and often with a strong feeling such as worry or sadness *The captured soldier pleaded for mercy. Dad pleaded with me not to go out in the rain. He had a pleading look in his eyes.*
2 if someone pleads guilty or not guilty in a court of law, they say whether they are guilty or not guilty of a crime

pleasant *adjective*
1 used for describing something that you like and that makes you happy *pleasant weather; a pleasant town*
2 used for describing someone that you like because they are friendly or helpful *Our teacher is very pleasant. My cousin is always pleasant to me.*
3 also used about someone's actions and behaviour *He gave me a pleasant smile.*

pleasantly *adverb*
1 in a way that you think is good and that makes you happy *a pleasantly warm day; I was pleasantly surprised.*
2 in a friendly way *She smiled pleasantly.*
3 in an attractive way *The flowers were pleasantly arranged.*

please *interjection*
1 used when asking or telling someone something when you want to be more polite *Could you help me, please? Come here, please! Please close the window.*
2 used when saying yes to something politely *'Do you want an ice cream?' – 'Yes, please.' 'More cake?' – 'Please.'*

please *verb*
pleases, pleasing, pleased
1 to make someone happy *Jack is very hard to please.*
2 used for saying that someone can do or have anything they want *You can take whatever you please and go wherever you please. My parents say I can come and go as I please.*

pleased *adjective*
1 used when you think something or someone is good and you're happy about that *Ms Patel is pleased with my homework. I was pleased to hear that my sister passed her exam. Seema was looking pleased with herself* (happy because something good has happened).
2 if you're pleased to do something, you want to do it or are ready to do it *John said he'd be pleased to teach me to swim.*

SIMILE 'as pleased as Punch' means very pleased. *Punch comes from the name of a puppet in an old-fashioned puppet show called Punch and Judy.*

pleasing *adjective*
1 another way of saying pleasant *a pleasing shape*
2 making you happy *The results were very pleasing.*

pleasurable *adjective*
making you feel very happy *a pleasurable experience*

pleasure *noun*
1 a feeling of being very happy *He smiled with pleasure.*
2 (plural **pleasures**) something that makes you feel very happy *Granddad prefers simple pleasures such as walking and watching TV.*
3 **with pleasure** a polite way of saying that you are very happy to do something that someone has asked you to do *'Will you help me across the road?' – 'With pleasure.'*

SYNONYM for sense 3: gladly

pleat *noun* **pleats**
a fold made in a piece of clothing or in something such as a curtain. It is pressed into the cloth in a special way or sewn into it so that it stays there.

pleated *adjective*
used for describing cloth that has pleats in it *a pleated skirt*

plectrum *noun* **plectrums**
a small flat piece of plastic or metal that you hold between your thumb and fingers and use for playing the strings of a musical instrument such as a guitar

SYNONYM pick

pledge *noun* **pledges**
1 a serious promise, for example to do something or give money
2 an amount of money that someone has promised

pledge *verb*
pledges, pledging, pledged
1 to promise something or to promise to do something in a very serious way, often when talking about important people *The head teacher pledged her support. The prime minister pledged to help young people find jobs.*
2 to promise to give money *Britain pledged millions of pounds to fight diseases in Africa.*

plentiful *adjective*
if something is plentiful, there is a lot of it *a plentiful supply of cakes; Apples are plentiful this year.* **plentifully** *adverb*

plenty *pronoun & adverb*
1 a lot of something *There are plenty of books in the school library. I've got plenty more to do. My bike cost my dad plenty.*
2 enough or more than enough of something *You've got plenty of time to finish your homework. There's plenty for everyone. 'More ice cream?' – 'No, thanks, I've still got plenty.'*

pliable *adjective*
used about a substance that is easy to bend or twist without breaking

pliers ['ply-ers] *noun plural*
a small metal tool with two handles at one end like scissors and flat parts at the other end. Pliers are used for holding things tightly, bending or cutting things such as wire and pulling out nails.

plight *noun*
an extremely bad and sad situation *The United Nations is looking at the desperate plight of refugees in Africa.*

plimsoll *noun* **plimsolls**
plimsolls are soft shoes that are made with strong cloth called canvas and that have rubber soles. They are used especially for playing sports.

plod *verb*
plods, plodding, plodded
1 to walk slowly and with short heavy steps, for example for a long way or because walking is difficult *We plodded through the streets in the rain until finally we reached Granddad's house.*
2 to work slowly and in a steady way, especially doing something that needs a lot of time and is often boring
3 to make slow progress with something even though you try *Andy has been plodding along at school for ages.*

plodder *noun* **plodders**
someone who works slowly and makes slow progress, for example because they are not very intelligent

plodding *adjective*
1 if something such as a book or film is plodding, it is slow and boring
2 if someone is plodding, they are usually not very intelligent and they work slowly and make slow progress

plonk *verb* (informal)
plonks, plonking, plonked
to put something or someone somewhere, for example carelessly or without thinking *I plonked my schoolbag on the floor and went out to play. Ethan plonked himself in front of the TV and refused to move.*

plop *noun* **plops**
the gentle sound made by something small falling into a liquid

plop *verb*
plops, plopping, plopped
1 to fall into a liquid with the gentle sound that something makes when it does this *I threw a stone and it plopped into the water.*
2 (informal) to put or drop something gently or carelessly somewhere
3 (informal) if someone plops themselves down somewhere, they go and sit or lie down there, for example carelessly

plot *noun* **plots**
1 a secret plan to do something, usually something bad, which is made by two or more people
2 the main events in a book, film or play that make up the story
3 a plot or plot of land is a small piece of land, for example for building on or growing plants on

plot *verb*
plots, plotting, plotted
1 if two or more people plot something, they make a secret plan to do something, usually something bad
2 to make a mark on a map to show the position or route of something
3 to draw points or lines on a graph (mathematical diagram)

plotter *noun* **plotters**
one of two or more people who take part in a plot (secret plan)

359

plough–plunge

plough noun ploughs
a piece of farm equipment with blades for breaking up the soil so that seeds can be planted. Ploughs are usually pulled over the ground by tractors or, especially in the past, by people, horses or oxen.

plough verb
ploughs, ploughing, ploughed
1 to plough land is to break up the soil with a plough so that seeds can be planted *We saw some farmers ploughing their fields.*
2 if you plough through something that there is a lot of or something that is large, you deal with it even though it takes a lot of time and needs a lot of effort *I have loads of emails to plough through. I'm still ploughing through my Harry Potter book* (reading it even though it is long).

LANGUAGE EXTRA be careful to write *plough*, not *plow*. Plow is the American spelling.

ploughman's noun ploughman's
1 a ploughman's or ploughman's lunch is a small meal of bread, cheese, salad and pickle (sauce made from vegetables), often eaten in a pub
2 also used for describing any type of sandwich made with cheese, salad and pickle

plover [rhymes with 'cover'] noun **plovers**
a bird with a short beak and short tail, long legs and long pointed wings. Plovers usually live near the sea.

ploy noun **ploys**
a trick or plan to secretly get something that you want

pluck verb
plucks, plucking, plucked
1 to pull something very quickly from something *Dad plucked a grey hair from his head. My big sister plucks her eyebrows* (pulls out hairs from them to make them thinner).
2 to pull or take someone very quickly away from a place, for example somewhere dangerous *A helicopter plucked the drowning boy from the water.*
3 if someone plucks a bird such as a chicken or turkey, they pull off its feathers so that it can be cooked and eaten
4 to pluck a flower or fruit is to cut it or break it off a plant or tree

SYNONYM to pick

5 to pluck the string of a musical instrument such as a guitar is to use your fingers or a plectrum (small flat piece of plastic or metal) to pull the string then let it go to produce a sound
6 **to pluck up courage** to be brave enough to do something, for example something that you were afraid to do before

pluck noun
the special quality of someone who is not afraid to face danger or difficult things

SYNONYM courage

plucky adjective **pluckier, pluckiest**
1 if someone is plucky, they are not afraid to face danger or difficult things and they won't let anything stop them

2 also used about someone's behaviour *That was a very plucky thing to do.*

SYNONYM brave

plug noun **plugs**
1 a small plastic or rubber object that has two or three metal pins or prongs (thin pieces of metal) sticking out and is fixed at the end of a wire. It is used for connecting electrical equipment such as TVs and computers to the electricity to make them work. The plug is pushed into a special opening, for example in a wall, that is called a socket.
2 an informal word for the special opening that a plug is pushed into *Do you have a plug in your room that I can use for my hairdryer?*
3 a circle of rubber, plastic or metal that covers a hole in a sink or bath (called a plughole) and stops the water from flowing out
4 any object or material used for stopping up a hole
5 an earplug (material you put into your ear to protect it)

plug verb
plugs, plugging, plugged
1 to plug a hole in a container is to stop up the hole so that no liquid can flow out
2 if someone such as an actor or writer plugs something such as a film or book, they talk about it, for example on TV, to make people interested
3 if you plug something in, you connect it to the electricity with a plug or you connect it to a piece of equipment such as a computer *At the back of the laptop there's a hole for plugging in a microphone.*
4 if something plugs in, it connects to the electricity or to a piece of equipment *The keyboard plugs in here.*

plug and play noun
a technology that allows equipment to be connected to a computer and to start working straightaway because the computer automatically installs any software that is needed

LANGUAGE EXTRA usually spelt *plug-and-play* when used in front of a noun, for example *a plug-and-play webcam*

plughole noun **plugholes**
a hole at the bottom of a sink or bath where the water flows out

plug-in noun **plug-ins**
a small computer program that adds something extra to another program or to a web browser (software for looking at sites on the internet)

plum noun **plums**
a small round fruit with a red, purple or yellow skin, soft flesh and a hard seed inside called a stone

plumage ['ploo-mij'] noun
the feathers of a bird

plumb verb
plumbs, plumbing, plumbed
if someone such as a plumber plumbs in a washing machine or dishwasher, they connect it to the pipes of a building so that water can flow into and out of it

plumb adverb (informal)
exactly in a particular position *The snowball hit me plumb in the middle of my forehead.*

plumber noun **plumbers**
someone whose job is to connect and repair water pipes and things that use water pipes to make them work, such as sinks, baths and toilets

plumbing noun
1 all the water pipes in a particular building and things connected to them
2 the work of connecting and repairing water pipes and the things that use water pipes
3 the job of a plumber

plume noun **plumes**
1 a large feather, for example one that someone wears as a decoration on a hat
2 a thick cloud of something shaped like a feather that rises up into the air *a plume of smoke*

plummet verb
plummets, plummeting, plummeted
to fall suddenly and quickly

plump adjective **plumper, plumpest**
1 having a pleasant round shape *plump cheeks*
2 a plump person or animal has a body that is heavy in a pleasant way

plump verb
plumps, plumping, plumped
1 to plump for something or someone is to choose them, often after thinking carefully first
2 (informal) if you plump something down somewhere, you put it down there carelessly or heavily
3 (informal) if someone plumps themselves down somewhere, they go and sit or lie down there carelessly

plum tomato noun **plum tomatoes**
a large tomato shaped like an egg

plunder noun
1 things stolen from a place, usually valuable things
2 the action of stealing things from a place

plunder verb
plunders, plundering, plundered
to steal things from a place, as soldiers sometimes do in a war *Many buildings were plundered during the civil war. Gold and silver were plundered from the royal palace.*
plunderer noun

plunge verb
plunges, plunging, plunged
1 to fall suddenly from a high place *A car plunged off the cliff and into the water.*
2 to jump quickly into water *Mum saw a girl fall into the river and plunged in to rescue her.*
3 to put someone or something suddenly into a particular situation or thing *There was a loud bang and we were plunged into darkness. First plunge the spaghetti into boiling water. She plunged the knife* (pushed it hard) *into the orange.*
4 to move somewhere quickly *When he saw the giant coming, he plunged under the table.*
5 to become lower suddenly *The temperature has plunged to minus five.*

360

plunge–point

6 to plunge something such as a sink is to get rid of dirt from it by using a plunger (tool with a handle fixed to a piece of curved rubber)

plunge noun **plunges**
1 a sudden fall, for example from a high place or in the level or value of something
2 when someone jumps into the water, for example to go for a swim

plunger noun **plungers**
a small tool with a handle fixed onto a piece of rubber called a suction cup, which is shaped like the top of a ball. It is used for getting rid of dirt from sinks, baths and toilets when the dirt is stopping the water from flowing out. It works by creating a vacuum (space without air) to suck up the dirt.

plural noun **plurals**
in grammar, the plural is the form of a word that you use when you mean more than one thing or person. Nouns, pronouns and verbs all have plural forms. The singular is the form used when you mean only one.

> **LANGUAGE EXTRA** the *plural* of nouns is usually formed by adding -s to the singular, for example *cups, trees*. Some nouns form their plural by adding -es, for example nouns ending in -ch, -sh, -x and -s (*bunches, dishes, foxes, buses*). With nouns ending in -o, the plural is usually -es (*potatoes*) but sometimes either -es or -s (*mosquitoes* or *mosquitos*).
> Nouns ending in -y where the letter in front of the -y is not a vowel (*a, e, i, o, u*) usually change *y* to *i* before adding -es (*one baby, two babies*). Nouns that end in -f change the *f* to *v* before adding -es (*one leaf, two leaves*).
> Some nouns have plurals that do not follow a particular rule (*one child, two children; one mouse, two mice*), and a small number have plurals that follow unusual rules (*one cactus, two cacti* or *two cactuses; one crisis, two crises*). A few nouns are the same in the plural and the singular (*one sheep, two sheep; one aircraft, two aircraft*). Finally, many nouns have no plural form at all (*dust, furniture*).
> In this dictionary the plural is shown for all noun headwords (nouns that you look up) if they have a plural.
> A plural pronoun is a word like *we, us, they* or *them* that refers to more than one person. If you mean one person only, you use singular words such as *I, me, he* or *him* or *she* or *her*.
> A plural verb is a word like *walk* (*we walk, they walk*). The singular form is usually the same as the plural in verbs (*I walk*) except for the third person of the present tense (*he walks, she walks*).

plural adjective
used for describing a noun, pronoun or verb that is used in the plural *'Books' is a plural noun. 'We' is a plural pronoun. 'Are' is a plural form of the verb 'to be'.*

plus preposition
1 used for showing that you are adding a number to another number. It is written as the symbol +. *Eight plus two equals ten (8 + 2 = 10).*
2 used for adding something extra to what you say or for mentioning someone else *You can't play outside now – it's raining, plus it's very late. Sophie came to my party with her sister plus her parents.*
3 the plus sign is the symbol + used instead of the word 'plus' when numbers are used

plus noun **pluses**
something good and useful about something or someone *Your new school is within walking distance, so that's a plus.*

plush adjective
very expensive and comfortable *a plush hotel*

plutonium ['ploo-toh-nee-erm'] noun
a chemical element used in nuclear weapons and as a fuel in producing nuclear power

plywood noun
a strong wood made by fixing thin layers of wood together with glue, used for making boxes, shelves and furniture, for example

p.m.
used for showing the time after midday and before midnight *It's 8.00 p.m.*

> **ORIGIN** from Latin *post meridiem* 'after midday'

pneumatic ['nyoo-mat-ik'] adjective
made to work by air that is kept under pressure *They were digging the road with pneumatic drills* (powerful tools for breaking up hard surfaces).

pneumonia ['nyoo-moh-nee-er'] noun
a serious illness of the lungs usually caused by an infection that makes you cough, causes pain in the chest and makes it difficult to breathe

poach verb
poaches, poaching, poached
1 to cook food using gently boiling water, for example an egg without its shell, sometimes in a special pan called a poacher
2 to kill or catch animals on land that belongs to someone else without their permission *He was caught poaching rabbits. They come out at night to poach.*

poacher noun

pocket noun **pockets**
1 a small cloth bag for carrying things that is fixed inside a piece of clothing such as a jacket, coat or pair of jeans. There is usually a pocket on either side of the piece of clothing towards the middle of the body so that you can easily put your hand in it. Some pieces of clothing have pockets in other places too.
2 any small bag for putting things in that is fixed inside or outside a larger object, for example a suitcase, handbag, backpack or vehicle seat
3 any object that has the shape of a pocket *A kangaroo pouch is a pocket of skin.*
4 an area where something happens or that is different from the area around it *Outside the city centre there are some more pockets of crime.*
5 used for talking about money for buying things *We have to pay for the school uniform out of our own pocket* (with our own money). *If Dad buys everyone an ice cream, he'll be out of pocket* (he'll have less money than before).

pocket adjective
small enough to carry in your pocket *a pocket dictionary*

pocket verb
pockets, pocketing, pocketed
1 to take money and keep it for yourself, for example money that doesn't belong to you or money that you win as a prize
2 to put something in your pocket

pocketbook noun **pocketbooks**
an American word sometimes used for a handbag

pocketful noun **pocketfuls**
an amount of something you can put in your pocket *a pocketful of coins*

pocket money noun
money that you are given by your parents or by the people who look after you, for example every week, so that you can spend it or save it

pod noun **pods**
1 a long narrow container for seeds that grows on some plants, for example bean plants or lupins (garden plants with long stems)
2 a long narrow container that is fixed to the outside of a space vehicle or aircraft and can be separated from it

podcast noun **podcasts**
a radio programme that you can download from the internet and listen to on a computer or media player such as an iPod

> **ORIGIN** from *iPod* and *broadcast*

podgy adjective **podgier, podgiest**
slightly fat, for example in a way that looks pleasant

poem noun **poems**
a piece of writing arranged in lines, usually with a particular beat (regular pattern of sounds). The lines often end with words that rhyme.

poet noun **poets**
someone who writes poems

poetic or **poetical** adjective
1 connected with poems that people write *the poetical works of Edward Lear*
2 connected with a quality of beauty and imagination and expressing strong feelings in a beautiful way *The film is full of powerful poetic images.*

poetically adverb

poetry noun
1 the poems that someone writes *a book of poetry*
2 poems as a form of literature that you study *Poetry is my favourite subject.*
3 a quality of great beauty and imagination and one that expresses strong feelings in a beautiful way *The book is beautifully written and has a certain poetry.*

po-faced adjective
used for describing someone who looks too serious and whose face shows no expression or feelings, for example because they dislike something or someone

point noun **points**
1 the sharp end of something such as a needle or pencil
2 a particular place or spot *The two lines cross at this point.*

361

point–police constable

3 an exact moment in time *At this point in the game, Ben scored another goal.*
4 a point or decimal point is a dot in a decimal number, for example 3.5 (three point five)
5 a number used for counting in a game or competition. You get a point each time you do something right, for example answering a question correctly in a quiz or winning a part of a tennis match. The numbers are added up at the end to make your score. *Mohammed won the quiz by 90 points to 50.*
6 the reason for something *There's no point in talking about this any more.*
7 something that someone says or writes, for example an idea or fact *That's a good point you made about pupils having too much homework. Chloe's dad has a point* (an idea worth considering).
8 the meaning of something *Thank you for explaining this to me – I get the point. Please get to* (or *come to*) *the point* (say what you really mean).
9 an important part or quality of something or someone *My laptop is very cheap but it does have its good points* (there are good things about it). *Maths is Amy's strong point* (she's good at maths).
10 the points of a compass are the directions marked on a compass, for example north, south, north-east, south-west
11 the points on a railway track are the places where the rails are moved so that trains can change from one track to another
12 to make a point of doing something is to make sure that you do something or pay attention to doing something
13 to be on the point of doing something is to be going to do it straightaway *Granddad is on the point of leaving.*
14 up to a point partly *What you say is true up to a point.*

point *verb*
points, pointing, pointed
1 to hold out your first finger (or something else such as a stick) towards something to show someone where it is *I pointed to the library across the road. It's rude to point!*
2 to move or turn something so that it is facing in a particular direction *Don't point that stick at me.*
3 to be turned in a particular direction *The gun was pointing towards me.*
4 to show something or a particular direction *The arrow points to the exit. The needle on the dial is pointing to number 6.*
5 if someone points something out, they tell you about it or show it to you *My parents pointed out the dangers of eating too many sweets.*

point-blank *adverb & adjective*
1 in a very direct and rude way *He refused point-blank to help me. It was a point-blank refusal.*
2 used about a gun that is fired very close to someone or something

pointed *adjective*
1 with a point at the end *The magician was wearing a pointed hat.*

SYNONYM **pointy**

2 very direct and said or done to upset someone *a pointed remark*

pointer *noun* **pointers**
1 any object used for pointing or showing something clearly, such as a needle in a measuring tool or a stick
2 a symbol or image, for example an arrow or a hand with a pointing finger, used for pointing to something on a computer screen and often controlled by a computer mouse
3 a helpful piece of information or advice *Can you give me a few pointers to help me make up my mind?*
4 something that tells you something about a situation or a sign that something is true
5 a dog used in hunting that stands still and points with its nose towards birds and animals when it finds them

pointless *adjective*
if something is pointless, it has no meaning or purpose or it is a waste of time doing it *It's pointless waiting any longer – he's not going to come.* **pointlessly** *adverb*

point of view *noun* **points of view**
1 the way someone thinks about something based on one particular part of a situation *The Mars landing was important from a scientific point of view. The story is told from the point of view of the little boy.*
2 someone's opinion about something *We should respect other people's points of view.*

pointy *adjective* **pointier, pointiest**
with a point at the end *a pointy hat*

SYNONYM **pointed**

poise *noun*
1 a careful and gentle way of moving your body, standing or sitting
2 a pleasant and relaxed way of behaving that people respect because you control your feelings

poised *adjective*
1 completely still and ready to do something *The cat was poised, ready to jump as soon as it saw the mouse.*
2 ready for something or ready to do something *The employers are poised to begin talks with the workers.*
3 behaving in a pleasant and relaxed way and controlling your feelings *He appeared calm and poised.*

poison *noun* **poisons**
1 a substance that kills people and animals or makes them ill if they eat it, drink it or breathe it in
2 a substance used by animals and insects to kill you or make you ill if they bite or sting you

poison *verb*
poisons, poisoning, poisoned
1 to kill a person or animal or make them ill by giving them poison
2 to put poison into something that a person or animal eats or drinks

poisonous *adjective*
1 containing poison *a poisonous mushroom; a poisonous gas*
2 using poison *a poisonous snake*

poke *verb*
pokes, poking, poked
1 to push something or someone with your finger or with something long or pointed like a stick *He poked me in the ribs with his elbow.*
2 to push something long or pointed into something or someone or through something *I poked my hand into the bird's cage. He poked his finger through the curtain.*
3 to appear from somewhere or make something appear *Jamie's head was poking out of the window. Poppy poked out her tongue.*

SYNONYM **to stick out**

4 if you poke around somewhere, you look for something there, for example by moving lots of things around *Who's been poking around in my drawer?*
5 if you poke fun at someone or something, you think they're silly and you say something unkind about them
6 if you poke a hole in something, you make a hole in it by pushing something through it

poke *noun* **pokes**
1 a push with your finger or with something long or pointed *He gave me a poke in the ribs.*
2 to have a poke around is to look for something somewhere

poker *noun*
1 a game that grown-ups play with playing cards, in which they try to win money
2 (*plural* **pokers**) a metal stick for stirring a fire (moving the pieces of coal around to make it burn better)

poky *adjective* **pokier, pokiest**
an informal way of saying small and uncomfortable *a poky little house*

LANGUAGE EXTRA also spelt *pokey*

Poland *noun*
a country in Central Europe

polar *adjective*
1 connected with the area near the North Pole or South Pole *the polar regions*
2 a polar bear is a large white bear that lives near the North Pole

pole *noun* **poles**
1 a long thin and usually round piece of wood or metal. It is often used for supporting something such as a tent or plant. *a runner bean pole; a telegraph pole* (for supporting phone wires)
2 each of the ends of a magnet or battery
3 the North Pole and South Pole are the places on the surface of the earth that are the furthest north and south
4 the pole vault is a sport in which someone uses a long pole to help them jump from the ground over a high bar

Pole *noun* **Poles**
someone from Poland

police *noun*
1 the men and women who have the job of making sure that people obey the law and who are responsible for dealing with crimes and accidents
2 the organisation that these men and women belong to *George's dad is thinking of joining the police.*

police constable *noun* **police constables**
an ordinary police officer

362

police force *noun*
the police in charge of a particular country or area

police officer *noun* **police officers**
a member of the police. A male police officer is also called a policeman and a female police officer is also called a policewoman.

police station *noun* **police stations**
the place where police officers work

policy *noun* **policies**
1 something that someone does in a particular situation, especially something included in a plan made by people in charge of an organisation or business *The school's policy is to always have a teacher on duty during playtime.*
2 someone's policy on a particular subject is the way they feel about it and the way they behave because of this, especially when this is part of a plan *What is the mayor's policy on transport?*
3 an insurance policy is a document from an insurance company giving details of the agreement with the customer and explaining what is insured

polio ['poh-lee-oh'] *noun*
a very serious disease that affects the brain and muscles and can make it impossible for someone to move part or all of their body
short for: poliomyelitis

polish ['pol-ish'] *verb*
polishes, polishing, polished
1 to rub something, for example with a cloth or brush, to make it shiny *Dad was polishing my shoes for school.*
2 (informal) to polish something off is to finish it quickly, for example food or work *Hasan has polished off all the cake!*

polish ['pol-ish'] *noun*
1 a substance you rub on something such as shoes or furniture to make it shiny *shoe polish*
2 when you rub something to make it shiny *My shoes need a quick polish.*

Polish ['poh-lish'] *adjective*
connected with Poland or the Polish language

Polish ['poh-lish'] *noun*
the language people speak in Poland

polished *adjective*
1 shiny because of being rubbed with polish *a polished floor*
2 doing something with great skill, or done with great skill *a polished actor; a polished performance*

polite *adjective* **politer, politest**
1 if you're polite, you behave in the nice way you should behave towards other people and you use kind and pleasant words because you respect other people's feelings *Isla is always polite to her teachers.*
2 also used about what you do or say *a polite smile; a polite apology*

ANTONYM **rude**

ORIGIN from Latin *politus* 'polished'

politely *adverb*
1 in a way that shows respect towards other people, for example using kind and pleasant words *I asked her politely to be quiet.*
2 in the nice way that you should behave towards other people to show that you respect their feelings *Seema smiled politely – she always behaves politely towards grown-ups. He sang very badly but we all clapped politely* (without enthusiasm and just to be nice).

ANTONYM **rudely**

politeness *noun*
1 the behaviour or special quality of someone who is nice towards other people and respects their feelings
2 if you talk about the politeness of what someone says or does, you mean that what they say or do is kind or pleasant and shows respect

ANTONYM **rudeness**

political *adjective*
connected with the power of being in charge of a country, area or organisation, or connected with governments or parties *political power; a political party* (people who try to win votes in elections to control a government); *a political leader* (in charge of a government or party) **politically** *adverb*

politician *noun* **politicians**
someone who works in politics, for example a member of a government or parliament

politics *noun*
1 the activities connected with getting and using power in order to be in charge of a country, area or organisation, for example the activities of a government or party such as the Labour or Conservative Party
2 work as a politician *My uncle wants to go into politics.*
3 the study of how to get and use power in a country, area or organisation *My brother wants to study politics at university.*

polka ['pol-ker'] *noun* **polkas**
1 a lively dance from Eastern Europe that was popular in the 19th century
2 the music played when people dance the polka

polka dot ['poh-ker' or 'pol-ker'] *noun* **polka dots**
a small round spot that is one of a pattern of spots, for example on clothes

LANGUAGE EXTRA usually spelt *polka-dot* when used in front of a noun, for example *a polka-dot dress*

poll *noun* **polls**
1 an occasion when people vote in an election
2 the polls are the places where people vote *Yesterday the country went to the polls* (went to vote).
3 a poll or opinion poll is when people are asked to give their opinion about something, for example by a company or political group, and their opinions are carefully considered

pollen *noun*
1 a powder produced by the stamens (male parts) of a flower. It is carried by insects or the wind to another flower where it helps the female part of that flower to produce seeds.
2 a pollen count is a measurement that shows the amount of pollen in the air. It is mentioned on the radio or on TV, for example, and is useful as a warning for people who suffer from illnesses such as hay fever (caused by breathing in pollen).

pollinate *verb*
pollinates, pollinating, pollinated
if an insect or the wind pollinates a flower, it carries pollen from that flower to another where the pollen helps to produce seeds
pollination *noun*

pollutant *noun* **pollutants**
a chemical or other substance that pollutes

pollute *verb*
pollutes, polluting, polluted
to make water, land or the air dirty or dangerous, for example by putting chemicals or waste matter from the body into it *a polluted beach*

pollution *noun*
1 damage done to water, land or the air by chemicals or other substances
2 chemicals or other substances that make water, land or the air dirty or dangerous

polo *noun*
a game between two teams, usually of four players, riding on horses. Each team tries to hit a small hard ball into the other team's goal using a mallet (long stick with a wooden part at the end like a fat tube).
compare: **hockey**

polo neck *noun* **polo necks**
a sweater with a high collar that is folded over and fits tightly around the neck

LANGUAGE EXTRA usually spelt *polo-neck* when used in front of a noun, for example *a polo-neck jumper*

poltergeist ['geist' rhymes with 'sliced'] *noun* **poltergeists**
a type of ghost that can do strange things such as move objects through the air while making a lot of noise

ORIGIN from German *Poltergeist* 'noisy ghost'

poly- *prefix*
used with nouns and adjectives to mean many *polygon* (shape with many sides); *polysyllabic* (with many syllables)

polyester *noun*
a light cloth that is made in a special way by machines, used for example for making clothes

polygon *noun* **polygons**
a flat shape with three or more straight sides, for example a triangle, square, hexagon or octagon

polyhedron ['pol-ee-hee-drern'] *noun* **polyhedra** or **polyhedrons**
a solid or 3-D shape with a number of flat faces (or surfaces), for example a pyramid or cube

polymer ['pol-ee-mer'] *noun* **polymers**
a chemical substance made up of large molecules (groups of atoms) that are made from joining together many small molecules. Polymers include many different materials such as plastics, nylon, rubber and silk.

polystyrene – popular

polystyrene ['pol-ee-stye-reen'] *noun*
a light, usually white, plastic material that is used for many different things. For example, it is often used for wrapping around delicate products such as computers or cameras to protect them when they are put in boxes and sent through the post, or for putting around something to stop it losing heat or for making ceiling tiles. *a polystyrene cup*

polythene ['pol-ee-theen'] *noun*
a plastic used especially for making thin soft sheets, for example for wrapping around things such as food. It is also used for making thin soft bags mainly for carrying food and keeping food fresh or dry.

pomegranate ['pom-ee-gran-it'] *noun* **pomegranates**
a large red fruit with a hard skin and many large juicy seeds inside that you eat

pomp *noun*
used about the special actions and the beautiful and colourful clothes and decorations connected with something such as an important occasion *The coronation ceremony took place with great pomp.*

pompom *noun* **pompoms**
1 a small fluffy ball made from pieces of fabric such as wool, usually worn as a decoration, for example on the top of a soft hat or slipper
2 in American English, a pompom is a ball made of loose strips, usually of paper, cloth or plastic, that is held in each hand and waved at a sports event by a cheerleader (someone who gets a crowd to cheer loudly)

LANGUAGE EXTRA also spelt *pompon*

pompous *adjective*
someone who is pompous thinks that they are more important than other people and behaves and speaks in a very serious way that is not very natural *My cousin's teacher uses long and old-fashioned words in a very pompous way.* **pomposity** *noun* **pompously** *adverb*

poncho *noun* **ponchos**
a piece of clothing made from a rectangle of cloth or plastic with a hole in the middle for your head. You wear it over your other clothes, for example to protect you from the rain.

ORIGIN from Spanish *poncho* (from *pontro* 'woollen blanket' in the Mapuche language of Chile and Argentina)

pond *noun* **ponds**
an area of water, much smaller than a lake, that is either natural or made by people

ponder *verb*
ponders, pondering, pondered
to think carefully about something, often for a long time

ponderous *adjective*
1 heavy, slow and clumsy *the ponderous steps of an elephant*
2 used for describing what someone writes or says that is long, difficult and boring **ponderously** *adverb*

pong *noun* **pongs**
a slang way of saying a very bad smell
pong *verb* **pongy** *adjective*

pony *noun* **ponies**
a small horse belonging to one of many different breeds (types with their own special qualities) with a strong thick body and thick tail

ponytail *noun* **ponytails**
used for describing someone's long hair that is tied at the back of the head and hangs down, like the tail of a pony

pony-trekking *noun*
the activity of riding on ponies through the countryside

poodle *noun* **poodles**
a dog with thick curly hair. Poodles can be big or small and their hair is often cut into different shapes.

ORIGIN from German *Pudelhund* 'water dog' (from *pudeln* 'to splash about' and *Hund* 'dog'), because poodles were trained to fetch birds or fish from the water

pool *noun* **pools**
1 another word for a swimming pool
2 a small area of liquid lying somewhere such as on the ground *After the rain there were pools of water in the road. They saw a dead soldier in a pool of blood.*
3 a game played on a cloth-covered table in which players use a cue (long stick) to hit 16 balls into holes
compare: **snooker** and **billiards**
4 something such as money or equipment that people share *The school keeps a pool of laptops for pupils to borrow.*
5 a group of people who are ready and able to do a particular job *a pool of plumbers*

pool *verb*
pools, pooling, pooled
if a group of people pool something such as money, equipment or knowledge, they share it, for example to help each other do something better

poor *adjective* **poorer, poorest**
1 if someone is poor, they have very little money or no money at all
2 also used for describing a place where poor people live *Odongo comes from a poor village in Africa.*
3 used for saying that you feel sorry for someone *Poor Kayla, she's fallen over again!*
4 used for saying that something is not of good quality or not of a good standard *very poor results*; *a poor excuse*
5 doing something badly *a poor runner*; *Ben is really poor at maths.*

SIMILE 'as poor as a church mouse' means very poor (sense 1)

poorly *adverb*
not very well *poorly dressed*; *poorly paid*

poorly *adjective*
not feeling well *Seema went home as she was feeling poorly.*

pop *verb*
pops, popping, popped
1 (informal) to go or come somewhere quickly and for a short time *Mum and Dad have popped out to the supermarket. Can I pop in for a minute?*
2 (informal) to put something somewhere *Pop the biscuits into the jar.*
3 to pop up is to appear, for example suddenly or in unexpected places *When I press Enter, a message pops up on my screen.*
4 if something such as a balloon pops or you pop it, it bursts with a short loud noise
5 if the cork in a bottle pops or you pop it, it comes out of the bottle with a short loud noise
6 if your eyes pop, you look very surprised or excited

pop *noun*
1 pop or pop music is modern music with short songs and a simple pattern of strong sounds. It is often played with electric or electronic equipment. *a pop group*; *a pop star* (famous singer or musician)
2 (plural **pops**) a short loud noise like a very small explosion
3 an old-fashioned word for a fizzy drink (one with lots of bubbles in it)

popcorn *noun*
a food made from the yellow seeds of a plant called maize that are heated until they burst open, often with a 'pop' sound, and become soft enough to eat. Popcorn is usually eaten as a snack, for example in the cinema or while watching TV.

Pope *noun* **Popes**
the religious title of the person in charge of the Roman Catholic Church

poplar *noun* **poplars**
a tall thin tree with triangular leaves that fall off in the autumn and fruits called catkins (fluffy flowers hanging down from the branches). It is often planted along the sides of roads and fields.

poppadom *noun* **poppadoms**
a type of very thin round bread cooked in hot oil. It is like a large dry biscuit and is eaten with food from India such as curry or as a snack between meals.

LANGUAGE EXTRA also spelt *poppadum*

poppy *noun* **poppies**
1 a plant with a long thin stem and large delicate flowers, usually red, with small black seeds inside
2 an artificial red poppy flower, usually made of wire and cloth and pinned to a piece of clothing. It is worn on Poppy Day or Remembrance Day (an occasion in November when people remember all soldiers who have died).

Popsicle *noun* (trademark)
the American word for an ice lolly

popular *adjective*
1 if something or someone is popular, lots of people like them *a popular teacher*; *This book is very popular with young people.*
2 believed, supported or felt by many or most people *a popular belief*; *popular support*
3 for or connected with ordinary people *popular music*; *a popular newspaper*

ORIGIN from Latin *popularis* 'belonging to the people' (from *populus* 'people')

popularise *verb*
popularises, popularising, popularised
1 to make something easy to understand for ordinary people
2 to make something known to lots of people and liked by them

> LANGUAGE EXTRA also spelt *popularize*

popularity *noun*
when something or someone is popular with lots of people *The popularity of our school continues to grow.*

popularly *adverb*
by lots of people or most people *Jacob is popularly known as Jack.*

populated *adjective*
used for describing a place that has people living there *a populated area* (for example a town); *London was less populated at that time.*

population *noun* populations
1 all the people who live in a particular place such as a country, region, town or neighbourhood
2 all the people or animals belonging to a certain group that live somewhere *How big is the French-speaking population of Switzerland?*

populous *adjective*
used for describing a place that has lots of people living there *a populous country*

pop-up *adjective*
1 a pop-up book is a particular type of children's book with pictures inside. The pictures are partly cut from the pages so that they stand up when you open the book.
2 a pop-up menu on a computer screen is a menu that appears on the screen, for example when you click something with your mouse

pop-up *noun* pop-ups
a pop-up or pop-up ad is an advert that suddenly pops up (or appears) in front of you on a web page as a new window

porcelain ['por-ser-lin'] *noun*
a hard shiny white substance made by heating a type of clay. It is used for making things such as cups, plates and bowls as well as artistic objects such as vases and figurines (small models of people or animals).

porch *noun* porches
a small shelter with a roof that is usually built outside the front door of a building as part of the building. A porch is either open or has walls and a door.

porcupine *noun* porcupines
a small animal that has quills (long stiff hairs with sharp points) on its back. It makes its quills stick up when it is in danger.

> ORIGIN from Old French *porc espin* 'prickly pig'

pore *noun* pores
one of the tiny holes in your skin that sweat passes through, for example when you do exercises or when you are hot or frightened

pore *verb*
pores, poring, pored
to pore over something such as a document is to read it or study it very carefully

pork *noun*
1 the meat from a pig that is eaten as food
2 a pork chop is a small piece of meat from a pig, with the bone in it

porous *adjective*
used for describing something that has lots of tiny holes in it so that liquid or air can pass through *porous soil*

porpoise ['por-pers'] *noun* porpoises
a large sea animal like a fish with teeth. It is similar to a dolphin but has a rounder nose and is slightly smaller.

porridge *noun*
a thick soft food made by boiling oats (crushed seeds of the oat plant) with milk or water. It is usually eaten hot for breakfast.

port *noun* ports
1 an area next to the sea where ships stop, for example for goods and passengers to be taken on and off, and where ships can be left safely. A port often has buildings and equipment such as cranes and is usually larger than a harbour.
2 a town or city that has a port *Dover is a busy port.*
3 a place on the outside of a computer for connecting another piece of equipment, for example a keyboard, mouse or printer, using a cable *a USB port*
4 used for describing the left side of a ship or aircraft from the position of someone who is on board and facing forward *The ship was damaged on its port side.*
compare: **starboard**
5 a strong sweet Portuguese wine that is usually red. It originally came from the Portuguese city of Oporto.

portable *adjective*
used for describing something that you can carry around with you, for example a mobile phone or tablet computer

portal *noun* portals
1 a website that has links to other sites on the internet and helps you find information there
2 a large and important-looking doorway or entrance

portcullis *noun* portcullises
a heavy iron gate made of metal bars hanging above the entrance to a medieval castle. It comes down and blocks the entrance if the castle is attacked.

porter *noun* porters
1 someone whose job is to carry your luggage, for example at an airport or railway station
2 someone whose job is to move patients around a hospital, for example between a ward (room with beds) and an operating theatre
3 someone who stands in front of the main door of a building such as a hotel to help people when they go in and come out
4 someone who works at a place such as a college, school or block of flats and deals with many different things such as looking after buildings, sorting letters and providing information *a porter's lodge*

porthole *noun* portholes
a small window, usually round, in the side of a ship or aircraft

portion *noun* portions
1 a part of something
2 an amount of food suitable for one person *Could you give me an extra portion of chips?*

portly *adjective* portlier, portliest
if someone is portly, they have a body that is heavy in a way that makes them look serious and important *a rich and portly old man*

portrait *noun*
1 (*plural* **portraits**) a painting, drawing or photo of a person, especially just the face or the face and top part of the body
2 (*plural* **portraits**) a description of something or someone, for example in a book
3 a way of printing a document from a computer in which the short sides of the page are at the top and bottom. If the long sides are at the top and bottom, it is called landscape.

portray *verb*
portrays, portraying, portrayed
1 to describe or show something or someone in a particular way
2 to show something or someone in a painting, drawing, book, play or film *The book portrays the First World War.*
3 to play the part of a particular character in a play or film

portrayal *noun* portrayals
when someone describes or shows something or someone, or the particular way something or someone is described or shown *The film is an excellent portrayal of life in the 1960s.*

Portugal *noun*
a country in South-West Europe

Portuguese *adjective*
connected with Portugal or the Portuguese language

Portuguese *noun*
1 the language people speak in Portugal and Brazil
2 the Portuguese are people from Portugal

pose *noun* poses
1 a particular position into which you move your body so that someone can paint or draw you or take your photo
2 behaviour that does not seem right or natural, for example when someone pretends to have qualities they don't really have

pose *verb*
poses, posing, posed
1 to move your body into a particular position and stay there so that someone can paint or draw you or take your photo *Would you pose in front of the school gate?*
2 if something or someone poses something such as a problem, danger or risk, they are considered to be or to cause that problem, danger or risk *These bullies pose a danger to the whole school. Going to that country poses a serious risk for our team.*
3 if someone poses a question, they ask someone a question

posh–post

4 if someone poses as someone else, they pretend to be that person, for example to trick someone *Someone came to the door posing as a police officer.*

posh *adjective* **posher, poshest** (informal)
1 expensive and fashionable *a posh hotel; My cousin lives in a posh part of Leeds.*
2 used for describing someone who belongs to a high class in society or their way of speaking or behaving *Our teacher has a posh accent.*

position *noun* **positions**
1 an exact place, for example where something is or should be *We're trying to locate the ship's position. Put the books back in the right position on the shelf.*
2 a particular type of place *Plant the tree in a sunny position in the garden.*
3 a particular way in which someone's body or an object is held or put, for example standing, sitting or lying flat *I was sitting in an uncomfortable position. Put the box in an upright position.*
4 used for talking about the order in which people complete a race or competition *Seema finished the race in third position.*
5 a particular point that has been reached, for example in a queue or book *I'm in second position in the queue.*
6 a seat, for example in a cinema *Can we swap positions?*
7 someone's particular situation *I would say yes if I were in your position. I'm not in a position to help her* (not able to help her).
8 a job, or someone's place in an organisation *My brother has applied for lots of positions. My mum has a position of responsibility in the NHS.*
9 an opinion or point of view

position *verb*
positions, positioning, positioned
to put something or someone in a particular place, for example carefully so that they are in the exact place they are supposed to be *Cut out these shapes and position the triangle on top of the square.*

positive *adjective*
1 if you're positive about something, you know it is true *I'm positive Ollie left for school without his coat.*

> SYNONYM **certain**

2 showing that something is true *positive proof; This is a positive sign that he's still alive.*
3 good, or making you feel good things about someone or something *a positive influence; Abdhul has very positive feelings towards school* (he likes it).
4 feeling or saying good things about someone or something *We're positive about the future. Indira's parents are very positive. I received a very positive reply to my email. I asked her to help me and she gave me a positive answer* (said yes).
5 very strong *Our teacher took positive action to deal with the bully.*
6 a positive number is one that is more than zero
7 used for describing the result of a medical test that someone has, for example to see if they are ill. A positive result means that the test has found something bad or different from usual.
8 used for describing a type of electrical charge that protons have. In a battery, for example, there is a positive pole (end) and a negative pole. Electrons flow from the negative pole to the positive pole.
compare: **negative**

positively *adverb*
1 in a good way, or in a way that makes you feel good things about someone or something *Sanjay has worked very positively this term.*
2 in a way that will produce good results in the future *We have to deal with this problem positively.*
3 in a way that shows something or someone is good or that shows someone likes something *I hope you will look at my suggestion positively. She replied positively to my email. I asked Tom if he wanted more ice cream and he answered positively* (said yes).
4 in a way that shows that something is true *She said positively that the mobile phone I had found was hers.*
5 used for giving extra importance to a word *Your friend was positively rude* (extremely rude).

posse ['poss-ee] *noun* **posses**
1 a group of people who move around together *a posse of journalists*
2 in the past, a group of people in the US who helped a sheriff (important police officer) to catch a criminal or search for someone

possess *verb*
possesses, possessing, possessed
1 if you possess something, for example something very good, big or valuable, it belongs to you *My uncle possesses a big house in the country. Do you possess the winning ticket?*
2 used for talking about something such as a quality or power that something or someone has *This TV possesses good picture quality. Do you possess the knowledge to fix my laptop?*

possessor *noun*

possessed *adjective*
if someone is possessed, they behave as if they are controlled by a very strong feeling or power, often a very bad or strange one *He was running about shouting and hitting people as if he were possessed.*

possession *noun*
1 (*plural* **possessions**) something that belongs to you *Granddad lost all his possessions in a fire.*
2 a situation where something belongs to you *Our school took possession of some land to build a gym.*

possessive *adjective*
1 wanting to keep things for yourself and not share them with other people
2 wanting to control someone that you love and not letting them show friendship to other people
3 used in grammar for showing who or what something or someone belongs to or is connected with. For example, 'my' and 'your' are possessive adjectives and 'mine' and 'yours' are possessive pronouns.

possibility *noun*
1 when something might happen or be true *There's a possibility I might be selected for the school team.*
2 (*plural* **possibilities**) something that might happen or be true *If you ski too fast, getting injured is a real possibility.*
3 (*plural* **possibilities**) a possible choice *Taking the bus to school is one possibility.*

possible *adjective*
1 if something is possible, it can be done or can happen *It's not possible to do your homework and watch TV at the same time!*

> ANTONYM **impossible**

2 used for saying that something could be true or correct or might exist *a possible explanation; It's possible she forgot. There's just one possible problem.*
3 suitable for something *This is a possible place for a picnic.*
4 used when asking someone something politely *Is it possible to close the window?*
5 as . . . as possible used when you mean the most someone or something can do or be *I ran as fast as possible* (as fast as I could). *Please come as soon as possible* (as soon as you can). *My teacher tries to be as helpful as possible* (as helpful as he or she can be).

possibly *adverb*
1 used for saying that something is possible or could be true but is not certain *Mohammed is possibly the best player on the team.*
2 used when answering a question when you don't want to say yes or no *'Can I come round to your house on Saturday?' – 'Possibly.'*
3 used when asking someone something politely *Could you possibly make a bit less noise?*
4 used for giving extra importance to something you say, for example to show how surprised you are or how much you can do something *You can't possibly have eaten all that cake! I ran as fast as I possibly could.*

post *noun* **posts**
1 a system for sending or receiving letters and parcels. To send them, you usually stick stamps on them and put them in a postbox or take them to a post office. *We sent Grandma a present by post.*

> SYNONYM **mail**

2 letters and parcels (or a letter or parcel) sent or received by post

> SYNONYM **mail**

3 when a postman or postwoman brings a letter or parcel, for example to someone's home *The post is late today.*
4 when letters or parcels are collected from a postbox or post office *The last post is at 5.30 p.m.*
5 a piece of written information such as a message or blog entry that you put on a website *Click here to read the next post.*
6 a long thick piece of wood, concrete or metal that is fixed upright in the ground, for example as part of a fence or part of a goal in football
7 a thin pole in a horse race that shows where the race ends or starts *They're very close to the winning post.*
8 an important job *a teaching post*

9 the place that someone such as a soldier or guard is supposed to protect

post *verb*
posts, posting, posted
1 to send something to someone by post
2 to put a letter in a postbox or take a parcel to a post office *I posted your letter in the postbox on the corner.*
3 to put up a notice where everyone can see it *The exam results are posted on the wall opposite the staff room.*
4 to post something on a website is to write information there, such as a message or blog, or to put an image or video there
5 to send someone such as a soldier or guard to watch over and protect a place *Two police officers were posted outside the house.*
6 to send someone somewhere as part of their job
7 to keep someone posted about something is to make sure they know about it *Keep me posted when you know what's happening.*

post- *prefix*
used with words such as adjectives and nouns to mean after or later than *post-war*; *This changed post-1990.*

postage *noun*
1 the money you pay to send a letter or parcel by post, for example using stamps
2 a postage stamp is a stamp you stick on a letter or parcel showing the amount paid to send it by post

postal *adjective*
connected with the sending of letters and parcels through the post *the postal service*; *a postal worker*

postbag *noun* postbags
a large strong bag used by postal workers for carrying letters and parcels

postbox *noun* postboxes
a container, for example in a street or inside the wall of a post office, that is used for posting letters in. Postboxes in the street are usually tall, round and painted red.

postcard *noun* postcards
a small card that you write a message on and send to someone by post without an envelope. It usually has a picture on one side.

postcode *noun* postcodes
a group of letters and numbers that are part of an address and show exactly where a place is

poster *noun* posters
a large piece of printed paper with a picture or words on it that is put up somewhere such as on a wall. Posters are used as decoration or for advertising something such as a film or concert.

posthumous ['pos-tyoo-mers'] *adjective*
happening after someone has died but often connected with something good they did when they were alive *The soldier was given a posthumous medal for bravery.*
posthumously *adverb*

ORIGIN from Latin *postumus* 'last one to be born', referring to someone born after the death of their father

postie *noun* posties
an informal word for a postman or postwoman

posting *noun* postings
1 a piece of written information such as a message or blog entry that you put on a website

SYNONYM post

2 a job in which someone is sent to another country or town as part of their work

Post-it *noun* Post-its (trademark)
1 a small piece of coloured paper, often yellow or green, with a sticky strip on the back. It is used for writing a message on and sticking onto something, for example as a reminder to do something.
2 a program that puts a small window that looks like a Post-it onto your computer screen for you to type messages and reminders into

LANGUAGE EXTRA also called a *Post-it note* or *sticky note*

postman *noun* postmen
a man whose job is to deliver letters and parcels to people's homes and businesses

postmark *noun* postmarks
an official mark put on something sent by post showing the place, date and time when it was posted **postmark** *verb*

postmaster *noun* postmasters
a man or woman in charge of a post office

post-mortem *noun* post-mortems
an examination of someone's dead body to find out how they died

SYNONYM autopsy

post office *noun* post offices
a place where people buy stamps, send letters and parcels and make and receive different kinds of payments

postpone *verb*
postpones, postponing, postponed
if someone postpones something such as a meeting or event, they say it will happen at a later time and not at the time it was supposed to happen *The school play has been postponed until after Christmas.*

SYNONYM to put off

postponement *noun*

postscript *noun* postscripts
1 a short extra message that you write at the end of a letter or email after the place where you sign your name. It is usually abbreviated to PS.
2 an extra piece of information at the end of something such as a story

ORIGIN from Latin *post scriptum* 'written after' (from *post* 'after' and *scribere* 'to write')

posture *noun* postures
the particular way someone holds their shoulders and back when they are standing, walking or sitting *Ellie has good posture* (her shoulders and back are straight).

post-war *adjective*
happening or existing after a war, especially the Second World War *The post-war period was very difficult.*

LANGUAGE EXTRA also spelt *postwar*

postwoman *noun* postwomen
a woman whose job is to deliver letters and parcels to people's homes and businesses

posy *noun* posies
a small bunch of flowers

pot *noun* pots
1 a deep round container, usually with a lid, for cooking things in
2 a container with a handle and lid for making and serving coffee or tea *a coffee pot*; *a pot of tea*
3 the hot coffee or tea that is in a pot *I drank two pots of tea.*
4 a container, usually round, for storing liquids or food or for growing plants in, or something that is in the container *a pot of paint*; *a pot of yoghurt*; *a pepper pot* (for shaking pepper onto food); *a plant pot*; *I've eaten two whole pots of yoghurt.*
5 (informal) if someone has pots of something such as money, they have lots of it
6 (informal) if something is going to pot, it is getting worse or becoming spoilt because no-one is looking after it

pot *verb*
pots, potting, potted
if you pot a plant, you put it into a container so that it will grow there *a potted plant* (one in a container)

potassium *noun*
a soft silver-white chemical element, used for example for adding to the soil to help plants grow

potato *noun* potatoes
a hard round brown, yellowish or reddish vegetable that grows under the ground as a tuber (thick part of the root). It is white or yellow inside and you cook it to make it soft before eating it.

ORIGIN from Spanish *patata* 'potato' (the potato was introduced into England from Spain in the 16th century)

potbelly *noun* potbellies
a large round stomach **potbellied** *adjective*

potent *adjective*
1 very powerful *a potent symbol*
2 having a very strong effect *a potent medicine*
potency *noun* **potently** *adverb*

potential *adjective*
1 used for describing something that may happen, exist or be true in the future *a potential danger*
2 used for describing what someone may be in the future *David is a potential chess champion.*

potential *noun*
1 the qualities that someone or something has that may allow them to become successful in the future *Anne has great potential as a singer.*
2 the possibility that something may happen, exist or be true in the future

potentially *adverb*
used for saying that something may happen, exist or be true in the future *This situation is potentially serious. Potentially, she could be a great singer.*

pothole – powerful

pothole noun **potholes**
1 a hole in the surface of a road
2 a hole or cave formed deep under the ground by the action of water

potholing noun
the activity of going into underground holes or caves **potholer** noun

potion noun **potions**
a special type of drink, for example one that is poisonous, is used as a medicine or has a magical effect *He drank the magic potion and was turned into a frog.*

pot luck noun
a situation where you take a chance without knowing if you're going to be lucky and get something good *I don't know what these dishes are on the menu – we'll have to take pot luck* (choose anything or be given something and hope it's good).

LANGUAGE EXTRA also spelt *potluck*

potter noun **potters**
someone who makes objects out of clay

potter verb
potters, pottering, pottered
if you potter around (or about), you spend your time happily doing small jobs around your home or garden

pottery noun
1 the activity of making objects out of clay using your hands
2 cups, plates, pots, vases and other objects made out of clay and baked in an oven called a kiln to make them hard
3 (plural **potteries**) a place where pottery is made

potty adjective **pottier, pottiest** (informal)
1 slightly crazy
2 to drive someone potty is to annoy them or make them angry

potty noun **potties**
a small container shaped like a bowl that a very small child sits on and uses as a toilet

pouch noun **pouches**
1 a small soft bag for keeping things in, made of cloth, leather or plastic
2 a pocket of skin at the front of the body of a female animal such as a kangaroo where it carries its baby

poultry ['pol-tree'] noun
1 birds such as chickens, turkeys and geese that people keep for their eggs and meat
2 the meat of birds such as chickens, turkeys and geese eaten as food

pounce verb
pounces, pouncing, pounced
1 to jump on someone or on an animal quickly to catch or attack them, for example from a hidden place *The cat pounced on the mouse.*
2 to move quickly to catch or hold someone *At that moment the police pounced.*

pound noun **pounds**
1 a unit of money in the UK. There are 100 pence in a pound and its symbol is £.
2 a unit for measuring weight, equal to about 454 grams. There are 16 ounces in a pound.

pound verb
pounds, pounding, pounded
1 to hit something or someone hard many times, for example making a lot of noise *We heard someone pounding on the door.*
2 to hit or press something many times until it becomes a powder or broken into tiny pieces
3 if your heart pounds, it beats very quickly, for example when you are nervous or excited
4 to move somewhere with heavy loud steps *Sam pounded angrily out of the classroom.*
5 to attack a place many times with bombs, big guns or tanks *The town has been pounded by jets for two weeks.*

pounding noun
1 when a place is attacked many times, for example with bombs or big guns *London took a pounding during the Second World War.*
2 when someone loses very badly, for example in a game or battle *Our football team took a real pounding.*

pour verb
pours, pouring, poured
1 if you pour something such as a liquid or powder, you make it flow from its container, especially into another container *Can you pour me a lemonade? Dad poured out the tea* (poured it from the teapot into the cups). *If you don't want your tea, just pour it away* (get rid of it by pouring it somewhere such as into a sink).
2 if something such as a liquid or powder pours somewhere, large amounts of it flow *Blood was pouring out of the animal's wound. Tears were pouring down his face.*
3 if people or things pour somewhere, large numbers or amounts of them go there *Visitors were pouring into the museum. Emails are pouring into the BBC about yesterday's programme. I opened the curtains and light came pouring into the room.*
4 to rain very heavily *Don't go out – it's pouring. It's been pouring with rain all day.*

pout verb
pouts, pouting, pouted
to push out your lips, especially your bottom lip, for example to show that you're not happy about something

poverty noun
the situation of someone who has very little money or no money at all *Many people in that country are poor and have always lived in poverty.*

powder noun
1 (plural **powders**) a soft dry substance made up of lots of tiny grains, for example flour, dust or ground coffee
2 a powder used as a make-up on someone's face to make their skin look less oily and more attractive

powder verb
powders, powdering, powdered
1 to put powder on someone's skin, especially the face
2 powdered milk is milk with the liquid removed and made into a powder so that it can last a long time. You add water to it to make milk that you can drink.

powdery adjective
like powder *powdery snow*

power noun **powers**
1 being able to do something *the power of speech; These doctors have the power to do good. Chloe has great powers of concentration. The wizard gave the princess special powers* (for example to perform magic).
2 being able to make people do what you want *He's an old-fashioned teacher who likes to have power over the class. The United States has lots of power in the world.*
3 being in charge of something such as a country, town or organisation, being able to make the people there do what you want and being able to influence actions and events *All politicians want power. Dad doesn't like the government in power* (in charge of the country). *A new government has come to power* (started to be in charge).
4 something that someone is allowed to do *The police have been given special powers to search inside the museum.*
5 something such as electricity or gas, used for example for making equipment work or providing heat or light *solar power* (power from the sun); *nuclear power* (power from changing the structure of an atom); *Plug in the computer and turn on the power.*
6 strength *Footballers need a lot of power in their muscles.*
7 when a vehicle or piece of equipment is able to work well and fast *Your laptop is slow – it doesn't have enough power.*
8 a country with a lot of influence in the world *Britain is an important power.*
9 in maths, the power of a number shows you how many times to multiply that number by itself. It is written as a small number (called the exponent) to the right of the number you are multiplying. For example, 5^3 (or 5 to the power of 3) means $5 \times 5 \times 5$, which equals 125.

power verb
powers, powering, powered
1 to provide a vehicle or piece of equipment with the power it needs to make it work *a nuclear-powered submarine; The computer mouse is powered by two small batteries.*
2 if you power up a computer or power down a computer, you turn it on or off

power cut noun **power cuts**
a short period when the electricity in a building is cut off

LANGUAGE EXTRA also called a *power failure*

powerful adjective
1 if a person or something such as a group or country is powerful, they have the power to strongly influence people, actions and events *a powerful prime minister*
2 if something such as an idea, argument, belief or reason is powerful, it strongly influences people's minds *Religion is very powerful in that part of the world.*
3 having a lot of strength *A footballer needs powerful muscles. My brother's motorbike has a powerful engine.*
4 done or produced with a lot of strength *Someone gave him a powerful blow on the head.*
5 working very well and producing very good results, for example because of having the latest equipment inside or the latest software *a powerful computer* (working very fast); *a powerful telescope* (showing images very big); *a very powerful software program* (big and with lots of features)

6 having a strong effect on someone *a powerful medicine* (for example one that changes something in the body); *a powerful smell* (for example a very bad or strong one)
7 making you feel very strong feelings such as fear, shock or happiness *a powerful film; a powerful image*

powerfully *adverb*
in a very strong way *Shakespeare expresses this idea powerfully. My dad is powerfully built* (has a big and strong body).

powerless *adjective*
having no power to do something such as stopping something bad from happening *The police were powerless to stop the looters.* **powerlessly** *adverb*

power line *noun* **power lines**
a wire that carries electricity. Usually the wire is high above the ground.

power point *noun* **power points**
a place, for example on a wall, where you connect a piece of electrical equipment

power station *noun* **power stations**
a building where electricity is produced

practical *adjective*
1 good at dealing with problems because you look at real situations and not ideas
2 good at using your hands, for example to make or fix things
3 useful because connected with real situations *My brother has practical experience as a carpenter. These shoes are practical if you do a lot of walking.*
4 likely to be successful because connected with real situations *a practical solution; Jamie's plan isn't very practical.*
5 if you play a practical joke on someone, you do something to trick them

practical *noun* **practicals**
a class or examination in which you do or make something, for example a scientific experiment or a model of something

practically *adverb*
another way of saying almost or nearly *I've practically finished.*

practice *noun*
1 when you do an activity lots of times to get better at it and get more knowledge and skill *You need lots of practice to speak a foreign language well.*
2 (*plural* **practices**) a particular time that you spend doing an activity you want to get better at *We have football practice tonight.*
3 (*plural* **practices**) something that people do regularly *Setting homework is common practice in schools. The police are trying to stop these criminal practices.*
4 used when talking about someone actually doing something *Are you going to put these ideas into practice?* (do what you say)
5 (*plural* **practices**) the business of a professional person such as a doctor or lawyer
6 in practice used when talking about a real situation *Children are supposed to tell a teacher if they are bullied but in practice not many do.*

7 out of practice used when you mean you haven't done an activity enough and so you've lost some of your skill *Tom played really badly – he must be out of practice.*

practise *verb*
practises, practising, practised
1 to do an activity lots of times to get better at it and get more knowledge and skill *Shreya practises the piano every day. Andrew doesn't practise much.*
2 to do something regularly such as a hobby *My brother practises karate.*
3 to follow something such as a religion or idea *Buddhism is practised in China.*
4 to work at a particular job *My cousin practises as a doctor. My mum practises law* (is a lawyer).

LANGUAGE EXTRA be careful to spell the noun with *-ice* at the end (*practice*) and the verb with *-ise* (*practise*)

practising *adjective*
used for describing someone who follows a religion *a practising Catholic*

prairie *noun* **prairies**
a very large area of flat land, mainly covered by long or short grass, in the USA and Canada

praise *verb*
praises, praising, praised
1 to say something good about someone, for example because they have done something well or done good things *Ms Singh praised me for my homework.*
2 to say something good about something *People praised the book for being honest and well written.*

praise *noun*
words that say something good about someone or something *The head teacher was full of praise for our cricket team.*

pram *noun* **prams**
a small vehicle on wheels for carrying a young baby around when you are walking. It is a kind of bed that the baby lies or sits in and it has a cloth hood hanging over it to protect the baby against the wind and rain.
compare: pushchair

prance *verb*
prances, prancing, pranced
1 to walk or jump about with a lot of energy and moving your body a lot, for example in a silly way *The actors were prancing about on the stage.*
2 to walk or move about in a way that shows you want people to look at you *Dylan was prancing around in his new suit.*
3 if an animal such as a horse prances, it moves about quickly, lifting its front legs very high

prank *noun* **pranks**
a trick that you play on someone for fun and to make them look silly
prankster *noun*

prawn *noun* **prawns**
a small greyish sea animal with a shell, a long body and 10 legs. It can be eaten as food and turns pink when it is cooked. Prawns look like large shrimps.

pray *verb*
prays, praying, prayed
1 to speak to someone or something such as God or a particular god or saint, for example using the special words of a prayer *She put her hands together to pray for her sick daughter to get better.*
2 to wish or hope very strongly that something will happen *We're all praying for good weather for tomorrow's sports day.*

prayer *noun*
1 (*plural* **prayers**) the words that someone says when they pray, for example the special words written in the prayer book of a particular religion *I'm meeting Ahmed after Friday prayers* (religious ceremony where people say prayers).
2 the action of praying *The bishop knelt in prayer.*

pre- *prefix*
used with words such as adjectives and nouns to mean before or earlier than *pre-existing; pre-war; Things were different pre-2010.*

preach *verb*
preaches, preaching, preached
1 to talk to people about a religious subject (used especially about someone in the Christian religion such as a priest)
2 to give someone advice in an annoying way about how to behave or what to believe *I wish Mum would stop preaching at me about the clothes I wear.*
3 to say that you strongly support something *Gandhi preached tolerance.*
preacher *noun*

precarious ['prer-kair-ee-ers'] *adjective*
1 if something or someone is precarious, they are in a dangerous place or situation where they can easily fall *Your cup's a bit precarious on the edge of the table.*
2 used for describing something bad that can easily get much worse or a situation where nothing about the future is certain *The life of a homeless person is precarious.*
precariousness *noun*

precariously *adverb*
1 in a dangerous way where something can easily fall *Your tablet is precariously perched on the edge of your desk.*
2 in a way that shows that things can easily get much worse or that nothing about the future is certain *These refugees live precariously in camps along the border.*

precaution *noun* **precautions**
something that someone does to stop bad things happening in the future, for example things being damaged or people being hurt *There's a snowstorm coming so we're taking precautions.*

precede *verb*
precedes, preceding, preceded
1 to happen or exist before something or someone *My birthday precedes yours. Shakespeare preceded Dickens.*
2 to come or go in front of something or someone *Adjectives precede nouns in English but not in French. Elsie preceded me into the room.*

LANGUAGE EXTRA be careful not to confuse *precede* with *proceed* (continue)

preceding–prejudiced

preceding *adjective*
used about something or someone that comes before or is earlier than something or someone else *the preceding pages* (the pages before this one); *the preceding week*; *The preceding monarch was Henry the Fifth.*

precinct ['pree-sinkt'] *noun* **precincts**
1 a part of a town with shops where vehicles are not allowed so that people can walk there *a pedestrian precinct*; *a shopping precinct*
2 an area around a large building such as a prison or cathedral, usually with a wall surrounding it
3 a part of a city in the USA with its own police and fire service

precious *adjective*
1 worth a lot of money, for example because of being rare and beautiful *a precious metal* (for example gold or silver); *a precious stone* (for example a diamond or emerald used for making jewellery)
2 used for describing something or someone that is very special and important to you *a precious memory*; *I love my baby sister – she's very precious to me.*
3 used for describing something that shouldn't be wasted because there isn't enough of it *Water is precious. Your teacher's time is very precious.*

precipice ['press-ip-iss'] *noun* **precipices**
a very steep cliff or side of a mountain

precis ['pray-see'] *noun* **precis** ['pray-seez']
a shorter version of a piece of writing or a speech. A precis mentions only the main ideas of the longer version.

> **LANGUAGE EXTRA** also spelt *précis*, from the French for 'precise'

precise *adjective*
1 correct in every detail *precise instructions*; *Can you be more precise?* (give more details)
2 used about something when you mean just that thing and no other *This is the precise spot where I last saw him. At that precise moment, Dad came into the room.*
3 very careful in the way you do something and paying attention to details *When using the mouse you have to be precise and click on one of the small icons.*
4 also used about something that you do very carefully *Sewing patterns onto cloth is very precise work.*

precisely *adverb*
1 in every way or detail *Tell me precisely how it happened.*
2 used when you mean no more and no less than a particular number or amount *I left for school at precisely eight o'clock.*
3 used when you mean a particular thing and no other *My parents bought me precisely the bike I wanted.*
4 very carefully and paying attention to details *You have to cut very precisely along the dotted line.*
5 very clearly *I can understand my French teacher because he speaks very precisely.*
6 used when you agree with what someone says *'We should have less homework.' – 'Precisely!'*

precision *noun*
1 the quality of being very careful in the way you do something and of paying attention to details *Making model planes needs a lot of precision.*
2 the quality of being correct or clear in every way or detail *She told me with great precision how it happened.*
3 a precision instrument is a piece of equipment such as a microscope, watch or measuring gauge that is made in a very delicate way using special tools and with careful attention to small details

predator ['pred-er-ter'] *noun* **predators**
an animal that hunts other animals to kill and eat them, for example a lion or tiger
predatory *adjective*

predecessor ['pree-diss-ess-er'] *noun* **predecessors**
1 a person who had the job or who did the work that someone else is doing now
2 something that came before something else *This computer is a lot faster than its predecessor.*

> **ANTONYM** successor

predicament ['prer-dik-er-mernt'] *noun* **predicaments**
a difficult situation

predicate ['pred-ik-ert'] *noun* **predicates**
in grammar, the predicate is the part of a sentence containing the verb and all the words that give information about the verb except the subject. For example, in 'Josh does his homework every day', 'does his homework every day' is the predicate and 'Josh' is the subject.

predict *verb*
predicts, predicting, predicted
to say that something is likely to happen in the future

predictable *adjective*
1 happening in exactly the way you would expect *The ending of the book was so predictable.*
2 behaving as you would expect and in the same way as always *You're completely predictable, Ben!*
predictably *adverb*

prediction *noun* **predictions**
what you say is likely to happen in the future *Arun made a prediction that we would win tomorrow's match.*

predominant *adjective*
1 most common or important *The predominant colour of our classroom is green.*
2 more important than others *My cousin plays a predominant part in the school play.*
predominance *noun*

predominantly *adverb*
mainly or mostly *a predominantly young audience*

predominate *verb*
predominates, predominating, predominated
used about things or people that are the most common or important in a particular place or situation *In this part of Brussels French speakers predominate. In this Picasso painting it's the blue that predominates.*

preen *verb*
preens, preening, preened
if a bird preens or preens itself, it cleans and tidies its feathers using its beak

prefab *noun* **prefabs**
a small house built quickly and cheaply from parts made in a factory, especially one built soon after the Second World War

preface ['pref-iss'] *noun* **prefaces**
something written at the beginning of a book that gives information such as what it is about and why it was written

prefect *noun* **prefects**
an older student in a school who is chosen to help the teachers in many different ways, for example by making younger students obey the rules of good behaviour

prefer *verb*
prefers, preferring, preferred
1 to like something or someone better than something or someone else *I prefer dogs to cats.*
2 to like something or someone best *I prefer Mary. In my spare time I prefer to read.*

preferable *adjective*
better than something or someone else *Being in Mrs Ravinder's class is preferable to being in Mr Brown's.*

preferably *adverb*
used for saying what you would like best *Could I have a tea, please, preferably with lots of milk?*

preference *noun* **preferences**
1 liking something or someone better than something or someone else *There's lemonade or orange juice – do you have a preference?*
2 liking something or someone best *When it comes to food, what are your preferences?*
3 in a computer program, preferences are choices on a menu that allow you to decide what parts of the program you want to use

prefix *noun* **prefixes**
in grammar, a prefix is a part added to the beginning of a word to change its meaning and make a new word. For example, 'un-' can be added to 'lucky' to make 'unlucky'. *compare*: **affix** and **suffix**

pregnant *adjective*
if a woman is pregnant, there is a baby developing inside her body. If a female animal is pregnant, there is a baby animal developing inside its body. **pregnancy** *noun*

prehistoric *adjective*
connected with the period of time in the past since life first appeared on earth until the time when information started to be written down *Dinosaurs are prehistoric monsters.*

prejudice *noun* **prejudices**
a feeling of strong dislike or fear towards a person or thing without any good reason, for example towards someone who has a different religion or comes from a different country

prejudiced *adjective*
1 if someone is prejudiced against someone or something, they dislike them strongly or fear them without any good reason

2 also used about someone's feelings or what someone does or says *a prejudiced opinion*

preliminary *adjective*
happening or coming before the main part of something *Our parents have had preliminary talks with the head teacher.*

prelude ['prel-yood'] *noun* **preludes**
1 a short piece of music, for example one that comes before a longer piece
2 something such as an event that comes before something more important

premature *adjective*
1 happening or done too soon *premature death*
2 born before the proper time *a premature baby*

premier ['prem-ee-er'] *noun* **premiers**
the leader of a government in some countries *the French premier*

premiere ['prem-yair'] *noun* **premieres**
the first occasion when a play is performed or a film is shown in public

LANGUAGE EXTRA also spelt *première*

premises ['prem-er-siss'] *noun plural*
the building (or buildings) used by a company or organisation and the land surrounding it

premium ['pree-mee-erm'] *noun* **premiums**
1 an amount of money that someone pays to an insurance company, for example to protect them or their property if something bad happens
2 a Premium Bond is a document with a number on it that you buy from the government. Every month some numbers are chosen by special equipment to win some money.

premium ['pree-mee-erm'] *adjective*
used for describing something of better quality or more expensive than something else *premium petrol; a premium phone number*

premonition *noun* **premonitions**
a very strong feeling that something bad is going to happen

preoccupation *noun*
1 (*plural* **preoccupations**) something that is important to you and that you think about very much, for example something that worries you *Our main preoccupation is getting the children home safely.*
2 when you think about something all the time and don't pay attention to anything else *I'm upset by my brother's preoccupation with computer games.*

preoccupied *adjective*
if someone is preoccupied, they think about something all the time and don't pay attention to anything else

prep *noun*
a word used in some schools for schoolwork that students do at home or outside normal school hours

preparation *noun*
1 the work of getting something or someone ready *Learning grammar is good preparation if you want to study French.*
2 preparations are things you do to get ready for something *We're making preparations for our holiday.*

preparatory *adjective*
done in order to get ready for something *preparatory work*

prepare *verb*
prepares, preparing, prepared
1 to get something or someone ready *Dad's preparing the meal. Ms Butler is preparing us for the exams. Prepare yourself for a big surprise.*
2 to get ready for something *We're preparing for our visit to the museum. I'm just preparing to go out.*

prepared *adjective*
1 ready for something *The storm is coming but we're prepared. The birthday party starts in two hours and the table is prepared.*
2 if you are prepared to do something, you are happy to do it or you will do it if you have to *You can see the dentist today if you're prepared to wait. My parents said they're prepared to see the head teacher if the bully can't be stopped.*

preposition *noun* **prepositions**
a word used for showing the connection between a noun or pronoun and another word or part of a sentence, for example 'in', 'on' or 'with'

LANGUAGE EXTRA there are many kinds of *prepositions*, for example showing where (*in, on, at, under, around, by*), where to (*to, towards*), when (*before, after, during*) or how (*with, by*). The preposition *of* shows a connection between a noun and another noun (*the top of the table*), and *for* often shows who or what gets something (*I've got a present for you*).
Prepositions usually come before a noun or pronoun (*I sat under a tree*) but can sometimes follow (*This is the tree I sat under*).
Sometimes a preposition is made up of more than one word (*out of, next to, on top of*).

preposterous *adjective*
very stupid and not making any sense

SYNONYM absurd

prep school *noun* **prep schools**
a private school in the UK for children aged from about 7 or 8 to 11 or 13

Presbyterian *noun* **Presbyterians**
a Christian belonging to a group that shares the beliefs of the 16th-century religious scholar John Calvin
Presbyterian *adjective*

Presbyterianism *noun*
the religion and beliefs of Presbyterians

prescribe *verb*
prescribes, prescribing, prescribed
if a doctor prescribes a medicine, he or she says you need it and gives you a prescription for it

prescription *noun* **prescriptions**
1 a piece of paper that a doctor gives you with the name of your medicine (or medicines) written on it. You take it to the chemist, who prepares the medicine for you.
2 an electronic document with the name of your medicine (or medicines) on it. A doctor sends it to a chemist, who prepares the medicine for you.

presence *noun*
1 when someone or something is in a particular place *They didn't notice my presence.*
2 **in the presence of someone** used for saying that something happens or someone does something while someone else is there in the same place *Please don't do that in my presence!*

present ['prez-ernt'] *noun*
1 (*plural* **presents**) something that someone gives to someone, usually for a special occasion or to say thank you *a birthday present; a thank-you present*

SYNONYM gift

2 the time that is happening now *The action of the play takes place in the present. Seema is on holiday at present* (now).
3 in grammar, the present is another way of saying the present tense

present ['prez-ernt'] *adjective*
1 existing or happening now *Who's the present head of your school? At the present time I have a lot of homework.*
2 if you are present somewhere, you are in that place *Ben has been present in class all week.*
3 connected with the present tense *'Are' is one of the present forms of the verb 'to be'.*

present ['pri-zent'] *verb*
presents, presenting, presented
1 to give someone something, for example something to think about such as an idea, reason or document *My parents presented the teacher with a few suggestions but she didn't like them.*
2 to give someone something such as a prize at a special ceremony *She was presented with an Olympic gold medal for swimming.*
3 to describe something or someone or make them known *Many people at that time presented London as a dangerous place. Chapter 2 of the book presents the main character.*
4 if someone presents a TV or radio programme, they are in charge of it. For example, for a documentary they say the words explaining and describing what is happening; for a quiz programme or chat show they ask the questions; for a news programme they read and discuss the news. *a documentary about the kings and queens of England presented by a famous professor*
5 to put on or show something such as a play or exhibition *Our school is presenting 'Matilda'.*
6 to show someone something such as a ticket or passport so that it can be checked
7 to show something for people to look at and enjoy, such as a new product or artistic creation *That company is presenting its latest range of trainers.*
8 to tell someone's name to another person or to other people when they meet for the first time *The teacher presented Declan to the class.*

SYNONYM to introduce

presentable – presumption

9 if something or someone presents something such as a problem, they are considered to be that problem or they cause that problem *Don't ride your bike like that – you'll present a danger to others.*
10 to make something happen or become possible *The school's closed today but that presents a good opportunity for you to finish your homework.*

presentable *adjective*
1 good or tidy enough for people to see *You can invite your friends – the house looks presentable.*
2 dressed in a pleasant way *You look very presentable in your uniform.*

presentation *noun*
1 (*plural* **presentations**) a short talk giving information about something *Jo's giving a little presentation about dinosaurs.*
2 the way something is arranged or shown *Your maths homework is excellent but the presentation is a bit messy.*
3 (*plural* **presentations**) a ceremony where someone gives someone something such as a prize *an award presentation*
4 showing something such as a play or ticket

presenter *noun* **presenters**
someone who presents a TV or radio programme, for example a documentary

presently *adverb*
1 at this time *Mr Sinclair is presently the head of our school.*
2 in a short time *The doctor will see you presently.*

present participle *noun*
present participles
a form of a verb that ends in '-ing' and is used with the verb 'to be' for making present and past tenses (for example 'I am walking', 'she was swimming'). It is also used for forming adjectives, as in 'an amazing book'.

present tense *noun* **present tenses**
a form of a verb that shows what is happening or what exists now, or what happens or exists regularly or all the time. For example, the following verbs are all in the present tense. 'am walking' ('I am walking'), 'likes' ('he likes music'), 'play' ('we play football a lot') and 'live' ('they live in York').

preservative *noun* **preservatives**
a chemical added to food to stop it from going bad, for example so that it lasts a long time

preserve *verb*
preserves, preserving, preserved
1 to keep something safe and stop it from being damaged or destroyed
2 to stop food from going bad, for example by adding chemicals to it
preservation *noun*

preserve *noun* **preserves**
1 a sweet food such as jam or marmalade, made by boiling fruit with sugar
2 a food such as pickle or chutney, made by boiling vegetables with salt or vinegar (sour liquid made from wine)

preside ['pri-zyde'] *verb*
presides, presiding, presided
if someone presides over a meeting or ceremony, they are in charge of it

presidency *noun*
1 the job of being a president
2 the period of time that someone has this job for

president *noun* **presidents**
1 a person in charge of a country that does not have a king or queen, usually the person with the most power and the leader of the government *the President of the United States*
2 the title given to someone in charge of a country *President Lincoln*
3 a person in charge of a club, organisation or business

presidential *adjective*
1 connected with a president *the presidential palace*
2 looking serious and important like a president

press *verb*
presses, pressing, pressed
1 to push something hard, for example with your finger *I pressed the doorbell. Press here to switch on your TV.*
2 to push something against something else *Ed pressed his face against the window. Abigail pressed down with her feet on the pedals.*
3 to be pushed against something *A part of the shoe is pressing on my toe.*
4 to hold something tightly and move the sides of it closer together or move your fingers closer together around it *Press the lemon hard to get out all the juice. She pressed my arm gently.*

SYNONYM to squeeze

5 to press clothes is to make them smooth using an iron (heated electric tool with a flat part underneath)

SYNONYM to iron

6 to try to make someone do something or tell you something *My teacher pressed me for an answer. Dad was pressing me to tell him the name of the bully.*

press *noun*
1 the action of pushing something or pushing against something *Give the button a press.*
2 the action of moving the sides of something closer together *I gave her hand a press.*
3 the action of making clothes smooth *Give my trousers a press.*
4 newspapers, magazines and the people who work for them, such as journalists and photographers *Our school was mentioned in the press last week.*
5 (*plural* **presses**) a machine used especially in the past for printing things such as books and newspapers by pressing ink onto paper *a printing press*
6 (*plural* **presses**) a business that prints and sells books
7 (*plural* **presses**) a machine or piece of equipment for making clothes smooth *a trouser press*

press-up *noun* **press-ups**
an exercise in which you lie on the ground with your face looking downwards and push your body up off the ground using your arms

pressure *noun*
1 when something such as a weight or force pushes something or pushes against something *Don't put any pressure on my arm – I've just had a vaccination.*
2 the force produced by a liquid or gas when it pushes against a surface or area *water pressure; air pressure* (air in the earth's atmosphere)
3 when someone tries to make someone do something or tell them something *My teacher is putting pressure on me to finish my homework.*
4 (*plural* **pressures**) used for talking about difficult situations, for example when someone has too much work or the work is too hard *the pressures of life; Our teacher has been under pressure this week because of the exams.*

pressurise *verb*
pressurises, pressurising, pressurised
to make someone (or try to make someone) do something by telling them that they have to do it *My cousin pressurised me into selling him my bike.*

LANGUAGE EXTRA also spelt *pressurize*. You can also say *to pressure someone*.

pressurised *adjective*
used for talking about air pressure, for example in an aircraft or submarine, that is made the same as it is near the ground so that people can breathe *a pressurised aircraft cabin*

LANGUAGE EXTRA also spelt *pressurized*

prestige ['press-teej'; 'j' has the middle sound of 'pleasure'] *noun*
the high quality that someone or something has, for example because of their importance, influence or success, that makes you feel great respect for them *Doctors have a lot of prestige in this country.*

prestigious ['press-tij-ers'] *adjective*
used for describing something or someone that you feel great respect for, for example because of their high quality, success, influence or importance *a prestigious school*

presto *interjection*
a word used when something happens so quickly that it seems like magic

SYNONYM hey presto

presumably *adverb*
used for saying something that you think is probably true even though you are not certain

presume *verb*
presumes, presuming, presumed
1 if you presume something is true, you think it is probably true even though you are not certain *I presume the person next to you in the photo is your sister.*
2 if someone presumes to do something, they do something they should not do and behave in a way that does not show enough respect *I wouldn't presume to tell you how to do your job.*

presumption *noun*
1 (*plural* **presumptions**) something that you think is probably true even though you are not certain

2 when someone does something they should not do, because it is not their business to do it, and behaves in a way that does not show enough respect to people

presumptuous *adjective*
if someone is presumptuous, they are rude because they do something they should not do and behave in a way that does not show enough respect

pretence *noun*
when you make someone believe something that isn't true *She smiled at me and called me her friend but it was just a pretence.*

pretend *verb*
pretends, pretending, pretended
to behave so as to make someone believe something that isn't true or make them think you are different from the way you really are, usually to trick them or as part of a game *I didn't want to do PE so I pretended I had a bad leg. He pretended to be a doctor. He's not hurt – he's only pretending.*

pretender *noun* **pretenders**
someone who says they are the true king or queen of a country instead of the king or queen who already rules that country

pretext *noun* **pretexts**
a false reason that someone gives for something instead of the real reason

pretty *adverb*
1 not very but still quite a lot *I'm getting pretty tired. I saw him pretty soon afterwards* (not very soon afterwards but not a long time either).

SYNONYMS quite, rather, fairly

2 another way of saying very *Five in the morning really is pretty early.*
3 **pretty much** or **pretty well** not completely but almost, or not always but almost always *I've pretty much finished my homework. We play football pretty well every day.*

pretty *adjective* **prettier, prettiest**
very pleasant to look at *a pretty baby*
prettily *adverb* **prettiness** *noun*

SIMILE 'as pretty as a picture' means very pretty

prevail *verb*
prevails, prevailing, prevailed
1 to be successful or to be more successful than something or someone else, usually after trying hard, for example in a game or argument *It was a difficult match but our team prevailed.*
2 to have more influence than something else or to have the most influence *Reason finally prevailed.*
3 to be usual and to exist at a particular time *This is the situation that prevails in Scotland. These opinions prevail among visitors to the country.*

prevailing *adjective*
usual and existing at a particular time *Prevailing conditions in some schools are terrible. What's the prevailing mood among students?*

prevalent *adjective*
happening a lot or existing in large numbers *These mistakes are prevalent among people who learn English.*

prevent *verb*
prevents, preventing, prevented
1 to stop someone from doing something *The snow prevented us from going to school.*
2 to stop something from happening *Cross at the crossing to prevent accidents. Something is preventing the window from closing.*
preventable *adjective* **prevention** *noun*

preventive *adjective*
used for describing something that is supposed to stop something bad from happening or getting worse *The storm is coming but people have taken preventive action* (for example covering their windows with boards).

preview *noun* **previews**
1 a showing of something such as a play, film or art exhibition before the public are officially allowed to go and see it
2 a part of a computer program that allows you to look at something such as a document before printing it (print preview) or before opening it on your computer (for example using a preview pane)

preview *verb*
previews, previewing, previewed
to look at something such as a document on a computer, for example to see how it will look when you print it

previous *adjective*
used about something or someone that comes before or is earlier than something or someone else *Grandpa had come over the previous day* (the day before). *There's a mistake on the previous line. The previous head teacher came from Wales.*

previously *adverb*
used for talking about the time before the present time or before a particular time in the past *My dad's a teacher but previously he was a bus driver.*

prey ['pray'] *noun*
an animal (or animals) that another animal catches and kills for food

prey ['pray'] *verb*
preys, preying, preyed
1 if an animal preys on another animal, it catches it and kills it for food
2 if a person preys on another person, he or she finds someone weaker and behaves towards them in a criminal or dishonest way, for example by stealing from them or attacking them
3 if something preys on your mind, you worry about it all the time

price *noun*
1 (*plural* **prices**) the money that you pay to buy something *The price of school meals has gone up again. In the shops today there were lots of price cuts* (prices made lower than usual).
2 used for talking about something unpleasant that someone must accept, for example because of something they have done or if they want to do or have something *Being sent home was a high price to pay for talking in class. Bad teeth is the price to pay if you eat too many sweets. Hard work is the price of success.*

3 **at any price** used when you mean you will do anything to get or do something *I wanted that bike at any price. He wants to win at any price.*

priced *adjective*
if something is priced at a particular amount, that is what you have to pay for it *Tickets are priced at £10 each.*

priceless *adjective*
1 worth so much that it is impossible to say what the price is *The crown jewels are priceless.*
2 worth a lot of money and impossible to replace, for example because of being very special or important *The thieves stole my dad's priceless stamp album.*
3 extremely useful and important *priceless information*
4 an informal way of saying extremely funny

pricey *adjective* **pricier, priciest**
costing a lot of money

SYNONYM expensive

LANGUAGE EXTRA also spelt *pricy*

prick *verb*
pricks, pricking, pricked
1 to make a tiny hole or tiny holes in something with something sharp *Mum pricked the potatoes with a fork and put them in the oven.*
2 to hurt someone or to hurt yourself by sticking something sharp into the skin *I pricked my finger on a piece of wire and it's bleeding.*
3 if someone pricks up their ears, they start listening very carefully
4 if an animal such as a rabbit or dog pricks up its ears, it puts its ears up straight so that it can listen better

prick *noun* **pricks**
1 a sudden slight pain when something sharp such as a needle is stuck into your skin
2 a tiny hole made by something sharp *It's nothing – just a pin prick.*

prickle *noun* **prickles**
one of the sharp points on a plant (such as on the stem of a rose) or on an animal (such as on the body of a hedgehog)

prickle *verb*
prickles, prickling, prickled
to make a part of your body feel as if small sharp points are touching it *This wool scarf is prickling my neck.*

prickly *adjective* **pricklier, prickliest**
1 covered with prickles *a prickly hedgehog*
2 giving you a prickly feeling *a prickly sweater*

pricy *adjective* **pricier, priciest**
costing a lot of money

SYNONYM expensive

LANGUAGE EXTRA also spelt *pricey*

pride *noun*
1 a strong feeling of happiness about something or someone because you think they're good or because they have done something good *My parents were full of pride watching me in the school play.*

2 a feeling of respect that you have for yourself and a feeling that you want to be treated with respect by other people and don't want them to think you're less good than they are *Losing the World Cup has hurt the country's pride* (made it lose respect for itself).
3 a feeling that you're more important than other people *People disliked him because of his pride.*
4 (plural **prides**) a group of lions
5 to take pride in to feel extremely happy about something or someone, for example something you have done well or something or someone you like or love *Our team took pride in their success. I always take pride in my work* (I'm happy doing it and try to do it well). *My sister takes pride in her two children* (she's happy about them and looks after them well).
6 the pride of something that makes you feel very happy, for example because it's the best part of something *The new sports centre is the pride of our school.*
7 pride and joy something that belongs to you that makes you feel very happy *My bike is my pride and joy.*

pride *verb*
prides, priding, prided
if you pride yourself on something good that you do or on a skill or quality that you have, you are very happy about it or very happy to tell other people about it *My sister prides herself on her knowledge of French.*

priest *noun* **priests**
a person who does religious duties, especially in the Christian church
priestly *adjective*

priestess *noun* **priestesses**
a woman who does religious duties in a religion that is not a Christian one

prig *noun* **prigs**
an insulting word for someone who thinks they are much better than other people because they always follow rules of correct behaviour **priggish** *adjective*
priggishness *noun*

prim *adjective* **primmer, primmest**
1 if someone is prim, their behaviour is too careful and correct and they are shocked by other people's bad behaviour or language
2 used for describing someone's appearance that is too neat and tidy *She wore a prim little hat.*
primly *adverb* **primness** *noun*

primary *adjective*
1 most important *The primary reason I came to this school was to get a good education.*

SYNONYM main

2 connected with the teaching of children in primary schools *primary education*

primary colour *noun* **primary colours**
one of the three colours that can be mixed together to make any other colour. When you are mixing paints, the three colours are red, blue and yellow. For example, mixing blue and yellow makes green, and mixing red and yellow makes orange.

primary school *noun* **primary schools**
a school for children between the ages of about 4 and 11

primate *noun* **primates**
an animal that belongs to a class of animals that includes humans, monkeys and apes. Primates have large brains, hands and feet made for climbing and walking, and excellent eyesight.

prime *adjective*
1 most important *Winning tomorrow's match is our team's prime concern.*

SYNONYM main

2 most likely *'Someone stole my phone.' – 'I think Tom is the prime suspect.'*

SYNONYM main

3 used for describing something that is the best or of the best quality *My laptop is in prime condition. This is a prime spot for building a house.*
4 a prime example a very good example of something or someone

ORIGIN from Latin *primus* 'first'

prime *noun*
used for talking about the best part of someone's life when they are strongest and most active *My mum and dad are in their prime* (for example around the ages of 35 to 45).

prime *verb*
primes, priming, primed
1 to prepare someone for a particular situation
2 to prepare something so that it can be used

prime meridian ['mer-rid-i-ern'] *noun*
an imaginary line that goes around the earth from the North Pole to the South Pole and passes through Greenwich in South London. The prime meridian shows zero degrees longitude on a map and is the standard for measuring all other longitudes.

LANGUAGE EXTRA also called the *Greenwich meridian*

prime minister *noun* **prime ministers**
someone who is in charge of a government, for example in the UK and some other countries

LANGUAGE EXTRA also spelt *Prime Minister*

prime number *noun* **prime numbers**
a number that can be divided exactly only by 1 or by itself. For example, 2, 3, 5 and 7 are prime numbers.
compare: **composite number**

primer *noun* **primers**
an old-fashioned word for a book that contains the main information you need to know about a subject you are studying *a Latin primer*

primeval ['pryme-ee-verl'] *adjective*
connected with the earliest time in the history of the world when the earth had just started to exist *primeval rocks*

primitive *adjective*
1 connected with a very early time in the history of the world before machines or ways of writing *a primitive tribe*; *a primitive tool*
2 a primitive animal or plant is one that has a simple form, for example because it is at a very early stage of its development
3 very simple or made in a very simple way *a primitive telescope*; *The sailor made a primitive boat out of logs.*
4 very simple and uncomfortable compared to the way things are in modern times *Conditions in the huts were primitive.*

primrose *noun* **primroses**
a small plant that grows wild and has flowers that are usually pale yellow

ORIGIN from Latin *prima rosa* 'first rose', called 'first' because it flowers in early spring

prince *noun* **princes**
1 a son or grandson of a king or queen *Prince Harry*
2 a man or boy closely related to a king or queen *Prince Philip*
3 a male ruler of a small country such as Monaco

princely *adjective*
1 used for describing an amount of money that is small and that you think should be bigger *I tidied up my uncle's garden for the princely sum of £2.*
2 connected with a prince or suitable for a prince, for example extremely good, large or beautiful *a princely meal*

princess *noun* **princesses**
1 a daughter or granddaughter of a king or queen *Princess Anne*
2 a woman or girl closely related to a king or queen *Princess Margaret*
3 the wife of a prince

principal *adjective*
1 most important *My principal ambition is to become a teacher.*
2 most likely *What would be the principal outcome of losing the match?*

principal *noun* **principals**
a teacher in charge of a school or college

principally *adverb*
mainly *This dictionary is written principally for children aged between 9 and 13.*

principle *noun* **principles**
1 a rule that someone has about the right way to behave *Answering a teacher back would be against my principles* (not the right way for me to behave).
2 a basic rule, idea or law that explains something *scientific principles*; *These two machines work on different principles* (different rules explain how they work).
3 in principle used for talking in a very general way about something someone does, believes or agrees, without considering any of the details *I think you have the right idea in principle.*

print *verb*
prints, printing, printed
1 if you print words, numbers or images, you put them usually onto paper using a computer printer or other equipment *I printed out a poem from the internet. The number is printed on the ticket. Press here to print.*
2 if something such as a printer prints or prints something, it produces something usually on paper *It's still printing. My printer printed some funny lines.*

3 to make lots of copies of something such as a book, newspaper or magazine
4 to include something such as a letter or picture in a newspaper or magazine
5 to write something by hand without joining up the letters of each word *Print your name in capitals in this space.*

print *noun* **prints**
1 a mark left on a surface by something being pressed on it *There was a hand print on the window.*
2 words, letters or numbers in a book, newspaper or magazine *I can't read this article – the print is too small.*
3 a photo produced on paper
4 a picture made by cutting a design into the surface of wood or metal, putting ink on the design and then pressing it onto paper *a Rembrandt print*
5 a copy of a painting
6 a cloth or piece of clothing with a pattern on it, or the pattern itself *a dress with a floral print*
7 in print used about a book that you can still buy new in the shops or on the internet
8 out of print used about a book that you can no longer buy new

printable *adjective*
1 used for describing something that can be printed with a printer connected to a computer, for example text or an image from a web page *printable vouchers*
2 good enough or suitable to be printed in something such as a newspaper

printer *noun* **printers**
1 a piece of equipment connected to a computer that uses ink for copying information from a computer screen onto paper
2 someone whose job is to print things such as books, newspapers and documents

printing *noun*
the activity or business of putting words, numbers or images onto paper, for example with a computer printer or, in the past, with a printing press (machine that presses ink onto paper)

printout *noun* **printouts**
a paper document or image produced by a printer connected to a computer

LANGUAGE EXTRA also spelt *print-out*

print preview *noun*
a part of a computer program that allows you to see how something such as a document will look before you print it

priority *noun*
1 (*plural* **priorities**) something that must be dealt with before other things because it is very important *Getting ready for the exams is my priority this term.*
2 special importance given to someone or something so that they can be dealt with first or in a better way or so that they can do something first *The music teacher will give priority to students who want to learn the piano. In traffic, police cars and ambulances have priority* (they are allowed to go first).
3 if something takes priority over something else, it is more important and should be dealt with first

prise *verb*
prises, prising, prised
to use force to open something or to move something away from something else *Dad prised open the lid with a penknife.*

prism *noun* **prisms**
1 in maths, a prism is a solid object that has two identical ends and flat sides. The ends of the prism are polygons (flat shapes such as triangles, squares or hexagons). The polygons can be regular (with all sides equal) or irregular.
2 a piece of glass or plastic shaped like a triangular prism that you can see through. It is used for separating light into the different colours of the rainbow.

prison *noun* **prisons**
a place where criminals are kept to punish them

SYNONYM jail

prisoner *noun* **prisoners**
1 a criminal kept in a prison
2 someone kept in a prison during a war or because a government does not like their political ideas *a prisoner of war*; *a political prisoner*
3 someone taken by force and kept in a place that they cannot escape from *He was held prisoner in a dark room for a week.*

pristine ['pris-teen'] *adjective*
new or like new *My laptop is a year old but it's in pristine condition.*

privacy *noun*
1 being alone without other people seeing you or hearing what you are doing *I share my bedroom with my sister so I don't have much privacy.*
2 keeping things in your life secret, for example feelings, information or behaviour, because they have nothing to do with anyone else *This software is intended to protect your privacy.*

private *adjective*
1 connected with or belonging to a particular person or group of people and having nothing to do with anyone else *a private road*; *a private conversation*; *This bike is my private property.*
2 used for describing a place where there are no other people and where someone cannot be seen or heard *We're looking for a private spot where we can talk.*
3 used for describing things in someone's life away from school or work that should be kept secret and that have nothing to do with anyone else, for example feelings, ideas, information or behaviour *I write my private thoughts in a diary. What I say to my friends is private.*
4 belonging to and paid for by a group of people and not controlled by the government *a private school*; *a private hospital*
5 used for describing something that someone pays for themselves and that isn't provided or paid for by the government *a private lesson*; *private education*
6 used for describing someone who pays for something themselves instead of having it provided or paid for by the government *a private patient* (one who pays for medical or dental treatment); *a private student* (for example one who pays for private lessons)
7 used for describing someone who doesn't work for an organisation that is controlled by or paid for by the government, so their work is paid for by individual people, not by the government *a private teacher*; *a private detective* (one that you pay to find information)
8 in private used about something someone does without anyone else being there or knowing what is happening *My teacher asked to speak to my parents in private.*

private *noun* **privates**
a soldier who has the lowest rank in the army

privately *adverb*
1 without anyone else being around or knowing what is happening *Can we go somewhere to talk privately?*
2 used about the thoughts and feelings someone really has that they don't tell anyone about *Some people hoped privately that our team wouldn't win.*
3 used about individual people rather than businesses or the government, when talking about paying for, selling or owning something *Jack bought his bike privately* (from a person not a shop). *My sister is privately educated* (at a school our parents pay for, not one controlled by the government). *This company is privately owned* (it belongs to a group of people, not the government).

privatise *verb*
privatises, privatising, privatised
if a government privatises a business, industry or service that it controls, it sells it so that it is no longer the property of the country **privatisation** *noun*

LANGUAGE EXTRA also spelt *privatize* and *privatization*

compare: **nationalise**

privet *noun* **privets**
a bush with small dark green leaves that stay green all year round. Privet bushes are usually grown together for making hedges, for example around gardens.

privilege *noun*
1 (*plural* **privileges**) something good and special given to one person or group of people but not to everyone *Pupils who work hard will be given extra privileges. In Britain we enjoy many privileges compared with other countries.*
2 something good and special that happens to you, or a good and special opportunity that you have *Ms Patel said she was lucky to have the privilege to teach in our school.*
3 used for talking about the good things that rich people enjoy as part of their way of life *He was a lord who lived a life of privilege.*

privileged *adjective*
1 having good and special opportunities that most people do not have *Students at these schools are a privileged group.*
2 connected with rich people and the good things they have in their lives *She comes from a privileged background.*
3 if you are privileged to do or have something, you are very happy about it because it is good and special

prize–procrastinate

prize noun **prizes**
1 something you get for winning in a game or competition or for doing very good work *a prize winner; a prize draw* (a competition in which tickets are picked by chance to win a prize)
2 something important or of great value that you must work hard to get *Becoming an American citizen was his prize.*

prize verb
prizes, prizing, prized
to consider something to be important or of great value *My bike is my prized possession.*

prize-giving noun **prize-givings**
a ceremony where prizes are given for good work, usually in a school

pro noun **pros**
1 someone who gets money for playing a sport *a tennis pro*
short for: **professional**
2 used when you mean one of the good things about something *What are the pros and cons* (good and bad things) *of living in London?*

pro- prefix
supporting something or someone *pro-European*

ANTONYM anti-

proactive adjective
1 if someone is proactive, they deal with things and make things happen rather than wait for problems to happen first and then have to deal with them
2 also used about something such as a way of dealing with things *proactive measures; a proactive approach*

probability noun
1 the chance that something will happen or be true *There's a strong probability of rain for tomorrow's match.*

SYNONYM likelihood

2 (plural **probabilities**) something that is almost certain to happen or be true
3 in maths, a probability scale is a line marked with a zero (meaning impossible) at one end and the number 1 (meaning certain) at the other end, and divided into fractions in between the two ends. It is used for showing how probable it is that something will happen.
4 **in all probability** used for saying that you think something is almost certain to happen or be true

probable adjective
if something is probable, it is almost certain to happen or be true *It's probable that it will snow tomorrow.*

SYNONYM likely

probably adverb
used for saying that something is almost certain to happen or be true *It will probably snow tomorrow.*

probation noun
1 a period of time when someone guilty of committing a crime is allowed to stay out of prison if they agree to commit no more crimes and to have someone watch their behaviour *My cousin is on probation* (someone is watching his behaviour carefully).

2 a probation officer is someone whose job is to watch the behaviour of someone who is on probation to make sure they commit no more crimes

probe noun **probes**
1 a search to find out the truth about something or someone

SYNONYM investigation

2 a long thin instrument used by doctors for looking inside a part of the body
3 a probe or space probe is a small vehicle that travels in space and sends information back to scientists on earth

probe verb
probes, probing, probed
1 to try to find out about something or someone, for example by asking lots of questions *The police were probing into his past life.*
2 to examine something carefully to try to find something
3 to look inside a part of the body with a probe

problem noun **problems**
1 something difficult or bad that needs to be understood and dealt with *I'm having problems with my mobile.*
2 a mathematical question that needs to be solved
3 if you say something is not your problem, you mean it has nothing to do with you and you don't want to know about it *'I don't have enough money for the bus.' – 'That's not my problem.'*
4 **No problem!** used for saying you're happy about something or happy to do something *'Can I borrow your bike?' – 'No problem!'*
5 **No problem!** also used for replying to someone who has thanked you for something or said sorry to you

problematic adjective
if something is problematic, it is a problem for someone

procedure noun **procedures**
a usual or correct way of doing something *If the fire alarm goes off, you must follow the emergency procedures.*

proceed verb
proceeds, proceeding, proceeded
1 to continue to happen, to do something or to be done *The building work on the new library is proceeding well. The school is proceeding with the trip to the museum despite the snow.*
2 to continue on to something such as a higher level *The winners will proceed to the semi-final.*
3 to move in a particular direction *Passengers for flight 105 should proceed to gate 7.*
4 to start doing something *I want to download the file from the internet but I don't know how to proceed.*

LANGUAGE EXTRA be careful not to confuse *proceed* with *precede* (happen before or go in front)

proceedings noun plural
1 an event, especially the series of actions that make up that event *We watched the proceedings from an upstairs window.*
2 actions taken in a court of law to decide a matter, for example when someone is accused of doing something wrong *criminal proceedings*

proceeds noun plural
the money someone makes, especially from selling something or organising an event such as a concert or school play

process noun **processes**
1 a series of actions or events that produce a particular result *Learning to speak French properly is a slow process.*
2 a series of changes that happen naturally *the body's ageing process*
3 a way of doing something or of making a product or chemical, for example in a factory or laboratory (room with scientific equipment)
4 if someone or something is in the process of doing something, they have started doing it and are busy doing it now

process verb
processes, processing, processed
1 to process something such as a document is to deal with it in an official way *New passports take a month to process* (to be produced).
2 to add chemicals to a substance in order to change it or to food to make it last longer *processed cheese*
3 if a computer processes information, or if someone processes information using a computer, the computer changes the information and organises it to produce a particular result *My laptop is taking a long time to process this image* (to display it).

processing noun
processing or data processing is organising, storing and finding information using a computer

procession noun **processions**
a group of people or vehicles moving slowly and in an organised way, usually through the streets, for example as part of a celebration or funeral ceremony *Thousands of people were walking in procession through the centre of Belfast.*

processor noun **processors**
a very small piece of electronic equipment made up of chips (pieces of silicon with electrical connections). It forms the main part of a computer (or other equipment) and makes it work.

SYNONYM microprocessor

see: **food processor** and **word processor**

proclaim verb
proclaims, proclaiming, proclaimed
1 to say in an official way that something is true *She proclaimed that she was innocent.*
2 to make something known in an official way *India proclaimed its independence in 1947.*

proclamation noun **proclamations**
an official or public announcement

procrastinate verb
procrastinates, procrastinating, procrastinated
to wait until a later time before doing something, usually because you don't want

procure–profitable

to do it *When Dad asks you to do your homework, you keep procrastinating* (you don't do it). **procrastination** noun

ORIGIN from Latin *procrastinare* 'to put off until tomorrow' (from *pro-* 'forward' and *cras* 'tomorrow')

procure verb
procures, procuring, procured
to get something, especially something difficult to get

SYNONYM to obtain

prod verb
prods, prodding, prodded
1 to push something or someone with something long like a stick or finger *I gently prodded the hedgehog to see if it was alive.*
2 to get someone to do something, especially when they are being slow or don't really want to do it *Mum always has to prod my brother into doing his homework.*

prod noun prods
1 a push with something long *I gave him a prod with my elbow to wake him up.*
2 the action of getting someone to do something *Joseph is very slow – he needs a bit of a prod to work faster.*

prodigal adjective
spending much too much money without thinking about the future

prodigy noun prodigies
someone with a much higher level of intelligence or skill than other people, which appears when they are very young *a musical prodigy*; *Mozart was a child prodigy.*

produce ['prer-jooss'] verb
produces, producing, produced
1 to make something *This factory produces hundreds of bicycles every year. Bees produce honey.*
2 to cause something or make something happen *This illness produces a high fever. Mixing these two colours produces an interesting result.*
3 to design, invent, write or paint something using skill *Shakespeare produced many beautiful sonnets. Hannah has produced a very nice portrait of our teacher.*

SYNONYM to create

4 used when talking about something such as heat, light, sound or a smell that spreads from a particular thing or place that makes it *Computers produce a lot of heat. Our smoke alarm produces a loud noise if there's smoke in the house.*
5 used when talking about someone or something that has come out of a particular place *Turner is one of the greatest painters the country has produced.*
6 to grow something *This marigold produces bright yellow flowers. These insects produce wings.*
7 to take something out of where it is hidden so that someone can see it *Dad produced a £5 note from his pocket.*
8 to show something *You have to produce your ticket on the train.*
9 to produce something such as a film, play or TV or radio programme is to organise the way it is made

produce ['proj-ooss'] noun
food such as fruit and vegetables grown by farmers

producer noun producers
1 a person, business or country that makes goods or grows food
2 in biology, a producer is a plant that produces food for animals to eat
compare: **consumer**
3 someone who organises the way something such as a film, play or TV or radio programme is made

product noun products
1 something that is made, for example in a factory, and is sold to people *a software product*; *dairy products* (butter, cheese and other things made from milk)
2 something you put on your skin or hair such as a liquid or cream *beauty products*
3 something that happens or exists, or someone who is the way they are, as a result of something else *The dislike between the two countries is the product of years of war. He often misbehaves – he's the product of a violent home.*
4 in maths, a product is the answer you get when you multiply two or more numbers together. For example, in 5 × 3 = 15, 15 is the product.

production noun
1 the action of making things, for example in a factory, or growing things, for example on a farm *Production starts next week on the new car. When does the new microchip go into production?* (start being made)
2 the amount of things being made or grown *The country has to increase its wheat production.*
3 used for talking about a play or show or the way it is performed *What a terrific production! We're going to see a school production of 'The Wizard of Oz'.*

productive adjective
1 producing a large amount of something *productive land* (lots of plants for food); *a productive factory* (lots of goods); *a productive author* (lots of books)
2 producing good results *Our meeting was very productive.*

productively adverb

productivity noun
the speed at which goods are produced and work is done

profess verb
professes, professing, professed
to say that something is true even though it may not be true *My brother professes to know a lot about computers but hardly knows anything.*

profession noun professions
an important job that needs a lot of education and training to do, for example the job of a teacher, doctor, dentist or lawyer

professional adjective
1 connected with the job of someone such as a teacher, doctor or lawyer who needs a lot of education and training *We respect our doctor's professional opinion. With his suit and tie he looked very professional* (like someone with an important job).
2 playing a game or sport or doing an activity as a job to earn money *a professional footballer*

ANTONYM amateur

3 showing a very high standard, or behaving in a way that shows very high standards *Dad made a professional job of painting the kitchen. The soldiers were very professional at all times.*

professional noun professionals
1 someone who plays a game or sport or does an activity as a job to earn money

ANTONYM amateur

2 someone such as a teacher, doctor or lawyer who does a job needing a lot of education and training
3 someone who has a lot of skill in their job

professionally adverb
1 done by someone who has been trained *This carpet needs to be professionally cleaned.*
2 in a way that shows very high standards *The police officers behaved very professionally.*
3 used for talking about someone's job or about something someone does as their job *My mum is successful professionally. Our cousin plays tennis professionally.*

professor noun professors
a teacher of the highest rank at a university

proficiency noun
the skill that someone has to be able to do something very well

proficient adjective
if someone is proficient, they are very good at doing something that needs a lot of skill *a proficient swimmer*; *Sophie is proficient in French.*

proficiently adverb
extremely well *Granddad speaks Spanish proficiently.*

profile noun profiles
1 the shape of your face when someone looks at it from the side *This is a picture of my sister in profile.*
2 a short description of someone or something that gives the most important details about them

profit noun profits
money that someone earns, usually in a business, by selling something for more than it costs them to make it or buy it *My brother bought his bike for £50 and sold it at a profit for £70.*

profit verb
profits, profiting, profited
if someone profits from something, they get something good from it, for example from an experience or from something bad that happens to someone *She profited from her sister's mistakes.*

profitable adjective
1 used for describing a business or something connected with it that makes money

377

profound–promise

2 used for describing something useful or an occasion when something good happens to you *I spent a profitable day in the library.*
profitably adverb

profound adjective
1 very great *The Battle of Hastings was of profound importance.*
2 a profound feeling is one that is very strong *We all felt profound disappointment.*

> SYNONYM **deep**

3 showing intelligence, great knowledge and serious thought *This film by Hitchcock is very profound.*

profoundly adverb
1 very *Dad was profoundly unhappy with the results.*
2 very much *That book influenced me profoundly.*

> SYNONYM **deeply**

profuse ['prer-fyooss'] adjective
used for describing a large amount of something or something done lots of times *profuse bleeding; profuse apologies*

profusely adverb
a stronger way of saying 'very much' or 'in large amounts' *He was bleeding profusely. She thanked me profusely.*

program noun **programs**
a piece of software containing instructions for performing particular actions on a computer *Mum installed a new word-processing program.*

program verb
programs, programming, programmed
to give instructions to a computer or another piece of equipment to perform particular actions

programme noun **programmes**
1 something that you watch on TV or listen to on the radio
2 a plan of things to be done, made up of a series of different actions
3 a piece of paper, thin book or computer document with information about what happens in an event such as a play or concert *a theatre programme*
4 a series of organised events or activities *a programme of music*
5 a series of actions done by a piece of equipment such as a washing machine

programme verb
programmes, programming, programmed
if you programme a piece of equipment such as a remote control, you give it instructions to perform a particular action

programmer noun **programmers**
someone who writes computer programs as their job

programming noun
the job of writing computer programs *Java is a programming language.*

progress ['proh-gress'] noun
1 when someone gets better at doing something, for example by developing their skills and knowledge *Kareem has made excellent progress this term.*
2 when someone feels less ill than they were *Granddad's in hospital but he's making good progress* (he's getting better).

3 when things change and become better with time *scientific progress*
4 when something moves closer to the time when it is finished *The two countries have made progress towards a solution.*
5 when something or someone moves forward *The crowd were making slow progress through the snow.*

progress ['prer-gress'] verb
progresses, progressing, progressed
1 to continue slowly, for example towards a situation that is better or towards a time when something is finished *Jamie is progressing nicely in maths. Work is progressing on the new sports hall. The illness is progressing* (getting slowly worse).
2 to move forward *The ship progressed with difficulty through the ice.*

progression noun
1 when something or someone continues or changes slowly, for example from one situation to another
2 used for talking about a number of things that come one after the other *a mathematical progression* (for example the series of numbers 2, 4, 6, 8)

progressive adjective
1 used for describing someone who thinks and behaves in a modern way *Our school has a progressive head teacher.*
2 used for describing ideas, actions and ways of behaving that are new and modern *Our school has introduced some progressive measures to stop bullying.*
3 continuing slowly *a progressive disease*
4 in grammar, the progressive form of the verb is made from the auxiliary verb 'to be' and a present participle (for example 'I am running', 'you were working', 'it has been snowing', 'I'll be sleeping'). It shows that an action is, was, has been or will be continuing. This form is also called the continuous form.

prohibit verb
prohibits, prohibiting, prohibited
1 to say that something is not allowed or is against the law *Riding a bike without a helmet is strictly prohibited.*
2 to tell someone that they are not allowed to do something *The law prohibits people from smoking on the trains.*

prohibition noun

prohibitive adjective
much too expensive for someone or for most people *The costs of travelling by train are getting prohibitive.*

prohibitively adverb
if something is prohibitively expensive, it is much too expensive

project ['proj-ekt'] noun **projects**
1 a long piece of schoolwork where you find out information about a subject *We're doing a class project on jungle animals.*
2 a piece of important work that a person, organisation or country plans to do *China has given details of a project to build the tallest building in the world.*

project ['prer-jekt'] verb
projects, projecting, projected
1 to show an image on a screen or wall, usually using a piece of equipment called a projector

2 if someone projects a particular quality, that is the quality that you notice most clearly
3 to stick out *A drainpipe was projecting from the roof.*

projection noun **projections**
1 when an image or film is shown on a screen or wall
2 an image that is shown on a screen or wall
3 something that sticks out
4 a calculation about something that you expect to happen in the future

projector noun **projectors**
a piece of equipment for showing images or films on a screen or wall. It works by displaying images from your computer or (especially in the past) by shining light through a strip of film or piece of photographic film.
compare: **overhead projector**

prolific adjective
producing a lot of something *Dickens was a prolific writer* (he wrote lots of books and articles).

prologue ['proh-log'] noun **prologues**
a piece of writing at the beginning of something such as a book, play or long poem that gives information about the story
compare: **epilogue**

prolong verb
prolongs, prolonging, prolonged
to make something last longer

prolonged adjective
lasting a long time *a prolonged period of rain*

promenade ['prom-er-nahd'] noun **promenades**
a place for people to walk along beside the sea, usually a wide concrete path

prominent adjective
1 important and well-known *She's a prominent actor.*
2 important *I'm going to play a prominent part in the school play.*
3 easy to see, for example because of sticking out from somewhere *My uncle has a prominent chin. My picture was displayed in a prominent position above the teacher's desk.*

prominence noun

prominently adverb
1 in a way that is easy to see *Nisha's project was displayed prominently.*
2 very much and in an important way *The name of the author's home town appears prominently in his novels.*

promise verb
promises, promising, promised
1 to tell someone that you will definitely do something (or not do it) or that something will definitely happen (or not happen) *Mum promises to help me if I get stuck. I promise that my dog won't bother you any more.*
2 to tell someone you will definitely give them something *Dad promised me a bike for my birthday.*
3 used about something that seems likely to happen *The school concert promises to be very exciting.*

promise noun **promises**
1 when you say that you will definitely do something (or not do it) or that something

378

will definitely happen (or not happen) *My sister will help me with my maths – she made a promise. She always keeps her promises* (does what she says she will do).
2 used for showing that something or someone is likely to be successful or much better in the future *Alex shows lots of promise as a footballer. Your future is full of promise.*

promising *adjective*
likely to be successful or much better in the future *a promising musician; The weather looks promising for our picnic.*

promontory ['prom-ern-tree'] *noun* **promontories**
a high piece of land or rock that sticks out into the sea or a lake

promote *verb*
promotes, promoting, promoted
1 to give someone a more important job, or to give a soldier or police officer a higher rank, for example because they have done good work or been working for many years *My sister has been promoted to head nurse.*
compare: **demote**
2 to move a sports team up into a higher division
compare: **relegate** and **demote**
3 to make something more likely to happen or to help it to happen *Eating fruit every day promotes good health.*
4 to tell people about a product or event to try to make them buy the product or go to the event *The author is coming to the school to promote her new book.*
promoter *noun*

promotion *noun* **promotions**
1 if someone gets a promotion, they are given a more important job or a higher rank
2 if a sports team is given a promotion, they are moved up into a higher division
3 making something more likely to happen
4 getting people to buy a product or go to an event, or a particular activity that gets people to do this *There are lots of sales promotions at the supermarket today.*

prompt *adjective* **prompter, promptest**
1 done very quickly or without any delays *I got a prompt reply to my email. We got prompt attention at the hospital.*
2 doing something very quickly *Simon is always prompt to reply.*
3 arriving exactly at a particular time *The coach leaves at nine o'clock – try to be prompt.*
promptness *noun*

prompt *verb*
prompts, prompting, prompted
1 to make something happen *What prompted such an angry email from Granddad?*
2 to make someone do or say something *It was disappointment that prompted her to say that.*
3 if someone prompts an actor who has forgotten the words to say during a play, they tell him or her which words to say

promptly *adverb*
1 very quickly or without any delays
2 exactly at a particular time *The lesson finished promptly at three o'clock.*

prone *adjective*
1 likely to do something or suffer from something *Joseph is prone to falling over* (often falls over). *I'm prone to headaches. My brother is accident prone* (has lots of accidents).
2 if someone is prone, they are lying flat with their face downwards. If they have their face upwards, they are supine.

prong *noun* **prongs**
1 one of the sharp points at the end of a fork for sticking into the food that you eat
2 one of the sharp points at the end of a garden fork for digging into the earth
3 one of the long pointed metal parts sticking out from an electric plug, used for connecting the plug to the electricity

pronoun *noun* **pronouns**
a word used instead of a noun, for example 'I', 'me', 'she', 'her', 'they', 'them', or a word used for referring to a noun that has come before in the sentence, for example 'who', 'which' or 'that'

LANGUAGE EXTRA a *pronoun* is a word you use when you don't want to repeat a noun. For example, instead of saying *Dad took the dog to the park and Dad let the dog run around*, it is easier to say *Dad took the dog to the park and he let it run around*. The words *he* and *it* are pronouns standing for *Dad* and *the dog*.
There are many types of pronouns. Some of the most important types are: personal pronouns (such as *I, me, she, her, they* or *them*) referring to a person, possessive pronouns (such as *mine, my, your* or *theirs*) showing who or what something or someone belongs to, and relative pronouns (such as *who, which* or *that*) referring to an earlier noun or sentence.
Pronouns can be singular (for example *she, I, him*) or plural (*they, we, our*). The pronoun *you* (or *your*) can be both singular and plural.

pronounce *verb*
pronounces, pronouncing, pronounced
1 if you pronounce a word or letter, you make the sound of it in a particular way *Pronounce 'aisle' to rhyme with 'pile'.*
2 to say officially that something is true *My cousin was pronounced the winner of the whole competition.*

pronounced *adjective*
very easy to see or notice *a pronounced limp; Claude speaks with a pronounced French accent.*

pronouncement *noun* **pronouncements**
something that people say in an official way

pronunciation ['prer-nun-see-**ay**-shern'] *noun* **pronunciations**
1 the way a word or letter is pronounced
2 the way the words of a language are pronounced *French pronunciation is very difficult.*

LANGUAGE EXTRA be careful to say and write this word in the correct way, with -nun- in the middle, not -noun-. Do not say or write *pronounciation*, which is wrong.

proof *noun* **proofs**
1 information that shows something is true or exists *There's no proof that Harry broke the window.*
2 a document showing something is true or exists *proof of identity* (saying who you are, for example a passport)
3 **proofs** a piece of writing that is specially printed so that mistakes, for example in punctuation and spelling, can be corrected before the final copy is printed *Our teacher is reading the proofs of the school newsletter.*

-proof *suffix*
protecting against something or someone *a bulletproof jacket; a waterproof coat; a childproof lock*

proofread *verb*
proofreads, proofreading, proofread
to read a piece of written work and correct the mistakes in it, for example in punctuation and spelling **proofreader** *noun*

prop *verb*
props, propping, propped
to put something somewhere or on something or against something so that it is supported *I propped my bike up against the fence. Mum propped up the baby's head with a pillow.*

prop *noun* **props**
1 an object or piece of furniture used by actors in a play or film *The only stage props were a table and chair.*
2 a piece of wood or metal for supporting something

propaganda *noun*
information that is spread by an organisation or country to influence people's opinions. The information is often false or made to seem more important than it really is.

propel *verb*
propels, propelling, propelled
1 to make something move in a particular direction, often very fast *The spacecraft was propelled towards Mars.*
2 to push or throw something or someone very hard *The bully grabbed my schoolbag and propelled it across the room.*
3 to provide the power that makes something work and moves it forward *a rocket-propelled grenade*

propeller *noun* **propellers**
a piece of equipment made up of two or more blades (long flat parts that go round), used for making a plane, helicopter or ship move

proper *adjective*
1 used for describing something you should do or have, the position or situation where something should be or the time when something should be done *What's the proper way to hold a fork? I don't have the proper tools. Put all your toys back in their proper place. This isn't the proper time.*

SYNONYM right

2 real and acceptable *Crisps aren't a proper meal. My sister has never had a proper job.*
3 used for talking about good behaviour *It's not proper to talk with your mouth full of food.*

379

proper fraction – Protestantism

4 used for giving extra importance to a word *He's a proper idiot.*

proper fraction *noun* **proper fractions**
in maths, a fraction in which the numerator (top number) is smaller than the denominator (bottom number), for example $\frac{1}{8}$. Proper fractions are worth less than one whole.
compare: **improper fraction** and **equivalent fractions**

properly *adverb*
1 in the right way, or in the way something should happen or be done *You haven't shut down your laptop properly. I haven't been eating properly this week.*
2 completely *My egg isn't properly cooked.*

proper noun *noun* **proper nouns**
a noun that names particular people or places, for example Amy, York, Scotland. Proper nouns are written with a capital first letter.

property *noun*
1 something that belongs to someone or to a group such as a club, school or government *These two bikes are my property.*
2 all the things that belong to someone or to a group *Please respect school property.*
3 (plural **properties**) buildings or land, or one building, belonging to someone *My cousin owns a property in Scotland.*
4 (plural **properties**) a special quality that shows what something is like and that makes it different from other things *Solids and liquids have different properties – solids are hard and liquids are runny.*

prophecy ['prof-er-see'] *noun*
1 (plural **prophecies**) something that someone says will happen in the future because they believe it very strongly
2 the magic power of knowing what will happen in the future *Merlin had the gift of prophecy.*

prophesy ['prof-er-sye'] *verb*
prophesies, prophesying, prophesied
to say that you strongly believe something will happen in the future

prophet *noun* **prophets**
1 someone who says what will happen in the future
2 in many religions a prophet is a person with special powers who tells people what God or a god wants them to do

prophetic *adjective*
used for saying what will happen in the future, especially when what is said happens to be true *The author's predictions about the internet were prophetic.*

proportion *noun* **proportions**
1 a part of the total amount of something *Girls make up the largest proportion of the class.*
2 a number of people or things compared to the total number of them *This year a higher proportion of students want to study French.*
3 used about an amount or number compared to another amount or number *The proportion of boys to girls in the school is roughly equal.*

4 used about the correct relationship in size or importance between different things *The artist painted everything completely in proportion. I like your drawing but the feet are out of proportion with the rest of the body* (for example, they are too big or too small).
5 the proportions of something are its size *Oak trees can grow to huge proportions.*

proportional or **proportionate** *adjective*
1 having the correct size or amount when compared to something else *How much people pay is proportional to what they can afford.*
2 equivalent in importance to something else *The punishment should be proportionate to the crime.*
proportionally *adverb*
proportionately *adverb*

proposal *noun* **proposals**
1 a suggestion for something
2 when someone asks someone else if they will get married to them

propose *verb*
proposes, proposing, proposed
1 to suggest something such as an idea or plan for someone to think about
2 if someone proposes doing something, they intend to do it
3 if someone proposes to someone else, they ask them if they will get married to them

proprietor ['prer-pry-er-ter'] *noun* **proprietors**
someone who owns a business such as a shop or restaurant

propulsion *noun*
the force or power that makes something work and moves it forward *jet propulsion* (used in a jet engine for making a jet aircraft fly)

prose *noun*
any kind of writing or speaking in ordinary sentences with normal grammar. Prose is different from poetry, which usually has rhymes and different grammatical rules.

prosecute *verb*
prosecutes, prosecuting, prosecuted
to accuse someone of a crime in a court of law so that they can be judged
prosecution *noun*

prospect ['pros-pekt'] *noun*
1 (plural **prospects**) the possibility that something will happen in the future, often something good *Is there any prospect that the sun will come out for our trip to the seaside?*
2 the idea of something that you know will happen in the future *I'm not looking forward to the prospect of going to the dentist next week.*
3 someone's prospects are their chances of being successful, for example in a job

prospect ['prers-pekt'] *verb*
prospects, prospecting, prospected
to search in the ground or under the sea for something such as gold or oil
prospector *noun*

prospectus *noun* **prospectuses**
a small book or part of a website that gives you information about something such as a school or college

prosper *verb*
prospers, prospering, prospered
to be successful, for example by making lots of money *My mum's restaurant is prospering.*

prosperity *noun*
a situation in which people are successful and have lots of money

prosperous *adjective*
rich and successful

prostrate *adjective*
if someone is prostrate, they are lying flat with their face downwards, for example because they are praying or feeling ill

protagonist *noun* **protagonists**
the main character in a book, story or film

protect *verb*
protects, protecting, protected
1 to keep a person, place or thing safe from harm or danger *This parasol will protect you from the sun.*
2 to keep something safe in case it is lost or stolen *You have to install antivirus software to protect your files.*
protector *noun*

protection *noun*
1 when someone or something keeps a person, place or thing safe *A bus shelter offers protection against the wind and rain.*
2 something that protects *If you ride a bike, a helmet is an essential protection for your head.*

protective *adjective*
1 wanting to protect someone you love or like by looking after them and making sure nothing bad happens to them *Our parents have always been very protective towards us. Chloe's mother is over-protective* (for example, she doesn't let Chloe go out in case something bad happens).
2 used for describing something such as clothing or equipment that is meant to protect someone *protective goggles*

protein ['proh-teen'] *noun* **proteins**
a substance that exists in all living things and that is needed by the body to help it grow and stay healthy. You get protein from food such as meat, fish, eggs and cheese.

protest ['prer-test'] *verb*
protests, protesting, protested
if someone protests, they show they are not happy about something, for example by complaining, shouting or walking with other people through the streets

protest ['proh-test'] *noun* **protests**
1 something someone says or does that shows they are not happy about something *The factory workers went on strike in protest at the manager's decision.*
2 an event in which people join together to show that they are not happy about something

Protestant ['prot-is-ternt'] *noun* **Protestants**
a Christian who belongs to a large group that separated from the Catholic Church in the 16th century **Protestant** *adjective*

Protestantism *noun*
the religion of Protestants

protester – prune

protester *noun* **protesters**
someone who shows they are not happy about something by joining with other people, for example to walk through the streets

proton *noun* **protons**
a part of an atom that has a positive electrical charge
compare: **electron** and **neutron**

prototype *noun* **prototypes**
the first model of a product such as a machine or vehicle that is produced before other examples of the same product are made

protractor *noun* **protractors**
a flat instrument shaped like half a circle or a full circle, used for drawing and measuring angles. It is marked with the degrees of a circle and is usually made from clear plastic.

protrude *verb*
protrudes, protruding, protruded
to stick out from somewhere, often in a way that is ugly or not pleasant *He had protruding teeth.*

protrusion *noun*
1 (*plural* **protrusions**) something that sticks out
2 when something sticks out from somewhere

proud *adjective* **prouder, proudest**
1 feeling extremely happy about something or someone because you think they're good *Hannah is proud of her new bike. Oliver's proud of his baby brother.*
2 feeling extremely happy about someone because of what they've done *Her parents are proud of her. I came top of the class and I feel very proud* (happy about what I've done). *Coming top gave me a really proud feeling.*
3 feeling that you're important enough to be treated with respect and not wanting people to think you're less good than they are *Granddad is too proud to ask for help. The Scots are a proud people.*
4 feeling that you're more important than other people *Your uncle looks down on me – he's too proud. His behaviour is always so proud.*

> SIMILE 'as proud as a peacock' means very proud (sense 4)

proudly *adverb*
1 in a way that shows you feel extremely happy about something or someone *'Our team has won,' he said proudly.*
2 in a way that shows you want to be treated with respect and don't want to appear less good than other people *She proudly refused the help they offered.*

prove *verb*
proves, proving, proved
1 to provide information to show that something is true or exists
2 used about something that after a certain time happens to be true or to be just as described, although you didn't know earlier that it really would be true *My choice proved to be a good one* (happened to be good). *The jumble sale proved a success.*
3 to prove yourself is to show that you're good at something

proverb *noun* **proverbs**
a short well-known sentence that tells you something about life or gives you useful advice, for example 'Practice makes perfect.'

proverbial *adjective*
1 used for showing that you are using a proverb *An Englishman's home is his proverbial castle.*
2 well-known *At school, people talk about my brother's proverbial laziness.*

proverbially *adverb*

provide *verb*
provides, providing, provided
1 to give something to someone or something, for example something that they need *Our teacher provided us with exercise books. This plant provides all the food these animals need.*
2 to get and bring something *The children must provide their own pens and pencils.*
3 to cause something or make something happen *The trip to the coast provided a lot of excitement.*
4 to make or do something *Bees provide honey. This charity provides a lot of help for elderly people.*
5 to show something *The bus conductor asked me to provide my ticket.*
6 to say or write something *In the next part of the quiz, you have to provide the missing word.*
7 to have something for people to use *Our school provides a room where parents can wait.*
8 to provide for someone is to give them the things they need to live, for example food and money
9 to provide for something is to take something into consideration, for example in order to deal with it

provided or **providing** *conjunction*
used for talking about something that must happen first before something else can be done *I'll help you with your homework provided you let me ride your bike.*

> LANGUAGE EXTRA you can also use 'that' after *provided* or *providing*, for example *You can come with me providing that you behave.*

province *noun* **provinces**
1 one of the areas that some countries are divided into, for example Canada, Spain, Belgium or Italy
2 the provinces are the parts of some countries outside the capital city or main towns *Chantal lives in the provinces, in the west of France.*
3 a particular subject that someone knows a lot about *Maths is not my province.*

provincial *adjective*
1 connected with a province *a provincial government*
2 connected with a part of a country outside the capital city or main towns *a provincial town in Ireland*

provision *noun*
1 when something is provided *Most parents think the provision of food in our canteen is excellent.*
2 when something is taken into consideration *The school doesn't have enough provision for pupils with learning difficulties.*

provisional *adjective*
1 used for describing something or someone that exists for a certain time only, usually a short time *a provisional government; Our school has a provisional head teacher.*
2 used about something that is not certain and might change at a later time *The provisional date of my birthday party is 9th May.*

provisionally *adverb*

provisions *noun plural*
food and drink, for example for taking on a journey

provocation *noun*
1 when someone deliberately wants to make you angry
2 (*plural* **provocations**) something someone says or does that is likely to make you angry

provocative *adjective*
used for describing something such as a remark or behaviour that is likely to make someone angry

provoke *verb*
provokes, provoking, provoked
1 if you provoke someone, you deliberately want to make them angry
2 to cause a strong feeling or action *The rise in prices provoked anger among the people.*

prow *noun* **prows**
the front part of a ship or boat

prowl *verb*
prowls, prowling, prowled
1 if someone prowls around, they walk around somewhere quietly and slowly as if they are going to do something bad
2 if an animal prowls, it walks around quietly and slowly looking for other animals to catch and kill

prowl *noun*
on the prowl prowling around *There's a fox on the prowl.*

prowler *noun* **prowlers**
someone who prowls around, for example at night, in order to do something bad such as frighten someone or steal from them

proximity *noun*
used for talking about how near something is to something else *What's good about my house is its proximity to the school.*

prudent *adjective*
sensible and wise, for example in the judgements and decisions that you make *a prudent businesswoman; a prudent decision; It would be prudent to leave now before it gets dark.* **prudence** *noun*
prudently *adverb*

prune *noun* **prunes**
a plum that is dried (the water has been removed from it). It is often eaten cooked. *stewed prunes*

> ORIGIN from Old French *prune* and Latin *prunum* 'plum'

prune–puddle

prune *verb*
prunes, pruning, pruned
1 if you prune a tree, bush or plant, you cut off some of the branches, leaves, stems or flowers to make it grow better
2 pruning shears are a tool used by gardeners for cutting the stems, leaves and flowers of plants. They look like a strong pair of scissors with two short sharp blades and with handles connected by a spring.

pry *verb*
pries, prying, pried
to try to find out things about someone or something that are private and that you shouldn't know about *You don't want strangers prying into your business. My uncle found some Roman coins but managed to keep them away from prying eyes* (not let people see them or find out about them).

PS
used when you write a short extra message at the end of a letter or email after the place where you sign your name
short for: postscript

psalm ['sahm'] *noun* psalms
a religious song or poem, especially one from the Bible (the holy book of the Christian and Jewish religions)

pseudonym ['soo-der-nim'] *noun*
pseudonyms
a name that someone uses instead of their real name when they write something such as a book, article or blog

psst *interjection*
a sound people make when they are trying to get someone's attention

psychiatrist ['sye-kye-er-trist'] *noun*
psychiatrists
a doctor who treats people with a mental illness (illness of the mind)

psychiatry ['sye-kye-er-tree'] *noun*
the treatment or study of mental illnesses
psychiatric *adjective*

psychic ['sye-kik'] *adjective*
if someone is psychic or has psychic powers, they know what people are thinking and what will happen in the future

psychological ['sye-ker-loj-ik-erl'] *adjective*
connected with the mind *My cousin has psychological problems.*

psychology ['sye-kol-er-jee'] *noun*
the study of the mind and feelings and the reasons for people's behaviour
psychologist *noun*

PTA *noun* PTAs
a group of parents and teachers who work together to help their school, for example by organising activities that bring in money for the school
short for: parent-teacher association

pterodactyl ['terr-oh-dak-til'] *noun*
pterodactyls
a large flying reptile that lived millions of years ago. Pterodactyls had very long wings and a long mouth with many sharp teeth.

PTO
an abbreviation written at the bottom of a page of a document to show that there is something written on the other side too
short for: please turn over

pub *noun* pubs
a place where adults go to meet friends, buy drinks such as beer or wine and eat light meals

puberty ['pyoo-ber-tee'] *noun*
a time in the life of a child when his or her body changes and becomes more like the body of an adult. These changes happen between the ages of about 10 and 17.

public *noun*
1 used when you mean all the people in a particular place or all the people everywhere *A famous film star was walking down the street but the public ignored him. The museum is open to the public every day.*
2 **a member of the public** an ordinary person in a particular place
3 **in public** in front of other people *You shouldn't behave like that in public.*

public *adjective*
1 used for describing something that belongs to everyone or that everyone can use *a public toilet*; *public transport* (for example buses and trains); *You should behave properly in a public place* (for example anywhere where there are people, such as in the street or park, at a beach, station, cinema or shopping centre); *This land is public property.*
2 used for describing something that everyone can go to or take part in *a public meeting*; *The concert is a public event.*
3 used for describing something that everyone can see, hear or know about *a public apology*; *a public announcement*; *The name of the new school has been made public.*
4 connected with lots of people *public support*; *public opinion* (the opinions of most people, for example in a country)
5 belonging to, controlled by or supported by the government, not by a particular group of people *The museums get a lot of public money.*

publication *noun*
1 (*plural* **publications**) a book, magazine or newspaper that is printed or that you can read on the internet or on a device such as an e-reader
2 when something such as a book is produced and it is ready for people to buy or to read on the internet or on a device such as an e-reader *Today is the publication date of my uncle's novel.*
3 when something is made known to the public *Everyone's waiting for the publication of the exam results.*

public holiday *noun* public holidays
a special day when you don't have to go to school and when most people don't have to go to work *New Year's Day is a public holiday.*

publicise *verb*
publicises, publicising, publicised
to tell people about something, for example by giving information in newspapers or on the internet

LANGUAGE EXTRA also spelt *publicize*

publicity *noun*
information that is given on TV, on the internet or in newspapers, for example, so that people know about something or someone *There has been a lot of publicity about the dangers of drinking.*

publicly *adverb*
1 if something is done publicly, it is done so that everyone knows about it *The head teacher has apologised publicly.*
2 in front of other people *You shouldn't use that word publicly.*
3 by the government, not by a particular group of people *The NHS is publicly owned.*

public school *noun* public schools
1 a private school in England and Wales for students aged from about 13 to 18. Public schools charge fees (money) and belong to a small group made up of the oldest and most well-known of private schools.
2 a school controlled by the government in many countries, for example Scotland, Australia and the USA

publish *verb*
publishes, publishing, published
1 to produce something such as a book or newspaper and make it ready for people to buy or to read on the internet or on a device such as an e-reader
2 to write something such as a letter, article or story that is printed somewhere such as in a newspaper or produced on the internet
3 to make something known to the public *The photos were published on the internet.*

publisher *noun* publishers
a company or person that produces things such as books, newspapers or software

publishing *noun*
1 the business of producing things such as books, newspapers or software
2 desktop publishing is the use of computers for producing documents containing words and pictures, for example for a newspaper or magazine

puck *noun* pucks
a small disc made of hard rubber used in ice hockey. Players try to hit the disc along the ice into the other team's goal using a special stick that is curved at one end.

pucker *verb*
puckers, puckering, puckered
1 if you pucker your lips, you squeeze them together
2 if you pucker your face or forehead, you make small folds or lines appear in it
3 if your skin, face or forehead puckers, small folds or lines appear in it

pudding *noun*
1 (*plural* **puddings**) a sweet dish made from flour, fat, sugar and water, milk or eggs mixed with different things such as bread, rice or fruit *a Christmas pudding*
2 (*plural* **puddings**) a hot dish made with meat or vegetables *a steak and kidney pudding*
3 something sweet that you eat at the end of a meal as a dessert

puddle *noun* puddles
a small area of water on the ground, usually left after it has rained

pudgy *adjective* **pudgier, pudgiest**
slightly fat, for example in a way that looks pleasant

puerile *adjective*
1 behaving like a silly child *He's very puerile.*
2 silly in a way that makes you think of a child *puerile behaviour*

SYNONYM childish

Puerto Rico *noun*
an island and country in the West Indies
Puerto Rican *adjective & noun*

puff *verb*
puffs, puffing, puffed
1 to breathe in and out loudly and with difficulty, for example after running or doing exercise
2 to blow air and smoke out of the mouth *You often see Churchill puffing on a cigar.*
3 to make something blow out such as smoke or steam *All around, chimneys were puffing smoke. Steam trains used to puff through this station.*
4 if you puff out your cheeks or chest, you fill them with air so that they look bigger

puff *noun* **puffs**
1 a small amount of something such as smoke, air or steam that comes out of something and goes up into the air *I felt a puff of warm air on my neck.*
2 when someone breathes something in such as medicine or smoke from a cigarette *My sister has asthma and takes two puffs a day from her inhaler. The waiter went outside to take a puff.*
3 a sound like the sound of someone or something blowing out air
4 a type of light pastry (flour, water and fat) that is filled with something soft such as cream, jam or cheese

puffed out *adjective* (informal)
if someone is puffed out, they have trouble breathing, for example after doing exercise or making an effort

SYNONYM short of breath

puffin *noun* **puffins**
a large black and white bird with a strong body and brightly coloured beak. Puffins live by the sea and eat fish.

puffy *adjective* **puffier, puffiest**
1 if a part of your body is puffy, it looks larger and rounder than it should *puffy eyes*

SYNONYM swollen

2 (informal) another way of saying puffed out

SYNONYM short of breath

pull *verb*
pulls, pulling, pulled
1 to take something or someone, usually with your hand, and move them towards you or into a different position, often quickly or by using a lot of strength *I pulled one end of the Christmas cracker. Stop pulling my hair! My baby sister pulled some wallpaper away from the wall. I helped to pull Granddad up out of his chair.*
2 to move something along in the same direction so that it follows from behind, for example something on wheels *The engine was pulling the train.*
3 if you pull a muscle, you hurt it by stretching it too much
4 used about a vehicle that moves somewhere *The bus pulled away* (went away) *before I could get on it. Let's pull in* (stop) *at the next garage. The train's just pulling in* (arriving). *Don't pull out* (move onto a road where there's traffic) *until it's all clear. Mum pulled over* (stopped at the side of the road) *to look at the map. The coach pulled up* (stopped) *in front of the school gates.*
5 to pull a face is to put a funny expression on your face, usually to show you dislike something or someone
6 to pull someone's leg is to tell someone something that isn't true as a joke
7 to pull at something is to pull it and often to keep pulling it *Stop pulling at my sleeve.*
8 to pull down something such as a building or wall is to completely destroy it
9 to pull off something that is difficult to do is to be successful in doing it *Our team almost beat Woodford County High but couldn't quite pull it off* (succeed).
10 to pull out of something such as a race, competition or business is to stop taking part in it or having anything to do with it
11 to pull through after you've been ill or injured is to stay alive and not die

pull *noun* **pulls**
the action of pulling something or someone *I gave my sister's ponytail a little pull.*

pull-down menu *noun* **pull-down menus**
a list of detailed things in a computer program that you can ask a computer to do. When you choose a word or name from the menu bar (strip usually at the top of the screen listing the main things the computer can do), the list is pulled down (or appears) under the word or name.

SYNONYM drop-down menu

pulley *noun* **pulleys**
a piece of equipment used for moving heavy objects up and down. It is made up of a metal bar supporting a wheel with a groove (long narrow space) around it. A rope or chain is put around the groove and attached to the object that you want to move.

pullover *noun* **pullovers**
a piece of knitted clothing without buttons that you wear over a shirt or T-shirt to keep the top of your body warm

pulp *noun*
1 a very soft substance made by crushing something, for example wood or cloth for making paper
2 a soft wet substance inside a fruit or vegetable such as a tomato or melon

pulpy *adjective*

pulp *verb*
pulps, pulping, pulped
to crush something until it becomes very soft

pulpit ['pul' rhymes with 'pull'] *noun* **pulpits**
a small raised structure inside a church where a priest stands and speaks to the people who take part in his or her service

pulse *noun*
1 the regular beat that you can feel as your heart pumps blood around your body. The pulse can be felt in several parts of the body such as the wrist or neck.
2 if someone such as a doctor or nurse takes your pulse, he or she feels the pulse in a place such as your wrist or neck in order to measure your pulse rate (count how many times your heart beats in a minute)

pulses *noun plural*
1 small seeds that are dried (water is removed) and then cooked and eaten as vegetables. They grow inside pods (long narrow containers). Lentils and some types of beans and peas are pulses.
2 the plants that produce these seeds

pulverise *verb*
pulverises, pulverising, pulverised
1 to hit something many times until it becomes a powder or broken into tiny pieces
2 to beat someone easily or completely, for example in a game or battle

LANGUAGE EXTRA also spelt *pulverize*

puma *noun* **pumas**
a big wild animal of the cat family. It has yellow-brown or greyish fur and lives mainly in North and South America.

pumice stone *noun* **pumice stones**
a grey stone used for rubbing your skin clean. It is very light in weight and comes from the rock that is thrown out by a volcano.

pump *noun* **pumps**
1 a piece of equipment for forcing liquid, air or gas out of something or into something *a bicycle pump* (for putting air into a bicycle tyre); *a petrol pump* (for putting petrol into a vehicle)
2 a piece of equipment for getting water out of the ground
3 one of a pair of soft light flat shoes used for doing exercise or dancing, for example

pump *verb*
pumps, pumping, pumped
1 to force liquid, air or gas out of something or into something
2 to pump something up is to fill it with air or gas using a pump *I had a flat tyre so I had to pump it up.*

pumpkin *noun* **pumpkins**
a large round orange or yellow fruit. It has a hard skin with lines on it going from top to bottom and lots of seeds inside. Pumpkins are cooked and eaten as a vegetable. *a pumpkin pie*

pun *noun* **puns**
a joke that someone makes by using a word that has more than one meaning or a word that has the same sound as another one (for example 'red' and 'read') but a different meaning. An example of a pun is 'There's no **point** in writing with a broken pencil'.

punch – pure

punch *verb*
punches, punching, punched
1 if someone punches someone or something, they hit them with their fist (hand with closed fingers)
2 to make a hole in something using a punch *This machine punches your ticket. I punched two holes in the paper before putting it in the binder.*
3 to press something hard such as a button on a piece of equipment or a key on a keyboard
4 to punch the air is to close your hand into a fist and hit the air, usually above your head, to show that you're very happy about something that has just happened

punch *noun*
1 (*plural* **punches**) the action of hitting someone or something with the fist (hand with closed fingers) *The bully gave me a punch in the ribs.*
2 (*plural* **punches**) a tool or piece of equipment for making holes in something *a paper punch*
3 a sweet drink made from fruit juice that can be mixed with pieces of fruit such as lemon and with spices and alcohol. It is usually made in a large bowl called a punch bowl.

punchbag *noun* **punchbags**
a large heavy bag shaped like a cylinder (tube with flat ends shaped like circles) that usually hangs from a rope attached to a frame. It is filled with soft material and is used by boxers to practise their punches.

LANGUAGE EXTRA also spelt *punch bag*

punchline *noun* **punchlines**
the last part of a joke that explains the joke and makes it funny

LANGUAGE EXTRA also spelt *punch line*

punch-up *noun* **punch-ups**
an informal word for a fight

punctual *adjective*
1 arriving somewhere at the right time and not late *Our teacher likes all pupils to be punctual. Trains to Leeds are usually punctual.*
2 happening at the right time and not late *punctual service*
punctuality *noun*

punctually *adverb*
at the right time and not late *The lesson started punctually at nine o'clock.*

punctuate *verb*
punctuates, punctuating, punctuated
to put the correct punctuation marks such as commas, full stops and question marks into a piece of writing *The last sentence isn't clear because it's badly punctuated.*

punctuation *noun*
1 the use of special symbols called punctuation marks in writing. Punctuation makes it easier to understand written sentences. *We're studying punctuation at school.*
2 the punctuation marks themselves *Jack's email has no punctuation.*

punctuation mark *noun*
punctuation marks
a special symbol used in writing that makes it easier to understand written sentences. Punctuation marks include commas, full stops, colons, dashes, apostrophes, question marks and exclamation marks.

puncture *noun* **punctures**
a small hole in a tyre made by accident by something sharp such as a nail or piece of glass *Dad had a puncture on the motorway.*

pungent *adjective*
used for describing a smell or taste that is very strong or too strong

punish *verb*
punishes, punishing, punished
1 to make someone suffer because they have done something wrong, for example by making them do something they don't want to do or by not giving them something that they want
2 to make someone suffer because they have done something bad or against the law, for example by sending them to prison, making them pay money or hurting them

punishment *noun*
1 (*plural* **punishments**) a way of punishing someone *My punishment was to sweep the classroom.*
2 the action of punishing someone *He deserves punishment.*

punk *noun*
1 punk or punk rock is a type of loud fast music with short songs played in a simple way. It was popular in the 1970s and 80s.
2 (*plural* **punks**) someone who likes punk music and often wears clothes and hairstyles that shock people

punnet *noun* **punnets**
a small square or rectangular container for selling fruit in, for example strawberries or raspberries

punt *noun* **punts**
a long narrow boat with square ends and a flat bottom. Someone stands at the end of the boat and moves it through the water using a pole with a metal piece at the end. Punts are used especially on small rivers such as the Cam in Cambridge and the Cherwell in Oxford.

punt *verb*
punts, punting, punted
to move a punt along through the water using a pole **punter** *noun*

puny ['pyoo-nee'] *adjective* **punier, puniest**
1 used for describing a person, animal or part of the body that is small and weak *As a boy my dad was thin and puny-looking.*
2 used for describing something that is not good enough or something that is too small *a puny effort; Despite Adam's puny size, he could run faster than me.*

pup *noun* **pups**
1 a young dog
2 a young animal like a dog *a wolf pup*
3 a young seal

pupa ['pyoo-per'] *noun* **pupae** ['pyoo-pee']
a part of the life cycle of some insects, such as butterflies, between the time when they are a larva (after first coming out of the egg) and the time when they change into their adult form. During this time the insect does not move but stays inside a cocoon (silky covering).

ORIGIN from Latin *pupa* 'doll'

pupil *noun* **pupils**
1 someone who is being taught in a school, for example a child in a primary school
2 someone who is being given lessons by someone or who learns a skill from someone *Many seventeenth-century artists were pupils of Rembrandt.*

ORIGIN from Latin *pupillus* 'young orphan' (from *pupus* 'boy')

pupil *noun* **pupils**
the small black circle in the middle of your eye that allows light into the eye. The large coloured circle around the pupil is called the iris.

ORIGIN from Latin *pupilla* 'little girl doll' (from *pupa* 'doll' or 'girl'), because you can see an image of yourself (like a little doll) when you look at the pupils of someone's eyes

puppet *noun* **puppets**
1 a toy model of a person or animal that you move by pulling strings or wires attached to different parts of its body
2 a toy model of a person or animal made of cloth that you move by putting your hand inside. It is also called a glove puppet.

ORIGIN from Old French *poupette* 'little doll' (from *poupée* 'doll' and from Latin *pupa* 'doll' or 'girl')

puppy *noun* **puppies**
a young dog

purchase *verb*
purchases, purchasing, purchased
another way of saying to buy *We've already purchased the tickets for the concert.* **purchaser** *noun*

purchase *noun*
1 (*plural* **purchases**) something that you buy
2 when you buy something *How do you make an online purchase?*
3 a tight hold on something, for example with your hands or feet *The climber couldn't get a purchase on the rope.*

pure *adjective* **purer, purest**
1 not mixed with anything else, for example so that something is of the best quality *pure apple juice; pure gold*
2 clean and not containing anything harmful *This mountain air is so pure.*
3 used for saying that something happens completely by accident *That's a pure coincidence. It was pure chance I bumped into her at the bus stop.*
4 used for giving extra importance to a word, for example when you mean that something is as great as can be *Relaxing on the beach was pure bliss!*
5 used for describing something such as a colour or sound that is clear and beautiful *She dreamt of the pure white beaches of a desert island.*
6 used for describing something such as someone's body, mind or life that is completely good and without evil

purely–put

purely *adverb*
used when you mean one thing only and nothing else *Dad is organising the Christmas party purely to help the school. I found my glasses under the cushion purely by chance.*

SYNONYM *only*

purge *verb*
purges, purging, purged
to get rid of someone or something because they are not wanted, for example people in an organisation or bad qualities or feelings
purge *noun*

purifier *noun* **purifiers**
a piece of equipment or a substance that gets rid of dirty or harmful substances from something *an air purifier*

purify *verb*
purifies, purifying, purified
1 to get rid of dirty or harmful substances from something, for example from water or the air, to make it clean and pure
2 to remove all bad things such as evil thoughts and germs from someone's body, for example by washing or bathing as happens in many religions
purification *noun*

puritan *noun* **puritans**
someone who believes in very strict standards of good behaviour **puritanical** *adjective*

purity *noun*
the quality of being pure *the purity of a mountain stream*

purple *adjective*
having a colour between red and blue

purple *noun*
the colour purple

purpose *noun*
1 (*plural* **purposes**) the reason for doing something *What's the purpose of your parents' visit to the school? Use this cream for medical purposes only.*
2 (*plural* **purposes**) the reason why something exists, for example what something is used for *What's the purpose of the Shift key on my laptop? Cycle helmets serve a useful purpose* (they do something useful). *Follow your dreams or your life has no purpose.*
3 a strong feeling of knowing what you want *Football has given me a purpose in life* (or *a real sense of purpose*).
4 **on purpose** used for saying that something is done because someone wants to do it and not because it happens by chance *You knocked over the glass on purpose – I saw you!*

SYNONYM for sense 4: *deliberately*

purposely *adverb*
to do something purposely is to do it because you want to

SYNONYMS *on purpose, deliberately*

purr *verb*
purrs, purring, purred
when a cat purrs, it makes a quiet continuous sound in its throat because it's happy
purr *noun*

purse *noun* **purses**
1 a very small bag for carrying your money
2 the American word for a woman's handbag

purse *verb*
purses, pursing, pursed
if you purse your lips, you press them together to make a small round shape, for example because you're angry

pursue *verb*
pursues, pursuing, pursued
1 to follow someone or something quickly to try to catch them

SYNONYM *to chase*

2 to do something (or to continue doing something) such as a course of study, activity or investigation *Ava wants to pursue French until she can speak it fluently.*
3 to achieve (or to try to achieve) something such as an aim or objective
4 to produce or develop something such as a plan or idea
pursuer *noun*

pursuit *noun*
1 the action of following someone or something quickly to try to catch them
2 the action of trying to achieve something *the pursuit of knowledge*
3 pursuits are activities someone likes doing when they are not at school or work *Sita enjoys outdoor pursuits.*

pus *noun*
a yellowish liquid that forms inside a place on your skin that is infected (has germs in it), for example a boil or cut

push *verb*
pushes, pushing, pushed
1 if you push something or someone, you move them away from you or you move them into a different position with your hands, another part of your body or an object, often using a lot of strength *I pushed the door open. The bully jumped on him but he pushed him off with both hands. Holly pushed me over* (made me fall over by pushing me hard). *Push down hard to get all your toys in the box.*
2 if you push something or someone somewhere, you move them there *I pushed my nose against the window. She pushed me into the water.*
3 if someone or something pushes something on wheels, they move it along in the same direction in front of them *Mum was pushing my baby brother in his buggy. A large engine was pushing the train.*
4 if you push a button, you put your finger on it hard to make a piece of equipment work
5 if someone is pushing, they're using their hands and arms to get people to move out of the way *Stop pushing and shoving!*
6 to make someone do something they don't want to do *I didn't want to learn the piano but Dad pushed me.*
7 to push someone around is to keep telling them what to do
8 to push in is to go and stand in front of people who are waiting in a queue
9 to push off is to go away from a place *Push off and leave me alone!*
10 to push on is to continue with a journey or activity *There's still a long way to go so let's push on.*

push *noun*
1 (*plural* **pushes**) the action of pushing someone or something *Can you give me a push on the swing?*
2 words or actions that help or force someone to do something *Dad says I always need a push to do my homework.*
3 if someone is given the push, they are told to leave a group or their job because they are not wanted

push-bike *noun* **push-bikes**
another word for a bicycle

LANGUAGE EXTRA also spelt *pushbike* or *push bike*

push-button *noun* **push-buttons**
a small switch that you press on a piece of equipment to make it work or perform a particular action *a push-button phone*

pushchair *noun* **pushchairs**
a chair with wheels for pushing a baby or young child in when you are walking. It usually has a cloth hood hanging over it to protect the baby or child against wind and rain. When it is not being used, it folds down to take up less room.
compare: **pram**

pushed *adjective* (informal)
if you're pushed, you don't have enough of something, especially time

push pin *noun* **push pins**
a small metal pin with a top shaped like a tiny ball or cylinder (tube), used for fixing a piece of paper or card to a wall or noticeboard

LANGUAGE EXTRA also spelt *pushpin*

compare: **drawing pin**

push-up *noun* **push-ups**
an exercise in which you lie on the ground with your face looking downwards and push your body up off the ground using your arms

LANGUAGE EXTRA also called a *press-up*

pushy *adjective* **pushier, pushiest**
if someone is pushy, they try very hard to get what they want in an unpleasant or rude way

puss *noun* **pusses**
an informal word for a cat

LANGUAGE EXTRA you can also say *pussy* or *pussycat*

put *verb*
puts, putting, put
1 to move something somewhere *I put my hands in my pockets.*
2 to take or get something or someone and move them somewhere *Could you put some sugar in my tea? Please put my book on the table. I'm going to put a cushion underneath.*
3 to change the situation that someone or something is in *If you make a noise, you'll put us all in danger. Put these pictures in the right order. The music put me in a good mood.*

385

putt–python

4 used with adjectives to show a change in a situation or position *Can you put the clock right? The picture was crooked so I put it straight.*
5 to make someone go somewhere *The doctor had to put me in hospital.*
6 to write something *Did you put my name on the list?*
7 to say something, for example in a particular way *Your answer is correct but you have a funny way of putting it!*
8 to build something *They're putting a block of flats next to the school.*
9 to put something away is to put it in the place where you keep it when you're not using it
10 to put something back is to put it in the place where it was before
11 to put back something such as an event or meeting is to change the date or time so that it happens at a later time
12 to put the clocks back is to change the clock time in October by turning clocks and watches one hour back
13 to put something down is to put something you're holding onto a surface or onto the floor
14 to put your hand down is to move it to a lower position *Ms Blake wasn't answering any more questions so I put my hand down.*
15 to put down an animal such as a dog or cat is to get a vet (animal doctor) to kill it, for example because it is very ill
16 to put down a price is to make it less
17 if someone puts your name down, your name is written on a list of people who want to do something or go somewhere *Dad put my name down for the trip to the British Museum.*
18 to put forward something such as an idea or suggestion is to tell it to someone so that they can think about it
19 to put the clocks forward is to change the clock time in March by putting clocks and watches one hour ahead
20 to put something off is to change the date or time so that it happens at a later time, for example a party, concert or meeting
21 to put off doing something or going somewhere is to wait longer before deciding to do it or go there *You can't put off the dentist any longer!*
22 to put someone off is to make them not want to do something or make them not like something or someone *This awful smell has put me off my food. What you said about living in the countryside has put me off.*
23 to put someone off is also to stop someone doing something such as working or concentrating, for example by making a noise
24 to put someone off somewhere is when a car or bus stops so that someone can get out *Mum put me off in front of the school gates.*
25 to put on clothes is to start wearing them
26 to put something such as paint, powder or a cream on something is to spread it there *My sister is putting on her make-up. Don't forget to put jam on my toast.*
27 to put on something such as a piece of equipment is to make it start working by switching it on *Put the light on, please.*
28 to put on something such as music or a film is to make it play, for example on a computer, DVD player or TV
29 to put on something such as a play, exhibition or course is to do it and organise it for people to go to
30 to put on a TV or radio programme is to show it on TV or broadcast it on the radio
31 to put on something such as an accent or way of speaking is to start doing it *Can you put on that funny voice, Mum?*
32 to put out something such as a fire or candle is to make it stop burning
33 to put out a light is to switch it off
34 to put someone out is to cause a problem or extra work for them *Sorry, I didn't mean to put you out. When I asked him to help me he looked put out* (upset because this was a problem for him).
35 if you put your back, shoulder or wrist out, one of the bones comes away from its normal place
36 to put something together such as an exhibition, document or plan is to produce it
37 to put something together such as a meal, team or piece of furniture is to make it from different parts
38 to put something together that is broken is to fix it
39 to put something up is to move it to a higher position *Put your hand up if you know the answer.*
40 to put something up is also to build it or make it stand straight up *They're putting up houses and a fence around them. Let's put up our tent by the river.*
41 to put up something such as a picture, notice or shelf is to fix it to a wall or other surface *We're putting up the decorations on the ceiling.*
42 to put up a price or amount of money is to increase it
43 to put someone up is to let them stay in your home
44 if you put up with someone or something unpleasant, you accept them without getting angry because you know you can't change them

putt *verb*
putts, putting, putted
in golf, to putt the ball is to hit it softly with a putter (thin metal stick) when the ball is on the short grass near the hole, so that it rolls into or towards the hole

putt *noun*

putty *noun*
a soft grey oily substance like clay, used for fixing glass into window frames made of wood. Putty becomes hard when it is dry.

puzzle *noun* **puzzles**
1 something that is difficult to understand *Her strange behaviour at the party is a bit of a puzzle.*
2 a picture game where a picture has been cut up into lots of tiny pieces with different shapes. You have to fit the pieces together to make the whole picture appear.

SYNONYM **jigsaw**

3 a word game where you have to find answers to questions or solve problems
compare: **crossword**

4 a difficult question that you have to find an answer to or a problem that you have to solve

puzzle *verb*
puzzles, puzzling, puzzled
1 to make someone confused because they don't understand something or someone *I was puzzled by what she did.*
2 if you puzzle over something, you try to understand it by thinking about it a lot

puzzled *adjective*
confused because you don't understand something

puzzling *adjective*
difficult to understand

pyjamas *noun plural*
1 soft loose clothes that you wear in bed, made up of trousers (or bottoms) and a jacket (or top) *a pyjama jacket; pyjama bottoms*
2 soft loose clothes, usually made up of bottoms and a top in many different styles, worn during the daytime in Asian countries such as India and China

ORIGIN from Urdu *pay-jama* 'leg clothing'. Pyjamas were loose trousers tied round the waist, first worn in India.

pylon *noun* **pylons**
one of many tall metal towers, used for holding electric wires. The wires go from pylon to pylon and carry electricity around the country.

ORIGIN from Greek *pylon* 'gateway' or 'gate tower', referring to one of the sloping towers in front of an ancient Egyptian temple

pyramid *noun* **pyramids**
1 a solid pointed shape with flat sides and a flat base (or bottom). Each side is a triangle that slopes inwards towards the point at the top. The most common type of pyramid has a square base and four triangular sides.
2 a large stone building in the shape of a pyramid with a square base and four sides, such as one built in ancient Egypt as a tomb

python *noun* **pythons**
a very large snake that kills other animals for food by wrapping a part of its body around them and squeezing them. Pythons live mainly in Africa, Asia and Australia.

q Q

ORIGIN the shape of our letter Q was already clear from the Phoenician letter *qoph* (pronounced 'kof'), which meant 'monkey'. This letter looked like a circle with a vertical line through the middle that stuck out like a tail. To some people it looked like a monkey's face and tail, to others like a knot. The sound of the letter was similar to 'k'. By the time the letter had passed into the Greek and Etruscan alphabets, there was no more line through the centre, leaving a shape like a lollipop on a stick. The Etruscans called their letter *qu* (pronounced 'koo'). When the Romans borrowed the shape, the tail was made shorter and moved to the right, producing the Q shape we use today. The Romans were the first to join Q to U for their 'kw' sound in words such as *quinque* 'five' (pronounced '**kwin**-kway') – the main use of Q in modern English too.

quack verb
quacks, quacking, quacked
when a duck quacks, it makes a loud rough sound that sounds like the word 'quack'
quack noun

quad noun quads (informal)
1 short for **quadrangle**
2 short for **quadruplet**

quadrangle noun quadrangles
a square or oblong area surrounded by buildings, for example in a school or university, especially an old one

quadrant noun quadrants
1 a shape that is a quarter of a circle. It is made from a quarter of the circumference (curved line that forms the outside of the circle) and two straight lines drawn from the centre of the circle to the circumference.
compare: **semicircle**
2 a square shape that you get by dividing a square into four equal parts

quadrilateral noun quadrilaterals
any flat shape with four straight sides such as a square, rectangle or rhombus (diamond) **quadrilateral** adjective

quadruped ['kwod-roo-ped'] noun quadrupeds
an animal that has four legs
compare: **biped**

quadruple adjective
four times the amount or size or number of something *The snow that fell in March was quadruple the amount in February.*
quadruple noun

quadruple verb
quadruples, quadrupling, quadrupled
1 to become four times as big or as much *The number of cars on the road has quadrupled in the last few years.*
2 to make something four times as big or as much *The museum is trying to quadruple the number of visitors.*

quadruplet noun quadruplets
each one of four babies who are born at the same time and have the same mother

quail noun quails
a small bird with a round body, short tail and small head. It is hunted for food or sport, and people sometimes eat its eggs.

quail verb
quails, quailing, quailed
to show great fear, for example by shaking slightly with your whole body

quaint adjective quainter, quaintest
if something such as a place, building, costume or tradition is quaint, it is pleasant, attractive and interesting and usually has an old-fashioned quality *a quaint seaside town* **quaintly** adverb **quaintness** noun

quake verb
quakes, quaking, quaked
to shake, for example because you are very frightened

quake noun quakes (informal)
a sudden and violent shaking of the ground that usually causes a lot of damage
short for: **earthquake**

Quaker noun Quakers
someone belonging to a religious group called the Society of Friends. It is a mainly Christian group and was started by George Fox in the 17th century. Quakers have very simple religious services and are against violence and war.

qualification noun qualifications
1 the special skill, knowledge or quality that someone needs to be able to do a particular job or activity *An excellent knowledge of French and lots of patience are the best qualifications for a French teacher.*
2 an official piece of paper that someone gets when they have passed an exam (or exams) or followed a course. It shows they have the skill or knowledge to do a particular job or activity. *My dad left school without any qualifications.*

qualified adjective
1 having passed an exam (or exams) or followed a course *My mum is a qualified teacher.*
2 having the skill, knowledge or quality that you need to be able to do something *I'm not qualified to say whether you have a good accent in French.*

qualify verb
qualifies, qualifying, qualified
1 to have passed an exam (or exams) or followed a course that shows you have the skill or knowledge to do a particular job or activity *My brother has just qualified as a doctor.*
2 to be allowed to have, do or take part in something *Students who don't have enough money will qualify for a grant. To qualify for the team you must be over 12.*
3 to make it possible for someone to have, do or take part in something *Having a learning difficulty qualifies you for lots of extra help.*
4 to reach a high enough level in a competition to go on to the next stage of the competition *The school football team qualified for the finals.*

quality noun
1 how good or bad something is *Jack's work is always of very good quality. We were surprised by the poor quality of the food.*
2 when something is very good *Always aim for quality when you do your homework.*
3 (plural **qualities**) used for describing something and showing what kind of thing it is, what it does or how it looks *Sita's voice has a friendly and gentle quality. Some plants have medicinal qualities* (they help to treat illnesses).
4 (plural **qualities**) used for showing what kind of person someone is, especially when you notice good things about them or about their character or appearance, for example being friendly, honest, hard-working or attractive *Daniel has the right qualities to become a successful actor. What quality do you like best in your sister?*

ORIGIN from Latin *qualis* 'of what kind'

quantity noun quantities
1 how much there is of something or how many particular things there are *Use this jug for measuring the quantity of water you'll need. There was a large quantity of bread and cakes on the table.*
2 when there is a lot of something or when there are many things of a particular kind *Look at the quantity of apples on our tree!*

ORIGIN from Latin *quantus* 'how much'

quarantine ['kwo-rern-teen'] noun
1 when an animal is kept in a special place away from other animals to make sure that it doesn't have a disease
2 when a person who has an illness is kept away from other people to make sure that the illness doesn't spread
3 a period of time when a quarantine lasts

ORIGIN from Italian *quarantina* 'forty', referring to a period lasting forty days

quarrel noun quarrels
an argument that you have with someone because you're angry about something

quarrel verb
quarrels, quarrelling, quarrelled
to have an argument with someone *My brother and sister are always quarrelling* (having arguments).

quarrelsome adjective
a quarrelsome person often quarrels with people

SYNONYM argumentative

quarry noun
1 (plural **quarries**) a large hole in the ground that people dig to remove things such as stone or rock and use them for building *a marble quarry*
2 an animal (or animals) or person (or people) that another animal or person hunts and tries to catch

quart ['kwort'] noun quarts
a unit for measuring liquid, equal to about 1.14 litres. There are four quarts in a gallon.

CULTURE NOTE in the USA, a *quart* is equal to about 0.95 litres

quarter–quick

quarter *noun* **quarters**
1 one of the four equal parts that make up the whole of something *I've eaten a quarter of the cake.*
2 a quarter of an hour is 15 minutes *We waited an hour and a quarter. The film lasted an hour and three quarters* (one hour and 45 minutes).
3 a small part of a town or city where a particular group of people live *Soho in London is the Chinese quarter.*
4 a coin worth a quarter of a dollar (25 cents) in the USA or Canada
5 **quarters** a place where someone lives, for example soldiers (and sometimes their families) or servants

quarter *adverb*
1 slightly and about a quarter of the way *The window was a quarter open.*
2 **quarter past** (or **a quarter past**) used when you mean 15 minutes later than a particular hour *I got to school at quarter past nine.*
3 **quarter to** (or **a quarter to**) used when you mean 15 minutes before a particular hour *It's quarter to four.*

quarter-final *noun* **quarter-finals**
one of four games played near the end of a competition to decide the winner (or winners) who will take part in the semi-finals (the two games before the final)

quarterly *adjective*
1 happening once every three months *quarterly payments*
2 lasting three whole months *a quarterly season ticket*

quarterly *adverb*

quartet *noun* **quartets**
1 a group of four musicians playing together or four singers singing together
2 a piece of music for four musicians

quartz ['kwortz'] *noun*
a hard stone or crystal (mineral like glass that you can see through) often used in making electronic clocks and watches *a quartz watch*

quaver *verb*
quavers, quavering, quavered
if someone's voice quavers, it sounds shaky, for example because they are frightened, nervous or worried *Oliver Twist asked for more in a quavering voice.*

quaver *noun*
1 (plural **quavers**) a very short musical note played for one eighth of the time of a whole note. It is half as long as a crotchet.
2 a shaky sound in someone's voice

quay ['kee'] *noun* **quays**
a long flat area next to the sea or a river where boats stop for goods and passengers to be taken on and off and where boats can be left safely

quayside ['kee-side'] *noun* **quaysides**
a quay and the area all around it

queasy *adjective* **queasier, queasiest**
if you feel queasy, you feel as if you are going to be sick **queasiness** *noun*

queen *noun* **queens**
1 a woman who rules a country, usually because she is the daughter of the person who ruled the country before. She is made the ruler by having a crown put on her head in a special ceremony called a coronation. *Queen Elizabeth I*
2 a woman who is married to a king
3 a woman who is the most important one of a group or the best at doing a particular thing *She was the queen of Bollywood. She's the queen of rock music.*
4 in the game of chess, the queen is the most powerful piece because she can move in any direction on the board
5 in a game of cards, a queen is a card with a picture of a queen on it. It has a value less than an ace and a king but more than a jack. *the queen of diamonds*
6 in a group of insects such as bees or ants, a queen is a large female insect that produces eggs *a queen bee*

queenly *adjective*
connected with a queen or like a queen

Queen Mother *noun*
the mother of the king or queen of a particular country

queer *adjective* **queerer, queerest**
(old-fashioned)
1 strange or unusual
2 feeling slightly ill

quench *verb*
quenches, quenching, quenched
if you quench your thirst, you drink until you are no longer thirsty

query ['kweer-ee'] *noun* **queries**
another word for a question

query ['kweer-ee'] *verb*
queries, querying, queried
to ask a question (or questions) about something to make sure it is true or correct

quest *noun* **quests**
a long search for something that is difficult to find or get

question *noun* **questions**
1 a sentence, phrase or word that you say to someone when you want information or when you want to see how much they know. If the question is written, it ends with a question mark. If it is spoken, it ends with your voice rising (becoming higher).
2 a problem or subject that someone needs to think about and deal with *The fight in the playground raises* (makes people think about) *the question of what to do about bullies.*
3 used when someone has a feeling of not being sure about something *There's some question of closing the school if it snows* (the school might close or it might not). *There's no question of that happening* (I'm sure that won't happen). *Seema is without question my best friend* (I'm sure about it).
4 **out of the question** used for saying that something is not possible and you are sure about it *Leaving your homework until tomorrow is out of the question!*

question *verb*
questions, questioning, questioned
1 to ask someone questions to find out information
2 if someone questions something (or if something someone says or writes questions something), they show that they are not sure whether something is true or how good something is *My stepdad's email to the school questions my teacher's decision to punish me.*

questionable *adjective*
1 if something is questionable, it may be true or it may happen or may not happen, but it is more likely that it won't be true or won't happen *It's questionable whether Hannah will pass her exams.*
2 used about something that is not likely to be good or reasonable *questionable behaviour*

questioning *noun*
when the police take someone to a police station to ask them questions about a crime

question mark *noun* **question marks**
a punctuation mark like this ? used after a question in a sentence

> **LANGUAGE EXTRA** you use a *question mark* after a word (*What?*), phrase (*How many?*) or sentence (*Where do you live?*) for showing that you are asking someone a direct question. If the question is read aloud, the question mark tells you there must be rising intonation (your voice becomes higher at the end).

question master *noun* **question masters**
a person who asks people questions in a quiz (competition)

questionnaire *noun* **questionnaires**
a written list of questions that lots of people are asked to reply to in order to get information about something such as people's opinions or behaviour

queue ['kyoo'] *noun* **queues**
1 a group of people waiting for something one behind the other *We stood in the queue waiting for a bus. There's a queue of traffic stretching all the way down the road.*
2 a lot of people wanting to have or do something *There's a long queue for places at our school.*
3 a lot of people waiting to speak to someone on the phone
4 a group of actions that a piece of equipment is waiting to do *The printer is showing three more jobs in the queue.*

queue ['kyoo'] *verb*
queues, queuing, queued
to wait for something in a queue *We queued up to get into the British Museum.*

quibble *verb*
quibbles, quibbling, quibbled
to quibble over something is to argue about it or complain about it even though it is not important **quibble** *noun*

quiche ['keesh'] *noun* **quiches**
an open pie that has a pastry base (made from a mixture of flour, water and fat) and a top part made by mixing eggs and milk with cheese, vegetables or meat

> **ORIGIN** from French *quiche* and German *Küche* 'little cake'

quick *adjective* **quicker, quickest**
1 lasting a short amount of time *I took a quick look at your book. Which is the quickest way to school?*
2 doing something in a short amount of time *You're really quick – you've finished already! I'm a quick learner.*

388

quick – quote

3 moving or operating with a lot of speed *I tried to catch him but he was too quick for me. My new computer is very quick. Quick – we'll miss the train!*
4 happening with a lot of speed *I hope you make a quick recovery. We got quick results in our experiment.*

quick *adverb* (informal)
with a lot of speed *Granddad walks pretty quick for an older person.*

SYNONYM quickly

SIMILES 'as quick as a flash', 'as quick as lightning' and 'as quick as a wink' mean very quickly

quicken *verb*
quickens, quickening, quickened
1 to make something become quicker *He quickened his pace.*
2 to become quicker

quickly *adverb*
1 with a lot of speed *You're walking too quickly.*

SYNONYM fast

2 in or after a short amount of time *Let me tell you quickly what I mean. I sent her an email and she replied quickly.*

quicksand *noun*
a dangerous area of loose wet sand that people and objects can sink into

LANGUAGE EXTRA also called *quicksands*

quid *noun* quid
a slang word for a pound (£1)

quiet *adjective* quieter, quietest
1 not making any noise or much noise *Please be quiet – I can't hear the film. Kayla always speaks in a quiet voice.*
2 without any noise, activity or excitement *I spent a quiet day relaxing in the garden. Life is very quiet in our village.*
3 a quiet person is one who doesn't talk much *Sayed is very quiet today.*
4 if you keep quiet about something or keep something quiet, you don't tell anyone about it

SIMILE 'as quiet as a mouse' means very quiet (sense 1)

quiet *noun*
a time, situation or place in which everything is quiet *Amy loves the quiet of the countryside. I want a few minutes of peace and quiet.*

quieten *verb*
quietens, quietening, quietened
1 to make someone or something less noisy *Dad is trying to quieten down the baby.*
2 to become less noisy

quietly *adverb*
1 without making any noise or much noise *We tiptoed quietly out of the room.*
2 without any noise, activity or excitement *She was sitting quietly in a corner.*

quill *noun* quills
1 a large feather with the end made into a point, used in the past for writing with ink
2 quills are the long stiff hairs that a porcupine has on its back

quilt *noun* quilts
1 another word for a duvet (bed cover filled with feathers or other soft materials, used instead of a blanket)
2 a large piece of cloth put together from lots of smaller pieces, often square ones, that are sewn together in a pattern to make something such as a cover for a bed or decoration for a wall

quilting *noun*
the activity of making decorative quilts

quinoa ['keen-wah'] *noun*
a plant from South America. It produces seeds that are crushed, cooked and eaten as a healthy food.

quintet *noun* quintets
1 a group of five musicians playing together or five singers singing together
2 a piece of music for five musicians

quip *verb*
quips, quipping, quipped
to say something intelligent and funny and sometimes unpleasant

quip *noun*

quirky *adjective* quirkier, quirkiest
unusual or strange in an interesting way

quit *verb*
quits, quitting, quit
1 to stop doing something *My big sister has quit smoking.*
2 to leave something and go away *The captain of our football team has quit. My brother has quit his job.*
3 to close a computer program *Click on the X to quit.*

quite *adverb*
1 not very but still enough or a certain amount *It's quite cold today* (not very cold or too cold but cold enough). *I've been waiting quite a long time* (not very long or too long but long enough).

SYNONYMS fairly, rather

2 completely or very *We're quite lost. It really was quite dark. I quite agree.*
3 used when you mean almost but not completely *I don't quite have enough money to get a bike.*
4 used for giving special importance to a phrase such as 'a lot' or 'a few' *I see my grandparents quite a lot* (very many times). *Sophie has quite a few friends* (very many friends). *It happened quite a long time ago* (very long ago) *in ancient Greece.*

quits *adjective* (informal)
if two or more people are quits, no-one owes anything to anyone else *I paid for the ice cream and you paid for the sweets so we're quits.*

quitter *noun* quitters
someone who gives up easily, for example starting an activity but not finishing it or not trying very hard to be successful

quiver *verb*
quivers, quivering, quivered
to shake very slightly, for example because of a strong feeling such as excitement, fear or anger *Dad was quivering with rage.*

quiver *noun*
1 a slight shaking movement
2 (*plural* quivers) a long container for carrying arrows for shooting, often worn on your back

quiz *noun* quizzes
a competition or game where you answer questions to show how much you know. There are many different types of quizzes, for example TV quizzes or school quizzes, where someone called a question master asks the questions, or magazine or internet quizzes where the questions are written down.

quiz *verb*
quizzes, quizzing, quizzed
to ask someone lots of questions *When I arrived home late from school, Dad quizzed me to find out where I'd been.*

quizzical *adjective*
showing that someone is surprised and confused because they don't understand something strange or unusual *She gave me a quizzical look.* **quizzically** *adverb*

quota *noun* quotas
a fixed amount or number of something that is officially allowed *Our school isn't allowed to have any more computers – it has filled its quota.*

quotation *noun* quotations
1 a sentence or phrase that someone has said or written before, taken from a book, poem, film or play or from a speech
2 a document that lets you know how much it is going to cost to do a piece of work, for example to fix something or build something

quotation marks *noun plural*
punctuation marks like this ' ' or this " "

LANGUAGE EXTRA you use either single ' ' or double " " quotation marks around words to show they are the exact words that someone is using (*'I'm tired,' said Josh. "Where are we?" asked Bimla*).
Quotation marks can also be used around titles, for example of books, films or paintings (*We're reading 'Oliver Twist'. "Starry Night", a famous painting by Van Gogh*).
You also use them to show that words have a meaning that is slightly different from their usual meaning (*I don't like the look of this 'food' you've put on my plate*).
Quotation marks can also be called *inverted commas* or *speech marks*.

quote *verb*
quotes, quoting, quoted
to repeat words that someone else has said or written *Ms Singh quoted a few lines from Shakespeare. Our history teacher often quotes Churchill.*

quote *noun* quotes
1 another word for a quotation, for example from a book or play
2 another word for a quotation when you mean a document telling you how much a piece of work will cost
3 quotes another word for quotation marks *This sentence from Dickens should be in quotes.*

389

quotient–rack

quotient ['kwoh-shernt'] *noun* **quotients**
in maths, a quotient is the answer you get when you divide one number (called the dividend) by another number (called the divisor)

Qur'an ['kor-ahn'] *noun*
the Qur'an is the holy book of Islam (the religion of Muslims)

LANGUAGE EXTRA also spelt *Koran*

ORIGIN from an Arabic word meaning 'reading'

r R

ORIGIN the letter R started life in ancient Egyptian hieroglyphics as a picture of a person's head looking left. The letter was called *resh* (pronounced 'raysh'), which also meant 'head'. When the letter passed into the Phoenician alphabet, it looked like a P facing left – the loop being the head and the straight line being the neck. When the letter passed into the Greek and Roman alphabets, the loop was turned around to the right so it looked more or less exactly like a P. To make it look different from P, the Romans added a small foot to the loop ending in mid-air and later continued the foot downwards until it was level with the bottom of the straight line – producing the R shape we use today.

rabbi ['bi' rhymes with 'by'] *noun* **rabbis**
a Jewish religious leader and teacher

ORIGIN from Old Hebrew *rabbi* 'my master'

rabbit *noun*
1 (*plural* **rabbits**) a small furry animal with long ears and big front teeth. It lives in a burrow (hole in the ground) or is kept as a pet.
2 the meat from a rabbit that is eaten as food

rabbit *verb* (informal)
rabbits, rabbiting, rabbited
if someone rabbits on about something, they keep on talking about it in a boring way

rabble *noun*
a crowd of very noisy or violent people

rabid ['rab-id' or 'ray-bid'] *adjective*
1 strongly interested in something, usually in an unreasonable way *a rabid football fan*
2 expressing or showing strong and unreasonable feelings *a rabid anti-religious point of view*
3 a rabid animal is one that has rabies

rabies ['ray-beez'] *noun*
a very serious disease of animals, especially dogs, that makes them go mad and die. Humans can get rabies if they are bitten by an animal that has the disease.

raccoon *noun* **raccoons**
a medium-sized animal with grey or brown fur on its body, black and white fur on its face and a thick tail with stripes on it. Raccoons live mainly in North America.

LANGUAGE EXTRA also spelt *racoon*

race *noun* **races**
1 a competition to see who or which animal is the fastest, for example at running, or who is the first to do something *a horse race*; *a race against time* (doing something quickly because there isn't much time to do it)
2 a group of people who are or who look similar in some way, for example because they share the same ancestors
3 **the human race** all the people in the world as one group

race *verb*
races, racing, raced
1 to take part in a race against a person or animal *I'll race you to the end of the playground. My uncle's horse is racing against nine others.*
2 to put an animal or vehicle in a race *My dad spends every Saturday racing cars.*
3 to move or do something very fast *We raced down the street to try to catch the bus. Don't race through your homework – take your time.*
4 to move something or someone very fast *My brother was racing his bike up and down the garden.*

racecourse *noun* **racecourses**
a wide path, usually shaped like an oval and covered with grass, where horse races take place

racehorse *noun* **racehorses**
a horse that runs very fast and is used in races

racetrack *noun* **racetracks**
a wide path or road with a hard surface, usually shaped like a circle or oval, where races between runners, cars or bicycles take place

LANGUAGE EXTRA also called a *racing track*

racial *adjective*
connected with people's race (the group of people they belong to because they are or look similar in some way) *a racial group*

racing *noun*
1 a sport in which animals or vehicles race against each other around a racecourse or racetrack *horse racing*; *motorcycle racing*
2 a racing car is a fast car used for racing
3 a racing driver is someone who drives a racing car

racist *adjective*
1 If someone is racist, they dislike people of different races (people who are or look different from them, for example because they share different ancestors)
2 also used about someone's feelings or what someone does, says or writes *a racist attack*; *a racist book*
racism *noun* **racist** *noun*

rack *noun* **racks**
1 a frame, often made of bars, or a small piece of furniture with open sections in it, used for keeping things in or holding things *a magazine rack*; *a towel rack*
2 a type of shelf or frame for keeping things on or carrying things *a luggage rack* (on a train, bus or bicycle)
3 the rack was a type of wooden frame used in the past for punishing people by tying their body to it and pulling their arms and legs in different directions
4 **to go to rack and ruin** used for saying that something such as a building or country that is in a bad condition is getting much worse

rack – ragged

rack verb
racks, racking, racked
1 if you rack your brains, you think very hard, for example to try to remember something or find an answer
2 if someone is racked with something such as pain or illness or a feeling such as doubt, they suffer badly because of it

racket noun
1 an informal word for a loud and unpleasant noise *Stop making that terrible racket!*
2 (plural **rackets**) an oval-shaped frame with strings going across and down it like a net and with a long handle. The frame and handle are made of wood or man-made materials. Rackets are used for hitting the ball in games such as tennis, squash and badminton.
3 (plural **rackets**) an informal word for a dishonest way of making money

racoon noun racoons
a medium-sized animal with grey or brown fur on its body, black and white fur on its face and a thick tail with stripes on it. Racoons live mainly in North America.

LANGUAGE EXTRA also spelt *raccoon*

radar ['ray-dar'] noun
a way of using radio signals for showing the position or speed of moving objects such as aircraft and ships when you cannot see them

ORIGIN an acronym from *radio detection and ranging*

radiant adjective
1 extremely happy, and often beautiful and healthy
2 very bright or filled with bright light
radiance noun **radiantly** adverb

radiate verb
radiates, radiating, radiated
1 to spread out in all directions from a point in the middle of something, like the spokes (thin metal pieces) of a wheel *Many avenues radiate out from the Arc de Triomphe in Paris.*
2 if someone radiates a quality or feeling (or if it radiates from them), they show it clearly *Grandma radiates joy and friendliness wherever she goes.*
3 if something radiates heat, light or energy (or if heat, light or energy radiates from something), it produces it and spreads it in all directions *Heat radiates from the sun.*

radiation noun
1 dangerous energy that comes from a radioactive substance (produced when the structure of an atom is changed by dividing its nucleus or central part)
2 energy such as heat or light that comes from something such as the sun

radiator noun radiators
1 a metal container filled with something such as hot water or oil, used for heating a room or part of a building. Radiators filled with water are connected by pipes under the floor and are fixed to a wall. Radiators filled with oil can be moved around and have a wire that is plugged into the electricity.
2 a piece of equipment inside the engine of a vehicle or aircraft that keeps the engine cool

radical adjective
1 very big and important because of being connected to the most important parts of something *The head teacher wants to make radical changes to the timetable. There are radical differences between our two countries on the question of education.*
2 very new and different and likely to cause lots of changes *radical ideas; a radical solution to a problem*
3 wanting to make big and important changes *Our head teacher is very radical.*

radical noun radicals
someone who has very new and different opinions and wants to make important changes, especially in politics

radically adverb
completely, or in very important ways *Things are radically different now.*

radii ['ray-dee-eye']
plural of **radius**

radio noun
1 (plural **radios**) a piece of electronic equipment with knobs or switches for listening to broadcast programmes *Mum bought me a digital radio.*
2 a system for sending special energy waves over a long distance and turning them into sounds that you can hear *The pilots spoke to each other by radio. Mobile phones use radio signals.*
3 the system that uses energy waves to broadcast programmes that you listen to on a radio *Do you prefer radio or TV? The news is on the radio at six o'clock.*
4 also used for talking about the programmes that you listen to *Let's listen to the radio. There's a good radio play on.*
5 (plural **radios**) a piece of electronic equipment, usually held in your hand, for sending and receiving spoken messages *a two-way radio*

radioactive adjective
1 a radioactive substance is a dangerous substance produced when the structure of an atom is changed by dividing its nucleus (or central part)
2 used for describing something that contains or produces a dangerous radioactive substance (or substances) *The whole area was radioactive.*
radioactivity noun

radio-controlled adjective
used for describing a piece of equipment such as a model aircraft that works by receiving radio signals from someone who is in another place

radio station noun radio stations
1 a place or building where radio programmes are made and broadcast from
2 a place on a radio that broadcasts these programmes *Could you put another radio station on?*

radish noun radishes
a small hard round or long vegetable, usually red on the outside and white inside. Radishes have a very strong taste and are eaten raw in salads. They are the roots of a plant that grow in the ground.

radius ['ray-dee-ers'] noun
radii ['ray-dee-eye'] or radiuses
1 a line or distance from the middle of a circle to the circumference (or edge) of the circle. It is half the diameter of a circle.
2 the length of this line
3 a particular distance from a certain place going in any direction *Most students live within a radius of two miles of the school.*

ORIGIN from Latin *radius* 'spoke of a wheel' or 'ray of light' (both describing lines spreading out from a particular point)

RAF noun
the air force of the UK (part of the UK's fighting force of soldiers that uses planes) short for: *Royal Air Force*

raffia noun
a kind of straw made from large leaves, used for making things such as baskets and mats. It comes from a particular type of palm tree.

raffle noun raffles
a competition in which you buy one or more tickets with a number on. You win a prize if any of the tickets with your number is chosen.

raffle verb
raffles, raffling, raffled
to offer something to be given as a prize in a raffle

raft noun rafts
1 a simple flat boat usually made from pieces of wood, logs or barrels (metal or plastic containers) tied together
2 a small rubber or plastic boat

rafter noun rafters
one of the long pieces of wood that support a sloping roof

rag noun rags
1 an old piece of cloth, usually used for cleaning things or wiping things up
2 a rag doll is a soft toy that looks like a person and is made from lots of pieces of cloth
3 **rags** old clothes that are often torn or dirty *We saw a beggar dressed in rags.*

ragamuffin noun ragamuffins
a child who is not looked after very well and who wears dirty or torn clothes

rage noun
1 a strong feeling of anger *Dad flew into a rage (became very angry).*
2 **all the rage** very fashionable and popular *Pointed shoes were all the rage.*

rage verb
rages, raging, raged
1 if something such as a fire, storm or battle rages, it happens or continues in a very strong way, for example for a long time *Fires were raging through the dry forests.*
2 if someone rages, they show that they are very angry, for example by shouting at someone *'You're an idiot!' he raged.*

ragged ['rag-id'] adjective
1 old and torn and usually dirty *a pair of ragged trousers*

391

raid – ram

2 wearing clothes that are old and torn and usually dirty *a ragged beggar*
3 not smooth or regular *a ragged edge*; *a ragged line*

raid *noun* **raids**
1 a sudden attack, for example by soldiers, planes or ships *an air raid* (by planes with bombs)
2 an attack by criminals who go into a place to steal money or goods *a bank raid*
3 an unexpected visit by police who go into a place to look for something or someone

raid *verb*
raids, raiding, raided
1 to attack a place suddenly, usually causing damage *A group of soldiers raided the building.*
2 to go into a place to steal money or goods *Our post office was raided last night.*
3 if police raid a place, they go there to look for something or someone

raider *noun*

rail *noun*
1 (*plural* **rails**) a horizontal metal, plastic or wooden bar for hanging things on *a curtain rail*
2 (*plural* **rails**) a long bar, usually of metal or wood, that goes along or around something. Rails are used, for example, for holding on to so you don't fall or for stopping you from going somewhere. *Hold on to the rail as you go down the stairs. The football supporters were kept behind a thick rail.*
3 (*plural* **rails**) a long metal bar that is usually one of two that trains travel on
4 trains as a way of travelling *We went to Birmingham by rail.*
5 used for talking about things connected with trains *a rail ticket*; *rail fares*

rail *verb*
rails, railing, railed
if someone rails against something, they complain about it in a very angry way

railcard *noun* **railcards**
a card that you buy that allows you to get cheaper tickets when you travel by train

railings *noun plural*
1 a fence made of metal bars
2 the metal bars that this fence is made of *He got his head caught in the railings.*

railroad *noun* **railroads**
the American word for railway

railway *noun*
1 (*plural* **railways**) the metal tracks (long metal bars) that trains travel on *The railway goes from Grantham to York.*
2 trains as a way of travelling *I prefer the railway to going by car or flying.*
3 used for talking about things connected with trains *a railway station*; *a railway line* (tracks that a train travels on)
4 (*plural* **railways**) an organisation that controls the trains in a particular area and the tracks they travel on *Northern Ireland Railways*

rain *noun*
water that falls from the clouds in small drops *It looks like rain* (it's very likely it's going to rain).

392

rain *verb*
rains, raining, rained
1 if it rains or is raining, small drops of water come down from the clouds
2 used for talking about things when there are lots of them and they hit something or someone from high up *Bombs rained down on London during the Second World War.*
3 used for talking about things when someone sends lots of them down to hit something or someone *The bully rained blows onto my head.*

rainbow *noun* **rainbows**
a curved line in the sky made up of different colours. A rainbow appears when the sun shines while it is raining. The sun produces the colours of the rainbow (red, orange, yellow, green, blue, indigo and violet) as it shines through the rain.

raincoat *noun* **raincoats**
a coat that you wear to protect you when it rains. It is made of material that is waterproof (the rain cannot go through).

raindrop *noun* **raindrops**
a tiny ball of rain that falls from the clouds

rainfall *noun*
the amount of rain that falls, for example in a particular place or at a particular time

rainforest *noun* **rainforests**
a thick forest with tall trees in a hot part of the world where it rains a lot *a tropical rainforest*

LANGUAGE EXTRA also spelt *rain forest*

rainstorm *noun* **rainstorms**
a period of very heavy rain with strong winds

rainswept *adjective*
used for describing a place where it is raining heavily *She hurried through the rainswept streets of Edinburgh.*

LANGUAGE EXTRA also spelt *rain-swept*

rainwater *noun*
water that falls to the ground as rain

rainy *adjective* **rainier, rainiest**
used for describing a time or the weather when it rains a lot *a rainy day*; *June was very rainy.*

raise *verb*
raises, raising, raised
1 to move something to a higher position or to a high or upright position *I raised the cup to my lips. Raise your hand if you know the answer.*
2 to make something bigger, higher, better or stronger *They've raised prices again. The head teacher wants to raise standards* (make the quality of our schoolwork better). *Don't raise your voice* (don't speak louder).
3 to collect money from people, often to do good things *The parents raised £500 to buy more books for the school.*
4 to cause something or make something happen, for example fears, doubts, suspicions or expectations *This good news raised our hopes. My question raised a smile* (made people smile).
5 to mention or suggest something *Put your hand up if you want to raise a question.*

6 to raise a child is to take care of and educate the child until he or she is grown up
7 to raise animals such as sheep or pigs is to keep them for food and make them produce baby animals
8 to raise the alarm is to warn people that something bad might happen

raise *noun* **raises**
the American word for a rise (an increase in the money someone gets for doing their job)

raised *adjective*
1 higher when compared to other things *A platform is a raised structure. My cousin reads by touching the raised dots in her braille book.*
2 in a high or upright position *raised flags*; *I can see lots of raised hands.*
3 bigger, more, better or stronger *raised temperatures*; *raised voices* (loud voices, for example people shouting)

raisin *noun* **raisins**
a grape that is dried (water has been removed)

rake *noun* **rakes**
a garden tool with a long thin handle fixed to a row of short metal points, used for example for making the earth level or for removing dead leaves

rake *verb*
rakes, raking, raked
1 to rake the earth is to make it level with a rake
2 to rake leaves is to remove them with a rake
3 to rake around for something is to search for it carefully

rally *noun* **rallies**
1 a large meeting of people who come together to show that they support something or someone (or to show that they don't support them) *an anti-war rally*
2 a car or motorcycle race on public roads, usually over a long distance
3 a period of time in a game such as tennis when the players hit the ball to each other without stopping

rally *verb*
rallies, rallying, rallied
1 to come together (or to bring people together) to support something or someone *The prime minister's supporters rallied round. The general rallied his men. The King sent out a rallying call* (a word or phrase to make people want to support him by taking action).
2 to get stronger or start to get better *Our team rallied in the last few minutes of the match.*

ram *verb*
rams, ramming, rammed
1 to hit something very hard *A van rammed into the back of my dad's car. The car was rammed from behind.*
2 to push something very hard, often in an unpleasant way *The thieves rammed a handkerchief into his mouth and tied him up.*

ram *noun* **rams**
a male sheep. A female sheep is called a ewe.

RAM noun
a type of computer memory for storing programs and information while your computer is switched on and working. The information can be changed but it is lost when the computer is switched off.
short for: random access memory
compare: ROM

Ramadan ['ram-er-dan' or 'ram-er-**dan**'] noun
the ninth month of the Muslim calendar, which is considered a holy month. During this time, Muslims do not have anything to eat or drink during the hours of daylight.

ramble noun rambles
a long walk in the countryside done for pleasure and without hurrying

ramble verb
rambles, rambling, rambled
1 to walk for pleasure in the countryside
2 to talk or write for a long time without making much sense, for example because you are talking about other things, not what you should be talking about
rambler noun **rambling** noun

rambling adjective
1 if something that someone writes or says is rambling, it is very long and does not make much sense *a rambling speech*
2 if a building is rambling, it is very large with lots of parts that have different shapes and go in different directions

ramp noun ramps
a sloping surface, usually joining two levels when one is higher than the other *The museum has a ramp at the front for people with wheelchairs.*

rampage ['ram-payj'] noun
to go on the rampage used about a group of people who run through an area such as a town breaking things and causing damage

rampage ['ram-payj'] verb
rampages, rampaging, rampaged
to run through an area breaking things and causing damage

ramparts noun plural
high hills or stone walls built in the past around a castle or town to protect it

ramshackle adjective
used for describing a building in a very bad condition

ran
past tense of **run**

ranch noun ranches
a large farm, especially in North America, where animals such as cows, horses and sheep are kept *a cattle ranch* **rancher** noun

rancid adjective
if food such as butter or milk is rancid, it smells and tastes bad because it is not fresh

random adjective
1 done or happening without any particular plan or pattern or for no particular reason *Be sure to buy a ticket as there are random checks on the train* (some people are checked but not others). *The books on the shelf are in random order* (no particular order). *Choose a random number* (it's not important which one).
2 (informal) used for describing something that you're not expecting and that is slightly strange *He made a completely random comment about not liking animals. Lucy said I wasn't her friend any more – that was a bit random!*
3 (informal) used for describing someone you don't know and who is a complete stranger *Some random boy came up to me in the street and asked me for money.*
4 **at random** without any particular plan or pattern or for no particular reason *My name was chosen at random* (by chance). *I'm going to open one of my presents at random* (without knowing which one).
randomly adverb

rang
past tense of **ring**

range noun ranges
1 a group of different things of the same kind *These shirts come in a wide range of colours.*
2 the distance within which a sound can be heard *We can't hear the music as we're out of range* (too far away).
3 the distance within which something or someone can be reached or seen *The town was in range of the enemy guns.*
4 the distance a plane can fly or a gun can shoot
5 all of the values within a group of numbers, amounts, ages or measurements, from the lowest to the highest *This dictionary is for children in the 9 to 13 age range. That mountain bike isn't within my dad's price range* (it costs more than any of the prices my dad can afford).
6 in maths, the range of a group of numbers is the difference (or amount) between the lowest and highest values
7 in a spreadsheet, a range is a group of cells (small squares) that contain information
8 in music, a range is all the notes that someone can sing or an instrument can play, from the highest to the lowest
9 a group of mountains or hills *a mountain range*
10 an area where people practise shooting guns *a rifle range*
11 an old-fashioned cooker with more than one oven that is heated with wood or coal, used especially in the past
12 a range cooker is a large cooker with more than one oven and many burners

range verb
ranges, ranging, ranged
1 used for saying that things such as numbers, prices, ages or sizes include the lowest and the highest or the biggest and the smallest and everything in between *Prices range from £5 to £100. Jeans sizes range between very small and extra large.*
2 used for saying that something includes different types of things or qualities *This shop sells everything ranging from computers to toys. In summer the weather ranges between very wet and very hot.*
3 to put things in a particular position *Chairs were ranged against the wall.*
4 to move around freely *Elephants range throughout this part of Africa.*

ranger noun rangers
someone in charge of something such as a forest or large park

Ranger noun Rangers
a girl who belongs to the section of the Guides (or Guide Association) for girls aged about 14 to 19

rank noun ranks
1 someone's position or job in an organisation, such as the army or police, or in a sporting competition. Their rank shows how important or how good their position or job is when compared to those of other people. *My uncle reached the rank of captain in the navy.*
2 the position that something has reached, usually given as a number, when compared to other things of the same kind *This book has reached the third rank among this week's bestsellers.*
3 a line or row of people, such as soldiers or police officers, or of things, such as trees or computers
4 a place in the street where taxis wait for people *a taxi rank*

rank verb
ranks, ranking, ranked
1 to be higher or lower than someone else, for example when you look at someone's position or job in an organisation, or to consider someone to be higher or lower *A captain ranks above a sergeant in the army. The tennis star was ranked number two in the world.*
2 to be described in a certain way, for example more (or less) important or better (or worse), when compared to other things or people *Paris ranks as one of the most beautiful cities in Europe.*
3 to describe something or someone in a certain way when comparing them to other things or people *My sister ranks 'Matilda' as the best book she's read.*
4 to give something a number to show what position it has reached compared to other things of the same kind *This book is ranked seven in the bestseller list.*

rank adjective
if something is rank or has a rank smell, it smells very bad

ranking noun rankings
the position or level that someone or something has reached, for example in a sporting competition, when compared to other people or things

ransack verb
ransacks, ransacking, ransacked
to search through a place such as a house or office, stealing things, causing damage and making a mess

ransom noun ransoms
1 money that someone asks for when they are keeping a person as a prisoner or when they have stolen something. They will not set the person free or give back what they have stolen until they are paid this money. *The millionaire is being held to ransom for £10000* (being kept as a prisoner until someone pays that money).
2 money someone pays to someone who is keeping a person as a prisoner or who has stolen something from them, so as to get that person set free or to get back what was stolen

ransom *verb*
ransoms, ransoming, ransomed
1 if someone ransoms someone, such as a member of their family, they pay money to someone who is keeping that person as a prisoner in order to get that person set free
2 if a criminal ransoms someone they are keeping as a prisoner, they ask for money and will not set that person free until they receive it *The kidnappers are ransoming their hostage for a million pounds.*

rant *verb*
rants, ranting, ranted
to complain about something in a loud and angry way **rant** *noun*

rap *verb*
raps, rapping, rapped
1 to hit something, often lots of times and quickly, in order to make a noise *Someone was rapping on the door.*
2 to perform rap music by saying the words of a rap song

rap *noun*
1 (plural **raps**) the sound or action of someone hitting something quickly
2 rap or rap music is a type of popular music with words that are not sung but spoken fast and with a strong beat (regular pattern of sounds) *a rap artist*

rapid *adjective*
happening or done quickly *rapid change*; *rapid movements* **rapidity** *noun*

rapidly *adverb*
another way of saying quickly

rapids *noun plural*
a dangerous part of a river where the water moves very fast because the river goes down a slope and usually flows over rocks

rapier ['ray-pi-er'] *noun* **rapiers**
a long thin sword with a very sharp point

rapper *noun* **rappers**
a musician who performs rap music (popular music with words that are not sung but spoken fast)

rare *adjective* rarer, rarest
1 not happening often *Spelling mistakes are rare in your homework.*
2 not existing in large numbers or not seen much *Butterflies are rare at this time of year.*
3 valuable, good or interesting because of not being seen much or not happening often *a rare book*; *Josh has a rare gift for telling jokes.*

rarebit *noun*
Welsh rarebit is toast with melted cheese on it

rarely *adverb*
not often

raring *adjective*
if someone is raring to do something, they are very excited about it and really want to start doing it

rarity *noun*
1 (plural **rarities**) something or someone that you don't see much, for example something that is valuable, good or interesting *These old stamps are rarities.*
2 something that doesn't happen often

rascal *noun* **rascals**
someone who behaves badly, especially someone you like even though they behave this way *Up to bed now, you little rascal!*

rash *noun*
1 (plural **rashes**) an area on your skin with lots of small red spots on it. A rash is usually caused by an illness or allergy (when you eat, drink or touch something). *a nappy rash* (when a baby wears a wet and dirty nappy); *a heat rash* (from too much sun)
2 a group of things, usually unpleasant things, all happening at about the same time *There's been a rash of attacks on British soldiers this week.*

rash *adjective* rasher, rashest
1 done too quickly and without thinking *a rash decision*; *Don't do anything rash!*
2 doing things too quickly and without thinking *Sam was rash to invite her friends over without asking her parents first.*
rashly *adverb* **rashness** *noun*

rasher *noun* **rashers**
a slice of bacon (meat from a pig)

raspberry *noun* **raspberries**
1 a small soft dark red fruit that you eat. Raspberries grow on bushes.
2 (informal) a rude sound made when someone pokes their tongue out and then blows out air *My brother didn't like my suggestion so he blew a raspberry.*

Rastafarian ['ras-ter-**fair**-ree-ern'] *noun* **Rastafarians**
a member of a religious group that started in Jamaica in the 1930s. Rastafarians worship Haile Selassie, who ruled Ethiopia between 1930 and 1974.
Rastafarianism *noun*

rat *noun* **rats**
1 a furry animal that has a long tail and looks like a large mouse
2 an informal word for a horrible person, especially someone you can't trust

rate *noun* **rates**
1 the speed at which something happens *These plants grow at a very fast rate.*
2 the number of times something happens in a certain period of time *The doctor measured my pulse rate* (the number of times my heart beats in a minute).
3 an amount of money that someone pays for something or is paid for doing something *postal rates* (the money it costs to send a letter or parcel); *My brother works for a low rate of pay.*
4 **at any rate** another way of saying anyway *I don't know what time Dad will be back, but he'll be home to cook dinner at any rate.*
5 **at this rate** or **at that rate** used for saying what will happen if a situation doesn't change and things continue the same way *You're so slow, Phoebe – at this rate you'll never finish your homework.*

rate *verb*
rates, rating, rated
1 to consider someone or something as having a particular quality or value *Miss Novak rates Seema's work highly* (in her opinion it's very good). *'How do you rate that film?' – 'I think it's fantastic.'*
2 to consider something or someone in a certain way when compared to other things or people *Our school has been rated number two in the league tables. It's a highly rated school* (people think it's very good).
3 to say what you think of something or someone, especially on the internet, for example by giving them a particular rating (measurement showing how good something or someone is) *'Thank you for visiting our restaurant. Click here to rate our service.'*
4 to consider a film or video to be suitable only for people of a particular age *'Willy Wonka and the Chocolate Factory' is rated 12.*
5 to be good or important enough for something *Our school play rated a lovely mention in the local paper.*

-rate *suffix*
used especially with words such as 'first' or 'second' for saying how good or bad you think something or someone is *first-rate* (very good and of the highest standard); *tenth-rate* (very bad and of the lowest standard)

rather *adverb*
1 not very but still enough *Dad's rather late* (not very late or too late but late enough). *My brother walks rather fast.*

> SYNONYM quite

2 very or very much *You're rather young to be going out by yourself. There were rather a lot of people in the park. I rather agree.*

> SYNONYM quite

3 used for saying something less strongly *I was rather hoping you would say yes.*
4 used for saying something more clearly or correctly or in a different way *Mr Jones is my teacher – or rather was my teacher until last year.*

> SYNONYM anyway

5 if someone would rather do something, that is the thing they prefer to do or want to do most *I'd rather go by bike than take the bus. 'Close the window.' – 'I'd rather not.'* (I prefer not to)
6 **rather than** instead of *I chose to study Spanish rather than French.*

rating *noun* **ratings**
a measurement showing how good something or someone is, for example when compared to other things or people

ratio ['ray-shee-oh'] *noun* **ratios**
an amount or number that is compared to another amount or number to show the different sizes of two things or groups *The ratio of girls to boys in the school is roughly three to one* (for every group of three girls there is one boy). *Our school has a high teacher–pupil ratio* (lots of teachers compared to the number of pupils).

ration ['rash-ern'] *noun* **rations**
a small amount of something that someone is allowed to have, for example because there isn't very much of it *Prisoners had a weekly ration of butter.*

ration – reaction

ration ['rash-ern'] *verb*
rations, rationing, rationed
to give someone a small and fixed amount of something *Mum has rationed me to two bags of crisps a week* (I'm only allowed two bags of crisps). *Eggs, cheese and butter were rationed during the Second World War.* **rationing** *noun*

rational ['rash-ern-erl'] *adjective*
1 based on an intelligent way of thinking or behaving, not on feelings or imagination *a rational explanation*; *rational behaviour*
2 a rational person is someone who is reasonable and who uses their mind to make judgements, not their feelings or imagination

ANTONYM irrational

rationally ['rash-ern-er-lee'] *adverb*
in a way that is intelligent or reasonable *Henry hasn't been behaving rationally this week.*

rattle *verb*
rattles, rattling, rattled
1 if something rattles, it makes the sound of things knocking against each other, for example when it is moved or shaken *The cups and saucers rattled as I carried them on the tray. The windows rattled in the wind.*
2 to rattle something is to make it rattle *I rattled the moneybox to see how much was inside.*
3 to rattle someone is to make them feel nervous or worried

rattle *noun* rattles
1 a toy for a baby that makes the sound of things knocking against each other when you shake it
2 a wooden object with a handle, used for example at football matches. It makes a clicking sound when you swing it around.
3 a sound of things knocking against each other

rattlesnake *noun* rattlesnakes
a poisonous snake in the USA and Mexico that makes a type of clicking sound with the end of its tail

ratty *adjective* rattier, rattiest (informal)
if someone is ratty, they become angry very easily

raucous *adjective*
1 loud in an unpleasant way *raucous laughter*
2 noisy in an unpleasant way *a raucous crowd of football fans*

ravage *verb*
ravages, ravaging, ravaged
to damage something very badly or destroy it almost completely *Our country was ravaged by war.*

rave *verb*
raves, raving, raved
1 to talk or shout in a loud or crazy way, for example because you are ill or angry *Granddad was ranting and raving about how bad the food was.*
2 if you rave about something or someone, you say or write things that show how much you like them *Arun spent weeks raving about his holidays.*

rave *noun* raves
a wild party, usually in a large empty building, where people dance and listen to loud music

raven *noun* ravens
a very large bird with shiny black feathers and a heavy sharp beak. It makes a loud rough noise and belongs to the same family as crows. Ravens usually live in areas where there are lots of hills and mountains.

ravenous ['rav-er-ners'] *adjective*
if a person or animal is ravenous or has a ravenous appetite, they are extremely hungry

ravenously *adverb*
in a way that shows that a person or animal is extremely hungry *He ate ravenously as if he hadn't eaten for days.*

ravine ['rer-veen'] *noun* ravines
a narrow valley with steep sides, usually made by a river

raving *adjective*
talking or behaving in a crazy way *If you think I'm going to Hari's party, you're a raving lunatic!* (you're talking nonsense because I'm not going)

ravioli ['ra-vee-oh-lee'] *noun*
a food made from small squares of pasta with meat, vegetables or cheese inside and usually eaten with a sauce

ORIGIN from Italian *ravioli*

ravishing *adjective*
extremely beautiful

raw *adjective* rawer, rawest
1 if food is raw, it is not cooked *raw meat*
2 if a part of the body is raw, it is red and painful because the skin has come off *Dad's been digging the garden and his hands are raw* (or *red raw*).
3 used for describing substances (such as sugar or cotton) and materials (such as iron or coal) as they are found in nature before people make other things with them or change them into other things *raw cotton* (fibres from the cotton plant)
4 used for describing weather that is very cold *A raw wind was blowing.*
5 without any experience or skill in a job *a raw recruit* (for example someone who has just joined the army)

ray *noun* rays
1 a long line of light, heat or energy that comes from something such as the sun *A ray of sunlight was shining through the curtains.*
2 a small amount of something good *a ray of hope*
3 a large flat fish with a long pointed tail. Rays live mainly at the bottom of the sea, often close to the coast.

rayon *noun*
a light shiny and smooth cloth made from fibres (long thin threads) from plants or wood

razor *noun* razors
1 a small tool with a sharp blade (or blades) used for shaving (removing hair from your skin). There are different types of razors, for example with the blade fixed at the end of a handle and with the blade that folds into the handle.
2 a piece of electrical equipment used for shaving *an electric razor*

re- *prefix*
used for giving a word the meaning of 'again' *reapply*; *redecorate*; *reheat*

reach *verb*
reaches, reaching, reached
1 to reach a place is to get there from somewhere else *We reached London at ten o'clock. Rain will reach the south coast by the evening.*
2 to take or touch something, for example by stretching out your arm *Can you reach that book on the top shelf? I reached out with both hands to catch the ball. He reached for a tissue to blow his nose.*
3 to get to someone or something, for example when talking about something that is sent or thrown *Your email hasn't reached me yet. The blow reached him just below the eye.*
4 to get to something such as a level, amount, age or situation *The temperature reached 30 degrees. I'm so tired that I've reached the point where I can't carry on.*
5 to be long enough to touch something or get to something *The ladder's too short – it won't reach. The ladder reached the roof.*
6 to continue for a distance as far as a particular place *These fields reach all the way to the river.*
7 to reach something such as a decision or agreement is to make it after thinking about it carefully
8 to reach someone by phone or email, for example, is to manage to speak to them or get a message to them *You can always reach me on my mobile.*

reach *noun*
1 the distance within which you can put out your hand and take or touch something *I always keep my phone within reach* (close by). *Mum put the sweets out of reach* (in a place where you can't get them).
2 the distance you travel to go somewhere easily *We live within reach of the school* (not far from the school).
3 the reaches of a river or area of land are the parts furthest away *the upper reaches of the Nile* (the part furthest from the sea); *The spaceship is travelling to the outer reaches of space.*

react *verb*
reacts, reacting, reacted
1 to react to something is to immediately do something or behave in a certain way when something else is done or happens *When she called me an idiot, I reacted by slamming the door. I reacted badly to the medicine* (I was ill or felt sick, for example).
2 if one chemical reacts with another, they form a different substance when they are put together

reaction *noun* reactions
1 something you do, a particular way you behave or a feeling you have immediately something else is done or happens *His reaction to the news was to burst out laughing.*

reactor–realm

2 an illness or bad feeling caused by eating, drinking or touching something or breathing something in *an allergic reaction to milk*
3 a change that happens when one chemical is put together with another
4 being able to think and move quickly when something suddenly happens, for example something bad or dangerous *Cyclists need quick reactions.*

reactor noun **reactors**
a reactor or nuclear reactor is a large structure that produces nuclear energy, usually to make electricity

read ['reed'] verb
reads, reading, read ['red']
1 if you read something that is written, you look at it and understand what it means and your eyes follow the words, often as an activity that you like doing *Can you read that road sign, Dad? I love reading books.*
2 to look at something written and say the words out loud so that other people can hear them *Mum read me a bedtime story.*
3 to learn something by reading, for example in a book or newspaper *We were reading about the solar system at school. I'm reading up on King Henry VIII* (learning about him by reading a lot).
4 to look at and usually write down the number or amount shown on a piece of measuring equipment *Someone came to read the meter.*
5 to show a particular measurement or show particular words *The thermometer reads 15 degrees. The label on the jar reads 'Best before 6 June'.*
6 to read music is to understand the symbols that represent particular musical sounds and patterns
7 if a computer or other device reads something, it takes information from it and copies it to a place where it can be used. For example, a computer takes information from a disk and copies it into its memory so that it can be used by a program.
8 to read someone's mind is to guess or to know what they are thinking

readable adjective
1 pleasant or easy to read *a very readable short story*
2 used for describing something that is clear enough to be read *Your handwriting isn't very readable.*

reader noun **readers**
1 someone who reads something or who likes reading a lot *My brother is a keen reader of comics.*
2 a book for children who are learning to read
3 someone who reads a piece of measuring equipment such as an electricity meter *a meter reader*

readily adverb
1 in a way that shows someone wants to do something *Dad said he would readily give me some advice.*
2 quickly and without stopping to think *When the bully hit me I readily handed over my mobile.*
3 easily *This information is readily available on the internet.*

readiness noun
being ready for something

reading noun
1 the activity or skill of reading books *I do a lot of reading. Ethan is good at reading.*
2 (plural **readings**) a number or amount shown on a piece of measuring equipment *a meter reading*

readme file noun **readme files**
a computer file that contains useful information about a piece of software

LANGUAGE EXTRA also spelt *read me file*

ready adjective **readier, readiest**
1 able to do something immediately, for example because you've finished doing something else *All of us are ready to watch the film except George who's talking on his mobile. Are you ready for bed now? My sister's getting ready to go out* (for example, she's finishing getting dressed before she can go out).
2 if something is ready, someone has finished doing something to it so that it can be used in a particular way *Lunch is ready* (we can eat it now). *The classroom is ready* (we can go in now). *The tickets are ready* (we can pick them up now).
3 happy to do something *Josh is always ready to help.*
4 wanting to have something *Are you ready for a cup of tea?*
5 having the quality, knowledge or experience needed for something or to do something *My sister says she's not ready to get married. Our class isn't ready for the test yet.*
6 likely to do something, or just about to do something *He looked as if he was ready to cry. Mum walked in just as I was ready to leave.*
7 quick, for example in answering someone *Dad has a ready answer to every question.*
8 **Ready, steady, go!** used for telling people that they can start a race

ready-made adjective
used for describing something that you buy that has already been made and is ready to be used *ready-made meals*

real adjective
1 existing as a person or thing in the world and not in someone's imagination *Dad, are goblins real? These things don't happen in real life* (life as it really is rather than in the imagination or in stories).
2 based on facts and not on what people think *What's the real reason you stayed at home yesterday? That's my real name.*

SYNONYM true

3 used for describing something that is not made by people or that is not a copy of something but is the proper thing *real leather; a real diamond*

SYNONYM genuine

4 used for describing something or someone that has the qualities they are supposed to have or that is what they are supposed to be *My sister has never had a real job. A real film star came to our school. These are my real feelings.*
5 used for giving special importance to a word *You're a real friend, Ava. It's a real problem.*

realise verb
realises, realising, realised
1 to know or know about something and to understand it or understand how important it is *I realise it's raining heavily. Do you realise your mistake? The dog ran out without anyone realising* (knowing).
2 to suddenly understand or notice something that you didn't know before or that you didn't know about before *As soon as I got home I realised I'd lost my pencil case. She suddenly realised her mistake.*
3 to achieve something or make something come true, for example a hope or ambition
realisation noun

LANGUAGE EXTRA also spelt *realize* and *realization*

realist noun **realists**
1 someone who looks at real situations and not ideas and who only does what is possible or sensible
2 an artist or writer who shows things as they are in real life
realism noun

realistic adjective
1 if someone is realistic, they look at real situations and not ideas and they only do things that are possible or sensible
2 possible or sensible because of being based on real situations and not ideas *a realistic solution*
3 showing things existing or happening as in real life *a realistic painting of Tower Bridge; These dinosaurs look very realistic.*

realistically adverb
used for talking about what is possible in a real situation *Realistically, our team can't win. How can you realistically expect me to finish my homework today?*

reality noun
1 things as they are or the true way things are, rather than based on the imagination *My brother plays video games all day – he's lost touch with reality.*
2 (plural **realities**) something that really exists or really happens *Her dream of being a teacher has become a reality.*

really adverb
1 used for saying what the truth about something is *Tell me what really happened.*
2 used for giving special importance to a word or for showing that you definitely mean something *They really don't know what to do. I really enjoyed the book* (enjoyed it very much).
3 another way of saying very, but more strongly *You're really late! George has been working really hard.*
4 used for saying something less strongly *I don't really want to go but I will if I have to. You don't really expect me to go home by myself, do you?*
5 used for showing that you're surprised about something or interested in it *'I have a new baby sister.' – 'Really?'*

realm ['relm'] noun **realms**
1 a particular area of activity or knowledge

396

2 another word for a kingdom (country ruled by a king or queen)

reap verb
reaps, reaping, reaped
1 if a farmer reaps a crop such as wheat, he or she cuts it, usually with an old-fashioned cutting tool such as a scythe (curved blade fixed to a long handle), and collects it
2 to get something good, such as a reward, usually by working hard for it
reaper noun

reappear verb
reappears, reappearing, reappeared
to appear again *Chloe went missing but reappeared a few minutes later.*
reappearance noun

rear adjective
at the back of something *the rear wheels of the car*

rear noun
the back part of something *We're at the rear of the queue.*

rear verb
rears, rearing, reared
1 to take care of a child or animal until they are fully grown
2 to rear animals such as cattle or sheep is to keep them for food and make them produce baby animals
3 if a horse rears (or rears up), it stands on its back legs and kicks its front legs up into the air
compare: **buck**

rearrange verb
rearranges, rearranging, rearranged
if you rearrange things such as furniture or flowers, you put them in a different order or place **rearrangement** noun

reason noun
1 (plural **reasons**) the reason for something is why someone does it or why it happens *Can you tell me the reason why you haven't done your homework? She walked out of the room without giving a reason* (without saying why).
2 (plural **reasons**) a fact or situation that explains why something is true *What's the reason plants are green?*
3 used about a situation that makes it right, sensible or normal to do something or to feel in a certain way *You have a good reason to be angry and complain. He had no reason to call me lazy* (it wasn't right to call me lazy because I'm not lazy).
4 the power to think about things in an intelligent way and make sensible decisions *People should always be guided by reason.*
5 the idea of behaving in a sensible way and doing what is right *George walked home by himself and wouldn't listen to reason* (he did not behave sensibly). *Mum said I can have more sweets but within reason* (being sensible about it, for example not too many).

reason verb
reasons, reasoning, reasoned
1 to decide something or make a judgement about something after considering all the facts in a logical way *'Mum's plane gets in at ten o'clock so she won't be home before midnight,' he reasoned.*
2 to reason with someone is to talk to them and try to persuade them to be more sensible

reasonable adjective
1 sensible because you use good judgement *Speak to your teacher – she's very reasonable.*
2 sensible because of being based on good judgement *reasonable behaviour*; *It's reasonable to think this will happen.*
3 suitable because of being right for a particular situation *a reasonable offer*
4 good enough but not extremely good *The quality is reasonable.*
5 used for describing something that is neither too much or too little nor too big or too small *Cambridge is a town of reasonable size. We live within a reasonable distance of the school* (not too far away or too close). *Prices in this shop are reasonable* (not too high but not cheap).

reasonably adverb
1 not very but still enough or quite a lot *Your handwriting is reasonably good* (not very good but good enough). *She sings reasonably well* (well enough but not very well).

SYNONYMS fairly, quite, rather

2 in a sensible way *Let's sit down and talk about this reasonably.*

reasoning noun
the skill of thinking about information in a logical way so that you can use that skill to solve problems and make decisions

reassurance noun
1 (plural **reassurances**) words that make someone feel less worried *My parents needed reassurances before they would let me go on the trip.*
2 when someone makes you feel calmer and less worried *Babies need lots of love and reassurance.*

reassure verb
reassures, reassuring, reassured
1 to make someone feel less worried *I feel reassured when all the doors are locked.*
2 to say something to stop someone worrying *He reassured me that my sister was safe.*

reassuring adjective
used for describing something or someone that makes you feel less worried *a reassuring smile* **reassuringly** adverb

rebel ['reb-erl'] noun rebels
1 someone such as a soldier or politician who fights against a government or leader *rebel soldiers*
2 someone who refuses to obey people in charge *At home Tom is a bit of a rebel.*

rebel ['ri-bel'] verb
rebels, rebelling, rebelled
1 to start to fight against a government or the leaders in charge of something such as a political party or an army
2 to refuse to obey people in charge such as parents or teachers *My brother has started to rebel against the family.*

rebellion noun
1 (plural **rebellions**) a fight against a government or the leaders in charge of something such as a political party or an army
2 not wanting to obey people in charge such as parents or teachers

rebellious adjective
1 used about someone such as a soldier or politician who is fighting or ready to fight against a government or leader
2 used about someone who does not want to obey people in charge such as parents or teachers *a rebellious teenager*

reboot verb
reboots, rebooting, rebooted
if you reboot a piece of equipment such as a computer or router (for connecting a computer to the internet), or if the equipment reboots, it starts working again after being turned off

rebound verb
rebounds, rebounding, rebounded
if a ball or another object rebounds, it springs back after hitting a surface such as a wall

SYNONYM to bounce back

rebuff verb
rebuffs, rebuffing, rebuffed
to refuse to accept something such as an offer or suggestion, usually in an unfriendly way

rebuild verb
rebuilds, rebuilding, rebuilt
to build something again, usually after it has been damaged or destroyed

rebuke ['ri-byook'] verb
rebukes, rebuking, rebuked
to tell someone you are angry with them because they have done something bad

recall verb
recalls, recalling, recalled
1 to remember someone or something
2 to make you think of something *What you just said recalls something that happened last month.*
3 to tell someone to come back
4 if a shop or company recalls a product, they ask people to return it because there is something wrong with it

recap verb
recaps, recapping, recapped
to repeat the most important details of something that has just been said or written
short for: recapitulate

recapture verb
recaptures, recapturing, recaptured
1 to catch a person or animal that has escaped from somewhere
2 to take control of something belonging to an enemy in war after losing control of it *The rebel soldiers recaptured the airport.*

recede verb
recedes, receding, receded
1 to go further away into the distance
2 to go down from a higher level *The flood waters have receded.*
3 if someone's hair recedes, it stops growing at the front of their head *a receding hairline* (line of hair)

receipt ['ri-seet'] noun
1 (plural **receipts**) a piece of paper or electronic document that shows the price of something someone has bought and that proves it has been paid for
2 the action of receiving something

receive–recollect

receive *verb*
receives, receiving, received
1 to be given something or to get something *I received lots of presents for my birthday. Our school received a visit from the prime minister.*
2 to get something that someone has sent you *Have you received my email?*
3 to greet or welcome a visitor *Our teacher stood by the classroom door to receive the parents. Mum and Dad were received warmly* (in a friendly way).
4 to get sounds or pictures on equipment such as a TV or mobile phone *If you're in a tunnel you can't always receive a signal on your phone.*

receiver *noun* receivers
1 the part of a landline phone (fixed in one place) that you hold in your hand next to your ear and mouth. It is used for listening and for speaking into. *The phone rang and I picked up the receiver.*
2 a piece of equipment in something such as a TV, radio or mobile phone that receives signals and changes them into sounds or pictures

recent *adjective*
used for describing something that happened, appeared, started to exist or was done a short time ago *a recent change; a recent book; a recent email* (sent or written a short time ago); *a recent photo* (taken a short time ago); *I haven't seen her in recent weeks* (in the last few weeks).

recently *adverb*
1 at the time just before the present time *I saw him recently. I haven't seen him recently* (I haven't seen him for quite a long time).
2 starting to happen from a short time ago *My aunt's been ill recently* (and she's still ill).

receptacle *noun* receptacles
something that you use for keeping things in, such as a box

> SYNONYM container

reception *noun*
1 the place in a building such as an office or hospital where visitors go, for example when they arrive or leave, and where there is someone who helps them *the reception desk*
2 the place in a hotel where guests go, for example to check in or out (sign their name in the register when they arrive or leave)
3 the way someone is greeted or welcomed somewhere *The parents got a warm reception at the school.*
4 (*plural* receptions) an important or official event such as a special meal to welcome someone or celebrate something *a wedding reception*
5 used about the quality of the signals that a piece of equipment such as a TV or mobile phone receives in order to work *The reception isn't very good in this part of Scotland.*
6 a reception class is a class for children aged four to five in England and Wales. It is the first year of primary school.

receptionist *noun* receptionists
someone who works in a place such as an office or hotel and who helps visitors or guests, for example when they arrive or leave, and does other things such as answering the phone

receptive *adjective*
if someone is receptive, they are ready to listen and pay attention or to accept new ideas

recess ['ree-sess] *noun* recesses
1 a recess in a room is a small extra area made when part of a wall is built further back from the rest of the wall
2 a short time when an official organisation such as a parliament stops working
3 the American word for a school break (short time between classes)

recession *noun* recessions
a period of time when there is less business activity in a country and when many people become poorer and lose their jobs

recharge *verb*
recharges, recharging, recharged
to recharge a battery is to put electricity into a special kind of battery using a piece of equipment called a charger

rechargeable *adjective*
used for describing a special kind of battery that you put electricity into when it is used up or something that uses this kind of battery *a rechargeable torch*

recipe ['ress-er-pee] *noun* recipes
instructions for cooking something such as a cake or meal and a list of the ingredients (different foods) you need to make it

recipient *noun* recipients
someone who receives something

recital *noun* recitals
a performance of music, poetry or dance by one person or a small number of people *a piano recital*

recite *verb*
recites, reciting, recited
if you recite a poem or story, you say it out loud to people after learning it word for word

reckless *adjective*
1 if someone is reckless, they do something dangerous without thinking about the bad things that might happen
2 also used about someone's behaviour or actions *reckless driving*
recklessly *adverb* **recklessness** *noun*

reckon *verb*
reckons, reckoning, reckoned
1 an informal way of saying to think or of saying that something is your opinion *It's too dark to play outside, I reckon. He's reckoned to be the most famous footballer alive.*
2 an informal way of saying to expect *I'm reckoning to finish* (or *on finishing*) *my homework by tonight.*
3 to calculate an amount or number *I'm not good at maths so I have to reckon things up on my fingers.*

reclaim *verb*
reclaims, reclaiming, reclaimed
1 to get something back from someone, for example something that you've lost or that was taken away from you
2 to get back your luggage at an airport when you've been on a flight
3 to make an area of land suitable for building or growing things on, for example land that is very wet or dry *Holland has reclaimed large amounts of land from the sea.*

reclaim *noun*
baggage reclaim is the area in an airport where you go to get your luggage back when you've been on a flight

recline *verb*
reclines, reclining, reclined
1 to lean back so that the top half of your body is at an angle or lying almost flat and you are in a comfortable position *Mum was reclining on the sofa.*
2 if a chair reclines or if you recline it, you move the back part of the chair backwards so that you can lean back in it

recognisable *adjective*
if someone or something is recognisable, they are easy to recognise *The film star has a face recognisable to millions of people.*

> LANGUAGE EXTRA also spelt *recognizable*

recognise *verb*
recognises, recognising, recognised
1 if you recognise someone, you know who they are because you've seen them before or, for example, because you've been told about them or heard their voice before *From the author's description it's easy to recognise the main character.*
2 if you recognise something, you know what it is because you've seen it, heard it or have been told about it before *I recognised her face and voice.*
3 to know or say that something is true or exists *We all recognise that there's a problem. I recognise how serious things are.*
4 to know or say that something is good or important *My teacher said she recognises the hard work we've put into the school project.*
5 to consider something as being official or trusted *This exam is recognised all over the world.*
6 to say that something is your fault *I recognise my mistake.*

> LANGUAGE EXTRA also spelt *recognize*

recognition *noun*
1 when you recognise someone or something *a smile of recognition*
2 when you know that something is true or exists
3 praise given to someone for doing something good or to something for being good *After writing many books, she finally got the recognition she deserved* (people realised her books were good).

recoil *verb*
recoils, recoiling, recoiled
if someone recoils, they move their body quickly away from someone or something because they are shocked or frightened *When he saw the dead pigeon, he recoiled in horror.*

recollect *verb*
recollects, recollecting, recollected
1 another way of saying to remember *I don't recollect ever seeing that film.*

398

recollection – recruit

2 used for showing the words someone speaks when they remember something *'That was the happiest time of my life,' she recollected.*

recollection *noun*
1 (*plural* **recollections**) something you remember from the past

SYNONYM memory

2 when you remember something *I have no recollection of seeing that film.*

recommend *verb*
recommends, recommending, recommended
1 to tell someone that something or someone is good *Can you recommend a book for me to read over the holidays?*
2 to tell someone to do something because you think they should do it *The doctor recommended that I should stay in bed for a few days.*
3 to tell someone that something is necessary, or a very good idea, if they want to do something *The school recommends strong shoes for the trip to Parker's Farm.*

recommendation *noun* **recommendations**
1 when someone tells you that something or someone is good *We went to see the film on Laura's recommendation.*
2 something that someone tells you is good *'Treasure Island' is at the top of his list of recommendations.*
3 when someone tells you to do something because they think you should do it *The doctor made several recommendations.*

reconcile *verb*
reconciles, reconciling, reconciled
1 to make people friendly again after a serious argument or fight *After many years the two brothers were reconciled* (became friends again).
2 if you are reconciled to a bad situation, you accept it because you can't change it *Our school is reconciled to being near the bottom of the league tables this year.*

reconciliation *noun*

reconditioned *adjective*
if a piece of equipment such as a computer is reconditioned, it is not completely new but has been repaired and is cheaper to buy

reconsider *verb*
reconsiders, reconsidering, reconsidered
to think about changing something such as a decision you've made or an opinion you have *I said I would join the football team but I might reconsider.*

reconstruct *verb*
reconstructs, reconstructing, reconstructed
1 to build something again

SYNONYM to rebuild

2 if someone reconstructs something, for example a crime, accident or battle, they show how it must have happened based on the information they have found out about it

reconstruction *noun*
1 the action of building something again
2 (*plural* **reconstructions**) an event showing how something must have happened in the past based on the information people have found out about it *Actors took part in several reconstructions of the robbery.*

3 the action of showing this type of event *The police did a reconstruction of the crime.*

record ['rek-ord'] *noun* **records**
1 used for talking about something that is the best that anyone has ever done, for example a result or performance, especially in a sport *He broke the record for the fastest time* (was faster than anyone had ever been) *in the cross-country race.*
2 used for talking about something that is, for example, the best or worst, biggest or smallest, fastest or slowest *The amount the National Gallery paid for this painting was a record* (the most anyone had ever paid). *The Guinness World Records website lists all the greatest records in the world. Holly finished her homework in record time* (faster than ever before).
3 used for talking about past actions, events or qualities connected with someone or something *Mohammed has an excellent school record* (he has always been very good at school). *This type of car has a good safety record* (it has usually been safe).
4 information written down and kept so that it can be used in the future *Your doctor keeps your medical records. Keep a record of* (write down) *how much you spend.*
5 a round flat piece of vinyl (a kind of plastic) that music is stored on, used especially in the past. The music is played on a piece of equipment called a record player.
6 on record used for saying that something is, for example, the biggest or smallest, best or worst, hottest or coldest that has ever been written about *This summer was the wettest on record.*

record ['ri-kord'] *verb*
records, recording, recorded
1 to store sounds or moving pictures on a piece of equipment such as a video camera or on a disc such as a CD or DVD *Mum often records her favourite TV programmes so she can watch them again later.*
2 if a piece of equipment records, sounds or pictures are being stored on it *Is the DVD player recording?*
3 if a musician, singer or band records an album, they perform the music so that it can be stored, for example on a CD, and later sold
4 to write down information on paper or on a computer and store it so that it can be used at a later time
5 to show a particular measurement *Low temperatures have been recorded in Scotland.*

recorded *adjective*
1 if something such as a concert or TV programme is recorded, it has been stored on a piece of equipment so that it can be watched or listened to at a later time

ANTONYM live

2 recorded delivery is a way of sending a letter or parcel by post. When someone receives it, they write their name somewhere so that you know they have received it.

recorder *noun* **recorders**
1 a musical instrument made up of a long plastic or wooden tube with holes in it. You play it by blowing into the tube and covering the holes with your fingers to change the notes.

2 a piece of equipment that records sounds or pictures, for example a DVD recorder

recording *noun*
1 (*plural* **recordings**) words, music or moving pictures that have been recorded, for example on a video camera or DVD *We watched a video recording of the prize-giving.*
2 the action or business of recording sounds, pictures or music *a television recording studio*

record player *noun* **record players**
a piece of equipment, used especially in the past, for playing music on records (flat round pieces of a plastic called vinyl)

recount ['ri-count'] *verb*
recounts, recounting, recounted
to tell someone something or about something that actually happened *He recounted how he rode on an elephant in India. Our teacher recounted the story of her trip around America.*

recount ['ree-count'] *noun* **recounts**
a type of text in which you tell the reader about something that actually happened. For example, a personal recount is about something that happened to you, and a factual recount is when you describe an event.

recover *verb*
recovers, recovering, recovered
1 to get better after you've been ill or injured *Has your brother recovered from the flu yet?*
2 to deal successfully with something bad that happens to you and then return to the way you were before *Dad lost his job but he's recovered from the shock* (for example, he's no longer sad or angry).
3 to get something back that you once had, for example something you lost *The police recovered my stolen mobile.*

recovery *noun*
1 when you feel better after being ill or injured *We hope our teacher will make a speedy recovery* (gets better fast).
2 when you get something back that you once had
3 in business, a recovery is a situation in which things return to normal after a difficult period when not much money has been made *Business is showing signs of recovery.*

recreation ['rek-ree-ay-shern'] *noun*
1 doing activities in your spare time to enjoy yourself *Dad doesn't have much time for recreation.*
2 (*plural* **recreations**) an activity that you do in your spare time to enjoy yourself *My favourite recreation is swimming.*

recreational *adjective*

recruit *noun* **recruits**
someone who has just joined a group or organisation such as the army

recruit *verb*
recruits, recruiting, recruited
1 to get someone to join an organisation or to work for a company
2 to get someone to take part in an activity or to help you *The school is recruiting volunteers to help at the fête.*

399

rectangle – reek

rectangle *noun* **rectangles**
a flat shape with four straight sides and four right angles (angles of 90 degrees). Opposite sides have the same length as each other but two of the opposite sides may be longer than the other two. A square is a special type of rectangle where all four sides are the same length.
compare: **oblong**

ORIGIN from Latin *rectus* 'straight' and *angulus* 'angle'

rectangular *adjective*
shaped like a rectangle

rectify *verb*
rectifies, rectifying, rectified
to put right something that is wrong or bad, for example a mistake or situation

rectum *noun* **rectums**
the tube inside your body that carries solid waste to the opening in your bottom where the waste comes out when you go to the toilet

recuperate *verb*
recuperates, recuperating, recuperated
if someone recuperates, they gradually get their health and strength back after being ill or injured

recur *verb*
recurs, recurring, recurred
if something recurs, it happens again or it happens several times *My phone often stops working – it's a recurring problem.*
recurrence *noun*

recycle *verb*
recycles, recycling, recycled
1 to deal with used materials such as paper, plastic, glass or cloth in a special way so that they can be used again
2 to deal with used equipment or objects such as TVs, computers or furniture so that the parts they are made up of can be used again
recycling *noun*

recycle bin *noun* **recycle bins**
1 a container for used materials such as paper or plastic that will be recycled later
2 a place on a computer where you store deleted documents, folders and programs until you decide to delete them permanently

recycling centre *noun* **recycling centres**
a place where people take things that they don't want, for example from their home or garden, to be recycled or thrown away

SYNONYM rubbish dump

red *adjective* **redder, reddest**
1 having the colour of blood or a tomato that is ripe (soft and ready to eat)
2 red hair is an orange-brown or reddish-brown colour
3 if you go red, your face becomes red, for example because you are ashamed or shy
4 a red blood cell is a cell (tiny unit of living matter) that carries oxygen in the blood
5 red meat is meat that has a dark red colour before it is cooked, for example meat from a cow (such as beef) or sheep (such as lamb)

red *noun* **reds**
1 the colour red
2 if you see red, you become very angry

redcurrant *noun* **redcurrants**
a very small soft and round red fruit

redden *verb*
reddens, reddening, reddened
to become red

reddish *adjective*
slightly red

redeem *verb*
redeems, redeeming, redeemed
1 if you redeem something such as a voucher (special piece of paper instead of money), you use it, for example in a shop, in order to pay for something
2 to do something to make something bad seem less bad *The film was terrible and even the good acting couldn't redeem it. The new boy is lazy and rude and seems to have no redeeming qualities* (nothing good that can make up for his bad character).
3 if you redeem yourself, you do something good to make up for the bad things you have done
4 in religion, to redeem someone is to save them from being punished for their sins

red-handed *adjective*
if you catch someone red-handed, you find them doing something wrong, for example committing a crime *My cousin was caught red-handed stealing a book from the library* (someone saw him stealing and stopped him).

redhead *noun* **redheads**
someone who has orange-brown or reddish-brown hair **red-headed** *adjective*

red herring *noun* **red herrings**
something completely unimportant that takes someone's attention away from what is really important in a particular situation *The police followed that clue but it was a red herring* (it wasn't connected with the crime).

ORIGIN a herring is a silver-coloured fish that turns red when it is cured (hung in smoke). The smell of these *red herrings* was used in the past to train dogs for chasing foxes in a hunt.

red-hot *adjective*
extremely hot *Be careful, the plate's red-hot from the oven.*

redial *verb*
redials, redialling, redialled
to press the buttons again on a phone to make a call, for example because the line was busy before

redirect *verb*
redirects, redirecting, redirected
1 to make something go in a different direction *A police officer was redirecting traffic away from the town centre.*
2 to change the purpose of something *Dad told me to redirect all my energy into my schoolwork.*
3 if you redirect a letter or parcel, you send it on to someone at a different address

redness *noun*
1 a red area, for example on the skin *I still have some redness on my shoulder from carrying my heavy schoolbag.*
2 a red colour *the redness of the evening sky*

redo *verb*
redoes, redoing, redid, redone
1 to do something again, for example in a different or better way *My teacher said my homework wasn't good enough and I had to redo it.*
2 if you redo an action on a computer, you do something such as press a key or click on an icon to bring back a change in a document or program that you had cancelled
compare: **undo**

reduce *verb*
reduces, reducing, reduced
1 to make something less or smaller *Drivers reduce their speed as they get close to the school.*
2 to make the price of something less *Everything is reduced in the sale. These jeans were reduced to £10.*
3 to force someone or something into a bad situation *He was reduced to tears* (so upset that he cried). *The building has been reduced to ruins. I had no money for the bus so I was reduced to walking home.*

reduction *noun* **reductions**
1 when someone makes something less or when something becomes less *There's been a reduction in the number of complaints.*
2 the amount by which the price of something is less *They're offering a reduction of 10 per cent on all mobile phones. Are there any reductions for children?*

SYNONYM discount

3 a photo or document that has been copied to make it smaller than the original

ANTONYM enlargement

redundant *adjective*
1 if someone who has a job is made redundant, they are told to leave their job because there is no more work for them
2 used for describing something that is not needed or useful (or no longer needed or useful) *redundant details; old redundant buildings; redundant skills*
3 in grammar, if something such as a word or expression is redundant, it is not needed because it repeats a meaning that is already given. For example, in the sentence 'He lives in a huge enormous house', either 'huge' or 'enormous' is redundant.
redundancy *noun*

reed *noun* **reeds**
1 a tall stiff type of grass that grows in wet places such as marshes (ground near rivers, lakes or the sea)
2 a thin strip of wood, metal or plastic at the top of a musical instrument such as a clarinet or saxophone. It vibrates to produce a sound when you blow air over it.

reef *noun* **reefs**
a line of rocks just below the surface of the sea, often made of coral (a hard substance from the bones of small sea creatures)

reef knot *noun* **reef knots**
a type of knot that is tied twice so that it is difficult to untie

reek *verb*
reeks, reeking, reeked
to have a very strong and unpleasant smell *His clothes reeked of fish.*

reel noun reels
1 an object that has the shape of a wheel or cylinder (tube with flat ends shaped like circles), around which something is rolled, for example string, cotton or cables (electrical wires) *a cotton reel* (for sewing); *a hose reel* (for a hosepipe); *a reel of film* (for example in an old-fashioned projector); *a fishing reel* (for the string on a fishing rod)
2 a fast Scottish or Irish traditional dance, or the music played for it

reel verb
reels, reeling, reeled
1 to move or walk in a way that looks as if you are going to fall over, for example like someone who is drunk or has been punched
2 to feel shocked or upset *People are still reeling at the news of the film star's death.*
3 to reel off things such as names or dates is to say them quickly from memory

refectory noun refectories
a large room, for example in a school or university, where people have their meals

refer verb
refers, referring, referred
1 to refer to someone or something is to talk or write about them or to describe them *I promise not to refer to this again. We refer to Granddad as 'Pop'.*
2 to refer to something such as a book is to look for information there *To find out what a word means, refer to a dictionary or the internet. I referred to my notes from class.*
3 to send or give something to someone else to be dealt with *I couldn't answer the question so I referred it to my teacher.*

referee noun referees
someone in charge of a game such as a football, rugby or boxing match who makes sure the rules are obeyed
compare: **umpire**

referee verb
referees, refereeing, refereed
to referee a game or match is to be the referee

reference noun references
1 words that you say or write about someone or something *There's a reference to his new bike in his email.*
2 when you talk or write about someone or something *In my homework I made reference to Shakespeare lots of times. 'I'm writing in reference to your email of 5 July.'*
3 a place where information can be found *I use the internet as my main reference* (or *source of reference*). *Our school has lots of reference books* (or *reference works*) (for example dictionaries and encyclopedias for getting information).
4 when you look for information somewhere *This is a useful book that you should keep for future reference.*
5 a number, word or symbol used for finding information such as who someone is or what something is *What's your customer reference number?*
6 a group of letters and numbers that shows where something is on a map *Norwich is at map reference G8.*
7 a letter or email about someone's character, skills or work they've done. It is usually used by someone who applies for a job, to show that they are suitable.

referendum ['ref-er-ren-derm'] noun
referendums
a vote in which all the people in a country or region are asked to give their opinion about an important question

refill ['ree-fil'] verb
refills, refilling, refilled
to fill something again, for example a glass, cup or bottle

refill ['ree-fil'] noun refills
1 an amount of something needed to fill a container that has become empty *I have no lemonade left – can you give me a refill?*
2 a container, for example of liquid, used for filling something that has become empty *My fountain pen needs a refill – do you have an ink cartridge?*

refine verb
refines, refining, refined
1 to make something better by making small changes to it *Sita has written a poem and she's still refining it.*
2 to remove bad or unwanted substances from something such as sugar or oil so that its quality is better and purer

refined adjective
1 if someone is refined, they are very polite, show good judgement and know the rules of how to behave towards other people
2 with the bad or unwanted substances removed *refined sugar*

refinement noun
1 (*plural* **refinements**) a small change made to something to make it better
2 (*plural* **refinements**) something that has been changed slightly to make it better
3 the special quality of someone who is refined *Our teacher is a person of great refinement.*
4 the action of removing bad or unwanted substances from something such as sugar or oil

refinery noun refineries
a factory where bad or unwanted substances are removed from something *an oil refinery*

reflect verb
reflects, reflecting, reflected
1 if a surface reflects something such as light or sound (or if light or sound reflects off a surface), the light or sound bounces off it and does not pass through *I couldn't see because the cars reflected the sunlight into my eyes. The bright light reflected off the snow.*
2 to show the image of something on the surface of something shiny such as water or a mirror *I could see my face reflected in the shop window.*
3 in maths, if you reflect a shape, you produce its mirror image
4 to show or be a sign of something *What my sister says doesn't reflect my own opinion.*
5 to think about something carefully

reflection noun reflections
1 an image of something that you see in a mirror, on water or on a shiny surface
2 in maths, a reflection is the way a shape is moved so that it is the mirror image of another shape. A shape has reflection symmetry when it has one or more lines of symmetry (lines that divide the halves or parts of a shape that are mirror images of each other).
compare: **rotation** (sense 3) and **translation** (sense 3)
3 a sign or description of something *The silence in the hall when the head teacher spoke was a reflection of our respect for her.*
4 careful thought about something

reflective adjective
1 used for describing something that reflects light and can be easily seen *Cyclists often wear reflective jackets.*
2 thinking carefully or showing signs of careful thought *a reflective mood*

reflector noun reflectors
a small piece of plastic or glass, for example on a bicycle, that reflects the light at night to make it easier for someone to be seen

reflex ['ree-fleks'] noun reflexes
1 a movement of your body that you cannot control, for example blinking or shivering
2 a reflex action is one that you do without thinking about it *When the doorbell rang I jumped – it was a reflex action.*
3 in maths, a reflex angle is one that is between 180 and 360 degrees
compare: **acute**, **obtuse** and **straight**

reflexive adjective
used in grammar for describing a pronoun such as 'myself', 'herself' or 'yourself' that shows that the person who does the action of a verb is also the person who receives the action, for example 'I hurt myself'. It is also used for describing a verb (such as 'to hurt yourself' or 'to enjoy yourself') that contains a reflexive pronoun.

reform verb
reforms, reforming, reformed
1 to improve someone or someone's behaviour by getting them to stop doing bad things
2 if someone reforms, they change their behaviour and stop doing bad things
3 to reform something such as an organisation or law is to change it and improve it

reform noun
1 (*plural* **reforms**) a change made to improve something *educational reforms*
2 when someone makes changes to improve something *Do our schools need more reform?*

Reformation ['ref-er-may-shern'] noun
a period of English history in the 16th century when some Christians separated from the Catholic Church and the Protestant Church was started

reformer noun reformers
someone who tries to change and improve things

refrain verb
refrains, refraining, refrained
if someone refrains from doing something, they do not do it *Please refrain from talking during the lesson.*

refrain noun refrains
a part of a song or poem that you repeat after each of the main parts (or verses)

refresh verb
refreshes, refreshing, refreshed
1 to give someone more energy and make them feel less tired *Mum needs a coffee to refresh her. I feel refreshed after my sleep.*

401

refreshing – registration

2 to make someone feel cooler when they are feeling too hot *I had a shower to refresh me.*
3 to refresh someone's memory is to help them remember something
4 in computing, if you refresh something such as a web page, you get the most recent information by performing an action such as clicking on or touching an icon (picture or symbol) on the screen

refreshing *adjective*
1 used for describing something that gives you more energy or makes you feel cooler *a refreshing drink of lemonade*; *a refreshing swim*
2 used for describing something pleasant and different *a refreshing change*

refreshments *noun plural*
things to eat and drink that people buy or are given, for example on a journey or at a party, concert or meeting *a refreshment area*

refrigerate *verb*
refrigerates, refrigerating, refrigerated
to keep food or drinks cold and fresh by putting them in a fridge

refrigerator *noun* refrigerators
a piece of equipment like a large box with shelves and a door, used for keeping food cold

SYNONYM fridge

refuel *verb*
refuels, refuelling, refuelled
to put more fuel into an aircraft or vehicle so that it can continue its journey

refuge ['ref-yooj'] *noun*
1 (*plural* **refuges**) a place where someone is safe from danger or a home for people or animals that need protection *a refuge for the homeless*
2 protection from danger or from something bad *Where can we go to take refuge from the storm?*

SYNONYM shelter

refugee ['ref-yoo-jee'] *noun* refugees
someone who leaves their own country, for example because of a war, not having enough food or being treated in a cruel way *a refugee camp*

refund ['ree-fund'] *noun* refunds
money that someone gives you back *If you don't use your ticket, you'll get a refund.*

refund ['ri-fund'] *verb*
refunds, refunding, refunded
to give someone their money back, for example because they no longer want something they've bought *Customers were refunded. Can you refund my money?*
refundable *adjective*

refurbish *verb*
refurbishes, refurbishing, refurbished
1 to repair and improve a building
2 to clean and repair a piece of equipment so that it is like new *Dad bought a refurbished bike because it was cheaper.*

refusal *noun* refusals
when someone refuses something or refuses to do or give something

refuse ['ri-fyooz'] *verb*
refuses, refusing, refused
1 if you refuse to do something, you say you won't do it *I refuse to say sorry.*
2 if something refuses to do something, it doesn't do it *My tablet refuses to start.*
3 to say that you don't want something *She offered me a chocolate but I refused.*
4 to say that you won't give or allow something *Dad refused me permission to watch TV after ten o'clock.*

refuse ['ref-yooss'] *noun*
another word for rubbish *a refuse collector* (someone who comes to your house to get rid of rubbish)

regain *verb*
regains, regaining, regained
to get something back, for example a quality or an ability to do something *The teacher has regained control of the class.*

regard *verb*
regards, regarding, regarded
1 to consider something or someone in a particular way *I regard the whole thing as a joke.*
2 to consider someone or something as being very good *My cousin is a highly regarded painter.*

regard *noun*
1 attention that you give to something or someone *Oliver rode his bike without regard to other children's safety.*
2 behaviour that shows that you think about other people's feelings *Emilia has no regard for older people.*
3 when you consider someone or something as being very good *Most parents have a high regard for the head teacher.*
4 regards good wishes that you give or send to someone *Regards to your mum and dad!*
5 with regard to used when mentioning a particular subject

regarding *preposition*
used when mentioning a particular subject *He wouldn't say anything regarding what happened.*

regardless *adverb*
used for saying that something you mention, for example something bad, does not stop something else happening *My feet were hurting but I carried on walking regardless. I'm going to school tomorrow regardless of the weather.*

regatta ['rig-at-er'] *noun* regattas
a series of races in which rowing boats or sailing boats take part

regenerate *verb*
regenerates, regenerating, regenerated
1 to grow another body part (used about animals or in science fiction)
2 to make something such as an area or business as good and successful as it was before *They're regenerating our town centre* (for example by repairing and repainting buildings, putting up new buildings and creating parks).

reggae ['reg-ay'] *noun*
a type of music with a strong beat (regular pattern of sounds). It started in Jamaica in the 1960s.

regiment *noun* regiments
a very large group of soldiers. A regiment usually contains several battalions and is part of a division. It is often made up of soldiers from a particular part of the country. The person in charge of a regiment is called a colonel.

regimental *adjective*
connected with a regiment *a regimental flag*

region *noun* regions
1 a part of a country or of the world *the mountainous regions of Pakistan*
2 a part of the universe *the furthest regions of the galaxy*
3 a particular part of the body *Granddad has pains in the lower back region.*
4 in the region of used with numbers for saying that something is not exact but roughly correct *Dad paid in the region of £100 for my bike.*

regional *adjective*
connected with a particular region *a regional newspaper*

register *verb*
registers, registering, registered
1 to put your name or someone else's name on an official list in order to be able to do something, for example study at a school or visit a doctor *We registered with Dr Patel when we moved here.*
2 to put the details of something on an official list *All new cars must be registered.*
3 to give your name, email address and other information about yourself to someone on the internet, for example so that you can use their website or another service that they provide *Click here to register for a Twitter account.*
4 to register software or a product is to give your name, address and other information to the company you bought it from, for example so they can send you updates or fix problems
5 to show a particular measurement *The earthquake registered 5 on the Richter scale.*
6 used about something that someone understands or realises *I told Mum I failed my maths test but it didn't seem to register* (she didn't seem to understand).
7 to register a letter or parcel is to send it by registered post
8 registered post is a way of sending a letter or parcel with special care. When someone receives it, they write their name somewhere, usually on an electronic device, so that you know they have received it.

register *noun* registers
1 a book or electronic document containing an official list of names *All guests must sign the hotel register.*
2 a book or electronic document containing the names of all the students in a class *The teacher called the register* (read out the name of each student to check who was present and who was absent).
3 the register of a voice or musical instrument is the particular range of notes that someone can sing or an instrument can play

registration *noun*
1 when someone registers a name or the details of something on an official list or gives information about themselves to a company on the internet

registration number – rekindle

2 the time when a teacher reads out the names of students on the register to check who is present and who is absent
3 (*plural* **registrations**) another way of saying registration number

registration number *noun*
registration numbers
the numbers and letters at the front and back of a road vehicle that show who it belongs to
compare: **number plate**

registry office *noun* registry offices
a place where people can go to get married officially and where official information is kept about births, deaths and marriages

regret *verb*
regrets, regretting, regretted
1 to feel sorry or sad about something *We regret the trouble this is going to cause.*
2 to feel sorry about something that you wish you hadn't done or said (or about something that you didn't do or say but wish you had) *I regret calling him an idiot. I regret not doing my homework this week.*

regret *noun* regrets
1 a feeling of sadness about something
2 when you feel sorry about something that you wish you hadn't done or said (or about something that you didn't do or say but wish you had) *I chose to study French and I have no regrets* (I'm happy that I did this).

regretful *adjective*
feeling or showing sadness about something *a regretful smile*

regretfully *adverb*
1 used about something you are sorry to mention *Regretfully, there's no money left to buy you a new bike.*

SYNONYM regrettably

2 in a way that shows you are sad or sorry about something *'I can't help you any more,' he said regretfully.*

regrettable *adjective*
used about something you are sorry to mention because it is unpleasant or bad and you wish the situation were different *a regrettable mistake*; *It's regrettable that the school hasn't dealt with that bully.*

regrettably *adverb*
used about something you are sorry to mention *Regrettably, I wasn't invited.*

SYNONYM regretfully

regular *adjective*
1 happening with equal periods of time in between *a regular heartbeat*; *You should stop and rest at regular intervals.*
2 used for describing objects or things such as shapes or patterns that have the same size or position or equal spaces in between *regular teeth*; *the regular shape of the statue's head*; *a scarf with a regular pattern of squares and circles*
3 in maths, a regular shape is one where all sides are equal, for example a square
4 happening, doing something or going somewhere often, for example on the same day each week or at the same time each day *regular exercise*; *a regular customer*; *I pay regular visits to my grandparents.*

5 flat and smooth *a regular surface*
6 not changing *a regular temperature*; *regular habits*
7 lasting a long time *My sister has a regular job.*
8 normal or usual *Can we see our regular dentist? It was a regular Tuesday morning.*
9 used for describing a standard size that is not big or small or for describing something that has this size *a regular cappuccino*; *Do you want regular or large fries?*
10 following the usual patterns of grammar *'To jump' is a regular verb. 'Books' is the regular plural of 'book'.*
regularity *noun*

ORIGIN from Latin *regula* 'rule'

regularly *adverb*
1 often or all the time *I regularly look up words in the dictionary.*
2 with equal periods of time in between *Take this medicine regularly three times a day. We go to the seaside regularly once a year.*
3 evenly or with equal amounts of space in between *Plant the bushes so they're regularly spaced along the wall.*

regulate *verb*
regulates, regulating, regulated
1 to control something, for example so that it works properly or in a particular way *Turn this knob to regulate the temperature in all the rooms.*
2 to control something officially, such as an activity, company, bank or industry, by using rules

regulation *noun*
1 (*plural* **regulations**) an official rule *building regulations* (rules about how to build things properly)
2 when something is controlled, for example a piece of equipment or an activity or company

rehearsal *noun* rehearsals
a time when people practise something such as a play, piece of music or dance so that they're ready to perform it

rehearse *verb*
rehearses, rehearsing, rehearsed
to practise something such as a play, piece of music, dance or speech so that you're ready to perform it *Don't make a noise – they're rehearsing. Let's rehearse the last act of the play again.*

reign [rhymes with 'rain'] *noun* reigns
the period of time when a king or queen rules a country or when someone such as an emperor or pope rules an area

reign [rhymes with 'rain'] *verb*
reigns, reigning, reigned
1 to rule a country or area *Queen Victoria reigned from 1837 to 1901. This pharaoh reigned over the whole of Egypt.*
2 to be the main thing or most important person at a particular time *Confusion reigned the whole afternoon. She's the reigning tennis champion* (the champion now).

reindeer *noun* reindeer
a large wild animal like a deer with very big antlers (twisted horns on its head). Reindeer live in very cold areas, especially the Arctic (region at the most northern point of the world).

reinforce *verb*
reinforces, reinforcing, reinforced
1 to make something stronger, for example by adding something extra to it or adding more of the same thing *The buildings in Tokyo are reinforced so they don't fall down in an earthquake. The troops need to be reinforced along the border.*
2 to make something such as an idea or feeling stronger

reinforcements *noun plural*
extra soldiers or police officers sent somewhere because more are needed

reins *noun plural*
1 leather straps that you hold in your hand, used for controlling a horse. The reins are fixed to the horse's bridle (leather strips around its head).
2 a series of straps around a baby or young child who has just started walking, used for keeping them safe and stopping them from falling

reject ['ri-jekt'] *verb*
rejects, rejecting, rejected
1 if you reject something such as an offer, idea or suggestion, you don't accept it, for example because you don't want it or don't agree with it
2 to reject someone is not to choose them, for example someone who wants something such as a job or who wants to do something such as study somewhere or join a team or group *My sister applied to Oxford but they rejected her. I wanted to join the football team but was rejected as I wasn't good enough.*
3 to reject goods is to say you don't want them because they're damaged, have something wrong with them or aren't what you asked for
4 to reject someone who wants to be liked or loved is to treat them cruelly and tell them you do not like or love them
5 to say that something such as a book, poem, play or piece of music is not good enough, for example to be printed or performed
6 if a machine rejects something such as a coin or card, you put the coin or card into the machine to make it work but it comes out again and the machine doesn't work
rejection *noun*

reject ['ree-jekt'] *noun* rejects
something that is damaged or has something wrong with it *Mum bought these dishes cheaply because they're rejects.*

rejoice *verb*
rejoices, rejoicing, rejoiced
to show how happy you are about something *We all rejoiced at the good news. People were rejoicing in the streets* (for example singing, dancing and shouting happily).

rejoicing *noun*
when people show how happy they are about something *There was rejoicing in every town and village.*

rekindle *verb*
rekindles, rekindling, rekindled
to make someone have a feeling, idea or memory that they had in the past *Watching the Olympics on TV has rekindled my interest in sport.*

relate – relevance

relate *verb*
relates, relating, related
1 to be connected in some way with something *This description relates to an event that happened earlier in Shakespeare's life.*
2 to see or show a connection between things *The head teacher relates bad behaviour in school to parents not being strict enough.*
3 to tell someone something or about something *Sam related a story about his childhood dreams.*

related *adjective*
1 belonging to the same family *Elvie and Grace are related. Elvie is related to Grace.*
2 connected in some way *These two events are related.*

relation *noun* **relations**
1 a connection between things
2 someone who belongs to your family *I have lots of relations in Ireland.*

> SYNONYM relative

3 relations between people or groups are the way they behave towards each other *There are very friendly relations between Britain and France.*

relationship *noun* **relationships**
1 the way things are connected
2 the way people or groups behave towards each other and how friendly they are to each other *She has a close relationship with her sister* (they like each other very much).
3 the way someone is related to someone else in their family *'What's the relationship between you and Jack?' – 'He's my cousin.'*
4 if two people have a relationship, they have feelings of love and respect for each other and spend time together, especially when this continues for a long time

relative *noun* **relatives**
someone who belongs to your family *She's a close relative* (someone such as a mother, father, brother or sister who is directly related to someone).

> SYNONYM relation

relative *adjective*
compared to something else such as other similar things or another situation, or compared to what is normal *Granddad lives in relative comfort* (for example compared to other people or compared to his situation before).

relative clause *noun* **relative clauses**
a clause (part of a sentence) that starts with a relative pronoun (for example 'that', 'which' or 'who') and adds information about a noun or sentence. For example, in the sentence 'I showed my teacher the picture that I drew', the relative clause is 'that I drew' because it adds some information about 'picture'.

> LANGUAGE EXTRA a *relative clause* is so called because it *relates to* (or refers to) a noun or sentence

relatively *adverb*
1 compared to something else, for example a situation that existed before, or compared to what is normal *Breakfast at nine o'clock would be relatively late for me.*
2 to a certain extent but not completely *This week's homework was relatively easy.*

> SYNONYMS for sense 2: fairly, rather

relative pronoun *noun* **relative pronouns**
a pronoun such as 'that', 'which' or 'who' that refers to an earlier noun or sentence. For example, 'that' in the sentence 'I showed my teacher the picture that I drew' is a relative pronoun because it refers to 'picture'.

> LANGUAGE EXTRA a *relative pronoun* is so called because it *relates to* (or refers to) a noun or sentence

relax *verb*
relaxes, relaxing, relaxed
1 to spend time doing something that makes you feel happy or good or to spend time not doing anything *Granddad was relaxing in his armchair. Relax and watch the film!*
2 to make someone feel happy or good *That hot shower has really relaxed me.*
3 to stop being worried *You can relax now – we've found your cat and he's safe.*
4 to stop being excited or angry *Relax for a moment and stop running around and shouting!*

> SYNONYM to calm down

5 to make something less tight, or to become less tight, for example a part of the body *Relax your muscles. Just let your arm relax. Relax your grip on the handlebars.*
6 to make something less strict or strong, for example a rule, law or your control over something *The head teacher has relaxed the rules on school uniforms.*

relaxation *noun*
doing something that makes you feel happy or good *What do you do for relaxation?*

relaxed *adjective*
1 happy or feeling good *You look more relaxed after your bath.*
2 used for showing that someone is happy or feels good *relaxed behaviour*
3 not feeling or looking worried *The tennis champion seemed relaxed at the start of the game.*
4 used for showing that someone is not worried *He had a relaxed smile on his face as the doctor examined him.*
5 not worrying or caring too much about something, for example the way people behave *My parents are relaxed about me going out by myself. They have a relaxed attitude to everything.*
6 used for describing a situation or place where people are friendly and where there are no strict rules about how to behave *the relaxed atmosphere of a British pub*
7 slow and pleasant, or done without hurrying *We were walking at a relaxed pace.*

relaxing *adjective*
making you feel happy or good *a relaxing bath; a relaxing evening*

relay ['ree-lay] or [ri-lay] *verb*
relays, relaying, relayed
1 to send out something such as a radio or television programme using radio waves

> SYNONYM to broadcast

2 to send on information, news or a message to someone, usually as soon as you receive it

relay ['ree-lay] *noun* **relays**
1 a relay or relay race is a running or swimming race between teams in which each person does only one part of the race
2 if people do something in relays, they work in groups. One group does something, then another group does it, until the activity is finished.

release *verb*
releases, releasing, released
1 to stop keeping a person or animal as a prisoner and let them go free
2 to allow someone to leave hospital
3 to stop holding something or someone *Release my arm! Don't release the brake or the car will roll backwards.*
4 to release something such as a film, CD or piece of software is to make it ready so that people can see it or buy it *He's just released a new album* (songs or music, for example as a file or on a CD).
5 to release information is to allow it to become known *The police released the names of the crash victims.*
6 if something releases something such as a chemical substance or energy, it allows that substance or energy to flow out from it *How is heat released from the sun?*

release *noun*
1 when someone or something is released *his release from prison; the release of gases into the atmosphere*
2 (*plural* **releases**) something such as a new film, piece of software or CD that is ready for people to see or buy

relegate *verb*
relegates, relegating, relegated
1 to move a sports team down into a lower division
compare: **promote**
2 to give something or someone a less important position than before *My dad's desk at work was relegated to a corner of the office.*

relegation *noun*

relent *verb*
relents, relenting, relented
if someone relents, they change their mind and allow someone to do something or allow something to happen that they wouldn't allow before

relentless *adjective*
1 used about something that never stops or gets weaker *relentless heat* (very strong and continuing all the time); *relentless criticism*
2 used about someone who never stops doing something *The police were relentless in hunting down the criminals.*

relentlessness *noun*

relentlessly *adverb*
without stopping and in a very strong way *The sun was beating down relentlessly.*

relevance ['rel-er-verns] *noun*
when something is connected with what someone is talking about or when something is important in a particular situation *I don't see the relevance of what you're saying.*

404

relevant ['rel-er-vernt'] *adjective*
important, useful or correct in a particular situation, or connected with what someone is talking about *relevant facts; Who is the relevant person to write to? That's not relevant to the question.*

reliable *adjective*
1 if someone is reliable, you can trust them to behave well or work well, always do what they should do, and do what you ask them to do *a reliable friend; a reliable plumber*
2 if something such as a piece of equipment, method or test is reliable, you can trust it to work well *Our car is very reliable. Is the local bus service reliable?*
3 used for describing something such as information or a book that you can trust to be good and correct *reliable facts; a reliable dictionary*
reliability *noun*

reliably *adverb*
1 by someone that you can trust *Parents have been reliably informed that the new head starts next Monday.*
2 in a way that you can trust *The figures haven't yet been reliably calculated.*

reliant *adjective*
if you are reliant on someone or something, you need them to help you, for example in order to live or to be successful *Holly is reliant on her wheelchair.* **reliance** *noun*

relic *noun* **relics**
a thing that has survived from the past, usually an object or tradition

relief *noun*
1 the happy feeling that you get when something bad doesn't happen or stops happening *It's a relief to know the coach has arrived safely. We all gave a sigh of relief – it had finally stopped raining!*
2 used when talking about getting rid of something bad such as pain or suffering or making it less strong *I took a painkiller to give me some relief from my back pain.*
3 used when talking about getting away from something unpleasant or difficult for a short time *Where can we go to get some relief from the heat and noise?*
4 help given to people who badly need things such as food, medicines and clothes *Our country sent relief to the earthquake victims. They need more relief workers.*
5 a person or group of people that takes over a job from another person or group for a period of time during the working day *The train driver was waiting for his relief. She's a relief driver on the tube.*
6 a way of making designs that are made up of raised parts on a flat surface *a relief map* (with raised parts or with different colours for low and high areas such as valleys, hills and mountains)
7 (*plural* **reliefs**) a design such as a stone or wooden sculpture made up of raised parts that stick out from a flat surface or background

relieve *verb*
relieves, relieving, relieved
1 to get rid of pain, suffering or a bad feeling or make it less strong *This medicine helps to relieve stress.*
2 to make a problem or situation less serious *The government wants to relieve poverty* (make people less poor). *We played games to relieve the boredom* (so we were less bored).
3 to take over a job or task from someone for a time *I've been painting this wall for an hour – can you relieve me?*
4 if someone relieves you of something heavy or difficult, they take it from you in order to help you *May I relieve you of your coat?*

relieved *adjective*
happy because something bad hasn't happened or has stopped happening

religion *noun* **religions**
1 people's beliefs about the existence of God or gods and about the meaning of life and the universe *science and religion*
2 the particular beliefs of people about God (for example the beliefs of Christians, Muslims or Jews) or gods (for example the beliefs of Hindus) *What's your religion?*

religious *adjective*
1 connected with religion or with a particular religion *religious beliefs*
2 if someone is religious, they believe strongly in their religion and obey its rules and traditions

religiously *adverb*
1 in a way that is connected with religion
2 (informal) very carefully, seriously or regularly *Follow this diet religiously.*

relish *noun*
1 a feeling of great pleasure
2 a great liking for something

relish *verb*
relishes, relishing, relished
to like or enjoy something very much

reluctant *adjective*
if someone is reluctant, they don't want to do something *I was reluctant to complain.*
reluctance *noun*

reluctantly *adverb*
if you do something reluctantly, you do it even though you don't want to *Dad reluctantly agreed.*

rely *verb*
relies, relying, relied
1 if you rely on someone, you can trust them to do something, for example to work or behave well or to help you *We can rely on our plumber to do a good job. If you have a problem, you can always rely on me* (you can be sure I will help you).
2 if you rely on someone or something, you need them to help you to live or be successful *Now that I've broken my leg, I have to rely on my crutches to get me around. Edinburgh relies on tourists.*
3 if you rely on something such as information, your memory or judgement, or a dictionary, you have a strong feeling that they are good and can be trusted

remain *verb*
remains, remaining, remained
1 to continue to be somewhere when everything or everyone else has gone or been dealt with *Jack ate most of the cake but there's one slice remaining* (left over). *One big problem remains.*
2 to continue as before in the same place or situation *Isaac has to remain in hospital. Temperatures remained low the whole month.*

remainder *noun* **remainders**
1 something or someone that is still there when everything or everyone else has gone or been dealt with *The remainder of the group chose to learn the violin.*
2 in maths, a remainder is the amount left over after you divide a number by a smaller number when the larger number cannot be divided exactly by the smaller one *13 divided by 4 is 3 remainder 1.*

remaining *adjective*
used for describing something or someone that is still there when everything or everyone else has gone or been dealt with *There's one remaining problem.*

remains *noun plural*
1 the parts of something such as a building or meal that are still there when the rest of it has gone, for example having been destroyed, eaten or used up *We visited the remains of Tintern Abbey. The remains of a meal were still on the table.*
2 the dead body of a person or animal

remark *noun* **remarks**
something that you say, for example giving an opinion or mentioning a fact

remark *verb*
remarks, remarking, remarked
1 to say something *Dad remarked that it was late.*
2 if you remark on something, you say a few words about something that you notice *My friends remarked on my new haircut.*

remarkable *adjective*
1 unusual and very good or great *Dan has a remarkable talent for playing the guitar. Ms Clarke is a remarkable teacher.*
2 very surprising *It's remarkable that no-one saw what happened.*

remarkably *adverb*
1 extremely *a remarkably successful book*
2 extremely and not what you normally expect *Great-Grandma is remarkably active for her age.*
3 in a way that is surprising, usually when talking about something good that happens *Remarkably, we all arrived on time.*

remedy *noun* **remedies**
something that cures an illness or pain or makes a problem or difficulty go away *This is a good remedy for toothache.*

remedy *verb*
remedies, remedying, remedied
to put something right that is wrong *These mistakes can easily be remedied.*

remember *verb*
remembers, remembering, remembered
1 to have an idea still in your mind of something or someone that you knew or knew about in the past *I remember you but I can't remember your name.*
2 to suddenly think of something from the past or someone you knew in the past *As soon as I got to school, I remembered that I'd left my homework at home. When I saw that old car, I remembered my granddad.*

remembrance – renown

3 not to forget something, for example something to bring with you, or not to forget to do something, for example something that you should do *Remember your key. I must remember to text Dad.*
4 to keep something important in your mind *Remember to behave at the party.*
5 to think about someone who has died (or about a past event) and show respect for them, for example in a special ceremony

remembrance noun
1 when you remember someone who has died and show respect for them *a service of remembrance* (a religious ceremony, for example for people who have died in a war)
2 Remembrance Day or Remembrance Sunday is an occasion in November when people remember all soldiers who have died

remind verb
reminds, reminding, reminded
1 to make someone think of someone or something *Seema reminds me of my sister. That reminds me – I still haven't done my homework.*
2 to put an idea back in someone's mind about something or someone that they knew or knew about in the past *I don't remember your name – can you remind me?*
3 to make someone remember something or to help them remember it, for example something to bring with them or something that they should do *Remind me to take my umbrella. The note on the door is to remind me to brush my teeth. Mum reminded me of my promise.*

reminder noun reminders
1 something that makes you remember something or helps you remember it *I have to write Grandma's birthday card – give me a reminder tomorrow.*
2 something that makes you think of something or someone from the past
3 a letter or message that tells you something that you've forgotten or forgotten to do *This email contains your password reminder. Dad got a reminder to pay the rent.*

reminisce ['rem-in-iss'] verb
reminisces, reminiscing, reminisced
to talk or think about things that happened to you or people you knew in the past in a way that gives you pleasant memories

reminiscences noun plural
pleasant memories about things that happened to you or people you knew in the past *My uncle wrote a book about his reminiscences as a child in India.*

reminiscent adjective
if something is reminiscent of something or someone, it makes you remember them or think of them

remiss adjective
if someone is remiss, they are careless because they have not done something that they should have done or they have done something that they should not have done

remix noun remixes
a piece of music that you change, for example using a computer, in order to make a different piece of music

remnant noun remnants
a small piece or amount of something that is left over *Old remnants of cloth were piled up in a corner.*

remorse noun
a strong feeling that someone has when they are sorry for something bad they have done *The killer was full of remorse.*

remorseful adjective
if someone is remorseful, they feel very sorry for something bad they have done
remorsefully adverb

remorseless adjective
1 if someone is remorseless, they are very cruel and show no feelings towards other people, for example by not feeling sorry for something bad they have done
2 if something is remorseless, it never stops or gets weaker *the remorseless rise in the cost of food*
remorselessly adverb

remote adjective
1 far away from other places *We live in a remote village in Scotland.*
2 far away from where you are *a remote galaxy; I'd like to travel to remote countries.*

SYNONYM distant

3 far away in the past or the future *Dinosaurs lived on earth in the remote past.*

SYNONYM distant

4 very small or slight *The chances of winning are remote.*
5 not friendly or not wanting to be with other people

SYNONYM distant

remoteness noun

remote noun remotes
another word for a remote control

remote control noun
1 (plural **remote controls**) a piece of equipment for making something such as a television work from a short distance away. It uses radio or electrical waves, for example.

SYNONYM remote

2 the way that something works using this equipment *My model car works by remote control.*

remote-controlled adjective

remotely adverb
1 slightly *Megan was only remotely interested in what the teacher was saying.*
2 used in negative sentences to make the meaning stronger *I don't look remotely like my dad.*

removal noun
1 the action of removing something or someone *the removal of a stain*
2 (plural **removals**) the action or business of moving furniture from one building to another *a removal van; My dad's firm does house removals.*

remove verb
removes, removing, removed
1 to take something or someone away from somewhere *Please remove your foot from the seat.*
2 to take off something that you're wearing, such as clothes, shoes or glasses *Remove your hat before you go inside.*
3 to get rid of something *How do you remove soup stains?*

rename verb
renames, renaming, renamed
to give something a different name *Rename the file before saving it. Rhodesia was renamed Zimbabwe.*

render verb
renders, rendering, rendered
1 used for describing how or what something or someone becomes *The flood rendered lots of people homeless* (they became homeless).

SYNONYM to make

2 to give someone something such as help *Britain rendered assistance to the earthquake victims.*

rendezvous ['ron-day-voo'] noun
rendezvous ['ron-day-vooz']
1 a meeting with someone at a particular place and time
2 a meeting place

ORIGIN from 17th-century French *rendez-vous*, an order for someone to go somewhere

renew verb
renews, renewing, renewed
1 to start or do something again *I haven't seen Mohammed for months and I want to renew our friendship.*
2 to make something official, such as a passport or ticket, last longer than the date written on it, for example by getting another one *My brother's student card expired so he renewed it. I'm going to renew my library books* (ask to be allowed to borrow them for more time).
3 to change something that is damaged, old or used up and put something new in its place *My bike got a puncture so I had to renew the tyre. You need to renew the battery in your phone.*

renewable adjective
1 used for describing something such as an official document that can be made to last longer than the date written on it *a renewable work permit*
2 connected with materials, such as wood, or with types of energy, such as wind or sunlight, that go on existing and are never used up *renewable energy*

renewal noun
1 when something starts again or when you start something again
2 when something official such as a passport or ticket continues past the date written on it *My library card is coming up for renewal* (the date when I can no longer use it is soon so I need to get another one).

renovate verb
renovates, renovating, renovated
to repair and decorate something old such as a building in order to make it look like new again

renown noun
when someone is famous and people respect them, for example for the quality of their work *a pianist of great renown*

renowned *adjective*
famous, usually for something good *a renowned painter*; *a renowned restaurant*

rent *noun*
money that someone pays for living in a house, flat or room or for using a shop or office that belongs to someone else. Rent is often paid every month or week.

rent *verb*
rents, renting, rented
1 if someone rents something such as a house or shop (or rents something from someone), they pay money to the person who owns it in order to live there or to use it
2 if someone rents something such as a house or shop to someone else, they allow that person to live there or use it if that person pays them money *My parents are renting* (or *renting out*) *a room to a student.*
3 if someone rents a car or piece of equipment, they borrow it for a short time and pay to use it

SYNONYM for sense 3: to hire

rental *noun* rentals
1 when someone pays money to rent a car or piece of equipment *My aunt used to have a TV rental business.*

SYNONYM hire

2 the amount of money someone pays to rent something such as a car or piece of equipment

rented *adjective*
used for describing something that someone pays rent for *rented rooms*; *a rented car*

reorganise *verb*
reorganises, reorganising, reorganised
to change the way something is organised to make it better **reorganisation** *noun*

LANGUAGE EXTRA also spelt *reorganize* and *reorganization*

rep *noun* reps
someone who sells the products or services of a company to people or other companies by travelling around visiting them
short for: sales representative

repair *verb*
repairs, repairing, repaired
to make something work again or to make something as good as it was before *Mum repaired my bike. Dad repaired the damaged roof.*

SYNONYM to fix

repair *noun* repairs
1 work needed to repair something *Mum's car is in the garage for repairs. The TV is beyond repair* (it can't be repaired).
2 a part of something that has been repaired *I can't see the repair in the vase.*
repairer *noun*

repairman *noun* repairmen
a man whose job is to make things that are broken work again *a TV repairman*

repairwoman *noun* repairwomen
a woman whose job is to make things that are broken work again *a computer repairwoman*

repay *verb*
repays, repaying, repaid
1 to give someone back the money that you borrow from them *When will you repay my £20? I repaid Mum last week.*

SYNONYM to pay back

2 to do something good for someone when they do something good for you *You've been kind to me – how can I repay you?*

repayment *noun*
1 the action of paying money back
2 (*plural* **repayments**) an amount of money that someone pays back to someone else

repeat *verb*
repeats, repeating, repeated
1 to say something again *Can you repeat the last word?*
2 to do something again *Try not to repeat this mistake.*
3 to tell someone something that someone else has told you *Never repeat what I just told you.*
4 if food repeats on you, you still taste it in an unpleasant way after eating it, for example because it makes you burp (air comes up from your stomach) or because a chemical (stomach acid) comes up into your mouth

repeat *noun* repeats
1 when something happens or is done again *The fight between the two boys is a repeat of what happened last week. The group are giving a repeat concert on Saturday.*
2 a TV or radio programme that has already been shown on TV or listened to on the radio

repeated *adjective*
done many times *repeated warnings*

repeatedly *adverb*
many times, for example talking about something bad *He hit me repeatedly.*

repel *verb*
repels, repelling, repelled
1 if something or someone repels you, they produce a strong feeling of dislike or horror in you, for example so that you don't want to be near them or look at them *The giant's ugly face repelled her.*
2 to keep something away *This cream repels insects.*
3 to make something or someone move away or to push them away *Turn this magnet around to repel the other magnet. The police repelled the protesters.*

repellent *noun* repellents
a substance for keeping insects or animals away from you *a mosquito repellent*

repellent *adjective*
extremely horrible and unpleasant

repent *verb*
repents, repenting, repented
to say or show that you are sorry for something bad you have done, for example something against the rules of your religion

repentant *adjective*
sorry for something bad that you have done
repentance *noun*

repercussions *noun plural*
something that influences something else in a bad way or causes something bad to happen to someone or something *Matt's behaviour on the trip had repercussions for the whole school* (for example, the school was punished because of Matt's bad behaviour).

repetition *noun*
1 when you say or do something again, or when something is said or done again *This paragraph has too much repetition.*
2 (*plural* **repetitions**) something that happens again or has been said or done before

repetitive *adjective*
used for describing something in which the same thing is done or said too often *a boring and repetitive job*; *a repetitive tune*

rephrase *verb*
rephrases, rephrasing, rephrased
to say or write something using different words

replace *verb*
replaces, replacing, replaced
1 to put something back where it was before *Please replace the cup on the hook.*
2 to get rid of something and put something different or new in its place *I'll soon have to replace my old bike. Mum replaced the battery in my phone with a second-hand one. Search for the word 'Jack' in your document and replace it with 'George'.*
3 if one thing replaces another, it does what the other thing did before or is used instead of the other thing *Computers replaced typewriters a long time ago.*
4 if one person replaces another, he or she does what the other person did before, for example in a job *Who's going to replace Ms Green when she leaves?*
5 used when you mean that nothing or no-one can be as special and important to you as something or someone else *Nothing can replace the precious gold ring that I lost.*

replacement *noun*
1 (*plural* **replacements**) something that does what something else did before or is used instead of something else *This bike is a replacement for the one that was stolen.*
2 (*plural* **replacements**) someone who does what someone else did before, for example in a job *They had trouble finding a replacement for our teacher.*
3 when something or someone is replaced with another *The battery in my laptop needs replacement.*

replay ['ree-play'] *noun* replays
1 a game played a second time because no-one wins the first game, used especially about a football match that ends in a draw (with both sides having the same number of goals)
2 something such as a film, DVD, piece of music or action in a sports game that is played again

replay ['ree-play'] *verb*
replays, replaying, replayed
1 to play a game a second time because no-one wins the first game

replenish – reproduction

2 to play something again, such as a film, DVD, piece of music or action in a sports game

replenish *verb*
replenishes, replenishing, replenished
to make something as full or complete as it was before *Can I replenish your glass of lemonade?*

replete *adjective*
filled with something *It's a book about Scotland, replete with interesting facts and stories.*

replica *noun* replicas
an exact copy of something *a replica gun*

reply *noun* replies
1 something you say when someone asks you a question
2 something you write back to someone, for example when they send you a letter or email or when you're dealing with an advertisement

reply *verb*
replies, replying, replied
1 to reply to someone or to a question is to say something to someone after they have said something to you or asked you a question *Have you replied to your teacher yet about your homework? 'Where are you going?' – 'To the shop,' I replied.*
2 to reply to something such as a letter, email or advertisement is to write back to it

report *noun* reports
1 a description of something that happened *Dad read the police report on the accident. Have you seen the news report on TV?*
2 a report or school report is a document written by teachers showing how well a student has worked and behaved at school. Reports are usually given to parents two or three times a year.
3 an official or scientific document *a government report*
4 a piece of information that may or may not be true *There are reports of a fight in the playground.*

report *verb*
reports, reporting, reported
1 to give information about something that has happened or is happening now *The film star's accident was reported in the newspapers and on TV. A neighbour reported* (said) *that he saw flames coming from the building. I have nothing to report* (nothing new to say).
2 to tell someone in charge such as a police officer or teacher about something *Dad reported the theft of my mobile to the police. Adam's dog has been reported missing* (for example, the police have been told it is lost).
3 to complain to someone in charge about someone *Sam swore in class so Miss Turner reported him to the head.*
4 to report somewhere or to someone is to go there or go to them for a particular reason such as to start work *My sister reports for work at nine o'clock every day. Students must report to the nurse's office for their measles vaccination.*
5 if you report back to someone, you go and find something out then tell them what you have found out *My teacher told me to report back to her after my internet search.*

reported speech *noun*
in grammar, reported speech refers to the words that someone says when they are written down or spoken by someone else. The form of the words is changed slightly in reported speech, for example if Lydia says 'I don't feel well' (direct speech), this changes to 'Lydia said that she didn't feel well' (reported speech). Reported speech is also called indirect speech.
compare: **direct speech**

reporter *noun* reporters
someone who writes about the news for a newspaper or magazine or for TV or radio

represent *verb*
represents, representing, represented
1 to form part of the whole of something *Boys represent over half the class.*

SYNONYM to make up

2 to be considered to be something *Teaching French and Spanish represents a big change for the school.*

SYNONYM to be

3 to be an example of something *The good exam results represent a lot of hard work by students.*
4 to mean or show something or be a symbol of something *The blue lines on the map represent rivers. A smile often represents happiness.*
5 to be someone from a group of people who does something good for the whole group (such as take part in a game or competition) when they have been asked or chosen to *Jacob is representing the school in the chess competition. They've selected a new football team to represent England.*
6 to officially express the opinions and wishes of a person or group and do good things for them to help them get what they want *My cousin is the MP who represents our town in Parliament. An ambassador is someone who represents his or her country.*

representation *noun* representations
1 a symbol or picture of something
2 when someone shows or describes something or someone, or the particular way in which something or someone is shown or described *The book gives a fascinating representation of life during the Victorian period.*

representative *noun* representatives
1 someone who officially does things for a person or group to help them get what they want
2 someone from a group of people who does something good for the whole group
3 a sales representative is someone who sells the products or services of a company to people or other companies by travelling around visiting them
4 a Representative is a member of the US House of Representatives (one of the two parts of the US Congress or government)
compare: **congressman**, **congresswoman** and **senator**

representative *adjective*
used about something or someone that is similar to or the same as most others of the same type *This is a representative example of Lowry's work at that period* (similar to other examples of his work then).

repress *verb*
represses, repressing, repressed
1 to stop yourself from having or showing a feeling or something such as a memory or smile
2 to control something or someone using force

repression *noun*

reprieve *verb*
reprieves, reprieving, reprieved
1 to officially stop a prisoner from being killed as his or her punishment *The murderer has been reprieved.*
2 to officially stop something bad that was going to happen

reprieve *noun* reprieves
1 an official decision, for example by a judge, that stops a prisoner from being killed as his or her punishment
2 an official decision that stops something bad from happening *Our local library isn't going to close after all – it's had a reprieve.*

reprimand *verb*
reprimands, reprimanding, reprimanded
to tell someone in a very serious way that you are not happy with them because they have done something wrong

reprimand *noun*

reprisals ['ri-prize-erlz'] *noun plural*
violent actions done to someone, for example in a war, by a group or enemy because of something bad that was done to them first

reproach *verb*
reproaches, reproaching, reproached
1 to tell someone that they have done something wrong or not done something they should have done, in a way that shows you are unhappy with them *Mum reproached my sister for not helping me.*
2 to reproach yourself is to feel bad because you have done something wrong *You have nothing to reproach yourself for* (you've done nothing wrong so don't feel bad).

reproach *noun*
1 when someone tells you that you have done something wrong and shows that they are unhappy with you *Her voice was full of reproach. A police officer must be beyond reproach* (so good that there can be nothing at all bad about him or her).
2 (*plural* **reproaches**) words telling someone that they have done something wrong

reproduce *verb*
reproduces, reproducing, reproduced
1 to copy something such as a picture, sound or document *The artist's design is reproduced on this T-shirt.*
2 to produce or do something again in the same way *Will our team ever reproduce the success they had last week?*
3 used about animals that produce baby animals and humans that produce babies, or about plants that produce new plants usually by making seeds *How do turtles reproduce?*

reproduction *noun*
1 when or how babies, baby animals or new plants are produced
2 when someone copies something such as a picture, sound or document
3 (*plural* **reproductions**) a copy of something, for example a painting

reproductive–reside

reproductive *adjective*
connected with producing babies, baby animals or new plants

reptile *noun* **reptiles**
an animal like a crocodile, lizard or snake, with a body that is covered in hard flat pieces called scales. Its body temperature changes with the temperature outside and it lays eggs to produce young animals.

ORIGIN from Latin *repere* 'to crawl'

republic *noun* **republics**
a country that has a leader such as a president that people vote for instead of a king or queen

republican *adjective*
connected with a republic

republican *noun* **republicans**
1 someone who thinks the idea of a republic is very important
2 a Republican in the USA is someone who supports the Republican Party (one of the two main US political parties)
compare: **Democrat**

repugnant *adjective*
bad enough to really upset or shock you

SYNONYM **disgusting**

repulsion *noun*
a very strong feeling of dislike about something or someone

SYNONYM **disgust**

repulsive *adjective*
bad enough to really upset or shock you

SYNONYM **disgusting**

reputation *noun* **reputations**
the opinion that people have about someone or something, for example how good or bad they are or what they are like *Our school has an excellent reputation* (people think it is excellent). *Aaron has a reputation for working hard* (people know he works hard).

request *verb*
requests, requesting, requested
1 to ask for something politely or officially *The police officers requested extra help.*
2 to ask someone politely or officially to do something (or not to do something) *'Pupils are requested not to run in the corridor.'*

request *noun* **requests**
1 when someone politely or officially asks for something or for someone to do something *Our teacher made repeated requests for Tim and Oliver to stop talking.*
2 something that someone asks for *Your request has been accepted.*
3 a request stop is a bus stop where the buses only stop if someone waiting puts out their arm as a sign that they want to get on, or if someone on the bus wants to get off

require *verb*
requires, requiring, required
1 if someone or something requires something, they need it *If I'm going to finish my homework by tomorrow, I'll require a lot of help. This film requires concentration.*
2 to officially make someone do something or have something, for example because a rule or the law says so *Car passengers are required to wear a seat belt. The school requires all students to do PE once a week.*

required *adjective*
used about something that you must do or have, for example for a particular purpose or because a rule or the law says so *required reading* (a book or books you must read, for example when studying a subject); *Have you put the required amount of sugar into the cake?*

requirement *noun* **requirements**
1 something that someone or something must have or do *Cyclists must wear a helmet – it's a requirement. Food and water are basic requirements.*
2 something that someone wants, for example to be happy or successful *This new laptop meets all my requirements – it's fast, reliable and cheap.*

reread ['ree-reed] *verb*
rereads, rereading, reread ['ree-red]
to read something again, for example because you didn't understand it properly the first time or because you have forgotten it

rescue *verb*
rescues, rescuing, rescued
to save someone or something from a dangerous or bad situation *A woman jumped in the water and rescued the boy from drowning.* **rescuer** *noun*

rescue *noun* **rescues**
when someone or something is saved from a dangerous or bad situation *a rescue attempt*; *A kind person came to my rescue* (saved me or helped me).

research *noun*
when someone studies a subject in a very detailed way to find out new information and improve their knowledge *scientific research* **research** *verb* **researcher** *noun*

resemblance ['ri-zem-blerns] *noun*
being like someone or something in a certain way, for example looking like them *There's a slight resemblance between Paul and his brother.*

resemble ['ri-zem-berl] *verb*
resembles, resembling, resembled
to resemble someone or something is to be like them, for example to look like them *You resemble your sister. A hamster resembles a mouse.*

resend *verb*
resends, resending, resent
to send something again, especially an email that you've sent to someone and that they haven't received

resent ['ri-zent] *verb*
resents, resenting, resented
to feel angry and upset about something or with someone, for example because you think you have been treated unfairly or wrongly *I resent all the attention my baby sister is getting. You shouldn't resent your new baby sister.* **resentful** *adjective*

resentment ['ri-zent-mernt] *noun*
feeling angry and upset about something or with someone, for example because of being treated unfairly or wrongly

reservation *noun* **reservations**
1 when you arrange for something to be kept for you, for example a room in a hotel or table in a restaurant *Mum made a reservation for four people at the restaurant.*

SYNONYM **booking**

2 an area of land specially kept for a group of people to live in, especially an area for Native Americans in the US
3 if someone has reservations about something such as an idea or plan, they have serious doubts about whether it is right or good

reserve *verb*
reserves, reserving, reserved
1 to arrange to have something kept for you to use at some future time, for example a room in a hotel, seat in a theatre or table in a restaurant *My parents reserved tickets to see the dinosaur exhibition.*

SYNONYM **to book**

2 to keep something for someone so that it can't be used by anyone else *The seats in the front row are reserved for parents.*

SYNONYM **to save**

3 to keep something for a particular purpose *On sports day, the school reserved one of the classrooms as a cloakroom.*
4 to keep something for when you need it at some future time *They reserved some of the pie for later.*

SYNONYM **to save**

reserve *noun* **reserves**
1 something that can be used at some future time when it is needed *The country has reserves of natural gas. My parents have some money in reserve for an emergency.*
2 an extra player in a sports team who is asked to play in a game only if he or she is needed *a reserve goalkeeper*
3 a reserve or nature reserve is an area of land that is exactly as it exists in nature and where wild animals and plants are kept and protected
4 the quality that someone has of not showing or talking about their feelings

reserved *adjective*
1 kept for someone, for example to be used at some future time or by a particular person *reserved tickets*; *This train seat is reserved.*
2 if someone is reserved, they don't show their feelings or talk about their feelings or opinions

reservoir ['rez-erv-wah] *noun* **reservoirs**
a lake, usually man-made (built by people instead of being natural), used for storing the water that goes to people's homes

reset *verb*
resets, resetting, reset
if you reset a piece of equipment, you press a button so that it starts working again or is ready to start working again *Press this button to reset the timer to zero.*

reside *verb*
resides, residing, resided
to live somewhere, for example in a particular house, town or country

residence – respectable

residence *noun*
1 (*plural* **residences**) a building where someone lives, often a large and expensive building
2 when someone lives somewhere *a place of residence*; *a hall of residence* (building where university students live)

resident *noun* **residents**
1 someone who lives in a particular place *French residents in London*
2 someone who is staying in a particular hotel *The restaurant is open to residents only.*

resident *adjective*
living in a particular place *We've been resident in Leeds for 10 years.*

residential *adjective*
a residential area is one that only has houses or flats where people live. It doesn't have offices or factories, for example.

resign *verb*
resigns, resigning, resigned
1 if someone resigns, they leave their job, for example because they no longer want to do it or are no longer allowed to do it
2 to resign yourself to something is to accept something unpleasant because you cannot change it

resignation *noun*
1 (*plural* **resignations**) when someone leaves their job
2 (*plural* **resignations**) a letter to someone such as an employer in which someone says they are leaving their job
3 the feeling that you have when you accept something unpleasant because you cannot change it

resin ['rez-in'] *noun* **resins**
a sticky substance usually taken from plants and trees. It is used for making things such as glue and varnish (liquid for covering surfaces and making them shiny).

resist *verb*
resists, resisting, resisted
1 to stop yourself doing something that you want to do or having something that you want to have *I couldn't resist jumping on the bouncy castle. Ben can't resist chocolate biscuits* (can't stop himself eating them).
2 to refuse to accept something, or try to stop something from happening *Lots of people resist change. We wanted the bully to say sorry but she resisted* (did not want to).
3 to fight against something or someone *This medicine will help you resist infection. The country needs more weapons to resist its enemies.*
4 to not be harmed by something *How does the earth resist the heat from the sun?*

resistance *noun*
1 when someone refuses to accept something *There was no resistance to the head teacher's plan* (everyone accepted it).
2 when someone or something fights against someone or something *The protesters put up a lot of resistance. Vitamins strengthen your body's resistance to infection.*
3 a force that makes an object or vehicle move more slowly

4 a property (special quality) that a particular material has to stop electricity from passing through it *Copper has low resistance* (it allows electricity to pass through it).
5 a secret organisation that fights against an enemy that has taken control of a country or area

resistant *adjective*
1 not harmed by something *These insects are resistant to pesticides.*
2 refusing to accept something *Granddad is very resistant to change.*

-resistant *suffix*
not harmed or damaged by something *a fire-resistant material*; *a heat-resistant surface*

resistor *noun* **resistors**
an object in an electrical circuit that controls the electricity passing through it or changes it into another form of energy such as heat or light

resit *verb*
resits, resitting, resat
if someone resits a test or exam, they take it again because they did not pass the first time **resit** *noun*

SYNONYM **to retake**

resize *verb*
resizes, resizing, resized
to change the size of something, especially the size of an image on a computer screen *Click on the arrows and drag them to resize the window.*

resolute *adjective*
if someone is resolute, they really want to do something and nothing will stop them
resolutely *adverb*

SYNONYM **determined**

resolution *noun*
1 (*plural* **resolutions**) an important decision to do something, often something good *George made a New Year resolution to do more exercise* (decided to do more exercise starting from 1 January).
2 (*plural* **resolutions**) an official decision made by an organisation *a United Nations resolution*
3 when someone deals successfully with something such as a disagreement
4 the quality of not letting anything stop you from doing what you want to do

SYNONYM **determination**

5 the resolution of a story is the part towards the end when the problems and puzzles of the story are solved
6 the resolution on a computer screen or in a digital camera is the amount of detail in an image. The more pixels (dots) there are in the image, the higher (or better) the resolution.

resolve *verb*
resolves, resolving, resolved
1 to deal successfully with something such as a disagreement or problem by finding an answer to it or putting an end to it
2 to resolve to do something is to decide to do it, for example after thinking about it carefully

resort *noun* **resorts**
1 a place where people go for a holiday, for example by the sea or in the mountains *a seaside resort*; *a ski resort*
2 **as a last resort** used about a particular action that should only be done if everything else fails *We could ask Granddad to help us as a last resort.*

resort *verb*
resorts, resorting, resorted
to resort to something is to do something bad or serious because that is the only way you can get what you want *He's a drug addict who often resorts to violence.*

resound ['ri-zownd'] *verb*
resounds, resounding, resounded
to be filled with sound, or to fill a place with sound *The hall resounded with cheers. Cheers resounded through the hall.*

resource ['ri-zors'] *noun* **resources**
1 something important that a person, country or organisation has and that they can use *The country has lots of natural resources* (for example fresh water, forests, coal, metals, salt, animals or fish).
2 something that can be used to help you, for example to get information *teaching resources* (for example books or software); *The internet is an excellent resource.*

respect *noun*
1 a way of treating someone politely because you have a good opinion of them, for example because of their good qualities, their knowledge or skills or the good things they have done *We all have great respect for our teacher.*
2 polite behaviour that shows that you think about other people's feelings *Chloe always shows respect towards older people. Simon has no respect for people's feelings.*
3 when you think that something has good or important qualities, for example something that deserves to be treated well *respect for the environment*; *We should show respect for other people's religions. I have no respect for that point of view.*
4 (*plural* **respects**) used when talking about a particular detail of something or way of looking at something *Our school is different from yours in many respects* (in lots of different ways).
5 **with respect to** used when mentioning a particular subject

respect *verb*
respects, respecting, respected
1 to have respect for someone or something, for example because of their good or important qualities *I respect my teachers. We should all respect the environment. My aunt is a highly respected lawyer.*
2 to obey something such as a rule, the law or someone's wishes because you think it is important to do this

respectable *adjective*
1 used about someone who follows standards of good behaviour or about something that shows this *He's a respectable citizen who leads a respectable life. This is a very respectable neighbourhood.*
2 used about something that is fairly good or more than good enough *My spelling test results were perfectly respectable.*
respectability *noun* **respectably** *adverb*

respectful–restore

respectful *adjective*
showing respect *She kept a respectful distance from him. We should all be respectful of the environment.*
respectfully *adverb*

respective *adjective*
connected with each one of the people or things mentioned *Sophie and Holly played together in the playground then went to their respective classrooms* (Sophie went to her classroom and Holly went to hers).

respectively *adverb*
used for showing that a particular order is the same order as the people or things mentioned *Ed and Sam are eight and nine respectively* (Ed is eight and Sam is nine).

respiration *noun*
1 used for describing the way animals, humans and plants use oxygen (a gas needed to live and grow). Animals and humans get their oxygen by breathing.
2 artificial respiration is when someone blows into someone else's mouth to try to make them start breathing again after they have stopped breathing, for example after an accident

respirator *noun* respirators
a piece of equipment that helps someone to breathe

respiratory ['ri-spir-er-tree'] *adjective*
connected with breathing *a respiratory illness*

respond *verb*
responds, responding, responded
1 to give a written or spoken answer *I sent him an email but he didn't respond. Has she responded to your letter?*

SYNONYM to reply

2 to do something or behave in a certain way when something else is done or happens *She responded to the news by starting to cry. I touched the frog but it didn't respond – it was dead.*

SYNONYM to react

3 used for showing that a sick person is getting better because the treatment is working *My stepdad has a sore throat but he's responding well to the antibiotics.*

response *noun* responses
1 something you do, a particular way you behave or a feeling you have when something else is done or happens *There was an angry response from Dylan when they told him he wasn't on the team.*

SYNONYM reaction

2 a written or spoken answer *Have you received a response to your email?*

SYNONYM reply

responsibility *noun*
1 being responsible for someone or something *Who has responsibility for the dog when you're on holiday? Teachers have lots of responsibility* (for example, they have to make important decisions about children).
2 (plural **responsibilities**) something someone has to do because it is an important part of their job or of a particular activity or because they think it is the right thing to do *If you join the football team, you have to take on lots of responsibilities.*
3 used when saying that someone has done something bad or when you tell someone that you have done something bad *You were the one who broke the window – that's your responsibility. John took responsibility for the broken window* (said he did it and agreed to be punished in some way).

responsible *adjective*
1 if you are responsible for someone or something, it is your job to make decisions about them and to make sure they are safe and that nothing bad happens to them *Mr Patel will be responsible for a group of five children on the trip. If you take your phone with you, you'll have to be responsible for it.*
2 if you are responsible for something or for doing something, it is your job to do it and to make sure you do it properly *Dad is responsible for washing the dishes.*
3 to be responsible for something is also to make it happen or cause it, often something bad *Jo was responsible for breaking the window. My teacher is the one responsible for saving me from drowning. A fallen tree was responsible for his injury.*
4 if you hold someone responsible for something, you want them to be punished in some way if something bad happens in a particular situation or if they cause something bad to happen *If any of my books are missing when I get back, I'm holding you responsible.*
5 used for describing someone that you can trust to behave well and to make sensible and good decisions *She's only seven but she's very responsible.*
6 sensible and good *responsible behaviour*
7 used about something such as a job or task where you have to make important decisions yourself *Pippa was given the responsible job of locking up the classroom at the end of the day.*

responsibly *adverb*
in a sensible way that shows you can be trusted to behave well and make good decisions *Sayed always behaves responsibly.*

rest *noun* rests
1 a quiet time when you stop doing something and do nothing or when you relax and do something that makes you feel happy *You should take a rest from your homework. Mum says she's really tired and needs a few days' rest.*
2 a period of sleeping *Have you had a good night's rest?*
3 a silence between notes in music or the sign that represents this silence
4 an object that supports something *Put the guitar back on its rest.*
5 **the rest** used about the part of something that is still there or that has not been mentioned or dealt with *I spent the morning helping Dad and the rest of the day playing. I ate the rest of the cake.*
6 **the rest** also used about the other people or things in a group that are still there or that have not been mentioned or dealt with *George and Dan will stay here and the rest of you will come with me.*

rest *verb*
rests, resting, rested
1 to spend time doing nothing or very little, for example because you're tired or ill
2 to not use a part of your body *I've been running so I need to rest my legs.*
3 to rest something on or against something is to put it there so that the other thing can support it in its position *I rested my elbows on the desk. Rest the ladder against the side of the shed.*
4 if something rests on or against something, it is in a position where the other thing supports it so that it doesn't fall or move *Fran's bike was resting against a wall.*
5 to be happy about something and stop worrying *I won't rest until I know he's safe.*
6 if your eyes rest on something or someone, you look at them
7 if something such as a hope or argument rests on something, it depends on it *Our team's hopes rest on this one player.*

-rest *suffix*
used for making nouns that refer to objects supporting something *an armrest; a footrest; a headrest*

restart *verb*
restarts, restarting, restarted
1 if something restarts, or if you restart it, it starts again after it has stopped
2 if you restart a computer, you make it turn off (but not shut down completely) and then start up again automatically

restaurant *noun* restaurants
a place where you buy a meal and eat it sitting at a table

rested *adjective*
feeling or looking better and full of energy because you've had a rest *I needed that sleep – I feel rested.*

restful *adjective*
making you feel less tired and more relaxed *a restful holiday*

resting place *noun* resting places
a place where a dead person is buried

restless *adjective*
1 moving about a lot rather than staying still in one place, for example because you're bored, excited or worried *On the long bus journey to the seaside the children got very restless.*
2 unhappy with things and wanting to do something new
3 if you have a restless night, you don't sleep very well
restlessly *adverb* **restlessness** *noun*

restore *verb*
restores, restoring, restored
1 to bring something back that existed before *The police tried to restore law and order. Make a backup of your important files so you can restore them if they get deleted.*
2 to give someone something back that they had before *Yesterday's win has restored our team's confidence. Someone found the dog and restored it to its owner.*
3 to make something the way it was before, for example by repairing it *Someone damaged the painting but the museum managed to restore it.*
restoration *noun*

restrain verb
restrains, restraining, restrained
1 to stop someone (or yourself) from doing something *The bully was going to hit me but the teacher restrained him. When we saw so many toys we just couldn't restrain ourselves* (for example, we couldn't stop ourselves from playing with them).
2 to control something bad such as your anger

restraint noun
when you show control over your feelings

restrict verb
restricts, restricting, restricted
1 to make sure the amount or number of something does not get bigger than a particular amount or number *The school has restricted the number of pupils studying French to no more than 50.*
2 to stop someone or something going beyond a certain amount or number *Try to restrict yourself to no more than two hours of TV a day. The school restricted the list to just 10 names.*
3 to make something less, fewer or worse *That country restricts opportunities for people to travel abroad. Our view of the stage is restricted by this pillar. Adjectives restrict the meaning of nouns.*

restriction noun
1 (plural **restrictions**) a rule that stops someone doing or having certain things or that stops certain things happening *There are restrictions on what you can wear to school. They've brought in new parking restrictions near the school* (parents are only allowed to park in certain places).
2 when something is restricted, for example an amount or number

restroom noun **restrooms**
a room with a toilet in it in a public place such as a restaurant (especially in American English)

result noun **results**
1 something that happens or exists because of something else that happened before *My broken leg is the result of an accident* (was caused by it).
2 the final points or score at the end of a game, competition or race or at the end of an election or vote, often given with the name of a winner (or winners) *The result of the match was: Arsenal 3, West Ham 2.*
3 a piece of information that you find out after examining or studying something *I'm waiting for the results of my blood test.*
4 a situation that exists at the end of something *What was the result of your mum's meeting with your teacher?*

SYNONYM outcome

5 the mark that you get in a test or exam that shows how well you've done
6 in maths, a result is the answer to a calculation *If you divide 10 by 5, the result is 2.*
7 **results** used when you mean things that someone does successfully *Miss Wood always gets results from her pupils* (her pupils always do well).

result verb
results, resulting, resulted
1 to happen or exist because of something else that happened before *The floods resulted from weeks of heavy rain.*
2 if something results in something, it makes it happen or that thing happens at the end of it *The crash resulted in many injuries. The match resulted in a draw.*

resume ['ri-zyoom'] verb
resumes, resuming, resumed
1 if you resume an activity, or if it resumes, it starts again after stopping *We resumed our reading. The match has resumed.*
2 if you resume your place or seat, you go back to it

resumption noun

resuscitate ['ri-suss-it-ayt'] verb
resuscitates, resuscitating, resuscitated
to make someone who is unconscious start to breathe and come alive again

retail adjective
connected with the business of selling goods to the public, for example from shops. Selling goods to shops, for example from factories, is called wholesale. *retail sales; What's the retail price of this TV?* (What is the price it is sold for?) **retailer** noun

retain verb
retains, retaining, retained
1 to keep something or continue to have it *Retain your ticket and put it in the machine when you get off the train.*
2 to remember something *It's getting harder for Great-Granddad to retain facts.*

retake verb
retakes, retaking, retook, retaken
if someone retakes a test or exam, they take it again because they did not pass the first time

SYNONYM to resit

retaliate verb
retaliates, retaliating, retaliated
to do something bad to someone because they have done something bad to you

reticent adjective
if someone is reticent, they don't want to talk about something, for example about their life or their feelings

retina ['ret-in-er'] noun **retinas**
the part at the back of your eye that is sensitive to light. An image of what you look at is created on the retina and a message is sent to the brain so that you can see the image.

retire verb
retires, retiring, retired
1 if someone retires, they leave their job and stop working, usually because they have reached the official age for stopping work *My grandparents retired to Spain* (left their jobs and went to live in Spain).
2 to stop taking part in a race or sports competition, for example because you are injured, ill or tired
3 to leave a place and go somewhere, often somewhere quieter *Jenny retired to her bedroom.*

retired adjective
if someone is retired, they have left their job and stopped working *Grandma is a retired teacher.*

retirement noun **retirements**
1 when someone leaves their job and stops working *Granddad took early retirement* (stopped working before reaching the official age for stopping work).
2 the period of time after someone has stopped working *We all wished Granddad a long and happy retirement.*

retiring adjective
if someone is retiring, they don't like talking to other people because they easily get frightened or upset

retort verb
retorts, retorting, retorted
to reply quickly to someone, usually in an angry or clever way

retort noun **retorts**
an angry or clever reply

retrace verb
retraces, retracing, retraced
1 if you retrace your steps, you go back along the same path that you took, for example in order to look for something
2 if you retrace something such as someone's movements, you repeat or study the actions that they made in the past, for example to find out what they did and where they went *Our class project is to retrace the voyage of Christopher Columbus.*

retrain verb
retrains, retraining, retrained
1 to learn a new skill *Dad is retraining as a plumber.*
2 to teach someone a new skill

retreat verb
retreats, retreating, retreated
if someone retreats, they move away from a place where they are in danger or to avoid a difficult situation *The defeated soldiers retreated to the safety of the castle. I didn't want to face the bully so I retreated into the classroom.*

retreat noun **retreats**
1 when soldiers move away from a place because they are in danger or have lost a battle *Napoleon's retreat from Russia in 1812.*
2 a quiet place you go to where you can get away from other people *a country retreat*

retrieve verb
retrieves, retrieving, retrieved
to find something and bring it or get it back *The dog retrieved the ball. Seema deleted an important file but managed to retrieve it from the Recycle Bin.* **retrieval** noun

retriever noun **retrievers**
a large dog used by hunters for finding and bringing back birds or other animals that the hunters have shot

return verb
returns, returning, returned
1 to go or come back to a place where you were before *Mia returned to school.*
2 to come back from a place where you were before *What time does Mum return from work?*
3 to give, send, bring or take something back to the person or place where it was before *Have you returned your library book?*

4 to put something back where it was before
5 if something that has happened before returns, it happens again *The cold weather has now returned.*
6 to go back to the way something was before *After the snow, the trains have returned to normal.*
7 to do something because the same thing has been done to you *Jack helped me with my homework so I returned the favour.*

return *noun*
1 when someone returns from somewhere to somewhere else *On my return from school I found the door locked. Her return to Edinburgh was a happy occasion.*
2 when someone gives, sends, brings, takes or puts something back *Your library book is due for return at the end of the month.*
3 when something happens again *At last it's the return of the good weather.*
4 (*plural* **returns**) a ticket that allows you to travel somewhere, for example by train, and come back again *a day return* (when you go somewhere and come back on the same day)
compare: **single**
5 on a computer keyboard, return is a key that you press to make the computer perform an action. It is also called the enter key. *Press Return to start a new line.*
6 in return used when talking about something that you do because something has been done to or for you *I gave her a present in return for her kindness.*
7 many happy returns used as a greeting when you want someone to have a happy birthday and many more happy ones in the future

return *adjective*
1 connected with travelling to and from a place, for example by train *The return trip lasts two hours* (it takes two hours to go there and come back).
2 connected with travelling back from a place, for example by plane or train *I felt ill on the return flight.*

return match *noun* **return matches**
a second match between players or teams who have already played against each other

LANGUAGE EXTRA also called a *return game*

return ticket *noun* **return tickets**
a ticket that allows you to travel to a place, for example by train, and come back again
compare: **single ticket** and **one-way ticket**

return visit *noun* **return visits**
1 when you visit a place or person that you have already visited
2 when you visit a person who has already come to see you.

retweet *noun* **retweets**
a short message that you see on Twitter (an internet messaging service) and send again using Twitter, for example because you think it is interesting or useful **retweet** *verb*

reunion *noun* **reunions**
1 a meeting between people who have not seen each other for a long time

2 a special occasion such as a party when people come together after they have not seen each other for a long time

reunite *verb*
reunites, reuniting, reunited
to bring people together again, for example people who have been away from each other for a certain time *Ava got lost in the zoo but was quickly reunited with her parents.*

rev *verb* (informal)
revs, revving, revved
if a car or motorcycle driver revs an engine, he or she presses the accelerator pedal (in a car) or turns the throttle (on a motorcycle) to make the engine go faster while the vehicle is not moving *My brother likes revving up on his motorbike.*

Rev
short for **Reverend**

LANGUAGE EXTRA also spelt *Rev.*

reveal *verb*
reveals, revealing, revealed
1 to make something known, for example something that was secret *Why don't you reveal the truth about what happened?*
2 to show something that couldn't be seen before *Dad took off his hat and revealed his bald patch* (area with no hair on it).

revel ['rev-erl'] *verb*
revels, revelling, revelled
if someone revels in something, they get a lot of pleasure from it

revelation *noun*
1 (*plural* **revelations**) a piece of information that is made known, for example something secret or surprising *These revelations about the film star are shocking.*
2 when something is made known *The footballer resigned following the revelation of his bad behaviour.*
3 if something or someone is a revelation, they are surprising or extremely good or interesting in a surprising way *Isabella's singing was a revelation.*

reveller ['rev-er-ler'] *noun* **revellers**
revellers are people who enjoy themselves in a noisy way, for example by singing, dancing and drinking alcohol
revelry *noun*

revenge *noun*
used about something bad that you do to someone or that you want to do to someone because they have done something bad to you *Tom took revenge on the person who broke his smartphone* (did something bad to that person).

revenue ['rev-er-nyoo'] *noun* **revenues**
1 money that a business receives from selling things
2 money that a government receives from taxes

revere ['ri-veer'] *verb*
reveres, revering, revered
to have the greatest possible respect for someone or something *Nelson Mandela is revered in South Africa.*

reverence ['rev-er-erns'] *noun*
a feeling of great respect for someone or something

Reverend *noun*
a title given to important leaders in some religions, for example in the Christian and Jewish religions *Reverend Green*

reverent *adjective*
showing great respect *'I agree,' he said, in a reverent tone of voice.* **reverently** *adverb*

reverential *adjective*
full of or caused by great respect *reverential fear*

reversal *noun*
a complete change in something so that it becomes the opposite *the reversal of a decision* (not doing what was decided)

reverse *noun*
1 the reverse of something is the opposite of it *Many people think George is clever but the reverse is true.*
2 the reverse of something such as a coin or piece of material is the opposite side of it
3 reverse or reverse gear is the part of a vehicle that makes it move backwards when a driver moves that part by hand *Dad put the car in reverse.*

reverse *adjective*
opposite *Put the letters of this word in reverse order.*

reverse *verb*
reverses, reversing, reversed
1 to change something completely so that it becomes the opposite, for example so that it follows the opposite order or goes in the opposite direction *If you reverse the word 'book', you get 'koob'. The head said the school would be closed because of the snow but she reversed her decision* (the school will not be closed).
2 if a driver reverses, or reverses a car, he or she makes the car go backwards using the reverse gear

reversible *adjective*
1 if a situation is reversible, it can be changed to how it was before
2 if clothes are reversible, they can be worn on both sides, for example the inside becomes the outside
3 in science, a reversible change is one that can be made to go backwards, such as freezing and melting (you can freeze water to make ice then heat it so it becomes water again)

revert *verb*
reverts, reverting, reverted
if someone or something reverts to something, they go back to a situation or way of doing things that existed in the past *Alain often reverts to using French when speaking to his cousins.*

review *noun* **reviews**
1 a description of something artistic such as a book, film, play or piece of music, in which someone gives their opinion about it
2 a careful examination of something, for example to see if changes or improvements can be made
3 an examination of all the information connected with a particular subject

review–rhyme

review *verb*
reviews, reviewing, reviewed
1 if someone reviews something artistic such as a book, film or piece of music, they give their opinion about it, usually by writing an article, for example in a newspaper or on the internet
2 to examine or consider something carefully, for example to see if you can make changes, improve things or learn from it *Our teacher reviews our progress regularly.*

reviewer *noun*

revise *verb*
revises, revising, revised
1 to get yourself ready for a test or exam by looking at all the work that you've done for it and reading your notes *My sister is revising for her English test on Friday. Next week she'll be revising maths.*
2 to change something to make it better or more accurate *Now that I know Holly better, I've revised my opinion of her. Don't forget to buy this revised edition of the dictionary.*

revision *noun*
1 work that you have to do when getting ready for a test or exam, for example going over exercises and reading notes *I'm not going out this week – I've got revision.*
2 (*plural* **revisions**) a change made to something, or something that has been changed *I made a few small revisions to the text.*
3 when you change something to make it better or more accurate

revive *verb*
revives, reviving, revived
1 to make something or someone strong, healthy or successful again *Put the roses in water to revive them. One of the boys fainted but they soon revived him. Wales is trying to revive this old tradition. My interest in chess has recently been revived.*
2 to become strong, healthy or successful again *The flowers haven't revived yet.*

revival *noun*

revolt *verb*
revolts, revolting, revolted
1 to start to fight against people in charge or to refuse to obey them or their laws and decisions *The army revolted against the government.*

SYNONYM to rebel

2 to make someone feel very shocked or upset *That behaviour revolts me.*

SYNONYM to disgust

revolt *noun* revolts
a fight against people in charge or a refusal to obey them or their laws and decisions *the Peasants' Revolt of 1381; Many students were in revolt against university tuition fees.*

revolting *adjective*
1 bad enough to make you feel sick *a revolting smell*
2 bad enough to really shock you or upset you *That was a revolting thing to say.*

SYNONYM disgusting

revolution *noun* revolutions
1 a political event in which ordinary people get rid of the ruler or government of their country by force, completely change the way the country is organised and put new people in charge *the French Revolution of 1789*
2 a complete change in what people think and the way things are done *The internet caused a revolution in most people's lives.*
3 the movement of something, for example in a circle, around something else *the revolution of the earth around the sun*
4 one complete turn of something such as a wheel moving in a circle

revolutionary *adjective*
1 completely different from anything that has existed or been done before *a revolutionary idea; revolutionary change*
2 connected with a political revolution *a revolutionary leader*

revolutionary *noun* revolutionaries
someone who takes part in a revolution

revolutionise *verb*
revolutionises, revolutionising, revolutionised
to change something completely

LANGUAGE EXTRA also spelt *revolutionize*

revolve *verb*
revolves, revolving, revolved
1 to go round and round a central point, for example in a circle *The planets revolve around the sun.*
2 to revolve around something or someone is to have that thing or person as the main subject of interest or the main purpose *David's life seems to revolve around football.*

SYNONYM for sense 2: to centre around

revolver *noun* revolvers
a small gun that is held in one hand. It holds several bullets so it can be fired several times.

revolving *adjective*
used for describing something that goes round and round in a circle *a revolving door* (for example for going into a large building)

reward *noun* rewards
1 something good that you get because you have done something good or because of your good behaviour *My reward was a trip to London, extra spending money and lots of praise.*
2 money that someone gets from the police for information that helps them to solve a crime
3 money that someone gets from someone for finding something lost or stolen *Mum offered a reward of £50 for the return of her handbag.*

reward *verb*
rewards, rewarding, rewarded
to give someone a reward *Dad rewarded me for my good work with a new bike.*

rewarding *adjective*
if an activity is rewarding, it makes you happy because it gives you what you want or because you feel it is useful or important

rewind *verb*
rewinds, rewinding, rewound
to press a button or click an icon to make something such as a video or DVD go backwards to another position or to the beginning without playing it

ANTONYM to fast-forward

reword *verb*
rewords, rewording, reworded
to say or write something such as a sentence or question using different words to make it clearer or better

rewrite *verb*
rewrites, rewriting, rewrote, rewritten
to write something again, such as a story or speech, for example to make it better or add things to it

rhetorical question *noun*
rhetorical questions
a question you ask that is not meant to be a true question because it doesn't need an answer, for example 'How should I know?' (another way of saying 'I don't know')

rheumatism ['roo-mer-tiz-erm'] *noun*
a medical problem that makes the joints (places where two bones meet) and the muscles painful and swollen

rhino *noun* rhinos
short for **rhinoceros**

rhinoceros *noun* rhinoceroses or rhinoceros
a very heavy animal with thick skin, short legs and a large head with one or two horns on its nose. Rhinoceroses live in Africa and Asia and feed on plants and grass.

ORIGIN from the Greek words *rhinos* 'nose' and *keras* 'horn' (a nose with a horn on it)

rhododendron ['roh-der-**den**-drern'] *noun*
rhododendrons
a large bush with big pink, purple or white flowers on it. It usually has leaves that stay green all year round.

ORIGIN from Greek *rhodon* 'rose' and *dendron* 'tree'

rhombus *noun* rhombuses
a flat shape with four equal straight sides. A rhombus is usually shown as a diamond shape, with sloping sides and no right angles (angles of 90 degrees), but it can also be a square with four right angles.

rhubarb *noun*
a plant with large dark green leaves and thick pink or red stems. The stems are cooked, usually with sugar, and eaten as a sweet dish at the end of a meal, for example in a pie.

rhyme *noun*
1 (*plural* **rhymes**) a word with the same last sound as another word, for example 'make' and 'bake'
2 (*plural* **rhymes**) a short poem that has lines that end with the same sound *a book of rhymes*
3 when you use words with the same sound at the end of lines *a poem written in rhyme*

rhyme – ridiculously

rhyme *verb*
rhymes, rhyming, rhymed
1 if words rhyme, they have the same sound at the end *'Face' rhymes with 'place'*.
2 if poems rhyme, they have lines with the same sound at the end
3 if someone rhymes one word with another, they put words together with the same sound at the end *In this poem, Jamie rhymes 'dad' with 'mad'*.

rhythm *noun* rhythms
1 a regular pattern of sounds or movements, for example in music or poetry
2 a regular pattern of changes *the rhythm of the seasons*

rhythmic or **rhythmical** *adjective*
used for describing a sound or movement that is repeated following a regular pattern *rhythmic dancing* **rhythmically** *adverb*

rib *noun* ribs
one of the long curved bones in humans and animals that go round the chest from the back and form a structure that protects the heart and lungs. Humans have 24 ribs.

ribbon *noun* ribbons
1 a narrow piece of thin cloth for tying around something such as your hair or a present. It is used for many other things, for example as a decoration, as a symbol of something or for showing support for something.
2 in computing, the ribbon is the long strip, usually at the top of a computer screen, where the commands (or instructions) for a computer program are organised in groups to make them easy to find

rice *noun*
1 small white or brown seeds from a tall plant that is similar to grass. The seeds are usually boiled in water and eaten when they are soft. Boiled rice is sometimes fried afterwards.
2 a rice paddy is a field where rice is grown in water

rich *adjective* richer, richest
1 if someone is rich, they have lots of money or valuable things
2 used for describing a place where rich people live *The rich countries should help the poor ones.*
3 producing lots of money or valuable things *This computer company is the richest in the world.*
4 containing a lot of something good and useful *rich soil* (with substances that help plants to grow); *Oranges are rich in vitamin C.*
5 containing a lot of interesting and important things *the rich history of Scotland*
6 if food is rich, it contains lots of something such as fat, eggs, oil or spices so you feel full very quickly when you eat it
7 used for describing a sound, colour, taste or smell that is very strong but in a pleasant way
8 very beautiful and costing a lot of money *rich satin fabrics*
richness *noun*

riches *noun plural*
1 lots of money or valuable things
2 a large amount of something important *It's a country with lots of oil riches.*

richly *adverb*
1 in a very strong but pleasant way *richly flavoured food*
2 in a very beautiful and expensive way *a richly decorated room*
3 very much or completely *She was richly rewarded for her hard work. His punishment was richly deserved.*

Richter scale ['rik-ter] *noun*
a system for measuring the strength of an earthquake using a number from 0 to over 8

rickety *adjective*
if something is rickety, it is not strong or steady and looks like it might break or fall down, for example because it is old *We climbed the rickety stairs.*

rickshaw ['rik-shor] *noun* rickshaws
a small vehicle, usually with a roof, used for carrying one or two passengers. It is pulled by someone walking or is driven by someone riding a tricycle (type of bicycle with three wheels).

> **ORIGIN** from Japanese *jinrikisha* 'human power vehicle'. Rickshaws were first used in Japan in the 19th century.

ricochet ['rik-er-shay] *verb*
ricochets, ricocheting, ricocheted
if an object such as a ball or bullet ricochets off a surface, it hits the surface and bounces off it at a different angle

rid *verb*
rids, ridding, rid
1 if you get rid of something, you make it go away or you do something to make sure you don't have it any longer, for example because it's bad or you don't want it *I can't get rid of this cough. Get rid of that dead spider* (take it away). *The school is getting rid of its old books* (for example by throwing or giving them away or selling them).
2 if you get rid of someone, you make them go away, for example because you don't like them or want them or they do bad things to you
3 to rid someone or something of a person or bad thing is to make that person go away or to stop the bad thing from happening *The head teacher said we must rid the school of bullies. Is it possible to rid the world of disease?*

riddance *noun*
good riddance used for saying in a very strong way that you're glad someone or something bad has gone away *The bully was thrown out of school – good riddance!*

ridden
past participle of **ride**

riddle *noun* riddles
1 a difficult or funny question that you have to guess the answer to
2 something that is difficult to understand, for example a problem that has not been solved

riddle *verb*
riddles, riddling, riddled
1 to make lots of holes in something, especially with bullets *The building was riddled with bullet holes.*
2 to be riddled with something bad is to be full of it *Alfie's homework is riddled with spelling mistakes.*

ride *verb*
rides, riding, rode, ridden
1 to sit on a vehicle such as a bicycle or motorcycle and make it move *Can you ride a bike?*
2 to sit on a large animal such as a horse and make it move *I'm learning to ride a horse. Arjun has ridden on an elephant. My sister enjoys riding.*
3 to go somewhere or go a certain distance on a vehicle such as a bicycle or motorcycle *Amy rides to school. She rides two miles every day. Peter delivered the newspaper and rode off* (went away).
4 to travel as a passenger in a vehicle such as a bus or car *I walked to school while my brother rode on the bus.*
5 to travel for fun in a machine that moves you around, for example at a fair or amusement park *Let's ride on the merry-go-round.*

ride *noun* rides
1 a journey somewhere, for example on a horse or bicycle or in a car or bus *Let's go for a ride.*
2 the action of riding on something such as a horse or bicycle *Can I have a ride of your bike?*
3 a journey in a car or other vehicle that you don't have to pay for *My cousin gave me a ride to school.*

> **SYNONYM** lift

4 a machine that moves you around for fun, for example a merry-go-round or Ferris wheel at a fair or amusement park
5 the action of travelling for fun in a machine that moves you around *Do you want to have a ride on the Ferris wheel?*

rider *noun* riders
someone who rides a horse, bicycle or motorcycle

ridge *noun* ridges
1 a long narrow raised part going along a flat surface *The plough made ridges in the ground.*
2 a long narrow pointed part going along the top of a mountain or group of mountains *a mountain ridge*

ridicule *verb*
ridicules, ridiculing, ridiculed
if you ridicule someone or something, you think they are silly and you laugh at them and say unkind things

ridicule *noun*
unkind words or actions that make someone or something seem silly

ridiculous *adjective*
completely stupid or unreasonable *a ridiculous hat; a ridiculous idea*

> **ORIGIN** from Latin *ridiculus* 'making you laugh' (from *ridere* 'to laugh')

ridiculously *adverb*
1 in a way that seems completely stupid *She had ridiculously long hair.*
2 in a way that seems completely unreasonable *My laptop was ridiculously cheap.*

riding–rightly

riding *noun*
the activity of riding a horse *horse riding; a riding stable*

rifle *noun* **rifles**
a gun with a very long barrel (tube through which the bullet comes out). It is held against the shoulder when it is fired.

rifle *verb*
rifles, rifling, rifled
if someone rifles through something, they search through it because they want to find or steal something *Someone has rifled through my drawer.*

rift *noun* **rifts**
1 a large gap or hole in something such as the ground or the clouds
2 a bad quarrel between people or groups that destroys the friendship between them

rig *verb*
rigs, rigging, rigged
1 if someone rigs something such as a competition or election, they cheat and produce results that are different from what they should be, usually so that they can win
2 if someone rigs something up, they make it quickly or put it quickly somewhere *They rigged up a shelter out of leaves and branches to protect them from the rain.*
3 if you are rigged out, or if you rig yourself out, in a particular way, you wear clothes of that particular type

rig *noun* **rigs**
a structure with equipment for drilling under the ground or sea for something such as gas or oil (thick liquid, for example for making petrol) *an oil rig*

rigging *noun*
the ropes and chains on a boat or ship that support the masts (poles for holding up the sails)

right *adjective*
1 your right side or your right hand, leg, arm, ear or eye are on the side of your body that has the hand that most people write with
2 on the right side of something. In the number 46, 6 is on the right side of 4. *Walk past the school then take a right turn.*
3 with no mistakes, or completely true *That's the right answer. 'Are you leaving now?' – 'Yes, that's right'.*

SYNONYM **correct**

4 used for talking about something you should do or have, the position or situation in which something or someone should be or the time when something should be done *You made the right decision. Do you have the right shoes for running? This is the right way to shut down your laptop. Put the book back in the right place. He's walking in the right direction. This isn't the right time.*

SYNONYM **correct**

5 if you say someone is right, you mean that what they say is completely true and based on facts *'It's snowing!' – 'Yes, you're right.'*
6 if you say someone is right to do something, you agree with them and think they should do it, for example because it's sensible or reasonable *You were right to say no. Seema is right to be upset.*

7 having the particular qualities needed for something *Is Oliver the right person to be captain of the team?*
8 used for talking about standards of good behaviour *It's not right to steal. Do the right thing and say you're sorry.*
9 used for saying that something or someone is normal or the way they should be *That noise from the TV isn't right* (it's unusual). *I don't feel quite right* (healthy). *You don't look right in that jacket* (you look odd). *Let's try and put things right* (make things better and the way they should normally be).
10 if something such as a piece of equipment isn't right, it doesn't work properly *My mobile hasn't been right for ages.*
11 a slang way of showing how bad something or someone is *We're in a right mess! You're a right idiot!*
12 **the right way up** in the normal position with the top part showing at the top

ANTONYM **upside down**

13 **the right way round** in the normal position with the front part showing at the front

SIMILE 'as right as rain' means healthy or normal (sense 9)

right *adverb*
1 towards the right side *I turned right at the end of the road.*
2 exactly at a particular place or time *I was right at the front of the queue. The phone rang right in the middle of the film.*
3 all the way, for example up to, through or around something *We walked right up to the top of the building. He poked his finger right through the hole.*
4 in the way that something should happen or be done *I'm doing my homework again as I didn't do it right. Nothing is going right today.*
5 completely *We're right out of time.*
6 immediately without any waiting *Mum went into the garden and came right back* (straight back). *Leave right now.*
7 **right away** immediately without any waiting

right *noun*
1 the right side or direction *My classroom is the second one on the right.*
2 (*plural* **rights**) something that the law or a rule allows you to do or have or that you should be allowed to do or have *In this country we have the right to say what we want. The workers fought for their rights.*
3 when you are allowed to do or have something or to be a certain way *I have the right to stand here if I want to. You don't have the right to be nasty to me.*
4 a reason for something *You have no right to be angry with me.*
5 good behaviour *He doesn't know the difference between right and wrong.*
6 **the right** or **the Right** political groups who believe that property and businesses should be owned by people and not by the government, and that money and power should not be shared between more people in society

right *interjection*
1 used for getting someone's attention *Right, let's begin!*
2 used for agreeing to something *'Don't forget to take your umbrella.' – 'Right!'*
3 used for asking someone if what you say is true or if they agree with what you say *You're playing football with us tomorrow, right?*

right *verb*
rights, righting, righted
1 if something rights itself, it returns to its normal position or situation *Don't turn the tortoise upside down – it will have trouble righting itself.*
2 to right a wrong is to make a bad situation good again

right angle *noun* **right angles**
in maths, a right angle is one that has exactly 90 degrees, like the angles of a square or rectangle

right-angled *adjective*
with one angle that has exactly 90 degrees *a right-angled triangle*

right-click *verb*
right-clicks, right-clicking, right-clicked
to press the right button on your computer mouse to make your computer do something *If you select a word and right-click on it, a menu of options opens.*

righteous ['rye-chers'] *adjective*
1 if someone is righteous, they behave in a good way, for example following the standards of their religion
2 used for describing feelings you have or actions you do when you know that you are right and behaving in a good way *righteous anger* (for example when something bad has happened to you that you don't deserve)

rightful *adjective*
1 correct, especially in an official way *I put the book back in its rightful place on the library shelf.*
2 the rightful owner of something is the person it belongs to according to the law

rightfully *adverb*
used for saying strongly that something belongs to someone, for example according to the law *Give me back the stuff you took that is rightfully mine.*

right-hand *adjective*
on the right side of something *There's a picture of the poet on the right-hand page.*

right-handed *adjective*
if someone is right-handed, they use their right hand for writing and most other things

right-handed *adverb*
with your right hand *Leah writes right-handed.*

rightly *adverb*
1 used for talking about a good reason for something and when you think someone is right about something *Mum and Dad are rightly proud of both of us. Quite rightly, our teacher talked to the head about the bully.*
2 in a correct way, or in a way that is completely true *It's very late, as you rightly say. She lives in Clarendon Avenue, if I remember rightly. I don't rightly know* (I'm not certain).

rigid – rise

3 **rightly or wrongly** used for saying that something may or may not be a good thing but it is true *Rightly or wrongly, many students choose not to study a foreign language at school.*

rigid *adjective*
1 if an object is rigid, you cannot bend it, or bend it easily, or move it into a different position

SYNONYM **stiff**

2 if something such as a rule or timetable is rigid, changes to it are not allowed

SYNONYM **strict**

3 if someone is rigid, their ideas, opinions or behaviour do not change
rigidity *noun*
rigidly *adverb*
1 strictly and completely *Follow these rules rigidly.*
2 without moving, for example while in an upright position *The soldiers stood rigidly in front of the palace.*

rigorous *adjective*
1 done with or doing something with a lot of attention to small details *a rigorous medical examination*; *The police were very rigorous.*
2 very strict *rigorous safety standards*
rigorously *adverb*

rim *noun* **rims**
1 the edge that goes around the top of a container such as a cup or glass
2 the outside edge of something round or curved *the rim of a wheel*; *My dad wears glasses with gold rims.*

rind [rhymes with 'mind'] *noun*
1 the thick layer on the outside of some foods such as cheese or bacon. It is not a part of the food that you can eat.
2 the thick skin on some fruits such as lemons or melons that you remove before eating them

ring *noun* **rings**
1 a small circle of metal that you wear on a finger *Mum has a gold wedding ring.*
2 an object, for example of metal, plastic or wood, that has the shape of a circle *a shower ring* (for hanging a shower curtain); *a key ring* (metal ring for keys); *a gas ring* (metal ring that produces a flame for cooking, for example on a cooker)
3 anything that has the shape of a circle *Mark drew a ring in the sand. Our teacher told us to sit in a ring on the ground.*
4 a small area with ropes around it where boxers fight each other in a match
5 the area of a circus where the show takes place in front of an audience
6 a group of people who work together secretly or do things against the law *a spy ring*
7 the sound of something ringing, such as a doorbell or phone *Was that a ring at the door?*
8 when you make a phone call to someone *I'll give you a ring on Monday.*

ring *verb*
rings, ringing, rang, rung
1 to ring a bell is to make it produce its usual sound *Our teacher is ringing the school bell. Someone's at the door – they just rang.*
2 if a bell or phone rings, it produces its usual sound
3 to ring someone is to call them on the phone *I rang Mum on my mobile to say I'd be late. Ring up when you get home.*

SYNONYM **to phone**

4 to ring off is to stop speaking to someone on the phone
5 to ring something such as a word, picture or sentence is to draw a circle around it *Ring the correct answer with a pencil.*

SYNONYM **to circle**

6 to surround something or someone *The building was ringed by armed police officers.*

ring binder *noun* **ring binders**
a type of binder (cardboard or plastic cover) with metal rings inside for holding loose papers together. The rings go through punched holes in the papers.

ringleader *noun* **ringleaders**
someone who leads a group of people who commit crimes or cause trouble

ringlet *noun* **ringlets**
a long piece of hair with a spiral curl in it that hangs down from someone's head

ringmaster *noun* **ringmasters**
someone in charge of a circus show who introduces the performers

ring road *noun* **ring roads**
an important road that goes round a town so that traffic does not need to go into the town centre

ringtone *noun* **ringtones**
the sound that a phone makes (especially a mobile phone) when someone calls you, for example a short piece of music or series of ringing sounds

rink *noun* **rinks**
1 a rink or ice rink is a floor of ice, usually inside a building, for people to skate on using ice skates (special shoes with a metal blade at the bottom)
2 an area with a hard surface for people to skate on using roller skates (special shoes with wheels at the bottom)

rinse *verb*
rinses, rinsing, rinsed
1 to wash something, often quickly, using clean water, for example to get rid of soap or something dirty *Wash your hair with shampoo then rinse it thoroughly. Please can you rinse out these dirty glasses?*
2 to wash something with a liquid to make it clean *Rinse your mouth out with mouthwash to keep it nice and fresh.*

rinse *noun* **rinses**
1 when you wash something, often quickly, using clean water *These plates don't look very clean – please could you give them a quick rinse?*
2 rinse aid is a chemical used in dishwashers that helps to keep glass objects clean and shiny

riot *noun* **riots**
an event in which a large group of people behave in a violent and angry way in a public place, for example by damaging and burning things

riot *verb*
riots, rioting, rioted
to behave in a violent and angry way in a public place **rioter** *noun* **rioting** *noun*

riotous *adjective*
1 violent in a public place *riotous behaviour*
2 very noisy, lively and wild *a riotous party*

rip *verb*
rips, ripping, ripped
1 to make a hole in something such as cloth or paper, or to pull it apart into two or more pieces, often with a lot of force *I ripped my shirt climbing over the wall. Holly was so angry she ripped up the letter.*

SYNONYM **to tear**

2 if something rips, a hole gets made in it *My jeans ripped as I bent down.*

SYNONYM **to tear**

3 to remove something, often with a lot of force or quickly *Someone has ripped some pages out of my book.*

SYNONYM **to tear**

4 (informal) if someone rips you off, they cheat you, for example by making you pay too much for something
5 if something such as a bomb or fire rips through something, it does a lot of damage to it or destroys it completely

rip *noun* **rips**
a hole that has been made in something such as cloth or paper *Don't buy that umbrella – there's a big rip in it.*

ripe *adjective* **riper, ripest**
used for describing fruit or vegetables that have grown enough and are ready to be eaten *Very ripe bananas are yellow with spots on them.* **ripeness** *noun*

ripen *verb*
ripens, ripening, ripened
1 if fruit or vegetables ripen, they gradually change until they are ready to be eaten, for example by becoming less green, softer or sweeter *Grapes ripen in the sun.*
2 if you ripen fruit or vegetables, you wait until they are ready to be eaten, for example by keeping them somewhere such as in the sun

rip-off *noun* (informal)
when someone is cheated, for example by being made to pay too much for something

ripple *noun* **ripples**
a small wave on the surface of water, caused for example by something falling into it or by the wind blowing

ripple *verb*
ripples, rippling, rippled
to move in small waves *Look how the water ripples. A gentle breeze rippled the lake.*

rise *verb*
rises, rising, rose, risen
1 if something rises, it moves upwards or goes higher *We could see smoke rising into the air. The road starts to rise on the other side of town. The tower rises to a height of 1000 feet* (is 1000 feet high).
2 if the sun rises, it appears in the sky in the early morning *The sun rises in the east and sets in the west.*

417

rise–roar

3 to become bigger, higher, better or stronger, for example when talking about amounts, levels, numbers or standards *Prices are always rising. The marks I've been getting for my homework have risen this term.*
4 if your voice rises, you speak louder
5 another way of saying to stand up *The children rose when the teacher came in.*
6 another way of saying to get up out of bed *The soldiers rose at dawn.*
7 to rise up against (or to rise against) someone or something such as a leader or government is to start to fight against them

> SYNONYM to rebel

8 if a river rises somewhere, that is the place where it begins to flow *The Mississippi River rises in Minnesota.*
9 if bread or cakes rise when they are baked, they swell up and become softer because yeast or baking powder has been used

rise *noun*
1 (*plural* **rises**) an increase in something such as an amount, number, level or standard *price rises; a rise in temperature*
2 (*plural* **rises**) an increase in the money someone gets for doing their job
3 when something or someone becomes powerful or successful *the rise of communism in China; the rise to fame of Charles Dickens* (when Dickens became famous)
4 to give rise to something is to cause it

risk *noun* **risks**
1 the chance that something bad or dangerous might happen *Don't poke your finger into the cage – there's a risk the hamster might bite.*
2 something bad or dangerous that might happen *This toy is a fire risk* (something in it could start to burn).
3 if you take a risk, you do something even though something bad or dangerous might happen
4 **at risk** in danger *Riding your bike with no brakes puts your life at risk.*

risk *verb*
risks, risking, risked
1 to put yourself in a situation where something bad might happen if you do something (or if you don't do something that you should do) *If I don't do my homework, I risk being told off.*
2 if you risk something important such as your life or your money, you go ahead and do something even though you might lose it *My friend risked her life to save me* (she could have died trying to save me).

risky *adjective* **riskier, riskiest**
if something is risky, it is dangerous or something bad might happen because of it

risotto ['ri-zot-oh'] *noun* **risottos**
an Italian food containing rice cooked with meat, fish or vegetables

rite *noun* **rites**
a ceremony, for example in a particular religion

ritual *noun* **rituals**
1 a ceremony with regular activities and words always done and said in the same way *religious rituals*

2 something that someone does regularly and always in the same way

rival *noun* **rivals**
1 a person, group or business that does the same activity as another but tries to do things better or get more things *The two schools have always been rivals in trying to attract the best students. Frankie and I are rivals for the first prize* (both of us want to get it). *There was a fight in the street between two rival gangs* (for example, both gangs want to control the same area).
2 something that is the same type of thing as something else *This dictionary is better than its rivals* (other similar dictionaries).

> ORIGIN from Latin *rivalis* 'someone sharing the same stream as you' (from *rivus* 'stream'). A rival is someone who wants to use more of the stream than someone else.

rival *verb*
rivals, rivalling, rivalled
to be as good as something or someone else *The beauty of the Scottish Highlands rivals anything you see in Europe.*

rivalry *noun* **rivalries**
when people, groups or businesses try to do things better or get more things than others *There's a lot of rivalry between me and my brother.*

river *noun* **rivers**
1 a wide or narrow area of fresh water that flows in a long line across the land and into the sea, a lake or another river *The River Thames flows through London.*
2 used for describing something that flows like a river *Rivers of lava flowed downhill from the volcano.*
3 a river bed is the bottom of a river

riverside *noun*
the land along the side of a river *a riverside restaurant*

rivet ['ri-vit] *noun* **rivets**
a thick metal pin with a round top, used for joining one piece of metal to another

rivet ['ri-vit] *verb*
rivets, riveting, riveted
1 to join pieces of metal together with metal pins
2 if someone is riveted, they are really interested in something or someone and give complete attention to them *We listened to the story of Rumpelstiltskin, completely riveted.*
3 if you are riveted to something or your eyes are riveted to it, you cannot stop looking at it, for example because you are so interested or frightened *Time for bed – you've been riveted to the TV all evening.*

riveting *adjective*
really interesting

> SYNONYM fascinating

Riviera ['riv-ee-air-rer] *noun*
the area of a country next to the sea where it is warm and where there are lots of beaches and holiday towns *the French Riviera* (part of the Mediterranean coast near the Italian border)

road *noun* **roads**
1 a long piece of ground with a hard surface that cars, buses, lorries, bicycles and other vehicles travel on *a road accident; a road sign* (with information on it at the side of a road); *Be careful crossing the road.*
2 a street with houses or buildings on it *My grandparents live on a quiet road with trees on both sides. Ollie lives in Acacia Road.*
3 a way that leads to a particular result *the road to recovery*
4 **by road** travelling by car, bus, bicycle or another vehicle
5 **down** (or **up** or **along**) **the road** a short distance away on the same road *My best friend lives down the road.*
6 **over** (or **across**) **the road** on the opposite side of the road

roadblock *noun* **roadblocks**
1 a place on a road where police officers or soldiers stop vehicles in order to check them
2 the structure or objects used for stopping vehicles on a road *Police have set up roadblocks around the town.*

> LANGUAGE EXTRA also spelt *road block*

road rage *noun*
angry or violent behaviour by the driver of one vehicle towards the driver of another

road safety *noun*
knowing how to behave safely, or ways of behaving safely, when crossing the road, driving a car or riding a bike

road sense *noun*
if someone has road sense, they know how to behave in a safe and sensible way when they walk along roads, drive a car or ride a bike

roadside *noun*
the area along the side of a road *a roadside café*

roadway *noun* **roadways**
the part of a road that traffic travels along

roadworks *noun plural*
work being done to repair a road, or the place in a road where the work is being done

roadworthy *adjective*
safe to be used on the road *My old bike isn't roadworthy any more.*

roam *verb*
roams, roaming, roamed
1 to walk or travel around without going in any particular direction and without doing anything in particular *You should be at school, not roaming around the streets.*

> SYNONYM to wander

2 if animals roam, they move around freely *The farmers let their sheep roam freely across the meadow.*

roar *verb*
roars, roaring, roared
1 when a lion roars, it makes a loud deep noise that is its own special sound
2 if a person roars, he or she says something in a loud deep or angry voice *'Sit down at once!' he roared.*
3 to laugh out loud *The audience roared with laughter.*

418

roar – role

4 if something such as thunder, the wind or an engine roars, it makes a lot of noise *Planes were roaring overhead.*
5 to go somewhere very fast making a lot of noise *I watched my cousin roar past on his motorcycle.*

roar *noun* roars
1 a loud deep noise that a lion makes
2 a loud deep or angry sound made by someone's voice
3 a loud noise made by something such as thunder, the wind or an engine *the roar of traffic*
4 the sound of a person or many people laughing

roast *verb*
roasts, roasting, roasted
to cook meat or vegetables in an oven or over a fire *Dad roasted a chicken. The potatoes are still roasting.*

roast *adjective*
cooked in an oven or over a fire *roast chicken*

roast *noun* roasts
a large piece of meat that has been cooked in an oven, or one that is going to be cooked in an oven

roasting *adjective*
very hot *I'm roasting.*

rob *verb*
robs, robbing, robbed
to steal something from someone or from a place such as a bank, shop or company *Our local bank has been robbed. My sister was robbed of her mobile phone* (it was stolen from her).

robber *noun* robbers
someone who steals from someone or somewhere *a bank robber*

robbery *noun* robberies
the crime of stealing from someone or somewhere *armed robbery* (done by someone carrying a gun)

robe *noun* robes
1 a long loose piece of clothing worn over other clothes by people such as judges, kings and queens, usually in official ceremonies and duties
2 a soft loose coat that people wear indoors, for example before or after a shower
short for: **bathrobe**
3 the American word for a dressing gown

robin *noun* robins
a small brown or grey bird that has an orange or red neck and front

CULTURE NOTE the *robin* is considered to be a friendly bird and a symbol of Christmas. It doesn't leave Britain in winter like many other birds do and can be seen in gardens around Christmas time. Known as *robin redbreast*, it often appears on Christmas cards and decorations.

robot ['roh-bot'] *noun* robots
a piece of equipment controlled by a computer that can move and perform actions in a similar way to humans

robust *adjective*
1 strong and healthy *a robust child*
2 strong and not likely to break or be damaged easily *a robust pair of shoes*
3 used about something done, shown or expressed with a lot of energy *robust opinions*

robustly *adverb* **robustness** *noun*

rock *noun*
1 the stone that the earth is made of *They dug through the rock to try to rescue the trapped miners.*
2 (*plural* rocks) a large mass of stone, for example in the sea, sticking out of the ground or lying on the ground *The ship hit some rocks.*
3 (*plural* rocks) a stone, often one that someone throws *The protesters threw rocks at the police.*
4 a very hard sweet shaped like a solid tube. You often buy it at the seaside and it has the name of a town going all the way through the tube. *a stick of Brighton rock*
5 rock or rock music is modern music with a simple pattern of strong sounds and songs that are easy to remember. It is often played with electric guitars and drums. *a rock group*; *a rock star* (famous singer or musician)

rock *verb*
rocks, rocking, rocked
1 to move backwards and forwards or from side to side, or to move someone in this way *I rocked gently in the chair as I read my book. Dad was rocking the baby to sleep.*
2 to shake violently *A bomb rocked the whole building. There was an earthquake and the whole house rocked.*

rock and roll *noun*
a type of music for young people that was popular in the 1950s. It had simple tunes and a simple pattern of strong sounds. It was often played on electric guitars.

rockery *noun* rockeries
an area in a garden (or a whole garden) where stones or small rocks have been carefully arranged so that plants grow among them and over them

LANGUAGE EXTRA also called a *rock garden*

rocket *noun* rockets
1 a vehicle for travelling in space. It is shaped like a large tube with a point at the top.
2 a weapon shaped like a long tube with a point at the top that is fired into the air and explodes when it hits something
3 a type of firework, usually a small tube on a stick. It is fired into the air where it explodes and produces lots of coloured lights.
4 a vegetable eaten in salads. It has dark green leaves with a very strong taste.

rocket *verb*
rockets, rocketing, rocketed
1 to increase a lot very quickly *The price of mobile phones has rocketed.*
2 to become successful very quickly *His album has rocketed to number one in the charts* (lists of the most popular music).

rocking chair *noun* rocking chairs
a chair with arms and with two curved pieces fixed to the bottom of its legs so that you can move backwards and forwards when you sit in it

rocking horse *noun* rocking horses
a toy horse usually with two curved pieces fixed to the bottom of its legs so that you can move backwards and forwards when you sit on it

rocky *adjective* rockier, rockiest
1 used for describing something made of rocks or with lots of rocks on it *a rocky path*; *the rocky surface of Mars*
2 (*informal*) used for describing situations where there are problems *Things are a bit rocky between my brother and his girlfriend.*

rod *noun* rods
1 a long thin and usually round piece of wood, plastic or metal *a curtain rod* (for holding up curtains)
2 a fishing rod is a long thin pole for catching fish, usually made from glass fibres (long thin threads) or bamboo (grass with hard hollow stems). It has a string attached to it with a hook at the end.

rode
past tense of **ride**

rodent *noun* rodents
an animal such as a mouse, rat, hamster or squirrel. It has long sharp front teeth that it uses for gnawing (biting on things many times).

ORIGIN from Latin *rodere* 'to gnaw'

rodeo ['roh-dee-oh' or 'roh-**day**-oh'] *noun* rodeos
a sports event, usually in the US, in which people try to control wild horses by riding them or other animals such as cows or bulls by lassoing them (catching them with a long rope with a loop at the end)

roe *noun*
a mass of eggs inside a female fish, for example a salmon or cod, that is used as food

rogue *noun* rogues
1 someone who behaves badly, especially someone you like even though they behave in this way

SYNONYM rascal

2 someone who behaves in a dishonest or criminal way

roguish *adjective*
used about what someone does or says or about the way someone looks when you think they might be doing something slightly bad or wrong *roguish behaviour*; *a roguish grin*

SYNONYM mischievous

role *noun* roles
1 a role in a play or film is the character that an actor plays, or all the words and actions of a character that an actor plays *I played the role of the prince in the school play.*

SYNONYM part

2 used for showing that something or someone is connected with something, or used about the influence that something or someone has on something *The internet*

419

role-play–roof

plays an important role in people's lives (has an influence on people's lives). *The bully admitted his role in the attack.*

SYNONYM part

3 what someone is supposed to do because it's their responsibility to do it *It's the teacher's role to make sure everyone does their homework.*

SYNONYM job

4 a role model is someone people try to be like because they respect them very much

role-play noun role-plays
an activity in which you act the part of another person, for example to help you learn a new skill or a foreign language
role-play verb

roll verb
rolls, rolling, rolled
1 if something rolls, it turns round and round like a ball or wheel as it moves along *The coin rolled under my desk.*
2 if you roll something, you make it move in this way *If your suitcase has wheels, you can roll it along the ground.*
3 to move somewhere without stopping *Tears were rolling down his cheeks.*
4 to move from side to side *The ship was rolling dangerously in the storm.*
5 to make something into the shape of a tube or ball, for example by wrapping it around itself or pushing the parts of it together *The teacher rolled up the map and put it back in the drawer. You make a snowball by rolling the snow into a ball.*
6 to make a substance flat by pressing something heavy all over it *Dad was rolling the pastry to make the pie.*
7 to produce a series of long low sounds, used for example when talking about drums or thunder
8 if you roll over while lying down, you change the position of your body, for example from being on your back to being on your front
9 if you roll up your sleeves or something such as your trousers, you fold the sleeves or the trouser legs over several times to make them shorter *My brother rolled up his jeans and went for a paddle.*
10 if you roll a car window up or down, you turn a handle or push a button to make it move up or down
11 (informal) if someone rolls up somewhere, they arrive there

roll noun rolls
1 a tube of something such as paper or cloth. It is made by wrapping the paper, cloth or other material around the tube or around itself. *a roll of wallpaper; a toilet roll* (roll of toilet paper)
2 a small amount of bread, usually made in a round shape but sometimes in a long shape. It is cut in half and buttered and often filled with food. *a cheese and tomato roll*

LANGUAGE EXTRA also called a *bread roll*

3 a long low sound *a drum roll*
4 an official list of names *a roll of honour* (names of people who have done good and important things)

roller noun rollers
1 a piece of equipment (or a part of a piece of equipment) that is made of metal, plastic or wood and shaped like a tube. It is used for rolling over a surface to make it flat or to crush it, or for spreading something such as paint over it. Rollers are also used in a conveyor belt (long flat band) for moving objects along.
2 a small thick wheel shaped like a tube that is fixed to the bottom of something such as a piece of furniture for moving it around
3 a small plastic tube for rolling hair around to make curls
4 a big wave that comes onto the seashore

SYNONYM breaker

5 in an amusement park, a roller coaster is a kind of small railway that you ride on for fun. It goes up and down along steep slopes and round bends that change direction suddenly.

Rollerblade noun Rollerblades (trademark)
a special shoe with a single line of four wheels at the bottom for skating on a hard surface **rollerblade** verb

roller skate noun roller skates
a special shoe with two pairs of wheels at the bottom for skating on a hard surface

roller-skate verb
roller-skates, roller-skating, roller-skated
to skate on a hard surface using roller skates **roller-skating** noun

rollicking noun rollickings (informal)
if someone gives you a rollicking, they speak to you in an angry voice because you've done something wrong

rolling adjective
1 rolling hills are hills that are small with gentle round slopes. They are usually pleasant to look at.
2 a rolling pin is a piece of wood or plastic shaped like a long tube. It is used for rolling over dough (flour and water) to make it flat before cooking it.

ROM noun
a type of computer memory for storing important information that your computer needs, for example the instructions for starting up. You cannot change this information or add more information to it.
short for: read only memory
compare: RAM

Roman noun Romans
someone from Rome, especially ancient Rome

CULTURE NOTE the ancient *Romans* lived from about 800 BC to about AD 500 and ruled a very large area including most of Europe, known as the Roman Empire. In AD 43, the Romans conquered Britain and ruled for nearly 400 years.

Roman adjective
connected with Rome, especially ancient Rome and the ancient Romans *a Roman road; the Roman Empire*

Roman Catholic noun Roman Catholics
a Christian who is a member of the Roman Catholic Church. Roman Catholics accept the Pope as their leader.
Roman Catholic adjective

Roman Catholicism noun
the religion of Roman Catholics

romance noun
1 (*plural* romances) a short love relationship with someone *My sister had a holiday romance.*
2 the strong feeling that someone has when they have a love relationship with someone
3 a strong feeling of excitement connected with a new or unusual activity or a new, beautiful or mysterious place *the romance of flying in a hot-air balloon; My sister lives in Paris because she loves the romance of the place.*
4 (*plural* romances) a book, film or play about love between two people

Romania noun
a country in South-East Europe

Romanian adjective
connected with Romania or the Romanian language

Romanian noun
1 the language people speak in Romania
2 (*plural* Romanians) someone from Romania

Roman numeral noun Roman numerals
any one of the written letters I, V, X, L, C, D and M that are used instead of numbers or words, for example page XV (page 15) or Henry VIII (Henry the Eighth). The numerals were first used by the ancient Romans.
compare: Arabic numeral

romantic adjective
1 connected with love or making someone have feelings of love or think about love *romantic music; a romantic novel*
2 very exciting, for example because of being new, unusual, beautiful or mysterious *a romantic journey by boat around England; the romantic landscape of the Highlands of Scotland*
3 not connected with real situations but based on imagination *My cousin has this romantic idea that he's going to be a film star.*
romantically adverb

romp verb
romps, romping, romped
if people or animals romp, they play happily and with lots of energy, often in a noisy way

rompers noun plural
1 a piece of clothing for babies and very young children that covers the body, legs and sometimes arms
2 a piece of clothing for women and girls that covers the body and the top of the legs

LANGUAGE EXTRA also called a *romper suit*

roof noun roofs
1 a covering that forms the top part of a building, vehicle or structure such as a tent or shelter
2 the highest part of an area under the ground such as a cave or tunnel
3 the hard top part inside your mouth

420

4 **under the same roof** in the same home or building as someone else

LANGUAGE EXTRA *roofs* is the usual plural of *roof*, but the plural *rooves* is sometimes used instead

roofer noun roofers
someone who repairs roofs or puts new roofs on buildings

roof-rack noun roof-racks
a metal frame fixed to the top of a car, used for carrying luggage or a large object such as a bicycle

rooftop noun rooftops
the top surface of the roof of a building

rook noun rooks
1 a large black bird that is a type of crow. Groups of rooks build their nests together at the tops of trees.
2 a piece in the game of chess that is shaped like a round castle and also called a castle. It can only move in a straight line across the board.

room noun
1 (plural **rooms**) a place inside a house, flat or building that has its own walls, floor, ceiling and door (or doors)
2 (plural **rooms**) a room in a house, flat or hotel with a bed or beds for sleeping in *I'm in my room doing my homework.*
3 all the people in a room *The whole room burst out laughing.*
4 the space that is needed for someone or something *Is there enough room for me at the table? I made room on the shelf for the extra books* (moved things so there was enough space for them).
5 used when you mean it's possible for something to happen or exist *Your homework is good but there's still room for improvement* (it's possible for you to improve it). *In the exam there's no room for mistakes* (you shouldn't make mistakes).

roomful noun roomfuls
the number of people or things, or the amount of something, that a room can hold *a roomful of children*

roomy adjective roomier, roomiest
1 if something such as a house or car is roomy, there's plenty of room inside
2 if a piece of clothing is roomy, it is not tight against your body and you have plenty of room to move *I like my sweaters and jeans roomy.*

roost verb
roosts, roosting, roosted
if a bird roosts somewhere, it goes there to rest or sleep

roost noun roosts
a place such as a branch where a bird rests or sleeps

rooster noun roosters
a male chicken

SYNONYM cock

root noun roots
1 the part of a plant that grows under the ground. Roots hold the plant in the soil and take in water and food from the soil.
2 the part of something such as a tooth or hair that grows under the skin

3 the cause of something, usually something bad *They're trying to get to the root of the problem.*
4 in maths, the root of a number is the number that you multiply by itself a certain number of times to get a bigger number. For example, a square root is a number multiplied by itself (3 is the square root of 9, which is 3 × 3) and a cube root is a number multiplied by itself twice (2 is the cube root of 8, which is 2 × 2 × 2).
5 in grammar, a root or root word is the part of a word that contains the meaning. You can add other parts to it, such as a prefix (at the beginning) or suffix (at the end), to make a new word. For example, 'dis-' can be added to the root word 'appear' to make 'disappear'.
6 **roots** where something or someone comes from, or where something starts to exist *This music has its roots in Eastern Europe. Dad traced his roots to Ireland.*

SYNONYM origins

7 **to take root** to be accepted by lots of people *These ideas began to take root in England in the 1960s.*
8 **to take root** also used about plants when you mean they grow roots somewhere

root verb
roots, rooting, rooted
1 to grow roots in the ground *The runner beans are beginning to root.*
2 to search for something by moving things around or turning things over *The foxes have been rooting around in the dustbins.*
3 to root for someone is to support them, for example in a sports competition
4 to root something or someone out is to find them and get rid of them *Our school needs to root out the bullies.*

rope noun ropes
1 a thick string made by twisting together lots of thinner strings. Ropes are used for many things such as tying, lifting or pulling large or heavy objects.
2 to learn or know the ropes is to learn or know how to do something
3 to show or teach someone the ropes is to show or teach them how to do something

rope verb
ropes, roping, roped
1 to tie people or things together with ropes
2 (informal) if you rope someone in, you get them to do something, usually with other people and when they don't want to do it *I got roped in to tidying up the house after all the guests had left.*
3 if police officers or soldiers rope off a place, they put ropes around it to stop people going there or coming from there

ropey adjective ropier, ropiest (informal)
1 slightly ill *I'm feeling ropey today.*
2 in bad condition *a ropey old pair of jeans*
3 bad *Jo's spelling is pretty ropey.*

LANGUAGE EXTRA also spelt *ropy*

rose noun
1 (plural **roses**) a beautiful flower, usually red, pink or white, that has a sweet and pleasant smell and thorns (sharp points) along its stem *a bunch of roses*

2 (plural **roses**) a rose or rose bush is the plant that produces roses *Please can you water the roses?*
3 a pink or dark pink colour

rose adjective
having a pink or dark pink colour

rose
past tense of **rise**

rosette noun rosettes
1 a decoration shaped like the flower of a rose and made out of cloth, usually with two ribbons hanging down from it. It is often given to someone who has won a prize or worn by someone to show that they support a team or group.
2 any design or decoration shaped like a rose

Rosh Hashanah ['rosh-ha-sha-ner'] noun
the Jewish New Year holiday. It usually takes place in September.

rostrum noun rostrums
a raised structure for someone to stand on, for example when talking to an audience or conducting an orchestra

rosy adjective rosier, rosiest
1 pink in a way that looks attractive *rosy cheeks*
2 if a situation is rosy, it is likely to be good and successful or it is full of hope *a rosy future*

rot verb
rots, rotting, rotted
1 if something rots, it goes bad because tiny organisms feed off it *The wood around the windows is starting to rot. There are rotting bananas in the fruit bowl.*

SYNONYM to decay

2 to make something go bad *These sweets will rot your teeth.*
3 if someone rots or is left to rot in prison, they grow old there and are forgotten about

rot noun
1 when something goes bad because tiny organisms feed off it
2 the part of something that has gone bad
3 an informal word for nonsense (stupid words or ideas)

rota noun rotas
a list of people's names that shows when each of them is supposed to do a particular task

rotate verb
rotates, rotating, rotated
1 to go round and round with a circular movement *The blades of the fan are rotating.*
2 to move something round in a circular direction *Can you rotate your wrist? Click on the arrow to rotate the photo clockwise.*
3 in maths, if you rotate a shape such as a square, you take one of its corners and keep turning the shape round so that it fits a certain number of times into the same shape that has been drawn somewhere
4 if a job rotates, or if a group of people doing a job rotate or someone rotates them, people take it in turns to do the job at different times

rotation noun
1 when something goes round and round with a circular movement *the rotation of the earth*
2 (plural **rotations**) one complete circular movement
3 in maths, a rotation is the way a shape is moved so that it fits a certain number of times into the same shape that has been drawn somewhere. A shape has rotation symmetry when it fits into its drawn shape in two or more ways, for example a square fits into a square in four separate ways. The number of times a shape can be made to fit in this way is called an order of rotation symmetry. For example, a square has an order of 4.
compare: **reflection** (sense 2) and **translation** (sense 3)

rotor noun **rotors**
a part of a piece of equipment that goes round and round, especially one of the blades (long flat parts) of a helicopter

rotten adjective
1 if something such as a fruit is rotten, it has gone bad because of tiny organisms feeding off it
2 an informal way of saying very bad or unpleasant *rotten weather*; *I'm a rotten swimmer. Don't be rotten to your sister.*
3 an informal way of giving extra importance to a word when you're very angry or upset *I didn't want to go to your rotten party anyway!*
rottenness noun

Rottweiler noun **Rottweilers**
a large strong dog that has short black hair with several small brown areas. It is often used for guarding buildings, as a guide dog (helping someone who cannot see) or by the police, for example to help rescue people in accidents.

rouble ['roo-berl'] noun **roubles**
a unit of money in Russia

> **LANGUAGE EXTRA** also spelt *ruble*, especially in American English

rough adjective **rougher, roughest**
1 not flat or smooth but full of bumps or hard parts *rough ground*; *a rough mountain road*
2 not feeling smooth or soft when you touch something *rough skin*; *a rough edge*
3 if the sea is rough, it has lots of big waves because the weather is stormy
4 if someone is rough, they use too much strength and energy and they are not careful or gentle in their movements *Don't play with the rough boys in your class.*
5 also used about the actions and behaviour of rough people *rough behaviour*; *rough play*
6 used for describing a place where there is a lot of rough behaviour or crime *a rough part of town*; *a rough school*
7 a rough voice is one that is unpleasant and loud or angry
8 not exactly right but mostly correct *What's the rough amount of time this homework should take? Give me a rough idea when you'll be home.*
9 not completely finished or not containing many details *a rough drawing*; *rough notes*; *a rough plan*
10 used for describing something such as paper or an exercise book where you write down useful things such as notes and ideas *I did my maths homework first on rough paper.*
11 (informal) if someone looks rough, they look very bad, for example because they are ill, tired, dirty or injured
12 (informal) if someone such as a criminal or bully looks rough, they look very unkind and unpleasant
13 an informal way of saying very difficult *We've had a rough time this week.*
roughness noun

roughage noun
a substance in fruit, vegetables and grains that your body cannot digest (change in the stomach). Roughage is useful because it helps food pass more quickly through the body.

> **SYNONYM** fibre

roughen verb
roughens, roughening, roughened
to make something rough

roughly adverb
1 not exactly but slightly more or less *roughly 20 minutes*; *roughly half the class*
2 also used when talking about slight differences *We had roughly the same idea.*
3 with too much strength and energy and without being gentle in any way *George pushed me roughly in the playground.*

roulette ['roo-let'] noun
a game played in a casino (where people try to win money). A small ball is thrown onto a moving wheel with numbers marked around it. A player chooses a number and wins money if the ball stops at that particular number when the wheel stops.

round adjective **rounder, roundest**
1 shaped like a circle *a round table*
2 shaped like a ball, either exactly or roughly *A football is round. I have a round face.*
3 shaped like a curve or part of a circle *a round arch*; *a square table with round corners*
4 a round number or figure is one given as a whole number, often ending in zero, and not as a fraction
5 a round trip is a journey to a place and back again, for example by train or car

round preposition & adverb
1 moving in a circular way like a wheel or in a roughly circular way *You have to keep turning the handle round and round. The earth goes round the sun.*
2 on all sides of something or someone *There's a wall round the garden. It goes all the way round. Gather round, children!*
3 in or to lots of different places *I love walking round Edinburgh. He's always rushing round somewhere. The teacher showed us round the school.*
4 to lots of different people *Hand the chocolates round.*
5 in a particular direction or in the opposite direction *Granddad has just gone round the corner. She turned round when I called her.*
6 near to somewhere *There are no shops round here. If you're going out on your bike, don't go far – stay round the house.*
7 to someone's home *Can you come round on Sunday?*
8 **round about** slightly more or less than something such as a number, amount or time *round about 20 people*; *round about six o'clock*

round noun **rounds**
1 a part of a competition or sports event *Daniel reached the third round of the quiz.*
2 an event such as a meeting or discussion that is a part of a series of events *There'll be another round of talks between teachers and parents tomorrow.*
3 the job of making regular visits to people or places *The doctor is on her rounds* (visiting patients at home or in hospital).
4 the job of delivering things such as letters or newspapers to houses or buildings *a delivery round* (delivering the post or newspapers); *a paper round* (delivering newspapers)
5 a slice of bread, or a sandwich made from two slices of bread *a round of toast* (one whole slice of toast); *a round of cheese sandwiches* (one whole sandwich, usually cut into two or four pieces)
6 a round of drinks is a number of drinks such as beers that someone buys for every person in a group
7 a bullet or bullets fired from a gun
8 a type of song in which two or more people sing the same tune but start at different times in the song
9 a round of applause is a time when an audience shows that they like a performance by clapping their hands

round verb
rounds, rounding, rounded
1 to go round something such as a corner or bend
2 if you round a number up or down, you make it more or less by choosing a whole number or number ending in zero (or two or three zeros) that is close to it. You round a number to get a quick idea of the number, for example before doing a calculation. *187 can be rounded up to 200. $21\frac{1}{4}$ can be rounded down to 21 or to 20.*
3 if you round something off, for example an event or activity, you finish it in a pleasant way *We rounded off the evening with a stroll through the park.*
4 if you round up people or animals, you find them and bring them together
5 if police or soldiers round people up, for example criminals, they find them and take them away

roundabout noun **roundabouts**
1 a big circle where three or more roads join each other. Vehicles drive round the circle in one direction until they get to the road that they want to drive into.
2 a round machine, for example in a playground, that you sit or stand on while someone pushes it to make it go round and round
3 another word for a merry-go-round

roundabout adjective
1 not going straight from one place to another *a roundabout route*
2 not saying what you think in a clear or honest way *He answered the question but in a roundabout way.*

> **SYNONYM** indirect

rounded *adjective*
shaped like a curve or part of a circle *My smartphone has rounded edges.*

rounders *noun*
a game played by two sides with a bat and ball. Players have to hit a ball and run round four sides of a square.

Roundhead *noun* **Roundheads**
someone who supported the Parliament and fought against King Charles I in the English Civil War of the 17th century
compare: **Cavalier**

roundly *adverb*
strongly or completely *The head teacher has been roundly criticised.*

round-up *noun* **round-ups**
1 when police or soldiers find people such as criminals and take them away
2 a short report giving the main news or facts about something *a news round-up*

rouse *verb*
rouses, rousing, roused
1 to cause something such as a strong feeling or attitude *Feelings of suspicion have now been roused.*
2 to make someone want to do something *They were roused to action.*
3 to wake someone up

rousing *adjective*
making someone have strong feelings such as excitement or anger *a rousing speech*

rout [rhymes with 'shout'] *verb*
routs, routing, routed
to win very strongly against someone, for example in a battle, game or competition *Our team was completely routed in the quiz.*
rout *noun*

route ['root'] *noun* **routes**
1 the roads or paths that someone uses to get from one place to another *Today I took a different route to school.*
2 a way that buses, trains, planes or ships travel regularly *Our school is on a bus route* (the buses go past the school).
3 a way that leads to a particular result *Hard work is the route to success.*

router ['roo-ter'] *noun* **routers**
a piece of electronic equipment that connects a computer to the internet, to other computers and to other pieces of equipment such as a printer. A router can be wireless (using radio waves instead of wires) or wired (using wires and cables).

routine *noun*
the usual way that you do things, for example always at the same time or in a particular order *Jack's routine is to get up at 7.00 a.m., have breakfast at 7.30 and leave for school at 8.00 a.m.*

routine *adjective*
used about something that happens or is done regularly and is not unusual in any way *I went to the dentist for a routine check-up.*

routinely *adverb*
happening or done regularly and in a way that is not unusual *The police routinely ask these sorts of questions.*

rove *verb*
roves, roving, roved
1 to travel or move around from one place to another
2 if your eyes rove around, you look around in different directions

rover *noun* **rovers**
1 a vehicle that travels over and explores the surface of a planet or moon. It is controlled by scientists or used by astronauts.
2 someone who travels or moves around

row [rhymes with 'flow'] *noun* **rows**
1 a line of things or people next to each other *People stood in a row watching the carnival. At school I usually sit in the back row* (line of desks at the back of a classroom).
2 a line of seats in a cinema or theatre *What row are you in?*
3 a line of numbers or words written next to each other, for example in a spreadsheet or table
compare: **column** (sense 4)
4 a street, for example a narrow one with houses on both sides *36 Savile Row*
5 if things happen in a row or if you do things in a row, they happen or you do them one after the other *Our captain scored three goals in a row.*

row [rhymes with 'cow'] *noun* (informal)
1 (*plural* **rows**) a noisy argument or serious disagreement with someone *Grandma and Granddad had a terrible row.*
2 a loud and unpleasant noise *The kids are making an awful row.*

row [rhymes with 'cow'] *verb* (informal)
rows, rowing, rowed
if people row, they have a noisy argument

row [rhymes with 'flow'] *verb*
rows, rowing, rowed
to move a boat through the water using oars (long poles with a flat part at one end) *We rowed across the lake. Can your dad row a boat?* **rower** *noun*

rowdy *adjective* **rowdier, rowdiest**
1 noisy and often behaving badly *a group of rowdy boys; a rowdy class*
2 rowdy behaviour is noisy and often bad
3 also used about an event or place that is full of noisy people, often people who behave badly *a rowdy party; a rowdy pub*

rowing [rhymes with 'flowing'] *noun*
1 the activity or sport of rowing a boat (moving it through the water using long poles called oars)
2 a rowing boat is a small open boat for rowing, used by one or two people, or a medium-sized boat used by a small group of people

royal *adjective*
1 connected with a king or queen or a member of their family *the royal family*
2 **Royal Highness** a title used for a royal person, especially a prince or princess
3 **Royal Mint** the place where UK coins are produced

royalty *noun*
one or more members of a royal family

rub *verb*
rubs, rubbing, rubbed
1 to move something against something else many times, for example pressing hard with an up-and-down or circular movement *I rubbed my knee with my hand to try and make the pain go away. Rub this cloth over the screen to get rid of the dust. She was rubbing her hands together to keep warm.*
2 to press against something else many times *The cat was rubbing against my leg. My shoes are rubbing* (hurting my feet).
3 to spread something such as a liquid or substance onto something *Rub this cream onto your blister.*
4 if you rub something off or if it rubs off, you get rid of it by rubbing or it disappears by rubbing *I rubbed the dirt off with a cloth. These dirt marks wouldn't rub off.*
5 if you rub out something written in pencil, you remove it using a rubber *If you make a mistake, just rub it out.*

rub *noun* **rubs**
the action of rubbing something *I banged my head – can you give it a rub?*

rubber *noun*
1 a strong but soft material that stretches or bends and is waterproof (does not let water pass through it). It is used for making many things, for example tyres, boots, gloves and balloons. Rubber comes from the liquid inside a tree that grows in hot countries or it is produced with chemicals. *a rubber ball; Our garden hose is made of rubber.*
2 (*plural* **rubbers**) a small piece of special rubber, or rubber mixed with other substances, for getting rid of pencil marks from paper

SYNONYM **eraser**

3 a **rubber band** is a thin ring of rubber that stretches, used for holding things together such as sheets of paper

SYNONYM **elastic band**

4 a **rubber dinghy** is a small open boat made of rubber. It is filled with air to make it float.
5 a **rubber stamp** is a small tool with a handle fixed to a flat part that has rubber letters, numbers or pictures on it. It is used for printing things such as dates or names on paper. The flat part is usually pressed onto an ink pad (soft material with ink on it) and then pressed onto the paper.

rubbery *adjective*
if something feels or looks rubbery, it feels or looks strong and soft like rubber *a rubbery material; a rubbery omelette* (unpleasant because of not being soft enough)

rubbish *noun*
1 things that are not wanted that you throw away *Put all your rubbish in the bin.*
2 things that are of no use that are left lying around, for example old or broken toys or electrical goods, old papers or empty containers *My room is full of rubbish.*

SYNONYM **junk**

3 things that are no good because they are of really bad quality *My sister watches rubbish on TV. This film is rubbish. Peter eats loads of rubbish* (unhealthy food).
4 words or ideas that are stupid or not true *Don't talk rubbish!*

SYNONYM **nonsense**

5 a **rubbish dump** (or **tip**) is a place where people take things that they don't want, for example from their home or garden, to be recycled (used again) or thrown away

SYNONYMS junkyard, recycling centre

rubbish adjective (informal)
1 really bad at doing something because you have no skill *I'm rubbish at maths.*
2 really bad *Chloe got a rubbish mark in French.*

rubbishy adjective (informal)
of very bad quality *a rubbishy book; a rubbishy computer*

rubble noun
broken materials such as stones, bricks, wood, glass and metal from a building that has been damaged or destroyed

Rubik's Cube noun Rubik's Cubes (trademark)
a plastic cube used as a puzzle (problem to solve). Each of the six sides of the cube is made up of nine squares with different colours. You have to move each of the squares until only one colour is showing on each side of the cube.

ruby noun
1 (*plural* **rubies**) a dark red jewel
2 ruby or ruby red is a dark red colour

rucksack noun rucksacks
a bag that you carry on your back. It has straps that go over your shoulders.

SYNONYM backpack

ORIGIN from German *Rucksack* 'back sack' (*Rücken* 'back' and *Sack* 'sack')

rudder noun rudders
a flat part at the back of a ship, plane or submarine. It is moved from side to side to make the ship, plane or submarine go in a particular direction.

ruddy adjective ruddier, ruddiest
if someone's face or cheeks are ruddy, they are red in a way that looks healthy

rude adjective ruder, rudest
1 if you're rude, you don't show respect towards people and you upset them, for example by not behaving in the nice way you should behave or by saying unkind things *Anthony is always rude to me.*

ANTONYM polite

2 also used about what you do or say *rude behaviour; a rude remark; It's rude to poke your tongue out at your brother.*

ANTONYM polite

3 connected with parts of the body in a way that makes people feel upset or angry *a rude joke; a rude gesture*
4 used for describing something that is sudden and unpleasant and affects you strongly *a rude shock*

rudely adjective
1 in a way that doesn't show respect towards other people *'What's your name?' he asked rudely. She always behaves rudely to her teachers.*

ANTONYM politely

2 in a way that is sudden and unpleasant *I was woken up rudely by a very loud noise.*

rudeness noun
1 behaviour towards other people that doesn't show respect towards them
2 if you talk about the rudeness of what someone says or does, you mean that what they say or do is unpleasant or unkind and doesn't show respect

ANTONYM politeness

rudimentary adjective
1 forming the most important or most needed part of something *My sister has a rudimentary knowledge of Chinese.*
2 very simple *This insect has rudimentary wings.*

SYNONYM basic

ruffian noun ruffians
a violent and unpleasant person, for example a member of a gang

ruffle verb
ruffles, ruffling, ruffled
1 to move, touch or rub something so that it is no longer smooth, flat or tidy *A gentle breeze ruffled the surface of the lake. She ruffled my hair then took a photo.*
2 if a bird ruffles its feathers, it makes them stand out on its body, for example when cleaning them
3 to ruffle someone is to make them upset or angry

rug noun rugs
1 a piece of thick material like a small carpet, used for covering part of a floor to protect it or as a decoration
2 a thick soft cover like a small blanket for keeping warm, often worn over the knees

rugby noun
a type of football played by two teams of 13 or 15 players. Points are scored by carrying an oval-shaped ball down the field or pitch (ground covered in grass) and past a particular point or by kicking the ball over a goal shaped like an H.

ORIGIN from the name of *Rugby School*, a well-known private school in Warwickshire, where it was first played and where the first rules were made

rugged ['rug-id] adjective
1 bumpy or full of hard parts such as rocks *the rugged surface of Mars; a rugged coastline*
2 not regular or smooth but in an attractive way *a strong rugged face*
ruggedness noun

rugger noun
an informal word for rugby

ruin verb
ruins, ruining, ruined
1 to damage something badly or destroy it completely *The flood ruined my garden. Too much drinking ruined his health.*
2 to spoil something completely, for example by making it unpleasant or ugly or by stopping it from happening *Chloe's behaviour ruined our visit to the museum. These tall buildings are ruining our town. You almost ruined our plans.*
3 to make someone lose all their money *If my mum bought that car, it would ruin her. A fire destroyed my uncle's shop and now he's ruined.*

ruin noun
1 (*plural* **ruins**) used about the part or parts of a building or town left when the rest has been destroyed *The old house is now a ruin. We visited the ruins of a Roman amphitheatre.*
2 when something is badly damaged or destroyed *The bomb caused the ruin of the whole village.*
3 when something is spoilt completely *Their friendship is going to ruin. This computer error meant the ruin of two days' work.*
4 when someone loses all their money, or the reason for this *Nothing can save the film star from ruin. Too much drinking was his ruin.*
5 **in ruins** used for describing something that has been badly damaged or destroyed or has been spoilt completely *The old house is in ruins. Our plans are now in ruins.*

rule noun rules
1 something that says what you can, should or must do (or cannot, should not or must not do) in a particular situation or place. People often make rules to organise the way things are done or to control other people's behaviour. *There are lots of rules in our house, such as when we can watch TV and when we have to go to bed. You'll be punished if you break the rules* (if you do something that you should not or must not do). *Playing football in the corridor is against the rules* (something you must not do).
2 something that says what you must or must not do in the way you play a game or sport, learn a language, study maths or science or do an activity, for example dancing or handwriting *You can't play chess unless you know the official rules* (how to play it properly). *Our class is learning the rules of grammar* (the correct way to use words in English). *It is difficult to understand these number rules* (things you have to do in maths to solve a problem).
3 something that says what you should do to be successful in a particular situation *A good rule is to eat lots of fruit if you want to be healthy. The rule in chess is to guess what the other player is thinking.*
4 when someone controls a place or country *A long time ago India was under British rule.*
5 the usual way something is *Fights in the playground used to be the rule in our school.*
6 a straight line, for example one that is drawn on paper
7 **as a rule** usually *As a rule, I go to bed at nine o'clock.*

rule verb
rules, ruling, ruled
1 to be in charge of an area, country or group of people *Henry VIII ruled England for nearly 40 years. Until India became independent in 1947, it was ruled over by Britain.*
2 to be more important or successful than anything or anyone else *At that time the dinosaurs ruled. Football seems to rule John's life.*

3 to decide something officially *The judge ruled that the thief was not guilty.*
4 to rule something out is to say that it should not be considered, for example because it is not possible or not good *The police ruled out bad weather as the cause of the crash. The school ruled out increasing the cost of the uniform.*
5 to rule someone out is to stop them from being connected with something, for example because they are not suitable *William has been ruled out as the next captain of the football team.*

ruled *adjective*
used for describing writing paper that has straight lines on it for you to write on

ruler *noun* **rulers**
1 a flat narrow piece of plastic, wood or metal with straight edges marked with centimetres or inches. It is used for measuring things or drawing straight lines.
2 someone in charge of an area or country, for example a king, queen, emperor or president

ruling *noun* **rulings**
an official decision, for example one made by a court or judge

rum *noun* **rums**
an alcoholic drink made from the juice of sugar cane (the hollow stem of the plant that sugar comes from)

rumble *noun* **rumbles**
a long low sound, often one that goes on and on, for example the sound of thunder or of big heavy vehicles moving

rumble *verb*
rumbles, rumbling, rumbled
1 to make a long low sound, used for example when talking about thunder or about a big heavy vehicle moving, such as a train, lorry or plane *After two hours the thunder was still rumbling. In the distance we heard trains rumbling through the countryside.*
2 if your stomach rumbles, it makes long low sounds, for example because you're hungry

rummage *verb*
rummages, rummaging, rummaged
to search for something, for example by moving things around *Dad was rummaging in the drawer for a pair of socks.*

rummy *noun*
a simple card game in which players collect cards of the same value, for example three aces, or cards of the same type, for example diamonds, with numbers that follow each other

rumour *noun* **rumours**
something that people talk about, for example a piece of news or a story, that is often not true *There's a rumour that our teacher is leaving.*

rump *noun*
1 (*plural* **rumps**) the round part of an animal's body above its back legs
2 meat from this part of an animal *a rump steak* (from a cow's rump)

run *verb*
runs, running, ran, run
1 if a person or animal runs, they move, or they go somewhere, very quickly on their legs, going faster than walking *It hurts my legs when I run. Fatima ran to the end of the playground. Lewis ran down the road.*
2 to travel a particular distance while running *I ran half a mile in the rain.*
3 to run as a sport or take part in a race *My mum runs every Saturday.*
4 to hurry somewhere because you want to get there quickly *When I heard a loud bang I ran over to the window.*

SYNONYM **to rush**

5 to go or move or to make something go or move *The ball ran off the end of the table. Dad ran his fingers through his hair. Strange thoughts kept running through my mind.*
6 if something such as a road or railway runs somewhere, for example through or along a place, it is built starting somewhere and ending somewhere else *The railway runs through the forest. The path runs along the river.*
7 used for saying that a vehicle such as a bus, train or plane travels at a certain time or in a certain way, or for saying that someone makes this happen *Buses run every 10 minutes to the school. Because of the crowds, they're running extra train services to Leeds.*

SYNONYM **to operate**

8 if someone runs you somewhere, for example by car, they take you there *'Can you run me to school, Dad? I'm late.'*
9 used for saying that something such as a piece of equipment, vehicle or computer program works or works in a certain way, or for saying that someone makes this happen *My laptop is running on the battery. Mum left the car engine running. This program runs in the background* (is always working on the computer). *Run a scan to see if you have a computer virus.*
10 to be in charge of something such as a business, shop or sports team and organise the way it works *Granddad used to run a language school.*
11 to run something such as a course or exhibition is to do it and organise it for people to go to
12 to flow or make something flow *Blood was running from the animal's wound. You left the tap running. Mum's going to run a bath for me after dinner.*
13 if your nose runs, liquid comes out of it, for example because you have a cold
14 if the colour of a piece of clothing runs, some of the colour comes out when it gets wet, usually when it is washed
15 to continue *The film ran for five weeks in the cinemas.*
16 to become, often when talking about something becoming less and not being enough *We're running short of exercise books. The printer is running low on ink. The river ran dry.*
17 if something or someone runs late, they happen, do something or arrive somewhere later than expected *All the trains are running late today. I was supposed to finish my homework yesterday but I'm running late.*
18 if you run a risk, you do something even though something bad might happen
19 to run across someone or something is to meet someone or find something by chance

SYNONYM **to come across**

20 to run after someone or something is to follow them quickly, for example to catch them or stop them

SYNONYM **to chase**

21 to run away is to go away from a place or person quickly, for example to escape from something bad
22 if someone in a vehicle runs someone down, they hit them
23 to run into someone is to meet them accidentally

SYNONYM **to bump into**

24 if something such as a passport or ticket runs out, it cannot be used later than the date written on it

SYNONYM **to expire**

25 if you run out of something, you have no more left *We've run out of apples and milk.*
26 if someone in a vehicle runs someone over, they hit them and injure or kill them

run *noun* **runs**
1 when you go somewhere by running *Dad goes for a run every morning.*
2 a short journey somewhere, for example in a car, bus, boat or plane *the school run* (to and from school by parents in their car); *Mum took Gran out for a run in the car to see the sea.*
3 a run in cricket is a point scored when a batsman hits the ball and runs between two places called wickets
4 a period when good or bad things happen one after another *We had a run of good luck. What a run of awful luck!*
5 a long thin hole in a pair of tights or a stocking

SYNONYM **ladder**

6 (*informal*) if someone has the runs, they have diarrhoea (an illness that makes you go to the toilet often)
7 in the long run used for talking about a time in the future *What's going to happen to the rainforests in the long run?*
8 on the run used about someone who has escaped from somewhere *He's a criminal on the run from the police.*
9 up and running used about something such as equipment or software or about a group or organisation to say it is ready and working *The engineer has set up our PC and it's up and running.*

runaway *noun* **runaways**
someone who has left their home without telling anyone and disappeared, usually because they are unhappy there

run-down *adjective*
1 very tired and slightly ill, for example because of working or studying too much
2 used for describing a building in very bad condition because no-one has looked after it or a place that has lots of these buildings *Granddad lives in a run-down part of London.*

rung
past participle of **ring**

rung noun **rungs**
one of the bars or steps joining the two long pieces of wood or metal of a ladder. You use the rungs to climb up and down the ladder.

runner noun **runners**
1 a person or animal that runs *My brother's a really fast runner.*
2 a person or animal that runs in a race *a long-distance runner*
3 a bar of metal, wood or plastic under something such as a sledge, used for sliding it on the ground. Runners are also used with something such as a drawer so that the drawer can slide in and out.
4 a runner bean is a long flat green bean that grows on a climbing plant. It is cooked and eaten as a vegetable.

runner-up noun **runners-up**
1 a person or team that comes second in a race or competition
2 a person or team that does not come first in a race or competition but gets a prize anyway *Each of the five runners-up received £100.*

running noun
1 the sport of moving very quickly on your legs, going faster than walking *running shoes*; *Running is good exercise.*
2 running water is water that flows through the pipes in a building. You use it for drinking or washing. *All the bedrooms have hot and cold running water.*

running adverb
used about periods of time or events to say that they happen one after another *Daniel has won the quiz for the third year running.*

SYNONYM in a row

runny adjective **runnier, runniest**
1 if your nose is runny, liquid comes out of it, for example because you have a cold
2 if a substance is runny, for example a sauce or omelette, it flows like liquid or has liquid in it

runway noun **runways**
a long wide piece of ground with a hard surface that planes use for taking off from and landing on

rupee ['roo-pee'] noun **rupees**
a unit of money in India, Pakistan and some other countries

rural adjective
connected with the countryside, not towns *a rural part of Scotland* (an area in the countryside)

ruse ['rooz'] noun **ruses**
a trick or plan to secretly get something that you want

SYNONYM ploy

rush verb
rushes, rushing, rushed
1 to do something or go somewhere quickly *I don't like rushing when I do my homework. I had to rush to catch the train. Don't rush off yet* (don't leave suddenly).
2 to make someone do something or go somewhere quickly *Don't rush me!*
3 to take or send someone or something somewhere quickly *Grandma was rushed to hospital.*
4 to make something go faster *If you rush your food, you'll get hiccups.*

rush noun
1 when people move quickly or try to do something at the same time *There was a mad rush for the door. There's been a rush to buy tickets for the Bruegel exhibition.*
2 used about the crowds of people who travel on trains, buses or in their cars, or who do something such as shopping, at the busiest times of the day *If you come home at three o'clock, you can avoid the evening rush.*
3 a sudden strong movement by the air or by water *When I opened the door, there was a rush of wind that blew Dad's papers off the table.*
4 if you do something in a rush, you do it quickly because you don't have time to do it properly
5 if you are in a rush, you want to get somewhere or do something quickly
6 **no rush** used for telling someone that they don't need to do something quickly

rushed adjective
1 if something is rushed, it is done quickly because there isn't time to do it properly
2 if someone is rushed, they feel that they have to do something quickly or they want to get somewhere quickly

rushes noun plural
plants like grass with tall hollow stems that grow in wet places. The stems are sometimes used for making things such as baskets and mats.

rush hour noun
the rush hour is a busy time of the day when very many people travel on trains, buses or in their cars

rusk noun **rusks**
a kind of hard dry biscuit used by babies for biting on and eating when they are growing their teeth

Russia noun
a country in North-East Europe and North Asia

Russian adjective
connected with Russia or the Russian language

Russian noun
1 the language people speak in Russia
2 (plural **Russians**) someone from Russia

rust noun
a reddish-brown substance that forms on iron or steel. It is caused by the air or by water and it damages the surface of the metal.

rust verb
rusts, rusting, rusted
if iron or steel rusts, it becomes covered by or damaged by rust

rustic adjective
simple or old-fashioned in a way that makes you think of the countryside *a rustic garden bench made of logs*

rustle verb
rustles, rustling, rustled
1 if something dry and light rustles, it makes the soft gentle sound of leaves rubbing against each other in the wind or paper being moved, folded or crushed
2 to make something make this sound *Stop rustling the pages of your newspaper – I'm trying to sleep.*
3 to rustle farm animals such as horses, cows or sheep is to steal them
4 to rustle something up such as a meal or sandwich is to make it quickly, often using whatever food you can find to make it with

rustle or **rustling** noun
the soft gentle sound made by the movement of something such as leaves or paper

rusty adjective **rustier, rustiest**
1 if something made of iron or steel is rusty, it is covered by or damaged by rust *a rusty old bike*
2 if a particular skill is rusty, it is not as good as it was because you haven't been practising
3 if someone is rusty, they haven't been practising a particular skill so they are not as good as they were *I'm a bit rusty in French.*

rustiness noun

rut noun
1 a bad situation that has been the same for a long time and that you cannot change *My sister's in a rut – she hates her job but can't find another one.*
2 (plural **ruts**) a deep narrow mark in the ground, especially one made by a wheel

ruthless adjective
1 if someone is ruthless, they do not care about the pain they cause people and they do everything they can to get what they want
2 also used about someone's actions, feelings and behaviour *the ruthless treatment of prisoners*

ruthlessly adverb **ruthlessness** noun

rye noun
a plant that produces grain (seeds) that people use for making food such as bread or flour *rye bread*

S s

ORIGIN the letter S comes from a zigzag shape that the Phoenicians called *shin* ('tooth'). It looked like an English W and had the sound of 'sh', not 's'. An earlier form looked like two U shapes put together and opened out – a shape that some people think represented an archer's bow made from two animal horns joined together. The Greeks copied the letter to use as their 's' sound and made the W shape simpler by getting rid of one of its four lines and making it zigzag up into the air on its side, almost like a Z. The Romans turned the shape to face right instead of left and turned the three lines and two pointed ends into regular curves to make the letter S we recognise today.

Sabbath noun
the Sabbath is a special day of the week for praying to God and for resting, especially in the Christian and Jewish religions. For Christians the special day is usually Sunday and for Jews it is Saturday.

ORIGIN from Hebrew *shabat* 'to rest'

sabotage ['sa-ber-tahj'; 'j' has the middle sound of 'pleasure'] noun
the deliberate damaging or destruction of equipment or property, for example to stop an enemy or employer from using it

sabotage verb
sabotages, sabotaging, sabotaged
if someone sabotages equipment or property, they deliberately damage or destroy it to stop an enemy or employer from using it or because they are angry about something *Groups of workers who had been fired sabotaged the machines in the factory.*

ORIGIN from French *saboter* 'to do something badly or carelessly'

saboteur ['sa-ber-terr'] noun saboteurs
someone who deliberately damages or destroys equipment or property, for example so that an enemy or employer can no longer use it

sabre ['say-ber'] noun sabres
1 a heavy sword, usually with a curved blade. Sabres were used in the past by soldiers, especially soldiers who rode on horses.
2 a light sword using for fencing (the sport of fighting with swords)

sac noun sacs
a part inside an animal or plant that is like a small bag. It often contains liquid.

saccharin noun
a chemical used instead of sugar for making food taste sweet. It is usually put in tea or coffee. *a saccharin tablet*

ORIGIN from Latin *saccharum* 'sugar'

sachet ['sash-ay'] noun sachets
a small closed plastic or paper bag, usually containing liquid or powder *a sachet of shampoo; a sachet of ketchup*

ORIGIN from French *sachet* 'little bag'

sack noun sacks
1 a large bag without handles, made of strong cloth, plastic or paper. It is used for carrying or storing heavy things such as potatoes or flour.
2 a sack race is a race in which you stand inside a cloth sack that you hold up with both hands and move along by jumping forwards
3 **the sack** used when telling someone to leave their job *If my brother keeps on being late, his boss will give him the sack. There wasn't enough work so my dad got the sack* (was told to leave his job).

sack verb
sacks, sacking, sacked
1 to tell someone to leave their job *My uncle's been sacked for being late.*

SYNONYM to fire

2 if people such as soldiers sack a place or building, they steal things from it using violence and causing damage, usually during a war *Rome has been sacked on many occasions.*

sacred ['say-krid'] adjective
1 considered holy or important in a particular religion *Cows are sacred to Hindus.*
2 connected with religion *sacred music*

sacrifice verb
sacrifices, sacrificing, sacrificed
1 to stop having or doing something important so that you or someone else can have or do something that is even more important *My uncle decided to sacrifice his job for his children* (for example, he gave up his job to look after his children). *The brave soldier sacrificed his life* (was killed for the important reason of defending his country). *It's a cheap computer but quality hasn't been sacrificed* (the quality is still good even though being cheap is more important).
2 if someone sacrifices an animal or person, they kill them as part of a religious ceremony as a way of pleasing a god. This happened especially in the past.

sacrifice noun sacrifices
1 when someone stops having or doing something important so as to have or do something even more important *All parents have to make sacrifices* (for example, not buy things they want so that their children have what they need). *It's a cheap computer but there has been no sacrifice of quality.*
2 the killing of an animal or person as part of a religious ceremony, especially in the past

sacrificial adjective

sad adjective sadder, saddest
1 if someone is sad, they have the unpleasant feeling you get when something bad has happened or when a situation, person or thing is bad
2 used about something that gives you this unpleasant feeling or that shows you have this feeling *the saddest day of my life; The story is very sad. It was sad to see our team lose. He had a sad look on his face.*
3 (informal) used for showing that you have no respect for someone or something because they are not fashionable, up to date or interesting *I love collecting stamps but my sister thinks I'm so sad. Dad thinks collecting stamps is cool, not sad.*

sadden verb
saddens, saddening, saddened
to make someone feel sad

saddle noun saddles
1 a seat, usually made of leather, for riding on a horse or other animal. It is fixed to the animal's back using straps.
2 a seat on a bicycle or motorcycle

saddle verb
saddles, saddling, saddled
1 to put a saddle on the back of a horse or other animal *Indira saddled her horse and rode off. Let's saddle up.*
2 to give someone something difficult or unpleasant to deal with *My teacher has been saddled with the responsibility of organising the fire drill.*

sadly adverb
1 used when talking about something bad happening that makes you sad *Sadly, our team lost the match.*
2 in a sad way *'Has your dog died?' – 'Yes,' she said sadly.*
3 very or very much, in a way that makes you sad *Our teacher is leaving and she will be sadly missed. I thought my uncle would help me but I was sadly mistaken* (completely wrong).

sadness noun
the feeling of being sad

safari ['ser-fah-ree'] noun safaris
1 a trip to see wild animals and take photos of them or, especially in the past, to hunt them. Most safaris are in Africa.
2 a safari park is an area of land where wild animals such as lions and elephants are kept and move around freely. Visitors drive through the park in their cars to watch the animals and take photos of them.

ORIGIN from *safari* 'long journey' in the East African language Swahili

safe adjective safer, safest
1 used about a place where something bad or dangerous does not or will not happen *This part of town is safe. I put my passport in a safe place* (for example where it won't be stolen or lost).
2 used about something that does not or will not cause any harm or danger or make anything bad happen *a safe car; The ladder is perfectly safe. Is it safe to eat this runny egg?*
3 used about someone or something protected from anything bad happening to them *All children are safe in school. Your passport will be safe in that drawer. In my brother's car I don't feel safe* (for example, I might be hurt in an accident because he's a bad driver or his car does not work properly).

427

4 without being harmed or damaged *We had a party to celebrate Dad's safe return. Your parcel has arrived – it's quite safe.*
5 used when you mean that you are careful and not wanting to take any risks that something bad might happen *My dad's a safe driver. Let's be safe and choose the easiest solution. You've made a safe decision. It's a safe bet* (pretty certain) *that Mohammed will pass his exams.*
6 a slang word that means good or OK *I like your friend – he's safe.*
7 to be on the safe side in case something bad might happen or in case you should do or need something *Take your umbrella to be on the safe side* (in case it rains). *To be on the safe side, hand your homework in today* (it's possible it needs to be handed in today so you should hand it in).
8 safe and sound without being harmed *The missing schoolboy has been found safe and sound.*

> SIMILE 'as safe as houses' means very safe (senses 1 & 3)

safe *noun* **safes**
a strong metal box for keeping money or valuable things in to protect them. The box is locked so that it can only be opened using a special key or, for example, by turning a dial (round part) to choose particular numbers or letters.

safeguard *verb*
safeguards, safeguarding, safeguarded
to keep a person, place or thing safe from harm or danger

> SYNONYM to protect

safeguard *noun* **safeguards**
something such as a rule or plan that protects someone or something from harm or danger

safekeeping *noun*
used when talking about keeping something safe from harm or danger *I gave my passport to my mum for safekeeping.*

safely *adverb*
1 in a way that does not or will not cause any harm or danger or make anything bad happen *You can safely drink the water from the tap.*
2 in a way that shows that someone or something is protected from anything bad happening to them *The children are safely in their classrooms.*
3 without being harmed or damaged *You can go out safely at night in our town. Your present arrived safely.*
4 in a way that is careful or that shows you don't want to take any risks that something bad might happen *My parents always drive safely. I put my money safely in the bank.*
5 without being wrong *I can safely say that our team is going to win tomorrow.*

safety *noun*
1 a situation of being protected from harm or danger or from anything bad happening *Our school pays great attention to the safety of children.*
2 ways of behaving in order to be protected from harm or danger *The head teacher gave us a talk about safety.*

3 a situation of not causing any harm or danger *The firefighters are worried about the safety of the building* (about how safe the building is).
4 a place where you are protected from harm or danger *After walking for two days we finally reached safety.*

safety belt *noun* **safety belts**
a strap that you put around your body to hold you safely in your seat, for example on a plane

safety net *noun* **safety nets**
a large net that is put below someone, for example an acrobat in a circus, to catch them if they fall

safety pin *noun* **safety pins**
a type of pin that is bent into a V shape, used especially for holding pieces of cloth together. It has a round part at one end and a sharp point at the other end. You stick the sharp point through the cloth and then fit the point into the round end.

safety record *noun* **safety records**
1 used for describing how safe something or a particular type of thing is *The London tube has an excellent safety record. Mum bought this car because of its good safety record* (this type of car has usually been safe).
2 used for describing how safely someone does something *The circus has a bad safety record* (for example, animals or performers often get hurt).

sag *verb*
sags, sagging, sagged
1 to bend downwards in the middle instead of being fairly hard or straight *The shelf was sagging under the weight of my books.*
2 to hang down, for example because of being loose or soft *Granddad has sagging skin on his face.*

saga ['sah-ger] *noun* **sagas**
a story that describes events and the adventures of people over a long period of time

> ORIGIN from Icelandic *saga* 'story'. A *saga* was a long story about ancient Scandinavian history or about Viking battles and adventures.

sage *noun*
1 a plant with flat light green leaves used for giving a stronger taste to food *chicken with sage and onion stuffing*
2 (*plural* **sages**) a very wise person

saggy *adjective* **saggier, saggiest**
used for describing something that hangs down, for example because of being loose or soft *saggy skin*

said
past tense & past participle of **say**

sail *verb*
sails, sailing, sailed
1 if a boat or ship (or someone in a boat or ship) sails somewhere, they travel there on the water *We watched a canoe sailing down the river. Christopher Columbus sailed to America.*
2 if a boat or ship (or someone in a boat or ship) sails from somewhere or at a particular time, they start their journey *Our ship sails from Dover. We sail at three o'clock.*

3 to control a boat that has sails and make it go somewhere, especially as a sport *My uncle sailed the yacht around the island. My sister loves to go sailing.*
4 to move or do something quickly and easily *The ball sailed across the pitch and landed straight in the goal. Sita sailed through her exams* (she was successful and had no problems).

sail *noun*
1 (*plural* **sails**) a large piece of strong cloth fixed onto a mast (tall pole) on a boat or ship. The wind blows the sail, which moves the boat or ship through the water.
2 a journey in a boat or ship that has sails *Let's go for a little sail.*
3 to set sail to start travelling somewhere on the water *Our boat sets sail tomorrow morning.*

sailboard *noun* **sailboards**
a long board with a sail fixed to a pole, used for windsurfing (the sport of standing on a board and letting the wind blow you across the water)

> SYNONYM windsurfer

sailing *noun*
1 the sport or activity of controlling a boat with sails, for example a yacht, and making it go somewhere
2 a sailing boat or ship is a boat or ship that uses sails to move through the water

sailor *noun* **sailors**
1 someone who works on a boat or ship
2 someone who sails a boat such as a yacht

saint *noun* **saints**
1 a special honour and title given, especially by Christians, to a person who has lived his or her life in a very good and holy way
2 someone who is very good, kind or patient

Saint Bernard *noun* **Saint Bernards**
a very large dog with brown and white fur and a long heavy tail. It was originally used for helping to rescue people lost in the mountains, especially in the Swiss and Italian Alps.

> LANGUAGE EXTRA usually shortened to *St Bernard* in writing

saintly *adjective* **saintlier, saintliest**
very good or holy

Saint Valentine's Day *noun*
Saint Valentine's Days
a special day (14 February) when people give cards and presents to people they have (or would like to have) a love relationship with

> LANGUAGE EXTRA also called *Valentine's Day*

sake *noun*
1 for the sake of something used for showing a reason or purpose *You should eat lots of fruit for the sake of your health.*
2 for the sake of someone used for showing that something helps someone *I have to tidy up my room for my parents' sake.*

salad–samurai

salad *noun* **salads**
1 a dish made of raw vegetables such as lettuce, cucumber and tomatoes, often mixed with other things like eggs, cheese or chicken. It is eaten either on its own or as part of a meal with other food.
2 salad cream is a pale yellow sauce that you put on a salad. It is made from oil, vinegar (sour liquid made from wine) and the yellow parts of eggs.
3 a salad dressing is a sauce that you put on a salad, for example made from oil, vinegar and spices

salamander *noun* **salamanders**
a small animal like a lizard with four short legs and a long body and tail. Salamanders have wet skin and live in water and on land.

salami *noun* **salamis**
a large sausage made from meat and spices. It usually has a strong taste and is cut into slices and eaten cold.

salary *noun* **salaries**
the money that someone is paid for the work they do in their job. People usually receive their salary every month.

ORIGIN from Latin *salarium* 'money given to a Roman soldier to buy salt' (from *sal* 'salt')

sale *noun* **sales**
1 when someone sells something for money and someone else buys it *Sales of tickets for the school concert have been good* (lots of tickets have been sold).
2 a time when things are sold in shops or online at a lower price than usual *Avi bought a new smartphone in the sales* (or *on sale*). *Sale prices are much better in January.*
3 an event at which particular things are sold *Our library is holding a book sale this Saturday.*
4 a sales assistant is someone who sells things to customers in a shop
5 **for sale** ready for someone to buy, when talking about something that belongs to someone *Seema's bike is for sale.*
6 **on sale** ready for someone to buy, in a place such as a shop or theatre *Tickets are on sale at the box office.*

salesperson *noun* **salespeople**
someone who sells things, for example to customers in a shop, by phoning people or by travelling around visiting people

LANGUAGE EXTRA you can also say *salesman* and *saleswoman*

saline ['say-line'] *adjective*
used for describing a liquid or substance that contains salt

saliva ['ser-lye-ver'] *noun*
the watery liquid inside your mouth that helps you swallow food and digest it (change it so that your body can use it)

sallow *adjective* **sallower, sallowest**
used for describing someone's skin or face that is slightly yellow and does not look healthy

sally *verb*
sallies, sallying, sallied
if someone sallies forth, they go somewhere quickly and with lots of energy

salmon *noun* **salmon**
a large fish that has pink flesh and silver skin and is used as food. Salmon live in the sea but produce their eggs in rivers.

salon *noun* **salons**
1 a shop where a hairdresser cuts and arranges your hair *a hair salon*
2 a shop where people go to get their face, skin or hair treated with products to make them look more attractive *a beauty salon*

saloon *noun* **saloons**
1 a car with a fixed roof, seats for four or five people, and a boot (covered place for luggage at the back)
2 a comfortable room in a pub or hotel, where drinks are served
3 a place where drinks are served, especially in the past in the west of the US

salsa *noun*
1 a sauce with a strong taste made from tomatoes, onions and chilli peppers. It is used mainly with Spanish and Mexican food.
2 (plural **salsas**) a type of Latin American dance
3 a type of music with a strong pattern of sounds that is played with this dance

salt *noun*
1 a white substance used for giving a flavour to food. It is produced from sea water or from rocks under the ground.
2 (plural **salts**) in science, one of the chemical substances formed when an acid and an alkali or base are mixed

salt *verb*
salts, salting, salted
to put salt on or in food, for example to give it a flavour or make it last longer *salted peanuts*

salty *adjective* **saltier, saltiest**
if something is salty, it tastes of salt or contains salt

salute *noun* **salutes**
1 a sign of respect that someone makes by touching the side of their head with their right hand, especially when a soldier shows respect for another soldier
2 an official occasion when soldiers fire a gun into the air as a sign of respect for someone

salute *verb*
salutes, saluting, saluted
to touch the side of your head with your right hand to show respect for someone *They saluted the general as he walked past. Soldiers must salute when they see an officer.*

salvage *verb*
salvages, salvaging, salvaged
to save something or parts of something from being destroyed or damaged *They managed to salvage all the computers from the fire. A special team salvaged the ship, which sank 200 years ago.* **salvage** *noun*

salvation *noun*
1 something or someone that helps you by saving you from a bad or dangerous situation *When I fell into the river my life jacket was my salvation.*
2 the action of saving something or someone from a bad or dangerous situation
3 the Salvation Army is a Christian organisation that helps people who are poor. Members wear uniforms like soldiers and often play music during meetings.

same *adjective & pronoun*
1 used about something or someone that is in every way what something or someone else is *I go to Acacia High and my brother goes to the same school* (also Acacia High). *My birthday is on 9th May – the same day as my sister's* (my sister and I both have 9th May as our birthday).
2 used about something or someone that is in every way what something or someone was in the past or will be in the future *My brother has the same curly hair as when he was a boy* (his hair has not changed). *I wonder if London will look the same in 10 years' time* (if London will have changed).
3 used about something when you mean just that kind of thing and no other kind *Elvie was wearing the same hat as me* (the same kind of hat). *Anyone would do the same if they'd lost their ticket.*

same *adverb*
in the same way *Myra dresses the same as her sister. Alfie behaved badly, same as always.*

samosa *noun* **samosas**
an Indian food like a small pie in the shape of a triangle. Samosas are filled with vegetables such as potatoes and onions, or with meat. They are baked in an oven or fried.

sample *noun* **samples**
1 a small amount of something larger that shows you what the rest of it is like or that gives you information about the rest of it *Anisha brought some samples of her homework to show her new teacher. The doctor took a blood sample from my dad* (to get information about his blood). *My dentist gave me a free sample of toothpaste* (she wanted me to try it and buy more if I liked it).
2 a small number of things or people chosen from a larger group, often providing information about the whole group *These opinions come from a sample of nine-year-olds at our school. The mayor asked a random sample of schools to take part in the concert.*
3 in pop music, a sample is a piece of music borrowed from someone else that is used as part of a new song

sample *adjective*
showing you what something is supposed to be like *a sample exam question; a sample email*

sample *verb*
samples, sampling, sampled
1 to taste a small amount of something, for example to see what it is like *I sampled some of the ice cream but I didn't like it.*
2 to try something such as an activity or experience to see what it is like *Granddad sampled life in London but didn't much like it. We sampled the delights of driving around the Kent coastline.*
3 to test a small amount of something larger, for example to get information or find out what it is like *Scientists keep sampling the river to check for pollution.*

samurai *noun* **samurai**
a soldier of high social rank who lived in Japan in the past

sanctuary – satellite

sanctuary noun
1 (plural **sanctuaries**) a place where someone is safe from harm or danger, usually someone who is being hunted or attacked
2 when someone is kept safe from harm or danger *The students took sanctuary in the US embassy.*
3 (plural **sanctuaries**) an area of land where birds and animals are kept and protected, for example to stop them being hunted or becoming extinct (with no more living examples) *a wildlife sanctuary* (for wild animals and birds)

sand noun
1 a substance like powder, formed mainly from tiny pieces of rock. It is usually yellow or pale yellow brown. Many beaches and deserts are made up of sand.
2 an area of sand, usually on a beach *I like walking along the sand.*
3 **sands** a large area of sand on a beach *Cornwall has miles of golden sands.*

sand verb
sands, sanding, sanded
to make something smooth, especially something made of wood or metal, by rubbing it with sandpaper (strong paper with a special rough surface) *Before I painted my rusty bike, I had to sand it down.*

sandal noun **sandals**
a light shoe with an open top or sides, often with straps to fix it to your foot

sandbag noun **sandbags**
a sack filled with sand or earth. Sandbags are used for building walls to protect people against things such as floods or bullets from heavy guns.

sandcastle noun **sandcastles**
a model made of wet sand, for example shaped like a tower or castle. You usually build sandcastles on a beach.

sand dune noun **sand dunes**
a hill of sand formed by the wind on a beach or in a desert

sandpaper noun
a type of very strong paper with one side covered by a special rough material, made for example from minerals. It is used for rubbing on surfaces such as wood or metal to make them smooth. **sandpaper** verb

sandpit noun **sandpits**
a container or area filled with sand for children to play in

sandstone noun
a type of rock made from grains of sand and other minerals. It is mainly used for building things such as houses and walls.

sandwich noun **sandwiches**
two pieces of bread, usually with butter or margarine on them, that you put food in between, for example slices of cheese or chicken. Sandwiches are eaten as a light meal. *a cheese and tomato sandwich*

> ORIGIN named after John Montagu, an 18th-century nobleman (someone with a high rank in society). His title was the Earl of *Sandwich* (from the town of *Sandwich* in Kent). Montagu played card games for money and used to ask his servant to bring him meat between two pieces of bread so he could carry on playing while eating.

sandwich bar noun **sandwich bars**
a restaurant or shop where you can buy sandwiches

sandwiched adjective
if someone or something is sandwiched between other people or things, they are in a very small space between them or are stuck between them so that it is hard to move *I stood on the crowded train sandwiched between two grown-ups.*

sandy adjective **sandier, sandiest**
1 if something is sandy, it is made up mainly of sand or has lots of sand in it or on it *a sandy beach*
2 having a yellowish brown or light yellow colour *sandy hair*

sane adjective **saner, sanest**
1 if someone is sane, they have a healthy mind and they behave in a reasonable and normal way
2 sensible and reasonable *a sane decision*

sang
past tense of **sing**

sanitary adjective
1 connected with keeping things clean and keeping people healthy *The sanitary conditions of London improved with the building of underground sewers* (pipes carrying away dirty water and waste matter).
2 clean and free of germs *Their school toilets were not very sanitary.*
3 a sanitary towel or pad is a piece of soft material used by a woman to absorb (take in) blood during a period (natural bleeding that happens every month)

sanitation noun
things provided for keeping people's bodies clean and healthy, especially the equipment for bringing clean water to people's homes and removing dirty water and waste products

sanity noun
1 when someone has a healthy mind and behaves in a reasonable and normal way *Grandma lives alone but does a lot of reading to keep her sanity.*
2 the quality of being sensible and reasonable

sank
past tense of **sink**

Sanskrit noun
an ancient language of India, used for example in Hindu religious ceremonies and in literature

Santa Claus ['san-ter-klorz'] or **Santa** noun
an imaginary man with a red coat and white beard who brings presents to children at Christmas. He is often called Father Christmas.

sap noun
a liquid inside a plant or tree that carries water and food to all parts of the plant or tree

sap verb
saps, sapping, sapped
to make something less or weaker *The heat sapped my energy* (made me feel weaker).

sapling noun **saplings**
a young tree

sapphire noun **sapphires**
a bright blue jewel

sarcasm noun
a way of speaking that shows you mean the opposite of what you are saying or something different from what you are saying. People often speak in this way to be unpleasant to someone or to be funny in an unkind way, for example because they are angry or upset. If you say 'Now that's a surprise' when someone who often does bad things does something bad again, you are using sarcasm.
compare: **irony**

> ORIGIN from Greek *sarkasmos* 'saying unkind things' (from *sarkazein* 'to tear the flesh off')

sarcastic adjective
1 if someone is sarcastic, they say something that is the opposite of or different from what they really mean, for example to be unpleasant to someone or to be funny in an unkind way
2 also used about what someone says or does *a sarcastic remark*; *His email was very nasty and sarcastic.*
sarcastically adverb

sardine noun **sardines**
a small silver-coloured sea fish with oily flesh. Sardines can be bought fresh and cooked, or bought in tins ready to eat.

sari ['sah-ree'] noun **saris**
a type of dress, worn especially by women from India or Pakistan. It is made from a long piece of thin cloth that is wrapped around the body.

sarong ['ser-rong'] noun **sarongs**
a long piece of thin cloth that is wrapped around the waist, worn by men and women in many countries, especially in South-East Asia

sash noun **sashes**
a long wide piece of thin cloth that someone wears over the shoulder or round the waist, for example as a decoration or as part of a uniform

sat
past tense & past participle of **sit**

Satan ['say-tern'] noun
an evil being that exists in some religions such as Christianity

satchel noun **satchels**
a bag shaped like a rectangle, used for carrying things such as schoolbooks. It has a long strap for carrying it over your shoulder or on your back, and can also have a handle for carrying it in your hand.

> ORIGIN from Old French *sachel* 'little bag' (from Latin *saccus* 'sack' or 'bag')

satellite noun **satellites**
1 a piece of equipment or a vehicle that is sent into space to orbit (go round) the earth or another planet. Satellites are used for many reasons such as collecting information and sending it back to scientists on earth or providing signals for communicating, for example by radio or television. *a weather satellite* (for collecting information about the weather); *a satellite phone* (that uses satellite signals)

430

satin – savage

2 a natural object in space that moves round a planet *The moon is the earth's satellite.*
3 a satellite dish is a round piece of equipment shaped like a dish, used for receiving TV signals from satellites
4 satellite navigation is a computer system that uses information from satellites to tell you where someone or something is or to help you find your way, for example if you are travelling by car

LANGUAGE EXTRA you can also say *satnav* for short

5 satellite TV or satellite television is a way of broadcasting TV programmes using signals from satellites

satin noun
a smooth cloth that is shiny on one side, often made from silk

satire noun
1 a style of writing in which you say unkind or funny things about the faults that people have (things wrong with their character) and the bad things that people do, so that everyone will laugh at them. Satire is often used as a way of trying to make bad situations better.
2 (plural **satires**) something such as a book or play that uses this style of writing
3 (plural **satires**) a painting or drawing in which an artist shows people's faults and the bad things they do, so that everyone will laugh at them
satirist noun

satirical adjective
using satire as a way of laughing at people *a satirical poem* **satirically** adverb

satisfaction noun
1 a feeling of being happy because you have what you want, need or expect *Sanjay gets lots of satisfaction from studying Shakespeare.*
2 (plural **satisfactions**) something that makes you feel happy
3 providing what is needed *the satisfaction of customers' needs* (giving customers what they need)

satisfactory adjective
1 good or fairly good *Abdul's homework is quite satisfactory.*
2 good enough to be accepted or to give someone what they want, need or expect *Your behaviour in class isn't always satisfactory. Did you get a satisfactory reply to your email?*
satisfactorily adverb

satisfied adjective
1 used for describing someone who is happy because they have what they want, need or expect *a satisfied customer*
2 if you're satisfied with something or someone, you think they are good or fairly good *Ms Driscoll was satisfied with my homework.*
3 if you're satisfied that something is true, you have all the information you need to be sure it's true *I was satisfied (sure) that the box was empty.*

satisfy verb
satisfies, satisfying, satisfied
1 to make someone happy because they get what they want, need or expect or because they get enough of something *The school test results satisfied most parents. There wasn't enough food at the party to satisfy all the hungry children.*
2 to do or provide what is needed, for example so that something can happen *The new gym satisfies all the school's needs. Ice creams are delicious but they don't satisfy your hunger* (they don't fill you up so that you're no longer hungry). *Anika peeked into the box to satisfy her curiosity* (so that she would know what was in it).
3 to give someone the information they need to make sure that something is true *Jo's explanations completely satisfied our teacher. I opened the box to satisfy myself that it was empty* (so that I'd know for sure that it was empty).

satisfying adjective
1 used for describing something that makes you happy because it gives you what you want, need or expect *a satisfying result; a satisfying job*
2 used for describing a meal that makes you feel that you've eaten well *The breakfast was very satisfying.*

satnav noun
1 (plural **satnavs**) a piece of equipment in a car that uses information from satellites to tell the driver and passengers where they are and to help them find their way
2 the system of satellites that this equipment uses *Dad used satnav to find his way to Granddad's new house.*
short for: satellite navigation

satsuma noun **satsumas**
a fruit like a small orange with a soft skin

saturate verb
saturates, saturating, saturated
1 to make something or someone completely wet *I was caught in the rain and my clothes got saturated.*
2 to fill something completely with something or with many things or people *The shops seem to be saturated with products from China.*
saturation noun

Saturday noun **Saturdays**
the day of the week between Friday and Sunday. Saturday and Sunday make up the weekend.

ORIGIN from Old English *Sæterdæg* 'day of the planet Saturn'. It was named after Saturn, the Roman god of agriculture.

Saturn noun
the sixth planet from the sun, after Jupiter and before Uranus. Saturn is surrounded by a very large number of rings made of ice and has many moons.

sauce noun
1 (plural **sauces**) a hot or cold liquid used for putting on food to give it a flavour
2 an old-fashioned word for rude behaviour or talk that shows no respect to the person you are speaking to

saucepan noun **saucepans**
a metal container for cooking things in. Saucepans usually have one long handle but sometimes have two short round ones.

saucer noun **saucers**
a small round object like a plate with slightly curved sides, used for putting a cup of tea or coffee on, usually a matching cup (with the same colour and pattern as the saucer)

saucy adjective saucier, sauciest
an old-fashioned word meaning not polite or not showing respect *George can be quite saucy in class.*

Saudi ['Sau' rhymes with 'how'] noun **Saudis**
someone from Saudi Arabia

Saudi ['Sau' rhymes with 'how'] adjective
connected with Saudi Arabia

Saudi Arabia noun
a country in South-West Asia
Saudi Arabian adjective & noun

sauna ['sor-ner'] noun **saunas**
1 a special room filled with steam and heated to a high temperature. People sit in the room without clothes on in order to sweat (produce liquid through the skin) and feel healthy.
2 the action of sitting and sweating in a sauna *Grandma sometimes goes for a sauna.*

ORIGIN from Finnish *sauna* referring to the traditional Finnish bath of steam

saunter verb
saunters, sauntering, sauntered
to walk without hurrying, in a relaxed way *I sauntered up to the table and took another sandwich.* **saunter** noun

sausage noun **sausages**
1 a food shaped like a thin tube, made for example of animal skin and filled with very small pieces of meat or vegetables that have been cooked with other things such as fat and spices. Some sausages are eaten hot and others, such as salami, are eaten cold. *a pork sausage; a vegetarian sausage*
2 a sausage roll is a small tube of light pastry (flour, water and fat) filled with the meat from a sausage

savage adjective
1 very violent, in a way that frightens and upsets you *The poor cat was hurt in a savage attack. The hound was a savage beast.*
2 used for describing something that someone says or does that is very unpleasant and cruel *a savage remark; My dad had to accept a savage cut to his salary.*
savagely adverb **savagery** noun

savage noun **savages**
a very violent and frightening person *This attack was the work of savages.*

savage verb
savages, savaging, savaged
1 if a person or animal is savaged by an animal, they are attacked and badly injured or killed
2 to say bad things about something or someone using very unpleasant and cruel words *The author's latest book was savaged by the critics.*

savannah–scale

savannah ['ser-van-er'] noun **savannahs**
a very large area of flat land covered by long or short grass and usually without many trees. Savannahs exist in hot parts of the world such as Africa, South America and Australia.

> **LANGUAGE EXTRA** also spelt *savanna*

save verb
saves, saving, saved
1 to get or keep someone or something away from a dangerous or bad situation, for example by stopping them from being killed or destroyed *The firefighters ran into the house and saved the family from the fire. Antibiotics save many people's lives* (stop them from dying).
2 to keep something and not use it so that you or someone else can have it or use it in the future *I've saved you some cake. My sister saves her red dress for special occasions.*
3 to use less of something such as money, time or space *If you buy your new smartphone before the weekend, you'll save £30* (you'll pay £30 less). *Taking the plane saves three hours.*
4 to collect things by adding more things to them gradually *If you save 10 tokens, you can get a free ice cream.*
5 to keep your money and keep adding more money to it, for example by putting it in a bank, so that you can do or buy something in the future *Jack has saved £300 for a new computer. We're saving up to go on holiday. Holly saves money every week by putting it in the bank.*
6 to stop someone from having to do something that doesn't need to be done *If you get some bread on the way home, that will save me having to go out specially to buy some later.*
7 to stop something from happening that doesn't need to happen *Tidy your room before you go to bed – that will save a lot of arguments with Mum.*
8 to keep something for someone so that it can't be used by anyone else *Could you save my place in the queue?*
9 to save information on a computer is to store it onto the hard disk (inside the computer) or onto something such as a DVD or flash drive (small object that plugs into the computer). You do this, for example, by clicking with your mouse or pressing certain keys. *Save your homework so you can carry on working on it tomorrow. It's sensible to save every few minutes.*
10 in a game such as football, if a goalkeeper saves the ball, he or she stops it from going into the goal

save noun **saves**
when a goalkeeper saves the ball in a game such as football

saver noun **savers**
someone who saves money, usually by putting it regularly in a bank

saving noun **savings**
1 an amount of money that you do not need to spend *If you buy your ticket early, you'll make a big saving.*
2 your savings are the money you have saved up, for example in a bank, so that you can use it in the future

saviour noun **saviours**
a person who saves someone or something from danger, harm or evil

savour verb
savours, savouring, savoured
to enjoy having a particular feeling or experience, or to enjoy eating or drinking something, and let the pleasure continue for a certain amount of time *Anika sipped her smoothie, savouring every moment.*

savoury adjective
having a salty or spicy taste, not a sweet taste. For example, crisps and pizzas are savoury and cakes and doughnuts are sweet.

saw
past tense of **see**

saw noun **saws**
1 a tool for cutting wood or other materials. It is made up of a handle and long blade with sharp teeth (points) along one edge. You push the blade backwards and forwards by hand.
2 a tool for cutting wood or other materials with a circular blade worked by a motor

saw verb
saws, sawing, sawed
to cut something with a saw

sawdust noun
a powder and tiny pieces of wood produced when wood is cut with a saw or rubbed with sandpaper (strong rough paper), or when holes are made in wood with a drill

saxophone noun **saxophones**
a musical instrument, usually made of brass (a yellowish metal). It is shaped like a long tube that is bent at the top and that curves upwards at the bottom like the letter U. You play it by blowing into it over a reed (thin strip of wood that vibrates) and by pressing keys (small buttons or levers) along the tube to change the notes. The saxophone is often used for playing jazz music. **saxophonist** noun

> **ORIGIN** from the name of Adolphe *Sax*, a 19th-century Belgian musician and designer of instruments

say verb
says, saying, said
1 if you say something, you use words to tell someone something, for example by using your voice or writing it down *'I'm tired,' he said. What did Seema say in her email? Can you say a few words about your trip to China?*
2 to give an opinion about something *I want to go swimming tomorrow, Dad – what do you say? People say our school is the best in Essex.*
3 to repeat the words of something *It's time to say a little prayer.*
4 used for talking about information given by something, for example something written such as a book, notice, email, rule or instruction *The rules say the ball must not hit the net. Uncle Jacob's letter says he wants to visit us in the spring.*
5 used for showing a particular measurement or number *The clock says six o'clock.*
6 to mean something *'I've broken your bike.' – 'What are you saying?'* (What do you mean?)
7 used for giving an example or suggestion *Can you come to my house tomorrow, say, at six o'clock?*

say noun
used for talking about giving or having an opinion *It's time for Granddad to have his say* (give his opinion).

saying noun **sayings**
a short sentence that most people know and believe is true and that often tells you something about life, for example 'There's nothing new under the sun.'

scab noun **scabs**
a hard area of dry blood that forms on your skin over a cut or graze while it is getting better

scabbard noun **scabbards**
a cover that goes over the blade of a sword or dagger (short pointed knife)

scaffold noun **scaffolds**
1 a raised structure for workers to stand on while working on the outside of a building, for example doing repairs. It is made up of long flat pieces of wood and metal poles joined together.
2 a raised structure on which criminals were killed in the past, for example by hanging them (putting a rope around their neck)

scaffolding noun
a framework of metal poles that cross over each other and are joined together and fixed to long flat pieces of wood. Scaffolding is used for making a raised structure for workers to stand on while working on the outside of a building.

scald ['skold'] verb
scalds, scalding, scalded
if you scald yourself or a part of your body, you burn your skin with very hot liquid or steam

scald ['skold'] noun **scalds**
a burn on the skin caused by very hot liquid or steam

scale noun **scales**
1 a series of marks along something such as a ruler or thermometer that you use when measuring *The scale on my ruler is in centimetres and millimetres.*
2 all of the values within a group of numbers, amounts or measurements, from the lowest to the highest *The price scale for this type of bike goes from £100 to £500. How bad is your headache on a scale of 1 to 10?*
3 used for showing how a distance or the size of something is connected to that particular distance or size when it is represented on a map or drawing or in a model *The scale of the map is two centimetres to the kilometre* (each two centimetres on the map represents one kilometre). *It's a scale model of the Eiffel Tower* (a model where every part represents the same part as in the real Eiffel Tower but smaller).
4 the size or amount of something, often a large size or amount *Many people were surprised by the scale of the damage. Toys*

scale–scarcely

are being made in China on a large scale (lots of toys are being made). *We don't know the scale of the problem* (how big or bad the problem is).
5 in music, a scale is a group of different notes, beginning at a particular note and going up or down in order
6 a hard white material that forms inside water pipes and kettles. It is also called limescale.
7 a hard substance that forms on the surface of people's teeth when they are not cleaned properly
8 one of the small flat hard parts that form the skin on the body of a fish or of a reptile such as a snake *fish scales; dinosaur scales*

scale verb
scales, scaling, scaled
1 to climb to the top of something high such as a mountain or the outside of a building
2 to climb over something high such as a wall or fence
3 if you scale something down, you make it smaller or less than it was in the past

scalene ['skay-leen'] adjective
a scalene triangle has three sides of different lengths and three angles of different degrees
compare: **equilateral** and **isosceles**

scales noun plural
1 a piece of equipment used for weighing things or people. Scales come in different shapes and sizes. For example, kitchen scales usually have a bowl for weighing ingredients and bathroom scales are for people to stand on to check their weight. A pair of scales is usually made up of an upright bar in the middle that supports another bar across with a little tray hanging from each end.
2 the skin on the body of a fish or of a reptile such as a snake. It is made up of many small parts that are flat and hard.

scallop ['sko-lerp' or 'ska-lerp'] noun
scallops
a shellfish that you can eat. It lives inside a shell made up of two parts joined together.

scalp noun
the skin on the part of your head that is covered by hair

scalpel noun **scalpels**
a small very sharp knife used by a doctor during an operation

scaly adjective **scalier, scaliest**
1 covered with scales like a fish or reptile
2 if your skin is scaly, it is dry and small thin pieces of it often come off

scam noun **scams**
a trick or dishonest plan for getting money from someone, or for not paying money that you should pay, for example by telling someone something that isn't true *an income tax scam* (trick for not paying tax)

scamper verb
scampers, scampering, scampered
to run or move somewhere quickly and with light steps *I saw a mouse scamper across the room.*

scampi noun plural
large prawns (sea animals with a shell and long body) that can be eaten as food, usually fried

scan verb
scans, scanning, scanned
1 to use a scanner to copy something from paper, such as a picture or piece of text, and save it as a digital file on a computer *I scanned in my latest school report.*
2 to use a scanner to see inside something such as luggage or a part of the body so that it can be examined carefully
3 if someone or a piece of equipment scans something such as a card or passport, or shopping in a supermarket, the equipment checks it carefully to get information from it *Remember to scan your library card in the machine if you want to take out a book. Don't remove your credit card, Mum – the machine is still scanning. Scan the barcode of each thing you want to buy before you put it in the trolley.*
4 if a computer program scans, or scans something, it checks something carefully because it is looking for something *The antivirus software is scanning for viruses. It scans my laptop once a day.*
5 to look through a piece of writing quickly, for example because you are trying to find something or want to have an idea of what it is about
6 to look at something carefully, usually because you are looking for something or someone *I scanned the crowd to see if I could see Gran.*
7 if a poem scans, it has a regular pattern of sounds

scan noun **scans**
1 an examination of the inside of something, especially a part of the body, using a scanner, or the picture produced by a scanner *Jon went to the hospital for a brain scan. There will be a scan of all luggage at the airport. What do the scans show?*
2 when you use a scanner to copy something from paper to a computer *I did a scan of my school report.*
3 when someone or a piece of equipment checks something to get information from it or to look for something *This equipment does a scan of your passport. Before I shut down my laptop I'll do a virus scan.*
4 a quick look through a piece of writing *I gave the book a quick scan but it didn't look interesting.*
5 a careful look at something *Using his telescope, Dad did a thorough scan of the night sky.*

scandal noun **scandals**
1 a situation where someone does something very bad that shocks people and means people no longer have respect for them
2 words that people say or write about someone who does something very bad *a newspaper full of scandal*
3 a very bad situation that makes people angry *It's a scandal that there are so many people who don't have enough to eat.*

scandalous adjective
1 used for describing something so bad that it shocks people or makes them angry *scandalous behaviour; It's scandalous that our school doesn't have enough computers.*
2 used about the words that people say or write about someone who does something very bad *a scandalous story*

scandalously adverb

Scandinavia noun
Sweden, Norway and Denmark considered as a group. Sometimes Finland and Iceland are also included.

Scandinavian adjective
connected with Sweden, Norway and Denmark, and sometimes also Finland and Iceland

Scandinavian noun **Scandinavians**
someone from Scandinavia

scanner noun **scanners**
1 a piece of equipment that copies something from paper, such as a picture or writing, and saves it as a digital file on a computer
2 a piece of equipment that examines the inside of something, for example a part of the body, and produces a picture of it *an ultrasound scanner; an airport luggage scanner*
3 a piece of equipment that checks something such as a barcode, card or passport to get information from it
4 a piece of equipment for receiving special signals such as radio waves

scant adjective
used when you mean very little of something or almost none of it at all *Simon paid scant attention to what the teacher said.*

scantily adverb
if someone is scantily dressed, they are not wearing enough clothes

scanty adjective **scantier, scantiest**
1 used when you mean a smaller amount of something than you need or than there should be *The soldiers received scanty supplies of food.*
2 used for describing a small piece of clothing that does not cover enough of the part of the body that it is supposed to cover *a scanty bikini*

scapegoat noun **scapegoats**
someone who gets the blame for something bad that someone else has done or for a bad situation that they have not caused *Noah made Emily a scapegoat for his mistakes* (Noah didn't want to be blamed so he made people blame Emily instead).

scar noun **scars**
a mark left on your skin after something such as a cut or burn has got better

scar verb
scars, scarring, scarred
if an injury scars you, it leaves a scar on your skin *Lila's leg was scarred in a road accident. Jesse has a scarred cheek* (with a scar or scars on it).

scarce adjective **scarcer, scarcest**
1 used for describing something when there is not enough of it or for describing things or people when there are not enough of them *Water is scarce. Good teachers are scarce.*

> ANTONYM **abundant**

2 (informal) if you make yourself scarce, you go away from somewhere or someone, for example to avoid a bad situation

scarcely adverb
1 almost not at all *I've scarcely watched any TV this week. My brother scarcely ever* (almost never) *plays any sport.*

scarcity–school

2 only just *I can scarcely see the house next door in this fog. Dad had scarcely left the house when it started to rain.*
3 definitely not *You can scarcely blame Sam for that.*

SYNONYM hardly

scarcity *noun*
a situation where there is not enough of something *a scarcity of water*

scare *verb*
scares, scaring, scared
another way of saying to frighten *I'm scared to go out after dark. Don't make that funny face – it scares me! I'm scared of him* (he frightens me). *You scared my cat away* (made it run away).

scare *noun*
1 a sudden strong feeling of being frightened *You gave me a real scare.*
2 (plural **scares**) a situation that makes people very worried about something *a health scare* (for example when people are ill and other people are worried about getting ill)

scarecrow *noun* **scarecrows**
a model of a person, often wearing old clothes, that a farmer puts in a field to frighten the birds away, for example to stop them eating the plants or seeds

scarf *noun* **scarves** or **scarfs**
1 a long piece of cloth that you wear around your neck to keep you warm or to make you look nice
2 a square or strip of cloth worn especially by girls and women over the head or head and shoulders. A scarf worn over the head is also called a headscarf.

scarlet *adjective*
bright red **scarlet** *noun*

scary *adjective* **scarier, scariest**
an informal word for frightening
scarily *adverb*

scathing ['skay-thing'; 'th' has the beginning sound of 'this'] *adjective*
showing in a strong or angry way that you dislike something or someone or that you think they are bad or wrong *a scathing remark; My dad was scathing about the school uniform rules* (he thought they were wrong and used strong or angry words to tell people).

scatter *verb*
scatters, scattering, scattered
1 to throw or drop things in lots of different places *The lorry crashed and scattered potatoes all over the road.*
2 to cover an area by throwing or dropping things in different places over it *Mum was scattering the earth with grass seeds.*
3 to move away quickly in different directions or to make people or animals do this *The crowd scattered when they saw the police officers. The children ran towards the chickens and scattered them.*

scatterbrain *noun* **scatterbrains**
(informal)
someone who keeps on forgetting things or who doesn't have a sensible or intelligent way of thinking

scattered *adjective*
1 used for describing things or people that are in different places, for example over a large area *My toys were scattered all around my room. My relatives are scattered around the country.*
2 happening in some places but not others *scattered showers*

scavenge *verb*
scavenges, scavenging, scavenged
1 if an animal or person scavenges, they search through rubbish for food or things that might be useful *The foxes scavenged through our dustbin during the night.*
2 to scavenge food or useful things is to find them by searching through rubbish *The boys scavenged some chairs from the rubbish tip.*
scavenger *noun*

scene *noun* **scenes**
1 a place where something happens, usually something bad *the scene of a crime; An ambulance was on the scene in 10 minutes.*
2 a short part of something such as a play, film or book in which a part of the action happens *The scene is a room in a Glasgow hotel. Act 2, Scene 1.*
3 used when someone describes the place that they see *a peaceful country scene; When the soldiers reached the town they found scenes of destruction.*
4 used when someone describes an event or activity that they see *There were scenes of rejoicing in the streets. The paintings show scenes from everyday life.*
5 when someone suddenly becomes angry with someone and talks to them loudly in a public place *Dad didn't let my sister have an ice cream so she made a scene.*

scenery *noun*
1 all the natural things in an area, such as hills, mountains, rivers, trees, forests and valleys, that people usually think are attractive to look at
2 the large painted pictures and all the furniture and structures that make the stage of a theatre look like a real place

scenic *adjective*
used for describing something that provides beautiful views of nature *a scenic route*

scent *noun* **scents**
1 a pleasant smell, such as the smell of a flower
2 the smell of an animal or person that some animals such as dogs can smell and follow
3 another word for perfume (liquid with a pleasant smell that is put on the skin)

scented *adjective*
used for describing something that has or has been given a pleasant smell *scented notepaper*

sceptic ['skep-tik'] *noun* **sceptics**
someone who is not sure about something or not sure whether something is true

sceptical ['skep-tik-erl'] *adjective*
if someone is sceptical, they are not sure about something or not sure whether something is true *I'm sceptical about our team's chances of winning.* **scepticism** *noun*

schedule ['shed-yool' or 'sked-yool'] *noun* **schedules**
1 a list of things to do and events to go to, including dates or times *Our head teacher has a busy schedule* (many things to do and events to go to).
2 used for talking about the date or time when someone must finish doing something *The building of the new gym is on schedule* (will be finished at the expected time). *The school roof was repaired ahead of schedule* (before the expected time).

scheme *noun* **schemes**
a plan for doing something, for example an official plan or a plan that is clever, secret or dishonest *a government training scheme for young people; It's a scheme to make money fast.*

scheme *verb*
schemes, scheming, schemed
to make a secret plan to do something, for example something bad or dishonest
schemer *noun*

scholar *noun* **scholars**
1 someone who knows a lot about a subject, for example because they have studied it at university *a history scholar*
2 someone who receives a scholarship (money) to study at a school or university

scholarly *adjective*
1 used about someone who knows a lot about a subject or many subjects *Our teacher is very scholarly.*
2 used about someone who studies a lot and likes studying *My sister has always been very scholarly.*
3 used about something written by a scholar *a scholarly book*

scholarship *noun*
1 (plural **scholarships**) money that a person, government or organisation gives you to study at a school or university
2 the serious study of a subject and the knowledge you get through studying *a work of scholarship; a woman of great scholarship*

school *noun*
1 (plural **schools**) a place where children go to learn things *My brother's at school now.*
2 the time that you spend at school or the activities that you do there *School starts at half past eight. My sister has left school* (no longer goes to school, for example because she has reached the age of 18). *I love school.*
3 all the children and teachers in a school *I sang a song in front of the whole school.*
4 (plural **schools**) a place that teaches a particular subject or skill *a language school* (where you learn a foreign language); *a riding school* (where you learn to ride a horse)
5 (plural **schools**) in American English, a school is a college or university

ORIGIN from Greek *skhole* 'free time for talking and learning'

school *noun* **schools**
a large group of fish or other sea animals such as whales or dolphins that swim together

ORIGIN from Old English *scolu* 'group of fish'

school–scoreboard

school *adjective*
connected with school *the school year* (period from autumn to summer when children go to school); *children of school age* (between the ages of about 5 and 18 when children go to school or college); *school dinner* (a meal that you eat at school in the middle of the day)

schoolbag *noun* **schoolbags**
a bag for carrying things such as schoolbooks, for example a backpack (carried on your back) or a satchel (shaped like a rectangle, often carried over your shoulder)

schoolbook *noun* **schoolbooks**
a book used in school, for example for studying a particular subject or for doing your schoolwork in

schoolchild *noun* **schoolchildren**
a child who goes to school. A boy who goes to school is also called a schoolboy and a girl is called a schoolgirl.

schooling *noun*
the education that you get at school

school-leaver *noun* **school-leavers**
a boy or girl who has just left school, usually around the age of 16 or 18

schoolmaster *noun* **schoolmasters**
a man who teaches in a school, especially a private school

schoolmistress *noun* **schoolmistresses**
a woman who teaches in a school, especially a private school

schoolteacher *noun* **schoolteachers**
a teacher who works in a school

schoolwork *noun*
the work that you do in school or that you do for school at home

schoolyard *noun* **schoolyards**
the American word for a playground at school

schooner ['skoo-ner'] *noun* **schooners**
a fast-moving sailing ship with two or more masts (poles for holding up the sails)

science *noun*
1 knowledge about the structure and behaviour of the natural world (for example air, land, water, plants, animals, substances and forces) that you get from studying nature carefully and doing experiments
2 the study of the structure and behaviour of the natural world *a science teacher*; *Science is one of the subjects we do at school.*
3 (*plural* **sciences**) a particular type of science *computer science*; *medical science*

ORIGIN from Latin *scientia* 'knowledge'

science fiction *noun*
a particular kind of story, for example in books, films or comics, about imaginary events, people and things, usually in the future or on other planets. Science fiction includes space travel, travelling back or forward in time, and alien creatures (beings from other planets).

scientific *adjective*
1 connected with science or used in science *a scientific instrument*; *This area is of great scientific interest.*
2 done in a very careful and detailed way to learn about nature and everything connected with it *scientific research*; *a scientific experiment*

scientifically *adverb*

scientist *noun* **scientists**
an expert in science or someone who studies one of the sciences *a nuclear scientist*

scissors *noun plural*
scissors (also called a pair of scissors) are used for cutting things such as paper, card, hair, nails and cloth. They are made up of two blades, joined together in the middle, that can be opened and closed. Each blade has a handle at the end with a hole to put your fingers through.

scoff *verb*
scoffs, scoffing, scoffed
1 to show that you think someone or something is silly or bad by saying something unkind *When I showed Oliver my painting he just scoffed. He scoffed at my attempt to paint a picture of Tower Bridge.*
2 (informal) to eat a lot of something, often quickly *My brother scoffed the whole pizza.*

scold *verb*
scolds, scolding, scolded
to tell someone in an angry voice that you are not happy with them because they have done something wrong

scone ['skohn' or 'skon'] *noun* **scones**
a small round cake for one person. It is usually cut in half and buttered or spread with jam. It is sometimes eaten as part of a cream tea (small meal of scones, jam, cream and a pot of tea).

scoop *noun* **scoops**
1 a tool with a bowl shape at one end for pushing into something soft such as ice cream or flour and picking it up
2 an amount of something picked up by a scoop *Two scoops of mashed potato, please.*
3 a piece of news that one particular news group discovers and makes known to the public before others have a chance to print or broadcast it *Yet another scoop for our local newspaper!*

scoop *verb*
scoops, scooping, scooped
to pick up or remove something soft using something such as a spoon or scoop or your curved hands *Dad scooped up some ice cream from the tub. I scooped out the water from the boat with my bare hands.*

scoot *verb* (informal)
scoots, scooting, scooted
to go somewhere quickly *I have to scoot off to the library to pick up a book.*

scooter *noun* **scooters**
1 a type of vehicle like a motorcycle with two small wheels, a low seat and a flat board for resting your feet on. It has less power than a motorcycle.
2 a toy for children to ride on. It has a narrow flat board with two small wheels and a tall upright handle. You stand on the board with one foot and move the scooter along by pushing with the other foot against the ground.

scope *noun*
1 used for talking about all the different things that something is supposed to deal with or include *The scope of the police investigation is very wide* (the police are investigating many things). *This subject is beyond* (or *outside*) *the scope of the book* (the book is not supposed to deal with this subject because it is not connected with the main subject).
2 used when you mean it is possible for something to happen or exist *There's plenty of scope for improvement in your schoolwork* (it's possible to make it much better).

scorch *verb*
scorches, scorching, scorched
1 to burn something slightly and make it go brown *I accidentally scorched my shirt with the iron.*
2 if something hot scorches a part of your body, it burns it slightly and causes pain *My neck has been scorched by the sun.*

scorcher *noun* **scorchers**
an informal way of saying a very hot day *Yesterday was a scorcher.*

scorching *adjective*
very hot *The weather was scorching.*

score *noun* **scores**
1 the number of points that a person or team gets in a game, sport or competition, for example the number of goals in a football match or runs in a cricket match *In the school quiz Daniel got a high score* (lots of points). *Leah's going to keep score* (keep a note of each person's score during a game, usually by writing it down).
2 the number of points or marks someone gets for giving correct answers in a test or exam *What score did you get in your exam? I got a good score in maths* (for example 18 out of 20).
3 the music for a film, play or other performance *He's a musician who has written many film scores.*
4 a piece of written music showing the parts for the instruments and voices
5 used when you mean 20 (or about 20) things or people *A score of countries voted yes.*
6 **scores of** lots of *I've been to Edinburgh scores of times. Scores of people came to my party.*

score *verb*
scores, scoring, scored
1 to get a point in a game, sport or competition, for example a goal in football or a run in cricket *Sanjay scored two goals. Our team hasn't scored yet.*
2 to get a point or mark in a test or exam *You score two marks for every correct answer. Seema scored 100 per cent in her maths test.*
3 to be worth a certain number of points *Every correct answer scores three points.*
4 to be successful in doing something *Our team scored a victory.*
5 to make a mark or cut in the surface of something

scorer *noun*

scoreboard *noun* **scoreboards**
a large flat surface or piece of electronic equipment where the scores of sports matches and other competitions are displayed

435

scorn–scraper

scorn noun
a strong feeling of dislike towards someone or something because you have no respect for them and think there is nothing good about them *He treated me with scorn. They poured scorn on my suggestion* (showed no respect towards it because they thought it was bad).

scorn verb
scorns, scorning, scorned
to show no respect for something or someone because you think there is nothing good about them

scornful adjective
showing no respect and a strong feeling of dislike *a scornful look; She was scornful of my ideas.*

scorpion noun scorpions
an animal like a big insect with eight legs, a long curved tail and two claws (pointed parts) at the front of its body. At the end of its tail there is a poisonous sting.

Scot noun Scots
someone from Scotland

Scotch egg noun Scotch eggs
a hard-boiled egg covered with chopped meat and breadcrumbs (tiny pieces of dry bread) and then fried. It is usually eaten cold.

Scotland noun
a country in North-West Europe. Scotland is a part of the island of Great Britain together with England and Wales.

Scotland Yard noun
1 the main office of the police force in London
2 the police officers who work there

Scotsman noun Scotsmen
a man from Scotland

Scotswoman noun Scotswomen
a woman from Scotland

Scottish adjective
connected with Scotland

scoundrel noun scoundrels
someone who behaves badly or in a dishonest way

scour verb
scours, scouring, scoured
1 to search through a place or thing carefully because you are looking for something or someone *The police scoured the woods for the missing boy.*
2 to clean something such as a saucepan by rubbing it hard with something such as a scouring pad (piece of rough material)

scouring pad noun scouring pads
a small piece of rough material for cleaning, made of pieces of wire or plastic threads twisted together

> LANGUAGE EXTRA you can also say *scourer*

Scout noun Scouts
a Scout or Boy Scout is a boy, usually aged 11 to 18, who belongs to the Scouts (or Scout Association). This organisation teaches boys useful skills.

scout noun scouts
1 someone, for example from a group of soldiers, who is sent ahead of the group to get information about the people they are fighting, such as where they are and how many there are
2 a search of a place *Dad had a scout around the town but couldn't find a good place to eat.*

scout verb
scouts, scouting, scouted
1 to try to find something by looking in different places *We've been scouting around for the best place to put up our tent.*
2 to search a place to try to find something *We scouted the whole area looking for a shady spot for our picnic.*

scowl verb
scowls, scowling, scowled
to look very angry, for example by frowning (moving your eyebrows closer together) or pursing your lips (pressing them tightly together) *Stop scowling at me!*

scowl noun scowls
a very angry look on someone's face

scrabble verb
scrabbles, scrabbling, scrabbled
to make lots of small quick movements with your fingers, hands or feet, for example to try to find something or get somewhere *He was scrabbling around for his glasses on the floor of the dark room.*

Scrabble noun (trademark)
a game you play on a square board on which you form words by putting together different letters that are marked on small plastic blocks called tiles

scraggly adjective scragglier, scraggliest (informal)
untidy and growing in an uneven way *a scraggly beard*

scraggy adjective scraggier, scraggiest
very thin so that you can see the shape of the bones *a scraggy neck*

scramble verb
scrambles, scrambling, scrambled
1 to move or climb somewhere quickly and with difficulty, often using your hands and feet *We saw some old men scrambling up a hill.*
2 to rush somewhere or rush to get or do something (used when you mean there are lots of other people who also want to do these things) *When the bell went off, the children scrambled for the door* (for example, they pushed each other to get there as fast as possible). *People are scrambling to buy tickets for our school play.*
3 if you scramble eggs, you mix the white and yellow parts together and cook them, for example in a frying pan or saucepan *I had toast and scrambled eggs for breakfast.*

scramble noun
1 a difficult climb or walk, often using your hands and feet
2 a mad rush somewhere or to get or do something *There was a scramble for the best seats in the hall.*

scrap noun
1 (plural scraps) a small piece of something *I wrote my phone number on a scrap of paper.*
2 old metal from vehicles or machines that can be recycled (used again after being dealt with in a special way) *Mum sold my old bike for scrap. My uncle is a scrap metal dealer.*
3 scraps are pieces of food from a meal that have not been eaten. Scraps are usually thrown away or given to an animal to eat.
4 (plural scraps) an informal word for a fight or argument *Jack has got into a scrap again.*

scrap verb
scraps, scrapping, scrapped
1 to stop doing something *The school trip to Gibraltar has been scrapped.*
2 to get rid of something because it is no longer useful *Some parents want to scrap the school uniform altogether.*

scrapbook noun scrapbooks
a book with empty pages for sticking things in, such as pictures, greetings cards or newspaper articles. The cover and pages of the scrapbook are often decorated with different designs and materials.
scrapbooking noun

scrape verb
scrapes, scraping, scraped
1 to accidentally rub the surface of something and cause damage *I fell over and scraped my knee, making it bleed. Dad drove too close to a bus and scraped the side of the car. My new boots have been scraping against my ankles.*
2 to rub the surface of something with something rough or sharp, especially to get rid of something *You have to scrape the wood hard to get the paint off. Scrape the carrots before cooking them* (get rid of the skin with a tool or knife).
3 to get rid of something from a surface by rubbing it off *I scraped the mud off my shoes.*
4 to move something hard or sharp along a surface *Stop scraping your chair across the floor.*
5 used when talking about being successful in doing something but almost not being successful because it is so difficult *Jack scraped through his maths exam* (he passed but only just). *My parents scraped together the money to buy me a bike* (had just enough money to buy it). *I can just about scrape by on my pocket money* (the money is only just enough to pay for the things I need).

scrape noun scrapes
1 a mark on the surface of something where it is rubbed against something *a scrape on the side of the car*
2 a place on your body where the skin has been accidentally rubbed
3 the noise of something hard or sharp moving along a surface
4 the action of rubbing something with something rough or sharp *Give your muddy boots a good scrape.*
5 (informal) a difficult or dangerous situation *Lana has got herself into another scrape!*

scraper noun scrapers
a tool with a handle and a sharp edge for getting rid of things by scraping
a wallpaper scraper

436

scrap paper – script

scrap paper noun
old paper, or paper that has been written or drawn on, that you use for writing or drawing things on

scrappy adjective **scrappier, scrappiest**
used for describing something that is badly organised or not put together carefully *a scrappy piece of homework*

scrapyard noun **scrapyards**
a place where people take old or broken vehicles or machines so that their parts can be recycled (used again after being dealt with in a special way)

scratch verb
scratches, scratching, scratched
1 to rub your skin, usually with your nails, to get rid of an itch (an uncomfortable feeling that you think will only go away if you rub it) *I was scratching my leg. This insect bite makes me want to scratch.*
2 to rub or touch the surface of something and cause damage *The cat scratched my leg* (cut my leg with its claws). *I dropped my pen and it scratched my tablet screen.*
3 to move something hard against a surface and make a noise *We heard mice scratching* (moving their bodies against something). *Someone was outside scratching with their nails against the window.*
4 if you scratch something off, you get rid of it, for example by rubbing it with something hard *My brother had a big scab which he scratched off. Please scratch my name off the list.*
5 if someone scratches their head about something, they don't understand it and they think about it to try to find an answer

scratch noun **scratches**
1 a small place on your body where the skin has been accidentally rubbed or cut *I've got a scratch on my knee. My uncle crashed his car but escaped without a scratch* (wasn't hurt at all).
2 a small mark on the surface of something where it has been rubbed against something or where something has touched it *There are some scratches on my glasses.*
3 when you rub your skin to get rid of an itch *I'm just going to have a scratch.*
4 **from scratch** used when talking about doing or starting something from the beginning *I learnt French from scratch in two years* (without knowing any French when I started).
5 **up to scratch** used for saying that something or someone is as good as they should be *Sayed's work has been up to scratch this term.*

scratchy adjective **scratchier, scratchiest**
1 if a piece of clothing is scratchy, it is slightly uncomfortable and gives you a feeling that makes you want to scratch your skin
2 if you have a scratchy throat, your throat is slightly painful
3 if something such as an old record or recording is scratchy, the sound is very rough and unclear

scrawl verb
scrawls, scrawling, scrawled
to write something quickly in a careless or untidy way, often something unpleasant *Someone had scrawled a rude word on the classroom door.*

scrawl noun **scrawls**
careless or untidy writing *I can't read the doctor's scrawl.*

scrawny adjective **scrawnier, scrawniest**
very thin in a way that doesn't look healthy *a scrawny neck*

scream verb
screams, screaming, screamed
to make a loud high noise with your voice, usually because you're frightened, hurt, angry or excited *We screamed when we heard the sound of the guns. When the rock star came on the stage, the fans started screaming. 'Leave me alone,' he screamed.*

scream noun **screams**
1 a loud high noise that you make, usually because you're frightened, hurt, angry or excited
2 (informal) **to be a scream** to be extremely funny

screech verb
screeches, screeching, screeched
if something or someone screeches, they make a loud high noise that is very unpleasant to hear *The driver put her foot on the brakes and the bus screeched to a halt.*

screech noun **screeches**
a loud high noise that is very unpleasant *We heard a screech of tyres.*

screen noun **screens**
1 the flat surface on a piece of equipment such as a computer or television that shows the pictures or words
2 in a cinema, the large flat area against the wall where you see the film
3 the pictures or words shown on a computer screen *Click this icon to print the screen.*
4 a frame or thin wall that you can move around, made of material such as wood, plastic or cloth. It is used for putting round things or people to hide them or protect them or for separating one area from another.
5 a wire net put over a window or door for stopping insects coming in

screen verb
screens, screening, screened
1 to screen people is to examine them by doing medical tests on them to see if they have anything wrong with them *All patients were screened for signs of infection.*
2 to screen things is to check them to see if there is a problem with them *Your luggage will be screened at the airport.*
3 to hide something or someone from something else, for example to protect them *I screened my eyes from the sun. A row of tall trees screen the house from view.*
4 to separate one area from another with a screen *One part of the hall was screened off for students to take their exams.*
5 to show a film or TV programme
6 to screen people who apply for a job is to find out information about them to make sure they are good enough and can be trusted

screensaver noun **screensavers**
a computer program that makes the screen go black or that shows moving images or patterns when you are not using the computer. In the past, screensavers were used for protecting the screen from damage but now they are mainly for decoration.

LANGUAGE EXTRA also spelt *screen saver*

screw noun **screws**
a small thin piece of metal with a twisted raised edge going along and around it in a spiral. It has a point at one end and a flat or round top with a narrow line or cross shape cut in it. A screw is used for joining something to wood or plastic. You turn the top of it round and round with a screwdriver so that the pointed end goes into the wood or plastic.

screw verb
screws, screwing, screwed
1 to fix something with a screw or screws, for example to a piece of wood *I screwed the coat hook onto the door. If the handle gets loose, you'll have to screw it in.*
2 to put something into its position by turning it round and round *Screw the lid on the jar as tightly as you can. Dad screwed in the light bulb.*
3 to screw up something such as paper is to crush it or twist it so that it becomes smaller *The wastepaper basket was full of screwed up pieces of paper.*
4 if you screw up your eyes, you almost close them by tightening the muscles, usually because the light is too bright
5 if you screw up your face, you show for example that you're in pain or unhappy about something, by tightening the muscles
6 (slang) if you screw something up, you do it badly or spoil it *Josh screwed up all our plans.*

screwdriver noun **screwdrivers**
a tool made up of a long thin piece of metal with a handle at one end and a small flat or shaped part at the other end. You fit this part into the cut at the top of a screw and turn the screw round and round to fix it into wood or plastic.

screwy adjective **screwier, screwiest**
(informal)
very strange or stupid

scribble verb
scribbles, scribbling, scribbled
1 to write something quickly in a careless or untidy way *Dad just had time to scribble an absence note before I went off to school.*
2 to make untidy marks or drawings with a pencil or pen *My baby sister scribbled all over my homework.*

scribble noun

scribe noun **scribes**
a person who in the past copied the words of books or documents by hand, especially before printing was invented

script noun **scripts**
1 the written words of something such as a film, play or speech. A script of a film or play tells the story through dialogue (words spoken by the characters) and stage directions.
2 the letters and symbols used for writing a language *Russian uses a different script from English.*

SYNONYM alphabet

437

scripture–seafront

3 the way someone writes using a pen or pencil

SYNONYM handwriting

scripture *noun* **scriptures**
the holy book or books of a religion *Hindu scripture*

scroll *verb*
scrolls, scrolling, scrolled
to move words or pictures up, down, right or left on a computer screen so that you can see all of them when not all of them fit on the screen at the same time *I scrolled down to the bottom of the page.*

scroll *noun* **scrolls**
1 a long roll of paper or other material such as parchment (dried skin of animals), used especially in the past for writing or drawing on
2 an object made up of two long rolls of paper or other material joined together *a scroll of a book of the Bible*
3 a design that has the curved shape of a roll of paper or that is made up of lots of different curved shapes

scrollbar *noun* **scrollbars**
a long strip along the side or bottom of a computer screen, with an icon on it that you drag up, down, right or left, for example using a mouse, to move words or pictures up, down or across the screen

LANGUAGE EXTRA also spelt *scroll bar*

scrooge *noun* **scrooges**
someone who has money but doesn't like spending it or giving any to other people to help them

SYNONYM miser

ORIGIN from Ebenezer *Scrooge* in the story *A Christmas Carol* by Charles Dickens

scrounge *verb* (informal)
scrounges, scrounging, scrounged
to ask someone to give you something because you cannot or do not want to pay for it *My dad scrounged some money off Granddad to pay for my music lessons.*
scrounger *noun*

scrub *verb*
scrubs, scrubbing, scrubbed
1 to clean something by rubbing it hard, for example with a hard brush, soap and water *a scrubbing brush*; *Mum wants me to scrub the kitchen floor to get rid of the grease.*
2 to scrub something off is to get rid of it by rubbing it hard
3 (informal) to get rid of something, or to stop doing something that was planned such as a visit or match

scrub *noun*
1 the action of cleaning something by rubbing it hard *Give your dirty hands a good scrub.*
2 bushes and small trees that grow especially on land of bad quality and in places without much rain
3 scrub or scrubland is land of bad quality where bushes and small trees grow

scruff *noun* **scruffs**
1 an informal word for a dirty and untidy person
2 **by the scruff of the neck** by the back of the neck *Dad grabbed me by the scruff of the neck.*

scruffy *adjective* **scruffier, scruffiest**
dirty and untidy *a scruffy old pair of jeans*
scruffiness *noun*

scrum *noun* **scrums**
in rugby, a scrum is a group of players from both teams who come together with their arms joined and heads down. Each team pushes against the other and tries to get the ball.
short for: scrummage

scrumptious *adjective* (informal)
if something is scrumptious, it tastes very good

SYNONYM delicious

scrunch *verb*
scrunches, scrunching, scrunched
1 to scrunch something up, such as paper or cloth, is to squeeze it into a smaller shape, for example like a ball
2 if an animal or person scrunches themselves up, they bring their legs (or their legs and arms) closer to their body than normal so that they take up less space *There isn't much room on the back seat so you'll have to scrunch yourselves up.*

scrutinise *verb*
scrutinises, scrutinising, scrutinised
to look at something carefully

LANGUAGE EXTRA also spelt *scrutinize*

scrutiny *noun*
when someone looks at something, or when a group of official people look at something, in a careful way *Our school's rules about uniforms have come under scrutiny* (people such as teachers and parents are looking at the rules, for example to see if they are good).

scuba diving *noun*
the activity of swimming under the water using a container of air on your back, with a tube fixed to it for breathing through. You wear flippers (flat wide rubber shoes) on your feet to help you move through the water. **scuba diver** *noun*

ORIGIN an acronym from *self-contained underwater breathing apparatus*

scuffle *noun* **scuffles**
a short fight, often a fight that is not serious and happens suddenly between groups of people *Scuffles broke out between students and police.*

scuffle *verb*
scuffles, scuffling, scuffled
to fight, often in a way that is not serious

sculptor *noun* **sculptors**
someone who creates sculptures

sculpture *noun*
1 (*plural* **sculptures**) a work of art that someone makes out of stone, metal or wood by cutting it with special tools
2 the art or work of creating sculptures

scum *noun*
1 a thick unpleasant substance that forms on the top of a liquid
2 a very insulting word for people you have no respect for and think are very bad

scurry *verb*
scurries, scurrying, scurried
to run or move somewhere quickly, often with short steps *We could hear mice scurrying under the floorboards.*

scuttle *verb*
scuttles, scuttling, scuttled
1 to run or move somewhere quickly with short steps, for example to get away from something or someone *The children scuttled off as soon as they heard someone coming.*
2 to scuttle a ship is to sink it on purpose, usually by making holes in it
3 if someone scuttles something such as a plan or deal, they stop it from being successful

scuttle *noun* **scuttles**
a scuttle or coal scuttle is a bucket, often shaped like a cylinder (tube) with a big sloping top, used especially in the past for carrying coal and pouring it onto a fire in a fireplace

scuzzy *adjective* **scuzzier, scuzziest**
a slang word for dirty

scythe ['scy' is pronounced like 'sigh'] *noun* **scythes**
a tool with a long curved blade fixed to a long handle that is held with both hands. It was used especially in the past, for example by farmers, for cutting grass or wheat.
scythe *verb*
compare: sickle

sea *noun*
1 the water that covers most of the surface of the world, or a small area of this water *Most of our planet is covered by sea. Dad visited many countries by sea* (in a boat or ship). *I love swimming in the sea. The ship is at sea* (on the sea away from land).
2 (*plural* **seas**) a very large area of water with land around most or all of it *the Mediterranean Sea*
3 **a sea of** an area covered with a large amount of something *We looked into the crowd and saw a sea of flags.*

seabed *noun*
the seabed is the ground at the bottom of the sea

LANGUAGE EXTRA also spelt *sea bed*

seabird *noun* **seabirds**
a bird that lives near the sea or that flies out a long way from the coast. Gulls, penguins, puffins and albatrosses are seabirds.

seafaring *adjective*
connected with travelling by sea *Britain is a seafaring nation.* **seafarer** *noun*

seafood *noun*
food from fish and from animals that live in the sea, especially animals with shells such as crabs, lobsters and oysters

seafront *noun*
1 a part of a town next to the sea, for example with houses and hotels facing the sea

438

2 a road going along the edge of the sea for people to walk along

seagull *noun* seagulls
a big grey and white bird with long wings that lives near the sea

SYNONYM gull

seahorse *noun* seahorses
a small fish with a long head that looks like a horse's head and a long curly tail. It swims upright in the water.

seal *verb*
seals, sealing, sealed
1 to close something tightly, for example so that no air or liquid can get in or out *The lid on the jar is not properly sealed. Dad sealed up the parcel with tape and took it to the post office.*
2 if you seal an envelope, you close it by sticking it down
3 if police officers, firefighters or soldiers seal off an area, building or road, they surround it or block it off to stop people going there or getting past *The dangerous building was sealed off with ropes.*

seal *noun* seals
1 a piece of material for keeping something tightly closed. There are many different types of seals. For example, there are plastic or rubber seals going around the tops of containers so that no air or liquid can get in or out or so that the things inside can be kept safe. There are also rubber seals going around openings such as doors or windows so that no air or liquid can get in or out. *Don't buy that pot of yoghurt – the seal is broken. The seal round the car window is loose and rain is getting in.*
2 an official design or mark on a document to show that it really comes from the person it is supposed to come from. In the past, seals were often made using wax (a substance like fat that is soft when hot and hard when cold). *This letter bears the seal of the president of the United States.*

ORIGIN from Latin *sigillum* 'small picture' (from *signum* 'mark' or 'sign')

seal *noun* seals
a sea animal that eats fish and also lives on the land. Seals have round faces with holes instead of ears, and long heavy bodies with a tail and flippers (body parts like arms for swimming). Some seals have smooth bodies and others are covered with fur, especially white fur.

sealant *noun* sealants
a liquid that is put onto a surface or a substance that is put into small holes or gaps along a surface, for example around a window or door, to protect the surface from water or dampness

sea level *noun*
the height of the sea, used for measuring the height of places or objects on the land *Ben Nevis in Scotland is over 1300 metres above sea level.*

sea lion *noun* sea lions
a sea animal like a large seal that eats fish and also lives on the land. Sea lions have round faces, small ears and long heavy bodies with very big flippers (body parts like arms) that they use for swimming and walking.

seam *noun* seams
1 a line where two pieces of cloth are joined together by sewing
2 a long thin layer of rock, especially coal, under the ground

seaman *noun* seamen
another word for a sailor

seaplane *noun* seaplanes
a plane that can take off from water and land on water. Some seaplanes have two long hollow structures at the bottom for floating on the water.

seaport *noun* seaports
a town or city with a port (area next to the sea where ships stop)

search *verb*
searches, searching, searched
1 to try to find something or someone by looking somewhere carefully *I've searched the house but can't find my mobile. Dad knocked on the neighbours' doors searching for my sister. We've searched everywhere but we can't find the answer.*
2 if someone official such as a police officer searches a person, they look in that person's pockets, bags and clothes to try to find something hidden *The head teacher searched the bully to see if he was carrying a weapon.*
3 to look for information on the internet by going to a web page (or pages) or to look for information stored on a computer *Search the BBC site for the dates and times of programmes. I searched my document for the word 'green' and replaced it with 'blue'.*

search *noun* searches
1 when you try to find something or someone by looking carefully *After a long search I found my glasses.*
2 when someone official such as a police officer tries to find something hidden, for example in a building, vehicle or someone's clothes *The police carried out a search of the thief's house.*
3 when you look for information on the internet or stored on a computer *I did a search to find out the difference between a seal and a sea lion.*
4 a search engine is a computer program that finds information on the internet when you type a word (or words) into a blank space called a search box

searching *adjective*
used for describing something that is meant to find out the truth about something or someone or that shows that you really want to know the truth *Jess always asks searching questions* (for example difficult and important ones, to find out how things work). *She gave me a searching look* (for example trying to find out what I was thinking).

searchlight *noun* searchlights
a large lamp with a strong beam (long line of light) that can be turned to shine in different directions, used for example for finding people at night or for lighting up the sky for decoration
compare: **floodlight** and **spotlight**

search party *noun* search parties
a group of people who go searching for a missing person or for missing people in an organised way

seashell *noun* seashells
1 an empty shell from a small sea animal such as a clam, oyster, mussel or scallop that you find on the beach
2 a design or pattern that looks like a seashell

seashore *noun*
the piece of land, made up of sand and rocks, that runs along the edge of the sea *We often go for walks along the seashore.*

seasick *adjective*
someone who is seasick feels ill when they travel by boat or ship or by a sea vehicle such as a hovercraft **seasickness** *noun*

seaside *noun* seasides
a place by the sea where people go for a holiday or for a day trip *We go to the seaside every year. Southwold is a seaside town.*

season *noun* seasons
1 spring, summer, autumn and winter are the four seasons of the year. The seasons are the periods that the year is divided into depending on the type of weather and the time of the year.
2 a period of the year when something happens, usually something that happens in the same way every year *September is the rainy season. The football season starts in August.*
3 a period when a series of events, shows or programmes are organised in a particular place or on TV or radio *a season of Harry Potter films at our local cinema; a season of new TV documentaries*
4 season's greetings used at Christmas or New Year to send someone good wishes, for example on a greetings card or in an email

season *verb*
seasons, seasoning, seasoned
to put something such as salt, pepper, spices or herbs (plants) on food to make it taste better

seasonal *adjective*
1 happening only at a particular time of the year *Strawberry picking is seasonal work.*
2 connected with a particular time of the year *seasonal changes in temperature; seasonal vegetables* (for example ready now to buy in the shops)
3 usual for a particular time of the year *This cold weather is not very seasonal for August.*

seasoning *noun* seasonings
something such as salt, pepper, spices or herbs (plants) that you put on food to make it taste better

season ticket *noun* season tickets
a special ticket you buy that allows you to use it lots of times within a certain period, for example to travel by train or to go to a football match, so that you don't have to pay every time. Buying a season ticket is cheaper than paying for a separate ticket every time.

seat *noun* seats
1 an object for sitting on, such as a chair, or a place where you sit, for example in a car, on a bike or on a toilet

2 a place that you pay for and sit in, for example to travel in a bus, train or plane or to watch a film in a cinema
3 the bottom part of something used for sitting on *The seat of the armchair is all sticky.*
4 the official position of someone as a member of a group, for example a political group or a group of people in charge of an organisation or business *How many seats in Parliament do the Labour Party have? My mum has a seat on the school board* (group in charge of the school).
5 the main place where an organisation operates from or where something important happens *London is the seat of government.*
6 if you take or have a seat, you sit down somewhere *'Come in and have a seat,' said the head teacher.*

seat verb
seats, seating, seated
1 to give someone a seat somewhere *I asked to be seated next to the window on the plane.*
2 if you seat yourself somewhere, you sit down there, and if you are seated somewhere, you are sitting there
3 if something such as a vehicle, theatre or stadium seats a certain number of people, that is the number it has room for on its seats *This minibus seats 12 people.*

seat belt noun **seat belts**
a strap that you put around your body to hold you safely in your seat, for example in a car or plane

LANGUAGE EXTRA also spelt *seatbelt*

seating noun
1 places to sit *There's not enough seating on the coach for everyone in the class.*

SYNONYM seats

2 the way seats are arranged *They've changed the seating in the canteen.*

seaweed noun
a green, brown or dark red plant that grows in the sea or on rocks by the sea

seaworthy adjective
safe to be used on the sea *My uncle's boat isn't seaworthy any more.*

secateurs ['sek-er-**terrz**] noun plural
a tool used by gardeners for cutting the stems, flowers and leaves of plants. Secateurs look like a strong pair of scissors with two short sharp blades and with handles connected by a spring.

SYNONYM pruning shears

secluded adjective
1 used for describing a place that has no people or places such as buildings or roads nearby, or a place that is hidden from other people *We found a quiet secluded beach. Grandma's garden is secluded* (for example hidden by trees).
2 without contact with other people *a secluded life*
seclusion noun

second adjective
1 coming next after the first one *You're the second person to ask me that question.*

2 another *I tried a second time. Can you speak a second language?*
3 next after the first when talking about the importance, quality or size of something or someone *Your first duty is to your parents and your second duty is to your grandparents. Is Birmingham still the UK's second biggest city?*
4 **every second . . .** happening once out of two possible times, or affecting one thing or person but not the next, as part of a regular pattern *I have music lessons every second Monday* (one Monday in two). *Every second girl was red-headed* (only the second, fourth, sixth girl and so on).
5 **to have second thoughts** to make a different decision or the opposite decision, or to no longer be sure about something *I said I would go to Lily's party then I had second thoughts* (I decided not to go). *James is having second thoughts about studying German* (he's not sure he wants to study it).

second adverb
next after the first person or thing *Hannah came second in the race. Tidy your room first and watch TV second!*

second noun
1 the person who comes next after the first person or who does something after the first person *Leo was the second to go in.*
2 the thing that comes next or happens after the first thing *That loud bang was the second we heard that evening.*
3 (plural **seconds**) a very short period of time that is one of the 60 parts that a minute is divided into
4 (plural **seconds**) used when talking about any very short period of time or the exact time when something happens *Wait here – I'm going into my room for a second. Dad will be back any second* (very very soon). *A boy climbed onto a desk but just at that second our teacher walked in.*
5 a second hand is a long thin part that moves around the face (front part) of a clock or watch and shows the time passing in seconds
6 seconds are products that you buy cheaply because they have something wrong with them, such as being slightly damaged or having a mistake in their pattern or colour *These cups are seconds.*
7 **seconds** an informal word for a second amount of the food you've just eaten *May I have seconds, please?*

second verb
seconds, seconding, seconded
1 to officially support an idea suggested by someone else at a meeting
2 used for saying you agree with something or someone *'I think we should have an ice cream.' – 'I'll second that!'*

secondary adjective
1 less important than something else *Having good teachers is important – how old they are is of secondary importance.*
2 connected with the teaching of students in secondary schools *secondary education*

secondary school noun
secondary schools
a school for students between the ages of 11 and 18

second class noun
a way of sending something by post or travelling somewhere, for example by train or plane, that is less expensive than first class *If you use second class, your letter will take two or three days to arrive. We always travel in second class although it's less comfortable than first.*

second class adverb
used about a second-class way of sending something or travelling *to send a letter second class; to travel second class*

second-class adjective
1 used for describing something that is not of good quality or not of a good standard *second-class goods*
2 connected with the less expensive way of sending something by post or travelling somewhere, for example by train or plane *a second-class stamp; a second-class ticket*

second cousin noun **second cousins**
a son or daughter of your mother's or father's cousin

second-hand adjective & adverb
1 used for describing something that is not new because it belonged to someone else before *My stepdad sometimes buys second-hand clothes. Jack bought his bike second-hand.*
2 selling things that are not new *a second-hand bookshop* (where you buy second-hand books)
3 if you get second-hand information, or get information second-hand from someone, you don't get it directly through speaking to someone but indirectly from other people

second-in-command noun
seconds-in-command
a person who has the second highest rank to someone in charge of a group, for example in the army

secondly adverb
used when talking about the second thing that happens or that you want to say *Firstly, tell us why you did it, and secondly, apologise.*

second name noun **second names**
1 family name (last name that you share with people in your close family). A second name is also known as a surname.
2 middle name (middle part of a name after the first name and before the family name)

second-rate adjective
used for describing a level, quality or person that is not of a good standard *a second-rate cricket team*

secrecy noun
when something is kept secret so that no-one knows anything about it

secret noun
1 (plural **secrets**) something that only one person or a few people know about and that should not be told to other people *I'll tell you her name if you can keep a secret* (not tell anyone else).
2 (plural **secrets**) something that is not known and has not been explained *the secrets of life and the universe*
3 the particular way someone has of being successful in achieving something

Dad knows the secret of a good cup of tea (for example, he knows how to make it). *Grandma can run faster than me – what's her secret?* (How does she do it?)
4 an open secret is something that no-one is supposed to know about but that lots of people do know about
5 in secret without anyone else knowing

secret *adjective*
1 used about something or someone that other people are not supposed to know or know about *Mum hides her jewellery in a secret place under the floorboards. My brother has a secret girlfriend.*
2 used about something that you don't tell anyone else *I keep my opinions secret.*
3 used about someone who does something that they don't want other people to know *My sister is a secret chocolate lover.*
4 a secret service is a part of a government that protects a country's secrets and tries to find out the secrets of other countries using spies called secret agents

secretary *noun* **secretaries**
1 a person who works for someone in an office and does things such as answering the phone, typing emails, arranging meetings and keeping records of documents
2 a member of a government in charge of an important section called a department *the Foreign Secretary* (dealing with foreign countries)
secretarial *adjective*

secrete ['sik-reet'] *verb*
secretes, secreting, secreted
1 to produce a liquid (used about a part of the body or a plant) *Glands in the mouth secrete saliva.*
2 to hide something in a secret place

secretive *adjective*
1 not telling people about anything or anyone *Their club is very secretive. He's secretive about his friends.*
2 not showing people your feelings or thoughts *secretive behaviour*; *She's quiet and secretive.*
secretively *adverb*

secretly *adverb*
1 without anyone else knowing *The police officer secretly recorded their conversation.*
2 used about the private thoughts and feelings someone has that they don't tell anyone about *Many people secretly hoped our team would lose.*

sect *noun* **sects**
a group of people with particular religious or political beliefs that some people think are unusual

section *noun* **sections**
1 one of the separate things that the whole of something is divided into *Passengers sit in the middle section of the plane. This section of the playground is for ball games. Dad's reading the sports section* (in a newspaper or on a website).
2 some of a particular thing but not the whole of it *A section of the motorway has been closed because of an accident.*
3 a drawing or model of something such as a machine or building that shows how it would look inside if it were cut in half

section *verb*
sections, sectioning, sectioned
if someone sections one area off from another, they separate it *This part of the pavement is dangerous and has been sectioned off with ropes.*

sector *noun* **sectors**
1 a part of something such as a country's business activity or an area or town *the manufacturing sector*; *This sector of Berlin was controlled by Russia.*
2 in maths, a sector is an area of a circle made by drawing two lines (or radiuses) from the middle to the circumference (or edge). A sector is sometimes called a pie slice or pizza slice.

ORIGIN from Latin *sector* 'someone who cuts' (from *secare* 'to cut')

secure *adjective*
1 protected from anything bad happening *We feel secure in school. Are my earrings secure in that box? Keep your computer files secure by backing them up online. Our website is secure* (for example, people can buy things without getting their money stolen).

SYNONYM safe

2 not likely to move, break or fall down *The ladder was wobbly but it's now secure. Don't walk on the ice – it's not secure.*

SYNONYM safe

3 fixed tightly to something *Make sure the windows and doors are secure* (for example locked). *The lid on the paint tin is quite secure.*
4 good and successful now and going on into the future *Mum has a secure job. The future of the school's football team looks secure.*
5 having good feelings about yourself and not feeling worried about life or the future *The Polish families feel very secure in our village.*
6 used about a place that is difficult to get into or out of, for example because people guard it or there are locked doors *This is a secure area of the airport* (where people are not allowed to go).

secure *verb*
secures, securing, secured
1 to get something, often after a lot of difficulty *My sister managed to secure a place in a good school.*
2 to fix or join something strongly to something else *Dad secured the luggage to the roof-rack with some heavy straps.*

securely *adverb*
1 in a way that protects something or someone from anything bad happening *My passport is kept securely in a locked drawer. I've backed up my computer files securely.*

SYNONYM safely

2 tightly or in a way that stops something from moving, breaking or falling down *The doors are securely locked* (for example so that the house is safe). *Hold the ladder securely while I'm on it.*

security *noun*
1 a situation of being protected from anything bad happening *Security in the classroom is very important.*
2 things done officially to protect people, places, buildings and organisations, for example against crimes or terrorist attacks *airport security*; *a security alert* (warning about a possible danger such as a bomb)
3 a group of people whose job is to protect something such as a building or airport and the people in it *a security guard* (for example who protects a building, stops people stealing things or transports money between banks)
4 when someone has good feelings about themselves and does not feel worried about life or the future

sedan chair *noun* **sedan chairs**
a type of box with a seat for carrying an important person around, used especially in the 17th and 18th centuries. The box was carried by two people holding two poles fixed to either side of the box.

sedate ['ser-date'] *adjective*
1 quiet and serious *a sedate village*; *Grandma is a very calm and sedate person.*
2 slow or relaxed *We continued our journey at a sedate pace.*
sedately *adverb*

sedate ['ser-date'] *verb*
sedates, sedating, sedated
to give a medicine to a person or animal to make them calm down or go to sleep

sedative ['sed-er-tiv'] *noun* **sedatives**
a medicine that makes someone calm down or go to sleep

sediment *noun*
1 a soft substance that falls to the bottom of a liquid and forms a layer there
2 (*plural* **sediments**) sand, stone, mud and other materials carried by water or the wind to the bottom of rivers or the sea

sedimentary *adjective*
used for describing rocks formed by sand, stone, mud and other materials at the bottom of rivers or the sea

see *verb*
sees, seeing, saw, seen
1 to take the image of something or someone into your brain through your eyes *I can see a fox in the garden. The sun shone in my eyes and I couldn't see.*
2 to meet someone and speak to them *The head teacher wants to see you. I'm going to see the doctor tomorrow.*
3 to watch something such as a film, TV programme or sports match *Did you see the quiz last night?*
4 to understand something *Thanks for explaining – I see what you mean. We have a big problem – don't you see?*
5 to find something out *Go and see who's at the door. I'll see if the windows are closed* (and close them if they are not).
6 to make sure something happens or is done *Please see that Jack gets this message. I won't do it now but I'll see to it later.*
7 to look at or imagine something or someone in a particular way, for example when giving your opinion *I can't see George being the captain of the football team. Sophia's lazy so can you see her passing her exam?*

seed – self-conscious

8 to see someone off somewhere is to go with them there and say goodbye to them *We saw Granddad off at the station.*
9 to see someone to a place is to go with them there *Dad saw me to the bus. Can my mum see you home?*
10 I'll see or **we'll see** used for saying that you're not sure about something and you'll decide later *'Are you going to Seema's party?' – 'I'll see.'*
11 See you later! an informal way of saying goodbye

seed *noun* **seeds**
a small hard part, usually round or oval, that is produced by a plant and that grows into a new plant when it is put into the ground. Some seeds, such as peas or sunflower seeds, can be eaten. The seeds of many fruits, such as apples and oranges, are called pips.

seedless *adjective*
not containing any seeds *seedless grapes*

seedling *noun* **seedlings**
a very young plant that has grown from a seed

seedy *adjective* **seedier, seediest** (informal)
1 looking unpleasant or dirty *a seedy hotel*
2 connected with bad or dishonest activities *a seedy character*

seeing *conjunction* (informal)
used for mentioning an important fact or situation that influences what you say or gives the reason for something *Let's go swimming, seeing as* (or *seeing that*) *there's no school today.*

seek *verb*
seeks, seeking, sought
1 to try to get something, or to ask for something *You should seek help and advice. Do I need to seek permission?*
2 to look for something or someone *This tube line isn't working so passengers should seek other routes. The rescue workers are seeking survivors of the crash.*
3 if you seek to do something, you try to do it

seem *verb*
seems, seeming, seemed
1 used when you think that what you say about something or someone is true although it may not be true *This poem seems difficult to understand. Your sister seems like a nice person. It seems to be getting colder* (for example, that's my opinion). *It seems as if our teacher is leaving* (for example, that's what people say or what someone has told me).
2 used for saying something in a polite way *Sorry, I seem to have lost my library card.*

seemingly *adverb*
used for saying that something seems to be true but may not be true *The universe is seemingly endless.*

seen
past participle of **see**

seep *verb*
seeps, seeping, seeped
to flow into, out of or through something very slowly *Rain was seeping through the roof.*

seesaw *noun* **seesaws**
a long board for two children to play on. The middle of the board is fixed to the ground on a support that allows each end to go up and down. The children sit at either end of the board and take it in turns to push the ground with their feet to make the seesaw go up and down.

> ORIGIN from a rhyme sung in the past by two people using a big saw in a backwards and forwards movement when cutting logs of wood

seethe *verb*
seethes, seething, seethed
1 to be full of anger or another strong feeling such as envy, sometimes without showing your feelings *My brother went up to his room, seething with anger.*
2 if something is seething with people or animals, there are lots of them everywhere *The whole town was seething with tourists.*

seething *adjective*
1 used about someone who is very angry or about the strong feelings someone has *seething anger* (very great anger); *seething jealousy*
2 used about people or animals when there are lots of them *a seething crowd of children*

segment ['seg-mernt'] *noun* **segments**
1 a part of something *There's a segment of the book about climate change.*
2 one of the natural parts that something is divided into, for example an orange or grapefruit or the body of an insect
3 in maths, a segment is an area of a circle made by drawing a straight line across the circle from one part of the circumference (or edge) to another

> ORIGIN from Latin *segmentum* 'piece cut off' (from *secare* 'to cut')

segment ['seg-ment'] *verb*
segments, segmenting, segmented
1 to divide something into separate parts
2 to break down a word into its separate sounds *The word 'chat' can be segmented into 'ch-a-t'.*
compare: **blend**

segregate *verb*
segregates, segregating, segregated
to keep people belonging to different groups apart from each other *In the refugee camps the men and women were segregated.*

segregation *noun*

seize *verb*
seizes, seizing, seized
1 to take something quickly and roughly with your hand or hands *The police officer seized the knife from the bully's hand.*
2 to put your hand or hands on someone quickly and roughly *She seized me by the arm.*
3 to take control of something in a violent way *Enemy soldiers have seized* (or *seized control of*) *the airport. The army seized power in Bolivia* (took control of the country).
4 to take away something that it is against the law for someone to have *The police seized a large amount of stolen goods.*
5 if you seize an opportunity, you quickly decide to do something you want to do while it is still possible for you to do it
6 if something seizes up, it suddenly stops moving or working properly

seizure *noun* **seizures**
a sudden illness in which someone becomes unconscious for a short time *an epileptic seizure*

> SYNONYM fit

seldom *adverb*
not very often *Great-Granddad seldom goes out in this cold weather.*

select *verb*
selects, selecting, selected
1 if you select something or someone from among two or more things or people, you decide which of them you want *My parents selected a good school for me. Mohammed was selected as captain of the team.*
2 if you select something on a computer screen, you mark it in some way or you choose it from a menu of options *Select the word by highlighting it with your mouse. I selected the print option.*

select *adjective*
1 used for describing something, or a small group of people or things, that is of very high quality *Olivia goes to a select school. Dan has a select group of friends.*
2 if something such as a club, hotel or part of a town is select, it is very expensive and suitable only for people who have lots of money

selected *adjective*
used for describing a small number of things that have been specially chosen by someone, for example because they are more important than other things *a book of selected poems by A. A. Milne; These jeans are available in selected stores only.*

selection *noun* **selections**
1 the action of selecting something or someone *I haven't made my selection yet.*
2 a number of different things someone can select from *The school library has a good selection of books on science.*
3 something that someone selects *Here's the book I bought for you – are you happy with my selection?*
4 a number of different things that someone selects *a selection of poems by Robert Louis Stevenson*

self *noun* **selves**
used for talking about what someone is usually like or really like as a person *Ruby's been ill but now she's back to her old self* (she's the same as she was before she became ill). *My brother never lets people see his true self.*

self-centred *adjective*
only interested in yourself, not in other people

self-confident *adjective*
knowing very well how to do things successfully and behaving boldly and calmly
self-confidence *noun*

self-conscious *adjective*
worried about your appearance and about what other people think about you

self-contained *adjective*
having everything that is needed to be complete or to work properly *a self-contained flat* (for example with its own kitchen, bathroom and entrance)

self-control *noun*
being able to control your feelings and behaviour, for example by not showing that you are angry or excited

self-defence *noun*
1 if you act in self-defence, you do something to protect yourself when you are being attacked, for example hitting someone back
2 the skill of protecting yourself if you are attacked *My sister goes to a self-defence class.*

self-destruct *verb*
self-destructs, self-destructing, self-destructed
if something such as a spaceship self-destructs, it destroys itself automatically using a built-in program

self-discipline *noun*
the control over your behaviour or mind that you need to make yourself do something that you should do, for example study, work or practise something
SYNONYM discipline

self-employed *adjective*
used for describing someone who has a job working for themselves and not for a company or another person

self-esteem *noun*
a good feeling that someone has about themselves, for example because they are happy with their qualities, mind and appearance *Simon has low self-esteem* (a bad feeling about himself).

self-evident *adjective*
very easy to see or understand and not needing any explanation
SYNONYM obvious

selfie *noun* selfies (informal)
1 a photo that you take of yourself (or of yourself and other people) using a digital camera or a piece of equipment with a camera inside such as a mobile phone
2 a selfie stick is a long pole, usually of metal, used with a mobile phone or camera fixed onto the end. You use it to take a photo of yourself (or yourself and others) from a better angle than if you hold the phone or camera in your hand.

self-important *adjective*
behaving as if you are more important than other people

selfish *adjective*
1 if someone is selfish, they only care about themselves and do not care about other people
2 also used about something that shows that someone is selfish *selfish behaviour*; *He did that for selfish reasons.*
selfishly *adverb* **selfishness** *noun*

selfless *adjective*
showing that you care about the needs or happiness of other people rather than caring about yourself *She jumped into the river to save the little boy – a selfless thing to do.* **selflessly** *adverb*

self-portrait *noun* self-portraits
a picture or drawing that an artist does of himself or herself

self-raising flour *noun*
flour that contains a powder called baking powder that makes cakes or bread swell up (or rise) when they are baked

self-respect *noun*
a good feeling that someone has about themselves because they know that what they do is good or right or that their life has important qualities

self-righteous ['self-rye-chers'] *adjective*
feeling or showing that you are always right in the way you behave, and in what you think, and that other people are wrong
self-righteousness *noun*

self-satisfied *adjective*
used for describing someone who is unpleasant because they are too pleased with their own qualities or things they have done or with the things that they have *a self-satisfied smile*; *a self-satisfied politician* **self-satisfaction** *noun*

self-service *adjective*
used about a place such as a garage or restaurant where customers serve themselves, for example by filling their own car with petrol and then paying someone, or by choosing their food, paying for it and taking it to their table

self-sufficient *adjective*
providing everything needed without help from anyone else *The country is self-sufficient in food.* **self-sufficiency** *noun*

sell *verb*
sells, selling, sold
1 to give someone something when they give you money for it *Amy sold me her guitar.*
2 to provide something for people to buy *Do you sell coloured pencils?*
3 if something sells, people buy it *These jeans are selling very well. The paperbacks sell for £5 each.*
4 if a shop or person sells out of something, they have no more left to sell *They've sold out of ice lollies.*
5 if something sells out, there is no more left to sell *All the tickets have sold out.*

seller *noun* sellers
1 someone who sells something
2 something that people buy *The dictionary is a very good seller* (lots of people buy it).

Sellotape *noun* (trademark)
a clear thin plastic material that is sticky on one side, usually used for sticking pieces of paper together. It is sold as a long strip wrapped around a cardboard or plastic ring to make a roll.

semaphore *noun*
a method of sending messages, especially in the past, using two flags, one held in each hand. The flags are moved to different positions to represent the letters of the alphabet.

semester *noun* semesters
one of the two parts that a school or college year is sometimes divided into

semi- *prefix*
used with nouns and adjectives to mean half or partly *semicircle* (half a circle); *semi-naked* (partly naked)

semibreve ['sem-ee-breev'] *noun* semibreves
a whole note in music that is half as long as a breve and equal to four crotchets or eight quavers

semicircle *noun* semicircles
1 a shape that is half of a circle. It is made from a half of the circumference (curved line that forms the outside of the circle) and a straight line drawn across the circle through its centre.
compare: **quadrant**
2 a shape that looks like half a circle, especially its curved outer edge *The children were sitting in a semicircle listening to the storyteller.*
semicircular *adjective*

semicolon *noun* semicolons
a punctuation mark consisting of a dot above a comma, like this ;

LANGUAGE EXTRA you can use a *semicolon* instead of a full stop for separating two sentences whose meanings are closely related (*I heard a loud bang; it frightened me*). You often do this when the second sentence starts with an adverb (*I like apples and oranges; however, I prefer pears*).
You can also use a semicolon instead of a comma in a long or complicated list of words or sentences where a comma would not be clear enough (*The menu gave us a choice between these dishes: fish, chips and peas; vegetarian lasagne with salad; chicken curry, rice and naan bread; lamb kebabs with chilli mayonnaise*).

semi-detached *adjective*
a semi-detached house is one that is joined to another house on one side only
compare: **terraced house** and **detached house**

semi-final *noun* semi-finals
one of two games played near the end of a competition. The semi-finals decide the winner (or winners) who will take part in the final (last game).

semi-finalist *noun* semi-finalists
a player or team that reaches the semi-final in a competition

semi-skimmed milk *noun*
milk from which half of the cream (thick fat substance that forms on the top of it) is removed so that there is much less fat in it. Skimmed milk has had all the cream removed.

semitone *noun* semitones
the smallest difference between the sound of any two musical notes that are next to each other, equivalent to a half tone on a musical scale

semolina *noun*
a powder made from grains of wheat. It is cooked with milk and sugar and is usually eaten as a pudding or breakfast cereal.

senate – sensitive

senate noun senates
1 one of the two parts of a parliament or government in some countries
2 the Senate is one of the two parts of the US Congress (or government)

senator noun senators
a man or woman who is a member of a senate, for example the US Senate
compare: **congressman**, **congresswoman** and **Representative**

send verb
sends, sending, sent
1 to make something go somewhere, for example by post, by the internet or using a messenger *I sent Grandma a present. Have you sent* (or *sent off*) *your email? The satellite sends signals back to earth* (using radio waves).
2 to tell someone to go somewhere or to make someone go somewhere *Dad sent me to my room. I hope they send me to a good school. The UK is sending more troops.*
3 to tell someone something as a message *Mum and Dad send their love.*
4 to make something or someone move or go somewhere quickly *She kicked the ball and sent it straight into the goal. A loud bang sent people running in all directions. The explosion sent huge flames into the air.*
5 to make someone do something or behave in a certain way *Dad sings to my sister to send her to sleep. The fire sent us all into a panic.*
6 to send back something that you buy is to send it by post or messenger to the place that it came from, for example because there's something wrong with it *We bought a printer online but had to send it back.*
7 to send for someone is to ask them to come to you *Can you send for the paramedics?*
8 to send for something is to ask someone to get something for you *Please send for help.*
9 to send off or away for something is to write to someone to ask for something by post *I sent off for a book I needed for my school project.*
10 if someone is sent off in a sports game, the referee makes them leave the game because they have done something against the rules
11 if you send on something such as a letter, email or piece of information, you send it to another person or place, for example by post or the internet
12 if you send out for something, you ask a shop or restaurant to bring food to your home *Mum sent out for a pizza.*
13 (informal) if you send someone or something up, you make fun of them, for example by copying someone's behaviour or way of speaking

sender noun senders
someone who sends something such as a letter or email

senile adjective
if someone old is senile, their mind does not work as it should, for example they can't remember things or make decisions, and they often behave strangely

senior adjective
1 older, or for or connected with older people *a senior student*; *the senior cricket team*
2 having a higher position in a job than someone else, for example because of having been in the job for longer *a senior teacher*
3 a senior citizen is an older person, for example someone who is more than 65 years old

senior noun seniors
1 someone who has a higher position in their job than someone else
2 an older person, for example someone who is more than 65 years old
3 an older student or pupil
4 if you are someone's senior, you are older than they are

sensation noun sensations
1 when you are able to touch things or feel something with your body *Since Ava's accident, she doesn't have much sensation in her right leg.*

> SYNONYM feeling

2 something that exists in your body and makes you feel or behave in a certain way *I had a burning sensation in my hand.*

> SYNONYM feeling

3 a general idea or feeling about someone or something that you can't explain *I had this weird sensation that the room was getting smaller.*
4 very great excitement or interest, or someone or something that causes this *The book caused a sensation when it came out. The Beatles were a sensation in the 1960s.*

sensational adjective
1 extremely good *It was a really sensational piece of music.*
2 extremely good and exciting *The captain scored a sensational goal.*
3 extremely attractive *Your sister looks sensational in that dress.*
4 causing very great excitement or interest *a sensational piece of news*

sense noun
1 an ability to make good and sensible decisions because you have a good understanding of people and situations *Kate had the sense to wait patiently until it was safe to cross the road.*
2 an ability to understand something or to do something well *Mohammed has a good musical sense* (he understands music, for example how the sound patterns work). *I have a good sense of direction* (I know which way to go in a new place and I don't get lost). *My dad has a great sense of humour* (knows how to see the funny side of things). *My sister has a good sense of fun* (knows how to enjoy herself and that things don't have to be serious).
3 a general idea or opinion about something *Street cameras can give you a sense of security. Manuel gave the class a sense of what life in Valencia is like.*
4 (plural **senses**) a natural ability that people (and many animals) have to see, hear, smell, touch (or feel) and taste things. The five senses are sight (or vision), hearing, smell, touch and taste. *My sense of smell is bad compared to my dog's.*
5 (plural **senses**) the meaning of something *The word 'great' has lots of different senses.*
6 (plural **senses**) a particular way of looking at a situation *Our school is, in every sense, the best in the county. In a sense, Jo is right* (not completely but only in a certain way).
7 to make sense to be easy to understand and have a meaning that is clear *Your last sentence doesn't make sense.*
8 to make sense also used when you mean that something is sensible or there is a good reason for it *It makes sense to go home now before it starts snowing.*
9 to make sense of to understand something difficult *I've been trying to make sense of this poem by Wilfred Owen.*

sense verb
senses, sensing, sensed
1 to have a general idea or feeling about something that you can't explain *I sensed that someone was following me. When I said no, I sensed his disappointment.*
2 if something such as a scientific instrument senses something, it finds it and often records it

senseless adjective
1 if something is senseless, it has no meaning or it happens or is done for no reason *the senseless killing of a swan*
2 unconscious *He was beaten senseless.*

sensible adjective
1 if someone is sensible, they make good decisions and do the right things because they think about people and situations in an intelligent way *We often leave Paul alone in the house – he's very sensible* (he behaves well and in a responsible way).
2 if something is sensible, it is based on reason, good decisions or an intelligent way of behaving *a sensible decision* (very good decision); *sensible advice*; *Wouldn't it be sensible to wait till it stops raining before we go out?*
3 sensible clothes are useful and suitable for a particular purpose rather than fashionable *Wear sensible shoes in this rain.*

sensibly adverb
1 in a way that shows that you make good decisions and do the right things *Behave sensibly when you're out with your friends. My sister always eats sensibly* (for example, she eats healthy food and not too much).
2 if you dress sensibly, you wear sensible clothes

sensitive adjective
1 if someone is sensitive about something, they get upset or angry if someone talks about it, for example because they are worried about what the other person thinks *Ben is very tall and is sensitive about his height. Don't be so sensitive.*
2 showing that someone understands the feelings and situation of someone else *Ms Patel is very kind and sensitive. Our school is sensitive to all our needs* (understands them and deals with them).
3 easily hurt or damaged, and often needing to be protected from something *sensitive skin*; *I wore dark glasses as my eyes were sensitive to the light. The neck is a sensitive part of the body.*
4 slightly painful *My gums are feeling quite sensitive.*
5 used about something affected in a strong way by something else, for example

noise or cold *My sister has sensitive hearing* (she hears small sounds loudly). *My teeth are sensitive to very cold food.*
6 used about something such as a piece of equipment that is made in a very delicate way, is strongly influenced by something such as air, light, heat or sound and can do very complicated things in a careful way *sensitive scientific instruments* (for example, they pick up and measure tiny changes); *a sensitive camera* (that takes very detailed pictures); *This microphone is very sensitive* (it picks up tiny sounds). *This gadget has a sensitive switch* (for example, it starts when you put your hand anywhere near it).

sensitively *adverb*
in a way that shows that someone understands the feelings and situation of someone else *Our teacher dealt with Chloe's problem sensitively.*

sensitivity *noun*
1 when you get upset or angry if someone talks about something, for example because you are worried about what they think *I didn't know Ollie had this sensitivity about his height.*
2 when you understand the feelings and situation of someone else *She dealt with the bullying situation with sensitivity.*
3 when something is easily hurt or damaged and often needs to be protected from something *He doesn't go out much because of the sensitivity of his eyes to sunlight.*
4 when something is affected strongly by something else, for example noise or cold *the sensitivity of the baby's hearing*
5 when something such as a piece of delicate equipment is strongly influenced by something such as air, light, heat or sound and can do very complicated things in a careful way *the sensitivity of a scientific instrument*

sensor *noun* **sensors**
a piece of sensitive equipment that finds, measures or records something such as light or heat *This camera has an infra-red sensor for seeing at night.*

sent
past tense & past participle of **send**

sentence *noun* **sentences**
1 a group of words, usually containing a verb, that express a complete thought or idea
2 a punishment given in a court of law by a judge to someone guilty of a crime. The guilty person is usually sent to prison.

> **LANGUAGE EXTRA** a *sentence* starts with a capital letter. There are four main types: statements, questions, commands and exclamations.
> Statements give information or an opinion: *I play football*. They usually have a subject and verb (here *I* is the subject and *play* is the verb) and usually end in a full stop.
> Questions ask for information or an opinion and end in a question mark: *How do you like your teacher?*
> Commands tell people what to do. They end in either an exclamation mark or a full stop: *Sit down! Come here.*
> Exclamations show feelings such as anger or surprise or show that you like something or someone very much: *What a lovely house!*

sentence *verb*
sentences, sentencing, sentenced
if a judge sentences a guilty person in a court of law, the judge decides what punishment he or she will get *The thief was sentenced to three months in prison.*

sentiment *noun*
1 (plural **sentiments**) an opinion or feeling about something
2 feelings such as love, sadness or pity *When you make your decision, there is no room for sentiment.*

sentimental *adjective*
1 showing or connected with feelings such as love, great liking or pity *My dad's very sentimental about animals. I keep these old glasses for sentimental reasons* (for example because I like them so much and they bring back happy memories).
2 showing too many feelings such as love between people, especially in a way that you think is silly *My sister is reading a sentimental love story.*
sentimentality *noun*

sentinel *noun* **sentinels**
another word for a sentry

sentry *noun* **sentries**
1 a soldier who guards a place, usually the entrance to a building
2 a sentry box is a small shelter with an open front where a sentry stands while guarding a building

sepal *noun* **sepals**
a part of a plant that supports the petals of the flower and that protected the flower when it was a bud

separate ['sep-er-ert'] *adjective*
1 if two or more things are separate from each other, they have their own existence or quality, for example they are not joined or put together or touching each other *Keep the meat and fish separate in the fridge. My sister and I have separate bedrooms* (we each have our own, not the same one). *You should each write your name on a separate piece of paper. The word 'cat' has three separate sounds.*
2 not connected, for example happening at a different time or being different from something *Mum complained to the teacher on four separate occasions. That's a completely separate problem. My uncle and aunt lead separate lives* (they don't do things together).

separate ['sep-er-rayt'] *verb*
separates, separating, separated
1 to take, put or keep people or things away from each other *Ms Grey separated Emily and Harriet because they wouldn't stop talking. Can you separate the red beads from the blue ones?*
2 if something separates, it stops being joined to something *Under the weight of the books, the shelf has separated from the wall.*
3 to be between two people, things or places, for example so that they are kept away from each other or not near each other *A high wall separates our garden from next door's. The two countries are separated by a desert and a distance of 1000 miles. Only three points separate the two teams.*
4 to put people or things into two or more groups, or to make things go into two or more parts *Mr Watson separated the class into three groups. Look at the list and separate the words into nouns, verbs and adjectives.*
5 to go into different groups or go away from each other *We separated into three small groups. They walked together for a mile then separated at the station.*
6 if a married man and woman, or two married partners, separate, they stop living together *Eve's parents separated a year ago* (or *have been separated for a year*).

separately *adverb*
1 not together, for example not at the same time or not in the same place *My brother and sister turned up separately at the party. Cook the potatoes and peas separately* (by themselves).
2 not with something else *The matter needs to be considered separately* (by itself).

separation *noun*
1 when people or things are separated or kept separate from other people or things *This wall marks a line of separation between the two communities.*
2 when a married man and woman, or two married partners, stop living together

September *noun*
the ninth month of the year, between August and October. September has 30 days.

> **ORIGIN** from Latin *septem* 'seven', because it was the seventh month of the ancient Roman year

septic *adjective*
infected with germs *Put a plaster over your cut so it doesn't go septic.*

> **ORIGIN** from Greek *septos* 'rotten'

sequel ['see-kwerl'] *noun* **sequels**
1 a book, film, play, piece of music or video game that continues the story from an earlier one
2 an event that happens after another event or because of it

sequence *noun* **sequences**
1 a series of things such as events or numbers that follow each other in a particular order *The driver described the sequence of events leading up to the crash.*
2 the order in which things happen or must be done *Put these letters into the correct sequence to make a word.*
3 a part of a film that shows one particular event or scene

sequin ['see-kwin'] *noun* **sequins**
one of the small shiny discs of plastic sewn as decoration onto clothes such as dresses or other things such as shoes or bags

Serb *noun* **Serbs**
someone from Serbia

Serbia *noun*
a country in South-East Europe
Serbian *adjective & noun*

serene ['ser-reen'] *adjective*
1 calm and quiet *a serene evening*
2 not worried or excited *Her face was serene.*
serenely *adverb* **serenity** *noun*

sergeant–service provider

sergeant ['sah-jernt'] *noun* **sergeants**
1 a soldier of middle rank in the army or air force, just above a corporal
2 a police officer of low rank, above a constable and below an inspector
3 a sergeant major is a soldier in the army above a sergeant

serial *noun* **serials**
1 a television or radio programme that tells a story in a number of separate parts that are broadcast at regular times, for example every week
2 a story in a magazine, in a newspaper or online that appears in separate parts over a period of time
3 a serial number is a number put on a product, for example a computer, phone or camera, so that it can be recognised. Each serial number is different.

series *noun* **series**
1 a number of things or events that follow one another *Sayed asked the teacher a series of interesting questions.*
2 a television or radio programme in a number of parts. Each part tells a separate story but with the same characters, or deals with the same subject in a different way or with different subjects that are related to each other. *A long time ago the BBC broadcast a series called 'Walking with Dinosaurs'.*

serious *adjective*
1 causing big problems or making you sad, upset or worried, for example because of being very big or bad *a serious mistake*; *a serious crime* (for example killing someone or robbing a bank); *a serious illness* (for example when someone can die)
2 used for saying that you really mean something *I want to learn Chinese next term – I'm serious. Is your brother serious about leaving his job?*
3 not funny or joking *One minute he's making jokes and the next he's very serious.*
4 showing that you think carefully about things *My uncle is always very serious. He has a serious look on his face.*
5 used about something or someone you should think carefully about because they deserve your attention, or about someone or something that makes you think carefully *a serious artist* (important and good); *a serious book* (for example dealing with an important subject); *a serious question*; *Mum and I had a serious talk. I gave the matter serious thought* (thought about it carefully).
6 connected with the way people feel and behave at a particular time when they show respect and do not show their other feelings *The atmosphere at school after the accident was very serious.*
7 used when you mean a lot of something *I've got some serious work to do to finish my school project.*
seriousness *noun*

seriously *adverb*
1 another way of saying very or very much, but more strongly *seriously ill*; *Mum is seriously worried about me. Was he seriously hurt?*
2 in a way that shows you are thinking carefully about something, for example something you want to do *My sister is seriously thinking of writing a book.*
3 in a way that shows that you really mean something or that you are not joking *Are you seriously saying you don't want to be my friend? Seriously, you should apologise to your parents.*
4 if you take something or someone seriously, you think they are important enough to pay attention to

sermon *noun* **sermons**
a talk usually given by a religious leader as part of a religious ceremony

serpent *noun* **serpents**
another word for a snake, especially a large one or when a snake is used as a symbol, for example in a religion

serrated *adjective*
if an object such as a knife or blade has a serrated edge, it has lots of pointed parts along the edge

servant *noun* **servants**
someone employed in someone else's home to do work such as cleaning and cooking, especially in the past

serve *verb*
serves, serving, served
1 to give or bring food or drink to someone at a meal *Mum served us our dinner in the garden. In the canteen you have to serve yourself* (choose your own food and take it to your table). *Sit down – Dad's ready to serve up.*
2 if someone serves you in a shop, they help you choose or find things to buy and they bring you the things you ask for *The manager is serving a customer. The shop assistant is busy serving.*
3 to work for an organisation, a person or your country, doing responsible and useful work *My brother is serving in the army. Ms O'Connor served our school as a teacher for many years.*
4 to do the job of a particular thing *This sofa also serves as a bed.*
5 to be useful in a particular way *Josh was sent home for being rude – that should serve as a warning to you all. Punctuation marks serve a useful purpose* (they are useful and important). *Alice won't be coming – it serves no purpose waiting* (it makes no sense and is a waste of time).
6 to provide someone or something with something that they need *Our area is served by excellent schools, shops and hospitals. Our school serves the needs of dyslexic children very well.*
7 if someone serves in tennis, they hit the ball to the other player with their racket (frame with strings and a handle) to start a game
8 if you say it serves someone right, you mean they deserve the bad thing that happens to them *'I failed the maths test.' – 'It serves you right for not doing any work for it.'*

serve *noun* **serves**
when a player serves the ball in tennis

> SYNONYM **service**

server *noun* **servers**
1 a computer used only for storing programs and providing information to other computers on a network
2 a player who serves the ball in tennis

service *noun* **services**
1 when someone brings you food or drink, for example in a restaurant, or when someone helps you, for example in a shop or hotel, and brings you the things you ask for *The service is bad in that café* (for example, people wait a long time for food or the people who work there are rude).
2 an organisation or group that provides things that people need, or the work that is done by this organisation or group *the police service*; *the civil service* (different sections of a country's government); *The postal service is good in this part of Cornwall.*
3 used for talking about a vehicle such as a bus, train or plane that makes regular journeys or about the journeys made by these vehicles *Is there a bus service that goes to your school? There's a shuttle service to the airport.*
4 when someone works for an organisation, a person or their country, doing responsible and useful work, or the period of time someone works *These soldiers do a great service for our country. Our teacher left after 10 years' service to the school.*
5 used for talking about the work done to a vehicle or piece of equipment to fix it or to make sure that it stays in good condition. The work is usually done regularly, for example once a year or once every two or three years. *My mum's car needs to go in for a service* (be taken to a garage for work to be done to it).
6 a religious ceremony *They held a service at the Cenotaph for soldiers killed in wars.*
7 a small amount of money added on to a bill in a restaurant to give to the waiter or waitress
8 a service or dinner service is a number of plates and dishes with the same design, used when serving a meal
9 when a player serves the ball in tennis

> SYNONYM **serve**

10 the work done for customers in a particular business such as banking or insurance, for example providing customers with information or advice or helping them with their money
11 a country's services are its army, navy and air force
12 a person's services are his or her particular skills *Our school needs the services of a plumber.*
13 services or motorway services are places beside motorways where drivers can stop to buy petrol, eat food, rest or go to the toilet

service *verb*
services, servicing, serviced
if someone services a vehicle or piece of equipment, they fix it or do things to it to make sure it stays in good condition. This is usually done regularly, for example once a year or once every two or three years.
servicing *noun*

serviceman *noun* **servicemen**
a man who belongs to a country's army, navy or air force

service provider *noun* **service providers**
a company that provides customers with a connection to the internet

> LANGUAGE EXTRA also called an *internet service provider* (or *ISP*)

446

service station *noun* **service stations**
1 a place with fuel pumps where someone goes to buy petrol or diesel for their vehicle
2 a motorway service station is a place beside a motorway where drivers can stop to buy petrol, eat food, rest or go to the toilet

servicewoman *noun* **servicewomen**
a woman who belongs to a country's army, navy or air force

serviette *noun* **serviettes**
a square piece of paper or cloth used when you eat a meal for keeping your clothes clean and wiping your mouth and hands on

SYNONYM napkin

ORIGIN from French *serviette* 'towel' or 'napkin' (from *servir* 'to serve')

serving *noun* **servings**
an amount of food for one person

SYNONYM portion

sesame ['ses-er-mee'] *noun*
a plant used in cooking for its seeds and oil. Sesame seeds are used for giving extra taste to bread and cakes.

session *noun* **sessions**
1 a period of time for doing a particular activity *a training session*; *After the head teacher's talk there'll be a question-and-answer session.*
2 an official meeting, for example of a parliament or court of law
3 a whole period of time when official meetings take place *This session of parliament lasts for about a year.*
4 a period of time at school, for example a part of the school day or year *There was a fire drill during the morning session.*
5 a school teaching year *Next session begins on 7 September.*

set *verb*
sets, setting, set
1 to get something such as a piece of equipment ready to do something or operate in a certain way *Mum set the alarm for seven o'clock* (for example, pressed buttons on the alarm clock to make it ring at that time). *Set the temperature in the room to 20 degrees.*
2 if you set a table, you put things on it to make it ready for a meal, for example a tablecloth, knives, forks and plates
3 if you set fire to something or set something alight, you make it start burning
4 if the sun sets, it disappears from the sky in the evening *The sun rises in the east and sets in the west.*
5 to set something such as a standard or record is to do or achieve it and often other people copy or follow it *The swimmer set a new record* (for example, finished the race faster than anyone else had ever done). *Anisha sets a good example to the class* (behaves in a way the class should copy).
6 to set a person or animal free is to allow them to leave or escape from a place such as a prison or cage
7 if a liquid or something soft sets, it becomes hard and solid *Leave the jelly to stand for an hour to set.*
8 to give someone something that they must do, for example a test or task *Our teacher has set us a lot of homework. He set the class a maths problem* (gave it to them to solve). *Ollie set himself the target of reading a book every month.*
9 if something such as a film, play or book is set somewhere or at a particular time, that is where and when the story happens *The action is set in Aberdeen around the year 2000.*
10 if someone sets to work, they start working
11 another way of saying to put *Just set your schoolbag down on the floor. How much time should I set aside for my homework?*
12 to decide a date or time for something *Has your sister set a date for the wedding?*
13 to make someone start doing something or to make something start happening or working *What he said set me thinking. Press this button to set the robot in motion.*
14 to set about something is to start doing it *How do we set about finding the right answer?*
15 to set someone or something back is to make someone lose time or to make something go more slowly *The heavy rain set the farmers back a few weeks.*
16 to set off or out is to start on a journey *We're setting off* (or *out*) *for Scotland in the morning.*
17 to set off an alarm is to make it start working
18 to set off something such as a firework or bomb is to make it explode
19 to set out things such as plans, ideas, facts or reasons is to explain them or make them known clearly
20 to set out to do something is to start doing it with a particular idea in your mind *If you set out to become a film star, you'll have to work hard and have lots of luck.*
21 to set up something is to build it or put it somewhere *The army set up roadblocks. The children set up their tent in the garden.*
22 to set up something is also to start something such as a group or business *The school is going to set up a playgroup.*
23 to set up something such as a meeting or event is to organise it
24 to set up something such as a piece of equipment or a software program is to get it ready so that it can be used *The engineer has set up my stepmum's computer* (for example, changed or installed programs or connected wires so that everything works).

set *adjective*
1 ready to do something *Get set to leave in five minutes. I'm all set to leave right now. Ready, get set, go!* (said to runners at the start of a race)
2 used for describing something that does not or will not change, for example something decided or planned earlier *a set routine*; *I spend a set number of hours on my homework every day.*
3 if you are dead set against something, you are completely against it and do not support it or want it *Dad is dead set against the idea of going on holiday to Greece.*
4 a set book, play or text is a book, play or piece of writing that you must study when you have an exam because there will be questions about it
5 a set meal is a meal in a canteen or restaurant made up of different kinds of food that you don't choose yourself. It costs less than choosing your own food. A set menu lists the different kinds of food included in the set meal.

set *noun* **sets**
1 a group of things that belong together or are used together *a set of four kitchen chairs*; *a chess set* (all the pieces used in the game of chess)
2 a number of things that are considered together, for example rules, ideas or facts *Every school has a set of rules you must follow.*
3 in maths, a set is a group of objects that are similar kinds of things or a group of similar numbers. For example, carrots, cucumbers and cabbages belong to a set of vegetables, and the numbers 1, 3, 5 and 7 belong to a set of odd numbers. The study of sets is called set theory.
4 a piece of equipment for receiving television or radio programmes *a TV set*
5 in tennis, a set is a group of six or more games that form part of a match
6 the place where a part of a film or TV programme is made *Actors spend at least 10 hours a day on the set.*
7 the painted pictures and the furniture, buildings and structures used for making a film or TV programme or putting on a play

setback *noun* **setbacks**
a problem that makes progress happen more slowly *Ethan was about to leave hospital but has suffered a setback.*

set square *noun* **set squares**
a tool, usually made of plastic, shaped like a right-angled triangle (with one angle that has exactly 90 degrees). It is used for drawing straight lines and angles, usually angles of 30, 45 or 60 degrees.

sett *noun* **setts**
a hole in the ground built by a badger (a grey animal that lives under the ground and comes out at night)

settee *noun* **settees**
a soft seat with a back and arms. It is made for more than one person to sit on.

SYNONYMS couch, sofa

setting *noun* **settings**
1 the place where something is or happens, including the area all around *Their house is in a beautiful country setting. What a great setting for an open-air concert!*
2 the place or time when the action of a play, film or story happens *The setting is London in 1850.*
3 a setting on a machine or piece of equipment is a particular position on its controls (the buttons or switches that you press, turn or move to operate it) *If it's cold put the radiator on the highest setting.*
4 a place in a computer program or in the software of a device such as a smartphone that makes the program work in the way you want *To change the brightness of your screen, go to settings.*
5 a setting or place setting is the dishes, glasses, knives, forks, spoons and other things used by one person at a meal

447

settle *verb*
settles, settling, settled
1 to decide what should be done about something, for example when talking about arguments, problems or differences between people *Mia and George have settled their argument* (they've put an end to it by agreeing with each other). *OK, that's settled – you're coming over to my house on Sunday.*
2 to get into a comfortable position *Dad settled into his armchair to watch TV. I settled down on the sofa.*
3 to go and live somewhere *My parents came over from Ireland and settled in York.*
4 to move down onto something and stay there, for example onto a surface or the ground *In summer, dust is quick to settle on the furniture. The snow is heavy but it's not settling* (it melts when it reaches the ground). *A pigeon settled on Mum's hand.*
5 to move down to the bottom of a liquid *The mud settles at the bottom of the river.*
6 to pay money that you owe *Dad settled the restaurant bill.*
7 if someone settles down, they start to live a quiet or more ordinary life, for example by buying a house or getting married

settlement *noun* **settlements**
1 a group of homes built by people who have come to live in a place from somewhere else, for example from another country *a Roman settlement near Norwich*
2 an official agreement that puts an end to an argument or problem

settler *noun* **settlers**
someone who goes to live in a different place and builds their home there, usually a place where no-one or few people have lived before *Who were the first settlers in America?*

set-top box *noun* **set-top boxes**
a piece of equipment that allows a television set to receive particular signals, for example through a cable in the ground or from a satellite dish, so that you can watch cable or satellite TV

set-up *noun* **set-ups**
1 the way something is organised
2 equipment organised in a particular way *Our school has an excellent computer set-up.*
3 getting a piece of equipment or a software program ready to be used *The engineer wanted £50 for set-up* (for example for getting everything ready so you can use a new computer or TV). *To install this program, double-click on the set-up file.*
4 an organisation or group of people

LANGUAGE EXTRA also spelt *setup*

seven *adjective & noun* **sevens**
the number 7

seventeen *adjective & noun* **seventeens**
the number 17

seventeenth *adjective & noun*

seventh *adjective & noun*
1 used about something or someone that comes in place number 7 *on the seventh day*
2 (*plural* **sevenths**) one of 7 equal parts of something *a seventh of the amount*

seventy *adjective & noun* **seventies**
1 the number 70
2 the seventies are the seventieth to seventy-ninth years of a century, for example 1970 to 1979

3 if someone is in their seventies, they are between 70 and 79 years old
seventieth *adjective & noun*

sever *verb*
severs, severing, severed
1 to cut something off or to cut completely through something so that it is no longer joined to the other part of it *Be careful not to sever the lawn mower wire when you're cutting the grass.*
2 to end something such as a friendship or contact with someone

several *adjective & pronoun*
more than two or three but not very many *There were several people waiting to see the doctor. Several of my friends have read the book already.*

severe *adjective* **severer, severest**
1 extremely bad and often worrying *Your laptop has some severe problems. Severe weather conditions are on the way.*
2 used for describing something unpleasant when there is a lot of it or when it is very big *severe pain* (very great pain); *severe damage; severe delays* (big or long delays); *In parts of Africa there are severe shortages of food* (hardly any food at all).
3 used for describing something such as a punishment or criticism that is very strong or someone who punishes or criticises in a very strong way *Twenty years in prison is a very severe sentence. This judge is very severe on drunken drivers.*
4 used for describing someone who is not friendly, kind or understanding, or the way they look or behave *My great-aunt is a very severe person. Dad had a severe look on his face.*

severely *adverb*
1 another way of saying very or very much, but more strongly *severely damaged; The flu outbreak severely affected our school.*
2 in a very strong way *He was severely punished.*
3 in a way that is not friendly or kind *She looked at me severely.*

severity *noun*
1 used for showing how bad or strong something is, for example a problem, punishment or damage
2 the quality of being severe *the severity of her expression; We were shocked by the severity of our head teacher.*

sew ['soh'] *verb*
sews, sewing, sewed, sewn *or* **sewed**
1 to make, repair or decorate something such as a piece of clothing or a curtain using a needle and thread *My mum taught me to sew by hand and with a machine. There's a hole in my sock – please can you sew it up?*
2 to join something onto a piece of cloth using a needle and thread *Dad sewed my button onto my shirt.*

LANGUAGE EXTRA be careful not to confuse *sew* with *sow* (to put seeds into the ground)

sewage ['soo-ij'] *noun*
dirty water and waste matter from people's bodies that is removed from buildings through drains (pipes) and carried by sewers (large pipes), usually to a place where it is specially treated

sewer ['soo-er'] *noun* **sewers**
a large pipe or group of pipes that go under the ground and take sewage (dirty water and waste matter) from buildings, usually to a place where it is specially treated

sewing *noun*
1 the activity of making, repairing or decorating things such as clothes by sewing
2 something that you're sewing at the moment
3 a sewing machine is a piece of equipment used for sewing

sewn
a past participle of **sew**. You can also say 'sewed'.

sex *noun*
1 being a girl or woman or being a boy or man *Write your name, date of birth and sex on the form.*
2 being a male or female animal *What sex is that panda?*
3 one of the two groups that people and animals are divided into based on how they produce babies or baby animals *Our school has separate play areas for each sex* (one for boys and one for girls). *David is shy when he talks to members of the opposite sex.*
4 when people come together, for example to produce babies, or when animals come together to produce baby animals *sex education; Have the pandas had sex?*

sexist *adjective*
1 if a boy or man is sexist, he does not treat girls or women in a fair and equal way or he uses words that do not show respect to girls or women. If a girl or woman is sexist, she behaves in this way towards boys or men.
2 also used about someone's feelings or what someone does, says or writes *a sexist remark*
sexism *noun* **sexist** *noun*

sextant *noun* **sextants**
a tool for measuring angles by looking at distant objects such as stars and the sun. It is used by people such as sailors for calculating the position of ships or astronomers for calculating the position of planets.

sextet *noun* **sextets**
1 a group of six musicians playing together or six singers singing together
2 a piece of music for six musicians

sexual *adjective*
1 connected with being a girl or woman, boy or man, or male or female animal *sexual development; sexual discrimination* (when girls and women, or boys and men, are treated badly)
2 connected with coming together, for example to produce babies or baby animals *sexual activity; sexual reproduction*
sexually *adverb*

sexy *adjective* **sexier, sexiest**
1 very attractive *a sexy film star*
2 very interesting *a sexy job as an airline pilot*
sexily *adverb*

sh *interjection*
used for telling someone to be quiet

LANGUAGE EXTRA also spelt *shh* and *ssh*

shabby *adjective* **shabbier, shabbiest**
1 in bad condition, for example because of being old or used a lot *An old man in shabby clothes was sitting on the bench. We stayed in a shabby hotel room.*
2 not looking nice because of wearing old and used clothes *She wore an old coat and looked rather shabby.*
3 not kind, reasonable or honest *a shabby trick; shabby treatment*
shabbily *adverb* **shabbiness** *noun*

shack *noun* **shacks**
a small building built in a simple way, for example from wood or metal, and often not built very well

shade *noun* **shades**
1 an area where the light from the sun does not reach. It is slightly darker and cooler than areas that are in the sun. *We had a picnic in the shade of an oak tree. This horse chestnut tree gives a lot of shade* (creates a darker and cooler area around it).
2 a colour of a particular type, for example blue or green, but it is lighter or darker, for example a lighter blue or darker green *We painted the walls in two different shades of blue.*
3 a cover for an electric light bulb, used for making the light less bright or for decoration

SYNONYM **lampshade**

4 a cover that can be pulled over a window, used for example for stopping the light from coming in
5 **shades** an informal word for sunglasses
6 **shades** used for talking about the slightly different types of something *In the meeting the parents expressed different shades of opinion. The word 'great' has many shades of meaning* (slightly different meanings).

shade *verb* **shades, shading, shaded**
1 to stop the sun or a bright light from shining onto someone or onto or into something *This big tree will shade us from the sun. She shaded her eyes from the dazzling headlights.*
2 to make a part of a drawing darker, for example with lots of pencil lines *We shaded in all the circles and squares. What do the shaded parts of the map represent?*

shading *noun*
the part or parts of a computer image or drawing that have been made darker, for example by using an instruction such as 'Fill' or by using a pencil to make lots of lines

shadow *noun* **shadows**
1 a dark shape, on the ground or a wall for example, that something or someone makes when they get in the way of the light *In the late afternoon sun, the tree cast a long shadow on the ground.*
2 a dark area where the light does not reach *Jack frightened me by jumping out of the shadows. I couldn't see who it was – their face was in shadow.*
3 a substance for colouring the eyelids (skin above and below your eyes). It is also called eye shadow.

shadow *verb* **shadows, shadowing, shadowed**
to follow someone closely and watch everything they do

shadowy *adjective*
1 dark or hidden by shadows *He hid in a shadowy corner of the room.*
2 very mysterious *the shadowy world of spies*

shady *adjective* **shadier, shadiest**
1 used about a place where there is shade because the light from the sun does not reach there *a cool shady spot in the garden*
2 used about something that gives shade and protects you from the sun *a big shady oak tree*
3 dishonest or likely to be dishonest *a shady deal*
shadiness *noun*

shaft *noun* **shafts**
1 a long narrow space or structure, for example inside a building or the ground, for something to move through *a lift shaft; a ventilation shaft* (for air)
2 the long narrow part of something such as a weapon *the shaft of an arrow*
3 the handle of a tool *the shaft of a hammer*
4 a long line of light *a shaft of light*

shaggy *adjective* **shaggier, shaggiest**
1 used about something such as hair or fur that is long and thick and sometimes untidy *a horse with a shaggy mane; a shaggy hairstyle*
2 used about an animal or person with shaggy hair *a shaggy dog*

shake *verb* **shakes, shaking, shook, shaken**
1 to move quickly from side to side, backwards and forwards or up and down with lots of small movements, or to make something or someone do this *The whole building shook when the lorry rumbled past. I was so scared I was shaking* (making small movements I couldn't control). *Shake the bottle before pouring the juice. My brother shook me by the shoulders.*
2 to make someone very upset, often causing suffering for a long time *The news of the accident shook the whole school. We were all shaken up by what happened.*
3 to make something less or weaker, for example someone's belief or confidence *The problem shook our faith in our teacher.*
4 if your voice shakes, it sounds weak and is difficult to hear, for example because you are frightened, upset, worried or angry
5 if you shake someone's hand, you take their right hand in your right hand and move it up and down in a friendly way, for example when you first meet them or as a way of saying goodbye *My dad and the teacher shook hands.*
6 if you shake your fist at someone, you close your hand (bend your fingers and thumb into the palm) and shake it towards someone to show that you are angry
7 if you shake your head, you move it from side to side, for example as a way of saying no or to show that you do not believe or like something or that you are sad about something
8 if you shake something or someone off, you get rid of them *I've got a nasty cold that I can't shake off.*

shake *noun* **shakes**
1 a quick and small movement from side to side, backwards and forwards or up and down *Give the bottle a good shake. 'No,' he said, with a shake of his head.*
2 a thick drink made from milk and ice cream

SYNONYM **milkshake**

3 (informal) **in two shakes** in a very short time *I'll be back in two shakes.*

shaken *adjective*
very upset, often used about someone who suffers for a long time because of something that suddenly happens and who is not able to behave normally or sensibly *Everyone was shaken and crying when they heard the terrible news. After our car hit a tree we were very shaken up for quite a while.*

shaky *adjective* **shakier, shakiest**
1 weak and shaking slightly, for example because someone is ill, nervous or old *a shaky voice; shaky handwriting* (done by someone whose hand shakes); *Grandma's feeling shaky.*
2 if an object is shaky, it is not strong or steady and looks as if it might fall down *an old shaky chair*
3 not very good, for example because you are not sure about something *shaky memories; My Urdu is a bit shaky.*
4 not very successful *After a shaky start, our team played a very good match.*
5 if a photo is shaky, it is slightly unclear because the camera has been shaken *a shaky old picture of Dad on a bicycle*
shakiness *noun*

shall *verb*
1 used with 'I' and 'we' for making suggestions, asking about what to do or asking for advice *Shall we have pizza tonight? Shall I close the door? How shall I colour in the drawing?*
2 used with 'I' and 'we' for saying what you are going to do in the future *We shall be taking a few days' holiday. I shan't forget to do my homework.*
3 an old-fashioned way of saying that something will definitely happen in the future or of telling someone to do something *One day you shall be king. You shall leave at once!*

shallot *noun* **shallots**
a type of small onion

shallow *adjective* **shallower, shallowest**
1 not going very far down from the ground or from the top of something *a shallow hole; a shallow bowl; the shallow end of the swimming pool*
2 not serious, or not having any serious ideas or strong feelings *a shallow book*
shallowness *noun*

sham *noun*
something or someone that is not what they are supposed to be *He goes to church every week but it's just a sham* (he is not religious at all).

shamble *verb* **shambles, shambling, shambled**
to walk slowly and in a clumsy way, only slightly lifting your feet

shambles *noun*
1 an untidy place *The house is a real shambles at the moment. What a shambles!*

2 something that is not well organised, or a situation with lots of problems *The railways are in a shambles in this country.*

shambolic *adjective* (informal)
1 badly organised *The trip to the museum was really shambolic. My dad's too shambolic to organise a birthday party.*
2 untidy *My room is always shambolic.*

shame *noun*
1 used for saying that someone is sad and disappointed about something *It's a shame I didn't say goodbye to Granddad before he left. What a shame!*

SYNONYM pity

2 the sad and embarrassed feeling someone has about something bad they've done, or that someone else has done, or about a particular thing or situation they don't like *I felt nothing but shame about my brother's behaviour. I would die of shame if my friends and family knew that I'd cheated in the test.*
3 when someone no longer has the respect of other people because of what they've done or what they do *There's no shame in coming second.*

shame *verb*
shames, shaming, shamed
to make someone feel sad and embarrassed about something they've done or that someone else has done *Your behaviour has shamed the whole family. Our school will name and shame parents who park in front of the gates.*

shameful *adjective*
if something is shameful, it is so bad that people should feel sad and embarrassed about it *a shameful secret; I've never seen such shameful manners.*

shamefully *adverb*

shameless *adjective*
1 used about someone who doesn't feel sad or embarrassed about their behaviour, although they should *You're shameless!*
2 also used about the thing that someone doesn't feel sad or embarrassed about, although they should *shameless greed; a shameless way of behaving*

shamelessly *adverb*

shampoo *noun* shampoos
1 a soapy liquid for washing your hair
2 a soapy liquid for cleaning carpets and furniture such as sofas and armchairs
3 the action of washing the hair with shampoo *The hairdresser is giving Mum a shampoo.*

shampoo *verb*
shampoos, shampooing, shampooed
to wash something with shampoo, especially your hair

ORIGIN from the Hindi command *champo* 'press!', referring to pressing the muscles or massaging the body

shamrock *noun* shamrocks
a plant that has leaves made up of three round parts of the same size

CULTURE NOTE the *shamrock* is a national symbol of Ireland

shandy *noun*
1 an alcoholic drink usually made by mixing beer and lemonade
2 (*plural* shandies) a glass of shandy

shan't
short for 'shall not'

shanty *noun* shanties
a small house built from pieces of wood, metal, plastic or cardboard where poor people in some countries live, usually just outside a big town

ORIGIN from Canadian French *chantier* 'cabin for lumberjacks' (people who cut down trees in the forest)

shanty *noun* shanties
a shanty or sea shanty is a song that sailors sang in the past while they were working

ORIGIN from the French command *chantez* 'sing!' (from *chanter* 'to sing')

shantytown *noun* shantytowns
an area just outside a big town in some countries, where poor people live in shanties (small houses made of pieces of wood, metal, plastic or cardboard)

shape *noun* shapes
1 what something or someone looks like when you look at their outside edges or surfaces *The shape of a giraffe's neck is very long. An orange is round in shape.*
2 something that is arranged in a particular way when you look at its lines, angles, curves and surfaces. Shapes can be flat, such as squares and circles, or 3-D, such as cubes and pyramids. *I drew a cat in my exercise book and cut out its shape.*
3 something or someone that you cannot see clearly *We could make out a shape moving towards us in the fog.*
4 used for saying how good or bad something is compared to how it should be, or for saying how healthy someone is *It's a very old bike but it's in good shape* (for example, it works well and looks good). *My dog was in bad shape when we took her to the vet.*
5 **in shape** healthy because you do exercises to keep your body strong
6 **out of shape** unhealthy because you don't do exercises
7 **out of shape** also used for describing something that no longer has its normal shape *The coat hanger was bent out of shape.*
8 **to take shape** to become clearer, more complete or more organised *My ideas are beginning to take shape.*

shape *verb*
shapes, shaping, shaped
1 to make something into a particular shape or give it a particular shape *We were shaping little animals out of clay. The artist was carefully shaping the wood.*
2 if something is shaped in a particular way, that is the shape it has *The centre of a daffodil is shaped like a trumpet. A cornet is a cone-shaped container for ice cream.*
3 to shape up is used for saying how well or badly something or someone is progressing *My sister's studies are shaping up nicely.*
4 to shape up is also to improve your behaviour or work *Ms Riley says I must shape up this term.*

shapeless *adjective*
1 not having a shape that is clear and easy to see *a shapeless lump of clay*
2 not attractive or pleasant because of not having a proper shape *a shapeless sweater*

shapely *adjective* shapelier, shapeliest
attractive because of having a very pleasant shape *shapely legs*

shard *noun* shards
a broken piece of something hard, usually glass, pottery or stone

share *verb*
shares, sharing, shared
1 to have or use something at the same time as someone else *I share a room with my sister. There wasn't enough room so I shared a seat with Oliver* (sat in the same seat as Oliver).
2 to let someone have or use something that is yours *Razia is happy to share her toys. My brother doesn't like sharing.*
3 to have the same thing or things as someone or something else *My friends and I share the same hobbies and interests. I don't share your opinion. Chloe shares her love of music with her mum. French and Spanish share a lot of the same words.*
4 if you share something such as information, thoughts or ideas with someone, you tell it to them *I shared this information with the whole class. Seema and Emma share their secrets* (tell each other their secrets).
5 to give a person, or two or more people, some of something or an amount or part of something so that every person has some *I shared the biscuits and the cake with my brother* (I gave him some and I had some). *We shared* (or *shared out*) *the money between us* (we both or all had some).
6 if you share something such as a task or piece of work with a person, or with two or more people, you do it together with them *George and I shared the job of tidying up the classroom after school.*
7 if two or more people share the blame for doing something, they are both or all responsible for doing it

share *noun*
1 a part of the whole of something that you share with someone or with two or more people *That slice is your share of the cake.*
2 a part of something such as a task or piece of work that someone does together with another person or other people *You haven't done your share of tidying up the house.*
3 an amount of something that is considered reasonable to expect *I've had my fair share of problems at school.*
4 a part of the responsibility for doing something *Jack must accept his share of the blame.*
5 (*plural* shares) in business, a share is one of the many equal parts that the property of a company is divided into. People buy shares in the company as a way of owning a part of it and trying to make money.

shareware–sheen

shareware *noun*
computer software that you can get free, for example by downloading it from the internet. If you want to use it for a long time or upgrade it, you have to pay for it.
compare: freeware

shark *noun* **sharks**
a very large fish with sharp teeth and a large fin (thin flat part) on its back that can be seen when it swims close to the surface of the water

sharp *adjective* **sharper, sharpest**
1 if something such as a knife or blade is sharp, it has a thin edge for cutting and it cuts well *a sharp pair of scissors*
2 if something such as a pencil or an animal's claw is sharp, it has a point (or points) that can make a hole or cause an injury, for example *sharp teeth; Don't climb on those rocks – they're sharp.*
3 happening quickly and strongly, for example when something changes very much *a sharp drop in temperature*; *a sharp bend in the road* (changing direction quickly); *a sharp pain* (coming and going quickly and hurting very much)
4 clear and easy to see *The picture on your TV is very sharp. There's a sharp contrast between the two men in the painting.*
5 quick to notice, understand or learn things *Sayed has a sharp mind. You need sharp eyes to spot the difference. Granddad is old but he's still very sharp.*
6 quick and loud *a sharp knock on the door*
7 having a slightly strong taste, for example like a cooking apple, or a very strong taste, for example like a lemon or mustard *These plums are quite sharp.*
8 very cold *a sharp wind*
9 unfriendly or angry *'Come here,' he said in a rather sharp voice.*
10 used about someone's face when it is not round or gentle but has parts that are square or straight *He has very sharp features* (for example a square chin and straight nose).
11 in music, a note that is sharp is one that is played or sung slightly higher than the correct note. A note that is slightly lower is called flat.

SIMILE 'as sharp as a razor' means very sharp (senses 1 & 2)

sharp *adverb*
1 used when you mean exactly at a particular time *The bus leaves at nine o'clock sharp.*
2 used for talking about a strong change of direction *Turn sharp right at the traffic lights.*

sharp *noun* **sharps**
a musical note that is slightly higher than the correct note

ANTONYM flat

sharpen *verb*
sharpens, sharpening, sharpened
1 to sharpen a pencil is to make the end of it very pointed so that it writes properly, usually by using a pencil sharpener
2 to sharpen something such as a knife or scissors is to make its cutting edge sharper using a special tool

sharpener *noun* **sharpeners**
1 a sharpener or pencil sharpener is a tool for making the ends of pencils more pointed so that they write properly
2 a tool for making the cutting edges of things such as knives or scissors sharper

sharply *adverb*
1 quickly and strongly *Temperatures have risen sharply. The river bends sharply just north of the town.*
2 clearly and in a way that is easy to see *With my new glasses I can see everything sharply.*
3 another way of saying very or very much, but more strongly *Jo was sharply criticised for being late all week. The painter uses sharply contrasting colours.*
4 in an unfriendly or angry way *'Sit down,' she said sharply.*

sharpness *noun*
the quality of being sharp (for example when talking about a blade, a pain, a picture or someone's mind)

shatter *verb*
shatters, shattering, shattered
1 if something shatters or if someone or something shatters it, it breaks into lots of tiny pieces *The glass shattered when it fell to the ground. A stone shattered the car windscreen.*
2 to take something away by destroying it completely, for example someone's hopes or confidence *Grandma has many shattered dreams. The accident shattered all his hopes.*
3 to make someone very upset or shocked *Everyone was shattered by the news of the crash.*

shattered *adjective*
1 very upset or shocked
2 very tired *I feel shattered.*

shattering *adjective*
1 very upsetting or shocking *shattering news*
2 very tiring *The journey was completely shattering.*

shave *verb*
shaves, shaving, shaved
1 if a man or young man shaves, he cuts the hair off his face by scraping his skin with a razor
2 if someone shaves something such as their head or leg, they cut the hair off it using a razor
3 if someone shaves hair off, they get rid of it by shaving *Granddad has shaved off his beard.*
4 if someone shaves off a thin piece of something, they remove it by cutting or scraping

shave *noun* **shaves**
1 the action of shaving the hair on your face *Dad's having a shave.*
2 if you say that something was a close shave, you mean that something bad or dangerous almost happened

shaver *noun* **shavers**
a piece of electrical equipment used for shaving

shavings *noun plural*
thin strips cut off the surface of something, especially wood, with a sharp tool such as a plane or chisel

shawl *noun* **shawls**
1 a piece of cloth that girls and women wear around their shoulders and arms and sometimes over their head
2 a piece of cloth for wrapping around a baby to keep it warm

she *pronoun*
a female person or animal that someone has mentioned before, for example in an earlier sentence *She's my friend.*

sheaf *noun* **sheaves**
1 a bunch made of many stems of grain, for example corn or wheat, that have been cut and tied together *sheaves of corn*
2 a bunch of papers, sometimes tied together

shear *verb*
shears, shearing, sheared, sheared or shorn
1 to shear a sheep is to cut off its wool
2 to shear someone's hair off is to cut it off
3 if something such as a piece of metal shears off or is sheared off, it breaks off *The top of the bus was sheared off when it hit the bridge.*

shearer *noun*

LANGUAGE EXTRA be careful not to confuse *shear* and *sheer*. *Sheer* has different meanings, for example *sheer hard work* means very hard work and *sheer cliffs* are very steep cliffs.

shears *noun plural*
1 a tool like a big pair of scissors, used for cutting things outdoors such as grass and bushes
2 a piece of equipment or a pair of special blades for cutting the wool off sheep

sheath [rhymes with 'teeth'] *noun*
sheaths [rhymes with 'seethes']
1 a cover for something such as a knife or sword that protects you from the blade
2 a cover or material that fits tightly around something and protects it
an umbrella sheath

sheaves
plural of **sheaf**

shed *noun* **sheds**
a small building, usually built out of wood, used for storing things such as garden tools or bicycles. It is also used for other purposes such as working in. *a garden shed*

shed *verb*
sheds, shedding, shed
1 to lose something that falls off or comes out in a natural way *The trees were shedding their leaves. Snakes shed their skin. In the riots a lot of blood was shed* (many people were killed or injured).
2 to get rid of something that is not wanted *Dad says he's overweight and needs to shed a few kilos.*
3 to shed light on something is to make it easier for someone to understand it by providing new information
4 to shed tears is to cry or to feel sad

she'd
short for 'she had' or 'she would'

sheen *noun*
a smooth shiny surface or appearance *hair with a soft sheen*

451

sheep–shift

sheep *noun* **sheep**
an animal that people keep on farms and use for getting wool from and for providing meat, called mutton. A young sheep is a lamb. The sound a sheep makes is a bleat (or baa).

sheepdog *noun* **sheepdogs**
a dog used by a shepherd for controlling sheep

sheepish *adjective*
slightly embarrassed, for example because you feel silly or have done something silly or wrong **sheepishly** *adverb*

sheer *adjective*
1 used for giving extra importance to a word *She had a look of sheer horror on her face. By sheer hard work, Jack caught up with the rest of the class.*
2 very steep *a sheer cliff face; It's a sheer drop of 100 metres to the sea.*
3 sheer cloth is so thin and light that you can almost see through it

LANGUAGE EXTRA be careful not to confuse *sheer* and *shear*. *Shear* has different meanings, for example to cut wool off a sheep or to cut someone's hair off.

sheer *adverb*
almost straight up or down *There were cliffs rising sheer above the clouds.*

sheet *noun* **sheets**
1 a large piece of thin cloth for a bed, used for lying on or for covering yourself
2 a thin flat piece of paper, usually shaped like a rectangle, for example used for printing or writing on
3 a thin flat piece of material such as glass, metal or plastic, shaped like a square or rectangle
4 a large area or amount of something, for example something lying on top of a surface or something that makes you think of a wall *There was a thin sheet of ice covering the road. A sheet of fire was moving closer to our village.*

sheikh ['shayk' or 'sheek'] *noun* **sheikhs**
an Arab man who is a leader in charge of a group of people or who is a religious expert

LANGUAGE EXTRA also spelt *sheik*

ORIGIN from Arabic *shaykh* 'old man'

shelf *noun* **shelves**
1 a long flat piece of wood, glass, plastic or metal for putting things on. It is fixed to a wall, frame or piece of furniture or fixed inside a cupboard. *a shelf full of books; supermarket shelves; Put your bag on the shelf underneath the table.*
2 something that sticks out like a shelf, for example a piece of rock on a cliff or under the sea

shell *noun* **shells**
1 the hard part on the outside of an animal such as a snail, turtle or crab that protects its body
2 the hard outside part of a nut or bird's egg *There are bits of shell in my omelette.*
3 a design or object that looks like a shell, usually a seashell *pasta shells*
4 the main structure of something such as a building, ship or vehicle, for example that still exists after a fire or explosion *The house was just a shell – only the outer walls were standing.*
5 a metal container filled with a substance that explodes. It is fired from a large gun.

shell *verb*
shells, shelling, shelled
1 to attack something or someone by firing shells at them *The army was shelling the centre of town.*
2 to remove the hard outside part of a nut such as a peanut or a vegetable such as a pea
3 (informal) if you shell out money, you spend a lot of it on something

she'll
short for 'she will'

shellfish *noun* **shellfish**
a sea animal that has a shell, for example a crab, mussel or clam

shelter *noun*
1 (*plural* **shelters**) a small building or place with a roof that protects someone from bad weather or danger *a bus shelter; a bomb shelter*
2 protection from bad weather or danger *It's raining hard and there's nowhere to take shelter (to protect ourselves). The hikers found shelter in an abandoned farmhouse.*
3 (*plural* **shelters**) a home for people or animals that need protection *a shelter for the homeless*

shelter *verb*
shelters, sheltering, sheltered
1 to go somewhere to keep yourself safe from bad weather or danger *I sheltered from the rain in a shop doorway.*

SYNONYM to take shelter

2 to protect someone or something from bad weather or danger *These tall trees shelter the campers from the wind.*

shelve *verb*
shelves, shelving, shelved
1 if someone shelves something such as a plan or idea, they say it will no longer happen or it will happen at a later time
2 to put something on a shelf *All the books on this table need to be shelved.*

shelves
plural of **shelf**

shelving *noun*
shelves on a wall *The classroom doesn't have enough shelving.*

shepherd *noun* **shepherds**
1 a person who looks after sheep
2 shepherd's pie is a pie made of minced meat, for example lamb or beef, with mashed potato on top. It is baked in an oven.

LANGUAGE EXTRA a *shepherd* can be a woman or girl as well as a man or boy. A *shepherdess* is an old-fashioned word for a woman or girl who looks after sheep.

shepherd *verb*
shepherds, shepherding, shepherded
to guide a group of people somewhere in a careful way so that they go where you want them to go

sherbet *noun*
a powder with a fruit flavour that you eat as a sweet or mix with water to make a fizzy drink (drink with lots of bubbles in it)

ORIGIN from Arabic *sharbah* 'drink'

sheriff *noun* **sheriffs**
1 in the US, a sheriff is the main person chosen to make sure people obey the law in a town or county
2 in Scotland, a sheriff is a judge in a court of law who deals with less serious crimes and decides whether someone is guilty or not
3 in England and Wales, a sheriff is someone connected with a court of law who represents the king or queen. A sheriff's job is mainly to go to official ceremonies.

sherry *noun* **sherries**
a strong Spanish wine that is usually brown. It originally came from the town of Jerez de la Frontera in southern Spain.

she's
short for 'she is' or 'she has'

shh *interjection*
used for telling someone to be quiet

LANGUAGE EXTRA also spelt *sh* and *ssh*

shield *noun* **shields**
1 a large piece of metal, leather or wood that soldiers carried in the past to protect the front of their bodies when fighting. Shields come in different shapes and sizes, for example with straight sides and a straight top and a pointed or round bottom part.
2 a large piece of strong plastic that police officers carry to protect themselves

LANGUAGE EXTRA also called a *riot shield*

3 something that protects someone or something from harm or damage *a heat shield (protecting a person or equipment from the heat)*
4 a design like a soldier's shield
5 an object that looks like a soldier's shield that you get as a prize, for example in a sports competition

shield *verb*
shields, shielding, shielded
to protect someone or something from something dangerous, harmful or bad *I shielded my eyes from the sun.*

shift *verb*
shifts, shifting, shifted
1 to change the position of something or take it from one place to another *Shift your chair – I can't see the TV. I shifted the boxes into the corner of the room.*
2 if someone or something shifts, they change their position *I was bored and kept shifting about in my seat. The dot on the screen keeps shifting.*
3 to change *The action of the play shifts from 1950 to the present day.*
4 to make something happen in a different way or go in a different direction *Please shift your attention away from football and on to your schoolwork. Don't try to shift the blame onto me.*
5 (informal) to get rid of something, for example a dirty mark or a cold

shift – shockingly

shift *noun* **shifts**
1 a period of time when a group of people do their work, for example in a factory or hospital. When they finish, another group comes and does the same kind of work. *My dad's on the night shift this week – he doesn't like shift work* (working sometimes at night and sometimes during the day).
2 the group of people who work during a particular period of time *The night shift has gone home but the day shift hasn't arrived yet.*
3 a change of position or direction *There's been a shift in what people think about the internet.*
4 a woman's dress that is straight and hangs down loosely from the shoulders
5 on a computer keyboard, shift or the shift key is a key that you press and hold down, for example when you want to write a capital letter or highlight a piece of text

shilling *noun* **shillings**
a unit of money in the UK until 1971. There were 20 shillings in a pound.

shimmer *verb*
shimmers, shimmering, shimmered
if something shimmers, it shines with a soft light that looks as if it is shaking slightly and quickly *The sea was shimmering in the moonlight.* **shimmer** *noun*

shin *noun* **shins**
the front part of your leg that goes from your knee to your ankle

shine *verb*
shines, shining, shone
1 to produce light, for example when talking about the sun, a lamp or a torch *The sun shone brightly. The light was shining in my eyes.*
2 to make a light go in a particular direction *I shone the torch on the pavement, looking for my lost keys.*
3 to reflect the light *Dad polished his car until it shone.*
4 *(past tense & past participle* **shined***)* to make something reflect the light by rubbing it *Mum shined my shoes for the party.*

SYNONYM **to polish**

5 if someone's eyes shine, they have a happy look on their face
6 to do well or be good at something *When it comes to sport, Yussuf really shines.*

shine *noun*
1 the bright appearance of something when it reflects the light *The polished glass had a beautiful shine.*
2 when you rub something until it reflects the light *Could you give my shoes a shine?*

shingle *noun*
a mass of small stones that cover a beach or the edge of a river

shiny *adjective* **shinier, shiniest**
1 used for describing something that reflects the light *shiny shoes; shiny smooth hair*
2 (informal) used for describing something that is new *My parents have bought a shiny new TV.*

ship *noun* **ships**
a large boat that travels on the sea or on a large river or lake

ship *verb*
ships, shipping, shipped
1 if a company or shop ships something that someone has bought, for example on the internet, or if something ships, the company or shop sends it to the person who has bought it *When will they ship my laptop? It shipped yesterday.*
2 to send something by ship *Food and blankets have been shipped to Bangladesh.*

shipload *noun* **shiploads**
a large number of people or amount of things that are carried in a ship

shipment *noun* **shipments**
an amount of goods that are sent somewhere, for example by plane, ship or train

shipping *noun*
1 when a company or shop sends something to the person who has bought it, for example on the internet, or the cost of sending it *Shipping is free this week.*
2 ships, for example all the ships of a country or all the ships sailing in a particular place
3 the business of carrying goods by ship *a shipping company*

shipshape *adjective*
neat and tidy with everything in the right place

shipwreck *noun* **shipwrecks**
1 an accident that happens to a ship while it is sailing, for example hitting rocks
2 a ship that has been badly damaged or destroyed in an accident, for example after hitting rocks

shipwrecked *adjective*
if someone is shipwrecked, they have had an accident in a ship, and the ship has been badly damaged or destroyed

shipyard *noun* **shipyards**
a place in a harbour where people build and repair ships

SYNONYM **dockyard**

shirk *verb*
shirks, shirking, shirked
if someone shirks something such as their duty or a task, they do not do it, or do not want to do it, for example because they think it is unpleasant or they just do not care *By not cleaning out your hamster's cage, you are shirking your responsibilities* (not doing what you should do). **shirker** *noun*

shirt *noun* **shirts**
1 a piece of clothing, usually made of thin cloth, that boys and men wear on the top half of their body. It has a collar, buttons going down the front and usually sleeves.
2 a similar piece of clothing worn by girls and women, sometimes called a blouse
3 a shirt with short sleeves that people wear for playing football. It has the particular colours of a football team.

shirtsleeve *noun* **shirtsleeves**
1 a sleeve of a shirt
2 if someone is in their shirtsleeves, they are wearing a shirt but no jacket

shish kebab *noun* **shish kebabs**
a food made up of small pieces of meat and vegetables cooked on a stick called a skewer

ORIGIN from Turkish *sis* 'skewer' and *kebap* 'roast meat'

shiver *verb*
shivers, shivering, shivered
if you shiver, your body shakes slightly because you're cold, frightened or ill *Put on your coat – you're shivering.*

shiver *noun* **shivers**
1 a slight shaking movement that your body makes, for example because you're frightened or excited *He felt a sudden shiver of horror.*
2 **the shivers** a feeling of being frightened or of being cold because you're ill *Don't make that funny face – it gives me the shivers* (frightens me). *Jo has a temperature and the shivers.*

shivery *adjective*
if you feel shivery, you can't stop shivering, for example because you're cold or ill

shoal *noun* **shoals**
a large group of fish swimming together

shock *noun* **shocks**
1 something bad that happens and makes you feel very upset and surprised *News of our teacher leaving came as a real shock. It was a shock to find out that Nandita was to blame for breaking the window.*
2 a feeling of being very upset and surprised because something bad has happened *I could see the shock on Dad's face when I told him the news.*
3 a medical problem that makes someone feel very weak, for example because of an injury *Khalid is in hospital suffering from shock.*
4 a strong movement of something hitting something else or of something shaking *We felt quite a shock when my dad's car hit the tree. The shock of the explosion could be felt for miles.*
5 a shock or electric shock is a pain that you get in your body if you touch a dangerous electric wire or electrical object. The pain is caused by electricity passing through the body.
6 a shock of hair is a lot of thick hair on someone's head

shock *verb*
shocks, shocking, shocked
1 to make someone feel very upset and surprised *The news of the crash shocked the whole school. We were all shocked.*
2 to make someone feel angry, embarrassed or ill, for example by saying or doing something rude or against the usual standards of behaviour *Lila shocked the teacher when she swore.*

shocker *noun* **shockers** (informal)
something really shocking

shocking *adjective*
1 making you feel upset and surprised *the shocking news of the crash*
2 making you feel angry, embarrassed or ill *shocking behaviour*
3 extremely bad *shocking weather; I have a shocking memory.*

shockingly *adverb*
1 extremely (used when you think something is bad) *shockingly bad handwriting; We're shockingly late.*
2 extremely badly *I think our team played shockingly.*

453

shockproof–short

shockproof *adjective*
if something is shockproof, it is not easy to break it if it is dropped or hit *a shockproof watch*

shoddy *adjective* **shoddier, shoddiest**
if something is shoddy, it is bad or made or done badly *shoddy goods; shoddy work*

shoe *noun* **shoes**
1 a strong covering for your foot below the ankle, which you usually wear over a sock. Shoes are usually made from leather, cloth or plastic and often have rubber soles (bottom parts).
2 a piece of metal shaped like the letter U that is fixed to the bottom of a horse's hoof to protect it

SYNONYM horseshoe

3 to be in someone's shoes to be in the situation that someone else is in *What would you do if you were in my shoes?*

shoe *verb*
shoes, shoeing, shod
to shoe a horse is to put horseshoes on its feet

shoebox *noun* **shoeboxes**
an oblong cardboard box for holding a pair of shoes when you buy them

shoelace *noun* **shoelaces**
a piece of material like string that you put through holes at the top of your shoe. You use it to tie your shoe to your foot.

shoestring *noun*
on a shoestring with very little money *This film was made on a shoestring.*

shone
a past tense & past participle of **shine**

LANGUAGE EXTRA when *shine* means to make something reflect the light by rubbing it, the past tense and past participle are *shined*

shoo *interjection*
used for telling a person or animal to go away **shoo** *verb*

shook
past tense of **shake**

shoot *verb*
shoots, shooting, shot
1 if someone shoots, they make something such as a bullet (or bullets) come out of a gun by pressing and sometimes holding the trigger (part of the gun that makes the bullet come out) *Don't shoot! Someone was shooting at the police with an air gun. Soldiers were shooting with automatic machine guns.*
2 if someone shoots a gun or shoots something from a gun, for example a bullet (or bullets), they make the bullet (or bullets) come out of the gun by pressing the trigger *In the army my brother learnt how to shoot a gun. The boy was shooting pellets into the wall with his air gun.*
3 to make an arrow come from a bow *The soldier shot an arrow into the tree. They were shooting with arrows.*
4 to make something dangerous come out of somewhere, like a bullet from a gun *The dragon shot flames from its mouth. The zoo-keeper shot a dart into the lion to send it to sleep.*
5 if someone shoots a person or animal, they injure them or kill them with a bullet (or bullets) from a gun or with something from another weapon, for example an arrow from a bow or a pellet from an air gun *The police officer was shot in the leg. If they find the criminal, they will shoot him* (kill him with bullets). *King Harold was shot by an arrow in 1066.*
6 to move suddenly and quickly *When Ms Spencer asked the question, everyone's hands shot up. Tom suddenly shot out of the room.*
7 to take moving pictures of something for a film or take photos of something *Spielberg shot this film in California. They start shooting tomorrow.*
8 in a sport such as football, to hit or kick a ball at a goal in order to score a goal or point *She shot the ball straight into the goal. When you're ready, shoot!*
9 to shoot down is to make someone or something fall to the ground by shooting something at them *He was shot down in the street* (killed by a bullet). *The plane was shot down by a missile.*
10 (informal) **to shoot off** is to leave a place suddenly *I have to shoot off now!*
11 to shoot up is to grow quickly *Your sister has shot up since I last saw her.*
12 to shoot up is also to increase by a large amount *Ticket prices have shot up in the last month.*

shoot *noun* **shoots**
1 a new stem, with a leaf or leaves on it, that grows on a plant
2 the first part of a plant that grows from a seed and appears above the ground
3 when someone takes moving pictures for a film or takes a series of photos

shooting *noun* **shootings**
when someone is injured or killed by a bullet (or bullets) from a gun *There have been two fatal shootings in this part of town.*

shooting star *noun* **shooting stars**
a small meteor (piece of rock from space) that burns with a bright light when it enters the earth's atmosphere

shop *noun* **shops**
1 a place where you buy something or pay for a service. A shop can be a building, a room in a large building such as a shopping centre or a place on the internet.
2 a place where something is made or repaired *a motorcycle repair shop*
3 when you go shopping, or the amount that you buy *Dad does the shop once a week. This week's shop seems bigger than last week's.*
4 a shop assistant is someone who serves customers in a shop

shop *verb*
shops, shopping, shopped
1 to buy things somewhere, for example in a shop (or shops) *This is the supermarket where we shop. Mum prefers shopping at the market.*
2 if someone shops around, they compare prices in different places to try to find the cheapest price

shopkeeper *noun* **shopkeepers**
someone who owns a shop or is in charge of one, usually a small shop

shoplifting *noun*
the crime of stealing things from a place such as a shop or store **shoplifter** *noun*

shopper *noun* **shoppers**
someone who goes somewhere to buy things, for example to a shop or store (or shops or stores)

shopping *noun*
1 when people go to buy things in places such as shops, stores or markets or on the internet *late night shopping* (when shops and stores are open late); *internet shopping; My parents go shopping once a week.*
2 the things that people buy, for example from shops or stores *a supermarket trolley full of shopping; a shopping bag*

shopping basket *noun*
shopping baskets
1 a container with a handle (or handles) for carrying your shopping, for example in a supermarket. It is often made from thin pieces of wire twisted together or from plastic, usually with holes in the sides.
2 the place on a shopping website where you put the things you want to buy

shopping centre *noun* **shopping centres**
a large building or group of buildings with lots of shops and restaurants and often a cinema

shore *noun*
the piece of land that runs along the edge of the sea, a lake or large river *The sailors managed to swim to the shore. We stayed in a hut on the shores of Lake Geneva.*

shorn
a past participle of **shear**. You can also say 'sheared'.

short *adjective* **shorter, shortest**
1 measuring a small amount of space from one end to the other *Ducks have short legs. We walked a short distance* (a small amount of space).
2 not lasting much time *a short walk; She waited a short time* (a small amount of time).
3 if someone is short, they are not as tall as most people
4 used about something that does not have many pages or words *a short book; a short email*
5 used for talking about something when there is not enough of it, or about things or people when there are not enough of them *Food is short. We're short of time. I'm a bit short* (I don't have enough money). *Do you want to be in the team? – We're two people short* (or *we're short of two people*) (we need two more people).
6 if a word is short for another word (or other words), it means the same but uses fewer letters *CD is short for compact disc.*
7 if you are short with someone, you don't say much to them and your voice is slightly angry
8 for short used for describing a shorter way of saying something *We call Daniel Dan for short.*
9 in short used for saying something that you've already said but in a different way using very few words
10 short of breath having trouble breathing, for example because you are ill or old or after doing exercise
shortness *noun*

454

short – shove

short *adverb*
1 without reaching a particular place or level but almost reaching it *The plane crashed just short of the runway.*
2 before the time that something is supposed to end *We cut short our holiday because I was ill.*
3 suddenly *Our teacher stopped short when the head came into the room.*
4 if you go short of something, you have less than you need *Poor people often go short of food.*
5 if you run short of something, you don't have enough left *We're running short of biscuits.*

shortage *noun* **shortages**
a situation where there is not enough of something *There's a serious shortage of computers in our school.*

shortbread *noun*
a sweet biscuit, made mainly from butter, flour and sugar, that crumbles easily (breaks into pieces) when eaten

shortcake *noun*
1 a type of cake made of layers of fruit and cream and with fruit and cream on top
2 another word for shortbread

short circuit *noun* **short circuits**
a fault in a piece of electrical equipment, caused by too much current in a circuit (path of an electric current), for example because of a damaged wire. The short circuit stops the equipment from working.

shortcomings *noun plural*
things that are wrong with the character of someone or the quality of something *I like my cousin despite all his shortcomings.*

SYNONYM faults

shortcut *noun* **shortcuts**
1 a quicker way of getting somewhere or doing something than the usual way *I often take a shortcut across the fields to my house.*
2 a quick way of doing something on a computer *a keyboard shortcut* (pressing one or more keys to perform an action, for example Alt + F4 to exit a program); *Don't forget to put a shortcut to the program on the desktop* (an icon that you click on or touch to start a program quickly).

LANGUAGE EXTRA also spelt *short cut*

short division *noun*
in maths, short division is a way of dividing one number by another, especially when dividing a long number by a very short one, and showing the different parts of the calculation in short easy steps
compare: **long division**

shorten *verb*
shortens, shortening, shortened
to make something shorter, or to become shorter *His name is Christopher but he usually shortens it to Chris. It's September and the days are shortening.*

shorthand *noun*
a type of handwriting made up of special symbols that represent words or parts of words. It is used for writing down the words someone says as quickly as they say them.

short-handed *adjective*
if a group of people are short-handed, they do not have enough people to help them with something or enough workers to do a particular job

shortly *adverb*
1 soon, or a short time before or after something *Mum will be home shortly. It happened shortly before nine o'clock.*
2 in a slightly angry way *'Wait here,' he said rather shortly.*

shorts *noun plural*
1 short trousers with legs that stop above or at the knee. Shorts are worn by boys and men as well as by girls and women.
2 another way of saying boxer shorts (cotton underwear for men, looking like short trousers)

short-sighted *adjective*
1 able to see things clearly when they are close but not when they are far away

ANTONYM long-sighted

2 used about someone who does not have the good judgement to think about things that may happen in the future, or used about the actions, plans or ideas of someone like this *That's a very short-sighted way of looking at the problem.*

short-sightedness *noun*

short-tempered *adjective*
getting angry very easily

shot
past tense & past participle of **shoot**

shot *noun* **shots**
1 when someone shoots something such as a bullet from a gun or an arrow from a bow *You've hit the tree – that was a good shot.*
2 a bullet shot from a gun *He was wounded by a shot to his leg.*
3 the noise a gun makes when someone shoots *We were woken up by a loud shot coming from the street.*
4 used for saying how good or bad someone is at shooting a gun *Granddad used to be an excellent shot.*
5 when someone hits or kicks a ball in a sport such as football or tennis *What a great shot from Murray!*
6 a photo, or a short part of a film usually showing one action *This is a nice shot of Mum in her red coat. We see a shot of his hands trembling with fear.*
7 when you try to do something *I'm going to have a shot at swimming a whole length.*

SYNONYM go

8 an injection to stop you from getting ill *a flu shot*

SYNONYM jab

9 (informal) **like a shot** very quickly *When Sita heard the phone ring, she ran downstairs like a shot.*

shotgun *noun* **shotguns**
a long gun that fires small round bullets and is held against the shoulder when it is fired. It is often used for shooting birds and animals.

should *verb*
1 used for saying what you think is right, sensible or important *It's ten o'clock so you should be in bed.*
2 used for asking someone if something is right, sensible or important *Should we tell him our secret?*
3 used for saying that something is likely to happen (or to have happened) or to be true *Dad left work early today so he should be home any minute. If you get the next question right, you should be the winner.*
4 used for making a suggestion *You should come round to my house one day.*
5 used for showing what might happen or be true, for example following 'if' *If you should need my help, just phone me.*
6 used after 'that' with adjectives that show how you feel (such as sad, happy, surprised or angry) *I'm very disappointed that you should behave this way.*
7 used after 'that' for showing the importance of something *It's essential that you should finish your homework today.*
8 used in a very polite way for asking for something or expressing a wish *I should like a cup of tea. I should love to be your friend.*
9 used for expressing an opinion or hope *'Is your sister going to Ali's party?' – 'I should think so.' 'My brother never behaves badly.' – 'I should hope not.'*

shoulder *noun* **shoulders**
1 the part of your body between your neck and the top of your arm
2 your **shoulder blade** is the flat bone at the back of your shoulder
3 the **hard shoulder** is an area at the side of a motorway where a driver can stop in an emergency

shoulder *verb*
shoulders, shouldering, shouldered
to accept something difficult such as a responsibility or the blame for something

shouldn't
short for 'should not'

shout *verb*
shouts, shouting, shouted
1 to speak in a loud voice *We could hear people shouting in the next classroom. I shouted for help.*
2 to say something in a loud voice, for example an order, insult or particular word *Someone shouted* (or *shouted out*) *my name in the playground.*
3 to be angry with someone or speak loudly to them because you're angry *My dad will shout at me if I get home late.*

shout *noun* **shouts**
1 the sound of someone speaking in a loud voice, for example because they're angry or excited
2 (informal) to **give someone a shout** is to let them know something *Give me a shout when you've finished.*

shove *verb*
shoves, shoving, shoved
1 to push someone or something, often roughly or with a lot of strength *The bully shoved me against the door. Stop pushing and shoving* (pushing people with your hands and arms to get them to move out of the way).
2 (informal) to put something somewhere, often quickly *Dad shoved a pizza into the oven.*
3 to **shove someone around** is to keep telling them what to do

shove–shrewd

4 (informal) to shove off is to go away from a place *We'll be shoving off in five minutes.*
5 if you shove over or up, for example when you're sitting somewhere, you move along to make room for someone to sit next to you

SYNONYMS for sense 5: to move over, to move up

shove noun **shoves**
the action of shoving someone or something *The door was stuck but it opened when I gave it a shove.*

shovel noun **shovels**
1 a tool like a spade with a long wooden or metal handle fixed to a flat metal part, usually with slightly curved sides. It is used for digging, lifting and moving things such as earth, snow or sand.
2 a part on a big vehicle that looks like a large basket. It is used for lifting and moving things such as earth or rocks.

shovel verb
shovels, shovelling, shovelled
to lift and move something such as snow or earth using a shovel

show verb
shows, showing, showed, shown
1 to let someone see something, for example by giving it to them, taking it out from somewhere, taking someone to it or pointing to it *Show me the photo. They took us in the car and showed us where it happened. I showed her the house where I was born.*
2 to let someone see someone *Show me your dad in the photo* (for example by pointing). *Show us the prisoners* (for example by bringing them to us or taking us to see them).
3 to be able to be seen, or to make something able to be seen *The stain on your shirt hardly shows. The shiny table top shows every little mark.*
4 to teach someone how to do something by letting them watch you and explaining it to them *Can you show me how to shut down the laptop properly?*
5 to give information so that you can **see** something or see that something is true *The clock is showing midday. Ben's high marks show that he's been working hard. The map shows that Glasgow isn't far from Edinburgh.*
6 to have something such as a feeling, quality or skill that people can see clearly *Seema shows respect for her teachers. George showed no interest in his schoolwork. His eyes showed his disappointment. Her surprise showed on her face.*
7 to take someone somewhere or help them to go somewhere *The waiter showed us to our table. The prefects showed the parents around the school.*
8 if someone shows something for people to look at and enjoy, such as an artistic creation, people can see it somewhere such as in a cinema, on TV or in an exhibition *What film are they showing on TV tonight? My mother is showing her paintings in a London gallery. I don't know what's showing at the cinema this week.*
9 if someone shows off, they try to make people think how good or clever they are, for example by talking about what they've done, how much they know or how much money they have
10 if someone shows something or someone off, they are proud of them and want other people to see them *My sister was showing off her new bike.*
11 (informal) to show up is to come to a place where someone is expecting you *We waited all morning for the plumber but no-one showed up.*
12 (informal) if someone shows you up, they make you feel embarrassed, for example because of their bad behaviour or because of knowing how to do something better than you

show noun **shows**
1 a programme that you watch on TV or listen to on the radio *It's a show about dinosaurs.*
2 a performance, for example acting, singing or dancing, in a place such as a theatre or club *The show has just opened* (started).
3 an event where people go to look at things such as paintings, sculptures, flowers or clothes *a flower show; a fashion show*
4 an occasion when someone shows a particular feeling, behaviour or action *Our team badly needs a show of support. Extra soldiers were sent to the capital as a show of force.*
5 **a good** (or **bad**) **show** something well (or badly) done *That was a very good show by your team.*
6 **on show** being shown for people to look at and enjoy *There are more paintings on show in the next gallery.*

show business noun
the business of people who entertain the public, for example people who work in films, the theatre, television and radio

shower noun **showers**
1 a sudden fall of rain or snow that doesn't last for very long *We were caught in a shower.*
2 a piece of equipment with a water pipe that you stand under to wash yourself. The pipe has a flat piece at the end with holes in it that spray water onto your body.
3 the small room or area that contains this equipment *I'm in the shower.*
4 the action of washing yourself in the shower, or the water you wash yourself with *to have a shower; The shower wasn't hot enough.*
5 a large number of small things or drops of liquid falling through the air like rain *a shower of petals; a shower of water*

shower verb
showers, showering, showered
1 to wash yourself by having a shower
2 used about small things or drops of liquid that fall through the air like rain, or about someone or something that makes this happen *Arrows showered down on the enemy soldiers. The window shattered and showered us with glass.*
3 to give someone lots of something *My grandparents showered me with gifts.*

showery adjective
used for describing a time or the weather when there are some showers or a lot of showers *a showery afternoon; It's often showery in May.*

show jumping noun
a sport in which someone riding a horse shows their skill at making the horse jump over objects such as fences and walls
show jumper noun

showman noun **showmen**
someone who is good at entertaining people in a lively and interesting way

LANGUAGE EXTRA if you mean a woman or girl, you can also say *show-woman*

showmanship noun
the skill of entertaining people in a lively and interesting way

shown
past participle of **show**

show-off noun **show-offs**
someone who tries to make people think how good or clever they are, for example by talking about what they've done, how much they know or how much money they have

showroom noun **showrooms**
a building or large room where people go to look at and buy products such as cars, furniture, carpets or electrical goods *a car showroom*

showy adjective **showier, showiest**
if something is showy, it attracts your attention, for example because of its bright colours or large size or because it has lots of decorations **showiness** noun

shrank
past tense of **shrink**

shrapnel noun
small sharp pieces of metal from a bomb when it explodes. People are sometimes injured or killed by shrapnel.

shred noun **shreds**
1 a tiny strip of cloth or paper that is torn or cut off from something *Dad was so angry that he ripped the letter to shreds.*
2 a tiny amount of something *There isn't a shred of truth in what she says.*

shred verb
shreds, shredding, shredded
to tear or cut something into tiny strips *These papers need to be shredded* (so that no-one can read them).

shredder noun **shredders**
a piece of equipment that cuts papers into tiny strips so that no-one can read them

shrew noun **shrews**
a small animal that looks like a mouse with a long pointed nose and very small eyes

shrewd adjective **shrewder, shrewdest**
1 if someone is shrewd, they are clever and make good decisions and judgements
2 also used about someone's actions, ideas or judgements *a shrewd plan; a shrewd decision*
shrewdly adverb **shrewdness** noun

456

shriek *verb*
shrieks, shrieking, shrieked
to make a short, loud and high noise with your voice, for example because you are in pain, excited, surprised or happy

shriek *noun* **shrieks**
the noise you make when you shriek *shrieks of laughter and delight*

shrill *adjective* **shriller, shrillest**
used for describing a sound or voice that is high and loud and often unpleasant to listen to **shrillness** *noun*

shrimp *noun* **shrimps**
a small sea animal with a shell, a long body that has a tail and 10 legs, and long antennae (feelers). It looks like a small prawn and can be eaten as food.

shrine *noun* **shrines**
a place where people go to pray because it is connected with a holy person such as a saint or prophet or with a god

shrink *verb*
shrinks, shrinking, shrank, shrunk
1 to become smaller, for example when talking about clothes that you wash *My socks have shrunk. The rainforests are shrinking every year.*
2 to make something smaller *Don't put my jeans in the washing machine or you'll shrink them.*
3 if someone shrinks from something, they do not do it or deal with it, for example because it is unpleasant or dangerous *The president said he would not shrink from using force.*

shrinkage *noun*
when something becomes smaller *Expect some shrinkage each time you wash your jeans.*

shrink-wrapped *adjective*
if a product that you buy is shrink-wrapped, it is tightly wrapped in thin transparent plastic, for example so you know it has not been used before *a shrink-wrapped DVD*

shrivel *verb*
shrivels, shrivelling, shrivelled
1 if something shrivels or shrivels up, it becomes smaller and weaker and lines often appear on it, for example because it is old, dry or burnt *shrivelled leaves*; *These sausages look a bit shrivelled up.*
2 to make something shrivel *The hot weather has shrivelled all the plants.*

shroud *noun* **shrouds**
1 a piece of cloth that is wrapped around a dead body
2 a layer or area of something that covers or hides something *There was a shroud of mist hanging over the town.*

shroud *verb*
shrouds, shrouding, shrouded
to cover or hide something *a mountain top shrouded in mist*; *What happened that night is shrouded in mystery* (strange and mysterious).

Shrove Tuesday *noun*
the day before the start of the Christian period of Lent (a period lasting 40 days before Easter) when pancakes are often eaten. It is also called Pancake Day.

shrub *noun* **shrubs**
a plant like a very small tree with lots of branches growing closely together. Shrubs are smaller than bushes and often grow in gardens and parks.

shrubbery *noun* **shrubberies**
a part of a garden or park where lots of shrubs grow

shrug *verb*
shrugs, shrugging, shrugged
if you shrug or shrug your shoulders, you move your shoulders up and then down again as a sign that you don't know something or don't care

shrug *noun* **shrugs**
the action of shrugging your shoulders *When I asked John if he was interested, he gave a shrug.*

shrunk
past participle of **shrink**

shrunken *adjective*
used for describing something or someone that is smaller and less attractive than before *She looked old and shrunken.*

shudder *verb*
shudders, shuddering, shuddered
to shake suddenly for a short time, for example because you're frightened or cold or because you have an unpleasant feeling or thought *I shuddered when I heard his name.* **shudder** *noun*

shuffle *verb*
shuffles, shuffling, shuffled
1 to walk slowly by sliding your feet along the ground instead of lifting them *My aunt shuffled into the room with her walking stick.*
2 to shuffle the cards in a game of cards is to mix them up by dividing the pack (total number of cards) into two parts and sliding cards from each part into the other part
3 to shuffle things around is to move them around into different positions in no particular order
4 to shuffle music tracks (songs or pieces of music), for example in a software program or on a media player, is to allow the program or equipment to play the tracks in no particular order

shuffle *noun*
1 a slow way of walking by sliding your feet along the ground
2 (plural **shuffles**) the action of shuffling the cards in a game of cards *Give the cards a shuffle first.*
3 **lost in the shuffle** used about something that you don't do when you should or about someone that you don't pay attention to when you should, especially when there are lots of other things you have to do *I didn't phone Granddad today – it got lost in the shuffle.*

shun *verb*
shuns, shunning, shunned
to avoid someone or something

shunt *verb*
shunts, shunting, shunted
1 to move a train or carriage from one railway line onto another
2 to move or send someone or something from one place to another, for example because they are not wanted

shush [rhymes with 'push'] *interjection*
used for telling someone to be quiet

shut *verb*
shuts, shutting, shut
1 another way of saying to close *I shut my eyes. The door shut behind me. The library shuts at eight o'clock.*
2 to shut someone or something somewhere (or shut them away or up somewhere) is to put them there, for example to hide them or keep them away from other people *They shut him* (or *shut him up*) *in his room all day. Mum shut the cakes away in the cupboard so we couldn't have any more.*
3 if you shut down a piece of equipment or a computer (or computer program), or if it shuts down, you make it stop working *My laptop takes a long time to shut down.*
4 if a shop, company or public building shuts down, it stops doing business and will not open again
5 if you shut something or someone in something, they get stuck or held somewhere *I shut my finger in the door. We were shut in the lift for 10 minutes.*
6 if you shut something off such as a car engine or tap, or if something shuts off, it stops working
7 to shut someone or something out is to stop them getting in somewhere *My brother accidentally shut me out of the house. Close the curtains to shut out the light.*
8 to shut up is to stop talking or stop making a noise, and to shut someone up is to make them stop talking or making a noise *Shut up – I'm doing my homework! If I give him some sweets, that might shut him up.*
9 to shut something up such as a house, flat or shop is to lock all the doors and windows *Don't forget to shut up the house when you go away on holiday.*

shut *adjective*
another way of saying closed *Was the window shut? The shops are shut today.*

shutters *noun plural*
1 metal or wooden covers that usually go over the outside of a window, for example to protect it or keep out the light and noise
2 metal covers that are pulled down over the front part of a shop to protect it when it is closed

shuttle *noun* **shuttles**
1 a train, plane, bus or other vehicle that takes people on regular journeys between two places, often a short distance apart *We took the shuttle from Victoria to Gatwick airport* (regular train service). *The company operates a shuttle service between Oxford and Cambridge.*
2 a shuttle or space shuttle is a spacecraft that travels into space and comes back to earth. It is used several times for making this journey.

shuttle *verb*
shuttles, shuttling, shuttled
to go on regular journeys between two places or take people on regular journeys *My parents have been shuttling to and from the hospital to visit Ibrahim.*

shuttlecock–sideshow

shuttlecock noun shuttlecocks
a light object with sloping sides like a cone, made from a piece of round cork or plastic at the bottom with feathers or long strips of plastic sticking out. It is used instead of a ball in the game of badminton and is hit over a net.

shy adjective shyer, shyest
1 if you're shy, you don't like being with people or talking to them, or doing anything with people or in front of them, because they make you feel uncomfortable and embarrassed *She's too shy to sing to us.*
2 also used about something that shows that you're shy *shy behaviour*; *a shy smile*
3 if an animal is shy, it is frightened of people and hides from them
shyly adverb **shyness** noun

shy verb
shies, shying, shied
to shy away from something is to avoid it or avoid doing it, for example because it is difficult or you are afraid *My brother never shies away from a good fight in the playground.*

sibling noun siblings
your siblings are your brothers and sisters

sick adjective sicker, sickest
1 if a person or animal is sick, they are ill *Iqbal is very sick in hospital.*
2 also used about a person or animal when the food they have eaten suddenly comes up from their stomach and out of their mouth, for example because they are ill or have eaten too much *The cat was sick all over the carpet.*
3 if you feel sick, you have an unpleasant feeling in your stomach and a feeling that food might come up out of your mouth
4 if you're sick of something or someone (or sick and tired of them), you're angry or bored about something, for example something that has been going on for a long time and that you think should stop *Jo's been playing that music all day – I'm sick and tired of it! You're not my friend any more – I'm sick of you!*
5 (slang) very unhappy or disappointed about something

> SIMILES 'as sick as a dog' and 'as sick as a parrot' mean very sick (senses 1, 2 & 3); 'as sick as a parrot' also means very unhappy or disappointed (sense 5)

sick noun (informal)
the food from someone's stomach that comes out of their mouth

sick verb (informal)
sicks, sicking, sicked
used about a person or animal when the food they have eaten suddenly comes up from their stomach and out of their mouth *The baby sicked up some milk over the high chair.*

sickbay noun sickbays
a room, for example in a school or on a ship, where someone goes for medical treatment when they are ill

sicken verb
sickens, sickening, sickened
1 if something or someone sickens you, they are so horrible that they make you feel very shocked, upset and angry

2 (old-fashioned) if someone is sickening for something, they are starting to become ill with a particular illness, for example the flu *You look pale – are you sickening for something?*

sickening adjective
bad enough to make you feel very shocked, upset and angry *sickening behaviour*

sickle noun sickles
a tool with a short blade, often shaped like a semicircle, fixed to a short handle that is held with one hand. It was used especially in the past, for example by farmers, for cutting grass or wheat.
compare: **scythe**

sickly adjective sicklier, sickliest
1 ill and weak *She looked pale and sickly.*
2 often getting ill *When he was young he was a sickly child.*
3 used for describing something such as a smell or taste that gives you an unpleasant feeling in your stomach and makes you feel sick

sickness noun
1 when someone is ill *There's a lot of sickness around in the school.*

> SYNONYM illness

2 (plural sicknesses) a particular health problem *travel sickness*

> SYNONYM illness

3 a feeling of being sick *It was that awful smell that caused my sickness.*

sick note noun sick notes
a short letter, usually from a parent or doctor, saying you cannot go to school because of illness, or from a doctor saying someone cannot go to work because of illness

side noun sides
1 the part at the end of something where it stops or the surface on the outside of something, for example the part or surface that is not the back, front, top or bottom *There's a label on the side of the box. The side of the cup has a crack in it.*
2 the surface of something thin that is made up of two main surfaces, for example a page, card, coin, piece of cloth or slice of bread *The paper was printed on both sides. You've burnt one side of the toast.*
3 one of the lines that make up a 2-D shape *A triangle has three sides.*
4 one of the flat surfaces of a 3-D shape *A cube has six equal square sides.*
5 one of two parts that something could be divided into *The boys stood on the left side of the room and the girls on the right side. Chloe lives on the other side of the road.*
6 a part of an area such as a town or village *We live on the north side of town.*
7 the slope of something such as a mountain or hill *a hut on the side of the mountain*
8 the place next to something or someone *There are banisters to hold on to on both sides of the stairs. Come and sit by my side.*
9 the left or right part of your body from the place where your arm joins your shoulder down to your hip *I have a terrible pain in my side.*

10 a group, team or country, for example playing against each other in a competition or fighting against each other in an argument or war (or playing or fighting together or supporting each other) *Neither side has scored a goal yet. In the Second World War, America was on our side* (fought with us and supported us). *He doesn't like to take sides* (support one person or group in an argument).
11 another word for a television or radio station *I don't like this programme – please change sides.*
12 a part of someone's family *Please send my best wishes to your side of the family.*
13 **to one side** out of the way *He ran past me and pushed me to one side. Put your homework to one side and help me in the kitchen.*
14 **side by side** next to each other *Mohammed and I were walking side by side.*

side adjective
1 on the side of something *a side door*
2 a side effect is something bad that happens, for example something that is not supposed to happen, when someone takes a medicine
3 a side street is a small street connected to a main street

side verb
sides, siding, sided
to side with someone is to support them in an argument instead of supporting someone else *Dad always sides with my sister rather than me.*

sideboard noun sideboards
1 a piece of furniture with drawers and cupboards, usually used in a dining room for storing things you need for a meal such as plates, knives and forks, and glasses. It has a flat top for putting things on and stands about three or four feet high.
2 sideboards is another word for sideburns

sideburns noun plural
hair that a man grows down the sides of his cheeks, for example like a long strip

> ORIGIN from the name of a 19th-century US army general Ambrose *Burnside* who wore *burnsides* (thick hair at the sides of his face). *Burnsides* gradually got turned around and became *sideburns*.

sidecar noun sidecars
a seat with a wheel, fixed to the side of a motorcycle. It is used for carrying an extra passenger.

-sided suffix
1 used with numbers for making adjectives that show how many sides something has *A hexagon is a six-sided shape.*
2 used for showing what kind of sides something has *a glass-sided building*

sideline noun sidelines
an activity that someone does as well as their main job or activity, for example to earn extra money

sideshow noun sideshows
a small show for entertaining people at a circus or fair that is not part of the main show

sidewalk – significance

sidewalk noun sidewalks
the American word for a pavement

sideways adverb & adjective
used when talking about the side of something or someone, for example towards one side, not forwards or backwards *Turn your head sideways, towards the window. Crabs walk sideways. She gave me a sideways glance.*

siding noun sidings
a short railway track beside the main track, where trains are kept when they are not being used or where goods are taken on or off trains

sidle verb
sidles, sidling, sidled
to walk somewhere slowly and nervously, for example because you don't want to be seen *Someone sidled up to me and tapped me on the shoulder.*

siege ['seej'] noun sieges
when an army or the police surround a place to stop the people inside from getting food and to make them stop fighting and come out

siesta ['see-es-ter'] noun siestas
a short sleep that someone has, usually in the afternoon

sieve ['siv'] noun sieves
a round container with lots of tiny holes in it that allow only liquids and very small things to pass through. Sieves are used for separating solids from liquids and hard things from soft ones. They are usually used in the kitchen, for example to remove lumps from a sauce, or in the garden, for example to remove stones from the earth.

sift verb
sifts, sifting, sifted
1 to put a soft or powdery substance such as flour, sand or earth through a sieve to separate the hard or larger parts from the soft or smaller parts
2 to examine every part of something very carefully *After the fire, the police sifted through the ashes looking for clues.*

sigh verb
sighs, sighing, sighed
to make a low sound when you breathe out as a way of showing a particular feeling such as being happy or relaxed or being disappointed, annoyed or bored

sigh noun sighs
the low sound you make when you sigh *He gave a sigh of relief.*

sight noun
1 the natural ability you have to see *Great-Grandma's sight is getting worse.*
2 when you see something or someone *The sight of all the family together made Granddad very happy. The squirrel has disappeared from sight* (can no longer be seen).
3 something or someone that you see *Rabbits are a common sight around here.*
4 the sights of a place are the interesting places to see *The children want to visit the sights of London.*
5 someone or something that looks ridiculous, unusual or unpleasant *You're wet and dirty – you look a real sight!*
6 (*plural* **sights**) the part of a gun that you look through to aim it at something

7 **to catch sight of** to see someone or something for a very short time only
8 **in sight** used about something or someone that you can see *Everybody in sight was waving flags.*
9 **out of sight** used about something or someone that you can no longer see *The plane flew behind a cloud and out of sight. Watch the baby and don't let her out of your sight* (make sure you can see her at all times).

sight verb
sights, sighting, sighted
to see something, for example something difficult to see or something you have been looking hard for *The captain sighted the enemy ship two miles away.*

sightseeing noun
when you travel around somewhere such as a town or country visiting interesting places, for example buildings, parks or zoos
sightseer noun

sign noun signs
1 something that provides information, for example a piece of wood, plastic, metal or paper with words or pictures on it *a road sign; a 'no smoking' sign; The sign in the shop window says 'closed for lunch'.*
2 an action or movement that has a certain meaning for someone or tells someone what they should do *We came running when Dad gave the sign* (for example a movement of the hand). *She smiled – it was a sign she wasn't angry.*
3 something that shows that something else exists, is happening or is about to happen *Daffodils are a sign of spring. If you have a runny nose, it's a sign you have a cold. These clouds are a sign of rain. We went to Granddad's flat but there was no sign of him* (he wasn't there).
4 a mark or symbol that represents something *a plus sign (+); a minus sign (−); a pound sign (£)*

sign verb
signs, signing, signed
1 if you sign a piece of paper, a card or electronic document, you write your name there in your own special way *Don't forget to sign your library card on the back.*
2 if you sign your name, you write your name somewhere in your own special way *Ask Mum to sign her name here. Sign on the dotted line.*
3 if people sign, they use sign language (hand movements instead of words and sounds) to talk to people who cannot hear
4 if you sign for a letter or parcel, you sign your name somewhere when it is given to you to show that you have officially received it
5 if you sign in to a website or computer program, you start using it, for example after typing a password. If you sign out, you stop using it, for example by clicking on an icon or button. *If you've already registered, you can sign straight in.*

SYNONYMS to log in, to log out

6 if you sign in somewhere such as an office or hotel, you write your name and the time, for example on a piece of paper, to say you have arrived. If you sign out, you write your name and the time to say you are leaving.

7 if someone signs on, they go to a government Jobcentre because they are looking for work and they receive money from the government until they find a job
8 to sign up (or to sign someone up) is to provide information about yourself (or someone else) such as a name and address so that you can do a particular activity, for example study on a course or use a particular website or internet service *My older sister has signed up for evening classes* (for example, she has given her name and address and paid her money). *Have you signed up for email?*
9 to sign someone up is also to get them to work for a company, join a sports team or join the army by signing an official agreement *Manchester United have signed up two new players.*

signal noun signals
1 an action, movement, sound or light that tells someone something or tells someone what they should do *When I give you the signal I want you all to start cheering.*
2 a series of radio or electrical waves sent and received by electronic equipment such as mobile phones, TVs and computers. The signals provide the sounds, pictures and information to make the equipment work. *I can't use my phone on the tube because there's no signal.*
3 a piece of information sent from one place to another in a particular system *These nerves send signals to the brain.*
4 a piece of equipment with different coloured lights that tells road vehicles or trains when to stop or go *traffic signals* (traffic lights); *You have to stop – the signal's red.*
5 something that shows that something else is about to happen or exists *There were warning signals but we missed them. This is a clear signal that things are not working.*

signal verb
signals, signalling, signalled
1 to do something such as make a movement or sound that has a certain meaning for someone or tells someone what they should do *With a wave of her hand she signalled for us to come into the room. Turn right at the traffic lights and don't forget to signal* (make your lights flash on one side of the car).
2 to show that something exists or is about to happen *Losing the match signalled the end of our team's hopes.*

signal box noun signal boxes
a small building beside a railway track where signals for trains are operated and tracks are controlled

signalman noun signalmen
a man who operates railway signals that tell trains when to stop and when to go, and who controls points (places where rails are moved so that trains can change tracks)

LANGUAGE EXTRA a woman who does this work is called a *signalwoman*

signature noun signatures
your name when you write it in your own special way

significance noun
1 the great importance of something or someone

459

significant – similarly

2 the meaning of something *None of us realised the significance of the ribbon she was wearing.*

significant *adjective*
1 very important *1066 is a significant date in British history.*
2 very large *You can save a significant amount of time by taking the bus instead of walking.*

significantly *adverb*
1 very much *Alfie's work has improved significantly this term.*
2 used for showing that you think something is very important *Sayed has been accepted into the football team and, more significantly, he's been made captain.*

signify *verb*
signifies, signifying, signified
1 to mean something *What do these Latin words signify?*
2 to be a sign of something *The blue lines on the map signify rivers.*
3 to show something *The audience signified their enthusiasm by cheering and clapping.*

sign language *noun* **sign languages**
a special language for people who cannot hear. Instead of using words and sounds, people make movements with their hands and arms.

> LANGUAGE EXTRA also called *signing*

signpost *noun* **signposts**
a pole, usually next to a road, with signs at the top showing the names of places and often how far away they are, and pointing in the direction of each place

signposted *adjective*
used for describing something such as a road that has signposts showing the directions to places

Sikh ['seek'] *noun* **Sikhs**
someone who follows the religion of Sikhism
Sikh *adjective*

Sikhism *noun*
one of the main religions of India. Sikhism started in the 15th century. It is based on a belief in one God only.

silence *noun*
1 when nothing or no-one makes any noise *We all sat in silence.*
2 (*plural* **silences**) a period of time when no-one speaks *When I speak to Uncle Alan on the phone there are lots of awkward silences.*
3 when someone doesn't want to talk about something *What are George's plans? – It's time for him to break his silence* (start talking about them).
4 to observe silence is to be silent for a short while

silence *verb*
silences, silencing, silenced
to silence someone is to stop them from speaking or making a noise

silencer *noun* **silencers**
1 a part fixed to a gun that makes it quieter
2 a part that makes the noise of a car or motorcycle engine quieter. It is fixed to the exhaust (gas pipe).

silent *adjective*
1 not making any noise *The old house was dark and silent. I want you to be silent when the play starts.*

2 not talking about something *Granddad has been silent about his plans.*
3 not talking very much *Raj is one of the silent ones.*
4 done without making any noise *It's time for a period of silent reading.*
5 a silent letter in a word is a letter that is included in the spelling of the word but has no sound when you pronounce the word *The word 'knee' has a silent k.*

> SIMILE 'as silent as the grave' means completely silent (sense 1)

silently *adverb*
1 without making any noise or much noise *I crept silently upstairs.*
2 without saying anything *We sat silently on the bus home.*

silhouette ['sil-oo-et'] *noun* **silhouettes**
a dark image showing only the shape of a person or thing that you see against the light

silicon *noun*
a grey substance found in rocks and sand, used especially for making microchips (small objects with electrical connections that make electronic equipment work)

silk *noun*
1 a thin, smooth and shiny cloth for making things such as shirts, scarves and ties. It comes from the threads of an insect called a silkworm.
2 fine threads produced by a silkworm to make its cocoon (covering for its body before it changes into a moth)

silkworm *noun* **silkworms**
a caterpillar that produces fine threads that silk is made from. The silkworm uses the threads to make its cocoon (covering for its body).

silky *adjective* **silkier, silkiest**
soft, smooth and shiny *silky hair*

sill *noun* **sills**
a narrow shelf at the bottom of a window

> SYNONYM *windowsill*

silly *adjective* **sillier, silliest**
1 if someone is silly, they are not very clever and don't think carefully about things or make good decisions and judgements *You're silly to leave your homework till the last minute.*
2 also used about someone's actions, ideas or judgements to show they are not very clever or good *a silly mistake; It's silly to go walking in the rain.*
3 feeling or looking uncomfortable and awkward, or likely to make someone feel or look this way *I feel silly in these pink spotty trousers. Do I look silly? What a silly hat!*
4 behaving in a way that is not very clever or good, for example like a child who doesn't know any better *Get down from that tree and stop being silly!*
5 not very serious, important or useful *You'll never get all your clothes into that silly little suitcase! Considering all the walking she does, she wears very silly shoes.*
6 used for describing something that annoys you *Stop that silly moaning!*
7 (informal) if you do something such as laugh, shout or eat yourself silly, you do those things as much as you can until you can't do them any more *My sister isn't back from school yet and my parents are worrying themselves silly.*

silliness *noun*

> SIMILE 'as silly as a goose' means very silly (sense 1)

silver *noun*
1 a valuable light grey metal, used for example for making jewellery, coins and medals or knives, forks and spoons
2 a light grey colour
3 coins made of silver or coins that have a silver colour *Dad has a pocketful of silver.*
4 knives, forks and spoons made of silver

silver *adjective*
1 made of silver or a metal that has a silver colour *silver earrings; silver coins*
2 having the light grey colour of silver *We painted the gate silver. Grandma has silver hair.*
3 a silver medal is given to the person who comes second in a race or competition. A gold medal goes to the winner and a bronze one to the person who comes third.
4 silver paper is very thin, shiny and silver-coloured paper made from aluminium (a silver-coloured metal). It is used, for example, in cooking and for wrapping around things such as food or sweets.

silver-plated *adjective*
covered with a very thin layer of silver

silverware *noun*
objects such as knives, forks and spoons that are made of silver or covered with a thin layer of silver

silvery *adjective*
1 having the light grey colour of silver *silvery hair*
2 shiny like silver *a silvery light*

SIM card *noun* **SIM cards**
a small piece of plastic inside a mobile phone with a microchip (electrical connections) in it. It stores information about the phone and the person using it.
short for: *subscriber identity module card*

similar *adjective*
1 used about something or someone that has many things the same as something or someone else but also has things that are different *Tortoises and turtles are similar animals. They are similar to each other.*
2 in maths, a similar shape is one that has exactly the same shape as another shape but is either larger or smaller

similarity *noun*
1 when something or someone is similar to something or someone else *There's some similarity between a guitar and a banjo.*
2 (*plural* **similarities**) something that is similar to something or someone else *There are quite a few similarities between football and rugby.*

similarly *adverb*
1 in a way in which many things are the same but not everything *The twins are dressed similarly.*
2 used when comparing things that happen in a similar way *Rachel came first in the maths exam and, similarly, she was top in English.*

simile ['sim-er-lee] *noun* **similes**
a way of describing something or someone by comparing them to something else, using the words 'as' or 'like'. For example, 'Henry is as hungry as a wolf' or 'Henry eats like a wolf' are similes because you are comparing Henry to a wolf.
compare: **metaphor**

simmer *verb*
simmers, simmering, simmered
1 if a liquid (or food with liquid in it) simmers, or if someone simmers it, it boils very gently on a low flame *Let the spaghetti simmer for about 10 minutes.*
2 if someone simmers down, they become less excited or angry

SYNONYM for sense 2: to calm down

simple *adjective* **simpler, simplest**
1 easy to do, understand or deal with *This phone is simple to use. Can you explain how to do it in simple English?*
2 not complicated *The solution is simple. My grandparents live a simple life in the country. A hammer is a simple tool.*
3 quick *There are no simple answers or solutions.*
4 not special or different in any way but completely normal and ordinary *Although he was a simple man from a quiet little village, he was also a brilliant scientist. Granddad likes simple old-fashioned pop songs.*
5 used for saying that something is exactly what it is and nothing else *It's just a simple cold. Just tell me the simple truth!*
6 without any or very much decoration or without any or very many details *a simple green dress; a simple drawing of a person's head; The book had a simple dedication – it just said 'To Mum'.*
7 providing just what someone needs without anything extra *simple food* (for example bread, eggs, fruit and vegetables); *The student rooms are very simple* (for example with just a bed, table and chair).
8 in maths, the simplest form of a fraction is when you divide the numerator (top number) and denominator (bottom number) by the largest number possible. For example, the simplest form of $\frac{6}{24}$ is $\frac{1}{4}$ because you divide both 6 and 24 by 6.
9 (old-fashioned) used about someone who has a disability and finds it difficult to learn new things

simpleton *noun* **simpletons**
an old-fashioned word for someone who has a disability and finds it difficult to learn new things

simplicity *noun*
the quality of being simple *I like the simplicity of this phone. She leads a life of great simplicity. The best thing about Mum's car is the simplicity of the design.*

simplify *verb*
simplifies, simplifying, simplified
to make something easier for someone or easier to do or understand
simplification *noun*

simply *adverb*
1 used for giving special importance to a word *Simply phone me and I'll come straight over. These pears are simply delicious!*
2 only *I didn't visit Grandma, simply because I had too much homework.*
3 in a way that is easy to understand *Can you explain simply what a metaphor is?*
4 in a way that is very ordinary and not at all special *He was simply dressed* (for example, he didn't wear a suit or tie). *They live simply in the country* (for example, they eat simple food and go for walks).

simulate *verb*
simulates, simulating, simulated
1 to copy a type of situation that happens in real life or to produce a situation that might happen, for example using a computer. Simulating a situation is often a way of studying it. *The scientists have simulated conditions deep under the sea.*
2 to pretend to have a particular feeling or medical problem *He simulated illness.*
simulation *noun*

simultaneous *adjective*
happening at the same time *People heard two simultaneous loud bangs in different parts of the city.* **simultaneously** *adverb*

sin *noun* **sins**
1 an action or type of behaviour that is wrong or bad because it is against the laws of a religion or against the standards of how to behave
2 if someone commits a sin, they do something wrong or bad that is a sin

sin *verb*
sins, sinning, sinned
to do something wrong or bad that is a sin

since *conjunction & preposition*
1 used for showing that a situation that started at a particular time in the past continues until now *It's a long time since I've been to London. Where are you? – We've been waiting for you since this morning.*
2 used for showing that something has happened between a particular time in the past and now *You've grown since I last saw you. Since then I've learnt how to ride a bike.*
3 another word for because *You have to go to bed since it's so late.*

since *adverb*
1 from a particular time onwards or from then until now *We went on holiday to Spain five years ago and have been going back regularly ever since.*
2 at a later time *I didn't know Seema last year but she's since become my best friend.*

sincere *adjective* **sincerer, sincerest**
1 if someone is sincere, they mean what they say and show what they really feel *I don't think he was completely sincere when he said sorry.*
2 used about feelings, actions or words that show what someone really feels *a sincere apology; Give your parents my sincere good wishes.*
3 showing that someone is honest and good and that you can trust them *Bimla's a very sincere person, always ready to listen to you and to help.*
4 real or true *He made sincere efforts to try to solve the problem.*
sincerity *noun*

sincerely *adverb*
1 really, and in a way that shows what you really feel or want *I sincerely believe you're wrong. I sincerely hope so.*
2 **Yours sincerely** used before your name at the end of a letter as a polite way of saying goodbye

sinew ['sin-yoo] *noun* **sinews**
a strong substance in the body made of many threads joining a muscle to a bone

SYNONYM tendon

sinful *adjective*
1 used about something that is wrong or bad because it is a sin
2 used about someone who does something wrong or bad that is a sin
sinfully *adverb* **sinfulness** *noun*

sing *verb*
sings, singing, sang, sung
1 to make musical sounds with your voice *My sister is good at singing.*
2 if you sing something, you produce the words of a song using musical sounds *They all sang 'Happy Birthday' to me.*
3 if birds or insects sing, they make pleasant high sounds
singer *noun*

Singapore *noun*
a country and city in South-East Asia
Singaporean *adjective & noun*

singe ['sinj'] *verb*
singes, singeing, singed
to burn the surface or end of something slightly, when talking about a flame *My hair went too close to the candle and got accidentally singed.*

single *adjective*
1 used when you mean only one thing, person or animal *She didn't say a single word. I don't have one single friend at my new school. Can you park on a single yellow line?*
2 for one person only *a single bed; a single hotel room*
3 used for giving extra importance to a word *You ask me the same question every single time!*
4 if someone is single, they are not married
5 for or about a journey to a place but not back again, for example when you travel by train *a single fare; a single trip*
6 **in single file** standing one behind the other in a line

single *noun* **singles**
1 a ticket that allows you to travel to a place, for example by train, but not to come back again

SYNONYM one-way ticket

compare: **return**
2 one song or piece of music as a computer file, on a CD or, especially in the past, on a cassette or record *The band has just released a new single.*
compare: **album**
3 if you play singles in tennis, you play against one other person only. If you play with someone else against two other people, you play doubles.

single *verb*
singles, singling, singled
if someone singles out a person in a group, they pay special attention to that person, either for a good or a bad reason *The teacher singled out Nisha for special praise. Alfie was singled out for criticism.*

single-decker – site

single-decker *noun* **single-deckers**
a bus that has only one level where people sit
compare: **double-decker**

single-handed *adverb & adjective*
used about something that you do on your own without anyone helping you *Her mum's a single parent who brought up two children single-handed. My uncle took part in a single-handed yacht race.*
single-handedly *adverb*

single-minded *adjective*
showing that you give all your attention to one particular thing and that nothing will stop you from doing what you really want

single parent *noun* **single parents**
a parent who looks after their child or children alone because he or she does not have a husband, wife or partner

single ticket *noun* **single tickets**
a ticket for a journey to a place but not back again, for example when you travel by train. It is also called a one-way ticket.
compare: **return ticket**

singly *adverb*
one at a time, or separately and not together *Ms Bates said we could work on our project singly or in pairs.*

singular *noun* **singulars**
in grammar, the singular is the form of a word that you use when you mean only one thing or person. Nouns, pronouns and verbs all have singular forms. The plural is the form used when you mean more than one.

> **LANGUAGE EXTRA** the *singular* of nouns is the form that does not have a plural ending such as *-s* or *-es*. For example, the singular of *books* is *book* and the singular of *matches* is *match*. Sometimes there are other differences between singular and plural. For example, the singular of *leaves* is *leaf* and the singular of *men* is *man*.
> A singular pronoun is a word like *I, me, he, him, she* or *her* that refers to one person. If you mean more than one person, you use plural words such as *we, us, they* or *them*.
> A singular verb is a word like *jump* (*I jump*) or *jumps* (*he* or *she jumps*) that refers to one person. The plural form is usually the same as the singular in verbs (*we jump, they jump*) except for the third person of the present tense (*jumps*).

singular *adjective*
used for describing a noun, pronoun or verb that is used in the singular *'Cat' is a singular noun. 'She' is a singular pronoun. 'Is' is a singular form of the verb 'to be'.*

sinister *adjective*
1 if someone is sinister, they look as if they might do something bad
2 if something is sinister, it makes you feel that something bad might happen *a sinister laugh*

> **ORIGIN** from Latin *sinister* 'on the left side'. The Romans thought that the left was unlucky and bad but the right was lucky and good.

sink *noun* **sinks**
a large bowl with taps that is fixed to a wall in a kitchen or bathroom. You use it for washing dishes in or for washing your hands and face.

sink *verb*
sinks, sinking, sank, sunk
1 to go down slowly under the water (or under another liquid) and disappear *The boat hit a rock and sank.*
2 to make something sink, usually by firing weapons at it *The enemy sank two of our ships.*
3 to go down below the surface of something soft *The tyres of my bike just sank into the mud.*
4 to let yourself fall to the ground or onto something such as a seat *He sank to his knees and asked the King to forgive him. Mum sank down into her armchair and went to sleep.*
5 to become slowly lower *The sun was sinking below the horizon.*
6 to move slowly into a worse situation *When Granddad died, Grandma sank into depression* (became ill because she was so sad).
7 if something sinks in, you understand how important it is to you *My parents won the lottery but the news hasn't sunk in yet.*
8 if someone sinks something into something, they make something sharp go deeply into it *The lion sank its teeth into its prey.*

sinkhole *noun* **sinkholes**
a large hole that opens up in the ground, often suddenly. It is usually caused by water making the surface of the ground so wet that it sinks.

sinner *noun* **sinners**
someone who does something wrong or bad that is a sin

sinuous *adjective*
having or moving with lots of twists and turns *a sinuous path; the sinuous shape of the letter S* **sinuously** *adverb*

sinus ['sigh-ners'] *noun* **sinuses**
one of the spaces in the bones of your face, behind your nose

sip *verb*
sips, sipping, sipped
to drink something slowly, a small amount at a time

sip *noun* **sips**
a small amount of something that you drink at one time *The tea's too hot so I just took a sip.*

siphon ['sigh-fern'] *noun* **siphons**
a bent tube used for moving liquid from one container to another

siphon *verb*
siphons, siphoning, siphoned
to move liquid from one container to another with a siphon

sir *noun*
1 a polite word to call a man when you don't know his name, used for example in a shop or restaurant *What would you like, sir?*
2 a title that children use when they talk to a man teacher *Please, sir, may I leave the room?*
3 Sir is the title of a man given a special honour, called a knighthood, by the British government *Sir Winston Churchill*
compare: **Dame**

siren *noun* **sirens**
a piece of equipment that makes a very loud high sound as a warning or signal, for example on an emergency vehicle such as a police car *We could hear the ambulance siren wailing. The workers used to rush home when they heard the factory siren.*

sirloin *noun* **sirloins**
a piece of meat of the best quality taken from the top part of a cow's back

sister *noun* **sisters**
1 a girl or woman who has the same parents as you
2 a female nurse in charge of a hospital ward (room with beds)
3 the title given to someone such as a nun who belongs to a Christian religious group *Sister Angela*

sister-in-law *noun* **sisters-in-law**
someone's sister-in-law is their brother's wife, or the sister of their own husband or wife, or the wife of their husband's brother or of their wife's brother

sit *verb*
sits, sitting, sat
1 to rest the part of your body at the bottom of your back on something such as a chair or the ground and keep the top half of your body fairly straight *We were sitting on the floor. Go and sit down on that chair.*
2 to be in a particular situation, usually sitting *We sat in silence next to each other on the bus. Mum spends an hour a day sitting in traffic* (for example driving her car slowly in a long line of vehicles). *He's been sitting at home for days doing nothing.*
3 to make someone sit somewhere *Dad sat the baby on his lap.*
4 if an animal such as a dog or cat sits, it rests the bottom of its body usually on the ground with its front legs straight
5 to be in a particular place *The jam had been sitting in the fridge for weeks.*
6 to sit an exam is to do it by answering questions to find out your knowledge of a subject
7 if something such as a parliament or court of law sits, that is the period of time when official meetings take place *Their parliament sits from October to June.*
8 (informal) to sit for someone is to look after their child (or children) when that person goes out

> **SYNONYM** to babysit

9 to sit around or about is to spend time doing nothing
10 to sit up is to get into a sitting position after you've been lying down or to put your back straight without leaning or bending *Sit up, Ollie, you're always slouching.*

site *noun* **sites**
1 a place on the internet where you find information about something or someone *Our school's site has just been updated.*

> **SYNONYM** website

2 a piece of land that people are building on, or where something was built, could be built or will be built *This will be the site of our new gym.*
3 a place used for something *a camping site; a helicopter landing site*
4 a place where something happens or happened in the past, often something important *We visited the site of the Battle of Hastings. The children were playing on a bomb site* (an area where a building was destroyed by a bomb).
5 a place where something important exists or existed in the past, for example a building *Their village was the site of a Roman cemetery and is now the site of a nuclear plant.*

site *verb*
sites, siting, sited
if something is sited somewhere, it is built there

sitemap *noun* sitemaps
a page on a website that lists all the pages of that website in a clear and organised way so that you can find the page you are looking for

LANGUAGE EXTRA also spelt *site map*

sitter *noun* sitters
an informal word for a babysitter

sitting *noun* sittings
a time when a meal is served, for example at a party or in a school canteen, usually when there isn't enough room for everyone to eat at the same time

sitting room *noun* sitting rooms
the main room in a house or flat, for example where you can relax, sit and talk or watch TV

SYNONYM living room

situated *adjective*
if a building or place is situated somewhere, that is where it is *Our school is situated near the centre of town.*

situation *noun* situations
1 used for saying what is happening to someone or something at a particular time or the way things are at a particular time *We don't want to get into that kind of situation* (we don't want those kinds of things to happen to us).
2 used for saying where something is, such as a building or town, when talking about the places surrounding it *The house has a beautiful situation on a hillside.*

six *adjective & noun* sixes
the number 6

sixpence *noun* sixpences
a coin used in the UK until 1971. It was worth half a shilling or six old pence.

sixteen *adjective & noun* sixteens
the number 16 **sixteenth** *adjective & noun*

sixth *adjective & noun*
1 used about something or someone that comes in place number 6 *That's the sixth time it's happened.*
2 (*plural* **sixths**) one of 6 equal parts of something *a sixth of the cake*

sixth form *noun* sixth forms
the two last years of school for students between the ages of 16 and 18

sixty *adjective & noun* sixties
1 the number 60
2 the sixties are the sixtieth to sixty-ninth years of a century, for example 1960 to 1969
3 if someone is in their sixties, they are between 60 and 69 years old
sixtieth *adjective & noun*

size *noun*
1 (*plural* **sizes**) how big something or someone is, for example when you look at the distance from one end to the other and from one side to the other *pens of all shapes and sizes; Our classroom is a good size* (fairly big). *A bee is similar in size to a wasp.*
2 when something or someone is very big *Look at the size of that tree!*
3 (*plural* **sizes**) a particular number or letter given to things that you buy, such as clothes, for showing what they measure *size 6 shoes; a size L shirt* (L for large)

size *verb*
sizes, sizing, sized
if you size someone or something up, you consider them carefully and give an opinion about them

sizeable *adjective*
fairly big *I spend a sizeable amount of my pocket money on books.*

LANGUAGE EXTRA also spelt *sizable*

-sized *suffix*
used for making adjectives and nouns that show how big or small something is or what the size of something is *large-sized; small-sized; pocket-sized*

sizzle *verb*
sizzles, sizzling, sizzled
if something sizzles, it makes the short loud noises of food cooking in hot fat or oil *The sausages were sizzling in the pan.*

skate *noun* skates
1 a special shoe with a metal blade at the bottom for moving or dancing on ice

SYNONYM ice skate

2 a special shoe with two pairs of wheels at the bottom for moving on a hard surface

SYNONYM roller skate

skate *noun* skate
a large flat fish that lives in the sea. It has flesh that is almost white and is used as food.

skate *verb*
skates, skating, skated
1 to move or dance on ice using ice skates

SYNONYM to ice-skate

2 to move on a hard surface using roller skates

SYNONYM to roller-skate

skateboard *noun* skateboards
a long flat piece of wood with four small wheels at the bottom and ends that are curved slightly upwards. You stand on it and ride it as a sport by pushing yourself along with one foot. **skateboarder** *noun* **skateboarding** *noun*

skater *noun* skaters
someone who skates on ice or a hard surface

skating *noun*
1 the sport of moving around using ice skates or roller skates
2 a skating rink is a floor of ice for skating on using ice skates or a hard surface for skating on using roller skates

skeletal *adjective*
1 so thin that you can see the shape of the bones *a skeletal dog*
2 connected with skeletons *skeletal remains* (a dead body that is no more than a skeleton)

skeleton *noun* skeletons
1 a structure made of all the bones that support a person's body or the body of an animal
2 the main structure of something such as a building, book or plan

sketch *noun* sketches
1 a drawing that you do quickly and without all the details
2 a short description without many details
3 a short piece of acting that is part of a longer show, for example on TV or the radio. Sketches are usually funny. *a comedy sketch*

sketch *verb*
sketches, sketching, sketched
1 to draw something or someone quickly and without all the details
2 to give a short description of something without many details *I've sketched out an idea for a short story.*

sketchbook *noun* sketchbooks
another word for a sketchpad

LANGUAGE EXTRA also spelt *sketch-book*

sketchpad *noun* sketchpads
a number of pieces of paper fixed together for drawing on

LANGUAGE EXTRA also spelt *sketch-pad*

sketchy *adjective* sketchier, sketchiest
containing very few details *Information about the accident is sketchy.*

skewer *noun* skewers
a long thin stick, usually made of metal, for holding together pieces of meat while they are being cooked

ski *noun* skis
a long thin piece of wood, plastic or metal that you wear under a boot on each foot for moving quickly over the snow, for example in the sport of skiing

ski *adjective*
connected with skiing *ski boots; ski slopes*

ski *verb*
skis, skiing, skied
to move over the snow wearing skis
skier *noun*

skid *verb*
skids, skidding, skidded
if a vehicle skids, its wheels move forward or to the side without turning, for example on ice or a wet road, and the driver can no longer control it *Dad skidded into a tree.*

skid–skull

skid noun skids
a skidding movement that cannot be controlled *The motorbike was going too fast on the icy road and went into a skid.*

skiing noun
the sport of moving over the snow on skis *My cousins go skiing every year. My mum's a skiing instructor.*

skilful adjective
1 good at doing something because you've practised *a skilful piano player*
2 used for describing something that you do well because you've practised *skilful piano playing*
skilfully adverb

ski lift noun ski lifts
a piece of equipment with seats that hang down from a wire, used for carrying people with skis up a slope so that they can ski down it

skill noun
1 (plural **skills**) an activity that you learn and know how to do well, for example an activity that is useful *a practical skill*; *My sister is studying French and computer programming to learn new skills.*
2 when you do something well, for example because you've had a lot of practice or you have a lot of knowledge *Amy plays football with great skill.*

skilled adjective
showing that you have the special knowledge needed to do something well *a very skilled plumber*; *Repairing computers is skilled work.*

skim verb
skims, skimming, skimmed
1 to move quickly just above a surface or just touching a surface *The plane flew low, skimming the tops of trees.*
2 to skim through something such as a book is to look at it quickly, for example to understand the main ideas but not the details
3 to remove something floating on the surface of a liquid *I skimmed the fat off the chicken soup with a big spoon.*

skimmed milk noun
milk from which the cream (thick fat substance that forms on the top of it) is removed so that there is no fat left. Semi-skimmed milk has had half the cream removed.

skimp verb
skimps, skimping, skimped
if you skimp on something, you do, use or give less of it than is necessary *Mum doesn't have much money but she doesn't skimp on food* (for example, she doesn't give us less food than we need). *Buy a good mobile phone – don't skimp* (for example, don't buy a worse phone than you need).

skimpy adjective skimpier, skimpiest
skimpy clothes are small and do not cover much of the body *a skimpy dress*

skin noun skins
1 the outside layer of the body of a person or animal
2 the skin (or skin and fur) of a dead animal, for example a cow, tiger or crocodile, used for making things such as leather or rugs
3 the outside layer of a fruit or vegetable, for example a banana or tomato
4 a thin layer that forms on the top of a liquid such as hot milk
5 a thin piece of a special plastic material that is stuck or pressed onto the top or back of a piece of equipment such as a laptop or mobile phone. Skins are used as decoration.
6 if someone has thick skin, they do not get angry or upset if people say bad or unkind things about them

skin verb
skins, skinning, skinned
to remove the skin from a dead animal or from a fruit or vegetable

skin diving noun
the activity of swimming under the water, usually with very simple breathing equipment and without wearing any special clothes to protect you **skin diver** noun

> LANGUAGE EXTRA also spelt *skin-diving* and *skin-diver*

skinhead noun skinheads
1 a young person with very short hair, or with hair completely cut off, who belongs to a group who behave in a violent way and without respect for other people
2 a hairstyle in which someone's hair is cut very short

-skinned suffix
used with adjectives for describing skin *a fair-skinned baby*; *a smooth-skinned fruit*

skinny adjective skinnier, skinniest
1 very thin *My brother has skinny legs.*
2 an informal word for describing a hot drink such as coffee made with semi-skimmed or skimmed milk (milk with less fat or no fat in it) *One skinny cappuccino, please!*

skint adjective (slang)
if you're skint, you have no money

skip verb
skips, skipping, skipped
1 to move along quickly making small jumping steps, first with one leg and then the other *I was so happy that I went skipping down the street.*
2 to jump over a rope while holding one end of it in each hand and turning it above your head and then under your feet, often many times. Each time the rope goes towards your feet, you jump up so that it goes underneath them.
3 to not do or have something or not go to something *Ismail was late for school so he skipped breakfast. I think I'll just skip my homework this week. My brother is always skipping lessons.*
4 to not read, watch, listen to or mention something but to go on to the next thing instead *Skip the first few pages and begin on page 7. Just skip over the boring bits and start telling us about your adventure. Click the icon to skip the ad and go straight to the video.*
5 to accidentally miss something out, for example because you don't notice it *I think you must have skipped a page, Dad, when you were reading us the story.*
6 to go quickly from one thing to another, usually in a way that is not careful or organised *Mum kept skipping from one subject to another. Dad wanted to spend the holiday skipping around from one place to another.*
7 (informal) to leave a place quickly and often secretly *The thieves have already skipped the country.*

skip noun skips
1 a skipping movement
2 a very large metal container with an open top used for putting rubbish in, for example when repairs are done to a building. The skip is brought empty to where it is needed and taken away full by a special lorry.

ski pants noun plural
1 tight trousers, mainly for women and girls, made from a material that stretches easily and with a thin strip of cloth called a stirrup fixed to the bottom of each leg. You put the stirrup under your foot when you wear them.
2 thick trousers worn by men and women when skiing

skipper noun skippers
1 someone in charge of a small ship or aircraft
2 someone in charge of a sports team, such as a football or cricket team

skipping rope noun skipping ropes
a rope with a handle at each end that you use for jumping over. You make the rope turn above your head and under your feet.

skirmish noun skirmishes
a small fight, often between several people

skirt noun skirts
a piece of clothing that girls and women wear, hanging down from the waist and over the legs. Skirts can be short (reaching above or below the knees) or long (reaching to the ankles or the ground).

skirt verb
skirts, skirting, skirted
to go around the edge of something

skirting board noun skirting boards
a narrow piece of wood fixed along the bottom of a wall inside a room. It covers the place where the wall meets the floor, protects the wall from kicks and is used as decoration.

skit noun skits
a short piece of acting or writing that makes fun of someone or something

skittish adjective
1 if a person or animal is skittish, they are easily frightened and likely to behave in an unexpected way *a skittish horse*
2 used about someone who is playful or not serious and is likely to change their opinion often

skittle noun skittles
a wooden object shaped like a bottle, used in a game such as bowling or in the game called skittles. People try to knock the skittles down with a large heavy ball that they roll along the ground.

skulk verb
skulks, skulking, skulked
if someone skulks, they move around or wait somewhere trying not to be seen, for example because they want to do something bad

skull noun skulls
1 a structure made of all the bones in a person's head or in the head of an animal

2 an informal or impolite word for your head or brain *Try and get that idea into your skull* (try to understand it).
3 a skull and crossbones is a picture of a human skull with two long bones forming a cross under it. It was used in the past on the Jolly Roger (the black flag of a pirate ship). It is often used now as a symbol of danger, for example on a container with poison inside.

skunk noun skunks
a black and white North American animal, usually the size of a cat, with thick fur and a long thick tail. It produces a very unpleasant smell when it is attacked or frightened.

sky noun
1 the space above the earth where you can see the clouds, sun, moon and stars
2 **skies** used for talking about the weather in a particular place *the sunny skies of Italy*

skydiving noun
the sport of jumping out of a plane and letting yourself fall for as long as possible before opening your parachute **skydiver** noun

sky-high adjective
extremely high *sky-high prices*

skylark noun skylarks
a small brown bird that sings as it flies high in the air

SYNONYM lark

skylight noun skylights
a window that is built into a roof

skyline noun skylines
the shape that is formed by buildings when you see them against the sky *the London skyline*

Skype noun (trademark)
a phone and video service that allows people to speak to each other and to see each other using a computer connected to the internet

skype verb
skypes, skyping, skyped
to speak to someone using Skype *We're going to skype Granddad in America. We spent two hours skyping.*

skyrocket verb
skyrockets, skyrocketing, skyrocketed
to increase a lot very quickly *The number of children getting flu this year has skyrocketed.*

skyscraper noun skyscrapers
a very tall building in a city, usually with offices

slab noun slabs
1 a large flat piece of something very hard such as stone, usually shaped like a square or rectangle *a slab of concrete*
2 a large flat piece of food such as meat

slack adjective slacker, slackest
1 used about something such as a rope or wire that is not pulled tight

SYNONYM loose

2 used about a period of time or a business when things are not busy and there isn't much work *Mondays are slack in my dad's shop* (there aren't many customers).

3 used about something that is not very strong or not controlled in the way it should be *slack discipline; Standards are quite slack in our school.*

SYNONYM lax

4 if someone is slack, they don't do something with much energy or enthusiasm or they don't work hard at something *We lost the match because some of our players were very slack.*
slackly adverb **slackness** noun

slack verb
slacks, slacking, slacked
to work less hard than usual or with less effort than you should *We all slack off a bit when it comes to Friday afternoon.*

slacken verb
slackens, slackening, slackened
1 to make something less tight, or to become less tight *Slacken the rope a bit. His grip slackened.*
2 to make something slower or less strong, or to become slower or less strong *He slackened his pace* (walked more slowly). *Alfie's revision work slackened off as the weather improved.*

slacks noun plural
comfortable trousers for men or women that are worn in relaxed situations and are not part of a suit

slag heap noun slag heaps
a hill made from waste materials from something such as a coal mine or steel factory

slain
past participle of **slay**

slam verb
slams, slamming, slammed
1 to close something with a loud noise *Don't slam the door.*
2 if something such as a door slams, it closes with a loud noise *The gate slammed shut behind me.*
3 to hit something hard, or to put something somewhere quickly using a lot of strength *George was so angry he slammed down the phone. Dad slammed on the brakes. The bully slammed his fist into my face.*
slam noun

slang noun
1 a type of language that you use when speaking or writing to friends or people in your family. Slang words and expressions are normally more interesting, expressive and unusual than informal words but they are often impolite or vulgar, for example 'pongy' (very smelly), 'humongous' (very big), 'lurgy' (an illness that you might catch), 'not much cop' (not very good).
2 a type of language used by particular groups of people, for example teenagers or criminals, or people who work at particular jobs *playground slang; internet slang; sailors' slang*

slangy adjective
1 containing a lot of slang *a slangy short story*
2 using a lot of slang *a slangy writer*

slant verb
slants, slanting, slanted
1 if something slants or is slanting, it is not straight but leans over or moves at an angle *Italic letters slant to the right. Most people have slanting handwriting.*

2 if information is slanted, someone leaves out some parts of it and gives extra importance to other parts. The information is then not completely true but shows someone's point of view.

slant noun
1 the particular angle that something leans over at or moves at *the slant of a roof; the slant of the sun's rays*
2 a particular way of giving information that is not completely true because it shows someone's point of view

slap verb
slaps, slapping, slapped
1 to hit someone with the flat part of your hand or to hit a part of someone's body such as the face *I called her a liar and she slapped me* (slapped my face or cheek because she was angry). *He slapped me on the back* (for example as a way of saying hello or well done).
2 to put something somewhere quickly and often carelessly or noisily *William slapped the book down on the desk. My sister slapped some make-up on and rushed out.*

slap noun slaps
the action or noise of hitting someone with the flat part of your hand *He gave me a slap on the face.*

slap bang adverb (informal)
1 used about something that hits something else hard *A lorry went slap bang into the back of Dad's car.*
2 exactly at a particular place or time *My cousins arrived slap bang in the middle of dinner.*

LANGUAGE EXTRA also spelt *slap-bang*

slapdash adjective
1 doing things too quickly and not carefully *Ava's a bit slapdash when it comes to homework.*
2 done too quickly and not carefully *a slapdash piece of work*

slapstick noun
1 a style of acting in plays or films that makes people laugh because the actors perform silly actions such as falling over, throwing things at each other or bumping into things *We went to see a Buster Keaton slapstick comedy.*
2 a style of writing plays or films that are funny because of the actors' silly actions

slash verb
slashes, slashing, slashed
1 to cut something deeply using a blade or knife with a quick and violent action *Someone slashed the tyres on my uncle's car.*
2 to make something such as a price much less than before or to make things such as jobs much fewer than before *The government has slashed the amount of money it pays to families with children.*

slash noun slashes
1 a long deep cut
2 a straight line that slopes at an angle so that it is neither horizontal nor vertical. A slash is used in writing for separating words or letters (and/or, c/o) and numbers, for example in fractions or dates (1/4, 25/10/2015). Another important use is for separating the different parts of a web address (www.schofieldandsims.co.uk/about/).

slat noun slats
a thin piece of wood, metal or plastic. Slats are used for making something such as a window blind or fence or for supporting the mattress of a bed. *a fence of overlapping slats*

slate noun
1 a dark grey rock that breaks easily into thin flat pieces
2 (plural **slates**) a small flat piece of slate, made into a regular shape such as a rectangle. Slates are used for covering roofs.

slaughter verb
slaughters, slaughtering, slaughtered
1 to kill many people or animals in a violent way
2 to kill a farm animal such as a cow or sheep for food

slaughter noun
1 the violent killing of many people or animals *the slaughter of baby seals*
2 the killing of a farm animal for food

slaughterhouse noun slaughterhouses
a place where farm animals are killed for food

Slav noun Slavs
someone from a country such as Russia, Poland or the Czech Republic who speaks a Slavonic language **Slavic** adjective

slave noun slaves
a person belonging to someone else as their property, especially in the past. Slaves must obey the person who owns them and work for them without getting paid.

slave verb
slaves, slaving, slaved
to work very hard *I've been slaving over my homework all day. Dad's been slaving away in the kitchen getting dinner ready.*

slavery noun
1 the activity of owning and keeping slaves, especially in the past *the abolition of slavery*
2 when someone is a slave *He was sold into slavery in 1790.*

Slavonic adjective
connected with a group of languages from Central and Eastern Europe, for example Russian, Polish and Czech

slay verb
slays, slaying, slew, slain
an old-fashioned word for to kill *St George slew the dragon.*

sleazy adjective sleazier, sleaziest
(informal)
1 very unpleasant and connected with things that are against the usual standards of behaviour *a sleazy part of town; a sleazy magazine*
2 bad and dishonest *a sleazy businessman*

sledge noun sledges
a simple vehicle for travelling over snow, with two long pieces of wood or metal at the bottom instead of wheels. Small sledges are used for sliding down hills as a sport or for fun and large sledges are often pulled along by horses or dogs.

> LANGUAGE EXTRA also called a *sled*

sledgehammer noun sledgehammers
a large heavy hammer that is held with both hands, usually used for breaking things such as rocks or concrete walls

sleek adjective sleeker, sleekest
smooth, and often shiny, in a way that looks attractive *the beautiful sleek hair of a racehorse; the sleek shape of a sports car*

sleep noun
1 a natural period of rest in which your eyes are closed, your body is relaxed and your mind is not conscious of what is happening around you *I need plenty of sleep. What time do you go to sleep? This music sends me to sleep* (makes me start sleeping).
2 a period of sleeping *I had a good sleep. The baby has just woken up from his sleep.*

sleep verb
sleeps, sleeping, slept
1 to rest with your eyes closed and body relaxed without being conscious of what is happening around you *She slept well in her new bed. I slept 10 hours.*
2 if you sleep (or sleep over or sleep the night) at someone's house, you stay there during a whole night and sleep there
3 if you sleep in, you stay in bed in the morning longer than usual

> SYNONYM to lie in

4 if someone sleeps rough, they live and sleep outside because they have no home and no money

sleeper noun sleepers
1 someone who sleeps, usually in a particular way *I'm a light sleeper* (I wake up easily). *My sister is a heavy sleeper* (she doesn't wake up easily).
2 a heavy piece of wood or concrete that is one of many used for supporting a railway track. The two rails (long metal bars) of a railway line are fixed across the top of the sleepers.
3 a railway carriage with beds for sleeping in
4 a train that has carriages for sleeping in

sleeping bag noun sleeping bags
a large thick bag like a blanket folded in half and sewn together, used for sleeping in, for example when you go camping

sleepless adjective
without sleep or without being able to sleep *I spent a sleepless night in a strange bed.*

sleepover noun sleepovers
when you spend the night at someone's home, for example when you are invited to a party there

sleepwalk verb
sleepwalks, sleepwalking, sleepwalked
to walk around while you are still asleep
sleepwalker noun **sleepwalking** noun

sleepy adjective sleepier, sleepiest
1 tired and wanting to sleep
2 a sleepy place such as a town or village is one where nothing much happens
sleepily adverb **sleepiness** noun

sleepyhead noun sleepyheads
1 someone who is tired and wants to sleep
2 someone who is still asleep when they should be awake or who has only just woken up

sleet noun
rain and snow mixed together

sleet verb
sleets, sleeting, sleeted
if it sleets or is sleeting, rain and snow mixed together come down from the sky

sleeve noun sleeves
1 the part of a piece of clothing such as a coat or sweater that covers your arm
2 a paper or plastic cover that protects something such as a CD or DVD or, especially in the past, a record
3 if you have something up your sleeve, you're keeping something secret for when you need it, for example an idea, plan or surprise

-sleeved suffix
used for making adjectives that show what type of sleeve a piece of clothing has *a short-sleeved shirt; a long-sleeved top*

sleeveless adjective
not having sleeves *a sleeveless dress*

sleigh ['slay'] noun sleighs
a simple vehicle for travelling over snow, with two long pieces of wood or metal at the bottom instead of wheels. Sleighs are usually pulled along by horses or dogs.

sleight of hand ['sleight' rhymes with 'slight'] noun
skilful use of your hands when performing a magic trick

slender adjective slenderer, slenderest
1 tall and thin or long and thin in a very pleasant way *My sister has a slender build. Jack has long slender fingers.*
2 very small *The chances of success are slender.*

slept
past tense & past participle of **sleep**

slew
past tense of **slay**

slice noun slices
1 a flat piece of food, such as bread, cheese or meat, that you cut from a larger piece *a thick slice of bread; thin slices of chicken*
2 a piece of food shaped like a wedge (a triangle shape with one wide end and one pointed end) that you cut from a larger piece *a slice of cake; Cut the pizza into slices.*

slice verb
slices, slicing, sliced
to cut something such as bread or cake into slices

slick adjective slicker, slickest
1 clever and done with skill but often not based on any serious ideas *a slick advertisement*
2 clever and skilful but not honest *a slick salesperson*

slick noun slicks
a slick or oil slick is a layer of oil floating on the sea or a lake. The oil usually comes from a ship that has had an accident.

slide verb
slides, sliding, slid
1 if something or someone slides along a surface, they move smoothly and easily along while keeping in contact with the surface *I lost my balance and slid down the slippery slope.*

2 to move something along a surface smoothly and easily *If your suitcase is too heavy, just slide it along the ground.*
3 to put something somewhere quickly and easily *I slid the £10 note secretly into my pocket.*
4 to go somewhere quickly and easily *Seema slid out of the room without anyone noticing.*

slide noun **slides**
1 a structure, for example in a playground or fairground, with steps on one side for going up and a slope on the other side that you slide down for fun
2 a sliding movement
3 a piece of photographic film that you shine a light through using a projector to show the picture much larger on a screen or wall
4 a small thin piece of glass for putting something on that you look at under a microscope
5 a slide or hair slide is a small plastic or metal object such as a clip that girls and women put in their hair to make it look pretty or to keep it out of their eyes
6 a slide show on a computer is a piece of software that shows different pictures on the screen one after the other

slight adjective **slighter, slightest**
1 very small *a slight problem; a slight breeze*
2 not very easy to see, hear, smell, taste or feel *a slight outline; a slight noise; a slight smell of fish; a slight taste of garlic; a slight feeling of dizziness*
3 not going up very high or very steeply *a slight slope*
4 if someone is slight, they have a thin body shape and small bones
5 not the slightest used for making a particular meaning stronger *She wasn't the slightest bit worried* (not worried at all). *You don't have the slightest chance of winning* (no chance at all). *I don't have the slightest idea* (I really don't know).

slightly adverb
1 a little but not very much *slightly better; He was slightly hurt. I'm slightly late for school.*
2 if someone is slightly built, they have a thin body shape and small bones

slim adjective **slimmer, slimmest**
1 thin in a very pleasant way *My sister is slim and my brother also has a fairly slim build.*
2 very small *Your chances of being selected for the team are slim.*
3 a slim book is one that doesn't have many pages *a slim volume of poetry*

slim verb
slims, slimming, slimmed
to try to become thinner and healthier by eating less food or special food or by doing more exercise **slimmer** noun

slime noun
1 any unpleasant wet substance, often sticky or thick *a pond full of green slime*
2 a sticky liquid produced by the body of an animal such as a snail or slug and left behind as it moves along a surface

slimy adjective **slimier, slimiest**
1 covered in slime *a slimy pond*
2 like slime *a slimy liquid*
sliminess noun

sling verb
slings, slinging, slung
1 to throw something somewhere hard or carelessly *He came in from school and just slung his bag on the floor. Dad slung out his old computer magazines* (threw them away).
2 to put something somewhere so that it hangs down *Sling the bag over your shoulder. Granddad wears his glasses on a string slung around his neck.*
3 (informal) to make someone leave a place or go somewhere when they don't want to *My cousin was slung out of school. The murderer was slung into prison.*

sling noun **slings**
1 a piece of cloth tied around your neck for supporting your arm when it is injured *I have my arm in a sling.*
2 a piece of cloth tied around someone's shoulder and back for carrying a baby at the front of their body
3 a simple weapon used in the past for throwing stones. It was made from a piece of rope or leather with a pocket in the middle for holding each stone before throwing it.

slink verb
slinks, slinking, slunk
to move somewhere slowly and quietly, for example because you don't want anyone to see you or you're embarrassed or ashamed *I was bored so I just slunk out of the room. Ollie knocked over a vase and then slunk off sheepishly.*

slip verb
slips, slipping, slipped
1 if you slip, you fall over or you almost fall, because your feet suddenly move smoothly along a surface, especially one that is wet, icy, greasy or very smooth *I was running to catch the bus and almost slipped.*
2 if something slips from the place where it is, it falls smoothly into a lower position *The pen slipped out of my hand and onto the floor. My satchel strap keeps slipping off my shoulder.*
3 to move somewhere quickly and quietly, for example without anyone noticing *I slipped out of the classroom while Ms Harris wasn't looking.*
4 to put something somewhere quickly or smoothly *Slip your mobile phone back into your bag. Sita slipped some good metaphors into her story.*
5 to get free from something *The dog slipped its lead and ran off.*
6 if something slips someone's mind, they forget to do it or forget about it *I was supposed to see the head today but it slipped my mind.*
7 if someone slips a piece of clothing on or off, they put it on or take it off quickly or gently
8 if someone slips up, they make a mistake

slip noun **slips**
1 a small piece of paper *Write your answer on a slip of paper.*
2 a slipping movement *One slip and the acrobat will fall off the rope.*
3 a small mistake
4 a piece of underwear like a thin skirt or dress that girls and women wear under a skirt or dress
5 a slip of the tongue something that you say by accident when you mean to say something else
6 to give someone the slip to escape from someone, for example someone following you or waiting for you

slipper noun **slippers**
a type of soft loose shoe that you wear at home

slippery adjective
1 if something such as a road or floor is slippery, it is difficult to move on it, for example because it is smooth, wet, icy or greasy *My feet were sliding all over the place on the slippery pavement.*
2 if an object or the surface of an object is slippery, it is difficult to hold, for example because it is smooth, wet or greasy *The soap was slippery and kept sliding out of my hand. This frog has a green slippery skin.*
slipperiness noun

slip road noun **slip roads**
a short road where vehicles join or leave a motorway

slipshod adjective
1 done in a careless way *slipshod repairs*
2 doing things in a careless way *a slipshod worker*

slip-up noun **slip-ups**
a careless mistake

slit verb
slits, slitting, slit
to make a long thin cut in something, for example to open something *Slit the bag along the top.*

slit noun **slits**
1 a narrow space or opening *I watched him through a slit in the curtains.*
2 a long thin cut

slither verb
slithers, slithering, slithered
1 to move along the ground smoothly and quickly, often twisting and turning like a snake *I slithered down the slippery slope.*
2 if a snake slithers, it moves along the ground smoothly in a twisting way

sliver noun **slivers**
a small thin piece of something *Can you put a sliver of cheese on my toast?*

slobber verb
slobbers, slobbering, slobbered
to let liquid come out of the mouth *The bulldog was slobbering over the floor.*

slog verb (informal)
slogs, slogging, slogged
1 to work hard at something *I've been slogging away all day learning how to do fractions.*
2 to walk somewhere with a lot of effort, for example in the mud, rain or snow *We slogged through the snow for miles until we reached our camp.*
3 if you slog a ball, for example while playing cricket, you hit it very hard

slog–slur

slog noun (informal)
1 something that is very hard work *I learnt all my times tables but it was a slog.*
2 a long and tiring journey *It was a long slog to the top of the hill.*

slogan noun **slogans**
a short phrase that is easy to remember, for example used in an advertisement or by a political group

slop verb
slops, slopping, slopped
if a liquid slops, or if you slop it, it spills over the edge of a container because it is shaken about

slope noun **slopes**
1 a straight surface that is higher at one end than it is at the other *Our road is built on a slope.*
2 the angle formed by this kind of surface *The roof has a slope of 45 degrees.*
3 the side of a mountain or hill
4 ski slopes are sides of mountains covered with snow that people ski on

slope verb
slopes, sloping, sloped
1 if something slopes, it goes upwards or downwards because one end is higher than the other *The path slopes up to the house. The path slopes down to the river.*
2 used about something that isn't upright but leans over at an angle *My handwriting slopes slightly to the left.*

sloping adjective
used for describing something where one end is higher than the other or something that leans over *a sloping ceiling*; *sloping shoulders* (leaning forwards)

sloppy adjective **sloppier, sloppiest**
1 if something is sloppy, it is done carelessly without someone paying much attention to it *a sloppy piece of work*
2 if someone is sloppy, they do something carelessly or they usually do things carelessly *My brother's a sloppy eater. Sorry – I was a bit sloppy pouring the tea!*
3 if clothes are sloppy, they are loose so there is lots of room around the body *a sloppy sweatshirt*
4 if something such as food is sloppy, it is too wet and has too much liquid in it
5 showing feelings such as love between people in a silly way *a sloppy Valentine's card*

sloppily adverb **sloppiness** noun

slops noun plural
liquid waste, for example containing food or drink

slosh verb
sloshes, sloshing, sloshed
if a liquid sloshes around, or if you slosh it around, it is shaken about, for example in a container, or it splashes over the edge of the container *As he ran with the bucket, some of the water sloshed onto the ground.*

slot noun **slots**
1 a small narrow hole for putting things into, such as coins into a machine or moneybox
2 a large narrow hole for putting things into or through, such as letters into a postbox or through the door of a house or flat
3 a special place inside a computer for fitting a particular part that the computer needs to work *This laptop has two memory slots.*
4 a particular time when something is planned, for example in a series of events

slot verb
slots, slotting, slotted
to put something into a place where it fits neatly into something else *I slotted the two Lego pieces together.*

sloth [rhymes with 'both'] noun
1 (plural **sloths**) a medium-sized furry animal from South America with a small head and long claws (curved nails) on its hands and feet. Sloths live in trees, move slowly and sleep a lot.
2 another word for laziness

slot machine noun **slot machines**
1 a machine for playing a game to win money. When you put a coin in the slot, three pictures appear and if they are the same you win.

SYNONYM fruit machine

2 a machine that you put a coin into to buy something such as a sandwich or drink

slouch verb
slouches, slouching, slouched
if someone slouches or is slouching, they sit or stand with their shoulders and head leaning forwards in a lazy way

Slovak noun **Slovaks**
someone from Slovakia

Slovakia noun
a country in Central Europe
Slovakian adjective & noun

Slovene noun **Slovenes**
someone from Slovenia

Slovenia noun
a country in Central Europe
Slovenian adjective & noun

slovenly ['sluv-ern-lee'] adjective
untidy and careless and often lazy *slovenly habits*; *My sister is very slovenly.*

slow adjective **slower, slowest**
1 taking a long time over something *I'm a bit too slow when I do my homework. He's a slow reader.*
2 lasting a long time *a slow journey*; *I'm going to have a slow walk to school because I've got so much to carry.*
3 moving or operating without much speed *Snails are very slow. If you're too slow you won't win the race. My laptop is pretty slow.*
4 happening without much speed *Progress is very slow. King Harold died a slow death.*
5 if a watch or clock is slow, the time it shows is earlier than the correct time

slowness noun

slow adverb
without much speed *Go slow when you see the traffic lights. Grandma walks slower than me.*

slow verb
slows, slowing, slowed
1 to go more slowly *Traffic slowed to a halt. Progress has slowed this month.*
2 to make something go more slowly *These pills slow the spread of the illness.*
3 to slow down is to go more slowly or make someone or something go more slowly *Slow down – you're walking too fast. This fog is slowing us down.*

slowcoach noun **slowcoaches** (informal)
someone who moves, works or does something too slowly *Come on, slowcoach – we don't have all day!*

slowly adverb
1 in a way that shows that someone or something moves or does something without much speed *Rebecca walks slowly. The door opened slowly.*
2 in a way that shows that something happens without much speed, for example gradually over a period of time *Things slowly began to get better.*

slow motion noun
a way of showing a short piece of film at a slower speed than normal *They showed the captain scoring the goal in slow motion.*

sludge noun
any thick and dirty wet substance, for example removed from sewage pipes (that take waste matter from buildings)

slug noun **slugs**
1 a very small animal like a snail without a shell. Slugs have long soft bodies without legs and move slowly, leaving behind a sticky liquid called slime.
2 an informal word for a bullet

sluggish adjective
moving, operating or happening more slowly than normal *I've been feeling sluggish all day* (for example because I've been tired). *This old laptop is very sluggish.*
sluggishly adverb

slum noun **slums**
a poor part of a town where the houses are old or badly built and have not been looked after and where too many people live *an inner-city slum*; *My parents used to live in the slums of Glasgow.*

slumber noun
another word for sleep **slumber** verb

slump verb
slumps, slumping, slumped
1 to fall or sit down suddenly, often making the sound of something heavy falling *He fainted and slumped to the floor.*
2 to lean in a heavy way *The police found the injured driver slumped over the steering wheel.*
3 if something such as a price or value slumps, it falls suddenly and often by a large amount

slump noun **slumps**
a sudden and often large fall, for example in the price or value of something

slung
past tense & past participle of **sling**

slunk
past tense & past participle of **slink**

slur verb
slurs, slurring, slurred
if someone slurs their words, they do not pronounce them clearly, for example because they are ill or tired *In the hospital, my dad's speech was slurred.*

slur noun **slurs**
something unpleasant that you say to make people have a bad opinion of someone *Is that a slur on our teacher's character?*

468

slurp–smell

slurp *verb*
slurps, slurping, slurped
to drink something and make loud sucking noises at the same time *Please don't slurp your soup!* **slurp** *noun*

slush *noun*
snow on the ground or a surface that is slowly melting and becoming dirty
slushy *adjective*

sly *adjective* slyer, slyest
1 if someone is sly, they are clever at hiding their true thoughts and feelings and at making people believe things that aren't true in order to get what they want
2 showing that you know something that other people don't know *a sly look*
3 **on the sly** in a way that is secret because you don't want anyone else knowing
slyly *adverb* **slyness** *noun*

SIMILE 'as sly as a fox' means very sly

smack *verb*
smacks, smacking, smacked
1 to hit someone with the flat part of your hand or to hit a part of their body, for example as a punishment
2 to hit something against or into something else *He smacked the ball straight into the goal.*
3 to hit something with a loud noise *A lorry smacked into the back of my brother's car.*

smack *noun* smacks
the action or noise of hitting someone with the flat part of your hand *Teachers in the UK are no longer allowed to give a naughty child a smack.*

smack *adverb* (informal)
1 exactly at a particular place *We're stuck smack in the middle of a traffic jam.*
2 used about something or someone that hits something hard *I wasn't looking and went smack into a tree.*

LANGUAGE EXTRA you can also say *smack bang* or *smack-bang*

small *adjective* smaller, smallest
1 less than the normal size *a small piece of bread; small feet*
2 less than the normal amount or number *a small amount of money; a small number of people*
3 less important than normal *a small difference; a small mistake*
4 very young *There were lots of small children at the party.*
5 used for describing a letter of the alphabet that is not a capital (or large) letter, for example *a* or *p*
6 used when you mean someone doesn't do something very much *I'm a small eater.*

smallpox *noun*
a very serious illness that produces a high temperature and lots of pink spots on the skin that leave deep scars. Smallpox was common in the past.

smart *adjective* smarter, smartest
1 if someone is smart, they are dressed in nice clothes, often new, that are arranged carefully and they look pleasant and attractive *Charlotte looks so smart in her new dress.*
2 used about clothes that are attractive, carefully arranged and often new *My dad was wearing a smart suit.*
3 used about a place such as a restaurant, hotel or neighbourhood that is fashionable and expensive and connected with rich and successful people
4 intelligent and good at using your mind *Daniel is the smartest person in the class.*
5 showing that someone is intelligent *a smart question; a smart answer*
6 making good judgements in particular situations and clever at getting what you want, or showing that someone can do these things *a smart politician; a smart move* (something you do that shows a good judgement); *'Everyone was panicking so I used my mobile to call for help!' – 'Smart idea!'*
7 quick and full of energy *We walked home at a pretty smart pace.*
8 controlled by a computer *a smart washing machine; a smart card* (small plastic card that stores information a computer can read)
9 used about a computer or program that performs complicated calculations and does clever things *Computers are smarter now than they were five years ago.*
10 (informal) a **smart alec** is someone who tries to show people how clever they are in a very annoying way
smartness *noun*

smart *verb*
smarts, smarting, smarted
if a part of your body smarts, it makes you feel sudden sharp pains *Our eyes were smarting from the smoke.*

smarten up *verb*
smartens up, smartening up, smartened up
1 to improve the appearance of something or someone *The hotel looks shabby so they're going to smarten it up. My dad smartened himself up for his new job.*
2 to improve your appearance *It's time to smarten up a bit.*

smartly *adverb*
1 if someone is dressed smartly, they are wearing nice clothes and they look pleasant and attractive
2 if someone moves smartly, they move quickly and with lots of energy

smartphone *noun* smartphones
a mobile phone that also works as a computer, for example for connecting to the internet or sending emails

LANGUAGE EXTRA also spelt *smart phone*

smash *verb*
smashes, smashing, smashed
1 to break something into lots of pieces, often with a loud noise, by hitting or dropping it *One of the boys accidentally smashed the window with a cricket ball.*
2 to be broken into lots of pieces, often with a loud noise, for example by being dropped *The glass slipped out of my hand and smashed into pieces.*
3 to hit something hard against something else *Smash the egg against the side of the bowl. Don't run or you could fall and smash your head.*
4 to smash a record is to do something better than anyone has done it before *He smashed the Olympic record for fastest time.*
5 if someone smashes down a door, they make it fall down by hitting it hard and often
6 if something smashes into something, or if someone smashes something into something, the first thing hits the second thing with a loud noise *A lorry smashed into the back of a coach. I smashed my bike into a tree.*
7 if someone smashes up an object or a place, they deliberately break it into pieces or break things in it into pieces *A burglar smashed things up in our neighbour's house. The house was completely smashed up.*

smash *noun* smashes
1 an accident caused by a car, bus, lorry or motorcycle hitting something

LANGUAGE EXTRA you can also say *smash-up*

2 a loud noise of something breaking into lots of pieces

smashing *adjective*
an old-fashioned way of saying very good or attractive *We had a smashing day at the seaside.*

smear *verb*
smears, smearing, smeared
1 to spread something soft, sticky or liquid on a surface *He smeared jam on his toast. I smeared my face with sun cream.*
2 to make something dirty *Mum cleaned the car windscreen as it was quite smeared.*

smear *noun* smears
a dirty mark on the surface of something

smell *verb*
smells, smelling, smelt or smelled
1 to notice the special quality something has when you breathe through your nose *Can you smell the garlic bread? I have a bad cold and can't smell. Compared to dogs, humans don't smell very well* (don't have the ability to smell things well).
2 if something smells, it has a special quality that you notice when you breathe through your nose *Do these carnations smell?*
3 to have a particular way of showing this quality *Dinner smells delicious. The whole kitchen smelt of onions.*
4 to show this quality in an unpleasant way, for example used about food that is not fresh *This yoghurt has gone bad and really smells. Open the door – it smells in here.*
5 (informal) if you smell trouble or danger, you have a feeling that trouble or danger is going to happen
6 (informal) if something smells fishy, you have a feeling that there is something wrong or dishonest about it

smell *noun*
1 (*plural* **smells**) the special quality that something has when you breathe through your nose close to it or not far away from it *Roses have a beautiful smell.*
2 (*plural* **smells**) this special quality when you think it is unpleasant *There's a smell coming from the drains.*
3 the natural ability you have to smell *Do you have a good sense of smell?*
4 when you use your nose to smell something *Have a smell of this daffodil.*

469

smelly–smudge

smelly *adjective* **smellier, smelliest**
if something or someone is smelly, they have a very unpleasant smell

smelt *verb*
smelts, smelting, smelted
to produce a metal such as iron or copper from rock by heating the rock and using special chemicals

smile *verb*
smiles, smiling, smiled
to make an expression with your face and mouth, usually with the ends of your lips curved upwards, to show that you're happy or being friendly or that you think something is pleasant or slightly funny *I started smiling when the shop assistant showed me these jeans* (showing that I liked them). *'Your homework is the best,' Ms Green said, smiling at me. All the children had smiling faces* (showing that they were happy).

smile *noun* **smiles**
a happy or friendly expression on your face that you make by stretching the muscles of your mouth, usually with the ends of your lips curved upwards and your teeth showing

smiley *adjective* (informal)
used for describing something such as an expression on your face that shows you're happy *Yasmin always has a smiley face.*

smiley *noun* **smileys**
1 a symbol of a smiling face that you put into an email, text message or computer document to show that you are happy or being friendly, for example ☺ or :-)
2 another name for an emoticon (any symbol in an email, text message or computer document that shows how you feel)

smirk *verb*
smirks, smirking, smirked
to smile with a smirk

smirk *noun* **smirks**
an unpleasant or silly smile, usually without showing your teeth. A smirk is a false smile rather than a happy and friendly one, for example a smile you make when something bad happens to someone else or a smile that shows you think you are better than someone else

smite *verb* (old-fashioned)
smites, smiting, smote, smitten
1 to hit someone or something very hard
2 to kill or injure a person or animal by hitting them very hard, for example with a stick or weapon *The prince smote the dragon with his sword.*

-smith *suffix*
used for making nouns that refer to people who make or repair things made of metal or iron *a blacksmith*; *a goldsmith* (things made of gold); *a locksmith* (locks)

smithereens *noun plural*
to smithereens used about something or someone destroyed by being broken into tiny pieces *The plate fell on the floor and smashed to smithereens. If someone steps on a landmine they could be blown to smithereens.*

smock *noun* **smocks**
1 a piece of clothing like a long loose shirt that girls and women wear on the top half of their body
2 a long loose shirt worn over other clothes, for example to protect them *an artist's smock*
3 a type of light and loose jacket, worn for example for doing outdoor sports such as running

smog *noun*
dirty air caused by smoke and chemicals mixing with fog. Smog hangs close to the ground, especially in large cities, makes it difficult to see and is dangerous to your health.

ORIGIN from *smoke* and *fog*

smoke *noun*
a cloud of grey, black or white gases and chemicals produced when something burns

smoke *verb*
smokes, smoking, smoked
1 to produce lots of smoke *You can see factory chimneys smoking in the distance.*
2 to have a cigarette, cigar or pipe in your mouth and breathe in the smoke from it *Granddad was smoking a pipe. A few people were smoking* (for example, had cigarettes in their mouths). *No smoking* (sign in a building or bus, for example).
3 to use cigarettes, cigars or a pipe in this way as a habit *My parents don't smoke.*
4 to preserve food such as fish and give it a special taste by hanging it up in the smoke from burning wood *smoked salmon*

smoke alarm *noun* **smoke alarms**
a piece of equipment for finding smoke in a building and warning people that there is a fire by making a loud noise

LANGUAGE EXTRA you can also say *smoke detector*

smoker *noun* **smokers**
someone who smokes cigarettes, cigars or a pipe as a habit

smokestack *noun* **smokestacks**
a tall chimney that gets rid of smoke, for example from a factory

smoky *adjective* **smokier, smokiest**
1 full of smoke *a smoky room*
2 tasting or smelling of smoke *smoky bacon crisps*

smokiness *noun*

smooth *adjective* **smoother, smoothest**
1 if something is smooth, it has no bumps, hard parts or holes and is often flat *a smooth piece of wood*; *a baby's smooth skin*; *The pebble was round and smooth.*
2 a smooth liquid or substance has no lumps in it *a smooth paste*
3 if something such as a journey, for example by car, plane or boat, is smooth, it is pleasant because there are no bumps and you are not shaken about *The flight was smooth and the landing too.*
4 without any problems or difficulties *Installing the new software was very smooth.*
5 moving or changing in a slow and steady way *a smooth curve*; *smooth movements*
6 pleasant to listen to, and making you feel relaxed *a smooth voice*

smoothness *noun*

SIMILE 'as smooth as silk' means very smooth (sense 1)

smooth *verb*
smooths, smoothing, smoothed
to make something flat and smooth, for example with your hand or a tool *I smoothed out the letter that had been folded several times. The carpenter smoothed down the door with sandpaper before painting it.*

smoothie *noun* **smoothies**
a cold drink made from different fresh fruits mixed together, sometimes with milk or ice cream added

smoothly *adverb*
1 without any problems or difficulties *My brother has organised my birthday party – I hope everything goes smoothly.*
2 in a steady way without stopping or making sudden movements or changes *The water is flowing smoothly from the tap again.*
3 without any bumps or shaking *Our plane landed smoothly.*
4 in a way that produces a flat surface without bumps or hard parts *I sanded down my rusty bike smoothly.*

smote
past tense of **smite**

smother *verb*
smothers, smothering, smothered
1 to cover something or someone with too much of something *a cake smothered in chocolate*; *My dad smothers his meat in gravy.*
2 to stop someone from breathing and kill them by covering their nose and mouth
3 to make someone unhappy by giving them too much love and attention *My cousin says she feels smothered by her parents.*
4 to stop a fire burning by covering the flames with something, for example with a thick piece of cloth

smoulder *verb*
smoulders, smouldering, smouldered
to burn slowly without a flame but usually with smoke *The fire was so strong that the building was still smouldering the next day.*

SMS *noun*
1 a system for sending written messages from one mobile phone to another one
2 (*plural* **SMSs**) the message you send
short for: short message service

SMS *verb*

smudge *noun* **smudges**
a dirty mark where something has been accidentally rubbed, for example ink when you are writing

smudge *verb*
smudges, smudging, smudged
1 to rub something accidentally, such as ink or paint, and make a dirty mark *Write your name again because you've smudged it.*
2 to put a dirty mark (or dirty marks) on or in something in this way *I smudged my exercise book in a few places.*
3 if something smudges, it makes a dirty mark *I don't like this fountain pen – the ink always smudges.*

smudgy *adjective* **smudgier, smudgiest**
if something is smudgy, it has dirty marks on it, for example from ink, and is not very clear to see or to read *The first page of your homework is a bit smudgy.*

LANGUAGE EXTRA you can also say *smudged*

smug *adjective* **smugger, smuggest**
1 used when you think someone is unpleasant because they are too pleased with their own qualities or things they have done or with the things that they have *Don't look so smug. I don't like my uncle – he's rich and smug.*
2 also used about the way someone looks, which you think is unpleasant *a smug grin; He had a smug look on his face.*

smugly *adverb* **smugness** *noun*

smuggle *verb*
smuggles, smuggling, smuggled
to take something or someone into or out of a country secretly and in a way that is not allowed by the law **smuggler** *noun*

smuggling *noun*

snack *noun* **snacks**
1 a small meal that is easy to make, for example a sandwich
2 snacks are small foods that you eat between your regular meals, for example crisps, peanuts or apples
3 a snack bar is a place inside a building or a small restaurant that sells small meals such as sandwiches, foods such as crisps, apples or biscuits and drinks such as lemonade or fruit juice

snack *verb*
snacks, snacking, snacked
to eat small amounts of food between meals *My brother likes snacking on crisps and sweets.*

snag *noun* **snags**
1 a problem, usually a slight or unexpected one *The plans for a new school have hit a snag.*
2 a tear or hole in a piece of clothing caused by something sharp or hard

snag *verb*
snags, snagging, snagged
to damage or tear a piece of clothing when it accidentally touches something sharp or hard *I snagged my sweater on a piece of wire.*

snail *noun* **snails**
a very small animal with a shell on its back and two feelers (long thin parts) on its head. Snails have long soft bodies without legs and move slowly, leaving behind a sticky liquid called slime.

snake *noun* **snakes**
1 an animal that has a long thin body with smooth skin and no legs. It moves along the ground by twisting and turning. Some snakes are poisonous.
2 snakes and ladders is a game you play with dice on a square board that has pictures of snakes and ladders on it. You move pieces around the board from a starting to a finishing place. If your piece stops on a snake, you go down the snake to go back, and if it stops on a ladder, you go up the ladder to go forward.

snake *verb*
snakes, snaking, snaked
if something such as a river, road or queue of people snakes somewhere, it has lots of twists and turns in it *The queue for tickets snaked all the way round the corner.*

snap *verb*
snaps, snapping, snapped
1 if something snaps, or if someone or something snaps it, it suddenly breaks into two pieces with a short loud noise *The young tree snapped in the wind. Dad was so angry he snapped the ruler in half.*
2 to quickly put something in a particular position with a short loud noise, or to move into a particular position *I snapped the book shut. The lid snapped shut.*
3 to speak or say something in an angry way *'Where are you going?' she snapped.*
4 if an animal snaps, it tries to bite someone *The bulldog was snapping at my heels.*
5 if someone snaps their fingers, they make a short loud sound by suddenly hitting their forefinger (next to the thumb) or middle finger against their thumb
6 (informal) to snap someone or something with a camera or mobile phone is to take a picture of them

snap *noun*
1 the noise of something snapping *I broke the stick in half with a snap.*
2 (plural **snaps**) an informal word for a photo *holiday snaps*
3 a card game in which you shout 'snap' when you see two cards that are the same
4 (plural **snaps**) a cold snap is a sudden short period of cold weather
5 a snap decision is a decision that you make suddenly without thinking about it properly

snappy *adjective*
to make it snappy to do something or go somewhere quickly *Make it snappy – we don't want to miss the bus.*

snapshot *noun* **snapshots**
another word for a photo

snare *noun* **snares**
a trap for catching animals

snare *verb*
snares, snaring, snared
to catch an animal using a snare

snarl *verb*
snarls, snarling, snarled
1 if an animal such as a dog snarls, it shows its teeth and makes a low, rough and frightening sound
2 to speak angrily to someone *'Leave me alone!' he snarled.*

snarl *noun* **snarls**
a snarling sound

snatch *verb*
snatches, snatching, snatched
1 to take something quickly and roughly with your hand or hands *He snatched the pen from my hand.*
2 an informal way of saying to get *Let's snatch a bite to eat.*

snatch *noun* **snatches**
1 a short part of a song or conversation or a short piece of music *I heard snatches of the conversation.*
2 the action of snatching or trying to snatch something

sneak *verb*
sneaks, sneaking, sneaked
1 if you sneak somewhere, you go there quietly, for example trying not to be seen
2 (informal) to tell someone such as a teacher that someone else has done something wrong *He's always sneaking on the other boys.*

sneak *noun* **sneaks** (informal)
someone who sneaks on other people

sneaker *noun* **sneakers**
a soft sports shoe (used mainly in American English)

sneaky *adjective* **sneakier, sneakiest**
if someone is sneaky, they behave in a dishonest way and do things secretly rather than openly

sneer *verb*
sneers, sneering, sneered
if you sneer at someone or something, you talk about them in a way that shows you have no respect for them

sneer *noun* **sneers**
an expression on your face or something you say that shows you have no respect for someone or something

sneeze *verb*
sneezes, sneezing, sneezed
1 to make a loud noise by suddenly blowing air out through your nose
2 (informal) if you say that something is not to be sneezed at, you mean it's very good or worth having

sneeze *noun* **sneezes**
the sound or action of someone sneezing

sniff *verb*
sniffs, sniffing, sniffed
1 to make a noise by breathing in through your nose, usually with lots of short breaths
2 if you sniff something, you smell it and breathe in noisily at the same time

sniff *noun* **sniffs**
the sound or action of someone sniffing

sniffle *verb*
sniffles, sniffling, sniffled
to breathe in quickly and noisily through your nose, for example because you have a cold or are crying

sniffle *noun* **sniffles** (informal)
if you have a sniffle or the sniffles, you have a slight cold

snigger *verb*
sniggers, sniggering, sniggered
to laugh in a quiet or silly way because you have no respect for someone or something *What are you sniggering at?* **snigger** *noun*

snip *verb*
snips, snipping, snipped
to cut something, usually with scissors and in one quick action

snip *noun* **snips**
1 the action of snipping something
2 a small cut made in something, usually with scissors
3 (informal) something of good value that you buy cheaply *That coat's a snip at £30.*

sniper–soapsuds

sniper *noun* **snipers**
someone who shoots at people from a place where they cannot be seen

snippet *noun* **snippets**
a small piece of something such as news or information

snivel *verb*
snivels, snivelling, snivelled
if someone snivels, they cry and sniff or they complain in a way that you think is annoying

snob *noun* **snobs**
someone who thinks they are better than other people, for example because they have lots of money or a high position in society or because they have more intelligence or better interests than other people **snobbery** *noun* **snobbish** *adjective*

snooker *noun*
a game played on a cloth-covered table in which players use a cue (long stick) to hit 21 coloured balls into holes
compare: **billiards** and **pool**

snoop *verb*
snoops, snooping, snooped
1 to go around a place secretly trying to find out information *There was a strange man snooping around the playground.*
2 if you snoop on someone, you try to find out things about them that are private and that you shouldn't know about

snore *verb*
snores, snoring, snored
to make a loud breathing noise as you sleep

snore *noun* **snores**
the sound of someone snoring

snorkel *noun* **snorkels**
a tube used for breathing through when swimming with your face under the water. It has one end that stays above the water.

ORIGIN from German slang *Schnorchel* 'nose'

snorkel *verb*
snorkels, snorkelling, snorkelled
to swim under the surface of the water using a snorkel **snorkelling** *noun*

snort *verb*
snorts, snorting, snorted
1 if an animal or person snorts, they make a loud noise by breathing out through their nose
2 to make a loud noise in this way because you are angry or you think that something is funny or unimportant *'You're an idiot!' she snorted.*

snort *noun* **snorts**
the sound of an animal or person snorting

snout *noun* **snouts**
the long nose and mouth of an animal such as a pig

snow *noun*
frozen water that falls from the sky as small soft white pieces

snow *verb*
snows, snowing, snowed
1 if it snows or is snowing, snow falls from the sky
2 if someone is snowed in, they cannot leave a place because there is too much snow
3 if someone is snowed under, they have too much work or too many things to do

snowball *noun* **snowballs**
snow pressed into the shape of a hard ball for throwing

snowdrop *noun* **snowdrops**
a small white flower that starts growing at the end of winter

snowfall *noun* **snowfalls**
an amount of snow that falls at a particular time or place

snowflake *noun* **snowflakes**
a piece of falling snow or a piece of snow that has fallen

snowman *noun* **snowmen**
a shape made out of snow that looks like a person

snowplough *noun* **snowploughs**
a large vehicle used for pushing snow off places such as roads, runways or railway lines

snowshoe *noun* **snowshoes**
a special shoe for walking in deep snow, often made of a metal or plastic frame that you fasten to your foot

snowstorm *noun* **snowstorms**
a storm when a lot of snow falls and there are strong winds

snowy *adjective* **snowier, snowiest**
1 used for describing a time or the weather when it snows a lot *a snowy afternoon; snowy winter weather*
2 covered with snow *the snowy peaks of Mount Everest*

snub *verb*
snubs, snubbing, snubbed
to behave rudely towards someone, for example by pretending not to see them or by paying no attention to them **snub** *noun*

snub-nosed *adjective*
a short nose, often flat, that is turned up at the end

snuff *verb*
snuffs, snuffing, snuffed
if someone snuffs out a flame, they stop it burning, for example by covering it with something *Granddad snuffed out the candle with his fingers.*

snug *adjective* **snugger, snuggest**
1 comfortable, warm and protected *My little sister was snug in her bed.*
2 if a piece of clothing is snug, it fits tightly on the body *a snug pair of jeans*
snugly *adverb*

SIMILE 'as snug as a bug in a rug' means very snug (sense 1)

snuggle *verb*
snuggles, snuggling, snuggled
to put yourself into a position where you are comfortable and warm, for example by moving your body closer to someone *My little brother snuggled up to me in bed.*

so *conjunction*
used for giving a reason *It's dark so we should close the curtains.*

so *adverb*
1 another way of saying very or very much, when you want to give special importance to a word *I'm so tired I just want to go to bed. There was so much noise and there were so many children at the party! You're walking so fast I can't keep up.*
2 used for giving a short answer to a question when you don't want to repeat a sentence *'Has he finished?' – 'I think so.'*
3 another way of saying also *'I like football.' – 'So do I.'*
4 **and so on** used at the end of a list to show that there are other things of the same type that you haven't mentioned
5 **or so** slightly more or less than a particular number or amount *There were 15 or so children at my party.*
6 **so as to** used for giving the reason for something *I got up early so as not to miss the bus.*

SYNONYM in order to

7 **so that** used for giving the reason for something *I got up early so that I wouldn't miss the bus.*

SYNONYM in order that

8 **so that** also used for showing what the result of something is *The curtains were closed so that we couldn't see inside.*
9 **so far** up until now

soak *verb*
soaks, soaking, soaked
1 if you soak something, you put it in a liquid and leave it there for a time *You have to soak the beans before cooking them.*
2 to make someone or something very wet *I got soaked in the rain. My brother is also soaked.*
3 if something such as paper, cloth or a sponge soaks up a liquid, the liquid goes into it *These tissues will soak up the spilt tea.*
4 to go into or through something such as paper or cloth *The blood soaked through the bandages.*

soaking *adjective*
very wet *Come out of the rain – you're soaking wet.*

so-and-so *noun* **so-and-sos** (informal)
1 used for talking about someone when you don't remember their name *Mr So-and-so's at the door – our neighbour from across the road.*
2 an annoying or unpleasant person *Jack has been a naughty so-and-so.*

soap *noun* **soaps**
1 a substance you use with water for washing your body or other things. Soap can be hard or in liquid form. *a bar of soap; a box of luxury soaps*
2 a soap or soap opera is a TV or radio programme that tells the story of the everyday lives of a group of imaginary people. Soaps are broadcast at regular times, for example two or three times a week.
3 soap powder is a powder made from soap used for washing clothes in a washing machine

soapsuds *noun plural*
bubbles that you make when you mix soap and water

soapy *adjective* **soapier, soapiest**
full of soap or covered with soap

soar *verb*
soars, soaring, soared
1 to move upwards or go higher *The tower soars to a height of 500 feet.*
2 to fly high *Seagulls were soaring above our heads.*
3 to become much higher, for example when talking about amounts or numbers *The temperature is expected to soar this weekend.*

soaring *adjective*
very high *soaring temperatures; soaring prices*

sob *verb*
sobs, sobbing, sobbed
if someone sobs, tears come out of their eyes and they breathe with short breaths in a noisy way, for example because they are unhappy

sob *noun* **sobs**
the sound or action of someone sobbing

sober *adjective*
1 if someone is sober, they have not drunk any alcohol or they have not drunk too much alcohol so they can control their actions
2 serious and showing respect *She had a sober expression on her face. The atmosphere at the funeral was sober.*
3 simple and not bright *sober colours*
soberly *adverb*

SIMILE 'as sober as a judge' means completely sober (sense 1)

so-called *adjective*
1 used when you think that a word or expression used for describing someone or something is wrong or may be wrong *I bumped into your so-called friend Jaimie.*
2 used when someone or something is often described in a particular way *King Alfred lived during the so-called Dark Ages.*

soccer *noun*
a game in which two teams of 11 players kick a ball around a pitch (ground covered in grass) and try to kick it into the other team's goal

SYNONYM football

sociable *adjective*
if someone is sociable, they are friendly and like to be with other people
sociably *adverb*

social *adjective*
1 connected with society and the way people live and behave *social problems; a social group*
2 connected with meeting other people to enjoy yourself when you are not working or studying *a social club*
3 living in groups *Ants are very social insects.*

socialism *noun*
a political belief that people should share the money and opportunities of a country equally and that important businesses and industries should be owned by the government, not by private individuals

socialist *noun* **socialists**
someone who believes in socialism
socialist *adjective*

socially *adverb*
1 connected with situations where you meet other people to enjoy yourself *My parents are friendly towards my teacher but they never see each other socially.*
2 connected with society *Bad behaviour is not socially acceptable.*

social media ['mee-di-er'] *noun*
websites and computer programs that allow you to share information with and speak to other people over the internet. Examples of social media are Facebook and Twitter.

social work *noun*
work helping people with problems, for example people who are very poor or who have difficulties with their families
social worker *noun*

society *noun* **societies**
1 all the people who live together as a group in a place or country *Bad drivers are a danger to society* (everyone in a country).
2 a group of people interested in the same thing *a local history society*

sociology *noun*
the study of society and the behaviour of people in society **sociological** *adjective*
sociologist *noun*

sock *noun* **socks**
1 a piece of clothing that you wear on your foot inside your shoe
2 (informal) if someone pulls their socks up, they try harder to work or to behave better

sock *verb* (slang)
socks, socking, socked
if someone socks someone, they hit them with their fist (hand with closed fingers)

socket *noun* **sockets**
an object with holes or a hole in it for connecting electrical equipment to the electricity. For example, you push a plug into a wall socket to make something such as a TV or computer work, or you push or screw a light bulb into a light socket to make a light work.

soda *noun*
water with lots of small bubbles in it that is mixed with drinks such as fruit juice

LANGUAGE EXTRA you can also say *soda water*

sodium *noun*
a silver-white chemical element that is found in salt and food

sofa *noun* **sofas**
a soft seat with a back and arms. It is made for more than one person to sit on.

SYNONYMS couch, settee

soft *adjective* **softer, softest**
1 if something is soft, it can be pressed in easily when you touch it, for example a cushion, a sponge, clay or cotton wool
2 pleasant to touch and not rough or hard *soft skin; a soft brush*
3 if food is soft, it is easy or ready to eat *a soft pear*
4 very quiet *Lucy speaks in a soft voice.*
5 pleasant to look at and not bright *soft colours*
6 not strict but kind towards someone, for example someone who does something wrong *Her parents are very soft on her.*
7 a soft drink is one that does not contain any alcohol, for example lemonade

soften *verb*
softens, softening, softened
1 to become softer or make something softer *Butter softens* (or *softens up*) *quickly in a warm room.*
2 to become more pleasant or make something more pleasant *After a while Dad softened his tone. His voice softened.*

softly *adverb*
1 quietly *Close the door softly. Grandma always speaks softly.*
2 not brightly or strongly *a softly lit room*

software *noun*
the information needed for making a computer and programs work. The equipment that makes up a computer, for example silicon chips, the hard disk or the monitor, is the hardware.

soggy *adjective* **soggier, soggiest**
very wet and soft in an unpleasant way *The ground is too soggy to play football.*

soil *noun*
the substance on and under the surface of the ground that plants and trees grow in

soil *verb*
soils, soiling, soiled
to make something dirty

solar *adjective*
1 connected with the sun *solar rays; solar energy* (power from the sun to produce electricity)
2 a solar eclipse is a period of darkness when the moon moves between the earth and the sun
3 a solar panel is a piece of equipment that changes energy from the sun into electricity that can be used in a building, for example
4 the solar system is the sun and the group of planets that go round it. The planets are: Mercury, Venus, Earth, Mars, Jupiter, Saturn, Uranus and Neptune.

sold
past tense & past participle of **sell**

solder *verb*
solders, soldering, soldered
to join pieces of metal together using solder

solder *noun*
a soft metal that becomes liquid when it is heated and hard when it cools down. It is used for joining together two pieces of metal with a tool called a soldering iron.

soldier *noun* **soldiers**
a man or woman who belongs to an army and fights in a war

sole *noun*
1 (plural **soles**) the flat part underneath your foot that you stand and walk on
2 (plural **soles**) the flat part of a shoe that is under your foot *rubber soles*
3 (plural **sole**) a flat fish that lives in the sea and is used for food

sole *adjective*
used when you mean only one person or thing *He was the sole survivor of the train crash.*

solely–somewhat

solely *adverb*
1 only *At home we speak solely in Hindi.*
2 connected with only one person or thing *Jacob is solely to blame.*

solemn *adjective*
1 serious and important *a solemn occasion; Everybody looked solemn.*
2 done in a serious way *a solemn promise*
solemnly *adverb*

solicitor *noun* **solicitors**
someone who gives people advice about the law and who prepares documents for them connected with the law

solid *adjective*
1 if something is solid, it is hard and it is not a liquid or gas *a solid block of ice; The river had frozen solid.*
2 strong and not likely to break *The chair seems pretty solid. My new mobile is more solid than my old one.*
3 without any empty spaces inside or not made up from other pieces joined together *a nest made from a solid mass of leaves and twigs; The door was made from one solid piece of wood.*
4 without any spaces or stops in between *a solid line*
5 used about something that continues without stopping or for the whole of a period of time *It rained for two solid days* (or *for two days solid*).
6 made from one substance only, for example with nothing else added *This chain is made of solid gold.*
7 used about something or someone you can trust to be good *solid facts; Our family has given the school solid support.*
8 used in maths about a shape such as a cube that is not flat but has length, width and height
solidity *noun*

> SIMILE 'as solid as a rock' means very solid (senses 1 & 2)

solid *noun* **solids**
1 a hard substance or object that has its own particular shape and is neither a liquid nor a gas. Solids, liquids and gases are the three states of matter (what everything in the world is made of).
2 food that a baby can eat that is not liquid, for example bread or potatoes *My little sister is on solids* (eating solid food).
3 in maths, a solid is an object that is not flat but has length, width and height, for example a cube

solidify *verb*
solidifies, solidifying, solidified
if something solidifies, it changes from a liquid to a solid

solidly *adverb*
1 continuing without stopping *It's been raining solidly for two days.*
2 strongly *a solidly built house; My brother solidly supports Manchester United.*

soliloquy ['ser-lil-er-kwee'] *noun* **soliloquies**
a speech in a play in which an actor speaks to himself or herself while alone on the stage

solitary *adjective*
1 used when you mean only one person, animal or thing *There was one solitary visitor in the whole museum. He didn't say a single solitary word all day.*
2 used about an activity that you do by yourself *Granddad likes to go for solitary walks in the country.*
3 spending a lot of time by yourself *She's shy and solitary and doesn't have many friends.*

solitude *noun*
being on your own, especially when you think this is pleasant

solo *noun* **solos**
a performance, usually of a piece of music, done by one person only

solo *adjective & adverb*
connected with or done by one person only *a solo album; a solo artist; Who was the first person to fly solo across the Channel?*

soloist *noun* **soloists**
a musician who performs a solo

solstice *noun* **solstices**
the summer and winter solstices are the two times of the year when the sun is furthest from the Equator. In the northern half of the world, the summer solstice is around 21 June (when the sun is furthest north and there are the most hours of daytime) and the winter solstice is around 21 December (when the sun is furthest south and there are the most hours of night-time).

soluble *adjective*
1 if a substance is soluble, it will dissolve in a liquid
2 if a problem is soluble, it is possible to solve it

solution *noun* **solutions**
1 an answer to a problem
2 a liquid that has a substance dissolved in it

solve *verb*
solves, solving, solved
1 to find an answer to something such as a problem or question
2 to find an explanation for something such as a mystery
3 to solve a crime is to find out the person responsible for doing it

solvent *noun* **solvents**
a liquid used for dissolving other substances so they become part of the liquid

solvent *adjective*
if someone is solvent, they have enough money to pay their debts (the money they owe other people)

Somalia *noun*
a country in East Africa
Somali *adjective & noun*

sombre ['som-ber'] *adjective*
1 dark, often in a way that makes you feel sad *sombre colours*
2 serious and sad *Our team lost the match and we were all in a sombre mood.*

some *adjective*
1 used about a certain number of things or people, usually a small number *I read some books during the holidays. Jo has some friends but not many.*
2 used about a certain amount of something, usually a small amount *Could you bring me some bread?*
3 used about someone or something without saying or knowing exactly who or what *Some boy came up to me in the street. For some reason my phone isn't working.*
4 used about a large number of things or large amount of something *It was some years before we saw each other again. I won't be finishing my homework for some time.*

some *pronoun*
used when you mean a part of a larger number of things or group of people or part of a larger amount of something *I left some of the books on the table. He only ate some of the cake. Some of the girls behaved badly.*

somebody *pronoun*
used when you mean a certain person but you don't know or say exactly who

> SYNONYM **someone**

someday *adverb*
at some time in the future but you don't know or say when

somehow *adverb*
1 in one way or another but you don't know exactly how *There are no buses today but I'll get to school somehow.*
2 for some reason or other but you don't know why *Somehow I don't think that's a good idea.*

someone *pronoun*
used when you mean a certain person but you don't know or say exactly who *Someone's at the door. I'll ask someone else* (some other person).

> SYNONYM **somebody**

someplace *adverb*
an American way of saying somewhere

somersault *noun* **somersaults**
1 a movement in which you make your body into a ball shape and roll it along the ground
2 a movement in which you make your body turn through the air with your feet going over your head
somersault *verb*

something *pronoun*
1 used when you mean a certain thing but you don't know or say exactly what *Is there something bothering you? I want to read something else* (some other thing).
2 **something to do with** connected in a certain way with something or someone *My sister's job is something to do with computers.*

sometime *adverb*
at some time in the future or the past but you don't know or say when

sometimes *adverb*
some of the time or at some times but not always or often *I sometimes go to bed after ten o'clock.*

somewhat *adverb*
1 not very but still enough *You look somewhat tired.*
2 very or very much *You're somewhat young to be surfing the internet by yourself. I can't keep up – you walk somewhat faster than me.*
3 used for saying something less strongly *I was somewhat hoping he wouldn't come.*

> SYNONYM **rather**

somewhere-soul

somewhere *adverb*
1 in or to some place but you don't know or say where *My friend lives somewhere near the station. Let's go somewhere else* (to some other place).
2 a certain place *I'm looking for somewhere to sit.*

son *noun* **sons**
the son of a mother or father is their male child

sonar ['soh-nahr'] *noun*
equipment on a ship that uses sound waves for finding the position of objects under the water or for measuring how deep the water is

> ORIGIN an acronym from **so**und **na**vigation and **r**anging

song *noun* **songs**
1 words of a tune that you sing
2 the activity of singing *The crowd suddenly burst into song* (started singing).
3 the pleasant musical sounds that a bird makes

songbird *noun* **songbirds**
a bird that produces pleasant musical sounds like singing. There are many different types of songbirds.

sonic *adjective*
connected with sound waves *a sonic boom* (loud sound made by a plane that starts to go faster than the speed of sound)

son-in-law *noun* **sons-in-law**
the husband of someone's daughter

sonnet *noun* **sonnets**
a poem of 14 lines with a fixed pattern of rhymes

soon *adverb*
1 in a short amount of time from now *I'll start my homework soon.*
2 after a short amount of time *I started to learn German but gave up soon after.*
3 early *It's too soon to go to bed.*
4 quickly *How soon can you get here? Can't you finish any sooner?*
5 **as soon as** at the same time as or immediately after something else *As soon as Mum went out, it started to rain.*
6 **as soon as possible** as quickly as someone can *We'll go and visit Granddad as soon as possible.*
7 **(just) as soon** used for saying that you would like to do or have something just as much as something else *'Do you want to go swimming?' – 'I'd just as soon watch TV.'*
8 **sooner or later** at some time in the future but you don't know or say exactly when

soot *noun*
a black powder that is left, for example in a chimney, when people burn something such as coal or wood **sooty** *adjective*

soothe *verb*
soothes, soothing, soothed
1 to make someone feel less upset, worried or angry *soothing words*
2 to make a part of the body or a pain hurt less *Use this cream to soothe your back. This hot-water bottle is very soothing.*

sophisticated *adjective*
1 clever and knowing a lot about difficult and complicated subjects *When it comes to computers, most of the children in the class are very sophisticated.*
2 well-educated, knowing a lot about things such as literature, painting and music, and knowing the rules of how to behave towards other people
3 if something such as a piece of equipment is sophisticated, it is at a high level of progress and able to do very clever and complicated things
sophistication *noun*

sopping *adjective*
if someone or something is sopping or sopping wet, they are very wet *sopping wet clothes*

soppy *adjective* **soppier, soppiest**
(informal)
1 showing feelings such as love, great liking or pity *My brother's soppy about cats.*
2 showing feelings such as love between people in a silly way *She's reading a soppy love story.*

soprano ['ser-prah-noh'] *noun* **sopranos**
a girl, boy or woman with a high singing voice

sorbet ['sor-bay'] *noun* **sorbets**
a kind of frozen ice cream made from water and fruit

sorcerer *noun* **sorcerers**
in stories, someone who has magic powers and who often uses them to do evil things
sorcery *noun*

sorceress *noun* **sorceresses**
in stories, a woman who has magic powers and who often uses them to do evil things

sordid *adjective*
1 very dirty *sordid conditions*
2 unpleasant and dishonest

sore *adjective* **sorer, sorest**
1 painful *I have a sore throat.*
2 an informal way of saying angry or upset, especially in American English *Are you still sore at me?*

sore *noun* **sores**
a painful place on your skin, usually where you have an infection (illness caused by germs) **soreness** *noun*

sorely *adverb*
very or very much *I was sorely tempted. Grandma will be sorely missed.*

sorrow *noun*
1 a feeling of being very sad
2 (plural **sorrows**) something that makes you feel very sad

sorrowful *adjective*
very sad **sorrowfully** *adverb*

sorry *adjective*
1 if you're sorry about something, you're sad about something you've done (or not done) or something that has happened and you wish things were different *I'm sorry I didn't go swimming with the rest of the class. We're sorry to hear your cousin's in hospital.*
2 you say sorry to someone when you want them to forgive you for something you've done (or not done) or when you want to be polite after doing something such as accidentally bumping into them *Sorry, I won't do this again. Sorry I'm late!*
3 used when you want someone to repeat something *Sorry, could you say your name again, please?*
4 if you feel sorry for someone, you think what is happening to them is not pleasant and you feel sad and upset about that

sort *noun* **sorts**
1 a group of things or people that are similar to each other and different from other groups *Classical and pop are different sorts of music. There were all sorts of interesting things to see.*

> SYNONYM kind

2 used for describing or asking about what someone or something is like *What sort of weather did you have? Seema is a very hard-working sort of girl.*

> SYNONYM kind

3 **sort of** used when you don't want to use a word or phrase in its exact meaning because it is too strong *These plans of yours are sort of silly. He may be naughty but I sort of like him.*

> SYNONYM kind of

sort *verb*
sorts, sorting, sorted
1 to arrange things neatly in a certain way, for example in groups or in a particular order, or to separate things into different groups *I sorted the shells into big ones and small ones. Can you sort all these words into alphabetical order? Sort out the clothes you want to wear to the party.*
2 to sort something out, such as a problem or something broken, untidy or badly organised, is to make it better, for example by solving it, fixing it or organising it *If something is worrying you, your teacher will help you to sort it out. My mobile wasn't working properly but Dad sorted it out. Your room's messy – please sort it out before you go to bed.*
3 (slang) to sort someone out, such as a bully or someone you don't like, is to do something to them such as punishing them or hitting them

sorting diagram *noun* **sorting diagrams**
a diagram in maths that helps you to organise and show information. The two main types are Venn diagrams and Carroll diagrams.

SOS *noun*
a signal or call from someone in danger, for example on a ship or plane, who needs urgent help

> ORIGIN from Morse code (a way of sending messages using signals as dots and dashes). S and O were the easiest letters to send because S is three small dots and O is three long dashes.

sought
past tense & past participle of **seek**

soul *noun* **souls**
1 the part of a person that is not their body or mind and that some people think continues to live after the body dies

sound–space

2 another word for a person *There wasn't a soul in the street. I haven't seen a living soul all day.*

sound *noun* **sounds**
1 energy that travels through the air (or water) and is taken into your brain through your ears. The energy is produced by vibrations (quick shaking movements) that travel as waves (particular patterns). *sound waves*; *We live in a world of sound.*
2 something you can hear *There was a strange sound coming from the TV.*
3 a long narrow area of water
4 the sound of used for showing what you think of something, for example based on what someone else says or on what you can see *'Ice cream for dessert?' – 'I like the sound of that.'* (for example, I think that's good); *From the sound of it, I think she'll be late for the party.*

sound *verb*
sounds, sounding, sounded
1 used for showing that what you say about something or someone is probably true, for example when someone tells you something *That sounds like a good idea* (I think your idea is good). *Your sister sounds cool from what you say. You sound as if you have a cold* (based on the noises you're making, I think you have a cold). *Dad sounds angry* (his voice and expression are angry).
2 if something such as a bell, whistle, horn or trumpet sounds, it makes a noise *The fire alarm sounded and we all went into the playground.*
3 to make something such as a bell or whistle sound is to make a noise with it *The referee sounded his whistle.*
4 to sound a letter is to say it *In the word 'knee', the k is not sounded.*
5 to sound someone out is to find out someone's opinion about something

sound *adjective* **sounder, soundest**
1 in good condition, for example not broken or damaged *Your laptop is quite sound.*
2 healthy *Granddad is old but his body and mind are sound.*
3 very good and full *My mum has a sound knowledge of computers.*
4 used about something you can trust to be good and correct or sensible *sound facts*; *sound advice*; *a sound argument*
5 deep *Grandma's a sound sleeper* (she doesn't wake up easily).
soundness *noun*

> SIMILE 'as sound as a bell' means very sound (senses 1 & 2)

sound effects *noun plural*
the sounds used in a film or in a TV or radio programme, for example a door closing or a glass breaking

soundly *adverb*
1 if you sleep soundly, you sleep very well and do not wake up easily
2 completely *Our team was soundly beaten.*
3 strongly and very well *a soundly built house*

sound patterns *noun plural*
the different ways sounds are used and arranged in a poem. Sound patterns include rhymes, rhythms, alliteration and onomatopoeia.

soundtrack *noun* **soundtracks**
the music used in a film or TV programme

soup *noun* **soups**
a hot liquid food made by cooking vegetables, meat or fish, for example with water

sour *adjective* **sourer, sourest**
1 having a very strong taste, for example like a lemon *This apple is green and sour.*
2 having an unpleasant taste, for example because of not being fresh *This milk has turned sour.*
3 unfriendly and unpleasant *He made a really sour face.*
sourly *adverb* **sourness** *noun*

source *noun* **sources**
1 where something comes from *This leaky pipe is the source of the problem.*
2 something that provides what you need *The sun is a source of energy. Orange juice is a good source of vitamin C.*
3 the place where a river or stream starts to flow from

south *noun*
1 the direction on your right if you face the sun as it rises in the east. On most maps the south is at the bottom.
2 the part of a country or town that is in the south *My cousins live in the south of Scotland.*
3 the South is the southern part of England. It includes cities such as London, Oxford and Southampton.

south *adverb*
towards the south *Our house faces south.*

south *adjective*
in or from the south *the south coast*; *a south wind*

South Africa *noun*
a country at the southern tip of Africa
South African *adjective & noun*

South America *noun*
the part of the American continent that contains countries such as Brazil, Chile and Argentina
South American *adjective & noun*

south-east *noun, adjective & adverb*
the direction that is between south and east

> LANGUAGE EXTRA also spelt *southeast*

southerly *adjective*
towards or from the south *a southerly wind*

southern *adjective*
in or connected with the south *southern Italy*

southerner *noun* **southerners**
someone from the southern part of a country or region

South Korea ['ker-ee-er'] *noun*
a country in East Asia
South Korean *adjective & noun*

South Pole *noun*
the place on the surface of the earth that is the furthest south

southwards *adverb*
towards the south **southward** *adjective*

south-west *noun, adjective & adverb*
the direction that is between south and west

> LANGUAGE EXTRA also spelt *southwest*

souvenir ['soo-ver-**neer**' or '**soo**-ver-neer'] *noun* **souvenirs**
something that you keep that makes you think about a place, person or special event

> ORIGIN from French *(se) souvenir* 'to remember'

sovereign ['sov-rin'] *noun* **sovereigns**
1 another word for a king or queen
2 an old British gold coin that was worth one pound

sow ['soh'] *verb*
sows, sowing, sowed, sown or **sowed**
if you sow seeds, you put them into or on the ground so that they will grow

> LANGUAGE EXTRA be careful not to confuse *sow* with *sew* (to make, repair or decorate with a needle and thread)

sow [rhymes with 'cow'] *noun* **sows**
a female pig

soya bean ['soy' rhymes with 'boy'] *noun* **soya beans**
a small bean that can be eaten. It is used for making oil and flour.

spa *noun* **spas**
1 a town where water comes out of the ground. People go there to improve their health, for example by bathing in the water or drinking it. *Harrogate is a spa town in the north of England.*
2 a place such as a building with a swimming pool and sauna (steam room) where people go to do exercises and improve their health *a health spa*

space *noun*
1 the area of the universe that is outside the earth's atmosphere (air and gases around the earth) or the area further away from the earth, for example where the moon, sun, stars and all the other planets are *The probe is travelling through space to Mars.*
2 (*plural* **spaces**) an empty place for something or someone *There's only one space left in the car park. Parking spaces are hard to find. Leave a space for your name.*
3 the amount of a place that is needed for someone or something *Is there space for one more person on the bus?*

> SYNONYM room

4 the area all around us and above the ground *Mark was just staring into space.*
5 (*plural* **spaces**) the part of a place used for a special purpose *Mum really liked the kitchen space in my uncle's house.*
6 a private place where someone is free to do what they want and develop and grow *'Give me some space,' shouted Luke.*
7 when you think that something is big and there is plenty of room *There's a feeling of space in this flat.*
8 used when you mean a period of time *It all happened in the space of a few minutes. In a short space of time Yussuf had become my best friend.*

space–sparkle

9 open spaces land with no buildings on it, for example gardens, parks and plains

space *verb*
spaces, spacing, spaced
if someone spaces things out, they organise them so as to leave a space or a period of time in between *Space out the plants so there's 10 centimetres between them. We spaced out our visits to Gran over the week.*

space bar *noun* **space bars**
a long piece of plastic on a computer keyboard below the letter keys. You press the space bar to make a space between words.

spacecraft *noun* **spacecraft**
a vehicle that travels in space

spaceman *noun* **spacemen**
an informal word for a man who travels in space

spaceship *noun* **spaceships**
a vehicle that carries people in space

space station *noun* **space stations**
a large spaceship that goes round the earth and is usually used by astronauts as a place to stay and do research

spacesuit *noun* **spacesuits**
a piece of clothing that covers the whole body and is used by astronauts for protection when they are outside their spacecraft

spacewoman *noun* **spacewomen**
an informal word for a woman who travels in space

spacing *noun*
the spacing between lines or words on a page is the amount of space between them *I wrote my homework in double spacing* (with an empty line after each line of writing).

spacious *adjective*
if something such as a room or car is spacious, it is large and there's plenty of room inside **spaciousness** *noun*

spade *noun* **spades**
1 a large tool used for digging. It has a long handle fixed to a flat or slightly curved part that is usually made of metal. *a garden spade*
2 a small tool for digging in the sand. It is usually made of plastic and has a short handle fixed to a flat part with curved edges. *We were playing with our buckets and spades.*
3 a shape like a pointed black leaf on a stem. A spade is one of the four types of playing cards. The other three types are diamonds, hearts and clubs.

spaghetti *noun*
a food made from long thin strings of pasta

LANGUAGE EXTRA remember to write *spaghetti* with the letter *h* after the *g*

ORIGIN from Italian *spaghetti* 'long thin strings'

Spain *noun*
a country in South-West Europe

spam *noun*
an email (or emails) that you have not asked for and that you don't want, often an advertisement for something to buy or containing something that harms your computer *My parents get lots of spam.*

span *noun* **spans**
1 the period of time that something lasts or is supposed to last *You must finish your homework within a time span of two weeks. George doesn't have a very good attention span* (the period he can pay attention for).
2 the distance from one end of something to the other end when it is stretched out *This eagle has wings with a span of over four feet.*
3 the distance from the tip of your thumb to the tip of your little finger when your hand is stretched out

span *verb*
spans, spanning, spanned
1 to last for a particular period of time, usually a long one *Queen Victoria's reign spanned nearly 64 years.*
2 to deal with or include a particular period of time or area *The book tells the story of Charles Dickens and spans 30 years of his life. Spain's influence spanned the globe.*
3 if a bridge spans something such as a river, it goes across it *How many bridges are there spanning the Thames?*

Spaniard *noun* **Spaniards**
someone from Spain

spaniel *noun* **spaniels**
a dog with long ears that hang down and often soft or shiny hair

Spanish *adjective*
connected with Spain or the Spanish language

Spanish *noun*
1 the language people speak in Spain and many countries in Central and South America such as Mexico, Argentina and Chile
2 the Spanish are people from Spain

spank *verb*
spanks, spanking, spanked
to hit someone with the flat part of your hand, usually on the bottom, as a punishment **spank** *noun*

spanner *noun* **spanners**
a metal tool with a shaped part at one or both ends. The shaped part fits round a nut (metal ring with six sides) and turns it to make it tighter or looser.

spar *verb*
spars, sparring, sparred
to practise boxing with someone without hitting them hard

spare *adjective*
1 used when talking about other things of the same kind that are ready to use if you need them *a spare pair of glasses; All cars carry a spare tyre.*
2 used about something that is not being used at the present time *a spare room; spare tickets*
3 used about money you can give to someone or about time you can spend with someone or doing something *Do you have any spare cash, Mum? Have you got a few spare minutes to help me with my homework? Sorry, I have no spare time today. He spends every spare moment playing chess.*
4 thin and often tall *My aunt is tall and spare.*
5 **spare time** time when you are not working or studying and can do what you like, such as relax and enjoy yourself *I play the guitar in my spare time.*

spare *verb*
spares, sparing, spared
1 to have money you can give to someone or spend on something *All I can spare is £20. Mum said there's no money to spare this month.*
2 to have time you can spend with someone or for doing something *Can you spare half an hour? We can't spare any time for a holiday. They got to the station with time to spare* (early, with extra time for doing something).
3 if you can (or can't) spare someone, you can (or can't) carry on as usual without them, for example when they are sent to work or help somewhere else *No teachers can be spared from the school at the present time.*
4 to stop someone from having an unpleasant experience or feeling *I wanted to spare you the trouble of making an extra journey to school. Please spare me the details* (don't tell me the unpleasant details).
5 to not harm or kill someone or damage something *The soldiers spared the children. During the earthquake not many buildings were spared.*
6 if you spare no effort, you do everything you can to do something
7 if you spare no expense, you spend as much money as you need to make sure something is good

spare *noun* **spares**
a piece that is the same as another piece in a car or machine and is needed to make it work. You keep it ready to use in case the other piece gets broken.

LANGUAGE EXTRA you can also say *spare part*

sparing *adjective*
using or giving only very small amounts of something *Mum is very sparing with the salt.*

sparingly *adverb*
in very small amounts *Use this cream sparingly.*

spark *noun* **sparks**
1 a tiny piece of fire that jumps out from something burning or is produced when two hard surfaces rub against each other
2 a tiny flash of electricity, for example when you unplug a piece of equipment quickly
3 a small amount of something such as a feeling or quality *a spark of enthusiasm*

spark *verb*
sparks, sparking, sparked
1 to produce sparks *The plug sparked as I pulled it out.*
2 to make something start or happen *A cigarette end sparked a fire. The president's speech sparked off demonstrations.*

sparkle *verb*
sparkles, sparkling, sparkled
1 to shine with flashes of light *sparkling diamonds; The stars sparkled in the sky.*
2 if someone's eyes sparkle, they show a feeling such as excitement or happiness
sparkle *noun*

477

sparkler – specification

sparkler noun **sparklers**
a firework that you hold in your hand. It looks like a thick wire and produces lots of tiny sparks as it burns.

sparkling adjective
a sparkling drink is one that has lots of small bubbles in it *sparkling mineral water*

sparrow noun **sparrows**
a small brown-grey bird with a short strong beak and short tail

sparse adjective
used about something when there is not much of it or about things when there are not many of them, often spread over a large area *The audience at the play was sparse. Houses are sparse in this remote part of the country.* **sparseness** noun

sparsely adverb
used when there is not very much of something *a sparsely populated region* (with only a few people)

spasm ['spaz-erm] noun **spasms**
a movement in your body in which a muscle suddenly becomes tight and painful

spat
past tense & past participle of **spit**

spate noun
a group of things, usually unpleasant things, all happening at about the same time *There was a spate of attacks on banks last month.*

spatter verb
spatters, spattering, spattered
to accidentally get drops of a liquid or bits of dirt onto someone or something, usually in lots of different places *The bus spattered us with water as it drove past. Take off those mud-spattered boots before you come in!*

spatula noun **spatulas**
a kitchen tool with a wide flat part at one end and a handle at the other end. It is used for lifting and spreading food.

spawn noun
the eggs of fish, frogs and other water animals

spawn verb
spawns, spawning, spawned
when fish, frogs and other water animals spawn, they produce eggs

speak verb
speaks, speaking, spoke, spoken
1 to use your voice to say something *My little brother is just beginning to speak. Mum spoke to the head teacher.*
2 to speak a language is to know how to use it and say words in it *Rosie speaks French fluently.*
3 to say things to a group of people about a particular subject *A famous author is coming to speak at our school.*
4 to speak out is to tell people your opinion in a very strong way, usually to show you agree or do not agree with something
5 to speak up is to speak louder

speaker noun **speakers**
1 someone who is speaking or who speaks to a group of people about a particular subject

2 someone who speaks a language *José is a Spanish speaker.*
3 a piece of equipment that the sound comes out of, for example in a computer, television or radio

spear noun **spears**
a long pole with a pointed end used for throwing. It was used in the past as a weapon for fighting or a tool for hunting.

spear verb
spears, spearing, speared
to throw or push a spear or pointed object into something or someone

spearmint noun
a plant with a strong fresh smell whose leaves are used for giving flavouring to food and toothpaste *spearmint chewing gum*

special adjective
1 used about something or someone different from usual and often better or more important than usual *a special gift; a special occasion; a special friend; Granddad is very special to me* (very important in my life).
2 used about something that is more than usual *a special effort; Pay special attention in class today. Take special care.*
3 used about something connected with one person, group or thing and no other *Ava sang the song in her own special way. Our teacher has special tickets for us to see the exhibition early.*
4 used about a price in a shop or supermarket that is lower than usual for a short time or for a particular reason, for example because you're a student or you buy a large amount *Special prices in store today! Special prices for children! I bought a lot of books so they gave me a special price. Today the fruit juice is on special offer* (at a lower price).

special delivery noun
a way of sending a letter or parcel by post. Special care is taken to deliver it the day after you post it and the letter or parcel is given a special number so that you can track it (follow each part of its journey online).

special effects noun plural
unusual images or sounds in a film or TV programme that are specially created by technical experts

specialise verb
specialises, specialising, specialised
1 to spend your time studying a particular subject or doing a particular type of work *My brother specialises in computers* (he's an expert who knows about computers).
2 to be known for something special such as producing and selling a particular product or doing a particular activity *This restaurant specialises in seafood.*
specialisation noun

> LANGUAGE EXTRA also spelt *specialize* and *specialization*

specialist noun **specialists**
someone who knows a lot about a particular subject

speciality noun **specialities**
1 a particular product, for example a food or drink, or activity that a person or place

is known for *Haggis is a Scottish speciality. This artist's speciality is painting bowls of fruit.*
2 a subject that someone spends their time studying *My mum's a teacher and her speciality is maths.*

specially adverb
1 for a particular reason or person and no other *Mum went out specially to buy some milk. It's specially for you.*

> SYNONYM especially

2 used for saying something is more true about one particular person or thing than it is about others *We all liked the film, specially Mum.*

> SYNONYMS particularly, especially

3 used for giving more importance to a word *This is specially good ice cream* (really good ice cream). *I'm specially upset about that. I've been waking up specially early this week* (much earlier than usual).

> SYNONYMS particularly, especially

4 **not specially** not really *'Did you like the book?' – 'Not specially.'*

special needs noun plural
the particular things that someone needs to help them keep well and happy, or to help them with their learning, when they have a medical problem that affects the way they use their body or mind *My brother's disabled so he's a special needs student.*

species ['spee-shiz] noun **species**
1 a group of animals that share similar qualities and can produce young animals together *a rare species of tiger*
2 a group of plants with similar qualities that can produce young plants together

specific adjective
1 used when you mean a particular thing or person *I don't know what I was doing at that specific moment. Is there a specific teacher you prefer?*
2 clear and correct in every detail *I followed the specific instructions. Can you be more specific?* (give more details)

specifically adverb
1 for a particular reason and no other *Mum bought me this dress specifically to wear to your party.*

> SYNONYM specially

2 clearly and correctly in every detail *Could you describe specifically what happened?*
3 used for giving special importance to a word, for example when you are upset or angry about something *'You're not in bed yet – I specifically told you to be in bed by nine o'clock!'*

specification noun **specifications**
1 a detailed description of something, for example showing how it is made or should be made
2 **specifications** a list of the main parts inside a machine or piece of equipment. For example, in a computer the specifications include the hard drive, memory, processor and type of operating system. *My parents bought me a computer with better specifications* (with better parts inside).

specify–spell

specify *verb*
specifies, specifying, specified
to say or explain something clearly or give exact information about something *Oliver said he'd be coming round tomorrow but didn't specify a time. The rules specify the exact size of the ball. You must hand in your homework by the specified date* (that particular date and no other).

specimen *noun* **specimens**
1 an example of what kind of thing something is, for example a plant, animal or object that people study *The museum has some interesting dinosaur specimens. This isn't a real £10 note – it's a specimen.*
2 a small amount of something that shows people what the rest of it is like *The nurse took a blood specimen from Grandma* (to get information about her blood).

speck *noun* **specks**
a very small mark or piece of something *a speck of dust; From up here on top of the hill, the people below look like tiny specks.*

speckled *adjective*
covered with small marks of a different colour *a speckled hen; a bird with speckled wings*

speckles *noun plural*
small marks of a different colour *This egg is white with brown speckles.*

specs *noun plural*
1 short for **spectacles** (glasses)
2 short for **specifications** (list of the main parts, for example in a computer)

spectacle *noun* **spectacles**
1 something such as an event or view that is exciting or unusual to watch *the spectacle of a king's coronation; An eclipse of the sun is a stunning spectacle.*
2 something that you look at that is stupid or ridiculous *Don't make a spectacle of yourself* (don't behave in a stupid way so that people will look at you).

spectacles *noun plural*
two pieces of special glass or plastic fixed to a frame that you wear in front of your eyes to see better

SYNONYM glasses

spectacular *adjective*
1 extremely beautiful or exciting to look at *spectacular scenery; You get a spectacular view from the top of the London Eye.*
2 used when you mean a very large amount of something or something very large *spectacular success; A spectacular crowd was marching towards the centre of town.*
3 extremely good or important *'Guernica' is a spectacular painting by Picasso.*

spectacularly *adverb*

spectator *noun* **spectators**
someone who watches an event, especially a sporting event

spectre ['spek-ter] *noun* **spectres**
another word for a ghost (image of a dead person)

spectrum *noun* **spectra**
1 the different colours that light can be separated into, for example when it goes through a prism (glass or plastic triangle) or a drop of water. The colours are red, orange, yellow, green, blue, indigo and violet (the colours of the rainbow).
2 used for talking about all the different things of the same kind, for example opinions, ideas or feelings *The children in my class have a wide spectrum of interests* (lots of different interests).

sped
a past tense & past participle of **speed**

LANGUAGE EXTRA when *speed* means to drive too quickly or when you use the phrase *speed up*, the past tense and past participle are *speeded*

speech *noun*
1 (*plural* **speeches**) an occasion when someone speaks in front of a group of people, or the words they say *At the prize-giving the head teacher gave a long speech.*
2 (*plural* **speeches**) a part of a play when an actor spends a long time speaking
3 the way that you speak or the sounds you make when you speak *When I'm tired my speech isn't very clear.*
4 the power to be able to speak *After his illness Granddad lost his speech.*
5 the language that you use for speaking, not for writing *Slang words are mainly used in speech.*

speechless *adjective*
if someone is speechless, they cannot speak because they are so surprised, angry or upset about something

speech marks *noun plural*
punctuation marks like this ' ' or this " "

LANGUAGE EXTRA you use either single ' ' or double " " *speech marks* around words to show they are the exact words that someone is using (*'Is it raining?' asked Eva. "Sit down, please," said Alex*).
   Speech marks can also be used around titles, for example of books, films or paintings (*I'm reading 'Matilda'. "Jaws", a famous film by Spielberg*).
   You also use them to show that words have a meaning that is slightly different from their usual meaning (*I really didn't like that 'song' he wrote*).
   Speech marks can also be called *quotation marks* or *inverted commas*.

speed *noun*
1 (*plural* **speeds**) how quickly or slowly something or someone moves or something happens *a speed of 20 miles an hour; Children can do the exercise at their own speed* (however quickly or slowly they want).
2 movement that is very fast *The cause of many road accidents is speed* (drivers going very fast). *The train is picking up speed* (or *gathering speed*) (going faster). *The coach was travelling at speed* (or *at high speed*) (very fast). *The athlete put on a burst of speed* (suddenly went faster).
3 used about how fast sound and light travel through the air *the speed of sound* (about 770 miles an hour); *the speed of light* (about 670 million miles an hour)
4 (*plural* **speeds**) the part of a bicycle used for controlling how fast the wheels turn *a 10-speed bike*

speed *verb*
speeds, speeding, sped or **speeded**
1 (*past tense & past participle* **sped**) to go somewhere quickly *The car sped round the corner.*
2 (*past tense & past participle* **sped**) to take someone somewhere quickly *The train speeds passengers to the airport in half an hour.*
3 (*past tense & past participle* **speeded**) to drive somewhere too quickly *My dad was fined for speeding.*
4 (*past tense & past participle* **speeded**) to speed up is to go, do something or happen more quickly *The bus is beginning to speed up. Speed up or you'll never finish your homework. The action speeds up halfway through the film.*
5 (*past tense & past participle* **speeded**) to speed something up is to make it go or happen more quickly *Knowing how to type has really speeded up my work.*

speedboat *noun* **speedboats**
a boat with an engine that goes very fast

speed bump *noun* **speed bumps**
a slightly raised part that is built across a road to make people drive more slowly

speedily *adjective*
very quickly

speeding *noun*
driving too quickly in a vehicle. Speeding is against the law.

speed limit *noun* **speed limits**
the fastest speed someone is allowed to drive by law

speedometer ['spee-dom-it-er] *noun* **speedometers**
a piece of equipment in a vehicle that shows how quickly it is travelling

speedy *adjective* **speedier, speediest**
1 done very quickly or without any delays *a speedy reply; We wished Grandma a speedy recovery.*
2 doing something very quickly *'Finished already? You're a speedy worker!'*

spell *verb*
spells, spelling, spelt or **spelled**
1 to say or write the correct letters of a word in the right order or in a particular way *Can you spell 'enough'? You spell the word 'knock' with a silent k. Please spell out your name again.*
2 to know the correct way words are written *David is very clever but he can't spell.*
3 if letters spell a particular word, they make that word *T-E-N spells 'ten'.*
4 used for showing that something bad happens or is going to happen, for example as a result of something else *If we lose the match, that will spell the end for our football team.*
5 to spell something out is to explain it in a very simple way
speller *noun*

479

spell–spindle

spell *noun* **spells**
1 special words or actions that make magic things happen, usually bad things *The witch cast a spell on the King* (made something magic happen to him by saying special words or doing special actions).
2 the influence that these special words or actions have on someone *The King was under a spell. The Queen tried to break the spell* (stop the bad influence of the spell from continuing).
3 a short period of time *My aunt has just had a spell in hospital.*
4 a short period when there is a particular type of weather *cold and rainy spells*; *We had a spell of sunny weather.*
5 a short period when you have a particular feeling *My sister suffers from dizzy spells.*

spellcheck *verb*
spellchecks, spellchecking, spellchecked
to use a spellchecker to check the spelling of something you write on a computer, for example an email or document, and correct mistakes in it

spellcheck *noun* **spellchecks**
another word for a spellchecker

spellchecker *noun* **spellcheckers**
a computer program that checks your spelling in something you write and helps you to correct any mistakes

spelling *noun*
1 the knowledge of how to write the letters of a word in the right way and in the correct order *My spelling isn't very good.*
2 the rules for writing the letters of a word in the right way and in the correct order *English spelling is very difficult. I've made lots of spelling mistakes in my homework.*
3 (*plural* **spellings**) the way of writing a word correctly *The word 'adviser' has two spellings – you can also write 'advisor'.*

spelt
a past tense & past participle of **spell**. You can also say 'spelled'.

spend *verb*
spends, spending, spent
1 to use money to buy something or pay for something *I spent my pocket money on a new schoolbag. My dad spends £50 to travel on the tube every week.*
2 to do something or stay somewhere for a certain amount of time *I spent an hour texting my friends. Mohammed spent a week in Spain.*
3 to stay somewhere or do something during a particular period *We plan to spend our holidays in Wales. I'll spend next term working harder on maths. Lily spent the whole journey sleeping.*
4 to use your energy or effort to do something *Ms Clark has spent all her energy marking exam papers.*

spending *noun*
1 money spent, for example by a family on things such as food, clothes and rent or by a government on things such as education or people's health *spending cuts* (when less money is spent on important things)
2 spending money is money that someone such as your mother or father gives to you to spend on anything you like

spendthrift *noun* **spendthrifts**
someone who spends too much money

spent
past tense & past participle of **spend**

sperm *noun* **sperms** or **sperm**
a small cell (smallest unit of living matter) produced by a male person or animal. A sperm goes into an egg in a woman or female animal and makes a new person or animal grow.

spew *verb*
spews, spewing, spewed
1 to spew out something such as a liquid, smoke or fire is to make a lot of it come out quickly *The volcano was spewing out ash and rock.*
2 if something spews out, a lot of it comes out quickly *Smoke spewed out from factory chimneys.*

sphere *noun* **spheres**
1 a perfectly round object shaped like a ball. Every point on its surface is the same distance away from the centre.
2 a particular subject, activity or type of work *The UK needs to do more work in the scientific sphere.*

ORIGIN from Greek *sphaira* 'ball' or 'globe'

spherical ['sfair-rik-erl'] *adjective*
perfectly round like a ball

sphinx ['sfinks'] *noun* **sphinxes**
1 in ancient Egyptian and Greek stories, an imaginary creature with the head of a person and the body of a lion
2 a statue of a sphinx

spice *noun* **spices**
a powder that you put on or into food to give it more taste. It is made from parts of plants such as their fruits, seeds or roots that are dried (the water is removed).

spice up *verb*
spices up, spicing up, spiced up
to spice something up is to make it more exciting and interesting

spick and span *adjective*
completely tidy and clean

spicy *adjective* **spicier, spiciest**
used about food that has a strong taste from spices **spiciness** *noun*

spider *noun* **spiders**
a small creature with eight long thin legs. Spiders spin webs to catch insects for their food.

spied
past tense & past participle of **spy**

spike *noun* **spikes**
1 a long or thin piece of metal with a sharp point *Around our school there are railings with spikes on top.*
2 any long thin object with a sharp point that sticks out from somewhere *He wore his hair in spikes.*

spiked *adjective*
1 having a sharp point or points *spiked railings*
2 spiked hair is the same as spiky hair

spiky *adjective* **spikier, spikiest**
1 covered with or having lots of sharp points *spiky leaves*
2 spiky hair is fairly short with sharp points that stick up all over the head

spill *verb*
spills, spilling, spilt or spilled
1 if you spill something such as a liquid or powder, you accidentally make some of it or all of it come out of its container *I spilt lemonade over the floor.*
2 if something such as a liquid or powder spills somewhere, some of it or all of it accidentally comes out of its container *I knocked over the sugar and it spilt onto the chair.*
3 if objects spill out of a container, or if you make them do this, they come out of the container *When I opened the box, lots of tennis balls spilled out.*
4 if people spill out of somewhere, they all come out at the same time *As soon as the match had finished, crowds spilled out onto the streets.*

spill *noun* **spills**
an amount of a liquid that has accidentally come out of a container *an oil spill* (thick liquid from under the ground that has flowed somewhere such as into the sea from a ship); *Can you wipe up that spill?*

spin *verb*
spins, spinning, spun
1 if something or someone spins, they turn round and round, often very quickly *The earth spins on its axis. We watched the ballet dancer spinning. The car hit a tree and spun round* (turned right round once or more than once).
2 to spin something is to make it turn round and round *Do you know how to spin a coin?*
3 to turn your head round quickly *I called her name and she spun round to face me.*
4 when a washing machine spins, the round container inside it (called a drum) turns round very quickly to squeeze water out of the clothes
5 to make threads for producing cloth by twisting together pieces of something such as cotton or wool using a special machine *The picture shows an old lady spinning on her spinning wheel.*
6 when a spider spins a web, it produces special threads from its body and twists them into a net (with tiny spaces between the threads) to catch insects for food
7 if your head is spinning, you feel dizzy (as if things are going round and round)

spin *noun* **spins**
1 a spinning movement *Give the wheel a spin with your hand. The car hit a lamp-post and went into a spin.*
2 a short journey in a car or on a motorbike, often for fun *Dad asked if we wanted to go for a spin.*

spinach ['spin-ij' or 'spin-itch'] *noun*
a vegetable with large dark green leaves that are eaten cooked or uncooked, for example in salads

spinal *adjective*
connected with the spine (backbone) *a spinal injury*

spindle *noun* **spindles**
1 an object shaped like a stick with a disc at one end. It is used for twisting

threads round when spinning something such as cotton or wool. Spindles were used especially in the past.
2 a long thin part, usually made out of metal, that turns round inside a piece of equipment, or a part that something else turns round on, for example a knob or wheel

spindly *adjective* **spindlier, spindliest**
long and thin, and often looking weak *spindly legs*

spine *noun* **spines**
1 the long row of bones down the middle of your back

SYNONYM backbone

2 the narrow part of a book cover where the pages are joined. The title of the book and the writer's name are usually printed on the spine.
3 a thin pointed part sticking out from the body of an animal such as a hedgehog or porcupine or from a plant such as a cactus

spine-chilling *adjective*
if something such as a film, book or story is spine-chilling, it is very frightening

spinning wheel *noun* **spinning wheels**
a small wooden machine with a wheel, used especially in the past for twisting together materials such as wool or cotton to make threads for producing cloth. Someone sits next to the machine and uses their foot to make the machine work.

spin-off *noun* **spin-offs**
1 something useful that happens or is made unexpectedly when someone does or makes something else, for example a useful product, material or situation *These robots are a spin-off from space research.*
2 something such as a film, book, TV programme or video game that has some of the same things as an earlier film, book, programme or game, for example the same characters or situations

spinster *noun* **spinsters**
an old-fashioned word for a woman who has never been married and will probably never get married, usually an older woman
compare: **bachelor**

spiny *adjective* **spinier, spiniest**
covered with spines (thin pointed parts) *a spiny animal*; *a spiny cactus*

spiral *noun* **spirals**
1 a curve that goes round and round a central point, getting further away from it as it goes
2 a curve that goes round and round a central point in three dimensions, staying the same distance from the central point, like a coil or screw thread. This type of spiral is also called a helix.

ORIGIN from Greek *speira* 'coil' or 'twist'

spiral *adjective*
shaped like a spiral *a spiral staircase*; *a spiral seashell*

spiral *verb*
spirals, spiralling, spiralled
1 to go round and round in a spiral shape, usually upwards or downwards *The plane spiralled down and crashed to the ground.*
2 to keep on getting higher or worse *Prices are spiralling and so is crime.*

spire *noun* **spires**
a tall pointed part on the top of a church tower or on the top of a building. It is shaped like a cone (with round sloping sides) or a pyramid (with flat sides like triangles).

spirit *noun* **spirits**
1 the part of a person that is not their body or mind and that some people think continues to live after the body dies

SYNONYM soul

2 someone's special qualities, for example their character or personality *My mum's an artist – she has a very creative spirit.*
3 (*plural* **spirits**) a creature or form such as a ghost, often with the power to do good or bad things
4 (*plural* **spirits**) the way someone feels and behaves, for example being happy or sad *in good spirits* (feeling happy); *in high spirits* (feeling excited and lively); *Our spirits were low* (we felt sad). *Try and get into the spirit of the party* (enjoy it by joining in with others). *All countries should live together in a spirit of respect and understanding.*
5 enthusiasm for doing something or for being part of a group *team spirit* (for example when players enjoy being in a team and play well together); *Can you all sing up with a bit more spirit?*
6 (*plural* **spirits**) a strong alcoholic drink

spiritual *adjective*
1 religious *The Pope is the spiritual leader of the Catholic Church.*
2 connected with deep feelings and beliefs rather than with the body or with things *spiritual values* (important beliefs that influence people's behaviour)
spiritually *adverb* **spirituality** *noun*

spiritual *noun* **spirituals**
a type of religious song, often sung by African Americans in the USA

spit *verb*
spits, spitting, spat
1 if someone spits, they quickly make the saliva (liquid inside the mouth) come out of their mouth *Granddad has the flu and keeps spitting into the sink.*
2 if someone spits something out, they quickly make it come out of their mouth *If you have a fish bone, just spit it out.*
3 to be spitting is to be raining very slightly *You don't need your umbrella – it's only spitting.*

spit *noun*
1 liquid from your mouth that has been spat out
2 (*plural* **spits**) a long thin metal stick for holding and turning meat while it is being cooked over a fire
3 (*plural* **spits**) a long thin strip of land sticking out into the sea or a lake

spite *noun*
1 an angry feeling towards someone that makes you want to upset them or cause them problems *He threw my schoolbag into someone's garden out of spite.*
2 **in spite of** used for saying that something you mention does not stop something else happening *In spite of the heavy rain, the plane landed safely* (the rain did not stop the plane landing safely).

SYNONYM for sense 2: despite

spiteful *adjective*
1 if someone is spiteful, they are angry and do bad things to someone to upset them and cause them problems
2 also used about something someone does or says *Simon sent me a very spiteful text.*
spitefully *adverb*

spitting image *noun*
to be the spitting image of someone is to look exactly like them *Sarah is the spitting image of her mum.*

spittle *noun*
an old-fashioned word for liquid that has been spat out of your mouth

SYNONYM spit

splash *verb*
splashes, splashing, splashed
1 to get drops of a liquid or bits of something wet onto someone or something *Seema splashed me with water. A motorbike splashed mud all over us as it turned the corner.*
2 if a liquid splashes somewhere, lots of drops of it go onto something or someone, often making a noise *Dad was carrying a tin of paint and some of it splashed on the floor.*
3 to make a noise as you move in water or in something wet *I love to splash about in the sea* (for example hitting the water with my arms and legs). *We walked home, splashing through the mud and puddles.*

splash *noun* **splashes**
1 the sound of something or someone hitting a liquid *We heard a splash and saw a person in the river.*
2 the sound of a liquid hitting something or someone *A huge wave hit the ship with a splash.*
3 an amount of a liquid that has splashed somewhere *My brother cleaned up the splashes of paint on the floor. Splashes of red and yellow make my painting look friendly.*

splatter *verb*
splatters, splattering, splattered
1 if a liquid or a wet substance splatters somewhere, some of it goes onto something *Hail was splattering noisily on the roof.*
2 to get drops of a liquid or bits of something wet onto someone or something *The lorry splattered us with mud as it drove past.*

splendid *adjective*
1 very beautiful or attractive to look at and deserving great respect *My brother looks splendid in his new suit.*
2 extremely good *a splendid piece of homework*; *Our school has some splendid teachers.*

splendidly *adverb*
1 in a very beautiful or attractive way *The palace rooms were splendidly decorated.*

splendour–spoon

2 extremely well *Kya plays the violin splendidly.*

splendour noun
1 the great beauty of something that deserves respect *the splendour of the Swiss Alps*
2 the splendours of something are its beautiful qualities *the splendours of the King's court*

splint noun splints
a flat piece of wood, plastic or metal tied to the broken bone of an arm or leg to support it while it gets better

splinter noun splinters
a small thin piece of wood or glass that has broken off something and is sharp and dangerous *Mum used tweezers to take out a splinter* (tiny piece of wood) *from my finger.*

splinter verb
splinters, splintering, splintered
to break something into tiny pieces or be broken into tiny pieces *The mirror fell to the ground and splintered into a thousand pieces. A heavy blow splintered the wood.*

split verb
splits, splitting, split
1 if something splits, it breaks or tears and a long thin hole or line appears in it *My schoolbag was so full that it split down the side. When Dad knocked in the nail, the wood split in two.*
2 to break or tear something and make a long thin hole or line in it *I split my jeans bending over. Ollie fell over and split his lip* (made a thin cut in it).
3 to separate something into two or more parts *Ms Patel split the class into two.*
4 to form two or more separate parts *We split up into different groups.*
5 to share something *They split the money between them.*
6 if married people or people such as a boyfriend and girlfriend split up, they stop living together or going out with each other

split noun splits
1 a long thin hole or line in something, for example in cloth, plastic or wood, where it has got torn or broken
2 when something such as a group is separated into two or more parts
3 a difference between people's opinions *There was a split between the boys and the girls about what poem to read in class.*
4 the splits a difficult exercise in which someone sits on the floor and stretches out their legs in opposite directions as far as they can go

split second noun split seconds
a very short amount of time *For a split second I thought I saw my teacher standing there. In football you often have to make split-second decisions* (very quick ones).

splitting adjective
if you have a splitting headache, you have a very bad pain in your head

splutter verb
splutters, spluttering, spluttered
1 to make a noise with your mouth as if you are spitting or finding it hard to breathe, or to say something in a confused way while making this noise *Granddad has been coughing and spluttering all day. 'Er . . . , um . . . , well, I don't know!' he spluttered.*
2 if something such as an engine splutters, it makes lots of short loud sounds, for example because it is not working properly

spoil verb
spoils, spoiling, spoilt or spoiled
1 to make something less good, attractive or interesting, for example by damaging it *These paint stains spoil your tablecloth. That ugly pylon spoils the view.*
2 to stop someone doing something that they like or want to do *The rain spoilt our day at the beach. Charlie's terrible behaviour spoilt our enjoyment* (we didn't enjoy ourselves).
3 to stop something from happening in the way it is supposed to *My sister's illness spoilt our holiday plans.*
4 to let a child do and have everything he or she wants. When children are spoilt, it makes them think only about themselves and expect to always do and get what they want. *Katie behaved like a spoilt child and screamed when Mum asked her to share the sweets.*
5 to treat someone very well or too well, for example by giving them lots of things *'More chocolates?' – 'You're spoiling me!'*

spoils noun plural
valuable things taken by an army that has won a war or by thieves who have done a robbery *the spoils of war*

spoilsport noun spoilsports
someone who stops other people from having fun, for example by saying they are not allowed to do something

spoke
past tense of **speak**

spoke noun spokes
one of the long thin pieces of metal that connect the middle of a wheel to the rim (outside edge). In wooden wheels, for example old-fashioned cart wheels, the spokes are made of wood. *bicycle wheel spokes*

spoken
past participle of **speak**

spokesperson noun spokespersons or spokespeople
someone who officially represents a particular group or person and makes announcements for them. A male spokesperson is also called a spokesman and a female is called a spokeswoman.

sponge noun sponges
1 a special kind of soft material with lots of tiny holes in it for soaking up liquid. It is used for washing and cleaning things such as your body. *a bath sponge*
2 the action of washing and cleaning something with a sponge *Give your face a good sponge.*
3 a sea animal with a soft body used for making sponges for washing and cleaning
4 a sponge or sponge cake is a soft light cake made from eggs, sugar, flour and sometimes fat

sponge verb
sponges, sponging, sponged
1 to wash and clean something with a sponge
2 to sponge up liquid is to soak it up with a sponge
3 (informal) if someone sponges off someone, they ask them for money to live instead of getting a job *My cousin is lazy and sponges off his parents.* **sponger** noun

spongy adjective spongier, spongiest
1 soft and able to take in water easily *spongy ground*
2 soft and able to keep its shape after being pressed *spongy rubber*
sponginess noun

sponsor verb
sponsors, sponsoring, sponsored
1 if a business or organisation sponsors someone or something such as a group, event, website or TV programme, it supports them by giving money or help, often so that it can get free advertising *The football match was sponsored by a big bank.*
2 to give money to someone who takes part in something such as a race, a long walk, swim or other activity. The person you sponsor gives the money to a charity (group helping people who need help). *I'm taking part in the marathon – will you sponsor me?*

sponsor noun sponsors
a person, group, business or organisation that gives money to support someone or something

sponsorship noun
money given to support someone or something

spontaneous ['spon-**tay**-nee-ers] adjective
used about something that happens or is done in a natural way, suddenly and without thinking about it *When our football team came onto the pitch, there was spontaneous cheering.*

spontaneously adverb
in a natural way, suddenly and without thinking *As soon as he saw me, he spontaneously grabbed my hand and thanked me for my help.*

spook verb (informal)
spooks, spooking, spooked
to frighten someone, for example when something strange happens

spooky adjective spookier, spookiest (informal)
strange and frightening *There was a knock at the door but when I opened it no-one was there – spooky!*

spool noun spools
an object like a tube around which something is rolled, for example film, wire or cotton for sewing. It usually has round parts that stick out at each end.

spoon noun spoons
something used for eating liquids such as soup or soft food such as cereals, or for mixing, measuring or serving soft food or liquids. It has a handle at one end and a small bowl shape at the other end.

spoon verb
spoons, spooning, spooned
to pick up or serve liquids or soft food with a spoon *Dad spooned some more stewed apple onto my plate.*

spoonful–spread

spoonful *noun* **spoonfuls**
an amount of something that is contained in a spoon

sporran *noun* **sporrans**
a small bag made of fur or leather that hangs at the front of a kilt (kind of heavy skirt for men and boys worn in Scotland)

sport *noun*
1 (*plural* **sports**) an activity in which you use your body, for example to keep healthy or for fun. Sports need effort and skill. They are usually done outside and include games such as football, tennis and cricket that you play with other people and try to win. *Golf is my favourite sport. Boxing is an indoor sport.*
2 different kinds of sport *Do you like sport?* (for example cycling, swimming, football or cricket)
3 (*informal*) a sport or good sport is someone you respect because they are pleasant, friendly, fair and reasonable, and they do not complain about things

sport *verb*
sports, sporting, sported
to wear something, especially something you want people to notice *Granddad came into the room sporting a yellow tie.*

sporting *adjective*
1 connected with sport *a sporting event*
2 showing respect for people by being pleasant, friendly, fair and reasonable *Giving up your seat is very sporting of you.*
3 interested in sport
sportingly *adverb*

sports *adjective*
1 connected with sport *a sports club*; *sports fans*; *a sports centre* (building where people do indoor sports); *sports day* (when children at school do different sports such as racing against each other while parents watch)
2 a sports car is a small fast car with seats for two people and often with a roof that opens
3 a sports jacket is a jacket that a man or boy wears in relaxed situations with trousers of a different colour and cloth

sportsman *noun* **sportsmen**
a man who plays a lot of sport, especially as his job

sportsmanship *noun*
in sport, the behaviour of someone who is pleasant, friendly, fair and reasonable and who shows respect to other players

sportswear *noun*
clothes for people who play sport

sportswoman *noun* **sportswomen**
a woman who plays a lot of sport, especially as her job

sporty *adjective* **sportier, sportiest**
1 a sporty person is someone who likes playing sport
2 sporty clothes are like clothes you wear for doing sport, for example bright and comfortable

spot *noun* **spots**
1 a particular place *I showed Mum the spot where I lost my mobile. I have a sore spot on my foot.*
2 a small round mark or shape with a different colour from the area around it *Leopards have yellow fur with black spots.*
3 a small round swelling on your skin such as a pimple or red mark, for example in a rash (area of red marks caused by an illness) *Try not to scratch your chickenpox spots!*
4 a dirty mark on something *There's a spot of grease on my shirt.*
5 (*informal*) a small amount of something *I felt a few spots of rain on my head. Is there time for a spot of TV before bed? I'm having a spot of bother with my tablet.*

SYNONYM **bit**

6 **on the spot** immediately *You don't have to make a decision on the spot.*
7 **on the spot** also used when you mean at the place where something is happening or where someone is *Mum called an ambulance for Granddad and it was on the spot in five minutes. In PE today we did running on the spot* (without moving from our places).

spot *verb*
spots, spotting, spotted
to see or notice something or someone, especially when this happens suddenly or when it is not easy to do *I spotted Mohammed coming out of the library. These mistakes are difficult to spot.*

spotless *adjective*
extremely clean and tidy

spotlessly *adverb*
if something is spotlessly clean, it is extremely clean

spotlight *noun* **spotlights**
1 a lamp with a strong beam (line of light) that can be turned to shine in different directions. It is used for shining on a small area, for example on actors on a stage.
2 the light from this type of lamp *The actor stood in the spotlight and made a speech.*
compare: **floodlight** and **searchlight**

spotted *adjective*
marked or covered with spots or with a pattern of spots *a blouse spotted with grease*; *Shall I wear the striped socks or the spotted ones?*

spotter *noun* **spotters**
someone who watches and studies things such as trains or birds, usually as a hobby *a train spotter*

spotty *adjective* **spottier, spottiest**
marked or covered with spots or with a pattern of spots *a spotty face*; *a spotty dress*

spouse [rhymes with 'house'] *noun* **spouses**
someone's spouse is their husband or wife

spout *noun* **spouts**
1 a part shaped like a tube at or near the top of something such as a kettle, used for pouring liquids
compare: **lip**
2 a strong stream of something such as liquid

spout *verb*
spouts, spouting, spouted
1 if something such as liquid spouts from somewhere, a strong stream of it comes out or keeps coming out
2 if something spouts something such as liquid, a lot of it comes out quickly and strongly
3 (*informal*) if someone spouts something, they say something or talk about something in a way that you do not think is true or good *Is Dad spouting nonsense again?*
4 (*informal*) to talk in a boring way, often for a long time *Has Ben been spouting on about his new house again?*

sprain *verb*
sprains, spraining, sprained
to accidentally hurt your ankle or wrist by turning it or stretching it too much

sprain *noun* **sprains**
an injury caused to your ankle or wrist by spraining

sprang
past tense of **spring**

sprawl *verb*
sprawls, sprawling, sprawled
1 to sit or lie somewhere with your arms and legs spread out in a comfortable, careless or untidy way *My brother was sprawling on the armchair watching TV.*
2 if something is sprawled somewhere, it is spread out in different places in an untidy way *Books and comics were sprawled across the floor.*
3 if something such as a town sprawls somewhere, it gets bigger and bigger and covers a lot of the area all around it *London is a huge sprawling city.*

sprawl *noun*
the part of a town that covers the area around it as it gets bigger

spray *verb*
sprays, sprayed, spraying
1 to make tiny drops of liquid or a substance such as foam come out of a container through a hole and into the air or onto something or someone *The boys were spraying paint onto the wall. The firefighters sprayed the flames with foam.*
2 if a liquid or substance sprays, or if it sprays something or someone, tiny drops of it go into the air or onto something or someone *Water from the fountain sprayed us as we passed.*
3 if someone sprays bullets, or if someone sprays something or someone with bullets, they shoot lots of bullets

spray *noun*
1 tiny drops of liquid in the air that come from somewhere such as a container or the sea
2 (*plural* **sprays**) a container with a liquid in it for spraying, or the liquid inside the container *a hair spray* (liquid sprayed on your hair for keeping it tidy); *a spray can*
3 (*plural* **sprays**) a small bunch of flowers or a small branch with flowers or leaves on it

spread *verb*
spreads, spreading, spread
1 to put something over something else to cover all or most of it *Spread the blanket over the bed. I spread jam on my toast. Spread the top of the cake with icing.*
2 to arrange something or open something out so that it covers a larger area *Mum spread the photos out on the table so we could all see them. The bird spread its wings and flew off. Spread your fingers* (move them apart to leave spaces in between).

483

spread – spurt

3 to affect, reach or cover a larger area, for example when something gets worse or bigger or when there is more of it *Rain is spreading from the west. The fire spread to our village. The King tried to stop the fighting from spreading* (for example, tried to stop people in other places from fighting against him).
4 to make something affect, reach or cover a larger area *The wind is spreading the fire. Don't touch the tablecloth or you'll spread dirty marks on it. Pollen is spread by insects and the wind.*
5 to affect or influence more and more people or have something to do with them in some way *The illness is beginning to spread* (more people are beginning to catch it). *The use of computers spread very fast in the 1990s.*
6 to make something affect or influence more and more people *Sneezing spreads germs. No-one likes my uncle – he spreads fear* (makes people afraid of him).
7 if something such as information or news spreads, it becomes known by lots of people or by more and more people *There's a rumour spreading that Ms Greene is leaving.*
8 to make something such as information become known to people *There are people spreading stories about me.*
9 to arrange something so that it covers a larger amount of time *Dad bought me a bike and spread the payments over 20 months. My sister's exams are spread over two weeks.*
10 if people in a group spread out, they move away from each other so that each person has plenty of room *Spread out a bit, boys, you're all bunched up at one end of the room.*
11 if someone spreads out or is spread out, they stretch their arms and legs, for example to be comfortable *My brother was spread out on the sofa watching TV.*

spread *noun*
1 (*plural* **spreads**) a soft food that you put on something such as bread, toast or biscuits *a cheese spread*
2 when something spreads, for example covering a larger area or affecting more people *Computers help the spread of information. How do you stop the spread of the disease?*
3 (*plural* **spreads**) an informal word for a large meal

spreadsheet *noun* **spreadsheets**
a piece of computer software for showing information or doing calculations with numbers. The information or numbers are written in cells (small squares) in rows and columns (lines next to or under each other).

spree *noun* **sprees**
a short period when someone spends a lot of money *My big sister went on a shopping spree.*

sprig *noun* **sprigs**
a small piece of a plant with leaves on it

sprightly *adjective* **sprightlier, sprightliest**
full of energy and able to walk about easily, used mainly about older people *Grandma is 80 but still very sprightly.*

spring *noun* **springs**
1 the season between winter and summer when leaves, plants and flowers start to grow again and the weather starts to get warm *The crocuses come up in spring.*
2 a thin piece of wire curved into small spiral loops. It goes back to its normal shape after it is pressed, pulled or bent. *bed springs*
3 a small river or pool formed from water that comes out of the ground *a hot spring; Spring water is good to drink.*
4 a sudden movement, for example upwards

spring *verb*
springs, springing, sprang, sprung
1 to move suddenly and quickly *The alarm went and I sprang out of bed. Sayed sprang to his feet* (stood up quickly). *When you open the box, the jack-in-the-box springs up.*
2 to do something suddenly *It's time to spring into action.*
3 to appear, usually suddenly *Tell me if anything springs to mind* (if you think of something). *New buildings are springing up all over London. These ideas spring from Jo's imagination.*
4 to do something suddenly, for example give someone something or tell them something *My parents sprang a surprise on me. I'm sorry to spring this news on you. The pipe has sprung a leak* (made a sudden hole that liquid comes out of).

springboard *noun* **springboards**
1 a long narrow piece of special metal or plastic hanging over a swimming pool. It is used for diving into the water from.

SYNONYM **diving board**

2 a narrow piece of plastic or wood placed on the ground, used for jumping higher when doing gymnastics

spring-clean *verb*
spring-cleans, spring-cleaning, spring-cleaned
to clean all parts of a place completely, for example a house, flat or office, often in the springtime **spring-clean** *noun*

spring onion *noun* **spring onions**
a small white onion with long green leaves coming out of it. The onion and leaves are usually eaten uncooked in salads.

springtime *noun*
the season of the year when it's spring

springy *adjective* **springier, springiest**
if something is springy, it is soft enough to be pressed, pulled or bent but goes back to its normal shape afterwards *springy sports shoes; a springy pillow* **springiness** *noun*

sprinkle *verb*
sprinkles, sprinkling, sprinkled
to gently throw small amounts of something such as a liquid or powder onto something *Can you sprinkle some sugar on the cake? I sprinkled my chips with vinegar.*
sprinkle *noun*

sprinkler *noun* **sprinklers**
a piece of garden equipment with lots of holes in it fixed to the end of a hose (long tube of rubber or plastic), used for watering plants and grass

sprint *noun* **sprints**
1 a race that people run, going very fast over a short distance
2 a very fast run *I was late for school so I went into a sprint when I got off the bus.*

sprint *verb*
sprints, sprinting, sprinted
to run very fast for a short distance
sprinter *noun*

sprout *noun* **sprouts**
1 a vegetable like a very small cabbage

SYNONYM **Brussels sprout**

2 a new stem or leaf on a plant

sprout *verb*
sprouts, sprouting, sprouted
1 if a plant sprouts, new leaves, stems or flowers begin to grow from it *You can't use these potatoes – they're sprouting.*
2 if a plant sprouts something such as new leaves, it begins to grow them
3 to grow, or to grow something *The old man had a few hairs sprouting from his chin. If you chop off the monster's arm, it sprouts a new one.*
4 to appear suddenly *In this part of the country new buildings sprout up almost overnight.*

spruce *noun* **spruces**
a kind of very large fir (tall tree with thin pointed leaves that stay green in winter)

spruce *adjective* **␣sprucer, sprucest**
tidy and looking clean and pleasant, used when talking about a person or house, for example

spruce up *verb*
spruces up, sprucing up, spruced up
if you spruce something or someone up, you make them look tidier, cleaner and better *They've spruced up the school for our open day. Go and spruce yourself up before Uncle George gets here.*

sprung
past participle of **spring**

spud *noun* **spuds**
an informal word for a potato

spun
past tense & past participle of **spin**

spur *noun* **spurs**
1 a sharp metal object fixed to the heels of boots worn by horse riders. The riders hit the sides of the horse with their spurs to make it go faster.
2 **on the spur of the moment** used about something that you do suddenly without thinking about it *The sun came out and my parents decided on the spur of the moment to take us to the seaside.*

spur *verb*
spurs, spurring, spurred
to make someone more likely to do something or make them want to do something *The thought of getting another bad school report spurred me on to work harder.*

spurt *verb*
spurts, spurting, spurted
1 if something such as a liquid or steam spurts or spurts out, a lot of it comes out suddenly *Water spurted out from the broken pipe.*

2 to make a lot of something come out suddenly *I hit my head, spurting blood from my nose.*

spurt noun **spurts**
1 an amount of liquid that suddenly comes out from somewhere
2 a short period when someone suddenly does something faster or tries harder to do something *If you want to finish your homework before bedtime, you'll have to put a spurt on* (work faster and harder).

spy noun **spies**
someone who tries to find out secret information about someone or something and passes that information to someone else, for example an enemy

spy adjective
1 connected with spies *a spy novel*
2 used for spying *a spy plane*

spy verb
spies, spying, spied
1 to work as a spy *They were accused of spying for Russia.*
2 to spy on someone or something is to watch them secretly to try to get information about them
3 to spy someone or something is to suddenly see or notice them

spying noun

spyware noun
a bad piece of computer software that collects secret information such as someone's passwords or the websites they visit
compare: **adware** and **malware**

squabble verb
squabbles, squabbling, squabbled
to argue with someone about something that is not important *Fran and Sita are always squabbling.*

squabble noun **squabbles**
an argument over something unimportant

squad noun **squads**
a group of people who do a particular job or activity, for example soldiers, police officers or sports players *the bomb squad* (soldiers who find bombs and stop them from exploding); *the Olympic squad* (team of players or athletes who take part in the Olympics)

squadron noun **squadrons**
a group of aircraft, ships or soldiers in an air force, navy or army

squalid adjective
1 very dirty *He lived in a squalid little room.*
2 unpleasant and dishonest

squalor noun

squall noun **squalls**
1 a sudden strong wind, usually with rain
2 a noisy and unpleasant cry or shout

squall verb
squalls, squalling, squalled
to cry or shout noisily and in an unpleasant way *squalling babies*

squally adjective
if the weather is squally, there are strong winds and rain *squally showers*

squander verb
squanders, squandering, squandered
1 if you squander something such as money or time, you use it or spend it in a bad or careless way *My sister squandered her pocket money on sweets.*
2 if you squander an opportunity, you don't use it and are not successful, for example because of something bad or careless you've done *Mark behaved badly and squandered his chances of getting selected for the team.*

square noun **squares**
1 a flat shape with four straight sides that are all the same length and with four right angles (angles of 90 degrees)
2 a piece of something shaped like a square *a square of cheese*
3 an open area in a town, often shaped like a square, surrounded by buildings *We visited Trafalgar Square in London.*
4 in maths, the square of a number is the number you get when you multiply that number by itself. For example, the square of 3 is 9 (3 × 3) and 9 is a square number.
5 in maths, the square root of a number is the number that you multiply by itself to get the bigger number. For example, the square root of 9 is 3.

square adjective
1 shaped like a square, either exactly or roughly *a square window*; *a square bottle*
2 shaped exactly or roughly like part of a square, for example with straight edges or right angles *a square arch*; *My dad has a square jaw.*
3 used in maths for measuring the total area (amount of space) that something covers. For example, a square metre is the area of a square where each side is one metre long; 100 square miles is the area of a surface that measures 10 × 10 miles (= 100) or 20 × 5 miles (= 100) or 50 × 2 miles (= 100) and so on.
4 (informal) if two people are square, they don't owe each other anything

square verb
squares, squaring, squared
1 in maths, if you square a number, you multiply that number by itself. For example, 2 squared is 4 (2 × 2).
2 to agree with something or make something agree *Your story doesn't square with the facts. How can you square these words with what you said yesterday?*
3 if you square something with someone, you get their permission *Come to my house tomorrow but square it with your parents first.*

squarely adverb
directly *Aim the camera squarely at the actor's head.*

squash verb
squashes, squashing, squashed
1 to press or push something hard so that it loses its shape, for example by becoming flatter, softer or damaged *Don't sit on my hat or you'll squash it. The tomatoes got squashed at the bottom of the bag.*
2 to hurt someone by pressing or pushing them hard *Get off my foot – you're squashing me!*
3 to push someone or something into a place where there isn't enough room *Six children were squashed together on the sofa.*

squash noun
1 an indoor sport played in a court (area marked with special lines), usually between two people. You hit a rubber ball against the walls of the court with a racket (frame with strings and a handle).
2 a drink made from fruit juice, sugar and water. You pour a small amount into a glass and add water before drinking it. *a glass of orange squash*
3 (plural **squashes**) a large hard vegetable like a marrow. There are many different types such as long ones or round ones and they have skins of different colours such as brown or yellow.

squashy adjective **squashier, squashiest**
if something is squashy, it is very soft and easy to press in when you touch it *a squashy pear*

squat verb
squats, squatting, squatted
1 to bend your legs and lower your body with your bottom close to the ground and the weight of your body on your feet *I was lying on the beach when my brother came and squatted down next to me. The prisoners were squatting in a corner.*
2 to live in someone's empty house or building without paying them money or asking permission **squatter** noun

squat adjective **squatter, squattest**
short and wide *a row of squat houses*; *My brother is rather squat.*

squawk verb
squawks, squawking, squawked
to make a loud unpleasant noise like a parrot or seagull **squawk** noun

squeak verb
squeaks, squeaking, squeaked
to make a short high sound *My new shoes are squeaking. Did you hear a mouse squeak?* **squeak** noun

squeaky adjective **squeakier, squeakiest**
if something is squeaky, it makes a short high sound *a squeaky door*

squeal verb
squeals, squealing, squealed
if something or someone squeals, they make a loud high sound *The tyres squealed as Dad went round the corner. Some of the children were squealing with excitement.* **squeal** noun

squeamish adjective
if you are squeamish, you feel sick or upset when you see or think about unpleasant things such as blood coming out of someone's body

squeegee noun **squeegees**
a tool with a long rubber edge and a short handle, used for removing water from something such as a window that has just been washed

squeeze verb
squeezes, squeezing, squeezed
1 to hold something tightly and move the sides of it closer together or move your fingers closer together around it *Squeeze the sponge to get all the water out. Hold my hand but don't squeeze it too hard.*
2 to make something go somewhere by squeezing it *I squeezed some toothpaste onto my brush.*
3 if you squeeze a fruit such as an orange or lemon, you get the juice out by pressing its sides closer together

485

squeeze–staggering

4 to press something against something else *I squeezed my face against the window.*
5 to go somewhere where there isn't much room by pushing yourself or pressing your body hard *Lots of people tried to squeeze onto the bus. Move over and let me squeeze in.*
6 to get something or someone to go somewhere where there isn't much room, for example by pushing or pressing hard *She squeezed the package through the letterbox. How did you squeeze so many children into the tent?*

squeeze *noun*
1 the action of squeezing something *He gave my arm a gentle squeeze.*
2 (informal) if you say it's a squeeze, you mean there isn't enough room to fit someone easily in a particular place *Jump on the bus, but it's going to be a tight squeeze!*

squelch *verb*
squelches, squelching, squelched
to make a soft sound by pressing down on something very wet, for example when walking through mud *To reach the house we had to squelch across a soggy lawn.*

squelch *noun*

squid *noun* **squid** or **squids**
a sea creature that has a long body with eight short arms and two long ones called tentacles around its mouth. Squid can be eaten as food.

squidgy *adjective* **squidgier, squidgiest**
(informal)
soft and often wet *These kiwi fruits are a bit too squidgy.*

squiggle *noun* **squiggles**
a line with curves in it that is written or drawn somewhere *The head teacher's signature is just a squiggle.*

squiggly *adjective*

squint *noun* **squints**
a medical problem in which someone's eyes look in different directions

squint *verb*
squints, squinting, squinted
1 to close your eyes slightly to see better when something is not clear enough or when there is too much light
2 to have eyes that look in different directions
3 to look sideways, for example because you think something is bad or wrong *Why are you squinting at me like that?*

squirm *verb*
squirms, squirming, squirmed
to twist and turn your body, for example because you're uncomfortable, nervous or in pain

squirrel *noun* **squirrels**
a small grey or red-brown animal with a long thick tail and large eyes. Squirrels live in trees and eat nuts and seeds.

squirt *verb*
squirts, squirting, squirted
1 if a liquid squirts, a thin or heavy flow of it comes out quickly from something *When I opened the tube, some ketchup squirted onto my shirt.*
2 to make a liquid come out quickly from something or come out quickly onto someone or something *Squirt some lemon juice into my tea. Andy grabbed his water pistol and squirted me with water. He squirted his water pistol at me.*

squirt *noun*

Sri Lanka *noun*
a country in South Asia
Sri Lankan *adjective & noun*

ssh *interjection*
used for telling someone to be quiet

> LANGUAGE EXTRA also spelt *sh* and *shh*

st
short for **stone** or **stones** in weight

St
short for **street** or **saint** *34 Oakdale St; St John*

stab *verb*
stabs, stabbing, stabbed
to push a knife or something sharp into someone or something *A homeless person was stabbed in the street* (injured or killed by someone with a knife). **stabbing** *noun*

stab *noun* **stabs**
1 the action of stabbing *He died of a stab wound.*
2 a stab of pain is a sudden sharp pain

stabilise *verb*
stabilises, stabilising, stabilised
if someone stabilises something, or if something stabilises, it stops changing or stops getting worse

> LANGUAGE EXTRA also spelt *stabilize*

stabilisers *noun plural*
two small wheels fixed next to the back wheel of a bicycle. They stop you from falling over when you are learning to ride.

> LANGUAGE EXTRA also spelt *stabilizers*

stability *noun*
when something is not likely to change

stable *adjective*
1 staying the same or continuing in the same way and not likely to change *stable prices; The UK has a stable government. Granddad is ill but his condition is stable* (he's not getting better or worse).
2 strong and safe and not likely to fall down or break *The ladder is quite stable.*
stably *adverb*

stable *noun* **stables**
a building where people keep horses

stack *noun* **stacks**
1 a lot of things on top of each other, either arranged carefully or put together in an untidy way *There's a neat stack of books on the teacher's desk. Dad cleared away the stack of rubbish in the garden.*
2 an informal way of saying a lot of something *I have a stack of* (or *stacks of*) *things to do. Granddad has stacks of money.*
3 a chimney stack is the part of a chimney that sticks out above the roof of a building

stack *verb*
stacks, stacking, stacked
1 to put things on top of each other *Stack the boxes neatly in the corner. A lot of rubbish was stacked up against the kitchen wall.*
2 to put lots of things onto or into something *Dad was stacking the shelves with tins of food.*
3 to put lots of things next to each other or in front of each other so that they are standing neatly *Supermarket trolleys were stacked against a wall.*

stadium *noun* **stadiums**
a large building, usually without a roof, formed by a sports ground with rows of seats all around. People go to stadiums to watch sports events such as football or other big events such as concerts.

> ORIGIN from Greek *stadion*, a measure of length of about 600 feet. This was the size of the track used for foot races at Olympia in ancient Greece.

staff *noun*
1 the people who work in a place such as an office, shop or hospital
2 the teachers who work in a school, college or university *Ms Lawrence is a member of the teaching staff.*
3 (*plural* **staffs**) a group of five lines for writing musical notes on

> SYNONYM stave

4 (*plural* **staffs**) an old-fashioned word for a strong stick, used for example for walking

stag *noun* **stags**
an adult male deer. It has big twisted horns on its head called antlers.

stage *noun* **stages**
1 a raised structure for standing on, for example in a theatre or concert hall, where people such as actors, musicians or dancers perform *The singer is on stage for one hour.*
2 a period that is one part of a longer period or one part of a particular activity *In the early stages of the game we thought we could win. Granddad has reached a stage of his life where he likes to relax.*
3 one part of a journey *The first stage of our trip begins in Edinburgh.*
4 **in stages** gradually, one bit at a time *The changes will happen in stages.*

stage *verb*
stages, staging, staged
1 to stage something such as an event, play or exhibition is to put it on, show it or organise it for people to go to
2 to stage something such as a demonstration or strike is to organise it and take part in it *Some parents staged a protest outside the head teacher's office.*

stagecoach *noun* **stagecoaches**
a vehicle pulled by two, four or six horses, used especially in past times to carry people, goods and letters

stagger *verb*
staggers, staggering, staggered
1 to move or walk in a way that looks as if you are going to fall over
2 to surprise someone very much *We were staggered by the huge number of people who turned up for the concert.*
3 to make things happen at different times, not at the same time *Lunch breaks are being staggered so the canteen won't get too crowded.*

staggering *adjective*
very surprising *Prices have gone up by a staggering amount.* **staggeringly** *adverb*

486

stagnant *adjective*
not flowing or fresh and often dirty *stagnant water*

stain *noun* stains
1 a dirty mark on something such as clothes that is difficult to remove *There's a ketchup stain on my shirt.*
2 something that makes people have a bad opinion about someone *My cousin stole some money so he now has a stain on his reputation.*

stain *verb*
stains, staining, stained
to make a dirty mark on something *I spilt my tea and it stained the carpet. The carpet is stained.*

stained-glass window *noun*
stained-glass windows
a window made of pieces of coloured glass. The pieces of glass are joined together to make a picture, often a religious picture in a church.

stainless steel *noun*
a metal that does not rust (its surface is not damaged by air or water), used for example for making knives, forks and spoons *a stainless steel knife*

stair *noun* stairs
1 stairs are the long narrow surfaces that you walk up or down when you want to go to a different level in a building *Wait for me at the foot of the stairs* (the bottom level). *The stair carpet is getting dirty.*
2 a stair is one of these long narrow surfaces, usually made of wood or stone *The top stair is broken.*

staircase *noun* staircases
a group of stairs between one floor of a building and the next, including the banister (rail at the side for holding on to)

stairway *noun* stairways
a group of stairs, usually in a public building, connecting different parts of the building

stake *noun* stakes
1 a thick stick with a pointed end that is hammered into the ground, used for example as a support or as part of a fence
2 a tall thick pole used in the past for tying someone to and burning them as a punishment *Joan of Arc was burnt at the stake in France in 1431.*
3 a part of a business that someone owns because they have put money into it
4 an amount of money that someone pays when they try to guess who will win in a sport or competition. If they guess correctly, they get more money, but if they are wrong, they lose the money they pay.
5 **at stake** used about a situation where something bad can happen, for example things can be lost or damaged or people can be harmed, if an action is not done or is not successful *We must act now – lives are at stake* (people are in danger). *There's a lot of money at stake* (people could lose money).

stake *verb*
stakes, staking, staked
if someone stakes money on something, for example on whether someone will win in a sport or competition, they pay money and hope to get more money if they are right *My parents staked £20 on our team winning.*

stalactite *noun* stalactites
a long pointed piece of rock that hangs down like an icicle from the roof of a cave, formed from chemicals and water over a long period of time

stalagmite *noun* stalagmites
a long pointed piece of rock that rises up like a column from the floor of a cave, formed from chemicals and water over a long period of time

stale *adjective* staler, stalest
1 if food is stale, it is not good to eat because it has been kept for too long. For example, stale bread or cakes are hard or dry.
2 used about something in the air that does not have a pleasant or clean smell *stale cigarette smoke*; *The air in the locked room was stale.*
3 used about something such as news or a joke that is not new
staleness *noun*

stalemate *noun*
1 in chess, stalemate is when neither player can win the game, for example because one player is unable to move any pieces *compare*: **checkmate**
2 a situation in which progress cannot be made because no-one can agree

stalk *noun* stalks
the long thin stem of a plant that supports the leaves, flowers or fruit

stalk *verb*
stalks, stalking, stalked
1 to follow an animal or person closely without being seen, for example to catch them or attack them
2 to follow or watch someone for a long period of time in a frightening way or in a way that shows no respect to them *Don't go into a chatroom if you're afraid of being stalked online.*
3 to walk in a stiff way, for example because you are angry *When I told him it was his fault, he stalked out of the room.*

stall *noun* stalls
1 a table used for displaying things to sell or a very small shop that is open at the front and sides and usually has a cloth roof, for example in a market or street *a flower stall*; *a market stall selling clothes*
2 a small area inside a farm building for one animal such as a horse or cow
3 the stalls in a cinema or theatre are the seats on the ground floor at the same level as the stage

stall *verb*
stalls, stalling, stalled
1 if a vehicle or engine stalls, the engine suddenly stops working *My brother's motorbike stalled when he put the brakes on.*
2 to not do something you are supposed to do so that you have more time to do it, for example because you are not ready *Stop stalling and give me an answer now!*

stallion *noun* stallions
an adult male horse

LANGUAGE EXTRA an adult female horse is called a *mare*

stamen ['stay-mern'] *noun* stamens
one of the thin stems inside a flower. The top part of the stamen, called an anther, produces pollen.

stamina ['sta-min-er'] *noun*
the energy that you need to do something difficult for a long time *Playing football four times a week needs plenty of stamina.*

stammer *verb*
stammers, stammering, stammered
to repeat the sounds of some words lots of times as you speak, for example because you are nervous or have a medical problem
stammerer *noun*

SYNONYM to stutter

stammer *noun* stammers
a problem in speaking that makes you repeat the sounds of words *Peter has a slight stammer.*

SYNONYM stutter

stamp *noun* stamps
1 a small piece of paper with a design on it that you stick on an envelope or parcel. It shows the amount you have paid to send the envelope or parcel by post.

SYNONYM postage stamp

2 a small tool with a design, words or numbers on it for printing, usually on paper. The side with the design, words or numbers is pressed onto an ink pad (soft material with ink on it) and then pressed onto the paper. *a date stamp*
3 a mark such as a design, words or numbers made on something such as paper with a stamp *Chloe has lots of stamps in her passport.*
4 when you stamp your foot on the ground *He put his foot down with an angry stamp.*
5 stamp collecting is the hobby of collecting postage stamps, usually from different countries, and displaying them, usually in a book called an album

stamp *verb*
stamps, stamping, stamped
1 to put your foot down hard on the ground or move it up and down on the ground, usually making a noise *Why did you stamp on that spider? I was stamping my feet to keep warm while waiting for the bus. Dad stamped his foot angrily and we all stopped talking.*
2 if you stamp something such as paper, you press a mark on it with ink using a stamp *The date was stamped in my library book.*
3 if you stamp an envelope or parcel, you stick a postage stamp on it *This envelope isn't stamped.*
4 to stamp something out is to get rid of something bad or dangerous, for example bullying or racism

487

stampede–star

stampede noun **stampedes**
when people or wild animals suddenly start to run in the same direction, for example because they are frightened, excited or trying to escape *When the fire broke out, there was a stampede from the stadium.*
stampede verb

> ORIGIN from Mexican Spanish *estampida*, taken from Spanish *estampido* 'loud bang'

stand verb
stands, standing, stood
1 if you stand or are standing, your feet are on something such as the ground and your body and legs are straight *Go and stand by the window. We had to stand* (or *stand up*) *as there weren't enough seats on the bus.*
2 to change from a sitting position to a standing position *We all stood* (or *stood up*) *when the head teacher came in. Stand up!*
3 if you stand something somewhere, you put it there in an upright position *You can stand your bike against the front wall.*
4 if something stands somewhere, that is where it is *Our house stands halfway up a hill. The train stood at the platform for an hour* (it was there for an hour without moving).
5 to move away from somewhere *Stand back and let the ambulance pass. I'm coming through – stand aside!*
6 used for describing how something such as a building or vehicle is, for example when it is empty or neglected *The train stood empty on the platform.*
7 used for describing how someone is or how they behave *I stand ready to help.*
8 to be unchanged or in the same position as before *Does your offer still stand? After the storm only a few trees were left standing.*
9 to be strong enough to support something *If you do any climbing, make sure the rope can stand your weight.*
10 if you say you can't stand someone or something, it means you hate them *Ben can't stand his uncle. I just can't stand this noise. We can't stand running for the bus or being late for school.*
11 to stand a chance or hope of doing something is to be likely to do it *Our team is awful and stands no chance of winning.*
12 if someone stands in an election, they want people to vote for them, for example to be a member of parliament
13 if someone stands around, they do nothing, for example when they should be studying or working
14 to stand by is to be ready for action *Ambulance crews are standing by.*
15 to stand by is also to do nothing when you should be doing something *I couldn't just stand by and watch the bully hit her.*
16 to stand by someone is to help and support them
17 to stand for something is to mean or represent something *The letters UK stand for United Kingdom.*
18 if you stand for something unpleasant such as bad behaviour, you accept it without doing anything about it *My teacher said she won't stand for my lateness any more* (for example, she will punish me).
19 to stand in for someone is to take someone's place or do someone's job for a certain period of time
20 to stand out is to be easy to see *The police officers stood out in the crowd because of their fluorescent jackets. Simon stands out as the cleverest one in the class.*
21 to stand up to someone is to not let yourself be treated badly by them *Well done, George, for standing up to the bully.*
22 to stand up for someone or something is to defend or support them, for example when they are being attacked or criticised

stand noun **stands**
1 a very small shop that is open at the front and sides or a table used for displaying things to sell or look at, for example in a street or fair *a hot dog stand; Visit our stand at the book fair.*
2 an object or piece of equipment for holding or storing something *an umbrella stand; a music stand* (for holding printed sheets of music)
3 a building at a sports ground that is open at the front and has rows of seats. People sit or stand there and watch sports events.
4 an opinion or point of view

standard noun **standards**
1 the good or bad quality of something *The standard of Ed's schoolwork is very high. My piano playing isn't good but I'm working hard to get up to standard* (to reach a good enough quality).
2 something used for measuring something or judging someone *The metre is a standard of measurement. Harry isn't a very good player by Alfie's standards.*
3 standards are levels of good behaviour *Granddad is someone of high standards.*

standard adjective
1 normal or usual *These gloves come in standard sizes.*
2 accepted as normal and correct by most people *standard English*
3 a standard book or text is one that is read and respected by most people

standardise verb
standardises, standardising, standardised
to change things so that they are all dealt with in the same way or have the same qualities *Don't forget to standardise the spelling in your homework* (for example, always use 'clip art' or 'clipart' but not both).

> LANGUAGE EXTRA also spelt *standardize*

standard lamp noun **standard lamps**
an electric light fixed to a pole that stands on a base (bottom part) on the floor. The light has a lampshade (cover) over it.

standby noun **standbys**
1 something or someone that is always ready to be used or ready to do something if they are needed, for example in an emergency
2 **on standby** ready to be used or ready to do something if needed *The doctor is on standby in case Granddad gets worse.*

standpoint noun **standpoints**
the particular way you think about something

> SYNONYM point of view

standstill noun
when something stops completely *The trains are at a standstill because of the bad weather. The snow brought the traffic to a standstill* (made it stop moving).

stank
a past tense of **stink**. You can also say 'stunk'.

stanza noun **stanzas**
a group of lines that form one section of a poem

> ORIGIN from Italian *stanza* 'stopping place'

staple noun **staples**
a small strip of thin metal used for holding pieces of paper together. You press the staples through the paper using a tool called a stapler.

staple verb
staples, stapling, stapled
to fasten pieces of paper together with a staple using a tool called a stapler

staple adjective
1 used about food that is the most important and most needed part of what people eat *Bread, milk and eggs are staple foods.*
2 used about food that someone eats all the time *Chips and crisps seem to be Luke's staple food.*

stapler noun **staplers**
a tool used for fastening pieces of paper together with metal staples. It presses the staples through the paper and bends the ends of the metal over to hold the pieces of paper together.

star noun **stars**
1 a small bright light that you see in the sky at night. Stars are large balls of hot gas that appear as billions of small points of light when you look at them from earth.
2 someone famous such as an actor, for example in films or on TV, or a sports player or musician *a film star; a football star*
3 the main actor in a film, play or TV programme *Who's the star of the show?*
4 a flat shape or an object that has five or more points sticking out from its centre. For example, a six-pointed star can be made by placing a triangle upside down over another triangle of the same size.
5 a piece of paper shaped like a coloured star that a teacher gives you for good work or behaviour
6 a star symbol given to a hotel or restaurant to show how good it is *a four-star restaurant* (one that has high quality)
7 someone who is the best in a particular group *Seema always comes top – she's the star of our class. She's a star pupil.*

star verb
stars, starring, starred
1 to be the main actor or one of the main actors in something such as a film or play *Daniel Radcliffe stars in 'Harry Potter and the Goblet of Fire'.*
2 if something such as a film or play stars someone, that person is the main actor or one of the main actors in it *'Harry Potter and the Goblet of Fire' starring Daniel Radcliffe*

starboard–state

starboard noun
used for describing the right side of a ship or aircraft from the position of someone who is on board and facing forward *Planes have a green light shining on their starboard side.*
compare: **port** (sense 4)

starch noun
1 a white substance that exists in plants and vegetables and foods made from them, for example in potatoes, rice and bread. Starch is a carbohydrate (it gives heat and energy to your body).
2 a substance, for example a powder or spray, that is used for making cloth stiffer. It is made from vegetable starch.

starchy adjective **starchier, starchiest**
used for describing food or a meal that has a lot of starch in it

stare verb
stares, staring, stared
to look at someone or something for a long time without moving your eyes *Why are you staring at that boy? It's bad manners to stare.*

stare noun **stares**
a long look at someone or something *She gave me a long frightening stare.*

starfish noun **starfish** or **starfishes**
a sea animal that has the shape of a star formed by five arms that grow from its body

stark adjective **starker, starkest**
1 very unpleasant *a stark choice*
2 very easy to see (often used about something unpleasant) *There's a stark contrast between David and his brother.*
3 without any decoration or colour (often when something looks unpleasant) *a stark room*; *a stark white wall*
4 if someone is stark naked, they are completely naked

starling noun **starlings**
a small or medium-sized bird, often with dark shiny feathers. Starlings make a noisy sound and live together in large groups.

starlit adjective
lit up with the light from the stars *a starlit sky*

starry adjective **starrier, starriest**
full of stars *a starry sky*

Stars and Stripes noun
the flag of the United States

starship noun **starships**
in science fiction and in video games, a starship is a spaceship that travels between stars

start verb
starts, starting, started
1 if someone or something starts or starts something, they do something that they were not doing before or something happens or exists that was not happening before or did not exist before *I've started my homework. Lucy hasn't started yet. Ollie started crying. The ball started to roll down the hill. We start school at eight o'clock. Someone has started a fire. Where did the fire start?*
2 if a vehicle or a piece of equipment starts or you start it, it works or you make it work *My tablet started up first time. Mum couldn't start the car.*
3 used for talking about the first part of something that you deal with in a particular way or about something that happens or exists in a particular way and changes later *Start a new sentence with a capital letter. Dad started as an office junior and ended up as the boss. The day started off rainy. Prices start at £20.*
4 to go on a journey *They started out* (or *off*) *early in the morning. Let's start after breakfast.*
5 to make a sudden movement with your body because you are surprised or frightened *The knock on the door made me start.*

SYNONYM to jump

6 to get started is to start doing something or to start being done *What time shall we get started? The lesson hasn't got started yet.*

start noun **starts**
1 the first part of something such as an activity, period or event. It is the point at which that particular thing exists when it did not exist before. *Tomorrow is the start of the holidays. I missed the start of the film. The start of the race is in five minutes.*
2 when something exists or happens for the first time *That was the start of our worries. I've made a start on the washing-up* (started doing it).
3 the way that something exists or happens for the first time, or the way that someone makes something happen *This was an excellent start to the day. I've made a good start on my homework* (started doing quite a lot of it and doing it well).
4 when you go on a journey *We made an early start the next day.*
5 a sudden movement with your body because you are surprised or frightened *You gave me a start when you banged on the door.*
6 the place where a race happens *The runners are waiting at the start.*
7 something useful that helps you to be more successful in something such as a race, for example extra time or being put in front of someone else *The children were given a two-minute start.*
8 **for a start** used when mentioning the first thing that you want to say, for example the main reason for something *I can't come to your party – for a start I've got the flu.*
9 **from the start** from the time that something first happens and all the time that follows *I liked my teacher right from the start* (for example from when I first saw her).
10 **in fits and starts** stopping and starting lots of times *I can only work in fits and starts because I get tired.*

starter noun **starters**
1 a person, animal or vehicle that is in a race when it starts *Only three of the starters finished the race.*
2 the first part of a meal
3 something that someone says or does to start an activity or game, for example the first question in a quiz

starting point noun **starting points**
the place where you start something, for example a journey or activity *This is a good starting point for our discussion about dinosaurs.*

startle verb
startles, startling, startled
to make a person or animal feel slightly frightened when you do something suddenly or when something happens suddenly *I didn't see you standing there – you startled me. I was startled by the doorbell ringing.*

startling adjective
very surprising and unusual *startling results*

start-up noun **start-ups**
a new business that someone has just started

LANGUAGE EXTRA also spelt *startup*

starve verb
starves, starving, starved
1 if someone starves, they suffer or die because they don't have enough food *Many people in the Middle Ages starved to death.*
2 to make someone suffer or die by not giving them enough food
3 (informal) to be starving is to be very hungry
4 to starve someone of something is to not give them something they need, for example money or love

starvation noun

stash verb (informal)
stashes, stashing, stashed
to hide something or keep something in a secret place, usually something valuable

state noun **states**
1 the state of something or someone is how they are, for example how good or bad they are, or what they are like compared to how they should be *Your bike's in a rusty old state. After the accident he was in a state of shock. What's Granddad's state of health?* (How healthy is he?)
2 in science, a state is whether a substance is a solid, liquid or gas. Solids, liquids and gases are the three states of matter (what everything in the world is made of). Matter can change states, for example from a liquid (water) to a solid (ice).
3 another word for a country
4 another word for the government of a country *Does your dad get any help* (money) *from the state?*
5 a part of a country such as the United States that has its own government *the state of Florida*
6 (informal) **in a state** used about someone or something that is in a bad state, for example someone nervous, upset, messy or injured, or something messy or broken *I was in a state before my exams. My room is always in a state.*
7 **the States** an informal way of saying the United States of America

state verb
states, stating, stated
to say or write something, especially in an official way *The rules state that no more than four people can play.*

stately–steady

stately *adjective* statelier, stateliest
1 looking beautiful or powerful in a way that deserves great respect *a stately mansion*
2 serious and important *a stately procession*
3 moving slowly because of being serious and important *The procession continued at a stately pace.*
4 a stately home is a large old house in the countryside, usually with an interesting history, that belonged (or still belongs) to a noble family. People pay to visit stately homes, for example to look at the furniture and architecture (style and design of the house).

statement *noun* statements
1 something that someone says or writes, especially in an official way or on an important subject *The head teacher is going to make a statement about the mayor's visit to the school.*
2 an official description of what happened, given to a police officer investigating a crime
3 a piece of paper or an electronic document that shows how much money someone has put into and taken out of their bank account
4 in grammar, a statement is a type of sentence that gives information or an opinion. For example: 'Our dog is old.' 'Lucy went to bed.' 'I think you look tired.' It usually ends in a full stop and does not end in a question mark or exclamation mark.

state school *noun* state schools
a school that provides free education to children because its money comes from the government

statesman *noun* statesmen
an important male politician that many people respect

stateswoman *noun* stateswomen
an important female politician that many people respect

static *adjective*
1 not changing *static temperatures*
2 not moving *These rain clouds look fairly static.*
3 static electricity is an amount of electricity produced when certain kinds of things such as metal objects and the human body come into contact with each other

station *noun* stations
1 a place where trains, buses or coaches stop for people to get on and off, and the area around it including places such as a ticket office, waiting rooms, shops and toilets *a railway station* (or *train station*); *a bus station*
2 a building or place used for a particular service to the public or type of work *a police station* (where police officers work); *a fire station* (where firefighters work and fire engines are kept); *a space station* (spaceship where astronauts do research)
3 a place or building where radio or TV programmes are made and broadcast from, or the organisation that broadcasts these programmes *My mum works for a TV station. Please change the station.*

ORIGIN from Latin *stationem* 'standing' and later 'place for standing' (from *stare* 'to stand')

station *verb*
stations, stationing, stationed
1 to send someone such as a soldier to work somewhere for a period of time *My uncle was stationed in Cyprus.*
2 to send someone somewhere to do something or to stand there *A police officer was stationed outside the house* (for example to protect someone).
3 if you station yourself somewhere, you go and stand there to do something *Our teacher stationed himself by the window to watch over us.*

stationary *adjective*
not moving *a stationary car*

LANGUAGE EXTRA be careful not to confuse *stationary* (ending in *-ary*) with the next word *stationery* (ending in *-ery*)

stationery *noun*
1 things you need for writing and printing, sending by post and doing general office work, for example paper, pens, pencils, rubbers, envelopes, CDs, DVDs and flash drives (for storing computer information) or ink cartridges (for printers)
2 paper used for writing letters *My parents received a letter written on school stationery.*

statistic *noun* statistics
a piece of information shown by a number *Official statistics show that more school places will be needed next year.*
statistical *adjective*

statue *noun* statues
a model of a person or animal, usually made out of stone or metal. Statues are usually the same size as a person or animal or larger.

status ['stay-ters'] *noun* statuses
1 someone's position in society or in a group that shows how important they are compared to other people *A doctor's status is very high.*
2 the high position that someone has in society or in a group that makes you feel great respect for them *My dad dreams of a job with status.*
3 the status bar is a long strip along the bottom of a computer screen with information about the program you are using

staunch *adjective* stauncher, staunchest
1 showing that you strongly support and greatly respect someone or something *a staunch friend*; *She's a staunch supporter of Manchester United.*
2 showing that you have strong feelings or opinions *a staunch opponent* (being strongly against someone or something)
staunchly *adverb*

stave *verb*
staves, staving, staved
to stave something off is to stop it happening or keep it away so that it doesn't cause harm or problems *Ms Gold managed to stave off a crisis in the classroom. I ate an apple to stave off my hunger.*

stave *noun* staves
a group of five lines for writing musical notes on

SYNONYM staff

stay *verb*
stays, staying, stayed
1 to continue as before in the same place or situation *I'm going to stay at home today because I have a cold. The weather stayed rainy all week.*
2 to live somewhere or with someone for a certain amount of time *How long did you stay at the hotel? I'm going to stay with Granddad for a few days.*
3 if you stay away from something or someone, you don't go near them *Stay away from the edge of the platform. Stay away from that bully.*
4 if you stay behind, you stay somewhere when everyone else has left
5 if you stay in, you stay at home without going out
6 if you stay over, you stay at someone's house overnight *Can I stay over at Laura's?*
7 if you stay up, you don't go to bed *Please let me stay up a bit longer.*

stay *noun* stays
a period of time that you spend living somewhere or with someone *Ishaan has just come back from a short stay in India.*

St Bernard *noun* St Bernards
a very large dog with brown and white fur and a long heavy tail. It was originally used for helping to rescue people lost in the mountains, especially in the Swiss and Italian Alps.

steadily *adverb*
1 in a way that stays the same or that doesn't change much *Granddad is breathing steadily.*
2 in a way that happens slowly and all the time without stopping *Jack has been steadily making progress all term. The river has been rising steadily.*
3 in a way that shows that something or someone doesn't move, shake or fall down *Can you hold this pen steadily? Granddad walks more steadily now. He was looking at me steadily* (without moving his head).

steady *adjective* steadier, steadiest
1 not moving or shaking and likely to stay in one position *Grandma has a steady hand. Hold the ladder steady.*
2 not shaking, or not likely to fall over *Granddad is very steady on his feet. This tree sways in the wind and doesn't look steady.*
3 staying the same or not changing much *a steady temperature*; *a steady heartbeat*; *The train travelled at a steady speed of 60 miles an hour.*
4 happening slowly and all the time without stopping *a steady increase*; *steady progress*; *There was a steady flow of visitors to the museum.*
5 lasting a long time *My brother has a steady job.*
6 used about someone who is sensible and works well *Dexter's a clever pupil and a steady worker.*

SIMILE 'as steady as a rock' means very steady (senses 1 & 2)

steady *verb*
steadies, steadying, steadied
1 to make something or someone stop moving or shaking *Dad held the ladder with both hands to steady it.*

2 to stop someone (or yourself) from falling over *I slipped on the stairs but steadied myself by grabbing the banister.*

steady interjection
used for telling someone to be careful *Steady – you almost hit me in the eye!*

steak noun steaks
a thick flat piece of meat, usually from a cow, that is fried or grilled (cooked close to a flame or heat)

steal verb
steals, stealing, stole, stolen
1 to secretly take something that belongs to someone else and keep it *Keep your mobile safe or it might get stolen.*
2 to move somewhere quietly and secretly, for example without anyone noticing *I stole out of the room.*
3 to do something quickly *He stole a glance at her* (looked at her quickly).

stealth [rhymes with 'health'] noun
when someone does something or moves somewhere quietly and secretly

stealthy adjective stealthier, stealthiest
showing that someone does something or moves somewhere quietly and secretly, for example so as not to be seen or heard
stealthily adverb

steam noun
1 a substance formed from tiny drops of water when you heat the water up. Steam is neither solid nor liquid.
2 tiny drops of water formed on glass or walls when warm air changes into liquid

SYNONYM condensation

3 power produced from steam, used for example in the past to make engines work *a steam engine*; *a steam train*
4 to let off steam to get rid of your energy or feelings of anger by doing an activity such as running about

steam verb
steams, steaming, steamed
1 to produce steam *The kettle is steaming.*
2 to cook food using steam, for example in a steamer *steamed fish*
3 to move somewhere using the power of steam *The old boat steamed out of the harbour.*
4 to steam up is to become covered with steam and to steam something up is to cover it with steam *When I walked into the kitchen my glasses steamed up. The warm air steamed up my glasses.*

steamer noun steamers
1 a saucepan for steaming food such as fish or vegetables
2 another word for a steamship

steamroller noun steamrollers
a vehicle with wheels that are wide heavy cylinders (tubes with flat ends shaped like circles). It is used for making surfaces such as roads flat when they are being built or repaired. In the past steamrollers were moved by steam.

steamship noun steamships
a ship that moves using the power of steam

steamy adjective steamier, steamiest
1 full of steam *a steamy bathroom*
2 covered with steam *steamy windows*

steed noun steeds
an old-fashioned word for a horse that you ride, especially a strong and fast one

steel noun
1 a very strong metal made mainly from iron. It is used for making many things such as vehicles, bridges and buildings as well as cutlery (knives, forks and spoons).
2 a steel band is a group of musicians who play steel drums
3 a steel drum is a metal musical instrument, used for example in West Indian music

steel verb
steels, steeling, steeled
to steel yourself is to make yourself ready to deal with something unpleasant or to do something difficult

steely adjective steelier, steeliest
showing that someone's character is strong and hard *a steely voice*

steep adjective steeper, steepest
1 if something such as a hill or slope is steep, it goes up or down quickly at an angle so it is difficult to climb up or down *a steep climb*; *a steep flight of stairs* (group of stairs)
2 sudden and big *a steep rise in prices*
steepness noun

steep verb
steeps, steeping, steeped
1 to be steeped in something such as history or tradition is to be deeply connected with it or have lots of it *York is steeped in history.*
2 to put something in a liquid and leave it there for a time *a fruit salad steeped in apple juice*

steeple noun steeples
a tower on the top of a church with a pointed top called a spire

steeply adverb
1 in a way that goes up or down quickly at an angle *The road rises steeply towards the other side of town.*
2 suddenly and a lot *Prices are increasing steeply.*

steer verb
steers, steering, steered
1 to control the direction a vehicle or ship goes in by using a wheel, for example a steering wheel *Mum steered the car slowly out of the garage.*
2 to move someone or something in a particular direction, or show someone a particular direction *Can you steer me in the right direction?*

steer noun steers
a young bull (male cow) that is used for its meat

steering wheel noun steering wheels
a wheel inside a vehicle that a driver uses for controlling its direction

stegosaurus noun stegosauruses
a large plant-eating dinosaur with a small head and two rows of large spikes going along its back

stem noun stems
1 the long thin part of a plant that supports the leaves and flowers. The stem has small tubes inside that carry water from the soil up to the leaves.
2 the long thin upright part of something such as a wine glass or vase
3 in grammar, a stem is the main part of some words that you can add an ending to (last letter or letters) to change their meaning. For example, in 'walks', 'walking', 'walked' and 'walker', the stem is 'walk' and the endings are 's', 'ing', 'ed' and 'er'.

stem verb
stems, stemming, stemmed
1 if something stems from something else, that is where it started or what caused it *These problems stem from Granddad's bad decision.*

SYNONYM to come from

2 to stop something from continuing to happen *The doctor bandaged my finger to stem the flow of blood.*

stench noun stenches
a very bad smell

stencil noun stencils
a thin piece of plastic, card or metal with shapes or letters cut out of it. You put it onto something such as paper and paint over it to produce a shape or letter.
stencil verb

step noun steps
1 a movement you make when you put one foot in front of the other to walk or run *Take two steps back.*
2 the sound of someone walking or running as their feet or shoes touch the ground

SYNONYM footstep

3 the short distance you move when you take a step *My house is just a few steps away from the school.*
4 a particular movement with your foot when you dance *These dance steps are difficult.*
5 a flat surface, for example made of wood, metal or concrete, that you use for walking up or down to a different level. A step is usually one of many in something such as a ladder or stairs. *A flight of steps* (group of stairs) *led down to the cellar. Mind the step!*
6 a small raised surface outside the front door of a building

SYNONYM doorstep

7 a way of dealing with a situation or solving a problem *Our teacher took steps to make sure the bully wouldn't misbehave again.*

SYNONYM measure

8 one thing you do out of a number of different things to get something done *Make your own puppet in five easy steps! I followed your instructions step by step.*
9 if you watch your step, you are very careful about something, for example where you walk or how you behave

step verb
steps, stepping, stepped
1 to walk or move, or to go somewhere by walking *I stepped onto the bus. Step back* (or *aside*) *and let them pass.*
2 to put your foot or feet on something *You're stepping on my toes.*

491

stepbrother–stick figure

3 if someone steps down, they leave their job

SYNONYM to resign

4 if someone steps in, they do something to change a bad situation, for example to stop it from continuing *There was a fight between David and Tom – the teacher had to step in.*

stepbrother *noun* **stepbrothers**
the son of someone's stepmother or stepfather

stepchild *noun* **stepchildren**
the child of someone's husband or wife from an earlier marriage

stepdad *noun* **stepdads**
an informal word for a stepfather

stepdaughter *noun* **stepdaughters**
the daughter of someone's husband or wife from an earlier marriage

stepfather *noun* **stepfathers**
the man who is married to your mother but is not your father

stepladder *noun* **stepladders**
a small ladder made up of two parts joined at the top. It can stand on its own and be folded flat so that you can carry it.

stepmother *noun* **stepmothers**
the woman who is married to your father but is not your mother

stepmum *noun* **stepmums**
an informal word for a stepmother

stepping-stone *noun* **stepping-stones**
1 something used as a way of making progress and going on to something better, for example in your studies or a job *Is studying computing a stepping-stone to a good job?*
2 one of a number of flat stones in a river that you walk on to cross to the other side

steps *noun plural*
a small ladder made up of two parts joined at the top. It can stand on its own and be folded flat so that you can carry it.

SYNONYM stepladder

stepsister *noun* **stepsisters**
the daughter of someone's stepmother or stepfather

stepson *noun* **stepsons**
the son of someone's husband or wife from an earlier marriage

stereo *noun*
1 (*plural* **stereos**) a piece of equipment for playing music or listening to the radio, with two or more speakers that the sound comes out of. Stereos were used especially in the past.
2 a system for listening to sound using two or more speakers *The sound is in stereo.*

stereo *adjective*
using sound that comes from two or more speakers *stereo sound*

sterile *adjective*
1 completely clean and without germs *a sterile bandage*
2 a sterile person is not able to produce babies, and a sterile animal cannot produce young animals

ANTONYM fertile

3 sterile land is bad for growing things, especially plants for food

ANTONYM fertile

sterility *noun*

sterilise *verb*
sterilises, sterilising, sterilised
1 to kill all the germs in or on something so that it is completely clean
2 to perform an operation on the body of a person or animal so that they can no longer produce babies or baby animals

sterilisation *noun*

LANGUAGE EXTRA also spelt *sterilize* and *sterilization*

sterling *noun*
the unit of money in the UK. There are 100 pence in a pound sterling. *Dad paid for the hotel in sterling.*

stern *adjective* **sterner, sternest**
1 not friendly, kind or understanding but very serious *Mum had a stern look on her face.*
2 very strong and unpleasant *a stern warning*

sternly *adverb*

stern *noun* **sterns**
the back part of a boat

LANGUAGE EXTRA the front part of a boat is called the *bow* (rhymes with 'brow')

stethoscope *noun* **stethoscopes**
a piece of equipment used by doctors and nurses to listen to your heart and breathing. It usually has a disc at one end that is placed against your body. The disc is connected to a tube with two end pieces that are placed in the doctor's or nurse's ears.

ORIGIN from Greek *stethos* 'chest' and *skopein* 'to look at'

stew *noun* **stews**
vegetables with meat or fish cooked slowly in liquid, usually water, and served as a meal

stew *verb*
stews, stewing, stewed
to slowly cook vegetables, meat, fish or fruit in liquid, usually water *We had stewed apples for dessert.*

steward *noun* **stewards**
1 someone who helps and looks after people on a plane, ship or train and serves them with food
2 someone who helps to control people at a public event such as a football match or concert

stewardess *noun* **stewardesses**
an old-fashioned word for a woman who is a flight attendant (someone who helps and looks after people on a plane)

stick *noun* **sticks**
1 a thin piece of wood, usually long, that has come off a tree or bush
2 a long thin piece of wood, or another material, used for many different things, for example hitting a ball in sports, supporting something such as a plant or balloon, or as a weapon. Sticks come in many different shapes and sizes. *a hockey stick* (curved at one end); *an ice lolly stick* (small and flat, for holding a lolly); *a memory stick* (short and narrow or square and flat, for plugging into a computer and storing information on)

3 a long thin piece of wood, usually with a curved handle, used by people to help them walk

SYNONYM walking stick

4 a long thin piece of something *a stick of celery*; *We bought a stick of rock at the seaside.*

stick *verb*
sticks, sticking, stuck
1 to fix something onto something else, for example with glue, tape or paste or with another substance or material such as Blu-Tack or Velcro, or by using something with a special power such as a magnet *Stick the stamp on the envelope. Mum stuck the broken pieces of the vase together. I bought a fridge magnet to stick on the fridge.*
2 if something sticks to (or on) something, it becomes fixed to it *The eggs stuck to the frying pan. My wet shirt was sticking to my body. The magnet sticks on the fridge.*
3 to push something long and thin into something or someone or through something *The doctor stuck a needle in my arm. Don't stick your finger through the paper.*
4 if something long and thin is sticking in something, a part of it has been pushed into that thing *There was a knife sticking in the tree.*
5 if something sticks or is stuck, it becomes fixed in one position and is difficult to move or cannot move *My laptop lid was sticking so I had to pull hard. The drawer's stuck.*
6 an informal way of saying to put *Amy stuck the book back on the shelf. Don't forget to stick my name on the list.*
7 another way of saying to stay *Stick with me – I don't know my way around. Our teacher told us to stick together and not wander off. Stick around* (don't go away). *Dad was wearing a funny hat – that's what sticks in my mind* (that's what I remember).
8 (informal) if you say you can't stick someone or something, it means you hate them *I just can't stick that boy! The film was so bad we walked out – we couldn't stick it any more* (we hated the film and couldn't watch it any longer).
9 if something sticks out, you can see it easily because it goes out further than the edge of something or goes out further from a surface than it should *My feet were sticking out from under the blanket. George's ears stick out.*
10 if a person or animal sticks something out, they put it out further from the place where it usually is *The dog stuck its tongue out. Don't stick your arm out of the window.*
11 if something sticks up, it goes up higher or further than a surface or edge *My brother has spiky hair that sticks up on his head.*
12 to stick up for someone or something is to defend or support them, for example when they are being attacked or criticised

sticker *noun* **stickers**
a piece of paper or plastic with a picture or message on it that you stick onto something

stick figure *noun* **stick figures**
a simple drawing of a man or woman with lines for the body, arms and legs and a circle for the head

sticking plaster–sting

sticking plaster noun sticking plasters
a small piece of thin material that you stick over a cut or injury on your skin to protect it

stick insect noun stick insects
a long thin insect with long thin legs. It is difficult to see because it looks like a small stick from a tree. Stick insects usually live in warm places such as South America and Australia.

sticky adjective stickier, stickiest
1 used about something that has something on it that sticks to things *Don't touch my book with your sticky fingers* (for example, your fingers have jam or grease on them). *The kitchen floor was wet and sticky. The paint's still a bit sticky* (not quite dry).
2 made of something that sticks to things that touch it *sticky clay; This Blu-Tack is fresh and sticky.*
3 if paper or plastic is sticky, one side of it has a special substance on it that makes it stick to things that touch it *a roll of sticky tape* (for example for sticking papers together or to something else); *Post-it notes have a sticky strip on the back.*
4 if the weather is sticky, the air is hot and slightly wet in an unpleasant way *It was a sticky summer's day in Athens.*
5 if you feel sticky, your skin feels hot and sweaty
6 (informal) used about a difficult or unpleasant situation *Andy is going through a sticky patch at school.*
stickiness noun

sticky note noun sticky notes
1 a small piece of coloured paper, often yellow or green, with a sticky strip on the back. It is used for writing a message on and sticking onto something, for example as a reminder to do something.
2 a program that puts a small window that looks like a sticky note onto your computer screen for you to type messages and reminders into

SYNONYM Post-it note

stiff adjective stiffer, stiffest
1 if something is stiff, you cannot bend it easily or move it into a different position because it is fairly hard *a stiff cardboard box; a stiff leather schoolbag; Rub off the dirt with a stiff brush.*
2 if a part of your body is stiff, or if you feel stiff, you have a pain in a muscle (or muscles) when you move *I've got a stiff neck. Granddad has been stiff all week* (for example with pains in his leg, shoulder or neck muscles).
3 used about something that you cannot move easily when it should be easy to move *This door is really stiff.*
4 if a substance is stiff, it is very thick *a stiff paste*
5 very difficult to do or deal with *a stiff maths test; There's stiff competition for the top prize.*
6 very strong, for example when talking about a punishment or criticism *The thief received a stiff prison sentence.*
7 unfriendly and not showing any happy or pleasant feelings *a stiff tone of voice; Our new teacher seems rather stiff.*
stiffly adverb **stiffness** noun

SIMILE 'as stiff as a board' means very stiff (senses 1 & 2)

stiff adverb
very or very much *Craig often gets bored stiff in class. After an hour playing in the snow, Ben was frozen stiff.*

stiffen verb
stiffens, stiffening, stiffened
1 to make something stiff *He stiffened his muscles.*
2 to become stiff *Mix the paste until it stiffens.*
3 to stop moving and make your body straight, for example because you are afraid

stifle verb
stifles, stifling, stifled
1 to stop yourself from doing something such as sneezing, yawning or laughing *I stifled a sneeze so as not to wake Grandma up.*
2 to stop something good from happening *Schools should not stifle children's imagination.*

ANTONYM to encourage

3 to have trouble breathing, for example because it is too hot *Open the windows – I'm stifling in here.*
4 to make it difficult for someone to breathe or to kill someone by stopping them from breathing *They were stifled by the fumes.*

stifling adjective
1 so hot that you have trouble breathing *The underground trains are stifling on a summer's day.*
2 used about something such as a situation or atmosphere where you are not allowed to do what you want or to develop

stigma noun stigmas
1 a female part of a plant at the top of the style (stalk that grows from the ovary or part that produces seeds). The stigma receives pollen from another flower.
2 used when you think something is wrong or bad and someone should feel ashamed about it *There's no stigma attached to being dyslexic* (it's nothing to be ashamed of).

stile noun stiles
a structure with two or three steps built over a fence or wall and sometimes beside a gate, for example at the edge of a field. You climb over the stile to get to the other side.

still adverb
1 used for saying that a situation has not changed up to the present time or up to a particular time, for example something continues to happen or exist or someone continues to do or be something *It's still snowing. I was still looking for my glasses when Mum came home. Jack is still my best friend.*
2 used for saying that something someone has just mentioned does not stop something else from happening or being true, usually something surprising or contrasting *I haven't started my homework yet but I can still finish it before tomorrow. It's cold and rainy. – Still, you can go out and play if you want to.*

SYNONYM nevertheless

3 when comparing things, used for saying that something is more than something else or more than before *I play the piano well but Leah plays better still. December was cold but January was colder still.*

SYNONYM even

4 used for giving extra importance to a word or words *There's still plenty of time. We still have two other books to read this term.*

still adjective
1 used for describing a person or animal that doesn't move about but stays in the same position, for example sitting or standing *Sit still and pay attention! When the bell goes, stand still. Declan is so fidgety he just can't keep* (or *stay*) *still for a minute.*
2 used for describing something such as air or water that doesn't move *the still night air; the still water of a pond*
3 without any noise or activity *It was night and the whole town was still.*

SYNONYMS quiet, peaceful

4 a still drink is one that does not have any small bubbles in it *still mineral water*

ANTONYMS fizzy, carbonated

stilts noun plural
1 two long poles with places for your feet to stand on, used for walking above the ground *We saw a circus clown on stilts.*
2 long poles made of wood or metal for supporting a house, for example a house built on soft ground or water, so that it stays high above the ground or water

stimulate verb
stimulates, stimulating, stimulated
1 if something stimulates you, it keeps your attention and makes you excited *Children need lots of books to stimulate them. Mum finds her new job really stimulating* (interesting and exciting).
2 to make something stronger, more active or work better *These exercises stimulate the mind and the imagination. They say that coffee stimulates the brain!*
3 to make something happen *The TV show stimulated a lot of discussion and exciting ideas.*
stimulation noun

stimulus ['stim-yoo-lers'] noun
stimuli ['stim-yoo-lee' or 'stim-yoo-lie']
1 something that makes you want to do something *Books for me were a real stimulus* (for example, they made me want to learn and read more).
2 something that makes something stronger, more active or work better *The imagination needs some sort of stimulus.*
3 something that makes something happen *The head teacher's actions will provide a stimulus to change.*

sting verb
stings, stinging, stung
1 if an insect or animal stings you, it makes a substance go into your skin from a pointed part of its body and causes you pain *I was stung by a bee.*

493

sting–stocking

2 if a plant stings you, it hurts you when a chemical that it produces touches your skin *Be careful of the nettles – they sting.*
3 if a part of your body stings, it makes you feel sudden sharp pains *This shampoo makes my eyes sting.*

sting *noun* **stings**
1 a pointed part of an insect's or animal's body that it uses for making a substance go into your skin and cause you pain
2 the pain that you feel when an insect, animal or plant stings you
3 the place on your skin where an insect, animal or plant stings you

stingray *noun* **stingrays**
a large flat fish with a long pointed tail that can sting. Stingrays live mainly at the bottom of the sea.

stingy ['stin-jee] *adjective*
stingier, stingiest
1 not wanting to spend money or give money to other people *Granddad is very stingy.*

SYNONYM mean

2 used about something someone gives that shows how stingy they are *a stingy gift*
3 not wanting to give things or share things with other people *Don't be stingy with the sweets* (for example, give me lots of them or some of them).

stinginess *noun*

stink *noun*
1 (*plural* **stinks**) a very bad smell
2 (informal) when someone shows how angry they are or complains about something *My teacher will make* (or *kick up*) *a stink if I'm late today.*

stink *verb*
stinks, stinking, stank or **stunk, stunk**
1 to smell very bad *Your feet stink.*
2 to smell very bad with a particular smell *The whole house stank of fish.*
3 (informal) to be very bad *Your idea stinks!*
4 (informal) to stink a place out is to make it smell very bad *My uncle's cigarettes stank the whole room out.*

stinking *adjective*
1 smelling very bad *piles of stinking rubbish*
2 an informal way of saying very bad *We had stinking weather in Italy.*

stinky *adjective* **stinkier, stinkiest**
(informal)
1 smelling very bad *a stinky toilet*
2 very bad *a stinky piece of homework*

stint *noun* **stints**
a period of time that you spend doing something such as working somewhere

stint *verb*
stints, stinting, stinted
if you don't stint on something, you give someone lots of something or you use lots of something *Please don't stint on the ice cream. Dad didn't stint on the salt in this omelette* (he used lots of salt).

stir *verb*
stirs, stirring, stirred
1 to move a liquid, something soft or the parts of something round and round with a circular movement *Give me a spoon to stir my tea. Dad stirred some cream into his coffee* (put some cream in and moved it round).
2 to move slightly *My brother was stirring in his sleep. We could hear a breeze gently stirring the leaves.*
3 to start to move, or to get someone to move, for example after being asleep or very still in one position for a long time *The alarm clock went off but she didn't stir from her chair. He's so fast asleep that I just can't stir him* (wake him up or make him move).
4 to cause a particular feeling such as fear or anger
5 if someone stirs up trouble, they cause problems and behave badly

stir *noun*
1 (*plural* **stirs**) the action of stirring something such as a liquid *Give the soup a good stir before you serve it.*
2 when people are very interested in something or someone or are surprised or angry about them *Our teacher left suddenly, which caused quite a stir.*

stir-fry *verb*
stir-fries, stir-frying, stir-fried
to cook small pieces of vegetables and meat by moving them around in hot oil, for example in a wok (frying pan like a bowl)

stir-fry *noun*

stirrup ['sti-rerp] *noun* **stirrups**
1 a metal loop that a horse rider rests his or her foot on. It hangs down from a strap fixed to each side of a horse's saddle (seat for riding a horse).
2 a thin strip of cloth fixed to the bottom of each leg of tight trousers such as ski pants or leggings. You put the stirrup under your foot when you wear these trousers.

stitch *noun* **stitches**
1 a short piece of thread on cloth, where the cloth has been sewn. The thread is usually made of cotton or nylon.
2 a short loop of wool made by a knitting needle (pointed stick for knitting). Stitches are joined together in rows to make things such as clothes.
3 a way of using a needle when you sew or knit *My sister knows some fancy stitches.*
4 a piece of special thread that a doctor or nurse uses for joining together the edges of someone's skin when it has been cut *Jack fell over and needed stitches to his knee.*
5 a sudden pain in your side when you do exercises such as running or swimming or when you laugh too much
6 in stitches used for describing someone laughing a lot

stitch *verb*
stitches, stitching, stitched
1 to join pieces of cloth together with a needle and thread *Mum stitched the button back onto my shirt.*
2 to repair or decorate something with a needle and thread *Dad has stitched up your jeans.*

stitching *noun*
a row of stitches in a piece of cloth

stoat *noun* **stoats**
a small animal like a weasel with a long body and tail. It has brown fur on its body with white fur on the front and underneath, and black fur on the end of its tail. Stoats often turn white in winter. They kill other animals such as mice, rabbits and birds for food.

stock *noun* **stocks**
1 all the goods that you can buy from a shop, store or factory *Our supermarket has new stock arriving every day. The shoes I wanted are out of stock* (there are no more left to buy). *When will they be back in stock?* (ready to buy)
2 an amount of something that you keep and that is ready to be used *Our teacher keeps a stock of pens in a drawer.*
3 a liquid made by boiling meat, animal bones or vegetables in water, usually used for making soups and stews or for adding flavour to soups and stews
4 used in business for talking about the equal parts that the property of a company is divided into. People buy stocks as a way of owning a part of a company and trying to make money.
5 the country, family or group that someone comes from
6 farm animals such as cows, pigs and sheep
7 the stocks were a type of wooden frame used in the past for punishing people. There were holes in the frame for fixing people's hands, feet or head so that they could not move.

stock *verb*
stocks, stocking, stocked
1 if a shop, store or factory stocks something, they have it ready for people to buy
2 to fill or provide something with things that are needed *My brother works in a supermarket stocking shelves* (filling them with food and goods when they become empty). *My parents have stocked up the fridge* (filled it with lots of food).
3 if you stock up, you buy a large amount of something you need so that you can use it later *We always stock up on paper for the printer.*

stockade *noun* **stockades**
a fence made of stakes (thick sticks with pointed ends), used for example around gardens or for protection around buildings

stockbroker *noun* **stockbrokers**
someone who buys and sells parts of companies' property (called shares) for people. People who buy the shares do this as a way of owning parts of companies and trying to make money.

stock car *noun* **stock cars**
an ordinary car that has been changed to make it stronger and faster. It is used in special races where cars are allowed to hit each other.

stock exchange *noun* **stock exchanges**
a place where shares in a company (parts of its property) are bought and sold

stocking *noun* **stockings**
1 a covering made of very thin material that women wear on their legs and feet
2 a stocking or Christmas stocking is a large sock to receive Christmas presents in. You hang it up somewhere, for example beside your bed, the day before Christmas before you go to sleep.

494

stock market–stopover

stock market noun stock markets
the business of buying and selling shares in a company (parts of its property)

stockpile noun stockpiles
a large amount of something, such as food or goods, that you keep until it is ready to be used **stockpile** verb

stocky adjective stockier, stockiest
1 short with a strong and heavy body *I'm rather stocky.*
2 short, strong and heavy *stocky legs*; *My dad has a stocky build.*

stodgy adjective stodgier, stodgiest
1 used for describing food that is heavy, hard to eat and makes you feel very full *a stodgy pizza*
2 used about something or someone that is boring or does not show any imagination *a stodgy book*; *an old-fashioned and stodgy teacher*

stodginess noun

stole
past tense of **steal**

stole noun stoles
a piece of cloth that women wear around their shoulders, usually on special occasions and made from expensive cloth such as silk

stolen
past participle of **steal**

stomach noun stomachs
1 the soft front part of your body below your chest that reaches to the top of your legs

SYNONYM abdomen

2 the organ inside this soft front part of your body where the food goes after you have eaten it and where food starts to be digested (changed into substances that your body can use)

stomach verb
if you say that you can't stomach someone or something or that someone or something is hard to stomach, it means you really dislike them or you can't accept them because they are so unpleasant or bad

LANGUAGE EXTRA used especially in negative sentences (*can't* or *won't stomach*) or questions

stomachache noun stomachaches
a pain in the stomach (front part of the body below the chest)

LANGUAGE EXTRA also spelt *stomach ache*

stone noun stones
1 the hard substance found in the ground that is often used for building or making things. Rocks are made of stone. *The house had a stone floor.*
2 a small piece of this substance *We threw stones in the water.*
3 a piece of this substance shaped or used for a particular purpose *a paving stone* (block of stone for walking on); *People danced around the stones of the prehistoric monument. The old cemetery was full of broken stones* (gravestones).
4 a special stone used as a jewel *a crown of diamonds, rubies and other stones*
5 the hard, often large, seed inside a fruit such as a cherry, plum or avocado
compare: **pip**
6 **a stone's throw** a short distance away *My best friend lives a stone's throw from my house.*
7 **to leave no stone unturned** to try as hard as you can to be successful in doing something *The police left no stone unturned in looking for the missing boy.*

stone noun stone
a unit for measuring weight, equal to about 6.35 kilos. There are 14 pounds in a stone.

stone verb
stones, stoning, stoned
1 to kill or hurt someone by throwing stones at them *In the past, people were sometimes stoned to death in some countries* (killed with stones as a punishment).
2 to throw stones at something
3 to remove the stone from a fruit such as a cherry or plum

stone adverb
completely *stone deaf*; *stone dead* (used for saying that a person or animal is definitely dead); *stone broke* (having no money at all)

Stone Age noun
the Stone Age is the period when people used stone to make tools and weapons. It lasted about three million years until the start of the Bronze Age around 4000 BC.

stone-cold adjective
extremely cold, usually when describing something that should be warm *Your dinner's stone-cold.*

Stonehenge noun
a monument about 4000 years old in the south-west of England. It consists of a circle of very tall stones.

stonemason noun stonemasons
someone whose job is to cut and use stone for building things

SYNONYM mason

stony adjective stonier, stoniest
1 full of or containing lots of stones *a stony beach*
2 if something such as someone's expression or welcome is stony, it is very unfriendly and does not show any kind or pleasant feelings *He was angry and gave me a stony stare. We sat in stony silence.*

stood
past tense & past participle of **stand**

stool noun stools
a piece of furniture for one person to sit on. It has three or four legs (supports) but doesn't have a back or arms (side parts for resting your arms on).

stoop verb
stoops, stooping, stooped
1 to stand or walk with your head and shoulders bent forwards and down *I'm very tall and often stoop.*
2 to move the top of your body forwards and down to do something *The doorway was so low we all had to stoop. Seema stooped down to stroke the cat.*
3 if someone stoops to something, they behave badly by doing something they know is completely wrong *I didn't think my sister would stoop to stealing money from Granddad.*

stoop noun
the way that someone stands or walks with their head and shoulders bent forwards and down *Grandma walks with a stoop.*

stop verb
stops, stopping, stopped
1 if someone stops, or stops doing something, they don't do something any more *That noise is awful – please stop! I've stopped taking the bus to school.*
2 if something stops, or stops doing something, it doesn't happen any more *Has the rain stopped? The alarm bell finally stopped ringing.*
3 to make sure that something doesn't happen any more *Put on this cream to stop the pain. The referee stopped the game.*
4 to make sure that someone doesn't do something or do it any more *She was about to hit me but I stopped her. Dad stopped me falling* (or *from falling*). *I will go to Ollie's party and you can't stop me! How do you stop a bully?*
5 to not move any more *The train will stop at the next station. I walked to the middle of the playground then stopped. We stopped at the stop sign.*
6 to make sure something or someone doesn't move any more *Mum stopped the car at the traffic lights. I stopped my teacher in the playground to ask a question.*
7 to do a different activity for a short time or stay somewhere for a short time *We stopped* (or *stopped off*) *to buy sweets on the way home. Let's stop for lunch. Uncle John is here but he's not stopping* (not staying long).
8 to not work any more or to make something not work *My watch has stopped. Press this button to stop the machine.*
9 **to stop by** is to visit someone or something for a short time *I'm going to stop by Granddad's house tomorrow.*
10 **to stop short** is to suddenly stop doing something
11 **to stop something up** is to block it, for example so that nothing can go through *Dad stopped up the hole so that mice can't get in. The sink is stopped up with hairs. My ears are stopped up* (I can't hear well, for example because of wax).

stop noun stops
1 the action of not moving or happening any more *The ball rolled across the playground and came to a stop in the grass. That terrible noise came to a stop after a few minutes.*
2 the action of making sure something doesn't happen any more *It's time to put a stop to your bad behaviour.*
3 when you stop somewhere (or when a vehicle stops) on a journey, or the time you spend there *The minibus has two more stops to make. We left after a short stop for lunch.*
4 the place where you stop on a journey *Our first stop will be York.*
5 a place where a bus or train is supposed to stop *We're getting off at the next stop.*

stopover noun stopovers
when you stay somewhere for a short time during a journey *On the way to Chile we had a stopover in Washington.*

495

stoppage–straight

stoppage noun **stoppages**
1 a situation when people stop doing their job to show that they are unhappy about something
2 a short period when a game such as football has to stop, for example because of bad weather

stopper noun **stoppers**
something that goes into the top of a bottle to stop the liquid coming out

stop sign noun **stop signs**
a sign at the side of a road or on a road that tells traffic to stop

stopwatch noun **stopwatches**
a small clock that you hold in your hand and that you can start and stop. It is used for measuring the time it takes to do something, for example how long it takes someone to complete a race.

storage noun
1 space where you put things to use later *There's plenty of storage under the stairs.*
2 when you put things somewhere to use later *Granddad is moving house and his furniture is in storage.*
3 somewhere for storing computer information, for example a piece of equipment or a place online

store noun **stores**
1 a large shop that sells lots of different things *a furniture store; a department store*
2 a shop of any size *a village store*
3 a place on the internet where you can buy lots of different things *an app store* (where you download apps, for example for smartphones and tablets)
4 an amount of something that you keep and that is ready to be used *Mum keeps a store of eggs in the fridge.*
5 a place where particular goods are kept *a grain store*
6 **in store** used about something that will happen to someone soon or in the future *Mum and Dad have a surprise in store for you. Ed soon found out there was trouble in store.*

store verb
stores, storing, stored
1 to keep something so that you can use it later *Store the vegetables in the fridge. Mum stores up all her old magazines.*
2 to keep information somewhere, for example in a computer's memory, online, or on a DVD or flash drive (object that plugs into a computer) so that you can use the information later *I've stored these files in a folder called 'school stuff' on the desktop.*

storey noun **storeys**
one level or floor in a building *a 10-storey building*

LANGUAGE EXTRA be careful not to confuse *storey* with *story* (description of something)

stork noun **storks**
a large bird with long legs, a long neck and a long straight pointed beak. Storks live near water.

CULTURE NOTE in old stories from the past, a new baby would be brought by a white *stork* flying through the air

storm noun **storms**
1 a period of very bad weather with lots of rain and wind and often with thunder and lightning
2 a situation that causes strong feelings in people, for example making them very angry or upset *The head teacher's new rules caused a storm of protest. The celebrity's tweet caused a Twitter storm* (a lot of interest or strong feelings on the Twitter social media website)
3 **a storm in a teacup** used when someone gets angry or worried about something that is not important

storm verb
storms, storming, stormed
1 if people storm a place, they attack it suddenly using violence *The police stormed the building where the gunman was hiding.*
2 to quickly go somewhere with a heavy step and in an angry way *She stormed out of the room.*
3 to shout something in an angry way *'Get out of here!' he stormed.*

stormy adjective **stormier, stormiest**
1 used for describing a time or the weather when there is a lot of rain and wind and often thunder and lightning *a stormy night; November was very stormy.*
2 a stormy sea has lots of big waves because there is a lot of rain and wind
3 if a situation is stormy, people are angry and argue a lot *a stormy meeting*

story noun **stories**
1 a description of events, imaginary or true, that someone writes or tells to entertain people *a book of short stories; an adventure story; Mum read me a bedtime story.*
2 a description of something that happens to someone or of how something happens *Tell my friend the story about when you rode on a camel. This TV programme tells the story of the Battle of Hastings* (is about that subject). *Don't change your story or Dad will get suspicious.*
3 something someone says that is not true, for example an explanation or excuse *He said he couldn't come to my party because he was ill but I don't believe that story. She's always telling stories* (lies).
4 something that lots of people talk about that is often not true *There's a story going round the school that Ms Seymour is leaving.*

SYNONYM rumour

5 a piece of news, for example on TV or in a newspaper *The film star's death was an important news story.*

LANGUAGE EXTRA be careful not to confuse *story* with *storey* (floor in a building)

storyboard noun **storyboards**
a series of drawings or pictures in boxes showing the main events of a story. A storyboard is often used during the planning of a film.

storybook noun **storybooks**
a book of stories for children

storyline noun **storylines**
the main events in a book, film or play that make up the story

SYNONYM plot

storytelling noun
the activity of telling or writing stories
storyteller noun

stout adjective **stouter, stoutest**
1 having a thick heavy body (used sometimes as a polite way of saying fat) *a stout elderly gentleman*
2 thick, heavy and often strong *stout legs; a stout stick*
3 strong and brave *Our teacher put up a stout defence of her opinions.*
stoutly adverb **stoutness** noun

stove noun **stoves**
1 a large piece of equipment with an oven and burners that provide heat for cooking food

SYNONYM cooker

2 a small piece of equipment with one or two burners for cooking food *a camping stove*
3 a large piece of equipment that burns gas, wood or coal, used for heating a room

stow verb
stows, stowing, stowed
1 to put something somewhere until you need it *My sleeping bag is stowed away under my bed.*
2 if someone stows away, for example on a ship, plane or train, they hide somewhere there so that they can travel without paying or because they are running away from something

stowaway noun **stowaways**
someone who stows away, for example on a ship, plane or train

straddle verb
straddles, straddling, straddled
1 to have or put one leg on either side of something *My brother climbed up and straddled his motorbike* (sat with one leg either side of the saddle).
2 to be on both sides of something at the same time *Our village straddles the border between England and Wales.*
3 to go across something *There are many bridges straddling the River Ouse.*

straggle verb
straggles, straggling, straggled
1 to move somewhere slowly in small groups or more slowly than others in a group *In the cross-country race, some runners were straggling a long way behind.*
2 to spread out or grow in an untidy way in different directions *The house was a ruin with ivy straggling up walls and across windows and doors.*

straggler noun **stragglers**
1 a person or animal that does not keep up with the rest of a group *A few stragglers in the marathon still haven't finished.*
2 someone who is one of the last people to leave a place *The party is finished but there are still some stragglers who haven't left.*

straggly adjective **stragglier, straggliest**
growing or spreading in an untidy way *straggly hair*

straight adjective **straighter, straightest**
1 going in one direction like one side of a square and not turning like the edge of a circle *a straight line; Do you prefer curly hair or straight?*

496

2 not leaning over to one side or not having one part or end higher than the other *straight teeth*; *The picture on the wall is crooked – can you put it straight? Your tie isn't straight.*
3 going upwards (or downwards) from a surface like one side of a square *It was a straight drop to the sea. The cliff was almost straight.*
4 not bent, curved or twisted *I was lying on my bed with my legs straight. Dad needs a straight piece of wire to fix the fence.*
5 going exactly to the correct place *It's a straight road from here to Leeds. She gave me a straight punch to the face.*
6 honest and saying what you really think *He gave me a straight answer to a straight question. My older brother is never straight with me.*
7 looking nice and tidy *You have one hour to get your room straight.*
8 correct *When you do your school project, make sure that you get your facts straight* (that your facts are correct). *Let's get this straight – you want to stay at Amy's house overnight?* (Have I understood correctly what you mean?)
9 a straight person is someone who is not gay and who has or wants a love relationship with a person of the opposite sex
10 in maths, a straight angle is an angle of 180 degrees
compare: **acute**, **obtuse** and **reflex**
11 a straight face an expression on your face showing that you're not laughing or smiling *My sister told us a really funny joke with a straight face* (without laughing herself). *We couldn't keep a straight face* (couldn't help laughing).

SIMILE 'as straight as an arrow' means very straight (senses 1, 4 & 6)

straight *adverb*
1 going to a place without stopping anywhere else *I went straight home without popping in to Grandma's house.*
2 going in only one direction to a place, without turning to go in other directions *This road goes straight to Leeds.*
3 in a straight line *Go straight on past the library, then turn right. The school is straight ahead. Straight in front of us was the tallest building we'd ever seen.*
4 immediately *We went swimming straight after school. It's your turn to see the doctor so go straight ahead.*
5 without including anything or anyone else *Mum bought it straight from the factory.*
6 with your body or a part of your body in a position that is not bent or leaning to one side *Sit up straight! Stretch your arms out straight. He was so tired he couldn't walk straight* (he was leaning and looked as if he would fall over).

straightaway *adverb*
right now without any waiting, or at a particular time without any waiting

SYNONYMS at once, immediately

LANGUAGE EXTRA also spelt *straight away*

straighten *verb*
straightens, straightening, straightened
1 to make something straight, for example so that it isn't bent, curved, twisted, leaning to one side or the wrong shape *I sat on the chair and straightened my legs. Can you straighten out this crumpled piece of paper? I go to the orthodontist to get my teeth straightened.*
2 to become straight *The road has a lot of bends in it here but straightens out when it crosses the plain. Straighten up, Chris, you're slouching again!*
3 to make something tidy *Straighten out your room before Dad gets home.*
4 to deal with a problem or confused situation *Our teacher tried to straighten out the muddle.*

straightforward *adjective*
1 easy to do *Downloading this app is straightforward.*
2 easy to understand *He sent me a straightforward text message.*
3 honest and saying what you really think *Can't you give me a straightforward answer?*
straightforwardly *adverb*

strain *verb*
strains, straining, strained
1 to hurt a part of your body such as a muscle or your back by stretching it or using it too much *George had a strained neck. I strained my wrist playing tennis.*
2 to try as hard as you can to do something, for example by pulling or stretching a part of your body *I was straining* (or *straining my neck*) *to see what was going on as there were lots of tall people in front of me. I had to strain my eyes to see the writing on the screen* (for example because the words were too small).
3 if you strain food or liquid, you put it through a strainer or sieve (containers with holes in) to separate the liquid from the solid parts
4 to pull or push very hard *My dog was straining at the lead.*

strain *noun*
1 (*plural* **strains**) an injury to a part of your body such as a muscle or your back, caused by stretching it or using it too much
2 when something such as a weight or force pulls or pushes something and can cause damage to it *The bridge collapsed under the strain* (fell down, for example because of too much traffic on it). *All this exercise puts a lot of strain on the heart.*
3 (*plural* **strains**) used for talking about a difficult situation that causes someone problems and worry, for example because they have too much to do or something that is too hard to do *Can our teacher cope with the strain of having so many boys behaving badly in the class? My brother is tired out under the strain of the exams.*

strainer *noun* **strainers**
a round metal or plastic container with holes in it. It is used in the kitchen for removing solid parts from liquid (for example when making tea with tea leaves) or for removing liquid from food (such as pasta that has been boiled).

strait *noun* **straits**
a narrow area of the sea that joins two large areas of the sea

LANGUAGE EXTRA often used in the plural, for example the *Straits of Gibraltar*

straits *noun plural*
if someone is in dire straits, they are in a very serious situation, usually because they don't have enough money

strand *noun* **strands**
a very thin piece of something such as rope, thread or hair *The sailor was making rope by twisting the strands around each other.*

stranded *adjective*
1 if someone is stranded somewhere, they are stuck there and cannot leave *Because of the bad weather, we were stranded in Glasgow* (for example, the trains, buses and planes were not working).
2 if a ship is stranded, it is stuck on the land or on rocks and cannot move back into the water

strange *adjective* **stranger, strangest**
1 different from what is usual, for example in a way that is surprising or that you don't understand *She had a strange look on her face. It's strange that he hasn't texted yet.*

SYNONYMS odd, unusual

2 used about someone whose behaviour is different and not normal *He's a very strange man.*
3 used about something or someone you don't know or have never seen before *a strange town*; *I saw many strange faces at the party. There's a strange man at the door.*
4 used about a feeling you've never had before *I've got a strange pain in my knee.*
strangeness *noun*

strangely *adverb*
1 in a way that is different from usual *She was behaving rather strangely.*
2 used for saying that something is surprising or is definitely true even though it seems surprising *Strangely enough, once I was in the dentist's chair I wasn't scared any more.*

stranger *noun* **strangers**
1 someone that you don't know
2 someone who is in a place that they don't know or don't know very well *I'm a stranger to Edinburgh.*

strangle *verb*
strangles, strangling, strangled
if someone strangles someone, they kill them by pressing their throat to stop them from breathing **strangler** *noun*
strangulation *noun*

strap *noun* **straps**
1 a long thin piece of material, usually cloth, leather or plastic. You use straps for many different things, for example for holding or carrying something such as a bag or camera, for holding something on your body such as a dress, watch or shoe, or for putting round something such as a suitcase. *a watch strap*; *a shoulder strap* (that goes over your shoulder)
2 an object that hangs from the ceiling of a vehicle such as a train or bus and that you hold on to so that you don't fall

strap *verb*
straps, strapping, strapped
to put a strap or straps round something or someone *Mum strapped the baby into the car seat. Dad strapped the luggage to the roof of the car. Are you strapped in?* (wearing your seat belt, for example in a car)

strategy *noun*
1 (*plural* **strategies**) a plan or plans for doing something important that needs a lot of careful thinking over a long period of time
2 the skill or activity of making important plans, for example in a game of chess or a computer game
strategic *adjective*

stratosphere *noun*
the stratosphere is the air and gases in the atmosphere around the earth, between 10 and 50 kilometres above the earth

stratum ['strah-term'] *noun*
strata ['strah-ter']
in geology, a stratum is a layer of rock or earth

straw *noun*
1 the dry cut yellow stems of some plants that produce grain such as wheat or oats. Straw is used, for example, for making things such as mats and baskets, for giving to animals such as cows to eat or sleep on, and for wrapping around things to protect them. *an old mattress filled with straw; a straw hat*
2 (*plural* **straws**) a long thin tube of plastic or paper that you use for drinking cold drinks by sucking the liquid up into your mouth *He was drinking lemonade through a straw.*
3 **the last straw** or **the final straw** used about another bad thing that someone has just done or that has just happened, which makes someone decide they can no longer put up with a bad situation *This is the seventh day you've behaved badly and that's the last straw – no pocket money for two weeks!*

strawberry *noun* **strawberries**
a small soft red fruit that you eat. It has lots of yellow dots on its skin that look like seeds. Strawberries grow on plants close to the ground.

stray *verb*
strays, straying, strayed
1 if a person or animal strays, they move away from the place where they should be or from the path they should be following *Don't stray too far from the campsite. Your dog has strayed into our garden.*
2 to talk about something different from what you should be talking about *We seem to have strayed from the subject.*
3 to think about something different from what you should be thinking about *I was bored in class and my mind kept straying.*
4 to move somewhere or move about without any real reason *My eyes strayed onto a picture hanging on the wall.*

stray *adjective*
1 used about an animal that is lost and has no home *a stray dog*
2 used about something that is not where it should be *You have a few stray hairs that need combing. A passer-by was accidentally killed by a stray bullet.*

stray *noun* **strays**
an animal, especially a cat or dog, that is lost and has no home

streak *noun* **streaks**
1 a thin mark or line of a different colour from the areas next to it *The singer had streaks of pink in her hair.*
2 used for talking about one particular quality of someone's character, often an unpleasant one *My uncle has a mean streak.*
3 used for talking about the number of times someone wins or loses, for example in a game or sport, when these happen one after the other *Our team had a lucky* (or *winning*) *streak* (for example, won several matches one after the other). *Dad's playing cards and he's on a losing streak.*

streak *verb*
streaks, streaking, streaked
1 to make thin marks or lines of a different colour go onto or into something *cheeks streaked with tears; My dad has black hair streaked with grey. My sister had her hair streaked* (the hairdresser put coloured lines in it using special chemicals).
2 to move somewhere very fast

streaky *adjective* **streakier, streakiest**
1 marked with streaks *streaky windows*
2 streaky bacon is bacon (meat from a pig) with thin lines of fat in it

stream *noun* **streams**
1 a small narrow river
2 used about something that keeps moving or flowing without stopping, for example water in a pipe or traffic on a road *A stream of water was pouring out of the gutter. There's been a steady stream of visitors going into the exhibition.*

stream *verb*
streams, streaming, streamed
1 used about a liquid that flows strongly and without stopping *Tears were streaming down her face. Blood streamed from the soldier's wounded leg.*
2 if people or things stream somewhere, large numbers or amounts of them go there quickly and without stopping *Football fans were streaming out of the stadium. Emails are streaming into the BBC about last night's film. Sally opened the curtains and sunlight came streaming into the room.*
3 if you stream something such as a film, programme or song on your computer, you watch or listen to it straight from the internet instead of downloading it first, or you watch or listen to it at the same time as it is being downloaded *Click on this icon to start streaming the song. Don't disconnect the router – my film is streaming.*

streamer *noun* **streamers**
streamers are long strips of coloured paper used for decoration, for example at a birthday party, or for throwing at people to celebrate something

streamlined *adjective*
if something is streamlined, it has a very smooth shape so that it can move easily through the water or the air *a streamlined submarine*

street *noun* **streets**
1 a road in a town or village with houses, buildings or shops on it, usually on both sides *a busy street; a street map* (map of the streets of a particular town); *I was walking down the street. Sayed lives in York Street.*
2 **down** (or **up** or **along**) **the street** a short distance away in the same street *My uncle lives down the street.*
3 **across the street** on the opposite side of the street
4 (*informal*) **up your street** used about something such as an activity that you know a lot about and that you are interested in

streetcar *noun* **streetcars**
the American word for a tram

streetlight *noun* **streetlights**
a light at the top of a tall post that stands at the side of a street

> LANGUAGE EXTRA you can also say *streetlamp*

strength *noun*
1 the power you have to do things with your body such as lift, move, push and pull heavy things or hit things hard, or the power that a part of your body has to do these things *My sister kicked me with all her strength. The lion killed the antelope because of its greater strength. Look at the strength of the boxer's arms. I didn't have the strength to get up from the chair.*
2 the power something has to move or hold something heavy or to be treated roughly without breaking or getting damaged *We used ropes of great strength to hold down the sails. Because of its strength, the fence didn't fall down in the wind.*
3 having a lot of something such as heat, light, speed or sound *the strength of the sun's rays; the strength of the wind; The boat capsized because of the strength of the current.*
4 the influence that someone or something has *The strength of the Labour Party is mainly in the north of England.*
5 (*plural* **strengths**) a good quality that someone or something has *Being able to run fast is one of David's strengths* (one of the things he's good at). *My new tablet has more strengths than weaknesses.*

strengthen *verb*
strengthens, strengthening, strengthened
1 to make something or someone stronger *Cycling is good for strengthening your leg muscles. If I stay over at Ben's, it will help to strengthen our friendship.*
2 to become stronger *The wind strengthened during the night.*

strenuous *adjective*
needing or showing a lot of hard work and energy *strenuous exercises; They made strenuous efforts* (tried very hard) *to put out the fire.*

strenuously *adverb*
1 in a way that shows you have strong feelings about something *He strenuously denied breaking the window.*

> SYNONYM strongly

2 with a lot of hard work and energy *Dad was exercising strenuously.*

stress *noun*
1 (*plural* **stresses**) great worry caused by having a problem (or problems) in your life, for example too much work or not enough money *My brother has headaches because of the stress of being bullied at school. My mum's under a lot of stress at work* (has lots of problems that make her very worried).
2 (*plural* **stresses**) when you say one part of a word more strongly because that is the correct way to say it, or when you say a whole word more strongly because you want people to take notice of it *In 'computer' you put the stress on the 'u'. 'I LOVE ice cream,' he said, with clear stress on the verb.*

> LANGUAGE EXTRA this dictionary uses **bold** in pronunciations to show when you say part of a word more strongly. For example, ['**roh**-bot'] shows that you say 'roh' more strongly than 'bot'.

3 extra importance given to something *My parents put a lot of stress on eating healthy food.*
4 in science, stress is a force that pushes against something and can change its shape or cause damage to it

stress *verb*
stresses, stressing, stressed
1 to say a part of a word, or a whole word, more strongly *In the word 'fantastic' the second syllable is stressed. 'I did NOT do it,' she said, stressing the 'not'.*
2 to say or mention something strongly because it is especially important *Miss Katz stressed that we must arrive early at school on Tuesday for the trip. Dad stressed the dangers of talking to strangers.*
3 if something stresses you out, or if you're stressed (or stressed out), you feel very worried because of a problem (or problems) in your life

stressful *adjective*
if something is stressful, it causes a lot of worry or is full of problems that make you worried *I had a stressful day at school. Chloe finds school very stressful* (for example because there's too much work).

stretch *verb*
stretches, stretching, stretched
1 if you stretch something, you pull it and make it longer or wider
2 if something stretches, it becomes longer or wider, for example when you pull it
3 to make your body or part of your body straighter and longer *For this exercise you have to stretch* (or *stretch out*) *your arms and legs. I always stretch when I wake up* (make my arms and legs straighter and longer).
4 if you stretch out your hand, for example to reach or take something, you move it away from your body
5 if you stretch your legs, you go for a walk
6 if something stretches somewhere, it continues over a certain distance or goes all the way there *The forest stretched for miles. These hills stretch to the Scottish border.*
7 to continue for a long period of time *My sister's birthday party stretched well into the night.*

stretch *noun* **stretches**
1 the action of stretching *Granddad got out of bed and had a good stretch* (stretched his arms and legs).
2 a period of time that you spend doing something *My brother often spends three hours at a stretch surfing the internet.*
3 an area of land or water *There's fog along some stretches of the motorway.*

stretcher *noun* **stretchers**
a kind of bed for carrying an injured, sick or dead person. Some stretchers are made of a piece of cloth with poles fixed to each side and are carried by two people. Others are made of a thin mattress built on a frame with wheels (called a trolley).

strewn *adjective*
used about things that have been thrown or dropped in lots of different places or about something covered with these things *Toys were strewn all over the floor. The floor was strewn with toys.*

stricken *adjective*
suffering from something such as fear, panic or grief (great sadness) or from an illness or bad situation *Tom was stricken with terror when he saw the bully looking at him. Grandma was stricken with gout.*

-stricken *suffix*
used for making adjectives that describe people or places suffering from something bad such as panic, horror, grief or poverty *horror-stricken; poverty-stricken*

strict *adjective* **stricter, strictest**
1 used about someone who has strong rules about how to behave that they want you to obey and who punishes you if you don't obey *a strict teacher; My parents have never been strict with us.*
2 used about something that you must obey, for example a rule, law or instructions *Discipline in our school is very strict. During the war there were strict controls on what food you could buy.*
3 correct and exact *My mum's a dentist, so she's not a doctor in the strict meaning of the word.*

strictness *noun*

strictly *adverb*
1 in such a way that you must obey someone or something *My cousin was brought up strictly.*
2 used for giving special importance to a word *Throwing things on the pitch during a game is strictly forbidden.*

> SYNONYM **completely**

3 used when you mean one thing only and nothing else *This class is strictly for students learning French.*

> SYNONYM **only**

4 used for talking about the exact meaning of a word when you are trying to be as correct as possible *That's not strictly true* (it's nearly true but not completely). *Strictly speaking, a tomato is a fruit, not a vegetable.*

stride *verb*
strides, striding, strode, stridden
to walk somewhere with long steps, often quickly and with lots of energy *The head teacher strode across the playground.*

stride *noun* **strides**
1 a long step that you take in walking or running
2 to make strides is to make fast progress in something
3 if someone takes something in their stride, they deal with a problem without letting it worry them too much

strife *noun*
fighting or arguing between people or groups

strike *verb*
strikes, striking, struck
1 to hit something or someone *I slipped and my head struck the floor. Someone threw a stone that struck me on the arm. The tree was struck by lightning.*
2 used when talking about something such as an idea that you suddenly think of *When I was on the bus it struck me that I'd left my schoolbag at home.*
3 used when saying that you think of something or someone in a particular way *Your uncle strikes me as being slightly strange. This week's homework strikes me as difficult.*
4 if workers strike, for example people who work in a factory or office, they stop working because they are angry about something such as not being paid enough money
5 if a clock strikes a particular time, it makes a ringing sound a number of times to show what the time is *The clock struck seven* (it rang seven times to show it was seven o'clock).
6 if something bad strikes someone or something, it happens suddenly to them *The next morning, disaster struck.*
7 to attack someone or something suddenly *The soldiers struck at dawn.*
8 to strike a match is to produce a flame by rubbing it against something
9 to strike gold or oil is to find lots of it in the ground
10 to strike something up is to start it, for example a conversation or friendship with someone

strike *noun* **strikes**
1 a period of time when workers stop working because they are angry, for example about not getting enough money or having to work too hard *The whole factory went on strike* (stopped working).
2 an attack by planes, by weapons such as missiles or by soldiers *an air strike* (when bombs are dropped)
3 a hit *a lightning strike*
4 when you find something in the ground such as gold or oil *an oil strike*

striker *noun* **strikers**
1 a worker, for example in a factory or office, who stops working because they are angry about something
2 a player in a team such as a football team whose job is to attack and score goals

striking *adjective*
1 used about something that is very easy to see, for example because it is unusual, big or great *a painting of striking beauty*; *My sister has a striking talent for languages.*
2 looking very attractive, important or interesting, especially in a way that makes you feel great respect *a very striking woman*; *A tall striking figure wearing a soldier's uniform entered the room.*

string *noun* **strings**
1 a long thin material made from fibres (long thin threads) that are twisted together. String is used for tying or holding things. *a ball of string*; *Pull the strings to make the puppets work.*
2 a long thin piece of nylon, wire or other material on a musical instrument such as a guitar, harp or violin. You use the strings for making the sounds. For example, you pull the strings of a guitar or harp with your fingers, and you touch the strings of a violin with a special stick called a bow.
3 a group of things of the same kind, for example that come one after the other *a string of questions*; *A string of taxis arrived at the school.*
4 a group of things joined together, for example on a string *a string of pearls*
5 in an orchestra, the strings are the people who play stringed instruments such as violins or cellos, or they are the instruments themselves

string *verb*
strings, stringing, strung
1 to hang something somewhere with string *Balloons were strung all around the room for my party.*
2 to tie things together with string, for example by putting a string through them *Do you know how to string beads?*
3 to put strings on a musical instrument such as a guitar or violin or on a racket such as a tennis racket
4 to string something out such as a speech or lesson is to make it last longer than it is supposed to
5 if things are strung out, they are spread out, for example in a line *There were plane trees strung out all along the road.*
6 a stringed instrument is a musical instrument that has strings, for example a violin, cello, guitar or banjo

string bean *noun* **string beans**
a long thin green bean that is cooked and eaten as a vegetable

SYNONYM green bean

stringent ['strin-jernt'] *adjective*
used about things such as rules, laws or controls that are very strict and must be obeyed

stringy *adjective* **stringier, stringiest**
1 if food such as meat is stringy, it is difficult to eat because it has lots of long thin hard parts
2 long and thin like a string or strings and usually looking unpleasant *stringy hair*

strip *noun* **strips**
1 a long narrow piece of something or a long narrow area *a strip of cloth*; *He tore the sheet of paper into thin strips. This strip at the top of the computer screen is for the program's menus.*
2 clothes that people in a sports team wear when they are playing. It shows the colours and patterns of their team.
3 a thin layer of magnetic substance, for example on a credit card, for storing information on
short for: **magnetic strip**
4 a comic strip is a series of drawings inside little boxes that tell a funny story, for example in a newspaper

strip *verb*
strips, stripping, stripped
1 to remove the things that cover something *Dad stripped the walls before putting up the new wallpaper. He stripped off the old wallpaper. The hospital strips the beds every day* (removes the bedclothes and puts on new ones).
2 to remove everything from something or somewhere *The caterpillars stripped the trees bare* (for example, ate all the leaves and fruits). *Burglars got into my uncle's house and stripped it* (stole everything).
3 to take your clothes off, or take the clothes off someone *It was so hot Granddad was stripped to the waist* (had no clothes on the top half of his body). *After the match the players strip off and have a shower.*
4 to take something away from someone *They stripped the criminal of his passport.*

stripe *noun* **stripes**
1 a line or long straight area that has a different colour from the areas next to it *A zebra has black and white stripes.*
2 a small strip of cloth that is sewn onto the sleeve of a uniform, for example of a soldier or police officer, for showing his or her rank or position *A sergeant has three V-shaped stripes.*

striped *adjective*
if something is striped, it has a pattern of stripes on it *a striped shirt*

LANGUAGE EXTRA you can also say *stripy* or *stripey*

strive *verb*
strives, striving, strove, striven
to try very hard to do or get something *My brother always strives to please his teacher.*

strobe light *noun* **strobe lights**
a very bright light that flashes quickly on and off or produces a beam (long line) that flashes on and off

strode
past tense of **stride**

stroke *verb*
strokes, stroking, stroked
to move your hand gently over a part of an animal's or person's body such as their hair or head, for example to show your love or to be friendly *Our dog loves to be stroked.*

stroke *noun* **strokes**
1 the action of moving your hand gently over something *Give the cat's head a little stroke.*
2 a particular way of swimming using your hands and legs *The crawl is my favourite stroke.*
3 the action of hitting something, for example hitting the ball in a sport such as tennis
4 a mark or line made with a brush, pen or pencil, or the action of moving a brush, pen or pencil to do this
5 a ringing sound made by a clock to show the hours *They arrived at the stroke of ten* (at exactly ten o'clock).
6 a sudden serious illness caused by blood not reaching the brain properly because a blood vessel (narrow tube) is blocked or has burst. It often makes people unable to speak or unable to move all or part of their body.
7 **a stroke of luck** a lucky event that happens to someone

stroll *verb*
strolls, strolling, strolled
to walk slowly in a very relaxing way *I was strolling along enjoying the warm sunshine.*

stroll *noun* **strolls**
a slow and relaxing walk

stroller *noun* **strollers**
the American word for a pushchair

strong *adjective* **stronger, strongest**
1 if a person or animal is strong, they have the power to do things with their body such as lift, move, push and pull heavy things or hit things hard *Granddad is old but strong. Footballers need strong legs* (for example for kicking the ball or running fast).
2 if something is strong, it has the power to move or hold something heavy or to be treated roughly without breaking or getting damaged *a strong rope*; *a strong fence*; *This plastic is very strong.*
3 done with a lot of power *a strong kick*; *Give the rope a strong pull.*
4 used for showing that someone has a lot of something or that there is a lot of something *Ben is dyslexic and gets strong support from his teacher. The artist uses strong colours* (for example reds, blues and greens with a lot of colour in them so they are bright or dark). *Alain has a strong French accent* (one that you can easily hear).
5 having a lot of heat, light, speed, sound or energy *a strong current* (with water flowing fast); *a strong explosion* (very loud); *a strong signal*; *strong winds*; *The sun's rays were strong* (very hot). *The light's too strong* (there's too much light).
6 having a lot of taste, flavour or smell *a strong taste of salt* (you can taste the salt very easily); *a strong smell of fish* (you can smell the fish very easily); *a strong tea* (you can taste the tea easily, for example because there is not much milk)
7 having the power to influence lots of people, actions and events *a strong leader*; *The head teacher took strong measures to deal with the problem.*
8 having a great effect on someone *a strong medicine*; *These are strong words* (for example bad things said in an angry way). *The film uses strong language* (rude words). *The bully received a strong punishment* (one that made him or her suffer badly).
9 used for showing that something or someone is extremely good, successful and

stronghold–stuck

of a high standard *Our school has a strong football team with four or five very strong players. The actors gave a strong performance. Always choose a strong password* (one that is difficult to guess).
10 used about something that is based on sensible and intelligent ideas *That's a strong argument for wearing a seat belt. I didn't have a strong reason to say no.*
11 used about something that is very likely to happen *There's a strong chance I'll be staying over at Harry's on Saturday.*
12 used for showing how many people or animals there are in a group, especially when you think there are a lot of them *The crowd was about 200 strong.*
13 used about something that someone thinks deeply about and believes a lot, for example something that is very special and important to them *I have a strong belief in friendship. My brother has a strong opinion about his new teacher* (for example, he thinks the teacher is very good or very bad and he won't change his mind).
14 strong feelings are feelings such as anger, excitement, sadness, love and hatred that people feel very deeply *When the footballer missed the goal, the crowd shouted insults to show their strong feelings* (for example anger and disappointment). *Grandma and Granddad have strong feelings for each other* (they love each other very much).
15 a strong point is a good quality that someone or something has
16 going strong used about something that is still good, successful or working well, or about someone who is still healthy, successful or doing well

SIMILE 'as strong as an ox' means very strong (sense 1)

stronghold *noun* **strongholds**
a place or strongly built building that can be defended against enemies who attack

strongly *adverb*
1 used for showing that you believe something very much or for saying that something is definitely true *I strongly believe* (or *I feel strongly*) *that you're wrong. Jack strongly denied breaking the window.*
2 used as a way of saying 'very much' or of giving special importance to a word *This pasta tastes strongly of garlic. I strongly recommend you pay more attention in class. My parents are strongly opposed to the new head teacher. 'I LOVE ice cream,' I replied, saying the verb strongly so that Dad would take notice.*
3 using the strength of your body *She hit the ball strongly.*
4 used about something that is made or built in a way that shows it is strong and not easily broken or damaged *a strongly built house; The chair was strongly padded with thick foam.*
5 used for showing that someone has a big strong body *Dave is strongly built.*
6 extremely well and successfully *The team performed very strongly. Mum's tomato plants are growing strongly.*

stroppy *adjective* **stroppier, stroppiest** (informal)
angry and very unpleasant to other people

strove
past tense of **strive**

struck
past tense & past participle of **strike**

structure *noun* **structures**
1 something that is made, built or organised using different parts, for example a building, monument or bridge *A pier is a narrow structure built out into the sea.*
2 the way in which the parts of something are put together and organised *the structure of the brain; Miss Roberts talked about the structure of the poem.*
structural *adjective* **structurally** *adverb*

structure *verb*
structures, structuring, structured
to organise something *The lesson was well structured.*

strudel ['stroo-derl'] *noun* **strudels**
a cake made from pieces of fruit rolled up in layers of pastry (flour, water and fat) and baked in an oven *an apple strudel*

struggle *noun* **struggles**
1 a fight, for example one in which someone tries to get away from someone else
2 something that you try very hard to do, get or stop *It was a struggle just to get out of bed. Maths is a real struggle* (very hard) *for some pupils. The story told of a struggle for good against evil.*

struggle *verb*
struggles, struggling, struggled
1 to try very hard to do something difficult *I'm struggling to finish my homework before tomorrow. Chloe is struggling with her maths* (finds maths very hard). *Ben has been struggling all term* (trying very hard to make progress).
2 to try very hard to stop something bad or to get something you want *He struggled with illness and depression all his life. We were struggling for breath.*
3 to have a lot of trouble moving your body or moving something *Granddad often has to struggle up the stairs. Help me – I'm struggling with these heavy boxes.*
4 to fight someone, for example to get away from them *The bully jumped on me but I managed to struggle free.*

struggling *adjective*
used for describing someone who has problems, especially someone who doesn't have enough money *My mum's a struggling author.*

strum *verb*
strums, strumming, strummed
if you strum an instrument such as a guitar, you move your fingers or a plectrum (flat piece of plastic) across some or all of the strings

strung
past tense & past participle of **string**

strut *verb*
struts, strutting, strutted
to walk around looking as if you're more important than other people

strut *noun* **struts**
a long piece of wood or metal for supporting something such as a part of a building

stub *verb*
stubs, stubbing, stubbed
1 if you stub your toe, you hurt it by accidentally hitting it against something hard
2 to stub out a cigarette or cigar is to make it stop burning by pressing the end of it against something hard

stub *noun* **stubs**
1 the part of something such as a pencil, candle or cigarette that is left over after the rest is used or has burnt
2 the part of a ticket that you keep after giving the main part to someone

stubble *noun*
1 the short hairs that grow on a man's face when he doesn't shave for a few days
2 the short stems of plants such as wheat or barley left in the ground after the plants have been cut

stubborn *adjective*
1 if someone is stubborn, they have an idea in their mind about something they really want to do (or something they really don't want to do) and nothing will make them change their mind or behave in a different way
2 also used about someone's actions and feelings *She had a stubborn look on her face. It was a stubborn refusal to accept the results.*

SYNONYM obstinate

3 difficult to get rid of *a stubborn cough*
stubbornness *noun*

SIMILE 'as stubborn as a mule' means very stubborn (sense 1)

stubbornly *adverb*
in a way that shows nothing will make someone change their mind and behave in a different way *She stubbornly refused to say sorry.*

stuck
past tense & past participle of **stick**

stuck *adjective*
1 fixed in one position and not able to move or be moved *The window's stuck. I got stuck trying to get through a hole in the fence. Be careful not to get your finger stuck in the drawer* (hurt as you close the drawer).
2 in an unpleasant situation that you can't escape from *stuck in traffic* (in a vehicle that doesn't move much because of so much traffic); *I've been stuck in bed with flu all day. Tom was stuck doing the washing-up* (had to do it even though he didn't want to). *I got stuck with boring Uncle Alan* (had to be with him even though I didn't want to).
3 not able to continue or make progress because of a problem or because you don't understand something *I don't know what to do in my maths homework – I'm really stuck. When I was reading 'The Hobbit', I got stuck on some long words* (I didn't know what they meant).

501

stuck-up – stupidly

stuck-up *adjective* (informal)
someone who is stuck-up thinks they are more important than other people and has no respect for them

stud *noun* **studs**
1 a small piece of metal jewellery that someone wears through a small hole made in a part of their body such as their ear or nose *stud earrings*
2 a small piece of metal fixed to something, especially to cloth or leather as a decoration
3 one of the small pieces of plastic, rubber or metal at the bottom of something such as a football boot or running shoe to stop you from slipping

studded *adjective*
1 decorated with studs *a studded belt*
2 if something is studded with things, there are lots of them everywhere *The sky was studded with stars.*

student *noun* **students**
someone who is being taught in a school or university

studio *noun* **studios**
1 a room where people make radio or TV programmes and where they broadcast these programmes from
2 a room where people record music
3 a place where people make films or a company that makes films
4 a room where a painter, photographer or sculptor works

studious ['styoo-dee-ers'] *adjective*
used for describing someone who spends a lot of time reading and studying in a very careful way **studiously** *adverb*

study *verb*
studies, studying, studied
1 to learn a subject or subjects (or learn about a subject or subjects), usually by reading yourself or when someone else teaches you *I'm studying French at school and the violin at home. We're studying the English Civil War. My sister studies in Edinburgh* (goes to a school or university there). *My brother is studying hard* (he spends a lot of time learning). *Some pupils were studying quietly in the library* (for example, they were reading or doing their homework).
2 to try to learn and understand things, for example by examining something carefully *The doctors studied Granddad's X-rays. To understand chimpanzees you have to study their behaviour.*

study *noun* **studies**
1 the activity of learning (or learning about) a subject or subjects *Maths is the study of numbers. After lunch there was a period of quiet study. My sister's studies are very hard* (the work she has to do, for example at college).
2 a room for doing quiet work such as reading, writing or working on a computer
3 an office *The head teacher called us into her study.*

stuff *noun* (informal)
used when you mean any thing or things without saying exactly what it is or what they are *What's that sticky stuff* (substance) *on your shirt? Put your school stuff* (belongings) *down in the corner. I have lots of stuff* (work) *to do. Ms Maynard wrote some stuff* (words) *on the whiteboard. If your order hasn't arrived, go to 'Where's my stuff?'* (goods ordered online)

stuff *verb*
stuffs, stuffing, stuffed
1 to fill something completely *Granddad's pockets were stuffed with tissues.*
2 to fill meat such as a turkey or a vegetable such as a pepper with other food before cooking it *stuffed peppers*
3 to push something into something else, usually quickly or carelessly *She stuffed the money into her bag and ran out. Don't stuff the whole sandwich in your mouth at once.*
4 (informal) if you stuff yourself, you eat lots of food
5 if you are stuffed up or if your nose is stuffed up, your nose is blocked and you have trouble breathing because you have a cold *Have you got a stuffed-up nose?*

stuffing *noun*
1 soft material used for filling something such as a cushion, mattress or toy
2 food such as bread, onions and herbs cut into small pieces. It is put inside meat such as turkeys or vegetables such as peppers before cooking them.

stuffy *adjective* **stuffier, stuffiest**
1 if a room or building is stuffy, it is too warm or hot because there is no fresh air
2 if someone is stuffy, they are old-fashioned, boring or too serious
3 if your nose is stuffy, it is blocked and you have trouble breathing because you have a cold
stuffily *adverb* **stuffiness** *noun*

stumble *verb*
stumbles, stumbling, stumbled
1 to lose your balance and fall or start to fall when walking or running *I stumbled over a piece of tree root* (hit my foot on it and fell or nearly fell).
2 to walk with difficulty, nearly falling
3 to make a mistake (or mistakes) when speaking or reading aloud *Naomi stumbled over some difficult words.*
4 to stumble across someone or something is to meet someone or find something by chance

stump *noun* **stumps**
1 the part of something that is left after most of it has been removed *a tree stump*
2 in cricket, a stump is one of the three upright wooden sticks of the wicket, used for throwing the ball at

stump *verb*
stumps, stumping, stumped
if you are stumped by something such as a question or problem, it is too difficult for you to answer or solve

stun *verb*
stuns, stunning, stunned
1 to make someone feel surprised and shocked, for example when talking about something bad *The news of the accident stunned the whole class. I was stunned when I heard the news.*
2 to make someone feel surprised and amazed, for example when talking about something good, big or beautiful *Her brilliant acting stunned the whole audience. We were stunned by the size and beauty of the building.*
3 to make someone unconscious for a short period, usually by hitting them on the head

stung
past tense & past participle of **sting**

stunk
past tense & past participle of **stink**. In the past tense, you can also say 'stank'.

stunning *adjective*
1 beautiful *You look stunning in that dress.*
2 really good *a stunning performance; a stunning stroke of luck*
3 really great or large *a stunning effort; a stunning victory*
4 really surprising *It's a stunning fact that some pupils never eat breakfast.*

stunningly *adverb*
1 extremely *stunningly beautiful; You played stunningly well yesterday.*
2 extremely well *She danced absolutely stunningly.*
3 in a way that is surprising *He's stunningly tall for his age.*

stunt *noun* **stunts**
1 a dangerous action that someone does that needs a lot of skill. A stunt is usually done by someone in a film.
2 an interesting or unusual action that someone does to attract people's attention *a publicity stunt*

stupendous *adjective*
1 really large or great *a stupendous amount of money; a stupendous effort*
2 really good *a stupendous performance; stupendous news*
3 very attractive *You look stupendous in your new outfit.*
stupendously *adverb*

stupid *adjective* **stupider, stupidest**
1 if someone is stupid, they are not very clever and don't think carefully about things or make good decisions and judgements *I was stupid to believe what he said.*
2 used about someone's actions, ideas or judgements to show they are not very clever or good *a stupid mistake; Going out without a coat in this weather is stupid.*
3 slow to learn and understand things *I know what you're up to – I'm not stupid.*
4 feeling or looking uncomfortable and awkward, or likely to make someone feel or look this way *I look stupid in these shoes. What a stupid hat!*
5 used for describing an unpleasant expression on someone's face that seems to show no intelligence *He said he didn't understand and gave me one of his stupid looks.*
6 used for describing something that annoys you or something that you think is not very serious, important or useful *Take your stupid hands out of your pockets! I can't fit all my books in that stupid little bookcase!*

stupidity *noun*

stupidly *adverb*
1 in a stupid way *Fran always behaves stupidly at parties.*
2 used for saying that you've done something stupid *Stupidly, I walked into the wrong classroom.*

sturdy–submissive

sturdy adjective sturdier, sturdiest
1 strong and not likely to break or be damaged easily *a sturdy pair of boots*; *a sturdy fence*
2 strong and healthy *sturdy legs*; *Great-Granddad is 90 but very sturdy.*
sturdily adverb **sturdiness** noun

SIMILE 'as sturdy as an oak' means very sturdy (sense 2)

stutter verb
stutters, stuttering, stuttered
to repeat the sounds of some words lots of times as you speak, for example because you are nervous or have a medical problem

SYNONYM to stammer

stutter noun
a problem in speaking that makes you repeat the sounds of words *Jo has a bad stutter.*

SYNONYM stammer

St Valentine's Day noun
St Valentine's Days
a special day (14 February) when people give cards and presents to people they have (or would like to have) a love relationship with

sty noun sties
a place on a farm where pigs live

sty or **stye** noun sties or styes
a small painful swelling on your eyelid (skin above and below your eyes) caused by an infection

style noun styles
1 a special way of doing something that someone or something has or that you see at a particular time or place *Picasso's style of painting*; *Roald Dahl's style of writing*; *The Gothic style of building was common in the 16th century.*
2 the way something is made or designed and how it looks *Do you like this style of shoe? The styles of mobile phones have started to change this year.*
3 another way of saying fashion *These jeans are the latest style. Long hair isn't in style now.*
4 another word for hairstyle (the way your hair is cut and shaped)
5 a special quality that someone has when they are attractive, well-dressed and behave in a pleasing and controlled way
6 a special quality that something has when it is attractive, fashionable and of a high standard *This hotel has real style.*
7 one of the female parts of a plant. The style is a stalk that grows from the ovary (part that produces seeds).
8 **in style** in a big and important way, for example when doing something or going somewhere *Granddad celebrated his birthday in style* (for example in a fashionable place with lots of expensive food). *Ollie likes travelling in style* (for example in great comfort).

style verb
styles, styling, styled
to shape something in a particular way to make it look attractive *My big sister has had her hair styled.*

stylish adjective
1 fashionable and attractive *a stylish pair of jeans*; *Grandma has always been a very stylish person.*
2 of high quality *The captain of the team did some very stylish playing.*
stylishly adverb

stylus noun styluses
an object shaped like a pen that you use with a computer for selecting information on the screen or for putting information into the computer

sub- prefix
used with nouns and adjectives to mean below or under *sub-zero temperatures* (below zero); *submarine* (under the water); *subway* (under the ground)

subcontinent noun subcontinents
a large area of land that is part of a continent and is made up of different countries *the Indian subcontinent*

subdivide verb
subdivides, subdividing, subdivided
to divide something into smaller parts *The book is divided into chapters and each chapter is subdivided into sections.*
subdivision noun

subdue verb
subdues, subduing, subdued
1 to control (or start to control) a person or group *Many police officers were needed to subdue the crowd. It took three teachers to subdue the bully* (by holding him or her down).
2 to stop something such as a feeling from happening by controlling it *Dad was trying to subdue his anger.*

subdued adjective
1 if someone is subdued, they are quieter than usual, for example because they are worried or sad
2 not very bright *subdued colours*; *a subdued light*
3 not very loud *subdued voices*

subheading noun subheadings
a word or words in a piece of writing such as a section of a book, used for describing what that part of it is about. A subheading is used when the piece of writing already has a main heading and needs to be divided into smaller parts.

LANGUAGE EXTRA also spelt sub-heading

subject ['sub-jekt] noun subjects
1 one of the areas of knowledge such as English, maths or science that you are taught, for example at school
2 what someone talks about or what they write about, for example in a story or letter *Our teacher spoke about the subject of road safety. Simon wanted to change the subject* (talk about something else). *Let's drop the subject* (stop talking about something completely).
3 the main thing, person or idea in a painting or photo
4 someone who lives in a country ruled by a king or queen *a British subject*
5 in grammar, the subject of a verb is the noun or pronoun that does the action of the verb, for example 'Emily' in 'Emily helped me' or 'I' in 'I heard a noise'
compare: **object** (sense 4)

subject ['serb-jekt] verb
subjects, subjecting, subjected
1 to subject someone to something is to make them experience something unpleasant *The prisoners were subjected to a lot of cruelty. Sorry to subject you to such a long wait.*
2 to subject something to something is to make something happen to it *All new medicines are subjected to years of testing.*

subjective adjective
1 showing that you are influenced by your own feelings and ideas and not by facts. Objective means not influenced by feelings or ideas but only by facts. *Write a few words about your family and try not to be too subjective.*
2 existing in your mind only *subjective feelings*
subjectively adverb **subjectivity** noun

subject line noun subject lines
the place in an email where you write what the email is about

subject matter noun
what someone writes about, for example in a book, article or email, or what someone talks about, for example in a conversation or speech

subject to ['sub-jekt] preposition
1 in a way that depends on something *Our trip to the seaside is subject to the weather being fine.*
2 in a way that is affected by something *These plans are subject to change* (they can change).
3 likely to suffer from something *I'm especially subject to colds in the winter.*

subjunctive noun subjunctives
in grammar, a particular form of a verb used for expressing a wish ('I wish I were taller') or for talking about a situation that you don't think will happen ('if I were taller'). The verb 'were' instead of 'was' in these examples is in the subjunctive (or subjunctive form).

submarine ['sub-mer-reen'] noun submarines
a ship with a long smooth shape that travels under the surface of the sea
submariner ['sub-ma-rin-er'] noun

submerge verb
submerges, submerging, submerged
1 if something such as a submarine submerges, it goes completely under the surface of some water
2 to submerge something is to put it completely under the surface of some water or another liquid *Floods have submerged large parts of the countryside. Most of the land around the village is submerged.*

submission noun
1 (plural **submissions**) something such as a document that someone gives or sends to someone for them to look at
2 the action of submitting something *Friday is the deadline for submission of homework.*
3 when a person or group obeys someone and allows themselves to be controlled by them

submissive adjective
if someone is submissive, they do what they are told to do and allow themselves to be controlled easily

503

submit–suburb

submit *verb*
submits, submitting, submitted
1 to give or send something to someone for them to look at and make a decision about *You should submit your homework by Monday. My brother has submitted an application for a new job.*
2 if someone submits to something, they accept it or allow it to happen to them even though they don't want to *At the airport we had to submit to a body search.*
3 if a person or group submits to someone such as an enemy, they obey them and allow themselves to be controlled by them

subordinate ['ser-bor-din-ert'] *adjective*
not as important as something or someone else, for example in a job or group *a subordinate officer in the army; a subordinate role; In Britain, Parliament is not subordinate to the king or queen.*

subordinate ['ser-bor-din-ert'] *noun*
subordinates
someone who is not as important as someone else

subordinate ['ser-bor-din-ayt'] *verb*
subordinates, subordinating, subordinated
to consider something or someone as less important than something or someone else
subordination *noun*

subordinate clause *noun*
subordinate clauses
a part of a sentence that does not make sense by itself because it is not a complete sentence. For example, in the sentence 'I love playing outside when it snows', the subordinate clause is 'when it snows'.
compare: **main clause**

subscribe *verb*
subscribes, subscribing, subscribed
1 if someone subscribes to a product such as a magazine or to a service such as a TV channel or phone line, they pay money to receive it regularly or to be able to use it
2 if someone subscribes to a group or club, they pay money to be a member
3 if someone subscribes to something on the internet, they give their name and email address to someone in order to receive messages or to be able to download software *Click here to subscribe and receive daily emails. Visit the BBC website to subscribe to the podcast.*
compare: **unsubscribe**

subscriber *noun* subscribers
someone who pays money to receive something such as a product or service *phone and broadband subscribers*

subscription *noun* subscriptions
1 money that someone pays to receive something such as a product or service or to be a member of a club or group *Broadband subscription charges have gone up.*
2 an agreement someone makes to pay this money *It's time to renew your magazine subscription.*

subsection *noun* subsections
one of the smaller parts that the main parts (or sections) of something are divided into, especially a document or book. A subsection usually has a subheading (a word or words describing what that part is about).

LANGUAGE EXTRA also spelt *sub-section*

subsequent *adjective*
used about something that comes after or is later than something else *The author corrected these mistakes in a subsequent book.*

ANTONYM previous

subsequently *adverb*
used for talking about the time after the present time or after a particular time in the past *My dad was a bus driver but subsequently became a teacher.*

ANTONYM previously

subset *noun* subsets
in maths, a subset is a set (group of similar things) contained in another set

subside *verb*
subsides, subsiding, subsided
1 to become less or less strong *The wind has subsided. The noise gradually subsided. The flood waters have begun to subside* (go lower).
2 if a building subsides, it slowly sinks into the ground

subsidise *verb*
subsidises, subsidising, subsidised
1 to pay a part of the cost of a product or service so that people pay less for it when it is sold *The school subsidises meals in the canteen so they are cheaper now. Travel on the buses and trains is subsidised by the government.*
2 to pay a subsidy to a person or group *The government subsidises farmers but not artists or writers.*

LANGUAGE EXTRA also spelt *subsidize*

subsidy *noun* subsidies
money that a government or organisation gives to a person or group to help them provide their products or services and to make the price of the products or services lower for the public

substance *noun*
1 (*plural* **substances**) any kind of liquid, solid, powder or gas with particular qualities *a sticky substance; Concrete is a hard substance for building things. Your stomach changes food into substances your body can use.*
2 the most important part of something such as what someone says or writes *That was the substance of his email.*

substandard *adjective*
used about something that is of bad quality and not as good as it should be *Megan's work this term has been substandard.*

substantial *adjective*
1 used when you mean a lot of something or something very large *a substantial amount of money; a substantial size; The cat was in substantial pain. The meal was substantial* (there was a lot of food).
2 used when you mean a large number of things *My brother has substantial problems with his reading.*
3 important *'Mona Lisa' is a substantial painting by Leonardo da Vinci.*
4 strongly built *This table seems fairly substantial.*

substantially *adverb*
1 a lot *The weather is substantially cooler today. My little brother has grown substantially.*
2 mainly or almost completely *These two words mean substantially the same thing. The details are substantially correct.*

substitute *verb*
substitutes, substituting, substituted
1 to use something or someone instead of something or someone else *If you don't want to make the cake with butter, you can always substitute margarine.*
2 to get rid of something and put something different in its place *I substituted Seema's name for mine on the list* (got rid of my name and put Seema's instead).
3 if someone substitutes for someone else, they do their job or work for a period of time *Who will substitute for Mrs Turner when she's on maternity leave?*
substitution *noun*

substitute *noun* substitutes
1 something used instead of something else
2 someone who does someone else's job or work for a period of time *a substitute teacher*
3 a player in a team who takes the place of another player during a match

subtitles *noun plural*
the words people speak in a film or TV programme that are translated into a different language at the bottom of the screen or written there for people who cannot hear or have trouble hearing *a French film with English subtitles*

subtle ['sut-erl'] *adjective* subtler, subtlest
1 not easy to see, hear, smell or taste and hard to describe *a subtle difference* (slight but important); *a subtle taste of vanilla* (not strong but noticeable); *The blues of the painting were quite subtle* (not bright and with only slight differences between them).
2 not showing what you mean in an obvious or direct way but in a way that shows you pay attention to small details *He's a very subtle comedian* (uses words very cleverly, for example with hidden meanings). *His jokes are subtle. I gave him a subtle reminder about the money he owed me* (I did not mention money to him directly).
3 organised in a clever way and with attention to small details *a subtle plan*
subtly *adverb* **subtlety** *noun*

subtotal *noun* subtotals
an amount you get by adding some numbers together. You add another number (or other numbers) to it to get the total.

subtract *verb*
subtracts, subtracting, subtracted
to take one number away from another number *If you subtract five from twenty, you get fifteen* (20 − 5 = 15).

subtraction *noun* subtractions
the action or result of taking one number away from another number in maths

suburb *noun* suburbs
an area outside the centre of a town, or a part of a town away from the centre, with lots of houses where people live *Edgware is a suburb of London. We live in the suburbs.*

504

suburban – suffer

suburban *adjective*
used about something that is in or connected with the suburbs of a town *a big suburban house; a map of suburban Leeds*

subway *noun* **subways**
1 a tunnel under the ground, usually under a street, used by people for walking through
2 the American word for a railway that goes under the ground, usually in a big town. The usual British English word is 'underground'.

succeed *verb*
succeeds, succeeding, succeeded
1 to do or get something you wanted to do or get *I'm happy because I've succeeded in learning my times tables. Jo succeeded in getting good marks this time.*

ANTONYM to fail

2 to do something well or be good at something, for example in school or in a job or activity *I've been trying to learn the violin but I'm not really succeeding.*
3 if something succeeds, what you wanted to happen does happen, for example it produces good results or does what it is supposed to do very well *Our plans have succeeded. The author's second book didn't succeed as well as the first one* (for example, it was less popular).

ANTONYM to fail

4 to come after someone and take their place in an important job or position *Queen Elizabeth II succeeded George VI.*

success *noun*
1 a situation in which someone is successful in doing or getting something they wanted or in which someone does something well *Our talks ended in success. I've been trying to learn the violin but I haven't had much success. They sent me a card to wish me success in my exam.*
2 (*plural* **successes**) someone or something that is successful *As a writer and artist, Beatrix Potter was a great success* (was very popular and made lots of money). *The talks were a success* (produced good results).

ANTONYM failure

successful *adjective*
1 used for showing that something that happens is what you wanted to happen or that something you get is what you wanted to get *Our team was hoping to beat yours and we were successful. My brother was successful in his exams* (he got the good results he wanted).
2 used for showing that you do something well or are good at something *Oliver hasn't been as successful in his schoolwork as the other boys. My mum is a successful teacher* (a very good teacher who cares about her students). *My aunt is a successful businesswoman* (she makes lots of money). *My brother sings in a successful band* (a famous band).
3 used for describing something that produces good results or does what it is supposed to do very well *a successful plan; a successful film* (popular and making a lot of money); *The computer updates were successful* (correctly installed).

successfully *adverb*
1 in a way that shows that something that happens is what you wanted to happen or something you get is what you wanted to get *I successfully got rid of the ink stains. Mum successfully dealt with the problem* (she solved the problem as she wanted to do).
2 in a way that shows that you do something well or are good at something *Dad has been teaching successfully for years.*
3 in a way that shows that something does what it is supposed to do very well *The plane landed successfully* (correctly and properly).

succession *noun*
1 (*plural* **successions**) a number of things or people coming one after another *Our school has had a succession of different head teachers. We've had six rainy days in succession.*
2 when someone such as a king or leader comes after someone and takes their place *He is third in order of succession to the British throne.*

successive *adjective*
coming immediately one after the other *three successive wins; Our class won the school quiz for the third successive year.*
successively *adverb*

successor *noun* **successors**
1 a person who comes after someone and takes their place in an important job or position *Who will be the successor to Miss Williams as head teacher?*
2 something that comes after something else *This computer is fast but its successor will be even faster.*

ANTONYM predecessor

succulent *adjective*
if food is succulent, it tastes good and is juicy *a succulent pear*

such *adjective*
1 used when you mean something or someone of that kind or of the same kind *I've never done such a thing before. Have you ever seen such a tall building? In our school there is no such teacher as Ms Parker* (no teacher of that name).
2 another way of giving special importance to a word, for example when you mean very or very much *I forgot my schoolbag as I was in such a hurry* (I was hurrying very much). *It was such a windy day* (a very windy day). *That's such a shame* (a very great shame). *Your parents are such kind people* (very kind people).
3 **such as** used for giving an example or for showing something or someone of the same kind *You use a bat for hitting the ball in games such as cricket and table tennis. A chance such as this won't happen again.*

SYNONYM like

4 **such and such** used when you mean a certain thing without saying exactly what it is *She told me to arrive at such and such a time and not be late.*

suck *verb*
sucks, sucking, sucked
1 to suck a liquid is to take it into your mouth by breathing inwards *I was sucking orange juice through a straw.*
2 to move something about in your mouth, or to put or have something in your mouth and pull on it with your tongue and lips *I was sucking a sweet. My baby brother sucks his thumb.*
3 if air or water sucks something or someone somewhere, for example into or out of something, it pulls them with great force *Dad's £10 note got sucked into the hoover. I was almost sucked under the boat by the current. A vacuum cleaner uses air to suck up the dust and dirt.*
4 (*slang*) used when someone thinks that something or someone is really bad *My brother says school sucks! I really suck at computer games* (I'm bad at them).
suck *noun*

suction *noun*
1 the force that pulls something into a space when air or liquid is removed
2 the force that makes two surfaces stick together when air is removed between them
3 a suction cup or pad is a circular piece of rubber that you press onto a surface to remove the air. It is usually used for sticking on a surface, for example to hold something there.

Sudan *noun*
a country in North-East Africa
Sudanese *adjective & noun*

sudden *adjective*
1 if something is sudden, it happens quickly and without any warning that it is going to happen *None of us were expecting such a sudden change in the weather.*
2 **all of a sudden** suddenly
suddenness *noun*

suddenly *adverb*
happening without any warning and often quickly *He suddenly stopped talking. It all happened suddenly.*

suds *noun plural*
bubbles that you make when you mix soap and water **sudsy** *adjective*

sue *verb*
sues, suing, sued
if someone sues someone, they ask a court of law to decide whether that person should pay them money because they say that person has done something bad to them

suede ['swayd'] *noun*
leather with a surface that is soft and slightly rough, often used for making shoes or jackets

ORIGIN from the French word *Suède* 'Sweden', because gloves made from suede material first came from Sweden

suffer *verb*
suffers, suffering, suffered
1 if a person or animal suffers, they feel pain in their body or mind *I have a headache and I'm suffering badly. The cat died but suffered no pain.*
2 to have something wrong with you *I'm suffering from a cold.*

505

suffering–summon

3 used for talking about something bad that happens to you *You'll really suffer if you miss too much school. Our team suffered a few problems last year.*
4 to become worse *My brother's schoolwork has suffered this term.*
sufferer *noun*

suffering *noun*
1 great pain that a person or animal feels in their body or mind
2 great problems that cause unhappiness *The floods caused suffering to local people.*

sufficient *adjective*
as much or as many as needed *I didn't have sufficient time to answer all the questions.*

SYNONYM enough

sufficiently *adverb*
as much as needed *You've studied sufficiently today.*

SYNONYM enough

suffix *noun* **suffixes**
in grammar, a suffix is a part added to the end of a word to change its meaning and make a new word. For example, '-ly' can be added to 'pleasant' to make 'pleasantly'.
compare: **affix** and **prefix**

suffocate *verb*
suffocates, suffocating, suffocated
1 to die because there isn't enough air to breathe
2 to feel bad because you have trouble breathing
3 to make it difficult for someone to breathe or to kill someone by stopping them from breathing *The fumes were suffocating us. It's suffocating in here.*
suffocation *noun*

sugar *noun*
1 a sweet substance made up of tiny white or brown pieces, used for making food or drinks taste sweeter. It is produced from sugar cane (the hollow stem of a plant) or sugar beet (a plant that grows under the ground).
2 (*plural* **sugars**) an amount of sugar in a teaspoon or a lump of sugar *How many sugars do you take in your coffee?*
3 a sugar cube or sugar lump is a small hard cube (shape with six square sides) made from pieces of sugar, used for putting in hot drinks such as tea

sugary *adjective*
if food is sugary, it tastes sweet from sugar

suggest *verb*
suggests, suggesting, suggested
1 to mention something such as an idea, plan or action for someone to think about as a possible thing to do *I suggest we go to the park.*
2 to tell someone about something or someone that you think is good, or to tell someone to do something that you think is good *Could you suggest a good book to read? I suggest you help me do the washing-up.*
3 to make someone think that something is true *His name suggests that he's French.*

suggestion *noun*
1 (*plural* **suggestions**) something that you mention such as an idea, plan or action for someone to think about

2 (*plural* **suggestions**) something or someone that you think is good and that you tell someone about *'Stig of the Dump' by Clive King would be my suggestion.*
3 a reason to think that something is true *Was there any suggestion that Jack was to blame?*
4 a small amount of something

suicidal *adjective*
if someone is suicidal, they want to kill themselves

suicide *noun* **suicides**
the action of a person who kills himself or herself deliberately *The police thought he had committed suicide* (killed himself).

suit *noun* **suits**
1 clothes made from the same cloth and worn together, such as a jacket and trousers, sometimes including a waistcoat, or a jacket and skirt
2 a piece of clothing used for a particular activity *a diving suit; a ski suit*
3 one of the four groups that the 52 playing cards of a pack are divided into. The four suits are called hearts, diamonds, spades and clubs.

suit *verb*
suits, suiting, suited
1 to be right or good for someone or something *This weather suits us very well. Mum bought a bigger car to suit our needs.*
2 to make someone look good *That skirt suits you.*

suitable *adjective*
used about something that is right or good for someone or for a particular purpose *Come and see me at midday if that's suitable. Bring suitable shoes for walking.*
suitability *noun*

suitably *adverb*
1 in a way that is right or good for a particular purpose *We're going to a wedding and have to be suitably dressed.*
2 used about feelings that people are supposed to show in a particular situation *Josh showed us his new bike and we were suitably impressed.*

suitcase *noun* **suitcases**
a container made of cloth, leather or plastic and shaped like a rectangle, used for carrying things such as clothes when you're travelling. You hold it by a handle or push it along on wheels.

suite ['sweet'] *noun* **suites**
1 a group of three pieces of furniture of the same style made up of a sofa and two armchairs *a three-piece suite*
2 a group of rooms in a hotel
3 a group of computer programs that are connected and work together *an antivirus suite*
4 a piece of music made up of different pieces of music for the same instruments

sulk *verb*
sulks, sulking, sulked
to show that you're angry about something by looking unhappy and not wanting to talk to anyone

sulky *adjective* **sulkier, sulkiest**
used for describing someone who is sulking or who often sulks *You look very sulky today* (angry and unhappy). **sulkily** *adverb*
sulkiness *noun*

sullen *adjective*
looking sad and not wanting to talk to anyone, for example because you're angry
sullenly *adverb* **sullenness** *noun*

sulphur ['sul-fer'] *noun*
a yellow chemical with a strong smell when it burns. It is often used for making medicines.

sultan *noun* **sultans**
the title of a ruler in some Muslim countries

sultana *noun* **sultanas**
a light-coloured grape without seeds that is dried (water has been removed) and eaten, for example as a snack or in cakes

sum *noun* **sums**
1 an amount of money
2 the total that you get when you add numbers together *The sum of 9 and 3 is 12.*
3 a simple calculation in maths, for example adding, taking away, multiplying or dividing numbers *Sanjay is good at sums.*

sum *verb*
sums, summing, summed
to sum up is to mention the most important details of something or ideas about something, for example something that has just been said or written *Ms Hawkins summed up the main points of the lesson.*

SYNONYM to summarise

summarise *verb*
summarises, summarising, summarised
to mention the most important details of something or ideas about something, for example something that has just been said or written

SYNONYM to sum up

LANGUAGE EXTRA also spelt *summarize*

summary *noun* **summaries**
a short description that mentions the most important details of something or ideas about something

summer *noun* **summers**
1 the season between spring and autumn when the weather is warmest
2 a summer camp is a place where children can stay during the summer holidays and take part in sports and other activities

summertime *noun*
the season of the year when it's summer

summery *adjective*
1 suitable for summer *a summery dress*
2 having the usual qualities of summer *summery weather*

summit *noun* **summits**
1 the top of something such as a mountain
2 a meeting between leaders of different countries to discuss important questions

summon *verb*
summons, summoning, summoned
1 to order someone to come to a particular place or to see a particular person *The head teacher summoned me to his office.*
2 to ask for something or someone *When Granddad felt dizzy, Mum summoned an ambulance.*

3 if you summon something up such as strength or courage, you try very hard to have those qualities *At last I summoned up the courage to ask a question.*

summons *noun* **summonses**
an official document ordering someone to appear in a court of law

sumptuous *adjective*
1 very expensive and showing that someone is rich *a sumptuous palace*
2 of high quality and much more, greater or bigger than normal *a sumptuous meal*
sumptuously *adverb*

sun *noun*
1 the yellow ball of matter in the sky that gives light and heat to the earth. The sun is a star that the earth goes round once a year.
2 the light and heat that you get from the sun *There's not enough sun today. Nisha was sitting in the sun.*
3 (*plural* **suns**) any star that has a planet that goes round it

sun *verb*
suns, sunning, sunned
if you sun yourself, you sit or lie somewhere in the sun

sunbathe *verb*
sunbathes, sunbathing, sunbathed
to sit or lie in the sun without many clothes on, for example so that your skin gets darker

sunbed *noun* **sunbeds**
a piece of equipment that someone lies on while a sunlamp shines on their skin to make it go darker

sunblock *noun*
a cream that you rub onto your skin to stop it from getting burnt by the sun

SYNONYM sunscreen

sunburn *noun*
a medical problem in which your skin is red and painful because you've spent too long in the sun

sunburnt *adjective*
1 red and painful from being in the sun for too long *My arms are badly sunburnt.*
2 having a darker skin colour from being in the sun *She came back from her holiday looking happy and sunburnt.*

SYNONYM suntanned

LANGUAGE EXTRA you can also say **sunburned**

sundae ['sun-day'] *noun* **sundaes**
a food made from ice cream mixed with fruits, nuts and cream and with a sweet sauce on it. It is usually eaten in a tall glass.

Sunday *noun* **Sundays**
the day of the week between Saturday and Monday. Saturday and Sunday make up the weekend.

ORIGIN from Old English *Sunnandæg* 'day of the sun'

Sunday school *noun*
religious lessons for children that are given on Sundays

sundial *noun* **sundials**
an instrument used when the sun shines for showing the time of day, made of a pointed metal piece that sticks up on a flat piece of stone. The metal piece makes a shadow on the stone and the position of the shadow shows the time.

sunflower *noun* **sunflowers**
a very tall plant that has large round yellow flowers with a brown centre that make people think of the sun

sung
past participle of **sing**

sunglasses *noun plural*
two pieces of special dark glass or plastic fixed to a frame that you wear in front of your eyes to protect them from the sun

sunk
past participle of **sink**

sunlamp *noun* **sunlamps**
a special lamp that someone uses for shining on their skin to make it go darker

sunlight *noun*
the light from the sun

sunlit *adjective*
lit up with the light from the sun *a sunlit room*

sunny *adjective* **sunnier, sunniest**
1 used for describing the weather or a time when the sun shines a lot *a sunny day; August is often very sunny.*
2 having lots of light from the sun *a sunny room*

sunrise *noun*
1 the beginning of the day when the sun rises and it starts to get light
2 (*plural* **sunrises**) the colours that appear in the sky when the sun rises *It was a beautiful sunrise.*

SYNONYMS dawn, daybreak

ANTONYMS sunset, dusk

sunscreen *noun*
a cream that you rub onto your skin to stop it from getting burnt by the sun

SYNONYM sunblock

sunset *noun*
1 the end of the day when the sun sets and it starts to get dark
2 (*plural* **sunsets**) the colours that appear in the sky when the sun sets *What a gorgeous sunset!*

SYNONYM dusk

ANTONYMS sunrise, dawn, daybreak

sunshade *noun* **sunshades**
any object used for protection against the sun, for example an umbrella that you hold over your head or fix over a table, or a piece of cloth above the door or window of a building

sunshine *noun*
the light and heat of the sun

sunspot *noun* **sunspots**
in science, a sunspot is a dark area that appears on the surface of the sun

sunstroke *noun*
a medical problem caused by being in the sun for too long

SYNONYM heatstroke

suntan *noun* **suntans**
1 a darker skin colour from being in the sun
2 a suntan lotion is a thick liquid that you put on your skin to protect it from the sun

suntanned *adjective*
having a darker skin colour from being in the sun *suntanned arms; Sarah was really suntanned.*

super *adjective*
an informal way of saying excellent *a super meal; We saw a really super film.*

super- *prefix*
used with nouns, adjectives and verbs to mean more, better, bigger or faster than normal *superhero; supersonic; superstore*

superb *adjective*
extremely good and of the highest quality

superbly *adverb*
extremely well and in the best possible way *a superbly written poem*

superficial *adjective*
1 if something such as an injury or damage is superficial, it is not deep but is on the surface or the outside only *The cut on my finger is superficial* (not serious because it is on the skin only).
2 used about something that does not include any details and is not very serious or good *a superficial piece of homework* (not showing any careful thought); *I have a superficial knowledge of Spanish* (I know a little bit of Spanish). *The police officers made a superficial examination of the car* (they did not examine it carefully).
3 if someone is superficial, they do not think carefully about things or care about people

superficially *adverb*
1 slightly *He was only superficially aware of what was going on.*
2 used about the way something seems from the outside although this may not be the way something really is *Superficially, she seemed friendly and relaxed.*
3 not very well or with any detail *The head teacher mentioned the school's problems very superficially. He only looked at my passport superficially.*

superfluous ['soo-**perr**-floo-ers'] *adjective*
used for describing something that is not needed or useful (or no longer needed or useful) *superfluous details*

superhero *noun* **superheroes**
a person in a cartoon, film or book who has special strength or a special quality and uses it to help people

superhuman *adjective*
1 used about something such as a quality or effort that is much greater than normal *He lifted the rock with superhuman strength.*
2 used about someone who has greater strength than normal or a special quality that other people don't have

507

superintendent–support

superintendent noun **superintendents**
1 a police officer above the rank of chief inspector
2 someone in charge of something, for example a park or building

superior adjective
1 better than something or someone else *My sister's school marks are always superior to mine. They make computers of superior quality.*
2 more or greater than something else *They won the battle because of their superior strength.*
3 if someone feels superior, they think they are more important than other people
4 having a higher position or rank than someone else *a superior officer*

superior noun **superiors**
someone who has a higher position or rank than someone else

superiority noun
1 when something or someone is better than something or someone else
2 when someone feels they are more important than other people

superlative ['soo-**perr**-ler-tiv] adjective
used about something or someone of the highest quality *a superlative piece of homework*; *a superlative teacher*
superlatively adverb

superlative ['soo-**perr**-ler-tiv] noun **superlatives**
the form of an adjective or adverb that is used for comparing three or more things (or people) when one of those things (or people) has the most of a particular quality

> **LANGUAGE EXTRA** to form the *superlative* of adjectives and adverbs, you add *-est*, for example *small – smallest, fast – fastest*. If a word ends in *-y* (like *happy*), then you change *y* to *i* (*happiest*). Words that end in a single consonant (for example *big, hot* or *thin*) usually double that consonant before *-est* (*biggest, hottest, thinnest*).
> Some very common words are exceptions to this *-est* rule: for example, *good* changes to *best*, not *goodest*!
> For longer adjectives and for adverbs ending in *-ly*, you usually put 'most' before the word, for example *difficult – most difficult, slowly – most slowly*.

compare: **comparative**

superman noun **supermen**
a man who has greater strength than normal or a special quality that other people don't have

supermarket noun **supermarkets**
a large shop that sells food and other goods. You take what you want from the shelves, put it in a basket or trolley and pay for it when you are ready to leave.

supernatural adjective
used about something that the natural laws of science cannot explain *The wizard had supernatural powers. I had a dream about ghosts, spirits and other supernatural beings.*

supersonic adjective
faster than the speed of sound (how fast sound travels through the air) *a supersonic jet*

superstar noun **superstars**
someone very famous such as a film star, sports player or musician

superstition noun **superstitions**
a belief that things are influenced by special powers such as magic or luck instead of being based on reason or science

superstitious adjective
1 believing in superstitions *Granddad is very superstitious.*
2 based on or connected with superstitions *superstitious beliefs*

superstore noun **superstores**
a very large shop selling many different types of goods

supervise verb
supervises, supervising, supervised
to be in charge of something or someone, for example to make sure they are safe or that things are done properly *The teaching assistant was supervising the class.*
supervision noun

supervisor noun **supervisors**
someone who is in charge of something or someone, for example a worker in charge of a group of other workers in an office

superwoman noun **superwomen**
a woman who has greater strength than normal or a special quality that other people don't have

supine adjective
if someone is supine, they are lying flat with their face upwards. If they have their face downwards, they are prone.

supper noun **suppers**
a meal that you eat in the evening. It is either the main meal of the day or a smaller meal such as a snack.

suppertime noun
the time in the evening when people usually have supper or when someone is having their supper

supple adjective **suppler, supplest**
1 if something such as a part of the body is supple, it bends and moves easily *supple fingers*
2 if a material such as leather is supple or if someone's skin is supple, it is not stiff but soft and smooth
3 if someone is supple, they can bend and move their body easily
suppleness noun

supplement noun **supplements**
1 something extra added to something *vitamin supplements* (extra vitamins that someone takes, usually as tablets)
2 an extra amount of money that someone pays for something
3 a separate part of a newspaper or magazine *Mum was reading the colour supplement* (the free magazine that comes with a newspaper).
4 an extra section in a book, usually at the end

supplementary adjective
1 used about something that is extra or added to something else
2 in maths, supplementary angles are two angles that together come to 180 degrees
compare: **complementary angles**

supply verb
supplies, supplying, supplied
1 to give something to someone or something, for example something that they need *This website doesn't supply enough information. The school supplies all students with pens and paper.*
2 to sell something to someone who needs it *My dad's shop supplies the school with uniforms.*
3 to get and bring something *Children must supply their own packed lunch for tomorrow's trip.*
4 to say or write something *For this exercise you have to supply the missing words.*

supply noun **supplies**
1 an amount of something that is ready to be used *I keep a supply of paper in my drawer. The fish tank needs a constant supply of fresh water.*
2 the action of supplying something *the supply of oxygen to the brain*
3 all the things such as pipes and cables that supply water, gas and electricity to people in homes and buildings *They've cut off the water supply.*
4 supplies are things such as food, medicine, blankets and equipment that people need for living *The lorries brought supplies of food to the refugees.*

supply teacher noun **supply teachers**
a teacher who does the job of another teacher when the other teacher is not able to work, for example because of illness

support verb
supports, supporting, supported
1 to hold the weight of something or someone so that they don't fall *Granddad walks with a stick to support him.*
2 to help someone, for example to help them to be successful or do what they want to do *My teachers have always supported me by being kind and understanding.*
3 to think that something or someone is good and, for example, want them to be successful *I don't support these ideas. Who do your parents support in the election? I asked Tom which football team he supports* (which one he wants to win).
4 to provide someone with the things they need to live, for example food, clothes and money *My parents have a large family to support.*
5 to support something such as a computer program is to provide information and software to allow it to keep working properly *Your version of the program is too old to be supported.*

support noun
1 words or actions that help someone, for example to be successful or do what they want to do *I had a lot of trouble at school but my parents gave me plenty of support.*

> **SYNONYM** encouragement

2 when you think that something or someone is good and, for example, want them to be successful *Our school doesn't show much support for those ideas. Which team do you give your support to?*

3 (*plural* **supports**) something that stops something or someone from falling by holding their weight *The bridge is held up by six large supports.*
4 money and help given to a person or group
5 help and information someone provides to make sure that something such as a computer or computer program is working properly *Dad had a problem with his tablet so he phoned technical support* (the people who provide help and information).

supporter *noun* **supporters**
someone who gives support, for example someone who watches a particular football team and wants them to win

suppose *verb*
supposes, supposing, supposed
1 to think that something is probably true even though you are not certain *I suppose you must be tired. You're tired, I suppose. 'Is it late?' – 'I suppose so.'*
2 another way of saying to think, when you're not completely happy about a situation *I suppose I should leave now* (I don't really want to leave). *It was quite an interesting film, I suppose* (but I didn't really like it). *'Can I come to your party?' – 'I suppose so.'* (yes, you can but I don't really want you to)
3 used for suggesting an idea or possible situation *Suppose we go swimming this afternoon!*

supposed *adjective*
1 used for saying you expect something to happen or someone to do something *You're supposed to wait here* (that's what you should do). *The computer is supposed to turn itself off. Mum was supposed to be home an hour ago* (she should have been home an hour ago). *You were supposed to do the washing-up, not watch TV* (you should have been doing the washing-up).
2 used for saying what people think about someone or something even though this may not be true *My cousin is supposed to be very clever. The British Museum is supposed to get more visitors than any other museum. Shakespeare is the supposed author of this poem.*
3 used for showing what something or someone is and the qualities they should have because of this *You're supposed to be my best friend* (you're my best friend and you should behave like one). *Our school is supposed to be a model for all the others in the county* (it should have the qualities of a model school).
4 used for describing the way something or someone is even though the description may not be true *This mobile phone is supposed to be unbreakable.*
5 if someone is not supposed to do something, they are not allowed to do it *You're not supposed to talk in the library.*

supposedly ['ser-poh-zid-lee'] *adverb*
used for saying what people think about someone or something even though this may not be true *My cousin is supposedly very clever.*

supposing *conjunction*
used for suggesting a possible situation or an idea *Supposing you were rich, what would you do? Supposing we go to the park this afternoon!*

SYNONYM suppose

suppress *verb*
suppresses, suppressing, suppressed
1 to put an end to something or stop something happening by using force *In some countries, people's freedom is suppressed.*
2 to stop yourself from doing something such as laughing or yawning *I suppressed a yawn.*
3 if someone suppresses information, they stop people from knowing that information
suppression *noun*

supremacy *noun*
when someone or something has more power and influence than anyone or anything else

supreme *adjective*
1 used for describing something or someone that has the greatest importance or the highest level *a supreme ruler*
2 very great *supreme courage*

supremely *adjective*
extremely *My teacher has been supremely patient with me.*

sure *adjective* **surer, surest**
1 if you're sure about something, you know it has happened or is true or correct (or you know or believe it will happen) *I'm sure I left my schoolbag on the stairs. I'm sure of her address. Dad is sure we'll win the match tomorrow. 'Are you coming to my party?' – 'I'm not sure.'* (I don't know)
2 used about something that is or was very likely to happen or to be true or correct *Daniel is sure to be chosen as head boy. You're sure of some freshly baked biscuits if you visit Grandma this weekend! When they took that turning, they were sure to get lost. One thing is sure – he knows where you live. It's a sure sign* (true and definite sign) *that things are getting better.*
3 if you make sure of something or make sure you do something (or if you want to be sure of something), you do what needs to be done so that something can happen or be true *Arrive early to make sure* (or *be sure*) *of a good seat* (or *of getting a good seat*). *Make sure you arrive early* (or *be sure to arrive early*) *to get a good seat. Close the door to make sure the dog doesn't get out.*
4 to make sure (or be sure) you do something also means to pay attention to doing it so that you know it definitely happens *Make sure* (or *be sure*) *you close the front door* (check carefully so you know it is definitely closed).
5 for sure used when you mean that something you know, say or do is really true or will happen (or has happened) *I'll email you later for sure* (definitely). *I can't say for sure* (exactly) *where I left my bag.*

sure *adverb*
1 used for saying yes to someone or for giving permission *'Can I have some more ice cream?' – 'Sure.' Sure, you can stay over at Erin's house tomorrow.*
2 sure enough used for saying that something happens exactly as you expected it to happen *I thought it would snow and sure enough it did.*

surely *adverb*
1 used for saying something will or did happen or is probably true *Our team will surely win on Saturday. Surely we've met before.*
2 used for showing surprise about something *Surely you're not going out in that silly hat!*

surf *noun*
1 large waves in the sea as they move onto the beach
2 the white foam (bubbles) produced by these waves

surf *verb*
surfs, surfing, surfed
1 to ride on the large waves in the sea using a surfboard (long narrow piece of wood or plastic)
2 if you surf the internet, you spend time looking at different websites on the internet
surfer *noun*

surface *noun* **surfaces**
1 the outside part or top part of something *the surface of the earth*; *The road surface was full of holes.*
2 the flat top part of something such as a table or desk that you use for working on *You need a large kitchen surface to prepare this meal.*
3 used for describing the way someone or something looks, which is different from the way they really are *Mr Clark always seemed relaxed but beneath the surface he was very unhappy.*
4 in maths, one of the sides of an object such as a cube or pyramid
5 in maths and physics, a surface area is the area (amount of space) of all the sides of a shape such as a cube or pyramid

surface *verb*
surfaces, surfacing, surfaced
1 if something such as a submarine or someone such as a diver surfaces, they come up to the surface from under the water
2 to surface something such as a road or path is to put a new layer of hard material over the top of it
3 to appear suddenly *New information has surfaced about the missing plane.*

surfboard *noun* **surfboards**
a long narrow piece of wood or plastic that you stand on and use for riding on large waves in the sea

surfing *noun*
the sport of riding on large waves in the sea using a surfboard (long narrow piece of wood or plastic)

surge *verb*
surges, surging, surged
1 to move forward strongly and quickly *The crowd surged forward when the film star appeared. After lagging behind, Ben surged ahead to win the race.*
2 to increase suddenly and very much *Support for the head teacher's plans has surged in the last month.*

surge noun
1 a sudden big increase in something *a surge in popularity*
2 a strong sudden movement forward, for example by a group of people
3 (plural **surges**) a surge of electricity is a sudden short increase in an electrical current, caused for example by lightning *My computer was damaged by a power surge.*

surgeon noun **surgeons**
a doctor who performs surgery (cutting into someone's body to remove or repair an injured or diseased part)

surgery noun
1 (plural **surgeries**) a room or place where a doctor or dentist sees patients
2 the period of time when patients can see their doctor or dentist *Morning surgery is from 8.00 to 11.00 a.m.*
3 the medical operation done by a surgeon when he or she cuts into someone's body to remove or repair an injured or diseased part

surgical adjective
1 used in medical operations *surgical gloves*
2 connected with medical operations *surgical treatment*

surly adjective **surlier, surliest**
if someone is surly, they are unfriendly, rude and in a bad mood

surname noun **surnames**
the last part of your name that you share with the people in your close family. Your surname is also called your family name or last name.

surpass verb
surpasses, surpassing, surpassed
1 to be or do better than something or someone *This year's exam results have surpassed last year's.*
2 to be more than a particular number or amount *The population of the country has surpassed 60 million.*

surplus ['serr-plers'] noun **surpluses**
used about things, people or an amount of something that is not needed *Our school has a surplus of PE teachers* (too many of them). *There's a lot of food left over from the party – what shall we do with this surplus?*

surprise noun **surprises**
1 something that happens or something you find out that you don't expect *Our team won – what a lovely surprise! The news was a complete surprise to us* (no-one was expecting it). *We received a surprise visit from Uncle Harry* (an unexpected visit from him).
2 something that you get that you don't expect, for example a present or letter *The email came as a complete surprise.*
3 the feeling you have when something unexpected happens or when you get something unexpected *You could see the look of surprise on their faces as they opened their presents.*
4 if you catch someone by surprise, you find them when they are not expecting to be found
5 if something such as an event, storm or news catches you by surprise, it happens unexpectedly and you are not ready for it

surprise verb
surprises, surprising, surprised
1 to give someone a feeling of surprise when something unexpected happens or when they get something unexpected *I was surprised at the way he behaved. It surprised me to hear that Ava couldn't ride a bike.*
2 to find someone when they are not expecting it, often when they are doing something they are not supposed to do *We got home early and surprised a burglar.*
3 to attack someone without warning

surprising adjective
used about something that makes you feel surprised because it is unexpected or unusual *The news was surprising. To be a teacher you need a surprising amount of energy* (more energy than you would expect).

surprisingly adverb
in a way that is unexpected or unusual *You were surprisingly lucky. Surprisingly, our team won the match.*

surrender verb
surrenders, surrendering, surrendered
1 if you surrender, you stop trying to fight someone and you tell them officially that you've been beaten *The leaders of the gang surrendered to the police.*
2 to give something to someone because you have to *The soldiers surrendered their weapons.*

surrender noun **surrenders**
when someone surrenders

surround verb
surrounds, surrounding, surrounded
1 to be or go all the way round something or someone *Our school is surrounded by a wall. The police surrounded the building* (police officers stood on all sides of it so that no-one could escape).
2 if you're surrounded by people such as friends or things such as books or toys, you have lots of them near you *Granddad was in hospital surrounded by all the family.*

surroundings noun plural
all the things that are around someone or something in a particular place *the castle and its surroundings* (for example the countryside all around); *My cousin moved to Leeds but hasn't yet got used to her new surroundings* (for example the town, the people and the house where she lives).

survey ['serr-vay] noun **surveys**
1 a detailed examination of a subject, for example one made by asking people questions about their opinions or behaviour
2 a quick and general examination of a subject
3 a detailed examination of a building or area of land

survey ['ser-vay] verb
surveys, surveying, surveyed
1 to examine something, usually in a detailed way
2 to look at something

surveyor noun **surveyors**
someone whose job is to examine buildings carefully to check the condition they are in

survival noun
a situation in which someone or something continues to live or exist *a struggle for survival*

survive verb
survives, surviving, survived
1 if someone survives, they continue to live after something bad happens to them that almost kills them or could have killed them *The plane crashed but all the passengers survived. They all survived the crash.*
2 if something survives, it continues to exist after something bad happens that almost destroys it or could have destroyed it *The library was burnt down and none of the books survived.*
3 to continue to live or exist in a very difficult situation *My grandparents don't have much money and it's hard for them to survive. These plants can survive in very cold temperatures.*
4 to continue to exist after a long period of time *Most of the author's books are lost but two of them survive.*
5 if someone survives someone else, they continue to live after that person has died

survivor noun **survivors**
someone who continues to live after something bad happens to them that almost kills them or could have killed them

sushi ['soo-shee] noun
a Japanese food made from cold rice shaped into a ball or square, with raw fish or other ingredients on top or inside

suspect ['suss-pekt] noun **suspects**
someone that people think has probably done something wrong or committed a crime

suspect ['sers-pekt] verb
suspects, suspecting, suspected
1 to think that something is likely to be true or likely to happen, often something bad *If you suspect a crime, call the police. Holly isn't back from school yet – I suspect she's taking shelter from the rain.*
2 to suspect someone is to think they've probably done something wrong *Mum suspects me of breaking the window.*

suspend verb
suspends, suspending, suspended
1 to stop something, or stop something happening, for a short period of time *Flights were suspended because of bad weather.*
2 to stop someone from going to school, doing their job or taking part in an activity for a short period because they have done something wrong *My brother was suspended for a week for fighting in the classroom.*
3 to hang something from something else *Christmas decorations were suspended from the ceiling.*

suspenders noun plural
1 straps that hang down from a belt worn by women for holding up their stockings, especially in the past
2 the American word for braces (straps for holding up trousers)

suspense noun
1 a feeling of great worry and excitement someone has while waiting for something to happen or waiting for news about something or someone *Do you have any news of the missing boy? – Don't keep us in suspense* (tell us and stop us being worried).

2 the feeling of great excitement, interest and pleasure someone gets, for example when they read a book or watch a film, when they don't know what is going to happen next or what will happen at the end

suspenseful *adjective*
used for describing things such as books and films that keep you interested and excited while you wait to know what is going to happen next

suspension *noun*
1 when something is stopped for a short period
2 (*plural* **suspensions**) when someone is stopped from doing something for a short period, such as going to school or work *a one-week suspension for bad behaviour*
3 in a vehicle, the suspension is the equipment that makes the ride smoother and more comfortable, for example springs and connecting parts
4 a suspension bridge is a bridge supported by cables that hang from two structures, called towers, at either end of the bridge

suspicion *noun* **suspicions**
1 a feeling that someone has done (or will do) something wrong or bad *Don't do anything to arouse suspicions* (make people think you've done something wrong).
2 a feeling that you do not trust someone, for example because they might do something bad *The children from the other school were treated with suspicion.*
3 a feeling that something may be true, usually something bad *I have a suspicion that we've got on the wrong train.*

suspicious *adjective*
1 used when you think there is something wrong or bad about something, or when you think someone has done (or will do) something wrong or bad *suspicious behaviour* (when someone looks as if they are doing something wrong); *a suspicious package* (one that could be dangerous); *a suspicious-looking man* (looking as if he is about to do something wrong); *I heard a noise that made me suspicious.*
2 used for showing that you do not trust someone or something *Some people were suspicious of Oscar because he was new.*

suspiciously *adverb*
1 in a way that makes you think someone has done (or will do) something wrong or bad *Two people were acting suspiciously outside the bank.*
2 in a way that makes you think there is something wrong about something or that there is something bad or strange happening *The class was suspiciously quiet.*

sustain *verb*
sustains, sustaining, sustained
1 to keep doing something or allow something to keep going *I'm running as fast as I can but I can't sustain this speed. Teachers should try to sustain pupils' interest in their lessons.*
2 to give someone energy, strength or support *You need more than a bag of crisps to sustain you at lunchtime. It was the thought of seeing my family again that sustained me when I was in hospital.*
3 used for talking about something bad that happens to someone or something *Ed sustained a leg injury playing football.*

swagger *verb*
swaggers, swaggering, swaggered
to walk around looking as if you're more important than other people

Swahili ['swah-**hee**-lee'] *noun*
a language that people speak in East Africa

swallow *verb*
swallows, swallowing, swallowed
1 to make food or drink go down your throat and into your stomach
2 to swallow something or someone up is to make them disappear, for example so they are completely destroyed *The whole village was swallowed up by the earthquake.*

swallow *noun* **swallows**
a small bird with very long pointed wings and a tail that is divided into two points. A swallow looks similar to a swift.

swam
past tense of **swim**

swami ['swah-mee'] *noun* **swamis**
a Hindu religious teacher

ORIGIN from Hindi *svami* 'master'

swamp *noun* **swamps**
flat ground that is very wet and muddy, where trees and plants grow
swampy *adjective*

swamp *verb*
swamps, swamping, swamped
1 to be too much or too many for someone to deal with *Our school has been swamped with calls from people wanting to help.*
2 to cover something with water

swan *noun* **swans**
a large white bird with a long thin neck. Swans live near and on lakes and rivers.

swanky *adjective* **swankier, swankiest**
an informal word used about something such as a restaurant or hotel that is fashionable and expensive

swap *verb*
swaps, swapping, swapped
1 to give something to someone and get something else back from them *The two girls swapped email addresses.*

SYNONYM to exchange

2 if you swap places or seats with someone, you let them sit in your seat and you go and sit in theirs

SYNONYM to change

3 to put something or someone in the place of something or someone else *I didn't want to wear my red T-shirt so I swapped it* (or *swapped it over*) *for my blue one.*
4 to do something that someone else has been doing and let them do what you've been doing *I'll throw the ball and you bat it, then after a while we'll swap* (or *swap over*) (then I'll bat the ball and you throw it).

swap *noun*
1 the action of swapping something or someone *I like your hat and you prefer mine so let's do a swap.*
2 (*plural* **swaps**) something you get from someone when you give them something else

swarm *verb*
swarms, swarming, swarmed
1 to move somewhere in large numbers *Children swarmed out of school.*
2 if insects or animals swarm somewhere, they fly or move there in large numbers *There were wasps swarming around the dustbins.*
3 if something is swarming with insects, animals or people, there are lots of them everywhere *The whole area was swarming with police.*

swarm *noun* **swarms**
1 a swarm of bees, ants or other insects is a large number of them flying or moving together
2 a large number of people

swastika ['swos-tik-er'] *noun* **swastikas**
an ancient symbol used in many different countries. It is shaped like a cross with each of its four ends bent over at an angle of 90 degrees.

CULTURE NOTE in the 20th century it was used as a symbol by the Nazis (rulers of Germany for a few years before and during the Second World War)

swat *verb*
swats, swatting, swatted
to hit and kill an insect such as a fly, usually with something flat, for example a folded newspaper or your hand

swatter *noun* **swatters**
a fly swatter is a plastic tool with a long handle fixed to a flat part, used for hitting and killing flies

sway *verb*
sways, swaying, swayed
to move gently from side to side, or to make something move this way *The sunflowers were swaying in the breeze. The rock star was swaying his hips.*

swear *verb*
swears, swearing, swore, sworn
1 if someone swears, they use a very bad and rude word (or words), for example because they are angry
2 to promise someone something in a very serious way *I swear to tell the truth.*
3 to say that something is definitely true *I didn't break the window – I swear!*
4 if you are sworn to secrecy, you promise not to tell anyone what someone else has told you
5 (informal) if you swear by something, you are sure it really does something useful and good *My mum takes lots of vitamins to stay healthy – she swears by them.*

swear word *noun* **swear words**
a very bad and rude word that someone says, for example because they are angry

LANGUAGE EXTRA also spelt *swearword*

sweat *verb*
sweats, sweating, sweated
to produce liquid through tiny holes in your skin called pores when you do exercises or when you are hot, frightened, nervous or ill

sweat *noun*
liquid that comes through your skin, for example when you are hot or do exercises

sweater–swimming

sweater noun sweaters
a piece of knitted clothing that you wear over a shirt or T-shirt to keep the top of your body and arms warm

> SYNONYMS jumper, jersey

sweatshirt noun sweatshirts
a piece of clothing made from soft thick cotton for keeping the top of your body and arms warm, used for example when playing sport or for relaxing in. Some sweatshirts have a hood.

sweaty adjective sweatier, sweatiest
1 covered with sweat *sweaty hands*; *My shirt was all sweaty.*
2 making you sweat *sweaty work*

swede noun swedes
a hard round vegetable with yellow flesh and a purple skin that grows under the ground. It is usually boiled and eaten mashed (crushed into a soft mass).

> ORIGIN from *Swedish turnip* (a large white vegetable growing under the ground) because it came from Sweden in the 18th century

Swede noun Swedes
someone from Sweden

Sweden noun
a country in Northern Europe

Swedish adjective
connected with Sweden or the Swedish language

Swedish noun
the language people speak in Sweden

sweep verb
sweeps, sweeping, swept
1 to clean something with a broom or brush by pushing all the dirt off it *Dad was sweeping the kitchen floor.*
2 to remove something such as dirt by pushing it, usually with a broom or brush *I swept up the pieces of broken glass. Stephen swept the crumbs off the table with his hand.*
3 to move or go quickly and smoothly or with a lot of energy *A strong wind swept through the village. He just swept into the room, said goodbye and ran out again.*
4 to move or push something or someone quickly or with a lot of energy *The waves nearly swept us overboard. Our dustbin got swept away in the wind. The bridge was swept away in the flood* (completely destroyed and taken away by the flood).
5 to spread *This is the latest craze sweeping through the country. The fire swept quickly though the whole building.*

sweep noun sweeps
1 the action of sweeping *I gave the room a good sweep.*
2 a quick movement that is smooth or done with a lot of energy *He showed us what he meant with a sweep of his arm.*

sweeper noun sweepers
something or someone that sweeps *a carpet sweeper*; *My cousin is a road sweeper.*

sweet adjective sweeter, sweetest
1 used about food or drink that has the taste of sugar *This cake is very sweet* (it has lots of sugar in it).

> ANTONYMS sour, bitter

2 having a strong and usually pleasant smell *These hyacinths smell sweet.*
3 pleasant and beautiful *a sweet baby*; *a sweet face*; *I like the sweet sounds of this music.*
4 pleasant and friendly *Your sister is really sweet.*

sweetness noun

> SIMILES 'as sweet as honey' (senses 1, 3 & 4) and 'as sweet as pie' (senses 3 & 4) mean very sweet

sweet noun sweets
1 a small piece of food made from sugar with other ingredients such as flavourings (substances that give flavour) and colourings (substances that give colour). It is not part of a meal but eaten for pleasure.
2 something sweet such as a cake that you eat at the end of a meal as a dessert

sweetcorn noun
the yellow seeds of the maize plant that can be cooked and eaten

sweeten verb
sweetens, sweetening, sweetened
to make something taste sweet or sweeter, usually by adding sugar

sweetener noun sweeteners
a substance added instead of sugar to drinks and to foods such as yoghurt, to make them taste sweet

sweetheart noun sweethearts
someone you love very much

sweetly adverb
1 in a pleasant and friendly way *She smiled sweetly.*
2 in a pleasant and beautiful way *He sings very sweetly.*

sweet pea noun sweet peas
a climbing plant with blue, pink, purple and white flowers that have a strong pleasant smell

sweet potato noun sweet potatoes
a vegetable that looks like a long potato, often with a pink skin and yellow flesh inside. It has a slightly sweet taste.

swell verb
swells, swelling, swelled, swollen or swelled
1 if something swells, it gets bigger than it normally is *A bee stung my finger and it swelled up. The wood has swollen because of the heavy rain.*
2 to make something bigger than it normally is *The rain has swollen the river.*

swell noun
1 the movement of the waves in the sea that go up and down
2 (plural swells) the waves themselves that go up and down

swelling noun
1 (plural swellings) a place on your body that has got bigger than it normally is, for example because of an injury or illness
2 when a part of your body gets bigger *Put this cream on the bite to stop the swelling.*

sweltering adjective
so hot that you feel uncomfortable *It's sweltering today. I'm sweltering.*

swept
past tense & past participle of **sweep**

swerve verb
swerves, swerving, swerved
to move suddenly to the left or right when going forward, for example in a vehicle or on a bike or while running *The bus swerved to avoid hitting a dog in the road.*

swerve noun swerves
a sudden movement to the left or right

swift adjective swifter, swiftest
happening or moving quickly *a swift reply*; *The current is swift in this part of the river.*
swiftness noun

swift noun swifts
a brown bird with pointed wings that are long and curved for fast flying and a tail that is divided into two points. A swift looks similar to a swallow.

swiftly adjective
quickly

swill verb
swills, swilling, swilled
1 to move liquid around inside something, for example to clean it *I swilled my mouth out with mouthwash.*
2 if liquid swills, it moves around inside something *Water was swilling about inside the sinking boat.*
3 if someone swills something, they drink a lot of it quickly

swill noun
waste food in water, given to pigs for eating
short for: pigswill

swim verb
swims, swimming, swam, swum
1 to move through the water using parts of your body, for example your arms and legs *I'm learning to swim. Lucy swam to the end of the pool. Dogs swim by walking in the water.*
2 to swim as a sport or for pleasure *My dad swims every Saturday.*
3 to travel a particular distance or from one side of something to another while swimming *I can swim 200 metres. You need lots of energy to swim the Channel.*
4 if fish swim, they move in the water using their fins and tail
5 if something is swimming in a liquid, it has too much of it *My potatoes are swimming in gravy.*
6 if something you look at swims, it seems to be moving *I was so tired that everything was swimming around me.*
7 if your head is swimming, you can't see clearly, for example because everything seems to be moving, or you can't think clearly. This usually happens when you're ill or very tired.

swim noun swims
the action of swimming, or a time when you swim *to have a swim*; *I've been for two swims today.*

swimmer noun swimmers
someone who swims *I'm a good swimmer. I can see two swimmers in the water.*

swimming noun
1 when you swim as an exercise or activity done for pleasure or as a sport *My brother goes swimming every Monday.*
2 a swimming costume is a piece of clothing for swimming in, usually worn by girls and women

512

swimsuit–swung

3 a swimming pool is an area of water specially built inside a building or outside for people to swim in *an outdoor swimming pool*
4 swimming trunks are a piece of clothing that covers the lower part of the body, used by boys and men for swimming in

swimsuit *noun* swimsuits
a piece of clothing for swimming in, usually worn by girls and women

swindle *verb*
swindles, swindling, swindled
to cheat someone in order to get money out of them **swindler** *noun*

swindle *noun* swindles
a trick or dishonest plan for getting money out of someone

swine *noun*
1 (plural **swine**) an old-fashioned word for a pig
2 (plural **swine** or **swines**) an insulting word for a very unpleasant person

swing *verb*
swings, swinging, swung
1 to move backwards and forwards or from one place to another through the air, usually while hanging from somewhere or being fixed to something *Dad's arms were swinging as he walked. The monkey was swinging from branch to branch. I pressed a button and the door swung open.*
2 to make something move backwards and forwards or from one place to another through the air *Don't swing that stick – you could hurt someone.*
3 to turn or move suddenly or smoothly, or to make something do this *I swung round when I heard footsteps behind me. Dad slammed on the brakes when a lorry swung out in front of him. Granddad swung the car gently left into the garage.*

swing *noun* swings
1 a seat hanging from chains or ropes on a bar fixed to a metal frame. You sit on the seat and move backwards and forwards, usually with someone pushing you.
2 a swinging movement *the swing of a pendulum*
3 a ride on a swing *It's my turn to have a swing.*
4 a sudden change, for example in people's opinions or in someone's mood
5 in full swing used about an event that has started and has been going on for a long while *You're late – my birthday party is in full swing.*

swipe *verb*
swipes, swiping, swiped
1 if someone swipes a card, they put a plastic card with electronic information on it through a special piece of equipment that reads the information. They do this to pay for something or open a door, for example.
2 an informal way of saying to steal
3 to hit something or someone, or try to hit them, using something such as a stick and with a swinging movement of your arm

swipe *noun*

swirl *verb*
swirls, swirling, swirled
to move round and round quickly, or to make something do this *The bath water swirls round as it goes down the plughole. My little brother was swirling the paint around with his finger.*

swirl *noun* swirls
1 a movement or pattern of something that goes round and round *a dress with swirls on it*
2 an object with a swirling pattern *Please could you put a swirl of cream on top of my cake?*

swish *verb*
swishes, swishing, swished
if something swishes, it makes a soft gentle sound as it moves, for example the sound of a cloth being waved in the air or water going through a pipe **swish** *noun*

swish *adjective* swisher, swishest
an informal word for something that looks expensive and fashionable *a swish restaurant*

Swiss *adjective*
connected with Switzerland

Swiss *noun*
the Swiss are people from Switzerland

switch *noun* switches
1 a small object of plastic or metal, often on the outside of a piece of equipment, used for turning it on or off by closing or opening the gap in the circuit or loop of electricity. Switches come in different shapes. They can be pushed up and down with your finger, pressed like a button or turned like a knob. *a light switch*
2 a change from one thing to another, often a sudden one

switch *verb*
switches, switching, switched
1 to switch something on or off, such as a piece of equipment, is to make it start or stop working by pushing a switch up or down or by pressing or turning a switch *Switch the light on. Dad stopped the car and switched off the engine. Switch off before you go to bed* (for example, switch off all the equipment that's on). *The printer switches off by itself after one hour.*

SYNONYMS 'to turn on' and 'to turn off' mean the same as 'to switch on' and 'to switch off'

2 to stop one thing and start, go to or start doing something else instead *I don't like this TV programme – let's switch channels. Our teacher switched her attention to another matter.*
3 to put something in the place of something else *If your phone doesn't work, try switching the battery. Someone switched our exercise books – I've got yours and you have mine!*
4 to switch planes or trains is to get off one and get on another *We switched planes at New York.*

SYNONYM to change

5 to switch places with someone is to let them sit in your seat while you go and sit in theirs

SYNONYM to change

switchboard *noun* switchboards
1 a piece of equipment that is a part of a phone system, used especially in the past for directing phone calls in a building such as an office or hotel
2 a switchboard operator is someone who works a switchboard. He or she connects people calling to the people they want to speak to.

Switzerland *noun*
a country in Western Europe

swivel *verb*
swivels, swivelling, swivelled
to turn round, or make something turn round, often round a central point *The head teacher swivelled his chair to face me.*

swollen *adjective*
if something is swollen, it is bigger than it normally is, for example because of an injury or illness *a swollen knee; a swollen river* (because of rain or snow)

swollen
a past participle of **swell**. You can also say 'swelled'.

swoon *verb* (old-fashioned)
swoons, swooning, swooned
to suddenly feel very weak and become unconscious for a short period

SYNONYM to faint

swoop *verb*
swoops, swooping, swooped
1 to move down quickly from the air, for example to attack something or someone *The eagle swooped down on the rabbit and carried it away.*
2 to move quickly to catch or attack someone *The police swooped on the building where the robbers were hiding.*

swoop *noun* swoops
1 a quick movement down from the air
2 an attack or raid, especially by the police

swop *verb*
swops, swopping, swopped
another spelling of **swap**

sword *noun* swords
a weapon with a long pointed blade fixed to a handle, used in the past by soldiers or used in the sport of fencing

swordfish *noun* swordfish
a large fish with a long pointed mouth like a sword and usually with white flesh that is used as food

swore
past tense of **swear**

sworn
past participle of **swear**

swot *verb*
swots, swotting, swotted
to study, usually for an exam, by learning a lot of information quickly *My sister is in her room swotting* (or *swotting up*) *for her GCSEs.*

swot *noun* swots
someone who studies too much

swum
past participle of **swim**

swung
past tense & past participle of **swing**

513

sycamore–systematic

sycamore *noun* **sycamores**
a tall tree with large leaves that have five points like a star. It has seeds that are shaped like two small wings.

syllable *noun* **syllables**
a word or part of a word that has one vowel sound. For example, 'dog' has one syllable, 'tiger' has two syllables (ti-ger) and 'hippopotamus' has five syllables (hip-po-pot-am-us). **syllabic** *adjective*

syllabus *noun* **syllabuses**
a plan of what students study at school or university, including the subjects and books *'A Christmas Carol' by Charles Dickens is on my brother's GCSE syllabus* (he must study this book for this exam).

symbol *noun* **symbols**
a mark, shape, letter or number that has a special meaning or is used instead of a particular quality or idea *The plus sign is the symbol for addition. A heart shape is the symbol of love.*

symbolic *adjective*
1 representing something important but often something that does not have any real influence on a situation *Suspending the bully from school for a week was a symbolic gesture by the school* (it didn't really make the situation better).
2 if something is symbolic of something else such as a quality or idea, it shows the particular meaning of it or is used instead of it *A heart shape is symbolic of love.*
symbolically *adverb*

symbolise *verb*
symbolises, symbolising, symbolised
to be a symbol of something

> SYNONYM to represent

> LANGUAGE EXTRA also spelt *symbolize*

symbolism *noun*
the use of symbols to represent ideas, for example in art or poetry

symmetrical *adjective*
if a shape is symmetrical, it has symmetry (it can be divided into two parts or halves that are mirror images of each other)
symmetrically *adverb*

symmetry *noun*
when two parts or halves of a shape are exactly equal to each other (or mirror images of each other) on either side of a dividing line called a line of symmetry
see: **reflection** (sense 2) and **rotation** (sense 3)

sympathetic *adjective*
showing or feeling sympathy and understanding for someone *My teacher was sympathetic when I said I had a bad back. She sent me a very sympathetic letter.*
sympathetically *adverb*

sympathise *verb*
sympathises, sympathising, sympathised
if you sympathise with someone, you show them that you feel sympathy and understanding for them

> LANGUAGE EXTRA also spelt *sympathize*

sympathy *noun*
1 a feeling that shows you understand another person's feelings and opinions and care about that person's problems or suffering
2 a sympathy card is a card you send to tell someone you are sorry that a member of their family or a friend has just died

> ORIGIN from a Greek word meaning 'suffering together' (*syn-* 'together' and *pathos* 'suffering')

symphony *noun* **symphonies**
a long piece of music for a large orchestra. It is usually divided into four parts called movements. **symphonic** *adjective*

symptom *noun* **symptoms**
a medical problem that is a sign that you have a particular illness *Symptoms of flu include a cough, headache and temperature.*

synagogue *noun* **synagogues**
a building where Jewish people pray and celebrate their religion

synchronise *verb*
synchronises, synchronising, synchronised
1 to make something happen or work at the same time as something else *In the film, the voices of the actors were not synchronised with the image. We synchronised our watches* (adjusted them to show exactly the same time).
2 to happen or work at the same time as something else *Click here to make sure the files on your laptop and tablet synchronise* (are updated and are exactly the same).
synchronisation *noun*

> LANGUAGE EXTRA also spelt *synchronize* and *synchronization*

synonym *noun* **synonyms**
a word that has the same meaning or almost the same meaning as another word *'Fast' is a synonym of 'quickly'.*

> ORIGIN from Greek *syn-* 'together' or 'same' and *onoma* 'name'

synonymous *adjective*
if words are synonymous, they have the same meaning or almost the same meaning *'Fast' is synonymous with 'quickly'.*

synopsis ['sin-op-siss'] *noun*
synopses ['sin-op-seez']
a short description that mentions the most important details of a piece of writing such as a book or play

> SYNONYM summary

synthesiser *noun* **synthesisers**
a piece of electronic equipment for producing and copying different sounds, especially musical sounds. It is usually used as a musical instrument.

> LANGUAGE EXTRA also spelt *synthesizer*

synthetic *adjective*
produced from different chemical substances, not made from natural substances that come from plants, trees or animals *synthetic rubber* **synthetically** *adverb*

Syria *noun*
a country in South-West Asia
Syrian *adjective & noun*

syringe *noun* **syringes**
a tube with a needle fixed into one end and a part that is pushed up or down at the other end. It is used by a doctor or nurse for putting medicines into your body or for taking blood from your body.

syrup *noun* **syrups**
1 a thick liquid made by cooking sugar and water. Substances are often added to it to give it a flavour.
2 any sweet and thick or sticky liquid *a cough syrup* (for helping you to stop coughing); *maple syrup* (from the maple tree and eaten with pancakes)

> ORIGIN from Arabic *sharab* 'wine' or 'drink'

system *noun* **systems**
1 all the things that work together or are connected to each other in different ways to make something happen *a central heating system* (pipes, radiators and other equipment); *the digestive system* (stomach, tubes and other parts of the body for digesting food); *the solar system* (the sun and planets that go round it); *Britain's motorway system* (all the country's motorways connected to each other)
2 a computer including all the equipment connected to it *system requirements* (the software and hardware needed for a program to work); *If you get an error message, turn off your system.*
3 a way of doing things that is organised and follows a plan or rules *a filing system; the Scottish education system; the decimal system* (a way of counting using the number 10); *the metric system* (a way of measuring using units such as metres, kilos and litres)

systematic *adjective*
1 if someone is systematic, they do things in an organised and careful way
2 also used about someone's actions *She's a scientist making a systematic study of the behaviour of chimpanzees.*
systematically *adverb*

t T

ORIGIN the shape of the letter T has only changed slightly since it began as a cross in the Phoenician alphabet. The Phoenicians called the letter *taw*, which meant 'mark' or 'sign', for example a sign shown by two sticks lying across each other to mark a place. The Greeks used the letter as their T sound, changing the cross into a T shape by getting rid of the top part of the upright line. The shape passed into the Etruscan and Roman alphabets unchanged to make the letter we recognise today.

tab *noun* tabs
1 a small flat or thin part that sticks out from the edge of something made of paper, metal, plastic or cloth. It is used for many things, for example it can be pulled to open something (such as a packet or can) or it can have information written on it about the thing it is fixed to.
2 a tab on a computer screen is a small button or strip at the top of the screen in a program such as a browser (for looking at sites on the internet). You click on a tab to do something such as open a different web page or document.
3 on a computer keyboard, tab (or the tab key) is a key that you press to do something such as move forward a few spaces to another position when typing. You can also use it to go to the next position when keying information such as your name or password into a web document.
4 if you keep tabs on someone, you watch them carefully

tabby *noun* tabbies
a brown or grey cat with darker stripes, curved lines and other small marks on its fur. It is also called a tabby cat.

ORIGIN from *Attabiyah*, a place in Baghdad, capital of Iraq, where a striped cloth called *tabby* used to be made. Because of its striped pattern, *tabby* was also used for describing this kind of cat.

table *noun* tables
1 a piece of furniture with a flat top and legs (supports) used for putting things on or for sitting at, for example to eat a meal *Help me lay* (or *set*) *the table* (put things on it such as knives, forks and plates for a meal). *Granddad cleared the table* (took things away after the meal).
2 a list showing the results of multiplying one number by another between 1 and 12 *I've just learnt my six times table.*

SYNONYM multiplication table

3 a list of words or numbers on a page, arranged in rows (lines written next to each other) and columns (lines written under each other). Tables are used for showing information clearly.

tablecloth *noun* tablecloths
a large piece of cloth used for covering a table, for example during a meal

tablespoon *noun* tablespoons
1 a large spoon, used for example for serving or measuring food. A tablespoon is bigger than a dessertspoon.
2 the amount of food or liquid that a tablespoon can hold

LANGUAGE EXTRA in sense 2, you can also say *tablespoonful*

tablet *noun* tablets
1 a small hard flat piece of medicine that you swallow with water. Tablets are usually round.
2 a flat piece of something hard, often square or rectangular *a stone tablet* (with words cut into it); *a clay tablet* (used by the ancient Egyptians for writing on)
3 a small computer that you carry around with you and can use for connecting to the internet. It uses a screen that you touch with your finger or with a special pen (called a stylus) to make programs work.
4 a graphics tablet is a piece of equipment with a flat surface that is connected to a computer. You draw on the surface with a special pen (called a stylus) to put a picture into the computer.

table tennis *noun*
a game like tennis that is played indoors on a table. One or two players stand at either end of the table holding wooden bats. They use the bats for hitting a small ball to each other across a low net in the middle of the table.

LANGUAGE EXTRA also called *ping-pong*

tabloid *noun* tabloids
a newspaper with small pages and lots of pictures, short news reports and many stories about famous people

taciturn *adjective*
used for describing someone who doesn't talk much and who seems unfriendly

tack *noun*
1 (*plural* tacks) a short nail with a flat top, used for example for fixing carpets to the floor
2 equipment used for riding horses, for example saddles, harnesses and bridles
3 a particular way of doing something when there are several other ways of doing it *OK, let's change tack* (let's do something in a different way).

tack *verb*
tacks, tacking, tacked
1 if someone tacks pieces of cloth together, they sew them quickly with big stitches to hold them before sewing them together properly
2 to fix something somewhere using tacks
3 if a boat tacks, it sails somewhere by turning many times so that the wind is always blowing onto its sails
4 if someone tacks something on to something else, they add it on as extra, often in a careless way

tackle *verb*
tackles, tackling, tackled
1 if someone tackles someone from the opposite team in football or hockey, they try to take the ball away from them
2 if someone tackles someone who is running, for example a player in rugby or a thief, they catch them and knock them to the ground
3 to deal with something difficult or bad *Let's tackle one problem at a time. The firefighters tackled the huge blaze.*

tackle *noun*
1 the special equipment you need for doing an activity such as fishing or climbing *fishing tackle*
2 (*plural* tackles) the action of tackling someone in a sport such as football or rugby

tacky *adjective* tackier, tackiest
1 used about something such as paint or varnish that is not completely dry and is sticky when you touch it
2 (*informal*) used about something that is cheap in quality, badly done or badly made *tacky souvenirs*; *a tacky novel*
tackiness *noun*

tact *noun*
skill in dealing with other people by speaking and behaving in a way that keeps them happy and does not upset them, especially in difficult situations

tactful *adjective*
showing skill in dealing with other people by keeping them happy and not saying or doing something wrong or unkind that might upset them *Miss Patel is always tactful when I make a mistake* (for example, she never says anything bad to me).
tactfully *adverb*

tactics *noun plural*
1 things that someone does or needs to do to get what they want *You'll have to change your tactics and stop misbehaving if you want a bike for your birthday.*
2 careful ways of planning and organising, for example in a battle or sport

tactless *adjective*
showing no skill in dealing with other people, for example often upsetting them by saying or doing something wrong or unkind
tactlessly *adverb*

tadpole *noun* tadpoles
a tiny baby frog or toad before its legs and body start to grow. It has a round black or brown head and a long tail and lives in water.

ORIGIN from 15th-century English *taddepol* 'toad head' (from *tadde* 'toad' and *pol* 'head')

tag *noun* tags
1 a piece of paper, cloth or other material that is fixed to something and gives information about it *Where's the price tag on this coat?*

SYNONYM label

2 a name tag is a small piece of paper, plastic or metal with your name on it that you wear for showing people who you are
3 a series of letters, numbers or symbols added to a piece of electronic information that tells a computer how to deal with that information
4 a game in which one child chases other children and tries to touch one of them

515

tag–take

tag verb
tags, tagging, tagged
1 to put a tag on something to give information about it
2 to mark a piece of electronic information with letters, numbers or symbols so that a computer can deal with it in a particular way
3 if someone tags along, they go somewhere with someone even though no-one has asked them to
4 if someone tags something on, they add it on as something extra, often in a careless way

Tahiti ['tah-**hee**-tee' or 'ter-**hee**-tee'] noun
an island in the South Pacific
Tahitian adjective & noun

tail noun **tails**
1 the part of the body of an animal, bird or fish that sticks out at the back, often a long or short narrow part
2 the long thin end or back of something *the tail of a comet*; *The British Airways plane has its colours painted on the tail* (part that sticks up at the back).
3 the tail end of something is the very last part of it *We were standing right at the tail end of the queue.*
4 **tails** used when throwing a coin in the air to decide something. Tails is the side of a coin that doesn't have a picture of someone's head on it. The side with the picture of a head is called heads. *'Tails!' he shouted, after tossing the coin.*

tail verb
tails, tailing, tailed
1 to follow and watch someone without them seeing you
2 if something tails off, it gradually becomes less *Towards the evening, the traffic tails off* (there is less traffic).

tailback noun **tailbacks**
a long line of traffic that is moving slowly or has stopped moving because of a problem somewhere on the road ahead

tailor noun **tailors**
someone who makes and repairs clothes, especially suits and coats

Taiwan noun
a country in East Asia

Taiwanese adjective
connected with Taiwan

Taiwanese noun
the Taiwanese are people from Taiwan

take verb
takes, taking, took, taken
1 if you take something, you stretch out your arm (or arms), put it in your hand (or hands) and move it from where it is *Take a chocolate. I took the book off the table. I took the pen out of my pocket and my teacher took it away from me. The police officer took out her notebook.*
2 to move something somewhere with your hands *Take these toys into your room. Can you take the ball outside? I have to take the book back to the library.*
3 to put your arms around someone, for example to move them somewhere *Mum took my baby sister into her arms. Grandma has trouble walking so Dad took her up the steps.*

4 to move something or someone somewhere in a vehicle *I was late so Mum took me to school in the car. Dad took the rubbish to the dump.*
5 to go with someone somewhere, often being responsible for them or paying for them *My teacher took me across the road. Can you take your little sister for a walk? Granddad took Grandma on holiday to Italy.*
6 to move something from its place, without asking permission, so that it is no longer there *Someone has taken my ruler. Thieves broke into our flat and took our TV* (they stole it). *Be careful that criminals don't take money from your bank account.*
7 to eat or drink something *Don't forget to take your medicine. Do you take sugar in your tea?*
8 to go somewhere by travelling on something such as a bus, plane or train or along a particular road *We took the train to Bristol. Take the first turning on the right. You can get to Cambridge by taking the M11 motorway.*
9 if something such as a road or journey takes you somewhere, it makes you go there *Follow this path and it will take you straight to the school.*
10 used for talking about a particular action or thing that you do *to take a shower; to take a look; It's time to take a rest. Where are you taking your holidays this year? Take a seat* (sit down). *I'm taking Spanish lessons. I took a picture* (or *photo*) *of Tower Bridge. Mum took my temperature* (used a thermometer to measure how hot my body was).
11 used for talking about what is needed to do something *The journey between Glasgow and Edinburgh takes an hour. It takes courage to stand up to a bully. It took three teachers to carry the heavy box. Chloe is taking a long time to do her homework.*
12 to accept something or say yes to something *Please take my advice. My brother took the job. 'Do you want to buy that teddy bear?' – 'Yes, I'll take it.' Holly can't take a joke* (accept that something is funny without getting angry).
13 to write something down *During the lesson we all took notes. The police officer took down our names and addresses.*
14 to win something *Mohammed took first prize.*
15 to be in charge of something or someone *Ms Turner took the class when our teacher was sick. Mr Harding takes us for maths* (teaches us maths).
16 to wear a particular size of clothes or shoes *What size trainers do you take?*
17 to have enough room for a certain number of people or things *The school bus can only take 35 children.*
18 if you take one number from (or away from) another number, you make the second number smaller by the amount of the first number *Taking four from* (or *away from*) *twelve leaves eight* (12 − 4 = 8).

SYNONYM to subtract

19 if you take an exam or test, you do it by answering questions to find out how much you know about a subject or how well you do an activity

20 to feel something good such as pride or pleasure *My sister takes pride in her schoolwork. My brother takes no interest in sport.*
21 to put up with something unpleasant without getting angry or upset *The sun is very hot but I can take it. I can't take all this shouting!*
22 to start controlling a place, for example a place belonging to an enemy in war *By dawn the soldiers had taken the town.*
23 to take after someone you're related to is to be like them or look like them *My brother takes after Granddad.*
24 if you take something away, you make it go away by putting it in your hand and moving it or you make it disappear *I've finished my dinner – can you take my plate away, please? I need some medicine to take the pain away.*
25 if you take away (or take out) food or drink from a restaurant, you carry it with you and eat it somewhere else
26 if you take something back, you make sure it goes to the place it was before *Take your library book back by the end of the week.*
27 if you take down something such as a picture or notice, you take it off the wall or surface it is fixed to *It's time to take down the Christmas decorations.*
28 if you are taken in by someone, they make you believe something that isn't true
29 if you take something in, you understand it and remember it *I paid attention in class but I didn't take everything in.*
30 to take off clothes is to stop having them on your body *Simon took his jacket off.*
31 if an aircraft takes off, it leaves the ground and goes up into the air
32 if someone in an aircraft takes off, they start their journey *We took off from Heathrow at noon.*
33 if you take a period of time off, you don't go to school or work *I took yesterday off because I wasn't well.*
34 to take someone or something on is to accept them *The bus stops here to take on passengers. Dad can't take on any more work this week. Our school is taking on two more teachers* (will give them a job).
35 to take out money is to take it from a bank account, for example using a card at a cash machine
36 if a doctor or dentist takes something out, he or she removes it from your body
37 to take over is to do something after someone else stops doing it *When our teacher was called to the head's office, Mrs Hobbs took over.*
38 to take something over, for example something that belongs to someone else, is to take control of it
39 to take part in something is to do or be in an activity together with other people, for example a race or conversation *The quiz is tomorrow – do you want to take part?*
40 to take place is to happen
41 to take up space or time is to use it or fill it *This table takes up a lot of room. My parents don't want to take up too much of the teacher's time.*
42 to take up something such as an activity or hobby is to start doing it *Granddad has taken up swimming.*

takeaway–tangle

takeaway noun takeaways
1 a meal that you buy from a shop or restaurant and take somewhere else to eat, for example to your home *a Chinese takeaway*
2 the place that you buy the takeaway meal from

taken adjective
if a seat is taken, for example on a train or in a cinema, someone is sitting in it now or is soon going to be sitting in it

take-off noun take-offs
when an aircraft leaves the ground and goes up into the air

ANTONYM landing

takeout noun takeouts
the American word for a takeaway (meal or restaurant)

takings noun plural
all the money that a shop or business gets from its customers for a particular period *This week's takings were good.*

talcum powder noun
a powder that you put on a baby's body or your own body, for example after a bath, to keep the skin dry and smooth

LANGUAGE EXTRA you can also say *talc*

tale noun tales
1 a story, especially one that is imaginary, full of action or hard to believe *a fairy tale* (in which magic things happen); *Great-Granddad told us some tales about when he was in the jungle.*
2 if someone tells tales, they say things that aren't true, usually about someone else

talent noun talents
a special skill that someone is born with that makes them very good at doing something *Yussuf has a talent for drawing* (he's good at drawing).

talented adjective
if someone is talented, they are very good at doing something *a talented musician*

talk verb
talks, talking, talked
1 to use your voice to say something *My little sister is just learning to talk. Jo and Brad are always talking in class. Come here and talk to me.*
2 to say things to a group of people about a particular subject *A famous footballer is coming to talk at our end-of-term assembly.*
3 to say things to someone to try to solve a problem (or problems) *The two sides in the war have decided to talk.*
4 if someone talks nonsense or rubbish, they say words that are stupid or not true
5 to talk about something or someone is to make them the subject of or reason for what you're saying *We were just talking about George.*
6 to talk about something or doing something is to think about doing it in the future *My parents are talking about moving to Scotland.*
7 if you say you don't know what someone is talking about, you mean you don't understand what they mean
8 to talk back is to answer someone by saying something rude *Don't talk back to your teacher!*
9 if someone talks down to you, they talk to you as if they are better or more intelligent than you are
10 to talk someone into something is to persuade them to do it by giving them good reasons why they should do it *I talked Ben into lending me his bike.*
11 to talk something over is to say things about a situation or problem and get someone else's opinions about it *I sat down with Dad to talk over my problems at school.*

talk noun talks
1 when two or more people talk to each other *Mum and I had a long talk.*

SYNONYM conversation

2 when someone talks on a particular subject to a group of people *They invited the mayor to the school to give a talk.*

talkative adjective
used for describing someone who talks a lot

talk show noun talk shows
a television or radio programme where someone called a host asks famous people questions about themselves

SYNONYM chat show

tall adjective taller, tallest
1 if someone is tall, their head is a long way up from the ground *Kareem is very tall for his age.*

ANTONYM short

2 if something is tall, its top part is a long way up from the ground *a tall building*
3 used for saying the measurement of something or someone from the ground *a wall 10 metres tall; Sarah is four feet tall.*
4 a tall story is a story that is difficult to believe

tallness noun

tally verb
tallies, tallying, tallied
if something tallies with something else or if two things tally, the two things are closely connected because something in one of them is similar to or the same as something in the other *Your story doesn't tally with Emma's. These two totals should tally* (be the same).

tally noun tallies
in maths, a tally is an upright or slanting line used for showing one thing in a table called a tally chart

tallying noun
a method of showing data (or information) in a table called a tally chart, in which every short straight line stands for one thing. You draw these lines in groups of five. The first four lines are upright or slanting and the fifth is drawn across the other four.

talon noun talons
a sharp claw (curved nail) on the foot of a bird of prey such as an eagle or hawk

tambourine noun tambourines
a round musical instrument that you hold in your hand. It has the shape of a drum or ring with small metal discs round the edge of it. You play the tambourine by shaking it or hitting it with your hand to make the metal discs ring.

tame adjective tamer, tamest
1 used for describing an animal that is happy to be with people and doesn't run away

ANTONYM wild

2 not very exciting or interesting *The film was rather tame. Life in our village is pretty tame.*

tamely adverb **tameness** noun

tame verb
tames, taming, tamed
if someone tames an animal, they train it to be happy being with people **tamer** noun

tamper verb
tampers, tampering, tampered
if someone tampers with something such as a piece of equipment, they make harmful changes to it, for example to damage it or stop it working

tampon noun tampons
a piece of soft material that a woman puts into her body to absorb (take in) blood during a period (natural bleeding that happens every month)

tan noun
1 (plural **tans**) a darker skin colour from being in the sun
2 a light yellow-brown colour

tan adjective
having a light yellow-brown colour *a pair of tan shoes*

tan verb
tans, tanning, tanned
1 if you tan, or if the sun tans your skin, the sun makes your skin darker *I tan easily.*
2 to make an animal's skin into leather by using chemicals **tanner** noun

tandem noun tandems
a long bicycle for two people, with pedals for each person. One person sits behind the other.

ORIGIN from Latin *tandem* 'at length' or 'at last', referring to the long shape

tandoori noun
an Indian way of cooking food in a large clay oven *tandoori chicken*

tang noun tangs
a very strong but pleasant taste or smell

tangerine noun tangerines
a type of small orange with loose skin that is easy to peel

ORIGIN from *Tangier*, a seaport in Morocco, because the oranges were sent from there to other parts of the world

tangle verb
tangles, tangling, tangled
if something tangles or becomes tangled, or if you tangle it, it becomes twisted round itself or round something else in an untidy way *The wires to my mum's computer are all tangled. A bird got tangled in the net.*

tangle noun tangles
used about things that have become twisted round themselves or round something else in an untidy way *I used a stiff comb to straighten a tangle of hair.*

tangy–target

tangy *adjective* **tangier, tangiest**
having a very strong but pleasant taste or smell *This drink has a tangy lemon flavour.*

tank *noun* **tanks**
1 a large container for liquid or gas *a petrol tank* (for example in a car); *an oxygen tank* (for example for a diver)
2 the amount that a tank holds *We drove to Wales on one tank of petrol.*
3 a container with glass sides for keeping fish in *a fish tank*
4 a heavy vehicle used by soldiers. It has a large gun on the top and metal belts (called tracks) over its wheels for travelling over rough or soft ground.

tankard *noun* **tankards**
a large metal mug with a handle, used for drinking beer

tanker *noun* **tankers**
1 a very large ship for carrying oil, petrol or gas
2 a large truck for carrying a liquid such as petrol or water

tanned *adjective*
having a darker skin colour from being in the sun *a tanned face*; *Jack looked quite tanned.*

Tannoy *noun* (trademark)
equipment for making sounds louder, used in a public place for making announcements

> LANGUAGE EXTRA also spelt *tannoy*

tantalise *verb*
tantalises, tantalising, tantalised
to annoy someone or make them suffer by showing them something that they cannot have and making them want to have it *The shop window had a tantalising display of expensive toys* (for example, I wanted to buy one but we didn't have enough money).

> LANGUAGE EXTRA also spelt *tantalize*

> ORIGIN from Greek King *Tantalos* who was punished by being made to stand in a river under branches of fruit. The water and the fruit moved away from him whenever he tried to drink or eat.

tantrum *noun* **tantrums**
a short period when someone suddenly becomes very angry and cannot control their anger

> LANGUAGE EXTRA you can also say *temper tantrum*

Tanzania ['tan-zer-**nee**-er'] *noun*
a country in East Africa
Tanzanian *adjective & noun*

tap *noun* **taps**
1 a piece of equipment with a handle or knob that you turn to control how much water, liquid or gas comes out of a pipe or container
2 a gentle touch or hit *a tap on the shoulder*
3 the sound of something gently hitting something else *We heard a few taps on the window.*
4 an informal word for tap dancing

tap *verb*
taps, tapping, tapped
1 to touch or hit someone or something gently *Someone tapped me on the shoulder.*
2 to hit something gently against something else, usually several times and with short soft sounds *She was nervously tapping her fingers on the table. I heard someone tapping but there was no-one at the door.*
3 to tap someone's phone is to hide a tiny microphone in it or close to it to listen to what people are saying

> SYNONYM to bug

4 to put information such as numbers or letters into a piece of equipment such as a computer by pressing buttons or keys *Tap in your password. You've tapped the wrong number into your phone.*
5 to touch a screen on a computer or other device such as a mobile phone to make something work
6 to use something that will help you and be good for you, for example a source of energy or someone's knowledge *Solar panels tap energy from the sun.*

tap dancing *noun*
a type of dancing in which you wear special shoes with pieces of metal on the toes and heels to make tapping sounds to the music
tap-dance *verb* **tap dancer** *noun*

tape *noun* **tapes**
1 a thin plastic material that is sticky on one side, used for sticking something to something else. It is sold in a roll as a long strip. *My broken glasses are held together by sticky tape.*
2 a thin narrow strip of material, usually plastic, used for example for tying things together, for showing the place where a race finishes, or by the police for keeping people away from a place where a crime happened
3 a thin plastic strip covered with a special substance with magnetic properties, used especially in the past for recording sounds, images or computer information *Great-Gran had some Beatles music on tape.*
4 a small flat plastic container with magnetic tape inside for playing and recording sounds and pictures, used especially in the past *Great-Granddad used to listen to tapes.*

tape *verb*
tapes, taping, taped
1 to stick something using tape that is sticky on one side *I taped a message to the door. Tape the envelope down so it doesn't come unstuck.*
2 to put tape on or around something *Tape up the package carefully. The police taped the area where the crime took place.*
3 to record sounds or moving pictures on magnetic tape, for example using a video recorder or tape recorder, especially in the past
4 if a piece of equipment tapes, sounds or pictures are being recorded on it *Is the VCR still taping?*

tape measure *noun* **tape measures**
a strip of cloth, thin plastic or metal with centimetres or inches marked along its edges, used for measuring things. It is usually rolled up when it is not being used.

taper *verb*
tapers, tapering, tapered
if something tapers, one end of it gradually gets thinner *Grandma has long tapering fingers.*

taper *noun* **tapers**
1 a long thin piece of string covered with wax (a substance like fat that is soft when hot and hard when cold). It is used for lighting things such as candles.
2 a type of long candle with one end that gradually gets thinner

tape recorder *noun* **tape recorders**
a piece of equipment for playing sounds such as music that have been recorded on magnetic tape and for recording sounds on tape, used especially in the past
tape recording *noun*

tapestry ['**tap**-er-stree'] *noun* **tapestries**
a piece of heavy cloth with pictures or patterns in it. Tapestries are often hung on walls as decoration.

tapeworm *noun* **tapeworms**
a type of long flat worm that can live inside a person's or animal's bowels (tubes carrying food from the stomach)

tapir ['**tay**-per'] *noun* **tapirs**
an animal like a large pig with a long nose that bends and very short hair of different colours, often brown, black, or black and white. Tapirs live in South and Central America and South-East Asia.

tar *noun*
a thick black sticky substance usually made from coal, used for making roads and other surfaces

tar *verb*
tars, tarring, tarred
to put tar on the surface of something, usually a road *Some roads in this part of the country are not tarred.*

taramasalata ['ta-rer-mer-ser-**lah**-ter'] *noun*
a soft Greek food made from fish eggs. It has a pink or beige colour.

tarantula ['ter-ran-**tyoo**-ler'] *noun* **tarantulas**
a large spider with a hairy body and hairy legs. Tarantulas live in hot countries in many parts of the world and some types are poisonous.

> ORIGIN from the town of *Taranto* in the south of Italy where these spiders are common

Tardis *noun*
used about a place or thing that is much bigger on the inside than it looks from the outside

> ORIGIN from the name of the time machine in the TV series *Doctor Who*. It looks like an old-fashioned police telephone box from the outside but is a huge spaceship on the inside.

target *noun* **targets**
1 something that someone hopes or tries to get or reach *Our school has set a target of raising £10000 for the new sports centre.*
2 an object that someone tries to hit in a game or sport such as darts or archery (shooting with a bow and arrow) or when practising shooting with a gun

3 a place, object or person that someone attacks (or intends to attack), for example with weapons such as guns or bombs
4 a person, object, place or something such as an idea or action that something bad is directed at *My brother was the target of Dad's anger. The school's exam results were the target of a lot of criticism.*

target *verb*
targets, targeting, targeted
1 to attack (or intend to attack) a particular place, object or person *The terrorists targeted the president's palace.*
2 to aim something such as a weapon at a particular place, object or person *The soldiers targeted their rockets across the border into Syria. The missiles were targeted at the refugees.*
3 to say, write, do or make something for a particular person or group *This dictionary is targeted at schoolchildren.*

tarmac *noun* (trademark)
1 a material for making roads and other hard surfaces, made from tar (thick black substance made from coal) mixed with small stones
2 the tarmac is the part of an airport where planes are kept, for example where passengers get on and off

tarnish *verb*
tarnishes, tarnishing, tarnished
1 if a metal tarnishes, or if something tarnishes it, its colour becomes less bright and it often looks dirty or damaged
2 if something tarnishes someone's reputation, good name or image, it makes people have less respect for them and like them less than before *The footballer's bad behaviour has tarnished his reputation among the fans.*

tarpaulin *noun* tarpaulins
a large piece of plastic or other material that water cannot go through, used for covering something to protect it

tart *noun* tarts
a large or small pie with a pastry base (made from flour, water and fat) and an open top. It is usually filled with fruit such as apples or blueberries. *an apple tart; a jam tart*

tart *adjective* tarter, tartest
used about food or drink that has a very strong taste, for example like a lemon or an apple that isn't ripe

SYNONYM sour

tartan *noun* tartans
1 a pattern of coloured stripes that cross each other to make squares and rectangles *My sister wore a tartan skirt.*
2 a woollen cloth that has this pattern, used especially for making Scottish kilts (heavy skirts for men and boys)

task *noun* tasks
1 a piece of work that needs to be done or has just been done *Learning French is no easy task.*
2 a task force is a group of people who come together, or are chosen, to do a special piece of work

taskbar *noun* taskbars
a long strip along the bottom, side or top of a computer screen with symbols or icons that you click on or touch, for example to move between different programs

tassel *noun* tassels
a group of strings tied together at the top. Tassels are used as decorations that hang down from things such as curtains, hats or clothes.

taste *verb*
tastes, tasting, tasted
1 to eat or drink something and let it produce a certain feeling on your tongue that you either like or don't like *You can taste the garlic in this soup. I've never tasted such a delicious cake.*
2 to eat or drink a small amount of something, for example to try it and see what it's like *Do you want to taste my ice cream?*
3 if something tastes in a particular way, that is the feeling it produces on your tongue *The bread tasted salty. This tea tastes like rotten eggs.*
4 also used for showing what you think about the feeling that something produces on your tongue *The bread tastes delicious but the jam tastes awful.*

taste *noun*
1 (plural **tastes**) the special quality that food or drink produces on your tongue that tells you what it is, lets you decide whether you like it or not, and lets you enjoy (or not enjoy) the feeling of eating or drinking it *the sweet taste of honey; This apple has a lovely taste. I don't like the taste of salt.*
2 a small amount of food or drink that you try *Have a taste of this ice cream.*
3 the natural ability you have to taste things *To be a chef you need to have a good sense of taste.*
4 a feeling that you like something or someone *Seema has a taste for classical music. This kind of music isn't to my taste* (I don't like it).
5 your tastes are the things that you like *What are your tastes in books? My brother has expensive tastes* (likes things that cost a lot of money).
6 a new experience of something that someone has *Today is Rupa's first taste of freedom after being in hospital for a month.*
7 the special quality that someone has to make good decisions about things and to choose or do only the best things *My sister loves Shakespeare – she has taste* (or *good taste*). *Granddad's flat is decorated with taste* (in the best possible way).

taste buds *noun plural*
the tiny areas on the surface of your tongue that allow you to recognise different tastes and enjoy them (or not enjoy them)

tasteful *adjective*
showing that someone has the special quality of choosing only the best things *Grandma's furniture is very tasteful.*
tastefully *adverb*

tasteless *adjective*
1 not having any taste *This orange is tasteless.*
2 showing that someone has bad judgement, for example because they choose things that are not attractive or fashionable *His arms were covered in big tasteless tattoos.*
tastelessly *adverb*

tasty *adjective* tastier, tastiest
having a very pleasant taste *a tasty meal*
tastiness *noun*

tattered *adjective*
badly torn *old tattered clothes*

tatters *noun plural*
if something is in tatters, it is badly torn *My jeans are old and in tatters.*

tattoo *noun* tattoos
a picture, pattern or words drawn on someone's skin using a special needle and ink

> **ORIGIN** from Tahitian *tatau* 'tattoo'. Sailors introduced the word into English in the 18th century.

tattoo *verb*
tattoos, tattooing, tattooed
if someone tattoos someone or a part of their body, they put a tattoo onto their skin *a sailor with tattooed arms* **tattooist** *noun*

tattoo *noun* tattoos
an outdoor event in which soldiers march, perform exercises and play music in bands

> **ORIGIN** from Dutch *tap toe* 'turn off the tap'. In 17th-century Holland, groups of musicians were sent into towns every day playing drums to tell soldiers to return to barracks (the place where they lived). *Tap toe* was an order for the people in charge of pubs to stop selling beer to soldiers and to send them home.

tatty *adjective* tattier, tattiest
in bad condition because of being old or used a lot *a tatty hotel; tatty clothes*

SYNONYM shabby

taught
past tense & past participle of **teach**

taunt *verb*
taunts, taunting, taunted
to say unkind or insulting things to someone, for example because of the way someone looks *She taunted me because of my big ears.*

taunt *noun* taunts
an unkind or insulting thing said to someone to upset them

taut *adjective* tauter, tautest
stretched or pulled very tight *taut muscles; Make sure the rope is taut.* **tautly** *adverb*
tautness *noun*

tavern *noun* taverns
an old-fashioned word for a place where adults go to buy drinks such as beer or wine and eat meals

tawny *adjective* tawnier, tawniest
having a light brown or yellow-brown colour

tax *noun* taxes
money that people have to pay to the government, for example some of the money they earn or some of the money it costs to buy something. Taxes pay for things such as schools, roads, doctors and police officers.

tax–tea towel

tax *verb*
taxes, taxing, taxed
if someone or something is taxed, or if the government taxes someone or something, a certain amount of money must be paid to the government, for example some of the money that people earn or that they pay when they buy something *Most people who earn money are taxed. Petrol is heavily taxed* (people pay a lot of tax when they buy petrol).

taxation *noun*
1 the system that the government uses to collect taxes from people
2 the money that the government collects as taxes

taxi *noun* **taxis**
1 a car with a driver that you pay to take you where you want to go. You pick up a taxi in the street and you can often call for one by phone.
2 a taxi rank is a place in the street where taxis wait for people

taxi *verb*
taxis, taxiing, taxied
used about an aircraft that moves slowly along the ground, for example after landing or while waiting to take off

taxpayer *noun* **taxpayers**
someone who pays taxes to the government

TB *noun*
a serious illness that affects people's lungs
short for: tuberculosis

tea *noun*
1 a drink made by pouring hot water onto the leaves of a tropical plant, usually the tea bush, after the leaves have been dried (water has been removed) *a cup of tea; camomile tea*
2 the dried leaves used for making this drink *a packet of tea*
3 (*plural* **teas**) a cup or mug of tea *Three teas, please.*
4 the tea bush or the leaves that grow on this bush *They grow tea in hot countries like India. We saw a group of tea pickers.*
5 a cooked meal that you eat in the early evening *What did you have for tea?*
6 a small meal that you eat in the afternoon or evening, for example a pot of tea with sandwiches or cakes, biscuits and scones *a cream tea* (with scones, jam and cream)

ORIGIN from Chinese *t'e* (pronounced 'tay' or 'cha')

teabag *noun* **teabags**
a small bag made of paper with tea leaves inside. You put it in hot water to make a cup of tea.

tea break *noun* **tea breaks**
a time when you have a short rest from your work or lessons to have a cup of tea and often something to eat

teacake *noun* **teacakes**
a small sweet round bread roll with raisins in it or other dried fruit (fruit with the water removed). You usually cut it in half, toast it and eat it with tea.

teach *verb*
teaches, teaching, taught
1 to make someone understand and remember something by giving them information *My brother taught me a few words of Spanish. My dad teaches maths in a school* (gives information about this subject in lessons). *My mum also teaches. Uncle George taught me a new skill.*
2 to let someone watch you do something and explain to them how to do it *Can you teach me how to swim?*
3 if someone or something teaches you a lesson, you change your behaviour in the future because of it *Jack was hit by a bike – that taught him a lesson* (he'll be more careful crossing the road next time).

teacher *noun* **teachers**
someone who teaches people, usually in a school or college

teaching *noun*
1 the job or activity of being a teacher, usually in a school or college *My big sister wants to go into teaching. Teaching can be fun.*
2 a teaching assistant is someone who is paid to help a schoolteacher in the classroom, for example by helping students with their lessons

tea cloth *noun* **tea cloths**
another word for a tea towel

tea cosy *noun* **tea cosies**
a cloth cover you put over a teapot to stop the tea from getting cold too quickly

teacup *noun* **teacups**
a small round container with a handle, used for drinking tea

teak *noun*
a strong yellow-brown wood from a large tree that grows in hot countries. It is often used for making furniture.

team *noun* **teams**
1 a group of people who play a game or sport together against other people *a football team; Sanjay is on our team.*
2 a group of people who work together *Granddad is being looked after by a team of doctors.*

teamwork *noun*

team up *verb*
teams up, teaming up, teamed up
if you team up with someone, you join them to do an activity together or to work together *My brother teamed up with his best friend to form a band. The two singers will team up on a new song.*

teapot *noun* **teapots**
a container for making and serving tea. It has a handle and a lid, and you pour the tea into a cup through a spout (part shaped like a tube).

tear ['teer'] *noun* **tears**
tears are drops of liquid that come out of your eyes when you cry *I saw him hiding behind a tree in tears* (crying). *When Jo told me the news, I burst into tears* (started crying).

tear ['tair'] *noun* **tears**
a hole that has been made in something such as cloth or paper where something or someone has torn it

tear ['tair'] *verb*
tears, tearing, tore, torn
1 to make a hole (or holes) in something such as cloth or paper, for example by accidentally pulling it too much or cutting it on something *I tore my shirt when I caught it on a nail.*
2 to pull something apart into two or more pieces *I tore the paper in half. Elena didn't like her photo so she tore it up.*
3 if something tears, a hole gets made in it (or holes get made in it) *My trousers tore when I bent over. This headscarf is delicate – it tears easily.*
4 to pull or remove something, often quickly or with a lot of force *Jack was so angry he tore the picture down from the wall. The wind tore the roof off.*
5 to move somewhere very quickly *My brother tore down the street on his new motorbike. I've been tearing around the school looking for my pencil case.*
6 to tear down something such as a building or wall is to completely destroy it

tearful ['teer-ferl'] *adjective*
1 used about someone who is crying or who cries *He always gets tearful when we say goodbye.*
2 also used about the actions of someone who is crying or who cries *a tearful voice; a tearful goodbye*

tearfully *adverb*

tear gas ['teer'] *noun*
a chemical weapon that makes people's eyes hurt. It is usually used by the police or soldiers to control violent crowds.

tease *verb*
teases, teasing, teased
1 to say unkind things to someone in a cruel way to upset them or in a friendly way as a joke *I'm always teasing my best friend about her accent.*
2 to do something to an animal to make it slightly angry, such as pulling its tail or hitting it gently with your hand

tease *noun*
1 someone who teases you, usually in a friendly way
2 something that someone says or does to tease you

teaspoon *noun* **teaspoons**
1 a very small spoon, used for example for putting sugar into hot drinks such as tea and stirring them, or for eating with. A teaspoon is much smaller than a dessertspoon.
2 the amount of food or liquid that a teaspoon can hold

LANGUAGE EXTRA in sense 2, you can also say *teaspoonful*

teat *noun* **teats**
1 a small rubber object on the end of a baby's feeding bottle that a baby sucks to drink milk or juice
2 teats are the small circular parts on a female animal's body that her baby animals drink milk through

teatime *noun*
the time in the afternoon or evening when people usually have tea or when someone is having their tea

tea towel *noun* **tea towels**
a cloth for drying plates, knives, forks and spoons, and other kitchen objects after they have been washed

LANGUAGE EXTRA you can also say *tea cloth*

techie – telescopic

techie *noun* **techies**
someone who knows a lot about computers and how they work, especially as their job

technical *adjective*
1 connected with technology and the special knowledge of how equipment, machines and software work *a technical expert* (for example someone who knows how a particular piece of equipment or computer software works)
2 connected with equipment, machines and software and how they work *Dad had lots of technical problems installing the new router.*
3 connected with the special knowledge or skills people have in a particular area *He's a story writer of great technical skill* (he writes very good stories). *Here is a list of technical terms used in Latin grammar* (difficult words for explaining things in Latin grammar).

technicality *noun* **technicalities**
a small detail of something such as a rule or how something works

technically *adverb*
1 connected with equipment, machines and software *The UK is technically very advanced.*
2 showing special knowledge or skills in a particular area *He's a technically brilliant pianist.*
3 used for talking about the exact meaning of a word, especially when the real meaning is different from this *It's technically possible to change schools* (this can happen but is unlikely). *Technically, he broke the law* (he did do this but no-one will do anything about it).

technician *noun* **technicians**
someone who does work that needs the special knowledge of how to use particular equipment or machines *a laboratory technician*

technique ['tek-neek'] *noun* **techniques**
a particular way of doing something that needs a lot of skill and practice

technological *adjective*
connected with technology *technological progress* **technologically** *adverb*

technology *noun*
knowledge about how equipment, machines and software work and using this knowledge to make more and better equipment, machines and software *computer technology*

teddy bear *noun* **teddy bears**
a small soft toy shaped like a bear

ORIGIN from the name of US President Roosevelt at the beginning of the 20th century. His first name was Theodore, which was *Teddy* for short, and he was a hunter of *bears*.

tedious ['tee-dee-ers'] *adjective*
very boring, for example because of being too long or because the same thing is done or said too often *a tedious lesson*; *a tedious journey* **tediously** *adverb* **tediousness** *noun*

tedium ['tee-dee-erm'] *noun*
when something is very boring *I hate the tedium of Mr Fraser's classes.*

teem *verb*
teems, teeming, teemed
1 if something is teeming with people, animals or insects, there are lots of them everywhere *The centre of town was teeming with shoppers.*
2 to rain very heavily *It's teeming down outside.*

teenage *adjective*
1 used about someone between the ages of 13 and 19 *My aunt and uncle have one teenage son.*

LANGUAGE EXTRA you can also say *teenaged*

2 connected with teenagers *a teenage magazine*

teenager *noun* **teenagers**
a young person between the ages of 13 and 19

teens *noun plural*
the years when someone is between the ages of 13 and 19 *I'm nine but my sister is in her teens.*

teeny *adjective* **teenier, teeniest**
an informal word for very small

LANGUAGE EXTRA you can also say *teeny-weeny*

teepee *noun* **teepees**
a tent shaped like a cone (sloping sides, point at the top and circle at the bottom) that Native Americans lived in in the past

LANGUAGE EXTRA also spelt *tepee*

tee shirt *noun* **tee shirts**
a piece of clothing made of thin cloth that you wear on the top half of your body. It has short sleeves and no collar or buttons.

LANGUAGE EXTRA also spelt *T-shirt*

teeter *verb*
teeters, teetering, teetered
to move or stand in an unsteady way and look as if you are about to fall

teeth
plural of **tooth**

teethe *verb*
teethes, teething, teethed
if a baby is teething, its first teeth are starting to grow, usually causing pain

tele- *prefix*
at or over a long distance *telescope*; *telephone*

ORIGIN from Greek *tele* 'far'

telecommunications *noun plural*
the science of sending information over long distances, for example by phone, satellite or radio

telegram *noun* **telegrams**
a piece of paper with a message written on it sent by telegraph. Telegrams were used in the past as a way of sending messages over long distances.

telegraph *noun*
1 a method of sending information over long distances using electrical wires and radio signals, used in the past
2 a telegraph pole is a tall wooden pole for carrying phone wires high above the ground

telepathy ['ter-lep-er-thee'] *noun*
being able to communicate with someone by using your thoughts rather than words or signals **telepathic** *adjective*

telephone *noun*
1 (*plural* **telephones**) a piece of electronic equipment for speaking to someone in another place *I'm on the telephone* (talking to someone using a telephone). *The telephone is off the hook* (the part that you hold next to your ear and mouth is not in its place).
2 a system for talking to someone who is in another place *Dad got in touch with the school by telephone.*

ORIGIN from Greek *tele* 'far' and *phone* 'sound' or 'voice'

telephone *verb*
telephones, telephoning, telephoned
to speak to someone using a telephone *Telephone the doctor if you need advice. No-one telephoned while you were out.*

telephone book *noun* **telephone books**
another word for a telephone directory

telephone booth *noun* **telephone booths**
a very small structure with walls, a roof and a door, or a structure that is partly open, with a telephone inside that people pay to use

telephone box *noun* **telephone boxes**
a very small structure with walls, a roof and a door, and with a telephone inside that people pay to use

telephone call *noun* **telephone calls**
when you speak to someone on the telephone *George makes lots of telephone calls.*

telephone directory *noun*
telephone directories
a book that lists the telephone numbers of people and businesses, together with their names and addresses

telephone number *noun*
telephone numbers
the number that you dial (press buttons on a telephone) to connect to another telephone that belongs to the person you want to speak to

telephonist ['ter-lef-er-nist'] *noun*
telephonists
an old-fashioned word for a switchboard operator (someone who connects people making phone calls to the people they want to speak to)

telescope *noun* **telescopes**
a piece of equipment shaped like a tube that someone looks through with one eye. It has lenses (curved pieces of glass) and mirrors inside for making objects far away look bigger and appear closer.

ORIGIN from Greek *tele* 'far' and *skopein* 'to look at'

telescopic *adjective*
1 used about something that makes faraway objects look bigger *telescopic sight* (part of a gun that you look through to aim it)

521

televise – tendency

2 used about an object that has different sections that can be pushed or folded into each other to make it smaller *a telescopic ladder; a telescopic umbrella*

televise *verb*
televises, televising, televised
to film something and show it on television *The cup final will be televised live.*

television *noun*
1 (*plural* **televisions**) a piece of electronic equipment with a screen for watching broadcast programmes *Turn the television off.*

LANGUAGE EXTRA you can also say *television set*

2 a system for sending special energy waves over a long distance and turning them into pictures and sounds that you can see and hear on a television set *The match will be on television tomorrow. I prefer radio to television.*
3 also used for talking about the programmes that you watch *I'm watching the television. Television is good in this country. It's a new television series.*

television station *noun*
television stations
a place or building where television programmes are made and broadcast from *My aunt works for a television station.*

tell *verb*
tells, telling, told
1 to use words to give someone information or opinions *Tell me where he is. Could you tell me the way to the library? People tell us our school is the best in the city.*
2 to say or give the words of something to someone, for example the words of a story or joke *Mum told me a story before bed. The book tells the tale of a very old king.*
3 if something tells you something, it gives you information or shows you that something is true *The clock tells us that it's midday. This funny noise tells me there's something wrong with my computer.*
4 to tell someone to do something is to say to them that they must do it *Mum told me to switch the TV off.*
5 to know or recognise something or someone *It's hard to tell when you're joking. Can you tell the difference between a seal and a sea lion? Ed couldn't tell the two sisters apart.*
6 to tell someone a secret is to let someone know what the secret is *Don't tell anyone my secret. Of course, I'll never tell.*
7 to tell tales is to say things that aren't true, usually about someone else, for example telling a teacher that someone has done something bad
8 to tell the truth (or a lie) is to say something that is true (or is not true) *I always tell the truth* (say true things).
9 to tell the time is to understand what the numbers mean on a clock or watch and to know what the positions of the hour hand and second hand mean
10 (informal) to tell someone off is to say something to them in an angry voice because they've done something wrong *If you play football in the corridor, you'll get told off.*

11 (informal) to tell on someone is to tell an important person such as a teacher that someone has done something wrong

telling-off *noun* **tellings-off** (informal) when someone says something to you in an angry voice because you've done something wrong *My mum gave me a good telling-off.*

telltale *noun* **telltales**
1 a boy or girl who tells an important person such as a parent or teacher about something bad that someone has done
2 a boy or girl who says things that aren't true, usually about someone else

telltale *adjective*
showing information about something, for example something that is supposed to be secret *Lucy's eyes were red – a telltale sign that she was working too hard.*

telly *noun* **tellies**
an informal word for television *The telly's broken. What's on the telly tonight?*

temper *noun*
1 the way someone feels and behaves at a particular time, especially when they are angry *Holly has quite a temper* (or *can't control her temper*) (she gets angry very quickly). *Tom's in a bad temper* (he's angry).
2 if you lose your temper, you become angry

temperament *noun* **temperaments**
the special qualities that someone is born with, for example that make them feel and behave in a certain way *My brother has a nervous temperament.*

temperamental *adjective*
1 if someone is temperamental, they easily become angry or excited or their mood often changes
2 if a piece of equipment or vehicle is temperamental, it doesn't always work the way it should or it often stops working

temperate *adjective*
used for describing a climate or region that is neither too hot nor too cold

temperature *noun*
1 (*plural* **temperatures**) a measurement that shows how hot or cold something is or how hot someone's body is *Water boils at a temperature of 100 degrees. The doctor took my temperature* (used a thermometer to measure how hot my body was).
2 when someone is ill because their body is too hot *I have a temperature. David was off school with a temperature.*

tempest *noun* **tempests**
a bad storm with very strong winds and lots of rain

temple *noun* **temples**
1 a word used in some religions for a building where people pray to a god or gods *a Hindu temple; an ancient Greek temple*
2 your temple is the flat part on each side of your face between your forehead and the top of your ear

tempo *noun* **tempos**
1 the speed that a piece of music is played at
2 the speed at which something happens

temporarily *adverb*
for a certain time only, usually a short time *The library has closed temporarily.*

ANTONYM permanently

temporary *adjective*
existing or lasting for a certain time only, usually a short time *a temporary classroom; While Ms Fuller is away, we have a temporary teacher.*

ANTONYM permanent

tempt *verb*
tempts, tempting, tempted
1 to get someone to want to do, have or try something that they shouldn't do, have or try *'Have another cake.' – 'Don't tempt me.' He was so annoying I was tempted to hit him* (I wanted to hit him even though I knew I shouldn't).
2 to get someone to want to do, have or try something that would make them very happy *The sight of the children splashing about tempted me into the water. Ferndale School offered me a place, which I was tempted to accept* (I wanted to accept it because it was a very good thing).

temptation *noun*
1 a strong feeling of wanting to do, have or try something, especially something that you shouldn't do, have or try
2 (*plural* **temptations**) something that you want to do, have or try that you shouldn't do, have or try

tempting *adjective*
used for describing something that would make you very happy, for example if you had it or did it *Those chocolates look tempting. 'Shall we go swimming?' – 'That sounds tempting.'*

ten *adjective & noun* **tens**
1 the number 10
2 in maths, tens are the numbers from 1 to 9 used in sums that include numbers above nine. The numbers are written in the tens column to the left of the units (whole numbers from 0 to 9). For example, 57 is made up of five tens and seven units, and 20 is two tens and no units.

tenant *noun* **tenants**
someone who pays money (called rent) to a person (called a landlord or landlady) for letting them live in a house, flat or room or for letting them use a building or piece of land that belongs to that person
tenancy *noun*

tend *verb*
tends, tending, tended
1 used about something that is likely to happen or about the way something is likely to be *It tends to rain a lot in April. April tends to be rainy.*
2 used about someone who is likely to do or have something or about the way someone is likely to be *Dad tends to get angry if you interrupt him. My sister tends to be moody.*
3 if someone tends to something or someone, they take care of them *Grandma likes to tend to her garden* (she looks after it so that it stays in good condition). *The doctor tended to the injured soldier* (dealt with his injuries to make them better).

tendency *noun* **tendencies**
1 something that is likely to happen or the way something is likely to be *There's a tendency for April to be wet.*

522

tender–termite

2 something that someone is likely to do or the way someone is likely to be *My brother has a tendency to be naughty and do silly things.*
3 something that has started to happen and is likely to continue happening *In our school there's been a tendency to ask parents to pay for schoolbooks.*

tender *adjective* tenderer, tenderest
1 if a part of your body is tender, it hurts slightly when you touch it

SYNONYM sensitive

2 if food is tender, for example meat or vegetables, it is soft and easy to cut and eat
3 if something such as a smile, touch or kiss is tender, it shows kindness and love in a very pleasant way
tenderness *noun*

tender *verb*
tenders, tendering, tendered
to officially offer something to someone, usually in writing, for example an apology

tenderly *adverb*
with kindness and love *We hugged each other tenderly.*

tendon *noun* tendons
a strong substance in the body made of many threads joining a muscle to a bone

SYNONYM sinew

tendril *noun* tendrils
a long thin stem on a climbing plant that twists itself around something to help the plant to support itself

tenement *noun* tenements
a large and usually old building containing flats, especially in towns in Scotland

tenner *noun* tenners (informal)
a piece of paper money worth £10

tennis *noun*
a game played on a rectangular area called a court, usually outside. One or two players stand at either end of the court holding rackets (frames with strings across fixed to a handle). They use the rackets for hitting a small ball to each other across a low net in the middle of the court.

tenor *noun* tenors
1 a man with a fairly high singing voice, higher than a baritone
2 a tenor voice or musical instrument

tenpin bowling *noun*
an indoor game in which people roll a large heavy ball down a narrow track to knock down wooden objects called pins (or tenpins), which are shaped like bottles

tense *adjective* tenser, tensest
1 if someone is tense, they are worried about something and are not relaxed *The parents were tense as they waited for news of the missing boy.*
2 showing that someone is worried and not relaxed *He had a tense expression on his face.*
3 making someone feel worried and not relaxed *a tense situation*
4 if your body or a part of it such as a muscle is tense, it is stretched tight
tensely *adverb* **tenseness** *noun*

tense *verb*
tenses, tensing, tensed
1 if you tense a part of your body such as a muscle, you make it tight
2 if you tense up, you become tense and worried

tense *noun* tenses
in grammar, a tense is the form of a verb that shows you when something happens or exists, for example whether it happens or exists now, whether it happened or existed in the past or whether it will happen or exist in the future

LANGUAGE EXTRA the *present tense* of a verb shows what is happening or what exists now, or what happens or exists regularly or all the time, for example *sing* (*I sing*), *sings* (*she sings*), *am singing* (*I am singing*), *are singing* (*they are singing*).
 The *past tense* shows what happened or existed before the present time, for example *sang* (*I sang*), *sung* (*I have sung*), *was singing* (*he was singing*), *were singing* (*we were singing*).
 The *future tense* shows what is going to happen but has not yet happened, for example *will sing* (*he will sing*), *shall sing* (*I shall sing*), *will be singing* (*they will be singing*).

tension *noun*
1 a feeling of being worried and not relaxed, for example while waiting for something to happen
2 (*plural* tensions) anger and unfriendly feelings between people or groups who do not trust each other *In Jo's house there are a lot of family tensions.*
3 a feeling of fear and excitement created in a film, play or book as the story develops and you don't know what is going to happen next
4 when something such as a rope, string or muscle is stretched tight

tent *noun* tents
a shelter made from strong cloth that can be folded or rolled up and carried around. The cloth is opened out and fixed to the ground with poles, ropes and pegs (sticks of metal). Tents are usually used for sleeping in and as protection against the weather, for example by campers or soldiers.

tentacle *noun* tentacles
one of the long thin arms of a sea creature such as an octopus or squid

ORIGIN from Latin *tentare* 'to feel'

tenterhooks *noun plural*
on tenterhooks worried about something that is going to happen *The whole class was waiting on tenterhooks for the results of the maths test.*

ORIGIN from the name of the special hooks used in the past for stretching cloth. If someone is *on tenterhooks*, they feel like stretched cloth!

tenth *adjective & noun*
1 used about something or someone that comes in place number 10 *in the tenth month*
2 (*plural* tenths) one of 10 equal parts of something *one tenth of the money*

tepid *adjective*
slightly warm, sometimes when you want something to be warmer *The bath water was tepid.*

terabyte *noun* terabytes
a piece of information used by a computer, for example for measuring the size of a program or hard disk. A terabyte is made up of 1024 gigabytes (or a million million bytes).

term *noun* terms
1 one of the parts that the school or college year is divided into. In the UK, these parts are usually the autumn term, spring term and summer term. *My brother is at boarding school during term time.*
2 a word or expression with a special meaning, usually in a subject that needs a special knowledge or skill *a slang term; That's a technical term used by pilots. What's the medical term for chickenpox?*
3 a period of time that someone official such as a politician spends in their job *The mayor was elected for a term of one year.*
4 a period of time someone spends in prison *He served a prison term of two years* (spent two years in prison).
5 the terms of an agreement are the conditions that you must agree to *To use this software, click here to accept the terms.*
6 if you are on good terms (or bad terms) with someone, you behave towards them in a friendly (or unfriendly) way

term *verb*
terms, terming, termed
to describe something or someone using a particular word or phrase *My teacher termed my homework a disaster.*

terminal *noun* terminals
1 a building at an airport, used by passengers when they arrive and leave *Terminal 3 is for international flights.*
2 a building in a town from where passengers are taken by bus to an airport terminal
3 a place where a ship, bus or train begins or ends its journey *a ferry terminal*
4 a computer screen and keyboard connected to a large computer system
5 a place in an electrical circuit (the path a current travels round) where something such as a battery or wire connects to the electricity

terminal *adjective*
used about an illness that cannot be cured. A person who has a terminal illness will die from it.

terminate *verb*
terminates, terminating, terminated
to end or stop, or make something end or stop *This tube train terminates at Tower Hill. Mum terminated her magazine subscription.* **termination** *noun*

terminus *noun* terminuses or termini
the station at the end of a bus route or railway line

termite *noun* termites
a small insect like an ant that lives in large groups under the ground in hot countries. Termites eat wood and damage buildings.

523

terrace – text

terrace noun **terraces**
1 a flat area outside a restaurant or house where you sit, for example to relax or eat
2 a row of houses joined to other houses on both sides
3 a street made up of houses joined on both sides *We live at 8 Fern Terrace.*
4 the terraces at a football ground are the wide steps where you stand and watch the match

terraced adjective
a terraced house is one that is joined to another house on both sides
compare: **semi-detached house** and **detached house**

terrapin noun **terrapins**
a small turtle that lives in warm countries, in water and on land

terrible adjective
1 extremely bad *a terrible mistake; a terrible film*
2 ill *I have a headache and feel terrible.*
3 sad *I feel terrible about what my brother said.*
4 frightening *The noise of the explosion was terrible.*
5 used for saying how much of something there is *It's a terrible shame. I've got a terrible amount of homework this week.*
6 ugly *That's a terrible dress she's wearing.*

terribly adverb
1 extremely *I'm terribly sorry.*
2 very much *Would you mind terribly if I closed the window?*
3 extremely badly *Our team played terribly.*

terrier noun **terriers**
a small energetic dog that people keep as a pet. There are many different types of terriers.

terrific adjective
1 very good *a terrific book; Rashid's coming to my party – that's terrific!*
2 very big *Polar bears travel terrific distances looking for food. Space rockets reach terrific speeds.*
3 used when you mean a lot of something *I'm in terrific pain. I have a terrific amount of work to do.*

terrifically adverb
1 extremely *She's terrifically happy.*
2 extremely well *You danced terrifically in the show.*

terrify verb
terrifies, terrifying, terrified
1 to frighten someone very much *The loud bang terrified me. Everyone on the bus was terrified.*
2 if you're terrified of something or someone, they frighten you very much *I'm terrified of spiders.*

terrifying adjective
extremely frightening **terrifyingly** adverb

territory noun **territories**
1 an area of land controlled by a particular country *This region is French territory.*
2 an area connected with someone, for example an area that they are responsible for or that they control *The soldiers deliver aid to a territory the size of Wales. The gang leader told me to keep off his territory.*
3 an area that an animal lives in and controls *Cats don't usually wander far from their territory.*

territorial adjective

terror noun
1 a very strong feeling of being frightened, for example when you are in danger *People screamed in terror when the bomb went off.*
2 violent action that causes fear among people *a campaign of terror; a terror attack*
3 (plural **terrors**) a boy or girl who behaves badly *You little terror!*

terrorise verb
terrorises, terrorising, terrorised
to frighten people, for example by telling them you will hurt them if they don't do what you want them to do *The gang terrorised the whole neighbourhood.*

> LANGUAGE EXTRA also spelt *terrorize*

terrorism noun
the use of violent actions to create fear among people and make governments change things

terrorist noun **terrorists**
someone who uses violent actions such as putting a bomb somewhere or holding someone hostage (as a prisoner). Terrorists do this to create fear among people and to make governments change things and give them what they want.

tessellation noun **tessellations**
in maths, a tessellation is a pattern of shapes that fit together without leaving any gaps in between

test noun **tests**
1 a series of questions to answer or something you do to find out how much you know about a subject or how well you do an activity *a maths test; a reading test*
2 an examination by someone such as a doctor to get information about your body (or a part of your body) and how healthy it is *a hearing test* (to find out how well you can hear); *an eye test; My sister had a test for diabetes* (to find out if she has that illness).
3 when someone performs a series of actions on something to find something out, for example whether it is working properly or how good it is *a safety test* (to see how safe something is, such as a car); *Every computer has to pass a test before it is sold* (all the actions performed on it must be successful). *The scientists are carrying out tests on the bones* (for example to see how old they are).
4 short for **test match** (game of cricket or rugby between teams from two countries)

test verb
tests, testing, tested
1 to give someone a test to find out how much they know about a subject or how well they do an activity *Tomorrow Ms Rogers will be testing us in French.*
2 to give something a test to find out if it is working properly and how good it is *All the toys are tested before they leave the factory.*
3 to examine someone or a part of someone's body to see how healthy they are *I need to get my eyes tested.*
4 to examine something scientifically to get information about it *They tested the lunar rocks in the lab to see what they were made of.*
5 to try something to see whether it is how it should be *Test the bath water with your wrist to make sure it's not too hot.*

Testament noun
the Old and New Testaments are the first and second parts of the Christian Bible (holy book of the Christian religion). The first part tells the story of the Jewish people and the second describes the life of Jesus Christ.
see: **Old Testament** and **New Testament**

testicle noun **testicles**
one of the two bags of skin on the body of a male person or animal that produce sperm (cells for making a new person or animal grow)

testify verb
testifies, testifying, testified
if someone testifies, usually in a court of law, they give information about something after they have promised to tell the truth about it *The witness testified that she saw the two men running away.*

testimony noun

testimonial noun **testimonials**
a letter or email describing someone's character or skills, for example one written by a person that someone has worked for

test match noun **test matches**
a game of cricket or rugby played between two teams from different countries

test tube noun **test tubes**
a small glass container shaped like a thin tube, used for scientific and medical experiments

testy adjective **testier, testiest**
slightly angry, or getting angry easily *a testy old person* **testily** adverb

tetanus ['tet-er-ners'] noun
a serious illness caused by germs getting into the body through a deep cut. It makes the muscles of the jaw and other parts of the body very stiff.

tetchy adjective **tetchier, tetchiest**
easily upset or annoyed *When I spoke to him he sounded rather tetchy.*

tether verb
tethers, tethering, tethered
to tie something to something else *The farmer tethered his goat to the fence.*

tether noun **tethers**
1 a rope or chain for tying something to something else, for example for tying a horse to a post
2 **to be at the end of your tether** to not have the strength or energy to deal with a difficult situation any longer

tetrahedron ['tet-rer-hee-drern'] noun
tetrahedra or **tetrahedrons**
a solid or 3-D shape with four flat faces (or surfaces). Each face is a triangle, usually an equilateral triangle (with sides the same length and angles of 60 degrees).

text noun **texts**
1 the main written part in something such as a book, magazine, poem or essay. The text does not include extra things such as pictures, notes at the bottom of the page or an index at the end.

2 any words that are written somewhere *The text of your email isn't clear. Here's the text of the head teacher's talk* (a copy of the words he or she said). *To remove a block of text from your document, highlight it and press the delete key.*
3 a book, story, play or poem that you study, for example as classwork or for an exam *'Animal Farm' is a set text this year* (a book you study for your exam).
4 short for **text message**
5 a text box is a space for writing in, usually with lines round it, on a printed page or web page or in a computer document

ORIGIN from Latin *textus* 'something woven or joined together', which comes from *texere* 'to weave' or 'to join'. The words 'textiles' and 'texture' also come from *texere*.

text *verb*
texts, texting, texted
to send a text message to someone on their mobile phone *I texted Mum to say that I had to stay late at school.* **texting** *noun*

textbook *noun* **textbooks**
a book used in school for studying a particular subject *a maths textbook*

textiles *noun plural*
different kinds of cloth, for example knitted cloth (made by joining loops of wool into rows) or woven cloth (made by crossing threads over each other)

text message *noun* **text messages**
a message that you send or receive on a mobile phone. Text messages can include pictures.

texture *noun* **textures**
the way that something feels when you touch it, for example how hard or soft or how rough or smooth it is

Thai *adjective*
connected with Thailand or the Thai language

Thai *noun*
1 the language people speak in Thailand
2 (*plural* **Thais**) someone from Thailand

Thailand *noun*
a country in South-East Asia

Thames *noun*
a long river that flows from the west of England, through Oxford, Reading and London, and into the North Sea

than *conjunction & preposition*
1 used when you compare things *Seema is taller and more intelligent than me. I can run faster than my brother. You're later than you should be. The taste is more like pear than peach.*
2 used with numbers for showing they are above or below other numbers *More than 20 carrots were used to make this soup. It took less than two hours.*

thank *verb*
thanks, thanking, thanked
to show someone that you're happy about something they've done for you or given you by expressing your feelings of happiness to them *I thanked my parents for the present and for their help.*

thankful *adjective*
happy about something, for example something good that happens or something unpleasant that doesn't happen *We were thankful that the rain stopped before our match.*

thankfully *adverb*
used for saying that you're happy about something good happening or something unpleasant not happening *Thankfully no-one was injured.*

SYNONYM **fortunately**

thankless *adjective*
used about an activity that is unpleasant or difficult and that other people are not likely to praise you for *Washing the dishes is a thankless task.*

thanks *noun plural*
words that you say or write to someone to tell them you're happy about something they've done or given you *a letter of thanks; Give my thanks to Aunt Amy.*

thanks *interjection*
used as another way of saying thank you *'I'll get you a glass of water.' – 'Thanks.'*

LANGUAGE EXTRA you can also say *thanks very much*, *thanks a lot* or *many thanks*

Thanksgiving *noun*
a public holiday in the United States during November and in Canada during October

ORIGIN from the time when people used to thank God for the crops and celebrate the harvest (when farmers collected their crops from the fields)

thanks to *preposition*
used for giving a reason for something, often something good that happens *Our team won, thanks to the goal we scored in the last 10 minutes. It's thanks to his doctor that Granddad's still alive.*

SYNONYM **because of**

thank you *interjection*
1 used as a polite way of thanking someone for something *'Here's your ice cream.' – 'Thank you.' Thank you for helping me.*
2 used as a polite way of saying yes to someone who asks you if you want something or who offers you something *'Do you want an ice cream?' – 'Thank you, I'd love one.' 'Would you like to come to my party?' – 'Thank you very much, I would.'*
3 also used as a polite way of saying no *'More cake?' – 'Thank you, I've already taken some.'*

LANGUAGE EXTRA you can also say *thanks*

that *adjective*
1 used about something or someone already mentioned or known about, or something or someone that you can see but that is not near you *We're reading that book in school. Do you know that boy over there? I want this one, not that one.*
2 used about something that is not near you in time *Where did you go that day? By that time I will have finished my homework.*

LANGUAGE EXTRA the plural is *those*, for example *We're reading those books in school.*

that *pronoun*
1 used about something or someone already mentioned or known about, or something or someone that you can see but that is not near you *That's the book we're reading in school. Is that the boy you saw?*

LANGUAGE EXTRA the plural is *those*, for example *Those are the books we're reading in school.*

2 used for saying something about something or someone *Show me the text message that you just received. Who's the girl that you were talking to? I'm waiting for the bus that goes to Leeds.*

LANGUAGE EXTRA *that* is often left out in sense 2, for example *Who's the girl you were talking to?*

that *conjunction*
used for introducing a clause (part of a sentence with a verb) after many types of verbs (for example 'say', 'tell', 'know', 'think', 'wish', 'hope'), adjectives (for example 'true', 'possible', 'angry', 'sorry', 'such') or nouns (for example 'idea', 'thought', 'fact', 'news') *I know that it's late. It's possible that it might rain. Dinesh was in such a hurry that he forgot his schoolbag. I was so tired that I fell asleep on the floor. The news that Ms Patel is leaving is sad.*

LANGUAGE EXTRA *that* is often left out, for example *I know it's late.*

that *adverb*
1 used for talking about the way something is or happens or about the size or amount of something *Slow down! – I can't walk that fast* (as fast as you). *The fish I caught was that big* (for example showing its size with your hands).
2 **not that** used when you mean 'not very' *The book wasn't that good* (wasn't very good). *You're not that clever.*

thatch *noun*
dry plants such as straw or reeds (types of grass) used for covering the roof of a house

thatch *verb*
thatches, thatching, thatched
to cover a roof with something such as straw or reeds *a thatched cottage*
thatcher *noun*

thaw *verb*
thaws, thawing, thawed
1 if snow or ice thaws, it slowly turns into liquid because the weather gets warmer
2 to make snow or ice turn into liquid *The sun has completely thawed the ice.*
3 if you thaw frozen food, or if it thaws, it warms up slowly so that it is not frozen any more. You thaw food by leaving it in a warm kitchen or using a microwave oven.

thaw *noun*
a period of warmer weather when snow and ice turn into liquid

the *definite article*
1 used for describing something or someone already known or talked about *The school is closed today. I asked the teacher.*

525

theatre–they'd

2 used before a singular noun when you mean any thing or person of that kind *The dog is a friendly animal. The teacher is someone to be respected.*
3 each of something *There are nearly two dollars to the pound.*

LANGUAGE EXTRA *the* is pronounced 'ther' before a consonant or consonant sound (*the girl, the house, the university, the last egg*) but it is pronounced 'thee' before a vowel or vowel sound (*the egg, the umbrella, the hour, the only time*)

theatre noun
1 (plural **theatres**) a place with a stage where you go to see plays or other shows (for example singing or dancing)
2 the activity of writing and performing plays *the theatre of Shakespeare*
3 plays in general that you see in a theatre *My parents love the theatre.*
4 (plural **theatres**) an operating theatre is a room in a hospital where doctors operate on patients

theatregoer noun **theatregoers**
someone who goes to the theatre to see plays

theatrical adjective
connected with the theatre, plays or acting
theatrically adverb

thee pronoun
an old word for 'you', used when talking to one person *I know thee.*

theft noun **thefts**
the action or crime of stealing *There have been some thefts in the school. Shoplifting is theft.*

their adjective
belonging to or connected with the people, things or animals that someone has just mentioned *My cousins will be bringing their friends.*

theirs pronoun
used about something belonging to or connected with the people, things or animals that someone has just mentioned *Theirs can be seen later. This house is theirs.*

them pronoun
the people, things or animals that someone has just mentioned *I can hear them. We were walking behind them.*

theme noun **themes**
1 the main idea, thing or person that someone deals with, talks about or writes about *What's the theme of the book? Sunflowers are the theme of several of Van Gogh's paintings.*
2 a short piece of music played at the beginning and end of a film or a TV or radio programme

LANGUAGE EXTRA you can also say *theme music* or *theme tune*

3 a theme park is a large outside area, based on one theme (idea), where people go to enjoy themselves. There are games to play, machines such as merry-go-rounds and Ferris wheels for riding on and other activities such as riding in trains, on roller coasters and on boats.

themselves pronoun
1 used when people, things or animals that someone has just mentioned do an action and that action is also directed back onto them *They fell down and hurt themselves. They gave themselves a treat. The computers turn themselves off.*
2 used when you mean particular people, things or animals that someone has just mentioned and no-one else *Sayed and Aisha came themselves.*
3 **by themselves** without anyone else being there, or without the help of anyone else *The children went to the shops all by themselves. As you walk up to the doors, they open by themselves.*

then adverb
1 used for talking about a particular time in the past or future *We were living in Wales then* (at that time). *Tuesday is fine – I'll see you then. Mum will be home before then.*
2 coming next, after something *I had a snack and then went to bed.*
3 because of a particular situation *'There isn't any lemonade.' – 'I'll have water then.'*
4 used about a particular situation that may or may not be true *If there isn't any lemonade then I'll have water.*
5 because of something someone has just said or done *You're not coming to my party then?*

theology noun
the study of religion and people's beliefs

theoretical adjective
based on or connected with theories, ideas or possibilities rather than real situations

theory noun
1 (plural **theories**) an idea (or ideas) for explaining something, for example how or why something happens or exists *Darwin's theory of evolution*
2 the ideas and rules that a particular subject or skill is based on *music theory*
3 **in theory** used when talking about a situation that is supposed to happen or be true *In theory, the journey should take an hour but it's usually much longer.*

therapy noun **therapies**
treatment to help someone get better from an illness of the body or mind without having an operation **therapist** noun

there adverb
1 in, at or to that place or a particular place that is not near you *We went to Glasgow to see our friends there. What did you do over there?*
2 at a particular point while doing something *Could you stop there and tell us some more stories tomorrow?*
3 used for telling someone that something exists or happens *There's a question I want to ask. There was a loud noise. There has been an accident.*
4 used for attracting someone's attention to something or someone *There's my cousin – wave to him! There goes my sister on her bike.*

thereabouts adverb
1 near the place mentioned *Granddad used to work in Cardiff or thereabouts.*
2 used about a number, amount or time that is not exactly right but roughly correct *Thirty children or thereabouts will be going on the trip.*

therefore adverb
for this reason *Harry's only seven and therefore too young to play in the school team.*

thermal adjective
1 connected with heat *thermal energy*
2 used about clothes that keep you warm *thermal underwear*

thermometer noun **thermometers**
an instrument or piece of equipment for measuring how hot or cold something is, for example the air in a room, or how hot or cold someone's body is

Thermos noun **Thermoses** (trademark)
a Thermos or Thermos flask is a container shaped like a tube, with hollow walls that have no air between them. It is used for keeping liquids hot or cold.

SYNONYM vacuum flask

thermostat noun **thermostats**
a piece of equipment that controls the temperature of something, for example a room or engine, by switching itself on when it is too cold and off when it is too hot

thesaurus ['ther-sor-ers'] noun **thesauruses** or **thesauri** ['ther-sor-eye']
a type of dictionary where words with similar meanings are put together in groups but the meanings are not given. A thesaurus helps you to build your vocabulary (to learn more words) and choose the best words to express your ideas.

ORIGIN from Greek *thesauros* 'treasure' or 'treasure store'

these adjective plural
1 used about things or people already mentioned or known about, or things or people that are near you *These websites are interesting. I want these ones, not those ones.*
2 near you in time *Where have you been these last few days?*

LANGUAGE EXTRA the singular is *this*, for example *This website is interesting.*

these pronoun plural
used about things or people already mentioned or known about, or things or people that are near you *These are interesting websites.*

LANGUAGE EXTRA the singular is *this*, for example *This is an interesting website.*

they pronoun
1 the people, things or animals that someone has mentioned before, for example in an earlier sentence *They've arrived.*
2 people in general *They say our teacher is going to leave.*
3 important and official people *They've banned smoking on buses and trains* (the government has banned it). *They say you should eat lots of fruit and vegetables* (for example, doctors say this).

they'd
short for 'they had' or 'they would'

they'll
short for 'they will'

they're
short for 'they are'

they've
short for 'they have'

thick adjective thicker, thickest
1 if something is thick, there is a big space or distance from one side of it to the other side *a thick slice of bread*; *thick fingers*; *thick curtains* (made from cloth that weighs a lot)
2 used for saying the measurement of something from one side to the other side *a wall two metres thick*
3 made up of many things close together, for example growing together *thick hair*; *a thick forest* (lots of trees); *a thick wad of banknotes* (lots of them pressed or held together)
4 used about something such as smoke or fog that is difficult to see through because there is so much of it *There are thick clouds today* (you can't see the sky).
5 used about a liquid or substance that doesn't flow easily *thick soup*; *a scone with jam and thick cream*
6 used about clothes that keep you warm because they are made from cloth that weighs more than usual *a thick sweater*
7 used about a book that has lots of pages
8 an informal word for stupid
9 an informal word for friendly, when talking about someone you don't like *Josh is thick with the class bully*.

SIMILES 'as thick as a brick' means very stupid (sense 8); 'as thick as thieves' means very friendly (sense 9)

thicken verb
thickens, thickening, thickened
to become thick or thicker, or to make something thick or thicker *The fog thickened during the night. Thicken* (or *Thicken up*) *the soup with barley.*

thicket noun thickets
a group of trees or bushes growing closely together

thickly adverb
1 in a way that makes thick pieces *Cut the bread thickly.*
2 in a way that makes a thick layer, for example because a lot of something is used *Spread the jam thickly. My coat is thickly padded with wool to keep me warm. The snow was falling thickly.*
3 made up of many things close together, for example growing together *My baby sister's hair is growing thickly. The orchard was thickly planted with apple trees.*

thickness noun
the thickness of something is how thick it is *This wall is two metres in thickness.*

thick-skinned adjective
not getting angry or upset if people say bad or unkind things about you

thief noun thieves
someone who steals *a bicycle thief*

thieving adjective (informal)
used about someone who steals or tries to steal something *a group of thieving boys*

thigh noun thighs
the thick part of your leg above your knee

thimble noun thimbles
a small metal or plastic cover that you wear on the end of your finger to protect it when you're sewing

thin adjective thinner, thinnest
1 if a person or animal is thin, they have a body that doesn't have much flesh on it and doesn't weigh much
2 if something is thin, there is not much space or distance from one side of it to the other side *a thin slice of tomato*; *thin legs*; *thin curtains* (made from cloth that doesn't weigh much)
3 used about clothes that are easy to wear or keep you cool because they are made from cloth that doesn't weigh much *a thin summer dress*
4 used about a book that doesn't have many pages
5 used about a liquid that flows easily, for example because there is a lot of water in it *This sauce is very thin.*
6 used about something when there is not much of it and it is not made up of many parts *My dad's hair is getting thin. The audience for the school play was a bit thin* (there were not many people).
7 delicate or small, often in an attractive way *Chloe has a thin mouth. The baby has soft thin hair.*

SYNONYM fine

8 easy to see through *a thin mist*
9 if something or someone disappears into thin air, they disappear suddenly and mysteriously and cannot be found

thinness noun

SIMILE 'as thin as a rake' means very thin (sense 1). A rake is a garden tool with a long thin handle.

thin verb
thins, thinning, thinned
1 to make a liquid less thick by adding another liquid to it
2 if someone's hair thins, there is less of it as it grows *My dad's hair has started thinning.*
3 to gradually become less or smaller *The fog is beginning to thin out. The crowd is thinning out.*

thine pronoun
an old word for 'yours', used when talking to one person *These books are thine.*

thing noun things
1 anything that you can touch or see, when you don't use its exact name *Give me that thing over there. Your drawings are beautiful things.*
2 anything that you do or think about or any kind of situation, event, fact or quality *I have one more thing to say. A strange thing happened. There are many things to remember. Things are difficult for Olivia at school. What was the best thing about your holiday?*
3 **things** objects that belong to you or are needed for a particular activity *Don't forget your school things* (for example schoolbooks, lunchbox, clothes for playing sports). *Dad put the breakfast things away* (for example bowls, cups, spoons).

think verb
thinks, thinking, thought
1 to have an idea in your mind that you are fairly sure is true *I think the school is closed today. Do you think so? The homework took me longer than I thought* (I was fairly sure it wouldn't take so long).
2 to have an opinion about something or someone based on your feelings or beliefs *I think my teacher is very nice. 'What did you think of the book?' – 'It was interesting.'*
3 to use your mind or have ideas in your mind *Go away – I'm thinking. I was just thinking how silly I was to go swimming when I had so much homework. You look sad – what are you thinking about?*
4 to pay attention to something *Sorry, when I said those words I wasn't thinking! It's time to think about your birthday party* (for example to do something about it).
5 to be kind to someone, for example by showing an interest in them and helping them *That was a lovely gift you sent – thanks for thinking of me. You never think about* (or *think of*) *your little brother.*
6 to plan or intend to do something *I think I'll go swimming tomorrow.*
7 if you're thinking of or about doing something, you are likely to do it but you haven't decided yet *I'm thinking of going swimming tomorrow.*
8 to remember something *I can't think where I left my phone. Sorry, I just can't think of your name.*
9 if you think a lot of someone or think highly of them, you think they are very good and you respect them
10 if you think something out, for example a plan or answer to a problem, you pay careful attention to all of its details *Molly's reply to my email was very well thought out.*
11 if you think something over, for example a decision or what someone says, you have ideas about it that you consider carefully
12 if you think something up or think of something, for example a plan, excuse or reason, you produce a new plan, excuse or reason in your mind *Think up an excuse quickly! Ben thought of a story for the school magazine.*

thinker noun thinkers
someone who produces new ideas in a serious subject such as science or philosophy *Einstein was a great thinker.*

thinly adverb
1 in a way that makes thin pieces *Slice the bread thinly.*
2 in a way that makes a thin layer, for example because not much of something is used *Spread the ointment very thinly. The ground was thinly covered in snow.*
3 in a way that shows that something isn't growing very much *My brother's hair is growing thinly.*
4 with only a small number of people or things *The Highlands are thinly populated* (not many people live there).

third adjective
1 coming after the second person or thing *She was the third girl to finish the race. I sat in the third row.*

third–thoughtful

2 next after the second when talking about the importance, quality or size of something or someone *What is the third largest skyscraper in London? The blue shirt would be my third preference.*
3 every third happening once out of three possible times, or affecting one thing or person in every three, as part of a regular pattern *I have football practice every third Friday* (one Friday in three). *Every third boy wore glasses* (the third, sixth, ninth boy and so on).

third *adverb*
after the second person or thing *Sita came third in the test.*

third *noun*
1 (*plural* **thirds**) one of the three equal parts that make up the whole of something *A third of nine is three. Two thirds of the class were away sick.*
2 the thing that happens or comes after the second thing *That accident was the third I've seen today.*
3 the person who comes after or does something after the second person *Mohammed was the third to leave.*

thirdly *adverb*
used when talking about the third thing that happens or that you want to say *Firstly, tell me where you went, secondly what you did and thirdly why you did it.*

Third World *noun*
the Third World is an old-fashioned word for the poor countries of the world, for example in Africa or Asia, that do not produce many goods and services

> **LANGUAGE EXTRA** people today talk instead about *developing countries* (countries starting to produce goods and services themselves as a way of earning more money)

thirst *noun*
1 the feeling you have when you need to drink something
2 not having enough to drink *The soldier died of thirst in the desert.*

thirsty *adjective* **thirstier, thirstiest**
1 feeling that you need to drink something or drink some more
2 thirsty work is hard work that makes you feel thirsty
thirstily *adverb*

thirteen *adjective & noun* **thirteens**
the number 13
thirteenth *adjective & noun*

thirty *adjective & noun* **thirties**
1 the number 30
2 the thirties are the thirtieth to thirty-ninth years of a century, for example 1930 to 1939
3 if someone is in their thirties, they are between 30 and 39 years old
thirtieth *adjective & noun*

this *adjective*
1 used about something or someone already mentioned or known about, or something or someone that is near you *This website is interesting. Does this girl usually sit next to you? I want this one, not that one.*

2 used about something that is near you in time *This month we're going on holiday. We have English this afternoon. By this time you should be in bed.*

> **LANGUAGE EXTRA** the plural is *these*, for example *These websites are interesting.*

this *pronoun*
used about something or someone already mentioned or known about, or something or someone that is near you *This is an interesting website. Is this the girl who sits next to you?*

> **LANGUAGE EXTRA** the plural is *these*, for example *These are interesting websites.*

this *adverb*
as much as this, when talking about the way something is or about the size or amount of something *I didn't think maths would be this easy* (as easy as this). *The fish Jack caught was this big* (for example showing its size with your hands).

thistle *noun* **thistles**
a wild plant with thick round purple flowers. It has leaves and stems with sharp points on them.

thorn *noun* **thorns**
one of the sharp points on a plant, for example on the stem of a rose
thorny *adjective*

thorough *adjective*
1 done very carefully so that no details or parts are left out *a thorough piece of homework; a thorough investigation*
2 very great and good and including every detail *Paul has a thorough knowledge of French.*
3 used for giving extra importance to a word, for example when you mean that something is as big or as much as can be *a thorough waste of time; Jo's room was in a thorough mess.*

> **SYNONYM** complete

4 if someone is thorough, they do things very carefully so that no details or parts are left out *I've always been a thorough worker* (for example doing my schoolwork very carefully).
thoroughness *noun*

thoroughbred *noun* **thoroughbreds**
a horse that is of very high quality and is produced from parents of high quality. Thoroughbreds are used mainly in horse racing.

thoroughly *adverb*
1 extremely or in every way *I was thoroughly disappointed.*
2 very much or in every way *We thoroughly enjoyed ourselves. The paint takes a long time to dry thoroughly.*
3 very carefully so that no details or parts are left out *The police searched the house thoroughly.*

those *adjective plural*
1 used about things or people already mentioned or known about, or things or people that you can see but are not near you *Those websites are interesting. I want these ones, not those ones.*

2 not near you in time *What was she doing those last few months?*

> **LANGUAGE EXTRA** the singular is *that*, for example *That website is interesting.*

those *pronoun plural*
used about things or people already mentioned or known about, or things or people that you can see but are not near you *Those are interesting websites.*

> **LANGUAGE EXTRA** the singular is *that*, for example *That is an interesting website.*

thou *pronoun*
an old word for 'you', used when talking to one person *Thou shalt not steal.*

though *conjunction*
used for connecting two parts of a sentence when the second part introduces a different idea from the first part, for example a surprising idea *We've travelled around Scotland though we've never been to Edinburgh. My sister is intelligent though lazy.*

> **SYNONYM** although

though *adverb*
used for connecting two ideas when the second one is different from the first, for example in a surprising way *My sister is intelligent – she's lazy though. Granddad is coming tomorrow – I don't know what time though.*

thought
past tense & past participle of **think**

thought *noun*
1 (*plural* **thoughts**) something such as an image, word, plan or opinion that you have in your mind *That was the first thought that came into my mind* (the first thing I thought of). *The head teacher had some thoughts* (a plan) *on how to attract more students. What are your thoughts about this book?* (What is your opinion of it?)
2 when you use your mind to think about something, for example to understand something or deal with a problem *the power of thought; I was deep in thought, doing my homework. Mum gave the matter a lot of thought.*
3 (*plural* **thoughts**) behaviour that shows you think about other people's feelings, for example by wanting to help other people *Granddad thanked Dad for his kind thoughts and for sending a card when he was in hospital.*

thoughtful *adjective*
1 used about someone who thinks about other people's feelings, for example being very pleasant towards other people and wanting to help them

> **SYNONYMS** kind, considerate

2 also used about something someone says or does that shows they think about other people's feelings *a thoughtful gift; She sent me a thoughtful email.*
3 used about someone who uses their mind for thinking carefully or deeply about things *Yusuf is a serious and thoughtful student. You look rather thoughtful.*

thoughtfully – throb

4 also used about something that shows someone is thinking carefully or deeply *a thoughtful expression; a thoughtful discussion*
thoughtfulness *noun*

thoughtfully *adverb*
1 in a way that shows you think about other people's feelings, for example by wanting to help them *Dad thoughtfully brought a chair so Grandma could sit down.*
2 in a way that shows you are thinking carefully or deeply *He was looking thoughtfully into the distance.*

thoughtless *adjective*
1 used about someone who doesn't think about other people's feelings, for example not thinking about whether what they say or do might upset other people
2 also used about someone's behaviour *You didn't text to say you'd be late – that was thoughtless.*
thoughtlessly *adverb*
thoughtlessness *noun*

thousand *noun* **thousands**
1 the number 1000
2 thousands of used when describing very large numbers of people, animals or things *Thousands of people marched through the streets. 'How many times have I told you?' – 'Thousands!'*
thousandth *adjective & noun*

thrash *verb*
thrashes, thrashing, thrashed
1 to hit someone or something very many times *The farmer was thrashing the poor donkey with a stick.*
2 to move from one side to the other in a violent way *The fish were thrashing about on the floor of the boat. The bully was thrashing his arms and legs about so the teacher couldn't hold him down.*
3 to beat someone completely in a game or competition

thrashing *noun* **thrashings**
1 when someone or something is hit very many times *I got a thrashing from the class bully.*
2 when someone loses badly, for example in a game or competition *Our team got a real thrashing.*

thread *noun* **threads**
1 a long and very thin piece of a substance such as cotton, nylon or wool, used for sewing or making cloth *cotton thread*
2 the threads of a spider are the long and very thin pieces of the substance that it uses to make its web
3 the thread of a screw or bolt is the twisted raised edge that curves round and round it in a spiral
4 used in computing to mean all the messages on a particular subject, for example on a message board (web page where you leave someone a message)

thread *verb*
threads, threading, threaded
1 to put something long and thin, such as a thread, through a small hole or something very narrow *I threaded the needle and sewed on the button. You have to thread the cotton through the hole.*
2 to join things together by putting something such as string through them *Mum was threading beads to make me a necklace.*

threadbare *adjective*
used for describing cloth or a piece of clothing that has become so thin from being used that you can see the threads in it *a threadbare carpet*

threadworm *noun* **threadworms**
a type of small thin worm that can live inside a person's or animal's bowels (tubes carrying food from the stomach)

threat *noun* **threats**
1 when someone tries to frighten you by saying they will do something bad if you don't do what they want *Alice was expelled for making threats against her teacher.*
2 something or someone likely to make bad things happen *These bullies are a real threat to our school.*
3 the possibility that something bad might happen *The threat of war hung over Europe at that time.*

threaten *verb*
threatens, threatening, threatened
1 if someone threatens you, they try to frighten you by saying or showing that they will do something bad to you unless you do what they want (or stop doing something) *The bully threatened the boy with a knife. Ethan threatened to tell the teacher if Lydia swore at him again.*
2 used for saying that something bad is likely to happen or that something is likely to make something bad happen *The fight between the two boys was threatening to become serious. These phone masts are threatening the neighbourhood* (for example making it look ugly).

threatening *adjective*
1 making you think that someone is likely to do something bad *a threatening look*
2 making you think that something bad is likely to happen *threatening skies* (showing that rain or a storm is likely)
threateningly *adverb*

three *adjective & noun* **threes**
the number 3

three-D *adjective*
used about a film you watch with special glasses that make the images seem not flat but real and moving towards you or away from you, just like when you look at real things

LANGUAGE EXTRA *three-D* is usually shortened to *3-D*. It is short for *three-dimensional*.

three-dimensional *adjective*
used about an object or image that is not flat but has the three dimensions of length, width and height, for example a cube, sphere or pyramid

three-quarters *noun*
1 three of the four equal parts that make up the whole of something *Three-quarters of the cake is still left.*
2 three-quarters of an hour is 45 minutes *I waited three-quarters of an hour.*

LANGUAGE EXTRA you can also write *three quarters* without a hyphen

three-star *adjective*
of fairly high quality *a three-star hotel*

three-wheeler *noun* **three-wheelers**
a type of bicycle or car with three wheels

thresh *verb*
threshes, threshing, threshed
to separate the grain (or seeds) from a plant such as wheat or rice, usually with a machine called a thresher

threshold *noun* **thresholds**
1 the floor at the bottom of a door where you go into a building *He crossed the threshold and entered the palace.*
2 if someone is on the threshold of something, that particular thing is about to happen *The scientists are on the threshold of an important discovery.*

threw
past tense of **throw**

thrift *noun*
the habit of being careful with money and not wasting any

thrifty *adjective* **thriftier, thriftiest**
used for showing that someone is careful about how they spend money and doesn't waste any *a thrifty shopper; thrifty habits*
thriftily *adverb*

thrill *noun* **thrills**
1 a feeling of great excitement or a strong feeling of pleasure *We loved the thrill of flying in a plane.*
2 something that gives you this feeling *Winning the race was a real thrill.*

thrill *verb*
thrills, thrilling, thrilled
to make someone very excited or extremely pleased *The roller coaster ride really thrilled us. I was thrilled with my birthday presents.*

thriller *noun* **thrillers**
a book, film, play or video game about a crime or murder *a spy thriller; We were watching a thriller by Alfred Hitchcock.*

thrilling *adjective*
extremely exciting

thrive *verb*
thrives, thriving, thrived
1 to grow well and strongly *Children thrive on healthy food. Plants thrive in the sunlight.*
2 to be very successful *Our school is thriving.*

thriving *adjective*
very successful *a thriving business*

throat *noun* **throats**
1 the part of the body at the back of your mouth where food goes down into your stomach *I have a sore throat* (painful infection in the throat).
2 the front part of your neck *The bully grabbed me by the throat.*
3 if you clear your throat, you cough slightly, often a few times, so that it is easier for you to speak

throb *verb*
throbs, throbbing, throbbed
1 if a part of your body throbs, you get slight pains there that keep happening all the time in a regular pattern *My head is throbbing* (I have a headache).
2 if your heart throbs, it beats more strongly than usual

throb–thunder

3 if music throbs, or if something such as an engine or machine throbs, it makes a low sound that keeps repeating itself in a regular pattern

throb noun **throbs**
1 the sound or action of something throbbing *the throbs of the engine*
2 a slight pain in a part of your body as it throbs

throne noun **thrones**
1 a special chair for someone very important to sit on during ceremonies, for example a king, queen, bishop or emperor
2 the throne the position of being a king or queen *In 1850 Queen Victoria was on the throne* (she was queen).

throng noun **throngs**
a large crowd of people

throng verb
throngs, thronging, thronged
if people throng somewhere, they go there in large numbers *Crowds thronged the central square. Tourists are thronging to see the new exhibition.*

throttle noun **throttles**
a piece of equipment that controls the fuel going into the engine of a vehicle, such as a motorbike, for example to make it start to move, go faster or go slower

throttle verb
throttles, throttling, throttled
to hurt or kill someone by pressing their throat to stop them from breathing

through preposition & adverb
1 from one side or end of something to the other *The cat got in through the window. The police are not letting anyone through.*
2 going towards something and then further on *Drive through the gates and park in front of the school. The cyclist went through a red light* (didn't stop at a red traffic light). *We didn't stop in York – we drove straight through.*
3 from the beginning to the end of something *I've read through the whole book. I've read it through. George slept through the film.*
4 moving around or going everywhere in something or someone *Birds fly through the air. The boat was moving through the water. My cousin is travelling through America. The police are searching through the house. Panic spread through the passengers. An idea went through my mind* (or *head*) (I thought of something).
5 because of something or someone *I made myself ill through eating too much ice cream. It's through you that I was late for school!*
6 with the help of someone or something *Dad got his new job through a friend of his.*
7 using a certain way of doing something *I bought the books through the school website. Granddad sent me a present through the post.*
8 connected by phone to someone *Mum phoned the school but couldn't get through. She's through now* (connected and speaking to someone by phone).
9 completely and including all the parts of something *The meat wasn't cooked through. My clothes are wet through.*
10 (informal) finished *Are you through yet?*
11 until and including the last day, time or number mentioned (used mainly in American English) *My dad's shop is open Monday through Saturday.*

through adjective
1 a through train travels all the way to a particular place without passengers having to change trains
2 a through road is a road that is not closed at one end so that traffic can pass through

throughout preposition & adverb
1 in all parts of something *There was a lot of excitement throughout the school.*
2 during the whole of a period of time *She was complaining throughout the journey. The film was good but you slept throughout!*

throw verb
throws, throwing, threw, thrown
1 to make something that you're holding in your hand go through the air by pushing it and letting go of it quickly *Rick threw the ball to me.*
2 to put something somewhere or in a particular position quickly or carelessly *Holly came in and threw her school things on the floor. Mum threw open the window.*
3 to move a part of your body somewhere quickly *He threw his arms around me.*
4 to make someone suddenly move somewhere *The driver put the brakes on and the passengers were thrown forward. The bully threw me to the ground.*
5 to cause something bad to happen to someone or something *They threw him into prison. Our teacher has fallen ill so the plans for the school trip have been thrown into confusion.*
6 to throw something away or out is to get rid of it because you don't want it, for example by putting it in the dustbin
7 to throw someone out is to make them leave a place or group, for example because they have behaved badly *If you keep behaving like that, you'll get thrown out of school.*
8 (informal) if someone throws up, the food they have eaten suddenly comes up from their stomach and out of their mouth

throw noun **throws**
1 the action of throwing something *That was a good throw.*
2 a piece of cloth for covering something such as an armchair or bed to make it look more attractive

thrush noun **thrushes**
a brown bird, usually with spots on its front, known for its pleasant singing

thrust verb
thrusts, thrusting, thrust
to push something somewhere roughly or with a lot of strength *Someone thrust a piece of paper into my hands.* **thrust** noun

thud noun **thuds**
a low sound made by something heavy falling or hitting something *Martin fainted and there was a dull thud as he fell to the floor.*

thud verb
thuds, thudding, thudded
to make the low sound of a thud when falling or hitting something

thug noun **thugs**
a violent and unpleasant person, for example a member of a gang

thumb noun **thumbs**
1 the part at the side of your hand that is like a short thick finger. The thumb is next to your index finger but is lower down on your hand.
2 the thumbs up a sign you make to show someone that you like something and think it's good or that everything is OK *Dad gave my plan the thumbs up* (he accepted it).

LANGUAGE EXTRA the opposite of *thumbs up* is *thumbs down*

thumb verb
thumbs, thumbing, thumbed
to thumb through something such as a book is to look at it quickly

thumbnail noun **thumbnails**
1 the hard smooth part at the end of your thumb
2 a small picture of something on a computer screen

thumbtack noun **thumbtacks**
an American word for a drawing pin

thump verb
thumps, thumping, thumped
1 to hit something or someone hard, for example with your hand closed *The bully thumped me over the head.*
2 to hit something hard against something else, often with a heavy noise *Simon was angry and thumped his fist on the table. Someone was thumping loudly on the door. I fell down and thumped my head* (for example, accidentally hit my head on the floor).
3 if your head thumps, you get strong pains in it that keep happening all the time in a regular pattern
4 if your heart thumps, it beats much more strongly than usual

thump noun **thumps**
1 the action of thumping something or someone *I'll give you a thump if you don't leave me alone.*
2 the noise of something hard hitting something or falling *My schoolbag fell off the table with a thump.*

thumping adjective (informal)
1 very big *That was a thumping defeat for our team.*
2 very painful *a thumping headache*

thumping adverb (informal)
extremely *We heard a thumping great bang.*

thunder noun
the loud noise you hear in the sky after lightning (a flash or flashes of bright light), usually during a storm. Thunder is the sound made by lightning.

thunder verb
thunders, thundering, thundered
1 if it thunders or is thundering, you hear thunder in the sky
2 if someone thunders, they say something in a very loud and usually angry voice *'Take your hands out of your pockets!' he thundered.*
3 to move very fast with a lot of noise *The train thundered past.*

thunderbolt *noun* **thunderbolts**
a flash of lightning (bright light) followed immediately by the loud noise of thunder

thunderclap *noun* **thunderclaps**
a sudden loud noise made by thunder

thunderous *adjective*
extremely loud *a thunderous explosion*; *thunderous applause* (for example because an audience really likes something)

thunderstorm *noun* **thunderstorms**
a storm with thunder and lightning as well as lots of rain and wind

thunderstruck *adjective*
extremely surprised

thundery *adjective*
used for describing the weather when there is a lot of thunder *thundery showers*

Thursday *noun* **Thursdays**
the day of the week between Wednesday and Friday

ORIGIN from Old English *Thursdæg* 'Thor's day'. In Old Norse, Thor was the god of thunder.

thus *adverb*
1 in this way *To make a paper hat you fold the paper thus.*
2 used for showing a reason for something or why something happens *My sister knows French and thus watched the film without subtitles. I left the door open, thus letting the dog run out into the street.*

thwack *noun* **thwacks**
a short loud sound made by something flat hitting something *She gave me a thwack over the head with a book.* **thwack** *verb*

thy *adjective*
an old word for 'your', used when talking to one person *Here is thy book.*

tic *noun* **tics**
a small movement of a muscle, usually in your face, that you cannot control

tick *noun* **ticks**
1 a mark ✓ that you write against something you check, for example an answer, to show that it is correct, or that you write against something on a list to show that it has been done or chosen
2 the sound that a clock, watch or timer makes *The school clock has a loud tick.*
3 an informal way of saying a very short time *I'll be back in a tick.*

tick *verb*
ticks, ticking, ticked
1 to mark something with a tick, for example to show that it is correct or has been done or chosen *Ms McKay ticked the right answers and put a cross against the wrong ones. I ticked off my name on the list. Tick here if you want to download the latest version.*
2 when a clock, watch or timer ticks, it makes short hard sounds as it marks the time
3 (informal) to tick someone off is to say something to them in an angry voice because they've done something wrong

SYNONYM for sense 3: to tell off

ticket *noun* **tickets**
1 a piece of paper or a card that allows you to do something such as travel on a bus, train or plane, go into a place such as a cinema, theatre or museum, or go and watch something such as a sports event *a train ticket*; *a free ticket*; *You can buy tickets for the match online.*
2 a small piece of paper that you buy with a number on it. You win money or a prize in a game or competition if your number is chosen. *a lottery ticket*; *a raffle ticket*
3 an official piece of paper showing that a driver must pay money for doing something against the law, for example parking in a bad place or going too fast *a parking ticket*; *a speeding ticket*
4 a ticket office is a place where you buy tickets, for example in a railway station

tickle *verb*
tickles, tickling, tickled
1 if you tickle someone, you touch them lightly many times with your fingers or with something soft and light, such as a feather, to produce a feeling that makes them laugh
2 if something soft and light tickles you, it produces a slightly uncomfortable feeling against your skin *Your beard is tickling me. It really tickles.*
3 if a part of your body tickles, it produces a slightly uncomfortable feeling that makes you want to stop it happening *My throat was tickling so I drank some water.*
4 (old-fashioned) to make someone pleased about something

tickle *noun*

ticklish *adjective*
1 if someone is ticklish, they laugh very easily when you tickle them
2 making you feel slightly uncomfortable on your skin or a part of your body *a ticklish feeling*; *a ticklish cough*

LANGUAGE EXTRA you can also say *tickly*

3 used about a situation or problem that is slightly difficult to deal with

tidal *adjective*
connected with tides or affected by tides *a tidal river*; *a tidal wave* (huge wave that moves onto the land with the tide)

tiddler *noun* **tiddlers** (informal)
1 a very small fish
2 something or someone very small

tiddlywinks *noun*
a game in which you press a small plastic disc (called a tiddlywink) onto another disc to make the other disc fly into the air and fall into a container

tide *noun* **tides**
the level of the sea that goes up and down at the coast twice every day *The tide is coming in* (or *going out*) (the level is going up or going down). *It's high tide* (or *low tide*) (when the sea reaches its highest or lowest level).

tide *verb*
tides, tiding, tided
to tide someone over is to give them something, usually money, to help them for a short period of time

tidily *adverb*
very carefully so that things look nice or well organised *Put your books back tidily on the shelf.*

tidings *noun plural*
an old-fashioned word for news *The messenger brought us good tidings.*

tidy *adjective* **tidier, tidiest**
1 arranged or done in a careful way and looking nice *Your room looks tidy. Abdul's hair isn't very tidy.*
2 a tidy person is someone who likes things arranged in a careful way *Dad told me to be more tidy* (for example to put things back where they belong).
3 (informal) used for describing an amount of money that is large or fairly large *a tidy sum of money*

tidiness *noun*

tidy *verb*
tidies, tidying, tidied
to arrange things carefully somewhere such as in a room or on a desk *We're tidying the house* (for example putting things back where they belong). *Please tidy up your toys and games. I'm tidying out my desk* (arranging things and removing things I don't want).

tie *verb*
ties, tying, tied
1 to fix or hold something or someone to something with string, rope or another piece of long thin material *We tied the balloons to the door with ribbon. The thief tied him to a chair.*
2 to fix things together, for example with string or rope *Tie up all the books so they're easier to carry. The climbers were tied together with ropes.*
3 to put something such as string around something *I tied the parcel with string.*
4 to make a knot or bow (knot with loops and loose ends) in something such as a piece of string or a ribbon *I tied a big knot at the end of the string. Can you tie a ribbon? I can't tie my shoelaces yet.*
5 to close something by joining the two ends of it together and making a knot, or to be closed in this way *Please tie my apron. This dress ties up at the back.*
6 if two or more players or teams in a game tie, they end the game with the same number of points *England tied with France in the cup final.*

tie *noun* **ties**
1 a narrow piece of cloth with a knot in it. It is worn around the neck under the collar of a shirt and hangs down at the front of the body.
2 the result of a game between two or more players or teams in which they both (or all) have the same number of points
3 a sports match in which the winners go on to the next part of the competition

tiebreaker *noun* **tiebreakers**
an extra part of a game used for deciding the winner when the result is a tie (when players or teams have the same number of points)

LANGUAGE EXTRA you can also say *tiebreak*

tiff
the ending of a computer filename. A .tiff contains an image (or images) such as a photo.
short for: Tagged Image File Format

LANGUAGE EXTRA also spelt *tif*

tiff – time

tiff *noun* **tiffs**
a slight argument, for example between friends

tiger *noun* **tigers**
a large wild animal of the cat family with yellow-orange fur and black stripes. Tigers live in parts of Asia.

tight *adjective* **tighter, tightest**
1 used about clothes that you wear very close against your body *a pair of tight jeans*
2 used about clothes that are not comfortable because they are too close against your body *These shoes are too tight.*
3 used about something that is fixed in its place and is hard to move *This jam jar lid is very tight. Tie your shoelaces and make sure the knot is tight. Use this screwdriver to make the screws tight – we don't want them to come loose.*
4 used about something such as rope or wire that is pulled as much as possible *Make sure the rope is tight.*
5 done with a lot of strength *a tight grip*
6 used when you mean a lot of something, for example control or security *Security at the airport was tight. My mum keeps a tight control over my pocket money.*
7 an informal word for mean (not wanting to spend money or give money to other people) *My uncle is very tight with money.*

tightness *noun*

tight *adverb*
1 very strongly and pressing hard *She held my hand tight. Hold on tight as we go round the bend.*
2 pulled as much as possible *Take the other end of the blanket and stretch it tight.*
3 very closely against your body *I like wearing my jeans tight.*

tighten *verb*
tightens, tightening, tightened
1 to make sure something is fixed in its place and hard to move *You need a smaller screwdriver to tighten these screws.*
2 to make sure something is pulled as much as possible or as close to something as possible *Pull the rope to tighten it. Tighten the string around the parcel. I tightened my seat belt.*
3 to make sure something is stronger or done in a controlled way *I tightened my grip on the handlebars of my bike. The police have tightened security at the match. If you don't tighten up your computer settings, you could easily get a virus.*
4 to become tight or tighter, for example used about a muscle in the body or someone's grip

tightly *adverb*
1 very strongly and pressing hard *Hold me tightly in case I fall!*
2 completely *My eyes were tightly closed. Fasten your seat belt tightly. Use of the school's computers is tightly controlled.*
3 in a way that is fixed and hard to move *a tightly tied knot; Put the lid on the jar tightly.*
4 with people or things very close together *a tightly packed train*
5 very closely against your body *He wore his scarf wrapped tightly around his neck.*

tightrope *noun* **tightropes**
a rope or wire fixed high above the ground, usually in a circus. It is used for walking on by acrobats, who often carry a long stick to help them balance.

tights *noun plural*
a piece of clothing that girls and women wear closely against their body from the waist to the feet, with separate parts for each leg

tigress *noun* **tigresses**
a female tiger

tile *noun* **tiles**
1 a thin piece of clay baked in an oven called a kiln to make it hard. Tiles are used for covering roofs.
2 a thin, flat and square piece of baked clay or other material used for covering walls or floors *bathroom tiles; a ceiling covered with polystyrene tiles*
3 a small flat piece or block used in games such as Scrabble
4 in maths, a tile is one of the flat shapes that fit together in a pattern without leaving gaps in between
5 in computing, a tile is a shape such as an image of a file or folder. Tiles are arranged on a screen so that you can see them all next to each other.

tile *verb*
tiles, tiling, tiled
1 to cover something with tiles, for example a roof, wall or floor *a tiled bathroom*
2 to arrange images or windows on a computer screen so that you can see them all next to each other

tiler *noun* **tiling** *noun*

till *preposition & conjunction*
used for saying that something continues to happen or is done up to the time mentioned *Jo slept till noon. Wait till the end. Stay here till I get back. The library doesn't close till eight o'clock* (it stops being open at that time).

till *noun* **tills**
a piece of equipment used in a shop or supermarket for adding up the money customers pay and for keeping the money safe *a till receipt*

till *verb* (old-fashioned)
tills, tilling, tilled
if someone such as a farmer tills the land, they break up or dig the soil so that seeds can be planted

tiller *noun* **tillers**
a long handle at the back of a boat, used for turning the rudder (flat part at the back of the boat, in the water) to make the boat go in a particular direction

tilt *verb*
tilts, tilting, tilted
if you tilt something, or if it tilts, it moves into a position with one side higher than the other *Tilt your bowl forward to eat the rest of your soup. The car seat tilts back for extra comfort.*

tilt *noun* **tilts**
the position of something that has one side higher than the other

timber *noun*
1 wood for building houses or making furniture
2 timbers are long pieces of wood for building houses or ships *roof timbers*

time *noun*
1 the part of existence that is measured using units such as seconds, minutes, hours, days, weeks, months and years *Time passes slowly when you're bored. Spend a bit more time doing your homework. I have plenty of time.*
2 the hour and minute of the day that is measured by a clock or watch *What time is it? What's the time? Come to my house this time tomorrow. I've learnt how to tell the time* (I know what the clock numbers and positions of the clock hands mean).
3 a particular point when something happens or exists (used about the past, present or future) *At that time, dinosaurs lived on earth. Granddad phoned around breakfast time. Are you enjoying your time at school? Come back in an hour's time. I was interested in football for a time* (for a short period).
4 used about one example of something happening or being done or about how many occasions something happens or is done *This is the first time I've eaten a pizza. Sally texted me three times. I'll be more careful next time. Eat the sweets one at a time* (one sweet and then another sweet).
5 a suitable moment for something to happen or be done *It's time to do your homework. Ask me later – now isn't the time.*
6 the speed at which you play a piece of music or sing *The singers kept in time with the piano* (they sang at the same speed as the tune was being played on the piano).
7 **to have a good time** to enjoy yourself doing something or being somewhere
8 **to take time** or **to take your time** to do something carefully without hurrying *I took time over this week's homework. There's no hurry so please take your time.*
9 **all the time** very often *My brother goes swimming all the time.*
10 **all the time** also used about something that continues happening *It's been raining all the time. All the time Grandma was here, Ashraf stayed in his room.*
11 **at times** or **from time to time** sometimes but not often
12 **for the time being** used about a situation that exists now but could change soon
13 **in time** not too late for something *Sayed came home in time for dinner.*
14 **on time** arriving somewhere or happening at the right time, not early and not late *The train from Huddersfield is on time. The lesson started on time.*
15 **time after time** very often
16 **time off** time when someone is not at school or work and is not doing any activity such as studying *I've been doing homework all day – I need some time off* (some rest).
17 **times** used in comparisons with adjectives and adverbs or with words such as 'more', 'much' and 'many' for showing differences or amounts *My cousin's school is four times bigger than mine. She's read three times more books than me but I have three times as many friends.*
18 **times** also used in maths when you mean 'multiplied by'. The symbol for this is ×. *Three times four is twelve (3 × 4 = 12).*

time *verb*
times, timing, timed
1 to use a watch or clock to measure how long something takes or how long someone takes to do something *Dad used a stopwatch to time me running.*
2 to make sure something happens at a particular time *We timed our visit to the museum to avoid the crowds. Their new album was timed to come out just before Christmas. Our trip to Bristol was badly timed* (made at the wrong time).

time limit *noun* **time limits**
a particular amount of time that someone is allowed for doing something

timeline *noun* **timelines**
a way of showing the order of particular events that happen over a period of time, for example a line showing important dates in history

timely *adjective* **timelier, timeliest**
happening at the right time

timer *noun* **timers**
1 a piece of equipment for measuring time. It makes a sound after a particular amount of time that you choose. Timers are used in cooking, for example.
2 a piece of equipment that makes another piece of equipment start working or stop working at a particular time that you choose

timescale *noun* **timescales**
the amount of time it takes for something to happen or for someone to do something

LANGUAGE EXTRA also spelt *time scale*

times table *noun* **times tables**
a list showing the results of multiplying one number by another between 1 and 12

SYNONYM multiplication table

timetable *noun* **timetables**
1 a list of times and dates showing when things happen *a school timetable* (showing the times and days of lessons)
2 a list of times and dates showing when trains, buses, planes and boats arrive and leave

time zone *noun* **time zones**
an area of the world with its own clock time that is different from the area next to it, usually by one hour. There are 24 main time zones.

timid *adjective*
1 if someone is timid, they are afraid of people and have no feelings of confidence
2 also used about something that shows someone is timid *a timid smile*
3 if an animal is timid, it is frightened of people and hides from them
timidity *noun* **timidly** *adverb*

SIMILES 'as timid as a mouse' and 'as timid as a rabbit' mean very timid (sense 1)

timing *noun*
1 the time when something happens
2 the skill of doing something at exactly the right time *a good sense of timing*
3 a situation when something happens at a particular time, either a good or bad time *Here's Ava – perfect timing as Dad is just dishing up dinner!*

tin *noun* **tins**
1 a soft silvery-white metal *a tin roof*
2 a sealed metal container that you buy food in, often shaped like a cylinder (tube with flat ends like circles). You open it with a tin opener or by pulling a small ring. *a tin of sardines; a tin of baked beans*
3 a metal container with a lid, usually for storing things in. It is often round like a cylinder but it can have any shape, for example a rectangle or oval. *a tin of paint; a biscuit tin*
4 something in a tin *Do you want a tin of soup?*
5 a metal container for cooking food in, usually without a lid *Pour the mixture into a cake tin and bake for 30 minutes.*

LANGUAGE EXTRA in senses 2, 3 and 4, you often use *can* instead of *tin*, for example *a can of sardines*

tinfoil *noun*
1 sheets of metal that are as thin as paper, used for example for wrapping food to keep it fresh
2 a piece of tinfoil *Dad wrapped my sandwiches in tinfoil.*

SYNONYM foil

ting-a-ling *noun*
the noise that a small bell makes

tinged ['tinjd'] *adjective*
if something is tinged with something, it has a small amount of that particular thing *The evening sky was tinged with red.*

tingle *verb*
tingles, tingling, tingled
to have the feeling of small sharp points touching your body, often caused by cold, fear or excitement *The snow made my fingers tingle.* **tingle** *noun*

tinker *verb*
tinkers, tinkering, tinkered
if someone tinkers or tinkers around with something such as a machine or engine, they spend time doing things to it such as trying to repair it

tinkle *verb*
tinkles, tinkling, tinkled
if something such as a small bell tinkles, it makes a high ringing sound **tinkle** *noun*

tinned *adjective*
tinned food is food that is put in a sealed metal container to preserve it *tinned peaches*

tinny *adjective* **tinnier, tinniest**
1 used about sounds that are unpleasant and very high *Your radio sounds a bit tinny.*
2 used about metal objects that are thin and of bad quality *a tinny washing machine*

tin opener *noun* **tin openers**
a tool used for opening tins of food

tinsel ['tin-serl'] *noun*
long pieces of thread covered with small coloured strips of shiny plastic material. Tinsel is used as decoration, for example at Christmas time.

ORIGIN from Old French *estincelle* 'spark' or 'flash'

tint *noun* **tints**
1 a small amount of a particular colour, usually a light colour *a white shirt with a yellowish tint*
2 a colour put in someone's hair with a special liquid
3 the action of putting a colour in someone's hair *My sister is going for a tint.*

tint *verb*
tints, tinting, tinted
to put a slightly different colour into or onto something *tinted paper* (for example light blue or green); *a car with tinted windows* (dark windows so that people cannot see inside); *My sister has had her hair tinted* (with a special liquid).

tiny *adjective* **tinier, tiniest**
extremely small *a tiny house; a tiny amount of snow*

tip *noun* **tips**
1 the end of something, usually something long and thin *I touched the tip of my nose with the tip of my finger. The rubber tip on Granddad's walking stick has fallen off.*
2 a small piece of information about something useful *Dad gave me some tips on how to stay safe when surfing the net.*
3 a place where people take rubbish to be recycled (used again) or thrown away

SYNONYMS dump, recycling centre

4 (informal) an untidy place with lots of things left lying around *Your bedroom's a real tip.*

SYNONYM dump

5 extra money given to someone such as a waiter, waitress or taxi driver to thank them *The waiter was so helpful that Mum left him a large tip.*
6 on the tip of your tongue used about something that you know and want to tell someone but that you can't remember although you think you will remember soon

tip *verb*
tips, tipping, tipped
1 to make something fall by moving it so that one side is higher than the other, or to fall by being moved in this way *Ravinder accidentally tipped the chair over by leaning back too far. I tipped up the box and the sewing things fell out. The chair tipped over and fell onto the floor.*
2 to move something from a level or upright position so that one side of it is higher than the other, or to move in this way *Tip the jug slightly to pour the milk. The plane seats tip back for extra comfort.*
3 to empty something from a container *If you don't want your lemonade, tip it out into the sink.*
4 to tip rubbish is to leave it somewhere to get rid of it *No tipping* (sign saying no-one should leave rubbish here).
5 to tip someone such as a waiter, waitress or taxi driver is to give them a tip (extra money to thank them)
6 to tip someone off is to give them secret information about something or someone

tipped *adjective*
used for describing something with a tip (end) covered in a particular way *a walking stick tipped with metal; a poison-tipped arrow*

tipsy *adjective* **tipsier, tipsiest** (informal)
if someone is tipsy, they have drunk a bit too much alcohol such as beer or wine

tiptoe *noun*
on tiptoe standing or walking with only your toes on the ground *I had to stand on tiptoe to get the book down from the top shelf.*

tiptoe *verb*
tiptoes, tiptoeing, tiptoed
to walk carefully on your toes, for example so as not to make any noise *We tiptoed down the stairs.*

tip-top *adjective*
an informal word for excellent *My computer is old but it's in tip-top condition.*

tire *verb*
tires, tiring, tired
1 to make someone feel tired *All this walking has tired me out.*
2 to become tired *Granddad tires very easily.*
3 to tire of something or someone is to become bored with them

tired *adjective*
1 if you're tired, you feel that you need to rest or sleep
2 if a part of your body is tired, you feel that you need to rest it *My feet are tired and achy.*
3 if you're tired of something or someone, you're unhappy or slightly angry and you don't want a situation to continue, especially when it has been going on for a long time *I'm tired of telling you to tidy up your room. I don't want Harry to be my friend any more – I'm sick and tired of him* (very angry and bored with him).

tireless *adjective*
1 having lots of energy and working all the time *a tireless worker*
2 also used about someone's actions *tireless efforts; tireless energy*
tirelessly *adverb*

tiresome *adjective*
making you feel slightly angry or bored *It's rather tiresome doing the same work every day.* **tiresomely** *adverb*

tiring *adjective*
making you feel tired

tissue *noun*
1 soft paper used especially for wiping things or for blowing your nose
2 (plural **tissues**) a piece of this paper, usually shaped like a square or rectangle *a box of tissues*
3 tissue or tissue paper is very thin paper that is often used for wrapping delicate things to stop them getting damaged or broken
4 a group of cells (smallest units of living matter) in humans, animals or plants *brain tissue*

titbit *noun* **titbits**
1 a small piece of interesting information or news
2 a small piece of food

titch *noun* **titches**
an informal word for a small child or person

titchy *adjective*
an informal word for small

title *noun* **titles**
1 the name of a piece of writing such as a book or story or something artistic such as a painting, film or piece of music
2 a word used in front of someone's name as a sign of respect (for example Mr, Miss, Ms, Mrs) or for showing that someone has a particular job or special honour *Mr Clark* (before a man's name); *Dr Lambeth* (for showing that a man or woman is a doctor); *Lord* (or *Lady*) *Armstrong* (for showing that a man or woman has a high rank in British society)
3 the position of being the winner in a sports event *Our football team has won another important title.*

title bar *noun* **title bars**
a long strip along the top of a computer screen that shows the name of the document you're working on or the program you have open

titled *adjective*
if someone is titled, they have a title in front of their name, such as Lord or Lady, that shows they have a special honour

titter *verb*
titters, tittering, tittered
to laugh quietly in a nervous way
titter *noun*

to *preposition*
1 used for showing the direction that someone or something goes in *We're off to school. The ball rolled to the bottom of the hill. I turned to the left.*
2 reaching as far as something *My hair hangs down to my shoulders. The fire spread to the garage.*
3 used for showing the position of something or someone *She stood to my right. I had my back to the window.*
4 used for showing something that is fixed or joined *a shelf fixed to the wall; a computer connected to the internet; We tied the balloons to the door handle.*
5 up until something *from Monday to Friday; It's only a week to my birthday. The film was exciting from beginning to end.*
6 used with many verbs (such as 'give', 'send', 'show', 'write', 'listen' and 'talk') for showing the person or thing that receives the action of the verb, for example the person or thing that is given or sent something *I sent a text to Arun. Show it to me. He listened to his mum.*
7 used for making the infinitive (basic form) of a verb or used instead of a verb *Do you want to go home? No, I don't want to* (for example, I don't want to go home).
8 used after an adjective or noun before a verb *Sophie was afraid to speak. I don't have the skill to create a website.*
9 used for showing how someone or something is treated *Ms Miller is always kind to me. Be nice to the cat.*
10 used for talking about the time on the clock when you mean a certain number of minutes before the hour *It's five to nine.*
11 used for showing a relationship between people *Who is he married to?*
12 used for comparing things or people *We won three goals to two. I prefer English to maths.*
13 used for showing how many parts make up something *There are 100 pence to a pound.*
14 belonging to something *Where's the lid to this jar?*
15 also used in many idiomatic expressions such as: *to my surprise* (showing someone's surprise); *to pieces* (showing something torn, smashed or separated into small parts); *back to front* (the wrong way round); *to have something all to yourself* (be the only one to have something and not have to share it)

to *adverb*
1 into a position where something is closed *Push the door to.*
2 **to and fro** backwards and forwards

toad *noun* **toads**
a small brown jumping animal with a rough dry body and big eyes. Toads look similar to frogs but are larger and live mainly on land.

toadstool *noun* **toadstools**
a small wild plant with a short stem and a body (main part) that is usually shaped like the top of a ball. Toadstools are similar to mushrooms but are often poisonous.

toast *noun*
1 bread heated up under a grill or in a toaster until it turns brown and hard *a slice of toast*
2 (plural **toasts**) when someone toasts someone by holding a glass of something such as wine in their hand and saying a few kind words *We drank a toast to my brother, who had just got married.*

toast *verb*
toasts, toasting, toasted
1 to heat something such as bread under a grill or in a toaster until it turns brown and hard *toasted muffins*
2 to hold a glass of something such as wine in your hand and drink it after saying a few kind words to someone on an important occasion, for example to wish them a happy birthday or lots of success in a new job *All the family toasted Granddad on his seventieth birthday.*

toaster *noun* **toasters**
a piece of electrical equipment for making toast

tobacco *noun*
the leaves of the tobacco plant that are dried (water is removed from them) and used for making cigarettes and cigars or for putting into pipes for smoking

tobacconist *noun* **tobacconists**
someone who works in a shop that sells tobacco and other things for smoking such as cigarettes and pipes

toboggan *noun* **toboggans**
a small simple vehicle for travelling over snow, with two long pieces of wood or metal at the bottom instead of wheels. Toboggans are often used for sliding down hills as a sport or for fun.

tobogganing *noun*
the sport or activity of sliding down hills on a toboggan

today *adverb*
1 on this day *There's no school today.*
2 at the present time when compared to the past *Cars today are safer.*

today *noun*
1 this day *today's lessons; Today is Friday.*
2 the present time *Today's cars are safer.*

534

toddle–tone

toddle verb
toddles, toddling, toddled
to walk with short unsteady steps *Look at my two-year-old sister toddling around the room!*

toddler noun toddlers
a very young girl or boy who is just learning to walk

toe noun toes
1 one of the five long thin parts at the end of your foot
2 the part of a sock or shoe that goes round your toes *a shoe with pointed toes*
3 **on your toes** active, energetic or ready to deal with anything that might happen *A class full of intelligent pupils keeps our teacher on her toes.*

toenail noun toenails
the hard smooth part at the end of each of your toes

toffee noun
1 a hard sticky brown food made by boiling sugar, water and butter
2 (plural **toffees**) a sweet made from a piece of toffee
3 a toffee apple is an apple covered with toffee. It is fixed to a stick that you hold when you eat it.

tofu ['toh-foo'] noun
a soft white food made from soya milk (a liquid produced from soya beans)

toga ['toh-ger'] noun togas
a long piece of clothing worn loosely around the body, especially in ancient Rome

together adverb
1 used for saying that someone is with someone else or does something with someone else, or that people are with each other or do something with each other *Jess and Seema walk to school together. I took the bus together with my friends. Lots of children were playing together. At the show, Mum and Dad sat together* (next to each other).
2 used for talking about two or more things that are put with each other, joined to each other or made to touch each other *Mix all the ingredients together. I clipped the two sheets of paper together. The pages are stuck together. Press the two blades of the scissors together. Add 3, 5 and 7 together.*
3 at the same time *Please don't all speak together. Everyone happened to arrive together.*

toggle noun toggles
an on/off key on a computer keyboard or button in a computer program that lets you make something happen by selecting it once and make it stop happening by selecting it again

toggle verb
toggles, toggling, toggled
to move backwards and forwards between two operations or programs on a computer by using a toggle

toil verb
toils, toiling, toiled
1 to work very hard *Mum's been toiling away in the office all day.*
2 to move somewhere slowly with a lot of effort *The climbers were toiling their way up the steep hill.*

toil noun

toilet noun toilets
1 a seat with a large hole in it that you use for getting rid of waste from your body *a toilet bowl*
2 a room with a toilet (or toilets) in it *public toilets*
3 if you go to the toilet, you get rid of waste from your body
4 toilet paper is soft thin paper for cleaning yourself after going to the toilet
5 a toilet roll is a tube with soft thin toilet paper wrapped around it

token noun tokens
1 a round piece of metal or plastic used instead of money, for example to make a piece of equipment work
2 a piece of paper or an electronic card used instead of money, for example in a shop, to buy something *a book token; My parents gave me a £20 gift token for my birthday* (so I could spend £20 on buying something).
3 a piece of paper or card that you collect when you buy something. When you have collected a certain number of them, you get something such as a free gift. *I cut out the token printed on the side of the cereal packet.*
4 something you give to someone or do for someone to thank them or as a sign of your special feelings for them *My best friend bought me a scarf as a token of his friendship.*

told
past tense & past participle of **tell**

tolerable adjective
1 used about something that someone can deal with or accept without complaining although it is unpleasant *The heat was just about tolerable.*
2 used about something that is reasonable although not very good *The food was tolerable.*

tolerably adverb
reasonably but not very well *Our captain played tolerably well but he should have played better.*

tolerant adjective
1 if someone is tolerant, they understand and accept other people who have ideas or behaviour different from their own or who have faults and problems *Dad is very tolerant towards our noisy neighbours.*
2 showing that someone is tolerant *a tolerant attitude*

tolerance noun

tolerate verb
tolerates, tolerating, tolerated
1 to accept someone or something even if you don't like them, for example by allowing someone to do something or allowing something to happen or exist *Why does Miss Williams tolerate such bad behaviour?*
2 to be able to deal with or accept something unpleasant *These penguins have to tolerate very low temperatures in winter.*

toll noun
1 (plural **tolls**) money that someone pays to use something such as a road or bridge *a motorway toll charge; a toll road*
2 the number of people killed or injured at a particular time *The death toll in the tsunami was huge.*

toll verb
tolls, tolling, tolled
if a bell tolls, it rings slowly and loudly, for example when someone dies

tomahawk ['tom-er-hork'] noun tomahawks
a small axe (tool with a metal blade fixed to a wooden handle). It was often used in the past as a weapon by Native Americans (people living in America before Europeans arrived).

tomato noun tomatoes
a soft red round fruit that is very juicy. You usually cut it into slices and eat it raw, for example in salads or sandwiches.

ORIGIN from *tomatl* 'tomato' in a Mexican Native American language. The tomato came to Europe from Mexico in the 16th century.

tomb [rhymes with 'doom'] noun tombs
a place in the ground where a dead person is buried, usually with a structure such as a monument built above it

tombstone ['tomb' rhymes with 'doom'] noun tombstones
a piece of stone standing next to a grave or tomb. It has on it the name of the person buried there and the dates when he or she lived.

tomcat noun tomcats
a male cat

LANGUAGE EXTRA also called a *tom*

tome noun tomes
a very large and heavy book

tomorrow adverb
1 on the day after today *I'll do my homework tomorrow.*
2 in the future *Things will be better tomorrow.*

tomorrow noun
1 the day after today *tomorrow's football match; Tomorrow is Saturday.*
2 the future *The computers of tomorrow will need to be much faster.*

tom-tom noun tom-toms
a small drum that you play by hitting it with your hands

ton noun tons
1 a unit for measuring weight, equal to 2240 pounds or 1016 kilos
2 (informal) used when you mean a lot of something *I've got a ton of homework to do. My sister has tons of friends.*

tone noun tones
1 the particular sound of someone's voice that shows what they are feeling *'Sit down,' he said in an angry tone.*
2 the particular quality of a musical sound *the sad tones of the violin*
3 the particular sound made by the signal in a piece of equipment such as a phone *the dialling* (or *dial*) *tone* (when you pick up a phone to make a call); *the engaged tone* (when you phone someone who is already speaking to someone else)

535

tone–top

4 the particular feeling you get from something, for example a book, place or event *The tone of the story was very jokey.*
5 a colour of a particular kind
6 the largest difference between the sound of any two musical notes that are next to each other on a musical scale

tone *verb*
tones, toning, toned
1 to tone something down is to make it less strong, for example less unpleasant or upsetting *The colour is too bright – tone it down a bit. The parents have toned down their criticism of the head teacher.*
2 if something tones in with something else, their colours look good or attractive together

tone-deaf *adjective*
if someone is tone-deaf, they cannot hear the difference between musical notes so they cannot sing correctly and sometimes cannot play music correctly

toner *noun*
an ink in the form of a powder used in laser printers and photocopiers

tongs *noun plural*
a small tool made up of two long thin parts (called arms) joined at the top. Tongs are used for picking things up by pushing the two parts together. *sugar tongs*

tongue *noun* **tongues**
1 the long soft part inside the mouth, used for example for tasting and swallowing food and in humans for speaking
2 another word for a language *English is my mother tongue* (the language I started learning as a baby).
3 a thin flat piece of leather under the part of a shoe or boot where you fasten the laces

tongue-tied *adjective*
if someone is tongue-tied, they cannot speak, for example because they are nervous, shy, afraid or ashamed

tongue twister *noun* **tongue twisters**
a sentence or word that is difficult to say because it contains difficult sounds or many sounds that are almost the same and difficult to pronounce quickly

tonic *noun* **tonics**
1 a medicine that gives you energy
2 a tonic or tonic water is a type of drink with lots of small bubbles in it and a bitter taste

tonight *adverb*
on this day in the evening or at night *My brother came home from work late tonight. Tonight I'll be staying at Seema's house.*

tonight *noun*
this day in the evening or at night *tonight's TV programmes; Tonight will be the last time I see him.*

tonne *noun* **tonnes**
a unit for measuring weight in the metric system. A tonne is equal to 1000 kilos.

LANGUAGE EXTRA also called a *metric ton*

tonsillitis *noun*
an illness in your throat caused by germs making your tonsils red and painful

tonsils *noun plural*
the two small lumps of soft flesh inside your mouth at the sides of your throat

too *adverb*
1 used when you mean something or someone extra or for adding something extra to what you say *Can I come too? It's late and it's raining too.*

SYNONYM also

2 used when you mean that the same thing is true about something or someone else *I go swimming every Saturday and my sister does too.*

SYNONYM also

3 more than someone needs or wants, more than something or someone should be or more than should be happening *Turn the TV down – it's too loud. You're working too hard. I've eaten too much cake. There are too many cars on the road.*
4 used when you mean a quality is so great or there is so much of something that something else is not possible *Granddad can't play football – he's too old. He's too old to play. It's raining too much for us to go out and play.*
5 **not too** not very *I'm not too worried.*

took
past tense of **take**

tool *noun* **tools**
1 a piece of equipment that you hold in your hand and use for doing a particular kind of job, for example a hammer (for knocking in nails) or a spade (for digging)
2 a tool kit is a container for tools used for repairing or making something

toolbar *noun* **toolbars**
a long strip, usually at the top of a computer screen, with icons that show the different actions you can perform in a program or document

toot *verb*
toots, tooting, tooted
if a car horn toots, or if someone toots it, it makes a short high sound **toot** *noun*

tooth *noun* **teeth**
1 one of the hard white parts in your mouth that you use for biting and chewing. Your teeth have roots that grow out of your gums (the pink fleshy parts of the mouth).
2 one of the points along the edge of a tool or object such as a saw or comb *a row of teeth*
3 if a sound sets your teeth on edge, it is very unpleasant and makes you feel very uncomfortable

toothache *noun*
a pain in one of your teeth

toothbrush *noun* **toothbrushes**
a small brush with a long handle, used for cleaning your teeth with toothpaste

tooth fairy *noun* **tooth fairies**
an imaginary creature that comes during the night and takes away a child's tooth that has been left under the pillow before the child goes to sleep. The tooth fairy leaves some money there instead.

toothpaste *noun*
a soft substance that you put on your toothbrush when you clean your teeth

top *noun* **tops**
1 the highest part of something *the top of the head; He stood at the top of the stairs.*
2 the flat outside surface of something, for example a table or box *Can you wipe down the table top?*
3 the end of something, such as a street or garden, that is furthest away from you *My uncle lives at the top of the road.*
4 a cover for a container such as a bottle, tin, jar or saucepan *a bottle top*
5 a piece of clothing that covers the body from the neck to the waist, for example a T-shirt or sweater *a pyjama top*
6 a toy that spins round and round when you move a handle up and down *a spinning top*
7 **the top** the most important position in something such as a job, group or team *At the top of the school is the head teacher.*
8 **at the top of your voice** very loudly
9 **on top** on something, when talking about its highest part or outside surface *a cake with chocolate on top* (covering its surface); *There's a pile of books on my desk – put this one on top.*
10 **on top of** on something or someone, or covering something or someone *I left your watch on top of the fridge. Put a plate on top of your food to keep flies off. The books were in a pile on top of each other. The toys on the shelf fell on top of me* (fell onto my head and body).
11 **on top of** also used when you mean something extra *On top of all his problems, Dad's just lost his job.*
12 **on top of** also used for showing that you deal with a situation correctly *At first I didn't know what was happening but now I'm on top of things. It's a big problem but don't let it get on top of you* (don't let it continue without dealing with it).

top *adjective*
1 highest or in the highest place or position *the top shelf; I came top in the exam* (I came first). *I got top marks. The train was travelling at top speed.*
2 used for describing something or someone that is the most important or best (or one of the most important or best) *the top prize* (for the person or thing that wins a competition); *The head teacher has the top job. We go to a top school. He's a top football player. Sayed's work is always of top quality.*

top *verb*
tops, topping, topped
1 to be in the highest position on a list *The band's last album topped the charts last week* (they sold more music than anyone else). *In that year the Conservatives topped the poll* (got more votes than anyone else).
2 to be more than a particular amount or number *The temperature topped 30 degrees.*
3 if food is topped with something, it has that particular thing covering the top of it *a pizza topped with mushrooms*
4 to top something up such as a kettle or cup of tea is to fill it with more liquid
5 to top something up such as a mobile phone or smart card is to pay more money so that you can continue using it

top hat *noun* **top hats**
a tall black hat shaped like a tube, worn by men in the past or on special occasions

topic *noun* **topics**
something that you talk or write about or something that you study *We're learning about the topic of the First World War.*

SYNONYM subject

topical *adjective*
connected with something that people are talking about at the present time *a topical subject; a book of topical interest*

topicality *noun*

topless *adjective*
not wearing clothes on the top half of your body

topmost *adjective*
highest *the topmost leaves of a tree*

topping *noun* **toppings**
food that is put on top of other food such as a pizza, cake or ice cream *a pizza with a cheese and tomato topping; an apple pie with a topping of hot custard*

topple *verb*
topples, toppling, toppled
1 to fall over by becoming less steady and moving from an upright position *The tree toppled over in the wind. George toppled over backwards in his chair.*
2 to make something or someone fall in this way *The crowds toppled the statue of the cruel King.*
3 to get rid of someone such as a ruler or government by taking away their power, usually by force

top secret *adjective*
used for describing information or an action that is very important and must be kept completely secret *a spy on a top-secret mission*

topsy-turvy *adjective* (informal)
very confused and not organised

top-up *noun* **top-ups**
1 when you add more liquid to something such as someone's drink or a kettle *I've finished my lemonade – please can you give me a top-up?*
2 when you pay more money to continue using something such as a mobile phone or smart card *a top-up card* (for paying more money, for example to use a phone); *My phone needs a top-up.*

Torah *noun*
the laws and main ideas of the Jewish religion

torch *noun* **torches**
1 a small electric light that you carry in your hand. It gets its power from batteries.
2 a long piece of wood with a flame at the end of it, used for giving light or setting fire to something, especially in the past

torch *verb*
torches, torching, torched
to set fire to something in order to destroy it

tore
past tense of **tear**

torment ['tor-ment'] *noun* **torments**
great pain and suffering

torment ['tor-ment'] *verb*
torments, tormenting, tormented
1 to cause a lot of suffering to a person or animal *He was tormented by guilt.*
2 to do something to a person or animal to make them upset or angry

torn
past participle of **tear**

tornado ['tor-nay-doh'] *noun*
tornadoes or **tornados**
a very strong and dangerous wind that blows in a circle and moves along the ground in a huge cloud or tall column

ORIGIN from Spanish *tronada* 'thunderstorm'

torpedo *noun* **torpedoes**
a bomb shaped like a long tube that travels under the water to destroy ships and submarines

torpedo *verb*
torpedoes, torpedoing, torpedoed
to hit a ship or submarine with a torpedo

torrent *noun* **torrents**
1 a large amount of water that moves or flows very fast *Heavy rain turned the stream into a torrent.*
2 a large amount of something unpleasant *a torrent of abuse*

torrential *adjective*
used for describing rain that is very heavy

torso *noun* **torsos**
the main part of the body without the head, arms and legs

tortilla *noun* **tortillas**
a type of thin round bread from Mexico that is usually rolled or folded and eaten with food such as meat, cheese or beans inside

tortoise *noun* **tortoises**
an animal with a hard shell on its back that it pulls its head and legs into for protection. It walks slowly along the ground, eats plants and flowers, and hibernates (spends the winter sleeping).

tortuous *adjective*
having lots of twists and turns *a tortuous path* **tortuously** *adverb*

torture *verb*
tortures, torturing, tortured
to make someone suffer a lot of pain as a punishment or to get them to tell you something you want to know
torturer *noun*

torture *noun*
1 the action of torturing someone
2 (informal) a very unpleasant or uncomfortable feeling *Sitting through one of Miss Dawson's lessons is sheer torture!*

Tory *noun* **Tories**
another word for a Conservative (member or supporter of the Conservative Party in the UK)

toss *verb*
tosses, tossing, tossed
1 to throw something somewhere or to someone, often gently or carelessly *Can you toss me my purse? Toss out your tea if it's gone cold.*
2 to move or be thrown from side to side or up and down *The boat was tossed about in the storm. I was tossing and turning all night* (moving my head from side to side in bed, for example because I was worried or ill).
3 to toss (or toss up) or to toss a coin is to throw a coin into the air to see which side it comes down so that you can decide something, for example who will win or lose *'Heads!' he shouted, after tossing the coin. Let's toss up to see who goes first.*

SYNONYM for sense 3: to flip a coin

toss *noun* **tosses**
1 the action of tossing a coin
2 the action of throwing something

total *noun* **totals**
the final amount you get when you add two or more smaller numbers together *Five and nine make a total of fourteen.*

total *adjective*
1 used for describing the whole of something and not just part of it *What's the total amount?*
2 used for giving extra importance to a word, for example when you mean that something or someone is as big or as great as can be *total silence; The school play was a total disaster.*

SYNONYM for sense 2: complete

total *verb*
totals, totalling, totalled
1 if you total numbers (or total numbers up), you add the numbers together to make a final amount
2 if something totals a particular amount, that is the amount it reaches when everything is added together *The earnings from Dad's two jobs total £500.*

totalitarian *adjective*
connected with a political belief that there should be only one political party and that it should have total control over people's lives

totally *adverb*
1 used for giving special importance to a word or for saying that something is very true *I totally agree with you. He's totally confused.*
2 in every way or when talking about every part of something *I blame you totally. These two books are totally different.*

SYNONYMS completely, entirely

totem pole ['toh-term'] *noun* **totem poles**
a tall wooden pole or tree trunk with symbols and images carved into it or painted on it, made by Native Americans (people living in America before Europeans arrived)

totter *verb*
totters, tottering, tottered
to move or walk in an unsteady way *Granddad was tottering about with his walking stick.*

toucan ['too-kan'] *noun* **toucans**
a large bird with a large, curved and colourful beak and a body that is black with areas of bright colours. Toucans live in Central and South America.

touch *verb*
touches, touching, touched
1 to put your fingers or hand or a part of your body on something or someone *Can you touch the ceiling? Touch the screen here to open the program.*
2 if something touches something else, it goes onto it or against it and then moves away from it *My sleeve touched the wet paint. Our shoulders touched as we ran.*
3 if something is touching (or touches) something else or if things are touching (or they touch), their surfaces come together and there is no space in between *The back of the computer was touching the wall. Push all the chairs together so they touch* (or *so they're touching*).
4 to go near something and do something with it, for example to use it, play with it or work on it *Don't touch my books when I'm away. Someone's touched my toys. You haven't touched your homework all week.*
5 to eat or drink something or start to eat or drink something *Vijay hasn't touched his dinner.*
6 to reach a certain amount *Last summer, temperatures touched 35 degrees.*
7 to have a strong influence on someone's feelings, for example by making them very happy or sad *I was very touched by the head teacher's kind words.*
8 if an aircraft or spacecraft touches down, it comes down to the ground from the air

SYNONYM to land

9 if you touch something up, you make small changes to it that make it look better

touch *noun*
1 the natural ability you have to feel things with your hands or through your skin *the sense of touch; It was cold to the touch.*
2 (*plural* **touches**) when you put your hand or a part of your body on something or someone or when something goes onto or against your skin *I felt a touch on my shoulder. The door opens at the touch of a button. I don't like the rough touch of this scarf against my neck.*
3 (*plural* **touches**) a small detail or quality that makes something better *Having a magician at your party was a nice touch.*
4 a touch of something is a small amount of it *There's a touch of frost tonight.*
5 used for talking about seeing someone or exchanging information with them, for example by phoning or writing *My mum is in touch with her school friends* (she sees or phones them or writes to them). *I've lost touch with my cousins* (or *My cousins and I are out of touch*) (we don't see or phone each other or write to each other any more).
6 used for talking about understanding people or knowing what is happening *Dad thinks our head teacher is out of touch* (doesn't understand the students or know what's going on). *Our class teacher is young and is very much in touch.*
7 the area outside the playing area in football or rugby *He kicked the ball into touch.*
8 if you put the finishing touches to something, for example a story or painting, you do the final things needed to complete it

touching *adjective*
making someone have strong feelings such as sadness or great happiness *a touching story*

touchpad *noun* **touchpads**
a small area, usually on a laptop, that you touch to move the cursor and perform other actions on the screen

touch screen *noun* **touch screens**
a screen on a computer, or on other equipment such as a mobile phone, that you touch to make programs work

LANGUAGE EXTRA also spelt *touchscreen*

touchy *adjective* **touchier, touchiest**
if someone is touchy, they very quickly get upset or angry

tough *adjective* **tougher, toughest**
1 if something is tough, it is strong and difficult to break or damage *a tough pair of shoes*
2 if someone is tough, they are strong, for example they can accept suffering and pain or are good at dealing with difficult situations *He's a very tough boxer. You need to be tough to be a police officer.*
3 difficult and needing a lot of effort to do or deal with *a tough race; a tough question; The work is very tough.*
4 if food such as meat is tough, it is hard and difficult to cut or eat
5 used for describing a place where there is a lot of violent behaviour or crime *a tough part of town*
6 used for describing someone who is bad and violent *a tough criminal*
7 with lots of problems *Life is tough if you are very poor.*
8 dealing with people and things in a very strict way *tough measures* (for example to make sure bad things never happen); *These rules aren't tough enough. Our teacher is tough on bullies* (punishes them a lot).
toughly *adverb* **toughness** *noun*

SIMILES 'as tough as old boots' and 'as tough as nails' mean very tough (sense 2)

toughen *verb*
toughens, toughening, toughened
1 to make something stronger or harder, or to become stronger or harder *Cooking the beans too long will toughen the skins.*
2 to make someone stronger and better at dealing with difficult situations, or to become stronger and better at dealing with difficult situations *School will toughen him up. Gang members toughen up as they get older.*
3 to do something in a stricter way, or to be done in a stricter way *The government has toughened up the law.*

tour *noun* **tours**
1 a journey for pleasure, when you visit different places
2 a short journey to visit different parts of a building or town, for example to learn things about it *We went on a guided tour of Buckingham Palace* (someone showed us around the building).
3 a journey to different places for a special purpose, for example to take part in an event or to meet people *The musicians are on tour in Scotland. The prince made a tour of Canada.*
4 a tour guide is someone who shows people interesting places in a town, country or building

tour *verb*
tours, touring, toured
to go on a tour somewhere *We toured Italy* (or *around Italy*). *Parents will tour the school at three o'clock.*

tourism *noun*
1 the activity of travelling for pleasure
2 the business of providing things that tourists need such as hotels, transport and places to visit

tourist *noun* **tourists**
someone who travels somewhere for pleasure, for example on holiday

touristy *adjective* (informal)
if an area is touristy, it has too many tourists or is too full of the places that people think tourists like to go to

tournament *noun* **tournaments**
a competition or sports event divided into different games. The winners of each game play against each other in the next game until only one winner is left. *a tennis tournament*

tow *verb*
tows, towing, towed
1 to pull something such as a vehicle or boat with a rope, chain or cable *You need a heavy car to tow a caravan.*
2 to tow a vehicle away is to lift it onto a lorry and take it away, for example because someone has left it parked in the wrong place
tow *noun*

towards *adverb*
1 going, facing or looking in the direction of something or someone *She ran towards me. I had my back towards the window. He glanced towards the pile of books.*
2 near a particular place or time *We sat towards the back of the cinema. It's my birthday towards the end of the year.*
3 used for showing the way someone or something is treated or someone's feelings about someone or something *Grandma was always kind towards me. Sophie behaves badly towards her parents.*
4 used for saying that something helps to get a particular result *Mum gave me £50 towards my tablet* (to help me buy it). *I haven't made much progress towards finishing my homework.*

LANGUAGE EXTRA you can also say *toward*, especially in American English

towel *noun* **towels**
1 a soft piece of cloth for wiping your hands or body until they are dry *a bath towel* (large towel used after a bath or shower)
2 paper or very soft material used in the kitchen, for example for wiping things *a roll of kitchen towel*
3 a sanitary towel is a piece of soft material used by a woman to absorb (take in) blood during a period (natural bleeding that happens every month)

towelling *noun*
a soft thick material used for making towels and clothes such as dressing gowns or socks

538

tower *noun* towers
1 a tall narrow building *a clock tower; Blackpool Tower*
2 a tall narrow part of a building such as a castle or church *The church tower has a very tall spire on top.*
3 a tower block is a tall building with lots of flats or offices

tower *verb*
towers, towering, towered
1 to be much taller than someone else *Sam towers above his brother.*
2 to be much higher than something else *The skyscraper towers above all the buildings nearby.*

Tower Bridge *noun*
a bridge across the River Thames in London. It has two towers and a section in between that opens to let ships pass. People often think of it as a symbol of Britain.

Tower of London *noun*
a castle beside the River Thames in London. The building was started in 1066 during the Norman Conquest (when the Normans from northern France took control of England).

town *noun*
1 (*plural* towns) a place where thousands or millions of people live and work. Towns are bigger than villages and smaller than cities.
2 the town where you live *Granddad lives in another part of town. Mum is out of town* (not at home but in another place).
3 the main part of a town where places such as the shops, cinemas and restaurants are *Let's go into town.*
4 the people who live in a town *The whole town was talking about it.*

town hall *noun* town halls
a building that contains the offices of the local council (people in charge of a town or county and who control public services)

toxic *adjective*
if a substance or chemical is toxic, it is poisonous and harmful to humans and animals *toxic fumes*

toy *noun* toys
1 something that you play with. Toys include teddy bears, dolls, spinning tops, Lego (plastic blocks for building things) and model animals, cars, trains and planes. *toy soldiers; toy dinosaurs*
2 a toy shop is a shop where you buy toys

toy *verb*
toys, toying, toyed
if you toy with an idea, you think about it but not very seriously

trace *noun* traces
1 a sign left behind by something or someone that shows they existed or were in a particular place *Our dog has disappeared without trace. We searched all over the house but there was no trace of little Billy.*
2 a very small amount of something *The police found traces of blood in the sink.*

trace *verb*
traces, tracing, traced
1 to find something or someone by looking for them carefully *The airline couldn't trace my lost luggage. The police traced the missing girl to a house in Glasgow.*
2 to find where something comes from *Many people trace their family back to the seventeenth century.*
3 to describe something that happens over a long period of time *The book traces the history of the royal family.*
4 if you trace a picture or pattern, you copy it using tracing paper (a special paper you can see through) by drawing over the lines of the picture or pattern with a pencil

traceable *adjective*
able to be traced and found *My mobile phone is marked with a special ink so it's traceable.*

tracing paper *noun*
special paper that you can see through, used for copying. You put the paper on top of the picture or pattern you want to copy and draw over the lines of the picture or pattern with a pencil.

track *noun* tracks
1 a path with lots of bumps in it, made by people or animals walking or by cars *a mountain track; a dirt track*
2 a mark left on the ground, for example by the feet of an animal or person or the tyres of a car *tyre tracks; We followed the elephant's tracks.*
3 the two long metal bars that trains or trams travel on *a railway track; The train was coming down the track. We had to leave the train and walk along the tracks* (or *track*).
4 a wide path or road with a hard surface, usually shaped like a circle or oval, where races between runners, cars or bicycles take place

> **LANGUAGE EXTRA** also called a *racing track* or *racetrack*

5 a long straight area or strip, for example in tenpin bowling, for rolling the ball down
6 a song or piece of music, for example on a CD or piece of electronic equipment such as an iPod
7 a metal belt around the wheels of a tank, tractor or bulldozer for travelling over rough or soft ground
8 **to keep track of** to know all about what is happening to someone or something or where they are
9 **on the right track** doing something correctly that will lead to a good result *The police don't have all the answers yet but they're on the right track* (they will have the answers soon).

track *verb*
tracks, tracking, tracked
1 to follow the signs showing where a person or animal has been in order to find them *The police tracked the criminals to the south of England.*
2 to use electronic equipment to follow something or someone as they move *Scientists are tracking the satellite as it orbits the earth.*
3 if you track a letter or parcel, you follow each part of its journey online using a tracking number (special number you are given when you post the letter or parcel)
4 to track someone or something down is to find them as part of a long and difficult search

trackball *noun* trackballs
a small ball on a piece of equipment such as a mouse that you touch with your thumb to move the cursor on a computer screen

tracksuit *noun* tracksuits
a loose warm top and trousers that you wear for doing exercises such as jogging or for relaxing in

tract *noun* tracts
1 a large area of land
2 a short piece of writing, for example on a political or religious subject

tractor *noun* tractors
a heavy vehicle with large back wheels. Tractors are used on farms for pulling things along, for example equipment such as a plough.

trade *noun*
1 the business of buying and selling goods and services *There's a lot of trade between the UK and the rest of Europe.*
2 (*plural* trades) a particular area of business *Dad works in the building trade.*
3 (*plural* trades) a job, often one that needs skill using your hands *He's a tailor by trade.*

trade *verb*
trades, trading, traded
1 to buy or sell goods or services
2 if someone trades in an old product (such as a computer or car) for a new or different one, they give a company the old product towards the cost of buying the other one. This means that the product they are buying costs them less.
trading *noun*

trademark *noun* trademarks
a name or symbol that shows that a product belongs to a particular company and to no-one else

trader *noun* traders
someone who buys and sells things *a market trader* (someone who sells things in a market)

tradesperson *noun* tradespeople
someone with a job that needs skill using their hands such as a builder, carpenter or plumber

trade union *noun* trade unions
an organisation of workers in a particular job. It helps the workers with things such as getting better working conditions and more money from the people they work for.

tradition *noun*
1 (*plural* traditions) a way of doing things or behaving that has existed for a very long time and is accepted as normal among a group of people *Parliament follows traditions that go back hundreds of years.*
2 used for talking about traditions in general *My parents are great lovers of tradition. By tradition, most Americans celebrate Thanksgiving.*

traditional *adjective*
1 used about something that has existed or been done for a very long time and is accepted as normal *a traditional family meal; At school we study new subjects like coding as well as traditional ones like English and maths.*
2 used about clothes that are the same as clothes that people wore a long time ago *The flamenco dancers wore traditional Spanish costumes.*
3 used about something or someone that follows older ways of doing things rather than modern ways *a traditional school; Granddad's opinions are very traditional.*

traditionally – tranquilliser

traditionally *adverb*
1 in a way that has happened or been done for a very long time *The festival traditionally takes place in August.*
2 in the same sort of clothes that people wore a long time ago *The dancers were dressed traditionally in the costumes of their country.*

traffic *noun*
1 all the cars and other vehicles that travel along a road at the same time *The traffic is heavy* (there are lots of vehicles).
2 the amount of aircraft, ships and trains travelling at the same time *There's a lot of air traffic between London and Edinburgh.*
3 the movement of signals and messages in an electronic system *internet traffic*
4 the buying and selling of things such as stolen goods, which is against the law

traffic island *noun* **traffic islands**
a small piece of pavement in the middle of a road, where you can stand safely while crossing the road

traffic jam *noun* **traffic jams**
a long line of vehicles close together that cannot move or can only move slowly

traffic lights *noun plural*
red, green and orange lights, usually on a long post, for controlling road traffic. The lights are often at dangerous places along a road, such as where roads join each other, and they tell the traffic when to stop (red) and go (green).

traffic warden *noun* **traffic wardens**
an official who checks vehicles to see if they are parked in the correct place and for the correct amount of time, and who gives drivers tickets (official pieces of paper telling drivers they must pay money for parking in a bad place)

tragedy *noun* **tragedies**
1 a very bad and sad event that causes one or more people to die or suffer greatly *The boat trip ended in tragedy* (someone died or was injured).
2 a very bad and sad situation *It's a tragedy that your brother left school without any qualifications.*
3 a play or film about suffering and unhappy events in which one or more people die at the end

tragic *adjective*
1 used about something that is very sad because it is connected with people suffering and dying, often dying suddenly or at an early age *a tragic accident*; *the tragic death of the 10-year-old boy*
2 used about a very bad and sad situation *It's tragic that the school doesn't have enough money to give us free music lessons.*
3 connected with plays and films that are tragedies *a tragic actor*

tragically *adverb*
used for showing that people suffer or die *Granddad fell over and tragically died. The boat trip ended tragically.*

trail *noun* **trails**
1 a path through the countryside, usually for walking or cycling along *a nature trail* (with signs telling you about animals and plants)
2 a long line of marks or series of signs left behind by a person or animal as they move along *a trail of blood*; *You've left a trail of muddy footprints on the carpet.*
3 if you are on the trail of someone or something, you are trying hard to find them

trail *verb*
trails, trailing, trailed
1 to pull something along the ground or be pulled along the ground *He was walking along trailing his scarf behind him. His scarf was trailing in the dirt.*
2 to move slowly behind someone *Simon never keeps up with me – he's always trailing behind.*
3 to hang down *Her golden hair was trailing over her shoulders.*
4 to be losing to someone, for example in a sport or competition *Our team are trailing by a few points.*

trailer *noun* **trailers**
1 a container or vehicle pulled by a car *We carry our luggage in a trailer.*
2 the separate back part of an articulated lorry (made up of two parts) that is pulled by the cab (front part) and used for carrying heavy things
3 a short film made up of a small part (or small parts) of a film or TV programme. It is shown to people to make them want to see the whole film or programme.
4 the American word for a caravan (vehicle that people live in)

train *noun* **trains**
1 a long thin vehicle made up of carriages (for passengers) or containers (for goods) and pulled by an engine that provides power
2 the long back part of a dress such as a wedding dress, or of another loose piece of clothing such as a bishop's robe, that the person wearing it pulls along the ground as they walk
3 a series of connected events or thoughts
4 a line of people, animals or vehicles slowly moving together, for example through the desert *a camel train*
5 a train set is a small model train and track that you play with as a toy

train *verb*
trains, training, trained
1 to learn a particular job or skill *My sister is training to be a dentist.*
2 to teach someone a job or skill *Why don't they train more teachers? They're training us in how to build a computer.*
3 to do a sports activity lots of times to get better at it *We're training for next week's football match.*
4 to help someone practise a sports activity *My uncle's a coach who trains Olympic athletes.*
5 to teach an animal to obey you or perform tricks
6 to point something such as a light or camera at someone or something

trainer *noun* **trainers**
1 a person who trains someone, for example in a sport, or who trains an animal
2 one of a pair of soft shoes with rubber soles used for running and playing sports or for wearing in relaxed situations

training *noun*
1 the activity of learning or teaching someone a job or skill *a training course*; *Doctors need a lot of training.*
2 when you do a sports activity lots of times to get better at it or the time you spend doing it *I haven't done any football training this week. We have an hour's rugby training after lunch.*

trainspotting *noun*
the activity of watching and studying trains, usually as a hobby

traitor *noun* **traitors**
someone who stops supporting a group or country and goes over to the enemy's side or gives information away to the enemy

tram *noun* **trams**
a large vehicle that travels along rails in the road, used for carrying passengers

tramlines *noun plural*
the rails in the street that trams travel along

tramp *noun*
1 (*plural* **tramps**) a person with no home or job who walks around begging for food and money
2 a long walk, especially one that makes you tired
3 the sound of someone walking slowly and with heavy steps

tramp *verb*
tramps, tramping, tramped
1 to walk slowly with heavy steps
2 to walk a long distance *We've been tramping around Manchester all day.*

trample *verb*
tramples, trampling, trampled
1 if a person or animal tramples something (or tramples on something), they put their feet down hard on it and cause damage *Someone's trampled on the daffodils. Cats trampled all over our tomato plants.*
2 if someone is trampled, they are injured or killed by animals or people running or walking over them *Many people were trampled in the stampede.*

trampoline *noun* **trampolines**
a piece of sports equipment made up of a metal frame with strong material fixed to it with springs, used for jumping up and down on

trance *noun*
a type of sleep in which you can still hear sounds and see things, and you answer questions and do what someone tells you to do *The magician hypnotised me and put me into a trance.*

tranquil ['tran-kwil'] *adjective*
without any noise, activity or excitement *It's tranquil in this part of the park.*
tranquillity *noun*

> SYNONYMS peaceful, quiet

tranquilliser *noun* **tranquillisers**
a chemical substance that makes a person or animal calm down or go to sleep

> LANGUAGE EXTRA also spelt *tranquillizer*

540

trans--trap

trans- *prefix*
1 connected with something that goes from one side to another *a transcontinental railway* (across continents); *a transatlantic flight* (across the Atlantic)
2 connected with change *to translate* (change words from one language to another)

transaction *noun* transactions
when someone performs a business action such as buying or selling something, taking money from a bank account or putting money into a bank account

transatlantic *adjective*
1 going across the Atlantic Ocean *a transatlantic flight*
2 connected with countries on either side of the Atlantic Ocean *a transatlantic phone call* (for example one between the UK and the US)

transfer ['trans-ferr'] *verb*
transfers, transferring, transferred
1 to move someone or something from one place to another *My dad has been transferred to a different hospital. Mum transferred £50 to my bank account.*
2 to go to or be moved to another place *Amy doesn't like our school and wants to transfer to Park Hill. Passengers had to transfer to another flight.*

transfer ['trans-fer'] *noun* transfers
1 the action of moving someone or something from one place to another *bank transfers* (money moved from one account to another); *The transfer of my files to the internet took all day.*
2 a piece of paper with a picture or pattern on it that can be moved onto another surface as a decoration using heat or water, for example pressed onto a T-shirt using a hot iron

transferable *adjective*
if a ticket or a card such as a library card is transferable, it can be used by someone else

transform *verb*
transforms, transforming, transformed
to change something or someone completely, often so that they are better *The internet has transformed the way people work and communicate. The wizard transformed the frog into a prince.*

transformation *noun* transformations
1 a complete change in something or someone
2 in maths, transformations are the different ways of changing or moving a shape, for example reflection, rotation and translation

transformer *noun* transformers
a piece of equipment that changes the force of an electrical current, for example so that different types of equipment can be used

transfusion *noun* transfusions
when someone such as a doctor puts blood from one person into the body of another person, for example when the other person has lost blood in an accident or is very ill

LANGUAGE EXTRA you can also say *blood transfusion*

transistor *noun* transistors
1 a small piece of electronic equipment for controlling an electric current, used for example in radios and computers
2 a transistor or transistor radio is a small radio with transistors inside that you can carry around, used especially in the past

transit ['tran-zit'] *noun*
when someone passes through one country on the way to another *a transit lounge* (room in an airport where you wait for a flight to another country)

transition *noun* transitions
a change from one situation to another *China is a country in transition* (it is changing).

transitional *adjective*
used for describing something that exists for a short time only because things are changing *a transitional period*; *a transitional government*

transitive *adjective*
in grammar, a transitive verb is one used with a direct object (a noun or pronoun that receives the direct action of the verb) and an intransitive verb is one used on its own without an object. For example, 'bring' is transitive ('Lucy brought her books') and 'look' is intransitive ('I looked out of the window'). Many verbs are both transitive and intransitive. For example, 'change' is transitive in 'I changed my shirt' but intransitive in 'Shreya has changed'.

translate *verb*
translates, translating, translated
if someone translates something, they write or say the meaning of the words in a different language *Can you translate 'My name is Daniel' into Spanish? This book has been translated into many languages.*

translator *noun*

translation *noun* translations
1 used for talking about a text whose words have been changed into the words of a different language with the same or a similar meaning *This song is a translation from Italian. The word 'school' is a translation of the French 'école'.*
2 the activity of translating something into a different language
3 in maths, translation is a way of moving a shape without turning it, for example so that it fits over another shape. A translation can be vertical, horizontal or diagonal.
compare: **reflection** (sense 2) and **rotation** (sense 3)

translucent *adjective*
if something such as glass is translucent, it allows light to pass through but you can't see through it clearly
compare: **transparent**

transmission *noun*
1 when something is transmitted, for example an electronic signal or a disease
2 (*plural* transmissions) a radio or television programme that is broadcast

transmit *verb*
transmits, transmitting, transmitted
1 to send out an electronic signal *The spacecraft transmits signals back to the scientists on the ground.*
2 to send out a radio or television programme using radio waves *The latest episode was transmitted to many countries.*

SYNONYM to broadcast

3 to pass or spread something to someone *Diseases like malaria are transmitted by mosquitoes.*

transmitter *noun* transmitters
a piece of equipment for broadcasting radio or television signals or for sending other types of signals such as mobile phone signals

transparency *noun*
1 the quality of being easy to see through *the transparency of glass*
2 (*plural* transparencies) a piece of photographic film or special plastic that you shine a light through using a projector to produce an image on a screen

transparent *adjective*
if an object or substance such as glass or plastic is transparent, you can see through it

ANTONYM opaque

transpire *verb*
transpires, transpiring, transpired
1 another way of saying to happen
2 used about something secret or not known about that becomes known *It transpired that Harry was the thief after all* (we now know he was the thief although we didn't know this before).

transplant *noun* transplants
1 an operation in which a doctor removes a part of someone's body and puts it into someone else's body *a kidney transplant*
2 a part of the body that has been transplanted

transplant *verb*
transplants, transplanting, transplanted
1 to remove a part of someone's body, for example a kidney or heart, and put it into someone else's body
2 to remove a plant from the place where it is growing and put it somewhere else

transport *noun*
1 a way of travelling from one place to another, for example using a road vehicle, train, plane or boat, or the vehicles, trains, planes or boats used for travelling somewhere *Dad gave Grandma a lift as she doesn't have transport* (for example a car). *'Do you have transport?' – 'Yes, I have a bike.' I often go by public transport* (for example by bus or train).
2 the action of transporting things, people or animals

transport *verb*
transports, transporting, transported
to move things, people or animals from one place to another, usually using a road vehicle, train, plane or boat

trap *noun* traps
1 something used for catching animals, for example an object with a spring that closes over the animal or a hole in the ground that the animal falls into *The rabbit was caught with its leg in a trap.*

541

trap – treasure

trap
2 a clever plan to trick someone or to catch or attack them *Don't answer that question – it's a trap. The soldiers were lured into a trap and captured.*
3 a bad situation that someone can't escape from *Borrowing more money than you can pay back is a trap you can easily fall into.*

trap verb
traps, trapping, trapped
1 if someone is trapped somewhere, they can't move or get out *When the building caught fire, some people were trapped inside.*
2 if you trap something somewhere, or if something is trapped somewhere, that thing is stuck and can't move *I trapped my coat in the door. They rescued a man whose legs were trapped under a fallen tree.*
3 to catch an animal using a trap
4 to stop someone you're trying to catch from leaving a place *The police trapped the criminal in an alleyway.*
5 to trick someone, for example to make them do or say something *They trapped me into making a confession.*
6 to stop something such as air, water or heat from escaping from a place *Solar panels trap energy from the sun.*

trapdoor noun **trapdoors**
a small door in a ceiling or floor or on a stage

trapeze ['trer-peez'] noun **trapezes**
a bar hanging from two ropes or straps from a support in a circus. It is used by acrobats to perform movements such as swinging and flying. *a trapeze artist*

trapezium ['trer-peez-ee-erm'] noun **trapeziums**
a flat shape with four straight sides. Two of its sides are parallel to each other but of different lengths.

trapezoid ['trap-i-zoyd'] noun **trapezoids**
a flat shape with four straight sides but no two sides are parallel

trash noun
1 something such as a book, play, film or programme that is of very bad quality *I wish you would read a good book instead of this trash!*
2 things that are not wanted that you throw away *All this trash goes straight into the bin. Chuck this broken radio out – it's trash. This old laptop is fit for the trash heap* (should be thrown away).
3 a place on a computer for storing files or emails that have been deleted
4 in American English, a trash can is a container for putting trash in, especially a dustbin

trash verb (informal)
trashes, trashing, trashed
to make a lot of mess in something such as a room, building or car by destroying or damaging things

trashy adjective **trashier, trashiest** (informal)
of bad quality *a trashy book; Your new mobile phone feels a bit trashy.*
trashiness noun

traumatic ['tror-mat-ik'] adjective
if something that happens to someone is traumatic, it makes them very upset and causes them a lot of suffering, often for a long time

traumatised ['tror-mer-tyzed'] adjective
if someone is traumatised, something happens to them that is so bad that they suffer very much and often for a long time

LANGUAGE EXTRA also spelt *traumatized*

travel verb
travels, travelling, travelled
1 to go from one place to another *Mum travels to work every day on the tube.*
2 to go visiting different places *Seema spent a month travelling around Spain. Do you like travelling?*
3 to go a particular distance *We travelled 50 miles to get there.*
4 to go or move somewhere at a particular speed or through or in something *The train was travelling at 100 miles an hour. Does sound travel through water?*
5 if something such as news or information travels, it becomes known by lots of people *Rumours travel fast.*

travel noun
1 when you go from one place to another or visit different places *I enjoy foreign travel* (going to different countries). *Where did you go on* (or *in*) *your travels?*
2 a travel agent is someone whose job is to organise people's journeys or holidays

traveller noun **travellers**
1 someone who is travelling somewhere or who travels a lot *rail travellers*
2 someone who doesn't live in one place but travels around and lives in a vehicle such as a caravan

travel-sick adjective
someone who is travel-sick feels ill when they travel, for example by car or plane
travel sickness noun

travolator ['trav-er-lay-ter'] noun **travolators**
a type of moving pavement that takes people from one place to another in a large building such as an airport or shopping centre

LANGUAGE EXTRA also spelt *travelator*

trawl verb
trawls, trawling, trawled
1 to search through something to try to find information about something or someone *I've been trawling the internet looking for stuff for my school project.*
2 if a boat trawls for fish, it pulls a large net behind it through the water

trawler noun **trawlers**
a boat for catching fish. It uses a large net that it pulls behind it through the water.

tray noun **trays**
1 a flat piece of wood, plastic or metal for carrying food and the things used for eating food. It has raised edges to stop things falling off.
2 a flat container with raised edges, for example for holding paper in a printer

treacherous adjective
1 very dangerous *The roads are treacherous* (for example because they are covered in ice).
2 if someone is treacherous, they say they support you but they do not and instead cause harm to you by helping an enemy
3 also used about something someone does or says *treacherous behaviour*
treacherously adverb

treachery noun
the behaviour of someone who is treacherous

treacle noun
a thick sweet dark-coloured liquid used in cooking, for example for making cakes and puddings. It is made from sugar when sugar is being refined (having unwanted substances removed to make its quality better).

tread verb
treads, treading, trod, trodden
1 to put your foot or feet on something *You're treading on my toe. Take off your shoe – you've trodden in some chewing gum.*
2 to leave dirty marks on something such as a carpet by pressing something into it with your foot or feet *The children have trodden mud into the new rug.*

tread noun
1 (plural **treads**) the tread of a stair or step is the flat top surface where you walk
2 (plural **treads**) the tread of a tyre or shoe is the pattern of lines cut into the rubber to stop it from slipping along the ground
3 the sound of someone putting their foot or feet down as they walk *We heard the giant's heavy tread.*

treason noun
the crime of doing something to harm your country, for example by helping an enemy, taking away the power of a government or killing a ruler

treasure noun **treasures**
1 a store of valuable things such as jewels or gold or silver coins that is hidden somewhere, for example under the ground in a big box called a treasure chest *The soldiers were digging for buried treasure.*
2 treasures are valuable works of art or things of historical importance *the treasures of the British Museum*
3 something or someone that is very special and important to you *This comic in Granddad's collection is his greatest treasure. Our teaching assistant is a real treasure – she helps me with my reading.*
4 a treasure hunt is a game or activity in which people look for a hidden treasure
5 a treasure trove is something or someone that provides a large amount of something valuable or good *This website is a treasure trove of information.*

treasure verb
treasures, treasuring, treasured
1 to consider something to be very special and important to you *I will always treasure my memories of Grandma.*
2 to look after something carefully because it is very special and important to you *Amy treasures the teddy bear that Granddad gave her for her birthday.*

treasurer *noun* **treasurers**
someone in charge of the money in a club or organisation

Treasury *noun*
the department of a government in charge of money and taxes

treat *verb*
treats, treating, treated
1 to behave in a certain way towards someone or something *I always treat Miss Dobson with respect. Treat your phone well and it will last for years.*
2 to deal with something in a particular way *I treated what he said as a joke.*
3 to give someone medical care *My uncle is being treated in hospital for a heart attack.*
4 to deal with an illness or injury so as to make it better or try to make it better *Diabetes can be treated with medicines or injections.*
5 to give, buy or do something special for someone or for yourself *Gran treated me to an ice cream. Tom had been working hard so he treated himself to a day off.*
6 to put a chemical substance onto or into something to change it in some way, for example to protect it or preserve it

treat *noun* **treats**
1 something special to enjoy that you give, buy or do for someone or for yourself *Going to the theatre was a real treat.*
2 when you pay for something for someone *'Lunch is my treat,' said Aunt Rose.*

treatment *noun* **treatments**
1 medical care, for example medicines and actions to deal with an illness or injury so as to make it better or try to make it better
2 the way you behave towards someone or something
3 a way of dealing with something
4 when a chemical substance is put onto or into something

treaty *noun* **treaties**
an agreement between countries that is made by the leaders of the countries signing their names on an official document

treble *adjective & adverb*
three times the amount or size or number of something *My mum earns treble what my dad earns.*

treble *noun*
1 something that is three times the amount or size or number of something *That pocket money just isn't enough – I need treble!*
2 used for talking about the highest notes in music

treble *verb*
trebles, trebling, trebled
1 to become three times as big or three times as much *The price of some foods has almost trebled.*
2 to make something three times as big or three times as much *Think of a number, then treble it.*

treble clef *noun* **treble clefs**
a symbol at the beginning of a line of music that shows the high pitch (or quality) of the notes

tree *noun* **trees**
a very tall plant with a thick stem made of wood (called a trunk), lots of branches with leaves growing on them and roots that grow deep into the ground

tree-lined *adjective*
used for describing something such as a street that has a line of trees, usually going along both sides of it

treetops *noun plural*
the highest branches in a group of trees

trek *verb*
treks, trekking, trekked
to walk somewhere or go on a journey somewhere, usually when talking about a long or difficult walk or journey *We spent all day trekking through the woods.*

trek *noun* **treks**
a walk or journey, usually a long or difficult one

trellis *noun* **trellises**
a framework of long strips of wood crossed over each other with spaces in between, used for supporting climbing plants

tremble *verb*
trembles, trembling, trembled
1 if someone or something trembles, they shake slightly *He was so scared he was trembling. They were trembling with cold. As Great-Gran got older, her hands started to tremble.*
2 if someone's voice trembles, it sounds weak and is difficult to hear, for example because they are afraid or upset

tremble *noun*

tremendous *adjective*
1 used when you mean a lot of something *a tremendous amount of homework; The dog was in tremendous pain.*
2 very good *a tremendous meal; You have some really tremendous friends.*
3 very big *a tremendous distance; a tremendous success*

tremendously *adverb*
1 extremely *My teacher was tremendously proud of me.*
2 very much indeed *We enjoyed the play tremendously.*
3 extremely well *Your team played tremendously last night.*

tremor *noun* **tremors**
1 a slight shaking movement, for example in your body or voice
2 a small earthquake

trench *noun* **trenches**
a long deep hole that is dug in the ground

trend *noun* **trends**
1 used for talking about the direction something such as a situation or activity is going in or about the way something is happening *In schools there seems to be a trend towards more tests and exams. What are the latest trends in music?*
2 another word for fashion (clothes worn at a particular time)

trend *verb*
trends, trending, trended
if a word or subject is trending on an internet messaging service such as Twitter, it is being mentioned lots of times

trendy *adjective* **trendier, trendiest**
an informal way of saying fashionable and popular, for example when describing something many people do, wear, go to or are interested in *a trendy haircut; a trendy pair of jeans; a trendy restaurant; These ideas are very trendy now.* **trendiness** *noun*

trepidation *noun*
great fear that something bad might happen

trespass *verb*
trespasses, trespassing, trespassed
to go onto an area of ground or into a building that belongs to someone, without asking their permission *Walkers trespassed on the farmer's land. No trespassing* (sign on a building or gate to a field, for example). **trespasser** *noun*

tresses *noun plural*
long hair that hangs down the back of a woman or girl

trestle *noun* **trestles**
a frame made up of a flat piece of wood fixed at each end to an object shaped like the letter A. Two or more trestles are used together for supporting a board to make a table.

trial *noun* **trials**
1 when a judge or jury in a court of law hears all the facts and sees all the objects connected with a crime and decides whether or not someone is guilty of that crime *He was on trial for hacking into people's computers.*
2 when something or someone is tested over a period of time to see how good they are so that someone can make a decision about them *a one-month trial period; Our teacher is on trial for six months* (being tested for six months to see if she is a good teacher). *My brother took the motorcycle on a trial run* (tested it to see how good it was).
3 in sport, trials are tests for finding the best players, usually for a particular event *Olympic trials*
4 **by trial and error** by trying out different ways of doing something until you find the best way or right way of doing it

triangle *noun* **triangles**
1 a flat shape with three straight sides and three angles
see: **equilateral**, **isosceles** and **scalene**
2 a piece of something shaped like a triangle *a cheese triangle*
3 a musical instrument made from a metal bar bent into the shape of a triangle. The triangle is not completely closed because the two ends of the bar do not touch each other. You play it by hitting it with a straight metal bar.

triangular *adjective*
shaped like a triangle *A pennant is a triangular flag.*

triathlon ['try-ath-lon] *noun* **triathlons**
a sports competition where someone takes part in three different sports, usually swimming, cycling and running
compare: **decathlon** and **pentathlon**

tribe *noun* **tribes**
a group of people in some countries, usually families that are related, who live in the same area far away from towns, share the same language and traditions and are ruled by a chief *The Apaches were a Native American tribe.* **tribal** *adjective*

tributary ['trib-yoo-tree] *noun* **tributaries**
a stream or river that flows into a larger river or a lake

543

tribute – triple

tribute *noun* **tributes**
something special that you do, say or make as a sign of the great respect you have for someone *The concert was a tribute to the life and work of the musician who recently died. Many people came to the cathedral to pay tribute to the dead and injured soldiers* (to show respect and hear people say kind things about them).

triceratops ['try-serr-er-tops'] *noun* **triceratops**
a large plant-eating dinosaur with two large horns on the top of its head and one small horn on its nose

trick *noun* **tricks**
1 something bad that you do to try to get something from someone or to make them believe something that isn't true *That was a nasty trick to get me to reveal my password.*
2 something that you do to laugh at someone or to make them look silly *Dad was annoyed by the trick I played on him.*
3 a clever action that needs a lot of skill, done in front of people to entertain them *a magic trick*; *a card trick*
4 a special way of doing something *Mum showed me a few little tricks to help me with my maths.*
5 a trick question is one that seems easy to answer but is really very difficult or complicated

trick *verb*
tricks, tricking, tricked
1 to make someone believe something that isn't true *He tricked me into believing there was no school today.*
2 to behave in a dishonest way towards someone, for example to get something from them *The bully tricked me out of my pocket money.*

trickery *noun*
bad behaviour when you try to get something from someone or make them believe something that isn't true

trickle *verb*
trickles, trickling, trickled
1 to flow somewhere slowly and in a thin line *The sweat was trickling down my forehead.*
2 to go somewhere gradually and in small numbers *People were beginning to trickle out of the concert hall.*
3 to happen or come in gradually and in small amounts *Money had started to trickle in.*

trickle *noun* **trickles**
1 a slow flow of something
2 a small number of people going somewhere
3 a small amount of things happening or coming in

tricky *adjective* **trickier, trickiest**
1 if something is tricky, it needs a lot of effort and skill to deal with or do *a tricky question*; *Tying your shoelaces can be a bit tricky.*

SYNONYM **difficult**

2 (informal) used for describing someone dishonest who is likely to trick you

tricycle *noun* **tricycles**
a type of bicycle with three wheels that children use to ride on

tried
past tense & past participle of **try**

trifle *noun* **trifles**
1 a cold sweet dish made from layers of different ingredients that include fruit, custard, jelly, cream and sponge cake (soft light cake), eaten at the end of a meal as a dessert
2 used when you mean something that is not very important or not worth very much *A thousand pounds is a mere trifle to my rich uncle.*
3 **a trifle** a little but not very much *I was a trifle disappointed.*

SYNONYM for sense 3: **slightly**

trifle *verb*
trifles, trifling, trifled
if you trifle with someone or something, you treat them without respect because you think they are not important enough to pay attention to *Your head teacher is not a person to be trifled with* (he or she is important and should be treated with respect).

trifling *adjective*
small and not very important *a trifling detail*

trigger *noun* **triggers**
a small bar of metal on a gun that someone presses with their finger to fire the gun (make the bullet come out)

trigger *verb*
triggers, triggering, triggered
to make something happen or start *Spending too much time in front of a computer can trigger a headache.*

trillion *noun* **trillions**
1 a million million or a thousand billion (1 000 000 000 000)
2 a really huge number of something *My brother has trillions of friends on Facebook.*

trilogy *noun* **trilogies**
a series of three works of art, usually books, films, plays or video games, that are connected, for example they have the same characters and settings (places where the action happens)

trim *verb*
trims, trimming, trimmed
1 to make something shorter by cutting the ends or edges off it, for example to make it look better or tidier *My brother has gone to the barber's to get his hair trimmed.*
2 to cut off a part of something that is not wanted *Dad trimmed the fat off the meat.*
3 to decorate something along its edges *Her dress was trimmed with lace.*

trim *noun*
1 the action of trimming something to make it shorter *Dad says the lawn needs a trim. My sister went to the hairdresser for a trim.*
2 material used for decorating the edges of something
3 **in trim** healthy because you do exercises to keep your body strong

trim *adjective* **trimmer, trimmest**
1 if someone is trim, they are healthy and thin in an attractive way
2 if something is trim, it is tidy and carefully looked after *a row of trim little houses*

trimming *noun* **trimmings**
1 material added as a decoration along the edges of something
2 the trimmings are all the extra things you have, for example for a special occasion or the extra dishes you eat with a special meal

Trinity *noun*
in the Christian religion, the Trinity is the name given to the three different forms of God – the Father, the Son and the Holy Spirit

trinket *noun* **trinkets**
something small and of not much value such as a piece of jewellery or an object used as a decoration

trio *noun* **trios**
1 a group of three people who play music or sing in front of an audience
2 a piece of music for three people to play or sing
3 a group of three people or things

trip *verb*
trips, tripping, tripped
1 to lose your balance and fall, or almost fall, when walking or running because your foot knocks against or touches something *Don't trip on the broken paving stone.*
2 if someone trips you, or trips you up, they make you fall or almost fall, by putting something in front of your feet when you're walking or running *He stuck his foot out and tripped me up.*
3 to trip someone up is also to make them make a mistake
4 to walk somewhere with short quick steps *The children tripped off down the corridor.*

trip *noun*
1 (plural **trips**) when you travel from one place to another *a coach trip*; *a day trip* (travelling and coming back the same day); *Tomorrow we're going on a trip to the Natural History Museum.*
2 when you fall, or almost fall, by tripping on something

tripe *noun*
1 (informal) words or ideas that are stupid or not true

SYNONYM **nonsense**

2 the stomach of a farm animal such as a cow or sheep, used as food

triple *adjective*
1 three times the amount or size or number of something *The number of mistakes in your homework is nearly triple what it was last time.*
2 used for describing something made up of three parts or something that happens three times *a triple somersault*; *a triple victory*

triple *verb*
triples, tripling, tripled
1 to become three times as big or three times as much *The price has tripled in a month.*

544

triplet – trough

2 to make something three times as big or three times as much *Being signed by Picasso triples the value of the painting.*

triplet *noun* **triplets**
each one of three babies who are born at the same time and have the same mother

tripod ['try-pod] *noun* **tripods**
a stand with three legs for supporting something such as a camera

triumph *noun*
1 (*plural* **triumphs**) a great success, for example after winning a competition or fight
2 the feeling of happiness someone gets after a great success *The football team returned in triumph.*

triumph *verb*
triumphs, triumphing, triumphed
to win or be successful, for example after a lot of effort

triumphant *adjective*
1 successful and feeling happy because of this *The soldiers came back triumphant.*
2 showing that someone is successful and feeling happy *After many years she made a triumphant return to the stage.*

triumphantly *adverb*
in a way that shows someone is happy because of their great success

trivial *adjective*
1 not important *a trivial detail*
2 not big or serious *a trivial amount of money*; *My uncle had an accident but his injuries were trivial.*

triviality *noun*
1 the quality of being trivial
2 trivialities are things that are not important

trod
past tense of **tread**

trodden
past participle of **tread**

Trojan *noun* **Trojans**
a software program that harms your computer, for example by deleting information or by allowing someone to take control of your computer. Trojans often look like useful programs to trick people into downloading them.

troll *noun* **trolls**
1 someone who behaves very badly on the internet, for example by sending rude, cruel or upsetting messages to websites such as Facebook or Twitter or to forums and chat rooms
2 in stories, an ugly imaginary creature that looks like a person and is either as tall as a giant or as small as a dwarf. Trolls sometimes live in caves and rocks.

troll *verb*
trolls, trolling, trolled
to behave very badly towards someone on the internet, for example by sending rude, cruel or upsetting messages to them

trolley *noun* **trolleys**
1 a large metal container with wheels, which you move by pushing it. Trolleys are used for carrying things, for example at a supermarket or airport.
2 a bed with wheels used at a hospital for carrying sick or injured people
3 a small table with wheels, used for serving food and drinks

trolleybus *noun* **trolleybuses**
a bus that uses electricity from wires high above the road. The wires are connected to posts at the side of the road.

trolling *noun*
the very bad behaviour of an internet troll (someone who sends rude, cruel or upsetting messages)

trombone *noun* **trombones**
a musical instrument made of brass (a yellowish metal) and shaped like a trumpet. It has a long U-shaped tube that you blow into and slide backwards and forwards to change the notes. **trombonist** *noun*

troop *noun* **troops**
1 a group of soldiers or Scouts
2 a group of people or animals
3 troops are soldiers *American troops*

troop *verb*
troops, trooping, trooped
to walk somewhere as part of a group *When the fire alarm went off, we all trooped into the playground.*

trophy *noun* **trophies**
an object such as a silver cup that you get as a prize when you win a competition or sports event

tropical *adjective*
connected with the hottest parts of the world in the tropics *tropical plants*; *tropical heat*; *tropical Africa*

tropics *noun plural*
the hottest region of the world between two imaginary lines round the earth called the Tropic of Cancer (23 degrees north of the Equator) and the Tropic of Capricorn (23 degrees south of the Equator)

trot *verb*
trots, trotting, trotted
1 if a horse trots, it runs slowly but goes faster than when it walks. It runs more slowly than when it canters and much more slowly than when it gallops.
2 to run slowly with short steps *We were trotting along behind our teacher.*
3 (informal) if you trot out something such as an idea, fact or excuse, you repeat it even though you have said it many times before

trot *noun*
1 the slowest speed that a horse can run
2 (*plural* **trots**) a slow run with short steps *I went for a trot around the park.*
3 (informal) **on the trot** one after the other *Our team won four matches on the trot.*

trouble *noun*
1 (*plural* **troubles**) a problem or problems *Seema is having some trouble with her mobile phone. Our troubles aren't over yet. My stepdad suffers from back troubles.*
2 when you make an effort to do something difficult *I had a lot of trouble doing this week's spelling test.*
3 fighting between people or angry words being said *There's some trouble in the playground between two groups of boys.*
4 a special effort you make for someone, for example to help them *My teacher took the trouble to go over the maths lesson with me. She went to a huge amount of trouble.*
5 used for saying there is something you don't like about something or someone or there is something bad about them *Your trouble is you're too lazy. The trouble with our house is it's a bit small.*
6 a bad, difficult or dangerous situation *If the brakes on your bike don't work, you're in trouble. The swimmer went out too far into the sea and got into trouble.*
7 a situation where you do something wrong that you can be blamed or punished for *My cousin is in trouble with the police. I got into trouble for being late* (for example, I was told off or punished). *If you misbehave again, you'll get the whole class into trouble* (we'll all be punished).

trouble *verb*
troubles, troubling, troubled
1 if something troubles you, it makes you worried or upset or it causes you a problem *My parents were really troubled by what the head teacher said.*
2 to cause someone pain *My shoulder's troubling me.*
3 to make someone slightly angry by interrupting them, pestering them or using up their time *Sorry to trouble you – could I get past?*
4 used as a polite way of asking someone for something or to do something *Could I trouble you for a knife and fork? May I trouble you to close the window?*
5 to make an effort to do something *My aunt left without troubling to say goodbye.*

troubled *adjective*
1 worried or upset *Hasan looks rather troubled.*
2 with lots of problems *We used to live in a troubled neighbourhood.*

trouble-free *adjective*
if something is trouble-free, it doesn't have any problems *My new tablet has been trouble-free so far.*

troublemaker *noun* **troublemakers**
someone who causes problems, especially by behaving in a very bad or violent way

troubleshoot *verb*
troubleshoots, troubleshooting, troubleshot
to solve problems, for example in an organisation or piece of software, by carefully examining every detail of the problem

troubleshooter *noun* **troubleshooters**
1 someone whose job is to solve problems in an organisation
2 a piece of software used for solving a computer problem

troublesome *adjective*
1 causing a problem or problems *a troublesome pupil*; *a troublesome journey*
2 causing pain *a troublesome cough*; *Grandma's back has been troublesome.*

troubling *adjective*
making you feel worried or upset

trough ['trof'] *noun* **troughs**
1 a long narrow container made of stone, metal or wood, for animals to eat and drink out of

545

2 the lowest point at the bottom of a wave. The top of a wave is called the crest.

trounce verb
trounces, trouncing, trounced
to easily beat someone in a competition or game and become the winner

trousers noun plural
a piece of clothing that you wear from the hips to the feet with separate parts for each leg

trout noun trout
a fish that lives in rivers and lakes and can be eaten although it has many bones

trowel noun trowels
1 a tool like a small spade, used in gardens for digging small holes or for digging plants or weeds out of the ground. It has a short handle fixed to a slightly curved part that is usually made of metal.
2 a small tool with a short handle fixed to a flat pointed metal part. It is used for spreading something such as cement or plaster, for example onto walls or bricks.

truant noun truants
1 someone who stays away from school without permission
2 if you play truant, you don't go to school when you should go to school
truancy noun

truce noun truces
an agreement between two countries, groups or people to stop fighting each other for a short period of time *Russia and Ukraine called a truce* (agreed to stop fighting for a time).

truck noun trucks
1 a large road vehicle for carrying goods

SYNONYM lorry

2 a railway vehicle for carrying goods or animals, often one that is open at the top *a coal truck*

trudge verb
trudges, trudging, trudged
to walk slowly with a lot of effort *We were trudging through the deep snow.*

true adjective truer, truest
1 used for describing something that is based on a real situation or real information or that really happened, not something that only exists in your mind *a true story*; *What I'm telling you is true.*
2 used for describing something or someone that has the qualities they are supposed to have or that is what they are supposed to be *You're a true friend. He never shows his true feelings. A tomato isn't a true vegetable.*

SYNONYM real

3 if you are true to someone or something, you stay with them and support them because they are important to you *Dexter always stays true to his friends.*
4 **to come true** to really happen (often used about someone's hopes or dreams) *My dream of having my own bike has come true.*

truly adverb
1 used for showing that you definitely mean something or for giving special importance to a word *I truly believed it was Ollie who broke the window. The meal was truly delicious* (extremely delicious). *We truly enjoyed the film* (enjoyed it very much). *I'm really and truly sorry* (very sorry indeed).

SYNONYM really

2 used about something or someone that is what they are supposed to be *You truly are a friend. That country is now truly independent.*

SYNONYM really

3 used for saying what the truth about something is *Tell me truly what happened.*

trump noun trumps
in a game of cards, a trump is a card belonging to one of the four groups (hearts, diamonds, spades and clubs) that people give the highest value to in a particular game

trumpet noun trumpets
a musical instrument made of brass (a yellowish metal) that has the shape of a long curved tube with a very wide end. You play it by blowing into the small end of the tube and pressing three buttons on the top to change the notes.
trumpeter noun

trumpet verb
trumpets, trumpeting, trumpeted
1 if someone trumpets something, they mention it to lots of people in a very enthusiastic way
2 when an elephant trumpets, it makes a very loud high noise that is its own special sound

truncheon noun truncheons
a short thick stick that a police officer carries as a weapon

trundle verb
trundles, trundling, trundled
1 if something that has wheels such as a road vehicle or train trundles somewhere, it moves slowly and noisily
2 if someone trundles something somewhere, for example a wheelbarrow, they move it slowly and noisily

trunk noun trunks
1 the thick wooden stem of a tree that the branches grow from *a tree trunk*
2 the long nose of an elephant
3 a large strong box with a lid, used for keeping things in or for carrying things on a journey
4 in American English, the trunk of a car is the boot (place for luggage at the back)

trunks noun plural
a piece of clothing that covers the lower part of the body, worn by boys and men, usually for swimming in

trust verb
trusts, trusting, trusted
1 if you trust someone, you have a feeling that makes you sure they are good and honest, behave well and would not do anything bad *I'll lend you my bike if I can trust you to return it tomorrow. Don't tell Ollie any secrets – you can't trust him* (for example, he will tell other people).

2 if you trust something such as information or an opinion, you are sure it is extremely good and correct *This is a dictionary you can trust. My brother's judgement isn't to be trusted.*
3 if you trust something such as a piece of equipment, a service or someone's way of doing something, you are sure it works well or is safe *You can't trust the bus service to school* (for example, the buses are late or slow). *I don't trust my brother's driving.*
4 if you trust someone with something, you let them look after it, use it or deal with it because you are sure they are good and honest
5 a polite way of saying to hope *I trust you and the family are well.*

trust noun
1 a strong feeling that someone is good and honest, behaves well and would not do anything bad
2 a strong feeling that something is good and correct or safe *You can put your trust in this dictionary. You need to have trust in your antivirus software.*
3 used about the responsibility given to someone because they are good and honest *Being head teacher is a position of trust.*
4 a trust fund is money that someone looks after for someone else, for example a young child until he or she becomes an adult

trusting adjective
if someone is trusting, they are ready to trust other people, often when this is not a sensible thing to do

trustworthy adjective
1 if someone or someone's behaviour is trustworthy, they can be trusted, for example because they are good and honest
2 if something is trustworthy, it can be trusted, for example because it is good and correct or safe *trustworthy information*; *a trustworthy car*
trustworthiness noun

truth noun
1 used for talking about a real situation or real information or something that really happened *I want you to tell the truth.*
2 the quality of something that is true *Are you certain of the truth of what you're saying?*
3 (plural **truths**) an idea that people accept as being true

truthful adjective
1 if someone is truthful, they tell the truth *I want you to be truthful with me* (to tell me the truth).
2 if something is truthful, it is completely true and based on the truth *a truthful answer*
truthfully adverb

try verb
tries, trying, tried
1 to do a particular action and hope it will succeed *I tried to turn on my tablet but it wouldn't work. I phoned Jude but he didn't answer – I'll try again tomorrow.*
2 to behave in a certain way and hope this will be successful *Can you try and be more careful in the future? Miss Patel told me to try harder* (for example to work harder to be more successful).

try–tumble drier

3 to do or use something, for example to see if it's good or useful, if it works or if you like it *I tried lots of bikes before I found the right one. Have you ever tried bungee jumping? Try it and see what happens.*
4 to eat or drink something to see what it's like or if you like it *Can I try some of Dad's sponge cake?*
5 to go or look somewhere and hope to find something or someone there *'I can't find my keys in my bag.' – 'Have you tried your coat pockets?'*
6 to ask someone to help you with something *I don't know anything about computers but have you tried Dan?*
7 if someone is tried for a crime, they are judged in a court of law to see whether or not they are guilty
8 if you try clothes on, you put them on to see if they fit you and if you like them
9 if you try something out, you use it, for example to find out if it's good or useful, if it works or if you like it *Tomorrow I'll try out my new tablet. You can always try out your French on Pierre.*

try noun
1 when you try to do something *I'll have a try* (or *give it a try*). *It's worth a try.*
2 (plural **tries**) an action in rugby when a player scores points by putting the ball on the ground behind the line where the other team's goal stands

trying adjective
if something or someone is trying, they are very difficult because they cause a lot of worry or are full of problems *The whole situation was trying. Your two-year-old brother is very trying* (he causes problems and makes me tired).

tsar ['zahr'] noun **tsars**
the name given to the emperor of Russia until 1917

LANGUAGE EXTRA also spelt *czar*

ORIGIN from the Latin name *Caesar*, first used in Russia by Emperor Ivan IV in 1547

T-shirt noun **T-shirts**
a piece of clothing made of thin cloth that you wear on the top half of your body. It has short sleeves and no collar or buttons.

LANGUAGE EXTRA also spelt *tee shirt*

tsunami ['tsoo-nah-mee'] noun **tsunamis**
a huge wave or series of waves moving onto the land with the tide, often caused by an earthquake

tub noun **tubs**
1 a small plastic or paper container with a lid, used for holding food *an ice cream tub*; *a tub of margarine*
2 something in a tub, such as ice cream *I ate the whole tub myself.*
3 a large container without a lid, usually round, used for example for growing plants in or washing clothes in
4 a tub or hot tub is a large bath for relaxing in with hot water that flows in through small holes
5 short for **bathtub** (the American word for a bath or water container that you wash yourself in)

tuba noun **tubas**
a very large musical instrument made of brass (a yellowish metal), used for playing very low notes. It looks similar to a trumpet and has a long curved tube and an extremely wide end. You play it by blowing into the small end of the tube and pressing buttons to change the notes.

tubby adjective **tubbier, tubbiest**
(informal)
used for describing someone or a part of someone's body that is slightly fat

tube noun **tubes**
1 a long hollow object shaped like a cylinder (with ends that are circles of the same size), usually used for liquids, gas or air to flow along. Tubes are made of many different materials such as plastic, metal, rubber or glass.
2 a long narrow container made of soft metal or plastic with a soft substance inside. You squeeze the container to make the substance come out through an opening at the top. *a tube of toothpaste*
3 a long narrow part inside the body that is shaped like a tube
4 the tube is the railway that goes under the ground in London *a tube station*; *I bumped into my teacher on the tube.*

LANGUAGE EXTRA also spelt *Tube*

5 also used when you mean one of the trains on the London railway *Stand back, the tube's coming.*
6 in American English, the tube is an informal word for television

tuber noun **tubers**
a thick round part on the root or stem of a plant that grows under the ground. Tubers can grow into new plants. A potato is an example of a tuber.

tubing noun
material such as plastic or metal that has the shape of a tube

tubular adjective
shaped like a tube

tuck verb
tucks, tucking, tucked
1 to put something somewhere because you think it's a good, safe or comfortable place to put it *Tuck your mobile phone into your top pocket. Granddad used to carry his newspaper tucked under his arm. Tuck your earrings away safely in your drawer.*
2 to push or fold a part of something somewhere so that it's tidy or so that you can't see it *Tuck your shirt in* (put the end of it inside your trousers). *Tuck the flap into the envelope. Mum tucked the edges of the sheet tightly under the mattress.*
3 to put a part of your body into a certain position, for example where it doesn't stick out *Please tuck your legs in – we don't want anyone tripping over. Stand up straight and tuck your tummy in.*
4 if something is tucked away somewhere, it is hidden there *My aunt's house is tucked away behind a clump of trees.*
5 if you tuck someone in or up, you make them comfortable in their bed by putting the bedclothes carefully round them
6 if someone tucks in, they start eating food with great enjoyment

tuck noun **tucks**
1 a fold that is sewn into a piece of material or clothing, for example as a decoration
2 a tuck shop is a small shop that sells sweets, cakes and snacks, for example inside a school

Tudor adjective
connected with the period between 1485 and 1603, including the reigns of Henry VIII and Elizabeth I

Tuesday noun **Tuesdays**
the day of the week between Monday and Wednesday

ORIGIN from Old English *Tiwesdæg* 'Tiw's day'. In Old English, Tiw was the god of war.

tuft noun **tufts**
a bunch of things such as hair, grass, feathers or threads joined together or growing together at the bottom

tug verb
tugs, tugging, tugged
to pull something with a lot of effort or with a quick strong movement *The little girl was tugging at her mum's skirt* (pulling it with lots of strong pulls).

tug noun **tugs**
1 a quick strong pulling movement
2 a strong boat with a powerful engine used for pulling larger boats, for example into and out of harbours

tug-of-war noun **tugs-of-war**
a competition between two teams pulling opposite ends of a rope. The winning team is the one that pulls the other team across a line marked between them on the ground.

tuition noun
1 when a teacher teaches a particular subject to one person or a small group *private tuition* (teaching that you pay for)
2 tuition fees are money that you pay to be taught. You can also say tuition. *Dad has just paid next year's tuition fees* (or *tuition*).

tulip noun **tulips**
a plant that appears in spring with flowers of many bright colours such as red or yellow. It has oval petals growing close together in an egg shape. A tulip grows from a bulb (root shaped like an onion).

ORIGIN from Turkish *tuliband* 'turban', because people thought a tulip looked like a turban

tumble verb
tumbles, tumbling, tumbled
to fall down *I slipped and tumbled down the stairs. Several roof tiles came tumbling down in the storm.* **tumble** noun

tumbledown adjective
a tumbledown building is old and in very bad condition

tumble drier noun **tumble driers**
a piece of equipment that uses hot air for drying material such as clothes, sheets and blankets that have been washed in a washing machine. The clothes are spun around inside a large drum (round container).

LANGUAGE EXTRA also spelt *tumble dryer*

547

tumbler–turn

tumbler *noun* **tumblers**
an ordinary glass for drinking out of that has no handle or stem (thin upright part at the bottom)

tumbleweed *noun*
any plant that grows like a bush in desert areas and breaks off from its root when it dies. It rolls along the ground like a ball in the wind.

tummy *noun* **tummies**
an informal word for your stomach (the soft part of your body below your chest)

tumour *noun* **tumours**
a lump growing inside or on the body

tumult ['tyoo-mult] *noun*
1 loud and unpleasant noises produced by a crowd of people
2 a situation of great confusion and excitement

tumultuous ['tyoo-mul-tyoo-ers] *adjective*
1 noisy and showing great happiness and excitement *a tumultuous welcome; tumultuous applause*
2 showing great confusion and lots of sudden changes *the tumultuous period of the English Civil War*
tumultuously *adverb*

tuna ['tyoo-ner] *noun* **tuna**
a large fish that lives in warm parts of the sea. It has oily flesh and a strong flavour and is used as food. *a tuna steak*

tundra ['tun' rhymes with 'bun'] *noun*
a very large area of flat land in the cold northern parts of the world where trees do not grow and where the ground is always frozen

tune *noun* **tunes**
1 a group of musical notes that sound pleasant together
2 a song or short piece of music
3 **in tune** used about a person or instrument that produces the correct musical notes *She sang perfectly in tune.*
4 **out of tune** producing the wrong musical notes

tune *verb*
tunes, tuning, tuned
1 to change the position of parts of a musical instrument so that it produces the correct notes, for example to make the strings of a guitar tighter or looser
2 if a TV or radio is tuned to a programme or station, that is the programme or station you are watching or listening to
3 to tune (or tune up) an engine, for example of a car or motorbike, is to make small changes to it so that it works better

tuneful *adjective*
having a pleasant tune or sound *a tuneful melody* **tunefully** *adverb*

tunic *noun* **tunics**
1 a piece of clothing with no sleeves, loosely covering the top half of the body almost as far as the knees and usually worn with a belt. It was worn mainly in ancient Rome and Greece.
2 a similar piece of clothing with or without a belt that is worn by girls and women
3 the top part of a uniform of a police officer or soldier

Tunisia *noun*
a country in North Africa
Tunisian *adjective & noun*

tunnel *noun* **tunnels**
1 a passage under the ground for vehicles or trains to travel through
2 a passage under the ground for people to walk through
3 a long hole in the ground dug by an animal such as a rabbit or fox

tunnel *verb*
tunnels, tunnelling, tunnelled
to dig a tunnel

turban *noun* **turbans**
a long piece of cloth that is wrapped around the head, worn mainly by men or boys in some religions. For example, Sikhs, Muslims and Hindus wear turbans.

turbine *noun* **turbines**
an engine or machine that uses water, gas, air or steam as energy to produce power and turn a wheel

turbulence *noun*
violent changes in the flow of air or water, for example when air affects an aircraft and makes the flight less smooth

turbulent *adjective*
1 used about a situation, period or place where there is a lot of confusion, change and violence *the turbulent years of the Second World War*
2 very rough *turbulent seas*

turf *noun*
1 short thick grass, including its roots and the earth it grows in
2 (*plural* **turfs** or **turves**) a small rectangular piece of this grass used with other pieces to make a lawn
3 an area of ground covered with this grass, used especially for sports, for example tennis

Turk *noun* **Turks**
someone from Turkey

turkey *noun*
1 (*plural* **turkeys**) a bird similar to a large chicken that people keep on farms and use for providing meat
2 the meat of the turkey. People often eat turkey at Christmas.

> **ORIGIN** from the name of the country *Turkey*, from where it was brought to Europe. Originally it meant a different kind of bird, not a turkey.

Turkey *noun*
a country in West Asia and South-East Europe

Turkish *adjective*
connected with Turkey or the Turkish language

Turkish *noun*
the language people speak in Turkey

turmoil *noun*
a situation where everything is confused *The whole school was in turmoil because of the two girls who had gone missing.*

turn *verb*
turns, turning, turned
1 to move in a circle round a central point *The wheel was turning. I saw the door handle turn.*
2 to make something move in a circle round a central point *She turned the key and opened the door.*
3 to move your head or your body so that you're facing in a different direction or in the opposite direction *He turned when he heard me come in. Don't turn your head when I'm speaking to you.*
4 to change direction *Walk to the corner then turn left. The bus turned at the traffic lights. The path twists and turns up the hill.*
5 to make something move or face in a different direction *Turn the laptop so I can see the screen. Dad turned the car into the drive.*
6 to become something or change in some way, for example when talking about a different colour, situation or appearance *The tomatoes are turning red. The weather turned cold. It has just turned midnight. I turn nine tomorrow* (I'll be nine years old). *Caterpillars turn into butterflies.*
7 to make something or someone become something or change in some way *The mud has turned the water brown. My parents have turned the garden into a play area. The witch turned the prince into a frog.*
8 if you turn a page, you move it to the other side so you can read the next page
9 if you turn to a particular page, you go to it
10 if you turn the corner, you go to the end of the road and then turn left or right, or you turn left or right into a side road
11 to point or direct something somewhere *Don't turn that torch on me. It's time to turn our attention to the six times table.*
12 if you turn around or turn round, you move your head or your body so that you're facing in the opposite direction
13 if you turn away, you look in a different direction
14 if you turn someone away, you tell them they are not allowed to go into a place or to have something
15 if you turn back, you go back in the same direction you came from
16 if you turn something down on a piece of equipment, for example the sound, heat or light, you make it less (for example quieter, colder or darker). If you turn it up, you make it more (for example louder, hotter or lighter). *The TV is too loud – turn it down. I turned the volume up on the radio.*
17 if you turn down something such as an offer or invitation, you don't accept it
18 if a vehicle or someone in a vehicle turns off, they leave the road they're travelling on and start travelling on another road
19 if you turn something on or off, such as a piece of equipment, you make it start or stop working by pushing a switch up or down, pressing it or turning it *Turn the tap on and let the water run. The printer turns itself off after two hours.*

> **SYNONYMS** to switch on, to switch off

20 if something turns out in a particular way, it happens that way or happens to be true *The weather turned out to be rainy that day. Your idea turned out to be excellent.*
21 if people turn out somewhere, they appear or arrive there

22 if you turn out a light, you switch it off
23 if you turn something over, you change its position so that the other side of it is facing the top *Turn your book over so I can see the front cover.*
24 if you turn to someone, you go to them to get help or advice
25 if you turn up, you arrive somewhere *We've been waiting all day but Granddad still hasn't turned up.*
26 if something lost turns up, someone finds it *'I don't know where my gloves are.' – 'They'll turn up soon.'*

turn noun **turns**
1 someone's turn is the time when they must do something such as play in a game after other people have played, or the time when they must do something because it's their responsibility to do it after other people have done it *It's your turn to play now. I did the washing-up yesterday so today it's your turn. Be patient and wait your turn* (wait until the time comes for you to do it).
2 a change of direction *The bus made a left turn at the lights.*
3 a place where something such as a road or river bends *There's a sharp turn just past the library. The river is full of twists and turns.*
4 a turning movement or the action of turning something *She made a turn towards me. Give the wheel a few turns.*
5 (informal) a time when you suddenly feel ill *Auntie Grace had a funny turn* (or *a bit of a turn*) (she felt ill or dizzy).
6 a good turn something you do to help someone
7 in turn one after the other, following a particular order *The teacher asked the children to say their names in turn* (for example starting with someone in the front row then going to the person sitting next to them and so on).
8 to take turns or **to take it in turns** used when people do something with first one person doing it then the other *My dad and my brother took it in turns to push the heavy suitcase.*

turning noun **turnings**
another word for a road, especially a road that leads away from another road *Take the first turning on the left.*

turnip noun **turnips**
a hard round vegetable that grows under the ground, usually with a white and purple skin. It is often boiled or baked.

turnover noun **turnovers**
a small pie for one person, often shaped like a triangle and filled with fruit such as apples or cherries *an apple turnover*

turnstile noun **turnstiles**
a type of metal gate with a bar or bars that you push to get into or out of a place such as a football stadium or the London Underground. The gate lets one person through at a time.

turntable noun **turntables**
a flat round surface on a record player that you put a record on to play it

turn-up noun **turn-ups**
the end part of the leg of a pair of trousers that is folded over for decoration

turquoise ['terr-kwoyz'] noun
1 a blue-green colour that can go from light to medium blue-green
2 a blue-green jewel

turquoise ['terr-kwoyz'] adjective
having a blue-green colour

turret noun **turrets**
1 a small tower that sticks out from the wall of a building such as a castle
2 a high structure in a ship or vehicle such as a tank. It contains a big gun that can be moved to face in any direction.

turtle noun **turtles**
an animal that lives mainly in the sea and looks like a tortoise. It has a hard shell on its back and four legs like flippers (parts for swimming) that it also uses for walking along the ground.

turtleneck noun **turtlenecks**
a sweater with a high collar that fits tightly around the neck

tusk noun **tusks**
one of the two very long pointed teeth that stick out from the mouth of an animal such as an elephant, walrus or boar

tussle noun **tussles**
a short fight over something between two or more people

tussle verb
tussles, tussling, tussled
to fight with someone over something

tutor noun **tutors**
1 a teacher who gives lessons to one student only or to a small group. The students pay for the lessons themselves. *a private tutor* (one that you pay to teach you)
2 a teacher in a school in charge of a particular class (or form) who sometimes stays with that class until the students leave school *a form tutor*
3 a teacher at a university or college, for example one who looks after the studies, health and safety of particular students

tutor verb
tutors, tutoring, tutored
to give lessons to someone, which that person has to pay for

tutorial noun **tutorials**
1 a website, document or book that teaches you a skill, such as how to use a computer program, by explaining every detail clearly
2 a lesson where one student or a small group is taught a particular subject such as maths or English, usually a lesson that has to be paid for
3 a class at a university or college where a small group of students talk about a subject with a teacher

tut-tut interjection
used in writing for showing the sound people make when they don't like something *'You're late, Billy – tut-tut,' said my teacher.*

TV noun **TVs**
short for **television** *a TV programme; The TV's not working. There's nothing much on TV today. I like watching TV online.*

tweak verb
tweaks, tweaking, tweaked
1 to make small changes to something, for example something you've written or a piece of software or equipment, usually to make it better or correct
2 to twist or pull a part of someone's body such as their nose, ear or cheek

tweak noun **tweaks**
1 a small change to something
2 a twist or pull

tweed noun
a thick rough cloth made from wool, using threads of different colours twisted together *a tweed jacket*

tweet noun **tweets**
1 a short message that you send using Twitter (an internet messaging service)
2 the short high sound that a small bird makes

tweet verb
tweets, tweeting, tweeted
to send a message to people using Twitter *The head teacher tweeted that the school will be closed tomorrow because of the snow.*

tweezers noun plural
a small tool made of two metal pieces joined at the top, which you press together with your fingers. Tweezers are used for picking up and holding small things or for pulling out small things such as hairs or splinters (pieces of wood or glass).

twelfth adjective & noun
1 used about something or someone that comes in place number 12 *on the twelfth day of the month*
2 (plural **twelfths**) one of 12 equal parts of something *one twelfth of the population*

twelve adjective & noun **twelves**
the number 12

twenty adjective & noun **twenties**
1 the number 20
2 the twenties are the twentieth to twenty-ninth years of a century, for example 1920 to 1929
3 if someone is in their twenties, they are between 20 and 29 years old
twentieth adjective & noun

twice adverb
1 two times *It was so icy I slipped over twice.*
2 two times the amount or size or number of something *You have twice the number of friends I have.*
3 if you think twice about something, you think carefully before deciding to do it, for example because doing it might be a bad idea *You should think twice about inviting to your party someone who has bullied you in school.*

twiddle verb
twiddles, twiddling, twiddled
1 to keep moving or touching something with your fingers, usually by twisting or turning it
2 to keep turning a switch on a piece of equipment *I twiddled the knob on the radio until I found BBC Radio 2.*
3 if someone is twiddling their thumbs, they have nothing to do and are bored

twig–typist

twig *noun* **twigs**
a small thin branch from a tree or bush, usually without leaves on it

twig *verb* (informal)
twigs, twigging, twigged
to understand or realise something that you didn't know before *I suddenly twigged what he meant.*

twilight *noun*
1 the part of the evening when the sun has set but it is not completely dark
2 the light from the sky at this time of the evening *I could just about see our farmhouse in the twilight.*

twin *noun* **twins**
1 each one of two babies who have the same mother and are born at the same time *My aunt has just had twins.*
2 if two people are twins, they have the same mother and were born at the same time *Holly introduced me to her twin. She has a twin sister. Kuldip and I are identical twins* (born from the same egg and looking the same).
3 each one of two things of the same kind that are used together *a plane with twin engines*; *twin beds* (two separate beds in a bedroom); *My sister found one of her lost earrings but she's still looking for its twin.*

twin *verb*
twins, twinning, twinned
if two towns or cities in different countries are twinned, there is a friendly agreement between them to work together, for example to encourage visits and business between them *Bristol is twinned with Bordeaux in France.* **twinning** *noun*

twine *noun*
strong string made from twisting two or more pieces of string together *a ball of garden twine*

twinge *noun* **twinges**
1 a sudden slight pain *I had a few twinges in my knee.*
2 a sudden slight feeling, especially an unpleasant feeling *a twinge of sadness; a twinge of guilt*

twinkle *verb*
twinkles, twinkling, twinkled
1 if a light or star twinkles, it shines with a flash of light then stops shining then starts to shine again and continues doing this
2 if your eyes twinkle, they have a look of excitement or fun or they show that you aren't being serious
twinkle *noun*

twirl *verb*
twirls, twirling, twirled
to turn round and round, or to make something do this *The skaters were twirling around on the ice. Dad twirled his moustache.*

twirl *noun* **twirls**
a twirling movement

twist *verb*
twists, twisting, twisted
1 to turn something round with your fingers, often lots of times *If your ring is too tight, keep twisting it and it will come off. I twisted the cap off the bottle. Twist the knob to open the door.*
2 to turn something round and round something else, or to turn things round and round each other *The nurse twisted the bandage round my leg. You form plaits by twisting together many threads of hair.*
3 to turn your body, or a part of your body such as your head, so that it faces in a different direction *I had to twist my head slightly to see above the crowd.*
4 to move your body from side to side lots of times *You were twisting and turning in your sleep.*
5 to bend something so that no longer has its normal shape *I hit a tree on my bike and twisted the front wheel. The magician twisted the wire into the shape of a swan.*
6 if something such as a road or river twists, it changes direction lots of times *The path twists around the side of the mountain.*
7 if you twist your ankle, wrist or knee, you hurt it by accidentally turning it too much

twist *noun* **twists**
1 a twisting movement
2 a place in something such as a road or river where it changes direction *The Thames has lots of twists and turns.*

> SYNONYM bend

3 used about something unexpected that happens in a situation or story *This sad story has taken another twist.*

twister *noun* **twisters**
an informal word for a tornado (wind that blows along the ground in a cloud)

twit *noun* **twits**
an informal word for a very stupid person

twitch *verb*
twitches, twitching, twitched
if a part of your body twitches, it moves with a short sudden movement (or movements) that you cannot control *Her face kept twitching.* **twitch** *noun*

twitter *verb*
twitters, twittering, twittered
when a small bird twitters, it makes a short high sound **twitter** *noun*

Twitter *noun* (trademark)
an internet service for sending short messages

two *adjective & noun* **twos**
the number 2

two-dimensional *adjective*
used about an object or image that is flat and has the two dimensions of length and width. For example, a drawing of a square or triangle on a whiteboard or piece of paper is two-dimensional.

> LANGUAGE EXTRA sometimes shortened to 2-D or two-D

two-star *adjective*
of medium quality *a two-star hotel*

two-faced *adjective*
used for describing someone you cannot trust because they do not mean what they say, for example they say different things to different people about the same subject

txt
the ending of a computer filename. A .txt file contains text only.
short for: text

-ty *suffix*
used for making nouns that show a quality *loyalty; certainty*

tying
present participle of **tie**

type *noun* **types**
1 a group of things or people that are similar to each other and different from other groups *My dad's shop sells all different types of pasta. What type of dog do you like best?*
2 letters printed in a book or written document. You use this word when talking about the size or design of letters. *The heading is in bold type* (printed in a thicker way than other letters).

type *verb*
types, typing, typed
1 to write something, for example using a computer keyboard or phone keypad, so that it appears on a screen *I'm typing an email to my best friend. Type in your password. Tom's learning how to type* (to write correctly using a keyboard).
2 to write something using a typewriter
typing *noun*

typeface *noun* **typefaces**
the letters and numbers of a particular design and size, used for computer documents and in printing *Change the typeface from Verdana to Arial.*

typewriter *noun* **typewriters**
a machine used in the past to type words straight onto a sheet of paper. It has long metal parts with letters at the end, which hit the paper when you press keys (buttons).

typewritten *adjective*
written using a computer or typewriter *a typewritten letter*

typhoon *noun* **typhoons**
a bad storm with winds that go round in circles. Typhoons happen between July and October in countries such as China and Japan.

typical *adjective*
1 used about something or someone that has all the qualities you would expect them to have *He's noisy and angry just like a typical teenager. We went to a village café for some typical French food.*
2 used about something that is normal and as you would expect *Monday was a typical day at school. Snow is typical at this time of year. Nan helped me with her typical enthusiasm. Such kindness is typical of her.*

typically *adverb*
1 normally *The headaches typically last for about an hour.*
2 in a way that shows the qualities you would expect *Sayed's homework is of a typically high standard.*
3 in a way that shows someone's normal behaviour *Typically, my brother went to school without his lunchbox.*

typist *noun* **typists**
1 someone whose job is to type documents using a computer or, in the past, using a typewriter
2 someone who has the special skill of knowing how to type, for example on a computer *My brother is a very fast typist.*

tyrannosaurus–umpire

tyrannosaurus ['ti-ran-er-**sohr**-ers'] *noun* **tyrannosauruses**
a very large and tall dinosaur with a large head and long heavy tail. It had two short front legs and two very strong back legs that it walked on. It ate other animals, not plants.

LANGUAGE EXTRA also called *Tyrannosaurus rex* (*rex* is the Latin for 'king')

tyranny ['ti-rer-nee'] *noun*
1 a very cruel way of ruling a country
2 someone's very cruel behaviour towards someone else

tyrant ['ty-rernt'] *noun* **tyrants**
1 someone who rules a country with complete power in a very cruel way
2 someone who controls someone else and behaves in a very cruel way towards them

tyre *noun* **tyres**
a thick rubber ring filled with air that fits around the wheel of a vehicle or bicycle

u U

ORIGIN U, F, V and W all come from the same letter in the Phoenician alphabet – a shape that looked like the letter Y and represented either a peg or a hook. It had the sound of 'w' and was called *waw*. When the letter passed into Latin, the Romans removed the stem from the Y to create a V shape which had either a 'u' sound, as in *TEMPVS* ('time'), or a 'w' sound, as in *VIDI* ('I saw'). Eventually the V was rounded at the bottom to make writing it easier and became the letter U we know today. In Latin, U and V were used in the same way to represent both the 'u' and the 'w' sounds. In English, when U is used with Q (as in QU), it is still pronounced with a 'w' sound: 'kw'.

udder *noun* **udders**
a soft part of the body of a female animal such as a cow or goat, where milk is produced for baby animals. It is shaped like a bag and hangs down between the animal's back legs.

UFO ['**yoo**-foh' or 'yoo-ef-**oh**'] *noun* **UFOs**
a strange object that someone sees flying in the sky, which they think could be a spacecraft from another planet
short for: unidentified flying object

Uganda ['yoo-**gan**-der'] *noun*
a country in East Africa
Ugandan *adjective & noun*

ugh ['err' or 'ug'] *interjection*
a word used for showing that you think something is unpleasant or disgusting *Ugh, what a horrible smell!*

ugly *adjective* **uglier, ugliest**
1 really horrible to look at *an ugly face; an ugly building*
2 very unpleasant *That was an ugly thing to say!*
3 very unpleasant, angry and violent *The crowd turned ugly.*
ugliness *noun*

ORIGIN from Old Norse *ugga* 'fear'

UK *noun*
short for **United Kingdom**

Ukraine ['yoo-**krayn**'] *noun*
a country in Eastern Europe
Ukrainian *adjective & noun*

ukulele ['yoo-ker-**lay**-lee'] *noun* **ukuleles**
a musical instrument with four strings. A ukulele looks like a small guitar.

LANGUAGE EXTRA also spelt *ukelele*

ulcer *noun* **ulcers**
a place on your body where the skin is broken or inside the body where a surface is damaged or infected (with germs in it)

ultimate *adjective*
1 coming at the end of something or after many things happen, or after considering everyone or everything else *My sister's ultimate ambition is to become a teacher* (for example after her studies and after she has done other activities). *Parents have ultimate responsibility for their children* (parents have the main responsibility, not teachers or anyone else).

SYNONYM final

2 used for describing something that is the most extreme, for example the best or most or the worst or least *Skydiving is the ultimate challenge. Failing all your exams is the ultimate nightmare.*
3 used for describing the very first place where something comes from *The sun is the ultimate source of life.*

ultimately *adverb*
1 coming at the end of something *My sister was ultimately successful.*

SYNONYM finally

2 after considering all other things *Ultimately, you must decide what you want to do. Life depends ultimately on the sun.*
3 after considering everyone else *Ultimately, it's your decision, not your mum's or your dad's.*

ultra- *prefix*
1 used with adjectives to mean extremely or more than *ultra-modern*
2 used with adjectives and nouns to mean beyond *ultraviolet*

ultrasound *noun*
a medical examination of the inside of a part of someone's body. It uses sound waves to produce an image on a screen, for example the image of a baby inside its mother's body.

ultraviolet *adjective*
used for describing light that humans cannot see because it is beyond violet in the spectrum (the last of the seven colours that light can be separated into). Ultraviolet light in sunlight makes light skin become darker.

umbilical cord ['um-**bil**-ik-erl'] *noun* **umbilical cords**
a long soft tube that joins a foetus or baby to its mother's placenta (organ inside the body) and is cut away when the baby is born

umbrella *noun* **umbrellas**
1 an object that you hold above your head to keep the rain off. It is made of a frame of long thin pieces of metal covered with a special cloth or plastic and fixed to a long handle. When you're using it, you unfold the frame and push the parts out so that it is shaped like the top of a ball. When you're not using it, you fold the frame down or push the parts together. *a telescopic umbrella*
2 a similar object that you use for protection against the sun. You hold it over your head or it is fixed to the ground. This type of umbrella is also called a parasol. *a beach umbrella*

ORIGIN from Latin *umbrella* 'little shade'

umpire *noun* **umpires**
someone in charge of a game such as cricket, tennis or baseball who makes sure the rules are obeyed
compare: **referee**

551

umpire–uncooked

umpire *verb*
umpires, umpiring, umpired
to be the umpire of a game such as cricket

un- *prefix*
used for giving a word the meaning of 'not' or for giving the opposite meaning of a word *unafraid*; *unfashionable*; *unimaginative*; *unhappiness*; *unlock*; *undelete*; *unfortunately*

UN ['yoo-en] *noun*
an international organisation made up of countries of the world. Its job is to help countries solve problems such as war and disease in a peaceful way.
short for: **United Nations**

unable *adjective*
not able to do something *George is unable to keep a secret.*

unacceptable *adjective*
1 used for describing something that is so bad or so much that it shouldn't be allowed or allowed to continue *unacceptable behaviour*; *For a top restaurant the food was unacceptable. Is there an unacceptable amount of violence in some films?*
2 not good enough to be accepted by someone *Chloe offered me £10 for my bike but that was unacceptable to me.*

unaided *adjective*
without any help *Great-Granddad can no longer walk unaided* (for example, he needs a stick).

unanimous ['yoo-**nan**-i-mers] *adjective*
used for saying that everyone agrees about something *a unanimous decision*; *The whole class was unanimous – we all wanted to visit the Science Museum.*
unanimously *adverb*

unarmed *adjective*
if someone is unarmed, they are not carrying a gun

unattended *adjective*
not being watched or looked after *Don't leave your luggage unattended.*

unavoidable *adjective*
if something bad is unavoidable, it cannot be stopped from happening *unavoidable delays* **unavoidably** *adverb*

unaware *adjective*
to be unaware of something is not to know about it or not to notice it *They were unaware of the danger. I was unaware that he was behind me.*

unawares *adverb*
if something such as an event, storm or question catches you unawares, it happens unexpectedly and you are not ready for it

unbearable *adjective*
if something is unbearable, it is so bad that you just can't deal with it *unbearable pain*; *The heat was unbearable.*
unbearably *adverb*

unbeatable *adjective*
if someone is unbeatable in a game or competition, no-one can do better than they can because they are the best

unbeknown to *preposition*
used for showing that something happens or is done without you knowing about it *Unbeknown to me, my friends organised a little party.*

> **LANGUAGE EXTRA** you can also say *unbeknownst to*

unbelievable *adjective*
1 almost impossible to believe *an unbelievable story*
2 extremely surprising, for example because of being unexpected or unusual *It was unbelievable how much time this week's homework took me.*
3 extremely good *You have an unbelievable gift for languages. The singing and acting were unbelievable.*
4 extremely great or large *an unbelievable bang*; *an unbelievable amount of money*
5 extremely bad *unbelievable conditions*; *Jack let us all down – his behaviour was unbelievable.*

unbelievably *adverb*
1 extremely, often in a way that is unexpected or unusual *My mum works unbelievably hard.*
2 used when something is almost impossible to believe *Unbelievably, my brother came top of the class.*
3 extremely well *He sang truly unbelievably.*

unblock *verb*
unblocks, unblocking, unblocked
1 if someone unblocks something such as a pipe or sink, they get rid of whatever is stopping the water from flowing through it or out of it
2 to allow someone or something to reach you, for example online, by email or by phone, when you had blocked them before (stopped them from reaching you) *Now that Andy and I are friends, I've unblocked him on Facebook.*

unborn *adjective*
not yet born *an unborn baby*

unbreakable *adjective*
used about something that you cannot break because it is made of strong material *an unbreakable toy*

unbroken *adjective*
continuing for a long time without any gaps *six hours of unbroken sunshine*

unbutton *verb*
unbuttons, unbuttoning, unbuttoned
to undo the buttons on something such as a shirt

uncalled for *adjective*
used about something that should not have happened or should not have been done, for example because it was cruel, wrong or insulting

> **LANGUAGE EXTRA** usually spelt *uncalled-for* when used in front of a noun, for example *an uncalled-for remark*

uncanny *adjective* uncannier, uncanniest
strange and difficult to understand or explain **uncannily** *adverb*

uncertain *adjective*
1 not sure about what to do *I'm uncertain as to how to reply to her email.*
2 used about something that is not known or understood, or used when you are not sure what is going to happen *a word of uncertain origin*; *It's uncertain what position Ollie will play in the football team.*
3 not known but likely to be bad or get worse *The weather is uncertain today. The refugees face an uncertain future.*

uncertainty *noun*
1 when you are not sure about something *There's a lot of uncertainty about what happened.*
2 when you are not sure about things and you think bad things might happen *There was a lot of uncertainty in this country in 1939.*
3 (*plural* **uncertainties**) something you are not sure about

uncle *noun* uncles
someone's uncle is the brother of their father or mother, or the husband of their aunt

unclear *adjective*
1 not easy to understand *The instructions are unclear.*
2 not understanding something *I'm unclear about what to do.*
3 not easy to see or hear *The picture is very unclear and so is the sound.*

uncomfortable *adjective*
1 not feeling good and relaxed, for example because there is something hurting you or worrying you or because you are sitting on something hard
2 if something such as a piece of clothing or a chair is uncomfortable, it gives you an unpleasant feeling in a part of your body, for example because it is rough or hard
3 feeling nervous, worried or upset, for example because you don't like doing something or being somewhere *I feel uncomfortable standing up in class and having to read aloud.*
uncomfortably *adverb*

uncommon *adjective*
1 not happening often *an uncommon mistake*
2 not existing in large numbers *Wasps are uncommon at this time of year.*
uncommonly *adverb*

unconscious *adjective*
1 not knowing what is happening around you because you're not awake and you can't see or hear, usually because you're ill or injured
2 to be unconscious of something is not to notice it or know about it

unconsciously *adverb*
if you do something unconsciously, you don't know you're doing it *Looking at his watch every minute is something my brother does unconsciously.*

uncontrollable *adjective*
used for describing something you can't control or stop *uncontrollable laughter*; *uncontrollable bleeding*
uncontrollably *adverb*

uncooked *adjective*
used about food that you don't heat up before you eat it or that has not been heated up yet *Tomatoes are usually eaten uncooked. Don't put the cooked and uncooked meat next to each other in the fridge.*

> **SYNONYM** raw

uncool *adjective* (informal)
1 not cool, modern or fashionable *an old-fashioned and uncool pair of trainers; You look uncool in that suit.*
2 not good or interesting *That idea is pretty uncool.*

uncooperative *adjective*
not wanting to work with other people or to help them

SYNONYM unhelpful

uncountable *adjective*
in grammar, an uncountable noun is one that isn't used in the plural, for example bread or rugby

ANTONYM countable

uncouth ['un-kooth'] *adjective*
1 if you are uncouth, you behave in a way that is rough and doesn't show respect towards people
2 also used about what you do or say *uncouth behaviour; an uncouth remark*

ANTONYM polite

uncover *verb*
uncovers, uncovering, uncovered
1 to find something or find out something that has been hidden or kept secret *Dad tried to uncover the truth about what happened. The police have uncovered some old documents.*
2 to remove something such as a lid, top or piece of material that is covering something
3 to find something that has been under the ground for a very long time

undamaged *adjective*
not damaged or spoilt in any way *The parcel arrived undamaged.*

undecided *adjective*
if you are undecided about something, you are not sure what to do so you haven't made a decision about it yet

undelete *verb*
undeletes, undeleting, undeleted
to perform a computer action to bring back something that has been deleted, such as a file or program, so that you can use it again

undeniable *adjective*
used about something that is completely true, usually in a way that everyone can see clearly *Einstein was a man of undeniable intelligence.* **undeniably** *adverb*

under *preposition*
1 lower than something *There's a pile of books under the table. The saucer goes under the cup.*
2 below the surface of something *under the ground; under the water; The floor was under a foot of water.*
3 on the lowest part of something (the part that is normally facing the ground) *There's a lot of rust under the car.*
4 less than something *I've read under 10 pages. The race is open to kids under the age of 15. It took me under five minutes.*
5 used for showing that someone is in charge of someone or something, or that someone controls or rules someone or something *Life was hard under Queen Victoria* (during her reign). *My uncle is a manager with three people under him.*
6 in a particular situation *The road is under construction* (being built). *My laptop is under repair* (being repaired). *The soldiers were under attack. During exam times, teachers are under a lot of pressure.*
7 in a particular part of a book *Look under 'badminton' in the dictionary to find out the origin of that word.*
8 using a particular name *The author sometimes writes under a different name.*

under *adverb*
1 less than something *Children aged 15 and under.*
2 lower than something *Sit on this chair and tuck your legs under so that no-one trips over your feet.*
3 below the surface of something *The ship went under* (sank under the water).

under- *prefix*
1 used with verbs, adjectives and nouns to mean not enough *to undercook; underfed; underpaid; underpayment*
2 used with nouns and adjectives to mean below the surface of something *underground; underwater*
3 used with nouns to mean less than *There's free entry to the museum for the under-fives* (children aged five and under).

undercarriage *noun* undercarriages
the wheels of an aircraft and the other parts that support it when it is moving along the ground before taking off and after landing

undercharge *verb*
undercharges, undercharging, undercharged
if someone undercharges you, for example in a shop, they accidentally ask you to pay less money than you should pay

undercover *adjective*
working secretly or done secretly to get information or catch criminals *an undercover police officer; an undercover investigation* **undercover** *adverb*

underdeveloped *adjective*
1 if a part of your body is underdeveloped, it has not grown as big or as strong as it should have grown *underdeveloped muscles*
2 an underdeveloped country or region is poor, for example because there are not enough people making goods in factories and not enough modern equipment and machines

underdog *noun* underdogs
in a competition, an underdog is a person or team that is not likely to win because they are the least good

underdone *adjective*
used for describing food that has not been cooked long enough

underestimate *verb*
underestimates, underestimating, underestimated
1 if someone underestimates something, they think it is smaller, less strong or less important than it really is *Don't underestimate the importance of plenty of sleep if you want to do well at school.*
2 if you underestimate someone, you think they are less good or less strong than they really are

underfed *adjective*
not given enough food

underfoot *adverb*
on the ground where you walk or stand *The pavement was wet underfoot. People rushing from the building were trampled underfoot* (injured by people walking or running over them).

undergo *verb*
undergoes, undergoing, underwent, undergone
if someone or something undergoes something, it happens to them or is done to them *My mum underwent a serious operation. Our school is undergoing lots of changes* (it is changing). *My bike is undergoing repairs* (being repaired).

undergraduate ['un-der-**grad**-joo-ert'] *noun* undergraduates
someone who is studying for a degree at a university or college

underground *adjective & adverb*
1 under the surface of the ground *an underground car park; Miners work underground.*
2 secret and often against the law *an underground movement* (a group of people fighting for something)

underground *noun*
a railway that goes under the ground in tunnels, usually in a big town

CULTURE NOTE the *underground* in London is often called the *tube*. You can also write *Underground* or *Tube*.

undergrowth *noun*
small thick bushes that grow together, usually close to trees in a forest or jungle

underhand *adjective*
secret and dishonest

underlie *verb*
underlies, underlying, underlay, underlain
to be the cause of something or the reason for something *What really underlies our school's success?*

underline *verb*
underlines, underlining, underlined
1 to draw a line under something such as a word or sentence
2 to show that something is especially important, or to give extra importance to something *These mistakes in your homework underline the need for you to pay more attention to grammar.*

underlying *adjective*
used for describing something such as a cause or fact that is the real or most important cause or fact, although this is not easy to see *What were the underlying reasons for his terrible behaviour last night?*

undermine *verb*
undermines, undermining, undermined
1 to make something weaker or make someone feel weaker or less successful *If you keep criticising her, you'll undermine her confidence. Encourage your brother – don't keep undermining him.*
2 to make something less likely to be successful *You've done all you can to undermine my efforts to play for the team.*
3 to make something worse *Smoking will undermine your health.*

underneath–undoubted

underneath preposition & adverb
1 lower than something *The ball rolled underneath the table. Fold over the blanket and tuck it underneath.*
2 below the surface of something *The boat sank underneath the ice.*
3 on the lowest part of something (the part that is normally facing the ground) *Underneath Dad's car there's a lot of rust. Turn your laptop over and read what's written on the label underneath.*

underneath noun
the underneath of something is the part that is under it *The underneath of the radio is badly scratched.*

underpants noun plural
underwear for boys and men that covers the lower part of the body from the hips to the top of the legs

underpass noun underpasses
a tunnel or road under a street for people or vehicles to go from one side to the other

underprivileged adjective
connected with people who have less money, fewer good things in their lives and fewer chances to make their lives better than most other people *underprivileged children; George comes from an underprivileged background.*

undershirt noun undershirts
the American word for a vest

understand verb
understands, understanding, understood
1 to know what something means or the idea or information that something represents *I don't understand the question. This word is difficult to understand. Say that again – I didn't understand. Sorry, I don't understand what you mean.*
2 to know a lot about a subject or how something works *My sister understands maths better than me. Jo understands Spanish* (knows what the words mean). *I don't understand much about computers.*
3 to know the reason for something, the way that something happens or how something is *She came over to me and hit me – I didn't understand why. Do scientists understand how the universe started? I don't understand what you're doing here. We didn't understand how ill my aunt was.*
4 to understand someone is to know what they are saying or what they mean *The phone line isn't clear – I can't understand you. You're not getting any pocket money for a month – do you understand me?*
5 to understand someone is also to know what they are like, how they feel and how they behave, and usually to care about their feelings *Our teacher really understands children. My brother says no-one understands him.*
6 to understand someone's feelings, for example someone who has a problem or who feels anger or fear, is to know how they feel and to care about their feelings *The head says she understands the parents' worries about safety. I understand your disappointment.*
7 to believe that something is true, for example because someone has told you *'I understand you want to see the head teacher,' said the secretary.*

understandable adjective
1 completely normal and just as you would expect something to be *His behaviour was perfectly understandable. It's understandable to be upset if your team loses.*
2 used about something you can understand easily because it is easy to see what it means *Mr Grant explained in a very understandable way how computers work.*

understandably adverb
in a way that is completely normal and just as you would expect *We lost the match and so we were understandably disappointed.*

understanding noun
1 what you know about a subject, situation or things in general *I have a better understanding of computers than Rupa. Our teacher is a person of great understanding.*

SYNONYM knowledge

2 (plural **understandings**) a friendly agreement about something between people who trust each other *Dad and I have an understanding – if I help in the kitchen, he'll let me stay up late.*
3 a strong feeling that shows you care about people's feelings because you know how people feel and behave and you know about their problems *My teacher showed me a lot of kindness and understanding.*
4 when you don't get angry or upset when someone does something bad or wrong, because you care too much about that person's feelings *Holly's parents show too much understanding towards their children.*

understanding adjective
1 used for showing that someone is kind and helpful and cares about your feelings *Ms Singh was understanding when I missed school because I had to visit Nan in hospital.*
2 used for showing that someone is not angry or upset with someone who does something bad or wrong, because they care too much about that person's feelings *Ravinder's parents are very understanding.*

understudy noun understudies
an actor who learns the words and actions of a character in a play so that he or she can perform in the play if the usual actor is ill or away

undertake verb
undertakes, undertaking, undertook, undertaken
1 to do something or start to do something, especially something that needs a lot of responsibility *The police have decided to undertake an investigation.*
2 if you undertake to do something, you promise to do it

undertaker noun undertakers
someone who deals with the bodies of people who have just died and gets them ready to be buried or cremated

undertaking noun undertakings
1 a difficult or important piece of work, for example one that takes a long time to do
2 a promise to do something

underwater adverb
below the surface of the water *Can you swim underwater?*

underwater adjective
existing, done or used below the surface of the water *underwater rocks; an underwater camera*

underway adjective
used for describing an activity that has already started and is happening now *Rescue efforts got underway* (started) *as soon as news of the crash came in.*

LANGUAGE EXTRA also spelt *under way*

underwear noun
clothes that you wear next to your skin under your other clothes such as trousers or a skirt

underweight adjective
used about someone who weighs less than they should

underworld noun
1 used for talking about criminals and the place where criminals do their activities *He's a member of the London underworld.*
2 in stories, the underworld is a place deep under the ground where people go after they die

undesirable adjective
1 if something is undesirable, it is bad and you don't want it or like it *undesirable behaviour; The medicine had undesirable side effects. This part of town is undesirable* (people don't want to live there).
2 if someone is undesirable, you think they are unpleasant and cause trouble *He has some undesirable friends.*

undies noun plural
an informal word for underwear (clothes worn next to your skin), especially underwear for girls or women

undo verb
undoes, undoing, undid, undone
1 to open or remove something so that it is not joined, tied or connected to something *Undo your seat belt. He undid his coat and took it off. Get a screwdriver and undo the screws. I can't undo this knot.*
2 if you undo something that has been done, you do something to change a situation and make it go back to how it was before *The bully wished he could undo the trouble he'd caused. Builders are working on the school roof to undo the damage caused by the storm* (to repair the damage and make the roof as good as before).
3 if you undo a change to a computer document or program, you do something such as press a key or click on or touch an icon to make the document or program go back to how it was before you made the change
compare: **redo**

undone adjective
1 not joined, tied or connected to something *One of your buttons is undone. Your shoelace has come undone* (has got loose and is no longer tied).
2 not finished *You've left half your homework undone.*

undoubted adjective
used for saying that something is definitely true, usually in a way that everyone can see clearly *He was the undoubted star of the show.*

undoubtedly *adverb*
in a way that shows that something is definitely true *The two events are undoubtedly connected.*

SYNONYM certainly

undress *verb*
undresses, undressing, undressed
1 to take your clothes off
2 to take the clothes off someone such as a baby or doll

undressed *adjective*
1 not wearing any clothes
2 wearing the clothes you go to bed in, for example your pyjamas
3 to get undressed is to take your clothes off

undrinkable *adjective*
not good or safe to drink

unduly *adverb*
1 very or too *We're not unduly worried.*
2 very much or too much *This noise doesn't bother me unduly.*

unearth *verb*
unearths, unearthing, unearthed
1 to find something that has been hidden or put somewhere for a long time
2 to find something out that has been hidden or kept secret *The police are trying to unearth the truth.*
3 to find something in the ground by digging *The sailors unearthed some buried treasure.*

unearthly *adjective*
1 used for describing something that is mysterious and frightening, for example because it doesn't seem normal *an unearthly noise*
2 if you describe a particular time of the day as an unearthly hour, you mean it is extremely early in the morning

uneasily *adverb*
1 in a way that shows you feel worried, nervous or upset *She heard a noise and started looking around uneasily.*
2 in a way that shows a situation could get worse at any moment *The different religious groups in that country live uneasily together.*

uneasy *adjective* uneasier, uneasiest
1 feeling worried, nervous or upset, for example because you don't like doing something or being somewhere *I feel a bit uneasy if I have to read in class.*
2 used about something such as a feeling or action that shows you feel worried, nervous or upset *an uneasy smile*
3 also used about a situation that could change and get worse at any moment *an uneasy peace between the two countries*

uneducated *adjective*
an uneducated person is someone who has not received much school education (or any school education at all)

unemployed *adjective*
if someone is unemployed, they don't have a job

unemployment *noun*
1 a situation in which someone doesn't have a job
2 used for talking about the numbers of people who don't have a job *Unemployment has gone up this month.*
3 unemployment benefit is money someone gets from the government if they don't have a job

unending *adjective*
used for describing a very large number of things or amount of something continuing without stopping *There was an unending stream of visitors to see the Picasso exhibition.*

unequal *adjective*
1 different in size, number, quality or importance *two pieces of string of unequal length*
2 used about people who are treated in different ways, for example because someone thinks that some people are better than others *unequal treatment*; *In that country men and women were considered unequal.*

uneven *adjective*
1 not flat or smooth *The ground was uneven* (bumpy). *The edge of the paper was uneven* (for example torn or with cuts in it).
2 not having the same size and position *My teeth are very uneven.*
3 not following a regular pattern *uneven breathing*; *We were walking at an uneven pace.*
4 not equal or fair *an uneven share of the money*; *The contest is uneven* (for example, some players are strong and others weak).
5 having some good parts and some parts that are less good *Your work this term has been very uneven.*

unevenness *noun*

unevenly *adverb*
1 not in the same way in all parts *The butter was spread unevenly on the toast.*
2 not equally or fairly *He shared out the money unevenly.*
3 in a way that doesn't follow a regular pattern *unevenly spaced lines*; *Our dog was breathing unevenly.*

uneventful *adjective*
used about something such as a period of time or a journey where nothing interesting or unusual happens **uneventfully** *adverb*

unexpected *adjective*
if something is unexpected, it surprises you because you didn't know about it or know it was going to happen or be the way it was *an unexpected birthday present*; *My lost schoolbook turned up in an unexpected place.*

unexpectedly *adverb*
in a way that surprises you because you were not expecting it or were not expecting it to be the way it was *It was unexpectedly cold that day.*

unfair *adjective*
1 not reasonable or right *These rules seem unfair. It's unfair to suggest it's my fault.*
2 used about a situation where not all people are treated in the same reasonable way and where some people are treated better than others *unfair treatment*; *Dad helped Rashid with his homework but not me – that's so unfair!*
3 if something such as a fight, game or match is unfair, one person or player is strong and the other one weak (or some people or players are strong and others weak)

unfairness *noun*

unfairly *adverb*
in a way that is not reasonable or right, especially when not everyone is treated the same *I think Ms Taylor has been unfairly helping some of the children with their homework.*

unfamiliar *adjective*
1 if something or someone is unfamiliar, you don't recognise them or know them *an unfamiliar face*; *The rules are unfamiliar to me.*
2 if you're unfamiliar with something, you don't know it or know anything about it

unfasten *verb*
unfastens, unfastening, unfastened
to open something that is fastened by moving the part or parts that join it to something else *I unfastened my seat belt. This dress unfastens at the back.*

unfavourable *adjective*
1 not favourable or good *She made an unfavourable impression on me.*
2 not helping you *The weather was unfavourable so I didn't go jogging.*
3 used for showing that you don't like something *Most parents were unfavourable to the idea of starting school an hour earlier.*

unfavourably *adverb*
1 in a way that shows that someone doesn't like something *She replied unfavourably to my email.*
2 in a way that shows that something is not good *British food used to compare unfavourably to French food.*
3 in a very bad way *We were unfavourably treated.*

unfinished *adjective*
not finished, often when talking about something such as a work of art or piece of work *an unfinished novel*; *an unfinished meal*

unfit *adjective*
1 if someone is unfit, they are not in good health, for example because they do not exercise
2 not good enough for something *This meat is unfit to eat.*
3 not well enough to do something or go somewhere *I've got the flu and I'm unfit for school.*
4 not having the right qualities to do something *My cousin's been in prison so he's unfit to be a police officer.*

unfold *verb*
unfolds, unfolding, unfolded
1 to open something that is folded, such as a map or newspaper
2 if something such as an event, story or situation unfolds, it happens and more of it gradually becomes known *We watched on TV as the disaster unfolded.*

unforeseen *adjective*
used about something that is not expected and usually not wanted *The school play has been cancelled due to unforeseen circumstances.*

555

unforgettable – union

unforgettable *adjective*
used about something you will remember for a long time, usually something pleasant *Our holidays were unforgettable.*

unforgivable *adjective*
used about something that someone does or says that is so bad that you can never forgive them *an unforgivable mistake; unforgivable behaviour*

unfortunate *adjective*
1 not lucky *The unfortunate animal walked straight into the trap.*
2 used about something such as a situation or event that you are sad to mention because it is unpleasant or bad *an unfortunate mistake; It's unfortunate you won't be coming to my party tomorrow.*
3 used about someone who has worse things in their life than other people *The unfortunate people who live in that country don't have a chance to go to school.*

unfortunately *adverb*
used when talking about something bad or unpleasant happening that you are sad to mention *Unfortunately, I slipped and bruised my knee.*

unfriend *verb*
unfriends, unfriending, unfriended
if you unfriend someone on an internet site such as Facebook, you remove them from your list of friends

SYNONYM to defriend

unfriendly *adjective*
unfriendlier, unfriendliest
not friendly, kind or helpful towards someone *an unfriendly shop assistant; an unfriendly voice* **unfriendliness** *noun*

unfurl *verb*
unfurls, unfurling, unfurled
if you unfurl something that is rolled up or folded, for example a flag or sail, you open it out

ungainly *adjective*
moving in a way that is awkward or clumsy

ungrammatical *adjective*
not obeying the rules of grammar *That sentence is ungrammatical.*

ungrateful *adjective*
not wanting to thank someone who has helped you or been kind to you **ungratefulness** *noun*

unhappily *adverb*
used when talking about something unpleasant or bad happening that makes you sad *Unhappily, our team wasn't successful.*

unhappiness *noun*
1 another way of saying sadness
2 the feeling you have when you don't think something or someone is good *Our teacher's unhappiness with the results was plain to see from the look on his face.*

unhappy *adjective* unhappier, unhappiest
1 another way of saying sad *I was very unhappy when my dog died. The story had an unhappy ending. I failed and I'm unhappy about it.*
2 used when you mean something is unpleasant or bad and you're sad that it has happened *an unhappy coincidence; You're in a very unhappy situation.*
3 if you're unhappy with something or someone, you don't think they are good or you don't like them *Alia is unhappy with her marks.*

unhealthily *adverb*
in a way that shows you don't pay much attention to staying well *My brother eats very unhealthily.*

unhealthy *adjective*
unhealthier, unhealthiest
1 not well or strong or showing good health *unhealthy skin; You look pale and unhealthy.*
2 not good for you *unhealthy food; Smoking is unhealthy and can cause illness and death.*

unheard-of *adjective*
used about something that never happens or has never happened before *It's unheard-of for someone to get full marks in the maths test.*

unhelpful *adjective*
1 if something is unhelpful, it is not useful and doesn't make a situation better *That was a rather unhelpful suggestion.*
2 if someone is unhelpful, they don't want to help you *an unhelpful bus driver*

unhurt *adjective*
not injured in any way *They escaped from the car crash unhurt.*

unhygienic *adjective*
1 very dirty and likely to make you ill *an unhygienic toilet*
2 doing things in a way that can make you ill *Eating food with dirty fingers is unhygienic.*

unhygienically *adverb*

uni ['yoo-nee'] *noun* unis
an informal word for university *My big sister's at uni.*

uni- *prefix*
connected with one thing only *unicycle* (cycle with one wheel); *unicorn* (creature with one horn)

unicorn ['yoo-ni-korn'] *noun* unicorns
in stories, an imaginary animal like a beautiful white horse. It has a long straight horn growing out of the front of its head.

uniform *noun* uniforms
clothes of a special colour and design that certain groups of people wear, for example children who go to the same school or people who work together such as police officers, nurses or soldiers *On the bus we saw a soldier in uniform* (wearing a uniform).

uniform *adjective*
used for describing something that is the same in all parts or all the time *The sky was a uniform blue* (it was the same blue everywhere). *The train was travelling at a uniform speed* (the speed didn't change).
uniformity *noun* **uniformly** *adverb*

uniformed *adjective*
wearing a uniform *a uniformed police officer*

unify *verb*
unifies, unifying, unified
1 to join or bring different things or people together to form a single thing or group *The different lines of the London Underground have been unified into one system. The people chose a new leader to unify the country.*
2 to join or come together *The two halves of Germany unified in 1990.*
unification *noun*

unimaginable *adjective*
used about something that is almost impossible to understand or imagine, for example because it is so bad, so good or so big *the unimaginable horrors of war; unimaginable success*

unimportant *adjective*
used about something or someone that is not important, for example without much value or influence or not worth paying attention to *an unimportant job; an unimportant decision*

uninhabitable *adjective*
if a place is uninhabitable, it is not suitable to be lived in *The storm did so much damage that it made the house uninhabitable.*

ANTONYM habitable

uninhabited *adjective*
used for describing a place where no-one lives

uninstall *verb*
uninstalls, uninstalling, uninstalled
to remove a program or piece of software from a computer using a special program that removes it completely

unintelligible *adjective*
if something such as a word or answer is unintelligible, it is impossible to understand

unintentional *adjective*
not done on purpose but happening by chance **unintentionally** *adverb*

uninterested *adjective*
not interested in something *Our teacher was explaining the reasons for the Second World War but the class seemed totally uninterested.*

LANGUAGE EXTRA be careful not to confuse *uninterested* with *disinterested*, which means 'able to give a fair opinion about something'

uninteresting *adjective*
used about something or someone that is not at all interesting *an uninteresting book; an uninteresting writer*

union *noun* unions
1 an organisation of workers in a particular job. It helps the workers with things such as getting better working conditions and more money from the people they work for. *My dad's a union official.*

LANGUAGE EXTRA also called a *trade union*

2 a group of countries that have joined together *the European Union*
3 when two or more groups, countries or people join together *France wants closer union with Germany.*
4 a group of people with the same aims who have joined together
5 in the American Civil War (1861–65), the Union was the group of northern states that fought the southern states *the Union flag*

compare: **Confederacy**

556

Union Jack noun Union Jacks
the flag of the United Kingdom

unique ['yoo-neek'] adjective
1 used about something or someone that is the only one of their kind *Every person's fingerprints are unique.*
2 used when describing something good that is very special and unusual *I had the unique chance to meet the prime minister.*
3 if something is unique to something or someone, it is connected only with that thing or person *Speaking, writing and reading are skills that are unique to humans.*
uniqueness noun

uniquely adverb
1 in a way that makes someone or something very special and different from all other people or things *Mozart was a uniquely gifted musician.*
2 only *This plant is found uniquely in the north of Scotland.*

unisex adjective
for both men and woman or boys and girls *unisex clothes*

unison ['yoo-ni-sern'] noun
if people do something in unison, they do it all together at the same time

unit noun units
1 an amount used for measuring things or for counting money *A metre is a unit for measuring length in the metric system. A pound is a unit of money.*
2 a single complete thing that is often a part of something larger *A cell is the smallest unit of living matter.*
3 a group of people who work together as a part of something larger, or the place where they do a particular type of work *an army unit; an intensive care unit in a hospital*
4 a piece of furniture that fits together with another piece of the same type *kitchen units* (cupboards)
5 one of the parts that a book such as a textbook (one for studying a particular subject) is divided into
6 a machine or piece of equipment that performs a particular action *the central processing unit of a computer*
7 in maths, a unit is any whole number for counting up to 9 (0, 1, 2, 3, 4, 5, 6, 7, 8, 9). In sums, the numbers above nine are called tens and are written in the tens column to the left of the units. For example, 46 is made up of four tens and six units, and 30 is three tens and no units.
8 in maths, a unit fraction is a fraction where the numerator (top number) is 1, for example $\frac{1}{2}$ or $\frac{1}{4}$

unite verb
unites, uniting, united
1 to join or bring things or people together to become one single thing or group *The country needs a leader who can unite people of different religions and backgrounds. The two girls are united by a very strong friendship.*
2 if people or groups unite, they join or come together, for example to do something as a group *All the neighbours have united to fight crime in the area.*
3 to bring people together who have been away from each other for a certain time *Joseph was united with his father, who was separated from him during the Second World War.*

United Kingdom noun
a country in North-West Europe that consists of England, Scotland, Wales and Northern Ireland

LANGUAGE EXTRA also called the *UK*

United Nations noun
an international organisation made up of countries of the world. Its job is to help countries solve problems such as war and disease in a peaceful way.

LANGUAGE EXTRA also called the *UN*

United States noun
a country in North America

LANGUAGE EXTRA also called *America*, the *United States of America*, the *US* and the *USA*

unity noun
1 when people or things are together as one single thing or group, or when people work together as a group *family unity; European unity*
2 when something is complete and all its parts fit together in an attractive way *There's no sense of unity in your painting.*

universal adjective
1 including or connected with everyone *There should be universal access to the internet* (access for everyone). *This music has universal appeal* (everyone likes it).
2 true everywhere and at all times *a universal truth*

universally adverb
1 by everyone, for example when talking about something that has been agreed, accepted or recognised *The results are universally accepted.*
2 everywhere and at all times *These DVDs don't work universally.*

universe noun
1 used for talking about all the planets and stars and everything that exists in space and in the world *The earth is a tiny part of the universe.*
2 used for talking about people's lives and all the things that happen to them and to people they know *In this book, Dickens creates a very bleak universe.*

university noun universities
a place where students study subjects at a high level or where they carry out research (detailed studies of a particular subject) in order to get a qualification. Students usually go to university soon after they leave school but sometimes they go when they are older.

unjust adjective
1 if something is unjust, it is not reasonable or right *an unjust decision*
2 if someone is unjust, they do not treat people in a good and reasonable way *an unjust ruler*
unjustly adverb

unkind adjective unkinder, unkindest
1 if someone is unkind, they are unpleasant, unfriendly or cruel
2 also used about someone's words or actions *an unkind remark*
unkindly adverb **unkindness** noun

unknowingly adverb
if you do something unknowingly, you do it without knowing it or noticing it

unknown adjective
used about someone or something that people don't know or don't know anything about *An unknown number of people were hurt in the crash. He's an unknown actor* (not famous). *A few years ago this problem was unknown* (it didn't exist). *These facts were unknown to most people.*

unleaded adjective
used for describing petrol that is less harmful because it does not contain any added chemical substances made from lead (a metal). Lead can cause pollution.

unless conjunction
used for saying that something must happen before something else can happen *I won't tell you my secret unless you tell me yours.*

unlike preposition
1 used for showing that something or someone is different from something or someone else *The book was unlike anything I'd read before. You're really unlike your dad. Unlike me, Seema can play the piano.*
2 used about something that someone does or says or something that happens that you wouldn't expect *It's very unlike Jon to forget his schoolbag.*

unlike adjective
different *My brother and I are as unlike as can be.*

unlike verb
unlikes, unliking, unliked
if you unlike something on a website such as Facebook, you click on or touch an icon to show that you no longer think it is good or interesting

unlikely adjective unlikelier, unlikeliest
1 if something is unlikely, it will probably not happen or it is probably not true *It's unlikely that I'll finish my homework before the weekend. What an unlikely excuse!*
2 used about something or someone that you wouldn't normally think of, for example as being suitable for something *an unlikely place to build a house; an unlikely candidate for a job; an unlikely cause*

unlimited adjective
used when you mean that as much of something as possible exists or is allowed (or as many things as possible exist or are allowed) *a ticket for unlimited travel on the underground; unlimited access to the internet; Be quick – my time is not unlimited.*

unload verb
unloads, unloading, unloaded
1 if you unload something such as a car or ship, you take the things it is carrying out of it or off it
2 if you unload things such as boxes or goods, you take them out of or off something such as a car or ship

unlock–unskilled

3 to take something out of a piece of equipment, for example when you've finished using it *I unloaded the washing machine* (took out the clothes). *The soldiers unloaded their guns* (took out the bullets).

unlock *verb*
unlocks, unlocking, unlocked
if you unlock something such as a door or suitcase, you open it by turning the key in the lock

unluckily *adverb*
used about something bad or unpleasant that happens *Unluckily for Oliver, there weren't any chocolates left.*

unlucky *adjective* **unluckier, unluckiest**
1 having a bad thing or bad things happen to you for no particular reason *We were unlucky with the weather – it rained all day.*
2 happening because of bad luck *Slipping on the ice was an unlucky accident.*
3 bringing bad luck *Thirteen is my unlucky number.*

unmistakable *adjective*
used about something that you recognise very easily because it is different from all other things *I heard Emma's unmistakable voice.* **unmistakably** *adverb*

unnatural *adjective*
used for describing something that is very strange and doesn't seem normal
unnaturally *adverb*

unnecessary *adjective*
1 used about something that is not needed or that doesn't have to happen or be done *an unnecessary journey*; *I got rid of the unnecessary files on my computer.*
2 used about something that should not be done, said or used because it is unkind or not right *That remark was unnecessary.*
unnecessarily *adverb*

unnoticed *adverb*
without being noticed *I got back into the classroom unnoticed.*

unoccupied *adjective*
1 used about something such as a room, building or toilet that is not being used by anyone
2 used about a seat that no-one is sitting in

unofficial *adjective*
1 used about something that does not have proper permission or agreement from important people such as people in a government, a school or the police *unofficial test results*
2 done by important people but not as part of their job *The prime minister paid an unofficial visit to Spain.*

unpack *verb*
unpacks, unpacking, unpacked
to take things out of a container such as a suitcase or bag *We haven't unpacked the bags yet. Have you unpacked the shopping?*

unpaid *adjective*
1 used for describing someone who doesn't get paid for something or hasn't been paid yet *an unpaid helper*
2 used for describing something such as work that you are not paid for *unpaid work*

unpin *verb*
unpins, unpinning, unpinned
on a computer, if you unpin an icon or symbol from a part of the screen such as a taskbar (strip along the bottom), you remove it from there so that it can no longer be used as a shortcut to open a program

unpleasant *adjective*
1 used about something you don't like or you don't think is good *The weather was unpleasant.*
2 not friendly or helpful *Your friend was unpleasant to me.* '*No,' he said in an unpleasant voice.*
3 angry or violent *Someone threw a stone and things got unpleasant.*
unpleasantly *adverb*

unpleasantness *noun*
a situation where people are angry, upset or violent

unplug *verb*
unplugs, unplugging, unplugged
if you unplug something such as a piece of equipment, you remove the plug that connects it to the electricity or to another piece of equipment

unpopular *adjective*
if something or someone is unpopular, not many people like them
unpopularity *noun*

unpredictable *adjective*
1 used about something that keeps changing without following any regular pattern *unpredictable weather*
2 used about someone when you don't know how they will behave in a certain situation, or about the behaviour of this type of person

unravel *verb*
unravels, unravelling, unravelled
1 if you unravel something such as a piece of clothing or string, you separate the threads it is made of
2 if something unravels, the threads become separated *My sock is beginning to unravel.*
3 if you unravel something such as a mystery or problem, you solve it by gradually understanding more about it

unread ['un-red'] *adjective*
used about something such as a book or email that has not been read *You have two unread messages in your inbox.*

unreal *adjective*
1 used about something that is very strange or unusual, as if it exists only in the imagination
2 not connected to any real situation *unreal expectations*
3 (informal) used about something or someone that you think is really good or really surprising *That film was unreal!*

unreasonable *adjective*
used about something that is not based on good judgement or someone who is not sensible or fair *unreasonable behaviour*; *Don't be so unreasonable.*
unreasonably *adverb*

unreliable *adjective*
1 if someone is unreliable, you can't trust them to behave well or work well or do what they should do *This plumber is very unreliable.*

2 if something such as a piece of equipment, method or test is unreliable, you can't trust it to work well *an unreliable bus service*
3 used for describing something such as information or a book that you can't trust to be good or correct *unreliable facts*

unrest *noun*
a situation in which people are angry or violent

unroll *verb*
unrolls, unrolling, unrolled
to open something that is rolled up and make it flat, for example a piece of carpet or a sleeping bag

unruly *adjective* **unrulier, unruliest**
if someone is unruly, or if their behaviour is unruly, they behave badly and are difficult to control *an unruly class*
unruliness *noun*

unsafe *adjective*
1 used about a place where something bad or dangerous can happen *This park is unsafe after dark.*
2 used about something or someone that can cause harm or danger or make something bad happen *an unsafe car*; *an unsafe driver*; *It's unsafe to eat a raw egg.*
3 used about someone or something not protected from bad things happening to them *We were unsafe travelling in that old lorry.*

unsanitary *adjective*
dirty and likely to make you ill *unsanitary toilets*; *unsanitary conditions*

unsatisfactory *adjective*
not good enough or not as good as expected *unsatisfactory homework*; *unsatisfactory behaviour*

unscrew *verb*
unscrews, unscrewing, unscrewed
1 to unscrew something such as the lid of a jar or the top of a bottle is to turn it until it comes off
2 to unscrew something that is fixed with screws is to turn the screws until they come out

unseemly *adjective*
not right or polite, or not suitable for a particular occasion *unseemly behaviour*; *He left in unseemly haste* (rushed off quickly in a way that seemed rude).

unseen *adjective & adverb*
1 not seen
2 without being seen *I crept out of the room unseen.*

unselfish *adjective*
1 if someone is unselfish, they care more about other people than about themselves
2 also used about something that shows that someone is unselfish *unselfish behaviour*
unselfishly *adverb* **unselfishness** *noun*

unsightly *adjective*
not pleasant to look at *There were unsightly piles of rubbish in the front garden.*

unskilled *adjective*
1 not having any special knowledge or skill *an unskilled worker*

2 not needing people with special knowledge or skill *unskilled work*

unsound *adjective*
1 used about something that you cannot trust to be good or correct *unsound advice; an unsound argument*
2 not in good condition *Poor Mr Chopra's heart is unsound.*

unspeakable *adjective*
if something is unspeakable, it is so bad that it is impossible to describe it in words

unsteady *adjective*
unsteadier, unsteadiest
1 moving or shaking and not likely to stay in one position *Great-Granddad's hand is very unsteady.*
2 shaking or likely to fall over *an unsteady ladder; My baby sister is unsteady on her feet.*
3 not following a regular pattern *unsteady breathing; an unsteady voice*
unsteadily *adverb*

unsubscribe *verb*
unsubscribes, unsubscribing, unsubscribed
if someone unsubscribes from an internet mailing list (list of people that emails are sent to), they remove their email address so as not to receive any more messages
compare: **subscribe** (sense 3)

unsuccessful *adjective*
1 used for showing that something that happens is not what you wanted to happen or that something you get is not what you wanted to get *Dad tried starting the car in the snow but was unsuccessful.*
2 used for showing that you don't do something well or are not good at something *My uncle was an unsuccessful businessman.*
3 used about something that produces bad results or doesn't do what it is supposed to do very well *an unsuccessful plan; an unsuccessful book*
unsuccessfully *adverb*

unsuitable *adjective*
used about something that is not right or good for someone or for a particular purpose *You're wearing unsuitable clothes for this weather.* **unsuitably** *adverb*

unsupported *adjective*
if something such as a computer program is unsupported, software updates (improvements) are no longer provided to keep it working properly

unsure *adjective*
if you're unsure about something, there is something about it that you don't know, for example if it has happened or if it is true or correct or the reason for it or whether you should do it *I'm unsure about the date. I'm unsure whether or not to go to Tim's party.*

unthinkable *adjective*
if something is unthinkable, it is so unlikely, bad or strange that you can't imagine it happening, being done or being accepted *Such bad test results would have been unthinkable at my old school.*

untick *verb*
unticks, unticking, unticked
to remove the tick from something such as a piece of software or web page, usually to show that you don't want something

untidy *adjective* untidier, untidiest
1 not arranged or done in a careful way and not looking very nice *an untidy room*
2 an untidy person is someone who does not like to arrange things in a careful way *Sam is really untidy* (for example leaving things lying around in different places).
untidily *adverb* **untidiness** *noun*

untie *verb*
unties, untying, untied
1 to take out the knot that is tying something *I untied my shoelaces and took off my shoes. Can you untie this knot?*
2 to remove the string, ribbon or rope that is tying something or someone *I untied my birthday present. Untie the prisoner and let him go free.*

until *preposition & conjunction*
1 continuing to happen or be done up to the time mentioned *We played football until two o'clock. Wait until I get back.*
2 continuing up to a particular place *Stay on this train until York.*

untimely *adjective*
1 used for describing something bad that happens earlier than it should *an untimely death*
2 used for describing something that happens at a bad time *an untimely visit*

untold *adjective*
1 used for saying that something is really bad *Smoking can cause untold damage.*
2 used for saying there is so much of something that it cannot be described or there are such large numbers that they cannot be counted *Scotland has untold riches. Untold numbers of people have been killed in wars.*

untoward *adjective*
unexpected and usually unpleasant *Nothing untoward happened.*

untrue *adjective*
used for describing something that is not based on a real situation, or for describing something that did not happen *These facts are untrue. It's untrue to say that I don't like maths.*

unusable *adjective*
not good enough to be used *This mobile phone is old and unusable.*

unused ['un-yoozd'] *adjective*
if something is unused, it has never been used or is not used now *unused tickets; This part of the school is unused.*

unused ['un-yoost'] *adjective*
if you are unused to something, it feels strange to you or you are not sure about it or not sure what to do, for example because you have never done it or known it before *We were unused to the hot Spanish summers.*

unusual *adjective*
1 different from what is normal or expected *I heard an unusual noise. It's unusual for Razia to be late.*
2 different in a way that is interesting, or different from and better than other things or people *Her dress has an unusual pattern. Einstein was a man of unusual intelligence.*

unusually *adverb*
1 showing the way something is when it is different from what is normal or expected (for example bigger or smaller, higher or lower), or showing the way someone is when they have more of a quality than is normal or expected *an unusually cold winter; an unusually intelligent person*
2 showing something that doesn't normally happen *Unusually for this time of year, people were walking around in shorts.*

unwanted *adjective*
used about something you don't want *an unwanted gift; Do you know how to block unwanted emails?*

unwelcome *adjective*
1 used about something unpleasant that you don't want or like *an unwelcome visit from a police officer*
2 used about someone that you don't want to come, for example to your home, or that you don't want to be with *an unwelcome guest*

unwell *adjective*
feeling ill

unwieldy *adjective*
heavy or large and difficult to move or carry *an unwieldy package*

unwilling *adjective*
if you are unwilling to do something, you don't want to do it **unwillingness** *noun*

unwillingly *adverb*
if you do something unwillingly, you do it even though you don't want to

unwind ['wind' rhymes with 'kind'] *verb*
unwinds, unwinding, unwound ['wound' rhymes with 'sound']
1 if you unwind something such as a cable or bandage, you undo it and stop it from being wrapped or twisted around something
2 if something unwinds, it becomes undone and stops being wrapped or twisted around something
3 (informal) if you unwind, you relax, usually after working hard or after a difficult or worrying period

unwise *adjective*
1 used about something that is not sensible or based on reason *un unwise decision*
2 used about someone who does something that is not sensible *She was very unwise to accept that invitation.*
unwisely *adverb*

unwittingly *adverb*
if you do something unwittingly, you do it without knowing it or without realising it is happening to you

unworthy *adjective*
1 not deserving something, or not good enough to have something good happen to you *That bully is completely unworthy of respect. I came top in the test but I feel unworthy because I didn't work much.*
2 used for talking about something that is not good enough or suitable for someone *This behaviour is completely unworthy of you, Jacob.*

unwrap *verb*
unwraps, unwrapping, unwrapped
to remove something such as the paper, plastic or cloth that covers something *It's time to unwrap your birthday presents.*

unzip – upright

unzip verb
unzips, unzipping, unzipped
1 if you unzip something such as a suitcase or dress, or if it unzips, you open it by undoing the zip (object with tiny points that fit together to close something)
2 to unzip a computer file is to make it go back to its full size after it has been made smaller using a special program

up adverb & preposition
1 to a higher position or level *You're slouching – sit up! I climbed up the ladder.*
2 in a higher position or level *The tent is up again. We're up the hill.*
3 to or in a standing position *Stand up! I saw her standing up by the door.*
4 not in bed any more *Will you get up now? I've been up for ages.*
5 going close to or all the way to something or someone *I walked up to the window. A stranger came up to me in the street.*
6 used about a place that is close by *There were lots of police officers up at the cinema.*
7 along *I bumped into my teacher walking up Charing Cross Road.*
8 towards the north *My friend is up from Brighton* (has travelled from Brighton to a place that is north of Brighton).
9 all the way to a particular time, number or amount *We lived in Paris from May up to August* (or *up until August*). *Can you count up to a hundred?*
10 used when you mean something is more than before *Turn the TV up* (make it louder). *I turned the heating up* (made it warmer). *Prices have gone up* (they are higher).
11 used for saying that someone does something completely, for example so there is nothing left, or that something happens completely *Eat up the rest of your ice cream. You've used up the battery. My cut has healed up* (there is no mark left to see).
12 in pieces *Dad tore up the letter. Cut up your old library card when you get the new one.*
13 used about a period of time that is finished *Time's up – hand in your maths tests now!*
14 (informal) used for saying that something is happening or for asking about something happening *There's nothing up. What's up?*
15 (informal) used when talking or asking about something bad such as a problem or pain *Chloe's crying. – What's up with her?* (What's wrong with her?)
16 if you say something is up to someone, you mean it will happen only if that person makes a decision and allows it to happen *'Shall we go swimming or play football?' – 'That's up to you.'*
17 (informal) **to be up to something** to be doing something, often something you think might be secret or bad *What are those two boys up to?*
18 up against something or **someone** in a difficult situation where you must deal with big problems if you want to be successful *Our team is up against the best footballers in the county.*
19 up to date very modern or using the most modern equipment and latest ideas, or using or having the latest information *The school's computers are up to date. The prices on the website are up to date* (the latest prices). *My parents are up to date with the latest news about the accident.*

up noun
ups and downs used for talking about both the good and the bad things that happen in a particular situation or period or in someone's life

upbringing noun
used for talking about the way a child's parents, or someone else in charge of a child, has taken care of the child and educated him or her *Patrick had a Catholic upbringing.*

update ['up-dayt'] verb
updates, updating, updated
1 to make something more modern, for example a document, website or piece of software, by adding the latest information or design *Click here to update your program to the latest version.*
2 to become more modern by adding the latest information or design *The software updates automatically.*
3 to make something more modern by adding or buying new parts or products *Our school has just updated all the computers* (for example, it has bought more modern ones or changed an old operating system to a new one). *Mum and Dad are updating our kitchen* (for example, they are buying a new fridge and a more modern microwave).
4 to give someone the latest information about something *Please update me about what's happening.*

update ['up-dayt'] noun updates
1 used for talking about new information about something *There are regular news updates about the crash. We don't know what's happening – please give us an update.*
2 a piece of software with the latest changes and improvements to a program *The updates to your operating system have been installed successfully.*
3 making something more modern by adding or buying new parts or products *Our kitchen has just had an update.*

upgrade ['up-grayd'] verb
upgrades, upgrading, upgraded
1 to add parts or information to something such as a piece of equipment or software to make it more powerful or work better *Dad upgraded my laptop memory* (installed more memory).
2 to make something more modern, for example by getting new computers or better equipment *Our school's network is being upgraded. Daljit has upgraded his flat by getting new windows.*

upgrade ['up-grayd'] noun upgrades
1 a piece of software or equipment for making something such as a computer or program more powerful or work better
2 making something more modern *Daljit's flat has had an upgrade.*

upheaval noun upheavals
a very big change that causes problems and confusion

uphill adjective & adverb
1 up a slope *an uphill climb; Running uphill is hard work.*
2 needing a lot of effort to be successful *For Harry, learning maths is an uphill struggle.*

uphold verb
upholds, upholding, upheld
to support something because you think it is good or right *The judge upheld the jury's decision. It's a police officer's duty to uphold the law.*

upholstery noun
the cloth, leather and all the soft material that covers furniture such as armchairs and sofas

upkeep noun
1 work done to look after something such as a building so that it stays in good condition, and the cost of doing this
2 the cost of providing a person or animal with what they need to live *Even though Dad doesn't live with us, he pays towards our upkeep.*

uplands noun plural
an area of land with lots of hills

upload ['up-lohd'] verb
uploads, uploading, uploaded
if you upload software or if software uploads, you copy it or move it from your computer to the internet or to another computer

upload ['up-lohd'] noun uploads
uploading a file or program *The upload was successful.*

upon preposition
1 another way of saying on *There was snow upon the ground. Upon hearing the news we all started clapping.*
2 used for showing a large number of something *We saw nothing but fields for mile upon mile* (miles and miles of fields).

upper adjective
1 above something of the same kind *the upper lip*
2 used about the top part of something *the upper floors of the building*

upper case noun
letters of the alphabet that are written as capital (or large) letters (for example A, B, C, D), not as small letters *Always use an upper case letter at the start of a new sentence.*
compare: **lower case**

upper class noun
a group of people in society who have the highest rank and who have lots of money and land **upper-class** adjective

> LANGUAGE EXTRA you can also say *upper classes*

compare: **middle class** and **working class**

upper school noun upper schools
a school (or part of a school), in some parts of the UK, for students between the ages of about 14 and 18

upright adverb
1 standing or sitting with your back straight *I was standing upright in front of the mirror.*
2 pointing straight up *The bottle is lying on its side – can you put it upright?*

upright – USB

upright *adjective*
1 standing straight up *an upright post*
2 if someone is upright, they are honest and follow standards of good behaviour

uprising *noun* **uprisings**
a fight against a government or against the leaders in charge of a country or region

uproar *noun*
1 a loud and unpleasant noise produced by people shouting because they are very angry about something
2 a feeling of great anger shown by many people

uproot *verb*
uproots, uprooting, uprooted
to pull a plant or tree out of the ground with its roots *There were many trees uprooted by the hurricane.*

upset ['up-set'] *adjective*
1 unhappy, worried or slightly angry *Ruby was upset when her budgie died. I was upset (disappointed) about getting a bad mark in the spelling test. Calling me an idiot made me really upset (angry).*
2 if you have an upset stomach (or tummy), you feel slightly ill because of something you've eaten or drunk

upset ['up-set'] *verb*
upsets, upsetting, upset
1 to make someone unhappy, worried or slightly angry *Her unkind words really upset me. His behaviour was very upsetting.*
2 to accidentally knock over a container and make the liquid or things inside it come out *I upset a glass of milk all over the floor.*
3 to stop something such as a plan from happening in the way it is supposed to *Our holiday plans were upset by my illness* (we had to delay or cancel our holiday because I was ill).

upset ['up-set'] *noun* **upsets**
1 something such as a problem or situation that makes you feel unhappy, worried or slightly angry
2 a feeling of unhappiness, worry or anger
3 an unexpected result in a competition or sport
4 a stomach (or tummy) upset is a slight illness caused by something you've eaten or drunk

upshot *noun*
the final result of something such as a meeting or discussion *Your dad had a word with the head – what was the upshot of that?*

SYNONYM outcome

upside down *adjective & adverb*
1 if something is upside down, the part that should be at the top is at the bottom and the bottom part is at the top *The picture was hanging upside down.*
2 if someone turns a place upside down, they make it very untidy, usually when looking for something or someone

upstairs *adverb*
to or on a higher floor of a building
upstairs *adjective*
upstairs *noun*
the higher floor (or floors) of a building

upstart *noun* **upstarts**
someone new in a job or group who behaves as if they are more important than anyone else

upstate *adjective*
connected with the northern part of a state in the United States *upstate New York*

upstream *adverb*
in the opposite direction to the way that a river flows

upsurge *noun*
a sudden increase in something, for example crime or interest

upthrust *noun*
in science, an upthrust is the upward force from a liquid on the object that floats in it. An object floats when the upthrust balances the weight.

uptight *adjective* (informal)
nervous, worried and often angry *My sister gets really uptight just before exams.*

up-to-date *adjective*
1 very modern or using the most modern equipment and latest ideas *up-to-date computers and software*; *an up-to-date hospital*
2 having or using the latest information *Check the website for up-to-date prices* (the latest prices).

upturned *adjective*
1 pointing upwards *an upturned nose*
2 having the part that should be at the top at the bottom and having the bottom part at the top

SYNONYM for sense 2: upside down

upward *adjective*
going towards a higher level *an upward climb*

upwards *adverb*
towards a higher level *We looked upwards.*

uranium ['yoor-ayn-i-erm'] *noun*
a metal used for producing nuclear energy (energy produced when the structure of an atom is changed by dividing its nucleus)

Uranus ['yoor-er-ners'] *noun*
the seventh planet from the sun. It comes between Saturn and Neptune and is the second furthest one away from the sun.

urban *adjective*
connected with a town or with towns *an urban area*

urchin *noun* **urchins**
used especially in the past for describing a young child, usually one dressed in rags in the street

Urdu ['oor-doo' or 'err-doo'] *noun*
a language similar to Hindi. It is the official language of Pakistan and is spoken also in India.

urge *verb*
urges, urging, urged
1 to tell someone what you think they should do or to say what you think should happen *My parents are urging me to work harder to get better marks. 'Help your sister,' he urged.*
2 to urge someone on is to use words of support and encouragement to tell them to continue doing something

urge *noun* **urges**
a sudden strong feeling of wanting to do something *I felt an urge to yawn.*

urgency *noun*
the need to deal with something or do something immediately or very quickly *He was taken to hospital as a matter of urgency* (immediately).

urgent *adjective*
if something is urgent, you need to deal with it or do it immediately or very quickly *an urgent message*; *The school has an urgent need for textbooks.* **urgently** *adverb*

urinate *verb*
urinates, urinating, urinated
to get rid of liquid waste from the body by going to the toilet

urine ['yoor-in'] *noun*
the liquid waste that your body gets rid of from your bladder

URL ['yoo-ahr-el'] *noun* **URLs**
in computing, a URL is a series of letters, numbers and symbols used for finding a website
short for: uniform (or universal) resource locator

LANGUAGE EXTRA also called a *web address*

urn *noun* **urns**
1 a large metal container used for making tea or coffee and keeping it hot. It is shaped like a cylinder (tube with flat ends shaped like circles) and has a tap on the side for pouring the tea or coffee.
2 a container shaped like a vase, used for storing the ashes of someone who has been cremated (their dead body has been burnt in a special way)

Uruguay ['yoor-er-gwye'] *noun*
a country in South America
Uruguayan *adjective & noun*

us *pronoun*
a word that you use when you are talking about yourself and you also include one or more other people *He didn't see us. Joe was walking in front of us.*

US *noun*
a country in North America
short for: **United States**

USA *noun*
a country in North America
short for: **United States of America**

usable *adjective*
suitable to be used or good enough to be used *The battery is still usable.*

usage *noun* **usages**
1 the way words are used when you speak and write. The rules you use when you speak and write are known as grammar.
2 a particular meaning of a word
3 the amount of something that is used or the way it is used

USB ['yoo-es-bee'] **USBs**
1 a place on the outside of a piece of equipment such as a computer, used for connecting something such as a printer, keyboard or camera using a special cable *a USB port*; *a USB stick* (for plugging into a computer and storing information on)

561

use – U-turn

2 a way of connecting this cable to a computer
3 an informal word for a small piece of equipment such as a flash drive that you plug into a computer using a USB connection
short for: universal serial bus

use ['yooz'] *verb*
uses, using, used
1 if you use something, you do something with it to make something happen *Use this knife to slice the cucumber. We use words for speaking and writing. I use the bus to get to school* (travel on the bus). *Most children know how to use a computer* (make it work). *I'd like to use your idea in my story* (include it).
2 to say or write something such as a particular word or type of language *'Ugly' is a horrible word to use. You use the plural when you mean more than one thing or person.*
3 to take a certain amount of something so the thing it is taken from becomes less *I've used some of the orange juice but left some for you. My laptop uses either electricity or a battery.*
4 if you use something up, you use all of it so there is nothing left *I've used up all my pocket money* (spent it).

use ['yooss'] *noun* **uses**
1 when you use something *The use of a calculator during the test is not allowed. This phone number is for use in emergencies. I went to France to make use of my French* (to use it).
2 the purpose that something is used for *Smartphones have lots of different uses. I don't have any further use for these books.*
3 the way you use something *The word 'take' has many uses.*
4 how much you use something *Our TV has had a lot of use.*
5 used for talking about something useful that helps someone *This old tablet is of no use to me* (it isn't useful). *Is it any use to you?*
6 **no use doing something** used for saying that trying to do something will not be successful *It's no use complaining* (for example because no-one will listen). *They tried to rescue the dog from the sea but it was no use* (for example because they couldn't reach it so it drowned).

used ['yoost'] *verb* (only used in the past)
if something used to happen, it happened in the past, often lots of times or for a certain period of time *I used to play chess on Saturdays. My teacher used to live in Australia.*

used ['yoost'] *adjective*
1 if you are used to something, you think it is normal because you have done it or seen it many times before or have known it for a long time *My sister is a good student and is used to hard work* (or *to working hard*). *I'm used to the damp British winters. I'm getting used to my new school* (it doesn't seem so strange to me any more).
2 if you are used to someone, you have got to know them, for example because you have seen them many times before *My cousin Sharif comes over every day so we're all used to him now.*

used ['yoozd'] *adjective*
if something is used, someone has had it before and used it *a used bike; used clothes*

useful *adjective*
1 if something is useful, it helps you in some way or it helps you a lot *a useful website; We hope this dictionary is very useful. Knowing Spanish might come in useful* (might help in a particular situation).
2 if someone is useful, they help you *My mum was useful to the police officer because she speaks Hindi. Make yourself useful* (do something to help).
usefully *adverb* **usefulness** *noun*

useless *adjective*
1 if something is useless, it doesn't help you in any way, for example because it doesn't do what it is supposed to do or it is not successful *a useless tool; a useless piece of advice; Your phone is useless* (for example because it doesn't work). *I went on a useless trip to the library – it was closed.*
2 if someone is useless, they don't or won't help you *Don't ask Ava – she's useless.*
3 if someone is useless at doing something, they are very bad at doing it *I'm useless at netball.*
uselessly *adverb* **uselessness** *noun*

user *noun* **users**
1 someone who uses something *computer users; Regular users of this dictionary will find lots of fascinating information inside. Our school has a special ramp for wheelchair users.*
2 a user guide is a document that shows you how to use something such as a computer, printer or camera

user-friendly *adjective*
if something such as a computer, website or guidebook is user-friendly, it is easy to use and understand

username *noun* **usernames**
a name or special word that you use with a password to get into a particular website or computer

LANGUAGE EXTRA also spelt *user name*

usher *noun* **ushers**
someone who shows people where to sit, for example in a cinema or theatre or at a wedding

usher *verb*
ushers, ushering, ushered
to make someone go somewhere, usually by going with them *The head teacher ushered us into her office.*

usual *adjective*
1 used for describing something that happens most often or that you do most often *This kind of behaviour is usual in teenagers. I went for my usual walk through the park. This ice cream is smaller than usual* (for example smaller than other ice creams I've bought). *I went to school by bus as usual* (as I do most often).
2 used for describing something or someone that is the same as always *Dad likes to sit in his usual chair. Dr Patel's my usual doctor.*

SYNONYM normal

usually *adverb*
in the way that happens most often *I usually play netball on Saturdays.*

SYNONYM normally

usurp ['yoo-**zerrp**' or 'yoo-**serrp**'] *verb*
usurps, usurping, usurped
to take control of something such as someone's power, job or property by using force *The king's cousin usurped his throne.*

utensil ['yoo-**ten**-serl'] *noun* **utensils**
an object or tool that you use in your home, usually for cooking or eating with. Utensils include knives, forks, spoons, frying pans and saucepans.

utilise *verb*
utilises, utilising, utilised
another way of saying to use
utilisation *noun*

LANGUAGE EXTRA also spelt *utilize* and *utilization*

utmost *adjective*
1 used for talking about the greatest amount of something or for saying how important or serious something is *This message is of the utmost importance. Carry these glasses into the kitchen with the utmost care.*
2 if you do or try your utmost, you try as hard as you can

utopia ['yoo-**toh**-pee-er'] *noun* **utopias**
an imaginary place where everything is perfect and everyone is happy
utopian *adjective*

ORIGIN from the name made up by Sir Thomas More in his 17th-century book *Utopia*

utter *verb*
utters, uttering, uttered
to say a word or make a sound *He left without uttering a word. The dying animal uttered a long cry of pain.*

utter *adjective*
used for giving extra importance to a word, for example when you mean that something or someone is as big or as great as can be *That lesson was an utter waste of time. You're an utter fool!*

SYNONYM complete

utterly *adverb*
used for giving special importance to a word or for saying that something is very true *It's utterly ridiculous. I said hello to him but he utterly ignored me.*

SYNONYM completely

U-turn ['yoo-**terrn**'] *noun* **U-turns**
1 a complete turn someone makes when driving a vehicle or riding a bike, so that they go back in the direction they came from. They turn in half a circle like the letter U.
2 a complete change in someone's ideas or plan

V

V v

ORIGIN V, F, U and W all come from the same letter in the Phoenician alphabet – a shape that looked like the letter Y and represented either a peg or a hook. It had the sound of 'w' and was called *waw*. The shape of the letter V has not changed much since then. When the Phoenician Y passed into Latin, the Romans removed its stem to create the V shape we know today. It had either a 'u' sound, as in *TEMPVS* ('time'), or a 'w' sound, as in *VIDI* ('I saw'). In Latin, V and U had the same 'u' and 'w' sounds so the Romans could also write *TEMPUS* and *UIDI*.

V
the Roman numeral for the number 5

vacancy *noun* **vacancies**
1 a room that is not being used, for example in a hotel, so that someone can stay there *No vacancies* (sign at a hotel showing that it's full).
2 a job, for example in an office, shop or factory, that is not being done by anyone so someone needs to be found who will do it *There's a vacancy for a maths teacher in our school.*

vacant *adjective*
1 used about something such as a room, toilet or hospital bed that is not being used
2 used about a seat that no-one is sitting in
3 used about a job that no-one is doing and that needs someone to do it
4 used about an empty or stupid look on someone's face that shows they are not interested in anything or thinking about anything in particular *Granddad was looking out of the window with a vacant stare.* **vacantly** *adverb*

vacate *verb*
vacates, vacating, vacated
1 to leave something such as a room or seat so that someone else can use it or sit in it
2 to leave a job so someone else needs to be found who will do it

vacation *noun* **vacations**
a holiday *the summer vacation*; *Ravi's going on vacation to Florida.*

LANGUAGE EXTRA used especially in American English

vaccinate ['vak-sin-ayt'] *verb*
vaccinates, vaccinating, vaccinated
if a doctor or nurse vaccinates you, they stop you from getting an illness by putting a vaccine (weak form of the germ that causes the illness) into your body, usually by touching your skin with a special needle *Have you been vaccinated against measles?*
vaccination *noun*

vaccine ['vak-seen'] *noun* **vaccines**
a substance that contains a weak form of the germ that causes a particular illness. It is put into people's bodies to stop them from getting the illness.

ORIGIN from Latin *vaccina* 'connected with cows' (Latin *vacca* 'cow'). In the 18th century, Dr Edward Jenner used cows to make a vaccine to protect people against smallpox.

vacuum ['vak-yoo-erm'] *noun* **vacuums**
1 a space that contains no air or any other gas so that it is completely empty
2 a vacuum cleaner is a piece of equipment for cleaning carpets and floors. It uses air to suck up dust and dirt.

SYNONYM hoover

3 a vacuum flask is a container shaped like a tube, with hollow walls that have no air between them. It is used for keeping liquids hot or cold.

SYNONYM Thermos flask

vacuum ['vak-yoo-erm'] *verb*
vacuums, vacuuming, vacuumed
to clean a carpet or floor with a vacuum cleaner

SYNONYM to hoover

vagina ['ver-jye-ner'] *noun* **vaginas**
a passage in the body of a female person or animal that goes from the outside of the body to the womb (the part where babies develop)

vague *adjective* **vaguer, vaguest**
1 used about something that is not explained clearly or is not easy to understand *The instructions are a little vague.*
2 used when you are not certain about something *a vague memory*; *vague suspicions*; *I'm still a bit vague about which way to go.*
3 not telling someone much about something *Dad's answer was very vague.*
4 used about something such as a feeling that you have only slightly *a vague feeling of dizziness*
vagueness *noun*

vaguely *adverb*
1 in a way that is not clear, for example when you are not certain about something or when something is not easy to understand *I only vaguely remember her. She explained the instructions so vaguely that we still didn't know what to do.*
2 slightly *It was vaguely embarrassing.*
3 without paying attention to what you are doing or saying *He vaguely mentioned something about coming round to see us.*

vain *adjective* **vainer, vainest**
1 someone who is vain has too high an opinion of their own qualities. For example, they think they are very attractive or very intelligent.
2 used about something such as an action, attempt or hope that does not produce the sort of result you want *Dad jumped into the water in a vain effort to save the dog* (his efforts were unsuccessful).
3 **in vain** without having any success *We waited in vain for the bus* (it didn't come).
4 **in vain** also used when you mean for no reason or purpose *The sick boy did not die in vain* (for example, doctors learnt things that helped them cure other people).

vainly *adverb*
1 without having any success *I vainly tried to reinstall the software.*
2 in a way that shows someone thinks too highly about their own qualities *He was looking at himself vainly in the mirror.*

Vaisakhi ['vy-sa-kee'] *noun*
a Sikh festival that takes place in April to celebrate the new year

LANGUAGE EXTRA also spelt *Baisakhi*

valentine *noun* **valentines**
1 a card that someone sends on Valentine's Day
2 the person that someone sends a card to on Valentine's Day

Valentine's Day *noun* **Valentine's Days**
a special day (14 February) when people give cards and presents to people they have (or would like to have) a love relationship with

LANGUAGE EXTRA also called *Saint Valentine's Day*

valiant *adjective*
used about someone (or someone's efforts) to show that they are very brave and that nothing will stop them from doing something that needs to be done *Mum made a valiant attempt to rescue the drowning dog.* **valiantly** *adverb*

valid *adjective*
1 if a document or card or something such as a ticket or passport is valid, it can be officially used and accepted because it has all the correct and latest information on it. It usually has a date on it showing the latest time it can be used. *Your library card isn't valid – it's expired.*
2 allowed by the law or the rules *a valid agreement*; *That's not a valid move in chess.*
3 if something such as a password or filename is valid, it works correctly on a computer
4 if something such as a reason, argument or idea is valid, it is reasonable and acceptable to most people *Oversleeping isn't a valid excuse for being late for school.*
validity *noun*

validate *verb*
validates, validating, validated
1 if someone validates something such as a ticket, token or piece of software, they make it valid so it can be used *You have to validate your bus ticket by putting it in a special machine before you travel.*
2 to show or check that something is true *Ed showed his passport to validate his age.*

valley *noun* **valleys**
a long low area of land between hills, often with a river running through it

valour *noun*
when someone is not afraid to face danger, especially in a battle or war

SYNONYM bravery

valuable – Vaseline

valuable adjective
1 worth a lot of money *a valuable watch*
2 very important and useful *Knowing a foreign language is a valuable skill.*

valuables noun plural
small things that belong to you that are worth a lot of money, for example your watch or your mobile phone

value noun **values**
1 the amount of money that you can get for something *The value of our house has gone up. Property values have fallen. This painting is of great value* (worth a lot of money).
2 used for showing how good or useful something is, especially when you think something is very good or useful or can have a lot of influence *My parents believe in the value of education. A dictionary is a tool of great value. The education at that school is of poor value* (not very good).
3 a value in maths is a number or amount that is represented by a letter or symbol
4 a value in maths is also another way of saying a place value (what a single number is worth depending on its position in a group of numbers)
5 a value in music is the amount of time a note lasts for
6 someone's values are the things or ideas that are very important to them in influencing their behaviour *Dad's values include hard work and respect for others.*

value verb
values, valuing, valued
1 to consider that something is very important and worth having or doing *If you value your health, don't eat so many sweets.*
2 to decide how much money something is worth, for example someone's house or flat

valueless adjective
used about something that is not worth any money (or is hardly worth any money)

valve noun **valves**
1 something that opens and closes to control the flow of liquid or air, usually in a piece of equipment *a safety valve* (letting steam, gas or air escape when there is too much of it)
2 a tube that controls the flow of electricity in old equipment such as radios and TVs

vampire noun **vampires**
in horror stories or films, a dead person who comes out of the grave at night to find living people and to suck their blood

van noun **vans**
a vehicle larger than a car and smaller than a lorry, used for carrying goods or people. It is shaped like a box, usually without any windows in the sides of the back half or at the back. *a delivery van*; *a police van* (for carrying prisoners)

vandal noun **vandals**
someone who deliberately breaks and damages things, for example public buildings such as libraries or phone boxes or vehicles such as trains

> **ORIGIN** the *Vandals* were a group of tribes from Scandinavia who destroyed the city of Rome in the 6th century

vandalise verb
vandalises, vandalising, vandalised
to deliberately break or damage something such as a building or vehicle
vandalism noun

> **LANGUAGE EXTRA** also spelt *vandalize*

vanilla noun
a substance for giving flavour to sweet foods. It comes from the bean of a tropical plant. *vanilla ice cream*

> **ORIGIN** from Spanish *vanilla* 'little pod' (container for seeds on a plant)

vanish verb
vanishes, vanishing, vanished
if someone or something vanishes, they go somewhere where you can't see or find them any more, usually suddenly *Someone rang our doorbell and then mysteriously vanished.*

> **SYNONYM** to disappear

vanity noun
behaviour that shows that someone has too high an opinion of their own qualities. For example, they think they are very attractive or very intelligent.

vanquish verb
vanquishes, vanquishing, vanquished
1 to win a battle or war against someone
2 to do better than someone in a game or competition
3 to deal successfully with something bad *Malaria has not yet been vanquished.*

vaporise verb
vaporises, vaporising, vaporised
to turn from liquid or solid form into a vapour, or to make something do this

> **LANGUAGE EXTRA** also spelt *vaporize*

vapour noun **vapours**
1 tiny drops of liquid in the air, for example made by heating up a liquid or solid
2 a vapour trail is a long white line made by a plane, usually seen against a blue sky. It is made of water vapour.

variable adjective
used about something that changes often or is likely to change *Temperatures have been variable this week.*

variable noun **variables**
1 something that can easily change in a particular situation
2 in maths, a variable is a letter (such as *x* or *y*) or a symbol that represents a number that is not known
3 in science, a variable is something that you can control or change, for example a particular object that you use or something that you do in an experiment

variation noun **variations**
1 a change or difference, for example in an amount or level of something *There are surprising price variations between the different supermarkets. There's a wide variation in the height of my classmates.*
2 used when you mean the same thing as something else but in a slightly different form *The breakfast we had in Spain was a variation on* (or *of*) *the usual one I have at home.*
3 used in biology for talking about the differences between animals or plants of the same species (group). For example, eye colour and hair colour are examples of variation in humans.

varied adjective
1 made up of many things, for example of different types, sizes or amounts *a varied diet* (lots of different types of food); *There were many varied opinions.*
2 made up of many different types of people *a varied group of students*

variety noun
1 a group of different things of the same type *Leeds has a wide variety of good places to eat. Aziz wants to change schools for a variety of reasons* (for many different reasons).
2 used for talking about different types of activities or situations, for example when you mean not always doing or having the same thing *It was an adventure holiday full of variety. Our lessons are boring – we need more variety in them.*
3 (plural **varieties**) a particular type of something that is different from other types *Nan planted three varieties of apple tree in her garden.*
4 a type of show, for example in a theatre or on TV, that includes many short performances, for example of singing, dancing, magic and acting

various adjective
used when you mean several different things or people *Pupils at our school come from various countries. Various people were waiting to get on the bus.*

variously adverb
in different ways *Our teacher has been described variously as hard-working, understanding and strict.*

varnish noun **varnishes**
a transparent liquid that you paint onto wood and other materials to make them look shiny and attractive and to protect them *For special occasions, Mum paints her nails with nail varnish.*

varnish verb
varnishes, varnishing, varnished
to paint something with varnish, for example wood

vary verb
varies, varying, varied
1 if things of the same type vary, they are different from each other *Prices vary in different parts of the country.*
2 if something varies, it changes or changes often *Temperatures vary a lot from day to day.*
3 if you vary something, you change it or change it often *It's healthy to vary your diet* (eat lots of different things).

vase noun **vases**
a container for holding flowers that have been cut from a plant. Vases come in different colours, shapes and sizes, for example round and bulging like a bulb.

Vaseline ['vas-er-leen' or 'vas-er-**leen**'] noun (trademark)
an oily substance that you rub onto your skin, for example if your skin is dry or sore

564

vast – vent

vast *adjective*
extremely large *The universe is vast. The vast majority of people* (almost everyone) *in that country are poor.* **vastness** *noun*

vastly *adverb*
1 extremely *My brother and I are vastly different from each other.*
2 very much *My sister is vastly more intelligent than I am.*

vat *noun* **vats**
a large container for storing liquid, for example in a factory

VAT ['vat' or 'vee-ay-tee'] *noun*
a tax on things that you buy
short for: value-added tax

Vatican *noun*
the home in Rome of the Pope (person in charge of the Roman Catholic Church) and the centre and main offices of the Roman Catholic Church

ORIGIN from Latin *mons Vaticanus* 'Vatican hill' – the hill where the Pope's palace stands

vault *noun* **vaults**
1 a room with thick walls and a strong door, usually in a bank, for storing money, valuable objects such as jewellery, and important documents
2 a roof or ceiling with a curved top, for example in a cathedral
3 a room underneath a church or in a cemetery where people are buried *a family vault*
4 the action of jumping over something, using your hands or a pole to push yourself over it

vault *verb*
vaults, vaulting, vaulted
to jump over something by running towards it and putting your hands on it or using a pole to push yourself over it *Raj vaulted over a fallen tree trunk.*

VCR *noun* **VCRs**
a piece of electrical equipment for recording TV programmes and playing them back or for playing videos (magnetic tapes with sounds and pictures), especially films. VCRs were used mainly in the past.
short for: video cassette recorder

veal *noun*
the meat from a calf (young cow) that is eaten as food. Veal comes mainly from male calves.

Veda ['vay-der'] *noun* **Vedas**
an ancient piece of writing that is an important part of the Hindu religion

veer *verb*
veers, veering, veered
to change direction or move to the left or right, usually suddenly, used for example when talking about a vehicle or the wind *A motorbike veered across the road right in front of us.*

veg ['vej'] *noun plural*
an informal word for vegetables

vegan ['vee-gern'] *noun* **vegans**
someone who doesn't eat meat or fish or any food that comes from animals or insects such as eggs, milk, butter or honey. Vegans don't use any animal products such as leather (from the skin of cows or other animals) or silk (from the threads of silkworms).

vegetable *noun* **vegetables**
a plant or a part of a plant (such as a seed or root) that is used as food, for example a potato, cabbage or carrot

vegetarian *noun* **vegetarians**
someone who doesn't eat meat or fish

vegetarian *adjective*
1 connected with food that doesn't contain meat or fish *a vegetarian diet* (for example fruit and vegetables)
2 connected with people who don't eat meat or fish *a vegetarian restaurant*

vegetation *noun*
plants and trees that are growing somewhere

veggie burger *noun* **veggie burgers**
a round flat cake made from tiny pieces of vegetables pressed together. It is fried and eaten in a bread roll.

vehicle *noun* **vehicles**
a machine with wheels and an engine, used for carrying people or things from one place to another, usually on a road or track. Cars, buses, lorries, motorcycles and trains are vehicles.

veil [rhymes with 'sail'] *noun* **veils**
a piece of cloth that covers a woman's face or head. Veils are made of thin cloth that you can see through or heavy cloth that hides the face and head completely.

veiled [rhymes with 'sailed'] *adjective*
covered with a veil *a veiled woman*

vein *noun* **veins**
1 a very thin tube that carries blood around your body and to your heart
2 a thin line on a leaf or on an insect's wing
3 a line or curve that is of a different colour from the areas next to it, for example on marble, cheese or wood
4 a layer of something such as metal inside a rock

Velcro *noun* (trademark)
a special cloth used for opening and closing something such as a piece of clothing or a bag. It consists of two separate strips, one like velvet and the other made of tiny hooks. You press the two strips together to make them stick to each other.

ORIGIN from French *velours* 'velvet' (Vel) and *crochet* 'hook' (cro)

velociraptor ['ver-los-ee-rap-ter'] *noun* **velociraptors**
a small dinosaur that moved very fast. It stood and walked on its two back legs and had a very long tail. It ate other animals, not plants.

velocity *noun*
the speed at which something moves. You use this word especially in science. *wind velocity*

ORIGIN from Latin *velox* 'quick'

velodrome *noun* **velodromes**
a building or track used for cycle racing

velvet *noun*
a cloth, made for example from cotton or silk, that is soft and thick on one side and smooth on the other

velvety *adjective*
if something is velvety, it feels very soft and pleasant

vendetta *noun* **vendettas**
a very bad and often violent quarrel between two people or groups that lasts for a long time

ORIGIN from Italian *vendetta* 'revenge'

vending machine *noun*
vending machines
a machine that you put a coin (or coins) into to buy something, for example a sandwich, drink, ticket or newspaper

vendor *noun* **vendors**
someone who sells something, often in the street *an ice cream vendor*

venerable *adjective*
1 if someone is venerable, they are usually old and people respect them because of their importance, wisdom or excellent character
2 if something is venerable, it is usually old and people respect it because of its high quality *a venerable tradition*

Venezuela ['ven-er-zway-ler'] *noun*
a country in South America
Venezuelan *adjective & noun*

vengeance *noun*
1 used about something very bad that you do to someone or that you want to do to someone because they have done something bad to you
2 **with a vengeance** in a very strong way or much more strongly than expected *The rain stopped in the morning but in the afternoon it came back with a vengeance* (it rained much more heavily).

vengeful *adjective*
wanting to do something very bad to someone because they have done something bad to you

venison *noun*
the meat from a deer that is eaten as food

Venn diagram *noun* **Venn diagrams**
a diagram in maths that uses a circle or circles inside a rectangle for grouping numbers or objects and showing how they are connected to each other. The circles often overlap (part of one covers part of another) to show numbers and objects that belong together.
compare: Carroll diagram

ORIGIN invented by the mathematician John *Venn* in about 1904

venom *noun*
1 a substance produced by certain animals and insects, for example snakes, scorpions and spiders, to kill or harm other animals or insects by biting or stinging them
2 a feeling of great anger towards someone
venomous *adjective*

vent *noun* **vents**
1 a small hole in something such as a wall or container that allows air, smoke, gas or smells to escape or allows fresh air to come in *My bedroom has two air vents.*

565

vent – vertigo

2 to give vent to something to show a feeling strongly, especially a feeling of anger *The football fans gave vent to their anger by stamping their feet and shaking their fists.*

vent *verb*
vents, venting, vented
to show a strong feeling, especially one of anger, and direct that feeling onto someone *He vented his anger on me.*

ventilate *verb*
ventilates, ventilating, ventilated
to allow fresh air to get into a room or building, for example by keeping windows and doors open **ventilation** *noun*

ventilator *noun* **ventilators**
1 a piece of equipment that helps someone to breathe by pushing air into and out of their lungs
2 a machine or object for allowing fresh air into a room or building

ventriloquist ['ven-tril-er-kwist'] *noun* **ventriloquists**
someone who performs in front of an audience by speaking without moving their lips and making it appear that the words are spoken by a puppet or dummy (toy model of a person or animal)
ventriloquism *noun*

venture *noun* **ventures**
a new, exciting and important activity or piece of work that someone starts, especially one where someone is not sure what is going to happen in the future

venture *verb*
ventures, venturing, ventured
1 to go somewhere when it could be dangerous *My sister doesn't like to venture out at night because our road has no streetlights.*
2 to go somewhere you don't usually go, for example somewhere you're not allowed to go or somewhere unusual or unpleasant, especially when you need to be brave to go there *Mum doesn't want anyone venturing into Dad's study while he's working. It was exciting venturing into a museum for the first time on our own.*

venue ['ven-yoo] *noun* **venues**
a place where an event or activity happens *The school has changed the venue of tonight's concert.*

Venus *noun*
one of the planets. It is the second closest one to the sun, between Mercury and the earth.

veranda ['ver-ran-der] *noun* **verandas**
an area with a roof along the outside wall of a house. A veranda is either open or has a wall or a low wooden structure like a fence going round it.

> **LANGUAGE EXTRA** also spelt *verandah*

> **ORIGIN** from Hindi *veranda* 'railing' or 'veranda'

verb *noun* **verbs**
a word used for showing what someone or something does (for example 'jump', 'eat', 'touch'), what happens or exists (for example 'happen', 'be', 'have') or what goes on in the mind (for example 'think', 'feel', 'know')

> **LANGUAGE EXTRA** verbs have different forms depending on how they are used. For example, they can be used in the singular (*my hat is red, I have an idea, she has an idea*) or the plural (*my hats are red, they have an idea*). They can also be used in the present tense (*I work, he works, I am working, he is working*), past tense (*we worked, we were working*) or future tense (*they will work, they will be working*).
> Verbs can be used in a transitive or intransitive way. A transitive verb has a direct object (noun or pronoun that receives the direct action), for example *I heard a noise*. An intransitive verb has no object, for example *I can't hear*.

verbal *adjective*
1 used about something that is said or spoken but not written *a verbal warning*
2 connected with words *verbal skills*
3 verbal reasoning is the skill of thinking in a logical way about how words are used in a piece of writing. You use this skill to do things such as understand meanings and grammar and make correct decisions about the writing. There are exercises to help you develop this skill and tests to help teachers find out how good your skill is.

verbally *adverb*
using spoken words, not writing *Ms Patel warned the class verbally about the dangers of swimming in deep water.*

verdict *noun* **verdicts**
1 a decision about whether someone is guilty or not guilty, made by a jury or judge at the end of a trial in a court of law
2 an official decision made by someone
3 a decision someone makes or an opinion someone gives about something after thinking about it carefully

verge *noun* **verges**
1 an area along the side of a road or path that is covered with grass *a grass verge*
2 **on the verge of** used for saying that something is likely to happen very soon *He was so upset he was on the verge of tears* (about to start crying).

verge *verb*
verges, verging, verged
if something verges on something else, it comes very close to being that particular thing, often something bad *His behaviour towards the teacher was verging on disrespect.*

verify *verb*
verifies, verifying, verified
1 to show that something is true or correct *I presented my passport to verify that I was British. When you sign into the school's website, you have to verify who you are* (show that you are who you say you are).
2 to check to see whether something is true or correct *When you sign up for the school's email, they need to verify your name and address.*
verification *noun*

vermin *noun*
insects or small animals that destroy things such as food or plants or that spread disease. Fleas, cockroaches, mice and rats are vermin.

verruca ['ver-roo-ker] *noun* **verrucas**
a type of wart (hard lump) that grows on your foot or toe, usually on the sole (flat part underneath the foot)

versatile ['verr-ser-tile] *adjective*
1 used about someone who has different skills and can do lots of things *a versatile musician* (for example who can play different instruments and different types of music)
2 used about something that can be used for different things, for example a tool, computer program or piece of clothing *a versatile jacket that can be used in summer or winter*
versatility *noun*

verse *noun* **verses**
1 a group of lines that form one section of a poem or song
2 one of the divisions of a chapter in a holy book, such as the Bible or the Koran, made up of a small group of lines or sentences with a number next to it
3 a piece of writing arranged in lines with a regular pattern of sounds. The lines often end with words that rhyme. *The play is written in verse.*

version *noun* **versions**
1 a form of something that is different from other forms of the same thing *The version of the story that is used in the film is slightly different from the original book.*
2 someone's particular description of something that happens *Let's listen to Yasmin's version of what happened.*

versus ['verr-sis' or 'verr-sers'] *preposition*
used for saying that two people, groups or teams are playing against each other in a game or match *Tomorrow's match will be Chelsea versus Manchester United.*

vertebra ['verr-ter-brer] *noun*
vertebrae ['verr-ter-bray]
one of the small round bones that form the backbone (row of bones down the middle of the back)

vertebrate ['verr-tib-rert' or 'verr-tib-rayt'] *noun* **vertebrates**
an animal with a backbone (row of bones down the middle of the back). Vertebrates include humans, mammals, birds and fish.
compare: **invertebrate**

vertex *noun*
vertices ['verr-ti-seez] or **vertexes**
in maths, a vertex is a corner or point where two or more straight lines meet in a shape such as a square, triangle or cube

vertical *adjective*
pointing or going straight up from a surface. Something is horizontal when it is straight and goes in the same direction as a level surface or the ground. *a vertical line; a vertical take-off* (when a plane moves straight up into the air) **vertically** *adverb*

vertigo *noun*
a feeling as if things are going round and round in your head and that you might fall. It is caused by being in a place that is high up such as the top of a tall building.

very *adverb*
used in front of an adjective or adverb to make its meaning stronger and to say it is more or greater in some way. For example, if you are 'very pleased', you are more pleased than just 'pleased'. *a very clever pupil*; *very slowly*; *That was the very first thing we did.*

very *adjective*
1 used about something or someone when you mean exactly that thing or person and no other *Here's the very boy I want to talk to. Those were his very words.*
2 if someone or something is the very opposite, they are completely different *I'm the very opposite of my sister.*
3 used when you mean exactly at a particular place or time, usually right at the end or beginning *I was at the very back of the queue. At the very start there were not many people at the party.*
4 used for making a meaning stronger, for showing the importance of something or for showing that something is really true *His very life was in danger. The very thought of that house makes me tremble.*

Vesak ['ves-ak'] *noun*
an important Buddhist festival in April or May. It celebrates the birth and death of the Indian philosopher Siddhartha Gautama (563–483 BC), also known as Buddha, who founded Buddhism.

LANGUAGE EXTRA also spelt *Wesak*

vessel *noun* **vessels**
1 a ship or large boat
2 a container for liquids, for example a bowl, pot or cup
3 a vessel or blood vessel is one of the narrow tubes in your body that blood flows through

vest *noun* **vests**
1 a piece of underwear for the top half of your body, usually without sleeves, worn for example under a shirt
2 the American word for a waistcoat (clothing without sleeves worn over a shirt)

vestige ['vest-ij'] *noun* **vestiges**
a small amount of something that still exists after most of the rest of it has disappeared

vestments *noun plural*
special clothes worn by a Christian priest during a ceremony in a church

vestry *noun* **vestries**
a room in a church where priests put on their special clothes and where they store the things they need for ceremonies

vet *noun* **vets**
a doctor for animals
short for: veterinary surgeon

veteran *noun* **veterans**
1 someone who has been doing a particular job or activity for a very long time *a veteran film-maker*
2 someone who was in a country's army, navy or air force in the past, especially during a war

veterinary *adjective*
connected with the medical treatment of animals *a veterinary hospital* (one for animals)

veto ['vee-toh'] *noun* **vetoes**
1 an official refusal to allow something to happen
2 the right that someone has to officially refuse to allow something to happen

veto ['vee-toh'] *verb*
vetoes, vetoing, vetoed
to officially refuse to allow something to happen, for example a plan or suggestion

ORIGIN from Latin *veto* 'I forbid' or 'I say no'

vex *verb*
vexes, vexing, vexed
to make someone slightly angry, worried or confused **vexation** *noun*

via [rhymes with 'higher'] *preposition*
1 going through one place to get to another *We travelled to Wales via Bristol.*
2 using a particular way of doing something *Let's keep in touch via email.*

viaduct ['via' rhymes with 'higher'] *noun*
viaducts
a long high bridge, usually built with arches or posts. A viaduct carries a road or railway across a valley, river, road or low ground.

vibrate *verb*
vibrates, vibrating, vibrated
to shake with lots of small quick movements *When lorries go past our house, the floor seems to vibrate. My mobile vibrates when someone phones me.*

vibration *noun* **vibrations**
1 a small quick shaking movement
2 a sound of something shaking with lots of small quick movements *My phone vibrations are too loud.*

vicar *noun* **vicars**
a Christian priest in charge of a parish (an area with its own church)

vicarage *noun* **vicarages**
the house where a vicar lives

vice *noun*
1 (*plural* **vices**) something someone does or the way someone behaves that shows a very bad quality in their character *Is smoking a vice? Pride and envy are two big vices.*
2 criminal activities or very bad behaviour that is against the usual standards of behaviour *Vice should be punished.*
3 (*plural* **vices**) a metal tool with jaws (parts that open and close) for holding something tightly such as wood while you work on it

vice- *prefix*
used in front of the name of a job with a very high rank for showing that someone is the second most important person in that job and is in charge when the most important person is not there *vice-president*; *the vice-captain of a football team*

vice versa ['vye-ser-**verr**-ser] *adverb*
used when you mean that something you say is true and the opposite is also true *British people are allowed to work in France and vice versa* (French people are allowed to work in Britain).

vicinity *noun* **vicinities**
the area around a particular place *There are lots of shops in the vicinity of the school* (near the school).

vicious *adjective*
1 violent and cruel *a vicious attack*; *a vicious bully*
2 dangerous *a vicious dog*
3 very unpleasant in a way that frightens and upsets you *a vicious remark*; *Your brother has a vicious temper.*
viciously *adverb* **viciousness** *noun*

victim *noun* **victims**
1 someone who has something bad done to them. Victims include people who are hurt or killed, for example in a crime, accident or disaster or because of an illness, and people who have something that belongs to them stolen or damaged. *Grandma was the victim of a robbery. My uncle was a polio victim. There were thousands of flood victims.*
2 someone who suffers because of the beliefs or bad behaviour of someone else *Joel was the victim of a racist remark.*

victimise *verb*
victimises, victimising, victimised
if someone victimises someone, they treat them in a bad way without any good reason, for example because they don't like them or their opinions or because they come from a different country
victimisation *noun*

LANGUAGE EXTRA also spelt *victimize* and *victimization*

victor *noun* **victors**
the winner, for example in a game, competition or war

Victorian *adjective*
connected with the time of Queen Victoria (1837–1901) *a large Victorian house*

victorious *adjective*
if someone is victorious, they have won a game or competition or a battle, war or fight *a victorious team*; *a victorious army*

victory *noun* **victories**
when someone wins a game or competition or a battle, war or fight *the British victory at Trafalgar in 1805*

video *noun* **videos**
1 a digital recording of something such as an event *She uploaded a video from her mobile phone to the school website.*
2 a system of recording pictures and sounds digitally (by using electronic signals) or onto a magnetic tape
3 a film or programme recorded onto a magnetic tape, which you watch on a TV screen. Videos were used especially in the past.
4 a piece of equipment for recording and playing these films and TV programmes, used especially in the past

SYNONYM VCR

5 a plastic container with magnetic tape inside for playing and recording films and TV programmes, used especially in the past

video *verb*
videos, videoing, videoed
1 to film something using a video camera
2 to record a TV programme onto magnetic tape using a VCR

ORIGIN from Latin *video* 'I see'

567

video camera–violet

video camera noun video cameras
a camera for recording pictures and sounds. Smartphones and tablets usually have a small video camera built into them.

video game noun video games
a game you play using electronic equipment to move images on a screen

video recorder noun video recorders
a piece of electrical equipment for recording TV programmes and playing them back or for playing videos, used especially in the past

SYNONYM VCR

videotape noun videotapes
a thin plastic strip with magnetic properties inside a plastic container, used for recording images and sounds, especially in the past

Vietnam noun
a country in South-East Asia
Vietnamese adjective & noun

view noun views
1 what you can see from a particular place, for example from a high place or through a window *From the top of the building there's a beautiful view of the lake.*
2 being able to see something from a particular place *Please move aside – you're blocking my view.*
3 what someone thinks or says that shows their feelings or beliefs *In my view, you're wrong. What are your parents' views about the new head teacher?*

SYNONYM opinion

4 **in view of** used for giving a reason for something *The match was called off in view of the bad weather.*

SYNONYM because of

5 **on view** used about something that is being shown so that everyone can see it *There were 10 paintings by Turner on view in the gallery.*

view verb
views, viewing, viewed
1 to consider something or someone in a particular way *Mia is lazy and seems to view her schoolwork as a big joke.*
2 to look at something *You can view the match from our balcony. This image has been viewed by thousands of people online.*

viewer noun viewers
1 someone who watches television or a particular television programme
2 a computer program that allows you to look at images or text stored on a computer or on a device such as a phone
3 a piece of equipment that allows you to look at slides (photographic films). It is also called a slide viewer.

viewpoint noun viewpoints
1 the way someone thinks about something based on one particular part of a situation *Try and think about this poem from a child's viewpoint.*

SYNONYM point of view

2 a place from where you can look at something and see it clearly, for example a beautiful part of the countryside

vigilant adjective
if you are vigilant, you pay careful attention to a situation so you will notice any dangers or problems as soon as they happen **vigilance** noun **vigilantly** adverb

vigorous adjective
1 needing a lot of energy *vigorous exercise*
2 having a lot of energy *Granddad is old but still vigorous.*
3 showing strong feelings *a vigorous discussion*

vigorously adverb
with a lot of energy

vigour noun
great energy and strength

Viking noun Vikings
the Vikings were people from Scandinavia who sailed in boats to many places in Northern and Central Europe during the 8th to 11th centuries. They attacked and destroyed villages but also bought and sold goods, for example cloth, wool, silk, glass and spices. **Viking** adjective

vile adjective viler, vilest
extremely bad, for example bad enough to really upset you or make you feel sick *vile behaviour; a vile smell; vile weather*

villa noun villas
a house, for example in the countryside or near the sea, often one that you use for spending your holidays in *My aunt has a villa in the South of France.*

village noun
1 (plural **villages**) a group of houses and other buildings, usually in the countryside. Villages are smaller than towns.
2 the people who live in a village *The whole village came out to cheer our cricket team.*

villager noun villagers
someone who lives in a village

villain ['vil-ern'] noun villains
1 someone who behaves very badly, for example by harming people, or who behaves in a dishonest way
2 the main bad person in a film, play or book
villainous adjective

villainy ['vil-er-nee'] noun
very bad or dishonest behaviour

vindaloo ['vin-der-loo'] noun vindaloos
an Indian food usually made with chicken or lamb and eaten with rice. It is a type of curry with a sauce that has a very strong taste.

vindictive adjective
1 if someone is vindictive, they do bad things (or want to do bad things) to someone to upset them or harm them, often because someone has done bad things to them
2 also used about something someone does or says *vindictive behaviour; a vindictive remark*

vine noun vines
1 a climbing plant that produces grapes. It grows by attaching itself to a pole.
2 any climbing plant *We bought some tomatoes on the vine* (still attached to the stems of the plant).

vinegar noun
a sour liquid made from wine. It is used for giving taste to food, for example chips, for preserving food (stopping it from going bad) or for making salad dressings (sauces for putting on salads).

vinegary adjective
if food is vinegary, it tastes sour like vinegar

vineyard ['vin-yard'] noun vineyards
an area of land where vines grow, used for producing grapes to make wine

vintage noun vintages
used for talking about wine made in a particular year, usually when it is of good quality *a wine of 2010 vintage*

vintage adjective
1 used for talking about something from the past that has the best qualities of its kind *a vintage Hollywood film; a vintage car* (one built before 1930)
2 used for talking about a good quality wine made in a particular year *a vintage wine*

vinyl ['vye-nerl'] noun
a kind of strong plastic that bends easily, used for example for covering floors, making wallpaper or making records (flat discs that music is stored on)

viola ['vee-oh-ler'] noun violas
a musical instrument that is slightly larger than a violin and produces a deeper sound

violate verb
violates, violating, violated
1 to not obey something such as a law, or to not do what something such as an agreement says you should do
2 to go somewhere without permission *A Russian aircraft violated Turkish airspace.*
3 to treat something such as a holy place with no respect
violation noun

violence noun
1 when someone uses force to hurt or attack people *The protesters used violence against the police.*
2 used when you mean the great energy of something such as a storm or explosion that often causes a lot of damage

violent adjective
1 if someone is violent, they use force to hurt or attack people *a violent bully; a violent criminal*
2 also used about the behaviour and actions of violent people *violent clashes between demonstrators and police; violent crime*
3 used about something that is caused by violent people or by force being used *a violent death*
4 used about something that shows violent people *a violent film*
5 used about something such as a storm or explosion that often causes a lot of damage
6 used about something that is very strong and unpleasant, for example a pain, feeling or argument *a violent headache; Jo has a violent dislike of people who don't say please and thank you.*
violently adverb

violet adjective
having a colour between blue and purple

violet – vocal

violet *noun*
1 the colour violet
2 (*plural* **violets**) a small plant usually with purple or blue-purple flowers of different shapes

violin *noun* **violins**
a musical instrument with four strings that you play by holding it under your chin and moving a special stick (called a bow) across the strings to produce the sounds. It has a main part (or body) that is shaped like the number eight and a long narrow top part (called a neck).

violinist *noun* **violinists**
someone who plays the violin

VIP ['vee-eye-pee'] *noun* **VIPs**
an important or famous person who is treated differently from and better than ordinary people wherever he or she goes
short for: very important person

viper *noun* **vipers**
a small poisonous snake with long fangs (pointed teeth)

viral *adjective*
1 caused by or connected with a virus *a viral infection*
2 used about something such as an image, video or piece of computer information that is seen by very many people on the internet *It wasn't long before the photo of the celebrity went viral.*

virgin *noun* **virgins**
1 someone who has never had sex
2 **the Virgin Mary** the mother of Jesus Christ. Jesus Christ was the founder of the Christian religion

LANGUAGE EXTRA *the Virgin Mary* is also called *the Virgin* or *the Blessed Virgin*

virtual *adjective*
1 used for saying that something should be considered as being true because it is almost true, although not completely true *He was a virtual prisoner in his own house. We sat in virtual silence* (almost complete silence).
2 used for describing something that does not really exist but has been created by computer software to look like something that does exist *a virtual museum* (pictures of all the things in a museum that you can click on or touch in order to see them on your computer); *I went to the website and took a virtual tour of Paris.*

virtually *adverb*
1 another way of saying almost *It's virtually impossible to get to school in this snow.*
2 in a way that is not real but produced by computer software *I've never been to York but have visited it virtually by taking an online tour.*

virtual reality *noun*
images and sounds produced by computer software to make them look like a situation that really exists and to make you feel as if you are really a part of that situation

virtue *noun*
1 (*plural* **virtues**) something someone does or the way someone behaves that shows a very good quality in their character *Patience is a great virtue.*
2 behaviour showing that you do what is good and right and avoid what is bad and wrong *Virtue should be praised.*
3 (*plural* **virtues**) a good or useful quality that something has *One of the virtues of a tablet computer is that it's easy to carry around.*

virtuous *adjective*
1 if someone is virtuous, they behave in a way that is good and right
2 also used about the behaviour and actions of virtuous people *a virtuous life*
virtuously *adverb*

virus *noun* **viruses**
1 a tiny living thing that makes people ill when it gets into the body
2 an illness caused by a virus *I've been ill all week with a virus.*
3 a computer program that contains instructions that harm your computer, for example by stopping it from working properly or deleting information *This virus is spread by email.*
4 a problem a computer has that is caused by a virus *My laptop has a virus.*

ORIGIN from Latin *virus* 'poison' or 'slime'

visa ['vee-zer'] *noun* **visas**
an official mark that is put in someone's passport and gives them permission to enter or leave a particular country *I needed a visa from the Australian embassy to go to Sydney.*

visibility *noun*
how far you can see in particular weather conditions *The sun was shining and visibility was good* (you could see things far away clearly).

visible *adjective*
if something is visible, you can see it

visibly *adverb*
in a way that you can see easily *Laura was visibly upset.*

vision *noun*
1 the natural ability a person or animal has to see *Cats have good night vision.*
2 (*plural* **visions**) an idea in your mind about something in the future, for example what things could be like
3 the power to think for yourself, produce new and exciting ideas and plan for the future *Our new head teacher is a woman of vision.*

visit *verb*
visits, visiting, visited
1 to go to see someone and spend time with them *I visit Nan once a week. My cousins from Australia are coming to visit.*
2 to go to a place or website and spend time there
3 to go to see someone such as a doctor or accountant to get treatment or advice

visit *noun* **visits**
when you go to see someone or something for a short or long period of time *My friend from Scotland paid us a visit* (came to see us). *We went on a short visit to Ireland.*

visitor *noun* **visitors**
someone who visits a person, place or website

vista *noun* **vistas**
a pleasant view that you can see from a particular place, for example a view of the countryside

ORIGIN from Italian *vista* 'sight'

visual *adjective*
1 connected with seeing or with things you can see *a visual image; a visual handicap* (a problem with seeing things)
2 a visual aid is something such as a film, picture or map that you look at to help you understand something
visually *adverb*

visualise *verb*
visualises, visualising, visualised
to form a picture of something or someone in your mind

LANGUAGE EXTRA also spelt *visualize*

vital *adjective*
1 if something is vital, it is very important, for example you must do it, have it or use it *A secure password is vital. It was vital to get my cat to the vet quickly. The passer-by gave the police vital information.*
2 used for describing something needed for someone to be able to live *vital organs* (for example the heart, brain and lungs)

vitality *noun*
great energy and strength

vitally *adverb*
extremely *vitally important*

vitamin *noun* **vitamins**
a natural substance in food that your body needs to keep it healthy. There are different vitamins in different types of foods such as fruit, vegetables, fish and meat.

vivid *adjective*
1 producing clear and detailed pictures in someone's mind *vivid memories; The book gives a vivid description of life during the Second World War.*
2 used for describing a colour that is strong and bright *a vivid blue sky*
vividness *noun*

ORIGIN from Latin *vividus* 'living'

vividly *adverb*
1 clearly and with lots of details *I remember David's birthday party vividly.*
2 brightly *The light shone quite vividly.*

vivisection *noun*
using living animals for scientific experiments

vixen *noun* **vixens**
a female fox

vocabulary *noun* **vocabularies**
1 used about all the words that someone knows in a particular language *My sister has a bigger vocabulary than me* (knows more words than me). *Our teacher has a wide vocabulary* (knows lots of words).
2 used about all the words of a particular language *a vocabulary book* (giving some of the most important words of a language or in a particular subject); *I'm working hard to improve my French vocabulary.*

vocal *adjective*
1 used about someone who makes their opinions known in a strong way

vocalist–vote

2 also used about what someone does or says, to show that it is done strongly *There was vocal opposition to the head teacher's plan.*
3 connected with the voice *vocal cords* (thin skin in your throat for making sounds)
vocally *adverb*

vocalist *noun* **vocalists**
a singer, especially in a band that plays pop or rock music

vocation *noun* **vocations**
1 a job or activity that you think is right for you and that you want to do very much, often a job or activity that people respect *My dad's vocation is teaching.*
2 a strong feeling that makes you want to do a particular job or activity because you think it is right for you

vocational *adjective*
used about something or someone that teaches someone the skills they need for a particular job *a vocational course*; *vocational training*

vodka *noun* **vodkas**
a strong alcoholic drink, usually made from grains such as wheat or rye or from potatoes. It comes originally from Russia.

voice *noun* **voices**
1 the sound you make when you speak or sing *My brother usually speaks in a loud voice.*
2 the ability someone has to speak or sing *Seema has a lovely singing voice. I've lost my voice* (I can't speak, for example because of a sore throat).
3 someone's opinion about a subject, or being allowed to have an opinion about a subject *Parents should have a voice in how to run the school.*
4 in grammar, the active voice describes a verb where the subject does the action, for example 'Ranjit kicked the ball.' The passive voice describes a verb where the subject receives the action, for example 'The ball was kicked by Ranjit.'

voice *verb*
voices, voicing, voiced
to let someone know something or know about something by saying what you think or feel *May I voice an opinion on the subject? Let him voice his anger.*

SYNONYM to express

voicemail *noun*
1 a system for sending and storing spoken messages using a phone
2 (*plural* **voicemails**) a spoken message you send to someone's phone

voice recorder *noun* **voice recorders**
a piece of electronic equipment that records someone's voice so that you can listen to it later

void *adjective*
used for describing something that is not officially acceptable, for example a document or agreement

void *noun*
1 (*plural* **voids**) an extremely large empty space
2 a feeling of emptiness, for example caused by losing something or when someone dies

volcano *noun* **volcanoes**
a mountain that opens at the top and throws rocks, lava (hot liquid rock) and ash (grey powder from crushed rocks) high into the air **volcanic** *adjective*

ORIGIN from *Vulcan*, the Roman god of fire

vole *noun* **voles**
a small animal like a mouse but with a thicker body. Voles live near water and in fields.

volley *noun* **volleys**
1 a large number of bullets or missiles fired at the same time
2 a large number or amount of something happening at the same time *a volley of questions*
3 in games such as tennis or football, a volley is the action of hitting or kicking the ball before it touches the ground

volleyball *noun*
1 a game in which two teams use their hands to hit a ball over a high net without letting the ball touch the ground
2 (*plural* **volleyballs**) the large ball used in the game of volleyball

volt *noun* **volts**
a unit for measuring the strength of an electric current

ORIGIN from Alessandro *Volta*, French 18th-century scientist who invented the first battery

voltage *noun* **voltages**
the strength of an electric current measured in volts

volume *noun*
1 the amount of sound produced by a piece of equipment such as a TV, radio or computer *Press this button on your mobile phone to turn the volume up* (to make it louder).
2 an amount of something, usually a large amount *the volume of cars on the road*; *We expect an increase in the volume of work.*
3 the amount of space inside a 3-D object, for example a cube or pyramid
4 (*plural* **volumes**) a book, or one book in a series of books *Volume 1 contains the poet's best work.*

voluntarily *adverb*
in a way that shows you want to do something *Harry left voluntarily – we didn't ask him to leave.*

voluntary *adjective*
1 used about something that you do or are connected with because you want to, not because someone tells you to *Mr Grey's poetry course is voluntary – you don't have to go.*
2 used about something such as work that you do without getting paid because you want to do it *My dad does voluntary work at the hospital.*
3 used about someone who does work without getting paid for it *a voluntary worker*
4 used about a group or organisation where people work to help other people, usually without getting paid *My aunt works for charities and other voluntary organisations.*

volunteer *noun* **volunteers**
1 someone who does work without getting paid for it, because they want to do it
2 someone who does something because they want to, not because they have to *Any volunteers to read out John Agard's poem?*

volunteer *verb*
volunteers, volunteering, volunteered
1 to do something (or say you will do something) because you want to do it, not because you have to *My brother volunteered to wash Mum's car. Will anyone volunteer?* (for example, say they are ready to do something such as help)
2 to do work without getting paid, because you want to do it *My cousin volunteers as a helper in the local football club.*
3 to give or tell someone something without being asked to *Our neighbour volunteered some information to the police. Many parents volunteered their time to help during the concert.*

vomit *verb*
vomits, vomiting, vomited
used for saying that the food someone eats or the liquid someone drinks suddenly comes up from their stomach and out of their mouth, for example because they are ill *The baby vomited on the carpet.*

vomit *noun*
the food or liquid from someone's stomach that comes out of their mouth

voracious ['ver-ray-shers'] *adjective*
showing that someone does something a lot or likes to do a lot of something *Paul has a voracious appetite* (eats a lot of food). *Sita is a voracious reader* (reads lots of books).

vote *verb*
votes, voting, voted
1 to choose someone or something, for example the person or thing that you want to do something for you or to win a prize. You usually vote by looking at a list of people or things on a piece of paper and putting a cross beside the name of the person or thing that you choose, or by putting up your hand when a name is called. *Everyone in the school is allowed to vote for head boy and head girl. Who was voted best actor? This book was voted the best children's novel of the year.*
2 to give an opinion about something by saying you want to do something (or don't want to do something) *The workers voted to accept a pay rise* (said they would accept one). *Most teachers voted against a strike* (said they didn't want one).

vote *noun*
1 (*plural* **votes**) a choice you make or the action of making a choice. You usually make this choice by looking at a list of people or things on a piece of paper and putting a cross beside the name of the person or thing that you choose, or by putting up your hand when a name is called. *How many votes did they get? Grandma has gone out to cast her vote* (choose someone in an election by voting for them).
2 the total number of votes in an election *Labour's share of the vote has gone up.*
3 being allowed to vote in an election *In the past, women did not have the vote.*

voter *noun* **voters**
someone who votes, usually to choose a government or leader in an election

vouch *verb*
vouches, vouching, vouched
1 if you vouch for someone, you say you know they have a good character and that they will behave well and do things well *Zaheera is a good babysitter – I can vouch for her. If I ask Dad to let your friend come to the party, will you vouch for her?* (be responsible for her because you know she has a good character)
2 if you vouch for something, you say you know it is good, correct or true *This is a first-class dictionary – I can vouch for that. I can vouch for the fact that Joel has been with me all evening.*

voucher *noun* **vouchers**
1 something used instead of money, for example a piece of paper in a shop or a special code online *a gift voucher* (one that someone gives you to buy something with)

LANGUAGE EXTRA *a gift voucher* is also called *a gift card* or *gift certificate*

2 a piece of paper that allows you to pay less for something or to get something for nothing *a discount voucher for 10 per cent off*; *a voucher for a free cup of coffee*

SYNONYM coupon

vow *verb*
vows, vowing, vowed
to make a serious promise or a serious decision to do something *She vowed to help me improve my grades. I vowed to work harder this term.*

vow *noun* **vows**
a serious promise or decision to do something

vowel *noun* **vowels**
any of the letters of the alphabet *a, e, i, o, u* and sometimes *y*

LANGUAGE EXTRA the *vowels* in English are sounds that you make without closing your mouth or throat. The *consonants* are the following letters: *b, c, d, f, g, h, j, k, l, m, n, p, q, r, s, t, v, w, x, y* and *z*. The letter *y* can be both a vowel and a consonant – it is a vowel in 'hilly' and a consonant in 'yes'.
 A consonant sound is made when the air through your mouth is blocked so the sound cannot last very long, as a vowel sound can. For example, the 'i' sound of 'rip' can be made to last longer but the 'r' and the 'p' sounds cannot: 'r-i-i-i-i-i-p'.

ORIGIN from Latin *vocalis*, short for *littera vocalis* 'voice letter' (from *vox* 'voice')

voyage *noun* **voyages**
a journey someone makes by boat or in a spacecraft **voyager** *noun*

vulgar *adjective*
1 if someone is vulgar, they are rude and unpleasant and they upset people *Don't be so vulgar.*
2 also used about something such as a remark or picture, to show that it is rude and unpleasant *He's always telling vulgar jokes.*
3 used about someone who does not have good manners or who cannot recognise things of good quality, or about something such as their behaviour *Those clothes make her look vulgar. Your accent is really vulgar.*
vulgarly *adverb* **vulgarity** *noun*

vulgar fraction *noun* **vulgar fractions**
in maths, a fraction written with one number above the line and one number below it, not written as a decimal (as a dot followed by one or more numbers). For example, $\frac{1}{2}$ and $\frac{3}{4}$ are vulgar fractions.

vulnerable *adjective*
1 used about someone who can be hurt or influenced easily, for example because they have no protection or because they are weak or very old or very young *a vulnerable old man*
2 used about something or someone that is easy to attack *This part of the border is vulnerable. The soldiers were in a vulnerable position.*

vulture *noun* **vultures**
a large bird that eats dead animals. It has no feathers on its head or neck.

W w

ORIGIN W, U, V and F all come from the same letter in the Phoenician alphabet. The letter looked like a Y and it represented either a peg or a hook. It had the sound of 'w' and was called *waw*. When the letter passed into Latin, it was written as a V shape, which was later rounded at the bottom into a U shape to make writing it easier. The Romans wrote one U next to another to make their 'w' sound, as in *EQUUS* ('horse') where *QU* makes the 'kw' sound. When Roman UU entered English, printers found it easier to change the letters by writing VV – two Vs next to each other. In about 1700 they changed the shape again into the W we know today – but the letter was still called a 'double u'.

wacky *adjective* **wackier, wackiest** (informal)
slightly strange and often funny *Your uncle's a bit wacky. Leo has a wacky sense of humour.*

LANGUAGE EXTRA you can also say *wacko*

wad *noun* **wads**
a wad of something soft such as paper or cotton wool or of things such as banknotes or tissues is an amount of them pressed or held together *Granddad showed me a wad of money in his wallet.*

waddle *verb*
waddles, waddling, waddled
to walk with short steps and move slightly from side to side like a duck
waddle *noun*

wade *verb*
wades, wading, waded
1 to walk in or through something liquid or soft such as water or mud *We waded across the river.*
2 if you wade through something such as information or a book, you spend a lot of time reading it and dealing with it

wafer *noun* **wafers**
a thin light biscuit, often eaten with ice cream *a wafer biscuit*; *an ice cream wafer* (or *ice cream wafer sandwich*) (a small block of ice cream in between two pieces of wafer)

wafer-thin *adjective*
extremely thin

waffle *noun*
1 (informal) something someone says or writes that uses lots of words but doesn't give anyone any useful or interesting information
2 (plural **waffles**) a type of flat cake, usually square, with a pattern of square holes in it

waffle *verb* (informal)
waffles, waffling, waffled
to talk or write a lot without saying anything useful or interesting

waft–wall

waft *verb*
wafts, wafting, wafted
if a smell or sound wafts through the air, it reaches you from somewhere *Pleasant smells of Chinese cooking wafted out into the street.*

wag *verb*
wags, wagging, wagged
1 if a dog wags its tail, or if its tail wags, it moves it from one side to the other, for example because it is happy
2 if someone wags their finger, they move it up and down or from one side to the other, for example because they are angry
wag *noun*

wage *noun* wages
the money someone gets paid for doing their job *My dad's wages are low. He's on a daily wage. Ask for a wage increase.*

wage *verb*
wages, waging, waged
to start or to take part in something such as a war or battle against an enemy *In 1939 Britain waged war on Germany.*

wager *verb*
wagers, wagering, wagered
to pay money, for example to choose the winner of a race, and hope to win more money **wager** *noun*

SYNONYM to bet

waggle *verb*
waggles, waggling, waggled
if you waggle something, you move it up and down or from one side to another, and if something waggles, it moves in this way *Can you waggle your toes?*

wagon *noun* wagons
1 a vehicle with four large wheels pulled by horses or oxen, used especially in past times to carry people and goods *American settlers travelled west in covered wagons.*
2 a large container with wheels pulled by a train, used for carrying goods
3 an open container with four wheels that is pulled along by a person, used for carrying goods

wail *verb*
wails, wailing, wailed
1 if someone wails, they cry or shout loudly, for example because they are sad or in pain
2 if something such as an alarm bell wails, it makes a long loud high sound *Police sirens were wailing.*
wail *noun*

waist *noun* waists
the narrow part in the middle of your body above your hips

waistcoat *noun* waistcoats
a piece of clothing without sleeves and with buttons down the front. It is worn over a shirt.

wait *verb*
waits, waiting, waited
1 to stay somewhere until someone or something arrives, until something happens or until you can do something *We're waiting for our teacher. Wait – I have something to tell you. Granddad is waiting to leave. Please wait a minute.*
2 to stay somewhere until someone is ready for you *The doctor kept me waiting.*
3 to be ready for someone *The doctor is waiting for you. There was a letter waiting when Mum got home.*
4 to not happen or to not be done or dealt with until a later time *Your questions will have to wait – I'm too busy to answer them now. I have to see you now – it can't wait* (it's urgent).
5 to hope for something to happen *These are the results we were waiting for.*
6 to serve food or drinks as a waiter *How many people will be waiting on the guests at your party?*
7 if you say that someone can't wait, you mean they are very excited about something and want it to happen very soon *Our holidays start tomorrow – I can't wait!*
8 to wait behind is to stay somewhere when everyone else has left
9 to wait in is to stay at home until someone or something comes *I waited in all day for Nan's phone call.*
10 to wait up for someone is to not go to bed until someone gets home

wait *noun* waits
1 an amount of time that you spend waiting *The wait was more than three hours.*
2 the action of waiting *We had a long wait to see the doctor.*

waiter *noun* waiters
a man who works in a restaurant or café and brings food or drinks to people's tables

waiting list *noun* waiting lists
a list of people who are waiting for something, for example medical treatment or a place in a particular school

waiting room *noun* waiting rooms
a room where people sit and wait, for example at a station until the train arrives or in a hospital until the doctor is ready to see them

waitress *noun* waitresses
a woman who works in a restaurant or café and brings food or drinks to people's tables

wake *verb*
wakes, waking, woke, woken
1 if you wake or wake up, you stop sleeping *Wake up – it's time for school.*
2 to wake someone or wake someone up is to make them stop sleeping *Don't wake Granddad. The noise woke the baby up.*

wake *noun* wakes
1 an area of water behind a boat or ship that is moved about as the boat or ship travels through the water
2 an occasion when friends and relatives of someone who has just died get together, for example to think about the dead person or to watch over their body
3 **in the wake of** used for saying that something such as damage is left by something or someone as they move along *The storm left destruction in its wake.*

waken *verb*
wakens, wakening, wakened
to wake up or wake someone up

LANGUAGE EXTRA in everyday language, you use *wake up* rather than *waken*. For example, you say *I woke him up at eight o'clock* rather than *I wakened him at eight o'clock.*

Wales *noun*
a country in North-West Europe. Wales is a part of the island of Great Britain together with England and Scotland.

walk *verb*
walks, walking, walked
1 if a person or animal walks, they move, or they go somewhere, at a normal speed, putting one foot in front of the other *It's hard to walk in these shoes. Walk – don't run! I walk to school every day. I opened the door and he walked out* (he left).
2 to travel a particular distance while walking *We walked two miles to the nearest supermarket.*
3 if you walk someone somewhere, you walk with them to keep them safe or show them the way *Dad walked Grandma to the station.*
4 if you walk a dog, you walk with it so that it gets some exercise
5 if someone walks off or away with something, they steal it or they win it

walk *noun* walks
1 a journey you make by walking *It's a long walk to school. Let's go for a walk. Lily took the dog for a walk.*
2 the action of walking *We started by running then slowed down to a walk.*
3 the way that you walk *I recognised Oliver by his walk.*

SYNONYM gait

4 a way or route that people follow by walking, for example around a town or through the countryside *There are some pleasant walks around York.*
5 **from all walks of life** or **from every walk of life** used for talking about someone's place in society based on things such as their job and education *My parents have friends from all walks of life.*

walker *noun* walkers
1 someone who walks or who walks in a particular way *There's a new path along the coast for walkers. I'm a slow walker.*
2 a special frame that someone uses to help them walk, for example an old person

walkie-talkie *noun* walkie-talkies
a small radio that you speak into like a phone, used for speaking to someone who has the same kind of radio. You hold it in your hand and carry it around.

walking stick *noun* walking sticks
a long thin piece of wood, usually with a curved handle, used by people to help them walk

SYNONYM cane

walkway *noun* walkways
1 a passage or path for walking along, usually one that is raised above the ground and connects two buildings
2 a moving walkway is a type of moving pavement that takes people from one place to another in a large building such as an airport or shopping centre. It is also called a travolator.

wall *noun* walls
1 one of the sides of a room or a building *A picture hung on the wall* (inside the room). *Someone wrote graffiti on the school wall* (outside the building).

572

2 a structure, usually of bricks or stone, that is built around or along one or more sides of an area such as a garden or playground, or all around a place such as a prison or castle *York city walls*
3 the surface of a hollow part inside the body, for example the stomach

wall *verb*
walls, walling, walled
1 if someone walls something in, they put a wall around it
2 if someone walls something up, for example a window or door, they block it up by filling it with bricks or pieces of wood

wallaby ['wol-er-bee'] *noun* **wallabies**
an animal like a kangaroo but much smaller. It has a long tail, two short front legs and two long back legs. A female wallaby carries its baby in a pocket of skin called a pouch at the front of its body.

wallet *noun* **wallets**
1 a small flat folding case made of leather or plastic, used for carrying money and keeping important things in such as a passport, ID card or credit card. It is usually carried in someone's pocket or bag.
2 a document wallet is a large thin cardboard or plastic case for carrying things such as papers

wallflower *noun* **wallflowers**
a garden plant with orange, yellow, red, purple or white flowers that grow in groups and have a pleasant smell

wallop *verb* (informal)
wallops, walloping, walloped
1 to hit someone or something very hard
2 to beat someone completely in a game or competition
wallop *noun* **walloping** *noun*

wallow *verb*
wallows, wallowing, wallowed
1 if an animal or person wallows in something such as mud or water, they roll their body slowly about in it, for example for pleasure or to keep cool
2 if someone wallows in something, for example a feeling or luxury, they get pleasure from it

wallpaper *noun* **wallpapers**
1 thick paper with a pattern on it, used for decorating a wall inside a room or building. You stick it onto the wall using a special paste (thick substance made from water and powder).
2 an electronic image or pattern used as decoration on a screen, for example a computer screen or mobile phone screen *Click here to change your desktop wallpaper.*

wally *noun* **wallies** (informal)
someone who behaves in a silly way or who looks silly *You look like a wally in that hat.*

walnut *noun* **walnuts**
a large round brown nut that you can eat. It has an uneven shape made up of lots of lumps and grows inside a hard light brown shell that is divided into two halves.

walrus *noun* **walruses**
a sea animal with a long heavy body and flippers (parts like arms for swimming). It looks like a large seal but has smaller eyes and two long tusks (pointed teeth) that grow downwards from its mouth.

waltz *noun* **waltzes**
1 a dance, usually one in which two people hold each other and move along while turning round and round following a particular rhythm
2 the music for this dance

waltz *verb*
waltzes, waltzing, waltzed
to dance a waltz

wan [rhymes with 'gone'] *adjective*
1 pale, for example because of illness or tiredness *a wan face*
2 pale and weak *a wan light*

WAN [rhymes with 'man'] *noun* **WANs**
a way of connecting computers together over a wide area, for example in different parts of the country, so that information and equipment can be shared
short for: wide area network

wand *noun* **wands**
a wand or magic wand is a thin straight stick used by someone such as a wizard, magician or fairy for performing magic or doing magic tricks

wander *verb*
wanders, wandering, wandered
1 to walk around in a relaxed way, often without any particular reason for going to the places you go to *We were bored so we went wandering around the shops.*
2 to travel around visiting different places for pleasure, often without any particular plan *My aunt and uncle spent their holiday wandering around Scotland.*
3 to move away from the place where you should be or the path that you should be following *Ms Hobbs told us to stay together and not wander off. Your dog has wandered into our garden.*
4 to talk about something different from what you should be talking about *You seem to have wandered off the subject.*
5 to think about something different from what you should be thinking about *I couldn't concentrate on my homework – my mind kept wandering.*

wander *noun*
when you walk around somewhere in a relaxed way *We went for a wander around the village.*

wanderer *noun* **wanderers**
someone who travels around visiting different places

wane *verb*
wanes, waning, waned
1 to become less or weaker *My interest in cricket is beginning to wane. The influence of traditional religion is waning.*
2 if the moon is waning, it appears to get smaller every day after a full moon (when it is a complete circle). When it appears to be getting bigger, it is waxing.

wane *noun*
on the wane becoming less or weaker *The popularity of desktop computers is on the wane.*

wangle *verb* (informal)
wangles, wangling, wangled
to get something you want in a clever way, for example by persuading someone, being nice to them or being slightly dishonest *My dad will see if he can wangle an extra invitation to the party.*

want *verb*
wants, wanting, wanted
1 to have a feeling that you must or should have or do something or that it's a good idea to have or do something *We want more time. I want a glass of water. Do you want to go swimming?*
2 to have a feeling that something should or must happen or that someone should or must do something *I want my laptop to be repaired, not thrown away. Our teacher wants everyone to arrive early tomorrow.*
3 to have a feeling that someone or something should be a certain way *We all want Miss Murray as our teacher. I want my homework to be as good as it can be.*
4 used for saying that something should be done or should happen or that someone or something should have something or someone *The kitchen floor wants a clean. The grass is long – it wants cutting. He wants a good telling-off. We want Daniel on our side. Plants want rain and sun to grow.*
5 to ask for someone because you must or should speak to them *The head teacher wants you in her office. Mum, you're wanted on the phone.*

want *noun*
1 when you don't have enough of something *My parents couldn't send me on the trip for want of money. If Ollie doesn't succeed, it won't be for want of trying (he's tried very hard).*
2 someone's wants are the things they want or need

wanted *adjective*
1 if someone is wanted, the police are trying to find them because they think they might be connected with a crime or might have committed a crime
2 if someone feels wanted, they know that other people love them and understand their good qualities

war *noun*
1 when two or more countries or different groups of people in the same country disagree with each other and use violence and weapons to hurt and attack each other *The two countries are at war* (fighting each other with weapons). *In 1939 Britain went to war* (started fighting in a war).
2 (plural **wars**) a particular time when countries or groups fight each other in this way *The war lasted six years.*
3 a great effort to deal with something bad and stop it from happening *the war on drugs*

> **CULTURE NOTE** important *wars* of the past include the *First World War* (1914–18) and the *Second World War* (1939–45)

warble *verb*
warbles, warbling, warbled
if a bird warbles, it makes pleasant singing sounds with notes that keep changing
warble *noun*

warbler *noun* **warblers**
a small bird, often brown or brightly coloured, that makes pleasant singing sounds

ward–wary

ward *noun* **wards**
1 a large room with beds in a hospital. People stay there to receive medical care, for example people who are ill or women who are having a baby.
2 a child, such as one whose parents have died, who is looked after and protected by a person called a guardian

ward *verb*
wards, warding, warded
if someone wards something off, they stop something from harming them *I put my hands over my head to ward off the bully's blows.*

-ward or **-wards** *suffix*
used for making adjectives or adverbs showing a particular direction *forward; downwards; eastwards*

warden *noun* **wardens**
1 short for **traffic warden** (someone who checks vehicles to see if they are parked in the correct place)
2 someone in charge of a building such as a block of flats, old people's home or youth hostel (place where young people can stay cheaply)

wardrobe *noun* **wardrobes**
1 a tall piece of furniture with a door in the front, used for hanging clothes in. Wardrobes are sometimes built into the wall of a room. *Nasreen always puts her dresses on hangers in the wardrobe.*
2 used when you mean all the clothes someone has

> ORIGIN from Old French *garderobe* 'place where clothes are kept' (from *garder* 'to keep' and *robes* 'long outer garments')

warehouse *noun* **warehouses**
1 a large building where goods are stored, for example before they are sent to the shops where people buy them
2 a large building where people go to buy particular goods more cheaply than in shops *a furniture warehouse*

wares *noun plural*
goods that someone sells, for example in a market

warfare *noun*
1 fighting in a war
2 fighting between different groups *gang warfare*

warhead *noun* **warheads**
the front part of a weapon such as a missile that explodes when it hits the place it has been aimed at *a nuclear warhead*

warlike *adjective*
1 used for describing a person or country that likes fighting in wars
2 also used for describing something they do or say *a warlike speech*

warm *adjective* **warmer, warmest**
1 if something is warm, its temperature is not too high and it feels pleasant *a warm day; a glass of warm milk; warm hands*
2 if something is very warm or too warm, it is hot and has a high temperature *The climate is very warm at the Equator. It's too warm to go out.*
3 used about something that has a low temperature but is not cold *The toast is still warm. The side of my laptop feels slightly warm.*
4 if someone is warm, they feel comfortable because the surrounding temperature is not too low or too high or because of clothes or blankets that help the body not to lose heat *I feel nice and warm in the house. This coat keeps me warm. Are you warm enough in bed?*
5 warm clothes are thick and make you feel comfortable because they help the body not to lose heat *a warm pair of socks*
6 showing friendliness and kindness *My dad's a very warm person. The head teacher gave us a warm welcome.*
7 warm colours are colours that have red, yellow or brown in them
8 (informal) close to getting the right answer to a question or problem or to finding something hidden *You're getting warm!*

> SIMILE 'as warm as toast' means very warm (sense 4)

warm *noun*
1 a warm place *Stay indoors in the warm.*
2 warm weather *I like the warm, not the cold.*

warm *verb*
warms, warming, warmed
1 to make something or someone warm *Put on the radiator to warm the room* (or *warm up the room*). *I need a hot tea to warm me up.*
2 to become warm *Seema went over to the fire to warm up* (or *to warm herself up*). *The flat takes an hour or so to warm up.*
3 if a piece of equipment or a vehicle warms up or if someone warms it up, someone switches it on and waits until it is ready to be used
4 if someone warms up while waiting to take part in a sport, they do exercises such as stretching their muscles

warm-blooded *adjective*
if an animal is warm-blooded, its body stays warm and its temperature does not change to match its surroundings. Mammals and birds are warm-blooded.
compare: **cold-blooded**

warming *noun*
when something becomes warm or warmer
see: **global warming**

warmly *adverb*
1 in a way that keeps you warm *Dress warmly if you're going to play in the snow.*
2 in a friendly and kind way *They welcomed us warmly.*
3 with lots of energy *The audience clapped warmly.*

warmth *noun*
1 when something makes you feel warm or keeps you warm *the warmth of the sun; the warmth of a blanket*
2 the friendliness and kindness of someone or something *the warmth of the welcome*

warn *verb*
warns, warning, warned
to tell someone that something bad might or will happen, for example so that they keep away from it or deal with it in some way or so that they won't do something they shouldn't do *The weather report warned us that rain was on the way.* *Mum warned me not to go out without a coat* (for example because it could rain). *Our teacher warned us of the dangers of wandering off.*

warning *noun* **warnings**
1 something that tells someone that something bad might or will happen *Dad gave me a warning about speaking to strangers. The label carries a warning that smoking is bad for your health. No talking during the lesson – this is your final warning* (for example, don't talk or you'll be punished).
2 something that shows that something bad is happening *This beeping sound is a warning that there is something wrong with your phone. The warning light on my laptop tells me when the battery is low.*
3 information that something is going to happen *Granddad dropped in yesterday without warning* (without telling anyone he was going to come). *My tablet stopped working, completely without warning* (suddenly and without anyone knowing this would happen).

warp *verb*
warps, warping, warped
1 if something such as wood or plastic warps or is warped, it becomes bent out of shape, usually because of heat or water *The back door of our house is slightly warped.*
2 to affect something such as someone's mind or character in a bad way, for example so that their ideas or behaviour appear strange or worrying *His mind was warped by years spent in prison. That comedian has a warped sense of humour* (his jokes are strange and worrying).

warrant *noun* **warrants**
an official document that is agreed by a judge and gives the police permission to do something such as arrest someone or search a building

warrant *verb*
warrants, warranting, warranted
if something warrants something, it needs it because there is a good reason for it *These matters warrant an investigation. This sort of behaviour is not warranted* (there is no good reason for it).

warren *noun* **warrens**
a group of holes and tunnels under the ground (called burrows) where rabbits live

warrior *noun* **warriors**
used especially in the past for describing a soldier or someone who is skilled in fighting

warship *noun* **warships**
a very large ship with guns, used for fighting in wars

wart *noun* **warts**
a small hard lump that grows on your skin, for example on your hands or face. It is caused by a virus.

wary *adjective* **warier, wariest**
careful about something or someone because you want to avoid danger, problems or mistakes *I'm wary of strangers* (I keep away from them to avoid danger). *When I asked Mum to do my homework for me, she gave me a wary look* (for example, she thought this was wrong and didn't want to). **warily** *adverb* **wariness** *noun*

was
first and third person singular past tense of **be**

wash *verb*
washes, washing, washed
1 to clean something with water and usually soap *Wash your hands. My jeans need washing* (by hand or in a washing machine). *Don't forget to wash out your mug.*
2 if someone washes (or washes themselves), they clean themselves with soap and water
3 if the sea washes something or someone somewhere, it makes them move there *Lots of jellyfish were washed up on the shore. A sailor was washed overboard.*
4 to wash up is to wash things such as plates, bowls, knives, forks and spoons after a meal

wash *noun*
1 (*plural* **washes**) the action of washing something *My jeans are dirty – please give them a wash. I'll put them in the wash* (with the other clothes to be washed in the washing machine). *Dad has already done two washes* (washed two lots of clothes in the washing machine).
2 the action of washing yourself, for example at a sink *I'm having a wash.*
3 an area of the sea or a river that is moved about by a boat or ship travelling through it

washable *adjective*
if cloth or a piece of clothing is washable, you can wash it without causing any damage to it *This skirt is machine washable* (it can be washed safely in a washing machine).

washbasin *noun* **washbasins**
a large container for washing your hands and face, for example one with taps that is fixed to a wall in a bathroom

washer *noun* **washers**
a small ring of rubber or metal that is put between two surfaces, such as on a bolt before the nut is screwed on. It is used for keeping the surfaces tightly together, for example to stop water dripping from a tap.

washing *noun*
1 things such as clothes, towels or sheets that are dirty and need to be washed or that have just been washed *a washing basket* (container for keeping dirty or clean washing in)
2 the action of washing things such as clothes, towels or sheets *Nan has done the washing today.*
3 a washing line is a long rope that you put outdoors for hanging wet clothes on when they have just been washed

> **SYNONYM** clothesline

4 a washing machine is a large piece of equipment where you put things such as dirty clothes to be washed

washing-up *noun*
1 the action of washing things such as plates, bowls, knives, forks and spoons after a meal *It's your turn to do the washing-up, Shanti.*
2 all the things such as plates, knives and forks that are dirty and need to be washed after a meal *a huge pile of washing-up*

washout *noun* **washouts** (informal)
if an event is a washout, it is completely unsuccessful

> **LANGUAGE EXTRA** also spelt *wash-out*

wasn't
short for 'was not' *He wasn't ready.*

wasp *noun* **wasps**
a flying insect that can sting. It has black and yellow stripes like a bee but a longer body than a bee.

wastage *noun*
when something is wasted, or the amount of it that is wasted *We should try and cut down on food wastage.*

waste *verb*
wastes, wasting, wasted
1 to use more of something than you need to, especially when there isn't enough of it *There isn't much water left so don't waste it.*
2 to leave something unused because there is more of it than you need or want *I hope you're not going to waste your potatoes. Mum doesn't like wasting food* (for example having food left over from meals and throwing it away).
3 to not use something fully or to do something that does not have a successful result *I didn't win the competition so all my hard work was wasted* (it was done for nothing). *What a lot of wasted effort! My sister's talents are wasted in that job* (the job isn't suitable for her because people are not using her talents). *It's too late to join the football team – another opportunity wasted!*
4 if you waste time, money or energy, you use it in a bad or careless way, for example doing something that is not useful, important or successful *You've wasted two hours watching that silly TV programme! Don't waste money on that phone – it looks cheap.*
5 if something is wasted on someone, they don't understand or enjoy its good qualities *My brother likes rock music – classical music is wasted on him.*
6 if someone wastes away, they slowly become thinner and weaker, for example because they are ill

waste *adjective*
1 used about something such as a substance that is got rid of or thrown away because it is no longer useful or needed *waste food; waste paper*
2 used about land that is not used or looked after by anyone *a piece of waste ground*

waste *noun*
1 when something is not fully used or when something is done that does not have a successful result *The maths test was cancelled so I did all that work for nothing – what a waste! Finish off the cake or it will go to waste* (it won't be used and will be thrown away).
2 when time, money or energy is used in a bad or careless way and doesn't produce a good result *It's a waste of time trying to get Dad to come to the party* (he will not come). *Buying that dress is a waste of money – it's much too expensive.*
3 something such as a substance that is got rid of or thrown away because it is no longer useful or needed *garden waste*
4 wastes are large areas of land where there are very few people, animals, plants and trees, for example in a desert

wasteful *adjective*
1 used for saying that more of something is used than needs to be used or that something is not used in a successful way *Leaving the lights on all day is wasteful.*
2 if someone is wasteful, they use more of something than they need to, or they use things in a careless way, for example they throw good things away
wastefully *adverb*

wastepaper basket *noun*
wastepaper baskets
an open container for rubbish such as used paper. It is kept on the floor, for example in the corner of a room.

> **LANGUAGE EXTRA** you can also say *wastepaper bin*

watch *noun*
1 (*plural* **watches**) a small clock that you carry with you. It is tied around your wrist with a strap (called a watch strap) or, especially in the past, fixed to a chain and carried in a pocket.
2 the action of paying attention to something or someone, for example to make sure nothing bad happens *Dad kept watch on us while we were playing in the park.*
3 the activity of keeping a person or place safe, usually by standing somewhere and paying attention to what is happening around you *A soldier stood watch by the door.*
4 (*plural* **watches**) the period of time when someone keeps a person or place safe *The police officer's watch has just ended.*

watch *verb*
watches, watching, watched
1 to look at something or someone, especially when you pay attention as you look *I was watching TV. She watched me walk down the street.*
2 to look after someone or something, for example to make sure they are safe *A babysitter is coming to watch my little brother.*
3 to be careful about something or someone *Watch your head as you get into the car. Watch out for* (or *watch for*) *broken glass. Watch out – there's a motorbike coming! Watch your step as you get off the bus* (for example so as not to fall).
4 to pay careful attention to a situation so that you will notice someone or something as soon as they appear *Keep watching out for the thief in the crowd.*
5 to watch over someone or something is to look after them and protect them

watchable *adjective*
if something such as a film or TV programme is watchable, it is pleasant to watch but often not of excellent quality

watchdog *noun* **watchdogs**
1 a dog that looks after a place or building
2 an official person or organisation that makes sure businesses and other organisations do not do things that are wrong or against the law

575

watchful–wax

watchful *adjective*
paying careful attention to someone or something so that you will notice any dangers, problems or changes as soon as they happen **watchfully** *adverb* **watchfulness** *noun*

watchman *noun* watchmen
a watchman or night watchman is an old-fashioned word for a security guard whose job is to protect a building at night

water *noun*
1 the transparent liquid that falls from the clouds as rain, is in seas, rivers, lakes and pools and is used for drinking and washing
2 an area of water such as a sea, lake, river or pool *I dived into the water.*

water *verb*
waters, watering, watered
1 to give water to something such as a plant or garden, for example by pouring water over it *It's fun to water the grass.*
2 if your mouth waters when you see or smell food, it produces saliva (watery liquid) and makes you want to eat the food because you think it will be delicious *The smell of Mum's stew made my mouth water.*
3 if your eyes water, tears come out of them, for example because you have a cold or a strong wind is blowing
4 if you water down a liquid, you make it weaker by adding water to it

water biscuit *noun* water biscuits
a very thin dry biscuit that is not sweet. It is often eaten with butter or cheese.

watercolour *noun* watercolours
1 watercolours are paints that are mixed with water and used for painting pictures
2 a painting done with watercolour paints

watercress *noun*
a small plant that grows in water. Its leaves are eaten raw in salads.

water cycle *noun*
the series of events that happen when water evaporates (changes into vapour), for example from the sea or rivers, then produces clouds and finally falls to the ground as rain or snow

waterfall *noun* waterfalls
a place where water from a river or stream falls off the edge of a cliff or rock

waterfront *noun* waterfronts
an area of land next to the sea or a river or lake, for example with houses and restaurants on it

waterhole *noun* waterholes
a small area of water in a dry place such as a desert, where animals go to drink

watering can *noun* watering cans
a container with a long spout (tube) for giving water to plants to make them grow

waterlogged *adjective*
used about ground that is so wet that it can't hold any more water, so that you can't walk on it or play sports on it

water main *noun* water mains
a large pipe that carries water to a building, usually under the ground

576

watermark *noun* watermarks
a pattern or picture in paper, which you can only see when you hold the paper close to light. It is often used to stop people copying an important piece of paper or document in a dishonest way, for example a banknote or passport.

watermelon *noun* watermelons
a large round fruit with a hard green skin. It is soft, red and juicy inside and has lots of small black seeds.

water pistol *noun* water pistols
a small toy gun that shoots out water

waterproof *adjective*
1 not letting water or rain pass through *a waterproof jacket*
2 not damaged by water *a waterproof watch*

water skiing *noun*
the sport of being pulled through the water by a boat while standing on special skis called water skis **water-ski** *verb*

watertight *adjective*
1 if an object is watertight, it is so tightly closed (or it can be closed so tightly) that water can't get into or out of it *a watertight flask*
2 if something such as an excuse or argument is watertight, every detail has been thought about carefully and no-one can find anything wrong with it

waterway *noun* waterways
a narrow area of water such as a river or canal that boats and ships sail along

waterworks *noun*
a place or building with equipment for storing and treating water and with pipes for supplying water to a particular area

watery *adjective*
1 used about food or drink that has a lot of or too much water in it *watery soup; a watery cup of tea*
2 used about something that is full of water or looks like water *watery eyes; Saliva is the watery liquid inside your mouth.*

watt *noun* watts
a unit for measuring electrical power *a 60-watt light bulb*

ORIGIN named after James *Watt*, Scottish 18th-century engineer. Watt invented the unit (called 'horsepower') for measuring the power of an engine.

wave *verb*
waves, waving, waved
1 to lift your hand (or hand and arm) and move it from side to side, usually as a way of saying hello or goodbye *Granddad waved to me as I got on the train. Suraj was waving his hands, trying to catch my attention. All the family waved goodbye to me.*
2 if you wave something, you move it from side to side or move it about in the air *Children were waving flags. The magician waved her magic wand.*
3 if something waves, it moves gently from side to side or in the air *The tall grass was waving in the breeze.*
4 to move your hand, for example from side to side or backwards and forwards, as a way of telling someone to move somewhere or do something *The police officers waved the bus driver on* (moved their hands to tell the driver to continue).

wave *noun* waves
1 a mass of higher water that moves across the surface of an area of water, usually the sea. Waves are caused by the wind blowing onto the surface of the water or by the tide (level of the sea going up and down at the coast). *After the storm, huge waves rolled onto the shore.*
2 the action of waving something, especially your hand *Mohammed greeted me with a friendly wave.*
3 a part of someone's hair that is slightly curved instead of being straight
4 in science, a wave is the particular form or pattern that types of energy such as sound, light or heat produce as they travel *Radio waves are a way of sending radio signals through the air.*
5 one group of a large number of people who arrive somewhere shortly after another group *Waves of demonstrators poured into Trafalgar Square.*
6 one amount of a large number of things that happen shortly after another amount *wave after wave of bombing*
7 a sudden increase in something *a crime wave* (lots of crimes suddenly happening)
8 a strong feeling that suddenly appears *a wave of anger*

wavelength *noun* wavelengths
1 in physics, the distance between the two peaks (highest points) of a sound or radio wave
2 the size of a radio wave that a radio station uses for broadcasting programmes

waver *verb*
wavers, wavering, wavered
1 if someone wavers, they are not sure about something, for example about what to do *My parents were wavering between buying me a tablet or getting me a bike.*
2 to be or become weak *He never wavered in his determination* (nothing stopped him doing what he was determined to do).
3 to shake slightly *Her voice wavered when she spoke to the head teacher.*

wavy *adjective* wavier, waviest
used for describing something such as someone's hair or a line that is not straight but has slight curves in it

wax *noun*
1 a substance like fat that is soft when heated up and hard when cold, used for making things such as candles, models, crayons and polish for furniture or cars. It comes from bees or is produced artificially. *a wax candle*
2 a soft yellow or brown substance that forms inside your ears

SYNONYM for sense 2: earwax

wax *verb*
waxes, waxing, waxed
1 to put wax on something to polish it or protect it *Dad was waxing the car.*
2 if the moon is waxing, it appears to get bigger every day until it becomes a full moon (complete circle). When it appears to be getting smaller, it is waning.

waxwork *noun*
1 (*plural* **waxworks**) a model made of wax, usually of a famous person and usually the same size as that person *The museum has a waxwork of Queen Victoria.*
2 a waxworks is a museum where you can see wax models of famous people

way *noun* **ways**
1 used for describing how something is done or what something is like *She said hello to me in a friendly way. I like the way you play the clarinet. Do it this way* (like this). *That's no way to speak to your teacher* (for example using bad words or an angry voice).
2 an imaginary line that someone or something goes along to get to a place *I think we're going the right way. Which way shall we walk? Tell me the way to the station.*

SYNONYM **direction**

3 a road or path for getting somewhere *This is the shortest way to school. Is there a way through the forest? The way in is over there and the way out is round the corner* (used for talking about the places where you go into and out of a building or room). *We live at 18 Acacia Way* (used in the name of roads).
4 if something or someone is (or gets) in the way or in someone's way, they stop someone from getting somewhere or doing something or they stop something from happening *You're standing in my way. We couldn't see the house – there were trees in the way. Mum's job gets in the way of picking me up from school.*
5 used when you mean a distance or period of time *It's a long way away. He's come all this way to see you. July is a long way off.*
6 used when you mean a particular position or the appearance of something *The painting was hanging the wrong way up* (with the top part at the bottom). *The car should be facing the other way round* (in exactly the opposite position). *Leave the room the way you found it* (looking how it was when you came into it). *The roof of the school is in a bad way* (in bad condition and needing to be fixed).
7 used when you mean a particular detail *My sister is different from me in every way. In some ways you're right.*
8 if someone is on their way to a person or place, they are coming (or going) and will arrive soon *I phoned the doctor and she's on her way. Mum's on her way back* (she's coming or going back).
9 **someone's ways** someone's particular behaviour *Your uncle has some strange ways.*
10 **by the way** used for adding something extra to what you've already said or written
11 **to get your own way** to make people let you do or have what you want
12 **to give way** to fall to the ground or break suddenly after becoming weak *The roof gave way under the weight of the snow. Grandma's legs just gave way.*
13 **to lose your way** to be lost and not know where you are
14 **to make your way** to go somewhere *I made my way over to the door.*
15 **to make way** to allow someone or something to get past, or to allow something to take the place of something *Stand up and make way for Charlie's wheelchair, please.. They knocked down a garage to make way for homes* (so that homes could be built instead).
16 (informal) **No way!** used when saying no very strongly *'Are you inviting Sam to your party?' – 'No way!'*

way *adverb*
1 (informal) used for giving extra importance to a word *These trousers are way too big for me. The exam had way more questions than last time.*

SYNONYMS **much, many**

2 used when talking about a long time in the past or future or a big distance in space *Nelson lived way back in the eighteenth century. Wait – you're way ahead of me!*

WC *noun* **WCs**
another word for a toilet, especially used as a sign in a public place

we *pronoun*
1 a word that you use when you are talking about yourself and you also include one or more other people *We're early.*
2 also used when you mean people in general *We should brush our teeth every day.*

weak *adjective* **weaker, weakest**
1 if a person or animal is weak, they don't have the power to do things with their body such as lift, move, push and pull heavy things or hit things hard *Great-Granddad is old and weak. My arms are too weak to pick up that heavy box.*
2 if something is weak, it doesn't have the power to move or hold something heavy, or it might break or get damaged if it is treated roughly *a weak roof; a weak fence; My tablet case is made out of weak plastic that doesn't protect it very well.*
3 done without much power, strength or energy *I gave a weak tug on the dog's lead but it barely noticed. She could only manage a weak smile.*
4 used for showing that someone doesn't have much of something or that something isn't much *Although Martine is dyslexic, the support she gets from her school is weak. I have a weak knowledge of French* (not much knowledge). *What a weak effort!*
5 not having much speed, light, heat or energy *a weak current* (with water flowing slowly); *a weak light; The sun's rays were weak* (not very hot). *The signal is weak here and I can't use my phone.*
6 not having much taste or flavour *a weak tea* (you can't taste the tea easily, for example because there is too much milk)
7 not having the power to influence people, actions or events *a weak leader; These measures are too weak to deal with such hurtful bullying.*
8 used for showing that something or someone is not very good, successful or of a high standard *Our school has a weak cricket team with one or two particularly weak players. I'm quite weak in maths. Don't choose a weak password* (one that is easy to guess).
9 used about something that is not based on sensible or intelligent ideas *a weak argument; a weak excuse*
10 a weak point is a bad quality that someone or something has, a bad part of something, or something that someone doesn't do or know very well *I'm good at maths but division is my weak point.*

SIMILE 'as weak as a kitten' means very weak (sense 1)

weaken *verb*
weakens, weakening, weakened
1 to make something or someone weaker *Heavy rain had weakened parts of the roof. The soldiers were weakened by months of war.*
2 to become weaker *Britain's influence in the area has been weakening.*

weakling *noun* **weaklings**
someone who is weak, usually having a weak or unhealthy body

weakly *adverb*
1 without much strength or energy *I hit the ball weakly over the net. Jake smiled weakly.*
2 not very well or successfully *Our team performed very weakly.*

weakness *noun*
1 the quality of being weak *the weakness of my legs; the weakness of an argument; My phone wouldn't work because of the weakness of the signal.*
2 (*plural* **weaknesses**) a bad quality that you have or that something has *I'm lazy – that's one of my weaknesses. Don't buy that laptop – it has more weaknesses than strengths.*
3 a feeling of really liking something or someone and not being able to stop yourself from liking them *I have a weakness for chocolate cake.*

wealth *noun*
1 lots of money or valuable things *My aunt is a person of great wealth* (a very rich person).
2 a large amount of something *The website gives a wealth of information about the school.*

wealthy *adjective* **wealthier, wealthiest**
1 if someone is wealthy, they have lots of money or valuable things
2 used for describing a place where wealthy people live *a wealthy neighbourhood*

weapon *noun* **weapons**
an object used for hurting people or causing damage, for example a gun, knife or bomb *a murder weapon; nuclear weapons*

wear *verb*
wears, wearing, wore, worn
1 if you wear something, you have it on a part of your body, usually as a piece of clothing, as a decoration or for protection *I'm wearing a blue shirt and glasses. Hannah was wearing earrings. He wore a strange expression on his face.*
2 to arrange your hair in a particular way *Maryam wears her hair in plaits.*
3 to become damaged or thinner by being rubbed or used a lot *The heels on my shoes are starting to wear* (or *wear out*).

wear – week

4 to damage something or make it thinner by rubbing it or using it *Riding your bike over rough ground all the time will wear* (or *wear out*) *your tyres. You've worn a hole in your jeans* (made a hole in them).
5 if a piece of clothing wears well, it lasts a long time without getting damaged
6 if something wears away, or if something wears it away, it becomes thinner or disappears, for example by being used a lot *The wind and rain have caused the letters on the sign to wear away over the years.*
7 if something wears off, it becomes less strong and disappears or it stops working *Soon after you leave the dentist's, the numb feeling in your mouth should begin to wear off. The anaesthetic has worn off.*
8 if someone or something wears you out, they make you very tired *All this studying has worn me out. You look worn out!*
9 if you wear something out, or if something wears out, you use it so much that it can't be used any more *In less than a year we've worn out our stair carpet! The batteries in my camera have worn out* (or *are worn out*) (they've stopped working because they are empty).

wear *noun*
1 used for talking about how much something is used or the damage caused to something by being used a lot *These boots are strong and can take a lot of wear* (can be worn a lot). *The carpets were old and there was a lot of wear on them.*
2 used for talking about particular types of clothes *children's wear; evening wear* (worn in the evening to go to important events)

weary ['weer-ee'] *adjective*
wearier, weariest
very tired *You look quite weary. I'm weary of listening to the same old excuse.*
wearily *adverb* **weariness** *noun*

weasel *noun* **weasels**
a small animal with a long body, short legs and a tail. Weasels usually have brown fur on their body with white fur on the front and underneath. They kill other animals such as mice and birds for food.

weather *noun*
1 used for talking about the conditions in the air at a particular time and place, such as the temperature and the amount of sun, rain, wind or snow there is *The weather is cloudy and rainy today.*
2 a weather forecast is a description of what the weather is likely to be at a particular time and place
3 **under the weather** feeling slightly ill *Jo has a cold and has been under the weather all week.*

weather *verb*
weathers, weathering, weathered
1 if something weathers, the sun, wind, rain and snow cause it to become worn or to change its appearance
2 if something such as the sun or wind weathers something, it becomes worn or its appearance changes *The sun and wind had weathered the old sailor's face.*
3 if someone weathers something bad or difficult, they are affected by it but they deal with it while it is happening and they carry on successfully once it has ended *The country has weathered difficult times. Our family has many problems but we must weather the storm* (deal with the problems now and carry on successfully afterwards).

weathercock *noun* **weathercocks**
a metal object fixed to the top of a building, usually shaped like a cockerel (male chicken) and standing on an arrow. It turns round as the wind blows and the arrow shows the direction the wind is coming from.

> **LANGUAGE EXTRA** you can also say *weathervane*

weatherproof *adjective*
if something is weatherproof, it is made from a material that protects it from the weather, for example from the rain and wind *a weatherproof jacket*

weave *verb*
weaves, weaving, wove, woven
1 to make cloth (or objects made of cloth) by putting long threads over and under each other using a special machine called a loom *Dad works in a factory where they weave carpets. In the past people spent a lot of time weaving.*
2 to make something by putting the stems of plants over and under each other, for example strips of wood from a willow tree *My sister weaves baskets.*
3 if someone or something weaves somewhere, they change direction lots of times *My brother was weaving in and out of the traffic on his motorcycle. The road weaves around the side of the mountain.*
weaver *noun*

web *noun* **webs**
1 a net of thin threads that a spider spins to catch insects for its food
2 a large amount or number of things that are connected to each other in a complicated way *a web of lies; We got lost in a web of streets in the old part of town.*
3 in computing, the web is a system that connects computers to each other all over the world and allows people to receive and share information, for example by using websites *a web-enabled computer* (one that can connect to this system)
4 the web is also used for talking about all the connected websites stored in this system *I was surfing the web.*
5 a web address is a series of letters, numbers and symbols used for finding a website. For example, you type it into your browser (program for looking at websites) and press the enter key.
6 a web page is a page that you read on a website

> **LANGUAGE EXTRA** in senses 3 and 4, it is also spelt *Web* and is short for *World Wide Web*

webbed *adjective*
if a bird such as a duck or animal such as a frog has webbed feet, its toes are joined by pieces of skin to help it swim

webcam *noun* **webcams**
a camera connected to or built into a computer. It takes moving pictures that you can see on the internet as they happen, for example using a phone and video service such as Skype.

website *noun* **websites**
a place on the internet where you find information about something or someone *Our school has a new website.*

wed *verb*
weds, wedding, wed or **wedded**
another way of saying to marry *The two actors will wed* (or *get wed*) *in the spring.*

we'd
short for 'we had' or 'we would'

wedding *noun* **weddings**
a ceremony in which two people get married, and the party or meal that happens afterwards *an invitation to the wedding; a wedding dress* (usually long and white, worn by a woman at her wedding); *a wedding ring* (worn by a man or woman to show they are married)

wedge *noun* **wedges**
1 an object, for example of wood, plastic or rubber, that is thin at one end and wider or thicker at the other end and looks like a triangle from the side. It is usually used for stopping something from moving by being pushed between that thing and something else. *I pressed the wedge under my door to stop it from closing.*
2 something shaped like a wedge *a wedge of cheese*

wedge *verb*
wedges, wedging, wedged
to hold something in a certain position, for example using a wedge *I wedged the door open with my doorstop.*

Wednesday *noun* **Wednesdays**
the day of the week between Tuesday and Thursday

> **ORIGIN** from Old English *Wodnesdæg* 'Woden's day'. In Old English, Woden was the chief of the gods.

wee *adjective*
a Scottish English word for little *a wee child; I had a wee nap.*

weed *noun* **weeds**
a wild plant that usually grows quickly in any type of soil and is often not wanted in places such as gardens and parks

weed *verb*
weeds, weeding, weeded
to remove weeds from something such as a garden or flowerbed

weedy *adjective* **weedier, weediest**
1 if someone is weedy, they are thin and weak
2 if something such as a path or area is weedy, it is full of weeds

week *noun* **weeks**
1 a period of time lasting seven days, starting from either Sunday or Monday *I'll finish my homework by the end of the week.*
2 any period of time that lasts seven days or about seven days *a week's holiday; I'll do it in a week. Come and see me a week on Friday* (or *Friday week*) (not this coming Friday but the one after that).
3 the five days from Monday to Friday when people go to work or to school *My mum works in Glasgow during the week.*

weekday *noun* **weekdays**
any one of the five days from Monday to Friday

weekend *noun* **weekends**
the two days of the week that consist of Saturday and Sunday and often Friday evening *What are you doing over the weekend?*

weekly *adjective*
1 happening once every week *a weekly visit*; *a weekly newspaper*
2 used for describing the total amount of something for a whole week *What's your brother's weekly pay?*
3 lasting a whole week *a weekly season ticket*

weekly *adverb*
happening once every week *We do the shopping weekly.*

weekly *noun* **weeklies**
a magazine that comes out once every week

weep *verb*
weeps, weeping, wept
if you weep, tears come out of your eyes, usually because you're unhappy or hurt

weeping willow *noun* **weeping willows**
a tree with long thin leaves and long thin branches that reach down to the ground. It often grows near water.

weigh *verb*
weighs, weighing, weighed
1 to measure how heavy something or someone is, usually using scales (a piece of equipment for weighing)
2 if something or someone weighs a certain amount, that's how heavy they are *I weigh about five stone.*
3 to weigh someone or something down is to make them heavier, for example so that they have trouble moving *Does that overcoat weigh you down?*
4 if something such as a problem or responsibility is weighing someone down, it is making them very worried
5 to weigh something up is to think about it carefully and then form an opinion about it

weight *noun*
1 how heavy something or someone is when this can be measured in pounds or kilos *Apples are sold by weight. My brother is the same weight as me.*
2 when something or someone is very heavy *This table can't support the weight of a computer. The rope gave way under the weight.*
3 (*plural* **weights**) any heavy object *I just can't lift this weight. Put some weights on those pieces of paper to stop them being blown away.*
4 if someone loses weight, they get thinner
5 if someone puts on (or gains) weight, they get fatter
6 a weight off your mind used when you mean something that you don't have to worry about any more

weight *verb*
weights, weighting, weighted
to weight something down is to make it heavier, for example by putting something heavy on it

weightless *adjective*
if an object or a person such as an astronaut is weightless, they seem to have no weight and they float about because they are not affected by the earth's gravity (force that pulls everything towards the earth) **weightlessness** *noun*

weightlifting *noun*
the sport or exercise of lifting heavy weights **weightlifter** *noun*

weighty *adjective* **weightier, weightiest**
1 very important and serious *a weighty subject*
2 very heavy *Grandma was in bed reading a weighty volume.*
weightiness *noun*

weir [rhymes with 'deer'] *noun* **weirs**
a structure such as a low wall built across a river or stream to control how the water flows

weird ['weerd'] *adjective* **weirder, weirdest**
very strange
weirdly *adverb* **weirdness** *noun*

weirdo ['weer-doh'] *noun* **weirdos**
an informal word for someone who is very strange

welcome *verb*
welcomes, welcoming, welcomed
1 to be friendly to someone when they arrive somewhere and make them feel comfortable, for example by saying how pleased you are to see them or by doing kind things *The head teacher welcomed us to our new school. When we got back from the trip, my stepmum welcomed us with a lovely meal.*
2 to be pleased to consider or accept something or someone *Our school welcomes new ideas. The club welcomes new members.*
3 to think that something is good *All the parents welcomed the decision.*

welcome *noun* **welcomes**
1 being friendly to someone when they arrive somewhere and making them feel comfortable *The head teacher gave us a warm welcome.*
2 the way someone is greeted somewhere *What sort of welcome did you get? The tennis champion got a hero's welcome.*

welcome *adjective*
1 used for saying that you're happy to see someone somewhere or to get something *a welcome visitor*; *We had a welcome visit from our cousin Martin. You'll always be welcome at our house. A cup of tea would be welcome.*
2 used for telling someone that they can do or have something if they want to and that you're happy about this *Nandita is welcome to borrow my book. You're welcome to have another ice cream.*
3 You're welcome! used as a polite reply when someone says thank you to you

welcome *interjection*
used as a friendly greeting to tell someone that you're happy to see them there *Welcome home! Welcome to York!*

welcoming *adjective*
1 friendly, for example to someone who has just arrived somewhere *a welcoming smile*
2 attractive in a friendly way *a welcoming hotel room*

weld *verb*
welds, welding, welded
to join two pieces of metal by heating them and pressing them together
welder *noun*

welfare *noun*
1 the health, comfort and safety of a person or animal *Great-Granddad's welfare is very important to Mum and Dad.*
2 help given by a country or organisation to people who need it, for example to people who are poor

well *adverb* **better, best**
1 in a way that is good *to sing well*; *to behave well*
2 very much or in every way *Shake the bottle well. We're well prepared. I know David well. It's well past midnight. The book was well worth reading.*
3 an informal way of saying very *I'm well pleased.*
4 used for saying that something could or might be true (or could have or might have been true) *You could well be right. I might well have left my sandwiches at home.*
5 if you say you can't very well do something, you mean it wouldn't be sensible to do it *I can't very well tell my teacher that he's wrong.*
6 if you say someone may (or might) as well do something, you mean that it seems like a good idea even though you're not sure what's going to happen, or you mean that someone should do something *The bus hasn't come but we may as well wait a bit longer* (it seems like a good idea to wait in case the bus comes soon). *'Can I finish the cake?' – 'You may as well.'*
7 as well used when you mean something or someone extra, or when you mean the same thing is true about something or someone else *Can I come as well? I love chess and Granddad does as well. I'm learning French as well as Spanish.*

> **SYNONYMS** too, also

8 to be doing well to be successful, or to be getting better after being ill or injured *My sister's doing well at school. Nan has left hospital and she's doing well.*
9 Well done! used for praising someone who has done something well or who has been successful
10 well off if someone is well off, they are rich or fairly rich

well *adjective* **better, best**
1 in good health *'How are you?' – 'I'm well.' She's not feeling well* (she's ill).
2 used for saying that a particular situation is good *All's well in Ms Taylor's class today.*
3 just as well used when you mean that it's a good thing something happens the way it does *It's just as well you didn't come to the party – it was boring.*

well *interjection*
a word used for many things, for example showing a feeling such as surprise, agreeing or disagreeing with someone, when you're not sure about something or when you start saying something after stopping for a short time *Well, I don't know. Well, well, look who's here!*

well–whack

well *noun* **wells**
1 a deep hole that is dug in the ground for people to get water from. A brick wall is usually built around the hole and there is often a small roof built over it.
2 a deep hole that is dug in the ground or sea for getting oil from *an oil well*

we'll
short for 'we will' or 'we shall'

well-behaved *adjective*
used for describing someone whose behaviour is good and polite *a well-behaved child*

well-being *noun*
someone's well-being is their health and happiness

well-built *adjective*
having a big and strong body *a well-built athlete*

well-dressed *adjective*
wearing clothes that are attractive and usually fashionable as well as clean and tidy

well-educated *adjective*
used for describing someone who has studied a lot in a school, college or university and knows a lot about many subjects

well-informed *adjective*
knowing a lot about something such as what's happening or about a particular subject

wellington *noun* **wellingtons**
one of a pair of tall rubber boots that do not let water pass through. Wellingtons are used for walking on wet or muddy ground or through water.

> ORIGIN named after the first Duke of *Wellington* (1769–1852) who wore these boots and made them popular in the countryside. The original boots were made of leather and were used by soldiers in battle.

well-known *adjective*
used about someone or something that lots of people know or know about *a well-known actor*; *a well-known fact*

well-mannered *adjective*
having good behaviour when you are with other people, especially being polite and showing respect

> ANTONYM bad-mannered

wellness *noun*
used for talking about people's good health and the things they do to stay healthy, for example taking exercise and eating good food *a wellness centre* (for example for learning about ways to stay healthy, receiving medical treatment or doing exercises)

well-off *adjective*
rich or fairly rich *We have some well-off neighbours.*

well-paid *adjective*
1 getting a lot of money from a job *a well-paid teacher*
2 paying you a lot of money *a well-paid job*

well-read *adjective*
used for describing someone who has read lots of books and knows a lot about many subjects

well-to-do *adjective*
rich (used for describing someone or the place where someone lives) *a well-to-do family*; *a well-to-do neighbourhood*

welly *noun* **wellies**
an informal word for a wellington boot

> LANGUAGE EXTRA also spelt *wellie*

Welsh *adjective*
1 connected with Wales or the Welsh language
2 Welsh rarebit is toast with melted cheese on it

Welsh *noun*
1 the language some people speak in Wales
2 the Welsh are people from Wales

Welshman *noun* **Welshmen**
a man from Wales

Welshwoman *noun* **Welshwomen**
a woman from Wales

wend *verb*
wends, wending, wended
if someone or something wends their way somewhere, they go there, often slowly or over a long distance

went
past tense of **go**

wept
past tense & past participle of **weep**

were
second person singular and first, second and third person plural past tense of **be**

weren't
short for 'were not' *They weren't at home.*

werewolf ['were' rhymes with 'where']
noun **werewolves**
in stories, a person who turns into a wolf at night when there is a full moon (when the moon appears as a complete circle)

Wesak ['ves-ak'] *noun*
an important Buddhist festival in April or May. It celebrates the birth and death of the Indian philosopher Siddhartha Gautama (563–483 BC), also known as Buddha, who founded Buddhism.

> LANGUAGE EXTRA also spelt *Vesak*

west *noun*
1 the direction that is straight ahead of you if you face the setting sun (as it disappears from the sky in the evening). The west is on your left if you face north and is also on the left of most maps, which have the north at the top.
2 the part of a country or town that is in the west *Hounslow is in the west of London.*
3 the West refers to the countries of Europe and North America

west *adverb*
towards the west *Our school faces west.*

west *adjective*
in or from the west *the west coast*; *a west wind*

West End *noun*
the West End is the main part of central London where there are lots of shops and stores, theatres and cinemas, tourist attractions and government offices. It is situated to the west of the City of London (the main banking centre).
compare: **East End**

westerly *adjective*
towards or from the west *a westerly wind*

western *adjective*
in or connected with the west *western Canada*

Western *adjective*
in or connected with the countries of Europe and North America *Western ideas and values*

western *noun* **westerns**
a film or story with action that happens in the west of the United States in the 19th and early 20th century. Westerns are about the lives of cowboys (men who ride horses, look after cows and do other things such as fight Indians or rob banks).

westwards *adverb*
towards the west *westward* *adjective*

wet *adjective* **wetter, wettest**
1 if something is wet, there is water, liquid or rain on it or in it *My jeans are wet through* (completely wet, for example because of being in the rain).
2 if someone is wet, they have water or rain on them *You'll get soaking wet if you go out without an umbrella in this rain.*
3 used about something such as paint or ink that has not become dry yet
4 used about the weather or about a place when you mean there is lots of rain *Tomorrow will be very wet. Glasgow is quite wet in winter.*
wetness *noun*

wet *noun*
1 liquid, especially water *Don't put your schoolbooks down in the wet.*
2 used for talking about the rain *Come in out of the wet.*

wet *verb*
wets, wetting, wetted or **wet**
to make something wet

wet suit *noun* **wet suits**
a piece of clothing made of rubber that people such as divers and windsurfers wear closely against their body to protect them from the water and keep them warm

> LANGUAGE EXTRA also spelt *wetsuit*

we've
short for 'we have'

whack *verb*
whacks, whacking, whacked
1 to hit something or someone hard *She whacked me with an exercise book. I fell and whacked my head.*
2 (informal) to put something somewhere, often quickly or carelessly *Dad whacked the pie in the oven.*

whack *noun* **whacks**
1 the action of whacking something or someone
2 the noise when something or someone is whacked

3 an informal word for a share of something, for example work *I'm not helping you any more – I've done my whack.*

whale *noun* **whales**
a sea animal that looks like a very large fish and breathes air through a hole in the top of its head called a blowhole. Whales are the largest animals that live in the sea.

whaling *noun*
the activity of hunting whales and killing them, for example to eat their meat

wham *interjection* (informal)
used for showing the loud noise something makes when it suddenly hits something else

wham *verb* (informal)
whams, whamming, whammed
to hit something or someone very hard

wharf *noun* **wharves**
a long flat area next to the sea or a river where boats stop for goods and passengers to be taken on and off and where boats can be left safely. A wharf often includes warehouses (buildings for storing goods in) and piers (structures built out into the sea).

what *pronoun*
1 used in questions when you want information about something or someone *What did you eat? What has she sent you? What are you doing?*
2 used for mentioning something such as an idea, action or situation without naming it *I saw what happened* (the thing that happened). *You didn't do what I asked* (the particular thing I asked). *What you say is right. I know what to do but Raj has no idea what to do.*
3 used when you mean all the things or the whole of something or any or every kind of thing *Lend me what you can. I ate what was on my plate. She always does what she wants.*

SYNONYM **whatever**

4 What about . . . ? used when you want someone to pay attention to something or someone *You've asked everyone else in the class if they want to go swimming! – So what about me?*
5 What about . . . ? also used for making a suggestion *What about a holiday in Ireland?*
6 What for? used for asking about or talking about the reason for something or when an explanation for something is needed *'Open the door.' – 'What for?' What did you do that for?*

SYNONYM **why**

7 What if . . . ? used for asking about something that could happen in a particular situation *What if there's a problem?*
8 (informal) **What's up?** used for asking someone what's happening or what they're doing, or for asking someone what's wrong
9 (informal) **What's up?** also used as a friendly way of saying hello to someone when you meet them

what *adjective*
1 used for asking for information about something or someone *What time is it? What's the time? What celebrities do you prefer? Tell me what kind of ice cream you want.*
2 used for mentioning something or someone without naming them *Dad knows what ice cream I like. I can guess what teachers you mean.*
3 used for giving extra importance to a word, for example when you mean how good or bad or how big or small something or someone is *What lovely weather we're having!* (we're having really lovely weather); *What a stupid mistake! What delicious cakes!*

what *interjection* (informal)
1 a way of asking someone to repeat something because you didn't hear or understand *'Pass me the chocolates.' – 'What?'*
2 used for showing surprise or a feeling such as anger or disappointment *What! – Is he still in bed? What! – Did you hit your sister again?*
3 used for asking someone what they want when they call your name *'Tom!' – 'What?'*

whatever *pronoun & conjunction*
1 used when you mean any or every kind of thing, situation, action or idea or the whole of something *On my birthday, my parents let me do whatever I want. He always eats whatever Mum puts on his plate.*

SYNONYMS **anything, everything**

2 used when you mean that something you do or something that happens is not important because it makes no difference to the situation *Whatever I do, I'll never be any good at French. Whatever happens, don't tell Dad.*

SYNONYM **no matter what**

3 used for showing something you don't know *He was waving a white flag at us, whatever that means.*
4 used for asking for information in a strong way, for example because you're angry or surprised *Whatever are you doing?*
5 or whatever used when you mean something of that kind *Rashid is in his room playing computer games or whatever.*

whatever *adjective & adverb*
1 used when you mean of any or every kind or when talking about two or more possibilities *Choose whatever chocolates you like. Whatever team finishes first is the winner. She has no reason whatever to complain* (no reason at all to complain).
2 used for describing something that is not important because it makes no difference to the situation *Every school, whatever its size* (or *whatever size it is*), *should have a music teacher.*
3 (informal) used for showing that you're slightly angry about something or when you don't want to give a proper answer to something *'Will you help me in the kitchen?' – 'Whatever.'*

whatsoever *adverb*
a stronger way of saying 'whatever', used in negatives (sentences with a word such as 'no', 'not' or 'never') *I've got no time whatsoever today* (no time at all). *'Are there any cakes left?' – 'None whatsoever.'* (none at all of any kind)

wheat *noun*
1 a tall plant with seeds used for making flour *a wheat field*
2 the seeds of this plant that are crushed to make flour for making bread, cakes and pasta *a sack of wheat*

wheel *noun* **wheels**
1 an object shaped like the letter O that is fixed to a vehicle, for example a car, train or bicycle, or to a container such as a suitcase or trolley. It turns round and round and makes the vehicle or container move along the ground. *a suitcase on wheels*
2 any round part that turns or makes something turn, either inside or connected to a machine or piece of equipment
3 a round part inside a vehicle that a driver uses for controlling its direction *I don't feel safe with my brother at the wheel* (driving the car).

SYNONYM **steering wheel**

4 a wheel clamp is a metal object put on one wheel of a car to stop someone driving it

wheel *verb*
wheels, wheeling, wheeled
1 to push something with wheels along the ground *Get off your bike and wheel it across the road.*
2 to push someone or something along the ground on or in something that has wheels *The porter wheeled me into the operating theatre* (on a bed with wheels on it).
3 to move in a circle around something or someone *Seagulls wheeled above us in the sky.*

wheelbarrow *noun* **wheelbarrows**
a container with one wheel at the front and two long handles at the back, used for carrying things outside, for example in a garden

wheelchair *noun* **wheelchairs**
a special chair with wheels, used by someone such as an injured or very old person who cannot walk. The person sits in the chair and uses it for moving around in or is pushed along by someone else.

-wheeled *suffix*
used for making adjectives showing a particular number or type of wheels *a three-wheeled pushchair; a big-wheeled truck*

wheelie bin *noun* **wheelie bins**
a large plastic container with wheels, used for putting rubbish in. Wheelie bins are kept outside, for example near a house, building or shop, and are usually shaped like a square or rectangle.

wheeze *verb*
wheezes, wheezing, wheezed
if someone wheezes, they make a high rough sound as they breathe because they have trouble breathing **wheeze** *noun*

wheezy *adjective* **wheezier, wheeziest**
used about someone who makes high rough sounds as they breathe or about the sound that they make

whelk *noun* **whelks**
a sea animal that has a soft body similar to a snail's body and lives inside a pointed shell with curves that go round and round like a spiral. Whelks are often eaten as food.

when – whine

when *adverb & conjunction*
1 used for asking about or talking about the time, date or day of something *When will I see you again?* (what date, day or time); *When is Harry's birthday?* (what date); *I don't know when this happened. Tell me when you see him* (immediately or soon after you see him). *I remember one summer when there were floods.*
2 used for asking about or talking about a particular situation and the time that it happens *When should you use an exclamation mark in a sentence? I never know when to call an adult by their first name.*
3 used for talking about two situations going on at the same time or two actions or events happening one after the other *When we lived in Scotland* (during the time we lived there), *I went to school in Perth. We went out when it stopped raining* (just after it stopped raining). *When he opened the door, no-one was there.*
4 used for connecting two parts of a sentence that show an important or surprising difference between two situations *I don't know why you walk to school when you could take the bus.*

whenever *adverb & conjunction*
1 used when you mean every time *Whenever Dad takes me to school, I arrive late.*
2 used when you mean at any time or in any situation *We can leave whenever you're ready. I help my brother with his reading whenever possible.*
3 used for mentioning a time that you don't know *I'll see you on Seema's birthday, whenever that is.*
4 used when you mean that the time something happens is not important because it makes no difference to the situation *Whenever I phone Uncle Vijay, I get the busy signal.*

SYNONYM no matter when

5 used for asking in a strong way about the time of something, for example because you're bored or angry *Whenever is this film going to end?*

where *adverb & conjunction*
1 used for asking about or talking about a place, for example what place something or someone is in or at, goes to or comes from *Where are you off to? Where's she from? I don't know where I put my glasses. Edinburgh is the city where I feel most at home.*
2 used for asking about or talking about a particular situation *I have a lot to say – so where should I begin? I don't understand where I went wrong. Dad reached the point where he could no longer read without his glasses.*

whereabouts *adverb*
used for asking about or talking about somewhere that is not an exact place but the rough place where something or someone is *Whereabouts did you leave your schoolbag?*

whereabouts *noun*
the place where something or someone is *My cousin is travelling around Italy but her exact whereabouts are* (or *is*) *not known.*

whereas *conjunction*
used for connecting two parts of a sentence that show an important difference between things, people or situations *I always get up late whereas my sister gets up early.*

whereupon *conjunction*
used for talking about something that happens immediately after something else, for example in stories *He rubbed the magic lamp, whereupon a genie appeared.*

wherever *adverb & conjunction*
1 used when you mean every place *Her cat follows her wherever she goes. Wherever I am in the country I always have my phone with me.*
2 used when you mean at any place or in any situation *You can put up your tent wherever you like. Tell us the whole story, beginning wherever you want to.*
3 used for mentioning a place that you don't know *He lives in a village called Upper Settlington, wherever that is.*
4 used when you mean that any place that you mention is not important because it makes no difference to the situation *Wherever you look you'll never find it.*

SYNONYM no matter where

5 used for asking in a strong way about a place, for example because you're surprised or angry *Wherever did you find my phone?*

whether *conjunction*
1 used when talking about two possible situations when you don't know which of them is true *I asked George whether he was tired* (is he tired or is he not tired?).

SYNONYM if

2 used when choosing between two possible situations *I'm not sure whether to laugh or cry.*
3 used when you mean that one situation or another situation makes no difference to a particular action *It's not Ava's job to cut the grass, whether now or in the future. I'm going to sit next to you whether you like it or not.*

whey ['way'] *noun*
the watery liquid left in milk when it becomes sour and after the curds (thick lumps) are removed

which *adjective & pronoun*
1 used in questions when you want exact information about something or someone that belongs to a group of similar things or people, usually a small group *Which shirt did she choose? Red, green or blue – which colour do you like? Which one do you want? Which is your house?*
2 used for mentioning something or someone from a particular group without naming them *I know which authors you mean. He showed me which football he wanted. There are so many pairs of trainers I can't decide which to buy. I don't remember which of the boys I spoke to.*
3 used for saying something about something *A beagle is one breed of dog which has long ears. Where's the pocket money which you promised me? We took the train which goes on to Norwich. Leeds is the city in which my dad was born.*
4 used after a comma for giving extra information about something *This book, which is about dinosaurs, was recommended by our teacher. Emma and Sita are best friends, which is why they always sit together.*

whichever *adjective & pronoun*
1 used when you mean 'of any kind' when talking about a group of similar things or when talking about two or more possibilities *You can borrow whichever book you want. Whichever side wins today goes through to the final. Have a look at these T-shirts and choose whichever you like. Whichever one you want, Dad will pay for.*
2 used when you mean that something is not important because it makes no difference to the situation *Whichever way you turn you can always see the mountains.*

SYNONYM for sense 2: no matter which

whiff *noun* whiffs
1 a smell of something that you smell for a short time *We caught a whiff of Chinese food as we walked past the restaurant.*
2 a slight amount of something

while *conjunction*
1 used for talking about two things that happen at the same time *We often watch TV while eating dinner.*
2 used for talking about something that happens at a certain time or during the time that something else is happening *Granddad came round while you were out. I hurt my knee while playing football.*
3 used for connecting two parts of a sentence that show an important difference between things, people or situations *In the south of the country it's very hot while in the north it's cold.*

SYNONYM whereas

4 another way of saying although *While I'm no good at maths, it's a subject I like.*

LANGUAGE EXTRA you can also say *whilst*

while *noun*
a period of time *This happened a long while ago. I'd like to stay here for a while* (for a short period of time).

while *verb*
whiles, whiling, whiled
if you while away the time, you spend it in a pleasant way without getting bored when you have nothing else to do *On the long plane journey I whiled away the time playing computer games.*

whim *noun* whims
a sudden strong feeling that you want to do or have something

whimper *verb*
whimpers, whimpering, whimpered
if a person or animal whimpers, they make soft quiet sounds such as small crying sounds, usually when they are hurt, frightened or sad **whimper** *noun*

whine *verb*
whines, whining, whined
1 if a person or animal whines, they make long high sounds that are unpleasant to listen to, for example because they are sad or hurt
2 to complain about something in a way that annoys someone
whine *noun*

582

whinge–whizz

whinge verb (informal)
whinges, whinging or whingeing, whinged
to complain, usually about something not important, in a way that annoys someone
whinger noun

whinny verb
whinnies, whinnying, whinnied
when a horse whinnies, it makes a gentle high noise **whinny** noun

whip noun whips
a long piece of leather or rope fixed to a handle. It is used for hitting or controlling animals, for example horses, to make them go faster or (especially in the past) for hitting people, usually to punish them.

whip verb
whips, whipping, whipped
1 to hit an animal or person with a whip
2 to mix food such as cream or eggs with a fork or piece of equipment such as a mixer until it becomes thick *whipped cream*
3 (informal) to take something or someone quickly away from or out of somewhere *I whipped off my socks and jumped into bed. She whipped out her pen and signed the card just before Mum walked in.*
4 (informal) to go or move quickly *Our teacher whipped through the lesson in about five minutes.*
5 an informal way of saying to steal
6 to whip something up is to cause a particular feeling or behaviour *The head teacher is trying to whip up support for the plan.*

whirl verb
whirls, whirling, whirled
1 to turn round and round, or to make something or someone do this *Leaves were whirling around in the wind. The dancer whirled his partner across the floor.*
2 used about something such as thoughts or ideas in your mind that often make you feel confused or uncomfortable *There were strange thoughts whirling around in my head.*

whirl noun whirls
a whirling movement

whirlpool noun whirlpools
1 a place in an area of water such as a river, lake or sea where the water goes round in a circle and pulls things towards it and under
2 a large bath for relaxing in. It has hot water that flows in through small holes and goes round in circles, producing lots of bubbles.

whirlwind noun whirlwinds
a strong wind that blows in a circle and moves along the ground in a tall column or huge cloud

whirr verb
whirrs, whirring, whirred
to make a continuous low sound, for example like the sound of something going round in a piece of equipment or an insect's wings moving quickly *Can you hear the DVD whirring in the drive?*

whirr noun
a whirring sound

whisk verb
whisks, whisking, whisked
1 to mix food such as eggs or cream with a fork or whisk, for example until it becomes thick
2 to move someone or something quickly *As soon as she felt chest pains, my aunt was whisked off to hospital.*
3 to go or move somewhere quickly

whisk noun whisks
a kitchen tool made up of curves of wire fixed to a handle. It is used for mixing food such as eggs or cream, for example until it becomes thick.

whisker noun whiskers
1 whiskers are the long strong hairs that grow above the mouth of an animal such as a cat or seal
2 whiskers are also the hairs that grow on the side of a man's face or on his chin

whisky noun whiskies
a strong alcoholic drink, usually made from the seeds of a plant called barley and produced in Scotland

whisper verb
whispers, whispering, whispered
to speak or say something in a very quiet way using your breath rather than your voice, usually on purpose so that other people can't hear *James and Eddie are always whispering. I whispered something into his ear.*

whisper noun whispers
a very quiet way of speaking using your breath rather than your voice *The two girls were speaking in a whisper.*

whist noun
a card game played by two groups of two players. Each side tries to win more cards than the other.

whistle verb
whistles, whistling, whistled
1 to produce a high sound by making your breath come out between your lips or teeth *When I whistle, my dog comes running.*
2 to produce musical notes by making your breath come out between your lips *Rosie was whistling a lovely tune. My brother loves whistling in the bath.*
3 if a piece of equipment whistles, or if something such as a boat or old-fashioned steam train whistles, it makes a loud high sound *The kettle whistles when the water is boiling.*
4 to move somewhere very quickly making a high sound *The wind was whistling through the trees. We could hear the Diwali fireworks whistling overhead.*
5 if birds whistle, they make pleasant high sounds

whistle noun whistles
1 a small metal or plastic object that you put in your mouth and blow into to produce a high sound, for example as a signal or warning *The referee blew the whistle to stop the game.*
2 a small piece of equipment in a kettle that makes a high sound when the water is boiled
3 a piece of equipment on something such as a boat or old-fashioned steam train or the roof of a factory that makes a very loud high sound, for example as a signal or warning
4 the sound of someone or something whistling *Amin gave a whistle when he saw me.*
5 the sound of someone blowing into a whistle *We stopped playing when we heard the whistle.*

white adjective whiter, whitest
1 having the lightest possible colour, like snow or milk
2 having less colour in your face than usual, for example because you're frightened or ill *When he saw the bully in the corridor, Ethan went white.*
3 having skin that is light-coloured, not dark
4 connected with people who have skin that is light-coloured *a white neighbourhood*
5 white coffee is coffee with milk in it
6 a white blood cell is a cell (tiny unit of living matter) that fights infection in the blood
7 a white lie is a small lie about something that is not important. Someone tells a white lie to be polite, especially when telling the truth would upset someone or cause a problem.
whiteness noun

SIMILES 'as white as a sheet' and 'as white as a ghost' mean very white (sense 2); 'as white as snow' means very white (sense 1)

white noun whites
1 the colour white
2 the white of an egg is the transparent liquid around the yolk (yellow part)
3 someone with light-coloured skin

whiteboard noun whiteboards
1 a large white surface, usually made of plastic, used for writing or drawing on with a special marker (pen with a thick soft point). The marks are rubbed away with a cloth or piece of soft material. Whiteboards are used by teachers in classrooms.
2 a large white screen for displaying images from a computer through a projector connected to the computer, used for helping teachers in classrooms. You can interact with the images in the same way as on a computer, for example by touching them with your finger or a special pen.

white-hot adjective
used for describing something such as metal or coal that is so hot that it becomes white

White House noun
1 the home of the president of the United States, in Washington, the capital city of the United States
2 the US president and the people who work for him or her

whitewash noun
a paint made from water and lime (a powdery substance from a rock called limestone). It is used for painting walls and ceilings white.

whitewash verb
whitewashes, whitewashing, whitewashed
to paint something white using whitewash, for example a wall or ceiling

whitish adjective
slightly white

Whitsun ['wit-sern'] noun
a Christian holiday in May or June on the seventh Sunday after Easter

whizz verb
whizzes, whizzing, whizzed
1 to move very fast *He whizzed past the house on his motorbike.*

who–why

2 to make the sound of something rushing through the air, for example a sound like 's' or 'sh' repeated lots of times
3 to do something very fast *My homework was easy – I whizzed through it in half an hour.*

LANGUAGE EXTRA also spelt *whiz*

who *pronoun*
1 used in questions when you want information about someone, for example what someone's name is *Who are these people? Who did you bump into?*

LANGUAGE EXTRA in the second example in sense 1, *whom* can be used instead of *who* when writing or speaking in a careful way

2 used for mentioning someone without naming them *I know who broke the window. Chloe didn't see who hit her.*
3 used for saying something about someone *He's an actor who's been in lots of films. Where's the teacher who you saw yesterday?*

LANGUAGE EXTRA in the second example in sense 3, *whom* can be used instead of *who* when writing or speaking in a careful way

4 used after a comma for giving extra information about someone *My brother, who is older than me, gets more pocket money.*
5 used before words such as 'know', 'care' or 'need' when you mean that no-one knows or cares or needs something. When you use it like this in a question, the question doesn't need an answer. *'Could he win?' – 'Who knows?' 'We're late.' – 'Who cares?' I don't know who needs a car in London!*

who'd
short for 'who had' or 'who would'

whoever *pronoun*
1 used when you mean any person, for example any person who does something (or any people who do something) *Whoever drew that picture is a true artist. Invite whoever you like to the party.*
2 used when you mean that it is not important which person (or people) you mention because it makes no difference to the situation *I don't want to speak to them, whoever they are. Whoever I ask tells me a different story.*

SYNONYM no matter who

3 used for asking for information about someone in a strong way, for example because you're angry or surprised *Whoever were you talking to just now?*

whole *adjective*
1 used for talking about something when you mean every part of it and not just one or more parts of it *I spent the whole day in bed.*
2 not broken or damaged, for example used about something that keeps its normal shape when something happens to it *The pelican swallowed the fish whole.*

584

3 used for giving extra importance to a word *Ibrahim has a whole lot of friends* (very many friends). *Kate complains the whole time* (every single moment). *You're the best dad in the whole world.*

whole *noun*
1 (plural **wholes**) one single thing or shape that has no parts missing from it *Two halves make a whole.*
2 if you talk about the whole of something, you mean every part of it and not just one or more parts of it *The whole of the classroom was painted blue.*

SYNONYM all of

3 on the whole considering everything about a particular situation without going into detail *On the whole, my teacher was pleased with my homework.*

whole *adverb*
an informal way of saying completely *This app gives me a whole new way of keeping in touch with friends.*

wholemeal *adjective*
used for describing bread or flour made from the seeds of a plant such as wheat, including the husk (outside covering of the seed)

whole number *noun* **whole numbers**
a number (such as 0, 1, 2, 3, 25, 481) that is not a fraction or decimal

wholesale *adjective & adverb*
1 connected with selling goods at low prices, for example from factories, to shops and businesses that sell them to customers at higher prices. Selling to customers from shops is called retail. *wholesale prices* (low prices, for example of goods sold from factories to shops); *Fatima bought her dress wholesale* (at a low price, for example directly from the factory).
2 used when you mean a very large amount of something or a very large number of things *wholesale destruction; wholesale changes*

wholesaler *noun*

wholesome *adjective*
1 good for your health *wholesome food; a wholesome climate*
2 good for you, or based on standards of good behaviour *The clowns at the circus provided some wholesome fun. He's a footballer who has a wholesome image.*

who'll
short for 'who will'

wholly *adverb*
1 used for giving special importance to a word or for saying that something is very true *That was wholly unexpected.*
2 in every way or when talking about every part of something *Hashim isn't wholly to blame.*

SYNONYM completely

whom *pronoun*
1 used instead of 'who' to say something about someone when 'who' is the object of a verb (receives the action of the verb). 'Whom' is also used instead of 'who' when it comes after a preposition. *the teacher whom I like best; the girl with whom I go swimming*

2 used instead of 'who' in questions when 'who' is the object of a verb *Whom did you see? Whom did he speak to?*

LANGUAGE EXTRA *whom* is used when writing or speaking in a careful or old-fashioned way. In everyday language, people usually use *who* instead.

whoop ['woop'] *noun* **whoops**
a sudden loud shout that you make because you're happy *There were whoops of delight from the children as they watched the clowns.* **whoop** *verb*

whoopee ['oo' in 'whoop' rhymes with 'u' in 'put'] *interjection*
used for showing the sudden sound people make when they're happy

whooping cough ['hoop-ing'] *noun*
an illness that causes a lot of bad coughing and makes you make a loud unpleasant noise when you breathe in after coughing

whoops *interjection*
used when you make a mistake or don't do something you should do or when a little accident happens, for example when you drop something *Whoops, I nearly forgot my lunchbox!*

whoosh *verb*
whooshes, whooshing, whooshed
to move quickly with a sound like 'sh' repeated lots of times, for example like the sound of water rushing or of something rushing through the air
whoosh *noun & interjection*

whopper *noun* **whoppers** (informal)
something very large that is much larger than other things of the same kind *Tyrannosaurus was a whopper compared to the other dinosaurs.*

whopping *adjective* (informal)
extremely large *My parents bought me a whopping great cake for my birthday.*

who's
short for 'who is' or 'who has'

whose *adjective & pronoun*
1 used when you ask who something or someone belongs to or is connected with *'Whose homework is this?' – 'It's mine.' Whose are these keys?*
2 used for mentioning who something or someone belongs to or is connected with but without naming them *I know whose dad you are.*
3 used for saying something about who something or someone belongs to or is connected with *Here's the boy whose uncle is a police officer. My best friend, whose house is around the corner, is moving to Scotland.*

LANGUAGE EXTRA be careful not to write *who's* ('who is' or 'who has') instead of *whose*

who've
short for 'who have'

why *adverb & conjunction*
1 used for asking what makes something happen or what makes someone do something when you want to know the reason for it or cause of it *Why are you late? 'Close the window.' – 'Why?'*

2 used for talking about what makes something happen or what makes someone do something when you know (or don't know) the reason for it or cause of it *I don't know why it's so dark. That's the reason why I'm angry.*
3 used with 'not' in a question for making a suggestion *Why don't we go swimming this afternoon?*
4 used with 'not' for showing that you're angry or upset *You've broken a glass – why can't you be more careful?*
5 Why not? used for saying yes to someone's suggestion *'Do you want a lift to school?' – 'Why not?'*

wick noun **wicks**
1 a piece of string that goes through the middle of a candle and sticks out at the top of the candle. It burns when you light it, for example with a match.
2 a strip of material inside an oil lamp that is used for lighting the lamp. The material absorbs the oil (takes it into itself) so that the lamp can continue to burn after it has been lit.

wicked adjective **wickeder, wickedest**
1 doing very bad and cruel things *a wicked witch*
2 also used about something that a wicked person does, says or has *a wicked attack; The bully had a wicked look in his eyes.*
3 very wrong and causing a lot of suffering *These rules are wicked.*
4 slightly bad, often in a way that shows you like having fun *My sister played a wicked little trick on me.*

SYNONYM mischievous

5 a slang word meaning very good *That film was wicked!*
wickedly adverb **wickedness** noun

wicker noun
thin strips of wood or hard material from the stems of plants that are twisted over and under each other to make things such as baskets and furniture *a wicker basket*

wicket noun **wickets**
1 in cricket, one of two small structures made of three upright wooden sticks (called stumps), which are stuck in the ground, and two small pieces of wood lying flat on top (called bails). A bowler bowls the ball (throws it in a special way) to try to hit one of the wickets.
2 the area of grass between the two wickets
3 a wicket keeper is someone who stands behind a wicket and is ready to catch the ball

wide adjective **wider, widest**
1 measuring a large amount of space from one side of something to the other side *a wide street*
2 used for saying the space that something measures from one side to the other *The box is nine inches wide.*
3 used about something that includes or affects lots of different things or people *a wide range of subjects; the wide influence of the internet; Plans for a new gym have wide support* (lots of people like the idea).
4 very large *a wide area; a wide gap in the fence; There's a wide difference of meaning between these two words.*

5 used for describing eyes that are open as much as possible, for example showing surprise

wide adverb
1 as much as possible or very much (used for talking about something that is open or moved apart) *The dentist told me to open my mouth wide. The door was wide open* (open completely or a lot).
2 not hitting something you are aiming at *He kicked the ball towards the goal but it landed wide.*
3 wide awake not sleeping and not feeling as if you want to go to sleep

widely adverb
1 in or to lots of places *These foods are widely available. My uncle has travelled widely.*
2 by lots of people *a widely used expression; Spanish is widely spoken in the US.*
3 very much *Prices vary widely from shop to shop.*
4 very *My sister and I have widely different opinions on the subject.*

widen verb **widens, widening, widened**
1 to make something wider, such as a road
2 to make something more or larger, for example so that it includes or affects more people or things *Scotland is trying to widen its influence. The supermarket must widen the choice it offers to customers.*
3 to become more or larger *The gap is widening.*

widespread adjective
1 by lots of people *the widespread use of smartphones; There was widespread anger about the way he dealt with the bully.*
2 happening in many places *widespread flooding*
3 happening a lot *widespread problems*

widget noun **widgets**
1 any very small piece of equipment or object, especially when you don't know what it is used for or what it is called
2 a software widget is a tiny program that displays something on your computer screen, for example a clock or the weather forecast

widow noun **widows**
a woman whose husband is dead and who has not got married again

widowed adjective
used about a woman whose husband is dead or a man whose wife is dead

widower noun **widowers**
a man whose wife is dead and who has not got married again

width noun **widths**
the width of something is the distance from one side of it to the other *The box is 10 centimetres in width.*

wield ['weeld'] verb **wields, wielding, wielded**
to hold something such as a tool or weapon and use it or be ready to use it *The police arrested a man who was wielding a knife.*

wife noun **wives**
a woman that a man is married to

ORIGIN from Old English *wif* 'woman'

Wi-Fi ['why-fye'] noun (trademark)
a system for connecting electronic equipment such as computers and smartphones to the internet and to each other using radio waves instead of wires *a wi-fi hotspot* (place for connecting to the internet without wires)

LANGUAGE EXTRA also spelt *wi-fi*

wig noun **wigs**
a covering of false or real hair that someone wears on their head if they have no hair of their own or want to cover their own hair

wiggle verb **wiggles, wiggling, wiggled**
1 if you wiggle something, you move it from side to side or up and down with lots of small movements *I was wiggling my toes to keep warm.*
2 if something wiggles, it moves in this way
wiggle noun

wiggly adjective (informal)
1 with lots of curves *a wiggly line*
2 moving from side to side or up and down with lots of small movements *a wiggly worm*

wigwam noun **wigwams**
a shelter, usually shaped like a dome (the top half of a ball), that Native Americans lived in in the past

wild adjective **wilder, wildest**
1 used for describing an animal that lives on its own away from people, for example in the countryside, a forest or a jungle *Tigers are wild animals.*

ANTONYM tame

2 used for describing a plant that grows on its own in a natural way and is not looked after by people *There are bluebells and other wild flowers growing at the end of the playground.*
3 used for describing a place or area where plants grow and animals live away from people in a natural way *the wild moors of Devon*
4 if someone is wild or their behaviour is wild, they behave in a way that is out of control, for example they behave badly or do whatever they want or they show their feelings in an excited way or with lots of energy *The children went wild as soon as the teacher left the room. When the celebrity appeared, there were wild cheers* (people cheered in a loud and excited way and showed their feelings strongly). *My big brother went to a wild party* (for example where people do what they want such as play loud music).
5 used for describing someone who is angry
6 if the weather is wild, it is extremely windy and rainy

SYNONYM stormy

7 (informal) if someone is wild about something or someone, they like them very much
wildness noun

wild adverb
1 in a way that shows that an animal lives on its own away from people *Lions roam wild in the jungle.*

wild – wind

2 in a way that shows that a plant grows on its own in a natural way *We saw daffodils growing wild.*
3 in a way that shows that someone's behaviour is out of control *Gangs of young people ran wild through the streets.*

wild *noun*
1 in the wild living in a natural way, for example in a forest, the countryside or a jungle *elephants in the wild*
2 the wilds an area where not many people live, far away from the nearest town *My aunt has a cottage in the wilds of Scotland.*

wildebeest ['wil-der-beest'] *noun* **wildebeest** or **wildebeests**
a large African animal with a heavy body, long legs, curved horns and a hairy tail. Wildebeest run very fast and live in herds (large groups).

wilderness ['wil-der-ners'] *noun*
an area of land where wild plants grow and wild animals live and where there are no houses or people

wild goose chase *noun*
when someone goes looking for something or someone without any success, for example because that thing or person doesn't exist or is somewhere else

wildlife *noun*
animals that live in a natural way, for example in the countryside. Wild plants are sometimes called wildlife too.

wildly *adverb*
1 in a way that is out of control, for example badly, in an excited way or with lots of energy *George behaved wildly at my birthday party. The children shouted wildly when the clowns appeared.*
2 extremely *Dad wasn't wildly enthusiastic about the idea.*

Wild West *noun*
the western part of the United States when people from the east first went there during the second half of the 19th century. There was a lot of fighting with Native Americans and often people did not obey the law.

wilful *adjective*
1 used for describing something bad or wrong that is done on purpose *wilful damage*
2 if someone is wilful, they do what they want and often do things that are bad or wrong

wilfully *adverb* **wilfulness** *noun*

will *verb*
1 used for saying what you are going to do or what is going to happen in the future *I will see you tomorrow. It'll* (it will) *be dark by five o'clock. They won't* (will not) *be coming to your party.*
2 used for asking someone something politely *Will you have a piece of cake? Ask Rohan if he will come for lunch.*
3 used for telling someone to do something *Will you sit down!*
4 used for saying that something will definitely happen in the future *Don't worry – I will never leave you.*
5 used about what something or someone can do or wants to do *My laptop won't shut down* (cannot shut down). *Yes, I will forgive you.*

6 used for saying that you think something is true but you are not completely sure *'There's someone at the door.' – 'That will be Granddad.'*

will *noun*
1 a strong feeling of wanting something and the power to control your actions to get what you want *Aishah works hard and has the will to succeed.*
2 what someone wants *Don't force your will on your little sister. I wouldn't do anything against your will* (anything that you didn't want me to do).
3 (*plural* **wills**) a legal document that says what will happen to someone's money and the things that belong to them after they die

willing *adjective*
happy to do something, for example when someone asks you *Are you willing to help me with my maths? People are more and more willing to visit museums and galleries.*

willingly *adverb*
in a way that shows you are happy to do something *I would willingly help you if I could.*

willingness *noun*
a feeling of being happy to do something *Harry has a willingness for hard work.*

willow *noun* **willows**
a tree with long thin leaves and long thin branches that can reach down to the ground. It often grows near water.

wilt *verb*
wilts, wilting, wilted
if a plant wilts, its stem and leaves hang down because it doesn't have enough water or is dying

wily ['why-lee'] *adjective* **wilier, wiliest**
if someone is wily, or if someone's behaviour is wily, they are clever at getting what they want, for example by making people believe things that aren't true

SYNONYM cunning

SIMILE 'as wily as a fox' means very wily

wimp *noun* **wimps** (informal)
someone who is weak, afraid of people and things, or not successful at doing things
wimpish *adjective*

win *verb*
wins, winning, won
1 to do better than everyone else or better than another person or side in something such as a game, race or battle, for example by being more intelligent, skilful, faster or stronger *Our team won the match. If I argue with my sister, she always wins. Who won the war?*
2 to get something such as a prize, for example by doing better than someone or because you're lucky *Mohammed won first prize in the competition. My aunt won some money on the lottery.*
3 to get something you want, for example by working hard *Luke won a scholarship to a private school. The head teacher is trying to win support for the idea.*

win *noun* **wins**
when someone wins, for example in a game, race or competition

wince *verb*
winces, wincing, winced
to make an unpleasant expression with your face, for example showing pain, dislike or worry or because you feel embarrassed

winch *noun* **winches**
a piece of equipment for lifting, pulling or lowering a person or object using a rope, cable or chain that is twisted round a tube

winch *verb*
winches, winching, winched
to lift, pull or lower someone or something with a winch *The drowning man was winched to safety by a helicopter.*

wind [rhymes with 'pinned'] *noun*
1 (*plural* **winds**) air that blows fast enough to make things move, such as the branches of a tree or the sails of a boat. A strong wind can cause problems or damage. *A gust of wind blew the dustbin over.*
2 air in your stomach or bowels (tubes that carry waste food out of the body). This air makes you feel uncomfortable.

SYNONYM gas

3 being able to breathe easily *After that long run I needed to get my wind back* (start breathing again normally).
4 a wind instrument is a musical instrument played by blowing through it, for example a trumpet or clarinet
5 in an orchestra, the wind section is the part where wind instruments are played

wind [rhymes with 'kind'] *verb*
winds, winding, wound [rhymes with 'sound']
1 to put something round something else, either once or lots of times *I wound a scarf around my neck.*
2 to put things round each other lots of times *Mum wound the wool into a ball.*
3 if something such as a road or river winds, or if a person or vehicle winds their way somewhere, they change direction lots of times *The path winds up and around the side of the mountain. The bus wound its way through the narrow streets of the old town.*
4 to press a button or click an icon to make something such as a video or DVD go backwards or forwards to another position without playing it *Please wind the film back to the beginning.*
5 if you wind a handle, you turn it or keep turning it
6 if you wind (or wind up) a watch or clock, you turn a part of it such as a knob to make it work
7 if you wind the window of a vehicle up or down, you close it or open it by making it move up or down, for example by pressing a button or turning a handle
8 if you wind something up, such as a lesson or meeting, you end it
9 if you wind up in a particular place or situation, you get to that place or situation although it is something you were not expecting to happen or something not wanted *We took the wrong train and wound up in Leeds.*

SYNONYM to end up

10 (informal) to wind someone up is to make them angry or upset, for example by saying unkind things to them

586

windfall *noun* windfalls
1 an amount of money someone suddenly receives that they are not expecting
2 a fruit such as an apple that has fallen off a tree and lies on the ground

wind farm *noun* wind farms
a group of wind turbines (tall structures with parts that turn in the wind, used for producing electricity)

windmill *noun* windmills
1 a tall building with four long flat parts at the front that look like a large cross. The flat parts are called sails. They turn in the wind to produce power for crushing grain to make flour (especially in the past).
2 a stick with a flower shape at the top made from curved pieces of plastic that turn in the wind or when you blow them. You can hold it in your hand and play with it as a toy.

window *noun* windows
1 a frame with glass in it in the wall of a room or building. It lets light and air come in and lets you see outside.
2 the glass part of a window *She threw a stone and broke the window.*
3 a space with glass in it in the side, front or back of a vehicle, for example a car, train, aircraft or ship, used for looking through
4 the front part of a shop, made of glass. A shop window is often used for displaying things that are sold in the shop.
5 an area on a computer screen that you can move or make smaller or bigger. It is used for showing or saving information on, for example in a program containing text or pictures or in a spreadsheet.
6 Windows (trademark) is a computer operating system (software that makes a computer work) used on millions of computers

windowpane *noun* windowpanes
a flat piece of glass in a window

windowsill *noun* windowsills
a narrow shelf at the bottom of a window

LANGUAGE EXTRA you can also say **window ledge**

windpipe *noun* windpipes
the tube in your body that carries air from your mouth or nose to your lungs
compare: **oesophagus**

windscreen *noun* windscreens
1 the large window at the front of a vehicle such as a car or lorry
2 a windscreen wiper is a long thin strip of rubber fixed to a metal part that moves backwards and forwards across a windscreen to wipe the rain away

windshield *noun* windshields
the American word for a windscreen

windsurfer *noun* windsurfers
1 a long board with a sail fixed to a pole, used for windsurfing

SYNONYM **sailboard**

2 someone who windsurfs

windsurfing *noun*
the sport of standing on a board with a sail fixed to a pole and letting the wind blow you across the water **windsurf** *verb*

windswept *adjective*
if a place is windswept, the wind blows strongly there, for example because there are no buildings or trees to protect it from the wind

wind turbine *noun* wind turbines
a tall structure with three long parts at the front, called blades, that turn in the wind to produce power for making electricity

windward *adjective*
the windward side of something such as a ship or hill is the side that faces the wind

ANTONYM **leeward**

windy ['win-dee] *adjective*
windier, windiest
used for describing a time, the weather or a place when the wind is blowing *a windy day; a windy corner; September was quite windy.*

windy ['win' rhymes with 'wine'] *adjective*
windier, windiest
if something such as a path or road is windy, it changes direction lots of times

wine *noun*
1 an alcoholic drink usually made from grapes
2 (*plural* wines) a type of wine or a glass of wine
3 a dark red colour

wing *noun* wings
1 one of the parts of the body of a bird or insect that it uses for flying, for example by moving it up and down
2 one of the long flat parts on either side of a plane that make it possible for it to fly
3 a part of a large building that is connected to the main building but is not a part of it, for example a part added to the main building later *the maternity wing of the hospital*
4 a corner part of a road vehicle that is above one of its wheels
5 a player in a game such as football who plays on the left or right side of the sports field
6 in a theatre, the wings are the areas beyond the left or right side of the stage that the audience cannot see
7 if someone takes you under their wing, they look after you and protect you

wing *verb*
wings, winging, winged
to go quickly *The eagle was winging its way across the sky. The prize money will be winging its way to you shortly.*

winged *adjective*
having wings *A griffin is an imaginary winged creature.*

wingspan *noun* wingspans
the distance from the end of one wing to the end of the other, usually when talking about the wings of a plane or bird

wink *verb*
winks, winking, winked
1 if someone winks, they close one of their eyes and then open it again quickly, for example to show that what they say is a joke or secret message *Josh winked at me when he said that.*
2 if a lamp or something shiny winks, it shines with a light that keeps going on and off (or it looks as though it is doing this) *The light on the printer is winking. In the distance, lights were winking through the fog* (seemed to be going on and off).

wink *noun* winks
1 the action of winking *She gave me a wink.*
2 to not sleep a wink to not get any sleep at all *My sister snored so loudly that I didn't sleep a wink last night.*

winkle *noun* winkles
a sea animal that has a soft body similar to a snail's body and lives inside a thick pointed shell. Winkles are eaten as food.

winkle *verb*
winkles, winkling, winkled
to get information from someone, usually after a lot of effort because they don't want to give you the information *Dad was trying to winkle the secret out of me.*

winner *noun* winners
1 a person, animal or team that does better than the others, for example in a game, race or competition
2 a successful thing or person *I think your idea is a real winner!*

winning *adjective*
1 used for describing someone who wins *the winning team*
2 used about something you do to win *Bimla scored the winning goal.*

winning post *noun* winning posts
a thin pole in a race, usually a horse race, that shows where the race ends. In a horse race, it has a red circle on the top with a white centre.
compare: **finishing line**

winnings *noun plural*
money that someone wins, for example in a horse race or card game

winter *noun* winters
the season between autumn and spring when the weather is coldest

wintertime *noun*
the season of the year when it's winter

wintry *adjective*
having the usual qualities of winter *wintry weather*

wipe *verb*
wipes, wiping, wiped
1 to rub something with a cloth, or with or against something soft, to clean it or make it dry *I came in from the rain and wiped my glasses. Wipe your hands!*
2 to remove something such as liquid or dirt with a cloth or your hands *Please wipe up the milk you spilt. I wiped the sweat off my forehead. You wash and I'll wipe* (dry the dishes).
3 to wipe something or someone out is to destroy them or get rid of them completely *An earthquake wiped out the whole village.*

wipe *noun* wipes
the action of wiping *Before setting the table, please give it a quick wipe.*

wiper *noun* wipers
short for **windscreen wiper**

wire–withdraw

wire noun wires
1 a long thin piece of metal that you can bend or cut *a wire fence*; *a wire coat hanger*
2 a long thin piece of metal that is easy to bend and has a layer of plastic around it, used for carrying electricity or phone signals

wire verb
wires, wiring, wired
1 to connect something with electrical wires *a badly wired light switch*; *a wired connection to the internet*; *The router isn't working because it hasn't been wired up properly. My dad is in hospital wired up to a heart monitor.*
2 to wire money is to send it directly from one bank to another using a computer

wireless adjective
used for describing equipment or systems that do not use wires but use radio waves instead, for example for connecting to the internet *a wireless network*; *a wireless hotspot*; *I connect to the internet using a wireless connection rather than a cable.*
wirelessly adverb

wireless noun wirelesses
an old-fashioned word for a radio

wiring noun
1 all the wires in a particular place or piece of equipment *The wiring in Granddad's house is very old.*
2 a piece of wire

wiry adjective wirier, wiriest
1 if someone is wiry, they are thin but strong
2 wiry hair is stiff and rough when you touch it

wisdom noun
1 the quality of being wise, for example having great knowledge and making good decisions *Grandma is a woman of great wisdom.*
2 used for talking about how sensible something is *I'm not sure about the wisdom of choosing such a difficult subject for your homework.*
3 a wisdom tooth is one of the four large teeth right at the back of the mouth that appear much later than the other teeth. Wisdom teeth grow on either side of your mouth at the top and bottom.

wise adjective wiser, wisest
1 if someone is wise, they are intelligent and make good decisions because they know a lot about things, for example things learnt through experience or from books *a wise old man with a beard*; *Your sister is very wise to continue her studies.*
2 if something is wise, it is sensible and based on good decisions *a wise choice*; *a wise decision*; *It's not very wise to go out in the rain without a raincoat.*
3 **none the wiser** or **not any the wiser** used when you mean someone knows no more about something now than before, or when someone doesn't know anything about something *Miss Singh explained the lesson to me but I'm none the wiser* (I still don't understand it). *If you clear up the broken glass, no-one will be any the wiser* (no-one will know that you broke a glass).

SIMILE 'as wise as an owl' means very wise

wisely adverb
in a way that is sensible and based on good decisions *George wisely deleted the spam email.*

wish verb
wishes, wishing, wished
1 to want something to be true even though that isn't likely or possible *I wish you would work harder in school. Granddad wishes he was 10 years younger.*
2 a polite way of saying to want *You may sit down if you wish. My dad wishes to speak to the head teacher.*
3 used when you mean you're sorry that something has happened (or you're sorry that something has not happened) *I wish I hadn't told you my secret. I wish I had warned you earlier.*
4 used when you mean you hope that someone will get something good such as a happy birthday, luck or success *We wished our teacher Happy New Year. I wish you well* (I hope good things happen to you).
5 to wish for something is to want it *The caravan has everything you could wish for. I couldn't wish for a better sister* (she's the best sister anyone could have).

wish noun wishes
1 something you want or a feeling of wanting something *The school always respects the wishes of parents.*
2 used for talking about what you would really like to happen or to have even though that isn't likely or possible *a secret wish*; *Close your eyes and make a wish. The wizard granted her three wishes* (things she wanted that would come true by magic).
3 **best wishes** used for saying you hope things are good for someone, for example as a friendly way of saying goodbye at the end of an email, letter or greetings card *Best wishes, Jack. Give my best wishes to Ollie.*

wishbone noun wishbones
a bone shaped like a V from the front part of a bird that people eat, such as a chicken, duck or goose

CULTURE NOTE when two people pull each of its ends, the *wishbone* breaks in two and the person with the larger piece is supposed to make a wish

wisp noun wisps
used for describing something long and thin, for example a line of smoke or a piece of hair *There were wisps of white cloud in the sky.* **wispy** adjective

wisteria ['wis-teer-ree-er] noun
a climbing plant with purple or white flowers that hang down in large bunches

wistful adjective
sad about something, for example something you had or did in the past but can no longer have or do, or something that you wanted to have or do but didn't *a wistful look*; *When she thinks about her life, Nan often gets wistful.* **wistfully** adverb
wistfulness noun

wit noun
1 the special quality of using words and ideas in a clever and funny way
2 (plural **wits**) someone who is good at using words and ideas in a clever and funny way
3 **wits** used for talking about the power to use your mind, understand things quickly and make good decisions in difficult situations or when playing games *Thanks to my quick wits I won the game.*
4 **to be at your wits' end** to not know how to solve a particular problem after you've tried many ways of dealing with it already
5 **to keep your wits about you** to pay attention to things so as to notice any problems or dangers as soon as they happen

witch noun witches
in stories, a woman who has magic powers and who usually uses them to do evil things

CULTURE NOTE people often think of a *witch* as an old woman wearing a pointed hat and flying on a broomstick

witchcraft noun
using magic powers, usually to do evil things

witch-doctor noun witch-doctors
a person who tries to cure people who are ill using magic powers or very old medical treatments, especially in some societies in Africa

with preposition
1 used for saying that something (or someone) and something else (or someone else) are together in the same place or doing something together at the same time *Put this book with the others on the shelf. I'm playing chess with Lila.*
2 used for saying what something or someone has *the house with the green door*; *the girl with an umbrella*
3 used for saying what something is used for *Dad sliced the melon with a sharp knife.*

SYNONYM using

4 used for saying what is in or on something *I filled my glass with lemonade. The ground was covered with snow.*
5 used for showing who you are fighting or arguing against *Don't start a fight with that bully.*
6 used for showing feelings towards someone *I'm angry with you.*
7 used for showing in what way someone does something or in what way something happens *Treat your computer with care. The box fell off the shelf with a loud noise.*
8 used for showing the cause or reason for something *She was trembling with cold. The air was thick with smoke.*
9 used for showing something connected with something or someone *Be careful with those glasses. What's the matter with you?*

withdraw verb
withdraws, withdrawing, withdrew, withdrawn
1 to stop taking part in an activity *Our captain withdrew from the match because of a leg injury.*
2 to move away from a place, for example because you are in danger or to avoid a difficult situation *The enemy soldiers were forced to withdraw from the town.*
3 to take money out of a bank account *Mum withdrew £20 from the cash machine.*

588

withdrawal–wonder

4 to stop giving, doing or selling something *The head teacher withdrew her support for the project. The supermarket has withdrawn its beef sausages from sale.*
5 to say that something you said is not true and show that you made a mistake by saying it *The prime minister withdrew his remarks.*

withdrawal noun
1 the action of withdrawing, for example moving away from somewhere, no longer taking part in something or no longer giving or doing something *the army's withdrawal from the battlefield; our team's withdrawal from the game; our sponsor's withdrawal of support*
2 (plural **withdrawals**) taking money out of a bank account, or an amount of money that someone takes out *Dad made a withdrawal so he could pay me my pocket money.*

withdrawn adjective
if someone is withdrawn, they are very quiet and don't talk to other people

wither verb
withers, withering, withered
if a plant withers, it becomes dry and weak and starts to die *Granddad forgot to water the violets and they withered* (became dry and died).

withhold verb
withholds, withholding, withheld
to not give someone something that they want or need, for example information, money or support *My parents withheld permission for me to go on the trip.*

within preposition
1 before the end of a period of time *The doctor will come back to see you within three days.*
2 during a particular period of time *Within the last few months Sayed has made a lot of progress at school.*
3 less than a particular distance *The school is within a mile of my house.*
4 less than the distance in which something or someone can be reached, seen or heard *The top shelf isn't within reach of my little brother. We were within earshot of the band playing in the park* (we could hear it). *The enemy tanks were within sight* (we could see them).
5 inside a particular place *We walked around the old part of town, within the city walls.*
6 inside the limits of what is possible, reasonable or allowed *I'll do what you ask within reason* (provided it is sensible). *Changing the date of tomorrow's match is not within my power* (I can't do that).

within adverb
inside something, for example a place or group *Our school had a bad report – it needs to change from within.*

without preposition
1 used for saying what something or someone doesn't have *a tree without leaves; I went out without my umbrella. Ismail can't see without glasses* (if he doesn't use them).
2 not in the same place as someone else, or not doing something together with someone *She was at the party without her mum. Don't leave without me.*

3 used for saying what someone or something doesn't do *We walked out of the shop without buying anything.*
4 used for saying what doesn't happen or exist *I accepted without hesitation. He told me the truth without any embarrassment. We had a whole month without problems.*
5 if you go or do without something, you carry on in the usual way even though you don't have something important *How long can you go without sleep?*

withstand verb
withstands, withstanding, withstood
1 to not be harmed or damaged by something *These plants are strong enough to withstand extremes of temperature.*
2 to deal with something difficult without letting it harm you *Celebrities have lots of pressures to withstand.*

witness noun **witnesses**
1 someone who sees something happen such as an accident or crime *There were many witnesses to the car crash.*
2 someone who tells a court of law what they know about a crime, event or person

witness verb
witnesses, witnessing, witnessed
to see something happen such as an accident or crime

witty adjective **wittier, wittiest**
using words and ideas in a clever and funny way *a witty author; a witty remark*
wittily adverb

wives
plural of **wife**

wizard noun **wizards**
1 in stories, a man who has magic powers and who uses them usually to do good things but sometimes to do evil things
2 a person who is very good at something or who knows all about something *a computer wizard; My sister is a wizard with numbers.*
3 a piece of software that helps you to do a particular task, for example to install a program, by giving you easy instructions to follow one at a time

wizardry noun
1 doing clever things with a computer *The police used their wizardry to track down the criminal.*
2 pieces of equipment that do clever things *The satellite is full of the latest technical wizardry.*

wobble verb
wobbles, wobbling, wobbled
if something wobbles, it moves slightly from side to side *The ladder is wobbling because it's not on a flat surface. Tap your jelly with a spoon and see it wobble.* **wobble** noun

wobbly adjective **wobblier, wobbliest**
1 if something is wobbly, it moves slightly from side to side *a wobbly chair* (for example because it is broken or not on a flat surface); *a wobbly tooth* (because it is loose)
2 if someone is wobbly, they are weak and shaking slightly and might fall over if they stand or walk

wodge noun **wodges**
an informal word for a large amount or piece of something

woe [rhymes with 'grow'] noun
1 an old-fashioned word for great sorrow or sadness
2 someone's woes are the problems they have and the bad things that happen to them

woeful ['woe' rhymes with 'grow'] adjective
1 very sad *a woeful expression*
2 very serious or bad *a woeful lack of respect*

woefully ['woe' rhymes with 'grow'] adverb
1 extremely, in a way that makes you feel sad because a situation is so bad *Our schoolbooks are woefully out of date.*
2 in a very sad way *The sick dog looked at me woefully.*

wok noun **woks**
a large frying pan shaped like a bowl, used for cooking pieces of vegetables and meat by moving them around in hot oil. Woks were first used in China.

woke
past tense of **wake**

woken
past participle of **wake**

wolf noun **wolves**
a wild animal that looks like a very large dog. Wolves live and hunt together in groups called packs. The sound they make is a howl.

wolf verb (informal)
wolfs, wolfing, wolfed
if you wolf something down, you eat it very quickly

woman noun **women**
1 a grown-up female person
2 a female person who works somewhere *She's the woman from the library. We took the computer to the repair woman.*

womankind noun
all the women in the world

womanly adjective
connected with women or having qualities that some people think women should have *a womanly voice; womanly looks*

womb ['woom'] noun **wombs**
1 the part in the body of a female person where babies develop
2 the part in the body of a female animal where baby animals develop

wombat ['wom-bat'] noun **wombats**
an animal with a thick hairy body and short legs. Wombats look like small bears and live in Australia.

women
plural of **woman**

won
past tense & past participle of **win**

wonder verb
wonders, wondering, wondered
1 used for saying that you want to know something that you don't know *I wonder what he's doing now. Don't you wonder why she left in a hurry? I wonder if Dad will be home late. Maths is my favourite subject – if you were wondering* (if you wanted to know).
2 used for saying that you haven't decided about something and you are still thinking about it *I'm wondering whether to go to Paul's party.*

589

wonder–wording

3 used for saying that you are surprised by something *I wonder you didn't hurt yourself when you slipped on the ice. I sometimes wonder how stupid these boys are.*
4 used for saying politely what you want or asking politely what someone wants *I wonder if I could have an ice cream and then go home. Mum was wondering if you wanted a cup of tea?*
5 if you wonder at something, for example something beautiful, large or good, you have and show a feeling of great respect for it and it gives you great pleasure

wonder noun
1 a feeling of great respect, pleasure and sometimes surprise, for example when you see something beautiful, large or good *The children's eyes were filled with wonder.*
2 (*plural* **wonders**) something that fills you with this feeling *the wonders of ancient Egypt*

SYNONYM marvel

3 it's a wonder used for saying that something is surprising *There was so much snow on the ground it's a wonder you got to school on time.*
4 no wonder used for saying that something is not surprising *No wonder you don't have any pocket money left – you spent it all on sweets.*

wonderful adjective
1 very good *wonderful weather; a wonderful dancer; I had a wonderful time.*
2 very beautiful *a wonderful dress; wonderful countryside*
3 very friendly and kind *Your mum's a wonderful person.*

wonderfully adverb
1 extremely well *The team played wonderfully.*
2 extremely *They were wonderfully happy in their new house.*

wonky adjective **wonkier, wonkiest** (informal)
1 not straight *wonky teeth; The picture on the wall looks wonky.*
2 shaking slightly or not fixed in one position *a wonky chair* (for example because it has one leg shorter than the others or is not on a flat surface); *This trolley has wonky wheels.*
3 weak, in bad condition or not working properly *a wonky knee; a wonky computer*
wonkiness noun

won't
short for 'will not' *I won't say a word.*

woo verb
woos, wooing, wooed
1 to try to get someone to support you, do things for you or buy things from you, for example by promising them something good *The airline is wooing passengers with cheap fares.*
2 (old-fashioned) if someone woos someone, they pay them a lot of attention, usually because they want to marry them

wood noun
1 the hard material that forms the main part of a tree, used for many things such as making furniture, floors and doors or for making a fire

2 (*plural* **woods**) an area where there are lots of trees growing together *I like going for walks with Mum in the wood* (or *woods*) *near the school.*

wooded adjective
used for describing a place where lots of trees grow *a wooded area*

wooden adjective
1 made of wood
2 if someone such as an actor or dancer is wooden, or if their actions are wooden, the way they move, behave or speak is awkward and doesn't show any natural human feelings

woodland noun
an area of land filled with lots of trees

LANGUAGE EXTRA you can also say *woodlands*

woodlouse noun **woodlice**
a tiny grey creature with a hard shell and many legs that looks like an insect. It lives in wet places in a house or garden and rolls itself into a small round shape if you touch it.

woodpecker noun **woodpeckers**
a bird that uses its strong pointed beak to make holes in the bark of trees and find insects there to eat. There are many kinds of woodpeckers with feathers of different colours.

woodwind noun
1 a woodwind instrument is a musical instrument played by blowing through it, for example a flute or clarinet
2 in an orchestra, the woodwind is a group of woodwind instruments or the musicians who play them

woodwork noun
1 making things out of wood *My older sister does woodwork at school.*
2 the parts of a building made out of wood

woodworm noun **woodworm** or **woodworms**
1 the young forms of many types of beetles that eat wood by making small holes in it. Woodworm usually eat the wood that is used in furniture or buildings.
2 damage caused to wood by woodworm making holes in it *a chair full of woodworm*

woody adjective **woodier, woodiest**
1 with lots of trees *a woody area*
2 used for describing the stem of a plant that is hard like wood or a plant that has a hard stem

woof ['oo' rhymes with 'u' in 'put'] noun
the sound a dog makes when it barks
woof verb

wool noun
1 the thick soft hair that grows on the body of a sheep or other animal such as a goat
2 cloth or thread made from this hair *a wool cardigan; a ball of wool*

woollen adjective
made from wool

woollens noun plural
clothes made from wool

woolly adjective **woollier, woolliest**
1 made from wool or from something that looks like wool *a woolly hat*
2 covered with wool or with hair that looks like wool *a woolly animal*
3 if something such as an idea or piece of writing is woolly, it is confused and not clear
4 if someone is woolly, what they say or think is confused and not clear
woolliness noun

word noun **words**
1 a part of a sentence with its own meaning and sound. A word is made up of a group of letters (for example 'happy') or just one letter (for example 'a' or 'I'). Written words are separated from each other by a space in between.
2 something that someone says *Ms Patel wants to say a word about* (or *a few words about*) *today's homework.*
3 something that someone says to someone *Could I have a word with you?*
4 news or a message about something or someone *Do you have any word about Granddad? Emily sent word that she would be home late.*
5 a promise that someone will do something (or not do something) *I won't tell anyone your secret – you have my word. I always keep my word* (do what I say I will do).
6 something that someone tells you to do *Start playing when I give* (or *say*) *the word* (when I tell you).
7 if someone gives you a word of something such as advice, warning, thanks or apology, they say that particular thing to you, for example they advise you, warn you, thank you or apologise to you *Dad gave me a word of advice. She left without a word of goodbye* (didn't say goodbye). *There was not one word of apology.*
8 word for word using the exact words someone said or wrote

word verb
words, wording, worded
to choose the right words when you say or write something *a thoughtfully worded birthday card; I'm having trouble wording this email to my teacher.*

word class noun **word classes**
one of the groups that the words of a language belong to, depending on how they are used in a sentence. The word classes in English are noun, verb, adjective, adverb, pronoun, preposition, conjunction and interjection.

SYNONYM part of speech

word family noun **word families**
a group of words that are related to each other because they share the same root (part of the word that contains the main meaning). For example, 'play', 'player', 'playful' and 'replay' belong to the same word family.

wording noun
the words that you choose when you say or write something *The wording of this sentence isn't very clear.*

word processing–worm

word processing *noun*
writing and printing documents using a computer

word processor *noun* **word processors**
a computer used for writing and printing documents

wordy *adjective* **wordier, wordiest**
using too many words or words that are very long *a wordy email*; *a wordy author*

wore
past tense of **wear**

work *verb*
works, working, worked
1 to spend time doing something that needs energy and attention *Faisal is working on his school project. My teacher told me to work harder in class* (pay more attention and try harder to learn).
2 to have a job that people pay you for *My brother works as a mechanic.*
3 to spend a particular time or amount of time working *Teachers work long hours. My mum works Sundays.*
4 if something such as a piece of equipment or a machine works, it does what it is supposed to do because all its parts move or connect correctly *I changed the battery in my phone and now it's working again. My brain's not working today!*
5 if you work a piece of equipment or a machine, you make it work *Do you know how to work the washing machine?*
6 if something such as a plan or medicine or particular action works, it produces good results and what you want to happen does happen *Do you think this idea will work? Being nice to him doesn't work – he still doesn't like me.*
7 to make something happen *They say she can work miracles. The wizard worked his magic on her.*
8 to move, or make something move, from one position to another *The knot has worked loose. The food works its way down the oesophagus.*
9 if you work at something, you work hard to be successful in something, for example by practising it *I've been working at my French all term.*
10 to work something out is to find the correct answer or the correct way of doing something, for example using numbers *Can you work out what sixty times seven is? I can't work out what to do next.*
11 to work something out is also to understand something *I was trying to work out what he meant.*
12 if something works out, it is successful *Things didn't work out at my new school.*
13 if something works out at a particular amount, it comes to that amount *I get £40 a month pocket money so that works out at £10 a week.*
14 if someone works out, they do exercises to keep fit

work *noun*
1 something someone does that needs energy and attention *She thanked me for my hard work. When do we start work? There's a lot of repair work to do in the house.*
2 another word for a job, the place where someone's job is or the time someone spends doing their job *What sort of work does your mum do? My uncle travels a long way to work. After work my brother went to a football match.*
3 something someone produces that they've been working on *Aziz's work was displayed on the classroom wall. What a lovely piece of work!*
4 (plural **works**) something produced by someone such as an author, painter or musician *a book of the complete works of Shakespeare; We're studying the work of Malorie Blackman. This painting is a work of art* (something of very high quality).
5 in science, work is a force applied to something over a certain distance to make it move
6 **at work** working or doing something *We watched the firefighters at work.*
7 **at work** also used when you mean at the place where someone works *Mum's not home yet – she's still at work.*
8 **in work** used for describing someone who has a job
9 **out of work** used for describing someone who doesn't have a job

workable *adjective*
likely to be successful *a workable plan*

SYNONYM **practical**

workbench *noun* **workbenches**
a heavy work table, for example where a carpenter makes things with tools

workbook *noun* **workbooks**
1 a book with school activities or exercises and blank spaces or pages for writing your work in
2 a computer program with exercises to do and spaces for writing your work in and sharing it, for example with a teacher

worked up *adjective*
worried, angry or upset about something

worker *noun* **workers**
1 someone who works, for example at a particular job *an office worker; Seema is a very good worker.*
2 someone who works with their hands at a particular job *a steel worker*
3 a female bee, ant or wasp that does the main work of the group but does not lay eggs

workforce *noun*
the total number of people who work for a particular company or in a particular country or place

working class *noun*
a group in society made up of people who do basic work, for example in factories and shops **working-class** *adjective*
compare: **middle class** and **upper class**

workman *noun* **workmen**
a man who works with his hands, for example building or repairing things

LANGUAGE EXTRA you can also say *worker*

workmanship *noun*
the skill used in making or doing something

workout *noun* **workouts**
a period when you do exercises, for example in a gym

works *noun plural*
1 a large factory or building for producing things *a steel works; a chemical works*
2 the parts of a clock or machine that work together

worksheet *noun* **worksheets**
1 a sheet of paper with questions and spaces for writing answers
2 one of the parts that a computer spreadsheet is divided into, used for showing one group of calculations

workshop *noun* **workshops**
1 an event where people go to learn about a subject and take part in practical work *a quilting workshop*
2 a building or room with equipment and tools for making or repairing things

workstation *noun* **workstations**
a desk with a computer for one person to work at in an office

world *noun* **worlds**
1 the planet that we live on *every country in the world; The world's climate is changing.*
2 people in all the countries of the planet *The whole world loves football.*
3 used for talking about another planet *creatures from other worlds*
4 a particular society or group of countries *the ancient Greek world; the English-speaking world*
5 used for talking about a particular subject, area of activity or group *the world of computers; the world of fashion; the animal world*

world *adjective*
1 connected with all countries or with very many countries of the world *a world championship; a world war; world-famous* (famous everywhere)
2 the World Cup is a football competition between many countries of the world that happens every four years

worldly *adjective* **worldlier, worldliest**
1 knowing a lot about the practical things of life and not upset or shocked by the way people behave
2 only interested in the ordinary things of life like money, possessions and pleasures
3 connected with the things of this world *worldly goods* (things that you own)
worldliness *noun*

World Wide Web *noun*
1 a system that connects computers to each other all over the world and allows people to receive and share information, for example by using websites
2 also used for talking about all the connected websites stored in this system *I found this information on the World Wide Web.*

worm *noun* **worms**
1 a small animal that has a long thin smooth body with no bones or legs. Worms usually live in the ground and move along by twisting and turning.
2 any small creature that looks like a worm

worm *verb*
worms, worming, wormed
1 to worm your way somewhere is to go there slowly and move with difficulty, for example twisting and turning your body *He wormed his way through the crowd.*

wormy – would

2 to worm something out of someone is to get information from them slowly and with difficulty
3 to worm your way into or out of something is to get something (or get into something) or avoid something (or avoid doing something) by being clever or dishonest *She wormed her way out of doing her homework.*

wormy *adjective* **wormier, wormiest**
if something is wormy, it has worms in it or has been damaged by worms *a wormy apple*

worn
past participle of **wear**

worn *adjective*
1 if something is worn, it is damaged or has become thinner by being rubbed or used a lot *shoes worn at the heels; worn tyres*
2 if something is worn out, it has been used so much that it can't be used any more
3 if someone is worn out, they are very tired

> **LANGUAGE EXTRA** *worn out* is usually spelt *worn-out* when used in front of a noun, for example *a worn-out battery, a worn-out teacher*

worried *adjective*
full of worry *She had a worried look on her face. Mum looked worried. We got worried when my sister didn't phone.*

worry *verb*
worries, worrying, worried
1 if you worry or if you're worried, you feel unhappy because you're thinking about a problem you have or about something bad that could happen *Don't worry (or be worried) about me taking the bus – I'll be fine. My dad's always worrying.*
2 to worry someone is to make them feel unhappy by causing them a problem or by making them think something bad could happen *Jason's behaviour was worrying us all. It worries me that you haven't started your homework yet.*

worry *noun*
1 the feeling of being unhappy because of a problem you have or because you're afraid of something bad happening *My parents were frantic with worry.*
2 (*plural* **worries**) something that makes you feel unhappy *If you have any worries, have a word with your teacher. My worry is that I won't have enough time.*

worrying *adjective*
giving someone a lot of worry *a worrying situation*

worse *adjective*
comparative of **bad**
1 more bad or less good *The weather's worse today. I'm worse at maths than you. Jack's behaviour is getting worse.*
2 of lower quality *Your school report is much worse than your brother's.*
3 more serious *The accident could have been worse.*
4 more ill than you were *My sore throat is bothering me – I'm worse today.*

worse *adverb*
comparative of **badly**
1 in a way that is more bad or less good *I play football worse than my sister.*

2 to feel worse is to feel more ill than you were
3 worse off used when you mean someone is in a worse situation or has less money *My cousin will be worse off living away from home than with her parents.*

worse *noun*
someone or something that is worse *The weather was bad today but worse is to come.*

worsen *verb*
worsens, worsening, worsened
1 to become worse *The weather's worsening.*
2 to make something worse *Doing that will only worsen the situation.*

worship *verb*
worships, worshipping, worshipped
1 to show love and respect for God or a god, for example by praying or singing religious songs *Many deities are worshipped in Hinduism.*
2 to go to a religious ceremony in a building such as a church or mosque
3 to love and respect someone very much *Our grandparents worship us.*

worshipper *noun*

worship *noun*
the activity of worshipping God or a god or going to a religious ceremony *The priest performs daily acts of worship. This mosque is one of several places of worship in the town.*

worst *adjective*
superlative of **bad**
worse than anything or anyone else *the worst teacher*

worst *adverb*
superlative of **badly**
in a way that is worse than anything or anyone else *Bristol was the worst affected town. Oliver plays the worst.*

worst *noun*
the person or thing that is worse than all the others *Our team has lots of bad players but Jacob is the worst.*

worth *adjective*
1 if something is worth a certain amount of money, that is the amount of money someone can sell it for *This old book is worth £50. How much is it worth?*
2 used for saying that something is good, important, useful, interesting or enjoyable enough for you to do something *The British Museum is worth a visit* (for example, it's important and interesting enough for you to visit it). *This film is worth seeing. Studying French is hard but it's worth it* (for example, French is useful and important and you should study it).

worth *noun*
1 used for showing an amount of something, for example when you mean how much money something costs, how much it weighs or how long it lasts *two pounds' worth of sweets; a kilo's worth of apples; We have three days' worth of food left* (enough food to last three days).

2 used for showing how good or useful something is or how much money you can get for something *a dictionary of great worth* (a very good and useful one); *What's the true worth of a huge house like that?*

> **LANGUAGE EXTRA** in sense 2, you can also say *value*

worthless *adjective*
if something is worthless, it has no value, for example it is not worth any money or it is completely useless *This old Roman coin is worthless. His promise turned out to be worthless.* **worthlessness** *noun*

worthwhile *adjective*
if something is worthwhile, it is good, important, useful, interesting or enjoyable enough for someone to do it, spend time on it or be connected with it *a worthwhile visit; The effort was worthwhile. Mum had a worthwhile meeting with my teacher. Helping homeless people is a worthwhile cause.*

worthy *adjective* **worthier, worthiest**
1 if someone or something is worthy, they have good or important qualities and deserve respect *Masud is a worthy winner. Grandma gives money to worthy causes* (for example to help people).
2 worthy of good or important enough to deserve something or someone *She is worthy of our respect and support. This painting isn't a masterpiece but it's worthy of our attention. Henry is Amy's friend but he's not worthy of her* (he's not good enough to be her friend).

worthily *adverb* **worthiness** *noun*

would *verb*
1 used after a verb in the past tense for talking about doing something or about something happening in the future *Rick said he would help me. I thought that would be a good idea.*
2 used for showing what will happen or be true if something else happens or is true *If I won the lottery, I'd buy a big house. If I were older, I would walk to school by myself. You would work better with a more up-to-date laptop.*
3 used for asking someone something very politely *Would you help me, please? Would you like another chocolate?*
4 used for politely telling someone to do something *Would you please sit down.*
5 used for saying that someone or something will not or cannot do something *He wouldn't help me. The car wouldn't start. She'd never do such a thing.*
6 used for talking about something that happened lots of times in the past *When Nan lived closer, she would come round every day.*

> **SYNONYM** used to

7 used for saying that you think something is true but you are not sure *'There's someone at the door.' – 'That would be Uncle Jack.'*

> **LANGUAGE EXTRA** *would* can be shortened to *'d*, for example *I'd* (I would), *you'd* (you would) and *they'd* (they would)

wouldn't – wristwatch

wouldn't
short for 'would not'

wound ['woond'] *noun* **wounds**
damage done to a part of a person's or animal's body, usually a hole in the skin made by a weapon *a stab wound; a bullet wound*

wound ['woond'] *verb*
wounds, wounding, wounded
1 to injure a person's or animal's body, usually by making a hole in the skin *a wounded soldier; Several people were wounded by the bomb.*
2 to make someone feel upset, for example by saying something unkind or rude to them or not showing respect

wound [rhymes with 'sound']
past tense & past participle of **wind**

wove
past tense of **weave**

woven
past participle of **weave**

wow [rhymes with 'now'] *interjection*
used for showing how happy or surprised you are about something or someone

WPC *noun*
a woman police officer *WPC Clarke gave a talk at our school.*
short for: woman police constable

PRONUNCIATION RULE when you see the letters **wr** at the beginning of a word, say 'r'. The **w** is silent.

wrap *verb*
wraps, wrapping, wrapped
1 if you wrap something or wrap something up, you put paper or another material round it *We spent an hour wrapping up the presents* (putting paper round them). *Dad wrapped the sandwiches in foil.*
2 if you wrap something round something else or round someone, you put cloth, paper or another material round them *I wrapped a towel around me when I got out of the shower. The nurse wrapped the bandage round my wrist.*
3 if something such as a snake or plant wraps itself around something else, it puts itself around it many times
4 if you wrap up or wrap yourself up, you put on warm clothes *Wrap up well when you go out.*

wrap *noun*
1 (*plural* **wraps**) a piece of cloth that girls and women wear around their shoulders
2 (*plural* **wraps**) a tortilla (thin round bread from Mexico) that has been wrapped or rolled around food such as meat, cheese or beans
3 gift wrap is attractive paper used for wrapping round something that you give as a gift

wrapper *noun* **wrappers**
a piece of paper or plastic that is wrapped round something you buy, especially food, to protect it *a sweet wrapper*

wrapping *noun*
paper or plastic that is wrapped round something to protect it *sandwiches in cellophane wrapping*

wrath [rhymes with 'moth'] *noun*
an old-fashioned word for anger
wrathful *adjective* **wrathfully** *adverb*

wreath [rhymes with 'teeth'] *noun*
wreaths [rhymes with 'seethes']
a circle made of flowers, leaves and branches tied together. It is used as a decoration, often at Christmas, or as a sign of respect for someone who has died, for example on their grave.

wreathed [rhymes with 'seethed'] *adjective* (old-fashioned)
covered or hidden in something *The city was wreathed in mist.*

wreck *verb*
wrecks, wrecking, wrecked
1 to destroy something or damage it very badly, for example so that it can't be used again or so that there isn't much of it left *A bomb wrecked the building.*
2 to spoil something completely *His behaviour wrecked our friendship. You've wrecked my plans!*

wreck *noun* **wrecks**
1 something such as a vehicle or ship that has been very badly damaged *The car was a burnt-out wreck.*
2 someone who feels or looks unhealthy, very tired or very worried *Waiting for news of the missing plane has made me a nervous wreck* (looking and feeling very worried).

wreckage *noun*
the parts of something such as a vehicle or plane that are left after it has been very badly damaged *Two survivors were pulled from the burning wreckage.*

wren *noun* **wrens**
a tiny brown bird with a short tail that points upwards and a loud singing voice

wrench *verb*
wrenches, wrenching, wrenched
1 to pull something with a violent and often twisting movement, for example to make it move or to take it away from someone *I said I wouldn't give him the book but he wrenched it out of my hands.*
2 to hurt a part of your body such as your ankle or wrist by twisting it

wrench *noun*
1 a violent pulling or twisting movement
2 (*plural* **wrenches**) a metal tool like a spanner with a shaped part at one end that fits round a nut (metal ring with six sides) and turns it to make it tighter or looser. The shaped part can be made wider or narrower to fit the particular size of the nut.

wrestle *verb*
wrestles, wrestling, wrestled
1 to wrestle with someone is to fight with them by holding them and pushing or throwing them to the ground, often as a sport
2 to wrestle with a problem or difficulty is to try very hard to deal with it

wrestling *noun*
a sport in which two people fight by holding each other and pushing or throwing each other to the ground
wrestler *noun*

wretch *noun* **wretches**
1 an unhappy or poor person that you feel sorry for *That beggar is a poor wretch.*
2 a horrible person

wretched ['retch-id'] *adjective*
1 used for talking about someone or something that annoys you *My wretched brother plays loud music all day. My wretched bike has a flat tyre.*
2 horrible *What a wretched life homeless people must have!*
3 poor *a wretched beggar*
4 ill *I have a bad cold and feel wretched.*
5 unhappy *I've been feeling wretched since our poor dog died.*

wriggle *verb*
wriggles, wriggling, wriggled
1 if a person or animal wriggles, they move their body from side to side lots of times *If the baby keeps wriggling, then he must be uncomfortable. The worm wriggled out of my hands.*
2 if someone wriggles out of something they don't want to do, they avoid doing it *How can I wriggle out of doing my homework?*

wriggly *adjective*

wring *verb*
wrings, wringing, wrung
1 if you wring something that is wet, you twist it hard to get the water out *Wring your wet towel out over the sink.*
2 if you wring something out of someone, you get something from them that is difficult to get, for example information or the truth about something
3 if someone or something is wringing wet, they are very wet

wrinkle *noun* **wrinkles**
1 a line on someone's skin, especially on their face, that appears as they start to get old
2 an accidental fold in something such as a piece of paper or cloth

wrinkle *verb*
wrinkles, wrinkling, wrinkled
1 to move part of your face such as your brow so that lines appear on it
2 if something such as your face or a piece of paper wrinkles, lines appear on it

wrinkled *adjective*
if someone or someone's face or skin is wrinkled, they have lots of wrinkles

LANGUAGE EXTRA you can also say *wrinkly*

wrist *noun* **wrists**
the part of your body where your arm joins your hand

wristband *noun* **wristbands**
1 a piece of material that you wear round your wrist, for example as decoration or for showing you support something such as an idea, group or charity (organisation for helping people)
2 a piece of leather, cloth or plastic that goes round your wrist and holds a wristwatch. It is also called a watch strap.

wristwatch *noun* **wristwatches**
a small clock that you carry with you and wear on your wrist

593

write *verb*
writes, writing, wrote, written
1 if you write, you make words, letters, numbers or symbols by marking them on a surface, for example on a computer screen or piece of paper, using something such as a keyboard, keypad, pen or pencil *My little sister is learning to read and write. You write on the whiteboard with a special pen called a marker.*
2 if you write something, you use words, letters, numbers or symbols to produce it or show it or to give information *Write your name here and then a short message. Please write your ideas and suggestions in an email. Historians write that the battle took place in 1066.*
3 to put words or other information on something such as an official document *Mum wrote a cheque for £50. Please can you write me an absence note?*

> SYNONYM to write out

4 to write a book, play or song, or something else that shows imagination and skill, is to put words together to create it so that people can read it, watch it or listen to it
5 to send someone a message in an email or letter *Write when you get to New York. Has Grandma written to you yet? Uncle Freddie writes that he'll be arriving next Sunday.*
6 used about something such as a pen for showing the way it works *My pen won't write. This marker writes too thickly.*
7 to write away or **off for something** is to write to someone to ask them to send you something *My parents wrote away for more information about Heather Lane School.*
8 to write back is to reply to someone's email or letter
9 to write something down is to write it somewhere so you will remember it
10 to write something out is to write it with all the details *Write out the poem neatly in your exercise books.*
11 to write something out is also to put words or other information on something such as an official document, for example a cheque or receipt

writer *noun* **writers**
1 someone who writes books, articles or stories
2 someone who writes a particular thing *Who's the writer of this email?*

writing *noun*
1 words that someone has written somewhere *There was writing on the whiteboard.*
2 the activity or skill of writing *Josh is better at reading than writing.*
3 the way someone writes using a pen or pencil *My writing* (handwriting) *isn't very easy to read.*
4 used for talking about things such as books, stories and articles *There's been a lot of writing about artificial intelligence.*
5 in writing written down, for example in a document or email

written
past participle of **write**

wrong *adjective*
1 if something is wrong, it has a mistake or mistakes in it *a wrong answer; I dialled the wrong number.*
2 not true *What Tara said was wrong – Rashid isn't my cousin.*
3 used for talking about something you should not do or have, the position or situation in which something or someone should not be, or the time when something should not be done *Telling lies is wrong. I made the wrong decision. That's the wrong way to shut down your tablet. I put the book back on the wrong shelf. Come and see me tomorrow – it's the wrong time now.*
4 if you say someone is wrong, you mean that what they say is not true or not based on facts *You're wrong – the capital of Spain is Madrid, not Barcelona.*
5 if you say someone is wrong to do something, you think they should not do it, for example because it's not sensible *George was wrong to say yes.*
6 not having the particular qualities needed for something *I think Sophie was the wrong person to be made head girl. You have the wrong sort of bike for riding on bumpy ground.*
7 if you say there is something wrong, you mean there is a problem or something bad happening, for example something isn't working or someone feels ill or unhappy *There's something wrong with the TV. You're crying – what's wrong? Your finger is bleeding – is there something wrong with it?*
8 the wrong way round in a position with the back part at the front and the front part at the back

> SYNONYM back to front

9 the wrong way up in a position with the top part at the bottom and the bottom part at the top

> SYNONYM upside down

wrong *adverb*
1 in a way that should not happen or be done *You've spelt my name wrong. You've done your maths homework all wrong – you must do it again.*
2 if something such as a piece of equipment goes wrong, it stops working or stops working properly
3 if something such as a plan or situation goes wrong, there are lots of problems that happen *Everything went wrong when I started my new school.*
4 if someone goes wrong, they make a mistake *You won't go wrong if you listen to Mum.*

wrong *noun*
1 behaviour that is wrong and bad *She doesn't know the difference between right and wrong. If you do wrong, you'll be punished.*
2 (*plural* **wrongs**) an action that is wrong and bad

wrong *verb*
wrongs, wronging, wronged
to treat someone badly and in an unfair way

wrongly *adverb*
in a way that should not happen or be done *The email was wrongly addressed. He was wrongly blamed* (blamed by mistake).

wrote
past tense of **write**

wrung
past tense & past participle of **wring**

wry *adjective* **wryer, wryest**
showing that you think a situation is funny even though you are disappointed or slightly angry *a wry smile* **wryly** *adverb*

www
short for **World Wide Web** (used mainly in internet addresses)

x X

ORIGIN the letter X has hardly changed its shape since it first appeared in ancient Greek and then in the Roman alphabet to represent the 'ks' sound – the sound in Latin words such as *rex* ('king'). When X entered English, it continued to be used for representing the 'ks' sound, for example in words like 'text'. It is now used in other ways too, such as for the 'gz' sound in 'exam' and for the 'z' sound in 'xylophone'.

X
the Roman numeral for the number 10

x-axis *noun*
one of the two lines of a graph or chart (mathematical diagrams) where the measurements are given. The other line is called the y-axis. The x-axis goes from left to right, for example along the bottom of the graph or chart, and the y-axis goes from top to bottom.

Xmas ['kris-mers' or 'eks-mers'] *noun* **Xmases**
an informal word for Christmas

X-ray *noun* **X-rays**
1 a special picture of the inside of something, for example a part of the body, using a type of radioactive energy called X-rays. X-rays go through something solid and allow hidden objects to be seen. *What do the X-rays show?*
2 an examination of the inside of something, for example a part of the body, using X-rays *Granddad is going for a chest X-ray.*

X-ray *verb*
X-rays, X-raying, X-rayed
to take an X-ray picture of the inside of something such as a part of the body so that it can be examined carefully

xylophone ['zye-ler-fohn'] *noun* **xylophones**
a musical instrument made up of a frame with narrow pieces of wood or metal of different lengths fixed to the top of it. You hit these pieces with a wooden hammer to produce a sound. The frame stands flat on the ground or rests on a table.

ORIGIN from Greek *xylon* 'wood' and *phone* 'sound'

y Y

ORIGIN the letter Y comes from a shape in the Phoenician alphabet that looked similar to a Y and represented either a peg or a hook. This shape changed in many ways after entering the Greek and Roman alphabets and different versions of these shapes became the English letters U, V, W and F. However, the Greeks also kept the Y shape unchanged to use as their letter *upsilon*, with a sound similar to 'oo'. The Romans borrowed this letter to use as their 'ee' sound in words that came from Greek such as *symmetria* ('symmetry'). When Y passed into English, it continued to be used as a vowel, usually with an 'ee' sound (as at the end of 'symmetry') or an 'i' sound (as in the first 'y' of 'symmetry'), but it took on extra work as a consonant too (as in 'yellow').

yacht [rhymes with 'pot'] *noun* **yachts**
1 a small or medium-sized boat with sails, used for racing or for sailing in for pleasure
2 a large or medium-sized boat with an engine, used for travelling in for pleasure

ORIGIN from Dutch *jaght* 'ship for hunting pirates'

yachtsman ['yacht' rhymes with 'pot'] *noun* **yachtsmen**
a man who sails in a yacht

yachtswoman ['yacht' rhymes with 'pot'] *noun* **yachtswomen**
a woman who sails in a yacht

yak *noun* **yaks**
a large animal like an ox or cow with long hair and large horns. Yaks live in Central Asia.

yam *noun* **yams**
a hard vegetable that grows under the ground and looks like a long potato

yank *verb* (informal)
yanks, yanking, yanked
to pull something or someone with a quick movement and a lot of strength *The drawer was stuck so my brother had to yank it open.* **yank** *noun*

Yankee *noun* **Yankees**
an informal or rude word for an American

LANGUAGE EXTRA you can also say *Yank*

yap *verb*
yaps, yapping, yapped
if a small dog yaps, it makes short loud high noises, often in an unpleasant way
yap *noun*

yard *noun* **yards**
1 an area of land next to a building, usually with a hard surface and a wall around it *a prison yard* (for example where prisoners do exercises); *There's a small yard behind the house.*
2 an area of land used for a special purpose *a builder's yard* (for example for storing bricks and building materials)
3 a unit for measuring length. There are 36 inches in a yard (about 91 centimetres).
4 in American English, a yard is a garden next to a house

Yard *noun*
the Yard is an informal name for Scotland Yard (the main office of the police force in London)

yarmulke ['yar-merl-ker'] *noun* **yarmulkes**
a small circle of cloth worn on the head at all times by Jewish men or boys who are religious and by other Jewish people when they pray

yarn *noun* **yarns**
1 a long thin twisted piece of material such as cotton, wool or nylon, used for many things such as making cloth, knitting and sewing
2 an informal word for a story or tale, often a long or exciting one or one that isn't true

yashmak *noun* **yashmaks**
a piece of thin cloth that covers most of the face. It is worn in public places by some Muslim women.

yawn *verb*
yawns, yawning, yawned
to open your mouth wide and breathe in and out deeply, usually because you are tired or bored

yawn *noun* **yawns**
the action of yawning or the sound of someone yawning *I gave a loud yawn.*

yawning *adjective*
very wide *a yawning chasm*

y-axis *noun*
one of the two lines of a graph or chart (mathematical diagrams) where the measurements are given. The other line is called the x-axis. The y-axis goes from top to bottom of the graph or chart, and the x-axis goes from left to right, for example along the bottom.

yay *interjection* (informal)
a word that you shout out to show you're very happy

yd
short for **yard** *1 yd of fabric*

LANGUAGE EXTRA the plural is *yds* or *yd*

ye ['yee'] *pronoun*
an old-fashioned word for 'you', especially when talking to more than one person

yeah ['yair'] *interjection*
an informal way of saying yes

year *noun* **years**
1 a period of 12 months or 52 weeks, measured from 1 January to 31 December. This is the time the earth takes to go once round the sun. *I'm changing schools later in the year.*
2 any period of time that lasts 12 months or about 12 months *I haven't seen her for a year. Grandma spent many years in America. My big brother's on his gap year* (doing something such as travelling or working for a year, after leaving school and before going to university).

595

yearbook–Yorkshire pudding

3 the period of time during the year when you go to school *The school year usually starts in September and ends in July.*
4 used for talking about the level that a pupil or student stays at for one year, for example at school or on a course *Mohammed is in my year. I'm a Year 5 pupil.*
5 used for talking about someone's age *an eight-year-old girl*; *I'm 10 years old.*
6 years used when you mean a very long time, for example three or more years *We haven't seen our uncle for years.*

> **LANGUAGE EXTRA** you can use *calendar year* when you mean the period from 1 January to 31 December

yearbook noun **yearbooks**
a book that comes out once every year and gives information, facts and details of activities and events connected with a school or organisation

yearn verb
yearns, yearning, yearned
to want something or someone very much *I yearned for some peace and quiet. They yearned to go home.*

> **SYNONYM** to long

yeast noun
a substance containing micro-organisms (tiny living things), used for example for making bread and some types of cakes rise (swell up and become softer)

yell verb
yells, yelling, yelled
1 to speak in a very loud voice *We could hear people yelling in the next room.*
2 to say something in a very loud voice *The bully was yelling insults at me.*
3 to speak very loudly to someone because you're angry *My mum will yell at me if I don't finish my homework.*

yell noun

yellow adjective **yellower, yellowest**
having the colour of a lemon or butter or the middle of an egg

yellow noun **yellows**
the colour yellow

yellowish adjective
slightly yellow

> **LANGUAGE EXTRA** you can also say *yellowy*

yelp verb
yelps, yelping, yelped
if a person or animal yelps, they make a short loud high sound (or sounds), for example because they are in pain or very excited *The puppy yelped when I stepped on its paw.*

yelp noun **yelps**
a yelping sound

Yemen ['**yem**-ern'] noun
a country in South-West Asia
Yemeni adjective & noun

yen noun
1 a strong feeling of wanting something

> **SYNONYM** hankering

2 (plural **yen**) a unit of money in Japan

yes adverb
1 used when what a question is asking is true or when you mean that what someone says is true *'Did you speak to Grandma?' – 'Yes.' 'It was a good film.' – 'Yes.'*
2 used for saying you will do something or have something *'Come over here.' – 'Yes.' 'I'm getting you an ice cream.' – 'Yes.'*
3 used for giving permission *'May I close the window?' – 'Yes.'*
4 used as a polite answer when someone calls you *'Megan?' – 'Yes!'*
5 used for saying the opposite of what someone says or for saying that what they say is not true *'You can't speak French.' – 'Yes, I can.'*
6 used for showing that you're very pleased about something *'Our captain just scored another goal!' – 'Yes!'*

yes noun **yeses**
an answer in which someone says yes *Was that a yes or a no?*

yesterday adverb
on the day before today *I finished my homework yesterday.*

yesterday noun
the day before today *yesterday's lessons*; *Yesterday was Tuesday.*

yet adverb
1 used for talking about something that hasn't happened or been true up to the present time or up to a particular time *Hannah hasn't come back yet. It was 1930 and computers hadn't been invented yet. This is your best homework yet. Is he here yet?*
2 used when you mean now or as early as this time *Can I go home yet? You can't have an ice cream yet.*
3 used for talking about a period of time from now on *I won't be finished for an hour or two yet. There's plenty of time yet* (for example before something needs to be done).
4 used for saying something could or will happen in the future *Leah could yet surprise us all.*
5 used for giving extra importance to a word or words *I don't want to read that book yet again. Yet more rain tomorrow!*

yet conjunction
used for saying that something you have just mentioned does not stop something else from happening or from being true *Our school is big yet friendly. My tablet is new yet I have lots of problems with it.*

> **SYNONYM** but

yeti ['**yet**-ee'] noun **yetis**
a frightening creature that some people believe looks like a hairy person and lives in the Himalayan mountains

yew noun
1 (plural **yews**) a tree with long flat pointed leaves that stay green in winter. It produces bright red fruits that are poisonous.
2 the wood of the yew tree, used for making things such as furniture

Yiddish noun
a language similar to German that was spoken in the past by Jewish people from Central and Eastern Europe and is still spoken today by many people such as religious Jews **Yiddish** adjective

yield verb
yields, yielding, yielded
1 to produce something such as information or a result *Our internet searches yielded nothing useful.*
2 to produce something such as fruit or vegetables or an amount of them *The orchard yielded a good crop of apples.*
3 to agree to do or accept something that you don't want to

> **SYNONYM** to give in

4 if something yields, it moves, bends or breaks, for example when something heavy pushes down on it

> **SYNONYM** to give way

yield noun **yields**
an amount of something produced *a high yield of wheat*

yippee interjection
a word that you shout out to show you're very happy

yodel ['**yoh**-derl'] verb
yodels, yodelling, yodelled
to sing by changing the pitch (quality) of your voice during a single note so that your voice goes between high and low sounds very quickly

> **ORIGIN** from German *jodeln* 'to shout yo'. In the Swiss Alps, shepherds used to shout this and other words to communicate between mountain villages.

yoga ['**yoh**-ger'] noun
a type of exercise in which you relax your body and mind by moving your body into different positions and controlling your breathing

yoghurt ['**yog**-ert'] **yoghurts**
a liquid food made from milk that is made thick by adding bacteria (tiny living things). It has a slightly sour taste that is often made sweeter by adding sugar, a fruit flavour or small pieces of fruit.

> **LANGUAGE EXTRA** also spelt *yogurt*

yoke noun **yokes**
a curved piece of wood fixed around the necks of two animals such as oxen to join them together when they are pulling something, for example a cart or plough
yoke verb

yolk [rhymes with '**yoke**'] noun **yolks**
the yellow middle part of an egg

Yom Kippur ['**yom**-ki-**poor**'] noun
the most important Jewish religious holiday of the year when people ask God to forgive them for their sins. It usually takes place in September or October.

yonder adverb & adjective
an old-fashioned word meaning over there *Look yonder!*

Yorkshire pudding noun
Yorkshire puddings
a food made from flour, milk (or milk and water) and eggs, mixed together and poured onto hot fat or oil then baked in an

oven, either in a large tin or in small round tins. It is often eaten with roast beef, for example as the main meal on a Sunday.

you *pronoun*
1 the person or people you are talking to or writing to *You are my best friend. You are all* (or *All of you are*) *my friends. I saw you in the park. They were sitting behind you.*
2 people in general *You never know what can happen.*
3 used when calling someone something, usually something unpleasant *You fool!*

you'd
short for 'you had' or 'you would'

you'll
short for 'you will'

young *adjective* **younger, youngest**
used for describing a person, animal or plant that has lived or has been living for a short time only *Playgroups are for very young children. A puppy is a young dog. I'm nine and I have a younger sister* (she is not as old as I am, for example she's seven).

young *noun plural*
1 baby animals or birds *A female kangaroo carries its young in a pocket of skin called a pouch.*
2 a word sometimes used for talking about young people *Things are tough for the young nowadays.*

youngster *noun* **youngsters**
a child or young person

your *adjective*
1 used when you are talking about something or someone belonging to or connected with the person or people you are talking or writing to *Kareem goes to your school.*
2 used about people in general *Satnav shows you how to get to your destination.*

you're
short for 'you are'

yours *pronoun*
1 used about something belonging to or connected with the person or people you are talking or writing to *Is this bike yours?*
2 **Yours sincerely** used before your name at the end of a letter as a polite way of saying goodbye

yourself *pronoun* **yourselves**
1 used when talking about an action done by the person or people you are speaking or writing to when that action is also directed back onto them *Did you hurt yourself? I see you've found yourselves some new friends.*
2 used when you mean the person or people you are speaking or writing to and no-one else *You came to see me yourself. You yourselves told me to choose Spanish instead of French.*
3 **by yourself** or **by yourselves** without anyone else being there, or without the help of anyone else *Have you spent the whole day by yourself? I can see you've done the work all by yourselves.*

youth *noun*
1 the time when someone is young *What did Granddad do in his youth?*
2 the quality of being and looking young *She has youth and beauty.*
3 (*plural* **youths**) a young man *a gang of youths*
4 young people in general

LANGUAGE EXTRA in sense 4, *youth* is used with a plural verb, for example *The youth of the country are smarter than their parents.*

youth club *noun* **youth clubs**
a place where older children go to take part in different activities and sports and to make friends

youthful *adjective*
1 behaving or looking as if you are younger than you really are *youthful looks*; *Grandma is very youthful.*
2 connected with young people *youthful energy*

youthfulness *noun*

youth hostel *noun* **youth hostels**
a building or large house where young people can stay cheaply for a short time, usually when travelling or on holiday

you've
short for 'you have'

yo-yo *noun* **yo-yos**
a small toy made up of a round plastic or wooden object with a piece of string wrapped round it. You tie the other end of the string round your finger and move the object quickly up and down by making the string unwrap itself and then wrap itself round again.

yuan ['yoo-an'] *noun* **yuan**
a unit of money in China

yuck *interjection*
an informal word used for showing that you think something is dirty, sticky or unpleasant

yucky *adjective* **yuckier, yuckiest**
an informal word for dirty, sticky or unpleasant *What's that yucky stuff on the window?*

Yuletide *noun*
an old-fashioned word for Christmas

yummy *adjective* **yummier, yummiest** (informal)
if something you eat or drink is yummy, it tastes very good

SYNONYM delicious

z Z

ORIGIN the letter Z comes from a shape in the Phoenician alphabet that looked like a capital I with a small line at the top and bottom – I. The Phoenicians called it *zayin* (with a 'z' sound) and it meant 'axe' or 'weapon'. It was the seventh letter of their alphabet. The Greeks copied the shape and gradually changed it from I to Z, using it as the sixth letter of their alphabet. They kept the 'z' sound and called the letter *zeta* – the word that has given Z the name we call it today: zed. The letter shape and sound passed into the Roman alphabet unchanged, mainly used in scientific words borrowed from Greek, but the Romans put Z at the end of their alphabet. There were no changes to the shape or sound of Z when it passed into English and its position remains the same as the final letter of our alphabet.

zany *adjective* **zanier, zaniest** (informal)
unusual, funny and imaginative *a zany sense of humour*

ORIGIN from Italian *zani* 'clown'

zap *verb* (informal)
zaps, zapping, zapped
1 to destroy something or someone, for example by using the most modern electronic equipment or some form of energy such as a laser beam
2 to use a remote control to go from one place to another, for example one TV channel or one part of a TV programme to another *Zap over to BBC to watch the news. I never watch the ads on TV – I just zap through them.*
3 to move or send something quickly *I zapped the file straight to the printer from my tablet.*

zapper *noun* **zappers**
an informal word for a remote control (equipment for making a TV work from a distance)

zeal ['zeel'] *noun*
great enthusiasm for doing something that you believe is important, for example in religion or politics

zealous ['zel-ers'] *adjective*
full of enthusiasm and energy *My teacher is a zealous supporter of educational reform.*
zealously *adverb*

zebra ['zeb-rer' or 'zee-brer'] *noun* **zebras**
1 a large wild animal of the horse family with black and white stripes on its body and legs. Zebras live in many parts of Africa.
2 a **zebra crossing** is a place in a road where people can cross the road safely. It has black and white stripes going across the road and vehicles must stop to allow people to cross.

597

zenith–zucchini

zenith noun
1 the highest point in the sky that the sun or moon reaches, which is directly above you
2 used for talking about the time when something or someone is at their most successful point

> ORIGIN from Arabic *samt* 'direction over the head'

zero noun
1 (*plural* **zeros**) the number 0, which means nothing
2 the temperature at which water freezes. This is equal to 0 in the Celsius system.
3 used when you mean nothing or none at all *Our chances of getting home before the snowstorm are zero.*

> ORIGIN from Arabic *sifr* 'empty'

zest noun
1 a feeling of pleasure and enthusiasm
2 the skin of an orange, lemon or lime, used for giving a flavour to food or drink

zigzag noun **zigzags**
a line that keeps changing direction, like lots of 'W's joined together

zigzag verb
zigzags, zigzagging, zigzagged
to move forward in a line that keeps changing direction, going one way and then another way *Look how that motorbike is zigzagging through the traffic.*

zillion noun **zillions**
an informal word for a really huge number of something *My sister has zillions of friends on Facebook.*

Zimbabwe ['zim-bahb-way'] noun
a country in southern Africa
Zimbabwean adjective & noun

Zimmer frame noun **Zimmer frames**
(trademark)
a special frame that someone uses to help them walk, for example someone with a medical problem that affects the way they use their body

> LANGUAGE EXTRA you can also say *Zimmer*

zinc noun
a shiny bluish-grey metal that is often mixed with other metals, for example mixed with copper to make brass

zip noun
1 (*plural* **zips**) a long object made of plastic or metal with two rows of tiny points. The rows of points fit together when you pull a small sliding piece along them. A zip is used for closing something such as a piece of clothing or a bag.
2 an informal word for energy

zip verb
zips, zipping, zipped
1 if you zip something (or zip something up), for example a suitcase or jacket, you close it using a zip
2 to zip a computer file is to make it smaller using a special program, for example to make it easier to download or to send by email

> SYNONYM to compress

3 (informal) to go or move quickly *Watch out for the cars zipping along these country lanes. Our teacher zipped through the lesson in 10 minutes.*

zip code noun **zip codes**
the American word for a postcode (group of numbers that are part of an address)

zipper noun **zippers**
the American word for a zip

zit noun **zits** (informal)
a small round swelling on your skin, such as a pimple or red mark

zodiac ['zoh-dee-ak'] noun
an imaginary area of the sky divided into 12 equal parts called the signs of the zodiac. Each part contains a group of stars. Some people think that the movements of the stars can influence people's lives.

zombie noun **zombies**
1 in stories, a zombie is a dead person who has come back to life
2 (informal) someone who is not interested in anything around them and moves about slowly as if they are almost asleep

zone noun **zones**
1 an area or place, for example one with a quality that makes it different from other areas *My cousins in California live in an earthquake zone. You can park only in a parking zone.*
2 an area that a larger area is divided into *The London Underground is divided into separate zones.*

zonked adjective
an informal word for very tired

zoo noun **zoos**
a place where wild animals are kept so that people can look at them or study them

zoo-keeper noun **zoo-keepers**
someone who looks after animals in a zoo

zoologist ['zoo-ol-er-jist'] noun **zoologists**
a scientist who studies animals

zoology ['zoo-ol-er-jee'] noun
the scientific study of animals
zoological adjective

zoom verb
zooms, zooming, zoomed
1 to go or move somewhere very fast *My brother spent two weeks zooming around Europe. The motorbike zoomed past the school* (went past it fast making a loud noise).
2 if you zoom in on something with a camera, or if a camera zooms in on something, it makes it look bigger
3 to make an image or text bigger on a computer screen, for example by clicking on or touching the symbol of a plus sign

zoom lens noun **zoom lenses**
a piece of equipment fixed to a camera, used for making something look bigger (and closer to you) or smaller (and further away)

zucchini ['zoo-kee-nee'] noun **zucchini** or **zucchinis**
the American word for a courgette

Parts of speech

The words of a language are divided into groups depending on how they are used in a sentence. These groups are called parts of speech or word classes. This page tells you about the main parts of speech.

Adjective

An adjective is a word that describes a noun or pronoun, for example *happy* or *short*. Adjectives come before a noun (*a small house*) or after a verb (*My house is small*).

There are many different kinds of adjectives, for example adjectives that describe size (*a big cat*); age (*an old man*); colour (*a blue shirt*); number or quantity (*nine boys*, *many books*); feelings (*an angry farmer*); opinions (*my favourite film*); state of health (*a sick girl*); qualities (*a clever son*); nationality (*an Italian singer*); what something is made of (*a plastic box*).

Many adjectives have two forms: the comparative and the superlative. The comparative is used for comparing two things: *This tree is taller than that one. Peter's drawing is good but Abdul's is better.* The superlative is used for describing the most of a particular quality: *This tree is the tallest one. Anne's is the best drawing in the class.*

Adverb

An adverb is a word that describes a verb, an adjective or another adverb or gives more information about them, for example *quickly, always, very*.

There are at least five different kinds of adverbs, showing: how (*I walked slowly*); when (*It rained yesterday*); where (*I hurt myself here*); how often (*Meena sometimes plays the piano*); to what extent (*He arrived very late*).

Most adverbs of the 'how' type are formed by adding *-ly* to an adjective, for example *brightly, softly, pleasantly*.

Article

An *article* is a word used for referring to a noun. An article is not usually considered as a part of speech but it is important to know what it is and how to use it.

There are two articles: the definite article and the indefinite article.

The definite article is the word *the*. It is called the definite article because it refers to a particular example of a noun, for example *the house* refers to a particular house, not just any house.

The indefinite article is the word *a* (or *an*). It is called the indefinite article because it does not refer to a particular example of a noun. For example, *a house* refers to any example of a house, not a particular house.

Conjunction

A conjunction is a word that joins other words or parts of a sentence together, for example *and* or *but*.

Conjunctions such as *and* and *or* are used for joining individual words together, for example *reading, writing and spelling*; *red or blue*. Conjunctions used for joining parts of sentences together include *and*, *or*, *but*, *because*, *that* and *so*, for example *I'm tired but I don't want to go to bed. She didn't go to school because she was ill.*

Interjection

An interjection is a word or words used for showing a feeling such as pain (*ouch*) or surprise (*oh dear*), when meeting someone (*hi*) or saying goodbye (*cheerio*), or for expressing unusual noises (*shh*, *oink*). Interjections are often followed by an exclamation mark (*ouch!*).

Noun

A noun is a word used as the name of a thing, place or person. There are many different kinds of nouns, for example common nouns and proper nouns.

Common nouns name things or people (*table, man, cat, happiness, anger*). They can be divided into concrete nouns, which name anything you can see, hear or touch (*table, man, cat*) and abstract nouns, which name ideas or feelings (*happiness, anger*).

Proper nouns (written with a capital first letter) name particular people or places (*George, Leeds, Ireland*).

Preposition

A preposition is a word used for showing the connection between a noun or pronoun and another word or part of a sentence, for example *in, on* or *with*.

There are many kinds of prepositions, for example showing where (*in, on, at, under, around, by*), where to (*to, towards*), when (*before, after, during*) or how (*with, by*). The preposition *of* shows a connection between a noun and another noun (*the top of the table*), and *for* often shows who or what gets something (*I've got a present for you*).

Prepositions usually come before a noun or pronoun (*I sat under a tree*) but can sometimes follow (*This is the tree I sat under*).

Sometimes a preposition is made up of more than one word (*out of, next to, on top of*).

Pronoun

A pronoun is a word used instead of a noun, for example *I, me, she, her, they, them*, or a word used for referring to a noun that has come before in the sentence, for example *who, which* or *that*.

You use a pronoun when you don't want to repeat a noun. For example, instead of saying *Dad took the dog to the park and Dad let the dog run around*, it is easier to say *Dad took the dog to the park and he let it run around*. The words *he* and *it* are pronouns standing for *Dad* and *the dog*.

There are many types of pronouns. Some of the most important types are: personal pronouns (such as *I, me, she, her, they* or *them*) referring to a person, possessive pronouns (such as *mine, my, your* or *theirs*) showing who or what something or someone belongs to, and relative pronouns (such as *who, which* or *that*) referring to an earlier noun or sentence.

Pronouns can be singular (for example *she, I, him*) or plural (*they, we, our*). The pronoun *you* (or *your*) can be both singular and plural.

Verb

A verb is a word used for showing what someone or something does (for example *jump, eat, touch*), what happens or exists (for example *happen, be, have*) or what goes on in the mind (for example *think, feel, know*).

Verbs have different forms depending on how they are used. For example, they can be used in the singular (*my hat is red, I have an idea, she has an idea*) or the plural (*my hats are red, they have an idea*). They can also be used in the present tense (*I work, he works, I am working, he is working*), past tense (*we worked, we were working*) or future tense (*they will work, they will be working*).

Verbs can be used in a transitive or intransitive way. A transitive verb has a direct object (noun or pronoun that receives the direct action), for example *I heard a noise*. An intransitive verb has no object, for example *I can't hear*.

Punctuation

Punctuation marks are special symbols used in writing. They make it easier to understand written sentences. This page tells you about the main punctuation marks.

Apostrophe '

You use an apostrophe for showing that one or more letters have been left out of a word, for example *I'm* (for *I am*) or *they'll* (for *they will*). The apostrophe stands for the missing part of the word.

An apostrophe is also used for showing that something belongs to someone or to something else – this is the possessive use of the apostrophe. In the sentence *This is the girl's book*, the *'s* shows that the book belongs to *the girl* (one girl), and in the sentence *These are the girls' books* the *s'* shows that the books belong to *the girls* (more than one girl). Be careful to put the apostrophe in the correct place – before the *s* when there is only one and after the *s* when there is more than one.

Take care also not to confuse *'s* with plural *s*. Write *I can see the girls*, not *I can see the girl's*.

Brackets ( ) [ ] { }

Brackets are used in pairs. You can put them around words to give extra information in a sentence, for example *My bike cost a lot of money (more than my parents could afford)*.

Capital letter

A *capital* or *capital letter* is a large letter (such as A, B or C). Capital letters are used at the beginning of names (for example *Alice, Manchester, Wales, Tuesday, August*). You always use a capital letter at the beginning of the first word of a sentence.

Capital letters are not punctuation marks but, like punctuation, they make it easier to understand written sentences. People don't always use capital letters in informal writing such as text messages, but in everyday and careful writing it is important to use them correctly.

Colon :

You use a colon before an explanation (*There's something I want you to know: I can't play chess*), a quotation (*It was Shakespeare who wrote: 'To be or not to be. That is the question'*) or a list of different things (*I speak three languages: English, French and Spanish*).

Comma ,

Commas help to make reading a sentence easier because they separate the different parts of the sentence (*As you can see, it's raining*).

Commas are also used for separating parts of a sentence that contain extra information about the main sentence (*My mobile phone, which I bought last week, doesn't work*). You can easily leave out the part between the commas without changing the basic meaning of the sentence.

You also use commas for separating different things in a list (*I love apples, pears, oranges and bananas*).

Dash –

A dash is slightly longer than a hyphen. You use it to separate parts of a sentence when you add an explanation or opinion or say something strongly.

You can use a dash on its own, for example *When I grow up, there's one thing I want to be – happy*. Or you can use two dashes in one sentence, for example *There is nowhere – nowhere in the world – I'd want to live except Scotland*.

A dash is used in a similar way to a comma but often separates a part of the sentence that is very different from the main sentence and doesn't belong to it (such as *nowhere in the world* in the last example).

Exclamation mark !

You use an exclamation mark after a word, phrase or sentence as a way of showing a particular feeling. For example, you can show that you are angry (*I'll never speak to you again!*); surprised (*Look at that!*); disappointed (*Pity!*); happy about something (*What a beautiful dress!*); unhappy about something (*Sorry!*); agreeing (*Yes!*) or disagreeing (*No!*).

You can also use an exclamation mark with a command (*Go away! Don't run! Help me!*) and to give special importance to a word or sentence (*I've been to Spain three times!*).

In informal writing, a number of exclamation marks can be used together to show that your feelings are very strong (*Your plan is completely crazy!!!*).

Full stop .

A full stop is used for showing the end of a sentence (but you do not use one after a question mark or exclamation mark). It is always followed by a capital letter at the beginning of the first word of the next sentence.

A full stop is sometimes used in words that have been shortened, for example *etc.* (short for Latin *et cetera* 'and so on') or *p.* (short for page).

Hyphen -

A hyphen is slightly shorter than a dash. It is used in writing for joining words or parts of words together (*old-fashioned, merry-go-round*).

It is also used when there is not enough room for a whole word at the end of a line of writing. The word then has to be divided into two parts: the first part is at the end of the line with a hyphen after it and the rest is at the beginning of the next line.

Question mark ?

You use a question mark after a word (*What?*), phrase (*How many?*) or sentence (*Where do you live?*) for showing that you are asking someone a direct question. If the question is read aloud, the question mark tells you there must be rising intonation (your voice becomes higher at the end).

Quotation marks ' ' " "

Quotation marks can also be called **inverted commas** or **speech marks**.

You use either single ' ' or double " " quotation marks around words to show they are the exact words that someone is using (*'I'm tired,' said Josh. "Where are we?" asked Bimla*).

Quotation marks can also be used around titles, for example of books, films or paintings (*We're reading 'Oliver Twist'. "Starry Night", a famous painting by Van Gogh*).

You also use quotation marks to show that words have a meaning that is slightly different from their usual meaning (*I don't like the look of this 'food' you've put on my plate*).

Semicolon ;

You can use a semicolon instead of a full stop for separating two sentences whose meanings are closely related (*I heard a loud bang; it frightened me*). You often do this when the second sentence starts with an adverb (*I like apples and oranges; however, I prefer pears*).

You can also use a semicolon instead of a comma in a long or complicated list of words or sentences where a comma would not be clear enough (*The menu gave us a choice between these dishes: fish, chips and peas; vegetarian lasagne with salad; chicken curry, rice and naan bread; lamb kebabs with chilli mayonnaise*).